Pub Guide 2012

AA Lifestyle Guides

15th edition September 2011.
© AA Media Limited 2011.

Assessments of AA inspected establishments are based on the experience of the Hotel and Restaurant Inspectors on the occasion(s) of their visit(s) and therefore descriptions given in this guide necessarily contain an element of subjective opinion which may not reflect or dictate a reader's own opinion on another occasion. See pages 6–7 for a clear explanation of how, based on our Inspectors' inspection experiences, establishments are graded. If the meal or meals experienced by an Inspector or Inspectors during an inspection fall between award levels the restaurant concerned may be awarded the lower of any award levels considered applicable.

Please contact:
Advertising Sales Department: advertisingsales@theAA.com
Editorial Department: lifestyleguides@theAA.com
AA Hotel Scheme Enquiries: 01256 844455

Every effort has been made to trace the copyright holders, and we apologise in advance for any unintentional omissions or errors. We would be pleased to apply any corrections in a following edition of this publication. Photographs in the gazetteer provided by the establishments.

AA Media Limited would like to thank the following photographers, companies and picture libraries for their assistance in the preparation of this book.
Abbreviations for the picture credits are as follows: (t) top; (b) bottom; (l) left; (r) right; (c) centre; (AA) AA World Travel Library.
Front Cover (t) The Tunnel House Inn; (bl) The Feathered Nest Inn; (br) foodfolio Alamy;
Back Cover (c) The White Hart Village Inn; (r) Charles Bathurst Inn.

Typeset/Repro: Wellcom London.
Printed and bound by Graficas Estella, Spain

Directory compiled by the AA Lifestyle Guides Department and managed in the Librios Information Management System and generated from the AA establishment database system.

Pub descriptions have been contributed by the following team of writers: Phil Bryant, Neil Coates, David Foster, David Halford, David Hancock, Felicity Jackson, Mark Taylor and Jenny White.

Published by AA Publishing, a trading name of AA Media Limited, whose registered office is Fanum House, Basing View, Basingstoke RG21 4EA. Registered number 06112600.
A CIP catalogue for this book is available from the British Library.
ISBN: 978-0-7495-7072-9
A04612

Maps prepared by the
Mapping Services Department of
AA Publishing.

Maps © AA Media Limited 2011.

Contains Ordnance Survey data
© Crown copyright and database right 2011.
Licence number 100021153.

Information on National Parks in England provided by the Countryside Agency (Natural England).

Information on National Parks in Scotland provided by Scottish Natural Heritage.

Information on National Parks in Wales provided by The Countryside Council for Wales.

Contents

1 LOCATION

Guide order Pubs are listed alphabetically by name (ignoring The) under their village or town. Towns and villages are listed alphabetically within their county (a county map appears at the back of the guide). The guide has entries for England, Channel Islands, Isle of Man, Scotland and Wales in that order. Some village pubs prefer to be initially located under the nearest town, in which case the village name is included in the address and directions.

Pick of the Pubs Over 700 of the best pubs in Britain have been selected by the editor and inspectors and these are highlighted. They have longer, more detailed descriptions and a tinted background. Over 150 of these have a full page entry and two photographs.

2 MAP REFERENCE

The map reference number denotes the map page number in the atlas section at the back of the book and (except for London maps) the National Grid reference. The London map references help locate their position on the Central and Greater London maps.

3 ESTABLISHMENT NAME AND SYMBOLS

See Key to symbols in the panel on page 5.

4 ADDRESS AND POSTCODE DETAILS

This gives the street name and the postcode, and if necessary the name of the village is included (see 1 above). This may be up to five miles from the named location.

☎ **Telephone number,** 🖷 **fax number, e-mail and websites:** Wherever possible we have included an e-mail address.

5 DIRECTIONS

Directions are given only when they have been supplied by the proprietor.

6 DESCRIPTION

Description of the pub and food.

7 OPEN

Indicates the hours and dates when the establishment is open and closed.

8 BAR MEALS

Indicates the times and days when proprietors tell us bar food can be ordered, and the average price of a main

1 **3** **4** **14** **5** **2**

SNAINTON   Map 17 SE98

The Coachman Inn ★★★★ RR ◉ ♟

Pickering Road West YO13 9PL
☎ 01723 859231 🖷 01723 850008
e-mail: info@coachmaninn.co.uk
web: www.coachmaninn.co.uk
dir: *5m from Pickering, off A170 onto B1258, 9m from Scarborough off the A170 onto B1258*

6

This imposing Grade II listed Georgian coaching inn on the road between York and Scarborough offers award-winning food and holds the coveted AA Rosette for culinary excellence. Food is served in the romantic candlelit Carriages Restaurant, cosy lounge or rustic Coachman Bar with its blazing log fire. Traditional beers are available and a wide selection of wines by the glass. Typical dishes include dressed crab and smoked salmon tian, herb salad and guacamole followed by pan-roast Goosnargh duck, potato terrine, spiced carrots, honey and black pepper jus. Outside, the tranquil gardens with large lawn and courtyard offer alfresco dining. Comfortable accommodation is available.

7   **Open** all wk noon-mdnt **Bar Meals** L served all wk 12-3   **8**
D served all wk 6.30-9 **Restaurant** L served all wk 12-3
D served all wk 6.30-9 booking required Av 3 course à la carte fr £25 ⊕ FREE HOUSE ◀ John Smith's, Wold Top, Guinness. ♟ 15 **Facilities** Children welcome Children's menu Children's portions Garden Parking Wi-fi **Rooms** 6

10 **9** **11** **12**

course as supplied by the proprietor. Please be aware that last orders could vary by up to 30 minutes.

9 RESTAURANT

Indicates the times and days when proprietors tell us food can be ordered from the restaurant. The average cost of a 3-course à la carte meal and a 3- or 4-course fixed-price menu are shown as supplied by the proprietor. Last orders may be approximately 30 minutes before the times stated.

10 BREWERY AND COMPANY

⬦ **The barrel symbol** indicates the name of the Brewery to which the pub is tied, or the Company that owns it. A free house is where the pub is independently owned and run.

◗ **The beer tankard symbol** indicates the principal beers sold by the pub. Up to five cask or hand-pulled beers are listed. Many pubs have a much greater selection, with several guest beers each week.

ō **The apple symbol** indicates that real cider is available and listed.

♟ **The wine glass symbol** followed by a number indicates the number of wines sold by the glass.

11 FACILITIES

Indicates if a pub has a children's menu, children's portions, a garden, children's play area, allows dogs on the premises, holds a beer festival (NEW for 2012), offers parking. For further information please phone the pub.

12 ROOMS

Only accommodation that has been AA inspected and rated is indicated, with the number of en suite bedrooms listed. Many pubs have rooms, but we only indicate those that are AA rated.

13 NOTES

As so many establishments take one or more of the major credit cards we only indicate if a pub does not take cards.

14 AA STARS/DESIGNATORS

AA Stars (and designators as appropriate) are shown at the beginning of an entry. The AA, in partnership with the national tourist bodies (VisitBritain, VisitScotland and VisitWales) has introduced new Quality Standards for inspected accommodation. See pages 6-7 for details of AA ratings.

AA Classifications & Awards

Many of the pubs in this Guide offer accommodation. Where a Star rating appears next to an entry's name in the Guide, the establishment has been inspected by the AA under common Quality Standards agreed between the AA, VisitBritain, VisitScotland and VisitWales. These ratings are for the accommodation, and ensure that it meets the highest standards of cleanliness, with an emphasis on professionalism, proper booking procedures and prompt and efficient services. Some of the pubs in this Guide offer accommodation but do not belong to a rating scheme. In this case the accommodation is not included in their entry.

AA recognised establishments pay an annual fee that varies according to the classification and the number of bedrooms. The establishments receive an unannounced inspection from a qualified AA inspector who recommends the appropriate classification. Return visits confirm that standards are maintained; the classification is not transferable if an establishment changes hands.

The annual *AA Hotel Guide* and *AA Bed & Breakfast Guide* give further details of recognised establishments and the classification schemes. Details of AA recognised hotels, guest accommodation, restaurants and pubs are also available at **theAA.com,** along with a useful Route Planner.

AA Hotel Classification

Hotels are classified on a 5-point scale, with one star ★ being the simplest, and five stars offering a luxurious service at the top of the range. The AA's top hotels in Britain and Ireland are identified by red stars. (★)

In addition to the main **Hotel** (HL) classification which applies to some pubs in this Guide, there are other categories of hotel which may be applicable to pubs, as follows:

Town House Hotel (TH) - A small, individual city or town centre property, which provides a high degree of personal service and privacy.

Country House Hotel (CHH) - Quietly located in a rural area.

Small Hotel (SHL) - Has fewer than 20 bedrooms and is owner managed.

Metro Hotel (MET) - A hotel in an urban location that does not offer an evening meal.

Budget Hotel (BUD) - These are usually purpose-built modern properties offering inexpensive accommodation. Often located near motorways and in town or city centres. **They are not awarded stars.**

AA Guest Accommodation

Guest accommodation is also classified on a scale of one to five stars, with one ★ being the most simple, and five being more luxurious. Yellow stars (★) indicate the very best B&Bs, Guest Houses, Farmhouses, Inns and Guest Accommodation in the 3, 4 and 5 star ratings. Stars have replaced the Diamond Classification for this type of accommodation, in accordance with Common Standards agreed between the AA and the UK tourist authorities of VisitEngland, VisitScotland and VisitWales. To differentiate them from Hotel Stars, they have been given a series of designators appropriate to the type of accommodation they offer, as follows:

Inn (INN) – Accommodation provided in a fully licensed establishment. The bar will be open to non-residents and provide food in the evenings.

Bed & Breakfast (B&B) – Accommodation provided in a private house, run by the owner and with no more than six paying guests.

Guest House (GH) – Accommodation provided for more than six paying guests and run on a more commercial basis than a B&B. Usually more services, for example dinner, provided by staff as well as the owner.

Farmhouse (FH) – B&B or guest house rooms provided on a working farm or smallholding.

Restaurant with Rooms (RR) – Destination restaurant offering overnight accommodation. The restaurant is the main business and is open to non-residents. A high standard of food should be offered, at least five nights a week. A maximum of 12 bedrooms. Most Restaurants with Rooms have been awarded AA Rosettes for their food.

Guest Accommodation (GA) – Any establishment which meets the entry requirements for the Scheme can choose this designator.

U A small number of pubs have this symbol because their Star classification was not confirmed at the time of going to press.

△ Refers to hotels rated by another organisation, eg VisitBritain.

Rosette Awards
Out of the thousands of restaurants in the British Isles, the AA identifies, with its Rosette Awards, around 2000 as the best. What to expect from restaurants with AA Rosette Awards is outlined here; for a more detailed explanation of Rosette criteria please see **theAA.com**

⊛ Excellent local restaurants serving food prepared with care, understanding and skill and using good quality ingredients.

⊛⊛ The best local restaurants, which consistently aim for and achieve higher standards and where a greater precision is apparent in the cooking. Obvious attention is paid to the selection of quality ingredients.

⊛⊛⊛ Outstanding restaurants that demand recognition well beyond their local area.

⊛⊛⊛⊛ Amongst the very best restaurants in the British Isles, where the cooking demands national recognition.

⊛⊛⊛⊛⊛ The finest restaurants in the British Isles, where the cooking stands comparison with the best in the world.

AA Pub of the Year

The AA Pub of the Year for England, Scotland and Wales have been selected with the help of our AA inspectors, we have chosen three very worthy winners for this prestigious annual award.

The winners stand out for being great all-round pubs or inns, combining a good pub atmosphere, a warm welcome from friendly, efficient hosts and staff, excellent food and well-kept beers.

ENGLAND

THE FEATHERED NEST INN ★★★★★ INN ◎◎
NETHER WESTCOTE, GLOUCESTERSHIRE Page 202

With marvellous views over the Evenlode Valley, The Feathered Nest Inn is set in the picturesque village of Nether Westcote on the Oxfordshire and Gloucestershire border. Proprietors Amanda and Tony Trimmer are charming and on hand daily. Originally an old malthouse, the pub has been updated and thoughtfully furnished whilst retaining the original character, especially in the cosy bar with its huge open fireplace, where Hook Norton Best is one of the real ales on offer. Awarded 2 AA Rosettes, a daily blackboard menu offers relaxed eating in the bar and the garden terrace when the weather allows. Many of the herbs and vegetables are grown in the kitchen garden, with local produce a backbone of the menu. A bar menu of classics like fish and chips, ploughman's and steak sandwiches is complemented by an interesting à la carte offering the likes of seared Cornish scallops with chicory salad and clementine purée or confit wood pigeon with seared foie gras, braised cabbage and parsnip purée. An impressive wine list offers some very unusual options featuring South Africa and Portugal. Individually decorated bedrooms furnished with antiques and comfortable beds are available.

SCOTLAND

THE CAFE ROYAL

EDINBURGH Page 550

A glorious example of Victorian and Baroque, little has changed at the Café Royal since it moved across the road from its original site in 1863. A stylish Parisian-style building designed by local architect Robert Paterson, entering the Café Royal is like stepping back in time. Elegant stained glass and fine late Victorian plasterwork dominate the building, as do irreplaceable Doulton ceramic murals in the bar and restaurant. The whole building and its interior were listed in 1970 so future generations will enjoy the unique building which still sticks to its early 19th century roots by serving local ales, wine, coffee and fresh oysters in the bar and restaurant. Friendly staff offer relaxed and informal service. Scottish produce dominates the menu, from starters of Stornoway black pudding and apple gratin or Scottish smoked salmon with lemon mayonnaise to main courses of fish stew or haggis and whisky cream pie with chips.

WALES

THE WHITE HART VILLAGE INN

LLANGYBI, MONMOUTHSHIRE Page 585

Situated in the beautiful Usk Valley in the pretty village of Llangybi, a warm welcome awaits at this picturesque, lovingly restored historic inn, where no less than eleven fireplaces can be found. Henry VIII became owner-by-default upon receiving it in the dowry of Jane Seymour, whilst arch-republican Oliver Cromwell based himself here during local Civil War campaigns. Add a priest hole, a wealth of exposed beams, precious Tudor plasterwork and a mention in a TS Eliot poem *Usk* and you've a destination to savour. Executive chef Michael Bates, formerly at Celtic Manor, is at the helm, offering village drinkers reliable beers from the likes of Tomos Watkins and Taffy Apple cider. It's the AA 2-Rosette menu that keeps visitors returning time-and-time-again, though. Using fresh local produce, and combining exciting ingredients and complementary flavours, head chef Adam Whittle prepares and presents dishes with the utmost care and attention to detail. In summer, head outside to the extensive seating area.

We aim to bring you the country's best pubs, selected for their atmosphere, great food and good beer. Ours is the only major pub guide to feature colour photographs, and to highlight the 'Pick of the Pubs', revealing Britain's finest hostelries. Updated every year, this edition includes lots of old favourites, as well as plenty of new destinations for eating and drinking, and great places to stay across Britain.

Who's in the Guide?

We make our selection by seeking out pubs that are worth making a detour - 'destination' pubs - with publicans exhibiting real enthusiasm for their trade and offering a good selection of well-kept drinks and good food. We also choose neighbourhood pubs supported by locals and attractive to passing motorists or walkers. Our selected pubs make no payment for their inclusion in our guide. They are included entirely at our discretion.

Tempting Food

We are looking for menus that show a commitment to home cooking, making good use of local produce wherever possible, and offering an appetising range of freshly-prepared dishes. Pubs presenting well-executed traditional dishes like ploughman's or pies, or those offering innovative bar or restaurant food, are all in the running. In keeping with recent trends in pub food, we are keen to include those where particular emphasis is placed on imaginative modern dishes and those specialising in fresh fish. Occasionally we include pubs that serve no food, or just snacks, but are very special in other ways.

That Special Place

We look for pubs that offer something special: pubs where the time-honoured values of a convivial environment for conversation while supping or eating have not been forgotten. They may be

attractive, interesting, unusual or in a good location. Some may be very much a local pub or they may draw customers from further afield, while others may be included because they are in an exceptional place. Interesting towns and villages, eccentric or historic buildings, and rare settings can all be found within this guide.

Pick of the Pubs and Full Page Entries

Some of the pubs included in the guide are particularly special, and we have highlighted these as Pick of the Pubs. For 2012 over 700 pubs have been selected by the personal knowledge of our editorial team, our AA inspectors, and suggestions from our readers.

These pubs have a coloured panel and a more detailed description. From these, over 150 have chosen to enhance their entry in the 2012 Guide by purchasing two photographs as part of a full-page entry.

Smoking Regulations

A law banning smoking in public places came into force in July 2007. This covers all establishments in this guide. Some pubs provide a private area in, for example an outbuilding, for smokers. If the freedom to smoke is important to you, we recommend that you check with the pub when you book.

Tell us what you think

We welcome your feedback about the pubs included and about the guide itself. We are also delighted to receive suggestions about good pubs you have visited and loved. A Reader Report form appears at the back of the book, so please write in or e-mail us at lifestyleguides@theAA.com to help us improve future editions.
The pubs also feature on the AA website, **theAA.com**, along with our inspected restaurants, hotels and bed & breakfast accommodation.

Own-Brew Pubs Revival

By MARK TAYLOR

*Like most rising trends, there is
nothing particularly new about pubs
brewing their own beer.*

The Three Tuns Inn,
Bishop's Castle, Shropshire

Before the rise and rise of large commercial breweries and pub companies, most beer would have been brewed on the premises of the pub where it was then dispensed into tankards for thirsty patrons.

One only has to look at traditional pub names – Coopers Arms, Hop Pole, Three Tuns (Bishop's Castle, Shropshire) for example – to trace the on-site brewing history of certain watering holes. These days, pubs brewing their own ale have less cryptic names – The Beer Engine in Newton St Cyres is one of the new wave of own-brew pubs, as is the Snowdonia Parc Brew-pub, which brews beer on the banks of the River Gwyrfai using clear Snowdonia water, and The Flower Pots in Cheriton, Hampshire.

Many of the original brew-pubs ended up closing or being bought out by larger breweries in the 1970s but there has been a resurgence in recent years. In much the same way that food lovers have rediscovered local, seasonal produce through farmers' markets and growing their own vegetables, discerning beer drinkers have embraced the new wave of micro-breweries popping up in independent free houses.

The oldest brew pub is The Blue Anchor Inn at Helston, Cornwall, which has been brewing its own beers for more than 600 years. Originally a monks' rest house which produced a strong honey-based mead, it now brews four 'Spingo' ales to traditional recipes. Their ales are soon to be available across Cornwall.

The return of own-brew pubs

A turning point for the renaissance of own-brew pubs came in the early 1980s with the Firkin pub chain, which started when David Bruce bought a few run-down London pubs from major brewers and turned them into brew pubs. The actual breweries were small and often located beneath or behind the pubs themselves, but many had viewing windows so drinkers could peer in and see the beer being made. The Firkin chain expanded rapidly until it was sold and eventually taken over by drinks giant Allied Domecq, but many beer-lover still have fond memories of the chain's famous Dogbolter – a dark porter which is still made by the award-winning Gadds' Brewery in Ramsgate, Kent. Thankfully, the Firkin's legacy remains and many trained brewers who worked for the chain went on to open their own brew pubs or micro-breweries.

The Beer Engine, Newton St Cyres, Devon

The revival of real ale and an increased interest in beer festivals has been mirrored by the rise in micro-breweries attached to pubs. (There is a list of pubs holding beer festivals on pages 23-25.) For the customer, it often means the opportunity to try ales exclusive to that pub and the fact they are brewed on the premises can often mean a saving of around 35p a pint – a considerable saving when many pubs charge up to £4 for a pint of mass-produced beer.

The Grainstore at Oakham is an award-winning own-brew pub and it goes from strength to strength. Using Maris Otter barley and English 'whole' hops such as Fuggle and Golding, the beers are sold in the adjacent Brewery Tap – recognised as one of the best brew-pubs in Britain. The pub also hosts the annual August Rutland Beer Festival featuring over 70 real ales and ciders.

Another fine example of a thriving own-brew pub is the Marble Arch Inn in Manchester, which is the main outlet for the highly acclaimed Marble Brewery. Many of the beers brewed here are organic and the copper and hot liquor tanks can be seen at the back of the pub via glass viewing windows.

It's this transparency when it comes to brewing that sets own-brew pubs apart from the pubs churning out mass-manufactured identikit beers, according to beer expert Melissa Cole, author of books such as *Taking the Beard Out of Beer* and *Let Me Tell You About Beer*. A member of the British Guild of Beer Writers, Cole says brew pubs are a great way of educating people about the beer-making process.

"With everyone being so much more in touch with where their food and drink comes from these days, a brew pub offers an ideal way for people to actually witness the alchemy of beer being made. It also demonstrates that the landlord has a genuine passion for beer so it means you're virtually guaranteed a good pint."

The John Thompson Inn and Brewery

One of the most established own-brew pubs in Britain is The John Thompson Inn & Brewery in Ingleby. Opened in 1968 when John and Ann Thompson converted their 15th century farmhouse into a public house, it was the first pub in Great Britain to be named after the licensee and owner. The pub's on-site brewery opened in 1977.

Thirty-five years later, The John Thompson is a highly acclaimed own-brew pub with extensive gardens set in idyllic countryside besides the banks of the River Trent. The pub serves four of its beers throughout the year, including the popular JTS, the Rich Porter and the best-selling Gold. At any one time,

there will be two of the pub's own beers on draught, alongside a nationally known brand such as Black Sheep or Timothy Taylor.

Owner Nick Thompson says that opening a brewery in a pub was a brave move in 1977, especially as the pub trade was a very different industry as it is today.

"Back in the 70s, you had ex-policemen taking early retirement to leasehold their local pub, kids used to have to stay in the car with a bottle of lemonade and the only food offering was eggs, whelks and cockles, all pickled from a jar. Back then, keg beers like Double Diamond and Worthington E were massive and the national brewers wanted the move to keg because they saw it as

less wastage and beers that travelled better and had a longer shelf life.

"It looked like the days of cask ales were numbered but then CAMRA (Campaign for Real Ale) set up and a ground swell for real ale started that continues today."

With all this in mind, and the 'error of judgment' of the national brewers in their focus on keg beers, The John Thompson Brewery re-introduced brewing to Derbyshire with an inaugural brew to celebrate the Silver Jubilee of 1977, with JTS XXX – a flagship beer still brewed, uninterrupted, to this day.

Advantages of own-brewing

With the rationalisation of the big brewers in nearby Burton-on-Trent, excellent brewing kit and brewers with committed skills were easy to procure for the Thompson family. Three decades on and the own-brewed beers at The John Thompson account for 50 per cent of all tap sales of beer, lager or cider. Thompson says the advantages of brewing your own beer for a pub are numerous.

"First and foremost is the USP of selling your own beer, although with almost 800 micro-breweries in the UK at present, I guess it is not so unique these days, which is great.

"There is still considerable interest and demand for the individuality of real ale. This has been enforced by the error of the national breweries in the 1970s to focus on the provision on homogenously bland products to be shipped out across the UK from Devon to Dumfries.

"The cost and profit factor of brewing your own is essential and highly beneficial, but the cost of raw ingredients has soared with poor harvests of previous years. The financial benefits are only evident if your production skills are

> ❝We're also getting back in contact with our beery roots again; after all it is our national drink❞

constant, the end product exceptional and your pub sales sufficient."

Thompson sees own-brew pubs and micro-breweries as a continuing trend, as more and more new ones open.

"There has been an exponential growth in the number of micro-breweries in recent times. I believe this can be chiefly associated with the change in duty and tax rates and PBD (progressive beer duty). Prior to 2003, beer duty was uniform across the board regardless of barrelage. Then duty decreased with the PBD for smaller breweries – even encompassing some regionals.

"This resulted in serious cost savings and was a significant turning point. People in the trade have now witnessed the financial benefits of brewing your own and more have seized on the opportunity of setting up their own grassroots production."

A growing trend

Beer writer Melissa Cole agrees that the own-brew revolution is a growing trend.

"As a country we're also getting back in contact with our beery roots again; after all it is our national drink. A lot of this, ironically, is from what people have seen in the USA and I think you'll see a lot more brew-pubs springing up all over the place, which is fantastic in my book.

"It's amazing how few people know how beer is actually made so brew pubs also have the opportunity to educate their customers. There's also the fact that a brewery in a pub just looks damn cool!"

Top left: Marble Arch Inn, Manchester

Above: The Old Inn, Gairloch, Highland

Opposite: The Black Sheep Brewery, Masham, North Yorkshire

Summer P

Above: The Bush, Ovington,
Hampshire

By CARINA SIMON

*If there's one thing that heralds the start of summer
along with that first strawberry or the first time you
leave the house without a jacket, it's welcoming in
the season with a cool drink outside your pub of*

grub all make your handcrafted ale or G&T taste even better. Here are some of our top suggestions to get your summer off to a flying start.

In the city

If you're heading for a pub in a city, be it to unwind at the end of a busy working day or if you're sightseeing, finding a pub with a lovely alfresco area is a bit of a treat, not least because it's a less common proposition than in the countryside. Portobello Gold in the heart of Notting Hill has a decidedly kitsch conservatory with a sliding glass roof and a tropical feel thanks to lots of plants. It's the perfect place to escape the hustle and bustle of the outside market and enjoy some Mediterranean grub. Also in West London, The Waterway is a smart pub in the aptly dubbed Little Venice area of Maida Vale. Everyone from trendy young things to relaxed families covets a place so its outdoor seating area with parasols to keep the sun at bay is always teaming. Set on the leafy canalside, it's an idyllic spot to watch the boats go by and is a great pit stop for those who want to follow the canal down to Camden Lock or Regent's Park. There are even central London pubs that have created small oases of calm. For instance, Westminster's traditional style Sherlock Holmes, packed with memorabilia, benefits from an intimate, covered roof garden - a lovely place to peruse the menu of themed dishes (The Illustrious Client, anyone?)

In the countryside

If you're out in the countryside it stands to reason you want to make the most of it, so why not combine fantastic views with some good food and drink? The family-friendly Sun in the Wood

in Berkshire's pretty Ashmore Green is nestled in the heart of the countryside surrounded by mature trees and woodland. Take a seat under a parasol on the decked terrace and soak up the view, enhanced by pots of flowers and lighting. Eating alfreso from the crowd-pleasing menu of pub classics is an attractive option here, be it in the large woodside garden or small child-free area. There's even a nine-hole woodland crazy golf pitch to help work up a thirst. Elsewhere in Berkshire, The Royal Oak Hotel in Yattendon has French windows leading to a walled garden with stylish outdoor furniture, a vine-laden trellis and a boules piste.

If there were a competition for the best alfresco pub views The Pheasant Inn in Higher Burwardsley would certainly be a front-runner. It benefits from a position nestled in the Peckforton Hills. A favourite with ramblers, it's a romantic place to enjoy the spectacular panoramic hill views. Also pretty special is the self-proclaimed 'best room in the house' at The Fox Goes Free in Charlton, West Sussex, that is the garden complete with apple trees and stunning views of the South Downs. If it's an English summer, there's heating under large umbrellas for cooler evenings and it's worth getting there early as there are no bookings for the outside area, it's strictly first come first served.

Meanwhile, at the heart of the Yorkshire Dales, The White Lion Inn in Cray commands great views thanks to its status as the highest pub in Wharfedale. Walkers heading to Buckden Pike often use this as a base and the garden, with its views of Cray Gill waterfall, is a lovely way to take in the views over a plate of good honest pub grub, which makes the most of local ingredients. Children have

Just as what you are drinking is likely to be a bit more sophisticated than it might have been a decade ago, recently pubs have been making more of their outside areas, which is great news for alfresco drinkers. Be it in space-poor cities or chocolate box villages, picturesque views, added entertainment and some great

their own menu. Also in the Dales, the 17th century former coaching inn The George and Dragon in Aysgarth boasts a lovely patio decorated with flowers and with great views of Pen Hill when the weather is clement. After exploring Wensleydale, treat yourself to a local ale from the Black Sheep Brewery or Yorkshire Dales Brewing Company and a plate of simple food from the crowd-pleasing menu.

By the water

There's something extremely calming about pulling up a chair by the water. The charming 13th century Pandora Inn in Mylor Bridge, Cornwall is also great for getting into the holiday spirit. Not only can you eat outside at the water's edge but there's even a pontoon for those who want to dine on the water itself. Another must in Cornwall is the Rashleigh Inn on the beach in Polkerris. Watch others sailing, surfing, rock pooling or playing on the golden sand from a table on the sunny multi-levelled terrace. Come evening, watch the sunset over the beach while digging into some hearty local fare.

There aren't many pubs in the UK where you might catch a glimpse of seals and otters from the garden but at Shieldaig Bar & Coastal Kitchen it's a distinct possibility. Take a seat in the courtyard beside Loch Shieldaig and enjoy some tempting local seafood while drinking in the view as well

Top left: Brackenrigg Inn,
Watermillock, Cumbria
Centre left: The Fox Goes Free,
Charlton, West Sussex
Left: Old Hall Inn, Chinley, Derbyshire
Right top: Steam Packet Inn,
Totnes, Devon
Right: Shieldaig Bar & Coastal Kitchen,
Shieldaig, Highland

> *There's something extremely calming about pulling up a chair by the water*

s a beer from the Black Isle or Isle of Skye breweries.

Meanwhile, it'd be a shame to go or something to eat and drink in the Lake District and not be able to see the main attractions. At Brackenrigg Inn in Watermillock, an elevated terrace and pretty gardens allow for superb views over Ullswater. For a different watery view, try Totnes in Devon for the family-owned Steam Packet Inn on the River Dart. Watch people fishing and boats sail

Above: Bear of Rodborough Hotel, Stroud, Gloucestershire

Right top: The Middle House, Mayfield, East Sussex

Right: Crown Inn at Pishill, Oxfordshire

If you can't choose between sea views or green and pleasant countryside, The Smugglers in Blue Anchor, Somerset is set between both. Sup a glass of Smugglers Otter – a beer produced specifically for the venue by local Otter Brewery - while looking out over the Exmoor Hills or the sea. Kids are well catered for with not just healthy meals but also a bouncy castle in the garden and a farm nearby so they can wave to the animals as they bounce and you relax.

Beautiful gardens

There are also plenty of pubs where eating and drinking outdoors becomes a bit of a treat because the outside space has been given lots of TLC with flowers and other little touches. The Swan Inn in Milton Keynes is a haven of tranquility thanks to its lovely orchard garden. A smart decked area, superb for alfresco eating leads out onto the lawn where tables are more rustic, lanterns hang from the trees and quirky sofas with cushions add to the relaxed vibe.

Picture postcard Chipping Campden in the Cotswolds is home to the 14th century traditional pub Eight Bells. The terraced garden overlooks almshouses and St James Church and was actually built to house the stonemasons as they built it. Heading south, Stroud's Bear of Rodborough Hotel enjoys lovely gardens

❝ *Eating and drinking outdoors becomes a bit of a treat because the outside space has been given lots of TLC* ❞

Drinking and dining alfresco

The Fox at Willian in Hertfordshire is a true locals pub and restaurant serving a decent selection of local ales with a sun terrace overlooking the village pond and a popular large garden. A lovely place to enjoy some impressive modern British food. It's easy to see why the Crown Inn at Pishill in Oxfordshire is such a hit with wedding parties. The 15th century coaching inn has a picturesque beer garden in which to admire the traditional build of the inn and adjacent thatched barn.

The Bat & Ball Freehouse in Farnham, Surrey, has plenty of interest inside with cricket memorabilia and oak beams. In the summer months eat or drink on the patio or garden where there's a children's play area and a vine-clad pergola overlooking the Bourne Stream. The patio is also the venue for the annual beer, cider and music festival.

Finally in Wales, Pant-yr-Ochain in Gresford, Wrexham, dates from the 1530s, complete with wattle and daub walls in the snug. Step outside into the award-winning gardens overlooking a lake, then relax and enjoy a meal or glass of Snowdonia Purple Moose or Taffy Apples cider. At the Caesars Arms in Cardiff, local Welsh produce rules. The farm shop is worth a visit for organic vegetables from

the gardens, honey from the beehives, smoked goods from the on-site smokery and a great selection of free-range meat and select wines and champagnes. After browsing, head for the heated dining terrace overlooking the vast gardens for some local seafood, delivered twice daily, or perhaps some Welsh Black beef and feel virtuous about the lack of air miles in your food while reveling in the view.

Why not spend less and relax more on UK breaks?

cottages4you
property ref: GRL

Make AA Travel your first destination and you're on the way to a more relaxing short break or holiday.

AA Members and customers can get great deals on accommodation, from B&Bs to farmhouses, inns and hotels.

You can also save up to 10% at cottages4you, enjoy a 5% discount with Hoseasons, and up to 60% off the very best West End shows.

Thinking of going further afield?

Check out our attractive discounts on car hire, airport parking, ferry bookings, travel insurance and much more.

Then simply relax.

These are just some of our well-known partners:

Visit theAA.com/travel

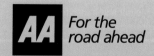

Beer festivals, or their equivalent, are as old as the hills. The brewing of hops goes back to the beginning of human civilisation, and the combination of common crop and a fermenting process that results in alcoholic liquid has long been a cause of celebration. Beer festivals officially began in Germany with the first Munich Oktoberfest in 1810. Wherever in the world beer is brewed, today and for the last few millennia, admirers, enthusiasts, aficionados – call them what you will – have gathered together to sample and praise its unique properties. It happens throughout Europe, in Australia and New Zealand, and in America and Canada, and annual events are held in pubs all over Britain.

Beer festivals are often occasions for the whole family, when entertainment is laid on for children as well as adults. Summer is naturally a popular season for festivals, when the action can be taken outdoors. Other festivals are held in October, traditionally harvest time, but they can be at any time of the year. Beer festivals are sometimes large and well advertised gatherings that attract a wide following for sometimes several days of unselfconscious consumption of unusual or award-winning ales; or they might be local but none the less enthusiastic get-togethers of neighbourhood or pub micro-breweries.

We list here the pubs that appear in this guide, who have told us they hold annual beer festivals.

For up-to-date information, please check directly with the pub.

We would love to hear from our readers about their favourite beer festivals. E-mail us at lifestyleguides@theAA.com

ENGLAND

BEDFORDSHIRE
The Globe Inn
LINSLADE, 01525 373338
The Bell
ODELL, 01234 720254 –
Summer

BERKSHIRE
Bird In Hand Country Inn
KNOWL HILL, 01628 826622
Jun & Nov
The Flowing Spring
READING, 0118 969 9878
Summer
The Bell
WALTHAM ST LAWRENCE
0118 934 1788
Annual - 30 Real Ales, 10 Ciders
The Broad Street Tavern
WOKINGHAM 0118 977 3706
4 per year

BRISTOL
The Albion
BRISTOL, 0117 973 3522
Annual beer and cider

BUCKINGHAMSHIRE
Hit or Miss Inn
AMERSHAM, 01494 713109
Middle wknd Jul
The King's Head
AYLESBURY, 01296 718812
2 per year
The Swan
CHESHAM, 01494 783075
May & Aug BHS
The Unicorn
CUBLINGTON, 01296 681261
May & Aug BHs
The Falcon Inn
DENHAM, 01895 832125
The Palmer Arms
DORNEY, 01628 666612
29-31 Jul
The White Horse
HEDGERLEY, 01753 643225
3 per year Easter, end of May BH & Aug BH
The Whip Inn
LACEY GREEN, 01844 344060
May & Sept
The Derehams Inn
LOUDWATER, 01494 530965
Annual
The White Hart
PRESTON BISSETT,
01280 847969
Spring BH
The Jolly Cricketers
SEER GREEN, 01494 676308
2 per year
The Chequers Inn
WHEELER END, 01494 883070
Whitsun BH

CAMBRIDGESHIRE
Cambridge Blue
CAMBRIDGE, 01223 471680
Feb, Jun, Oct
The Crown Inn
ELTON, 01832 280232
Summer
The Rupert Brooke
GRANTCHESTER, 01223 840295
The Cock Pub and Restaurant
HEMINGFORD GREY
01480 463609
Aug BH wknd
Red Lion
HISTON, 01223 564437
At Easter & 1st wk Sept
Pheasant Inn
KEYSTON, 01832 710241
Aug BH
The Horseshoe
OFFORD D'ARCY, 01480 810293
Mid-summer (on local green)
The White Hart
UFFORD, 01780 740250

CHESHIRE
The Bhurtpore Inn
ASTON, 01270 780917
Old Harkers Arms
CHESTER, 01244 344525
Early Feb
Swan Inn
KETTLESHULME, 01663 732943
1st wknd Sept
The Ship Hotel
PARKGATE, 0151 336 3931
April
The Bull
SHOCKLACH, 01829 250239
Easter wknd
The Bunbury Arms
STOAK, 01244 301665

CO DURHAM
The Morritt Arms Hotel
BARNARD CASTLE
01833 627232
Ship Inn
MIDDLESTONE, 01388 810904
May & Nov
The Stables Pub and Restaurant
STANLEY, 01207 288750
3rd wknd in Sept

CORNWALL & ISLES OF SCILLY
The Blisland Inn
BLISLAND, 01208 850739
May
Manor House Inn
CALLINGTON, 01579 362354
1st wknd Jul
The Smugglers' Den Inn
CUBERT, 01637 830209
May Day BH wknd
Godolphin Arms
MARAZION, 01736 710202

The Plume of Feathers
MITCHELL, 01872 510387
May
The Bush Inn
MORWENSTOW, 01288 331242
Old Mill House Inn
POLPERRO, 01503 272362
1st wknd in Oct
Driftwood Spars
ST AGNES, 01872 552428
Mini beer festival
The New Inn
TRESCO, 01720 422844
Mid May & early Sept

CUMBRIA
The Boot Inn
BOOT, 01467 23224
1st or 2nd wknd Jun
Brook House Inn
BOOT, 01467 23288
7-10 Jun
Hare & Hounds Country Inn
BOWLAND BRIDGE
015395 68333
Blacksmiths Arms
BROUGHTON-IN-FURNESS
01229 716824
1st wknd Oct
The Britannia Inn
ELTERWATER, 015394 37210
2 wks mid Nov
Three Shires Inn
LITTLE LANGDALE
015394 37215
May
The Wheatsheaf Inn
LOW LORTON, 01900 85199 &
85268 End Mar
Kirkstile Inn
LOWESWATER, 01900 85219
Newfield Inn
SEATHWAITE, 01229 716208
Oct
The Strickland Arms
SIZERGH, 015395 61010
Farmers Arms
ULVERSTON, 01229 584469
Wasdale Head Inn
WASDALE HEAD, 01947 26229
1st Sun Oct

DERBYSHIRE
Old Poets Corner
ASHOVER, 01246 590888
Mar & Oct, Thu-Sun
Rowley's
BASLOW, 01246 583880
Thornbridge Brewery annual beer and food evening
Red Lion Inn
BIRCHOVER, 01629 650363
Mid Jun
Old Hall Inn
CHINLEY, 01663 750529
3rd wknd Sept, 4th wknd Feb
The Alexandra Hotel
DERBY, 01332 293993
Annual

The Brunswick Inn
DERBY, 01332 290677
1st wknd Oct
Miners Arms
EYAM, 01433 630853
3 per year
Bentley Brook Inn
FENNY BENTLEY, 01335 350278
Annual - May
The Mill Wheel
HARTSHORNE, 01283 550335
The Royal Hotel
HAYFIELD, 01663 742721
1st wknd Oct
The Old Crown Inn
SHARDLOW, 01332 792392
Apr & Oct

DEVON
The Quarrymans Rest
BAMPTON, 01398 331480
May BH
The Fountain Head
RANSCOMBE, 01297 680359
Mid Jun
The Masons Arms
BRANSCOMBE, 01297 680300
15-17 Jul
Dartbridge Inn
BUCKFASTLEIGH, 01364 642214
Annual
Red Lion Hotel
CLOVELLY, 01237 431237
Late May BH
The Royal Oak Inn
MEAVY, 01822 852944
Cider fest, Aug BH. Cider & Beer fest, mid Nov. Real Ale 3rd wknd of June
The White Hart Hotel
MORETONHAMPSTEAD
01647 441340 Aug
The Wild Goose Inn
NEWTON ABBOT, 01626 872241
Early May BH wknd
The Blacksmiths Arms
PLYMTREE, 01884 277474
Biannual Jul
The Tower Inn
SLAPTON, 01548 580216
Steam Packet Inn
TOTNES, 01803 863880
Mid May (4 days)

DORSET
Stapleton Arms
BUCKHORN WESTON,
01963 370396
The Acorn Inn
EVERSHOT, 01935 83228
Cider & Beer festival
The Drovers Inn
GUSSAGE ALL SAINTS
01258 840084 Easter
The Hambro Arms
MILTON ABBAS,
01258 880233 Jul

The Three Elms
NORTH WOOTTON, 01935 812881
Summer
The Bankes Arms Hotel
STUDLAND 01929 450225
Annual
The Castle Inn
WEST LULWORTH,
01929 400311 Annual
The Ship Inn
WEST STOUR, 01747 838640
Annually with 20 ales and cider
The Square and Compass
WORTH MATRAVERS, 01929 439229
Beer & Pumpkin Festival 1st Sat Oct

ESSEX
The Bell Inn
CASTLE HEDINGHAM, 01787 460350
3rd wknd in Jul. Winter and Easter
The Chequers Inn
GOLDHANGER, 01621 788203
Mar & Sept
The Ducane
GREAT BRAXTED, 01621 891697
The White Hart Inn
MARGARETTING TYE, 01277 840478
Jul & Nov
The Duck Pub & Dining
NEWNEY GREEN, 01245 421894
Aug BH
The Hoop
STOCK, 01277 841137 Late May BH
Hurdlemakers Arms
WOODHAM MORTIMER
01245 225169 Last wknd Jun

GLOUCESTERSHIRE
The Gardeners Arms
ALDERTON, 01242 620257
Spring BH & Boxing Day
(both last 5 days)
The Royal Oak Inn
ANDOVERSFORD, 01242 820335
Summer
Catherine Wheel
BIBURY, 01285 740250
Aug BH
Craven Arms Inn
BROCKHAMPTON, 01242 820410
Sat & Sun Aug BH wknd
The Royal Oak Inn
CHELTENHAM, 01242 522344
Spring BH Beer festival, August BH
Cider festival
The Gloucester Old Spot
CHELTENHAM, 01242 680321
May Day BH
The Yew Tree
CLIFFORD'S MESNE,
01531 820719 Oct
The Tunnel House Inn
COATES, 01285 770280 29-31 Jul
The Old Spot Inn
DURSLEY, 01453 542870
3 times a year
The Trout Inn
LECHLADE ON THAMES
01367 252313 Jun

The George Inn
STONEHOUSE, 01453 822302
Aug BH

GREATER LONDON
The Five Bells
CHELSFIELD, 01689 821044
Easter & Oct

GREATER MANCHESTER
Marble Arch
MANCHESTER, 0161 832 5914
The Nursery Inn
STOCKPORT, 0161 432 2044
3 times a year
The Lord Raglan
BURY, 0161 764 6680
Summer & autumn

HAMPSHIRE
The Drift Inn
BEAULIEU, 023 8029 2342
The Three Tuns Country Inn
BRANSGORE, 01425 672232
Sept
The Red Lion
CHALTON, 023 9259 2246
End Jul beg Aug
The Flower Pots Inn
CHERITON, 01962 771318
Turfcutters Arms
EAST BOLDRE, 01590 612331
The Shoe Inn
EXTON, 01489 877526 Annual
The Hawkley Inn
HAWKLEY, 01730 827205
10-12 Jun
The Kings Head
HURSLEY, 01962 775208
2 per year - Aug BH & Dec
New Forest Inn
LYNDHURST, 023 8028 4690
2nd wknd Jul
The Red Lion
MORTIMER WEST END
0118 970 0169 3-4 Sept
The Fox
NORTH WALTHAM, 01256 397288
Late Apr
The White Horse Inn
PETERSFIELD, 01420 588387 Jun
The Fleur de Lys
PILLEY, 01590 672158 Jul
The Alice Lisle
ROCKFORD, 01425 474700
Three times a year in the summer
The Dukes Head
ROMSEY, 01794 514450 May & Sept
The Selborne Arms
SELBORNE, 01420 511247
1st wknd Oct
The Tichborne Arms
TICHBORNE, 01962 733760
3rd wknd Aug

HEREFORDSHIRE
England's Gate Inn
BODENHAM, 01568 797286 Jul
Live and Let Live
BRINGSTY, COMMON 01886 821462
Easter wknd

The New Harp Inn
HOARWITHY, 01432 840900 BH
The Grape Vaults
LEOMINSTER, 01568 611404
2nd Sat in Dec
The Crown Inn
WOOLHOPE, 01432 860468
May Day BH

HERTFORDSHIRE
The Valiant Trooper
ALDBURY, 01442 851203
The Fox & Hounds
BARLEY, 01763 849400
Every BH wknd
The Old Mill
BERKHAMSTED, 01442 879590
The Land of Liberty, Peace
and Plenty
HERONSGATE, 01923 282226
Winter ales, Easter, Aug BH
The Radcliffe Arms
HITCHIN, 01462 456111
2-3 per year
The Fox
WILLIAN, 01462 480233
Guinness & Oyster Festival Mar

ISLE OF WIGHT
Horse & Groom
NINGWOOD, 01983 760672 Sept
The Chequers
ROOKLEY, 01983 840314
Ryde Castle
RYDE, 01983 563755

KENT
The Red Lion
CANTERBURY, 01227 721339
Aug BH wknd
The Bowl Inn
CHARING, 01233 712256 Mid Jul
The White Horse
CHILHAM, 01227 730355 Summer
Rose & Crown
HALSTEAD, 01959 533120
Spring, Summer & Autumn
The Mundy Bois
PLUCKLEY, 01233 840048 Apr/May
The Bull
ROLVENDEN, 01580 241212
The Chequers Inn
SMARDEN, 01233 770217
The Coastguard
ST MARGARET'S BAY, 01304 853176
Historic Food Festival Sept

LANCASHIRE
Owd Nell's Tavern
BILSBORROW, 01995 640010
Oyster Festival 1st wk Sept;
Oktoberfest last wk Oct; Cider
Festival last wk Jul
The Sun Hotel and Bar
LANCASTER, 01524 66006
Summer festival
The Waterwitch
LANCASTER, 01524 63828 Seasonal
The Eagle & Child
PARBOLD, 01257 462297
1st May BH

The Royal Arms
TOCKHOLES, 01254 705373 Summer

LEICESTERSHIRE
The Swan in the Rushes
LOUGHBOROUGH, 01509 217014
End of May & mid Nov
Cow and Plough
OADBY, 0116 272 0852 Quarterly

LINCOLNSHIRE
The Jolly Miller
BRIGG, 01652 655658 Aug
The Victoria
LINCOLN, 01522 541000
Halloween & Winter
The Willoughby Arms
LITTLE BYTHAM, 01780 410276
Aug BH

LONDON
POSTAL DISTRICTS
The Peasant
LONDON EC1, 020 7336 7726
Spring & Autumn
Ye Olde Mitre
LONDON EC1, 020 7405 4751
May & Dec
The Charles Lamb
LONDON N1, 020 7837 5040
Spring BH (end May)
The Drapers Arms
LONDON N1, 020 7619 0348 Aug
The Queens
LONDON NW1, 020 7586 0408
During British Food Fortnight
The Prince Albert
LONDON NW1, 020 7485 0270
3 day Festival held 2-3 times a year
The Holly Bush
LONDON NW3, 020 7435 2892
The Junction Tavern
LONDON NW5, 020 7485 9400
2-3 per year & mini festivals
William IV Bar & Restaurant
LONDON NW10, 020 8969 5944
The White Horse
LONDON SW6, 020 7736 2115
4 per year.
The Alma Tavern
LONDON SW18, 020 8870 2537
Annual Youngs Mini Festival
The George
LONDON WC2, 020 7353 9638
March Real ale & Cider

NORFOLK
Chequers Inn
BINHAM, 01328 830297 4 per year
The Jolly Sailors
BRANCASTER STAITHE
01485 210314 10-12 Jun
The Brisley Bell Inn & Restaurant
BRISLEY, 01362 668686
The Crown
BURSTON, 01379 741257
2-3 per year
The Red Lion Food and Rooms
CROMER, 01263 514964
Annual - Autumn

Earle Arms
HEYDON, 01263 587376
St George's Day
The Hunny Bell
HUNWORTH, 01263 712300
Throughout Sept
The Stuart House Hotel, Bar &
Restaurant
KING'S LYNN, 01553 772169
Angel Inn
LARLING, 01953 717963 Early Aug
The Mad Moose Arms
NORWICH, 01603 627687 May & Oct
The Parson Woodforde
WESTON LONGVILLE, 01603 881675
Sept
Fishermans Return
WINTERTON-ON-SEA, 01493 393305
Aug BH

NORTHAMPTONSHIRE
The White Swan
HARRINGWORTH, 01572 747543
Welland Valley Beer Festival
The George
KILSBY, 01788 822229
St George's Day wknd
The Fox & Hounds
nr NORTHAMPTON, 01604 770651
The Chequered Skipper
OUNDLE, 01832 273494
The Great Western Arms
AYNHO, 01869 338288
1st wknd in Oct

NORTHUMBERLAND
The Lord Crewe Arms
BLANCHLAND, 01434 675251 Aug
The Feathers Inn
HEDLEY ON THE HILL, 01661 843607
Easter
Miners Arms Inn
HEXHAM, 01434 603909
The Bamburgh Castle Inn
SEAHOUSES, 01665 720283 Annual

NOTTINGHAMSHIRE
Victoria Hotel
BEESTON, 0115 925 4049
End Jan; Easter; last 2 wks July, Oct
The Dovecote Inn
LAXTON, 01777 871586
Last wknd Aug
Ye Olde Trip to Jerusalem
NOTTINGHAM, 0115 947 3171
2-3 per year

OXFORDSHIRE
The Elephant & Castle
BLOXHAM, 0845 873 7358 May
(part of Bloxfest Music Festival)
The Red Lion
BRIGHTWELL-CUM-SOTWELL
01491 837373 Beer & Live Music -
2 days in Summer
Horse & Groom
CAULCOTT, 01869 343257 Mid July
Fleur De Lys
DORCHESTER (ON THAMES)
01865 340502

The Woodman Inn
FERNHAM, 01367 820643 Annual
The Butchers Arms
FRINGFORD, 01869 277363 Jun
The White Hart
FYFIELD, 01865 390585
Early May BH & Aug BH
The Plough Inn
KELMSCOTT, 01367 253543
The Lamb at Satwell
HENLEY-ON-THAMES, 01491 628482
Autumn 2011
Plough Inn
WEST HANNEY, 01235 868674
May BH & Aug BH
The Three Horseshoes
WITNEY, 01993 703086
Annual - Aug BH

RUTLAND
Old White Hart
LYDDINGTON, 01572 821703
Summer
The Jackson Stops Country Inn
STRETTON, 01780 410237

SHROPSHIRE
The New Inn
BASCHURCH, 01939 260335
Annual - see website
The Three Tuns Inn
BISHOP'S CASTLE, 01588 638797
2nd wknd Jul involving all pubs
in town
The White Horse Inn
CLUN, 01588 640305 1st wknd Oct
The Sun Inn
CRAVEN ARMS, 01584 861239
The Ragleth Inn
LITTLE STRETTON, 01694 722711
1st wknd Jul
Fighting Cocks
STOTTESDON, 01746 718270

SOMERSET
The Globe Inn
APPLEY, 01823 672327
1st wknd Sept
The Star Inn
BATH, 01225 425072
2 annual Cornish beer festivals
The George Inn
CROSCOMBE, 01749 342306
Spring BH wknd
Ilchester Arms
ILCHESTER, 01935 840220
The Oakhill Inn
OAKHILL, 01749 840442 2 per year
Duke of York
SHEPTON BEAUCHAMP
01460 240314 Sept
The Hatch Inn
TAUNTON, 01823 480245 Jul
The Crown and Victoria Inn
TINTINHULL, 01935 823341
Crossways Inn
WEST HUNTSPILL, 01278 783756
Aug BH
The Rest and Be Thankful Inn
WHEDDON CROSS 01643 841222
2nd wknd Sept

STAFFORDSHIRE
Burton Bridge Inn
BURTON UPON TRENT
01283 536596 2 per year
Oddfellows in the Boat
SUMMERHILL, 01543 361692
The Hand & Trumpet
WRINEHILL, 01270 820048
Last wk in Jan

SUFFOLK
The Station Hotel
FRAMLINGHAM, 01728 723455
Mid Jul
The Kings Head (The Low House)
LAXFIELD, 01986 798395 May & Sept
The Lindsey Rose
LINDSEY TYE, 01449 741424
3 days in summer
Anchor Inn
NAYLAND, 01206 262313
Fathers Day, Octoberfest
The Rose & Crown
STANTON 01359 250236
The Anchor
WALBERSWICK, 01502 722112
Mid Aug

SURREY
The Jolly Farmers Deli Pub
& Restaurant
BUCKLAND, 01737 221355 Annual
The Sun
CARSHALTON, 020 8773 4549
Jun & Nov
The Bat & Ball Freehouse
FARNHAM, 01252 792108
2nd wknd June
The Bell
FETCHAM, 01372 372624
Cask Ale Festival in Autumn
The Keystone
GUILDFORD, 01483 575089
Cider Festival 21-24 July
The Surrey Oaks
NEWDIGATE, 01306 631200
Late May BH & Aug BH

SUSSEX, EAST
The Greys
BRIGHTON, 01273 680734
Aug BH
The Merrie Harriers
COWBEECH, 01323 833108
Aug BH
The Queen's Head
ICKLESHAM, 01424 814552
1st wknd Oct

SUSSEX, WEST
Duke of Cumberland Arms
HENLEY, 01428 652280 Dukefest
The Dog and Duck
KINGSFOLD, 01306 627295
Mid Jun.
The Lamb Inn
LAMBS GREEN, 01293 871336 Oct
The Gribble Inn
OVING, 01243 786893
Summer & winter

The Royal Oak
WINEHAM, 01444 881252
The Windmill Inn
LINTON, 01937 582209 Jul

WARWICKSHIRE
The Holly Bush
ALCESTER, 01789 762482 Jun & Oct
The Castle Inn
EDGEHILL, 01295 670255
The Red Lion, Hunningham
HUNNINGHAM, 01926 632715
The Red Lion Film & Beer Festival
Aug BH
The Almanack
KENILWORTH, 01926 353637
The Duck on the Pond
LONG ITCHINGTON. 01926 815876
1st May BH
White Bear Hotel
SHIPSTON ON STOUR, 01608 661558
Easter

WEST MIDLANDS
The Old Joint Stock
BIRMINGHAM 0121 200 1892
2 per year

WILTSHIRE
The Blue Boar
ALDBOURNE, 01672 540237
2 per year - Apr & Oct
The Quarrymans Arms
BOX, 01225 743569 Mini ale weeks
The Queens Head Inn
BROAD CHALKE, 01722 780344
Summer
Red Lion Inn
LACOCK, 01249 730456
The Smoking Dog
MALMESBURY, 01666 825823
Spring BH
The Malet Arms
NEWTON TONEY, 01980 629279 Jul
Old Mill
SALISBURY, 01722 327517
During Oct
The Somerset Arms
SEMINGTON, 01380 870067 May BH
The Cross Keys Inn
UPPER CHUTE, 01264 730295
2nd wknd Aug
Prince Leopold Inn
UPTON LOVELL, 01985 850460
The George Inn
LONGBRIDGE DEVERELL
01985 840396 Mid Aug
The Bridge Inn
WEST LAVINGTON, 01380 813213
Last Sun Aug

WORCESTERSHIRE
The Beckford
BECKFORD, 01386 881532 Summer
The Mug House Inn & Angry Chef
Restaurant
BEWDLEY, 01299 402543
May Day BH wknd
The Fleece Inn
BRETFORTON, 01386 831173
Mid-late Oct

The Talbot
KNIGHTWICK, 01886 821235
2nd wknd Oct
Nags Head
MALVERN, 01684 574373
St George's Day

YORKSHIRE,
EAST RIDING OF
The Old Star Inn
KILHAM, 01262 420619
Last wknd Sept

YORKSHIRE, NORTH
The Craven Arms
APPLETREEWICK, 01756 720270
Oct, 25+ beers
Ye Old Sun Inn
COLTON, 01904 744261 Summer
The New Inn
CROPTON, 01751 417330 Nov
The Bay Horse Inn
GREEN HAMMERTON
01423 330338 April
The Forresters Arms Inn
KILBURN 01347 868386
St George's Day
The Tennant Arms
KILNSEY, 01756 752301
North v South Easter 2011
The Shoulder of Mutton Inn
KIRBY HILL, 01748 822772
George & Dragon Hotel
KIRKBYMOORSIDE, 01751 433334
The George at Wath
RIPON, 01765 641324 BH

YORKSHIRE, SOUTH
Kelham Island Tavern
SHEFFIELD, 0114 272 2482
Mid summer

SCOTLAND

CITY OF DUNDEE
The Royal Arch Bar
BROUGHTY FERRY, 01382 779741
1st wknd Oct

CITY OF EDINBURGH
The Bow Bar
EDINBURGH, 0131 226 7667
End Jan & end Jul, 10 days each
The Bridge Inn
RATHO, 0131 333 1320

CITY OF GLASGOW
Bon Accord
GLASGOW, 0141 248 4427
4 per year, 90 different beers
and ciders

HIGHLAND
The Anderson
FORTROSE, 01381 620236
Burns Weekend Real Ale Festival in
Jan, Barley Wine Festival Dec-Mar
The Torridon Inn
TORRIDON, 01445 791242 Sept

NORTH LANARKSHIRE
Castlecary House Hotel CASTLECARY
01324 840233 TBA. Once or twice
a year, over a wknd

PERTH & KINROSS
Meikleour Hotel
MEIKLEOUR, 01250 883206
Last Sun in May

RENFREWSHIRE
Fox & Hounds
HOUSTON, 01505 612448
May & August

STIRLING
The Lade Inn
CALLANDER, 01877 330152
Aug-mid Sept

WEST LOTHIAN
The Four Marys
LINLITHGOW, 01506 842171
Last wknd in May & Oct

WALES

GWYNEDD
Snowdonia Parc Brewpub
& Campsite
WAUNFAWR, 01286 650409
Usually mid-May.

MONMOUTHSHIRE
Clytha Arms
ABERGAVENNY, 01873 840206
Whitsun BH, Aug BH
Goose and Cuckoo Inn
ABERGAVENNY, 01873 880277
End of May & end of Aug
Fountain Inn
TINTERN, 01291 689303
Easter & Sept
The Lion Inn
TRELLECH, 01600 860322
Jun & Nov

POWYS
The Coach & Horses
LLANGYNIDR, 01874 730245 Jul
The Harp
OLD RADNOR, 01544 350655 Jun
Star Inn
TALYBONT-ON-USK, 01874 676635
Mid Jun & mid Oct

RHONDDA CYNON TAFF
Bunch of Grapes
PONTYPRIDD 01443 402934
Every 2 months

SWANSEA
Kings Head
LLANGENNITH, 01792 386212
Last wknd of Nov

VALE OF GLAMORGAN
The Cross Inn
COWBRIDGE, 01446 772995
Mini Beer/Cider fest - late Apr
& Sept

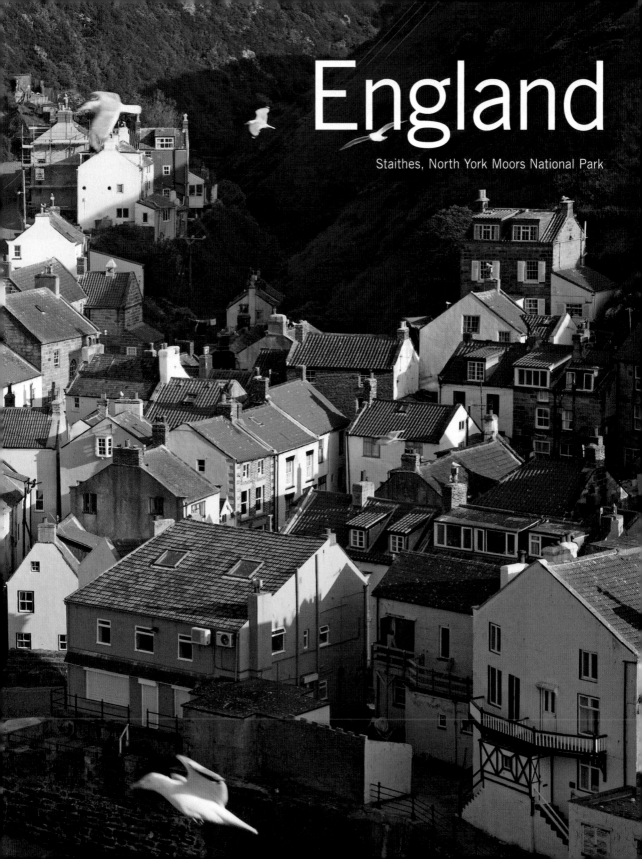

England

Staithes, North York Moors National Park

BEDFORDSHIRE

BEDFORD — Map 12 TL04

The Embankment ♥ NEW

6 The Embankment MK40 3PD ☎ 01234 261332
e-mail: embankment@peachpubs.com
dir: From M1 junct 13, A421 to Bedford. Left onto A6 to town centre. Into left lane on river bridge. Into right lane signed Embankment. Follow around St Paul's Square into High St, into left lane. Left onto The Embankment

Behind an outdoor terrace overlooking the River Great Ouse, this imposing mock-Tudor pub lies at the heart of Bedford's beautifully landscaped Embankment. Dating from 1891, the building has been renovated to create a relaxed, hospitable atmosphere that reflects its late-Victorian heyday. Sea bass with crushed potatoes and prawn butter sauce, and winter vegetable and mixed bean tagine are amongst the main course options on a varied menu that also includes sandwiches and deli boards.

Open all wk 7am-mdnt (Sat 7.30am-mdnt, Sun 7.30am-11pm) Closed: 25 Dec **Bar Meals** L served all wk 12-6 D served all wk 6-9.30 Av main course £10.50 food served all day **Restaurant** L served all wk 12-6 D served all wk 6-9.30 Av 3 course à la carte fr £25 food served all day ⊕ PEACH PUBS ◀ Young's, Eagle IPA, Wells Bombardier Ö Aspall. ♥ 13 **Facilities** Children welcome Children's menu Children's portions Dogs allowed Garden Parking Wi-fi

The Three Tuns ♥

57 Main Rd, Biddenham MK40 4BD ☎ 01234 354847
e-mail: enquiries@threetunsbiddenham.com
dir: On A428 from Bedford towards Northampton 1st left signed Biddenham. Into village, pub on left

In the heart of a beautiful village, this stone-built, thatched and recently refurbished pub has a large garden with a patio and decking, and a separate children's play area. Separating two parts of the garden is a long-disused morgue, the oldest building hereabouts and allegedly haunted. Home-cooked dishes on the regularly changing menus include rack of venison with honeyed parsnip purée; rabbit pasty with tempura langoustines; chargrilled turbot and oxtail with pappardelle; or pie of the day.

Open all day all wk **Bar Meals** L served all wk 12-2.30 D served Mon-Sat 6-9.30 **Restaurant** L served Mon-Sat 12-2.30, Sun 12-4 booking required D served Mon-Sat 6-9.30 booking required ⊕ GREENE KING ◀ Greene King IPA, Guinness, guest ale. **Facilities** Children welcome Children's portions Play area Family room Dogs allowed Garden Parking Wi-fi

BLETSOE — Map 11 TL05

PICK OF THE PUBS

The Falcon

Rushden Rd MK44 1QN
☎ 01234 781222 🖹 01234 781222
e-mail: thefalcona6@aol.com
dir: 9m from M1 junct 13, 3m from Bedford

The 17th-century Falcon stands in rolling downland, beside the River Great Ouse. Before becoming a coaching inn in 1727 it was a mill, and in 1859 Edward FitzGerald translated *The Rubaiyat of Omar Khayyam* here, describing The Falcon as 'The cleanest, the sweetest, the civilest, the quietest, the liveliest and the cheapest that was ever built'. Not one to prevaricate, then. Inside are an inglenook fireplace, beams galore, a splendidly oak-panelled restaurant and a secret tunnel to Bletsoe Castle. In winter, you can enjoy the crackling log fires and in summer there is a large riverside garden and marquee. Small and big appetites are catered for - 'Little Plates' choices include home-made soup of the day; moules marinière; and chicken liver pâté with confit de figues, cornichons and Melba toast. The 'Large Plates' could include creamy winter vegetable gnocchi with leeks, squash, carrots and sweet potato; oven baked monkfish on crushed new potatoes with caperberry and caviar sauce; slow roasted pork belly, colcannon, oven-baked brandied apples and Calvados cream.

Open all day all wk ⊕ CHARLES WELLS ◀ Wells Bombardier, Wells Eagle. **Facilities** Children welcome Children's menu Play area Garden Parking Wi-fi

BOLNHURST — Map 12 TL05

PICK OF THE PUBS

The Plough at Bolnhurst ◉ ♥

Kimbolton Rd MK44 2EX ☎ 01234 376274
e-mail: theplough@bolnhurst.com
dir: On B660 N of Bedford

Tiny windows, thick walls and mellow pitched roof typify this whitewashed Tudor country inn in north Bedfordshire. Low-beamed with great open fires and characterful decor, The Plough's impressive choice of real ales and inspired wine list is matched by a delicious menu prepared by Raymond Blanc-trained Martin Lee and his team of skilful chefs. The menu is driven by the freshest local and regional produce and specialist foods gathered from all corners. The result is an ever-changing choice of unique dishes which have gained The Plough an AA Rosette. Start with spinach ricotta ravioli, poached egg and sage butter sauce before sampling roast saddle of lamb, confit garlic, sautéed potatoes, spinach and thyme; grilled fillet of sea bass, cavolo nero, thyme roast potatoes and chilli, red pepper and coriander sauce; or an old favourite like deep-fried pollack in beer batter, mushy peas, tartare sauce and chips. But do leave room for the cheese board, with its astonishing choice of British, Italian and French varieties on offer.

Open Tue-Sat 12-3 6.30-11 (Sun 12-3) Closed: 1 Jan, 2wks Jan, Mon & Sun eve **Bar Meals** L served Tue-Sun 12-2 booking required D served Tue-Sat 6.30-9.30 booking required Av main course £17.50 **Restaurant** L served Tue-Sun 12-2 booking required D served Tue-Sat 6.30-9.30 booking required Fixed menu price fr £15 Av 3 course à la carte fr £30 ⊕ FREE HOUSE ◀ Adnams Broadside, Nethergate Azzanewt, Batemans XB, Village Bike Potton, Fuller's London Pride. ♥ 13 **Facilities** Children welcome Children's portions Dogs allowed Garden Parking Wi-fi

BROOM — Map 12 TL14

The Cock

23 High St SG18 9NA ☎ 01767 314411 🖹 01767 314284
dir: Off B658 SW of Biggleswade. 1m from A1

Unspoilt to this day with its intimate quarry-tiled rooms with latched doors and panelled walls, this 17th-century establishment is known as 'The Pub with no Bar'. Real ales are served straight from casks racked by the cellar steps. A straightforward pub grub menu includes ham off the bone, eggs and chips; breaded plaice filled with prawns and mushrooms; 3-egg omelettes; beef lasagne; battered fish medley (haddock, plaice, salmon and cod). There is a skittle room for hire and a camping and caravanning site at the rear of the pub.

Open 12-4 6-11 Closed: Sun eve ⊕ GREENE KING ◀ Greene King Abbot Ale, IPA, Ruddles County. **Facilities** Children welcome Children's menu Children's portions Play area Family room Dogs allowed Garden Parking

EATON BRAY — Map 11 SP92

The White Horse ♥

Market Square LU6 2DG
☎ 01525 220231 🖹 01525 222485
e-mail: davidsparrow@onetel.net
web: www.thewhitehorseeatonbray.co.uk
dir: A5 N of Dunstable onto A505, left in 1m, follow signs

Oak beams and horse brasses add to the traditional charms of this 300-year-old village inn. For around 20 years, David and Janet Sparrow have built its reputation on a warm and cosy atmosphere, great home cooked food and well kept real ales. There's a wide ranging menu including comfort food like chargrilled local bangers and mash, steaks with a choice of sauces to accompany and a daily updated specials board that always includes a fresh fish dish. It's worth booking for the restaurant, but the same menu is also available in the bar.

Save on hotels. Book at **theAA.com/hotel**

BEDFORDSHIRE 29 **ENGLAND**

Open all wk Closed: Sun eve Jan-Mar **Bar Meals** L served all wk 12-2.15 D served all wk 7-9.30 Av main course £9.50 **Restaurant** L served all wk 12-2.15 D served all wk 7-9.30 booking required Av 3 course à la carte fr £19.50 ⊕ PUNCH TAVERNS ◀ Greene King IPA, Shepherd Neame Spitfire Ò Aspall. ♥ 10 **Facilities** Children welcome Children's menu Children's portions Play area Family room Garden Parking

PICK OF THE PUBS

The Muntjac

71 High St MK43 7BJ ☎ 01234 721500
e-mail: muntjacharrold@hotmail.co.uk
dir: Telephone for directions

Fine wines and ales and fine Indian cuisine is not how an inn normally sets out its stall, but this 17th-century former coaching inn is quite happy to be a little unorthodox. Independently run Harrold's Indian Cuisine restaurant offers dishes cooked to order to eat in or take away, its extensive menu featuring all the popular fish, meat, poultry and vegetarian dishes, as well as the less often encountered tandoori chicken mossallam, duck Darjeeling, and tawa specialities cooked using a traditional iron plate. A few English dishes are also available. The bar serves Frog Island Best Bitter, Fuller's London Pride, regularly-changing guest ales from local breweries, and real cider from the village Calvados Society. Sports fans will appreciate the large-screen TVs. Members of the pub-sponsored local football team can often be found in the bar on Sunday lunchtimes after their match.

Open all wk Mon-Thu 5.30-11 (Fri 4-mdnt Sat noon-mdnt Sun 12.30-10.30) **Bar Meals** Av main course £12 **Restaurant** D served Mon-Sat 5.30-11, Sun 5.30-10 ⊕ FREE HOUSE ◀ Frog Island, Fuller's London Pride, Guest ales Ò Stowford Press, Harrold Calvados Society. **Facilities** Children welcome Children's portions Dogs allowed Garden Parking **Notes** ⊛

The Black Horse ♥

SG17 5QL ☎ 01462 811398 🖷 01462 817238
e-mail: countrytaverns@aol.com
dir: From S: M1 junct 12, A5120 to Flitwick. Onto A507 by Redbourne School. Follow signs for A1, Shefford (cross A6). Left onto A600 towards Bedford

Homely village-inn looks combine with a bright, airy, chic interior where a comfy mix of light and dark beams, inglenook fire and low ceilings invites you to tarry a little longer. The flower-rich garden and courtyard dining are popular in clement weather. Grab a pint of Adnams, or choose from the excellent wine list, and settle down to appreciate the tempting range of dishes – a starter of seared escalope of smoked salmon, perhaps, followed by cassoulet of duck and pork with cannellini beans.

Open all wk 12-3 6-12 (Sun noon-6pm) Closed: 25-26 Dec, 1 Jan **Bar Meals** L served Mon-Sat 12-2.30, Sun 12-5 booking required D served Mon-Sat 6.30-10 booking required Av main course £10.95 **Restaurant** L served Mon-Sat 12-2.30, Sun 12-5 booking required D served Mon-Sat 6.30-10 booking required Av 3 course à la carte fr £25.95 ⊕ FREE HOUSE ◀ London Pride, Adnams, St Austell Tribute Ò Westons Stowford Press. ♥ 20 **Facilities** Children welcome Children's portions Garden Parking

The Chequers

Pertenhall Rd, Brook End MK44 2HR ☎ 01234 708678
e-mail: chequers.keysoe@tesco.net
dir: On B660, 7m N of Bedford. 3m S of Kimbolton

This peaceful 15th-century country pub has been in the same safe hands for over 25 years. No games machines, pool tables or jukeboxes disturb the simple pleasures of well-kept ales and great home-made food. The menu offers pub stalwarts like ploughman's; home-made steak and ale pie; pan-fried trout, glazed lamb cutlets and a variety of grilled steaks, and a blackboard displays further choice plus the vegetarian options. For a lighter option try the home-made chicken liver pâté or soup, fried Brie with cranberries or plain or toasted sandwiches.

Open Wed-Mon 11.30-2.30 6.30-11 Closed: Mon eve & Tue **Bar Meals** L served all wk 12-2 D served all wk 6.30-9 Av main course £8.50 ⊕ FREE HOUSE ◀ Hook Norton Best, Fuller's London Pride Ò Stowford Press. **Facilities** Children welcome Children's menu Children's portions Play area Family room Garden Parking **Notes** ⊛

The Globe Inn ♥

Globe Ln, Old Linslade LU7 2TA
☎ 01525 373338 🖷 01525 850551
e-mail: 6458@greeneking.co.uk
dir: N of Leighton Buzzard

A very homely old pub, creaking with the character of the small Georgian farmhouse and stables it once was; beams, log fires, partial weatherboarding and a wrinkly roofline. Fronting the Grand Union Canal at the end of a no-through lane, it's a marvellous place to linger watching boating activity, supping on Greene King beers and choosing from a Pandora's Box of meals varying from traditional meaty favourites to engaging new dishes like ham hock and broad bean pie; fish dishes are a speciality. There's a well appointed restaurant, and children are made particularly welcome with a play area in the tree-shaded garden.

Open all day all wk 11-11 (Sun 11-10.30) **Bar Meals** L served all wk 12-10 D served all wk 12-10 food served all day **Restaurant** food served all day ⊕ GREENE KING ◀ Greene King Abbot Ale, Old Speckled Hen Ò Aspall, Suffolk. ♥ 16 **Facilities** Children welcome Children's menu Children's portions Play area Dogs allowed Garden Beer festival Parking

The Crown ♥

2 Ickwell Rd SG18 9AA
☎ 01767 627337 🖷 01767 626107
e-mail: victoria@doughtysbrasserie.com
dir: Next to church & village green

Adrian and Victoria Doughty took over this delightful 16th-century pub in 2010 and have given the place a total refurbishment and a new feel. Although locals can still enjoy a pint of Abbot Ale, the new Doughty's Brasserie is attracting those tempted by dishes such as seared fillet of hake, mash, green beans, clams and smoked bacon broth or home-made beef burger and hand cut chips. The garden has plenty of tables for alfresco eating.

Open all day all wk **Bar Meals** L served Mon-Fri 11-3, Sat-Sun 12-4 D served all wk 6.30-10 Av main course £12.50 **Restaurant** L served Mon-Fri 12-2.30, Sat-Sun 12-10.30 booking required ⊕ GREENE KING ◀ Greene King IPA, Abbot Ale, Old Speckled Hen, Olde Trip plus, Guest ales. ♥ 9 **Facilities** Children welcome Children's menu Children's portions Play area Garden Parking

The Bell ♥

Horsefair Ln MK43 7AU ☎ 01234 720254
dir: Telephone for directions

Stone walls, open fireplaces and exposed beams provide the character for this 16th-century thatched village pub, with a spacious garden leading down to the River Ouse adding even more. But it doesn't stop there, not when you factor in the quality home-cooked food, such as chargrilled steak with mushroom and white wine sauce; Moroccan lamb kebabs; breaded fillet of haddock with home-made tartare sauce; and broccoli and Stilton penne pasta. The new landlords have introduced a summer beer festival.

Open all wk Mon-Thu 11.30-3 5-11.30 (Fri-Sun all day) **Bar Meals** L served Mon-Sat 11.30-2.30, Sun 12-4.30 booking required D served Tue-Sat 6.30-9 booking required ⊕ GREENE KING ◀ Greene King IPA, Abbot Ale, Seasonal ales Ò Stowford Press. ♥ 8 **Facilities** Children welcome Children's menu Children's portions Dogs allowed Garden Beer festival Parking

OLD WARDEN   Map 12 TL14

PICK OF THE PUBS

Hare and Hounds ☻

SG18 9HQ ☎ **01767 627225** 🖹 **01767 627209**
dir: *From Bedford turn right off A603 (or left from A600) to Old Warden. Also accessed from Biggleswade rdbt on A1*

Situated in the charming Buckinghamshire village of Old Warden, this attractive 200 year-old building is part of the Shuttleworth estate, home to the famous collection of classic cars and vintage aeroplanes.The interiors of the bar and the three chic dining rooms feature timbered walls, warm red and cream colours, fresh flowers and contemporary furnishings. Wines include some from the local Warden Abbey vineyard, whilst cracking beers come courtesy of Charles Wells. Food is taken very seriously here; the printed menu lists a well balanced choice of rustic traditional dishes and more modern offerings, with every effort made to use local produce. Typical starters include local rabbit ravioli with baby spinach, basil pesto and Parmesan. For main course, try the pan-fried calves' liver with rösti potato, smoked bacon, red onion marmalade, sherry vinegar and sage sauce; or roasted butternut squash, black-eyed peas and tomato curry.

Open Tue-Sat 12-3 6-11 (Sun 12-10.30) Closed: 25 & 26 Dec, 1 Jan, Mon (ex BH) **Bar Meals** L served all wk 12-2 D served all wk 6.30-9 **Restaurant** L served all wk Mon-Sat 12-2, Sun 12-3.30 D served Mon-Sat 6.30-9 ⊕ CHARLES WELLS ◀ Wells, Young's, Eagle IPA. ☻13 **Facilities** Children welcome Children's portions Garden Parking

SALFORD   Map 11 SP93

PICK OF THE PUBS

The Swan ☻

2 Warendon Rd MK17 8BD ☎ **01908 281008**
e-mail: swan@peachpubs.com
dir: *M1 junct 13, follow signs to Salford*

The attractive village where you'll find the tile-hung, Edwardian-era Swan is a reminder of how this part of the county looked before modern Milton Keynes was built. Painted in rich reds, the lively bar makes you feel instantly at home, as does the eating area, whose big French doors can be thrown open to the garden. Peer through the feature window into the kitchen to watch the chefs preparing dishes from top, locally supplied ingredients, including sandwiches, deli boards and chargrills; supreme of cod bourguignonne; braised smoked pork belly; and saffron, date, cashew and parsnip tagine. A short, sensibly priced wine list offers plenty by the glass. The carefully restored barn with a large central dining table can be used as a memorable setting for a private dinner. With a busy social calendar of events, on the last Sunday of the month the Swan hosts a farmers' market.

Open all day all wk 11am-mdnt (Sun 12-10.30) Closed: 25 Dec **Bar Meals** L served all wk 12-6 D served Mon-Sat 6-9.45, Sun 6-9.30 Av main course £18 food served all day **Restaurant** L served all wk 12-3 D served Mon-Sat 6-9.45, Sun 6-9.30 booking required Av 3 course à la carte fr £23 ⊕ GREENE KING ◀ Bombardier, IPA ♂ Addlestones. ☻10 **Facilities** Children welcome Children's menu Children's portions Dogs allowed Garden Parking Wi-fi

SOULDROP   Map 11 SP96

The Bedford Arms ☻ NEW

High St MK44 1EY ☎ **01234 781384**
e-mail: thebedfordarms@tiscali.co.uk
dir: *From Rushden take A6 towards Bedford. In 6m right into Stocking Lane to Souldrop. Pub 50mtrs on right*

Thought to be over 300 years old, Souldrop's only pub has all the traditional attributes – low beams, horse brasses, tankards, skittles and dominoes. Then there are the four well kept real ales available in the bar with its cosy open fire in winter. Plus there is a pretty good selection of pub dishes too, served in the cottage-style dining room with its country prints and shelves of china - chicken (or vegetable) tikka masala; sausage, mash and onion gravy; mixed grill; chicken and ham pie; home-made cottage pie; battered cod; and leek and Stilton bread and butter pudding.

Open 12-3 6-11 (Fri-Sun 12-11) Closed: Mon (ex BHs) **Bar Meals** L served Tue-Sat 12-2 D served Tue-Sat 6.30-9 Av main course £9.25 **Restaurant** L served Tue-Sat, Sun 12-4 D served Tue-Sat 6.30-9 ⊕ FREE HOUSE ◀ Black Sheep, Phipps Red Star, Greene King IPA, guest ale ♂ Stowford Press. ☻9 **Facilities** Children welcome Children's menu Children's portions Dogs allowed Garden Parking

SOUTHILL   Map 12 TL14

The White Horse ☻

High St SG18 9LD ☎ **01462 813364**
e-mail: whitehorsesouthill@live.co.uk
dir: *Telephone for directions*

A country pub with traditional values, happily accommodating the needs of children in the large patio gardens and those who like to sit outside on cool days enjoying a well kept pint (the patio has heaters). Offering traditional English food, fish, vegetarian and children's dishes, grilled steaks are a big draw in the restaurant but other main courses from the extensive menu include rack of barbecue spare ribs; home-made game pie; home-made fisherman's pie; plus choices from the chef's specials board are worth a look at too.

Open all wk **Bar Meals** L served Mon-Fri 12-2.30, Sat-Sun 12-10 booking required D served Mon-Fri 6-10, Sat-Sun 12-10 booking required **Restaurant** L served Mon-Fri 12-2.30, Sat-Sun 12-10 booking required D served Mon-Fri 6-10, Sat-Sun 12-10 booking required ⊕ ENTERPRISE INNS ◀ Greene King IPA, Golden Fox, John Smith's, Sharp's Doom Bar. ☻8 **Facilities** Children welcome Children's menu Play area Dogs allowed Garden Parking Wi-fi

STANBRIDGE   Map 11 SP92

PICK OF THE PUBS

The Five Bells

Station Rd LU7 9JF ☎ **01525 210224**
e-mail: fivebells@fullers.co.uk
dir: *Off A505 E of Leighton Buzzard*

A stylish and relaxing setting for a drink or a meal is offered by this white-painted 400-year-old village inn, which has been delightfully renovated and revived. The bar features lots of bare wood as well as comfortable armchairs and polished, rug-strewn floors. The modern decor extends to the bright, airy 75-cover dining room. There's also a spacious garden with patio and lawns. The inn offers bar meals, set menus and a carte choice for diners. The bar menu typically includes dishes such as beer battered fish, chips and mushy peas; rib-eye steak with hand-cut chips; home-made beef and venison burger; red onion charlotte and roasted vegetable tart; and pan roasted duck breast with sour cherry sauce.

Open all day all wk 11-11 (Sun 12-10.30) ⊕ FREE HOUSE ◀ Fuller's London Pride, Fuller's Chiswick Bitter, Gales Seafairers ♂ Aspall. **Facilities** Children welcome Children's menu Children's portions Dogs allowed Garden Parking

SUTTON   Map 12 TL24

John O'Gaunt Inn ☻

30 High St SG19 2NE ☎ **01767 260377**
dir: *Off B1040 between Biggleswade & Potton*

Situated in one of Bedfordshire's most picturesque villages, the John O'Gaunt is a pretty village inn of character at the centre of the community and many rural walks. A guest ale features alongside the regular beers supplied in rotation from various breweries. Piped music is notable by its absence, though you may be encouraged to join in the regular folk music sessions; thirty different clubs and societies are hosted here. Good traditional fayre is on offer such as haddock in batter; chicken, spinach and mushroom lasagne; and beef with mustard sauce, plus various balti dishes. The pub has a large garden, and welcoming winter fires.

Open all wk 12-3 7-11 (Fri 12-3 6-11, Sun 12-5 7-11) **Bar Meals** L served all wk 12.30-1.45 D served all wk 7-9 ⊕ FREE HOUSE ◀ Rotating - Woodforde's Wherry, Black Sheep, London Pride, Potton's Porter ♂ Westons Old Rosie. ☻8 **Facilities** Dogs allowed Garden Parking Wi-fi **Notes** ☺

TILSWORTH
Map 11 SP92

The Anchor Inn

1 Dunstable Rd LU7 9PU ☎ 01525 211404
e-mail: graham.wilsher@btconnect.com
dir: *Exit A5 at Tilsworth. In 1m pub on right at 3rd bend*

The only pub in a Saxon village, The Anchor dates from 1878. The restaurant is a recent addition to the side of the pub, and the whole building has been refurbished. The licensees pride themselves on their fresh food and well-kept beers and guest ales. An acre of garden includes patio seating for alfresco dining, an adventure playground and a barbecue. Recent change of hands.

Open all day all wk noon-11.30pm **Bar Meals** L served all wk 12-8 D served all wk 12-8 food served all day **Restaurant** L served all wk 12-8 D served all wk 12-8 food served all day ⊕ GREENE KING ◀ Greene King IPA, Abbot Ale, Wadworth 6X, Guest ales. **Facilities** Children welcome Children's menu Children's portions Play area Family room Dogs allowed Garden Parking

WOBURN
Map 11 SP93

The Birch at Woburn ♥

20 Newport Rd MK17 9HX
☎ 01525 290295 📄 01525 290899
e-mail: ctaverns@aol.com
dir: *Telephone for directions*

A beautifully presented family-run establishment, The Birch is located opposite Woburn Championship Golf Course, close to Woburn Abbey and the Safari Park. It has built its reputation on the friendly service of freshly cooked food; the kitchen team is passionate about sourcing the freshest ingredients from local farms and estates. The menu offers a range of English and Continental dishes, and there is a griddle area where customers can choose their steaks and fish, which are then cooked to their preference by the chefs. The restaurant is air conditioned and alfresco dining is possible in the summer.

Open 12-3 6-12 Closed: 25-26 Dec, 1 Jan, Sun eve **Bar Meals** L served 12-2.30 booking required D served 6-10 Av main course £8.95 **Restaurant** L served 12-2.30 booking required D served 6-10 Av 3 course à la carte fr £25 ⊕ FREE HOUSE ◀ London Pride, Adnams, Guinness. ♥ 12 **Facilities** Children welcome Children's portions Parking

The Black Horse ♥ NEW

1 Bedford St MK17 9QB ☎ 01525 290210
e-mail: blackhorse@peachpubs.com
dir: *In town centre on A4012*

Plum in the middle of the pretty village of Woburn, this 18th-century inn cuts an elegant figure. Behind the Georgian frontage, the original coaching inn feel of the cosy bar has been retained and complemented with a chic, relaxed dining area where seasonal, locally sourced food drives the all-day menus. As well as sandwiches and deli boards to share, daily specials might include

venison hotpot; pork collar, chorizo and butter bean cassoulet; or pumpkin risotto.

Open all day all wk 11-11 (Sat 11am-11.30pm) Closed: 25 Dec **Bar Meals** L served all wk 12-6 D served all wk 6-9.45 Av main course £14 food served all day **Restaurant** L served all wk 12-3 D served all wk 6-9.45 Av 3 course à la carte fr £25 ⊕ PEACH PUBS ◀ Greene King IPA, Abbot Ale, guest ale Ö Aspall. ♥ 10 **Facilities** Children welcome Children's menu Children's portions Dogs allowed Garden Wi-fi

The Tavistock Bar & Lounge ♥ NEW

The Inn at Woburn, George St MK17 9PX
☎ 01525 290441
e-mail: inn@woburn.co.uk
dir: *M1 junct 13, left to Woburn, in Woburn turn left at T-junct*

The Inn at Woburn has been a welcome sight for travellers for nearly 300 years. Originally a coaching inn, it was a popular spot for Royal Mail coaches travelling from London to the north. The Tavistock bar offers an informal setting to enjoy real ales and a wide range of wines – including 25 by the glass. In addition, an all-day bar menu of light snacks and meals might feature croque-monsieur, steak baguette or venison burger.

Open all day all wk **Bar Meals** L served all wk 12-10 D served all wk 12-10 food served all day ⊕ FREE HOUSE ◀ Wells Bombardier, Eagle IPA. ♥ 25 **Facilities** Children welcome Children's menu Parking Wi-fi

BERKSHIRE

ALDERMASTON
Map 5 SU56

Hinds Head

Wasing Ln RG7 4LX ☎ 0118 971 2194 📄 0118 971 4511
e-mail: hindshead@fullers.co.uk
dir: *M4 junct 12, A4 towards Newbury, left on A340 towards Basingstoke, 2m to village*

This 17th-century inn with its distinctive clock and bell tower still incorporates the village lock-up, which was last used in 1865. The former brew house behind the pub has been refurbished to create an additional dining area. Menu choices range from jacket potatoes and filled baguettes to whole baked sea bass; carbonara pasta; and cauliflower cheese. Recent change of hands.

Open all wk Mon-Sat 12-3 6-9 (Sun 12-8) ⊕ FULLER'S BREWERY ◀ Fuller's HSB. **Facilities** Children's menu Children's portions Family room Dogs allowed Garden Parking Wi-fi

ALDWORTH
Map 5 SU57

PICK OF THE PUBS

The Bell Inn

RG8 9SE ☎ 01635 578272
dir: *Just off B4009 (Newbury to Streatley road)*

One might be surprised to discover that an establishment without a restaurant can hold its own in a world of smart dining pubs and modish gastro-pubs. Well, be surprised. The Bell not only survives, it positively prospers and, to be fair, it does serve some food, if only hot, crusty, generously filled rolls. And since it is one of the few truly unspoiled country pubs left, and serves cracking pints of Arkell's, West Berkshire and guest real ales plus ciders, this limitation has been no disadvantage. The Bell is old, very old, beginning life in 1340 as a five-bay cruck-built manor hall. It has reputedly been in the same family for 200 years: ask Mr Macaulay, the landlord - he's been here for more than thirty of them, and he has no plans to change it from the time warp it is. A 300-year-old, one-handed clock still stands in the taproom 'keeping imperfect time', and the rack for the spit-irons and clockwork roasting jack are still over the fireplace. Taller customers may bump their heads over the glass-panelled bar hatch.

Open Mon-Sat 11-3 6-11 (Sun 12-3 7-10.30) Closed: 25 Dec, Mon (BH Mon L only) **Bar Meals** L served Mon-Sat 11-2.30, Sun 12-2.30 D served Mon-Sat 6-9.30, Sun 7-9 ⊕ FREE HOUSE ◀ Arkell's Kingsdown, 3B, West Berkshire Old Tyler & Maggs Magnificent Mild, Guest ales Ö Uptons Farmhouse, Tutts Clump, Lilleys Pear & Apple. **Facilities** Children welcome Dogs allowed Garden Parking Notes ✉

ASCOT
Map 6 SU96

The Thatched Tavern

Cheapside Rd SL5 7QG
☎ 01344 620874 📄 01344 623043
e-mail: thethatchedtavern@4cinns.co.uk
dir: *Follow Ascot Racecourse signs. Through Ascot 1st left (Cheapside). 1.5m, pub on left*

Just a mile from the famous racecourse, a 17th-century building of original beams, flagstone floors and very low ceilings. In summer the sheltered garden makes a fine spot to enjoy real ales and varied choice of food; in the cooler months there is the cosy bar and warming fires. The kitchen brigade produces dishes like venison and mushroom pudding, seared calves' liver on bubble and squeak, and beef stew and dumplings.

Open all wk Mon-Thu 12-3.30 5.30-11 (Fri-Sun all day) ⊕ FREE HOUSE ◀ Fuller's London Pride, IPA, Guinness Ö Stowford Press. **Facilities** Children welcome Children's portions Dogs allowed Garden Parking Wi-fi

ASHMORE GREEN — Map 5 SU56

The Sun in the Wood ♥

Stoney Ln RG18 9HF ☎ **01635 42377** 📠 **01635 528392**
e-mail: info@suninthewood.co.uk
dir: *From A34 at Robin Hood Rdbt left to Shaw, at mini-rdbt right then 7th left into Stoney Ln 1.5m, pub on left*

Surrounded by beautiful mature trees and natural woodland, this award-winning Wadworth country pub and restaurant has an outstanding reputation, for which top licensees Philip and Lauren Davison share the honours. Inside, stone floors and wood panelling; outside, a country garden, decking and, unusually, a nine-hole crazy-golf course. Snacks include a dozen varieties of baguette, while a sample main menu promises lamb and mint pie, fillet of beef Wellington, and pan-fried sea bass on herb and potato cake.

Open noon-2.30 6-11 (Sat noon-11 Sun noon-5) Closed: Mon **Bar Meals** L served Tue-Fri 12-2, Sat 12-2.30, Sun 12-4 booking required D served Tue-Fri 6-9.30, Sat 5.30-9.30 booking required **Restaurant** L served Tue-Fri 12-2, Sat 12-2.30, Sun 12-4 booking required D served Tue-Fri 6-9.30, Sat 5.30-9.30 booking required ⊕ WADWORTH ◀ Wadworth 6X, Henrys Original IPA ♂ Westons Stowford Press. ♥ 15 **Facilities** Children welcome Children's menu Children's portions Play area Garden Parking

BOXFORD — Map 5 SU47

The Bell at Boxford ♥

Lambourn Rd RG20 8DD
☎ **01488 608721** 📠 **01488 658502**
e-mail: paul@bellatboxford.com
web: www.bellatboxford.com
dir: *M4 junct 14 onto A338 towards Wantage. Turn right onto B4000 to x-rds, signed Boxford; From junct 13 onto A34 to Hungerford, right at rdbt onto B4000. At x-rds turn right to Boxford, signed*

This mock Tudor country pub is at the heart of the glorious Lambourn Valley, noted for its pretty villages and sweeping Downland scenery. The main bar is located in the earliest part of the building, dating from the 17th century. There is also a patio, which is popular throughout the year with its array of flowers and outdoor heating, hog roasts, barbecues and parties. Menus might include rib-eye steak served with field mushroom and tomato on a bed of chips; tiger prawn linguini; or pan-fried lemon sole with lemon and caper sauce. Accommodation is available.

Open all wk 11-3 6-11 (Sun noon-10.30)
Bar Meals L served Mon-Sat 12-2, Sun 12-9 D served Mon-Sat 7-9.30, Sun 7-9 **Restaurant** L served Mon-Sat 12-2.30, Sun 12-7 D served Mon-Sat 7-9.30, Sun 7-9 ⊕ FREE HOUSE ◀ Bishop's Tipple, Henry's IPA, Guinness, 6X. ♥ 60 **Facilities** Children welcome Children's portions Dogs allowed Garden Parking Wi-fi

BRAY — Map 6 SU97

The Crown Inn ♥ NEW

High St SL6 2AH ☎ **01628 621936** 📠 **01628 623394**
dir: *M4 junct 8/9, exit to Maidenhead Central. At next rdbt, take exit to Bray & Windsor (A308). 0.5m, left at the Bray sign (B3028). In village, pub on left*

This 16th-century village pub was acquired in the summer of 2010 by chef Heston Blumenthal of the neighbouring Fat Duck restaurant. The original low beams and open fireplaces remain and guests can also dine outside in the courtyard with its overhanging grape vines. The modern British food includes mouthwatering lunchtime sandwiches and ploughman's, or hearty main courses such as baked suet steak and ale pie; lemon sole and potted shrimps; chargrilled Angus sirloin, marrowbone sauce and fries.

Open all wk 12-3 6-11 Closed: 26-27 Dec
Bar Meals L served Mon-Fri 12-2.30, Sat-Sun 12-3 D served all wk 6.30-10 Av main course £15
Restaurant L served Mon-Fri 12-2.30, Sat-Sun 12-3 booking required D served all wk 6.30-10 booking required ⊕ SCOTTISH & NEWCASTLE ◀ Courage Best, Directors, Shepherd Neame Spitfire. ♥ 13
Facilities Children welcome Children's menu Children's portions Dogs allowed Garden Parking

PICK OF THE PUBS

The Hinds Head ◉◉ ♥

High St SL6 2AB ☎ **01628 626151** 📠 **01628 623394**
e-mail: info@hindsheadbray.com
dir: *M4 junct 8/9 take exit to Maidenhead Central. Next rdbt take exit for Bray & Windsor. After 0.5m take B3028 to Bray*

Heston Blumenthal's boozy younger sibling to his eponymous Fat Duck restaurant next door has, not surprisingly, become a gastronomic destination, yet the former Tudor hunting lodge remains very much a village local. Expect an informal atmosphere in the traditional bar, with its beams, sturdy oak panelling, log fires, leather chairs, and pints of Rebellion available at the bar. On the ground floor is the main restaurant, while upstairs are two further dining areas, the Vicars Room, and the larger Royal Room. Having worked alongside the Tudor kitchens at Hampton Court Palace, Heston rediscovered the origins of British cuisine, and has reintroduced some classic recipes that echo the pub's Tudor roots. Top notch produce is used in dishes that are cooked simply and delivered in an unfussy manner by head chef Kevin Love. Take pea and ham soup, oxtail and kidney pudding, shepherd's pie with lamb breast and sweetbreads, smoked salmon and cod fishcakes, rump steak with bone marrow sauce and triple-cooked chips, and rhubarb trifle. Well selected, widely sourced wines complete the picture.

Open all wk Closed: 25 Dec **Bar Meals** L served Mon-Sat 12-2.30, Sun 12-4 D served Mon-Sat 6.30-9.30
Restaurant L served Mon-Sat 12-2.30, Sun 12-4 booking required D served Mon-Sat 6.30-9.30 booking required ⊕ FREE HOUSE ◀ Greene King IPA, Greene King Abbot Ale, Marlow Rebellion, Timothy Taylor Landlord, London Pride, Guest ales ♂ Stowford Press. ♥ 15 **Facilities** Children welcome Children's menu Parking

CHADDLEWORTH — Map 5 SU47

The Ibex

Main St RG20 7ER ☎ **01488 638311**
e-mail: inn@the-ibex.co.uk
dir: *A338 towards Wantage, through Great Shefford then right, then 2nd left, pub on right in village*

An award-winning hard-working community pub in a Grade II listed building with low beams. The only pub in the UK called The Ibex, it's the headquarters for local cricket teams; it has strong connections with horse-racing (it used to be run by ex-jockey Colin Brown of Desert Orchid fame); it has its own golf society; it runs film, quiz and curry nights; it sells home-made bread, free range eggs and local honey; it will even take your dry cleaning and deliver a bouquet. All this, and it serves with a smile Greene King ales and real ciders, and comprehensive menus of traditional pub grub. Change of hands in Nov 2010.

Open all wk 11-3 6-mdnt (all day Sat-Sun & BHs) ⊕ GREENE KING ◀ IPA, Morland Original, Guinness ♂ Tutts Clump, Stowford Press, Ciderworks.
Facilities Children welcome Children's menu Children's portions Dogs allowed Garden Parking Wi-fi

CHIEVELEY — Map 5 SU47

The Crab at Chieveley

★★★★ GA ◉◉ ♥

North Heath, Wantage Rd RG20 8UE
☎ **01635 247550** 📠 **01635 247440**
e-mail: info@crabatchieveley.com
dir: *M4 junct 13. 1.5m W of Chieveley on B4494*

This lovely old thatched dining pub has an award-winning seafood restaurant, which makes it the perfect place to break a tedious M4 journey. Specialising in fish dishes and with fresh deliveries daily, the continuously-changing menu in the maritime-themed restaurant offers mouth-watering starters such as Cornish crab gratin with thyme and tarragon gnocchi, followed by harissa salmon with butternut squash or lamb rump with black olive tapenade. Beers are from West Berkshire Brewery and 13 boutique bedrooms complete the package.

Open all day all wk 11-11 **Bar Meals** L served all wk 12-2.30 D served all wk 7-9.30 Av main course £17
Restaurant Fixed menu price fr £15.95 Av 3 course à la carte fr £45 ⊕ FREE HOUSE ◀ West Berkshire Brewery ♥ 20 **Facilities** Children welcome Children's menu Children's portions Garden Parking Wi-fi **Rooms** 13

COOKHAM DEAN   Map 5 SU88

PICK OF THE PUBS

The Chequers Brasserie ⚑

Dean Ln SL6 9BQ ☎ **01628 481232**   📠 **01628 481237**
e-mail: info@chequersbrasserie.co.uk
dir: *From A4094 in Cookham High St towards Marlow, over rail line. 1m on right*

Kenneth Grahame, who wrote *The Wind in the Willows*, spent his childhood in these parts. He would surely have enjoyed this historic pub, tucked away between Marlow and Maidenhead in one of the prettiest villages in the Thames Valley. Striking Victorian and Edwardian villas around the green set the tone, whilst the surrounding wooded hills and dales have earned Cookham Dean a reputation as a centre for wonderful walks. The bar presents a good selection of ales from Adnams, amongst others, backed by top-flight real ciders from the likes of Thatchers. The Anglo-French menu is dedicated to the use of fresh and high quality produce. Expect the likes of seared calves' liver with smoked bacon; and slow-cooked belly of Norfolk pork with crackling, Savoy cabbage and gratin potato. Accompanying children can be served smaller portions from the menu, and dogs are welcome in the garden.

Open all day all wk 11-11 **Bar Meals** L served Mon-Sat 12-2.30, Sun 12-9.30 D served Mon-Thu 6.30-9.30, Fri-Sat 6.30-10, Sun 12-9.30 **Restaurant** L served Mon-Sat 12-2.30, Sun 12-9.30 D served Mon-Thu 6.30-9.30, Fri-Sat 6.30-10, Sun 12-9.30 Fixed menu price fr £13.95 Av 3 course à la carte fr £25.95 ⊕ FREE HOUSE ◀ Guinness, Rebellion IPA, Adnams Bitter, Guest ales Ó Thatchers Cox, Thatchers Katy, Cotswold Cider. ⚑ 14 **Facilities** Children welcome Children's portions Garden Parking Wi-fi

CRAZIES HILL   Map 5 SU78

PICK OF THE PUBS

The Horns ⚑

RG10 8LY ☎ **0118 940 6222**
dir: *Off A321 NE of Wargrave*

The Horns is a beautifully restored 17th-century pub with oak beams, terracotta walls and stripped wooden floors. When Steve Wiltshire and his wife Dawn took it over, they set about turning the large garden into a paradise for children. Today it is home to two miniature Shetland ponies, a donkey, rabbits, guinea pigs, ducks and chickens. Inside are three interconnecting rooms full of old pine tables, warmed by open fires; a barn added 200 years ago forms the dining room. The peaceful atmosphere makes it a great place to enjoy a pint of Brakspear's bitter. The menu of pub favourites ranges from bar meals like chilli con carne or whole-tail scampi with chips; to starters such as Thai salmon and crab fishcakes served with a sweet chilli sauce; and main courses such as Cumberland sausage or marinated chicken breast. Look to the specials board for the likes of venison stew or fish pie.

Open 12-3 6-11 Closed: Mon **Bar Meals** L served Tue-Sun 12-2.30 D served Tue-Sun 6-9 **Restaurant** L served Tue-Sun 12-2.30 D served Tue-Sun 6-9 ⊕ BRAKSPEAR ◀ Brakspear Bitter, Oxford Gold. ⚑ 8 **Facilities** Children welcome Children's menu Children's portions Play area Family room Dogs allowed Garden Parking

CURRIDGE   Map 5 SU47

The Bunk Inn

RG18 9DS ☎ **01635 200400**
e-mail: thebunkinn@btconnect.com
dir: *M4 junct 13, A34 N towards Oxford. Take 1st slip road then right for 1m. Right at T-junct, 1st right signed Curridge*

Owned by the Liquorish family since 1991, this village free house is renowned for its cuisine and friendly atmosphere. Stay in the log fire-warmed bar in winter or, in summer, head for the attractive garden and patio. The only question is, where to dine - stylish restaurant or lovely conservatory? All food is fresh, and wherever possible, seasonal and local. An impressive carte menu, plus specials that usually include fresh Brixham fish.

Open all day all wk 11am-11.30pm ⊕ FREE HOUSE ◀ Fuller's London Pride, Good Old Boy Ó Stowford Press. **Facilities** Children welcome Children's menu Children's portions Play area Dogs allowed Garden Parking Wi-fi

EAST GARSTON   Map 5 SU37

PICK OF THE PUBS

The Queen's Arms Country Inn ★★★★ INN

RG17 7ET ☎ **01488 648757**
e-mail: info@queensarmshotel.co.uk
dir: *M4 junct 14, 4m onto A338 to Great Shefford, then East Garston*

This 18th-century inn is pleasantly located in a small village in the Lambourn Valley, home to many a racehorse. It is also an excellent area for walking, being quite close to the Ridgeway. Now part of the small and select Miller's Collection of inns, the Queen's

Arms offers a warm welcome in a stylishly traditional setting. The bar, with its horse racing theme, is one of the few places in the valley with mobile phone reception – a blessing for visitors from the racing fraternity. A good selection of country dishes is prepared from fresh ingredients sourced as locally as possible. The menu evolves with the seasons, and promises innovative modern cuisine in such dishes as pan-seared sea trout with crushed truffle purple potatoes and caviar cream; or spiced loin of venison with cauliflower and almond purée. The terrace and large garden are popular in the summer, and comfortable accommodation is available.

Open all day all wk **Bar Meals** L served all wk 12-2.30 D served all wk 6.30-9.30 Av main course £13.50 **Restaurant** L served all wk 12-2.30 D served all wk 6.30-9.30 Av 3 course à la carte fr £21 ⊕ FREE HOUSE ◀ Guinness, Wadworth 6X, Henry's IPA, guest ale. **Facilities** Children welcome Children's portions Dogs allowed Garden Parking Wi-fi **Rooms** 8

FRILSHAM   Map 5 SU57

PICK OF THE PUBS

The Pot Kiln ◉ NEW

RG18 0XX ☎ **01635 201366**   📠 **01635 201366**
e-mail: admin@potkiln.org
dir: *From Yattendon follow Pot Kiln signs, cross over motorway. Continue for 0.25m pub on right*

It takes a bit of seeking out, the 18th-century Pot Kiln country pub, but once found, never forgotten. It could be the commitment to real ale, with three on tap at any one time, from the award-winning West Berkshire Brewery (which originated at the pub, since relocated), but like-as-not it's the exceptional food which draws crowds to this former kiln-workers' old beerhouse secluded along back lanes in beautiful unspoilt countryside. Chef-patron Mike Robinson is renowned for shooting much of the game he then crafts into extraordinary dishes such as ragu of muntjac or roasted loin and leg of Berkshire rabbit. Signature dishes include warm salad of wood pigeon, bacon and black pudding and a pavé of wild venison. Local pike and trout and crayfish from the river Kennet may also feature. The small public bar serves excellent bar food including the pub's famous venison burgers and venison steak sandwiches.

Open Mon & Wed-Fri 12-3 6-11 (Sat-Sun 12-11) Closed: 25 Dec, Tue **Bar Meals** L served Wed-Mon 12-2.30 D served Wed-Mon 6.30-8.30 Av main course £8 **Restaurant** L served Wed-Mon 12-2 booking required D served Wed-Mon 7-9 booking required Fixed menu price fr £12.95 Av 3 course à la carte fr £25 ⊕ FREE HOUSE ◀ Brick Kiln, West Berkshire Brewery Mr Chubbs Ó Thatchers. **Facilities** Children welcome Children's menu Children's portions Play area Dogs allowed Garden Parking Wi-fi

HERMITAGE   Map 5 SU57

The White Horse of Hermitage

Newbury Rd RG18 9TB ☎ 01635 200325
e-mail: thewh@btconnect.com
dir: *5m from Newbury on B4009. Follow signs to Chieveley, right into Priors Court Rd, turn left at mini-rdbt, pub approx 1m*

The White Horse has achieved a solid reputation for its pub food, using the freshest and finest local produce to create a daily menu, including signature dishes such as BBQ babyback ribs. The interior bar and restaurant is contemporary in decor, and outside you choose between the Mediterranean-style patio or the large garden which is equipped with swings and a football area.

Open all wk noon-3 5-11 Closed: Mon (ex BH) ⊕ GREENE KING ◀ Abbot Ale, Greene King IPA, Guinness Ŏ Stowford Press. **Facilities** Children welcome Children's menu Play area Dogs allowed Garden Parking Wi-fi

HUNGERFORD   Map 5 SU36

PICK OF THE PUBS

The Crown & Garter ★★★★ INN ♀

Inkpen Common RG17 9QR ☎ 01488 668325
e-mail: gill.hern@btopenworld.com
dir: *From A4 to Kintbury & Inkpen. At village store left into Inkpen Rd, follow signs for Inkpen Common 2m*

This traditional 17th-century, family-run free house is said to have been used by James II on the way to visit one of his mistresses. Today, its historic charm is best seen in the bar, where there's a huge inglenook fireplace and criss-crossing beams, and which West Berkshire and Ramsbury breweries supply with their beers. You can eat in the bar, the wood-panelled restaurant, on the patio or even under an oak tree in the beer garden. The daily-changing menu might feature fried fillet of haddock with chips and mushy peas; curried chicken jalfrezi with basmati rice; and spinach and Stilton tart with tomato and basil salsa, while a typical dessert would be apple strudel with toffee ice cream. The spacious en suite bedrooms are built round a pretty cottage garden, making the inn a good base for cycling and walking, perhaps to Combe Gibbet on top of 975-feet Inkpen Beacon.

Open 12-3 5.30-11 (Sun 12-5 7-10.30, closed Mon & Tue lunch) Closed: Mon L & Tue L **Bar Meals** L served Wed-Sat 12-2, Sun 12-2.30 booking required D served Mon-Sat 6.30-9.30 booking required Av main course £15 **Restaurant** L served Wed-Sat 12-2, Sun 12-2.30 booking required D served Mon-Sat 6.30-9.30 booking required Fixed menu price fr £8.50 Av 3 course à la carte fr £25 ⊕ FREE HOUSE ◀ Mr Chubbs, Good Old Boy, Guinness, Moonlight, Ramsbury Gold. ♀ 9 **Facilities** Garden Parking Wi-fi **Rooms** 9

The Pheasant Inn ★★★★ INN ♀

Ermin St, Shefford Woodlands RG17 7AA
☎ 01488 648284   🖹 01488 648971
e-mail: enquiries@thepheasant-inn.co.uk
dir: *From M4 junct 14 take A338 towards Wantage. Left onto B4000 towards Lambourn*

Once called The Paraffin House (because that's what it was licensed to sell alongside beer), this old drovers' retreat now has eleven contemporary-styled bedrooms, but the beamed, wood-panelled and stone-floored old pub itself remains unchanged. The Berkshire Downs are horse-racing country, a fact more than hinted at in the bar/restaurant, serving Lambourn Valley wild garlic omelette; bavette of Scottish beef; and South Coast fish cakes. The scrumpy here is Pheasant Plucker — and so it should be.

Open all day all wk **Bar Meals** L served all wk 12-2.30 D served all wk 7-9 **Restaurant** L served all wk 12-2.30 D served all wk 7-9 ⊕ FREE HOUSE ◀ Wadworth, Sharp's Ŏ Pheasant Plucker. ♀ 12 **Facilities** Children welcome Children's portions Dogs allowed Garden Parking Wi-fi **Rooms** 11

PICK OF THE PUBS

The Swan Inn ★★★★ INN

Craven Rd, Lower Green, Inkpen RG17 9DX
☎ 01488 668326   🖹 01488 668306
e-mail: enquiries@theswaninn-organics.co.uk
web: www.theswaninn-organics.co.uk
dir: *S down Hungerford High St (A338), under rail bridge, left to Hungerford Common. Right signed Inkpen (3m)*

Organic beef farmers Mary and Bernard Harris preside over this rambling award-winning 17th-century free house, which stands in fine walking country just below Combe Gibbet and Walbury Hill. An attractive terraced garden sets the scene for alfresco summer dining, in contrast to the heavily beamed interior with its old photographic prints and open winter fires. Almost everything on the menu is prepared using their own fresh produce; meats – 100% organic and butchered on the premises – can be bought from the farm shop. The bar menu offers well kept ales and traditional English favourites, with beef and classic Italian dishes. Fresh pasta and bread are cooked daily on the premises. Even the wine is organic. There is an organic farm shop and butchery attached to the pub (Soil Association registered) to visit, and 10 en suite bedrooms available. (Current menus appear on the inn's website.)

Open all wk 12-2.30 7-10 (Sat noon-11pm Sun noon-4) Closed: 25-26 Dec **Bar Meals** L served all wk 12-2 booking required D served Mon-Sat 7-9.30 booking required Av main course £9.95 **Restaurant** L served Wed-Sun 12-2.30 booking required D served Wed-Sat 7-9.30 booking required Av 3 course à la carte fr £24.50 ⊕ FREE HOUSE ◀ Butts Traditional & Jester Bitter, Butts Blackguard, Guest ales. **Facilities** Children welcome Children's menu Children's portions Play area Garden Parking Wi-fi **Rooms** 10

HURLEY   Map 5 SU88

The Olde Bell Inn ★★★★★ INN ◉◉ ♀ NEW

High St SL6 5LX ☎ 01628 825881   🖹 01628 825939
e-mail: oldebellreception@coachinginn.co.uk
dir: *M4 junct 8/9 follow signs for Henley. At rdbt take A4130 to Hurley, turn right to Hurley, 800yds on right*

Heritage seeps from the very framework of this smart village inn, parts of which date to 1135 when it was a guesthouse for pilgrims to a nearby priory. Its charming old bar has seen a republican plot (appropriately, Rebellion beers are sold here) and wartime visits by Churchill and Eisenhower. Today's visitors are drawn by the superb accommodation and accomplished gastro-pub menu which may feature a starter of marinated octopus as prelude to braised ox cheek with roast butternut squash. The terrace and wildflower meadow-style beer garden are delightful.

Open all day all wk **Bar Meals** L served all wk 10-10 D served Mon-Sat 6-10, Sun 6-9.30 Av main course £10 **Restaurant** L served Mon-Sat 12.30-2.30, Sun 12.30-4 booking required D served Mon-Sat 6-10 booking required Fixed menu price fr £12.50 Av 3 course à la carte fr £30 ⊕ FREE HOUSE ◀ Rebellion. ♀ 10 **Facilities** Children welcome Children's portions Play area Dogs allowed Garden Parking Wi-fi **Rooms** 48

HURST   Map 5 SU77

The Green Man ♀

Hinton Rd RG10 0BP
☎ 0118 934 2599   🖹 0118 934 2939
e-mail: phil@thegreenman.uk.com
web: www.thegreenman.uk.com
dir: *Off A321, adjacent to Hurst Cricket Club*

The pub gained its first licence in 1602, and Brakspear purchased a 1,000 year lease on the building in 1646. The old black beams, low in places, are still to be seen

and the building has been developed to include all the old features, while newer areas reflect a similar theme. Inside you'll find open fires, hand drawn beer and good food, from sandwiches to Sunday roasts. With a change of hands in July 2010, there is now fish and chips available for takeaway, 7 days a week. The garden, open to fields and woodland, includes a children's play area.

Open all wk 11-3 5.30-11 (Sat all day, Sun noon-10.30) **Bar Meals** L served 12-2.30 D served 6-9.30 Av main course £8 **Restaurant** L served 12-2.30 D served 6-9.30 booking required ⊕ BRAKSPEAR ◀ Brakspear Bitter, Hobgoblin, seasonal ales. ₹ 8 **Facilities** Children welcome Children's menu Children's portions Play area Garden Parking Wi-fi

---

KINTBURY   Map 5 SU36

PICK OF THE PUBS

The Dundas Arms

53 Station Rd RG17 9UT
☎ **01488 658263** ▤ **01488 658568**
e-mail: info@dundasarms.co.uk
web: www.dundasarms.co.uk
dir: *M4 junct 13 take A34 to Newbury, then A4 to Hungerford, left to Kintbury. Pub 1m by canal & rail station*

On the banks of both the Kennet & Avon Canal and the River Kennet itself, this late-18th-century free house has been in the same family for more than forty years, with proprietor David Dalzell-Piper working and cooking here throughout that time. The bar offers beers from Adnams, West Berkshire and Ramsbury breweries, plus a guest, and a blackboard selection of food. When David received a real ale award in 2009, he said: "We do great food, but good beer has been the mainstay throughout good times and bad". You can watch narrowboats on the canal from the auberge-style restaurant, where a modern British starter of grilled goat's cheese on Italian bread and sweet tomato might be followed by roast duck breast with cider and apple sauce, or baked Orkney salmon with fennel and saffron risotto. By all means, take your drinks and food outside to the patio or canalside jetty.

Open all wk 11-2.30 6-11 Closed: 25 & 31 Dec, Sun eve **Bar Meals** L served Mon-Sat 12-2 D served Tue-Sat 7-9 Av main course £13 **Restaurant** L served Mon-Sat 12-2 D served Tue-Sat 7-9 booking required Av 3 course à la carte fr £26 ⊕ FREE HOUSE ◀ West Berkshire, Mr Chubbs Lunchtime Bitter, Adnams, West Berkshire Good Old Boy, Ramsbury Gold. **Facilities** Children welcome Children's menu Family room Parking

---

KNOWL HILL   Map 5 SU87

PICK OF THE PUBS

Bird In Hand Country Inn ₹

Bath Rd RG10 9UP
☎ **01628 826622** & **822781** ▤ **01628 826748**
e-mail: info@birdinhand.co.uk
web: www.birdinhand.co.uk
dir: *On A4, 5m W of Maidenhead, 7m E of Reading*

Proprietor Caroline Shone is a third-generation member of her family to run this part-14th-century inn, where some three centuries ago George III probably slipped in for a swift one while his horse was being re-shod at the forge next door. Had he still been waiting, his choice today of local real ales in the wood-panelled Oak Lounge bar would have been considerably wider. Or he could have selected one or two of the 20 wines by the glass from the 50-bin wine list, including some from nearby Stanlake Park vineyard. In the attractive restaurant, which overlooks a courtyard and fountain, the menu (also available in the bar) offers salads, vegetarian meze, jacket potatoes, omelettes and pizzas, with typical main meals of fresh salmon teriyaki with wild rice and stir-fried vegetables; home-made steak and kidney pudding; and slow-cooked shoulder of lamb. There are beer festivals in June and November. Accommodation available.

Open all day all wk **Bar Meals** Av main course £10.95 food served all day **Restaurant** Fixed menu price fr £10.95 Av 3 course à la carte fr £25 food served all day ⊕ FREE HOUSE ◀ Guest ales Ὄ Thatchers. ₹ 20 **Facilities** Children welcome Children's menu Children's portions Dogs allowed Garden Beer festival Parking Wi-fi

---

LECKHAMPSTEAD   Map 5 SU47

PICK OF THE PUBS

The Stag ₹

Shop Ln RG20 8QG ☎ **01488 638436**
dir: *6m from Newbury on B4494*

The white-painted Stag lies just off the village green in a sleepy downland village and close by are the Ridgeway long-distance path and Snelsmore Common, home to nightjar, woodlark and grazing Exmoor ponies. During the winter months the wood-burning stove is always ready. The bar and restaurant walls are painted in warm red, or left as bare brick, while old black and

---

white photographs tell of village life many years ago. Surrounding farms and growers supply all produce, including venison, pheasant and fresh river trout. Aberdeen Angus beef from cattle raised next door may also feature as a special, and those lucky enough to find it there agree that its taste and texture are sublime. Other possibilities are venison and redcurrant sausages with butternut squash mash, pork loin with creamy mushroom sauce, or traditional beer battered fish and chips with mushy peas. There are around 20 red and white wines, among them varieties from Australia, California and France.

Open all day 12-3 6-11 Closed: Sun eve & Mon L **Bar Meals** L served Tue-Sat 12-2, Sun 12-3.30 booking required D served Tue-Sat 6-9 booking required **Restaurant** L served Tue-Sat 12-2, Sun 12-3.30 booking required D served Tue-Sat 6-9 Fixed menu price fr £12 ⊕ FREE HOUSE ◀ Morlands Original, Good Old Boy, Guest ales Ὄ Aspall. ₹ 8 **Facilities** Children welcome Children's menu Children's portions Dogs allowed Garden Parking

---

MAIDENHEAD   Map 6 SU88

The George on the Green NEW

Holyport SL6 2JL ☎ **01628 628317**
e-mail: natalie@thegeorgeonthegreen.com
dir: *M4 junct 8/9, at rdbt 2nd exit onto A308(M). At rdbt 3rd exit onto A308. At rdbt take 2nd exit signed Holyport. Pub in village centre*

Facing the vast, eponymous green, this low-beamed 16th-century pub may possibly have played host to Charles II and Nell Gwynne when the actress lived locally. Today's locals can look forward to great beers from Rebellion Brewery in nearby Marlow Bottom coupled with a selective, well thought out menu; maybe baked crab gratin to start then smoked chicken, leek and butternut squash risotto or slow-roasted half shoulder of lamb with sweet potato boulangère. From outside tables, views stretch across the green to the tree-shaded village duck pond.

Open 12-3 5-11 (Sat 12-11 Sun 12-6) Closed: Mon **Bar Meals** L served Tue-Fri 12-2.30, Sat 12-4 D served Tue-Fri 5.30-9, Sat 6-9 Av main course £5-£7 **Restaurant** L served Tue-Fri 12-2.30, Sat 12-4 D served Tue-Fri 5.30-9, Sat 6-9 Fixed menu price fr £10 Av 3 course à la carte fr £22 ⊕ ENTERPRISE INNS ◀ Rebellion Mutiny, Rebellion IPA, Fuller's London Pride. **Facilities** Children welcome Children's portions Dogs allowed Garden Parking

MARSH BENHAM
Map 5 SU46

The Red House NEW

RG20 8LY ☎ **01635 582017**
e-mail: info@theredhousepub.com
dir: *5m from Hungerford, 3m from Newbury, 400yds off A4*

This thatched village local is set in beautiful countryside overlooking marshes. There is a bar with local ales and cosy log fire, a charming restaurant and a patio and garden for the summer. Run by experienced French chef/patron, Laurent Lebeau; his essentially British menu might include lamb's liver with crispy bacon; steak and kidney pudding; line-caught haddock in West Berkshire ale batter; crab gratin Thermidor; and grilled field mushroom, spinach and goat's cheese stack. As for the wines, Laurent chooses well.

Open all day all wk **Bar Meals** food served all day **Restaurant** Fixed menu price fr £12.95 Av 3 course à la carte fr £25 food served all day **Facilities** Children welcome Children's menu Children's portions Dogs allowed Garden Parking

MONEYROW GREEN
Map 6 SU87

The White Hart

SL6 2ND ☎ **01628 621460** 📄 **01628 621460**
e-mail: admin@thewhitehartholyport.co.uk
dir: *2m S from Maidenhead. M4 junct 8/9, follow Holyport signs then Moneyrow Green. Pub by petrol station*

With easy access from the M4, Maidenhead and Windsor, this traditional 19th-century coaching inn offers quality home-made food and real ales in a cosy atmosphere with an open fire. Typical mains are tortellini with pesto, rocket and Parmesan; Thai chicken curry; farmhouse cheese and tomato chutney tart; or chilli con carne. The wood-panelled lounge bar is furnished with leather Chesterfields and there are large gardens to enjoy in summer with a children's playground and petanque pitch.

Open all day all wk 12-11.30 (Fri-Sat noon-mdnt, Sun 12-11) **Bar Meals** L served Tue-Sat 12.2.30, Sun 12.30-4 D served Tue-Sat 6-9 Av main course £7.95 ⊕ GREENE KING ◀ Guinness, Morland Original, IPA, Ruddles Best, Old Speckled Hen Ö Stowford Press, Aspall. **Facilities** Children welcome Children's menu Children's portions Play area Dogs allowed Garden Parking Wi-fi

NEWBURY
Map 5 SU46

PICK OF THE PUBS

The Yew Tree Inn ◉ ☍

Hollington Cross, Andover Rd, Highclere RG20 9SE
☎ **01635 253360** 📄 **01635 255035**
e-mail: info@theyewtree.net
web: www.theyewtree.net
dir: *M4 junct 13, A34 S, 4th junct on left signed Highclere/Wash Common, turn right towards Andover A343, inn on right*

This fine 17th-century free house occupies a pleasant setting close to Highclere Castle. Full of charm and character, the pub blends original features like old beams, tiled floors, and logs smouldering in the inglenook fireplaces with the contemporary refinements of crisp linen and sparkling glassware. Several interconnecting rooms provide a choice of dining areas and unusual real ales, ciders and fifteen wines by the glass are served in the bar. The kitchen offers traditional British food and time-honoured classics from the French culinary canon. The Anglo-French cooking takes a brasserie approach, with the menu split into sections like hors d'oeuvres, fish and seafood, pies and puddings and roasts and grills, and delivers accomplished, well-presented dishes that are driven by quality ingredients. A memorable meal might kick off with potted duck with Agen prunes and Madeira jelly, before moving on to roast venison 'Pierre Koffmann' with chocolate sauce. The dessert menu could include blackberry and apple crumble or sherry trifle.

Open all day all wk **Bar Meals** L served Mon-Sat 12-2.30, Sun 12-3 D served Mon-Sat 6-9.30, Sun 6-9 Av main course £16 **Restaurant** L served Mon-Sat 12-2.30, Sun 12-3 D served Mon-Sat 6-9.30, Sun 6-9 Fixed menu price fr £16.50 Av 3 course à la carte fr £30 ⊕ FREE HOUSE ◀ Timothy Taylor, Adnams, Butt's Barbus Barbus, Black Sheep Ö Westons Old Rosie, Westons Bounds Brand. ☍ 15 **Facilities** Children welcome Children's portions Dogs allowed Garden Parking Wi-fi

PALEY STREET
Map 5 SU87

PICK OF THE PUBS

The Royal Oak Paley Street ◉◉◉ ☍

Littlefield Green SL6 3JN ☎ **01628 620541**
e-mail: info@theroyaloakpaleystreet.com
dir: *From Maidenhead take A330 towards Ascot for 2m, turn right onto B3024 signed Twyford, 2nd pub on left*

Set amidst cornfields, pocket woods and stock farms in deepest Berkshire, The Royal Oak plays it's traditional English role to the full, combining a decent pint of finest Fuller's London Pride beer with exemplary culinary offerings that manage both to reflect the old and offer stunning new flavours and combinations, gaining head chef Dominic Chapman 3 AA Rosettes. This stylish, oak-beamed 17th-century gastro-pub is run by Nick Parkinson, while co-owner Sir Michael Parkinson takes a distant back seat, where 25 wines by the glass (from a list of over 330) may accompany any of a galaxy of tempting treats from the thoughtfully crafted menu. A lasagne of rabbit with wild mushrooms and chervil, or a wood pigeon, ham and Middlewhite pithivier with green peppercorn sauce may in themselves sate some appetites. Magnificent mains may tempt, however: an inventive West Country brown hare and trotter pie or the pub's signature dish of peppered haunch of Denham Estate venison with creamed spinach and sauce poivrade, finishing in style with a soufflé of Yorkshire rhubarb. For a snack there is always the renowned Scotch egg.

Open 12-3 6-11 (Sun 12-4) Closed: Sun eve **Restaurant** L served Mon-Sat 12-3, Sun 12-4 booking required D served Mon-Thu 6.30-9.30, Fri-Sat 6.30-10 booking required Fixed menu price fr £17.95 Av 3 course à la carte fr £40 ⊕ FULLER'S ◀ Fuller's London Pride, Seafarers Ale. ☍ 25 **Facilities** Children welcome Children's portions Garden Parking

READING
Map 5 SU77

The Flowing Spring

Henley Rd, Playhatch RG4 9RB ☎ **0118 969 9878**
e-mail: info@theflowingspringpub.co.uk
web: www.theflowingspringpub.co.uk
dir: *3m N of Reading*

Some quirky furnishings and artefacts will make this rural Fullers' pub stick in the mind, as may the sloping floor, whilst families love the huge garden bounded by two streams, one of which emanates from a nearby spring, hence the name. Beams, open fires and a verandah balcony overlooking Thames Valley countryside are the accompaniment to the invigorating menu of pub classics and creative new dishes using locally sourced and foraged produce; the soups are particularly notable. A summer beer festival is planned.

Open all day all wk **Bar Meals** L served Mon-Sat 12-2.30, Sun 12-3 D served Tue-Sat 6-9.30 Av main course £8.95 **Restaurant** L served Mon-Sat 12-2.30, Sun 12-3 D served Tue-Sat 6-9.30 Av 3 course à la carte fr £17.50 ⊕ FULLER'S ◀ London Pride, ESB, Chiswick, Discovery Ö Aspall. **Facilities** Children welcome Children's portions Play area Dogs allowed Garden Beer festival Parking Wi-fi

See advert on opposite page

The Shoulder of Mutton

Playhatch RG4 9QU ☎ 0118 947 3908
e-mail: shoulderofmutton@hotmail.co.uk
dir: *From Reading follow signs to Caversham, then onto A4155 to Henley-on-Thames. At rdbt left to Binfield Heath, pub on left*

An inviting combination of rustic, cosy village inn and chic, contemporary dining in the airy conservatory restaurant draws in a dedicated crowd of regulars and appreciative diners keen to share head chef Alan Oxlade's passion for the finest local foodstuffs. The pub, true to its name, specialises in mutton dishes, and is proud to be a member of HRH The Prince of Wales' Mutton Renaissance Club. The signature dish is Welsh organic mountain mutton, slow roasted for seven hours so it just 'falls off the bone'. Other dishes that might tempt are 'Granchio torte' – Italian-style crab cakes with Avjar pepper sauce, or 'Farmyard Fracas' – pan-fried lambs' liver and bacon. The walled garden is a popular retreat, or relax by the open fire over a glass of Loddon ale.

Open 12-3 6-11 (Mon 12-3 7-11, Sat 12-3 6.30-11, Sun 12-3) Closed: 26-30 Dec, 1 Jan, Sun pm
Bar Meals L served all wk 12-2 booking required D served Mon-Sat 6.30-9 booking required Av main course £13 **Restaurant** L served all wk 12-2 booking required D served Mon-Sat 6.30-9 booking required Fixed menu price fr £20 Av 3 course à la carte fr £25 ⊕ GREENE KING ◀ Greene King IPA, Hullabaloo Loddon ♂ Aspall. **Facilities** Children welcome Children's portions Garden Parking

Buratta's at the Royal Oak ▼ NEW

Ruscombe Ln RG10 9JN ☎ 0118 934 5190
e-mail: enquiries@burattas.co.uk
dir: *From A4 (Wargrave rdbt) take A321 to Twyford (signed Twyford/Wokingham). Straight on at 1st lights, right at 2nd lights onto A3032. Right onto A3024 (Ruscombe Rd which becomes Ruscombe Lane). Pub on left on brow of hill*

Built in the 1880s, The Royal Oak was originally a one-bar pub, but it has been extended over the years and the old cottage next door is now the kitchen. With Binghams Brewery Twyford Tipple as a resident ale, the relaxed restaurant offers a wide range of meals, from hearty bar snacks to à la carte choices such as beef Stroganoff with rice. The pub even has its own antiques shop and everything in the pub is for sale - including the tables and chairs.

Open Tue-Sat 12-3 6-11 (Sun-Mon 12-3) Closed: Sun eve & Mon eve **Bar Meals** L served all wk 12-2.30 D served Tue-Sat 7-9.30 Av main course £8-£9.50 **Restaurant** L served all wk 12-2.30 D served Tue-Sat 7-9.30 booking required Av 3 course à la carte fr £20 ⊕ ENTERPRISE INNS ◀ Fuller's London Pride, Binghams Brewery Ales, Guest ales. ▼ 12 **Facilities** Children welcome Children's menu Children's portions Dogs allowed Garden

The Walter Arms ▼

Bearwood Rd RG41 5BP ☎ 0118 977 4903
e-mail: mail@thewalterarms.com
dir: *From Wokingham take A329 towards Reading. In 1.5m left onto B3030. 5m left into Bearwood Rd. Pub 200yds on left*

This popular dining pub, with its pleasing mix of chic modern and Edwardian overtones, is a pivotal point in the social life of the village. It was built in the 1850s for a member of the Walter family, founders of The Times newspaper; in fact the family built the village of Sindlesham. Diners can sample a diverse seasonal menu of traditional English, classic French and European dishes given an Asian twist, with choice smorgasbords, stone-baked pizzas and pasta dishes like crab and watercress linguine. The wrap-around beer garden is a good place to sample the reliable selection of real ales and cider on sunny summer days. There's also a good bin of wines.

Open all day all wk **Bar Meals** L served Mon-Fri 12-3, Sat 12-10, Sun 12-9 D served Mon-Fri 6-10, Sat-Sun all day **Restaurant** L served Mon-Fri 12-3, Sat 12-10, Sun 12-9 booking required D served Mon-Fri 6-10, Sat-Sun all day booking required ⊕ FREE HOUSE ◀ London Pride, Black Sheep Best ♂ Stowford Press. ▼ 10 **Facilities** Children welcome Children's menu Children's portions Garden Parking

The Bull Inn ▼ NEW

High St RG4 6UP ☎ 0118 969 3901 📠 0118 969 7188
e-mail: bullinn@fullers.co.uk
dir: *From Reading take A4 towards Maidenhead. Left onto B4446 to Sonning*

Two minutes' walk from the River Thames in the pretty village of Sonning, this olde worlde inn can trace its roots back 500 years or more; it can also boast a mention in Jerome K. Jerome's classic *Three Men in a Boat*. With Fuller's ales on tap and log fires in the grate, The Bull charms locals and visitors alike. It's a great place to eat too, with specials changing daily – perhaps 'fabulous fish stew' served with fresh crab dumplings and crispy bread; or cinnamon and apple spiced pork belly with mulled wine cabbage and roasted almonds.

Open all day all wk **Bar Meals** L served all wk 10-9.30 D served all wk 6.30-9.30 Av main course £14 food served all day **Restaurant** L served all wk 10-9.30 D served all wk 6.30-9.30 food served all day ⊕ FULLER'S ◀ London Pride, HSB, Chiswick, Discovery, Honey Dew. ▼ 24 **Facilities** Children welcome Children's portions Dogs allowed Garden Parking Wi-fi

The Flowing Spring
A Unique Pub with a Unique Name

The Flowing Spring nestles on the border of the Chilterns and the Thames Valley between Reading and Henley-On-Thames. It is a friendly country pub that serves fresh, home-made food, fine Fuller's ales and excellent wines. The entire pub is on a slant with almost a foot difference from one end of the bar to the other! There is a huge garden with streams on two sides, one of which is fed from the local spring. We hold barbecues, concerts, fun days, beer festivals and parties during the warmer months making it the perfect place to relax in beautiful surroundings. Walkers, cyclists, dogs and children are always welcome!

Meetings and buffets are catered for all year round and Wi-Fi is free. Open all day.

The Flowing Spring, Henley Road, Playhatch, near Reading, Oxfordshire RG4 9RB
Tel: 0118 969 9878 Web: www.theflowingspringpub.co.uk

STANFORD DINGLEY   Map 5 SU57

The Old Boot Inn ☖

RG7 6LT ☎ 0118 974 4292   📠 0118 974 4292
dir: M4 junct 12, A4/A340 to Pangbourne. 1st left to Bradfield. Through Bradfield, follow Stanford Dingley signs

The Middleton family were regulars at John Haley's 18th-century pub in the Pang Valley, which is why he was invited to Catherine's marriage to Prince William. John serves locally brewed beers in his bar, while his fresh seafood might include Guernsey oysters served with shallot red vinegar, and sea bass baked in a salt crust. Other possibilities are sweetbreads with chasseur sauce; seared pigeon breast; and fresh buffalo mozzarella with avocado, tomato and pesto.

Open all wk 11-3 6-11 **Bar Meals** L served all wk 12-2 D served all wk 7-9 **Restaurant** L served all wk 12-2 D served all wk 7-9 ⊕ FREE HOUSE ◖ Brakspear Bitter, Interbrew Bass, West Berkshire Dr Hexters, Archers Best, Thomas Hardy Royal Oak Ö Stowford Press. ☖ 10 **Facilities** Children welcome Children's menu Children's portions Play area Dogs allowed Garden Parking Wi-fi

SWALLOWFIELD   Map 5 SU76

PICK OF THE PUBS

The George & Dragon

Church Rd RG7 1TJ
☎ 0118 988 4432   📠 0118 988 6474
e-mail: dining@georgeanddragonswallowfield.co.uk
dir: M4, junct 11, A33 towards Basingstoke. Left at Barge Ln to B3349 into The Street, right into Church Rd

Here is an award-winning, country pub and restaurant with a sound reputation for real ales, excellent wines and great food, and has been under the same ownership for the last 16 years. Formerly a farm, it looks good too – stripped low beams, log fires, rug-strewn floors and warm earthy tones. Menus are internationally inspired, the chef setting great store on sourcing as much produce as possible from local suppliers. An unusual starter is bacalao, Spanish salt-cod fritters with dipping sauce; another is twice-baked Fourme d'Ambert blue cheese soufflé with toasted hazelnut and pear salad. Typical main courses include lightly roasted duck breast on sesame noodles with shredded cucumber, spring onions, plum sauce and crispy seaweed; and roast red snapper coated in harissa on wok-fried bok choi with fresh ginger and lime leaf. The garden overlooks beautiful countryside, and the pub makes a great place to ease up after a walk along the long-distance Blackwater Valley Footpath.

Open all day all wk **Bar Meals** L served Mon-Sat 12-2.30, Sun 12-3 booking required D served Mon-Sat 7-9.30, Sun 7-9 booking required Av main course £13 **Restaurant** L served Mon-Sat 12-2.30, Sun 12-3 booking required D served Mon-Sat 7-9.30, Sun 7-9 booking required Fixed menu price fr £25 Av 3 course à la carte fr £25 ⊕ FREE HOUSE ◖ Fuller's London Pride, Brakspears Ö Thatchers Gold. **Facilities** Children welcome Children's menu Children's portions Dogs allowed Garden Parking

WALTHAM ST LAWRENCE   Map 5 SU87

The Bell ☖

The Street RG10 0JJ ☎ 0118 934 1788
e-mail: scott@thebellinn.biz
dir: On B3024 E of Twyford. From A4 turn at Hare Hatch

This 14th-century free house is renowned for its ciders and an ever-changing range of real ales selected from small independent breweries. The building was given to the community in 1608 and profits from the rent still help village charities. With all charcuterie and preparation of game carried out in house, seasonal home-made dishes on the daily menu might include goose with apple sauce; pan-fried hake with salsa verde; or spinach and Parmesan tart with confit tomatoes. Don't miss the annual beer festival in June.

Open all wk 12-3 5-11 (Sat noon-11 Sun noon-10.30) **Bar Meals** L served Mon-Fri 12-2, Sat-Sun 12-3 D served all wk 7-9.30 Av main course £13 ⊕ FREE HOUSE ◖ 5 changing real ales Ö Pheasant Plucker, Old Rosie. ☖ 19 **Facilities** Children welcome Children's menu Children's portions Play area Dogs allowed Garden Beer festival Parking

WHITE WALTHAM   Map 5 SU87

The Beehive ☖ NEW

Waltham Rd SL6 3SH ☎ 01628 822877
e-mail: beehivepub@aol.com
dir: M4 junct8/9, A404, follow White Waltham signs

In an idyllic village location, overlooking the cricket pitch, The Beehive is a cracking country local, renowned locally for its relaxing atmosphere, four real ales, including local Loddon ales, and fresh seasonal food. Look to the chalkboard for the daily dishes, perhaps scallops and shrimps with chorizo, followed by braised oxtail with celeriac mash, and bread-and-butter pudding. On match days bag a table on the front terrace and watch an over or two with a pint of London Pride.

Open all wk 11-3 5-11 (Sat 11am-mdnt, Sun 12-10.30) Closed: 26 Dec **Bar Meals** L served Mon-Fri 12-2.30, Sat 12-9.30, Sun 12-8.30 D served Mon-Fri 5-9.30, Sat 12-9.30, Sun 12-8.30 Av main course £6.95 **Restaurant** L served Mon-Fri 12-2.30, Sat 12-9.30, Sun 12-8.30 booking required D served Mon-Fri 5-9.30, Sat 12-9.30, Sun 12-8.30 booking required Av 3 course à la carte fr £15 ⊕ ENTERPRISE INNS ◖ Brakspear, Fuller's London Pride, Abbot, Guest ale Loddon, Rebellion. ☖ 14 **Facilities** Children welcome Children's menu Children's portions Dogs allowed Garden Parking

WINKFIELD   Map 6 SU97

Rose & Crown

Woodside, Windsor Forest SL4 2DP
☎ 01344 882051   📠 01344 885346
dir: M3 junct 3 from Ascot Racecourse on A332 take 2nd exit from Heatherwood Hosp rdbt, then 2nd left

A 200-year-old traditional pub complete with old beams and low ceilings. Hidden down a country lane, it has a peaceful garden overlooking open fields where you can see horses and llamas at pasture. A typical menu may include pan-fried fillet steak with blue cheese gratin potatoes, with seasonal vegetables and a bourguignon sauce; pavé of halibut with rosemary sauté potatoes, chargrilled asparagus and baby leeks, with horseradish cream sauce; or asparagus tortellini with basil and Parmesan cheese. Recent change of hands.

Open all day all wk ⊕ GREENE KING ◖ Morland Original, Greene King IPA, guest ale. **Facilities** Children welcome Children's menu Children's portions Play area Garden Parking Wi-fi

WINTERBOURNE   Map 5 SU47

The Winterbourne Arms ☖

RG20 8BB ☎ 01635 248200   📠 01635 248824
e-mail: winterbournearms@tiscali.co.uk
dir: M4 junct 13 into Chieveley Services, follow Donnington signs to Winterbourne sign. Turn right into Arlington Ln, right at T-junct, left into Winterbourne

Only five minutes from the busy M4 yet steeped in 300 years of history, warmth and charm, this privately owned pretty black and white village pub offers a high standard from both the big and gusty food and range of drinks. Real ales may include Whistle Whetter, while ten wines served by the glass and 20 more by the bottle make for a comprehensive list. Traditional British menus include fresh Brixham fish and home-made pie of the week, which can be served in candlelight and by the winter fires or out in the large gardens in summer.

Open all wk noon-3 6-11 (Sun noon-10.30) **Bar Meals** L served all wk 12-2.30 D served all wk 6-10 **Restaurant** L served all wk 12-2.30 D served all wk 6-10 ⊕ FREE HOUSE ◖ Ramsbury Gold, Guinness, Whistle Wetter. ☖ 10 **Facilities** Children welcome Children's portions Dogs allowed Garden Parking

PICK OF THE PUBS

The Royal Oak Hotel ♟

YATTENDON   Map 5 SU57

The Square RG18 0UG
☎ **01635 201325** 📄 **01635 201926**
e-mail: info@royaloakyattendon.com
web: www.royaloakyattendon.co.uk
dir: *M4 junct 12, A4 to Newbury, right at 2nd rdbt to Pangbourne then 1st left. From junct 13, A34 N 1st left, right at T-junct. Left then 2nd right to Yattendon*

Formed out of a row of 16th-century cottages facing the village square, the wisteria-clad Royal Oak has a long, celebrated history: Oliver Cromwell and his Roundheads dined here and planned their strategy for the Battle of Newbury in 1664. Ironically, the pub was re-named in memory of King Charles who sought refuge here after the bloody confrontation. Today, the Royal Oak puts on a civilised face, tucked away in sleepy Yattendon deep in shooting country, and it wears its history well. Log fires blaze in the bar and the adjoining lounge and dining rooms, where the decor is all oak beams, quarry tiled and wood floors, and an assorted mix of pine and mahogany tables. The pub is rarely interrupted by anything more menacing than the clip-clop of passing horse riders, and owner Rob McGill offers tip-top real ales from the nearby West Berkshire Brewery (try a pint of Good Old Boy), and delicious home-cooked food. From the daily menu, order a sandwich, perhaps filled with steak, sweet onions and horseradish cream, or begin a leisurely meal with tarragon crab cake with caper and shallot relish, or oxtail soup with mustard croutons. For main course, choose seafood pie with smoked Cheddar mash and wild leaf salad, venison Wellington with red wine gravy, or opt for one of the fish specials. Round off with apple and rhubarb crumble with lemongrass custard or banana bread and butter pudding. Give four days notice and you can host your own dinner party in one of the private rooms, ordering a whole suckling pig with rosemary and cider sauce, or a rib of aged beef with all the trimmings. French windows lead to a walled rear garden with smart garden furniture and a vine-laden trellis, plus its own boules piste, the perfect spot for a summer drink or meal.

Open all day all wk **Bar Meals** L served Mon-Fri 12-2.30, Sat-Sun 12-3 D served Mon-Thu 7-9.30, Fri- Sat 7-10, Sun 7-9 Av main course £14 **Restaurant** L served Mon-Fri 12-2.30, Sat-Sun 12-3 D served Mon-Thu 7-9.30, Fri- Sat 7-10, Sun 7-9 Fixed menu price fr £11.95 Av 3 course à la carte fr £25 🍺 FREE HOUSE ◀ West Berkshire, Good Old Boy, Mr Chubbs, guest ale ♂ Stowford Press. ♟ 10 **Facilities** Children's menu Children's portions Dogs allowed Garden Parking Wi-fi

WOKINGHAM Map 5 SU86

The Broad Street Tavern ♀

29 Broad St RG40 1AU ☎ 0118 977 3706
e-mail: broadstreettavern@wadworth.co.uk
dir: *In town centre, adjacent to Pizza Express*

In a handsome detached period building fronted by elegant railings, the Wadworth-owned 'Tav' offers leather armchairs and sofas in the bar, and an extensive decked garden area with a summer bar and barbecues. Meals include sausages sizzler board to share; gammon and eggs; salmon and spinach in tarragon sauce; rib-eye steaks; and hand-made pies. Then there are deli plates, ciabattas and nibbles, such as spicy fries, lamb samosas and duck spring rolls; and quite a reputation for well-kept beers, Champagnes and cocktails too. The pub hosts four beer festivals a year.

Open all day all wk **Bar Meals** L served all wk 12-2.30 D served all wk 6-9.30 ⊕ WADWORTH & CO ◖ Wadworth 6X, Henrys IPA, Bishops Tipple ♂ Old Rosie. ♀ 17
Facilities Dogs allowed Garden Beer festival Wi-fi

YATTENDON Map 5 SU57

PICK OF THE PUBS

The Royal Oak Hotel ♀

See Pick of the Pubs on page 39

BRISTOL

BRISTOL Map 4 ST57

The Albion ♀ NEW

Boyces Av, Clifton BS8 4AA ☎ 0117 973 3522
e-mail: info@thealbionclifton.co.uk
dir: *From A4 take B3129 towards city centre. Right into Clifton Down Rd. 3rd left into Boyces Ave*

This handsome Grade II-listed coaching inn dates from the 17th-century and was refurbished by owner Owain George in 2005. It has become one of Bristol's premier dining destinations, as well as a popular pub to enjoy local ales and ciders. Perennially popular is the enclosed courtyard, where you can order jugs of Pimms in summer or sip mulled cider under heaters in the winter. The modern British cooking here takes on a 'nose to tail' approach, with much use of local produce in dishes such as Portland crab, mussel and saffron risotto; venison faggots with onion and mash; roast skate with bacon and peas; baked vanilla cheesecake with blood orange.

Open all day all wk Closed: 25 Dec **Bar Meals** L served all wk 12-3 D served all wk 7-9.30 **Restaurant** L served all wk 12-3 D served all wk 7-9.30 ⊕ ENTERPRISE INNS ◖ Butcombe Bitter, Otter Bitter, Sharp's Doom Bar ♂ Thatchers Cheddar Valley, Stowford Press. ♀ 12
Facilities Children welcome Children's menu Children's portions Dogs allowed Garden Beer festival Wi-fi

Cornubia

142 Temple St BS1 6EN
☎ 0117 925 4415 ▤ 0117 929 1523
e-mail: philjackithecornubia@hotmail.co.uk
dir: *Opposite Bristol Fire Station*

Hidden among tall office buildings in the centre of Bristol, this welcoming Georgian pub was originally built as two houses; with its name being the Latinised version for Cornwall. Local workers love it, not just because of its convenience, but also for its choice of seven changing real ales, including its own Cornubia, two draught ciders and a serious collection of malts and bottled beers. Weekday lunchtime bar snacks include baguettes, Phil's specials of the day, and the pub's famous pork pies. There is a raised decking area at the front and live entertainment every week.

Open all day Mon-Sat noon-11 Closed: 25-26 Dec, 1 Jan, Sun **Bar Meals** L served Mon-Sat 12-2.30 ⊕ FREE HOUSE ◖ Cornubia, Sunraker, Guest ales ♂ Cheddar Valley, Thatchers Gold, guest ciders. **Facilities** Dogs allowed Parking Wi-fi

The Hare on the Hill

41 Thomas St North, Kingsdown BS2 8LX
☎ 0117 908 1982
e-mail: harehill@bathales.co.uk
dir: *Telephone for directions*

If you can find it in the maze of streets that is Kingsdown, this is a gem – a small, street-corner local from the good old days, remaining close to the heart of the community. If all you want is a pint of one of Bath Ales award-winning brews, malt whisky or a European-style beer, come here. All food (except fresh fish) is sourced from within a 40-mile radius. Typical are BLT baguette; steak and Barnstormer pie; home-made faggots, mash and onion gravy; plus a roast on Sundays. Monday night quizzes and major sports fixtures shown on TV.

Open all wk 12-2.30 5-11 (Sat 12-11.30 Sun 12-11)
Bar Meals L served Mon-Sat 12-2 (Sun 12-4) D served Mon-Sat 6-9 ⊕ BATH ALES ◖ Gem, Spa, Barnstormer.
Facilities Children welcome Wi-fi

Highbury Vaults

164 St Michaels Hill, Cotham BS2 8DE
☎ 0117 973 3203
e-mail: highburyvaults@youngs.co.uk
dir: *Take A38 to Cotham from inner ring dual carriageway*

Once a turnpike station, this 1840s pub has retained much of its Victorian atmosphere. In days when hangings took place on nearby St Michael's Hill, many victims partook of their last meal in the vaults. Today, it's a business crowd by day and students at night feasting on chilli, meat and vegetable curries, casseroles, pasta dishes, and jacket potatoes. No fried foods, no music or fruit machines here, but a popular heated garden terrace. Look carefully and you'll spot a little train running the length of the pub.

Open all day all wk noon-mdnt (Sun 12-11)
Bar Meals L served Mon-Fri 12-2, Sat 12.30, Sun 12-4 D served Mon-Fri 5.30-8.30 Av main course £6.50 ⊕ YOUNG & CO BREWERY PLC ◖ Bath Ales Gem, St Austells Tribute, Brains SA, Young's Special & Bitter, rotating guest ales ♂ Addlestones, Thatchers Gold.
Facilities Children welcome Garden **Notes** ✉

PICK OF THE PUBS

The Kensington Arms ♀ NEW

35-37 Stanley Rd BS6 6NP ☎ 0117 944 6444
e-mail: info@thekensingtonarms.co.uk
dir: *From Redland Rail Station into South Rd, then Kensington Rd. 4th right into Stanley Rd*

A prominent Victorian corner pub in the heart of Bristol's leafy Redland district, The Kensington Arms is popular with locals as well as the many university students living in the streets surrounding it. Under the new owners, the pub has been smartened up and transformed into a smart bar and a dining room packed with mismatched antique furniture, Victorian prints and a window into the open kitchen. The modern British food utilises the very best local producers and the menu changes daily. In the bar, upmarket snacks include pig's cheeks and Scotch eggs, as well as the popular burger. The restaurant menu might start with Brixham mussel and sweetcorn chowder or breast of wood pigeon, pearl barley risotto, followed by confit leg of Creedy Carver duck with a ham hock and Toulouse sausage cassoulet or a simple, well-made fish pie.

Open all day all wk Closed: 26 Dec **Bar Meals** L served Mon-Fri 12-3 D served Mon-Sat 6-10 Av main course £13.95 **Restaurant** L served Mon-Fri 12-3, Sat 10-3, Sun 12-4 D served Mon-Sat 6-10 Av 3 course à la carte fr £22 ⊕ GREENE KING ◖ Morland, Greene King IPA, Ruddles County ♂ Stowford Press. ♀ 14
Facilities Children welcome Children's portions Dogs allowed Garden Wi-fi

Robin Hood's Retreat ♟

197 Gloucester Rd BS7 8BG ☎ 0117 924 8639
e-mail: info@robinhoodsretreat.gmail.com
web: www.robinhoodsretreat.co.uk
dir: *At main rdbt at Broad Mead take Gloucester Rd exit,*
St Pauls. Road leads into Gloucester Rd (A38)

In the heart of Bristol, this Victorian red-brick pub is
popular with real ale lovers, who usually have eight to
choose from. The interior has been superbly appointed,
with original features retained and with the addition of
richly coloured wood panelling and furniture. There's
plenty of attention to detail in the food too, which is all
prepared on the premises. Favourites are slow-cooked
British dishes such as braised brisket of salt beef with
toffee carrots and dripping roast potatoes, and several
seafood options.

Open all wk Sun-Wed noon-11pm (Thu-Sat noon-mdnt)
Closed: 25 Dec **Bar Meals** L served Mon-Fri 12-3, Sun
12-4 D served 6-9.30, Sun 7-9 **Restaurant** L served
Mon-Fri 6-9.30, Sun 7-9 D served 6-9.30, Sun 7-9
booking required ⊕ ENTERPRISE INNS ◀ Doom Bar,
Butcombe, Tribute, Tanglefoot ♂ Stowford Press. ♟ 15
Facilities Children welcome Children's portions Garden

AMERSHAM   Map 6 SU99

Hit or Miss Inn ♟

Penn Street Village HP7 0PX
☎ 01494 713109   🖷 01494 718010
e-mail: hit@ourpubs.co.uk
dir: *M25 junct 18, A404 (Amersham to High Wycombe*
road) to Amersham. Past crematorium on right, 2nd left
into Whielden Ln (signed Winchmore Hill). 1.25m, pub
on right

This 18th-century cottage-style dining pub overlooks the
cricket ground from which its name is taken. It has a
beautiful country garden with lawn, patio and picnic
tables for warmer days, while inside you'll find fires, old
world beams and a warm welcome from owners Michael
and Mary Macken. Home-cooked dishes range from
tempting sandwiches and light meals like mini game pie
to veal escalope with vegetable tagliatelle and basil
sauce or pork tenderloin stuffed with chestnuts and
mushrooms, plus daily specials and Sunday roasts, too.
There is a village beer festival in July.

Open all day all wk 11-11 (Sun 12-10.30)
Bar Meals L served Mon-Sat 12-2.30, Sun 12-8 D served
Mon-Sat 6.30-9.30, Sun 12-8 Av main course £12
Restaurant L served Mon-Sat 12-2.30, Sun 12-8 D served
Mon-Sat 6.30-9.30, Sun 12-8 Av 3 course à la carte fr
£23 ⊕ HALL & WOODHOUSE ◀ Badger Best, Tanglefoot,
Sussex, Hopping Hare ♂ Stowford Press. ♟ 10
Facilities Children welcome Children's menu Children's
portions Dogs allowed Garden Beer festival Parking Wi-fi

AYLESBURY   Map 11 SP81

The King's Head ♟ NEW

Market Square HP20 2RW
☎ 01296 718812   🖷 01296 428597
e-mail: info@farmersbar.co.uk
dir: *Access on foot only. From Market Square access*
cobbled passageway. Pub entrance under archway on
right

A well preserved coaching inn dating from 1455, with
many fascinating architectural features and, unusually,
a second-hand bookshop. Come at lunchtime for a beer-
bread sandwich and a Chiltern Brewery pint, perhaps in
the cobbled courtyard; or dine inside on pan-fried sea
bass with crayfish, steak and kidney pudding, or
vegetable pie. Rothschild's supplies the wines from its
former family seat at nearby National Trust-owned
Waddesdon Manor. Beer festivals are held twice a year.

Open all day all wk Closed: 25 Dec & Etr Sun
Bar Meals L served Mon-Fri 12-2, Sat 12-3 D served
Wed-Sat 6-9 Av main course £8 ⊕ CHILTERN BREWERY
◀ Beechwood Bitter, Chiltern Ale, 300s Old Ale
♂ Stowford Press, Westons Organic. ♟ 11
Facilities Children welcome Children's menu Children's
portions Family room Garden Beer festival

BEACONSFIELD   Map 6 SU99

PICK OF THE PUBS

The Royal Standard of England ♟

Brindle Ln, Forty Green HP9 1XT ☎ 01494 673382
e-mail: theoldestpub@btinternet.com
dir: *A40 to Beaconsfield, right at church rdbt onto*
B474 towards Penn, left onto Forty Green Rd, 1m

Ramblers can use the large car park here before
setting out on one of the circular walks around this
historic ale house, reputedly the oldest in England.
Situated in the beautiful Chilterns village of Forty
Green, it can trace its roots to Saxon times. It's no
surprise then that tales from its history abound, many
recounted on the back of the menu. Along with a good
selection of real ales and ciders, good hearty food is
the order of the day, served amid the striking stained
glass windows, beams and flagstone floors, and
around the large inglenook fireplace that warms the old
walls in winter. Seasonal wild game is a regular
feature on the specials board, supported by an
extensive bill of fare. Start, perhaps, with devilled
lamb's kidneys on fried toast; continue with roundhead
pork sausages made in the kitchen; and finish with
bread and butter pudding or treacle tart served with
custard, cream or ice cream.

Open all day all wk 11-11 **Bar Meals** Av main course
£11 food served all day **Restaurant** Av 3 course à la
carte fr £20 food served all day ⊕ FREE HOUSE
◀ Chiltern Ale, Brakspear Bitter, Rebellion IPA,
Theakston Old Peculier, Guest ales ♂ Cotswold Cider,
Orchard Pig Cider, Westons Perry. ♟ 11
Facilities Children welcome Children's portions Family
room Dogs allowed Garden Parking Wi-fi

PICK OF THE PUBS

The Crooked Billet ✿ ♥

BLETCHLEY — Map 11 SP83

2 Westbrook End, Newton Longville MK17 0DF ☎ **01908 373936**
e-mail: john@thebillet.co.uk
web: www.thebillet.co.uk
dir: *M1 junct 13, follow signs to Buckingham. 6m, signed at Bottledump rdbt to Newton Longville*

Timbers from a vessel surplus to requirements around the time of Sir Francis Drake were recycled to create the core of this magnificently thatched village pub, and it remained for centuries a farming community local in a rural village setting. Time and tide wait for no-one, however, and the countryside became part of greater Milton Keynes, Newton just remaining detached from the new town; Bletchley Park WWII code-breaking centre is just down the road. Fortunately, the soul of the rural alehouse remains; crackling winter log fires (the house bacon is smoked in the inglenook) cast flickering shadows across oak beams whilst a glimpse of village green life is recalled by the huge lawned gardens. Top sommelier John Gilchrist and wife/chef Emma took on the run down Billet a decade ago and realised their dream of running a high end destination dining pub together. Local foodies flock to the two intimate wine-themed dining rooms for Emma's menus, which are based on the finest, freshest ingredients from a multitude of small, local specialist food producers and suppliers. The emphasis is on taste, combined with modern presentation; a cosmopolitan mix of contemporary and classical with definite English and French influences. Set lunch and dinner menus change daily, whilst the carte selection reads like a gastronome's wish list; all meals are matched on the menus to particular wines, astonishingly well over 200 are listed, all available by the glass. An opening gambit could be truffle and thyme marinated pan-fried pigeon breast, pinot noir reduced Puy lentils, bacon and tarragon parsnip purée; paving the way for guinea fowl breast with spinach and roasted garlic stuffing, creamed pearl barley and chimney smoked bacon with leek gratin, roasted salsify and a port reduction; or pan-fried cod fillet and crispy squid linguini nero with lemon marinated fennel salad, chive and chervil cream. The sweets and cheeseboard are equally fulfilling, whilst evening taster menus, including vegetarian, are available.

Open noon-2.30 5-11 (Sun noon-4 7-10.30) Closed: 27-28 Dec, Mon L **Bar Meals** L served Tue-Sat 12-2, Sun 12-4 D served Mon-Sat 7-9 Av main course £10.75 **Restaurant** L served Tue-Sat 12-2, Sun 12-4 D served Mon-Fri 7-9.30, Sat 6.30-10 booking required Fixed menu price fr £19.50 Av 3 course à la carte fr £25 ⊕ GREENE KING ◀ Old Speckled Hen, Badger Tanglefoot, Hobgoblin, Ruddles County. ♥ 200 **Facilities** Children's portions Garden Parking

PICK OF THE PUBS

The Royal Oak ♛

BOVINGDON GREEN   Map 5 SU88

Frieth Rd SL7 2JF
☎ **01628 488611**   🖹 **01628 478680**
e-mail: info@royaloakmarlow.co.uk
web: www.royaloakmarlow.co.uk
dir: *From Marlow, take A4155. In 300yds right signed Bovingdon Green. In 0.75m pub on left*

On the edge of Marlow Common and glorious walking country, this lovely cream-painted cottage is part of David and Becky Salisbury's thriving mini-empire of pubs, which includes the Alford Arms at Frithsden, Hertfordshire and The Swan at Denham, Buckinghamshire (see entries). Literally, just up the hill and a world away from bustling Marlow, retreat here for the sunny summer terrace and the sprawling, flower-filled gardens, replete with petanque piste and, if you're lucky, red kites wheeling overhead. Inside, it's both spacious yet cosy, with dark floorboards, rich fabrics, terracotta and pale green walls and a wood-burning stove setting the upmarket tone, and the early evening regulars gather around the crossword. Meanwhile the kitchen team can offer something for everyone, the imaginative modern British menu making good use of fresh local produce, and an exclusively European wine list includes 21 by the glass. From the seasonal menu's 'small plates' section begin with rustic breads, roast garlic and olive oil, crab and coriander risotto, or a warm black

pudding, pork and sage Scotch egg. Main courses range from Amersham pork belly with butternut squash purée and sage potato cake, through pork and leek sausage and root vegetable cassoulet with Cheddar cheese champ, to sea bream with celeriac and apple mash and Thatcher's cider velouté. Leave room for sticky toffee pudding with toffee sauce and tonka bean ice cream, or a plate of British cheeses with spiced fruit chutney. The beers come from the Rebellion Brewery in Marlow Bottom, whilst free Wi-fi is available if you're planning a working lunch or dinner.

Open all day all wk 11-11 (Sun 12-10.30) Closed: 26 Dec **Bar Meals** L served Mon-Fri 12-2.30, Sat 12-3, Sun 12-4 D served Sun-Thu 6.30-9.30, Fri-Sat 6.30-10 Av main course £14.25 **Restaurant** L served Mon-Fri 12-2.30, Sat 12-3, Sun 12-4 D served Sun-Thu 6.30-9.30, Fri-Sat 6.30-10 booking required Av 3 course à la carte fr £26.25 ⊕ SALISBURY PUBS LTD ◀ Marlow Rebellion IPA, Marlow Rebellion Smuggler, Marlow Rebellion Mutiny Ŏ Thatchers. ♛ 21 **Facilities** Children's portions Dogs allowed Garden Parking Wi-fi

BLEDLOW   Map 5 SP70

The Lions of Bledlow ♥

Church End HP27 9PE
☎ 01844 343345   🖹 01844 343345
dir: *M40 junct 6, B4009 to Princes Risborough, through Chinnor into Bledlow*

A beautiful long, low pub dating back to the 1500s and with character to match, from the enormous fireplace to the low beams and careworn flooring. Popular for location filming, period furnishings add to the timeless feeling, as do steam trains chugging past on the nearby preserved railway beyond the village green. Sheltered below the wooded Chiltern scarp, beers from the likes of Loddon and Tring breweries welcome ramblers down from the hills; they can also top up on rustic home-made meals like chicken and ham pie or wild mushroom Stroganoff, boosted by daily changing specials.

Open all wk 11.30-3 6-11 (Sat 12-3 7-10.30 Sun noon-11 BHs & Summer Wknds all day) **Bar Meals** L served Mon-Sun 12-2.30 D served Mon-Sat 7-9.30, Sun 7-9 **Restaurant** L served Mon-Sun 12-2.30 D served Mon-Sat 7-9.30, Sun 7-9 ⊕ FREE HOUSE ◀ Wadworth 6X, Guest ales Ď Stowford Press. ♥ 12 **Facilities** Children welcome Children's menu Children's portions Family room Dogs allowed Garden Parking

BLETCHLEY   Map 11 SP83

PICK OF THE PUBS

The Crooked Billet ◉ ♥

See Pick of the Pubs on page 42

BOVINGDON GREEN   Map 5 SU88

PICK OF THE PUBS

The Royal Oak ♥

See Pick of the Pubs on page 43

BRILL   Map 11 SP61

The Pheasant Inn

Windmill St HP18 9TG ☎ 01844 239370
e-mail: info@thepheasant.co.uk
dir: *In village centre, by windmill*

High on the edge of Brill Common, this 17th-century beamed inn benefits from a large garden, and a veranda from which you can see the village windmill and across seven counties. A simple menu offers British, Mediterranean and Asian cooking, including starters of grilled lamb kofta kebabs and grilled sardines on toast; mains come in 'big or small' portions, such as Caesar salad (with or without chicken); smoked haddock, parsley and spring onion fishcakes with saffron butter sauce; rump steak beef Stroganoff. There are locally brewed ales on offer, plus many wines available from smaller vineyards.

Open all day all wk Mon-Thu noon-11pm (Fri-Sat noon-mdnt Sun noon-10.30) **Bar Meals** L served all wk 12-2 booking required D served all wk 6.30-9, Sun 12-7 booking required Av main course £12 **Restaurant** L served all wk 12-2 booking required D served all wk 6.30-9 booking required Av 3 course à la carte fr £24 ⊕ FREE HOUSE ◀ London Pride, Local Vale Ale Ď Thatchers. **Facilities** Children welcome Children's portions Garden Parking Wi-fi

BUCKINGHAM   Map 11 SP63

The Old Thatched Inn ♥

Main St, Adstock MK18 2JN
☎ 01296 712584   🖹 01296 715375
e-mail: manager@theoldthatchedinn.co.uk
dir: *Telephone for directions*

Dating back to 1702, this lovely old thatched and beamed inn still boasts the traditional beams and inglenook fireplace. The spacious interior consists of a formal conservatory and a bar with comfy furniture and a welcoming, relaxed atmosphere. Using the freshest, seasonal ingredients from local and regional suppliers, meat options might include country pork pâté and pan-fried Aylesbury duck breast, braised red cabbage and roast root vegetables. Other options might be beetroot cured salmon; pan-fried sea bass fillet; and courgette, lemon and Parmesan risotto. Belgian chocolate slice, honeycomb and vanilla ice cream will please a sweet tooth.

Open all wk noon-11 (Mon-Tue 12-2.30 6-11 Sun noon-10.30) **Bar Meals** L served Mon-Fri 12-2.30, Sat 12-3, Sun 12-8 D served Mon-Sat 6-9.30 ⊕ FREE HOUSE ◀ Hook Norton Best, Timothy Taylor, Old Speckled Hen, London Pride Ď Aspall. ♥ 14 **Facilities** Children welcome Children's menu Children's portions Dogs allowed Parking Wi-fi

CHALFONT ST GILES   Map 6 SU99

PICK OF THE PUBS

The Ivy House ♥

See Pick of the Pubs on opposite page

CHALFONT ST PETER   Map 6 TQ09

PICK OF THE PUBS

The Greyhound Inn ♥

SL9 9RA ☎ 01753 883404   🖹 01753 891627
e-mail: reception@thegreyhoundinn.net
dir: *M40 junct 1/M25 junct 16, follow signs for Gerrards Cross, then Chalfont St Peter*

Massive beams support the weight of this venerable old coaching inn, the brick chimneys of which have proved a village focal point for over 600 years. Oliver Cromwell and Winston Churchill have called in, whilst local landowner and Lord Chancellor of England George Jeffreys held some of his notorious assizes here, condemning many to gallows on the nearby riverbank in the 1680's. Establish a presence in the imposing panelled, flagstoned bar or chic, recently refurbished restaurant, chinwag with the locals over a Sharp's Doom Bar beer and look forward to choosing from the extensive modern British and continental gastro-pub menu, where a starter of leek tart warm poached egg or minted lamb ciabatta with red onion marmalade whets the appetite for a medley of venison, steak, confit and burger, Savoy cabbage, redcurrant and juniper berry sauce; or grilled fillet of sea bass on chorizo potato, guacamole, shallot and white wine sauce. Local cheeses, biscuits and quince jelly help clear the palate.

Open all day all wk Mon-Wed 6.30am-10.30pm (Thu 6.30am-11.30pm, Fri-Sat 6.30am-1am, Sun 8.30am-10.30pm) **Bar Meals** L served Mon-Sat 12-2.30, Sun 12-6 D served Mon-Sat 6-9.30 **Restaurant** L served Mon-Sat 12-2.30, Sun 12-6 booking required D served Mon-Sat 6-9.30 booking required Av 3 course à la carte fr £25 ⊕ ENTERPRISE INNS ◀ London Pride, Doom Bar, Adnams. ♥ 10 **Facilities** Children welcome Children's menu Children's portions Dogs allowed Garden Parking Wi-fi

PICK OF THE PUBS

The Ivy House 🍷

CHALFONT ST GILES   Map 6 SU99

London Rd HP8 4RS
☎ **01494 872184**   🖹 **01494 872870**
e-mail: ivyhouse@fullers.co.uk
dir: *On A413 2m S of Amersham & 1.5m N of Chalfont St Giles*

A beautiful 250-year-old brick and flint coaching inn, enjoying amazing views of the Chiltern Hills and set close to John Milton's cottage. In a great location for country walks as well as several nearby golf courses, the pub is well known for its friendly welcome, great food and extensive wine list. Old beams, open fires, comfy armchairs and brasses all give the place a welcoming, cosy atmosphere. Naturally there's the odd ghost story to be told, and whisky lovers will appreciate the range of over 30 malts, including some of the landlord's favourite rarities.

Meals are served in the bar, the former coach house and the restaurant, and in fine weather you can dine alfresco in the garden, with fantastic views over the Chiltern Hills. The fresh rustic menu changes every season, and also features daily specials, with the emphasis on quality local produce and fresh fish. and salads. The lunchtime bar menu brings a selection of sandwiches, salads, and good value hot dishes such as hand-carved honey roasted ham with free range eggs and hand-cut chips or beer-battered fish and chips.

More formal dining might begin with starters like chargrilled halloumi and chorizo with sweet red peppers, pan-fried curried mackerel, or duck liver, smoked duck and Cointreau pâté. Moving on, choose from squash, Parmesan and red onion marmalade tart; Buckinghamshire Country pork sausages with bubble and squeak; confit tuna Niçoise; or poached chicken and spring vegetable broth. Desserts include apricot bread and butter pudding, pecan pie, or rich chocolate and Amaretto truffle torte.

Open all day all wk **Bar Meals** L served Mon-Fri 12-2.45, Sat-Sun all day D served Mon-Fri 6-9.15, Sat-Sun all day **Restaurant** L served Mon-Fri 12-2.45, Sat-Sun all day booking required D served Mon-Fri 6-9.15, Sat-Sun all day booking required ⊕ FULLERS ◀ Fuller's London Pride, Guest ale ♻ Symonds Founders Reserve, Symonds Cider. 🍷 10
Facilities Children's menu Children's portions Dogs allowed Garden Parking Wi-fi

PICK OF THE PUBS

The Red Lion ♉

CHENIES Map 6 TQ09

WD3 6ED
☎ 01923 282722 📄 01923 283797
e-mail: theredlionchenies@hotmail.co.uk
web: www.theredlionchenies.co.uk
dir: *Between Rickmansworth & Amersham on A404, follow signs for Chenies & Latimer*

Set in the Chess Valley, in a picture-book village, complete with a pretty green and an ancient parish church, and just up the lane from Chenies Manor. The unassuming, white-painted Red Lion's owners Mike and Heather Norris have over 20 years' experience behind them, and they firmly believe the 17th-century inn's popularity stems from being a pub that serves good food, not a restaurant that serves beer. Expect a plain, simply furnished main bar, a charming, snug dining area housed in the original cottage to the rear with a tiled floor, old inglenook and rustic furniture, a new restaurant, and Mike talking passionately about his real ales. Lion's Pride, brewed by Rebellion in Marlow, is available here and here alone; other local beers come from Vale Brewery in Haddenham.

Heather cooks everything, including fresh daily pastas; bangers with bubble-and-squeak; big chunks of oven-baked leg of lamb (much like Greek kleftiko); roast pork belly on leek and potato mash; game pie;

fishcakes with horseradish and beetroot dip; Orkneys rump steak; curries; poached haddock with peppered red wine sauce; and sausage, apple and Cheddar pie. Speaking of pies, brace yourself for the famous lamb version, which a visiting American serviceman once declared beat a rival pub's pies hands down. Ever since, its entry on the menu has acquired an additional adjective every time it is rewritten. Today, therefore, it reads (take a deep breath) 'The awesome, internationally acclaimed, world-renowned, aesthetically and palatably pleasing, not knowingly genetically modified, hand-crafted, well-balanced, famous, original Chenies lamb pie'. Outside, on the pub's sunny side, is a small seating area.

Open all wk Mon-Sat 11-2.30 5.30-11 (Sun 12-3 6.30-10.30) Closed: 25 Dec
Bar Meals L served Mon-Sat 12-2, Sun 12-2.30 D served Mon-Sat 7-10, Sun 7-9.30 **Restaurant** L served Mon-Sat 12-2, Sun 12-2.30 D served Mon-Sat 7-10, Sun 7-9.30 booking required 🍺 FREE HOUSE
🍺 Wadworth 6X, Rebellion, Lion's Pride, Vale Best, plus guest ales 🍏 Thatchers Gold. ♉ 10 **Facilities** Dogs allowed Garden Parking

Save on hotels. Book at theAA.com/hotel

BUCKINGHAMSHIRE 47 ENGLAND

CHEDDINGTON · Map 11 SP91

The Old Swan ♀

58 High St LU7 0RQ ☎ 01296 668226
e-mail: oldswancheddington@btconnect.com
dir: *From Tring towards Marsworth take B489, 0.5m. Left towards Cooks Wharf onto Cheddington, pub on left*

Formed out of three cottages in the 15th century, this delightful thatched pub is known not only for its real ales and traditional charm but also for its food. Using fresh, locally sourced ingredients and game, fish and seafood supplies from sustainable sources, the menus offer modern British dishes. Lunchtime food ranges from hot paninis and ciabatta sandwiches to smaller and larger plates like steak and ale pie. Imaginative evening meals could be venison in a Shrewsbury sauce or lemon and garlic chargrilled chicken breast. Children are made very welcome and there's a good play area in the attractive garden.

Open all day all wk **Bar Meals** L served Mon-Thu 12-2.30, Fri-Sat 12-5, Sun 12-4 D served Mon-Thu 6-9, Fri-Sat 6-9.30 **Restaurant** L served Mon-Thu 12-2.30, Fri-Sat 12-5, Sun 12-4 D served Mon-Thu 6-9, Fri-Sat 6-9.30 ⊕ PUNCH TAVERNS ◀ St Austell Tribute, Spitfire, Adnams Broadside, Adnams Explorer Ŏ Stowford Press. ♀ 20 **Facilities** Children welcome Children's portions Play area Dogs allowed Garden Parking Wi-fi

---

CHENIES · Map 6 TQ09

PICK OF THE PUBS

The Red Lion ♀

See Pick of the Pubs on opposite page

CHESHAM · Map 6 SP90

The Black Horse Inn

Chesham Vale HP5 3NS ☎ 01494 784656
e-mail: mgoodchild@btconnect.com
dir: *A41 from Berkhamsted, A416 through Ashley Green, 0.75m before Chesham right to Vale Rd, at bottom of Mashleigh Hill, 1m, inn on left*

Set in some beautiful valley countryside, this 500-year-old pub is ideal for enjoying a cosy, traditional environment without electronic games or music. During the winter there are roaring log fires to take the chill off those who may spot one of the resident ghosts. An ever-changing menu includes an extensive range of snacks, while the main menu may feature steak and Stallion Ale pie, trout and almonds, various home-made pies, steaks and gammon, stuffed plaice, or salmon supreme.

Open all wk 11-3 5.30-11 (Sat-Sun all day) ⊕ PUNCH TAVERNS ◀ Adnams Bitter, Speckled Hen, Wadworth 6X, Guest ale Ŏ Stowford Press. **Facilities** Children welcome Dogs allowed Garden Parking Wi-fi

---

The Swan

Ley Hill HP5 1UT ☎ 01494 783075
e-mail: swanleyhill@btconnect.com
dir: *1.5m E of Chesham by golf course*

A beautiful 16th-century pub set in the delightful village of Ley Hill, this was once where condemned prisoners would drink a 'last and final ale' on the way to the nearby gallows. During World War II, Glen Miller and Clark Gable cycled here for a pint from their base. These days, it is a free-house offering a warm welcome, real ales and good food, plus a large inglenook fireplace and original beams. Pan-fried smoked haddock with leeks and mornay sauce, and slow-cooked pork belly with apple purée are typical choices. Look out for bank holiday beer festivals in May and August.

Open all wk 12-3 5.30-11 (Sun 12-10.30) **Bar Meals** L served all wk 12-2.30 D served Tue-Sat 6.30-9.30 **Restaurant** L served all wk 12-2.30 D served Tue-Sat 6.30-9.30 booking required ⊕ FREE HOUSE ◀ Adnams Bitter, St Austell Tribute, Timothy Taylor Landlord, Brakspears, Guest ales. **Facilities** Children welcome Children's menu Garden Beer festival Parking

---

CHOLESBURY · Map 6 SP90

PICK OF THE PUBS

The Full Moon ♀

Hawridge Common HP5 2UH
☎ 01494 758959 🖷 07092 875764
e-mail: annie@alberto1142.freeserve.co.uk
dir: *At Tring on A41 follow signs for Wiggington & Cholesbury. On Cholesbury Common pub by windmill*

When this 17th-century former coaching inn was first built, the local Chiltern Hills were overrun with alehouses. These days, only three remain. Fortunately the Full Moon, which graduated from the Half Moon in 1812, is something of an ideal country pub. Situated on the edge of Cholesbury Common, views to the windmill behind can be enjoyed from the large garden with heated paved patio, pergola and giant parasols. Inside are beams, flagstones, winter fires and six cask ales which include two weekly-changing guests. Comprehensive menus cover a range of possibilities, from sandwich of the day to farmhouse pâté; from bacon and black pudding in a mixed salad to beer-battered haddock fillet with rustic chunky chips. Finish with a raspberry and white chocolate crème brûlée. In 1907, the landlord was fined for permitting drunkenness on the premises; these days the clientele is much better behaved.

Open all day all wk 12-11 (Sun 12-10.30) Closed: 25 Dec **Bar Meals** L served Mon-Fri 12-2, Sat 12-9, Sun 12-8 D served Mon-Fri 6.30-9, Sat 12-9, Sun 12-8 **Restaurant** L served Mon-Fri 12-2, Sat 12-9, Sun 12-8 booking required D served Mon-Fri 6.30-9, Sat 12-9, Sun 12-8 booking required ⊕ ADMIRAL TAVERNS ◀ Brakspear, Adnams, Fuller's London Pride, Timothy Taylor Landlord, Guest ales. ♀ 9 **Facilities** Children welcome Children's menu Children's portions Dogs allowed Garden Parking Wi-fi

---

CUBLINGTON · Map 11 SP82

The Unicorn ◉◉ NEW

High St LU7 0LQ ☎ 01296 681261
e-mail: theunicornpub@btconnect.com
dir: *2m N of A418 (between Aylesbury & Leighton Buzzard). In village centre*

A cracker of a village local, overflowing with character from the low beamed bar, real fires and good beers (Bank Holiday beer festivals, too) to the scrubbed old tables, wooden floors and great atmosphere. Opposite the village church in a quiet corner of Aylesbury Vale, relax in the secluded garden of this 17th century freehouse with a pint of locally brewed ale. In the restaurant, keep an eye on the specials board for a dish of local game, complementing the regular menu of hearty pub staples and inspired dishes, such as wild mushroom and chestnut-stuffed cabbage with potato onion bake and mustard sauce, which have gained two AA Rosettes.

Open all day all wk 10.30am-11pm (Fri-Sat 10.30am-mdnt) **Bar Meals** food served all day **Restaurant** L served Mon-Sat 12-2.30, Sun 12-3 booking required D served Mon-Fri 7-9, Sat 7-9.30 booking required Fixed menu price fr £12.50 Av 3 course à la carte fr £18 ⊕ FREE HOUSE ◀ Brakspear, Spitfire Ŏ Stowford Press, Thatchers. **Facilities** Children welcome Children's menu Children's portions Play area Dogs allowed Garden Beer festival Parking Wi-fi

---

CUDDINGTON · Map 5 SP71

PICK OF THE PUBS

The Crown ♀

Spurt St HP18 0BB ☎ 01844 292222
e-mail: david@anniebaileys.com
dir: *Off A418 between Aylesbury & Thame*

Fans of the television series *Midsomer Murders* may recognise The Crown's thatched and whitewashed exterior, which has been used several times as a location. A Grade II listed building with bags of character, the pub plays a dual role as a popular local and a serious dining pub. The Crown's atmospheric interior includes a locals' bar and several low-beamed dining areas filled with charming prints and the glow of evening candlelight. Fuller's London Pride and Adnams are on tap, and there's also an extensive wine list. Sandwiches, pasta and salads are a constant feature, supported by appetising light bites and starters such as king prawn and smoked chicken linguini or spinach and sweet pepper risotto. Typical main courses include slow-roasted pork belly, cabbage, smoked bacon, mash and vanilla jus, or braised shank of lamb with caramelised shallots, red wine sauce. A small patio area provides an opportunity for alfresco dining.

Open all wk 12-3 6-11 (Sun all day) **Bar Meals** L served all wk 12-2.15 D served Mon-Sat 6.30-9.15 Av main course £12.95 **Restaurant** L served all wk 12-2.15 D served Mon-Sat 6.30-9.15 ⊕ FULLER'S ◀ Fuller's London Pride, Adnams, Guest Ales. ♀ 12 **Facilities** Children welcome Children's portions Garden Parking

PICK OF THE PUBS

The Swan Inn ♀

Village Rd UB9 5BH
☎ **01895 832085** 📄 **01895 835516**
e-mail: info@swaninndenham.co.uk
web: www.swaninndenham.co.uk
dir: *From A40 take A412. In 200yds follow Denham Village sign on right. Through village, over bridge, last pub on left*

Set in the picturesque and untouched village of Denham, The Swan may feel secluded and peaceful, but it is only minutes from the London suburbs and handy for two motorways. A double-fronted Georgian property covered in wisteria, the interior of this traditional country inn is cosily welcoming with a large log fire and a collection of pictures picked up at auction. Outside, a peaceful, sunny terrace and gardens are ideal for families with children. Though The Swan is still very much a pub, with locals drawn in by well kept pints of Marlow Rebellion IPA, the quality of the food is also a great attraction here. Fresh seasonal produce underpins a menu that re-invigorates some old favourites, and makes the most of market availability with a daily-changing specials board. For a starter or light meal, look to the 'small plates' section of the menu, which may feature deep-fried breaded Colston Bassett Stilton, roast pumpkin and hazelnut salad with balsamic dressing. Among the main courses you'll find plenty of variety, from crispy Stockings Farm pork belly with braised red cabbage, apple and sage gravy to Label Anglais free-range coq au vin with creamy mash and curly kale. Puddings are comforting classics with a twist. Poached rhubarb, for example, arrives with custard pannacotta; glazed vanilla rice pudding is served with fig compote. An interesting range of 'stickies' (dessert wines) has its own list, or you could round off with good coffee, tea or infusions. The whole experience is expertly managed by friendly, professional staff who are clearly well trained and enjoy working for the hands-on family that owns the pub. A private dining room is also available for family occasions or business meetings.

Open all day all wk 11-11 (Sun 12-10.30) Closed: 26 Dec **Bar Meals** L served Mon-Fri 12-2.30, Sat 12-3, Sun 12-4 D served Sun-Thu 6.30-9.30, Fri-Sat 6.30-10 **Restaurant** L served Mon-Fri 12-2.30, Sat 12-3, Sun 12-4 booking required D served Sun-Thu 6.30-9.30, Fri-Sat 6.30-10 booking required ⊕ SALISBURY PUBS LTD ◀ Wadworth 6X, Marlow Rebellion IPA ⬤ Thatchers. ♀ 20 **Facilities** Children's portions Dogs allowed Garden Parking Wi-fi

Save on hotels. Book at theAA.com/hotel

BUCKINGHAMSHIRE 49 ENGLAND

DENHAM
Map 6 TQ08

The Falcon Inn ★★★★ INN

Village Rd UB9 5BE ☎ 01895 832125
e-mail: mail@falcondenham.com
web: www.falcondenham.com
dir: M40 junct 1, follow A40/Gerrards Cross signs. Approx 200yds turn right onto Old Mill Rd. Pass church on right, enter village. Pub opposite village green

Located opposite the green in the pretty village of Denham, this historic 16th-century inn is an ideal place to refuel when exploring nearby Colne Valley Country Park. Expect excellent real ales and brasserie-style food: Cajun chicken fillets or mussels in white wine to start; and main courses such as ham, egg and chips; spaghetti Bolognese or chicken tikka masala. Desserts may include crème caramel or triple chocolate bavarois. Beamed bedrooms with original features are also available.

Open all wk 11-3 5-11 (Fri-Sun all day)
Bar Meals L served all wk 12-2.30 D served all wk 5-9.30 Av main course £8 **Restaurant** L served all wk 12-2.30 D served all wk 5-9.30 Av 3 course à la carte fr £16 ⊕ ENTERPRISE INNS ◄ Timothy Taylor Landlord, Bombardier, Archers, Brakspear & Guest ale Ò Stowford Press. **Facilities** Children welcome Children's menu Children's portions Dogs allowed Garden Beer festival Wi-fi **Rooms** 4

PICK OF THE PUBS

The Swan Inn ♥

See Pick of the Pubs on opposite page

DORNEY
Map 6 SU97

The Palmer Arms ♥

Village Rd SL4 6QW ☎ 01628 666612
e-mail: chrys@thepalmerarms.com
dir: From A4 take B3026, over M4 to Dorney

Engaging chickens take dust baths in the suntrap garden of this family-friendly community pub in pretty Dorney, just a short stroll from the Thames Path and Boveney Lock. Its 15th century origins are disguised behind contemporary decor and furnishings, with winter open fires adding atmosphere, whilst a thoroughly modern menu adds spice: walnut coated goat's cheese and pear salad may precede a main of macaroni cheese, asparagus, leeks and oven dried tomatoes or slow-roasted belly pork with celeriac dauphinoise. A summer beer festival features local beers and ciders.

Open all day all wk 11am-11.30pm (Sun 11-9)
Bar Meals L served all wk 11-9 D served all wk 11-9 Av main course £12 food served all day **Restaurant** L served all wk 11-11 D served all wk 11-11 Fixed menu price fr £20 Av 3 course à la carte fr £25 food served all day ⊕ GREENE KING ◄ Greene King Abbot Ale, IPA, Guinness Ò Aspall. ♥ 18 **Facilities** Children welcome Children's menu Children's portions Play area Dogs allowed Garden Beer festival Parking

EASINGTON
Map 5 SP61

PICK OF THE PUBS

Mole and Chicken NEW

HP18 9EY ☎ 01844 208387 📄 **01844 208250**
e-mail: enquiries@themoleandchicken.co.uk
dir: M40 juncts 8 or 8a, A418 to Thame. At rdbt left onto B4011 signed Long Crendon & Bicester. In Long Crendon right into Carters Lane signed Dorton & Chilton. At T-junct left into Chilton Rd signed Chilton. Approx 0.75m to pub

Set in rolling open country with magnificent views across Oxfordshire/Buckinghamshire countryside from the glorious terraced garden, this attractive end-of-terrace pub was built in 1831 as part of the workers' estate, later becoming the village store and pub that sold only beer and cider until 1918. Inside it's all exposed beams and unusual flagged floors, two roaring log fires, and a motley collection of oak and pines tables and chairs. Although self-styled as a restaurant with rooms, the atmosphere is informal and relaxed despite the emphasis on food, and local Hooky and Vale ales are served on tap. Modern pub food draws an appreciative crowd, the seasonal menu typically offering crab cakes with aioli, rocket and sweet chilli, or lentil and garlic soup, followed by lamb shank with bubble-and-squeak, shallots and garlic, or sea bream with creamed leeks. To finish there's caramelised apple tart or a plate of British cheeses.

Open all wk 12-close **Bar Meals** Av main course £15 **Restaurant** L served Mon-Sat 12-2.30, Sun all day booking required D served Mon-Sat 6-9, Sun all day booking required Fixed menu price fr £12.50 Av 3 course à la carte fr £30 ⊕ FREE HOUSE ◄ Old Hooky, Vale Best. **Facilities** Children welcome Children's menu Children's portions Garden Parking

---

FARNHAM COMMON
Map 6 SU98

The Foresters ♥

The Broadway SL2 3QQ
☎ 01753 643340 📄 **01753 647524**
e-mail: info@theforesterspub.com
dir: Telephone for directions

Dating from the 1930s, The Foresters' bright gastro-pub decor lends a great atmosphere to the interior; the gardens to front and rear complete this well presented hostelry. The bar stocks reliable ales from Fuller's and Young's, usually with a guest alongside. The bar menu offers the likes of potted pork; open tandoori marinated chicken sandwiches; and beer battered fish and chips; while the restaurant menu might feature prawn and crayfish cocktail; Thai spiced Mahi Mahi with coconut milk shot; aubergine and vegetarian haggis parcel. After lunch, head off for a walk in Burnham Beeches, the world's largest ancient beech woodlands.

Open all day all wk **Bar Meals** L served all wk 12-3 D served all wk 6.30-10 Av main course £12 **Restaurant** L served all wk 12-3 D served all wk 6.30-10 Fixed menu price fr £10 Av 3 course à la carte fr £23 ⊕ PUNCH TAVERNS ◄ Fuller's London Pride, Young's, Guest ales Ò Aspall. **Facilities** Children welcome Children's menu Children's portions Dogs allowed Garden Parking Wi-fi

FARNHAM ROYAL
Map 6 SU98

The Emperor ♥

Blackpond Ln SL2 3EG ☎ 01753 643006
e-mail: manager@theemperorfarnhamroyal.com
dir: Telephone for directions

With its log fire in winter and alfresco tables in the summer, this old inn is a pub for all seasons. A wealth of polished wood floors and original beams run through the bar, conservatory and refurbished barn. British food based on fresh seasonal fare drives the menu, which might include Asian duck salad or confit pork belly, creamed potato, apple sauce and crackling. Tuesday is steak night and might include kangaroo or ostrich.

Open all day all wk **Bar Meals** L served Mon-Thu 12-3, Fri-Sat 12-10, Sun 12-6 D served Mon-Thu 6-10, Fri-Sat 12-10, Sun 12-6 ⊕ OPENING COUNTY LEISURE ◄ London Pride, Timothy Taylor Landlord. ♥ 8 **Facilities** Children welcome Children's menu Children's portions Dogs allowed Garden Parking

FORD
Map 5 SP70

PICK OF THE PUBS

The Dinton Hermit
INN ☻

Water Ln HP17 8XH
☎ 01296 747473 📠 01296 748819
e-mail: relax@dintonhermit.co.uk
dir: Off A418 between Aylesbury & Thame

Deep in the Vale of Aylesbury, this traditional stone-
built inn is a comfortable and friendly place to pop in
for a quick drink in front of the open fire in winter.
You'll find guest beers and locally brewed ales at the
bar, as well as a wide selection of wines. In summer,
the large garden is just the place to enjoy the sunshine
in the peace and quiet of the Buckinghamshire
countryside. Both the restaurant and the bar menus
offer a range of quality dishes, with locally sourced
ingredients wherever possible. Menus change with the
seasons, but might include chargrilled lamb chops,
colcannon, roasted baby carrots and rosemary gravy;
baked vine tomato, olive and goat's cheese tart with
purple broccoli and new potatoes; grilled whole lemon
sole with purple potatoes and garlic caper butter. And,
if you can't bear to leave, just book into one of the
contemporary bedrooms. Recent change of hands.

Open all day all wk 10am-11pm (Sun noon-10.30pm)
Bar Meals food served all day **Restaurant** L served
Mon-Fri 12-2, Sat-Sun 12-3 D served all wk 6.30-8.45
⊕ FREE HOUSE ◀ Vale Best Bitter, Guest ales
♻ Stowford Press. ☻ 10 **Facilities** Children welcome
Children's menu Children's portions Dogs allowed
Garden Parking Wi-fi **Rooms** 13

FRIETH
Map 5 SU79

The Prince Albert ☻

RG9 6PY ☎ 01494 881683
dir: 4m N of Marlow. Follow Frieth road from Marlow.
Straight across at x-rds on Fingest road. Pub 200yds
on left

Set in the Chilterns, close to Hambleden and Marlow, this
traditional country pub dating back to the 1700s, prides
itself on old world values. There are no televisions, juke
boxes or games - just good conversation, great beers and
a welcoming atmosphere. With copper pots and pans and
jugs hanging in the bar, warming open fires enhance the
mood in winter and there is a garden with seating to
admire the views. Expect traditional pub food with jacket
potatoes and country pâté and toast among the small

bites, while the evening menu typically offers local cured
ham; Hambleden Valley steak burger; gammon steak with
egg (or pineapple) and chips; jumbo battered cod; lamb
shank; and home-made steak and kidney pie.

Open all day all wk 11-11 (Sun noon-10.30pm)
Bar Meals L served Mon-Sat 12.15-2.30, Sun 12.30-3
D served Fri-Sat 7.30-9.30 Av main course £9.25
⊕ BRAKSPEAR ◀ Brakspear Bitter, Brakspear seasonal
ales. ☻ 9 **Facilities** Children welcome Children's portions
Dogs allowed Garden Parking

FULMER
Map 6 SU98

PICK OF THE PUBS

The Black Horse ☻

See Pick of the Pubs on opposite page

GREAT HAMPDEN
Map 5 SP80

The Hampden Arms

HP16 9RQ ☎ 01494 488255 📠 01494 488094
dir: From M40 junct 4 take A4010, turn right before
Princes Risborough. Great Hampden signed

The large garden of this mock-Tudor free house on the
wooded Hampden Estate sits beside the common, where
you might watch a game of cricket during the season.
Chef proprietor Constantine Lucas includes some Greek
signature dishes such as moussaka and kleftico
alongside more traditional choices such as roasted
salmon and asparagus; venison bourguignon; and green
vegetable risotto. Guest ales support regular brews from
Adnams and Vale Brewery.

Open all wk noon-3 6-mdnt **Bar Meals** L served Mon-Sat
12-2, Sun 12-3 D served Mon-Sat 6-9.30 Sun 7-9.30 Av
main course £7.95 **Restaurant** Fixed menu price fr £10
Av 3 course à la carte fr £19.70 ⊕ FREE HOUSE
◀ Adnams Bitter, Guest ales, Vale Brewery, London Pride
♻ Addlestones. **Facilities** Children welcome Children's
portions Family room Dogs allowed Garden Parking

GREAT MISSENDEN
Map 6 SP80

PICK OF THE PUBS

The Nags Head ★★★★ INN ⑳ ☻

See Pick of the Pubs on page 52

PICK OF THE PUBS

The Polecat Inn ☻

170 Wycombe Rd, Prestwood HP16 0HJ
☎ 01494 862253 📠 01494 868393
e-mail: polecatinn@btinternet.com
dir: On A4128 between Great Missenden & High
Wycombe

John Gamble bought the closed and dilapidated Polecat
over 20 years ago, renovating and extending it to create
an attractive free house, while retaining many original
features. The inn dates back to the 17th century, and
its beautiful three-acre garden, set amidst rolling
Chilterns countryside, is part of its great attraction.
The small low-beamed rooms radiating from the
central bar give many options when it comes to
choosing where to sit and relax with a pint or a plate of
freshly cooked food. Dishes are prepared from local
ingredients, including herbs from the garden.
Lunchtime snacks (sandwiches, warm baguettes,
jackets and ploughman's) are backed by a main menu
ranging from half a pint of shell-on prawns for starters
to main courses such as fillet of beef Wellington or
braised lamb shank; and for pudding, almond and
apricot tart. Daily blackboard specials add to the
choice - pan-fried sea bass with cherries and Kirsch, or
daube of beef with parsnip gnocchi may be on offer.

Open 11-2.30 6-11 (Sun noon-3) Closed: 25-26 Dec,
1 Jan, Sun eve **Bar Meals** L served all wk 12-2 booking
required D served Mon-Sat 6.30-9 booking required Av
main course £12 **Restaurant** Av 3 course à la carte fr
£22 ⊕ FREE HOUSE ◀ Marston's Pedigree, Morland,
Old Speckled Hen, Interbrew Flowers IPA, Brakspear
Bitter. ☻ 16 **Facilities** Children welcome Children's
portions Play area Family room Garden Parking

GROVE
Map 11 SP92

Grove Lock ☻ NEW

LU7 0QU ☎ 01525 380940
dir: From A4146 (S of Leighton Buzzard) take B4146
signed Ivinghoe & Tring. Pub 0.5m on left

A recent refurbishment has transformed this pub next to
Lock 28 on the Grand Union Canal. Its lofty open-plan bar
has leather sofas, assorted tables and chairs and a
couple of old butcher's blocks. The restaurant, once the
lock-keeper's cottage, serves braised blade of beef; cod
and chips; and buck rarebit. Plenty of outdoor seating
means you can watch the barges, while enjoying a pint of
Fuller's. Catch a summer barbecue and hog roast.

Open all day all wk **Bar Meals** L served Mon-Sat 12-9
D served Sun 12-7 Av main course £9.95 food served all
day **Restaurant** L served Mon-Sat 12-9 booking required
D served Sun 12-7 booking required Av 3 course à la
carte fr £20 food served all day ⊕ FULLER'S ◀ Fuller's
London Pride, ESB, Chiswick Bitter, Discovery. ☻ 14
Facilities Children welcome Children's menu Children's
portions Garden Parking Wi-fi

PICK OF THE PUBS

The Black Horse ♉

FULMER   Map 6 SU98

Windmill Ln SL3 6HD
☎ **01753 663183** 📠 **01753 662778**
e-mail: info@blackhorsefulmer.co.uk
web: www.blackhorsefulmer.co.uk
dir: *A40 east of Gerrards Cross. Take
turning to Fulmer/Wexham. Pub in centre
of village after 1.5m*

A short hop from Central London, The Black
Horse is tucked away in the heart of Fulmer,
a pretty conservation village hidden in a
valley between Gerrards Cross and Slough.
Originally 17th-century cottages which
housed local craftsmen building the
Church of St James next door, the main
building is a warren of small rooms, which
have barely altered over the years. Now part
of the Salisbury Pubs group, its new owners
have placed the emphasis firmly on
recreating a proper village community pub
with a range of hand-pulled real ales, an
eclectic selection of European wines (21 of
them sold by the glass), and hearty 'British
Colonial' food. The pub is full of character
with antique furniture, rich fabrics and
pictures snapped up at local salerooms.
The garden is large enough to almost lose
children while you enjoy a glass of
something chilled on the peaceful terrace.
Happy, chatty waiting staff clearly enjoy
working here and there is a genuine
warmth whether you are a new customer or
a regular. The menu is driven by local
produce, including lamb from Coleshill and
seasonal game from around Marlow. The

chefs are also keen foragers so expect wild
garlic to pop up on the menu in spring and
berries in the autumn. For a light lunch or
starter, the range of 'small plates' are a
good starting point and may embrace
bubble and squeak with oak-smoked
bacon, free-range poached egg and
hollandaise sauce. Typical mains take in
slow-cooked shin of beef and oxtail suet
pudding with glazed Chantenay carrots, or
lemon and parsley crumbed hake fillet with
skinny chips, pea purée and tartare sauce.
Traditional puddings often come with a
twist: chocolate pot, for example, might be
served with mini sugared doughnuts;
classic spotted dick arrives with
cinnamon custard.

Open all day all wk Closed: 26 Dec
Bar Meals L served Mon-Fri 12-2.30, Sat
12-3, Sun 12-4 D served Sun-Thu

6.30-9.30, Fri-Sat 6.30-10
Restaurant L served Mon-Fri 12-2.30,
Sat 12-3, Sun 12-4 D served Sun-Thu
6.30-9.30, Fri-Sat 6.30-10 booking
required ⊕ SALISBURY PUBS LTD
🍺 Greene King IPA, Old Speckled Hen,
London Glory Ŏ Aspall. ♉ 21
Facilities Children welcome Children's
portions Dogs allowed Garden Parking Wi-fi

PICK OF THE PUBS

The Nags Head ★★★★ INN 🌹 🍷

GREAT MISSENDEN   Map 6 SP80

London Rd HP16 0DG
☎ **01494 862200** 📠 **01494 862685**
e-mail: goodfood@nagsheadbucks.com
web: www.nagsheadbucks.com
dir: *1m from Great Missenden on London
Rd. From A413 (Amersham to Aylesbury)
turn left signed Chiltern Hospital. After
500mtrs pub on corner of Nags Head Ln &
London Rd*

Having made a huge success of the
Bricklayers Arms in Flaunden,
Hertfordshire (see entry), Alvin Michaels
has worked his magic on this 15th-century
inn tucked away in the sleepy Missbourne
Valley deep in the Chiltern Hills. Originally
three small cottages and later converted
into a coaching inn, offering rest and
refreshment to weary travellers and their
horses, the Michaels family extensively
restored the inn in 2008 and, like the
Bricklayers, continues to gain a
formidable reputation for food and
hospitality, and The Nags Head offers five
beautifully refurbished and contemporary
bedrooms. Original features including the
low oak beams and inglenook fireplace
have been carefully retained as a
backdrop for the stylish new bar. The
dining room is decorated with limited
edition prints by the late Roald Dahl, the
children's author who lived locally and
who was a regular, and the pub features
in the film of his book *Fantastic Mr Fox*.
Food is a passion here, and executive head
chef Claude Paillet sources the finest
ingredients from local suppliers wherever
possible for the Anglo-French menu. Lunch
and dinner menus may offer starters like
seafood gratin with Chardonnay cream, or
chicken liver and wild mushroom parfait.
Main courses range from trio of lamb with
red onion jus, and duck breast with confit
onion mash and sherry sauce, to 21-day
aged beef fillet with duck liver and foie
gras mousse and a port jus, and steak
and ale pie with chive mash. Leave room
for a tempting pudding; typical choices
include chocolate fondant with vanilla ice
cream or the chef's trio of desserts –
crème brûlée, chocolate profiteroles and
bread and butter pudding. In summer,
relax over a drink or a meal whilst gazing
out over the Chiltern Hills from the pub's
lovely informal garden.

Open all day all wk **Bar Meals** L served
Mon-Sat 12-2.30, Sun 12-3.30 booking
required D served all wk 6.30-9.30
booking required Av main course £15.95
Restaurant L served Mon-Sat 12-2.30,
Sun 12-3.30 booking required D served all
wk 6.30-9.30 booking required Fixed menu
price fr £17.50 Av 3 course à la carte fr
£28 🌐 FREE HOUSE ◀ London Pride,
Rebellion, Tring, Vale Ö Aspall. 🍷 19
Facilities Children welcome Children's
portions Dogs allowed Garden Parking
Wi-fi **Rooms** 5

HAMBLEDEN   Map 5 SU78

The Stag & Huntsman Inn

RG9 6RP ☎ 01491 571227 📄 01491 413810
e-mail: pubmanager@culdenfaw.com
dir: *5m from Henley-on-Thames on A4155 towards Marlow, left at Mill End towards Hambleden*

Close to the glorious beech-clad Chilterns, this 400-year-old brick and flint village pub has featured in countless films and television series. Ever-changing guest ales are served in the public bar, larger lounge bar and cosy snug. Food is available in the bars as well as the dining room, from an extensive menu of home-made dishes prepared with local seasonal produce. Hambleden estate game features in season. Change of hands.

Open all wk 11-2.30 6-11 (Fri-Sat all day Sun 12-3 7-10.30) Closed: 25-26 Dec & 1 Jan evenings ⊕ FREE HOUSE ◀ Rebellion IPA, Sharp's Doom Bar, Loddon Hoppit, Guest ales ♂ Thatchers Gold, Thatchers Dry. **Facilities** Children welcome Dogs allowed Garden Parking

HEDGERLEY   Map 6 SU98

The White Horse ⚑

SL2 3UY ☎ 01753 643225
dir: *Telephone for directions*

An ale drinker's paradise if ever there was one, parts of which date back 500 years. With three beer festivals a year and barely a pause between them, this pub can almost claim to run a single year-long celebration, with over 1,000 real ales consumed annually. Real cider and Belgian bottled beers augment the already mammoth range. A large well-kept garden at the rear hosts summer barbecues; otherwise the menu of home-cooked pub favourites ranges from a salad bar with quiches, sandwiches and ploughman's through to curries, chilli, pasta dishes, pies and steaks (lunchtime only).

Open all wk 11-2.30 5-11 (Sat 11-11, Sun 11-10.30) **Bar Meals** L served Mon-Fri 12-2, Sat-Sun 12-2.30 ⊕ FREE HOUSE ◀ Regularly changing ♂ Regularly changing. ⚑ 10 **Facilities** Children welcome Children's portions Family room Dogs allowed Garden Beer festival Parking

HIGH WYCOMBE   Map 5 SU89

The Sausage Tree ⚑ NEW

Saffron Rd HP13 6AB ☎ 01494 452204
e-mail: sausagetreepub@hotmail.co.uk
dir: *M40 junct 4, take A404 signed Town Centre & Amersham. At rdbt 2nd exit signed Beaconsfield, Amersham, A404. At rdbt 2nd exit signed Beaconsfield. Left into Stuart Rd, left into Easton Terrace, left into Saffron Rd*

A touch of the exotic at the fringe of the Chilterns is championed at this street corner at the outskirts of High Wycombe. Grab a place at one of the chunky tables in the brightly decorated rooms and try to decide just which of the fifty-or-so types of sausage and mash will be your repast: kangaroo, Welsh rarebit, beef peri peri or the tempting pork, banana and honey combination just scratch the surface here. Maybe sip on one of their huge range of speciality bottled beers and plump instead for fish and chips or an ostrich burger, or experiment with a zebra steak on their specialist Black Rock Grill, cooked at your table on fearsomely hot volcanic rock platters.

Open 12-3 5-11 Closed: Sun **Bar Meals** L served Mon-Sat 12-3 D served Mon-Sat 5.30-10 Av main course £8.50-£11.50 **Restaurant** L served Mon-Sat 12-3 D served Mon-Sat 5.30-10 Av 3 course à la carte fr £19.50 ◀ Guest ales. **Facilities** Garden Wi-fi

LACEY GREEN   Map 5 SP80

The Whip Inn ⚑

Pink Rd HP27 0PG ☎ 01844 344060 📄 01844 346044
dir: *1m of A4010 (Princes Risborough to High Wycombe road). Adjacent to windmill*

A picturesque old smock windmill catches the breeze on the ridgetop where also stands this 150 year old pub, high above the Vale of Aylesbury; five counties are visible on clear days. Ramblers on The Chiltern Way join locals in appreciating some of 700 real ales offered each year, as well as real Millwhites cider. A robust menu of home-made classic favourites and seasonally based specials seals the deal at this rustic, music- and fruit-machine free country inn. The pub holds a beer festival in May and September.

Open all day all wk **Bar Meals** L served all wk 12-2.30 booking required D served all wk 6.30-9 booking required **Restaurant** L served all wk 12-2.30 booking required D served all wk 6.30-9 booking required ⊕ FREE HOUSE ◀ Over 700 different guest ales every year ♂ Thatchers, Millwhites. ⚑ 22 **Facilities** Children welcome Children's portions Dogs allowed Garden Beer festival Parking

LONG CRENDON   Map 5 SP60

PICK OF THE PUBS

The Angel Inn ◉ ⚑

47 Bicester Rd HP18 9EE
☎ 01844 208268 📄 01844 202497
e-mail: info@angelrestaurant.co.uk
dir: *M40 junct 7, A418 to Thame, B4011 to Long Crendon. Inn on B4011*

Dating from the 15th century, this smartly refurbished former coaching inn retains original fireplaces such as wattle and daub walls alongside modern features including an airy conservatory and tasteful natural materials and fabrics throughout. Set in a picturesque village on the Bucks and Oxfordshire borders, the inn's main focus is food but you'll also find local cask real ales on offer as well as cocktails, champagne, wine by the glass and an impressive selection of single malt whiskies. At lunch, choose between tempting sandwiches and the more substantial fare on offer, typically breast of wood pigeon on autumn vegetable rösti followed by Oxfordshire lamb on curly kale with boulangère potatoes, roast vegetables and rosemary sauce. Similar choices abound at dinner, along with a tasting menu offering the likes pork fillet wrapped in Parma ham with confit pork belly, black pudding croquette and sage and cider sauce. An impressive array of fish dishes might include crispy fillet of sea bass on chargrilled Mediterranean vegetables. In warmer weather, head for the heated alfresco terrace.

Open all day Closed: Sun eve **Bar Meals** L served all wk 12-3 D served Mon-Sat 7-10 Av main course £18.95 **Restaurant** L served all wk 12-3 D served Mon-Sat 7-10 Fixed menu price fr £15.50 Av 3 course à la carte fr £28 ⊕ FREE HOUSE ◀ Oxford Blue, IPA, Brakspear, Wychert ale. ⚑ 18 **Facilities** Children welcome Children's portions Garden Parking Wi-fi

LOUDWATER — Map 6 SU99

The Derehams Inn

5 Derehams Ln HP10 9RH ☎ **01494 530965**
e-mail: derehams@hotmail.co.uk
dir: *From A40 (London Rd) from High Wycombe towards Beaconsfield turn left onto Derehams Ln*

All low beams and brasses, panelling and pewter, The Derehams, which originated as 18th century farm cottages, shouts timeless English village pub loud and clear. A bevy of beer-wickets dispense a great range of local ales: Maggie's kitchen rustles up anything from light bites and sandwiches to goat curry and solid Sunday roasts. They also host an annual beer festival here and a classic car and bike meet every month.

Open all wk Mon-Thu 11.30-3.30 5.30-11 (Fri-Sun all day) ⊕ FREE HOUSE ◀ London Pride, Loddon, Brakspear, Guest ales. **Facilities** Children welcome Children's menu Children's portions Dogs allowed Garden Beer festival Parking Wi-fi

MARLOW — Map 5 SU88

PICK OF THE PUBS

The Hand and Flowers ◉◉◉ ♊

See Pick of the Pubs on opposite page

The Kings Head ♊

Church Rd, Little Marlow SL7 3RZ
☎ **01628 484407** 🖶 **01628 484407**
e-mail: clive.harvison@sky.com
dir: *M40 junct 4 take A4040 S, then A4155 towards Bourne End. Pub 0.5m on right*

This charming 16th-century pub forms part of an attractive group of buildings a few minutes' walk from a church dating back to 1400 and the Thames Footpath. It has an open-plan but cosy interior with original beams and warming fires, plus a large garden to enjoy in the summer. In addition snacks like hot-filled French bread and jacket potatoes, the traditional pub menu offers a range of more substantial meals, including breaded deep-fried Cornish sardine fillets; pan-fried lambs' liver and bacon with onion gravy; and smoked haddock and spring onion fishcakes. The Pavilion is available for private dining.

Open all day all wk **Bar Meals** L served Mon-Sat 12-2.15, Sun 12-7 booking required D served all wk 6.30-9.30 booking required Av main course £10 **Restaurant** L served Mon-Sat 12-2.15, Sun 12-7 booking required D served all wk 6.30-9.30 booking required Fixed menu price fr £10 ⊕ ENTERPRISE INNS ◀ Fuller's London Pride, Timothy Taylor Landlord, Adnams Broadside, Rebellion IPA, Rebellion Smuggler ♂ Aspall. ♊ 13 **Facilities** Children welcome Children's menu Children's portions Garden Parking

MENTMORE — Map 11 SP91

PICK OF THE PUBS

The Stag Inn ♊

The Green LU7 0QF
☎ **01296 668423** 🖶 **01296 660264**
e-mail: info@thestagmentmore.com
dir: *Telephone for directions*

High quality service is the keynote at the imposing Stag Inn, which offers a distinctive fusion of British and Mediterranean cuisine. The pub stands in a picture-postcard village overlooking the huge Elizabethan-style stately home of Mentmore Towers, which was built in 1855 for Baron Amschel de Rothschild. This idyllic area supplies head chef Mani Rebelo with fresh, seasonal produce to create his diverse range of popular dishes. An authentic selection of fresh pasta dishes complements the choice of home-made rustic pizzas (the pizza dough is made daily from a closely guarded secret recipe), with toppings that include The Stag's own combination of mozzarella, tomato, salami, onions, capers and fresh basil. For something a little more traditional, you could try a grilled Woburn venison steak with seasonal vegetables, or grilled sea bass with herbs and garlic. The full menu is available in the bar and restaurant, as well as in the pub's lovely summer garden.

Open all wk **Bar Meals** L served Mon-Fri 12-2.30, Sat all day, Sun 12-4.30 D served Mon-Fri 6-9.30 **Restaurant** L served Mon-Fri 12-2.30, Sat all day, Sun 12-4.30 D served Mon-Fri 6-9.30 ⊕ CHARLES WELLS ◀ Young's Bitter, Guinness, Bombardier. ♊ 8 **Facilities** Children welcome Children's portions Dogs allowed Garden Parking

MILTON KEYNES — Map 11 SP83

The Swan Inn

Broughton Rd, Milton Keynes Village MK10 9AH
☎ **01908 665240** 🖶 **01908 395091**
e-mail: info@theswan-mkvillage.co.uk
dir: *M1 junct 14 towards Milton Keynes. Pub off V11 or H7*

Everything you could wish for from an ancient thatched pub in the heart of the original Milton Keynes village. Sympathetically renovated, the interior is an eclectic mix of traditional charm and contemporary chic. Flagstone floors, an open fire in the inglenook in winter keep things cosy, and an orchard garden for those warmer days. Real ales and many served by the glass are backed by a range of organic fruit juices and lemonades. The open-plan kitchen creates simple yet creative dishes that change monthly according to availability of produce, which includes herbs from the pub's own garden.

Open all day all wk ⊕ FRONT LINE INNS ◀ Bombardier, Young's, Guest ales. **Facilities** Children welcome Children's portions Dogs allowed Garden Parking Wi-fi

MOULSOE — Map 11 SP94

The Carrington Arms ♊

Cranfield Rd MK16 0HB
☎ **01908 218050** 🖶 **01908 217850**
e-mail: carringtonarms@aol.com
dir: *M1 junct 14, A509 to Newport Pagnell 100yds, turn right signed Moulsoe & Cranfield. Pub on right*

Dating from 1860, this Grade II listed building is set in the picturesque village of Moulsoe. The Dodman family took over the pub in 2008 and have created a 'Best of British' restaurant offering seasonal menus. Customers can choose their own cuts of meat, fish and seafood from a special counter. Typical choices might be venison with chestnut mash, curly kale and blackberry sauce; roasted grey mullet on a herb crouton with shellfish ragout; or Bourbon-marinated steak.

Open all day all wk **Bar Meals** L served Mon-Fri 12-3, Sat-Sun all day D served Mon-Fri 6-10, Sat-Sun all day Av main course £13.25 **Restaurant** L served Mon-Fri 12-2.30, Sat-Sun all day D served Mon-Fri 6-10, Sat-Sun all day booking required Fixed menu price fr £13.95 Av 3 course à la carte fr £16.50 ⊕ FREE HOUSE ◀ London Pride, Guest ales ♂ Aspall. ♊ 10 **Facilities** Children welcome Children's menu Garden Parking Wi-fi

OVING — Map 11 SP72

The Black Boy ♊

Church Ln HP22 4HN
☎ **01296 641258** 🖶 **01296 641271**
e-mail: theblackboyoving@aol.com
dir: *4.6m N of Aylesbury*

Oliver Cromwell and his soldiers camped in The Black Boy's huge garden after sacking nearby Bolebec Castle during the Civil War. Today, the 16th-century pub is a rural oasis, with spectacular views over the Vale of Aylesbury to Stowe School and beyond. Choices at lunch include tomato and dry-cured bacon rarebit; smoked chicken and chorizo risotto; or home baked honey-glaze ham, two fried eggs and chips; then in the evening a vegetarian, fish or meat platter to share is popular.

Open all wk noon-3 6-11 (Sat all day, Sun noon-5) **Bar Meals** L served Mon-Sat 12-2, Sun 12-3 D served Mon-Thu 6.30-9, Fri-Sat 6-9.30 **Restaurant** L served Mon-Sat 12-2, Sun 12-3 D served Mon-Thu 6.30-9, Fri-Sat 6.9.30 ⊕ FREE HOUSE ◀ Hale Best, Guest ales ♂ Aspall. ♊ 10 **Facilities** Children welcome Children's portions Dogs allowed Garden Parking

PENN — Map 6 SU99

PICK OF THE PUBS

The Old Queens Head ♊

See Pick of the Pubs on page 56

PICK OF THE PUBS

The Hand and Flowers

MARLOW Map 5 SU88

126 West St SL7 2BP
☎ **01628 482277** 📄 **01628 401913**
e-mail:
theoffice@thehandandflowers.co.uk
web: www.thehandandflowers.co.uk
dir: *M4 junct 9, A404 N into Marlow,*
A4155 towards Henley-on-Thames. Pub on
outskirts on right

Tom and Beth Kerridge bought the lease of this whitewashed 18th-century pub in 2005 and it quickly became a destination for food lovers as much as locals in search of a pint of Abbot Ale and a pork pie. An unassuming pub on the outskirts of this upmarket town, The Hand and Flowers remains a class act and a gastronomic hotspot. Despite gaining three AA Rosettes in the first year, the pub remains a relaxed and unpretentious place, with flagstone floors, old beams and timbers, roaring winter log fires, walls lined with striking modern art, leather banquettes and cloth-less, smartly-set tables. A small bar area serves decent real ale, and a cracking set lunch that features dishes like tomato soup with basil pesto; crispy lamb breast with pomme boulangère; profiteroles with dark chocolate sauce. The friendly, knowledgeable service also helps to set the tone of the place. Tom's cooking is intelligently straightforward and elegant, with simplicity, flavour and skill top of his agenda. The style is broadly modern British, underpinned by classical French techniques, and the seasonally-changing menu is built around top notch produce. Considerable skill and confidence can be seen in dishes such as glazed omelette of smoked haddock and Parmesan; crispy pig's head with pickled rhubarb, pancetta and chickweed; fillet of lemon sole with beurre blanc, roast turnip and razor clams; loin of venison with beetroot tart, chestnuts, bacon and red wine chocolate sauce. Be wowed by desserts such as glazed Cox's apple tart with cinnamon ice cream, lavender pannacotta or warm pistachio cake with melon sorbet and marzipan. A few paces down the road, there are four stylish suites in two refurbished cottages. The Thames is close for revitalising river walks. The Hand and Flowers is the AA Restaurant of the Year for England 2011-2012.

Open 12-2.30 6.30-9.30 (Sun 12-3.30)
Closed: 24-26 Dec, 1 Jan Dinner, Sun eve
Bar Meals L served Mon-Sat 12-2.30
booking required D served Mon-Sat
6.30-9.30 booking required
Restaurant L served all wk 12-2.30
booking required D served all wk
6.30-9.30 booking required ⊕ GREENE
KING ◀ Abbot Ale, IPA, Morland Original.
🍷 11 **Facilities** Children's portions Garden
Parking Wi-fi

PICK OF THE PUBS

The Old Queens Head ♀

PENN Map 6 SU99

Hammersley Ln HP10 8EY
☎ **01494 813371** 📠 **01494 816145**
e-mail: info@oldqueensheadpenn.co.uk
web: www.oldqueensheadpenn.co.uk
dir: *B474 (Penn road) through Beaconsfield New Town towards Penn, approx 3m left into School Rd, left in 500yds into Hammersley Ln. Pub on corner opp church*

Sitting right on the border between the delightful villages of Penn and Tylers Green in rural South Buckinghamshire, The Old Queens Head has bags of character and atmosphere. The timber-built dining room dates from 1666 and although it has seen several additions since then, the cosy corners, uneven floors and real fires are reminders of its history. The owners have clearly spent many hours at local auctions finding lovely old furniture and pictures in keeping with the age of the pub, whose warm heritage colours harmonise well with the dark floorboards, flagstones, rugs and classic fabrics. A sunny terrace overlooks the village church, and there's a large garden in which to eat and drink. The kitchen team has created a modern British menu offering good choice, with starters such as warm Cornish crab thermidor tart with watercress salad; 'Amersham' pork rillettes with piccalilli and toasted onion bread; crispy Shropshire Blue cheese beignets with pickled red onion, rocket

and wholegrain mustard dressing. Main course options are similarly appetising; grilled Cornish haddock with free-range poached egg, Lyonnaise potatoes, curly kale and béarnaise sauce; pan-fried gnocchi with spinach, wild mushrooms, salsify and slow-roast garlic oil; braised Oxfordshire steak and kidney suet pudding with horseradish mash and purple sprouting broccoli are typical choices. Leave room for puddings like steamed treacle sponge pudding with clotted cream, or caramelised pineapple tarte Tatin with stem ginger ice cream. A well considered wine list includes 21 by the glass and 'stickies' (dessert wines) get a list of their own. Alternatively, you can snuggle up by the fire with a pint of Ruddles County or a mug of hot chocolate and marshmallows.

Open all day all wk 11-11 (Sun 12-10.30) Closed: 26 Dec **Bar Meals** L served Mon-Fri 12-2.30, Sat 12-3, Sun 12-4 D served Sun-Thu 6.30-9.30, Fri-Sat 6.30-10 **Restaurant** L served Mon-Fri 12-2.30, Sat 12-3, Sun 12-4 booking required D served Sun-Thu 6.30-9.30, Fri-Sat 6.30-10 booking required ⊕ SALISBURY PUBS LTD ◀ Ruddles County, Greene King IPA, Guinness Ŏ Aspall. ♀ 21 **Facilities** Children's portions Dogs allowed Garden Parking Wi-fi

PRESTON BISSETT　　Map 11 SP62

The White Hart

Pound Ln MK18 4LX ☎ 01280 847969
dir: *2.5m from A421*

Seek out this pretty thatched and timbered free house in the winter months for traditional game dishes from the local shoots. The Grade II listed building dates from the 18th century, has three cosy rooms warmed by a log fire and lies amid the rolling hills of rural Buckinghamshire. There's a good selection of wines and local real ales, and a small select menu that changes with the seasons; expect classic dishes like home-cooked ham, egg and chips or 10oz sirloin steak. There's a secluded garden and patio and a beer festival on Spring Bank Holiday.

Open 12-2.30 6-11 (Sat-Sun noon-11pm) **Closed:** Mon **Bar Meals** L served Tue-Sun 12-2.30 D served Tue-Sun 6-11 **Restaurant** L served Tue-Sun 12-2.30 booking required D served Tue-Sun 6-10 booking required ⊕ FREE HOUSE ◀ Hooky Best Bitter, Old Hooky, Timothy Taylor Landlord, Rev James, Tribute, Doom Bar.
Facilities Children welcome Children's menu Children's portions Dogs allowed Garden Beer festival Parking

RADNAGE　　Map 5 SU79

The Three Horseshoes Inn ♀

Horseshoe Rd, Bennett End HP14 4EB ☎ 01494 483273
e-mail: threehorseshoe@btconnect.com
dir: *From M40 junct 5, A40 towards High Wycombe, after unrestricted mileage sign turn left signed Radnage (Mudds Bank). 1.8m, 1st left into Bennett End Rd, inn on right*

When award-winning chef/patron Simon Crawshaw bought this beautiful old building in 2005, he knew it would be something special. Down a leafy lane, it is truly traditional – worn flagstones, blackened beams and original inglenook fireplace. On his modern English and European menu he typically offers roast Barbary duck breast with butternut squash purée; roast rump of local lamb with ratatouille; and pan-fried halibut with lobster risotto. Enjoy Marlow's Rebellion ale in the bar or in the lovely garden.

Open 12-3 6-11 (Sat all day, Sun 12-4) **Closed:** Sun eve, Mon L **Bar Meals** L served Tue-Sat 12-2.30, Sun 12-3 D served Mon-Sat 7-9.30 **Restaurant** L served Tue-Sat 12-2.30, Sun 12-3 D served Mon-Sat 7-9.30 booking required ⊕ FREE HOUSE ◀ Rebellion beers. ♀ 12
Facilities Children welcome Children's portions Dogs allowed Garden Parking Wi-fi

SEER GREEN　　Map 6 SU99

The Jolly Cricketers ♀ NEW

24 Chalfont Rd HP9 2YG ☎ 01494 676308
dir: *M40 junct 2, A355 signed Beaconsfield A40, Amersham. At Pyebush rdbt 1st exit, A40 signed Beaconsfield, Amersham, A355. At rdbt, A355 signed Amersham. Right into Longbottom Ln signed Seer Green. Left into Bottom Ln, right into Orchard Rd, left into Church Rd, right into Chalfont Rd*

A traditional, 19th-century, wisteria-clad free house set in the picture-postcard village of Seer Green, which Chris Lillitou and Amanda Baker have transformed to appeal to locals chatting over pints of Marlow Rebellion, quiz addicts on Sunday nights, live jazz fans, beer festival-goers, dog walkers... Their signature dish is ale-and cider-braised ham with crispy poached egg, pineapple chutney and triple-cooked chips, served on locally-crafted wooden boards. There's plenty more too, such as curried mussels, rabbit cannelloni, and gnocchi with sautéed wild mushrooms, with poached Yorkshire rhubarb or British cheeses to follow.

Open all day all wk **Bar Meals** L served Tue-Sat 12-2.30 D served Tue-Sat 6.30-9 Av main course £14 **Restaurant** L served Tue-Fri 12-2.30, Sat-Sun 12-3.30 D served Tue-Sat 6.30-9 Av 3 course à la carte fr £27 ⊕ FREE HOUSE ◀ Marlow Rebellion IPA, Fuller's London Pride, Chiltern Brewery Beechwood ♂ Millwhites, Artisan Bottle selection. ♀ 16 **Facilities** Children welcome Children's menu Children's portions Dogs allowed Garden Beer festival Parking Wi-fi

SKIRMETT　　Map 5 SU79

PICK OF THE PUBS

The Frog ♀

RG9 6TG ☎ 01491 638996 📠 01491 638045
e-mail: info@thefrogatskirmett.co.uk
web: www.thefrogatskirmett.co.uk
dir: *Turn off A4155 at Mill End, pub in 3m*

The Hamble Brook flows by behind the pub, whilst red kites float on thermals rising above the wooded hills at the heart of The Chilterns Area of Outstanding Natural Beauty. In summer the garden of this 300 year old pub is a relaxing place to be, perhaps resting from a ramble to the famous windmill on nearby Turville Hill, whilst winter warmth is guaranteed in the charming 18th century bar. Away from the bar, spacious dining rooms are a striking mix of opulence with contemporary design. Head chef and co-owner Jim Crowe has

developed excellent relationships with his suppliers, resulting in fantastic local produce to sate the most discerning of appetites. If the pub has a signature dish, then it must be one featuring local estate venison, perhaps roast loin with haggis, spinach and roast figs with redcurrant and juniper sauce; the cut and style will vary with the ever-changing menu. Jim's cooking is adventurous, modern European; a starter of local game terrine or watercress pancake filled with smoked haddock and saffron chive sauce sets the tone for mains that encompass roast fillet of cod with an anchovy crust or good old Lancashire hotpot with pickled red cabbage. Clean the palate with a wine list that includes English bins, or indulge in beers from Rebellion or Hook Norton breweries.

Open 11.30-3 6-11 **Closed:** Sun eve (Oct-Apr) **Bar Meals** L served all wk 12-2.30 D served all wk 6.30-9.30 Av main course £12.50 **Restaurant** L served all wk 12-2.30 D served all wk 6.30-9.30 Av 3 course à la carte fr £26.50 ⊕ FREE HOUSE ◀ Adnams Best, Hook Norton, Rebellion, Fuller's London Pride, IPA, Guest ale ♂ Thatchers Dry. ♀ 15 **Facilities** Children welcome Children's menu Children's portions Family room Dogs allowed Garden Parking

TURVILLE　　Map 5 SU79

PICK OF THE PUBS

The Bull & Butcher ♀

RG9 6QU ☎ 01491 638283
e-mail: info@thebullandbutcher.com
dir: *M40 junct 5 follow Ibstone signs. Right at T-junct. Pub 0.25m on left*

You'll probably recognise The Bull & Butcher, even if you've never been there before. For Turville, with its delightful 16th-century pub and 10th-century church, has won celebrity status in numerous film and television productions: *Midsomer Murders, The Vicar of Dibley, Goodnight Mr Tom,* and *Chitty Chitty Bang Bang.* After an exhilarating walk amid the glorious Chilterns scenery, drop down from the windmill on Turville Hill and unwind with a pint from a fantastic choice of real ales in the Well Bar or Windmill Lounge with their natural oak beams and open fires. There's also a function room ideal for leisure and corporate occasions, and a large garden and patio area. Menu choices begin with starters that include a platter of cured meats with olives and bread, whilst main course dishes range from cod, chips and mushy peas or pan-fried duck with rice and stir-fried vegetables to roasted vegetable cannelloni with spinach.

Open all day all wk noon-11 (Sat noon-1am) **Bar Meals** L served Mon-Fri 12-2.30, Sat 12-3.30 Sun 12-4 booking required D served Mon-Sat 6.30-9.30, Sun 7-9 booking required ⊕ BRAKSPEAR ◀ Brakspear Bitter, Oxford Gold, Brewers selections ♂ Addlestones. ♀ 36 **Facilities** Children welcome Children's menu Dogs allowed Garden Parking

WEST WYCOMBE — Map 5 SU89

PICK OF THE PUBS

The George and Dragon Hotel ☻

High St HP14 3AB ☎ 01494 535340
dir: *On A40*

Visitors to the area will enjoy exploring West Wycombe Caves, and the stately houses at Cliveden and Hughenden Manor. After a day's hard touring, a visit to this traditional coaching inn with 14th-century origins in a National Trust village will be nicely relaxing. It wasn't always the case – it was once a hideout for highwaymen stalking travellers between London and Oxford; indeed, one unfortunate guest robbed and murdered here is rumoured still to haunt its corridors. The hotel is reached through a cobbled archway and comprises a delightful jumble of whitewashed, timber-framed buildings. Reliable real ales include Tribute and Rebellion IPA. Also reliable is the varied menu which offers freshly-prepared dishes cooked to order such as beef and ale pie; beer battered haddock; a button mushroom, Brie and cranberry filo parcel; and succulent rib-eye steaks.

Open all wk noon-mdnt (Fri-Sat 12-1 Sun noon-11.30pm) **Bar Meals** L served 12-3 D served 6-9, Fri-Sun 6-9.30 **Restaurant** L served 12-3 D served 6-9 ⊕ ENTERPRISE INNS ◀ Tribute, Rebellion IPA, Guest ales. ☻ 9 **Facilities** Children welcome Play area Family room Dogs allowed Garden Parking Wi-fi

WHEELER END — Map 5 SU89

The Chequers Inn ☻

Bullocks Farm Ln HP14 3NH ☎ 01494 883070
e-mail: chequersinn2@btconnect.com
dir: *4m N of Marlow*

Styling itself 'a traditional village pub with old style values in an adult environment', this picturesque 17th-century inn, with its low beamed ceilings, roaring winter fires and two attractive beer gardens, is ideally located for walkers on the edge of Wheeler End Common. A solid choice of mouth-watering sandwiches and bar meals supplements the main menu, which features plenty of fresh fish and local estate game. Grilled witch sole, pork fillet with Stilton sauce, stuffed pheasant breast followed by a selection of home-made puddings all might tempt. There's a beer festival at Whitsun.

Open 12-3 6-11 (Sun 12-4) Closed: Mon L **Bar Meals** L served Tue-Sat 12-2, Sun 12-3.30 D served Tue-Sat 6.30-9 **Restaurant** L served Tue-Sat 12-2, Sun 12-3.30 D served Tue-Sat 6.30-9 ⊕ FULLER SMITH TURNER PLC ◀ Fuller's ESB, London Pride, Guest ale. ☻ 12 **Facilities** Children welcome Children's portions Dogs allowed Garden Beer festival Parking

WHITELEAF — Map 5 SP80

Red Lion

Upper Icknield Way HP27 0LL
☎ 01844 344476 🖷 01844 344476
e-mail: tim_hibbert@hotmail.co.uk
dir: *A4010 through Princes Risborough, turn right into The Holloway, at T-junct turn right, pub on left*

Family-owned 17th-century traditional country inn in the heart of the Chilterns, surrounded by National Trust land and situated close to the Ridgeway national trail. There are plenty of good local walks with wonderful views. A cosy fire in winter and a secluded summer beer garden add to the appeal. Hearty pub fare is served in the bar area and includes rib-eye steak, sausage and mash, vegetarian lasagne, haddock and chips, warm baguettes and jacket potatoes. You can also dine in the restaurant.

Open all wk 12-3 5-11 (Fri-Sun all day) ⊕ FREE HOUSE ◀ Brakspear Bitter, Hook Norton, Tribute, Guinness Ô Aspall. **Facilities** Children welcome Children's portions Family room Dogs allowed Garden Parking Wi-fi

WOOBURN COMMON — Map 6 SU98

PICK OF THE PUBS

Chequers Inn ★★★ HL ⊛ ☻

Kiln Ln HP10 0JQ ☎ 01628 529575 🖷 01628 850124
e-mail: info@chequers-inn.com
dir: *M40 junct 2, A40 through Beaconsfield Old Town towards High Wycombe. 2m from town left into Broad Ln. Inn 2.5m*

A perfect base for exploring Buckinghamshire's neck of the picturesque Thames Valley, this 17th-century inn is an absolute charmer; so you may wish to book one of the 17 beautifully appointed bedrooms. Oak posts and beams, flagstone floors and a wonderful open fireplace blackened by a million blazing logs characterize the pub's interior. It has been owned and run by the same family for over 35 years, ensuring a friendly, relaxed and welcoming atmosphere. There is an attractively decorated restaurant, and a refurbished lounge furnished with leather sofas and low tables. While the restaurant is ideal for both quick business lunches and long romantic dinners, eating options include an extensive bar menu which has a tempting list of small plates. Fresh, predominantly local ingredients are used in dishes such as fresh crab salad with lemon mayonnaise; a home-made burger served with bacon, cheese, chips, salad and coleslaw; and Cumberland sausages, mash and onion gravy. Outside, the large garden hosts summer barbecues.

Open all day all wk noon-mdnt **Bar Meals** L served Mon-Fri 12-2.30, Sat 12-10, Sun 12-9.30 D served Mon-Thu 6-9.30, Fri 6-10, Sat 12-10, Sun 12-9.30 Av main course £9.95 **Restaurant** L served all wk 12-2.30 booking required D served all wk 7-9.30 booking required Fixed menu price fr £13.95 Av 3 course à la carte fr £35 ⊕ FREE HOUSE ◀ IPA, Rebellion Smuggler, Old Speckled Hen Ô Stowford Press. ☻ 14 **Facilities** Children welcome Children's menu Children's portions Garden Parking Wi-fi **Rooms** 17

WOOBURN GREEN — Map 6 SU98

Old Bell ☻

Town Ln HP10 0PL ☎ 01628 520406
e-mail: peterlim@oldbell.co.uk
dir: *On A4094. Pub adjacent to church in village*

Right on the edge of the Chilterns, this almost 300-year-old village inn stands just a short distance from Burnham Beeches woods. In a former guise it was an oriental restaurant and bar; nowadays traditional English pub food is the mainstay, with a nod to contemporary European influences, plus Sunday roast. Tuck into starters of devilled whitebait or house pâté with toasted brioche and onion marmalade, followed perhaps by half a shoulder of lamb cooked in oregano and garlic or Cumberland sausages with mash, red wine and onion gravy.

Open all wk noon-3 5-11 **Bar Meals** L served Tue-Sat 12-2.30 D served Tue-Sat 6.30-9.30 **Restaurant** L served Tue-Sun 12-2.30 booking required D served Tue-Sat 6.30-9.30 booking required ⊕ ENTERPRISE INNS ◀ Young's Bitter, Timothy Taylor Landlord. ☻ 10 **Facilities** Children welcome Children's portions Garden Parking Wi-fi

CAMBRIDGESHIRE

BABRAHAM — Map 12 TL55

PICK OF THE PUBS

The George Inn at Babraham ☻

High St CB2 4AG ☎ 01223 833800
e-mail: info@thegeorgebabraham.co.uk
dir: *In High St, just off A11/A505 & A1307*

An 18th-century coaching inn once renowned for the Whitsun and May Day revels hosted here. Set in the heart of rural Cambridgeshire, it was devastated by fire in 2004 but new kitchens and three restaurant areas have restored this village dining pub to its former glory. Just four miles outside Cambridge, the George is a good reason for a stroll around the picturesque village of Babraham before taking your refreshment. Joanna Laurie now runs the pub full time, serving well kept Greene King beers and good home-cooked food. Exposed beams and brickwork characterise most areas, lending a friendly and relaxed air to the place. A mix of leather sofas and solid oak furniture add to the appeal, and the dining room has been refurbished. An attractive rear patio with heaters and parasols leads to a garden, and special culinary and music events are hosted throughout the year.

Open all wk Mon-Fri 12-3 5-11 (Sat-Sun all day) **Bar Meals** L served all wk 12-2 D served all wk 5.30-9 Av main course £9 **Restaurant** L served Mon-Fri 12-2, Sat-Sun 12-3 D served all wk 5.30-9 ⊕ GREENE KING ◀ Old Speckled Hen, Greene King IPA, Guest ale Ô Aspall. ☻ 8 **Facilities** Children welcome Children's menu Children's portions Dogs allowed Garden Parking Wi-fi

Save on hotels. Book at theAA.com/hotel

CAMBRIDGESHIRE 59 ENGLAND

BARRINGTON Map 12 TL34

The Royal Oak

31 West Green CB22 7RZ
☎ 01223 870791 📄 01223 870791
e-mail: info@royaloak.uk.net
dir: *From Barton off M11, S of Cambridge*

One of the oldest thatched pubs in England, this rambling, timbered 13th-century building overlooks one of the largest village greens in England. It's only six miles from Cambridge, three miles from the M11 and a mile from Shepreth Station. A wide range of fish dishes includes scallops, trout, scampi, tuna, swordfish, tiger prawns, squid and other seasonal offerings. There is also a carvery on Sunday which could be accompanied by a pint of IPA Potton Brewery or Young's Bitter. A change of hands took place in 2010.

Open all wk noon-2.30 6-11 (Sun noon-3 6.30-10.30) ⊕ FREE HOUSE ◧ IPA Potton Brewery, Adnams, Young's Bitter, Morland Original. **Facilities** Children welcome Children's menu Children's portions Dogs allowed Garden Parking

BROUGHTON Map 12 TL27

PICK OF THE PUBS

The Crown Inn ☙

Bridge Rd PE28 3AY ☎ 01487 824428
e-mail: info@thecrowninnrestaurant.co.uk
dir: *Just off A141 between Huntingdon & Warboys, by church in village centre*

In the mid-19th century, this picturesque village inn incorporated a saddler's shop, thatched stables and piggeries. The livestock has long gone, and today it focuses on being a popular village pub and restaurant at the heart of a thriving local community. The bar offers real ales from local breweries, and you'll also find Aspall cider. The restaurant combines a traditional pub look with contemporary design and it's here you'll be able to eat modern European dishes cooked using the best sustainable fish caught by day boats, the highest quality meats, and excellent seasonal vegetables. Menus change regularly, so when you visit you may find one offering starters of crispy duck salad or mussels cooked with bacon and beer. Typical main courses are slow-cooked blade of beef with horseradish mash, or braised rabbit in cream and rosemary with bubble and squeak. Round off with nougat parfait and berries or profiteroles. Now under new ownership.

Open all wk Mon-Sat 11.30-3 6.30-11 (Sun 11.30-8) **Bar Meals** L served all wk 12-2.30 D served all wk 6.30-9.30 Av main course £13 **Restaurant** L served all wk 12-2.30 D served all wk 6.30-9.30 Av 3 course à la carte fr £25 ⊕ FREE HOUSE ◧ Greene King IPA, Nethergate Sweeney Todd, Timothy Taylor Landlord, Adnams Bitter, Guest ales ☍ Aspall. ☙ 10 **Facilities** Children welcome Children's menu Children's portions Play area Dogs allowed Garden Parking

CAMBRIDGE Map 12 TL45

PICK OF THE PUBS

The Anchor ☙

Silver St CB3 9EL ☎ 01223 353554
e-mail: 7614@greeneking.co.uk
dir: *Telephone for directions*

Situated at the end of the medieval lane that borders Queens' College in the heart of the University city, this attractive waterside pub appeals to students and visitors alike. Hard by the bridge over the River Cam, in fine weather the riverside patio is an ideal spot for enjoying one of a range of guest beers while watching the activities on the water. The more adventurous can hire a punt for a leisurely trip to Grantchester (of Rupert Brooke and Jeffrey Archer fame), and on return sample a choice of hearty meals from a range that includes lasagne, home-made pie, and roast beef.

Open all wk Mon-Thu & Sun 11am-11pm (Fri-Sat 11am-mdnt) **Bar Meals** L served all wk 11am-10pm food served all day ⊕ GREENE KING ◧ Greene King, IPA, Abbot Ale, Old Speckled Hen, St Edmunds ☍ Aspall. ☙ 12 **Facilities** Children welcome Children's menu

PICK OF THE PUBS

Cambridge Blue ☙

85 Gwydir St CB1 2LG ☎ 01223 471680
dir: *In city centre. Access by car to Gwydir St from Mill Rd only (no access by car from Norfolk St). Gwydir St parking available*

A friendly 1860s backstreet pub, built to serve the terrace that housed railway workers, with an unexpected large suntrap garden and an amazing range of beers, from unusual bottled beers from around the world to a mind-boggling choice of 14 real ales from micro-breweries on handpump in the tap room – try a pint of Oakham Bishops Farewell or Woodforde's Wherry. Inside are two real fires, lots of memorabilia and a lively, buzzy vibe. Good value pub grub made on the premises comes in the form of steak and kidney pie, fish pie, sausages and mash, a daily curry and a range of filled ciabatta sandwiches and jacket potatoes (plus there are always vegetarian options). Don't miss the February, June and October beer festivals.

Open all day all wk Mon-Fri noon-11 (Sat 11-11, Sun noon-10.30) **Bar Meals** L served Mon-Sat 12-10, Sun 12-9 Av main course £8 food served all day ⊕ FREE HOUSE ◧ Woodforde's Wherry, Oakham Bishops Farewell, Guest ales ☍ Pickled Pig, Thatchers. ☙ 8 **Facilities** Children welcome Children's portions Family room Dogs allowed Garden Beer festival Wi-fi

Free Press ☙

Prospect Row CB1 1DU ☎ 01223 368337
dir: *Telephone for directions*

A pub for over 120 years, The Free Press gets its name from when part of it was a printing press which circulated a free Cambridge newspaper. Now a haunt for students, academics, locals and visitors, this atmospheric and picturesque back-street pub near the city centre has open fires and a beautiful walled garden - but no music, mobile phones or gaming machines. Punters are attracted by first-rate real ales and great home-made food such as toasted ciabattas; seafood platter; lamb's liver and bacon with bubble 'n' squeak and gravy.

Open all wk noon-2.30 6-11 (Fri noon-2.30 4.30-11, Sat noon-11, Sun noon-3 7-10.30) Closed: 25-26 Dec, 1 Jan **Bar Meals** L served Mon-Fri 12-2, Sat-Sun 12-2.30 D served Mon-Sat 6-9, Sun 7-9 Av main course £7.50 **Restaurant** Fixed menu price fr £10 ⊕ GREENE KING ◧ Greene King IPA, Abbot Ale, Dark Mild, Guest ales. ☙ 10 **Facilities** Children welcome Children's portions Dogs allowed Garden

The Old Spring ☙

1 Ferry Path CB4 1HB
☎ 01223 357228 📄 01223 357235
e-mail: theoldspring@hotmail.co.uk
dir: *Just off Chesterton Rd, (A1303) in city centre, near Midsummer Common*

In the leafy suburb of Defreville, just a short stroll from the River Cam and its many boatyards, the splendid decked patio of this bustling neighbourhood pub is a popular post-workout refreshment spot for rowers. The bright and airy interior offers rug-covered wood floors, comfy sofas and large family tables. Sip a pint of Abbot Ale or one of 20 wines by the glass while choosing from the array of freshly prepared food, perhaps corned beef, potato and red onion hash, battered haddock and hand-cut chips, or sirloin steak with pepper sauce.

Open all day all wk 11.30-11 (Sun 12-10.30) **Bar Meals** L served Mon-Fri 12-2.30, Sat-Sun 12-4 D served Mon-Fri 6-9.30 Av main course £10 ⊕ GREENE KING ◧ IPA, Abbot Ale, Olde Trip, Old Speckled Hen, Guest ales ☍ Aspall. ☙ 20 **Facilities** Children welcome Children's menu Children's portions Garden Parking Wi-fi

CAMBRIDGE *continued*

The Punter

3 Pound Hill CB3 0AE ☎ 01223 363322
e-mail: thepunter@hotmail.co.uk
dir: *Telephone for directions*

Just two minutes' walk from the city centre and popular with visitors, locals and students alike, this beautifully renovated old coaching house is furnished with an eclectic mix of pine furniture that creates a comfortable, relaxed ambience where drinkers can sit alongside diners and enjoy well-priced rustic food. The daily-changing seasonal menu includes a £5 set lunch, whilst other choices might include rabbit Caesar salad with bacon; potted shrimps with toast; guinea fowl breast with fondant potato, wild mushrooms and kale; pesto baked aubergine with Suffolk Gold cheese and stuffed cabbage; steamed lemon and ginger sponge and custard. In the delightful courtyard garden pots of home-grown produce are sold.

Open all day all wk Closed: 25 Dec **Bar Meals** L served Mon-Fri 12-3, Sat-Sun all day D served Mon-Fri 6-10, Sat-Sun all day **Restaurant** L served Mon-Fri 12-3, Sat-Sun all day D served Mon-Fri 6-10, Sat-Sun all day ◀ Adnams Explorer, Adnams Broadside Ö Aspall. **Facilities** Children welcome Children's portions Dogs allowed Garden Wi-fi

DUXFORD	Map 12 TL44

PICK OF THE PUBS

The John Barleycorn ♀

3 Moorfield Rd CB2 4PP
☎ 01223 832699 📄 01223 832699
e-mail: info@johnbarleycorn.co.uk
dir: *Exit A505 into Duxford*

Step through the door of this thatched and whitewashed 17th-century inn into the low-beamed and softly lit bar. There's a rustic mix of country furniture, a large brick fireplace and an old tiled floor, with cushioned painted pews and hop-adorned beams.

This is a cosy, comfortable and relaxing place in which to enjoy a hearty home-cooked meal, washed down with a cracking pint of Greene King Abbot or Old Speckled Hen. During World War II, it became a favourite watering hole for the brave young airmen of Duxford Wing. Lunchtime brings a varied menu that ranges from favourites like pies and burgers to slightly more adventurous fare such as Thai fish cakes or baked Camembert with apple chutney. An evening meal might begin with terrine of Gressingham duck, followed by fresh tagliatelle with wild mushrooms, lemon, tarragon and shaved Parmesan. Finish, perhaps, with a warm pear crumble slice. Summer alfresco eating can be enjoyed on the flower-festooned rear patio.

Open all day all wk **Bar Meals** L served all wk booking required D served all wk booking required Av main course £8.95 food served all day **Restaurant** Av 3 course à la carte fr £25 food served all day ⊕ GREENE KING ◀ Greene King IPA, Abbot Ale, Old Speckled Hen, Ruddles Best & County. ♀ 12 **Facilities** Children welcome Children's menu Children's portions Play area Garden Parking Wi-fi

ELSWORTH	Map 12 TL36

The George & Dragon ♀

41 Boxworth Rd CB3 8JQ
☎ 01954 267236 📄 01954 267080
e-mail: www.georgeanddragon-elsworth.co.uk
dir: *SE of A14 between Cambridge & Huntingdon*

Set in a pretty village just outside Cambridge, this pub offers a friendly, relaxed environment, great beers and a wide range of satisfying food for locals and visitors alike. Aberdeen Angus steaks and fish fresh from Lowestoft are a draw here on the seasonal menu. Look out for blue cheese and walnut terrine; chicken breast with wild mushroom and thyme farcie; Asian style glazed grilled salmon; and home-made fish pie. Friday night is steak night and there are special menus for occasions such as Valentine candlelit dinner and Mother's Day.

Open all wk 11-2.30 6-11 **Bar Meals** L served all wk 11-2.30 D served all wk 6-11 Av main course £10

Restaurant L served all wk 11-2.30 D served all wk 6-11 Fixed menu price fr £10 Av 3 course à la carte fr £20 ⊕ FREE HOUSE ◀ Greene King IPA, Ruddles County, Greene King Old Speckled Hen Ö Aspall. ♀ 13 **Facilities** Children welcome Children's menu Children's portions Garden Parking

ELTON	Map 12 TL09

PICK OF THE PUBS

The Black Horse ♀

14 Overend PE8 6RU ☎ 01832 280240 & 280875
e-mail: theblackhorseelton@gmail.com
dir: *Off A605 (Peterborough to Northampton road)*

Antique furnishings and open log fires crank up the old world charm in this 17th-century inn, while the delightful one-acre rear garden overlooks Elton's famous church and rolling open countryside. The real ales include Everards Tiger, seasonal brews, and Barnwell Bitter, which is brewed locally. The superb selection of food ranges from bar snacks to a full à la carte. Among the 'snacks' are sandwiches, filled baguettes, jacket potatoes, a home-made pie of the day, and seasonal salads. Or you might start with Portobello mushrooms topped with bacon and cheese gratin; or freshly dressed crab with brown bread and salad. Typical main courses include guinea fowl stuffed with black pudding and chorizo sausage, wrapped in Parma ham and served with a rich red wine jus; fillet of sea bass with braised pak choi, pesto and sun-blushed tomatoes; and bangers and mash.

Open all day Mon-Thurs noon-10pm (Fri-Sat noon-11pm, Sun noon-9pm) Closed: (Sun eve) **Bar Meals** L served Mon-Fri 12-2.30, Sat 12-9, Sun 12-8 D served Mon-Fri 6-9, Sat 12-9, Sun 12-8 **Restaurant** L served Mon-Fri 12-2.30, Sat 12-9, Sun 12-8 D served Mon-Fri 6-9, Sat 12-9, Sun 12-8 ⊕ FREE HOUSE ◀ Everards Tiger, Barnwell Bitter, Oakham JHB. ♀ 14 **Facilities** Children welcome Children's menu Play area Family room Dogs allowed Garden Parking

PICK OF THE PUBS

The Crown Inn ★★★★★ INN ◉

8 Duck St PE8 6RQ ☎ 01832 280232
e-mail: inncrown@googlemail.com
web: www.thecrowninn.org
dir: *A1(M) junct 17, W on A605 signed Oundle/ Northampton. In 3.5m right to Elton, 0.9m left signed Nassington. Inn 0.3m on right*

Tucked away behind a towering chestnut tree in an idyllic, picture-postcard setting by the village green, this stone-and-thatch 17th-century inn oozes atmosphere and charm – surely The Crown must be the quintessential English village inn. Click open the latch door to find oak beams and timbers aplenty, soothing pastel shades, natural wood and stone, and a crackling log fire in the inglenook in the time-honoured bar. Chef-patron Marcus Lamb places great emphasis on the food, with local produce forming the mainstay of his imaginative menus. You'll find ham hock terrine with beetroot relish, cod in beer batter with mushy peas and hand-cut chips, and roast beef and horseradish sandwiches on the lunchtime bar menu. At dinner there's pork belly with apple and pork samosa and cider sauce, and lamb rump with rosemary sauce, with baked lemon tart or a plate a cheese with home-made chutney for pudding. Annual treats include a May Day hog roast and a summer beer festival. There are five en suite bedrooms, each with its own individual appeal.

Open all wk noon-11 (Mon 5-11 (BH noon-11)) Closed: 1-7 Jan (Restaurant) **Bar Meals** L served Tue-Sun 12-2 D served Mon-Sat 6.30-8.45 **Restaurant** L served Tue-Sun 12-2 booking required D served Tue-Sat 6.30-8.45 booking required ⊕ FREE HOUSE ◀ Golden Crown Bitter, Greene King IPA, Adnams, Jeffrey Hudson Bitter, Black Sheep. **Facilities** Children welcome Children's portions Dogs allowed Garden Beer festival Parking Wi-fi **Rooms** 5
                    See advert on opposite page

ELY   Map 12 TL58

PICK OF THE PUBS

The Anchor Inn ★★★★ RR ◉ ♥

See Pick of the Pubs on page 62

FEN DITTON   Map 12 TL46

PICK OF THE PUBS

Ancient Shepherds ♥

High St CB5 8ST ☎ 01223 293280 🖨 01223 293280
e-mail: ancientshepherds@hotmail.co.uk
dir: *From A14 take B1047 signed Cambridge/Airport*

Located three miles from Cambridge in the riverside village of Fen Ditton, this heavily-beamed pub and restaurant provides a welcome escape for those who like to enjoy their refreshments without the addition of music, darts or pool. Easily recognised by its white washed walls and hanging baskets in summer, it was named after the ancient order of Shepherds who once met here; it was built originally as three cottages in 1540. The two bars, a lounge and a dining room all boast inglenook fireplaces. The menus range from filled baguettes, home-made soup, ploughman's, sausage and chips and the like for lunch, to specials such as seafood salad with new potatoes; moussaka; oyster, mushroom and champagne risotto; and home-made beef and Guinness pie. Desserts should get your attention too with home-made summer fruit Pavlova, strawberry and white chocolate cheesecake or tangy lemon tart being typical options.

Open noon-2.30 6-11 Closed: 25-26 Dec, 1 Jan, Sun eve, Mon eve **Bar Meals** L served all wk 12-2 Av main course £9.95 **Restaurant** L served all wk 12-2 D served Tue-Sat 6.30-9 booking required ⊕ PUNCH TAVERNS ◀ Adnams Bitter, Greene King IPA, London Pride ♂ Aspall. ♥ 8 **Facilities** Children welcome Children's portions Dogs allowed Garden Parking

---

FENSTANTON   Map 12 TL36

King William IV ♥

High St PE28 9JF ☎ 01480 462467
e-mail: kingwilliamfenstanton@btconnect.com
dir: *Off A14 junct 27 between Cambridge & Huntingdon*

Under new ownership since early 2011, this rambling 17th-century village-centre pub features oak beams, old brickwork and a wonderful central fireplace. In addition to bar food, there's a choice of classics, of the sausage, pasta and pie of the day variety; then there's lamb's liver and bacon or chilli con carne, or you can enjoy chicken breast stuffed with cream cheese and chilli; poached smoked haddock with bubble and squeak; or mushroom Stroganoff. There is live music on Wednesday evenings and twice monthly at Sunday lunchtimes.

Open all wk Mon-Thu 12-3 5-11 (Fri-Sun all day) **Bar Meals** L served all wk 12-2.30 D served Mon-Wed 6-9, Thu-Sat 5.30-9.30 Av main course £12 **Restaurant** L served all wk 12-2.30 D served Mon-Wed 6-9, Thu-Sat 5.30-9.30 Av 3 course à la carte fr £18 ⊕ GREENE KING ◀ Greene King Abbot Ale & IPA, Guest ales ♂ Aspall. ♥ 11 **Facilities** Children welcome Children's portions Dogs allowed Garden Parking

---

FORDHAM   Map 12 TL67

PICK OF THE PUBS

White Pheasant ♥

CB7 5LQ ☎ 01638 720414
e-mail: chef@whitepheasant.com
dir: *From Newmarket A142 to Ely, approx 5m to Fordham. Pub on left in village*

This 18th-century building stands in a fenland village between Ely and Newmarket. In recent years its considerable appeal has been subtly enhanced by improvements that preserve its period charm. You can enjoy locally brewed ale, a glass of wine, home-made lemonade or strawberryade while perusing the menus. Food is taken seriously here, with quality, presentation and flavour taking top priority, using produce sourced as locally as possible. Starters could be free range chicken terrine with cranberry and chervil; crispy whitebait with tartare sauce. Following on with pan-fried Suffolk-reared beef fillet, wild mushrooms and red wine with thick cut chips; roasted Gressingham duck breast, braised red cabbage with rapeseed oil mash; and buffalo mozzarella, plum tomato and Parmesan gratin tart. Honey and lavender pannacotta is among the desserts.

Open noon-3 6-11 (Sun 12-4) Closed: 26-29 Dec, 1 Jan, Sun eve **Bar Meals** L served Mon-Sat 12-2.30, Sun 12-3 booking required D served Mon-Sat 6-9.30 **Restaurant** L served Mon-Sat 12-2.30, Sun 12-3 booking required D served Mon-Sat 6-9.30 booking required ⊕ FREE HOUSE ◀ Rusty Bucket, Nethergate ♂ Aspall. ♥ 12 **Facilities** Children welcome Children's portions Garden Parking

---

FOWLMERE   Map 12 TL44

The Chequers ♥

High St SG8 7SR ☎ 01763 208369 🖨 01763 208944
e-mail: info@thechequersfowlmere.co.uk
web: www.thechequersfowlmere.co.uk
dir: *From M11, A505, 2nd right to Fowlmere. 8m S of Cambridge, 4m E of Royston*

The pub's sign - blue and red chequers - honours the British and American squadrons based nearby during World War II, though the pub dates from the 16th century and Samuel Pepys was a visitor in 1660. These days The Chequers is known for its imaginative dishes made from local produce, which are served in the galleried restaurant, conservatory, bar or attractive garden. Their

continued on page 63

PICK OF THE PUBS

The Anchor Inn ★★★★ RR ✿ 🍷

ELY Map 12 TL58

Sutton Gault CB6 2BD
☎ **01353 778537** 📄 **01353 776180**
e-mail: anchorinn@popmail.bta.com
web: www.anchorsuttongault.co.uk
dir: *From A14, B1050 to Earith, take
B1381 to Sutton. Sutton Gault on left*

Scrubbed pine tables on gently undulating tiled floors, antique prints and winter log fires lend character to the cosy, intimate atmosphere of this family-run free house. Sutton Gault lies on the western edge of the Isle of Ely, which until the 17th century stood with its ancient cathedral high above the surrounding swamps. Then, in 1630, the Earl of Bedford engaged the Dutch engineer Cornelius Vermuyden to drain the lawless and disease-ridden fens for agricultural use. The Anchor was originally constructed on the bank of the New Bedford River to accommodate Vermuyden's workforce - largely Scottish prisoners of war conscripted by Oliver Cromwell. Despite this rather grim provenance The Anchor has been a pub ever since, evolving over the last 350 years to combine modern comforts with timeless charm and character. The pub has won wide recognition for its stylish en suite accommodation and modern British cuisine. There's an emphasis on seasonal and traditional ingredients and, in summer, meals can be enjoyed on the terrace overlooking the New Bedford River.

Weekday lunch might begin with grilled dates in bacon on a mild grain mustard cream sauce; or smoked salmon blinis with lemon, horseradish and dill cream cheese. Main course options include pan-fried gilthead bream with herb crushed potatoes, butternut squash pureé and braised fennel; lamb rump with parsnip pancake, poached rhubarb, curly kale and balsamic jus; and roasted garlic, spinach and sun-blushed tomato tagliatelle with micro herb salad. Typical dessert choices range from lemon posset to double chocolate brownie with chocolate ice cream. The Anchor is ideally situated for exploring East Anglia; it is only 7 miles from the cathedral city of Ely, and less than half an hour from Cambridge. Newmarket and its racecourse are also within easy reach.

Open Mon-Fri 12-2.30 7-10.30 (Sat 12-3 6.30-11 Sun 12-4 6.30-10) Closed: 25-26 Dec eve **Restaurant** L served Mon-Sat 12-2, Sun 12-2.30 booking required D served Mon-Fri 7-9, Sat 6.30-9.30, Sun 6.30-8.30 booking required ⊕ FREE HOUSE ◼ Little Sharpie, Hobsons Choice. 🍷 12 **Facilities** Children's portions Garden Parking Wi-fi **Rooms** 4

FOWLMERE *continued*

wide-ranging menu might include a starter of Louisiana crab cakes with celeriac remoulade, and mains of pan-fried pork loin escalopes served on potato rösti with stir-fried cabbage and pancetta, or featherblade of beef braised in a Portobello mushroom, red wine and thyme sauce.

Open all wk 12-3 6-11 Closed: 25-26 Dec eve & 1 Jan eve **Bar Meals** L served Mon-Sat 12-2, Sun 12-3 D served Mon-Sat 7-9.30, Sun 7-9 Av main course £16 **Restaurant** L served Mon-Sat 12-2, Sun 12-3 D served Mon-Sat 7-9.30, Sun 7-9 Av 3 course à la carte fr £30 ⊕ FREE HOUSE ◄ Adnams, Buntingford, Sharp's, Fuller's ♻ Aspall. ♟ 19 **Facilities** Children welcome Garden Parking Wi-fi

GRANTCHESTER   Map 12 TL45

The Rupert Brooke ♟

2 Broadway CB3 9NQ ☎ 01223 840295
e-mail: info@therupertbrooke.com
dir: *M11 junct 12, follow Grantchester signs*

Only five minutes from the centre of Cambridge and the M11, yet set in an idyllic location overlooking the meadows close to the River Cam, sits The Rupert Brooke, named after the WWI poet. Inside, you'll find timber beams and winter log fires, with relaxing sofas and tub chairs, plus a good selection of real ales. Using local, seasonal produce and with regularly changing menus, watch the chefs at work in the theatre-style kitchen, creating their range of modern British dishes – Camembert soufflé; sea bass fillet with glazed crab mash, spinach and crab velouté; and almond pannacotta. The pub provides newspapers and Wi-fi.

Open all day all wk Mon-Thu 11.30-11 (Fri-Sat 11.30-mdnt, Sun 12-10.30) **Bar Meals** L served all wk 12-3 D served all wk 6-9.30 Av main course £10 **Restaurant** L served all wk 12-3 booking required D served all wk 6-9.30 booking required Fixed menu price fr £11 ⊕ ENTERPRISE INNS ◄ Harveys Sussex Best, Woodforde's Wherry, London Pride, Timothy Taylor Landlord, Sharp's Doom Bar, Flowers IPA ♻ Westons Stowford Press. ♟ 12 **Facilities** Children welcome Children's menu Children's portions Family room Dogs allowed Garden Beer festival Parking Wi-fi

GREAT CHISHILL   Map 12 TL43

The Pheasant

24 Heydon Rd SG8 8SR ☎ 01763 838535
dir: *Off B1039 between Royston & Saffron Walden*

Stunning views and roaring log fires characterise this traditional, beamed village free house, where Nethergates, Woodforde's Wherry and Greene King ales are some of the choices. There are no gaming machines or piped music to disturb the friendly, sociable bar, and children under 14 are not allowed in. In summer, bird song holds sway in the idyllic pub garden. Freshly-made sandwiches come complete with chips and salad garnish or there is a deal to include home-made soup as well, whilst home-made dishes like four-rib rack of lamb; calves' liver and bacon; and wild mushroom and tarragon linguini cater for larger appetites.

Open all wk noon-3 6-11 (Sat-Sun all day) ⊕ FREE HOUSE ◄ Nethergates, Greene King IPA, London Pride, Woodforde's Wherry, Oakham JHB ♻ Stowford Press. **Facilities** Dogs allowed Garden Parking

HEMINGFORD GREY   Map 12 TL27

PICK OF THE PUBS

The Cock Pub and Restaurant ♟

47 High St PE28 9BJ ☎ 01480 463609
e-mail: cock@cambscuisine.com
dir: *2m S of Huntingdon and 1m E of A14*

A pretty 17th-century pub in an idyllic village of thatched, timbered and brick cottages, with peaceful views across the willow-bordered Great Ouse river. It's a world away from the busy A14, just a mile away. Famished travellers should look for the turning for Hemingford Grey as the food on offer at this thriving dining pub is worth the detour – the set lunch menu is a steal. The stylishly revamped interior comprises a contemporary bar for drinks only, and a restaurant with bare boards, dark or white-painted beams, wood-burning stoves, and church candles on an eclectic mix of old dining tables. Cooking is modern British and fresh local produce is used in preparing the short, imaginative carte. A typical meal might kick off with pheasant and black pudding faggot with port sauce. Follow with bacon and sage wrapped chicken breast or sausages (made by the owner) and mash, then a sherry trifle to round everything off. The wine list specialises in the Languedoc. There is a beer festival every August Bank Holiday weekend.

Open all wk 11.30-3 6-11 **Restaurant** L served all wk 12-2.30 D served all wk 6.15-9.30 ⊕ FREE HOUSE ◄ Golden Jackal, Wolf Brewery, IPA, Great Oakley, Potbelly Brewery, Brewsters Hophead, Nethergate ♻ Cromwell. ♟ 18 **Facilities** Children welcome Children's portions Dogs allowed Garden Beer festival Parking

HILDERSHAM   Map 12 TL54

The Pear Tree Inn ♟

High St CB21 6BU ☎ 01223 891680
e-mail: peartreeinn@btconnect.com
dir: *5m E of Cambridge, take A1307 to Haverhill, turn left to Hildersham*

This has been a village pub for more than 200 years but became a free house in 2011 and now offers several real ales. Standing opposite the village green and close to a Roman road, the present building took over the Pear Tree name in the 19th century, and there's a picture of the former thatched pub in the bar. Home-cooked food includes steak and kidney pudding, rib-eye steaks, and beer-battered haddock with chips. There are excellent walks from the pub.

Open 6.30-11 (Fri 6-11, Sun 12-2.30 7-10.30) Closed: Mon & Tues **Bar Meals** L served Sun 12-2.30 D served Wed-Sat 6.30-9.30, Sun 7-9 Av main course £9 **Restaurant** Fixed menu price fr £13 Av 3 course à la carte fr £18.80 ⊕ FREE HOUSE ◄ Greene King IPA , Abbot Ale. ♟ 12 **Facilities** Children welcome Children's menu Children's portions Dogs allowed Garden Parking

HILTON   Map 12 TL26

The Prince of Wales ★★★ INN ♟

Potton Rd PE28 9NG ☎ 01480 830257
e-mail: bookings@thehiltonpow.co.uk
dir: *On B1040 between A14 & A428 S of St Ives*

The Prince of Wales is a traditional, 1830s-built, two-bar village inn with four comfortable bedrooms. Food options range from bar snacks to full meals, among which are grills, fish, curries brought in from a local Indian restaurant, and daily specials, such as lamb hotpot. Home-made puddings include crème brûlée and sherry trifle. The village's 400-year-old grass maze was where locals used to escape the devil.

Open 12-2.30 6-11 Closed: Mon L **Bar Meals** L served Tues-Sun noon-2 D served all wk 7-9 **Restaurant** L served Tues-Sun noon-2 D served all wk 7-9 ⊕ FREE HOUSE ◄ Adnams, Timothy Taylor Landlord, Guest ales. ♟ 9 **Facilities** Children's menu Children's portions Garden Parking Wi-fi **Rooms 4**

HINXTON   Map 12 TL44

PICK OF THE PUBS

The Red Lion Inn ★★★★ INN ⊕ ♟

32 High St CB10 1QY ☎ 01799 530601
e-mail: info@redlionhinxton.co.uk
dir: *N'bound only: M11 junct 9, towards A11, left onto A1301. Turn left to Hinxton. Or M11 junct 10, take A505 towards A11/Newmarket. At rdbt take 3rd exit onto A1301, right to Hinxton*

Lurking quietly in a pretty conservation village near the county border, this 16th-century pink-washed free house simply oozes charm. Many customers opt to eat informally on settles in the bar with its low ceilings and wooden floors. Others might choose from the wide-ranging modern British menu beneath the lofty ceilings and pegged oak rafters in the spacious, airy restaurant. Guests are encouraged to dine wherever they feel most comfortable – which, in summer, might include the lovely walled garden. Lighter options include baguettes and sandwiches as well as classic pub dishes like hand-cut Suffolk ham with egg and chips. A typical à la carte dinner might begin with pressed tomato terrine, followed by Denham Estate venison loin with basil purée; rounded off with individual berry Pavlova with whipped cream and raspberry sorbet. Eight purpose-built flint and brick guest rooms are set apart within a private garden area.

Open all wk Sun-Thu 11-3 6-11 (Fri-Sat all day) **Bar Meals** L served Mon-Thu 12-2, Fri-Sun 12-2.30 D served Sun-Thu 7-9, Fri-Sat 7-9.30 Av main course £10 **Restaurant** L served Mon-Thu 12-2, Fri-Sun 12-2.30 D served Sun-Thu 7-9, Fri-Sat 7-9.30 Av 3 course à la carte fr £23 ⊕ FREE HOUSE ◄ Adnams, Greene King IPA, Woodforde's Wherry, Rusty Bucket, Guest ales ♻ Aspall. ♟ 20 **Facilities** Children welcome Children's portions Dogs allowed Garden Parking Wi-fi **Rooms 8**

HISTON   Map 12 TL46

Red Lion NEW

27 High St CB24 9JD ☎ 01223 564437
dir: *M11 junct 14, A14 towards. Exit at junct 32 onto B1049 for Histon*

"A grown-up village local for grown-up people" says long-standing landlord Mark Donachy of his popular pub on Cambridge's northern fringe. A dyed-in-the-wool pub grub man, Mark's real ales include Tring Blonde and Oakham Bishops Farewell, as well as Pickled Pig Porker's Snout cider from Ely. There are also around two dozen Belgian bottled beers and three draft Belgian/German beers. Expect cheerful service, winter log fires and a good-sized neat garden. Food is served at lunchtimes only. Time a visit for the Easter or early September beer festivals.

Open all day all wk **Bar Meals** L only Av main course £7.25 ⊕ FREE HOUSE ◀ Batemans XB, Tring Blonde, Oakham Bishops Farewell Ale ♂ Pickled Pig Porker's Snout, Westons Perry. **Facilities** Children welcome Children's portions Garden Beer festival Parking **Notes** ⊛

HOLYWELL   Map 12 TL37

The Old Ferryboat Inn ★★★ INN

Back Ln PE27 4TG ☎ 01480 463227 📄 01480 463245
e-mail: 8638@greeneking.co.uk
dir: *From Cambridge on A14 right onto A1096, then right onto A1123, right to Holywell*

Renowned as England's oldest inn, built some time in the 11th century, but with a hostelry history that goes back to the 6th. In a tranquil setting beside the Great Ouse river, The Old Ferryboat has immaculately maintained thatch, white stone walls, cosy interior and bags of charm and character. A pleasant atmosphere - despite the resident ghost of a lovelorn teenager - in which to enjoy grilled bacon and warm poached egg salad; British beef and Ruddles ale pie, mash, seasonal vegetables and onion gravy; or sweet potato, chick pea and spinach curry. There are seven en suite bedrooms available.

Open all wk 11-11 (Sun noon-10.30) ⊕ OLD ENGLISH INNS & HOTELS ◀ Greene King Abbot Ale/IPA, Guest ales. **Facilities** Children welcome Garden Parking **Rooms** 7

HORNINGSEA   Map 12 TL46

The Crown & Punchbowl

CB5 9JG ☎ 01223 860643 📄 01223 441814
e-mail: info@thecrownandpunchbowl.co.uk
dir: *Telephone for directions*

First recorded as a coaching inn in 1764, this tile-roofed, whitewashed free house is ten minutes from Cambridge city centre. The soft colours and wooden floors create a warm and comfortable atmosphere. The low-beamed restaurant offers traditional English fare with a Mediterranean influence with produce sourced locally. Dishes include breast of duck with polenta-crusted chicken livers; pan-roasted hake with wild garlic and smoked bacon risotto; and vegetarian options. Fresh fish and a sausage board featuring three sausage, mash and gravy varieties also feature on the specials board.

Open noon-3 6.30-9.30 Closed: Sun eve & BH eve **Bar Meals** Av main course £13.95 **Restaurant** L served all wk 12-3 booking required D served Mon-Sat 6.30-9.30 booking required Av 3 course à la carte fr £24 ⊕ FREE HOUSE ◀ Hobson's Choice. **Facilities** Children welcome Children's portions Garden Parking

KEYSTON   Map 11 TL07

PICK OF THE PUBS

Pheasant Inn ◉ ♥

Village Loop Rd PE28 0RE ☎ 01832 710241
e-mail: info@thepheasant-keyston.co.uk
dir: *0.5m off A14, clearly signed, 10m W of Huntingdon, 14m E of Kettering*

At the heart of sleepy Keyston, beneath a huge sycamore tree, sits the award-winning Pheasant Inn, formed from classic 16th-century cottages with dark thatch, a mass of floral planters and tubs adorning the front and white-painted brickwork. Within, it's quintessentially 'olde England': oak beams, flagstone floor, stripped boards, brick inglenooks, simple wooden furnishings, and a comfortable, intimate and relaxed country feel. There's nothing 'olde worlde' about the cooking, however, the daily menu bristles with local produce, much of it sourced within a few miles of the pub, and the food is unpretentious British with more than a nod to Mediterranean shores. Crisp squid with aïoli and deep-fried parsley, fennel and saffron risotto with smoked haddock and poached egg, caramelised garlic tart with braised stuffed shallots, cod with warm potato salad, chorizo oil, herbs and aïoli, and caramel and amaretto parfait with peanut brittle show the imaginative style. A great list of wines, East Anglian ales and an August Bank Holiday beer festival complete the picture.

Open all day all wk **Bar Meals** L served Mon-Sat 12-2.30, Sun 12-12.30 booking required D served Mon-Sat 7-9.30 booking required Av main course £15 **Restaurant** L served all wk 12-2.30 booking required D served all wk 7-9.30 booking required Av 3 course à la carte fr £30 ⊕ FREE HOUSE ◀ Adnams, Village Bike Potton Brewery, Augustinian Nethergate Brewery. **Facilities** Children welcome Children's menu Children's portions Dogs allowed Garden Beer festival Parking Wi-fi

KIMBOLTON   Map 12 TL16

The New Sun Inn ♥

20-22 High St PE28 0HA
☎ 01480 860052 📄 01480 869353
e-mail: newsuninn@btinternet.com
dir: *From A1 N take B645 for 7m. From A1 S take B661 for 7m. From A14 take B660 for 5m*

This 17th-century inn enjoys a high street location close to Kimbolton Castle. As well as being a real ale pub, it offers both conservatory dining and a more formal restaurant. The lunchtime bar menu, the carte, tapas and specials board can be served throughout the building. Expect the likes of kiln-roasted salmon with potato, dill and horseradish salad, and garlic rabbit with chorizo and Puy lentils. A patio area at the rear is furnished with giant umbrellas.

Open all wk Mon-Thu 11.30-2.30 6-11 (Fri-Sun all day) **Bar Meals** L served Mon-Sat 12-2.15, Sun 12-2.30 D served Tue-Sat 7-9.30 Av main course £6 **Restaurant** L served Mon-Sat 12-2.15, Sun 12-2.30 D served Tue-Sat 7-9.30 Av 3 course à la carte fr £22 ⊕ CHARLES WELLS ◀ Wells Bombardier & Eagle IPA, Guest ales change weekly. ♥ 12 **Facilities** Children welcome Children's portions Dogs allowed Garden

LITTLE WILBRAHAM   Map 12 TL55

PICK OF THE PUBS

Hole in the Wall ◉ ♥

2 High St CB21 5JY ☎ 01223 812282
e-mail: jenniferleeton@btconnect.com
dir: *Telephone for directions*

This picturesque, heavily timbered village pub halfway between Cambridge and Newmarket dates back to the 15th century. As its name implies, there was once a hole in the wall of the main bar so the local farm workers could collect their beer when only the gentry were allowed in the pub. Nowadays, it welcomes all-comers for pints of Woodforde's Wherry and some first-class modern British cooking prepared from fresh local produce by chef-patron Chris Leeton. In a relaxing and comfortable setting of hop-adorned exposed beams, gleaming brass, roaring log fires and rustic country furnishings, you can choose from imaginative and sensibly short daily menus. Take eight-hour confit pork belly and apple terrine with home-made piccalilli, or seared smoked salmon with warm roasted beetroot and red onion and horseradish crème fraîche for starters, with main course options ranging from local rabbit, sage and bacon pie with honey glazed carrots, mash and Brussels sprouts and chestnuts to pan-fried Cornish mackerel with roasted new potatoes, sea salt, lemon, dill, purple sprouting broccoli. The one-AA Rosette menu also features puddings like winter-spiced Cambridgeshire burnt cream with mulled pear and mulled wine.

Open 11.30-3 6.30-11 Closed: 2wks Jan, 25 Dec, Mon (ex BH L), Sun eve **Bar Meals** L served Tue-Sun 12-2 booking required D served Tue-Sat 7-9 booking required Av main course £14 **Restaurant** L served Tue-Sun 12-2 booking required D served Tue-Sat 7-9 booking required Av 3 course à la carte fr £26 ⊕ FREE HOUSE ◀ Woodforde's Wherry, Cambridge Bitter, Sparta, Nelsons Revenge ♂ Stowford Press. ♥ 10 **Facilities** Children welcome Children's portions Dogs allowed Garden Parking

Save on hotels. Book at **theAA.com/hotel**

CAMBRIDGESHIRE 65 **ENGLAND**

PICK OF THE PUBS

The Three Horseshoes ₹

High St CB3 8AB ☎ 01954 210221 📠 **01954 212043**
e-mail: 3hs@btconnect.com
dir: M11 junct 13, 1.5m from A14

With its large garden overlooking meadowland and the local cricket pitch, this quintessential thatched village inn enjoys a picturesque location. Inside is a small, bustling bar serving a great selection of beers and twenty-two wines by the glass, and a pretty conservatory restaurant. Chef-patron Richard Stokes has eaten his way around the world, and his success can be gauged by the long queues for tables and prior booking is advisable. Richard's own style is a modern take on Italian cuisine, characterised by seasonal and imaginative dishes with intense flavours. After antipasti, you could try ribolita (classic winter Tuscan soup of cavolo nero, borlotti beans, root vegetables, bread and new season's olive oil); or pappardelle with cime di rape, ricotta, red chilli and pecorino, followed by roast fillet of monkfish with castelluccio lentils, cottechino sausage, spinach and salsa verde; or roast saddle of Scottish red deer with beetroot purée, potato fondant, Italian spinach, rosemary and red wine. Desserts might include pannacotta with caramelised quince.

Open all wk 11.30-3 6-11 (Sun 6-9.30)
Bar Meals L served Mon-Fri 12-2, Sat-Sun 12-2.30 D served all wk 6.30-9.30 Av main course £16 **Restaurant** L served all wk 12-2.30 D served Mon-Sat 6.30-9.30 Fixed menu price fr £19 Av 3 course à la carte fr £35 ⊕ FREE HOUSE ◀ Adnams Bitter, Hook Norton Old Hooky, Smile's Best, Cambridge Hobsons Choice, Guest ales ♂ Stowford Press. ₹ 22 **Facilities** Children welcome Children's portions Garden Parking

Waggon & Horses

39 High St CB24 6DF ☎ 01223 860313
e-mail: winningtons.waggon@ntlworld.com
dir: A14/A10 junct. Past Tesco, through village, approx 1m set back on left

Elgood Brewery's most southerly house, the pub is an imposing mock-Tudor building famed for its large collection of hats. As well as a great selection of ales served in the one room pub, real cider is also served, from local producer Cassells. A challenging quiz is set on Wednesday nights and baltis are the speciality on Thursdays. Bar billiards, shove ha'penny and darts are popular; outside there is a large child-safe garden. All meals are good value - haddock and chips, Cajun bean stew and Cornish pasty.

Open all wk noon-2.30 5-11 (Fri 5-mdnt, Sat noon-3 6-11.30, Sun noon-3 7.30-10.30) **Bar Meals** L served all wk 12-2 D served all wk 7-9 Av main course £6 ⊕ ELGOOD & SONS LTD ◀ Elgoods Cambridge Bitter, Black Dog Mild, Golden Newt, Seasonal Guest ales ♂ Cassells. **Facilities** Children welcome Children's portions Dogs allowed Garden Parking

PICK OF THE PUBS

The Queen's Head

Fowlmere Rd CB22 7PG ☎ 01223 870436
dir: 6m S of Cambridge on B1368, 1.5m off A10 at Harston, 4m from A505

For nearly 50 years now the Short family have owned and operated their tiny and very traditional village pub. Unchanging and unmarred by gimmickry, the simple, stone-tiled bars, replete with log fires, pine settles and old school benches, draw an eclectic clientele, from Cambridge dons to local farm workers, for tip-top Adnams ale direct from the drum, the friendly, honest atmosphere and straightforward pub food. It's all very simple – soup served in mugs, excellent sandwiches and Aga-baked potatoes at lunch, and just soup and cold platters (roast beef, smoked ham or cheese) in the evening. Village tradition is kept alive with time-honoured pub games – try your hand at dominoes, table skittles, shove ha'penny and nine men's Morris. There is a green opposite for summer sipping.

Open all wk 11.30-2.30 6-11 (Sun noon-2.30 7-10.30) Closed: 25-26 Dec **Bar Meals** L served all wk 12-2.15 D served all wk 7-9.30 ⊕ FREE HOUSE ◀ Adnams Southwold, Broadside, Fisherman, Bitter, Regatta ♂ Crones. **Facilities** Children welcome Children's portions Family room Dogs allowed Parking **Notes** ✉

The Horseshoe ₹ NEW

90 High St PE19 5RH ☎ 01480 810293
e-mail: info@thehorseshoeinn.biz
dir: Between Huntingdon & St Neots. 1.5m from Buckden on A1

Local boy Oliver Cromwell was 27 years old when, in 1626, a yeoman farmer built this house close to the River Ouse. Now a dining pub with two bars serving good local real ales, and a frequently changing menu. Chef Richard Kennedy and his team offer dishes such as tea-infused loin of wild venison; bacon-wrapped chicken with cider-and apple-creamed leeks; smoked haddock in bubble and squeak cake; and vegetarian tart of the day. A midsummer beer festival is held on the green.

Open all day all wk (12-2.30 4.30-close Jan-Mar) **Bar Meals** L served Mon-Sat 12-2.30 booking required D served Mon-Sat 6.30-9.30 booking required Av main course £10 **Restaurant** L served Mon-Sat 12-2.30, Sun 12-5.30 booking required D served Mon-Sat 6-9.30, Sun 12-5.30 booking required Fixed menu price fr £7.20 Av 3 course à la carte fr £25.50 ⊕ FREE HOUSE ◀ Fuller's London Pride, Sharp's Doom Bar, Potton Shannon IPA, Oakham JHB. ₹ 12 **Facilities** Children welcome Children's portions Play area Dogs allowed Garden Beer festival Parking Wi-fi

The Brewery Tap

80 Westgate PE1 2AA
☎ 01733 358500 📠 **01733 310022**
e-mail: brewerytap@hotmail.com
dir: Opposite bus station

This is the home of multi-award-winning Oakham Ales, moved here from their home in Rutland when Peterborough's spacious old labour exchange opened its doors as the Brewery Tap in 1998. Visitors to this striking pub can see the day-to-day running of the brewery through a glass wall spanning half the length of the bar. As if the appeal of the beer range were not enough, Thai chefs beaver away producing delicious snacks, soups, salads, stir-fries and curries. Look out for live music nights.

Open all day all wk noon-11pm (Fri-Sat noon-mdnt) Closed: 25-26 Dec, 1 Jan ⊕ FREE HOUSE ◀ Oakham Inferno, Jeffery Hudson Bitter, Bishops Farewell, White Dwarf, Elgoods Black Dog, 7 Guest ales ♂ Westons 1st Quality. **Facilities** Children welcome Children's portions Dogs allowed Wi-fi

Charters Bar & East Restaurant

Upper Deck, Town Bridge PE1 1FP
☎ 01733 315700 & 315702 (bkgs) 📠 **01733 315700**
e-mail: charters.manager@oakagroup.com
dir: A1/A47 towards Wisbech, 2m for city centre & town bridge (River Nene). Barge moored at Town Bridge (west side)

Moored in the heart of Peterborough on the River Nene, this 176-foot converted barge promises 'brews, blues and fine views'. It motored from Holland across the North Sea in 1991, and is now a haven for real ale and cider lovers. Twelve hand pumps dispense a continually changing repertoire of brews, while Friday and Saturday nights bring live blues music. The East part of the name applies to the oriental restaurant on the upper deck which offers a comprehensive selection of Asian dishes.

Open all day all wk noon-11pm (Fri-Sat noon-2am) Closed: 25-26 Dec, 1 Jan ⊕ FREE HOUSE ◀ Oakham JHB, Oakham Bishops Farewell, Abbeydale Absolution, Elgoods Black Dog ♂ Westons Old Rosie, Westons Traditional Draught Scrumpy. **Facilities** Children welcome Dogs allowed Garden Parking

REACH   Map 12 TL56

Dyke's End

CB25 0JD ☎ 01638 743816
dir: *Telephone for directions*

In 1996/7 villagers saved this pub from closure and ran it as a co-operative until 2003, when it was bought by Frank Feehan, who has further refurbished and extended it. Frank's additions include the Devil's Dyke microbrewery, which produces four real ales, including a strong mild. The pub's local reputation for the quality of its food means restaurant booking is strongly advised, particularly at weekends. A fenced front garden overlooks the village green.

Open 12-2.30 6-11 (Sat-Sun noon-11) Closed: Mon L ⊕ FREE HOUSE ◀ Devil's Dyke micro-brewery beer, Woodforde's Wherry, Adnams Bitter Ö Aspall, Old Rosie. **Facilities** Play area Family room Dogs allowed Garden Parking

STAPLEFORD   Map 12 TL45

The Rose at Stapleford ♥

81 London Rd CB22 5DE ☎ 01223 843349
e-mail: paulnbeer@aol.com
dir: *Telephone for directions*

Paul and Karen Beer made a success of The George and Dragon at Elsworth and now they're weaving their magic at The Rose, a traditional village pub close to Cambridge and Duxford Imperial War Museum. Expect a stylish interior, replete with low beams and inglenook fireplaces, and extensive menus that draw on local Suffolk produce, particularly meat, with fish from Lowestoft. Typical dishes include half a local pheasant braised in a port sauce; home-made steak and kidney pudding; and cod in ale batter with chips. Look out for special dining events.

Open 12-2.30 6-11 Closed: Sun eve **Bar Meals** L served all wk 12-2.30 D served Mon-Sat 6-9.30 Av main course £9 **Restaurant** L served all wk 12-2.30 D served Mon-Sat 6-9.30 Fixed menu price fr £11.50 Av 3 course à la carte fr £18 ◀ IPA, Tribute, Guest ale Ö Aspall. ♥ 13 **Facilities** Children welcome Children's menu Children's portions Dogs allowed Garden Parking

STILTON   Map 12 TL18

PICK OF THE PUBS

The Bell Inn Hotel ★★★ HL ◉ ♥

Great North Rd PE7 3RA
☎ 01733 241066 ▤ 01733 245173
e-mail: reception@thebellstilton.co.uk
dir: *From A1(M) junct 16 follow signs for Stilton. Hotel on main road in village centre*

Just off junction 16 of the A1 in the village of Stilton, The Bell Inn has stood on its present site since 1500 and the current buildings date from 1642. The Bell is famous as the birthplace of Stilton cheese, which was first served here in the early 1700s. Steeped in history and reputedly the oldest coaching inn on the Great

North Road, The Bell's impressive 16th-century stone façade hides a fine interior that boasts original features, including a grand stone fireplace in the Village Bar. In its time the inn has hosted highwayman Dick Turpin, Lord Byron and, more recently, Clark Gable and Joe Louis, who were stationed nearby in World War II. Imaginative modern British dishes are served in the atmospheric, galleried restaurant, the set menu offering white onion and Stilton soup; rack of spring lamb with roast garlic risotto; rhubarb parfait with warm rice pudding. Tuck into tagliatelle with lemon, oregano, broad beans and Parmesan or fillet of beef goulash with potato pancakes in the more informal bistro. Note the magnificent inn sign, it's a replica of the original weighing two and three quarter tonnes. There are 22 comfortable en suite rooms available.

Open all wk noon-2.30 6-11 (Sat 12-3 6-12, Sun noon-11) Closed: 25 Dec **Bar Meals** L served Mon-Sat 12-2.30, Sun all day D served all wk 6-9.30 Av main course £13.50 **Restaurant** L served Sun 12-2 booking required D served Mon-Sat 7-9.30 booking required Fixed menu price fr £19.95 Av 3 course à la carte fr £20.25 ⊕ FREE HOUSE ◀ Greene King Abbot Ale, Oakham JHB, Fuller's London Pride, Greene King IPA, Brewers Gold. ♥ 8 **Facilities** Children welcome Children's menu Children's portions Garden Parking Wi-fi **Rooms** 22

STRETHAM   Map 12 TL57

The Lazy Otter

Cambridge Rd CB6 3LU ☎ 01353 649780
e-mail: thelazyotter@btconnect.com
dir: *Telephone for directions*

Just off the A10 between Ely and Cambridge, The Lazy Otter stands overlooking the marina beside the River Great Ouse. There's been a pub on this site since the 18th century. Today, the large beer garden and riverside restaurant are popular summer attractions. Menus might feature steak and kidney pudding, seafood tagliatelle, or Thai green curry (both chicken a vegetarian varieties) plus grills, burgers, baguettes and Sunday roasts. Perhaps enjoy your meal with a glass of locally produced, award-winning Pickled Pig cider.

Open all day all wk 11-11 (Sun noon-10.30pm) ⊕ FREE HOUSE ◀ Greene King, IPA, Guest ales Ö Pickled Pig. **Facilities** Children welcome Children's menu Children's portions Play area Garden Parking

UFFORD   Map 12 TF00

The White Hart ★★★★ INN ♥ NEW

Main St PE9 3BH ☎ 01780 740250 ▤ 01780 740927
e-mail: Info@whitehartufford.co.uk
dir: *From Stamford take B1443 signed Barnack. Through Barnack and follow signs to Ufford*

Salvaged railway memorabilia and agricultural tools adorn the bar of this popular 17th-century country inn, where three real ales from the on-site micro-brewery join Aspall cider. Locally sourced produce, like game from local shoots and nearby farms, ends up on the seasonal menus in many ways: fillet of roasted sea bream on king prawns; braised leg of Tallington lamb; wild mushroom and goat's cheese risotto with pea shoot salad. Four individually-styled bedrooms are in the main building, two in the converted cart shed. Check out the beer festival.

Open all day all wk **Bar Meals** L served Mon-Sat 12-2.30 Av main course £10 **Restaurant** L served Mon-Sat 12-2.30, Sun 12-7 booking required D served Mon-Sat 6-9.30 booking required Fixed menu price fr £25 Av 3 course à la carte fr £30 ⊕ FREE HOUSE ◀ Ufford Ales White Hart, Golden Drop, Rupert's War Dog, Adnams Ö Aspall. ♥ 10 **Facilities** Children welcome Children's portions Play area Dogs allowed Garden Beer festival Parking Wi-fi **Rooms** 6

CHESHIRE

ALDFORD   Map 15 SJ45

PICK OF THE PUBS

The Grosvenor Arms ♥

Chester Rd CH3 6HJ
☎ 01244 620228 ▤ 01244 620247
e-mail: grosvenor.arms@brunningandprice.co.uk
dir: *On B5130, S of Chester*

This 'delight of higgledy-piggledy rooflines and soft, warm Cheshire brick' dates from 1864. The architect was John Douglas, locally infamous for adulterating many fine medieval buildings in and around Chester, supposedly in the name of progress. Its spacious, open-plan interior includes an airy conservatory and a panelled, book-filled library. Outside, a terrace leads into a small but pleasing garden, and on out to the village green. On the bistro-style menu are sandwiches, starters such as breaded Brie with apple chutney, or pork satay with spiced carrot salad; and light meals, typically crab linguine with ginger, red chilli and coriander. Main courses include braised shoulder of lamb; pork and chorizo meatballs with pappardelle pasta; and aubergine, spinach and lentil moussaka. This is a Brunning & Price pub, so expect lots of different real ales from small breweries around the country. No wonder the locals are fond of it.

Open all day all wk **Bar Meals** Av main course £10.95 food served all day ⊕ BRUNNING & PRICE ◀ Weetwood-Eastgate, Phoenix, Brunning & Price Original, Guest ales Ö Stowford Press, Aspall. ♥ 20 **Facilities** Children welcome Children's portions Dogs allowed Garden Parking

Save on hotels. Book at **theAA.com/hotel**

CHESHIRE 67 ENGLAND

PICK OF THE PUBS

The Bhurtpore Inn ♌

ASTON   Map 15 SJ64

Wrenbury Rd CW5 8DQ ☎ 01270 780917
e-mail: simonbhurtpore@yahoo.co.uk
web: www.bhurtpore.co.uk
dir: *Just off A530 between Nantwich &*
Whitchurch. Turn towards Wrenbury at
x-rds in village

A pub since at least 1778, when it was
called the Queen's Head, it subsequently
became the Red Lion, but it was Lord
Combermere's success at the Siege of
Bhurtpore in India in 1826 that inspired the
name that has stuck. Simon and Nicky
George came across it in 1991, boarded-up
and stripped-out. Simon is a direct
descendant of Joyce George, who leased the
pub from the Combermere estate in 1849,
so was motivated by his family history to
take on the hard work of restoring the
interior, and reopening in early 1992. Since
then, 'award winning' hardly does justice to
the accolades heaped upon this hostelry.

In the bar, eleven ever-changing real ales
are always available, mostly from local
micro-breweries, as are real ciders,
continental draught lagers and around 150
of the world's bottled beers. An annual beer
festival, reputedly Cheshire's largest, is in
its 16th year, with around 130 real ales to
be sampled. Beers are only part of the
story; the pub has been short-listed five
times for the 'National Whisky Pub of the
Year' award, and the soft drinks menu is as
long as your arm.

Recognition extends to the kitchen too,
where unfussy dishes of classic pub fare
are acceptable to both the palate and the
wallet. Among the hearty British ingredients
you'll find seasonal game, such as venison
haunch on cabbage with smoked bacon
and cream; and rabbit loin with a pork and
black pudding stuffing. As you might
expect, curries and balti dishes are always
to be found on the blackboard; these
usually comprise at least six options, based
on beef, mutton and goat, as well as
vegetables and quorn. Vintage vehicles
bring their owners here on the first
Thursday of the month, and folk musicians
play on the third Tuesday.

Open all wk 12-2.30 6.30-11.30 (Fri-Sat
12-12, Sun 12-11) Closed: 25-26 Dec,
1 Jan **Bar Meals** L served Mon-Fri 12-2
D served Mon-Fri 6.30-9.30 (Sat 12-9.30,
Sun 12-9) **Restaurant** L served Mon-Fri
12-2 D served Mon-Fri 6.30-9.30 (Sat
12-9.30, Sun 12-9) ⊞ FREE HOUSE
🍺 Salopian Golden Thread, Abbeydale
Absolution, Weetwood Oasthouse Gold,
Copper Dragon Golden Pippin, Hobson's
Mild ♺ Cheddar Valley, Moonshine,
Westons Old Rosie. ♌ 11
Facilities Children's menu Children's
portions Dogs allowed Garden Parking
Beer festival

ASTON — Map 15 SJ64

PICK OF THE PUBS

The Bhurtpore Inn ♟

See Pick of the Pubs on page 67

BOLLINGTON — Map 16 SJ97

The Church House Inn

Church St SK10 5PY
☎ 01625 574014 📄 01625 562026
e-mail: info@thechurchhouseinn-bollington.co.uk
dir: *From A34 take A538 towards Macclesfield. Through Prestbury, then follow Bollington signs*

Exposed beams, log fires and agricultural decorations lend a homely feel to this stone-built village free house, which hit the headlines when it was bought by a group of local residents. The varied menu includes home-made soup, the inn's own sausages and pies, and other traditional British favourites. Vegetarian options feature on the daily specials board. The pub also has a small enclosed beer garden.

Open all wk 12-3 5.30-11 (Sun 12-10.30) ⊕ FREE HOUSE
◀ Adnams, Timothy Taylor Golden Best, Duchess IPA.
Facilities Children welcome Children's menu Children's portions Parking Wi-fi

BROXTON — Map 15 SJ45

Egerton Arms ♟ NEW

Whitchurch Rd CH3 9JW
☎ 01829 782241 📄 01829 782530
e-mail: egertonarms@woodwardandfalconer.com
dir: *On A41 between Whitchurch & Chester*

A little gem in the heart of the rolling Cheshire plains, where the aim is to cosset customers with a combination of lovely ales, a wide selection of wines, food that hits the spot, and excellent service from the enthusiastic and friendly staff. With a pint of Piffle in hand, choosing a dish to tickle your taste buds is not a problem – the menu covers all preferences, from steak and kidney pie to lobster thermidor. The spacious gardens are another bonus, and occasional special events represent excellent value.

Open all day all wk Closed: 25 Dec & 1 Jan
Bar Meals L served all wk 12-5.30 D served Mon-Sat 5.30-9.30, Sun 5.30-9 food served all day
Restaurant L served all wk 12-5.30 D served Mon-Sat 5.30-9.30, Sun 5.30-9 food served all day ◀ Piffle Beer, Eastgate Ale, Theakston. ♟ 18 **Facilities** Children welcome Children's menu Children's portions Play area Garden Parking

BUNBURY — Map 15 SJ55

PICK OF THE PUBS

The Dysart Arms ♟

Bowes Gate Rd CW6 9PH
☎ 01829 260183 📄 01829 261286
e-mail: dysart.arms@brunningandprice.co.uk
dir: *Between A49 & A51, by Shropshire Union Canal*

A truly classic English village pub, with open fires, lots of old oak, full-height bookcases and a really pretty garden with views of two castles and the neighbouring parish church. Built as a farmhouse in the mid-18th century, licensed since the late 1800s, and once an abattoir, it was named after the local landowners, the Earls of Dysart, whose coat of arms is above the door. An ever-changing line-up of ales from small breweries around the country is served in the central bar, around which are several airy rooms perfect for drinking and eating. Starters include pan-fried scallops with carrot and cumin purée and crisp Parma ham, and venison faggot with juniper sauce. Among the main courses are Moroccan spiced lamb rump with apricot and date salad and chick pea cakes, and fisherman's pie with Cheddar cheese. Lack of parking space explains why there's a hitching-rail for horses!

Open all day all wk 11.30-11 (Sun noon-10.30)
Bar Meals L served all wk D served all wk food served all day **Restaurant** L served all wk D served all wk food served all day ⊕ BRUNNING & PRICE ◀ Weetwood, Best Cask, Timothy Taylor Landlord, Brunning ♂ Aspall.
♟ 17 **Facilities** Children welcome Children's portions Dogs allowed Garden Parking

BURLEYDAM — Map 15 SJ64

The Combermere Arms ♟

SY13 4AT ☎ 01948 871223 📄 01948 661371
e-mail: combermere.arms@brunningandprice.co.uk
dir: *From Whitchurch take A525 towards Nantwich, at Newcastle/Audlem/Woore sign, turn right at junct. Pub 100yds on right*

This classic 17th-century country inn is popular with local shoots, walkers and town folk alike. Its interior retains great character and warmth. Three roaring fires complement the wealth of oak, nooks and crannies, pictures and old furniture. Food options range from sandwiches and light bites such as crab linguine with ginger, red chilli and coriander through to a hearty meal of duck liver and port pâté with red onion marmalade followed by braised lamb shoulder with rosemary gravy and dauphinoise potatoes. There is a great choice of real ales and ciders, an informative wine list and impressive cheese list.

Open all day all wk 11.30-11 **Bar Meals** Av main course £11 food served all day **Restaurant** food served all day ⊕ BRUNNING & PRICE ◀ Woodlands Oak Beauty, Weetwood, Cheshire Cat, St Austells Tribute, B&P Original, Old Speckled Hen ♂ Weston Stowford Press, Thatchers Old Rascal, Aspall. ♟ 20 **Facilities** Children welcome Children's portions Dogs allowed Garden Parking

BURWARDSLEY — Map 15 SJ55

PICK OF THE PUBS

The Pheasant Inn ★★★★★ INN

See Pick of the Pubs on opposite page

CHESTER — Map 15 SJ46

PICK OF THE PUBS

Albion Inn

See Pick of the Pubs on page 70

Old Harkers Arms ♟

1 Russell St CH1 5AL
☎ 01244 344525 📄 01244 344812
e-mail: harkers.arms@brunningandprice.co.uk
dir: *From A56 towards city centre. At Hoole Way rdbt 1st exit onto A5268 signed Nantwich/Whitchurch. Left into Seller St, right into The Square, left into Canal Side, right into Russell St*

A buzzy meeting place with the feel of a gentlemen's club, this former Victorian chandler's warehouse on the Shropshire Union Canal is one of Chester's more unusual pubs. The bar offers over 100 malt whiskies (there's a helpful booklet to aid decision making), 15 wines by the glass, and hand pumps dispensing regular and guest ales mostly from local micro-breweries. The daily-changing menu runs from light dishes such as Welsh rarebit on granary toast or crab linguine through to main courses such as confit duck leg, bubble and squeak cake, caramelised plums and spiced redcurrant sauce. The pub holds events such as 'Pie & Ale Week'.

Open all day all wk 11.30-11 (Sun noon-10.30) Closed: 25 Dec **Bar Meals** L served all wk 12-9.30 booking required D served all wk 12-9.30 booking required Av main course £10.95 food served all day **Restaurant** L served all wk 12-9.30 booking required D served all wk 12-9.30 booking required Av 3 course à la carte fr £18.95 food served all day ⊕ FREE HOUSE ◀ Weetwood Cheshire Cat, Flowers Original, Titanic Stout, Spitting Feathers, Brunning and Price Original, Crouch Vale Brewers Gold ♂ Westons Organic, Scrumpy, Old Rosie, Broadoak Moonshine. ♟ 15 **Facilities** Dogs allowed Beer festival

PICK OF THE PUBS

The Pheasant Inn ★★★★★ INN

BURWARDSLEY   Map 15 SJ55

CH3 9PF
☎ **01829 770434** 🖷 **01829 771097**
e-mail: info@thepheasantinn.co.uk
web: www.thepheasantinn.co.uk
dir: *A41 (Chester to Whitchurch), after 4m left to Burwardsley. Follow 'Cheshire Workshops' signs*

Cheshire's sandstone spine is liberally dressed by thick woodlands and embellished by fortifications and castles dating back to the mists of time. At the heart of this verdant countryside lie the Peckforton Hills; high on the west-facing slopes of such is The Pheasant Inn. What began life as a sandstone and half-timbered farmhouse and barn perhaps 300 years ago is nowadays a secluded and sophisticated gastro-pub that also manages to cater for a passing trade of walkers on the increasingly popular Sandstone Trail, a challenging ramble from the Mersey to the Shropshire market town of Whitchurch. Since it became an alehouse in the mid-17th century, only five families have been licensees. Four real ales, usually drawn from the local Weetwood Brewery, are always on tap in the wooden-floored bar as well as a list of well chosen wines, where hefty beams support the storey above. Drinks are also to be enjoyed in the stone-flagged conservatory and flower-filled courtyard and terrace, from which sheltered spot can be glimpsed the towers of cathedrals at Chester and Liverpool as well as the shadowy mountains of Flintshire. In winter, vast open fires warm the cockles of the heart, perhaps quickened by the racy menu that is strong on produce of the local estates hereabouts. Various menus cater for appetites ranging from nibble to blow-out, with a strong nod to modern British and European dishes. Mull over your main course choice with a starter of local ham hock and Cheshire cheese pressing with a pommery mustard dressing, progressing then to lemon and thyme encrusted medallion of pork with dauphinoise potatoes and mustard jus or possibly lamb shank served on mustard mash with a Weetwood Bitter jus; vegetarians can enjoy spring onion, chilli and coriander potato cake with poached egg and glazed hollandaise. Stay overnight in the stylish accommodation and a filling Cheshire breakfast will kick start the day to a treat.

Open all day all wk **Bar Meals** L served all wk (no food Mon 3-6) D served all wk (no food Mon 3-6) food served all day **Restaurant** L served all wk (no food Mon 3-6) D served all wk (no food Mon 3-6) food served all day ⊕ FREE HOUSE ◀ Weetwood Old Dog, Eastgate, Best, Guest Bitter ♂ Kingstone Press. **Facilities** Children welcome Children's menu Children's portions Dogs allowed Garden Parking Wi-fi **Rooms** 12

PICK OF THE PUBS

Albion Inn

CHESTER   Map 15 SJ46

Park St CH1 1RN
☎ **01244 340345**
e-mail: christina.mercer@tesco.net
web: www.albioninnchester.co.uk
dir: *In city centre adjacent to Citywalls & Newgate*

The home fires still burn on winter nights at this living memorial to the Great War of 1914-18. With its splendid cast-iron fireplaces and original three-room layout, the pub is adorned with sepia photographs and prints, whilst leather sofas, enamelled advertisements and vintage artefacts from World War I complete the period look.

The lounge wallpaper was designed on the first day of the Great War, and other objects of interest include a 1928 Steck Duo Art player piano, which still performs on occasions. The Albion is the creation of Michael Mercer, who has run Chester's last Victorian street corner pub in the shadow of the city's Roman wall for over 40 years.

'Trench rations' are locally and regionally sourced wherever possible. Lunchtime choices include great British butties, both club and doorstep in concept, while Staffordshire oatcakes with various fillings, including vegetarian options, make for a lighter snack.

Hot dishes range from boiled gammon and pease pudding served with parsley sauce; Penrith Cumberland sausages with apple sauce, caramelised onions and gravy; McConichy's corned beef hash with pickled red cabbage; to lamb's liver, bacon and onions in a rich cider gravy; or fish pie with a mashed potato and Parmesan cheese topping served with a green salad.

Four cask ales are on tap, backed up by bottled organic cider from Westons, a good range of malts, and a decent list of New World wines. Please note that – in true wartime spirit – this is an adults-only pub.

Open all wk 12-3, Tue-Fri 5-11, Sat 6-11, Sun 7-10.30, Mon 5.30-11 Closed: 25-26 Dec, 1-2 Jan **Bar Meals** L served all wk

12-2 D served Mon-Sat 6-8.30 Av main course £10 **Restaurant** L served all wk 12-2 D served Mon-Sat 6-8.30 Fixed menu price fr £10 ⊕ PUNCH TAVERNS ◀ Black Sheep, Batemans, Deuchars, Adnams, Guest ales Ò Westons Organic bottled cider. **Facilities** Dogs allowed **Notes** ⊘

CHOLMONDELEY   Map 15 SJ55

PICK OF THE PUBS

The Cholmondeley Arms ♥

SY14 8HN ☎ 01829 720300 📠 **01829 720123**
e-mail: info@cholmondeleyarms.co.uk
dir: *On A49, between Whitchurch & Tarporley*

Quirky and eclectic; the decor and artefacts within this converted old estate village schoolhouse add tremendously to the atmosphere of the cavernous interior. No longer a draughty institute, today's attendees learn quickly to appreciate the terrific range of dishes that have gained Carolyn Ross-Lowe and her staff many accolades. After exploring the local countryside, visiting nearby Cholmondeley Castle, country seat of Lord and Lady Cholmondeley or the fabulous ruins at Beeston, stapled to Cheshire's hilly sandstone spine, it's the perfect place to unwind, sup a beer from the nearby Weetwood micro-brewery and taste the best of Cheshire's burgeoning high quality produce. Local estate pan-fried pheasant breast with Jerusalem artichoke risotto and sherry caramel or venison and parsnip stew with chestnut dumplings could catch the eye, or perhaps a plate of devilled kidneys on granary toast – school meals were never like this!

Open all day all wk Closed: 25 Dec **Bar Meals** L served all wk 12-9.30 D served all wk 12-9.30 Av main course £10 food served all day **Restaurant** food served all day ⊕ FREE HOUSE ◀ Weetwood Eastgate Ale, Salopian Gold, Black Sheep, Brakspear. ♥ 10 **Facilities** Children welcome Children's menu Children's portions Dogs allowed Garden Parking Wi-fi

CONGLETON   Map 16 SJ86

Egerton Arms Country Inn
★★★★ INN ♥ NEW

Astbury Village CW12 4RQ
☎ **01260 273946** 📠 **01260 277273**
e-mail: egertonastbury@totalise.co.uk
dir: *1.5m SW of Congleton off A34, by St Mary's Church*

A buzzing village local with a good name for dependable real ales and freshly prepared fodder – the lamb and mint suet pudding hits the spot. At the edge of one of Cheshire's picture-perfect villages, near the ancient church and flowery green, views from the peaceful beer-garden focus on the nearby Bosley Cloud hill; paths lead there or stroll along the Macclesfield Canal towpath. Stay awhile in the comfortable accommodation and you may meet the ghost, a local lady murdered next door in 1922!

Open all day all wk **Bar Meals** L served Mon-Sat 11.30-2, Sun 12-8 D served Mon-Sat 6-9, Sun 12-8 Av main course £9-£10 **Restaurant** L served Mon-Sat 12-1.45, Sun 12-8 D served Mon-Sat 6.30-8.45, Sun 12-8 Fixed menu price fr £13.95 Av 3 course à la carte fr £20 ⊕ ROBINSONS ◀ Robinsons Unicorn, Dizzy Blonde, Double Hop. ♥ 12 **Facilities** Children welcome Children's menu Children's portions Play area Garden Parking Wi-fi **Rooms** 6

The Plough At Eaton ★★★★ INN

Macclesfield Rd, Eaton CW12 2NH
☎ **01260 280207** 📠 **01260 298458**
e-mail: theploughinn@hotmail.co.uk
web: www.theploughinnateaton.co.uk
dir: *On A536 (Congleton to Macclesfield road)*

Set well back from the main road in the hamlet of Eaton, this old Cheshire-brick inn is a far cry from its genesis as a farmer's local in a 400-year-old farmhouse. It's now a popular destination gastro-pub with a very accomplished menu, available throughout the very traditional interior or in the restaurant housed in a remarkable cruck barn moved here from Wales. From bar snacks such as grilled fresh sardines, the choice of dishes balloons to include callops of monkfish or pink roasted duck breast, with additional changing specials. Handy for visiting Gawsworth Hall and Macclesfield's museums, the comfortable, en suite rooms are in a separate annexe. Beers are largely from local Cheshire craft breweries.

Open all day all wk 11am-mdnt ⊕ FREE HOUSE ◀ Hydes, Moore Houses, Storm Brew, Flowers, Guest ales. **Facilities** Children welcome Children's menu Garden Parking **Rooms** 17

FARNDON   Map 15 SJ45

The Farndon NEW

High St CH3 6PU ☎ 01829 270570 📠 **01829 272060**
e-mail: enquiries@thefarndon.co.uk
dir: *From Wrexham take A534 towards Nantwich. Follow signs for Farndon on left*

A family-run 16th-century coaching inn by the River Dee in delightful village surroundings, where the warmth of the welcome is matched by the log fire, lots of candles and an atmosphere of tasteful renovation. Several real ales and a cider are on tap, and menus change every month. The brasserie-style dishes, built around local produce, include starters that can also be ordered as main courses, or you could just settle for a hearty lamb hotpot topped with crisp potatoes and served with crusty bread.

Open all wk Mon-Fri 5-11 (Sat noon-11 Sun noon-10.30) **Bar Meals** L served Sat-Sun 12-9.30 D served Mon-Fri 6-9, Sat-Sun 12-9.30 Av main course £10 **Restaurant** D served Mon-Thu 6-9, Fri 6-9.30, Sat 12-9.30, Sun 12-8 Av 3 course à la carte fr £25 ◀ Timothy Taylor Landlord, Cheshire Cat, Spitting Feathers, Thirst Quencher, Sandstone, Eastgate. **Facilities** Children welcome Children's menu Children's portions Dogs allowed Garden Parking Wi-fi

GAWSWORTH   Map 16 SJ86

Harrington Arms ♥

Church Ln SK11 9RJ ☎ 01260 223325
dir: *From Macclesfield take A536 towards Congleton. Turn left for Gawsworth*

This memorable pub has been a licensed premise for over 300 years. It's part of a three-storey Cheshire brick farmhouse, with a warren of quirky little rooms, open fires, rustic furnishings; the hum of locals' conversations diverting from its bucolic location near to Gawsworth's wonderful old church, village ponds and magnificent half-timbered hall. On offer is good, filling pub food using the wealth of Cheshire produce available locally, including sandwiches, double egg and chips, fish and chips, steak, Harrington platters to share, vegetarian options and a specials board. Autumn sees the annual conker championship here.

Open all wk Mon-Sat noon-3 5-11.30 (Sun noon-4 7-11) **Bar Meals** L served Mon-Sat 12-2.30 Sun 12-3.30 D served Mon-Sat 5-8.30 Av main course £7 ⊕ ROBINSONS ◀ Unicorn, Hatters, Robinsons Seasonal Ale, Guinness ♂ Stowford Press. ♥ 8 **Facilities** Children welcome Children's portions Dogs allowed Garden Parking

HANDLEY   Map 15 SJ45

The Calveley Arms

Whitchurch Rd CH3 9DT
☎ **01829 770619** 📠 **01829 770901**
e-mail: calveleyarms@btconnect.com
dir: *5m S of Chester, signed from A41. Follow signs for Handley & Aldersey Green Golf Course*

Built as a coaching in the early 17th century, the smart black-and-white pub stands opposite the church with views of the distant Welsh hills. Chock full of old timbers, jugs, pots, pictures, prints and ornaments, the rambling bars provide an atmospheric setting in which to sample some good beers and pub food. Perhaps lamb cutlets on a sizzling platter; salmon teriyaki; chicken with a mild, creamy curry apricot sauce. A good section of pasta dishes, speciality salads and tempting sandwiches or baguettes are also available. There are spacious gardens to enjoy in summer.

Open all wk noon-3 6-11 (Sun noon-3 7-11) **Bar Meals** L served all wk 12-3 D served Mon-Sat 6-9, Sun 7-9 ⊕ ENTERPRISE INNS ◀ Castle Eden Ale, Marston's Pedigree, Black Bull, Bombardier, Greene King IPA. **Facilities** Children welcome Children's portions Play area Dogs allowed Garden Parking

HAUGHTON MOSS · Map 15 SJ55

The Nags Head ☏

Long Ln CW6 9RN ☎ 01829 260265 📄 01829 261364
e-mail: roryk1@btinternet.com
dir: Exit A49 S of Tarporley at Beeston/Haughton sign into
Long Ln. 1.75m to pub

Among the attractions at this 17th-century black-and-white timbered village pub are the glorious summer gardens, the sun-trap patios and the bowling green. In winter, retreat inside the former smithy to find cosy, low-ceilinged rooms with old beams, exposed brickwork and open log fires. Owners Rory and Debbie are committed to providing quality food and service in a warm and friendly atmosphere. The extensive menu offers wholesome, traditional dishes such as deep-fried whitebait, steak, ale and mushroom pie, and fish and chips, alongside beef Stroganoff, a hot lunchtime buffet, and popular Sunday roast lunches (booking essential).

Open all day all wk 11am-mdnt Bar Meals L served all wk 12-10 D served all wk 12-10 Av main course £10.95 food served all day Restaurant L served all wk 12-10 D served all wk 12-10 Fixed menu price fr £14.30 Av 3 course à la carte fr £21.95 food served all day ⊕ FREE HOUSE ◀ Flowers IPA, Wadworth 6X, Guest ales ♨ Stowford Press. ☏ 14 Facilities Children welcome Children's menu Children's portions Play area Dogs allowed Garden Parking Wi-fi

HUXLEY · Map 15 SJ56

Stuart's Table at the Farmer's Arms ☏

Huxley Ln CH3 9BG ☎ 01829 781342 📄 01829 781794
e-mail: stuart@stuartstable.com
dir: Telephone for directions

A pub since 1802, the Farmer's Arms stands in beautiful Cheshire countryside and prides itself on menus that reflect modern British flavours executed using classical cooking techniques. The best seasonal produce available is sourced from the pub's own vegetable patches, locally and from around the British Isles. Main courses might include succulent steaks; chicken, ham and leek pie; honey-roasted Goosnargh duck with creamy mashed potato; or stone bass with a mussel and clam bisque. There are monthly fine dining evenings and 30 wines by the glass.

Open all wk noon-3 5-11 (Fri-Sat noon-mdnt, Sun noon-10.30, Mon 5-11) Bar Meals L served Tue-Sat 12-2 Av main course £14 Restaurant L served Tue-Sat 12-2, Sun 12-4 D served Tue-Thu 6.30-9, Fri-Sat 6.30-9.30 booking required Fixed menu price fr £12 Av 3 course à la carte fr £25 ⊕ ADMIRAL TAVERNS ◀ Black Sheep, Adnams, guest ale. ☏ 30 Facilities Children welcome Children's menu Children's portions Dogs allowed Garden Parking

KETTLESHULME · Map 16 SJ97

Swan Inn

SK23 7QU ☎ 01663 732943
e-mail: the.swan.kettleshulme@googlemail.co.uk
dir: On B5470 between Whaley Bridge (2m) and
Macclesfield (5m)

A glorious, tiny 15th-century village inn huddled in the shadow of the craggy Windgather Rocks in the Cheshire Peak District. A consortium of locals bought the place in 2005 to save it from closure. Now safe and thriving in private hands again, the eclectic and robust menu is strong on seafood, including the special 'Zarzuela' seafood risotto: a 'Catalan symphony' of mussels, clams, tiger prawns and monkfish topped with a grilled oyster and scallop in its shell. Local craft beers keep ramblers and locals very contented, especially at the pub's beer festival on the first weekend in September.

Open all wk Mon 5-11 Tue 12-3 5-11 Wed-Sun all day Closed: 25-26 Dec, 1 Jan, Mon L Bar Meals L served Tue 12-2, Wed 12-9, Thu-Fri 12-7, Sat 12-9, Sun 12-4 booking required D served Tue 6.30-8.30, Wed 12-9, Thu-Fri 12-7, Sat 12-9 ⊕ FREE HOUSE ◀ Marstons, Marble, Thornbridge, Phoenix. Facilities Children welcome Children's portions Dogs allowed Garden Beer festival

KNUTSFORD · Map 15 SJ77

PICK OF THE PUBS

The Dog Inn ★★★★ INN ☏

Well Bank Ln, Over Peover WA16 8UP
☎ 01625 861421 📄 01625 864800
e-mail: thedoginnpeover@btconnect.com
web: www.doginn-overpeover.co.uk
dir: S from Knutsford take A50. Turn into Stocks Ln at
The Whipping Stocks pub. 2m

Serving ale since the beginning of the 19th century, this timbered inn has in its time been a row of cottages, a grocer's, a shoemaker's and a farm. Colourful flowerbeds, tubs and hanging baskets create quite a setting in summer, but the cask-conditioned ales from Hydes in Manchester and Weetwood's in Tarporley, large array of malt whiskies, and classic English food prepared from ingredients sourced largely within a six-mile radius provide all-year round appeal. Among the typical main courses in the olde worlde restaurant are pan-roasted chicken breast with wild mushroom sauce; grilled halibut steak on creamed spinach; pan-fried duck breast with apricot and ginger sauce; and mushroom Stroganoff. Ever popular

desserts include chocolate fudge cake and bread and butter pudding. For something lighter, choose from the excellent range of sandwiches and hot baguettes. There are six attractive guest rooms if you would like to stay over and explore the area.

Open all wk 11.30-3 4.30-11 (Sat-Sun all day) Bar Meals L served all wk 12-2.30 D served all wk 6-9 Restaurant L served all wk 12-2.30 D served all wk 6-9 ⊕ FREE HOUSE ◀ Hydes Traditional Bitter, Weetwood Best, Skipton Brewery, Moorhouses. ☏ 10 Facilities Children's menu Children's portions Dogs allowed Garden Parking Wi-fi Rooms 6

LACH DENNIS · Map 15 SJ77

The Duke of Portland

Penny's Ln CW9 7SY ☎ 01606 46264
e-mail: info@dukeofportland.com
web: www.dukeofportland.com
dir: M6 junct 19, A556 towards Northwich. Left onto
B5082 to Lach Dennis

Awards reflecting this family-run pub's commitment to its customers include one for best use of local produce. Indeed it should, since only highly regarded suppliers are listed. Try confit of Glyn Arthur Estate lamb, not least because you won't find it anywhere else; pan-fried organic Shetland salmon; or Cheshire blue cheese, leek, grelot onion and peppered mushroom pie. A sunny, landscaped garden complements the attractive building.

Open all day all wk Bar Meals L served all wk 12-3 booking required D served all wk 5.30-9.30 booking required Av main course £11.95 Restaurant L served all wk 12-3 booking required D served all wk 5.30-9.30 booking required Fixed menu price fr £10.95 Av 3 course à la carte fr £30 ⊕ MARSTONS ◀ Banks Cocker Hoop Original, Oxford Gold, Cumberland Ale ♨ Thatchers Gold. Facilities Children welcome Children's menu Children's portions Garden Parking Wi-fi

Save on hotels. Book at theAA.com/hotel

CHESHIRE 73 ENGLAND

LITTLE NESTON
Map 15 SJ27

The Harp Inn

19 Quay Side CH64 0TB
☎ 0151 336 6980   📄 0151 336 6980
e-mail: jonesalbert@sky.com
dir: From Neston town centre, at 2nd mini-rdbt, turn right onto Marshlands Rd. At bottom turn left, 200yds ahead

Popular with walkers, cyclists and bird-watchers, this isolated pub enjoys beautiful scenery and sunsets, with views over the River Dee and across to Wales. The building was formerly miners' cottages before becoming a pub 150 years ago; on the walls mining artefacts and pictures testify to its history. Although renovated over the years, it remains a simple two-roomed pub, with quarry-tiled floors and low beams. A good range of real ales is kept – six available all the time, and simple plates of food. There is a boules pitch in the beer garden.

Open all day all wk noon-mdnt Bar Meals L served Mon-Fri 12-2 Av main course £4.50 ⊕ ADMIRAL TAVERNS
◀ Joseph Holts, Timothy Taylor Landlord, Wadworth 6X, Guest ales. Facilities Children welcome Children's menu Children's portions Family room Dogs allowed Garden Parking Notes ⊛

MACCLESFIELD
Map 16 SJ97

The Windmill Inn ☕

Holehouse Ln, Whitely Green, Adlington SK10 5SJ
☎ 01625 574222
e-mail: mail@thewindmill.info
web: www.thewindmill.info
dir: Between Macclesfield & Poynton. Follow brown tourist signs on main road. Pub in 1.5m

In the heart of the east Cheshire countryside where the plain gives way to the hills of the Peak District; the large gardens (where there's a maze) make the most of this happy situation and the dining inn is a popular stop-off for boaters on the nearby canal and cyclists on the popular Middlewood Way trail. Local beers from Macclesfield's Storm Brewery set the agenda for the rest of the fare here, which draws much from the area's rich resources; a filling lunchtime snack may be a sandwich of fillet steak, Cheshire blue cheese and red onion jam, whilst larger appetites are challenged by spring lamb rump on a mixed warm salad of asparagus, green beans, sun-blush tomatoes and new potatoes.

Open all wk noon-3 5-11 (Fri-Sat noon-11, Sun noon-10.30) Bar Meals L served Mon-Fri 12-2.30, Sat-Sun 12-8 D served Mon-Fri 5-9.30, Sat-Sun 12-8
Restaurant L served Mon-Fri 12-2.30, Sat-Sun 12-8 D served Mon-Fri 5-9.30, Sat-Sun 12-8 ⊕ MOYO LTD
◀ Black Sheep, Old Speckled Hen, Bombardier, changing Storm Ales. ☕ 16 Facilities Children welcome Children's menu Dogs allowed Garden Parking

MARTON
Map 16 SJ86

PICK OF THE PUBS

The Davenport Arms ☕

Congleton Rd SK11 9HF
☎ 01260 224269   📄 01260 224565
e-mail: enquiries@thedavenportarms.co.uk
dir: 3m from Congleton on A34

As hereditary royal foresters, the Davenports once wielded considerable power, including the right to try, convict and execute highwaymen. Trials took place in an upstairs room of this old farm, those found guilty then hanged from a nearby gibbet. Today it's an independent free house with a traditional bar furnished with cushioned settles and leather armchairs around a log fire; a decommissioned well adds appeal of its own to the restaurant. Food, right down to the chutneys and sauces, is all freshly made on the premises using locally supplied ingredients. Specials change daily and there's always a good fresh fish selection dishes - fresh haddock with home-made chips, or seasonal pheasant breast with red wine, bacon and shallot gravy. The large garden contains a discreet play area for children, although they may also want to see the Marton Oak in the village. Looking somewhat ravaged – not surprisingly after more than 1200 years – this is possibly the oldest surviving tree in England.

Open noon-3 6-mdnt (Fri-Sun noon-mdnt) Closed: Mon L (ex BH) Bar Meals L served Tue-Sat 12-2.30, Sun 12-3 D served Tue-Fri 6-9, Sun 6-8.30
Restaurant L served Tue-Fri 12-2.30, Sat 12-9, Sun 12-8 booking required D served Tue-Fri 6-9, Sat 12-9, Sun 12-8 booking required ⊕ FREE HOUSE ◀ Copper Dragon, Storm Brewing, Directors, Weetwood, Theakstons. ☕ 9 Facilities Children welcome Children's menu Play area Garden Parking Wi-fi

MOBBERLEY
Map 15 SJ77

The Roebuck ☕

Mill Ln WA16 7HX ☎ 01565 873322
e-mail: mail@theroebuck.com
web: www.theroebuck.com
dir: Just off B5085 NE of Knutsford

Deep in the footballer belt of leafy north Cheshire, this white-painted Cheshire brick old village pub notches up the ticks for both food and beers, both of which are strong on local provenance. Great ales from Beartown and Storm detain patrons winding down in the secluded beer garden, whilst the gastro-pub menu introduces new twists to familiar dishes; wood pigeon and roasted

shallot puff pastry pie to kick in with Provencal-style Fleetwood fish stew with saffron potatoes, local crisp air-dried ham and Goostrey bread to follow.

The Roebuck

Open all wk 12-3 5-11 (Fri-Sun all day)
Bar Meals L served Mon-Thu 12-2.30, Fri-Sun all day D served Mon-Thu 5-9.30, Fri-Sun all day
Restaurant L served Mon-Thu 12-2.30, Fri-Sun all day booking required D served Mon-Thu 5-9.30, Fri-Sun all day booking required ⊕ FREE HOUSE ◀ Timothy Taylor Landlord, Tetley's cask, Guest ales. ☕ 12
Facilities Children welcome Children's menu Children's portions Garden Parking

MOULDSWORTH
Map 15 SJ57

PICK OF THE PUBS

The Goshawk ☕

Station Rd CH3 8AJ
☎ 01928 740900   📄 01928 740965
dir: A51 from Chester onto A54. Left onto B5393 towards Frodsham. Enter Mouldsworth, pub on left opposite rail station

This sturdy old railway inn has a hint of Edwardian grandeur whilst benefitting from contemporary comforts; print-clad walls and dado rails, comfy sofas and open fires. Its village setting makes the most of the area's delights, including the many miles of footpaths, cycle trails and mysterious meres of nearby Delamere Forest, one of the largest in northwest England, whilst historic Chester is just one stop away on the train. The terrace and large grassy beer garden offer views across the heart of Cheshire, and the local motor museum is an interesting diversion. Cheshire ales from Weetwood draw an appreciative crowd of locals, whilst the wide-ranging menu is matched by an extensive wine list. Starters tempt with sautéed chicken livers with Madeira cream or confit duck pancakes; mains browse a wide choice of traditional favourites often with a twist: smoked haddock rarebit with cured tomatoes and thermidor sauce, or chicken breast topped with goat's cheese and a beetroot risotto, plus the popular steak and kidney pie. There's a good range of vegetarian dishes and a choice of 21-day aged steaks.

Open all day all wk noon-11 (Sun noon-10.30) Closed: 25 Dec & 1 Jan Bar Meals food served all day Restaurant food served all day ⊕ WOODWARD & FALCONER PUBS ◀ Weetwoods Eastgate, Piffle. ☕ 14
Facilities Children welcome Children's menu Children's portions Play area Family room Garden Parking

NANTWICH Map 15 SJ65

The Thatch Inn

Wrexham Rd, Faddiley CW5 8JE ☎ 01270 524223
dir: *Follow signs for Wrexham from Nantwich, inn 4m from Nantwich on A534*

Believed to be the oldest (and one of the prettiest) pubs in south Cheshire, the black-and-white Thatch Inn has a three quarter acre garden, while inside there are plentiful oak beams, and open fires in winter. Starters might be salmon and spring onion fishcakes with dill crème fraîche or black pudding on wilted spinach and caramelised pear, topped with streaky bacon and creamy mustard sauce. For mains, perhaps slow roasted belly pork on red cabbage with a creamy cider sauce or posh sausages and chips. Children have their own menu.

Open Mon-Tue 6-11, Wed-Thu 12-3 6-11, Fri-Sat 12-11, Sun 12-10.30 Closed: Mon L & Tue L ⊕ ENTERPRISE INNS ◀ Timothy Taylor Landlord, Weetwoods.
Facilities Children welcome Play area Family room Garden Parking

NORTHWICH Map 15 SJ67

The Red Lion ★★★ INN NEW

277 Chester Rd, Hartford CW8 1QL ☎ 01606 74597
e-mail: cathy.iglesias@tesco.net
dir: *From A556 take Hartford exit. Red Lion at 1st junct on left next to church*

This engaging inn was the village fire station until a century or so ago; many artefacts remain from this era, whilst a warming winter fire tempts fate here at the heart of Cheshire. Hunker down with a pint of Black Sheep, tuck in to hearty pub grub like home-made lamb hotpot or take on the locals at darts or doms; this is a thriving community local where visitors to the nearby Delamere Forest or Oulton Park motor-racing circuit can also bed down in the en suite accommodation here.

Open all day all wk **Bar Meals** Av main course £5.50 food served all day **Restaurant** L served all wk 12-2 D served all wk 6-8 ⊕ PUNCH TAVERNS ◀ Marston's Pedigree, Black Sheep brewery. **Facilities** Children welcome Children's portions Family room Dogs allowed Garden Parking Wi-fi **Rooms** 3

PARKGATE Map 15 SJ27

The Boat House ⚑

1 The Parade CH64 6RN
☎ 0151 336 4187 📄 0151 336 4813
dir: *On B5135, 3m from Heswall*

Situated beside the RSPB's Parkgate Reserve, with magnificent views across the Dee estuary to Wales, this striking black-and-white timbered building is a haven for bird-watchers and food lovers. Eat in the airy dining room looking out across salt marshes, or in the cosy modernised bars. The extensive menu favours fresh fish and seafood, perhaps half a dozen oysters followed by monkfish wrapped in Parma ham. Alternatives include toad in the hole or chicken breast stuffed with haggis and wrapped in streaky bacon. Look out for the flooding, about four times a year, when the water laps right up to the walls of the pub.

Open all day all wk noon-11 (Sun noon-10.30) Closed: 25 Dec, 1 Jan **Bar Meals** L served Mon-Sat 12-9.30, Sun 12-9 D served Mon-Sat 12-9.30, Sun 12-9
Restaurant L served all wk 12-5 D served Mon-Sat 5-9.30, Sun 5-9 ⊕ FREE HOUSE ◀ Theakstons, John Smith's, Old Speckled Hen, Piffle Ale. ⚑ 17
Facilities Children welcome Children's portions Family room Garden Parking

The Ship Hotel ★★★ HL

The Parade CH64 6SA
☎ 0151 336 3931 📄 0151 203 1636
e-mail: info@the-shiphotel.co.uk
dir: *A540 (Chester towards Neston) left then immediately right onto B5136 (Liverpool Rd). In Neston town centre, left onto B5135. Follow to The Parade in Parkgate, hotel 50yds on right*

Although silting put paid to Parkgate's days as a thriving port, visitors to this old free house with rooms can still enjoy fine views across the wildlife-rich Dee estuary to the coast and mountains of North Wales. Home-made food on the daily menus is traditional in style — hot and cold sandwiches; cod in beer batter; and pan-fried liver and onions, with the specials board adding further choice. There's a beer festival in April.

Open all day all wk **Bar Meals** L served all wk 12-2.30 D served all wk 6-8.30 Av main course £6.95
Restaurant L served all wk 12-2.30 D served all wk 6-8.30 ⊕ FREE HOUSE ◀ Trapper's Hat, Storr, Oak Beauty, Peerless, Oast House Gold. **Facilities** Children welcome Dogs allowed Beer festival Parking Wi-fi **Rooms** 24

PLUMLEY Map 15 SJ77

The Golden Pheasant Hotel ⚑

Plumley Moor Rd WA16 9RX
☎ 01565 722261 📄 01565 723804
dir: *M6 junct 19, A556 signed Chester. 2m, left at Plumley/Peover signs. Through Plumley, pub 1m opp rail station*

Set in the beautiful Cheshire countryside, The Golden Pheasant is convenient for Chester and Manchester, with trains from the station opposite hourly. This 200-year-old, traditional wayside inn has a wealth of beams, low ceilings and a magnificent carved oak bar servery. Privately owned, the pub is proud of its great choice of real ales, extensive wine list and home-cooked, locally sourced food served in the more formal dining rooms and lounge bar area. There is wonderful fresh fish and Tabley Estate game to enjoy. Expect roaring log fires, comfy sitting areas, alfresco dining, a children's play area and a locals' bar with a darts board.

Open all day all wk 11-11 (Sun noon-10.30) **Bar Meals** Av main course £10.95 food served all day **Restaurant** Fixed menu price fr £17.95 Av 3 course à la carte fr £22.95 food served all day ⊕ J W LEES ◀ J W Lees Bitter, John Willies Bitter, Guinness, Great Budworth Best Bitter, Dragon's Fire. ⚑ 14 **Facilities** Children welcome Children's menu Children's portions Play area Garden Parking Wi-fi

The Smoker ⚑

WA16 0TY ☎ 01565 722338
e-mail: thesmokerinn@aol.com
dir: *From M6 junct 19 take A556 W. Pub 1.75m on left*

A 400-year-old thatched coaching inn named after a white racehorse bred by the Prince Regent and run by the same family for over 20 years. The pub's striking wood-panelled interior of three connecting rooms welcomes drinkers as well as diners, all enjoying the warm welcome of log fires, beams and copper kettles. The menu has an appealing and lengthy array of starters such as home-made chicken liver parfait, while main courses include a hearty mixed grill.

Open all wk 10-3 6-11 (Sun 10am-10.30pm)
Bar Meals L served Mon-Sat 10-2.30, Sun 10-9 D served Mon-Sat 6-9.30, Sun 10-9 Av main course £11
Restaurant L served Mon-Sat 10-2.30, Sun 10-9 booking required D served Mon-Sat 6-9.30, Sun 10-9 booking required Av 3 course à la carte fr £19.50 ⊕ FREDERIC ROBINSON ◀ Robinson's Best, Double Hop, Robinson's Smooth, Dizzy Blonde, Old Stockport, Hannibal's Nectar. ⚑ 10 **Facilities** Children welcome Children's menu Children's portions Play area Garden Parking

PRESTBURY
Map 16 SJ87

The Legh Arms ♥ NEW

The Village SK10 4DG
☎ 01625 829130 📠 01625 827833
e-mail: legharms@hotmail.co.uk
dir: On A538 (New Road)

An immensely characterful gabled, part-timbered old inn and restaurant at the heart of trendy Prestbury, where premiership footballers trip over each other on the pavements. They're fortunate in having The Legh Arms' exceptional menu to enjoy, with great local estate meat and game to take the edge off an appetite; excellent vegetarian and fish selections, too. Take time to acclimatise to the Cheshire Set in the very comfy, opulent rooms, lounging in easy chairs by log fires where you can enjoy fine ales from the nearby Robinsons Brewery.

Open all day all wk **Bar Meals** L served Mon-Fri 12-2, Sat-Sun 12-10 D served Mon-Fri 6-10, Sat-Sun 12-10 Av main course £10 **Restaurant** L served Mon-Fri 12-2, Sat-Sun 12-10 booking required D served Sat 12-10, Sun 12-9.30 booking required Fixed menu price fr £15 Av 3 course à la carte fr £25 ⊕ ROBINSONS ◀ Robinsons Hatters, Unicorn. **Facilities** Children welcome Children's portions Dogs allowed Garden Parking Wi-fi

SHOCKLACH
Map 15 SJ44

The Bull ♥

SY14 7BL ☎ 01829 250239
e-mail: info@thebullshocklach.com
dir: 12m S of Chester, 3m W of Malpas

A traditional village pub, set in a picturesque village a stones throw from the River Dee, with lots of old beams, a funky bar with an open fire and what the owners call 'unusual' furniture, in which hand pumps dispense local and national real ales. High quality, locally sourced ingredients are the basis for black pudding fritters with apple sauce; garlic and blue cheese mushrooms with sourdough bread; slow cooked shoulder of lamb with garlic mash; and butternut squash risotto. A growing single malt collection sits alongside an extensive wine list, and the pub organises various events including an Easter Ale Festival.

Open all wk Mon-Thu 12-3 5-11 (Fri-Sat noon-11 Sun noon-10.30) **Bar Meals** L served Mon-Fri 12-2.30, Sat 12-10, Sun 12-8 booking required D served Mon-Thu 6-9.30, Fri 6-10, Sat 12-10, Sun 12-8 booking required **Restaurant** L served Mon-Fri 12-2.30, Sat 12-10, Sun 12-8 booking required D served Mon-Thu 6-9.30, Fri 6-10, Sat 12-10, Sun 12-8 booking required ⊕ ADMIRAL TAVERNS ◀ Stonehouse Station Bitter, Guest ales. ♥ 9 **Facilities** Children welcome Children's menu Children's portions Dogs allowed Garden Beer festival Parking Wi-fi

STOAK
Map 15 SJ47

The Bunbury Arms ♥ NEW

Little Stanney Ln CH2 4HW ☎ 01244 301665
dir: From M53/M56 junct 11/15 take A5117. 1st left into Little Stanney Ln

This traditional Cheshire alehouse is off the beaten track in a small wooded hamlet. Extensive, well-tended gardens host summer barbecues, when asparagus peas, rainbow carrots, chillies and blue beans from the vegetable plot also appear on the menu. Inside, the snug is exactly that — with open fire, TV, board games and darts, not forgetting an award-winning selection of real ales, and a wine list with more than 20 served by the glass. There are daily specials including fresh fish, afternoon teas and Champagne breakfasts for those attending the Chester races. Handy for the Cheshire Oaks retail outlet, Chester Zoo, Canal Boat Museum and Blue Planet Aquarium.

Open all day all wk **Bar Meals** booking required food served all day **Restaurant** booking required food served all day ⊕ FREE HOUSE ◀ Robinsons Unicorn, Joseph Holt, JW Lees Coronation Street Bitter, Cains Brewery. ♥ 26 **Facilities** Children welcome Children's menu Children's portions Dogs allowed Garden Beer festival Parking Wi-fi

SUTTON LANE ENDS
Map 16 SJ97

The Hanging Gate Inn ♥ NEW

Meg Ln, Higher Sutton SK11 0NG ☎ 01260 252238
dir: From S of Macclesfield take A523 (signed Leek). At lights left into Byron's Lane signed Sutton, Langley & Wincle. Bear left into Jarman, left onto Ridge Hill, becomes Meg Lane. 2nd right to pub on left

Dating from 1621, this old drovers' inn is the highest pub in Cheshire, clinging to the hillside high above Rossendale, with breathtaking panoramas sweeping west across the Cheshire Plain into Wales. On a fine day bag a seat in the terraced garden or hunker down in winter by the fire in one of the three unspoilt rooms. Quaff a pint of Hydes Original and tuck into local game and farm produce, perhaps lamb Henry with spring onion mash and red wine jus, or venison and beef pie with braised red cabbage and hand-cut chips.

Open all wk 12-3 5-11 (Sat-Sun 12-11)
Bar Meals L served Mon-Fri 12-2.30, Sat-Sun 12-3.30 D served all wk 6-9 Av main course £7.95-£13.95 **Restaurant** L served Mon-Fri 12-2.30, Sat-Sun 12-3.30 D served all wk 6-9 ⊕ HYDES BREWERY ◀ Hydes Original, Craft Range, Manchester Finest. ♥ 10 **Facilities** Children welcome Children's menu Children's portions Family room Dogs allowed Garden Parking Wi-fi

PICK OF THE PUBS

Sutton Hall ♥

Bullocks Ln SK11 0HE
☎ 01260 253211 📠 01260 252538
e-mail: sutton.hall@brunningandprice.co.uk
dir: A523 from Macclesfield. At lights left into Byron's Lane (signed Sutton, Langley & Wincle) to village. Pub on left

A stunning half-timbered and gritstone manor lost deep within its own estate grounds; the Macclesfield Canal threads close by whilst the steeply wooded hills, crags and moors of Macclesfield Forest rise beyond the nearby picturesque stone hamlets of Gurnett and Langley. A Norman convent stood here, and today's Elizabethan house rose from the ruins of this, which eventually became a family seat to the Earls of Lucan; famously, the 6th Lord Lucan disappeared in 1974 leaving unresolved the mystery of his nanny's murder. It's now part of the respected Brunning and Price chain of destination dining pubs, so a great combination of beers and food is guaranteed. Expect to be startled by the range of beers; usually a few from very local breweries such as Wincle, Storm and Beartown will feature amongst at least five on tap; the wine list is equally gregarious and there are over 100 whiskies. Bag a table in the courtyard, garden or any of the fabulously characterful old rooms and look to hake fillet poached in cockle broth; pan-fried venison rump with juniper and single malt gravy; or leek risotto stuffed butternut squash to provide sustenance.

Open all day all wk Mon-Sat 11.30-11 (Sun noon-10.30) **Bar Meals** L served Mon-Sat 12-10, Sun 12-9.30 booking required D served Mon-Sat 12-10, Sun 12-9.30 booking required Av main course £11.95 food served all day **Restaurant** L served Mon-Sat 12-10, Sun 12-9.30 booking required D served Mon-Sat 12-10, Sun 12-9.30 booking required food served all day ⊕ FREE HOUSE ◀ Brunning & Price Original, Flowers Original, Wincle Lord Lucan Ò Aspall, Westons Organic. ♥ 28 **Facilities** Children welcome Children's portions Play area Dogs allowed Garden Parking

SWETTENHAM Map 15 SJ86

PICK OF THE PUBS

The Swettenham Arms 🍷

Swettenham Ln CW12 2LF
☎ 01477 571284 📠 01477 571284
e-mail: info@swettenhamarms.co.uk
dir: *M6 junct 18 to Holmes Chapel, then A535 towards Jodrell Bank. 3m right (Forty Acre Lane) to Swettenham*

Deep in the Dane Valley, this delightful 16th-century inn lies hard by the ancient parish church, with a lavender and sunflower meadow to the rear and a nature reserve and arboretum to the side. Run by the same owners for 17 years, it was once a nunnery, but before that probably provided funeral parties with bed and board; corpses were 'rested' too, in the underground passage linking the pub to the church. Recent mysterious sightings keep alive the legend that a nun was murdered here. Eyes peeled then as you enjoy high standards of locally sourced, home prepared food chosen from a short menu listing lunchtime sandwiches, platters and salads alongside day or evening options such as honey-glazed pork belly with apple and ginger purée followed by braised oxtail with smoked bacon, horseradish mashed potatoes and red wine sauce; or maybe a simple home-made burger with Cheshire cheese, bacon, home-made mayonnaise and hand-cut chips. If it's too warm for a log fire inside, sit outside on the flower-festooned patio.

Open all day all wk 11.30am-11pm (Sun noon-11pm) **Bar Meals** L served Mon-Fri 12-2.30, Sat-Sun 12-9.30 booking required D served Mon-Fri 5-9.30, Sat-Sun 12-9.30 booking required Av main course £13 **Restaurant** L served Mon-Fri 12-2.30, Sat-Sun 12-9.30 booking required D served Mon-Fri 5-9.30, Sat-Sun 12-9.30 booking required Fixed menu price fr £12.50 Av 3 course à la carte fr £25 FREE HOUSE Landlord, Hydes, Beartown, Sharp's Doom Bar, Bollington Best, Black Sheep, Directors, Pride of Penale Addlestones. 🍷 12 **Facilities** Children welcome Children's menu Children's portions Dogs allowed Garden Parking Wi-fi

TARPORLEY Map 15 SJ56

Alvanley Arms Inn ★★★★ INN 🍷

Forest Rd, Cotebrook CW6 9DS ☎ 01829 760200
e-mail: info@alvanleyarms.co.uk
dir: *On A49, 1.5m N of Tarporley*

A charming 16th-century, family-run coaching inn with shire horse-themed decor: rosettes, harnesses and horseshoes decorate the walls, linking the inn to the landlords' Cotebrook Shire Horse Centre next door. Hand-pulled ales in the oak-beamed bar complement a range of freshly prepared dishes, based on ingredients from local family businesses. Dishes range from traditional steak and ale pie or gammon steak with honey mustard glaze and chips to chef's own curry of the day and Stroganoff of mushrooms. Renovations uncovered original beams in the individually designed bedrooms. Recent change of hands.

Open all wk noon-3 5.30-11.30 (Sat-Sun noon-11) **Bar Meals** L served Mon-Sat 12-2, Sun 12-9 D served Mon-Sat 6-9, Sun 12-9 **Restaurant** L served Mon-Sat 12-2, Sun 12-9 D served Mon-Sat 6-9, Sun 12-9 booking required FREDERIC ROBINSON Robinsons Best, Guest ales. 🍷 12 **Facilities** Dogs allowed Garden Parking **Rooms** 7

The Swan, Tarporley 🍷 NEW

50 High St CW6 0AG ☎ 01829 733838
e-mail: info@theswantarporley.co.uk
web: www.theswantarporley.co.uk
dir: *From junct of A49 & A51 into Tarporley. Pub on right in village centre*

Home to the 250-year-old Tarporley Hunt Club, known as The Green Collars, this one-time coaching inn is full of nook-and-cranny-imbued character. Regulars favour the open-fired Pantry Bar and visitors will feel at home there too, but the Hayes and Pickering Rooms are also welcoming, the latter for locally sourced herb-crusted swordfish and slow-cooked beef brisket. Generate a thirst for Weetwood Best, or any of the four other real ales, with home-made pork scratchings.

Open all day all wk **Bar Meals** L served Mon-Sat 7am-9pm, Sun 8am-8pm D served Mon-Sat 7am-9pm, Sun 8am-8pm Av main course £12-£14 food served all day **Restaurant** L served Mon-Sat 7am-9pm, Sun 8am-8pm D served Mon-Sat 7am-9pm, Sun 8am-8pm food served all day FREE HOUSE Black Sheep, Weetwood Best Bitter & Eastgate Ale Westons Premium Cider, Stowford Press. 🍷 10 **Facilities** Children welcome Children's menu Children's portions Family room Garden Parking Wi-fi

TUSHINGHAM CUM GRINDLEY Map 15 SJ54

PICK OF THE PUBS

Blue Bell Inn

SY13 4QS ☎ 01948 662172 📠 01948 662172
dir: *A41, 4m N of Whitchurch, signed Bell O' the Hill*

In what must be a unique tale from the annals of pub-haunting, this inn reputedly has a ghost duck, whose spirit is sealed in a bottle buried in the bottom step of the cellar. Believe that or not, the Blue Bell remains a charming pub. A lovely black-and-white building that oozes character with its abundance of beams, open fires and horse brasses, its oldest part dates to approximately 1550, and the main building was completed in 1667. It has all the features you'd expect of a timber-framed building of this date, including one of the largest working chimneys in Cheshire and a priest hole. Curios that have been discovered from within the wall structure are on show in the pub. A menu of hearty, home-cooked pub food includes curries, steak and chips, and chilli with garlic bread. Drink options include well kept ales, real cider and a selection of wines.

Open noon-3 6-11.30 Closed: Mon (ex BH) **Bar Meals** L served Tue-Sun 12-2 D served Tue-Sat 6-9 **Restaurant** L served Tue-Sun 12-2 D served Tue-Sat 6-9 booking required FREE HOUSE Shropshire Gold, Oakham JHB, Guest ales Cheddar Valley. **Facilities** Children welcome Children's portions Family room Dogs allowed Garden Parking

WARMINGHAM Map 15 SJ76

PICK OF THE PUBS

The Bear's Paw ★★★★★ INN 🍷

See Pick of the Pubs on opposite page

WINCLE Map 16 SJ96

The Ship Inn 🍷 NEW

Barlow Hill SK11 0QE ☎ 01260 227217
e-mail: shipinnwincle@btconnect.com
dir: *From Buxton towards Congleton on A54 left into Barlow Hill at x-roads, follow signs for Wincle (0.75m) & Swythamley*

Dating back to the 17th-century, The Ship Inn is located in the small, vibrant village of Wincle in the heart of the Peak District National Park. With several circular trails nearby, walkers and their dogs are welcome in the flag-stoned tap room, as well as the beer garden with its splendid views. In the more formal dining area, enjoy a pint of JW Lees Coronation Street ale with an extensive menu that might include rabbit and cider pie or home-cooked ham, egg and chips.

Open 12-3 evening times vary Closed: Mon ex BHs **Bar Meals** L served Tue-Fri 12-2.30, Sat-Sun 12-3 D served Tue-Sat 7-9 Av main course £11.25 **Restaurant** L served Tue-Fri 12-2.30, Sat-Sun 12-3 D served Tue-Sat 7-9 Av 3 course à la carte fr £19.95 J W LEES J W Lees Bitter, Coronation Street. 🍷 11 **Facilities** Children welcome Children's portions Family room Dogs allowed Garden Parking

PICK OF THE PUBS

The Bear's Paw ★★★★★ INN ♉

WARMINGHAM   Map 15 SJ76

School Ln CW11 3QN ☎ 01270 526317
e-mail: info@thebearspaw.co.uk
web: www.thebearspaw.co.uk
dir: *M6 junct 18, A54, A533 towards*
Sandbach. Follow signs for village

The once faded and run down village free house was snapped up by Nelson Hotels, who also own The Pheasant at Burwardsley (see entry), in 2008 having seen its potential as being a thriving gastro-pub with rooms. With the refurbishment almost complete in May 2008, the pub suffered a devastating fire resulting in complete rebuild and an investment of £2.5 million before the doors of the spanking new Bear's Paw were pushed open in May 2009 revealing a vibrant and grand interior. Even with acres of reclaimed antique oak flooring, two huge fireplaces surrounded by leather sofas, bookshelves and hundreds of pictures and archive photos lining oak-panelled walls, it still successfully retains the charm and character of a traditional village pub. The bar (home to a carved wooden bear with a salmon in its mouth) plays host to no less that six cask ales from local micro-breweries, including the appropriately named Beartown in Congleton, and Weetwood in Tarporley. Whether you're sitting out front looking across to the churchyard or in the clubby interior, there is plenty of comfortable dining space in which to sample some

wholesome food from a wide-ranging menu that cleverly blends classics with modern twists. Take starters like ham hock terrine with home-made piccalilli or mussels in white wine, garlic and shallot cream sauce, and such main dishes as braised lamb shoulder with mustard mash, minted pea purée and juniper berry sauce, steak and Weetwood ale pie, or 28-day aged Bowland rib-eye steak with hand-cut chips. Great for sharing are the imaginative deli boards, which come laden with local cheeses, charcuterie or pickled and smoked fish, and don't miss the Sunday roast lunches. Upstairs, the 17 stylish bedrooms are a real treat, with funky fabrics, contemporary art and wallpaper, and sleek bathrooms with rain showers and posh toiletries.

Open all day all wk **Bar Meals** L served Mon-Thu 12-9.30, Fri-Sat 12-10, Sun 12-8 D served Mon-Thu 12-9.30, Fri-Sat 12-10, Sun 12-8 **Restaurant** L served Mon-Thu 12-9.30, Fri-Sat 12-10, Sun 12-8 D served Mon-Thu 12-9.30, Fri-Sat 12-10, Sun 12-8 ⊕ FREE HOUSE ◀ Weetwood, Beartown, Storm Brewery, Wincle, Titanic ♉ Westons Stowford Press. ♉ 10 **Facilities** Children welcome Children's menu Children's portions Dogs allowed Garden Parking Wi-fi **Rooms** 17

WRENBURY — Map 15 SJ54

The Dusty Miller ☕

CW5 8HG ☎ 01270 780537
dir: *Telephone for directions*

A beautifully converted 16th-century mill building beside the Shropshire Union Canal. A black and white lift bridge, designed by Thomas Telford, completes the picture postcard setting. With a good choice of real ales, the menu, which mainly relies on ingredients from the region, offers warm duck salad with pickled fennel; smoked haddock, prawn and caper risotto; slow roasted lamb shank with roast garlic mash, buttered Savoy cabbage and rosemary and redcurrant jus; honey glazed ham, eggs and hand-cut chips.

Open 12-3 6.30-11 (noon-mdnt summer) Closed: Mon in winter **Bar Meals** Av main course £9.95 ⊕ FREE HOUSE ◀ Robinson's Unicorn, Double Hop, Old Tom, Hatters Mild, Hartleys XB ♻ Stowford Press, Westons Traditional Scrumpy. ♥ 12 **Facilities** Children welcome Children's menu Children's portions Dogs allowed Garden Parking

WYBUNBURY — Map 15 SJ64

The Swan ☕

Main Rd CW5 7NA ☎ 01270 841280 📄 01270 841200
e-mail: jacqueline.harris7@btinternet.com
dir: *M6 junct 16 towards Chester & Nantwich. Turn left at lights in Wybunbury*

Set in the heart of the village with the church next door, The Swan is a relaxed, welcoming and popular public house that dates from 1580. Serving a variety of Robinsons ales, all the food is freshly prepared on the premises. Typical examples include starters of buttered monkfish on cherry tomato fondue with olive tapenade, and garlic king prawns with a chilli tomato compote; and mains such as half a crispy roast duck with wok-fried vegetables or local sausages on mash with onion gravy and vegetables. Sit in the garden overlooking the famous leaning church tower. Keep an eye out for music nights.

Open all wk noon-mdnt, (Mon 5-mdnt)
Bar Meals L served Tue-Sat 12-2, Sun 12-3.30 D served Mon-Sat 6.30-9.30, Sun 5-8 **Restaurant** L served Tue-Sat 12-2, Sun 12-3.30 booking required D served Mon-Sat 6.30-9.30, Sun 5-8 booking required ⊕ ROBINSON ◀ Unicorn, Cumbria Way, Guest ales ♻ Stowford Press. ♥ 9 **Facilities** Children welcome Children's menu Children's portions Dogs allowed Garden Parking Wi-fi

CORNWALL & ISLES OF SCILLY

BLISLAND — Map 2 SX17

The Blisland Inn

PL30 4JF ☎ 01208 850739
dir: *5m from Bodmin towards Launceston. 2.5m off A30 signed Blisland. On village green*

Beside the village green, this old stone inn hosts a beer festival each May when milds are promoted, augmenting the Cornish bitters, local ciders and countless guest beers that have gained the pub national recognition. Inside; beams, toby jugs, local photos, a huge collection of barometers and a slate floor produce a timeless atmosphere, whilst reliable pub grub includes home-made chicken and ham pie and bowls of thick soup, ideal for warming up after walking on nearby Bodmin Moor.

Open all day all wk **Bar Meals** L served all wk 12-2 D served all wk 6.30-9 booking required ⊕ FREE HOUSE ◀ Sharp's, Skinner's, Guest ales ♻ Cornish Orchard, Winkleigh, Haye Farm. **Facilities** Children welcome Children's portions Family room Dogs allowed Garden Beer festival

BODINNICK — Map 2 SX15

Old Ferry Inn ☕

PL23 1LX ☎ 01726 870237 📄 01726 870116
e-mail: royce972@aol.com
dir: *A38 towards Dobwalls, left onto A390. After 3m left onto B3359 then right to Bodinnick/Polruan for 5m*

This friendly family-run free house overlooks Dauphne du Maurier's former home and stands just 50 yards from the scenic River Fowey, where the car ferry still makes regular crossings to Fowey itself. Inside the 400-year-old building, old photographs and nautical bric-a-brac set the scene. Sample an ale, stout or continental lager while perusing the extensive lunchtime bar menu which embraces hot and spicy chicken wings, creamy garlic mushrooms, burgers, home-made chilli, and fresh pasta of the day. Daily specials and an evening carte serving local fish, meat and produce complete the dining options. There are superb sea views from the terraces.

Open all day all wk 11-11 (summer), noon-10 (winter) Closed: 25 Dec **Bar Meals** L served all wk 12-3 (summer), 12-2.30 (winter) D served all wk 6-9 (summer), 6.30-8.30 (winter) Av main course £9 **Restaurant** D served all wk 7-8.30 booking required Av 3 course à la carte fr £20 ⊕ FREE HOUSE ◀ Sharp's Bitter, Guinness ♻ Cornish Orchard. ♥ 12 **Facilities** Children welcome Children's menu Children's portions Family room Dogs allowed Garden Parking

BOLVENTOR — Map 2 SX17

Jamaica Inn *

PL15 7TS ☎ 01566 86250 📄 01566 86177
e-mail: enquiry@jamaicainn.co.uk
dir: *Follow A30 from Exeter. 10m after Launceston take Bolventor road, follow signs*

The setting for Daphne du Maurier's famous novel, this 18th-century inn stands high on Bodmin Moor. Its Smugglers Museum houses fascinating artefacts, while the Daphne du Maurier room honours the great writer. The place is big on atmosphere, with a cobbled courtyard, beamed ceilings and roaring fires, plus a children's play area and beautiful gardens. Breakfasts, mid morning snacks and lunches provide an inviting choice, while the evening menu offers steaks, fish, chicken and vegetarian options. This inn changed hands in 2010.

Open all day all wk 9am-11pm ⊕ FREE HOUSE ◀ Sharp's Doom Bar, Tribute, Jamaica Inn Ale. **Facilities** Children welcome Play area Dogs allowed Garden Parking

BOSCASTLE — Map 2 SX09

Cobweb Inn NEW

The Bridge PL35 0HE ☎ 01840 250278
e-mail: cobweb.inn@virgin.net
dir: *In village centre*

A short hop from the quaint harbour, this immense, five-storey old stone edifice was a bonded warehouse where customs agents guarded taxable goods imported through the port. Today's lucky patrons can freely indulge in north-Cornish real ales and farm ciders either in the ageless beamed, flag-floored interior (the eponymous cobwebs were mostly removed in 1947 when the bar was created!) or on a small terrace below the spectacular tree-hung gorge-side. Seafood features prominently on the wide-ranging menu, as bar meals or in the charming white-painted restaurant. Each Saturday sees a live music event here.

Open all day all wk **Bar Meals** L served all wk 11-2.30 D served all wk 6-9.30 **Restaurant** D served all wk 6.15-9 booking required ⊕ FREE HOUSE ◀ Sharp's Doom Bar, Tribute, Harbour Special, Guest ales ♻ Cornish Rattler, Stowford Press. **Facilities** Children welcome Children's menu Family room Dogs allowed Garden Parking Wi-fi

PICK OF THE PUBS

Cadgwith Cove Inn

CADGWITH   Map 2 SW71

TR12 7JX
☎ **01326 290513**   📄 **01326 291018**
e-mail: david@cadgwithcoveinn.com
web: www.cadgwithcoveinn.com
dir: *10m from Helston on main Lizard road*

Formerly the haunt of smugglers and now popular with coast path walkers and local fishermen, this 300-year-old pub is set in an unspoilt fishing hamlet of thatched cottages on the rugged Lizard coastline. In summer, ramblers mingle with tourists and locals on the sunny front patio, which affords views across the old pilchard cellar to the peaceful cove. The atmospheric, simply furnished bars are adorned with relics that record a rich seafaring history, and it's easy to imagine that the ghosts of smugglers still gather within these cosy walls.

The pub offers a warm welcome and authentic local colour – come on a Friday night and relax with pint of Sharp's Doom Bar and listening to sea shanties sung by the Cadgwith Singers late into the night. On Tuesday nights the inn hosts a thriving folk club when guests are invited to join in or just sit back and enjoy the music. On any night of the week you might find yourself swapping tales with one of the fishermen whose catches feature on the popular menus – their colourful boats rest on the shingle a few steps down the lane from the pub.

As may be expected, these are positively laden with seafood - lobster and crab of course, but also grilled red mullet or bass, moules marinière, the special Cadgwith fish casserole, and traditional fish and chips. Meat eaters and vegetarians are also well provided for, with ingredients coming from local butchers and surrounding farms. Meals can be served in the garden in clement weather, and the large terrace is also an ideal spot during the summer gig races, or for one of the regular seafood barbecues prepared by local fishermen.

Open all wk Mon-Thu 12-3 6-11 Winter (Fri noon-1am Sat noon-11pm Sun noon-10pm) Summer Mon-Sat noon-11pm **Bar Meals** L served all wk 12-2 D served all wk 7-9 **Restaurant** L served all wk 12-2 D served all wk 7-9 🍺 PUNCH TAVERNS ◧ Sharp's, Skinners, guest ales. **Facilities** Children welcome Children's menu Children's portions Family room Dogs allowed Garden Parking

BOSCASTLE *continued*

PICK OF THE PUBS

The Wellington Hotel ♥

The Harbour PL35 0AQ ☎ 01840 250202
e-mail: info@boscastle-wellington.com
dir: A30/A395 at Davidstowe follow Boscastle signs.
B3266 to village. Right into Old Rd

Known affectionately as 'The Welly' by both locals and
loyal guests, this listed 16th-century coaching inn with
its castellated tower nestles on one of England's most
stunning coastlines at the end of a glorious wooded
valley where the rivers Jordan and Valency meet. It was
fully refurbished after the devastating floods in 2004,
but retains much of its original charm, including
beamed ceilings and real log fires. The traditional
beamed bar complete with minstrels' gallery and log
fires proffers a good selection of Cornish ales and
ciders, malt whiskies and bar snacks, together with
pub favourites and a specials board - pan-fried
Cornish chicken supreme with spring onion mash,
Cornish red mullet with dill potato cake, or roast
butternut squash, pinenut and Parmesan risotto. There
is also a fine dining restaurant. There was a change of
hands in January 2011.

Open all day all wk 11am-11pm (Sun noon-10pm)
Bar Meals L served Mon-Fri 12-3, Sat-Sun 12-9
D served Mon-Fri 6-9, Sat-Sun 12-9
Restaurant D served Fri-Wed 6-9 ⊕ FREE HOUSE ◀ St
Austell Tribute, Skinner's Ales Spriggan, Betty Stogs,
Truro Harbour, Tintagel ♂ Rattler Apple, Rattler Pear,
Thatchers Dry. ♀15 **Facilities** Children welcome
Children's menu Children's portions Dogs allowed
Garden Parking Wi-fi

| CADGWITH | Map 2 SW71 |

PICK OF THE PUBS

Cadgwith Cove Inn

See Pick of the Pubs on page 79

| CALLINGTON | Map 3 SX36 |

The Coachmakers Arms

6 Newport Square PL17 7AS
☎ 01579 382567 ▤ 01579 384679
dir: Between Plymouth & Launceston on A388

There's plenty of choice on the menu at this traditional
stone-built pub, from chargrilled steaks, steak and kidney
pie or hot-pot, to oven-baked plaice, vegetable balti or
salads. Clocks, plates, pictures of local scenes, old cars
and antique trade advertisements contribute to the
atmosphere, as do the fish tank and aviary. Regulars
range from the local football team to the pensioners
dining club. On Wednesday there's a charity quiz night,
and Thursday is steak night.

Open all day all wk ⊕ ENTERPRISE INNS ◀ Sharp's Doom
Bar, Worthington Best Bitter, Bass. **Facilities** Children
welcome Children's menu Children's portions Dogs
allowed Parking

Manor House Inn

Rilla Mill PL17 7NT ☎ 01579 362354
e-mail: dcproctor@btinternet.com
dir: 5m from Callington, just off B3257

Set by the River Lynher on the edge of Bodmin Moor, the
Manor House Inn was originally a granary for the mill next
door. Today it offers real ales and ciders, a bespoke wine
list and a reasonably-priced selection of home-made
food. A new venture is the Black Rock Grill concept, when
customers cook their own food at the table on pre-heated
volcanic rocks; choices of raw ingredients include Cajun
chicken, Moroccan lamb skewers and monkfish, as well
as popular cuts of steak. All desserts are home made. A
beer festival is held on the first weekend in July.

Open Mon-Fri 11-3 5-11 (all day Sat-Sun) Closed: Mon L
Bar Meals L served Tue-Sun 11.30-2 D served Tue-Sun
6-9 Av main course £9 **Restaurant** L served Tue-Sun
11.30-2 D served Tue-Sun 6-9 Av 3 course à la carte fr
£21 ⊕ FREE HOUSE ◀ Sharp's Own & Special, Doom Bar,
Betty Stogs ♂ Thatchers Gold, Westons Scrumpy, Cornish
Rattler. **Facilities** Children welcome Children's menu
Children's portions Dogs allowed Garden Beer festival
Parking

| CONSTANTINE | Map 2 SW72 |

PICK OF THE PUBS

Trengilly Wartha Inn ♥

Nancenoy TR11 5RP
☎ 01326 340332 ▤ 01326 340332
e-mail: reception@trengilly.co.uk
dir: Follow signs to Constantine, left towards Gweek
until 1st sign for inn, left & left again at next sign,
continue to inn

In Cornish the name of this friendly free house means a
settlement above the trees – although it actually lies at
the foot of a densely wooded valley. William and Lisa
Lea have been here a dozen or so years, during which
they have turned it into one of Cornwall's leading
residential inns. Its black-beamed, cricketing
memorabilia-filled bar offers Skinner's Betty Stogs and
other local real ales and ciders, a stupendous wine list
with fifteen by the glass, and over forty malt whiskies.
In the small bistro, the menu and specials board
include Cornwall-raised meats and game, Helford
oysters and other regionally caught seafood, and
modern vegetarian dishes. A pretty beer garden and
vine-shaded pergola are surrounded by three meadows,
this land being part of the original smallholding that
predated the inn's early development in the 1950s.

Open all wk 11-3 6-12 **Bar Meals** L served all wk
12-2.15 D served all wk 6.30-9.30 **Restaurant** L served
all wk 12-2.15 booking required D served all wk
6.30-9.30 booking required ⊕ FREE HOUSE
◀ Skinner's Cornish Knocker, Betty Stogs, Sharp's
Doom Bar, Sharp's Edenale, Guest ales ♂ Cornish
Rattler, Thatchers Gold. ♀15 **Facilities** Children
welcome Children's menu Children's portions Play area
Family room Dogs allowed Garden Parking Wi-fi

| CRAFTHOLE | Map 3 SX35 |

The Finnygook Inn ♥ NEW

PL11 3BQ ☎ 01503 230338
e-mail: eat@finnygook.co.uk
dir: 10m W of Tamar Bridge take A374 S. 3m turn right
for Crafthole & follow pub signs. From Torpoint take
A374, 5m to Antony. Left in Antony, 1m to T-junct. 3m
to Crafthole

The ghost of smuggler Silas Finny walks abroad on the
cliffs and byways hereabouts; so, too, do ramblers and
visitors seeking to share the inspirational beers and food
available at this refurbished old coaching inn in a hamlet
above Portwrinkle's cove-nibbled coast. Peninsula-
brewed beers from the likes of Dartmoor Brewery set the
scene for tempting fodder featuring grilled mackerel and
ever-changing seafood dishes, backed by a host of
reliable pub favourites taken by the warming log fire, in
the library room or on the terrace with distant views up
the Tamar estuary.

Open all day Closed: Mon in Jan-Mar **Bar Meals** L served
all wk 12-9 D served all wk 12-9 booking required Av
main course £11 food served all day **Restaurant** L served
all wk 12-9 booking required D served all wk 12-9
booking required Av 3 course à la carte fr £20 food served
all day ⊕ FREE HOUSE ◀ Sharp's Doom Bar, Proper Job,
Dartmoor. ♀10 **Facilities** Children welcome Children's
portions Dogs allowed Garden Parking

| CUBERT | Map 2 SW75 |

The Smugglers' Den Inn ♥

Trebellan TR8 5PY ☎ 01637 830209 ▤ 01637 830580
e-mail: info@thesmugglersden.co.uk
web: www.thesmugglersden.co.uk
dir: From Newquay take A3075 to Cubert x-rds, then right,
then left signed Trebellan, 0.5m

Look to the blackboard for fish specials in this thatched
16th-century pub situated less than fifteen minutes from
Newquay; the table d'hôte menu includes catch of the day
too. Popular with locals and visitors alike, the pub
comprises a long bar, family room, children's play area,
courtyards and huge beer garden. Local suppliers are
listed at the bottom of the no-nonsense modern menu,
where a salmon and dill fishcake could be followed by a
chargrilled breast of Celtic Farm free-range chicken. A
real ale, cider and pie festival is held over the May Day
Bank Holiday weekend.

Save on hotels. Book at theAA.com/hotel

CORNWALL & ISLES OF SCILLY 81 ENGLAND

Open all wk 11.30-3 6-11 (Sat 11-3 6-mdnt, Sun & summer open all day) Closed: (Jan-Mar closed Mon-Tue L) **Bar Meals** L served all wk 12-2.30 (winter 12-2) D served all wk 6-9.30 (winter Sun-Thu 6-9, Fri-Sat 6-9.30) **Restaurant** L served all wk 12-2.30 (winter 12-2) booking required D served all wk 6-9.30 (winter Sun-Thu 6-9, Fri-Sat 6-9.30) booking required ⊕ FREE HOUSE ◀ Skinner's Smugglers Ale, Sharp's Doom Bar, St Austell Tribute, rotating Guest ales ♂ Healey's Cornish Rattler, Cornish Orchards. ♀ 10 **Facilities** Children welcome Children's menu Play area Family room Dogs allowed Garden Beer festival Parking Wi-fi

See advert below

See advert below

DUNMERE
Map 2 SX06

The Borough Arms

PL31 2RD ☎ 01208 73118
e-mail: boroughams@hotmail.co.uk
dir: *From A30 take A389 to Wadebridge, pub approx 1m from Bodmin*

Although it was built in the 1850s to refresh rail workers transporting china clay from the moors down to the port at Padstow, The Borough seems much older. These days walkers, cyclists, horseriders and summertime tourists drop in as they follow the now-disused railway line which has become the 17-mile Camel Trail. Food includes pub favourites (pie of the day; curries; scampi and sausage and mash) and dishes such as grilled goat's cheese and walnut salad, and herb-crusted salmon fillet are served all day, plus a carvery. Children's portions are marked on the menu.

Open all day all wk **Bar Meals** L served all wk 12-9 D served all wk 12-9 Av main course £7 food served all day **Restaurant** L served all wk 12-9 D served all wk 12-9 Fixed menu price fr £7 Av 3 course à la carte fr £15 food served all day ⊕ ST AUSTELL ◀ Tribute, IPA, Bass. **Facilities** Children welcome Children's menu Children's portions Play area Family room Dogs allowed Garden Parking

FEOCK
Map 2 SW83

The Punchbowl & Ladle ♀

Penelewey TR3 6QY
☎ 01872 862237   🖅 01872 870401
e-mail: punchbowlandladle@googlemail.com
dir: *From Truro take A39 Truro towards Falmouth, after Shell garage at Playing Place rdbt follow for King Harry Ferry signs. 0.5m, pub on right*

Old English roses clamber to the thatch of this charming country inn close to the King Harry Ferry; local rumour has it that the bar fireplace was used to burn contraband when customs officers used the building. Smuggle yourself into the sun-trap walled garden or stake out the patio with a glass of St Austell beer, or snuggle down in the comfy furnishings and settees in the low beamed bar to await your choice from the locally sourced menu, which features great comfort dishes such as fisherman's pie and mixed grills.

Open all day all wk 11.30am-11pm (Fri-Sat 11.30am-mdnt, Sun noon-11) **Bar Meals** L served 12-2.30 D served 6-9 Av main course £12 ⊕ ST AUSTELL BREWERY ◀ Tribute, Tinners, Proper Job, Cornish Cream. ♀ 8 **Facilities** Children welcome Children's portions Dogs allowed Garden Parking Wi-fi

FOWEY
Map 2 SX15

The Ship Inn

Trafalgar Square PL23 1AZ ☎ 01726 832230
e-mail: shipinnfowey@hotmail.com
dir: *From A30 take B3269 & A390*

One of Fowey's oldest buildings, The Ship was built in 1570 by John Rashleigh, who sailed to the Americas with Walter Raleigh. Given Fowey's riverside position, assume a good choice of fish, including River Fowey mussels, pan-fried scallops with mushrooms and bacon, and Ship Inn fish pie. Other options include beef and Guinness pie or local butcher's sausages and mash. St Austell ales, real fires and a long tradition of genial hospitality add the final touches. As we went to press, a change of hands was about to take place.

Open all day all wk 11am-mdnt (Fri-Sat 11am-1am) ⊕ ST AUSTELL BREWERY ◀ Tribute, Proper Job, Trelawny's ♂ Cornish Rattler, Pear Cider. **Facilities** Children welcome Children's menu Children's portions Family room Dogs allowed

GOLDSITHNEY — Map 2 SW53

The Trevelyan Arms

Fore St TR20 9JU ☎ 01736 710453
e-mail: mikehitchens@hotmail.com
dir: *5m from Penzance. A394 signed to Goldsithney*

The former manor house for Lord Trevelyan, this 17th-century property stands at the centre of the picturesque village just a mile from the sea. It has also been a coaching inn and a bank/post office in its time, but these days is very much the traditional family-run Cornish pub. Food is fresh and locally sourced, offering good value for money. Typical dishes are T-bone steaks, home-made pies and curries, pasta dishes and local fish.

Open all wk 4-mdnt (Sat-Sun noon-mdnt) ⊕ PUNCH TAVERNS ◗ Morland Speckled Hen, Guinness, St Austell Tribute ♂ Green Goblin. **Facilities** Children welcome Children's menu Children's portions Dogs allowed Garden Wi-fi

GUNNISLAKE — Map 3 SX47

The Rising Sun Inn

Calstock Rd PL18 9BX ☎ 01822 832201
dir: *From Tavistock take A390 to Gunnislake. Left after lights into Calstock Rd. Inn approx 500mtrs on right*

Located within walking distance of the High Peak Trail and Black Rocks and overlooking the stunning Tamar Valley, this traditional two-roomed picture-postcard pub is a popular stop for walkers, wildlife enthusiasts and cyclists. In warmer weather, enjoy a pint of real ale in the award-winning gardens or order from the simple menu of locally sourced, home-cooked food that also includes ploughman's and baguettes. Keep an eye out for beer festivals, hog roasts and live music evenings.

Open all wk 12-3 5-11 **Bar Meals** L served all wk 12-3 D served all wk 5-9 Av main course £8 ⊕ FREE HOUSE ◗ Otter, Skinner's Betty Stogs Bitter, Bass, Otter Amber, Skinner's Sprigan, Legend ♂ Stowford Press. **Facilities** Children welcome Children's menu Children's portions Dogs allowed Garden Parking

GUNWALLOE — Map 2 SW62

PICK OF THE PUBS

The Halzephron Inn ⛾

TR12 7QB ☎ 01326 240406 ▤ 01326 241442
e-mail: halzephroninn@tiscali.co.uk
web: www.halzephron-inn.co.uk
dir: *3m S of Helston on A3083, right to Gunwalloe, through village. Inn on left*

Once a haunt of smugglers, The Halzephron Inn stands just 300 yards from the famous South Cornwall footpath and is the only pub on the stretch between Mullion and Porthleven. The name of this ancient inn derives from Als Yfferin, old Cornish for 'cliffs of hell', an appropriate description of its situation on this hazardous stretch of coastline. Originally called The Ship, it changed its name in the late 1950s when it regained its licence after 50 'dry' years. Today it offers a warm welcome, a wide selection of ales including organic Halzephron Gold and whiskies, and meals prepared from fresh local produce. These may be served outside, with views of the countryside or the ocean, or in cosy nooks or the main dining area. Lunch and dinner bring a choice of fresh Cornish fare. Starters of grilled fillet of Cornish mackerel served on a tomato, red onion and chive salad or pan-seared pigeon breast with a beetroot, walnut and balsamic salad might be followed by chargrilled Cornish sirloin steak, hand cut chips, pancetta and peppercorn sauce or pan-seared corn-fed chicken breast with leek risotto and molten Brie.

Open all wk 11-3 6-11 Closed: 25 Dec
Bar Meals L served all wk 12-2 D served all wk 7-9 Av main course £12-£14 **Restaurant** L served all wk 12-2 booking required D served all wk 7-9 booking required Av 3 course à la carte fr £25 ⊕ FREE HOUSE ◗ Sharp's Own, Doom Bar & Special, St Austell Tribute, Skinner's Betty Stogs, Halzephron Gold ♂ Cornish Rattler, Press Gang. ⛾ 8 **Facilities** Children welcome Children's menu Children's portions Family room Dogs allowed Garden Parking Wi-fi

HELSTON — Map 2 SW62

The Queens Arms ★★★ INN **NEW**

Breage TR13 9PD ☎ 01326 573485
e-mail: chris-brazier@btconnect.com
dir: *Village off A394 (Penzance to Helston). Pub adjacent to church*

Built in the 15th-century to house workmen building the church of St Breacca next door, The Queens Arms is a traditional inn in a peaceful village near Helston. Enjoy Cornish ales in the large L-shaped bar area with its beamed ceilings and open log fires, or head for the restaurant where the simple, home-cooked food makes good use of local produce, including vegetables from the pub's own allotment at the back. The pretty beer garden even has a DIY barbecue – all you need do is bring and cook the food. Bedrooms are bright and comfortable.

Open all wk Mon-Thu 11.30-3 5-11.30 (Fri-Sun 11.30-11.30) **Bar Meals** L served all wk 12-2 D served Mon-Sat 6.30-9 Av main course £10 **Restaurant** L served all wk 12-2 D served Mon-Sat 6.30-9 (ex Tue Oct-Mar) ⊕ PUNCH TAVERNS ◗ Sharp's Doom Bar, Betty Stogs. **Facilities** Children welcome Children's menu Children's portions Play area Dogs allowed Garden Parking Wi-fi **Rooms** 2

KINGSAND — Map 3 SX45

The Halfway House Inn ⛾

Fore St PL10 1NA ☎ 01752 822279 ▤ 01752 823146
e-mail: info@halfwayinn.biz
dir: *From Torpoint Ferry or Tamar Bridge follow signs to Mount Edgcumbe*

Set among the narrow lanes and colour-washed houses of a quaint fishing village, this picturesque inn has been licensed since 1850. Its name comes from the fact that the stream at the rear of the premises once marked the border between Devon and Cornwall. The pleasant stone-walled bar with low-beamed ceilings and large central fireplace is ideal for a relaxing pint of real ale. Locally caught seafood is a feature of the small restaurant, whose menu includes a platter of smoked fish to start, and main courses such as garlic monkfish; whole sea bass with orange butter sauce; and sautéed scallops.

Open all wk **Bar Meals** L served all wk 11-2 D served all wk 6-9 **Restaurant** L served all wk 11-2 D served all wk 6-9 ⊕ FREE HOUSE ◗ Sharp's Doom Bar & Own, Guinness, Skinner's ♂ Stowford Press, Old Rosie. ⛾ 12 **Facilities** Children welcome Dogs allowed

LAMORNA   Map 2 SW42

Lamorna Wink

TR19 6XH ☎ 01736 731566
dir: *4m on B3315 towards Land's End, then 0.5m to turn on left*

This oddly-named pub was one of the original Kiddlywinks, a product of the 1830 Beer Act that enabled any householder to buy a liquor licence. Popular with walkers and not far from the Merry Maidens standing stones, the Wink provides a selection of local beers including Skinner's Betty Stogs. A simple menu includes sandwiches, jacket potatoes and fresh local crab. The management have been at the Wink for over thirty years and pride themselves on providing diners with as much local produce as possible.

Open all wk Mon-Sat 11-2.30 (Sun 12-2.30)
Bar Meals L served Mon-Sat 11-2, Sun 12-2 ⊕ FREE HOUSE ◀ Sharp's Doom Bar, Betty Stogs.
Facilities Children welcome Family room Dogs allowed Garden Parking **Notes** ✎

LANLIVERY   Map 2 SX05

PICK OF THE PUBS

The Crown Inn ✕✕✕✕ INN

See Pick of the Pubs on page 84

LOOE   Map 2 SX25

The Ship Inn ★★★ INN ⚑ NEW

Fore St PL13 1AD ☎ 01503 263124
dir: *In town centre*

This lively St Austell Brewery-owned pub with well-equipped bedrooms stands on a corner in the heart of this charming old fishing town, a minute's walk from the working harbour. Locals and tourists enjoy a range of dishes such as home-made fish pie, Tribute ale sausages and mash, cauliflower and broccoli cheese bake, plus burgers, baguettes and jacket potatoes. A quiz is held on Mondays throughout the year and live bands appear here regularly.

Open all day all wk **Bar Meals** Av main course £7 food served all day ⊕ ST AUSTELL BREWERY ◀ St Austell Brewery Tribute, Tinners, HSD ♂ Cornish Rattler.
Facilities Children welcome Children's menu Children's portions Family room Dogs allowed **Rooms** 8

LUDGVAN   Map 2 SW53

White Hart ⚑

Churchtown TR20 8EY ☎ 01736 740574
e-mail: info@whitehartludgvan.co.uk
dir: *From A30 take B3309 at Crowlas*

Built somewhere between 1280 and 1320, the White Hart is one of the oldest pub's in Cornwall. It sits opposite the church and retains the peaceful atmosphere of a bygone era, offering splendid views across St Michael's Mount and Bay. A great selection of real ales is sold from the back of the bar, with different guest ales every month, and the food is as popular as ever, offering snacks to fine dining. Perhaps choose home-made Thai fishcakes; local sausages, mash and onion gravy; grilled sea bass with prawns and lemon butter; or one of the vegetarian options. Now under new ownership.

Open all wk 12-3 6-late **Bar Meals** L served all wk 12-2.30 booking required D served all wk 6-9.30 booking required Av main course £11 **Restaurant** L served all wk 12-2.30 booking required D served all wk 6-9.30 booking required ⊕ PUNCH TAVERNS ◀ Sharp's Doom Bar, Betty Stogs ♂ Thatchers. ⚑ 8 **Facilities** Children welcome Children's portions Dogs allowed Garden Parking

MALPAS   Map 2 SW84

The Heron Inn ⚑

Trenhaile Ter TR1 1SL
☎ 01872 272773   📠 01872 272773
e-mail: theheron@hotmail.co.uk
dir: *From Trafalgar rdbt in Truro exit towards BBC Radio Cornwall, & pub sign. Follow Malpas Rd for 2m into village. Pub on left*

To overlook not one, not two, but three rivers is what helps to make The Heron such an attractive destination, for it's here that the Tresilian and Truro combine to become the Fal. Local produce features in pan-fried trio of haddock, lemon sole and monkfish; pork and St Austell's Tribute ale sausages; and mushroom, spinach and roasted tomato lasagne. There is a terrace area with wonderful views and the perfect place to enjoy a pint of ale from St Austell Brewery. Although walkable in 40 minutes from Truro, mooring the yacht at Malpas Marina is more stylish.

Open all wk 11.30-3 6-11 (Fri-Sat all day (Sun till 5) summer all day every day) **Restaurant** L served Mon-Thu 12-2, Fri-Sun 12-2.30 booking required D served Mon-Sat 6.30-9 booking required ⊕ ST AUSTELL BREWERY ◀ Tribute, IPA, Proper Job ♂ Cornish Rattler. ⚑ 11 **Facilities** Children welcome Children's menu Children's portions Garden Parking Wi-fi

MANACCAN   Map 2 SW72

The New Inn

TR12 6HA ☎ 01326 231323
e-mail: penny@stmartin.wanadoo.co.uk
dir: *7m from Helston*

This thatched village pub, deep in Daphne du Maurier country, dates back to Cromwellian times, although obviously Cromwell forbade his men to drink here. Attractions include the homely bars and large, natural garden full of flowers. At lunchtime you might try a locally made pasty or moules marinière, and in the evening perhaps sea bass and chive fishcakes with tomato coulis and sautéed vegetables, or slow-roasted lamb shank with red wine and redcurrant gravy.

Open all wk 12-3 6-11 (Sat-Sun all day in summer) ⊕ PUNCH TAVERNS ◀ Sharp's Doom Bar ♂ Stowford Press. **Facilities** Children welcome Children's menu Play area Dogs allowed Garden Parking

MARAZION   Map 2 SW53

PICK OF THE PUBS

Godolphin Arms ★★★★ INN

TR17 0EN ☎ 01736 710202   📠 01736 710171
e-mail: enquiries@godolphinarms.co.uk
dir: *From A30 just outside Penzance follow Marazion signs. Pub 1st large building on right in Marazion, opposite St Michael's Mount*

The Godolphin Arms stands atop the sea wall at the end of the causeway to St Michael's Mount. There are superb views across the bay from the traditional bar and beer terrace, as well as from the restaurant and many of the stylishly decorated bedrooms. With direct access to a large sandy beach where at low tide the causeway is revealed, the sea is so close that it splashes at the windows in winter as you watch the fishing boats returning with their catch. Seafood from the Newlyn fish market is listed on the daily specials board, whilst other options include traditional pub favourites like bangers and mash. Cornish steaks and chicken from the chargrill come with potatoes and fresh vegetables, and the Sunday carvery offers a choice of roasts as well as a vegetarian option. Breakfast, which includes everything from a full English to kippers on toast, is the highlight of any stay - unless, of course, you've come for the beer festival!

Open all day all wk 11am-mdnt (Sun noon-mdnt)
Bar Meals L served all wk noon-9 D served all wk noon-9 food served all day **Restaurant** food served all day ⊕ FREE HOUSE ◀ Special, St Austell Tribute, St Austell Tinners ♂ Cornish Rattler. **Facilities** Children welcome Dogs allowed Garden Beer festival Parking **Rooms** 10

PICK OF THE PUBS

The Crown Inn ★★★ INN

Map 2 SX05

PL30 5BT

☎ **01208 872707**

e-mail: thecrown@wagtailinns.com

web: www.wagtailinns.com

dir: *Signed from A390. Follow brown sign about 1.5m W of Lostwithiel*

Located in the historic village of Lanlivery, The Crown Inn is one of Cornwall's oldest pubs. Built in the 12th-century to house the stonemasons constructing the church of St Brevita just behind the pub, it has long served weary travellers using the ancient track known as the Saints' Way. This old coast-to-coast path links Padstow and Fowey and follows 30 miles of valleys, woodlands, pastures, moors and villages.

This ancient pub has been extensively, but sympathetically, restored over the years. The work uncovered a huge, deep well under the porch, which is now covered by glass enabling you to peer down as you walk over it. Needless to say, with such a history, everything about this charming pub oozes tradition - its thick stone walls, granite and slate floors, low beams, open fireplaces, and large, unusual bread oven.

Fowey harbour is only a few miles away, so expect the menu to offer fresh fish and seafood. Other local produce also features strongly and a typical meal might begin with local ham hock and leek terrine with home-made apple chutney and toast or deep-fried mini Fowey crab cakes, cauliflower purée and truffle oil. Main courses could include pea and mushroom risotto with pea shoots and truffle oil; fish pie with steamed broccoli; or Cornish beef, braised in Guinness, caramelised shallots, smoked bacon and fondant potatoes. At lunchtime, enjoy fresh handpicked Fowey crab sandwich or just a proper Cornish pasty from Tregonissey Butchers.

The beers come from Sharp's in Rock and Skinners of Truro, while a reasonably priced wine list offers seven wines by the glass. The pretty garden is a lovely spot to enjoy a summer evening, perhaps with a glass of Pimms. Attractive bedrooms are more contemporary and are impressively appointed.

Open all day all wk **Bar Meals** food served all day booking required Av main course £12 **Restaurant** food served all day booking required Av 3 course à la carte fr £18.85 ⊞ FREE HOUSE ◼ Sharp's Doom Bar, Skinners Betty Stogs, guest ales. **Facilities** Children's menu Children's portions Dogs allowed Garden Parking Wi-fi **Rooms** 9

MEVAGISSEY Map 2 SX04

The Ship Inn ♀

Fore St PL26 6UQ ☎ 01726 843324
dir: *7m S of St Austell*

This 400-year-old inn stands just a few yards from Mevagissey's picturesque fishing harbour, so the choice of fish and seafood dishes comes as no surprise on a menu of home cooked dishes: moules marinière, beer-battered cod, and oven-baked fillet of haddock topped with prawns and Cornish Tiskey cheese. The popular bar has low-beamed ceilings, flagstone floors and a strong nautical feel. The inn is host to local musicians in the winter months.

Open all day all wk **Bar Meals** L served all wk 12-3 D served all wk 6-9 ⊞ ST AUSTELL BREWERY ◀ St Austell Ales ♻ Rattler. ♀ 8 **Facilities** Children welcome Children's menu Dogs allowed

MITCHELL Map 2 SW85

PICK OF THE PUBS

The Plume of Feathers ★★★★ INN

TR8 5AX ☎ 01872 510387 ▤ 01637 839401
e-mail: enquiries@theplume.info
dir: *Exit A30 to Mitchell/Newquay*

This successful destination pub restaurant in the peaceful village of Mitchell dates from the 16th century and has welcomed various historical figures in its time - Sir Walter Raleigh lived nearby and John Wesley preached Methodism from the pillared entrance. Nowadays, with its roaring log fires, beamed ceilings and cosy ambience, it offers a choice of real ales, holds a beer festival every May, and the imaginative kitchen has an excellent reputation for its food. Based on a fusion of modern European and classical British dishes, with an emphasis on fresh fish and the best Cornish ingredients, expect starters such as sticky belly pork with parsnip purée; or home-smoked mackerel with warm potato and spring onion salad; followed by mains of Tresawle farm sausages and bubble and squeak, or braised beef and beer pie. Choose from a selection of desserts served with Cornish clotted cream or ice cream. Seven stylish bedrooms and a new conservatory complete the picture.

Open all day all wk 9am-11/mdnt (25 Dec 11-4) **Bar Meals** food served all day **Restaurant** food served all day ⊞ FREE HOUSE ◀ Doom Bar, John Smith's Smooth, Various Skinner's Ales. **Facilities** Children welcome Play area Dogs allowed Garden Beer festival Parking **Rooms** 7

MITHIAN Map 2 SW75

The Miners Arms NEW

TR5 0QF ☎ 01872 552375
e-mail: minersarms@live.co.uk
dir: *From A30 at Chiverton Cross rdbt take A3075 signed Newquay. At Pendown Cross left onto B3284 signed Perranporth. Left, left again to Mithian*

The curiously light interior of this historic old pub adds yet another layer of mystery to the legends of its past. Over the centuries it has served as a courthouse, a venue for inquests, a smugglers' lair and even a house of ill repute. Relax beneath the low beamed ceilings while admiring the wall paintings of Elizabeth I, and choose from the menu of dishes freshly cooked to order from local produce: mussels and Cornish hake in the Miners fish pie make it a must.

Open all day all wk **Bar Meals** L served all wk 12-2 D served all wk 6-9 booking required Av main course £9 **Restaurant** L served all wk 12-2 D served all wk 6-9 booking required ⊞ PUNCH TAVERNS **Facilities** Children welcome Children's menu Children's portions Dogs allowed Garden Parking

MORWENSTOW Map 2 SS21

PICK OF THE PUBS

The Bush Inn ♀

EX23 9SR ☎ 01288 331242
dir: *Exit A39, 3m N of Kilkhampton, 2nd right into village of Shop. 1.5m to Crosstown. Inn on village green*

The Bush is a 13th-century pub set in an isolated clifftop hamlet, close to a dramatic stretch of the north Cornish coast, a natural haunt for smugglers and wreckers a couple of centuries ago. The historic interior features stone-flagged floors, old stone fireplaces and a 'leper's squint', a tiny window through which food scraps were passed for the needy. Cornish ales are on tap, and menus featuring produce fresh from Devon's larder are served all day, every day. The pub's kitchen garden is becoming productive, and beef comes from the inn's own farm; seafood from home waters does not have far to travel. Game from local shoots is used in robust winter warmers such as venison stew, while summer days are ideal for a bowl of mussels and fresh salads. Among the fish dishes may be found beer-battered pollock or a whole roast John Dory. Desserts such as apple and cherry crumble can be served with clotted cream or local ice cream. The large garden overlooking the beautiful Tidna Valley and Atlantic Ocean has sturdy wooden play equipment for children.

Open all day all wk 11am-12.30am **Bar Meals** L served all wk D served all wk Av main course £12 food served all day **Restaurant** L served all wk D served all wk Fixed menu price fr £8 Av 3 course à la carte fr £19 food served all day ◀ St Austell HSD, Sharp's Doom Bar, Skinner's Betty Stogs, St Austell Tribute ♻ Thatchers & Cornish Orchard. ♀ 9 **Facilities** Children welcome Children's menu Children's portions Play area Dogs allowed Garden Beer festival Parking

MYLOR BRIDGE Map 2 SW83

PICK OF THE PUBS

The Pandora Inn ♀

Restronguet Creek TR11 5ST
☎ 01326 372678 ▤ 01326 378958
e-mail: info@pandorainn.com
dir: *From Truro/Falmouth follow A39, left at Carclew, follow signs to pub*

You can reach this thatched white-painted inn on foot, by bicycle or boat, as well as by car. Its breathtakingly beautiful situation, right on the banks of the Restronguet Creek, affords panoramic views across the water. You can even dine on the pontoon, where up to twenty boats can moor at high tide; inside, the Upper Deck restaurant offers a more traditional experience. The inn itself dates back in part to the 13th century, and its flagstone floors, low-beamed ceilings and thatched roof suggest little has changed. The name stems from the good ship Pandora, sent to Tahiti in 1790 to capture the Bounty mutineers. Sadly it was wrecked and the captain, court-martialled upon his return, reputedly bought the inn. The Pandora was badly damaged by fire in late March 2011. Owners of the building, St Austell Brewery, are committed to re-building the inn as soon as possible. Much of the historic ground floor of the building survived the fire relatively intact and it is hoped to return it to its former glory in 2012.

Open all day all wk 10.30am-11pm Closed: 25 Dec **Bar Meals** L served Sun-Thu 10.30-9, Fri-Sat 10.30-9.30 Av main course £12 ⊞ ST AUSTELL BREWERY ◀ St Austell Tinners Ale, HSD, Bass, Tribute. ♀ 15 **Facilities** Children welcome Children's menu Children's portions Dogs allowed Garden Parking Wi-fi

NEWQUAY Map 2 SW86

The Lewinnick Lodge Bar & Restaurant

Pentire Headland TR7 1NX
☎ 01637 878117 ▤ 01637 870130
e-mail: ask@lewinnick-lodge.info
dir: *From Newquay take Pentire Rd 0.5m, pub on right*

Originally built as a small stone cottage in the late 18th century, the Lodge enjoys stunning views of Cornwall's Atlantic coast. One of only two properties on the rugged Pentire Headland, the pub has established a great reputation, built up by the current owners over the last 20 years, with locals and visitors alike. Menu choices include smoked mackerel pâté and Cornish rarebit to begin, followed by chickpea, squash and oat burger; chargrilled Donald Russell rib-eye steak and hand-cut chips; and Cullumpton Farm chicken breast and roast potatoes. Relax outside on the patios and decks and enjoy those views.

Open all day all wk **Bar Meals** L served all wk 12-5 D served all wk 5-10 food served all day **Restaurant** L served all wk 12-5 D served all wk 5-10 food served all day ⊞ FREE HOUSE ◀ Sharp's Doom Bar, Skinner's Betty Stogs ♻ Cornish Orchards. **Facilities** Children welcome Children's menu Dogs allowed Garden Parking Wi-fi

PAR
Map 2 SX05

The Royal Inn ★★★★ INN ☐

66 Eastcliffe Rd PL24 2AJ
☎ 01726 815601 ☐ 01726 816415
e-mail: info@royal-inn.co.uk
dir: *A3082 Par, follow brown tourist signs for 'Newquay Branch line' or railway station. Pub opp rail station*

Travellers and employees of the Great Western Railway once frequented this 19th-century inn, which was named after a visit by King Edward VII to a local copper mine. These days it's much extended and smartly appointed, with an open-plan bar serving a variety of real ales. Leading off are the dining areas which comprise a cosy beamed room and the Ladybird conservatory. Pub classics include game terrine; battered cod with hand-cut chips; home-made sticky toffee pudding. Other interesting choices include navarin of venison two ways; and wild mushroom and leek risotto. Fifteen comfortable rooms are available.

Open all day all wk 11.30am-11pm (Sun 12-10.30) **Bar Meals** L served all wk 12-2 D served Mon-Sat 6.30-9, Sun 7-9 **Restaurant** L served all wk 12-2 D served Mon-Sat 6.30-9, Sun 7-9 booking required ⊕ FREE HOUSE ◀ Sharp's Doom Bar & Special Ale, Wells Bombardier, Shepherd Neame Spitfire, Cotleigh Barn Owl ♂ Cornish Rattler. ☐ 13 **Facilities** Children welcome Children's menu Dogs allowed Garden Parking Wi-fi **Rooms** 15

PENZANCE
Map 2 SW43

Dolphin Tavern ★★★ INN ☐

Quay St TR18 4BD ☎ 01736 364106
e-mail: dolphin@tiscali.co.uk
dir: *From rail station follow road along harbour. Tavern on corner opposite Scilonian Ferry Terminal*

Judge Jeffries held court in this harbourside pub during the 18th century. Back in 1585, Sir John Hawkins used the tavern as his headquarters when recruiting Cornishmen to fight in the Armada. Said to be the most haunted pub in Cornwall, The Dolphin now serves great home-made food accompanied by a full range of St Austell beers, plus accommodation. Fresh, locally caught fish features on the daily specials board, and the menu offers a tempting selection of meat, vegetarian and children's dishes prepared from the finest Cornish ingredients. Look out for real ale tasting evenings.

Open all day all wk Closed: 25 Dec **Bar Meals** food served all day **Restaurant** food served all day ⊕ ST AUSTELL ◀ St Austell HSD, Tinners Tribute ♂ Cornish Rattler. ☐ 10 **Facilities** Children welcome Children's menu Children's portions Play area Family room Dogs allowed Garden Wi-fi **Rooms** 2

The Turks Head Inn ☐

Chapel St TR18 4AF
☎ 01736 363093 ☐ 01736 360215
e-mail: turks@fsmail.net
dir: *Telephone for directions*

Dating from around 1233, making it Penzance's oldest pub, it was the first in the country to be given the Turks Head name. Sadly, a Spanish raiding party destroyed much of the original building in the 16th century, but an old smugglers' tunnel leading directly to the harbour and priest holes still exist. Typically available are fresh seafood choices like crab, ray wing, gurnard and tandoori monkfish, along with others such as pan-fried venison, chicken stir-fry, pork tenderloin, steaks, mixed grill and salads. A sunny flower-filled garden lies at the rear.

Open all day all wk **Bar Meals** L served all wk 12-2.30 booking required D served all wk 6-9.30 booking required Av main course £8.95 **Restaurant** L served all wk 12-2.30 booking required D served all wk 6-9.30 booking required Fixed menu price fr £12 ⊕ PUNCH TAVERNS ◀ Betty Stogs, 6X, Sharp's Doom Bar, Guest ale ♂ Thatchers. ☐ 22 **Facilities** Children welcome Children's menu Children's portions Family room Dogs allowed Garden

PERRANUTHNOE
Map 2 SW52

PICK OF THE PUBS

The Victoria Inn ★★★ INN ◎

TR20 9NP ☎ 01736 710309
e-mail: enquiries@victoriainn-penzance.co.uk
dir: *Off A394 (Penzance to Helston road), signed Perranuthnoe*

Offering easy access to a safe sandy beach and the coastal footpath, alongside imaginative pub food, this striking, pink-washed village inn is a favoured summer destination for rest and refreshment, so arrive early for a seat in the Mediterranean-style patio garden. Dating from the 12th century it is reputedly Cornwall's oldest inn. The typically Cornish stone-walled bar, adorned with various seafaring and fishing memorabilia, is popular with famished coast path walkers and families strolling up from the beach. Food is taken seriously here, with chef-patron Stewart Eddy cooking the best fish, seafood and seasonal ingredients with care and simplicity. The result is earthy, flavoursome dishes that pack a punch. At dinner, follow ham hock and green pea soup, with rib-eye steak with real chips, onion rings and aioli, and dark chocolate and orange pot. Add traditional lunch dishes and Sunday roasts, tip-top Doom Bar Bitter on tap, and two individually decorated, en suite bedrooms, and you have a cracking Cornish coastal gem.

Open 12-2 6.30-11 (all day Jun-Sep) Closed: 25-26 Dec, 1 Jan, Sun eve & Mon (off season) **Bar Meals** L served Mon-Sat 12-2, Sun 12-3 booking required D served all wk 6.30-11 booking required Av main course £15 **Restaurant** L served Mon-Sat 12-2, Sun 12-3 booking required D served all wk 6.30-11 booking required Av 3 course à la carte fr £25 ⊕ FREE HOUSE ◀ Doom Bar, Tribute ♂ Cornish Orchards. **Facilities** Children welcome Children's menu Children's portions Dogs allowed Garden Parking Wi-fi **Rooms** 2

PHILLEIGH
Map 2 SW83

Roseland Inn NEW

TR2 5NB ☎ 01872 580254
dir: *From Truro take A39 towards Falmouth. Turn left onto B3289 towards St Mawes. Turn left at sharp right bend for Philleigh*

Phil and Debbie Heslip take pride in the quality of their home-prepared modern British cooking at this highly appealing traditional rural 16th-century inn. The character of the interior owes much to the low-beamed ceilings, brassware, paintings and prints. Phil brews on-site his ornithologically themed Cornish Shag, Chough to Bits and High-as-a-Kite beers. So, in winter cosy up to the fire for a drink or a meal prepared using the best of local Cornish produce, or in warmer weather head outside to the picnic tables. Just to the west is the famous King Harry Ferry over the River Fal.

Open all wk 11-3 6-11.30 **Bar Meals** L served all wk 12-2.30 D served all wk 6-9 **Restaurant** L served all wk 12-2.30 D served all wk 6-9 ⊕ PUNCH TAVERNS ◀ Betty Stogs, Micro-brewed ale on site ♂ Stowford Press. **Facilities** Children welcome Children's menu Children's portions Dogs allowed Garden Parking Wi-fi

POLKERRIS
Map 2 SX05

The Rashleigh Inn

PL24 2TL ☎ 01726 813991 ☐ 01726 815619
e-mail: jonspode@aol.com
web: www.rashleighinnpolkerris.co.uk
dir: *Off A3082 outside Fowey*

Overlooking pretty Polkerris beach, this 300-year-old, stone-built building was once a boathouse and coastguard station. There are panoramic views across St Austell Bay from the multi-level heated and south west-facing terrace. In the bar there's an excellent real ale selection, with real cider and local organic soft drinks are also on offer. There's superb food too, using the best of locally sourced ingredients (suppliers listed on the menu): slow roasted belly pork with cider and mustard jus; venison and redcurrant burgers; River Fowey mussels steamed in cider and leeks.

Open all day all wk **Bar Meals** L served all wk 12-2 D served all wk 6-9 Av main course £8.95 **Restaurant** L served all wk 12-2 booking required D served all wk 6-9 booking required Fixed menu price fr £8.95 ⊕ FREE HOUSE ◀ Sharp's Doom Bar, Timothy Taylor Landlord, Skinner's Betty Stogs, St Austell HSD, Otter Bitter ♂ Stowford Press, Addlestones. **Facilities** Children welcome Children's menu Children's portions Dogs allowed Garden Parking

POLPERRO   Map 2 SX25

Old Mill House Inn ▾

Mill Hill PL13 2RP ☎ 01503 272362
e-mail: enquiries@oldmillhouseinn.co.uk
dir: *Telephone for directions*

In the heart of historic Polperro, this old inn was once the house and storage area of a grain mill built in the early 17th century. It has survived serious flood damage in the past – photographs recording the disaster can be seen on the walls. Here you can sample well-kept local ales and cider beside a log fire in the bar, or sit out over lunch in the riverside garden during fine weather. Local ingredients, with an emphasis on freshly caught fish, are the foundation of dishes on the restaurant menu. Traditional roasts are served on Sundays, and a beer festival is held on the first weekend in October.

Open all day all wk 10am-12.30am (Sun 10am-11.30pm) **Bar Meals** L served all wk 10-2.30 D served all wk 5.30-9 **Restaurant** D served all wk 5.30-9 ⊕ FREE HOUSE ◀ Skinner's, Skinner's Mill House Ale, Sharp's, Guest ales Ŏ Stowford Press, Old Rosie. **Facilities** Children welcome Children's menu Children's portions Dogs allowed Garden Beer festival Parking Wi-fi

PORT GAVERNE   Map 2 SX08

PICK OF THE PUBS

Port Gaverne Hotel ★★ HL ▾

PL29 3SQ ☎ 01208 880244   ▤ 01208 880151
e-mail: graham@port-gaverne-hotel.co.uk
dir: *Signed from B3314, S of Delabole via B3267 on E of Port Isaac*

This delightful 17th-century inn stands just up the lane from the secluded cove where women once loaded ships with slate from the great quarry at Delabole. All that ended after 1893, when the coming of the railway put paid to the port's prosperity. A meandering building with plenty of period detail, the hotel has long association with fishing and smuggling. As you might expect, locally supplied produce includes plenty of fresh fish, and it appears on all the menus. For example, besides the selection of ploughman's, you might fancy a starter of smoked mackerel pâté with hot toast and salad leaves, followed by Doom Bar battered fish of the day with chips and peas; smoked haddock, Mozzarella and spring onion fishcakes; or home-cooked ham with fried eggs and chips. Walkers from the Heritage Coast Path can pause for a pint in the comfortable bar, or in the small beer garden.

Open all day all wk **Bar Meals** L served all wk 12-2.30 D served all wk 6-9 Av main course £9.50 **Restaurant** D served all wk 7-9 Av 3 course à la carte fr £30 ⊕ FREE HOUSE ◀ Sharp's Doom Bar, Bass, St Austell Tribute. ▾ 9 **Facilities** Children welcome Children's menu Children's portions Dogs allowed Garden Parking Wi-fi **Rooms** 14

PORTHLEVEN   Map 2 SW62

The Ship Inn ▾

TR13 9JS ☎ 01326 564204   ▤ 01326 564204
e-mail: cjoakden@yahoo.co.uk
dir: *From Helston follow signs to Porthleven, 2.5m. On entering village continue to harbour. Take W road by side of harbour to inn*

Dating from the 17th century, this smugglers' inn is actually built into the cliffs, and is approached by a flight of stone steps. During the winter, two log fires warm the interior, while the flames of a third flicker in the separate Smithy children's room. Expect a good selection of locally caught fish and seafood, such as crab and prawn mornay, or the smoked fish platter, all smoked in Cornwall. The pub has declared itself a 'chip-free zone'.

Open all day all wk 11.30am-11.30pm (Sun noon-10.30) **Bar Meals** L served all wk 12-2 D served all wk 6.30-9 ⊕ FREE HOUSE ◀ Courage Best, Sharp's Doom Bar & Special, Guest ales Ŏ Cornish Orchard. ▾ 8 **Facilities** Children welcome Children's menu Family room Dogs allowed Garden

PORTREATH   Map 2 SW64

Basset Arms

Tregea Ter TR16 4NG ☎ 01209 842077
e-mail: bassettarms@btconnect.com
dir: *From Redruth take B3300 to Portreath. Pub on left near seafront*

Tin-mining and shipwreck paraphernalia adorn the low-beamed interior of this early 19th-century Cornish stone cottage, built as a pub to serve harbour workers. At one time it served as a mortuary for ill-fated seafarers, so there are plenty of ghost stories! The menu makes the most of local seafood, such as mussels and fries, and home-made fish pie, but also provides a wide selection of alternatives, including half chicken in barbecue sauce; 12oz gammon steak; curry of the day; and salads including crab, when available. Wash down your meal with a pint of Skinner's real ale.

Open all day all wk 11am-11pm (Fri-Sat 11am-mdnt, Sun 11-10.30) **Bar Meals** L served all wk 12-2 D served all wk 6-9 **Restaurant** L served all wk 12-2 D served all wk 6-9 ⊕ FREE HOUSE ◀ Sharp's Doom Bar, Skinner's Real Ales. **Facilities** Children welcome Children's menu Children's portions Play area Dogs allowed Garden Parking

RUAN LANIHORNE   Map 2 SW84

The Kings Head

TR2 5NX ☎ 01872 501263
e-mail: contact@kings-head-roseland.co.uk
dir: *3m from Tregony Bridge on A3078*

Expect a warm welcome at this traditional country pub set deep in the Roseland countryside. Roaring winter fires, beamed ceilings and mulled wine contrasts with summer days relaxing on the terrace with a jug of Pimms, a pint of Betty Stogs or Rattler Cornish cider. Whatever the time of year, the chef responds with seasonal dishes using the best of local produce, ranging from Cornish

smoked mackerel pâté, goat's cheese, beetroot and butternut salad to calves' liver and bacon, red onion gravy and mash. Look out for the signature dish, too - slow-roasted Terras Ruan duckling with pepper sauce.

Open 12-2.30 6-11 Closed: Sun eve, Mon (Oct-Etr) **Restaurant** L served all wk 12.30-2 booking required D served all wk 6.30-9 booking required Av 3 course à la carte fr £20 ⊕ FREE HOUSE ◀ Skinner's Kings Ruan, Cornish Knocker, Betty Stogs Ŏ Cornish Rattler. **Facilities** Children welcome Dogs allowed Garden Parking

ST AGNES   Map 3 SW75

PICK OF THE PUBS

Driftwood Spars ★★★★ GA ▾

Trevaunance Cove TR5 0RT ☎ 01872 552428
e-mail: info@driftwoodspars.co.uk
web: www.driftwoodspars.co.uk
dir: *A30 onto B3285, through St Agnes, down steep hill, left at Peterville Inn, onto road signed Trevaunance Cove*

Around here the ancient Celtic landscape of dramatic cliffs, crashing surf, small fields and moorland abounds with legend and intrigue; in spring, watch for the Giant Bolster who rears his head in search of the lovely maid St Agnes. Take refuge in this family-run pub which occupies a 300-year-old tin miners' store, chandlery and sail loft, complete with its own smugglers' tunnel; it takes its name from spars salvaged from nearby shipwrecks. Altogether this award-winning establishment comprises fifteen bedrooms; a dining room with sea view; two beer gardens; three bars sparkling with real fires, old brass and lanterns; a micro-brewery; and a shop. Two of the eight ales brewed are on sale at any one time, alongside guests and a 40-bin wine list. On the menu seafood figures strongly, in dishes such as Cornish ray wing with black olive and caper butter. Other local products can be found in grilled Cornish goat's cheese salad with roasted beetroot, and braised rump of Cornish beef with dauphinoise potatoes. Ice creams from Callestick Farm come in a variety of flavours.

Open all day all wk 11-11 (Fri-Sat 11-1am, 25 Dec 11am-2pm) **Bar Meals** L served all wk 12-2.30 D served all wk 6.30-9.30 (winter 6.30-8.30) Av main course £10 **Restaurant** L served Sun 12-2.30 booking required D served all wk 7-9, (winter Thu-Sat 7-8.30) booking required Av 3 course à la carte fr £25 ⊕ FREE HOUSE ◀ Blue Hills Bitter, Tribute, Betty Stogs, Doom Bar, Red Mission, Lou's Brew Ŏ Cornish Rattler, Thatchers. ▾ 35 **Facilities** Children welcome Children's menu Children's portions Dogs allowed Garden Beer festival Parking Wi-fi **Rooms** 15

ST AGNES (ISLES OF SCILLY)   Map 2 SV80

Turks Head

TR22 0PL ☎ 01720 422434
dir: By boat or helicopter to St Mary's & boat on to St Agnes

Named after the 16th-century Turkish pirates who arrived from the Barbary Coast, the Turks Head is Britain's most southwesterly inn. Noted for its atmosphere and superb location overlooking the island quay, this former coastguard boathouse is packed with fascinating model ships and maritime photographs. Lunchtime brings soup, salads and open rolls, while evening dishes might include blackened swordfish steak in Cajun spices, or sirloin steak with all the trimmings.

Open all wk Closed: Nov-Feb ⊕ FREE HOUSE ◖ Skinner's Betty Stogs, Sharp's Doom Bar, Ales of Scilly, Scuppered, Turks Ale. **Facilities** Children welcome Dogs allowed Garden

ST BREWARD   Map 2 SX07

The Old Inn & Restaurant ♓

Churchtown, Bodmin Moor PL30 4PP
☎ 01208 850711 ▤ 01208 851671
e-mail: theoldinn@macace.net
web: www.theoldinnandrestaurant.co.uk
dir: A30 to Bodmin. 16m, right just after Temple, follow signs to St Breward. B3266 (Bodmin to Camelford road) turn to St Breward, follow brown signs

On the edge of Bodmin Moor, this is not just Cornwall's highest inn, it's one of the oldest too, having been built in the 11th century for monks to live in. You can see ancient granite fireplaces and sloping ceilings in the bars, where Sharp's Doom Bar and Cornish Orchard cider are in the line-up. It is owned and run by local man Darren Wills, the latest licensee in its 1,000-year history. Mixed grills, over 25 daily changing specials, and all-day Sunday carvery are served in the bars, spacious restaurant or large garden.

Open all day all wk **Bar Meals** L served Sun-Fri 11-2, Sat 11-9 D served Sun-Fri 6-9, Sat 11-9 Av main course £9.95 **Restaurant** L served Mon-Fri 11-2, Sat-Sun 12-9 booking required D served Mon-Fri 6-9, Sat-Sun 12-9 booking required ⊕ FREE HOUSE ◖ Sharp's Doom Bar & Special, Guest ales ♓ Sharp's Orchard Cider. ♓ 15 **Facilities** Children welcome Children's menu Children's portions Family room Dogs allowed Garden Parking Wi-fi

ST EWE   Map 2 SW94

The Crown Inn

PL26 6EY ☎ 01726 843322 ▤ 01726 844720
e-mail: linda@thecrowninn737.fsnet.co.uk
dir: From St Austell take B3273. At Tregiskey x-rds turn right. St Ewe signed on right

The Crown's chef John Nelson co-founded and helped to restore the famous 'Lost Gardens of Heligan', just a mile from this delightful 16th-century inn. Hanging baskets add plenty of brightness and colour to the outside, while indoors you'll find well-kept St Austell ales complementing an extensive menu and daily specials. Expect cod in beer batter, local steaks, rack of lamb, and liver and bacon among other favourites. Try a glass of Polmassick wine from the vineyard only half a mile away.

Open all wk ⊕ ST AUSTELL BREWERY ◖ Tribute, Tinners, guest ale ♓ Cornish Rattler. **Facilities** Children welcome Children's menu Children's portions Play area Family room Dogs allowed Garden Parking

ST IVES   Map 2 SW54

The Sloop Inn ★★★ INN NEW

The Wharf TR26 1LP
☎ 01736 796584 ▤ 01736 793322
e-mail: sloopinn@btinternet.com
dir: On St Ives harbour by middle slipway

Right on the harbourside at the heart of old St Ives, parts of the inn date back 700 years. Slate floors, beamed ceilings and nautical artefacts dress some of the several bars and dining areas; the cellar bar has an exhibition of work by artists of the famous St Ives School of Painting. The cobbled forecourt is an unbeatable spot for people and harbour watching; sup a pint of Doom Bar and share in the delights of the excellent menu that is strong on local seafood, from a thick chowder to trio of gurnard, haddock and lemon sole. Most of the comfortably appointed accommodation rooms overlook the bay.

Open all day all wk **Bar Meals** L served all wk 12-3 D served all wk 6-10 **Restaurant** D served Mon-Sat 6-10 booking required ⊕ ENTERPRISE INNS ◖ Sharp's Doom Bar ♓ Thatchers Gold. **Facilities** Children allowed Wi-fi **Rooms** 18

The Watermill

Lelant Downs, Hayle TR27 6LQ ☎ 01736 757912
e-mail: watermill@btconnect.com
dir: Exit A30 at junct for St Ives/A3074, turn left at 2nd mini rdbt

Set in extensive gardens on the old St Ives coach road, with glorious valley views towards Trencrom Hill, The Watermill is a cosy, family friendly pub and restaurant created in the 18th-century Lelant Mill. The old mill machinery is still in place and the iron waterwheel still turns, gravity fed by the mill stream. Downstairs is the old beamed bar and wood-burning stove, while upstairs

in the open-beamed mill loft is the atmospheric restaurant where steaks and fish (sea bass, sardines and mackerel perhaps) are specialities.

The Watermill

Open all day all wk noon-11 **Bar Meals** L served all wk 12-2.30 D served all wk 6-9 **Restaurant** D served all wk 6-9 booking required ⊕ FREE HOUSE ◖ Sharp's Doom Bar, Skinner's Betty Stogs, Guest ales ♓ Cornish Rattler. **Facilities** Children welcome Children's menu Play area Dogs allowed Garden Parking

ST JUST (NEAR LAND'S END)   Map 2 SW33

PICK OF THE PUBS

Star Inn

TR19 7LL ☎ 01736 788767
dir: Telephone for directions

Plenty of tin mining and fishing stories are told at this traditional Cornish pub, located in the town of St Just, near Land's End. It dates back a few centuries, and was reputedly built to house workmen constructing the 15th-century church. John Wesley is believed to have been among the Star's more illustrious guests over the years, but these days the pub is most likely to be recognised for having featured in several television and film productions due to its character and immense charm. A choice of local beers is served, but there is no food. Monday night is folk night, and there's live music on Thursdays and Saturdays, too, in a whole range of styles.

Open all day all wk 11am-12.30am ◖ St Austell HSD, Tinners Ale, Tribute, Dartmoor ♓ Cornish Rattler. **Facilities** Children welcome Family room Dogs allowed Garden Notes ✉

The Wellington ★★ INN

Market Square TR19 7HD
☎ 01736 787319 ▤ 01736 787906
e-mail: wellingtonhotel@msn.com
dir: Take A30 to Penzance, then A3071 W of Penzance to St Just

Standing in the market square of an historic mining town, this family-run, stunning granite inn makes an ideal base for exploring the spectacular beaches and countryside - walking, climbing and bird-watching. Low ceilings, solid stonework and a secluded walled garden help evoke the atmosphere of Cornwall as it once was. St Austell beers and Cornish Rattler cider are served in the bar, while the kitchen specialises in fresh local produce. There are a selection of steaks, fish of the day from the specials board and the popular Welly burger. Accommodation is available.

Open all day all wk **Bar Meals** L served all wk 12-2 D served all wk 6-9 (winter 6-8.30) Av main course £8 **Restaurant** D served all wk 6-9 (summer) ST AUSTELL BREWERY St Austell Tinners, St Austell Tribute, HSD Cornish Rattler. **Facilities** Children welcome Children's menu Children's portions Play area Dogs allowed Garden Wi-fi **Rooms** 11

ST MAWES Map 2 SW83

PICK OF THE PUBS

The Victory Inn

Victory Hill TR2 5DQ
01326 270324 01326 270238
e-mail: contact@victory-inn.co.uk
web: www.victory-inn.co.uk
dir: *Take A3078 to St Mawes. Pub up Victory Steps adjacent to harbour*

Located near the harbour, this friendly fishermen's local is named after Nelson's flagship but adopts a modern approach to its daily lunch and dinner menus. You may eat downstairs in the traditional bar, or in the modern and stylish first-floor Seaview Restaurant, with a terrace that looks across the town's rooftops to the harbour and the River Fal. High on the list of ingredients is fresh seafood - all from Cornish waters, of course - the choice changing virtually daily to include crab risotto; fisherman's pie; and beer-battered cod and hand-cut chips, with chicken breast cordon bleu; lamb shank provençale; and curry or casserole of the day among the other favourites. Children are provided with paper, crayons and their own menu; dogs are given treats too. Wines are all carefully chosen and excellent in quality, as are the real ales from Cornwall's own Roseland, Sharp's and Skinners breweries. There is outside seating with views over the harbour.

Open all day all wk 11am-mdnt **Bar Meals** L served all wk 12-3 D served all wk 6-9.30 booking required **Restaurant** L served all wk 12-3 D served all wk 6-9.15 booking required PUNCH TAVERNS Sharp's, Bass, Wadworth 6X, Roseland Brewery Cornish Shag, Skinner's Betty Stogs. **Facilities** Children welcome Children's menu Children's portions Dogs allowed Garden Wi-fi

ST MAWGAN Map 2 SW86

PICK OF THE PUBS

The Falcon Inn ★★★★ INN

TR8 4EP 01637 860225 01637 860884
e-mail: thefalconinnstmawgan@gmail.com
web: www.thefalconinnstmawgan.co.uk
dir: *From A30 (8m W of Bodmin) follow signs to Newquay/St Mawgan Airport. After 2m right into village, pub at bottom of hill*

You'll find this pub nestling in the sheltered Vale of Lanherne, in a village of outstanding tranquility and natural beauty. Nearby, traces of a 6th-century Celtic monastery can be found in what became the Arundel family manor house – today a convent housing nuns and friars. The wisteria-covered Falcon has a large attractive garden, magnificent magnolia tree and cobbled courtyard. The interior is cosy and relaxed, with flagstone floors and log fires in winter; plus comfortable accommodation is available. Beers from St Austell Brewery are augmented by Rattler cider, and a dozen wines are served by the glass. At lunchtime home-made soups, sandwiches, jacket potatoes, and main courses such as chicken and mushroom pie are the order of the day. An à la carte evening menu is served in the more formal restaurant. Main courses always include fresh fish options, and vegetarians are well catered for. Two en suite bedrooms are available.

Open all wk 11-3 6-11 (Jul-Aug open all day) Closed: 25 Dec (open 12-2) **Bar Meals** L served all wk 12-2 D served all wk 6-9 **Restaurant** L served all wk 12-2 D served all wk 6-9 ST AUSTELL BREWERY St Austell HSD, Tinners Ale, Tribute, Proper Job IPA Cornish Rattler. 12 **Facilities** Children welcome Children's menu Children's portions Dogs allowed Garden Parking Wi-fi **Rooms** 2

ST MERRYN Map 2 SW87

PICK OF THE PUBS

The Cornish Arms

Churchtown PL28 8ND
01841 532700 01841 532942
e-mail: reservations@rickstein.com
dir: *From Padstow follow signs for St Merryn then Churchtown*

When Rick and Jill Stein took over this ancient village pub, situated across the road from the parish church and overlooking a peaceful valley, the locals feared their treasured boozer would become a fancy gastro-pub. Luckily, the Steins' loved their local pub just as it was, a traditional pub, replete with slate floors, beams and roaring log fires, and have kept the food offering equally traditional, the chalkboard listing simple pub classics prepared from fresh produce. Wash down ham, egg and chips, battered cod with chips and mushy peas, or a fresh crab salad with a decent pint of St Austell Tribute ale, or a glass of Chalky's Bite, named after his much-missed rough-haired Jack Russell.

Open all day all wk 11am-11pm **Bar Meals** L served all wk 12-3 D served all wk 6-8.30 Av main course £9 **Restaurant** L served all wk 12-3 D served all wk 6-8.30 Av 3 course à la carte fr £19.50 ST AUSTELL BREWERY St Austell Tribute, Proper Job, Tinners, Cornish Rattler. 15 **Facilities** Children welcome Children's menu Children's portions Dogs allowed Garden Parking

SALTASH Map 3 SX45

The Crooked Inn ★★★★ INN

Stoketon Cottage, Trematon PL12 4RZ
01752 848177 01752 843203
e-mail: info@crooked-inn.co.uk
dir: *Telephone for directions*

Overlooking the lush Lyher Valley and run by the same family for 25 years, this delightful inn once housed staff from Stoketon Manor, whose ruins lie on the other side of the courtyard. It is set in 10 acres of lawns and woodland, yet only 15 minutes from Plymouth. There is an extensive menu including evening specials with plenty of fresh fish and vegetarian dishes. The children's playground has friendly animals, swings, slides, a trampoline and a treehouse. Spacious bedrooms are individually designed and decorated.

Open all day all wk Closed: 25 Dec **Bar Meals** L served all wk 11-2.30 D served all wk 6-9.30 FREE HOUSE Hicks Special Draught, Dartmoor Jail Ale, Skinner's Thatchers Gold. **Facilities** Children welcome Children's menu Play area Dogs allowed Garden Parking Wi-fi **Rooms** 18

SENNEN   Map 2 SW32

The Old Success Inn

Sennen Cove TR19 7DG
☎ **01736 871232**   🖹 **01736 871457**
e-mail: oldsuccess@staustellbrewery.co.uk
dir: *Telephone for directions*

Once the haunt of smugglers and now a focal point for the Sennen Lifeboat crew, this 17th-century inn enjoys a glorious location overlooking Cape Cornwall. Its name comes from the days when fishermen gathered here to count their catch and share out their 'successes'. Fresh local seafood is to the fore, and favourites include cod in Doom Bar batter, steaks, chilli, and vegetable lasagne. Live music every Saturday night in the bar. Change of hands in Oct 2010.

Open all wk Mon-Sat 10am-11pm (Sun 12-10.30) ⊕ ST AUSTELL BREWERY ◀ Tribute, HSD, Proper Job ♂ Rattler. **Facilities** Children welcome Children's menu Dogs allowed Garden Parking

TINTAGEL   Map 2 SX08

The Port William

Trebarwith Strand PL34 0HB
☎ **01840 770230**   🖹 **01840 770936**
e-mail: theportwilliam@btinternet.com
dir: *Off B3263 between Camelford & Tintagel, pub signed*

Occupying one of the best locations in Cornwall, this former harbourmaster's house lies directly on the coastal path, 50 yards from the sea. There is an entrance to a smugglers' tunnel at the rear of the ladies' toilet! Focus on the daily-changing specials board for such dishes as artichoke and roast pepper salad, warm smoked trout platter, and spinach ricotta tortelloni. There has been a change of hands.

Open all wk Mon-Sat 10am-11pm ⊕ ST AUSTELL BREWERY ◀ Tribute, Tinners, Guest ales ♂ Cornish Rattler. **Facilities** Children welcome Family room Dogs allowed Garden Parking

TORPOINT   Map 3 SX45

PICK OF THE PUBS

Edgcumbe Arms ☘

Cremyll PL10 1HX ☎ **01752 822294**
dir: *Telephone for directions*

The inn, now under new ownership, dates from the 15th century and is located right on the Tamar estuary, next to the National Trust Park, close to the foot ferry from Plymouth. Views from the bow window seats and waterside terrace are glorious, taking in Drakes Island, the Royal William Yard and the marina. Real ales from St Austell like Proper Job, plus Cornish Rattler cider, and quality home-cooked food (the same menu is offered throughout) are served in a series of rooms, which are full of character with American oak panelling and stone flagged floors. The inn has a first-floor function room with sea views, and a courtyard garden.

Open all day all wk 11am-11pm Closed: Nov, Jan-Feb Mon-Tue eve **Bar Meals** Av main course £7.95 food served all day **Restaurant** food served all day ⊕ ST AUSTELL BREWERY ◀ Tribute HS, Proper Job ♂ Cornish Rattler. ☘ 10 **Facilities** Children welcome Children's menu Children's portions Dogs allowed Garden Parking Wi-fi

TREBARWITH   Map 2 SX08

PICK OF THE PUBS

The Mill House Inn

See Pick of the Pubs on opposite page

TREBURLEY   Map 3 SX37

PICK OF THE PUBS

The Springer Spaniel

See Pick of the Pubs on page 92

TREGADILLETT   Map 3 SX28

Eliot Arms

PL15 7EU ☎ **01566 772051**
dir: *From Launceston take A30 towards Bodmin. Then follow brown signs to Tregadillett*

The extraordinary decor in this charming creeper-clad coaching inn, dating back to 1625, includes Masonic regalia, horse brasses and grandfather clocks. It was believed to have been a Masonic lodge for Napoleonic prisoners, and even has its own friendly ghost! Customers can enjoy real fires in winter and lovely hanging baskets in summer. Food, based on locally sourced meat and fresh fish and shellfish caught off the

Cornish coast, is served in the bar or bright and airy restaurant. Expect home-made soups, pie and curry of the day; steak and chips; chargrills; and home-made vegetarian dishes.

Open all day all wk 11.30-11 (Fri-Sat 11.30am-mdnt, Sun noon-10.30) ⊕ FREE HOUSE ◀ Sharp's Doom Bar, Courage Best. **Facilities** Children welcome Family room Dogs allowed Parking

TRESCO (ISLES OF SCILLY)   Map 2 SV81

PICK OF THE PUBS

The New Inn ✦✦✦✦ INN ◉ ☘

New Grimsby TR24 0QQ
☎ **01720 422844**   🖹 **01720 423200**
e-mail: newinn@tresco.co.uk
dir: *By New Grimsby Quay*

As the sole survivor of the once-thirteen island pubs this has to be, as landlord Robin Lawson says, the 'Best Pub on Tresco'. Everywhere you look is maritime history, much of it, such as the signboard, mahogany bar and wall-planking, salvaged from wrecks. An AA Rosette recognises the quality of food in the quiet restaurant, the livelier Driftwood Bar, the Pavillion, and outside, all singing from the same menu. Accompany a lunchtime grilled pollock and chips with a pint of Scillonian real ale or Cornish Rattler cider. For dinner, seek out salmon fishcakes with spinach and white wine cream; braised Cornish pork sausages with creamed mash and onion gravy; or roasted red pepper, pear, walnut and goat's cheese gnocchi. Traditional roasts are served on Sundays. Some of the comfortable rooms available have ocean views. There are beer festivals in mid May and early September. A 10:10 signatory, the New Inn is aiming for a ten per cent carbon emissions cut this year.

Open all wk all day (Apr-Oct) phone for winter opening **Bar Meals** L served all wk 12-2.15 D served all wk 6.30-9 Av main course £13 **Restaurant** D served all wk 6.30-9 booking required Av 3 course à la carte fr £21 ⊕ TRESCO ESTATE ◀ Skinner's Betty Stogs Bitter, Tresco Tipple, Ales of Scilly Scuppered & Firebrand, St Austell IPA ♂ Cornish Rattler, Pear Rattler. ☘ 13 **Facilities** Children welcome Children's menu Children's portions Garden Beer festival Wi-fi **Rooms** 16

PICK OF THE PUBS

The Mill House Inn

TREBARWITH   Map 2 SX08

PL34 0HD
☎ **01840 770200**   📠 **01840 770647**
e-mail:
management@themillhouseinn.co.uk
web: www.themillhouseinn.co.uk
dir: *From Tintagel take B3263 S, right
after Trewarmett to Trebarwith Strand.
Pub 0.5m on right*

The surfing beach at Trebarwith Strand, half a mile from The Mill House, is one of the finest in Cornwall. Also close by is Tintagel Castle, famously associated with the legend of King Arthur, standing on its 'island' at the bottom of a neighbouring valley. This charming 18th-century corn mill dates from 1760, and was still working in the late 1930s. Then it became successively a private house, a guest house and finally, in 1960, a pub. Set in seven acres of wooded gardens on the north Cornish coast, it's a beautifully atmospheric stone building, with log fires in the residents' lounge and an informally furnished, slate-floored bar, where wooden tables and chapel chairs help create a relaxed, family-friendly feel. Locally brewed real ales are furnished by Sharp's, Skinner's and Tintagel, and ciders from Cornish Orchards and Rattler haven't travelled far either. The cosmopolitan wine list is to everyone's taste, and features an especially good choice of half bottles. Lunches, evening drinks and barbecues are particularly enjoyable out on the attractive split-level terraces, while dinner in the restaurant over the millstream is an intimate and romantic experience. Regularly changing dishes use the best fresh fish, meat, vegetables and other ingredients that North Cornwall can supply. The bar menu lists home-made meatball linguine in a spicy tomato and basil sauce; or Cornish crab salad with a lemon and dill dressing. A typical dinner might start with harissa marinated baby monkfish with a courgette and chick pea falafel. A Cornish duck breast and home-made duck black pudding with smoked Sarladaise potatoes and cherry jus may remind you of France; so could the cheeseboard were it not for the fact that they too are local. Carpaccio of mango, chilli and pineapple sorbet with coconut tuile is representative of the exquisite desserts.

Open all day all wk 11-11 (Fri-Sat 11am-mdnt, Sun noon-10.30)
Bar Meals L served Mon-Sat 12-2.30, Sun 12-3 D served all wk 6.30-8.30
Restaurant D served all wk 7-9
🍺 FREE HOUSE ◀ Sharp's Doom Bar, Skinner's Cornish Knocker, Tintagel Brewery Harbour Special 🍏 Cornish Orchards, Cornish Rattler.
Facilities Children's menu Children's portions Play area Family room Dogs allowed Garden Parking Wi-fi

PICK OF THE PUBS

The Springer Spaniel

TREBURLEY Map 3 SX37

PL15 9NS
☎ **01579 370424**
e-mail:
enquiries@thespringerspaniel.org.uk
web: www.thespringerspaniel.org.uk
dir: *On A388 halfway between Launceston & Callington*

The creeper-clad walls of this 200 year-old free house shelter a cosy bar with high-backed wooden settles, farmhouse-style chairs and a wood-burning stove. You can bring your dog, join in with the chat, read the papers or cast an eye over the many books in the snug. Owner-managers Roger and Lavinia Halliday aim to provide the best that a traditional Cornish hostelry can offer - reliable ales, delicious food, fine wines and friendly service.

The restaurant is full of plants and flowers, with flickering candles in the evenings adding to the romantic atmosphere. In summer the landscaped, sheltered garden is a great place to relax and enjoy the sunshine with a pint of St Austell Tribute. The fully stocked bar also includes other local brews and guest ales, as well as a wine list designed to complement the food on offer.

Food is a big draw here, with beef from the owners' neighbouring organic farm supplementing ingredients from the best local suppliers. Bar lunches range from the ever-popular ploughman's, and a selection of hot filled foccacias; to pub favourites like organic beef sausages and mash. Meanwhile a three-course meal might begin with warm butternut squash salad or game and bacon terrine, before moving on to grilled coriander and lime chicken or pan-fried local scallops with pancetta and white wine sauce. Desserts include Springer bread and butter pudding with creamy custard or brandy snap basket with chunky ginger ice cream. Children are always welcome, and will enjoy the 'Little Jack Russell' menu which serves up soft drinks, organic burgers and sausages, as well as a seasonal vegetable pasta bake.

Open all wk noon-2.30 6-10.30
Bar Meals L served all wk 12-1.45
D served all wk 6.15-8.45 Av main course
£14 **Restaurant** L served all wk 12-1.45
D served all wk 6.15-8.45 ⊕ FREE HOUSE
🍺 Sharp's Doom Bar, Skinner's Betty Stogs, St Austell Tribute, guest ale
🍏 Cornish Orchards. **Facilities** Children's menu Children's portions Family room Dogs allowed Garden Parking

TRURO   Map 2 SW84

Old Ale House

7 Quay St TR1 2HD ☎ **01872 271122** 📠 **01872 271817**
e-mail: old.ale.house@btconnect.com
dir: In town centre

Olde-worlde establishment with a large selection of real
ales on display, as well as more than twenty flavours of
fruit wine. Lots of attractions, including live music and
various quiz and games nights. Food includes 'huge
hands of hot bread', oven-baked jacket potatoes,
ploughman's lunches and daily specials. Vegetable stir
fry, five spice chicken and sizzling beef feature among
the sizzling skillets.

Open all wk 11-11 (Fri-Sat 11am-mdnt Sun 12-10.30)
Closed: 25-26 Dec, 1 Jan ⊕ ENTERPRISE INNS
◀ Skinner's Kiddlywink, Shepherd Neame Spitfire,
Courage Bass, Greene King Abbot Ale, Fuller's London
Pride. **Facilities** Children welcome

The Wig & Pen Inn

Frances St TR1 3DP
☎ **01872 273028** 📠 **01872 277351**
dir: In city centre near Law Courts. 10 mins from rail
station

Tim and Georgina Robinson took over the reins of this
Truro city centre pub in January 2011, bringing with them
their respective skills in the kitchen and top quality front-
of-house experience. Locals are now enjoying a menu full
of modern pub classics, hand-made on the premises
whenever possible – even the baguettes and crisps. The
wine list is currently being overhauled and expanded,
while the St Austell ales are as reliable as ever.

Open all day all wk Closed: 25 Dec **Bar Meals** L served all
wk 12-2.30 D served all wk 6-9.30 Av main course £10
⊕ ST AUSTELL BREWERY ◀ Tribute, HSD.
Facilities Children welcome Children's portions Dogs
allowed Garden

VERYAN   Map 2 SW93

The New Inn ♟

TR2 5QA ☎ **01872 501362**
e-mail: newinnveryan@gmail.com
dir: From St Austell take A390 towards Truro, in 2m left to
Tregony. Through Tregony, follow signs to Veryan

In the centre of a pretty village on the Roseland
Peninsula, this unspoiled, part-thatched pub has been in
new hands since early 2011. Comprising a pair of 16th-
century cottages, it has a single bar, open fires, a
beamed ceiling and a warm, welcoming atmosphere. The
emphasis is on good ales and home cooking. Sunday
lunch is a speciality; other choices during the week might
include hand-breaded Cornish Brie with redcurrant jelly
followed by home-made steak and St Austell ale pie;
home-made lasagne with garlic bread; or hand-carved
Cornish ham with egg and fries.

Open all day all wk **Bar Meals** L served all wk 12-2
D served all wk 6.30-9 **Restaurant** L served all wk 12-2
D served all wk 6.30-9 booking required
booking required D served all wk 6.30-9 booking required
⊕ ST AUSTELL BREWERY ◀ St Austell, Tribute, Tinners,
Proper Job Ŏ Cornish Rattler. **Facilities** Children welcome
Children's menu Children's portions Dogs allowed Garden
Wi-fi

WADEBRIDGE   Map 2 SW97

The Quarryman Inn

Edmonton PL27 7JA ☎ **01208 816444**
e-mail: thequarryman@live.co.uk
dir: Off A39 opposite Royal Cornwall Showground

Close to the famous Camel Trail, this friendly 18th-
century free house has evolved from a courtyard of
cottages once home to slate workers from the nearby
quarry. Several bow windows, one of which features a
stained-glass quarryman panel, add character to this
unusual inn. The pub's signature dishes are chargrilled
steaks served on sizzling platters and fresh local
seafood; puddings are on the blackboard. The first
Tuesday night of the month features curries made to
authentic recipes.

Open all day all wk noon-11pm Closed: 25 Dec
Bar Meals L served all wk 12-2.30 booking required
D served all wk 6-9 booking required ⊕ FREE HOUSE
◀ Sharp's, Skinner's, Timothy Taylor Landlord, Alton's
Pride, Guest ales Ŏ Stowford Press. **Facilities** Children
welcome Children's menu Children's portions Dogs
allowed Garden Parking Wi-fi

Swan ♟

9 Molesworth St PL27 7DD
☎ **01208 812526** 📠 **01208 812526**
e-mail: reservations@smallandfriendly.co.uk
dir: In centre of Wadebridge on corner of Molesworth St
& The Platt

Set alongside the Camel Trail, this family friendly, white-
painted, town centre corner hotel is an ideal base for
exploring north Cornwall and cycling the famous route.
Full of life and at the heart of the local community, the
main bar provides a comfortable place to relax and enjoy
a drink or a meal. Typical pub food includes home-made
steak and Tribute ale pie, home-made lasagne and
Cornish pasties. There's also a good selection from the
char-grill and light meals ranging from burgers to
salads. Recent change of hands.

Open all day all wk **Bar Meals** L served all wk 12-9 food
served all day **Restaurant** D served all wk 6.30-9 booking
required ⊕ ST AUSTELL BREWERY ◀ Tribute, IPA,
Guinness Ŏ Rattler. ♟ 13 **Facilities** Children welcome
Children's menu Children's portions Family room Dogs
allowed Garden Wi-fi

WIDEMOUTH BAY   Map 2 SS20

Bay View Inn ♟

Marine Dr EX23 0AW ☎ **01288 361273**
e-mail: thebayviewinn@aol.com
dir: On Marine Drive adjacent to beach in Widemouth Bay

True to its name, this welcoming, family-run pub has
wonderful views of the rolling Atlantic from its restaurant
and the large raised decking area outside. Dating back
about a hundred years, it was a guesthouse for many
years before becoming an inn in the 1960s. The menu
makes excellent use of local produce, as in the signature
dish of Exmoor fillet steak on sweet potato dauphinoise
with wilted spinach, wild mushroom pâté and an onion
and red wine reduction. Other choices include home-
made pies, stews and bistro-style burgers.

Open all day all wk **Bar Meals** L served Mon-Fri 12-2.30,
Sat-Sun 12-9 D served Mon-Fri 6-9, Sat-Sun 12-9 Av
main course £11 **Restaurant** L served Mon-Fri 12-2.30,
Sat-Sun 12-9 D served Mon-Fri 6-9, Sat-Sun 12-9
⊕ FREE HOUSE ◀ Sharp's Doom Bar, Skinner's Betty
Stogs, Spriggan Ale Ŏ Stowford Press. ♟ 14
Facilities Children welcome Children's menu Children's
portions Play area Dogs allowed Garden Parking Wi-fi

ZENNOR
Map 2 SW43

PICK OF THE PUBS

The Gurnard's Head
INN ⊛ �P

Treen TR26 3DE ☎ 01736 796928
e-mail: enquiries@gurnardshead.co.uk
dir: *5m from Penzance. 5m from St Ives on B3306*

In a fabulous location, remote amidst a latticework of stone-walled pastures atop the high cliff of Gurnard's Head, thrust out into the North Atlantic and with fabulous views across the Penwith peninsula. This rugged setting is more than matched by the robust meals created under the tutelage of head chef Bruce Rennie. Choose a table in the strikingly decorated, multi-roomed interior, all colourwash, scrubbed tables, rugs and local art and contemplate a fare that kicks in with adventurous starters like wood pigeon, nettles, leeks and mushroom jus with a main of gurnard, leeks, Puy lentils and curry velouté to follow. The 'Kitchen Garden' vegetarian options are equally striking; sample gnocchi with samphire, cherry tomatoes, olives and a basil dressing. Cornish beers and a cider brewed locally at St Buryan wet the whistle of diners and walkers, whilst there's also an extraordinary wine list, with sixteen by the glass. Accommodation is available if you would like to stay over and explore the area.

Open all day all wk 11am-11pm Closed: 24-25 Dec, **Bar Meals** L served Mon-Sat 12.30-2.30, Sun 12-2.30 booking required D served all wk 6.30-9.30 booking required **Restaurant** L served Mon-Sat 12.30-2.30, Sun 12-2.30 booking required D served all wk 6.30-9.30 booking required ◀ St Austell Tribute, Skinner's Betty Stogs, Heligan Honey Ŏ Stowford Press, Press Gang, Local cider. �P 16 **Facilities** Children welcome Children's menu Children's portions Dogs allowed Garden Parking **Rooms** 7

PICK OF THE PUBS

The Tinners Arms �P

TR26 3BY ☎ 01736 796927
e-mail: tinners@tinnersarms.com
dir: *Take B3306 from St Ives towards St Just. Zennor approx 5m*

D H Lawrence reputedly stayed here during WW1, when he was writing *Women in Love*. The only pub in the village, this 13th-century granite-built free house is close to the South West coastal path, so walkers taking a well earned rest are usually found among its clientele. Built around 700 years ago to accommodate masons working on the church next door, it has changed little over the years: its stone floors and low ceilings are warmed by open fires in winter, when cushioned settles and mixed chairs around solid wood tables greet locals and visitors alike; outside is a large terrace with sea views. The dinner menu, based on ingredients from local suppliers, might propose pan-fried woodcock breast with croûtons, tarragon, white truffle oil and game jus; braised lamb neck with boulangère potatoes and spinach; and treacle tart with clotted cream.

Open all wk Bar Meals L served all wk 12-2.30 D served all wk 6.30-9 (ex Sun & Mon eve winter) ⊕ FREE HOUSE ◀ Zennor Mermaid, Tinners Ale, Sharp's Own Ŏ Burrow Hill. �P 10 **Facilities** Children welcome Children's menu Children's portions Family room Dogs allowed Garden Parking

CUMBRIA

AMBLESIDE
Map 18 NY30

PICK OF THE PUBS

Drunken Duck Inn
★★★★★ INN ⊛ ⊛ �P

See Pick of the Pubs on opposite page

Wateredge Inn ★★★★ INN �P

Waterhead Bay LA22 0EP
☎ 015394 32332 📄 015394 31878
e-mail: stay@wateredgeinn.co.uk
dir: *M6 junct 36, A591 to Ambleside, 5m from Windermere station*

With large gardens and plenty of seating running down to the shores of Lake Windermere, the Wateredge Inn has been run by the same family for over 27 years. The inn was converted from two 17th-century fishermen's cottages, and now offers a stylish bar/restaurant and pretty, spacious en suite bedrooms. The extensive menus range from local favourites like Cumberland sausage, to more contemporary dishes including mixed bean, celery and coriander chilli; and poached smoked haddock on wilted spinach.

Open all day all wk 10.30-11 Closed: 24-26 Dec **Bar Meals** L served all wk 12-8.30 D served all wk 12-8.30 food served all day ⊕ FREE HOUSE ◀ Theakstons, Barngates ales, Colly Wobbles, Tag Lag, Cat Nap Ŏ Simmons. �P 15 **Facilities** Children welcome Children's menu Children's portions Dogs allowed Garden Parking Wi-fi **Rooms** 22

APPLEBY-IN-WESTMORLAND
Map 18 NY62

The Royal Oak Appleby �P

Bongate CA16 6UN ☎ 017683 51463 📄 017683 52300
e-mail: jan@royaloakappleby.co.uk
dir: *M6 junct 38, B6260 to Appleby-in-Westmorland. Through square, over bridge, right onto B6542, Pub in 0.25m. Or from A66 take B6542 through Appleby, pub on left*

Parts of this award-winning former coaching inn date back to 1100, with 17th-century additions. The building has been sympathetically and painstakingly refurbished to provide a classic dog-friendly tap-room with blackened beams, an oak-panelled lounge with open fire, and a comfortable restaurant. The modern British menu uses the best of local ingredients and features dishes like rosemary and garlic studded lamb shank; stuffed chicken

fillet with celery, onion and peppers; and sun-dried tomato, roasted red pepper and goat's cheese tart. Enjoy your visit with a pint of Hawkshead.

Open all day all wk **Bar Meals** L served Mon-Fri 8-3, Sat-Sun all day D served Mon-Fri 5-9, Sat-Sun all day **Restaurant** L served Mon-Fri 8-3, Sat-Sun all day D served Mon-Fri 5-9, Sat-Sun all day ⊕ FREE HOUSE ◀ Hawkshead, Black Sheep, Timothy Taylor, Copper Dragon. �P 9 **Facilities** Children welcome Children's menu Children's portions Dogs allowed Garden Parking Wi-fi

PICK OF THE PUBS

Tufton Arms Hotel �P

Market Square CA16 6XA
☎ 017683 51593 📄 017683 52761
e-mail: info@tuftonarmshotel.co.uk
dir: *In town centre*

Appleby-in-Westmorland is a medieval market town nestling in the heart of a valley so magically unspoilt that the only possible name for it is Eden. The Milsom family have lovingly restored the Tufton Arms to its former Victorian splendour with rich drapes, period paintings and antique furniture. The elegant conservatory restaurant overlooks a cobbled mews courtyard; light and airy in the daytime, this room takes on an attractive glow in the evening when the curtains are closed and the lighting is low. Chef David Milsom and his kitchen team have won many accolades for their superb food, which comprises a selection of delicious dishes made from the finest and freshest local ingredients. Typical starters include creamy garlic mushrooms or a platter of oak-smoked salmon. Move on to roast rack of Eden Valley lamb; loin of pork chop; or baked cod steak. Round off with home-made lemon cheesecake or brandy snap basket filled with chocolate mousse.

Open all day all wk 7.30am-11pm Closed: 25-26 Dec **Bar Meals** L served all wk 12-2 D served all wk 6-9 **Restaurant** L served all wk 12-2 D served all wk 6-9 ⊕ FREE HOUSE ◀ Tufton Arms Ale, Corby Ale. �P 15 **Facilities** Children welcome Dogs allowed Parking

Save on hotels. Book at **theAA.com/hotel**

CUMBRIA 95 ENGLAND

PICK OF THE PUBS

Drunken Duck Inn ★★★★★ INN 🌸🌸 🍷

AMBLESIDE Map 18 NY30

Barngates LA22 0NG
☎ **015394 36347** 📄 **015394 36781**
e-mail: info@drunkenduckinn.co.uk
web: www.drunkenduckinn.co.uk
dir: *From Kendal on A591 to Ambleside, then follow Hawkshead sign. In 2.5m inn sign on right, 1m up hill*

There are fabulous views towards Lake Windermere from this 17th-century inn, which stands at a lonely crossroads close to Tarn Hows in glorious Lakeland countryside between Ambleside and Hawkshead. In the same ownership since the mid-1970s, the 'Duck' continues to offer good service, with excellent food and drink in a friendly, relaxed atmosphere. The amusing title dates back to Victorian times, when the landlady found her ducks motionless in the road. Thinking that they were dead, she began to pluck them for the pot, unaware that they were merely legless from drinking beer that had leaked into their feed. Legend has it that after the ducks recovered on their way to the oven, the good lady knitted them waistcoats to wear until their feathers grew back. No such risk today - the adjoining Barngates Brewery takes good care of its award-winning real ales, which are served in the oak-floored bar with its open fire, leather club chairs and beautiful

slate bar top. Excellent, locally sourced food is served in three informal restaurant areas. Lunchtime brings a range of soups and sandwiches, as well as hot dishes like pumpkin and sage risotto; fisherman's pie; and braised beef shin with garlic mash and red wine jus. At dinner, begin with seared scallops with tomato, crab and coriander broth, followed by lamb rump with braised sweet red cabbage. Leave room for prune and Armagnac soufflé with vanilla ice cream. Each of the seventeen bedrooms comes complete with antique furniture, prints and designer fabrics. After an invigorating walk there's nothing better than relaxing on the front verandah with a pint of Barngates Cracker Ale, whilst soaking up the view to Lake Windermere.

Open all day all wk Closed: 25 Dec **Bar Meals** L served all wk 12-4 Av main course £10.95 **Restaurant** D served all wk 6-9.30 booking required Av 3 course à la carte fr £30 🛢 FREE HOUSE ◼ Barngates Cracker Ale, Chesters Strong & Ugly, Tag Lag, Catnap, Mothbag, Westmorland Gold, Guest ale. 🍷 17 **Facilities** Children's portions Garden Parking Wi-fi **Rooms** 17

ARMATHWAITE — Map 18 NY54

The Dukes Head Inn ★★★ INN

Front St CA4 9PB ☎ 016974 72226
e-mail: info@dukeshead-hotel.co.uk
dir: *9m from Penrith, 10m from Carlisle between junct 41 & 42 of M6*

First licensed when the Carlisle to Settle railway was being built, this homely, whitewashed inn stands in the heart of a tiny village in the beautiful Eden Valley. Follow a fabulous walk along the banks of the River Eden with a pint of Black Sheep and a hearty meal in the civilised lounge bar, with its stone walls, open fires and sturdy oak settles and tables. Follow hot potted Solway shrimps, with venison, pheasant and rabbit hotpot with pickled red cabbage, or steak, kidney and pie, leaving room for sticky toffee pudding with toffee sauce. There are five comfortable bedrooms available.

Open all wk 11am-mdnt (Fri-Sat 11am-12.30pm) Closed: 25 Dec ⊕ PUNCH TAVERNS ◀ Jennings Cumberland Ale, Black Sheep Bitter, Black Cat Mild, Lancaster Blonde Ŏ Aspall Premier Cru, Westons, Thatchers. **Facilities** Children welcome Children's menu Children's portions Dogs allowed Garden Parking Wi-fi **Rooms** 5

BAMPTON — Map 18 NY51

PICK OF THE PUBS

Mardale Inn

CA10 2RQ ☎ 01931 713244
e-mail: info@mardaleinn.co.uk
dir: *Telephone for directions*

Found on the rural eastern edge of the Lake District, in perfect walking, biking and fishing country, the Mardale Inn forms part of a terrace of 18th-century cottages in a small farming village. The spruced up interior is a refreshing mix of flagstone floors, exposed stone and brick, old beams, open fireplaces and rustic furniture and more modern colours and design. Expect to find a great selection of Cumbrian real ales, perhaps Dent Aviator or Hesket Newmarket High Pike, to enjoy while perusing the menu. At lunch refuel on decent sandwiches and classic pub meals prepared from locally sourced produce. At dinner, typically tuck into Morecambe Bay potted shrimps, or caramelised onion tart, followed by lamb cutlets with minted pea mash and braised beetroot, or sea bass with fennel and dill sauce, and bread-and-butter pudding for dessert. Dogs are welcome in all public areas, and fans of cult movie, *Withnail and I*, will find plenty of the film's locations in the area.

Open all wk 11-11 **Bar Meals** L served all wk 12-6 D served all wk 6-9 food served all day ⊕ FREE HOUSE ◀ Coniston Bluebird, Timothy Taylor Landlord, Hesket Newmarket High Pike, Dent Aviator, Tirril Ŏ Westons Scrumpy. **Facilities** Children welcome Children's menu Children's portions Dogs allowed Parking Wi-fi

BARBON — Map 18 SD68

The Barbon Inn ☻

LA6 2LJ ☎ 015242 76233 📄 051242 76574
e-mail: info@barbon-inn.co.uk
dir: *3.5m N of Kirkby Lonsdale on A683*

In a magnificent setting between the River Lune and the looming fells rising to Whernside, this whitewashed small village inn oozes the character only centuries of heritage can generate. The cosy Coach Lamp bar is particularly welcoming, with its vast fireplace, old furnishings and huge stuffed fish above the mantle. The Oak Room restaurant is equally enticing; secure one of the polished old settles and contemplate the very best that Cumbria, Yorkshire and Lancashire can provide, from grand beers brewed in Dent and Kirkby Lonsdale to Lunesdale lamb shank or three counties sausage with mash and onion gravy.

Open all wk 12-2 6-11 (Sun 6-10.30) Closed: 25 Dec **Bar Meals** L served all wk 12-2 D served all wk 6-9 Av main course £10 **Restaurant** L served all wk 12-2 booking required D served all wk 6-9 Av 3 course à la carte fr £25 ⊕ FREE HOUSE ◀ York Brewery, Dent, Tirril, Kirby Lonsdale. ☻ 20 **Facilities** Children welcome Children's portions Dogs allowed Garden Parking

BASSENTHWAITE — Map 18 NY23

PICK OF THE PUBS

The Pheasant ★★★ HL ◉ ☻

See Pick of the Pubs on opposite page

BEETHAM — Map 18 SD47

PICK OF THE PUBS

The Wheatsheaf at Beetham ☻

LA7 7AL ☎ 015395 62123 📄 015395 64840
e-mail: info@wheatsheafbeetham.com
dir: *On A6 5m N of junct 35*

Run with passion and enthusiasm by the Skelton family, this atmospheric 16th-century former coaching inn stands in the heart of Beetham close to the River Bela. Inside, expect to find wood panelling, low lighting, period pictures and floral displays with the small bar counter screened from the lounge featuring lots of polished wood. Jennings Cumberland Ale heads up the choice of three real ales, while ten wines by the glass span classic European with New World offerings. As far as possible, seasonal menus use the freshest and finest local produce. Lunchtime light meals include hot and cold sandwiches, and simple dishes such as potted shrimps and tomato, rocket and Parmesan tart with basil dressing. At dinner, start with chicken liver and garlic pâté with apple marmalade, moving on to minted lamb Henry, or halibut with garlic prawns, lemon and white wine risotto and scallop cream. Finish with rich chocolate pot or sticky toffee pudding with caramel sauce.

Open all day all wk noon-11pm Closed: 25 Dec **Bar Meals** L served Mon-Sat 12-9, Sun 12-8.30 D served Mon-Sat 12-9, Sun 12-8.30 food served all day ⊕ FREE HOUSE ◀ Jennings Cumberland Ale, Wainwright, Queen Jean Ŏ Kingstone Press. ☻ 10 **Facilities** Garden Parking

BLENCOGO — Map 18 NY14

The New Inn

CA7 0BZ ☎ 016973 61091 📄 016973 61091
dir: *From Carlisle take A596 towards Wigton, then B5302 towards Silloth. After 4m Blencogo signed on left*

This late Victorian sandstone pub has superb views of the north Cumbrian fells and Solway Plain. It is located in a farming hamlet, and the impressive menu makes good use of produce from the region - perhaps chargrilled tenderloin of pork topped with apricot and herb crust; fresh salmon served with hollandaise sauce and asparagus; or yellow-fin tuna with mild curried mango and Armagnac sauce. A selection of malt whiskies is kept.

Open 6.30-11 Closed: 1st 2wks Jan, Mon-Wed ⊕ FREE HOUSE ◀ Boddingtons, Guest ales. **Facilities** Children welcome Garden Parking

BLENCOWE — Map 18 NY43

The Crown Inn

CA11 0DG ☎ 017684 83369
e-mail: crowninn@talktalk.net
dir: *From Penrith take B5288. Approx 3m turn right, follow Blencowe signs. Pub in village centre*

Parts of this traditional village free house date from the 16th century, and the inn enjoys far reaching views to the Pennines and Northern fells being situated just outside the Lake District National Park. Very much part of the community, the inn offers a good selection of well kept cask ales and a comprehensive wine list. Choices from the modern British menu might include herb stuffed chicken with roasted vegetables and red pesto drizzle; salmon fillet with black pepper crust, rosemary and baby tomato; spinach and ricotta cannelloni; or game dishes when in season. There are also regular themed dining nights like Celebration of Cumbrian beef.

Open 12-2 5-close (Tue eve 6-close) Closed: Mon **Bar Meals** L served Wed-Sun 12-2 D served Wed-Sun 6-8.30 **Restaurant** L served Wed-Sun 12-2 D served Wed-Sun 6-8.30 ⊕ FREE HOUSE ◀ Small Local Breweries. **Facilities** Children welcome Children's menu Children's portions Dogs allowed Parking

PICK OF THE PUBS

The Pheasant ★★★ HL

BASSENTHWAITE LAKE   Map 18 NY23

CA13 9YE
☎ 017687 76234   📄 017687 76002
e-mail: info@the-pheasant.co.uk
web: www.the-pheasant.co.uk
dir: *A66 to Cockermouth, 8m N of Keswick on left*

First a farmhouse, then a coaching inn, this 500-year-old Lake District favourite is surrounded by lovely gardens and today combines the role of traditional Cumbrian hostelry with that of an internationally renowned modern hotel. Even so, you still sense the history the moment you walk through the door – the legendary foxhunter John Peel, who's "view halloo would awaken the dead", according to the song, was a regular. In the warmly inviting bar, with polished parquet flooring, panelled walls and oak settles, hang two of Cumbrian artist and former customer Edward H Thompson's paintings. Here, order a pint of Cumberland Ale from Jennings, the Cockermouth brewery that resumed production within weeks of catastrophic flood damage in November 2009, or cast your eyes over the extensive selection of malt whiskies.

The high standard of food, recognised by an AA Rosette, is well known for miles around; meals are served in the attractive beamed restaurant, bistro, bar and lounges overlooking the gardens. Light lunches served in the lounge and bar include open sandwiches, ploughman's, home-made pork pie, and chicken Caesar. A three-course dinner in the restaurant could feature crab and cucumber cannelloni with soy marshmallow and chilled cucumber velouté; fillet of smoked haddock with creamed leeks; slowly cooked loin of wild Cumbrian venison with creamy pearl barley, jellied balsamic, beetroot and peanut butter; or poached breast of wood pigeon with apricot chutney, watercress, cumin jus and natural yoghurt. Treat the family to afternoon tea with home-made scones and rum butter. A private dining room is available for small parties, and there are individually decorated en suite bedrooms with beautiful fabrics, antique pieces and impressive bathrooms.

Open all wk Mon-Thu 11-2.30 5.30-10.30 (Fri-Sat 11-2.30 5.30-11 Sun 12-2.30 6-10.30) Closed: 25 Dec **Bar Meals** L served all wk 12-2 D served all wk 6-9 **Restaurant** L served Sun 12.30-1 booking required D served all wk 7-8.30 booking required ⊕ FREE HOUSE ◀ Coniston Bluebird, Interbrew Bass, Jennings Cumberland Ale ♂ Thatchers Gold. ♟12 **Facilities** Children's portions Dogs allowed Garden Parking Wi-fi **Rooms** 15

BOOT
Map 18 NY10

PICK OF THE PUBS

The Boot Inn

CA19 1TG ☎ 019467 23224
e-mail: enquiries@bootinn.co.uk
dir: From A595 follow signs for Eskdale then Boot

The charming Eskdale village of Boot lies at the bottom of Hardknott Pass, the steepest road in the Lake District. Surrounded by glorious peaks on every side, the area contains some of England's finest walking country. Scafell Pike, England's highest mountain, and Wastwater, England's deepest lake, are within rambling distance and, naturally enough, the pub attracts many hikers and climbers. Whether you are in the bar with its log fire, in the conservatory, from which there are splendid views, outside, or in the 16th-century beamed Burnmoor Room restaurant, Caroline and Sean will provide you with a hearty, unfussy meal, at lunch or dinner. Starters of prawn cocktail or home-made pâté might be followed by mains of chilli con carne; mutton and black pudding hot pot; or curry of the day. The Boot's annual June beer festival is a great event for all the family.

Open all wk Closed: 25 Dec Bar Meals L served all wk 12-3 (ex Nov, Jan & mid Feb 4pm-late) D served all wk 6-8.30 Av main course £9 Restaurant D served all wk 6-8.30 (ex Nov, Jan & mid Feb 4pm-late) booking required Fixed menu price fr £9 ⊕ ROBINSONS ◀ Double Hop, Unicorn, Dizzy Blonde, Dark Hatters ᗏ Westons Stowford Press Organic. Facilities Children welcome Children's menu Children's portions Play area Family room Dogs allowed Garden Beer festival Parking Wi-fi

PICK OF THE PUBS

Brook House Inn ★★★★ INN ♀

CA19 1TG ☎ 019467 23288 📠 019467 23160
e-mail: stay@brookhouseinn.co.uk
dir: M6 junct 36, A590 follow Barrow signs. A5092, then A595. Past Broughton-in-Furness then right at lights to Ulpha. Cross river, next left signed Eskdale, & on to Boot. (NB not all routes to Boot are suitable in bad weather conditions)

One of the most enviably-sited inns in the country, with the Lakeland fells rising behind the inn to England's highest peak, whilst golden sunsets illuminate tranquil Eskdale. Footpaths string to nearby Stanley Ghyll's wooded gorge with falls and red squirrels; whilst the charming La'al Ratty narrow gauge railway steams to and from the coast. It's a magnet for ramblers and cyclists, so a small drying room for wet adventurers is greatly appreciated. Up to seven real ales are kept, including Yates' Bitter and Langdale from Cumbrian Legendary Ales, and an amazing selection of 170 malt whiskies. Award-winning home-made food prepared from Cumbria's finest (ducks and saddleback pigs reside beside the inn) is available in the restaurant, bar and snug all day. Temper the local drizzle with a

rewarding starter of black pudding tower (with Wensleydale cheese, melted orange and parsley butter); then indulge in smoked haddock on mash, with leeks in a cream cheese and prawn sauce; or feta cheese and spinach pie. Much too much for one day, so stay in the light, airy bedrooms before exploring the mountain roads across to Wordsworth's favourite Duddon valley. This great community pub also takes a full role in the famous Boot Beer Festival each June.

Open all day all wk Closed: 25 Dec Bar Meals Av main course £12 food served all day Restaurant L served by arrangement booking required D served 6-8.30 Av 3 course à la carte fr £25 ⊕ FREE HOUSE ◀ Hawkshead Bitter, Jennings Cumberland, Yates, CLA Langdale, Guest ales ᗏ Westons Old Rosie. ♀ 10 Facilities Children welcome Children's menu Family room Dogs allowed Garden Beer festival Parking Wi-fi Rooms 8

BORROWDALE
Map 18 NY21

The Langstrath Country Inn ♀

CA12 5XG ☎ 017687 77239
e-mail: info@thelangstrath.com
dir: B5289 past Grange, through Rosthwaite, left to Stonethwaite. Inn on left after 1m

Nestling in the stunning Langstrath valley, this lovely family-run inn dates back to the 16th century and was originally a miner's cottage. Refurbishments over the years include the addition of a restaurant ideally placed to make the most of the spectacular views. A meal here could start with Cumbrian cheese soufflé, followed by breast of Lowther free-range corn-fed chicken wrapped in Cumbrian pancetta and served with Cumberland mustard and white wine cream, and finishing with sticky toffee pudding. The bar offers decent ales and an extensive wine list. Set on the coast-to-coast and Cumbrian Way walks, this is an ideal spot for hikers.

Open noon-10.30 Closed: Jan, Mon Bar Meals L served Tue-Sun 12-2.30 D served Tue-Sun 6-9 Restaurant L served Tue-Sun 12-2.30 D served Tue-Sun 6-9 ⊕ FREE HOUSE ◀ Jennings Bitter, Black Sheep, Hawkshead Bitter, Cocker Hoop ᗏ Thatchers Gold. ♀ 9 Facilities Children welcome Children's menu Children's portions Dogs allowed Garden Parking Wi-fi

BOUTH
Map 18 SD38

The White Hart Inn ♀

LA12 8JB ☎ 01229 861229 📠 01229 861836
e-mail: nigelwhitehart@aol.com
dir: 1.5m from A590. 10m from M6 junct 36

Lying more or less midway between the southern tips of Lake Windermere and Coniston Water, this 17th-century free house serves a village where locals once made gunpowder. When the factory closed in 1928, they turned to woodland industries and agriculture – you can see some of their tools inside. Peruse the simple menu over a pint of Ulverston or Jennings in the upstairs restaurant that looks out over the fells, or in the horseshoe-shaped bar.

Open all day all wk noon-11 (Sun noon-10.30) Bar Meals L served Mon-Fri 12-2 booking required D served all wk 6-8.45 booking required Av main course £12 Restaurant L served Mon-Fri 12-2 booking required D served all wk 6-8.45 booking required ⊕ FREE HOUSE ◀ Black Sheep Best, Jennings Cumberland Ale, Coniston Bluebird, Ulverston. Facilities Children welcome Children's menu Dogs allowed Garden Parking

BOWLAND BRIDGE
Map 18 SD48

PICK OF THE PUBS

Hare & Hounds Country Inn ♀

LA11 6NN ☎ 015395 68333 📠 015395 68777
e-mail: info@hareandhoundsbowlandbridge.co.uk
dir: M6 onto A591, left after 3m onto A590, right after 3m onto A5074, after 4m sharp left & next left after 1m

This 17th-century coaching inn is set in the pretty little hamlet of Bowland Bridge, not far from Bowness; there are gorgeous views all round, especially of Cartmel Fell. A traditional country pub atmosphere is fostered by the flagstone floors, exposed oak beams, ancient pews warmed by open fires, and cosy niches. A quiz night every Thursday capitalises on the fun family feel, as does the popular garden in summer, when the children's play area and swings come into their own. A recent change of ownership and refurbishment has refocussed the genuine Lake District experience of tarrying here, whether just for a coffee and a browse through the papers, a local ale or a plate of home-made food. Typical of these is Cumberland sausage and black pudding terrine with rustic bread; fell-bred lamb hotpot with home-pickled red cabbage; and seasonal fruit crumble. The excellent children's menu is based on the adult version.

Open all day all wk 11am-11pm Bar Meals L served Mon-Sat 12-2, Sun 12-8.30 D served Mon-Sat 6-9 Av main course £10.95 ⊕ MARSTONS ◀ Jennings, Marstons Pedigree, Cumberland Ale, guest beers. ♀ 10 Facilities Children welcome Children's menu Children's portions Play area Family room Dogs allowed Garden Beer festival Parking

BRAITHWAITE
Map 18 NY22

Coledale Inn

CA12 5TN ☎ 017687 78272
e-mail: info@coledale-inn.co.uk
dir: M6 junct 50, A66 towards Cockermouth for 18m. Turn to Braithwaite then towards Whinlatter Pass. Follow sign on left, over bridge to Inn

Dating from about 1824, the Coledale Inn began life as a woollen mill. Today, the interior is attractively decked out with Victorian prints, furnishings and antiques, whilst footpaths leading off from the large gardens make it ideal for exploring the nearby fells. Two homely bars serve a selection of local ales. A traditional lunch and dinner menu is served in the dining room. Typical choices include roast lamb shoulder with red wine and rosemary; salmon with watercress sauce; and aubergine and tomato bake.

Open all day all wk **Bar Meals** L served all wk 12-2 D served all wk 6-9 Av main course £9.95 ⊕ FREE HOUSE ◀ Yates, Jennings, Keswick, Tirril, Corby Ale, Hesket Newmarket. **Facilities** Children welcome Children's menu Children's portions Play area Dogs allowed Garden Parking Wi-fi

The Royal Oak ★★★ INN ♉

CA12 5SY ☎ **017687 78533** ⊟ **017687 78533**
e-mail: tpfranks@hotmail.com
dir: Exit M6 junct 40, A66 to Keswick, 20m. Bypass Keswick & Portinscale juncts, take next left, pub in village centre

The Royal Oak is set in the centre of the village in a walkers' paradise surrounded by high fells and beautiful scenery. The interior is all oak beams and log fires, and the menu offers hearty pub food, such as giant Yorkshire pudding with home-made Cumberland sausage casserole or steak and kidney suet pudding (including a section for smaller appetites) in the bar area or restaurant, served alongside local ales, such as Jennings Lakeland or Cocker Hoop. Visitors can extend the experience by staying over in the comfortable en suite bedrooms, some with four-poster beds.

Open all day all wk **Bar Meals** L served all wk 12-2 D served all wk 6-9 Av main course £10 **Restaurant** L served all wk 12-2 D served all wk 6-9 ⊕ MARSTONS ◀ Jennings Lakeland Ale, Cumberland Ale, Cocker Hoop, Sneck Lifter. ♉ 8 **Facilities** Children welcome Children's menu Children's portions Dogs allowed Garden Parking Wi-fi **Rooms** 10

| BRAMPTON | Map 21 NY56 |

Blacksmiths Arms ★★★★ INN ♉

Talkin Village CA8 1LE
☎ **016977 3452** ⊟ **016977 3396**
e-mail: blacksmithsarmstalkin@yahoo.co.uk
web: www.blacksmithstalkin.co.uk
dir: From M6 take A69 E, after 7m straight over rdbt, follow signs to Talkin Tarn then Talkin Village

This attractive 18th-century free house stands in some of northern Cumbria's most scenic countryside, within easy reach of the Borders, Hadrian's Wall and the Lakes. The original smithy, dating from 1700, remains part of the inn along with the bar, Old Forge Restaurant and comfortable accommodation. A traditional menu of good home cooking is backed by a daily-changing specials list which may include goujons of plaice with tartare sauce to start; and creamy chicken and ham pie or duck breast in port and plum sauce to follow.

Open all wk noon-3 6-mdnt **Bar Meals** L served all wk 12-2 D served all wk 6-9 Av main course £9.25 **Restaurant** L served all wk 12-2 booking required D served all wk 6-9 booking required Av 3 course à la carte fr £18.95 ⊕ FREE HOUSE ◀ Yates, Brampton, Black Sheep, Getsdale Cold Fell. ♉ 16 **Facilities** Children welcome Children's menu Children's portions Garden Parking Wi-fi **Rooms** 8

| BROUGHTON-IN-FURNESS | Map 18 SD28 |
| **PICK OF THE PUBS** | |

Blacksmiths Arms

See Pick of the Pubs on page 100

| BUTTERMERE | Map 18 NY11 |

Bridge Hotel

CA13 9UZ ☎ **017687 70252** ⊟ **017687 70215**
e-mail: enquiries@bridge-hotel.com
dir: M6 junct 40, A66 to Keswick. Continue on A66 to avoid Keswick centre, exit at Braithwaite. Over Newlands Pass, follow Buttermere signs. (if weather bad follow Whinlatter Pass via Lorton). Hotel in village

An 18th-century former coaching inn set between Buttermere and Crummock Water in an outstandingly beautiful area, surrounded by the Buttermere Fells. There are wonderful walks right from the front door. Good food and real ales are served in the character bars (Cumberland sausage, rainbow trout or Scottish salmon), and a four-course dinner in the dining room - including, perhaps, roast Lakeland lamb with Cumberland sauce and crispy leeks, or venison braised with mushrooms and Old Peculier jus.

Open all day all wk 10.30am-11.30pm ⊕ FREE HOUSE ◀ Jennings Cumberland Ale, Yates Corby Blonde, Guinness, Jennings Smooth. **Facilities** Children welcome Children's menu Children's portions Garden Parking Wi-fi

| CALDBECK | Map 18 NY34 |

Oddfellows Arms

CA7 8EA ☎ **016974 78227** ⊟ **016974 78056**
dir: Telephone for directions

Popular with coast-to-coast cyclists and walkers on the Cumbrian Way, this 17th-century former coaching inn is in the scenic conservation village of Caldbeck. A tied house, it serves real ales from Jennings in Cockermouth, and lunchtime snacks include jacket potatoes and sandwiches. The main menu always includes local Gilcrux trout, Cumbrian steaks, and beef and ale pie, as well as vegetarian dishes and blackboard specials. Admire the views of the northern fells from the peaceful beer garden.

Open all wk all wk **Bar Meals** L served all wk 12-2 D served all wk 6.15-8.30 Av main course £9 **Restaurant** L served all wk 12-1.30 booking required D served all wk 6.15-8.30 booking required Av 3 course à la carte fr £17 ⊕ MARSTONS ◀ Jennings Bitter, Cumberland Ale. **Facilities** Children welcome Children's menu Children's portions Dogs allowed Garden Parking

| CARTMEL | Map 18 SD37 |
| **PICK OF THE PUBS** | |

The Cavendish Arms ♉

LA11 6QA ☎ **015395 36240**
e-mail: food@thecavendisharms.co.uk
dir: M6 junct 36, A590 signed Barrow-in-Furness. Cartmel signed. In village take 1st right

Situated within the village walls, this 450-year-old coaching inn is Cartmel's longest-surviving hostelry. Many traces of its history remain, from the mounting block outside the main door to the bar itself, which used to be the stables. Oak beams, uneven floors and an open fire create a traditional, cosy atmosphere, and outside a stream flows past a tree-lined garden. The food, from the lunchtime sandwiches to the cheeses served at the end of dinner, owes much to its local origins (and, of course, to the skilled kitchen team). Perhaps begin your meal with seafood chowder or mushroom and feta cheese risotto. Then move on to supreme of chicken with cherry tomato, mushroom and air-dried ham sauce; steak and ale pie; or goat's cheese lasagne. Desserts include sticky toffee pudding with butterscotch sauce and tiramisu. The owners have teamed up with a local company that offers carriage tours of the village. This popular area is ideal for walking, horse riding, visiting Cartmel races, Lake Windermere and car museum.

Open all day all wk 9am-11pm **Bar Meals** L served Mon-Fri 12-2, Sat-Sun 12-9 D served Mon-Fri 6-9, Sat-Sun 12-9 **Restaurant** L served Mon-Fri 12-2, Sat-Sun 12-9 D served Mon-Fri 6-9, Sat-Sun 12-9 ⊕ FREE HOUSE ◀ Theakstons, Deuchars IPA, Jennings Cumberland, Corby Ale, Symonds. ♉ 8 **Facilities** Children welcome Children's menu Children's portions Dogs allowed Garden Parking

PICK OF THE PUBS

Blacksmiths Arms

BROUGHTON-IN-FURNESS   Map 18 SD28

Broughton Mills LA20 6AX
☎ **01229 716824**
e-mail: blacksmithsarms@aol.com
web: www.theblacksmitharms.com
dir: *A593 from Broughton-in-Furness towards Coniston, in 1.5m left signed Broughton Mills, pub 1m on left*

Built as a farmhouse in the 16th century, this whitewashed country local stands in the secluded Lickle Valley, with miles of glorious walks radiating from the front door. Owners Michael and Sophie Lane's long-departed predecessors learnt their landlordly ropes serving home brews to travellers and local farmers, and by 1748 the house was formally recorded as an inn. The Lanes took over in 2004, Michael dividing his time between the kitchen and the bar, Sophie running front of house. The interior is largely original, with four log fires, including one in the massive old range, low beams, oak-panelled corridors, and worn slate floors; if the electricity fails, gaslights in the dining room and bar are lit. The bar is reserved for drinking only, with Jennings Cumberland Ale from Cockermouth always available, supported by the output of local micro-breweries and a summer farmhouse cider.

Freshly cooked food makes good use of local produce from quality Cumbrian suppliers, Herdwick lamb from the valley, for example, often appearing on the menu in a variety of award-winning ways. Lunchtime brings sandwiches, light

meals, starters such as salt and pepper calamari rings with chorizo, potato and spinach salad, and main course options of beer-battered hake, Cumberland sausage and steaks. The evening menu features shin of beef, mushroom and ale pie; baked salt cod loin with cockle chowder; and butternut squash, roasted garlic and thyme risotto. Look too for specials of whole spatchcock partridge, and roasted breast of pheasant. For dessert, maybe vanilla pannacotta with Cointreau-flamed strawberries and balsamic vinegar, or double chocolate tart with honey and yoghurt ice cream. The sheltered, flower-filled front patio garden is great for warm-weather dining. Visit the pub during the first weekend in October and catch the Broughton beer festival.

Open all wk Mon 5-11 Tue-Fri 12-2.30 5-11 (Sat-Sun noon-11pm) Closed: 25 Dec, Mon Lunch **Bar Meals** L served

Tue-Sun 12-2 booking required D served all wk 6-9 booking required Av main course £12.50 **Restaurant** Av 3 course à la carte fr £21 ⊕ FREE HOUSE ◀ Jennings Cumberland Ale, Dent Aviator, Barngates Tag Lag, Moorhouses Pride of Pendle, Hawkshead Bitter. **Facilities** Children's menu Dogs allowed Garden Beer festival Parking

Save on hotels. Book at **theAA.com/hotel**

CUMBRIA 101 ENGLAND

CLIFTON Map 18 NY52

PICK OF THE PUBS

George and Dragon ♀ NEW

CA10 2ER ☎ 01768 865381
e-mail: enquiries@georgeanddragonclifton.co.uk
dir: *M6 junct 40, A66 towards Appleby-in-Westmorland, A6 S to Clifton*

The historic Lowther Estate fringes the eastern Lake District near Ullswater; the ruined castle-mansion is set at the heart of pasture, woodland and fells alongside the rushing River Lowther and pretty villages of Askham and Clifton. The latter saw the last battle to take place on British soil, when in 1745 the retreating army of Bonnie Prince Charlie was defeated here; behind the inn is the Rebel Oak, marking the burial place of some of the victims. It's more peaceful today; in 2008 the failing village pub was bought by the Estate and meticulously renovated in sympathy with the Georgian building, creating a traditional inn with contemporary comforts. There's an extremely comfortable menu, too, overseen by respected chef Paul McKinnon and majoring on the bountiful produce of the Estate. Beef is from pedigree shorthorns; pork from home-reared rare breed stock; game and most fish from local waters. Settle in with a pint of Hawkshead Bitter and secure a starter of smoked eel with warm potato salad, leading up to medallions of Lowther venison, mash, spring greens and wild mushroom cream. The menu changes monthly, as do the daily specials. There is a secluded stone-walled courtyard and garden for the summer.

Open all day all wk Closed: 26 Dec **Bar Meals** L served all wk 12-2.30 booking required D served all wk 6-9 booking required **Restaurant** L served all wk 12-2.30 booking required D served all wk 6-9 booking required ⊕ FREE HOUSE ◀ Lancaster Blonde, Hawkshead Bitter ♻ Stowford Press. **Facilities** Children welcome Children's menu Children's portions Dogs allowed Garden Parking Wi-fi

---

COCKERMOUTH Map 18 NY13

The Trout Hotel ★★★★ HL

Crown St CA13 0EJ ☎ 01900 823591 ▤ 01900 827514
e-mail: enquiries@trouthotel.co.uk
dir: *In town centre*

Overlooking the River Derwent, The Trout's well appointed rooms make a good base for horse riding, cycling, fell walking, climbing and fishing trips. The patio of the Terrace Bar and Bistro, with its large heated parasols, offers alfresco dining any time of the year, while the Derwent Restaurant, dominated by a classic fireplace and ornate mirrored sideboard, offers daily-changing menus featuring the best local produce, such as pheasant and pigeon breast, grilled sea bass, and mushroom risotto.

Open all day all wk ⊕ FREE HOUSE ◀ Jennings Cumberland Ale, Theakston Bitter, Marston's Pedigree, Courage Directors. **Facilities** Children welcome Children's menu Garden Parking **Rooms** 49

CONISTON Map 18 SD39

PICK OF THE PUBS

The Black Bull Inn & Hotel ♀

1 Yewdale Rd LA21 8DU
☎ 015394 41335 & 41668 ▤ 015394 41168
e-mail: i.s.bradley@btinternet.com
dir: *M6 junct 36, A590. 23m from Kendal via Windermere & Ambleside*

All the beers, stout and lager served at this 400-year-old coaching inn are produced at the pub's own on-site micro-brewery. Set at the foot of the Old Man of Coniston and adjacent to Coniston Water, The Black Bull with its open fires, uneven floors and oak beams is a cosy refuge in the heart of the Lake District that has been in the same ownership for 35 years. In its time it has welcomed some famous faces. These include Coleridge and Turner, as well as Donald Campbell when attempting his water speed records, and Anthony Hopkins who starred in the film of Campbell's last 60 days. Hungry ramblers calling in at lunchtime will find an unfussy range of snacks and daily specials, whilst the restaurant menu might feature local crispy duckling with fruit sauce; fresh haddock and chips with home-made tartare sauce; or grilled gammon with eggs, mushrooms and tomatoes.

Open all day all wk Closed: 25 Dec **Bar Meals** food served all day **Restaurant** D served all wk 6-9 booking required ⊕ FREE HOUSE ◀ Coniston Bluebird, Old Man Ale, Opium, Blacksmith, XB, Oatmeal Stout. ♀ 10 **Facilities** Children welcome Children's menu Children's portions Family room Dogs allowed Garden Parking

---

PICK OF THE PUBS

The Sun, Coniston

LA21 8HQ ☎ 015394 41248 ▤ 015394 41219
e-mail: info@thesunconiston.com
dir: *From M6 junct 36, A591, beyond Kendal & Windermere, then A598 from Ambleside to Coniston. Pub signed from bridge in village*

In an enviable Lakeland location, set above Coniston village, yet below the famous Old Man mountain, this 16th-century inn and hotel makes the most of its stunning location, with both the conservatory dining room and large garden enjoying wonderful fell views. The refurbished old pub oozes traditional charm, boasting beams and timbers, stone walls and floors, a blazing fire in the Victorian range, and eight real ales on tap, including Cumbrian brewed Coniston Bluebird and Hawkshead Bitter. From an eclectic menu, which makes sound use of quality local ingredients, start with devilled whitebait with paprika, horseradish and garlic mayonnaise or guinea fowl and pistachio terrine with red onion marmalade, then follow with lamb shank with minted stout gravy, braised beef with red wine and caper sauce, or sea bass with garlic sautéed potatoes. Finish with sticky toffee pudding or a plate of Cumbrian cheeses.

Open all day all wk 11am-mdnt **Bar Meals** L served all wk 12-2.30 D served all wk 5.30-8.30 Av main course £14.95 ⊕ FREE HOUSE ◀ Coniston Bluebird, Hawkshead, Copper Dragon, 4 guest ales. **Facilities** Children's menu Children's portions Play area Family room Dogs allowed Garden Parking Wi-fi

---

CROOK Map 18 SD49

The Sun Inn

LA8 8LA ☎ 01539 821351 ▤ 01539 821351
dir: *Off B5284*

A welcoming inn which has grown from a row of cottages built in 1711, when beer was served to travellers from a front room. The same pleasure is dispensed today by the winter fires or on the summer terrace. The bar and regular menus feature steak and mushroom pie, beer battered cod and chips, curries, steaks, salads and vegetarian dishes. Enjoy dining in the restaurant for that special occasion. The seasonal menus use locally sourced produce.

Open all wk Mon-Fri 12-2.30 6-11 (Sat 12-11 Sun 12-10.30) ⊕ SCOTTISH & NEWCASTLE ◀ Theakston, Courage Directors, Coniston Bluebird, Hawkshead. **Facilities** Children welcome Children's menu Children's portions Dogs allowed Garden Parking

CROSTHWAITE — Map 18 SD49

PICK OF THE PUBS

The Punch Bowl Inn

INN ◎◎ ♈

LA8 8HR ☎ 015395 68237 📄 015395 68875
e-mail: info@the-punchbowl.co.uk
web: www.the-punchbowl.co.uk
dir: *M6 junct 36, A590 towards Barrow, A5074 & follow signs for Crosthwaite. Pub by church on right*

Set near the head of the Lyth Valley amidst crimped limestone knolls, verdant pastures and damson orchards, this notable, destination dining inn has been awarded two AA Rosettes for the fabulous menu created by Richard Rose and his team. The elegantly furnished, light and contemporary interior; the slate bar-top, wood-burner stoves, fresh flowers and restrained decor reflect the care and attention to detail that ensure clients return time-and-again to this bolt-hole (with sumptuous, individually designed residential rooms available) just a few miles from Windermere's wooded shores. Drawing heavily on the area's estates, farms and nearby coastal villages for the raw materials, the carte menu is available throughout the bar and restaurant rooms; prepare to be tempted by starters such as woodpigeon, lentil casserole, root vegetables and balsamic or glazed Lancashire cheese soufflé, leading into roasted skate with shrimp and brown butter sauce, almonds and capers, or a hearty dish of Cumberland sausages, mash and red onion gravy; finishing on lemon cream with poached rhubarb and cinder toffee. The owners are great supporters of Cumbrian micro-breweries, so expect bitters from Barngates and Hawkshead breweries.

Open all day all wk **Bar Meals** L served all wk noon-9 booking required D served all wk noon-9 booking required **Restaurant** L served all wk noon-9 booking required D served all wk noon-9 booking required ⊕ FREE HOUSE ◀ Westmorland Gold, Coniston Bluebird, Hawkshead Gold ☼ Thatchers Gold. ♈14 **Facilities** Children welcome Children's portions Dogs allowed Garden Parking Wi-fi **Rooms** 9

ELTERWATER — Map 18 NY30

PICK OF THE PUBS

The Britannia Inn

LA22 9HP ☎ 015394 37210 📄 015396 78075
e-mail: info@britinn.co.uk
dir: *In village centre*

This whitewashed free house stands in the centre of Elterwater village amidst the imposing mountains of the Langdale valley. It was built around 500 years ago as a gentleman farmer's house, and within its thick stone walls the bar seating areas are a cluster of small and cosy rooms with low-beamed oak ceilings and winter coal fires. There's generally a quiz night on Sundays, and this popular pub really comes to life in summer when colourful hanging baskets dazzle the eye. Dent Aviator and Hawkshead bitter are amongst the six hand pulled ales, whilst committed drinkers should head for the two-week beer festival that starts on 13th November. The inn offers a wide choice of fresh, home-cooked food, and a typical evening meal might begin with home-made Cumberland pâté, followed by grilled sea bass with a basil and Parmesan crust. Round off with a poached pear in mulled wine. Morris dancers visit the inn at Easter and in the summer.

Open all day all wk 10am-11pm **Bar Meals** L served all wk 12-9.30 D served all wk 12-9.30 Av main course £9.50 food served all day **Restaurant** D served all wk 6.30-9.30 booking required ⊕ FREE HOUSE ◀ Jennings Bitter, Coniston Bluebird, Thwaites Wainwright, Dent Aviator, Hawkshead Bitter. **Facilities** Children welcome Children's menu Children's portions Dogs allowed Garden Beer festival Parking Wi-fi

ENNERDALE BRIDGE — Map 18 NY01

PICK OF THE PUBS

The Shepherd's Arms Hotel

CA23 3AR ☎ 01946 861249 📄 01946 861249
e-mail: shepherdsarms@btconnect.com
dir: *A66 to Cockermouth (25m), A5086 to Egremont (5m) then follow sign to Ennerdale*

Located on one of the most beautiful stretches of Wainwright's Coast to Coast footpath, this informal free house is a favourite with walkers. The bar has a long serving counter, a long case clock and wood-burning stove below a large beam hung with copper and brass. The main area has an open log fire and comfortable seating, and is a venue for local musicians; it opens into a small conservatory with tables and an additional outdoor sitting area. Shepherd's Arms own brew heads a list of beers that includes Jennings Bitter and a regular guest ale. A nicely varied menu is served throughout, with plenty of choice for vegetarians, as well as daily specials and carte options in the dining room. Using locally sourced produce where possible, dinner might begin with fresh home-made soup, or deep-fried Brie with a hot

redcurrant sauce, before moving on to nut and mushroom fettuccine; Herdwick lamb half shoulder slow cooked in a mint and garlic jus; grilled swordfish; or local sirloin steak with brandy and black pepper sauce.

Open all wk Mon-Fri 12-2 6-11 (Winter) noon-11 (Summer) **Bar Meals** L served all wk 12-2 D served all wk 6-9 **Restaurant** L served all wk 12-2 D served all wk 6-9 ◀ Jennings Bitter, Cumberland, Guest ales. **Facilities** Children welcome Dogs allowed Garden Parking

ESKDALE GREEN — Map 18 NY10

PICK OF THE PUBS

Bower House Inn

CA19 1TD ☎ 019467 23244 📄 019467 23308
e-mail: info@bowerhouseinn.co.uk
dir: *4m off A595, 0.5m W of Eskdale Green*

A traditional Lake District hotel tucked away in the gloriously unspoilt Eskdale Valley, the appeal of this 17th-century inn finds favour with an eclectic clientele, from walkers and tourists to business folk and wedding parties. Less than four miles from the Cumbrian coast road, it is ideally placed for visitors heading to the western lakes – and has been welcoming people through its door for over 400 years. Oak beams, ticking clocks, crackling log fires and local Coniston, Hawkshead and Jennings ales are on tap in the bar, which opens out on to a delightful enclosed garden. The restaurant is a charming room with candlelit tables, exposed stone, log fires and equestrian pictures. Here, typical starters may include sage and onion hash brown with mustard cream, which might be followed by pan-fried sea bass with basil pesto risotto. Why not time your visit to coincide with one of the special events running throughout the year?

Open all day all wk **Bar Meals** L served Mon-Fri 12-2, Sat-Sun 12-9 D served Mon-Fri 6-9, Sat-Sun 12-9 food served all day **Restaurant** D served all wk 6-9 ⊕ FREE HOUSE ◀ Theakston Bitter, Ennerdale, Yates. **Facilities** Children welcome Children's menu Children's portions Dogs allowed Garden Parking

FAUGH   Map 18 NY55

The String of Horses Inn ▼

CA8 9EG ☎ 01228 670297
e-mail: info@stringofhorses.com
dir: *M6 junct 43, A69 towards Hexham. In 5-6m right at 1st lights at Corby Hill/Warwick Bridge. 1m, through Heads Nook, in 1m bear sharp right. Left into Faugh. Pub on left down hill*

Tucked away in a sleepy village close to Talkin Tarn, this traditional Lakeland inn oozes old world charm. It dates from the 17th century, when it was a packhorse inn. The bar and restaurant have oak beams, roaring log fires, wood panelling and oak settles. You'll find a good range of real ales and imaginative pub food on offer – maybe moules marinière followed by sizzling fajitas. This is the perfect base for exploring the North Lakes.

Open Tue-Sun 6-11pm Closed: Mon **Bar Meals** D served Tue-Sun 6-8.45 Av main course £8.95
Restaurant D served Tue-Sun 6-8.45 Av 3 course à la carte fr £19 ⊕ FREE HOUSE ◀ Brampton Bitter, Theakston Best, John Smith's, Guinness. ▼ 8
Facilities Children welcome Children's menu Parking

GRASMERE   Map 18 NY30

The Travellers Rest Inn ▼

Keswick Rd LA22 9RR
☎ 015394 35604 📠 017687 72309
e-mail: stay@lakedistrictinns.co.uk
dir: *From M6 take A591 to Grasmere, pub 0.5m N of Grasmere*

Located on the edge of picturesque Grasmere and handy for touring and exploring the ever-beautiful Lake District, The Travellers Rest has been a pub for more than 500 years. Inside, a roaring log fire complements the welcoming atmosphere of the beamed and inglenook bar area. Along with ales like Sneck Lifter, an extensive menu of traditional home-cooked fare is offered, ranging from Westmorland terrine and eggs Benedict, to wild mushroom gratin and rump of Lakeland lamb.

Open all day all wk Mon-Sat 11-11 (Sun noon-10.30)
Bar Meals Av main course £11-£13 food served all day
Restaurant food served all day ⊕ FREE HOUSE
◀ Jennings Bitter & Cocker Hoop, Cumberland Ale, Sneck Lifter, Guest ales. ▼ 10 **Facilities** Children welcome Children's menu Children's portions Family room Dogs allowed Garden Parking Wi-fi

GREAT LANGDALE   Map 18 NY20

The New Dungeon Ghyll Hotel ★★ HL ▼

LA22 9JX ☎ 015394 37213 📠 015394 37666
e-mail: enquiries@dungeon-ghyll.com
dir: *From Ambleside follow A593 towards Coniston for 3m, at Skelwith Bridge right onto B5343 towards 'The Langdales'*

Traditional Cumberland stone hotel standing in its own lawned grounds in a spectacular position beneath the Langdale Pikes and Pavey Ark. The hotel dates back to medieval times, and is full of character and charm. Local specialities, expertly cooked, are served in the bar and smart dining room. A sample dinner menu might include breaded lentil chilladas with tomato and chilli dip, roasted chicken breast with mushroom, brandy and cream sauce, then apple and red berry pie or baked American vanilla cheesecake. The bar menu offers home-made seafood bake and lasagne.

Open all day all wk **Bar Meals** food served all day
Restaurant D served all wk 6-8.30 booking required
⊕ FREE HOUSE ◀ Thwaites Bitter, Langdale Tup
Ō Kingstone Press, Wainwrights. ▼ 8 **Facilities** Children welcome Children's menu Children's portions Dogs allowed Garden Parking Wi-fi **Rooms** 20

GREAT SALKELD   Map 18 NY53

PICK OF THE PUBS

The Highland Drove Inn and Kyloes Restaurant ▼

See Pick of the Pubs on page 104

HAWKSHEAD   Map 18 SD39

Kings Arms ★★★ INN

The Square LA22 0NZ
☎ 015394 36372 📠 015394 36006
e-mail: info@kingsarmshawkshead.co.uk
dir: *M6 junct 36, A590 to Newby Bridge, right at 1st junct past rdbt, over bridge, 8m to Hawkshead*

Overlooking the picturesque square at the heart of this virtually unchanged Elizabethan Lakeland village, made famous by Beatrix Potter who lived nearby, this 16th-century inn throngs in summer. In colder weather, bag a table by the fire in the traditional carpeted bar, quaff a pint of Hawkshead bitter and tuck into lunchtime light bites such as minute steak and sautéed red onion jacket; alternatively try main courses like steak and Hawkshead ale pie, or the chef's home-made gourmet lamb and mint burger. Look out for the carved figure of a king in the bar. Cosy, thoughtfully equipped bedrooms are available.

Open all day all wk 11am-mdnt **Bar Meals** L served all wk 12-2.30 D served all wk 6-9.30 **Restaurant** L served all wk 12-2.30 booking required D served all wk 6-9.30 booking required ⊕ FREE HOUSE ◀ Tetley Bitter, Black Sheep Best, Hawkshead Gold, Hawkshead Bitter, Coniston Bluebird, Guest ales. **Facilities** Children welcome Children's menu Dogs allowed Garden Wi-fi **Rooms** 8

PICK OF THE PUBS

The Queen's Head ★★★★ INN ⊛ ▼

Main St LA22 0NS
☎ 015394 36271 📠 015394 36722
e-mail: enquiries@queensheadhotel.co.uk
dir: *M6 junct 36, A590 to Newby Bridge, 1st right, 8m to Hawkshead*

Surrounded by fells and forests, a stone's throw from Esthwaite Water, the Queen's Head is the perfect base for exploring the Lakes. This 16th-century inn is located in a village with impressive literary links - William Wordsworth attended the local grammar school and Beatrix Potter lived just up the road. Behind the pub's flower-bedecked exterior, there are low oak-beamed ceilings, wood-panelled walls, slate floors and welcoming fires. Real ales and an extensive wine list are offered, plus a full menu and an ever-changing specials board of quality local produce. For lunch try sandwiches, salads or light bites. An evening meal might open with venison and wild mushroom terrine, or steamed mussels with Chardonnay, garlic and parsley sauce, followed by slow roasted shoulder of lamb with rosemary and red wine reduction; Hartley's beer battered haddock, home-cut chips and mushy peas; or perhaps the vegetarian option of potato, pea and cauliflower curry. Thirteen very attractive en suite rooms are available.

Open all day all wk 11am-11.45pm (Sun 12-11.45)
Bar Meals L served 12-2.30, Sun 12-5 D served all wk 6.15-9.30 Av main course £14 **Restaurant** L served 12-2.30, Sun 12-5 D served all wk 6.15-9.30 booking required Av 3 course à la carte fr £32.20 ⊕ FREDERIC ROBINSON ◀ Hartleys Cumbria Way, Double Hop, Guest ale. ▼ 16 **Facilities** Children welcome Children's menu Family room Garden Wi-fi **Rooms** 13

The Sun Inn ★★★★ INN

Main St LA22 0NT ☎ 015394 36236 📠 015394 36155
e-mail: rooms@suninn.co.uk
dir: *N on M6 junct 36, A591 to Ambleside, B5286 to Hawkshead. S on M6 junct 40, A66 to Keswick, A591 to Ambleside, B5286 to Hawkshead*

You'll find this listed 17th-century coaching inn at the heart of the charming village where Wordsworth went to school. Inside are two resident ghosts - a giggling girl and a drunken landlord - and outside is a paved terrace with seating. The wood-panelled bar has low, oak-beamed ceilings, and hill walkers and others will enjoy the log fires, real ales and locally-sourced food. Choices range from lunchtime sandwiches through bar snacks such as Whitby scampi and chips to fell-reared local steak and salad. There are 8 modern bedrooms, including a four-poster room.

Open all day all wk 11am-11pm (Sun noon-10.30pm)
Bar Meals L served all wk 12-2.30 D served all wk 6-9 Av main course £9.95 ⊕ FREE HOUSE ◀ Jennings, Cocker Hoop, 2 guest ales. **Facilities** Children welcome Children's menu Children's portions Dogs allowed Garden Wi-fi **Rooms** 8

PICK OF THE PUBS

The Highland Drove Inn and Kyloes Restaurant ♟

GREAT SALKELD　　　Map 18 NY53

CA11 9NA
☎ 01768 898349　📄 01768 898708
e-mail: highlanddrove@kyloes.co.uk
web: www.kyloes.co.uk
dir: *Exit M6 junct 40, take A66 E'bound then A686 to Alston. After 4m, left onto B6412 for Great Salkeld & Lazonby*

Nestling on an old drove road by a village church deep in the lovely Eden Valley, Donald and Christine Newton's 300-year-old country inn is named after the original Highland cattle that were bred in the Western Isles and then driven over the short channels of water to the mainland. Looking more like an old farmhouse, the pub is a great all-rounder with a well deserved reputation for high quality food and conviviality. Despite the excellence of the food, The Highland Drove is still an award-winning pub where locals come to enjoy the wide range of cask-conditioned real ales, and a good selection of wines. Inside, there's an attractive brick and timber bar, old tables and settles in the main bar area, and a lounge with log fire, dark wood furniture and tartan fabrics. The upstairs restaurant has a unique hunting lodge feel, with a veranda and lovely country views.

Menus list traditional local dishes, alongside daily specials reflecting the availability of local game and fish, and meat from herds reared and matured in Cumbria. Typical meals might be black pudding and apple fritter on sweet potato and parsnip purée with whole grain mustard sauce; twice-baked goat's cheese soufflé with a roasted tomato and garlic sauce; fillet of beef on a turnip fondant with pomme purée, leek and haggis cannelloni served with a rich Madeira sauce; curried aubergine and mushrooms with a potato and pea samosa, braised onion rice and spiced cauliflower. Leave room for steamed chocolate sponge pudding with chocolate and mint sauce or home-made lemon tart and raspberry coulis.

Open all wk noon-2 6-late (Closed Mon L) Closed: 25 Dec **Bar Meals** L served Tue-Sun 12-2 D served all wk 6-9 Av main course £8.95 **Restaurant** L served Tue-Sun 12-2 D served all wk 6-9 Av 3 course à la carte fr £18 ⊕ FREE HOUSE
◀ Theakston Black Bull, John Smith's Cask, John Smith's Smooth, Theakston Best, Theakston Mild, guest ale. ♟ 10
Facilities Children welcome Children's menu Children's portions Dogs allowed Garden Parking Wi-fi

Save on hotels. Book at **theAA.com/hotel**

CUMBRIA 105 ENGLAND

PICK OF THE PUBS

The Horse & Farrier Inn ♀

KESWICK Map 18 NY22

Threlkeld Village CA12 4SQ
☎ **017687 79688** 📄 **017687 79823**
e-mail: info@horseandfarrier.com
web: www.horseandfarrier.com
dir: *M6 junct 40 follow Keswick (A66) signs, after 12m turn right signed Threlkeld. Pub in village centre*

For over 300 years this solid Lakeland inn has seen poets, playwrights and lead miners wending their way along the Glenderamackin Valley. This ancient route between Keswick and Penrith in the northern outpost of the Lake District National Park is tucked beneath the challenging mountains of Blencathra, Skiddaw and Helvellyn. Little wonder that it's a hot-spot for serious walkers, who take their rest in the beer garden here – a case of up hill and down ale, perhaps. Within the thick, whitewashed stone walls of this long, low old building you'll find slate-flagged floors, beamed ceilings and crackling log fires, with hunting prints decorating the traditional bars and a memorable panelled snug.

The inn has an excellent reputation for good food, from hearty Lakeland breakfasts to home-cooked lunches and dinners served in either the bar or the charming period restaurant. The chefs make full use of local and seasonal produce. The lunchtime bar menu has all the old favourites, from home-made curry of the day to steak and kidney pie in rich ale gravy. In the restaurant, starters embrace a seared trio of fresh Morecambe Bay scallops served on a roulade of black pudding; or a broader medley of seafood in a puff pasty case finished with fresh dill. Look for the local produce in the main courses. There are pan-fried sirloin or fillet steaks cooked to your liking; slow roasted belly pork served on a cushion of grain mustard mash; and a pan-griddled duo of Cumberland sausages made with beef, pork, and the pub's own blend of herbs and spices. If your visit coincides with teatime, you could ask for a round of cheese or Cumbrian ham sandwiches, with scone, jam and cream; or the home-made soup of the day with a hot Cumbrian rarebit.

Open all day all wk 7.30am-mdnt
Bar Meals food served all day
Restaurant food served all day
🌐 JENNINGS BROTHERS PLC 🍺 Jennings Bitter, Cocker Hoop, Sneck Lifter, Cumberland Ale, guest ale. 🍷 10
Facilities Children welcome Children's menu Children's portions Family room Dogs allowed Garden Parking Wi-fi

HESKET NEWMARKET Map 18 NY33

The Old Crown ▼

CA7 8JG ☎ 016974 78288
e-mail: edna.theoldcrown@btinternet.com
dir: From M6 junct 41, B5305, left after 6m towards
Hesket Newmarket

Regulars here can sleep soundly, in the knowledge that
their favourite beers will always be waiting for them.
That's because the pub and its associated micro-brewery,
which stands at the rear, are owned by a dedicated co-
operative of local people and they sell only Hesket
Newmarket Brewery real ales. The traditional home-
cooked food includes steak and Hesket ale pie; lamb
shank slow cooked in garlic, mint and honey; and breaded
Whitby scampi and tartare sauce.

Open all wk 5.30-11 (Fri-Sat 12.30-2.30 5.30-11) Closed:
25 Dec eve, Mon-Thu L ex Wed-Thu sch hols
Bar Meals L served Fri-Sun 12.30-2 D served all wk
6.30-9 Av main course £9 ⊕ FREE HOUSE ◀ Doris,
Skiddaw, Blencathra, Catbells, Great Cockup, Old Carrock
◗ Stowford Press. ▼ 11 Facilities Children welcome
Children's portions Play area Family room Dogs allowed
Garden

KESWICK Map 18 NY22

Farmers Arms ▼

Portinscale CA12 5RN ☎ 017687 72322
e-mail: thefarmers.arms@hotmail.co.uk
dir: M6 junct 40, A66, bypass Keswick. After B5289
junct turn left to Portinscale

Set in the pretty village of Portinscale not far from
Keswick, this historic pub has traditional decor and long-
standing ties with the local hunt. Ben and Sharon
welcome warmly their locals and touring visitors, serving
good quality, well-kept ales, and traditional home-cooked
food. Typical of the menu are mushrooms in creamy
pepper sauce on garlic bruschetta topped with Stilton;

and local grilled rainbow trout. Favourites from the
dessert menu such as sticky toffee pudding round things
off nicely. There is a two-course meal special from
Sunday to Thursday.

Open all day all wk Bar Meals L served all wk 12-2
D served all wk 6-9 Av main course £8
Restaurant L served all wk 12-2 D served all wk 6-9
⊕ MARSTONS ◀ Jennings Bitter, Jennings Cumberland
Ale, Jennings Cocker Hoop, Jennings Sneck Lifter, guest
ale. Facilities Children welcome Children's menu
Children's portions Family room Dogs allowed Garden
Parking Wi-fi

The George ★★★ INN ▼

3 St John's St CA12 5AZ
☎ 017687 72076 🖹 017687 75968
e-mail: rooms@thegeorgekeswick.co.uk
dir: M6 junct 40 onto A66, take left filter road signed
Keswick, pass pub on left. At x-rds turn left onto Station
St, 150 yds on left

Keswick's oldest coaching inn is a handsome 17th-
century building in the heart of this popular Lakeland
town. Restored to its former glory, retaining its traditional
black panelling, Elizabethan beams, ancient settles and
log fires, it makes a comfortable base from which to
explore the fells and lakes. Expect to find local Jennings
ales on tap and classic pub food prepared from local
ingredients. Typical dishes include Cumberland ale
battered haddock and chips, Borrowdale rainbow trout
with herb butter, venison casserole, cow (steak) pie, and
sticky toffee pudding. There are 12 comfortable bedrooms
available.

Open all day all wk Bar Meals L served Mon-Thu 12-2.30,
Fri-Sun 12-5 D served all wk 5.30-9 Restaurant L served
Mon-Thu 12-2.30. Fri-Sun 12-5 booking required D served
all wk 5.30-9 booking required ⊕ JENNINGS BROTHERS
PLC ◀ Jennings, Cumberland, Sneck Lifter, Cocker Hoop,
Guest ales. ▼ 10 Facilities Children welcome Children's
menu Dogs allowed Garden Parking Rooms 12

PICK OF THE PUBS

Keswick Lodge ★★★★ INN NEW

Main St CA12 5HZ ☎ 017687 74584
e-mail: info@keswick.co.uk
dir: M6 junct 40 (Penrith), A66 to Keswick town centre
to x-roads (war memorial) on right. Left into Station St.
Lodge 100yds on right

Located on the corner of Keswick's vibrant market
square, this large, friendly 18th-century coaching inn
combines contemporary comfort with a charming
account of local history. It is understandably popular
with walkers – it's within a few strides of England's
three highest peaks; dogs are permitted in the bar,
restaurant area and some of the bedrooms, an
important consideration for many. Wainwright is one of
the Thwaites ales on tap, but there are guests from
Cumbrian brewers too. Good wholesome home-cooked
food is based on locally supplied produce, with a
specials board offering the best of the season. Nibbles
like pigs in blankets and black pudding fritters, plus
deli sandwiches, classic pub fare and grills are
complemented by the taste of Cumbria fare such as

Fellside lamb hot pot and platters of Mackenzie's Smoke House oak-smoked chicken Caesar salad. If you decide to stay over in one of the cosy rooms, a wholesome Cumbrian breakfast awaits.

Open all day all wk **Bar Meals** L served Mon-Sat 11-9.30 D served Sun 12-9 Av main course £8.95 food served all day **Restaurant** food served all day ⊕ THWAITES ◀ Wainwright & Original, Lancaster Bomber. **Facilities** Children welcome Children's menu Children's portions Dogs allowed **Rooms** 19

See advert on opposite page

PICK OF THE PUBS

The Kings Head ♀

Thirlspot CA12 4TN
☎ 017687 72393 ☎ 017687 72309
e-mail: stay@lakedistrictinns.co.uk
dir: *From M6 take A66 to Keswick then A591, pub 4m S of Keswick*

Standing at the foot of Helvellyn near the shores of Lake Thirlmere, this 17th-century coaching inn offers spectacular views towards Blencathra and Skiddaw. On warmer days the garden is the best place to enjoy a meal or drink, whilst indoors the traditional bar features old beams and inglenook fireplaces. Popular real ales include beers from the Jennings Brewery in nearby Cockermouth, and there is a fine selection of wines and malt whiskies. The flexible and extensive menu begins with lunchtime soups and sandwiches, whilst in the elegant restaurant you can linger over a four-course seasonal menu of traditional English dishes and local specialities. A steak menu is offered during the week, and booking is advisable to enjoy the choice of roasts on Sunday lunchtimes.

Open all day all wk **Bar Meals** Av main course £11 food served all day **Restaurant** D served all wk 7-8.30 booking required Av 3 course à la carte fr £20 ⊕ FREE HOUSE ◀ Jennings Bitter, Cumberland Ale, Sneck Lifter, Cocker Hoop, Guest ales. ♀ 9 **Facilities** Children welcome Children's menu Family room Dogs allowed Garden Parking Wi-fi

Pheasant Inn ♀

Crosthwaite Rd CA12 5PP ☎ 017687 72219
dir: *On A66 Keswick rdbt towards town centre, 60yds on right*

Famous local artist John William Wilkinson – 'Wilk' – would sit in the corner here near the open fire, sketching the locals; some of his work is still on display. The Pheasant is also widely known hereabouts for its range of Jennings ales on tap, Cocker Hoop and Cumberland being two of the most popular. It's always been associated with the local hunt, which continues to meet here on Boxing Day to enjoy a pint or a local whisky. The kitchen produces seasonal and local food of excellent quality in dishes such as cod and chorizo fishcake with Cajun yoghurt dressing; pan-fried duck breast with prune and

cherry brandy thyme sauce; and spicy vegetable and bean goulash. New for 2011 – an afternoon lite bite menu and a larger beer garden.

Open all day all wk **Bar Meals** Av main course £10.95 food served all day **Restaurant** food served all day ⊕ JENNINGS ◀ Jennings Bitter, Cumberland, Cocker Hoop, Sneck Lifter. ♀ 10 **Facilities** Children welcome Children's menu Dogs allowed Garden Parking

The Swinside Inn

Newlands Valley CA12 5UE ☎ 017687 78253
e-mail: swinsideinn@btconnect.com
dir: *1m from A66, signed for Newlands/Swinside*

Situated in the quiet Newlands Valley, the Swinside Inn is a listed building dating back to about 1642. From the pub there are superb views of Causey Pike and Cat Bells among other landmarks. The pub has been refurbished and there is a new lounge bar and landscaped beer garden. Inside you'll find traditional open fires and oak-beamed ceilings, and from Easter to late October food is served all day. Extensive bar menu may offer lamb Henry, Cumberland sausage, Swinside chicken, and fresh, grilled Borrowdale trout. Recent change of hands.

Open all wk 11-3 6-11 winter (all day summer) ⊕ SCOTTISH & NEWCASTLE ◀ Jennings Cumberland Ale, John Smith's Smooth, Deuchars, Guest ales. **Facilities** Children welcome Children's menu Children's portions Dogs allowed Garden Parking

KIRKBY LONSDALE   Map 18 SD67

PICK OF THE PUBS

The Pheasant Inn ♀

Casterton LA6 2RX
☎ 01524 271230 📧 01524 274267
e-mail: info@pheasantinn.co.uk
web: www.pheasantinn.co.uk
dir: *M6 junct 36, A65 for 7m, left onto A683 at Devils Bridge, 1m to Casterton centre*

A whitewashed 18th-century coaching inn, The Pheasant nestles beneath the fells in the quiet hamlet of Casterton, just a mile from the market town of Kirkby Lonsdale in the beautiful Lune Valley. The Dixon family and staff ensure a warm welcome and traditional food is served daily in both the oak-panelled restaurant and the bar, where beams and open fireplaces add to the relaxing atmosphere. Local ales, malt whiskies and a broad choice of wines can be sampled while perusing the menu of quality produce sourced from the valley

farms. Dishes may include smoked mackerel mousse; home-made pâté; and prawn and apple cocktail Marie-Rose to start, followed by traditional Cumberland sausage with onion rings and a fried egg; beef Stroganoff; seafood mixed grill; steak and ale pie; or spinach, feta and mushroom strudel. In fine weather you can sit outside and enjoy the lovely views of the fells.

Open all wk noon-3 6-11 Closed: 2wks mid Jan **Bar Meals** L served Tue-Sun 12-2 D served all wk 6-9 **Restaurant** L served Tue-Sun 12-2 booking required D served all wk 6-9 booking required ⊕ FREE HOUSE ◀ Theakston Best & Cool Cask, Black Sheep Best, Dent Aviator, Timothy Taylor Landlord. ♀ 8 **Facilities** Children welcome Children's portions Garden Parking

PICK OF THE PUBS

The Sun Inn ★★★★★ INN ⊛ ♀

Market St LA6 2AU
☎ 01524 271965 📧 01524 272485
e-mail: email@sun-inn.info
dir: *From M6 junct 36 take A65 for Kirkby Lonsdale. In 5m left signed Kirkby Lonsdale. At next T-junct turn left. Right at bottom of hill*

You'll find this welcoming 17th-century free house in the heart of Kirkby Lonsdale, just a few minutes' walk from the famous Ruskin's View. Natural stone walls, oak floors, log fires and furniture hand-made by the landlady's father, a cabinet maker, create a relaxed atmosphere in the bar. The selection of cask ales is backed by an extensive wine choice with helpful tasting notes. 'Meats, fishes, loaves and dishes' is the carte to look for if all you want is a starter-size meal for grazing or nibbling; served between midday and 10pm, you'll find the likes of sausages with mustard dips, haddock goujons with herb mayonnaise, and an award-winning pork and damson pie. The restaurant menu changes seasonally. Starters may embrace French onion soup, while hearty main courses such as rump of venison or duo of lamb keep the customers replete. Eleven de luxe bed and breakfast rooms blend modern comforts with character and charm, making The Sun an ideal base from which to explore the Lake District and Yorkshire Dales.

Open all wk Mon 3-11, Tue-Sun 10am-11pm **Bar Meals** L served Tue-Sun 12-10 D served Mon 4-10, Tue-Sun 12-10 Av main course £8 food served all day **Restaurant** L served Tue-Sun 12-2.30 D served all wk 7-9 Av 3 course à la carte fr £25 ⊕ FREE HOUSE ◀ Timothy Taylor Landlord, Thwaites Wainwright, Hawkshead Best Bitter. ♀ 9 **Facilities** Children welcome Children's menu Children's portions Dogs allowed Wi-fi **Rooms** 11

KIRKBY LONSDALE *continued*

The Whoop Hall ★★ HL

Skipton Rd LA6 2HP
☎ 015242 71284 📄 015242 72154
e-mail: info@whoophall.co.uk
dir: *From M6 junct 36 take A65. Pub 1m SE of Kirkby Lonsdale*

This 16th-century converted coaching inn was once the kennels for local foxhounds. In an imaginatively converted barn you can relax and enjoy Yorkshire ales and a good range of dishes based on local produce. Oven baked fillet of sea bass with tagliatelle verde and tiger prawns, and stir-fried honey roast duck with vegetables and water chestnuts are among the popular favourites. The bar offers traditional hand-pulled ales and roaring log fires, while outside is a terrace and children's area.

Open all wk ⊕ FREE HOUSE ◀ Black Sheep, Greene King IPA, Tetley Smooth Ѻ Thatchers Gold. **Facilities** Children welcome Play area Family room Dogs allowed Garden Parking **Rooms** 24

LITTLE LANGDALE | Map 18 NY30

PICK OF THE PUBS

Three Shires Inn ★★★★ INN

LA22 9NZ ☎ 015394 37215 📄 015394 37127
e-mail: enquiry@threeshiresinn.co.uk
dir: *Turn off A593, 2.3m from Ambleside at 2nd junct signed 'The Langdales'. 1st left 0.5m. Inn in 1m*

Named after its situation near the meeting point of three county shires - Westmorland, Cumberland and Lancashire – this recently refurbished, traditional Cumbrian slate and stone inn enjoys a stunning location in the beautiful Little Langdale Valley and has been personally run by the Stephenson family since 1983. It's the perfect pit-stop for lunch on walks through the Langdale valleys and for travellers negotiating the Wrynose and Hardknott passes. In winter cosy up by the fire in the traditional beamed bar, while the landscaped garden with its magnificent fell views is the place to savour a pint of Barngates Tag Lag in summer. Food is locally sourced and ranges from light lunches of filled crusty cob rolls (ham with Cumberland sauce), beef and ale pie and baked salmon with lemon mayonnaise, to evening dishes like braised lamb shank with sweet potato purée, and Holker Hall venison with Bordelaise sauce. The ten prettily furnished bedrooms offer a high standard of accommodation, with lovely views of the valley. There is a Langdale beer festival in May.

Open all wk 11-3 6-10.30 Dec-Jan, 11-10.30 Feb-Nov (Fri-Sat 11-11) Closed: 25 Dec **Bar Meals** L served all wk 12-2 (ex 24-25 Dec) D served all wk 6-8.45 (ex mid wk Dec-Jan) booking required Av main course £13 **Restaurant** D served all wk 6-8.45 (ex mid wk Dec-Jan) booking required Av 3 course à la carte fr £23 ⊕ FREE HOUSE ◀ Jennings Best & Cumberland, Coniston Old Man, Hawkshead Bitter, Ennerdale Blonde, Melbreak Bitter, Barngate Tag Lag. **Facilities** Children welcome Children's menu Children's portions Dogs allowed Garden Beer festival Parking Wi-fi **Rooms** 10

LOWESWATER | Map 18 NY12

PICK OF THE PUBS

Kirkstile Inn ★★★★ INN ♥

CA13 0RU ☎ 01900 85219
e-mail: info@kirkstile.com
web: www.kirkstile.com
dir: *From A66 Keswick take Whinlatter Pass at Braithwaite. Take B5292, at T-junct left onto B5289. 3m to Loweswater. From Cockermouth B5289 to Lorton, past Low Lorton, 3m to Loweswater. At red phone box left, 200yds*

The Kirkstile has offered shelter and hospitality amidst the stunning Cumbrian fells for some 400 years. Tucked away next to an old church and a stream, it's just half a mile from the Loweswater and Crummock lakes, and makes an ideal base for walking, climbing, boating and fishing. The whole place has an authentic, traditional and well looked after feel – whitewashed walls, low beams, solid polished tables, cushioned settles, a well-stoked fire and the odd horse harness remind you of times gone by. You can call in for afternoon tea, but better still would be to taste one of the Cumbrian ales brewed by landlord Roger Humphreys in Esthwaite Water near Hawkshead. The dining room dates back to 1549 and is the oldest part of the inn, facing south down the Buttermere Valley. Regular menus and the daily-changing blackboard specials offer local produce in traditional dishes, some with a modern twist: examples are steak and ale pie, chicken, leek and chorizo pudding, and sticky toffee pudding.

Open all day all wk Closed: 25 Dec **Bar Meals** L served all wk 12-2 booking required D served all wk 6-9 booking required Av main course £8.95 **Restaurant** D served all wk 6-9 booking required Av 3 course à la carte fr £20 ⊕ FREE HOUSE ◀ Kirkstile Gold, Yates Bitter, Melbreak, Grasmoor Ale, LPA Ѻ Stowford Press. ♥ 9 **Facilities** Children welcome Children's menu Children's portions Family room Dogs allowed Garden Beer festival Parking **Rooms** 10

LOW LORTON | Map 18 NY12

The Wheatsheaf Inn NEW

CA13 9UW ☎ 01900 85199 & 85268
e-mail: j.williams53@sky.com
dir: *From Cockermouth take B5292 to Lorton. Right onto B5289 to Low Lorton*

Hidden away in the Vale of Lorton, yet close to the Whinlatter Forest and it's walking and mountain biking trails, The Wheatsheaf is a friendly and welcoming village local, popular for its Jennings ales and traditional pub food. Seek it out for its stunning setting and savour the panoramic views of the Lakeland fells with a pint of Cumberland Ale in the peaceful garden. The menu ranges from sandwiches and pub classics to fresh fish nights (Thursday & Friday) and hearty Sunday roasts. Camping facilities.

Open Tue-Sun Closed: Mon & Tue eve in Jan & Feb **Bar Meals** L served Fri 12-2, Sat 12-3, Sun 12-8.30 D served Mon-Sat 6-8.30, Sun 12-8.30 Av main course £9-£15 **Restaurant** L served all wk D served Mon-Sat 6-8.30, Sun 12-8.30 ⊕ MARSTONS ◀ Jennings Bitter, Cumberland Ale, Pedigree, Oxford Gold. **Facilities** Children welcome Children's menu Children's portions Family room Dogs allowed Garden Beer festival Parking

---

LUPTON | Map 18 SD58

PICK OF THE PUBS

The Plough Inn ♥ NEW

Cow Brow LA6 1PJ ☎ 015395 67700
e-mail: info@theploughatlupton.co.uk
dir: *M6 junct 36, A65 towards Kirkby Lonsdale. Pub on right in Lupton*

In an audacious move, the owners of the renowned Punch Bowl at Crosthwaite took on this failing country pub and have transformed it into a sublime dining establishment. Located in the hills between Kendal and Kirkby Lonsdale, the immense limestone whaleback of Farleton Fell rises behind the inn, whilst the sunset view across towards Morecambe Bay and the lower Furness Fells can be stunning. Beers, including tasty Lancaster Amber, are available to deserving ramblers who've tackled the fell, but this is primarily a top-notch food destination, where uniformed staff carry meals to diners enjoying antique furniture or comfy sofas in the roomy, airy, very spacious wood-floored inn. Log burners blaze, country prints decorate and quirky stuffed creatures take the eye momentarily from a menu that delivers with a punch, from simple small plate light bites (roll mops or lamb koftas) to filling mains of venison sausages or pumpkin risotto, complemented by ever-changing blackboard specials. Sweets such as a crumble or baked pear with hazelnut ice cream complete the feast, possibly accompanied by a wine chosen from the magnificent list kept in rustic 'wine caves' viewable to the rear.

Open all day all wk **Bar Meals** L served all wk 12-9 D served all wk 12-9 Av main course £9.95 food served all day **Restaurant** L served all wk 12-9 D served all wk 12-9 Av 3 course à la carte fr £21 food served all day ⊕ FREE HOUSE ◀ Kirkby Lonsdale Monumental, Jennings Cumberland Ale, Lancaster Amber ♂ Thatchers Gold, Westons Organic. **Facilities** Children welcome Children's menu Children's portions Dogs allowed Garden Parking Wi-fi

MILNTHORPE　　　　Map 18 SD48

The Cross Keys ★★★★ INN

1 Park Rd LA7 7AB ☎ 015395 62115 📱 015395 62446
e-mail: stay@thecrosskeyshotel.co.uk
dir: *M6 junct 35, to junct 35A then A6 N of Milnthorpe; or M6 junct 36, A65 towards Kendal. At Crooklands left onto B6385 to Milnthorpe. Pub at x-rds in village centre*

In the heart of Milnthorpe village, this imposing former coaching inn makes a good pit-stop for comfortable accommodation, cask conditioned ales and hearty pub food. Levens Hall, Leighton Moss Nature Reserve and Morecambe Bay are all nearby. Served in the traditional bar and dining room, menus offer sandwiches, salads and pub favourites like curry; steak and ale pie; Cumberland sausages in Yorkshire pudding with gravy; and locally reared sirloin steak with peppercorn sauce. Puddings are a speciality – look out for the local favourite, sticky toffee.

Open all day all wk **Bar Meals** L served Mon-Fri 12-2 Sat-Sun all day D served Mon-Fri 5.30-8.30 Sat-Sun all day Av main course £8 **Restaurant** L served Mon-Fri 12-2 Sat-Sun all day D served Mon-Fri 5-8.30 Sat-Sun all day ⊕ ROBINSONS ◀ Hartley XB, Dizzy Blond, Veltins, Guest ale ♂ Stowford Press. **Facilities** Children welcome Children's menu Children's portions Dogs allowed Garden Parking Wi-fi **Rooms** 8

NEAR SAWREY　　　　Map 18 SD39

PICK OF THE PUBS

Tower Bank Arms

LA22 0LF ☎ 015394 36334
e-mail: enquiries@towerbankarms.com
dir: *On B5285 SW of Windermere.1.5m from Hawkshead. 2m from Windermere via ferry*

This 17th-century Lakeland inn stands next to Beatrix Potter's home, Hill Top, now owned by the National Trust. Follow a visit to Hill Top, which featured in the *Tale of Jemima Puddleduck*, with lunch at this traditional and delightfully unspoilt little pub - but time your arrival carefully as it can get swamped during the summer months. Its rustic charm is best enjoyed out of season, when you can relax and soak up atmosphere in the low-beamed main bar with its slate floor, crackling log fire, fresh flowers and ticking grandfather clock. Tip-top local ales on handpump include Hawkshead Bitter, Barngates Tag Lag and Cumbrian Legendary, and hearty country food makes good use of local produce. Tuck into a bowl of steamed

mussels with white wine, garlic and cream followed by Cumbrian beef and ale stew or maybe shoulder of Cumbrian lamb with creamy mash and mint and rosemary jus. For vegetarians there is mushroom Stroganoff or Mediterranean pasta. Puddings include traditional sticky toffee pudding and a slate of local cheeses.

Open all wk all day Etr-Oct **Bar Meals** L served all wk 12-2 D served Mon-Sat 6-9, Sun & BH 6-8 (Mon-Thu in winter) Av main course £10.50 **Restaurant** D served Mon-Sat 6-9, Sun & BH 6-8 (Mon-Thu in winter) Av 3 course à la carte fr £19.30 ⊕ FREE HOUSE ◀ Barngates Tag Lag, Hawkshead Bitter, Brodies Prime, Ulverston, Cumbrian Legendary ♂ Westons Organic Vintage, Old Rosie. **Facilities** Children welcome Children's portions Dogs allowed Garden Parking

OUTGATE　　　　Map 18 SD39

Outgate Inn ♀

LA22 0NQ ☎ 015394 36413
e-mail: info@outgateinn.co.uk
dir: *Exit M6 junct 36, by-passing Kendal, A591 towards Ambleside. At Clappersgate take B5285 to Hawkshead then Outgate 3m*

A 17th-century Lakeland inn with oak beams, once a mineral water manufacturer and now part of Robinson's and Hartley's Brewery. During the winter there's a real fire, while the secluded beer garden at the rear is a tranquil place to enjoy the summer warmth. Pub lunches range from sandwiches and jackets to hot plates such as home-made beef and Guinness casserole and locally produced Cumberland sausages, while dinner choices continue the traditional route: pan-fried rump steak medallions, perhaps, or poached chicken supreme in a chasseur sauce. Recent change of hands.

Open all day all wk **Bar Meals** L served all wk 12-9 D served all wk 12-9 food served all day **Restaurant** L served all wk 12-9 booking required D served all wk 12-9 booking required Fixed menu price fr £15 food served all day ⊕ FREDERIC ROBINSON ◀ Hartleys XB, Dizzy Blonde, seasonal guest ales ♂ Stowford Press. ♀ 14 **Facilities** Children welcome Children's menu Children's portions Dogs allowed Garden Parking Wi-fi

PENRITH　　　　Map 18 NY53

Cross Keys Inn ♀ NEW

Carleton Village CA11 8TP
☎ 01768 865588 📱 01768 866422
e-mail: crosskeys@kyloes.co.uk
dir: *From A66 in Penrith take A686 to Carleton Village, inn on right*

This much-refurbished old drovers and coaching inn at the edge of Penrith offers patrons sweeping views to the nearby North Pennines from the upstairs restaurant where timeless, traditional pub meals are the order of the day; local Cumberland sausage or T-bone steak for

example. Kyloes Grill here is particularly well thought of, with only Cumbrian meats used. Beers crafted in nearby Broughton Hall by Tirril brewery draw an appreciative local clientele, warming toes by the ferocious log-burner or laying a few tiles on the domino tables.

Open all wk Mon-Fri 12-2.30 5-12 (Sat-Sun all day) **Bar Meals** L served Mon-Sat 12-2.30 Av main course £9.95 **Restaurant** L served all wk 12-2.30 D served Sun-Thu 6-9, Fri-Sat 5.30-9 ⊕ FREE HOUSE ◀ Theakston Black Bull, Tirril 1823, guest ale. ♀ 10 **Facilities** Children welcome Children's menu Children's portions Dogs allowed Garden Parking Wi-fi

RAVENSTONEDALE　　　　Map 18 NY70

PICK OF THE PUBS

The Black Swan　　　　INN ♀

See Pick of the Pubs on page 110

PICK OF THE PUBS

The Fat Lamb Country Inn ★★ HL

See Pick of the Pubs on page 111

SEATHWAITE　　　　Map 18 SD29

Newfield Inn ♀ NEW

LA20 6ED ☎ 01229 716208
dir: *From Broughton-in-Furness take A595 signed Whitehaven & Workington. Right into Smithy Lane signed Ulpha. Through Ulpha to Seathwaite*

Paul Batten's 16th-century cottage-style pub can be found tucked away in the peaceful Duddon Valley. Wordsworth's favourite valley is also popular with walkers and climbers and the slate-floored bar regularly throngs with parched outdoor types quaffing pints of Cumberland Ale and Cumbrian Dickie Doodle. Served all day, food is hearty and traditional and uses local farm meats, the choice ranging from fresh rolls, salads and lunchtime snack like ham, egg and chips, to steak pie, sirloin steak and chips, and home-made bread-and-butter pudding. Escape to the garden in summer and savour cracking fell views.

Open all day all wk **Bar Meals** Av main course £9 food served all day **Restaurant** Av 3 course à la carte fr £25 food served all day ⊕ FREE HOUSE ◀ Jennings Cumberland Ale, Cumbrian Legendary Ales Dickie Doodle. ♀ 8 **Facilities** Children welcome Children's portions Play area Dogs allowed Garden Beer festival Parking

PICK OF THE PUBS

The Black Swan ★★★★ INN 🍷

RAVENSTONEDALE   Map 18 NY70

CA17 4NG ☎ 015396 23204
e-mail: enquiries@blackswanhotel.com
web: www.blackswanhotel.com
dir: *M6 junct 38 take A685 E towards Brough*

The Black Swan is set in this pretty little village that nestles below Wild Boar Fell beside the frothy headwaters of the appropriately named River Eden. The enterprising owners of this family-run residential inn, which has gained 4 AA Highly Commended Yellow Stars for the quality of the individually-styled bedrooms and Breakfast and Dinner awards for the food, have placed themselves right at the heart of the community, with the on-site village store being opened by HRH Prince Charles in 2008; part of the 'Pub is the Hub' campaign and specialising in locally produced foods and goodies. The imposing Victorian inn's tranquil riverside garden is home to red squirrels, which will let you share their space to relax in after you've walked the Howgill Fells, explored the Lakes or toured the Yorkshire Dales, all of which are on the doorstep. The ever-changing selection of northern beers includes ales from the likes of Dent, Hesket Newmarket and Tirril breweries. This local pride ethos is also strongly evident in the choice of dishes, with all

meat traceable locally and detailed for lucky guests to contemplate. The menu might include a starter of layered terrine of smoked trout, mackerel and salmon, wrapped in smoked salmon with horseradish and artisan bread, a robust precursor to steak, venison and ale cobbler with a choice of potato accompaniment. Vegetarians may relish the vegetable Wellington stuffed with celeriac, broccoli and spinach in a creamy cheese sauce accompanied by braised red cabbage, chestnuts and new potatoes. Making the most of the local country's largesse, menus tend to be seasonal with daily-changing specials; there's also a good choice of snacks and light bites.

Open all day all wk 8am-11.30pm
Bar Meals L served all wk 12-2 D served all wk 6-9 Av main course £12

Restaurant L served all wk 12-2 booking required D served all wk 6-9 booking required Av 3 course à la carte fr £20 ⊕ FREE HOUSE ◉ Black Sheep Ale, Black Sheep Bitter, John Smith's, Dent, Tirril Brewery, Hawkshead Brewery, Hesket Newmarket, Cumberland Brewery, Guinness, Guest ales ⊘ Thatchers Gold. **Facilities** Children welcome Children's menu Children's portions Dogs allowed Garden Parking Wi-fi **Rooms** 14

Save on hotels. Book at **theAA.com/hotel**

CUMBRIA 111 ENGLAND

PICK OF THE PUBS

The Fat Lamb Country Inn ★★ HL

RAVENSTONEDALE Map 18 NY70

Crossbank CA17 4LL
☎ **015396 23242** 📄 **015396 23285**
e-mail: enquiries@fatlamb.co.uk
web: www.fatlamb.co.uk
dir: *On A683 between Sedbergh & Kirkby Stephen*

From The Fat Lamb's gardens, your gaze will fall on some of England's most precious, under-visited and remote countryside. So it's no surprise that ramblers and country lovers compete to stay in the comfy AA-rated en suite bedrooms at this stone coaching inn high above the green meadows of Ravenstonedale in the furthest corner of old Westmorland. Modern amenities blend with old fashioned hospitality at this 350-year-old free house. An open fire in the traditional Yorkshire range warms the bar in winter; this is the oldest part of the building and was converted from the former kitchen and living area. Here, visitors and locals mingle and natter without the intrusion of electronic entertainments. Snacks and meals are served both here and in the traditional and relaxed restaurant, which is decorated with old prints and plates. Bar snacks take the form of sandwiches and warm baguettes, plates of Cumberland sausage, best Whitby scampi, and salads. The five-course table d'hôte menu may offer seared pigeon breast with carrot purée and sage

sauce, followed by a home-made soup and then assiette of local fell-bred lamb. If you go à la carte, salt and pepper squid with wasabi mayonnaise and sweet chilli sauce makes an excellent start, which could be followed by pavé of wild Cumbrian venison with a green peppercorn sauce. Alternatively, check out the day's specials board. Whatever you choose, it will have been prepared on site using the best available local ingredients. A short, post-prandial constitutional could take you through the inn's own nature reserve – seven acres of open water and wetlands, surrounded by flower rich meadows. Over 80 species of bird have been recorded, sharing their glorious surroundings with badgers, foxes, otters, roe deer and bats.

Open all day all wk **Bar Meals** L served all wk 12-2 booking required D served all wk 6-9 booking required Av main course £9.80 **Restaurant** L served all wk 12-2 booking required D served all wk 6-9 booking required Fixed menu price fr £24 Av 3 course à la carte fr £15.50 🛢 FREE HOUSE ◼ Black Sheep Bitter Ö Stowford Press. **Facilities** Children's menu Children's portions Play area Dogs allowed Garden Parking Wi-fi **Rooms** 12

SIZERGH Map 18 SD48

PICK OF THE PUBS

The Strickland Arms ♥ NEW

LA8 8DZ ☎ 015395 61010 📠 015395 61068

e-mail: thestricklandarms@yahoo.co.uk

dir: From Kendal A591 S. At Brettargh Holt junct branch left, at rdbt 3rd exit onto A590 (dual carriageway) signed Barrow. Follow brown signs for Sizergh Castle. Into right lane, turn right across dual carriageway. Pub on left

Beside the lane leading to the National Trust's Sizergh Castle and just a stride from paths alongside the lively River Kent, this slightly severe-looking building (also NT owned) slumbers amidst low hills above the Lyth Valley at the southern fringe of the Lake District National Park. Visitors to the valley's renowned damson blossom extravaganza (April) can enjoy produce gleaned from this bounteous harvest, maybe including a damson beer from one of the local micro-breweries whose ales stock the bar here; an annual beer festival scoops many more Lake District breweries into the fold. The essentially open-plan interior is contemporary-Edwardian, with high ceilings, flagstoned floors, grand fires and Farrow & Ball finish to the walls creating an instantly welcoming atmosphere. Re-opened after years of closure just a couple of seasons ago, the great beers and fine food made an immediate impact, and the inn is a popular destination dining pub. Home-made chicken liver and brandy pâté with Hawkshead damson chutney, salad and crusty bread is a good foundation for a main of sweet cured pork loin steak with black pudding and free range eggs; all local produce when possible.

Open all wk Mon-Thu 11.30-3 5.30-11 (Fri-Sun all day) Closed: 25 Dec Bar Meals L served Mon-Fri 12-2, Sat 12-2.30, Sun 12-8.30 D served Mon-Sat 6-9, Sun 12-8.30 Av main course £11.75 Restaurant L served Mon-Fri 12-2, Sat 12-2.30, Sun 12-8.30 D served Mon-Sat 6-9, Sun 12-8.30 Fixed menu price fr £19.95 Av 3 course à la carte fr £19.75 ⊕ FREE HOUSE ◀ Thwaites Langdale Tup, Bomber, Coniston Bluebird, Loweswater Gold, Kirkby Lonsdale Monumental. ♥ 9 Facilities Children welcome Children's menu Children's portions Dogs allowed Garden Beer festival Parking Wi-fi

TEMPLE SOWERBY Map 18 NY62

The Kings Arms Hotel ★★ HL NEW

CA10 1SB ☎ 017683 62944

e-mail: enquiries@kingsarmstemplesowerby.co.uk

dir: M6 junct 40, E on A66 to Temple Sowerby. Hotel in town centre

Just nine miles from Penrith, this 400-year-old coaching inn was where William Wordsworth and Samuel Coleridge set off for their exploration of the Lake District. Acquired by new owners in 2009, it has been fully refurbished as a traditional inn with rooms. The kitchen serves a mix of old pub favourites (Cumberland bangers and mash) and à la

carte choices such as venison steak with blackcurrant and sherry reduction, as well as Black Sheep ale.

Open all wk 10-3 6-11 Bar Meals L served all wk 12-2 D served all wk 6-9 Av main course £9.50 Restaurant L served all wk 12-2 booking required D served all wk 6-9 booking required Fixed menu price fr £18 Av 3 course à la carte fr £18 ⊕ FREE HOUSE ◀ Black Sheep, Guest ales ♺ Stowford Press. Facilities Children welcome Children's menu Children's portions Dogs allowed Garden Parking Wi-fi Rooms 9

TIRRIL Map 18 NY52

PICK OF THE PUBS

Queen's Head Inn ♥

CA10 2JF ☎ 01768 863219

e-mail: bookings@queensheadinn.co.uk

dir: A66 towards Penrith then A6 S towards Shap. In Eamont Bridge turn right just after Crown Hotel. Tirril in 1m on B5320

Situated on the edge of the Lake District National Park, this traditional English country inn dates from 1719 and is chock-full of beams, flagstones and memorabilia as you would expect from an old inn. While enjoying a pint of Unicorn, Cumbrian Way and Dizzy Blonde in the bar, look for the Wordsworth Indenture, signed by the great poet himself, his brother, Christopher, and local wheelwright John Bewsher, to whom the Wordsworths sold the pub in 1836. You can eat in the bar or restaurant, and a meal might include bacon and black pudding salad; oven-baked chicken stuffed with Blengdale Blue and spinach; and chocolate and orange tart. In August every year the Cumbrian beer and sausage festival is held here. The village shop is located at the back of the inn.

Open all day all wk Sun-Thurs noon-11pm, Fri-Sat noon-mdnt Bar Meals L served all wk 12-2.30 D served all wk 5.30-8.30 Restaurant L served all wk 12-2.30 D served all wk 5.30-8.30 ⊕ ROBINSONS ◀ Unicorn, Cumbria Way, Dizzy Blonde, XB Smooth, Guest ales ♺ Stowford Press. ♥ 10 Facilities Children welcome Children's portions Dogs allowed Parking

TORVER Map 18 SD29

Church House Inn

LA21 8AZ ☎ 01539 441282

e-mail: churchhouseinn@hotmail.co.uk

dir: Take A539 from Coniston towards Broughton-in-Furness. Inn on left in Torver before junct with A5084 towards Ulverston

Footpaths wind to the bank of Coniston Water whilst the ridges of the Coniston Horseshoe mountains rise steeply from sloping pastures opposite. Sitting plum in the middle, the 15th century Church House Inn revels in this idyllic location, offering a great range of Lakeland beers and satisfying meals sourced from local farms and estates; Cumberland Tattie hot pot based on slow braised Herdwick lamb hits the spot, enjoyed in the olde-worlde rambling interior or sheltered beer garden.

Open all day all wk (Dec-Mar noon-3 5-11) Closed: Dec-Mar Mon-Tue fr 5pm, Wed-Thu noon-3 5-mdnt ⊕ ENTERPRISE INNS ◀ Hawkshead Bitter, Hawkshead Gold, Tag Lag, Loweswater Gold. Facilities Children welcome Children's portions Family room Dogs allowed Garden Parking Wi-fi

TROUTBECK Map 18 NY40

PICK OF THE PUBS

Queen's Head ★★★★ INN ♥

Townhead LA23 1PW

☎ 015394 32174 📠 015394 31938

e-mail: reservations@queensheadtroutbeck.co.uk

web: www.queensheadtroutbeck.co.uk

dir: M6 junct 36, A590/591, W towards Windermere, right at mini-rdbt onto A592 signed Penrith/Ullswater. Pub 2m on left

Nooks and crannies, low beams stuffed with old pennies by farmers on their way home from market, and a log fire throughout the year make this smart 17th-century coaching inn hard to beat when it comes to old world charm. The lovely undulating valley of Troutbeck, with its maze of footpaths and stunning felltop views, is a magnet for ramblers. True to its roots, this inn offers sustenance and comfortable accommodation to the weary and footsore. The bar is perhaps its most remarkable feature, carved from a four-poster bed that once resided in Appleby Castle. Robinson's Brewery furnishes the likes of Cumbria Way, Old Tom and Dizzy Blonde at the pumps, while the chef's reputation for accomplished cooking is well established. The menu proffers hearty international fare ranging from a mezze of nuts, olives, feta and deep-fried halouni to a starter of home-made black pudding with scallops, crispy bacon and mustard sauce followed by venison and Guinness cottage pie or moules marinière. Typical desserts include lemon posset and sticky toffee pudding.

Open all day all wk Bar Meals food served all day Restaurant booking required food served all day ⊕ FREDERIC ROBINSON ◀ Hartleys XB, Cumbria Way, Double Hop, Old Tom, Dizzy Blonde. ♥ 8 Facilities Children welcome Children's menu Dogs allowed Parking Wi-fi Rooms 15

See advert on opposite page

Save on hotels. Book at theAA.com/hotel

CUMBRIA 113 ENGLAND

ULVERSTON   Map 18 SD27

Farmers Arms �

Market Place LA12 7BA
☎ 01229 584469 📠 01229 582188
dir: *In town centre*

A warm welcome is extended at this lively 16th-century inn located at the centre of the attractive, historic market town. Visitors will find a comfortable and relaxing beamed front bar with an open fire in winter. Landlord Roger Chattaway takes pride in serving quality ales and food. His Sunday lunches are famous locally, and there's a varied and tempting specials menu, deli boards to share, pub classics, chargrilled steaks and seafood delights like crab cakes with sweet chilli salsa. Pizzas have now made an appearance on the menu; perhaps Pizza de la Mer, American Hot, or the vegetarian option Vitabella.

Open all day all wk **Bar Meals** L served all wk 9-3 booking required D served all wk 6-9 booking required Av main course £9.99 ⊕ FREE HOUSE ◀ Hawkshead Best Bitter, John Smith's, Directors, Yates ♂ Symons. ♟12 **Facilities** Children welcome Children's menu Children's portions Garden Beer festival Wi-fi

The Stan Laurel Inn NEW

31 The Ellers LA12 0AB ☎ **01229 582814**
e-mail: thestanlaurel@aol.com
dir: *M6 junct 36, A590 to Ulverston. Straight on at Booths rdbt, left at 2nd rdbt in The Ellers, pub on left after Ford garage*

In 1890, when the old market town of Ulverston's most famous son, the comic actor Stan Laurel, was born, this town-centre pub was still a farmhouse with two cottages surrounded by fields and orchards. Owners Trudi and Paul Dewar provide a selection of locally brewed real ales and a full menu of traditional pub food plus a specials board, including sandwiches and baguettes, salads, grills and old favourites like fisherman's pie; chilli tortilla stack; steak and ale pie; chicken curry; and vegetable and Stilton crumble.

Open 12-2.30 6-12 Closed: Mon L **Bar Meals** L served Tue-Sat 12-2, Sun 12-8 booking required D served Tue-Sat 6-9, Sun 12-8 booking required **Restaurant** L served Tue-Sat 12-2, Sun 12-8 booking required D served Tue-Sat 6-9, Sun 12-8 booking required ⊕ FREE HOUSE ◀ Thwaites Original, Ulverston Brewing Co, Barngates Brewery, Salamander Brewing Co. **Facilities** Children welcome Children's menu Children's portions Dogs allowed Parking Wi-fi

WASDALE HEAD   Map 18 NY10

Wasdale Head Inn ★★★ INN

CA20 1EX ☎ **019467 26229** 📠 019467 26054
e-mail: reception@wasdale.com
dir: *From A595 follow Wasdale signs. Inn at head of valley*

Famous historic inn dramatically situated at the foot of England's highest mountain, adjacent to England's smallest church and not far from her deepest lake. With views to Great Gable, Kirk Fell and Yewbarrow, this is reputedly the birthplace of British climbing — photographs decorating the oak-panelled walls reflect the passion for this activity. Real ales are local, and a beer festival on the first Sunday in October is a great reason to hang up the climbing boots for a day and maybe stay over in one of the comfortable bedrooms. A menu speciality is Herdwick lamb and mutton, when available.

Open all day all wk **Bar Meals** L served all wk 12-9 D served all wk 12-9 Av main course £9 food served all day **Restaurant** D served all wk 7-8 booking required Fixed menu price fr £33 Av 3 course à la carte fr £33 ⊕ FREE HOUSE ◀ Yates Best Bitter, Loweswater Gold, Yewbarrow, Gable, Jennings. **Facilities** Children welcome Children's menu Children's portions Dogs allowed Garden Beer festival Parking **Rooms** 10

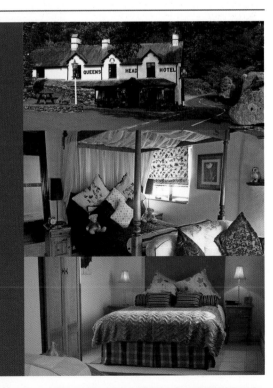

PICK OF THE PUBS

Brackenrigg Inn ★★★ INN 🍷

WATERMILLOCK   Map 18 NY42

CA11 0LP
☎ **017684 86206** 📠 **017684 86945**
e-mail: enquiries@brackenrigginn.co.uk
web: www.brackenrigginn.co.uk
dir: *M6 junct 40 take A66 signed Keswick. Then A592 signed Ullswater. Right at lake. Inn 6m from M6 & Penrith*

The long, white-washed inn was once a farm and dates from the 18th century. Its elevated position overlooking the stunning landscape of Ullswater and the surrounding fells is beyond compare.

A traditional walkers' inn, the Brackenrigg retains an appealing homely feel. The attractive panelled bar with polished wooden floor, open log fires, and separate dining room with polished mahogany furniture, along with that view, creates the perfect retreat. Expect a good choice of real ales such as Coniston Bluebird and Black Sheep. The wine list too is balanced and full of interest, with a choice of fifteen wines by the glass and helpful suggestions on tasting.

The menu caters for all tastes, and meals are freshly prepared from local produce, ranging from traditional dishes to those that belie the nature of a traditional walkers' inn, and can be enjoyed in the restaurant or bar. Typical starters include potted hoi sin duck, sesame prawn toast with a tomato chilli jam, pan-seared

scallops, white chocolate and truffle oil risotto, and Brackenrigg twice-baked cheese soufflé. For main course, try the roast rump of Lakeland lamb, goat's cheese mashed potato, spinach and red wine rosemary jus; braised leeks, sautéed mushrooms and potatoes with Welsh rarebit; or pan-fried sea bass, lemon mashed potato, curly kale and truffle cream. If time is short the Light Bites and Snacks menu offers decent sandwiches, a selection of ciabattas and a range of lighter snacks including a walkers' ploughman's lunch.

Finally, if you can't tear yourselves away from the peace and beauty of this place, then make yourself at home in one of the inn's 17 bedrooms, some housed on the ground floor in Stable Cottages. It makes

a superb base for exploring the delights of the north Lakes, which include walking, climbing, watersports and golf, as well as simply touring by car.

Open all day all wk **Bar Meals/ Restaurant** Light Bites and Snacks 12-6 served all week Menu served all week 12-9.30 🌐 FREE HOUSE 🍺 Coniston Bluebird, Tirril, Black Sheep, Cumbrian Legendary Ales, Cumberland Ales 🍎 Westons. 🍷 15 **Facilities** Children's menu Dogs allowed Garden Parking Wi-fi **Rooms** 17

WATERMILLOCK   Map 18 NY42

PICK OF THE PUBS

Brackenrigg Inn ★★★ INN ♥

See Pick of the Pubs on opposite page

WINDERMERE   Map 18 SD49

The Angel Inn ♥

Helm Rd LA23 3BU ☎ 015394 44080
e-mail: rooms@the-angelinn.com
dir: *From Rayrigg Rd (parallel to lake) into Crag Brow, then right into Helm Rd*

Situated in the centre of Bowness-on-Windermere within its own gardens and grounds, five minutes' walk from Lake Windermere, this family owned and run gastro-pub offers plenty of city chic style. Unusual local ales vie with international beers at the bar, and good food based on local produce is available throughout the day from a choice of menus: breakfast/brunch; sandwiches and light lunches; starters, nibbles and salads; main courses – try braised shoulder of Lune Valley lamb or Cartmel Valley duck and chilli sausage – desserts and a children's menu. Enjoy fantastic views from the garden terrace in summer.

Open all day all wk 9am-11pm Closed: 25 Dec
Bar Meals L served all wk 9.30-4 D served all wk 5-9
Restaurant L served all wk 9.30-4 D served all wk 5-9
⊕ FREE HOUSE ◀ Coniston Bluebird Bitter, Hawkshead Bitter, Tirril Old Faithful, Stringers West Coast Blonde.
♥ 12 Facilities Children welcome Children's menu Children's portions Dogs allowed Garden Parking Wi-fi

Eagle & Child Inn

Kendal Rd, Staveley LA8 9LP ☎ 01539 821320
e-mail: info@eaglechildinn.co.uk
dir: *M6 junct 36, A590 towards Kendal then A591 towards Windermere. Staveley approx 2m*

The rivers Kent and Gowan meet at the gardens of this friendly inn, and it's surrounded by miles of excellent walking, cycling and fishing country. Several pubs in Britain share the same name, which refers to a legend of a baby found in an eagle's nest. With a good range of beers to chose from, dishes include Fleetwood mussels in tomato, garlic and white wine sauce, local rump steak braised with onions; and roast cod loin in anchovy and parsley butter.

Open all day all wk ⊕ FREE HOUSE ◀ Coniston, Hawkshead Bitter, Dent Ales, Yates Bitter, Tirril Brewery Ò Westons, Ancient Orchard, Cumbrian.
Facilities Children welcome Children's menu Children's portions Dogs allowed Garden Parking Wi-fi

WORKINGTON   Map 18 NY02

The Old Ginn House

Great Clifton CA14 1TS
☎ 01900 64616   📠 01900 873384
e-mail: enquiries@oldginnhouse.co.uk
dir: *Just off A66, 3m from Workington & 4m from Cockermouth*

When this was a farm, ginning was the process by which horses were used to turn a grindstone that crushed grain. It took place in the rounded area known today as the Ginn Room and which is now the main bar, serving Jennings and Bluebird beers. The dining areas, all butter yellow, bright check curtains and terracotta tiles, rather bring the Mediterranean to mind, although the extensive menu and specials are both cosmopolitan and traditional.

Open all day all wk Closed: 24-26 Dec, 1 Jan
Bar Meals L served all wk 12-2 D served all wk 6-9.30 Av main course £8 Restaurant L served all wk 12-2 D served all wk 6-9.30 Av 3 course à la carte fr £16 ⊕ FREE HOUSE ◀ Jennings Bitter, John Smith's Bitter, Local Bluebird.
Facilities Children welcome Children's menu Children's portions Garden Parking

YANWATH   Map 18 NY52

PICK OF THE PUBS

The Yanwath Gate Inn ♥

CA10 2LF ☎ 01768 862386
e-mail: enquiries@yanwathgate.com
web: www.yanwathgate.com
dir: *Telephone for directions*

To one horizon rise the lofty North Pennines; to another the hills and moors bounding nearby Ullswater draw the eye. In between is the Eden Valley, source of much of the food prepared at this well respected dining inn. Evolving over centuries from a toll gate, or 'yat', on the long road from Kendal to Scotland, today's incarnation is a classy mix of traditional pub and fine restaurant; timeless ambience (the pub is around 330 years old) and top notch dishes, where free range and organic are words constantly at the forefront of Matt Edwards' mantra. Lunch and evening menus will vary, and content depends on seasonal or specialist availability, but could encompass starters of seafood ceviche or black pudding rarebit with watercress and chestnut salad, setting the scene for venison burger on home-baked focaccia or braised belly of saddleback pork with apricot and spinach forcemeat stuffing. To accompany, there's an extraordinarily wide list of bins, or take a

leaf out of locals' and Matt's book and indulge in a beer from one of the reliable craft breweries within a few miles of the inn, perhaps a pint from Hesket Newmarket's range.

Open all day all wk Bar Meals L served all wk 12-2.30 booking required D served all wk 6-9 booking required Restaurant L served all wk 12-2.30 booking required D served all wk 6-9 booking required ⊕ FREE HOUSE ◀ Hesket Newmarket, Tirril, Loweswater, Keswick Ò Westons Old Rosie. ♥ 12 Facilities Children welcome Children's menu Dogs allowed Garden Parking Wi-fi

DERBYSHIRE

ASHBOURNE   Map 10 SK14

Barley Mow Inn

Kirk Ireton DE6 3JP ☎ 01335 370306
dir: *Telephone for directions*

Built on the edge of the Peak District National Park by the Storer family of yeomen farmers in the 16th century, the building became an inn during the early 1700s. The imposing free house has remained largely unchanged over the years, and has been run by Mary Short since 1976. Six nine-gallon barrels of beer stand behind the bar, with cheese and pickle or salami rolls and bar snacks on offer at lunchtime. Close to Carsington Water, there are good walking opportunities on nearby marked paths.

Open all wk noon-2 7-11 (Sun noon-2 7-10.30) Closed: 25 Dec, 1 Jan ⊕ FREE HOUSE ◀ Changing micro-breweries Ò Thatchers. Facilities Children welcome Dogs allowed Garden Parking Wi-fi Notes ◉

ASHOVER   Map 16 SK36

Old Poets Corner NEW

Butts Rd S45 0EW ☎ 01246 590888
dir: *From Matlock take A632 signed Chesterfield. Right onto B6036 to Ashover*

Ale aficionados and traditional cider drinkers flock to this traditional village local, a 'true' free house dispensing eight ciders and ten cask ales, two of which (Light Rale and Poet's Tipple) are brewed in the Ashover Brewery behind the pub. Wash down hearty home-made pub dishes, perhaps beef stew, liver and onions or ham, egg and chips, then head off into the beautiful Derbyshire countryside as miles of lovely walks radiate from the front. Don't miss the March and October beer festivals – up to 40 ales!

Open all day all wk Bar Meals L served Mon-Fri 12-2, Sat-Sun 12-3 D served Mon-Thu 6.30-9, Fri-Sat 6-9.30, Sun 7-9 Av main course £7.50 Restaurant L served Mon-Fri 12-2, Sat-Sun 12-3 booking required D served Mon-Thu 6.30-9, Fri-Sat 6-9.30, Sun 7-9 booking required Av 3 course à la carte fr £15 ⊕ FREE HOUSE ◀ Ashover Brewery ales. Facilities Children welcome Family room Dogs allowed Beer festival Parking

BAKEWELL — Map 16 SK26

PICK OF THE PUBS

The Bull's Head

Church St, Ashford-in-the-Water DE45 1QB
☎ 01629 812931
e-mail: bullshead.ashford@virgin.net
dir: Off A6, 2m N of Bakewell, 5m from Chatsworth Estate

A 17th-century, family-run coaching inn with oak beams, open fires, carved settles, and jazz playing quietly in the background. Debbie Shaw's family have run this busy country pub for over fifty years; Debbie and husband/chef Carl have been in charge for twelve years, earning some impressive accolades along the way. With a clear preference for using local produce, Carl develops appealing menus that always feature steak and Old Stockport ale pie, and may well include calves' liver with bubble and squeak; monkfish baked with sweet chilli sauce; and fennel and smoked cheese tartlet with salad. The sticky toffee pudding here, which comes with black treacle sauce and fresh cream, has acquired quite a reputation, but there are tasty alternatives, such as Stilton and Manchego cheese with grapes and Scottish oatcakes. A snack or sandwich in the beautiful beer garden, followed by a game of boules or Jenga, is worth contemplating.

Open all wk 11-3 (summer) noon-3 (winter) 6-11 (Sun noon-3 7-10.30) Bar Meals L served all wk 12-2 D served Mon-Sat (ex Thu in winter) 6.30-9, Sun 7-9 ⊕ ROBINSONS ◄ Old Stockport, Unicorn, seasonal ales. Facilities Children welcome Children's portions Family room Dogs allowed Garden Parking

PICK OF THE PUBS

The Monsal Head Hotel ★★ HL ◉ ♀

Monsal Head DE45 1NL
☎ 01629 640250 📱 01629 640815
e-mail: enquiries@monsalhead.com
dir: A6 from Bakewell towards Buxton. 1.5m to Ashford. Follow Monsal Head signs, B6465 for 1m

A ten-minute drive from Chatsworth House and Haddon Hall, this distinctive, balconied free house is set in the heart of the Peak District National Park and offers commanding superb views over Monsal Dale. The hotel's real ale pub, the Stable Bar, reflects its earlier role as the home of railway horses, which collected passengers from Monsal Dale station. Today, this delightful venue features original flagstone floors, winter fires and a range of cask ales. Food is served all day in the bar and Longstone Restaurant, or in fine weather you may prefer to eat in the large enclosed garden. Expect lunchtime sandwiches and jacket potatoes, but for something more ambitious, head for the restaurant, where French fish soup might be followed by grilled fillet of sea bass with prawn, scallop and vegetable spring rolls. Lime cheesecake is a typical dessert, or you might opt for a selection of farmhouse cheeses.

Open all day all wk 8am-11pm Bar Meals L served Mon-Sat 12-9.30, Sun 12-9 D served Mon-Sat 12-9.30, Sun 12-9 food served all day Restaurant L served Mon-Sat 12-9.30, Sun 12-9 D served Mon-Sat 12-9.30, Sun 12-9 food served all day ⊕ FREE HOUSE ◄ Bradfield ales, Lloyds Monsal, Thornbridge ales, Abbeydale, Peakstones Black Hole. ♀ 17 Facilities Children welcome Children's menu Children's portions Dogs allowed Garden Parking Rooms 7

BAMFORD — Map 16 SK28

PICK OF THE PUBS

Yorkshire Bridge Inn ★★★★ INN ♀

Ashopton Rd S33 0AZ
☎ 01433 651361 📱 01433 651361
e-mail: info@yorkshire-bridge.co.uk
dir: A57 from M1, left onto A6013, pub 1m on right

In the heart of wonderful Peak District walking country, this inn dates from 1826 and is named after an old packhorse bridge over the River Derwent. Views from the beamed and chintz-curtained bars take in the peak of Whin Hill, a beautiful setting in which to enjoy a pint of Chatsworth Gold and some good quality, freshly made pub food using local produce. The main menu lists sandwiches, salad platters and filled jacket potatoes, plus grills and other hot dishes, including steak and kidney pie and lasagne. In addition, daily specials may take in pan-fried duck with orange and cranberry sauce, chargrilled minted lamb chops, and battered haddock with chips and mushy peas. For dessert, you could try chocolate sponge pudding or local Bradwell's ice creams. The en suite bedrooms, including one with a four-poster, and self-catering apartments over the road make a good base for touring the nearby attractions of Chatsworth, Dovedale and Bakewell.

Open all day all wk Bar Meals L served Mon-Sat 12-2, Sun 12-8.30 D served Mon-Thu 6-9, Fri-Sat 6-9.30, Sun 12-8.30 ⊕ FREE HOUSE ◄ Bakewell Best, Pale Rider, Scotts 1816, Chatsworth Gold, Easy Rider. ♀ 11 Facilities Children welcome Children's menu Children's portions Garden Parking Wi-fi Rooms 14

BARLOW — Map 16 SK37

The Trout at Barlow ♀

33 Valley Rd S18 7SL
☎ 0114 289 0893 📱 0114 289 0893
e-mail: mikenorie@btconnect.com
dir: From Chesterfield follow the Newbold Rd B619 for 4.5m

With an open fire in winter, this country pub is a few miles outside Chesterfield at the start of the Peak District. There's a Jazz Club every five weeks, steak night on a Thursday, quiz night on a Wednesday, and the Barlow Proms in the village every June. A weekly-changing choice of two real ales along with regulars is

offered and plenty of freshly prepared, home-cooked food at good prices. All special occasions are catered for, such as weddings and parties.

Open all day all wk Bar Meals Av main course £8.95 Restaurant L served Mon-Sat 12-2, Sun 12-2 booking required D served Mon-Sat 6-9 booking required ⊕ MARSTONS ◄ Marstons Pedigree, Mansfield Smooth, Marston's Finest Creamy, Guest ales. ♀ 9 Facilities Children welcome Children's menu Children's portions Dogs allowed Garden Parking

BARROW UPON TRENT — Map 11 SK32

Ragley Boat Stop ♀

Deepdale Ln, Off Sinfin Ln DE73 1HH ☎ 01332 703919
e-mail: ragley@king-henrys-taverns.co.uk
dir: Telephone for directions

This spacious pub has a lovely garden that slopes down to the Trent and Mersey Canal, lots of relaxing sofas, many eating areas and a huge balcony overlooking the gardens and canal for enjoying a drink and just watching the world go by. The menu of freshly prepared dishes has choices for small and large appetites alike. Choose from steaks, fish and seafood, rumpburgers, traditional favourites, and international and vegetarian dishes.

Open all day all wk 11.30am-11pm Bar Meals Av main course £7.00 food served all day Restaurant food served all day ⊕ KING HENRY TAVERNS ◄ Greene King IPA, Marstons Pedigree, Guinness. ♀ 16 Facilities Children welcome Children's menu Children's portions Garden Parking

BASLOW — Map 16 SK27

PICK OF THE PUBS

Rowley's ◉◉ ♀

Church Ln DE45 1RY ☎ 01246 583880
e-mail: info@rowleysrestaurant.co.uk
dir: A619/A623 signed Chatsworth. Baslow on edge of Chatsworth Estate

Set in a peaceful village overlooking the church, the former Prince of Wales pub was transformed into this modern bar and restaurant by the team behind Fischer's Restaurant in nearby Baslow Hall. The sibling venue offers an informal mix of stone-flagged bar area, where you can sup a pint of local Thornbridge ale, alongside the chic, more contemporary feel of its three dining areas upstairs. Very much a dining destination (the food has been awarded two AA Rosettes), menus feature an appealing mix of modern and traditional British, with an emphasis on quality local produce. At lunch, simply presented dishes may take in light bites of Rowley's venison burger in a freshly baked sesame bun, or a poached salmon sandwich with dill mayonnaise. Main courses range from chargrilled dry-aged bavette of beef with braised red cabbage and gratin dauphinoise, to oven-roasted wood pigeon or pan-fried brill. Children's choices are home made by the chefs too.

Open all day Closed: Sun eve **Bar Meals** L served Mon-Sat 12-2.30, Sun 12-3 D served Mon-Thu 5.30-7.30 Av main course £12 **Restaurant** L served Mon-Sat 12-2.30, Sun 12-3 D served Mon-Thu 5.30-9, Fri-Sat 6-10 Fixed menu price fr £21 Av 3 course à la carte fr £27.70 ⊕ FREE HOUSE ◀ Thornbridge, Abbeydale Brewery, Buxton Brewery. ♇ 10 **Facilities** Children welcome Children's menu Children's portions Beer festival Parking Wi-fi

The Devonshire Arms at Beeley
★★★★ INN ◉◉ ♇ NEW

Devonshire Square DE4 2NR
☎ 01629 733259   📠 01629 734542
e-mail: res@devonshirehotels.co.uk
dir: *B6012 towards Matlock, pass Chatsworth House. After 1.5m turn left, 2nd entrance to Beeley*

A lovely mellow-stone village inn set between the Derbyshire Wye and the wooded edges of the eastern Peak District. On the Chatsworth Estate, and handy for the stately home, the inn draws heavily on the area's bountiful produce, from beers brewed at Chatsworth's brewery to the sublime dishes which have gained chef-patron Alan Hill two AA Rosettes. Stay in the ultra-traditional pubby side or plump for the chic brasserie area, a great menu mixes old favourites with gastro fare. Long evenings spent at this National Park situated inn may extend overnight at the comfortable accommodation here.

Open all day all wk **Bar Meals** L served all wk 12-3 D served all wk 6-9.30 Av main course £14 **Restaurant** L served all wk 12-3 D served all wk 6-9.30 Av 3 course à la carte fr £30 ⊕ FREE HOUSE ◀ Chatsworth Gold, Peak Ales, Buxton Blonde, Buxton Brewery, Thornbridge Brewery Jaipur. ♇ 10 **Facilities** Children welcome Children's menu Children's portions Garden Parking Wi-fi **Rooms** 8

PICK OF THE PUBS

The Druid Inn

Main St DE4 2BL ☎ 01629 650302
e-mail: thedruidinn@hotmail.com.uk
dir: *From A6 between Matlock & Bakewell take B5056 signed Ashbourne. Approx 2m left to Birchover*

Built in 1607, this family-run gastro-pub offers freshly prepared traditional and contemporary food, largely sourced from within the Peak District. You can choose from four different dining areas: lunch (and maybe a pint of Druid Bitter) in the bar and snug; a more formal meal in the upper or lower restaurant; or outside on the terrace, from where you can survey the surrounding countryside. Each dining area has the same varied and ever-changing menu, ranging from light bites and sandwiches to two- and three-course meals. A starter such as Bakewell black pudding with streaky bacon,

onions and poached free-range egg could precede classic coq au vin; curried smoked haddock and garden pea risotto; or penne pasta creamed with wild mushrooms and Stilton. End with chocolate marquise, or crumble of the day. If you want to walk up on the moors behind the inn, it's best to do that first.

Open Mon-Sat 11-11 (Sun 11-5) Closed: 25 Dec, Sun eve **Bar Meals** L served Mon-Sat 12-2.30, Sun 12-3 booking required D served Mon-Thu 6-9, Fri-Sat 6-9.30 booking required **Restaurant** L served Mon-Sat 12-2.30, Sun 12-3 booking required D served Mon-Thu 6-9, Fri-Sat 6-9.30 booking required ⊕ FREE HOUSE ◀ Druid Bitter, Guest ale. **Facilities** Children welcome Children's menu Children's portions Garden Parking

PICK OF THE PUBS

Red Lion Inn

Main St DE4 2BN ☎ 01629 650363
e-mail: red.lion@live.co.uk
dir: *5.5m from Matlock, off A6 onto B5056*

Originally a farmhouse and recently refurbished, The Red Lion was built in 1680, and gained its first licence in 1722, and its old well, now glass-covered, still remains in the Tap Room. Follow a walk to nearby Rowter Rocks, a gritstone summit affording stunning valley and woodland views, cosy up in the character bar, with its old oak beams, exposed stone walls, scrubbed oak tables, worn quarry-tiled floor, and welcoming atmosphere. Quaff a pint of locally brewed Swift Nick or one of the other real ales on tap that change from week to week, and refuel with a plate of home-cooked food prepared from local ingredients. Start with a Sardinian speciality from owner Matteo Frau's homeland, perhaps courgette, tomato and pecorino rösti with pickled onion chutney and pistoccu, or a prosciutto, melon, mozzarella and tomato platter, then follow with roast rack of lamb with roasted pear and cannonau wine sauce or prickly pear glazed pork belly with Spam and black pudding. Don't miss the Sunday lunches and the Sardinian nights in winter.

Open 12-2.30 6-11.30 (Sat & BH Mons noon-mdnt Sun 12-11) Closed: Mon in winter **Bar Meals** L served Tue-Sat 12-2, Sun 12-7(winter) D served Tue-Sat 6-9 Av main course £11.95 **Restaurant** L served Tue-Sat 12-2, Sun 12-7(winter) D served Tue-Sat 6-9 Fixed menu price fr £10.95 Av 3 course à la carte fr £14.95 ⊕ FREE HOUSE ◀ Nine Ladies, Swift Nick, Ichinusa (Sardinian), Peakstone's Rock Brewery Bitters, Buxton Brewery, Thornbridge Brew Ó Westons Scrumpy, Perry, Old Rosie. **Facilities** Children welcome Children's portions Dogs allowed Garden Beer festival Parking

PICK OF THE PUBS

The Waltzing Weasel Inn ♇

New Mills Rd SK22 1BT ☎ 01663 743402
e-mail: waltzingweasel@mailauth.co.uk
dir: *Village at junct of A6015 & A624, halfway between Glossop & Chapel-en-le-Firth*

Dramatic views of Kinder Scout set this 400-year-old quintessential English inn apart from the crowd. Situated beside the Sett Valley trail, it is an ideal spot for walkers. Although refurbished, the bar is still warmed by a real fire and furnished with country antiques, while the restaurant enjoys more of those wonderful views from its mullioned windows. No games machines or piped music sully the atmosphere, so sit back with a pint of Marston's and choose from a menu of robust and reasonably priced dishes. In addition to soups, filled jackets, sandwiches and light bites, the lunch menu embraces starters such as button mushroom and blue cheese bake; or corned beef hash with soft poached egg. Main courses include proper steak and ale pie in a puff pastry case; and chargrilled gammon steak with hand-cut chunky chips.

Open all day all wk **Bar Meals** L served Mon-Fri 12-2, Sat-Sun all day D served Mon-Fri 6-9.30, Sat-Sun all day **Restaurant** L served Mon-Fri 12-2, Sat-Sun all day D served Mon-Fri 6-9.30, Sat-Sun all day ⊕ FREE HOUSE ◀ Marston's Best & Pedigree, Jennings Sneck Lifter, Greene King IPA, Old Speckled Hen, Worthingtons, Guest ales. ♇ 10 **Facilities** Children welcome Children's menu Children's portions Garden Parking Wi-fi

Ye Old Bowling Green Inn

Smalldale S33 9JQ ☎ 01433 620450
e-mail: dalesinns@aol.com
dir: *Off A623 onto B6049 to Bradwell. Onto Gore Ln by playing field to Smalldale & inn*

An early 16th-century coaching inn with impressive views over glorious Hope Valley and Win Hill, and reports of a resident ghost or ghosts. With its old world atmosphere and warming winter fires, the pub is popular with the locals who discuss all kinds of matters especially those ghosts. Traditional country cooking features pub classics such as BBQ chicken breast with bacon and cheese; home-made pie of the day (look out for Desperate Dan Pie); a range of steaks from the griddle plus sandwiches, baguettes, salads and light bites. This is a great place for setting out for a walk or hike.

Open all day all wk ⊕ ENTERPRISE INNS ◀ Copper Dragon, Black Sheep, John Smith's, Hobgoblin. **Facilities** Children welcome Children's menu Children's portions Play area Garden Parking Wi-fi

BRASSINGTON   Map 16 SK25

PICK OF THE PUBS

Ye Olde Gate Inne

Well St DE4 4HJ ☎ 01629 540448   📠 01629 540448
e-mail: info@theoldgateinnbrassington.co.uk
dir: *2m from Carsington Water off A5023 between Wirksworth & Ashbourne*

Built in 1616 out of local stone and timbers allegedly salvaged from the wrecked Armada fleet, this venerable inn stands beside an old London to Manchester turnpike in the heart of Brassington, a hill village on the southern edge of the Peak District. Oak beams, black cast iron log burner, an antique clock, charmingly worn quarry-tiled floors and a delightful mishmash of polished furniture give the inn plenty of character. Hand-pumped Jennings Cumberland takes pride of place behind the bar, alongside other Marston's beers and guest ales. The menu offers firm lunchtime favourites, such as steak and Guinness pie with vegetables and home-made chips; or locally caught trout when in season. In the evening you may find a duo of pork: slowly cooked belly and roasted fillet with an apple and mustard jus; or a whole fillet of sea bass stuffed with a fish mousseline. Desserts range from a traditional Bakewell tart to a white chocolate and pine nut torte.

Open Tue eve-Sun Closed: Mon (ex BH), Tue L
Bar Meals L served Wed-Sat 12-1.45, Sun 12.30-2.30 booking required D served Tue-Sat 6.30-8.45 booking required Av main course £11.95 ◀ Marston's Pedigree, Jennings Cumberland, Guest ales. **Facilities** Children welcome Children's portions Family room Dogs allowed Garden Parking

CASTLETON   Map 16 SK18

The Peaks Inn

How Ln S33 8WJ ☎ 01433 620247
e-mail: enquiry@peaksinn.com
dir: *On A6187 in centre of village*

Standing below the ruins of Peveril Castle, after which Castleton is named, this attractive, stone-built village pub is an ideal place to recover after a country walk. Recently refurbished and with new owners, its bar is warm and welcoming, with leather armchairs and open log fires plus a great range of real ales, malt whiskies, vodkas and gins. The menu offers old favourites of lasagne; bangers and mash; The Peak all-day breakfast; and home-made pie of the day. There is a new beer garden with heaters and lighting, and the coffee shop next door is part of the pub.

Open all day all wk **Bar Meals** L served Sun-Thu noon-7, Fri-Sat noon-9 Av main course £7 ⊕ PUNCH TAVERNS ◀ Kelham Island Easy Rider, Old Speckled Hen, Guest ale 🍎 Westons Old Rosie, Westons Traditional Scrumpy on rotation. **Facilities** Children welcome Children's menu Dogs allowed Garden Parking Wi-fi

Ye Olde Nags Head

Cross St S33 8WH ☎ 01433 620248
e-mail: info@yeoldenagshead.co.uk
dir: *A625 from Sheffield, W through Hope Valley, through Hathersage & Hope. Pub on main road*

A traditional 17th-century coaching inn in grey stone situated in the heart of the Derbyshire Peak District National Park, close to Chatsworth House and Haddon Hall. Miles of wonderful walks and country lanes favoured by cyclists bring thirsty visitors seeking a warm welcome and refreshment in the cosy bars warmed by open fires. A recent refurbishment now offers a mix of contemporary and traditional dining options complete the picture: expect the likes of chef's home-made game pie or a sizeable bacon chop.

Open all day all wk **Bar Meals** food served all day **Restaurant** food served all day ⊕ FREE HOUSE ◀ Black Sheep, Guinness, Timothy Taylor Landlord, Kinder Sunset, Moonshine, Riders on the Storm. **Facilities** Children welcome Children's menu Children's portions Dogs allowed Parking

CHELMORTON   Map 16 SK16

The Church Inn

SK17 9SL ☎ 01298 85319
e-mail: justinsatur@tiscali.co.uk
dir: *From A515 or A6 take A5270 between Bakewell & Buxton. Chelmorton signed*

Pennine Way walkers take note of this 18th-century stone inn between Buxton and Bakewell for the long-distance trail passes the front door. Time your visit for opening time and rest weary legs in the warm and welcoming bar, where the modern decor combines well with period features. Refuel from a menu listing freshly prepared pub favourites, perhaps braised beef in Guinness with Stilton dumplings, fish pie, and fresh battered haddock and chips, all best washed down with a foaming pint of Pedigree.

Open all wk 12-3 6-12 (Fri-Sun noon-mdnt)
Bar Meals L served Mon-Thu 12-2.30, Fri-Sun 12-9 D served all wk 7-9 Av main course £8.50
Restaurant L served Mon-Thu 12-2.30, Fri-Sun 12-9 D served all wk 7-9 ⊕ FREE HOUSE ◀ Marstons Best Bitter, Pedigree, Adnams Best Bitter, Local ales.
Facilities Children welcome Children's menu Dogs allowed Garden Wi-fi

CHESTERFIELD   Map 16 SK37

PICK OF THE PUBS

Red Lion Pub & Bistro ♀

Darley Rd, Stone Edge S45 0LW
☎ 01246 566142   📠 01246 591040
e-mail: redlionpubandbistro@yahoo.com
dir: *Telephone for directions*

On the edge of the Peak District National Park, the Red Lion dates back to 1788. Although it has seen many changes, including the opening of a new boutique hotel in April 2011, it has retained much of its character. The original wooden beams and stone walls are now complemented by discreet lighting and comfy leather armchairs which add a thoroughly contemporary edge. Striking black and white photographs decorate the walls, whilst local jazz bands liven up the bar on Thursday evenings. Meals are served in the bar and bistro, or beneath umbrellas in the large garden. Seasonal produce drives the menu and the chefs make everything, from sauces to the hand-cut chips. Typical choices might start with pan-seared king scallops with black pudding and pea purée, followed by roast pepper and Brie tart with red onion, tomato and herb salad, or Manor Farm lamb shank with creamed potato, caramelised onions and braised red cabbage. Leave space for desserts like caramelised apple tart with Chantilly cream and mango coulis.

Open all day all wk **Bar Meals** Av main course £13.75 food served all day **Restaurant** food served all day ⊕ FREE HOUSE ◀ Black Sheep. **Facilities** Children welcome Children's menu Children's portions Garden Parking Wi-fi

Save on hotels. Book at **theAA.com/hotel**

DERBYSHIRE 119 ENGLAND

The Old Hall Inn

Whitehough, Chinley, High Peak SK2 6EJ

Tel: 01663 750529 • **Web:** www.old-hall-inn.co.uk • **E-mail:** info@old-hall-inn-co.uk

We are a small family run, 16th Century Inn, located in the heart of the stunning Peak District. We are the quintessential English country pub, with an award winning selection of local ales, menus prepared fresh daily from the best local produce and comfortable homely accommodation. All this with a friendly team that have our customers returning again and again.

We stand out above the rest not only for the informal hospitably that you will receive but the delight of being attached to Whitehough Hall, where the traditional cosy country pub opens up into the old manor houses' Minstrels Gallery, open for dining and breakfast.

CHINLEY
Map 16 SK08

PICK OF THE PUBS

Old Hall Inn ☻

Whitehough SK23 6EJ ☎ 01663 750529
e-mail: info@old-hall-inn.co.uk
web: www.old-hall-inn.co.uk
dir: *From Chapel-en-le-Frith take B5470 W. Right into Whitehough Head Ln. 0.8m to inn*

Smack in the heart of prime walking country, with Kinder Scout, Mam Tor and Stanage Edge all within easy reach, this family-run establishment is part traditional coaching inn, part medieval manor house – Whitehough Hall complete with minstrels' gallery. With a drinks list as long as your arm, you are bound to find your refreshment of choice. The impressive range of local cask ales and ciders is backed by all manner of bottled beers and spirits, and this makes no mention of around 80 wines and extensive non-alcoholic infusions. Two annual beer and cider festivals (third weekend in September, fourth weekend in February) confirm the Old Hall's commitment to serving the best of Derbyshire's micro-breweries. But don't miss the opportunity to eat here too. The kitchen prides itself on making all its own chutneys, pickles and sauces, along with plates of good food made from fresh local produce: sandwiches, home-made Scotch eggs, chicken curry of the day, and steak and kidney pudding are some examples.

Open all day all wk **Bar Meals** L served Mon-Sat 12-2, Sun 12-7.30 booking required D served Mon-Thu 5-9, Fri-Sat 5-9.30, Sun 12-7.30 booking required Av main course £10 **Restaurant** L served Mon-Sat 12-2, Sun 12-7.30 booking required D served Mon-Thu 5-9, Fri-Sat 5-9.30, Sun 12-7.30 booking required Fixed menu price fr £10 Av 3 course à la carte fr £19 ⊕ FREE HOUSE ◀ Marstons, Thornbridge, Phoenix, Abbeydale, Storm, Kelham Island ♂ Thatchers, Sheppy's, Westons. ☻ 12 **Facilities** Children welcome Children's menu Children's portions Dogs allowed Garden Beer festival Parking Wi-fi

See advert on page 119

DERBY
Map 11 SK33

The Alexandra Hotel

203 Siddals Rd DE1 2QE ☎ 01332 293993
e-mail: alexandrahotel@castlerockbrewery.co.uk
dir: *150yds from rail station*

Built in 1871, this small hotel is named after the Danish princess who married the Prince of Wales, later Edward VII. It was also known as the Midland coffee house after the Midland railway company, one of Derby's major employers. It is noted for its real ales from seven hand pumps, and an annual beer festival confirms its serious approach to the amber liquid; real ciders, and bottled and draught continental beers complete the line-up at the bar. Freshly-made and filled cold cobs and hot pies are served all day.

Open all day all wk noon-11pm (Fri noon-mdnt Sat 11am-mdnt) **Bar Meals** food served all day ◀ Castle Rock, Elsie Mo, Harvest Pale ♂ Old Rosie, Stowford Press. **Facilities** Children welcome Children's portions Dogs allowed Garden Beer festival Parking

---

THE HARDWICK INN

The Hardwick Inn is a delightful 15th-century building built using locally quarried sandstone, situated on the south gate of Hardwick Park. The Hardwick has been in the Batty family for three generations, and landlords Peter and Pauline take pride in providing efficient, friendly service to customers old and new. When you step over the threshold, you'll feel like you've stepped back in time; the historic surroundings create a comfortable, friendly atmosphere. In winter, the inn is kept cosy with open fires, while in summer customers can enjoy two large beer gardens.

Diners come from miles around to sample the Hardwick's delicious homemade food. The bar menu includes Steaks, Fish dishes, homemade pies, local game as well as a snack menu and a extensive specials board. The excellent range of drinks include five real ales and over 200 malt whiskys. The carvery restaurant boast beautiful views of the garden and serves local roast meats as well as the a la carte menu.

Hardwick Inn, Hardwick Park, Doe Lea, Nr. Chesterfield S44 5QJ
Tel: 01246 850245   E-mail:Batty@Hardwickinn.co.uk

Save on hotels. Book at **theAA.com/hotel**

DERBYSHIRE 121 **ENGLAND**

The Brunswick Inn

1 Railway Ter DE1 2RU
☎ 01332 290677 🖹 01332 370226
e-mail: thebrunswickinn@yahoo.co.uk
dir: *From rail station turn right. Pub 100yds*

Built in 1841 by the railway, this Grade II listed building is the oldest brewery in Derby producing its own range of traditional Everards ales. There are sixteen handpumps – six Brunswick ales and ten guest beers. Food is served Monday to Saturday with cobs and snacks on Sundays. So choose your ale and sit back with a pint and relax by the cosy coal fire. On the first weekend in October the pub holds a beer festival.

Open all day all wk **Bar Meals** L served Mon-Wed 11.30-2.30, Fri-Sat 11.30-5, Sun 12-4 ⊕ EVERARDS BREWERY ◀ Various ales and Guests ♻ Westons Old Rosie, Westons 1st Quality. **Facilities** Children welcome Children's portions Family room Dogs allowed Garden Beer festival **Notes** ⊛

| **DOE LEA** | **Map 16 SK46** |

Hardwick Inn ☐

Hardwick Park S44 5QJ
☎ 01246 850245 🖹 01246 856365
e-mail: batty@hardwickinn.co.uk
web: www.hardwickinn.co.uk
dir: *M1 junct 29 take A6175. 0.5m left (signed Stainsby/Hardwick Hall). After Stainsby, 2m, left at staggered junct. Follow brown tourist signs*

Dating from around 1600 and built of locally quarried sandstone, this striking building was once the lodge from Hardwick Hall (NT) and stands at the south gate of Hardwick Park. Own by the Batty family for three generations, the pub has a rambling interior and features period details such as mullioned windows, oak beams and stone fireplaces. Traditional food takes in a popular daily carvery roast, a salad bar, hearty home-made pies and casseroles, and beer-battered cod. A handy pit-stop for M1 travellers.

Open all day all wk **Bar Meals** food served all day **Restaurant** L served Tue-Sat 12-2, Sun 12-1 & 4-5.30 booking required D served Tue-Sat 6.30-8.30 booking required ⊕ FREE HOUSE ◀ Theakston Old Peculier & XB, Black Sheep, Bombardier, Bess of Hardwick ♻ Westons, Addlestones. ☐ 10 **Facilities** Children welcome Children's portions Play area Family room Garden Parking

See advert on opposite page

| **EYAM** | **Map 16 SK27** |

Miners Arms

Water Ln S32 5RG ☎ 01433 630853
dir: *Off B6521, 5m N of Bakewell*

This welcoming 17th-century inn (and restaurant) was built just before the plague hit Eyam; the village tailor brought damp cloth from London and hung it to dry in front of the fire so releasing the infected fleas. The pub gets its name from the local lead mines of Roman times. Now owned by Greene King, there's always the option to pop in for a pint of their IPA, Old Speckled Hen or Ruddles Best Bitter or enjoy a meal. A beer festival is held three times a year.

Open all day all wk Closed: 26 Dec eve **Bar Meals** L served Mon-Sat 12-2, Sun 12-3 D served Mon 6-8, Tue-Fri 6-9, Sat 7-9 **Restaurant** L served Mon-Sat 12-2, Sun 12-3 D served Mon 6-8, Tue-Fri 6-9, Sat 7-9 ⊕ GREENE KING ◀ Greene King IPA, Old Speckled Hen, Ruddles Best. **Facilities** Children welcome Children's menu Children's portions Dogs allowed Garden Beer festival Parking

| **FENNY BENTLEY** | **Map 16 SK14** |

PICK OF THE PUBS

Bentley Brook Inn ★★★ INN ☐
See Pick of the Pubs on page 122

The Coach and Horses Inn

DE6 1LB ☎ 01335 350246
e-mail: coachandhorses2@btconnect.com
dir: *On A515 (Ashbourne to Buxton road), 2.5m from Ashbourne*

A cosy refuge in any weather, this family-run, 17th-century coaching inn stands on the edge of the Peak District National Park. Besides the beautiful location, its charms include stripped wood furniture and low beams, real log-burning fires plus a welcoming and friendly atmosphere. Expect a great selection of real ales and good home cooking that is hearty and well cooked using the best of local produce. Expect local specials and dishes like slow cooked beef in red wine puff pastry pie. Hot and cold sandwiches and baguettes provide lighter options.

Open all day all wk 11-11 (Sun 12-10.30) **Bar Meals** food served all day **Restaurant** food served all day ⊕ FREE HOUSE ◀ Marston's Pedigree, Oakham JHB, Peak Ales Swift Nick, Whim Ales Hartington Bitter, Derby Brewing Co. **Facilities** Children welcome Children's menu Family room Garden Parking

| **FOOLOW** | **Map 16 SK17** |

The Bulls Head Inn ★★★★ INN

S32 5QR ☎ 01433 630873 🖹 01433 631738
e-mail: wilbnd@aol.com
dir: *Just off A623, N of Stoney Middleton*

Set against a backdrop of rolling hills, this 19th-century former coaching inn is tucked away in a conservation village high up in the Peak District. Open fires, oak beams, flagstone floors, great views and good food are among the attractions. It provides a welcome pit-stop for walkers and visitors for lunchtime sandwiches, bar meals such as turkey, leek and ham pie washed down with a pint of Black Sheep, or restaurant choices like roast sea bass with fennel, or venison medallions in a Cumberland sauce. Bedrooms are comfortable and well equipped.

Open 12-3 6.30-11 (Sun all day) Closed: Mon (ex BH) **Bar Meals** L served Tue-Sun 12-2 D served Tue-Sun 6.30-9 **Restaurant** L served Tue-Sun 12-2 D served Tue-Sun 6.30-9 ⊕ FREE HOUSE ◀ Black Sheep, Peak Ales, Adnams, Tetley. **Facilities** Children welcome Children's menu Children's portions Dogs allowed Parking **Rooms** 3

| **FROGGATT** | **Map 16 SK27** |

PICK OF THE PUBS

The Chequers Inn ★★★★ INN ⊛ ☐

Froggatt Edge S32 3ZJ
☎ 01433 630231 🖹 01433 631072
e-mail: info@chequers-froggatt.com
dir: *On A625, 0.5m N of Calver*

The Chequers is an excellent base for exploring the Peak District, with Chatsworth House in close proximity. Originally four stone-built 18th-century cottages, this traditional country inn nestles below beautiful Froggatt Edge. A haven for walkers, its westward panorama is reached by a steep, wild woodland footpath from the elevated secret garden. The comfortable interior of wooden floors, antiques and blazing log fires is perfect for a relaxing pint of Bakewell Best Bitter or your choice from an innovative modern European menu. The food is prepared from locally sourced produce, ranging from sandwiches and salads through to starters as varied as game terrine with pear jelly, and smoked haddock and blue cheese soufflé with pea purée. Mains take in pot-roasted lamb shank with braised winter vegetables, and slow-cooked pork shoulder with parsley mash and apple and vanilla compote. Finish with blackcurrant and elderflower mousse. There are five en suite bedrooms available.

Open all wk 12-2 6-9.30 (Sat 12-9.30, Sun 12-9) Closed: 25 Dec **Bar Meals** L served Mon-Fri 12-2, Sat 12-9.30, Sun 12-9 D served Mon-Fri 6-9.30, Sat 12-9.30, Sun 12-9 ⊕ FREE HOUSE ◀ Kelham Island Easy Rider, Bakewell Best Bitter, Bombardier, changing guest ales. ☐ 10 **Facilities** Children welcome Children's menu Children's portions Garden Parking Wi-fi **Rooms** 5

PICK OF THE PUBS

Bentley Brook Inn ★★★ INN ♀

FENNY BENTLEY Map 16 SK14

DE6 1LF
☎ 01335 350278 📠 01335 350422
e-mail: all@bentleybrookinn.co.uk
web: www.bentleybrookinn.co.uk
dir: *Telephone for directions*

Admiral Lord Nelson was seeing off the French fleet at Trafalgar when this substantial farmhouse was created in 1805 from the shell of a medieval building that served the local manor. Vestiges of the latter survive nearby, whilst the fascinating village church has memorials to the Beresford family, including one who fought at Agincourt. Between the World Wars, two elderly ladies lived here in considerable style, attended to by five servants, a gardener, an under-gardener and a coachman. It became a restaurant in 1954, a full drinks licence was granted in the early 1970s, and in 2006/7 it was completely restored and refurbished. There's a civilised, secluded feel to the inn which is approached up a long drive from the village, revealing the substantial, gabled, timbered frontage surveying three acres of gardens and grounds. Eleven well appointed and thoughtfully equipped bedrooms make this inn the ideal base for exploring nearby Dovedale, the White Peak and the peaceful Derbyshire Dales. Those with energy to spare may be interested in the World Toe-wrestling championship held here each June, whilst beer fans will revel in the annual May beer festival,

featuring beers from Leatherbritches Brewery, which originated here before relocating to Ashbourne. You can all too easily settle by the central open log fire in the bar and play dominoes, cards or chess, or peruse the menu. In the restaurant, which overlooks the terrace and garden, locally sourced, seasonal menus provide lunches and dinners that might begin with deep-fried Dovedale Blue cheese with home-made Cumberland sauce or salmon fishcake on tomato salsa. Mains might include free-range chicken breast in pesto with tagliatelle; home-made steak and ale pie with suet pastry crust; or roasted vegetable tartlet with goat's cheese and home-made red onion marmalade. The Sunday carvery offers a choice of traditional roast meats, fish and vegetarian options; during the summer the barbecue in the garden is fired up.

Open all day all wk **Bar Meals** L served all wk 12-9 (Oct-Mar 12-3) booking required D served all wk 12-9 (Oct-Mar 6-9) booking required Av main course £7.95 **Restaurant** L served all wk 12-9 (Oct-Mar 12-3) booking required D served all wk 12-9 (Oct-Mar 6-9) booking required ⊕ FREE HOUSE ◀ Leatherbritches Bespoke, Leatherbritches Hairy Helmet, Goldings, Marstons Pedigree. ♀ 10 **Facilities** Play area Dogs allowed Garden Beer festival Parking Wi-fi **Rooms** 11

Save on hotels. Book at **theAA.com/hotel**

DERBYSHIRE 123 **ENGLAND**

The Queen Anne Inn ★★★ INN ☕

SK17 8RF ☎ **01298 871246** 🖹 01298 873504
e-mail: angelaryan100@aol.com
dir: A623 onto B6049, turn off at Anchor pub towards
Bradwell, 2nd right to Great Hucklow

Enjoy stunning open views from the sheltered south-
facing garden of this traditional country free house. The
inn dates from 1621; a licence has been held for over 300
years, and the names of all the landlords are known.
Inside you'll find an open fire in the stone fireplace, good
food using locally sourced produce, and an ever-changing
range of cask ales. Dishes include beer-battered haddock
and chips, and Gressingham duck breast with orange,
sherry and pomegranate. There is a child-friendly south-
facing garden and two guest bedrooms available.

Open noon-2.30 5-11 (Fri-Sun noon-11) Closed: Mon
Bar Meals L served Tue-Sun 12-2 D served Tue-Thu
6-8.30, Fri-Sat 6-9, Sun 6-8 **Restaurant** L served Tue-
Sun 12-2 D served Tue-Thu 6-8.30, Fri-Sat 6-9, Sun 6-8
⊕ FREE HOUSE ◀ Tetleys Cask Ales, Copper Dragon,
Peak Ales, Brampton, Theakstons ♂ Stowford Press. ☕ 9
Facilities Children welcome Children's menu Children's
portions Family room Garden Parking **Rooms** 2

PICK OF THE PUBS

The Maynard ★★★ HL ◎◎

Main Rd S32 2HE ☎ **01433 630321** 🖹 01433 630445
e-mail: info@themaynard.co.uk
dir: From M1 junct 30 take A619 into Chesterfield, then
onto Baslow. A623 to Calver, right into Grindleford

Nestled below the steep, wooded crags of Froggatt
Edge and close to the moorland acres of the National
Trust's Longshaw Estate, this imposing stone hotel
guarantees guests indulging in the capacious beer
garden some stunning panoramas of the eastern Peak
District and the deep valley of the River Derwent.
Continuing the Peakland theme, beer from
Chatsworth's own estate brewery may be sampled in
the Longhaw Bar, where a good value lunch menu
might include twice baked smoked salmon soufflé, or
fish and garden pea pie. For some of the best cuisine
in the Midlands, however, head for the Maynard
Restaurant where chef Ben Hickinson creates menus
which have gained two AA Rosettes; smoked chicken
and broad bean ballotine with rhubarb and red onion
salsa a fascinating starter before the main event
which might be pan-roast duck breast with plum
tomato cassoulet and winter greens; ribeye of local
beef with mushroom and tomato galette: or sweet
potato tagine with marinated pepper couscous and
mint yoghurt.

Open all day all wk 11-9 **Bar Meals** L served all wk
12-2 D served all wk 7-9 **Restaurant** L served all wk
12-2 D served all wk 7-9 ⊕ FREE HOUSE ◀ Abbey Dale
Moonshine, Bakewell Bitter. **Facilities** Children
welcome Dogs allowed Garden Parking **Rooms** 10

The Mill Wheel ★★★★ INN

Ticknall Rd DE11 7AS
☎ **01283 550335** 🖹 01283 552833
e-mail: info@themillwheel.co.uk
dir: M42 junct 2 follow signs for A511 to Woodville, left
onto A514 towards Derby to Hartshorne

This building's long life has included stints as a corn mill
and an iron furnace. Its huge mill wheel has survived for
some 250 years. In 1945 a dispute over water rights cut
off the supply and the site became derelict, but since
being restored in 1987, the wheel has been slowly turning
once again, and is very much the focus of attention in the
bar and restaurant. Mill Wheel Bitter is available along
with dishes such as mussels with a shallot, garlic and
white wine cream or lamb cutlets with braised shoulder,
Lyonnaise potatoes and kale. If you want to stay over,
there are modern bedrooms available.

Open all wk (all day Sat-Sun) **Bar Meals** L served Mon-
Sat 12-2.30, Sun 12-7 D served Mon-Thu 6-9.15, Fri-Sat
6-9.30, Sun 12-7 **Restaurant** L served Mon-Sat 12-2.30,
Sun 12-7 D served Mon-Thu 6-9.15, Fri-Sat 6-9.30, Sun
12-7 ⊕ FREE HOUSE ◀ Abbot Ale, Summer Lightning,
Bass, Pedigree, Mill Wheel Bitter. **Facilities** Children
welcome Children's portions Garden Beer festival Parking
Wi-fi **Rooms** 4

Eyre Arms ☕

DE45 1NS ☎ **01629 640390**
e-mail: nick@eyrearms.com
dir: On B6001 N of Bakewell

Formerly a farmstead and 17th-century coaching inn,
this traditional ivy-clad free house has been run with
courtesy and pride by the same family for seventeen
years. Views of rolling Peak District countryside from the
secluded garden can only be improved with a pint of
Bakewell Best in hand, brewed on the nearby Chatsworth
estate. Oak settles, low ceilings and cheery log fires
create a cosy atmosphere, ideal surroundings for enjoying
a rabbit pie cooked with cider and bacon from the
specials board.

Open all wk 11-3 6.30-11 Closed: 25 Dec
Bar Meals L served all wk 12-2 D served all wk 6.30-9 Av
main course £10 ⊕ FREE HOUSE ◀ Marston's Pedigree,
Black Sheep Special, Bakewell Best Bitter ♂ Westons
Stowford Press. ☕ 9 **Facilities** Children welcome
Children's menu Garden Parking

Millstone Inn

Sheffield Rd S32 1DA
☎ **01433 650258** 🖹 01433 650276
e-mail: enquiries@millstoneinn.co.uk
dir: Telephone for directions

Striking views over the picturesque Hope Valley are
afforded from this former coaching inn, set amid the
beauty of the Peak District yet convenient for the city of

Sheffield. The atmospheric bar serves six traditional cask
ales all year round and the menu offers a good choice of
dishes prepared from local produce, including a popular
Sunday carvery of freshly roasted joints.

Open all day all wk 11.30am-11pm ◀ Timothy Taylor
Landlord, Black Sheep, Guest ales. **Facilities** Children
welcome Dogs allowed Garden Parking

PICK OF THE PUBS

The Plough Inn ★★★★ INN ⊛ ☕

Leadmill Bridge S32 1BA
☎ **01433 650319** & 650180 🖹 01433 651049
e-mail: sales@theploughinn-hathersage.co.uk
web: www.theploughinn-hathersage.co.uk
dir: M1 junct 29, take A617W, A619, A623, then B6001
N to Hathersage

The lively waters of Highlow Brook were once harnessed
here to drive waterwheels which turned stones, first to
grind corn and later crushers to release lead ore from
rock mined in the hills of the surrounding Peak District.
Trains of packhorses would have moved the ore;
perhaps the overseers had home-brewed beer here
three centuries ago, starting a tradition which has
culminated in today's notable roadside inn near the
banks of the glorious River Derwent; the inn's nine-
acre riverside estate stretches to the old bridge
carrying the Derwent Valley Heritage Way across the
rapids here. An exceptional menu has achieved the
award of one AA Rosette for Bob Emery and his
enthusiastic team. A homely bar and restaurant,
cobbled courtyard or glorious beer garden; all great
locations to settle at and anticipate dishes which may
begin with a leek and potato soup with smoked
haddock, preceding a choice from around 40 mains;
perhaps fillet of bream with braised baby leeks,
crushed potato and vanilla jus, or tagliatelli with
walnuts in a spinach and Gorgonzola cream. Guests
can stroll through the landscaped grounds before
retiring to the beautifully appointed accommodation in
the inn or converted barns across the secluded
courtyard.

Open all day all wk 11-11 (Sun noon-10.30pm) Closed:
25 Dec **Bar Meals** booking required food served all day
Restaurant booking required food served all day
⊕ FREE HOUSE ◀ Adnams, Black Sheep, Timothy
Taylor, Bass Smooth. ☕ 15 **Facilities** Children welcome
Children's portions Dogs allowed Garden Parking Wi-fi
Rooms 5

HATHERSAGE *continued*

The Scotsmans Pack Country Inn ★★★★ INN ⓣ

School Ln S32 1BZ ☎ 01433 650253 📠 01433 650712
e-mail: scotsmans.pack@btinternet.com
web: www.scotsmanspack.com
dir: *Hathersage is on A625 8m from Sheffield. Pub near church and Little John's Grave*

Just a short walk away from Hathersage church and Little John's Grave, this traditional inn is ideally placed for walking and touring the Peak District, and has five individually designed en suite bedrooms for those who wish to stay. Set in the beautiful Hope Valley on one of the old packhorse trails used by Scottish 'packmen' or travelling drapers, it offers hearty pub dishes such as gammon, egg and chips or home-made lasagne alongside a lengthy specials board. Wash your meal down with a great choice of real ales. Weather permitting, head outside onto the sun trap patio, next to the trout stream.

Open all day all wk 11-3 6-mdnt (Fri-Sun all day) **Bar Meals** L served Mon-Fri 12-2 booking required D served Mon-Fri 6-9, Sat-Sun 12-9 booking required Av main course £8.95 **Restaurant** Fixed menu price fr £10.95 ⊕ MARSTONS PLC ◀ Jennings Cumberland, Pedigree, Mansfield Bitter. ⓣ 10 **Facilities** Children welcome Children's menu Children's portions Family room Garden Parking Wi-fi **Rooms** 5

The Royal Hotel ⓣ

Market St SK22 2EP ☎ 01663 742721
e-mail: enquiries@theroyalhayfield.co.uk
dir: *Off A624*

Dating from 1755, this is a fine-looking former vicarage in an attractive High Peak village. The oak-panelled bar offers Hydes' and guest ales, and traditional snacks and light dishes; the Dining Room offers a good choice from the carte. Or you could try the family lounge, popular with the local cricket team whose ground is next door. From the patio, the windswept plateau of Kinder Scout looks impressive. A beer festival is held in October.

Open all day all wk 9am-mdnt **Bar Meals** L served Mon-Fri 12-2.30, Sat 12-9, Sun 12-6 D served Mon-Fri 6-9, Sat 12-9, Sun 12-6 **Restaurant** L served Mon-Fri 12-2.30, Sat 12-9, Sun 12-6 D served Mon-Fri 6-9, Sat 12-9, Sun 12-6 ⊕ FREE HOUSE ◀ Hydes, Guest Ales Ö Stowford Press. **Facilities** Children welcome Children's menu Children's portions Family room Dogs allowed Garden Beer festival Parking Wi-fi

The Red Lion Inn ⓣ

Main St DE6 1PR ☎ 01335 370396 📠 01335 370396
e-mail: redlion@w3z.co.uk
web: www.redlionhognaston.org.uk
dir: *From Ashbourne take B5035 towards Wirksworth. Approx 5m follow Carsington Water signs. Turn right to Hognaston*

This 17th-century pub is one of the original destination gastro-pubs and still does the business with a great rack of specials that change frequently and feature the best Derbyshire produce. Work up an appetite with a walk at the nearby Carsington Water, bag a fireside seat in the antique-rich, rustic bar, chinwag with the locals and look forward to local wild mushrooms on toast with melted Dovedale Blue Stilton followed by Derbyshire extra matured sirloin steak, or Gressingham duck breast with port and black cherry sauce. In summer, you can enjoy a Derbyshire beer in the tranquil garden.

Open all wk 12-3 6-11 **Bar Meals** L served all wk 12-2.30 D served all wk 6.30-9 Av main course £10.95 **Restaurant** L served all wk 12-2.30 D served all wk 6.30-9 Av 3 course à la carte fr £25 ⊕ FREE HOUSE ◀ Marston's Pedigree, Guinness, Ruddles County, Derbyshire Brewing Co, Black Sheep Ö Old Rosie. ⓣ 9 **Facilities** Children welcome Children's portions Dogs allowed Garden Parking Wi-fi

Cheshire Cheese Inn

Edale Rd S33 6ZF ☎ 01433 620381
e-mail: info@cheshirecheeseinn.co.uk
dir: *On A6187 between Sheffield & Chapel-en-le-Frith, turn off at Hope Church down Edale Rd*

Originally a farm, this 16th-century inn stands on the old trans-Pennine salt route in the heart of the Peak District, and owes its name to the tradition of accepting cheese as payment for lodgings. It has a reputation for good home-made food and a great selection hand-pulled beer served in a relaxed atmosphere with open fires. There is a choice of light bites and main meals, ranging from toasted sandwiches or jacket potatoes to Aberdeen Angus lasagne or steak and ale pie. Recent change of hands.

Open all day Sat-Sun Closed: Mon ⊕ ENTERPRISE INNS ◀ Golden Pippin, Copper Dragon, Swift Nick, Deuchars IPA, Farmers Blonde, Young's Best. **Facilities** Children welcome Children's portions Dogs allowed Garden Parking

The John Thompson Inn & Brewery ⓣ NEW

DE73 7HW ☎ 01332 862469 📠 01332 865647
e-mail: nick@johnthompsoninn.com
dir: *From A38 between Derby and Burton upon Trent take A5132 towards Barrow upon Trent. At mini-rdbt right onto B5008 (signed Repton). At rdbt 1st exit into Brook End. Right onto Milton Rd. Left, left again to Ingleby*

In 1968, John and Ann Thompson converted their 15th century farmhouse into the first pub in Britain to be named after the licensee and owner. Now run by son Nick, this traditional brew pub is set in idyllic countryside beside the banks of the River Trent with views of the neighbouring National Forest. This relaxed inn has a wealth of original features and is a friendly place to enjoy a pint of home-brewed JTS XXX and tuck into sarnies, jacket potatoes or order from the carvery menu. (See also Own-Brew Pubs Revival on page 12)

Open Tue-Fri 11-2.30 6-11 (Sat-Sun 11-11 Mon 6-11) Closed: Mon L **Bar Meals** L served Tue-Sun 12-2 Av main course £7.45 **Restaurant** L served Tue-Sun 12-2 Fixed menu price fr £10 ⊕ FREE HOUSE ◀ John Thompson Brewery JTS XXX, St Nick's, Gold, Rich Porter. ⓣ 9 **Facilities** Children welcome Children's portions Family room Dogs allowed Garden Parking Wi-fi

Lantern Pike

45 Glossop Rd SK22 2NG ☎ 01663 747590
e-mail: sales@lanternpikeinn.co.uk
dir: *On A624, between Glossop and Chapel-en-le-Frith*

Peak District beers major here in this creeper-clad, convivial pub amidst the striking, knolly countryside at the fringe of mighty Kinder Scout. Paths and bridleways thread to the door, where hungry ramblers and riders indulge in reliable pub stalwart dishes such as braised liver or Stilton vegetable bake. Moor-up in the patio-garden with its grand vista of Lantern Pike hill, or indulge in a bit of 'Corrie' nostalgia – it was here that Tony Warren created the series; the original Rover's Return swing doors adorn the bar.

Open Mon 5-mdnt, Tue-Fri noon-3 5-mdnt (Sat-Sun all day) Closed: 25 Dec, Mon L **Bar Meals** L served Tue-Fri 12-2.30, Sat-Sun 12-8.30 D served Tue-Fri 5-8.30, Sat-Sun 12-8.30 booking required Av main course £10 **Restaurant** L served Tue-Fri 12-2.30, Sat-Sun 12-8.30 D served Tue-Fri 5-8.30, Sat-Sun 12-8.30 booking required Av 3 course à la carte fr £17 ⊕ ENTERPRISE INNS ◀ Timothy Taylor Landlord, Hartington Bitter, Lord Marples. **Facilities** Children welcome Children's menu Children's portions Garden Parking

LITTON   Map 16 SK17

Red Lion Inn

SK17 8QU ☎ **01298 871458**   🖷 **01298 871458**
e-mail: theredlionlitton@yahoo.co.uk
dir: *Just off A623 (Chesterfield to Stockport road), 1m E of Tideswell*

The Red Lion is a beautiful, traditional pub on the village green, very much at the heart of the local community. It became a pub in 1787 when it was converted from three farm cottages. With its wood fires, selection of well kept real ales and friendly atmosphere, it's a favourite with walkers and holiday-makers too. The menu offers hearty pub food at reasonable prices, such as Thai fishcakes with sweet chilli dip to start; Derbyshire lamb hotpot; steak and kidney pie; or South African bobotie to follow; and apple and berry crumble with custard to finish. A gluten-free menu is available.

Open all day all wk ⊕ ENTERPRISE INNS ◀ Barnsley Bitter, Abbeydale, Absolution, Guest ales.
Facilities Children's portions Dogs allowed

MATLOCK   Map 16 SK35

The Red Lion ★★★ INN

65 Matlock Green DE4 3BT ☎ **01629 584888**
dir: *From Chesterfield, A632 into Matlock, on right just before junct with A615*

This friendly, family-run free house makes a good base for exploring local attractions like Chatsworth House, Carsington Water and Dovedale. Spectacular walks in the local countryside help to work up an appetite for bar lunches, or great tasting home-cooked dishes in the homely restaurant. On Sunday there's a popular carvery with freshly cooked gammon ham, beef, pork, lamb and turkey. In the winter months, open fires burn in the lounge and games room, and there's a boules area in the attractive beer garden for warmer days. There are six comfortable bedrooms.

Open all day all wk **Bar Meals** L served Tue-Fri 12-2 **Restaurant** L served Sun 12-2.45 D served Tue-Sat 7-9 ⊕ FREE HOUSE ◀ Pedigree, Old Speckled Hen, Peak Ales, Guest ales. **Facilities** Garden Parking Wi-fi **Rooms** 6

MELBOURNE   Map 11 SK32

The Melbourne Arms ★★★ INN ♟

92 Ashby Rd DE73 8ES
☎ **01332 864949** & 863990   🖷 **01332 865525**
e-mail: info@melbournearms.co.uk
dir: *Telephone for directions*

This Grade II 18th-century inn on the village outskirts was tastefully converted about 14 years ago. There are two bars, a coffee lounge and a traditionally decorated restaurant - no, not red flock wallpaper - where an extensive menu of authentic Indian dishes is offered. With a range of English fare and a children's menu too,

there's no reason why the whole family can't find plenty to enjoy. You can stay over in one of the modern, thoughtfully equipped bedrooms.

Open all day all wk 11.30am-11.30pm ◀ Pedigree, Tetley's Smooth, Guinness. ♟ 12 **Facilities** Children welcome Children's menu Play area Family room Garden Parking **Rooms** 9

MILLTOWN   Map 16 SK36

The Nettle Inn ♟

S45 0ES ☎ **01246 590462**
e-mail: marcus.sloan@thenettleinn.co.uk
dir: *Telephone for directions*

A 16th-century hostelry on the edge of the Peak District, this inn has all the traditional charm you could wish for, from flower-filled hanging baskets to log fires and a stone-flagged taproom floor. Expect well-kept ales such as Bakewell Best, and impressive home-made food using the best of seasonal produce. Typical bar options are Armstrong's sausage butty or hot roast meat baguette, while on the restaurant menu dishes such as braised wild rabbit may tempt.

Open all wk Sat-Sun all day **Bar Meals** Av main course £15 food served all day **Restaurant** Av 3 course à la carte fr £28 food served all day ⊕ FREE HOUSE ◀ Swift Nick, Bakewell Best, Derbyshire Pale Ale. ♟ 9
Facilities Children welcome Children's menu Children's portions Dogs allowed Garden Parking Wi-fi

NEW MILLS   Map 16 SK08

Pack Horse Inn ♟ NEW

Mellor Rd SK22 4QQ
☎ **01663 742365**   🖷 **01663 741674**
e-mail: info@packhorseinn.co.uk
dir: *From A6 at Newtown take A6015 to New Mills. At lights left into Union Rd (B6101) signed Marple. At mini rdbt right into Market St, becomes Spring Bank Rd. Approx 1m left into Mellor Rd. 0.5m to pub*

Overlooking the valley of the River Sett, with views towards Kinder Scout, The Pack Horse is situated in the heart of the Peak District. This former farmhouse is an ideal base to explore the surrounding countryside or a pleasant pit stop between Sheffield and Manchester. The pub uses as much local produce as possible and the enticing menu might include Peak-reared lamb cutlets, mushrooms, tomatoes and peas or local butchers' sausages with onion gravy and mash.

Open all wk 12-3 5-11 (Sat 12-12, Sun 12-10.30)
Bar Meals L served Mon-Fri 12-2, Sat-Sun all day fr noon D served Mon-Fri 5-9.30, Sat until 9.30pm, Sun until 8.30pm Av main course £10 **Restaurant** L served Mon-Fri 12-2, Sat-Sun all day fr noon booking required D served Mon-Fri 5-9.30, Sat until 9.30pm, Sun until 8.30pm booking required Fixed menu price fr £10 ⊕ FREE HOUSE ◀ Phoenix Brewery Arizona, 2 guest ales. ♟ 14
Facilities Children welcome Children's menu Children's portions Garden Parking Wi-fi

PILSLEY   Map 16 SK27

The Devonshire Arms at Pilsley

★★★ INN **NEW**

High St DE45 1UL ☎ **01246 583258**
e-mail: res@devonshirehotels.co.uk
dir: *From A619, in Baslow, at rdbt take 1st exit onto B6012. Follow signs to Chatsworth, 2nd right to Pilsley*

Here is a fabulous old stone pub nestling in an estate village amidst the rolling parkland surrounding Chatsworth House, the 'Palace of The Peaks'. Such provenance also oozes from the food and drink on offer here; Peak Ales from the estate's brewery can accompany meats, game and greens from the adjacent estate shop, all sourced from these productive acres at the heart of the Peak District. A roast Chatsworth Estate Barnsley chop is a filling repast after a day's exploration of the area and prior to stopping-over at the luxurious accommodation, individually designed by The Duchess of Devonshire.

Open all day all wk **Bar Meals** L served all wk 12-2.30 D served all wk 5-9 Av main course £10 ⊕ FREE HOUSE ◀ Thornbridge Jaipur, Peak Ales Chatsworth Gold, Guest ales. **Facilities** Children welcome Children's menu Children's portions Parking **Rooms** 7

ROWSLEY   Map 16 SK26

The Grouse & Claret ★★★★ INN ♟

Station Rd DE4 2EB
☎ **01629 733233**   🖷 **01629 735194**
dir: *On A6 between Matlock & Bakewell*

A popular venue for local anglers, this 18th-century pub takes its name from a fishing fly. Situated at the gateway to the Peak District National Park, it is handy for touring the Peak District or visiting the stately homes of Haddon Hall and Chatsworth House. With an eye on healthy eating, a meal from the varied menu might include chicken Parmesan burger; sea bass with spiced tomato and pepper sauce; or wild mushroom tortellini. For the more traditionally minded, pub favourites include ham, egg and chips or a trio of mini pies. Comfortable accommodation is available.

Open all day all wk **Bar Meals** L served Mon-Sat 12-9, Sun 12-8 D served Mon-Sat 12-9, Sun 12-8 Av main course £5.50 food served all day **Restaurant** L served Mon-Sat 12-9, Sun 12-8 D served Mon-Sat 12-9, Sun 12-8 food served all day ⊕ WOLVERHAMPTON & DUDLEY BREWERIES PLC ◀ Marston's Pedigree, Mansfield, Bank's Bitter. ♟ 16 **Facilities** Children welcome Children's menu Children's portions Play area Garden Parking Wi-fi **Rooms** 8

The Old Crown Inn

Cavendish Bridge DE72 2HL ☎ 01332 792392
e-mail: the.oldcrowninn@btconnect.com
dir: *M1 junct 24 take A6 towards Derby. Left before river, bridge into Shardlow*

Up to nine real ales are served at this family-friendly pub on the south side of the River Trent, where there's a beer festival twice a year. Built as a coaching inn during the 17th century, it retains its warm and atmospheric interior. Several hundred water jugs hang from the ceilings, while the walls display an abundance of brewery and railway memorabilia. Traditional food is lovingly prepared by the landlady; main meals focus on pub classics such as home-made steak and kidney pie, ham, eggs and chips, lasagne, curry, steaks and daily specials. Monday night is quiz night, and there's folk music every Tuesday.

Open all day all wk 11am-11.30pm (Fri-Sat 11am-12.30am, Sun 11am-11pm) **Bar Meals** L served Tue-Fri 12-2, Sat 12-8, Sun 12-3 D served Tue-Fri 5-8, Sat 12-8 Av main course £6.50 **Restaurant** L served Tue-Fri 12-2, Sat 12-8, Sun 12-3 D served Tue-Fri 5-8, Sat 12-8 ⊕ MARSTONS ◀ Marston's Pedigree, Jennings Cocker Hoop, Marston's Empire, Guest ales. **Facilities** Children welcome Children's menu Children's portions Play area Dogs allowed Garden Beer festival Parking

The Flying Childers Inn NEW

Main Rd DE4 2LW ☎ 01629 636333
web: www.flyingchilders.com
dir: *From A6 (between Matlock & Bakewell) follow Youlgrave signs. Onto B5056 to Ashbourne. Follow Stanton in Peak signs*

Named after a champion racehorse owned by the 4th Duke of Devonshire, this stone-built pub has evolved over the years from a row of cottages. Set in the pretty village of Stanton in Peak close to Stanton Moor, it is now a cosy bolt hole offering real ales, a well-considered wine list and reasonably priced lunchtime food such as home-made soup, mouthwatering filled cobs (hot roast beef, black pudding and bacon) and toasties. Canine visitors are treated just as well as their owners with doggy bar snacks. Head outside to the lovely beer garden in summer.

Open all wk Wed-Fri 12-2 7-close (Sat-Sun 12-3 7-close) **Bar Meals** L served Wed-Sun 12-2 Av main course £3.80 ⊕ FREE HOUSE ◀ Wells Bombardier, Guest ales. **Facilities** Children welcome Dogs allowed Garden Parking **Notes** ⊛

The George Hotel ♥

Commercial Rd SK17 8NU
☎ 01298 871382   ▤ 01298 871382
e-mail: simon@tght.co.uk
dir: *A619 to Baslow, A623 towards Chapel-en-le-Frith, 0.25m*

Built in 1730, this delightful stone-built coaching inn stands in the shadow of St John the Baptist's church, known locally as the Cathedral of the Peak. It is conveniently placed for exploring the National Park and visiting Buxton, Chatsworth and Eyam. Since taking over the licence in 2010, Simon Easter has introduced a distinctive range of 'volcanic grills' served whilst still cooking on smooth slabs of hot volcanic rock. Other food options include sandwiches, filled jacket potatoes, stone-baked pizzas and pub favourites. There's a special children's selection, and traditional Sunday roasts.

Open all day all wk **Bar Meals** L served all wk 12-2.30 D served all wk 6-9 Av main course £8.95 **Restaurant** L served all wk 12-2.30 D served all wk 6-9 ⊕ GREENE KING ◀ Greene King IPA, Old Speckled Hen, Abbot Ale. ♥ 8 **Facilities** Children welcome Children's menu Children's portions Dogs allowed Parking Wi-fi

---

Three Stags' Heads

Wardlow Mires SK17 8RW ☎ 01298 872268
dir: *At junct of A623 (Baslow to Stockport road) & B6465*

A remarkable survivor, this 17th-century moorland longhouse features a stone-flagged bar and huge range fire. It is designated by English Heritage as one of over 200 heritage pubs throughout the UK. The bar counter, a 1940s addition, sells Abbeydale beers, including the hefty Black Lurcher, which commemorates a now-departed canine resident, and several real ciders. Hearty food includes chicken and spinach curry; and pork, leek and Stilton pie. Restricted hours allow owners Geoff and Pat Fuller time to make pottery, which you can buy. Sorry, it's not a pub for children.

Open all day noon-mdnt (Fri 7-mdnt) Closed: Mon-Thu (ex BH) **Bar Meals** L served Sat-Sun 12-3.30 D served Fri-Sun 6-9.30 Av main course £8.50 **Restaurant** L served Sat-Sun 12-2.30 D served Fri-Sun 6-9.30 ⊕ FREE HOUSE ◀ Abbeydale Matins, Absolution, Black Lurcher, Brimstone Bitter Ŏ Black Fox, Kingston Black, Yarlington Mill. **Facilities** Dogs allowed Parking **Notes** ⊛

The Three Horseshoes

The Green DE55 6DQ ☎ 01773 834854
dir: *A615 towards Matlock, 3m after Alfreton, 5m before Matlock*

This late-17th-century, stone-built coaching inn and blacksmith's forge in a village on the edge of the Peak District once traded horses over the bar. These days it serves what one regular customer called the 'best meat and potato pie in Derbyshire'. He would undoubtedly enthuse in similar vein about the creamy curries; liver and onions; ham, egg and chips; and lamb hot pot. A Thai cook takes over on Saturday evenings; the Sunday carvery usually includes beef, pork and/or turkey, with a vegetarian option. There are several walks that start or end at the pub.

Open all day all wk **Bar Meals** L served all wk 12-2.30 D served all wk 5-8 ⊕ GREENE KING ◀ Guinness, Hardys & Hansons Olde Trip, guest ale. **Facilities** Children welcome Children's menu Play area Dogs allowed Garden Parking

The Rising Sun ★★★★ INN ♥

Woodland TQ13 7JT ☎ 01364 652544
e-mail: admin@therisingsunwoodland.co.uk
dir: *From A38 E of Ashburton take lane signed Woodland/Denbury. Pub on left, approx 1.5m*

A former drovers' inn, largely rebuilt following a fire in 1989, The Rising Sun is set in beautiful and peaceful Devon countryside. Owner Paul is the chef and is dedicated to using local and seasonal produce on his menus. There's a good choice of fish from Brixham – baked sea bass - and excellent West Country cheeses, plus home-made puddings and children's menu too. The pub is well known for its home-made pies (perhaps mixed game or beef and blue cheese) and regularly-changing ales. There are five en suite bedrooms available, including a family room.

Open all wk noon-3 6-11 (Sun noon-3 6.30-11, all day mid Jul-mid Sep) Closed: 25-26 Dec **Bar Meals** L served Mon-Sat 12-2.15, Sun 12-2.30 D served Mon-Sat 6-9.15, Sun 6.30-9.15 **Restaurant** L served Mon-Sat 12-2.15, Sun 12-2.30 D served Mon-Sat 6-9.15, Sun 6.30-9.15 ⊕ FREE HOUSE ◀ Princetown Jail Ale, Guest Ales Ŏ Thatchers. ♥ 16 **Facilities** Children welcome Children's menu Children's portions Play area Family room Dogs allowed Garden Parking Wi-fi **Rooms** 5

AVONWICK　　　　　　　Map 3 SX75

The Avon Inn

TQ10 9NB ☎ **01364 73475**
dir: *Telephone for directions*

A handsome whitewashed free house, just off the Exeter to Plymouth trunk road, run since 2010 by the Needs family, whose mission statement is "Real ales, real food, real pub". The real ales come from Devon and Cornwall and are looked after by owner Gary and son Brad, the real food is honest-to-goodness pub grub with Karen at the helm, offering dishes such as cottage pie; 'gigantic' meat and vegetable pasty; pizzas; beer-battered cod; and vegetable carbonara. Sit outside in the large beer gardens in summer.

Open all day all wk 11am-12.30am (Sun noon-11.30pm) **Bar Meals** Av main course £7.95 food served all day **Restaurant** food served all day ⊕ FREE HOUSE ◀ Otter, Doom Bar, Hunters Gold ♂ Thatchers Gold. **Facilities** Children welcome Children's menu Children's portions Play area Dogs allowed Garden Parking Wi-fi

PICK OF THE PUBS

The Turtley Corn Mill ▼

TQ10 9ES ☎ **01364 646100** 🖿 **01364 646101**
e-mail: eat@turtleycornmill.com
dir: *From A38 at South Brent/Avonwick junction, take B3372, then follow signs for Avonwick, 0.5m*

You'll find plenty of newspapers and books to browse through while supping a pint of Tribute or Tamar Ale at this sprawling old free house. Not surprisingly, the building began life as a corn mill, then spent many years as a chicken hatchery before being converted to a pub in the 1970s. The six-acre site is bordered by a river and includes a lake with its own small island, whilst the interior is light and fresh with old furniture and oak and slate floors. The daily-changing modern British menus are extensively based on local produce from around the pub's idyllic South Hams location. Pork rillettes with toasted brioche are amongst the interesting starters, whilst main course choices include Niçoise-style griddled salmon on dressed leaves, and vegetarian Somerset stew with creamy mash. Dark chocolate torte is a typical dessert.

Open all day all wk Closed: 25 Dec **Bar Meals** L served all wk 12-10 booking required D served all wk 12-10 booking required Av main course £12 food served all day **Restaurant** L served all wk 12-10 booking required D served all wk 12-10 booking required Fixed menu price fr £11.95 Av 3 course à la carte fr £24 food served all day ⊕ FREE HOUSE ◀ Tamar Ale, Jail Ale, Tribute, Sharp's Doom Bar, IPA, Guest ales ♂ Thatchers. ▼ 8 **Facilities** Children welcome Children's portions Dogs allowed Garden Parking Wi-fi

AXMOUTH　　　　　　　Map 4 SY29

PICK OF THE PUBS

The Harbour Inn

Church St EX12 4AF ☎ **01297 20371**
dir: *Main street opposite church, 1m from Seaton*

The River Axe meanders through its valley into Lyme Bay, but just before they meet is Axmouth harbour, which accounted for one sixth of Devon's trade during the 16th century. This cosy, oak-beamed, harbourside inn was built four centuries earlier, however. Local ingredients are sourced for the food here. Bar and bistro menu offers scampi and chips, lasagne, sausages or faggots with mash and gravy, jacket potatoes, baguettes and sandwiches. From a daily updated blackboard menu, you might want to consider pork tenderloin with prunes and bacon. The Harbour makes a great stop if you are walking the South West Coast Path between Lyme Regis and Seaton. Change of hands.

Open all wk 11am-11pm (Fri-Sat 11am-mdnt, Sun 11am-10.30pm) **Bar Meals** L served all wk 12-9.30 food served all day **Restaurant** L served all wk 12-9.30 food served all day ⊕ HALL & WOODHOUSE ◀ Badger 1st Gold, Tanglefoot, Sussex ♂ Stowford Press, Applewood. **Facilities** Children welcome Children's menu Children's portions Play area Dogs allowed Garden Parking

The Ship Inn

EX12 4AF ☎ **01297 21838**
dir: *1m S of A3052 between Lyme & Sidmouth. Signed to Seaton at Boshill Cross*

There are long views over the Axe estuary from the beer garden of this creeper-clad family-run inn. It was built soon after the original Ship burnt down on Christmas Day 1879, and is able to trace its landlords back to 1769. Well kept real ales complement an extensive menu including daily blackboard specials where local fish and game feature, cooked with home-grown herbs. The pub has a skittles alley. Change of hands December 2010.

Open all day all wk ⊕ PUNCH TAVERNS ◀ Otter Bitter, Guinness, Sharp's Doom Bar ♂ Stowford Press. **Facilities** Children welcome Children's menu Children's portions Play area Family room Dogs allowed Garden Parking

BAMPTON　　　　　　　Map 3 SS92

The Quarrymans Rest ★★★★ INN ⊛ ▼
NEW

Briton St EX16 9LN ☎ **01398 331480**
e-mail: info@thequarrymansrest.co.uk
dir: *M5 junct 27 towards Tiverton on A361, at rdbt right signed Bampton. At next rdbt take 2nd exit signed Bampton, on right*

Workers quarrying stone nearby in the 18th century gave this pub its name. Sited at the top of town opposite the old toll house, it has a small seating area at the front and a patio and grassed area to the rear. The cosy bar serves ales such as Exmoor Gold, with comfy seats next to wood burners and tables suitable for informal eating. A separate dining room offers a quieter place to enjoy the likes of Cornish sardine fillets, slow-cooked pork belly from Hills Farm, and luscious home-made desserts. A beer festival is held during the May Bank Holiday and well equipped rooms are available.

Open all day all wk **Bar Meals** L served all wk 12-2 booking required D served all wk 6-9.30 booking required Av main course £12 **Restaurant** L served all wk 12-2 booking required D served all wk 6-9.30 booking required Fixed menu price fr £10.95 Av 3 course à la carte fr £23 ⊕ FREE HOUSE ◀ Sharp's Doom Bar, Otter, Exmoor Gold ♂ Cornish Rattler, Winkleigh Cider. **Facilities** Children welcome Children's portions Dogs allowed Garden Beer festival Parking Wi-fi **Rooms** 3

BEER　　　　　　　Map 4 SY28

Anchor Inn ★★★★ INN ▼

Fore St EX12 3ET ☎ **01297 20386** 🖿 **01297 24474**
e-mail: 6403@greeneking.co.uk
dir: *A3052 towards Lyme Regis. At Hangmans Stone take B3174 into Beer. Pub on seafront*

Fish caught by local boats feature strongly on the menu at this pretty colour-washed inn, which overlooks the sea in the picture-perfect Devon village of Beer. Starters to tempt might be oven baked spinach and goat's cheese tart with red onion marmalade or traditional prawn cocktail, followed by barbecue chicken breast with bacon, melted Cheddar and fries, or large fillet of beer battered cod, chips and mushy peas. There are six comfortable guest rooms available.

Open all day all wk 8am-11pm **Bar Meals** L served Mon-Fri 11-2.30, Sat-Sun 11-4 D served Sun-Thu 6-9, Fri-Sat 6-9.30 **Restaurant** L served Mon-Fri 12-2.30, Sat-Sun 12-3 D served Sun-Thu 6-9, Fri-Sat 6-9.30 ⊕ GREENE KING ◀ Otter Ale, Greene King IPA, Abbot Ale ♂ Aspall. ▼ 14 **Facilities** Children welcome Children's menu Dogs allowed Garden Wi-fi **Rooms** 6

BEESANDS — Map 3 SX84

PICK OF THE PUBS

The Cricket Inn ★★★★ INN ⊛ ☻
NEW

TQ7 2EN ☎ 01548 580215
e-mail: enquiries@thecricketinn.com
dir: From Kingsbridge take A379 towards Dartmouth. At Stokenham mini rdbt turn right to Beesands

In the small South Hams fishing village of Beesands, The Cricket Inn first opened its doors in 1867 and is only metres from the sloping beach and clear waters of Start Bay. Fishing was the main source of employment here until the early 1970s but there are still three trawler captains living in the village, plus fishermen who bring their catch straight to The Cricket. The dog-friendly bar is the place to enjoy Otter Ale or Heron Valley cider but the newly extended restaurant with its sea views is the place to sample crab, lobster and scallops caught in the bay outside. Locally grown vegetables and meat from the local butcher means a menu that is dictated by what's best on the day. Handpicked Start Bay crab sandwiches or fish pie make for a light lunch option, with diver caught Beesands scallops with shitake mushrooms, cauliflower purée and crispy Parma ham, followed by whole lemon sole with lemon and chive butter, two of the choices at dinner. Bright and airy accommodation is available.

Open all wk 11-3 6-11 (May-Sep all day)
Bar Meals L served all wk 12-3 D served all wk 6-9
Restaurant L served all wk 12-3 D served all wk 6-9
⊕ HEAVITREE BREWERY ◀ Otter Ale & Bitter, Tribute Ale ♉ Aspall, Heron Valley. ☻ 10 Facilities Children welcome Children's menu Children's portions Dogs allowed Garden Parking Wi-fi Rooms 8

BICKLEIGH — Map 3 SS90

Fisherman's Cot ☻

EX16 8RW ☎ 01884 855237 ▤ 01884 855241
e-mail: fishermanscot.bickleigh@marstons.co.uk
dir: Telephone for directions

Well-appointed thatched inn by Bickleigh Bridge over the River Exe with food all day and beautiful gardens, just a short drive from Tiverton and Exmoor. The Waterside Bar is the place for doorstep sandwiches, pies, snacks and afternoon tea, while the restaurant incorporates a carvery (on Sunday) and carte menus. Expect dishes such as farmhouse pâté; deep-fried baby squid; Thai red fish curry; slow-cooked pork shank; venison pie; and forest fruit crumble. Children's menu available.

Open all day all wk 11am-11pm (Sun noon-10.30pm)
Bar Meals Av main course £9 food served all day
Restaurant food served all day ⊕ MARSTONS
◀ Ringwood, Hobgoblin. ☻ 8 Facilities Children welcome Children's menu Children's portions Dogs allowed Garden Parking

BIGBURY-ON-SEA — Map 3 SX64

Pilchard Inn

Burgh Island TQ7 4BG
☎ 01548 810514 ▤ 01548 810243
e-mail: reception@burghisland.com
dir: From A38 turn off to Modbury then follow signs to Bigbury & Burgh Island

The Pilchard must be unique – an atmospheric 14th-century smugglers' inn located on a tiny island off the Devon coast that's cut off by the tide twice a day and only accessible at low tide by foot or via a hydraulic 'sea tractor' when the water is up. Expect beams, flagstones and blazing log fires in the bar, picnic tables by the water's edge, lovely coastal views and invigorating cliff walks. Simple bar food is served at lunchtime only, except for the set curry night menu on Fridays (booking advisable).

Open all day all wk Bar Meals L served Mon-Sun 12-3 Av main course £4.95 Restaurant D served Fri 7-9 (curry buffet) booking required Fixed menu price fr £18.75 ⊕ FREE HOUSE ◀ Pilchard, XSB, Hopnosis ♉ Thatchers Gold. Facilities Children welcome Dogs allowed

BLACKAWTON — Map 3 SX85

PICK OF THE PUBS

The Normandy Arms ☻ NEW

Chapel St TQ9 7BN ☎ 01803 712884
e-mail: info@normandyarms.co.uk
dir: From Dartmouth take A3122 towards Halwell. Turn right at Forces Tavern to Blackawton

Venture well off-the-beaten track down narrow winding country lanes into sleepy Blackawton village to locate this revamped 16th-century inn, named in honour of the Normandy landings, for which training exercises took place on nearby Slapton beach. Landlord Nick Crosley took over in January 2010, immediately spruced up the beamed and slate-floored bar and the relaxing dining room, both with warming log-burning stoves, and added chef Roger Hawkshaw, formerly at the renowned New Angel restaurant in Dartmouth, to the team. Expect imaginative seasonal menus that draw on top-notch South Hams produce, perhaps including ham hock terrine with apple chutney and pan-fried scallops with black pudding and truffled celeriac purée among the starters. Main dishes may take in daube of beef, shoulder of Blackawton lamb with couscous, harissa and red pepper fondue, or beer battered 'day boat' fish with triple-cooked chips and tartare sauce, while puddings could feature warm orange Bakewell tart. The 2-course Thursday night menus are a steal at £10.

Open 10.30-3 5-11 Closed: 2 Jan-1 Feb, Sun eve & Mon Bar Meals L served Tue-Sun 12-2.30 D served Tue-Sat 6-9.30 booking required Av main course £9.50 Restaurant L served Tue-Sun 12-2.30 booking required D served Tue-Sat 6-9.30 booking required Fixed menu price fr £15.50 Av 3 course à la carte fr £25 ⊕ FREE HOUSE ◀ Dartmoor Brewery Legend, Cotleigh Brewery ♉ Orchard Pig, Cheddar Valley. ☻ 12 Facilities Children welcome Children's menu Children's portions Dogs allowed Garden Parking Wi-fi

BRAMPFORD SPEKE — Map 3 SX99

The Lazy Toad Inn ☻

EX5 5DP ☎ 01392 841591 ▤ 01392 841591
e-mail: thelazytoadinn@btinternet.com
dir: From Exeter take A377 towards Crediton 1.5m, right signed Brampford Speke

There's much to commend this 19th-century country inn just a short drive from Exeter. It stands in a sleepy thatched village in peaceful countryside, close to the Exe Valley Way and glorious riverside walks, and Clive and Mo Walker's smallholding behind the pub supplies the soft fruit, herbs, vegetables, lamb and eggs to the kitchen, while meat and fish are cured in the pub smokery. Bag a table by the fire in one of the cosy beamed rooms, or outside in the courtyard or walled beer garden, and tuck into potted crab, rabbit confit with tarragon chips, and gooey treacle tart. Cracking ales and ciders complete the promising picture.

Open 11.30-2.30 6-11 (Sun 12-3) Closed: 3wks Jan, Sun eve & Mon Bar Meals L served Tue-Sun 12-2 D served Tue-Sat 6.30-9 Av main course £12.50 Restaurant Av 3 course à la carte fr £24 ⊕ FREE HOUSE ◀ Exmoor Ale, Otter Ale & Bitter, Exe Valley Exeter Old, Bays Topsail ♉ Sandford Devon Red, Traditional Farmhouse, Sandford Devon Mist. ☻ 12 Facilities Children welcome Children's menu Children's portions Family room Dogs allowed Garden Parking

BRANSCOMBE — Map 4 SY18

The Fountain Head NEW

EX12 3BG ☎ 01297 680359
dir: From Seaton on A3052 towards Sidmouth left at Branscombe Cross to pub

A true 500-year-old rural survivor tucked away in a peaceful Devon village a short walk from the coastal path. The old forge and cider house is often rammed with walkers and locals, drawn by the traditional charm of worn flagstones, crackling log fires, rustic furnishings, village brewed beers (Branscombe Vale), and the chatty atmosphere – no intrusive music or electronic games here. Hearty pub food includes local crab salad, ham, egg and chips, cod and chips, and beef and mushroom pie. Don't miss the mid-summer beer festival.

Open all wk 11-3 6-11 (Sun 12-3 6-10.30)
Bar Meals L served all wk 12-2 D served all wk 6.30-9 Av main course £7.50 Restaurant L served all wk 12-2 D served all wk 6.30-9 ⊕ FREE HOUSE ◀ Branscombe Vale Branoc, Jolly Geff, Summa That ♉ Thatchers Cheddar Valley. Facilities Children welcome Children's menu Children's portions Family room Dogs allowed Garden Beer festival Parking

PICK OF THE PUBS

The Masons Arms ♟

EX12 3DJ ☎ 01297 680300 📠 01297 680500
e-mail: reception@masonsarms.co.uk
dir: Turn off A3052 towards Branscombe, down hill, hotel at bottom of hill

Once a haunt of smugglers, this creeper-clad inn stands in the picturesque village of Branscombe, just a ten-minute stroll from the beach. The building dates from 1360, when it was a cider house squeezed into the middle of a row of cottages. Today, that row of cottages is a family-run pub with peaceful gardens with sea views across the valley. The bar has hardly changed in 200 years, with stone walls, ancient ships' beams, slate floors, and a splendid open fireplace used for spit-roasts, including Sunday lunchtimes. Five real ales are always available, including several that are locally brewed. Food is a serious business here; where possible all ingredients are grown, reared or caught locally, especially lobster and crab. Expect starters such as steamed West Country mussels and main choices of grilled pork loin steak with leek mash and Devon Blue cheese rarebit; followed, perhaps, by honey and mascarpone cheesecake. A three-day beer festival is held in the middle of July.

Open all day all wk **Bar Meals** L served Mon-Fri 12-2.30, Sat-Sun 12.30-2.15 booking required D served all wk 6.30-9 booking required Av main course £15 **Restaurant** D served all wk 7-9 booking required Fixed menu price fr £29.95 Av 3 course à la carte fr £29.95 ⊕ ST AUSTELL BREWERY ◀ Tribute, Branscombe, Proper Job, Guest ales. ♟ 14 **Facilities** Children welcome Children's menu Children's portions Dogs allowed Garden Beer festival Parking Wi-fi

BRAUNTON   Map 3 SS43

The Williams Arms

Wrafton EX33 2DE ☎ 01271 812360 📠 01271 816595
e-mail: info@williamsarms.co.uk
dir: On A361 between Barnstaple & Braunton

Owned by the Squire family since 1976 and refurbished in January 2011, this postcard-pretty thatched pub dates back to the 16th century. Its prime location beside the popular Tarka Trail sees weary walkers, cyclists and local diners pile in for the pub's famous daily carvery, which always features locally-reared meat. Alternatively, you can try venison braised in red wine, steak and ale pie, or lighter options like salad Niçoise and a bacon and Brie panini, perfect washed down with a pint of Sharp's Doom Bar.

Open all day all wk 8.45am-11pm **Bar Meals** food served all day **Restaurant** L served Mon-Sat noon-2, Sun 12-3 D served all wk 6-9 ⊕ FREE HOUSE ◀ Guinness, Creamflow, Doom Bar ♙ Thatchers. **Facilities** Children welcome Children's menu Children's portions Play area Garden Parking

BRENDON   Map 3 SS74

Rockford Inn

EX35 6PT ☎ 01598 741214
e-mail: enquiries@therockfordinn.com
dir: A39 through Minehead follow signs to Lynmouth. Turn left off A39 to Brendon approx 5m before Lynmouth

This traditional 17th-century free house stands in the heart of Exmoor and on the banks of the East Lyn river, and is handy for several Exmoor walking routes. Thatchers ciders complement local ales served from the cask, and there's a choice of good home-made pub meals. Game pie, salmon with shrimps, capers and parsley, and wild mushroom crumble are typical menu choices; the specials board changes daily. Eat in the garden in fine weather, or come indoors to the open fire as the nights draw in.

Open all day Closed: Mon L **Bar Meals** L served Tue-Sun 12-3 D served Tue-Sun 6-8.30 booking required Av main course £9 ⊕ FREE HOUSE ◀ Barn Owl, Tribute, Cotleigh 25, Exmoor, Proper Ansome, Devon Darter, Real Smiler ♙ Thatchers, Addlestones. **Facilities** Children welcome Children's menu Children's portions Dogs allowed Garden Parking Wi-fi

BROADHEMPSTON   Map 3 SX86

The Monks Retreat Inn

The Square TQ9 6BN ☎ 01803 812203
dir: Exit A381 (Newton Abbot to Totnes road) at Ipplepen, follow for Broadhempston signs for 3.5m

Apparently a friendly ghost of a monk inhabits this 1456 inn, formerly called Church House Inn. Certainly it's the sort of place you'd want to linger in: the building (listed as of outstanding architectural interest) is full of fascinating features, including a panelled oak screen typical of ancient Devon houses. Sit by one of the cosy log fires and enjoy a pint of Otter Bitter or Jail Ale or some good food at this popular locals pub.

Open Tue-Sun Closed: Mon **Bar Meals** L served Tue-Sun 12-1.45 D served Tue-Sun 6.30-9 **Restaurant** L served Tue-Sun 12-1.45 booking required D served Tue-Sun 6.30-9 booking required ⊕ ENTERPRISE INNS ◀ Jail Ale, Otter Bitter ♙ Thatchers Gold. **Facilities** Children welcome Dogs allowed

BUCKFASTLEIGH   Map 3 SX76

Dartbridge Inn ♟

Totnes Rd TQ11 0JR
☎ 01364 642214 📠 01364 643839
e-mail: 6442@greeneking.co.uk
dir: From Exeter A38, take 1st Buckfastleigh turn, then left to Totnes. Inn on left

Wooden floors, leather chairs, sofas and real fires define the ambience in the spacious bar of the Dartbridge, where various guest ales vie for your trade; a dozen wines are served by the glass too. Outside, there are views through trees to the River Dart, and a prettily furnished terrace with parasols. Menus comprise fairly priced pub favourites made with good quality produce, such as farm-assured chicken and bacon rigatoni; and smoked haddock, spinach and West Country Cheddar florentine bake. Children's choices comprise smaller portions of dishes selected from the adult menu. Accommodation available.

Open all day all wk **Bar Meals** Av main course £7 food served all day **Restaurant** food served all day ◀ Abbot Ale, IPA, Ruddles County, Old Speckled Hen, Guest ales. ♟ 12 **Facilities** Children welcome Children's menu Children's portions Beer festival Parking Wi-fi

BUCKLAND MONACHORUM   Map 3 SX46

Drake Manor Inn ♟

The Village PL20 7NA
☎ 01822 853892 📠 01822 853892
e-mail: drakemanor@drakemanorinn.co.uk
dir: Off A386 near Yelverton

In the 12th century, when nearby St Andrew's church was being built, the masons needed a house to live in. Today's licensee of that now very old house is Mandy Robinson, who prides herself on running a 'proper pub', where her locally sourced menu includes bar snacks, vegetarian options, steaks and fresh fillet of smoked haddock on pea risotto, as well as pub favourites, such as home-made steak and kidney pie and chicken supreme. The sunny cottage garden is appealing.

Open all wk 11.30-2.30 6.30-11 (Fri 6.30-11.30, Sat 11.30am-11.30pm, Sun noon-11) **Bar Meals** L served all wk 12-2 D served Mon-Sat 7-10, Sun 7-9.30 Av main course £8.50 **Restaurant** L served all wk 12-2 D served Mon-Sat 7-10, Sun 7-9.30 ⊕ PUNCH TAVERNS ◀ John Smith's & Courage Best, Sharp's Doom Bar, Jail Ale, Otter Ale. ♟ 9 **Facilities** Children welcome Children's portions Family room Dogs allowed Garden Parking

BUTTERLEIGH
Map 3 SS90

The Butterleigh Inn

EX15 1PN ☎ 01884 855407 📠 **01884 855600**
dir: *3m from M5 junct 28 turn right by Manor Hotel in Cullompton. Follow Butterleigh signs*

Located within rolling countryside, this 400-year-old traditional free house sits opposite a pretty 13th-century church. There is a mass of local memorabilia throughout this friendly local, where customers can choose from a selection of real ales including O'Hanlon's Yellow Hammer, and ciders including Sam's Medium from Winkleigh Cider. On fine days, the peaceful garden with its huge flowering cherry tree is very popular. Home-made dishes and daily specials are always available in the bar and restaurant. Expect choices such as fish pie; beef or five-bean chilli; sausage and mash; and steak and ale pie.

Open 12-2.30 6-11 (Fri-Sat 12-2.30 6-12 Sun 12-3) Closed: Sun eve Nov-Apr **Bar Meals** L served Mon-Sat 12-2 D served Mon-Sat 7-9 Av main course £9.50 **Restaurant** L served Mon-Sat 12-2 D served Mon-Sat 7-9 ⊕ FREE HOUSE ◀ Cotleigh Tawny Ale, Yellow Hammer, Otter Ale, Otter Amber, guest ale ♂ Sams Medium, Thatchers Gold. **Facilities** Children welcome Children's menu Children's portions Dogs allowed Garden Parking Wi-fi

CADELEIGH
Map 3 SS90

The Cadeleigh Arms NEW

EX16 8HP ☎ 01884 855238
e-mail: info@thecadeleigharms.co.uk
dir: *M5 junct 27, A361 onto A396 signed Tiverton & Bickleigh A396. In Bickleigh at Fisherman's Cot right signed Crediton & Cadeleigh. 1st right immediately after humped-backed bridge signed Cadeleigh. 1.75m to pub in village centre*

Devon beer, Devon wine and Devon beef keep the scattered rural community returning to this flagstone-floored, fine food haven in tiny Cadeleigh, where farming talk is disturbed by the topple of alley skittles, whilst occasional local theatre and art classes emphasise the strong bonds between the licensees and their supportive locals. Meals appeal to traditionalists as well as those looking for alternative cuisine with a twist; but beef and Otter pie definitely isn't exactly what it says on the specials board!

Open 12-2 6-11 Closed: Sun eve & Mon **Bar Meals** L served Tue-Sun 12-2 booking required D served Tue-Sat 7-9 booking required Av main course £9.95 **Restaurant** L served Tue-Sun 12-2 booking required D served Tue-Sat 7-9 booking required Av 3 course à la carte fr £20 ⊕ FREE HOUSE ◀ Otter Bitter ♂ Sandford Orchards. **Facilities** Children welcome Children's portions Dogs allowed Garden Parking Wi-fi

CHAGFORD
Map 3 SX78

PICK OF THE PUBS

Sandy Park Inn ♥

TQ13 8JW ☎ 01647 433267
e-mail: sandyparkinn@btconnect.com
dir: *From A30 exit at Whiddon Down, turn left towards Moretonhampstead. Inn 5m from Whiddon Down*

Everything about the thatched Sandy Park is just as it should be: dogs are frequently to be found slumped in front of the fire, while homely horse brasses and sporting prints adorn the walls. The beamed bar attracts locals and travellers alike, all happily setting the world to rights with the help of an eclectic wine list and good range of traditional local ales like Otter and Dartmoor Legend. You can eat in the bar, snug or candlelit dining room. Menus of home-made dishes change with the seasons, blending pub classics with modern fusion and vegetarian options; a range of gourmet stone-baked pizzas is especially popular. Sandwiches and salads are perfect for summer lunchtimes, when they can be served in the garden with its views towards the Castle Drogo estate and deer park. Monthly open mic nights attract musicians, poets and story tellers.

Open all day all wk noon-11pm **Bar Meals** L served all wk 12-2.30 booking required D served all wk 6-9 booking required Av main course £10.50 **Restaurant** L served all wk 12-2.30 booking required D served all wk 6-9 booking required Fixed menu price fr £9 Av 3 course à la carte fr £20 ⊕ FREE HOUSE ◀ Otter Ale, O'Hanlons, Dartmoor Legend ♂ Pound House. ♥ 8 **Facilities** Children welcome Children's portions Family room Dogs allowed Garden Parking Wi-fi

CHARDSTOCK
Map 4 ST30

The George Inn

EX13 7BX ☎ 01460 220241
e-mail: info@george-inn.co.uk
dir: *A358 from Taunton through Chard towards Axminster, left at Tytherleigh. Signed from A358*

A glorious, thatched 15th century village inn with superb oak panelling removed from a ship, a ghostly parson named Copeland and robust, long-standing locals who preside in 'Compost Corner', perhaps ruminating over local ales or awaiting a feast from the kitchen, anything from filled baguettes to home-made pies and slow-roast belly of pork with cider sauce, before tackling a game of skittles against visiting foes. As we went to press a change of hands was taking place.

Open all wk 11.30-3 6-12 (Sat-Sun all day) ⊕ FREE HOUSE ◀ Otter Bitter, Sharp's Doom Bar, Guest ales ♂ Stowford Press. **Facilities** Children welcome Children's menu Children's portions Dogs allowed Garden Parking

CHERITON BISHOP
Map 3 SX79

PICK OF THE PUBS

The Old Thatch Inn ♥

See Pick of the Pubs on opposite page

CLAYHIDON
Map 4 ST11

PICK OF THE PUBS

The Merry Harriers ♥

Forches Corner EX15 3TR
☎ 01823 421270 📠 **01823 421270**
e-mail: peter.gatling@btinternet.com
dir: *M5 junct 26 towards Wellington A38, turn onto Ford Street (marked by brown tourist sign). At top of hill turn left, 1.5m on right*

Set in beautiful countryside high on the Blackdown Hills, this free house stands on the once notorious Forches Corner, which was the scene of ambushes during the 17th-century Monmouth Rebellion. Highwaymen were reputedly hanged outside the pub – which might explain why it's said to be haunted. Originally a Devon longhouse dating from 1492, the black and white building features beamed ceilings, a cosy inglenook and attractive dining areas, whilst the large mature garden is popular during the summer months. Peter and Angela Gatling have worked tirelessly to build the local drinks trade and expand the food operation. More than 90 per cent of kitchen ingredients come from the surrounding hills or further afield in the West Country. A bar lunch might feature local steak and kidney pie with rich Otter Ale gravy, or for lighter appetites there are filled baguettes. In the evening you could try oven-roasted pigeon breast on honey-glazed baby vegetables followed by West Country chicken and tomato tagine.

Open noon-3 6.30-11 Closed: Sun eve & Mon **Bar Meals** L served Tue-Sat 12-2, Sun 12-2.15 booking required D served Tue-Sat 6.30-9 booking required Av main course £9 **Restaurant** L served Tue-Sat 12-2, Sun 12-2.15 booking required D served Tue-Sat 6.30-9 booking required Fixed menu price fr £9 Av 3 course à la carte fr £16 ⊕ FREE HOUSE ◀ Otter Head, Cotleigh Harrier, Exmoor Gold, St Austell Tinners, Otter Amber ♂ Thatchers Gold, Bollhayes. ♥ 14 **Facilities** Children welcome Children's menu Children's portions Play area Family room Dogs allowed Garden Parking Wi-fi

Save on hotels. Book at **theAA.com/hotel**

DEVON 131 ENGLAND

PICK OF THE PUBS

The Old Thatch Inn ♀

CHERITON BISHOP   Map 3 SX79

EX6 6HJ ☎ 01647 24204
e-mail: mail@theoldthatch.f9.co.uk
web: www.theoldthatchinn.com
dir: *0.5m off A30, 7m SW of Exeter*

This charming 16th-century free house is just outside the eastern border of Dartmoor National Park. Stagecoaches would stop here when the old road to Cornwall went through the village, but today the pub stands half a mile away from its successor, the A30 dual-carriageway that takes holiday traffic to and from all points west. For a time during its long history the inn was in private hands, then became a tea room, before its licence was renewed in the early 1970s. Following a fire, major refurbishment was necessary in 2007, but it was carried out thoughtfully and sympathetically so as not to compromise its period appeal. At least four real ales are served in the bar and there's an extensive wine list.

Owners David and Serena London are proud of their high standards, and prepare all their food from fresh, regionally sourced ingredients, with seafood featuring strongly. Light snacks at lunchtime include filled pumpkin and sunflower seed mini-loaves, and soup of the day with ciabattas. Main menu starters include warm pigeon breast rocket salad with strawberry and balsamic dressing; terrine of wild boar, red onion confit, toasted bread; Bantry Bay mussels with white wine and garlic cream sauce; Cornish crab gateau, cucumber and lemon mayonnaise; and buffalo mozzarella and beef tomato, black olive and pesto dressing.

Appearing as main courses may be fillet of beef medallions layered with fresh spinach with sautéed potatoes and wild mushroom and port sauce; sirloin steak with pan-fried cherry tomatoes, mushrooms and chips; pan-fried calves' liver with celeriac mash, caramelised red onion and balsamic jus; fresh sea bass fillets on a bed of pak choi, new potatoes and crab bisque; and goat's cheese and asparagus filo parcel with tomato coulis.

Open all wk 11.30-3 6-11 Closed: 25-26 Dec, Sun eve **Bar Meals** L served Mon-Thu 12-2, Fri-Sat 12-2.30, Sun 12-3 D served Mon-Thu 6.30-9, Fri-Sat 6.30-9.30 **Restaurant** L served Mon-Thu 12-2, Fri-Sat 12-2.30, Sun 12-3 D served Mon-Thu 6.30-9, Fri-Sat 6.30-9.30 ⊕ FREE HOUSE ◼ Otter Ale, Port Stout, O'Hanlon's Storm Stay, Sharp's Doom Bar, Yellowhammer, Dartmoor Legend ♻ Thatchers. ♀ 9
Facilities Children's menu Children's portions Family room Dogs allowed Garden Parking

CLEARBROOK · Map 3 SX56

The Skylark Inn

PL20 6JD ☎ **01822 853258**
e-mail: skylvic@btinternet.com
dir: *5m N of Plymouth on A386 towards Tavistock. Take 2nd right signed Clearbrook*

The Skylark is set in the Dartmoor National Park just ten minutes from Plymouth and the area is ideal for cyclists and walkers. The beamed bar with its large fireplace and wood-burning stove characterises this attractive village inn, where good wholesome food is served from an extensive menu. Dishes include classics like ham and eggs; gammon steak; or a mixed grill.

Open all wk 11.30-3 6-11.30 ⊕ UNIQUE PUB CO LTD
◀ Otter Ale, St Austell Tribute, Dartmoor Best Bitter.
Facilities Play area Family room Dogs allowed Garden Parking

CLOVELLY · Map 3 SS32

PICK OF THE PUBS

Red Lion Hotel ★★ HL

The Quay EX39 5TF
☎ **01237 431237** 🖅 **01237 431044**
e-mail: redlion@clovelly.co.uk
dir: *From Bideford rdbt, follow A39 to Bude for 10m. At Clovelly Cross rdbt turn right, follow past Clovelly Visitor Centre entrance, bear to left. Hotel at bottom of hill*

This charming whitewashed hostelry sits right on the quay in Clovelly, the famously unspoilt 'village like a waterfall', which descends down broad steps to a 14th-century harbour. Guests staying in the whimsically decorated bedrooms can fall asleep to the sound of waves lapping the shingle and wake to the cries of gulls squabbling for scraps. Originally a beer house for fishermen and other locals, the Red Lion has plenty of character and offers Cornish ales such as Doom Bar in its snug bar, where you can rub shoulders with the locals. Alternatively, you could settle in the Harbour Bar, which, as it name suggests, is a perfect place to watch the comings and goings of this busy fishing village. Seafood, unsurprisingly, is a priority on the modern menu since fresh fish is landed daily right outside the door, plus local organic vegetables and produce and venison and game from Clovelly estate are also featured in the seasonal dishes. There is an annual beer festival late May Bank Holiday.

Open all day all wk **Bar Meals** L served all wk 12-2.30 D served all week 6-8.30 **Restaurant** D served all wk 7-9 booking required ⊕ FREE HOUSE ◀ Doom Bar, Guinness, Clovelly Cobbler ♂ Thatchers, Sam's Poundhouse. **Facilities** Children welcome Children's menu Children's portions Family room Beer festival Parking Wi-fi **Rooms** 11

CLYST HYDON · Map 3 ST00

PICK OF THE PUBS

The Five Bells Inn ♟

EX15 2NT ☎ **01884 277288**
e-mail: info@fivebellsclysthydon.co.uk
web: www.fivebellsclysthydon.co.uk
dir: *B3181 towards Cullompton, right at Hele Cross towards Clyst Hydon. 2m turn right, then sharp right at left bend at village sign*

Originally a 16th-century farmhouse, this attractive country pub takes its name from the five bells hanging in the village church tower: the pub was located next to the church and moved to its present location in the 1880s. It's increasingly popular thanks to its family-friendly owners and a focus on excellent real ales, good food and cheerful hospitality. The roof was re-thatched in 2010, and the well-maintained garden is a colourful all year round and a delight in summer, with 20 tables enjoying lovely views of the rolling east Devon countryside, and a children's play area. The interior boasts two wood fires, numerous prints and watercolours, and brass and copper artefacts. In addition to real ales, there are draught lagers, cider and bottled beers. Tuck in to mains of sliced duck breast with blackcurrant sauce; or steak and kidney suet pudding; or choose something like oven-baked monkfish with a white wine, cream and dill sauce from the specials board.

Open 11.30am-3 6.30-11pm Closed: Mon L
Bar Meals L served Tue-Sun 11.30-2 D served all wk 6.30-9 Av main course £11 **Restaurant** Fixed menu price fr £7.95 Av 3 course à la carte fr £20 ⊕ FREE HOUSE ◀ Cotleigh Tawny Ale, Otter Bitter, O'Hanlon's.
♟ 10 **Facilities** Children welcome Play area Family room Garden Parking

COCKWOOD · Map 3 SX98

PICK OF THE PUBS

The Anchor Inn ♟

EX6 8RA ☎ **01626 890203** 🖅 **01626 890355**
dir: *Off A379 between Dawlish & Starcross*

Reputedly over 450 years old, this former Seamen's Mission overlooks a small landlocked harbour on the River Exe; expect tales of smugglers and even a friendly ghost with his dog. In summer customers spill out onto the veranda and harbour wall, while real fires and low beams make the interior cosy in winter. Nautical bric-a-brac abounds, with lights inside divers' helmets, ropes and pulleys, binnacles, and a wall displaying over 200 cast ship badges. The addition of the Wheel House five years ago doubled capacity, and allowed space for live music and entertainment about twice per week. An excellent range of draught ales is backed by popular 'home-made' wines. For fish lovers, the comprehensive menu will challenge the indecisive – there are 30 different ways to eat mussels, a menu dedicated to scallops, and fish dishes include snapper and swordfish. Meat eaters and vegetarians are not forgotten, and most people cannot resist one of the twelve varieties of treacle tart.

Open all day all wk 11-11 (Sun noon-10.30, 25 Dec 12-2) **Bar Meals** Av main course £8.95 food served all day **Restaurant** L served all wk 12-2.15 D served Mon-Sat 6.30-10, Sun 6.30-9.30 booking required Av 3 course à la carte fr £30 ⊕ HEAVITREE ◀ Interbrew Bass, Timothy Taylor Landlord, Fuller's London Pride, Otter Ale, Abbot, Adnams Broadside. ♟ 20
Facilities Children's menu Dogs allowed Garden Parking

COLEFORD · Map 3 SS70

PICK OF THE PUBS

The New Inn ★★★★ INN ♟

EX17 5BZ ☎ **01363 84242** 🖅 **01363 85044**
e-mail: enquiries@thenewinncoleford.co.uk
dir: *From Exeter take A377, 1.5m after Crediton turn left for Coleford, 1.5m to inn*

The ancient slate floored bar with its old chests and polished brass blends effortlessly with fresh white walls, original oak beams and simple wooden furniture in the dining room of this pretty 13th-century inn. Set beside the babbling River Cole, the riverside garden is perfect for alfresco summer dining, when you can ponder on the pub's history: it was used by travelling Cistercian monks long before Charles I reviewed his troops from a nearby house during the English Civil War. Menus change regularly, and special events such as 'pie week' or 'sea shanty night' are interspersed throughout the year. Home-made bar food includes a range of soups, omelettes and platters, while a full three-course meal could start with deep-fried Brie wedge in crispy breadcrumbs; continue with sautéed black pudding and grilled bacon with rosemary mash;

Save on hotels. Book at **theAA.com/hotel**

DEVON 133 **ENGLAND**

and finish with olde English apple tart and cream. The pub's Amazon Blue parrot, called Captain, has been a famous fixture here for nearly 30 years, greeting bar regulars and guests booking into the six well-appointed bedrooms.

Open all wk 12-3 6-11 (Sun 7-10.30 winter) Closed: 25-26 Dec **Bar Meals** L served all wk 12-2 D served all wk 6.30-9.30 Av main course £12 **Restaurant** L served all wk 12-2 D served all wk 6.30-9.30 Av 3 course à la carte fr £22 ⊕ FREE HOUSE ◀ Doom Bar, Otter Ale, Exmoor Ale, Spitfire, Rev James Ò Thatchers, Winkleigh Sam's. ♚ 20 **Facilities** Children welcome Children's menu Children's portions Dogs allowed Garden Parking **Rooms** 6

COLYFORD   Map 4 SY29

The Wheelwright Inn

Swanhill Rd EX24 6QQ
☎ 01297 552585 📄 01297 553841
e-mail: gary@wheelwright-inn.co.uk
dir: *Telephone for directions*

This pretty thatched inn has earned a reputation for outstanding food and service since the current landlords took over. The exterior of the 17th-century building belies the contemporary interior, but the low beams, wooden floors and log fire ensure that it retains its authentic country feel. Well kept beers include Badger First Gold and Hopping Hare. Expect a varied modern menu, including well-filled sandwiches on locally baked bread; local pork cutlet with creamy potato and swede mash; and moules marinière with crusty bread.

Open all day all wk Closed: 26 Dec ⊕ HALL & WOODHOUSE ◀ Badger First Gold, Hopping Hare, Guinness, Sussex Ò Stowford Press. **Facilities** Children welcome Children's menu Children's portions Family room Dogs allowed Garden Parking

---

DALWOOD   Map 4 ST20

PICK OF THE PUBS

The Tuckers Arms ♚

EX13 7EG ☎ 01404 881342 📄 01404 881138
e-mail: tuckersarms@tuckersarms.com
dir: *Off A35 between Honiton & Axminster*

An 800-year-old, family-run Devon longhouse in a pretty setting between two ridges of the Blackdown Hills, a tranquil landscape of high plateaux, valleys and springs, dotted with farms and villages. Some sources suggest that the pub was built as living accommodation for the labourers constructing St Peters church across the way, although at least one other source credits the Duke of Beaulieu for building it as a hunting lodge. The interior is everything you would expect of a traditional, thatched inn – inglenook fireplaces, low beams and flagstone floors. Local ales on tap come from the Otter and Branscombe breweries. As the pub is only fifteen minutes from the coast at Lyme Regis, fish and seafood have only a short

---

distance to travel, so its freshness is assured. At lunchtime, chose beer-battered catch of the day with hand-cut chips and pea purée, or maybe prime beefburger topped with cheese. The evening menu offers Thai crab linguine, slow-roast pork belly, West Country ham, eggs and chips, or a 10oz gammon steak.

Open all wk 11.30-3 6.30-11 **Bar Meals** L served all wk 12-2 D served all wk 7-9 **Restaurant** L served all wk 12-2 D served all wk 7-9 ⊕ FREE HOUSE ◀ Otter Bitter, Branoc Ale, Guest Ales. ♚ 8 **Facilities** Children welcome Children's menu Children's portions Dogs allowed Garden Parking Wi-fi

---

DARTMOUTH   Map 3 SX85

PICK OF THE PUBS

Royal Castle Hotel ★★★ HL ♚

11 The Quay TQ6 9PS
☎ 01803 833033 📄 01803 835445
e-mail: becca@royalcastle.co.uk
dir: *In town centre, overlooking inner harbour*

Five hundred years of history surround visitors to this ancient coaching inn, overlooking Dartmouth's inner harbour. A century after two merchants built adjacent quayside houses during the 1630s, one had become The New Inn and was later joined by its neighbour to become The Castle Inn. Further rebuilds resulted in the battlemented cornice and the front entrance with its Doric columns. Tudor fireplaces, spiral staircases and priest holes are other intriguing features, along with fine antique pieces including four-poster beds. The contemporary Nu first floor restaurant looks out over the river and is open to non-residents. A supporter of Taste of the West's 'buy local' campaign, the hotel offers an extensive seasonal menu that might include Dartmoor venison loin, South Hams beef or Dartmouth crab. Lunchtime sandwiches, jacket potatoes and ploughman's are also served in the bar, supported by a good selection of hot dishes. Curry night is every Tuesday and salt beef lunch every Saturday in the Galleon lounge.

Open all day all wk 8am-11.30pm **Bar Meals** L served all wk 11.30am-10pm D served all wk 11.30am-10pm food served all day **Restaurant** L served all wk 12-2 D served all wk 6-9 ⊕ FREE HOUSE ◀ Jail Ale, Bays Gold, Doom Bar Ò Thatchers Gold, Orchards Cider. ♚ 29 **Facilities** Children welcome Children's menu Children's portions Family room Dogs allowed Parking Wi-fi **Rooms** 25

DENBURY   Map 3 SX86

The Union Inn

Denbury Green TQ12 6DQ
☎ 01803 812595 📄 01803 814206
e-mail: enquiries@theunioninndenbury.co.uk
dir: *2m from Newton Abbot, signed Denbury*

The Union Inn is at least 400 years old and counting. Inside are the original stone walls that once rang to the hammers of the blacksmiths and cartwrights who worked here many moons ago. Choose freshly prepared, mouth-watering starters such pea and ham soup, crayfish cocktail and spiced smoked duck breast with pink ginger, and follow with beer battered cod and hand-cut chips; venison sausage toad-in-the-hole; or wild mushroom risotto. The guest ale is changed on a keg-by-keg basis. Change of hands.

Open all wk noon-3 6-11.30 (Thu-Sun 11-11) ⊕ ENTERPRISE INNS ◀ Otter Bitter, Denbury Dreamer, rotating guest ales Ò Westons. **Facilities** Children welcome Children's menu Children's portions Dogs allowed Garden Parking Wi-fi

---

DITTISHAM   Map 3 SX85

PICK OF THE PUBS

The Ferry Boat ♚

Manor St TQ6 0EX ☎ 01803 722368
e-mail: simonfbi@hotmail.co.uk
dir: *Telephone for directions*

The only pub situated on the River Dart, the Ferry Boat Inn dates back 300 years and the pontoon outside the entrance means that you can still arrive here by boat. Tables at the front of this waterside pub enjoy views across the river to Greenway House and Gardens, the National Trust property that used to be Agatha Christie's home. The pub has plenty of marine connections, being just a few miles upriver from the Royal Naval College in Dartmouth. The pontoon guarantees popularity with the boating fraternity, but the pub is also a favourite with walkers and families. With its year-round selection of four or five real ales, and open log fires crackling in the grates in winter, this really is a pub for all seasons. Menus of home-cooked food vary seasonally, based on fresh fish and seafood, and local meats and cheeses. Typical dishes might include home-made smoked haddock chowder, seafood linguine with tiger prawns and mussels or fresh crab salad. A beach barbecue in summer is often accompanied by live music from local musicians.

Open all day all wk **Bar Meals** L served all wk 12-2.30 booking required D served all wk 7-9 booking required ⊕ PUNCH TAVERNS ◀ Otter ale, St Austell Tribute, IPA, Sharp's Doom Bar, Guest ales Ò Addlestones Cloudy, Old Rosie. ♚ 10 **Facilities** Children welcome Children's menu Children's portions Family room Dogs allowed

DODDISCOMBSLEIGH
Map 3 SX88

PICK OF THE PUBS

The Nobody Inn ★★★★ INN ♥

See Pick of the Pubs on opposite page

DOLTON
Map 3 SS51

Rams Head Inn ♥

South St EX19 8QS ☎ 01805 804255 📠 01805 804509
e-mail: ramsheadinn@btopenworld.com
dir: *8m from Torrington on A3124*

This 15th-century free house has retained much of its
original character with huge old fireplaces, bread ovens
and pot stands. The inn's central location places it on
many inland tourist routes, whilst the Tarka Trail and
Rosemoor Gardens are both nearby. Expect a selection of
cask ales on tap, accompanied by popular and traditional
meals on the restaurant menu, served at lunchtime and
in the evening.

Open all wk 10-3 5-11 (Fri-Sat noon-mdnt Sun noon-4
6-11) Bar Meals food served all day Restaurant food
served all day ⊕ FREE HOUSE ◀ Flowers IPA Cask,
Trophy, Sharp's Own ♂ Winkleigh. ♥ 14
Facilities Children welcome Dogs allowed Garden Parking

DREWSTEIGNTON
Map 3 SX79

PICK OF THE PUBS

The Drewe Arms ♥

The Square EX6 6QN
☎ 01647 281224 📠 01647 281179
e-mail: mail@thedrewearms.co.uk
dir: *W of Exeter on A30 for 12m. Left at Woodleigh
junct follow signs for 3m to Drewsteignton*

In a sleepy village square, this traditional thatched pub
lies just within Dartmoor National Park. Built in 1646,
it used to be the Druid Arms, but in the 1920s the
Drewe family, who had commissioned Sir Edwin
Lutyens to design nearby Castle Drogo, persuaded the
brewery to change the pub's name. The Drewe's
contribution? They paid for a pub sign showing the
family coat of arms. Real ales are served from the cask
in the tap room and served through a hatchway into the
bar. Dine in The Dartmoor or Card Rooms, or in Aunt
Mabel's Kitchen, named after Mabel Mudge, landlady
for 75 years from 1919 to 1994. Enjoy grilled steaks;
pizzas; fillet of cod; steak and kidney pudding; fresh
mussels cooked several ways; and Teign Valley venison
pie, as well as sandwiches and ploughman's lunches.
In summer relax in the attractive gardens or enjoy a
game of boules.

Open all day all wk 11am-mdnt (winter 11-3 6-mdnt)
Bar Meals L served all wk 12-10 (winter 12-2.30)
D served all wk 12-10 (winter 6-9.30) food served all
day Restaurant L served all wk 12-10 (winter 12-2.30)
D served all wk 12-10 (winter 6-9.30) food served all
day ⊕ FREE HOUSE ◀ Otter Ale, Regional Guest Ales
♂ Winkleigh Autumn Scrumpy. ♥ 10 Facilities Children
welcome Children's menu Children's portions Dogs
allowed Garden Parking Wi-fi

EAST ALLINGTON
Map 3 SX74

Fortescue Arms

TQ9 7RA ☎ 01548 521215
e-mail: info@fortescue-arms.co.uk
dir: *Telephone for directions*

Run by Werner Rott, the Austrian chef/proprietor and
spare-time sculptor, this charming old country inn is the
only pub in the village and very much the centre of the
community. In the flagstone-floored bar Werner offers
Butcombe Bitter, guest real ales and a short menu. In the
restaurant, expect the likes of cock-a-leekie soup or
sliced, sautéed wild boar and apple sausage on creamy
sauerkraut, followed by fillet steak with Stilton and port
sauce or salmon en croûte with dill cream sauce. For
dessert, maybe warm apple strudel with crème pâtissière.

Open 12-2.30 6-11 Closed: Mon lunch Bar Meals L served
all wk 12-2.30 booking required D served all wk 6.30-10
booking required Av main course £9.85
Restaurant L served all wk 12-2.30 booking required
D served all wk 6.30-10 booking required Av 3 course à la
carte fr £28 ⊕ FREE HOUSE ◀ Butcombe Bitter, Dartmoor
IPA, Guinness, Guest ales ♂ Ashton Press.
Facilities Children's menu Children's portions Family
room Dogs allowed Garden Parking Wi-fi

EXETER
Map 3 SX99

The Hour Glass ♥ NEW

21 Melbourne St EX2 4AU ☎ 01392 258722
e-mail: ajpthehourglass@yahoo.co.uk
dir: *From M5 junct 30, A370 signed Exeter. At Countess
Weir rdbt 3rd exit onto Topsham Rd (B3182) signed City
Centre. In approx 2m left into Melbourne St*

This distinctively-shaped back street pub has built up a
reputation for its friendly service and inventive food, not
to mention its impressive range of local real ales. Expect
beams, wood floors, an open fire and resident cats in the
bar, where handpulled pints of Otter Bitter or St Austell
Proper Job can be enjoyed with curried eggs and
watercress, or lamb, quince and Rioja stew with anchovy
dumplings.

Open 12-3 5-close (Sat-Sun all day, Mon 5-close) Closed:
25-26 Dec, Mon L Bar Meals L served Tue-Fri 12.30-2.30,
Sat-Sun 12.30-3 D served Mon-Sat 7-9.30, Sun 6-9
booking required Av main course £13 Restaurant L served
Tue-Fri 12.30-2.30, Sat-Sun 12.30-3 D served Mon-Sat
7-9.30, Sun 6-9 Av 3 course à la carte fr £23
⊕ ENTERPRISE INNS ◀ Otter Bitter, Exeter Brewery
Ferryman, Bath Ales Spa ♂ Burrow Hill. ♥ 24
Facilities Dogs allowed Wi-fi

Red Lion Inn ♥

Broadclyst EX5 3EL ☎ 01392 461271
dir: *On B3181 (Exeter to Cullompton)*

A 16th-century listed building set at the heart of a
delightful village in the National Trust's Killerton Estate.
The interior boasts a wealth of beams and warming open
fires, where pints of Exmoor and Yellowhammer are
cheerfully served and supped. The menu offers light bites
such as a spicy hot chicken stir fry wrap, or savoury
bacon and Cheddar melt. Otherwise turn to the classic
dishes among which lamb's liver, onion and bacon
casserole may be found, or pot-roasted lamb shank.

Open all wk 11-3.30 5.30-11.30 (Sat 11am-11.30pm Sun
noon-11) Bar Meals L served Mon-Fri 12-2.30, Sat-Sun
12-9 D served Mon-Fri 6-9, Sat-Sun 12-9 Av main course
£5 Restaurant L served Mon-Fri 12-2.30, Sat-Sun 12-9
D served Mon-Fri 6-9, Sat-Sun 12.9 Fixed menu price
fr £9 Av 3 course à la carte fr £25 ⊕ FREE HOUSE
◀ Fuller's London Pride, O'Hanlons Yellowhammer, Old
Speckled Hen, Exmoor Ale. ♥ 8 Facilities Children
welcome Children's menu Children's portions Dogs
allowed Garden Parking

EXTON
Map 3 SX98

PICK OF THE PUBS

The Puffing Billy ♥

Station Rd EX3 0PR ☎ 01392 877888
e-mail: enquiries@thepuffingbilly.co.uk
dir: *A376 signed Exmouth, through Ebford. Follow signs
for Puffing Billy, turn right into Exton*

Acquired in September 2009 by an expanding Devon-
based hotel and restaurant group, the 16th-century
Puffing Billy overlooks the Exe estuary near its
confluence with the River Clyst. Local Otter Brewery
supplies the real ales to the smartly designed bar,
while the contemporary restaurant serves food from a
modern British seasonal menu using local, seasonal
produce. Begin with the popular sharing platter – duck
liver parfait, ham hock, braised pork rillette and Parma
ham – or starters of pan-fried local pigeon breast with
fig purée or smoked salmon with quail egg dressing.
Main courses might include fresh, locally caught fish in
light beer batter with chips, garden peas and home-
made tartare sauce; ballantine of chicken stuffed with
wild mushrooms; seared calves' liver and crisp smoked
bacon; or roasted butternut squash and Jerusalem
artichoke pan-fry. All the wines are personally chosen.
Watch the river traffic go by from the secluded garden.
Booking is essential.

Open all wk noon-3 6-11 (all day Apr-Sep) Closed:
selected days over Xmas Bar Meals L served Mon-Sat
12-2 Av main course £12.50 Restaurant L served
Mon-Sat 12-2 (Sun 12-2.30) booking required D served
Mon-Sat 6.30-9.30 (Sun 6-9) booking required
⊕ FREE HOUSE ◀ Otter Ale, Otter Bitter,
Yellowhammer. ♥ 15 Facilities Children welcome
Children's menu Children's portions Garden Parking

Save on hotels. Book at **theAA.com/hotel**

DEVON 135 ENGLAND

PICK OF THE PUBS

The Nobody Inn ★★★★ INN 🍷

EX6 7PS ☎ **01647 252394**
e-mail: info@nobodyinn.co.uk
web: www.nobodyinn.co.uk
dir: *3m SW of Exeter Racecourse (A38)*

The Nobody Inn is set in a pretty cottage garden in rolling countryside between the Haldon Hills and the Teign Valley. Although its history can be traced back to 1591, it was another two centuries before it became an inn and a further 160 years before it was renamed 'The No Body Inn'. For many years this late 16th-century free house served as the village's unofficial church house and meeting place, becoming a de facto inn along the way. It was officially licensed as the New Inn in 1838, and acquired its unusual name after an unfortunate incident following the innkeeper's death in 1952. His corpse was accidentally left in the mortuary while the funeral took place around an empty coffin with 'no body'.

The present owners - only the fifth since 1838 - have refurbished the pub, but have wisely bypassed the bar, which retains its traditional ambience. Here, the low ceilings, blackened beams, inglenook fireplace and antique furniture all contribute to the timeless atmosphere, and you can sample some 260 wines and 230 whiskies in addition to an ever-changing range of real ales.

Fresh fish is delivered daily from Brixham and imaginative bar meals are served every lunchtime and evening from a regularly changing menu. Dinner might begin with pan-fried pigeon breast with rocket and walnut dressing or game terrine with red onion marmalade and toast, continuing with venison steak with mandarin and chocolate sauce, sautéed herb potatoes; or Creedy Carver duck with gooseberry sauce; and finish with steamed spotted dick and custard or a board of West Country cheeses. A small bar shop sells some of the items you are likely to have enjoyed in the pub. Five attractive bedrooms are available.

Open all day all wk 11-11 (Sun 12-10.30) Closed: 25-26 Dec, 1 Jan
Bar Meals L served Mon-Sat 12-2, Sun 12-3 booking required D served Sun-Thu 6.30-9, Fri-Sat 6.30-9.30 booking required
Restaurant D served Tue-Thu 6.30-9, Fri-Sat 6.30-9.30 booking required
⊕ FREE HOUSE ◀ Branscombe Nobody's Bitter, guest ales ♂ Brimblecombes local cider, Cornish Rattler, Thatchers Gold.
🍷 28 **Facilities** Children welcome Children's portions Dogs allowed Garden Parking Wi-fi **Rooms** 5

GEORGEHAM — Map 3 SS43

The Rock Inn ♀ NEW

Rock Hill EX33 1JW ☎ 01271 890322
e-mail: therockgeorgeham@gmail.com
dir: *From A361 at Braunton follow Croyde Bay signs. Through Croyde, 1m to Georgeham. Pass shop & church. Inn on right*

A great watering hole for walkers and cyclists, this old inn is also handy for the famous surfing beaches at Woolacombe. Its friendly atmosphere, comprising a mix of happy banter from the locals and gentle jazz played at lunchtime, adds to the enjoyment of a pint selected from the five ales on offer. Choose between the traditional bar, the slightly more contemporary lower bar, or a bright conservatory decorated with local art. The tasty menu is hard to resist, extending from door-step sandwiches and omelettes to pan-fried pheasant breast or a pavé of local venison.

Open all day all wk **Bar Meals** L served all wk 12-2.30 D served all wk 6-9.30 Av main course £11 **Restaurant** L served all wk 12-2.30 D served all wk 6-9.30 Av 3 course à la carte fr £24 ⊕ PUNCH TAVERNS ◀ Timothy Taylor Landlord, Exmoor Gold, Fuller's London Pride, Tribute, Sharp's Doom Bar ♂ Thatchers Gold. ♀ 12 **Facilities** Children welcome Children's menu Children's portions Dogs allowed Garden Parking Wi-fi

HARBERTON — Map 3 SX75

The Church House Inn ♀

TQ9 7SF ☎ 01803 863707
e-mail: info@churchhouseharberton.co.uk
dir: *From Totnes take A381 S. Turn right for Harberton, pub by church in village centre*

Nestled in the beautiful South Devon countryside, this 13th-century inn is tucked away but easily accessible from Totnes. Built to house masons working on the church next door around 1100, the inn's historic features include a fine medieval oak screen separating the long bar with its wood burners from the comfortable family room. In addition to a menu of popular favourites, the blackboard displays daily specials such as steak and kidney pie and Sunday roasts. There has been a change of hands.

Open all day all wk Closed: 25 Dec eve, 1 Jan eve **Bar Meals** L served all wk 12-2 D served all wk 6.30-9 Av main course £9.50 **Restaurant** L served all wk 12-2 booking required D served all wk 6.30-9 booking required ⊕ FREE HOUSE ◀ Skinner's, Dartmoor IPA, Legend, Guest ales. ♀ 10 **Facilities** Children welcome Children's menu Children's portions Family room Dogs allowed Wi-fi

HAYTOR VALE — Map 3 SX77

PICK OF THE PUBS

The Rock Inn ★★ HL ◉

See Pick of the Pubs on opposite page

HOLSWORTHY — Map 3 SS30

The Bickford Arms

Brandis Corner EX22 7XY
☎ 01409 221318 ▤ 01409 220085
e-mail: info@bickfordarms.com
dir: *On A3072, 4m from Holsworthy towards Hatherleigh*

This pub stood on the Holsworthy to Hatherleigh road for 300 years before it was gutted by fire in 2003. Although totally rebuilt, it retains much period charm, with beams, a welcoming bar and two fireplaces. The bar, which serves both real ales and ciders, and restaurant menu offers food prepared with locally-sourced ingredients - perhaps free-range Devon duck breast with redcurrant and red wine sauce or home-made steak and ale pie. Change of hands 2010.

Open all wk 11-11 (11-3 5.30-11 winter) ⊕ FREE HOUSE ◀ Skinner's Betty Stogs, Sharp's Doom Bar, Dartmoor legend ♂ Rattler. **Facilities** Children welcome Children's menu Children's portions Garden Parking Wi-fi

HONITON — Map 4 ST10

PICK OF THE PUBS

The Holt ◉ ♀

178 High St EX14 1LA ☎ 01404 47707
e-mail: enquiries@theholt-honiton.com
dir: *Telephone for directions*

In the heart of Honiton, The Holt is run by brothers Joe and Angus McCaig, whose family has been in the brewing business for three generations. Enjoy the full range of the family's Otter ales in the downstairs bar, busy with timeworn pub tables and chairs and a spread of sofas. The open-plan kitchen provides plenty of buzz; in the candlelit dining area upstairs tables look down on the bar below, so you can still feel totally involved. The pub also has its own smokery, where locally sourced poultry, meats, game, fish, shellfish and cheese are prepared. The frequently-changing menu is supplemented by daily specials and tapas; such inventive cooking has gained The Holt an AA Rosette. A starter of smoked prawns, fresh herb mayonnaise, parsley and shallots might precede a seared beef skirt steak with ox tongue, walnut and beetroot salad, and end with rhubarb and almond cake.

Open 11-3 5.30-mdnt Closed: 25-26 Dec, Sun & Mon **Bar Meals** L served Tue-Sat 12-2 D served Tue-Sat 6.30-9 Av main course £12 **Restaurant** L served Tue-Sat 12-2 booking required D served Tue-Sat 7-9.30 booking required Av 3 course à la carte fr £24 ⊕ FREE HOUSE ◀ Otter Bitter, Otter Ale, Otter Bright, Otter Amber, Otter Head. ♀ 9 **Facilities** Children welcome Children's portions Dogs allowed Wi-fi

HORSEBRIDGE — Map 3 SX47

The Royal Inn

PL19 8PJ ☎ 01822 870214
e-mail: paul@royalinn.co.uk
dir: *S of B3362 (Launceston-Tavistock road)*

The pub, with a façade enlivened by superb pointed arched windows, was once a nunnery until Henry VIII dissolved the monastery. Standing near a bridge built over the Tamar in 1437 by Benedictine monks, it became the Packhorse Inn until Charles I pitched up one day - his seal is in the doorstep. Beef for the steaks, casseroles and stews, and the pheasant and venison on the specials board are all locally supplied. Chilli cheese tortillas are much appreciated; so is the absence of noisy machines.

Open all wk noon-3 6.30-11pm ⊕ FREE HOUSE ◀ Dartmoor Jail Ale, Dartmoor Legend, Bass, Skinner's, St Austell Proper Job ♂ Cornish Rattler, Thatchers Gold. **Facilities** Children welcome Dogs allowed Garden Parking

ILFRACOMBE — Map 3 SS54

The George & Dragon

5 Fore St EX34 9ED ☎ 01271 863851
e-mail: linda.quinn5@btinternet.com
dir: *Telephone for directions*

The oldest pub in town, The George & Dragon dates from 1360 and is reputedly haunted. The food is of the simple, no-nonsense variety - typical examples include home-cooked boozy beef; chicken curry; mixed grills; and home-cooked crab from the harbour when available. No fruit machines or pool table, but if you are lucky there will be a little home-produced background music, along with a good choice of real ales and ciders.

Open all day all wk 10am-mdnt (Sun noon-mdnt) ⊕ PUNCH TAVERNS ◀ Spitfire, Betty Stogs, Courage Best ♂ Aspall. **Facilities** Children welcome Children's menu Children's portions Dogs allowed **Notes** ◉

KINGSBRIDGE — Map 3 SX74

The Crabshell Inn ♀

Embankment Rd TQ7 1JZ
☎ 01548 852345 ▤ 01548 852262
e-mail: info@thecrabshellinn.com
dir: *A38 towards Plymouth, follow signs for Kingsbridge*

A traditional sailors' watering hole on the Kingsbridge estuary quayside (arrive by boat and you may moor free). As you would expect, the views from the outside tables, where you can enjoy a glass of Shingle Bay ale or a meal, and from the first-floor restaurant are wonderful. The extensive menu and specials board use locally-sourced produce and might include moules marinière, scallop mornay, Crabshell chowder, pan-fried sea bass fillet or Aune Valley rib-eye steak.

Open all day all wk **Bar Meals** Av main course £11 food served all day **Restaurant** food served all day ⊕ FREE HOUSE ◀ Shingle Bay, Doom Bar, Otter Ale ♂ Addlestones, Stowford Press. **Facilities** Children welcome Children's menu Children's portions Play area Family room Dogs allowed Garden Parking

Save on hotels. Book at **theAA.com/hotel**

DEVON 137 ENGLAND

PICK OF THE PUBS

The Rock Inn ★★ HL 🏵

HAYTOR VALE Map 3 SX77

TQ13 9XP
☎ **01364 661305** 📠 **01364 661242**
e-mail: inn@rock-inn.co.uk
web: www.rock-inn.co.uk
dir: *A38 from Exeter, at Drum Bridges rdbt take A382 for Bovey Tracey, 1st exit at 2nd rdbt (B3387), 3m left to Haytor Vale*

Sheltering below the Haytor Rocks, this beamed and flagstoned 18th-century inn is an oasis of calm and comfort on wild and windy Dartmoor. This old coaching inn occupies a stunning location just inside Dartmoor National Park, with wonderful surrounding walks, and the nine, upgraded and comfortable en suite bedrooms, all named after Grand National winners, make this well established, family-run inn a peaceful base for exploring Dartmoor and South Devon's superb coastline. The old stables recall the pub's strategic position on the road between Widecombe-in-the-Moor and Newton Abbot. The characterful, traditional beamed interior has sturdy old furnishings, plenty of antique tables, settles, prints and paintings, a grandfather clock, and various pieces of china over the two fireplaces, where logs crackle constantly on wild winter days and make a welcome respite from Dartmoor's wilderness.

Both the classic main bar and the attractive adjoining rooms are popular settings in which to appreciate some solid modern British cooking, using top notch local produce in attractively presented dishes. After a day walking on the moor, healthy appetites can be satisfied with tempura king prawns with sweet chilli and ginger dip; grilled plaice fillets on wilted spinach with herb-crushed potatoes and chive hollandaise; pan-fried rump steak with garlic butter, chunky chips and salad garnish. Leave room for a steamed chocolate pudding with chocolate sauce and vanilla ice cream or home-made rice pudding with berry compote.

Simpler, more traditional lunch dishes include steak and ale pie, cheese ploughman's with chutneys, pickles and crusty bread - best enjoyed alfresco in the sheltered courtyard or in the peaceful garden across the lane. Devon cheese is a particular feature, alongside wine from the Sharpham Vineyard in Totnes and local ales, including Dartmoor Jail Ale or Otter Bright.

Open all day all wk 11-11 (Sun noon-10.30) Closed: 25-26 Dec **Bar Meals** L served all wk 12-2 booking required **Restaurant** D served all wk 7-9 booking required ⊕ FREE HOUSE 🍺 Otter Bright, Dartmoor Brewery's Jail Ale. **Facilities** Children's menu Children's portions Family room Garden Parking **Rooms** 9

KINGSKERSWELL   Map 3 SX86

Barn Owl Inn

Aller Mills TQ12 5AN ☎ **01803 872130**
e-mail: barnowl.allermills@hall-woodhouse.co.uk
dir: *Telephone for directions*

Flagged floors, a black-leaded range and oak beams are amongst the many charming original features at this 16th-century former farmhouse. The renovated building, which is handy for Dartmoor and the English Riviera towns, also boasts a high-vaulted converted barn with a minstrels' gallery. Lunchtime snacks include toasties, wraps and baguettes, while the main menu features plenty of traditional pub favourites all washed down with a pint of Tanglefoot or Badgers First Gold. Recent change of hands.

Open all day all wk noon-11 (Sun noon-10.30) Closed: 26 Dec ⊕ WOODHOUSE INNS ◀ Tanglefoot, Badger First Gold. **Facilities** Children welcome Children's menu Children's portions Dogs allowed Garden Parking

PICK OF THE PUBS

Bickley Mill Inn ♥

TQ12 5LN ☎ **01803 873201**
e-mail: info@bickleymill.co.uk
dir: *From Newton Abbot on A380 towards Torquay. Right at Barn Owl Inn, follow brown tourist signs*

Tucked away in the wooded Stoneycombe Valley, close to Torquay and Newton Abbot, this former flour mill dates from the 13th-century. Now a family-owned free house, the spacious property blends old and new in a fresh contemporary style. It comprises an attractive bar with roaring log fires and comfy sofas, and a restaurant separated into three areas – The Fireside, The Mill Room and The Panel Room. While perusing the appealing menu enjoy a pint of Otter or Teignworthy ale. Dishes are freshly prepared using quality produce from the local area. Fish from Brixham is a feature of the daily specials, along with regulars like smoked duck breast, orange, watercress and pine nut salad; pan-fried field mushrooms, garlic and tarragon cream on toast; whole grilled plaice, caper and parsley butter, chargrilled lemon, new potatoes; roast pork belly, black pudding and bacon potato cake with cider gravy; rum and raisin cheesecake. An 18th-century former barn has been transformed into a function room catering for groups of 25 to 125 guests. There is outside decking and a tranquil garden for the warmer weather.

Open all day all wk Mon-Sat 11.30-3 6.30-11 (Sun 6-10.30) Closed: 27-28 Dec & 1 Jan **Bar Meals** L served Mon-Sat 12-2 (Sun 12-2.30) D served Mon-Sat 6.30-9.15 (Sun 6-8.30) Av main course £9.95 **Restaurant** L served Mon-Sat 12-2 (Sun 12-2.30) D served all wk 6.30-9.15 booking required ⊕ FREE HOUSE ◀ Otter Ale, Teignworthy, Bays. ♥ 9 **Facilities** Children welcome Children's menu Children's portions Dogs allowed Garden Parking Wi-fi

KINGS NYMPTON   Map 3 SS61

PICK OF THE PUBS

The Grove Inn ♥

EX37 9ST ☎ **01769 580406**
e-mail: enquiry@thegroveinn.co.uk
web: www.thegroveinn.co.uk
dir: *2.5m from A377 (Exeter to Barnstaple road)*

At the vanguard of the localisation movement, mine hosts at The Grove have been working closely with north Devon farmers for nearly a decade to source truly fresh, seasonal produce from just down the lane. The rare-breed sausages hail from Highlands Farm whilst the pheasant (breast wrapped in bacon and stuffed with spinach) is from a local estate, both close-by this picturesque thatched inn which shares listed status with the generous array of thatched cottages in this secluded village. Add wild rabbit stew or perhaps a duo of north Devon trout, with local cheeses and chutney to finish and there's something for most palates. Lucky locals and visitors can indulge in memorable Devon farmhouse ciders or beers from micro-breweries such as Jollyboat's Mainbrace. The setting is suitably cosy and welcoming – beamed and stone-walled bar and dining areas with rustic furnishings, flagstoned floor and blazing winter log fires. Look for the the hundreds of bookmarks on the bar beams.

Open noon-3 6-11 (BH noon-3) Closed: Mon L ex BH **Bar Meals** L served Tue-Sat 12-2 **Restaurant** L served Tue-Sun 12-2 booking required D served Tue-Sat 7-9 booking required ⊕ FREE HOUSE ◀ Exmoor Ale, Bath Gem Ale, Mainbrace, Sharp's Own, Dympsy Ò Winkleigh, Sams Dry. ♥ 26 **Facilities** Children welcome Children's menu Children's portions Dogs allowed Garden

KINGSTON   Map 3 SX64

The Dolphin Inn

TQ7 4QE ☎ **01548 810314**   📄 **01548 810314**
e-mail: info@dolphininn.eclipse.co.uk
dir: *From A379 (Plymouth to Kingsbridge road) take B3233 for Bigbury-on-Sea. Follow brown inn signs*

Off the beaten track just a mile from the beaches of the South Hams and the beautiful Erme Estuary, this area is popular with walkers, golfers and water sports enthusiasts. The 16th-century inn was originally built as cottages for stone masons working on the adjacent village church. Then it was used by fishermen's families

at a time when the village was self-sufficient. All the food is home made and ranges from 'soup and a sarnie' to slow-roasted belly pork and daily seafood specials.

Open noon-3 6-11 (Sun noon-3 7-10.30) Closed: Sun eve winter **Bar Meals** L served Mon-Fri 12-2 (Sat-Sun 12-2.30) D served all wk 6-9 (closed Sun & Mon eve winter) Av main course £9.95 **Restaurant** L served Mon-Fri 12-2 (Sat-Sun 12-2.30) D served all wk 6-9 (closed Sun & Mon eve winter) ⊕ PUNCH TAVERNS ◀ Teignworthy Springtide, Courage Best, Sharp's Doom Bar, Otter Ò Westons Scrumpy. **Facilities** Children welcome Children's menu Children's portions Play area Family room Dogs allowed Garden Parking Wi-fi

LIFTON   Map 3 SX38

PICK OF THE PUBS

The Arundell Arms ★★★ HL ⊚⊚ ♥

PL16 0AA ☎ **01566 784666**   📄 **01566 784494**
e-mail: reservations@arundellarms.com
web: www.arundellarms.com
dir: *1m off A30 dual carriageway, 3m E of Launceston*

One of England's classic country inns; travellers through Devon have been stopping off here for nigh-on 300 years. Today's discerning visitors enjoy the first rate accommodation and exceptional menus, respite from the countless activities which make the inn a destination of choice for lovers both of countryside and country sports. With some of Devon's most unspoilt countryside on the doorstep, walkers and horse-riders have much to explore, whilst the inn's own 20 miles on the Tamar and tributaries attract flyfishers keen to tangle with trout, sea-trout (an annual sea-trout festival is held in July), grayling and fresh-run salmon. Local farms and estates host shoots for woodcock, snipe, duck and partridge as well as raising livestock which features in the dishes that have gained AA 2 Rosette recognition for head chef Steve Pidgeon and his team. Intimate dining areas and restaurants are weaved into the elegant interior of the solid old stone inn, which is richly furnished with antiques and country artefacts. Here too can be found robust indoor sports such as alley skittles, where villagers sampling St Austell Tribute and guest ales mingle with pre-prandial diners at the Courthouse Bar. The bar menu here is good robust bar food, including Devon ruby beef burgers, pan-fried lambs' liver or roasted fillet of hake. Restaurant diners may enjoy pan-fried Falmouth Bay scallops with haricot beans, chorizo, cream and chives.

Open all wk 12-3 6-11 **Bar Meals** L served all wk 12-2 D served all wk 6-9.30 ◀ Tribute, Guest ales Ò Thatchers, Cornish Rattler. ♥ 9 **Facilities** Children welcome Dogs allowed Garden Parking **Rooms** 21

Save on hotels. Book at **theAA.com/hotel**

DEVON 139 **ENGLAND**

LITTLEHEMPSTON
Map 3 SX86

Tally Ho Inn

TQ9 6NF ☎ 01803 862316   📄 01803 862316
e-mail: inn.matters@blueyonder.co.uk
dir: *Off A38 at Buckfastleigh. A381 between Newton Abbot & Totnes*

A traditional, family-owned 14th-century thatched inn in a pretty village, with inglenook fireplaces, a flower-filled patio and real ales from Devon breweries. Local suppliers are the mainstay of seasonal menus offering home-made crêpe filled with bacon, mushrooms and Parmesan sauce; a foil parcel baked salmon steak with white wine, lemon and thyme; home-made steak and kidney pie and chips; or falafel served with salad, pitta bread and dipping sauces. The specials board has temping dishes too.

Open noon-3 6.30-11 Closed: 25 Dec, Sun eve (winter) **Bar Meals** L served all wk 12-2 booking required D served all wk 6.30-9 booking required Av main course £10 ⊕ FREE HOUSE ◀ Exmoor Ale, Teignworthy Brewery Ales, Guinness, Hunters Brewery Local Ale, Guest ales ♻ Thatchers Gold. **Facilities** Children welcome Children's menu Children's portions Dogs allowed Garden Parking

LUSTLEIGH
Map 3 SX78

The Cleave Pub NEW

TQ13 9TJ ☎ 01647 277223
e-mail: ben@thecleavelustleigh.com
dir: *From Newton Abbot take A382, follow Bovey Tracey signs, then Moretonhampstead signs. Left to Lustleigh*

Thatched and dating from the 16th century, this friendly, family-run pub is the only one in the village and is adjacent to the cricket pitch. It has a traditional snug bar, with beams, granite flooring and log fire; to the rear, formerly the old railway station waiting room, is a refurbished light and airy dining area leading to a lovely cottage garden. All dishes are under a tenner, including lamb tagine with couscous; ribs 'n' wings; and fresh fish and seafood, depending on the catch. The Cleave hosts regular films, quizzes, Wii nights, concerts and live music.

Open all day all wk 11-11 **Bar Meals** L served all wk all day D served all wk all day Av main course £9.95 food served all day **Restaurant** L served all wk all day D served all wk all day food served all day ⊕ HEAVITREE BREWERY ◀ Otter Ale, Otter Bitter ♻ Aspall Suffolk. **Facilities** Children welcome Children's menu Children's portions Dogs allowed Garden Parking Wi-fi

LUTON (NEAR CHUDLEIGH)
Map 3 SX97

The Elizabethan Inn ⬤

Fore St TQ13 0BL ☎ 01626 775425   📄 01626 775151
e-mail: elizabethaninn@btconnect.com
web: www.elizabethaninn.co.uk
dir: *Between Chudleigh & Teignmouth*

Good honest Devon food and drink attract diners and drinkers alike to this welcoming 16th-century free house, known locally as the Lizzie. There's a choice selection of Devon ales, as well as Thatcher's Gold and local Reddaways cider to drink beside a log fire in winter or in the pretty beer garden on warmer days. The pub prides itself on using the best of local ingredients and the specials board might include home-made lamb, venison or pork sausages flavoured with fresh herbs; local venison, pheasant and steaks; traditional fisherman's pie; as well as a choice of vegetarian dishes such as risotto-stuffed pepper on a red pepper sauce. A take-away menu is available.

Open all wk 12-3 6-11.30 (Sun all day) Closed: 25-26 Dec, 1 Jan **Bar Meals** L served Mon-Sat 12-2, Sun 12-9 booking required D served all wk 6-9.30, Sun 12-9 booking required Av main course £10 **Restaurant** L served Mon-Sat 12-2, Sun 12-9 booking required D served all wk 6-9.30, Sun 12-9 booking required Fixed menu price fr £12.99 ⊕ FREE HOUSE ◀ London Pride, Teignworthy Reel Ale, Otter Ale, O'Hanlon's Yellowhammer, Dartmoor IPA ♻ Thatchers Gold, Local Reddaways. ♟ 11 **Facilities** Children welcome Children's menu Children's portions Dogs allowed Garden Parking

LYDFORD
Map 3 SX58

PICK OF THE PUBS

Dartmoor Inn ⬤⬤

EX20 4AY ☎ 01822 820221   📄 01822 820494
e-mail: info@dartmoorinn.co.uk
dir: *On A386 S of Okehampton*

Owners Karen and Philip Burgess have made their mark at this distinctive free house, which Charles Kingsley almost certainly described in his novel *Westward Ho!* The stylish, restrained decor extends through the cosy dining rooms and small bar, where real ales and high class pub classics are on offer. Food is based on seasonal ingredients, sourced locally, and turned into top-notch dishes. In the New England-style restaurant you might start with corned beef terrine with mustard dressing, followed by pan-fried lamb's

kidneys, bacon, black pudding and red wine sauce. After your meal, you can even browse for beautiful accessories and home ware in the inn's own boutique.

Open all day 11-3 6-11 Closed: Sun eve, Mon L ex BHs **Bar Meals** L served Tue-Sun 12-2.30 D served all wk 6.30-9.15 **Restaurant** L served Tue-Sun 12-2.30 D served all wk 6.30-9.15 ⊕ FREE HOUSE ◀ Otter Ale, Tribute. **Facilities** Children welcome Dogs allowed Garden Parking

LYMPSTONE
Map 3 SX98

The Globe Inn ⬤

The Strand EX8 5EY ☎ 01395 263166
dir: *Telephone for directions*

Set in the estuary village of Lympstone, this traditional beamed, friendly village inn has a good local reputation for food and drink. Well-kept Bass, Otter and London Pride are the ales on offer in the bar. Look out for bass fillets with plum sauce; monkfish kebabs; seafood platter; and seafood grill on the menu. Occasional music nights and Tuesday is quiz night. The pub has now changed hands.

Open all day all wk **Bar Meals** L served all wk 12-2 D served all wk 6.30-9 **Restaurant** L served all wk 12-2 D served all wk 6.30-9 ◀ London Pride, Otter, Bass ♻ Aspall, Addlestones. ♟ 10 **Facilities** Children welcome Dogs allowed

LYNMOUTH
Map 3 SS74

PICK OF THE PUBS

Rising Sun Hotel ★★ HL ⬤

Harbourside EX35 6EG
☎ 01598 753223   📄 01598 753480
e-mail: reception@risingsunlynmouth.co.uk
dir: *From M5 junct 25 follow Minehead signs. A39 to Lynmouth*

Overlooking Lynmouth's tiny harbour and bay is this 14th-century thatched smugglers' inn. In turn, overlooking them all, are Countisbury Cliffs, the highest in England. The building's long history is evident from the uneven oak floors, crooked ceilings and thick walls. Literary associations are plentiful: R D Blackmore wrote some of his wild Exmoor romance, *Lorna Doone*, here; the poet Shelley is believed to have honeymooned in the garden cottage, and Coleridge stayed too. Immediately behind rises Exmoor Forest and National Park, home to red deer, wild ponies and birds of prey. With moor and sea so close, game and seafood are in plentiful supply; appearing in dishes such as braised pheasant with pancetta and quince and Braunton greens; and roast shellfish – crab, mussels, clams and scallops in garlic, ginger and coriander. At night the oak-panelled, candlelit dining room is an example of romantic British inn-keeping at its best.

Open all day all wk 11am-mdnt Closed: 25 Dec **Bar Meals** L served all wk 12-2.30 D served all wk 6-9 **Restaurant** D served all wk 7-9 booking required ⊕ FREE HOUSE ◀ Exmoor Gold, Fox, Exmoor Antler ♻ Thatchers Gold. **Facilities** Dogs allowed **Rooms** 14

MARLDON
Map 3 SX86

The Church House Inn ♥

Village Rd TQ3 1SL ☎ 01803 558279 📠 01803 664865
dir: *Take Torquay ring road, follow signs to Marldon & Totnes, follow brown signs to pub*

This ancient country inn dates from 1362, when it was a hostel for the builders of the adjoining village church. It was rebuilt in 1740 and many features from that period still remain including beautiful Georgian windows; some of the original glass still remains despite overlooking the cricket pitch. These days it has an uncluttered, contemporary feel. Typical evening offerings include crab bisque; baked Blue Vinny and pear tartlet; followed by cornfed chicken supreme; chargrilled loin of pork with sweet 'n' sour sauce; and salmon fillet with pearl barley and crab butter.

Open all wk 11.30-2.30 5-11 (Fri-Sat 11.30-2.30 5-11.30 Sun 12-3 5.30-10.30) **Bar Meals** L served all wk 12-2 D served all wk 6.30-9.30 Av main course £14 **Restaurant** L served all wk 12-2 D served all wk 6.30-9.30 Av 3 course à la carte fr £26 ⊕ FREE HOUSE ◀ Dartmoor Best, Bass, Old Speckled Hen, Greene King IPA, London Pride. ♥ 12 **Facilities** Children welcome Children's portions Dogs allowed Garden Parking

MEAVY
Map 3 SX56

The Royal Oak Inn ♥

PL20 6PJ ☎ 01822 852944
e-mail: info@royaloakinn.org.uk
dir: *B3212 from Yelverton to Princetown. Right at Dousland to Meavy, past school. Pub opposite village green*

This traditional 15th-century inn is situated by a village green within Dartmoor National Park. Flagstone floors, oak beams and a welcoming open fire set the scene at this free house popular with cyclists and walkers. Local cask ales, ciders and fine wines accompany the carefully sourced ingredients in a menu ranging from lunchtime light bites to steak and ale pie, home-cooked ham, egg and chips, or local bangers and mash. Look out for cider and beer festivals during the year.

Open all wk Mon-Fri 11-3 6-11 (Sat-Sun & Apr-Oct all day) **Bar Meals** L served Mon-Fri 12-2.30, Sat-Sun 12-3 D served all wk 6-9 Av main course £8 **Restaurant** L served Mon-Fri 12-2.30, Sat-Sun 12-3 D served all wk 6-9 Fixed menu price fr £10 ⊕ FREE HOUSE ◀ Dartmoor Jail Ale, Dartmoor IPA, St Austell Tribute, Sharp's Doom Bar, Guest ales ♂ Westons Scrumpy, Old Rosie, Thatchers Gold. ♥ 12 **Facilities** Children welcome Children's menu Children's portions Dogs allowed Garden Beer festival

MODBURY
Map 3 SX65

PICK OF THE PUBS

California Country Inn
See Pick of the Pubs on opposite page

MORETONHAMPSTEAD
Map 3 SX78

PICK OF THE PUBS

The White Hart Hotel ★★★ HL ⊛ ♥

The Square TQ13 8NF
☎ 01647 441340 📠 01647 441341
e-mail: enquiries@Whitehartdartmoor.co.uk
dir: *From A30 at Whiddon Down take A382 for Chagford & Moretonhampstead. Pub in village centre. Parking in 20yds*

The White Hart has been at the heart of village life since 1639. Set in the centre of Dartmoor National Park, the Grade II-listed building has a recently had a refurbishment of its bar, lounge and contemporary brasserie restaurant area complete with oak tables, wooden floors and stag's antler chandelier. Locally brewed ales and a wide selection of malt whiskies are served alongside locally sourced food. Exciting dishes include pear and Exmoor Blue tarte Tatin with port wine reduction; tea-smoked duck salad with blackberries; pressed terrine of Old Spot belly pork and oxtail with thyme toast; rump of Dartmoor lamb with mini moussaka and feta. Customers can also call in for morning coffee or afternoon tea, and walkers, cyclists and dogs are welcome. A pleasant courtyard garden makes for a tranquil place to enjoy a pre-dinner drink or a quality cigar purchased from the bar.

Open all day all wk 11-11 **Bar Meals** L served all wk 12-2.30 D served all wk 6-9.30 Av main course £11.95 **Restaurant** L served all wk 12-2.30 D served all wk 6-9.30 booking required ⊕ FREE HOUSE ◀ St Austell Tribute, Otter Ale ♂ Thatchers. ♥ 10 **Facilities** Children welcome Children's menu Children's portions Dogs allowed Garden Beer festival Wi-fi **Rooms** 28

NEWTON ABBOT
Map 3 SX87

The Wild Goose Inn ♥

Combeinteignhead TQ12 4RA ☎ 01626 872241
dir: *From A380 at Newton Abbot rdbt take B3195 (Shaldon road), signed Milber, 2.5m into village, right at sign*

Originally licensed as the Country House Inn in 1840, this inn was renamed in the 1960s when nearby geese began intimidating the pub's customers. Set in the heart of the village at the head of a long valley, it's a charming free house that boasts a sunny garden sheltered by the adjacent 14th-century church tower. A good range of real ales and ciders accompanies home-made pub food prepared from local ingredients. Expect starters such as coquilles St Jacques, followed perhaps by Betty Stogs

steak and ale pie. There is a village store and deli within the pub selling local produce, plus a beer festival every May Day weekend.

Open all wk 11-3 5.30-11 (Sun 12-3 7-11) **Bar Meals** L served all wk 12-2 D served all wk 7-9.30 booking required **Restaurant** L served all wk 12-2 D served all wk 7-9.30 booking required ⊕ FREE HOUSE ◀ Otter Ale, Cotleigh, Sharp's Bitter, Skinner's Bitter, Teignworthy, Branscombe, Exe Valley ♂ Skinners Press Gang, Wiscombe Suicider, Milltop Gold. ♥ 10 **Facilities** Children welcome Children's menu Children's portions Family room Dogs allowed Garden Beer festival Parking

NEWTON ST CYRES
Map 3 SX89

The Beer Engine

EX5 5AX ☎ 01392 851282 📠 01392 851876
e-mail: info@thebeerengine.co.uk
web: www.thebeerengine.co.uk
dir: *From Exeter take A377 towards Crediton. Signed from A377 towards Sweetham. Pub opp rail station over the bridge*

Originally opened as a railway hotel in 1852, this pretty whitewashed free house sits opposite the Tarka line on the banks of the River Creedy, much favoured by dogs and their walkers. The Beer Engine is also home to one of Devon's leading micro-breweries, producing ales delighting in names such as Rail Ale and Sleeper Heavy. Freshly baked bread uses the wort (beer yeast) from the brewery; dishes may include cod in Beer Engine batter or Sleeper ale steak pie; and vegetarians will rejoice in the range of soups and bakes.

Open all day all wk 11am-11pm (Sun noon-10.30) **Bar Meals** L served all wk 12-2.15 D served Tue-Sat 6.30-9.15, Sun-Mon 6.30-8.15 **Restaurant** L served all wk 12-2.15 booking required D served Tue-Sat 6.30-9.15, Sun-Mon 6.30-8.15 booking required ⊕ FREE HOUSE ◀ Engine Ales: Piston Bitter, Rail Ale, Sleeper Heavy, Silver Bullet ♂ Stowford Press, Dragon's Tears Cyder. **Facilities** Children welcome Children's portions Dogs allowed Garden Parking Wi-fi

Save on hotels. Book at **theAA.com/hotel**

DEVON 141 ENGLAND

PICK OF THE PUBS

California Country Inn

MODBURY   Map 3 SX65

California Cross PL21 0SG
☎ 01548 821449   📠 01548 821566
e-mail:
enquiries@californiacountryinn.co.uk
web: www.californiacountryinn.co.uk
dir: *Near Modbury on B3392, follow brown tourist signs for California Cross*

This centuries old inn stands in some of the most tranquil countryside in southern England, just a few miles from Dartmoor to the north and the cliffs and estuaries of the coast to the south. In fact, this Area of Outstanding Natural Beauty encompasses the hills and vales which can be seen from the pub's landscaped and lawned gardens. Dating from the 14th century, its unusual name is thought to derive from local adventurers in the mid-19th century who heeded the call to 'go west' and waited at the nearby crossroads for the stage to take them on the first part of their journey to America's west coast. They must have suffered wistful thoughts of home when recalling their local pub, with its wizened old beams, exposed dressed-stone walls and a fabulous, huge stone fireplace. Old rural prints and photographs, copper kettles, jugs, brasses and many other artefacts add to the rustic charm of the whitewashed pub's atmospheric interior. A family-run free house, the beers on tap are likely to include Sharp's and Fuller's, the wine list has award-winning Devon wines from

nearby Sharpham Vineyard, and the good value house wines come from – you guessed – California. Having won accolades as a dining pub, head chef Tim Whiston's food is thoughtfully created and impressively flavoursome. Most ingredients are sourced from the bounty of the local countryside and waters, with meats from a supplier in nearby Loddiswell and fish from the renowned 'Catch of the Day' in Kingsbridge. Meals can be taken from the bar menu, but why not indulge in the à la carte menu from the inn's dining room? Appetizing starters include five spiced duck salad, and seafood pancake. The main course selection may include local guinea fowl (leg confit and pan-fried breast) with creamed wild mushrooms, or pan-fried sea bass fillets. Specials and desserts can be found on the ever-changing blackboards.

Open all day all wk **Bar Meals** L served Mon-Sat 12-2, Sun 12-2.30 D served Mon-Sat 6-9, Sun 6-8.30 **Restaurant** L served Sun 12-2 D served Wed-Sun 6-9 booking required ⊕ FREE HOUSE
🍺 Guinness, Otter Bitter, London Pride, Doom Bar. **Facilities** Children's menu Children's portions Family room Dogs allowed Garden Parking Wi-fi

NORTH BOVEY — Map 3 SX78

PICK OF THE PUBS

The Ring of Bells Inn ♥

TQ13 8RB ☎ 01647 440375 📠 01647 440746
e-mail: mail@ringofbells.net
dir: *1.5m from Moretonhampstead off B3212. 7m S of Whiddon Down junct on A30*

Set in idyllic North Bovey, this 13th-century building was originally built to house the stonemasons building the parish church. Overlooking the green in this pretty village, the Ring of Bells is the hub of the community and draws Dartmoor visitors and walkers in for good food and locally brewed ales. The kitchen uses fresh, locally sourced produce and menus reflect the changing seasons; suppliers are proudly listed. Served in cosy low-beamed bars, with heavy oak doors, rustic furnishings, crackling winter log fires and evening candlelight, the short daily menu may list smoked haddock, leek and sweetcorn chowder or venison, pistachio and juniper berry terrine for starters, followed by hearty main dishes such as a steaming bowl of Exmouth mussels finished with double cream, or baby monkfish tails with Thai green curry. Round off with English Victoria plum and almond tart with vanilla ice cream, or North Bovey honey cheesecake with comb honey and baked figs.

Open all day all wk Closed: 25 Dec drinks only **Bar Meals** L served all wk 12-2.30 booking required D served all wk 6-9 booking required Av main course £12 **Restaurant** L served all wk 12-2.30 booking required D served all wk 6-9 booking required ⊕ FREE HOUSE ◀ Otter Ale, St Austell Tribute, Sharp's Doom Bar. ♥ 15 **Facilities** Children welcome Children's portions Family room Dogs allowed Garden

NOSS MAYO — Map 3 SX54

PICK OF THE PUBS

The Ship Inn ♥

PL8 1EW ☎ 01752 872387 📠 01752 873294
e-mail: ship@nossmayo.com
dir: *5m S of Yealmpton on River Yealm estuary*

A popular haunt for sailing enthusiasts, this beautifully renovated free house occupies a lovely spot on Noss Mayo's tidal waterfront on the south bank of the stunning Yealm estuary. Walkers, too, throng the bar, and dogs are allowed downstairs. The deceptively spacious building, refurbished using reclaimed materials such as local stone and English oak, remains cosy thanks to its wooden floors, old bookcases, log fires and dozens of local pictures. Local ales such as Proper Job and Jail Ale are complemented by an ever-changing menu of home-made dishes majoring on local produce, especially fish. Order chicken curry or home-made steak and kidney pie from the bar menu or dive into the main menu for dishes such as breast of

duck with dauphinoise potatoes and plum sauce, or seared scallops with bacon and sautéed potato salad. Round off with bread and butter pudding and custard.

Open all day all wk **Bar Meals** L served Mon-Sat 12-9.30, Sun 12-9 D served Mon-Sat 12-9.30, Sun 12-9 Av main course £13.50 **Restaurant** L served Mon-Sat 12-9.30, Sun 12-9 D served Mon-Sat 12-9.30, Sun 12-9 Av 3 course à la carte fr £25 ⊕ FREE HOUSE ◀ Jail Ale, Dartmoor IPA, Tribute, Otter, Proper Job, Jail Ale, Palmers. ♥ 13 **Facilities** Children welcome Children's portions Dogs allowed Garden Parking

OTTERY ST MARY — Map 3 SY19

The Talaton Inn

Talaton EX5 2RQ ☎ 01404 822214 📠 01404 822214
dir: *Take A30 to Fairmile, then follow signs to Talaton*

Run by a brother and sister partnership, this well-maintained, timber-framed 16th-century inn offers a good selection of real ales and malts, and a fine collection of bar games. Specials set menus are available at lunch from Tuesdays to Saturdays. Dishes might include crispy bacon, chicken and Brie Caesar salad, braised lamb steak with rosemary, red wine and chive sauce, with Eton mess to finish. At Sunday lunchtimes (booking advisable), as well as the popular roast, there is also a pie and vegetarian choice. There is a patio for summer dining and themed food nights.

Open all wk 12-3 7-11 Closed: Mon in winter **Bar Meals** L served Tue-Sun 12-2 D served Tue-Sun 7-9 Av main course £11 **Restaurant** L served Tue-Sun 12-2 D served Tue-Sun 7-9 ⊕ FREE HOUSE ◀ Otter, Bright Bitter Ö Stowford Press. **Facilities** Children welcome Children's menu Children's portions Dogs allowed Garden Parking

PARRACOMBE — Map 3 SS64

PICK OF THE PUBS

The Fox & Goose ♥

See Pick of the Pubs on page 144

PETER TAVY — Map 3 SX57

Peter Tavy Inn ♥ NEW

PL19 9NN ☎ 01822 810348
e-mail: chris@wording.freeserve.co.uk
dir: *From Tavistock take A386 towards Okehampton. In 2m right to Peter Tavy*

A pub since the 15th century, it is thought The Peter Tavy Inn was originally built to accommodate stonemasons rebuilding the church in this pretty village on the western flanks of Dartmoor. It is now as much a draw for its range of local real ales and ciders as it is its food, much of it sourced locally. Wash down game casserole or steak and Stilton pie with pints of Dartmoor Jail Ale or Sam's Poundhouse Dry Cider. Ask about the pub's link to a past notorious criminal.

Open all wk 12-3 6-11 (Sun 12-3 6-10.30) Closed: 25 Dec **Bar Meals** L served all wk 12-2 D served all wk 6.30-9 Av main course £8.95 **Restaurant** L served all wk 12-2 D served all wk 6.30-9 Av 3 course à la carte fr £17.95 ⊕ FREE HOUSE ◀ Dartmoor Brewery Jail Ale, Sharp's Doom Bar, Otter Bright Ö Sam's Poundhouse Dry Cider, Poundhouse Crisp. ♥ 10 **Facilities** Children welcome Children's menu Children's portions Dogs allowed Garden Parking Wi-fi

PLYMOUTH — Map 3 SX45

The Fishermans Arms ♥

31 Lambhay St, The Barbican PL1 2NN
☎ 01752 661457
e-mail: info@thefishermansarms.com
dir: *At top of Lambhay Hill turn right, pass large car park, 2nd right into Lambhay St*

Plymouth's second oldest pub stands in the Barbican, the city's historic Elizabethan quarter, and one wall is the only surviving part of Plymouth Castle, which was demolished in the 15th century. There is also a 3ft wide tunnel underneath the bar which runs to the shoreline — smugglers perhaps? Devoid of modern-day intrusions, it's a bustling local with log fires, regular quiz nights, tip-top St Austell ales, and good pub food cooked by a finalist in the Great British Pie Competition. Dishes range from pork and leek sausages, olive oil and parsley mash to 100% local beef fillet burger with triple cooked chunky chips.

Open all wk Mon 6pm-11pm Tue-Thu noon-3 6-11 Fri-Sun all day from noon **Bar Meals** L served Tue-Sat 12-2, Sun 12-3 D served Tue-Sat 6.30-9.30 Av main course £10 **Restaurant** L served Tue-Sat 12-2, Sun 12-3 D served Tue-Sat 6.30-9.30 Av 3 course à la carte fr £21 ⊕ ST AUSTELL ◀ Tribute, HSD, Proper Job, Dartmoor Best Ö Rattler Apple. ♥ 12 **Facilities** Children welcome Children's portions Dogs allowed

PLYMTREE — Map 3 ST00

The Blacksmiths Arms ♥

EX15 2JU ☎ 01884 277474
e-mail: blacksmithsplymtree@yahoo.co.uk
dir: *From A373 (Cullompton to Honiton road) follow Plymtree signs. Pub in village centre*

Situated in an idyllic Devon village, this traditional yet stylish freehouse with exposed beams, large oak mirrors, log fire and sofa seating has a reputation for serving quality freshly prepared food using local ingredients, well kept local ales and a fine selection of world wines. Portions are generous and flavours punchy on the seasonal menu and daily-changing pub favourites board. A large colourful beer garden with boules piste, children's play area and alfresco dining area complete the picture at this vibrant proper West Country pub.

Open all wk Mon-Fri 6-11 Sat noon-11 Sun noon-10 (Sun noon-4 Oct-Mar) Closed: Mon (Apr-Sep) **Bar Meals** L served Sat-Sun 12-2 D served Tue-Sun 6-9 Av main course £5.50 **Restaurant** L served Sat-Sun 12-2 D served Tue-Sun 6-9 Av 3 course à la carte fr £18.90 ⊕ FREE HOUSE ◀ O'Hanlons, Otter, Exe Valley, Bays,

Exmoor Ales Ö Stowford Press, Cornish Rattler. ♀ 8
Facilities Children welcome Children's menu Children's
portions Play area Family room Dogs allowed Garden Beer
festival Parking Wi-fi

PORTGATE   Map 3 SX48

PICK OF THE PUBS

The Harris Arms ♀

EX20 4PZ ☎ 01566 783331   ▤ 01566 783359
e-mail: info@theharrisarms.co.uk
dir: *From A30 at Broadwoodwidger/Roadford Lake exit
follow signs to Lifton then for Portgate*

Located on the old A30 close to the boundary between
Devon and Cornwall, this 16th-century inn has
wonderful views to Brent Tor. It's an accessible spot for
honest food with substance and style, plus real ales
and excellent wines – the pub certainly lives up to its
promotional strapline: 'Eat real food and drink real
wine'. Owners Rowena and Andy Whiteman have
previously run vineyards in France and New Zealand, so
their wine list, with over 150 wines, is both eclectic
and extensive. The pub's reputation for excellent food,
which reaches far beyond the local area, has picked up
many awards. The menu is built on exact cooking and
locally sourced ingredients. Examples from the à la
carte may include starters such as prawns piri-piri;
pressed ham hock and prune terrine; pork cheeks with
sweet potato and mushroom hash. Main dishes
continue the emphasis on good ingredients with roast
breast of guinea fowl with braised red cabbage,
fondant potato, spinach mousse and Madeira sauce,
plus pub classics of Devon faggots. In warmer weather,
enjoy a meal or drink outside on the decked patio.

Open Tue-Sun L Closed: Mon & Sun eve
Bar Meals L served Tue-Sun 12-2 booking required
D served Tue-Sat 6.30-9 booking required
Restaurant L served Tue-Sun 12-2 booking required
D served Tue-Sat 6.30-9 booking required ⊕ FREE
HOUSE ◀ Sharp's Doom Bar, Otter Ale, Bays Best. ♀ 20
Facilities Children welcome Children's menu
Children's portions Dogs allowed Garden Parking

POSTBRIDGE   Map 3 SX67

Warren House Inn NEW

PL20 6TA ☎ 01822 880208
dir: *On B3212 between Moretonhampstead & Princetown*

Isolated high on Dartmoor, the Warren House (named
after the prolific rabbit activity all around) has no mains
services; it uses generators for electricity and gravity-fed
water from a spring. It was built to service the local tin
mines, and furnishes the same warm hospitality today –
the fire in the hearth is said to have been burning
continuously since 1845. Four real ales and scrumpy
cider are served, along with a menu of good home-cooked
food: hearty soups, selection of pies, beef and lamb
raised on the moor, and vegetables supplied by local
farms.

Open all day all wk 11-11 (winter Mon-Tue 11-5)
Bar Meals L served all wk 12-9, Mon-Tue in winter
11-4.30 D served all wk 12-9, Mon-Tue in winter 11-4.30
Av main course £8.50 food served all day
Restaurant L served all wk 12-9, Mon-Tue in winter
11-4.30 D served all wk 12-9, Mon-Tue in winter 11-4.30
food served all day ⊕ FREE HOUSE ◀ Otter Ale, Sharp's
Doom Bar, Guest ales Ö Countryman Cider, Ashton Press.
Facilities Children welcome Children's menu Family room
Dogs allowed Garden Parking

RATTERY   Map 3 SX76

Church House Inn ♀

TQ10 9LD ☎ 01364 642220   ▤ 01364 642220
e-mail: ray.hardy@btconnect.com
web: www.thechurchhouseinn.co.uk
dir: *1m from A38 Exeter to Plymouth Rd & 0.75m from
A385 Totnes to South Brent Rd*

This venerable inn dates from 1028 and its interior
burgeons with brasses, bare beams, large fireplaces and
other historic features. Some customers encounter the
wandering spirit of a monk; fortunately he seems to be
friendly. In the character dining room, the menu includes
fresh fish (local smoked trout fillet; whole sea bream), as
well as spinach and ricotta cannelloni; pork loin cutlets
in apple and sage sauce; citrus and olive lamb shank;
and creamy coconut chicken curry. There is a large lawn
beer garden and patio where you can enjoy a pint of
Dartmoor ale in warmer months.

Open all wk 11-2.30 6-11 (Sun noon-3 6-10.30)
Bar Meals L served Mon-Sat 11.30-2, Sun 12-2 booking
required D served all wk 6.30-9 booking required
Restaurant L served Mon-Sat 11.30-2, Sun 12-2 booking
required D served all wk 6.30-9 booking required ⊕ FREE
HOUSE ◀ Dartmoor Jail Ale, Dartmoor Legend, Otter Ale,
George Gale Seafarers Ö Thatchers Gold, Thatchers Katy.
♀ 10 **Facilities** Children welcome Children's menu
Children's portions Dogs allowed Garden Parking

ROCKBEARE   Map 3 SY09

PICK OF THE PUBS

Jack in the Green Inn ◉◉ ♀

See Pick of the Pubs on page 145

SALCOMBE   Map 3 SX73

PICK OF THE PUBS

The Victoria Inn ♀

Fore St TQ8 8BU ☎ 01548 842604   ▤ 01548 844201
e-mail: info@victoriainn-salcombe.co.uk
dir: *In town centre, overlooking estuary*

Tim and Liz Hore run this friendly and inviting pub in
the centre of town, keeping the log fire roaring in
winter, and in milder weather welcoming mums, dads,
children and pets to the huge family garden with its
shady terrace and enclosed children's play area. The
bar presents a veritable smörgåsbord of St Austell
ales, in addition to a diverse selection of wines and
spirits; if you have something to celebrate, champagne
is served by the glass as well as the bottle. The first-
floor restaurant gives stunning views of the pretty
harbour and fishing boats bringing in the catch of the
day. So expect to find an open sandwich of Salcombe
white crabmeat; starters such as smoked haddock
kedgeree or pan-fried West Country scallops; and a
heart-warming selection of main dishes: sautéed pork
fillet; chef's own steak and kidney pudding; and the
inn's own 'scrummy' fish pie.

Open all day all wk 11.30am-11pm (Fri-Sat 11.30am-
11.30pm) Closed: 25 Dec pm **Bar Meals** L served all wk
12-2.30 D served all wk 6-9 ⊕ ST AUSTELL BREWERY
◀ St Austell Tribute, Black Prince, Proper Job IPA
Ö Rattler. ♀ 20 **Facilities** Children welcome Children's
portions Play area Dogs allowed Garden Wi-fi

SHEBBEAR   Map 3 SS40

The Devil's Stone Inn NEW

EX21 5RU ☎ 01409 281210
e-mail: churst1234@btinternet.com
dir: *From Okehampton right opposite White Hart, follow
A386 towards Hatherleigh. At rdbt outside Hatherleigh
take Holsworthy road to Highampton. Just after
Highampton right, follow signs to Shebbear*

A farmhouse before it became a coaching inn some 400
years ago, this inn is reputedly one of England's top
dozen most haunted pubs. That does not deter the
country sports lovers who use it as a base for their
activities; it is especially a haven for fly fishermen, with
beats, some of which the pub owns, on the middle and
upper Torridge. The beamed and flagstone floored interior
has several open fires. Locally-sourced and home-cooked
food, a selection of real ales and ciders, a games room,
separate dining room and large garden complete the
picture.

Open all wk 12-3 6-11 (Fri-Sun all day fr 12)
Bar Meals L served all wk 12-2.30 D served all wk 6-9.30
Restaurant L served all wk 12-2.30 D served all wk
6-9.30 booking required ⊕ FREE HOUSE ◀ Sharp's Doom
Bar, HSD, Tribute, Black Prince Ö Cornish Rattler,
Thatchers Gold, Brothers Pear Cider. **Facilities** Children
welcome Children's menu Children's portions Play area
Dogs allowed Garden Parking

PICK OF THE PUBS

The Fox & Goose ♟

PARRACOMBE
Map 3 SS64

EX31 4PE
☎ 01598 763239 📄 01598 763621
web: www.foxandgooseinnexmoor.co.uk
dir: *1m from A39 between Blackmoor Gate (2m) & Lynton (6m). Signed to Parracombe. Fox & Goose sign on approach*

This imposing Victorian building was once just a couple of tiny thatched cottages serving the local farming community. Transformation into a hotel took place when a narrow-gauge railway arrived in 1898 to link Parracombe with the outside world, represented by Lynton and Barnstaple. The line closed in the 1930s, although a short section was reopened a few years ago. Decorating the pub's interior are farm memorabilia, a scarf-wearing stag's head and photographs of villagers who now drink in more celestial surroundings; here beer drinkers have a choice of local Cotleigh and Exmoor, Otter from South Devon and cider from Winkleigh, just north of Dartmoor.

Good home-made food comes from constantly changing blackboard menus that are likely to feature seasonal game from surrounding farms and estates, as well as fish and shellfish caught off the North Devon coast. Examples include bouillabaisse; pan-fried skate wing with brown shrimp and capers; brill fillets poached in red wine; and roast cod wrapped in bacon with Puy lentils. Among the meat choices are trio of venison sausages with creamy mash and gravy; fillet steak with sautéed mushrooms and cherry vine tomatoes; and confit of duck with juniper and port sauce. For vegetarians there are mushroom Stroganoff with cream, mustard and Cognac; and pearl barley risotto with roasted squash and sage. To follow, there's a good board of South West cheeses; brioche bread and butter pudding; and lemon posset with vanilla sablé biscuits. A newish addition to the repertoire is eat-in or takeaway pizzas. Children and dogs are welcome and, if they want, they can let off steam in the paved courtyard garden overlooking the river.

Open all day all wk **Bar Meals** L served all wk 12-2 D served Mon-Sat 6-9, Sun 7-9 Av main course £12.95
Restaurant L served all wk 12-2 D served Mon-Sat 6-9, Sun 7-9 ⊕ FREE HOUSE
🍺 Cotleigh Barn Owl, Exmoor Fox, Otter Ale, Guinness Ö Winkleigh. ♟ 10
Facilities Children's menu Children's portions Dogs allowed Garden Parking Wi-fi

PICK OF THE PUBS

Jack in the Green Inn

ROCKBEARE Map 3 SY09

London Rd EX5 2EE
☎ **01404 822240** 🖹 **01404 823445**
e-mail: info@jackinthegreen.uk.com
web: www.jackinthegreen.uk.com
dir: *From M5 take old A30 towards Honiton, signed Rockbeare*

Passionate foodie Paul Parnell has owned this unassuming, white-painted roadside inn for nearly two decades and continues to work tirelessly at developing the 'Jack's' well-deserved reputation for upmarket modern pub food and his links with local artisan producers. Top-drawer, locally sourced raw ingredients underpin chef Matthew Mason's innovative menus, be it game from local shoots, or salad leaves and seasonal vegetables grown within six miles of the pub. So, it's a cracking award-winning dining destination with two AA Rosettes and a simple philosophy to serve the best of Devon's produce in stylish surroundings - neat open-plan bar with wood-burning stoves and leather armchairs, and a warren of cosy dining rooms adorned with fresh flowers and Simon Drew prints. Simple pub classics are deliciously updated, even the humble ploughman's is given the VIP treatment, and a prawn cocktail, for example, is poshed-up with slow-roasted tomatoes and 'Bloody Mary' sauce, with other bar dishes taking in spicy red Thai chicken, traditional fish and chips, and chicken, smoked ham hock and leek pie. For a

'Totally Devon' experience, kick off with creamed Vulscombe goat's cheese and home-made gingerbread, then follow with loin of Kenniford Farm pork with smoked paprika, black pudding, pistachio and apple, and finish with Exmoor blue cheese and pickled blackberries. Alternatives may include main course options like Exmoor venison loin and braised shoulder, and chump of lamb with chorizo and white beans. Why not push the boat out and experience the tasting menu, delve into the excellent value wine list, and dine alfresco in the revamped rear courtyard. There is live jazz on the second Friday of the month from May to September.

Open all wk 11-3 5.30-11 (Sun noon-11) Closed: 25 Dec-5 Jan **Bar Meals** L served Mon-Sat 12-2, Sun 12-9 D served Mon-Sat 6-9.30, Sun 12-9 Av main course £17.50

Restaurant L served Mon-Sat 12-2, Sun12-9 D served Mon-Sat 6-9.30, Sun 12-9 Fixed menu price fr £25 Av 3 course à la carte fr £30 ⊕ FREE HOUSE ◀ Otter Ale, Sharp's Doom Bar, Butcombe Bitter ♂ Dragon Tears, Luscombe, St Georges. ♀ 12 **Facilities** Children welcome Children's menu Children's portions Family room Garden Parking Wi-fi

SIDBURY — Map 3 SY19

The Hare & Hounds NEW

Putts Corner EX10 0QQ ☎ 01404 41760
e-mail: contact@hareandhounds-devon.co.uk
dir: *From Honiton take A375 signed Sidmouth. In approx 0.75m pub at Seaton Rd x-rds*

Behind the whitewashed walls of this traditional Devon free house you'll find a comfortable interior with wooden beams and winter log fires. There's also a large garden with fantastic views down the valley to the sea at Sidmouth. Besides the daily carvery, the extensive menu features classic pub dishes and snacks. Main course options include beef in Guinness with roast potatoes, as well as fish dishes and vegetarian options. Three cask ales are on offer; they are brewed less than 10 miles away by Otter and Branscombe Breweries.

Open all day all wk 10am-11pm (Sun 11-10.30)
Bar Meals L served Mon-Sat 12-9 D served Mon-Sat 12-9
Restaurant L served Mon-Sat 12-2, Sun 12-9 D served Mon-Sat 6-9, Sun 12-9 ⊕ FREE HOUSE ◀ Otter Bitter, Branscombe Branoc ♂ Wiscombe Suicider.
Facilities Children welcome Children's menu Children's portions Play area Dogs allowed Garden Parking Wi-fi

SIDMOUTH — Map 3 SY18

PICK OF THE PUBS

Blue Ball Inn — INN ♀

See Pick of the Pubs on opposite page

PICK OF THE PUBS

Dukes ★★★★ INN ♀

See Pick of the Pubs on page 148

SLAPTON — Map 3 SX84

PICK OF THE PUBS

The Tower Inn

Church Rd TQ7 2PN ☎ 01548 580216
e-mail: towerinn@slapton.org
web: www.thetowerinn.com
dir: *Off A379 S of Dartmouth, turn left at Slapton Sands*

Visitors exploring Slapton Ley Nature Reserve and Slapton Sands should venture inland to seek out this ancient inn. Tucked away behind the church and standing beside the dramatic, ivy-clad ruins of the chantry tower, the 14th-century Tower Inn is a truly atmospheric village pub, built to accommodate the artisans working on the monastic college next door. Six hundred years on and guests continue to be warmly welcomed and refreshed with local ales and a good choice of modern pub food in the rambling bar and dining rooms characterised by stone walls, open fires, low beams, flagstone floors, and scrubbed oak tables topped with church candles. Menus are based around local ingredients, including Devon beef, estate-reared venison, and fish from Dartmouth. Dishes range from local crab sandwiches and Thai fishcakes at lunchtime to rabbit terrine with fig chutney and pork belly and cheek stew at dinner. There's a splendid landscaped garden with church and tower views.

Open 12-2.30 (12-3 Summer) 6-11 Closed: 1st 2wks Jan, Sun eve during Winter **Bar Meals** L served all wk 12-2.30 D served all wk 6.30-9.30 Av main course £12.95 **Restaurant** L served all wk 12-2.30 D served all wk 6.30-9.30 Av 3 course à la carte fr £25 ⊕ FREE HOUSE ◀ Butcombe Bitter, Otter Bitter, St Austell Proper Job, Sharp's Doom Bar ♂ Addlestones, Sharps Orchard. **Facilities** Children welcome Children's menu Children's portions Dogs allowed Garden Beer festival Parking Wi-fi

SOURTON — Map 3 SX59

The Highwayman Inn

EX20 4HN ☎ 01837 861243 🖹 01837 861196
e-mail: info@thehighwaymaninn.net
dir: *On A386 (Okehampton to Tavistock road). Exit A30 towards Tavistock. Pub 4m from Okehampton, 12m from Tavistock*

Undoubtedly one of Britain's most unusual inns. The Highwayman is indeed a fascinating place, full of legend, strange architecture, eccentric furniture and obscure bric-a-brac, with roots going back to 1282. Since 1959 Welshman John 'Buster' Jones has been working on his vision – features include part of a galleon, wood hauled from Dartmoor's bogs, and Gothic church arches; the entrance is through the old Okehampton-Launceston coach. Popular with holidaymakers and international tourists, the Highwayman refreshes one and all with drinks which include real farmhouse cider and interesting bottled beers from local breweries; great pasties and pies are always available.

Open 11.30-2 6-10.30 (Sun 12-2 7-10.30) Closed: 25-28 Dec **Bar Meals** L served all wk 12-1.45 D served all wk 6-9 Av main course £5 ⊕ FREE HOUSE ◀ St Austell Duchy ♂ Grays. **Facilities** Family room Dogs allowed Garden Parking Wi-fi **Notes** ⊛

SOUTH POOL — Map 3 SX74

The Millbrook Inn ♀

TQ7 2RW ☎ 01548 531581
e-mail: info@millbrookinnsouthpool.co.uk
dir: *Take A379 from Kingsbridge to Frogmore then E for 2m to South Pool*

A brook complete with white Aylesbury ducks runs past the rear terrace of this quaint 16th-century village pub. Set at the head of South Pool creek, summer barbecues and paellas in the pretty front courtyard attract small boat owners from Salcombe and Kingsbridge when the tide is right. The interior is cosy and unspoilt, with open fires, fresh flowers, cushioned wheelback chairs, and beams adorned with old banknotes and clay pipes. Two real ales and food ingredients are all local, while the award-winning French chef brings his country's influence to bear on the menus. On Sundays, the speciality is rib of beef with slow-braised ox cheek, followed by live music.

Open all wk 12-11 (Sun 12-10.30) **Bar Meals** L served all wk 12-2 D served all wk 7-9 Av main course £15 **Restaurant** L served Mon-Sat 12-2, Sun 12-3 D served all wk 7-9 Av 3 course à la carte fr £30 ⊕ FREE HOUSE ◀ Redrock, Otter Ale ♂ Thatchers Heritage. ♀ 10 **Facilities** Children welcome Children's portions Dogs allowed Garden Wi-fi

Save on hotels. Book at **theAA.com/hotel**

DEVON 147 ENGLAND

PICK OF THE PUBS

Blue Ball Inn ★★★★ INN ♀

SIDMOUTH   Map 3 SY18

Stevens Cross, Sidford EX10 9QL
☎ 01395 514062   📄 01395 519584
e-mail: rogernewton@blueballinn.net
web: www.blueballinnsidford.co.uk
dir: *M5 junct 30 exit to A3052. Through Sidford towards Lyme Regis, on left after village, approx 13m*

Painstakingly rebuilt after a disastrous fire in 2006, this marvellous 14th-century thatched, cob-and-flint pub has been run by generations of the Newton family since 1912. Roger and Linda Newton sourced old furniture, pictures and memorabilia to re-capture the unique atmosphere of the original inn. They also added nine contemporary en suite bedrooms, including one on the ground floor suitable for disabled people, as well as a function room with full conference facilities. The new-look inn is a hugely attractive and lovingly maintained building, festooned with colourful hanging baskets in summer, when the patio and landscaped gardens come into their own. Arrive early in winter to bag a seat by one of the three log fires within the rambling carpeted bars, which specialise in hand-pumped cask conditioned ales. The food bar and large dining area offer extensive menus of family favourites interspersed with dishes for the more sophisticated palate. So a starter like potted Lyme Bay crab with cucumber salad and warm toast, for

example, could be followed by local Chinns of Crediton pork sausages, mashed potatoes and onion with a grain mustard sauce; or honey-glazed ham from Drews of Sidbury, served with two Greendale Farm eggs, chips and peas. Don't forget to check out the specials too, or you may miss the seared pigeon breast with black pudding, pancetta and garden leaves; or pan-fried lamb's liver and bacon with bubble and squeak, buttered fine beans and an onion and mustard sauce. Within easy reach of the M5, A303 and Exeter, and just minutes from stunning walks along the coast, the Blue Ball's AA-rated accommodation provides an ideal base for exploring the county, or for a night's stay en route to the southwest.

Open all day all wk Closed: 25 Dec eve
Bar Meals L served all wk 12-2.30 booking recommended D served all wk 6-9 booking recommended Av main course £10
Restaurant L served all wk 12-2.30
D served all wk 6-9 🍺 PUNCH TAVERNS
🍺 Otter Bitter, Tribute, Doom Bar, Guest Ale ♂ Stowford Press, Taunton Traditional.
♀ 13 **Facilities** Children's menu Children's portions Play area Family room Dogs allowed Garden Parking Wi-fi **Rooms** 9

PICK OF THE PUBS

Dukes ★★★★ INN ♆

The Esplanade EX10 8AR
☎ **01395 513320** 🖹 **01395 519318**
e-mail: dukes@hotels-sidmouth.co.uk
web: www.hotels-sidmouth.co.uk
dir: *M5 junct 30 onto A3052, take 1st exit to Sidmouth on right then left onto Esplanade*

In the heart of Sidmouth town centre on the beautiful Regency Esplanade, Dukes might be a contemporary inn but its values are traditional. The interior is stylish and lively, with a relaxed continental feel in the bar and public areas. In fine weather the patio garden overlooking the sea is perfect for a mid-morning freshly ground Italian coffee and home-baked pastry. Later on, soak up the sun while sipping a pint of O'Hanlon's Firefly or a Burrow Hill cider; wine choice, too, is excellent, with around 20 to choose from by the glass. Varied menus include traditional English-style favourites, fresh fish from Brixham and Lyme Bay, and prime meats from West Country farms. Lunch options include game pie; breaded salmon goujons; and a beef and horseradish burger garnished with salad and chips. If you just want a snack, possibilities range from stone-baked pizzas to sandwiches made from hand-cut locally baked white or granary bread: roast chicken and pesto mayonnaise; roasted pepper and houmous; and honey-roast gammon with cider chutney are three options. Loaded nachos, home-made

jacket wedges and garlic bread are always popular, but it may be wise to hold back for a Devon cream tea later. After a day breathing sea air, the dinner choices can be as robust as your appetite. You could start with chicken, bacon and asparagus terrine, or baked Cornish camembert. Continue with a prime West Country steak served with grilled tomatoes, mushrooms and a choice of potatoes. Desserts, such as toffee and pecan tart or steamed mocha sponge, are all made on the premises and served with clotted cream or Yarde Farm ice cream. Alternatively, look to the cheeseboard of local varieties, where you may find Cornish Yarg, a goat's cheese from Somerset, and Exmoor Blue. Refurbished bed and breakfast accommodation is available, with most rooms overlooking the bay; all are en suite and have free Wi-fi.

Open all day all wk **Bar Meals** L served Sun-Thu 12-9, Fri-Sat 12-9.30 D served Sun-Thu 12-9, Fri-Sat 12-9.30 **Restaurant** L served Sun-Thu 12-9, Fri-Sat 12-9.30 booking required D served Sun-Thu 12-9, Fri-Sat 12-9.30 booking required ⊕ FREE HOUSE ◀ Branscombe Vale Branoc & Summa That, O'Hanlon's Firefly, Otter Ale, Yeovil Ale ♂ Stowford Press, Burrow Hill. ♆ 20 **Facilities** Children's menu Children's portions Play area Dogs allowed Garden Parking Wi-fi **Rooms** 13

SOUTH ZEAL   Map 3 SX69

Oxenham Arms ★★★★ INN ▾

EX20 2JT ☎ 01837 840244   📠 01837 840791
e-mail: relax@theoxenhamarms.co.uk
dir: *Just off A30 4m E of Okehampton, in village centre*

Although the imposing Tudor porch prepares you for antiquity, you may not guess that the Ox, as it is affectionately known, was probably built by monks as long ago as the 12th century. Situated on the edge of Dartmoor, turn left into the unchanged bar, where Sharp's Doom Bar and Otter form part of the real ale line-up, or right into Burgoyne's restaurant. There's a third choice – up the oak staircase to one of the individually decorated bedrooms, many with four-poster beds.

Open all wk 10.30-3.30 5-11 **Bar Meals** L served all wk 12-2.30 D served all wk 6-9.30 Av main course £10 **Restaurant** L served all wk 12-2.30 D served all wk 6-9.30 Av 3 course à la carte fr £20 ⊕ FREE HOUSE ◀ Sharp's Doom Bar, Otter, guest. ▾ 8 **Facilities** Children welcome Children's portions Dogs allowed Garden Parking Wi-fi **Rooms** 7

SOWTON   Map 3 SX99

The Black Horse Inn

Old Honiton Rd EX5 2AN ☎ 01392 366649
e-mail: blackhorse@wadworth.co.uk
dir: *On old A30 from Exeter towards Honiton, 0.5m from M5 junct 29; 1m from Exeter International Airport. Inn between Sowton & Clyst Honiton*

Recent refurbishment has seen this village roadside pub emerge as a fresh, contemporary dining inn, with crisp decor and a relaxed atmosphere. Using produce from local suppliers, the menu offers great specials adding to a base of wholesome favourites. Pan-fried Lyme Bay scallops are the lead-in to supreme of guinea fowl on a confit of leek and bacon with cider and wholegrain mustard sauce; or perhaps a panini or a lamb balti will hit the spot. Try the local ale while sitting on the terrace on warmer days. Change of hands.

Open all wk 11am-11pm (Fri-Sat 11am-mdnt) ⊕ FREE HOUSE ◀ Wadworth IPA, 6X, Guest ales ○ Thatchers. **Facilities** Children welcome Children's menu Garden Parking

SPREYTON   Map 3 SX69

PICK OF THE PUBS

The Tom Cobley Tavern

EX17 5AL ☎ 01647 231314
dir: *From A30 at Whiddon Down take A3124 N. Take 1st right after services then 1st right over bridge.*

It was from this peaceful, whitewashed pub, one day in 1802, that a certain Thomas Cobley and his companions set forth for Widecombe Fair, an event immortalised in song, and his cottage still stands in the village. This pub draws the crowds in summer due

to its name and associations with Widecombe Fair. It stands in a sleepy Dartmoor village and remains a traditional village local; the unspoilt main bar has a roaring log fire, cushioned settles and dispenses a mind-boggling range of 20 tip-top real ales straight from the cask, for which it has won many awards. The pub also offers a great range of real ciders. Typically, order a pint of Cotleigh Tawny Ale or Sharp's Doom Bar to accompany some hearty pub food, which ranges from simple bar snacks to decent pies, salads, duck and fish dishes, as well as a good vegetarian selection. Finish off with one of the great ice creams or sorbets. Summer alfresco drinking can be enjoyed on the pretty flower-decked gravel terrace or in the rear garden with its far-reaching views.

Open 12-3 6-11 (Sun 12-4 7-11 Mon 6.30-11 Fri-Sat 12-3 6-1am) Closed: Mon L **Bar Meals** L served Tue-Sun 12-2 booking required D served all wk 7-9 booking required **Restaurant** L served Tue-Sun 12-2 booking required D served all wk 7-9 booking required ⊕ FREE HOUSE ◀ Cotleigh Tawny Ale, Doom Bar, Otter Brewery, Sharp's Doom Bar, St Austell Tribute, Proper Job, Dartmoor Brewery Jail Ale, Legend, Guest ales ○ Winkleigh Cider, Stowford Press, Healey's Cornish Apple Rattler, Pear Rattler, Sandford Orchards Devon Scrumpy. **Facilities** Children welcome Children's menu Children's portions Dogs allowed Garden Parking

STAVERTON   Map 3 SX76

Sea Trout Inn NEW

TQ9 6PA ☎ 01803 762274
e-mail: info@theseatroutinn.co.uk
dir: *From A38 take A384 towards Totnes. Follow Staverton & Sea Trout Inn sign*

With a cracking locals' bar, stylish restaurant and 600 years of history, this characterful village inn ticks all the right boxes. The throaty cough of a steam train on the South Devon Railway may drift across the pretty Dart Valley to enhance a tranquil moment on the terrace, agonising over the fine menu choice, prepared in a modern British style; sea trout, of course, or perhaps a venison casserole with herb dumplings, with Palmers perfect ales the icing on the cake.

Open all day all wk **Bar Meals** L served Mon-Fri 12-2, Sat 12-2.30, Sun 12-3 booking required D served Mon-Thu 6-9, Fri-Sat 6-9.30 booking required **Restaurant** L served Mon-Fri 12-2, Sat 12-2.30, Sun 12-3 booking required D served Mon-Thu 6-9, Fri-Sat 6-9.30 booking required ⊕ PALMERS ◀ Palmers 200, Copper, Best ○ Thatchers. **Facilities** Children welcome Children's menu Children's portions Dogs allowed Garden Parking Wi-fi

STOKE FLEMING   Map 3 SX84

The Green Dragon Inn ▾

Church Rd TQ6 0PX
☎ 01803 770238   📠 01803 770238
e-mail: pcrowther@btconnect.com
dir: *Off A379 (Dartmouth to Kingsbridge coast road) opposite church*

A tunnel leading from Blackpool Sands to the pub's cellars may have been a smugglers route to this medieval inn in the beautiful South Hams. The seafaring connection remains; the current landlord, a keen solo sailor, has turned the interior into a haven of boating memorabilia, including charts, flags, sextants and sailing pictures. Devon-made beers and wine, and Somerset scrumpy slake the thirst of walkers from nearby Dartmouth, whilst the great value bar meals can satisfy the largest of appetites with lamb and aubergine pie or sausage and pork cassoulet.

Open all wk 11.30-3 5.30-11 **Bar Meals** L served all wk 12-2 D served all wk 6.30-8.30 Av main course £10 ⊕ HEAVITREE ◀ Otter, Tribute, guest ale ○ Aspall, Addlestones. ▾ 10 **Facilities** Children welcome Children's portions Play area Dogs allowed Garden Parking

STRETE   Map 3 SX84

PICK OF THE PUBS

Kings Arms ◉

Dartmouth Rd TQ6 0RW
☎ 01803 770377   📠 01803 771008
e-mail: kingsarms_devon_fish@hotmail.com
dir: *On A379 (Dartmouth-Kingsbridge road), 5m from Dartmouth*

You can't miss this striking, 18th-century pub, with its unique cast-iron balcony, as it stands smack beside the coast road and the South West coast path passes the front door. Pop in for a pint of Otter Ale, bag a seat by the fire in the traditional, terracotta-walled bar, or head up the few steps into the light and airy contemporary-styled restaurant, replete with modern artwork and stunning views across Start Bay. Chef Rob Dawson's motto is 'keep it fresh, keep it simple' and on his daily lunch and dinner menus you'll find wonderfully fresh seafood, simply prepared with some modern twists, including crab, lobster and fish from a local boat (the boat trawls exclusively for the pub once a week). At lunch, tuck into delicious fish soup with saffron and rouille, a plate of smoked sprats, or smoked haddock and rocket fishcake with wholegrain mustard sauce. Evening choices extend to cod with local clams, peas and asparagus, red gurnard with scallion mash and roasted red pepper cream, and sirloin steak with Café de Paris butter. In summer, head for the flower-filled garden and dine alfresco overlooking the bay.

Open 11.30-3 6-11 (Sat-Sun 11.30-11) Closed: Mon winter ⊕ HEAVITREE ◀ Otter Bitter, Adnams Bitter, Guinness ○ Aspall. **Facilities** Children welcome Dogs allowed Garden Parking

PICK OF THE PUBS

The Golden Lion Inn ♟

TIPTON ST JOHN   Map 3 SY09

EX10 0AA ☎ **01404 812881**
e-mail: info@goldenliontipton.co.uk
web: www.goldenliontipton.co.uk
dir: *Telephone for directions*

It's eight years and counting for Michelle and Francois Teissier, who took over this inviting village pub in 2003. So many things contribute to its traditional feel – the low wooden beams and stone walls, the winter log fire, the Art Deco prints and Tiffany lamps, not to mention the paintings by Devonian and Cornish artists. And there's the bar, of course, where locally brewed Otter ales are the order of the day.

Chef/patron Franky (as everyone calls him) trained in classical French cooking at a prestigious establishment in the Loire Valley, a grounding that accounts today for his rustic French, Mediterranean and British menus. Their delights may include moules marinière; chunky fish soup; coq au vin; magret de canard with oriental plum sauce; grilled goat's cheese with Italian ham; and steak and kidney pudding. From the specials selection look for chicken Breton with leeks, venison pie, braised pheasant, and fresh fish and seafood, your choice of which, given that the genteel seaside town of Sidmouth is just down the road, will depend totally on that day's catch – cod, hake and sea bass are all candidates. For vegetarians there's

likely to be vegetable lasagne; deep-fried Brie with cranberry sauce; and butter bean cassoulet. Tempting white and granary bread sandwiches are filled with roast beef; chicken and mayonnaise; home-made gravadlax with honey and mustard dressing; or fresh Lyme Bay crab. The Sunday lunch menu (half price for children) offers roast West Country beef with Yorkshire pudding; roast lamb with mint sauce; and winter vegetable crêpe. As Michelle sums up: "With a menu that changes seasonally, we're lucky that Devon offers such good quality and variety of produce." Outside there is a grassy beer garden and terracotta-walled terrace area with tumbling grapevines. On summer evenings you can listen to jazz.

Open all wk 12-2.30 6-11 (Sun 12-2.30 7-10.30) **Bar Meals** L served all wk 12-2 D served Mon-Sat 6.30-8.30, Sun 7-8.30 booking required Av main course £11 **Restaurant** L served all wk 12-2 Fixed menu price fr £12.50 Av 3 course à la carte fr £25 ⊕ HEAVITREE ◀ Otter Ale, Bass, Otter Bitter. ♟ 12
Facilities Children's menu Children's portions Garden Parking

THURLESTONE   Map 3 SX64

The Village Inn

TQ7 3NN ☎ 01548 563525
e-mail: enquiries@thurlestone.co.uk
dir: *Take A379 from Plymouth towards Kingsbridge, at Bantham rdbt straight over onto B3197, then right into a lane signed Thurlestone, 2.5m*

Built in the 16th century as a farmhouse, this old pub prides itself on good service, well-kept ales and decent food. Like the nearby Thurlestone Hotel, it has been owned by the Grose family for over a century. Seafood is a speciality, with Salcombe crabmeat, River Exe mussels and other local fish and shellfish to choose from on the seasonal menus. Other possibilities are Cajun roasted chicken breast, sirloin and rump steaks, and beef burgers.

Open all wk 11.30-3 6-11.30 (Sun & summer all day) ⊕ FREE HOUSE ◀ Palmers IPA, Interbrew Bass, Sharp's Doom Bar, guest ale ♂ Heron Valley. **Facilities** Children welcome Children's menu Family room Dogs allowed Garden Parking

TIPTON ST JOHN   Map 3 SY09

PICK OF THE PUBS

The Golden Lion Inn ☕

See Pick of the Pubs on opposite page

TOPSHAM   Map 3 SX98

PICK OF THE PUBS

Bridge Inn

Bridge Hill EX3 0QQ ☎ 01392 873862
e-mail: su3264@eclipse.co.uk
dir: *M5 junct 30 follow Sidmouth signs, in approx 400yds right at rdbt onto A376 towards Exmouth. In 1.8m cross mini-rdbt. Right at next mini rdbt to Topsham. 1.2m, cross River Clyst. Inn on right*

This 'museum with beer' is substantially old 16th century, although its constituent parts vary considerably in age. Most of the fabric is local stone, while the old brewhouse at the rear is traditional Devon cob. Four generations of the same family have run it since great-grandfather William Gibbings arrived in 1897, and it remains eccentrically and gloriously old fashioned – mobile phones are definitely out. Usually around ten real ales from local and further flung breweries are served straight from their casks, the actual line-up varying by the week. There are no lagers and only a few wines, two from a local organic vineyard. Traditional, freshly prepared lunchtime bar food includes granary ploughman's, pies and pasties, sandwiches, all made with local ingredients. Queen Elizabeth II visited in 1998, believed to be the only time she has officially stepped inside an English pub.

Open all wk 12-2 6-10.30 (Sun 12-2 7-10.30)
Bar Meals L served all wk 12-2 Av main course £7 ⊕ FREE HOUSE ◀ Branscombe Vale-Branoc, Adnams Broadside, Exe Valley, O'Hanlons, Teignworthy, Jollyboat Plunder, Otter Amber. **Facilities** Children welcome Dogs allowed Garden Parking Wi-fi Notes ☺

TORCROSS   Map 3 SX84

Start Bay Inn ☕

TQ7 2TQ ☎ 01548 580553   🖨 01548 581285
e-mail: clair@startbayinn.co.uk
dir: *Between Dartmouth & Kingsbridge on A379*

The fishermen working from the beach in front of this 14th-century pub deliver their catch direct to the kitchen; so does a local crabber, who leaves his catch at the back door to be cooked and picked by the pub. The former landlord (father of landladies Clair and Gail) continues to dive for scallops. Be in no doubt therefore about the freshness of the seafood on the specials board. Look also for Dartmouth Smokehouse products, locally sourced steaks, burgers from the village butcher, and Salcombe Dairy ice creams. Ales, cider, juices and spring water have not travelled far either.

Open all day all wk 11.30am-11.30pm
Bar Meals L served all wk 11.30-2.15 D served all wk 6-9.30 winter, 6-10 summer Av main course £9 ⊕ HEAVITREE ◀ Bass, Otter Ale, Otter Bitter ♂ Heron Valley. ☕ 8 **Facilities** Children welcome Children's menu Children's portions Family room Garden Parking

TORQUAY   Map 3 SX96

PICK OF THE PUBS

The Cary Arms ★★★★★ INN ☕

Beach Rd TQ1 3LX
☎ 01803 327110   🖨 01803 323221
e-mail: enquiries@caryarms.co.uk
dir: *From Exeter A380 towards Torquay. Left onto B3192. On entering Teignmouth, at bottom of hill at lights, right signed Torquay/A379. Cross River Teign. At mini rdbt follow Babbacombe/Seafront signs. Pass Babbacombe Model Village & Bygones, through lights, left into Babbacombe Downs Rd, left into Beach Rd*

So much more than just an inn on the beach, this classic English pub tempts with boutique-style luxury accommodation – the en suite rooms are sea facing and most have a balcony. In the stone-walled bar, perhaps with a pint of Doom Bar in hand, you'll stand on planked floors beneath beamed ceilings contemplating the views across the bay and perusing the seasonal menu. If it's a glorious summer's day, you will unquestionably wish to eat on one of the terraces that lead down to the water's edge; this is when the barbecue and wood-fired oven come into their own. Catch of the day from Brixham will be a must for fish lovers – perhaps a dressed crab salad, or a simple fillet of fresh fish enclosed in crisp Otter ale batter and served with proper chips and crushed peas. Award-

winning roasted Creedy duck breast on sweet potato mash with a bacon, shallot and red wine sauce is equally hard to resist. Jazz, gastro, quiz and steak nights punctuate the year.

Open all day all wk noon-11pm **Bar Meals** L served all wk 12-3 booking required D served all wk 6.30-9 booking required ⊕ FREE HOUSE ◀ Otter Ale, Bays Top Sail, Sharp's Doom Bar ♂ Thatchers Gold, Addlestones. ☕ 14 **Facilities** Children welcome Children's menu Children's portions Family room Dogs allowed Garden Wi-fi **Rooms** 8

TOTNES   Map 3 SX86

PICK OF THE PUBS

The Durant Arms ☕

See Pick of the Pubs on page 152

Royal Seven Stars Hotel ☕

The Plains TQ9 5DD
☎ 01803 862125   🖨 01803 867925
e-mail: enquiry@royalsevenstars.co.uk
dir: *From A382 signed Totnes, left at 'Dartington' rdbt. Through lights towards town centre, through next rdbt, pass Morrisons car park on left. 200yds on right*

This Grade II listed property in the heart of Totnes features an accommodating front terrace, where both food and drink are served in fine weather. Inside two traditional bars are warmed by log fires. The focus on 'local' ranges from the ales, ciders and soft drinks to the meats and fish on the menu. Home-cooked bar meals available all day include sandwiches, starters and sharing platters, and extend to chef's famous fish pie or a full-blown Devonshire sirloin or fillet steak with all the trimmings.

Open all day all wk **Bar Meals** L served all wk 11-9.30 D served all wk 11-9.30 Av main course £10.95 food served all day **Restaurant** L served Sun 12-2.30 booking required D served all wk 6.30-9.30 booking required Av 3 course à la carte fr £24.95 ⊕ FREE HOUSE ◀ Jail Ale, Doom Bar, Bays Gold, Courage Best, Dartmore Legend ♂ Thatchers, Orchards, Ashridge. ☕ 26 **Facilities** Children welcome Children's menu Children's portions Family room Dogs allowed Parking Wi-fi

Rumour ☕

30 High St TQ9 5RY ☎ 01803 864682
dir: *Follow signs for Totnes castle/town centre. On main street up hill above arch on left. 5 min walk from rail station*

This 17th-century building has a chequered history including stints as a milk bar, restaurant and wine bar. Named after Fleetwood Mac's landmark 1977 album, it is now comprehensively refurbished, with innovative heating and plumbing systems which reduce its environmental footprint. Hospitable staff add to its charm. Food offerings include an extensive hand-made

continued on page 153

PICK OF THE PUBS

The Durant Arms 🍷

Ashprington TQ9 7UP
☎ **01803 732240**
e-mail: info@durantarms.co.uk
web: www.durantarms.co.uk
dir: *Exit A38 at Totnes junct, to Dartington & Totnes, at 1st lights right for Kingsbridge on A381, in 1m left for Ashprington*

Under new ownership since March 2011, this award-winning 18th-century pub set in the picturesque village of Ashprington stands in the shadow of a beautiful 16th century church and has stunning views of the River Dart. Located just outside the Elizabethan town of Totnes, in the heart of the South Hams, the building was originally the counting house for the neighbouring 500-acre Sharpham Estate. Formerly known as The Ashprington Inn, the small bar is fitted out in a traditional style, with work by local artists on display alongside the horse brasses, ferns and cheerful red velvet curtains – the perfect place to enjoy local Sharpham Vineyard wines or local real ales and ciders.

All dishes at The Durant are cooked to order, using locally sourced ingredients wherever possible. Typical dishes from the daily-changing blackboard menu include pub favourites such as home-cooked ham, eggs and chips, pan-fried lambs' liver with onions and shepherd's pie with a cheese topping. A more formal meal might begin with Brie and spinach tart or sautéed scallops with black pudding and wholegrain mustard sauce. Follow on, perhaps, with chicken supreme filled with Brie and wrapped in Parma ham; fillet of venison with red berry sauce; or sea bass fillet with roasted cherry tomatoes and spring onion. Leave space for desserts such as blackberry and apple pie, plum and apple crumble or passionfruit cheesecake. The little courtyard to the rear provides a cosy spot to linger over a summer meal.

Open all wk Sat-Sun all day
Bar Meals L served all wk 12-2 D served all wk 7-9.15 **Restaurant** L served all wk 12-2 D served all wk 7-9.15
🍺 FREE HOUSE ◀ Dartmoor Bitter, Tetley, Tribute ○ Luscombe. 🍷 10
Facilities Children welcome Children's menu Children's portions Family room Dogs allowed Garden Parking Wi-fi

TOTNES *continued*

pizza menu alongside more formal à la carte options; maybe grilled goat's cheese with roasted beetroot and truffle honey dressing followed by pork sausages braised in red wine, shallots and mushrooms served with mash.

Open all wk Mon-Sat 10-11 (Sun 6-11)
Bar Meals L served Mon-Sat 12-3 D served all wk 6-10 booking required **Restaurant** L served Mon-Sat 12-3 D served all wk 6-10 booking required ⊕ FREE HOUSE ◄ Erdinger, Abbots Ale, Half Bore ♂ Thatchers. ♥ 12
Facilities Children welcome Children's portions

Steam Packet Inn ★★★★ INN ♥

St Peter's Quay TQ9 5EW
☎ 01803 863880   ▤ 01803 862754
e-mail: steampacket@buccaneer.co.uk
web: www.steampacketinn.co.uk
dir: *Exit A38 towards Plymouth, 18m. A384 to Totnes 6m. Left at mini-rdbt, pass Morrisons on left, over mini-rdbt, 400yds on left*

Named after the passenger, cargo and mail steamers that once plied the Dart, this riverside pub, with four en suite rooms, makes full use of its riverside position. Great views, particularly from the conservatory restaurant, and plenty of seating on the heated, extensive waterside patio contribute to its popularity. Choices at lunch and dinner might include fresh Dartmoor Ale-battered cod; slow-cooked belly pork; or steak and kidney suet pudding. You're welcome to moor your boat alongside the inn. Look our for the beer festival in mid May.

Open all day all wk **Bar Meals** L served Mon-Fri 12-2.30, Sat-Sun 12-3 D served Mon-Sat 6-9.30, Sun 6-9 Av main course £9.95 **Restaurant** L served Mon-Fri 12-2.30, Sat-Sun 12-3 D served Mon-Sat 6-9.30, Sun 6-9 Av 3 course à la carte fr £16.50 ⊕ BUCCANEER HOLDINGS LTD ◄ Sharp's Doom Bar, Otter Ale, Jail Ale, Guest ale ♂ Stowford Press, Ashridge Organic. ♥ 11
Facilities Children welcome Children's menu Dogs allowed Garden Beer festival Parking Wi-fi **Rooms** 4

PICK OF THE PUBS

The White Hart ♥

Dartington Hall TQ9 6EL
☎ 01803 847111   ▤ 01803 847107
e-mail: bookings@dartingtonhall.com
dir: *From A38 take Totnes turn onto A384. Turn by Dartington church into Dartington Hall Estate*

Surrounded by landscaped gardens and an ancient deer park, the White Hart stands within the courtyard of the magnificent 14th-century Dartington Hall.

Ancient tapestries hang above the original kitchen fire in the main restaurant, recently fully refurbished, which is floored with flagstones and oak, lit by gothic chandeliers, and furnished with limed oak settles. Otter real ales are available in the bar, again with a fire, and there's a patio for the warmer weather. The daily changing bar and restaurant menu uses fresh, seasonal ingredients from South Devon and the estate itself – single-suckled beef, grass-reared lamb, additive-free and free-range chickens and eggs, and fish. Typical dishes might be grilled field mushroom burger with caramelised onions, beefsteak tomato and goat's cheese; confit of free-range Crediton duck leg with apple and celeriac purée, and cranberry and balsamic compote; and grilled salmon fillet with sautéed spinach and garlic, and herb butter sauce.

Open all day all wk Mon-Sat 10am-11pm, (Sun 10am-10.30pm) Closed: 24-29 Dec **Bar Meals** L served all wk 12-2.30 booking required D served all wk 6-9 booking required **Restaurant** L served all wk 12-2.30 booking required D served all wk 6-9 booking required ⊕ FREE HOUSE ◄ Otter Brewery Ale & Bitter ♂ Addlestones. ♥ 14 **Facilities** Children welcome Children's portions Garden Parking

---

TRUSHAM   Map 3 SX88

PICK OF THE PUBS

Cridford Inn ♥

See Pick of the Pubs on page 154

TUCKENHAY   Map 3 SX85

The Maltsters Arms ♥

TQ9 7EQ ☎ 01803 732350   ▤ 01803 732823
e-mail: pub@tuckenhay.demon.co.uk
dir: *A381 from Totnes towards Kingsbridge. 1m, at hill top turn left, follow signs to Tuckenhay, 3m*

Once owned by flamboyant TV chef, the late Keith Floyd, this 18th-century stone inn is accessible only along high-banked lanes, or by boat either side of high tide. The daily-changing menu may feature lambs kidneys in sherry and wholegrain mustard; wild River Dart sea trout with lemon and herb butter; pork and cider casserole, washed down with Maltsters Ale or Heron Valley cider. Famous for summer barbecues and music events.

Open all day all wk 11-11 (25 Dec 12-2)
Bar Meals L served all wk 12-3 D served all wk 7-9.30
Restaurant L served all wk 12-3 booking required D served all wk 7-9.30 booking required ⊕ FREE HOUSE ◄ Princetown Dartmoor IPA, Teignworthy Maltsters Ale, Sharp's Doom Bar ♂ Westons Perry, Heron Valley 'Shag', Bays Breaker Yarde Dry. ♥ 18 **Facilities** Children welcome Children's menu Children's portions Family room Dogs allowed Garden Parking

---

TYTHERLEIGH   Map 4 ST30

Tytherleigh Arms Hotel

EX13 7BE
☎ 01460 220400 & 220214   ▤ 01460 220814
e-mail: tytherleigharms@aol.com
dir: *Equidistant from Chard & Axminster on A358*

Situated on the borders of Devon, Dorset and Somerset, this family-run 16th-century former coaching inn boasts beamed ceilings and huge roaring fires. It's a food-led establishment that takes pride in sourcing local ingredients, with seafood and steaks a speciality. Fish dishes might include pan-seared salmon with light lemon sauce, whilst other choices could be lamb shanks with honey and cider jus. There's also a comprehensive children's menu and a selection of delicious home-made puds. If you are just popping for a drink, there are some great local ales on offer, like Butcombe Bitter or Otter.

Open 11-2.30 6.30-11 Closed: Sun Eve winter
Bar Meals L served all wk 11-2.30 booking required D served all wk 6.30-9 booking required Av main course £10.95 **Restaurant** L served all wk 11-2.30 booking required D served all wk 6.30-9 booking required ⊕ FREE HOUSE ◄ Butcombe Bitter, Otter, Murphy's ♂ Ashton Press. **Facilities** Children welcome Children's menu Children's portions Garden Parking

---

UMBERLEIGH   Map 3 SS62

PICK OF THE PUBS

The Rising Sun Inn

EX37 9DU ☎ 01769 560447
dir: *On A377 (Exeter-Barnstaple road) at junct with B3227*

Idyllically set beside the River Taw and with a very strong fly fishing tradition, The Rising Sun dates back in part to the 13th century. The traditional flagstoned bar is strewn with comfortable chairs and adorned with fishing memorabilia; daily papers and magazines put the finishing touches to a relaxing atmosphere. Outside is a sunny raised terrace with beautiful views over the valley, and the riverside walk is enjoyable before or after a meal. A choice of à la carte restaurant or bar menus feature the best of West Country produce, with seasonal delights like seafood from the North Devon coast, salmon and sea trout from the Taw, game from Exmoor, and local cheeses. The daily changing specials board could be the best place to start looking. Change of hands.

Open all day all wk 11.30-11 **Bar Meals** L served Mon-Sun 12-2.30 D served Mon-Sat 6-9, Sun 6-8.30 **Restaurant** L served Mon-Sun 12-2.30 D served Mon-Sat 6-9, Sun 6-8.30 ⊕ FREE HOUSE ◄ Guest ales ♂ Thatchers Gold. **Facilities** Children welcome Children's menu Children's portions Dogs allowed Garden Parking

PICK OF THE PUBS

Cridford Inn 🍷

TRUSHAM   Map 3 SX88

TQ13 0NR
☎ **01626 853694**
e-mail:
reservations@vanillapod-cridfordinn.com
web: www.vanillapod-cridfordinn.com
dir: *A38 take junct for Teign Valley, turn right follow signs Trusham for 4m*

Heritage enthusiasts will be in seventh heaven here, where researchers have pieced together a remarkable history dating back over a thousand years, putting a 9th-century longhouse on the site before a modern rebuild took place in the 13th century. A mosaic floor in the Vanilla Pod restaurant and what is probably the oldest surviving window frame in a secular building add immense warmth and character, as do the rough stone walls, old fireplaces and the general atmosphere of this architectural treasure, which has medieval masons' marks still visible above the bar. The only chill in the air may be from the ghost of a nun (the place also served as a nunnery), whilst the shade of a cavalier is also occasionally spotted abroad.

This picturesque thatched inn crouches like an owl below towering trees near a brook in the Teign Valley just a brace of miles from Dartmoor National Park; a pretty terrace is an ideal summertime spot to mull over the alfresco lunchtime dishes with a pint of local Teignworthy bitter.

Quite apart from the fine destination dining of the chic Vanilla Pod restaurant, the bar menu boasts dishes prepared from the finest Devonshire ingredients and changes regularly to reflect seasonal largesse – chargrilled 8oz prime Ivybridge rump steak with Teignworthy real ale battered onion rings, and slow-roasted Beadon Farm belly of pork on black garlic mash. In the Vanilla Pod, start with avocado, Brixham crab and prawn cocktail, followed by estate game such as pan-fried haunch of Teign Valley venison with braised red cabbage and red wine and thyme jus, or pan-fried local sea bass with fennel chips and tomato relish. Specials and vegetarian choices are on the blackboard near the bar.

Open all wk 11-3 6.15-11 (Sat 11am-11pm Sun noon-10.30)
Bar Meals L served all wk 12-2.30 D served all wk 7-9.30 Av main course £10
Restaurant L served Sun 12-1 booking required D served Tue-Sat 7-9.30 booking required Fixed menu price fr £26.50 Av 3 course à la carte fr £28.50 ⊕ FREE HOUSE ◀ Doom Bar, Otter Ale, Teignworthy Ales, Bays ♂ Thatchers. 🍷 10
Facilities Children's menu Children's portions Family room Garden Parking

Save on hotels. Book at **theAA.com/hotel**

DEVON 155 ENGLAND

PICK OF THE PUBS

The Digger's Rest

WOODBURY SALTERTON   Map 3 SY08

EX5 1PQ
☎ **01395 232375**   📄 **01395 232711**
e-mail: bar@diggersrest.co.uk
web: www.diggersrest.co.uk
dir: *2.5m from A3052. Signed from Westpoint Showground*

Standing in the delightful East Devon village of Woodbury Salterton, this picturesque free house is just a few minutes drive from the Exeter junction of the M5. The 500-year-old building with its thatched roof, thick stone and cob walls, heavy beams and log fire was originally a cider house. Today the choice on the bar is much wider but cider is still well represented with Westons Scrumpy and Stowford Press. Real ales feature Otter Bitter from Devon with guest appearances from other West Country brewers such as Exmoor, St Austell and Sharp's. Wine fans will appreciate the wine list which has been created by the independent Wine Merchant, Tanners of Shrewsbury.

Food here features fresh ingredients, simply cooked. The menus are created to make the best of seasonal produce. Sourcing locally plays a big role in freshness and quality control, and English and West Country produce is used wherever possible. Menus feature fish landed at Brixham and Looe, West Country

beef hung for 21 days and pork from a farm just up the road. Buying organic whenever possible, the kitchen is also committed to supporting farmers who practice good husbandry. As well as the main menu there is a blackboard which features special dishes the chef has created from prime cuts or rarer seasonal ingredients he has found.

Many of the dishes can be served as smaller portions for children, and there is also a children's menu. Whether you want to check your emails (free Wi-fi), have a drink, snack or a full meal, you will find a warm welcome at The Digger's Rest.

It's also worth checking the website for details of food clubs, quizzes and events.

Open all wk 11-3 5.30-11 (Sun 12-3.30 5.30-10.30) **Bar Meals** L served Mon-Sat noon-2.15, Sun 12-2.15 D served Mon-Sat 6.30-9.15, Sun 6.30-9 ⊕ FREE HOUSE ◀ Otter Bitter, guest ales from Exmoor, St Austell, Sharp's ♉ Westons Scrumpy, Stowford Press. **Facilities** Children's menu Children's portions Dogs allowed Garden Parking Wi-fi

Rose & Crown

Market Street, Yealmpton, Devon

01752 880223 • www.theroseandcrown.co.uk

*T*he Rose & Crown is an award winning food pub in Yealmpton and is one of the most popular eating-out places in Devon, offering excellent food, real ales and an extensive wine list. Our pub reflects the modern British Pub by offering a stylish and skilled approach to your pub experience. Our focus lies heavily on serving high quality 'restaurant standard' pub food that is affordable and satisfying, whilst adopting a village life approach to our main bar area. From the freshest local fish to the highest quality local meat the Rose & Crown really is an exceptional place to dine out in Devon. We recommend reservations in the dining area but also have a welcoming bar and garden for those who just want to pop in. We have a large car park and are disabled friendly! Yealmpton is a lovely Devon village a few miles outside Plymouth, just inside the South Hams and a short drive from some beautiful beaches. The Rose & Crown offers comfy sofas, a log fire and a welcoming atmosphere.

WIDECOMBE IN THE MOOR   Map 3 SX77

The Old Inn

TQ13 7TA ☎ 01364 621207 ▤ 01364 621407
e-mail: oldinn.widecombe@hall-woodhouse.co.uk
dir: *Telephone for directions*

Set in the heart of Dartmoor, this 600-year-old inn is a pub for all seasons and the ideal place for walkers. Sit outside in summer and admire the views, or enjoy the five log fires when the weather turns cold. Award-winning cask ales include seasonal guests, with plenty of wines by the glass. Lunchtime brings baked jackets and baguettes with a range of fillings, while those with larger appetites can tuck into plates of bangers and mash, chicken tikka masala, or grilled tuna steak.

Open all day all wk ⊕ HALL & WOODHOUSE ◖ Badger, Guest ales ♂ Applewood. **Facilities** Children welcome Children's menu Children's portions Dogs allowed Garden Parking

PICK OF THE PUBS

The Rugglestone Inn ♟

TQ13 7TF ☎ 01364 621327
e-mail: enquiries@rugglestoneinn.co.uk
dir: *From village centre take road by church towards Venton. Inn down hill on left*

With mighty Haytor to one horizon and shapely Hound Tor to another, this refreshingly unaltered old Dartmoor inn makes the most of its position at the heart of this enchanting wilderness. The Rugglestone itself rises behind the pub, whilst Widecombe's famous church acts as a beacon for ramblers and riders seeking out the inn's village location. Cosy little rooms, log fires and beers such as O'Hanlon's Yellowhammer and farmhouse ciders tapped straight from barrels stillaged behind the snug bar draw an appreciative crowd of regulars and thankful visitors. They are doubly-rewarded by the filling fare, a decent mix of rip-roaring pub staples and savoury dishes aimed at taking away the winter nip or fulfilling a summer eve's promise in the streamside beer garden. Smoked duck with plum sauce and salad; beef and ale, fish or chicken and leek pies; pan-fried lamb's liver or roasted vegetable lasagne are an essential part of the Dartmoor experience.

Open all wk Sat-Sun all day & BH **Bar Meals** L served all wk 12-2 D served all wk 6.30-9 **Restaurant** L served all wk 12-2 D served all wk 6.30-9 ⊕ FREE HOUSE ◖ Dartmoor Bitter, Butcombe, O'Hanlons Yellowhammer, Blackawton Original, Otter Bitter ♂ Ashton Press, Lower Widdon Farm, Ashridge Farm. ♟ 10 **Facilities** Children welcome Children's menu Children's portions Dogs allowed Garden Parking

WINKLEIGH   Map 3 SS60

PICK OF THE PUBS

The Duke of York ♟

Iddesleigh EX19 8BG
☎ 01837 810253 ▤ 01837 810253
dir: *Telephone for directions*

The atmosphere of this venerable thatched inn is blissfully unsullied by juke box, fruit machine or karaoke. Set deep in rural mid-Devon in a small hamlet, it was originally three cottages housing craftsmen who were rebuilding the parish church; local records accurately date this work to 1387. All the timeless features of a classic country pub remain - heavy old beams, scrubbed tables, farmhouse chairs and a huge inglenook fireplace with winter fires. Popular with all, it offers decent real ales (Cotleigh Tawny, for example) and hearty home cooking, with everything freshly prepared using local produce such as meat reared on nearby farms. Examples of bar meals taken from the large blackboard menu include rainbow trout, liver and bacon, and casseroles. From the dining room menu could come Dartmouth smokehouse salmon, followed by pork loin with port and tarragon sauce, then a choice of more than a dozen classic home-made desserts.

Open all day all wk 11am-11pm **Bar Meals** L served all wk 11-10 D served all wk 11-10 food served all day ⊕ FREE HOUSE ◖ Adnams Broadside, Cotleigh Tawny, Guest ales ♂ Winkleigh. ♟ 10 **Facilities** Children welcome Children's portions Dogs allowed Garden

The Kings Arms

Fore St EX19 8HQ ☎ 01837 83384 ▤ 01834 83055
e-mail: kingsarmswinkleigh@googlemail.com
dir: *Village signed from B3220 (Crediton to Torrington road)*

Traditional pub games are encouraged at this ancient thatched country inn situated in the centre of the village. Scrubbed pine tables, military memorabilia and traditional wooden settles set the scene, and wood-burning stoves warm the beamed bar and dining rooms in winter. The freshly made, locally sourced food ranges from sandwiches and hot snacks, to dishes like pork medallions in bacon, Lucy's fish pie, and steak and kidney parcels. The village's own Winkleigh cider is available and Devon cream teas are served every day.

Open all day all wk 11-11 (Sun noon-10.30)
Bar Meals L served Mon-Sat 11-9.30, Sun 12-9 D served Mon-Sat 11-9.30, Sun 12-9 food served all day
Restaurant L served Mon-Sat 11-9.30, Sun 12-9 D served Mon-Sat 11-9.30, Sun 12-9 food served all day ⊕ ENTERPRISE INNS ◖ Butcombe Bitter, Sharp's Doom Bar, Otter Bitter ♂ Winkleigh Cider. **Facilities** Children welcome Children's portions Dogs allowed Garden

WOODBURY SALTERTON   Map 3 SY08

PICK OF THE PUBS

The Digger's Rest

See Pick of the Pubs on page 155

YEALMPTON   Map 3 SX55

PICK OF THE PUBS

Rose & Crown

Market St PL8 2EB ☎ 01752 880223
e-mail: info@theroseandcrown.co.uk
web: www.theroseandcrown.co.uk
dir: *Telephone for directions*

From its classic brown and cream decor to the comfy leather sofas and open fire, the interior of this stylish bar-restaurant in the South Hams reflects a perfect balance between contemporary and traditional. When owner Simon Warner took it over a few years ago, he aimed to preserve the 'village local' atmosphere in the bar while serving restaurant standard food at affordable prices. A grand selection of real ales is backed by wines that are few in number but high on quality. The menu is also short, with nine or ten choices at each stage, but it proffers traditional classics with an extra touch of class, allowing the kitchen's focus on quality, freshness and local supply to be maintained. A typical three-course choice could start with smoked ham hock and wild mushroom terrine; continue with Brownstone pheasant breast wrapped in bacon with wholegrain mustard mash, buttered kale and onion gravy; and finish with dark chocolate tart with kumquats compôte and orange sorbet. The famous 'Old Mother Hubbard' cottage is directly opposite.

Open all wk Mon-Sat 12-2.30 6-11 (Sun all day)
Bar Meals L served all wk 12-2.30 D served all wk 6.30-9.30 Av main course £14 **Restaurant** L served all wk 12-2.30 booking required D served all wk 6.30-9.30 booking required Av 3 course à la carte fr £22 ⊕ FREE HOUSE ◖ Doom Bar, London Pride, Courage Best, IPA Greene King, Otter, Tribute ♂ Thatchers Gold. **Facilities** Children welcome Children's menu Children's portions Dogs allowed Garden Parking Wi-fi

See advert on opposite page

DORSET

ASKERSWELL · Map 4 SY59

The Spyway Inn ★★★★ INN ♥ NEW

DT2 9EP ☎ 01308 485250
e-mail: spywayinn@sky.com
dir: *From A35 follow Askerswell sign, then follow Spyway Inn sign*

This old beamed country inn, where smugglers plied their trade in Georgian times, undulates beside a high-hedged lane threading down from the spectacular Eggardon Hill hill fort to the Jurassic Coast World Heritage Site at nearby West Bay. Glorious Dorset countryside envelops the landscaped, sloping beer garden, a great locale to enjoy Otter Ales and sample locally sourced, home cooked fare like Dorset Smokies or fresh-baked pies. Handy for Dorchester and Bridport, the inn has attractive accommodation for those tempted to explore deepest rural England.

Open all wk 12-3 6-close **Bar Meals** L served all wk 12-3 D served all wk 6.30-9 **Restaurant** L served all wk 12-3 D served all wk 6.30-9 ⊕ FREE HOUSE ◄ Otter Ale & Bitter. **Facilities** Children welcome Children's menu Children's portions Play area Garden Parking Wi-fi **Rooms** 3

BISHOP'S CAUNDLE · Map 4 ST61

The White Hart ♥

DT9 5ND ☎ 01963 23519
e-mail: info@whitehartbishopscaundle.co.uk
dir: *From Salisbury take A3030 towards Sturminster Newton*

Deep in Blackmore Vale with views across rolling countryside from its garden, this 17th-century village pub has seen its fortunes restored following the arrival of new tenants in 2009. In a setting of thick stone walls, original old beams and a roaring log fire, you can quaff Hall & Woodhouse beers and tuck into some good pub food that utilises the best local seasonal produce, notably fresh fish. Typical dishes include black pudding and apple fritters; potted trout; local beer-battered fish and home-made chips; and home-made pies. There is a large pub garden and events throughout the year.

Open 12-2.30 5.30-11 Closed: Mon (seasonal closures) **Bar Meals** L served all wk 12-2.30 D served all wk 6.30-9.30 **Restaurant** L served all wk 12-2.30 booking required D served all wk 6.30-9.30 booking required ⊕ HALL & WOODHOUSE ◄ Badger 1st Gold, Tanglefoot, Seasonal ales, Fursty Ferret Ò Stowford Press. ♥ 20 **Facilities** Children welcome Children's menu Children's portions Play area Dogs allowed Garden Parking Wi-fi

BLANDFORD FORUM · Map 4 ST80

The Anvil Inn ★★★★ INN

Salisbury Rd, Pimperne DT11 8UQ
☎ 01258 453431   ▤ 01258 480182
e-mail: theanvil.inn@btconnect.com
dir: *Telephone for directions*

A thatched roof, crooked beams and a cavernous fireplace are just a few of the rustic charms of this family-run 16th-century inn located in the pretty village of Pimperne, two miles from Blandford Forum. The two bars offer a range of real ales and light bites, while the charming beamed restaurant with log fire offers a full menu using ingredients from local Dorset producers and growers as well as fresh fish landed on the Dorset coast. Try the Dorset sausages with garlic mash and onion gravy, or pan-fried salmon with lemon herb butter. In summer months, meals can be enjoyed outside. There are 12 en suite bedrooms available.

Open all wk **Bar Meals** L served all wk 12-9.30 D served all wk 12-9.30 Av main course £13 food served all day **Restaurant** L served all wk 12-9.30 D served all wk 12-9.30 Av 3 course à la carte fr £25 food served all day ⊕ FREE HOUSE ◄ Guinness, London Pride, IPA, Copper Ale. **Facilities** Children welcome Dogs allowed Garden Parking **Rooms** 12

Crown Hotel ♥

West St DT11 7AJ ☎ 01258 456626   ▤ 01258 451084
e-mail: crownhotel.blandford@hall-woodhouse.co.uk
dir: *M27 junct 1 W onto A31 to A350 junct, right to Blandford Forum. 100mtrs from town bridge*

Enjoying views across the water meadows of the River Stour and the Dorset market town of Blandford Forum, this 18th-century coaching inn replaces the original inn destroyed by fire in 1731. A more modern refurbishment has lost none of the historic character of this charming inn. An extensive bar menu includes sandwiches and light bites. In the restaurant, expect duck and herb pâté with fig relish to start. Mains might include Stargazy pie of crayfish, prawns, scallops, monkfish and smoked haddock, or lemon and garlic roast chicken. There is a classic formal garden to enjoy in summer.

Open all wk 10am-11.30pm (Sun 12-10.30) **Bar Meals** L served all wk 12-3 D served all wk 6-9 **Restaurant** L served all wk 12-3 D served all wk 6-10 ⊕ HALL & WOODHOUSE ◄ Badger Tanglefoot, Badger 1st Gold. ♥ 12 **Facilities** Children welcome Children's menu Children's portions Dogs allowed Garden Parking Wi-fi

BOURTON · Map 4 ST73

The White Lion Inn

High St SP8 5AT ☎ 01747 840866
e-mail: office@whitelionbourton.co.uk
dir: *Off A303, opposite B3092 to Gillingham*

Dating from 1723, the White Lion is a beautiful, stone-built, creeper clad Dorset inn. The bar is cosy, with beams, flagstones and an open fire, and serves a range of real beers and ciders. Imaginative menus draw on the wealth of quality local produce, and dishes range from twice-baked Cheddar soufflé or duck rillette to Moroccan tagine or roast venison.

Open all wk Mon-Thu noon-3 5-11 (Fri-Sat Sun all day) ⊕ ADMIRAL TAVERNS ◄ Otter Amber, Sharp's Doom Bar, St Austell Tribute Ò Thatchers. **Facilities** Children welcome Children's menu Children's portions Dogs allowed Garden Parking Wi-fi

BRIDPORT · Map 4 SY49

The George Hotel

4 South St DT6 3NQ ☎ 01308 423187
dir: *In town centre, 1.5m from West Bay*

Handsome Georgian town house, with a Victorian-style bar and a mellow atmosphere, which bustles all day, and offers a traditional English breakfast, decent morning coffee and a good menu featuring fresh local plaice, natural smoked haddock, avocado and bacon salad, and the famous rabbit and bacon pie. Everything is home cooked using local produce and can be enjoyed with a selection of Palmers real ales.

Open all wk 10am-11.30pm (Fri-Sat 10am-12.30am Sun noon-10.30) ⊕ PALMERS ◄ Palmers - IPA, Copper & 200, Tally Ho. **Facilities** Children welcome Children's portions Family room Dogs allowed **Notes** ⊛

Save on hotels. Book at **theAA.com/hotel**

DORSET 159 **ENGLAND**

PICK OF THE PUBS

The Shave Cross Inn INN 🍷

Shave Cross, Marshwood Vale DT6 6HW
☎ 01308 868358 📠 01308 867064
e-mail: roy.warburton@virgin.net
dir: *From Bridport take B3162. In 2m left signed 'Broadoak/Shave Cross', then Marshwood*

During the long and troubled reign of Edward III, the landlord of the day acted as both victualler and barber, shaving the heads of monks before they visited the nearby shrine to St Candida and St Cross. Perhaps they and passing pilgrims also tarried a while at the skittles alley at the foot of the garden; it's believed to be of Saxon origin and the oldest in the Kingdom. Dorset thatch roofs the alley and the ancient inn itself, secluded along lanes in Marshwood Vale deep in Thomas Hardy country. Ducking your head to avoid the low beams, notice the fossils embedded in the flagstoned floors here near the commanding inglenook fireplace. A look at the bar is rewarded with pump-clips announcing the wares of Dorset micro-breweries; real ciders too are a draw. The food here is both unusual and inspirational, with a strong Caribbean influence together with dishes originating as far afield as Fiji. A 'Genesis' starter can be seared local scallops with a banana relish and basil oil, leading into the menu of mains, featuring Louisiana blackened chicken with cream and pepper sauce or Zarzuela, a seafood medley in a mild coconut curry sauce. There are individually designed luxury bedrooms here.

Open 11-3 6-11.30 Closed: Mon (ex BH)
Bar Meals L served Tue-Sun 12-2.30 D served Tue-Sun 6-7 **Restaurant** L served Tue-Sun 12-2.30 booking required D served Tue-Sun 6-9 (closed Sun eve winter) booking required ⊕ FREE HOUSE ◀ Local guest ales, Branoc (Branscombe Vale), Quay Dorset Brewing Co ♂ Old Rosie, Thatchers, Gold Pitfield. 🍷 8
Facilities Children welcome Children's menu Children's portions Play area Dogs allowed Garden Parking Wi-fi **Rooms** 7

The West Bay

Station Rd, West Bay DT6 4EW
☎ 01308 422157 📠 01308 459717
e-mail: pcrisp.thewestbayhotel@google.com
dir: *From A35 (Bridport by-pass) take B3157 (2nd exit) towards West Bay. After mini-rdbt 1st left (Station Road). Pub on left*

Built in 1739, this traditional bar/restaurant lies at the foot of East Cliff, part of the impressive World Heritage Jurassic Coast, and in the picturesque harbour of West Bay. The pub specialises in fish and seafood with the latest catch shown as blackboard specials. Perhaps choose Thai crab cakes with sweet chilli prawn butter; then bouillabaisse with a hot baguette. For meat eaters there's a good choice of steaks or maybe pot-roasted pork belly and cider jus. Palmers Brewery in Bridport furnishes the real ales, or you can ring the changes with a pint of Thatcher's Gold cider.

Open all wk Mon-Thu noon-3 6-11 (Fri-Sun all day)
Bar Meals L served all wk 12-2.30 D served all wk 6-9
Restaurant L served all wk 12-2.30 booking required D served all wk 6-9 booking required ⊕ PALMERS ◀ Palmers IPA, Palmers Copper, Palmers 200, Guinness, Tally Ho! ♂ Thatchers Gold. **Facilities** Children welcome Children's portions Dogs allowed Garden Parking

BUCKHORN WESTON Map 4 ST72

PICK OF THE PUBS

Stapleton Arms 🍷

Church Hill SP8 5HS ☎ 01963 370396
e-mail: relax@thestapletonarms.com
dir: *3.5m from Wincanton in village centre*

Stylish but unstuffy, the Stapleton Arms is a new style country pub with rooms, tucked away in a pretty village on the Somerset, Wiltshire and Dorset border. There's an elegant dining room, secluded garden and a spacious bar offering real ales such as Butcombe and Moor's Revival. In addition, the specialist cider and apple juice list includes draught ciders like Cheddar Valley and Thatcher's Gold. The freshest seasonal ingredients from local producers lie behind an innovative modern menu. Starters like ham hock and apricot terrine with green tomato chutney herald main course offerings that might include slow cooked Old Spot pork belly with Bramley apple mash, cauliflower purée, black pudding and mustard gravy. Pannacotta with stewed stoned fruits is a typical dessert. As well as regular beer tastings, festivals and events, there are some great walks in the area, and picnics and maps can be provided by the helpful staff.

Open all wk 11-3 6-11 (Sun noon-10.30)
Bar Meals L served all wk 12-3 D served all wk 6-10 Av main course £12.50 **Restaurant** L served all wk 12-3 booking required D served all wk 6-10 booking required Av 3 course à la carte fr £25 ⊕ FREE HOUSE ◀ Butcombe, Moor's Revival ♂ Thatchers Cheddar Valley, Orchard Pig, Thatchers Gold. 🍷 30
Facilities Children welcome Children's menu Children's portions Play area Dogs allowed Garden Beer festival Parking Wi-fi

BUCKLAND NEWTON Map 4 ST60

PICK OF THE PUBS

Gaggle of Geese 🍷

DT2 7BS ☎ 01300 345249
e-mail: goose@thegaggle.co.uk
web: www.thegaggle.co.uk
dir: *On B3143 N of Dorchester*

An extraordinary village inn with a heart of gold, the Gaggle harks back to times past when many villages could claim such a retreat. Now as rare as hen's teeth (there's a twice-yearly poultry auction here, so who knows...); step from the lane into the large front parlour, complete with sofas, wingbacks in front of the welcoming fire, bookshelves, matchboarding and scrubbed tables. A glance at the bar reveals well lubricated handpumps dispensing beers from Hop Back and Otter breweries, farmhouse ciders and a perry from the local Bridge Farm. The treats continue with a skittles alley, whilst the grounds host a cricket pitch, croquet lawn and orchard. Just like the Tardis, the inside expands to reveal a sizeable, well appointed restaurant, where top-notch meals include many sourced from the home farm of landlord Mark Hammick. Be tempted by a starter of Pecker's pan-fried pigeon breast with poached egg, lardons and pan juices, but do leave room for pan-fried loin and fillet of Cheselbourne venison with miniature venison cottage pie, braised red cabbage and fondant potato; or crispy skinned sea bass with green Thai butternut squash broth, completing with mulled wine poached pear with Blue Vinny ice cream.

Open all wk 10-3 6-11.30 (Sat-Sun all day in summer)
Bar Meals L served Mon-Sat 12-2, Sun 12-3 booking required D served Mon-Sat 7-9, Sun 6.30-8.30 booking required **Restaurant** L served Mon-Sat 12-2, Sun 12-3 booking required D served Mon-Sat 7-9, Sun 6.30-8.30 booking required ⊕ FREE HOUSE ◀ Ringwood, Proper Job, Tribute, Hop Back Summer Lightning, Otter Amber ♂ Thatchers Gold, Lulworth Skipper, Bridge Farm Perry. 🍷 10 **Facilities** Children welcome Children's portions Play area Dogs allowed Garden Parking Wi-fi

BURTON BRADSTOCK — Map 4 SY48

PICK OF THE PUBS

The Anchor Inn ♀

High St DT6 4QF ☎ 01308 897228
e-mail: info@dorset-seafood-restaurant.co.uk
web: www.dorset-seafood-restaurant.co.uk
dir: 2m SE of Bridport on B3157 in centre of Burton Bradstock

The Southwest Coastal Path threads along the coast close to this homely old inn; ramblers who've just challenged the famous Chesil Beach or families catching the sun on the lovely beaches of the Jurassic Coast World Heritage Site willingly travel slightly inland for the fabulous range of seafood dishes for which The Anchor is widely renowned. The decor is distinctly maritime, exampling the many and varied ways that the wealth of the sea is harvested for the benefit of diners keen to sample the very best Dorset can provide. Mussels are a favourite, whilst fishermen deliver the freshest lobsters, crab and soles to the door. A particular favourite is a dish of hand-dived scallops, harvested from nearby West Bay and served with bacon and mushroom sauce or tangy salsa. Mike Harris, the long-serving head chef, relishes creating new dishes, including fillets of red mullet with a chilli prawn and white bean cassoulet. Barbary duck or Cajun blackened fillets are amongst the meat options, accompanied by beers from the likes of Otter Brewery or a glass from a well-balanced selection of wines.

Open all wk 11.30-3 5.30-12 (Sat-Sun 11.30am-mdnt) **Bar Meals** L served all wk 12-2 booking required D served all wk 6-9.30 booking required **Restaurant** L served all wk 12-2 booking required D served all wk 6-9.30 booking required ⊕ PUNCH TAVERNS ◀ Otter Bitter, Tribute, Theakston Best Bitter, John Smith's Ŏ Thatchers Traditional. ♀ 10 **Facilities** Children welcome Children's menu Children's portions Dogs allowed Parking Wi-fi

CATTISTOCK — Map 4 SY59

Fox & Hounds Inn

Duck St DT2 0JH ☎ 01300 320444 📠 01300 320444
e-mail: lizflight@yahoo.co.uk
dir: On A37, between Dorchester & Yeovil, follow signs to Cattistock

This attractive award-winning 17th-century inn is situated in a picturesque village. Expect a bar full of locals; children, dogs and even chickens under foot; and a traditional atmosphere engendered by ancient beams, open fires in winter and huge inglenooks, one with an original bread oven. Palmers ales are on tap, along with Thatchers ciders, while home-made meals embrace dressed Portland crab salad with fries; grilled sea bass; and slow-roast pork belly with cauliflower cheese.

Open 12-2.30 7-11 (Thu-Sat 12-2.30 6-11) Closed: Mon L **Bar Meals** L served Tue-Sun 12-2 D served Tue-Sat 7-11 booking required Av main course £8.95 **Restaurant** L served Tue-Sun 12-2 D served Tue-Sat 7-11 booking required ⊕ PALMERS ◀ Palmers IPA, Copper Ale, Palmers 200, Dorset Gold Ŏ Thatchers Traditional, Thatchers Gold. **Facilities** Children welcome Children's portions Play area Dogs allowed Garden Parking Wi-fi

CHEDINGTON — Map 4 ST40

Winyards Gap Inn ♀

Chedington Ln DT8 3HY ☎ 01935 891244
e-mail: enquiries@winyardsgap.com
dir: 5m S of Crewkerne on A356

This family-run free house enjoys stunning views from its location, tucked beneath an ancient earthwork and surrounded by National Trust property. Sitting in the beamed bar with a pint of Piddle ale (named after a Dorset river) in one hand, menu in the other, choose pan-fried calves' liver with smoked bacon on bubble and squeak with sage and roasted shallot sauce; sweet potato, leek, spinach and feta cheese bake with Macadamia nut crumble and Evershot bread; or 21-day matured West Country beef with chips, field mushroom, slow-dried tomatoes and garlic butter. There are regular quiz and jazz nights held. The terraced garden is a picturesque spot in summer.

Open all wk 11.30-3 6-11 (Sat-Sun 11.30-11) Closed: 25 Dec **Bar Meals** L served Mon-Sat 12-2 D served all wk 6-9 **Restaurant** L served all wk 12-2 booking required D served all wk 6-9 booking required ⊕ FREE HOUSE ◀ Doom Bar, Exmoor Ale, Otter Ale, Dorset Piddle Ŏ Thatchers Gold, Old Rosie, 1st Quality Cider. ♀ 8 **Facilities** Children welcome Children's menu Children's portions Dogs allowed Garden Parking Wi-fi

CHIDEOCK — Map 4 SY49

The Anchor Inn

Seatown DT6 6JU ☎ 01297 489215
dir: On A35 turn S in Chideock opp church & follow single track rd for 0.75m to beach

Originally a smugglers' haunt, The Anchor has an incredible setting in a little cove surrounded by National Trust land, beneath Golden Cap. The large sun terrace and cliff-side beer garden overlooking the beach make it a premier destination for throngs of holidaymakers in the summer, while on winter weekdays it is blissfully quiet. The wide-ranging menu starts with snacks and light lunches - three types of ploughman's and a range of sandwiches might take your fancy. For something more substantial choose a freshly caught fish dish accompanied with one of the real ales or ciders.

Open all wk 11.30am-10.30pm ⊕ PALMERS ◀ Palmers 200 Premium Ale, IPA, Copper Ale Ŏ Thatchers Tradition, Thatchers Pear. **Facilities** Children welcome Children's menu Children's portions Family room Dogs allowed Garden Parking

CHRISTCHURCH — Map 5 SZ19

The Ship In Distress

66 Stanpit BH23 3NA
☎ 01202 485123 📠 01202 483997
e-mail: enquiries@theshipindistress.com
web: www.theshipindistress.com
dir: Telephone for directions

Local fish and seafood dominates the imaginative menu at this 300-year-old smugglers' pub close to Mudeford Quay and Stanpits Nature Reserve. Naturally, both cosy bars and the restaurant are awash with nautical memorabilia to keep its smuggling history alive. Bag a seat by the woodburner, sup a pint of local Ringwood ale and tuck into traditional fish and chips or cottage pie, or head next door for scallops in garlic and herb butter, or sea bass with samphire and saffron cream sauce, followed by sticky toffee pudding. In summer make the most of the Shellfish Bar on the sun-trap terrace.

Open all day all wk 11am-mdnt (Sun 11-11) **Bar Meals** L served Mon-Fri 12-2, Sat-Sun 12-2.30 D served Sun-Thu 6.30-9, Fri-Sat 6.30-9.30 Av main course £5.95 **Restaurant** L served Mon-Fri 12-2, Sat-Sun 12-2.30 D served Sun-Thu 6.30-9, Fri-Sat 6.30-9.30 Av 3 course à la carte fr £29.50 ⊕ PUNCH TAVERNS ◀ Ringwood Best, Fortyniner, Adnams Broadside, Guest ales. **Facilities** Children welcome Children's menu Children's portions Dogs allowed Garden Parking Wi-fi

CHURCH KNOWLE   Map 4 SY98

The New Inn ⚐

BH20 5NQ ☎ 01929 480357 🖷 01929 480357
e-mail: maurice@newinn-churchknowle.co.uk
web: www.newinnchurchknowle.co.uk
dir: *From Wareham take A351 towards Swanage. At Corfe Castle turn right for Church Knowle. Pub in village centre*

At the heart of the Isle of Purbeck, views from the grassy garden of this part-thatched village inn stretch across the Corfe Valley towards lofty Swyre Head, whilst the mellow ruins of Corfe Castle are an easy walk away. Dressed stone walls and an open fire feature in the lofty, convivial bar, where Dorset Beers from Weymouth are a favoured tipple; locally-made elderflower bubbly also features and there's a great walk-in wine cellar. The freshest home-cooked food includes catch of the day from local boats, or perhaps Poacher's casserole to tempt; smaller appetites may snack on Dorset Blue Vinny soup, laced with wine and cream.

Open 11-3 6-11 Closed: Mon eve Jan & Feb
Bar Meals L served all wk 12-2.15 booking required D served all wk 6-9.15 booking required Av main course £10 **Restaurant** L served all wk 12-2.15 booking required D served all wk 6-9.15 booking required Fixed menu price fr £9.70 ⊕ PUNCH TAVERNS ◀ Old Speckled Hen, Jurassic, St Austell Tribute, changing guest ales Ŏ Old Rosie, Stowford Press. ⚐ 10 **Facilities** Children welcome Children's menu Children's portions Family room Garden Parking

CORFE CASTLE   Map 4 SY98

The Greyhound Inn

The Square BH20 5EZ
☎ 01929 480205 🖷 01929 480205
e-mail: eat@greyhoundcorfe.co.uk
dir: *W from Bournemouth, take A35 to Dorchester, after 5m left onto A351, 10m to Corfe Castle*

A classic pub set beneath the ruins of Corfe Castle, the Greyhound warmly welcomes locals and visitors, children and pets. Its large sun-drenched beer garden with views of Swanage Steam Railway is ideal for sampling a summer ale or cider. Food for all the family make it a popular choice for walkers, cyclists and nearby campsites, but emphasis is nonetheless put on sourcing and cooking fresh seasonal produce in dishes such as Dorset crab salad; prime Dorset beef steaks; and home-cooked Wiltshire ham. The pub hosts food, beer and cider festivals throughout the year.

Open all day all wk ⊕ ENTERPRISE INNS ◀ Ringwood Best, Sharp's Doom Bar, London Pride Ŏ Westons Organic, Stowford Press, Thatchers Gold.
Facilities Children welcome Children's menu Children's portions Play area Family room Dogs allowed Garden Wi-fi

CORFE MULLEN   Map 4 SY99

The Coventry Arms ◉

Mill St BH21 3RH ☎ 01258 857284
e-mail: info@coventryarms.co.uk
dir: *On A31 (Wimborne-Dorchester road)*

Built in the 13th-century, this friendly pub was once a watermill with its own island. Beer is served direct from the cask, while an annual spring seafood festival attracts many visitors. The inn specialises in fish and game from local estates, and most of the produce is sourced from within the area. Expect such creative dishes as open ravioli of monkfish medallions and mussels; or pan-seared Sika deer's liver with smoked bacon. There's a lovely garden to enjoy in warmer weather. Change of hands.

Open all wk 11am-11pm ⊕ ENTERPRISE INNS ◀ Timothy Taylor Landlord, Guest ales Ŏ Stowford Press.
Facilities Children welcome Children's menu Children's portions Dogs allowed Garden Parking

EAST MORDEN   Map 4 SY99

PICK OF THE PUBS

The Cock & Bottle

BH20 7DL ☎ 01929 459238
dir: *From A35 W of Poole turn right B3075, pub 0.5m on left*

A cob-walled Dorset longhouse built some 400 years ago, the pub acquired a brick skin around 1800 and remained thatched until 1966. The original interiors are comfortably rustic with quaint, low-beamed ceilings, attractive paintings and lots of nooks and crannies around the log fires. Additional to the lively locals' bar are a lounge bar and modern rear restaurant extension. Lovely pastoral views over farmland include the pub's paddock, where vintage car and motorcycle meetings are occasionally hosted during the summer. Bar and light lunch menus are supported by a daily carte and Badger ales, and a children's choice is also available.

Open all wk 11.30-2.30 6-11 (Sun noon-3 7-10.30)
Bar Meals L served all wk 12-2 D served Mon-Sat 6-9 (Sun 7-9) **Restaurant** L served all wk 12-2 booking required D served Mon-Sat 6-9 (Sun 7-9) booking required ⊕ HALL & WOODHOUSE ◀ Badger Dorset Best, Tanglefoot & Sussex. **Facilities** Children welcome Children's menu Dogs allowed Garden Parking

EVERSHOT   Map 4 ST50

PICK OF THE PUBS

The Acorn Inn ★★★★ INN ◉ ⚐

DT2 0JW ☎ 01935 83228 🖷 01935 83707
e-mail: stay@acorn-inn.co.uk
web: www.acorn-inn.co.uk
dir: *A303 to Yeovil, Dorchester Rd, on A37 right to Evershot*

The Sow and Acorn in Thomas Hardy's *Tess of the D'Urbervilles* was based on this rural 16th-century village inn. Surrounded by unspoiled countryside, The Acorn is an excellent base from which to explore Hardy Country and many of the comfortable bedrooms boast four-poster beds. Throughout the oak-panelled bars and elegantly decorated dining areas, both warmed by blazing winter log fires, there's some imaginative food to choose from. Using local, seasonal produce from local farms and estates, the modern British repertoire takes in twice-baked Dorset goat's cheese soufflé with walnuts and grapes; woodland mushroom risotto with Parmesan and truffle oil; braised belly of pork with apple mash, glazed carrots, spinach and sage jus; casserole of Melbury Estate venison en croute with truffle mash and winter vegetables. More rustic and traditional bar meals include ploughman's, beef burger and chips, and steak and kidney pudding. There are some wonderful walks from the front door so don't forget to pack your boots. Look out for annual beer and cider festivals.

Open all day all wk 11am-11.30pm **Bar Meals** L served all wk 12-2 D served all wk 7-9 Av main course £10 **Restaurant** L served all wk 12-2 booking required D served all wk 7-9 booking required Av 3 course à la carte fr £30 ⊕ FREE HOUSE ◀ Sharp's Doom Bar, Otter Ŏ Thatchers Gold, Thatchers Scrumpy. ⚐ 11 **Facilities** Children welcome Children's portions Family room Dogs allowed Garden Beer festival Parking Wi-fi **Rooms** 10

FARNHAM — Map 4 ST91

PICK OF THE PUBS

The Museum Inn ♀

DT11 8DE ☎ 01725 516261
e-mail: enquiries@museuminn.co.uk
dir: *From Salisbury take A354 to Blandford Forum, 12m. Farnham signed on right. Pub in village centre*

An award-winning free house and restaurant set in the heart of rural Dorset, this part-thatched country inn has attracted Hollywood celebrities and top chefs alike. It was built in the 17th century by the father of modern archaeology, General Pitt-Rivers, who established one of his museums nearby. Today's sympathetically refurbished traditional inn retains original features like the inglenook fireplace and flagged stone floors and, liberally endowed with antique furniture, the atmosphere is warm and relaxing. In the kitchen, head chef Ricky Ford sources seasonal produce locally for the modern British dishes served in both the bar and The Shed restaurant, open Friday and Saturday nights and for Sunday lunch. Slow-cooked Gloucestershire Old Spot pork belly; Ashcombe hare and venison pie; pan-roasted fillet of brill; and wild mushroom lasagne are among dishes listed. Twelve of the cellars' excellent wines are served by the glass, and there are locally brewed real ales including the inn's own ale.

Open all wk noon-3 6-11 **Bar Meals** L served all wk 12-2 D served all wk 7-9 Av main course £10 **Restaurant** L served Sun 12-3 booking required D served Fri-Sat 7-9.30 booking required Av 3 course à la carte fr £27 ⊕ FREE HOUSE ◀ Sixty, Double Drop, House ale Both Barrels Ŏ Stowford Press, Westons Organic. ♀ 12 **Facilities** Children welcome Children's menu Children's portions Dogs allowed Garden Parking

GILLINGHAM — Map 4 ST82

The Kings Arms Inn ♀

East Stour Common SP8 5NB ☎ 01747 838325
e-mail: nrosscampbell@aol.com
dir: *4m W of Shaftesbury on A30*

This family-run village inn makes a great base for exploring Dorset's countryside and coast. A 200-year-old free house, it has a public bar with a log fire, several dining rooms and an enclosed acre of attractive beer garden. The menus offer an extensive choice of restaurant fare and traditional pub grub. Choices might include Devon free-range duck breast, gratin potatoes and black pepper sauce; traditional Greek spanakopita; slow braised shank of new season lamb with light grain mustard mash; pan-fried sea bass with sautéed king prawns. Look to the blackboard specials for the range of home made desserts.

Open all wk **Bar Meals** L served Mon-Sat 12-2.30, Sun 12-9.15 booking required D served Mon-Sat 5.30-9.15, Sun 12-9.15 booking required Av main course £11 **Restaurant** L served Mon-Sat 12-2.30, Sun 12-9.15 booking required D served Mon-Sat 5.30-9.15, Sun 12-9.15 booking required Av 3 course à la carte fr £22 ⊕ FREE HOUSE ◀ Copper Ale, Tribute, Wadworth 6X. **Facilities** Children welcome Children's menu Children's portions Family room Dogs allowed Garden Parking Wi-fi

GUSSAGE ALL SAINTS — Map 4 SU01

The Drovers Inn ♀

BH21 5ET ☎ 01258 840084
e-mail: info@thedroversinn.biz
dir: *A31 Ashley Heath rdbt, right onto B3081 follow signs*

A rural 16th-century pub with fine terrace and wonderful views from the garden, so it's something of a surprise to know it was rescued from closure in 2000. Its refurbished interior retains plenty of traditional appeal with flagstone floors and oak furniture. Landlords Jo and Jason are proud of the welcome they provide – ensuring, for example, that drinkers are never moved from tables to accommodate diners. Ales from Ringwood include seasonal guests, and the menu features carefully chosen rare breed meats, vegetables from new Covent Garden via a local supplier, and fresh seafood from Poole. There is a beer festival around Easter time.

Open all wk 12-3 6-12 (Sat-Sun & BH all day) Closed: 26 Dec **Bar Meals** L served all wk 12-2 D served all wk 6-9 Av main course £9.50 **Restaurant** L served all wk 12-2 D served all wk 6-9 ⊕ RINGWOOD BREWERY ◀ Ringwood Best, Old Thumper, Ringwood seasonal ales, Fortyniner, Guest ales Ŏ Thatchers Gold, Thatchers Traditional. ♀ 10 **Facilities** Children welcome Children's menu Children's portions Dogs allowed Garden Beer festival Parking Wi-fi

KING'S STAG — Map 4 ST71

The Greenman

DT10 2AY ☎ 01258 817338 🖹 01258 818358
dir: *E of Sherborne on A3030*

Legend has it that King's Stag in the Blackmore Vale owes its name to Henry III's favourite white hart, hunted down and killed by a local nobleman. Built around 1775 and full of oak beams, the pub has five separate dining areas where you can order anything from a snack to a banquet. The Sunday carvery offers a choice of five meats and eight vegetables - booking is essential. Children will enjoy the play area while parents can relax and enjoy a drink. Recent change of hands.

Open all wk 11-3 5.30-11 ⊕ ENTERPRISE INNS ◀ Exmoor, Spitfire, HBC, London Pride, Old Speckled Hen. **Facilities** Children welcome Play area Family room Dogs allowed Garden Parking

LODERS — Map 4 SY49

Loders Arms ♀

DT6 3SA ☎ 01308 422431
e-mail: mike.webb@orange.net
dir: *Off A3066, 2m NE of Bridport*

This 17th-century, creeper-covered local, tucked away in a pretty village near the Dorset coast, is run by long-term Palmers Brewery tenants, Mike and Julie Webb. Child- and dog-friendly, it has a patio and garden with views over Boarsbarrow Hill. Alternatively, bag a seat in the long cosy bar with warming winter fires or in the homely

dining room for beef and Stilton pie, home-cooked ham with egg and chips, or Brie, mushroom and nut Wellington, all prepared with the best of local produce. Look out for theme evenings and summer barbecues.

Open all wk **Bar Meals** L served all wk 12-2 booking required D served all wk 6.30-9 Av main course £12.50 **Restaurant** L served all wk 12-2 D served all wk 6.30-9 Fixed menu price fr £12.50 ⊕ PALMERS ◀ Palmers Copper, Palmers IPA, Palmers 200, Tally Ho Ŏ Taunton Traditional. ♀ 8 **Facilities** Children welcome Children's menu Children's portions Dogs allowed Garden Parking Wi-fi

LOWER ANSTY — Map 4 ST70

The Fox Inn ★★★★ INN ♀

DT2 7PN ☎ 01258 880328 🖹 01258 881440
e-mail: fox@anstyfoxinn.co.uk
web: www.anstyfoxinn.co.uk
dir: *A35 from Dorchester towards Poole for 4m, exit signed Piddlehinton/Athelhampton House, left to Cheselbourne, then right. Pub in village opposite post office*

The 250-year-old house was built for Charles Hall, later to co-found Blandford's Hall & Woodhouse Brewery. When Ansty's original Fox burnt down in 1915, the Woodhouse family decided to move it to the family home. Badger beers are, naturally enough, served in the bar. The oak-panelled main restaurant is now augmented by a light and airy garden eatery. Restaurant food proffers terrine of pressed pigeon, pheasant and hock with fig chutney; seafood and shellfish pie; and roast butternut squash, cherry tomato and Parmesan risotto. Comfortable accommodation is available.

Open all day all wk **Bar Meals** L served all wk 12-2.30 D served all wk 6.30-9 **Restaurant** L served all wk 12-2.30 D served all wk 6.30-9 ⊕ HALL & WOODHOUSE ◀ Badger Tanglefoot, Badger Best, Badger Smooth, seasonal guest ale. ♀ 12 **Facilities** Children welcome Children's menu Children's portions Dogs allowed Garden Parking Wi-fi **Rooms** 11

Save on hotels. Book at **theAA.com/hotel**

DORSET 163 **ENGLAND**

The Mariners ★★★★ INN ◉ NEW

Silver St DT7 3HS ☎ 01297 442753
e-mail: enquiries@hotellymeregis.co.uk
dir: *From A35 onto A3052 to Lyme Regis. In town bear right into Silver St. 350mtrs to establishment*

This 17th-century coaching inn is steeped in Lyme's fossiling history. Beatrix Potter is said to have stayed here and taken inspiration from her stay to write *Little Pig Robinson* – The Mariners is pictured in the book. Recently refurbished, the building combines traditional character with modern style. Enjoy pints of Otter Bright in the comfortable bar or local fish and seafood in the restaurant – mussels Provençale might be followed by slow roasted pork belly with grain mustard mash and Calvados sauce. Many of the guest rooms have views over the bay.

Open all day all wk **Bar Meals** L served all wk 12-2 D served all wk 6.30-9 Av main course £9.50 **Restaurant** L served all wk 12-2 D served all wk 6.30-9 booking required Fixed menu price fr £14.95 Av 3 course à la carte fr £19.95 ⊕ FREE HOUSE ◀ Otter Bright, Mighty Hop Mighty Red IPA ♂ Thatchers.
Facilities Children welcome Children's menu Children's portions Garden Parking Wi-fi **Rooms** 14

Pilot Boat Inn ♥

Bridge St DT7 3QA ☎ 01297 443157
dir: *Telephone for directions*

Old smuggling and sea rescue tales are associated with this busy town centre pub, close to the seafront. However its biggest claim to fame is as the birthplace of the original Lassie, Hollywood's favourite collie. Along with Palmers ales, there is a good range of food on regularly changing menus. Sandwiches, salads and cold platters are offered, plus local crab, real scampi and chips, and other fresh fish as available. There's also a good vegetarian choice.

Open all day all wk Closed: 25 Dec **Bar Meals** food served all day **Restaurant** food served all day ⊕ PALMERS ◀ Palmers, IPA, 200, Bridport Bitter. ♥ 9
Facilities Children welcome Children's menu Children's portions Dogs allowed Garden

The Hambro Arms ♥

DT11 0BP ☎ 01258 880233
e-mail: info@hambroarms.co.uk
dir: *A354 (Dorchester to Blandford road), turn off at Royal Oak*

The thirty-six identical cottages lining the village street were built in 1780 to replace an original settlement that interfered with the view of Lord Milton, the local landowner. The pub, dating from the same time, is owned by a village partnership devoted to providing exceptional, largely locally sourced food. Their classics include ploughman's, home-made steak and Guinness pie, ale-battered cod and chips, and Piddle ale pork and leek sausages. A beer festival is held in July.

Open all wk 11.30-3 6-11 (Sat-Sun 11.30am-11.30pm) **Bar Meals** L served Mon-Fri 12-2.30, Sat-Sun 12-3 D served Mon-Thu 6-9, Fri-Sat 6-9.30 Av main course £9.50 **Restaurant** L served Mon-Fri 12-2.30, Sat-Sun 12-3 D served Mon-Thu 6-9, Fri-Sat 6-9.30 ◀ Ringwood, Piddle Ales, Durdle Door ♂ Stowford Press. ♥ 8
Facilities Children welcome Children's menu Garden Beer festival Parking

The Coppleridge Inn ★★★ INN ♥

SP7 9HW ☎ 01747 851980 📄 01747 851858
e-mail: thecoppleridgeinn@btinternet.com
web: www.coppleridge.com
dir: *Take A350 towards Warminster for 1.5m, turn left at brown tourist sign. Follow signs to inn*

Formerly a working farm, this 18th-century building still retains plenty of traditional features, including flagstone floors and log fires. Run by the Goodinge family for nearly 20 years, it offers an excellent range of real ales and a constantly-changing menu of sophisticated pub dishes such as grilled local brown trout with a rocket and Parmesan salad, or tenderloin of pork stuffed with mozzarella and pesto and wrapped in bacon. Outside there is a large garden and terrace with views of Blackmore Vale, and a secure children's playground. There are ten spacious bedrooms available situated around a converted courtyard. Look out for speciality food nights.

Open all wk 11-3 5-11 (Sat 11am-mdnt Sun noon-11) **Bar Meals** L served all wk 12-2.30 D served all wk 6-9 Av main course £9 **Restaurant** L served all wk 12-2.30 D served all wk 6-9 Av 3 course à la carte fr £23 ⊕ FREE HOUSE ◀ Butcombe Bitter, Wadworth 6X, Fuller's London Pride, Sharp's Doom Bar, Ringwood Best ♂ Ashton Press. ♥ 10 **Facilities** Children welcome Children's menu Children's portions Play area Family room Dogs allowed Garden Parking Wi-fi **Rooms** 10

See advert below

NETTLECOMBE   Map 4 SY59

Marquis of Lorne

DT6 3SY ☎ 01308 485236
e-mail: info@themarquisoflorne.co.uk
dir: From A3066 (Bridport-Beaminster road) approx 1.5m
N of Bridport follow Loders & Mangerton Mill signs. At
junct left past Mangerton Mill, through West Milton. 1m to
T-junct, straight over. Pub up hill, approx 300yds on left

A 16th-century farmhouse converted into a pub in 1871,
the Marquis of Lorne is family friendly with beautiful
gardens. A change of hands in 2010 thankfully left the
Palmers ales on tap, but renewed the focus on local
produce throughout the menus. Roast Dorset scallops
and black pudding are presented on mash with garlic
and parsley cream, while continental and oriental
influences can be found in dishes such as 'sticky' beef
with Indonesian salad; and tenderloin of Dorset pork
wrapped in Serrano ham. There are various special dinner
evenings to look out for.

Open all wk 12-2.30 6-11 **Bar Meals** L served all wk 12-2
D served all wk 6-9 Av main course £13
Restaurant L served all wk 12-2 D served all wk 6-9 Av 3
course à la carte fr £25 ⊕ PALMERS ◀ Palmers Copper,
IPA, 200 Premium Ale. **Facilities** Children welcome
Children's menu Children's portions Play area Dogs
allowed Garden Parking Wi-fi

NORTH WOOTTON   Map 4 ST61

The Three Elms

DT9 5JW ☎ 01935 812881
dir: From Sherborne take A352 towards Dorchester then
A3030. Pub 1m on right

On the edge of the beautiful Blackmore Vale, with views
of Bulbarrow Hill, this family-friendly pub and restaurant
is a clever mix of original and contemporary features. The
bar is well stocked with real ales, ciders and local beers.
Freshly cooked British classics are served at candlelit
tables, including Sunday roasts and weekly changing
blackboard specials. A typical meal might be West
Country sardines, followed by liver, bacon and onions,
and a home-made dessert to finish. The large beer garden
hosts summer BBQs and beer festivals. Recent change of
hands.

Open all wk 11-2.30 6.30-11 (Sun noon-3 7-10.30)
Closed: 25-26 Dec ⊕ FREE HOUSE ◀ Butcombe Bitter,
Otter Bitter, Tribute Ö Thatchers Burrow Hill, Thatchers
Dry, Ashton Press. **Facilities** Children welcome Children's
menu Children's portions Dogs allowed Garden Beer
festival Parking

OSMINGTON MILLS   Map 4 SY78

The Smugglers Inn

DT3 6HF ☎ 01305 833125
e-mail: smugglersinn.weymouth@hall-woodhouse.co.uk
dir: 7m E of Weymouth towards Wareham, pub signed

Set on the cliffs at Osmington Mills with the South Coast
Footpath running through the garden, the inn has
beautiful views across Weymouth Bay. In the late 18th
century (the inn dates back to the 13th century) it was
the base of infamous smuggler Pierre La Tour who fell in
love with the publican's daughter, Arabella Carless, who
was shot dead while helping him to escape during a raid.
Things are quieter now and you can enjoy a pint of
Tanglefoot or one of the guest ales like Pickled Partridge.
On the menu typical dishes are smoked haddock
Benedict; venison sausages and mash; and steak and
Tanglefoot pie.

Open all wk 11-11 (Sun noon-10.30) ⊕ HALL &
WOODHOUSE ◀ Badger, Tanglefoot, guest ale.
Facilities Children welcome Children's menu Children's
portions Play area Dogs allowed Garden Parking

PIDDLEHINTON   Map 4 SY79

The Thimble Inn

DT2 7TD ☎ 01300 348270
e-mail: thimbleinn@googlemail.com
dir: A35 W'bound, right onto B3143, Piddlehinton in 4m

Friendly village local with open fires, traditional pub
games and good food cooked to order. The pub stands in
a pretty valley on the banks of the River Piddle, and the
riverside patio is popular in summer. Along with an
excellent range of beers, the extensive menu ranges from
sandwiches, ploughman's and jacket potatoes to
special's such as pigeon, beef and mushroom pudding;
fish crumble topped with cheesy mash; pheasant breast
casserole; and a vegetarian option of three bean smoky
chilli with basmati rice. Change of hands.

Open all wk 11.30-2.30 6-11 Closed: 25 Dec ⊕ FREE
HOUSE ◀ Ringwood Best, Palmer Copper Ale & Palmer
IPA, Ringwood Old Thumper, Summer Lightning
Ö Thatchers Gold, Thatchers Dry. **Facilities** Children
welcome Children's menu Children's portions Dogs
allowed Garden Parking

PIDDLETRENTHIDE   Map 4 SY79

The European Inn ☙

DT2 7QT ☎ 01300 348308
e-mail: info@european-inn.co.uk
dir: 5m N of Dorchester off A35 on B3143

This Georgian inn dates back to the first landlord's return
from the Crimean War, known as the European War, when
he named the pub after it. Close to the Jurassic Coast in
Thomas Hardy walking country, the pub provides great
real ales and ciders, splendid wines and good food, with
produce as fresh, seasonal and local as possible.
Mismatched tables, fitted settles with bright cushions

and fresh flowers set the scene for seasonal British
menus. Starters include Lyme Bay scallops with lemon
butter sauce, and pigeon and smoked bacon salad. To
follow, try confit shoulder of Dorset Down lamb with
Piddle honey-glazed carrots, or West Country brill fillet
with triple-cooked chips. Head outside in warmer weather
to the garden or decked area.

Open all day Closed: 25 Dec, Sun eve **Bar Meals** L served
all wk 2.30-5.30 Av main course £6.50
Restaurant L served all wk 12-2 D served Mon-Sat 7-9
booking required Fixed menu price fr £19.95 Av 3 course
à la carte fr £30 ⊕ FREE HOUSE ◀ Otter Ale, Sharp's
Doom Bar, St Austell's Tribute, Purbeck Fossil Fuel
Ö Burrow Hill, Thatchers Gold, Perrys Original. ☙ 12
Facilities Children welcome Children's portions Dogs
allowed Garden Parking Wi-fi

The Piddle Inn ★★★★ INN

DT2 7QF ☎ 01300 348468   📠 01300 348102
e-mail: piddleinn@aol.com
web: www.piddleinn.co.uk
dir: 7m N of Dorchester on B3143, in village centre

Smirks at the name turn into rumblings of pleasure upon
discovering this idyllic, partly creeper-clad village inn,
secluded in the valley of the eponymous chalk stream
that courses behind the inn. Ramblers and visitors
exploring the enfolding Dorset Area of Outstanding
Natural Beauty just north of historic Dorchester can enjoy
the comfortable accommodation here, relaxing with
gravity-dispensed beers from Dorset Piddle Brewery and
indulging in meals created from the best local produce;
lamb rump, Lyme Bay scallops or venison sausages and
daily-changing fish specials.

Open all day all wk **Bar Meals** L served all wk 12-2
D served all wk 6.30-9 **Restaurant** L served all wk 12-2
D served Mon-Sat 6.30-9, Sun 7-9 booking required
⊕ FREE HOUSE ◀ St Austell Tribute, Dorset Piddle
Ö Thatchers Gold, Cornish Rattler. **Facilities** Children
welcome Children's menu Children's portions Dogs
allowed Garden Parking Wi-fi **Rooms** 3

The Poachers Inn

DT2 7QX ☎ 01300 348358   📠 01300 348153
e-mail: info@ thepoachersinn.co.uk
dir: 6m N from Dorchester on B3143. At church end of
village

Saxon King Ethelred's wife Emma founded the village;
Thomas Hardy loved it and today's licensees at The
Poachers continue this deeply ingrained sense of heritage

with a comfortably welcoming, traditional inn beside the River Piddle. Classic pub meals (steak and ale pie) vie with contemporary alternatives (yellow fin sole with brown butter) in the fashionably furnished bar and restaurant, or relax in the pool-side beer garden with a glass of local Palmers bitter.

Open all day all wk 8am-mdnt ⊕ FREE HOUSE ◀ Wadworth 6X, Palmers Copper Ale, Guinness, John Smith's, Tinners, Doom Bar ♂ Thatchers Gold. **Facilities** Children welcome Children's menu Children's portions Dogs allowed Garden Parking Wi-fi

---

PLUSH　　　　　Map 4 ST70

The Brace of Pheasants ▾

DT2 7RQ ☎ 01300 348357 📠 01300 348959
e-mail: info@braceofpheasants.co.uk
dir: *A35 onto B3143, 5m to Piddletrenthide, then right to Mappowder & Plush*

Tucked away in a fold of the hills in the heart of Hardy's beloved county is this pretty 16th-century thatched village inn. With a welcoming open fire, oak beams and fresh flowers, it's an ideal place to start or end a walk. Along with a good selection of real ales and ciders and 18 wines by the glass, a menu might offer ginger, chilli and lime marinated squid; pan-fried guinea fowl breast with cider, bacon and Camembert sauce; and roast red pepper stuffed with cream cheese, mushrooms and herbs.

Open all wk noon-3 7-11 Closed: 25 Dec **Bar Meals** L served Tue-Sun 12-2.30 D served Tue-Sun 7-9 **Restaurant** L served Tue-Sun 12-2.30 D served Tue-Sun 7-9 ⊕ FREE HOUSE ◀ Palmers, Dorset Piddle, Sharp's Doom Bar, Flack Manor, Double Drop ♂ Sharp's Orchard, Westons Traditional Scrumpy. ▾ 18 **Facilities** Children welcome Children's portions Dogs allowed Garden Parking Wi-fi

---

POOLE　　　　　Map 4 SZ09

The Cow NEW

58 Station Rd, Parkstone BH14 8UD
☎ 01202 749569 📠 01202 307493
e-mail: info@thecowpub.co.uk
dir: *From A35 into Station Rd. Pub at Parkstone rail station*

Although still an old-fashioned local with cosy open fires and wood floors, this busy and vibrant free house boasts an award-winning bistro where the excellent food is matched by more than 100 wines. Expect pub classics on the lunch menu and à la carte choices such as roast whole plaice; slow-cooked lamb shank; or pepper-crusted venison loin in the evening. The pub also loves its rugby and shows all the big games.

Open all day all wk **Bar Meals** L served all wk 12-2.30 Av main course £8 **Restaurant** L served all wk 12-2.30 D served Mon-Sat 7-9.30 Av 3 course à la carte fr £25 ⊕ FREE HOUSE **Facilities** Children welcome Children's menu Children's portions Dogs allowed Parking

---

The Guildhall Tavern

15 Market St BH15 1NB ☎ 01202 671717
e-mail: sewerynsevfred@aol.com
dir: *2 mins from Quay*

Standing in the heart of Poole's old town and just two minutes from the historic quay, this former cider house has been stunningly refurbished without losing its traditional charm. Beautifully fresh seafood reflects the owners' Gallic roots, so you could start with pan-fried soft herring roes on toast, followed by monkfish medallions sautéed in garlic and crayfish butter. Other main course options might include Dorset rack of lamb with rosemary jus; or a mixed vegetable pancake. French themed evenings are held every month.

Open Tue-Sat Closed: 1st 2wks Nov, Mon, Sun **Bar Meals** L served Tue-Sat 11.30-3 **Restaurant** L served Tue-Sat 11.30-3 D served Tue-Sat 6-10 ⊕ PUNCH TAVERNS ◀ Ringwood Best. **Facilities** Children welcome Children's menu Children's portions Dogs allowed Parking

---

PICK OF THE PUBS

The Rising Sun ◉◉ ▾

3 Dear Hay Ln BH15 1NZ ☎ 01202 771246
e-mail: paul@risingsunpoole.co.uk
dir: *7m from Wimborne B3073, A349 take A350 signed Poole/Channel Ferries*

Once a pub better known for its Thai food, this 18th-century pub just off the High Street in Poole has been spruced-up and reinvented as a stylish, light and modern gastro-pub. A warm and relaxing atmosphere is guaranteed, whether you are popping for a pint of Ringwood Best in the elegant lounge bar, or heading for the charming restaurant to explore Greg Etheridge's innovative menus (two AA Rosettes). Both lunch and dinner menus successfully combine traditional pub classics with more adventurous dishes and make sound use of fresh local ingredients. Lunch offers salads, inventive sandwiches, starters like cold shellfish platter with lemon and herb mayonnaise, a tapas board of cured meat, cheese and olives, and main courses like beer-battered cod fillet, chunky chips, pea purée and tartare sauce. Evening extras may include chargrilled Honeybrook Farm bacon steak, pineapple, fried egg, Cajun new potato wedges and garlic butter, or honey and mustard glazed spatchcocked baby chicken. Round off, perhaps, with dark chocolate fondant.

Open all day Closed: 25 Dec, Sun **Bar Meals** L served Mon-Sat 12-2.30 D served Mon-Sat 6-9.30 booking required Av main course £10 **Restaurant** L served Mon-Sat 12-2.30 booking required D served Mon-Sat 6-10 booking required Av 3 course à la carte fr £20 ⊕ ENTERPRISE INNS ◀ Ringwood Best Bitter ♂ Stowford Press. ▾ 12 **Facilities** Children welcome Children's portions Garden Parking Wi-fi

---

POWERSTOCK　　　　　Map 4 SY59

PICK OF THE PUBS

Three Horseshoes Inn

DT6 3TF ☎ 01308 485328 📠 01308 485229
e-mail: threehorseshoespowerstokc@live.co.uk
dir: *3m from Bridport off A3066 (Beaminster road)*

A pretty Victorian inn belonging to Bridport's Palmers Brewery in idyllic west Dorset countryside. The patio and terraced garden look out over the village, which lies at the foot of Eggardon hill fort, from which you can see Start Point in South Devon on a clear day. A reputation for excellent cooking owes much to the kitchen's devotion to baking its own bread from organic flour, and making its own ingredients from scratch, including stocks, sausages and ice creams. There is also a focus on local produce, especially game in winter and fresh fish in the summer. Typical starters of pickled day-boat mackerel with horseradish ice cream, or rabbit, pork and bacon terrine could be followed by steamed steak and kidney pudding; a spring lamb burger with hand-cut chips; or one of the seafood specials: deep-fried hake in beer batter; half a Portland Bay lobster; or smoked eel, fennel and bacon pie with sea vegetables.

Open 12-3 6.30-11.30 (Sun noon-3 6.30-10.30pm) Closed: Mon L **Bar Meals** L served Tue-Sat 12-2.30, Sun 12-3 D served Tue-Sat 7-9, Sun 7-8.30 Av main course £12 **Restaurant** L served Tue-Sat 12-2.30, Sun 12-3 D served Tue-Sat 6.30-9.30 Fixed menu price fr £12 Av 3 course à la carte fr £23 ⊕ PALMERS ◀ Palmer's IPA, Copper Ale ♂ Thatchers Gold. **Facilities** Children welcome Children's portions Play area Dogs allowed Garden Parking Wi-fi

---

PUNCKNOWLE　　　　　Map 4 SY58

The Crown Inn

Church St DT2 9BN ☎ 01308 897711
e-mail: crownpuncknowle@btinternet.com
dir: *From A35, into Bridevally, through Litton Cheney. From B3157, inland at Swyre*

There's a traditional atmosphere within the rambling, low-beamed bars at this picturesque 16th-century thatched inn, which was once the haunt of smugglers on their way from nearby Chesil Beach to visit prosperous customers in Bath. Food ranges from light snacks and sandwiches to home-made dishes like lamb chops with mint sauce and tuna steak with basil and tomato sauce. Accompany your meal with a glass of real ale or one of the wines by the glass.

Open 12-3 6-11 Closed: Sun eve in winter ⊕ PALMERS ◀ Palmers IPA, 200 Premium Ale, Copper, Tally Ho! ♂ Thatchers Gold. **Facilities** Children's menu Children's portions Family room Dogs allowed Garden Parking

SHAPWICK — Map 4 ST90

The Anchor Inn

West St DT11 9LB ☎ 01258 857269
e-mail: anchor@shapwick.com
dir: *From Wimborne or Blandford Forum take B3082. Pub signed. From A31, A350 towards Blandford Forum, turn right to Sturminster Marshall then follow Shapwick signs*

Situated in the heart of the village, this welcoming pub has been updated to make it more comfortable, without compromising its rural feel. So you can still sit by an open fire, or head outside where there is seating at the front and back of the pub, and a waitress will bring you great pub food made from fresh local produce. Being a free house, the bar offers a selection of real ales, with regular guests, and ciders. Recent change of hands.

Open noon-3 6-11 Closed: Sun eve ⊕ FREE HOUSE
◀ Ringwood Best, Keystone, Palmers, Guest ales
Ŏ Thatchers, Rosie, Orchard Pig. **Facilities** Children welcome Children's portions Play area Dogs allowed Garden Parking Wi-fi

SHERBORNE — Map 4 ST61

PICK OF THE PUBS

The Kings Arms ★★★★★ INN ♈

North Rd, Charlton Horethorne DT9 4NL
☎ 01963 220281 📠 01963 220496
e-mail: admin@thekingsarms.co.uk
web: www.thekingsarms.co.uk
dir: *On A3145, N of Sherborne. Pub in village centre*

A beautiful Edwardian building, with an imposing façade, totally renovated and restored by owners Tony and Sarah Lethbridge a couple of years ago, and now a country pub, modern restaurant and boutique hotel. The bar, whose chic soft furnishings and pretty fabrics blend with natural slate and oak, has become one of Dorset's more fashionable meeting places. A wide walkway leads past a theatre-style kitchen and a

display of local artwork to the Georgian-mirrored dining room, from which doors open on to an extensive terrace overlooking a croquet lawn and the countryside. Classically trained chefs use locally sourced, seasonal ingredients to prepare traditional and modern British dishes, such as Thai-scented Lyme Bay mussels; chicken breast, roasted in a Josper charcoal oven, with Jerusalem artichoke risotto and truffle mascarpone; pan-fried sea bass with crushed new potatoes, fennel confit and black olive and feta cheese salad; and smoked haddock kedgeree. There are stylish bedrooms available replete with marble bathrooms.

The Kings Arms

Open all day all wk **Bar Meals** L served all wk 12-2.30 booking required D served Mon-Thu 7-9.30, Fri-Sat 7-10, Sun 7-9 booking required **Restaurant** L served all wk 12-2.30 booking required D served Mon-Thu 7-9.30, Fri-Sat 7-10, Sun 7-9 booking required ⊕ FREE HOUSE
◀ Butcombe, Kings Arms Tipple, Sharp's Doom Bar
Ŏ Lawrences. ♈ 13 **Facilities** Children welcome Children's menu Children's portions Dogs allowed Garden Parking Wi-fi **Rooms** 10

See advert below

Queen's Head

High St, Milborne Port DT9 5DQ ☎ 01963 250314
e-mail: info@queenshead.co.uk
dir: *On A30, 2.5m W of Sherborne towards Salisbury*

Milborne Port has no facilities for shipping, the suffix being Old English for 'borough', a status it acquired in 1249. The building came much later, in Elizabethan times, although no mention is made of it as a hostelry until 1738. This popular old inn offers great real ales and dishes along the lines of grilled pork loin steaks with gin and coriander sauce; red snapper supreme with vegetable risotto; crispy battered cod; curry of the day; and vegetable paella. Recent change of hands.

Open all wk 11-2.30 5.30-11.30 (Fri-Sat 11am-mdnt)
⊕ ENTERPRISE INNS ◀ Butcombe Bitters, Fuller's London Pride, Hop Back Summer Lightning. **Facilities** Children welcome Dogs allowed Garden Parking

SHROTON OR IWERNE COURTNEY — Map 4 ST81

PICK OF THE PUBS

The Cricketers

DT11 8QD ☎ 01258 860421 📠 01258 861800
e-mail: info@thecricketersshroton.co.uk
web: www.heartstoneinns.co.uk
dir: *7m S of Shaftesbury on A350, turn right after Iwerne Minster. 5m N of Blandford Forum on A360, past Stourpaine, in 2m left into Shroton. Pub in village centre*

Set in beautiful Dorset countryside at the foot of Hambledon Hill, known for its Iron Age hill forts, this welcoming English pub was built at the turn of the 20th century. It's a real community pub with themed nights and regular events, and you are very likely to meet the village cricket team here in the summer months. The pub is also popular with hikers, lured from the Wessex Way, which runs conveniently through the garden. The comfortable open plan interior is light and

Save on hotels. Book at **theAA.com/hotel**

DORSET 167 **ENGLAND**

airy with views over the attractive well-stocked garden. In winter there is a roaring log fire. The menu changes with the seasons and the dishes feature home cooking using locally sourced ingredients. There is also an ever-changing specials board and in the summer barbecues are sometimes held in the garden. Butcombe and Tribute are among the real ales on offer, while wine lovers will find an interesting wine list, with many available by the glass.

The Cricketers

Open all wk Mon-Sat 11-3- 6-11 (Sun 11-10.30)
Bar Meals L served Mon-Sun 12-2.30 D served Mon-Sat 6.30-9.30 **Restaurant** L served Mon-Sun 12-2.30 D served Mon-Sat 6.30-9.30 ⊕ FREE HOUSE ◀ Butcombe, Tribute ○ Stowford Press. **Facilities** Children welcome Children's menu Children's portions Garden Parking

---

STRATTON   Map 4 SY69

Saxon Arms ♟

DT2 9WG ☎ **01305 260020**
e-mail: rodsaxonlamont1@yahoo.co.uk
dir: *3m NW of Dorchester on A37. Pub between church & village hall*

With its solid oak beams, log-burning stove and flagstone floors, this pretty thatched flint-stone free house makes a great first impression. Popular with the local community, fishermen and cycling clubs, the pub is also handy for riverside walks. It remains true to the principles of the traditional English pub with its hearty welcome, wholesome pub food and real ales. Menu choices include Dorset Blue Vinny rarebit; local faggots with onion gravy; red onion tart Tatin with crumbled goat's cheese; and chef's chicken and ham pie.

Open all wk 11-3 5.30-late (Sat-Sun 11am-late)
Bar Meals L served Mon-Sat 11-2.15, Sun 12-9 booking required D served Mon-Sat 6-9.15, Sun 12-9 booking required Av main course £9.95 **Restaurant** L served Mon-Sat 11-2.15, Sun 12-9 booking required D served Mon-Sat 6-9.15, Sun 12-9 booking required Fixed menu price fr £10.95 ⊕ FREE HOUSE ◀ Fuller's London Pride, Palmers IPA, Ringwood, Timothy Taylor, Butcombe, Abbot, Ruddles, Otter ○ Stowford Press. ♟ 15 **Facilities** Children welcome Children's menu Children's portions Dogs allowed Garden Parking

---

STUDLAND   Map 5 SZ08

The Bankes Arms Hotel

Watery Ln BH19 3AU
☎ **01929 450225** 📠 **01929 450307**
dir: *B3369 from Poole, across on Sandbanks chain ferry, or A35 from Poole, A351 then B3351*

Close to sweeping Studland Bay, across which can be seen the prime real estate enclave of Sandbanks, is this part 15th-century, creeper-clad inn, once a smugglers' dive. It specialises in fresh fish and seafood, but also offers game casserole, lamb noisettes in mint, honey and orange sauce, and spicy pork in chilli, coriander and caper sauce. The annual beer festival held in its large garden showcases 60 real ales, music, Morris dancing and stone carving.

Open all day all wk 11-11 (Sun 11-10.30) Closed: 25 Dec ⊕ FREE HOUSE ◀ Isle of Purbeck Fossil Fuel, Studland Bay Wrecked, Solar Power, IPA ○ Westons Old Rosie, Thatchers Cheddar Valley. **Facilities** Children welcome Children's menu Dogs allowed Garden Beer festival Parking

---

SYDLING ST NICHOLAS   Map 4 SY69

PICK OF THE PUBS

The Greyhound Inn ♟

DT2 9PD ☎ **01300 341303**
e-mail: info@dorsetgreyhound.co.uk
dir: *Off A37 (Yeovil to Dorchester road), turn off at Cerne Abbas/Sydling St Nicholas*

Tucked away in a tranquil village in a glorious valley north of Dorchester, the 17th-century Greyhound Inn is the perfect pub from which to explore Hardy Country. Visit postcard-pretty Cerne Abbas or head to the coast for an invigorating cliff path walk, before returning to relax in the neat open-plan bar, replete with traditional pine and darkwood furnishings and country prints, with a pint of local Palmer's IPA. The food will not disappoint either, the modern British menu and interesting daily specials make sound use of local produce. Best enjoyed in the warmly decorated dining room, the choice may include scallops with pea shoot and pancetta salad for starters, with rack of lamb with pea and mint purée or monkfish with chorizo, fresh basil, cherry tomatoes and sherry for main course. Super, sun-trap front terrace for summer alfresco dining. Change of hands.

Open 11-3 6-11 Closed: Sun eve **Bar Meals** L served Mon-Sat 12-2, Sun 12-2.30 booking required D served Mon-Sat 6-9 booking required **Restaurant** L served Mon-Sat 12-2, Sun 12-2.30 booking required D served Mon-Sat 6-9 booking required ⊕ FREE HOUSE ◀ St Austell Tinners, Butcombe, Guest ales ○ Thatchers Gold. ♟ 12 **Facilities** Children welcome Children's menu Children's portions Play area Dogs allowed Garden Parking Wi-fi

---

TARRANT MONKTON   Map 4 ST90

PICK OF THE PUBS

The Langton Arms ★★★★ INN

DT11 8RX ☎ **01258 830225** 📠 **01258 830053**
e-mail: info@thelangtonarms.co.uk
dir: *A31 from Ringwood, or A357 from Shaftesbury, or A35 from Bournemouth*

Surrounded by countryside immortalised in Thomas Hardy's novels, this attractive 17th-century thatched inn sits close to the village church. The award-winning pub has two bars, the Farmers and the Carpenters, both relaxing places for drinkers and diners. An ever-changing supply of outstanding real ales is served from four pumps. The carte and traditional pub dishes are served in the bars, as well as in the Stables restaurant and conservatory. Expect choice West Country traditional fare: Langton Arms steak pie; local wild duck confit with braised red cabbage; whole baked sea bass from Poole quay; or venison bourguignon; followed by apple and blackberry crumble with custard, or sticky toffee pudding and home-churned vanilla ice cream. There's also a choice of light bites and sharing platters, and a children's menu. All the comfortable and well-equipped bedrooms are on the ground floor situated around an attractive courtyard.

Open all day all wk **Bar Meals** L served Mon-Fri 12-2.30, Sat-Sun all day D served Mon-Thu 6-9.30, Fri 6-10, Sat-Sun all day Av main course £14.95 **Restaurant** L served Mon-Fri 12-2.30, Sat-Sun all day D served Mon-Thu 6-9.30, Fri 6-10, Sat-Sun all day Av 3 course à la carte fr £27 ⊕ FREE HOUSE ◀ Guest ales (all local). **Facilities** Children welcome Children's menu Children's portions Play area Family room Dogs allowed Garden Parking Wi-fi **Rooms** 6

TRENT
Map 4 ST51

PICK OF THE PUBS

Rose & Crown Trent ♥

DT9 4SL ☎ 01935 850776 📄 01935 850776
e-mail: dine@roseandcrowntrent.co.uk
dir: *Just off A30 between Sherborne & Yeovil*

This ivy-clad, thatched inn is situated in the conservation village of Trent. The original building dates from the 14th century, when workers erecting the spire of the church opposite lived in it, although the structure as it is now is 18th century, and was first a farmhouse before becoming an inn. Recently refurbished, the interior still speaks eloquently of its past, especially in the Trent Barrow Room, which has a massive open fire, plenty of seating, old bottles, books and walls that must resonate with whatever a former landlord called Buff Biggins got up to that made him 'infamous'. Generations of farmers have beaten a path here for a pint, these days brewed by Wadworth in Devizes. Apart from the restaurant, which has wonderful views, you can eat in the beer garden, or at the front of the pub. Look out for the popular sausage menu.

Open noon-3 6-11 (Sat-Sun noon-11) Closed: Mon
Bar Meals L served Tue-Sun 12-3 booking required
D served Tue-Sat 6-9 booking required
Restaurant L served Tue-Sun 12-3 D served Tue-Sat
6-9 booking required ⊕ WADWORTH ◀ 6X, Henry's IPA,
Horizon, Bishops Tipple, guest ale ♂ Stowford Press,
Thatchers Gold. ♥ 8 **Facilities** Children welcome Family
room Dogs allowed Garden Parking

WEST BEXINGTON
Map 4 SY58

The Manor Hotel

DT2 9DF ☎ 01308 897660
e-mail: themanorhotel@btconnect.com
dir: *On B3157, 5m E of Bridport*

Overlooking the Jurassic Coast's most famous feature, Chesil Beach, parts of this ancient manor house date from the 11th century. It offers an inviting mix of flagstones, Jacobean oak panelling, roaring fires and a cosy cellar bar serving Dorset beer and organic cider, and locally sourced dishes. There has been a recent change of hands and renovation work has begun, so watch this space.

Open all day all wk 11.30am-10.30pm
Bar Meals L served all wk 12-2 D served all wk 6.30-9
⊕ FREE HOUSE ◀ Guest ales. **Facilities** Children
welcome Children's menu Play area Family room Dogs
allowed Garden Parking Wi-fi

WEST LULWORTH
Map 4 SY88

The Castle Inn ♥

Main Rd BH20 5RN ☎ 01929 400311 📄 01929 400415
e-mail: office@lulworthinn.com
dir: *Follow village signs from A352 (Dorchester to Wareham road). Inn on right on B3070 through West Lulworth. Car park opposite*

This award-winning thatched rural 16th-century pub in the heart of the Purbecks near Lulworth Cove offers 13 real ciders and six real ales (complete with a booklet of tasting notes) in its traditional, friendly bars, and holds a beer festival every year. Outside, you'll find large tiered gardens packed with plants, and in summer there's a giant outdoor chess set. The wide-ranging menu includes beef bourguignon, pork medallions in cream and Calvados sauce, and scampi and scallop Provençal. This is a dog-friendly inn.

Open all wk 12-2.30 7-11 Closed: 25 Dec
Bar Meals L served all wk 12-2 D served all wk 7-10 Av
main course £9.90 ⊕ FREE HOUSE ◀ Sharp's, Isle of
Purbeck, Piddle Ales, Palmers, Plain Ales, Flack Manor
♂ Westons Old Rosie, 1st Quality, Country Perry, Hecks
Kingston Black, Hecks Blakeney Red. ♥ 8
Facilities Children welcome Children's menu Children's
portions Dogs allowed Garden Beer festival Parking Wi-fi

Lulworth Cove Inn ★★★ INN ♥

Main Rd BH20 5RQ ☎ 01929 400333 📄 01929 400453
e-mail: inn@lulworth-cove.com
web: www.lulworth-cove.com
dir: *From A352 (Dorchester to Wareham road) follow Lulworth Cove signs. Inn at end of B3070, opposite car park*

Many of the bedrooms at this 400-year old inn have memorable views of Dorset's Jurassic Coast, whilst Lulworth Cove's famous horseshoe bay is just steps away from the front door. It was once a distribution point for the royal mail arriving by stage coach, plus many smugglers stories can be heard. Ramblers can sate their appetites from the extensive menu, which features light bites, filled baguettes and jacket potatoes, as well as main course dishes like steak and kidney suet pudding; spinach and ricotta cannelloni; and beer battered cod with chips and mushy peas.

Open all day all wk **Bar Meals** L served all day Etr-Oct
(winter Mon-Fri 1-3) D served all day Etr-Oct (winter
Mon-Fri 6-9) **Restaurant** L served all day Etr-Oct (winter
Mon-Fri 1-3) D served all day Etr-Oct (winter Mon-Fri 6-9)
⊕ HALL & WOODHOUSE ◀ Badger Ales, HB Extra Cold, HB
Export, HB Premium ♂ Applewood. ♥ 10
Facilities Children welcome Children's menu Children's
portions Dogs allowed Garden Wi-fi **Rooms** 13

WEST STOUR
Map 4 ST72

The Ship Inn NEW

SP8 5RP ☎ 01747 838640
e-mail: mail@shipinn-dorset.com
dir: *On A30, 4m W of Shaftesbury (4m from Henstridge)*

A privately-owned coaching inn built in 1750 set in picturesque Dorset countryside. The main bar has a traditional flagstone floor, low ceiling and welcoming log fire, while the lounge bar has stripped oak floorboards and chunky farmhouse furniture. Menus are extensive and include daily-changing fish specials such as Cajun-spiced swordfish; or whole bream with green beans, thyme and fennel. Home-made desserts may include rhubarb and apple crumble with vanilla pod custard. Outside a sun-trap patio and large child-friendly garden host an annual festival showcasing up to 20 real ales and ciders.

Open all wk 12-3 6-11.30 **Bar Meals** L served all wk
12-2.30 D served all wk 6-9 Av main course £10-£15
Restaurant L served all wk 12-2.30 booking required
D served all wk 6-9 booking required Fixed menu price fr
£10 Av 3 course à la carte fr £20 ⊕ FREE HOUSE
◀ Palmers IPA, Sharp's Doom Bar, Dartmoor Ale,
Ringwood Fortyniner ♂ Cheddar Valley, Stowford Press.
Facilities Children welcome Children's menu Children's
portions Dogs allowed Garden Beer festival Parking Wi-fi

WEYMOUTH
Map 4 SY67

The Old Ship Inn

7 The Ridgeway DT3 5QQ ☎ 01305 812522
e-mail: theoldshipinn@googlemail.com
dir: *3m from Weymouth town centre, at bottom of The Ridgeway*

Thomas Hardy refers to this pub in his novels *Under the Greenwood Tree* and *The Trumpet Major*. It is the oldest pub in the village and has been welcoming travellers for 400 years. Copper pans, old clocks and a beamed open fire create just the right atmosphere inside, while outside the garden offers views over Weymouth. With a frequently changing menu, you will find good home cooked pub food here along with great real ales and traditional ciders. Change of hands.

Open all day all wk ⊕ PUNCH TAVERNS ◀ Otter, Jurassic,
Sharp's Doom Bar, Guest ales ♂ Westons Old Rosie,
Scrumpy. **Facilities** Children welcome Children's menu
Children's portions Dogs allowed Garden Parking Wi-fi

WIMBORNE ST GILES
Map 5 SU01

The Bull Inn ♥ NEW

Coach Rd BH21 5NF ☎ 01725 517300
e-mail: bullwsg@btconnect.com
dir: *From Salisbury take A354 towards Blandford Forum. Left onto B3081. Follow signs to Wimborne St Giles*

Situated in the heart of the Shaftesbury estate on the edge of Cranborne Chase, there are three shoots within a five-minute drive of this award-winning pub, plus chalkwater stream fishing in the village. Much of the local produce ends up on the acclaimed menu – pigeon breast with smoked black pudding and apple salad might be followed by pork belly with bubble and squeak and rocket – all washed down with local Badger ales.

Open all wk 12-3 6-11 **Bar Meals** L served all wk 12-2.30 booking required D served all wk 6.15-9.30 booking required Av main course £14 **Restaurant** Av 3 course à la carte fr £26 ⊕ HALL & WOODHOUSE ◀ Tanglefoot, Sussex Ale, Hopping Hare ○ Orchard Pig. ♥ 28 **Facilities** Children welcome Children's portions Dogs allowed Garden Parking Wi-fi

---

WINTERBORNE ZELSTON   Map 4 SY89

Botany Bay Inne ♥

DT11 9ET ☎ 01929 459227
dir: *A31 between Bere Regis & Wimborne Minster*

Built in the 1920s as the General Allenby, the pub's name was changed during the 1990s in belated recognition of prisoners from Dorchester jail who spent their last nights in the area before transportation to Australia. Today this hard-working pub welcomes all-comers with or without children and dogs, with Hall and Woodhouse ales and menus of pleasing pub fare made using local ingredients: breaded whitebait with lemon mayonnaise, or Dorset field mushrooms topped with Stilton and apricot cream, are easily followed by slow-roasted lamb shank, or steak and kidney pudding.

Open all wk 10-3 6-11.30 **Bar Meals** L served all wk (bkfst)10-12, (lunch)12-2.15 D served all wk 6.30-9.30 **Restaurant** L served all wk (bkst)10-12, (lunch) 12-2.15 booking required D served all wk 6.30-9.30 booking required ⊕ HALL & WOODHOUSE ◀ Badger First Gold, Tanglefoot, Guest ales. ♥ 10 **Facilities** Children welcome Children's menu Children's portions Dogs allowed Garden Parking

---

WORTH MATRAVERS   Map 4 SY97

PICK OF THE PUBS

The Square and Compass

BH19 3LF ☎ 01929 439229
dir: *Between Corfe Castle & Swanage. From B3069 follow signs for Worth Matravers*

Overlooking the English Channel, an unspoilt stone-built pub which has been run by the Newman family since 1907. A book on sale in the bar captures its fascinating history, and is crammed with stories, anecdotes and pictures collected during the 'Newman century'; its simple interior – there is no bar, just a serving hatch – can have seen few radical changes in that time. Stone flags on the floor come from local quarries, there's a wood-burner in the tap room, an open fire in the oak-panelled larger room, and a museum of local artefacts (some dating from Roman times) together with a collection of fossils from the nearby Jurassic Coast. Award-winning Wessex and West Country beers come straight from the barrel; real ciders include an award-winning seasonal traditional

cider home-pressed by landlord Charlie Newman. Any of these will perfectly accompany a traditional hot pasty or pie with various fillings, these being the only food options. Live music is played in the evenings throughout the year, and on the first Saturday in October there's a beer and pumpkin festival.

Open all wk 12-3 6-11 (12-11 in summer) **Bar Meals** L served all wk D served all wk ⊕ FREE HOUSE ◀ Palmer's Copper Ale & Dorset Gold, RCH Pitchfork, Hop Back Summer Lightning ○ Hecks Farmhouse, Single Variety, Seasonal home-produced. **Facilities** Children welcome Dogs allowed Garden Beer festival **Notes** ⊛

DURHAM, CO

AYCLIFFE   Map 19 NZ22

The County ★★★★ RR ♥

13 The Green, Aycliffe Village DL5 6LX
☎ 01325 312273 📄 01325 317131
e-mail: info@thecountyaycliffevillage.com
dir: *Off A167 into Aycliffe Village. Off Junct 59 A1(M)*

This award-winning restaurant with rooms overlooks the pretty village green. Within doorstep distance are top quality suppliers of fish, meat, game and many of the other ingredients that make up the seasonal menus and daily specials - steaks with field mushrooms and peppercorn sauce; salmon fillet with crab and sweet chilli linguine; home-made turkey and ham pie; and chicken breast with baby leeks, black pudding and Aspall cider cream. Bedrooms in the smart townhouse next door are all furnished to a high standard.

Open all wk 12-3 6-11 Closed: 25 Dec, 1 Jan **Bar Meals** L served Mon-Sat 12-2, Sun 12-2.30 D served all wk 6-9 Av main course £8.95 **Restaurant** L served Mon-Sat 12-2, Sun 12-2.30 D served all wk 6-9 Fixed menu price fr £9.95 Av 3 course à la carte fr £25 ⊕ FREE HOUSE ◀ Yorkshire Dales, Hawkshead, Jennings County Best Bitter, Black Sheep, Cocker Hoop ○ Aspall. ♥ 10 **Facilities** Children welcome Children's portions Parking **Rooms** 7

BARNARD CASTLE   Map 19 NZ01

PICK OF THE PUBS

The Morritt Arms Hotel ★★★★ HL ♥

Greta Bridge DL12 9SE
☎ 01833 627232 📄 01833 627392
e-mail: relax@themorritt.co.uk
dir: *At Scotch Corner take A66 towards Penrith, after 9m turn at Greta Bridge. Hotel over bridge on left*

This fine building dates from the late 17th century, when it served Carlisle- and London-bound coach travellers. Traditionally a fine-dining venue, the restaurant has been brought bang up to date with vibrant colours, a touch of black leather, comfortable armchairs, new lighting, silk blinds over window seats and works by local artists. This association with art

began in 1946, when local portraitist Jack Gilroy painted the mural of Dickensian characters you'll find in the bar. Here, the menu opens with seafood platter, before featuring Mediterranean vegetable risotto, Neasham pork and leek sausages, and beer-battered cod. In the restaurant, venison loin with beetroot risotto, butter-fried plaice fillets, and wild mushroom and vegetable Wellington may well appear. Major Morritt beer, named after the hotel's former owner and namesake, was introduced at the pub's first cask ale festival in 2010. En suite bedrooms help to make this a popular function and wedding choice.

Open all day all wk 7am-11pm (Sun 7-10.30pm) **Bar Meals** Av main course £9.50 food served all day **Restaurant** L served all wk 12-3 D served all wk 7-9.30 Fixed menu price fr £12 Av 3 course à la carte fr £23 ⊕ FREE HOUSE ◀ Timothy Taylor Landlord, 'Major Morritt', Thwaites. ♥ 19 **Facilities** Children welcome Children's menu Children's portions Play area Family room Dogs allowed Garden Beer festival Parking Wi-fi **Rooms** 27

CHESTER-LE-STREET   Map 19 NZ25

The Moorings Hotel ♥ NEW

Hett Hill DH2 3JU ☎ 0191 370 1597 📄 0191 370 3033
e-mail: info@themooringsdurham.co.uk
dir: *A1(M) junct 63 to Chester-le-Street. Take B6313. Hotel on left*

Handy for Beamish Museum and fellside walks at Waldridge, the old inn is now part of an exclusive hotel complex, yet retains a local feel and majors on some cracking local beers from Consett and Beamish breweries, enjoyed by ramblers and horse-riders with whom the inn is popular. Signature dishes feature local steaks and North-East whitefish and shellfish, and the kids are well catered for with a good choice of junior dishes. With a large patio and 3 acres of land, it's a peaceful spot to take time out at.

Open all day all wk **Bar Meals** L served all wk 11.30-9.30 D served all wk 11.30-9.30 Av main course £8.50 food served all day **Restaurant** L served Sun 11.30-4 booking required D served Thu-Sat 6.30-9.30 booking required Av 3 course à la carte fr £25 ⊕ FREE HOUSE ◀ Rudgate Battleaxe, Mordue Workie Ticket, Beamish Brown, Consett White Hot, Timothy Taylor Landlord. ♥ 10 **Facilities** Children welcome Children's menu Children's portions Garden Parking Wi-fi

COTHERSTONE — Map 19 NZ01

The Fox and Hounds

DL12 9PF ☎ **01833 650241**
e-mail: ianswinburn999@btinternet.com
dir: *4m W of Barnard Castle. From A66 onto B6277, signed*

Huddled above one of the village greens in pretty Cotherstone, at the heart of beautiful Teesdale and just a stone's throw from the river's wooded gorge. Beams, open fires and thickly cushioned wall seats tempt you to linger at this 360-year-old coaching inn, admiring the local photographs and country pictures while you sip a pint of Black Sheep. From the menu, tuck in to white Wensleydale cheese and hazelnut pâté served with crusty bread; or oven-roasted halibut steak with prawn and pesto dressing. When washing your hands say hello to Reva, the African grey parrot.

Open all wk 12-2.30 6.30-11 (Sun 6.30-10.30) Closed: 25-26 Dec **Bar Meals** L served all wk 12-2 D served all wk 6.30-9 **Restaurant** L served all wk 12-2 D served all wk 6.30-9 ⊕ FREE HOUSE ◀ Black Sheep Best, Village Brewer Bull Bitter, Black Sheep Ale, Daleside Special, Yorkshire Terrier ♂ Aspall. **Facilities** Children welcome Children's menu Children's portions Garden Parking Wi-fi

DURHAM — Map 19 NZ24

Victoria Inn

86 Hallgarth St DH1 3AS ☎ **0191 386 5269**
dir: *In city centre*

This unique listed inn has scarcely changed since it was built in 1899. Just five minutes' walk from the cathedral, it has been carefully nurtured by the Webster family for over 35 years. Small rooms warmed by coal fires and a congenial atmosphere include the unusual off-sales booth and tiny snug, where a portrait of Queen Victoria still hangs above the upright piano. You'll find a few simple snacks to tickle the taste buds, but it's the cracking well kept local ales, single malts, and over 40 Irish whiskeys that are the main attraction.

Open all wk 11.45-3 6-11 ⊕ FREE HOUSE ◀ Wylam Gold Tankard, Durham Magus, Big Lamp Bitter, Hambleton ♂ Scrumpy. **Facilities** Children welcome Family room Dogs allowed Parking Wi-fi

FIR TREE — Map 19 NZ13

Duke of York Inn

DL15 8DG ☎ **01388 767429** 📄 **01388 767429**
e-mail: markhardy69@live.co.uk
dir: *On A68, 12m W of Durham. From Durham take A690 W. Left onto A68 to Fir Tree*

A former drovers' and coaching inn dating from 1749, the Duke of York stands on the tourist route (A68) to Scotland. Refurbished inside and out to a high standard, keeping the traditional country feel with contemporary

touches. Typical dishes include steak and ale pie, and chicken with pepper sauce, plus choices from the carvery and grill. Change of hands.

Open all day all wk **Bar Meals** food served all day **Restaurant** food served all day ⊕ CAMERONS BREWERY ◀ Camerons Smooth, John Smith's, Guinness, Ruby Red Ale. **Facilities** Children welcome Children's menu Children's portions Dogs allowed Garden Parking Wi-fi

HUTTON MAGNA — Map 19 NZ11

PICK OF THE PUBS

The Oak Tree Inn @@

DL11 7HH ☎ **01833 627371**
dir: *From A1 at Scotch Corner take A66. 6.5m, right for Hutton Magna*

Expect great food, a superb selection of drinks and a warm welcome at this whitewashed, part 18th-century free house run by Alastair and Claire Ross. Alastair previously spent 14 years in London working at the Savoy, Leith's and, more recently, a private members' club on The Strand. The AA two-Rosette meals in the simply furnished dining room are based around the finest local ingredients, and dishes change daily depending on produce available. The fish choices, in particular, rely on what comes in on the boats. The refined cooking style combines classic techniques and occasional modern flavours: you could start with roast saddle of hare with teal and chicken liver pâté or steamed Shetland mussels with coconut, chilli, ginger and mint. After that, maybe fillet of John Dory with roast scallops, carrot and star anise sauce or best end of lamb with lamb and black pudding shepherd's pie and tenderstem broccoli. As well as fine real ales, there's a menu of bottled beers from around the globe, and a list of 20 malt whiskies.

Open 6-11 (Sun 5.30-10.30) Closed: Xmas & New Year, Mon **Restaurant** D served Tue-Sun 6-9 booking required Fixed menu price fr £18.50 Av 3 course à la carte fr £32 ⊕ FREE HOUSE ◀ Wells Bombardier, Timothy Taylor Landlord, Black Sheep Best. **Facilities** Dogs allowed Parking

MIDDLESTONE — Map 19 NZ23

Ship Inn ☛

Low Rd DL14 8AB ☎ **01388 810904**
e-mail: tony.theshipinn@googlemail.com
dir: *On B6287 (Kirk Merrington to Coundon road)*

A bustling local that knows how to generate community loyalty, not least through an ever-changing real ale portfolio and its May and November beer festivals. The lounge is all nautical memorabilia and walls festooned with old beer pump clips. At 550 feet above sea level the rooftop patio offers excellent views over the Tees Valley and Cleveland Hills. Home-cooked food is served in the bar and restaurant, using locally reared beef, pork and lamb. Look out for regular themed evenings, plus quiz night on Thursdays.

Open all wk 4-11 (Fri-Sun noon-11) **Bar Meals** L served Fri-Sun 12-2 D served Mon-Sat 6-9 Av main course £6.50 ⊕ FREE HOUSE ◀ 6 guest ales ♂ Westons. ☛ 9 **Facilities** Children welcome Children's menu Children's portions Play area Family room Dogs allowed Beer festival Parking Wi-fi

MIDDLETON-IN-TEESDALE — Map 18 NY92

The Teesdale Hotel ★★ HL

Market Place DL12 0QG
☎ **01833 640264** 📄 **01833 640651**
e-mail: enquiries@teesdalehotel.com
dir: *A1 to Scotch Corner, A66 to Barnard Castle, follow signs for Middleton-in-Teesdale*

In the quaint stone-built village of Middleton, this tastefully modernised, family-run former coaching inn sits amidst some of Britain's loveliest scenery. It has a striking 18th-century stone exterior and archway, while the interior is warm and friendly, with an open fire in the bar and well-kept real ales hand-pumped from the ancient cellar. Home-made food sourced from local produce results in heart-warming dishes such as black pudding with crispy bacon, followed by roast ham and pease pudding.

Open all day all wk **Bar Meals** L served all wk 12.30-2.30 D served all wk 7-9 **Restaurant** D served all wk 7-9 ⊕ FREE HOUSE ◀ Guinness, Jennings Smooth, Black Sheep Best Bitter, Bitburger ♂ Aspall. **Facilities** Children welcome Children's menu Children's portions Dogs allowed Parking Wi-fi **Rooms** 14

NEWTON AYCLIFFE — Map 19 NZ22

Blacksmiths Arms ☛

Preston le Skerne, (off Ricknall Lane) DL5 6JH
☎ **01325 314873**
dir: *Turn off A167 next to Gretna pub, into Ricknall Ln. Blacksmiths Arms 0.5m*

Enjoying an excellent reputation locally as a good dining pub, this former smithy dates from the 1700s, and is still relatively isolated in its farmland setting. The menu offers starters of hot smoked mackerel and potato salad; cod and prawn brandade; and chicken fillet goujons. Requiring their own page on the menu are fish dishes such as grilled halibut steak with risotto, and gingered salmon. There is an ever-changing selection of real ales served in the bar.

Open 11.30-2.30 6-11 Closed: 1 Jan, Mon **Bar Meals** L served Tue-Sun 11.30-2.30 D served Tue-Sun 6-9 **Restaurant** L served Tue-Sun 11.30-2.30 D served Tue-Sun 6-9 ⊕ FREE HOUSE ◀ Changing selection of real ales. ☛ 10 **Facilities** Children welcome Children's menu Play area Dogs allowed Garden Parking

PICK OF THE PUBS

Rose & Crown ★★★ HL ❀❀ ☐

ROMALDKIRK Map 19 NY92

DL12 9EB
☎ 01833 650213 📠 01833 650828
e-mail: hotel@rose-and-crown.co.uk
web: www.rose-and-crown.co.uk
dir: *6m NW from Barnard Castle on B6277*

No less than three greens meander through pretty Romaldkirk, set at the heart of Teesdale, greenest of the deep valleys which fracture the Durham Moors into memorable dales characterised by waterfalls, cataracts and timeless villages. Well loved local walks explore this Eden; one passes by the glorious gardens at nearby Eggleston Hall. Fringing one of these greens is a three-storey creeper-clad Georgian inn; stone-built like the adjoining cottages and across the green from the ancient Saxon church christened the Cathedral of the Dale. Step inside and you'll see fresh flowers, varnished oak panelling, old beams, gleaming copper and brass artefacts. Enter the quirky little bar, all oak settles and a fire crackling in the vast grate, timeless brasses, carriage lamps and rural artefacts, or retire to the secluded lounge behind, lulled by the ticking of a grandfather clock or maybe a glass of Allendale Ale whilst relaxing in the wing-back chairs. The more formal panelled, two AA Rosette restaurant is another option in this wonderful warren. The luck of Teesdale is its thriving farming community which produces some of the

best food in England, local sporting estates and the proximity of small fishing harbours. Making the most of this largesse, the chefs at the Rose & Crown create a thoughtful range of dishes, starting perhaps with potted rabbit and belly pork with apple and fig chutney and pork scratchings before sampling a main of pan-fried pink wood pigeon, bacon floddy, onion confit and juniper berry jus; for fish, enjoy smoked white haddock kedgeree, quails' eggs, prawns and garden herbs. Bar snacks include baguettes and a ploughman's based on the local Cotherstone cheese. Time for a stroll around the village before retiring to one of the comfortable bedrooms in the inn or courtyard-side contemporary suites.

Open all day all wk 11-11 Closed: 23-27 Dec **Bar Meals** L served all wk 12-1.30

D served all wk 6.30-9.30 Av main course £12 **Restaurant** L served Sun 12-1.30 D served all wk 7.30-8.45 Booking required Fixed menu price fr £35 ⊕ FREE HOUSE 🍺 Theakston Best, Black Sheep Best, Allendale ale. ☐ 14 **Facilities** Children's menu Children's portions Dogs allowed Parking Wi-fi **Rooms** 12

ROMALDKIRK — Map 19 NY92

PICK OF THE PUBS

Rose & Crown ★★★ HL ◉◉ ♥

See Pick of the Pubs on page 171

SEAHAM — Map 19 NZ44

The Seaton Lane Inn ★★★★ INN NEW

Seaton Ln SR7 0LP ☎ 0191 581 2036
dir: *S of Sunderland on A19 take B1404 towards Houghton-le-Spring. In Seaton turn left for pub*

Recently refurbished, with a traditional bar area as well as a stylish restaurant and lounge, this boutique-type inn offers three real ales to keep the regulars happy, served from the central bar. The menu proffers many pub favourites – hot sandwiches such as the traditional BLT are served with chips; pastas, tortilla wraps and warm salads are all here too. Fish dishes are a speciality in the restaurant: salmon pâté; seared scallops; mussels; oven-roasted cod; and a monkfish and mussel Thai red curry are some examples. Bedrooms are modern, spacious and smartly furnished.

Open all day all wk **Bar Meals** L served all wk 7am-9.30pm D served all wk 7am-9.30pm Av main course £7 food served all day **Restaurant** L served all wk 7am-9.30pm D served all wk 7am-9.30pm Fixed menu price fr £9.95 Av 3 course à la carte fr £15 food served all day ⊕ FREE HOUSE ◀ Timothy Taylor Landlord, Wells Bombardier, Theakston Bitter. **Facilities** Children welcome Children's menu Children's portions Dogs allowed Garden Parking Wi-fi **Rooms** 18

STANLEY — Map 19 NZ15

The Stables Pub and Restaurant ★★★★ CHH ♥ NEW

Beamish Hall Hotel, Beamish DH9 0YB
☎ 01207 288750 & 233733 📠 01207 299220
e-mail: info@beamish-hall.co.uk
dir: *A693 to Stanley. Follow signs for Beamish Hall Country House Hotel & Beamish Museum. Left at museum entrance. Hotel on left 0.2m after golf club. Pub within hotel grounds*

Creatively moulded from the estate workshops at a stunning country mansion - with excellent accommodation - adjoining the famous 'live' industrial and social museum at Beamish. From handpumps at the bar flow beers brewed on the premises, whilst from regional producers flow the best raw materials from which are crafted exemplary meals, appreciated in the timeless stone-floored, beamed bar or the sheltered courtyard. Snack on smoked ham and curried risotto or sink into slow roast belly pork with black pudding, creamed leeks, red wine sauce and English mustard cream.

Open all day all wk Mon-Thu 11-11 (Fri-Sat 11am-mdnt Sun 11-10.30) **Bar Meals** L served Mon-Thu 12-9, Fri-Sat 12-9.30, Sun 12-8 D served Mon-Thu 12-9, Fri-Sat 12-9.30, Sun 12-8 Av main course £5.95 food served all day **Restaurant** Av 3 course à la carte fr £15.95 food served all day ⊕ FREE HOUSE ◀ Beamish Hall Bitter, Old Miner Tommy, Silver Buckles, Beamish Burn Ò Gwynt Y Ddraig Haymaker & Pyder. **Facilities** Children welcome Children's menu Children's portions Play area Dogs allowed Garden Beer festival Parking Wi-fi **Rooms** 42

ESSEX

ARKESDEN — Map 12 TL43

PICK OF THE PUBS

Axe & Compasses ♥

See Pick of the Pubs on page 174

AYTHORPE RODING — Map 6 TL51

Axe & Compasses

Dunmow Rd CM6 1PP ☎ 01279 876648
e-mail: axeandcompasses@msn.com
dir: *From A120 take junct for Dunmow*

A weather-boarded, 17th-century pub where the owners like to create a 'nostalgic pub experience'. In the bar, ales from small regional brewers such as Nethergate Old Growler and Saffron Walden Gold are backed by Westons ciders. David, a skilled self-taught chef, uses the best of seasonal produce and loves to offer dishes such as pan-fried pigeon breast, bacon salad and parsnip crisp or Mersea oysters to start; then calves' liver, crispy bacon, sage mash and caper butter; and ginger parkin, toffee sauce and home-made brandy ice cream to finish.

Open all day all wk 11am-11.30pm (Sun noon-11) ⊕ FREE HOUSE ◀ Brentwood Best, Nethergate Old Growler, Crouch Vale Brewers Gold, Woodforde's Wherry, Saffron Walden Gold Ò Westons Old Rosie, Westons Scrumpy, Herefordshire Perry. **Facilities** Children welcome Children's portions Dogs allowed Garden Parking Wi-fi

BLACKMORE — Map 6 TL60

PICK OF THE PUBS

The Leather Bottle

The Green CM4 0RL ☎ 01277 823538
e-mail: leatherbottle@tiscali.co.uk
dir: *M25 junct 8 onto A1023, left onto A128, 5m. Left onto Blackmore Rd, 2m. Left towards Blackmore, 2m. Right then 1st left*

The charming and historic village of Blackmore is mentioned in the Domesday Book and there has been a pub on the site for over 400 years. According to local legend, Henry VIII used to stable his horses here when he came to visit his mistress. The original pub building burned down in 1954 and was rebuilt two years later. The stone-floored bar is a cosy, welcoming place to

savour real ales, while the restaurant is smart, with modern furnishings. There's also an airy conservatory which opens onto the spacious enclosed garden with covered patio area. There is always a good selection of real ales and ciders, and all food is prepared with the finest freshest ingredients mainly from local suppliers. Options include a very reasonably priced lunchtime menu, which might include salmon and basil fishcakes followed by slow cooked belly of pork with apple and cider sauce. Typical dishes at other times are honey-glazed duck breast served with parsnips, or wild boar sausages with mash and red wine jus. Friday night is fish and chips night with a pint or glass of wine included in the price.

Open all day all wk **Bar Meals** L served all wk 12-2 D served Mon-Sat 7-9, Sun 12-4 Av main course £10.95 **Restaurant** L served Mon-Sat 12-2, Sun 12-4 booking required D served Mon-Sat 7-9, Sun 12-4 booking required Fixed menu price fr £8.95 Av 3 course à la carte fr £20 ⊕ FREE HOUSE ◀ Adnams Best, Adnams Broadside, Sharp's Doom Bar, Woodforde's Wherry, Cottage Cactus Jack Ò Aspall, Westons Old Rosie. **Facilities** Children's portions Dogs allowed Garden Parking

BRIGHTLINGSEA — Map 7 TM01

The Rosebud

66-67 Hurst Green CO7 0EH ☎ 01206 304571
e-mail: mark@rosebudpub.co.uk
dir: *From Colchester take A120 towards Harwich. Right to Brightlingsea. Follow High St (away from war memorial). 0.5m to Hurst Green*

Apparently, only the locals know about this quaint little pub propping up a row of fishermen's cottages, named after a wrecked ship – at least until this entry appears! Opened in 1849 for the oyster fishermen, the pub has been in the same family for two generations. Expect fresh fish and seafood like seafood platter and moules marinière, plus meat from the local butcher; lamb's liver and bacon, gammon and steaks. Look for the recently found tail in a bottle behind the bar – some say it belonged to a cat on the doomed Rosebud. An on-site micro-brewery is planned.

Open all wk Mon-Thu 4.30-11 (Fri-Sat noon-11 Sun noon-7 open all day in Spring/Summer) ⊕ FREE HOUSE ◀ Guest ales. **Facilities** Children welcome Children's portions Garden

BURNHAM-ON-CROUCH — Map 7 TQ99

Ye Olde White Harte Hotel

The Quay CM0 8AS ☎ 01621 782106 📠 01621 782106
dir: *Along high street, right before clocktower, right into car park*

Directly overlooking the River Crouch and situated on the quay, the hotel dates from the 17th century and retains many original features, including original beams and fireplaces. It also has its own private jetty. Enjoy fresh local produce and local fish in The Waterside Restaurant,

Save on hotels. Book at **theAA.com/hotel**

ESSEX 173 ENGLAND

or bar meals in the bar or on the terrace - steak and kidney pie, ham and Stilton salad, and choices of locally caught fish and snacks. The dining room offers steaks, fish and roast of the day, plus vegetarian fare.

Open all day all wk **Bar Meals** L served all wk 12-2.15 D served all wk 6.30-9 Av main course £8.20 **Restaurant** L served all wk 12-2.15 D served all wk 7-9 Av 3 course à la carte fr £22 ⊕ FREE HOUSE ◄ Adnams Bitter, Crouch Vale Best. **Facilities** Children welcome Dogs allowed Parking

CASTLE HEDINGHAM Map 13 TL73

PICK OF THE PUBS

The Bell Inn

Saint James St CO9 3EJ ☎ **01787 460350**
e-mail: hedinghambell@zoho.com
web: www.hedinghambell.co.uk
dir: *On A1124 N of Halstead, right to Castle Hedingham*

Victorian Prime Minister Benjamin Disraeli honed his early debating skills in the barrel-ceilinged assembly room on the first floor of this notable Georgian coaching inn. He was a latecomer, for drinkers first rested easy here in the 15th century; beams and wattle and daub walls hark back to these medieval foundations. Settle at eye-catching period furniture by log fires or a shady spot on the patio and consider a wide-ranging menu of English favourites; all the meats come from welfare-accredited farms in Essex and Suffolk and go into the selection of pies available here; chicken and bacon or steak and ale for example. As an extraordinary counterpoint, The Bell's Turkish chef creates dishes inspired by his home country, from spicy minced lamb pizzas cooked in a wood-fired oven to exotic BBQ fish and red bean and roast aubergine chilli. Add their award-winning range of very local real ales (and 3 beer festivals a year), together with Delvin End cider and the experience is complete.

Open all wk 11.45-3 6-11 (Fri-Sat noon-mdnt Sun noon-11) Closed: 25 Dec eve **Bar Meals** L served Mon-Fri 12-2, Sat-Sun 12-2.30 D served Sun-Mon 7-9, Tue-Sat 7-9.30 Av main course £9 ⊕ GRAYS ◄ Mighty Oak Maldon Gold, IPA, Adnams Bitter, Guest ale Ö Aspall, Delvin End, Pheasant Plucker. **Facilities** Children welcome Children's menu Children's portions Play area Family room Dogs allowed Garden Beer festival Parking Wi-fi

CHAPPEL Map 13 TL82

The Swan Inn

CO6 2DD ☎ **01787 222353** 📠 **01787 220012**
e-mail: swan@cipubs.com
dir: *Pub visible just off A1124 (Colchester to Halstead road), from Colchester 1st left after viaduct*

This rambling low-beamed free house stands in the shadow of a magnificent Victorian railway viaduct, and boasts a charming riverside garden with overflowing flower tubs. Fresh meat arrives daily from Smithfield, and fish from Billingsgate. Typically the seafood may include crispy sole fillets or poached skate, while the grill comes into its own with prime steaks and platters of surf 'n' turf. There are daily vegetarian specials, and home-made desserts. The bar serves up a well-kept pint and offers plenty of wines by the glass.

Open all wk 11-3 6-11 (Sat 11-11 Sun noon-10.30) ⊕ FREE HOUSE ◄ Adnams Bitter, Broadside, Guest Ale Ö Aspall. **Facilities** Children welcome Children's menu Children's portions Play area Dogs allowed Garden Parking Wi-fi

CHELMSFORD Map 6 TL70

The Alma ♥

37 Arbour Ln CM1 7RG ☎ **01245 256783**
e-mail: alma@cipubs.com
dir: *Telephone for directions*

Named after the bloodiest battle of the Crimean War, The Alma was built in the late 19th century as an alehouse for soldiers recovering in the neighbouring hospital. The present owners have created a contemporary edge for the pub, and the menu follows suit with a stylish mix of traditional and modern dishes - perhaps pan-fried sea bass fillet with fennel and crayfish risotto and pesto dressing; chicken breast with tarragon and white wine sauce; or Stilton-stuffed fillet of beef with a rich red wine and mushroom sauce. There is a front patio and more secluded rear garden for alfresco dining.

Open all day all wk 11-11 (Fri-Sat 11-mdnt, Sun noon-10.30) **Bar Meals** L served Mon-Sat 12-2.30, Sun 12-8 D served Mon-Sat 6-9.30, Sun 12-8 Av main course £10 **Restaurant** L served Mon-Sat 12-2.30, Sun 12-8 D served Mon-Sat 6-9.30, Sun 12-8 Fixed menu price fr £10 Av 3 course à la carte fr £19 ⊕ FREE HOUSE ◄ Adnams Ö Aspall. ♥ 12 **Facilities** Children welcome Children's menu Children's portions Garden Parking Wi-fi

CLAVERING Map 12 TL43

PICK OF THE PUBS

The Cricketers ♥

See Pick of the Pubs on page 175

COLCHESTER Map 13 TL92

The Rose & Crown Hotel ★★★ HL

East St CO1 2TZ ☎ **01206 866677** 📠 **01206 866616**
e-mail: info@rose-and-crown.com
dir: *From M25 junct 28 take A12 N. Follow Colchester signs*

The Rose & Crown is a beautiful timber-framed building dating from the 14th century, believed to be the oldest hotel in the oldest town in England, just a few minutes' from Colchester Castle. The Tudor bar with its central roaring fire is a great place to relax with a drink. Food is served in the Oak Room or the Tudor Room brasserie, an informal alternative serving classic bar food. A meal might consist of smoked salmon and caperberries, followed by 28-day aged rump or sirloin steak, finishing with treacle tart with home-made marmalade ice cream.

Open all wk **Bar Meals** L served all wk 12-2.30 D served all wk 6.30-9.30 Av main course £9.95 ⊕ FREE HOUSE ◄ Tetley's Bitter, Rose & Crown Bitter, Adnams Broadside. **Facilities** Children welcome Family room Parking Wi-fi **Rooms** 39

DEDHAM Map 13 TM03

Marlborough Head Inn ★★★ INN

Mill Ln CO7 6DH ☎ **01206 323250**
e-mail: jen.pearmain@tiscali.co.uk
dir: *E of A12, N of Colchester*

Tucked away in glorious Constable Country, a 16th-century building that was once a clearing-house for local wool merchants. In 1660, after a slump in trade, it became an inn. Today it is as perfect for a pint, sofa and newspaper as it is for a good home-cooked family meal. Traditional favourites such as steak, Guinness and mushroom pie; and lamb shank with red wine and rosemary appear on the menu, plus fish is given centre stage on Fridays. There is a terrace and walled garden to enjoy in the warmer weather. Three en suite bedrooms are available.

Open all day all wk 11.30-11 ⊕ PUNCH TAVERNS ◄ Adnams Southwold, Greene King IPA, Woodforde's Wherry Ö Aspall. **Facilities** Children welcome Children's menu Children's portions Family room Dogs allowed Garden Parking **Rooms** 3

PICK OF THE PUBS

Axe & Compasses ♀

ARKESDEN   Map 12 TL43

High St CB11 4EX
☎ **01799 550272** 📄 **01799 550906**
*dir: From Buntingford take B1038 towards
Newport. Then left for Arkesden*

Sleepy Arkesden is full of white, cream
and pink-washed thatched cottages, the
stuff of English picture postcards.
Through the village runs gentle Wicken
Water, spanned by little footbridges. Right
in the centre is the Axe, its thatched
central part dating from 1650; the right-
hand extension was added during the
early 19th century and is now the public
bar. It's run by Themis and Diane Christou
from Cyprus, who between them have
knocked up a good few awards for the
marvellous things they do here, and who
have impressed at least one national
newspaper.

Easy chairs and settees, antique furniture,
clocks and horse brasses fill their
comfortable lounge and, in winter, there's
an open fire. The pumps of Greene King
hold sway in the bar, and it's with a pint
of Abbot Ale that you can have a sandwich
or light meal, such as monkfish served on
a roasted red pepper sauce. In the softly
lit restaurant area, which seats 50 on
various levels, and where agricultural
implements adorn the old beams, the
slightly Greek-influenced menus offer a
good selection of starters, including flat
field mushrooms baked with garlic, thyme,
lemon juice and olive oil; and avocado,
bacon and blue cheese crostini. There's a
good choice of main courses too, examples
being moussaka; supreme of chicken Kiev
with mushroom duxelles in puff pastry
and wholegrain mustard cream; tender
rump of lamb with mint and red wine
gravy; grilled halibut steak with creamed
leeks; and fried spinach and potato cakes
with tomato and basil sauce. Rounding off
the menu are desserts from the trolley,
such as trifle of the day, and summer
pudding. The wine list is easy to navigate,
with house reds and whites coming in at
modest prices. On fine days many drinkers
and diners head for the patio.

Open all wk noon-2.30 6-11 (Sun noon-3
7-10.30) **Bar Meals** L served all wk 12-2
D served all wk 6.45-9.30 booking
required **Restaurant** L served all wk 12-2
D served all wk 6.45-9.30 booking
required ⊕ GREENE KING ◀ Greene King
IPA, Abbot Ale, Old Speckled Hen. ♀ 14
Facilities Garden Parking

Save on hotels. Book at **theAA.com/hotel**

ESSEX 175 ENGLAND

PICK OF THE PUBS

The Cricketers ♟

CLAVERING   Map 12 TL43

CB11 4QT
☎ **01799 550442**   📠 **01799 550882**
e-mail: info@thecricketers.co.uk
web: www.thecricketers.co.uk
dir: *From M11 junct 10, A505 E. Then A1301, B1383. At Newport take B1038*

Rural Essex enfolds pretty Clavering, which seeps along lanes and byroads fronted by thatched cottages and dappled with pocket woodlands amidst rich arable farmland. The Cricketers (the pitch is just down the road) has served the local community for nigh-on 500 years; elements of this heritage remain amidst the beams, old fireplaces with cosy winter log fires; outside a wisteria girdles the door and tables dot a rose-fringed garden. Tasteful refurbishment and attention to decor has produced a relaxing destination dining pub, where customers dine amidst a forest of wooden pillars strikingly adorned with rural artefacts, brasses and other absolutes of the country pub. Head chef, Justin Greig, is passionate about quality local materials and developing his Italian-inspired seasonally changing menus and daily chalkboard specials. Jamie Oliver, son of the owners Trevor and Sally Oliver, supplies the pub with wonderful seasonal vegetables, herbs and salads from his certified organic garden nearby, perfectly complementing the fresh, organic produce which are at the heart of the memorable fare on offer here. Open the batting with breast of local pigeon, cooked pink and sliced onto a light pea purée topped with watercress salad and a little truffle oil before scoring with medallions of Priors Hall Farm pork, sautéed in garlic butter and served on potato rösti with black pudding and a rosemary jus; spicy venison meatballs with curly pappardelle and grated parmesan or home-made potato gnocchi with crushed butternut squash, goat's cheese and toasted walnuts. With a choice of 17 wines by the glass or beers from East Anglian breweries time passes easily at this, one of the very first good-food dining inns, under the same ownership for over 30 years and where children are particularly welcomed, with their own small, dedicated menu.

Open all day all wk Closed: 25-26 Dec **Bar Meals** L served all wk 12-2 D served all wk 6.30-9.30 **Restaurant** L served all wk 12-2 D served all wk 6.30-9.30 🍺 FREE HOUSE ◄ Adnams Bitter, Tetley Bitter, Greene King IPA, Adnams Broadside, Woodforde's Wherry, Nog ♂ Aspall. ♟ 17 **Facilities** Children's menu Children's portions Family room Garden Parking Wi-fi

PICK OF THE PUBS

The Swan at Felsted ♥

FELSTED   Map 6 TL62

Station Rd CM6 3DG
☎ **01371 820245**   📠 **01371 821393**
e-mail: info@theswanatfelsted.co.uk
web: www.thegreatpubcompany.co.uk
dir: *Exit M11 junct 8 onto A120 signed Felsted. Pub in village centre*

Venture through the door of this red brick-and-timber building and a pleasant surprise awaits. Rebuilt after a disastrous fire in the early 1900s, the building was formerly the village bank, then a run-down boozer. In 2002 it was rescued and stylishly refurbished by Jono and Jane Clark. Today it's very much a gastro-pub, with polished wood floors, leather sofas, chunky furnishings and colourful modern art, yet it successfully balances traditional pub attributes with a quality dining experience. There are roaring log fires in winter and a courtyard garden to enjoy in the warmer months. The atmosphere is friendly and informal and locals beat a path to the door for cracking Greene King ales and over a dozen world wines served by the glass; if sharing a bottle, allow time to peruse the 80-plus choices on the list. Seasonally changing food menus champion locally sourced produce. The à la carte menu offers an imaginative selection of modern European dishes whilst the lunch menu keeps them in touch with their pub roots. Tasters begin with olives or garlic bread, before brasserie starters such as smoked trout pâté and classic crayfish and prawn cocktail with Marie Rose sauce. Main courses cater to all tastes: slow roasted pork belly, apple mash, black pudding croquette, sprouts tops and jus; or grilled sea bass with chorizo sauce, crushed new potatoes and courgette spaghetti. Old favourites include pork sausages and creamy mash potato, and 100% minced rump steak burger, Gruyère, bacon and fries to name just two examples. Home-made treacle tart or Bramley apple and sultana crumble with crème anglaise may feature on the dessert list. Special offers and events, such as 3-course dinners for £15 on Tuesdays and live music every other Thursday, succeed in keeping the clientele coming. And with Stansted airport just 15 minutes away, The Swan makes a great last port of call before the holiday begins.

Open all wk 11.30-3 5-11 (Sun 11.30-6)
Bar Meals L served Mon-Sat 12-2.30, Sun 12-4 D served Mon-Thu 5.30-9.30, Fri-Sat 5.30-9.45 Av main course £12
Restaurant L served Mon-Sat 12-2.30, Sun 12-4 booking required D served Mon-Thu 5.30-9.30, Fri-Sat 5.30-9.45 booking required Fixed menu price fr £7.50 Av 3 course à la carte fr £27.50
⊕ GREENE KING 🍺 IPA, Prospect, Guinness, Guest ale Ö Stowford Press.
♟ 14 **Facilities** Children welcome Children's menu Children's portions Dogs allowed Garden Parking

Save on hotels. Book at **theAA.com/hotel**

ESSEX 177 ENGLAND

DEDHAM *continued*

PICK OF THE PUBS

The Sun Inn INN @ ♀

High St CO7 6DF ☎ 01206 323351
e-mail: office@thesuninndedham.com
dir: *From A12 follow signs to Dedham for 1.5m, pub on High Street*

The Sun has been transformed by owner Piers Baker into an inn of fine repute, with open fires, oak beams, a sun-trap terrace and walled garden. Here, a quiet pint goes hand in hand with robust food; there's a decent selection of real ales, with over twenty wines served by the glass. Locally sourced seasonal ingredients drive the daily-changing menu of Mediterranean-style dishes, many with a pronounced Italian flavour. Choose a plate of antipasti to share; or mussels and clams with white wine, parsley, garlic, chilli and lemon. Follow with Sutton Hoo chicken roasted with Mediterranean vegetables and grilled polenta, finishing with pannacotta with grappa and raspberries. If you can't quite tear yourself away, five en suite guest rooms with large comfy beds, crisp linen, character furniture and great showers are available. Look out for produce for sale at Victoria's Plums, and wine and food evenings from September to May.

Open all day all wk 11am-11pm Closed: 25-27 Dec **Bar Meals** L served Mon-Thu 12-2.30, Fri-Sun 12-3 D served Sun-Thu 6.30-9.30, Fri-Sat 6.30-10 Av main course £5 **Restaurant** L served Mon-Thu 12-2.30, Fri-Sun 12-3 D served Sun-Thu 6.30-9.30, Fri-Sat 6.30-10 Fixed menu price fr £12 Av 3 course à la carte fr £18 ⊕ FREE HOUSE ◀ Brewer's Gold Crouch Vale, Adnams Broadside, 2 Guest ales ♂ Aspall. ♀ 25 **Facilities** Children welcome Children's menu Children's portions Dogs allowed Garden Parking Wi-fi **Rooms** 5

FEERING Map 7 TL82

The Sun Inn ♀

Feering Hill CO5 9NH
☎ 01376 570442 ▤ 01376 570442
e-mail: sunninnfeering@live.co.uk
dir: *On A12 between Colchester & Witham. Village 1m*

Real ale and real food are at the heart of this pretty, timbered pub that dates from 1525. There's a large garden for the summer months, while winter warmth comes from two inglenook fireplaces. There are no TVs or games machines; instead the customers create the atmosphere. Food-wise, expect simple, seasonal dishes; perhaps tempura-battered prawns followed by fresh fish in a Spitfire ale batter with chips, peas and home-made tartare sauce, with plum crumble for pudding.

Open all wk Sat-Sun all day **Bar Meals** L served Mon-Sat 12-2.30, Sun 12-8 D served Mon-Sat 6-9.30, Sun 12-8 **Restaurant** L served Mon-Sat 12-2.30, Sun 12-8 D served Mon-Sat 6-9.30, Sun 12-8 ⊕ SHEPHERD NEAME ◀ Master Brew, Spitfire, Bishops Finger, seasonal ale, Guest ales. ♀ 10 **Facilities** Children welcome Children's menu Children's portions Dogs allowed Garden Parking

FELSTED Map 6 TL62

PICK OF THE PUBS

The Swan at Felsted ♀

See Pick of the Pubs on opposite page

FINGRINGHOE Map 7 TM02

The Whalebone ♀

Chapel Rd CO5 7BG ☎ 01206 729307
e-mail: vicki@thewhaleboneinn.co.uk
dir: *Telephone for directions*

This Grade II listed 18th-century free house enjoys breathtaking views from its position at the top of the Roman river valley. The unusual name comes from bones, once fastened above the door of the pub, which came from a locally beached whale. The converted barn has wooden floors, exposed beams, unique artwork and sculptures. Another unusual feature is the oak tree nearby; legend has it that the tree grew from an acorn in the mouth of a pirate executed and buried there some centuries ago. No acorns on the menu though, just hearty dishes prepared on the premises along with four cask ales.

Open all wk noon-3 5.30-11 (Sat-Sun 11 Sun noon-10.30) **Bar Meals** L served Mon-Sat 12-2.30, Sun 12-6.45 booking required D served Mon-Thu 6.30-9, Fri-Sat 6.30-9.30, Sun 12-6.45 booking required Av main course £12.95 **Restaurant** L served Mon-Sat 12-2.30, Sun 12-6.45 booking required D served Mon-Thu 6.30-9, Fri-Sat 6.30-9.30, Sun 12-6.45 booking required Av 3 course à la carte fr £24.95 ⊕ FREE HOUSE ◀ 4 Guest ales ♂ Aspall. ♀ 13 **Facilities** Children's menu Children's portions Play area Family room Dogs allowed Garden Parking

FULLER STREET Map 6 TL71

The Square and Compasses ♀

CM3 2BB ☎ 01245 361477 ▤ 01245 362633
e-mail: info@thesquareandcompasses.co.uk
web: www.thesquareandcompasses.co.uk
dir: *From A131 (Chelmsford to Braintree) take Great Leighs exit, enter village, turn right into Boreham Rd. Turn left signed Fuller St & Terling. Pub on left on entering hamlet*

Known locally as The Stokehole, this lovingly restored free house dates from about 1652. Originally two farm cottages, the building still retains its original exposed beams and inglenook fireplaces, with antique furnishings. Food is simple and straightforward, served alongside a good selection of cider and East Anglian ales. As well as pub classics, the daily-changing chalkboard specials might include pan-fried local pigeon, crispy black pudding and buttered swede; Essex coast skate wing with lemon and parsley butter; home-made lemon and lime cheesecake with lemon sauce. There is a picket fenced garden and Mediterranean-style decking area.

Open all wk 11.30-3 6-11 (Sat-Sun noon-11) **Bar Meals** L served Mon-Fri 12-2, Sat 12-2.30, Sun 12-6 D served Mon-Sat 6.30-9.30 booking required **Restaurant** L served Mon-Fri 12-2, Sat 12-2.30, Sun 12-6 D served Mon-Sat 6.30-9.30 booking required ⊕ FREE HOUSE ◀ Square and Compasses Stokers Ale, Essex ♂ Westons. ♀ 14 **Facilities** Children welcome Children's portions Dogs allowed Garden Parking

GOLDHANGER Map 7 TL90

The Chequers Inn ♀ NEW

Church St CM9 8AS ☎ 01621 788203 ▤ 01621 788500
e-mail: chequersgoldhang@aol.com
dir: *From B1026, 500mtrs to village centre*

Built in 1410 The Chequers can be found in the picturesque village of Goldhanger on the River Blackwater. The pub name comes from a chequerboard used by the tax collector in the pub many, many years ago. At around 30 feet above sea level, it reputedly has the 'lowest' bar in Britain where you can enjoy a pint of Nelson's Revenge. Pride is taken in the preparation and presentation of food. Lite bites may include moules marinière or local asparagus wrapped in smoked salmon. Main courses on the carte are reasonably priced: home-baked steak and stout pie; bacon, sage and onion pudding; and chicken and seafood paella. There is a beer festival in March and September.

Open all day all wk **Bar Meals** L served all wk 12-3 D served Mon-Sat 6.30-9 Av main course £9.25 **Restaurant** L served all wk 12-3 booking required D served Mon-Sat 6.30-9 booking required Av 3 course à la carte fr £17 ⊕ PUNCH TAVERNS ◀ Young's Bitter, Woodforde's Nelson's Revenge, Crouch Vale Brewers Gold, St Austell Tribute ♂ Westons Old Rosie & Traditional Perry. ♀ 13 **Facilities** Children welcome Children's menu Children's portions Dogs allowed Garden Beer festival Parking

GOSFIELD Map 13 TL72

The Green Man ♀

The Street CO9 1TP ☎ 01787 273608
e-mail: info@thegreenmangosfield.co.uk
dir: *Take A131 N from Braintree then A1017 to village*

Situated close to the picturesque Gosfield Lake, this pink-washed medley of buildings houses a village dining pub where all are welcome. At lunchtime, enjoy a pint of Abbot Ale or one of the guest ales with a choice of thick cut sandwiches and crusty filled baguettes, plus dishes such as breaded scampi and chips, and mussels in white
continued

GOSFIELD *continued*

wine, shallots and cream. Using the best of local produce, the dinner menu is based around classic British and international fare and offers the likes of Thai spiced chicken skewers with peanut and almond dipping sauce; crab, king prawn and crayfish linguini; and oven baked sea bass fillet with dill and caper cream.

Open all day all wk Mon-Thu 12-3 6-11 (Fri-Sat noon-mdnt Sun 12-10.30) **Bar Meals** L served Mon-Sat 12-2.30, Sun 12-4 D served Mon-Sat 6-9 Av main course £8.50 **Restaurant** L served Mon-Sat 12-2.30, Sun 12-4 D served Mon-Sat 6-9 Fixed menu price fr £10 Av 3 course à la carte fr £24 ⊕ GREENE KING ◀ Greene King IPA, Abbot Ale, Guest ales ♂ Aspall, Kopparberg. ♥ 16 **Facilities** Children welcome Children's menu Children's portions Dogs allowed Garden Parking Wi-fi

GREAT BRAXTED Map 7 TL81

PICK OF THE PUBS

The Ducane ♥

The Village CM8 3EJ
☎ 01621 891697 ▤ 01621 890009
e-mail: eat@theducane.co.uk
dir: *Great Braxted signed between Witham & Kelvedon on A12*

Forming part of a village that was displaced by Lord Du Cane in the 19th century, this friendly, modern-looking pub was built in 1935 and is the domain of award-winning chef Jonathan Brown. Refurbished with style and flair by Jonathan and partner Louise Partis, expect a warm welcome, local Maldon ales at the bar and innovative menus that champion local produce and local suppliers, including Braxted beef and lamb, Colchester oysters and seasonal goodies (plums, quince, pears and figs) from the gardens and allotments of local residents. Typical dishes may include sea bass with scallops and bean and herb salsa, beef fillet with creamed peppercorn and brandy sauce, rabbit pie, braised Wicks Manor pork belly, and chocolate terrine with chocolate sauce and walnut ice cream. Great value set menus and don't miss the roast on Sunday. One to watch…!

Open Tue-Fri 12-3 6-11.30 (Sat 12-3 6-12 Sun 12-4) Closed: Sun eve & Mon **Bar Meals** L served Tue-Sun 12-2.30 booking required D served Tue-Sat 7-9.30 booking required Av main course £12.50 **Restaurant** L served Tue-Sun 12-2.30 booking required D served Tue-Sat 7-9.30 booking required Fixed menu price fr £10 Av 3 course à la carte fr £25.50 ⊕ FREE HOUSE ◀ Adnams Bitter, Bass Bitter, Maldon Gold, Farmers Ales. ♥ 10 **Facilities** Children welcome Children's menu Children's portions Dogs allowed Garden Beer festival Parking

GREAT YELDHAM Map 13 TL73

PICK OF THE PUBS

The White Hart ★★★★ RR ◉◉

Poole St CO9 4HJ ☎ 01787 237250 ▤ 01787 238044
e-mail: mjwmason@yahoo.co.uk
dir: *On A1017 between Haverhill & Halstead*

Highwaymen were once locked up in a small prison beneath the stairs of this impressive 500-year-old timber-framed inn. Situated on the border of Essex and Suffolk, the White Hart enjoys a setting within four and a half acres of gardens, close to Heddingham Castle, the Colne Valley and Newmarket. With its blend of traditional and contemporary, it's a popular wedding venue on the one hand, and a great place to sample Brandon's Rusty Bucket on the other. The hard work put in by the establishment's owner, Matthew Mason, has resulted in many awards, including two AA Rosettes for its food. The express bar menu lists favourites such as Cumberland sausage ring with Cheddar mash and onion gravy, while the à la carte choice includes ballotine of Yeldham wood pigeon among its starters, and Auberies Estate roast loin of venison as a main course. For dessert there's baked Alaska or warm pear frangipane. Eleven en suite and fully equipped rooms complete the picture.

Open all day all wk **Bar Meals** L served all wk 12-6 **Restaurant** L served all wk 12-9.30 D served all wk 12-9.30 ⊕ FREE HOUSE ◀ Adnams Bitter, Black Sheep, Rusty Bucket, Doom Bar ♂ Aspall. **Facilities** Children welcome Children's menu Children's portions Play area Garden Parking Wi-fi **Rooms** 11

HASTINGWOOD Map 6 TL40

Rainbow & Dove ♥ NEW

Hastingwood Rd CM17 9JX ☎ 01279 415419
e-mail: rainbowanddove@hotmail.co.uk
dir: *Just off M11 junct 7*

A farmhouse before it became a pub, this beamed local can trace its origins back to the Domesday Book. Three real ales include a guest, and menus revolve around fresh produce. Fish from Billingsgate Market is bought, delivered and cooked all on the same day, so you may find skate, sea bass and bream on the blackboard. Other dishes for which the pub is famous are fresh crab sandwiches, hot salt-beef sandwiches, and the 'Over the Rainbow' burger, which has too many ingredients to list.

Open Mon-Sat 11.30-3.30 6-11 (Sun 12-4) Closed: Sun eve **Bar Meals** L served Mon-Sat 12-2.30, Sun 12-3.30 D served Mon-Sat 7-9.30 Av main course £8.50 **Restaurant** L served Mon-Sat 12-2.30, Sun 12-3.30 D served Mon-Sat 7-9.30 Av 3 course à la carte fr £17 ⊕ FREE HOUSE ◀ Adnams Broadside, Sharp's, Rainbow & Dove own brew, Guest ales ♂ Aspall. ♥ 10 **Facilities** Children welcome Children's menu Children's portions Dogs allowed Garden Parking

HORNDON ON THE HILL Map 6 TQ68

PICK OF THE PUBS

Bell Inn & Hill House ♥

See Pick of the Pubs on opposite page

INGATESTONE Map 6 TQ69

The Red Lion

Main Rd, Margaretting CM4 0EQ ☎ 01277 352184
e-mail: the_redlion@msn.com
dir: *From Chelmsford take A12 towards Brentwood. Margaretting in 4m*

The phrase 'quintessential English pub' is something of a cliché, but how else to describe the 17th-century Red Lion? The bar is decorated in burgundy and aubergine, the restaurant in coffee and cream. Seasonal highlights include spring onion, feta and courgette fritters; sausage and mustard mash; lamb hotpot; a daily roast; deep-fried Lowestoft cod and chips (or to take away); and aubergine, tomato and mozzarella pie. As we went to press a change of hands was taking place.

Open all wk 12-3 5.30-11.30 (Sat-Sun 11am-11pm) ⊕ GREENE KING ◀ Greene King IPA, Tribute, Abbot, Speckled Hen ♂ Aspall. **Facilities** Children welcome Children's menu Children's portions Play area Garden Parking Wi-fi

LANGHAM Map 13 TM03

The Shepherd and Dog

Moor Rd CO4 5NR ☎ 01206 272711 ▤ 01206 273136
dir: *A12 from Colchester towards Ipswich, take 1st left signed Langham*

Set in the attractive village of Langham deep in Constable country on the Suffolk/Essex border, this 1928 free house has all the classic styling of an English country pub. Widely renowned for its food, it serves an extensive variety of meat, fish and poultry dishes, plus a vegetarian selection and a children's menu. A typical meal could take in deep-fried Brie with cranberry sauce followed by home-made chicken curry or maybe pork fillet with creamy orange, cider and mushroom sauce.

Open all wk **Bar Meals** L served Mon-Fri 12-3, Sat-Sun 12-9.30 D served Mon-Fri 6-9.30, Sat-Sun 12-9.30 **Restaurant** L served Mon-Fri 12-3, Sat-Sun 12-9.30 D served Mon-Fri 6-9.30, Sat-Sun 12-9.30 ⊕ FREE HOUSE ◀ Greene King IPA, Abbot Ale, Guest ales. **Facilities** Children welcome Children's menu Children's portions Dogs allowed Garden Parking

PICK OF THE PUBS

Bell Inn & Hill House 🍷

HORNDON ON THE HILL Map 6 TQ68

High Rd SS17 8LD
☎ **01375 642463** 📠 **01375 361611**
e-mail: info@bell-inn.co.uk
web: www.bell-inn.co.uk
dir: *M25 junct 30/31 signed Thurrock*

Much of the structure of this historic free house was already complete when King Henry VII came to the throne in 1445. The Bell's longevity has clearly affected its proprietors, who have kept it in the same family since 1938. From its earliest days it served as a coaching inn, as witnessed by the archway through to the courtyard. From the first-floor gallery that runs above the courtyard, luggage would have been transferred to and from the top of the London stagecoaches. Once inside, look for the original king post that supports the inn's ancient roof timbers. You cannot help but notice hot cross buns hanging from the beams in the saloon bar. Every year the oldest willing villager hangs another, an unusual tradition that dates back about 100 years when the pub happened to change hands on a Good Friday; during the shortages of World War II the tradition was maintained with a bun of concrete. In the bars, regular brews like Greene King IPA and Crouchvale Brewers Gold are backed by a selection of guest ales that changes every few days. Many bottles from the extensive wine list are served by the glass. The lunchtime bar menu offers open sandwiches and a popular selection of light meals such as smoked haddock kedgeree with poached egg, and sautéed beef with Stilton and buttered onions. Booking is essential in the bustling, cosmopolitan restaurant, where the daily-changing modern British menu is built on fresh produce. A typical meal begins with deep-fried Tamworth Brie, aubergine caviar, smoked garlic and tomato jam; followed by oregano roasted chump of lamb on sweet potato hash, minted pea purée and tomato jus. Stylish puddings include mango mousse with coconut ice cream and spun sugar.

Open all wk Mon-Fri 11-3 5.30-11 (Sat 11-3 6-11 Sun 12-4 7-10.30)

Closed: 25-26 Dec **Bar Meals** L served all wk 12-1.45 D served Sun-Fri 6.30-9.45, Sat 6-9.45 Av main course £12.95 **Restaurant** L served Mon-Sat 12-1.45, Sun 12-2.30 booking required D served all wk 6.30-9.45 booking required Av 3 course à la carte fr £26.95 🛢 FREE HOUSE ⬛ Greene King IPA, Interbrew Bass, Crouchvale Brewers Gold, Ruddles County, Spitfire. 🍷 16 **Facilities** Children's portions Dogs allowed Garden Parking Wi-fi

LITTLE BRAXTED   Map 7 TL81

The Green Man NEW

Green Man Ln CM8 3LB
☎ 01621 891659   📠 01621 891659
e-mail: info@thegreenmanlittlebraxted.co.uk
dir: *From A12 junct 22 take unclassified road (Little Braxted Lane) through Little Braxted. Straight ahead into Kelvedon Rd. Right into Green Man Lane*

The real ales in this country pub, which has traded since the early 1700s, have won recognition for their quality. It's reckoned that over three-quarters of the monthly trade comprises of customers returning here from all over the county. Apart from the range of ales and lagers, its popularity stems from the full snack menu available at every session; and home-made specials such as steak and kidney pudding; braised lamb shank; and beef stew with dumplings. Haggis, too, is always available thanks to its introduction 25 years ago by the Scottish landlord. A large secluded garden eases summer congestion.

Open all wk Mon-Sat 11.30-3 5-11 (Sun 12-7)
Bar Meals L served Mon-Sat 12-2.30, Sun 12-6 D served Mon-Sat 6-9 Av main course £8.95 **Restaurant** L served Mon-Sat 12-2.30, Sun 12-6 D served Mon-Sat 6-9
Facilities Children welcome Children's menu Children's portions Dogs allowed Garden Parking

LITTLEBURY   Map 12 TL53

The Queens Head Inn ♥

High St CB11 4TD ☎ 01799 522251
e-mail: thequeenshead@fsmail.net
dir: *M11 junct 9A take B184 towards Saffron Walden. Right onto B1383, S towards Wendens Ambo*

A beautiful family-run former coaching inn with open fires, exposed beams and one of only two remaining full-length settles in England. Very much at the centre of the local community, the pub runs darts and football teams and pétanque competitions; a large beer garden with bouncy castle confirms its family-friendly credentials. The kitchen aims to produce good home-made pub grub at realistic prices, with a menu of popular favourites from pizzas to pies, ciabattas to curries.

Open all wk Mon-Thu 12-3 5.30-11 (Fri 12-3 5.30-mdnt Sat noon-mdnt Sun noon-10.30) **Bar Meals** L served all wk 12-2.30 D served all wk 6.30-9 **Restaurant** L served all wk 12-2.30 booking required D served all wk 6.30-9 booking required ⊕ GREENE KING ◖ Greene King IPA, Morland Old Speckled Hen, Guest ale ⦵ Stowford Press, Aspall. ♥ 9 **Facilities** Children welcome Children's menu Children's portions Play area Dogs allowed Garden Parking Wi-fi

LITTLE CANFIELD   Map 6 TL52

The Lion & Lamb ♥

CM6 1SR ☎ 01279 870257   📠 01279 870423
e-mail: info@lionandlamb.co.uk
web: www.lionandlamb.co.uk
dir: *M11 junct 8, B1256 towards Takeley & Little Canfield*

Ideal for business or leisure, this traditional country pub and restaurant was built as a coaching inn on what used to be the main East Coast road. Now bypassed, travellers on the way to Stansted airport seek it out for a last English pint before their trip, relaxing in the large and well-furnished garden. Inside are oak beams, winter log fires, an extensive food selection, real ales and up to eleven wines served by the glass. From the restaurant menu a starter of smoked trout fillet could be followed by roasted breast of Telmara duck with an apple and cream sauce.

Open all day all wk **Bar Meals** food served all day **Restaurant** food served all day ⊕ GREENE KING ◖ Old Speckled Hen, Greene King IPA, Old Bob, Guest ales. ♥ 11 **Facilities** Children welcome Children's menu Children's portions Play area Garden Parking Wi-fi

See advert on opposite page

LITTLE DUNMOW   Map 6 TL62

Flitch of Bacon

The Street CM6 3HT ☎ 01371 820323
dir: *B1256 to Braintree for 10m, turn off at Little Dunmow, 0.5m pub on right*

A charming 15th-century country inn, looking out over the fields, whose name refers to the ancient gift of half a salted pig, or 'flitch', to couples who have been married for a year and a day, and 'who have not had a cross word'. There are always two guest ales in addition to Greene King IPA. Children and dogs are welcome.

Open Mon eve-Sun Closed: Mon L **Bar Meals** L served Tue-Sun 12-2 D served Mon-Sat 6.30-9 ⊕ FREE HOUSE ◖ Greene King IPA, Guest ales. **Facilities** Children welcome Children's portions Family room Dogs allowed Garden Wi-fi **Notes** ⊜

MANNINGTREE   Map 13 TM13

PICK OF THE PUBS

The Mistley Thorn ⊚⊚ ♥

High St, Mistley CO11 1HE
☎ 01206 392821   📠 01206 390122
e-mail: info@mistleythorn.com
web: www.mistleythorn.com
dir: *From Ipswich A12 junct 31 onto B1070, follow signs to East Bergholt, Manningtree & Mistley. From Colchester A120 towards Harwich. Left at Horsley Cross. Mistley in 3m*

The Mistley Thorn has been standing in the Georgian village of Mistley since 1723, when it was purpose built as a coaching inn. During the 17th century, Witchfinder General Matthew Hopkins interrogated his unfortunate victims in a previous building on the site. The present interior is modish and clean-cut with a whiff of New England about it, and patrons can look forward to an eclectic menu that has gained two AA Rosettes for executive chef Sherri Singleton. Unsurprisingly, there's an emphasis on fresh fish, and local oysters and seafood take pride of place. Start, perhaps, with treacle-cured organic salmon, or chargrilled day boat squid, before moving on to sample Mistley fish cakes with hand-cut fries and leaves; or choose from the daily catch list. Duck 'shepard's pie' with creamy parsnip mash and roasted vegetables is amongst the alternatives to fish, whilst hazelnut semifreddo with honey-roasted pears makes a typical dessert.

Open all wk 12-2.30 6.30-9 (Sat-Sun all day)
Bar Meals L served Mon-Fri 12-2.30, Sat-Sun all day D served Mon-Fri 6.30-9, Sat 6.30-9.30
Restaurant L served Mon-Fri 12-2.30, Sat-Sun all day D served Mon-Fri 6.30-9, Sat 6.30-9.30 Fixed menu price fr £16.50 Av 3 course à la carte fr £22.50 ⊕ FREE HOUSE ◖ Mersea Bitter, Adnams Bitter. ♥ 17
Facilities Children welcome Children's menu Children's portions Dogs allowed Parking Wi-fi

Lion & Lamb | The White House

Restaurant and Bar now offering Accommodation in conjunction with
The White House Luxury Country House

A traditional country restaurant and bar complete with oak beams and a large secluded garden overlooking farmland. Side the B1256 (the old A120) 5 mins from M11–J8 and Stansted Airport is the Lion & Lamb, a traditional country pub combined with a restaurant serving very modern food all day long – kangaroo, grilled dover sole, pork belly and roasted loin with a pumpkin puree, parsnips and a tarragon jus and wild mushroom risotto are just some of the temptations that could be offered. With its oak beams and cosy fireplace, the Lion & Lamb dates back to the 16th century and is very inviting. Bar snacks are available and diners are welcome to eat in the bar, dining area or conservatory. Children are welcome, making the Lion & Lamb a popular choice for family groups.

This carefully refurbished family home displays many original 16th-century features alongside modern comforts. The Grade II listed building is close to Stansted Airport and is enclosed by extensive gardens. Accommodation is stylish with large beds and ensuite and there is a luxurious Victorian bathroom.

Served around one table in the farmhouse-style kitchen, the full cooked breakfast is a wholesome start to the day. For other meals a range of interesting dishes, using quality local ingredients, is available in the Lion and Lamb pub a mile up the road, which is owned by the same proprietors who offer free transport to and fro.

Stortford Road (B1256), Little Canfield, Dunmow, Near Takeley CM6 1SR
Tel: 01279 870257   Fax: 01279 870423
Email: info@lionandlamb.co.uk or enquiries@whitehousestansted.co.uk
www.lionandlamb.co.uk or www.whitehousestansted.co.uk

ROUTIERS Johansen Conde Nast

MARGARETTING TYE — Map 6 TL60

The White Hart Inn ♥ NEW

Swan Ln CM4 9JX ☎ 01277 840478
e-mail: enquiries@thewhitehart.uk.com
dir: *From A12 junct 15, B1002 to Margaretting. At x-roads in Margaretting left into Maldon Rd. Under rail bridge, left. Right into Swan Lane, follow Margaretting Tye signs. Follow to pub on right*

The owners of this part-weatherboarded pub, tucked in beside the village green, revel in offering a great choice of the best regional and local beers and cider; much anticipated spring and autumn beer festivals testify to the popularity of this approach. The pub's interior, all matchboarding, dark posts, pillars, beams and fireplaces, oozes character, whilst the solidly traditional menu shouts quality, the home-made deep-dish steak and ale pie and Arbroath smokie fishcakes are local favourites; a specials board adds to the fray.

Open all wk 11.30-3 6-mdnt (Sat-Sun noon-mdnt) Closed: 25 Dec **Bar Meals** L served Mon-Fri 12-2, Sat 12-2.30, Sun all day D served Tue-Sat 6-9, Sun 6.30-8.30 Av main course £9 **Restaurant** L served Mon-Fri 12-2, Sat 12-2.30, Sun all day D served Tue-Sat 6-9, Sun 6.30-8.30 Fixed menu price fr £18.95 ⊕ FREE HOUSE ◀ Adnams Best, Broadside, Mighty Oak IPA, Oscar Wilde Mild, Red Fox Hunter's Gold ♂ Aspall, Black Rat. ♥ 10 **Facilities** Children welcome Children's menu Family room Dogs allowed Garden Beer festival Parking Wi-fi

NEWNEY GREEN — Map 6 TL60

The Duck Pub & Dining ♥ NEW

CM1 3SF ☎ 01245 421894
e-mail: theduckinn1@btconnect.com
dir: *From Chelmsford take A1060 (Sawbridgeworth). Straight on at mini rdbt, 4th left into Vicarage Rd (signed Roxwell & Willingate), left into Hoe St, becomes Gravelly lane, left to pub*

A 17th-century inn formed from two agricultural cottages in the tiny hamlet of Newney Green, The Duck was taken over by the current owner in 2010 after years of neglect. Now fully restored, this friendly country inn offers up to six real ales, local ciders and menus that reflect the region's produce — there are even plans to create a kitchen garden. In the beamed dining room, popular dishes include classic steak and ale pie, and thickly cut loin of pork with caramelised apples. There is a garden with children's play area and an August Bank Holiday beer festival.

Open all day Closed: Mon **Bar Meals** L served Tue-Sun 12-9.30 D served Tue-Sun 12-9.30 Av main course £12 food served all day **Restaurant** L served Tue-Sun 12-9.30 D served Tue-Sun 12-9.30 Av 3 course à la carte fr £16 food served all day ⊕ FREE HOUSE ◀ Woodforde's Wherry, Muddy Duck, Adnams Broadside. ♥ 14 **Facilities** Children welcome Children's menu Children's portions Play area Family room Garden Beer festival Parking Wi-fi

NORTH FAMBRIDGE — Map 7 TQ89

The Ferry Boat Inn

Ferry Ln CM3 6LR ☎ 01621 740208
dir: *From Chelmsford take A130 S, then A132 to South Woodham Ferrers, then B1012. Turn right to village*

Popular with yachtsmen, walkers and visitors to the nearby wildlife reserve (Essex Wildlife Trust's 600-acre sanctuary), this 500 year-old weather-boarded free house is tucked away in a lovely village beside the River Crouch and marina. It started out as three fishermen's cottages and is believed to have been an inn for at least 200 years. Low beams and winter fires add character to the bars where tip-top Greene King ales are on tap. Menu choices include traditional pub fare such as baguettes, jacket potatoes and omelettes, plus favourites like steak and kidney pie or half a roast duck, chips and salad.

Open all wk 11.30-3 6.30-11 (Sun 12-4 6.30-10.30 & all day in summer) **Bar Meals** L served all wk 12-2 D served all wk 7-9.30 **Restaurant** L served all wk 12-2 booking required D served all wk 7-9.30 booking required ⊕ FREE HOUSE ◀ Greene King IPA, Abbot Ale, Morland. **Facilities** Children welcome Children's menu Children's portions Family room Dogs allowed Garden Parking

PATTISWICK — Map 13 TL82

PICK OF THE PUBS

The Compasses at Pattiswick ♥

See Pick of the Pubs on opposite page

PELDON — Map 7 TL91

The Peldon Rose ♥

Colchester Rd CO5 7QJ
☎ 01206 735248 📠 01206 736303
e-mail: enquiries@thepeldonrose.co.uk
dir: *On B1025 Mersea Rd, just before causeway*

This 500-year-old heavily beamed former smugglers' and coaching inn exudes character in spades. It boasts log fires in the bar in winter, original beams and leaded windows. With well kept real ales and a well sourced wine list, the menu features haddock in Adnams beer batter — the fish is from Mersea Island just a mile away; other dishes are Greek-style lamb casserole with lemon couscous; and vegetable samosa with spiced roasted sweet potato and raita. A conservatory, perfect for summer dining, leads to the garden.

Open all day all wk Closed: 25 Dec **Bar Meals** L served all wk 12-2.30 booking required D served all wk 6.30-9 booking required Av main course £11 **Restaurant** L served all wk 12-2.30 booking required D served all wk 6.30-9 booking required Fixed menu price fr £10 Av 3 course à la carte fr £10 ⊕ FREE HOUSE ◀ Adnams, Old Speckled Hen, Greene King IPA ♂ Aspall. ♥ 15 **Facilities** Children welcome Children's menu Children's portions Dogs allowed Garden Parking

STANSTED AIRPORT

See **Little Canfield**

STOCK — Map 6 TQ69

The Hoop

21 High St CM4 9BD ☎ 01277 841137
e-mail: thehoopstock@yahoo.co.uk
web: www.thehoop.co.uk
dir: *On B1007 between Chelmsford & Billericay*

This 15th-century free house on Stock's village green is every inch the traditional country pub. Expect a warm welcome, authentic pub interiors and a pleasing absence of music and fruit machines. Seasonal menus comprise high quality ingredients carefully prepared and presented. Its annual beer festival (late May Bank Holiday) has been going from strength to strength for over 30 years; you'll have over 200 real ales to choose from, not to mention fruit beers and perries, and a hog roast to soak it up.

Open all day all wk 11-11 (Sun 12-10.30) **Bar Meals** L served Mon-Sat 12-2.30, Sun 12-5 D served Mon-Sat 6-9 Av main course £9 **Restaurant** L served Tue-Fri 12-2.30, Sun 12-3 booking required D served Tue-Sat 6-9 booking required Av 3 course à la carte fr £25 ⊕ FREE HOUSE ◀ Adnams Bitter, 4 Guest ales ♂ Westons, Thatchers, Aspall. **Facilities** Children welcome Children's portions Dogs allowed Garden Beer festival

WOODHAM MORTIMER — Map 7 TL80

Hurdlemakers Arms ♥

Post Office Rd CM9 6ST
☎ 01245 225169 📠 01245 225169
e-mail: info@hurdlemakersarms.co.uk
dir: *From Chelmsford A414 to Maldon/Danbury. 4.5m, through Danbury into Woodham Mortimer. Over 1st rdbt, 1st left, pub on left. Behind golf driving range*

Formerly two cottages, this 400 year-old listed building has been a pub since 1837. The beamed interior still retains its open log fire and many original features, and real ale lovers will be delighted by the wide range of micro-brewery products and ciders on offer. Home-made specials might include Barnsley lamb chops, Tuscan vegetable tart, or smoked haddock Florentine. There are weekend summer barbecues in the large beer garden, and a beer festival on the last weekend in June.

Open all day Mon-Sat (Sun 12-9) **Bar Meals** L served Mon-Fri 12-3, Sat 12-9.30, Sun 12-8 D served Mon-Fri 6-9.30, Sat 12-9.30, Sun 12-8 **Restaurant** L served Mon-Fri 12-3, Sat 12-9.30, Sun 12-8 D served Mon-Fri 6-9.30, Sat 12-9.30, Sun 12-8 ⊕ GRAY & SONS ◀ Abbot, Mighty Oak, Crouch Vale, Farmers ales, Wibblers, Guest ales ♂ Old Rosie, Westons Scrumpy, Westons Organic. ♥ 8 **Facilities** Children welcome Children's menu Children's portions Play area Garden Beer festival Parking

PICK OF THE PUBS

The Compasses at Pattiswick 🍷

PATTISWICK   Map 13 TL82

Compasses Rd CM77 8BG
☎ 01376 561322 📄 01376 564343
e-mail:
info@thecompassesatpattiswick.co.uk
web: www.thegreatpubcompany.co.uk
dir: *From Braintree take A120 E towards Colchester. After Bradwell 1st left to Pattiswick*

Years ago, two farm-workers cottages were amalgamated to form this friendly pub, still surrounded by the meadows and pocket woodlands of the Holifield Estate, tucked away deep in the north Essex countryside. Connections with the estate run deeper than mere location, however: the pub's owners source some of the raw materials for the extensive menu direct from the estate, so you'll be confident in knowing just where your pheasant, venison, rabbit or partridge grew to maturity. Support for local producers is at the centre of the pub's ethos, with minimising food miles a guiding principle; hence meats are traceable to local farms and seafood comes from inshore fishermen on the Essex coast. Hearty rural recipes and uncomplicated cooking allow the dishes to do the talking; the monthly changing menu is supplemented by a daily specials board allowing the chefs to take full advantage of seasonal produce and the freshest ingredients - braised lamb shank with crushed root vegetables and creamy mashed potatoes or grilled

sea bass with chervil-crushed potatoes, watercress and a red pepper coulis. Specials will vary with the seasons. The wine list is very comprehensive, with 13 available by the glass, a generous range of old and new world bins and a fine wine list featuring some exclusive Bordeaux and Burgundies. A roaring log fire is a welcoming sight after a winter walk, while in summer the large garden is inviting. Families are very well catered for here, with a play area, child menus, a toy box to keep little diners entertained and family fun days in the summer with a beer tent.

Open all wk 11-3 5.30-11 (Sat 5.30-mdnt, Sun noon-4 5.30-9) **Bar Meals** L served all wk 12-3 D served Mon-Thu 5.30-9.30, Fri-Sat 5.30-9.45, Sun 5.30-9 Av main course £12 **Restaurant** L served Mon-Sat 12-3, Sun 12-4 booking required D served

Mon-Thu 5.30-9.30, Fri-Sat 5.30-9.45, Sun 5.30-9 booking required Fixed menu price fr £7.50 Av 3 course à la carte fr £27.50 🍺 FREE HOUSE ◀ Woodforde's Wherry, Adnams, Adnams Broadside, St Austell Tribute ♂ Aspall. 🍷 13 **Facilities** Children welcome Children's menu Children's portions Play area Dogs allowed Garden Parking Wi-fi

GLOUCESTERSHIRE

ALDERTON
Map 10 SP03

The Gardeners Arms

Beckford Rd GL20 8NL ☎ 01242 620257
e-mail: gardeners1@btconnect.com
web: www.gardenersarms.biz
dir: Telephone for directions

This charming family-run 16th-century thatched free house has always been a pub. The quiet Cotswolds village of Alderton was created when plague hit nearby Great Washbourne, so villagers moved up the road to a place that wasn't 'cursed'. Today you can play boules in the large beer garden, and traditional bar games in the stone-walled bar. Seasonal local produce underpins the menu, while weekly-changing specials include fresh fish dishes. The pub hosts two five-day beer festivals, one in May and the other at Christmas.

Open all wk 10-2 5.30-10 (Sun all day, Fri til mdnt)
Bar Meals L served all wk 12-2.15 D served all wk 5.30-9
Av main course £8.95 Restaurant L served Mon-Sat 12-2.15, Sun all day (until 9) booking required D served all wk 5.30-9 booking required ⊕ FREE HOUSE ◀ Sharp's Doom Bar, Butcombe Best, Courage Best, local Guest ales ♻ Westons Stowford. Facilities Children welcome Children's menu Children's portions Dogs allowed Garden Beer festival Parking Wi-fi

ALMONDSBURY
Map 4 ST68

The Bowl

16 Church Rd BS32 4DT
☎ 01454 612757 ▤ 01454 619910
e-mail: bowlinn@sabrain.com
dir: M5 junct 16 towards Thornbury. 3rd left onto Over Ln, 1st right onto Sundays Hill, next right onto Church Rd

Part of this pretty, whitewashed building dates from 1146, when monks were building the village church, so it was getting on when it became an inn in 1550. The Bowl nestles on the south-eastern edge of the Severn Vale, hence its name. It has an atmospheric interior with exposed stonework and a wood burner for winter warmth. A variety of freshly prepared food ranges from steaks to fresh fish and pasta – monkfish tail wrapped in prosciutto with white wine and tarragon sauce, blue goat's cheese and spinach lasagne.

Open all day all wk Bar Meals L served Mon-Thu 12-2.30, Fri-Sat 12-9.30, Sun 12-7.30 D served Mon-Thu 6-9.30 ⊕ BRAINS BREWERY ◀ Butcombe, Tribute, Brains ♻ Stowford Press. Facilities Children welcome Children's menu Children's portions Parking Wi-fi

ANDOVERSFORD
Map 10 SP01

The Royal Oak Inn ♥

Old Gloucester Rd GL54 4HR ☎ 01242 820335
e-mail: oakhouseinns@hotmail.com
dir: 200mtrs from A40, 4m E of Cheltenham

The 17th-century Royal Oak stands on the banks of the River Coln, in the heart of Andoversford. Originally a coaching inn, it has been sympathetically refurbished in recent times; its main dining room, galleried on two levels, occupies the converted former stables. Two log fires, three or more real ales and a draught cider are part of the allure, coupled with a restaurant menu of seasonal produce sourced locally; the specials board changes twice a week. Ask about meal deals, often on offer. The inn holds a beer festival each summer.

Open all day all wk Bar Meals L served all wk 12-2 D served all wk 7-9 Av main course £9.50
Restaurant L served all wk 12-2 D served all wk 7-9 Fixed menu price fr £9.75 ⊕ ENTERPRISE INNS ◀ Doom Bar, Butcombe ♻ Westons Vintage Organic. ♥ 13
Facilities Children welcome Children's menu Children's portions Dogs allowed Garden Beer festival Parking

ARLINGHAM
Map 4 SO71

PICK OF THE PUBS

The Old Passage Inn

RR ⊛⊛ ♥

Passage Rd GL2 7JR
☎ 01452 740547 ▤ 01452 741871
e-mail: oldpassage@ukonline.co.uk
dir: 5m from A38 adjacent M5 junct 13

Occupying a delightful location on the edge of the River Severn, surrounded by fields, this seafood restaurant-with-rooms has been an inn for centuries. It once provided refreshment to ferry passengers across the tidal river but now attracts people from afar for its quality food and air of tranquility. You will still find real ales like Wickwar and Westons Organic cider on tap, but the food and wine on offer may be too tempting to ignore. Eating in the open and airy dining room is a delight, as it's on the popular riverside terrace. Years ago the Severn would have supplied much of the fish, but its elvers and salmon are now in short supply and rarely feature on the menu; freshwater crayfish may turn up, though, and the inn's own saltwater tanks virtually guarantee Pembrokeshire or Cornish lobsters. Dishes include roast halibut with broccoli purée with celeriac fondant and whole roasted plaice with nut brown butter. Non-fish alternatives, such as slow roasted shoulder of pork with beer braised Savoy cabbage, are there if you want them. There are three modern en suite bedrooms here.

Open 10-3 7-finish (all day Etr-Sep) Closed: 25 Dec, Jan-Feb Tue & Wed eve, Sun eve & Mon
Bar Meals L served Tue-Sat 12-2, Sun 12-3 booking required D served Tue-Sat 7-9 Restaurant L served Tue-Sat 12-2.30, Sun 12-3 booking required D served Tue-Sat 6-9 booking required ⊕ FREE HOUSE ◀ Wickwar ♻ Westons Organic. ♥ 12
Facilities Children welcome Children's portions Dogs allowed Garden Parking Wi-fi Rooms 3

ASHLEWORTH
Map 10 SO82

Boat Inn

The Quay GL19 4HZ ☎ 01452 700272 ▤ 01452 700272
e-mail: elisabeth_nicholls@yahoo.co.uk
dir: From Gloucester take A417 towards Ledbury. At Hartpury follow signs for Ashleworth Quay

This picturesque pub on the banks of the Severn has been in the same family for over 400 years, and has changed very little in that time. Renowned for its real ales, serving them straight from the barrel, the beers are sourced from smaller, local and regional brewers and are changed frequently. The pub also has a great selection of ciders supplied by the local cider house, Westons. Traditionally filled rolls, perhaps with home-made tomato chutney, form the hub of the simple but delicious food offering, available only at lunchtimes.

Open Tue & Wed (eve)-Sun Closed: Mon & Wed L
Bar Meals L served Tue, Thu-Sun 12-2 ⊕ FREE HOUSE ◀ Wye Valley, Church End, Arkells, RCH Pitchfork ♻ Westons Stowford Press, Westons Old Rosie Scrumpy, Westons Stowford Export. Facilities Children welcome Garden Parking Notes ⊛

PICK OF THE PUBS

The Queens Arms ♥

The Village GL19 4HT ☎ 01452 700395
web: www.queensarmsashleworth.co.uk
dir: From Gloucester N on A417 for 5m. At Hartpury, opp Royal Exchange turn right at Broad St to Ashleworth. Pub 100yds past village green

It was 1998 when Tony and Gillian Burreddu opened the doors of their engaging 16th-century inn in this pretty Severn-side village. During the intervening years they have completed most of their planned alterations, while leaving the original beams and iron fireplaces well alone, simply complementing them with comfortable armchairs and antiques; plus most recently a gallery of local artists' work. It's one of those always-reliable locals, popular for all sorts of reasons, but especially because of ever-changing menus that typically have featured seared fresh tuna steak on salsa verde with chilli ginger and garlic dressing; Gressingham duck breast with hot black cherries and Kirsch and brandy sauce; and tomato bredie, a subtly spiced lamb stew from South Africa. From the peaceful garden behind 200-year-old clipped yews, enjoy views of the surrounding hills, in one hand a pint of Sharp's Doom Bar or dry white wine; in the other a ping pong ball for amusing Bonnie, the pub cat.

Open noon-3 7-11 Closed: 25-26 Dec & 1 Jan, Sun eve & Mon (ex BH wknds) **Bar Meals** L served Tue-Sun 12-2 booking required D served Tue-Sat 7-9 booking required Av main course £12.95 **Restaurant** L served Tue-Sun 12-2 booking required D served Tue-Sat 7-9 booking required Fixed menu price fr £6.95 Av 3 course à la carte fr £22.50 ⊕ FREE HOUSE ◀ Timothy Taylor Landlord, Donnington BB, S A Brain & Company Rev James, Shepherd Neame Spitfire, Sharp's Doom Bar Ö Stowford Press. ₹ 14 **Facilities** Children welcome Garden Parking

---

BARNSLEY   Map 5 SP00

PICK OF THE PUBS

The Village Pub ⊛ ⌕

GL7 5EF ☎ **01285 740421**   📄 **01285 740925**
e-mail: reservations@thevillagepub.co.uk
web: www.thevillagepub.co.uk
dir: On B4425 4m NE of Cirencester

Refurbished by new owners, this traditional 'Village Pub' is a far cry from the average local. Owned by the same team behind Calcot Manor Hotel and Barnsley House opposite, this chic pub-restaurant is at the heart of the charming Cotswold village. It has been beautifully refurbished, yet retains its polished flagstones, oak floorboards, exposed timbers and open fireplaces. Expect a civilised atmosphere in the five rambling dining rooms, which sport an eclectic mix of furniture, rug-strewn floors, oil paintings, cosy settles, warm terracotta walls and crackling log fires. Innovative modern British pub food draws a discerning

dining crowd, the daily menus featuring quality local ingredients, including traceable or organic meats, fresh seasonal fish and vegetables from the famous Barnsley House gardens. Starters may take in quail Scotch eggs, with main dishes ranging from braised lamb hotpot with Anna potatoes to Barbary duck breast with vegetable gratin.

Open all wk 11-11 (Sun 11-10) **Bar Meals** L served Mon-Fri 12-2.30, Sat-Sun 12-3 D served Mon-Thu 6-9.30, Fri-Sat 6-10, Sun 6-9 Av main course £14 **Restaurant** Av 3 course à la carte fr £25 ⊕ FREE HOUSE ◀ Hook Norton Bitter, Butcombe Traditional, Guest ales Ö Ashton Press. ₹ 10 **Facilities** Children welcome Children's portions Dogs allowed Garden Parking Wi-fi

---

BERKELEY   Map 4 ST69

The Malt House ★★★ INN

Marybrook St GL13 9BA
☎ **01453 511177**   📄 **01453 810257**
e-mail: the-malthouse@btconnect.com
dir: M5 junct 13/14, A38 towards Bristol. Pub on main road towards Sharpness

Within walking distance of Berkeley Castle and its deer park, this family-run free house is also handy for the Edward Jenner museum, dedicated to the life of the founding father of immunology. Inside the heavily beamed pub you'll find a varied selection of lunchtime bar food with a choice of real ales and ciders, as well as weekly home-made specials in the restaurant. Pub favourites like steak and ale pie rub shoulders with vegetarian stuffed peppers, and grilled halibut, butter and lime. Accommodation is available.

Open all wk Mon-Thu 4-11 (Fri 3-mdnt Sat noon-mdnt Sun noon-4) ⊕ FREE HOUSE ◀ Old Speckled Hen, Theakstons Best Ö Stowford Press, Thatchers Gold. **Facilities** Children welcome Children's menu Garden Parking **Rooms** 10

BIBURY   Map 5 SP10

Catherine Wheel

Arlington GL7 5ND ☎ **01285 740250**
e-mail: info@catherinewheel-bibury.co.uk
dir: On B4425, W of Bibury

This former blacksmiths has changed hands many times since J Hathaway opened it as an inn in 1856 but a warm welcome, good local ales and quality food remain its hallmarks. The beautiful Cotswold stone building, stable courtyard and orchard date back to the 15th century and plenty of historical features remain. The short but appetising menu might include seared scallops with crispy duck confit, squash purée and red wine syrup; pot-roasted chicken with truffle mash, smoked bacon, shallots and peas; and king prawn and mussel spaghetti. There is a beer festival held every August Bank Holiday.

Open all day all wk 10am-11pm **Bar Meals** L served 12-9.30 D served 6-9.30 Av main course £10 food served all day **Restaurant** L served 12-3 booking required D served 6-9.30 ⊕ WHITE JAYS LTD ◀ Hook Norton, Sharp's Doom Bar Ö Westons Stowford Press. **Facilities** Children welcome Children's menu Children's portions Dogs allowed Garden Beer festival Parking Wi-fi

---

BIRDLIP   Map 10 SO91

The Golden Heart ⌕

Nettleton Bottom GL4 8LA
☎ **01242 870261**   📄 **01242 870599**
e-mail: info@thegoldenheart.co.uk
dir: On A417 (Gloucester to Cirencester road). 8m from Cheltenham. Pub at base of dip in Nettleton Bottom

Enjoy glorious views from the terraced gardens of this centuries-old Cotswold stone inn. It probably started life as a drovers' resting place, and retains plenty of original features. The main bar is divided into five cosy areas with log fires and traditional built-in settles. Excellent local ales and ciders are backed by a good selection of wines, while the extensive menus demonstrate commitment to local produce, particularly prize-winning meat from the region's livestock markets and shows.

Open all wk 11-3 5.30-11 (Fri-Sun & summer holidays open all day) Closed: 25 Dec **Bar Meals** L served Mon-Sat 12-3, Sun all day D served Mon-Sat 6-10, Sun all day Av main course £11.25 **Restaurant** L served Mon-Sat 12-3, Sun all day D served Mon-Sat 12-3, Sun all day ⊕ FREE HOUSE ◀ Otter Bitter, Wickwar, Cotswolds Way, Wye Valley, Otter, Gold Festival Ö Westons, Henney, Thatchers. ₹ 10 **Facilities** Children welcome Family room Dogs allowed Garden Parking Wi-fi

BLAISDON — Map 10 SO71

The Red Hart Inn NEW

GL17 0AH ☎ 01452 830477
dir: *Take A40 (NW of Gloucester) towards Ross-on-Wye. At lights left onto A4136 signed Monmouth. Left into Blaisdon Lane to Blaisdon*

Expect a greeting from Spotty, the now-15-year-old Jack Russell, as you enter this low-ceilinged, beamed village pub. In the flagstoned bar with its cosy fire, real ales are taken seriously, as one guest ale finishes another, usually different, replaces it, and there's always a traditional cider. There are two restaurants where a comprehensive menu features chicken breast in creamy mustard seed and sherry sauce, and fresh local grilled trout with almonds. Among the specials are guinea fowl with apricot and pine nut stuffing, and pan-fried red snapper with caramelised peppers.

Open all wk 12-3 6-11.30 (Sun 12.30-4 7-11)
Bar Meals L served 12-2.15 D served 6.30-9.30
Restaurant L served 12-2.15 D served 6.30-9.30 ⊕ FREE HOUSE ◀ 4 Guest ales ♢ Stowford Press, Westons Traditional & 1st Quality. **Facilities** Children welcome Children's menu Children's portions Play area Dogs allowed Garden Parking Wi-fi

BLEDINGTON — Map 10 SP22

PICK OF THE PUBS

The Kings Head Inn ★★★★ INN ⊛ ♀

The Green OX7 6XQ
☎ 01608 658365 ▤ 01608 658902
e-mail: info@kingsheadinn.net
dir: *On B4450 4m from Stow-on-the-Wold*

Stone-built and dating back to the 15th century, this perfect country retreat facing the village green is the quintessential Cotswold inn. Much of the original structure has survived, leaving sturdy beams, low ceilings, flagstone floors, exposed stone walls, and inglenook fireplace. Archie and Nicola Orr-Ewing have worked hard to earn an excellent reputation built on well kept real ales, an extensive wine list and wonderful local produce in the kitchen. In the bar, Hook Norton Bitter is a mainstay, alongside guest ales from local micro-breweries, organic cider, local lagers, over 25 malt whiskies, and eight wines served by the glass. The menu is concise but some of the starters can be served as main courses, so choice is more than ample: asparagus, poached egg, whole grain mustard might be followed by confit duck leg, crushed potatoes, spring greens, broad beans and pancetta. Sticky ginger cake is one of the popular desserts.

Open all wk 11.30-3 6-11 (May-Sep Sat-Sun 11.30am-11pm) Closed: 25-26 Dec **Bar Meals** L served Mon-Fri 12-2, Sat-Sun 12-2.30 D served Sun-Thu 7-9, Fri-Sat 6.30-9.30 **Restaurant** L served Mon-Fri 12-2, Sat-Sun 12-2.30 D served Sun-Thu 7-9, Fri-Sat 6.30-9.30 ⊕ FREE HOUSE ◀ Hook Norton Bitter, Doom Bar, Vale Pale Ale, Wye Valley & Brakspear ♢ Stowford Press. ♀ 8 **Facilities** Children welcome Children's menu Children's portions Dogs allowed Garden Parking Wi-fi **Rooms** 12

BOURTON-ON-THE-HILL — Map 10 SP13

PICK OF THE PUBS

Horse and Groom ♀

GL56 9AQ ☎ 01386 700413 ▤ 01386 700413
e-mail: greenstocks@horseandgroom.info
dir: *2m W of Moreton-in-Marsh on A44*

Owned and run by the Greenstock brothers, the Horse and Groom is a honey-coloured Grade II listed Georgian building which combines a contemporary feel with original period features. It's both a serious dining pub and a friendly place for a drink. The beer selection mixes local brews and guest ales, and over twenty wines are served by the glass. The blackboard menu changes daily, providing plenty of appeal for even the most regular of diners. With committed local suppliers backed up by the pub's own vegetable patch, the kitchen has plenty of good produce to work with. A typical menu might feature home-cured salt cod fritters served with rouille, lemon and rocket; slow-cooked Middle White pork belly with Duncan's barbecue sauce; and puds such as pear and almond tart with Jersey cream. In summer, head for the mature garden with its panoramic hilltop views.

Open 11-3 6-11 Closed: 25 Dec, Sun eve
Bar Meals L served all wk 12-2 booking required D served Mon-Sat 7-9 booking required Av main course £13 **Restaurant** L served all wk 12-2 booking required D served Mon-Sat 7-9 booking required Av 3 course à la carte fr £21 ⊕ FREE HOUSE ◀ Wye Valley Bitter, Pure UBU, Goffs Jouster, Cotswold Wheat, Prescott Brewery's Track Record ♢ Westons Stowford Press. ♀ 21 **Facilities** Children welcome Children's portions Garden Parking Wi-fi

BROCKHAMPTON — Map 10 SP02

Craven Arms Inn ♀ NEW

GL54 5XQ ☎ 01242 820410
e-mail: cravenarms@live.co.uk
dir: *From Cheltenham take A40 towards Gloucester. In Andoversford, at lights, left onto A436 signed Bourton & Stow. Left, follow signs for Brockhampton*

Hidden away at the end of a village driveway a few miles from Cheltenham, this beautiful 16th-century Cotswold inn is full of warmth and character. Landlords Bob and Barbara Price have worked hard to build their trade through well-kept real ales and menus built on high quality seasonal ingredients. You can cook your own meat or fish at the table on hot grill stones; or choose specials such as whole baked Camembert to start, followed by pan-fried duck breast with potato purée and green peppercorn sauce. A beer festival is held on August Bank Holiday.

Open 12-3 6-11 Closed: Sun eve & Mon (in winter)
Bar Meals L served all wk 12-2 D served Mon-Thu 6.30-9, Fri-Sat 6.30-9.30 **Restaurant** L served Mon-Sat 12-2, Sun 12.30-5 D served Mon-Thu 6.30-9, Fri-Sat 6.30-9.30, Sun 12.30-5 ⊕ FREE HOUSE **Facilities** Children welcome Children's portions Dogs allowed Garden Beer festival Parking Wi-fi

CHEDWORTH — Map 5 SP01

PICK OF THE PUBS

Hare & Hounds ★★★★ INN ⊛ ♀

Foss Cross GL54 4NN ☎ 01285 720288
e-mail: stay@hareandhoundsinn.com
dir: *On A429 (Fosse Way), 6m from Cirencester*

A memorable mix of old world character and contemporary cuisine (gaining chef-patron Geraldo Ragosa one AA Rosette for the past decade); creepers cling to the sharply-pitched roofline of the 14th century inn, the old inn sign swings beneath a shading oak and a string of open fires welcome ramblers from the countless local walks, visitors to the nearby Roman villa complex or fans of the turf breaking away from Cheltenham's racecourse just a few miles distant. The interior is an eclectic marriage of original features and modern chic; the ideal foundation for relaxing with a glass of locally brewed Arkells bitter to accompany the accomplished menu which is strong on seafood dishes with a nod to world cuisine. Grilled fillet of halibut on a bed of mild spiced celeriac, or spiced tofu and grilled halloumi cheese on an oriental vegetable stir-fry could be on the regularly updated menu here. In summer eat alfresco in the sun-trap garden or stay over in one of the smart and comfortable rooms.

Open all wk Mon-Sat 11.30-2.30 6-close (Sun 11.30-2.30 7-close) **Bar Meals** L served all wk 12-2.30 booking required D served Mon-Sat 6.30-9.30, Sun 7-9 booking required Av main course £12.95 **Restaurant** L served all wk 12-2.30 booking required D served Mon-Sat 6.30-9.30, Sun 7-9 booking required Fixed menu price fr £16 Av 3 course à la carte fr £30 ⊕ ARKELLS ◀ Arkells 2B, 3B, Moonlight ♢ Stowford Press. ♀ 8 **Facilities** Children welcome Children's menu Children's portions Family room Dogs allowed Garden Parking Wi-fi **Rooms** 10

PICK OF THE PUBS

Seven Tuns ♀

See Pick of the Pubs on opposite page

PICK OF THE PUBS

Seven Tuns ♀

CHEDWORTH   Map 5 SP01

Queen St GL54 4AE ☎ 01285 720242
e-mail: theseventuns@clara.co.uk
dir: *Exit A429, turn off at junct to Chedworth. Approx halfway between Northleach & Cirencester, follow signs to pub*

Just over the hill in the Coln Valley is Chedworth Roman Villa, amongst the most spectacular of its kind. Equally notable in its genre, that of idyllic country pub, is this memorable Cotswold stone inn which has stood since 1610 above a vale famed for its lily-of-the-valley flowers. The pub's name is derived from the seven chimney pots that deck the roof. Creepers smother walls, roof and chimneys here; whilst opposite a path slinks up past beautiful cottages to the village church.

Bag a garden table beside the quiet byway, secure a glass of Young's Bitter or Bombardier and take a light lunch of a ploughman's, soup of the day or appealing Mediterranean dishes like melted Brie and ham croquet madame with a fried egg; goat's cheese bruschetta with black cherry compote; or courgette, garden pea and basil risotto.

Typical of a winter evening, when light from log fires dances across beams, stone walls and boarded floors, might be wild boar pâté with spiced apple chutney; braised oxtail and cranberry casserole with mustard mash; and rope mussels in creamy cider and white wine sauce. Enjoy your meal with one of the twelve wines available by the glass.

In the beer garden there's a revolving South African barbecue and a renovated skittle alley. Live music evenings are held.

Open all wk noon-3 6-11 (Sat noon-mdnt Sun noon-10.30pm) May-Sep all day
Bar Meals L served Mon-Fri 12-2.30, Sat-Sun 12-3 D served Mon-Sat 6.30-9.30, Sun 6.30-9 **Restaurant** L served Mon-Fri 12-2.30, Sat-Sun 12-3 D served Mon-Sat 6.30-9.30, Sun 6.30-9 ◖ Young's Bitter, Winter Warmer, Waggledance, Bombardier, Tribute Ŏ Stowford Press. ♀ 12
Facilities Children welcome Children's menu Children's portions Family room Dogs allowed Garden Parking Wi-fi

CHELTENHAM   Map 10 SO92

The Gloucester Old Spot NEW

Tewkesbury Rd, Piff's Elm GL51 9SY ☎ 01242 680321
e-mail: eat@thegloucesteroldspot.co.uk
web: www.thegloucesteroldspot.co.uk
dir: On A4019 on outskirts of Cheltenham towards
Tewkesbury

The Old Spot is just what you would expect from a
traditional farming pub – quarry tile floors, roaring log
fires and farmhouse furnishings. Real ales such as Purity
take centre stage at the bar, as do local ciders and
perries; there is a beer festival in May too. The baronial
dining room takes its inspiration from the local manor
and game and rare-breed pork make an appearance on a
menu that offers pork belly and black pudding with swede
and squash purée, and braised local pheasant with
chestnuts and herb dumplings.

Open all day all wk Closed: 25 Dec **Bar Meals** L served all
wk 12-2 D served all wk 6-9 Av main course £10.95
Restaurant L served Mon-Sat 12-2, Sun all day D served
Mon-Sat 6-9 Fixed menu price fr £12.50 Av 3 course à la
carte fr £24.50 ⊕ ENTERPRISE INNS ◀ Timothy Taylor
Landlord, Purity Mad Goose, Wye Valley HPA ◌ Thatchers,
Stowford Press, Black Rat, Gwynt y Ddraig.
Facilities Children welcome Children's menu Children's
portions Dogs allowed Garden Beer festival Parking Wi-fi

The Royal Oak Inn NEW

The Burgage, Prestbury GL52 3DL
☎ 01242 522344 ▤ 01242 577344
e-mail: eat@royal-oak-prestbury.co.uk
web: www.royal-oak-prestbury.co.uk
dir: From town centre follow signs for Winchcombe/
Prestbury & Racecourse. In Prestbury follow brown signs
for inn from Tatchley Lane

On the outskirts of Cheltenham, The Royal Oak is the
closest pub to the town's famous racecourse. Built in the
16th-century, the pub was once owned by England cricket
legend Tom Graveney and continues its sporting links to
this day. Enjoy well-kept local cask ales, real ciders and
delicious food in the snug, the comfortable dining room or
the heated patio overlooking a pretty beer garden. The
menu includes twice-baked smoked Applewood soufflé
and belly pork with chorizo and sweet chilli relish. There
is a beer festival at Whitsun and a cider one on August
Bank Holiday.

Open all day all wk Closed: 25 Dec **Bar Meals** L served
Mon-Sat 12-2 D served all wk 6.30-9 Av main course
£12.95 **Restaurant** L served Mon-Sat 12-2, Sun 12-9

booking required D served Mon-Sat 6.30-9, Sun 12-9
booking required Av 3 course à la carte fr £23
⊕ ENTERPRISE INNS ◀ Timothy Taylor Landlord, Purity
Mad Goose, Butcombe Bitter ◌ Thatchers Dry & Heritage,
Stowford Press, Black Rat Perry. **Facilities** Children
welcome Children's menu Children's portions Garden
Beer festival Parking Wi-fi

See advert below

CHIPPING CAMPDEN   Map 10 SP13

The Bakers Arms

Broad Campden GL55 6UR ☎ 01386 840515
e-mail: sally@bakersarmscampden.co.uk
dir: 1m from Chipping Campden

This traditional Cotswold free house dates back to the
early 1700s. There's a choice of five real ales in the
friendly bar, which has exposed stone walls, beams, a
large inglenook fireplace and a framed carpet presented
to the landlord in the 1960s by a happy customer. Choose
from ploughman's, warm baguettes and filled giant
Yorkshire puddings, or main courses such as wild boar
casserole cooked in red wine, beef and Guinness pie or
mariner's pie.

Open all wk 11.30-2.30 5.30-11 (Fri-Sun 11.30-11
Apr-Oct all wk 11.30-11) Closed: 25-26 Dec & 31 Dec eve
Bar Meals L served Mon-Fri 12-2, Sat 12-2.30, Sun 12-6
D served Mon-Sat 6-9 Av main course £8.25
Restaurant L served Mon-Fri 12-2, Sat 12-2.30, Sun 12-6
D served Mon-Sat 6-9 ⊕ FREE HOUSE ◀ Stanway Bitter,
Donnington BB, Hobsons, Wye Valley, Wickwar
◌ Thatchers Heritage. **Facilities** Children welcome
Children's menu Children's portions Play area Garden
Parking

PICK OF THE PUBS

Eight Bells ♟

See Pick of the Pubs on opposite page

PICK OF THE PUBS

Eight Bells ☐

CHIPPING CAMPDEN   Map 10 SP13

Church St GL55 6JG
☎ **01386 840371**   📄 **01386 841669**
e-mail:
neilhargreaves@bellinn.fsnet.co.uk
web: www.eightbellsinn.co.uk
dir: *8m from Stratford-upon-Avon, M40 junct 15*

Originally built in the 14th-century to house the stonemasons that built nearby St James' church, this lovely, flower basket-hung inn was later used to store the peel of eight bells that were hung in the church tower. Just off the bustling High Street of this showpiece Cotswold town, the Eight Bells was rebuilt in the 17th-century, using the rough-hewn stones and timbers you see around you today. The way in is through a cobbled entranceway leading into two atmospheric beamed bars with open fireplaces and, in the floor of one, a surviving priest's hole; outside is an enclosed courtyard and terraced garden overlooking the almshouses and church. The owners have gone to great lengths to avoid the Eight Bells turning into a gastro-pub. Although food is served, it's also a place to enjoy the Hook Norton and Purity (from Stratford-upon-Avon) real ales and freshly prepared, locally sourced dishes offered, such as lunchtime sandwiches on freshly baked ciabatta bread; home-made soup; fish pie topped with creamy mash; and

fresh tagliatelle with wild mushrooms and spinach in tomato sauce. From a main menu come starters of mature Cheddar cheese and spring onion fritters with sweet chilli dipping sauce. Appearing as a main course might be home-made, deep-filled chicken and leek shortcrust pastry pie; pan-fried medallions of pork with caramelised apples set on Lyonnaise potatoes with a grain mustard jus; seared lamb's liver served with bubble and squeak and bacon and shallot jus. Coffee crème brûlée with home-baked shortbread and white chocolate cheesecake with winter fruit compote are typical home-made desserts. Children will be tempted by their own menu.

Open all day all wk noon-11 (Sun noon-10.30) Closed: 25 Dec
Bar Meals L served Mon-Thu 12-2,

Fri-Sun 12-2.30 D served Mon-Thu 6.30-9, Fri-Sat 6.30-9.30, Sun 6.30-8.45 Av main course £12 **Restaurant** L served Mon-Thu 12-2, Fri-Sun 12-2.30 D served Mon-Thu 6.30-9, Fri-Sat 6.30-9.30, Sun 6.30-8.45 Fixed menu price fr £9 Av 3 course à la carte fr £25 ⊕ FREE HOUSE ◀ Hooky Best, Purity UBU, Purity Gold, Goffs Jouster, HPA Wye Valley ♂ Old Rosie Cider, Perry, Stowford Press. ☐ 8
Facilities Children's menu Children's portions Dogs allowed Garden Wi-fi

CHIPPING CAMPDEN *continued*

PICK OF THE PUBS

The Kings RR

The Square GL55 6AW
☎ 01386 840256 01386 841598
e-mail: info@kingscampden.co.uk
dir: *Telephone for directions*

A lovely old townhouse facing the square of one of England's prettiest towns. Sympathetically restored, yet packed with character, the oldest parts include the 16th-century stone mullioned windows on the first floor. The bar offers at least two real ales, including local Hook Norton, as well as daily papers and traditional pub games, but no noisy gaming machines. Bar snacks include a good range of sandwiches and baguettes, while main meals are served in the informal bar brasserie or more formal AA Rosette restaurant overlooking the square. The packed menu offers some imaginative delights: tian of Salcombe crab with cherry tomatoes and herb crème fraîche; braised shank of Lighthorne lamb with dauphinoise potatoes, roast root vegetables and rosemary sauce; risotto of the day. The large grassed garden and dining terrace is good to find in a town centre pub. Individually decorated bedrooms offer period features with plenty of modern comforts.

Open all day all wk 7am-11pm (Sat-Sun 8am-11pm) **Bar Meals** L served all wk 12-2.30 booking required D served all wk 6.30-9.30 booking required **Restaurant** L served all wk 12-2.30 booking required D served all wk 6.30-9.30 booking required FREE HOUSE Hooky Bitter Thatchers Gold. 10 **Facilities** Children welcome Children's menu Children's portions Garden Parking Wi-fi **Rooms** 19

PICK OF THE PUBS

Noel Arms Hotel ★★★ HL

High St GL55 6AT ☎ 01386 840317 01386 841136
e-mail: reception@noelarmshotel.com
web: www.noelarmshotel.com
dir: *On High St, opposite Town Hall*

One of the oldest hotels in the Cotswolds, the Noel Arms combines the traditional with the contemporary. Charles II stayed in this golden, Cotswold stone 16th-century coaching inn and it was through the carriage arch that packhorse trains used to carry bales of wool, the source of the town's prosperity, to Bristol and Southampton. Absorb the hotel's atmosphere with a pint of Wye Valley Butty Bach in front of the log fire in Dover's Bar; read the papers over a coffee and pastry in the coffee shop; and enjoy brasserie style food in the restaurant, with ingredients sourced from the surrounding area. Classic starters include crab and crayfish cocktail, crisp smoked ham hock or leek and wild mushroom tart. Main course choices might include Cotswold Coney (rabbit) pie; roast duck breast with bashed neeps, spinach, apple and cinnamon sauce or chef Indunil's award-winning Sri Lankan black lamb curry with yellow rice. Replete, you can retire to bed in a four-poster made in 1657.

Open all day all wk **Bar Meals** L served all wk 12-3 D served all wk 6-9.30 **Restaurant** L served all wk 12-3 D served all wk 6-9.30 FREE HOUSE Hook Norton Best Bitter, Guinness, Wye Valley Butty Bach, Purity Gold, UBU Westons Stowford Press. **Facilities** Children welcome Children's menu Children's portions Dogs allowed Garden Parking Wi-fi **Rooms** 28

PICK OF THE PUBS

Seagrave Arms INN NEW

Friday St, Weston Subedge GL55 6QH
☎ 01386 840192
e-mail: info@seagravearms.co.uk
dir: *From Moreton-in-Marsh take A44 towards Evesham. In approx 7m right onto B4081 signed Chipping Campden. Road becomes Sheep St. At junct with High Street left, into Dyers Ln. 0.5m over Dovers Hill, into Weston Subedge, road becomes Church St. Pub on left*

Set in a delectable honey-stoned village between the verdant Vale of Evesham and the golden scarp of The Cotswolds; the inn's reputation grows year-on-year. Stately Broadway Tower is on the horizon; the delights of Hidcote Manor and Garden just a short distance away and the remarkable, eccentric collections at Snowshill similarly handy; touring visitors are equally captivated by the luxurious AA 4-star accommodation here at the Seagrave. With the bountiful foodstuffs of the Cotswolds to choose from, the proprietors revel in selecting the best local produce and drinks to satisfy their restaurant's hard-won one-AA Rosette status. Outstanding beers from Purity and Cotswold breweries slake the thirst of locals and ramblers diverting from the nearby Cotswold Way footpath. Start with seared pigeon breast, butternut mousse, roasted red onions and cep mushrooms followed by braised rabbit with Dijon mustard, leeks and turnip or pan fried lamb sweetbreads with smoked chorizo, perhaps savoured with a sprightly Gloucestershire wine from Three Choirs vineyard and finish with a selection of cheeses from nearby villages.

Open all day Closed: Mon **Bar Meals** Av main course £7.95 food served all day **Restaurant** L served Tue-Sun 12-3 D served Tue-Sun 6-9.15 booking required Av 3 course à la carte fr £25 Hook Norton, Cotswold, Purity. **Facilities** Children welcome Children's portions Dogs allowed Garden Parking **Rooms** 6

The Volunteer Inn

Lower High St GL55 6DY ☎ 01386 840688
e-mail: info@thevolunteerinn.net
dir: *From Shipston on Stour take B4035 to Chipping Campden*

A 300-year-old inn where, in the mid-19th-century, the able-bodied used to sign up for the militia. Set in a peaceful location, ramblers can set off from here to walk the Cotswold Way. Food options are provided by the Pan-Asian Maharaja Restaurant serving a wide choice of popular and more unusual curries in the evenings. Volunteer Ale is among the regulars on offer. In summer, head out to the beer garden.

Open all day all wk **Bar Meals** Av main course £8 **Restaurant** D served all wk 5-10.30 booking required FREE HOUSE Hook Norton, Hobgoblin, Volunteer Ale. **Facilities** Children welcome Children's portions Play area Family room Dogs allowed Garden

Save on hotels. Book at **theAA.com/hotel**

GLOUCESTERSHIRE 191 ENGLAND

CIRENCESTER   Map 5 SP00

PICK OF THE PUBS

The Crown of Crucis ★★★ HL

Ampney Crucis GL7 5RS
☎ 01285 851806   📠 01285 851735
e-mail: reception@thecrownofcrucis.co.uk
dir: On A417 to Lechlade, 2m E of Cirencester

Overlooking the village cricket green, this refurbished 16th-century former coaching inn retains its historical charm while feeling comfortably up-to-date. The building stands beside the Ampney brook at the gateway to the Cotswolds, and the quiet stream meandering past the lawns creates a perfect picture of quintessential rural England. The name 'Crucis' refers to the Latin cross in the nearby churchyard. With its traditional beams, log fires and warm, friendly atmosphere, the bar has been recently restored. Bar food is served all day, along with a range of daily specials. The busy bar offers a large selection of draught and real ales and a choice of wines by the glass. The restaurant menu offers starters of pan-fried pigeon breast, and prawn and avocado cocktail; followed perhaps by peppered venison steak on garlic cream potatoes with rich red wine sauce, or ginger and spring onion risotto with infused lemon oil and Parmesan crisp. Round things off with Cotswold crème brûlée and home-made shortbread biscuits.

Open all day all wk 8am-11pm Closed: 25 Dec **Bar Meals** L served all wk 12-5 D served all wk 5-10 food served all day **Restaurant** D served all wk 7-9 booking required ⊕ FREE HOUSE ◀ Sharp's Doom Bar, Sharp's Seasonal Ales ♂ Stowford Press. **Facilities** Children welcome Dogs allowed Garden Parking **Rooms** 25

CLEARWELL   Map 4 SO50

The Wyndham Arms ★★★ HL ⚜ ♟
NEW

The Cross GL16 8JT ☎ 01594 833666   📠 01594 836450
e-mail: dine@thewyndhamhotel.co.uk
dir: M4 junct 21 onto M48 for Chepstow. Exit at junct 2 signed A48/Chepstow. At rdbt take A48 towards Gloucester. Take B4228 to Coleford & The Forest of Dean. 10m, through St Briavels, in 2m Clearwell signed on left

Between the beautiful Wye Valley and the Royal Forest of Dean, The Wyndham Arms offers the closest accommodation to Clearwell Castle. A cosy bar with oak floors and open fires is the perfect place to enjoy a pint of Humpty's Fuddle brewed by Kingstone brewery at nearby Tintern. The exciting menu in the stone walled Old Spot restaurant offers local venison and red wine casserole and old favourites like grilled gammon steak with fried eggs and chips.

Open all day all wk Closed: early Jan **Bar Meals** L served Mon-Sat 12-2, Sun 12-2.30 D served all wk 6.30-9 Av main course £11.50 **Restaurant** L served Mon-Sat 12-2, Sun 12-2.30 D served all wk 6.30-9 Av 3 course à la carte fr £25 ⊕ FREE HOUSE ◀ Kingstone Brewery Humpty's Fuddle ♂ Severn Cider. **Facilities** Children welcome Children's menu Children's portions Dogs allowed Parking Wi-fi **Rooms** 18

CLEEVE HILL   Map 10 SO92

The Rising Sun ★★★ INN ♟ NEW

GL52 3PX ☎ 01242 676281   📠 01242 673069
e-mail: 9210@greeneking.co.uk
dir: On B4632, 4m N of Cheltenham

A Victorian hotel on Cleeve Hill with views over Cheltenham and the Malverns. On a clear day you can see South Wales, so if you're looking to stay, why not ask for a room with a view. But if you're calling in just to relax, settle in the nicely modernised bar or, in summer, out in the verdant garden which is well furnished with trestle tables and benches. Food ranges from sandwiches and wraps to traditional English favourites served both at lunch and dinner, including a choice of gourmet burgers.

Open all day all wk **Bar Meals** Av main course £9.50 food served all day **Restaurant** Av 3 course à la carte fr £19 food served all day ⊕ GREENE KING ◀ IPA, Abbot ♂ Aspall. ♟ 15 **Facilities** Children welcome Children's menu Children's portions Family room Dogs allowed Garden Parking Wi-fi **Rooms** 24

CLIFFORD'S MESNE   Map 10 SO72

PICK OF THE PUBS

The Yew Tree ♟

GL18 1JS ☎ 01531 820719
e-mail: unwind@yewtreeinn.com
web: www.yewtreeinn.com
dir: From Newent High Street follow signs to Clifford's Mesne. Pub at far end of village on road to Glasshouse

Finding this welcoming pub may prove tricky. It's up a little lane on the slopes of the National Trust's May Hill, Gloucestershire's highest point, where horses and sheep graze wild. Formerly a cider press, The Yew Tree is pleasingly floored with quarry tiles, warmed by winter log fires, and proffers an excellent choice of locally brewed real ales and ciders; these and many more feature in the annual beer festival held here every October. Study the seasonal menu while you snack on

bowls of olives, roast garlic and baby peppers. Starters could include sardine pâté with toast, or a game duo of rabbit parfait and carpaccio of venison with Cumberland sauce and crusty bread. For a main course, consider seared duck breast with black cherry sauce and rösti potatoes, or roast belly of pork with apple and fennel confit and colcannon. A blackboard lists daily specials, and home-made desserts comprise the nation's favourites — everything from vanilla cheesecake to treacle and pecan tart.

Open 12-2.30 6-11 (Sun 12-5) Closed: Mon, Tue L, Sun eve **Bar Meals** L served Wed-Sat 12-2 booking required D served Tue-Sat 6-9 booking required Av main course £14 **Restaurant** L served Sun 12-4 booking required ⊕ FREE HOUSE ◀ Wye Valley HPA, Cotswold Spring Brewery Glory, Goffs, Spinning Dog, Local Ales ♂ Stowford Press, Lyne Downe, Black Dragon, Gwatkins. ♟ 12 **Facilities** Children welcome Children's menu Children's portions Play area Dogs allowed Garden Beer festival Parking Wi-fi

COATES   Map 4 SO90

PICK OF THE PUBS

The Tunnel House Inn ♟

See Pick of the Pubs on page 192

COLESBOURNE   Map 10 SP01

PICK OF THE PUBS

The Colesbourne Inn ♟

GL53 9NP ☎ 01242 870376
e-mail: colesbourneinn@wadworth.co.uk
dir: Midway between Cirencester & Cheltenham on A435

Sympathetically restored and dating back to 1827, the handsome, stone-built Colesbourne Inn stands north of Cirencester in a picturesque Cotswold Valley. The source of the River Thames is accessible on foot via field and meadow paths from the pub. Set in two acres, and now in new hands, the former coaching inn has a fine terrace and garden, where you can sit with a pint of Wadworth 6X and savour the glorious country views, and oozes historic charm and character inside the bar and dining area, where you'll find original beams and roaring log fires. Dishes on the chalkboard and seasonal menu combine traditional pub classics, including honey and mustard glazed ham with egg and chips, with modern ideas, perhaps sea bass with warm vegetable and pancetta salad, and beef bourguignon with dauphinoise potatoes and green beans. Rustic baguettes filled with smoked salmon and dill mayonnaise or steak and caramelised onions are also available.

Open all day all wk **Bar Meals** L served all wk 12-2.30 D served Mon-Sat 6-9.30, Sun 6-9 Av main course £12.75 **Restaurant** L served all wk 12-2.30 D served Mon-Sat 6-9.30, Sun 6-9 Fixed menu price fr £9.50 ⊕ WADWORTH ◀ Wadworth 6X, Henrys IPA, Horizon ♂ Stowford Press. ♟ 20 **Facilities** Children welcome Dogs allowed Garden Parking Wi-fi

PICK OF THE PUBS

The Tunnel House Inn ♟

COATES   Map 4 SO90

Tarlton Rd GL7 6PW
☎ **01285 770280** 📠 **01285 700040**
e-mail: info@tunnelhouse.com
web: www.tunnelhouse.com
dir: *From Cirencester on A433 towards Tetbury, in 2m turn right towards Coates, follow brown signs to Canal Tunnel & Inn*

Nestling between the Cotswold villages of Coates and Tarlton, the Tunnel House enjoys a glorious rural location down a bumpy track leading to the mouth of the two-mile long Sapperton Tunnel on the Thames and Severn Canal; the inn was built to accommodate navvies constructing the canal, and is not far from the source of the Thames. In appropriate weather the garden is an ideal place to relax with a pint of Wye Valley or Hook Norton and enjoy lovely views across the fields. In the winter months three log fires warm the welcoming bar, where oddities include an upside-down table on the ceiling. Food is served from noon onwards, every day. You may dine on simple, home-made cooking in the restaurant area or relax in the comfortable seating in the bar. Eat lightly at lunchtime with a hot panini stuffed with Cajun chicken and mozzarella, or a ploughman's with mature Cheddar or Stilton. In the evening, starters combine continental and traditional flavours in the likes of potted duck with rustic toast and piccalilli, or warm salad of pigeon breast with crispy Parma ham, black pudding and walnuts. Although built around traditional English ingredients, main dishes too introduce European flavours: rump or rib-eye steaks with beurre café de Paris, or monkfish wrapped in prosciutto on a lentil cassoulet. Purists may wish to stick to Wiltshire honey-roast ham with two eggs, coleslaw and mixed leaves, or Gloucester Old Spot sausages with creamed mashed potatoes and red onion marmalade. For vegetarians, the wild mushroom carbonara served with garlic and herb ciabatta will do nicely. All-year-round camping in the grounds, a beer festival in July, a kiddie's play area and spectacular walks in the surrounding countryside add to the pub's popularity, and dogs are welcome too.

Open all day all wk noon-late
Bar Meals L served noon-9.30 D served noon-9.30 Av main course £10 food served all day **Restaurant** food served all day
🍺 FREE HOUSE ◀ Uley Old Spot, Uley Bitter, Wye Valley Bitter, Hook Norton, Budding, Butcombe ♻ Cornish Rattler, Black Rat, Westons Organic. ♟ 9
Facilities Children's menu Children's portions Play area Family room Dogs allowed Garden Beer festival Parking Wi-fi

Save on hotels. Book at **theAA.com/hotel**

GLOUCESTERSHIRE 193 **ENGLAND**

PICK OF THE PUBS

The Green Dragon Inn ★★★★ INN

COWLEY Map 10 SO91

Cockleford GL53 9NW
☎ **01242 870271** 🖨 **01242 870171**
e-mail: green-dragon@buccaneer.co.uk
web: www.green-dragon-inn.co.uk
dir: *Telephone for directions*

This beautiful Cotswold-stone inn has surveyed the heart of the pretty little village of Cockleford for well over 300 years. Behind the striking, rose and creeper covered façade lies a stunning interior crafted at the workshops of Robert Thompson, the 'Mouse Man of Kilburn' (that's Kilburn, North Yorkshire, not London), so-called for his trademark mouse, after whom the popular Mouse Bar, with its stone-flagged floors, beamed ceilings and crackling log fires, is named. See if you can find the craftily hidden, playful little rodents carved into the Yorkshire oak. Once your eye is in, they're surprisingly easy to spot, aided by a glass of Butcombe bitter.

With comfy AA-listed accommodation on site, it's an ideal base for exploring the Cotswolds; Miserden Gardens and Chedworth Roman villa are a short way away and there are easy strolls in the Churn Valley. In summer the secluded patio garden overlooking a lake is a great space; colder times see the Mouse Bar and Lower Bar both busy with diners who make a bee-line for The Green Dragon from many miles around.

They arrive to experience the superb meals that cater for both snackers and indulgents keen to try the happy mix of traditional and modern cuisines. A light lunch could be granary or white sandwiches (except on Sundays); Cajun chicken and balsamic focaccia; a starter of smoked haddock fishcakes with dill and white wine cream sauce; or chicken Caesar salad with anchovies, croutons and parmesan shavings. Then perhaps a larger appetite braised faggots with bubble and squeak and onion gravy; vegetable curry with savoury rice; haddock fillet in lemon butter with fries and mushy peas; or pan-fried duck breast with sweet potato wedges and plum and port sauce.

Open all day all wk **Bar Meals** L served Mon-Fri 12-2.30, Sat 12-3, Sun 12-3.30 D served all wk 6-10 Av main course £14.50 **Restaurant** L served Mon-Fri 12-2.30, Sat 12-3, Sun 12-3.30 D served all wk 6-10 booking required
🌐 BUCCANEER 🍺 Hook Norton, Directors, Butcombe, Guest ale Ŏ Stowford Press.
Facilities Children's menu Dogs allowed Garden Parking Wi-fi **Rooms** 9

PICK OF THE PUBS

The New Inn At Coln ★★ HL ◉◉

GL7 5AN ☎ 01285 750651   📠 **01285 750657**
e-mail: info@thenewinnatcoln.co.uk
dir: *Between Bibury (B4425) & Fairford (A417), 8m E of Cirencester*

The setting for this handsome Elizabethan coaching inn is perfect: a sleepy Cotswold village close to the River Coln and historic Bibury, with a postcard-pretty frontage of flower baskets and ivy. Tastefully refurbished rooms within include the Courtyard Bar, with its old beams, tiled floor, stone walls and open fires, and the more intimate, red-walled dining room. Modern menus are built around fresh, high quality ingredients. In the bar, share a deli board of continental and cold meats and pickles, enjoy a a roast beef and horseradish sandwich, or the traditional English sausages, mash and onion gravy, or choose the great value set lunch menu. At dinner, order pressed pigeon and confit rabbit terrine, crispy fig salad and port syrup, follow with pan-fried gilthead bream fillet with caper and parsley new potatoes, and round off with iced banana and Bailey's parfait, glazed banana and chocolate sorbet. There is also a Little Adults and afternoon menu. You can also eat outside on the terrace. Individually designed bedrooms ooze comfort and style – each has a view, over the village, terrace or water meadows.

Open all day all wk 11-11 **Bar Meals** L served all wk 12.30-3 D served all wk 7-9 Av main course £12 **Restaurant** L served all wk 12.30-3 D served all wk 7-9 Av 3 course à la carte fr £30 ⊕ FREE HOUSE ◀ Old Hooky, Old King Coln. **Facilities** Children welcome Children's menu Children's portions Play area Dogs allowed Garden Parking Wi-fi **Rooms** 14

PICK OF THE PUBS

The Green Dragon Inn ★★★★ INN

See Pick of the Pubs on page 193

The Black Horse Inn ♟

GL4 8HP ☎ 01452 812217
dir: *A46 towards Stroud, follow signs for Cranham*

Set in a small village surrounded by woodland and commons, a mile from the Cotswold Way and Prinknash Abbey, this inn is especially popular with walkers, the pub cricket team and visiting Morris dancers. Home-cooked traditional pub food – faggots, toad-in-the-hole, pies (chicken, bacon and leek, beef and Guinness), melted Brie, bacon and walnut salad, and very popular

Sunday roasts – is on the menu. A great selection of real ales and ciders are served in the cosy bar with open fires in the colder weather. Recent change of landlord.

Open 12-2.30 6.30-11 (Sun 12-3.30 6.30-11) Closed: 25 Dec, Mon **Bar Meals** L served Tue-Sat 12-2, Sun 12-2.30 D served Tue-Sun 6.45-9 Av main course £10.50 **Restaurant** L served Sat 12-2, Sun 12-2.30 booking required D served Sat-Sun 6.45-9 booking required ⊕ FREE HOUSE ◀ Otter, Doom Bar, Hancocks HB, Guest ales Ö Thatchers Gold, Stowford Press, Westons Country Perry & Scrumpy. ♟ 9 **Facilities** Children welcome Children's portions Dogs allowed Garden Parking

PICK OF THE PUBS

The Old Spot Inn ♟

Hill Rd GL11 4JQ ☎ 01453 542870
e-mail: steveoldspot@hotmail.co.uk
dir: *From Tetbury on A4135 (or Uley on B4066) into Dursley, round Town Hall. Straight on at lights towards bus station, pub behind bus station. From Cam to lights in Dursley immediately prior to pedestrianised street. Right towards bus station*

This classic 18th-century free house is a former real ale pub of the year, so it's worth visiting to sample the eight tip-top real ales on handpump and to savour the cheerful buzzing atmosphere, as The Old Spot is a cracking community local. It sits smack on the Cotswold Way and was once three terraced farm cottages known as 'pig row.' It's apt, then that it should take its name from the Gloucestershire Old Spot Pig. As well as organising three real ale festivals a year, landlord Steve Herbert organises a host of events, including brewery visits, cricket matches and celebrity chef nights. Devoid of modern-day intrusions, the rustic and traditional low-beamed bars are havens of peace, with just the comforting sound of crackling log fires and the hubbub of chatting locals filling the rambling little rooms. Food is wholesome and home made, ranging from ploughman's lunches and doorstep sandwiches to cottage pie with home-made bread and salad; home-made steak and ale pie; or chicken fajitas. Puddings include treacle tart and blackberry and apple crumble. There's also a pretty garden for summer alfresco sipping.

Open all day all wk **Bar Meals** L served all wk 12-3 booking required Av main course £8 ⊕ FREE HOUSE ◀ Otter, Butty Bach, Golden Hare Ö Ashton Press, Happy Days, Stowford Press. ♟ 8 **Facilities** Children welcome Children's portions Family room Dogs allowed Garden Beer festival Parking Wi-fi

PICK OF THE PUBS

The Ebrington Arms ★★★★ INN ◉

See Pick of the Pubs on opposite page

The Wild Duck ★★ HL ♟

GL7 6BY ☎ 01285 770310   📠 **01285 770492**
e-mail: duckreservations@aol.com
web: www.thewildduckinn.co.uk
dir: *From Cirencester take A429 towards Malmesbury. At kemble left to Ewen. Inn in village centre*

This inn was built from honeyed Cotswold stone in 1563 and sits near to the source of the Thames. Family-owned for more than 20 years, it has a resident ghost, log fires and oak beams. Deep red walls lined with old portraits give the Post Horn bar a warm feel; the rambling restaurant offers seared tuna with black olive tapenade, dill mayonnaise, lemon and capers followed by pan-fried Cajun chicken, roasted corn on the cob, rice, peas and spicy salsa, while board specials include beer battered cod and chips and baked Camembert wrapped in Parma ham. There is a delightful garden plus comfortable rooms if you would like to stay over.

Open all day all wk Closed: 25 Dec (eve) **Bar Meals** L served Mon-Fri 12-2, Sat-Sun 12-10 booking required D served all wk 6.30-10 booking required Av main course £14.95 **Restaurant** L served Mon-Fri 12-2, Sat-Sun 12-10 booking required D served all wk 6.30-10 booking required Av 3 course à la carte fr £25 ⊕ FREE HOUSE ◀ Duckpond Bitter, Butcombe Bitter, Dorothy Goodbody, Abbot Ale, Old Speckled Hen, Sharp's Doom Bar Ö Ashton Press, Stowford Press, Aspall. ♟ 32 **Facilities** Children welcome Children's menu Children's portions Dogs allowed Garden Parking Wi-fi **Rooms** 12

PICK OF THE PUBS

The Ebrington Arms ★★★★ INN ❀

EBRINGTON	Map 10 SP14

GL55 6NH ☎ 01386 593223
e-mail: jim@theebringtonarms.co.uk
web: www.theebringtonarms.co.uk
dir: *Chipping Campden on B4035 towards*
Shipston on Stour. Left to Ebrington
signed after 0.5m, by village green

Every inch the real McCoy of a village pub, this award-winning hidden gem is in the Cotswolds – the hills look lovely from the walled beer garden. Built in 1640, its abundance of character owes much to the heavy beams and original flagstones in both the bar and Old Bakehouse dining room, and the large inglenook fireplaces, which recall the building's days as the village bakery. Very much the hub of community life, it's where lucky locals (and visitors too, of course) are spoilt for choice with several real ales, some from nearby breweries like Stroud and Uley, while cider drinkers can enjoy Thatchers, and even Cotswold-brewed lagers. Wine-wise, owners Jim and Claire Alexander researched the market thoroughly before plumping for local merchant Savage Wines, of whose proprietor wine critic Oz Clarke has said: "I don't think Mark Savage could buy a dull wine if he tried".

As for the food, chef James Nixon, having grown up in the area, knows how to get his hands on the best freshly harvested, organic produce, as most of it is grown or reared in fields around the pub. That his culinary talents are recognised with an AA Rosette should therefore come as no surprise. One of his typical evening meals could feature tuna carpaccio with radish, parmesan shavings and lemon olive oil; noisettes of Cotswold lamb topped with wild mushroom gratin, celeriac dauphinoise, roasted squash and thyme jus; and passionfruit and orange glaze. A vegetarian's first two courses on the other hand might be bruschetta of marinated wild mushrooms with feta, spinach and basil mousse; and roasted root vegetable cassoulet with rocket salad.

Music, games and quiz nights, and occasional themed food evenings are held. If you would like to stay, there are attractive en suite bedrooms available.

Open all day all wk noon-close
Bar Meals food served all day
Restaurant food served all day booking required ⊕ FREE HOUSE ◀ Butty Bach, Uley Bitter, Stroud Organic, Hobsons Bitter ♂ Thatchers Pear, Thatchers Gold.
Facilities Children's portions Dogs allowed Garden Parking Wi-fi **Rooms** 3

FORD · Map 10 SP02

PICK OF THE PUBS

The Plough Inn ★★★★ INN

GL54 5RU ☎ 01386 584215 📠 01386 584042
e-mail: info@theploughinnatford.co.uk
dir: *4m from Stow-on-the-Wold on B4077 towards Tewkesbury*

Trainers, jockeys and stable hands are often in the bar at this 16th-century inn, which is just across the street from the famous Jackdaws Castle racing stables and a short drive from Cheltenham racecourse. The interior decor celebrates the pub's love of all things racing; so committed is landlord Craig Brown that he rode as a novice at Aintree on Grand National day in April 2009. If you want to stay over after a day at the races, there are bedrooms situated in a restored stable block, adjacent to the large beer garden. It's a traditional English pub, with flagstone floors and log fires, sturdy pine furnishings, and remnants of the stocks that once held convicted sheep-stealers. Excellent Donnington Ales served in the bar are made from water drawn from a spring next to the brewery and hops which travel only from neighbouring Worcestershire. Meals are cooked to order from the best of local produce and typically include home-made Thai crab fishcakes with a sweet chilli dipping sauce; crispy roast duck with bubble and squeak and a traditional orange sauce; baked ham with colcannon mash, broad beans and parsley sauce; and game dishes in season.

Open all wk Closed: 25 Dec **Bar Meals** L served Mon-Fri 10-2, Sat-Sun all day D served Mon-Fri 6-9, Sat-Sun all day Av main course £11.95 **Restaurant** L served Mon-Fri 10-2, Sat-Sun all day D served Mon-Fri 6-9, Sat-Sun all day ⊕ DONNINGTON ◀ Donnington BB, SBA & XXX (summer only) ♻ Stowford Press. **Facilities** Children welcome Play area Garden Parking **Rooms** 3

FOSSEBRIDGE · Map 5 SP01

PICK OF THE PUBS

The Inn at Fossebridge ★★★★ INN

See Pick of the Pubs on opposite page

FRAMPTON MANSELL · Map 4 SO90

PICK OF THE PUBS

The Crown Inn ★★★★ INN ❦

GL6 8JG ☎ 01285 760601
e-mail: enquiries@thecrowninn-cotswolds.co.uk
dir: *A419 halfway between Cirencester & Stroud*

Once a simple cider house, this classic award-winning Cotswold stone inn is full of old world charm, with honey-coloured stone walls, beams and open fireplaces where log fires are lit in winter. A handsome 17th-century inn right in the heart of the village, it is surrounded by the peace and quiet of the Golden Valley. There is also plenty of seating in the large garden for the warmer months. Gloucestershire beers, such as Stroud Organic and Laurie Lee's Bitter, are usually showcased alongside others from the region, and a good choice of wines by the glass is served in the restaurant and three inviting bars. Fresh local food with lots of seasonal specials may include braised ham hock with pease pudding and toast or potted rabbit terrine and rabbit loin Wellington with apple chutney to start, followed by fish, chips and garden peas or rolled chicken with spinach, red wine sauce and sautéed potatoes. Comfortable annexe rooms are well appointed and ideal for both business and leisure guests.

Open all day all wk noon-11 **Bar Meals** L served Mon-Sat 12-2.30, Sun 12-8.30 booking required D served Mon-Sat 6-9.30, Sun 12-8.30 booking required Av main course £9.50 ⊕ FREE HOUSE ◀ Butcombe Bitter, Laurie Lee's Bitter, Stroud Organic, guest ale. ❦ 16 **Facilities** Children welcome Children's portions Dogs allowed Garden Parking Wi-fi **Rooms** 12

GLOUCESTER · Map 10 SO81

Queens Head ❦

Tewkesbury Rd, Longford GL2 9EJ
☎ 01452 301882 📠 01452 524368
e-mail: queenshead@aol.com
dir: *On A38 (Tewkesbury to Gloucester road) in Longford*

Under the same ownership since 1995, this 250 year-old pub/restaurant is just out of town but there's no missing it in summer when it is festooned with hanging baskets. Inside, there's a lovely old flagstone-floored locals' bar which proffers a great range of real ales, while two dining areas tempt with comprehensive menus. These may include home-made Ardennes pâté, toast and Cumberland port sauce; pan-fried chorizo flamed with Russian vodka served with crisp potatoes and tomato salsa; followed by a main course of pan-fried pheasant breast with 'rumble de thump' cheese roast.

Open all wk 11-3 5.30-11 **Bar Meals** L served all wk 12-2 D served all wk 6.30-9.30 Av main course £11 **Restaurant** D served all wk 6.30-9.30 booking required Fixed menu price fr £12.50 Av 3 course à la carte fr £18.95 ⊕ FREE HOUSE ◀ Butty Bach, Dursley Steam, Otter, Butcombe, Hobgoblin, Rev James ♻ Ashton Press, Stowford Press. **Facilities** Parking Wi-fi

---

GREAT BARRINGTON · Map 10 SP21

PICK OF THE PUBS

The Fox

OX18 4TB ☎ 01451 844385
e-mail: info@foxinnbarrington.com
dir: *3m W on A40 from Burford, turn N signed The Barringtons, pub approx 0.5m on right*

This picturesque 17th-century former coaching house is set in the heart of the Cotswolds. It has a delightful patio and large beer garden overlooking the River Windrush - on warm days a perfect summer watering hole and very popular with those attending Cheltenham racecourse. Built of mellow Cotswold stone and characterised by low ceilings, beams and log fires, the inn offers a range of well-kept Donnington beers and a select wine list. Enjoy a meal in the main bar or the riverside dining room. Wholesome food is prepared using produce from local suppliers. Expect dishes like beef in ale pie; local pigeon breasts casseroled with button mushrooms; chicken piri-piri; and Thai tuna steak.

Open all day all wk 11am-close **Bar Meals** L served Mon-Fri 12-2.30, Sat-Sun all day D served Mon-Fri 6.30-9.30, Sat-Sun all day **Restaurant** L served Mon-Fri 12-2.30, Sat-Sun all day D served Mon-Fri 6.30-9.30, Sat-Sun all day ⊕ DONNINGTON ◀ Donnington BB, SBA ♻ Stowford Press, Perry, Addlestones. **Facilities** Children welcome Children's portions Dogs allowed Garden Parking

---

GUITING POWER · Map 10 SP02

The Hollow Bottom ❦

GL54 5UX ☎ 01451 850392 📠 01451 850945
e-mail: hello@hollowbottom.com
dir: *Telephone for directions*

Often frequented by Cheltenham race-goers, this 18th-century Cotswold free house is decorated with all manner of horse-racing memorabilia – from badges and silks to framed newspaper cuttings. Its nooks and crannies are warmed by a blazing log fire and lend themselves to planning a punt with an intimate drink or meal; there's also a separate dining room, plus outside tables for fine weather. In addition to real ales and ciders, the bar proffers a grand selection of malt whiskies, wines and champagne. If you're after a snack, baked potatoes and freshly made baguettes have a choice of fillings. Other dishes of typical pub fare extend from chef's pâté to home-made pie or roast of the day, grilled gammon steak or a succulent steak.

Open all day all wk **Bar Meals** Av main course £11 food served all day **Restaurant** Av 3 course à la carte fr £22 food served all day ⊕ FREE HOUSE ◀ Hollow Bottom Best Bitter, Goffs Jouster, Donningtons SBA, Festival Gold ♻ Addlestones Cloudy, Stowford Press, Westons Organic. ❦ 9 **Facilities** Children welcome Children's menu Children's portions Play area Dogs allowed Garden Parking Wi-fi

PICK OF THE PUBS

The Inn at Fossebridge ★★★★ INN

FOSSEBRIDGE   Map 5 SP01

GL54 3JS ☎ 01285 720721
e-mail: info@fossebridgeinn.co.uk
web: www.fossebridgeinn.co.uk
dir: *From M4 junct 15, A419 towards*
Cirencester, then A429 towards Stow. Pub
approx 6m on left in dip

An 18th-century family-run free house set in extensive grounds with a lake. Its history stretches back over 300 years, when this old coaching inn on the ancient Fosseway was known as Lord Chedworth's Arms. Wealthy landowner Lord Chedworth still lends his name to the characterful old bar even though the hostelry changed its name in the early 19th century. Today it's a beautiful Cotswold retreat with wonderful accommodation; all nine bedrooms – named after local towns and villages – have been refurbished to a high standard with excellent shower and bathroom facilities. Two bars and a restaurant are divided by stone archways, with each area boasting exposed beams, stone walls, flagstone floors and open fires. They provide an idyllic setting for sampling a real ale chosen from the grand array of taps, including Bath Gem and Proper Job. A light lunch menu includes the likes of crispy-coated butterfly prawns with dressed mixed leaves and sweet chilli dipping sauce; and Coln Valley smoked salmon, with crème fraîche and cracked black pepper. Alternatively a warm bacon and egg sandwich made with farmhouse

white or granary bread may suffice. Otherwise look to the carte for both lunch and dinner options: a starter of breaded crab, cod and parsley fishcakes is served with lemon aïoli; smooth chicken liver and brandy pâté comes with red onion marmalade and toast. For a popular main course try the Cotswold saddle of lamb with a herb crust, baby root vegetables, roasted new potatoes and a rosemary jus. Or select one of the Fossebridge classics: chargrilled home-made burger with bacon, cheese, tomato relish and chips; or beer battered haddock with chips, garden peas and home-made tartare sauce. Puddings, home made in the kitchen, also follow classic lines: orange and vanilla crème brûlée or sticky toffee pudding with toffee sauce and Cotswold Company vanilla bean ice cream.

Open all day all wk noon-mdnt (Sun noon-11.30) **Bar Meals** L served Mon-Fri 12-2.30, Sat 12-3, Sun 12-3.30 **Restaurant** L served Mon-Fri 12-2.30, Sat 12-3, Sun 12-3.30 booking required D served Oct-Mar Mon-Sun 6-9, Apr-Sep Mon-Sun 6-10 booking required ⊕ FREE HOUSE ◗ Tribute, Proper Job, Hill Climb, Rev James, Bath Gem, Hook Norton ⬦ Stowford Press, Kingstone Press. **Facilities** Children's menu Children's portions Play area Dogs allowed Garden Parking Wi-fi **Rooms** 9

HINTON
Map 4 ST77

PICK OF THE PUBS

The Bull Inn ♥

SN14 8HG ☎ 0117 937 2332
e-mail: diserwhite@aol.com
dir: From M4 junct 18, A46 to Bath 1m, turn right 1m,
down hill. Pub on right

Tucked away in a sleepy village on the edge of the
Cotswolds, the 17th-century stone-built Bull Inn is run
with charm and personality by David and Elizabeth
White. Formerly a farm and dairy, the Wadworth-owned
pub retains original inglenook fireplaces and flagstone
floors in the beamed bar and dining room, which are
furnished by big oak tables and old pews. The sun-trap
south-facing terrace and garden are popular for
summer alfresco pints of 6X and meals, the latter
making good use of the home-grown fruit and
vegetables and the Old Spot pigs reared out back.
Short, seasonal menus may take in chicken liver pâté
served with red onion marmalade, the Bull burger –
½lb of prime beef in a bun with mayonnaise, lettuce,
relish and hand-cut fries – beef and ale pie, and pan-
fried lambs' liver and smoked bacon with creamy mash
and onion gravy. Puddings range from Bailey's and
banana bread-and-butter pudding to a trio of locally
made Marshfield Farm ice creams.

Open noon-3 6-11.30 (Sat-Sun & BH open all day)
Closed: Mon L (ex BH) **Bar Meals** L served Tue-Sat
12-2, Sun 12-8.30 D served Mon-Thu 6-9, Fri-Sat
6-9.30 Av main course £10.95 **Restaurant** L served
Tue-Sat 12-2, Sun 12-8.30 booking required D served
Mon-Thu 6-9, Fri-Sat 6-9.30 booking required
⊕ WADWORTH ◀ Wadworth 6X & Henrys IPA, Wadworth
Bishops Tipple, Wadworth Summersault, Guest ale
Ö Thatchers Gold, Stowford Press. ♥ 11
Facilities Children welcome Children's menu Play area
Dogs allowed Garden Parking Wi-fi

LECHLADE ON THAMES
Map 5 SU29

The Trout Inn ♥

St Johns Bridge GL7 3HA
☎ 01367 252313 📠 01367 252313
e-mail: chefpjw@aol.com
dir: A40 onto A361 then A417. From M4 junct 15, A419,
then A361 & A417 to Lechlade

In 1220, when workmen constructed a new bridge over
the Thames, they built an almshouse to live in. In 1472 it
became an inn, which it has been ever since. The bar, all
flagstone floors and beams, overflows into the old
boathouse, and serves a range of ales and 15 wines by
the glass. Look out for the locally sourced ingredients –
steaks, pork and Bibury trout. Other favourites such as
beef and ale stew with dumplings and beer battered hake
make a showing. This family-friendly pub has a large
garden which often pulsates with tractor and steam
events, and jazz and folk festival; plus there's a beer
festival in June.

Open all wk 10-3 6-11 (summer all wk 10am-11pm)
Closed: 25 Dec **Bar Meals** L served all wk 12-2 D served
all wk 7-10 Av main course £11.50 **Restaurant** L served
all wk 12-2 D served all wk 7-10 Fixed menu price fr
£8.40 ⊕ ENTERPRISE INNS ◀ Courage Best, Doom Bar,
Cornish Coaster, Guest ales. ♥ 15 **Facilities** Children
welcome Children's menu Children's portions Play area
Family room Dogs allowed Garden Beer festival Parking

LITTLETON-ON-SEVERN
Map 4 ST58

White Hart ♥

BS35 1NR ☎ 01454 412275
e-mail: whitehart@youngs.co.uk
web: www.whitehartbristol.com
dir: M48 junct 1 towards Chepstow left on rdbt, follow for
3m, 1st left to Littleton-on-Severn

Secluded in a hamlet close to the Severn Estuary, views
from the shrubby, suntrap beer garden of this lovely 17th
century inn encompass the distant wooded ridge of the
Forest of Dean. Defiantly olde world with all the timeless
trimmings, the enchanting beamed interior draws in
beer-lovers to sample beers from Bath Ales whilst diners
can expect a wide choice from an inspiring menu
featuring classic dishes alongside unusual home-made
pies such as stargazy (fish and shellfish) or Highland
venison and pheasant, with a local fruit crumble to finish.

Open all day all wk noon-11 **Bar Meals** L served Mon-Fri
12-2.30, Sun 12-8 D served Mon-Sat 6-9.30 ⊕ YOUNG'S
◀ Young's Bitter, Young's Special, Bath Ales Gem, Guest
ales Ö Thatchers Heritage, Thatchers Gold, Addlestones.
♥ 18 **Facilities** Children welcome Children's menu
Children's portions Family room Dogs allowed Garden
Parking

LITTLE WASHBOURNE
Map 10 SO93

The Hobnails Inn

GL20 8NQ ☎ 01242 620237
e-mail: enquiries@thehobnailsinn.co.uk
dir: M5 junct 9, A46 towards Evesham then B4077 to
Stow-on-the-Wold. Inn 1.5m on left

This charming 13th-century building, one of the oldest
inns in the county, sits in an idyllic rural setting. Inside
you'll find winter log fires, and you can tuck yourself into
a private corner, or relax with a pint of ale on one of the
leather sofas. In addition to a lunchtime carvery, there's
a great selection of English home-cooked classics and a
specials board for more contemporary seasonal dishes.
Try beef Stroganoff or braised lamb shank; non-meat

choices include vegetable lasagne or mushroom risotto.
Outside is a lovely large garden for warmer days with
views over surrounding countryside. The inn has recently
changed hands.

Open all wk 12-3 5.30-11 (Sun all day)
Bar Meals L served all wk 12-3 D served all wk 5.30-9
Restaurant L served all wk 12-3 D served all wk 5.30-9
⊕ ENTERPRISE INNS ◀ London Pride, Jouster Ö Stowford
Press. **Facilities** Children welcome Children's menu
Children's portions Dogs allowed Garden Parking Wi-fi

LONGHOPE
Map 10 SO61

The Glasshouse Inn ♥

May Hill GL17 0NN ☎ 01452 830529
e-mail: glasshouseinn@btconnect.com
dir: Village off A40 between Gloucester & Ross-on-Wye

The Glasshouse is unique and its popularity confirms the
need for traditional pubs with no gimmicks. The inn dates
back to 1450 and gets its name from Dutch glassmakers
who settled locally in the 16th century. It is located in a
wonderful rural setting with a country garden outside and
a tranquil and dignified interior. The inn serves a range of
real ales and home-cooked dishes. Remember to book for
Sunday lunch. Under fourteens are not allowed inside the
pub.

Open Mon-Sat 11.30-3 7-11 (Sun 12-3) Closed: Sun eve
Bar Meals L served all wk 12-2 (booking required for
parties of 6 or more) D served Mon-Sat 6.30-9 (booking
required for parties of 6 or more) ⊕ FREE HOUSE
◀ Butcombe, Spitfire, Black Sheep, London Pride, Greene
King Ö Stowford Press. ♥ 12 **Facilities** Garden Parking

LOWER ODDINGTON
Map 10 SP22

PICK OF THE PUBS

The Fox ♥

GL56 0UR
☎ 01451 870555 & 870666 📠 01451 870666
e-mail: info@foxinn.net
dir: A436 from Stow-on-the-Wold then right to Lower
Oddington

Fresh flowers and antique furniture create a period feel
in the bar of this stone-built and creeper-clad free
house. Set in a quintessential Cotswold village and
dating back to the 17th century, the interior boasts
polished flagstone floors, beams and log fires. The Fox's
reputation for well kept beers, good food and wine at
reasonable prices draws people in to enjoy the
atmosphere of a traditional English pub. The regularly
changing menus and the daily specials take full
advantage of seasonal local produce and freshly
caught Cornish fish. Starters like tarragon potted
shrimps with wholemeal toast herald main course
options that include rare roast Scottish beef sirloin
with Yorkshire pudding, and leek and Brie tart with
mixed leaves. Desserts such as raspberry cream pot
with a sablé biscuit provide a satisfying conclusion. In
summer, there's a heated terrace for alfresco dining,
as well as a pretty, traditional cottage garden.

Open all wk 12-2.30 6-11 or mdnt Closed: 25 Dec
Bar Meals L served Mon-Sat 12-2, Sun 12-4 booking
required D served Mon-Sat 6.30-10, Sun 7-9.30
booking required Av main course £13.50
Restaurant L served Mon-Sat 12-2, Sun 12-4 booking
required D served Mon-Sat 6.30-10, Sun 7-9.30
booking required Av 3 course à la carte fr £25 ⊕ FREE
HOUSE ◼ Hook Norton Best, Abbot Ale, Ruddles
County, Wickwar's Old Bob, Purity UBU ♂ Stowford
Press. ♗ 15 **Facilities** Children welcome Children's
portions Dogs allowed Garden Parking Wi-fi

MARSHFIELD Map 4 ST77

The Catherine Wheel

39 High St SN14 8LR ☎ 01225 892220
e-mail: roo@thecatherinewheel.co.uk
dir: *Between Bath, Bristol & Chippenham on A420. 5m
from M4 junct 18*

Simple, stylish decor complements the clean lines of this
impressive, mainly 17th-century inn on the edge of the
Cotswolds, with its exposed brickwork and large open
fireplaces. Menus are also simple and well presented,
with favourites at lunchtime including jacket potatoes
and ploughman's. In the evening look forward to duck
and pork pâté or grilled sardines for a starter, followed by
aromatic braised pork belly with stir-fry noodles; fish pie
with cheesy mash topping; or roast butternut squash
risotto. A small but sunny patio is a lovely spot for a
summertime pint brewed by nearby Cotswold and Bath-
based breweries.

Open all day all wk **Bar Meals** L served Mon-Fri 12-2
Sat-Sun 12-3 D served Mon-Thu 6.30-9 Fri-Sat 6.30-9.30
Sun 6-8.30 **Restaurant** L served Mon-Fri 12-2 Sat-Sun
12-3 D served Mon-Thu 6.30-9 Fri-Sat 6.30-9.30 Sun
6-8.30 ◼ Courage Best, Guest ales ♂ Stowford Press.
Facilities Children welcome Children's portions Dogs
allowed Garden Parking

The Lord Nelson Inn ★★★ INN ♗

1 & 2 High St SN14 8LP ☎ 01225 891820
e-mail: thelordnelsoninn.@btinternet.com
dir: *M4 junct 18 onto A46 towards Bath. Left at Cold
Ashton rdbt towards Marshfield*

A 17th-century coaching inn on the edge of the
Cotswolds, this pub is known for good home-made food
and quality cask ales. A spacious bar that provides a
chance to mix with the locals, candlelit restaurant, log
fires in winter and a patio for summer use complete its
attractions, along with comfortable accommodation in
peaceful village surroundings. With the food emphasis on
simplicity and quality, fish is sourced every Friday and
available over the weekend, along with a Sunday carvery.

Open all day all wk **Bar Meals** L served Mon-Sat 12-2,
Sun 12-3 booking required D served Mon-Sat 6.30-9, Sun
6-8 booking required Av main course £9.95
Restaurant L served Mon-Sat 12-2, Sun 12-3 booking
required D served Mon-Sat 6.30-9, Sun 6-8 booking
required Fixed menu price fr £13.95 Av 3 course à la
carte fr £20.95 ⊕ ENTERPRISE INNS ◼ Greene King IPA,
Bath Gem, Sharp's Doom Bar ♂ Stowford Press. ♗ 9
Facilities Children welcome Children's menu Children's
portions Play area Dogs allowed Garden **Rooms** 3

MEYSEY HAMPTON Map 5 SP10

The Masons Arms

28 High St GL7 5JT ☎ 01285 850164 📄 01285 850164
dir: *6m E of Cirencester off A417, beside village green*

Nestling alongside the green in the heart of the village,
this is a quintessential 17th-century stone-built
Cotswold inn. The hub of the community and welcoming
to visitors, it offers something for everyone, from a
warming log fire in the large inglenook to the range of
well-kept Arkell's ales and Westons cider served in the
convivial beamed bar. Good value home-made food.
Worth noting if visiting the Cotswold Water Park near by.
Change of hands in June 2010.

Open all wk 12-2 5.30-11 (Sat 12-11 Sun 12-10)
⊕ ARKELLS ◼ 3B's, 2B's, Kingsdown, SBA, Moonlight
♂ Westons Vintage, Perry. **Facilities** Children welcome
Children's portions Dogs allowed Parking Wi-fi

MINCHINHAMPTON Map 4 SO80

PICK OF THE PUBS

The Weighbridge Inn ♗

See Pick of the Pubs on page 200

MORETON-IN-MARSH Map 10 SP23

The Red Lion Inn ★★★ INN ♗

GL56 0RT ☎ 01608 674397
e-mail: info@theredlionlittlecompton.co.uk
dir: *Between Chipping Norton & Moreton-in-Marsh on A44*

A pretty Cotswold stone building quietly located on the
edge of the village, this is one of 15 pubs owned by
Donnington Brewery – a family concern that has been
brewing since 1865. Set in a large mature garden, the
building has exposed stone walls and beams, inglenook
fireplaces and real fires; there is comfortable, stylish-
presented accommodation, too. Public bar games include
darts, dominoes, a juke box and pool table. The
restaurant offers a seasonal menu and sensibly priced
daily-changing specials.

Open all wk 12-3 6-12 **Bar Meals** L served all wk 12-2
D served all wk 6-9 booking required Av main course £10
Restaurant L served all wk 12-2 booking required
D served all wk 6-9 booking required Fixed menu price fr
£10 ⊕ DONNINGTON BREWERY ◼ Donnington BB,
Donnington Double D. ♗ 10 **Facilities** Children welcome
Children's portions Dogs allowed Garden Parking Wi-fi
Rooms 2

NAILSWORTH Map 4 ST89

PICK OF THE PUBS

The Britannia ♗

Cossack Square GL6 0DG ☎ 01453 832501
e-mail: pheasantpluckers2003@yahoo.co.uk
dir: *From A46 S'bound right at town centre rdbt. 1st
left. Pub directly ahead*

This stone-built 17th-century former manor house
occupies a delightful position on the south side of
Nailsworth's Cossack Square. The interior is bright and
uncluttered with low ceilings, cosy fires and a blue
slate floor. Outside you'll find a pretty garden with
plenty of tables, chairs and parasols for sunny days.
Whether inside or out, a pint of well-kept ale is sure to
go down well. The brasserie-style menu offers an
interesting blend of modern British and continental
food, with ingredients bought from local suppliers and
from Smithfield Market. You can go lightly with just a
starter from a tapas-style list that includes houmous,
deep-fried Brie and moules marinière; or plunge into
hearty classics such as steak and ale pie or ham, egg
and chips. Other options include stone-baked pizzas
and impressive meat-free options such as butternut
squash and chilli risotto. Great wines, too.

Open all wk Mon-Thu 11-11 (Fri-Sat 11-mdnt Sun
11-10.30) Closed: 25 Dec **Bar Meals** L served Mon-Fri
11-2.45, Sat-Sun 11-10 D served Mon-Fri 5.30-10,
Sat-Sun 11-10 ⊕ FREE HOUSE ◼ Buckham, Otter,
Wickwar Bob, Doom Bar ♂ Ashton Press, Black Rat.
♗ 10 **Facilities** Children welcome Dogs allowed Garden
Parking

PICK OF THE PUBS

Egypt Mill

GL6 0AE ☎ 01453 833449 📄 01453 839919
e-mail: reception@egyptmill.com
dir: *M4 junct 18, A46 N to Stroud. M5 junct 13, A46 to
Nailsworth*

Situated in the charming Cotswold town of Nailsworth,
this converted corn mill contains many features of
great character, including the original millstones and
lifting equipment. The ground floor bar and bistro enjoy
a picturesque setting, and its views over the pretty
water gardens complete the scene. There is a choice of
eating in the bistro or restaurant, and in both there is
a good selection of wines by the glass. For those who
like to savour an aperitif before dining, try the large
Egypt Mill Lounge. Tempting starters might offer ham
hock and pea risotto; smoked salmon and avocado
parcels; and salmon and lobster sausages. Main
courses include the likes of saddle of lamb Greek style;
calves' liver and bacon; breast of duck with apple and
blackberry risotto; and Brixham fish and potato pie.

Open all day all wk 11am-11pm ⊕ FREE HOUSE
◼ Stroud Brewery, Nailsworth ♂ Stowford Press.
Facilities Children welcome Garden Parking

PICK OF THE PUBS

The Weighbridge Inn ☖

MINCHINHAMPTON — Map 4 SO80

GL6 9AL
☎ **01453 832520** 🖷 **01453 835903**
e-mail: enquiries@2in1pub.co.uk
web: www.2in1pub.co.uk
dir: *Between Nailsworth & Avening on B4014*

Parts of this beautifully positioned free house date back to the 17th century, when it stood adjacent to the original packhorse trail between Bristol and London. The trail is now a footpath and bridleway and the road in front (now the B4014) became a turnpike in the 1820s. The innkeeper at the time ran both the pub and the weighbridge for the local woollen mills – serving jugs of ale in between making sure tolls were paid.

Associated memorabilia and other rural artefacts from the time are displayed around the inn, which has been carefully renovated to retain original features. From the patios and sheltered landscaped garden the Cotswolds are in full view. Up in the restaurant, which used to be the hayloft, for example, the old roof timbers reach almost to the floor. The drinking areas are, as you would expect, tailor-made for a decent pint – Wadworth 6X, maybe – but if beer is not to your taste, a heady Wicked Witch cider.

The inn prides itself on the quality of its food, all cooked from scratch to appear on the regular menu as simple starter dishes of smoked salmon and scrambled eggs on truffle oil crostini and horseradish cream, for example. The hearty main courses include cauliflower cheese, cottage pie, bangers and mash from a local award-winning butcher or the popular Weighbridge burger. The Weighbridge is also the home of '2 in 1 pies', half containing one of seven fillings of your choice, the rest with home-made cauliflower cheese – also available to take away and bake at home. Typical desserts include treacle and hazelnut sponge with toffee sauce and local vanilla ice cream or cappuccino pannacotta. Lighter meals are available as salads, omelettes, jacket potatoes and filled baguettes.

Open all day all wk noon-11 (Sun noon-10.30) Closed: 25 Dec **Bar Meals** L served all wk 12-9.30 D served all wk 12-9.30 Av main course £12 food served all day **Restaurant** L served all wk 12-9.30 D served all wk 12-9.30 food served all day ⊕ FREE HOUSE ◼ Wadworth 6X, Uley Old Spot, Palmers IPA ♻ Wicked Witch, Westons Bounds Brand, Thatchers Gold. ☖ 15 **Facilities** Children's menu Children's portions Family room Dogs allowed Garden Parking Wi-fi

THE FEATHERED NEST COUNTRY INN

The Food   The Pint   The Pillow

Nether Westcote   Oxfordshire OX7 6SD | T 01993 833030 | info@thefeatherednestinn.co.uk

www.thefeatherednestinn.co.uk

NAILSWORTH *continued*

PICK OF THE PUBS

Tipputs Inn ♥

Bath Rd GL6 0QE ☎ 01453 832466
e-mail: pheasantpluckers2003@yahoo.co.uk
dir: *A46, 0.5m S of Nailsworth*

Mellow Cotswold stone and stripped floorboards blend nicely with modern, clean-lined furniture in this impeccably decorated 17th-century pub-restaurant. A giant candelabra adds a touch of grandeur. Located in the heart of the Cotswolds, the Tipputs Inn is owned by Nick Beardsley and Christophe Coquoin. They started out as chefs together more than 12 years ago, but admit to spending less time in the kitchen these days now that they have to create menus for this and their other Gloucestershire food pubs, plus they select and import some ingredients and wines direct from France. There are dishes for every eventuality, starting with tapas-style appetisers and extending through starters such as pan-fried halloumi or spicy prawn cocktail to pub classics (fish and chips; home-made burger and chips) and classy options such as confit duck leg with black pudding, mashed potato and seasonal vegetables or cherry tomato, basil and ricotta risotto. Classic desserts include Eton Mess and vanilla crème brûlée.

Open all wk 10-30am-11pm **Bar Meals** L served Mon-Fri 12-3, Sat-Sun all day D served Mon-Fri 6-10, Sat-Sun all day **Restaurant** L served Mon-Fri 12-3, Sat-Sun all day D served Mon-Fri 6-10, Sat-Sun all day ⊕ FREE HOUSE ◀ Stroud Brewery, Otter Ale ♂ Stowford Press. ♥ 12 **Facilities** Children welcome Children's menu Dogs allowed Garden Parking

NETHER WESTCOTE   Map 10 SP22

AA PUB OF THE YEAR FOR ENGLAND 2011-2012

PICK OF THE PUBS

The Feathered Nest Inn

INN ◉◉ ♥ NEW

OX7 6SD ☎ 01993 833030 🖨 01993 833031
e-mail: info@thefeatherednestinn.co.uk
web: www.thefeatherednestinn.co.uk
dir: *A424 between Burford & Stow-on-the-Wold, follow signs*

With marvellous views over the Evenlode Valley, The Feathered Nest Inn is set in the picturesque village of Nether Westcote, on the border of Gloucestershire and

Oxfordshire. Originally an old malthouse, the pub has been updated and thoughtfully furnished whilst retaining the original character, especially in the cosy log-fired bar, where Hook Norton Best is one of the real ales on offer. Awarded 2 AA Rosettes, a daily blackboard menu offers relaxed eating in the bar and the garden terrace when the weather allows. Many of the herbs and vegetables are grown in the kitchen garden, with local produce a backbone of the menu. A bar menu of classics like fish and chips, ploughman's and steak sandwiches is complemented by an interesting à la carte offering the likes of seared Cornish scallops with chicory salad and clementine purée or confit wood pigeon with seared foie gras, braised cabbage and parsnip purée. Individually decorated bedrooms furnished with antiques and comfortable beds are available.

Open all day Closed: 25 Dec, Mon **Bar Meals** L served Tue-Sun 12-2.30 D served Tue-Sun 6.30-9.30 **Restaurant** L served Tue-Sun 12-2.30 booking required D served Tue-Sun 6.30-9.30 booking required ⊕ FREE HOUSE ◀ Hook Norton Best, Wychwood Hobgoblin, Marston's Pedigree ♂ Thatchers Gold. ♥ 19 **Facilities** Children welcome Children's menu Children's portions Family room Dogs allowed Garden Parking Wi-fi **Rooms** 4   *See advert on page 201*

NEWLAND   Map 4 SO50

PICK OF THE PUBS

The Ostrich Inn

GL16 8NP ☎ 01594 833260
e-mail: kathryn@theostrichinn.com
dir: *Follow Monmouth signs from Chepstow (A466), Newland signed from Redbrook*

A 13th-century inn situated in a pretty village on the western edge of the Forest of Dean and adjoining the Wye Valley, both Areas of Outstanding Natural Beauty. To this day it still retains many of its ancient features, including a priest hole. With wooden beams and a welcoming log fire in the large lounge bar throughout the winter, visitors can enjoy a relaxed and friendly setting for a wide selection of cask-conditioned beers, real ciders and good food. Diners are served in the small, intimate restaurant, the larger lounge bar, the garden and the patio. In the bar expect simpler dishes, such as salmon spinach fishcakes or steak and ale pie. The monthly changing menu in the restaurant offers more sophistication in the form of slow-roasted spiced belly pork with pak choi; and supreme of Nile perch from Lake Victoria with black tiger prawns and chive cream sauce. No one will frown at your muddy boots.

Open all wk noon-3 (Mon-Fri 6.30-11.30, Sun 6.30-10.30) **Bar Meals** L served all wk 12-2.30 D served Sun-Fri 6.30-9.30, Sat 6-9.30 **Restaurant** L served all wk 12-2.30 D served Sun-Fri 6.30-9.30, Sat 6-9.30 ⊕ FREE HOUSE ◀ Timothy Taylor Landlord, Butty Bach, Pigs Ear, Old Hooky, Adnams, Guest ales ♂ Stowford Press, Old Rosie, Ty Gwyn, Severn Cider Perry. **Facilities** Children welcome Dogs allowed Garden

NORTH CERNEY   Map 5 SP00

PICK OF THE PUBS

Bathurst Arms ♥

GL7 7BZ ☎ 01285 831281
e-mail: james@bathurstarms.com
dir: *5m N of Cirencester on A435*

Set in the picturesque village of North Cerney, the 17th-century Bathurst Arms offers the intimacy of a traditional inn combined with high standards of food and drink. The rambling creeper-covered building stands on the Earl of Bathurst's estate, with a pretty flower-filled garden running down to the River Churn. The stone-flagged bar exudes character with its beams and log fires, and draws walkers and locals for pints of Hook Norton or Wickwar's IKB (named after Isambard Kingdom Brunel — a pint 'engineered to perfection'). Decent pub food prepared from locally sourced ingredients has starters such as creamy cauliflower and Stilton soup and ham hock and pea terrine. Main courses follow reliable lines, with the likes of Old Spot sausages and root vegetable mash, chargrilled Cotswold rump steak, and breaded wholetail scampi. For the sweet tooth, chocolate and hazelnut brownie with coffee liqueur and chocolate sauce will be irresistible.

Open all day all wk **Bar Meals** L served all wk 12-2 D served all wk 6-9 Av main course £7.50 **Restaurant** L served all wk 12-2 D served all wk 6-9 Av 3 course à la carte fr £20 ⊕ FREE HOUSE ◀ Hook Norton House Ale, Battledown Premium, IKB Wickwar, Stonehenge Heelstowe ♂ Stowford Press. ♥ 25 **Facilities** Children welcome Children's menu Children's portions Dogs allowed Garden Parking Wi-fi

OLDBURY-ON-SEVERN   Map 4 ST69

The Anchor Inn ♥

Church Rd BS35 1QA ☎ 01454 413331
e-mail: info@anchorinnoldbury.co.uk
dir: *From N A38 towards Bristol, 1.5m then right, village signed. From S A38 through Thornbury*

Located on the original river bank in the village of Oldbury-on-Severn, parts of this Cotswold stone pub date from 1540. The village has a long history dating back to the Iron Age, whilst the pub itself was formerly a mill. There is a large garden to enjoy, flower-filled in summer, and a boules area. A typical menu features dishes such as roast Severnvale topside of beef and Yorkshire pudding; smoked haddock and salmon fish pie; crispy belly of pork and black pudding; and pan-fried pheasant breast, chipolata and bacon.

Open all wk Mon-Fri 11.30-2.30 6-11 (Sat 11.30am-mdnt Sun noon-10.30) **Bar Meals** L served Mon-Fri 12-2, Sat 12-2.30, Sun 12-3 D served Sat-Sun 6-9 Av main course £9.75 **Restaurant** L served Mon-Fri 12-2, Sat 12-2.30, Sun 12-3 booking required D served Sat-Sun 6-9 booking required Av 3 course à la carte fr £18.95 ⊕ FREE HOUSE ◀ Interbrew Bass, Butcombe Best, Otter Bitter, Guest ales ♂ Ashton Press, Stowford Press, Ashton Still. ♥ 16 **Facilities** Children welcome Children's menu Family room Dogs allowed Garden Parking

Save on hotels. Book at **theAA.com/hotel**

GLOUCESTERSHIRE 203 ENGLAND

PICK OF THE PUBS

The Churchill Arms ★★★★ INN ✿✿

PAXFORD   **MAP 10 SP13**

GL55 6XH
☎ **01386 594000** 📠 **01386 594005**
e-mail: info@thechurchillarms.com
web: www.thechurchillarms.com
dir: *2m E of Chipping Campden, 4m N of Moreton-in-Marsh*

In the heart of the picture postcard village of Paxford, near the historical wool town of Chipping Campden, this unpretentious 17th-century pub is the quintessential Cotswold inn. Nestled among honey stone cottages, The Churchill Arms offers glorious views over the local chapel towards the rolling Cotswold countryside. The pub draws an eclectic mix of customers, including drinkers, well-informed foodies and muddy walkers - the starting point of the Cotswold Way is a short stroll away. Hook Norton, Purity and Wye Valley ales are on tap, among others, and an impressive list of wines ensures there's a tipple to suit every taste and pocket. The setting for savouring the imaginative food and tip-top ales is suitably cosy with a rustic interior - expect flagstones, a beamed ceiling and large inglenook fireplace with wood-burning stove.

The kitchen makes sound use of quality local supplies, and prepares innovative modern British dishes that evolve with the seasons, with clever twists on pub classics. Braised lamb's tongue with carrot and cumin purée might be followed by parsley-crusted turbot with mussels and chestnut mushrooms; cod with crushed black olive potatoes and pesto dressing; or venison with red cabbage and juniper berry jus. For traditionalists, there is real ale-battered fish and chips. Desserts are a strength here and might include sticky toffee pudding or roasted hazelnut parfait with banana curd and poached fig. There is free Wi-fi throughout and four comfortable en suite rooms complete the picture at a pub that is a perfect base for exploring the Cotswolds.

Open all wk 11-3 6-11 Closed: 25 Dec **Bar Meals** L served all wk 12-2 booking required D served all wk 7-9 booking required **Restaurant** L served all wk 12-2 booking required D served all wk 7-9 booking required ⊕ ENTERPRISE INNS ◀ Hook Norton Bitter, Butty Bach, Wye Valley, Mad Goose, Purity, London Pride Ŏ Stowford Press. **Facilities** Children's menu Children's portions Dogs allowed Garden Wi-fi **Rooms** 4

PAINSWICK   Map 4 SO80

The Falcon Inn

New St GL6 6UN ☎ 01452 814222 📄 01452 813377
e-mail: enquiries@falconinn-cotswolds.co.uk
dir: *On A46 in centre of Painswick*

Built in 1554, this former coaching inn has been licensed since the 17th century. It was a courthouse for over two hundred years, but today its friendly service extends to a drying room for walkers' gear. A good choice of real ales and food using local produce is available. The Falcon stands at the heart of the village opposite St Mary's church, famous for the 99 yew trees growing within its grounds. It makes an ideal base for exploring Painswick and the surrounding area. As we went to press a change of hands was about to take place.

Open all day all wk 10am-11pm ⊕ ENTERPRISE ◀ Otters Ale, Butcombe Blend, Butcombe Bitter ♻ Stowford Press, Ashton Press. **Facilities** Children welcome Children's portions Dogs allowed Garden Parking Wi-fi

PAXFORD   Map 10 SP13

PICK OF THE PUBS

The Churchill Arms ★★★★ INN ◉◉

See Pick of the Pubs on page 203

POULTON   Map 5 SP00

The Falcon Inn ♟ NEW

London Rd GL7 5HN ☎ 01285 851597 & 850878
e-mail: bookings@falconinnpoulton.co.uk
dir: *From Cirencester 4m E on A417 towards Fairford*

Husband and wife Gianni Gray and Natalie Birch bought this 300-year-old village pub in July 2010 and have put real ale and good food at the top of the agenda. Contemporary furnishings blend with original features and log fires to create an informal pub for locals who want to sup a pint of Hooky or one of the rotating guests beers, or diners tempted by rib-eye steak and chips, pork belly and mustard mash, and pear tarte Tatin with vanilla ice cream.

Open Tue-Sat 12-3 5-11, Sun 12-4 Closed: 25 Dec, Mon **Bar Meals** L served Tue-Sat 12-2.30, Sun 12-3 D served Tue-Sat 6-9 **Restaurant** L served Tue-Sat 12-2.30, Sun 12-3 booking required D served Tue-Sat 6-9 booking required Fixed menu price fr £12.50 Av 3 course à la carte fr £21 ⊕ FREE HOUSE ◀ Hooky, rotating guest beer ♻ Stowford Press. ♟ 11 **Facilities** Children welcome Children's menu Children's portions Dogs allowed Garden Parking Wi-fi

SAPPERTON   Map 4 SO90

PICK OF THE PUBS

The Bell at Sapperton ♟

GL7 6LE ☎ 01285 760298 📄 01285 760761
e-mail: thebell@sapperton66.freeserve.co.uk
dir: *From A419 halfway between Cirencester & Stroud follow signs for Sapperton. Pub in village centre near church*

Set in an idyllic village close to Cirencester Park, the 300-year-old Bell continues to wow Cotswold walkers, drinkers and diners. Built of mellow Cotswold stone, the pub is civilised in every way, attracting discerning folk from miles around for innovative pub food served throughout three cosy dining areas, where exposed stone walls, polished flagstones, bare boards, open log fires and individual tables and chairs set the style. Use of top-notch seasonal produce is key to the popularity of the menus and includes fish from Cornwall and organic and rare breed meats. Follow steamed River Fowey mussels in cider and smoked bacon sauce with pan-fried loin of Badminton Estate venison, beetroot jus and horseradish mash. Walkers calling in for a snack can tuck into a three-cheese ploughman's, washed down by a pint of local Uley Old Spot ale. There's a secluded rear courtyard and a landscaped front garden for alfresco dining.

Open 11-2.30 6.30-11 (Sun 12-10.30) Closed: 25 Dec, Sun eve in winter **Bar Meals** L served all wk 12-2.15 booking required D served all wk 7-9.15 booking required Av main course £15 **Restaurant** Av 3 course à la carte fr £35 ⊕ FREE HOUSE ◀ Uley Old Spot, Bath Ales, Otter Bitter, Cotswold Way ♻ Stowford Press. ♟ 20 **Facilities** Children's portions Dogs allowed Garden Parking

SHEEPSCOMBE   Map 4 SO81

PICK OF THE PUBS

The Butchers Arms

GL6 7RH ☎ 01452 812113 📄 01452 814358
e-mail: mark@butchers-arms.co.uk
web: www.butchers-arms.co.uk
dir: *1.5m S of A46 (Cheltenham to Stroud road), N of Painswick*

Tucked into the western scarp of the Cotswolds, pretty Sheepscombe radiates all of the mellow, sedate, bucolic charm you'd expect from such a haven. The village pub, dating from 1620 and a favourite haunt of

Cider with Rosie author Laurie Lee, lives up to such expectations and then some. Stapled to the steep, wooded valley-side, views from the gardens are idyllic whilst within is all you'd hope for; log fires, drunken beams, clean-cut rustic furnishings, village chatter backed up by Cotswold beers from the likes of Goff's Brewery. Walkers, riders, locals and tourists all beat an enthusiastic path to the door beneath the pub's famous carved sign showing a butcher supping a pint of ale with a pig tied to his leg. True to form, the fulfilling fodder here includes locally sourced meats; the chicken, broccoli and ham pie is a cracker, as is the pork, apple and cider sausage dish whilst the specials board slants the fare well towards fish and vegetarian choices. Nibblers can graze on great sandwiches like West Country Brie, apple and caramelised balsamic onions.

Open all wk 11.30-2.30 6.30-11 (Sat 11.30-11.30 Sun noon-10.30) **Bar Meals** L served Mon-Fri 12-2.30, Sat-Sun all day D served Mon-Sat 6.30-9.30, Sun 6.30-9 (ex Sun Jan & Feb) **Restaurant** L served Mon-Fri 12-2.30, Sat-Sun all day booking required D served Mon-Sat 6.30-9.30, Sun 6.30-9 (ex Sun Jan & Feb) booking required ⊕ FREE HOUSE ◀ Otter Bitter, Severn Vale, Butcombe Bitter, St Austell Proper Job, Wye Valley Dorothy Goodbody, Severn Vale ♻ Westons Stowford Press, Westons Traditional Scrumpy. **Facilities** Children welcome Children's menu Children's portions Dogs allowed Garden Parking

SOMERFORD KEYNES   Map 4 SU09

The Bakers Arms

GL7 6DN ☎ 01285 861298
dir: *Exit A419 signed Cotswold Water Park. Cross B4696, 1m, follow signs for Keynes Park & Somerford Keynes*

This beautiful chocolate box pub is built from Cotswold stone, with low-beamed ceilings and inglenook fireplaces. Dating from the 15th century, the building was formerly the village bakery and stands in mature gardens ideal for alfresco dining. Discreet children's play areas and heated terraces add to its broad appeal. Somerford Keynes is in the Cotswold Water Park, and the man-made beach of Keynes Park is within easy walking distance, while the nearby Thames Path and Cotswold Way make the pub popular with walkers. The food on offer runs along the lines of baguettes and pub favourites –marinated rack of pork ribs and Gloucester Old Spot sausages.

Open all day all wk 11-11 (Sun 12-10.30) **Bar Meals** L served 12-9 D served 12-9 food served all day **Restaurant** L served 12-9 D served 12-9 food served all day ⊕ ENTERPRISE INNS ◀ Courage Best, Butcombe Bitter, Stroud Budding ♻ Stowford Press. **Facilities** Children welcome Children's menu Children's portions Play area Dogs allowed Garden Parking

Save on hotels. Book at **theAA.com/hotel**

GLOUCESTERSHIRE 205 **ENGLAND**

SOUTH CERNEY   Map 5 SU09

The Old Boathouse ◉ ⚲ NEW

Cotswold Water Park Four Pillars Hotel, Spine Road East GL7 5FP ☎ 01285 864111
dir: *M4 junct 15/A419 to Cirencester, turn onto B4696 & follow signs for Cotswold Water Park Information Centre*

At the heart of the watery wonderland of the Cotswold Water Park, this ultra-modern gastro-pub is a relaxing spot at which to unwind after a day's hard touring honeyed villages or birdwatching amidst these flooded gravel pits. A robust menu includes a great game pie (venison, wild boar, rabbit, and pheasant), or simply nibble at a pigeon and quail terrine and enjoy the views from the terrace. A daily-changing specials board combines to earn this unusual destination bar an AA Rosette for head chef Marcus Stevenson and his team.

Open all day all wk **Bar Meals** Av main course £12 food served all day **Restaurant** Fixed menu price fr £10 Av 3 course à la carte fr £22 food served all day ⊕ FREE HOUSE ◀ Black Sheep, Fuller's London Pride, Guest ales. ⚲ 15 **Facilities** Children welcome Children's menu Children's portions Play area Dogs allowed Garden Parking

---

SOUTHROP   Map 5 SP10

PICK OF THE PUBS

The Swan at Southrop ◉◉

GL7 3NU ☎ 01367 850205 📄 01367 850517
e-mail: info@theswanatsouthrop.co.uk
dir: *Off A361 between Lechlade & Burford*

Occupying a lovely spot on the village green at Southrop, this creeper-clad early 17th-century Cotswold inn is run by Sebastian and Lana Snow, both protégés of celebrity chef Antony Worrall-Thompson. The interior - bar, snug and award-winning restaurant - is surprisingly light and airy for such an historic building, but homely too, especially when the log fire is ablaze. In the kitchen, impeccable local produce is used in the modern British cooking with Mediterranean touches. Relax with a glass of wine or Cotswold Way to peruse the menu. Typical of the starters are white bean, wild mushroom and truffle oil soup, and poached pear, Cashel blue, hazelnuts and chicory salad. Mains might include crisp confit of Kelmscott pork belly with artichokes and mushrooms; lamb, pearl barley and leek pudding with caramelised root vegetables; braised shin of beef with horseradish dumplings, carrots, chestnuts, parsnip mash and bone marrow crostini. The bar menu offers the likes of fish and chips; home-made burger; club sandwich with fries; moules marinière; whitebait; and home-made pork scratchings. There's a children's menu too.

Open all wk 12-3 6-11 Closed: Dec 25
Bar Meals L served all wk 12-3 D served Mon-Sat 6-10 Av main course £10 **Restaurant** L served all wk 12-3 booking required D served Mon-Sat 6-10 booking required Fixed menu price fr £13.50 Av 3 course à la carte fr £25 ⊕ FREE HOUSE ◀ Hook Norton, Wadworth 6X, Cotswold Way, Tribute, Doom Bar, guest ale ◐ Breton. **Facilities** Children welcome Children's menu Children's portions Family room Dogs allowed Garden Wi-fi

---

STONEHOUSE   Map 4 SO80

The George Inn ⚲

Peter St, Frocester GL10 3TQ
☎ 01453 822302 📄 01453 791612
e-mail: paul@georgeinn.co.uk
dir: *M5 junct 13, onto A419 at 1st rdbt 3rd exit signed Eastington, left at next rdbt signed Frocester. Approx 2m on right in village*

Look in vain for a fruit machine or jukebox in this family-run 18th-century former coaching inn; instead, enjoy what makes a pub good – a sensible choice of real ales and locally sourced, home-made food, which here means bacon-wrapped chicken breast; faggots; filled omelettes; and fish pie. The lovely courtyard garden is overlooked by the original coaching stables, while the Cotswold Way and a network of leafy paths help guide visitors to the August Bank Holiday village beer festival.

Open all day all wk 7.30am-mdnt **Bar Meals** L served all wk 12-9.30 D served all wk 12-9.30 Av main course £8.95 food served all day **Restaurant** L served all wk 12-9.30 D served all wk 12-9.30 Fixed menu price fr £8.95 Av 3 course à la carte fr £15.95 food served all day ⊕ ENTERPRISE INNS ◀ Timothy Taylor, Doom Bar, 3 guest ◐ Old Rosie, Stowford Press. ⚲ 10 **Facilities** Children welcome Children's menu Children's portions Play area Family room Dogs allowed Garden Beer festival Parking Wi-fi

---

STOW-ON-THE-WOLD   Map 10 SP12

The Eagle and Child

GL54 1HY ☎ 01451 830670 📄 01451 870048
e-mail: stay@theroyalisthotel.com
dir: *From Moreton-in-Marsh rail station take A429 to Stow-on-the-Wold. At 2nd lights left into Sheep St, A436. Establishment 100yds on left*

Reputed the oldest inn in England, dating back to 947 AD and once a hospice to shelter lepers, The Eagle and Child is part of the Royalist Hotel. The social hub of the hotel and village, serving local ales on handpump, it also delivers pub food that manages to be both rustic and accomplished. Informality and flexibility go hand-in-hand with flagstone floors, oak beams and rustic tables; the light-flooded conservatory offering a striking contrast to the character, low-ceilinged dining room. Expect range of pub classics, from Old Spot sausages with leek mash to steak and Guinness pie, and more innovative food like seafood and charcuterie deli plates. As we went to press a change of hands was taking place.

Open all wk Mon-Sat 11-11 (Sun 11-10.30) ⊕ FREE HOUSE ◀ Hook Norton, Goffs, Donnington, Jouster, Hooky ◐ Stowford Press. **Facilities** Children welcome Dogs allowed Garden Parking

---

The Unicorn

Sheep St GL54 1HQ ☎ 01451 830257 📄 01451 831090
e-mail: reception@birchhotels.co.uk
dir: *Telephone for directions*

Originally a coaching inn, this attractive 17th-century hotel of honey-coloured limestone, with hand-cut roof tiles and abundantly flowering window boxes, is set in the heart of Stow-on-the-Wold. The interior is stylishly presented with Jacobean pieces, antique artefacts and open log fires. The pub menu offers a good choice of dishes which can be served in the oak-beamed bar, the stylish contemporary restaurant or in the secluded garden if the weather is fine.

Open all wk **Bar Meals** Av main course £10.95 **Restaurant** L served all wk 12-2 D served all wk 7-9 Av 3 course à la carte fr £22.45 ⊕ FREE HOUSE ◀ Hook Norton, Dorothy Goodbody ◐ Westons. **Facilities** Children welcome Children's menu Children's portions Dogs allowed Garden Parking Wi-fi

---

White Hart Inn ⚲ NEW

The Square GL54 1AF ☎ 01451 830674
e-mail: info@theoldbutchers.com
dir: *From A429 into market square. Inn on left*

Many of the mellow stone buildings in this lovely Cotswold town date to the 12th century, including parts of the White Hart. Under the management of Louise and Peter Robinson since 2010, it has been refurbished throughout. Two cosy bars benefit from open fires, and an atmospheric dining room serves lunchtime snacks such as croque monsieur or croque madame. Dinner dishes range from home-made scotched egg with salad cream starter, following on with braised oxtail and shin of beef pie. The spacious car park is an added bonus.

Open all day Closed: 1 wk May & 1 wk Oct, Sun eve **Bar Meals** L served all wk 12-2.30 D served Mon-Sat 6.30-9 Av main course £11 **Restaurant** L served all wk 12-2.30 D served Mon-Sat 6.30-9 Av 3 course à la carte fr £23 ⊕ ARKELLS ◀ 3B, 2B, Kingsdown ◐ Stowford Press. ⚲ 11 **Facilities** Children welcome Children's menu Children's portions Dogs allowed Garden Parking Wi-fi

PICK OF THE PUBS

Bear of Rodborough Hotel ★★★ HL ♉

STROUD   Map 4 SO80

Rodborough Common GL5 5DE
☎ **01453 878522** 📄 **01453 872523**
e-mail: info@bearofrodborough.info
web: www.cotswold-inns-hotels.co.uk/bear
dir: *From M5 junct 13 follow signs for Stonehouse then Rodborough*

Standing 600 feet above sea level and surrounded by 300 acres of National Trust land, this 17th-century former Cotswolds alehouse takes its name from the bear-baiting that used to take place nearby. The hotel is worth seeking out for all sorts of reasons. There's the comfortable accommodation, open log fires, stone walls and solid wooden floors, as well as an interesting inscription over the front doors that reads 'Through this wide opening gate none come too early, none return too late'. The motto was reputedly carved by the renowned sculptor and typographer, Eric Gill.

A running bear design is incorporated into the ceiling beams in the elegant Box Tree restaurant and Tower Room, while the identity of a resident ghost is often discussed in the Grizzly Bar over pints of Butcombe, John Smith's or Tipster. Outside, there's a delightful York stone terrace, as well as a walled croquet lawn created in the 1920s by a former resident called Edmunds, a partner in a well-known firm of Stroud nurserymen.

The bar menu begins with an attractive range of hot and cold sandwiches, the former served with mixed leaf salad and spicy potato wedges. Then there are starters, salads and main course dishes like warm aubergine tart with Greek salad and tzatziki, and steak and Guinness pie with herb mash and vegetables. A full afternoon tea menu with cakes, scones and clotted cream fills in the time before dinner in the restaurant. Start, perhaps, with smoked salmon salad with purple rocket, Thai grass and parmesan; followed by a duet of guinea fowl, smoked bacon and Savoy cabbage, served with pear purée and roasted cocotte potato. Warm chocolate tart with English raspberries brings the meal to an appealing conclusion.

Open all day all wk 10.30am-11pm
Bar Meals L served all wk 12-2.30
D served all wk 6.30-10
Restaurant D served all wk 7-10 ⊕ FREE
HOUSE ◼ Butcombe, John Smith's, Tipster
♻ Ashton Press. ♉ 10
Facilities Children's portions Play area
Dogs allowed Garden Parking **Rooms** 46

Save on hotels. Book at theAA.com/hotel

GLOUCESTERSHIRE 207 ENGLAND

STROUD — Map 4 SO80

PICK OF THE PUBS

Bear of Rodborough Hotel ★★★ HL ☕

See Pick of the Pubs on opposite page

The Ram Inn

South Woodchester GL5 5EL
☎ 01453 873329 📠 01453 873329
e-mail: raminnwoodchester@hotmail.co.uk
dir: *A46 from Stroud to Nailsworth, right after 2m into South Woodchester, follow brown tourist signs*

From the plentiful seating on terrace of the 17th-century Cotswold stone Ram Inn, there are splendid views over five valleys, although proximity to the huge fireplace may prove more appealing in winter. Rib-eye steak, at least two fish dishes, home-made lasagne and Sunday roasts can be expected, washed down with a glass of Uley Old Spot or Stroud Budding and regularly changing guests. Enjoy a display by the Stroud Morris Men who regularly perform here.

Open all day all wk ⊕ FREE HOUSE ◀ Uley Old Spot, Stroud Budding, Butcombe Bitter, Guests.
Facilities Children welcome Children's menu Children's portions Family room Dogs allowed Garden Parking Wi-fi

PICK OF THE PUBS

Rose & Crown Inn

The Cross, Nympsfield GL10 3TU ☎ 01453 860240
dir: *M5 junct 13 off B4066, SW of Stroud*

An imposing, 400-year-old coaching inn of honey-coloured local stone that could well be the highest pub in the Cotswolds, a fact that hardly matters since the views over the Severn are stunning anyway. Occupying a central position in the village, the closeness of the Cotswold Way makes it a popular stop for hikers and bikers. Inside, the inn's character is preserved with natural stone, wood panelling, a lovely open fire and some local real ales, like Pig's Ear from the Uley brewery. In the galleried restaurant, the new owners offer fresh, home-made food cooked to order – steak and ale pie, T-bone steak, Gressingham duck, lamb rump and vegetarian options. In the large garden, children will enjoy the playground area, which has a swing, slides and a climbing bridge.

Open all day all wk noon-mdnt **Bar Meals** L served Mon-Fri 12-3, Sat 12-9, Sun 12-6 D served Mon-Fri 6-9, Sat 12-9 **Restaurant** L served Mon-Fri 12-3, Sat 12-9, Sun 12-6 D served Mon-Fri 6-9, Sat 12-9 ⊕ FREE HOUSE ◀ Uley Pigs Ear, Guest ales ♉ Stowford Press.
Facilities Children welcome Children's menu Children's portions Play area Dogs allowed Garden Parking

The Woolpack Inn

Slad Rd, Slad GL6 7QA ☎ 01452 813429
e-mail: info@thewoolpackinn-slad.com
dir: *2m from Stroud, 8m from Gloucester*

The Woolpack is a friendly local in the beautiful Slad Valley close to the Cotswold Way, an area immortalised by Laurie Lee; indeed, the author was a regular here. The place is popular with walkers, so muddy boots are not frowned upon, and children and dogs are welcome. The menu of honest and freshly prepared food from local suppliers may include roast red pepper and chilli soup; pork belly stuffed with black pudding and herbs, bubble and squeak potato cake and cider and honey velouté; and ginger pudding with butterscotch sauce.

Open all day all wk **Bar Meals** L served Mon-Sat 12-2, Sun 12-3.30 booking required D served Tue-Sat 6.30-9 booking required Av main course £11
Restaurant L served Mon-Sat 12-2, Sun 12-3.30 booking required D served Tue-Sat 6.30-9 booking required Av 3 course à la carte fr £20 ⊕ FREE HOUSE ◀ Uley Pig's Ear, Old Spot, Uley Bitter, Budding, Butcombe Bitter ♉ Old Rosie, Stowford Press. **Facilities** Children welcome Children's portions Dogs allowed Garden Parking Wi-fi

TETBURY — Map 4 ST89

PICK OF THE PUBS

Gumstool Inn ☕

Calcot Manor GL8 8YJ
☎ 01666 890391 📠 01666 890394
e-mail: reception@calcotmanor.co.uk
web: www.calcotmanor.co.uk
dir: *3m W of Tetbury*

Built in the 14th-century by Cistercian monks, this charming subtley refurbished country inn is part of Calcot Manor Hotel, which is set in 220 acres of Cotswold countryside. The hotel is a successful conversion of a stone farmhouse, set around a flower-filled courtyard. As a free house, the cheerful and cosy Gumstool Inn has a real English country pub atmosphere and stocks a good selection of some unusual real ales, mostly from the West Country, and an excellent choice of wines. Food is top notch gastro-pub quality - starters of poached free-range Sherston egg on brioche, buttered leeks, spinach and hollandaise or Cornish fish soup indicate the calibre. A section of the menu proffers light main courses such as grilled scallops in the half shell with garlic and parsley or duck confit salad with sweet and sour

dressing. Among the main courses may be found salmon and smoked haddock fishcakes with dill butter; crispy roasted and braised pork belly, mashed carrot and swede, cavolo nero; and roast and confit free-range chicken with dauphinoise potatoes. There is a pretty sun terrace, while winter evenings are warmed with cosy log fires.

Open all wk 11.30-2.30 5.30-11 **Bar Meals** L served all wk 11.30-2 booking required D served Mon-Sat 7-9.30, Sun 7-9 booking required Av main course £10.75 **Restaurant** L served all wk 12-2 booking required D served Mon-Sat 7-9.30, Sun 7-9 booking required Av 3 course à la carte fr £23 ⊕ FREE HOUSE ◀ Atlantic, Sharp's IPA, Matthews Bob Wool, Wickwar Cotswold Way, Butcombe Blonde. ☕ 21 **Facilities** Children welcome Children's menu Children's portions Play area Family room Garden Parking Wi-fi

PICK OF THE PUBS

The Priory Inn ★★★ SHL ☕

London Rd GL8 8JJ
☎ 01666 502251 📠 01666 503534
e-mail: info@theprioryinn.co.uk
dir: *M4 junct 17, A429 towards Cirencester. Left onto B4014 to Tetbury. Over mini-rdbt onto Long St, pub 100yds after corner on right*

Thriving gastro-pub, hotel and coffee bar at the centre of Tetbury life. The excellent selection of real ales from local breweries includes a premium lager from the Cotswold Brewing Company; real cider from Thatchers is also on tap; and a local bubbly from Bow in the Cloud vineyard near Malmesbury is sold by the glass. Since 2008 a '30-mile food zone' has demonstrated the pub's commitment to serving food and drink from farms and suppliers within a 30-mile radius. Children are particularly welcome, with a specialised menu of home-made dishes and junior cocktails, plus the opportunity to decorate a personalised wood-fired pizza. An evening meal could begin with smoked pigeon breast salad with bacon, beetroot and black pudding; and continue with a seven-ounce Willesley Farm beef burger with smoked tomato and cucumber salsa. Try an upside down apple tart with Ceri's vanilla ice cream for dessert; or a vanilla pannacotta with poached pear and hazelnut biscotti. There is live music every Sunday evening, and local ale and cider days twice a year.

Open all day all wk Mon-Thu 7am-11pm (Fri 7am-mdnt, Sat 8am-mdnt, Sun 8am-11pm)
Bar Meals L served Bkfst all wk 7-10.30, L all wk 12-3, Fri-Sun & BHs all day D served Mon-Thu 5-10, Fri-Sun & BHs all day **Restaurant** Bkfst all wk 7-10.30, L all wk 12-3, Fri-Sun & BHs all day booking required D served Mon-Thu 5-10, Fri-Sun & BHs all day booking required ⊕ FREEHOUSE ◀ Uley Bitter, two guest ales ♉ Thatchers Gold, Cotswold. ☕ 13 **Facilities** Children welcome Children's menu Children's portions Play area Family room Dogs allowed Garden Parking **Rooms** 14

TETBURY continued

Snooty Fox Hotel ★★★ SHL ☕ NEW

Market Place GL8 8DD
☎ 01666 502436 📠 01666 503479
e-mail: res@snooty-fox.co.uk
dir: In town centre opposite covered market hall

Slap bang in the centre of Tetbury, this 16th-century
coaching inn retains many of its original features. Sit in a
leather armchair in front of the log fire with a pint of
Butcombe Bitter and order from the extensive bar menu –
pint of prawns with lemon and garlic mayonnaise or
smoked chicken Caesar salad maybe. Alternatively, head
for the restaurant and enjoy the likes of rabbit terrine
with pear chutney; beef Wellington; or roast partridge
with whisky sauce, haggis, neeps and tatties.

Open all day all wk **Bar Meals** L served all wk 12-3,
snacks 3-6 D served all wk 6-9.30 Av main course £10
Restaurant L served all wk 12-3 booking required
D served all wk 6-9.30 booking required Av 3 course à la
carte fr £24 ⊕ FREE HOUSE ◀ Wadworth 6X, Butcombe
Bitter ⚙ Ashton Press cider. **Facilities** Children welcome
Children's portions Dogs allowed Wi-fi **Rooms** 12

PICK OF THE PUBS

The Trouble House ☕

Cirencester Rd GL8 8SG ☎ 01666 502206
e-mail: contact@troublehousetetbury.co.uk
dir: On A433 between Tetbury & Cirencester

Uniquely named after a series of unfortunate events at
the pub, namely agricultural riots, two suicides and a
disastrous fire, this historic inn stands beside the A433
between Tetbury and Cirencester and continues to
thrive as a destination dining pub under Shane and
Liam Parr (ex-Calcot Manor), who took over the
Wadworth pub in February 2010. The setting may be
rustic-chic, with scrubbed tables, wooden floors,
pastel-painted walls and three warming log fires, but
Liam's modern British cooking draws restaurant
tourists across the Cotswolds for a table – do book.
From simpler, more pubby dishes on the blackboard,
perhaps venison pie or rib of beef for two, the menu
may offer Salcombe crab gratin or roast pumpkin soup
to start, followed by seared mackerel with chorizo and
roast pepper stew, or braised blade of beef with confit
garlic mash. Leave room for spiced crème brûlée or a
plate of British cheeses.

Open 11.30-3 6.30-11 Closed: 25 Dec, 1st 2 wks Jan,
Sun eve, Mon (ex BHs open for lunch)
Bar Meals L served Tue-Fri 12-2 booking required Av
main course £14 **Restaurant** L served Tue-Sun 12-2
booking required D served Tue-Sat 7-9.30 booking
required Fixed menu price fr £12 Av 3 course à la carte
fr £26 ⊕ WADWORTH ◀ Wadworth 6X, Henrys IPA
⚙ Stowford Press. ☕ 12 **Facilities** Children welcome
Children's portions Dogs allowed Garden Parking

TODENHAM — Map 10 SP23

PICK OF THE PUBS

The Farriers Arms ☕

Main St GL56 9PF ☎ 01608 650901
e-mail: info@farriersarms.com
web: www.farriersarms.com
dir: Right to Todenham at N end of Moreton-in-Marsh.
2.5m from Shipston on Stour

Dating back to 1650 when it was a church house, this
Cotswold hostelry was also an ironworks and a smithy
before becoming a pub in 1830. It ticks all the country
pub boxes with its polished flagstone floors, exposed
stone walls, wooden beams, and large inglenook
fireplace with woodburner – perfect surroundings in
which to sample a pint of Goffs. Alternatively take your
drink outside to the landscaped walled garden and
suntrap patio at the rear, and enjoy the superb views to
the church and the Cotswold countryside. The
refurbished restaurant offers a daily-changing menu
packed with local produce. Starters range from apricot
and Stilton tart to a duo of Todenham sausages served
with a grain mustard sauce. Typical main courses are
pork tenderloin wrapped in Parma ham, and
Gressingham duck breast on braised red cabbage.
Leave space for a home-made dessert along traditional
lines: banoffee pie or white and dark chocolate tart.
Look out for the ghostlike figure of a priest with a pair
of dogs.

Open all wk noon-3 6-11 (Sun 6.30-11)
Bar Meals L served Mon-Sat 12-2, Sun 12-2.30
D served Mon-Sat 6-9, Sun 6.30-9 **Restaurant** L served
Mon-Sat 12-2, Sun 12-2.30 D served Mon-Sat 6-9, Sun
6.30-9 ⊕ FREE HOUSE ◀ Hook Norton Best, Wye Valley
Butty Bach, Black Sheep, Goffs Brewery Ales
⚙ Stowford Press. ☕ 10 **Facilities** Children welcome
Children's menu Children's portions Dogs allowed
Garden Parking

TORMARTON — Map 4 ST77

Best Western Compass Inn ☕

GL9 1JB ☎ 01454 218242 📠 01454 218741
e-mail: info@compass-inn.co.uk
dir: M4 junct 18, A46 N towards Stroud. After 200mtrs 1st
right towards Tormarton. Inn in 300mtrs

A charming 18th-century creeper-clad inn, set in six
acres of grounds in the heart of the Gloucestershire
countryside, right on the Cotswold Way. Light bites and
more filling meals can be taken in the bar where real ales
and cider are served. In the restaurant, dishes might
include home-made chicken Kiev; grilled lamb in mint
marinade; spinach and ricotta tortellini; and breaded
whole tail scampi.

Open all day all wk 7am-11pm (Sat-Sun 8am-11pm)
Closed: 25-26 Dec **Bar Meals** Av main course £9 food
served all day **Restaurant** Av 3 course à la carte fr £22
food served all day ⊕ FREE HOUSE ◀ Interbrew Bass,
London Pride, Butcombe ⚙ Ashton Press. ☕ 11
Facilities Children welcome Children's menu Children's
portions Dogs allowed Garden Parking Wi-fi

UPPER ODDINGTON — Map 10 SP22

PICK OF THE PUBS

The Horse and Groom Inn ☕

GL56 0XH ☎ 01451 830584
e-mail: info@horseandgroom.uk.com
dir: 1.5m S of Stow-on-the-Wold, just off A436

Located in a Cotswold conservation village just a mile
and a half from Stow-on-the-Wold, this stone-built inn
dates from the 16th century. It is immaculately kept,
with pale polished flagstone floors, beams, stripped
stone walls and log fires in the inglenook. Grape vines
grow outside and in fine weather you can enjoy the
terrace and gardens which are surrounded by dry stone
walls. A great selection of cask ales is offered from
local breweries and the wine list, including over twenty
available by the glass, is ever growing. Menus
comprise regional food sourced from as close to the
kitchen door as possible. Bread, for example, is made
daily from local flours. Local meat, such as outdoor
reared Old Spot pork, venison, pheasant, partridge,
pigeon and rabbit feature in dishes such as juniper
and spice braised Gloucester Old Spot pork belly, or
pan-fried breast of pheasant, confit leg, honey roast
parsnips and mustard mash. Fish for dishes like roast
haddock fillet with parsley and pine nut crust is
responsibly sourced from sustainable fisheries.

Open all wk noon-3 5.30-11 (Sun 6.30-10.30)
Bar Meals L served all wk 12-2 D served Mon-Sat
6.30-9, Sun 7-9 **Restaurant** L served all wk 12-2
D served Mon-Sat 6.30-9, Sun 7-9 ⊕ FREE HOUSE
◀ Wye Valley Best, Hereford Pale Ale, Wickwar Bob,
Goffs Tournament, Box Steam Chuffin Ale ⚙ Kingstone
Press. ☕ 25 **Facilities** Children welcome Children's
menu Children's portions Dogs allowed Garden Parking
Wi-fi

WINCHCOMBE   Map 10 SP02

The White Hart Inn and Restaurant ♥

High St GL54 5LJ ☎ 01242 602359 📠 **01242 602703**
e-mail: info@wineandsausage.com
dir: In centre of Winchcombe on B4632

The White Hart is a 16th-century inn in the heart of Winchcombe just outside Cheltenham, a small historic town set in the Cotswold countryside. Reopened at the end of 2006, it offers a new bar, restaurant and wine shop. Specialising in an amazing choice of wines, there are also plenty of real ales, and simple and unpretentious British food sourced from local suppliers. Popular with walkers, it's the perfect place to unwind in the cosy bar or intimate restaurant and enjoy traditional British food and a pint or glass of wine. Recent change of hands.

Open all day all wk 10am-11pm (Fri-Sat 10am-mdnt Sun 10am-10.30pm) **Bar Meals** L served all wk 12-3 D served all wk 6-9 **Restaurant** L served all wk 12-3 D served all wk 6.9 ⊕ FREE HOUSE ◀ Wadworth 6X, Old Speckled Hen, Butcombe, Otter, Jouster, Changing ales Õ Stowford Press, Addlestones. ♥ 8 **Facilities** Children welcome Dogs allowed Garden Parking

WOODCHESTER   Map 4 SO80

PICK OF THE PUBS

The Old Fleece ♥

Bath Rd, Rooksmoor GL5 5NB ☎ 01453 872582
e-mail: pheasantpluckers2003@yahoo.co.uk
dir: 2m S of Stroud on A46

Set amid beautiful countryside with miles of footpaths to explore, this delightful coaching inn was built in the 18th century from Cotswold stone and has a traditional stone roof. From the Old Fleece, you can walk to Rodborough, Minchinhampton and Selsley Commons, or go one step further and connect eventually with the scenic Cotswold Way long distance trail. The beautifully refurbished interior includes wooden floors, wood panelling and exposed stone, and the bar serves well kept Tom Long and Buckham Bitter. Predominantly French chefs offer a comprehensive menu of British and continental dishes, ranging from classics such as Old Spot sausage and mash with onion gravy to the likes of confit duck leg with hoi sin noodles, whole sea bream with braised fennel, or pork loin steak with apple and Calvados purée.

Open all day all wk 11-11 (Sun 11-10.30)
Bar Meals L served all wk 11am-10pm food served all day **Restaurant** L served all wk 11am-10pm food served all day ⊕ PHEASANT PLUCKERS LTD ◀ Buckham Bitter, Tom Long, Guest ales Õ Ashton Still. ♥ 12 **Facilities** Children welcome Dogs allowed Parking

GREATER MANCHESTER

ALTRINCHAM   Map 15 SJ78

PICK OF THE PUBS

The Victoria ♥

See Pick of the Pubs on page 210

BIRTLE   Map 15 SD81

Pack Horse Inn ♥

Elbut Ln BL9 7TU ☎ 0161 764 3620
e-mail: pack@jwlees.co.uk
dir: From Bury towards Rochdale take B6222 (Bury & Rochdale Old Rd). Left at Fairfield General Hospital

Just beyond the Pack Horse the lane gives way to marked moorland paths and tracks into the spectacular wooded chasm of the Cheesden Gorge. Ramblers in this heritage hotspot rest awhile at this converted farmhouse, which offers classic English pub meals and some interesting specials served in a comfy inn busy with artefacts. It is a great community pub with events all year through, also popular with families, and horse-riders hitch up here en route to the moorland bridle paths. Head out to the patio on warmer days with fine views over farmland high above Bury.

Open all day all wk 11.30am-11.30pm (Sun noon-10.30)
Bar Meals food served all day **Restaurant** food served all day ⊕ JW LEES ◀ JW Lees Bitter, Guvnor. ♥ 20
Facilities Children welcome Children's menu Children's portions Garden Parking

DENSHAW   Map 16 SD91

The Rams Head Inn ♥

OL3 5UN ☎ 01457 874802 📠 **01457 820978**
e-mail: ramsheaddenshaw@aol.com
dir: M62 junct 22, A672 towards Oldham, 2m to inn

From its position 1212 feet above sea level, this 400-year-old country inn offers panoramic views over Saddleworth. Log fires and collections of memorabilia are features of the interior, where blackboard menus list everything available and food is cooked to order. Game and seafood figure strongly, with dishes such as smoked Finnan haddock chowder, and pheasant Wellington with bacon and sage cream. Another attraction is The Pantry

(open 9am-4.30pm Tue-Sat, 11am-4.30pm Sun), a farm shop, deli, bakery, and coffee shop. There's a garden area to the rear of the inn with bench seating and panoramic views.

Open noon-2.30 6-11 Closed: 25 Dec, Mon (ex BH)
Bar Meals L served Tue-Sat 9-4.30, Sun 11-4.30
Restaurant food served all day ⊕ FREE HOUSE ◀ Timothy Taylor Landlord, Black Sheep Bitter Õ Thatchers Gold.
♥ 16 **Facilities** Children welcome Children's portions Garden Parking Wi-fi

DIDSBURY   Map 16 SJ89

PICK OF THE PUBS

The Metropolitan ♥

2 Lapwing Ln M20 2WS
☎ 0161 438 2332 📠 **0161 282 6544**
e-mail: info@the-metropolitan.co.uk
dir: M60 junct 5, A5103, right onto Barlow Moor Rd, left onto Burton Rd. Pub at x-rds. Right onto Lapwing Ln for car park

A former Victorian railway hotel, the 'Met' is well situated in the leafy suburb of West Didsbury. Originally a hotel for passengers riding the old Midland Railway into Manchester, the pub still punches above its weight architecturally - look in particular at the decorative floor tiling, the ornate windows and the delicate plasterwork. During the latter part of the 20th century the building became very run down, but it was given a sympathetic renovation in 1997, reopening as a gastro-pub. Its huge, airy interior is filled with antique tables and chairs, and deep sofas, which suit the mainly young, cosmopolitan clientele. Food ranges from starters and light bites (warm confit duck leg with watercress, steak sandwiches) to main courses such as rack of lamb with black olive crust and ratatouille, or fillet of sea trout with peas and asparagus. Spacious outside terraces buzz with drinkers and diners in the summer.

Open all day all wk 11.30-mdnt (Sun noon-11) Closed: 25 Dec **Bar Meals** L served Mon-Sat 12-7, Sun 12-6 D served Mon-Sat 6-9.30 food served all day **Restaurant** L served Mon-Sat 12-6, Sun 12-9 D served Mon-Thu 6-9.30, Fri-Sat 6-10, Sun 6-9 food served all day ◀ Timothy Taylor Landlord, Deuchars IPA, Guinness Õ Westons, Rekorderlig. ♥ 28
Facilities Children welcome Children's portions Garden Parking Wi-fi

PICK OF THE PUBS

The Victoria ♀

ALTRINCHAM Map 15 SJ78

Stamford St WA14 1EX ☎ 0161 613 1855
e-mail: the.victoria@yahoo.co.uk
dir: *From rail station, cross main road,*
turn right. 2nd left onto Stamford St

Playfully dubbed as a 'Gin Palace and
Dining Room' by owners Rachel Wetherill
and Kevin Choudhary, this compact, one-
roomed street-corner pub in trendy
Altrincham was a breath of fresh air for
drinkers and discerning diners when it
burst onto the scene in 2006. An old,
dilapidated town-centre drinking den had
been transformed into an airy destination
of choice; a stylish wood-panelled
drawing-room area set for dining twinned
with a chic, slate-floored area fronting the
bar, where bar-stools offer refuge for
those intent simply on a restful pint of
Jennings Cumberland bitter, just a step or
two away from Altrincham's shops and
galleries and handy too for the nearby
Metrolink tram and rail interchange. Their
aim, to offer a tranquil, adult's retreat
where home-cooked imaginative British
food with a strong traditional influence
takes the lead, paid dividends. The most
tasty of starters may (the menu changes
every 8 weeks) field rabbit and Cheshire
Smokehouse bacon hash, topped with a
poached egg served in a buttery tarragon
sauce; or perhaps a steaming bowl of
brown onion soup topped with Cheddar

cheese croutons. Such lead seamlessly to
a distinguished suite of mains: oven
roasted chicken breast on a smoked
applewood cheese and sweet red onion
pancake, with winter greens and port
gravy; a plate of Mutton Reform, pan-fried
breadcrumbed mutton chops with fondant
potato, wilted greens and a sweet
redcurrant gravy; or poached haddock
fillet on parsley and cabbage mashed
potato with a creamy cockle and ham hock
stew. To finish, what better than ice cream
made with Cheshire dairy produce at a
local farm or a trio of farmhouse cheeses
with black beer and raisin-soaked prunes.
For drivers, The Victoria has a temperance
bar offering Lancashire-made old
favourites like dandelion and burdock and
sarsaparilla.

Open all day all wk noon-11 (Sun noon-6)
Closed: 26 Dec & 1 Jan
Bar Meals L served Mon-Sat 12-3 D
served Mon-Sat 5.30-9 **Restaurant** L
served Mon-Sat 12-3, Sun 12-4 D served
Mon-Sat 5.30-9 ⊕ FREE HOUSE ◀ Old
Speckled Hen, Jennings Cumberland,
Flowers IPA Ö Westons Organic. ♀ 10
Facilities Children's portions

DOBCROSS   Map 15 SD90

Swan Inn

The Square OL3 5AA ☎ **01457 873451**
dir: *A62 outside Oldham. Follow brown tourist signs towards Saddleworth*

A picture-perfect South-Pennine weaving village in magnificent walking country, Dobcross was a main location for the 1979 film YANKS. Fronting the steeply sloping little cobbled square, the Swan is a commanding gritstone inn with a warren of characterful rooms off the passageway bar; think open fires, slabbed floors and centuries of service to discerning locals. Offering reliable real ales and robust, traditional pub grub (try the home-made pies), the inn is on the route of the remarkable Longwood Thump rushcart festival each August. Change of hands.

Open all wk Mon-Thu 12-3 5-11 (Fri 12-3 5-mdnt, Sat noon-11.30, Sun noon-11pm) ⊕ MARSTONS/JENNINGS ◀ Cumberland, Pedigree, Oxford Gold, Hobgoblin. **Facilities** Children welcome Children's menu Children's portions Family room Dogs allowed Garden

LITTLEBOROUGH   Map 16 SD91

The White House ▾

Blackstone Edge, Halifax Rd OL15 0LG ☎ **01706 378456**
dir: *On A58, 8m from Rochdale, 9m from Halifax*

A coaching house built in 1671, standing 1,300 feet above sea level on the Pennine Way, with panoramic views of the moors and Hollingworth Lake far below. Not surprising, then, that it attracts walkers and cyclists who rest up and sup on Theakstons and regular guest ales. It's been known as The White House for over 100 years and has been in the same hands for just over 27 of them. A simple menu of pub grub ranges from sandwiches and starters like garlic and herb mushrooms, to grills, curries, chillies and traditional plates of home-made steak and kidney pie. Plus fresh fish dishes are featured on the blackboard.

Open all wk Closed: 25 Dec **Bar Meals** L served Mon-Sat 12-2, Sun 12-9 D served Mon-Sat 6-9, Sun 12-9 Av main course £8 **Restaurant** L served Mon-Sat 12-2, Sun 12-9 D served Mon-Sat 6.30-9.30, Sun 12-9 ⊕ FREE HOUSE ◀ Timothy Taylor Landlord, Theakstons Bitter, Exmoor Gold, Black Sheep, Phoenix. **Facilities** Children welcome Parking

MANCHESTER   Map 16 SJ89

Dukes 92

14 Castle St, Castlefield M3 4LZ ☎ **0161 839 8646** 📄 **0161 832 3595**
e-mail: info@dukes92.com
dir: *In Castlefield town centre, off Deansgate*

Beautifully-restored 19th-century stable building with a vast patio beside the 92nd lock of the Duke of Bridgewater canal, opened in 1762. The interior is full of surprises, with minimalist decor downstairs and an upper gallery displaying local artistic talent. A grill restaurant supplements a lunchtime bar menu and evening pizza choices, as well as the renowned cheese and pâté counter with its huge range of British and continental cheeses which can be enjoyed with one of the wines served by the glass or a pint of Interbrew.

Open all day all wk Closed: 25-26 Dec, 1 Jan ⊕ FREE HOUSE ◀ Interbrew Boddingtons Bitter, Boddingtons ♻ Kopparberg. **Facilities** Children welcome Children's menu Children's portions Garden Parking

Marble Arch

73 Rochdale Rd M4 4HY ☎ **0161 832 5914** 📄 **0161 819 2694**
dir: *In city centre (Northern Quarter)*

A listed building with a strikingly original interior, the Marble Arch is a fine example of Manchester's Victorian heritage. Famous for its sloping floor, glazed brick walls and barrel-vaulted ceiling, the Marble Arch was designed by theatrical Victorian, Alfred Darbyshire. It was built in 1888 for the award-winning organic Marble Brewery and called the Wellington. These days there are six regular and eight seasonal house beers on offer. A comprehensive menu of hot and cold food is freshly prepared on the premises and served daily from lunchtime until mid evening.

Open all day all wk Closed: 25 Dec **Bar Meals** L served all wk 12-8 D served all wk 12-8 Av main course £10 **Restaurant** L served all wk 12-8 D served all wk 12-8 ⊕ FREE HOUSE ◀ Marble Manchester Bitter, Ginger Marble, Marble Lagonda IPA. **Facilities** Children welcome Dogs allowed Garden Beer festival

MARPLE BRIDGE   Map 16 SJ98

Hare & Hounds

19 Mill Brow SK6 5LW ☎ **0161 4274042**
e-mail: gmarsh@bwanorth.co.uk
dir: *From Marple Bridge travelling towards Mellor, turn left up Hollins Lane. Follow road to T junct with Ley Lane. Turn right, pub is 0.25m on left.*

Dating from 1805 the Hare & Hounds is a hidden gem in the beautiful hamlet of Mill Brow, a genuine village community in a great rural setting. It is a comfortable country pub with great atmosphere, roaring fires in winter and a get-away from loud music and big TV screens. You can enjoy a pint of real ale or cider here, or peruse the menu if you like. Freshly prepared food is offered using local ingredients where possible. Expect dishes like starters of pigeon breast with Bury black pudding, followed by slow roasted free-range Packington pork belly, sweet potato fondant and purée and pickled apple; or asparagus, broad bean and sun-dried tomato risotto.

Open all wk Mon-Thu 5-mdnt, Fri noon-3 5-mdnt, Sat-Sun noon-mdnt **Bar Meals** L served Fri-Sat 12-2, Sun 1-7 D served Wed-Sat 6-9.30 booking required Av main course £12 **Restaurant** L served Fri-Sat 12-2, Sun 1-7 D served Wed-Sat 6-9.30 booking required Av 3 course à la carte fr £25 ⊕ FREDERIC ROBINSON ◀ Unicorn Bitter,

Hatters Mild, Dizzy Blonde, Seasonal Ales ♻ Stowford Press. **Facilities** Children welcome Children's portions Dogs allowed Garden Parking Wi-fi

MELLOR   Map 16 SJ98

The Moorfield Arms ★★★★ INN ▾

Shiloh Rd SK6 5NE
☎ **0161 427 1580** 📄 **0161 427 1582**
e-mail: info@moorfieldarms.com
dir: *From Marple station down Brabyns Brow to lights. Right into Town St. 3m, left into Shiloh Rd. 0.5m, pub on left*

Magnificent views of Kinder Scout and Lantern Pike make this traditional old moorland pub an ideal Peak District base. The building dates from 1640 and retains plenty of old world charm and atmosphere. A bit of fell-walking should generate an appetite for a hot tandoori chicken sandwich; grilled gammon steak; savoury tortilla wrap; steak and ale pie; cod mornay; slow-roasted lamb Henry (the house signature dish); or one of the many specials. Situated in a barn conversion, en suite rooms are comfortable and stylish.

Open Mon-Sat 12-2.30 6-9.30 (Sun 12-9) Closed: Mon in winter **Bar Meals** L served Tue-Sat 12-2, Sun 12-9 D served Tue-Sun 6-9.30 Av main course £12 **Restaurant** L served Tue-Sun 12-2 D served Tue-Sun 6-9.30 Av 3 course à la carte fr £25 ⊕ FREE HOUSE ◀ Wychwood, Hobgoblin, Marstons EPA. ▾ 12 **Facilities** Children welcome Children's menu Garden Parking **Rooms** 4

OLDHAM   Map 16 SD90

The Roebuck Inn ▾

Strinesdale OL4 3RB
☎ **0161 624 7819** 📄 **0161 633 6210**
e-mail: sehoworth1@hotmail.com
dir: *From Oldham Mumps Bridge take Huddersfield Rd (A62), right at 2nd lights onto Ripponden Rd (A672), after 1m right at lights onto Turfpit Ln, follow for 1m*

Set high in the rugged Pennines, 1000 feet above sea level, this historic inn on the edge of Saddleworth Moor is said to be haunted by the ghost of a girl who drowned in the local reservoir. The menu offers an extensive choice ranging from traditional home-made pies or roast beef and Yorkshire pudding through to less traditional chicken fajitas with soured cream, guacamole and salsa. Food and drink can be enjoyed in the garden in the summer months.

Open all wk Mon-Thu noon-3 5-11, Fri-Sun noon-11 **Bar Meals** L served all wk 12-2.15 D served all wk 5-9.15 Av main course £11 **Restaurant** L served all wk 12-2.15 D served all wk 5-9.15 booking required Fixed menu price fr £6.95 Av 3 course à la carte fr £16 ⊕ FREE HOUSE ◀ Black Sheep Brewery. ▾ 9 **Facilities** Children welcome Children's menu Children's portions Play area Dogs allowed Garden Parking Wi-fi

OLDHAM *continued*

PICK OF THE PUBS

The White Hart Inn ◎ ⚲

Stockport Rd, Lydgate OL4 4JJ
☎ 01457 872566 📄 01457 875190
e-mail: bookings@thewhitehart.co.uk
dir: *From Manchester A62 to Oldham. Right onto bypass, A669 through Lees. In 500yds past Grotton, at brow of hill turn right onto A6050*

There's been a pub on this site – high on the hillside overlooking Oldham and Manchester – since 1788, when its vast cellars were used for brewing beer using water from the well. A barn added to house the local foxhounds later served as a police station, school and weaver's cottage. The Grade II listed coaching inn's ground floor became a smart bar and brasserie when current owner Charles Brierley took over in 1994, although still retaining its period charm of beams, exposed stonework and open fireplaces. The inn also has a contemporary restaurant, an intimate library dining area, and award-winning gardens. The cosmopolitan menu makes good use of local ingredients. A table d'hôte lunch in the brasserie could feature confit duck hash with fried duck egg and HP sauce, followed by poached fillet of salmon with crushed new potatoes. Book the restaurant for Sunday lunch or a mid-week dinner, when a natural smoked haddock scotch egg with chargrilled chorizo, roast red pepper purée and watercress salad would make a memorable start to your meal.

Open all day all wk Closed: 26 Dec **Bar Meals** L served Mon-Sat 12-2.30, Sun 12.30-8 booking required D served all wk 6-9.30 booking required Av main course £17 **Restaurant** L served Sun 12.30-3.30 booking required D served Mon 6-9.30, Wed-Sat 6-9.30 booking required Fixed menu price fr £19.95 Av 3 course à la carte fr £29.70 ⊕ FREE HOUSE ◀ Timothy Taylor Landlord, J W Lees Bitter, Copper Dragon, Golden Best. ⚲ 12 **Facilities** Children welcome Children's menu Dogs allowed Garden Parking Wi-fi

---

STALYBRIDGE   Map 16 SJ99

The Royal Oak

364 Huddersfield Rd, Millbrook SK15 3EP
☎ 0161 338 7118
dir: *From Stalybridge turn onto Huddersfield road, pub on right adjacent to Country Park*

This family-run pub, once a coroner's evidence room, was later owned by the late Jackie Blanchflower of Manchester United, who took it on in the 1960s, and rumour has it that the players used to drink here. It stands next to a country park, which is great for walks before or after eating. The food is Italian influenced, and everything is freshly prepared and cooked to order. The wine list is short but well chosen.

Open Wed-Fri 5.30-11 (Tue 6-9 only by prior reservation, Sat 4.30-11, Sun noon-10.30) Closed: 1 Jan, Mon ⊕ ENTERPRISE INN ◀ Boddingtons, John Smith's. **Facilities** Children welcome Children's menu Children's portions Garden Parking

---

Stalybridge Station Buffet Bar

The Railway Station, Rassbottom St SK15 1RF
☎ 0161 303 0007
e-mail: www.buffetbar.org
dir: *Telephone for directions*

Unique Victorian railway station refreshment rooms dating from May 1885, including original fittings such as the marble-topped bar and open fire. The first-class ladies' waiting room, with ornate ceiling, and a conservatory provide additional space. Decorated throughout with an ever-growing collection of railway memorabilia and photographs, the place is famous locally for its range of real ales, bottled foreign beers and draught cider, as well as simple home-cooked and inexpensive food: black pudding and black peas, pasta bake, pies, liver and onions, and sausages and mash.

Open all wk 11-11 (Sun noon-10.30) Closed: 25-26 Dec, 1 Jan **Bar Meals** L served 10-8 D served 10-8 food served all day **Restaurant** L served 10-8 D served 10-8 ⊕ FREE HOUSE ◀ Flowers IPA, Millstone, Phoenix. **Facilities** Children welcome Dogs allowed Garden Parking **Notes** ◎

STOCKPORT   Map 16 SJ89

The Arden Arms ⚲

23 Millgate SK1 2LX ☎ 0161 480 2185
e-mail: steve@ardenarms.com
dir: *M60 junct 27 to town centre. Across mini-rdbt, at lights turn left. Pub on right of next rdbt behind Asda*

The classic unspoilt layout and original tiled floors of this Grade II listed late Georgian coaching inn rank high among the country's timeless gems. The building was last modernised in 1908, giving drinkers the opportunity to order from the traditional curved bar before settling down by the coal fire in the tiny snug. These days, this historic inn offers great real ales plus guests, and good food. On offer are interesting sandwiches and home-made soup, a selection of hot dishes like seared gammon steak or grilled halloumi and vegetable kebabs, in addition to the daily-changing specials board. There's always a traditional Sunday roast, jazz nights and charity quizzes.

Open all wk noon-11.45 Closed: 25-26 Dec, 1 Jan **Bar Meals** L served Mon-Fri 12-2.30, Sat-Sun 12-4 Av main course £8.95 ⊕ ROBINSONS ◀ Unicorn Bitter, Hatters Mild, Double Hop, Old Town, seasonal ales. ⚲ 8 **Facilities** Children welcome Dogs allowed Garden

---

The Nursery Inn

Green Ln, Heaton Norris SK4 2NA
☎ 0161 432 2044 📄 0161 442 1857
e-mail: nurseryinn@hydesbrewery.com
dir: *Green Ln off Heaton Moor Rd. Pass rugby club on Green Ln, at end on right. Narrow cobbled road, pub 100yds on right*

Finding a pub with its own bowling green is challenging, but possible at this classic, unspoilt 1930s hostelry, down a cobbled lane in a pleasant Manchester suburb, which has one at the rear. In the rambling interior you can drink beers from Hydes and enjoy some good value, home-cooked lunchtime snacks and pub grub mains, like home-made pie or roast of the day. Eight guest real ales on hand-pump are served at the three annual beer festivals.

Open all day all wk **Bar Meals** L served Tue-Fri 12-2.30, Sat-Sun 12-4 Av main course £6.50 **Restaurant** L served Tue-Sun 12-2.30 ⊕ HYDES BREWERY ◀ Hydes Bitter, Hydes Jekylls Gold, Hydes Seasonal Ales, Guest ales. **Facilities** Children welcome Children's portions Dogs allowed Garden Beer festival Parking Wi-fi

---

WALMERSLEY   Map 15 SD81

The Lord Raglan ⚲ NEW

Nangreaves BL9 6SP ☎ 0161 764 6680
dir: *M66 junct 1, A56 to Walmersley. Left into Palatine Drive, left into Ribble Drive, left into Walmersley Old Rd to Nangreaves*

Set beside a cobbled lane high on the moors above Bury at the head of a former weaving hamlet, where lanes and tracks dissipate into deep, secluded gorges rich in industrial heritage. Beers brewed at the on-site Leyden Brewery may be taken in the garden, where the throaty cough of steam engines on the East Lancashire Railway echoes off the River Irwell's steep valley sides below the towering Peel Monument. Reliable, traditional pub grub takes the edge off walkers' appetites, whilst a frequently changing specials menu draws diners to the characterful dining room of this rambling, stone built pub.

Open all wk 12-2.30 6-11 (Fri 12-2.30 5-11, Sat-Sun all day) **Bar Meals** L served Mon-Fri 12-2, Sat 12-9, Sun 12-8 D served Mon-Thu 6-9, Fri 5-9, Sat 12-9, Sun 12-8 Av main course £10 **Restaurant** L served Mon-Fri 12-2, Sat 12-9, Sun 12-8 D served Mon-Thu 6-9, Fri 5-9, Sat 12-9, Sun 12-8 Av 3 course à la carte fr £15 ⊕ FREE HOUSE ◀ Nanny Flyer, Crowning Glory, Light Brigade, Black Pudding. ⚲ 10 **Facilities** Children welcome Children's menu Children's portions Dogs allowed Garden Beer festival Parking

HAMPSHIRE

ALTON   Map 5 SU73

PICK OF THE PUBS

The Anchor Inn   INN ☺☺ ♟

Lower Froyle GU34 4NA
☎ 01420 23261   📠 01420 520467
e-mail: info@anchorinnatlowerfroyle.co.uk
web: www.anchorinnatlowerfroyle.co.uk
dir: A31 signed Bentley, follow brown tourist signs to Anchor Inn

It's a bit of a timewarp, this ancient, tile-hung rural inn. Charmingly eccentric, the whiff of Edwardian England hangs heavy in the air. Shootin', horseracin', fly-fishin' and other noble pursuits blend easily with the upmarket gastro-pub (with 2 AA Rosettes) and classy accommodation at the fringe of quaint Lower Froyle. The intimate snug and saloon bar are decked out with low beams, open fires, wooden floors and lots of original features, generously dressed with antiques and old prints. In the dining room, candlesticks and polished wooden tables combine with the painted wall panelling to create a romantic interior. Beers from down the lane and a great list of bins set the scene for fare with a distinctly traditional English flavour. Cast off with pheasant and bacon terrine, braised leg and hazelnut salad before indulging in a warming beef shin and kidney pie with mash and braised red cabbage, or perhaps roast halibut, lentils, ham hock and spinach.

Open all day all wk **Bar Meals** L served all wk 12-2.30 D served all wk 6.30-9.30 **Restaurant** L served Mon-Sat 12-2.30, Sun 12-4 booking required D served Mon-Fri 6.30-9.30, Sat 6.30-10, Sun 7-9 booking required ⊕ THE MILLERS COLLECTION ◀ Alton's Pride Triple fff, Andwells King John ☼ Thatchers. ♟ 9
Facilities Children welcome Children's portions Dogs allowed Garden Parking Wi-fi **Rooms** 5

AMPFIELD   Map 5 SU42

White Horse at Ampfield ♟ NEW

Winchester Rd SO51 9BQ ☎ 01794 368356
e-mail: whitehorseinn@hotmail.co.uk
web: www.whitehorseampfield.co.uk
dir: From Winchester take A3040, then A3090 towards Romsey. Ampfield in 7m. Or M3 junct 13, A335 (signed Chandler's Ford). At lights right onto B3043, follow Chandler's Ford Industrial Estate then Hursley signs. Left onto A3090 to Ampfield

A majestic timber-framed 17th-century farmhouse inn mid-way between Winchester and Romsey. Under its old tiled roof will be found a public bar with darts and shove ha'penny, a lounge bar with comfortable seating, a restaurant, and two huge inglenook fireplaces — both always ablaze during winter. John and Gaye Armstrong have been in charge for over five years, steadily building a reputation for good food, service, ambience and reasonable prices. Typical of the carte are the Hursley butcher's champion sausages; pan-seared local mackerel; and apple pie with a jug of custard. The lovely garden looks across the village cricket ground on one side and a golf course on the other.

Open all day all wk **Bar Meals** L served Mon-Fri 12-2.30, Sat 12-9, Sun 12-7 booking required D served Mon-Fri 6-9, Sat 12-9, Sun 12-7 booking required Av main course £10.95 **Restaurant** L served Mon-Fri 12-2.30, Sat 12-9, Sun 12-7 booking required D served Mon-Fri 6-9, Sat 12-9, Sun 12-7 booking required Av 3 course à la carte fr £20 ⊕ GREENE KING ◀ Ringwood Best, Wadworth 6X, Old Speckled Hen. ♟ 14 **Facilities** Children welcome Children's menu Children's portions Play area Dogs allowed Garden Parking

ANDOVER   Map 5 SU34

Wyke Down Country Pub & Restaurant

Wyke Down, Picket Piece SP11 6LX
☎ 01264 352048   📠 01264 324661
e-mail: info@wykedown.co.uk
dir: 3m from Andover town centre/A303. Follow signs for Wyke Down Caravan Park

Combining a pub/restaurant with a caravan park and golf driving range, this establishment is a diversified farm on the outskirts of Andover. It still raises beef cattle, but the pub started in a barn over 25 years ago and the restaurant was built 13 years ago. Dishes range from salmon and broccoli fishcakes and coriander chicken skewers to main dishes like slow-roasted belly of pork on mustard mash, nut loaf or steaks from the griddle.

Open all wk noon-3 6-11 Closed: 25 Dec-2 Jan **Bar Meals** L served all wk 12-2 booking required D served all wk 6-9 booking required **Restaurant** L served all wk 12-2 booking required D served all wk 6-9 booking required ⊕ FREE HOUSE ◀ Guinness, London Pride. **Facilities** Children welcome Children's menu Children's portions Play area Garden Parking

BALL HILL   Map 5 SU46

The Furze Bush Inn

Hatt Common, East Woodhay RG20 0NQ
☎ 01635 253228   📠 01635 254883
e-mail: info@furzebushinn.co.uk
dir: From Newbury onto Andover Road (A343), signed

Tucked away in a glorious rural location, this whitewashed free house is handy for Highclere Castle, Newbury Races and walking on the Berkshire Downs. The bar menu features a good range of pub favourites, with more adventurous dishes like roast breast of duck with an orange and passionfruit sauce, or plaice fillets filled with shellfish mousse and wrapped in smoked salmon available in the restaurant. There's a large front garden, a rear patio with huge TV and parasol plus a children's play area. The pub is happy to cater for many different types of occasions, whether for business or for the family.

Open all day all wk **Bar Meals** L served Mon-Fri 12-2.30, Sat-Sun & BH all day D served all wk 6-9.30 Av main course £11 **Restaurant** L served Mon-Fri 12-2.30, Sat-Sun & BH 12-6 D served all wk 6-9.30 ⊕ FREE HOUSE ◀ London Pride, Greene King, Abbot Ale. **Facilities** Children welcome Children's menu Play area Dogs allowed Garden Parking Wi-fi

BAUGHURST — Map 5 SU56

PICK OF THE PUBS

The Wellington Arms ⊛⊛ ☂

Baughurst Rd RG26 5LP ☎ 0118 982 0110
e-mail: hello@thewellingtonarms.com
web: www.thewellingtonarms.com
dir: *M4 junct 12 follow Newbury signs on A4. At rdbt left signed Aldermaston. Through Aldermaston. Up hill, at next rdbt 2nd exit, left at T-junct, pub 1m on left*

Lost down a maze of lanes in peaceful countryside between Basingstoke and Newbury, the remodelled 'Welly', formerly a hunting lodge for the Duke of Wellington, draws discerning diners from miles around due to the combined efforts of Jason King and Simon Page, who have worked wonders with the place since taking over in 2006. Jason's daily chalkboard menus offer plenty of interest and imagination and much of the produce is organic and sourced within a five-mile radius of the pub, with salad leaves and vegetables from the pub's own polytunnel and three raised vegetable beds, eggs from their 100 rare breed and rescue hens, plus five Jacob sheep, four Tamworth pigs and three beehives. This translates to gazpacho of home-grown tomatoes, cucumbers and peppers, home-reared rack of pork with apple sauce, and chocolate and walnut brownie with raspberry ripple ice cream. Book ahead or arrive early as there are only 8 tables in the tastefully decorated single bar-cum-dining room.

Open 12-3.30 6-11 Closed: Sun eve
Restaurant L served all wk 12-2.30 booking required D served Mon-Sat 6-9.30 booking required ⊕ FREE HOUSE ◀ Wadworth 6X, West Berks Brewery, Good Old Boy. ☂ 11 **Facilities** Children welcome Children's portions Dogs allowed Garden Parking Wi-fi

BEAULIEU — Map 5 SU30

The Drift Inn NEW

Beaulieu Rd SO42 7YQ ☎ 023 8029 2342
e-mail: bookatable@driftinn.co.uk
dir: *From Lyndhurst take B3056 (Beaulieu Rd) signed Beaulieu. Cross railway line, inn on left*

Recently refurbished by owners New Forest Hotels, the Drift Inn is surrounded by glorious New Forest heath and forest and is named after the centuries-old practice of rounding up the ponies that roam the area, known locally as The Drift. Refuel after completing the Shatterford walk with a pint of locally-brewed Ringwood Best or Old Thumper and a hearty plate of food, perhaps ham, egg and chips, salmon and cod fishcakes with spicy tomato relish, or try one of the sharing platters laden with ham, pork pie, pâté, chutneys and breads.

Open all wk 11-3 6-11 (Fri 11-3 6-mdnt, Sat 11am-mdnt, Sun noon-10.30) **Bar Meals** L served all wk 12-3 winter, 12-9 summer D served all wk 6-9 winter, 12-9 summer **Restaurant** L served all wk 12-3 D served all wk 6-9 Av 3 course à la carte fr £14.85 ⊕ FREE HOUSE ◀ Ringwood Best, Old Thumper ☉ Thatchers.
Facilities Children welcome Children's menu Children's portions Play area Dogs allowed Garden Beer festival Parking

BEAUWORTH — Map 5 SU52

The Milburys

SO24 0PB ☎ 01962 771248 📠 01962 771910
e-mail: info@themilburys.co.uk
dir: *A272 towards Petersfield, after 6m turn right for Beauworth*

Taking its name from the Bronze Age barrow nearby, this rustic hill-top pub is noted for its massive, 250-year-old treadmill that used to draw water from the 300ft well in the bar. It's a historic site of interest, dating from the 17th century. In summer, sweeping views across Hampshire can be savoured from the lofty garden. Inside you will find a great selection of real ales with a guest one changing weekly which you can enjoy by the warming winter fires. Traditional pub food is served all week in the bar and restaurant. There's a skittle alley, and rallies and club meetings are held here.

Open all wk **Bar Meals** L served all wk 12-2.30 D served all wk 6-9.30 Av main course £8.95 **Restaurant** L served all wk 12-2.30 D served all wk 6-9.30 ⊕ FREE HOUSE ◀ Theakstons Old Peculier, Altons Pride Triple fff, Deuchars, Ale of Wight, Summer Lightning, Guest ale.
Facilities Children welcome Dogs allowed Garden Parking

BENTLEY — Map 5 SU74

The Bull Inn

GU10 5JH ☎ 01420 22156
dir: *2m from Farnham on A31 towards Winchester*

Open log fires, exposed beams and good food make this 15th-century coaching inn well worth a visit. Lunch brings light meals including jacket potatoes with interesting fillings and Welsh rarebit. More substantial offerings include ham, free-range eggs and chips, and local sausages with mash and onion gravy. There's a decent selection of wines, including as Châteauneuf du Pape, while beers include Alton's Pride and Moondance. Recent change of hands.

Open all day all wk 11-11 (Sun 12-10.30)
Bar Meals L served Mon-Sat 11-3, Sun 11-4 D served Mon-Sat 6-9.30 Av main course £10 **Restaurant** L served Mon-Sat 11-3, Sun 11-4 D served Mon-Sat 6-9.30 Fixed menu price fr £6.50 Av 3 course à la carte fr £30 ⊕ ENTERPRISE INNS ◀ Courage Best, Westcott Bitter, Moondance, Alton's Pride ☉ Thatchers Pear.
Facilities Children welcome Children's portions Dogs allowed Garden Parking

BENTWORTH — Map 5 SU64

PICK OF THE PUBS

The Sun Inn ☂

See Pick of the Pubs on opposite page

BOLDRE — Map 5 SZ39

The Hobler Inn ☂

Southampton Rd, Battramsley SO41 8PT
☎ 01590 623944
e-mail: hedi@alcatraz.co.uk
dir: *2m from Brockenhurst, towards Lymington on main road*

On the main road between Brockenhurst and Lymington, with a large grassed area and trestle tables ideal for families visiting the New Forest. The Hobler Inn is more London wine bar than local with stylish leather furniture, but still serves a well-kept pint of Ringwood. Hot lunchtime snacks like Welsh rarebit or Boston baked beans on toast are good value. Mains include a variation on the classic shepherd's pie but with added Nepalese spices.

Open all day all wk **Bar Meals** Av main course £12 food served all day **Restaurant** Fixed menu price fr £9.95 food served all day ◀ Ringwood, Ringwood Best, Timothy Taylor. ☂ 10 **Facilities** Children welcome Garden Parking Wi-fi

PICK OF THE PUBS

The Sun Inn ♥

BENTWORTH   Map 5 SU64

Sun Hill GU34 5JT
☎ **01420 562338**
e-mail: info@thesuninnbentworth.co.uk
web: www.thesuninnbentworth.co.uk
dir: *Telephone for directions*

Hidden down a tiny lane on the village edge, this pretty flower-decked and unspoilt rural pub dates from the 17th century when it was a pair of traditional cottages. Little has changed inside over the years, where brick and board floors are laid with a rustic mix of scrubbed pine tables, benches and settles, original beams are hung with sparkling horse brasses, walls are adorned with prints and plates, and tasteful cosmetic touches – magazines to peruse, fresh flowers, flickering candlelight – enhance the overall unblemished atmosphere. Crackling log fires warm the three inter-linked rooms and you can expect a friendly, relaxed atmosphere throughout.

As well as The Sun's charm, real ale and an extensive selection of hearty home-cooked dishes (listed on the changing chalkboard menu) are prime reasons for visiting. Dishes range from ploughman's lunches, home-made soup and sandwiches (chicken and avocado), to beef stew and dumplings, beer-battered cod, calves' liver and bacon, pork and Stilton pie, and half-shoulder of lamb with

redcurrant and mint gravy. Game in season includes venison, cooked in Guinness with pickled walnuts, and pheasant. For pudding, tuck into apple and raspberry crumble, white chocolate and strawberry cheesecake, or a warm chocolate brownie. A thriving free house, the bar groans with hand-pumps, dispensing Ringwood Fortyniner and Stone Henge Pigswill, plus Fuller's London Pride and regular guest beers.

There is much to see and do in the area: Gilbert White's House and the Oates Museum in Selborne are not far away, and neither are Jane Austen's House at Chawton, nor the Watercress Line at Alresford, where you can enjoy a 10-mile steam train ride through glorious Hampshire countryside to Alton.

Open all wk 12-3 6-11 (Sun 12-10.30) **Bar Meals** L served all wk 12-2 D served all wk 7-9.30 ⊕ FREE HOUSE ◀ Andwells Resolute, Ringwood Fortyniner, Sharp's Doom Bar, Stone Henge Pigswill, Fuller's London Pride, Black Sheep ♂ Aspall. ♥ 12 **Facilities** Children's menu Children's portions Family room Dogs allowed Garden Parking

BOLDRE *continued*

PICK OF THE PUBS

The Red Lion ⚲

Rope Hill SO41 8NE
☎ 01590 673177 📄 01590 674036
web: www.theredlionboldre.co.uk
dir: *1m from Lymington off A337. From M27 junct 1 through Lyndhurst & Brockenhurst towards Lymington, follow signs for Boldre*

A New Forest pub for all seasons, which sits at the crossroads in the centre of an ancient village. Consistent with 15th-century origins, its rambling interior contains beamed rooms, log fires and authentic rural memorabilia. So it's no surprise that Ringwood ales feature at the bar. Traditional home-made meals use the best of ingredients – the pub is renowned for its use of local produce. Chef's specials follow seasonal availability of local shellfish, whole fresh fish, venison and other game. Main menu choices could start with warmed Loosehanger Farm goat's cheese with home-made onion marmalade, or whole king prawns pan-fried with garlic and chilli. Next may come pan-fried local crab and spring onion fishcakes, or a substantial beef Wellington. In the summer, you can enjoy full table service outside while cooking your own meat or fish on a patio barbecue, next to the new herb garden.

Open all wk 11-3 5.30-11 (Winter Sun noon-4 6-10.30, Summer Sat 11-11 Sun noon-10.30)
Bar Meals L served Mon-Sat 12-2.30, Sun 12-3.30 (Summer Sat 12-9.30, Sun 12-9) D served Mon-Sat 6-9.30, Sun 6-9 (Summer Sat 12-9.30, Sun 12-9)
Restaurant L served Mon-Sat 12-2.30, Sun 12-3.30 (Summer Sat 12-9.30, Sun 12-9) D served Mon-Sat 6-9.30, Sun 6-9 (Summer Sat 12-9.30, Sun 12-9) ⊕ FREE HOUSE ◀ Ringwood Best, Ringwood Fortyniner, Marstons Pedigree, Guinness, Guest ales ⌕ Thatchers Gold. ⚲ 17 **Facilities** Children welcome Children's portions Dogs allowed Garden Parking

See advert below

BRANSGORE   Map 5 SZ19

PICK OF THE PUBS

The Three Tuns Country Inn ⊚⊚ ⚲

See Pick of the Pubs on opposite page

BUCKLERS HARD   Map 5 SU40

PICK OF THE PUBS

The Master Builders House Hotel
★★★ HL ⊚ ⚲

SO42 7XB ☎ 01590 616253 📄 01590 616297
e-mail: enquiries@themasterbuilders.co.uk
dir: *From M27 junct 2 follow signs to Beaulieu. Left onto B3056. Left to Bucklers Hard. Hotel 2m on left*

During the great age of sail, this 18th-century building was home to master shipbuilder Henry Adams, who oversaw construction of the navy's fleet. Situated on the banks of the River Beaulieu, in the famous shipbuilding village of Bucklers Hard, visitors can enjoy the New Forest National Park, Lord Montagu's Beaulieu Palace and the National Motor Museum all on the doorstep. Beams, open fires and maritime memorabilia set the scene in the Yachtsmans Bar where food includes game sausage roll, bucket of Atlantic prawns, or Godminster board served with a choice of real ales like Pugwash or wines. The refurbished Riverside Restaurant has a contemporary feel and tranquil river views. In summer, guests can dine on the terrace under the stars. The modern menu combines excellent local ingredients and innovative ideas to produce dishes such as roast fillet and belly of pork with black pudding, linguini with crab, mussels and prawns, and lemon sole with sprouting broccoli and new potatoes.

Open all day all wk 11-11 (Sun 11-10.30)
Bar Meals L served Mon-Fri 12-2.30, Sat-Sun 12-3 D served all wk 6-9.30 **Restaurant** L served Mon-Fri 12-2.30, Sat-Sun 12-3 booking required D served all wk 7-9.30 booking required ⊕ HILLBROOKE HOTELS ◀ Ringwood Best, Ringwood Boondoggle ⌕ Stowford Press. ⚲ 11 **Facilities** Children welcome Children's menu Dogs allowed Garden Parking Wi-fi **Rooms** 25

PICK OF THE PUBS

The Three Tuns Country Inn

BRANSGORE   Map 5 SZ19

Ringwood Rd BH23 8JH ☎ 01425 672232
e-mail: threetunsinn@btconnect.com
web: www.threetunsinn.com
dir: *1.5m from A35 Walkford junct. 3m*
from Christchurch & 1m from Hinton
Admiral railway station

One of the few remaining thatched pubs
in the New Forest National Park, this
picture-perfect, 17th-century survivor is
also immediately recognisable for another
reason — by the riot of flowers outside.
There are five distinct public areas: a
comfortable, music-, TV- and games-free
lounge bar (with a winter log fire); an oak-
beamed Snug, similarly warmed, and with
biscuits and water for the dog; a large
terrace with a water feature; a huge
south-facing garden, with over 2500
square metres of lawn (and not a bouncy
castle in sight, although on sunny days
out comes the barbecue), surrounded by
fields, trees and grazing ponies; and
finally, the 60-seat restaurant. Here, fresh
produce and seasonings from around the
world are transformed into award-winning
dishes and seasonal specials, recognised
for their quality by two AA Rosettes. The
menus offer something for everyone: if
there's time for just a pint of Ringwood
Best and a light bar snack, then maybe
what will do the trick is moules marinière;
six Dorset snails in garlic tarragon butter;
bangers and mash; venison pasty; deep-
fried cod and chips; or a sandwich. Or, for
those with more time to spend, the
specials menu offers pan-fried Mudeford
sea bass with a fricassée of squid,
tomatoes, olives and artichoke; Irish stew
with suet dumplings and pearl barley;
rabbit pie with penny bun mushrooms;
and truffle risotto with crispy egg. For
pudding, try the baked cheesecake with
preserved fruits, or a plate of British and
French artisan and farmhouse cheeses
with home-made pickles. A listed barn
provides space for functions.

Open all day all wk 11.30-11 (Sun
12-10.30) **Bar Meals** L served Mon-Fri
12-2.15, Sat-Sun 12-9.15 booking
required D served Mon-Fri 6.30-9.15,
Sat-Sun 12-9.15 booking required Av
main course £9.95-£18.95

Restaurant L served Mon-Fri 12-2.15,
Sat-Sun 12-9.15 booking required D
served Mon-Fri 6.30-9.15, Sat-Sun
12-9.15 booking required Fixed menu price
fr £10.95 Av 3 course à la carte fr £25
⊕ ENTERPRISE INNS ◧ St Austell Tribute,
Ringwood Best Bitter, Fortyniner, Exmoor
Gold, Timothy Taylor, Otter Bitter
♂ Thatchers Gold, New Forest Traditional
Farmhouse, Katy. ♀ 9 **Facilities** Children's
menu Children's portions Dogs allowed
Garden Beer festival Parking Wi-fi

BURGHCLERE — Map 5 SU46

PICK OF THE PUBS

Carnarvon Arms ♥

Winchester Rd RG20 9LE
☎ 01635 278222 📠 01635 278444
e-mail: info.carnarvonarms@bespokehotels.com
dir: *M4 junct 13, A34 S to Winchester. Exit A34 at Tothill Services, follow Highclere Castle signs. Pub on right*

Built in the 1800s as a coaching inn providing a stop off for travellers to nearby Highclere Castle, home to the present Lord and Lady Carnarvon, this Grade II listed coaching inn is steeped in history. It was the 5th Earl of Carnarvon who famously opened Tutankhamun's tomb in 1922, dying the following year and triggering suggestions of a Mummy's Curse. The large bar is all open plan, airy and fresh, tastefully appointed with leather sofas and chairs blending seamlessly with more traditional seating and screens dividing up the space. Here, a bar menu of inviting sandwiches and traditional bites like beer battered fish and chips will take the edge off an appetite. Modern British food, with a strong emphasis on seasonal ingredients, is the kitchen's objective. Kick in with a pea and ham velouté before progressing to smoked haddock and roasted beetroot risotto. Recent change of hands.

Open all day all wk 7.30am- late **Bar Meals** L served all wk 12-2.30 D served all wk 6.30-9 **Restaurant** L served all wk 12-2.30 D served all wk 6.30-9.30 ◄ Guinness, Guest ales ♂ Aspall. ♥ 15 **Facilities** Children welcome Children's menu Children's portions Dogs allowed Garden Parking Wi-fi

BURLEY — Map 5 SU20

The Burley Inn ♥

BH24 4AB ☎ 01425 403448
e-mail: info@theburleyinn.co.uk
dir: *4m SE of of Ringwood*

Once a GP's surgery, this fine Edwardian building makes a smart and atmospheric inn. Surrounded by an Area of Outstanding Natural Beauty, it sits on what was once a major smuggling route. Food is served all day, with a menu offering morning coffee, cream teas, freshly cut sandwiches, hot snacks, freshly baked pies, grills and vegetarian dishes. Take a glass of Ringwood Best Bitter or locally produced fruit wine out to the new patio and decking area and watch the ponies, donkeys and cattle wandering freely through the village.

Open all day all wk **Bar Meals** L served all wk 12-10 D served all wk 12-10 food served all day **Restaurant** L served all wk 12-10 D served all wk 12-10 food served all day ⊕ FREE HOUSE ◄ Ringwood Best, Ringwood Old Thumper, Gales HSB, Young's Special ♂ Thatchers Old Rascal. ♥ 10 **Facilities** Children's menu Dogs allowed Garden Parking Wi-fi

CADNAM — Map 5 SU31

Sir John Barleycorn ♥

Old Romsey Rd SO40 2NP ☎ 023 8081 2236
e-mail: hedi@alcatraz.co.uk
dir: *From Southampton M27 junct 1 into Cadnam*

This friendly thatched establishment is reputedly the oldest inn in the New Forest, formed from three 12th-century cottages, one of which was once home to the charcoal burner who discovered the body of King William Rufus. Its name comes from a folksong celebrating the transformation of barley to beer. The menu has something for everyone with quick snacks and sandwiches, a children's menu and traditional dishes like toad-in-the-hole; chicken, leek and bacon pie; and Thai chicken curry.

Open all day all wk 9am-11pm (Sat-Sun 11-11) **Bar Meals** L served all wk 12-9.30 Av main course £12 food served all day **Restaurant** L served all wk 12-3 booking required D served all wk 6-9.30 booking required Fixed menu price fr £11.95 ◄ Ringwood, Ringwood Fortyniner ♂ Stowford Press. ♥ 10 **Facilities** Children welcome Children's menu Garden Parking

CHALTON — Map 5 SU71

PICK OF THE PUBS

The Red Lion ♥

PO8 0BG ☎ 023 9259 2246 📠 023 9259 6915
e-mail: redlionchalton@fullers.co.uk
dir: *Just off A3 between Horndean & Petersfield. Follow signs for Chalton*

Ask someone who's never been to Britain to describe the typical English pub and the chances are it would be this one, all half-timbering, whitewash and thatch. Records show that it began life in 1147 as a residential workshop for the builders of St Michael's church opposite; by the time another three centuries had gone by church and civic dignitaries were lodging there, then in 1503 it was granted its first licence to sell alcohol to travellers on the old London to Portsmouth road. Well known for its excellent food, the kitchen sources locally for the daily-changing main and pub snack menus. The garden offers stunning views of the South Downs and a beer festival takes place during the last weekend of July.

Open all day all wk 11.30-11 (Sun 12-10.30) **Bar Meals** Av main course £4.95 food served all day **Restaurant** Fixed menu price fr £8.95 food served all day ⊕ FULLER, SMITH & TURNER PLC ◄ Fuller's, HSB, London Pride, Discovery, ESB, seasonal ales ♂ Kopparberg, Pear, Aspall. ♥ 20 **Facilities** Children welcome Children's portions Family room Dogs allowed Garden Beer festival Parking

CHARTER ALLEY — Map 5 SU55

The White Hart Inn

White Hart Ln RG26 5QA
☎ 01256 850048 📠 01256 850524
e-mail: enquiries@whitehartcharteralley.com
dir: *From M3 junct 6 take A339 towards Newbury. Turn right to Ramsdell. Right at church, then 1st left into White Hart Lane*

On the outskirts of the village overlooking open farmland and woods, this pub draws everyone from cyclists and walkers to real ale enthusiasts. Dating from 1818, it originally refreshed local woodsmen and coach drivers visiting the farrier next door. Today's more modern menu is likely to include Cornish crab rarebit; wood pigeon, pork and herb terrine; confit of duck leg; a variety of pies (maybe venison or lamb and potato); and roast pepper, leek and shallot risotto. Look to the blackboard for specials.

Open all wk noon-2.30 7-11 (Sun noon-10.30) Closed: 25-26 Dec, 1 Jan **Bar Meals** L served all wk 12-2 D served Tue-Sat 7-9 Av main course £10 **Restaurant** L served Tue-Sun 12-2 booking required D served Tue-Sat 7-9 booking required ⊕ FREE HOUSE ◄ Palmers IPA, Triple fff Alton Pride, Stonehenge Great Bustard, Loddon Ferryman's Gold, Bowmans Swift One. **Facilities** Children welcome Children's menu Children's portions Family room Dogs allowed Garden Parking Wi-fi

CHAWTON — Map 5 SU73

The Greyfriar

Winchester Rd GU34 1SB ☎ 01420 83841
e-mail: trevor@advantagecapitol.co.uk
web: www.thegreyfriar.co.uk
dir: *Just off A31 near Alton. Access to Chawton via A31/ A32 junct. Follow Jane Austen's House signs*

Fran and Trevor Jones arrived at this 16th-century pub, once a terrace of cottages, opposite Jane Austen's House Museum in 2010. With its friendly atmosphere and delightful village setting, the pub is Fuller's-owned and offers London Pride, Seafarers and ESB along with great food. The menu might include Hampshire-reared chicken with chasseur sauce; oven-baked loin of cod with pea and celeriac purée; and veggie burger with roasted aubergine, beef tomato, red onion marmalade and breaded goat's cheese.

Open all day all wk noon-11 (Sun noon-10.30) **Bar Meals** L served Mon-Sat 12-2.30, Sun 12-7 D served Mon-Sat 6-9.30 ⊕ FULLER'S ◄ Fuller's London Pride, Seafarers, ESB, Seasonal ales. **Facilities** Children welcome Children's menu Children's portions Play area Dogs allowed Garden Parking Wi-fi

CHERITON   Map 5 SU52

PICK OF THE PUBS

The Flower Pots Inn

SO24 0QQ ☎ 01962 771318
dir: A272 towards Petersfield, left onto B3046, pub 0.75m on right

Known almost universally as The Pots, this popular village pub used to be a farmhouse and home to the head gardener of nearby Avington Park. These days, there are two bars: one rustic and pine-furnished, with a glass-covered well, the other with a sofa; both have open fires when it's cold. Local beer drinkers know the pub well for its award-winning Flower Pots Bitter and Goodens Gold, brewed across the car park in the pub's own micro-brewery. Simple home-made food includes toasted sandwiches, jacket potatoes and different hotpots - chilli con carne, lamb and apricot, beef bourguignon - served with garlic bread, basmati rice or jacket potato. Ploughman's feature various cheeses, ham or beef, and baps come filled with Cheddar cheese; pork steak with onions and apple sauce; bacon and mushroom. A large, safe garden, with a covered patio, allows children to let off steam (under 14s are not allowed in the bar).

Open all wk noon-2.30 6-11 (Sun noon-3 7-10.30)
Bar Meals L served all wk 12-2 D served Mon-Sat 7-9 Av main course £8 ⊕ FREE HOUSE ◀ Flower Pots Bitter, Goodens Gold ♂ Westons Old Rosie.
Facilities Children welcome Children's portions Dogs allowed Garden Beer festival Parking **Notes** ⊛

CRAWLEY   Map 5 SU43

The Fox and Hounds ♥

SO21 2PR ☎ 01962 776006 📠 01962 776006
e-mail: liamlewisairey@aol.com
dir: A34 onto A272 then 1st right into Crawley

Rebuilt in impressive mock-Tudor style in 1910, this popular inn serves a well-to-do village close enough to affluent Winchester to attract its citizens too. Dining tables grouped round a central bar soon fill up for well prepared chicken with Stilton and mushroom sauce; cod with basil and Parmesan crust; home-made pies; and mushroom Stroganoff. To drink, there are 36 wines by the glass and the beers come from Ringwood, Wadworth and Wychwood. Just down the road is a proper village duckpond.

Open all wk 11-3 6-mdnt **Bar Meals** L served all wk 12-2 D served all wk 6.30-9 **Restaurant** L served all wk 12-2 booking required D served all wk 6.30-9.30 booking required ⊕ ENTERPRISE INNS ◀ Wadworth 6X, Ringwood Best, Ringwood Fortyniner, Hobgoblin ♂ Stowford Press. ♥ 36 **Facilities** Children welcome Children's menu Children's portions Play area Garden Parking

CROOKHAM VILLAGE   Map 5 SU75

The Exchequer ♥

Crondall Rd GU51 5SU ☎ 01252 615336
e-mail: inbox@theexchequer.co.uk
dir: M3 junct 5, A287 towards Farnham for 5m. Left to Crookham Village

A whitewashed free house just a stone's throw from the A287 in the beautiful setting of Crookham Village. Known as the George and Lobster in a previous life, today's Exchequer serves ales straight from the cask, popular Sunday roasts, and delicious hand-made and freshly cooked pies all year round. A specialist seafood menu in the summer months maintains the pub's ethos of keeping things simple, local where possible, and presented at value-for-money prices by a happy team of staff.

Open all wk Mon-Fri 12-3 6-11 (Sat-Sun noon-11)
Bar Meals L served Mon-Fri 12-2, Sat-Sun all day D served Mon-Fri 6.30-9, Sat-Sun all day booking required Av main course £12 **Restaurant** L served Mon-Fri 12-2, Sat-Sun all day D served Mon-Fri 6.30-9, Sat-Sun all day booking required ⊕ FREE HOUSE ◀ Exchequer Ale, Hogs Back TEA, Otter Ale ♂ Aspall. ♥ 15 **Facilities** Children welcome Children's menu Children's portions Dogs allowed Garden Parking

DOWNTON   Map 5 SZ29

The Royal Oak ♥

Christchurch Rd SO41 0LA ☎ 01590 642297
e-mail: royal.oak.downtown@gmail.com
dir: On A337 between Lymington & Christchurch

Fronted by a white-painted picket fence, this well renovated pub on the edge of the New Forest is a mile from the beach at Lymington, from where you can look across the Solent to the Isle of Wight and its famed Needles. With Ringwood's Best Bitter, the stronger Fortyniner or a weekly guest ale, the food changes daily on the chalkboard - traditional ploughman's or sandwich; local crab, lobster or fresh fish; steak or game in season; sausages from a butcher's in Sway; or a Sunday roast.

Open all day all wk 11am-11.30pm **Bar Meals** L served Mon-Fri 12-2.30, Sat-Sun all day D served Mon-Fri 6-9.30, Sat-Sun all day Av main course £8.95 **Restaurant** L served Mon-Fri 12-2.30, Sat-Sun all day booking required D served Mon-Fri 6-9.30, Sat-Sun all day booking required Fixed menu price fr £9.95 Av 3 course à la carte fr £24.95 ⊕ ENTERPRISE INNS ◀ Ringwood Best Bitter, Ringwood Fortyniner, Guest ales ♂ Thatchers Gold. ♥ 9 **Facilities** Children welcome Children's menu Children's portions Dogs allowed Garden Parking Wi-fi

DROXFORD   Map 5 SU61

PICK OF THE PUBS

The Bakers Arms ◉

High St SO32 3PA ☎ 01489 877533
e-mail: enquiries@thebakersarmsdroxford.com
dir: 10m E of Winchester on A32 between Fareham & Alton. 7m SW of Petersfield. 10m inland from Portsmouth

With an enviable position in the pretty Meon Valley in a lovely corner of rural Hampshire, this unpretentious, white-painted pub and restaurant is a perfect place to refuel. It has been opened up inside but still oozes country charm and character, the staff are friendly, and the locals clearly love the place. Over the big log fire a blackboard menu lists the simple, well cooked and locally sourced food, while in the bar customers make short work of its barrels of Wallops Wood from the village's own Bowman Brewery. They can snack, too, on home-made Cornish pasties, pickled eggs and onions, and hot filled baguettes. But the kitchen cooks to AA Rosette standard, so make the most of your visit if you're just passing through (much of the produce is grown or shot by the owner): smoked River Test eel with salad and horseradish dressing; slow-cooked pork belly, tagliatelle and creamy wild mushroom sauce; and Droxford blackberry and apple crumble with vanilla ice cream will make you wish every village had a pub like this.

Open 11.45-3 6-11 (Sun 12-3) Closed: Sun eve & Mon **Bar Meals** L served Tue-Sun 12-2 booking required D served Tue-Sat 7-9 booking required Av main course £13.95 **Restaurant** L served Tue-Sun 12-2 booking required D served Tue-Sat 7-9 booking required Fixed menu price fr £13 Av 3 course à la carte fr £27 ⊕ FREE HOUSE ◀ Bowman Swift One, Bowman Wallops Wood ♂ Stowford Press. **Facilities** Children welcome Children's portions Dogs allowed Garden Parking Wi-fi

DUMMER   Map 5 SU54

The Queen Inn

Down St RG25 2AD ☎ 01256 397367 📠 01256 397601
e-mail: richardmoore49@btinternet.com
dir: M3 junct 7, follow Dummer signs

Situated in the centre of a beautiful village, you can dine by candlelight from the restaurant menu at this 16th-century inn with its low beams and huge open log fire. Alternatively you'll find lunchtime savouries like jalapeno cheeseburger alongside sandwiches and jackets. The bar menu offers everything from starters and healthy options to flame grills, house favourites, and perhaps dishes like chicken and chorizo pasta, teriyaki salmon or chicken with noodles. Food can be washed down with a pint of Old Speckled Hen or one of the guest ales.

Open all wk 11-3 6-11 (Sun 12-3 7-10.30)
Bar Meals L served all wk 12-2.30 D served all wk 6.30-9.30 **Restaurant** L served all wk 12-2.30 booking required D served all wk 6.30-9.30 booking required ⊕ ENTERPRISE INNS ◀ Courage Best, Fuller's London Pride, Old Speckled Hen, Guest ales. **Facilities** Children welcome Children's menu Children's portions Garden Parking Wi-fi

DUMMER *continued*

The Sun Inn ◉ ♀ NEW

A30 Winchester Rd RG25 2DJ ☎ **01256 397234**
e-mail: thesuninndummer@live.co.uk
dir: *M3 junct 7, take A30 (Winchester Rd) towards
Basingstoke. Left onto A30 towards Winchester. Inn on
right*

Situated on the old Winchester road south of Basingstoke,
the Sun Inn's reputation as a child-friendly gastro-pub is
growing in the capable hands of head chef Justin Brown.
But drinkers are welcome too, and ales from the Triple fff
Brewery outside Alton do not have far to travel. The pub
has undergone an extensive refurbishment inside and
out, making a warm and pleasant environment in which
to enjoy British classic dishes such as pan-roasted
English sirloin steak with triple-cooked chips, followed
perhaps by a white chocolate cheesecake with vanilla
poached pear.

Open all day all wk **Bar Meals** L served all wk 12-2.30
D served all wk 6.30-9.30 Av main course £10
Restaurant L served all wk 12-2.30 D served all wk
6.30-9.30 booking required Fixed menu price fr £20 Av 3
course à la carte fr £25 ⊕ FREE HOUSE ◀ Alton's Pride,
Marston's Pedigree. ♀ 9 **Facilities** Children welcome
Children's menu Children's portions Play area Dogs
allowed Garden Parking Wi-fi

The Mill Arms ♀ NEW

Barley Hill SO51 0LF
☎ **01794 340401** 🖷 **01794 342281**
e-mail: millarms@btconnect.com
dir: *From Romsey take A3057 signed Stockbridge &
Winchester. Left onto B3084 through Awbridge to
Dunbridge. Pub on left before rail crossing*

This late 18th-century inn is close to the River Test, one
of the finest chalk streams in the world. Not surprisingly,
the pub is popular with fishermen the world over — ex-
President Jimmy Carter stayed and fished here once. A
traditional country inn with wood and stone floors, oak
beams and open fires, the menus combine old favourites
and contemporary dishes. Beer-battered haddock, chips
and peas, beef bourguignon and crab linguine are typical
main courses.

Open noon-2.30 6-11 (Sat noon-11, Sun winter noon-5,
Sun summer noon-10) Closed: winter only Sun fr 5pm &
Mon **Bar Meals** L served Mon-Fri 12-2.30, Sat 12-9.30,
Sun 12-4 D served Mon-Thu 6-9, Fri-Sat 6-9.30 Av main
course £9-£15 **Restaurant** L served Mon-Fri 12-2.30, Sat
12-9.30, Sun 12-4 booking required D served Mon-Thu
6-9, Fri-Sat 6-9.30 booking required Av 3 course à la
carte fr £20 ⊕ ENTERPRISE INNS ◀ Ringwood, Flack's
Double Drop, Sharp's Doom Bar. ♀ 10 **Facilities** Children
welcome Children's menu Children's portions Dogs
allowed Garden Parking Wi-fi

Turfcutters Arms NEW

Main Rd SO42 7WL ☎ **01590 612331**
e-mail: enquiries.turfcutters@gmail.com
dir: *From Beaulieu take B3055 towards Brockenhurst.
Left at Hatchet Pond onto B3054 towards Lymington, turn
left, follow signs for East Boldre. Pub approx 0.5m*

One of the last remaining 'Forest' pubs. In winter the
open fires warm the cockles, while the lovely garden
comes into its own in summer. Cyclists, ramblers, dog-
walkers and locals congregate here year-round to enjoy
cheerful banter, good beer, draught ciders and honest
pub grub. Among the favourites are pie of the day, home-
made lasagne, and Hampshire ham with free-range eggs
and chips. Children have their own menu, and doggie
treats are handed out at the bar.

Open all day all wk **Bar Meals** L served all wk 12-3
booking required D served all wk 6-9 booking required Av
main course £8.75 **Restaurant** L served all wk 12-3
booking required D served all wk 6-9 booking required
◀ Ringwood Best, Ringwood Fortyniner ♂ Thatchers
Gold. **Facilities** Children welcome Children's menu
Children's portions Play area Dogs allowed Garden Beer
festival Parking Wi-fi

PICK OF THE PUBS

The East End Arms ♀

Main Rd SO41 5SY
☎ **01590 626223** 🖷 **01590 626223**
e-mail: manager@eastendarms.co.uk
dir: *From Lymington towards Beaulieu (past Isle of
Wight ferry), 3m to East End*

Close to Beaulieu and historic Bucklers Hard, this New
Forest inn, owned by John Illsley, the bass player of Dire
Straits, combines the authenticity of a proper local with
a good reputation as a gastro-pub. Ringwood ales are
drawn straight from the wood in the Foresters Bar,
where stone floors and open fires create a homely,
traditional feel. The atmospheric lounge bar, with its
sofas and winter fires, is a comfortable setting for a
meal from the daily-changing brasserie-style menu.
Locally sourced fish/seafood make a strong showing in
dishes such as roast cod, creamy Savoy cabbage,
potato galette and smoked salmon gravadlax velouté.
Other dishes might be seared calves' liver with crisp
Parma ham, carpaccio of beetroot and creamed
potatoes, or curried mussels and saffron tart. The pub
is well worth the drive down country lanes, or a short
diversion from the nearby Solent Way long distance
footpath.

Open all wk 11.30-3 6-11 (Fri-Sun 11.30am-11pm)
Bar Meals L served Mon-Sat 12-2.30
Restaurant L served all wk 12-2.30 booking required
D served Mon-Sat 7-9.30 booking required ⊕ FREE
HOUSE ◀ Ringwood Best, Ringwood Fortyniner,
Andwell Brewery, Jennings, Cottage Brewing
♂ Thatchers, Katy Cider. **Facilities** Children welcome
Children's menu Children's portions Dogs allowed
Garden Parking

Ye Olde George Inn ♀

Church St GU32 1NH ☎ **01730 823481**
e-mail: yeoldegeorge@live.co.uk
dir: *S of A272 (Winchester/Petersfield). 1.5m from
Petersfield turn left opposite church*

The River Meon runs by this delightful 15th-century
coaching inn, which sits close to a magnificent Norman
church (where tapestry designs similar to Bayeux can be
found). If you want heavy beams, inglenook fireplaces
and wooden floors, look no further — they're all here,
making an ideal setting for a choice of real ales, freshly
prepared bar snacks and monthly changing menus. Tuck
into pan-fried scallops on baby leeks with chorizo oil;
steak and suet pudding with creamed mash, roasted
winter vegetables and red wine jus; or risotto of butternut
squash with ricotta, all made using local seasonal
produce. An ideal spot for walkers and cyclists.

Open all wk Mon-Sat 11-3 6-11 (Sun 11-10) Closed:
25 Dec **Bar Meals** L served Mon-Sat 12-2.30, Sun 12-3
D served Mon-Sat 6.30-9.30, Sun 6.30-9
Restaurant L served Mon-Sat 12-2.30, Sun 12-3 D served
Mon-Sat 6.30-9.30, Sun 6.30-9 ⊕ HALL & WOODHOUSE
◀ Badger Best, King & Barnes Sussex, Tanglefoot. ♀ 9
Facilities Children welcome Children's menu Children's
portions Dogs allowed Garden Parking Wi-fi

PICK OF THE PUBS

The Chestnut Horse ♀

SO21 1EG ☎ **01962 779257** 🖷 **01962 779037**
e-mail: info@thechestnuthorse.com
dir: *From M3 junct 9 take A33 towards Basingstoke,
then B3047. Take 2nd right, then 1st left*

This traditional English gem of a 16th-century pub is
hidden away in the idyllic village of Easton in the Itchen
Valley. Enjoying an abundance of old English heritage
character and atmosphere, it has old tankards hanging
from the low-beamed ceilings in the two bar areas, and
a large open fire that is the central focus through the
winter months. Award-winning English beers can be
enjoyed in the bar or the garden. A good-value set price
menu is offered Monday to Saturday lunchtime
(12-2pm) or Monday to Friday early evening (6-7.30pm).
This might include deep-fried bream fillet, crushed
potatoes and coriander sauce, or lamb lasagne with
garlic bread and salad. Typical à la carte menu choices
are slow-cooked Hampshire pork belly, red beef and
potato curry, or feta and chestnut ravioli with fine
ratatouille. Take your walking boots with you and you
can walk off any excesses on one of the enjoyable
countryside walks that start at the front door.

Open all wk noon-3.30 5.30-11 (Sun eve closed winter)
Bar Meals L served Mon-Sat 12-2.30, Sun 12-4 booking
required D served Mon-Sat 6-9.30 booking required Av
main course £12 **Restaurant** L served Mon-Sat 12-2,
Sun 12-4 booking required D served Mon-Sat 6-9.30
booking required Fixed menu price fr £12 Av 3 course à
la carte fr £24 ⊕ HALL & WOODHOUSE ◀ Chestnut
Horse Special, Badger First Gold, Tanglefoot ♂ Stowford
Press. **Facilities** Children welcome Children's portions
Dogs allowed Garden Parking Wi-fi

The Cricketers Inn ☕

SO21 1EJ ☎ **01962 779353**
dir: *M3 junct 9, A33 towards Basingstoke, right at Kingsworthy onto B3047. In 0.75m turn right. Pub signed*

Standing on a corner in the heart of a popular village, this 1904 pub is a real local, with a single L-shaped bar and cricketing memorabilia on the walls. Situated on the Pilgrims Way, it's a popular place for walkers seeking refreshment, and with the River Itchen running through the village, a fresh local trout can sometimes be found on the specials board. Otherwise expect pub dishes such as filled baked potatoes, baguettes, lasagne and chargrilled steaks, all freshly prepared. Recent change of hands.

Open all wk 12-3 6-11 **Bar Meals** L served all wk 12-2 D served Mon-Sat 6-8 Av main course £8 **Restaurant** Av 3 course à la carte fr £17 ⊕ MARSTONS ◀ Ringwood, Pedigree, Guest ales ♂ Thatchers Gold. ☕ 8 **Facilities** Children welcome Children's menu Children's portions Dogs allowed Garden Parking

EAST STRATTON   Map 5 SU54

Northbrook Arms ☕ NEW

SO21 3DU ☎ **01962 774150**
dir: *Follow brown pub sign from A33, 4m S of junct with A303*

Right opposite the green in the picturesque estate village of East Stratton, the Northbrook Arms has been in Lord Northbrook's family for many generations. Wendy, Nick and Sophie aim to deliver good beer, fun and food in equal measures, and their modern British menu incorporates ideas from around the globe. Expect lunchtime sandwiches and a special set menu; daily changing fish dishes; and main course choices such as Hampshire lamb rump with rosemary and garlic. Hampshire and Sussex ales are served along with wines from around the world.

Open 12-3 6-11 (all day Sun in summer) Closed: Sun pm (winter) & Mon **Bar Meals** L served Tue-Sun 12-2 D served Tue-Sat 6.30-9 Av main course £11 **Restaurant** Av 3 course à la carte fr £20 ⊕ FREE HOUSE ◀ Otter, Bowman Swift One, Cheriton Pots. ☕ 10 **Facilities** Children welcome Children's portions Dogs allowed Garden Parking Wi-fi

EAST TYTHERLEY   Map 5 SU22

PICK OF THE PUBS

The Star Inn Tytherley
★★★★ INN ⊛ ☕

SO51 0LW ☎ **01794 340225**
e-mail: info@starinn.co.uk
dir: *5m N of Romsey off A3057, left for Dunbridge on B3084. Left for Awbridge & Kents Oak. Through Lockerley then 1m*

The 16th-century Star Inn stands overlooking the village cricket green in the smallest village in the Test Valley. You'll find Andwell Brewery beers and other guest ales behind the bar, plus an extensive international wine list. Dine where you like, in the bar, at dark-wood tables in the main dining room, or outside on the patio in summer, where you can also play king-sized chess. Lunchtime brings a variety of platters (fish, Barkham Blue, or Winchester farmhouse cheese), sandwiches (perhaps smoked salmon, crème fraîche and dill, or Cumberland sausage with caramelised onion), and a good value two-course menu (stir-fried tiger prawns with chorizo and gremolata, and roast chicken supreme). The evening menu might offer crab soufflé with watercress and saffron cream, and braised belly pork with sage polenta and celeriac purée. There's a good choice at Sunday lunch, too, including traditional roasts.

Open 11-2.30 6-10 Closed: Sun eve & Mon (ex BH) **Bar Meals** L served Tue-Sun 12-2 booking required D served Tue-Sat 7-9 booking required **Restaurant** L served Tue-Sun 12-2 booking required D served Tue-Sat 7-9 booking required ⊕ FREE HOUSE ◀ Flax Brewery, Andwell Brewery, Guest ales ♂ Thatchers Gold. ☕ 8 **Facilities** Children welcome Dogs allowed Garden Parking **Rooms** 3

EMSWORTH   Map 5 SU70

The Sussex Brewery

36 Main Rd PO10 8AU
☎ **01243 371533** 📠 **01243 379684**
e-mail: info@sussexbrewery.com
dir: *On A259 (coast road), between Havant & Chichester*

The Sussex Brewery is set in the picturesque village of Emsworth, renowned for its annual food festival in September. This 17th-century pub upholds traditional values with its sawdust covered floors, real ales and open fires. The menu includes a large variety of sausages, from Cumberland and Lincolnshire to Cajun and Mexican (there's a good choice for vegetarians too). Other dishes include slow roasted belly of pork on pea mash with caramelised apple and cider sauce, or fillet steak stuffed with Stilton on a bed of truffle mash.

Open all day all wk 7am-mdnt ⊕ YOUNG & CO BREWERY PLC ◀ Young's Special, Young's Ordinary, Waggle Dance, Bombardier, Tribute ♂ Stowford Press. **Facilities** Children welcome Children's portions Dogs allowed Garden Parking

EVERSLEY   Map 5 SU76

The Golden Pot ☕

Reading Rd RG27 0NB ☎ **0118 973 2104**
e-mail: jcalder@golden-pot.co.uk
web: www.golden-pot.co.uk
dir: *Between Reading & Camberley on B3272 approx 0.25m from Eversley cricket ground*

Dating back to the 1700s, this well established and smartly turned out free house offers a fine selection of real ales from such brewers as Windsor and Eton, Bowman, and Crondall; nine wines are sold by the glass. A double-sided warming fire connects the bar and restaurant, while outside the Snug and Vineyard surrounded by colourful tubs and hanging baskets are just the ticket for summer relaxation. Monday evenings see live music performed for appreciative audiences, while they tuck into home-cooked food augmented by a unique rösti menu.

Open all wk 11.30-3 5.30-10.30 Closed: 25-26 & 31 Dec, 1 Jan, & Sun eve **Bar Meals** L served all wk 12-2.45 booking required D served Mon-Sat 6-9 booking required **Restaurant** L served all wk 12-2.45 booking required D served Mon-Sat 6-9 booking required ⊕ FREE HOUSE ◀ Andwell Brewery, Bowman Ales, Crondall Brewery, Ascot Ales, Rebellion Brewery, Windsor & Eton Brewery. ☕ 9 **Facilities** Children welcome Children's menu Children's portions Dogs allowed Garden Parking

EXTON   Map 5 SU62

The Shoe Inn ☕

Shoe Ln SO32 3NT ☎ **01489 877526**
e-mail: theshoeexton@googlemail.com
dir: *Exton on A32 between Fareham & Alton*

In the heart of the Meon Valley, a popular village pub maintaining its appeal since Annabel Terry took it over. Food is key – local ingredients include those from its ever-expanding herb and organic vegetable garden. A typical selection of dishes could include home-made Hampshire haslet with piccalilli, or king prawn, sweet potato purée with garlic, lemon and herb butter and crispy bacon. The bar offers well-kept Wadworth ales and over a dozen wines served by the glass. Enjoy the views of Old Winchester Hill from the garden on warmer days. There is a beer festival each year.

Open all wk 11-3 6-11 Closed: 25 Dec **Bar Meals** L served all wk 12-2.15 **Restaurant** L served all wk 12-2.15 D served all wk 6-9 ⊕ WADWORTH ◀ Wadworth 6X, IPA, Bishops Tipple ♂ Stowford Press. ☕ 13 **Facilities** Children welcome Children's menu Children's portions Dogs allowed Garden Beer festival Parking

FORDINGBRIDGE   Map 5 SU11

The Augustus John

116 Station Rd SP6 1DG ☎ 01425 652098
e-mail: enquiries@augustusjohnfordingbridge.co.uk
dir: *12m S of Salisbury on A338 towards Ringwood*

The Welsh post-impressionist painter Augustus John
ended his days in nearby Fordingbridge, yet chose to
drink in this former station pub, run since 2009 by
Lorraine Smallwood after fourteen years as a member of
staff. Ringwood real ales are one reason why today's
locals and visitors enjoy coming here; another is the food,
typically tagliatelle carbonara; fillet steak au poivre;
seared duck breast with plum sauce; honey roast ham,
egg and chips; and pan-fried chicken supreme.

Open all wk Mon-Sat 11.30-3 6.30-11.30 (Sun noon-3
7-11.30) **Bar Meals** L served all wk 12-2.30 D served all
wk 6.30-9 (Sun 7-9) (booking advised Fri-Sun)
Restaurant L served all wk 12-2.30 D served Mon-Sat
6.30-9 (Sun 7-9) (booking advised Fri-Sun) ⊕ MARSTONS
◀ Ringwood Best, Fortyniner Ö Thatchers Gold.
Facilities Children welcome Children's menu Children's
portions Dogs allowed Garden Parking Wi-fi

FRITHAM   Map 5 SU21

The Royal Oak

SO43 7HJ ☎ 023 8081 2606 📄 023 8081 4066
e-mail: royaloak-fritham@btopenworld.co.uk
dir: *M27 junct 1, B3078 signed Fordingbridge. 2m, then
left at x-rds signed Ocknell & Fritham. Then follow signs
to Fritham*

An award-winning small traditional thatched pub and
working farm dating from the 15th century, deep in the
New Forest. Walkers, cyclists and horse-riders delight in
the large garden overlooking woodland. Unaltered for 100
years and with no jukebox or fruit machine, the three
small bars focus on serving a great selection of good real
ales and draught ciders. Simple plates of food include
quiches, sausages, pork pies and sausage rolls, all home
made using the farm's pigs.

Open all wk all day wknds & Jul-Sep ⊕ FREE HOUSE
◀ Ringwood Best & Fortyniner, Hop Back Summer
Lightning, Palmers Dorset Gold, Bowman Ales Swift One
Ö Aspall, Thatchers. **Facilities** Children welcome Dogs
allowed Garden **Notes** ✆

HAMBLE-LE-RICE   Map 5 SU40

PICK OF THE PUBS

The Bugle ⊚ ♥

High St SO31 4HA
☎ 023 8045 3000 📄 023 8045 3051
e-mail: manager@buglehamble.co.uk
dir: *M27 junct 8, follow signs to Hamble. In village
centre turn right at mini-rdbt into one-way cobbled
street, pub at end*

Matthew Boyle, owner of the White Star Tavern in
Southampton (see entry) rescued this famous
waterside pub from proposed demolition in 2005 and
lovingly refurbished it using traditional methods and
materials. Old features include exposed beams and
brickwork, natural flagstone floors and the wonderful
oak bar, while among the new is a large heated terrace
with lovely views over the River Hamble - perfect for
outdoor dining. A pint of locally-brewed ale makes an
ideal partner for one of the deli boards (great for
sharing), a roast beef, horseradish crème fraîche and
rocket sandwich, or a pub classic like fish pie with
buttered greens. From the dining room menu, go for
ham hock terrine with home-made piccalilli to start,
then order the whole Torbay sole with garlic sauté
potatoes and bisque vièrge, and round off with a
seasonal fruit crumble with thick custard. For private
dining, there is the Captain's Table upstairs.

Open all day all wk **Bar Meals** L served Mon-Thu
12-2.30, Fri 12-3, Sat 12-10, Sun 12-9 D served
Mon-Thu 6-9.30, Fri 6-10, Sat 12-10, Sun 12-9
Restaurant L served Mon-Thu 12-2.30, Fri 12-3, Sat
12-10, Sun 12-9 D served Mon-Thu 6-9.30, Fri 6-10,
Sat 12-10, Sun 12-9 ⊕ FREE HOUSE ◀ Rotating locally
brewed ales, Courage Best. ♥ 10 **Facilities** Children
welcome Children's portions Wi-fi

HANNINGTON   Map 5 SU55

PICK OF THE PUBS

The Vine at Hannington ♥

RG26 5TX ☎ 01635 298525
e-mail: info@thevineathannington.co.uk
web: www.thevineathannington.co.uk
dir: *Hannington signed from A339 between
Basingstoke & Newbury*

Set in rolling countryside that typifies the North Wessex
Downs Area of Outstanding Natural Beauty, this gabled
old inn is popular with ramblers and cyclists; the views
from nearby White Hill sweep across the chalk downs
and rich farming countryside where the Vine and
Craven Hunt, after which the pub is named, once
trailed. The colourwashed Victorian country inn exudes
warmth, partly from the woodburning stove, partly the
restrained rural artefacts and partly the eclectic mix of
soft and traditional pub furnishings, a jigsaw that sets
the scene for an indulgence in real ales from the likes
of Hog's Back and Sharp's breweries. A good, solid
menu of pub favourites may feature dishes such as

grilled sea bass fillets with tomato and herb dressing,
a fulfilling home-made Cornish pasty, or pork, honey
and Hampshire watercress sausages. There's a large,
shrubby garden out back, or choose to eat in the airy
conservatory.

Open 12-3 6-11 (Sat-Sun all day) Closed: 25 Dec, Mon
Bar Meals L served Tue-Fri 12-2, Sat-Sun 12-2.30
D served all wk 6-9 **Restaurant** L served Tue-Fri 12-2,
Sat-Sun 12-2.30 D served all wk 6-9 ⊕ PUNCH
TAVERNS ◀ Sharp's Doom Bar, Ringwood Best, Hogs
Back TEA Ö Aspall. ♥ 11 **Facilities** Children welcome
Children's portions Play area Family
room Dogs allowed Garden Parking Wi-fi

HAVANT   Map 5 SU70

The Royal Oak ♥

19 Langstone High St, Langstone PO9 1RY
☎ 023 9248 3125
e-mail: 7955@greeneking.co.uk
dir: *Telephone for directions*

Occupying an outstanding position overlooking Langstone
Harbour, this historic 16th-century pub is noted for its
rustic, unspoilt interior. Flagstone floors, exposed beams
and winter fires contrast with the waterfront benches and
secluded rear garden for alfresco summer drinking. The
comprehensive dinner menu includes British beef and
Ruddles Ale pie; slow cooked New Zealand lamb shank;
Punjabi chicken tikka curry; aubergine, feta and beetroot
cannelloni; steaks and gourmet burgers.

Open all day all wk 11-11 **Bar Meals** L served all wk 12-5
D served all wk 5-9 Av main course £9
Restaurant L served all wk 12-5 D served all wk 5-9
⊕ GREENE KING ◀ Greene King IPA, Ruddles County,
Ruddles Best, Abbot Ale, Speckled Hen. ♥ 16
Facilities Children welcome Children's menu Children's
portions Family room Dogs allowed Garden Wi-fi

HAWKLEY   Map 5 SU72

The Hawkley Inn ★★★ INN **NEW**

Pococks Ln GU33 6NE ☎ 01730 827205
e-mail: info@hawkleyinn.co.uk
dir: *A3 Liss rdbt towards Liss B3006. Right at Spread
Eagle, 2.5m turn left at Pococks Ln*

Described as 'quirky' by the landlord, The Hawkley
welcomes 'most children' and 'well-behaved dogs', as
well as their owners. Two real fires simmer away, one of
them warming a moose head mounted above the hearth.
Awaiting ale lovers are seven brews on tap, and almost
as many ciders; a beer festival in early June in this
peaceful corner of East Hampshire is an idyllic way to
celebrate these amber liquids. Daily changing menus of
good home-cooked food proffer the likes of warm lamb
rillettes, followed by filleted mackerel with fresh
horseradish mash; lunchtime ciabattas and baguettes
are available on weekdays. Contemporary accommodation
is available.

Open all wk Mon-Fri 12-3 5.30-11 (Sat-Sun all day)
Bar Meals L served Mon-Sat 12-2, Sun 12-4 D served
Mon-Sat 7-9 **Restaurant** L served Mon-Sat 12-2, Sun
12-4 D served Mon-Sat 7-9 ⊕ WISHBOURNE INNS ⬛ 7
beers on tap, Guest ales ♂ Mr Whiteheads, Brothers
Toffee Apple Cider, Westons Bounds Brand.
Facilities Children welcome Children's portions Dogs
allowed Garden Beer festival Wi-fi **Rooms** 5

HERRIARD   Map 5 SU64

The Fur & Feathers NEW

Herriard Rd RG25 2PN ☎ **01256 384170**
e-mail: peter@franskitchen.co.uk
dir: *From Basingstoke take A339 towards Alton. After
Herriard follow pub signs. Turn left to pub*

The Fur and Feathers reopened under new owners Fran
and Peter Whitehead at the end of 2010. The couple have
retained the pub's high-ceilinged Victorian charm and
enhanced it with new log-burning fireplaces at each end
of the bar. There is an emphasis on sourcing ingredients
and ales from within 20 miles of the pub and this is
reflected in the extensive menu, which includes local
game and meat, all cooked by Fran and her team –
venison steak in a rich chilli and chocolate sauce, whole
roasted sea bass with ginger, lemon and lime.

Open Tue-Thu 12-3 6-11 (Fri-Sat 12-11 Sun 12-6)
Closed: Sun eve & Mon **Bar Meals** Av main course £14
Restaurant L served Tue-Sat 12-2.30, Sun 12-3 booking
required D served Tue-Sat 7-9.30 booking required
⊕ FREE HOUSE ⬛ Local ales ♂ Westons Cider Ice,
Westons Seasonal Hand Pump Cider, Mr Whiteheads.
Facilities Children welcome Children's menu Children's
portions Dogs allowed Garden Parking

HOLYBOURNE   Map 5 SU74

The White Hart Hotel ♀

139 London Rd GU34 4EY ☎ **01420 87654**
e-mail: whitehart-holybourne@btconnect.com
dir: *From M3 junct 5 follow Alton signs (A339). In Alton
take A31 towards Farnham. Follow Holybourne signs*

Rebuilt in the 1920s on the site of the original inn, the
White Hart has been recently refurbished to create a
comfortable, welcoming setting for a well kept pint of
Greene King IPA or a hearty meal. The village of
Holybourne is steeped in history: an old Roman fort lies
under the cricket field, and the village also stands on the
Pilgrims' Way. Expect a daily-changing selection of
freshly cooked dishes that includes plenty of fresh fish
and shellfish, local farm and smallholding beef, pork and
lamb, vegetarian choices, mid-week and Sunday roasts.

Open all day all wk **Bar Meals** L served all wk 12-3
D served all wk 6.30-9.30 Av main course £8.50
Restaurant L served all wk 12-3 D served all wk
6.30-9.30 Fixed menu price fr £5.50 ⊕ GREENE KING/
MERLIN INNS ⬛ Courage Best, Greene King IPA, 2 guest
ales, 1 mild ale. ♀ 10 **Facilities** Children welcome
Children's menu Children's portions Play area Dogs
allowed Garden Parking Wi-fi

HOOK   Map 5 SU75

Crooked Billet

London Rd RG27 9EH
☎ **01256 762118** 📠 **01256 761011**
e-mail: richardbarwise@aol.com
web: www.thecrookedbillethook.co.uk
dir: *From M3 take Hook ring road. At 3rd rdbt turn right
onto A30 towards London, pub on left 0.5m by river*

A hostelry has stood on this site since the 1600s, though
the present pub only dates back to 1935. The family-
friendly pub has a lovely river garden and children's play
area. There is food to suit all appetites, including a
children's menu. Expect sirloin steak, tomato and
mushrooms; honey-glazed ham, local eggs and chips; or
home-made chilli with rice or tortilla chips and melted
cheese. There's also a range of ploughman's and open
sandwiches, all to be washed down with beers from
Andwells Brewery. The pub is home to the Hook Eagle
Morris Men.

Open all wk Mon-Fri 11.30-3 6-12 (Sat-Sun 11.30-mdnt)
Bar Meals L served Mon-Fri 12-2.30, Sat 12-8 booking
required D served Mon-Fri 6.30-9.30, Sat 6.30-10 booking
required Av main course £10 ⊕ FREE HOUSE ⬛ Courage
Best, Andwells Brewery, Sharp's Doom Bar ♂ Thatchers.
Facilities Children welcome Children's menu Children's
portions Play area Dogs allowed Garden Parking

The Hogget ♀

London Rd, Hook Common RG27 9JJ ☎ **01256 763009**
e-mail: home@hogget.co.uk
dir: *M3 junct 5, A30, 0.5m, between Hook & Basingstoke*

Close to the M3 motorway, The Hogget's relaxed,
contemporary atmosphere is just the place to enjoy good
food and drink. Guest ales support regular beers from
Ringwood, Jennings and Marston's, whilst the sensible
wine list offers plenty of choice by the glass. Lunchtime
brings freshly-cut doorstep sandwiches, and named local
suppliers provide the ingredients for menu choices like
slow-roast belly pork with cider cream sauce, and grilled
John Dory on creamed leeks. A heated outdoor seating
area completes the picture.

Open all day all wk Closed: 25 Dec **Bar Meals** L served all
wk 10-6.30 booking required D served all wk 6.30-9
booking required Av main course £12 food served all day
Restaurant L served all wk 10-6.30 booking required
D served all wk 6.30-9 booking required food served all
day ⊕ MARSTONS PUB COMPANY ⬛ Ringwood Best,
Jennings Sneck Lifter, Marston's Pedigree, Guest ales
♂ Thatchers Gold. ♀ 16 **Facilities** Children welcome
Children's menu Children's portions Dogs allowed Garden
Parking

HURSLEY   Map 5 SU42

The Dolphin Inn ♀

SO21 2JY ☎ **01962 775209**
e-mail: mandy@dolphininn.demon.co.uk
dir: *Telephone for directions*

Reputedly built from the timbers of an early HMS Dolphin,
hence the pub name, the roadside village inn dates from
the 16th century and was once a thriving coaching inn.
Follow a stroll through nearby Farley Mount Country Park
with a traditional pub lunch in the mature garden or in
the beamed bars. Quench your thirst with a cold glass of
Summer Lightning, while the children enjoy the play area.
Pub favourites include steak and Guinness pie; ham, egg
and chips; and warm Cajun salad. Thursdays is quiz
night and on Fridays a meat draw is held.

Open all wk Mon-Sat 11-11 (Sun 12-10.30)
Bar Meals L served Mon-Thu 12-2, Fri-Sat 12-2.30, Sun
12-8.30 booking required D served Mon-Thu 6-9, Fri-Sat
6.30-9.30, Sun 12-8.30 booking required ⊕ ENTERPRISE
INNS ⬛ Ringwood, Summer Lightning, HSB ♂ Thatchers
Dry, Thatchers Premium. ♀ 12 **Facilities** Children
welcome Children's menu Children's portions Play area
Family room Dogs allowed Garden Parking

The Kings Head ★★★★ INN ♀ NEW

Main Rd SO21 2JW ☎ **01962 775208**
e-mail: info@kingsheadhursley.co.uk
dir: *On A3090 between Winchester & Romsey*

In 2009, five local farming families pooled their resources
and bought this former coaching inn, extensively
refurbished it and asked pub regular Alan Rodbourne,
who began work on the Hursley Estate in 1946, to
officially reopen it. The decor and furniture was chosen by
the farmers' wives to reflect the inn's Georgian origins,
while bedrooms take their names from previous
incumbents of the Estate. Beer festivals are held on
August Bank Holiday and in December. Stylish,
individually designed bedrooms available.

Open all day all wk **Bar Meals** L served Mon-Sat 12-2,
Sun 12-3 D served all wk 6-9 Av main course £9.95
Restaurant L served Mon-Sat 12-2, Sun 12-3 D served all
wk 6-9 Av 3 course à la carte fr £20 ⊕ FREE HOUSE
⬛ Sharp's Doom Bar, Ringwood, 5 Local Ales. ♀ 10
Facilities Children welcome Children's menu Children's
portions Dogs allowed Garden Beer festival Parking Wi-fi
Rooms 8

IBSLEY
Map 5 SU10

Old Beams Inn ☂

Salisbury Rd BH24 3PP
☎ **01425 473387** 📄 **01202 743080**
e-mail: oldbeams@alcatraz.co.uk
dir: *On A338 between Ringwood & Salisbury*

Old Beams is a beautiful 13th-century thatched and timber-framed village inn located at the heart of the New Forest, with views of lovely countryside and the famous native ponies. It has a beer garden with a decked area and patio, and a cosy old world interior. Pub food favourites, based on local and New Forest produce, dominate the menu, and on Friday night (fish night) there's a large selection.

Open all wk 11am-11.30pm **Bar Meals** Av main course £10 food served all day **Restaurant** Fixed menu price fr £9.95 Av 3 course à la carte fr £25 food served all day ⊕ ALCATRAZ ◄ IPA, Old Speckled Hen. ☂ 10 **Facilities** Children welcome Children's menu Garden Parking Wi-fi

ITCHEN ABBAS
Map 5 SU53

The Trout

Main Rd SO21 1BQ ☎ **01962 779537** 📄 **01962 791046**
dir: *M3 junct 9, A34, right onto A33, follow signs to Itchen Abbas, pub 2m on left*

This 19th-century coaching inn is situated in the picturesque Itchen Valley close to the river itself. Originally called the Plough, it is said to have been the location that inspired Charles Kingsley to write *The Water Babies*. Freshly cooked, locally sourced produce is served in the bar and restaurant: watercress soup, of course, smoked trout from the Avington fishery, hand carved ham, egg and chips, and Hursley Butcher's champion sausages and mash - ideal for hungry walkers. A lunchtime selection of light meals includes baguettes, sandwiches, omelettes and salads. Check out the special board for other interesting options.

Open all wk 12-3 6-11 **Bar Meals** booking required Av main course £9.50 **Restaurant** booking required Fixed menu price fr £9.95 ⊕ GREENE KING ◄ Greene King IPA, Abbot Ale, Olde Trip. **Facilities** Children welcome Children's menu Children's portions Play area Dogs allowed Garden Parking Wi-fi

LEE-ON-THE-SOLENT
Map 5 SU50

The Bun Penny ☂ NEW

36 Manor Way PO13 9JH ☎ **023 9255 0214**
e-mail: bar@bunpenny.co.uk
dir: *From Fareham take B3385 to Lee-on-the-Solent. Pub 300yds before High St*

Prominently positioned on the road into Lee-on-the-Solent, this former farmhouse is a short walk from the waterfront. It looks every bit the classic country free house, and has charm and character to match. A large patio at the front and an extensive back garden are ideal for summer relaxation, while real fires and cosy corners are welcome in winter. Otter beer is sold direct from the cask, backed by hand-pulls for a rotating selection of ales which include the local Oakleaf Brewery. Seasonally changing menus and the specials board feature fresh local produce.

Open all day all wk 11-11 (Fri-Sat 11am-mdnt, Sun 12-10.30) **Bar Meals** L served Mon-Sat 12-2.30, Sun 12-9 D served Mon-Sat 6-9, Sun 12-9 **Restaurant** L served Mon-Sat 12-2.30, Sun 12-9 D served Mon-Sat 6-9, Sun 12-9 ⊕ FREE HOUSE ◄ Otter Bitter, Oakleaf Brewery Whole Hearted, Guest ales ♻ Westons Scrumpy. ☂ 13 **Facilities** Children welcome Children's menu Children's portions Dogs allowed Garden Parking Wi-fi

LINWOOD
Map 5 SU10

PICK OF THE PUBS

The High Corner Inn ☂

BH24 3QY ☎ **01425 473973** 📄 **01425 480015**
e-mail: highcorner@wadworth.co.uk
dir: *From A338 (Ringwood to Salisbury road) follow brown tourist signs into forest. Pass Red Shoot Inn, after 1m turn down gravel track at Green High Corner Inn*

Lost down a quarter-mile gravel track a mile from the village of Linwood, this much extended and modernised, early 18th-century inn is set in seven beautiful acres of woodland deep in the heart of the New Forest. The cluster of rambling buildings began life as a farm in the early 1700s. A quiet hideaway in winter, mobbed in summer, it is a popular retreat for families with its numerous bar-free rooms, flower-filled terrace, large garden, an outdoor adventure playground and miles of wildlife-rich forest and heathland walks and cycle trails. The beamed bars, replete with roaring winter log fires and the full range of Wadworth ales on tap, and the lovely forest garden are very agreeable

settings for sampling an extensive range of home-cooked meals and bar snacks; daily specials are shown on chalkboards and a carvery is available on Sunday. Rest and refuel during or following a forest ramble with a refreshing pint of 6X and a bowl of home-made soup or a ploughman's lunch, or tuck into something more substantial from the traditional pub menu.

Open all wk Mon-Fri noon-3 6-11 (Sat 11am-11pm, Sun 11-10.30, all day summer & school holidays) **Bar Meals** L served Mon-Fri 12-2.30, Sat 12-9, Sun 12-8 D served Mon-Fri 6-9, Sat 12-9, Sun 12-8 **Restaurant** L served Mon-Fri 12-2.30, Sat 12-9, Sun 12-8 D served Mon-Fri 6-9, Sat 12-9, Sun 12-8 ⊕ WADWORTH ◄ Wadworth 6X, Horizon, Henry's IPA, Wadworth Seasonal Ales ♻ Westons, Thatchers Gold. ☂ 14 **Facilities** Children welcome Children's menu Play area Dogs allowed Garden Parking

LISS
Map 5 SU72

The Jolly Drover ☂ NEW

London Rd, Hill Brow GU33 7QL ☎ **01730 893137**
e-mail: thejollydrover@googlemail.com
dir: *From station in Liss at mini-rdbt right into Hill Brow Rd (B3006) signed Rogate, Rake, Hill Brow. At junct with B2071 pub opposite. Cross dual carriageway*

Built nearly two hundred years ago by a drover, to offer cheer and sustenance to other drovers on the old London road. It has been run for the last seventeen years by Anne and Barry Coe, who welcome all-comers with a large log fire, secluded garden, a covered and heated patio, a choice of real ales, and home-cooked food. The same menu is served in the bar and restaurant. Snacks include loaded nachos and potato skins, or choose from the English favourites such as prawn cocktail; pollock goujons; locally-reared pheasant breast with redcurrant sauce; beef lasagne; or the house mixed grill.

Open all wk 11-3 6-11 Closed: 25-26 Dec, 1 Jan **Bar Meals** L served all wk 12-2 D served all wk 7-9.30 Av main course £11 **Restaurant** L served all wk 12-2 D served all wk 7-9.30 ⊕ ENTERPRISE INNS/WHITBREAD ◄ Alton's Pride, Fuller's London Pride, Sharp's Doom Bar. ☂ 10 **Facilities** Children welcome Children's portions Garden Parking Wi-fi

LITTLETON   Map 5 SU43

PICK OF THE PUBS

The Running Horse ★★★★ INN ⊛ ♀

88 Main Rd SO22 6QS
☎ 01962 880218   📠 01962 886596
e-mail: runninghorseinn@btconnect.com
web: www.runninghorseinn.co.uk
dir: 3m from Winchester, signed from Stockbridge Rd

Just three miles from Winchester's city centre, this
attractive food pub is a popular pit stop for locals and
visitors alike. The quality accommodation of the nine
en suite rooms is matched by the highly rated food, but
the bar draws those interested in sampling locally
brewed beers such as Flowerpots and Ringwood Best. The
bar with its limestone counter is a successful
blend of the traditional and the modern, with stripped
wooden floor, leather tub chairs around an original
fireplace, and white walls. The rear garden and the
patio to the front are large and peaceful, and are
perfect for summer dining or simply relaxing with a
drink. The focus here is undoubtedly on good eating,
and the chefs' sourcing of seasonal produce helped
The Running Horse to gain its AA Rosette for the quality
of its contemporary cuisine. Main courses include
grilled calves' liver with mash, confit of onion, crispy
pancetta and Cumberland sauce, or duo of Stockbridge
rabbit wrapped in Parma ham with Puy lentil ragout,
wild mushroom and tarragon-braised leg pithivier.

Open all day all wk Bar Meals L served all wk 12-2
D served all wk 6-9.30 Av main course £10
Restaurant L served all wk 12-2 D served all wk 6-9.30
Fixed menu price fr £12.50 Av 3 course à la carte fr
£25 ⊕ FREE HOUSE ◀ Ringwood Best, Flowerpots
Ở Aspall. ♀ 10 Facilities Children welcome Children's
portions Dogs allowed Garden Parking Wi-fi Rooms 9

LONGPARISH   Map 5 SU44

PICK OF THE PUBS

The Plough Inn

SP11 6PB ☎ 01264 720358
e-mail: eat@theploughinn.info
dir: M3 junct 8, A303 towards Andover. In approx 6m
take B3048 towards Longparish

This charming old 18th-century inn stands close to the
centre of Longparish, just a few minutes' drive from
Andover. The nearby River Test is one of southern
England's finest chalk streams and the Test Way
footpath runs through the inn's car park. This
delightful location makes The Plough a popular stop for
walkers, as well as for the fishermen and cyclists who
are also drawn to this lovely valley. Expect Hampshire
ales from the Ringwood and Itchen Valley breweries,
and a food offering that encompasses fish specials
and pub classics as well as the à la carte menu.
Typical dishes include duo of duck on rösti potato with
sautéed Savoy cabbage and five spice jus; award-
winning local sausages with mash and onion gravy;

grilled goat's cheese and pimento polenta with
balsamic glazed rocket; and locally-smoked trout on
toasted brioche with creamed leeks and dill dressing.

Open Mon-Sat noon-2.30 6-9.30 (Sun noon-8 summer,
noon-4 winter) Closed: Sun eve in winter
Bar Meals L served all wk 12-2.30 booking required D served
6-9.30 booking required Restaurant L served 12-2.30
booking required D served 6-9.30 booking required
⊕ ENTERPRISE INNS ◀ Itchen Valley, Black Sheep,
Flacks Double Drop Ở Thatchers. Facilities Children
welcome Children's portions Dogs allowed Garden
Parking Wi-fi

LOWER SWANWICK   Map 5 SU40

Old Ship ♀

261 Bridge Rd SO31 7FN ☎ 01489 575646
e-mail: simonoldship@gmail.com
dir: Telephone for directions

A 17th-century inn of great character on the banks of the
Hamble River, which makes it popular with sailing types.
There are open fires in winter, dark wood panelling and
beams, and a bar serving well-kept Fuller's beers. The
spacious, candlelit restaurant has a high-vaulted ceiling
and nautical paraphernalia. In addition to light bites and
snacks, the menu includes freshly cooked home-made
chilli, curry, lamb's liver and bacon, cottage pie, steaks
and burgers from the grill, and salmon fillet with lemon
sauce. Chef's specials appear on the blackboard. There is
a waterside patio for warmer weather.

Open all day all wk Bar Meals L served all wk 12-2.15
booking required D served all wk 6.30-9.30 booking
required Restaurant L served all wk 12-2.15 booking
required D served all wk 4.30-9.30 booking required
⊕ MERLIN INNS / FULLER'S ◀ HSB. Facilities Children
welcome Children's menu Children's portions Family
room Dogs allowed Garden Parking

LOWER WIELD   Map 5 SU64

PICK OF THE PUBS

The Yew Tree ♀

SO24 9RX ☎ 01256 389224   📠 01256 389224
dir: Take A339 from Basingstoke towards Alton. Turn
right for Lower Wield

This free house first served ale in 1845, when the
eponymous, now 650-year-old yew tree was just getting
into its stride. Set in glorious countryside, opposite a
picturesque cricket pitch, the popular landlord's simple
mission statement promises 'Good honest food; great
local beers; fine wines (lots of choice); and, most
importantly, good fun for one and all'. Triple fff is the
house beer, with 20 guest ale brewers on rotation,
including Bowman Ales and Hogs Back TEA. Most of
the seasonal food is sourced from Hampshire or
neighbouring counties, while keeping the regular
favourites 'to avoid uproar'. Sample dishes include
whole sea bass topped with dill and sun-dried tomato
butter; ham hock roasted with honey and mustard and

served with a leek, Cheddar and parsley sauce; and
roasted pepper with a leek, butternut squash and
tomato ragout topped with Applewood cheese. The
wines are mainly New World, but with some classic
Burgundies and plenty available by the glass. There is
an annual cricket match and sports day in summer,
and 'silly' quiz nights in winter.

Open Tue-Sat 12-3 6-11 (Sun all day) Closed: 1st 2wks
Jan, Mon Bar Meals L served Tue-Sun 12-2 D served
Tue-Sat 6.30-9, Sun 6.30-8.30 Av main course £10.50
Restaurant L served Tue-Sun 12-2 D served Tue-Sat
6.30-9, Sun 6.30-8.30 ⊕ FREE HOUSE ◀ Cheriton
Pots, Bowman Ales Swift One, Triple fff Moondance,
Hogs Back TEA, GFB Hop Back, Andwell Gold Muddler.
♀ 14 Facilities Children welcome Children's menu
Children's portions Dogs allowed Garden Parking

LYMINGTON   Map 5 SZ39

Mayflower Inn ♀

Kings Saltern Rd SO41 3QD
☎ 01590 672160   📠 01590 679180
e-mail: info@themayflower.uk.com
dir: A337 towards New Milton, left at rdbt by White Hart,
left to Rookes Ln, right at mini-rdbt, pub 0.75m

A favourite with yachtsmen and dog walkers, this solidly
built mock-Tudor inn overlooks the Lymington River, with
glorious views to the Isle of Wight. There's a magnificent
garden with splendid sun terraces where you can enjoy a
pint of Goddards Fuggle Dee Dum, a purpose-built play
area for children and an on-going summer barbecue in
fine weather. Menu prices are reasonable, with dishes
that range from light bites like lemon and pepper
monkfish goujons or a sharing platter to main courses of
black bean stir fry chicken or sea bass fillet with prawn
and saffron risotto.

Open all day all wk Bar Meals food served all day
Restaurant food served all day ⊕ ENTERPRISE INN/
COASTAL INNS & TAVERNS LTD ◀ Ringwood Best, Fuller's
London Pride, 6X, Goddards Fuggle Dee Dum
Ở Thatchers. ♀ 9 Facilities Children welcome Children's
menu Children's portions Play area Dogs allowed Garden
Parking Wi-fi

LYNDHURST
Map 5 SU30

New Forest Inn

Emery Down SO43 7DY ☎ 023 8028 4690
e-mail: info@thenewforestinn.co.uk
dir: M27 junct 1 follow signs for A35/Lyndhurst. In Lyndhurst follow signs for Christchurch, turn right at Swan Inn towards Emery Down

An inn which prides itself on its friendliness, great local atmosphere, and relaxed attitude to dogs. Located in the heart of the New Forest, with ponies often trying to come in through the front door, the pub has oak beams and floors, two open fires in feature fireplaces and three seating areas. At least two guest cask ales are on offer throughout the year, in addition to the regular Ringwood brews; a beer festival here on the second weekend in July makes great use of the lovely garden. Home-cooked meals comprise everybody's favourites, from steak and ale pie to pan-fried lamb's liver with sautéed potatoes.

Open all day all wk **Bar Meals** Av main course £9 food served all day **Restaurant** Fixed menu price fr £9.95 food served all day ⊕ ENTERPRISE INNS ◄ Ringwood Best, Ringwood Fortyniner, Guest ales ⓒ Stowford Press.
Facilities Children welcome Children's menu Children's portions Dogs allowed Garden Beer festival Parking

The Oak Inn ♟

Pinkney Ln, Bank SO43 7FE
☎ 023 8028 2350   📠 023 8028 4601
e-mail: oakinn@fullers.co.uk
dir: From Lyndhurst signed A35 to Christchurch, follow A35 1m, turn left at Bank sign

New Forest ponies, pigs and deer graze outside this small, but perfectly formed former cider house, behind whose bay windows lie a traditional woodburner, antique pine and bric-a-brac galore. With a wide range of wines and well kept Fuller's ales changing regularly, your can enjoy your glass with lunchtime doorstep sandwiches filled with crayfish and rocket; beef and horseradish; ham, cheese and chutney. Typical menu dishes feature

pan-fried calves' liver and bacon, and chargrilled rib-eye steak. The pub is popular with walkers, cyclists and horse riders, and dogs love the large beer garden.

Open all wk Mon-Fri 11.30-3.30 6-11 (Sat 11.30-11 Sun 12-10.30) **Bar Meals** L served Mon-Sat 12-2.30, Sun 12-9 booking required D served Mon-Sat 6-9.30, Sun 12-9 booking required **Restaurant** L served Mon-Sat 12-2.30, Sun 12-9 booking required D served Mon-Sat 6-9.30, Sun 12-9 booking required ⊕ FULLER'S BREWERY ◄ London Pride, Fuller's HSB, Gale's Seafarer Ale ⓒ Aspall. ♟ 9
Facilities Children welcome Children's menu Dogs allowed Garden Parking

MAPLEDURWELL
Map 5 SU65

PICK OF THE PUBS

The Gamekeepers ♟

Tunworth Rd RG25 2LU
☎ 01256 322038 & 07786 998994 📠 01256 322038
e-mail: info@thegamekeepers.co.uk
web: www.thegamekeepers.co.uk
dir: M3 junct 6, take A30 towards Hook. Turn right after The Hatch pub. The Gamekeepers signed

The Gamekeepers, with its large secluded garden, sits in the idyllic rural village of Mapledurwell; this 19th-century pub/restaurant with an indoor well was known as the Queen's Head 150 years ago. Relax on a leather settee with a pint of Hall and Woodhouse ale, enjoy the cosy atmosphere of low beams and flagstone floors, and make your selection from the daily changing menu. Contemporary in style yet home made, dishes are based

on seasonal produce. An example is the impressive range of game (pheasant, venison, wild boar) that goes into the slow-cooked game hotpot, baked in ale with rosemary and thyme, sliced potatoes and seasonal vegetables. The truly hungry could start with grilled sardines presented on mixed leaves and red chard, with marinated red peppers and black olive tapenade. Children are welcome and eat the same food as their parents, in smaller portions.

Open all wk Mon-Fri 11-3 5.30-mdnt (Sat 11-mdnt Sun 11-11) **Bar Meals** L served Mon-Fri 11-2.30, Sat-Sun 11-9.30 booking required D served Mon-Fri 5.30-9, Sat-Sun 11-9.30 booking required Av main course £10 **Restaurant** L served Mon-Fri 11-2.30, Sat-Sun 11-9.30 booking required D served Mon-Fri 5.30-9, Sat-Sun 11-9.30 booking required Fixed menu price fr £35 Av 3 course à la carte fr £35 ⊕ HALL & WOODHOUSE ◄ Badgers First Gold, Tanglefoot, Fursty Ferret, Hopping Hare, Firkin Fox, Pickled Partridge ⓒ Stowford Press, Applewood Cider. ♟ 10 **Facilities** Children welcome Children's portions Dogs allowed Garden Parking Wi-fi

See advert below

MICHELDEVER
Map 5 SU53

The Dove Inn ★★★★ INN ♟ NEW

Andover Rd, Micheldever Station SO21 3AU
☎ 01962 774288
e-mail: info@the-dove-inn.co.uk
dir: M3 junct 8 merge onto A303, take exit signed Micheldever Station, follow station signs onto Andover Rd, on left

Built in 1840 as a coaching inn when neighbouring Micheldever station served distant Andover. A changing roster of three real ales is the norm in the recently refurbished bars and eating areas, where menus feature home-made, locally sourced crispy shoulder of lamb with Mediterranean vegetable couscous; whole grilled plaice with lemon and caper butter; creamy saffron, leek and Winchester Cheddar tartlet; and pub classics. Overnight stays in the comfortable bedrooms include a good breakfast.

Open all wk 11-3 6-11 **Bar Meals** L served all wk 12-2 D served Sun-Thu 6.30-9, Fri-Sat 6.30-9.30 Av main course £10.95 **Restaurant** L served all wk 12-2 D served Sun-Thu 6.30-9, Fri-Sat 6.30-9.30 Av 3 course à la carte fr £25 ⊕ FREE HOUSE ◀ Ringwood Best, Hobgoblin, Itchen Valley Ö Aspall. ♚14 **Facilities** Children welcome Children's portions Dogs allowed Garden Parking Wi-fi **Rooms** 5

Half Moon & Spread Eagle

Winchester Rd SO21 3DG ☎ 01962 774339
dir: *From Winchester take A33 towards Basingstoke. In 5m turn left after small car garage. Pub 0.5m on right*

Old drovers' inn located in the heart of a pretty thatched and timbered Hampshire village, overlooking the cricket green. The pub, comprising three neatly furnished interconnecting rooms, has a real local feel, and a few years back reverted to its old name having been the Dever Arms for eight years. An extensive menu ranges through Sunday roasts, fresh battered cod, and half shoulder of minted lamb. Recent change of hands.

Open all wk 13-3 6-11 (Sun 12-3) ⊕ GREENE KING ◀ Greene King IPA, Abbot Ale, Guest ales.
Facilities Children welcome Children's menu Children's portions Play area Dogs allowed Garden Parking

MORTIMER WEST END   Map 5 SU66

The Red Lion

Church Rd RG7 2HU ☎ 0118 970 0169
e-mail: red-lionwestend@hotmail.co.uk
dir: *Telephone for directions*

Dating back to 1650, this traditional pub has a profusion of original oak beams and an inglenook fireplace. A range of real ales are served, plus stylish, unfussy cooking. Where possible produce is locally sourced, including free-range chicken and eggs, and English beef hung for 21 days. A bar menu offers traditional favourites while restaurant fare might start with jellied pork meat with home-made pickles and toast, followed by confit duck legs with fondant potato, orange purée and glazed chicory, then treacle tart and clotted cream. Look out for authentic Czech dishes.

Open all day all wk **Bar Meals** Av main course £11 food served all day **Restaurant** L served all wk 12-3 D served all wk 6.30-9 Av 3 course à la carte fr £22 ⊕ HALL & WOODHOUSE ◀ Tanglefoot, Badger First Gold, Guinness, Sussex Ö Stowford Press. **Facilities** Children welcome Children's menu Children's portions Play area Family room Dogs allowed Garden Beer festival Parking Wi-fi

NEW ALRESFORD   Map 5 SU53

The Bell Inn ♚

12 West St SO24 9AT ☎ 01962 732429
e-mail: info@bellalresford.com
dir: *In village centre*

A restored 17th-century former coaching inn situated in the heart of a picturesque Georgian town in the peaceful Itchen Valley. Take a steam train ride on the Watercress Line, browse the boutiques and galleries, or enjoy a

riverside stroll, then rest and refuel in the homely bar and candlelit restaurant at The Bell. Follow devilled kidneys on brioche, with slow roast honey-glazed pork belly, pan-seared partridge breasts, braised cabbage and red wine sauce. Round off with plum and cinnamon crumble or treacle and walnut tart. Wash down with tip-top pint of Itchen Valley Winchester Bitter or Heart of Hampshire cider.

Open all day Closed: Sun eve **Bar Meals** L served all wk 12-3 D served Mon-Sat 6-9 Av main course £14 **Restaurant** L served Mon-Sat 12-3, Sun 12-4 D served Mon-Sat 6-9 Fixed menu price fr £10 ⊕ FREE HOUSE ◀ Sharp's Doom Bar, Winchester, Otter, Resolute, Upham Ale Ö Mr Whiteheads, Heart of Hampshire, Scrumpy. ♚18 **Facilities** Children welcome Children's portions Dogs allowed Garden Parking Wi-fi

NORTHINGTON   Map 5 SU53

PICK OF THE PUBS

The Woolpack Inn   INN ⊛⊛ ♚

Totford SO24 9TJ
☎ 0845 293 8066   🖷 0845 293 8055
e-mail: info@thewoolpackinn.co.uk
dir: *From Basingstoke take A339 towards Alton. Under motorway & turn right (across dual carriageway) onto B3036 signed Candovers & Alresford. Pub between Brown Candover & Northington*

Brian and Jarina Aherne's old drovers' inn stands in a tiny hamlet in the peaceful Candover Valley north of Alresford, close to The Grange (summer opera) and within easy reach of Winchester. Sympathetically smartened up, creating a sense of calm modernity while still retaining the classic feel of a country pub, The Woolpack is once again thriving, drawing walkers in for pints of Flower Pots Bitter and local foodies for Brian's cracking pub food, while the seven stylish rooms in the spruced up cottages out back are popular with visitors seeking a quiet rural base. Eat in the traditional bar, where rugs on tiled or wood floors, a roaring log fire, rustic pine tables and the daily papers create a relaxing atmosphere, or head for the smart dining room. The menu ranges from pub classics like ham, egg and chips and 32-day aged Longhorn rump steak with chips and horseradish relish, to pork belly with bubble-and-squeak and roast garlic sauce and seasonal game shot on the Candover Estate. Excellent Sunday roasts – booking essential.

Open all day all wk Closed: 25 Dec eve
Bar Meals L served all wk 12-3 D served Mon-Sat 6-close, Sun 6-8.30 Av main course £10
Restaurant L served all wk 12-3 D served Mon-Sat 6-close, Fixed menu price fr £14.95 Av 3 course à la carte fr £25 ⊕ FREE HOUSE ◀ Palmers Copper, The Woolpack Ale, Otter Bitter, Flower Pots Ö Thatchers Gold. ♚12 **Facilities** Children welcome Children's menu Children's portions Play area Dogs allowed Garden Parking Wi-fi **Rooms** 7

NORTH WALTHAM   Map 5 SU54

PICK OF THE PUBS

The Fox ♚

See Pick of the Pubs on page 228

OVINGTON   Map 5 SU53

PICK OF THE PUBS

The Bush ♚

See Pick of the Pubs on page 229

PETERSFIELD   Map 5 SU72

The Good Intent ♚

40-46 College St GU31 4AF ☎ 01730 263838
e-mail: info@goodintentpetersfield.co.uk
web: www.goodintentpetersfield.co.uk
dir: *Telephone for directions*

Candlelit tables, original oak beams, open fires, an inglenook fireplace and well-kept ales characterise this 16th-century pub, and in summer, flower tubs and hanging baskets festoon the front patio. Menus feature starters such as crab soufflé or home-made duck and chicken liver pâté; followed by O'Hagans sausages and mash; ham (home prepared), free range egg and hand cut chips; pan-fried salmon fillet with orange and vanilla sauce; or rack of lamb with caramelised apple and potato cake. Sandwiches and baguettes are also available at lunchtime. Sunday evening is live music night.

Open all wk 11-3 5.30-11 (Sun 12-3 7-11)
Bar Meals L served all wk 12-2.30 D served Sun-Mon 7-9, Tue-Sat 6.30-9.30 ⊕ FULLER'S BREWERY ◀ Fuller's HSB, London Pride, Guest ales. ♚9 **Facilities** Children welcome Children's menu Children's portions Dogs allowed Garden Parking Wi-fi

PICK OF THE PUBS

The Fox ♀

NORTH WALTHAM   Map 5 SU54

RG25 2BE ☎ **01256 397288**
e-mail: info@thefox.org
web: www.thefox.org
dir: *M3 junct 7, A30 towards Winchester. North Waltham signed on right. Take 2nd signed road*

Why pull off at a service station on the M3 when, two miles from Junction 7, down a quiet country lane, is this peaceful village pub? Built as three farm cottages in 1624, The Fox welcomes families, as the children's adventure play area in the extensive beer garden testifies. The garden has other attractions too, as it fair blazes with colour in summer when the pretty flower borders and hanging baskets are in bloom. In the bar, in addition to landlord Rob MacKenzie's passionately cared for real ales, is an ever-growing collection of over 1,100 spirit miniatures, to which visitors' additions are always welcome. Obviously, these aren't for sampling, but anything from the malt whisky selection (AnCnoc, Dalwhinnie and Old Pulteney, for example) is available on conventional pub terms. Rob's wife Izzy is responsible for dishes on the monthly menus and daily specials boards, which, from the basics like mayonnaise, are prepared in her kitchen. A simple bar menu offers pie of the day; ham, egg and chips; and chicken breast schnitzel, while in the tartan-carpeted restaurant there's a wider choice. Begin with crispy duck cakes with sweet mango and coriander salsa; Scottish smoked salmon; or cheese soufflé; then continue with herb-crusted loin of cod, new potatoes, spinach and parsley; Hampshire venison with glazed shallots, field mushrooms and creamed swede; steak and kidney pudding with mash and vegetables; or Stilton and wild mushroom Wellington. Home-made desserts sound tempting too – the red berry Pavlova comes with coulis and whipped cream. The Fox's well-known events calendar features a late-April annual oyster festival, with a beer tent.

Open all day all wk 11-11
Bar Meals L served all wk 12-2.30
D served all wk 6-9.30 Av main course
£8.10 **Restaurant** L served all wk 12-2.30
booking required D served all wk 6-9.30
booking required Av 3 course à la carte fr
£23.25 ⊕ FREE HOUSE ◄ Ringwood Best
Bitter, Brakspear, West Berkshire Good Old
Boy, guest ale Ở Aspall, Thatchers Gold,
Old Rosie. ♀ 14 **Facilities** Children's
menu Children's portions Play area Dogs
allowed Garden Beer festival Parking

PICK OF THE PUBS

The Bush ♟

SO24 0RE
☎ **01962 732764** 📄 **01962 735130**
e-mail: thebushinn@wadworth.co.uk
web: www.thebushinn@wadworth.co.uk
dir: *A31 from Winchester, E to Alton &
Farnham, approx 6m turn left off dual
carriageway to Ovington. 0.5m to pub*

Located just off the A31 on a peaceful
lane, this unspoilt 17th-century rose-
covered cottage enjoys an enviable
picturesque setting, close to one of
Hampshire's famous chalk trout streams
– the River Itchen. Gentle riverside strolls
are very popular, as are the rustic bars
and bench-filled garden of this one-time
refreshment stop on the Pilgrim's Way
between Winchester and Canterbury, both
of which are often crammed with people
replenishing their energy after a walk,
especially on fine summer weekends.

Don't expect to find a juke box or fruit
machine, the intimate, softly-lit and
atmospheric rooms boast dark-painted
walls, an assortment of sturdy tables,
chairs and high-backed settles and a
wealth of old artefacts, prints and stuffed
fish. On cold winter nights the place to sit
with a pint of traditional ale is in front of
the roaring log fire.

The regularly-changing menu is based on
the freshest food the owners, Nick and
Cathy Young, can source, including local
farm cheeses, meats from Wiltshire,

Hampshire and Scotland, and fish from
the Dorset and Cornish coasts. Choices
range from sandwiches, ploughman's
lunches and other bar snacks, through to
satisfying meals such as chicken liver
pâté with grape chutney, or local smoked
trout mousse; followed by Chinese-style
braised belly pork with spring onions, pak
choi and apple purée; and a daily
seasonal special like Italian sausages on
cannellini bean and potato mash, or
vegetarian baked potato stuffed with leek
and Gruyère cheese on tomato sauce.
Finish with sticky toffee pudding with
caramel sauce, or Valrhona dark chocolate
and raspberry crème brûlée.

You will certainly find a wine to suit your
palate, including from among the nineteen
served by the glass. Real ales keep their
end up too, with Wadworth 6X and guest

ales. Traditional afternoon tea is available
on Fridays and every weekend throughout
the year.

Open all day all wk **Bar Meals** L served all
wk 12-2.30 D served all wk 7-9
Av main course £12.60 ⊞ WADWORTH
◀ Wadworth 6X, IPA, Farmers Glory, Old
Timer, Horizon, guest ales. ♟ 19
Facilities Children's menu Children's
portions Family room Dogs allowed Garden
Parking Wi-fi

PICK OF THE PUBS

The Rose & Thistle 🍷

ROCKBOURNE Map 5 SU11

SP6 3NL ☎ 01725 518236
e-mail: enquiries@roseandthistle.co.uk
web: www.roseandthistle.co.uk
dir: *Follow Rockbourne signs from A354 (Salisbury to Blandford Forum road), or from A338 at Fordingbridge follow signs to Rockbourne*

Standing at the top of a fine main street lined with picture postcard period houses, this pub was originally two 17th-century thatched cottages. A delightful, long and low whitewashed pub located in one of Hampshire's most picturesque downland villages, it is quintessentially English with its stunning rose arch, hanging baskets around the door and a quaint dovecot in the glorious front garden. Country-style fabrics, impressive floral arrangements and magazines to peruse are tasteful touches in the charming beamed bars, which boast a collection of polished oak tables and chairs, carved settles and benches, and two huge fireplaces with blazing winter log fires - perfect to hunker down beside following a breezy downland walk. Expect a relaxing atmosphere, Palmers Copper Ale on tap and interesting pub food from well balanced lunch and dinner menus, and daily dishes that favour fresh fish and local game in season. Bar snacks take in smoked salmon and watercress sandwiches; bacon and mushroom on granary toast; pork and leek sausages with mash and

red wine gravy. From the main menu, order crevettes in hot garlic butter or roasted squash, Stilton and honey-roasted walnut salad for starters. Follow with confit duck on spring onion and chive mash with port gravy; tagliatelle with mushrooms, spinach, garlic and herb butter with crispy Parmesan; peppered New Forest sirloin steak with roasted garlic cloves, red wine and shallot sauce, or one of the fish specials. Round off with bread and butter pudding or spiced orange pannacotta with marsala raisins and toasted almonds. The pub is conveniently placed for visiting Rockbourne's Roman Villa, the New Forest, Salisbury and Breamore House.

Open all wk 11-3 6-11 (Sat 11-11 Sun 12-8) **Bar Meals** L served all wk 12-2.30 booking required D served Mon-Sat 7-9.30

booking required **Restaurant** L served all wk 12-2.30 booking required D served Mon-Sat 7-9.30 booking required
🍺 FREE HOUSE ◀ Fuller's London Pride, Palmers Copper Ale, Timothy Taylor Landlord ⚙ Westons Scrumpy, Black Rat.
🍷 12 **Facilities** Children welcome Children's portions Dogs allowed Garden Parking Wi-fi

PETERSFIELD *continued*

PICK OF THE PUBS

The Trooper Inn ♥

Alton Rd, Froxfield GU32 1BD
☎ 01730 827293   📠 01730 827103
e-mail: info@trooperinn.com
dir: *From A3 take A272 Winchester exit towards Petersfield (NB do not take A272). 1st exit at mini-rdbt for Steep. 3m, pub on right*

Rescued from closure by the present owners in the mid-1990s, this 17th-century free house stands in an isolated location at one of Hampshire's highest points. Said to have been a recruiting centre at the outset of the Great War, The Trooper now boasts winter log fires, spacious bar and a charming restaurant with a vaulted ceiling and wooden settles. Expect seasonal country cooking with fresh fish and game, much of it from local suppliers and producers. Lunchtime sandwiches and baguettes are served with chips and salad, whilst baked fennel, pecan and watercress filo pie; free range chicken breast with Madeira and spiced kumquats; and slow roasted lamb half shoulder of lamb with rich honey and mint gravy are typical main course choices. The inn backs onto Ashford Hangers National Nature Reserve, and is also well positioned for the South Downs National Park, Jane Austen's Chawton and Gilbert White's Selborne.

Open noon-3 6-11 Closed: 25-26 Dec & 1 Jan, Sun eve & Mon L **Bar Meals** L served Tue-Sat 12-2, Sun 12-2.30 booking required D served Mon-Thu 6.30-9, Sat 7-9.30 booking required **Restaurant** L served Tue-Sat 12-2, Sun 12-2.30 booking required D served Mon-Fri 6.30-9, Sat 7-9.30 booking required ⊕ FREE HOUSE ◀ Ringwood Best, Ballards, local guest ales. **Facilities** Children welcome Children's menu Children's portions Dogs allowed Garden Parking Wi-fi

The White Horse Inn

Priors Dean GU32 1DA
☎ 01420 588387   📠 01420 588387
e-mail: details@pubwithnoname.co.uk
dir: *A3/A272 to Winchester/Petersfield. In Petersfield left to Steep, 5m then right at small x-rds to East Tisted, take 2nd drive on right*

Also known as the 'Pub With No Name' as it has no sign, this splendid 17th-century farmhouse was originally used as a forge for passing coaches. The blacksmith sold beer to the travellers while their horses were attended to. Today there is an excellent range of beers including No Name strong, and for something a little different there's rhubarb, damson and elderflower wines too. Menus offer the likes of Hampshire smoked platter; fishcakes; home-made pie of the day; selection of O'Hagans sausages with bubble and squeak. The pub holds a beer festival each June.

Open all wk Mon-Wed 12-3 6-12 (Thu-Sun all day) **Bar Meals** L served all wk 12-2.30 D served all wk 6-9.30 **Restaurant** L served all wk 12-2.30 booking required D served all wk 6-9.30 booking required ⊕ FULLER'S BREWERY ◀ No Name Best, No Name Strong, Ringwood Fortyniner, Sharp's Doom Bar, Seafarers, London Pride. **Facilities** Children welcome Children's menu Children's portions Family room Dogs allowed Garden Beer festival Parking

---

PILLEY Map 5 SZ39

The Fleur de Lys ♥

Pilley St SO41 5QG ☎ 01590 672158
e-mail: a.p.rainford@gmail.com
dir: *From Lymington A337 to Brockenhurst. Cross Ampress Park rdbt, right to Boldre. At end of Boldre Ln turn right. Pub 0.5m*

The Fleur de Lys isn't just the oldest pub in the New Forest – parts of the building originate from 1014 and pre-date the forest that surrounds it. Now in new hands, the pub has been serving ales since 1498 and it remains a traditional thatched pub with open fires and two wood-burning stoves. Outside is a large landscaped garden with wooden tables and chairs. The emphasis here is on simple home-cooked food and the pies are especially popular. There is a beer festival in July.

Open all day all wk 11am-11pm **Bar Meals** Av main course £9 food served all day **Restaurant** food served all day ⊕ ENTERPRISE INNS ◀ Ringwood Best, Guest ales ♒ Stowford Press. ♀ 10 **Facilities** Children welcome Children's menu Children's portions Family room Dogs allowed Garden Beer festival Parking Wi-fi

---

ROCKBOURNE Map 5 SU11

PICK OF THE PUBS

The Rose & Thistle ♥

See Pick of the Pubs on opposite page

ROCKFORD Map 5 SU10

The Alice Lisle ♥

Rockford Green BH24 3NA ☎ 01425 474700
e-mail: alicelisle@fullers.co.uk
dir: *From Ringwood A338 towards Fordingbridge after 1m turn right into Ivy Lane at end turn left cross cattle grid. Inn on left*

Well known New Forest pub with a beautiful garden overlooking a lake, popular with walkers and visitors to the region. It was named after the widow of one of Cromwell's supporters who gave shelter to two fugitives from the Battle of Sedgemoor. Fuller's beers are on offer here with a choice of 10 wines by the glass. Choose from a varied menu which might include jellied New Forest ham and parsley terrine, shellfish bouillabaisse, or one of the walkers' boards. The majority of produce is sourced from New Forest Marque suppliers. Three beer festivals take place in the summer.

Open all day all wk 10am-11pm **Bar Meals** L served Mon-Fri 12-2.30, Sat 12-4, Sun 12-6 D served Mon-Fri 6-9, Sat 5-9 Av main course £10 **Restaurant** L served Mon-Fri 12-2.30, Sat 12-4, Sun 12-6 booking required D served Mon-Fri 6-9, Sat 5-9 Av 3 course à la carte fr £21 ⊕ FULLER'S ◀ HSB, London Pride, Gales Seafarers ♒ New Forest Traditional. ♀ 10 **Facilities** Children welcome Children's menu Children's portions Play area Dogs allowed Garden Beer festival Parking Wi-fi

---

ROMSEY Map 5 SU32

The Cromwell Arms ♥ NEW

23 Mainstone SO51 8HG
☎ 01794 519515   📠 01794 519514
e-mail: dining@thecromwellarms.com
dir: *From Romsey take A27 signed Ringwood, Bournemouth, Salisbury. Cross River Test, pub on right*

With Broadlands, former home of Lord Mountbatten, as its neighbour, The Cromwell Arms derives its name from Romsey's links with the English Civil War. Its Hampshire-skewed offering of real ales includes Double Drop from the town's Flack Manor brewery, which began production in 2009, and a diverse selection of wines. With some unique twists on traditional gastro-pub favourites, typical locally sourced dishes are braised belly of pork; home-cooked honey-roast ham; whole roasted partridge; fillet of wild sea bass; smoked haddock on Cheddar mash; and butternut squash tarte Tatin.

Open all day all wk **Bar Meals** L served Mon-Sat 12-9.30, Sun 12-8.30 D served Mon-Sat 12-9.30, Sun 12-8.30 Av main course £15 food served all day **Restaurant** L served Mon-Sat 12-9.30, Sun 12-8.30 D served Mon-Sat 12-9.30, Sun 12-8.30 Av 3 course à la carte fr £26 food served all day ⊕ FREE HOUSE ◀ Flack Manor Brewery Double Drop, Andwell Brewery Ruddy Darter, Ringwood Best ♒ Thatchers Gold. ♀ 17 **Facilities** Children welcome Children's menu Children's portions Dogs allowed Garden Parking Wi-fi

PICK OF THE PUBS

The Dukes Head ♥

Greatbridge Rd SO51 0HB ☎ 01794 514450
dir: *Telephone for directions*

Dating back to 1468 and close to the Test Way long-distance walk, this rambling, cream-painted pub, festooned with flowers in the summer, nestles in the Test Valley just a stone's throw from England's foremost trout river. There are large gardens at the front and a rear terrace, while inside there's a beamed bar with a big winter log fire, a cosy snug and four other comfortable rooms. Since taking over in 2009, Karen Slowen has built a strong customer base for her range of real ales - at least four guests beers change on a weekly basis – and the enjoyable food she offers at lunch and dinner. Fresh fish and shellfish appear on the daily specials board, with lobster and crab favourites during the summer months. On the supper menu you'll find 'Things you expect on a pub menu' such as the Dukes' burger; other main courses take in pork belly with roast onion mash and black pudding, and desserts such as treacle tart. There is a beer festival in May and September.

Open all day all wk Closed: 25 Dec **Bar Meals** L served all wk 12-2.30 booking required D served all wk 6-9.30 booking required Av main course £11 **Restaurant** L served all wk 12-2.30 booking required D served all wk 6-9.30 booking required ⊕ ENTERPRISE INNS ◀ Fuller's London Pride, Ringwood Best Bitter, Fortyniner, Summer Lightning, Guinness, 4 guest ales. ♀ 10 **Facilities** Children welcome Children's menu Children's portions Dogs allowed Garden Beer festival Parking Wi-fi

ROMSEY *continued*

The Three Tuns ♀

58 Middlebridge St SO51 8HL ☎ 01794 512639
e-mail: manager@the3tuns.co.uk
dir: *Romsey bypass, 0.5m from main entrance of Broadlands Estate*

Brimming with authentic charm, vintage chandeliers, beams, open fireplaces and eye-catching botanical prints, this old inn stands close to the River Test and fabulous riverside walks; its handy, too, for Broadlands, home to the Mountbatten family, and the pretty town centre. New owners carefully balance the appeal of a traditional pub (with Bath Ales amongst those on offer) with hearty pub food; robust classics, sharing platters and Sunday roast amongst them, based on local produce.

Open all day all wk 12-3 5-11 (Fri-Sun noon-11pm) summer all day (Sun 11-10.30) Closed: 25 Dec
Bar Meals L served Mon-Thu 12-2.30, Fri 12-3, Sat-Sun 12-4 D served Mon-Thu 6-9, Fri-Sat 6-9.30, Sun 12-4 Av main course £10 **Restaurant** L served Mon-Thu 12-2.30, Fri 12-3, Sat-Sun 12-4 D served Mon-Thu 6-9, Fri-Sat 6-9.30, Sun 12-4 Av 3 course à la carte fr £22
◀ Ringwood Best, Bath Gem, 2 changing guest ales ♂ Stowford Press. ♀ 10 **Facilities** Children welcome Children's portions Dogs allowed Garden Parking

ST MARY BOURNE   Map 5 SU45

The Bourne Valley Inn ♀

SP11 6BT ☎ 01264 738361 📄 01264 738126
e-mail: enquiries@bournevalleyinn.com
dir: *Telephone for directions*

This popular, traditional inn is an oasis of tranquillity surrounded by fields on the outskirts of St Mary Bourne. Smartly furnished throughout, it has a large character bar with plenty of guest ales and a more intimate dining area, as well as a riverside garden abounding with wildlife where children can let off steam in the special play area. At lunch you could enjoy a filled baguette or old favourites such as ham, egg and chips. The evening menu offers home-made lasagne or steak and Guinness pie alongside chef's specials like slow-roasted belly of pork with redcurrant jus.

Open all day all wk **Bar Meals** L served all wk 12-2.30 D served all wk 6-9 Av main course £9
Restaurant L served all wk 12-2.30 D served all wk 6-9 ⊕ FREE HOUSE ◀ Guest ales. ♀ 12 **Facilities** Children welcome Children's menu Children's portions Play area Dogs allowed Garden Parking Wi-fi

SELBORNE   Map 5 SU73

The Selborne Arms ♀

High St GU34 3JR ☎ 01420 511247 📄 01420 511754
e-mail: info@selbornearms.co.uk
dir: *From A3 follow B3006, pub on left in village centre*

Nick and Hayley Carter's traditional and simply furnished local stands in the heart of Selborne village, famous for its connections with the pioneer naturalist Gilbert White, and the surrounding walks through glorious beech 'hangers'. Walkers and visitors fill the two homely bars, which sport hop-strewn beams and a huge fireplace with a roaring winter log fire, the draw being the local micro-brewery ales and the freshly prepared food. Making sound use of locally sourced produce the menu takes in Hampshire hog beef burger, oxtail and kidney pudding, whole grilled plaice, and traditional fish pie. Don't miss the early October beer festival.

Open all wk 11-3 6-11 (Sat-11-11, Sun 12-11)
Bar Meals L served all wk 12-2 D served Mon-Sat 7-9, Sun 7-8.30 **Restaurant** L served all wk 12-2 D served Mon-Sat 7-9, Sun 7-8.30 ⊕ FREE HOUSE ◀ Courage Best, Ringwood Fortyniner, Suthwyk Old Dick, Local guest ales ♂ Mr Whiteheads. ♀ 10 **Facilities** Children welcome Children's menu Children's portions Play area Garden Beer festival Parking

SILCHESTER   Map 5 SU66

Calleva Arms ♀

Little London Rd, The Common RG7 2PH
☎ 0118 970 0305
dir: *A340 from Basingstoke, signed Silchester. M4 junct 11, 20 mins signed Mortimer then Silchester*

Overlooking the common, this pub is the perfect starting (or finishing) point for visitors to Calleva Atrebatum, a Roman town whose surviving wall is one of the best in Britain. Two bar areas, with a log burner in the middle, lead to a pleasant conservatory and large enclosed garden. A comprehensive menu lists steaks, ribs, chicken balti, battered jumbo cod, teriyaki vegetable stir-fry and daily specials, with roasts every Sunday. Guest beers change frequently.

Open all wk 11-3 5.30-11.30 (Sat 11am-11.30pm Sun noon-11) **Bar Meals** L served al wk 12-2 D served all wk 6.30-9 **Restaurant** L served all wk 12-2 D served all wk 6.30-9 ◀ London Pride, HSB, Guinness, Butser Bitter. ♀ 8 **Facilities** Children welcome Children's portions Dogs allowed Garden Parking

SOUTHAMPTON   Map 5 SU41

The White Star Tavern, Dining & Rooms ★★★★★ INN ⚜⚜ ♀

28 Oxford St SO14 3DJ
☎ 023 8082 1990 📄 023 8090 4982
e-mail: reservations@whitestartavern.co.uk
dir: *M3 junct 13, take A33 to Southampton, towards Ocean Village & Marina*

The illustrious White Star shipping line is the inspiration for this stylish gastro-pub and boutique inn, set in Southampton's cosmopolitan Oxford Street. With two AA Rosettes, the restaurant provides modern British cooking typified by shallot tarte Tatin with truffled mash and organic spinach; and pan-fried bream fillet with Scottish mussels and whipped chorizo mash. Watch the world go by from the pavement tables, or stay a little longer in one of thirteen smart and comfortable bedrooms.

Open all day all wk 7am-11pm (Fri 7am-mdnt, Sat 8.30am-mdnt, Sun 8.30am-10.30pm) Closed: 25 Dec
Bar Meals L served Mon-Thu 7-2.30, Fri 7-3, Sat 9-3, Sun 9-4 D served Mon-Thu & Sat 6-9, Fri 6-10, Sun 6-9.30 **Restaurant** L served Mon-Thu 12-2.30, Fri-Sat 11-3, Sun 12-8 D served Mon-Thu 6-9.30, Fri-Sat 6-10 ⊕ ENTERPRISE INNS ◀ London Pride, Ringwood, Swift One. ♀ 11 **Facilities** Children welcome Children's menu Children's portions Wi-fi **Rooms** 13

SPARSHOLT   Map 5 SU43

PICK OF THE PUBS

The Plough Inn ♀

See Pick of the Pubs on opposite page

Save on hotels. Book at **theAA.com/hotel**

HAMPSHIRE 233 ENGLAND

PICK OF THE PUBS

The Plough Inn ♟

SPARSHOLT
Map 5 SU43

Main Rd SO21 2NW
☎ **01962 776353** 📠 **01962 776400**
dir: *From Winchester take B3049 (A272) W, left to Sparsholt, Inn 1m*

In beautiful countryside, just a few miles out of Winchester, this popular village pub has been a local winner for years. It was built about 200 years ago as a coach house to serve Sparsholt Manor opposite, but within 50 years it had become an alehouse. Inside, the main bar and dining areas blend harmoniously together, with judiciously placed farmhouse-style pine tables, wooden and upholstered seats, and miscellaneous agricultural implements, stone jars, wooden wine box end-panels and dried hops. Wadworth of Devizes supplies all the real ales, and there's a good wine selection.

The dining tables to the left of the entrance look over open fields to wooded downland, and it's at this end of the pub you'll find a blackboard offering dishes such as salmon and crab fishcakes with saffron sauce; lamb's liver and bacon with mash and onion gravy; beef, ale and mushroom pie; and whole baked camembert with garlic and rosemary. The menu board at the right-hand end of the bar offers the more substantial venison steak with celeriac mash and roasted beetroot; roast pork belly with bubble-and-squeak, five spice and sultana gravy; chicken breast filled with goat's cheese mousse; and fillet of sea bass with olive mash. Lunchtime regulars know that 'doorstep' is a most apt description for the great crab and mayonnaise, beef and horseradish and other sandwiches, plus good soups and chicken liver parfait. Puddings include sticky toffee pudding and crème brûlée. The Plough is very popular, so it's best to book for any meal.

The delightful flower- and shrub-filled garden has plenty of room for children to run around and play in. There's a jazz night on the first Sunday in August and carol singing with Father Christmas on 23rd December.

Open all wk 11-3 6-11 (Sun 12-3 6-10.30) Closed: 25 Dec **Bar Meals** L served all wk 12-2 booking required D served Sun-Thu 6-9, Fri-Sat 6-9.30 booking required **Restaurant** L served Mon-Sun 12-2 booking required D served Sun-Thu 6-9, Fri-Sat 6-9.30 booking required 🍺 WADWORTH 🍺 Wadworth Henry's IPA, 6X, Old Timer, JCB. ♟ 15 **Facilities** Children's menu Children's portions Play area Family room Dogs allowed Garden Parking

STEEP
Map 5 SU72

PICK OF THE PUBS

Harrow Inn

GU32 2DA ☎ 01730 262685
dir: *A3 to A272, left through Sheet, take road opposite church (School Ln) then over A3 by-pass bridge*

This 16th-century tile-hung gem is situated in a lovely rural location and has changed little over the years. The McCutcheon family has run it since 1929; sisters Claire and Nisa, both born and brought up here, are now the third generation with their names over the door. Tucked away off the road, it comprises two tiny bars - the 'public' is Tudor, with beams, tiled floor, inglenook fireplace, scrubbed tables, wooden benches, tree-trunk stools and a 'library'; the saloon (or Smoking Room, as it is still called) is Victorian. Beers are dispensed from barrels, there is no till and the toilets are across the road. Food is in keeping: ham and pea soup; hot scotch eggs (some days); Cheddar ploughman's; and various quiches. The large garden has plenty of tables surrounded by country-cottage flowers and fruit trees. Quiz nights raise huge sums for charity, for which Claire's partner Tony grows and sells flowers outside.

Open all wk 12-2.30 6-11 (Sat 11-3 6-11 Sun 12-3 7-10.30) Closed: Sun eve in winter **Bar Meals** L served all wk 12-2 D served all wk 7-9 Av main course £9.50 ⊕ FREE HOUSE ◀ Ringwood Best, Palmers Best, Hop Back GFB, Bowman Ales, Otter Ale Ö Thatchers Heritage. **Facilities** Dogs allowed Garden Parking **Notes** ☺

STOCKBRIDGE
Map 5 SU33

PICK OF THE PUBS

The Greyhound Inn ☺☺ ♥

31 High St SO20 6EY ☎ 01264 810833
e-mail: enquiries@thegreyhound.info
dir: *In village centre*

Refurbished and remodelled in recent years, this classy 15th-century village inn stands in the heart of fly-fishing country midway between Winchester and Salisbury. It backs on to the River Test and the beautiful riverside garden is one of only a handful to be found along its length; the inn has fishing rights on this stretch of the magnificent chalk stream. The history-steeped bar and more contemporary lounge sport polished wood floors, old beams and timbers, subtle spot-lighting, open log fires, and scatter cushions on deep comfy sofas. You could pop in for a pint of Ringwood, but most people are drawn by the first-class modern British cooking, with occasional influences from France and Italy. Simplicity is key to the kitchen's approach, delivering cracking modern dishes with care, finesse and thoughtful composition. Try fresh sage linguini with roasted butternut, pine

nuts and Parmesan; or a piece of halibut, pan-fried to perfection, served with bubble and squeak, wild mushrooms and smoked bacon vinaigrette.

Open all day Closed: 24-26 & 31 Dec, 1 Jan, Sun eve **Bar Meals** L served Mon-Thu 12-2, Fri-Sat 12-2.30 booking required Av main course £15 **Restaurant** L served Mon-Thu 12-2, Fri-Sun 12-2.30 booking required D served Mon-Thu 7-9, Fri-Sat 7-9.30 booking required Av 3 course à la carte fr £30 ⊕ FREE HOUSE ◀ Ringwood Best, Spitfire Bitter. ♥ 8 **Facilities** Children welcome Children's portions Dogs allowed Garden Parking Wi-fi

Mayfly ♥

Testcombe SO20 6AZ ☎ 01264 860283
dir: *Between A303 & A30, on A3057*

Situated right on the banks of the swiftly flowing River Test, this beamed old farmhouse has a traditional bar, a bright conservatory and a splendid riverside terrace. This idyllic, tranquil setting makes the Mayfly a popular drinking spot so arrive early on warm summer days to sup a pint of Adnams Best on a waterside bench. All-day bar food includes salmon and monkfish terrine; spinach and mascarpone lasagne; roasted rack of lamb, spring onion mash and rich minted gravy; and Mexican beef chilli with tortillas. Barry and Julie Lane are celebrating running The Mayfly for 25 years.

Open all day all wk 10am-11pm **Bar Meals** L served all wk 11.30-9 D served all wk 11.30-9 Av main course £9.95 food served all day **Restaurant** food served all day ⊕ FREE HOUSE ◀ Adnams Best, 6X, Fuggle Dee Dum, Summer Lightning, Palmers Gold, Flack's Double Drop Ö Aspall, Green Goblin, Thatchers Gold. ♥ 20 **Facilities** Children welcome Children's portions Dogs allowed Garden Parking

PICK OF THE PUBS

The Peat Spade ☺ ♥

Longstock SO20 6DR ☎ 01264 810612
e-mail: info@peatspadeinn.co.uk
web: www.peatspadeinn.co.uk
dir: *Telephone for directions*

The Peat Spade sits on the banks of the river Test in a corner of Hampshire countryside famed for being the fly-fishing capital of the world. Unusual paned windows overlook the peaceful village lane and idyllic heavily thatched cottages at this striking, redbrick and gabled

Victorian pub. Located between Winchester and Salisbury, this classy country inn is a reminder of a bygone England and its country sport traditions. You will find a relaxed atmosphere in the cosy fishing and shooting themed bar and dining room, and a simple, daily-changing menu listing classic English food. Using locally-sourced produce, including allotment fruit and vegetables and game from the Leckford Estate, the choice may take in crisp pork belly, rocket, capers and lemon dressing for starters, with main dishes ranging from locally shot pheasant with pan-fried bread sauce and braised red cabbage to Test Valley trout and pan-roasted beetroot, watercress and horseradish cream. To drink, there's Ringwood Fortyniner on tap and a choice of 10 wines by the glass – quaff them on the super summer terrace.

Open all day all wk 11am-11pm (Sun 11am-10.30pm) Closed: 25 Dec **Bar Meals** L served all wk 12-2 booking required D served all wk 7-9 booking required Av main course £15 **Restaurant** L served all wk 12-2 booking required D served all wk 7-9 booking required Av 3 course à la carte fr £25 ⊕ MILLER'S COLLECTION ◀ Ringwood Best, Ringwood Fortyniner, Guest ales. ♥ 10 **Facilities** Children welcome Dogs allowed Garden Parking Wi-fi

PICK OF THE PUBS

The Three Cups Inn
INN ♥

High St SO20 6HB ☎ 01264 810527
e-mail: manager@the3cups.co.uk
dir: *M3 junct 8, A303 towards Andover. Left onto A3057 to Stockbridge*

The pub's name apparently comes from an Old English phrase for a meeting of three rivers, although there's only one river here. That river happens to be the Test, generally regarded as the birthplace of modern fly fishing. One of these channels flows through the delightful rear garden of this 15th-century, timber-framed building, where brown trout may be spotted from the patio. The low-beamed bar to the right of the front door can be warmed by the centrally placed log fire; Itchen Valley and Flower Pots, all Hampshire real ales, and a guest, are served here. You can eat in the bar, but the main, candlelit dining area is at the other end of the building. Modern European and traditional selections blend fresh regional ingredients to create starters such as smoked salmon and crème fraîche terrine with citrus dressing; and main courses of rabbit leg braised in sherry, saffron, Savoy cabbage and wild mushroom tortellini. Accommodation suites provide Egyptian cotton sheets and real ground coffee.

Open all day all wk 10am-10.30pm **Bar Meals** L served all wk 12-2.30 D served all wk 6-9.30 **Restaurant** L served all wk 12-2.30 D served all wk 6-9.30 ⊕ FREE HOUSE ◀ Fagin's Itchen Valley, Young's Best Bitter, Flower Pots, Guest ales Ö Stowford Press. **Facilities** Children welcome Children's portions Dogs allowed Garden Parking **Rooms** 8

Save on hotels. Book at **theAA.com/hotel**

HAMPSHIRE 235 **ENGLAND**

SWANMORE	Map 5 SU51

The Rising Sun ♀ NEW

Hill Pound SO32 2PS ☎ 01489 896663
dir: *From M27 junct 10 take A32. Through Wickham towards Alton. Turn left onto Bishop's Wood Rd, right at x-rds into Mislington Rd to Swanmore*

Walkers exploring the beautiful Meon Valley regularly beat a path to the door of this appealing brick and beamed village pub for refreshing pints of Ringwood Best and Sharp's Doom Bar, which are best enjoyed in the secluded rear garden on warm sunny days. Home-cooked food makes good use of locally sourced ingredients, the choice ranging from pub classics in the bar to venison medallions with redcurrant jelly and mustard sauce, and pan-fried halibut with pesto dressing in the cosy dining room and vaulted brick cellar.

Open all wk Mon-Sat 11.30-3 5.30-11 (Sun 12-4 5.30-10.30) **Bar Meals** L served Mon-Sat 12-2, Sun 12-2.30 D served Mon-Sat 6-9, Sun 6-8.30 Av main course £9.75 **Restaurant** L served Mon-Sat 12-2, Sun 12-2.30 D served Mon-Sat 6-9, Sun 6-8.30 Fixed menu price fr £9.40 Av 3 course à la carte fr £25 ⊕ FREE HOUSE ◀ Sharp's Doom Bar, Ringwood Best, Summer Lightning, Marston's Pedigree. ♀ 13 **Facilities** Children welcome Children's menu Children's portions Dogs allowed Garden Parking

TANGLEY	Map 5 SU35

The Fox Inn ♀

SP11 0RU ☎ 01264 730276 📄 01264 730478
e-mail: info@foxinntangley.co.uk
dir: *A343, 4m from Andover*

A 300-year-old brick and flint cottage that has been the Fox since 1830. It stands on a small crossroads, miles, it seems, from anywhere. There is plenty of parking, a front terrace with giant parasol and heater, and another terrace at the back. The interior comprises several different rooms, including the comfortable bar with sofas, chairs and dining tables, and a dedicated dining room. Authentic Thai cuisine is prepared by Thai chefs, with traditional English dishes also available.

Open all day all wk noon-11 (Sun noon-10.30) Closed: 25 Dec, 1 Jan **Bar Meals** L served Mon-Sat 12-2.30, Sun 12-2.45 booking required D served Mon-Sat 6-9.45, Sun 6-8 booking required Av main course £10.95 **Restaurant** L served Mon-Sat 12-2.30, Sun 12-2.45 booking required D served Mon-Sat 6-9.45, Sun 6-8 booking required Av 3 course à la carte fr £18.95 ⊕ FREE HOUSE ◀ London Pride, Ramsbury. ♀ 12 **Facilities** Children welcome Children's menu Children's portions Dogs allowed Garden Parking Wi-fi

TICHBORNE	Map 5 SU53

PICK OF THE PUBS

The Tichborne Arms ♀

SO24 0NA ☎ 01962 733760 📄 01962 733760
e-mail: tichbornearms@xln.co.uk
dir: *Off A31 towards Alresford, after 200yds right at Tichborne sign*

Three pubs have been built on this site, the first in 1429, but each has been destroyed by fire; the present free house is a red-brick building erected in 1939. It sits in an idyllic rural hamlet deep in the heart of the Itchen valley, which was dramatised in a feature film titled *The Tichborne Claimant*. The film told the story of a butcher's boy from Australia who impersonated the son of Lady Tichborne to claim the family title and estates. The pub's picturesque thatched exterior is matched by the eclectic mix of artefacts inside, from stuffed animals and antiques to a chiming grandfather clock. Glowing fires in both bars match the warmth of the welcome from owners Patrick and Nicky Roper, who cook to order daily changing menus of fresh local and seasonal produce. So expect a wide range of game dishes in winter; the fish menu is also extensive. A beer festival is held on the third weekend in August.

Open all wk 11.30-3 6-11.30 (Sat open all day) **Bar Meals** L served all wk 11.30-2 booking required D served all wk 6.30-9 booking required ⊕ FREE HOUSE ◀ Hop Back Brewery, Palmers, Bowman, Sharp's Downton ⋆ Mr Whitehead's Cirrus, Mr Whitehead's Strawberry. ♀ 10 **Facilities** Children welcome Children's portions Dogs allowed Garden Beer festival Parking Wi-fi

UPPER FROYLE	Map 5 SU74

The Hen & Chicken Inn ♀

GU34 4JH ☎ 01420 22115
e-mail: info@henandchicken.co.uk
dir: *2m from Alton, on A31 next to petrol station*

Situated beside the A31 between Alton and Farnham, this 18th-century former coaching inn was once a favoured resting stop for bishops travelling from Winchester to Canterbury. A traditional atmosphere pervades the open-plan bar and dining areas and you'll find a large inglenook fireplace complete with empty post boxes above, plus plenty of wood panelling and beams. Quaff a pint of Hall and Woodhouse Tanglefoot and refuel with a classic steak and kidney pudding, local game and winter vegetable stew, or a big bowl of mussels. There's a children's play area in the garden.

Open all wk Mon-Thu 10-3 5.30-12 (Fri 10-3 5-12 Sat-Sun all day) **Bar Meals** L served all wk 10-2.30 D served all wk 6-9 Av main course £10 **Restaurant** L served all wk 10-2.30 booking required D served all wk 6-9 booking required Fixed menu price fr £9.95 Av 3 course à la carte fr £25 ⊕ HALL & WOODHOUSE ◀ Tanglefoot, Badger, K & B Sussex ⋆ Stowford Press. **Facilities** Children welcome Children's menu Children's portions Play area Dogs allowed Garden Parking Wi-fi

WARNFORD	Map 5 SU62

The George & Falcon ★★★★ INN ♀ NEW

Warnford Rd SO32 3LB
☎ 01730 829623 📄 01730 352222
e-mail: reservations@georgeandfalcon.com
dir: *M27 junct 10, A32 signed Alton. Approx 10.5m to Warnford*

An 18th-century inn reputedly where Colonel Butler refreshed his men before meeting Charles II on Winchester Hill. Today the proximity of the South Downs Way means this watering hole is ideally sited for walkers planning a stop; muddy boots and dogs are always welcome, and six en suite rooms make it perfect for an overnight stay. Marston's ales are on tap, while the menu ranges from lunchtime hot ciabattas to an evening course or two such as farmhouse pâté followed by chicken roly-poly. The beautiful garden leads down to the River Meon.

Open all day all wk **Bar Meals** L served all wk 11-3 D served all wk 6-9.30 Av main course £9.95 **Restaurant** L served all wk 12-3 booking required D served all wk 6-9.30 booking required Fixed menu price fr £12.95 Av 3 course à la carte fr £21 ⊕ MARSTON'S ◀ Ringwood Best & Fortyniner ⋆ Thatchers Gold. ♀ 9 **Facilities** Children welcome Children's menu Children's portions Family room Dogs allowed Garden Parking Wi-fi **Rooms** 6

WARSASH	Map 5 SU40

The Jolly Farmer Country Inn ♀

29 Fleet End Rd SO31 9JH
☎ 01489 572500 📄 01489 885847
e-mail: mail@thejollyfarmeruk.com
dir: *Exit M27 junct 9 towards A27 Fareham, right onto Warsash Rd. Follow for 2m, left onto Fleet End Rd*

The multi-coloured classic cars lined up outside make it hard to miss this friendly country inn. Farming equipment decorates the rustic-style bars, whilst the patio, beer garden and children's play area are popular on warmer days. The comprehensive menu ranges from sandwiches, grills and pub favourites to home-made dishes like vegetable stir-fry, poached salmon in lemon and prawn sauce, and lamb cutlets in port and red wine. There's also a chalkboard menu and children's specials.

Open all day all wk 11am-11pm **Bar Meals** L served Mon-Sat 12-2.30 (Sun all day) D served Mon-Sat 6-10 (Sun all day) **Restaurant** L served all wk 12-2.30 D served all wk 6-10 ⊕ WHITBREAD ◀ Fuller's London Pride & HSB, Interbrew Flowers IPA. ♀ 14 **Facilities** Children welcome Children's menu Children's portions Play area Family room Dogs allowed Garden Parking Wi-fi

WELL   Map 5 SU74

The Chequers Inn ☻

RG29 1TL ☎ 01256 862605 🖹 01256 861116
e-mail: roybwells@aol.com
dir: *From Odiham High St turn right into Long Ln, follow for 3m, left at T-junct, pub 0.25m on top of hill*

Set deep in the heart of the Hampshire countryside, in the village of Well near Odiham, this 15th-century pub is full of charm and old world character, with a rustic, low-beamed bar, log fires, scrubbed tables and vine-covered front terrace. The menu offers good pub food such as sausage and mash with onion gravy; rib-eye steak, chips and béarnaise sauce; and lambs' liver and bacon. There is also an extensive vegetarian menu.

Open all wk noon-3 6-11pm (Sat noon-11pm Sun noon-10.30pm) **Bar Meals** L served Mon-Fri 12-2, Sat 12-3, Sun 12-6 booking required D served Mon-Thu 6.30-9, Fri-Sat 6.30-9.30 booking required Av main course £11 **Restaurant** L served Mon-Fri 12-2, Sat 12-3, Sun 12-6 D served Mon-Thu 6.30-9, Fri-Sat 6.30-9.30 ⊕ HALL & WOODHOUSE ◀ Badger First Gold, Tanglefoot, Seasonal Ales, Guinness Ŏ Stowford Press. 🍷 8 **Facilities** Children welcome Family room Dogs allowed Garden Parking

WEST MEON   Map 5 SU62

PICK OF THE PUBS

The Thomas Lord ☺☺ ☻ NEW

High St GU32 1LN ☎ 01730 829244
dir: *M3 junct 9, A272 towards Petersfield, right at x-roads onto A32, 1st left*

Named after the founder of Lords cricket ground, who is buried in the local churchyard, The Thomas Lord has remained very much a rustic country inn rather than another identikit gastro-pub. Hampshire beers such as Ringwood Best and Winchester Ale feature at a bar festooned with cricketing memorabilia, as do wines from local vineyards in the Test Valley. The pub's own stunning garden supplies the kitchen with many of the herbs, salads and vegetables, as do local farms and small-scale producers. The pub even uses eggs from its own hens and quails. The result is a very tempting menu of seasonal delights with starters such as Hammer Farm smoked trout pâté, asparagus tips and quail's eggs followed by Rother Valley lamb rump, garlic roasted potatoes and rosemary sauce. Finish, perhaps, with New Forest strawberry parfait or Hill Farm apple trifle.

Open Tue-Fri 12-3 5-11, Sat-Sun 12-11 Closed: Mon **Bar Meals** L served Tue-Fri 12-2, Sat-Sun 12-3 booking required D served Tue-Thu & Sun 7-9, Fri-Sat 7-9.30 booking required **Restaurant** L served Tue-Fri 12-2, Sat-Sun 12-3 booking required D served Tue-Thu & Sun 7-9, Fri-Sat 7-9.30 booking required ⊕ ENTERPRISE INNS ◀ Ringwood Best, Bowmans Wallops Wood, Winchester Ale, Swift One, Triple fff, Moondance Ŏ Westons Stowford. 🍷 12 **Facilities** Children welcome Children's portions Dogs allowed Garden Parking Wi-fi

WHITCHURCH   Map 5 SU44

Watership Down Inn

Freefolk Priors RG28 7NJ ☎ 01256 892254
e-mail: watershipdowninn@live.co.uk
dir: *On B3400 between Basingstoke & Andover*

Enjoy an exhilarating walk on Watership Down before relaxing with a pint of well-kept local ale at this homely 19th-century inn named after Richard Adams' classic tale of rabbit life. The pub offers a menu that includes scampi, chips and peas; steak and ale pie; Caribbean chicken; plus baguettes, sandwiches and jacket potatoes. All dishes are available in smaller portions for children, and as takeaways.

Open all day all wk ⊕ PUNCH TAVERNS ◀ Ringwood Best, Young's Special, Sharp's Doom Bar, Cumberland, Bombardier. **Facilities** Children welcome Children's portions Play area Dogs allowed Garden Parking Wi-fi

WICKHAM   Map 5 SU51

Greens Restaurant & Pub ☻

The Square PO17 5JQ ☎ 01329 833197
e-mail: DuckworthGreens@aol.com
dir: *2m from M27, on corner of historic Wickham Square. 3m from Fareham*

Set on a corner of Wickham's picturesque square, Frank and Carol Duckworth have been welcoming customers to award-winning Greens for 26 years. Drinkers will find local ales and high standards of customer service that ensure a warm and welcoming reception. Enjoy mulled wine and warming log fires in winter and head for the garden in warmer weather for Pimms and a barbecue. With a new chef at the helm, the modern British menu includes starters like spicy beef kofta with minted yoghurt, whilst main course options might include 21 day aged roast Hampshire beef sirloin, or pan-fried pigeon breast with red onion tart Tatin.

Open 10-3 6-11 (Sun & BH noon-5, May-Sep all day) Closed: 19-20 May, Sun eve & Mon **Bar Meals** L served Tue-Sat 12-2.30, Sun 12-5 booking required D served Tue-Sat 6.30-9.30 booking required **Restaurant** L served Tue-Sat 12-2.30, Sun 12-3 booking required D served Tue-Sat 6.30-9.30 booking required Fixed menu price fr £13.95 Av 3 course à la carte fr £27 ⊕ FREE HOUSE ◀ Hop Back Summer Lightning, Young's Special, Guinness, Timothy Taylor, Local ales. 🍷 10 **Facilities** Children welcome Children's portions Garden Parking Wi-fi

WINCHESTER   Map 5 SU42

The Bell Inn

83 St Cross Rd SO23 9RE ☎ 01962 865284
e-mail: the_bellinn@btconnect.com
dir: *M3 junct 11, B3355 towards city centre. Approx 1m pub on right*

Edge of town local that's worth noting as it stands close to the 12th-century St Cross Hospital, with its fine Norman church, and glorious walks through the River Itchen water meadows to Winchester College and the city centre. Very much a community local, with Greene King ales and good value food served in the main bar and the pine-furnished lounge, plus a warm welcome to families and dogs. Head for the sunny walled garden on warm summer days. Recent change of hands.

Open all day all wk 11-11 (Fri-Sat 11am-mdnt Sun noon-10.30) ⊕ GREENE KING ◀ IPA, 2 guest ales Ŏ Stowford Press. **Facilities** Children welcome Children's portions Play area Dogs allowed Garden Parking

The Golden Lion NEW

99 Alresford Rd SO23 0JZ ☎ 01962 865512
e-mail: derekandbrid@thegoldenlionwinchester.co.uk
web: www.thegoldenlionwinchester.co.uk
dir: *From Union St in Winchester town centre follow 'All other routes' sign. At rdbt 1st exit onto High St. At rdbt 1st exit onto Bridge St (B3404) signed Alton/Alresford, (becomes Alresford Rd)*

Award-winning flower baskets cover the frontage of Brid and Derek Phelan's 1932-built, but delightfully cottage style, award-winner of a pub on Winchester's eastern fringe. As well as Irish charm, expect main and specials menus offering plenty of straightforward steak and ale pie; gammon steak with egg or pineapple; tempura-battered hake fillet; and spinach and ricotta cannelloni. Soft cushions are provided in the 'treasure chest' by the back door for those sitting in the large beer garden.

Open all wk Mon-Sat 11.30-3 5.30-11 (Sun 12-10.30) **Bar Meals** L served all wk 12-2.30 booking required D served all wk 6-9 booking required Av main course £8.95-£15.45 **Restaurant** L served all wk 12-2.30 booking required D served all wk 6-9 booking required ⊕ WADWORTH ◀ 6X, Henry's IPA, seasonal ales Ŏ Stowford Press. **Facilities** Children welcome Children's menu Children's portions Dogs allowed Garden Parking Wi-fi

See advert on opposite page

Save on hotels. Book at **theAA.com/hotel**

HAMPSHIRE 237 ENGLAND

The Golden Lion

99 Alresford Road, Winchester, Hampshire, SO23 0JZ
Tel: 01962 865512 • **Web:** www.thegoldenlionwinchester.co.uk
E-mail: derekandbrid@thegoldenlionwinchester.co.uk

We warmly invite you to *The Golden Lion Pub*, Winchester, for our cosy vintage style interiors, excellent home cooked food and great Irish welcome! We are located just on the eastern edge of the city, within very easy reach of the M3, the A272 and the A34, just a 10 minute walk into the beautiful heart of the city with all of its historic attractions and wealth of independent shops. We have a large car park as well as patio areas and beer gardens to the front and back, including a special enclosed area for doggies to have a run. We are a TV and gaming machine free zone so that you can relax in our friendly atmosphere and enjoy our great music, and we also welcome children who are eating with their parents/ guardians.

We are very proud to have received many awards for the services that we offer, including 'The Casque Mark' and 'The Beer Master Award' for our real ales, the certification of 'Excellent' for our food hygiene and we have won many First Prizes for our floral displays and hanging baskets. We were also very honoured to have recently been awarded the Wadworth Brewery 'Best Pub of the Year' award.

We have regular live music sessions such as Bluegrass music on the last Tuesday and Irish music on the second Thursday evening of each month.

We are really pleased to receive regular visitors who return again and again for the traditional home-cooked food and the constantly changing daily specials menus – so much so that we would recommend booking a table to avoid disappointment! We can also offer to arrange all your party booking requirements, whether you are planning a formal sit-down meal, a more casual finger buffet or a barbecue in the summer under our recently installed canopied 'Garden Room'.

We very much look forward to welcoming you very soon!

WINCHESTER continued

The Old Vine ★★★★ INN ♥ NEW

8 Great Minster St SO23 9HA
☎ **01962 854616** 📄 **01962 854616**
e-mail: reservations@oldvinewinchester.com
dir: *M3 junct 11 towards St Cross, turn right at Green Man Pub, left onto Symonds St, left onto Little Minster St*

Facing Winchester's fine cathedral, this 18th-century pub takes its name from the elderly vine rambling over the street frontage, while the interior's vestigial doorways and other features in unexpected places suggest a complex architectural history. Freshly prepared, locally sourced British and European food is served in the restaurant, and Timothy Taylor Landlord vies with three Hampshire real ales in the oak-beamed bar. Beautifully presented accommodation features Georgian, Arts and Crafts, Victorian and Art Deco furniture.

Open all day all wk Closed: 25 Dec **Bar Meals** L served Mon-Thu 12-2.30, Fri-Sun 12-6 D served Mon-Sat 6.30-9.30, Sun 6.30-9 Av main course £10.90 **Restaurant** L served Mon-Thu 12-2.30, Fri-Sun 12-3 booking required Av 3 course à la carte fr £20 ⊕ ENTERPRISE INNS ◀ Ringwood Best, Timothy Taylor Landlord, Guest ales (1 local). ♥ 11 **Facilities** Dogs allowed **Rooms** 5

The Westgate Inn ★★★ INN

2 Romsey Rd SO23 8TP
☎ **01962 820222** 📄 **01962 820222**
e-mail: wghguy@yahoo.co.uk
dir: *On corner of Romsey Rd & Upper High St, opposite Great Hall & Medieval West Gate*

When the railway developed its routes to the west, brewer Eldridge Pope saw the potential to transport its ales to London and provide accommodation and refreshment to travellers since the 1850s. This listed Palladian building in Winchester's main shopping street was created from three buildings opposite the medieval West Gate. Impressive home-cooked meals, based on locally sourced ingredients, are served along with real ales and ciders, including succulent steaks, fish and chips and share platters. Attractive and good-sized accommodation is available.

Open all day all wk noon-11.30 **Bar Meals** L served all wk 7-2.30 D served all wk 6-9.30 Av main course £8.50 **Restaurant** L served all wk 12-2.30 D served all wk 6-9.30 ⊕ MARSTONS ◀ Jennings Cumberland, Banks Original, Marstons Burton Bitter, Guest ales Ŏ Thatchers Gold, Wychwood Green Goblin. **Facilities** Dogs allowed Wi-fi **Rooms** 8

PICK OF THE PUBS

The Wykeham Arms ♥

75 Kingsgate St SO23 9PE
☎ **01962 853834** 📄 **01962 854411**
e-mail: wykehamarms@fullers.co.uk
dir: *Near Winchester College & Winchester Cathedral*

A fine 270-year-old brick building located in the oldest part of the city between the cathedral close and Winchester's famous college. Full of character and always buzzing with activity it draws an eclectic mix of customers, from businessmen and barristers, clergy and college Dons to tourists and local drinkers and diners. The rambling series of character bars and eating areas are furnished with old pine tables and old-fashioned college desks, and boast four welcoming winter log fires and an impressive collection of hats, fascinating pictures and military memorabilia adorn every available wall space. Follow a town or water meadow stroll with a satisfying lunch from the modern, seasonal menu, perhaps a minute steak and Barkham Blue rarebit sandwich, or duck leg with bean cassoulet and spiced tomato coulis. Evening choices extend to Hursley venison Wellington and chargrilled Manor Farm rib-eye steak with Bordelaise sauce, with bitter chocolate tart for pudding. Wash down with a cracking pint of London Pride, or one of 20 excellent wines by the glass.

Open all day all wk 11-11 (Sun 11-10.30) **Bar Meals** L served all wk 12-3 Av main course £11 **Restaurant** L served all wk 12-3 booking required D served all wk 6-9.30 booking required Av 3 course à la carte fr £25 ⊕ FULLER'S ◀ HSB, London Pride, Chiswick, Seafarer, Bengal Lancer, Flowerpots, Guest ales Ŏ Aspall. ♥ 20 **Facilities** Dogs allowed Garden Parking Wi-fi

---

HEREFORDSHIRE

ASTON CREWS	Map 10 SO62

PICK OF THE PUBS

The Penny Farthing Inn

HR9 7LW ☎ **01989 750366** 📄 **01989 750366**
e-mail: thepennyfarthinginn@hotmail.co.uk
dir: *5m E of Ross-on-Wye*

This whitewashed 17th-century blacksmith's shop and coaching inn is located high above the Wye Valley, with stunning views of the Malvern Hills, the Black Mountains and the Forest of Dean. Inside are lots of nooks and crannies with oak beams, antiques, saddlery and warming log fires. The menu capitalises on the wealth of local vegetable and fruit growers' produce, and some of the best meat in the country. Begin with sauté king prawns in coriander batter with sweet chilli dip or creamy garlic mushrooms, then follow with slow roast belly pork with red wine gravy; pan-fried guinea fowl supreme with thyme and bacon gravy, or one of the daily chalkboard specials, perhaps medallions of

---

monkfish with king prawns in a saffron sauce. For those who want to pack their walking boots, footpaths radiate from the front door.

Open all wk Mon 6-11, Tue-Thu noon-3 6-11, Fri noon-3 6-mdnt, Sat noon-mdnt, Sun noon-10.30 **Bar Meals** L served Tue-Sun 12-2.30 D served Tue-Sat 6-9 Av main course £8.95 **Restaurant** L served Tue-Sun 12-2.30 D served Tue-Sat 6-9 ⊕ PUBFOLIO ◀ Hobgoblin, Black Sheep, 6X Ŏ Westons Stowford Press. **Facilities** Children welcome Children's menu Children's portions Play area Dogs allowed Garden Parking Wi-fi

AYMESTREY	Map 9 SO46

PICK OF THE PUBS

The Riverside Inn

See Pick of the Pubs on opposite page

BODENHAM	Map 10 SO55

England's Gate Inn

HR1 3HU ☎ **01568 797286** 📄 **01568 797768**
e-mail: englandsgate@btconnect.com
dir: *Hereford A49, turn onto A417 at Bosey Dinmore hill, 2.5m on right*

A pretty black and white coaching inn dating from around 1540, with atmospheric beamed bars and blazing log fires in winter. A picturesque beer garden attracts a good summer following, and so does the food. The menu features such dishes as slowly roasted shank of Ledbury lamb with parsnip and cardamom purée in red wine jus; baked fillet of cod topped with a garlic and herb crumble; or wholemeal pancakes filled with spinach and cream cheese served with ratatouille. The annual beer and sausage festival, featuring locally produced beer and cider, is a well-known local event with live bands playing in the garden.

Open all day all wk **Bar Meals** L served all wk 12-2.30 D served all wk 6-9.30 **Restaurant** L served all wk 12-2.30 D served all wk 6-9.30 booking required ⊕ FREE HOUSE ◀ Wye Valley Bitter, Butty Bach, Shropshire Lad, Guest ales. **Facilities** Children welcome Children's menu Children's portions Dogs allowed Garden Beer festival Parking Wi-fi

Save on hotels. Book at **theAA.com/hotel**

HEREFORDSHIRE 239 ENGLAND

PICK OF THE PUBS

The Riverside Inn

AYMESTREY   Map 9 SO46

HR6 9ST ☎ 01568 708440
e-mail: theriverside@btconnect.com
web: www.theriversideinn.org
dir: *On A4110, 18m N of Hereford*

On a still and foggy November night you may still hear the Roman infantry marching along Watling Street as it crosses the River Lugg beside this ancient free house. Built in 1580, the pub is halfway along the Mortimer Trail from Ludlow to Kington, and numerous circular walks, with plenty of wildlife to spot, start from the front door. Anglers are also drawn to stay at the inn, which offers its residents private fishing for brown trout and grayling. The wood panelled interior with its low beams and log fires engenders a relaxed atmosphere that reflects the pub's long history. Real ales and ciders, drawing on the Marches' tradition of brewing and cider making, include Wye Valley Bitter and Three Tuns XXX as well as Brooke Farm cider from nearby Wigmore. Owner Richard Gresko aims to offer seriously good food that's 'truly seasonal and truly local'. He encourages visitors to take a stroll round the pub's extensive vegetable, herb and fruit gardens; strung above the secluded riverside beer garden, these are some of the nicest that you'll find anywhere. Diners are promised classic British dishes with a modern twist, produced from the finest ingredients by an award winning team of

chefs. As you'd expect, the menus change constantly throughout the year, but a typical dinner might begin with pan-fried River Lugg trout with sweet garlic palette and a mint, parsley and caper dressing. Main course options could feature a rare-breed Herefordshire stew of best shin and oxtail with wild mushroom and garden kale, parsnip purée and parsnip crisps; or roasted winter root vegetables in a creamy spinach, mustard and local Monkland cheese sauce, with celeriac purée and frisée salad. Leave space for one of the tempting desserts such as garden rhubarb and apple hazelnut crumble with home-made elderflower ice cream.

Open 11-3 6-11 (Sun 12-3 6-10.30)
Closed: 26 Dec & 1 Jan, Sun eve, Mon
L, Mon eve in winter **Bar Meals** L served
Tue-Sun 12-2 booking required D served
Mon-Sat 7-9 booking required Av main
course £9.95 **Restaurant** L served
Tue-Sun 12-2 booking required D served
Mon-Sat 7-9 booking required Av 3 course
à la carte fr £22.50 ⊞ FREE HOUSE
◀ Wye Valley Bitter & Butty Bach,
Hobsons Best Bitter, Three Tuns XXX
Ŏ Brooke Farm Medium Dry, Westons
Stowford Press, Robinsons Flagon Cider.
Facilities Children's menu Children's
portions Dogs allowed Garden Parking
Wi-fi

BRINGSTY COMMON   Map 10 SO75

PICK OF THE PUBS

Live and Let Live

WR6 5UW ☎ 01886 821462
e-mail: theliveandletlive@tiscali.co.uk
dir: *From A44 (Bromyard to Worcester road) turn at sign with cat onto track leading to the common. At 1st fork bear right. Pub 200yds on right*

Secluded on Bringsty Common amidst bracken and old orchards, this lovely thatched cider house is one of the oldest buildings in the area. It was closed for eleven years while planning permission was sought and a complete renovation undertaken by owner Sue Dovery. It reopened in 2007 with its sand-blasted timber framing exposed for all to appreciate. Local Oliver's cider is joined by beers from various south Marches micro-breweries. Bar meals and the intimate Thatch restaurant major on seasonal food from the home area. A typical three-course meal could comprise bacon and black pudding salad with dressed mixed leaves topped with a poached egg; home-made steak and kidney pie with short-crust pastry, served with proper chips and garden peas; and dessert of milk chocolate and honeycomb truffle tart. A four-day beer and cider festival runs over the Easter weekend, when live music adds to the entertainment.

Open Tue-Thu 12-2.30 5.30-11 Fri-Sun all day (summer noon-11) Closed: Mon (ex BHs) **Bar Meals** L served all wk 12-2 D served all wk 6-9 Av main course £9.95 **Restaurant** D served all wk 6-9 Fixed menu price fr £10 ⊕ FREE HOUSE ◀ MHB, Ludlow, Wye Valley, Hobsons Ò Olivers, Robinsons. **Facilities** Children welcome Children's portions Dogs allowed Garden Beer festival Parking **Notes** ⊛

CAREY   Map 10 SO53

Cottage of Content NEW

HR2 6NG ☎ 01432 840242
dir: *From x-roads on A49 between Hereford & Ross-on-Wye. follow Hoarwithy signs. In Hoarwithy branch right, follow Carey signs*

Situated within beautiful, unspoilt countryside a short drive from Hereford and Ross-on-Wye, this 15th-century inn started life as three labourers' cottages. A popular spot for walkers and ramblers, the pub offers local Wye Valley ales and local ciders, plus a simple menu that appeals to all, with children well catered for. Popular meal options include Double Gloucester cheese and ale pot, followed by rib-eye of Herefordshire beef on grain mustard mash or local lamb and mint pie, finishing with spotted dick and custard.

Open 12-2 6.30-11 (times vary summer & winter) Closed: 1wk Feb, 1wk Oct, Sun eve, Mon, Tue L (winter only) **Bar Meals** L served Tue-Sat 12-2 Av main course £12.50 **Restaurant** L served Tue-Sun 12-2 D served Tue-Sat 6.30-9 Av 3 course à la carte fr £23.50 ⊕ FREE HOUSE ◀ Wye Valley Butty Bach, Hobsons Best Bitter Ò Broome Farm, Carey Organic, Stowford Press. **Facilities** Children welcome Children's menu Children's portions Dogs allowed Garden Parking Wi-fi

CRASWALL   Map 9 SO23

The Bulls Head

HR2 0PN ☎ 01981 510616
e-mail: info@thebullsheadcraswall.co.uk
dir: *From A465 turn at Pandy. Village in 11m*

Set in a remote spot at the foot of the Black Mountains, this old drovers' inn is not easy to find but well worth the effort. Just six miles from Hay on Wye, it is popular with walkers and riders, who tie their horses at the rail outside. Real ales and farmhouse ciders are served through the hole in the wall servery in the character bar with its flagstone floors and log fires in winter. Typical seasonal dishes include a starter of home-cured bresaola or roasted Piedmont pepper and feta cheese; followed by navarin of new season's Craswall lamb with summer vegetables or spaghetti with crab meat, cherry tomatoes and chillies.

Open 12-3 6.30-11 Closed: winter months, Mon-Wed **Bar Meals** L served 12-2 D served 6.30-8.30 Av main course £15 **Restaurant** L served 12-2 D served 6.30-8.30 Fixed menu price fr £26 Av 3 course à la carte fr £27.50 ⊕ FREE HOUSE ◀ Butty Bach, Wye Valley Bitter Ò Gwatkin's Farmhouse & Norman, Westons Old Rosie Scrumpy. **Facilities** Children welcome Dogs allowed Garden Wi-fi

DORSTONE   Map 9 SO34

PICK OF THE PUBS

The Pandy Inn

HR3 6AN ☎ 01981 550273
e-mail: info@pandyinn.co.uk
web: www.pandyinn.co.uk
dir: *Off B4348 W of Hereford*

The Pandy is one of the oldest inns in the country and has a fascinating history. One of the four Norman knights who killed Thomas à Becket in Canterbury Cathedral in 1170, Richard de Brito, built a chapel at Dorstone as an act of atonement after 15 years in the Holy Land. He also built the Pandy to house the workers, subsequently adapting it to become an inn. Later, during the Civil War in the 17th century, Oliver Cromwell is known to have taken refuge here. The ancient hostelry is located opposite the village green and part of it retains its original flagstone floors and beams. The large garden, which offers 19 tables and a children's playground, has views of Dorstone Hill. Food

is freshly prepared daily and the seasonal menu includes Pandy pies and home-made puddings. Farmhouse ciders are served alongside local cask ales.

Open Tue-Fri noon-3, 6-11 (Sat noon-11, Sun noon-3, 6.30-10.30) Closed: Mon Oct-Jun (ex BH & Mon eve in school summer hols) **Bar Meals** L served all wk 12-2 **Restaurant** L served all wk 12-2 D served all wk 6.30-9 ⊕ FREE HOUSE ◀ Wye Valley Butty Bach, Golden Valley Brewer's Choice Ò Stowford Press. **Facilities** Children welcome Children's menu Children's portions Play area Dogs allowed Garden Parking Wi-fi

HAMPTON BISHOP   Map 10 SO53

The Bunch of Carrots ♥

HR1 4JR ☎ 01432 870237 🖺 01432 870237
e-mail: bunchofcarrots@buccaneer.co.uk
dir: *From Hereford take A4103, A438, then B4224*

The pub's name has nothing to do with crunchy orange vegetables – it's a reference to a rock formation in the River Wye, which runs alongside this pub. It's a family-friendly place, with a children's play area outside. Inside are real fires, old beams and flagstones, ideal surroundings in which to sample a pint of Wye Valley. The extensive menu of pub favourites, backed by a daily specials board, centres around a carvery which operates seven days a week: two roast meats, sourced from Herefordshire, are accompanied by freshly prepared seasonal vegetables.

Open all wk **Bar Meals** L served Mon-Fri 12-2, Sat-Sun 12-9.30 D served Mon-Fri 5.30-9.30, Sat-Sun 12-9.30 Av main course £11 **Restaurant** L served Mon-Fri 12-2, Sat-Sun 12-9.30 booking required D served Mon-Fri 5.30-9.30, Sat-Sun 12-9.30 booking required Av 3 course à la carte fr £21 ⊕ FREE HOUSE ◀ Wye Valley Bitter, Doom Bar, Courage, Best Bitter Ò Westons Stowford Press. ♥ 10 **Facilities** Children welcome Children's menu Play area Dogs allowed Garden Parking Wi-fi

HOARWITHY   Map 10 SO52

The New Harp Inn ♥

HR2 6QH ☎ 01432 840900
e-mail: adrianchef@btinternet.com
dir: *From Ross-on-Wye take A49 towards Hereford. Turn right for Hoarwithy.*

Situated on the River Wye, this pub is popular with locals, fishermen, campers and visitors to the countryside. A real country pub, its slogan reads: 'kids, dogs and muddy boots all welcome'. Begin with a great choice of local real ale, an unusual foreign bottled beer or a home-produced cider. The menu includes tapas and nibbles such as peppers with feta or roasted tomatoes. After that, maybe Serrano ham and goat's cheese parcel with white balsamic and pine nuts followed by traditional steak and local ale cobbler topped with a Hereford cheese scone. Outside are extensive gardens and a real babbling brook. Look out for beer festivals on Bank Holidays.

Save on hotels. Book at **theAA.com/hotel**

HEREFORDSHIRE 241 **ENGLAND**

Open all wk Mon-Thu noon-3 6-11 (Fri-Sun all day)
Bar Meals L served all wk 12-3 D served all wk 6-9 Av
main course £7.95 **Restaurant** L served all wk 12-3
D served all wk 6-9 Fixed menu price fr £12 Av 3 course à
la carte fr £18 ⊕ FREE HOUSE ◂▪ Timothy Taylor
Landlord, Wye Valley, Malvern Pear, Wickwar BOB,
Holden's Best Bitter, Holden's Golden Glow Ō Stowford
Press, New Harp Reserve. ♇ 8-10 **Facilities** Children
welcome Children's menu Children's portions Play area
Dogs allowed Garden Beer festival Parking Wi-fi

KILPECK   Map 9 SO43

The Kilpeck Inn ♇ NEW

HR2 9DN ☎ **01981 570464**
e-mail: booking@kilpeckinn.com
web: www.kilpeckinn.com
dir: *From Hereford take A465 S. In 6m at Belmont rdbt
left towards Kilpeck. Follow church & inn signs*

Saved from redevelopment as a private dwelling in 2006,
the Red Lion — as it was known 250 years ago — reopened
as the Kilpeck Inn in 2010. Sensitive refurbishment
focussed on bestowing excellent green credentials:
underfloor heating is driven by a wood pellet burner;
rainwater is recovered to flush the loos; solar panels heat
the water; even food and staff miles are minimised by
sourcing people and ingredients as close to the pub as
possible. Wye Valley ales and Westons ciders from nearby
Much Marcle head the drinks list, while dishes range
from bar snacks to char-grilled steaks.

Open all wk **Bar Meals** L served all wk 12-2 D served all
wk 6-9 Av main course £15 **Restaurant** L served all wk
12-2 booking required D served all wk 7-9 booking
required Av 3 course à la carte fr £25 ◂▪ Butcombe Bitter,
Wye Valley Butty Bach, Golden Valley 410 Ō Stowford
Press. ♇ 9 **Facilities** Children welcome Children's
portions Dogs allowed Garden Parking Wi-fi

KIMBOLTON   Map 10 SO56

PICK OF THE PUBS

Stockton Cross Inn ♇

HR6 0HD ☎ **01568 612509**   🖹 **01568 620238**
e-mail: mb@ecolots.co.uk
web: www.stocktoncrossinn.co.uk
dir: *On A4112, 0.5m off A49, between Leominster &
Ludlow*

A drovers' inn dating from the 16th century, the
Stockton Cross Inn stands beside a crossroads where
witches, rounded up from the surrounding villages
such as Ludlow, were allegedly hanged. This grisly past
is at odds with the peace and beauty of the setting,
which includes a pretty country garden with umbrellas
and trees for shade. The building itself is regularly
photographed by tourists and featured on calendars
and chocolate boxes. Landlord Mike Bentley tends a
range of ales which include Wye Valley Butty Bach and
HPA, Flowers Best Bitter and guest ales. Children are
welcome and enjoy their own menu. In addition to the
specials board, dishes on the menu might include
smoked haddock and risotto cake; glazed goat's
cheese, black olive and sundried tomato salad and
basil pesto; beer battered fish and home made chips;
cottage pie and vegetables; locally made sausages
with mash and onion gravy. If you've room left, maybe
tuck into a dessert of rhubarb and apple crumble. All
meals are prepared on the premises using organic
produce wherever possible.

Open 12-3 7-11 Closed: Sun eve & Mon
Bar Meals L served Tue-Sun 12-2 D served Tue-Sat 7-9
Restaurant L served Tue-Sun 12-2 D served Tue-Sat
7-9 ⊕ FREE HOUSE ◂▪ Wye Valley Butty Bach & HPA,
Flowers Best Bitter, Guest ales Ō Robinsons Flagon,
Stowford Press. ♇ 8 **Facilities** Children welcome
Children's menu Children's portions Garden Parking
Wi-fi

KINGTON   Map 9 SO25

PICK OF THE PUBS

The Stagg Inn and Restaurant ⊛⊛ ♇

Titley HR5 3RL ☎ **01544 230221**   🖹 **01544 231390**
e-mail: reservations@thestagg.co.uk
dir: *Between Kington & Presteigne on B4355*

Titley stands amid unspoilt Welsh border countryside
at the junction of two drovers' roads. Wool would have
been weighed here – it was known as the Balance until
Eliza Greenley of Titley Court gave the building its brick
frontage and named it after her family crest in 1833;
where the second 'g' in the title came from is a
mystery. Farmhouse tables and crackling log fires
make for a relaxed atmosphere in the rambling dining
rooms and homely bar, where local farmers gather for
pints of Hobson's and local cider on draught, to
accompany bar snacks like devilled kidneys with rice.
Local boy and Roux-trained chef Steve Reynolds has a
passion for local produce, and his assured modern
approach to cooking allows key flavours to shine
through in such robust dishes as gnocchi with
Jerusalem artichoke, chicory and Caerphilly cheese,
and saddle of Marches venison. Cheese lovers should
allow time to choose between the twenty or so options
available.

Open Tue-Sun 12-3 (Tue-Sat 6.30-10.30) Closed:
25-27 Dec, 2wks Nov, 2wks Jan & Feb, Sun eve & Mon
Bar Meals L served Tue-Sat 12-2 booking required
D served Tue-Thu 6.30-9 booking required Av main
course £10.50 **Restaurant** L served Tue-Sun 12-2
booking required D served Tue-Sat 6.30-9 booking
required Av 3 course à la carte fr £26.50 ⊕ FREE
HOUSE ◂▪ Ludlow Gold, Hobson's Best Bitter
Ō Dunkertons, Westons, Ralph's. ♇ 12
Facilities Children's portions Dogs allowed Garden
Parking Wi-fi

LEDBURY   Map 10 SO73

The Farmers Arms

Horse Rd, Wellington Heath HR8 1LS ☎ **01531 632010**
dir: *Through Ledbury, pass rail station, right into
Wellington Heath, 1st right for pub*

Standing at the bottom of a country lane, this charming
country inn has an elevated position over the village
green. Wye Valley's Butty Bach and Sharp's Doom Bar are
among the beers in the bar. The comprehensive menu
makes good use of local produce, such as Pontypool loin
of lamb; grilled 12oz Hereford rib-eye steak; escalope of
Severn and Wye salmon; and Maynard Farm caramelised
ham. Heated, covered seating on the patio is tailor-made
for outdoor eating; there's a children's play area too.
Recent change of hands.

Open all wk ⊕ BERMILL LTD ◂▪ London Pride, Wye Valley,
Doom Bar, Guest ales. **Facilities** Children welcome
Children's menu Play area Dogs allowed Garden Parking

LEDBURY *continued*

Prince of Wales NEW

Church Ln HR8 1DL ☎ 01531 632250
e-mail: pebblewalk@gmail.com
dir: *M50 junct 2, A417 to Ledbury. Pub in town centre behind Market House (black & white building) on cobbled street (parking nearby)*

In an enchanting spot hidden between Ledbury's memorable half-timbered market house and the ancient church, a cobbled alley lined by eye-catching medieval houses hosts this cracking little pub. All low beams with bags of character, folk nights add to the craic at this half-timbered gem, where home-made pies or pork and beef sausages from a local butcher are firm favourites on the traditional pub menu. The local theme continues, with cider from Weston's at neighbouring Much Marcle and beers from Wye Valley Brewery just down the road complementing a huge range of guest ales.

Open all day all wk **Bar Meals** L served all wk 12-2.30 D served all wk 6-8.30 Av main course £6.25 ⊕ FREE HOUSE ◀ Hobsons Bitter, Sharp's Doom Bar, Wye Valley Butty Bach & HPA, Guest ales ♂ Westons First Quality & Vintage Organic. **Facilities** Children welcome Children's menu Dogs allowed Garden

The Talbot ♈

14 New St HR8 2DX ☎ 01531 632963 📄 01531 636107
e-mail: talbot.ledbury@wadworth.co.uk
dir: *Follow Ledbury signs, turn into Bye St, 2nd left into Woodley Rd, over bridge to junct, left into New St. Pub on right*

Right at the heart of medieval Ledbury, this multi-gabled, half-timbered coaching inn overflows with history (parts date from 1550), whilst panelled rooms and restaurant radiate character. After a stroll in the nearby Malvern Hills or Leadon Valley, retire to the bar, warm up by the log fire, sip a Herefordshire-brewed Wye Valley Butty Bach or, unusually, local Westons perry and share a platter of starters prior to a plate of speciality sausage and mash or seared lamb's liver, black pudding and bacon. There is a courtyard garden for the warmer weather.

Open all day all wk **Bar Meals** L served all wk 12-2.30 D served all wk 6-9.15 **Restaurant** L served all wk 12-2.30 D served all wk 6-9.15 ⊕ WADWORTH ◀ Wadworth 6X & Henrys Original IPA, Wye Valley Butty Bach, Wadworth guest ales ♂ Stowford Press, Westons Organic, Westons Perry. ♈ 15 **Facilities** Children's portions Garden Wi-fi

The Trumpet Inn

Trumpet HR8 2RA ☎ 01531 670277
e-mail: trumpet@wadworth.co.uk
dir: *4m from Ledbury, at junct of A438 & A417*

This former coaching inn and post house takes its name from the days when mail coaches blew their horns on approaching the crossroads. A traditional black and white building, it dates back to the late 14th century. The cosy bars feature a wealth of exposed beams, with open fireplaces and a separate dining area. There is Camembert or fisherman's platters to share, and main courses like Mr Waller's trio of sausages with mash and onion gravy, Angus beef burgers, or risotto or pie of the day.

Open all day all wk **Bar Meals** L served Mon-Sat 12-2.30, Sun 12-9 booking required D served Mon-Sat 6-9, Sun 12-9 booking required Av main course £10 **Restaurant** L served Mon-Sat 12-2.30, Sun 12-9 booking required D served Mon-Sat 6-9, Sun 12-9 booking required Fixed menu price fr £7.95 Av 3 course à la carte fr £20 ⊕ WADWORTH & CO LTD ◀ Wadworth 6X, Henrys IPA ♂ Stowford Press. **Facilities** Children welcome Dogs allowed Garden Parking Wi-fi

The Grape Vaults

Broad St HR4 8BS ☎ 01568 611404
e-mail: jusaxon@tiscali.co.uk
dir: *Telephone for directions*

This unspoilt pub is so authentic that even its fixed seating is Grade II listed. Its many charms include a small, homely bar complete with real fire. A good selection of real ale is a popular feature, and includes micro-brewery offerings. The food includes favourites like steak and ale pie and various fresh fish dishes. No piped music, gaming machines or alcopops! There is live music every Sunday and in December a beer festival takes place on the same day as the Victorian street market.

Open all day all wk 11-11 **Bar Meals** L served all wk 12-2 D served Mon-Sat 5.30-9 Av main course £7 ⊕ PUNCH TAVERNS ◀ Ludlow Best, Mayfields, 3 Tuns, Woods, Malvern Hills, Guest ales ♂ Stanford Press. **Facilities** Children's portions Dogs allowed Beer festival Wi-fi **Notes** ⊠

The Three Horseshoes Inn

HR7 4RQ ☎ 01885 400276 📄 01885 400276
e-mail: info@threehorseshoes.co.uk
dir: *Off A456 (Hereford/Bromyard). At Stokes Cross follow Little Cowarne/Pencombe signs*

They no longer shoe horses at the blacksmith next door, but this old ale house's long drinking pedigree - 200 years and counting - looks secure. Norman and Janet Whittall have seen over 20 years here and have redecorated throughout; their son Philip, the head chef, creates dishes sourced mainly from fresh, local ingredients; some are grown in the inn's garden. There's a good range of bar snacks but the restaurant menu could feature pork and pheasant pâté with pickled damsons; pan-fried Herefordshire venison with sloe gin sauce; or pheasant breast stuffed with spiced pear with elderberry sauce. Well travelled Philip turns his talents to more exotic dishes for an 'all you can eat' curry night each Wednesday.

Open 11-3 6.30-mdnt (Sun noon-4 7-mdnt) Closed: 25-26 Dec, 1 Jan & Sun eve in Winter ⊕ FREE HOUSE ◀ Greene King Old Speckled Hen, Wye Valley Bitter, Ruddles Best ♂ Stowford Press, Olivers Cider, Perry. **Facilities** Children's menu Children's portions Family room Garden Parking

The Comet Inn

Stoney St HR2 9NJ ☎ 01981 250600
e-mail: thecometinn-madley@hotmail.co.uk
dir: *6m from Hereford on B4352*

Set at a crossroads deep in rural Herefordshire, the space-age parabolic dishes of the Madley Earth Station and the distant smudge of the Black Mountains provide contrasting skylines visible from the large grounds of this convivial local. Within, it retains much of the character of the old cottages from which it was converted over 100 years ago. Vicky Willison, the enthusiastic and welcoming owner, serves a select range of Herefordshire and Worcestershire-brewed beers to accompany simple and hearty home-cooked pub food in the conservatory off the main bar, with smaller portions for smaller appetites if required. There is a large garden with children's play area.

Open all wk 12-3 6-11 (Fri-Sun all day) **Bar Meals** food served all day **Restaurant** food served all day ⊕ FREE HOUSE ◀ Wye Valley Bitter, Butty Bach, guest ales from St George's Brewery ♂ Stowford Press. **Facilities** Children welcome Children's menu Children's portions Play area Garden Parking Wi-fi

The Slip Tavern

Watery Ln HR8 2NG ☎ 01531 660246 📄 01531 660700
e-mail: thesliptavern@aol.com
dir: *Follow signs off A449 at Much Marcle junction*

Curiously named after a 1575 landslip which buried the local church, this country pub is delightfully surrounded by cider apple orchards. An attractive conservatory overlooks the award-winning garden, where summer dining is popular, and there's also a cosy bar with roaring fires in winter. Being situated next to Weston's Cider Mill, cider is a favourite in the bar along with real ales from the cask. There are regular jazz and folk evenings.

Open all wk Tue-Sun 12-3 6-11.30 Closed: Mon ⊕ FREE HOUSE ◀ John Smith's, Butcombe, Guest ales ♂ Stowford Press. Vintage Organic. **Facilities** Children welcome Children's portions Play area Dogs allowed Garden Parking

ORLETON　　　　Map 9 SO46

The Boot Inn

SY8 4HN ☎ 01568 780228
e-mail: thebootinn@villagegreeninns.com
web: www.thebootinnorleton.co.uk
dir: *Follow A49 S from Ludlow (approx 7m) to B4362 (Woofferton), 1.5m off B4362 turn left. Inn in village centre*

A black and white, half-timbered, 16th-century village inn characterised by a large inglenook fireplace, oak beams, mullioned windows, and exposed wattle and daub. Herefordshire real ales and Robinson's cider accompany dishes such as slow-cooked belly pork; line-caught sea bass; and wild mushroom and spinach linguine. In the back room is a painting from which the figure of one-time regular Joe Vale was obliterated after arguing with the landlord. Occasionally, old Joe's ghost returns...

Open all wk Mon-Thu 12-3 5.30-11 (Fri 12-3 5.30-12 Sat-Sun noon-mdnt) **Bar Meals** L served Mon-Sat 12-2, Sun 12-3.30 D served all wk 6.45-9 **Restaurant** L served all wk 12-3 D served all wk 6-9 ⊕ VILLAGE GREEN INNS ◀ Hobsons Best, Local real ales, Woods, Wye Valley ♂ Robinsons. **Facilities** Children welcome Children's menu Play area Dogs allowed Garden Parking

PEMBRIDGE　　　　Map 9 SO35

New Inn

Market Square HR6 9DZ
☎ 01544 388427　📠 01544 388427
dir: *From M5 junct 7 take A44 W through Leominster towards Llandrindod Wells*

Formerly a courthouse and jail, and close to the last battle of The War of the Roses, this 14th-century black and white timbered free house has been in the same ownership for 26 years. Worn flagstone floors and winter fires characterise the cosy bar, and in summer customers spill out into the pub's outdoor seating area in the Old Market Square. Home-cooked English fare might include seafood stew with crusty bread; beef steak and ale pie; or leek, mushroom and Shropshire Blue cheese croustade with salad.

Open all wk 11-2.30 6-11 (summer 11-3) Closed: 1st wk Feb **Bar Meals** L served all wk 12-2 D served all wk 6.30-9 booking required Av main course £11.50 **Restaurant** L served all wk 12-2 D served all wk 6.30-9 booking required ⊕ FREE HOUSE ◀ Bishops Castle Three Tuns, Ludlow Brewery, Hobsons Town Crier, Doom Bar, Hook Norton ♂ Stowford Press, Westons Organic, Dunkertons. **Facilities** Children welcome Children's portions Family room Garden Parking

ST OWENS CROSS　　　　Map 10 SO52

PICK OF THE PUBS

The New Inn ☉

HR2 8LQ ☎ 01989 730274　📠 01989 730557
e-mail: info@newinn.biz
web: www.newinn.biz
dir: *Off A4137 W of Ross-on-Wye*

A delightful, black and white half-timbered 16th-century inn situated in the rolling Herefordshire countryside. The spacious beer garden has views stretching to the Black Mountains in the distance and is ideal for alfresco dining, weather permitting. Thankfully recent interior refurbishments have preserved the character of features like the exposed beams and woodwork, creating a cosy and traditional backdrop for a drink, a quick snack or a leisurely meal. Among the changing selection of ales you might find Wychwood's Hobgoblin and Marstons Burton Bitter. The ever-changing menus reveal a keen sense of the seasons and a real commitment to sourcing excellent local ingredients. Ross-on-Wye is just four miles away, and the surrounding area includes countless other attractions such as Symonds Yat rock, Goodrich Castle and Hereford Cathedral, all of which are within easy reach.

Open all day all wk 11am-11pm **Bar Meals** L served Mon-Sat 12-9, Sun 12-8 food served all day **Restaurant** L served Mon-Sat 12-9, Sun 12-8 food served all day ⊕ MARSTONS ◀ Marstons Bitter, Hobgoblin ♂ Thatchers Gold. ☉ 8 **Facilities** Children welcome Children's menu Children's portions Play area Dogs allowed Garden Parking Wi-fi

SHOBDON　　　　Map 9 SO46

The Bateman Arms ★★★★ INN

HR6 9LX ☎ 01568 708374
e-mail: diana@batemanarms.co.uk
dir: *On B4362 off A4110 NW of Leominster*

An 18th-century three-storey coaching inn of striking appearance, with old cobbled paving lining its street frontage. Inside you can sit beneath ancient oak beams on 300-year-old wooden settles in the bar and enjoy a Herefordshire beefburger in a bun with mozzarella cheese, lettuce, tomato and chips. Pool and darts can be played in the games room, decorated with donated military paraphernalia. Keep going and you'll find yourself in the large beer garden, a pleasant spot in which to relax and taste one of the guest ales. There are comfortable en suite bedrooms available.

Open all day all wk **Bar Meals** L served all wk 12-2 D served Tue-Sat 7-9 Av main course £6.50 **Restaurant** L served all wk 12-2 D served Tue-Sat 7-9 Av 3 course à la carte fr £24 ⊕ FREE HOUSE ◀ John Smith's, Hobgoblin, Guinness, Guest ale ♂ Stowford Press, Robinsons Flagon. **Facilities** Children welcome Children's portions Dogs allowed Garden Parking **Rooms** 6

STAPLOW　　　　Map 10 SO64

PICK OF THE PUBS

The Oak Inn ★★★★ INN ☉

HR8 1NP ☎ 01531 640954
e-mail: oakinn@wyenet.co.uk
web: www.oakinnstaplow.co.uk
dir: *M50 junct 2, A417 to Ledbury. At rdbt take 2nd exit onto A449, then A438 (High St). Then take B4214 to Staplow*

Owners Hylton Haylett and Julie Woollard have sympathetically refurbished this lovely old 17th-century black and white free house in the heart of rural Herefordshire. The three cosy bar areas have log burning stoves, flagstone floors and old wooden beams. Four cask ales are on offer, including Wye Valley Bitter and Bathams Best Bitter. The open plan kitchen serves home-cooked, locally sourced food in the rustic restaurant. The traditional lunchtime menu offers tempting sandwiches; grilled ciabatta melts with chips and mixed salad; a deli board to share and a range of pub favourites that includes the ever-popular steak and kidney pie. Go à la carte in the evenings with braised venison casserole, mash and spicy red cabbage; lamb shank in port, rosemary and redcurrant sauce; pan-fried, herb crust fillet of pollack with a creamy watercress sauce and sauté potatoes. There is a large garden adjacent to orchards with lovely views. Four luxury en suite bedrooms make The Oak Inn an ideal base for exploring the Malvern Hills and the nearby market town of Ledbury.

Open all wk Mon-Sat noon-3 5.30-11 (Sun noon-3.30 7-11) **Bar Meals** L served all wk 12-2.30 D served all wk 6.30-9.30 **Restaurant** L served Mon-Sat 12-2.30, Sun 12-3 booking required D served Mon-Sat 6.30-9.30, Sun 7-9 booking required Av 3 course à la carte fr £25 ⊕ FREE HOUSE ◀ Marstons Pedigree, Wye Valley Bitter, Sharp's Doom Bar, Bathams Best Bitter ♂ Westons Stowford Press, Robinsons. ☉ 8 **Facilities** Children welcome Children's portions Dogs allowed Garden Parking Wi-fi **Rooms** 4

PICK OF THE PUBS

The Saracens Head Inn ★★★★ INN ♀

SYMONDS YAT (EAST) Map 10 SO51

HR9 6JL ☎ 01600 890435
e-mail: contact@saracensheadinn.co.uk
web: www.saracensheadinn.co.uk
dir: *From Ross-on-Wye take A40 to Monmouth. In 4m take Symonds Yat East turn. 1st right before bridge. Right in 0.5m. Right in 1m*

For centuries this former cider mill has occupied its spectacular position on the east bank of the River Wye, where the river flows into a steep wooded gorge. This is the yat, the local name for a gate or pass; it was named after Robert Symonds who was a Sheriff of Herefordshire in the 17th century. The inn's own ferry across the river still operates by hand, just as it has for the past 200 years. There's a relaxed atmosphere throughout the inn, from the flagstoned bar to the cosy lounge and stylish dining room, and you can also eat on one of the two sunny riverside terraces. Regularly changing menus and daily specials boards offer both the traditional: locally made faggots with mashed potato, garden peas and onion gravy, for example; and the modern: the sharing plate of charcuterie includes cecina de León, spicy chorizo, wild boar salami and Milano salami served with olives, balsamic onions and olive ciabatta. A typical three course meal might start with steamed River Teign mussels with local cider and creamed leeks, followed by chargrilled Welsh lamb chops with sautéed potatoes,

Savoy cabbage and rosemary jus. Complete your meal with one of the desserts on the blackboard, or you might opt for a slate of three local cheeses – Hereford Hop, Per Las and Golden Cenarth – served with grapes, crackers, and quince and rose petal jelly. The inn is situated in an Area of Outstanding Natural Beauty on the edge of the Royal Forest of Dean, so a stay in one of the ten en suite bedrooms is a must for exploring the unspoiled local countryside. Walking, cycling, mountain biking, canoeing, kayaking, climbing, abseiling and potholing are all available nearby, whilst fishing is free to residents.

Open all day all wk Closed: 25 Dec
Bar Meals L served all wk 12-2.30
D served all wk 6.30-9 **Restaurant**
L served all wk 12-2.30 D served all wk
6.30-9 ⊕ FREE HOUSE ◼ Theakstons Old Peculier, Old Speckled Hen, Wye Valley Hereford Pale Ale, Wye Valley Butty Bach, Butcombe Bitter ☍ Westons Organic, Stowford Press, Lyne Down's Roaring Meg. ♀ 10 **Facilities** Children's menu Children's portions Dogs allowed Garden Parking Wi-fi **Rooms** 10

Save on hotels. Book at **theAA.com/hotel**

HEREFORDSHIRE 245 ENGLAND

PICK OF THE PUBS

The Mill Race 🍷

WALFORD   Map 10 SO52

HR9 5QS ☎ 01989 562891
e-mail: enquiries@millrace.info
web: www.millrace.info
dir: *From Ross-on-Wye take B4234 to Walford. Pub 3m on right after village hall*

Walford nestles enviably between the silvery waters of the river Wye just above where it disappears into its fabulous twisting gorge and the dome-like wooded hills of the Forest of Dean, home to countless deer and wild boar, and laced by footpaths and cycle tracks. Add nearby Goodrich Castle and the scene is set for activity-filled days out building up an appetite for some good Herefordshire fare. The setting at The Mill Race is suitably cosy and welcoming – beamed and stone-walled bar and dining areas with rustic furnishings, flagstoned floor, and blazing winter log fires; a far cry from the dowdy Spread Eagle of old, it's a gastro-pub with heart. Relax on the terrace, idly watch buzzards drifting above, and sip at a pint of Wye Valley Bitter, looking forward to sharing in the pub's award winning cuisine. With a farm estate at nearby Bishopswood and a dedicated supply chain of ultra-local, ultra-reliable producers, Luke Freeman and his team here at The Mill Race can dedicate time and thought to producing fare recognised as amongst the best in the burgeoning Herefordshire Slow Food movement. Lunch and evening menus will vary; a typical

midday feast may start with deep-fried Ragstone goat's cheese, salsify and beetroot salad, before pie of the day with seasonal vegetables. The menus focus on seasonal local produce and game; fricassee of Bishopswood pheasant, prune and Stowford Press jus, or perhaps Madgetts Farm duck – confit leg, pan-fried breast and liver for example, with Rowlestone Farm ice cream or Herefordshire cheeses to follow. You'll also regularly find wines from Herefordshire and Monmouthshire. Wednesday nights are fish nights, and luxury hampers containing the best of The Mill Race's suppliers' produce are available.

Open all wk 11-3 5-11 (Sat-Sun all day) **Bar Meals** L served Mon-Fri 12-2, Sat 12-2.30 Sun all day D served Mon-Sat 6-9.30, Sun 6-9 booking required Av main

course £10 **Restaurant** L served Mon-Fri 12-2, Sat 12-2.30 Sun all day D served Mon-Sat 6-9.30, Sun 6-9 booking required Av 3 course à la carte fr £22 ⊞ **FREE HOUSE** ◀ Wye Valley Bitter, Guest Ales, Guinness Ö Westons, Stowford Press, Roaring Meg. ⚑ 14 **Facilities** Children welcome Children's menu & portions Garden Parking Wi-fi

SYMONDS YAT (EAST) Map 10 SO51

PICK OF THE PUBS

The Saracens Head Inn
★★★★ INN ♚

See Pick of the Pubs on page 244

TILLINGTON Map 9 SO44

The Bell

HR4 8LE ☎ 01432 760395 📠 01432 760580
e-mail: glenn@thebellinntillington.co.uk
dir: *NE Hereford, on road to Weobley via Burghill*

Run by the same family since 1988, The Bell offers something for everybody, with extensive gardens, patio, and grassed children's play area. Inside there is a separate dining room, lounge bar and eating area, and a comfortable public bar complete with oak parquet flooring, an open fire and dart board. The traditional British food is prepared and cooked on site using local ingredients. A lemon peppered sirloin steak on focaccia bread topped with sun blush tomato makes an ample bar snack, while traditional pub main courses include roast chicken with sage and onion stuffing.

Open all wk **Bar Meals** L served Mon-Sat 12-2.30, Sun 12-3 D served Mon-Sat 6-9.30 Av main course £14 **Restaurant** L served Mon-Sat 12-2.30, Sun 12-3 D served Mon-Sat 6-9.30 ◀ London Pride, Hereford Bitter, other local ales. **Facilities** Children welcome Play area Dogs allowed Garden Parking

WALFORD Map 10 SO52

PICK OF THE PUBS

The Mill Race ♚

See Pick of the Pubs on page 245

WALTERSTONE Map 9 SO32

Carpenters Arms

HR2 0DX ☎ 01873 890353
dir: *Off A465 between Hereford & Abergavenny at Pandy*

There's plenty of character in this 300-year-old free house located on the edge of the Black Mountains where the owner, Mrs Watkins, was born. Here you'll find beams, antique settles and a leaded range with open fires that burn all winter; a perfect cosy setting for enjoying a pint of Rambler's Ruin. Popular food options include beef and Guinness pie, beef lasagne and thick lamb cutlets. Ask about the vegetarian selection, and large choice of home-made desserts. There are a few tables outside which can be a sun trap in summer.

Open all day all wk noon-11pm Closed: 25 Dec **Bar Meals** food served all day ⊕ FREE HOUSE ◀ Wadworth 6X, Breconshire Golden Valley & Rambler's Ruin Ö Westons. **Facilities** Children welcome Children's portions Play area Family room Garden Parking **Notes** ⊜

WELLINGTON Map 10 SO44

The Wellington

HR4 8AT ☎ 01432 830367
e-mail: thewellington@hotmail.com
dir: *Off A49 into village centre. Pub 0.25m on left*

Owners Ross and Philippa Williams came from London to create one of Herefordshire's finest gastro-pubs. They've certainly made their mark and Ross has become an award-winning champion of food prepared from local, seasonal produce. In the bar you can sit by the fire and enjoy a pint of real ale or a glass of wine and enjoy a light meal from the bar menu. In the restaurant, start with twice-baked Hereford hop soufflé, followed by pan-roasted pork belly with curly kale, borlotti beans and pancetta, or grilled salmon fillet with pea and lemon risotto. Head outside to the attractive garden in the warmer months.

Open 12-3 6-11 Closed: 25-26 Dec, Sun eve, Mon L **Bar Meals** L served Tue-Sun 12-2 D served Mon-Sat 7-9 Av main course £9 **Restaurant** L served Tue-Sun 12-2 D served Mon-Sat 7-9 Av 3 course à la carte fr £25 ⊕ FREE HOUSE ◀ Hobsons, Wye Valley Butty Bach, Wye Valley HPA, Guest ales Ö Westons Scrumpy. **Facilities** Children welcome Children's portions Play area Dogs allowed Garden Parking

WEOBLEY Map 9 SO45

PICK OF THE PUBS

Ye Olde Salutation Inn

Market Pitch HR4 8SJ ☎ 01544 318443
e-mail: salutationweobley@btconnect.com
dir: *A44, then A4112, 8m from Leominster*

Proprietor Stuart Elder took over this 17th-century black and white timber-framed pub in March 2011 – 12 years after he worked here as a chef for the previous owners. The inn, sympathetically converted from an old ale house and adjoining cottage, is the perfect base for exploring the Welsh Marches and enjoying a host of leisure activities, including fishing, horse riding, golf, walking, and clay shooting. The book capital of Hay-on-Wye and the cathedral city of Hereford are close by, as are the Wye Valley and Black Mountains. The inn's restaurant offers a range of tempting dishes created with the use of locally sourced ingredients. Chef's specials and old favourites are also served in the traditional lounge bar with its welcoming atmosphere and cosy inglenook fireplace. Start, perhaps, with pork, liver and mushroom pâté and follow with salmon fillets poached in cider. Leave room for the Baileys cheesecake with butterscotch sauce.

Open all day all wk noon-11 (Sun noon-10.30) **Bar Meals** L served all wk 12-3 D served all wk 6-9.30 Av main course £10 **Restaurant** L served all wk 12-3 D served all wk 6-9.30 Fixed menu price fr £13 Av 3 course à la carte fr £25 ⊕ FREE HOUSE ◀ Hobsons, Thwaites Wainwright, Pedigree Ö Stowford Press. **Facilities** Children welcome Children's portions Dogs allowed Garden Parking Wi-fi

WHITNEY-ON-WYE Map 9 SO24

Rhydspence Inn

HR3 6EU ☎ 01497 831262 📠 01497 831751
e-mail: info@rhydspence-inn.co.uk
dir: *N side of A438, 1m W of Whitney-on-Wye*

Set in the heart of Kilvert country, with glorious views over the Wye Valley, the Rhydspence is a charming and well loved 14th-century inn with 17th and 20th century additions. It was most likely built to provide comfort for travellers and pilgrims from Abbey Cwmhir to Hereford Cathedral, but it later became a watering hole for drovers taking cattle, sheep and geese to market in London. Expect a delightful timbered interior, two attractive bars with real fires, old furniture and beams aplenty. Food is no longer available.

Open all wk 11-2.30 7-11 ⊕ FREE HOUSE ◀ Robinsons Best, Interbrew Bass. **Facilities** Children welcome Family room Garden Parking Wi-fi

WOOLHOPE Map 10 SO63

PICK OF THE PUBS

The Butchers Arms ◉◉ ♚

HR1 4RF ☎ 01432 860281 📠 01531 660461
e-mail: food@butchersarmswoolhope.co.uk
dir: *From Hereford take B4224 towards Ross-on-Wye. Follow signs for Woolhope on left in Fownhope.*

Set by a stream in an Area of Outstanding Natural Beauty, this picturesque, half-timbered black and white inn stands at the foot of the sublime Marcle Ridge at the heart of cider country. Dating from the 16th century, it was a butcher's shop that also brewed beer and baked the village's bread. Five real ales and seven local ciders are complemented by a well-considered wine list to match the accessible menu created by the renowned chef-patron Stephen Bull. The menus are strong on Herefordshire fare: slow-braised Longhorn brisket with red wine sauce or ballotine of Chepstow duck, potato rösti and caramelised shallot tart with bitter cherries might follow starters of smoked haddock tart or haggis fritters with piccalilli mayonnaise. Bull's famous puddings include warm ginger cake with treacle toffee ice cream and marmalade brioche and butter pudding.

Open 12-2.30 6.30-11 Closed: Sun eve, Mon (ex BHs) **Bar Meals** L served Mon-Sat 12-2, Sun 12-2.15 D served all wk 7-9 Av main course £12.50 **Restaurant** L served all wk 12-2 D served all wk 7-9 Av 3 course à la carte fr £19 ⊕ FREE HOUSE ◀ Local cask ales Ö Stowford Press, Olivers, Dragon, Orchard, Gwatkin. ♚ 10 **Facilities** Children welcome Children's portions Dogs allowed Garden Parking Wi-fi

The Crown Inn ♥

HR1 4QP ☎ **01432 860468** 🖥 **01432 860770**
e-mail: menu@crowninnwoolhope.co.uk
dir: *B4224 to Mordiford, left after Moon Inn. Pub in village centre*

Excellent food and drink are a priority at this village free house which features three good ales as well as a list of 23 local ciders and perries. Well supported by locals and visitors alike, the pub is host to many clubs and societies, and holds a beer and cider festival every May Day Bank Holiday. Food includes daily specials like sticky beef noodles, Woolhope pheasant and cider pie, and roasted butternut squash risotto. There are stunning views from the large garden, and there is an outside summertime bar on Saturday nights.

Open all wk noon-2.30 6.30-11 (Sat-Sun all day)
Bar Meals L served all wk 12-2 D served all wk 6.30-9 Av main course £10 **Restaurant** L served all wk 12-2 D served all wk 6.30-9 Av 3 course à la carte fr £19 ⊕ FREE HOUSE ◀ Wye Valley Best, Guest ales ♂ Westons Stowford Press, Country Perry, Bounds Brand Scrumpy, Local ciders. ♥ 8 **Facilities** Children welcome Children's menu Children's portions Garden Beer festival Parking Wi-fi

HERTFORDSHIRE

ALDBURY   Map 6 SP91

The Greyhound Inn ♥

19 Stocks Rd HP23 5RT
☎ **01442 851228** 🖥 **01442 851495**
e-mail: greyhound@aldbury.wanadoo.co.uk
dir: *Telephone for directions*

The village's ancient stocks and duck pond are popular with film-makers who frequently use Aldbury as a film location, allowing the pub's customers the chance to witness every clap of the clapperboard. In the oak-beamed restaurant, the comprehensive menu includes

rump of new season lamb on parmentier potatoes; crispy duck legs with a sesame salad; supreme of corn-fed chicken with creamy wild mushroom sauce; and pan-fried sea bass fillet with crayfish and fennel risotto. The bar snacks are a local legend, especially when accompanied by Badger Best or Tanglefoot ale.

Open all day all wk 11.30-11 (Sun noon-10.30) Closed: 25 Dec **Bar Meals** L served all wk 12-2.30 D served all wk 6.30-9.30 Av main course £12 **Restaurant** L served all wk 12-2.30 D served all wk 6.30-9.30 Av 3 course à la carte fr £22 ⊕ HALL & WOODHOUSE ◀ Badger Best, Tanglefoot, King & Barnes Sussex. ♥ 13
Facilities Children welcome Family room Dogs allowed Garden Parking Wi-fi

The Valiant Trooper

Trooper Rd HP23 5RW ☎ **01442 851203**
e-mail: info@thevalianttrooper.co.uk
dir: *A41 at Tring junct, follow rail station signs 0.5m, at village green turn right, 200yds on left*

Luckily locals have been enjoying this old pub in this quintessential village at the foot of the Chilterns beneath the beech woods of Ashridge Park for several centuries. Originally its name recalls times when the Duke of Wellington discussed strategy with his troops here; when the famous warrior died it was named in his honour. Expect starter dishes such as ham hock and leek terrine with perhaps fish pie with smoked Cheddar crust or Thai green chicken curry. Sandwiches, salads, ploughman's and lighter bites, such as fish platter, can be enjoyed with a glass of Tring Trooper.

Open all day all wk noon-11pm (Sun noon-10.30)
Bar Meals L served Mon-Fri 12-3, Sat 12-9, Sun 12-4.30 D served Mon-Fri 6.30-9, Sat 12-9 **Restaurant** L served Mon-Fri 12-3, Sat 12-9, Sun 12-4.30 D served Mon-Fri 6.30-9, Sat 12-9 ⊕ FREE HOUSE ◀ Fuller's London Pride, Tring Trooper Ale, Brakspear Bitter. **Facilities** Children welcome Children's menu Children's portions Play area Family room Dogs allowed Garden Beer festival Parking

ARDELEY   Map 12 TL32

Jolly Waggoner ♥

SG2 7AH ☎ **01438 861350** 🖥 **01438 861350**
dir: *From Stevenage take B1037, through Walkern, in 2m right to Ardeley*

With over 17 years of experience in the trade, new owners in 2010 restored the Jolly Waggoner name to this 500-year-old village pub, after a spell as the Rabbit's Foot. A large garden for the summer is matched by open fires for the winter. Buntingford and Woodforde breweries supply the regular real ales, alongside a guest. Fresh local ingredients are used in the seasonal menus to ensure main courses of rib-eye steak, fresh fish of the day, and mushroom, cherry tomato and pea risotto.

Open all wk 12-3 6-11 **Bar Meals** L served all wk 12-2 booking required D served Mon-Sat 6-9 booking required Av main course £8.50 **Restaurant** L served all wk 12-2 booking required D served Mon-Sat 6-9 booking required Fixed menu price fr £12 Av 3 course à la carte fr £20 ⊕ FREE HOUSE ◀ Buntingford Brewery, Highway Man, Woodforde's Wherry, Guest ale. ♥ 10 **Facilities** Children welcome Children's menu Children's portions Garden Parking Wi-fi

ASHWELL   Map 12 TL23

Three Tuns ♥

6 High St SG7 5NL ☎ **01462 742107** 🖥 **01462 743662**
e-mail: info@threetunshotel.co.uk
web: www.threetunshotel.co.uk
dir: *Telephone for directions*

The building, dating from 1806, replaced an earlier one first recorded as a public house in 1701. Original features survive in the two bars – a lounge bar with restaurant and a large public bar, both recently refurbished. The extensive menu offers devilled whitebait; moules marinière; scampi and chips; grilled sea bass with rosemary and lemon on steamed greens; pan-fried

continued

ASHWELL *continued*

pork fillet with Calvados sauce; and whole roast partridge with wild blackberry, apple and red wine jus; and fillet steak Diane. There is a large garden with mature borders and children's play area, and a patio.

Three Tuns

Open all day all wk 11am-11.30pm (Fri-Sat 11am-12.30am) **Bar Meals** L served Mon-Fri 12-2.30, Sat-Sun all day booking required D served Mon-Fri 6.30-9.30, Sat-Sun all day booking required Av main course £9.50 **Restaurant** L served Mon-Fri 12-2.30, Sat-Sun all day booking required D served Mon-Fri 6.30-9.30, Sat-Sun all day booking required Fixed menu price fr £9.50 Av 3 course à la carte fr £19 ⊕ GREENE KING ◖ Greene King IPA, Abbot, Guest ale Ò Aspall. ♀ 9 **Facilities** Children welcome Children's menu Children's portions Play area Family room Dogs allowed Garden Parking Wi-fi

See advert on page 247

AYOT GREEN   Map 6 TL21

The Waggoners ◉ ♀

Brickwall Close AL6 9AA ☎ 01707 324241
e-mail: laurent@thewaggoners.co.uk
web: www.thewaggoners.co.uk
dir: *Ayot Green on unclassified road off B197, S of Welwyn*

Built in the 17th century to house the workers at nearby Brocket Hall before becoming a thriving coaching inn, this dining pub overlooks the beautiful village green. In the cosy beamed bar and smart restaurant extension, experienced French owners offer an upmarket, French inspired menu alongside classic English ales. Accompany a pint of Adnams Broadside or one of the 25 wines by the glass with goats' cheese tart with red onion marmalade, confit duck leg with creamed mash, with winterberry cheesecake with blackberry coulis to finish. There is a sun-trap garden and sheltered terrace for summer alfresco dining.

Open all day Closed: Sun eve **Bar Meals** Av main course £8.95 food served all day **Restaurant** L served all wk 12-2.45 booking required D served all wk 6.30-9.30 Fixed menu price fr £13.95 Av 3 course à la carte fr £30 ⊕ PUNCH TAVERNS ◖ Fuller's London Pride, IPA, Tribute, Adnams Broadside Ò Stanford Press. ♀ 25 **Facilities** Children welcome Children's portions Dogs allowed Garden Parking Wi-fi

---

BARLEY   Map 12 TL43

The Fox & Hounds ♀

High St SG8 8HU ☎ 01763 849400   📧 01763 849400
e-mail: foxandhoundsbarley@hotmail.co.uk
dir: *A505 onto B1368 at Flint Cross, pub 4m*

Set in a beautiful and historic village in North Hertfordshire, this 17th-century Grade II listed former hunting lodge has a wealth of exposed beams, original fireplaces, wood-burners, original flooring and more nooks and crannies than you can shake a stick at. It's child- and dog-friendly too, and making a name for itself by serving top quality real ales from local micro-breweries. Home-cooked food, a dedicated restaurant, and beer festivals every Bank Holiday weekend complete the picture. Recent change of ownership.

Open 10-3 6-late (Sat 10am-late, Sun 10am-11pm) Closed: Mon ⊕ FREE HOUSE ◖ Adnams Best, Flowers IPA, Woodforde's Wherry, Falstaff Phoenix, Abbot Ale Ò Roaring Meg. ♀ 12 **Facilities** Children welcome Children's menu Children's portions Play area Dogs allowed Garden Beer festival Parking Wi-fi

---

BERKHAMSTED   Map 6 SP90

The Old Mill ♀ NEW

London Rd HP4 2NB ☎ 01442 879590
dir: *At east end of London Rd in Berkhamsted centre*

Perched on the Grand Union Canal, this restored pub has retained its original Georgian and Victorian features. Enjoy real ales and deli boards on big leather sofas in the low-beamed bar or head for the comfortable dining room for menus showcasing the best seasonal ingredients: crab linguine might be followed by slow-cooked pork belly, braised red cabbage and cider sauce. The canal-side garden is a perfect place for relaxed alfresco dining or a quiet pint.

Open all day all wk 10am-mdnt Closed: 25 Dec **Bar Meals** Av main course £13.50 food served all day **Restaurant** L served all wk 12-3 D served all wk 6-10 Av 3 course à la carte fr £22.50 ⊕ PEACH PUBS ◖ Greene King IPA, Old Speckled Hen, Side Pocket for a Toad Ò Aspall. ♀ 10 **Facilities** Children welcome Children's menu Children's portions Dogs allowed Garden Beer festival Parking Wi-fi

---

BUNTINGFORD   Map 12 TL32

The Sword Inn Hand ★★★★ INN

Westmill SG9 9LQ ☎ 01763 271356
e-mail: welcome@theswordinnhand.co.uk
dir: *Off A10 1.5m S of Buntingford*

Midway between London and Cambridge in the lovely award-winning village of Westmill, this inn has been welcoming travellers since the 14th century. Inside there are oak beams, flag floor and an open fireplace. It styles itself a 'real English', family-run pub offering a large selection of snacks, specials and a range of real ales. Fresh produce is delivered daily to create herb-crushed rack of lamb, sea bass fillet with stir-fry vegetables, escalope of veal with melted Brie, or Chef's cod and chips. There are four ground floor bedrooms available.

Open all wk 12-3 5-11 (Sun Sep-Apr 12-7, May-Aug 12-10) ⊕ FREE HOUSE ◖ Greene King IPA, Young's Bitter, Timothy Taylor Landlord, Guest ales Ò Aspall. **Facilities** Children welcome Play area Dogs allowed Garden Parking **Rooms** 4

COTTERED   Map 12 TL32

The Bull at Cottered

SG9 9QP ☎ 01763 281243
e-mail: cordell39@btinternet.com
dir: *On A507 in Cottered between Buntingford & Baldock*

Low-beamed ceilings, antique furniture, cosy fires and pub games typify this charming traditional village local. The setting is picturesque, and a well-tended garden offers an alternative dining venue in summer. The menu presents a classy and comprehensive carte of brasserie-style food which is all home made: typical are starters of fresh Devon crab, or wild mushroom risotto; and main courses such as fillet of pork stuffed with smoked bacon, or rack of lamb in herb breadcrumbs. Book ahead if you want to participate in the full diary of social events.

Open all wk 11.30-3 6.30-11 (Sun 12-10.30) **Bar Meals** L served Mon-Sat 12-2, Sun 12-4 D served Mon-Sat 6.30-9.30, Sun 6-9 Av main course £12 **Restaurant** L served Mon-Sat 12-2, Sun 12-4 D served Mon-Sat 6.30-9.30, Sun 6-9 booking required Fixed menu price fr £20 Av 3 course à la carte fr £25 ⊕ GREENE KING ◖ Greene King IPA, Abbot Ale. **Facilities** Children welcome Children's portions Garden Parking

---

DATCHWORTH   Map 6 TL21

The Tilbury ◉ ♀ NEW

Walton Rd SG3 6TB ☎ 01438 815550
e-mail: info@thetilbury.co.uk
dir: *A1(M) junct 7, A602 signed Ware & Hertford. At Bragbury End right into Bragbury Lane to Datchworth*

TV chef Paul Bloxham has revitalised this once-tired old village boozer and turned it into a notable dining pub. Bare brick walls, wooden floors and interesting art suit the mood for the simply cooked, seasonally inspired modern British food: deep-fried Tye Farm duck egg with house-cured bacon and dandelion might be followed by free-range Old Spot pork, sage and onion, Suffolk cider jus, or veal and ham pie. Puddings include lavender pannacotta with red wine roasted pears. A well selected wine list, real ales and ciders complete the picture.

Open 12-3 6-late Closed: Sun eve **Bar Meals** D served all wk 12-2 Av main course £10 **Restaurant** D served all wk 6-9.30 booking required Fixed menu price fr £12 Av 3 course à la carte fr £25 ⊕ BRAKSPEAR ◀ Brakspear Bitter, Oxford Gold ⚬ Westons Organic. ⏺ 30 **Facilities** Children welcome Children's menu Children's portions Garden Parking

---

EPPING GREEN   Map 6 TL20

The Beehive ⏺ NEW

SG13 8NB ☎ 01707 875959
e-mail: squirrell15@googlemail.com
dir: South of Hertford

A family-run free house full of traditional charms including exposed beams and a real fire, The Beehive has held its liquor license for over 200 years and featured in Catweazel in the 1970s. These days you can relax by the fire in winter or in the decked or grass areas in finer weather. The kitchen specialises in fresh fish from Billingsgate market – maybe poached fish pie or sea bass fillets with basil pesto. Alternatives include steak, mushroom and ale pudding, and Thai green chicken curry. At the bar you'll find two permanent ales and a changing guest.

Open all wk Mon-Sat 11.30-3 5.30-11 (Sun 11-11) **Bar Meals** L served Mon-Sat 12-2.30, Sun 12-4 booking required D served Mon-Sat 6-9.30, Sun 6-8.30 booking required Av main course £10.95 **Restaurant** L served Mon-Sat 12-2.30, Sun 12-4 booking required D served Mon-Sat 6-9.30, Sun 6-8.30 booking required ⊕ FREE HOUSE ◀ Greene King IPA, Old Speckled Hen, Guest ale. ⏺ 8 **Facilities** Children welcome Children's portions Garden Parking Wi-fi

---

FLAUNDEN   Map 6 TL00

PICK OF THE PUBS

The Bricklayers Arms ⏺

See Pick of the Pubs on page 250

HEMEL HEMPSTEAD   Map 6 TL00

PICK OF THE PUBS

Alford Arms ⏺

See Pick of the Pubs on page 251

HERONSGATE   Map 6 TQ09

The Land of Liberty, Peace and Plenty NEW

Long Ln WD3 5BS ☎ 01923 282226
e-mail: beer@landoflibertypub.com
dir: M25 junct 17, follow Heronsgate signs. 0.5m, pub on right

Named after a Chartist settlement established in Heronsgate in 1847, this pub is believed to have the second longest name in the British Isles. A traditional pub with a large garden and covered decked area, the cosy single bar has a buzz of conversation from locals. The focus here are the real ales and real ciders, all of which can be enjoyed with bar snacks of pork pies, pasties and pots of nuts. Regular events and beer festivals are held during the year.

Open all wk 12-11 (11am-mdnt Fri-Sat) **Bar Meals** food served all day ⊕ FREE HOUSE ◀ 6 guest ales ⚬ Millwhites, Westons. **Facilities** Dogs allowed Garden Beer festival Parking

---

HEXTON   Map 12 TL13

The Raven ⏺

SG5 3JB ☎ 01582 881209 📠 01582 881610
e-mail: theraven@emeryinns.com
dir: 5m W of Hitchin. 5m N of Luton, just outside Barton-le-Clay

This neat 1920s pub is named after Ravensburgh Castle in the neighbouring hills. Comfortable bars witness the serving of four weekly-changing guest ales, while outside a large garden with heated terrace and a play area ensure family friendliness. Comprehensive menus embrace ranges of wraps, baguettes, jackets and baps if a snack is required. For a full meal expect the likes of chilli and ginger chicken goujons to start, followed by a steak, mushroom and ale pudding; or a whole rack of barbeque spare ribs.

Open all day all wk Mon-Thu 11-3 6-11 (Fri-Sun all day) **Bar Meals** Av main course £9.95 food served all day **Restaurant** food served all day ⊕ FREE HOUSE ◀ Greene King, Old Speckled Hen, Fuller's London Pride, Greene King IPA, Landlord Ale, Doom Bar. ⏺ 24 **Facilities** Children welcome Children's menu Children's portions Play area Garden Parking

---

HITCHIN   Map 12 TL12

The Greyhound

London Rd, St Ippolyts SG4 7NL ☎ 01462 440989
e-mail: greyhound@freenet.co.uk
dir: 1.5m S of Hitchin on B656

On the outskirts of Hitchin and with easy access to the M1 and Luton Airport, there has been a pub on the site for 300 years although the current building dates from 1900. The pub prides itself on being a friendly, family-run hostelry, and is located in pleasant countryside and open farmland. The food is unpretentious, generous and competitively priced. Typical dishes might be lasagne or steak, ale and mushroom pie.

Open all wk 7am-2.30 5-11 (Sun 7am-8pm) **Bar Meals** L served Mon-Sat 7-2, Sun 7am-8pm D served Mon-Sat 5-9, Sun 7am-8pm **Restaurant** L served Mon-Sat 7-2, Sun 7am-8pm D served Mon-Sat 5-9, Sun 7am-8pm ⊕ FREE HOUSE ◀ Adnams, Guest ale. **Facilities** Children welcome Dogs allowed Parking

---

The Radcliffe Arms ⏺ NEW

31 Walsworth Rd SG4 9ST ☎ 01462 456111
e-mail: enquiries@radcliffearms.co.uk
dir: From Hitchin rail station turn left into Walsworth Rd (B656)

Named after a Lancastrian family who moved to Hitchin in the 16th-century, the red-brick Radcliffe Arms dates from 1855 and is located in the town's 'Victorian Triangle'. Restored to its former glory by new owners in 2009, this popular free-house now offers a range of local real ales, thirteen different gins and a comprehensive wine list to match daily specials such as beef medallions, herb mash and roasted root vegetables or sea bass fillet with beetroot risotto. Look out for the summer beer festivals.

Open all day all wk 8am-mdnt Closed: 26 Dec & 1 Jan **Bar Meals** Av main course £14 **Restaurant** L served Mon-Sat 12-2.30, Sun 12-3 booking required D served Mon-Sat 6-9.30, Sun 6.30-9 booking required Fixed menu price fr £18 Av 3 course à la carte fr £24 ⊕ FREE HOUSE ◀ Buntingford Brewery Twitchell, Polar Star, Grain Oak ⚬ Aspall. ⏺ 30 **Facilities** Children welcome Children's menu Children's portions Dogs allowed Garden Beer festival Parking Wi-fi

PICK OF THE PUBS

The Bricklayers Arms ♟

FLAUNDEN Map 6 TL00

Hogpits Bottom HP3 0PH
☎ **01442 833322** 📠 **01442 834841**
e-mail: goodfood@bricklayersarms.com
web: www.bricklayersarms.com
dir: *M25 junct 18 onto A404 (Amersham road). Right at Chenies for Flaunden*

Lost down leafy Hertfordshire lanes in a peaceful and inviting location, the creeper-clad Bricklayers Arms is a low, cottagey-tiled pub formed from a pair of 18th-century cottages. In summer, the flower-festooned garden is the perfect place to savour an alfresco pint or meal. It was in 1832 when Benskin's brewery converted one of them into an alehouse, which it remained until the 1960s, when the neighbouring cottage became part of the pub. Sympathetic conversion of an outbuilding and barn resulted in today's award-winning restaurant. Tucked away in deepest Hertfordshire, it has featured in many fictional film and TV programmes, and is a favourite with locals, walkers, horse-riders and, well, just about everyone. One reason for its success is an ivy-covered façade that gives way to an immaculate interior, complete with low beams, exposed brickwork, candlelight and open fires. Another is a happy marriage between traditional English and French fusion cooking. The Gallic influence comes from experienced head chef, Claude Paillet, and his team who use fresh organic produce from local suppliers to

create seasonal lunch and dinner menus, plus daily specials. For starters try pan-fried scallops with spicy tomato coulis, or a selection of home-smoked fish with lemon coriander butter and tomato chutney. To follow, opt for lamb shank with wholegrain mustard mash and rosemary jus; game pie with wild mushroom mash; or beer battered haddock with tartare sauce. But don't stop there, as the pub is also held in high esteem for its pudding menu, on which you're likely to find warm apple and rhubarb tart, and chocolate and honey fondant with pistachio ice cream. Choose one of the 120 wines from all corners of the world and, in the summer, enjoy it with your lunch in the terraced garden.

Open all day all wk noon-11.30 (25 Dec 12-3) **Bar Meals** L served Mon-Sat

12-2.30, Sun 12-3.30 booking required D served Mon-Sat 6.30-9.30, Sun 6.30-8.30 Av main course £15.95 **Restaurant** L served Mon-Sat 12-2.30, Sun 12-3.30 booking required D served Mon-Sat 6.30-9.30, Sun 6.30-8.30 Av 3 course à la carte fr £28 ⊕ FREE HOUSE ◀ Greene King IPA, London Pride, Jack O'Legs (Tring Brewery), Rebellion, Doom Bar Ꝋ Aspall. ♟ 16 **Facilities** Children welcome Children's portions Dogs allowed Garden Parking Wi-fi

Save on hotels. Book at **theAA.com/hotel**

HERTFORDSHIRE 251 ENGLAND

PICK OF THE PUBS

Alford Arms ♟

HEMEL HEMPSTEAD   Map 6 TL00

Frithsden HP1 3DD
☎ **01442 864480** 📠 **01422 876893**
e-mail: info@alfordarmsfrithsden.co.uk
web: www.alfordarmsfrithsden.co.uk
dir: *From Hemel Hempstead on A4146 take 2nd left at Water End. In 1m left at T-junct, right after 0.75m. Pub 100yds on right*

With historic Ashridge forest on the doorstep and a flower-filled garden overlooking the village green, The Alford Arms is one of those quintessential English village pubs rarely found these days. Set in the untouched hamlet of Frithsden and surrounded by National Trust woodland, this pretty Victorian pub is full of surprises. Cross the threshold and you'll immediately pick up on the warm and lively atmosphere, derived partly from the buzz of conversation and the background jazz music, and partly from the rich colours and eclectic mix of old furniture and antique pictures in the dining room and bar. The seasonal menus and daily specials balance innovative dishes with more traditional fare, and everything is prepared from fresh local produce whenever possible. There's a great choice of light dishes or 'small plates', from the warm soused mackerel with sweet beetroot purée to the crispy lamb breast with 'Alford' grain mustard. Main meals with a similarly imaginative approach include pan-roast cod fillet with kedgeree and soft poached duck egg; wild mushroom and Rebellion IPA pie with roast salsify and sprout tops; thyme roast Halsey Estate pheasant with boulangère parsnips, curly kale and juniper and blackberry jus. Puddings have an interesting tweak too, such as warm chocolate bread and butter pudding with marmalade sauce or Bramley apple tart with walnut crumble and English fudge ice cream. The British cheese plate is a tempting alternative to finish, with Alford oatcakes, sticky malt loaf and tomato chutney. The staff are renowned for their good humour, and they take the trouble to ensure that customers have an enjoyable experience.

Open all day all wk 11-11 (Sun 12-10.30) Closed: 26 Dec **Bar Meals** L served Mon-Fri 12-2.30, Sat 12-3, Sun 12-4 D served Mon-Thu 6.30-9.30, Fri-Sat 6.30-10, Sun 7-9.30 **Restaurant** L served Mon-Fri 12-2.30, Sat 12-3, Sun 12-4 booking required D served Mon-Thu 6.30-9.30, Fri-Sat 6.30-10, Sun 7-9.30 booking required ⊕ SALISBURY PUBS LTD 🍺 Marlow Rebellion IPA, Sharp's Doom Bar, Tring Brewery Side Pocket 🍏 Thatchers. ♟ 21 **Facilities** Children's portions Dogs allowed Garden Parking Wi-fi

HUNSDON
Map 6 TL41

PICK OF THE PUBS

The Fox and Hounds ☻

2 High St SG12 8NH ☎ 01279 843999
e-mail: info@foxandhounds-hunsdon.co.uk
dir: From A414 between Ware & Harlow take B180 in Stanstead Abbotts N to Hunsdon

Owned and run by chef James Rix, this renowned gastro-pub may be set in a sleepy Hertfordshire village, but it attracts food lovers from afar. There's an easy-going atmosphere thanks to a cosy winter fire warming the old bar, liberally supplied with Victorian-style furnishings. There is no pressure to do anything other than enjoy a glass of Adnams brewery beer, as the local drinkers do, but resistance is futile when you see the menu. There's no doubting that the food side of the pub is the main draw here, and lunch and dinner can be taken in the bar or elegant, chandeliered dining room. Kick off with spaghetti, clams, chilli, garlic and parsley before progressing to whole roast squab pigeon, potato gnocchi, pumpkin and leeks, or seared scallops, spinach and harissa butter. Finish with a calorific pudding such as hot chocolate fondant with espresso ice cream, accompanied by an impressive wine list. The tree-shaded garden, together with the heated, covered terrace is popular with both drinkers and alfresco diners.

Open noon-4 6-11 Closed: 26 Dec, Sun eve, Mon & BHs eve (Tue after BHs) **Bar Meals** L served Tue-Sun 12-3 D served Tue-Sat 6.30-9.30 Av main course £14 **Restaurant** L served Sun 12-3.30 booking required D served Fri-Sat 6.30-9.30 booking required Fixed menu price fr £12.50 Av 3 course à la carte fr £25 ⊕ FREE HOUSE ◀ Adnams Bitter, Adnams Broadside, Guinness Ö Aspall. ☻ 9 **Facilities** Children welcome Children's menu Children's portions Play area Dogs allowed Garden Parking Wi-fi

LITTLE HADHAM
Map 6 TL42

The Nags Head

The Ford SG11 2AX ☎ 01279 771555 ▤ 01279 771555
e-mail: paul.arkell@virgin.net
dir: M11 junct 8 take A120 towards Puckeridge & A10. Left at lights in Little Hadham. Pub 1m on right

Formerly a coaching inn, this welcoming 16th-century pub has also been a brewery, a bakery and Home Guard arsenal in its time. The 1960s folk-rock group Fairport Convention once performed in concert opposite and the pub ran dry! Open brickwork and an old bakery oven are among the features at this village inn, as well as the range of real ales behind the bar. The extensive menu specialises in fish dishes and the Sunday roasts are popular. Try perhaps prawn thermidor or smoked salmon pâté to start; then chicken au gratin or beef steak and ale pie. Sit out the front on a good day and enjoy the countryside.

Open all wk **Bar Meals** L served Mon-Sat 12-2, Sun 12-3 D served Mon-Sat 6-9, Sun 7-9 **Restaurant** L served Mon-Sat 12-2, Sun 12-3 booking required D served Mon-Sat 6-9, Sun 7-9 booking required ⊕ GREENE KING ◀ Greene King Abbot Ale, IPA, Old Speckled Hen & Ruddles County Ale, Marstons Pedigree. **Facilities** Children welcome Children's menu Children's portions Garden

NORTHAW
Map 6 TL20

The Sun at Northaw ☻ NEW

1 Judges Hill EN6 4NL ☎ 01707 655507
e-mail: reservations@thesunatnorthaw.co.uk
dir: From M25 junct 24, A111 to Potters Bar. Right onto A1000, becomes High Street (B156). Follow to Northaw, pub on left

A restored Grade II-listed building situated on a picturesque village green, The Sun at Northaw has gained a reputation for its real ale, with up to seven available at any time. There is also an excellent wine list to complement menus driven by local, seasonal produce from a number of artisan producers. Specials might include wild rabbit and smoked bacon terrine; braised beef shin and pickled walnut pie; duck egg custard tart with poached rhubarb.

Open all day Closed: Sun eve & Mon **Bar Meals** L served all wk 12-3 booking required D served all wk 6-10 booking required Av main course £15 **Restaurant** L served all wk 12-3 booking required Fixed menu price fr £13.50 Av 3 course à la carte fr £25 ⊕ FREE HOUSE ◀ Red Squirrel RSX, Grain Oak, Adnams Broadside Ö Millwhites Organic Single Orchard, Aspall Suffolk Cyder. ☻ 12 **Facilities** Children welcome Children's menu Children's portions Dogs allowed Garden Parking Wi-fi

PERRY GREEN
Map 6 TL41

The Hoops Inn NEW

SG10 6EF ☎ 01279 843568
e-mail: reservations@hoops-inn.co.uk
dir: From Ware on B1004 towards Bishop's Stortford right onto unclassified road to Perry Green

Perry Green was home to Henry Moore; his visionary sculptures dot the home estate, part of which is this comfortable dining inn. Country chic decor, a pleasant mix of woodburner and beams with contemporary furnishing and Moore-inspired artefacts, welcomes guests faced with a huge choice of dining, from small plates and an alfresco snacks menu to rich, good value mains like Suffolk ham hock with winter greens and fried duck egg. Excellent Sunday roasts can be walked off by visiting the Moore Foundation's estate just across the village green here. There is a large front terrace and back garden to enjoy in the warmer weather where regular barbecues and hog roasts take place.

Open all day 11.30-11 Closed: Mon **Bar Meals** Av main course £9.95 food served all day **Restaurant** L served Tue-Sun 12-2.30 booking required D served Tue-Sun 6-9.30 booking required Av 3 course à la carte fr £12.95 ⊕ FREE HOUSE ◀ Guinness, Adnams Best Bitter Ö Aspall, Thatchers. **Facilities** Children welcome Children's portions Garden Parking

POTTERS CROUCH
Map 6 TL10

The Holly Bush

AL2 3NN ☎ 01727 851792 ▤ 01727 851792
e-mail: info@thehollybushpub.co.uk
dir: Ragged Hall Ln off A405 or Bedmond Ln off A4147

Now refurbished after passing into the hands of the previous landlords' daughter and son-in-law, The Holly Bush is a picturesque country pub with a large enclosed garden. There is a delightfully welcoming atmosphere and traditional and modern pub fare is offered. At lunch there's ploughman's, jacket potatoes, salads, and various platters, plus toasted sandwiches, and on the evening menu there might be chicken and mushroom risotto; lamb cutlets with red onion confit and mash; warm duck salad; and cod and pancetta fishcakes. The pub is close to St Albans with its Roman ruins and good local walks.

Open all wk noon-2.30 6-11 (Sun noon-3) **Bar Meals** L served all wk 12-2, Sun 12-2.30 D served Wed-Sat 6-9 ⊕ FULLER SMITH TURNER PLC ◀ Fuller's Chiswick Bitter, Fuller's London Pride, ESB, seasonal ales. **Facilities** Garden Parking

RICKMANSWORTH
Map 6 TQ09

The Rose and Crown

Harefield Rd WD3 1PP ☎ 01923 897680
e-mail: roseandcrown@morethanjustapub.co.uk
dir: M25 junct 17/18, follow Northwood signs. Past Tesco, pub 1.5m on right

This 16th-century former farmhouse first became licensed in the mid-1700s. Around the wisteria-clad building, you'll find a large garden looking out across the lovely Colne Valley; the local stables, Field Ways, is popular with the film industry and Russell Crowe has enjoyed a pint here. The bar still retains its historic charm with low-beamed ceilings and real fires, while the kitchen prepares local produce such as meat from Daltons of Ickenham and Flexmore Farm. Lunchtime sandwiches and sharing platters are backed by favourite pies such as game or fish, while the dinner range broadens to include chargrilled steaks.

Open all day all wk 11am-11.30pm ⊕ MORE THAN JUST A PUB CO LTD ◀ London Pride, Deuchars IPA, Timothy Taylor Landlord. **Facilities** Children welcome Children's menu Children's portions Play area Dogs allowed Garden Parking Wi-fi

ROYSTON   Map 12 TL34

PICK OF THE PUBS

The Cabinet Free House and Restaurant �

High St, Reed SG8 8AH ☎ 01763 848366
e-mail: chefangusmartin@hotmail.com
dir: 2m S of Royston, just off A10

A cabinet used to be a small room used as a study or retreat, although little studying - and even less retreating - gets done these days at this 16th-century, white-painted clapboard inn. A cabinet could also be a meeting place, which is more like it, because people come here to drink and eat with their friends, enjoying a wide range of real ales beneath low-beamed ceilings. The pub is situated on a chalk ridge at almost the highest point in Hertfordshire, with the Roman Ermine Street passing just to the west. There has been a settlement here for centuries - the community is mentioned in the Domesday Book. Food is prepared from the best local produce, but draws inspiration from around the world. Starters include a crayfish Bloody Mary cocktail and might be followed by local hare with gnocchi tomatoes and curly kale. Finish with steamed jam suet pudding and custard.

Open 12-3 6-11 (Sat-Sun 12-11) Closed: 26 Dec, 1 Jan, Mon **Bar Meals** L served Tue-Sun 12-3 D served Tue-Sat 6-9 Av main course £15 **Restaurant** L served Tue-Sun 12-3 booking required D served Tue-Sat 6-9 booking required Fixed menu price fr £22 Av 3 course à la carte fr £35 ⊕ FREE HOUSE ◀ Woodforde's Wherry, Adnams, Old Speckled Hen, Nelson's Revenge, Timothy Taylor, Augustinian ○ Aspall. ♟ 12 **Facilities** Children welcome Children's portions Family room Dogs allowed Garden Parking Wi-fi

ST ALBANS   Map 6 TL10

Rose & Crown ♟

10 Saint Michael St AL3 4SG
☎ 01727 851903 📠 01727 761775
e-mail: ruth.courtney@ntlworld.com
dir: Telephone for details

Traditional 16th-century pub situated in a beautiful part of St Michael's 'village', opposite the entrance to Verulanium Park and the Roman Museum. It has a classic beamed bar with a huge inglenook, open fires in winter and a lovely sheltered walled garden. Along with a good selection of ales, the pub offers a distinctive range of American deli-style sandwiches, which are served with potato salad, kettle crisps and pickled cucumber. There is traditional folk music on Thursday nights, live music on Monday nights.

Open all day all wk 11.30-3 5.30-11 (Sat 11.30-11.30) **Bar Meals** L served Mon-Sat 12-3, Sun 12-5 D served Mon-Sat 6-9 ◀ Adnams Bitter, IPA, Courage Directors, Sharp's Doom Bar, Purity Mad Goose, Guest ales ○ Addlestones, Aspall. ♟ 12 **Facilities** Children welcome Children's menu Children's portions Dogs allowed Garden Parking

SARRATT   Map 6 TQ09

The Cock Inn NEW

Church Ln WD3 6HH ☎ 01923 282908
e-mail: enquiries@cockinn.net
dir: M25 junct 18, A404 signed Chorleywood, Amersham. Right follow signs to Sarratt. Pass church on left, pub on right

Originally called the 'Cock Horse' and dating from the 17th century, this traditional village pub stands opposite Sarratt's Norman church in the heart of the Chess Valley, a favoured walking area. Head-cracking low beams, an inglenook fireplace and Hall & Woodhouse ales await in the character bar, while the ancient timbered barn houses the restaurant. Expect classic home-cooked pub food, from steak and Badger ale pie and line-caught baked cod to lamb rump with port and redcurrant jus, and pan-fried calves' liver with roasted vine tomatoes, mash and port jus. Light bites and sandwiches are served in the bar.

Open all day all wk **Bar Meals** L served all wk 12-2.30 D served all wk 6-9 Av main course £9.95 **Restaurant** L served all wk 12-2.30 booking required D served all wk 6-9 booking required Av 3 course à la carte fr £22 ⊕ HALL & WOODHOUSE ◀ Badger, Tanglefoot, King and Barnes Sussex ○ Stowford Press. **Facilities** Children welcome Children's menu Children's portions Play area Dogs allowed Garden Parking

SHENLEY   Map 6 TL10

The White Horse, Shenley ♟ NEW

37 London Rd WD7 9ER ☎ 01923 853054
e-mail: 182036mgr@mbplc.com
dir: M25 junct 22, B556 then B5378 to Shenley

Bright, light and cheerful, with some quirky decor, The White Horse belies its 170-year-old foundation as a village pub, offering contemporary comforts and dining at the fringe of this green-belt village, with country walks to the Hertfordshire Way from the door. Sup a Sharp's Doom Bar bitter over a Sunday roast or crack a bottle from the extensive wine list and indulge in pan-fried grey mullet with a far-eastern touch then organic pork and sage sausages with colcannon mash; the menu is truly impressive and features tasty daily-changing specials, all home prepared.

Open all day all wk **Bar Meals** Av main course £10 food served all day **Restaurant** booking required Fixed menu price fr £12 Av 3 course à la carte fr £20 food served all day ⊕ MITCHELLS & BUTLERS ◀ Young's, Sharp's Doom Bar ○ Aspall. ♟ 24 **Facilities** Children welcome Children's portions Dogs allowed Garden Parking

STAPLEFORD   Map 6 TL31

Papillon Woodhall Arms ★★★ INN ♟

17 High Rd SG14 3NW
☎ 01992 535123 📠 01992 587030
e-mail: info@papillon-woodhallarms.com
dir: On A119, between A602 & Hertford

A pink-washed twin-gabled building behind a neat white picket fence, just a five-minute drive from the centre of Hertford. The bar serves well-kept ales in a welcoming atmosphere, plus a huge selection of snacks and pub lunches. Restaurant food includes plentiful fish dishes, such as duet of lightly poached lemon sole and salmon served in a prawn and crab sauce, or grilled halibut steak in a yogurt, mustard, almond and rocket sauce. The credit crunch menu is proving popular. Accommodation is available in ten en suite bedrooms.

Open all wk 12-2 6.30-10.30 (Sun 12-2.30 6.30-10.30) **Bar Meals** L served all wk 12-2 D served Sun-Fri 6.30-10 Av main course £8 **Restaurant** L served all wk 12-2 booking required D served all wk 6.30-10 booking required Fixed menu price fr £13.95 Av 3 course à la carte fr £25 ⊕ FREE HOUSE ◀ Greene King IPA, Young's Special, Black Sheep Brewery, Tribute ○ Thatchers. ♟ 10 **Facilities** Children welcome Children's menu Children's portions Family room Garden Parking Wi-fi **Rooms** 10

TRING   Map 6 SP91

The Cow Roast Inn NEW

Cow Roast, London Rd HP23 5RF ☎ 01442 822287
e-mail: cowroastinn@btconnect.com
dir: Between Berkhamstead & Tring on A4251

Originally called the Cow Rest, this former coaching inn dates back to the 16th century, when it was used by local farmers en route to the London markets. Before that, archaeological studies have found there was an important Roman settlement on the site. These days, the pub is an old fashioned village inn with a modern twist thanks to the addition of a full-blown Thai restaurant, although traditional pub meals can still be ordered in the bar.

Open all day all wk **Bar Meals** L served all wk food served all day **Restaurant** L served Mon-Sat 12-3, Sun 12-5 D served Mon-Sat 5-9 ◀ Abbot Ale, Side Pocket for a Toad, Guest ales ○ Westons. **Facilities** Children welcome Children's portions Dogs allowed Garden Parking Wi-fi

PICK OF THE PUBS

The Fox ❀ ♖

WILLIAN   Map 12 TL23

Baldock Ln SG6 2AE
☎ 01462 480233   🖹 01462 676966
e-mail: restaurant@foxatwillian.co.uk
web: www.foxatwillian.co.uk
dir: A1(M) junct 9 towards Letchworth, 1st
left to Willian, 0.5m on left

Not far from Hitchin, Letchworth and Junction 9 of the A1M, this popular award-winning destination dining pub draws locals, walkers and cyclists to its range of ales and menus of modern British cooking. A clean, crisp look defines the interior, with settees and cane chairs, themed paintings by local artists on the walls, and chunky wooden furniture; its glazed restaurant atrium and enclosed courtyard are both pleasant places to settle down with a menu. The imposing Georgian building sits opposite the village pond and right next door to the church, ideal aspects for the two beer gardens. The pub has answered to several names over the years, being the Orange Tree from around 1750, then until 1870 the Dinsdale Arms (after the family who owned the village), when it became for a while the Willian Arms. In 1907, after its first incarnation as the Fox, the People's Refreshment House Association took it over. It's now part of a select chain overseen by Cliff Nye, renowned for his Norfolk coast pubs. The choice of ales reflects this, with East Anglian brews from Woodforde's and Adnams to the fore, while a recently added fifth handpump is dedicated to rotating ales from the pub's own Brancaster Brewery. Young and friendly staff serve food from the daily-changing, AA Rosette menu, which includes fish and shellfish fresh from north Norfolk: Brancaster Staithe oysters feature in the oyster and Guinness festival held during March. At other times the menu may tempt with a pan-seared fillet of red gurnard with fondant potato, wilted red chard and garlic foam. Meat lovers are likely to plump for a roast breast of chicken with lemon and vegetable nage, or seared Sacombe Hill Farm loin of venison.

Open all day all wk Mon-Thu noon-11 (Fri-Sat noon-mdnt, Sun noon-10.30) **Bar Meals** L served Mon-Fri 12-2, Sat 12-6, Sun 12-3 D served Mon-Thu 6.30-9 Av main course £11 **Restaurant** L served Mon-Sat 12-2, Sun 12-3 D served Mon-Thu 6.45-9, Fri-Sat 6.30-9.15 Av 3 course à la carte fr £25 ⊕ FREE HOUSE ◀ Adnams Bitter, Woodforde's Wherry, Fuller's London Pride, Brancaster Brewery weekly changing guest ales ♂ Aspall ♛ 14 **Facilities** Children welcome Children's portions Dogs allowed Garden Beer festival Parking Wi-fi

WELWYN   Map 6 TL21

The White Hart ♥

2 Prospect Place AL6 9EN
☎ 01438 715353 📠 01438 714448
e-mail: bookings@thewhiteharthotel.net
web: www.thewhiteharthotel.net
dir: *Just off A1(M) junct 6. On corner of Prospect Place
(just past fire station)*

This neck of the old Great North Road was once Dick
Turpin's hunting ground. The White Hart's origins as a
17th-century coaching inn can still be seen its olde
worlde beams and inglenook fireplace, but today they
blend easily with contemporary wood floors, leather
chairs and bold artwork after an elegant refurbishment.
In keeping with the surroundings, menus mix modern and
innovative European style with the best of British
produce, so expect the likes of mustard and oat-crumbed
herrings; Wobbly Bottom Farm goat's cheese fritters;
roast pheasant breast with chestnut stuffing; and
monthly changing seasonal specials.

Open all day all wk 7am-mdnt (Sun 9am-10.30pm)
Bar Meals L served Mon-Sat 12-2.30 D served Mon-Sat
6.30-9.30 Av main course £6.50 **Restaurant** L served all
wk 12-2.30 booking required D served Mon-Sat
6.30-9.30, Sun 6-8.30 booking required Fixed menu price
fr £9.99 Av 3 course à la carte fr £25 ⊕ CHARLES WELLS
🍺 Eagle IPA, Bombardier, Young's ♂ Stowford Press.
♥ 14 **Facilities** Children welcome Children's menu
Children's portions Parking Wi-fi

See advert below

WELWYN GARDEN CITY   Map 6 TL21

The Brocket Arms ★★★★ INN

Ayot St Lawrence AL6 9BT
☎ 01438 820250 & 07984 282800
e-mail: bookings@brocketarms.com
dir: *A1(M) junct 4 follow signs to Wheathampstead, then
Shaw's Corner. Pub past Shaw's Corner on right*

Originally built as a monks' hostel, parts of The Brocket
Arms date back to 1378 but it didn't become a tavern
until the 1630s. Encircled by a picturesque village that
was once home to George Bernard Shaw, the pub was
refurbished and reopened in May 2009 by Howard and
Suzy Sharp. Huge oak beams and hefty hearths greet you
along with a great range of real ales and wines. Chef
Andrew Knight uses the best local seasonal ingredients
for his bar menu and modern British menu du jour. There
are also six comfortable bedrooms, each full of character
and charm.

Open all day all wk Mon-Sat noon-11, Sun noon-10.30
⊕ FREE HOUSE 🍺 Nethergate Brewery Brocket Bitter,
Greene King IPA, Sharp's Doom Bar, Guest ales ♂ Aspall.
Facilities Children welcome Children's portions Dogs
allowed Garden Parking Wi-fi **Rooms** 6

WILLIAN   Map 12 TL23

PICK OF THE PUBS

The Fox ⊛ ♥

See Pick of the Pubs on opposite page

KENT

BEARSTED   Map 7 TQ85

The Oak on the Green

Bearsted Green ME14 4EJ
☎ 01622 737976 📠 01233 820074
e-mail: headoffice@villagegreenrestaurants.com
dir: *In village centre next to green*

As its name suggests, this refurbished 17th-century pub
overlooks Bearsted's pretty green and the front terrace,
canopied under huge blue brollies, makes the most of its
pleasant location. Once the village courthouse and
prison, it is now a thriving gastro-pub. An eclectic
modern menu offers an extensive choice including
succulent steaks and pies (Kentish farmhouse chicken),
alongside classic dishes like steak and kidney pie; and
imaginative specials - seared squid with garlic, chilli
and coriander butter; and the 'wonderfully comforting
and rustic' slow roasted pork belly with sage mash,
crackling, French beans and rich gravy.

Open all day all wk **Bar Meals** L served Mon-Sat 12-5
booking required D served Mon-Sat 12-10.30, Sun
12-9.45 booking required Av main course £5 food served
all day **Restaurant** L served Mon-Sat 12-5 booking
required D served Mon-Sat 12-10.30, Sun 12-9.45 Av 3
course à la carte fr £20 food served all day ⊕ FREE
HOUSE 🍺 Fuller's London Pride, ESB, Old Thumper,
Beehead ♂ Biddenden. **Facilities** Children welcome
Children's menu Children's portions Dogs allowed Garden
Parking

BENENDEN — Map 7 TQ83

The Bull at Benenden NEW

The Street TN17 4DE ☎ 01580 240054
e-mail: enquiries@thebullatbenenden.co.uk
dir: From A229 onto B2086 to Benenden. Or from
Tenterden take A28 S towards Hastings. Right onto B2086

Dating from 1601, this award-winning village pub and
restaurant has been sympathetically renovated with
unusual chinoiserie windows and an eclectic array of
comfortable antique furniture. From the kitchen, expect
home-prepared, locally sourced food, with traditional
regulars like steak and kidney pudding, fresh cod in beer
batter, and wild rabbit stew. Daily specials include pan-
fried Rye Bay scallops and vegetable balti. The main bar,
centring on an inglenook with integral seats, is where
landlord Mark always presents a terrific local real ale,
cider and perry selection. In summer, head outside to the
secret garden or tables overlooking the cricket green.

Open all day all wk noon-2am Bar Meals L served
Mon-Sat 12-2.30, Sun 12-4 D served Mon-Sat 6-9.20
Restaurant D served Fri-Sun 6-9.20 ◀ Larkins, Harveys,
Dark Star Hop Head, Rother Valley Level Best, Guest ales.
Facilities Children welcome Children's menu Children's
portions Dogs allowed Garden Parking

BIDDENDEN — Map 7 TQ83

PICK OF THE PUBS

The Three Chimneys

Biddenden Rd TN27 8LW ☎ 01580 291472
dir: From A262 midway between Biddenden &
Sissinghurst, follow Frittenden signs. (Pub seen from
main road). Pub immediately on left in hamlet of Three
Chimneys

Worth remembering if visiting nearby Sissinghurst
Castle, this 15th-century timbered treasure that has
every natural advantage of being a classic country pub,
its original, small-roomed layout and old-fashioned
furnishings remain delightfully intact. There are old
settles, low beams, wood-panelled walls, worn brick
floors, crackling log fires, soft evening candlelight,
absence of music and electronic games – glorious.
Modern-day demand for dining space has seen the
addition of the rear Garden Room and a tasteful
conservatory, and drinkers and diners spill out onto the
secluded heated side patio and vast shrub-filled
garden, which are perfect for summer eating. Food is
bang up-to-date and listed on daily-changing
chalkboards. Tuck into a hearty ploughman's lunch or
salmon and smoked haddock fishcakes with tartare
sauce, or something more substantial, perhaps roast
duck with bubble-and-squeak and port jus, or pan-
fried rib-eye steak with garlic butter. If you have room
for a pudding, try the delicious sticky toffee pudding.
Adnams ales and the heady Biddenden cider are
tapped direct from cask.

Open all wk 11.30-3 5.30-11 (Sat-Sun 11.30-4,
5.30-11) Closed: 25 Dec Bar Meals L served all wk
12-2.30 booking required D served all wk 6.30-9.30
booking required Restaurant L served all wk 12-2.30
booking required D served all wk 6.30-9.30 booking
required ⊕ FREE HOUSE ◀ Adnams, Harveys Old,
Special ♂ Biddenden. Facilities Children welcome
Dogs allowed Garden Parking

BODSHAM GREEN — Map 7 TR14

PICK OF THE PUBS

Froggies At The Timber Batts

School Ln TN25 5JQ
☎ 01233 750237 📠 01233 750176
e-mail: joel@thetimberbatts.co.uk
web: www.thetimberbatts.co.uk
dir: 4m E of Wye

Named after a nearby wood yard, this delightful 15th-
century pub is set in unspoilt and spectacular Kent
countryside. French chef/proprietor Joel Gross built up a
great reputation for his former restaurant in Wye; now
he's built a similar one at this pub, built in the reign of
Henry VII. The beamed and timbered bar, serving three
real ales, has an inglenook fireplace the size of a small
room, while the restaurant has a huge fireplace of its
own, old pine tables and candles. Three different
menus - bar snacks, carte and daily specials - offer
locally sourced dishes, some classically French,
naturally. An economy with words on the bar menu
results in croque madame, omelette fromage, salade
Niçoise, for example. Restaurant favourites include duo
of scallops and gambas in garlic butter; duck leg
confit; grilled halibut vièrge sauce; pan-fried veal loin
in lardons, porcini and cream sauce. As for wines,
remember that Monsieur Gross is French, and his huge
wine list fairly bristles with his mother country's
products.

Open 12-3 6.30-close Closed: 24 Dec-2 Jan, Mon
(except BHs L) Bar Meals L served all wk 12-2.30
D served all wk 7-9.30 Restaurant L served all wk
12-2.30 booking required D served all wk 7-9.30
booking required ⊕ FREE HOUSE ◀ Adnams, London
Pride, Woodforde's Wherry. Facilities Children welcome
Children's portions Dogs allowed Garden Parking

BOSSINGHAM — Map 7 TR14

The Hop Pocket

The Street CT4 6DY ☎ 01227 709866 📠 01227 709866
dir: Telephone for directions

Birds of prey and an animal corner for children are among
the more unusual attractions at this family pub in the
heart of Kent. Canterbury is only five miles away and the
county's delightfully scenic coast and countryside are
within easy reach. As this is a free house there is a good
range of ales to accompany dishes like fish pie, supreme
of chicken, spicy salmon, Cajun beef, chilli nachos and
fish platter. There is also an extensive range of
sandwiches and omelettes.

Open all wk 11-3 6-mdnt (Sat & Sun all day)
Bar Meals L served all wk 12-2.30 D served Mon-Sat
7-9.30 Restaurant L served all wk 12-2.30 D served Mon-
Sat 7-9.30 ⊕ FREE HOUSE ◀ London Pride, Adnams,
Wadworth 6X, Purity Ales. Facilities Children welcome
Children's portions Play area Dogs allowed Garden
Parking Wi-fi

BRABOURNE — Map 7 TR14

The Five Bells Inn ₹

The Street TN25 5LP ☎ 01303 813334
e-mail: visitus@fivebellsinnbrabourne.com
dir: 5m E of Ashford

Alison and John Rogers took over this 16th-century free
house pub in April 2010. A wood-fired oven is central to
the new menu, with many of the 'small plate' starters
also available as main courses. Typical choices include
pie or chargrilled breast of chicken with home-made
barbecue sauce topped with Kentish cheese and streaky
bacon. The pub is surrounded by rolling hills and
orchards and it is the perfect pit stop for walkers and
cyclists where they can enjoy a glass of local beer, cider
and wine.

Open all day all wk Bar Meals L served Mon-Fri 12-2.30,
Sat-Sun all day D served Mon-Fri 6-9.30, Sat-Sun all day
Av main course £12 ⊕ FREE HOUSE ◀ Goachers,
Hopdaemon, Brabourne Stout, Guest ales ♂ Curious
Brew, Biddenden. ₹ All Facilities Children welcome Dogs
allowed Garden Parking Wi-fi

BROOKLAND — Map 7 TQ92

PICK OF THE PUBS

The Royal Oak ₹

High St TN29 9QR ☎ 01797 344215
e-mail: info@royaloakbrookland.co.uk
dir: A259, 5m E of Rye. In village by church

A Grade II-listed marshland pub, The Royal Oak has
been providing shelter and sustenance to locals and
visitors to Romney Marsh since 1736, although it dates
back as far as 1570. These days its uncluttered, smart
interior is a pleasing combination of original features
and modern furnishings. The menus cater for
everything from speedy lunchtime snacks to leisurely

Save on hotels. Book at **theAA.com/hotel**

KENT 257 **ENGLAND**

three-course dining. Regularly changing dishes draw on local, seasonal produce. Simple options are freshly made sandwiches; beer-battered south coast cod with hand-cut chips and garden peas; and the ploughman's platter with home-cooked smoked ham, Cheddar cheese, chutney and crusty bread. For dinner, choose from the likes of chicken, pork and pistachio terrine with pear and date chutney; grilled fillets of local mackerel glazed with chilli jam on whole grain mustard mash; and apple and cinnamon crumble with thick cream. A well-kept and tranquil garden borders the churchyard of St Augustine, one of only four churches in England with a separate bell tower.

Open 12-3 6-11 Closed: Sun eve & Mon eve **Bar Meals** L served Mon-Fri 12-2, Sat-Sun 12-2.30 D served Tue-Fri 6.30-9, Sat 6.30-9.30 **Restaurant** L served Mon-Fri 12-2, Sat-Sun 12-2.30 D served Tue-Fri 6.30-9, Sat 6.30-9.30 ⊕ ENTERPRISE INNS ◀ Harvey's Best Bitter, Adnams Best Bitter, Woodforde's Wherry, Guest ale Ö Westons Stowford Press. ♟ 20 **Facilities** Children's portions Dogs allowed Garden Parking

PICK OF THE PUBS

Woolpack Inn

See Pick of the Pubs on page 258

BURHAM Map 6 TQ76

The Golden Eagle

80 Church St ME1 3SD ☎ 01634 668975
e-mail: kathymay@btconnect.com
web: www.thegoldeneagle.org
dir: *S from M2 junct 3 or N from M20 junct 6 on A229, follow signs to Burham*

Commanding striking views across the Medway Valley, this traditional Kentish village pub, which dates from 1850, has been famous locally for 30 years for its authentic Malaysian food. Expect to find an extensive menu, enhanced by chef specialities on the chalkboard, and featuring king prawn sambal, wortip crispy chicken, sweet and sour crispy pork, pad Thai chicken, and traditional puddings like apple crumble.

Open all wk Closed: 25-26 Dec **Bar Meals** L served all wk 12-2 D served all wk 7-9.30 Av main course £8.95 **Restaurant** L served all wk 12-2 D served all wk 7-9.30 Fixed menu price fr £10.75 ⊕ FREE HOUSE ◀ Wadworth 6X Ö Stowford Press. **Facilities** Parking

---

CANTERBURY Map 7 TR15

The Chapter Arms ♟

New Town St, Chartham Hatch CT4 7LT
☎ 01227 738340
e-mail: info@chapterarms.com
dir: *3m from Canterbury. Off A28 in Chartham Hatch or A2 at Upper Harbledown*

This charming and picturesque free house sits on the North Downs Way in over an acre of gardens overlooking apple orchards and oast houses. It was once three cottages owned by Canterbury Cathedral's Dean and Chapter - hence the name. A comely choice of ales is offered in the bar, and food ranges from lunchtime specials (beef suet pudding; honey roast ham; egg and chips) to evening dishes such as honey-glazed confit duck leg with a truffle oil-dressed salad followed by slow braised lamb shank with root vegetable casserole and creamy mash. Desserts such as sticky toffee apple sponge are made on the premises.

Open all wk 11-3 6-11 (all day Fri-Sun Jun-Sep) **Bar Meals** L served all wk 12-2.30 D served Mon-Sat 6.30-9 **Restaurant** L served Mon-Sat 12-2.30 Sun 12-3 D served Mon-Sat 6.30-9 ⊕ FREE HOUSE ◀ Shepherd Neame Master Brew, Adnams, Harveys, Young's, Wells Bombardier, Greene King IPA, Guest ales. ♟ 10 **Facilities** Children welcome Children's menu Children's portions Play area Dogs allowed Garden Parking Wi-fi

PICK OF THE PUBS

The Dove Inn ◎

Plum Pudding Ln, Dargate ME13 9HB
☎ 01227 751360
e-mail: phillipmacgre@btconnect.com
dir: *5m NW of Canterbury. A299 Thanet Way, exit at Lychgate service station*

This award-winning vine-covered Victorian country gastro-pub is tucked away in a sleepy hamlet between Faversham and Whitstable, surrounded by orchards and farmland. It has established a reputation for well-kept Shepherd Neame ales and good food based on locally sourced ingredients. The interior is simple and relaxed with stripped wooden floors and scrubbed tables. Outside is a large formal garden where, appropriately, a dovecote and doves present an agreeably scenic backdrop for an alfresco meal or quiet pint. The Dove's menu is short but nonetheless offers something for most palates and appetites. After breads and olives, fish lovers could enjoy a whole plaice with capers and cockles; local cod with spinach Lyonnaise potatoes; or smoked haddock macaroni with a soft poached hen's egg. If you fancy something heartier, plump for confit pork belly with apple sauce and potato purée, or maybe Kentish pork and ale sausages and mash. For dessert, maybe choose sticky toffee pudding or crème brûlée. Children are offered smaller portions from the main menu. The Dove holds lots of events throughout the year.

Open noon-3 6-mdnt (Fri noon-mdnt Sun noon-9 (Apr-Oct) noon-4 (Nov-Mar)) Closed: Mon **Bar Meals** L served Tue-Sat 12-2.30 D served Tue-Thu 6.30-9 **Restaurant** L served Tue-Sun 12-2.30 booking required D served Tue-Sat 7-9 booking required ⊕ SHEPHERD NEAME ◀ Shepherd Neame Master Brew, Spitfire, seasonal ale. **Facilities** Children welcome Children's portions Dogs allowed Garden Parking Wi-fi

PICK OF THE PUBS

The Granville ◎

Street End, Lower Hardres CT4 7AL
☎ 01227 700402 📠 01227 700925
e-mail: info@thegranvillecanterbury.com
dir: *On B2068, 2m from Canterbury towards Hythe*

A light and airy destination dining pub with an eye-catching feature central fireplace/flue which draws the eye, at least temporarily, away from the series of roll-over art exhibitions and installations (lino cuts, photographs, sculptures) which add to the draw of this contemporarily-executed village pub outside Canterbury. With ample parking, a patio and large beer garden where summer barbecues take place, this Shepherd Neame pub is good for families and dogs, whilst locals indulge in a more traditional public bar. Don't, however, expect typical pub grub from the short, lively menu; the confident approach to utilising the best that Kent and the enfolding seas can provide has gained an AA Rosette for Gabrielle Harris and her team. The soup of the day may delight as a rabbit, smoked bacon and winter vegetable broth before progressing through the board with braised brill fillet with mussels and saffron or that fulfilling favourite, roast pork belly with crackling and apple sauce; every day brings a new dish or two to savour, finishing perhaps with a flourless chocolate cake with raspberry sorbet and cream.

Open noon-3 5.30-11 Closed: 26 Dec, Mon eve **Bar Meals** L served Tue-Sat 12-2 D served Tue-Sat 7-9 Av main course £15.95 **Restaurant** L served Tue-Sun 12-2 booking required D served Tue-Sat 7-9 booking required Av 3 course à la carte fr £27 ⊕ SHEPHERD NEAME ◀ Master Brew, seasonal ale. **Facilities** Children welcome Children's portions Dogs allowed Garden Parking

PICK OF THE PUBS

Woolpack Inn

BROOKLAND — Map 7 TQ92

Beacon Ln TN29 9TJ
☎ 01797 344321
web: www.thewoolpackbrookland.co.uk
dir: *1.5m past Brookland towards Rye on A259*

Partly built of old timbers salvaged from local shipwrecks and isolated down a lane deep in Kentish marshland, surrounded by dykes and reed beds, this low, white-painted 15th-century cottage oozes authentic character and charm. Built when smuggling was rife on Romney Marsh, it's rumoured that at one time the Woolpack had a secret tunnel used by smugglers to escape from the Excise men. The old spinning wheel mounted on the bar ceiling was used to divide up their contraband; but, nowadays, the pub is ideally situated for those who wish to explore this unique and beautiful area of Kent. There are many walks in the area to study nature at close quarters, go fishing, or just to stop and let the world go by. Open beams and a vast inglenook fireplace (you can sit in it!) add to the atmosphere, and the staff extend a warm welcome to all.

The chef makes extensive use of fresh produce including fish from the local fishermen. The menu offers a wide variety

of home-made meals, whilst dishes on the specials board make the most of seasonal produce. Lunchtime brings ploughman's, sandwiches and filled jacket potatoes (vegetable curry), and there are hog roasts and barbecues in the pub garden on summer evenings.

On the main menu, expect pub favourites like chicken Kiev, lamb shank and battered cod. There are also game and vegetarian dishes like whole partridge with red wine and cream sauce, and Stilton and vegetable bake. Finish with the likes of honey and cinnamon pudding, steamed spotted Dick, or bitter chocolate and orange sponge. Wash down with a cracking pint of Shepherd Neame Spitfire.

Open all wk Mon-Fri 11-3 6-11 Sat 11-11 Sun noon-10.30 **Bar Meals** L served Mon-Fri 12-2.30, Sat-Sun 12-9 D served Mon-Fri 6-9, Sat-Sun 12-9 (open all day BHs & school hols) ◗ Shepherd Neame Spitfire Premium Ale, Master Brew Bitter. **Facilities** Children's menu Children's portions Play area Family room Dogs allowed Garden Parking

CANTERBURY *continued*

PICK OF THE PUBS

The Red Lion

High St, Stodmarsh CT3 4BA ☎ 01227 721339
e-mail: ajtowse@hotmail.com
dir: *From Canterbury take A257 towards Sandwich, left into Stodmarsh Rd to Stodmarsh*

Built in 1475 and burnt to the ground in 1720, The Red Lion was rebuilt and has remained much as you'll find it today. Set in a tiny hamlet, it is surrounded by reed beds which are home to marsh harriers, bearded tits and bitterns. The pub's interior, warmed by two large log fires, is adorned with traditional hop garlands, curios, antiques and a collection of international menus. Outside is an extensive garden where an antique forge doubles as a barbecue during the summer months; here you'll find an abundance of flowers and hop bines, with ducks, chickens and rabbits wandering about. From the intently focussed kitchen expect a cosmopolitan and seasonally changing menu blended with local produce. Salads come from allotments and gardens, meats from Brogdale Farm, and wild mushrooms from surrounding woodland. Classic plates with a modern twist include oxtail stew, game pies, herb-crusted rump of salt marsh lamb, and dishes featuring fish from Whitstable.

Open all day 10.30am-11pm (Sun 10.30-4.30) Closed: Sun eve **Bar Meals** L served all wk 12-2.15 booking required D served Mon-Sat 7-9.15 booking required **Restaurant** L served all wk 12-2.15 booking required D served Mon-Sat 7-9.15 booking required ⊕ FREE HOUSE ◀ Greene King IPA, Ruddles County, Old Speckled Hen. **Facilities** Children welcome Children's portions Play area Family room Dogs allowed Garden Beer festival Parking

The White Horse Inn ⚑

53 High St, Bridge CT4 5LA ☎ 01227 830845
e-mail: info@whitehorsebridge.com
dir: *3m S of Canterbury, just off A2*

Built in 1500, this one-time staging post between London and Dover stands proudly in the centre of Bridge, just three miles south of Canterbury. The white-painted building wears its age well, looking very pretty in summer with an abundance of flower baskets, and there is a pleasant beer garden to the rear. An enormous log fire burns in the beamed bar during the winter months and Fuller's and Shepherd Neame are amongst the real ales served in the bar. New landlords continue the strong emphasis on food, with seasonal dishes created from the best local ingredients. Choose between the blackboard bar menu, and more formal dining in the Stables Restaurant.

Open Mon-Sun L Closed: Sun eve **Bar Meals** food served all day **Restaurant** food served all day ◀ Shepherd Neame Masterbrew, Greene King Abbot Ale, Fuller's London Pride, Greene King IPA, Gadds No. 5. ⚑ 10 **Facilities** Children welcome Dogs allowed Garden Parking

---

The Bowl Inn

Egg Hill Rd TN27 0HG
☎ 01233 712256   📠 01233 714705
e-mail: info@bowl-inn.co.uk
dir: *M20 junct 8/9, A20 to Charing, then A252 towards Canterbury. Left at top of Charing Hill down Bowl Rd, 1.25m*

Well known for its selection of real ales, all-day snack menu and speciality food nights, this whitewashed free house stands high on the North Downs in an Area of Outstanding Natural Beauty. Built as a farmhouse in 1512 and later converted to a brewhouse, it has been run by Alan and Sue Paine since 1992. It retains its old world charm with a large inglenook fireplace and warming winter fires. Expect a small but varied menu that includes Kent-cured ham, English Cheddar ploughman's, and hot bacon and sausage sandwiches. An annual beer festival takes place in mid-July.

Open all wk Mon-Sat noon-mdnt Sun noon-11 (Mon-Thu 4-11 Fri-Sun noon-mdnt winter) **Bar Meals** L served all wk 12-9.30 D served all wk 12-9.30 food served all day ⊕ FREE HOUSE ◀ Fuller's London Pride, Adnams Southwold, Harveys Sussex Best, Whitstable IPA, Young's Best. **Facilities** Children welcome Dogs allowed Garden Beer festival Parking Wi-fi

The Oak

5 High St TN27 0HU ☎ 01233 712612
e-mail: info@theoakcharing.co.uk
web: www.theoakcharing.co.uk
dir: *M20 junct 9, A20 towards Maidstone. 5m to Charing. Right into High St*

This gabled old inn in one of Kent's prettiest villages makes the most of its location, sourcing beers from Nelson's, across the North Downs in Chatham and harvesting produce from the bountiful surrounding acres of the Garden of England. High quality ingredients are sourced for the robust modern English menus. Fish from Hythe and Rye, pork and lamb from downland farms and vegetables from local growers feature in dishes such as pan-seared fillet of smoked haddock on sautéed leeks with crème fraîche mash.

Open all wk 11am-11pm (Sun noon-10.30) **Bar Meals** L served all wk 12-2.30, Sun 12-4 D served all wk 6-9 **Restaurant** L served all wk 12-2.30, Sun 12-4 D served all wk 6-9 booking required ⊕ FREE HOUSE ◀ Masterbrew, Nelson ð Thatchers Gold. **Facilities** Children welcome Children's menu Children's portions Dogs allowed Garden Parking Wi-fi

---

PICK OF THE PUBS

Castle Inn ⚑

TN8 7AH ☎ 01892 870247   📠 01892 871420
e-mail: info@castleinn-kent.co.uk
dir: *1.5m S of B2027 between Tonbridge & Edenbridge*

Located at the end of a unique, unspoilt row of Tudor timbered houses opposite the parish church, this historic tile-hung building dates from 1420 and boasts leaded casement windows and projecting upper gables. Both the pub and the village street are owned by the National Trust and regularly feature in period TV dramas and films. The charming interior has also remained delightfully unchanged; its two traditional bars have quarry-tiled floors and an old brick fireplace, as well as rustic wall benches in the classic public bar. When the sun shines head for the vine-hung courtyard or the peaceful, flower-filled garden. Chef-patron John McManus took over in August 2010 and has significantly improved the food offering, with dishes ranging from cottage pie and chicken Caesar salad to seared squid with smoked pancetta and tomato risotto cake, poussin with lemon and thyme butter, and treacle tart with almond and Chantilly cream. Larkins ales, nine wines by the glass and set Sunday lunches complete the picture.

Open all day all wk 11-11 (Sun 12-10.30) **Bar Meals** L served all wk 12-4 D served Mon-Sat 7-9.30 **Restaurant** L served Mon-Fri 12-2, Sat-Sun 12-4 D served Mon-Sat 7-9.30 ⊕ FREE HOUSE ◀ Larkins Traditional, Harveys Sussex, Larkins Porter, Larkins Blonde ð Stowford Press. ⚑ 9 **Facilities** Children welcome Children's menu Children's portions Dogs allowed Garden

CHILHAM   Map 7 TR05

PICK OF THE PUBS

The White Horse

The Square CT4 8BY ☎ 01227 730355
e-mail: info@thewhitehorsechilham.co.uk
dir: *Take A28 from Canterbury then A252, in 1m turn left*

Set next to St Mary's church and opposite the 15th-century village square where the annual May Fair is held, this is one of the most photographed pubs in Britain. The square is a delightfully haphazard mix of gabled, half-timbered houses shops and inns dating from the late Middle Ages, with the North Downs Way passing through. This flint and stone inn offers a traditional atmosphere and modern cooking from a monthly-changing menu based on fresh local produce, mainly organic. A meal might include smoked mackerel and couscous salad followed by meatballs in Biddenden wine and tomato sauce or Bluey's fish pie, with crème brûlée or apple pancake with toffee sauce and organic vanilla ice cream for dessert. There is a wide selection of real ales from local Kentish and more well known breweries. Look out for live music and quiz nights, plus a summer beer festival.

Open all day all wk noon-close Closed: 25 Dec
Bar Meals L served all wk 12-2.30 booking required
D served all wk 6.30-9 booking required Av main course
£12.95 ⊕ ENTERPRISE ◀ Masterbrew, Guest.
Facilities Children welcome Children's menu Children's portions Dogs allowed Garden Beer festival

CHILLENDEN   Map 7 TR25

PICK OF THE PUBS

Griffins Head ♀

See Pick of the Pubs on opposite page

CRANBROOK   Map 7 TQ73

The George Hotel ♀ NEW

Stone St TN17 3HE ☎ 01580 713348 📄 01580 715532
e-mail: georgehotel@shepherd-neame.co.uk
dir: *From A21 follow signs to Goudhurst. At large rdbt take 3rd exit to Cranbrook (A229). Hotel on left*

One of Cranbrook's landmark buildings, the 14th-century George Hotel traditionally served visiting buyers of locally made Cranbrook cloth. Magistrates held court here for over 300 years, and today the sophisticated interior retains a wealth of period features, making the hotel a comfortable base for exploring Kent and Sussex. There are separate brasserie and restaurant menus, whilst daily specials might include baked oysters with lime pancetta and Parmesan, or pan-roasted lamb steak with mixed bean casserole.

Open all day all wk **Bar Meals** L served Sun-Fri 12-3, Sat all day D served Mon-Sat 6-9.30, Sun 6-9 Av main course £15 **Restaurant** L served Sun-Fri 12-3, Sat all day D served Mon-Sat 6-9.30, Sun 6-9 Fixed menu price fr £18 Av 3 course à la carte fr £24 ⊕ SHEPHERD NEAME ◀ Masterbrew, Spitfire ♂ Thatchers. ♀ 16
Facilities Children welcome Children's menu Children's portions Dogs allowed Garden Parking

DARTFORD   Map 6 TQ57

The Rising Sun Inn ★★★ INN ♀

Fawkham Green, Fawkham, Longfield DA3 8NL
☎ 01474 872291 📄 01474 872779
web: www.risingsun-fawkham.co.uk
dir: *0.5m from Brands Hatch Racing Circuit & 5m from Dartford*

Standing on the green in a picturesque village not far from Brands Hatch, The Rising Sun has been a pub since 1702. Inside you will find a bar full of character, complete with inglenook log fire, and Inglenooks restaurant where home-made traditional house specials and a large fish menu, using the best local produce, are served. There is also a front patio and garden for alfresco dining in warmer weather, plus comfortable en suite bedrooms if you would like to stay over.

Open all day all wk **Bar Meals** food served all day
Restaurant L served all wk 12-3 D served all wk
6.30-9.30 ⊕ FREE HOUSE ◀ Courage Best, Courage Directors, London Pride, Timothy Taylor Landlord, Harveys. ♀ 9 **Facilities** Children's portions Garden Parking Wi-fi **Rooms** 5

DOVER   Map 7 TR34

The White Cliffs Hotel ★★★ HL ◉ ♀

High St, St Margaret's at Cliffe CT15 6AT
☎ 01304 852400 & 852229
e-mail: mail@thewhitecliffs.com
dir: *3m NE of Dover in centre of village*

A contemporary atmosphere and a refreshingly independent way of thinking characterise this traditional Kentish weather-boarded establishment. The hotel has a stylish, contemporary feel without compromising the charm of this delightful historic building, with its winter log fires and bar leading out onto the rose-filled summer garden. Gavin Oakley brings imagination and flair to menus at The Bay Restaurant, which has earned him an

AA Rosette, where main course offerings might include roasted corn-fed chicken breast with sweetcorn, rainbow chard and Madeira jus, and poached Hebridean loch salmon with chorizo, cannellini beans and mussels.

Open all wk **Bar Meals** L served all wk 11am-11pm
D served all wk 11am-11pm Av main course £7.95 food served all day **Restaurant** L served all wk 12-2.30
D served all wk 6.30-9 Fixed menu price fr £7.95 Av 3 course à la carte fr £25 ⊕ FREE HOUSE ◀ Adnams, Gadds ♂ Westons Organic, Aspall. ♀ 10
Facilities Children welcome Children's menu Children's portions Dogs allowed Garden Parking Wi-fi **Rooms** 15

FAVERSHAM   Map 7 TR06

PICK OF THE PUBS

Shipwright's Arms ♀

Hollowshore ME13 7TU ☎ 01795 590088
dir: *A2 through Ospringe then right at rdbt. Right at T-junct then left opposite Davington School, follow signs*

Built of homely brick and clad in weatherboard, this extraordinary creekside pub was first licensed in 1738. Standing in a remote location on the Swale marshes and once the haunt of pirates and smugglers, it is best reached on foot or by boat. The effort in getting here is well rewarded as this unspoilt tavern oozes historic character and charm. Step back in time in the classic bars, which boast nooks and crannies, original standing timbers, built-in settles, well-worn sofas, wood-burning stoves, a wealth of maritime artefacts, and a relaxed, no-frills but comfortable atmosphere. In time-honoured fashion, quaff locally-brewed Goachers and Whitstable ales tapped straight from the cask, and tuck into simple, traditional bar food: moules frites; Aberdeen Angus lasagne; home-cooked ham, egg and chips; and fresh fish caught by the local trawler.

Open 11-3 6-10 (Sat-Sun 11-4 6-11 in winter, Sat 11-11, Sun noon-10.30 in summer) Closed: Mon (Oct-Mar) **Bar Meals** L served Mon-Sat 11-2.30, Sun 12-2.30 D served Tue-Sat 7-9 (no food Tue-Thu eve in winter) Av main course £8.25 **Restaurant** L served Tue-Sat 11-2.30, Sun 12-2.30 D served Tue-Sat 7-9 (no food Tue-Thu eve in winter) ⊕ FREE HOUSE ◀ Local ales, Goachers, Hop Daemon, Whitstable Brewery. ♀ 12
Facilities Children welcome Children's menu Children's portions Family room Dogs allowed Garden Parking

Save on hotels. Book at **theAA.com/hotel**

KENT 261 ENGLAND

PICK OF THE PUBS

Griffins Head ♀

　　　Map 7 TR25

CT3 1PS

☎ 01304 840325　📄 01304 841290

dir: *A2 from Canterbury towards Dover, then B2046. Village on right*

Dating from 1286, the Griffins Head is an architectural gem of a building, a fine black-and-white half-timbered Wealden hall house, nestling in a tiny farming hamlet amid rolling open countryside south-east of Canterbury. Originally built as a farmhouse to serve the local estate, ale and cider were always brewed on the premises for the workers but it was only granted an ale licence in 1743. The present Tudor structure is built around the original wattle and daub walls, remains of which can be viewed in one of the three delightfully unspoilt rooms, which also feature flagstone floors, exposed brick walls and beams and a tasteful mix of furnishings, from old scrubbed pine tables and chairs to church pews.

Fine Shepherd Neame ales and home-made food have helped this old inn to make its mark with visitors as well as locals, among them Kent's cricketing fraternity. The constantly changing

seasonal menu is typically English, and specialises in game from local estates, and locally caught fish where possible. Typical dishes might include lamb stew; braised steak, onions and mash; warm salads with steak and roasted vegetables; or sautéed prawns and squid; and traditional pub dishes like cottage pie and ham, egg and chips. Desserts include apple crumble, or home-made ice creams like passionfruit, ginger, or raspberry and strawberry.

The pretty garden, full of rambling roses and clematis, is the setting for popular summer weekend barbecues.

Open all wk Closed: Sun pm
Bar Meals L served all wk 12-2 D served Mon-Sat 7-9.30 booking required
Restaurant L served all wk 12-2 D served Mon-Sat 7-9.30 booking required
🌐 SHEPHERD NEAME ☜ Shepherd Neame.
♀ 10 **Facilities** Garden Parking

FORDCOMBE   Map 6 TQ54

Chafford Arms ♥

TN3 0SA ☎ 01892 740267
e-mail: chaffordarms@btconnect.com
web: www.chaffordarms.com
dir: *On B2188 (off A264) between Tunbridge Wells, East Grinstead & Penshurst*

This visually striking country inn, with multiple gables and tall chimneys has hints of Arts and Crafts about it. Set in The Weald high above the Medway Valley, close to Penshurst Place and handy for Hever Castle, fine walking on the Weald Way is rewarded by the prospect of beers from local micro-breweries and a menu of comforting, home-made pub meals like fisherman's pie or Italian meatball linguini. Hunker down beside roaring log fires or rest awhile in the rose-scented garden, with great views of pretty countryside.

Open all day all wk 11am-mdnt **Bar Meals** L served Mon-Sat 12-9, Sun 12-8 D served Mon-Sat 12-9, Sun 12-8 food served all day **Restaurant** L served Mon-Sat 12-9, Sun 12-8 D served Mon-Sat 12-9, Sun 12-8 food served all day ⊕ ENTERPRISE INNS ◀ Larkins Bitter, Harvey's Best. ♥ 9 **Facilities** Children welcome Children's menu Dogs allowed Garden Parking

GOODNESTONE   Map 7 TR25

The Fitzwalter Arms

The Street CT3 1PJ ☎ 01304 840303
e-mail: thefitzwalter arms@gmail.com
dir: *Signed from B2046 & A2*

The 'Fitz', hostelry to the Fitzwalter Estate, has been a pub since 1702. Quintessentially English, it is a place of conviviality and conversation. Jane Austen was a frequent visitor to nearby Goodnestone Park after her brother, Edward, married into the family. On the menu, brawn with a radish, celery, parsley and caper salad; or mackerel tartare with an oyster fritter and bloody Mary sauce; followed by poached halibut fillet, asparagus and hollandaise sauce; or confit pork belly, crackling and rhubarb. Dessert might be rhubarb and ginger crumble with custard.

Open all wk Mon-Fri noon-3 6-11 (Sat-Sun noon-11) Closed: 25 Dec, 1 Jan ⊕ SHEPHERD NEAME ◀ Master Brew, Spitfire. **Facilities** Children welcome Dogs allowed Garden Wi-fi

GOUDHURST   Map 6 TQ73

Green Cross Inn

TN17 1HA ☎ 01580 211200   📄 01580 212905
dir: *A21 from Tonbridge towards Hastings turn left onto A262 towards Ashford. 2m, Goudhurst on right*

In an unspoiled corner of Kent, close to Finchcocks Manor, and originally built to serve the Paddock Wood-Goudhurst railway line, which closed in 1968, this thriving dining pub specialises in fresh seafood. Arrive early to bag a table in the dining room, prettily decorated with fresh flowers, and tuck into oysters, crab, mussels, smoked eel, whole Dover sole, or Rye Bay skate, or order the duck cassoulet, followed by hot chocolate soufflé with chocolate sauce; all prepared and supervised by chef/ owner who is Italian classically trained.

Open all wk noon-3 6-11 Closed: Sun eve ⊕ FREE HOUSE ◀ Harvey's Sussex Best Bitter, Guinness ♂ Biddenden. **Facilities** Children welcome Children's portions Garden Parking

PICK OF THE PUBS

The Star & Eagle ★★★★ INN ♥

High St TN17 1AL ☎ 01580 211512   📄 01580 212444
e-mail: starandeagle@btconnect.com
web: www.starandeagle.co.uk
dir: *Just off A21 towards Hastings. Take A262 into Goudhurst. Pub at top of hill next to church*

A commanding position at 400 feet above sea level gives the 14th-century Star & Eagle outstanding views of the orchards and hop fields that helped earn Kent the accolade 'The Garden of England'. The vaulted stonework suggests that this rambling, big-beamed building may once have been a monastery, and the tunnel from the cellars probably surfaces underneath the neighbouring parish church. The ten bedrooms and the public rooms boast original features and much character. Adnams and Harveys are the mainstays in the bar, and there's plenty of choice in wines served by the glass. While supping, unwind and enjoy choosing between the fine traditional and continental dishes prepared under the guidance of Spanish chef/proprietor Enrique Martinez. Typical dishes are moules marinière; salmon and cod fishcakes; poached hake Basque style; ginger chicken and rice; beef fillet Stroganoff; and sautéed calves' liver, bacon and crispy onions. Puddings might be apple, blackberry and hazelnut crumble with custard or crème brûlée.

Open all day all wk 11-11 (Sun 12-3 6.30-10.30) **Bar Meals** L served all wk 12-2.30 D served all wk 7-9.30 Av main course £12.50 **Restaurant** L served all wk 12-2.30 D served all wk 7-9.30 Av 3 course à la carte fr £28 ⊕ FREE HOUSE ◀ Adnams Bitter, Harvey's, Grasshopper. ♥ 14 **Facilities** Children welcome Children's menu Children's portions Family room Garden Parking Wi-fi **Rooms** 10

GRAVESEND   Map 6 TQ67

The Cock Inn

Henley St, Luddesdowne DA13 0XB
☎ 01474 814208   📄 01474 812850
e-mail: andrew.r.turner@btinternet.com
dir: *Telephone for directions*

Two traditional beamed bars with wood-burning stoves set the scene at this whitewashed free house in the beautiful Luddesdowne Valley. Seven hand pumps deliver a wonderful array of well-kept real beers, and there's not a fruit machine, jukebox or television in sight. The simple bar menu includes filled submarine rolls and basket meals, as well as home-made dishes like chilli con carne, lamb shank, and vegetarian risotto. No children allowed under 18.

Open all day all wk noon-11 (Sun noon-10.30) **Bar Meals** L served all wk 12-3 D served all wk 6-8 Av main course £6.50 ⊕ FREE HOUSE ◀ Adnams Southwold, Broadside, Lighthouse, Shepherd Neame Master Brew, Goacher's Real Mild Ale, Woodforde's Wherry. **Facilities** Dogs allowed Garden Parking

HALSTEAD   Map 6 TQ46

Rose & Crown ♥ NEW

Otford Ln TN14 7EA ☎ 01959 533120
e-mail: info@roseandcrownhalstead.co.uk
dir: *M25 junct 4, follow A21, London (SE), Bromley, Orpington signs. At Hewitts Rdbt 1st exit onto A224 signed Dunton Green. At rdbt 3rd exit into Shoreham Lane. In Halstead left into Station Rd, left into Otford Lane*

Handy for the M25 and tucked away in a North Downs village, this flint-built free house draws walkers and locals in for tip-top real ales, the choice including beer from local micro-breweries, notably Larkins Traditional and Whitstable East India Pale Ale. Regular events include seasonal beer festivals, summer barbecues, hog roasts and bat & trap competitions. This lively local also serves good traditional home-made pub food all day and booking is advisable for Sunday lunch.

Open all day all wk **Bar Meals** L served all wk 12-11 D served all wk 12-11 food served all day **Restaurant** L served all wk 12-11 D served all wk 12-11 food served all day ⊕ FREE HOUSE ◀ Larkins Traditional, Whitstable East India Pale Ale, Guest ales ♂ Westons. **Facilities** Children welcome Children's menu Children's portions Play area Dogs allowed Garden Beer festival Parking Wi-fi

Save on hotels. Book at theAA.com/hotel

KENT 263 ENGLAND

HARRIETSHAM
Map 7 TQ85

The Pepper Box Inn ♀

ME17 1LP ☎ **01622 842558**
e-mail: enquiries@thepepperboxinn.co.uk
web: www.thepepperboxinn.co.uk
dir: From A20 in Harrietsham take Fairbourne Heath turn.
2m to x-rds, straight over, 200yds, pub on left

High up on the Greensand Ridge this delightful 15th-
century country pub enjoys far-reaching views over the
Weald of Kent from its terrace. Run by the same family
since 1958, it takes its name from an early type of pistol,
a replica of which hangs behind the bar. Using the best
of local seasonal produce, food ranges from bar snacks
of ham, egg and chips or chicken curry through to tiger
prawns pan fried in garlic, chilli and ginger butter
followed by slow-roasted belly pork with cider, apples,
thyme and mashed potatoes.

Open all wk 11-3 6-11 **Bar Meals** L served all wk 12-2.15
D served Tue-Sat 7-9.45 Av main course £8.50
Restaurant L served Mon-Sat 12-2, Sun 12-3 booking
required D served Mon-Sat 7-9.45 booking required Av 3
course à la carte fr £25 ⊕ SHEPHERD NEAME
◀ Shepherd Neame Master Brew, Spitfire, Late Red. ♀ 10
Facilities Dogs allowed Garden Parking

HAWKHURST
Map 7 TQ73

The Black Pig at Hawkhurst NEW

Moor Hill TN18 4PF ☎ **01580 752306**
e-mail: enquiries@theblackpigathawkhurst.co.uk
dir: On A229, S of Hawkhurst

The once run-down Kent Cricketer pub on Moor Hill has
been refurbished and renamed by Mark and Lucy Barron-
Reid, who also own the hugely successful Bull at
Benenden (see entry) a few miles away. Like the Bull, the
ethos is to specialise in food and drink from Kent and
Sussex, so expect to find Copper Top ale from the Old
Dairy Brewery in Rolvenden, heady traditional cider from
Biddenden, and simple, home-cooked food prepared from
ingredients sourced from local farmers, growers and
artisan producers.

Open all day all wk 11am-mdnt **Bar Meals** L served
Mon-Sat 12-2.30, Sun 12-4 D served Mon-Sat 6.30-9.30
⊕ FREE HOUSE ◀ Harveys, Dark Star Hophead, Larkins
Traditional, Old Dairy Copper Top ○ Biddenden.
Facilities Children welcome Children's menu Children's
portions Dogs allowed Garden

PICK OF THE PUBS

The Great House ♀

Gills Green TN18 5EJ ☎ **01580 753119**
e-mail: enquiries@thegreathouse.net
dir: Just off A229 between Cranbrook & Hawkhurst

With its network of exposed beams, roaring log fires
and stone floors, this is a wonderfully atmospheric
16th-century free house. Serving traditional English
and regional French brasserie-style cuisine, its three
dining areas are complemented by the magnificent new
Orangery that opens on to a Mediterranean-style
terrace and a garden with a lych-gate, the ideal
backdrop for civil wedding photographs. The food is
fresh, seasonal and, in the case of the meat, organic
too. Perennial favourites include game and fish pies,
Harvey's beer-battered haddock and chicken Caesar
salad, while among the more sophisticated choices are
Sussex-reared, 28-day matured beef with gratin
dauphinoise; seared breast of wood pigeon with
pommes purée; pan-fried Loch Duart salmon; and
sweet and sour pumpkin risotto with Parmesan
crackling. Sharing boards offer three choices – fish,
charcuterie and Sicilian antipasti. Desserts range from
fruit sorbet to Kentish apple and cinnamon crumble
with honeycomb ice cream. Seventy world wines
include some from nearby Tenterden.

Open all day all wk 11.30am-11pm **Bar Meals** L served
Mon-Fri 12-3, Sat-Sun 12-9.45 D served Mon-Fri
6-9.45, Sat-Sun 12-9.45 Av main course £13
Restaurant L served Mon-Fri 12-3, Sat-Sun 12-9.45
D served Mon-Fri 6-9.45, Sat-Sun 12-9.45 Av 3 course
à la carte fr £23 ⊕ FREE HOUSE ◀ Harvey's, Guinness,
Young's ○ Biddenden. ♀ 20 **Facilities** Children
welcome Children's portions Dogs allowed Garden
Parking Wi-fi

HEVER
Map 6 TQ44

The Wheatsheaf

Hever Rd, Bough Beech TN8 7NU ☎ **01732 700254**
dir: M25 & A21 take exit for Hever Castle & follow signs.
1m past Castle on right

Originally built as a hunting lodge for Henry V, this
splendid creeper-clad inn has some stunning original
features, including a crown post revealed during
renovation in 1997. Timbered ceilings and massive Tudor
fireplaces set off various curios, such as the mounted jaw
of a man-eating shark, and a collection of musical
instruments. Food served all day encompasses light
lunches from Monday to Saturday; the daily board menu
may include houmous with olives and pitta bread
followed by lightly spiced pork casserole. Real ales
include Harvey's Sussex best and interesting ciders like
Kentish Biddenden cider served by handpump.

Open all day all wk 11am-11.30pm ⊕ FREE HOUSE
◀ Harveys Sussex Bitter, Grasshopper ○ Biddenden,
Westons Stowford Press. **Facilities** Children welcome
Children's menu Dogs allowed Garden Parking

HODSOLL STREET
Map 6 TQ66

The Green Man

TN15 7LE ☎ **01732 823575**
e-mail: the.greenman@btinternet.com
dir: On North Downs between Brands Hatch & Gravesend
off the A227

This 300-year-old, family-run pub is loved for its decent
food and real ales. It stands in the picturesque village of
Hodsoll Street on the North Downs, surrounded by
beautiful Kent countryside, with a large garden for the
warmer weather. Food is prepared to order using fresh
local produce, and includes a wide variety of fish such as
whole sea bass or salmon fillet with hollandaise sauce as
well as a range of steaks and grills, plus dishes like roast
duck with plum sauce and onion marmalade.

Open all wk 11-2.30 6-11 (Fri-Sun all day)
Bar Meals L served Mon-Fri 12-2, Sat 12-3, Sun all day
D served Mon-Sat 6.30-9.30, Sun all day
Restaurant L served Mon-Fri 12-2, Sat 12-3, Sun all day
D served Mon-Sat 6.30-9.30, Sun all day ⊕ HAYWOOD
PUB COMPANY LTD ◀ Timothy Taylor Landlord, Harvey's,
Old Speckled Hen, Guest ale. **Facilities** Children welcome
Children's menu Children's portions Play area Dogs
allowed Garden Parking

HOLLINGBOURNE
Map 7 TQ85

The Windmill NEW

32 Eyhorne St ME17 1TR ☎ **01622 880280**
e-mail: windmillinn123@btconnect.com
dir: M20 junct 8, A20 towards Lenham. Left into
Hollingbourne opposite Ramada Hotel. In village, pub
on right

Below the North Downs and near to Leeds Castle, this
solid old inn, with exposed timbers and slender
chimneystacks, has entertained passers-by for over 400
years. Draw close to the immense inglenook huddled
beneath a forest of blackened beams, sip on a pint of
Harveys beer and appreciate an extensive carte and
specials menu, strong on Kentish produce; stuffed field
mushroom and risotto cake stack or Kassler (smoked pork
loin) vie for attention. The large garden is very child
friendly.

Open all wk 12-3 5-11 (Sat 12-11.30, Sun 12-10.30)
Bar Meals L served Mon-Fri 12-2.30, Sat 12-5 Av main
course £9.95 **Restaurant** L served Mon-Fri 12-2.30, Sat
12-5 D served Mon-Fri 6-10, Sat 12-10, Sun 12-9.30
Fixed menu price fr £11.95 Av 3 course à la carte fr £20
⊕ ENTERPRISE INNS ◀ Harveys Sussex, Masterbrew,
Hobgoblin. **Facilities** Children welcome Children's menu
Children's portions Play area Dogs allowed Garden
Parking

PICK OF THE PUBS

The Plough at Ivy Hatch ♥

IVY HATCH Map 6 TQ55

High Cross Rd TN15 ONL
☎ **01732 810100**
e-mail: info@theploughivyhatch.co.uk
web: www.theploughivyhatch.co.uk
dir: *Off A25 between Borough Green &
Sevenoaks, follow signs to Ightham Mote*

This tile-hung 17th-century free house
stands in the picturesque village of Ivy
Hatch, just a short walk from the National
Trust's Ightham Mote, Britain's best
preserved medieval house. Owners Miles
and Anna have renovated the bar area,
conservatory and dining room to restore
the pub to the centre of its small
community. The Plough offers everything
from drinks for weary walkers to full meals
for hungry families – and the smart oak
flooring and seating area around the
fireplace make this the perfect spot for a
lingering lunch or supper. Beers are from
the Tunbridge Wells Brewery and the wine
list covers new and old world. The modern
British menu with its European highlights
aims to please all tastes and budgets.
Menus are updated daily, driven by locally
produced seasonal ingredients including
south coast seafood and seasonal game
from local shoots, and the food is freshly
cooked with no frozen or bought-in dishes.
The comfort food bar menu offers venison
liver and bacon with mash, local sausages
with black pudding, and brunch - bacon,
sausage, poached egg and trimmings.

Starters from the main menu might
include warm salad of foie gras, black
pudding, poached egg and curly endive, or
leek and potato soup. Moving on to the
main course, expect dishes like braised
oxtail, root vegetables with confit garlic
mash, or slow roast belly pork with
celeriac purée, apple compôte, Savoy
cabbage, bacon and red wine jus.
Desserts include Bramley apple and mixed
berry crumble with custard, and soft
chocolate pudding with mascarpone and
chocolate sauce. There is also a great
sweet and savoury pancake menu. With
lots of good walks in the area, there is no
need to worry about squelching back to
the pub in muddy boots, as the terrace
and garden are ideal for alfresco dining.

Open all wk noon-3 6-11 (Sat noon-11
Sun 10-6) Closed: 1 Jan
Bar Meals L served Mon-Sat 12-2.45, Sun
12-6 D served Mon-Sat 6-9.30 Av main
course £12 **Restaurant** L served Mon-Sat
12-2.45, Sun 12-6 D served Mon-Sat
6-9.30 Av 3 course à la carte fr £22
⊞ FREE HOUSE ◀ Tunbridge Wells
Brewery Royal, Dipper & Porter Ŏ Stowford
Press. ♥ 10 **Facilities** Children's
menu Children's portions Garden Parking
Wi-fi

ICKHAM
Map 7 TR25

The Duke William ★★★ INN ♀

The Street CT3 1QP ☎ 01227 721308
e-mail: goodfood@dukewilliam.biz
dir: A257 Canterbury to Sandwich. In Littlebourne turn left opposite The Anchor, into Nargate St. 0.5m turn right into Drill Ln, then right into The Street

Traditional, locally sourced and home-cooked food is the keynote at this whitewashed free house in the heart of Ickham village. Menu choices might be game terrine with red onion marmalade; sirloin steak and peppercorn sauce; or poached halibut with dill and Pernod sauce. The lovely garden features a covered patio, as well as a children's play area with a swing and slide. Four comfortable, well appointed, en suite bedrooms and free Wi-fi throughout complete the picture.

Open all day all wk **Bar Meals** L served all wk 12-3 booking required D served all wk 6.30-10 booking required **Restaurant** L served all wk 12-2.30 booking required D served all wk 6.30-10 booking required ⊕ FREE HOUSE ◀ Masterbrew, Harveys. ♀ 9 **Facilities** Children welcome Children's menu Children's portions Play area Dogs allowed Garden Wi-fi **Rooms** 4

IDEN GREEN
Map 6 TQ73

The Peacock

Goudhurst Rd TN17 2PB ☎ 01580 211233
dir: A21 from Tunbridge Wells to Hastings, onto A262, pub 1.5m past Goudhurst

A Grade II listed building dating from the 17th century with low beams, an inglenook fireplace, and ancient oak doors. Seasonal ales can be found amongst the Shepherd Neame handles in the convivial bar. Popular with families, the Peacock offers a wide range of traditional pub food; children may be served smaller portions from the main carte or choose from their own menu, and in summer they can use the large enclosed garden with fruit trees and picnic tables on one side of the building.

Open all day all wk 12-11 (Sun 12-6) ⊕ SHEPHERD NEAME ◀ Shepherd Neame Master Brew, Spitfire, seasonal ales. **Facilities** Children welcome Children's menu Children's portions Family room Dogs allowed Garden Parking Wi-fi

IGHTHAM
Map 6 TQ55

PICK OF THE PUBS

The Harrow Inn ♀

Common Rd TN15 9EB ☎ 01732 885912
dir: 1.5m from Borough Green on A25 to Sevenoaks, signed Ightham Common, turn left into Common Rd. Inn 0.25m on left

Tucked away down country lanes, yet easily accessible from both the M20 and M26, this creeper-hung, stone-built free house dates back to at least the 17th century. The two-room bar area has a great brick fireplace, open to both sides and piled high with logs,

while the restaurant's vine-clad conservatory opens on to a terrace that's ideal for a pint of Loddon Hoppit or Gravesend Shrimpers and warm weather dining. Menus vary with the seasons, and seafood is a particular speciality: fish lovers can enjoy dishes such as crab and ginger spring roll; swordfish with Cajun spice and salsa; or pan-fried fillets of sea bass with lobster cream and spinach. Other main courses may include baked sausage with gammon, fennel, red onions and garlic; and tagliatelle with wild mushroom, fresh herb, lemongrass and chilli ragout. The car park is fairly small, although there's adequate street parking.

Open noon-3 6-11 Closed: 1 wk between Xmas & New Year, Sun eve & Mon **Bar Meals** L served Tue-Sun 12-2 D served Tue-Sat 6-9 **Restaurant** L served Tue-Sun 12-2 booking required D served Tue-Sat 6-9 booking required ⊕ FREE HOUSE ◀ Loddon Hoppit, Gravesend Shrimpers. ♀ 9 **Facilities** Children welcome Children's portions Family room Garden Parking

IVY HATCH
Map 6 TQ55

PICK OF THE PUBS

The Plough at Ivy Hatch ♀

See Pick of the Pubs on opposite page

LEIGH
Map 6 TQ54

The Greyhound Charcott ♀

Charcott TN11 8LG ☎ 01892 870275
e-mail: ghatcharcott@aol.com
dir: From Tonbridge take B245 N towards Hildenborough. Left onto Leigh road, right onto Stocks Green road. Through Leigh, right then left at T-junct, right into Charcott (Camp Hill)

This cosy pub has been welcoming locals and visitors for around 120 years. Tony French, who took over six years ago, has maintained the traditional atmosphere in which music, pool table and fruit machine have no place. Winter brings log fires, while in summer you can enjoy the garden. Meals could include breast of pigeon with smoked bacon and Puy lentils; monkfish and crayfish risotto; a kilo of Scottish rope grown mussels with white wine, shallots, cream and garlic; and slow roasted pork belly with sage mash, alongside ploughman's, sandwiches and ciabattas. Enjoy your meal with a good selection of well-kept ales.

Open all wk noon-3 5.30-11 (Sat-Sun all day) **Bar Meals** L served Mon-Sat 12-2, Sun 12-3 D served Mon-Sat 6.30-9.30 **Restaurant** L served Mon-Sat 12-2, Sun 12-3 D served Mon-Sat 6.30-9.30 ⊕ ENTERPRISE INNS ◀ Harvey's, Woodforde's Wherry, Westerham British Bulldog Ö Stowford Press. ♀ 12 **Facilities** Children welcome Children's portions Dogs allowed Garden Parking Wi-fi

LINTON
Map 7 TQ75

The Bull Inn

Linton Hill ME17 4AW ☎ 01622 743612
e-mail: food@thebullatlinton.co.uk
dir: S of Maidstone on A229 (Hastings road)

Here since at least 1674, when the licensee was first listed, this old coaching inn stands high on the Greensand Ridge, with wonderful views over the Weald from the garden and large decked area. Inside there is a large inglenook fireplace and lots of beams, and a bar serving Kentish beers and a menu featuring four versions of Kentish ploughman's. Along with a popular Sunday carvery, the bistro dining area offers home-made pork, stuffing and leek pie; penne pasta with chorizo and bacon; beer-battered haddock and mushy peas; and Mexican fajitas.

Open all day all wk 11am-11.30pm (Sun noon-10.30pm) **Bar Meals** Av main course £10 food served all day **Restaurant** Av 3 course à la carte fr £25 food served all day ◀ Shepherd Neame Master Brew, Kent's Best, Late Red. **Facilities** Children welcome Children's menu Children's portions Dogs allowed Garden Parking Wi-fi

MAIDSTONE
Map 7 TQ75

The Black Horse Inn ★★★★ INN ♀

Pilgrims Way, Thurnham ME14 3LD
☎ 01622 737185 🖹 01622 739170
e-mail: info@wellieboot.net
dir: M20 junct 7, A249, right into Detling. Opposite Cock Horse Pub turn onto Pilgrim's Way

Smack beside the Pilgrim's Way and tucked just below the North Downs ridge, this popular free house was converted from a forge in the 18th century. Much extended, with stylish annexe bedrooms to the rear, you'll find a charming beamed bar with open fires for quaffing pints of Harveys Sussex Bitter and local Biddenden cider, and a candlelit restaurant serving a good range of imaginative food. Enjoy your drink or dine outside in the lovely garden with its fish and duck pond.

Open all day all wk **Bar Meals** L served all wk 12-6 D served all wk 6-10 Av main course £8.95 food served all day **Restaurant** L served all wk 12-6 D served all wk 6-10 Fixed menu price fr £14.95 Av 3 course à la carte fr £25 food served all day ⊕ FREE HOUSE ◀ Greene King IPA, Black Sheep, Hobgoblin, Grasshopper, Harveys Sussex Ö Biddenden. ♀ 21 **Facilities** Children welcome Children's menu Dogs allowed Garden Parking **Rooms** 30

MARKBEECH
Map 6 TQ44

The Kentish Horse

Cow Ln TN8 5NT ☎ 01342 850493
dir: 3m from Edenbridge & 7m from Tunbridge Wells. 1m S of Hever Castle

Surrounded by Kent countryside, this pub is popular with ramblers, cyclists and families, as well as having a strong local following. Situated in four acres with views over Ashdown Forest, there is an extensive garden and children's play area. The menu is cooked simply from fresh ingredients, and can be served anywhere in the pub or garden. Real ales always available are Harveys and locally-brewed Larkins.

Open all day all wk ∰ FREE HOUSE ◀ Harveys, Larkins. **Facilities** Children welcome Play area Dogs allowed Garden Parking

NEWNHAM
Map 7 TQ95

The George Inn

44 The Street ME9 0LL
☎ 01795 890237 📠 01795 890726
e-mail: hotcheifpaul@msn.com
dir: 4m from Faversham

The George is an attractive country inn with a large beer garden. Despite the passing of the centuries, the inn retains much of its historic character with beams, polished wooden floors, inglenook fireplaces and candlelit tables. Food is served in the bar and 50-seater restaurant. Bar snacks range from sandwiches to sausage and mash, while main meals could include pan-fried fillet of red snapper with crushed potatoes, baby fennel, fresh scampi and rosemary butter; or peppered duck breast with celeriac mash and cherry and port sauce. Regular events include live jazz, quizzes and murder mystery evenings. Recent change of hands.

Open all wk 11-3 6.30-11 (Sun noon-10) **Bar Meals** L served Mon-Sat 12-2.30, Sun 12-4.30 booking required D served Mon-Sat 7-9.30 booking required **Restaurant** L served Mon-Sat 12-2.30, Sun 12-4.30 booking required D served Mon-Sat 7-9.30 booking required ∰ SHEPHERD NEAME ◀ Shepherd Neame Master Brew, Kent Best, seasonal ale. **Facilities** Children welcome Children's menu Garden Parking

PENSHURST
Map 6 TQ54

PICK OF THE PUBS

The Bottle House Inn ☕

See Pick of the Pubs on opposite page

The Leicester Arms

High St TN11 8BT ☎ 01892 870551
dir: From Tunbridge Wells take A26 towards Tonbridge. Left onto B21765 towards Penshurst

A large and picturesque country inn at the centre of a picturesque village, the Leicester Arms stands in its own pretty gardens looking out over the River Medway. It was once part of the Penshurst Place estate. The wood-panelled dining room is worth a visit for the views over the weald and river alone. Dishes range from traditional pub food in the bar to the likes of pressed pork belly with crackling, chicken curry, or Moroccan vegetable tagine from the carte menu.

Open all wk 11am-mdnt ∰ ENTERPRISE INNS ◀ Harvey's Sussex Bitter, Shepherd Neame Master Brew, Sharp's Doom Bar ♂ Stowford Press. **Facilities** Children welcome Children's menu Dogs allowed Garden Parking

PICK OF THE PUBS

The Spotted Dog ☕

Smarts Hill TN11 8EE
☎ 01892 870253 📠 01892 870107
dir: Off B2188 between Penshurst & Fordcombe

Kentish ales from Larkins are just one excellent reason to rest awhile at The Spotted Dog, now under new ownership, nestled in the folds of The Weald close to two magnificent stately homes, Penshurst Place and Hever Castle. Years ago, a row of old cottages were converted into this low, weather-boarded old inn; open fires, a forest of low beams and oak-board floors recall the old days whilst the menu here is bang up to date, making the most of the produce grown in this richly endowed countryside. Sample a starter of baked field mushrooms stuffed with baby spinach and Stilton served with dressed leaves and apple and ale chutney, precursor to local sausages of the day, home-made steak and kidney pie or salmon and spinach Wellington with hollandaise sauce and sauté potatoes — traditional English with a twist, enhanced by a daily-changing specials board.

Open all day all wk **Bar Meals** L served Mon-Fri 12-2.30, Sat 12-9.30 D served Mon-Fri 6-9, Sat 12-9.30 Av main course £9.50 **Restaurant** L served Mon-Fri 12-2.30, Sat 12-9.30, Sun 12-5.30 D served Mon-Fri 6-9, Sat 12-9.30 Fixed menu price fr £9.95 Av 3 course à la carte fr £20 ∰ FREE HOUSE ◀ Sharp's Doom Bar, Larkins Traditional, Harveys, Guest ale ♂ Chiddingstone. ☕ 10 **Facilities** Children welcome Children's menu Children's portions Dogs allowed Garden Parking Wi-fi

PLUCKLEY
Map 7 TQ94

PICK OF THE PUBS

The Dering Arms ☕

Station Rd TN27 0RR ☎ 01233 840371
e-mail: jim@deringarms.com
dir: M20 junct 8, A20 to Ashford. Right onto B2077 at Charing to Pluckley

Pluckley's residents cherish its claim to fame as the most haunted village in England; they're also proud of its starring role in the 1990s TV series, *The Darling Buds of May*. The village was for centuries the home of the Dering family, hence the name. The impressive inn, originally an old hunting lodge, has two simply furnished traditional bars with mounted stags' heads and fishing rods, roaring fires in winter, an intimate restaurant, and a family room with a baby grand piano (there to be played). The extensive daily menus reflect the chef's love of fresh fish and seafood, as in starters of moules marinières, oysters from Cork, and pan-fried soft herring roes with crispy smoked bacon. One of chef/proprietor James Buss's favourites is the seafood special for two people — a platter overflowing with traditional fruits de mer, both hot and cold, served with fresh granary bread and three mayonnaise dips. There is a classic car meet on the second Sunday of the month.

Open Mon-Fri 11.30-3.30 6-11, Sat 9-11, Sun 9-5 Closed: 26-29 Dec, Sun eve **Bar Meals** L served Mon-Fri 12-2.30, Sat 9am-9pm, Sun 9-5 D served Mon-Sat 6.30-9 Av main course £12.50 **Restaurant** L served Mon-Sat 12-2.30, Sat 9am-9pm, Sun 9-5 D served Mon-Sat 6.30-9 Av 3 course à la carte fr £22.50 ◀ Goacher's Dering Ale, Maidstone Dark, Gold Star, Old Ale ♂ Biddenden. ☕ 8 **Facilities** Children welcome Children's portions Family room Dogs allowed Garden Parking

The Mundy Bois

Mundy Bois TN27 0ST ☎ 01233 840048
e-mail: info@mundybois.com
dir: From A20 at Charing exit towards Pluckley. Right into Pinnock at bottom of Pluckley Hill. Next right into Mundy Bois Rd. 1m left

An ale house since 1780, this creeper-clad pub is in the midst of 'Darling Buds of May' country in the Kentish Weald. The large family garden is an ideal place to savour a pint of ale from the Whitstable Brewery, weather permitting; in winter sit alongside the inglenook fireplace in the village bar. A menu of frequently changing dishes uses reputable local produce in starters such as Rye Bay scallops, and main dishes like best end of Smarden lamb with dauphinoise potatoes. The Mundy Bois runs a beer festival here in late Spring.

Open all wk 12-3 5.30-11 (Sun 12-7) **Bar Meals** L served Tue-Sun 12-3 D served Tue-Sun 6-9 Av main course £14 **Restaurant** L served Tue-Sat 12-3, Sun 12-4 D served Tue-Sat 6-9 Av 3 course à la carte fr £20 ∰ FREE HOUSE ◀ Tribute, Master Brew, Whitstable Brewery Real Ales ♂ Biddenden. **Facilities** Children welcome Children's menu Children's portions Play area Dogs allowed Garden Beer festival Parking

Save on hotels. Book at **theAA.com/hotel**

KENT 267 **ENGLAND**

PICK OF THE PUBS

The Bottle House Inn 🍷

PENSHURST   Map 6 TQ54

Coldharbour Rd TN11 8ET
☎ **01892 870306**   📄 **01892 871094**
e-mail:
info@thebottlehouseinnpenshurst.co.uk
web: www.thebottlehouseinnpenshurst.co.uk
dir: *From Tunbridge Wells take A264 W,*
then B2188 N. After Fordcombe left
towards Edenbridge & Hever. Pub 500yds
after staggered x-rds

Remotely situated on a country lane two miles southwest of Penshurst, The Bottle House Inn was built as a farmhouse in 1492, and later divided into two properties. Thomas Scraggs, 'a common beer seller of Speldhurst', leased one of them in 1806 and obtained a licence to sell ales and ciders. It was registered as an alehouse at each subsequent change of hands, at a time when hop-growing was the major local industry. During the 19th century it also housed a shop, a farrier and a cobbler, and there was a skittle alley at the back. The pub was said to be the originator of the ploughman's lunch, made with bread from the old bakery next door and cheese donated by Canadian soldiers billeted near by. The building was completely refurbished in 1938 and granted a full licence; it was reputedly named after all the old bottles discovered during these works. In the intervening decades further improvements have been tastefully executed, such that the inn's ancient beams and copper-topped counter give the bar a traditional warm and welcoming atmosphere. Choose between Harveys and local Larkins hand-pumped beers, or a wine from one of the eleven served by the glass, then settle at a bench seat on the patio or in the garden, perhaps to peruse the menu. It changes regularly to capitalise on the availability of seasonal produce, while the specials board is never the same from one day to the next. Light bites might include macaroni cheese with salad and garlic ciabatta; or butterflied sardines on granary toast. Starters are equally appealing – pan-fried salt and chilli squid or home-cured gravad lax are two examples. There are over a dozen main course options to choose from: honey and mustard baked ham served with fried eggs, chips and salad; coq au vin; and chargrilled swordfish among them. Of the desserts, look no further than the berry millefeuille with chocolate sauce.

Open all day all wk 11-11 (Sun 11-10.30) Closed: 25 Dec **Bar Meals** Av main course £13 food served all day **Restaurant** Fixed menu price fr £22.50 Av 3 course à la carte fr £22.50 food served all day 🍺 FREE HOUSE 🍺 Larkins Ale, Harveys Sussex Best Bitter. 🍷 11
Facilities Children's menu Children's portions Dogs allowed Garden Parking

PICK OF THE PUBS

The Coastguard

ST MARGARET'S BAY   Map 7 TR34

CT15 6DY

☎ **01304 853176**

e-mail: bookings@thecoastguard.co.uk
web: www.thecoastguard.co.uk
dir: *2m off A258 between Dover & Deal,
follow St Margaret's at Cliffe signs.
Through village towards sea*

Sitting on the suntrap terrace here, the hazy smudge on the horizon is likely to be the French coast, shimmering beyond the silently passing ferries and freighters. Crane your neck upwards and the view of Blighty's fine countryside is cut off by – well – Blighty's most famous natural feature; the White Cliffs of Dover thrust upwards behind this convivial waterside inn. The popular Heritage Coast footpath passes the door, whilst the watersport fans beach their kayaks here to indulge in a half of Gadd's of Ramsgate No. 5 bitter or a sip of Rough Old Wife cider; Loch Fyne Ales from western Scotland are also on handpump here, reflecting owner Nigel Wyndmus's roots.

The food from Nigel's wife Sam and her team is renowned for its wonderful flavours, and all freshly made on the premises from local produce as far as possible. Many dishes have a story behind them: they might be based on an old Roman recipe, a reworked classic dish, or perhaps an original creation in response

to something particularly outstanding that becomes available. The menus change twice daily, depending on the weather and what's available. Bar bites and starters feature local pork and cider pie; rabbit and mushroom parfait with truffle oil and Melba toast; or a smoked haddock, spinach and Cheddar omelette, enough for nibblers. Those with heartier appetites may progress to hot devilled crab topped with mature Cheddar, smoked haddock roasted with a Shetland mussel and saffron cider cream, or gratin of Kentish broccoli with cider, mushrooms and leeks. Calorific desserts abound, or tackle the pub's award-winning Waterloo cheeseboard.

Open all day all wk 11-11 (Sun 11-10.30)
Bar Meals L served all wk 12.30-2.45

D served all wk 6.30-8.45
Restaurant L served all wk 12.30-2.45
D served all wk 6.30-8.45 ⊕ FREE HOUSE
◀ Gadds of Ramsgate No 5, Loch Fyne Ales, Adnams ♂ Kent Cider, Rough Old Wife, Hogan's. **Facilities** Children welcome Children's portions Dogs allowed Garden Beer festival Parking Wi-fi

Save on hotels. Book at **theAA.com/hotel**

KENT 269 **ENGLAND**

ROLVENDEN
Map 7 TQ83

The Bull ♀ NEW

1 Regent St TN17 4PB ☎ 01580 241212
e-mail: thebullinnkent@yahoo.com
dir: *Just off A28, approx 3m from Tenterden*

This handsome, Kentish tile hung village inn dates, in part, back to the 13th century. It's close to the walled garden that inspired Frances Hodgson Burnet to write the classic tale *The Secret Garden* and handy, too, for steam trains of the Kent and East Sussex Railway. New owners here are making the most of local beers and produce, with a heartwarming, pubby menu enhanced by modern dishes like monkfish kebabs. There's a great beer garden overlooking the village cricket ground.

Open all day all wk **Bar Meals** Av main course £9 food served all day **Restaurant** L served Mon-Sat 12-2.30, Sun 12-4 D served Mon-Sat 6-9 ⊕ FREE HOUSE ♀ 12 **Facilities** Children welcome Children's menu Children's portions Dogs allowed Garden Beer festival Wi-fi

ST MARGARET'S BAY
Map 7 TR34

PICK OF THE PUBS

The Coastguard

See Pick of the Pubs on opposite page

SANDWICH
Map 7 TR35

George & Dragon Inn ♀

Fisher St CT13 9EJ ☎ 01304 613106
e-mail: enquiries@georgeanddragon-sandwich.co.uk
web: www.georgeanddragon-sandwich.co.uk
dir: *Between Dover & Canterbury*

Built in 1446, ale was first sold here in 1549, but was only licensed under the name of George & Dragon in 1615. This town centre pub oozes charm and character, with its wood floors and open fires, and makes a welcome pit-stop when exploring historic Sandwich on foot. Run by two brothers, you can refuel with a pint of well kept ale, including Shepherd Neame Master Brew or Wantsum. The lunch board includes dishes like grilled pork with root vegetable mash, or chicken and mushroom pie. On the monthly-changing evening menu, expect rump of lamb on curried chickpeas, or butternut squash tart with sage Parmesan crumble. Head outside to the picturesque sun-trap courtyard in summer.

Open all wk 11-3 6-11 (Sat 11-11 Sun 12-4) **Bar Meals** L served all wk 12-2 booking required D served Mon-Sat 6-9 booking required Av main course £13 **Restaurant** L served all wk 12-2 booking required D served Mon-Sat 6-9 booking required Av 3 course à la carte fr £18 ⊕ ENTERPRISE INNS ◀ Shepherd Neame Master Brew, Harvey's Sussex Best, Sharp's Doom Bar, Ringwood Best, Wantsum, Turbulent Priest. ♀ 9 **Facilities** Dogs allowed Garden Wi-fi

See advert below

SELLING
Map 7 TR05

The Rose and Crown

Perry Wood ME13 9RY ☎ 01227 752214
e-mail: info@roseandcrownperrywood.co.uk
dir: *From A28 right at Badgers Hill, left at end. 1st left signed Perry Wood. Pub at top*

Stroll through 150-acres of woodland to The Pulpit viewpoint and savour magnificent views across the Kent countryside, then return to this rambling 16th-century free house for a pint of Harveys Sussex or heady Biddenden cider and some traditional home-cooked pub food. Renowned for its green credentials, the cosy, low-beamed interior features exposed brick walls, inglenook fireplaces and is traditionally decorated with hop garlands, horse brasses and corn dollies. There's a delightful, flower-festooned garden for summer alfresco meals.

Open all wk noon-3 6.30-11 Closed: 25-26 Dec eve, 1 Jan eve, Mon eve **Bar Meals** L served all wk 12-2 D served Tue-Sat 6.30-9 Av main course £8 **Restaurant** L served all wk 12-2 D served Tue-Sat 6.30-9 ⊕ FREE HOUSE ◀ Adnams Southwold, Harvey's Sussex Best Bitter, guest ale Ö Stowford Press, Biddenden. **Facilities** Children welcome Children's menu Children's portions Play area Dogs allowed Garden Parking

SHIPBOURNE — Map 6 TQ55

PICK OF THE PUBS

The Chaser Inn ⚐ NEW

Stumble Hill TN11 9PE
☎ 01732 810360 📠 01732 811168
e-mail: enquiries@thechaser.co.uk
dir: N of Tonbridge take A227. Pub on left on main road

The award-winning Chaser Inn takes its name from the pub's long association with the nearby Fairlawne racing stable, where the late Peter Cazalet trained horses for the Queen Mother and other leading owners. Once a haunt for stars such as Richard Burton and Elizabeth Taylor, it is now an informal, relaxed village inn, next to the church and overlooking the common, with log fires, a lovely beer garden and a covered courtyard that comes into its own in the winter months. Well kept real ales, such as Old Speckled Hen, and forty wines by the glass are complemented by an extensive menu of sandwiches, light bites and main courses such as Irish lamb stew with root vegetables, pearl barley and Savoy cabbage; pan-roasted breast of chicken with bacon and mushroom risotto; and grilled High Field Farm sirloin of beef with grilled flat mushrooms, vine tomatoes, peppercorn sauce and chips.

Open all day all wk Bar Meals Av main course £9.95 food served all day Restaurant Av 3 course à la carte fr £21 food served all day ⊕ WHITING AND HAMMOND ◀ Abbot Ale, Greene King IPA, Old Speckled Hen, Guest ales. ⚐ 40 Facilities Children welcome Children's portions Dogs allowed Garden Parking Wi-fi

SMARDEN — Map 7 TQ84

PICK OF THE PUBS

The Chequers Inn

The Street TN27 8QA
☎ 01233 770217 📠 01233 770623
e-mail: spaldings@thechequerssmarden.com
dir: Through Leeds village, left to Sutton Valence/ Headcorn then left for Smarden. Pub in village centre

The former weavers' village of Smarden has around 200 buildings of architectural and historical interest; one of them is the clapboard façaded 14th-century Chequers. In its beautiful landscaped garden are a large carp pond and an attractive south-facing courtyard. Real ales brewed by Harveys and Adnams are served in the low-beamed bars, and seasonal menus and specials offer traditional and modern food. The bar menu has all the pub favourites, starting with a range of baguettes, and encompassing award-winning pork and leek sausages with mash, and home-made chilli con carne. The refurbished restaurant raises the bar with starters such as asparagus and poached quail's eggs dressed with lime hollandaise; and main courses like slow-cooked pork belly on bubble and squeak with a baked cider apple and gravy. The bar menu, carte and children's menu are all served on

Sundays too, when traditional beef, lamb and pork roasts are joined by gammon and turkey. Time your visit for a Thursday evening if the weekly steak, ribs and burger night appeals.

Open all wk Bar Meals L served all wk 12-3 D served all wk 6-9 Restaurant L served all wk 12-3 D served all wk 6-9 ⊕ FREE HOUSE ◀ Harvey's, IPA, Adnams, Hancock. Facilities Children welcome Children's menu Children's portions Dogs allowed Garden Beer festival Parking

SPELDHURST — Map 6 TQ54

PICK OF THE PUBS

George & Dragon ⚐

Speldhurst Hill TN3 0NN
☎ 01892 863125 📠 01892 863216
e-mail: julian@speldhurst.com
dir: Telephone for directions

Built around 1500, the award-winning George and Dragon is a venerable timber-clad village hostelry. Some say its origins are earlier, when Speldhurst would have seen archers departing for the Battle of Agincourt. At the beginning of the 17th century the curative powers of the village's iron-rich waters were discovered, which put nearby Tunbridge Wells on the map. Today's customers enjoy a modern gastro-pub, where just about every ingredient comes from within a 30-mile radius. The menu is not only seasonal but promises organic, free-range and GM-free produce whenever possible. British pub classics served only at lunchtime include a roast beef sandwich with horseradish and chips, and a Chart Farm venison burger with tomato salsa. Starters such as Speldhurst pigeon breasts with locally smoked bacon and Puy lentils are followed with half a dozen eclectic lunch/ dinner main course choices: typical are whole roasted Sussex coast John Dory; and chargrilled chicken salad with slow-roasted tomatoes. Refreshments include Larkins bitter, made about three miles away, and a range of local organic fruit juices.

Open all day all wk Bar Meals L served all wk 12-2.30 D served Mon-Sat 7-9.45 Av main course £13.50 Restaurant L served Sat 12-3, Sun 12-4 booking required D served Fri 7-10, Sat 6.30-10 booking required Av 3 course à la carte fr £28 ⊕ FREE HOUSE ◀ Harvey's Best, Larkins, Westerham Brewery George's Marvellous Medicine Ö Stowford Press. ⚐ 11 Facilities Children welcome Children's portions Family room Dogs allowed Garden Parking Wi-fi

STONE IN OXNEY — Map 7 TQ92

The Crown Inn NEW

TN30 7JN ☎ 01233 758302
e-mail: enquiries@thecrowninnstoneinoxney.co.uk
dir: From Tenterden take B2082 towards Rye. Through Wittersham, in approx 0.75m left towards Stone in Oxney. Inn in 1.5m at bottom of hill

Lost down lanes in a sleepy hamlet above Romney Marsh, this 300-year-old pub was locked and unloved for three years before Chris and Nicki Conrath saw its potential and revamped it in contemporary style. Expect to find Larkins ale and a big inglenook in the bar, and wooden floors and a light, airy feel in the dining room. Varied menus take in smoked haddock fishcakes, beef burger with Dijon mustard mayonnaise, home-made lasagne, tarte Tatin, and wood-fired pizzas to eat in or take away.

Open 12-3 6-11 (Sun 12-5) Closed: Jan, Sun eve & Mon Bar Meals L served Tue-Sat 12-2, Sun 12.30-2.30 booking required D served Tue-Sat 6.30-9 booking required Av main course £11 ⊕ FREE HOUSE ◀ Larkins Traditional, Spitfire, Shepherd Neame. Facilities Children welcome Children's portions Dogs allowed Garden Parking Wi-fi

TENTERDEN — Map 7 TQ83

White Lion Inn

57 High St TN30 6BD
☎ 01580 765077 📠 01580 764157
e-mail: whitelion.tenterden@marstons.co.uk
dir: On A28 (Ashford to Hastings road)

This 16th-century coaching inn stands on a broad tree-lined street in 'the Jewel of the Weald'. Renovated and rejuvenated, the pub combines its many original features with a contemporary look and feel. Reasonably priced fresh food ranges from starters of roasted Portobella mushrooms, or shredded duck in crisp filo pastry, to mains such as harissa lamb kebabs or chicken Caesar salad. Look out for special offers on pub classics served all day. Reliable Marston ales are the mainstay in the bar.

Open all wk 10am-11pm (wknds 10am-mdnt) Bar Meals L served Mon-Fri 12-9.30, Sat-Sun 12-10 D served Mon-Fri 12-9.30, Sat 12-10, Sun 12-8.30 Av main course £7.50 food served all day Restaurant L served Mon-Fri 12-9.30, Sat-Sun 12-10 booking required D served Mon-Fri 6-9.30, Sat 6-10, Sun 6-8.30 Fixed menu price fr £17.95 food served all day ⊕ MARSTONS ◀ Marstons Pedigree, Cumberland. Facilities Children welcome Children's menu Children's portions Garden Parking Wi-fi

TONBRIDGE

See Penshurst

TUNBRIDGE WELLS (ROYAL) — Map 6 TQ53

PICK OF THE PUBS

The Beacon   INN ⚐

See Pick of the Pubs on opposite page

Save on hotels. Book at **theAA.com/hotel**

KENT 271 ENGLAND

PICK OF THE PUBS

The Beacon ★★★★ INN ♀

TUNBRIDGE WELLS (ROYAL) Map 6 TQ53

Tea Garden Ln, Rusthall TN3 9JH
☎ **01892 524252** 📠 **01892 534288**
e-mail: beaconhotel@btopenworld.com
web: www.the-beacon.co.uk
dir: *From Tunbridge Wells take A264
towards East Grinstead. Pub 1m on left*

The house dates from 1895 and was built as the country home of Sir Walter Harris, a former lieutenant of the City of London. After Harris's death the house passed through various hands until, during World War II, it became a hostel for Jewish refugees. Standing in seventeen acres, The Beacon offers a host of impressive architectural features and the building still pulsates with country house charm; the bar, for example, with its moulded plaster ceiling, bookshelves and stained glass windows decidedly stands out from the crowd and is the perfect place to enjoy a pint of Harveys Best or Larkins Traditional real ale, or organic draught cider. Take it out to the terrace, from which there are truly glorious views. Food is served in both the bar and the restaurant, with its large fireplace, or in one of three private dining rooms. Menus take full advantage of seasonal local produce, to which, as a member of Kentish Fare, the kitchen is strongly committed, although fruit, vegetables and herbs are increasingly grown in The Beacon's own kitchen garden. Start perhaps with Brixham crab bound with a ginger mayonnaise, served with a lemon spiced warm water prawn and toast, or smoked ham hock terrine wrapped in Savoy cabbage with crisp pickled vegetables. Select a main dish of pan-roasted halibut with confit sweet cherry tomatoes and a creamy chanterelle and cider sauce, or Gressingham duck breast served with a celeriac spring roll, braised baby gem lettuce and a spiced apple and cherry sauce. A separate list of classic dishes includes Pembury Porker sausage on root vegetable mash and roasted garlic sauce, or fish of the day, spiced lemon tempura batter, crushed peas, hand-cut potato chips and gherkin mayonnaise. A good wine list offers plenty of choice by the glass. Why not stay over in one of the spacious, comfortably furnished bedrooms.

Open all day all wk 11-11 (Sun 12-10.30)
Bar Meals L served Mon-Thu 12-2.30, Fri-Sun 12-9.30 D served Mon-Thu 6.30-9.30, Fri-Sun 12-9.30
Restaurant L served Mon-Thu 12-2.30, Fri-Sun 12-9.30 D served Mon-Thu 6.30-9.30, Fri-Sun 12-9.30 🍺 FREE HOUSE ◀ Harveys Best, Timothy Taylor Landlord, Larkins Traditional Ò Stowford Press Draught Cider, Westons Organic Bottled Pear Cider. ♀ 12 **Facilities** Play area Garden Parking **Rooms** 3

TUNBRIDGE WELLS (ROYAL) continued

The Crown Inn

The Green, Groombridge TN3 9QH ☎ 01892 864742
e-mail: crowngroombridge@hotmail.co.uk
dir: *Take A264 W of Tunbridge Wells, then B2110 S*

Dating back to 1585, this charming free house was a favourite with the cast of *Pride and Prejudice* during filming nearby in 2004. Earlier, Groombridge Place was home to Sir Arthur Conan Doyle, who made The Crown his local. Earlier still, it was an infamous haunt for smugglers, who hid their casks of tea in the cellar. Today, its low beams and an inglenook fireplace are the setting for some great food and drink. Favourites include home-made pies and daily specials based on fresh local produce.

Open all wk 11-3 6-11 (Sat 11-11 Sun noon-10.30 Sun noon-5 winter) **Bar Meals** L served Mon-Fri 12-2.30, Sat-Sun 12-3 D served Mon-Thu 6.30-9, Fri-Sat 6.30-9.30 Av main course £10.50 **Restaurant** L served Mon-Fri 12-2.30, Sat-Sun 12-3 booking required D served Mon-Thu 6.30-9, Fri-Sat 6.30-9.30 booking required Av 3 course à la carte fr £20 ⊕ FREE HOUSE ◼ Harvey's Best, Tunbridge Wells Royal ♡ Stowford Press.
Facilities Children welcome Children's menu Children's portions Play area Dogs allowed Garden Parking

PICK OF THE PUBS

The Hare on Langton Green ♥

Langton Rd, Langton Green TN3 0JA
☎ 01892 862419 📄 01892 861275
e-mail: hare@brunningandprice.co.uk
dir: *From Tunbridge Wells follow A264 towards East Grinstead. The Hare is on the x-rds at Langton Green*

Situated on the edge of rolling Kent countryside, this site has been home to an inn since the 18th century. The current Hare's predecessor was extensively damaged in a fire in 1900, and the present Victorian-Tudor edifice was completed a year later in what is now a well-to-do suburb of Tunbridge Wells. The extensive menu changes daily. Starters might include sweet chilli chicken samosa with tzatziki and sesame noodle salad, followed by mains of sea bass with clams in a potato, leek, pea and saffron broth, or wild mushroom and lentil pie with sweet potato mash. There is also a choice of light bites and sandwiches. In addition to a choice of real ales and ciders, there's an impressive range of malt whiskies and wines by the glass. A woman holding a child is said to haunt the main staircase and cellar, though nobody has been able to identify the period she comes from.

Open all day all wk noon-11 (Fri-Sat noon-mdnt, Sun noon-10.30) **Bar Meals** Av main course £10.95 food served all day **Restaurant** Av 3 course à la carte fr £19.95 food served all day ⊕ BRUNNING & PRICE ◼ Greene King IPA, Abbot Ale, Morland Original, Ruddles Best, Olde Trip ♡ Westons Old Rosie, Westons Organic, Aspall Suffolk Cyder. ♥ 20 **Facilities** Children welcome Children's menu Children's portions Dogs allowed Garden Parking

---

WESTERHAM — Map 6 TQ45

The Fox & Hounds ♥

Toys Hill TN16 1QG ☎ 01732 750328
e-mail: hickmott1@hotmail.com
dir: *Telephone for directions*

Close to Chartwell, this late 18th-century ale house is set in an Area of Outstanding Natural Beauty high on Kent's Greensand Ridge, amidst National Trust land. A popular pub with walkers, it has a traditionally styled restaurant where all food is made on the premises from locally sourced produce. Starters might include chicken liver pâté or field mushrooms stuffed with Welsh rarebit, followed by steak and ale pie, home cooked honey-roast ham and eggs or fried lamb's liver with bacon, mash and red wine gravy.

Open 10-3 6-11 (Sat-Sun 10am-11pm) (all day in summer) Closed: 25 Dec, Mon eve **Bar Meals** L served Mon-Sat 12-2, Sun 12-3 D served Tue-Sat 6-9 Av main course £11.50 **Restaurant** L served Mon-Sat 12-2, Sun 12-3 booking required D served Tue-Sat 6-9 ⊕ GREENE KING ◼ Greene King IPA, Abbot Ale, Ruddles County, Morlands. ♥ 10 **Facilities** Children welcome Children's menu Dogs allowed Garden Parking

---

Grasshopper on the Green ♥

The Green TN16 1AS ☎ 01959 562926
e-mail: info@grasshopperonthegreen.com
dir: *M25 junct 5, A21 towards Sevenoaks, then A25 to Westerham. Or M25 junct 6, A22 towards East Grinstead, A25 to Westerham*

With its log fires, mulled wine and peaceful summer garden, this 700 year-old free house is an inn for all seasons. It takes its name from the heraldic crest of the local 16th-century merchant and financier Thomas Gresham, founder of the Royal Exchange. Enjoy Grasshopper Kentish Bitter alongside home-cooked dishes like floured herring roes on garlic toast, beer-battered calamari or lamb shank with vegetables and onion gravy.

Open all day all wk **Bar Meals** L served all wk 12-9 D served all wk 12-9 Av main course £10 food served all day **Restaurant** L served all wk 12-9 D served all wk 12-9 food served all day ⊕ FREE HOUSE ◼ Grasshopper Ale, Adnams Broadside, Harveys Sussex, Courage Best. ♥ 12 **Facilities** Children welcome Children's menu Children's portions Play area Dogs allowed Garden Parking Wi-fi

---

WEST MALLING — Map 6 TQ65

PICK OF THE PUBS

The Farmhouse ♥

97 The High St ME19 6NA
☎ 01732 843257 📄 01622 851881
e-mail: enquiries@thefarmhouse.biz
dir: *M20 junct 4, S on A228. Right to West Malling. Pub in village centre*

The Farmhouse is a handsome Elizabethan property in the heart of the beautiful old market town of West Malling. There's a friendly atmosphere in this modern gastro-pub's stylish bar and two dining areas. Outside is a pretty walled garden with an area of decking

---

overlooking 15th-century stone barns. Local seasonal ingredients are used to produce a range of menus with a strong French influence. Expect starters such as traditional Mediterranean fish soup, croûtons, cheese and rouille; or fillet of beef carpaccio, roasted pine nuts, rocket salad, shaved Parmesan and truffle oil; and mains like Sussex-reared beef with dauphinoise potatoes and green peppercorn sauce; and oven-roasted baby monkfish, crushed new potatoes, bean cassoulet and crab and herb sauce. There are stone-baked pizzas and toasted paninis alongside the blackboard menu which changes regularly.

Open all day all wk 11am-11pm **Bar Meals** L served Mon-Thu 12-3, Fri-Sat 12-9.45, Sun 12-9 D served Mon-Thu 6-9.45, Fri-Sat 12-9.45, Sun 12-9 Av main course £12 **Restaurant** L served Mon-Thu 12-3, Fri-Sat 12-7.45, Sun 12-9.45 D served Mon-Thu 6-9.30, Fri-Sat 12-9.45, Sun 12-9.45 Av 3 course à la carte fr £25 ⊕ ENTERPRISE INNS ◼ Harvey's, Guinness, Young's ♡ Biddenden. ♥ 20 **Facilities** Children welcome Children's portions Dogs allowed Garden Parking Wi-fi

---

WHITSTABLE — Map 7 TR16

PICK OF THE PUBS

The Sportsman ◉◉ ♥

Faversham Rd CT5 4BP ☎ 01227 273370
e-mail: contact@thesportsmanseasalter.co.uk
dir: *3.5m W of Whitstable, on coast road between Whitstable & Faversham*

The first evidence of an inn on this site dates back to 1642, but the surrounding area of Seasalter was entered in the Domesday book as belonging to the kitchens of Canterbury cathedral. Reached via a winding lane across open marshland from Whitstable, and tucked beneath the sea wall, The Sportsman has a rustic yet comfortable and welcoming interior, with wooden floors and stripped pine furniture. A new plaque on the wall commemorates the part played by the pub in a little known WWII episode. Called the Battle of Graveney Marshes, in 1940 a German Junkers 88 crashlanded near the pub, where a platoon of London Irish Rifles was billeted. After surrendering the Germans were taken to the pub for a pint to await the POW authorities. Today's range of Shepherd Neame ales would certainly have gone down well in 1940. The impressive daily menu is based on local produce from farms, boats and game suppliers. Seafood dishes might include Whitstable native oysters; rock oysters and hot chorizo; and mussel and bacon chowder. Other options embrace Monkshill Farm pork belly, and crispy duck, smoked chilli salsa and sour cream.

Open all wk noon-3 6-11 Closed: 25 Dec, 26 Dec, 1 Jan **Restaurant** L served Tue-Sun 12-2 booking required D served Tue-Sat 7-9 booking required Av 3 course à la carte fr £32 ⊕ SHEPHERD NEAME ◼ Shepherd Neame Late Red, Master Brew, Porter, Early Bird, Goldings, Whitstable Bay ♡ Thatchers Gold. ♥ 9
Facilities Children welcome Children's portions Family room Dogs allowed Garden Parking

Save on hotels. Book at **theAA.com/hotel**

KENT – LANCASHIRE 273 ENGLAND

WROTHAM   Map 6 TQ65

The Bull ★★★ INN ◉ ♥ NEW

Bull Ln TN15 7RF ☎ 01732 789800 📠 01732 886288
e-mail: info@thebullhotel.com
web: www.thebullhotel.com
dir: M20 junct 2, A20 (signed Paddock Wood, Gravesend
& Tonbridge). At rdbt 3rd exit onto A20 (signed Wrotham,
Tonbridge, Borough Green, M20 & M25). At rdbt take 4th
exit into Bull Lane (signed Wrotham)

An attractive three-storey building whose records can be
traced to 1385 and first licensed under Henry VII in 1495.
More recently, WWII pilots relaxed here; stamps on the
restaurant ceiling mark downed German planes, and
dozens of pictures of Spitfires decorate the place. Ales
from the award-winning Dark Star micro-brewery are ably
supported by a 70-bottle wine list, some of which are
personally imported by the owner. Food follows classic
lines, but as much as possible is sourced from local
growers and suppliers: Hartley Bottom beef fillet
carpaccio and Harvel House Farm rare breed pork steak
are two examples. Why not stay over and try the circular
walk from the pub?

Open all day all wk Bar Meals L served Mon-Sat 12-2.30
D served Mon-Sat 6-9 Av main course £9
Restaurant L served Mon-Sat 12-2.30, Sun 12-8 D served
Mon-Sat 6-9 booking required Fixed menu price fr £19.50
Av 3 course à la carte fr £24 ⊕ FREE HOUSE ◀ Dark Star
Best Bitter, Hop Head Ŏ Stowford Press. ♥ 8
Facilities Children welcome Children's portions Dogs
allowed Garden Parking Wi-fi Rooms 11

WYE   Map 7 TR04

The New Flying Horse ♥

Upper Bridge St TN25 5AN
☎ 01233 812297 📠 01233 813487
e-mail: newflyhorse@shepherd-neame.co.uk
dir: Telephone for directions

Originally a 17th-century posting house, this thatched
and refurbished village local has a rare bat and trap
game, and a stunning WWII 'Soldier's Dream of Blighty'
garden which won an award at the 2005 Chelsea Flower
Show; tea can be served here in the summer months. At
chillier times you can snuggle up to the log fire in the
timeless, cosy interior, savour an award-winning Kentish
ale, and select a couple of classics from the new owners'
menu, such as smoked mackerel rillettes followed by New
Romney lamb's liver.

Open all day all wk Bar Meals L served all wk 12-2
booking required D served all wk 6-9 booking required Av
main course £8.95 Restaurant L served all wk 12-2
booking required D served all wk 6-9 booking required Av
3 course à la carte fr £20 ⊕ SHEPHERD NEAME
◀ Masterbrew Spitfire, Late Red, Guest ales. ♥ 12
Facilities Children welcome Children's menu Children's
portions Play area Dogs allowed Garden Parking

LANCASHIRE

ALTHAM   Map 18 SD73

The Walton Arms ♥ NEW

Burnley Rd BB5 5UL ☎ 01282 774444
e-mail: info@waltonarms.com
dir: Just off M65 junct 8. On A678 between Accrington
& Padiham

This sturdy, stone-built dining pub oozes all the character
of a long-established way-station on an ancient highway
linking Yorkshire and Lancashire; pilgrims to Whalley
Abbey called at an inn here when Henry VII was king.
Beams and brasses, rustic furniture and slabbed stone
floors welcome today's pilgrims intent on sampling the
comprehensive menu, either as bar meal or in the
atmospheric dining room; succulent shoulder of local
lamb is the signature dish, aided and abetted by John
Willie Lees' best beers or one of the list of wines by the
glass.

Open all wk Mon-Sat 12-2.30 5.30-11 (Sun 12-10.30)
Bar Meals L served Mon-Sat 12-2, Sun 12-8.30 D served
Mon-Sat 6-9, Sun 12-8.30 Av main course £6.95
Restaurant L served Mon-Sat 12-2, Sun 12-8.30 D served
Mon-Sat 6-9, Sun 12-8.30 Fixed menu price fr £12.95 Av
3 course à la carte fr £16 ⊕ J W LEES ◀ Lees Bitter,
Coronation Street Ale. ♥ 16 Facilities Children welcome
Children's menu Children's portions Parking Wi-fi

BASHALL EAVES   Map 18 SD64

PICK OF THE PUBS

The Red Pump Inn ♥

Clitheroe Rd BB7 3DA ☎ 01254 826227
e-mail: info@theredpumpinn.co.uk
dir: 3m from Clitheroe, NW, follow 'Whitewell, Trough of
Bowland & Bashall Eaves' signs

There's some doubt about exactly when this old pub
was built, although 1756 would be a reasonable guess
since that's the date carved on a door lintel. It used to
be a coaching inn and the horses would quench their
thirst from the old red pump now in the bar. Real ales
drinkers can quench theirs from a line-up including
Timothy Taylor Landlord, Black Sheep and Moorhouses.
Of the restaurant side of things, owners Jonathan and
Martina Myerscough say: "We love good honest, tasty
food, prepared fresh from local-as-possible ingredients
and presented well with thought, but without too much
fuss". Either they, or their chefs, might change the
menus on a whim, as well as seasonally, to offer
typical mains of rich Lancashire ox-cheek pie; rabbit
loin casserole with rabbit haggis, carrot mash and
twice-fried chips; and linguini salsa verde. Look on the
specials board for fish. Children have their own menu.

Open noon-3 6-11 (Sun noon-9) Closed: 2wks early
Jan, Mon (ex BH) Bar Meals L served Mon-Fri 12-2, Sat
12-2.30, Sun 12-7 D served Mon-Sat 6-9, Sun 12-7
booking required Av main course £11
Restaurant L served Mon-Fri 12-2, Sat 12-2.30, Sun
12-7 booking required D served Mon-Sat 6-9, Sun 12-7
booking required Fixed menu price fr £10 Av 3 course à
la carte fr £15 ⊕ FREE HOUSE ◀ Black Sheep,
Moorhouses, Tirril Brewery. ♥ 10 Facilities Children
welcome Children's menu Children's portions Garden
Parking Wi-fi

BILSBORROW   Map 18 SD53

Owd Nell's Tavern ♥

Guy's Thatched Hamlet, Canal Side PR3 0RS
☎ 01995 640010 📠 01995 640141
e-mail: info@guysthatchedhamlet.com
dir: M6 junct 32 N on A6. In approx 5m follow brown
tourist signs to Guy's Thatched Hamlet

This country-style tavern is full of old-world charm, with
beams and flagstones aplenty. Run by the same family
for over 30 years, it forms part of Guy's Thatched Hamlet,
a cluster of eating and drinking venues beside the
Lancaster Canal. Expect excellent ales, such as Owd
Nell's Canalside Bitter or Pendle Witch, and an authentic
country pub ambience enhanced by flagged floors,
fireplaces and low ceilings. All-day fare is typified by
home-made soup, fish and chips and specials like beef
goulash. Children's menus are available.
There is a cider festival at the end of July, and several
others to look out for.

continued

BILSBORROW continued

Open all day all wk 7am-2am Closed: 25 Dec
Bar Meals L served all wk 12-9 D served all wk 12-9 Av main course £9 food served all day **Restaurant** L served Mon-Sat 12-2.30, Sun 12-10.30 D served Mon-Sat 5.30-10.30, Sun 12-10.30 Fixed menu price fr £9.95 Av 3 course à la carte fr £14 ⊕ FREE HOUSE ◀ Bowland, Copper Dragon, Black Sheep, Owd Nell's Canalside Bitter, Moorhouses Bitter, Pendle Witch, Thwaites, Hart ♂ Thatchers Heritage, Cheddar Valley. ☙ 20
Facilities Children welcome Children's menu Children's portions Play area Family room Dogs allowed Garden Beer festival Parking Wi-fi

BLACKBURN   Map 18 SD62

PICK OF THE PUBS

Clog and Billycock

See Pick of the Pubs on opposite page

The Fernhurst Lodge ★★★★ INN
NEW

466 Bolton Rd BB2 4JP
☎ 01254 693541 ▤ 01254 695004
e-mail: info@thefernhurst.co.uk
dir: M65 junct 4, A666 towards Blackburn. Pub on left in approx 0.5m

Just a mile from Blackburn town centre and directly opposite Blackburn Rovers Football Club, The Fernhurst was built by Daniel Thwaites in the late 1890s. A magnificent Victorian building retaining a number of architectural features, the pub offers accommodation as well as real ales and an all-day menu. Enjoy a pint of Thwaites beer with pub classics such as haddock and chips or steak and ale pie from the 'Taste of Lancashire' selection.

Open all day all wk **Bar Meals** Av main course £8 food served all day **Restaurant** Av 3 course à la carte fr £20 ⊕ THWAITES ◀ Thwaites Wainwright, Smooth ♂ Kingstone Press. **Facilities** Children welcome Children's menu Children's portions Parking Wi-fi **Rooms** 30

PICK OF THE PUBS

The Millstone at Mellor ★★ HL 🏠🏠 ☙

Church Ln, Mellor BB2 7JR
☎ 01254 813333 ▤ 01254 812628
e-mail: info@millstonehotel.com
web: www.millstonehotel.co.uk
dir: M6 junct 31, A59 towards Clitheroe, past British Aerospace. Right at rdbt signed Blackburn/Mellor. Next rdbt 2nd left. Hotel at top of hill on right

The river Ribble meanders lazily in its trough-like valley just to the north of this village. Near by are the impressive half-timbered mansion of Samlesbury Hall, Whalley's ancient abbey and the legend-wreathed slopes of Pendle Hill. All are excellent reasons to spend a couple of days at this lovely village inn and restaurant, with Thwaites Wainwright ale being the clincher. And did we mention the food? Classic and inventive dishes are created by chef/patron Anson Bolton, who has gained two AA Rosettes for each of the past eight years. You choose from the same menu whether you eat in the very English oak-panelled

Miller's restaurant or in the bar. Bowland beef is aged for 28 days before being carefully grilled to your liking. How considerate to see a lady's steak listed too – a six-ounce sirloin is nicely manageable. Gluten-free choices are plentiful, while vegetarians rejoice in the greengrocer's deli board. Sticky toffee pudding and vanilla crème brûlée head the short but sweet list of 'afters'.

Open all day all wk **Bar Meals** L served Mon-Sat 12-9.30, Sun 12-9 Av main course £12 food served all day ⊕ SHIRE HOTELS LTD ◀ Thwaites, Lancaster Bomber, Thwaites Original Cash Bitter, Wainwrights ♂ Kingstone Press. ☙ 10 **Facilities** Children's menu Children's portions Parking Wi-fi **Rooms** 23

See advert below

BLACKO   Map 18 SD84

Moorcock Inn

Gisburn Rd BB9 6NG
☎ 01282 614186 ▤ 01282 614186
e-mail: boo@patterson1047.freeserve.co.uk
dir: M65 junct 13, take A682 inn halfway between Blacko & Gisburn

Beyond the folly of Blacko Tower, high on the road towards Gisburn on the Upper Admergill area, lies this family-run, 18th-century inn with traditional log fires and splendid views towards the Pendle Way. With Thwaites Wainwright and Kingstone Press cider served in the bar, home-prepared dishes are a speciality, with a wide choice from the menu and specials board including salads and sandwiches, and vegetarian and children's meals. Main dishes are hearty and might include lasagne, various steaks, pork in orange and cider, and grilled trout.

Open 12-2 6-9 (Sat 12-9 Sun 12-6) Closed: Mon eve **Bar Meals** L served all wk 12-2 D served Tue-Sun 6-9 Av main course £9.50 **Restaurant** L served all wk 12-2 D served Tue-Sun 6-9 Fixed menu price fr £9.50 ⊕ FREE HOUSE ◀ Thwaites Wainwright, Smooth ♂ Kingstone Press. **Facilities** Children welcome Children's menu Children's portions Garden Parking

PICK OF THE PUBS

Clog and Billycock

BLACKBURN Map 18 SD62

Billinge End Rd, Pleasington BB2 6QB
☎ **01254 201163**
e-mail:
enquiries@theclogandbillycock.com
web: www.theclogandbillycock.com
dir: *M6 junct 29 onto M65 junct 3, follow
signs for Pleasington*

From the same stable as The Three Fishes
at Mitton and The Highwayman at Nether
Burrow, the team at Ribble Valley Inns
have taken a good and popular dining inn
and made it better still. In a village at the
fringe of Blackburn, its hillside setting is
in pleasantly wooded countryside with the
historic Hoghton Tower close by and walks
from the door to Witton Country Park,
Pleasington Old Hall and riverside rambles
through the striking gorge of the River
Darwen. Originally the Bay Horse Inn, a
century ago a new landlord took the reins;
his favoured attire was a billycock hat and
Lancashire clogs, his personality did the
rest and the 'new' name stuck! It's a
Thwaites' house, with their popular
Lancaster Bomber the pick of the beers,
whilst the wine list stretches to over 35
bins. Marry this to the well crafted menu
created by award-winning chef Nigel
Haworth and you've the start of a long
friendship with this mid-Victorian inn,
which is an engaging mix of contemporary
and traditional styles, with a surprisingly
airy interior, modern art and photos of
local food heroes. It's Lancashire produce

that Nigel concentrates on; commence
with warm Morecambe Bay shrimps or
organic day-old Lancashire curd, buttered
crumpet, Ashcroft's beetroot and salad.
Ideal bedfellows for mains that promise
heather-reared Lonk lamb Lancashire
hotpot with pickled red cabbage, or a
generous local seafood platter based on
Port of Lancaster Smokehouse beech and
juniper smoked salmon, seawater prawns,
hot smoked trout, smoked mackerel pâté
and dressings and relishes. Non-meat
options are weighty with Lancashire's
artisan cheese producers and the
bounteous vegetables of the region. For
afters, try Bramley apple pie with
Leagram's Lancashire cheese.

Open all wk noon-11 (Sun noon-10.30)
Closed: 25 Dec **Bar Meals** L served Mon-
Sat 12-2, Sun (& BHs) 12-8 (afternoon

bites Mon-Sat 2-5.30) D served Mon-Thu
5.30-8.30, Fri-Sat 5.30-9, Sun (& BHs)
12-8 Av main course £13.50 **Restaurant**
L served Mon-Sat 12-2, Sun (& BHs) 12-8
D served Mon-Thu 5.30-8.30, Fri-Sat
5.30-9, Sun (& BHs) 12-8 ⊕ FREE HOUSE
◀ Thwaites Bomber, Wainwright, Original.
Facilities Children's menu Children's
portions Dogs allowed Garden Parking

BURROW
Map 18 SD67

PICK OF THE PUBS

The Highwayman

LA6 2RJ ☎ **01524 273338**
e-mail: enquiries@highwaymaninn.co.uk
web: www.highwaymaninn.co.uk
dir: M6 junct 36, A65 to Kirkby Lonsdale. Then A683 S. Burrow approx 2m

The Highwayman, an 18th-century inn, is the sister pub to the Three Fishes at Mitton in Nigel Haworth's thriving Ribble Valley Inns empire of dining pubs. In a smart, civilised setting of stone floors, handsome wooden furniture, crackling log fires and wonderful terraced gardens you can sample cracking real ales and delicious food. Food is very much at the heart of the operation, and the head chef focuses on an attractive contemporary interpretation of traditional specialities using regional produce – the menu celebrates local food heroes on every line. The ingredients they supply appear in dishes such as crispy slow cooked saddleback pork belly with celeriac, salt-baked Hesketh Bank beets and winter herbs to begin. To follow, maybe Fleetwood caught battered scampi, crispy east coast squid with chips cooked in dripping; or Lake District Farmers Herdwick mutton pudding, Forager's mash potato, black peas and capers. Typical desserts are banana, chocolate and toffee knickerbocker glory. There are seasonal alternative menus, a very good children's menu and a gluten free one too. Lancaster Bomber and Thwaites supply the ales and there is a list of non-alcoholic alternatives.

Open all wk noon–11 (Sun noon-10.30) Closed: 25 Dec
Bar Meals L served Mon-Sat 12-2, Sun (& BHs) 12-8.30 (afternoon bites Mon-Sat 2-6) D served Mon-Fri 6-9, Sat 5.30-9, Sun (& BHs) 12-8.30 Av main course £13.50 food served all day ⊕ RIBBLE VALLEY INNS ◀ Lancaster Bomber, Wainwright, Thwaites Original Ŏ Kingstone. **Facilities** Children welcome Children's portions Dogs allowed Garden Parking

CARNFORTH
Map 18 SD47

The Longlands Inn and Restaurant

Tewitfield LA6 1JH ☎ **01524 781256** ▤ **01524 781004**
e-mail: info@longlandshotel.co.uk
dir: Telephone for directions

With its nooks and crannies, old beams and uneven floors, this family-run inn stands next to Tewitfield locks on the Lancaster canal. The bar comes to life with band night on Mondays, with a more relaxed feel during the rest of the week. The appetising menu includes slate platters with deli-style bread; and main course choices ranging from braised Silverdale lamb shank, and tamarind confit duck leg on Chinese noodles to the Longlands fish pie with melted cheese topping.

Open all day all wk 11am-11pm ⊕ FREE HOUSE ◀ Black Sheep, Amber Gold, Guest ales. **Facilities** Children welcome Children's menu Dogs allowed Garden Parking

CHIPPING
Map 18 SD64

Dog & Partridge

Hesketh Ln PR3 2TH ☎ **01995 61201** ▤ **01995 61446**
dir: M6 junct 31A, follow Longridge signs. At Longridge left at 1st rdbt, straight on at next 3 rdbts. At Alston Arms turn right. 3m, pub on right

Dating back to 1515, this pleasantly modernised rural pub in the Ribble Valley enjoys delightful views of the surrounding fells. The barn has been transformed into a welcoming dining area, where home-made food on the comprehensive bar snack menu is backed by a specials board featuring fresh fish and game dishes. A typical menu shows a starter of deep fried garlic mushrooms; then mains of braised pork chops with home-made apple sauce and stuffing or home-made steak and kidney pie.

Open 11.45-3 6.45-11 (Sat 11.45-3 6-11 Sun 11.45-10.30) Closed: Mon ⊕ FREE HOUSE ◀ Black Sheep. **Facilities** Children welcome Children's menu Children's portions Parking

CLITHEROE
Map 18 SD74

PICK OF THE PUBS

The Assheton Arms ?

Downham BB7 4BJ
☎ **01200 441227** ▤ **01200 440581**
e-mail: asshetonarms@aol.com
dir: A59 to Chatburn, then follow Downham signs

Originally a farmhouse brewing beer just for the workers, this stone building became the George and Dragon in 1872, then in 1950 was renamed in honour of the contribution Ralph Assheton, Lord Clitheroe, made to the war effort during WWII. The Assheton family owns the whole, TV aerial-free village and their coat-of-arms is on the sign above the door. Visitors to the pub that Wendy and David Busby have run since 1983 will find the single bar and little rooms, with original 1765 stone fireplace, attractively furnished with solid oak tables and wing-back settees. Real ales

from Thwaites of Blackburn include Lancaster Bomber and Wainwright, named after the famous fell walker. A large blackboard lists the range of daily specials, particularly fish and shellfish. Local and traditional favourites on the main menu include a roast of the day, chicken and mushroom pie and Lancashire hot pot. Children and dogs are welcome.

Open all wk Mon-Fri 12-3 6-11 (Sat-Sun noon-11pm) **Bar Meals** L served Mon-Sat 12-2, Sun 12-8 D served all wk 6-9 **Restaurant** L served Mon-Sat 12-2, Sun 12-8 D served all wk 6-9 ⊕ FREE HOUSE ◀ Thwaites, Lancaster Bomber, Wainwright Ŏ Kingstone Press. ? 20 **Facilities** Children welcome Children's menu Children's portions Dogs allowed Parking

DALTON
Map 15 SD40

The Beacon at Dalton ?

Beacon Ln WN8 7RR ☎ **01695 622771**
dir: M6 junct 26 onto M58 towards Skelmersdale. At junct 5 follow signs for Up Holland & Beacon Country Park. In Up Holland 1st left by Victoria pub into Mill Ln which becomes Beacon Ln in approx 2m. Pub on right on brow of hill

Nestling at the edge of a country park close to the renowned viewpoint of Ashurst's Beacon (look for Snowdonia and the Lakes on very clear days), this welcoming 300 year old pub is a true local serving the scattered Lancashire community and discerning diners who seek out such as pork fillet on a bed of Lancashire cheese and black pudding. The period 19th century dining room is most refreshing, reflecting the care taken in the comprehensive refurbishment here.

Open all day all wk 4-10 (Fri-Sat 1pm-mdnt, Sun 1-10)
Restaurant L served Sun 1-6 booking required D served Fri-Sat 6-9 booking required ⊕ MARSTONS ◀ Pedigree, Cumberland, Hobgoblin, Sneck Lifter. ? 10
Facilities Children welcome Children's menu Children's portions Play area Dogs allowed Garden Parking Wi-fi

ELSWICK
Map 18 SD43

The Ship at Elswick ? NEW

High St PR4 3ZB ☎ **01995 672777**
e-mail: mail@theshipatelswick.co.uk
dir: M55 junct 3, A585 signed Fleetwood. Right onto Thistleton Rd (B5269)

This reliable village local and dining inn lies in a quiet village on the Fylde, handy both for Blackpool and the quieter resorts of Cleveleys and Fleetwood. From the latter comes some of the fish inhabiting the very traditional menu here; Lancashire hot pot is another favourite or snack on a plate of Morecambe Bay shrimps. The owners are proud to use Lancashire produce in most of their dishes, although the standard beer is a fine pint of Yorkshire's Black Sheep bitter!

Open all day all wk **Bar Meals** Av main course £9 food served all day **Restaurant** food served all day ⊕ PUNCH TAVERNS ◀ Black Sheep, Jennings Cumberland, Guest ales. ? 8 **Facilities** Children welcome Children's menu Children's portions Play area Garden Parking Wi-fi

FENCE   Map 18 SD83

Fence Gate Inn ☻

Wheatley Lane Rd BB12 9EE
☎ 01282 618101   📠 01282 615432
e-mail: info@fencegate.co.uk
web: www.fencegate.co.uk
dir: *From M65 junct 13 towards Fence, 1.5m, pub set back on right opposite T-junct for Burnley*

Next to the village church at the edge of beautiful open countryside, this imposing building, dating back 300 years, was a private house until 1982 when today's comfortable inn was created. High quality furnishings, a brasserie and dining suites reveal its function as a foodie destination, but drinkers aren't forgotten, with a characterful wood-panelled bar and grand log fire where Lancashire-brewed beers are the order of the day. The Lancashire theme continues with the food; Bowland beef features strongly, home-made local pork sausages a speciality and Red Rose cheeses a fine final flourish to a meal.

Open all day all wk noon-close **Bar Meals** L served Mon-Sat 12-2.30, Sun 12-8 D served Mon-Sat 6-9, Sun 12-8 **Restaurant** L served Mon-Sat 12-2.30, Sun 12-8 D served Mon-Sat 6-9, Sun 12-8 ⊕ FREE HOUSE ◀ Theakston, Directors, Deuchars, Moorhouse, Bowland, changing guest ales ♻ Stowford Press. ☻ 10 **Facilities** Children welcome Children's menu Children's portions Dogs allowed Garden Parking Wi-fi

Ye Old Sparrowhawk Inn ☻

Wheatley Lane Rd BB12 9QG
☎ 01282 603034   📠 01282 603035
e-mail: mail@thesparrowhawk.co.uk
web: www.thesparrowhawk.co.uk
dir: *M65 junct 13, A6068, at rdbt take 1st exit 0.25m. Turn right onto Carr Hall Rd, at top turn left 0.25m, pub on right*

Set on a hillside above Nelson, views from the sloping beer garden here stretch across the hidden Calder Valley to the lofty heights of the South Pennines and Brontë

country, whilst famous Pendle Hill beckons to the north. Now in new hands, the eyecatching, half-timbered 17th century former farmhouse is a curious structure, with a novel stained-glass dome; nothing curious about the beers and food though, with beers from Bolton and Bashall Eaves and food from suppliers proud to be part of the Taste of Lancashire campaign. Port of Lancaster smoked haddock tart or local Goosnargh slow cooked duck leg are typical choices from the extensive menus.

Open all day all wk noon-11 (Sun noon-10)
Bar Meals L served Mon-Sat 12-2.30, Sun 12-8 booking required D served Mon-Sat 5.30-9.30, Sun 12-8 booking required **Restaurant** L served Mon-Sat 12-2.30, Sun 12-8 booking required D served Mon-Sat 5.30-9.30, Sun 12-8 booking required ⊕ MOYO LTD ◀ Thwaites Cask, Draught Bass, Greene King IPA, Banktop, Guest ales. ☻ 10 **Facilities** Children welcome Children's menu Children's portions Dogs allowed Garden Parking

FORTON   Map 18 SD45

PICK OF THE PUBS

The Bay Horse Inn ☻

LA2 0HR ☎ 01524 791204   📠 01524 791204
e-mail: yvonne@bayhorseinn.com
dir: *M6 junct 33 take A6 towards Garstang, turn left for pub, approx 1m from M6*

Mismatched furniture and a handsome stone fireplace with roaring winter log fire characterise this charming 18th-century pub in the Trough of Bowland. Expect a warm welcome and real cask beers, as well as an extensive wine list and a good selection of malt whiskies. Award-winning chef Craig Wilkinson specialises in simple, fresh and imaginative dishes, exercising his culinary skills on the very best of local ingredients to produce pub fare of unashamedly gastro standards. A fixed-price lunch carte offers two or three courses such as seafood salad with tarragon dressing; roast sirloin of beef with duck fat roast potatoes and Yorkshire pudding; and apple crumble with vanilla ice cream. Following Craig's 'taste is the philosophy' maxim, a dinner selection could comprise warm potted shrimps with herbs and spices, followed by Goosnargh chicken breast with wild mushrooms. The recently created herb garden and newly extended back garden also make an ideal setting in which to enjoy his excellent cooking.

Open noon-3 6.30-mdnt Closed: Mon (ex BH L)
Bar Meals L served Tue-Sat 12-1.45, Sun 12-3 D served Tue-Sat 6.30-9 booking required **Restaurant** L served Tue-Sat 12-1.45, Sun 12-3 D served Tue-Sat 6.30-9 booking required ⊕ FREE HOUSE ◀ Thwaites Lancaster Bomber, Moorhouses Pendle Witch, Masham Brewery, Black Sheep. ☻ 11 **Facilities** Children welcome Children's portions Garden Parking Wi-fi

GOOSNARGH   Map 18 SD53

The Stag's Head

990 Whittingham Ln, Whittingham PR3 2AU
☎ 01772 864071
e-mail: clare@thestagshead.co.uk
dir: *From A6 at Broughton take B5260 signed Longridge. 3m to pub*

The search continues here for a tunnel rumoured to link this part-18th-century village pub to haunted Chingle Hall. In the bar five guest ales are always on tap. Dishes relying on quality local suppliers include slow-cooked Goosnargh duck on toast; Curwen Hill beef and ale pie; Pendle lamb Lancashire hot pot; and battered deep-fried Fleetwood cod. The cheeseboard reflects the fact that this area is known as the Cheese Triangle. The surrounding countryside is a rambler's dream, with the pub a welcome stopping point. Change of hands.

Open all day Closed: Tue ⊕ SCOTTISH & NEWCASTLE ◀ Theakstons, John Smith's, Guest ales. **Facilities** Children welcome Children's menu Children's portions Dogs allowed Garden Parking

HESKIN GREEN   Map 15 SD51

Farmers Arms

85 Wood Ln PR7 5NP
☎ 01257 451276   📠 01257 453958
e-mail: andy@farmersarms.co.uk
dir: *On B5250 between M6 & Eccleston*

This fine 17th-century pub used to be called the Pleasant Retreat, but in 1902 the name was changed. Never mind, because this long, creeper-covered building is still pleasant, very pleasant actually, and its stone-flagged Vault Bar is still a retreat. The Rothwell family have been here for a quarter of a century, and Andrew Rothwell cooks hearty chicken au poivre; minted lamb cutlets; and grilled fresh plaice. Hand-pulled real ales include Silver Tally, named after the token that miners would exchange for a lamp.

Open all day all wk **Bar Meals** food served all day **Restaurant** food served all day ⊕ ENTERPRISE INNS ◀ Timothy Taylor Landlord, Pedigree, Black Sheep, Tetley, Silver Tally. **Facilities** Children welcome Children's menu Children's portions Play area Dogs allowed Garden Parking Wi-fi

HEST BANK   Map 18 SD46

Hest Bank Hotel

2 Hest Bank Ln LA2 6DN
☎ 01524 824339   📠 01524 824948
e-mail: chef.glenn@btinternet.com
dir: *From Lancaster take A6 N, after 2m left to Hest Bank*

Comedian Eric Morecambe used to drink at this canalside former coaching inn, first licensed in 1554. Awash with history and 'many happy ghosts', it now offers cask ales and a wide selection of meals all day, with local suppliers playing an important role in maintaining food quality.

continued

HEST BANK *continued*

The good value menu may range from a large pot of Bantry Bay mussels to the pub's own lamb hotpot made to a traditional recipe. The pub is family-friendly so perhaps while keeping an eye on the children you can enjoy a pint of Timothy Taylor Landlord or Black Sheep Bitter in the terraced garden.

Open all day all wk 11.30-11.30 (Sun 11.30-10.30) **Bar Meals** L served Mon-Sat 12-9, Sun 12-8 D served Mon-Sat 12-9, Sun 12-8 food served all day ⊕ PUNCH TAVERNS ◀ Timothy Taylor Landlord, Black Sheep Bitter, Guest ales. **Facilities** Children welcome Children's menu Children's portions Play area Garden Parking

LANCASTER	Map 18 SD46

PICK OF THE PUBS

Penny Street Bridge ★★★ TH ☕ NEW

Penny St LA1 1XT ☎ 01524 599900 📄 01524 599901
e-mail: relax@pennystreetbridge.co.uk
web: www.pennystreetbridge.co.uk
dir: In town centre

Originally the site of the Corporation Toll House before being replaced by two pubs in the early 1900s, this striking stone building stands in the heart of Lancaster and was transformed by Thwaites Brewery in 2007, creating a smart townhouse hotel with a lively bar and brasserie. Period features have been retained throughout – note the high ceilings, the stained glass windows, the servant bell hooks, and the listed staircase. The atmosphere is relaxed and informal, with wooden floors in the brasserie, tub chairs in the traditional bar, and a stylish, contemporary feel in the 28 refurbished bedrooms. Served all day, the seasonal menu makes the most of the excellent Lancashire produce available locally, from pea and ham soup, or crab cakes with brown shrimp and caper vinaigrette for starters to main courses like a classic steak and ale pie or daube of beef with mustard mash, and confit duck leg with beans, root vegetables and Puy lentil cassoulet. For pudding, try the chocolate brioche bread-and-butter pudding with custard.

Open all day all wk **Bar Meals** Av main course £10 food served all day **Restaurant** Av 3 course à la carte fr £20 food served all day ⊕ THWAITES INNS OF CHARACTER ◀ Wainwright, Smooth Ö Kingstone Press. ☕ 9 **Facilities** Children welcome Children's menu Children's portions Parking Wi-fi **Rooms** 28

See advert below

The Stork Inn

Conder Green LA2 0AN
☎ 01524 751234 📄 01524 752660
e-mail: tracy@thestorkinn.co.uk
dir: M6 junct 33 take A6 north. Left at Galgate & next left to Conder Green

White-painted coaching inn spread along the banks of the Conder Estuary, with a colourful 300-year-history that includes several name changes. The quaint sea port of Glasson Dock is a short walk along the Lancashire Coastal Way, and the Lake District is easily accessible. In the bar you will find local ales such as Lancaster Amber and Black. Seasonal specialities join home-cooked English and South African food like pan-fried chicken breast topped with Lancashire cheese and bacon; Boerewors - lightly spiced pure beef farmer's sausage, served with sweet potato mash and a balsamic, red onion and tomato relish; and minted pea risotto.

Open all day all wk 10am-11pm (Sat-Sun 8.30am-11pm) ⊕ ENTERPRISE INN ◀ Black Sheep, Timothy Taylor Landlord, Lancaster Amber, Lancaster Black, Marstons Pedigree. **Facilities** Children welcome Children's menu Children's portions Play area Dogs allowed Garden Parking Wi-fi

PICK OF THE PUBS

The Sun Hotel and Bar ☕

LA1 1ET ☎ 01524 66006 📄 01524 66397
e-mail: info@thesunhotelandbar.co.uk
dir: 6m from M6 junct 33

First licensed as 'Stoop Hall' in 1680, The Sun was formerly Lancaster's premier coaching inn. Generals from the occupying Jacobean Army lodged at The Sun in 1745, and the artist JMW Turner stayed here whilst making sketches of Heysham in 1812. Now famous for its hospitality and wide selection of cask ales and wines, its lovely old bar is frequented throughout the day; first arrivals are the hotel guests and business breakfasters, then shoppers and people checking their e-mails over coffee. At lunchtime it's busy with customers keen to tuck into the locally sourced good food on the main and daily changing specials menus. And in the evening there are the real ale enthusiasts, draught and bottled lager connoisseurs and wine lovers. The experienced kitchen brigade prepares home-cooked food, including the popular cheese, cold meat and pâté boards. There is a patio for alfresco dining in warmer weather and an annual beer festival in the summer.

Open all day all wk from 7.30am until late **Bar Meals** Av main course £8 food served all day ⊕ FREE HOUSE ◀ Thwaites Lancaster Bomber, Lancaster Amber, Timmermans Strawberry, Lancaster Blonde. ☕ 23 **Facilities** Children welcome Children's menu Children's portions Garden Beer festival

PICK OF THE PUBS

The Waterwitch

The Tow Path, Aldcliffe Rd LA1 1SU
☎ 01524 63828 📠 01524 34535
e-mail: thewaterwitch@mitchellsinns.co.uk
dir: *6m from M6 junct 33*

The Waterwitch takes its name from three longboats that worked the adjacent Lancaster canal in the late 18th century. It occupies an old stables, tastefully converted to retain original features such as stone walls and interior slab floors. In just a few years the pub has acquired celebrity status and a clutch of awards, yet it still remains a genuine pub with the broad appeal of a wine bar and restaurant. It is noted for its ever-changing selection of fine cask-conditioned real ales, impressive wine list and guest cheeses. The talented team of chefs work with locally sourced produce including fish that arrives daily from Fleetwood harbour.

Open all day all wk 11am-late **Bar Meals** food served all day **Restaurant** food served all day ⊕ MITCHELL'S OF LANCASTER BREWERY ◀ Thwaites Lancaster Bomber, York Brewery Ales, Guest ales Ö Westons Cider. **Facilities** Children welcome Children's menu Children's portions Garden Beer festival Wi-fi

---

LITTLE ECCLESTON   Map 18 SD44

PICK OF THE PUBS

The Cartford Inn

PR3 0YP ☎ 01995 670166
e-mail: info@thecartfordinn.co.uk
dir: *Off A586*

This 17th-century former coaching inn stands in an idyllic setting by the toll bridge over the tidal River Wyre. Enjoy imaginative food cooked with fresh local produce, and an extensive wine list, in the new dining area overlooking the river and surrounding countryside. In summer, the beer garden with views over the river to the shapely Lancashire fells is the perfect place to relax with a beer from Moorhouses, Bowland or Lakeland Breweries. Owners Julie and Patrick Beaume offer a pleasant mix of traditional and gastro elements; a timeless log fire still burns in the winter grate, while polished wood floors and chunky dining furniture are decidedly up-to-date. Imaginative food starts with a choice of nibbles, continues with wood platters of antipasti or seafood, and culminates in the full menu experience: the chef's signature dish of oxtail and beef in real ale suet pudding or Cartford Inn fish pie.

Open all day Closed: 25 Dec, Mon L **Bar Meals** L served Tue-Sat 12-2, Sun 12-8.30 D served Mon-Thu 5.30-9, Fri-Sat 5.30-10 **Restaurant** L served Tue-Sat 12-2, Sun 12-8.30 D served Mon-Thu 5.30-9, Fri-Sat 5.30-10 ⊕ FREE HOUSE ◀ Pride of Pendle Moorhouse, Lakeland Gold Hawkshead, New Harrier Bowland Brewery, Old Peculier Theakston. **Facilities** Children welcome Children's menu Children's portions Garden Parking Wi-fi

---

NEWTON-IN-BOWLAND   Map 18 SD65

Parkers Arms

BB7 3DY ☎ 01200 446236
e-mail: enquiries@parkersarms.co.uk
web: www.parkersarms.co.uk
dir: *From Clitheroe take B6478 through Waddington to Newton-in-Bowland*

Bowland's imposing fells swoop across the horizon above this refurbished dining inn just yards from the pretty river Hodder. It's the pub nearest to the geographical centre of the UK, and celebrates its rural location by serving the best of Lancashire produce. This includes ales from the Bowland Brewery, meats raised on the grassy hills all around, vegetables from Ribble Valley farms, and cheeses from local craft producers. Fresh fish from Fleetwood and seasonal fruits complete the focus on quality ingredients, presented without fuss or frills.

Open all wk Mon-Fri noon-3 6-mdnt (Sat-Sun noon-mdnt) (open all day in summer) **Bar Meals** L served Mon-Fri 12-3, Sat-Sun all day Av main course £12 **Restaurant** L served Mon-Fri 12-3, Sat-Sun all day D served Mon-Fri 6-9, Sat-Sun all day Fixed menu price fr £12.50 Av 3 course à la carte fr £21 ⊕ ENTERPRISE INNS ◀ Bowland Hen Harrier, Sawley Tempted, Lancaster Amber, Skipton Brewery Copper Dragon Ö Stowford Press. **Facilities** Children welcome Children's menu Children's portions Dogs allowed Garden Parking Wi-fi

---

PARBOLD   Map 15 SD41

PICK OF THE PUBS

The Eagle & Child

Maltkiln Ln, Bispham Green L40 3SG
☎ 01257 462297 📠 01257 464718
web: www.ainscoughs.co.uk
dir: *3m from M6 junct 27. Take A5209 to Parbold. Right onto B5246. 2.5m, Bispham Green on right*

An award-winning dining pub in a pretty and peaceful location, with outside seating positioned to enjoy bowling on the green during the summer months. The pub's unusual name derives from a local legend that Lord Derby's illegitimate son was discovered in an eagle's nest; a more prosaic local title is the Bird and Bastard. The bar maintains its traditional atmosphere by offering a choice of real ciders and regularly-changing guest ales from a dozen nearby micro-breweries; the annual early May Bank Holiday beer festival attracts up to 2,000 people to a huge marquee in the pub grounds. Menus for both bar and restaurant hinge on locally sourced and organic produce when possible. Typical of starters are flash-fried squid with fried lemon, pancetta and pangrattato, and chicken and pumpkin lasagne with tomato sauce and buffalo mozzarella. Follow up with sautéed strips of lamb rump with a rosemary, garlic and port sauce, or pan-fried wild duck breasts with parsnip tart.

Open all wk 12-3 5.30-11 (Fri-Sun noon-11pm) **Bar Meals** L served all wk 12-2 booking required D served Sun-Thu 5.30-8.30, Fri-Sat 5.30-9 booking required Av main course £12 **Restaurant** L served all wk 12-2 booking required D served Sun-Thu 5.30-8.30, Fri-Sat 5.30-9 booking required ⊕ FREE HOUSE ◀ Moorhouse Black Cat Mild, Thwaites Bitter, Southport Golden Sands, Guest ales Ö Kingstone Press Traditional Cider. **Facilities** Children welcome Children's menu Children's portions Family room Dogs allowed Garden Beer festival Parking

SAWLEY — Map 18 SD74

PICK OF THE PUBS

The Spread Eagle ¶

BB7 4NH ☎ 01200 441202 📠 01200 441973
e-mail: spreadeagle@zen.co.uk
dir: Just off A159 between Clitheroe & Skipton, 4m N of Clitheroe

Beautifully refurbished by Martin Clarkson in 2009, this handsome old stone inn stands on a quiet lane in the glorious Ribble Valley, flanked on one side by the impressive ruins of Sawley Abbey, and on other by the River Ribble. Inside, choose between the elegant, light-filled dining room with its lush river views through picture windows, or the charming 17th-century bar, where you'll find traditional stone-flagged floors, old oak furniture and roaring fires alongside trendy wallpaper, painted settles strewn with bright cushions, colourful upholstered chairs, eclectic objets d'art, and cool Farrow and Ball hues. The result is a cosy and relaxing setting for savouring a pint of Timothy Taylor Landlord and some decent modern pub food. Served throughout the inn and changing daily, the menu may include scallops and black pudding with saffron and orange dressing, a classic steak and kidney pudding, rib-eye steak with garlic butter and hand-cut chips, and warm chocolate brownie with maple ice cream. Don your boots and walk it all off in the Bowland hills.

Open all day all wk 11-11 (Sun noon-10.30)
Bar Meals L served Mon-Sat 12-2, Sun 12-7.30 D served Mon-Sat 6-9.30, Sun 12-7.30 Av main course £10 **Restaurant** L served Mon-Sat 12-2, Sun 12-7.30 D served Mon-Sat 6-9.30, Sun 12-7.30 Av 3 course à la carte fr £25 ⊕ INDIVIDUAL INNS ◀ Timothy Taylor, Wainwrights. ¶ 16 **Facilities** Children welcome Children's menu Children's portions Garden Parking

TOCKHOLES — Map 15 SD62

PICK OF THE PUBS

The Royal Arms NEW

Tockholes Rd BB3 0PA ☎ 01254 705373
dir: M65 junct 4 follow Blackburn signs. Right at lights, 1st left. Up hill left at 3B's Brewery into Tockholes Rd. Pub in 3m on left

An appealing, four-square old stone pub in a tiny fold of mill-workers cottages beside a winding back road high in the West Pennine Moors; walks from the door drop into the deer-haunted Roddlesworth Woods around a picturesque string of reservoirs, or climb to the imposing Jubilee Tower on nearby Darwen Hill, a popular local walk. Characterful, flag-floored, beamed little rooms with log fires; there's an engaging hotchpotch of furnishings, fascinating old photos of the local villages in their mill-town heyday and a bar rich with pickings from Lancashire micro-breweries. Take a glass of Hopstar or Tockholes Treacle out to tables on the lawn; listen to curlews call on the reedy moors and study the appealing, regularly changing

menu of home-cooked goodies, including cheeky leeky pie (chicken, leek and onion) and some great spicy dishes. Sunday roasts or a fulfilling steak and pepper pie take the chill off a bracing winter walk. A summer beer festival is planned.

Open all day Closed: Mon **Bar Meals** L served Tue-Fri 12-2, Sat 12-3, Sun 12-7 D served Wed-Sat 6-8.45, Sun 12-7 Av main course £7 ◀ Local micro breweries. **Facilities** Children welcome Children's menu Children's portions Dogs allowed Garden Beer festival Parking

TUNSTALL — Map 18 SD67

PICK OF THE PUBS

The Lunesdale Arms

LA6 2QN ☎ 015242 74203 📠 015242 74229
e-mail: info@thelunesdale.co.uk
dir: M6 junct 36. A65 Kirkby Lonsdale. A638 Lancaster. Pub 2m on right

Emma Gillibrand's bright, cheery and welcoming pub is set in a small rural village in the beautiful Lune Valley. Well established, with quite a reputation for its food, wines and fine regional beers (Black Sheep & Dent), it draws diners from far and wide for changing chalkboard menus that showcase locally sourced produce, including bread baked on the premises, meat from local farms and organically grown vegetables and salads. Both lunch and evening menus change on a daily basis according to the seasonality of ingredients and new ideas. Country terrine with medlar jelly; slow-roasted shoulder of lamb; butternut squash, sage and Lancashire blue cheese risotto; steak, Guinness and mushroom pie; and Yorkshire rhubarb pannacotta with poached rhubarb show the style. In winter, cosy up by the wood-burning stove in the light and airy bar, with its bare boards, stripped dining tables, comfortable sofas, and local artwork.

Open 11-3 6-close (Sat Sun & BHs 11-4 6-1am) Closed: 25-26 Dec, Mon (ex BH) **Bar Meals** L served Tue-Fri 12-2, Sat-Sun 12-2.30 booking required D served Tue-Sun 6-9 booking required **Restaurant** L served Tue-Fri 12-2, Sat-Sun 12-2.30 booking required D served Tue-Sun 6-9 booking required ⊕ FREE HOUSE ◀ Black Sheep, Dent Aviator, Guinness, Brysons Bitter Ŏ Stowford Press. **Facilities** Children welcome Children's portions Family room Dogs allowed Garden Parking

WHALLEY — Map 18 SD73

PICK OF THE PUBS

The Three Fishes @ ¶

See Pick of the Pubs on opposite page

WHEELTON — Map 15 SD62

The Dressers Arms ¶ NEW

Briers Brow PR6 8HD ☎ 01254 830041
e-mail: info@dressersarms.co.uk
dir: M61 junct 8, A674 to Blackburn. Follow sign for pub on right

Handy for the West Pennine Moors and the nearby scenic reservoirs at Anglezarke, this long, low, creeper-festooned old gritstone-built pub (until the 1960's the smallest in Lancashire) is crammed with local photos, collectables and artefacts spread through a clutch of separate drinking areas, featuring partly flagged floors and roaring fires for winter warmth. This winning combination is enhanced by a great range of beers and a reliable raft of home-made pubby grub (curries, suet puddings and Sunday carvery are all well thought of), boosted by specials including some good fish dishes. There is quiz night on Tuesday and steak night on Wednesday.

Open all day all wk **Bar Meals** Av main course £6.50 food served all day **Restaurant** Av 3 course à la carte fr £18.30 food served all day ⊕ FREE HOUSE ◀ Black Sheep, Dressers Bitter Ŏ Westons. ¶ 20 **Facilities** Children welcome Children's menu Children's portions Family room Dogs allowed Garden Parking Wi-fi

WHITEWELL — Map 18 SD64

PICK OF THE PUBS

The Inn at Whitewell

★★★★★ INN @ ¶

Forest of Bowland BB7 3AT
☎ 01200 448222 📠 01200 448298
e-mail: reception@innatwhitewell.com
dir: From B6243 follow Whitewell signs

Despite its splendid isolation amid the wild beauty of the Forest of Bowland, there's much to enjoy at this ancient stone inn. The whole complex embraces a wine merchant, an art gallery, a shop selling home-made goodies, and 23 individually decorated bedrooms - not to mention seven miles of fishing rights. The somewhat eccentric interior is packed with a random collection of furnishings, including a vast assortment of old prints and paintings. The cooking takes a simple modern British approach: bar lunch dishes might include smoked salmon with lemon and granary bread; or spicy fried squid with soft noodles, carrot and sweet ginger salad. Bar suppers follow similar lines, or you can choose à la carte starters like smoked Goosnargh chicken salad, followed by roast pork with pancetta and grain mustard mash. There's a constantly changing selection of traditional puddings and home-made ice creams to round off the meal. There are stunning walks from the front door.

Open all day all wk 10am-1am **Bar Meals** L served all wk 12-2 D served all wk 7.30-9.30 Av main course £11 **Restaurant** D served all wk 7.30-9.30 booking required Av 3 course à la carte fr £30 ⊕ FREE HOUSE ◀ Bowland Bitter, Copper Dragon, Timothy Taylor Landlord, Moorhouse Hawkshead Ŏ Dunkerton's Organic Premium. ¶ 16 **Facilities** Children welcome Children's portions Dogs allowed Garden Parking Wi-fi **Rooms** 23

PICK OF THE PUBS

The Three Fishes

WHALLEY   Map 18 SD73

Mitton Rd, Mitton BB7 9PQ
☎ 01254 826888   📄 01254 826026
e-mail: enquiries@thethreefishes.com
web: www.thethreefishes.com
dir: *M6 junct 31, A59 to Clitheroe. Follow
signs for Whalley, take B6246 for 2m*

The River Ribble loops energetically out of the Forest of Bowland at Mitton, picking up the tributary river Hodder in a landscape that inspired JRR Tolkien when he wrote parts of his spellbinding *Lord of the Rings* trilogy hereabouts. The old Three Fishes could have seeped from the pages of this epic; today's sublime inn, however, is a far cry from its foundation maybe 400 years ago above a ferry and bridge across the river. This relaxed country dining inn pushes the boundaries of cuisine and comfort, trumpeting its Lancashire roots and championing all that the Red Rose County can provide from its magnificent larder. This is the flagship — and first born — pub in celebrity chef Nigel Haworth's Ribble Valley Inns stable, a string of similar establishments dappled across Bowland and Ribblesdale. With Pendle Hill to one horizon; Longridge Fell to another, there are few more idyllic settings than to sit out at the terrace, contemplate the nearby medieval church and wonder at the breadth of dishes created from Lancashire's finest. A simple afternoon bite of an Elmwood seafood platter celebrates Morecambe Bay's provender,

with Port of Lancaster beech and juniper smoked salmon, hot smoked trout and smoked mackerel pâté amongst the fish delights. Or, for a winter warmer, nestle in the tasteful, contemporary, rambling interior next to log fires and lose yourself in a warming dish of heather-reared Lonk lamb Lancashire hotpot with pickled red cabbage, perhaps washed down with a glass of real ale from the local Bowland craft brewery. Haworth's menus and recipes have gained an AA Rosette for the inventive, inspirational ingredients and presentation; vegetarians will delight in dishes using Formby asparagus or Southport samphire, whilst indulgent meat-eaters can savour Forest of Bowland venison and pearl barley pudding, foragers mashed potato, roast onions and juniper berry sauce.

Open all day all wk Closed: 25 Dec
Bar Meals/Restaurant L served Mon-Sat 12-2, Sun 12-8 (afternoon bites Mon-Sat 2-5.30) D served Mon-Thu 5.30-8.30 Fri-Sat 5.30-9, Sun 12-8 Av main course £11 food served all day ⊕ FREE HOUSE 🍺 Thwaites Traditional, Thwaites Bomber, Bowland Brewery Hen Harrier. ♈ 13
Facilities Children welcome Children's menu Children's portions Dogs allowed Garden Parking

PICK OF THE PUBS

Freemasons at Wiswell 🍷

WISWELL   Map 18 SD73

8 Vicarage Fold BB7 9DF
☎ 01254 822218   📄 01254 824375
e-mail:
enquiries@freemasonswiswell.co.uk
web: www.freemasonswiswell.co.uk
dir: *M6 junct 31, A59 towards Clitheroe.*
A671 towards Whalley for 0.1m, turn left
for Wiswell. Pub opposite red phone box

A beautiful country inn in a picture-perfect village in the heart of the Ribble Valley. The inn was formerly three small cottages, one of which was a freemasons' lodge – hence the name. When the new owner along with chef/patron Steven Smith took it over, an exceptional renovation saw this rural village pub evolve into a stylish and inviting country dining inn, where great food is served in elegant and relaxed surroundings. Downstairs flagstone floors, roaring log fires, walls in muted heritage colours, antique rugs and furniture, period paintings and prints all unite to create a superbly warm and comfortable atmosphere. A period-style oak staircase leads guests up to the Derby room with its cast iron fireplace and an impressive collection of antique horse-racing prints. To the left is the Tudor room with oak tables and chairs, settles and Tudor artwork. The Portrait room has elegant Georgian furniture and period portraits. The magnificent Gun room is the place to relax with a post prandial coffee or liqueur. Steven Smith, a local man with

Gilpin Lodge and Box Tree Restaurant on his CV, has quickly established the Freemasons on the Ribble Valley food map. His confident, modern British approach to cooking starts with his passion for top-notch produce, and offers something for every taste. Typical of his starters are a fisherman's pie made with roast scallops, smoked bacon and celeriac, or leek and potato soup with smoked haddock fish fingers. The main event could comprise milk-poached calves' liver, or roasted loin of cod with olive oil poached squid. At the bar you will find several fine cask ales from independent brewers, plus an extensive list of 240 wines.

Open Tue-Fri 11.30-3 5.30-11 (Sat 11.30-mdnt, Sun 11.30-8) Closed: Jan 2-14, Mon
Bar Meals L served Tue-Sat 12-2.30, Sun

12-8 D served Tue-Sat 5.30-9.30 Av main course £15 **Restaurant** L served Tue-Sat 12-2.30 D served Tue-Sat 5.30-9.30 Fixed menu price fr £12.95 Av 3 course à la carte fr £27 🍺 FREE HOUSE 🍺 Tirrils, Moorhouses, Bowland, Bank Top, Skipton Brewery ♂ Aspall. 🍷 15
Facilities Children's menu Children's portions Dogs allowed Garden Wi-fi

WISWELL   Map 18 SD73

PICK OF THE PUBS

Freemasons at Wiswell ▾

See Pick of the Pubs on opposite page

LEICESTERSHIRE

BELTON   Map 11 SK42

PICK OF THE PUBS

The Queen's Head ★★★★ RR ◉◉ ▾

2 Long St LE12 9TP
☎ 01530 222359 📠 01530 224860
e-mail: enquiries@thequeenshead.org
web: www.thequeenshead.org
dir: *On B5324 between Coalville & Loughborough*

A contemporary, boutique-style pub with rooms in the centre of the picturesque village of Belton, this place has all-round appeal. The clean, uncluttered exterior suggests that its new owners might also have a fair idea of what constitutes good interior design. And so they have. Settle into a leather sofa in the contemporary bar, enjoy the food in the restaurant, garden or terrace, or stay overnight in a smartly designed bedroom. A Lite Bites/Classics menu incorporates club sandwiches; burger and chips; risotto of the day; and fish and chips with tartare sauce and minted peas. The modern British set menu offers starters of pan-fried squid with chorizo, confit potato and salsa verde or slow-cooked pork belly with apple and Swiss chard, with mains including mustard-glazed pork fillet, home-made sausage and gratin potato; pot-roasted pheasant with celeriac, pancetta and Brussels sprouts; or fillet of brill with mousseline, fennel and capers. The two AA Rosettes The Queen's Head has earned speak volumes.

Open all day all wk Closed: 25-26 Dec
Bar Meals L served all wk 12-2.30 D served all wk 6-9.30 **Restaurant** L served all wk 12-2.30 D served all wk 6-9.30 ⊕ FREE HOUSE ◀ Pedigree, Queens Special. ▾ 14 **Facilities** Children welcome Children's portions Play area Dogs allowed Garden Parking Wi-fi **Rooms** 6

BIRSTALL   Map 11 SK50

PICK OF THE PUBS

The White Horse

White Horse Ln LE4 4EF ☎ 0116 267 1038
e-mail: info@thewhitehorsebirstall.co.uk
dir: *M1 junct 21A, A46 towards Newark 5.5m. Exit A46 at Loughborough*

Little did the builders of the Grand Union Canal realise, but their local coal wharf serving the village of Birstall would one day become the tranquil garden of this old canal-workers beerhouse, which has matured over the years since it was rebuilt in the 1920's into today's restful retreat. Overlooking Watermead Country Park, The White Horse (formerly The Mulberry Tree) delivers the very best expected of a village inn; reliable beers, good company, garden with views and a sought-after range of dishes. Boaters and ramblers alike can look forward to venison pâté, ciabatta crisps and onion jam or goat's cheese and red onion tart to whet the appetite prior to wild mushroom and spinach pancakes with white wine and Parmesan sauce, a specialist stone-baked pizza or braised lamb shank, finishing with white chocolate bread and butter pudding or locally made ice cream. Or just follow the locals' lead and tuck in to the renowned pie of the week with all the trimmings.

Open all wk winter 12-3 5.30-11, summer all day, everyday **Bar Meals** L served Mon-Sat 12-2.30, Sun 12-4 D served Mon-Sat 6-9 **Restaurant** L served Mon-Sat 12-2.30, Sun 12-4 D served Mon-Sat 6-9 ⊕ TRUST INNS ◀ Timothy Taylor Landlord, Jennings Cumberland, Guest. **Facilities** Children welcome Children's menu Children's portions Play area Dogs allowed Garden Parking Wi-fi

BREEDON ON THE HILL   Map 11 SK42

The Three Horseshoes

Main St DE73 8AN ☎ 01332 695129
e-mail: ian@thehorseshoes.com
dir: *5m from M1 junct 23a. Pub in village centre*

Originally a farrier's, the buildings here are around 250 years old, but nobody knows how long it's been a pub: a gourmet food and gift shop and a chocolate workshop now occupy the smithy's and stables in the courtyard. In the pub, numerous original features and old beams are supplemented by antique furniture, and sea-grass matting completes the warm and welcoming atmosphere. Typical dishes range from sandwiches and salads to chicken breast with beetroot sauce, and lamb shank with parsnip mash.

Open Mon-Sun L Closed: 25-26, 31 Dec-1 Jan, Sun eve **Bar Meals** L served Mon-Sat 12-2 D served Mon-Sat 5.30-9.15 Av main course £9 **Restaurant** L served Mon-Sat 12-2, Sun 12-3 booking required D served Mon-Sat 6.30-9.15 booking required Av 3 course à la carte fr £30 ⊕ FREE HOUSE ◀ Marstons Pedigree. **Facilities** Children welcome Dogs allowed Garden Parking

BRUNTINGTHORPE   Map 11 SP68

Joiners Arms ▾

Church Walk LE17 5QH ☎ 0116 247 8258
e-mail: stephen@thejoinersarms.co.uk
dir: *4m from Lutterworth*

More restaurant than village pub, with restored natural oak beams, tiled floor, pleasant decor, and lots of brassware and candles. Menus change constantly, and quality ingredients are sourced – beef from Scotland, Cornish lamb, Portland crab. From an impressive menu, dishes might include king scallops, Clonakilty black pudding and garlic mash; melon in elderflower and ginger jelly; medallions of Scottish beef fillet with Diane sauce; butternut squash and blue cheese risotto; liquorish pannacotta with blackcurrant sorbet; or mango and passionfruit Pavlova. Every Tuesday there's a 3-course fixed menu 'Auberge Supper'.

Open 12-2 6.30-11 Closed: Mon **Bar Meals** L served Tue-Sun 12-2 booking required Av main course £12.50 **Restaurant** L served Tue-Sun 12-2 booking required D served 6.30-9.30 booking required Fixed menu price fr £10.95 Av 3 course à la carte fr £30 ⊕ FREE HOUSE ◀ Greene King IPA, John Smith's, Guinness. ▾ 16 **Facilities** Parking

BUCKMINSTER   Map 11 SK82

Tollemache Arms ▾

48 Main St NG33 5SA ☎ 01476 860477
e-mail: info@tollemache-arms.co.uk
dir: *From Melton Mowbray take B676 to Buckminster, approx 4m*

Sympathetically refurbished by two young couples in early 2010, this striking, 18th-century building on the Tollemache Estate is now a thriving pub, welcoming drinkers at the big oak bar for local Grainstore ales and diners in the stylish, oak-floored dining room and library for good modern British food. Using local seasonal produce, much of it from the estate, daily menus may feature spiced root vegetable soup, roast cod with cockle butter sauce, and chocolate and caramel tart with banana cream for pudding: Thursday evening is pie night. A community focused pub where dogs and children are most welcome.

Open all wk Tue-Sat noon-3 5-11, Sun noon-5 Closed: 27-28 Dec, 2-3 Jan, Sun eve, Mon **Bar Meals** L served Tue-Sat 12-2, Sun 12-3 booking required D served Tue-Sat 6.30-9 booking required Av main course £13 **Restaurant** L served Tue-Sat 12-2, Sun 12-3 booking required D served Tue-Sat 6.30-9 booking required Fixed menu price fr £24 Av 3 course à la carte fr £20 ⊕ FREE HOUSE ◀ Guinness, John Smith's, Ten Fifty, Red Star Ales, Guest ales, Local ales, Grainstore Brewery. ▾ 10 **Facilities** Children welcome Children's menu Children's portions Dogs allowed Garden Parking Wi-fi

COLEORTON Map 11 SK41

George Inn ♥ NEW

Loughborough Rd LE67 8HF ☎ 01530 834639
e-mail: janice@jwilkinson781.orangehome.co.uk
dir: *Just off A42 junct 13 on A512*

The 300-year-old George Inn is a family-run free house tucked away in rolling Leicestershire countryside close to Ashby-de-la-Zouch, yet is a handy pit-stop for both A42 and M1 travellers. Sympathetically refurbished in 2010, the traditional bar and homely lounge, with leather sofa and chairs fronting a wood-burning stove, provide a relaxing and comfortable setting for sampling some honest pub food. Typical dishes include lamb stew and dumplings, beef and ale pie, and fish and chips.

Open all day all wk **Bar Meals** L served Mon-Sat 12-4, Sun 12-3 booking required D served Mon-Thu 6-9, Fri-Sat 6-9.30 booking required **Restaurant** L served Mon-Sat 12-4, Sun 12-3 booking required D served Mon-Thu 6-9, Fri-Sat 6-9.30 booking required ⊕ FREE HOUSE ◀ Marston's Pedigree, Guest ales Ö Thatchers Gold. ♥ 12 **Facilities** Children welcome Children's portions Play area Dogs allowed Garden Parking Wi-fi

EVINGTON Map 11 SK60

The Cedars

Main St LE5 6DN ☎ 0116 273 0482
e-mail: thecedars@king-henrys-taverns.co.uk
dir: *From Leicester take A6 towards Market Harborough. Left at lights, onto B667 to Evington. Pub in village centre*

At The Cedars you can choose to eat in the bar restaurant or just enjoy a drink in the lounge bar with its leather sofas and relaxed atmosphere. King Henry's Taverns, the owners, offer something for everyone on their menu of freshly prepared dishes – for small and large appetites alike. Choose from steaks, fish and seafood, rumpburgers, traditional favourites, and international and vegetarian dishes. Panoramic windows in the main eating area overlook a fountain and pond, and the gardens are a great place for alfresco dining.

Open all day all wk 11.30am-11pm **Bar Meals** L served all wk 12-10 D served all wk 12-10 food served all day **Restaurant** L served all wk 12-10 D served all wk 12-10 food served all day ⊕ KING HENRY'S TAVERNS ◀ Guinness, IPA, Marstons Pedigree. **Facilities** Children welcome Children's menu Children's portions Garden Parking

GRIMSTON Map 11 SK62

The Black Horse

3 Main St LE14 3BZ ☎ 01664 812358
e-mail: amanda.wayne@sky.com
dir: *Telephone for directions*

Wayne and Amanda Sharpe's traditional 16th-century coaching inn overlooks the village green, and beyond that to the Vale of Belvoir, inspiration for the Belvoir Star Mild sold in the bar alongside real ales from Adnams, St

Austell and Marston's. Traditional main courses include pan-fried trio of lamb; sizzling Cajun chicken; lamb cutlets; and lasagne, as well as a daily specials board listing fresh fish and some less familiar dishes. The outdoor eating area is popular.

Open all wk 12-3 6-11 (Sun 12-6) **Bar Meals** L served all wk 12-2 D served all wk 6-9 **Restaurant** L served all wk 12-2 D served all wk 6-9 ⊕ FREE HOUSE ◀ Adnams, Marston's Pedigree, St Austell Tribute, Belvoir Mild, Guest ales Ö Thatchers Gold. **Facilities** Children welcome Children's portions Dogs allowed Garden

KNOSSINGTON Map 11 SK80

The Fox & Hounds

6 Somerby Rd LE15 8LY ☎ 01664 452129
dir: *4m from Oakham in Knossington*

High quality food and helpful, friendly service are the hallmarks of this 500-year-old pub. Set in the village of Knossington close to Rutland Water, the building retains lots of traditional features, and the large rear garden and sitting area are ideal for alfresco summer dining. A typical lunch menu might include grilled lamb rump with ratatouille and tapenade; vegetable tart with Stilton; or salmon with roasted aubergine, red pepper and coriander salsa.

Open noon-2.30 6.30-11 (Fri noon-3 5-11 Sun eve in summer) Closed: Mon, Tue L & Sun eve
Bar Meals L served Wed-Sun 12-2 booking required D served Tue-Sat 6.30-9 booking required Av main course £6.50 **Restaurant** L served Wed-Sun 12-2 booking required D served Tue-Sat 6.30-9 Av 3 course à la carte fr £25 ◀ Bombardier, London Pride, IPA.
Facilities Children's portions Dogs allowed Garden Parking

LEICESTER Map 11 SK50

The Almanack ♥ NEW

15 Bathhouse Ln, Highcross LE1 4SA ☎ 0116 216 0705
e-mail: hello@thealmanack-leicester.co.uk
dir: *In Highcross shopping centre (car parks nearby)*

In the heart of Leicester's trendy Highcross restaurant quarter, The Almanack is a modern British gastro-pub with dramatic floor-to-ceiling windows and a vintage-inspired interior. Take a place on one of the retro chairs or slide into a booth for a pint of Purity Gold and order from an extensive menu that includes deli boards, sandwiches and main dishes of steak and ale pie; pan-fried sea bass, Puy lentil and artichoke salad; coq au vin.

Open all day all wk 10am-mdnt Closed: 25 Dec
Bar Meals Av main course £15 food served all day
Restaurant Av 3 course à la carte fr £25 food served all day ⊕ PEACH PUBS ◀ Purity Gold, Purity UBU. ♥ 10
Facilities Children welcome Children's menu Children's portions Dogs allowed Wi-fi

LONG WHATTON Map 11 SK42

The Falcon Inn ★★★ INN

64 Main St LE12 5DG
☎ 01509 842416 📄 01509 646802
e-mail: enquiries@thefalconinnlongwhatton.com
web: www.thefalconinnlongwhatton.com
dir: *Telephone for directions*

Decked out with award-winning flower displays in summer, this traditional country inn is just ten minutes' drive from East Midlands airport and the M1. It offers great food, plus en suite accommodation in a converted stable and school house at the rear of the pub. Food choices range from classic pub favourites like home-made soup of the day, gammon steak, chips and peas, and steak and ale pie, to more exotic dishes including a choice of Lebanese wraps that reflect the traditions of Lebanese-born proprietor Jad Otaki. There is a beautiful terrace and special events throughout the year.

Open all day all wk **Bar Meals** L served Mon-Sat 12-2, Sun 12-4 D served Mon-Sat 6.30-9 Av main course £9.95 **Restaurant** L served Mon-Sat 12-2, Sun 12-4 D served Mon-Sat 6.30-9 booking required Fixed menu price fr £10.95 Av 3 course à la carte fr £9.95 ⊕ EVERARDS ◀ Tiger Best Bitter, Everards Original, Guest ale.
Facilities Children welcome Family room Garden Parking Wi-fi **Rooms** 11

PICK OF THE PUBS

The Royal Oak ★★★★★ INN ◉ ♥ NEW

26 The Green LE12 5DB ☎ 01509 843694
e-mail: enquiries@theroyaloaklongwhatton.co.uk
dir: *M1 junct 24, A6 to Kegworth. Right into Whatton Road (becomes Kegworth Lane) to Long Whatton. From Loughborough, A6 towards Kegworth. Left onto B5324, right into Hathern Rd leading to The Green*

Following extensive improvements, The Royal Oak reopened in 2010 as a self-styled gastro-pub, offering fresh, locally sourced good quality food. In the extremely smart bar, popular brews from St. Austell, Bass, Timothy Taylor, Blue Monkey Brewery and regular guests grace the counter along with a carefully selected wine list. In the equally clean-cut restaurant diners can expect to face some thought-provoking decisions: will it be assiette of pork – slow-roasted belly, pan-fried fillet and faggot with Sarladaise potato and red onion Tatin; confit of duck leg on butter bean, chick pea and chorizo stew; pan-roasted whole Cornish plaice with sautéed new potatoes, seasonal greens, capers, crayfish and herb butter; or steamed pumpkin with celeriac and wild butternut squash pudding? A 30-strong line-up of real ales and 10 real ciders keep the aficionados coming to the annual beer festival, held at the end of April. The comfortable and contemporary, impeccably furnished guest bedrooms are in a separate building.

Open all day all wk **Bar Meals** L served Mon-Sat 12-2.30, Sun 12-4 D served Mon-Sat 5.30-9.30. **Restaurant** L served Mon-Sat 12-2.30, Sun 12-4 D served Mon-Sat 5.30-9.30 Booking required. ⊕ FREE HOUSE ◀ St Austell Tribute, Bass, Timothy Taylor Landlord, Blue Monkey Brewery, Guest ales Ò Westons Old Rosie ♥ 9. **Facilities** Children's portions Dogs allowed Garden Beer festival Parking **Rooms** 7

LOUGHBOROUGH   Map 11 SK51

The Swan in the Rushes ♥

21 The Rushes LE11 5BE
☎ 01509 217014   📄 01509 217014
e-mail: swanintherushes@castlerockbrewery.co.uk
dir: *On A6 (Derby road). Pub in front of Sainsbury's, 1m from railway station.*

A 1930s tile-fronted real ale pub, it was acquired by the Castle Rock chain in 1986, making it the oldest in the group. There's a first-floor drinking terrace, a function room and bar that seats 80, and a family/dining area. This real ale pub with a friendly atmosphere always offers ten ales, including seven guests, a selection of real ciders and fruit wines. Expect traditional pub grub. Music nights, folk club and a skittle alley complete the picture. Beer festivals are held at the end of May and in mid November. There has been a change of hands.

Open all day all wk 11-11 (Fri-Sat 11-mdnt Sun noon-11) **Bar Meals** L served all wk 12-3 D served Mon-Fri 5-9.30, Sat 12-9.30 Av main course £5.95 ⊕ CASTLE ROCK ◀ Castle Rock Harvest Pale, Castle Rock Sheriff's Tipple, Adnams Bitter, Castle Rock Elsie Mo, 7 guests Ò Westons Old Rosie Scrumpy, Broadoak Moonshine. ♥ 12 **Facilities** Children welcome Children's portions Family room Dogs allowed Beer festival Parking Wi-fi

LUTTERWORTH   Map 11 SP58

Man at Arms ♥

The Green, Bitteswell LE17 4SB ☎ 01455 552540
e-mail: man@king-henrys-taverns.co.uk
dir: *From Lutterworth take Lutterworth Rd towards Ullesthorpe. Turn left at small white cottage. Pub on left after college on village green*

Named after a bequest left by the Dowse Charity to the nearby village of Bitteswell to provide a 'man at arms' in time of war, this was the first pub bought by the King Henry's Taverns group. Now, after 26 years, the pub shares a common menu with others in the group. Expect some sizeable options, including a pound of lamb chops; Superman's mixed grill; and Cajun chicken and ribs combo, along with plenty of choices for those with smaller appetites.

Open all day all wk 11.30am-11pm **Bar Meals** food served all day **Restaurant** food served all day ⊕ KING HENRY'S TAVERNS ◀ Greene King IPA, Guinness, Bass, Bombardier. ♥ 16 **Facilities** Children welcome Children's menu Children's portions Garden Parking

MOUNTSORREL   Map 11 SK51

The Swan Inn ★★★★ INN

10 Loughborough Rd LE12 7AT
☎ 0116 230 2340   📄 0116 237 6115
e-mail: swan@jvf.co.uk
dir: *On A6 between Leicester & Loughborough*

Originally two 17th-century terraced cottages, this Grade II listed free house stands on the banks of the River Soar in the pretty village of Mountsorrel. Exposed beams, flagstone floors and roaring winter log fires characterise the cosy bar and dining areas, while the secluded riverside garden is ideal for summer sipping. Cask-conditioned beers and fine wines accompany a varied menu of British and European classics: vodka-cured gravadlax with blinis followed by beef casseroled in Old Peculier are indicative of the standard. There is a luxury apartment available.

Open all wk 12-2.30 5.30-11 (Sat 12-11 Sun 12-3 7-10.30) **Bar Meals** L served all wk 12-2 D served Mon-Sat 6.30-9.30 Av main course £8 **Restaurant** L served all wk 12-2 D served Mon-Sat 6.30-9.30 Fixed menu price fr £10.90 Av 3 course à la carte fr £18 ⊕ FREE HOUSE ◀ Black Sheep Bitter, Theakston's XB, Old Peculier, Ruddles County, Abbot Ale. **Facilities** Dogs allowed Garden Parking **Rooms** 1

MOWSLEY   Map 11 SP68

PICK OF THE PUBS

The Staff of Life ♥

Main St LE17 6NT ☎ 0116 240 2359
dir: *M1 junct 20, A4304 to Market Harborough. Left in Husbands Bosworth onto A5199. In 3m turn right to pub*

Were they to return, the residents of this former well-proportioned private Edwardian house would surely be amazed by the transformation of their home into such an appealing community local. The bar retains some traditional features – the high-backed settles and flagstone floor, for example – along with a new large woodburning stove. If you look up you'll see not just a fine wood-panelled ceiling, but also, not quite where you'd expect, the wine cellar. Many of the wines are served by the glass, and there are Marston's and guest real ales to choose from. In the dining area, which overlooks the garden, carefully prepared dishes combine British and international influences - duo of local pheasant and pigeon breast; roasted Cornish hake; and penne pasta with roasted vegetables and pine-nuts. Desserts are made by Linda O'Neill, a former member of Ireland's Panel of Chefs. A small patio area lies to the front with additional outside seating in the rear garden.

Open Tue eve-Sun Closed: Mon & Tue L (ex BH) **Bar Meals** L served Wed-Sat 12-2.15, Sun 12-3.30 D served Tue-Sat 6.30-9.30 Av main course £15 **Restaurant** L served Wed-Sat 12-2.15, Sun 12-3.30 D served Tue-Sat 6.30-9.30 Fixed menu price fr £25 ⊕ FREE HOUSE ◀ Marstons, Guest ales Ò Thatchers. ♥ 19 **Facilities** Children's portions Garden Parking

NETHER BROUGHTON   Map 11 SK62

The Red House

23 Main St LE14 3HB
☎ 01664 822429   📄 01664 823805
e-mail: bernie@mulberrypubco.com
dir: *M1 junct 21A, A46. Right onto A606. Or take A606 from Nottingham*

The Red House is a fine mixture of a 300-year-old village pub (with log fires in winter) and light, contemporary design. The lounge bar opens into an airy restaurant, and a conservatory area overlooks the outdoor bar, terrace and courtyard grill. Immaculate gardens include a small play area and a permanent marquee for weddings, parties and corporate functions. Dishes range from a selection of sandwiches or hot dishes like Guinness and beef sausages with mash and stout gravy in the bar, to roast rump of English lamb, pea mash and confit carrots in the restaurant. An ideal spot for walking, fishing and bird-watching.

Open all wk Mon-Thu 7-3 5-11 (Fri-Sun all day) ⊕ MULBERRY PUB (UK) PLC ◀ Guinness, Belvoir Brewery Cask, Greene King IPA Ò Jacques. **Facilities** Children welcome Children's menu Children's portions Play area Dogs allowed Garden Parking Wi-fi

OADBY   Map 11 SK60

PICK OF THE PUBS

Cow and Plough ♥

Gartree Rd, Stoughton Farm LE2 2FB
☎ 0116 272 0852   📄 0116 272 0852
e-mail: cowandplough@googlemail.com
dir: *3m Leicester Station A6 to Oadby. Turn off to Spire Hospital, pub 0.5m beyond*

Occupying former Victorian farm buildings, this much-loved pub dates back to 1989, when licensee Barry Lount approached the owners of Stoughton Grange Farm, who were then in the process of opening the farm to the public. The farm park attraction has since closed, but the Cow and Plough continues to thrive, hosting functions and events such as beer and cider festivals. The pub also brews its own award-winning Steamin' Billy beers, named in honour of the owners' Jack Russell terrier. The interior is decorated with historic inn signs and brewing memorabilia, providing a fascinating setting in which to enjoy food from the regularly changing menus. Typical choices include grilled sardines with tomato and lime salsa, followed by fish with hand-cut chips and mushy peas, or something more imaginative like Broome Farm lamb rump with roasted vegetables and minted Puy lentils, with white chocolate bread-and-butter pudding with crème anglaise among the pudding choices.

Open all day all wk **Bar Meals** L served all wk 12-2.30 D served all wk 6-9 Av main course £7.95 **Restaurant** L served all wk 12-2.30 D served all wk 6-9 booking required Fixed menu price fr £13.95 Av 3 course à la carte fr £19.95 ⊕ FREE HOUSE ◀ Steamin' Billy Bitter, Steamin' Billy Skydiver, London Pride, Abbeydale, Batemans Mild. ♥ 10 **Facilities** Children welcome Children's menu Children's portions Family room Dogs allowed Garden Beer festival Parking

---

| OLD DALBY | Map 11 SK62 |

PICK OF THE PUBS

The Crown Inn ▼

Debdale Hill LE14 3LF ☎ **01664 823134**
e-mail: oldcrown@castlerockbrewery.co.uk
dir: *A46 turn for Willoughby/Broughton. Right into Nottingham Ln, left to Old Dalby*

A classic creeper-covered, country pub dating from 1509, set in extensive gardens and orchards, with small rooms, all with open fires. The owners have returned the pub to its former glory - traditional with a contemporary feel. They place a strong emphasis on fresh seasonal produce: if the food doesn't all come from Leicestershire, the county's suppliers are nonetheless wholeheartedly supported. Expect dishes like pan-fried sea bass with lemon and crayfish risotto, or oven roasted rack and braised shoulder of lamb with minted pea purée. There's a good choice of real ales to help wash down a meal, or to enjoy without food: Castle Rock Hemlock and Harvest Pale are among the selection.

Open 12-3 6-11 (Fri-Sun all day) Closed: Mon L **Bar Meals** L served Tue-Fri 12-2, Sat 12-3 D served Tue-Fri 6-9 **Restaurant** L served Tue-Fri 12-2, Sat 12-3 D served Tue-Fri 6-9 ⊕ FREE HOUSE ◖ Castle Rock, Hemlock, Beaver, Harvest Pale, Brewery Best Bitter, Guest ales ♂ Stowford Press. ▼ 10 **Facilities** Children welcome Family room Dogs allowed Garden Parking

---

| REDMILE | Map 11 SK73 |

Peacock Inn ★★★★ INN

Church Corner, Main St NG13 0GA
☎ **01949 842554** 🖷 **01949 843746**
e-mail: reservations@thepeacockinnredmile.co.uk
dir: *From A1 take A52 towards Nottingham. Turn left, follow signs for Redmile & Belvoir Castle. In Redmile at x-rds turn right. Pub at end of village*

Beamed ceilings, cosy open fires and a friendly atmosphere are the hallmarks of this 18th-century inn, just two miles from the picturesque Belvoir Castle. The Peacock provides a relaxed setting for wining and dining, and has a local reputation for home-made food and real ales. The appetising bar menu is based on local seasonal produce and includes shallot and goat's cheese tarte Tatin, and game pie with chips in dripping and seasonal vegetables. Ten en suite guest rooms offer a comfortable overnight stay.

Open all day all wk **Bar Meals** L served all wk 12-2.30 D served all wk 6-9 **Restaurant** D served all wk 6-9 ⊕ CHARLES WELLS ◖ Young's Bitter, Bombardier. **Facilities** Children welcome Children's portions Dogs allowed Garden Parking **Rooms** 10

| SILEBY | Map 11 SK61 |

The White Swan ▼

Swan St LE12 7NW ☎ **01509 814832** 🖷 **01509 815995**
e-mail: tamiller56@googlemail.com
dir: *From Leicester A6 towards Loughborough, turn right for Sileby; or take A46 towards Newark-on-Trent, turn left for Sileby*

Behind the unassuming exterior of this 1930s building, you'll find a free house of some character, with a book-lined restaurant and a homely bar with an open fire. A wide selection of home-made rolls, baguettes and snacks is on offer; menus change weekly, and there are blackboard specials, too. Typical main course choices include baked fillet of plaice with prawns and garlic butter; roast Gressingham duck breast with marmalade and whisky glaze; beef, ale and mushroom puff pastry pie. Save some room for desserts such as chocolate fudge cake or sticky toffee pudding.

Open Tue-Sun L Closed: 1-7 Jan, (Sat L, Sun eve & Mon) **Bar Meals** L served Tue-Sun 12-1.30 (ex Sat) D served Tue-Sat 7-8.30 Av main course £9 **Restaurant** L served Sun 12-1.30 D served Tue-Sat 7-8.30 Fixed menu price fr £10 Av 3 course à la carte fr £18 ⊕ FREE HOUSE ◖ Marston's Pedigree, Tetley's Cask, Ansells, Fuller's London Pride. ▼ 8 **Facilities** Children welcome Children's portions Garden Parking Wi-fi

---

| SOMERBY | Map 11 SK71 |

Stilton Cheese Inn ▼

High St LE14 2QB ☎ **01664 454394**
dir: *From A606 between Melton Mowbray & Oakham follow signs to Pickwell & Somerby. Enter village, 1st right to centre, pub on left*

This attractive 17th-century inn enjoys a good reputation for its food, and great selections of real ales, wines and malt whiskies. Built from mellow local sandstone, it stands in the centre of the village surrounded by beautiful countryside; nearby is Melton Mowbray, famous for its pork pies and Stilton cheese – hence the pub's name. Pub staples such as Somerby sausages and mash and home-made lasagne, are backed by an interesting range of regularly-changing specials, including vegetarian options like home-made butternut squash ravioli.

Open all wk 12-3 6-11 (Sun 7-11) **Bar Meals** L served all wk 12-2 D served Mon-Sat 6-9, Sun 7-9 Av main course £9 **Restaurant** L served all wk 12-2 D served Mon-Sat 6-9, Sun 7-9 ⊕ FREE HOUSE ◖ Grainstore Ten Fifty, Brewster's Hophead, Belvoir Star, Tetley's Cask, Marston's Pedigree ♂ Old Rosie, Westons Scrumpy, Bounds Brand. ▼ 15 **Facilities** Children welcome Children's menu Children's portions Family room Garden Parking

---

| STATHERN | Map 11 SK73 |

PICK OF THE PUBS

Red Lion Inn ▼

Red Lion St LE14 4HS
☎ **01949 860868** 🖷 **01949 861579**
e-mail: info@theredlioninn.co.uk
dir: *From A1 (Grantham), A607 towards Melton, turn right in Waltham, right at next x-rds then left to Stathern*

The Red Lion is located in the beautiful Vale of Belvoir and comprises a stone-floored bar, a comfortable lounge with plenty of reading material, an elegant dining room and an informal eating area. Whatever the season, there are treats to be enjoyed here: logs crackling in the stove, daily-changing specials boards, superb value lunch offers, cookery demonstrations, and wine evenings – all this and regional ales too. Menus change seasonally in accordance with locally supplied produce, and offer a mix of classic pub food and innovative country cooking. Typical of chef Sean Hope's dishes are ham hock with home-made piccalilli and Hambleton bakery sour dough; pigeon breast with Puy lentil, bacon and rocket salad; lamb faggots with Grasmere Farm black pudding and red cabbage; and Longhorn rump steak from Northfield Farm with all the trimmings. Desserts too reflect a serious attention to detail: quince brûlée with shortbread biscuit and Rearsby treacle tart with blackberry compôte are two examples.

Open 12-3 6-11 (Fri-Sat 12-11, Sun 12-7) Closed: Sun eve **Bar Meals** L served Tue-Sat 12-2, Sun 12-3 booking required D served Tue-Thu 5.30-9, Fri 5.30-9.30, Sat 7-9.30 booking required Av main course £7.50 **Restaurant** L served Tue-Sat 12-2, Sun 12-3 booking required D served Tue-Thu 5.30-9, Fri 5.30-9.30, Sat 7-9.30 booking required Fixed menu price fr £11.50 Av 3 course à la carte fr £19 ⊕ RUTLAND INN COMPANY LTD ◖ Grainstore Red Lion Ale, Brewster's Marquis, London Pride ♂ Aspall, Sheppy. ▼ 8 **Facilities** Children welcome Children's menu Children's portions Dogs allowed Garden Parking

---

| SWITHLAND | Map 11 SK51 |

The Griffin Inn ▼ NEW

174 Main St LE12 8TJ ☎ **01509 890535**
e-mail: thegriffininn@swithland.info
dir: *From A46 into Anstey. Right at rdbt to Cropston. Right at x-roads, 1st left, 0.5m to Swithland. Follow brown signs for inn*

A welcoming, traditional, family-run country inn with three cosy bar areas serving a range of real ales and ciders, two dining rooms, skittle alley and large patio. Monthly changing menus and a wide range of specials offer unfussy, good value food including mussels with home-made frites, Moroccan lamb tagine, creamy forest mushroom risotto, and Thai chicken and prawn curry. The area is popular with walkers heading for Swithland Woods, Beacon Hill and the Old John folly.

Open all day all wk **Bar Meals** L served Mon-Thu 12-2, Fri-Sun 12-9 D served Mon-Thu 6-9, Fri-Sun 12-9 Av main course £10 **Restaurant** L served Mon-Thu 12-2, Fri-Sun 12-9 booking required D served Mon-Thu 6-9, Fri-Sun 12-9 booking required Av 3 course à la carte fr £18.65 ⊕ EVERARDS ◀ Adnams Bitter, 2 Guest ales. ☙ 9 **Facilities** Children welcome Children's portions Garden Parking Wi-fi

THORPE LANGTON   Map 11 SP79

The Bakers Arms ☙

Main St LE16 7TS ☎ 01858 545201 📠 01858 545924
dir: Take A6 S from Leicester then left signed 'The Langtons', at rail bridge continue to x-rds. Straight on to Thorpe Langton. Pub on left

Set in a pretty village, this thatched pub offers plenty of period charm, with an enthusiastic following. An intimate atmosphere is created with low beams, rug-strewn quarry-tiled floors, large pine tables, and open fires. The modern pub food is one of the key attractions, with the menu changing from week to week; Thursday is fish night. Expect dishes like smoked salmon, smoked trout and prawn cocktail platter; confit of duck with red pepper and ginger marmalade; and vanilla brûlée with fresh strawberries. The area is popular with walkers, riders and mountain bikers.

Open 6.30-11 (12-2.30 wknds) Closed: 1-7 Jan, Sun eve-Mon **Bar Meals** Av main course £14.95 **Restaurant** L served Sat-Sun 12-2.30 booking required D served Tue-Sat 6.30-9.15 booking required Av 3 course à la carte fr £26.50 ⊕ FREE HOUSE ◀ Langton Brewery, Bakers Dozen Bitter. ☙ 9 **Facilities** Garden Parking

WELHAM   Map 11 SP79

The Old Red Lion ☙

Main St LE16 7UJ ☎ 01858 565253
e-mail: redlion@king-henrys-taverns.co.uk
dir: NE of Market Harborough take B664 to Weston by Welland. Left to Welham

This old country pub is part of the King Henry's Taverns group. It was once a coaching inn, and the small area opposite the main bar was originally the archway where the coaches would swing in to offload their weary passengers. In winter the leather chesterfields around the log fires create a cosy feel, while in summer take an evening stroll along one of the many footpaths and bridleways. The menu of freshly prepared dishes has choices for small and large appetites alike. Choose from steaks, fish and seafood, rumpburgers, traditional favourites, and international and vegetarian dishes.

Open all day all wk 11.30am-11pm ◀ Greene King IPA, Marstons Pedigree, Guinness. ☙ 15 **Facilities** Children welcome Parking

WOODHOUSE EAVES   Map 11 SK51

The Wheatsheaf Inn ★★★★ INN ☙

Brand Hill LE12 8SS ☎ 01509 890320
e-mail: richard@wheatsheafinn.net
dir: M1 junct 22, follow Quorn signs

Around the turn of the 19th century, when local quarrymen wanted somewhere to drink, they built themselves The Wheatsheaf. It's what locals call a Dim's Inn, a succession of pubs run by three generations of the Dimblebee family. With a good selection of real ales, food includes seasonal daily specials and tempting dishes such as smoked haddock, leek and Gruyère fishcakes; Lincolnshire sausage and mash; wild rice, spinach and honey nut roast; and venison bourguignonne. Modern en suite bedrooms are available in the adjacent cottage annexe.

Open Mon-Sun Closed: Sun eve in winter **Bar Meals** L served Mon-Fri 12-2, Sat 12-2.30, Sun 12-3.30 booking required D served Mon-Sat 6.30-9.15 booking required Av main course £10.25-£21.95 **Restaurant** L served Mon-Fri 12-2, Sat 12-2.30, Sun 12-3.30 booking required D served Mon-Sat 6.30-9.15 booking required ⊕ FREE HOUSE ◀ Greene King Abbot Ale, Timothy Taylor Landlord, Adnams Broadside, Tetley Smooth, guest ale, Marson's Pedigree. ☙ 16 **Facilities** Children welcome Children's portions Dogs allowed Garden Parking Wi-fi **Rooms** 2

LINCOLNSHIRE

ALLINGTON   Map 11 SK84

The Welby Arms ★★★★ INN ☙

The Green NG32 2EA
☎ 01400 281361 📠 01400 281361
web: www.thewelbyarmsallington.com
dir: From Grantham take either A1 N, or A52 W. Allington 1.5m

A lovely example of a traditional village inn, where the local Morris team dance, the resplendent creeper changes with the seasons and travellers through this rural part of south Lincolnshire can find a comfy bed for the night. Up to six real ales slake the thirst, whilst appetites are sated by a well balanced menu plus specials that may reveal a starter choice of pan-fried scallops, chorizo sausage and chilli sauce, leading to a wild mushroom Stroganoff with rice and vegetables, or braised lamb shank with redcurrant and mint sauce.

Open all wk 12-3 6-11 (Sun 12-10.30) **Bar Meals** L served Mon-Sat 12-2, Sun 12-8.30 D served Mon-Sat 6-9 **Restaurant** L served Mon-Sun 12-2, Sun

12-8.30 booking required D served Mon-Sat 6-9, booking required ⊕ ENTERPRISE INNS ◀ John Smith's, Interbrew Bass, Timothy Taylor Landlord, Jennings Cumberland Ale, Badger Tanglefoot, Adnams Broadside ○ Stowford Press. ☙ 22 **Facilities** Children welcome Children's menu Children's portions Garden Parking **Rooms** 3

See advert on page 288

ASWARBY   Map 12 TF03

The Tally Ho Inn

NG34 8SA ☎ 01529 455170
e-mail: info@thetallyhoinn.com
dir: 3m S of Sleaford on A15 towards Bourne/Peterborough

Built as a farm around 1750, this handsome, award-winning inn was until 1945 the home of the manager of the Aswarby Estate. In fact, like the surrounding parkland, it's still part of it. The old English garden, complete with fruit trees, overlooks the estate and grazing sheep. Among sturdy pillars, beams and exposed stonework, dine on freshly prepared modern British dishes, served perhaps with a fine hand-picked wine, are twice-cooked pork belly; Chianti-braised lamb shank; and grilled fillet of sea bass.

Open noon-2.30 5.30-11 (Tue 6-11 Sun noon-4) Closed: Tue L **Bar Meals** L served Mon & Wed-Sat 12-2.30, Sun 12-3.30 D served Mon-Sat 6-9.30 Av main course £9.75 **Restaurant** Fixed menu price fr £11.50 Av 3 course à la carte fr £24 ⊕ FREE HOUSE ◀ Timothy Taylor Landlord, Abbot Ale, Guest ales ○ Westons Organic. **Facilities** Children welcome Children's portions Play area Garden Parking Wi-fi

BARNOLDBY LE BECK   Map 17 TA20

The Ship Inn

Main Rd DN37 0BG ☎ 01472 822308
e-mail: the-ship-inn@btinternet.com
dir: M180 junct 5, A18 past Humberside Airport. At Laceby Junction rdbt (A18 & A46) straight over follow Skegness/Boston signs. Approx 2m turn left signed Waltham & Barnoldby le Beck

Set in a picturesque village on the edge of the Lincolnshire Wolds, this 300-year-old inn has always attracted an interesting mix of customers, from Grimsby's seafarers to aviators from the county's WWII airstrips. The bar is filled with maritime bric-à-brac and serves a grand choice of ales, and there's a beautiful garden outside. The Ship is perhaps best known for its menu of fresh seafood: Grimsby smoked haddock with poached egg makes a great starter, follow with pan-fried skate wing and caper butter.

Open 12-3 6-11 (Fri-Sat 12-3 6-12) Closed: Sun eve **Bar Meals** L served Mon-Sat 12-2, Sun 12-4.30 D served Mon-Sat 6.30-9.30 booking required Av main course £15 **Restaurant** L served Mon-Sat 12-2, Sun 12-4.30 booking required D served Mon-Sat 6.30 booking required Av 3 course à la carte fr £25 ⊕ INNOVATIVE SIGHT LTD ◀ Black Sheep Best, Tetley's Smooth, Guinness, Tom Woods Bomber County. **Facilities** Children welcome Children's portions Garden Parking

The Blue Bell Inn

1 Main Rd LN9 6LQ ☎ 01507 533602
dir: Off A153 between Horncastle & Louth

Darren and Shona Jackson have run this traditional countryside free house for the past seven years and offer a warm welcome. Located on the Viking Way in the heart of the Lincolnshire Wolds, expect comfy armchairs, well-kept real ales and a wide selection of wines. At lunchtime, choose between tempting ciabatta rolls and beef, Guinness and mushroom pie, whilst evening meals range from succulent steaks to saddle of venison with pumpkin, sage and smoked bacon risotto.

Open Tue-Sat 11.30-2.30 6.30-11 (Sun 12-4) Closed: 2nd & 3rd wk Jan, Sun eve-Mon **Bar Meals** L served Tue-Sun 12-2 D served Tue-Sat 6.30-9 **Restaurant** L served Tue-Sun 12-2 D served Tue-Sat 6.30-9 Fixed menu price fr £8.95 ⊕ FREE HOUSE ◀ Black Sheep, Timothy Taylor Landlord, Guest ale. **Facilities** Children welcome Children's menu Children's portions Garden Parking

The Wishing Well Inn

Main St, Dyke PE10 0AF
☎ 01778 422970 📠 01778 394508
e-mail: wishingwell@hotmail.com
dir: Take A15 towards Sleaford. Inn in next village

This Lincolnshire village free house started life in 1879 as a one-room pub called the Crown. Several extensions have since been sympathetically executed with recycled stone and timbers; the well that gives the pub its name, previously in the garden, is now a feature of the smaller dining room. Loyal customers return again and again to enjoy a comprehensive menu of traditional favourites in the warm and welcoming atmosphere. Outside, an attractive beer garden backs onto the children's play area.

Open all wk 11-3 5-11 (Fri-Sat 11-mdnt Sun & summer all wk 11-11) **Bar Meals** L served Mon-Thu 12-2.30, Fri-Sun 12-9 D served Mon-Thu 5.30-9, Fri-Sun 12-9 ⊕ FREE HOUSE ◀ Greene King Abbot Ale, Spitfire, 3 Guest ales. **Facilities** Children welcome Children's menu Children's portions Play area Dogs allowed Garden Parking Wi-fi

The Jolly Miller

Brigg Rd, Wrawby DN20 8RH ☎ 01652 655658
dir: 1.5m E of Brigg on A18, on left

This popular country inn in a village location a few miles south of the Humber Estuary is a family-run business. The pleasant bar and dining area are traditional in style, and there's a large beer garden where a beer festival is held in the summer, plus a play area for children. The menu offers a good range of food from bar snacks and a children's menu to main courses of Cajun chicken; steak and ale pie; and roast vegetable Wellington, washed down with a pint of Black Sheep. Coach parties accepted with advanced booking and there is a small caravan park. Recently changed hands.

Open all day all wk **Bar Meals** Av main course £6.95 food served all day **Restaurant** Fixed menu price fr £6 Av 3 course à la carte fr £18 food served all day ⊕ FREE HOUSE ◀ Guinness, John Smith's Extra Smooth, Black Sheep, Guest ales. **Facilities** Children welcome Children's menu Children's portions Play area Garden Beer festival Parking Wi-fi

Save on hotels. Book at theAA.com/hotel

LINCOLNSHIRE 289 ENGLAND

CONINGSBY — Map 17 TF25

The Lea Gate Inn

Leagate Rd LN4 4RS
☎ 01526 342370 📠 01526 345468
e-mail: theleagateinn@hotmail.com
dir: *Off B1192 just outside Coningsby*

The oldest licensed premises in the county, dating from 1542, this was the last of the Fen Guide Houses that provided shelter before the treacherous marshes were drained. The oak-beamed pub has a priest's hole and a very old inglenook fireplace among its features. The same family have been running the pub for over 25 years. Both the bar and restaurant serve food and offer seasonal menus with lots of local produce (including game in season) and great fish choices, such as freshwater trout and lobster.

Open all wk 11.30-3 6-11 (Sun 12-10.30) ⊕ FREE HOUSE ◀ Theakston's XB, Bombardier, Guest ales.
Facilities Children welcome Children's menu Play area Garden Parking

DRY DODDINGTON — Map 11 SK84

Wheatsheaf Inn ♥ NEW

NG23 5HU ☎ 01400 281458
e-mail: wheatsheafdrydoddington@hotmail.co.uk
web: www.wheatsheaf-pub.co.uk
dir: *From A1 between Newark-on-Trent & Grantham. Turn into Doddington Lane for Dry Doddington*

Church and inn face each other across the village green deep in the Lincolnshire countryside. Both are ancient, although the pub has fared better judging by the leaning church tower. Batemans XB is the beer of choice, whilst Lincolnshire produce takes pride of place on the traditional menu, enhanced by great specials. Crab and samphire salad breaks the ice, a precursor to roast chicken breast with wild mushroom gravy, enjoyed in the fire-warmed bar or sheltered beer garden.

Open 12-2.30 5-11 (Sat-Sun 12-close) Closed: Mon **Bar Meals** L served Tue-Sun 12-2 D served Tue-Sun 6-9 Av main course £6 **Restaurant** L served Tue-Sat 12-2, Sun 12-3 D served Tue-Thu 6-9, Fri-Sat 6-9.30, Sun 5-7 Fixed menu price fr £12 Av 3 course à la carte fr £22 ⊕ FREE HOUSE ◀ Timothy Taylor Landlord, Abbot Ale, Batemans XB. ♥ 12 **Facilities** Children welcome Children's menu Children's portions Dogs allowed Garden Parking Wi-fi

FROGNALL — Map 12 TF11

The Goat

155 Spalding Rd PE6 8SA ☎ 01778 347629
e-mail: graysdebstokes@btconnect.com
web: www.thegoatfrognall.com
dir: *A1 to Peterborough, A15 to Market Deeping, old A16 to Spalding, pub approx 1.5m from A15 & A16 junct*

Families are welcome at this cosy, friendly country free house, which has an open fire, a new spacious conservatory with its own courtyard (ideal for large parties and group bookings), beer garden and plenty to amuse the children. Main courses include beef Stroganoff; pork in sweet and sour sauce; leek and mushroom pie; and warm bacon and Stilton salad. Beer is taken seriously here, with five different guest ales each week and Westons Old Rosie and Broadoak ciders are available.

Open all wk 11.30-3 6-11.30 (Sun noon-11) Closed: 25 Dec, 1 Jan **Bar Meals** L served Mon-Sat 12-2 booking required D served Mon-Sat 6.30-9.30, Sun 12-9 booking required **Restaurant** L served Mon-Sat 12-2, Sun 12-9 booking required D served Mon-Sat 6.30-9.30, Sun 12-9 booking required ⊕ FREE HOUSE ◀ Guest ales: Elgoods, Batemans, Abbeydale, Nethergate, Hopshackle ♢ Westons Old Rosie, Broadoak Moonshine, Thatchers Cheddar Valley. **Facilities** Children welcome Children's menu Children's portions Play area Family room Garden Parking

GOSBERTON — Map 12 TF23

The Black Horse ♥ NEW

66 Siltside, Gosberton Risegate PE11 4ET
☎ 01775 840995
e-mail: cr8ion@theblackhorserestaurant.net
dir: *From Spalding take A16 towards Boston. Left onto A152. At Gosberton take B1397 to Gosberton Risegate. Pub set back from road*

Tucked away in a village amidst the fens outside Spalding, this lovely creeper-clad local is a showcase for Lincolnshire's wealth of food producers and brewers. Huddle up to the woodburning stove or catch the summer rays in the beer garden, sipping Tom Woods' Best Bitter and tuck into a Fen Farm venison sirloin or tackle scallops and king prawns cooked at the table on a Blackrock volcanic slab; the menu changes fortnightly and has Spanish and Indian influences. A take-away menu is available.

Open all day Tue-Sat 6-late (Sun noon-3 6-9, Tue-Thu summer 6-late, Fri-Sun summer noon-late) Closed: Mon **Bar Meals** L served Fri-Sun 12-4 (summer) D served Tue-Sun 6-10 (summer) Av main course £14.25 **Restaurant** L served Fri-Sun 12-3 D served Tue-Sun 6-10.30 booking required Av 3 course à la carte fr £23 ⊕ FREE HOUSE ◀ Black Sheep Best Bitter, Batemans XXXB, Tom Wood's Best Bitter, Tom Wood's Bomber County ♢ Thatchers Gold Apple. ♥ 9 **Facilities** Children welcome Children's menu Children's portions Dogs allowed Garden Parking Wi-fi

HOUGH-ON-THE-HILL — Map 11 SK94

The Brownlow Arms ★★★★★ INN ⊛

High Rd NG32 2AZ ☎ 01400 250234 📠 01400 251993
e-mail: armsinn@yahoo.co.uk
dir: *Take A607 (Grantham to Sleaford road). Hough-on-the-Hill signed from Barkston*

Named after the former owner Lord Brownlow, this 17th-century stone inn set in the heart of a picturesque village still looks like a well tended country house. Enjoy a glass of real ale in the friendly bar while perusing the impressive menu. Modern classic dishes include starters of seared scallops, Jerusalem artichoke purée, green beans, hazelnut vinaigrette; braised ox tongue with celeriac remoulade; baked crab Thermidor. These might be followed by main courses of loin of veal with creamed wild mushrooms; seared calves' liver, leek mash, back bacon and shallot gravy; or beer-battered cod with chunky chips and mushy peas. Leave room for desserts such as steamed treacle sponge pudding with golden syrup ice cream or caramelised lemon tart with blackcurrant sorbet. Alfresco dining can be enjoyed on the landscaped terrace. Take advantage of one of the en suite double bedrooms.

Open Tue-Sat 6pm-11pm, Sun L Closed: 25-27 Dec, 31 Dec-1 Jan, Mon, Sun eve **Restaurant** L served Sun 12-2.30 booking required D served Tue-Sat 6.30-9.30 booking required ⊕ FREE HOUSE ◀ Timothy Taylor Landlord, Marston's Pedigree. **Facilities** Garden Parking Wi-fi **Rooms** 5

INGHAM — Map 17 SK98

Inn on the Green ♥ NEW

34 The Green LN1 2XT ☎ 01522 730354
dir: *From Lincoln take A15 signed Scunthorpe. Left into Ingham Lane signed Ingham, Cammeringham. Right onto B1398 (Middle St), left to Ingham*

The name says it all about the location of this charming Grade II-listed country pub/restaurant, proud holder of many awards thanks to the endeavours of the owners. Impressive food is served in three bars - cosy entrance bar with sofas, front bar with roaring log fire plus one upstairs - and the first-floor restaurant. Cooking centres around seasonal, Lincolnshire produce: staples include home-made fishcakes with sweet chilli jam; seared salmon with bubble and squeak; steak and ale pie; braised shoulder of lamb; and vegetarian options. Nine wines by the glass and, as a free house, several cask ales complete the picture.

continued

INGHAM *continued*

Open Tue-Sat 11.30-3 6-11 (Sun noon-10.30) Closed: Mon **Bar Meals** L served Wed-Sat 12-2, Sun 12-5 D served Tue-Thu 6.30-9, Fri-Sat 6.30-9.30 Av main course £9.50 **Restaurant** L served Wed-Sat 12-2, Sun 12-5 booking required D served Tue-Thu 6.30-9, Fri-Sat 6.30-9.30 booking required Av 3 course à la carte fr £20 ⊕ FREE HOUSE ◀ Black Sheep, Adnams, Batemans 6X ♦ Stowford Press. ♀ 9 **Facilities** Children welcome Children's portions Garden Parking

---

KIRKBY LA THORPE   Map 12 TF04

Queens Head ♀ NEW

Church Ln NE34 9NU
☎ 01529 305743 & 307194 📄 01529 307194
e-mail: clrjcc@aol.com
web: www.thequeensheadinn.com
dir: *Just off A17 (dual carriageway). Pub signed from A17*

An ancient coaching inn whose interior has all the character you may expect – heavy beams, open log fires in winter, and an old English decor rich in antique furnishings, original watercolours, large flower arrangements, and the owner's collection of long case clocks. It's won awards as a destination dining pub; the chef-proprietor prepares everything on site, from breads to desserts, and is an enthusiastic ambassador for local products, including Lincoln red beef and fresh vegetables. As well as local cask ales, a delightful and refreshing touch is the home-made lemonade served in summer.

Open all wk Mon-Sat 12-3 6-11 (Sun 12-11) **Bar Meals** L served Mon-Sat 12-2.30, Sun 12-8.30 D served Mon-Fri 6-9.30, Sat 6-10, Sun 12-8.30 booking required Av main course £8.45-£14.95 **Restaurant** L served Mon-Sat 12-2.30, Sun 12-8.30 booking required D served Mon-Fri 6-9.30, Sat 6-10, Sun 12-8.30 booking required Fixed menu price fr £12.95 Av 3 course à la carte fr £25 ⊕ FREE HOUSE ◀ Batemans XB, Guest ales. ♀ 9 **Facilities** Garden Parking

---

KIRTON IN LINDSEY   Map 17 SK99

The George

20 High St DN21 4LX ☎ 01652 640600
e-mail: enquiry@thegeorgekirton.co.uk
dir: *From A15 take B1205, turn right onto B1400*

Lincoln and The Wolds are within easy reach of this extensively restored modern yet traditional styled pub run by Glen and Neil McCartney. The George is an 18th-century former coaching inn offering locally brewed Batemans ales and seasonally changing menus. Customers can dine in the informal atmosphere of the restaurant or comfortable bar area where the ever-changing specials and traditional bar meals are served. From pub classics like battered haddock, mushy peas and hand-cut chips, the choice extends to twice-baked Stilton soufflé; lamb rack with minted pea purée; and braised pigs' cheeks and all butter mash. A children's menu is available.

Open all wk Mon-Sat 5-11 (Sun noon-2.30) **Bar Meals** Av main course £10.95 **Restaurant** Av 3 course à la carte fr £25 ⊕ FREE HOUSE ◀ Batemans XB. **Facilities** Children welcome Children's menu Children's portions Play area Garden

---

LINCOLN   Map 17 SK97

Pyewipe Inn

Fossebank, Saxilby Rd LN1 2BG
☎ 01522 528708 📄 01522 525009
e-mail: enquiries@pyewipe.co.uk
dir: *From Lincoln on A57 past Lincoln/A46 Bypass, pub signed in 0.5m*

There's a great view of nearby Lincoln Cathedral from the 4 acres of grounds of this waterside inn, which takes its name from the local dialect for lapwing. Set in four wooded acres beside the Roman-built Fossedyke Navigation, it serves real ales and home-made, locally-sourced food. Expect dishes such as partridge and black pudding stack with a red wine sauce; pork belly with a cider and grain mustard sauce and mash; or loin of cod poached in Thai broth with noodles and stir-fried vegetables. There is a beer garden and riverside patio where you can enjoy your meal or one of the regularly changing beers such as Everards Tiger.

Open all day all wk 11-11 **Bar Meals** L served all wk 12-9.30 D served all wk 12-9.30 Av main course £12 food served all day **Restaurant** L served all wk 12-9.30 D served all wk 12-9.30 booking required Av 3 course à la carte fr £23 food served all day ⊕ FREE HOUSE ◀ Shepherds Neame Spitfire, Everards Tiger. **Facilities** Children welcome Children's portions Dogs allowed Garden Parking Wi-fi

---

The Victoria ♀

6 Union Rd LN1 3BJ ☎ 01522 541000
e-mail: jonathanjpc@aol.com
dir: *From city outskirts follow signs for Cathedral Quarter. Pub 2 mins' walk from all major up-hill car parks. Adjacent to the West Gate of Lincoln Castle*

Situated right next to the Westgate entrance of the Castle and within a stone's throw of Lincoln Cathedral, a long-standing drinkers' pub with a range of real ales, including six changing guest beers, ciders and perries. As well as the fantastic views of the castle, the pub also offers great meals made from home-prepared food including hot baguettes and filled bacon rolls, Saturday breakfast and Sunday lunches. House specials include sausage and mash, various pies, chilli con carne and home-made lasagne. There are Halloween and winter beer festivals.

Open all day all wk 11-mdnt (Fri-Sat 11-1am) **Bar Meals** L served all wk 12-2.30 Av main course £5.95 ⊕ BATEMANS ◀ Timothy Taylor Landlord, Batemans XB, Castle Rock Harvest Pale, Guest ales ♦ Westons. ♀ 10 **Facilities** Children welcome Children's portions Play area Dogs allowed Garden Beer festival

---

PICK OF THE PUBS

Wig & Mitre ♀

32 Steep Hill LN2 1LU
☎ 01522 535190 📄 01522 532402
e-mail: email@wigandmitre.com
dir: *At top of Steep Hill, adjacent to cathedral & Lincoln Castle car parks*

Standing on the Pilgrim Way in the heart of medieval Lincoln, the Wig & Mitre is a mix of the 14th and 16th centuries with some more recent additions. It's a reassuringly civilised free house that has been owned and operated by the same family since 1977. There's never any music, but you will find a reading room, and real ales like Batemans XB and Young's London Gold are on tap. Food includes a comprehensive breakfast menu served until noon. Hot and cold sandwiches are amongst the lighter options, which also include a plate of Scottish smoked salmon with lemon. Daily specials might begin with home-made corned beef with piccalilli and boiled egg, followed by mackerel fillets with sweet potato and chorizo salad and lime crushed peas. Round things off, perhaps, with dark chocolate torte and carrot sorbet.

Open all day all wk 8.30am-mdnt **Bar Meals** L served all wk 8.30am-10pm D served all wk 8.30am-10pm Av main course £13 food served all day **Restaurant** L served all wk 8.30am-10pm booking required D served all wk 8.30am-10pm booking required Fixed menu price fr £12.75 Av 3 course à la carte fr £25.40 food served all day ⊕ FREE HOUSE ◀ Black Sheep Special, Batemans XB, Young's London Gold. ♀ 24 **Facilities** Children welcome Children's menu Children's portions Dogs allowed

LITTLE BYTHAM — Map 11 TF01

The Willoughby Arms ☐

Station Rd NG33 4RA ☎ **01780 410276**
e-mail: info@willoughbyarms.co.uk
dir: B6121 (Stamford to Bourne road), at junct follow signs to Careby/Little Bytham, inn 5m on right

This beamed, traditional stone country inn started life as the booking office and waiting room for Lord Willoughby's private railway line. These days it has a fresher look whilst retaining its traditional charms. Expect a good selection of real ales - including several from local micro-breweries - with great, home-cooked food available every lunchtime and evening. Dishes range from sirloin steak topped with a Diane sauce to chargrilled tuna steak with lemon butter. There is a large beer garden with stunning views to enjoy on warmer days.

Open all day all wk noon-11 **Bar Meals** L served Mon-Sat 12-2, Sun 12-4 D served all wk 6-9 Av main course £8 ⊕ FREE HOUSE ◀ White Hart, Batemans XB, Absolution ♂ Bristol Port Cider, Broadoak Kingston Black. ☐ 10 **Facilities** Children welcome Children's menu Children's portions Dogs allowed Garden Beer festival Parking Wi-fi

MARKET RASEN — Map 17 TF18

The Black Horse Inn

Magna Mile LN8 6AJ
☎ **01507 313645** ▤ **01507 313645**
e-mail: info@blackhorseludford.co.uk
dir: In village on A631, between Louth & Market Rasen

Expect beers from Lincolnshire micro-breweries at village inn in the heart of the Lincolnshire Wolds. Comfy contemporary furnishings and open fires blend easily with displays recalling 101 Squadron, based at nearby Ludford Magna airfield in WWII. Food is a key part of the offering here. Diners can enjoy an eclectic menu of home-made, locally sourced meals: perhaps confit guinea fowl with white bean casserole followed by honey roast ham shank with pease pudding and parsley sauce. Finish with white chocolate rice pudding and apricot jam.

Open 12-2 6-10 (Sun 12-3) Closed: 2wks Jan, Sun eve, Mon **Bar Meals** L served Tue-Sat 12-2, Sun 12-3 D served Tue-Sat 6-10 Av main course £9.95 **Restaurant** L served Tue-Sat 12-2, Sun 12-3 D served Tue-Sat 6-10 Fixed menu price fr £10 Av 3 course à la carte fr £18.70 ⊕ FREE HOUSE ◀ Tom Woods Best, Great Newsome, Pricky Back Otchan, Poachers Monkey Hanger ♂ Westons Scrumpy, Skidbrooke Cyder. **Facilities** Children Children's portions Garden Parking

NEWTON — Map 12 TF03

The Red Lion

NG34 0EE ☎ **01529 497256**
dir: 10m E of Grantham on A52

Dating from the 17th century, the Red Lion is particularly popular with walkers and cyclists, perhaps because the flat Lincolnshire countryside makes for easy exercise. Low beams, exposed stone walls and an open fire in the bar help to create a very atmospheric interior. Popular dishes include haddock in beer batter, lemon sole with parsley butter sauce, breadcrumbed scampi, and home-made steak and ale pie. The carvery serves cold buffets on weekdays, hot ones on Friday and Saturday evenings, and Sunday lunchtime.

Open 12-3 6-11 Closed: Sun eve & Mon eve ⊕ FREE HOUSE **Facilities** Children welcome Dogs allowed Garden Parking

PARTNEY — Map 17 TF46

Red Lion Inn

PE23 4PG ☎ **01790 752271** ▤ **01790 753360**
e-mail: enquiries@redlioninnpartney.co.uk
dir: On A16 from Boston, or A158 from Horncastle

Warmed by wood burners, this welcoming village inn at the foot of the Lincolnshire Wolds is popular with walkers and cyclists who take refreshment here between visits to the nearby nature reserves and sandy beaches. Two real ales are always on tap, with ciders, lagers, and a good choice of wines too. The pub also has an excellent reputation for home-cooked food: maybe sugar-baked gammon and peaches, pheasant, venison and rabbit pie, or beef in beer with a garlic crust.

Open all wk Mon-Sat 12-2 6-11 (Sun 12-2 6-10.30) **Bar Meals** L served 12-2 D served 6-9 **Restaurant** L served 12-2 D served 6-9 ⊕ FREE HOUSE ◀ Black Sheep, Guinness, Tetley's, Guest ales ♂ Westons 1st Quality Draught. **Facilities** Children welcome Children's portions Garden Parking Wi-fi

POTTERHANWORTH — Map 17 TF06

The Chequers NEW

Cross St LN4 2DS ☎ **01522 790123**
e-mail: chequers-pub@btconnect.com
dir: From Lincoln take B1188. Through Branston. Turn left onto B1202 to Potterhanworth

First licensed in 1786, The Chequers would have welcomed workers from the local pottery industry; it was rebuilt in late Victorian times. Its current owner has refurbished and doubled its size with the addition of a large kitchen, where real food is prepared by real chefs. Examples from the menu include seared scallops with a minted pea purée; slow-braised belly pork in cider and sage; and orange filled profiteroles with a pecan and toffee sauce. Vegetarians and special diet requirements are also well catered for.

Open Tue-Sun Closed: Mon **Bar Meals** L served Tue-Sun 12-2.30 D served Tue-Sun 5.30-9.30 Av main course £11 **Restaurant** L served Tue-Sun 12-2.30 D served Tue-Sun 5.30-9.30 booking required Av 3 course à la carte fr £22 ⊕ FREE HOUSE **Facilities** Children welcome Children's portions Dogs allowed Garden Parking

RAITHBY — Map 17 TF36

Red Lion Inn

PE23 4DS ☎ **01790 753727**
dir: A158 from Horncastle, through Hagworthingham, right at top of hill signed Raithby

This traditional beamed village pub, parts of which date back 300 years, is situated on the edge of the Lincolnshire Wolds, a great place for walking and cycling. Inside is a wealth of character with log fires providing a warm welcome in winter. Dine in one of the four bars or on the comfort of the restaurant. A varied menu of home-made dishes is prepared using fresh local produce - sea bass with lime stir fry vegetables, roast guinea fowl with tomato, garlic and bacon, and medallions of beef with peppercorn sauce. Meals can be taken in the garden in the warmer months.

Open all wk 12-2 6-11 (Mon 6-11) **Bar Meals** L served Tue-Sun 12-2 D served Tue-Sat 7-8.30 **Restaurant** L served Tue-Sun 12-2 D served Tue-Sun 7-8.30 ⊕ FREE HOUSE ◀ Thwaites, Hardy & Hanson. **Facilities** Children welcome Children's menu Children's portions Garden Parking

SKEGNESS — Map 17 TF56

Best Western Vine Hotel ★★★ HL ☐

Vine Rd, Seacroft PE25 3DB
☎ **01754 763018** & **610611** ▤ **01754 769845**
e-mail: info@thevinehotel.com
dir: In Seacroft area of Skegness. S of town centre

Said to be the second oldest building in Skegness, the Vine remains largely unchanged since 1770. Set amid two acres of beautiful gardens, the ivy-covered hotel was bought by the brewer Harry Bateman in 1927. This charming hostelry offers comfortable accommodation and a fine selection of Bateman's own ales. Typical food choices include pasta dishes such as spinach and mushroom tortellini or lasagne, a selection from the grill, and main courses including ham, egg and chips, and chicken pot pie.

Open all day all wk **Bar Meals** L served Mon-Fri 12-2 D served all wk 6-9 Av main course £9.95 **Restaurant** L served Sun 12-2 booking required D served all wk 6-9 booking required Fixed menu price fr £22.50 ◀ Batemans XB & XXXB, Valiant, Black Sheep, Dixon's Ale. ☐ 8 **Facilities** Children welcome Children's menu Children's portions Dogs allowed Garden Parking **Rooms** 25

SOUTH RAUCEBY — Map 11 TF04

PICK OF THE PUBS

The Bustard Inn & Restaurant ◉ ⬩

44 Main St NG34 8QG ☎ **01529 488250**
e-mail: info@thebustardinn.co.uk
dir: *A15 from Lincoln. Right onto B1429 for Cranwell, 1st left after village, straight across A17*

Great Bustard won't have been on the menu for some time hereabouts, since the last indigenous specimen was shot nearby in 1845 by the local lord of the manor; the pub's name recalls this deed. Situated above Lincoln Edge and close to RAF Cranwell, the pub dates from 1860 and is an imposing building set at the heart of the pretty stone-built estate village. A well-cosseted beer garden wraps around the Gothic-style edifice; here locals indulge in the house beer Cheeky Bustard, brewed by a local micro. The light and airy interior is divided between the colourwashed bar and an elegant restaurant that makes the most of the stone construction, with dressed stone walls and tapestries adding much character. Chef Phil Lowe's gastro-pub menu draws on local produce where possible; poached egg Benedict a tasty inroad to the choice of mains which may feature loin of venison with fondant potato, red cabbage and port and peppercorn sauce or home-made linguini with baby chorizo sausage and roasted garlic king prawns, whilst Lincolnshire Poacher features on the cheese board. There is live jazz once a month and special food nights.

Open 12-3 5.30-11 (Sun 12-3.30) Closed: 1 Jan, Sun eve, Mon **Bar Meals** L served Tue-Sat 12-2.30, Sun 12-3 D served Tue-Sat 6-9.30 Av main course £17 **Restaurant** L served Tue-Sat 12-2.30, Sun 12-3 D served Tue-Sat 6-9.30 Fixed menu price fr £12.95 Av 3 course à la carte fr £26 ⊕ FREE HOUSE ◀ Batemans XXXB, Guinness, Cheeky Bustard, Guest ale. ⬩ 13 **Facilities** Children welcome Children's portions Garden Parking Wi-fi

SOUTH WITHAM — Map 11 SK91

Blue Cow Inn & Brewery ⬩

High St NG33 5QB ☎ **01572 768432** ▤ **01572 768432**
e-mail: enquiries@bluecowinn.co.uk
dir: *Between Stamford & Grantham on A1*

Named after the political allegiance of its erstwhile owner, the Duke of Buckminster, this partly medieval building has been a pub for over 400 years. Low beams, pillars, flagged floors and dressed-stone walls characterise its ancient interior, with crackling log fires to take the edge off the fenland breezes; any remaining chill may be generated by the pub's ghosts – a lady and a dog. Licensee Simon Crathorn brews his own award-winning ales, ideally consumed on the colourful beer garden patio.

Open all day all wk 11-11 **Bar Meals** Av main course £7.95 food served all day **Restaurant** Fixed menu price fr £5 Av 3 course à la carte fr £15 food served all day ⊕ FREE HOUSE ◀ Blue Cow. **Facilities** Children welcome Children's menu Children's portions Family room Dogs allowed Garden Parking Wi-fi

STAMFORD — Map 11 TF00

PICK OF THE PUBS

The George of Stamford ★★★ HL ◉ ⬩

71 St Martins PE9 2LB
☎ **01780 750750** ▤ **01780 750701**
e-mail: reservations@georgehotelofstamford.com
web: www.georgehotelofstamford.com
dir: *From Peterborough take A1 N. Onto B1081 for Stamford, down hill to lights. Hotel on left*

A gallows sign across the old A1 acting as a warning to highwaymen, a medieval crypt lurking under the Cocktail Bar, and a walled monastery garden that, curiously, monks never used, all contribute to this magnificent inn's historic charm. The London Room and York Bar once served as waiting rooms for passengers as the 'twenty up' and 'twenty down' daily stage coaches changed horses. Today's visitors, many reliant upon a different form of horsepower, can have a snack in the bar or lounge, a light meal in the Garden Room or cobbled courtyard, or something more traditional in the magnificent oak-panelled restaurant, such as table-carved English sirloin of beef, fillet of venison or grilled Dover sole. Those feeling particularly flush might be tempted by the Grand Brittany Platter of a half lobster and an abundance of other seafood. Each of the well-equipped bedrooms reflects the artistic skills of Julia Vannocci.

Open all day all wk 11-11 (Sun noon-11)
Bar Meals L served all wk 11.30-2.30 Av main course £7.95 **Restaurant** L served all wk 12-2.30 (Garden Room all wk 12-11) booking required D served all wk 7-10.30 booking required Fixed menu price fr £23 Av 3 course à la carte fr £34 food served all day ⊕ FREE HOUSE ◀ Adnams Broadside, Ruddles Bitter, Grainstore Brewery ♂ Aspall Suffolk Cider. ⬩ 19 **Facilities** Children welcome Children's portions Dogs allowed Garden Parking Wi-fi **Rooms** 47

PICK OF THE PUBS

The Tobie Norris ⬩

12 Saint Pauls St PE9 2BE ☎ **01780 482256**
e-mail: info@tobienorris.com
dir: *From A1 to Stamford on A6121, which becomes West St, then East St. After right bend turn right into Saint Pauls St*

Built in 1280 as a medieval hall and sympathetically restored and remodelled as pub in 2006, 12 St Pauls Street is named after a bell founder who lived in the property in the 16th century. The Tobie Norris has since won awards for its stunning renovation and the seven rooms set across three floors ooze atmosphere and charm. A free house it offers a fine range of micro-brewery real ales and one of them is always White Hart, brewed by Ufford Ales brewery at a sister pub (White Hart) six miles away. The kitchen specialises in stone-baked pizzas, cooked in specially imported Italian ovens, and you can choose your own toppings - anything from free-range chicken to black pudding and sun-dried tomatoes. There is also a full menu of seasonal Italian-inspired specials and typical dishes include lamb steak with garlic and rosemary, penne with tomato and basil sauce, and oven-roasted sea bass.

Open all day all wk **Bar Meals** L served all wk 12-2.30 D served Mon-Sat 6-9 ⊕ FREE HOUSE ◀ Ufford Ales White Hart, Adnams Bitter, Guest ales ♂ Aspall, Jollydale. ⬩ 18 **Facilities** Dogs allowed Garden Wi-fi

SURFLEET SEAS END — Map 12 TF22

The Ship Inn

154 Reservoir Rd PE11 4DH
☎ **01775 680547** ▤ **01775 680548**
e-mail: shipsurfleet@hotmail.com
dir: *Off A16 (Spalding to Boston). Follow tourist signs towards Surfleet Reservoir then The Ship Inn signs*

Not yet 10 years old, this successor to an earlier pub stands by two rivers, the Welland and the Glen, as well as Vernatti's Drain, named after an engineer who drained these fenlands in the mid-1600s. The bar is panelled in hand-crafted oak, while upstairs is the restaurant overlooking the flat surrounding land, which is only just above sea level. Locally sourced food includes beef and Batemans Ale suet pudding; pan-fried Barbary duck breast with chilli and orange marmalade; and vegetable lasagne.

Open all wk 11-3 5-mdnt (Sat-Sun 11am-mdnt) ◀ Hydes Smooth, local micro-breweries. **Facilities** Dogs allowed Parking

SUSWORTH   Map 17 SE80

The Jenny Wren Inn

East Ferry Rd DN17 3AS ☎ 01724 784000
e-mail: info@jennywreninn.co.uk
dir: Telephone for directions

It's easy to imagine an 18th-century farmer, tankard in
hand, in front of the open fire looking forward to his
simple supper in this beamed, wood-panelled former
farmhouse. Fast forward to what, for him, would be an
unimaginable choice: a pint of Theakston or Tom Wood,
with warm Cajun chicken salad; pan-fried salmon steak,
new potatoes and parsley sauce; leek and courgette
cottage pie. The pub is known for their fish dishes and for
reliance on locally sourced produce. The River Trent flows
passed the front.

Open all wk Mon-Thu 11.30-3 5.45-10.30 (Fri-Sun
11.30-10.30) **Bar Meals** L served Mon-Thu 12-2, Fri-Sun
12-9 booking required D served Mon-Thu 5.45-9, Fri-Sun
12-9 booking required Av main course £10
Restaurant L served Mon-Thu 12-2, Fri-Sun 12-9 booking
required D served Mon-Thu 5.45-9, Fri-Sun 12-9 booking
required Fixed menu price fr £9.95 Av 3 course à la carte
fr £15.50 ⊕ FREE HOUSE ◀ Old Speckled Hen, IPA Bitter,
Theakstons, Tom Wood. **Facilities** Children welcome
Children's menu Children's portions Family room Dogs
allowed Garden Parking Wi-fi

TIMBERLAND   Map 17 TF15

The Penny Farthing Inn ★★★★ INN

4 Station Rd LN4 3SA
☎ 01526 378359 📠 01526 378915
*dir: From Sleaford take A153, left onto B1189. At
junct with B1191 follow signs for Timberland*

Recently refurbished in a traditional style, this popular
and friendly pub is worth noting if you're looking for a
comfortable and informal base from which to explore
Lincoln and its cathedral. Located in a charming village
just outside Lincoln, its en suite rooms are well appointed
and equipped with flat-screen TV and Wi-fi. The seasonal
dinner menu is worth staying in for. Try twice-baked
cheese soufflé with a spinach and grain mustard velouté
followed by oven roasted belly pork with fennel and bacon
in cider jus. Finish with baked chocolate tart and ice
cream.

Open all day Closed: Mon **Bar Meals** L served Tue-Sun
12-2.30 D served Tue-Sun 5.30-9.30 Av main course £10
Restaurant L served Tue-Sun 12-2.30 D served Tue-Sun
5.30-9.30 booking required Av 3 course à la carte fr £22
⊕ FREE HOUSE ◀ Spitfire, John Smith's, Timothy Taylor
Landlord, Bombardier. **Facilities** Children welcome
Children's portions Dogs allowed Garden Parking Wi-fi
Rooms 7

WOODHALL SPA   Map 17 TF16

Village Limits Country Pub, Restaurant & Motel

Stixwould Rd LN10 6UJ ☎ 01526 353312
e-mail: info@villagelimits.co.uk
*dir: At rdbt on main street follow Petwood Hotel signs.
Motel 500yds past Petwood Hotel*

The pub and restaurant are situated in the original part
of the building, so expect bare beams and old world
charm. Typical meals, championing the ingredients of
many local Lincolnshire suppliers, include chicken and
avocado salad; or smoked trout and salmon pâté;
followed by home-made steak and ale pie; or slow roast
belly pork with plum and apple sauce. Finish with bread
and butter pudding. There's a good choice of real ales to
wash it all down.

Open 11.30-3 6.30-11 Closed: Mon L ⊕ FREE HOUSE
◀ Batemans XB, Tetley's Smooth Flow, Highwood Tom
Wood's Best, Fulstow IPA, Dixon's Major Bitter.
Facilities Children welcome Children's portions Garden
Parking Wi-fi

WOOLSTHORPE   Map 11 SK83

PICK OF THE PUBS

The Chequers Inn ☺

Main St NG32 1LU ☎ 01476 870701
e-mail: justinnabar@yahoo.co.uk
*dir: Approx 7m from Grantham. 3m from A607. Follow
heritage signs to Belvoir Castle*

The modern rubs along with the traditional just fine in
this 17th-century coaching inn next to the village
cricket pitch and from whose mature garden you can
see Belvoir Castle. Interior delights are the five real
fires, a bar that does a good line in real ales, namely
Woodforde's Wherry Bitter and Batemans, and the
Bakehouse Restaurant, where the oven from village
bakery days remains in situ. Expect sophisticated pub
food - monkfish pie with Gruyère and herb crust, or
pan-fried duck breast with sweet potato cake, sauté
spinach and cherry jus. There are pub classics too, like
beer-battered haddock and hand-cut chips, and
gammon steak with fried organic egg. If against your
chosen dish on the menu appear the words '7th
Heaven', it is one of seven served between six and
seven o'clock every day of the week for £7.

Open all wk Mon-Fri 12-3 5.30-11 (Sat-Sun all day)
Closed: 25 eve & 26 eve Dec, 1 Jan eve
Bar Meals L served Mon-Sat 12-2.30, Sun 12-4
D served Mon-Sat 6-9.30, Sun 6-8.30 Av main course
£10.50 **Restaurant** L served Mon-Sat 12-2.30, Sun
12-4 D served Mon-Sat 6-9.30, Sun 6-8.30 Fixed menu
price fr £16.50 Av 3 course à la carte fr £25 ⊕ FREE
HOUSE ◀ Woodforde's Wherry, Batemans ales
♙ Aspall, Old Rosie Scrumpy. ☺ 25 **Facilities** Children
welcome Children's menu Children's portions Family
room Dogs allowed Garden Parking

LONDON

E1

Town of Ramsgate ☺   PLAN 2 G3

62 Wapping High St E1W 2NP ☎ 020 7481 8000
e-mail: peter@townoframsgate.co.uk
dir: 0.3m from Wapping tube station & Tower of London

This 500-year-old, Grade II listed building is close to The
City, and decorated with bric-a-brac and old prints.
Judge Jeffries was caught here while trying to flee the
country and escape the kind of justice he dealt out. Press
gangs used to work the area, imprisoning men overnight
in the cellar. The owners continue to serve a good
selection of real ales and up to 13 wines by the glass.
The bar food offers good value for money, and can be
enjoyed on the decked terrace overlooking the River
Thames.

Open all day all wk noon-mdnt (Sun noon-11)
Bar Meals L served all wk 12-4 D served all wk 5-9 Av
main course £9.50 food served all day ⊕ FREE HOUSE
◀ Adnams, Young's, Fuller's London Pride ♙ Brothers
Pear Cider. ☺ 13 **Facilities** Children welcome Dogs
allowed Garden Wi-fi

E8

The Cat & Mutton ☺   PLAN 2 G4

**76 Broadway Market, Hackney E8 4QJ
☎ 020 7254 5599**
e-mail: catandmutton@yahoo.co.uk
dir: Telephone for directions

Formerly known as the 'Cattle & Shoulder of Mutton' the
pub was used by workers on their way to London's
livestock markets in the 17th century. Today, the
revamped building has been reinvented as one of East
London's busiest food pubs with the current owner in
place for the last seven years. At scrubbed tables in
trendy, gentrified surroundings, order steak tartare with
Melba toast; pan-fried sea trout Niçoise; or pot-roast
spring chicken with baby vegetables. There are well-kept
real ales and up to 12 wines are offered by the glass.

Open all day all wk noon-11 (Fri-Sat noon-1am) Closed:
25-26 Dec **Bar Meals** L served Mon-Fri 12-3 D served
Mon-Sat 6.30-10 booking required Av main course £9
Restaurant L served Mon-Sat 12-3, Sun 12-5 D served
Mon-Sat 6-10 booking required Fixed menu price fr
£12.50 Av 3 course à la carte fr £26 ⊕ SEAMLESS LTD
◀ Adnams Bitter, Shepherd Neame Spitfire, Deuchars IPA
♙ Westons, Addlestones. ☺ 12 **Facilities** Children
welcome Children's portions Dogs allowed Wi-fi

E9

PICK OF THE PUBS

The Empress of India ☂   PLAN 2 G4

130 Lauriston Rd, Victoria Park E9 7LH
☎ 020 8533 5123   020 7404 2250
e-mail: info@theempressofindia.com
dir: *From Mile End Station turn right onto Grove Rd, leads onto Lauriston Rd*

Built a few years after Queen Victoria became Empress of India, this classic East End pub has in its time been a nightclub, a print works and, more recently, a floristry training school. The beautifully styled interior includes a carpet with the pub's name woven into it. The bar serves classic cocktails, draught beers and fine wines from around the globe. Modern British food, served from the open kitchen, offers options throughout the day, including breakfast, lunch, dinner, bar snacks, kids' menu, afternoon tea and a feast menu. Rare breed meats, poultry and game are spit roasted daily; and shellfish figures prominently. In the evening, expect starters of deep-fried herring roes and sauce gribiche to be followed by slow-braised ox cheek, truffle mash, turnips, butterbeans, braising juices. Sunday lunchtime brings the likes of roast sirloin of Angus beef from the oven and whole roast Cumbrian chicken from the rotisserie.

Open all day all wk Closed: 25-26 Dec **Bar Meals** Av main course £4.75 food served all day **Restaurant** L served Mon-Fri 12-3, Sat 12.30-4, Sun 12.30-9 D served Mon-Sat 6-10, Sun 12.30-9 Av 3 course à la carte fr £20 ⊕ FREE HOUSE ○ Aspall. ☂ 19 **Facilities** Children welcome Children's menu Children's portions Dogs allowed Wi-fi

E14

PICK OF THE PUBS

The Grapes   PLAN 2 G3

76 Narrow St, Limehouse E14 8BP
☎ 020 7987 4396   020 7531 9264
dir: *Telephone for directions*

Immortalised as the Six Jolly Fellowship Porters in his novel *Our Mutual Friend*, this Thames-side pub used to be a haunt of Charles Dickens, who was made to stand on a table and sing here when he was a child. While the novelist might still recognise the interior of this award-winning 18th-century tavern, the surroundings have changed dramatically with the development of Canary Wharf and the Docklands Light Railway. However, old-fashioned values are maintained by the pulling of superb cask conditioned ales in the atmospheric dark timber-clad bar downstairs, while in the tiny upstairs restaurant only the freshest seafood is served. This is a fish lover's paradise, with a menu that includes whole sea bass oven baked with lemon and parsley, poached Loch Duart salmon and daily specials cooked to your liking. Nonetheless meat lovers and vegetarians should not be deterred from experiencing

this evocative slice of old Limehouse; traditional roasts are served on Sundays, and salads, bar meals and sandwiches are always available.

Open all day all wk noon-11 (Mon-Wed noon-3 5.30-11) Closed: 25-26 Dec, 1 Jan **Bar Meals** L served Mon-Sat 12-2.30, Sun 12-3.30 D served Mon-Sat 6.30-9.30 Av main course £7.90 **Restaurant** L served Mon-Fri 12-2.30 booking required D served Mon-Sat 6.30-9.30 booking required Fixed menu price fr £17.95 Av 3 course à la carte fr £28.50 ⊕ PUNCH ◀ Adnams, Marstons Pedigree, Timothy Taylor Landlord, Guest ales ○ Addlestones. **Facilities** Dogs allowed

PICK OF THE PUBS

The Gun ◉ ☂   PLAN 2 G3

27 Coldharbour, Docklands E14 9NS
☎ 020 7515 5222   020 7515 4407
e-mail: info@thegundocklands.com
dir: *From South Quay DLR, east along Marsh Wall to mini rdbt. Turn left, over bridge then 1st right*

The Gun stands on the banks of the Thames in an area once home to the dockside iron foundries which produced guns for the Royal Navy. The pub takes its name from the cannon fired to celebrate the opening of the West India docks in 1802; it was also, allegedly, where Nelson and Lady Hamilton sometimes met on their secret assignations. Destroyed by fire several years ago, the Grade II listed building re-opened in 2004 following painstaking restoration work. It offers adjoining main bar and restaurant, two private dining rooms, two snugs, and a stunning riverside terrace overlooking the Millennium Dome. Right next door is the pub's latest addition – A Grelha serves traditional southern Portuguese food straight from the barbecue. Back in The Gun, you can snack on oysters from Borough Market, lunch on a plate of devilled whitebait from the pub menu, or choose a restaurant main course such as roast breast of Yorkshire guinea fowl. There is a strong wine list featuring over 100 bins.

Open all wk 11am-mdnt (Sun 11-11) Closed: 25-26 Dec **Bar Meals** L served Mon-Sat 12-3, Sun 12-4 D served Mon-Sat 6-10.30, Sun 6.30-9.30 Av main course £9 **Restaurant** L served Mon-Sat 12-3, Sun 12-4 booking required D served Mon-Sat 6-10.30, Sun 6.30-9.30 booking required Fixed menu price fr £18 Av 3 course à la carte fr £24 ⊕ ETM GROUP ◀ Guinness, London Pride, Adnams ○ Aspall. ☂ 22 **Facilities** Children welcome Children's portions Dogs allowed Garden Wi-fi

EC1

PICK OF THE PUBS

The Bleeding Heart Tavern ◉ ☂   PLAN 1 E4

19 Greville St EC1N 8SQ ☎ 020 7242 8238
  020 7831 1402
e-mail: bookings@bleedingheart.co.uk
dir: *Close to Farringdon tube station, at corner of Greville St & Bleeding Heart Yard*

Standing just off London's famous Leather Lane, and dating from 1746, when Holborn had a boozer for every five houses and inns boasted that their customers could be 'drunk for a penny and dead drunk for twopence'. It traded until 1946, was a grill for 52 years, and reopened as The Tavern Bar in 1998. Today this Tavern offers traditional real ales and a light lunchtime menu if you're pressed for time. Downstairs, the warm and comforting dining room features an open rotisserie and grill serving free-range organic British meat, game and poultry alongside an extensive wine list. Typical menu choices might start with mackerel and whisky pâté as a prelude to braised beef in Adnams Ale with dumplings, or spit-roast suckling pig with sage apple and onion stuffing and crushed garlic potatoes. Desserts include steamed chocolate pudding, treacle tart and a jam roly-poly.

Open all day 7am-11pm Closed: BHs, 10 days at Xmas, Sat-Sun **Bar Meals** food served all day **Restaurant** L served Mon-Fri 12-2.30 booking required D served Mon-Fri 6-10.30 booking required ⊕ FREE HOUSE ◀ Adnams Southwold Bitter, Broadside, Fisherman, Mayday ○ Aspall. ☂ 17

PICK OF THE PUBS

Coach & Horses ☂   PLAN 1 E5

26-28 Ray St, Clerkenwell EC1 3DJ ☎ 020 7278 8990
e-mail: info@thecoachandhorses.com
dir: *From Farringdon tube station right onto Cowcross St. At Farringdon Rd turn right, after 500yds left onto Ray St. Pub at bottom of hill*

Located on the site of Hockley-in-the-Hole bear-baiting pit, this restored, wood panelled Victorian pub was built to serve the myriad artisans, many of them Italian, who once populated this characterful area. What is now the public bar used to be a sweet shop, people lived in the beer cellars, and there was a secret passage to the long-buried River Fleet, which runs underneath the pub and which can still be heard from the cellar and a drain outside the front entrance. Unsurprisingly there are a few ghosts, including an old man and a black cat. Among the reasonably priced dishes on the modern European menu, look for rabbit rillettes with piccalilli; beetroot risotto; slow-roast lamb with kale and pearl barley; buttermilk pudding with hazelnut and apple purée; and treacle tart with clotted cream. If you just want a snack, chose the famous Scotch eggs and enjoy them with a pint of Adnams

Bitter or a glass of wine from the great list. Over the road is the original Clerk's Well, from which this district takes its name.

Open all wk noon-11 (Sat 6-11 Sun 12.30-5) Closed: 24 Dec-1st Mon in Jan, BHs **Bar Meals** L served Mon-Fri & Sun 1-4 D served Mon-Sat 6-10 Av main course £13 **Restaurant** L served Mon-Fri 12-3, Sun 1-4 D served Mon-Sat 6-10 Av 3 course à la carte fr £24 ⊕ PUNCH PUBS ◀ Timothy Taylor Landlord, Adnams Bitter, London Pride ♂ Burrow Hill Farm. ♀ 14 **Facilities** Children welcome Children's portions Dogs allowed Garden Wi-fi

---

PICK OF THE PUBS

The Eagle ♀   PLAN 1 E5

159 Farringdon Rd EC1R 3AL ☎ 020 7837 1353
dir: *Angel/Farringdon tube station. Pub at north end of Farringdon Rd*

The Eagle, which is celebrating its 20th year anniversary, was a front-runner in the new breed of stylish eating and drinking establishments that we now know as gastro-pubs. Farringdon Road was more downbeat in those days but Clerkenwell is quite a trendy district now. The Eagle is still going strong, despite considerable competition, and remains one of the neighbourhood's top establishments. The airy interior includes a wooden-floored bar and dining area, a random assortment of furniture, and an open-to-view kitchen that produces a creatively modern, daily-changing menu which revels in cosmopolitan flavours. Typical of the range are smoked haddock and chorizo soup, with tomato, fennel, chilli and potato; bifeana – marinated rump steak sandwich; and pork and cockles Alentejo style (smoked paprika, cloves, garlic and white wine). The tapas selection includes oak-smoked salmon and horseradish mousse. Lemon and almond cake with mascarpone and berries is typical of the desserts.

Open all day Mon-Sat noon-11, Sun noon-5 Closed: BHs L (1wk Xmas), Sun eve **Bar Meals** L served Mon-Fri 12-3, Sat-Sun 12-3.30 D served Mon-Sat 6.30-10.30 **Restaurant** L served Mon-Fri 12-3, Sat-Sun 12-3.30 D served Mon-Sat 6.30-10.30 ⊕ FREE HOUSE ◀ Wells Eagle IPA, Bombardier ♂ Westons, Addlestones. ♀ 15 **Facilities** Children welcome Children's portions Dogs allowed

---

PICK OF THE PUBS

The Jerusalem Tavern   PLAN 1 E4

55 Britton St, Clerkenwell EC1M 5NA
☎ 020 7490 4281
e-mail: thejerusalemtavern@gmail.com
dir: *100mtrs NE of Farringdon tube station; 300mtrs N of Smithfield*

Now owned by St Peter's Brewery, this historic tavern has close links to Samuel Johnson, Oliver Goldsmith, David Garrick and the young Handel, who used to drink

here on his visits to London. Named after the Priory of St John of Jerusalem, founded in 1140, the pub can be traced back to the 14th century, having occupied several sites in the area including part of St John's Gate. The current premises date from 1720 although the shop frontage dates from about 1810, when it was a workshop for Clerkenwell's various watch and clock craftsmen. Its dimly lit Dickensian bar, with bare boards, rustic wooden tables, old tiles, candles, open fires and cosy corners, is the perfect film set - which is what it has been on many occasions. A classic pub in every sense, it offers the full range of cask and bottled beers from St Peter's Brewery, as well as a range of simple pub fare.

Open all day 11-11 Closed: 25 Dec-1 Jan, Sat-Sun **Bar Meals** L served Mon-Fri 12-3 Av main course £8.50 ⊕ ST PETER'S BREWERY ◀ St Peter's (complete range) ♂ Aspall. **Facilities** Dogs allowed Wi-fi

---

PICK OF THE PUBS

The Peasant ♀   PLAN 1 E5

240 Saint John St EC1V 4PH
☎ 020 7336 7726 📄 020 7490 1089
e-mail: eat@thepeasant.co.uk
dir: *Exit Angel & Farringdon Rd tube station. Pub on corner of Saint John St & Percival St*

In between Islington and Smithfield markets, this beautifully restored former gin palace offers a choice of great British bar food, or fine dining in the upstairs restaurant. Grade II listing acknowledges many original Victorian features, such as the lovingly restored mahogany horseshoe bar, inlaid mosaic floor, and the period chandeliers in the upstairs restaurant. Real ciders from Thatchers and Aspall supplement a good wine list and an extensive range of pumped and bottled beers that includes some Belgian Trappist varieties. Amid the cult band posters and old speedway billboards in the bar, you might opt for vegetable kedgeree; braised ox cheek with rapeseed oil mash; or one of the substantial sharing platters. Upstairs, a typical dinner in the circus art themed restaurant might kick off with honey-roasted parsnip soup and spiced chestnuts, followed by roast haunch of venison with redcurrant jelly. Dark chocolate ganache brings things to a sweet conclusion.

Open all day all wk Closed: 24 Dec-2 Jan **Bar Meals** L served all wk 12-11 D served all wk 12-11 Av main course £10.50 food served all day **Restaurant** D served Tue-Sat 6-11, Sun 12-3 Av 3 course à la carte fr £31 ⊕ FREE HOUSE ◀ Bombardier, Dekonick Belgian Ale, Crouch Vale, Brewers Gold, Staropramen ♂ Thatchers Pear & Katy, Aspall. ♀ 15 **Facilities** Children welcome Children's portions Dogs allowed Garden Beer festival

Ye Olde Mitre ♀   PLAN 1 E4

1 Ely Court, Ely Place, By 8 Hatton Garden EC1N 6SJ
☎ 020 7405 4751
e-mail: yeoldemitre@fullers.co.uk
dir: *From Chancery Lane tube station exit 3 walk downhill to Holborn Circus, left into Hatton Garden. Pub in alley between 8 & 9 Hatton Garden.*

Built in 1546 in the shadow of the palace of the Bishops of Ely, this quirky historic corner pub is still technically part of Cambridgeshire. Choose from at least five real ales in the magnificent wood-panelled rooms, with a limited range of bar snacks that includes toasted sandwiches, pork pies, scotch eggs, sausages and gherkins. Beer festivals are held in May, August and December, but the pub is closed at weekends and Bank Holidays.

Open all day Closed: 25 Dec, 1 Jan, BHs, Sat-Sun (ex 1st wknd Aug) **Bar Meals** L served Mon-Fri 11.30-9.30 D served Mon-Fri 11.30-9.30 food served all day ⊕ FULLER SMITH & TURNER ◀ Gales Seafarer, Fuller's London Pride, Deuchars IPA, Adnams Broadside, Guest ales. ♀ 8 **Facilities** Dogs allowed Garden Beer festival Wi-fi

---

EC2

Old Dr Butler's Head ♀   PLAN 1 F4

Mason's Av, Coleman St, Moorgate EC2V 5BT
☎ 020 7606 3504 📄 020 7600 0417
e-mail: olddoctorbutlers@shepherdneame.co.uk
dir: *Telephone for directions*

Dr Butler was Court Physician to King James I; his sometimes questionable cures included a 'medicinal ale', sold through his chain of alehouses of which this is the sole survivor, rebuilt after the Great Fire of 1666. Sandwiches are served in the Dickensian dark-panelled, gas-lit bar, while upstairs, the Chop House restaurant offers a lunchtime menu featuring favourites such as steak and kidney suet pudding, complementing the Shepherd Neame real ales and an extensive wine list. In common with many City pubs, Dr Butler's is closed at weekends but the bar is now open for dinner from 6-9pm during the week.

Open all day Closed: Sat-Sun **Bar Meals** L served Mon-Fri 12-3 D served Mon-Fri 6-9 Av main course £11 **Restaurant** L served Mon-Fri 12-3 booking required ⊕ SHEPHERD NEAME ◀ Shepherd Neame Spitfire, Bishops Finger Master Brew, Shepherd Neame Best. ♀ 12 **Facilities** Wi-fi

EC4

The Black Friar ☻
PLAN 1 E3

174 Queen Victoria St EC4V 4EG ☎ 020 7236 5474
dir: *Opposite Blackfriars tube station*

Space permitting, so much could be written about this 1875 pub and its later Art Nouveau interior celebrating the fanciful antics of the medieval Dominican monks, who once lived here, known as the Blackfriars. Real ales range from Adnams to Timothy Taylor's, via Fuller's, Sharp's and St Austell, with solid sustenance of sandwiches and pies; Cumberland sausage and mash; salmon and broccoli fishcakes; and roasted vegetable risotto. On a triangular site by Blackfriars tube station, it's popular with City suits.

Open all day all wk Mon-Sat 10am-11pm (Sun noon-10.30) Closed: 25 Dec **Bar Meals** L served all wk 10-5 D served all wk 5-10 Av main course £7.50 ⊕ MITCHELL & BUTLERS ◀ Fuller's London Pride, Adnams, Timothy Taylor, St Austell Tribute, Sharp's Doom Bar ☼ Westons Organic, Aspall. ☻ 14 **Facilities** Children welcome Garden

---

The Old Bank of England
PLAN 1 E4

194 Fleet St EC4A 2LT ☎ 020 7430 2255
e-mail: oldbankofengland@fullers.co.uk
dir: *Pub by Courts of Justice*

This magnificent building previously housed the Law Courts' branch of the Bank of England. Set between the site of Sweeney Todd's barbershop and his mistress' pie shop, it stands above the original bank vaults and the tunnels in which Todd butchered his unfortunate victims. Aptly, there's an extensive range of speciality pies including game, brandy and redcurrant, and lamb and red pepper, but other treats include roasted lemon and thyme chicken breast on a pearl barley broth, and caramelised onion and olive puff pastry tart.

Open all day Closed: BHs, Sat-Sun ⊕ FULLER SMITH TURNER PLC ◀ London Pride, ESB, Chiswick, Discovery, Seasonal. **Facilities** Garden Wi-fi

PICK OF THE PUBS

The White Swan ◉ ☻
PLAN 1 E4

108 Fetter Ln, Holborn EC4A 1ES
☎ 020 7242 9696 ▯ 020 7404 2250
e-mail: info@thewhiteswanlondon.com
dir: *Nearest tube: Chancery Lane. From station towards St Paul's Cathedral. At HSBC bank left into Fetter Lane. Pub on right*

Transformed from the old Mucky Duck pub, this is now a handsome, traditional city watering hole. Downstairs is the wood-panelled bar which serves a cosmopolitan selection of beers and lagers, and 22 wines by the glass. Its fresh cream coloured walls embrace leather covered bar stools and mixed wooden tables, chairs and banquettes; beneath your feet the reclaimed timber floorboards complete the sumptuous atmosphere. Upstairs on the mezzanine is a beautifully restored dining room with mirrored ceiling and linen-clad tables. Cooking is modern British in style: a baby

leek vinaigrette with grated egg and anchovy dressing is a sample starter. Fish fresh from Billingsgate each morning appears in main courses such as roast fillet of Atlantic halibut with leeks, mussels and crème fraîche. An alternative is rump of Scottish Blackface mutton with hedgehog mushrooms and fondant potatoes. To finish, the passionfruit cheesecake, apple and blackberry crumble, and home-made ice creams are all excellent.

Open 11am-mdnt (Fri 11-1am) Closed: 25-26 Dec, 1 Jan, Sat-Sun & BHs **Bar Meals** L served Mon-Fri 12-3 D served Mon-Fri 6-10 Av main course £14 **Restaurant** L served Mon-Fri 12-3 booking required D served Mon-Fri 6-10 booking required Fixed menu price fr £29.75 Av 3 course à la carte fr £30 ⊕ ETM GROUP ◀ London Pride, Guinness, Adnams ☼ Addlestones. ☻ 22 **Facilities** Children welcome Children's portions Wi-fi

---

N1

The Albion NEW
PLAN 2 F4

10 Thornhill Rd, Islington N1 1HW ☎ 020 7607 7450
e-mail: info@the-albion.co.uk
dir: *From Angel tube station, cross road into Liverpool Rd past Sainsbury's, continue to Richmond Ave. Left. At junct with Thornhill Rd turn right. Pub on right*

An award-winning hostelry in central Islington, just off Upper Street and within the Barnsbury conservation area. Its picturesque Georgian façade, spacious walled garden and wisteria-covered pergola prove irresistibly attractive to locals and city workers alike in summer; log fires warm the classic dark wood panels and tastefully furnished interior in winter. Brasserie-style food centres around the charcoal grill, where Tamworth pork chops and Blackface lamb leg steaks sizzle. Greene King and Black Sheep vie for your custom at the bar.

Open all day all wk **Bar Meals** L served Mon-Fri 12-3, Sat-Sun 12-4 D served Mon-Sat 6-10, Sun 6-9 Av main course £14 **Restaurant** L served Mon-Fri 12-3, Sat-Sun 12-4 D served Mon-Sat 6-10, Sun 6-9 Fixed menu price fr £28 Av 3 course à la carte fr £30 ◀ Greene King, Black Sheep. **Facilities** Children welcome Children's portions Dogs allowed Garden Wi-fi

PICK OF THE PUBS

The Barnsbury ☻
PLAN 2 F4

209-211 Liverpool Rd, Islington N1 1LX
☎ 020 7607 5519 ▯ 020 7607 3256
e-mail: thebarnsburypub@hotmail.com
dir: *Telephone for directions*

The Barnsbury, a 'free house and dining room' in the heart of Islington, is a welcome addition to the London scene. It's a gastro-pub where both the food and the prices are well conceived – and its walled garden makes it a secluded and sought-after summer oasis for alfresco relaxation. At least six guest ales are backed by an in-depth wine list. The food is cooked from daily supplies of fresh ingredients which have been bought direct from the market, itemised in refreshingly concise

terms on the menu. Starter dishes range from seared tuna on mouli and radish salad with citrus mayo or goat's cheese and red onion marmalade tart to ham hock terrine with piccalilli. Tempting mains might include glazed pigs' cheeks with thyme and bacon scented cabbage, mash and jus; pan-fried sea bream fillet with al forno potatoes and samphire; and wild mushroom, artichoke and blue cheese strudel.

Open all day all wk noon-11 (Sun noon-10.30) Closed: 25-26 Dec, 1 Jan **Bar Meals** L served Mon-Fri 12-3 **Restaurant** L served Sat-Sun 12-4 D served all wk 6.30-10 ⊕ FREE HOUSE ◀ Guest ales. ☻ 12 **Facilities** Children welcome Dogs allowed Garden

---

The Charles Lamb ☻ NEW
PLAN 2 F4

16 Elia St, Islington N1 8DE ☎ 020 7837 5040
e-mail: food@thecharleslambpub.com
dir: *From Angel station turn left, at junct of City Rd turn left. Pass Duncan Terrace Gdns, left into Colebrooke Row. 1st right*

Camille and MJ Hobby-Limon took over the former Prince Albert in 2005 and have breathed new life into this Islington favourite. Named after a local writer who lived in the area in the 1830s, the free house has built up a formidable reputation for its ever-changing range of ales from micro-breweries, as well as award-winning food which takes influence from Britain, France and Spain. The pub hosts an annual Bastille Day event complete with petanque competition.

Open all wk open from 4 Mon & Tue Closed: 23 Dec-1 Jan **Bar Meals** L served Wed-Fri 12-3, Sat 12-4, Sun 12-6 D served Mon-Sat 6-9.30, Sun 7-9 Av main course £12 ⊕ FREE HOUSE ◀ Dark Star Hophead, Triple fff Alton's Pride, Guest ales ☼ Thatchers. ☻ 9 **Facilities** Children welcome Dogs allowed Beer festival Wi-fi

---

The Compton Arms
PLAN 2 F4

4 Compton Av, Off Canonbury Rd N1 2XD
☎ 020 7359 6883
e-mail: andard07@btinternet.com
dir: *Telephone for directions*

George Orwell was once a customer at this peaceful pub, 'a country pub in the city', on Islington's back streets. The late 17th-century building has a rural feel, and is frequented by a mix of locals, actors and musicians. One local described it as 'an island in a sea of gastro-pubs'. Expect real ales from the hand pump, and good value steaks, mixed grills, big breakfasts and Sunday roasts. The bar is busy when Arsenal are at home.

Open all day all wk Closed: 25 Dec pm ⊕ GREENE KING ◀ Greene King IPA, Abbot Ale, Guest ale. **Facilities** Dogs allowed Garden

Save on hotels. Book at **theAA.com/hotel**

LONDON 297 **ENGLAND**

The Crown PLAN 2 F4

116 Cloudesley Rd, Islington N1 0EB ☎ **020 7837 7107**
e-mail: crown.islington@fullers.co.uk
dir: *From tube station take Liverpool Rd, 6th left into Cloudesley Sq. Pub on opposite side of Square*

A lovely Grade II listed Georgian building in the Barnsbury village conservation area of Islington, this pub boasts one of only two remaining barrel bars in London. It has a shaded outdoor area for good weather and a roaring log fire for winter. The pub specialises in quality gastro-pub food, along with Fuller's beers. The daily changing menu offers mezze-style options such as houmous and flatbread or various platters to share, and main meals along the lines of fishcakes or steak and ale pie. Change of hands.

Open all day all wk Closed: 25 Dec ⊕ FULLER'S BREWERY ◄ Fuller's London Pride, Organic Honeydew, ESB, London Porter Ö Aspall. **Facilities** Children welcome Children's portions Dogs allowed Garden Wi-fi

PICK OF THE PUBS

The Drapers Arms ◉ ♀ PLAN 2 F4

44 Barnsbury St N1 1ER ☎ **020 7619 0348**
e-mail: nick@thedrapersarms.com
dir: *Turn right from Highbury & Islington station, 10 mins along Upper St. Barnsbury St on right opposite Shell service station*

Built by the Drapers' Company in the 1830s, Nick Gibson's handsome Islington pub serves its local real ale and cider drinkers well, with Harveys Sussex, Sambrook's Wandle (named after a South London river), Truman's Runner, plus Aspall and Westons Organic cider. Thought clearly goes into the menus too, as testified by pleasingly different, hearty starters like cullen skink; haggis fritters with gribiche sauce; and potted beef with pickled red cabbage. The kitchen approaches mains in the same way, with kedgeree; grilled quail with braised red cabbage and prunes; and lentils with roast squash, chanterelles and chive crème fraîche; while a typical dessert might be burnt fennel and orange custard. The downstairs open-plan bar is illuminated by large picture windows, its unfussy interior furnished with a mix of squashy sofas and solid wooden tables. For a quieter pint, try the peaceful garden (yes, even in London). August beer festival details are on the website.

Open all day all wk **Bar Meals** L served Mon-Sat 12-3, Sun 12-4 D served Mon-Sat 6-11, Sun 6.30-9.30 Av main course £13 **Restaurant** L served Mon-Sat 12-3, Sun 12-4 D served Mon-Sat 6-11, Sun 6.30-9.30 Av 3 course à la carte fr £22 ⊕ FREE HOUSE ◄ Harveys Sussex, Sambrook's Wandle, Truman's Runner Ö Aspall, Stowford Press, Westons Organic. ♀ 18 **Facilities** Children welcome Children's menu Children's portions Dogs allowed Garden Beer festival Wi-fi

PICK OF THE PUBS

The Duke of Cambridge ♀ PLAN 2 F4

30 Saint Peter's St N1 8JT
☎ **020 7359 3066** ▤ **020 7359 1877**
e-mail: duke@dukeorganic.co.uk
dir: *Telephone for directions*

A multiple award-winning organic gastro-pub, where obsession with achieving the lowest possible carbon footprint has reached new heights. Everything possible is re-used or recycled and even the electricity is wind and solar generated. Sustainable, ethically-produced ingredients are approved by the Soil Association and Marine Conservation Society, and items such as bread, ice cream and pickles are all made on site. Beers from local micro-breweries, real ciders such as Luscombe's, and organic wines go hand-in-hand with a remarkable menu that may change twice daily; the chefs are ever-ready to utilise the freshest seasonal produce. A summer choice could be gazpacho with mint salsa, followed by a rack of lamb with Jersey Royals, runner beans and salsa verde. The winter menu may offer pigeon breast wrapped in bacon with Brussels sprouts and chestnuts, followed by darne of gurnard with roast butternut squash. Even desserts are allied to the seasons – an apricot cheesecake for sunny days, or a warming and filling mincemeat and almond tart when it's cold outside.

Open all day all wk Closed: 24-26 & 31 Dec, 1 Jan **Bar Meals** L served Mon-Fri 12.30-3, Sat-Sun 12.30-3.30 D served Mon-Sat 6.30-10.30, Sun 6.30-10 Av main course £15 **Restaurant** L served Mon-Fri 12.30-3, Sat-Sun 12.30-3.30 D served Mon-Sat 6.30-10.30, Sun 6.30-10 booking required Av 3 course à la carte fr £29 ⊕ FREE HOUSE ◄ Pitfield SB Bitter & Eco Warrior, St Peter's Best Bitter, East Kent Golding, Shoreditch Stout Ö Westons, Dunkertons, Luscombe Draft. ♀ 12 **Facilities** Children welcome Children's portions Dogs allowed Wi-fi

The House ♀ PLAN 2 F4

63-69 Canonbury Rd N1 2DG
☎ **020 7704 7410** ▤ **020 7704 9388**
e-mail: info@inthehouse.biz
dir: *Telephone for directions*

This successful gastro-pub has featured in a celebrity cookbook and garnered plenty of praise since it opened its doors a few years ago. Situated in Islington's prestigious Canonbury district but moments away from the hustle and bustle of Upper Street, expect a thoroughly modern, seasonal British menu at lunch and dinner. A winter menu showcases starters such as slow braised potted rabbit and juniper with celeriac remoulade. The mains might be Barnsley chop with potato and mint gratin, or roast pumpkin risotto with stuffed Portobella mushroom and Blue Wensleydale.

Open all day 10-11 Closed: Mon L (ex BH) **Bar Meals** Av main course £14-£18 **Restaurant** L served Tue-Fri 12-3, Sat-Sun 10-4 D served Mon-Fri 6-10.30, Sat-Sun 6-10 ⊕ PUNCH TAVERNS ◄ Adnams, Guinness Ö Aspall. ♀ 8 **Facilities** Children welcome Dogs allowed Garden

N6

PICK OF THE PUBS

The Flask ♀ PLAN 2 E5

77 Highgate West Hill N6 6BU ☎ **020 8348 7346**
e-mail: theflaskhighgate@london-gastros.co.uk
web: www.theflaskhighgate.com
dir: *Nearest tube: Archway/Highgate*

Dating from 1663 and made famous by Byron, Keats, Hogarth and Betjeman, and also arguably by hard-drinking Sixties rock stars, this Grade II listed pub in leafy Highgate has become a London landmark. It retains much of its character and cosy atmosphere despite refurbishments. A network of small rooms is served by two bars, one of which houses the original sash windows. Fuller's, Butcombe and guest real ales ensure that the hand-pumps are constantly on the move; there are also two dozen Belgian and worldwide bottled ales and ciders, and some modestly priced wines. Starters include balsamic duck liver with bacon and chicory, and smoked haddock with Parmesan cream, while typical mains are ale-battered coley; stuffed salt marsh lamb saddle; and mixed squash, walnut and marjoram risotto. For dessert, try apple, quince and redcurrant crumble and custard, or forced rhubarb and Drambuie jelly with lavender ice cream. Large gazebo-like structures out front increase capacity, but it can still get very busy, especially at weekends.

Open all day all wk 12-11 (Sun 12-10.30) Closed: 25 Dec **Bar Meals** L served Mon-Fri 12-3, Sat-Sun 12-4 booking required D served Mon-Sat 6-10, Sun 6-9 booking required ⊕ FULLER'S ◄ Fuller's London Pride, ESB, Discovery, Butcombe Bitter, Guest ales Ö Aspall. ♀ 13 **Facilities** Children welcome Dogs allowed Garden Wi-fi

See advert on page 298

N19

The Landseer
PLAN 2 F5

37 Landseer Rd N19 4JU ☎ 020 7263 4658
e-mail: info@thelandseer.wanadoo.co.uk
dir: *Nearest tube stations: Archway & Tufnell Park*

Leather sofas, chunky farmhouse-style tables and much indoor greenery characterise this airy gastro-pub. This is an ideal spot to relax with the weekend papers, or while away an evening with one of the pub's extensive library of board games. Snack from the bar, brunch or Tapas menu, indulge in chargrilled meat or fish steaks, or claim a classic sea bass with braised fennel; Sunday roasts are a major draw here. In warmer weather, enjoy a meal or a drink on the spacious patio.

Open all day all wk noon-mdnt (Mon-Tue & Sun noon-11) Closed: 25 Dec, 1 Jan ⊕ FREE HOUSE ◀ Staropramen, Guest ales ♂ Brothers Pear Cider, Aspall.
Facilities Children welcome Children's portions Play area Dogs allowed Wi-fi

NW1

The Chapel ♀
PLAN 1 B4

48 Chapel St NW1 5DP
☎ 020 7402 9220 📠 020 7723 2337
e-mail: thechapel@btconnect.com
dir: *By A40 Marylebone Rd & Old Marylebone Rd junct. Off Edgware Rd by tube station*

This award-winning gastro-pub takes its name from its Chapel Street location. Bright and airy with stripped floors and pine furniture, the informal open-plan building enjoys one of the largest gardens in central London with seating for over 60 customers. Fresh produce is delivered daily, and served in starters like cauliflower, ham and saffron soup, and mains such as thyme and honey-glazed pan-fried duck breast with Parmesan polenta, or poached sea bass with petit pois bonne femme. A children's menu is also available.

Open all day all wk Closed: 25-26 Dec, 1 Jan, Etr **Bar Meals** Av main course £13 **Restaurant** L served Mon-Sat 12-2.30, Sun 12.30-3 D served all wk 7-10 Av 3 course à la carte fr £25 ⊕ GREENE KING ◀ Greene King IPA, St Edmunds ♂ Aspall. ♀ 15 **Facilities** Children welcome Children's menu Children's portions Dogs allowed Garden

PICK OF THE PUBS

The Engineer ♀
PLAN 2 E4

65 Gloucester Av, Primrose Hill NW1 8JH
☎ 020 7722 0950 📠 020 7483 0592
e-mail: info@the-engineer.com
dir: *Telephone for directions*

Situated in a residential part of Primrose Hill close to Camden Market, this unassuming street corner pub is worth seeking out. Built by Isambard Kingdom Brunel in 1841, it attracts a discerning dining crowd who relish its imaginative and well-prepared food and friendly, laid-back atmosphere. Inside it is fashionably rustic, with a spacious bar area, sturdy wooden tables with candles, simple decor and changing art exhibitions in the restaurant area. A walled, paved and heated garden to the rear is popular in fine weather. In addition to cosmopolitan beers, the drinks list includes hand-crafted teas, freshly ground coffees, around 130 quirky and/or bio-dynamic wines, and a variety of whiskies. A regularly-changing menu features an eclectic mix of inspired home-made dishes using organic and free-range products: warm smoked river farm mackerel with bacon and Jerusalem artichokes, honey and harissa-roasted root vegetables, and spiced poached pear, chocolate custard and straciatella ice cream give a flavour of what to expect.

Open all day all wk 9am-11pm (Sun & BH 9am-10.30pm) Closed: 24-28 Dec **Bar Meals** Av main course £14 food served all day **Restaurant** L served Mon-Fri 12-3, Sat-Sun 12.30-4 booking required D served Mon-Sat 6.30-11, Sun & BH 6.30-10.30 booking required Av 3 course à la carte fr £30 ⊕ MITCHELLS & BUTLER ◀ Erdinger, Bombardier, Staropramen, St Peters ♂ Addlestones. ♀ 19 **Facilities** Children welcome Children's menu Children's portions Family room Dogs allowed Garden Wi-fi

The Globe ♀
PLAN 1 B4

43-47 Marylebone Rd NW1 5JY
☎ 020 7935 6368 📠 020 7224 0154
e-mail: globe.1018@thespiritgroup.com
dir: *At corner of Marylebone Rd & Baker St, opposite Baker St tube station*

Built in 1735, the same year as the neighbouring Nash terraces, the pub retains much of its period charm, including William, the ghost of a former landlord. The first omnibus service from Holborn stopped here and the Metropolitan line was constructed under the road a few feet from the tavern. Many famous and infamous characters have been patrons here including Charles Dickens. A good choice of real ales is offered alongside freshly cooked British pub food, such as toasted sandwiches, burgers, steaks, Whitby breaded scampi, rib of beef and pies. Roast of the day comes in two sizes.

Open all day all wk 10am-11pm (Fri-Sat 10am-11.30pm, Sun noon-10.30) Closed: 25 Dec **Bar Meals** L served Mon-Sat 10-10 D served Sun 12-9.30 Av main course £8.50 food served all day **Restaurant** food served all day ⊕ PUNCH PUB COMPANY ◀ Abbot, Bombardier, Young's, IPA, Old Speckled Hen, occasional guest ales. ♀ 13 **Facilities** Children welcome Wi-fi

---

The Flask

77 Highgate West Hill, City of London N6 6BU   Tel: 020 8348 7346
www.theflaskhighgate.com   Email: theflaskhighgate@london-gastros.co.uk

The Flask is a Grade 2 listed building dating from 1663 made famous by ghostly tales, legendary deeds and the heavy drinking of '60's rock stars. A modern British gastro menu & exceptional table service has again made *The Flask* one of the best venues in North London.

Byron, Shelley & Keats are among the famous Romantic writers reputed to have used the pub as a watering hole when visiting opium-addled Coleridge, who spent his last 18 years in the house opposite.

Satirist William Hogarth was a Flask patron and is said to have sketched a fight between two customers as they smashed each other with tankards. His portrait now sits in the old cellar room.

The Flask is located between Highgate Cemetery, resting place of Karl Marx and Douglas Adams, and Hampstead Heath, which contains one of the highest points in London offering views across the City.

PICK OF THE PUBS

The Lansdowne   PLAN 2 E4

90 Gloucester Av, Primrose Hill NW1 8HX
☎ 020 7483 0409
e-mail: info@thelansdownepub.co.uk
dir: Turn right from Chalk Farm tube station into Adelaide Rd, 1st left into Bridge Approach (on foot). Into Gloucester Ave, 500yds. Pub on corner

In 1992, Amanda Pritchett started The Lansdowne as one of the earliest dining pubs in Primrose Hill. Stripping the pub of its fruit machines, TVs and jukebox, she brought in solid wood furniture and back-to-basics decor; today, it blends a light, spacious bar and outdoor seating area with a slightly more formal upper dining room. All that apart, however, its success depends on the quality of its cooking. All food is freshly prepared on the premises, using organic or free-range ingredients wherever possible, and portions are invariably generous. The seasonal menu offers spiced red lentil soup with Greek yoghurt; home-cured bresaola with rocket, capers and Parmesan; pan-fried sardines on toast with watercress; confit pork belly with prunes, potatoes and lardons; poached sea trout with crushed herb potatoes; polenta with roast pumpkin, buffalo mozzarella and walnut.

Open all day all wk noon-11 (Sat 10-11 Sun 10am-10.30pm) Bar Meals L served Mon-Fri 12-10, Sat 12.30-10, Sun 12.30-9.30 food served all day Restaurant L served Tue-Sun 12-3 D served Tue-Sat 6-10, Sun 6-9.30 ⊕ FREE HOUSE ◄ Bombardier, Trumans ○ Aspall. Facilities Children welcome Dogs allowed

The Prince Albert ▼   PLAN 2 F4

163 Royal College St NW1 0SG
☎ 020 7485 0270   📠 020 7713 5994
e-mail: info@princealbertcamden.com
dir: From Camden tube station follow Camden Rd. Right onto Royal College St, 200mtrs on right

Standing solidly behind the picnic tables in its small, paved courtyard, The Prince Albert's welcoming interior features polished wooden floors and bentwood furniture. Twenty wines by the glass team with Adnams Broadside and Black Sheep bitters at the bar, whilst menu choices include crispy duck and five spice salad or sardines with rose harissa and couscous; followed by devilled lambs' kidneys and chorizo on toast, salmon fishcakes, and chargrilled 35-day aged rump steak. Two or three times a year the pub holds a three-day real ale festival.

Open all day all wk noon-11 (Sun 12.30-10.30) Closed: 25-30 Dec Bar Meals L served Mon-Sat 12-3, Sun 12.30-6 booking required D served Mon-Sat 6-10 booking required Av main course £13 Restaurant L served Mon-Sat 12-3, Sun 12.30-6 booking required D served Mon-Sat 6-10 booking required Fixed menu price fr £9.95 Av 3 course à la carte fr £25 ⊕ FREE HOUSE ◄ Black Sheep, Adnams Broadside, Hoegaarden, Staropramen, Kirin Ichiban ○ Brothers. ▼ 20 Facilities Children welcome Children's menu Children's portions Dogs allowed Garden Beer festival Wi-fi

The Queens ▼   PLAN 2 E4

49 Regents Park Rd, Primrose Hill NW1 8XD
☎ 020 7586 0408
e-mail: queens@youngs.co.uk
dir: Nearest tube - Chalk Farm

There's a traditional British menu at this cosy Victorian pub overlooking Primrose Hill, now in new hands. Located in one of London's most affluent and personality-studded areas, The Queens is steeped in celebrity history and is mentioned in many stars' autobiographies. The bar menu offers a range of sandwiches, supported by hot dishes like sausages, mash and onion gravy, and cod and chips in ale batter. Grab a seat on the terraced seating outdoors in good weather. An annual beer festival coincides with British Food Fortnight.

Open all day all wk 11-11 (Sun noon-10.30) Bar Meals L served Mon-Fri 12-3, Sat 12-10, Sun 12-8 D served Mon-Fri 6-10 Av main course £12.50 Restaurant L served Mon-Fri 12-3, Sat 12-10, Sun 12-8 D served Mon-Fri 6-10, Sat 12-10, Sun 12-8 booking required ⊕ YOUNG'S & CO ◄ Young's Bitter & Special, Bombardier, Guest ales. ▼ 20 Facilities Children welcome Children's portions Dogs allowed Beer festival Wi-fi

NW3

The Holly Bush ▼   PLAN 2 E4

Holly Mount, Hampstead NW3 6SG
☎ 020 7435 2892   📠 020 7431 2292
e-mail: hollybush@fullers.co.uk
dir: Nearest tube: Hampstead. Exit tube station onto Holly Hill, 1st right

The Holly Bush was once the home of English portraitist George Romney and became a pub after his death in 1802. The building has been investigated by 'ghost busters', but more tangible 21st-century media celebrities are easier to spot. Depending on your appetite, the menu offers 'to share' and snacks – a pint of King prawns, Cropwell Bishop and beetroot croquettes with candied walnuts, and Cumberland Scotch egg with onion jam. Main dishes might include corn fed chicken breast, clams, rouille, Savoy cabbage, bacon and fennel shoots, or fish pie with champ. There has been a change of hands.

Open all day all wk noon-11 (Sun noon-10.30) Bar Meals Av main course £12 ⊕ FULLER'S ◄ Harveys Sussex Best, Fuller's London Pride, Butcombe, ESB ○ Aspall. ▼ 10 Facilities Children welcome Children's portions Dogs allowed Beer festival Wi-fi

NW5

Dartmouth Arms ▼   PLAN 2 E5

35 York Rise NW5 1SP ☎ 020 7485 3267
e-mail: dartmoutharms@faucetinn.com
dir: 5 min walk from Hampstead Heath, 2 mins from Tufnell Park underground station

Open for breakfast from 10am at weekends, this welcoming local close to Hampstead Heath will happily serve you a Virgin Mary (a Bloody Mary without the vodka) along with your Bridge Farm organic pork and Westerham Ale sausages. Quiz nights every Tuesday are perhaps a better time to sample ales by Adnams and Fuller's, and there's a good choice of real ciders too. Sustenance takes the form of door-step sandwiches; sharing boards; plates of deep-filled cottage pie; and English-style tapas such as pig's cheek fritters with apricot chilli jam.

Open all day all wk 11-11 (Fri 11am-mdnt, Sat 10am-mdnt, Sun 10am-10.30pm) Bar Meals L served Mon-Fri 12-10, Sat-Sun 10-10 D served Mon-Fri 12-10, Sat-Sun 10-10 Av main course £9.50 food served all day Restaurant L served Mon-Fri 12-10, Sat-Sun 10-10 D served Mon-Fri 12-10, Sat-Sun 10-10 food served all day ⊕ FREE HOUSE ◄ Adnams, Fuller's London Pride, Titanic Stout ○ Westons, Dunkertons, Brook Farm. ▼ 10 Facilities Children welcome Children's portions Dogs allowed Wi-fi

PICK OF THE PUBS

The Junction Tavern ▼   PLAN 2 E4

101 Fortess Rd NW5 1AG
☎ 020 7485 9400   📠 020 7485 9401
dir: Between Kentish Town & Tufnell Park tube stations

Halfway between Kentish Town and Tufnell Park underground stations, this friendly local is handy for Camden and the green spaces of Parliament Hill and Hampstead Heath. The pub specialises in real ales, with five real ale pumps on the bar – Sambrook's Wandle included. Regular beer festivals celebrate the amber liquid, when enthusiasts in the conservatory or large heated garden choose from a range of up to 50 beers hooked to a cooling system and served straight from the cask. The seasonal menus change daily to offer interesting choices from brunch to dinner. Daytime options include toad-in-the-hole; linguine with chilli, garlic, parsley, rocket and Parmesan; and a char-grilled cheeseburger with hand-cut chips. In the evening, you could try caramelised onion and goat's cheese tart with walnut pesto followed by roast pork fillet, potato rösti, Swiss chard, black pudding and apple sauce. Finish with apple crumble or lemon polenta cake.

Open all day all wk noon-11 (Sun noon-10.30) Closed: 24-26 Dec, 1 Jan Bar Meals L served Mon-Fri 12-3, Sat-Sun 12-4 D served Mon-Sat 6.30-10.30, Sun 6.30-9.30 Restaurant L served Mon-Fri 12-3, Sat-Sun 12-4 booking required D served Mon-Sat 6.30-10.30, Sun 6.30-9.30 booking required Fixed menu price fr £16 Av 3 course à la carte fr £25 ⊕ ENTERPRISE INNS ◄ Sambrook's Wandle Ale, Guest ales ○ Westons Organic. ▼ 13 Facilities Dogs allowed Garden Beer festival Wi-fi

NW5 *continued*

The Lord Palmerston PLAN 2 E5

33 Dartmouth Park Hill NW5 1HU ☎ 020 7485 1578
e-mail: lordpalmerston@geronimo-inns.co.uk
dir: *From Tufnell Park Station turn right. Up Dartmouth Park Hill. Pub on right, on corner of Chetwynd Rd*

Stylishly revamped London pub in the Dartmouth Park conservation area. It has two open fires in winter and fully opening windows in summer, plus a large front terrace and rear garden for dining. Food is taken seriously, with dishes ranging from crisp fried salt and pepper squid, with tomato and sweet chilli salsa, to a dry-aged British rib eye steak, with asparagus flan, hand cut chips and 'maitre d'hotel' butter. Saturday brunch is served from noon until 4pm, when the fish finger baguette and pea purée may prove too tempting. Recent change of hands.

Open all day all wk 12-11 (Sun 12-10.30) ⊕ GERONIMO INNS LTD ◀ Adnams Best, Bombardier, Sharp's Doom Bar, Twickenham Naked Ladies Ö Aspall.
Facilities Children welcome Dogs allowed Garden

NW6

The Salusbury Pub and Dining Room 🍷 PLAN 2 D4

50-52 Salusbury Rd NW6 6NN ☎ 020 7328 3286
e-mail: thesalusburypub@btconnect.com
dir: *100mtrs left from Queens Park tube & train station*

A recently refurbished gastro-pub with a lively and vibrant atmosphere, offering a London restaurant-style menu without the associated prices. The award-winning wine list boasts more than a hundred wines including mature offerings from the cellar. The owners are appreciated by a strong local following for continuity of quality and service. Example dishes are roast sea bream with Roman artichokes, leg of duck confit with lentils and cotechino, and Angus rib-eye steak.

Open all day noon-11 (Thu-Sat noon-mdnt, Sun noon-10.30) Closed: 25-26 Dec, Mon L (Ex BHs)
Bar Meals L served Mon-Fri 12.30-3, Sat-Sun 12.30-3.30 D served 7-10.15 **Restaurant** L served Mon-Fri 12.30-3, Sat-Sun 12.30-3.30 D served 7-10.15 ⊕ FREE HOUSE ◀ Broadside, Bitburger, Guinness, Staropramen Ö Aspall. 🍷 13 **Facilities** Children welcome Family room Dogs allowed

NW8

The New Inn ★★★ INN 🍷 PLAN 2 E4
NEW

2 Allitsen Rd, St John's Wood NW8 6LA
☎ 020 7722 0726 📠 020 7722 0653
e-mail: thenewinn@gmail.com
dir: *Off A41 by St John's Wood tube station onto Acacia Rd, last right, to end on corner*

Guests staying overnight in the well-appointed rooms at this convivial Regency inn are well-placed for nearby Regent's Park, Lords (hence the background cricketing theme) and bustling Camden Lock and Market.

Voluminous flower baskets and troughs break the lines of this traditional street-corner local, where pavement tables are a popular retreat for locals supping Abbot Ale and diners indulging in some of the huge array of Thai meals (how does a roasted duck fancy sound?), offset by a solid, dependable English pub food selection. Live music at weekends.

Open all day all wk **Bar Meals** L served all wk 12-3 D served all wk 6-10 Av main course £7.75 ⊕ GREENE KING ◀ Abbot Ale, IPA. 🍷 14 **Facilities** Children welcome Children's portions Wi-fi **Rooms** 5

PICK OF THE PUBS

The Salt House 🍷 PLAN 2 E4

63 Abbey Rd, St John's Wood NW8 0AE
☎ 020 7328 6626
e-mail: salthousemail@majol.co.uk
dir: *Turn right outside St John's Wood tube. Left onto Marlborough Place, right onto Abbey Rd, pub on left*

Describing itself as a mere scuttle from The Beatles' famous Abbey Road zebra crossing, this 18th-century inn promises a two-fold commitment to good food: to source excellent ingredients and to home cook them. With the exception of the odd bottle of ketchup, everything – including bread, buns and pasta – is made on site. Meats are accredited by the Rare Breed Survival Trust, and most fish served has been caught by Andy in Looe. Representative starters are Thai-style fishcake with lemon aïoli, and pork pâté, with apple jelly and toast. Main courses include comfort dishes such as beer-battered fish and chips with pea purée, and pork and leek sausages with mustard mash. Warm pear and almond tart with Chantilly cream is a nice finish, or look to the cheeseboard for three varieties served with grapes, crackers and home-made chutney. A function room can be hired for larger parties, while outside heaters allow for alfresco dining even when the weather is inclement.

Open all day all wk 12-11 (Sat 12-12) **Bar Meals** food served all day ⊕ GREENE KING ◀ Abbot Ale, Guinness Ö Aspall. 🍷 14 **Facilities** Children welcome Family room Dogs allowed

NW10

William IV Bar & Restaurant PLAN 2 D4

786 Harrow Rd NW10 5JX
☎ 020 8969 5944 📠 020 8964 9218
e-mail: info@williamivlondon.com
dir: *Nearest tube: Kensal Green*

Character is everywhere in this large, rambling gastro-pub, happily co-existing with cosmopolitan Kensal Green's cafés, delis and antique shops. Music plays in the bar, but you can always chill out in the sofa area. Classic and modern European food is represented by duck breast with pickled cabbage, bok choi and anise jus; baked cod, chorizo and potato cake, green beans and sweet wine dressing; and courgette parcel stuffed with wild rice, and saffron cream sauce.

Open all day all wk 12-11 (Fri-Sun noon-1am)
Restaurant food served all day ⊕ FREE HOUSE ◀ Fuller's London Pride, IPA, Speckled Hen, Guest ales Ö Aspall.
Facilities Children welcome Children's menu Children's portions Dogs allowed Garden Beer festival Wi-fi

SE1

PICK OF THE PUBS

The Anchor & Hope ◎◎ PLAN 1 E3

36 The Cut SE1 8LP
☎ 020 7928 9898 📠 020 7928 4595
e-mail: anchorandhope@btconnect.com
dir: *Nearest tube: Southwark & Waterloo*

Now approaching its tenth anniversary and still very busy, this gastro-pub has picked up a long list of accolades. But it remains a down-to-earth and lively place with a big bar; children, parents, and dogs with owners are all welcome. In fine weather, pavement seating allows you to watch the world go by as you enjoy a pint of Young's. The wine list is notable for its straightforward pricing approach; many half bottles can be bought for half the cost of full ones – a factor much appreciated by the pub's faithful diners. The short menu, too, is refreshingly unembroidered, and may change twice daily according to demand. A heavy curtain separates the bar from the dining area which has an open kitchen. Expect robust, gutsy dishes along the lines of deep-fried calf's brain with radishes and gribiche; salt cod brandade; Spanish-style tripe and chips; or a brace of Orkney kippers. You could finish with a grappa pannacotta with Yorkshire rhubarb.

Open all day Closed: BH, Xmas, New Year, Sun eve, Mon L **Bar Meals** L served Tue-Sat 12-2.30, Sun 2pm fixed time D served Mon-Sat 6-10.30 Av main course £14 **Restaurant** Fixed menu price fr £30 Av 3 course à la carte fr £23 ⊕ FREE HOUSE ◀ Bombardier, Young's Ordinary, IPA, Erdinger, Kirin. **Facilities** Children welcome Dogs allowed

The Bridge House Bar & Dining Rooms 🍷 PLAN 1 G3

218 Tower Bridge Rd SE1 2UP
☎ 020 7407 5818 📠 020 7407 5828
e-mail: the-bridgehouse@tiscali.co.uk
dir: *5 min walk from London Bridge/Tower Hill tube stations*

There are great views of the Thames, the Gherkin and the ever-changing City skyline from this, the nearest pub to Tower Bridge. It comprises a bar, dining room and café, plus facilities for private functions. A range of Adnams and guest ales are accompanied by meals produced from ingredients bought at the local markets. Typical dishes include traditional shepherd's pie with cheesy mash; grilled sea bass with spinach; and confit lamb chump with Swiss chard and oyster mushrooms.

Save on hotels. Book at theAA.com/hotel

LONDON 301 ENGLAND

Open all day all wk Closed: 25-26 Dec **Bar Meals** L served all wk 12-4 D served all wk 5.30-10.30 Av main course £10 **Restaurant** L served all wk 12-4 D served all wk 5.30-10.30 Fixed menu price fr £5.50 Av 3 course à la carte fr £20 ⊕ ADNAMS ◄ Adnams Best Bitter, Adnams Broadside, Adnams Explorer, guest ale. ♀ 32
Facilities Children welcome Children's menu Children's portions Family room Wi-fi

PICK OF THE PUBS

The Fire Station ♀   PLAN 1 E3

150 Waterloo Rd SE1 8SB ☎ 020 7620 2226
e-mail: info@thefirestationwaterloo.com
dir: *Turn right at exit 2 of Waterloo Station*

Close to Waterloo, and handy for the Old Vic Theatre and Imperial War Museum, this remarkable conversion of an early-Edwardian fire station has kept many of its former trappings intact. The rear dining room faces the open kitchen, and there are bar snacks and light bites, lunch, pre-theatre, plates to share and restaurant menus. Take your pick from perhaps rabbit and grain mustard pâté, smoked eel with celeriac or devilled whitebait to start, then tagliatelle with sorrel, wild garlic leaf and courgette; salmi of wood pigeon, grilled crusts, chopped liver, parsley and lemon; pie of the day; or roast salmon fillet with dill potatoes and hollandaise. The handy location means it can get very busy, but the friendly staff cover the ground with impressive speed.

Open all day all wk 9am-mdnt (Sun 11am-11pm) Closed: 25-26 Dec, 1 Jan **Bar Meals** L served Mon-Sat 9am-11pm, Sun 11am-10pm D served Mon-Sat 9am-11pm, Sun 10am-11pm Av main course £9 food served all day **Restaurant** L served all wk 12-3 D served all wk 5-10.45 Fixed menu price fr £12.50 Av 3 course à la carte fr £22 ⊕ MARSTONS ◄ Fuller's London Pride, Ringwood, Marston's EPA. ♀ 32
Facilities Children welcome Children's portions Wi-fi

PICK OF THE PUBS

The Garrison ♀   PLAN 1 G2

99-101 Bermondsey St SE1 3XB
☎ 020 7089 9355 📄 020 7407 1084
e-mail: info@thegarrison.co.uk
dir: *From London Bridge tube station, E towards Tower Bridge 200mtrs, right onto Bermondsey St. Pub in 100mtrs*

Transformed a few years ago from a typical 'Sarf London' boozer, this busy, friendly neighbourhood gastro-pub may still look rather ordinary from the outside, but the cleverly restyled interior, with its delightful hotch-potch of decorative themes, has a French brasserie flavour. Antique odds and ends, including mismatched chairs and tables, add to the quirky charm. The place bounces with life from breakfast through to dinner and beyond, when the downstairs room doubles as a mini-cinema. Breakfast could be a croissant, porridge or a full cooked English; for lunch, maybe potted shrimp then pumpkin,

courgette and chickpea tagine; in the evening, try smoked ham hock and parsley terrine followed by pan-roasted venison pavé with courgette and potato rösti, caramelised onions and peppercorn sauce. On the side are dauphinoise potatoes, hand-cut chips, and various salads. Drinks include real ales from Adnams, Breton cider and a good few wines by the glass.

Open all day all wk 8am-11pm (Fri 8am-mdnt, Sat 9am-mdnt, Sun 9am-10.30pm) Closed: 25-26 Dec **Bar Meals** L served Mon-Fri 12-3, Sat-Sun 12.30-4 booking required D served Mon-Sat 6-10, Sun 6-9.30 booking required Av main course £14.50 **Restaurant** L served Mon-Fri 12-3, Sat-Sun 12.30-4 booking required D served Mon-Sat 6-10, Sun 6-9.30 booking required Fixed menu price fr £22.50 Av 3 course à la carte fr £22.50 ⊕ FREE HOUSE ◄ Adnams, Franziskaner, Staropramen ♻ Thatchers Pear Cider, Cidre Breton. ♀ 17 **Facilities** Wi-fi

The George Inn   PLAN 1 F3

77 Borough High St SE1 1NH
☎ 020 7407 2056 📄 020 7403 6956
e-mail: 7781@greeneking.co.uk
dir: *From London Bridge tube station, take Borough High St exit, left. Pub 200yds on left*

The only remaining galleried inn in London and now administered by the National Trust. This striking 17th-century black and white is mentioned by Dickens in *Little Dorrit* - his original life assurance policy is displayed along with 18th-century rat traps. The honestly-priced pub grub includes hot and cold sandwiches, salads and dishes like herbed crusted chicken with Puy lentils and Savoy cabbage; smoked salmon, Somerset Brie and chive fishcakes; and vegetable moussaka.

Open all day all wk 11-11 (Sun noon-10.30) Closed: 25-26 Dec **Bar Meals** L served Mon-Sun 12-9 food served all day **Restaurant** D served Mon-Sat 5-9 booking required ⊕ GREENE KING ◄ Greene King Abbot Ale, George Inn Ale, IPA, Old Speckled Hen, Royal London, Guest ale ♻ Aspall. **Facilities** Children welcome Garden Wi-fi

The Market Porter   PLAN 1 F3

9 Stoney St, Borough Market, London Bridge SE1 9AA
☎ 020 7407 2495 📄 020 7403 7697
dir: *Close to London Bridge Station*

Situated in the middle of bustling Borough Market, this traditional tavern is friendly and always bustling. You will find rustic wooden floors and traditional decor after a recent refurbishment. The pub was used as a location in *Lock, Stock and Two Smoking Barrels* and *Only Fools and Horses*. The exceptional choice of real ales is the draw here with beers changing many times a day. It is matched by a menu that includes sandwiches, bar snacks, bangers and mash, fish and chips and specials like baked chicken fillet with cep sauce and creamed cabbage mash. Early morning opening.

Open all day all wk ⊕ FREE HOUSE ◄ Harveys Best, wide selection of international ales.

SE5

The Sun and Doves ♀   PLAN 2 F3

61-63 Coldharbour Ln, Camberwell SE5 9NS
☎ 020 7733 1525
e-mail: mail@sunanddoves.co.uk
dir: *On corner of Caldecot Rd & Coldharbour Ln*

Recognized for food, drink and art, this attractive Camberwell venue mixes private views with wine tastings, jazz, film and music evenings. As London pubs go, it has a decent sized garden, planted in Mediterranean style, plus a paved patio where you can enjoy a pint or a choice of cocktails. The menu at this community pub is stylishly simple, with great brunches all weekend and wonderful Sunday roasts representing excellent value. Other choices range from toasted triple deck sandwiches to duck leg confit with cannellini bean stew or Franconian Sausage Company sausages, mash and onion gravy. There are interesting bar nibbles and all food can be take away.

Open all day all wk Closed: 25-26 Dec **Bar Meals** Av main course £8.50 food served all day **Restaurant** food served all day ◄ Old Speckled Hen, Adnams Broadside, Wandle, Adnams Ale ♻ Hogans Draught. ♀ 8 **Facilities** Children welcome Children's portions Dogs allowed Garden Wi-fi

SE10

The Cutty Sark Tavern ♀   PLAN 2 G3

4-6 Ballast Quay, Greenwich SE10 9PD
☎ 020 8858 3146
dir: *Nearest tube: Greenwich. From Cutty Sark ship follow river towards Millennium Dome (10 min walk)*

There's been a tavern on Ballast Quay for hundreds of years. The current building dates back to the early 1800s when it was called the Union Tavern. It was renamed when the world famous tea-clipper was dry-docked upriver in 1954. Inside there are low beams, creaking floorboards, dark panelling and, from the large bow window in the upstairs bar, commanding views of the Thames, Canary Wharf and the Millennium Dome. Well kept beers, wines by the glass and a wide selection of malts are all available, along with a choice of light bites, salads, classics like poacher's chicken, steak and ale pie and Hawaiian burger, as well as vegetarian and fish dishes, and a children's menu. Busy at weekends, especially on fine days.

Open all day all wk **Bar Meals** L served all wk 12-9 D served all wk 12-9 Av main course £9.95 food served all day **Restaurant** L served all wk 12-9 D served all wk 12-9 food served all day ⊕ FREE HOUSE ◄ Fuller's London Pride, Seafarers, Butcombe. ♀ 8
Facilities Children welcome Children's menu Children's portions Dogs allowed Garden

PICK OF THE PUBS

North Pole Bar & Restaurant ♟

131 Greenwich High Rd,
Greenwich SE10 8JA
☎ 020 8853 3020   📄 020 8853 3501
e-mail: natalie@northpolegreenwich.com
web: www.northpolegreenwich.com
dir: *From Greenwich rail station turn right, pass Novotel. Pub on right (2 min walk)*

Built in 1849, the pub's name originated with the Victorian obsession for polar exploration. The building was converted in 1998 to the stylish venue that it is today, offering a complete night out under one roof. Guests might begin their evening with a signature cocktail in the bar, then climb the spiral staircase to the stylish Piano Restaurant, where the resident pianist tinkles away on the ivories in the evenings from Thursday to Sunday. If at this point you happen to look up and see goldfish swimming around in the chandeliers, don't worry: they are real, and nothing to do with the cocktail you enjoyed earlier. In the basement you'll find the South Pole club, where you can dance until 2am. Completing the picture is a terrace, which makes an ideal spot for a glass of Pimms on a summer's evening.

An extensive bar menu is available daily from noon until 10pm. Choices include light bites, loosely defined as tapas — Chinese chicken satay with hoi sin sauce; Thai battered prawns with sweet chilli sauce; and houmous, tzatziki and baba

ghanoush dips with pitta bread are some examples. A selection of salads, wraps and baguettes also cater for smaller appetites. From the main menu, the North Pole burger is home made and served with chips and salad; other comfort dishes are fresh tagliatelle; steak and ale pie; and a half-pound sirloin steak. For the sweet tooth, one of half a dozen desserts will hit the spot: lemon and lime tart with fresh raspberries; a dark chocolate cheesecake; or a baklava in filo pastry with mixed nuts, dried fruit and vanilla syrup. Sundays bring roast dinners in the restaurant and live jazz, funk and Latin music downstairs — sophisticated tastes but children are nonetheless welcome. The bar features popular international beers such as Staropramen and Peroni.

Open all day all wk noon–2am
Bar Meals L served all wk 12–10 D served all wk 12–10 Av main course £6
Restaurant L served Sat–Sun 12–5 D served all wk 6–10.30 booking required Fixed menu price fr £16.95 Av 3 course à la carte fr £19.95 food served all day ⊕ FREE HOUSE ◀ Guinness, IPA, Staropramen, Peroni ♂ Aspall. ♟ 9
Facilities Children's menu Children's portions Dogs allowed Garden Wi-fi

Save on hotels. Book at **theAA.com/hotel**

LONDON 303 **ENGLAND**

SE10 *continued*

PICK OF THE PUBS

Greenwich Union Pub   PLAN 2 G3

56 Royal Hill SE10 8RT ☎ 020 8692 6258
e-mail: theunion@meantimebrewing.com
dir: *From Greenwich DLR & main station exit by main ticket hall, turn left, 2nd right into Royal Hill. Pub 100yds on right*

In the heart of Greenwich's bustling Royal Hill, this welcoming pub is a beer-drinker's idea of heaven. Comfortable leather sofas and flagstone floors help to keep the original character of this refurbished pub intact. Interesting beers from the award-winning Meantime Brewing Co, lagers and even freshly squeezed orange juice, along with a beer garden, make this a popular spot. The food is an eclectic range of traditional and modern dishes drawn from around the world. Everything is freshly prepared and sourced locally where possible; for example the fish comes straight from Billingsgate Market. The menu might include home-made pork and apple burger with chips and apple sauce, or pan-fried hake supreme with squid and black ink risotto. Try tempting bar snacks such as fish fingers with tartare sauce or a British cheese board. Round things off with bread pudding and chocolate ice cream.

Open all day all wk noon-11 (Sun noon-10.30)
Bar Meals Av main course £11 food served all day
Restaurant food served all day ⊕ FREE HOUSE
◀ Helles, Kolher, Wheat Stout, London Pale Ale
ᵔ Aspall, Thatchers. **Facilities** Children welcome Dogs allowed Garden

PICK OF THE PUBS

North Pole Bar & Restaurant ♀   PLAN 2 G3

See Pick of the Pubs on opposite page

SE21

The Crown & Greyhound ♀   PLAN 2 F2

73 Dulwich Village SE21 7BJ ☎ 020 8299 4976
dir: *Nearest train: North Dulwich*

With a tradition of service and hospitality reaching back to the 18th century, The Crown and Greyhound (nicknamed The Dog) counts Charles Dickens and John Ruskin amongst its celebrated patrons. In the olden days, the pub was split in two - The Crown served the gentry while The Greyhound housed the labourers. Modern day customers will find three bars and a restaurant in the heart of peaceful Dulwich Village. The weekly-changing menu might feature bean cassoulet with couscous, or an 8oz Angus burger with Cheddar cheese and potato wedges. There are daily salads, pasta and fish dishes, too.

Open all day all wk 11-11 (Thu-Sat 11am-mdnt Sun 11-10.30) **Bar Meals** Av main course £7.95 food served all day **Restaurant** Fixed menu price fr £9.99 food served all day ⊕ MITCHELLS & BUTLERS ◀ Fuller's London Pride, Harveys Sussex Best, Sharp's Doom Bar, Guest ales ᵔ Aspall, Thistley Cross. ♀ 15 **Facilities** Children welcome Children's menu Children's portions Family room Dogs allowed Garden

SE22

PICK OF THE PUBS

Franklins ⊛ ♀   PLAN 2 F2

157 Lordship Ln, Dulwich SE22 8HX ☎ 020 8299 9598
e-mail: info@franklinsrestaurant.com
dir: *0.5m S from East Dulwich station along Dog Kennel Hill & Lordship Lane*

Since 1999 this neighbourhood pub has built up a reputation as a reliable local restaurant that also happens to serve a good selection of real ales, ciders and lagers. Internal surfaces are stripped back and exposed, and the furnishings are smart, although the bar retains a more traditional appearance. Meats are rare breeds from farms in southern England and include Gloucester Old Spot pigs, Red Poll cattle and Oxford Down lambs; fish and shellfish are sourced from sustainable British stocks; game is from Yorkshire and the Scottish Highlands; vegetables are Kent grown; and the water, for those who avoid London tap, is bottled in the Garden of England. Start with pickled pigeon, beetroots and watercress, or soused herring, cucumber and yoghurt. Main courses include whole rainbow trout, clams and fennel; rabbit, white beans, carrots, turnips and cider; and spinach, wild mushroom, spring onion and St Tola (Irish organic goat's cheese) pasty.

Open all day all wk Closed: 25-26 & 31 Dec, 1 Jan
Bar Meals Av main course £15 food served all day
Restaurant Fixed menu price fr £13.95 Av 3 course à la carte fr £16.95 food served all day ⊕ FREE HOUSE
◀ Harveys, Guinness, Meantime Pale Ale, Shepherd Neame's Orginal Porter, Harveys ᵔ Westons, Aspall, Biddenden. ♀ 13 **Facilities** Children welcome Children's portions Dogs allowed Wi-fi

The Palmerston ⊛ ♀ NEW   PLAN 2 F2

91 Lordship Ln, East Dulwich SE22 8EP
☎ 020 8693 1629 ▤ 020 8693 9662
e-mail: info@thepalmerston.net
dir: *2m from Clapham, 0.5m from Dulwich Village, 10min walk from East Dulwich station*

A striking gastro-pub, heavy on the wood panelling, with much stripped floorboard and some great floor tiling. Occasional installations of photographic exhibitions add to the flair of this corner-plot destination dining pub in leafy Dulwich. Chef Jamie Younger's one AA Rosette results from his modern British menu with a Mediterranean twist; witness the mussel, bacon, dill and saffron chowder, offsetting roast rump of Dedham Vale lamb. Affable locals pop in for some flavoursome beers, too, from the likes of Sharp's and Harveys.

Open all day all wk **Bar Meals** L served Mon-Fri 12-2.30, Sat-Sun 12-3.30 booking required D served Mon-Sat 7-10, Sun 7-9.30 booking required Av main course £14 **Restaurant** L served Mon-Fri 12-2.30, Sat-Sun 12-3.30 booking required D served Mon-Sat 7-10, Sun 7-9.30 booking required Fixed menu price fr £12.50 Av 3 course à la carte fr £26 ⊕ ENTERPRISE INNS ◀ Sharp's Doom Bar, Harveys ᵔ Stowford Press. ♀ 16 **Facilities** Children welcome Children's portions

SE23

The Dartmouth Arms   PLAN 2 G2

7 Dartmouth Rd, Forest Hill SE23 3HN
☎ 020 8488 3117
e-mail: mail@thedartmoutharms.com
dir: *800mtrs from Horniman Museum on South Circular Rd*

The long-vanished Croydon Canal once ran behind this transformed old pub, and you can still see the towpath railings at the bottom of the car park. Smart bars serve snacks, traditional real ales, continental lagers, cocktails, coffees and teas, while the restaurant might offer devilled ox kidneys with black pudding or smoked haddock tart for starters, and mains might be pork belly with cannellini beans or scallops with cauliflower purée and crispy pancetta.

Open all wk Closed: 25-26 Dec, 1 Jan ⊕ ENTERPRISE INNS ◀ Fuller's London Pride, Timothy Taylor Landlord, Adnams Broadside. **Facilities** Children welcome Garden Parking Wi-fi

SW1

The Buckingham Arms   PLAN 1 D2

62 Petty France SW1H 9EU ☎ 020 7222 3386
e-mail: buckinghamarms@youngs.co.uk
dir: *Nearest tube: St James's Park*

Known as the Black Horse until 1903, this elegant, Young's pub is situated close to Buckingham Palace. Retaining its old charm, this friendly pub is popular with tourists, business people and real ale fans alike. With its etched mirrors, the long bar offers a good range of simple pub food, including the 'mighty' Buckingham burger, nachos with chilli, chicken ciabatta and old favourites like ham, egg and chips.

Open all day 11-11 (Sat noon-6, Sun noon-6 summer)
Closed: Sun (winter) ⊕ YOUNG & CO BREWERY PLC
◀ Young's Bitter, Special & Winter Warmer, Bombardier.
Facilities Dogs allowed Wi-fi

SW1 *continued*

PICK OF THE PUBS

Nags Head PLAN 1 B2

53 Kinnerton St SW1X 8ED ☎ 020 7235 1135
dir: *Telephone for directions*

With its Dickensian frontage and an interior like a well-stocked bric-à-brac shop, the award-winning Nags Head stubbornly resists any contemporary touches in its appearance. Compact and bijou, it's located in a quiet mews near Harrods, its front and back bars connected by a narrow stairway and boasting wooden floors, panelled walls, and low ceilings. It was built in the early 19th century to cater for the footmen and stable hands who looked after the horses in these Belgravia mews. The walls are covered with photos, drawings, mirrors, helmets, model airplanes; there are even penny-slot machines. The atmosphere is best described as 'entertaining' if you're in the right frame of mind. It's a mobile phone-free zone, too. The waist-high bar is another oddity, but the full Adnams range is served, along with a good value menu that includes sandwiches; a daily roast; and traditional pub favourites like shepherd's pie, and sausages and mash.

Open all day all wk **Bar Meals** food served all day **Restaurant** food served all day ⊕ FREE HOUSE ◀ Adnams Best, Broadside, Fisherman, Regatta Ö Aspall. **Facilities** Children welcome Dogs allowed

The Orange Public House & Hotel ☗ NEW PLAN 1 C1

37 Pimlico Rd SW1W 8NE
☎ 020 7881 9844 ▤ 020 7235 5377
e-mail: reservations@theorange.co.uk
dir: *Nearest tube stations: Victoria & Sloane Street*

Restored to its former glory, The Orange has a light and airy, rustic Tuscan feel about it with its muted colours and potted orange trees on stripped wooden boards. The well-heeled locals quaff English ales and Italian wines – perfect with pizzas cooked in the wood-fired oven; salad of buffalo mozzarella, bacon, rocket and honey dressing or a main course roast lamb with honey-glazed figs and rosemary sautéed potatoes.

Open all day all wk 8am-11.30pm (Sun 8am-10.30pm) **Bar Meals** L served all wk 12-6 D served all wk 6-10 Av main course £15 food served all day **Restaurant** L served all wk 12-3 booking required D served all wk 6-10 booking required Av 3 course à la carte fr £28 ⊕ FREE HOUSE ◀ Adnams, Meantime Wheat & Pale Ale Ö Aspall. ☗ 15 **Facilities** Children welcome Children's menu Children's portions Dogs allowed Wi-fi

The Wilton Arms PLAN 1 B2

71 Kinnerton St SW1X 8ED
☎ 020 7235 4854 ▤ 020 7235 4895
e-mail: wilton@shepherd-neame.co.uk
dir: *Between Hyde Park Corner & Knightsbridge tube stations*

Known locally as The Village Pub, this early 19th-century hostelry's other name is a reference to the 1st Earl of Wilton. In summer it is distinguished by fabulous flower-filled baskets and window boxes. High settles and bookcases create individual seating areas in the air-conditioned interior, and a conservatory covers the old garden. Shepherd Neame ales accompany traditional pub fare: scampi and chips; oversized burgers; or maybe a smoked salmon platter with brown bloomer bread.

Open all day all wk **Closed:** BHs **Bar Meals** L served Mon-Fri 12-4, Sat 12-3 D served Mon-Fri 5.30-9 Av main course £7 ● SHEPHERD NEAME ◀ Spitfire, Orangeboom, Bishops Finger. **Facilities** Children welcome Children's portions

SW3

The Admiral Codrington PLAN 1 B2

17 Mossop St SW3 2LY
☎ 020 7581 0005 ▤ 020 7589 2452
e-mail: admiral.codrington@333holdingsltd.com
dir: *Nearest tube stations: South Kensington & Sloane Square. Telephone for detailed directions*

To habitués of this smart South Ken gastro-pub, it's The Cod, which explains the whimsical item on the menu – Admiral's cod, served with tomato, mushroom and herb crust. It's one of many modern British options that also include slow-cooked shoulder of lamb, root vegetables and rosemary, and three-cheese macaroni with crispy bacon. The restaurant's glass roof retracts to give 'alfresco' dining, and the heated beer garden has an all-weather awning. Snacks are available in the bar.

Open all day all wk 11.30am-mdnt (Fri-Sat 11.30am-1am, Sun noon-10.30) **Bar Meals** L served all wk 12-2.30 Av main course £16 **Restaurant** L served all wk 12-2.30 D served all wk 6.30-11 Fixed menu price fr £15.95 Av 3 course à la carte fr £32 ⊕ FREE HOUSE ◀ Guinness, Black Sheep, Spitfire. **Facilities** Children welcome Children's menu Dogs allowed Garden Wi-fi

PICK OF THE PUBS

The Builders Arms PLAN 1 B1

13 Britten St SW3 3TY ☎ 020 7349 9040
e-mail: buildersarms@geronimo-inns.co.uk
dir: *From Sloane Square tube station down Kings Rd. At Habitat turn right onto Chelsea Manor St, at end turn right onto Britten St, pub on right*

Just off Chelsea's famous Kings Road, a three-storey Georgian back-street pub built by the same crew that constructed St Luke's church over the way. Inside, leather sofas dot the spacious informal bar area, where you can enjoy a pint of Cornish Coaster or London

Pride. A brief, daily changing menu offers a good choice of modern English food with a twist, but if further ideas are needed, consult the specials board and dine in the restaurant. Starters on the main menu might include mackerel and dill fishcake with spicy tomato ketchup; mussels and clams with cider, red onion and cream sauce; and sautéed chicken livers with smoked Black Forest bacon and broad beans. Typical main courses are baked codling fillet with Parmentier potatoes and mustard lentils; pan-fried sea bass with caramelised shallot and gremolata; and courgette, sun-blushed tomato and feta risotto. There are more than 30 bins, with French producers just about taking the lead, plus many wines by the glass. When the sun shines the outdoor terrace is highly popular.

Open all wk **Closed:** 25 Dec ◀ Adnams, London Pride, Sharp's Cornish Coaster Ö Aspall. **Facilities** Children welcome Dogs allowed

PICK OF THE PUBS

The Coopers of Flood Street ☗ PLAN 1 B1

87 Flood St, Chelsea SW3 5TB ☎ 020 7376 3120
e-mail: coopersarms@youngs.co.uk
dir: *From Sloane Square tube station, straight onto Kings Rd. Approx 1m W, opposite Waitrose, turn left. Pub half way down Flood St*

A quiet backstreet Chelsea pub close to the Kings Road and the river. Celebrities and the notorious rub shoulders with the aristocracy and the local road sweeper in the bright, vibrant atmosphere, while the stuffed brown bear, Canadian moose and boar bring a character of their own to the bar. Food is served here and in the quiet upstairs dining room, with a focus on meat from the pub's own organic farm. The fresh, adventurous menu also offers traditional favourites that change daily: seared king scallops and chorizo; grilled chicken, bacon, avocado and sunblushed tomato salad might precede chargrilled harissa lamb steak with Moroccan vegetable couscous; bangers and mash with onion gravy; and ricotta and spinach tortellini. Good staff-customer repartee makes for an entertaining atmosphere.

Open all day all wk noon-11 (Sun 12-10.30) **Bar Meals** L served Mon-Fri 12-3, Sat 12-10, Sun 12-9 D served Mon-Fri 5-10 **Restaurant** L served Mon-Fri 12-3, Sat 12-10, Sun 12-9 D served Mon-Fri 5-10 ● YOUNG & CO BREWERY PLC ◀ Young's Special, Young's Bitter, Wells Bombardier, Guinness. ☗ 15 **Facilities** Children welcome Children's portions Dogs allowed Garden

The Cross Keys ♥   PLAN 2 E3

1 Lawrence St, Chelsea SW3 5NB
☎ 020 7349 9111 📠 020 7349 9333
e-mail: info@thexkeys.co.uk
dir: *From Sloane Square walk down Kings Rd, left onto Old Church St, then left onto Justice Walk, then right*

This Chelsea pub established in 1765 can count JMW Turner, Whistler, DG Rossetti and Dylan Thomas among its previous customers. More recently it was co-owned by the sculptor Rudy Weller, who created the Horses of Helios and the Three Graces prominently displayed in Piccadilly Circus. While at the Cross Keys, Rudy created 'a magical kingdom' throughout its four rooms, which comprise the bar, conservatory restaurant, gallery and a room at the top. The modern European menu tempts with foie gras terrine; red snapper; and corn-fed Provençal chicken.

Open all day all wk Closed: 23-29 Dec, 1-4 Jan & BH **Bar Meals** L served Mon-Fri 12-3, Sat-Sun 12-10.30 D served Mon-Fri 6-10, Sat-Sun 12-10.30 **Restaurant** L served all wk12-3 D served all wk 6-10.30 ⊕ FREE HOUSE ◀ Directors, Guinness, Tiger, Doom Bar ♂ Aspall. ♥ 11 **Facilities** Children welcome Children's portions Dogs allowed Wi-fi

The Pig's Ear ♥   PLAN 1 E3

35 Old Church St SW3 5BS
☎ 020 7352 2908 📠 020 7352 9321
e-mail: thepigsear@hotmail.co.uk
dir: *Telephone for directions*

An award-winning gastro-pub off the King's Road, specialising in traditional beers like Pig's Ear and Sambrook's and continental cuisine, with food sourced from top quality suppliers. There is a traditional yet timeless feel to the bar and the oak-panelled dining room on the first floor. A menu might offer spiced parsnip soup, coriander and parsnip crisps; sautéed squid, chorizo parrilla dulce; line-caught whole sea bass 'en papillote'; fillet steak tartare with chips; or Kilravock Farm pressed slow-roasted pork belly with colcannon. Syllabub with poached rhubarb and shortbread or sticky toffee and banana pudding rounds things off nicely.

Open all wk **Bar Meals** L served Mon-Fri 12-3, Sat 12-4, Sun 12-9 D served Mon-Sat 6-10, Sun all day Av main course £12 **Restaurant** L served Mon-Fri 12-3, Sat 12-4, Sun 12-9 D served Mon-Sat 6-10, Sun all day Fixed menu price fr £30 Av 3 course à la carte fr £35 ⊕ FREE HOUSE ◀ Pig's Ear, Sambrook's, Guinness. ♥ 10 **Facilities** Wi-fi

SW4

The Windmill on the Common   PLAN 2 E2

Clapham Common South Side SW4 9DE
☎ 020 8673 4578 📠 020 8675 1486
e-mail: windmillhotel@youngs.co.uk
dir: *5m from London, just off South Circular 205 at junct with A24 at Clapham*

Crackling open fires in winter and soft leather sofas make this pub a popular place for friends to meet. The original part of the building was known as Holly Lodge and at one time was the property of the founder of Young's Brewery. The Windmill today offers a varied menu with something for all tastes and appetites: 'Young's own famous pies' including steak and ale or chicken, leek and ham; fresh fish, grilled or in Young's beer batter; sausage of the day; and poached pear with cinnamon pannacotta are typical.

Open all day all wk Mon-Sat 11am-mdnt Sun noon-10pm ⊕ YOUNG & CO BREWERY PLC ◀ Young's SPA & PA ♂ Rekorderlig, Kopparberg. **Facilities** Children welcome Garden Parking Wi-fi

SW6

The Atlas ♥   PLAN 2 E3

16 Seagrave Rd, Fulham SW6 1RX
☎ 020 7385 9129 📠 020 7386 9113
e-mail: theatlas@btconnect.com
dir: *2 mins walk from West Brompton tube station*

Just around the corner from West Brompton tube, The Atlas is one of only a handful of London pubs to have a walled garden. Located in a trendy part of town where a great many pubs have been reinvented to become diners or restaurants, here is a traditional, relaxed local that remains true to its cause with a spacious bar area split into eating and drinking sections. Lunch might feature starters such as sweet potato soup with pumpkin crisps, cumin and soured cream, and confit duck and spiced peach salad with balsamic molasses. Tempting mains continue the European influences in dishes such as wild mushroom and chestnut risotto with sage and mascarpone, or braised lamb shank with red wine, olives, nutmeg and creamy polenta. Leave room for chocolate torte with crème Anglaise. Real ales for the current season are listed on the menu along with the ales about to arrive.

Open all day all wk Closed: 24 Dec-1 Jan **Bar Meals** L served Mon-Fri 12-2.30, Sat 12-4, Sun 12-10 D served Mon-Sat 6-10, Sun 12-10 ⊕ FREE HOUSE ◀ Fuller's London Pride, Caledonian Deuchars IPA, Timothy Taylor Landlord, Guest ale. ♥ 15 **Facilities** Children welcome Dogs allowed Garden Wi-fi

The Jam Tree ♥ NEW   PLAN 2 E3

541 King's Rd SW6 2EB
☎ 020 3397 3739 📠 020 3397 2210
e-mail: info@thejamtree.com
dir: *Nearest stations: Imperial Wharf & Fulham Broadway*

Matching the quirky style and atmosphere of the original Jam Tree gastro-pub in Kensington, its King's Road sibling opened in March 2011. Antique mirrors, personalised art work, old Chesterfields and mismatched furniture, alongside roaring fires and a copper-topped bar give the bar and dining areas an eclectic and original feel. A diverse Colonial-style menu takes in Jamaican chicken curry, cod and prawn fishcakes, lamb rump with pea and mint jus, and jam roly-poly. A vast cocktail list, an outdoor barbecue, plasma screen and a DJ booth complete the picture.

Open all day all wk **Bar Meals** Av main course £14 **Restaurant** L served Mon-Fri 12-3, Sat 10am-10pm, Sun 10am-8pm D served Mon-Fri 6-10, Sat 10am-10pm, Sun 10am-8pm Av 3 course à la carte fr £26 ⊕ FREE HOUSE ◀ Greene King IPA ♂ Aspall. ♥ 9 **Facilities** Children welcome Children's menu Children's portions Dogs allowed Garden Wi-fi

The White Horse ♥   PLAN 2 E3

1-3 Parson's Green, Fulham SW6 4UL
☎ 020 7736 2115
e-mail: info@whitehorsesw6.com
dir: *140mtrs from Parson's Green tube*

An archetypal London corner pub – indeed, it was a Victorian gin palace – but it began life in the late 18th century as a coaching inn. These days it's a destination for lovers of traditional British pub food and interesting real ales and wines, with a restaurant in the former coach house, an upstairs bar, and a luxurious private dining area. The interior is a pleasing blend of polished mahogany and wooden and flagstone floors, open fires and contemporary lighting. For lunch, you might try Portland dressed crab salad, or sausage and mash; evening possibilities might be beer-battered Cornish haddock; braised lamb shank; pan-fried chicken in chestnut and cider sauce; or giant butternut squash, Jerusalem artichoke and ricotta cheese ravioli. Every dish comes with a recommended drink, such partnering forming part of the pub's Beer Academy Courses. Four annual beer festivals further demonstrate where the White Horse hangs its hat.

Open all day all wk **Bar Meals** L served all wk 12-10.30 D served all wk 12-10.30 Av main course £13 food served all day ⊕ MITCHELL & BUTLER ◀ Adnams Broadside, Harveys Sussex Best Bitter, Oakham JHB ♂ Aspall. ♥ 20 **Facilities** Children welcome Children's portions Dogs allowed Garden Beer festival Wi-fi

SW7

The Anglesea Arms
PLAN 1 A1

15 Selwood Ter, South Kensington SW7 3QG
☎ 020 7373 7960
e-mail: enquiries@angleseaarms.com
dir: Telephone for directions

Feeling like a country pub in the middle of South Kensington, the interior has barely changed since 1827, though the dining area has been tastefully updated with panelled walls and leather-clad chairs, plus there's outside seating. Lunch and dinner menus place an emphasis on quality ingredients, fresh preparation and cosmopolitan flavours. From the menu expect perhaps goat's cheese, spinach and fig tart; crispy fried baby squid with risotto nero; wild boar and apple sausages with mash, braised red cabbage and shallot gravy; pan-fried skate wing with hand-cut chips, watercress and aïoli; followed by rum pannacotta with rhubarb compôte. Sunday lunches are popular, booking is advisable.

Open all day all wk Closed: 25-26 Dec ⊕ CAPITAL PUB COMPANY ◀ Fuller's London Pride, Adnams Bitter, Broadside, Sambrooks Wandle, Sharp's Doom Bar ♂ Symonds. Facilities Children welcome Children's portions Dogs allowed Garden Wi-fi

SW8

The Masons Arms
PLAN 2 E3

169 Battersea Park Rd SW8 4BT
☎ 020 7622 2007 ▤ 020 7622 4662
e-mail: masons.arms@london-gastros.co.uk
dir: Opposite Battersea Park BR Station

This Fuller's gastro-pub breaks the mould, with live jazz, blues or folk at weekends adding a new dimension to the indoor-outdoor choice of where to eat and sup. Worn wooden floors, friendly, professional staff and a welcoming atmosphere, all equally suited for a quiet romantic dinner or a family outing. Food - British, with Italian and Asian influences, the menu changes daily – is freshly prepared in an open kitchen, a touch of theatre whilst awaiting perhaps squid stuffed with feta and chilli.

Open all day all wk noon-11 (Fri noon-mdnt Sun noon-10.30) Closed: 25 Dec ⊕ FULLER'S ◀ London Pride, Peroni, Staropramen, Fuller's Organic Honeydew.
Facilities Dogs allowed Garden Wi-fi

SW10

PICK OF THE PUBS

The Chelsea Ram ♥
PLAN 2 E3

32 Burnaby St SW10 0PL ☎ 020 7351 4008
e-mail: bookings@chelsearam.co.uk
dir: Telephone for directions

A popular neighbourhood corner gastro-pub and friendly local, The Chelsea Ram is located close to Chelsea Harbour and Lots Road, a little off the beaten track. There is a distinct emphasis on fresh produce in the monthly-changing menu, which includes fish and meat from Smithfield Market. Start with goat's cheese, spring onion and spinach tart; steamed Shetland mussels; or 'London cured' smoked salmon plate. Among the main courses might be slow braised pork belly and crackling; 'retro' chicken Kiev; or roasted butternut risotto, sage and walnut pesto. Finish with a traditional apple and pear crumble, or puff pastry mille feuille, toffee bananas, rum cream and chocolate and sea salt sauce. If you haven't a sweet tooth then a selection of English cheeses, wheat wafers, red grapes and home-made chutney will appeal. A stone's throw from the Kings Road, it is the ideal place to refuel after a shopping spree, or relax with a pint at the end of the day.

Open all day all wk 11-11 Bar Meals L served Mon-Sat 12-3, Sun 11-7 D served Mon-Sat 6.30-10, Sun 11-7 Restaurant L served Mon-Sat 12-3, Sun 11-7 D served Mon-Sat 6.30-10, Sun 11-7 ⊕ YOUNG & CO BREWERY PLC ◀ Young's Bitter, Bombardier, Guinness, Peroni. ♥ 14 Facilities Children welcome Children's portions Dogs allowed Wi-fi

PICK OF THE PUBS

The Hollywood Arms ♥
PLAN 1 A1

45 Hollywood Rd SW10 9HX ☎ 020 7349 7840
e-mail: hollywoodarms@youngs.co.uk
dir: 1 min from Chelsea & Westminster Hospital, 200mtrs down Hollywood Rd on right towards Fulham Rd

This listed building is one of Chelsea's hidden treasures. The interior has been elegantly refurbished, augmenting its original charm with rich natural woods, pastel shades and modern fabrics. The large upstairs lounge has elegant mouldings around the ceiling and large open fires at each end, with the bar centred on its length; four huge picture windows make the ambience light and airy. The ground floor pub and restaurant retains much of its traditional atmosphere. Here the chefs lovingly create menus from scratch using high quality ingredients; some, such as cheeses and cured meats, have won national or international recognition. Small plates will produce Rannoch Smokery smoked goose breast, or salt and pepper squid, while main courses offer the home-made half-pound beefburger and chips, Welsh lamb cutlets, or Muffs of Bromborough Old English herb sausages. Award-winning Burtree House Farm puddings are among the desserts. Change of hands.

Open all day all wk noon-11.30 (Thu-Sat noon-mdnt Sun noon-10.30) Bar Meals L served Mon-Fri 12-3, Sat-Sun 12-10 D served Mon-Fri 5-10, Sat-Sun 12-10 Restaurant L served Mon-Fri 12-3, Sat-Sun 12-10 D served Mon-Fri 5-10, Sat-Sun 12-10 ⊕ YOUNG & CO BREWERY PLC ◀ Young's Bitter, Wells Bombardier, Guinness, Guest ales ♂ Kopparberg. ♥ 12 Facilities Dogs allowed

PICK OF THE PUBS

Lots Road Pub and Dining Room
PLAN 2 E3

114 Lots Rd, Chelsea SW10 0RJ ☎ 020 7352 6645
e-mail: lotsroad@foodandfuel.co.uk
dir: 5-10 mins walk from Fulham Broadway Station

Located just off the bustling King's Road, opposite the entrance to Chelsea Harbour, the Lots Road is a real star of the gastro-pub scene, appealing to well-heeled locals for the relaxing vibe and a daily menu that lists imaginative, modern pub food. Expect a smart, comfortable, well-designed space, which segues smoothly between jaunty bar area and the more secluded dining area. Slate grey and cream walls and wooden tables create a light, pared-down feel, and attentive staff are set on making you feel comfortable. There's real ales, an excellent wine list, and cocktails both quirky and classic. Food takes in a mix of seasonal pub classics and more innovative dishes, perhaps pumpkin and ginger soup; or steamed Isle of Lewis mussels, white wine, garlic and shallots, followed by lamb shoulder shepherd's pie and curly kale; root vegetable and butter bean lasagne and French beans; then a pudding of sticky toffee pudding with honey pot ice cream; or chocolate mousse tart and orange syrup. Don't miss Saturday brunch and the Sunday family roasts.

Open all day all wk 11-11 (Sun noon-10.30) ⊕ FOOD AND FUEL ◀ Sharp's Doom Bar, Bombardier, IPA, Guinness. Facilities Children welcome Children's menu Children's portions Dogs allowed Wi-fi

SW11

The Bolingbroke Pub & Dining Room ♥ NEW
PLAN 2 E2

172-174 Northcote Rd SW11 6RE ☎ 020 7228 4040
e-mail: info@thebolingbroke.com
dir: Nearest stations: Clapham South; Clapham Junction

Named after Henry St John, 1st Viscount Bolingbroke, this refined contemporary dining pub stands at the end of Battersea Road that is more commonly known as 'Nappy Valley' due to its popularity with well-heeled young families. Not only does the pub cater admirably for them, it offers a weekly modern British menu, perhaps listing pigeon with wild mushroom and thyme jus, bowls of mussels in fennel and cider cream sauce, and lamb shank with mint sauce, alongside a more traditional bar menu.

Open all day all wk Closed: 25-28 Dec, 1 Jan Bar Meals L served Mon-Fri 12-3.30, Sat 10-4, Sun 12-9 booking required D served Mon-Sat 6-10.30, Sun 12-9 booking required Av main course £3.50-£10.50 Restaurant L served Mon-Fri 12-3.30, Sat 10-4, Sun 12-9 booking required D served Mon-Sat 6-10.30, Sun 12-9 booking required Av 3 course à la carte fr £21.50 ⊕ FREE HOUSE ◀ Timothy Taylor Landlord ♂ Aspall, Westons Organic. ♥ 13 Facilities Children welcome Children's menu Children's portions Dogs allowed Wi-fi

PICK OF THE PUBS

The Fox & Hounds ☕   PLAN 2 E2

66 Latchmere Rd, Battersea SW11 2JU
☎ 020 7924 5483 📠 020 7738 2678
e-mail: foxandhoundsbattersea@btopenworld.com
dir: *From Clapham Junction exit onto High St turn left, through lights into Lavender Hill. After post office, left at lights. Pub 200yds on left*

Just like the Queen Vic in *EastEnders*, this is one of those archetypal Victorian corner pubs that London still has in abundance. The style is simple, imparting the convivial feel of a true neighbourhood local, with bare wooden floors, an assortment of furniture, walled garden, extensive patio planting and a covered and heated seating area. Locals head here for the good selection of real ales and an international wine list; the menu suggests the' Wine of the Moment' with tasting notes. Fresh ingredients are delivered daily from the London markets, enabling the Mediterranean-style menu and specials to change accordingly; all prepared in the open-to-view kitchen. So, you might start with winter minestrone soup, Caesar salad, or pork terrine with pineapple chutney. Follow with pan-fried duck breast, celeriac gratin dauphinoise; Tuscan lamb shank with olives and rosemary; or salmon and dill fishcakes. A traditional British lunch is served on Sundays.

Open noon-3 5-11 (Mon 5-11 Fri-Sat noon-11 Sun noon-10.30) Closed: 24 Dec-1 Jan, 2nd Mon Aug, Mon L **Bar Meals** L served Fri 12.30-3, Sat 12.30-4, Sun 12.30-10 D served all wk 6-10 ⊕ FREE HOUSE ◀ Caledonian Deuchars IPA, Harveys Sussex Best Bitter, Fuller's London Pride, St Austell Tribute. ☕ 14 **Facilities** Children welcome Children's portions Dogs allowed Garden Wi-fi

SW13

The Bull's Head ☕   PLAN 2 D3

373 Lonsdale Rd, Barnes SW13 9PY
☎ 020 8876 5241 📠 020 8876 1546
e-mail: jazz@thebullshead.com
dir: *Telephone for directions*

Built right on the Thames in 1684, this is one of London's top jazz, blues and funk venues, with performances seven nights a week and during Sunday lunchtimes for over 50 years. Countless musicians have wet their whistles with the fine cask-conditioned ales from Wells and Young's – and so can you. Traditional bar lunches include haddock, crab, roasts and pies, while authentic Thai food is available throughout the pub in the evening.

Open all day all wk noon-mdnt Closed: 25 Dec **Bar Meals** L served all wk 12-3.30 Av main course £8 **Restaurant** D served all wk 6-10.30 ◀ Young's Special, Bitter, Winter Warmer, Bombardier, Ramrod, Guinness. ☕ 21 **Facilities** Children welcome Children's portions Family room Dogs allowed Garden Wi-fi

PICK OF THE PUBS

The Idle Hour ☕   PLAN 2 D2

62 Railway Side, Barnes SW13 0PQ ☎ 020 8878 5555
e-mail: theidlehour@aol.com
dir: *From Mortlake High St (A3003) into White Hart Ln. 5th left into Railway Side (at rail crossing). Pub just past school*

Built as a pub in 1864, this Victorian free house went through a number of guises before becoming the Idle Hour ten years ago. Though hidden away down an alleyway, the pub is noted for its cosy atmosphere with plenty of fresh flowers, candles, and clocks that tell the wrong time. As the name suggests, this is just the spot for whiling away an afternoon, while the stunning secluded garden is ideal for alfresco summer dining. The weekday menu changes regularly and features some traditional choices alongside more adventurous dishes. Typical starters include home-made mixed mushroom and herb soup; and grilled halloumi with chickpea salsa and harissa. Main course options might include seared sea bass fillets on Puy lentils with sweet potato; organic tagliatelle with lemon, peas, cream and Parmesan; or Moroccan-style organic lamb shank with couscous and spicy tomato sauce. The dessert menu features apple and pear crumble with vanilla custard.

Open all wk 5.30-mdnt (Sat-Sun noon-mdnt) ⊕ FREE HOUSE ◀ Adnams, Harveys Sussex. ☕ 10 **Facilities** Children welcome Dogs allowed Garden Wi-fi

SW14

The Victoria ☕ NEW   PLAN 2 C2

10 West Temple Sheen, East Sheen SW14 7RT
☎ 020 8876 4238 📠 020 8878 3464
e-mail: bookings@thevictoria.net
dir: *Nearest tube station: Mortlake*

Located in leafy Sheen close to Richmond Park, The Victoria is a warm, friendly and cosy pub. The large conservatory leads out into a fabulous garden with a safe children's play area. It was purchased in 2008 by TV chef Paul Merrett and restaurateur Greg Bellamy, so you can expect top notch food. Menus encompass casual bites like home-made Scotch egg with beetroot and green bean salad, as well as great choices such as smoked trout risotto with a crispy poached egg. Saturday brunch and Sunday lunch bring a change of pace, being particularly popular with families.

Open all day all wk **Bar Meals** L served Mon-Sat 12-10 D served Mon-Sat 12-10, Sun 6-8 Av main course £13 food served all day **Restaurant** L served Mon-Sat 12-2.30, Sun 12-6 D served Mon-Fri 6-10, Sat 6-10.30 Fixed menu price fr £12.50 Av 3 course à la carte fr £25.50 ⊕ ENTERPRISE INNS ◀ Fuller's London Pride, Timothy Taylor Landlord, Guest ale ♂ Westons Organic Cider. ☕ 28 **Facilities** Children welcome Children's menu Children's portions Play area Dogs allowed Garden Parking Wi-fi

SW15

PICK OF THE PUBS

The Spencer ☕   PLAN 2 D2

237 Lower Richmond Rd, Putney SW15 1HJ
☎ 020 8788 0640 📠 020 8788 2216
e-mail: info@thespencerpub.com
dir: *Corner of Putney Common & Lower Richmond Rd, opposite Old Putney Hospital*

The green and leafy expanse of Putney Common is the view from tables outside this long-established pub, out in the 'burbs and just a short stroll from the Thames Embankment; their beer garden is part of the Common. A light, bright and airy interior belies the rather traditional look of the place; revamped a few years ago, the emphasis is on good dining in a crisp, chic environment where locals are still welcomed to sup at the bar, with Sharp's Doom Bar or Fuller's London Pride the pick of the beers. Meals, in the bar or restaurant area, are a modern take on traditional favourites, such as a starter of Welsh rarebit with fresh beef tomato and pan-fried smoked bacon, or shredded duck, poached pear and walnut salad with Stilton dressing. Mains take on a seasonal look to reflect the desire to use only the freshest ingredients; look for a linguini of fresh crab, parsley, cherry tomatoes, garlic and chilli; grilled Mediterranean sea bass with Jerusalem artichoke purée and wilted spinach; or honey roast belly of pork, glazed apple and Puy lentils. Sunday roasts and rotisserie free-range chickens are a favourite with families.

Open all day all wk 10-mdnt Closed: 25 Dec **Bar Meals** L served Mon-Fri 12-3, Sat-Sun all day booking required D served Mon-Fri 6-10, Sat-Sun all day booking required Av main course £11.75 **Restaurant** L served Mon-Fri 12-3, Sat-Sun all day booking required D served Mon-Fri 6-10, Sat-Sun all day booking required Av 3 course à la carte fr £24 ⊕ FREE HOUSE ◀ Guinness, Fuller's London Pride, Sharp's Doom Bar, Peroni ♂ Aspall Draught, Peronelle's Blush, Westons Organic. ☕ 11 **Facilities** Children welcome Children's menu Children's portions Play area Dogs allowed Garden Wi-fi

The Telegraph NEW   PLAN 2 D2

Telegraph Rd, Putney Heath SW15 3TU
☎ 020 8788 2011
e-mail: info@thetelegraphputney.co.uk
dir: *Nearest tube: East Putney. Nearest rail station: Putney High St*

This pub was close to an Admiralty telegraph station between London and Portsmouth, and has been involved in the sale of beer since before 1856. Although it's only five minutes from the hustle and bustle of Putney High Street, the essence of The Telegraph is that of a country pub. Certainly the focus on well-kept real ales cannot be faulted, with Naked Ladies from Twickenham Fine Ales well worth a try. Plenty of food choices include grazing

continued

SW15 *continued*

boards and menus of typical pub fare such as grills, pizzas, fish pie, slow-roast chicken, and sausages of the day.

Open all day all wk **Bar Meals** L served all wk all day D served Mon-Thu until 9.30, Fri-Sat until 10, Sun until 9 Av main course £12.95 food served all day **Restaurant** L served all wk all day D served Mon-Thu until 9.30, Fri-Sat until 10, Sun until 9 booking required Av 3 course à la carte fr £21 food served all day ◀ Sharp's Doom Bar, Naked Ladies, Brakspear Bitter, Adnams Broadside. **Facilities** Children welcome Children's menu Children's portions Dogs allowed Garden Parking

SW18

PICK OF THE PUBS

The Alma Tavern ☻   PLAN 2 E2

499 Old York Rd, Wandsworth SW18 1TF
☎ **020 8870 2537**
e-mail: alma@youngs.co.uk
dir: *Opposite Wandsworth town rail station*

Vivid green tiles covering part of the curving frontage of this street-corner inn can't fail to catch the eye, as do the belvedere tower and the imposing balustrading of this impressive Young's establishment. Not far from the Thames or the greenery of Wandsworth Common, step inside to a well renovated Victorian town pub, complete with decorative plaster frieze, a superb island bar, mosaics and feature mahogany staircase; the latter leads to the Bramford Room which is licensed for weddings at this landmark London pub. The roomy bar has an interesting mix of highly polished wood and distressed tables, with lots of perching posts for those days when Twickenham hosts internationals; off this is a more peaceful dining room where an enthusiastic mix of traditional pub grub and gastro-pub dishes attract diners from a wide area. A twice-baked Cheddar soufflé or seared scallops with pea-mint purée set out the stall, followed by pan-fried fillet of line-caught mackerel, bacon and beetroot relish; Gressingham duck breast with Puy lentils and garlic mash; or an Alma burger with Somerset Brie, bacon and French fries giving a flavour of the mains. Beers from Young's stable, plus guests from local micro-breweries and a good list of bins, provide ample accompaniment.

Open all day all wk **Bar Meals** Av main course £10 food served all day **Restaurant** L served all wk 12-4 D served all wk 6-10 ⊕ YOUNG & CO BREWERY ◀ Young's PA, Special Sambrooks Wandle ♂ Addlestones. ☻ 10 **Facilities** Children welcome Children's portions Dogs allowed Beer festival Wi-fi

PICK OF THE PUBS

The Cat's Back   PLAN 2 E2

86-88 Point Pleasant, Putney SW18 1NN
☎ **020 8877 0818 & & 8874 2937**
e-mail: info@catsback.co.uk
dir: *2 min walk from Wandsworth Park, by river*

Some years ago, just before the landlord went on holiday, the pub cat disappeared, causing much concern among the regulars. A month later, after mine host's return, in strolled the wayward feline, prompting him to write a notice reading, somewhat prosaically, "The cat's back". Much relief all round. Built in 1865 for lightermen on the Thames and Wandle, this vestige of a once-busy riverside stands defiant among blocks of new apartments. Its eccentricity is exemplified by an old globe-topped petrol pump on the pavement, dodgy Victorian photographs, a Calypso fruit machine (one old penny a go), Barbie dolls in glass cases and more. The bar offers a wide range of tempting food including lamb stew; Cumberland sausages and mash; cheese ravioli; spaghetti Bolognese; beef Stroganoff; and vegetarian spring rolls. Food is also served in the ornate first-floor dining room. Live music, from jazz to West African, can break out spontaneously.

Open all day all wk 11am-mdnt (Fri-Sat 11am-2am) ⊕ FREE HOUSE ◀ Guinness, Staropramen ♂ Biddenden. **Facilities** Children welcome Dogs allowed Garden

PICK OF THE PUBS

The Earl Spencer   PLAN 2 E2

260-262 Merton Rd, Southfields SW18 5JL
☎ **020 8870 9244** 📠 **020 8877 2828**
e-mail: theearlspencer@hotmail.com
dir: *Exit Southfields tube station, down Replingham Rd, left at junct with Merton Rd, to junct with Kimber Rd*

A rare mix of community and gastro-pub only 10 minutes from the Wimbledon Tennis Centre. Edwardian pubby grandeur, log fires and polished wood furnishings offer a relaxed, informal atmosphere, whilst a good selection of wines and real ales draws in a dedicated bunch of regulars. It's child-friendly too, something of a rarity in establishments where food is taken seriously. The emphasis is on fresh cooking (even the bread is home baked) with an international cast of chefs; the menu changes daily and reflects seasonal produce. Kick in with poached salted ox tongue, lentils and green sauce or Normandy oysters, shallot vinegar and lemon before progressing to neck end of pork, root vegetable mash, buttered kale, cider and mustard, or whole lemon sole accompanied by ratte potatoes, braised leeks, chives and vermouth. Round off with Bramley apple and blackberry crumble or prune and Armagnac iced parfait. Events are catered for in a large, self-contained function suite, or simply unwind with a beer on the front patio.

Open all wk Mon-Thu 11am-11pm (Fri-Sat 11am-mdnt Sun noon-10.30pm) Closed: 25 Dec ⊕ ENTERPRISE INNS ◀ Guinness, Hook Norton, Fuller's London Pride, Sharp's Doom Bar ♂ Aspall. **Facilities** Children welcome Dogs allowed Garden Wi-fi

The Roundhouse ☻   PLAN 2 E2

2 Northside, Wandsworth Common SW18 2SS
☎ **020 7326 8580**
e-mail: roundhouse@sabretoothvintners.com
dir: *Telephone for directions*

Sambrook's Brewery in Battersea furnishes this pub with its Wandle and Junction ales, the former named after a nearby river and the latter for the famous station at Clapham. The young brewery's crafted ales fit well with the Roundhouse, which has undergone a renaissance in name, decor and management in recent years. But the ambience of a friendly local has been preserved, with a round black walnut bar, open kitchen, eclectic art on the walls, daily-changing menus and those lip-smacking Sambrook's ales. The concise menu takes in charcuterie board; home-made soup; lamb burger; beer battered hake; and mushroom, spinach and ricotta cannelloni.

Open all day all wk **Bar Meals** L served Sat-Sun 12-4 D served all wk 6-10 Av main course £12 **Restaurant** L served Sat-Sun 12-4 D served all wk 6-10 Av 3 course à la carte fr £20 ⊕ FREE HOUSE ◀ Wandle, Junction ♂ Westons Organic. ☻ 15 **Facilities** Children welcome Children's portions Dogs allowed Garden Wi-fi

PICK OF THE PUBS

The Ship Inn   PLAN 2 E2

Jew's Row SW18 1TB
☎ **020 8870 9667** 📠 **020 8874 9055**
e-mail: drinks@theship.co.uk
dir: *Wandsworth Town BR station nearby. On S side of Wandsworth Bridge*

Take the river walk to approach this famous Thames-side pub, which stands in the shadow of Wandsworth Bridge, and enter via the delightful, two-level terrace, complete with rose-covered rustic terrace, barbecue and summer bar; the pub really makes to most of its stunning riverside location. Within, you'll find a light, airy conservatory bar sporting bare boards, a central wood-burning stove, a motley collection of old wooden tables and chairs, and an open-plan kitchen that delivers some cracking pub food prepared from quality raw ingredients. On warm days when the barbecue is fired up, arrive early, grab a pint of Young's and enjoy lime, chilli and coriander marinated squid, whole sea bream with rocket, caper and green bean sauce, rack of West Country pork ribs with barbecue sauce, or 21-day aged rib-eye steak with hand-cut chips and watercress mayonnaise. With plenty of music and quiz nights as well, you won't want to leave this waterside gem.

Open all wk ◀ Young's: PA, SPA, Waggle Dance, Winter Warmer, Young's Limited Edition seasonal ales. **Facilities** Children welcome Dogs allowed Garden

Save on hotels. Book at **theAA.com/hotel**

LONDON 309 **ENGLAND**

SW19

The Brewery Tap ⚐　　　PLAN 2 D1

68-69 High St, Wimbledon SW19 5EE ☎ 020 8947 9331
e-mail: thebrewerytap@hotmail.com
dir: *Nearest tube station: Wimbledon*

A small, cosy one room pub, big on sports like football, rugby and cricket. It is also the closest pub to the Wimbledon tennis championships. Lighter meals take in platters, cold sandwiches, hot sandwiches like salt beef, jacket potatoes and salads. More substantial meals are cassoulet; Cumberland sausages, mash and rich onion gravy; chilli con carne; and lambs' liver, streaky bacon, bubble and squeak and black pudding. The pub's ploughman's is a 'big feast' for one person so it might be ideal for sharing.

Open all day all wk noon-11 (Fri-Sat noon-mdnt, Sun noon-10.30) **Bar Meals** L served Mon-Sat 12-2.30, Sun 12-4 D served Mon-Sat 7-9 Av main course £9 ⊕ ENTERPRISE INNS ◀ Fuller's London Pride, Deuchars, Guest ales Ò Aspall. ⚐ 14 **Facilities** Dogs allowed

W1

French House ⚐　　　PLAN 1 D4

49 Dean St, Soho W1D 5BG
☎ 020 7437 2477 📄 020 7287 9109
dir: *Telephone for directions*

This historic pub was patronised by General de Gaulle during the Second World War, and later by Dylan Thomas, Francis Bacon, Dan Farson and many other louche Soho habitués. Run by Lesley Lewis for 22 years, its bar serves only half pints. The new upstairs restaurant, Polpetto, offers Venetian small plates: maybe lamb and pistachio meatballs; rabbit and sage terrine; and warm lentils; and Jerusalem artichoke with radicchio and truffle vinaigrette. Finish with pannacotta, rhubarb and biscotti.

Open all day all wk noon-mdnt (Sun noon-10.30) Closed: 25 Dec **Bar Meals** L served Mon-Fri 12-4 **Restaurant** L served Mon-Sat 12-3 booking required D served Mon-Sat 5.30-11 booking required ⊕ FREE HOUSE ◀ Budvar, Kronenbourg, Leffe, Meteor, Guinness Ò Cidre Breton. ⚐ 22 **Facilities** Wi-fi

The Grazing Goat ⚐ NEW　　　PLAN 1 B4

6 New Quebec St WIH 7RQ ☎ 020 7724 7243
e-mail: reservations@thegrazinggoat.co.uk
dir: *Behind Marble Arch tube station, off Seymour St*

This classy, six-storey pub and hotel, featuring open fireplaces, oak floors and solid oak bars, has opened just minutes away from Oxford Street and Marble Arch. The name is not mere whimsy – goats did once graze around here because the first Lady Portman was allergic to cow's milk. Fresh, British, seasonal food is available in the ground and first floor dining rooms - classic British steak, mushroom and Guinness pie; beer-battered fish and chips; whole lemon sole; and pumpkin, spinach and goat's cheese tart. Floor-to-ceiling glass doors are opened in warmer weather for alfresco dining, plus there is an express lunch available.

Open all day all wk 8am-11.30pm (Sun 8am-10.30pm) Closed: Xmas & New Year **Bar Meals** Av main course £13.50 food served all day **Restaurant** L served all wk 12-3 booking required D served all wk 6-10 booking required Av 3 course à la carte fr £29 ⊕ FREE HOUSE ◀ Badger Dandelion Organic Ale, Shepherd Neame Whitstable Bay Ò Aspall. ⚐ 20 **Facilities** Children welcome Children's menu Children's portions Dogs allowed Wi-fi

W2

The Cow　　　PLAN 2 E4

89 Westbourne Park Rd W2 5QH
☎ 020 7221 5400 📄 020 7727 8687
e-mail: office@thecowlondon.co.uk
dir: *Telephone for directions*

Popular with the Notting Hill glitterati, this atmospheric Irish gastro-pub has a bustling downstairs bar and a tranquil first-floor dining room. 'Eat heartily and give the house a good name' is the sound philosophy here, and the stars of the show are oysters and Guinness. Daily specials include seafood plates and platters; bowls of whelks and winkles; and 'Cow classics' such as Londoner sausages with mash and gravy; hand-made taglioni with crab, tomato and chilli; or fish stew with rouille and croutons.

Open all day all wk Closed: 25 Dec **Bar Meals** L served Mon-Fri 12-3.30, Sat 12-10.30, Sun 12-10 D served Mon-Fri 6-10.30, Sat 12-10.30 Sun 12-10 Av main course £14 **Restaurant** L served Sat-Sun 12.30-3.30 booking required D served all wk 7-10.30 booking required Fixed menu price fr £22 Av 3 course à la carte fr £28.50 ⊕ FREE HOUSE ◀ Fuller's London Pride, Guinness, Courage Directors Bitter, De Konick.

The Prince Bonaparte　　　PLAN 2 E4

80 Chepstow Rd W2 5BE ☎ 020 7313 9491
e-mail: princebonaparte@realpubs.co.uk
dir: *Nearest tube: Notting Hill Gate*

A first-generation gastro-pub where Johnny Vaughan filmed the Strongbow ads. Renowned for its bloody Marys, good music and quick, friendly service, the pub proves popular with young professionals and has DJ nights on Fridays and Saturdays. The building is Victorian, with an airy and open plan interior. Typical meals include sausages and mash, tomato and mozzarella bruschetta and sea bass with spinach, and can be enjoyed with one of the wines served by the glass or a guest ale.

Open all day all wk Mon-Sat noon-11 (Sun noon-10.30) ⊕ REAL PUBS ◀ Sharp's Doom Bar, 2 Guest ales Ò Aspall. **Facilities** Children welcome Children's portions Dogs allowed Wi-fi

The Westbourne　　　PLAN 2 E4

101 Westbourne Park Villas W2 5ED
☎ 020 7221 1332 📄 020 7243 8081
dir: *On corner of Westbourne Park Rd & Westbourne Park Villas*

Bare floorboards and a long green and zinc bar characterise this classic Notting Hill gastro-pub, much favoured by its bohemian and celebrity clientele. The popular terrace is a sun trap in summer and heated in winter, attracting many locals and visitors to enjoy good food and drinks in a unique atmosphere. Daily-changing imaginative dishes are listed on a large blackboard above the bar, using fresh ingredients from leading independent suppliers. Dishes might include Gloucester Old Spot pork loin chop with chorizo and black cabbage.

Open Tue-Sat noon-11 (Sun noon-10.30, Mon 5-11) Closed: 24 Dec-2 Jan **Bar Meals** L served Tue-Sun 12.30-3.30 D served Tue-Sat 6.30-10, Sun 6.30-9.30, Mon 6.30-10.15 **Restaurant** L served Tue-Sun 12.30-3.30 D served Tue-Sat 6.30-10, Sun 6.30-9.30, Mon 6.30-10.15 ⊕ FREE HOUSE ◀ Leffe, Hoegaarden, Flowers, Deuchars, Staropramen Ò Breton. **Facilities** Children welcome Children's portions Dogs allowed Garden Wi-fi

W4　　　Map 6 TQ27

Sam's Brasserie & Bar ◉◉ ⚐ NEW　　　PLAN 2 D3

11 Barley Mow Passage, Chiswick W4 4PH
☎ 020 8987 0555 📄 020 8987 7389
e-mail: info@samsbrasserie.co.uk
dir: *Behind Chiswick High Rd, next to green, off Heathfield Terrace*

Once the Sanderson wallpaper factory, this large converted red-brick warehouse is a very unique space. Open all day from breakfast onwards, Sam's Brasserie covers all bases with its drink and AA 2-Rosette food offering. Enjoy a pint of London Pride and rock oysters in the bar or tuck in to main menu choices such as grilled pork chop with black pudding mash, winter greens and cider jus in the buzzy brasserie. Don't miss the Sunday roasts.

Open all day all wk Closed: 25-26 Dec **Bar Meals** Av main course £8 food served all day **Restaurant** L served Mon-Fri 12-3, Sat-Sun 12-4 booking required D served all wk 6.30-10.30 booking required Fixed menu price fr £13 Av 3 course à la carte fr £25 ⊕ FREE HOUSE ◀ Fuller's London Pride. **Facilities** Children welcome Children's menu Children's portions Wi-fi

W4 *continued*

PICK OF THE PUBS

The Swan ☻   PLAN 2 D3

1 Evershed Walk, 119 Acton Ln W4 5HH
☎ **020 8994 8262** 📄 **020 8994 9160**
e-mail: theswanpub@btconnect.com
dir: *Pub on right at end of Evershed Walk*

A friendly gastro-pub, The Swan is much appreciated
by locals for its international range of beers and
cosmopolitan atmosphere. A pub for all seasons, it has
a welcoming wood-panelled interior and a large lawned
garden and patio for summertime refreshments. Good
food is at the heart of the operation, and you can sit
and eat wherever you like. The menu of modern, mostly
Mediterranean cooking has a particular Italian
influence, and vegetarians are not forgotten. Start
perhaps with bruschetta di Pomodoro – grilled Pugliese
bread with vine tomatoes and basil; a vegetarian
option could be Turkish 'pizza' – feta, spinach, onion,
pine nuts and pomegranate. Next comes the main
course: penne with Italian sausage ragout, or
Andalusian oxtail casserole with judion beans, chorizo,
mushrooms and paprika. If you still have an appetite,
then finish off with apple and blackberry crumble with
ice cream, or pannacotta with orange compôte. Current
real ales are listed on the menu along with the next
guest ale and 'wine of the moment'.

Open all wk 5-11.30 (Sat noon-11.30, Sun noon-10.30)
Closed: 23 Dec-2 Jan, **Bar Meals** L served Sat 12.30-3,
Sun 12.30-10 D served Sun-Thu 6-10, Fri-Sat 6-10.30
⊕ FREE HOUSE ◀ Fuller's London Pride, Guinness,
Harvey's Sussex Best, St Austell Tribute, Otter Bitter
Ŏ Westons Organic. ♟ 12 **Facilities** Children welcome
Children's portions Dogs allowed Garden

W5

The Wheatsheaf   PLAN 2 C4

41 Haven Ln, Ealing W5 2HZ ☎ **020 8997 5240**
e-mail: wheatsheaf@fullers.co.uk
dir: *1m from A40 junct with North Circular*

Just a few minutes from Ealing Broadway, this large
Victorian pub has a rustic appearance inside. Ideal place
to enjoy a big screen sporting event and a drink among
wooden floors, panelled walls, beams from an old barn,
and real fires in winter. Fuller's beers and traditional pub
grub that includes Cumberland sausages and mash;
home-made fish pie; platters to share; Fuller's beer
battered cod and hand cut chips; and spaghetti
carbonara. There is a quiz night on Mondays. Change of
hands in March 2011

Open all day all wk noon-11 (Sun noon-10.30) ⊕ FULLER
SMITH TURNER PLC ◀ Fuller's London Pride, Discovery,
Chiswick, seasonal ales Ŏ Aspall Suffolk Draught.
Facilities Children welcome Children's portions Dogs
allowed Garden Wi-fi

W6

PICK OF THE PUBS

Anglesea Arms ⊛ ☻   PLAN 2 D3

35 Wingate Rd W6 0UR ☎ **020 8749 1291**
dir: *Telephone for directions*

A traditional corner pub close to Ravenscourt Park tube
station, and walkable from Goldhawk Road and
Hammersmith. It's whispered that the Great Train
Robbery was hatched here back in the 1960s, but who
knows. Today, real fires and a relaxed atmosphere are
the attraction, together with a terrace where drinks and
food can be served. Behind the Georgian façade, well
kept ales are dispensed from breweries as far apart as
Suffolk and Cornwall, and the place positively hums
with people eagerly seeking out the unashamedly
gastro-pub level food. Unusual dishes shine out,
including starters such as pig's head terrine or wolf
fish goujons, entrées for mains which may feature roast
pigeon with truffle mashed potato and braised endive,
or sea bass with braised fennel, lentils and gremolata.
There's a seriously impressive wine cellar here too, with
20 available by the glass.

Open all day all wk 11-11 (Sun noon-10.30) Closed:
25-27 Dec **Bar Meals** L served all wk 12.30-7 D served
Mon-Sat 7-10.30, Sun 6.30-9.30 Av main course
£16.50 **Restaurant** L served Mon-Fri 12.30-2.45, Sat
12.30-3, Sun 12.30-3.30 D served Mon-Sat 7-10.30,
Sun 6.30-9.30 Av 3 course à la carte fr £27
⊕ ENTERPRISE INNS ◀ Ringwood Fortyniner, St Austell
Tribute, Sharp's Cornish Coaster, Otter Ale, Otter Bitter,
Woodforde's Wherry Ŏ Westons Organic. ♟ 20
Facilities Children welcome Children's portions Dogs
allowed Garden

PICK OF THE PUBS

The Dartmouth Castle ☻   PLAN 2 D3

26 Glenthorne Rd, Hammersmith W6 0LS
☎ **020 8748 3614** 📄 **020 8748 3619**
e-mail: dartmouth.castle@btconnect.com
dir: *Nearest tube station: Hammersmith. 100yds from
Hammersmith Broadway*

While very much a place to relax over a pint or two, the
food is proving a great attraction at this corner pub.
The monthly-changing menu ranges from imaginative
sandwiches (mozzarella and slow roast tomatoes with
pesto; or marinated rump steak with onions, chilli and
red wine) to gutsy Mediterranean fare such as
gnoccheti sardi with wild boar; grilled Tuscan
sausages with garlic mashed potatoes; and braised
lamb shank with rosemary, olives and tomatoes.
Vegetarian aren't forgotten either, with choices like
wild mushroom and chestnut risotto with sage and
mascarpone. Typical desserts are apple and blackberry
crumble and home-made ice creams. The range of
beers includes at least two real ales on tap at any one
time, and there's a well-chosen international wine list
with 15 available by the glass. There's also a beer
garden for the summer months and a function room.

Open all day noon-11 (Sat 5-11, Sun noon-10.30)
Closed: Etr, 23 Dec-2 Jan & 2nd Mon Aug, Sat
afternoon **Bar Meals** L served Mon-Fri 12-2.30, Sun
12-9.30 D served Mon-Fri 6-10, Sat 6-10, Sun 12-9.30
Av main course £11.50 ⊕ FREE HOUSE ◀ Fuller's
London Pride, Guest ales Ŏ Aspall. ♟ 15 **Facilities** Dogs
allowed Garden Wi-fi

The Stonemasons Arms ☻   PLAN 2 D3

54 Cambridge Grove W6 0LA
☎ **020 8748 1397** 📄 **020 8846 9636**
e-mail: stonemasonsarms@london-gastros.co.uk
dir: *Hammersmith tube. Walk down King St, 2nd right up
Cambridge Grove, pub at end*

Fascinating menu options make this imposing corner
pub, just a short hop from Hammersmith tube station,
well worth finding; charcuterie plate or vegetarian mezze
plate to share and O'Hagan's American smokey sausages
with buttered vegetables, mash and onion gravy all
tantalise the tastebuds, enhancing the popularity of the
pub with local residents and business people alike.
During warmer months a decking area can be used for
alfresco dining, and there's a secluded, intimate
restaurant area. The pub carries an ever-changing
display of works by a local artist, whilst the upstairs
function room doubles as a tiny (and free) cinema on
Sunday afternoons.

Open all day all wk 11-11 (Sun noon-10.30)
Bar Meals L served Mon-Fri 12-3, Sat 12-10, Sun 12-9.30
D served Mon-Fri 6-10, Sat 12-10, Sun 12-9.30
Restaurant L served Mon-Fri 12-3, Sat 12-10, Sun
12-9.30 D served Mon-Fri 6-10, Sat 12-10, Sun 12-9.30
⊕ FULLER'S ◀ Fuller's London Pride & Organic
Honeydew, Guinness Ŏ Symonds Founder Reserve. ♟ 20
Facilities Children welcome Children's portions Garden
Wi-fi

W8

The Scarsdale ☻   PLAN 2 E3

23A Edwardes Square, Kensington W8 6HE
☎ **020 7937 1811** 📄 **020 7938 2984**
dir: *Exit Kensington High Street Station, turn left, 10 mins
along High St. Edwardes Sq next left after Odeon Cinema*

A 19th-century free-standing local with colourful hanging
baskets and window boxes spilling into the small terraced
patio, just off Kensington High Street. The Frenchman
who developed the site was supposedly one of
Bonaparte's secret agents. A planned refurbishment
worried the regulars, but the essence of the place has
hardly been interfered with at all. The kitchen was
updated though, allowing the introduction of a broader
menu of brasserie-style dishes. Examples are mussels
with lime and ginger, and char-grilled chicken sandwich
on ciabatta with red peppers, spinach and mayonnaise.

Open all day all wk noon-11 (Sun noon-10.30) Closed:
25-26 Dec **Bar Meals** Av main course £8 food served all
day **Restaurant** L served all wk 12-3 booking required
D served all wk 6-10 booking required ⊕ FULLER INNS
◀ Fuller's London Pride, Shepherd Neame Spitfire,
Seafarers, Bengal Lancer, Butcombe. ♟ 20 **Facilities** Dogs
allowed Garden

The Windsor Castle ♀   PLAN 2 E3

114 Campden Hill Rd W8 7AR ☎ 020 7243 8797
dir: From Notting Hill Gate, take south exit towards Holland Park, left onto Campden Hill Rd

Established in 1845, this pub takes its name from the royal castle, which could once be seen from the upper-floor windows. Unmodernised for at least 100 years, it boasts a large garden with its own bar, and oak panelling warmed by two gas fires within. Very much a drinker's pub, it serves 24 draught products including five cask ales and four real ciders. Daily specials include pig's cheeks, beef shin, speciality sausages and fresh fish.

Open all day all wk noon-11 (Sun noon-10.30)
Bar Meals Av main course £9.50 food served all day
Restaurant food served all day ⊕ MITCHELLS & BUTLERS
◀ Timothy Taylor Landlord, Greene King Abbot Ale, Sambrook's, Wandle Ŏ Westons Old Rosie Scrumpy, Addlestones, Aspall. ♀ 12 **Facilities** Dogs allowed Garden

W9

The Waterway ♀   PLAN 2 E4

54 Formosa St W9 2JU
☎ 020 7266 3557   📄 020 7266 3547
e-mail: info@thewaterway.co.uk
dir: From Warwick Ave tube, up Warwick Ave, turn left at Formosa St, pub is No. 54

Trendy Maida Vale restaurant and bar in a canalside setting with a fabulous outdoor terrace where popular barbecues are held. In colder weather, the bar is a great place to relax with its comfy sofas and open fires. There is a good choice of drinks, including cocktails and champagne by the glass. The restaurant menu offers modern European food – goat's cheese beignets with pear chutney and pistachio dressing; Moroccan lamb tagine; roast cod with chorizo and red peppers.

Open all day all wk noon-11pm (Sat 10.30am-11pm Sun 11am-10.30pm) **Bar Meals** L served all day D served all day Av main course £12 food served all day
Restaurant L served Mon-Fri 12-3.30, Sat-Sun 12-4 D served Mon-Sat 6.30-10.30, Sun 6.30-10 Av 3 course à la carte fr £25 ⊕ ENTERPRISE ◀ Guinness, Hoegaarden, Fuller's London Pride Ŏ Aspall. ♀ 16 **Facilities** Children welcome Children's menu Children's portions Garden Wi-fi

W11

Portobello Gold ♀   PLAN 2 E3

95-97 Portobello Rd, Notting Hill W11 2QB
☎ 020 7460 4900
e-mail: reservations@portobellogold.com
dir: From Notting Hill Gate Tube Station, follow signs to Portobello Market

In the heart of famous Portobello market, this quirky Notting Hill pub/wine bar/brasserie serves an interesting range of British ales and European beers, great wines and cocktails. Food is served all day in the bar and the Conservatory Restaurant and menus always list game

and seafood, including oysters, and dishes such as pasta, tortillas, burgers, bangers and steaks - all prepared from scratch on the premises. With the landlord's wife, Linda Bell, an established wine writer, 18 wines by the glass should be no surprise.

Open all day all wk **Bar Meals** L served all day D served all day Av main course £12 food served all day
Restaurant L served all day booking required D served all day food served all day ⊕ ENTERPRISE ◀ Guinness, Fuller's London Pride, Harveys Sussex Ales, Leffe, Meantime, Freedom Ŏ Thatchers Gold, Katy, Spartan.
♀ 18 **Facilities** Children welcome Children's portions Dogs allowed Wi-fi

W14

PICK OF THE PUBS

The Cumberland Arms ♀   PLAN 2 D3

29 North End Rd, Hammersmith W14 8SZ
☎ 020 7371 6806   📄 020 7371 6848
e-mail: thecumberlandarmspub@btconnect.com
dir: From Kensington Olympia, exit station, turn left, at Hammersmith Rd right, at T-junct (North End Rd) left, 100yds, pub on left

A popular gastro-pub close to Olympia, the Cumberland Arms has an attractive blue-painted façade with gold lettering and impressive floral displays in season. Pavement benches and tables help alleviate the pressure inside, where mellow furniture and stripped floorboards characterise its interior. Friendly staff, an affordable wine list and well-kept ales are the draw for those seeking after-work refreshment, but it is also a great place for flavoursome plates of unpretentious Mediterranean-style food offered from a monthly-changing menu. Hearty dishes range through roast courgette and white bean soup served with goat's cheese crostini; grilled lamb and red onion skewers; Tuscan rabbit casserole with prosciutto, thyme and tomato; and roast Italian sausages with mashed potatoes and sweet onion marmalade. Desserts and cheese revert to a more French/English style – bread and butter pudding with crème anglaise; and apple and mixed berry crumble with vanilla ice cream are two examples. Now stays open until midnight on Thursday and Friday evenings.

Open all day all wk noon-11 (Sun noon-10.30 Thu-Fri noon-mdnt) Closed: 23 Dec-2 Jan **Bar Meals** Av main course £14 **Restaurant** L served Mon-Sat 12-3, Sun 12.30-9.30 D served all wk 6-10 ⊕ THE PURPLE TIGER ◀ Fuller's London Pride, Exmoor Gold, Sharp's Doom Bar, Staropramen. ♀ 16 **Facilities** Children welcome Children's portions Dogs allowed Garden Wi-fi

The Havelock Tavern ♀   PLAN 2 D3

57 Masbro Rd, Brook Green W14 0LS ☎ 020 7603 5374
e-mail: enquiries@thehavelocktavern.co.uk
dir: Nearest tubes: Shepherd's Bush & Olympia

Despite being a gastro-pub for fifteen years, the award-winning Havelock is still run very much as a pub. It is situated in the quiet residential area of Brook Green and is popular with both lunchtime and evening customers who want a flavoursome plate of food before returning to work or home. They can choose from the twice daily changing menus with the likes of grilled sardines with rocket, broad bean and roast tomato salad; roast lamb rump with root vegetable purée and dauphinoise potatoes; and chocolate and mascarpone cheesecake. As well as real ales to enjoy, the pub has an extensive wine list.

Open all day all wk 11-11 (Sun 12-10.30) Closed: 25-26 Dec **Bar Meals** L served Mon-Sat 12-2.30, Sun 12.30-3 D served Mon-Sat 7-10, Sun 7.30-9.30 Av main course £13 ⊕ FREE HOUSE ◀ Fuller's London Pride, Sharp's Doom Bar, Sambrook's Wandle Ŏ Hogan's. ♀ 11 **Facilities** Children welcome Children's portions Dogs allowed Garden

The Jam Tree ♀ NEW   PLAN 2 D3

58 Milson Rd W14 0LB ☎ 020 7371 3999
e-mail: info@thejamtree.com
dir: Nearest stations: Shepherds Bush & Kensington (Olympia)

Tucked away behind Kensington Olympia, The Jam Tree's bar is furnished with an eclectic mix of chairs, tables and artworks; pavement tables add to its cosmopolitan appeal. Refreshments include a wide range of beers and spirits, and a wine list designed around menus that aim to set The Jam Tree apart from the usual gastro fare. So expect some spicy options among more familiar classics: a starter of curried Cornish crab samosas with cucumber raita could be followed by seared scallops with spicy coconut sauce, Malay potato cake and sautéed bok choy. Desserts too offer exotic possibilities: South African malva pudding with amarula cream is one option.

Open all day all wk **Bar Meals** L served Mon-Sat 12-3, Sun 12-8 D served Mon-Sat 6-10, Sun 12-8 Av main course £12 **Restaurant** L served Mon-Sat 12-3, Sun 12-8 D served Mon-Sat 6-10, Sun 12-8 ⊕ FREE HOUSE ◀ Old Speckled Hen, Greene King St Edmunds Ŏ Aspall. **Facilities** Children welcome Children's menu Children's portions Dogs allowed Wi-fi

WC1

PICK OF THE PUBS

The Bountiful Cow ♀   PLAN 1 E4

See Pick of the Pubs on opposite page

PICK OF THE PUBS

The Lamb ♀   PLAN 1 D5

94 Lamb's Conduit St WC1N 3LZ ☎ 020 7405 0713
e-mail: lambwc1@youngs.co.uk
dir: *Russell Square, turn right, 1st right, 1st left, 1st right*

This building was first recorded in 1729, was 'heavily improved' between 1836-1876, and frequented by Charles Dickens when he lived nearby in Doughty Street (now housing the Dickens Museum). This really is a gem of a place, with its distinctive green-tiled façade, very rare glass snob screens, dark polished wood, and original sepia photographs of music hall stars who performed at the nearby Holborn Empire. The absence of television, piped music and fruit machines allows conversation to flow, although there is a working polyphon. Home-cooked bar food includes a vegetarian corner (vegetable curry, or burger), a fish choice including traditional fish and chips; and steaks from the griddle, plus pies and baked dishes from the stove. Favourites are steak and ale pie (called the Celebration 1729 pie); sausage and mash; liver and bacon; and fried egg and chips. For something lighter, try a ploughman's or a vegetable samosa with mango chutney.

Open all day all wk noon-11 (Thu-Sat noon-mdnt, Sun noon-10.30) **Bar Meals** L served all wk 12-4 D served all wk 5-9 ⊕ YOUNG & CO BREWERY PLC ◁ Young's (full range). ♀ 11 **Facilities** Children welcome Garden

Norfolk Arms ♀ NEW   PLAN 1 D5

28 Leigh St WC1H 9EP ☎ 020 7388 3937
e-mail: info@norfolkarms.co.uk
dir: *Nearest tube stations: Russell Square, Kings Cross & Euston*

Located on a busy street corner within five minutes' walk of St Pancras International, the Norfolk Arms is one of London's newest gastro-pubs. Behind its Victorian frontage, the main bar and dining area are at ground level, with private dining on the first floor. An extensive menu features modern British food served in a tapas style that encourages sharing: typical choices include chickpea and tomato stew; grilled Shetland salmon; and barbeque chicken wings. A great choice of beers and ten wines by the glass complete the picture.

Open all day all wk Closed: 25 Dec, 1 Jan **Bar Meals** Av main course £11 food served all day **Restaurant** Av 3 course à la carte fr £23 food served all day ⊕ SCOTTISH & NEWCASTLE ◁ Theakstons XB, Greene King IPA. ♀ 10 **Facilities** Children welcome Children's portions Dogs allowed Wi-fi

WC2

The George ♀   PLAN 1 E4

213 Strand WC2R 1AP ☎ 020 7353 9638
e-mail: enquiries@georgeinthestrand.com
dir: *Opposite Royal Courts of Justice*

Facing the Royal Courts of Justice, The George was built as a coffee house in 1723, although the black and white façade is late Victorian. Once regulars included Horace Walpole and Samuel Johnson, today mingle with judges, barristers and court reporters over a pint of Sharp's Doom Bar or Black Sheep, a lunchtime salad, an open sandwich or hot wrap. For something more substantial, try chargrilled rib-eye steak; smoked poached haddock with bubble and squeak; traditional Irish lamb stew with dumplings; or the roast carvery. There's a real ale and cider festival every March.

Open all day all wk Closed: 25-26 Dec **Bar Meals** L served all wk 12-5 D served Mon-Sat 5-9, Sun 5-8 Av main course £8.95 **Restaurant** L served Mon-Fri 12-3 D served pre-booked only booking required ⊕ FREE HOUSE ◁ Sharp's Doom Bar, Hogsback TEA, Sussex Best, Sambrooks Wandle, Black Sheep, Purity UBU, Adnams bitter ♂ Aspall, Suffolk Cider. ♀ 12 **Facilities** Children welcome Dogs allowed Beer festival Wi-fi

The Lamb and Flag   PLAN 1 D3

33 Rose St, Covent Garden WC2E 9EB
☎ 020 7497 9504
dir: *Leicester Square, Cranbourne St exit, turn left into Garrick St, 2nd left*

Licensed during the reign of Elizabeth I, The Lamb and Flag exudes a strong atmosphere, with low ceilings, wood panelling and high-backed settles both striking features of the bar. In 1679 the poet Dryden was almost killed in a nearby alley. These days office workers and Covent Garden tourists throng the surrounding streets. Typical examples of the hot food served upstairs include Cumberland sausages, chips and beans; and roast beef, pork, lamb or chicken. There is a courtyard to enjoy in fine weather.

Open all day all wk 11-11 (Fri-Sat 11am-11.30pm, Sun 12-10.30) Closed: 25 Dec ⊕ FREE HOUSE ◁ Courage Best, Directors, Young's PA, Young's Special, Wells Bombardier, Harveys Best.

PICK OF THE PUBS

The Seven Stars   PLAN 1 E4

53 Carey St WC2A 2JB ☎ 020 7242 8521
e-mail: roxy@roxybeaujolais.com
dir: *From Temple N via The Strand & Bell Yard to Carey St. From Holborn SE via Lincoln's Inn Fields & Searle St to Carey St*

The Seven Stars may never have seen better days in its 410-year old history, because since Roxy Beaujolais took over this ancient Grade II listed pub, back of the Royal Courts of Justice, it has been delicately and undisruptively primped. The improvements were

managed with such tact by Roxy's architect husband that some even think his modern dumbwaiter is ancient. Strengthened by its ambience, The Seven Stars has bloomed into the ideal pub - the food is simple but well executed, the ales are kept perfectly, the wines are few but very good, and the staff are welcoming and efficient. In the last eleven years it has won many accolades. Roxy, sometime cookbook author and TV food show presenter, cooks herself most of the time. The dishes are always changing according to what's best in the market, and are listed on the blackboard. To the delight of barristers, journalists, BBC World Service staff and church music practitioners, Tom Paine the pub cat wears a chorister's ruff.

The Seven Stars

Open all day all wk 11-11 (Sat noon-11, Sun noon-10.30) Closed: 25-26 Dec, 1 Jan, Good Fri, Etr Sun **Bar Meals** L served Mon-Fri 12-3, Sat-Sun 12-9 D served Mon-Fri 5.30-9, Sat-Sun 12-9 Av main course £10 ⊕ FREE HOUSE ◁ Adnams Best, Adnams Broadside, Dark Star Best, Hophead, Sambrook's Wandle ♂ Aspall, Weston Organic Pear. **Facilities** Wi-fi

The Sherlock Holmes ♀   PLAN 1 D3

10 Northumberland St WC2N 5DB
☎ 020 7930 2644 ▤ 020 7839 0263
e-mail: 7967@greeneking.co.uk
dir: *From Charing Cross tube station exit onto Villiers St. Through 'The Arches' (runs underneath Charing Cross station) straight across Craven St into Craven Passage to Northumberland St*

Painted black with etched glass windows and colourful hanging baskets, this traditional corner pub is chock-full of Holmes memorabilia, including photographs of Conan Doyle, mounted pages from manuscripts, and artefacts and pieces recording the adventures of the Master Detective. There's even a replica of Holmes' and Watson's sitting room and study adjacent to the restaurant. This split level establishment has a bar on the ground floor and on the first floor an intimate covered roof garden and the restaurant. There's hot and cold bar food plus a themed à la carte menu offering such treats as Sir Arthur Conan Doyle's (roast topside of beef), and Dr. Watson's favourite (traditional Cumberland sausages).

Open all day all wk Closed: 25-26 Dec **Bar Meals** food served all day **Restaurant** booking required booking required food served all day ⊕ GREENE KING ◁ Sherlock Holmes Ale, Abbot Ale, Old Speckled Hen ♂ Aspall. ♀ 14 **Facilities** Children welcome Garden Wi-fi

Save on hotels. Book at theAA.com/hotel

LONDON 313 ENGLAND

PICK OF THE PUBS

The Bountiful Cow ♟

WC1   PLAN 1 E4

51 Eagle St, Holborn WC1R 4AP
☎ **020 7404 0200** 📠 **020 7404 8737**
e-mail: manager@roxybeaujolais.com
web: www.thebountifulcow.co.uk
dir: *230 mtrs NE from Holborn tube
station, via Procter St. Walk through 2
arches into Eagle St. Pub between High
Holborn & Red Lion Square*

Roxy Beaujolais, proprietor of the ancient
Seven Stars in WC2, found a 1960s pub
between Red Lion Square and High
Holborn and turned it into The Bountiful
Cow, 'a public house devoted to beef'. You
enter below green waterfalls of periwinkles
to find two floor levels that feel neatly
halfway between a funky bistro and a
stylish saloon. Walls are bedecked with
pictures of cows, bullfights, cowgirls,
meat cuts diagrams and cow-themed
films, presided over by a colourful poster
for *Cattle Queen of Montana* starring
Barbara Stanwyck and a former president
of the United States. The house seats 70
drinkers/diners; the music is jazzy but
discreet. Head Cook Roxy is author of the
pub cookbook *Home From the Inn
Contented* and was a presenter of the
BBC's *Full On Food*. Her menu, based on
beef sourced at Smithfield Market and
aged in-house, features exceptionally
large and well-made hamburgers, dubbed

Bountyburgers, and big steaks (rib-eye,
sirloin, T-bone, filet, rump, onglet) aged
many weeks and destined to be accurately
cooked by the grill chef, alongside cask-
conditioned ales and wines. Lunches are
of particularly notable value: the pub pays
homage to the Free Lunch tradition of US
pre-prohibition days with an Almost Free
Lunch. Memorable choices, including
vegetarian ones, are offered at 'nugatory',
i.e. low, prices, with the customer
requested to also buy a drink (it could be
a soft drink). A new, low cost Early Dinner
menu from 5 to 7pm offers some favourite
choices - steak sandwich, grilled pork
chop with apple sauce and mash,
mushroom risotto. The sights and tourist
destinations of central London are an
improving short walk away.

Open all day 11am-11pm (Sat
noon-11pm) Closed: 25-26 Dec, Good Fri,
Etr Sun, some BHs, Sun **Bar Meals** L
served Mon-Sat 12-3 D served Mon-Sat
5-10 **Restaurant** L served Mon-Sat 12-3
D served Mon-Sat 5-10 🍺 FREE HOUSE
🍺 Adnams Best, Adnams Broadside,
Timothy Taylor, Dark Star Hophead
🍏 Aspall. ♟ 9 **Facilities** Children's
portions Wi-fi

GREATER LONDON

CARSHALTON
Map 6 TQ26

The Sun ♀ NEW

4 North St SM5 2HU ☎ 020 8773 4549
e-mail: thesuncarshalton@googlemail.com
web: www.thesuncarshalton.com
dir: Off A232 (Croydon Rd) between Croydon & Sutton

Very much a family friendly pub, The Sun is nonetheless serious about its food and drink. Beer festivals with hog roasts and live music are held every June and November; at other times there are always five ales on the go. Menus of rustic comfort food with European influences use the freshest, seasonal, free-range and organic produce. The chefs move to the garden for summer barbecues, when the family bar, children's chalk board wall and sandpit come into their own. A popular stop after visiting Carshalton Ponds, The Sun has come a long way since its refurbishment in 2009.

Open all day **Closed:** Mon **Bar Meals** L served Tue-Sat 12-3, Sun 12-7 booking required D served Tue-Sat 6-9.30 booking required Av main course £10-£14 ⊕ FREE HOUSE ◀ Timothy Taylor Landlord, Rudgate Ruby Mild ☼ Westons. ♀ 14 **Facilities** Children welcome Children's menu Children's portions Play area Family room Dogs allowed Garden Beer festival Wi-fi

See advert below

CHELSFIELD
Map 6 TQ46

PICK OF THE PUBS

The Five Bells ♀

BR6 7RE ☎ 01689 821044 📄 01689 891157
dir: From M25 junct 4 take A224 towards Orpington. In approx 1m turn right into Church Rd. Pub on left

Conveniently located just inside the M25 at Junction 4, this family-run Grade II listed pub is situated in a protected conservation village, with many lovely walks in the area. Dating from 1668, the Five Bells takes its name from the magnificent St Martin of the Tours church just up the road. There are two bars: one is a dog-friendly front bar boasting an original inglenook fireplace; the other is larger and houses the restaurant area. This in turn leads to the patio and extensive garden, which comes complete with a swing and play area for the children. In the kitchen, chef Chris Miller's seasonal menu complements the real ales and wines on offer, and is particularly strong on gluten-free choices: garlic mushrooms, home-cured salmon, rump of lamb, and pan-fried sea bass are some examples. Home-made pizzas can be served at any time during pub opening hours, and beer festivals take place at Easter and in October along with monthly events.

Open all day all wk **Bar Meals** L served all wk 12-3 D served Thu-Sat 6.30-9 Av main course £10 **Restaurant** L served all wk 12-3 D served Thu-Sat 6.30-9 ⊕ ENTERPRISE INNS ◀ Courage Best, Sharp's Doom Bar, Guinness. ♀ 13 **Facilities** Children welcome Children's menu Children's portions Play area Dogs allowed Garden Beer festival Parking

HAM

Hand & Flower ♀ NEW
PLAN 1 C2

24 Upper Ham Rd TW10 5LA
☎ 020 8332 2022 📄 01923 711327
e-mail: info@handandflower.co.uk
dir: On A307

Originally the old toll house on the turnpike opposite Ham Common, the recently revamped Hand & Flower stands a short stroll from Richmond Park. Follow a good summer walk with lunch in the stunning, award-winning garden, replete with pond, private dining area and secluded tables away from the bustling patio. On inclement days head indoors to the modern and spacious dining area for all-day food, the daily menu ranging from home-made burgers and sandwiches to dressed crab, Caesar salad and sea bass with samphire, chilli and lime braised fennel, and vegetable and potato broth. Accompany with a pint of Pride or one of 15 wines by the glass.

Open all day all wk **Bar Meals** L served all wk 12-10 D served all wk 12-10 Av main course £10 food served all day **Restaurant** L served all wk 12-10 D served all wk 12-10 Av 3 course à la carte fr £18 food served all day ⊕ TOP TAVERNS LTD ◀ Fuller's London Pride, Harveys. ♀ 15 **Facilities** Children welcome Children's menu Children's portions Dogs allowed Garden Wi-fi

Save on hotels. Book at **theAA.com/hotel**

MERSEYSIDE 315 | ENGLAND

MERSEYSIDE

BARNSTON   Map 15 SJ28

Fox and Hounds ☺

Barnston Rd CH61 1BW
☎ **0151 648 7685** 📠 **0151 648 0872**
e-mail: ralphleech@hotmail.com
web: www.the-fox-hounds.co.uk
dir: *M53 junct 4 take A5137 to Heswall. Right to Barnston on B5138. Pub on A551*

The pub, located in a conservation area, became a centenarian in 2011, being built on the site of an alehouse and barn 100 years ago; its Edwardian character has been preserved in the pitch pine woodwork and leaded windows. The Snug is adorned with period fixtures and fittings, open fire and collections of 1920s/1930s memorabilia. A good selection of real ales is served alongside lunchtime salads, paninis, platters and traditional mains, while the specials board concentrates on beef and steak pie, lamb shank, lasagne, Somerset chicken, and battered fish and chips. The beautifully kept beer garden is a riot of colour in summer.

Open all day all wk 11-11 (Sun noon-10.30)
Bar Meals L served Mon-Sat 12-2, Sun 12-2.30 booking required D served Tue-Fri fr 5.30 booking required Av main course £6.95 ⊕ FREE HOUSE ◀ Websters, Theakston's Best, Old Peculier, Brimstage Trapper's Hat, Timothy Taylor Landlord, Guest ales. ☙ 12
Facilities Children welcome Children's portions Family room Dogs allowed Garden Parking Wi-fi

BROMBOROUGH   Map 15 SJ38

Dibbinsdale Inn ★★★★ INN

Dibbinsdale Rd CH63 0HJ
☎ **0151 334 9818** 📠 **0151 334 0097**
e-mail: info@thedibbinsdale.co.uk
dir: *M53 junct 5, A41 towards Birkenhead. In 2m left towards Bromborough rail station. Through 2 sets of lights. 2nd right into Dibbinsdale Rd. Inn 600yds on left*

When this urban-fringe pub was purchased by Thwaites a few years ago, the brewery gave it the contemporary makeover you see today, both inside and out, and now offers comfortable accommodation too. No prizes for guessing whose cask ales are sold, backed by guests and Kingstone Press cider. Sourcing ingredients from carefully chosen suppliers, the kitchen creates an ever-changing menu of traditional favourites: baked field mushrooms topped with Cheshire cheese is a typical starter, while grills, a daily roast with seasonal vegetables, and beer-battered haddock with thick-cut chips and mushy peas feature among the main courses.

Open all day all wk **Bar Meals** Av main course £8 food served all day **Restaurant** Av 3 course à la carte fr £20 food served all day ⊕ THWAITES ◀ Thwaites cask ales, Wainwright ♂ Kingstone Press. **Facilities** Children welcome Children's menu Children's portions Parking Wi-fi **Rooms** 11

GREASBY   Map 15 SJ28

Irby Mill ☺ NEW

Mill Ln CH49 3NT ☎ **0151 604 0194** 📠 **0151 604 0194**
e-mail: info@irbymill.co.uk
dir: *M53 junct 3, onto A552 signed Upton & Heswall. At lights onto A551 signed Upton & Greasby. At lights left into Arrowe Brook Rd. At rdbt 3rd exit into Mill Lane*

An eyecatching, solid, sandstone-block built old miller's cottage (the windmill was demolished in 1898, pub opened in 1980) just a short jog from the airy heights of Thurstaston Common at the heart of The Wirral Peninsula. One of the area's best choices of real ales meets an exceptional, very pubby menu strong on Wirral produce – steaks are from locally grazed Aberdeen Angus, sausages from an award-winning local butcher. Popular with ramblers and Sunday diners, there's a suntrap grassy garden for summer; log fire, low beams and York-stone floor for the winter.

Open all day all wk **Bar Meals** L served Mon-Sat 12-9, Sun 12-6 D served Mon-Sat 12-9, Sun 12-6 Av main course £8 food served all day **Restaurant** L served Mon-Sat 12-9, Sun 12-6 D served Mon-Sat 12-9, Sun 12-6 Av 3 course à la carte fr £18 food served all day ⊕ SCOTTISH & NEWCASTLE ◀ Wells Bombardier, Abbot Ale, Adnams Bitter, Jennings Cumberland Ale, 4 guest ales. ☙ 12
Facilities Children welcome Children's menu Children's portions Dogs allowed Garden Parking Wi-fi

HIGHTOWN   Map 15 SD30

The Pheasant Inn ☺

20 Moss Ln L38 3RA ☎ **0151 929 2106**
dir: *From A565 take B5193, follow signs to Hightown*

This former alehouse is just minutes from Crosby Beach, where sculptor Antony Gormley's 100 cast-iron figures gaze out to sea. Surrounded by fields and nearby golf courses, the pub retains an original brick in the restaurant wall dated 1719, when the pub was called the Ten Billets Inn. In the bar these days you'll find Timothy Taylor Landlord alongside Aspall ciders. The menu is changed twice a year so expect seasonal dishes like venison steak on honey-roasted root vegetables and butternut squash; or oyster mushroom and asparagus suet pudding with a cream sauce. There are also grill nights and Friday fish suppers to enjoy.

Open all day all wk noon-11pm (Sun noon-10.30pm)
Bar Meals food served all day **Restaurant** food served all day ⊕ MITCHELLS & BUTLERS ◀ Timothy Taylor Landlord ♂ Aspall Draught & Organic. ☙ 30 **Facilities** Children welcome Children's menu Garden Parking

LIVERPOOL   Map 15 SJ39

Everyman Bistro

9-11 Hope St L1 9BH
☎ **0151 708 9545** 📠 **0151 703 0290**
e-mail: bistro@everyman.co.uk
dir: *In front of Metropolitan Cathedral. Bistro in basement of Everyman Theatre*

Situated between the two cathedrals in the Georgian cultural quarter and celebrating 40 years in business, this is a favourite haunt of Liverpool's media, academic and theatrical fraternity - Bill Nighy and Julie Walters started out in the theatre above. The good value, twice-daily changing menus use the best of fresh local produce, and might include Tom's lamb scouse with beetroot and red cabbage, Thai spinach and mushroom curry and strawberry and rhubarb fruit crumble. Enjoy your meal with a pint of Black Sheep or Cains Bitter. Live music is performed occasionally often supporting new bands.

Open all day noon-mdnt (Fri-Sat noon-2am) Closed: Sun & BH **Bar Meals** food served all day **Restaurant** food served all day ⊕ FREE HOUSE ◀ Cains Bitter, Black Sheep, Derwent Pale Ale, Copper Dragon, Timothy Taylor Landlord. **Facilities** Children welcome Wi-fi

NORFOLK

BAWBURGH   Map 13 TG10

PICK OF THE PUBS

Kings Head ♀

Harts Ln NR9 3LS ☎ **01603 744977**
e-mail: anton@kingshead-bawburgh.co.uk
dir: From A47 W of Norwich take B1108 W

Run by Pam and Anton Wimmer for more than two decades, the 17th-century Kings Head stands opposite the village green, with the River Yare flowing close by. The pub is big on traditional charm with solid oak beams, bulging walls, wooden floors and comfy leather seating, making it the perfect place to be after a day exploring the delights of nearby Norwich. As a free house it serves real ales from East Anglia, as well as Aspall cider from Suffolk. Monthly menus and daily-changing specials firmly rooted in local markets offer a wide choice and the menu lists VIPs (Very Important Producers) who supply the kitchen. Recent menus include starters of pressed smoked chicken and Norfolk ham hock terrine, with main courses of Swannington rump steak, Binham Blue butter, Norfolk Dapple rarebit grilled mushroom and hand-cut chips. The dessert list might feature apple and date crumble with vanilla custard.

Open all day all wk Closed: 25-27 Dec eve, 1 Jan eve **Bar Meals** L served Mon-Sat 12-2, Sun 12-4 booking required D served Mon-Sat 5.30-9 booking required **Restaurant** L served Mon-Sat 12-2, Sun 12-4 booking required D served Mon-Sat 5.30-9 booking required ⊕ FREE HOUSE ◀ Adnams Best, Adnams Broadside, Woodforde's Wherry, Wadworths, IPA, Guest Ale ♂ Aspall, Aspall Blush. ♀ 11 **Facilities** Children welcome Children's menu Children's portions Dogs allowed Garden Parking Wi-fi

BINHAM   Map 13 TF93

Chequers Inn

Front St NR21 0AL ☎ **01328 830297**
e-mail: steve@binhamchequers.co.uk
dir: On B1388 between Wells-next-the-Sea & Walsingham

The Chequers is home to the Front Street Brewery, but even though they brew their own beer they still have regular Norfolk/East Anglian guest ales, and a large selection of bottled beers such as Old Tom. The pub has been owned by a village charity since the 1640s, and was originally a trade hall. Many stones from the nearby Binham Priory were used in its construction. The daily changing menu might include dishes such as butternut squash and roast pepper soup; grilled sea bass with sweet potato mash and pimento cream; minced beef, courgette and potato bake; cinnamon baked peaches and ice cream; and plum crumble. A beer festival is held four times a year.

Open all wk 11.30-2.30 6-11 (Fri-Sat 11.30-2.30 6-11.30 Sun noon-2.30 7-11) **Bar Meals** L served all wk 12-2 D served Mon-Sat 6-9, Sun 7-9 ⊕ FREE HOUSE ◀ Binham Cheer 3.9%, Callums Ale 4.3%, Unity Strong 5%, Seasonal specials, micro-brewery on site. **Facilities** Children welcome Children's menu Children's portions Garden Beer festival Parking Wi-fi

BLAKENEY   Map 13 TG04

PICK OF THE PUBS

The Blakeney White Horse ♀

4 High St NR25 7AL
☎ **01263 740574** ▤ **01263 741303**
e-mail: info@blakeneywhitehorse.co.uk
dir: From A148 (Cromer to King's Lynn road) onto A149 signed to Blakeney

This former 17th-century coaching inn is tucked away in the cluster of narrow streets lined with fishermen's cottages winding down to a small tidal harbour, with fabulous views over creeks, Glaven Valley estuary and vast marshes of sea lavender, samphire and mussel beds. Inside, the bar, dining room and airy conservatory are tastefully decorated in creams and darkwood and the informal bar is adorned with local artwork. The inn has a deserved reputation for its food, with lobster, crab and mussels sourced from local fishermen, meat and game from nearby Holkham Estate, and soft fruit, salads and vegetables from small farms and suppliers. From the appealing menu, choose potted Weybourne crab with curry spices and pickled courgettes, followed perhaps by navarin of Firs Farm lamb and steamed herb dumplings. An 80-bin wine list, 35 of them available by the glass, and a range of real ales complete the picture.

Open all day all wk 10.30am-11pm Closed: 25 Dec **Bar Meals** L served all wk 12-2.15 booking required D served Sun-Thu 6-9, Fri-Sat 6-9.30 booking required ⊕ FREE HOUSE ◀ Adnams Bitter, Woodforde's Wherry, Adnams Broadside, Yetmans ♂ Aspall. ♀ 35 **Facilities** Children welcome Children's menu Children's portions Family room Dogs allowed Garden Parking Wi-fi

The Kings Arms ♀

Westgate St NR25 7NQ
☎ **01263 740341** ▤ **01263 740391**
e-mail: kingsarmsnorfolk@btconnect.com
dir: From Holt or Fakenham take A148, then B1156 for 6m to Blakeney

A Grade II listed free house close to the north Norfolk coastal path, it's an ideal base for walks or a ferry trip to the nearby seal colony. Hosts Marjorie and Howard Davies settled here after long and successful showbiz careers, with their son Nic now handling the day-to-day running of the pub. An excellent selection of real ales is backed by menus featuring locally-caught fish and seasonal seafood – crab in summer and mussels in winter – together with game, home-made lasagne and steaks.

Open all day all wk **Bar Meals** food served all day ⊕ FREE HOUSE ◀ Greene King Old Speckled Hen, Woodforde's Wherry Best Bitter, Marston's Pedigree, Adnams Best Bitter. ♀ 10 **Facilities** Children welcome Children's menu Children's portions Play area Family room Dogs allowed Garden Parking

BLICKLING   Map 13 TG12

PICK OF THE PUBS

The Buckinghamshire Arms

Blickling Rd NR11 6NF ☎ **01263 732133**
e-mail: bucksarms@tiscali.co.uk
dir: A410 from Cromer exit at Aylsham onto B1354, follow Blickling Hall signs

A stunning late 17th-century coaching inn, 'The Bucks' stands by the gates of the National Trust's Blickling Hall. The lounge bar and restaurant, with their solid furniture and wood-burning stoves, have plenty of appeal. The Victorian cellar houses real ales from Norfolk's Wolf Brewery and Adnams in Suffolk. Meals can be taken in either the lounge bar or restaurant, with menus offering fresh local food served in both traditional and modern styles. Dishes from the dinner menu include starters of Mr Kew's Gunton venison sausage with braised Puy lentils, or gratin of smoked haddock and leek with brioche and Gruyère crust. Robust main courses might take in slow-roasted Old Spot pork belly with curly kale and sweet potato dauphinoise, or confit duck with thyme roasted red onion, celeriac mash and rich Madeira sauce. Vegetarians may select the creamy gnocchi with butternut squash, baby spinach and toasted pine nuts. This beautiful inn is said to be haunted by Anne Boleyn's ghost, who wanders in the adjacent courtyard and charming garden.

Open all day 11-11 summer (1-3 6-11 winter) Closed: 25 Dec, Sun eve **Bar Meals** L served Mon-Fri 12-2, Sat-Sun 12-2.30 booking required D served Tue-Sat 6.30-9 booking required Av main course £10.50 **Restaurant** L served Mon-Fri 12-2, Sat-Sun 12-2.30 booking required D served Tue-Sat 6.30-9 booking required Av 3 course à la carte fr £24 ⊕ FREE HOUSE ◀ Adnams Bitter & Regatta, Woodforde's Wherry, Nelson's Revenge, Wolf Coyote Bitter ♂ Aspall, Norfolk. **Facilities** Children welcome Children's portions Garden Parking Wi-fi

Save on hotels. Book at **theAA.com/hotel**

NORFOLK 317 **ENGLAND**

BRANCASTER — Map 13 TF74

PICK OF THE PUBS

The Ship Hotel ☻ NEW

Main Rd PE31 8AP ☎ 01485 210333
e-mail: thebar@shiphotelnorfolk.co.uk
dir: *On A149 in village centre*

TV chef and hotelier Chris Coubrough snapped up the faded and forlorn Ship Hotel, set in a prime coastal location opposite the access road to Brancaster beach, in 2009 to enhance his portfolio of chic inns along the north Norfolk coast. He embarked on a stunning refurbishment of the property, pushing open the doors in May 2010 and business has been brisk ever since. Coast path walkers, beach bums and families flock by to rest and refuel on some cracking modern pub food prepared from fresh produce sourced from local farmers and fisherman. Be tempted by a 'Ship Classic', perhaps braised gammon with new potatoes and parsley sauce, or tuck into sea bass with shellfish and tomato linguini, slow-cooked duck hash with fried duck egg and wild mushroom jus, or confit duck leg and balsamic jus. Wash down with a pint of Adnams and relax in the gorgeous bar and dining rooms, where you can expect rug-strewn wood floors, wood-burning stoves, contemporary Farrow and Ball hues, shelves full of books, quirky antiques, scrubbed wooden tables and a distinct nautical feel.

Open all day all wk **Bar Meals** L served 12-2.30 (school holidays, menu available 3-6) booking required D served 6.30-9.30 booking required **Restaurant** L served 12-2.30 (school holidays, menu available 3-6) booking required D served 6.30-9.30 booking required ⊕ FLYING KIWI INNS ◀ Adnams Bitter, Joc's Kiwi, Ale brewed by owner's wife ♂ Aspall. ☻ 14 **Facilities** Children welcome Children's menu Children's portions Dogs allowed Garden Parking Wi-fi

BRANCASTER STAITHE — Map 13 TF74

The Jolly Sailors ☻ NEW

PE31 8BJ ☎ 01485 210314
e-mail: info@jollysailorsbrancaster.co.uk
dir: *On A149 coast road between Hunstanton & Wells-next-the-Sea*

Recently restored to its former glory but retaining its unique charm and character, The Jolly Sailors is set in the hub of village life. The cover of the menu and wine list at this gem of an 18th-century free house shows a jolly Jack Tar dancing a hornpipe. Today's visitors should consider doing the same, not only because it's the brewery tap for the Brancaster micro-brewery, but also because it serves great pub food like mussels caught 'just over there'; Norfolk gammon with duck egg; and stone-baked pizzas. There are quiz, themed and local live music nights, and an annual beer festival in June.

Open all wk Mon-Thu 12-3 6-11, Fri 12-3 5-11, Sat 12-11, Sun 12-10.30 (all day spring & summer) **Bar Meals** L served (winter) Mon-Fri 12-2, Sat-Sun 12-9, all day spring & summer D served (winter) Mon-Fri 6-9, Sat-Sun 12-9, all day spring & summer Av main course £9.50 ⊕ FREE HOUSE ◀ Brancaster Brewery Malthouse Bitter, Woodforde's Wherry, Adnams Bitters, Guest ales ♂ Stowford Press. ☻ 10 **Facilities** Children welcome Children's menu Children's portions Play area Dogs allowed Garden Beer festival Parking Wi-fi

PICK OF THE PUBS

The White Horse ★★★ HL ◉◉ ☻

PE31 8BY ☎ 01485 210262 ▤ 01485 210930
e-mail: reception@whitehorsebrancaster.co.uk
dir: *A149 (coast road), midway between Hunstanton & Wells-next-the-Sea*

Run by the Nye family for the past 15 years, The White Horse occupies a spectacular coastal location overlooking the Norfolk Coast Area of Outstanding Natural Beauty. Enjoy the view of creeks, marshes and sandbars from the glass-screened viewing balcony edging the elevated sundeck terrace - also the place to head for to view inspiring sunsets over The Wash. Equally inspiring is the extensive, daily-changing conservatory restaurant menu at this two AA Rosette inn, where alfresco dining in the sunken garden is a popular warm-weather option, accompanied by Brancaster Best bitter or one of the other great real ales. Inside, scrubbed pine tables and high-backed settles help to create a welcoming atmosphere for diners eager to sample the freshest seafood, including seasonal fish and shellfish gathered from the village fishermen at the foot of the garden. Look forward to grilled whole plaice with crayfish and parsley butter and buttered new potatoes; local mussels with white wine, garlic and cream; meat-lovers can tuck in to 28 day matured 10oz Norfolk rump steak with garlic and rosemary butter, mushrooms and hand-cut chips, or local venison pie. Fifteen chic and comfortable en suite bedrooms complete the package.

Open all day all wk 11am-11pm (Sun 11am-10.30pm) (open from 9am for breakfast) **Bar Meals** L served all wk 11-9 D served all wk 11-9 Av main course £14 food served all day **Restaurant** L served all wk 12-2 booking required D served all wk 6.30-9 booking required Av 3 course à la carte fr £23.50 ⊕ FREE HOUSE ◀ Adnams Broadside, Woodforde's Wherry, Brancaster Best, Brancaster Malthouse, Brancaster The Wreck, Guest ales ♂ Aspall. ☻ 16 **Facilities** Children welcome Children's menu Children's portions Dogs allowed Garden Parking Wi-fi **Rooms** 15

BRISLEY   Map 13 TF92

The Brisley Bell Inn & Restaurant ★★★ INN

The Green NR20 5DW ☎ 01362 668686
e-mail: info@brisleybell-inn.co.uk
dir: On B1145, between Fakenham & East Dereham

The patio of this attractive 16th-century warm brick-built pub overlooks the largest piece of common land in Norfolk, amounting to some 200 acres. Inside you'll find a small refurbished bar serving reliable ales including their own Taverner's Tipple, with old beams, a large brick fireplace and exposed brick walls. There's a separate neatly laid-up dining room, and a wide-ranging menu that takes in bar snacks, fresh locally-sourced game, steaks, daily fish specials, and popular Sunday roasts. If you would like to stay over to explore the area, then there are comfortable bedrooms available.

Open all day all wk **Bar Meals** L served all wk 12-2.30 D served Mon-Thu & Sun 6-8, Fri-Sat 6-9 Av main course £5.95 **Restaurant** L served all wk 12-2.30 D served Mon-Thu & Sun 6-8, Fri-Sat 6-9 booking required Fixed menu price fr £7.95 Av 3 course à la carte fr £12.95 ⊕ FREE HOUSE ◀ Greene King IPA, Abbot, Olde Trip, Guinness Ö Aspall. **Facilities** Children welcome Children's menu Children's portions Dogs allowed Garden Beer festival Parking Wi-fi **Rooms** 3

BURNHAM MARKET   Map 13 TF84

PICK OF THE PUBS

The Hoste Arms ★★★ HL ◉◉ ℗

The Green PE31 8HD
☎ 01328 738777 🖷 01328 730103
e-mail: reception@hostearms.co.uk
web: www.hostearms.co.uk
dir: Signed off B1155, 5m W of Wells-next-the-Sea

Nelson's local, and one of Norfolk's most lauded and recognisable destination dining inns, with a magnificent combination of top-notch 2 AA Rosette food and distinctive accommodation, this old village manor house luxuriates in its location within the Norfolk Coast Area of Outstanding Natural Beauty, with the coastal path, marshlands, endless beaches and tremendous wildlife just a few minutes away from tranquil Burnham Market's green. The bar of the 371-year old inn retains a traditional feel with its lively atmosphere, open log fire and East Anglian ales; there's also a pretty walled garden tucked behind the Moroccan-themed terrace, as well as a relaxed conservatory where you can chill out and read the

papers over a cappuccino. The immense wine list is breathtaking, matching the notable surf and turf lunch menu available at the bar or in five restaurant areas, where the very finest Norfolk produce is gainfully employed in dishes such as Norfolk Coast assiette, just part of which includes soused mackerel, tempura oysters and Brancaster mussels, whilst home-made steak and kidney pud comes with honey-glazed parsnips and Chantenay carrots; there's a good clutch of vegetarian options too, completed by warm treacle tart and blackberry compote.

Open all day all wk **Bar Meals** L served all wk 12-2 D served all wk 6-9 Av main course £14 **Restaurant** L served all wk 12-2 booking required D served all wk 6-9 booking required ⊕ FREE HOUSE ◀ Woodforde's Wherry Best, Greene King Abbot Ale, Nelson's Revenge. ℗ 16 **Facilities** Children's menu Children's portions Dogs allowed Garden Parking Wi-fi **Rooms** 34

See advert on page 317

BURNHAM THORPE   Map 13 TF84

PICK OF THE PUBS

The Lord Nelson ℗

Walsingham Rd PE31 8HN
☎ 01328 738241 🖷 01328 738241
e-mail: simon@nelsonslocal.co.uk
web: www.nelsonslocal.co.uk
dir: B1355 (Burnham Market to Fakenham road), pub 9m from Fakenham & 1.75m from Burnham Market. Pub near church opposite playing fields

Opposite the delightful village cricket ground and bowling green, this pub started life in 1637 as The Plough. It was renamed The Lord Nelson in 1798, to honour Horatio Nelson who was born in the village. Visitors today can soak up an atmosphere that has changed little over the past 370 years; you can even sit on Nelson's high-backed settle. Drinks are served from the taproom, with real ales drawn straight from the cask. In the cosy bar you can also partake in unique rum-based tipples such as Nelson's Blood. The kitchen aims to cook dishes with balance between flavours, so that the quality of the ingredients shines. Lamb shank with rosemary sauce and sea bass with white wine sauce on bacon and leek mash are typical choices, with seasonal specialities such as Brancaster mussels and Cromer crab. Children will enjoy the huge garden. Walking tours of Nelson's village at weekends from May to September are organised.

Open all wk noon-3 6-11 (Jul-Aug noon-11pm) **Bar Meals** L served all wk 12-2.30 D served all wk 6-9 Av main course £12.95 **Restaurant** L served all wk 12-2.30 D served all wk 6-9 booking required Av 3 course à la carte £24.50 ⊕ GREENE KING ◀ Greene King Abbot Ale & IPA, Woodforde's Wherry, Nelson's Blood Bitter. ℗ 14 **Facilities** Children welcome Children's menu Play area Dogs allowed Garden Parking Wi-fi

BURSTON   Map 13 TM18

The Crown NEW

Mill Rd IP22 5TW ☎ 01379 741257
e-mail: enquiries@burstoncrown.com
dir: NE of Diss

Lost down winding lanes north of Diss, the 16th-century Crown is a cracking community pub set beside Burston's pretty green. Steve and Bev Kembery work hard to draw in the locals for top-notch ale and food, organising the village fete, hosting three beer festivals a year, a weekly busker's night and regular theme nights. As well as a decent pint of Adnams, you can tuck into hake in beer batter or Norfolk Platter for sharing in the bar, or look to the carte for tomato, potato and garlic soup, confit duck leg with braised Puy lentils, and whole baked sea bass. Well worth finding...!

Open all day all wk **Bar Meals** L served Mon-Sat 12-2, Sun 12-4 D served Mon-Sat 6.30-9 booking required Av main course £17 **Restaurant** L served Mon-Sat 12-2, Sun 12-4 D served Mon-Sat 6.30-9 Av 3 course à la carte fr £23 ⊕ FREE HOUSE ◀ Adnams Best Bitter, Adnams Old, Burston's Cuckoo, Abbot Ale, Elmtree Beers, Elgood & Sons Ö Aspall, Burnards Norfolk Cider. **Facilities** Children welcome Children's menu Children's portions Dogs allowed Garden Beer festival Parking Wi-fi

CLEY NEXT THE SEA   Map 13 TG04

PICK OF THE PUBS

The George Hotel ℗

High St NR25 7RN
☎ 01263 740652 🖷 01263 741275
e-mail: info@thegeorgehotelatcley.co.uk
dir: On A149 through Cley next the Sea, approx 4m from Holt

Located near the sea and marshes, The George is stands on historic Cley's winding High Street. The beer garden backs onto the marshes, from where you can see Cley's famous mill, while the lovely oak-floored bar provides a year-round welcome. You can snack in the lounge bar or dine in the light, painting-filled restaurant. At lunchtime the menu runs from sandwiches (hot chicken, avocado, crispy bacon and red pesto mayonnaise; or Brie, smoked ham and fresh mango) to starters and light meals such as warm pan-fried chicken liver, duck liver and rocket salad with balsamic dressing; or hearty main courses - perhaps home-made steak, kidney and suet pudding. Dinner brings starters of roast parsnip and honey soup laced

Save on hotels. Book at theAA.com/hotel

NORFOLK 319 ENGLAND

with cream, followed by braised pork belly with spiced red cabbage, wilted spinach and honey glaze. Seafood is a real strength.

Open all day all wk 10.30am-11.30am
Bar Meals L served Mon-Sat noon-2.15, Sun 12.30-2.30 D served Mon-Sat 6.30-9, Sun 6.30-8.30
Restaurant L served Mon-Sat noon-2.15, Sun 12.30-2.30 D served Mon-Sat 6.30-9, Sun 6.30-8.30
🍺 Yetmans ales, Adnams Broadside, Woodforde's Wherry, Guest ales Ö Aspall. 🍷 8 **Facilities** Children welcome Family room Dogs allowed Garden Parking

COLTISHALL   Map 13 TG21

Kings Head

26 Wroxham Rd NR12 7EA ☎ **01603 737426**
e-mail: contact@kingsheadcoltishall.co.uk
dir: A47 (Norwich ring road) onto B1150 to North Walsham at Coltishall. Right at petrol station, follow to right past church. Pub on right by car park

Standing on the banks of the River Bure, this 17th-century free house is right in the heart of the Norfolk Broads. Hire cruisers are available at nearby Wroxham, and fishing boats can be hired at the pub. If you prefer to stay on dry land you'll find a warm welcome at the bar, with a range of real ales that includes Adnams Bitter, Directors and Marston's Pedigree. There's an inviting menu, too, served in both the bar and the restaurant.

Open all wk 11-3 6-12 Closed: 26 Dec ⊕ FREE HOUSE 🍺 Adnams Bitter, Directors, Marston's Pedigree, Fuller's London Pride. **Facilities** Children welcome Children's menu Children's portions Parking

CROMER   Map 13 TG24

The Red Lion Food and Rooms ★★★★ INN 🍷 NEW

Brook St NR27 9HD ☎ **01263 514964** 📠 **01263 512834**
e-mail: info@redlion-cromer.co.uk
dir: From A149 in Cromer right into Church St, leads to Garden St. Right into Jetty St, left into Tucker St. Pub on corner of Brook St

Situated in the heart of Cromer, overlooking the pier and award-winning beach. The Red Lion was HQ of the area's coastal defences during WWII, and tunnels reputedly connected it to other strategic buildings in town. It was built in the late 1800s, and although refurbished it retains many original features. Beer options are an ale drinker's dream, and real ciders are planned. Short but high quality menus proffer the likes of terrine of spiced pork and Gunton venison casserole. There are light, comfortable rooms, many with sea views.

Open all day all wk **Bar Meals** L served all wk 12-2.30 D served all wk 6-9.30 Av main course £11
Restaurant L served all wk 12-2.30 D served all wk 6-9.30 booking required Av 3 course à la carte fr £20 ⊕ FREE HOUSE 🍺 Bees Brewery Wobble, Green Jack Brewery Lurcher, Woodforde's Nelson's Revenge, Humpty Dumpty Brewery Railway Sleeper, Adnams Broadside. 🍷 9 **Facilities** Children welcome Children's menu Children's portions Dogs allowed Beer festival Parking Wi-fi **Rooms** 12

DEREHAM   Map 13 TF91

Yaxham Mill

Norwich Rd, Yaxham NR19 1RP
☎ **01362 851182** 📠 **01362 691482**
e-mail: yaxhammill@hotmail.co.uk
dir: From Norwich take A47 towards Swaffham. At East Dereham take B1135. Yaxham 2m

A converted windmill in the middle of open Norfolk countryside and dating back to 1810. The miller's house and chapel were transformed into a restaurant and bar. Menus cater for all tastes, with grilled lemon sole, minted lamb steak, sweet and sour chicken, and chilli con carne among other dishes. Home-made pies, including steak and kidney and cottage, are something of a speciality.

Open all wk 🍺 Bombardier, Young's, 2 guest ales.
Facilities Garden Parking

EAST RUDHAM   Map 13 TF82

PICK OF THE PUBS

The Crown Inn 🍷

The Green PE31 8RD ☎ **01485 528530**
e-mail: reception@crowninnnorfolk.co.uk
dir: On A148, 6m from Fakenham on King's Lynn road

Standing at the head of the village green on the A149, the award-winning Crown at East Rudham is part of TV chef Chris Coubrough's thriving Flying Kiwi mini-empire of pubs along the Norfolk coast. It draws the crowds for its charming, spruced-up interior, which successfully blends traditional period features (low beams, rug-strewn wooden floor, open log fires) with contemporary comforts - cool Farrow & Ball colours, high-backed leather chairs at scrubbed tables, shelves of books, fresh flowers and chunky church candles. Equally bang up-to-date is the food, with the menu changing every two weeks listing good modern British dishes prepared from fresh Norfolk produce. Tuck into salmon and brown shrimp rillettes with toast and caper berries, then follow with roast chump of lamb with roast Mediterranean vegetables, crispy polenta and black olive jus, leaving room for raspberry brûlée tart. Expect decent lunchtime sandwiches and proper kids' food.

Open all day all wk **Bar Meals** L served all wk 12-2.30 D served all wk 6.30-9.30 **Restaurant** L served all wk 12-2.30 D served all wk fr 6.30 ⊕ FREE HOUSE 🍺 Adnams Bitter, Broadside, Flying Kiwi Homebrew Ö Aspall. 🍷 14 **Facilities** Children welcome Children's menu Children's portions Dogs allowed Parking Wi-fi

EAST RUSTON   Map 13 TG32

The Butchers Arms

Oak Ln NR12 9JG ☎ **01692 650237**
dir: From A149 SE of North Walsham follow signs for Briggate, Honing & East Ruston. Oak Ln off School Rd

Originally three terraced cottages built in the early 1800s, the middle one of which was a butcher's shop. Today it's a quintessential beamed village pub, without jukebox or pool table; you'll just find 'Mavis', a 1954 Comma fire engine, parked outside. Landlady Julie Oatham has been at the Butchers for over 20 years, and takes pride in creating a welcoming atmosphere, offering a good choice of real ales from local breweries, and serving traditional home-cooked favourites such as cottage pie, roast of the day, or vegetable lasagne. There is a beer garden and vine-covered patio for summer dining.

Open 12-2.30 6.30-11 Closed: Mon (Jan-Mar)
Bar Meals L served all wk 12-2 D served all wk 7-8.30 Av main course £7.75 **Restaurant** L served all wk 12-2 D served all wk 7-8.30 Fixed menu price fr £8 Av 3 course à la carte fr £12 ⊕ FREE HOUSE 🍺 Adnams, Woodforde's, Old Speckled Hen, Greene King IPA. **Facilities** Children welcome Children's menu Children's portions Dogs allowed Garden Parking **Notes** ⊜

EATON   Map 13 TG20

The Red Lion 🍷

50 Eaton St NR4 7LD
☎ **01603 454787** 📠 **01603 456939**
e-mail: redlioneaton@hotmail.co.uk
dir: Off A11, 2m S of Norwich city centre

This heavily-beamed 17th-century coaching inn has bags of character, thanks to its Dutch gable ends, panelled walls and inglenook fireplaces. The covered terrace enables customers to enjoy one of the real ales or sample a glass from the wine list outside during the summer months. The extensive menus offer everything from Hungarian beef goulash soup to pan-fried or deep-fried skate wing with capers, or Norfolk rabbit, bacon and leek puff pastry pie. There's a light meals and snack menu too.

Open all day all wk **Bar Meals** L served all wk 12-2.15 booking required D served all wk 6.15-9 booking required **Restaurant** L served all wk 12-2.15 booking required D served all wk 6.15-9 booking required 🍺 Adnams Bitter, Woodforde's Wherry, Fuller's London Pride. 🍷 10 **Facilities** Children welcome Children's menu Children's portions Garden Parking Wi-fi

ERPINGHAM   Map 13 TG13

PICK OF THE PUBS

The Saracen's Head

NR11 7LZ ☎ 01263 768909 📠 01263 768993
e-mail: info@saracenshead-norfolk.co.uk
dir: *From A140, 2.5m N of Aylsham, left, through Erpingham. Pass Spread Eagle on left. Through Calthorpe, 0.5m, pub on right*

The privately owned Saracen's Head is deep among the fields down country lanes — and you do find yourself wondering why there's a pub in such a lonely spot. The answer is that it was once a coach house, built in Tuscan farmhouse style in 1806 for neighbouring Wolterton Hall. Its arty, parlour room atmosphere is the legacy of the former owner, who has now been succeeded by Tim and Janie Elwes. You may eat in one of the bars, where Suffolk and Norfolk real ales are on hand pump, or in the restaurant, where a sample three-course meal might comprise grilled halloumi on lavender (a local crop) croute with sun-blushed tomatoes; roast Norfolk pheasant with Calvados and cream; or baked Cromer crab with apple and sherry; and poached pears in spicy red wine. For a really quiet drink or meal, sit out in the sheltered courtyard garden.

Open 11.30–3 6–11 (Sun noon–3 7–10.30) Closed: 25–29 Dec, Mon (ex BHs), Tue L (Oct–May)
Bar Meals L served 12–2 D served 6.30–8.30 booking required **Restaurant** L served 12–2 booking required D served 6.30–8.30 booking required ⊕ FREE HOUSE ◀ Adnams Best Bitter, Woodforde's Wherry, Guest ales. **Facilities** Children welcome Children's menu Children's portions Dogs allowed Garden Parking

FAKENHAM   Map 13 TF92

The Wensum Lodge Hotel

Bridge St NR21 9AY
☎ 01328 862100 📠 01328 863365
e-mail: enquiries@wensumlodge.fsnet.co.uk
dir: *In town centre*

Idyllically located by the River Wensum just three minutes walk from Fakenham, this lovely pub has a stream flowing through its garden and offers guests free fishing on the river. The building dates from around 1700, and was originally the grain store for the adjoining mill. Fine ales are complemented by home-cooked food prepared from locally supplied ingredients, with baguettes, jacket potatoes and an all-day breakfast on the light bite menu and a carte menu for heartier fare. An ideal base for cycling, bird-watching, fishing and horse-racing.

Open all wk ⊕ FREE HOUSE ◀ Greene King Abbot Ale & IPA, Old Mill Bitter. **Facilities** Children welcome Garden Parking

GREAT RYBURGH   Map 13 TF92

The Blue Boar Inn ♀

NR21 0DX ☎ 01328 829212
e-mail: blueboarinn@ryburgh.co.uk
dir: *Off A1067 4m S of Fakenham*

Tracing its roots back to 1685, this former coaching inn has been lovingly restored, retaining period features like the inglenook fireplace and tiled floors. The inn stands opposite the round towered Saxon church of St Andrew with the river Wensum flowing nearby. Nowadays the inn serves a good range of real ales alongside home-cooked, locally sourced food. Typical choices include four cheese quiche with salad; venison and pheasant casserole; and grilled cod with shrimp and Chablis beurre blanc.

Open 11.30–2.30 6.30–11.30 Closed: Tue
Bar Meals L served Wed-Fri 11.30–2.30, Sun 11.30–2.30 D served Wed-Mon 6.30–10.30 Av main course £9.95 **Restaurant** L served Wed-Fri 11.30–2.30, Sun 11.30–2.30 D served Wed-Mon 6.30–10.30 Av 3 course à la carte fr £19.95 ⊕ FREE HOUSE ◀ Adnams Bitter, Winters Golden, Winters Revenge, Guinness, Staropramen, Yetman's ♂ Addlestones, Stowford Press. ♀ 8 **Facilities** Children welcome Children's menu Children's portions Play area Family room Dogs allowed Garden Parking Wi-fi

HEVINGHAM   Map 13 TG12

Marsham Arms Freehouse

Holt Rd NR10 5NP ☎ 01603 754268
e-mail: info@marshamarms.co.uk
dir: *On B1149 N of Norwich airport, 2m through Horsford towards Holt*

Built as a roadside hostel for poor farm labourers by Victorian philanthropist and landowner Robert Marsham. Some original features remain, including the wooden beams and large open fireplace. There is a spacious garden with paved patio and dedicated family room. A good range of fresh fish dishes includes cod, haddock, sea bass, herrings and crab. With a popular 'help yourself' salad bar, other main courses might include braised beef with red wine and cranberry, locally sourced roast pheasant, and steaks. Look out for the monthly wine appreciation evenings.

Open all day all wk ⊕ FREE HOUSE ◀ Adnams Best, Woodforde's Wherry Best Bitter, Mauldens, Worthington, Broadside ♂ Aspall. **Facilities** Children welcome Children's menu Children's portions Play area Family room Dogs allowed Garden Parking Wi-fi

HEYDON   Map 13 TG12

Earle Arms ♀

The Street NR11 6AD ☎ 01263 587376
e-mail: hatthearlearms@aol.com
dir: *Signed between Cawston & Corpusty on B1149 (Holt to Norwich road)*

Horse-racing memorabilia adorn the walls of this 16th-century free house situated on the green in this pretty privately-owned village. One of the two rooms offers service through a hatch to the tables in the pretty back garden. Not only is it thought that Oliver Cromwell once stayed here, but Heydon itself is often used as a film location, so stars of stage and screen have enjoyed a good choice of dishes complemented by daily specials. There is a beer festival held on St George's Day.

Open 12–3 6–11 Closed: Mon **Bar Meals** L served Tue-Sun 12–2 booking required D served Tue-Sun 7–9 booking required Av main course £10 **Restaurant** L served Tue-Sun 12–2 booking required D served Tue-Sun 7–9 booking required ⊕ FREE HOUSE ◀ Adnams, Woodforde's Wherry, Black Sheep. ♀ 16 **Facilities** Children welcome Children's menu Children's portions Dogs allowed Garden Beer festival Parking

HINGHAM   Map 13 TG00

The White Hart Hotel **NEW**

3 Market Place NR9 4AF ☎ 01953 850214
e-mail: reception@whitehartnorfolk.co.uk
dir: *In market square on B1108*

In the midst of Norfolk at the heart of the peaceful town of Hingham, this long established coaching inn reopened in 2011 after extensive refurbishment. Elements of the old inn remain in the beams and open fireplaces; however this is unashamedly a gastro-pub drawing on the larder of East Anglia, twinned with contemporary design ideals, resulting in a memorable mix of retro rustic, exotic touches and cool chic. Part of a small, upmarket chain, one of the beers here is brewed by the owner's wife. The menu from TV chef Chris Coubrough is suitably inspiring; char-grilled quail or twelve-hour cooked brisket take the eye here.

Open all day all wk **Bar Meals** L served all wk 12–2.30 D served all wk 6.30–9.30 **Restaurant** L served all wk 12–2.30 D served all wk 6.30–9.30 ⊕ FREE HOUSE ◀ Adnams Bitter, Joc's Kiwi Ale, Guest ale ♂ Aspall. **Facilities** Children welcome Children's menu Children's portions Dogs allowed Garden Parking

Save on hotels. Book at theAA.com/hotel

NORFOLK 321 ENGLAND

HOLKHAM
Map 13 TF84

PICK OF THE PUBS

Victoria at Holkham ★★ SHL ◉◉ ▮

Park Rd NR23 1RG
☎ 01328 711008 📄 01328 711009
e-mail: victoria@holkham.co.uk
dir: On A149, 3m W of Wells-next-the-Sea

The Victoria stands at the gates of landlord Tom Coke's Palladian ancestral home, Holkham Hall, just minutes from the golden sands of Holkham Beach. Its opulent, colonial-style interior is full of furniture and accessories from Rajahstan and other exotic places. Outside is a courtyard where summer barbecues are popular. Tom Coke would argue that the Victoria's main attraction is what he calls 'some of the most consistently good food in North Norfolk'. Key words here are fresh, local and seasonal, whether it be shellfish, fish or samphire from the north Norfolk coast, beef from farms on the Holkham estate, organic chickens from a tenant farmer, venison from the herd of fallow deer or, in the winter, wild game from family shoots. Perhaps choices might be pumpkin and truffle risotto; slow braised beef with pomme purée; or Holkham venison with braised red cabbage; and chilled vanilla rice pudding with stewed English plums.

Open all day all wk 11-11 **Bar Meals** L served Mon-Fri 12-2.30, Sat -Sun 12-3 D served all wk 6.30-9 **Restaurant** L served Mon-Fri 12-2.30, Sat-Sun 12-3 booking required D served Sun-Thu 7-9, Fri-Sat 7-9.30 booking required ⊕ HOLKHAM ESTATE ◀ Adnams Best ♻ Aspall. ▮ 12 **Facilities** Children welcome Children's menu Children's portions Play area Dogs allowed Garden Parking Wi-fi **Rooms** 10

HOLT
Map 13 TG03

PICK OF THE PUBS

The Pigs ◉ ▮ NEW

Norwich Rd, Edgefield NR24 2RL ☎ 01263 587634
e-mail: info@thepigs.org.uk
dir: On B1149

A remarkable local pub where community spirit (the kids' cookery school is very popular) and culinary endeavour combine in a celebration of all things Norfolk. Perhaps chef/landlord Tim Abbott's AA Rosette should be dedicated to the porcine stars of the show; an amazingly versatile menu emerges from the kitchens, utilising oft-forgotten cuts of meat and produce of the pub's adjoining allotment gardens. Braised cheeks or the Pigs' signature dish of slow cooked belly with smoky bacon beans, black pudding and crackling should fit the bill. If pork-based treats aren't your thing, then Edgefield game casserole with liquorice and prunes may tempt, or how's about smoked eel with beetroot relish. The lovely tranquil setting at the fringe of the village allows for a peaceful garden (except when petanque is being played), whilst locals barter their plentiful fresh fruit and vegetables,

or maybe freshly caught mackerel or a hedgerow rabbit (the specials board reflects just what the regulars can come by!) for a pint or two, practice darts or bar billiards and quaff Wolf Brewery Old Spot Bitter – what else.

Open all wk Mon-Sat 11-2.30 6-11 (Sun & BHs 12-9) **Bar Meals** L served Mon-Sat 12-2.30, Sun & BHs 12-9 booking required D served Mon-Sat 6-9, Sun & BHs 12-9 booking required Av main course £10.25-£14.95 **Restaurant** L served Mon-Sat 12-2.30, Sun & BHs 12-9 booking required D served Mon-Sat 6-9, Sun & BHs 12-9 booking required Av 3 course à la carte fr £25 ⊕ FREE HOUSE ◀ Woodforde's Wherry, Abbot Ale, Wolf Brewery Old Spot, Adnams Broadside & Bitter. ▮ 17 **Facilities** Children welcome Children's menu Children's portions Play area Family room Dogs allowed Garden Parking

HORSEY
Map 13 TG42

Nelson Head

The Street NR29 4AD ☎ 01493 393378
dir: On B1159 (coast road) between West Somerton & Sea Palling

Located on a National Trust estate, which embraces nearby Horsey Mere, this 17th-century inn will, to many, epitomise the perfect country pub. It enjoys the tranquility of a particularly unspoilt part of the Norfolk coast - indeed, the Broads are ½ mile away and glorious beaches only a mile - and the sheltered gardens look out towards the dunes and water meadows. Haddock and chips, cottage pie and a selection of vegetarian choices are among the dishes available. Local beers are Woodforde's Wherry and Nelson's Revenge. Change of hands March 2011

Open all day all wk ⊕ FREE HOUSE ◀ Woodforde's Wherry, Nelson's Revenge ♻ Stowford Press. **Facilities** Children welcome Children's menu Play area Family room Garden Parking

HORSTEAD
Map 13 TG21

Recruiting Sergeant ▮

Norwich Rd NR12 7EE ☎ 01603 737077
dir: On B1150 between Norwich & North Walsham

Matthew and Nicola Colchester have developed an enviable local reputation for food at this award-winning colour-washed brick and flint free house. Fresh local produce is the foundation of their ever-changing menu, which might include Binham Blue salad with pickled pears; toasted steak sandwich, red onion marmalade and chips; chargrilled Cajun spiced swordfish and king prawn brochettes on Caesar salad; a giant bowl of Brancaster mussels.

Open all day all wk 11-11 (Sun noon-10.30) **Bar Meals** L served Mon-Sat 12-2, Sun 12-9 booking required D served Mon-Sat 6-9, Sun 12-9 booking required Av main course £12.95 **Restaurant** L served Mon-Sat 12-2, Sun 12-9 booking required D served Mon-Sat 6-9, Sun 12-9 booking required ⊕ FREE HOUSE ◀ Adnams, Woodforde's, Greene King Abbot Ale, Scottish Courage ♻ Aspall. ▮ 10 **Facilities** Children welcome Children's menu Children's portions Dogs allowed Garden Parking

HUNSTANTON
Map 12 TF64

The King William IV Country Inn & Restaurant ▮

Heacham Rd, Sedgeford PE36 5LU
☎ 01485 571765 📄 01485 571743
e-mail: info@thekingwilliamsedgeford.co.uk
dir: A149 to Hunstanton, right at Norfolk Lavender in Heacham onto B1454, signed Docking. 2m to Sedgeford

Tucked away in the village of Sedgeford and conveniently close to the north Norfolk coastline, this extensively refurbished and extended free house has been an ale house since 1836. Made cosy by winter log fires, it has four dining areas, plus a covered alfresco terrace for warmer months. At the height of the season, you'll find five real ales on tap, and extensive menus to please everyone: expect the likes of coquilles St Jacques; guinea fowl breast stuffed with a pork and sage sausagemeat; and treacle sponge served with cream, ice cream or custard. Accommodation available.

Open all day 11-11 (Sun 12-10.30) Closed: Mon L (ex BH) **Bar Meals** L served Tue-Sat 12-2, Sun 12-2.30 booking required D served all wk 6.30-9 booking required **Restaurant** L served Tue-Sat 12-2, Sun 12-2.30 booking required D served all wk 6.30-9 booking required ⊕ FREE HOUSE ◀ Woodforde's Wherry, Adnams Bitter, Greene King Abbot Ale, Old Speckled Hen, guest ale. ▮ 9 **Facilities** Children welcome Children's menu Children's portions Family room Dogs allowed Garden Parking Wi-fi

HUNWORTH — Map 13 TG03

PICK OF THE PUBS

The Hunny Bell ♀

The Green NR24 2AA ☎ 01263 712300
e-mail: hunnybell@animalinns.co.uk
dir: *From Holt take B1110. 1st right to Hunworth*

Niche Norfolk pub group Animal Inns spruced up and extended this 18th-century village gem in 2008. Set by the green in pretty Hunworth in the peaceful Glaven Valley, just two miles south of Holt, the neat, whitewashed pub provides a quiet haven away from the bustling beaches and villages on the coast. In-the-know foodies retreat from the salt marshes to the cosy snug and the rustic-chic beamed main bar, which successfully blend historic charm with a contemporary feel, for real coffee, pints of Wherry and some imaginative pub food. Kick off with twice-baked Norfolk Dapple soufflé with dressed leaves and balsamic vinaigrette, follow with braised Stody Estate venison with bubble-and-squeak, red cabbage and braising jus, and finish with apple and oak crumble with vanilla ice cream. Walkers will find excellent lunchtime sandwiches. Outside, there's a terrace overlooking the green, as well as a charming old-world English garden.

Open all wk noon-3 6-11 **Bar Meals** L served all wk 12-2.30 D served all wk 6-9 **Restaurant** L served all wk 12-2.30 D served all wk 6-9 ⊕ ANIMAL INNS ◀ Woodforde's Wherry, Adnams, Greene King, Elgoods, Oakham ♂ Aspall. ♀ 10 **Facilities** Children welcome Children's menu Children's portions Dogs allowed Garden Beer festival Parking Wi-fi

INGHAM — Map 13 TG32

The Ingham Swan ♀ NEW

Swan Corner, Sea Palling Rd NR12 9AB
☎ 01692 581099
e-mail: info@theinghamswan.co.uk
dir: *From A149 through Stalham to Ingham*

Built in the 14th-century, this beautifully preserved inn was originally part of Ingham Priory until its destruction in the 16th-century under Henry VIII. A sympathetic refurbishment has retained the building's heritage and blended it with contemporary decor. Chef-patron Daniel Smith used to work at Le Gavroche and Morston Hall and he sticks to his Norfolk roots with a menu packed with local produce. Starters of Brancaster mussels marinière with parsley and cream or twice-baked Montgomery Cheddar cheese soufflé with buttered spinach might precede honey and ginger roast guinea fowl breast with cocotte potatoes, roast beetroot, Savoy cabbage, carrot and rich orange jus. Round things off with dark chocolate Nemesis with amaretti mousse and honey ice cream, or Bakewell tart and fresh raspberries with raspberry ripple ice cream. Local ales such as Woodforde's Wherry are complemented by an interesting international wine list that boasts a number of notable bottles from France.

Open 11-3 6-11 Closed: 25-26 Dec, 2wks Jan, Mon **Bar Meals** Av main course £18 **Restaurant** L served Tue-Sun (all wk Apr-Oct) booking required D served Tue-Sat (all wk Apr-Oct) booking required Fixed menu price fr £14.95-£17.95 Av 3 course à la carte fr £34 ⊕ WOODFORDE'S ◀ Woodforde's Wherry, Nelson's Revenge, Nog, Sundew, Admiral's Reserve ♂ Aspall. ♀ 10 **Facilities** Children welcome Children's portions Garden Parking

ITTERINGHAM — Map 13 TG13

PICK OF THE PUBS

Walpole Arms ⊛ ♀

NR11 7AR ☎ 01263 587258
e-mail: goodfood@thewalpolearms.co.uk
dir: *From Aylsham towards Blickling. After Blickling Hall take 1st right to Itteringham*

A pub since 1836, the Walpole Arms is both a real pub and a dining destination. Now in new hands, both restaurant and oak-beamed bar offer a daily changing three-course carte and the kitchen team uses the best seasonal and local produce to create thoroughly modern dishes. Bar snacks are available but for those with a heartier appetite, main course choices take in traditional beer-battered coley fillet, hand-cut chips, home-made tartare sauce and watercress, or butternut squash risotto with Parmesan, rocket and vegetable crisps. Desserts are traditional and modern at the same time: pear and blackberry trifle with Pedro Ximenez custard typifies the kitchen's approach, and children get to choose from their own menu. Expect to find a dozen wines served by the glass, as well as Adnams Broadside and Woodforde's Wherry Best on tap. The pub was formerly owned by Robert Horace Walpole, a direct descendant of Britain's first prime minister.

Open all wk noon-3 6-11 (Sun noon-4) Closed: 25 Dec **Bar Meals** L served Mon-Sat 12-2, Sun 12-2.30 D served Mon-Sat 6-9.30 **Restaurant** L served Mon-Sat 12-2, Sun 12-2.30 D served Mon-Sat 6-9.30 ⊕ FREE HOUSE ◀ Adnams Broadside & Bitter, Woodforde's Wherry Best Bitter, Guest ales ♂ Aspall. ♀ 12 **Facilities** Children welcome Children's menu Play area Dogs allowed Garden Parking

KING'S LYNN — Map 12 TF62

The Stuart House Hotel, Bar & Restaurant ★★★ HL

35 Goodwins Rd PE30 5QX
☎ 01553 772169 ▤ 01553 774788
e-mail: reception@stuarthousehotel.co.uk
web: www.stuarthousehotel.co.uk
dir: *Follow signs to town centre, pass under Southgate Arch, immediate right, in 100yds turn right*

Situated within its own grounds, this hotel and bar is a short walk from Kings Lynn's historic town centre. Cask conditioned East Anglian ales and traditional dishes are served in the bar, and there is a separate restaurant offering a carte menu and daily specials. A programme of events includes regular live music, murder mystery dinners and an annual beer festival. The patio and beer garden are perfect places to relax in warmer months. Eighteen en suite bedrooms are available.

The Stuart House Hotel, Bar & Restaurant

Open all wk 5-11 **Bar Meals** D served all wk 6-9.30 **Restaurant** D served all wk 7-9.30 ⊕ FREE HOUSE ◀ Adnams, Woodforde's, Greene King, Oakham JHB, Timothy Taylor Landlord. **Facilities** Play area Garden Beer festival Parking **Rooms** 18

LARLING — Map 13 TL98

PICK OF THE PUBS

Angel Inn ♀

NR16 2QU ☎ 01953 717963
e-mail: info@angel-larling.co.uk
dir: *5m from Attleborough, 8m from Thetford. 1m from station*

On the edge of Breckland and Thetford Forest Park, this 17th-century former coaching inn has been run for more than 80 years by three generations of the Stammers family. There's a good, local feel to the heavily-beamed public bar, with juke box, dart board and fruit machine, while the oak-panelled lounge bar has dining tables with cushioned wheel-back chairs, an oak settle, a wood burner and a huge collection of water jugs. Five guest ales, including a mild, are served, as well as more than a hundred whiskies. Menus make good use of local ingredients, with lighter snacks including freshly-made sandwiches, jacket potatoes, ploughman's, burgers and salads. Typically among the mains are chicken and mushroom Stroganoff; lamb chops; red Thai prawn curry; salmon fillet with creamy white wine and dill sauce; and sweet pepper lasagne. Each August the Angel hosts Norfolk's largest outdoor beer festival, with over 70 real ales and ciders.

Open all day all wk 10am-mdnt **Bar Meals** L served Sun-Thu 12-9.30, Fri-Sat 12-10 booking required D served Sun-Thu 12-9.30, Fri-Sat 12-10 booking required Av main course £9.95 food served all day **Restaurant** L served Sun-Thu 12-9.30, Fri-Sat 12-10 booking required D served Sun-Thu 12-9.30, Fri-Sat 12-10 booking required food served all day ⊕ FREE HOUSE ◀ Adnams Bitter, Hop Back, Caledonian Deuchars IPA, Timothy Taylor Landlord, Mauldons ♂ Aspall. ♀ 10 **Facilities** Children welcome Children's menu Children's portions Play area Garden Beer festival Parking Wi-fi

Save on hotels. Book at **theAA.com/hotel**

NORFOLK 323 ENGLAND

| LETHERINGSETT | Map 13 TG03 |

PICK OF THE PUBS

The Kings Head ♀

Holt Rd NR25 7AR ☎ 01263 712691
e-mail: thebar@kingsheadnorfolk.co.uk
dir: *On A148, 1 mile from the town of Holt. Pub on corner*

Chris Coubrough's thriving Norfolk-based Flying Kiwi Inns snapped up this rather grand, manor-like building on the edge of upmarket Holt in 2009 and revamped it in impressive style. Expect an elegant, rustic-chic feel throughout the rambling dining areas that radiate from the central bar, with rugs on terracotta tiles, squashy sofas and leather chairs fronting blazing winter log fires, fat tables lamps, feature bookcases, warm heritage hues, and an eclectic mix of old dining tables. The atmosphere is informal, the beer is East Anglian brewed – try a pint of Adnams Broadside – and the food modern British and prepared from top-notch ingredients supplied by the pub's own herd of Dexter cows, local farmers, fisherman and artisan producers. This translates to ham hock, pistachio and mustard terrine with piccalilli, Norfolk duck cassoulet, sea bass with shellfish bouillabaisse, saffron potatoes and garlic rouille, and vanilla pannacotta with rhubarb. This award-winning gastro-pub has superb alfresco areas including an excellent children's garden and a gravelled front terrace with posh benches and brollies.

Open all day all wk **Bar Meals** L served all wk 12-2.30 D served all wk 6.30-9.30 booking required **Restaurant** L served all wk 12-2.30 D served all wk 6.30-9.30 booking required ⊕ FREEHOUSE ◀ Adnams Bitter, Flying Kiwi Homebrew Ⓞ Aspall. ♀ 14 **Facilities** Children welcome Children's menu Children's portions Play area Dogs allowed Garden Parking Wi-fi

| LITTLE FRANSHAM | Map 13 TF91 |

The Canary and Linnet

Main Rd NR19 2JW ☎ 01362 687027
dir: *On A47 between Dereham & Swaffham*

A pretty, former blacksmith's cottage fulfilling the key requirements of a traditional English country pub - low ceilings, exposed beams and an inglenook fireplace. Its sign once showed footballers in Norwich City (Canaries) and Kings Lynn (Linnets) strips, but now features two birds in a cage. Food offered throughout the bar, conservatory restaurant and garden includes smoked salmon and crayfish salad; tempura battered red mullet; vegetarian or traditional lasagne; pan-fried liver and smoked bacon; rack of lamb, served pink, with redcurrant and rosemary sauce.

Open all wk noon-3 6-11 (Sun noon-3 6.30-10.30) **Bar Meals** L served all wk 12-2 booking required D served all wk 6-9 booking required **Restaurant** L served all wk 12-2 D served all wk 6-9 ⊕ FREE HOUSE ◀ Greene King IPA, Adnams Bitter, Wolf Ⓞ Aspall. **Facilities** Children welcome Children's menu Dogs allowed Garden Parking

| MARSHAM | Map 13 TG12 |

The Plough Inn ♀

Norwich Rd NR10 5PS
☎ 01263 735000 🖷 01263 735407
e-mail: enq@ploughinnmarsham.co.uk
web: www.ploughinnmarsham.co.uk
dir: *On A140, 10m N of Norwich, 1m S of Aylsham*

A warm welcome is assured at this 18th-century countryside inn, ideally located for the North Norfolk coast and the Broads. The pumps in the friendly bar serve both real ales and cider, while menus based on local and seasonal produce include favourites such as ham hock and parsley terrine; steak and kidney pie; and slow cooked lamb shank. The chef's signature dishes are crab salad, slow-roasted belly of pork and Cheddar soufflé. There is a specials board, children's menu and a carvery on Sunday.

Open all wk 12-2.30 6-11 (all day summer) **Bar Meals** L served all wk 12-2.30 D served all wk 6-9 ⊕ FREE HOUSE ◀ IPA, Adnams, John Smith's Ⓞ Aspall. ♀ 10 **Facilities** Children welcome Children's menu Children's portions Garden Parking Wi-fi

| MUNDFORD | Map 13 TL89 |

Crown Hotel

Crown Rd IP26 5HQ
☎ 01842 878233 🖷 01842 878982
e-mail: info@the-crown-hotel.co.uk
web: www.the-crown-hotel.co.uk
dir: *A11 to Barton Mills junct, then A1065 to Brandon & onto Mundford*

Originally a hunting lodge, this historic hillside inn on the edge of Thetford Forest dates back to 1652. Traditional, home-cooked food is served in the bars and two restaurants; perhaps pan-fried supreme of salmon with warm cherry tomato and basil salad or Jimmy Butler's slow-roasted pork belly with apple brandy sauce, baked apple and dauphinoise potatoes. In addition to the real ales and wines, there is a choice of over 50 malt whiskies. Being on a hill, the garden is on the first floor.

Open all day all wk **Bar Meals** L served all wk 12-3 D served all wk 6.30-10 **Restaurant** L served all wk 12-3 D served all wk 6.30-10 booking required ⊕ FREE HOUSE ◀ Courage Directors, Ruddles County, Olde Tripp, Woodforde's Wherry, Guest ales. **Facilities** Children welcome Children's portions Dogs allowed Garden Parking Wi-fi

| NEWTON | Map 13 TF81 |

The George & Dragon ♀ NEW

Swaffham Rd PE32 2BX ☎ 01760 755046
e-mail: info@newtongeorge.co.uk
dir: *3m N of Swaffham on A1065*

Just north of the market town of Swaffham and a stone's throw from Castle Acre Priory, The George & Dragon has been refreshing weary travellers since 1740. These days, visitors can make use of the Wi-fi connection as they enjoy the pub's own Newton Bitter in the beamed bar or in the three acres of garden. The menu changes monthly and might include rare beef platter with chips and salad or smoked haddock, spinach and Cheddar pie.

Open 11-3 6-11 Closed: Sun eve & Mon L **Bar Meals** L served Tue-Sun 12-2 D served Mon-Sat 6-9 Av main course £10.50 **Restaurant** L served Tue-Sun 12-2 D served Mon-Sat 6-9 Av 3 course à la carte fr £20 ⊕ FREE HOUSE ◀ Newton Bitter, Guest ales Ⓞ Aspall. ♀ 13 **Facilities** Children welcome Children's menu Children's portions Play area Dogs allowed Garden Parking Wi-fi

NORWICH
Map 13 TG20

Adam & Eve ♥

Bishopsgate NR3 1RZ
☎ 01603 667423 📄 01603 667438
e-mail: theadamandeve@hotmail.com
dir: Behind the Anglican Cathedral, next to the Law Courts

Norwich's oldest pub, the Adam & Eve has been serving ale since 1249, when it was the lodging house for craftsmen building the Anglican cathedral next door. These days it remains a traditional pub undisturbed by TV or games machines, and counts a few ghosts among its regulars. Decked with award-winning flowers in summer, it offers real ales and plenty of traditional, home-made food with the likes of steak and kidney pudding, and pork ribs with chips and salad.

Open all day all wk 11-11 (Sun noon-10.30) Closed: 25-26 Dec, 1 Jan **Bar Meals** L served Mon-Sat 12-7, Sun 12-5 Av main course £8.95 ⊕ ENTERPRISE INNS
◀ Adnams Bitter, Theakston Old Peculier, Wells Bombardier, Mauldons Moletrap Ŏ Aspall. ♥ 11
Facilities Parking Wi-fi

PICK OF THE PUBS

The Mad Moose Arms ◉◉ ♥

2 Warwick St NR2 3LB
☎ 01603 627687 📄 01508 494946
e-mail: madmoose@animalinns.co.uk
dir: 1m from A11

Popular with the locals, this friendly neighbourhood gastro-pub offer the best of both worlds, with a stylish ground floor bar and a sophisticated upstairs dining room. Regulars know they can expect Norfolk real ales – Woodforde's Wherry and Wolf's Straw Dog - and a bar menu offering a variety of interesting sandwiches, light meals and salads; and main dishes such as duck hash; smoked haddock gratin and toad in the hole. On the first floor is the elegant, AA two-Rosette, 1Up restaurant with chandeliers, sea green drapes, and a feature wall depicting a fairytale forest. Confident and ambitious cooking is typified by a starter of seared scallops and chorizo, cauliflower beignets, quince purée, chorizo and lime oil. This might be followed by roast Norfolk venison loin, pomme sarladaise and baby onions, curly kale and mushroom jus. Among the desserts consider iced hazelnut parfait. There is a stylish outdoor patio for alfresco dining and beer festivals in May and October.

Open all day all wk noon-mdnt Closed: 25 Dec
Bar Meals L served all wk 12-2 D served all wk 5.30-9.30 **Restaurant** L served Sun 12-2.30 D served Mon-Sat 7-9 booking required ⊕ ANIMAL INNS
◀ Woodforde's Wherry, Straw Dog, Oakham Ŏ Aspall. ♥ 9 **Facilities** Children welcome Children's menu Children's portions Garden Beer festival

Ribs of Beef ♥

24 Wensum St NR3 1HY
☎ 01603 619517 📄 01603 625446
e-mail: roger@cawdron.co.uk
dir: From Tombland (in front of cathedral) turn left at Maids Head Hotel. Pub 200yds on right on bridge

Once used by the Norfolk wherry skippers, this welcoming riverside pub (celebrating 25 years) is still popular among boat owners cruising The Broads. Its structure incorporates remnants of the original 14th-century building, which was destroyed in the Great Fire in 1507. The pub is famous for its range of cask ales, excellent wines and traditional English food using locally sourced produce. The menu offers a wide range of tempting sandwiches, burgers and jacket potatoes, while larger appetites should be satisfied with dishes such as beef and ale stew; sausage platter; or retro chicken in a basket. Sit outside on the terrace in the warmer months.

Open all day all wk 11-11 (Fri-Sat 11am-1am)
Bar Meals L served Mon-Fri 12-2.30, Sat-Sun 12-5 Av main course £6 ⊕ FREE HOUSE ◀ Woodforde's Wherry, Adnams Bitter, Elgoods Mild, Oakham JHB, Fuller's London Pride Ŏ Kingfisher Norfolk Cider. ♥ 9
Facilities Children welcome Children's menu Children's portions Family room Wi-fi

RINGSTEAD
Map 12 TF74

PICK OF THE PUBS

The Gin Trap Inn ★★★★ INN ◉ ♥

6 High St PE36 5JU ☎ 01485 525264
e-mail: thegintrap@hotmail.co.uk
dir: A149 from King's Lynn towards Hunstanton. In 15m turn right at Heacham for Ringstead

The Peddars Way recreational path passes the door of this attractive pub in a pretty village just a couple of miles from the North Norfolk coast and its string of little ports, nature and bird reserves. Dating from 1667 and sympathetically upgraded over the years, it's a comfy base from which to explore this engaging countryside. The rustic bar has a relaxed and friendly atmosphere, exposed brickwork and beams, blazing log-burning stove for warmth throughout the winter, plus an intimate dining room and modern conservatory, and a pretty garden for summer alfresco drinking and dining. Walkers pop in for drinks (East Anglian real ales) and a meal to fortify them on their way, and dogs are very welcome - landlords Steve Knowles and Cindy Cook have two Great Danes. They pride themselves on the provenance of the produce that goes into the meals, much of which is extremely locally sourced. Carpaccio of beef with horseradish, celeriac rémoulade and micro herbs to start, followed by grilled hake with home-made egg noodles, razor fish chowder and lemon oil are fine examples from the inspired, one AA Rosette gastro-pub menu here.

Open all day all wk 11.30am-11pm (11.30-2.30 6-11 in winter) **Bar Meals** L served Mon-Fri 12-2, Sat-Sun 12-2.30 D served Sun-Thu 6-9, Fri-Sat 6-9.30 **Restaurant** L served Mon-Fri 12-2, Sat-Sun 12-2.30 D served Sun-Thu 6-9, Fri-Sat 6-9.30 ⊕ FREE HOUSE
◀ Adnams Best, Woodforde's Wherry, Guest ales Ŏ Aspall. ♥ 9 **Facilities** Children welcome Children's menu Children's portions Dogs allowed Garden Parking Wi-fi **Rooms** 3

SALTHOUSE
Map 13 TG04

The Dun Cow ♥

Coast Rd NR25 7XG ☎ 01263 740467
dir: On A149 (coast road). 3m E of Blakeney, 6m W of Sheringham

In an Area of Outstanding Natural Beauty and situated in a quiet coastal village, this ancient pub (under new owners since 2010) overlooks some of Britain's finest salt marshes, so expect to share it, particularly its front garden, with birdwatchers and walkers. Many original beams have been retained in the bar, formerly the village forge. There is a great range of real ales to choose from and the food is home cooked. For the warmer months, there is a walled rear garden.

Open all day all wk **Bar Meals** Av main course £9.95 food served all day **Restaurant** food served all day ◀ Adnams, Woodforde's Wherry, Guest ales in summer Ŏ Aspall. ♥ 19 **Facilities** Children welcome Children's menu Children's portions Family room Dogs allowed Garden Parking

SNETTISHAM
Map 12 TF63

PICK OF THE PUBS

The Rose & Crown ★★ HL ◉ ♥

Old Church Rd PE31 7LX
☎ 01485 541382 📄 01485 543172
e-mail: info@roseandcrownsnettisham.co.uk
dir: 10m N from King's Lynn on A149 signed Hunstanton. Inn in centre of Snettisham between market square & church

Anthony and Jeannette's splendid 14th-century inn was originally built to house the craftsmen who built the beautiful church up the road and is everything you'd expect from a Norfolk village inn. Beyond the rose-festooned façade lays twisting passages and hidden corners, leading to three charming bars, replete with heavy oak beams, uneven red-tiled floors, inglenook fireplaces, tip-top Adnams ale on tap, and an informal atmosphere. The menu makes good use of locally supplied produce – beef comes from cattle that grazed the nearby salt marshes; fishermen still in their waders deliver Brancaster mussels and Thornham oysters; and strawberries and asparagus are grown locally. Start with goat's cheese, caramelised onion and walnut tart, follow with gammon, egg and hand-cut chips, or pan-fried skate wing with curly kale and beurre noisette, leaving room for white chocolate and raspberry mousse with chocolate chip cookies. Stylish bedrooms offer excellent accommodation and the pretty walled garden was once the village bowling green.

Open all day all wk **Bar Meals** L served Mon-Fri 12-2, Sat-Sun 12-2.30 booking required D served Sun-Thu 6-9, Fri-Sat 6-9.30 booking required Av main course £11.50 **Restaurant** L served Mon-Fri 12-2, Sat-Sun 12-2.30 booking required D served Sun-Thu 6-9, Fri-Sat 6-9.30 booking required ⊕ FREE HOUSE ◖ Adnams Bitter & Broadside, Interbrew Bass, Fuller's London Pride, Greene King IPA. ♀ 12 **Facilities** Children welcome Children's menu Children's portions Play area Family room Dogs allowed Garden Parking Wi-fi **Rooms** 16

STOKE HOLY CROSS　　　Map 13 TG20

PICK OF THE PUBS

The Wildebeest Arms ◉◉ ♀

82-86 Norwich Rd NR14 8QJ
☎ 01508 492497　📠 01508 494946
e-mail: wildebeest@animalinns.co.uk
dir: *From A47 take A140, left to Dunston. At T-junct turn left, Wildebeest Arms on right*

This charming village local is the perfect retreat from the hustle and bustle of nearby Norwich. Tastefully modernised with a warm rustic chic look, expect thick, chunky wooden tables, wooden floors and oak beams, vases of fresh lilies, potted plants, crackling log fires and yellow rag-washed walls. What is striking is the quirky collection of African tribal art, which adds a touch of exoticism. Although the emphasis has been placed firmly on delivering great food, all are welcome to pop in for a pint of Adnams and a decent glass of wine (16 are available by the glass). The kitchen takes a modern approach - underpinned by a classical French theme. Kick off with warm pigeon and Parma ham salad and move on to grilled smoked haddock with garlic creamed potato and buttered spinach. Leave room for pistachio cake and pistachio parfait with boozy cherries.

Open all wk Closed: 25-26 Dec **Bar Meals** L served all wk 12-2.30 D served all wk 6-9 **Restaurant** L served all wk 12-2.30 booking required D served all wk 6-9 booking required ⊕ FREE HOUSE ◖ Adnams ♂ Aspall. ♀ 16 **Facilities** Children welcome Children's portions Garden Parking

---

STOW BARDOLPH　　　Map 12 TF60

PICK OF THE PUBS

The Hare Arms ♀

PE34 3HT ☎ 01366 382229　📠 01366 385522
e-mail: trishmc@harearms222.wanadoo.co.uk
dir: *From King's Lynn take A10 to Downham Market. After 9m village signed on left*

This attractive ivy-clad pub was built during the Napoleonic wars and takes its name from the surrounding estate, ancestral home of the Hare family since 1553. The Hare has preserved its appeal and become deservedly popular, thanks in no small part to Trish and David McManus, who have been licensees here

for 35 years. The L-shaped bar and adjoining conservatory are packed with decades-worth of fascinating bygones; the cat warms itself by the fire and peacocks wander around outside. An extensive menu of regular pub food is supplemented by daily specials, including the pub's award-winning and hugely popular steak and peppercorn pie. Other choices include lamb shank cooked with fennel, garlic, coriander, star anise and port. At the other end of the spectrum, the à la carte restaurant menu might offer lamb koftas followed by beef and venison casserole or Gressingham duck breast with a sticky pineapple and chilli chutney. Vegetarians are well catered for with dishes such as baby spring rolls and chilli dip, or deep fried jalapeno peppers filled with cream cheese.

Open all wk 11-2.30 6-11 (Sun noon-10.30) Closed: 25-26 Dec **Bar Meals** L served Mon-Sat 12-2, Sun 12-10 D served Mon-Sat 6.30-10, Sun 12-10 Av main course £10 **Restaurant** D served Mon-Sat 7-9 booking required Fixed menu price fr £16 Av 3 course à la carte fr £30 ⊕ GREENE KING ◖ Greene King Abbot Ale, IPA & Old Speckled Hen, St Edmunds, guest ale ♂ Aspall. ♀ 9 **Facilities** Children welcome Children's menu Children's portions Family room Garden Parking Wi-fi

---

SWANTON MORLEY　　　Map 13 TG01

Darbys Freehouse

1&2 Elsing Rd NR20 4NY
☎ 01362 637647　📠 01362 637928
e-mail: louisedarby@hotmail.co.uk
dir: *From A47 (Norwich to King's Lynn) take B1147 to Dereham*

A large country house, divided first into cottages in the late 19th century, then in 1988 converted into a pub. The old beams and inglenooks are still there, of course, while the spacious bar is furnished with stripped pine tables and benches, and stools are made from tractor seats. Mostly locally supplied, traditional pub food includes home-made curries; scampi and chips; chicken mozzarella melt; and vegetarian and children's selections. Guest ales join Norfolk and Suffolk regulars.

Open all wk Mon-Thu 11.30-3 6-11 (Fri-Sat 11.30-11, Sun 12-10.30). Food served all day Sat-Sun **Bar Meals** L served Mon-Fri 12-2.15, Sat 12-9.45, Sun 12-9 D served Mon-Fri 6.30-9.45, Sat 12-9.45, Sun 12-9 **Restaurant** L served Mon-Fri 12-2.15, Sat 12-9.45, Sun 12-9 booking required D served Mon-Fri 6.30-9.45, Sat 12-9.45, Sun 12-9 booking required ◖ Woodforde's Wherry, Adnams Broadside & Best, 2 Guest ales. **Facilities** Children welcome Children's menu Children's portions Play area Family room Dogs allowed Garden Parking

---

THOMPSON　　　Map 13 TL99

PICK OF THE PUBS

Chequers Inn ♀

See Pick of the Pubs on page 326

THORNHAM　　　Map 12 TF74

PICK OF THE PUBS

Lifeboat Inn ♀

Ship Ln PE36 6LT
☎ 01485 512236　📠 01485 512323
e-mail: reception@lifeboatinn.co.uk
web: www.lifeboatinn.co.uk
dir: *A149 from Hunstanton for approx 6m. 1st left after Thornham sign*

A perennial classic: the Lifeboat is a charming, whitewashed, 16th-century smugglers inn, set on the edge of an expanse of glorious, bird-rich salt marsh. The ramble of old rooms retain their original character, boasting low-beamed ceilings, rug-strewn tiled floors, low doors, half-panelled walls and a rustic array of furniture, from sturdy oak tables to antique settles and pews. Antique oil lamps suspended from the ceiling enhance the charm, while the adjoining conservatory is renowned for its ancient vine and there's an adjacent walled patio garden. Food ranges from roast beef and horseradish sandwiches and traditional fish and chips to lamb rump with pea purée and minted gravy. Perfectly placed for spending the day exploring the coast path, visiting Sandringham, Nelson's birthplace at Burnham Thorpe, and the coastal villages of Blakeney and Cley-next-the-Sea.

Open all day all wk **Bar Meals** food served all day **Restaurant** D served all wk 7-9.30 booking required ⊕ MAYPOLE GROUP PLC ◖ IPA, Abbot, Wherry, Adnams, Guest ales. ♀ 10 **Facilities** Children welcome Children's menu Children's portions Play area Dogs allowed Garden Parking Wi-fi

PICK OF THE PUBS

Chequers Inn ♀

THOMPSON   Map 13 TL99

Griston Rd IP24 1PX
☎ **01953 483360**   📠 **01953 488092**
e-mail: richard@thompsonchequers.co.uk
web: www.thompsonchequers.co.uk
dir: *Between Watton & Thetford off A1075*

Well off the beaten track, this splendid, long and low, thatched 17th-century inn is worth finding – a mile off the A1075 Watton to Thetford road along a tiny lane on the edge of the village – for its peaceful location and unspoilt charm. It takes its name from the chequered cloth used for counting money, wages and rents in medieval times. Manorial courts, held here from at least 1724, dealt with rents, letting of land, and petty crime. Beneath the steep-raked thatch of this ancient ale house, once a row of several cottages, lies a series of low-ceilinged inter-connecting rooms served by a long bar. Wonky wall timbers, low doorways, open log fires, a rustic mix of old furniture and old farming implements characterise the atmospheric interior.

Eat in the bar for pub favourites such as steak and kidney pudding, deep-fried cod and chips, and home-made vegetable curry. In the evenings, choose from pork medallions with Stilton and red onion, stuffed chicken breast with smoked salmon, sirloin steak with horseradish, brandy and mushroom sauce, or look to

the chalkboard for the day's fresh fish dishes, perhaps whole sea bream, and game in season. Round things off with home-made desserts like treacle and almond tart, or opt for a selection of English and continental cheeses served with grapes, celery and biscuits.

The inn is an ideal base for exploring the heart of Norfolk and the Peddars Way National Trail. Alternatively, the eight-mile Great Eastern Pingo Trail follows a succession of shallow depressions in the ground that were formed during the last Ice Age. Dogs are welcome in the large rear garden, which offers picnic tables and children's play equipment, as well as extensive views over the surrounding countryside.

Open all wk 11.30-3 6.30-11 **Bar Meals** L served all wk 12-2 D served all wk 6.30-9 **Restaurant** L served all wk 12-2 booking required D served all wk 6.30-9 booking required ⊕ FREE HOUSE 🛢 Fuller's London Pride, Adnams Best, Wolf Best, Greene King IPA, Woodforde's Wherry Best Bitter. ♀ 8 **Facilities** Children welcome Children's menu Children's portions Play area Dogs allowed Garden Parking Wi-fi

THORNHAM *continued*

PICK OF THE PUBS

The Orange Tree ☻

High St PE36 6LY
☎ 01485 512213   📠 01485 512424
e-mail: email@theorangetreethornham.co.uk
dir: *Telephone for directions*

This 400-year-old pub was once a smugglers' haunt, these days it has been restyled to a contemporary country pub, now run by Mark and Joanna Goode. It stands by the ancient Peddar's Way in a lovely coastal village. Along with a good choice of real ales, the award-winning chef changes his menus frequently, according to the season, while his specials vary from day to day. Bar classics include pan-fried ox liver and bacon, and black treacle roast ham and eggs. Naturally, the seafood on the main menu is the best, as it is fresh from the local fishing boats. With most of the meat coming from the Sandringham Estate, tempting possibilities include corn-fed chicken and wild mushroom pie with smoked pancetta mash; Moroccan spiced lamb rump with sweet potato fondant; and surf 'n' turf sizzler. Two large gardens add extra appeal.

Open all day all wk **Bar Meals** L served all wk 12-3 D served all wk 6-9.30 Av main course £16 **Restaurant** L served all wk 12-3 D served all wk 6-9.30 Av 3 course à la carte fr £29 ⊕ PUNCH TAVERNS ◀ Woodforde's Wherry, Adnams Best Bitter, Brewers Gold ⚫ Aspall. ☻ 21 **Facilities** Children welcome Children's menu Play area Dogs allowed Garden Parking Wi-fi

TITCHWELL   Map 13 TF74

PICK OF THE PUBS

Titchwell Manor Hotel ★★★ HL ☺☺ ☻

PE31 8BB ☎ 01485 210221   📠 01485 210104
e-mail: margaret@titchwellmanor.com
dir: *A149 between Brancaster & Thornham*

In a stunning location on Norfolk's north coast and run by the Snaith family for over 20 years, this Victorian manor looks out over an RSPB reserve to the sea beyond. The hotel has been tastefully updated with a mix of muted contemporary design and bold eye-catching colours. Popular with bird watchers and golfers, this is very much a dining venue, although you will find a log fire and two reliable Greene King beers in the bar, and eight wines served by the glass. Head for the new terrace in summer, or the air-conditioned conservatory restaurant for an à la carte meal. The cooking is skilled and interesting, using local and seasonal ingredients to produce imaginative and well-presented dishes. Indicative are starters such as diver scallops with oxtail, lentils and red wine, and Brancaster shellfish in the form of oysters, or mussels in white wine. Pies may include chicken with creamed leeks, while steaks from the grill are Red Poll beef from the Royal Sandringham Estate.

Open all day all wk **Bar Meals** Av main course £12 food served all day **Restaurant** Av 3 course à la carte fr £25 food served all day ⊕ FREE HOUSE ◀ Greene King IPA, Abbot. ☻ 8 **Facilities** Children welcome Children's menu Dogs allowed Garden Parking Wi-fi **Rooms** 26

WARHAM ALL SAINTS   Map 13 TF94

PICK OF THE PUBS

Three Horseshoes

NR23 1NL ☎ 01328 710547
dir: *From Wells A149 to Cromer, then right onto B1105 to Warham*

This gem of a pub first opened its doors in 1725. Its rambling old rooms, including a gas-lit main bar, are stone floored with scrubbed wooden tables; a grandfather clock ticks away in one corner, and a curious green and red dial in the ceiling turns out to be a rare example of Norfolk Twister, an ancient pub game. Vintage posters, clay pipes, photographs and memorabilia adorn the walls, while down a step are old one-arm bandits. Woodforde's Norfolk Wherry and guest ales are served from the cask through a hole in the bar wall. Home-made soups, pies and puddings dominate the menu, so start with beef and onion soup or cheesy mushroom bake; follow with game and wine pie or seafood and salmon pie; and finish with chocolate syrup sponge or bread and butter pudding. A no-chips policy applies, incidentally. Outside is a beer garden and covered courtyard.

Open all wk 12-2.30 6-11 **Bar Meals** L served all wk 12-1.45 D served all wk 6-8.30 ⊕ FREE HOUSE ◀ Greene King IPA, Woodforde's Wherry ⚫ Whin Hill Cider. **Facilities** Children welcome Children's portions Family room Dogs allowed Garden Parking **Notes** ☺

WELLS-NEXT-THE-SEA   Map 13 TF94

PICK OF THE PUBS

The Crown Hotel ☻

The Buttlands NR23 1EX
☎ 01328 710209   📠 01328 711432
e-mail: reception@crownhotelnorfolk.co.uk
dir: *10m from Fakenham on B1105*

Overlooking the tree-lined green known as The Buttlands, the striking contemporary decor of this 17th-century former coaching inn blends effortlessly with its old-world charm. Beneath the bar's ancient beams, East Anglian ales and Aspall real cider accompany bar menu dishes such as smoked salmon with pickled beetroot, and chicken breasts on roast root vegetables. Whether you eat here, more formally in the restaurant, in the cheerful Orangery, or outside with its great views, the main menu features traditional favourites, the best of modern British cuisine, and Pacific Rim influenced dishes. Perhaps fish in Thai watermelon curry with fragrant rice and coriander yoghurt; roast rack of lamb with roast vegetables and

tapenade jus; and pork and leek sausages with grain mustard mash and onion gravy. Try also a sampler of European and Asian appetizers served on a tile, or one of the seafood specials. A good few wines are available by the glass and there are a few half-bottles.

Open all day all wk **Bar Meals** L served all wk 12-2.30 D served all wk 6.30-9.30 **Restaurant** L served all wk 12-2.30 D served all wk 6.30-9.30 booking required ⊕ FREE HOUSE ◀ Adnams Bitter, guest ale, Kiwi Ale brewed by owner's wife ⚫ Aspall. ☻ 14 **Facilities** Children welcome Children's menu Children's portions Dogs allowed Garden Parking Wi-fi

The Globe Inn ☻ NEW

The Buttlands NR23 1EU
☎ 01328 710206   📠 01328 713249
e-mail: globe@holkham.co.uk
dir: *in village centre*

Overlooking the leafy village green, The Globe is a short stroll from Wells-next-the-Sea bustling quay. It has a warm, welcoming bar and comfortable restaurant, with a sunny courtyard for alfresco drinking and dining. The menus take full advantage of the abundance of local produce from both land and sea – such as tender asparagus in early summer and game from the Holkham Estate in winter. Morston mussels with garlic, cream and parsley served with rosemary bread makes a delicious starter for two.

Open all day all wk **Bar Meals** L served all wk 12-2.30 D served all wk 6.30-9 Av main course £14 **Restaurant** L served all wk 12-2.30 D served all wk 6.30-9 ⊕ FREE HOUSE ◀ Adnams ⚫ Aspall. ☻ 10 **Facilities** Children welcome Children's menu Children's portions Dogs allowed Garden Wi-fi

WEST BECKHAM   Map 13 TG13

The Wheatsheaf ☻

Manor Farm, Church Rd NR25 6NX ☎ 01263 822110
e-mail: wheatsheafnorfolk@gmail.com
dir: *2m inland from Sheringham on A148, turn opp Sheringham Park*

Situated in a quiet village just two miles from Sheringham and formerly known as the 'old manor farmhouse', this charming building was converted to a pub over 20 years ago and retains many original features. Sample one of the real ales from Woodforde's and relax in bar, one of the restaurants or the large garden. All food is made on the premises using fresh local produce. From the bar menu, dishes might include prime beef lasagne or steak and kidney suet pudding, while typical choices from the restaurant menu are minted lamb meatballs with tomato sauce; and local rabbit casseroled in wine and herbs. Change of hands.

Open 11.30-3 6.30-11.30 Closed: Mon **Bar Meals** L served Tue-Sun 12-2 D served Tue-Sun 6.30-9 Av main course £10 **Restaurant** L served Tue-Sun 12-2 D served Tue-Sun 6.30-9 ⊕ FREE HOUSE ◀ Woodforde's Wherry Best Bitter, Greene King IPA, Guest ales ⚫ Aspall. **Facilities** Children welcome Children's menu Children's portions Play area Dogs allowed Garden Parking

WESTON LONGVILLE — Map 13 TG11

The Parson Woodforde ♥ NEW

Church St NR9 5JU ☎ 01603 881675
e-mail: chef@theparsonwoodforde.com
dir: *From Norwich take A1067 (Fakenham road). After
Morton turn left in Marl Hill Rd to Weston Longville*

Situated in the village of Weston Longville, 20 minutes
from Norwich, this pub started life as the Five Ringers
back in 1845. Now a free house with a great selection of
real ales and a restaurant, it re-opened at the end of
2010 after an extensive refurbishment. A range of local
cask ales are on offer alongside a menu that showcases
Norfolk produce in dishes such as stuffed belly pork with
parsnip purée, Calvados and apple jus. A beer festival is
held in September.

Open all day all wk Closed: 25 Dec (drinks only 12-2.30)
Bar Meals Av main course £8.95-£11.95 food served all
day **Restaurant** L served Mon-Fri 12-2.30, Sat all day,
Sun 12-9 D served Sat 12-9.30, Sun 12-9 Fixed menu
price fr £15.95 Av 3 course à la carte fr £26 ⊕ FREE
HOUSE ◀ Grain Best Bitter, Wolf Brewery Straw Dog,
Adnam Best Bitter ♂ Aspall. ♥ 12 **Facilities** Children
welcome Children's menu Children's portions Dogs
allowed Garden Beer festival Parking Wi-fi

WINTERTON-ON-SEA — Map 13 TG41

Fishermans Return ♥

The Lane NR29 4BN ☎ 01493 393305
e-mail: enquiries@fishermansreturn.com
web: www.fishermansreturn.com
dir: *8m N of Great Yarmouth on B1159*

Long beaches and National Trust land are within 300
metres of this 350-year-old brick and flint pub – and it's
dog-friendly too, making it an ideal spot to finish a walk.
Behind the bar are Woodforde's Wherry, Norfolk Nog and
guest ales. Menus include popular favourites from
toasted sandwiches to cottage pie. But look to the daily-
changing blackboard for fish and seafood specials, when
freshly caught sea bass and mackerel may be on offer.
On August Bank Holiday the pub hosts a beer festival.

Open all wk 11-2.30 5.30-11 (Sat-Sun 11am-11pm)
Bar Meals L served all wk 12-2.30 D served all wk 6-9 Av
main course £8 **Restaurant** L served all wk 12-2.30
D served all wk 6-9 ⊕ FREE HOUSE ◀ Woodforde's
Wherry, Norfolk Nog, Guest ales ♂ Westons Stowford
Press, Old Rosie Scrumpy. ♥ 9 **Facilities** Children
welcome Children's menu Play area Family room Dogs
allowed Garden Beer festival Parking

WIVETON — Map 13 TG04

PICK OF THE PUBS

Wiveton Bell ☜ ♥

Blakeney Rd NR25 7TL ☎ 01263 740101
e-mail: enquiries@wivetonbell.co.uk
dir: *1m from Blakeney. Wiveton Rd off A149*

Just a mile from the salt marshes, this elegant,
18th-century pub overlooks Wiveton's green and church.
The interior is chic with earthy heritage-coloured walls,
greyish woodwork, stripped beams, chunky tables and
oak-planked floors. Further character is provided by the
bold, contemporary oil paintings by local artists that
line the walls of the cosy bar, where Adnams Broadside,
Aspalls cider and a carefully selected wine list hold
sway. If it's chilly outside, head for the tables close to
the inglenook fireplace and mingle with the locals. The
seasonal menu is bolstered by adventurous specials
that make good use of local fish, game and much more.
As well as classic bistro favourites, there's always a
daily fish special. Begin with ham hock terrine with
home-made piccalilli and follow with slow-roast Briston
pork belly with whole grain mash and Bramley apple
sauce, or pan-fried black bream, smoked bacon potato
cake and dill hollandaise.

Open all day all wk Closed: 25 Dec **Bar Meals** L served
all wk 12-2.15 booking required D served all wk 6-9
booking required Av main course £14.95
Restaurant L served all wk 12-2.15 booking required
D served all wk 6-9.15 booking required ⊕ FREE HOUSE
◀ Woodforde's Wherry, Adnams Broadside, Yetmans
♂ Aspall. ♥ 17 **Facilities** Children's menu Dogs
allowed Garden Parking Wi-fi

WOODBASTWICK — Map 13 TG31

The Fur & Feather Inn ♥

Slad Ln NR13 6HQ ☎ 01603 720003 📄 01603 722266
dir: *From A1151 (Norwich to Wroxham road), follow brown
signs for Woodforde's Brewery. Pub next to Brewery*

An idyllic thatched country pub ideal for beer lovers:
Woodforde's Brewery next door furnishes the ales which
are served straight from the cask; and there's not a juke
box, TV or pool table in sight. The pub was originally two
farm cottages, and now boasts three cosy bar areas and
a smart restaurant where you can enjoy traditional home-
made English fare. Word has it that the steak and kidney
pudding has a county-wide reputation; round off with
treacle tart.

Open all day all wk **Bar Meals** food served all day
Restaurant food served all day ◀ Woodforde's Wherry,
Sundew, Norfolk Nog, Nelsons Revenge, Adnam's Reserve.
♥ 10 **Facilities** Children welcome Garden Parking

NORTHAMPTONSHIRE

ASHBY ST LEDGERS — Map 11 SP56

The Olde Coach House Inn

CV23 8UN ☎ 01788 890349 📄 01788 891541
e-mail: info@oldecoachhouse.co.uk
dir: *M1 junct 18 follow A361/Daventry signs. Village
on left*

A carefully modernised former farmhouse with lots of
different eating and drinking areas, at least three real
ales, a good choice of wines, friendly staff, and plenty of
seating outside. The handsome creeper-clad stone inn is
furnished with all manner of chairs, squashy leather
sofas, pale wooden tables, large mirrors, hunting scenes,
an original old stove, and fresh flowers. Dining here is
popular too: expect the likes of smoked pigeon breast
with herb croûte; meat and fish grazing boards; and
lemon tart with raspberry sorbet.

Open all wk Mon-Fri noon-3 5.30-11 (Sat-Sun all day)
⊕ CHARLES WELLS ◀ Everards Tiger, Young's, Wells
Bombardier, Old Hooky. **Facilities** Children welcome
Children's menu Children's portions Play area Dogs
allowed Garden Parking

ASHTON — Map 11 SP74

The Old Crown ♥

1 Stoke Rd NN7 2JN ☎ 01604 862268
e-mail: bex@theoldcrownashton.co.uk
dir: *M1 junct 15. 1m from A508 from Roade*

A well-appointed homely village local in the small rural
community of Ashton. A pub for over 300 years old; its
pretty, sheltered gardens are a popular choice for summer
dining, or settle in to the beamed bar room and look
forward to choosing from the well thought out, balanced
menus while sipping a pint of well kept ale. Perhaps start
with deep-fried squid with aioli, followed by ginger and
soy marinated chicken breast with sticky coconut rice; or
trio of lamb (cutlet, mini shepherd's pie and slow cooked
shoulder); then spiced pecan and chocolate tart. There
are regular events held throughout the year.

Open Tue-Fri noon-3 6-11 (Sat noon-11.30 Sun
noon-10.30) Closed: Mon **Bar Meals** L served Tue-Fri
12-3, Sat 12-9.30, Sun 12-6 D served Tue-Fri 6-9.30, Av
main course £9 **Restaurant** Av 3 course à la carte fr £18
⊕ CHARLES WELLS ◀ IPA Eagle, Young's, Directors. ♥ 10
Facilities Children welcome Children's portions Dogs
allowed Garden Parking Wi-fi

AYNHO — Map 11 SP53

The Great Western Arms ♥ NEW

Station Rd OX17 3BP ☎ 01869 338288
e-mail: info@great-westernarms.co.uk
dir: *From Aynho take B4031 (Station Road) W towards
Deddington. Turn right to pub*

A double-sided fireplace in winter and a lovely courtyard
in summer are enduring attractions for customers drawn
to this well-run pub, situated between the Great Western

Save on hotels. Book at theAA.com/hotel

NORTHAMPTONSHIRE 329 ENGLAND

Railway and the Oxford Canal. Hook Norton ales are backed by an extensive selection of wines, whiskies and premium spirits. Lunch and dinner menus are full of good things, all prepared with pride by chef-patron Rene Klein. Half a grilled lobster followed by honey-roasted duck breast served with braised red cabbage and orange sauce would be a perfect dinner for that special occasion.

Open all day all wk Closed: 25 Dec **Bar Meals** Av main course £12 food served all day **Restaurant** Av 3 course à la carte fr £25 food served all day ⊕ HOOK NORTON ◀ Hooky Bitter, Ali's Ale, Twelve Days ♂ Westons Perry, Old Rosie, Stowford Press. ▼ 10 **Facilities** Children welcome Children's menu Children's portions Dogs allowed Garden Beer festival Parking Wi-fi

BULWICK   Map 11 SP99

PICK OF THE PUBS

The Queen's Head

Main St NN17 3DY ☎ 01780 450272
e-mail: queenshead-bulwick@tiscali.co.uk
dir: Just off A43, between Corby & Stamford

A 17th-century stone-built free house overlooking the village church, parts of The Queen's Head date back to 1400. Recently refurbished, the pub is a warren of small rooms with exposed wooden beams, four open fireplaces and flagstone floors. Relax by the fire or on the patio with a pint of real ale from the local Oakham or Rockingham breweries. Local shoots supply seasonal game such as teal, woodcock and partridge, and other ingredients often include village-grown fruit and vegetables brought in by customers and friends. Lunchtime brings a good selection of sandwich and snacks, and main dishes that have helped the pub to attract a string of awards. The evening menu might feature local pork sausages with mash and white onion and grainy mustard sauce. The menu is backed by a comprehensive wine list. The Queen's Head also has a new outdoor oven for outside dining.

Open 12-11 Closed: Mon **Bar Meals** L served Tue-Sun 12-2.30 booking required D served Tue-Sat 6-9.30 booking required **Restaurant** L served Tue-Sun 12-2.30 booking required D served Tue-Sat 6-9.30 booking required ⊕ FREE HOUSE ◀ Elland, Rockingham Ales, Newby Wyke, Thornbridge, Oakham. **Facilities** Children welcome Children's portions Dogs allowed Garden Parking

CASTLE ASHBY   Map 11 SP85

The Falcon ★★★ INN ▼

NN7 1LF ☎ 01604 696200 📠 01604 696673
e-mail: 6446@greeneking.co.uk
dir: From A428 follow Castle Ashby signs. Inn in village centre

Set in the idyllic hamlet of Castle Ashby, the 16th-century Falcon Inn seems a world away from the hustle and bustle of everyday life. The cellar bar menu offers pub

classics and lighter snacks, whilst restaurant choices include Welsh lamb rump with apple and mint mash; pan-seared citrus sea bass with dill and fennel cream; and vegetarian risotto with rocket leaves and Parmesan crisp. Sit outside in the garden in summer and enjoy a drink or meal. The inn's comfortable en suite bedrooms are individually decorated.

Open all day all wk **Bar Meals** L served all wk 12-3 D served all wk 6-9 Av main course £7.95 **Restaurant** L served all wk 12-3 booking required D served all wk 6-9 booking required Fixed menu price fr £12 Av 3 course à la carte fr £19.95 ⊕ GREENE KING ▼ 17 **Facilities** Children welcome Children's menu Children's portions Dogs allowed Garden Parking Wi-fi **Rooms** 15

CHACOMBE   Map 11 SP44

PICK OF THE PUBS

George and Dragon

Silver St OX17 2JR
☎ 01295 711500 📠 01295 710516
e-mail: georgeanddragonchacombe@googlemail.com
dir: M40 junct 11, A361 (Daventry road). Chacombe 1st right

Within easy reach of the Cotswolds and Silverstone racing circuit, this honey-stoned, 17th-century pub is tucked away beside the church in the pretty village of Chacombe. Situated in a Conservation Area, the pub retains a traditional, welcoming atmosphere: the three comfortable bars have an abundance of low beams, simple wooden chairs and settles, roaring log fires, and warm terracotta decor. The sun terrace is a good spot for sampling the cask ales in summer. The lunchtime menu offers sandwiches and baguettes with salad and tortilla chips or hand-cut chips; small bites such as soups, salads and fishcakes; and bigger bites like chilli con carne, beef burger and ratatouille vegetable lasagne, as well as a daily specials board. In the evening, the menu lists starters like Brixworth pâté with warm toast and red onion and port marmalade, followed by sirloin steak served with vine cherry tomatoes, mushroom, onion rings and hand-cut chips, or smoked haddock fillet on a bed of sautéed spinach served with creamy leek sauce

Open all day all wk noon-11 **Bar Meals** L served Mon-Thu 12-9, Fri-Sat 12-9.30, Sun 12-7 booking required D served Mon-Thu 12-9, Fri-Sat 12-9.30, Sun 12-7 booking required food served all day **Restaurant** L served Mon-Thu 12-9, Fri-Sat 12-9.30, Sun 12-7 booking required D served Mon-Thu 12-9, Fri-Sat 12-9.30, Sun 12-7 booking required food served all day ⊕ EVERARDS ◀ Everards Tiger, Everards Beacon, Guest ales. **Facilities** Children welcome Children's menu Children's portions Garden Parking Wi-fi

CRICK   Map 11 SP57

The Red Lion Inn

52 Main Rd NN6 7TX
☎ 01788 822342 📠 01788 822342
e-mail: ptm180@tiscali.co.uk
dir: From M1 junct 18, 0.75m E on A428, follows signs for Crick from new rdbt

Exposed beams, low ceilings and open fires rack up the rustic charm in this thatched 17th century coaching inn, which is easily accessible from the M1. The Marks family, landlords here for the last 31 years, give their regulars and visitors exactly what they want - a friendly atmosphere, real ales including a guest ale every week and traditional food. The daily home-made steak pie is a lunchtime favourite, while fillet and sirloin steaks are a speciality in the evening. Fish eaters will find trout, lemon sole, salmon and seafood platter.

Open all wk 11-2.30 6.15-11 (Sun noon-3 7-11) **Bar Meals** L served all wk 12-2 D served Mon-Sat 6.30-9 Av main course £7.50-£14 ⊕ FREE HOUSE ◀ Wells Bombardier, Greene King Old Speckled Hen, Deuchars IPA, guest ale. **Facilities** Dogs allowed Garden Parking

EAST HADDON   Map 11 SP66

The Red Lion ▼ NEW

Main St NN6 8BU ☎ 01604 770223
e-mail: nick@redlioneasthaddon.co.uk
dir: Just off A428

The Red Lion has undergone a complete refurbishment of kitchen, restaurant and bar during the four years since new owners arrived. The recent appointment of a high-profile partner/chef in 2010 signalled the intent to turn the venue into one of the county's top destination gastro-pubs. So expect a high standard of food, whether in snacks such as potted Northamptonshire trout to begin; main dishes like roasted bacon chop with bubble and squeak; and puddings along the lines of chocolate doughnuts with warm chocolate sauce. The newly landscaped gardens offer good views over rolling countryside.

Open all day all wk **Bar Meals** L served all wk 12-2.30 booking required D served all wk 6-10 booking required Av main course £13 **Restaurant** L served all wk 12-2.30 booking required D served all wk 6-10 booking required Av 3 course à la carte fr £23 ⊕ CHARLES WELLS ◀ Wells Bombardier, IPA, Young's London Gold. ▼ 14 **Facilities** Children welcome Children's portions Garden Parking Wi-fi

FARTHINGHOE   Map 11 SP53

The Fox ♀

Baker St NN13 5PH ☎ 01295 713965
e-mail: enquiries@foxatfarthinghoe.co.uk
dir: Follow A422, midway between Banbury & Brackley. On Baker Street directly off A422.

Reopening a few years ago after being derelict for five years, this Charles Wells pub brings its customers fresh, locally sourced food with friendly service, well kept beers and a relaxing village atmosphere. In practice this translates as a varied menu offering tempting sandwiches; charcuterie, seafood and vegetarian deli boards; cullen skink stack; goats' cheese and scallion tart; Brackley Butchers sausages and mash. There is even a take out menu. Ladies' Night on Wednesdays means three courses and a glass of wine for £15.

Open all wk 12-3 6-11 (Fri-Sun 12-11)
Bar Meals L served all wk 12-2.30 booking required D served all wk 6-9.30 booking required Av main course £10 **Restaurant** L served all wk 12-2.30 booking required D served all wk 6-9.30 booking required Av 3 course à la carte fr £20 ⊕ CHARLES WELLS ◀ Young's, Bombardier, Erdinger. ♀ 12 **Facilities** Children welcome Children's portions Garden Parking Wi-fi

FARTHINGSTONE   Map 11 SP65

PICK OF THE PUBS

The Kings Arms

Main St NN12 8EZ
☎ 01327 361604 ⧉ 01327 361604
e-mail: paul@kingsarms.fsbusiness.co.uk
dir: M1 junct 16, A45 towards Daventry. At Weedon take A5 towards Towcester. Right signed Farthingstone

This 300-year-old stone free house is tucked away in perfect walking country, close to the National Trust's Elizabethan mansion at Canon's Ashby. Paul and Denise Egerton grow their own salads and herbs in the pub's quirky garden, which is full of interesting recycled items as well as decorative trees and shrubs. The terrace is the place to enjoy alfresco drinking on warmer days with red kites and buzzards overhead; in winter, real fires warm the stone-flagged interior. The Kings Arms is a lively local and mainly a drinkers' pub, with up to five real ales and a cider on tap. But light lunches served in the bar at weekend lunchtimes feature quality fine foods such as fish from Cornwall and British cheeses which can be bought from the pub. Find out about summer barbecues or winter casserole evenings, when game, diced pork with ginger and garlic, or Moroccan vegetable stew may feature. Expect desserts such as Tunisian lemon pudding, raspberry meringue, and apple and strawberry slice.

Open 7-11.30 (Fri 6.30-12, Sat-Sun 12-3.30 7-11.30) Closed: Mon **Bar Meals** L served Sat-Sun 12-2.30 Av main course £8.95 ⊕ FREE HOUSE ◀ Thwaites Original, Adnams, St Austell Tinners, Young's Bitter, Hoggleys Northamptonshire Bitter ⓪ Westons Old Rosie. **Facilities** Children welcome Children's portions Family room Dogs allowed Garden Parking **Notes** ⊕

FOTHERINGHAY   Map 12 TL09

PICK OF THE PUBS

The Falcon Inn ◉ ♀

PE8 5HZ ☎ 01832 226254 ⧉ 01832 226046
e-mail: info@thefalcon-inn.co.uk
dir: N of A605 between Peterborough & Oundle

First the history: it was in this sleepy village that Richard III was born in 1452, and 115 years later Mary, Queen of Scots was beheaded. The attractive 18th-century, stone-built pub stands in gardens redesigned by award-winning landscape architect Bunny Guinness. It's a real local, the Tap Bar regularly used by the village darts team, their throwing arms lubricated by pints of Fool's Nook and Aspalls cider. The menus in both the bar and charming conservatory restaurant rely extensively on locally sourced ingredients, offering for example in the winter, cauliflower and Lincolnshire poacher soup; duck rillette with home-made piccalilli and toasted sourdough to start. Mains might be pan-fried sea bream with braised fennel, roast aubergine purée, black olive tapenade and crushed potatoes. For dessert, there's affogato (vanilla ice cream with expresso poured over); caramelised lemon tart with crème fraîche; and local cheeses. About fourteen wines and Champagnes are available by the glass.

Open all day noon-11 Closed: Sun eve Jan-Mar
Bar Meals L served Mon-Sat 12-2.15, Sun 12-3 D served Mon-Sat 6.15-9.15, Sun 6.15-8.30 Av main course £14 **Restaurant** L served Mon-Sat 12-2.15, Sun 12-3 D served Mon-Sat 6.15-9.15, Sun 6.15-8.30 Fixed menu price fr £12.50 Av 3 course à la carte fr £22 ⊕ FREE HOUSE ◀ Greene King IPA, Fool's Nook, Fuller's London Pride, Guest ales ⓪ Aspall. ♀ 14 **Facilities** Children welcome Children's menu Children's portions Dogs allowed Garden Parking Wi-fi

GRAFTON REGIS   Map 11 SP74

The White Hart ♀

Northampton Rd NN12 7SR ☎ 01908 542123
e-mail: alan@pubgraftonregis.co.uk
dir: M1 junct 15 onto A508 between Northampton & Milton Keynes

This thatched, stone-built property dating from the 16th century is the focal point for a friendly village with approximately 96 residents. In 1464 Edward IV married Elizabeth Woodville in this historic place. The pub has been owned by the same family for over 14 years and Alan, now the owner, is also chef. Menus change frequently according to available produce. Typical choices include salmon and monkfish mornay; home-made steak and kidney pie; and garlic mushroom tagliatelle. Well kept ales and fourteen wines by the glass complete the picture.

Open 12-2.30 6-11 Closed: Mon **Bar Meals** L served all wk 12-2 D served all wk 6-9.30 **Restaurant** D served all wk 6.30-9 booking required ◀ Greene King, Abbot Ale, IPA. ♀ 14 **Facilities** Children's portions Garden Parking

GREAT OXENDON   Map 11 SP78

PICK OF THE PUBS

The George Inn ♀

See Pick of the Pubs on opposite page

HARRINGWORTH   Map 11 SP99

The White Swan NEW

Seaton Rd NN17 3AF ☎ 01572 747543
e-mail: adam@whiteswanharringworth.co.uk
dir: From A47 between Uppingham & Duddington take B672 signed Coldacott & Seaton. Under Harringworth Viaduct to T-junct. Left signed Harringworth. Under viaduct again. Pub in village centre on left

A handsome, ironstone-built old coaching inn set in the verdant Welland Valley close to where it is crossed by England's longest railway viaduct, all 82 arches of it. The 16th century village centre inn is well respected for a wide variety of dishes created from produce of the area; wood pigeon, home-smoked trout or roast breast of guinea fowl may feature, rounded off by calorific pudding treats. Local beers and ciders are championed here, with the Welland Valley Beer Festival hosted each year.

Open 12-2.30 6.30-11 Closed: Sun eve & Mon L
Bar Meals L served Tue-Sun 12-2 D served Mon-Sat 6.30-9 Av main course £12 **Restaurant** L served Tue-Sun 12-2 D served Mon-Sat 6.30-9 Fixed menu price fr £10.95 Av 3 course à la carte fr £20 ◀ Adnams Bitter, Shepherd Neame Spitfire, Digfield Ales, Barnwell Bitter ⓪ Welland Vineyard Roundhead cider. **Facilities** Children welcome Children's menu Children's portions Beer festival Parking

KILSBY   Map 11 SP57

The George ♀ NEW

Watling St CV23 8YE
☎ 01788 822229 ⧉ 01788 822584
dir: M1 junct 18, follow A361/ Daventry signs. Pub at rdbt junct of A361 & A5

This traditional village pub, with its warm welcome and great local atmosphere, has a traditional public bar and a high-ceilinged wood-panelled lounge which opens into a smarter but relaxed area with solidly comfortable furnishings. The full menu might include Arbroath smokie fishcakes, chicken and bacon Caesar salad and up to 16oz steaks. Adnams, Fuller's, Old Speckled Hen and a guest real ale are well kept on hand pumps. Mondays are Pie and Pint Nights, Wednesdays are Steak and Wine, while Thursdays are devoted to burgers. There's a beer festival every St George's Day weekend.

Open all wk Mon-Sat 11.30-3 5.30-11.30 (Sun 12-5 6-11) **Bar Meals** L served Mon-Sat 12-2, Sun 12-4 booking required D served all wk 6-9 booking required Av main course £4.90 **Restaurant** L served Mon-Sat 12-2, Sun 12-4 booking required D served all wk 6-9 booking required Fixed menu price fr £9.50 ⊕ PUNCH TAVERNS ◀ Fuller's London Pride, Morland Old Speckled Hen, Adnams Bitter. ♀ 8 **Facilities** Children welcome Children's menu Children's portions Dogs allowed Garden Beer festival Parking Wi-fi

PICK OF THE PUBS

The George Inn 🍷

GREAT OXENDON   Map 11 SP78

LE16 8NA ☎ 01858 465205
e-mail:
info@thegeorgegreatoxendon.co.uk
web: www.thegeorgegreatoxendon.co.uk
dir: *A508 towards Market Harborough*

There's been a pub on the site here at the fringe of the little village of Great Oxenden for at least 500 years; some past patrons find it hard to leave and reports of ghostly apparitions add to the chatter at the welcoming bar, where beers from Timothy Taylor and Adnams are supplemented by regular guest ales. Perhaps some of these shades are veterans of the Battle of Naseby, that great Civil War confrontation that occurred just a few miles away in 1645, some of the Royalist troops are believed to have been billeted at The George.

Inside, the inn has been lovingly restored and refurbished over the years, retaining much character, with beams, open log fires and comfy furnishings setting the scene for an indulgence in the excellent cuisine prepared by chef-patron David Dudley. Diners will be in safe hands here; in the past David has prepared meals for HM The Queen, Nelson Mandela, Paul and Linda McCartney and Cher, although not at The George!

Choose the airy conservatory overlooking the gardens or hunker down near the fires and start with a light bite such as salmon, sweet potato and red pepper cake, or Gruyère fritters with cranberry sauce. Mains are a good mix of solid inn fare; braised beef with horseradish mash and red wine jus, or escalope of salmon on crushed potatoes with a tarragon velouté, with locally sourced specials that may include half a roast pheasant on mash with bourguignon sauce. Vegetarian options add fresh choice from a short menu offering up tortellini filled with Ricotta and spinach with a tomato and basil sauce. The wine list provides useful notes.

Open Mon-Sat 12-3 5.30-11 (Sun 12-3)
Closed: 25 Dec, Sun eve
Bar Meals L served all wk 12-2 D served Mon-Sat 6-9.30 **Restaurant** L served all wk 12-2 D served Mon-Sat 6-9.30
🛢 FREE HOUSE 🛢 Adnams Bitter, Timothy Taylor Landlord, guest ales. 🍷 10
Facilities Children welcome Children's portions Garden Parking

PICK OF THE PUBS

The Red Lion ♟

SIBBERTOFT Map 11 SP68

43 Welland Rise LE16 9UD
☎ **01858 880011**
e-mail: andrew@redlionwinepub.co.uk
web: www.redlionwinepub.co.uk
dir: *From Market Harborough take A4304, through Lubenham, left through Marston Trussell to Sibbertoft*

Andrew and Sarah Banks have rejuvenated this award-winning free house since taking it over in 2004. Wine is their special passion of the owner at this friendly 300-year-old pub and restaurant in the heart of rural Leicestershire, and over 200 bins appear on the ever-growing wine list with 20 served by the glass. Additionally all the wines can be bought at take-home prices - so having tasted a wine you can avoid the guesswork in a supermarket. When choosing a wine for dinner, allow time to absorb the useful guidelines on twinning food types with grape varieties; you'll also enjoy the humorous quotations, which reveal truths every wine lover will recognise. 'Nothing gets on the list unless I try it, quality reassurance guaranteed,' says Andrew. He also hosts fun and informative dinners during which his customers can listen to wine makers and suppliers. The pub offers an appealing blend of contemporary and classic decor, with oak beams, leather upholstery and a smartly turned-out dining room. In fine weather, meals are served in the quiet garden, which is a

favourite with local walkers and cyclists; there's also an outdoor play area for children. The same monthly-changing menu is served in all the pub's eating areas; local and seasonal produce is used wherever possible. The list of lunchtime snacks runs from curry of the day to thick ham, double egg and hand-cut chips. Freshly made baguettes or sandwiches include prawns Marie Rose or ham and English mustard fillings. A typical dinner could start with salmon, cod and coriander fishcake with warm tomato salsa. Meat from nearby farms butchered by Joseph Morris appears in main courses such as a 16oz côte de boeuf with chasseur sauce. Warm chocolate fondant with chocolate sauce and vanilla ice cream accompanied by one of Andrew's 'stickies' (dessert wines) makes for a happy ending.

Open noon-2 6.30-11 Closed: Mon L & Tue L, Sun eve **Bar Meals** L served Wed-Sun 12-2 booking required D served Mon-Sat 6.30-9.30 booking required Av main course £12.50 **Restaurant** L served Wed-Sun 12-2 booking required D served Mon-Sat 6.30-9.30 booking required Fixed menu price fr £9.95 Av 3 course à la carte fr £22 ⊕ FREE HOUSE ◀ Adnams, Timothy Taylor Landlord, Black Sheep ♂ Samuel Smiths Reserve. ♟ 20 **Facilities** Children's menu Children's portions Play area Garden Parking Wi-fi

Save on hotels. Book at theAA.com/hotel

NORTHAMPTONSHIRE 333 ENGLAND

NASSINGTON
Map 12 TL09

The Queens Head Inn ★★★★ INN ◉ ☂
NEW

54 Station Rd PE8 6QB ☎ 01780 784006
e-mail: info@queensheadnassington.co.uk
dir: *Exit A1 at Wansford, follow Yarwell & Nassington signs. Through Yarwell. Pub on left in Nassington*

Named after Mary, Queen of Scots, who was executed at nearby Fotheringhay Castle, this historic stone-built inn is situated on the banks of the River Nene in the picturesque village of Nassington. A range of comfortable and smart dining and seating areas is matched by a comprehensive menu, awarded an AA Rosette, that majors on fresh flavoursome local produce and makes good use of a Josper charcoal grill for steaks sourced from a local farm. Alfresco dining in warmer weather and nine en suite bedrooms complete the package.

Open all day all wk **Bar Meals** L served all wk 12-2 D served all wk 5.30-9.30 Av main course £13 **Restaurant** L served all wk 12-2.30 D served Mon-Sat 5.30-9.30 Fixed menu price fr £18.50 Av 3 course à la carte fr £19 ⊕ FREE HOUSE ◀ Greene King IPA, Oakham Ales JHB. ☂ 8 **Facilities** Children welcome Children's menu Children's portions Dogs allowed Garden Parking Wi-fi **Rooms** 9

NORTHAMPTON
Map 11 SP76

The Fox & Hounds ☂

Main St, Great Brington NN7 4JA
☎ 01604 770651 📄 01604 770164
e-mail: althorpcoachinginn@btconnect.com
dir: *From A428 pass main gates of Althorp House, left before rail bridge. Great Brington 1m*

A 16th-century stone and thatched coaching inn on the Althorp Estate, the Spencer ancestral home. A brick and cobbled courtyard is surrounded by stable rooms, and the enclosed flower garden is a wonderfully peaceful spot in which to sample one of the twelve real ales. A cellar restaurant specialises in traditional English cooking based on locally sourced ingredients. Look out for dishes such as seared Scottish scallops with sherry and chilli dressing; slow braised beef and Guinness casserole; and fillet of Gloucester Old Spot pork filled with apricots and sage with pear cider sauce.

Open all day all wk 11-11 **Bar Meals** L served all wk 12-3 D served Sun-Thu 6.30-9.30, Fri-Sat 6.30-10 Av main course £14 **Restaurant** L served all wk 12-3 D served Sun-Thu 6.30-9.30, Fri-Sat 6.30-10 ⊕ FREE HOUSE ◀ Greene King IPA, Fuller's London Pride, Abbot Ale, Cottage Puffing Billy, Tunnell Parish Ale, 5 guest ales Ŏ Farmhouse, Thatchers Heritage. ☂ 10 **Facilities** Children welcome Children's menu Children's portions Dogs allowed Garden Beer festival Parking Wi-fi

OUNDLE
Map 11 TL08

The Chequered Skipper ☂

Ashton PE8 5LD ☎ 01832 273494
e-mail: enquiries@chequeredskipper.co.uk
dir: *A605 towards Dundle, at rdbt follow signs to Ashton. 1m turn left into Ashton, pub in village*

The pub sign depicts a butterfly in honour of Dame Miriam Rothschild, a renowned entomologist who lived at the banking family's country house here. The little thatched village was built for the estate workers in the 1880's; huddled by the huge green the ironstone buildings are the epitome of rural England – the World Conker Championships are held here. The pub plays its part well, with timeless oak floor and beams and a collection of butterfly display cases diverting attention from a bar stocking locally brewed beers (two beer festivals a year); whilst the menu mixes speciality pizzas, traditional English and European dishes - smoked pigeon, pork and blueberry terrine, linguine with marinated artichokes and feta cheese may appear.

Open all wk 11.30-3 6-11 (Sat 11.30-11 Sun 11.45-11) **Bar Meals** L served Mon-Fri 12-2, Sat 12-2.30, Sun 12-3 D served Mon-Sat 6.30-9.30, Sun 6.30-9 Av main course £7 **Restaurant** L served Mon-Fri 12-2, Sat 12-2.30, Sun 12-3 D served Mon-Sat 6.30-9.30, Sun 6.30-9 Fixed menu price fr £10 Av 3 course à la carte fr £25 ⊕ FREE HOUSE ◀ Rockingham Ale, Oakham Ale, Brewsters Hophead. ☂ 8 **Facilities** Children welcome Children's portions Dogs allowed Garden Beer festival Parking Wi-fi

SIBBERTOFT
Map 11 SP68

PICK OF THE PUBS

The Red Lion ☂

See Pick of the Pubs on opposite page

STOKE BRUERNE
Map 11 SP74

The Boat Inn ☂

NN12 7SB ☎ 01604 862428 📄 01604 864314
e-mail: info@boatinn.co.uk
web: www.boatinn.co.uk
dir: *In village centre, just off A508 or A5*

A busy free house set on the banks of the Grand Union Canal, just across the lock from the National Waterways Museum. Run by the same family since 1877, you can 'have a drink on Jack Woodward' in the top canalside bar;

his ashes were interred under one of the flagstones there in 2008. The all-day bar menu proffers everything from hot baguettes to main courses such as beef stew and dumplings. For a more formal experience overlooking the peaceful waters, the Woodwards Restaurant offers à la carte and table d'hôte menus.

Open all day all wk 9.30am-11pm (Sun 9.30am-10.30pm) **Bar Meals** L served all wk 9.30am-9.30pm D served all wk 9.30am-9.30pm Av main course £8 food served all day **Restaurant** L served Tue-Sun 12-2 booking required D served all wk 7-9 booking required Fixed menu price fr £14.95 Av 3 course à la carte fr £23 ⊕ FREE HOUSE ◀ Banks Bitter, Marstons Pedigree, Frog Island Best, Marstons Old Empire, Wychwood Hobgoblin, Jennings Cumberland Ŏ Thatcher's Traditional. ☂ 10 **Facilities** Children welcome Children's menu Children's portions Dogs allowed Garden Parking

TITCHMARSH
Map 11 TL07

The Wheatsheaf at Titchmarsh ☂ NEW

1 North St NN14 3DH ☎ 01832 732203
e-mail: enquiries@thewheatsheafattitchmarsh.co.uk
dir: *From A14 junct 13 take A605 towards Oundle, right to Titchmarsh. Or from A14 junct 14 follow signs for Titchmarsh*

Darren and Amy Harding took over this stone-built village centre hostelry in 2010. After a refurbishment that didn't damage its character, The Wheatsheaf now sees Greene King and regularly changing guest ales dispensed at the bar, while food orders are taken and presented by friendly and efficient staff. The menu's variety sees most tastes catered for, from sandwiches and snacks to specials which may include the likes of pan-fried pigeon breast with sweet potato purée and bacon crisps; oven-roasted salmon fillet on a bed of creamy mash; and a traditional sweet such as plum jam sponge with vanilla custard.

Open 12-3 6.30-11 (Sat all day, Sun 12-6) Closed: Sun eve **Bar Meals** L served Mon-Fri 12-2.30, Sat 12-3, Sun 12-4 booking required D served Mon-Fri 6.30-9.30, Sat 6-9.30 booking required Av main course £10-£15 **Restaurant** L served Mon-Fri 12-2.30, Sat 12-3, Sun 12-4 booking required D served Mon-Fri 6.30-9.30, Sat 6-9.30 booking required Av 3 course à la carte fr £23 ⊕ FREE HOUSE ◀ Greene King IPA, Guest ales Ŏ Stowford Press. ☂ 9 **Facilities** Children welcome Children's portions Dogs allowed Garden Parking Wi-fi

PICK OF THE PUBS

The Crown

WESTON   Map 11 SP54

Helmdon Rd NN12 8PX
☎ **01295 760310** 📄 **01295 760310**
e-mail: info@thecrownweston.co.uk
web: www.thecrownweston.co.uk
dir: *Accessed from A43 or B4525*

Following the brutal murder of the children's nanny at his London house in 1974, Lord Lucan was never seen again. Or was he? Some say he had a pint the following day in this attractive 16th-century inn, unlikely as it may sound. What is certain is that the inn has been serving ale since the reign of Elizabeth I, the first recorded owner being All Souls College, Oxford. Latest in a long line of proprietors is Robert Grover, who took over The Crown in 2003. He has ensured that his pub continues to feature prominently in the life of the local community by hosting regular special events such as curry evenings. But it is perhaps better known for the provision of excellent beers, a short but elegant range of dishes based on high quality ingredients, welcoming staff and its family-friendly atmosphere. Real ales are a strength, at least four in number, and wines are reasonably priced, from the unashamedly gluggable to sophisticated gems from top producers. A selection of freshly made snacks at lunchtime may include half a dozen soft-boiled quail's eggs with celery salt and lemon mayonnaise, and sliced chorizo with houmous.

Move up in size to small plates — perhaps smoked eel with baby beetroots and horseradish cream; or roasted wild mushrooms with parsley, garlic and butter sauce. These can be served as large plates if you wish; alternatively choose from the range of seasonal main dishes: Elliots' rib-eye steak with home-made chips, watercress salad, béarnaise sauce and roasted garlic mushrooms; or linguini with rocket, roasted peppers, artichokes, parmesan and chilli. Round off with steamed orange syrup pudding with lemon posset, or spiced pineapple with vanilla and lemon sherbet. Traditional roasts on Sundays are popular all year round, with smaller portions for children. Nearby attractions include Sulgrave Manor, the ancestral home of George Washington, and Silverstone racing circuit.

Open all wk 6-11.30 (Fri-Sat noon-3.30 6-11.30 Sun noon-3.30 7-11) Closed: 25 Dec **Bar Meals** L served Fri-Sun 12-2.30 D served Tue-Sat 6-9.30 Av main course £11.50 🌐 FREE HOUSE 🛢 Greene King IPA, Hook Norton Best, Black Sheep, Landlord, Reservoir Hogs ☙ Stowford Press. **Facilities** Children's portions Family room Dogs allowed Garden Parking

TOWCESTER   Map 11 SP64

The Saracens Head

219 Watling St NN12 8BX
☎ 01327 350414   📠 01327 359879
e-mail: saracenshead.towcester@greeneking.co.uk
dir: *From M1 junct 15A, A43 towards Oxford. Take A5
signed Towcester*

This imposing building dates back over 400 years, and is
featured in Charles Dickens' first novel, *The Pickwick
Papers*. The same home comforts that Dickens enjoyed
when visiting Towcester have been updated to modern
standards, and discerning guests will find excellent service
in the restored hotel. Main menu choices include guinea
fowl stuffed with pancetta; baked salmon fillet with a
tomato, pepper and white wine Provençale sauce; and
Mediterranean vegetable lasagne with a dressed salad.

Open all day all wk ⊕ GREENE KING OLD ENGLISH INNS
◀ Abbot Ale, IPA, Guest ale. **Facilities** Children welcome
Children's menu Children's portions Garden Parking Wi-fi

WADENHOE   Map 11 TL08

PICK OF THE PUBS

The King's Head ♥

Church St PE8 5ST ☎ 01832 720024
e-mail: aletha@wadenhoekingshead.co.uk
dir: *From A605, 3m from Wadenhoe rdbt. 2m from Oundle*

A haven for travellers since the 17th century, The
King's Head is a stone-built partially thatched inn
situated at the end of a quiet country lane. Extensive
gardens overlook the tranquil River Nene; here,
customers can sit and watch the boats pass by as they
enjoy a pint of Barnwell bitter. The warm, welcoming
interior has quarry-tiled and bare-boarded floors, heavy
oak-beamed ceilings, pine furniture and open log fires.
Indeed, the pub has lost none of its old world charm
but offers most modern facilities. You can challenge
the locals to a game of Northamptonshire skittles – if
you dare. The lunchtime menu offers sandwiches, and
pies such as beef and ale or roast chicken and
mushroom; light bites take the form of sausages and
mash, or home-made burger with Cheddar cheese and
hand-cut chips. In the evening you can dine regally on
fresh mussels cooked in white wine and cream,
followed by pan-fried calves' liver on creamy mash.

Open all day 11-11 (Sun noon-10, winter 11-2.30
5.30-11 Sun noon-6) Closed: Sun eve in winter
Bar Meals L served all wk 12-9 food served all day
Restaurant food served all day ⊕ FREE HOUSE
◀ Kings Head Bitter, Barnwell Bitter ♻ Westons
Stowford Press. ♥ 15 **Facilities** Children welcome
Children's portions Dogs allowed Garden Parking

WESTON   Map 11 SP54

PICK OF THE PUBS

The Crown

See Pick of the Pubs on opposite page

WOLLASTON   Map 11 SP96

PICK OF THE PUBS

The Wollaston Inn

87 London Rd NN29 7QS ☎ 01933 663161
e-mail: info@wollaston-inn.co.uk
dir: *From Wellingborough, onto A509 towards
Wollaston. After 2m, over rdbt, then immediately left.
Inn at top of hill*

Back in the late Sixties and early Seventies, when this
was the Nags Head, the late John Peel was the resident
Sunday night DJ here. Then, in 2003, it was reinvented
as a restaurant within a pub. Renamed and restored,
the 350-year-old building's interior provides a
commendable backdrop to soft Italian leather sofas,
casual tables and chairs, ambient lighting and gentle
background music. The menus are prepared every day
from only fresh ingredients and everything, from the
bread and infused oils to the ice creams and chocolate
truffles, is made on the premises. The daytime menu
offers antipasti, soup, burgers and club sandwiches,
while the evening carte moves with the seasons to offer
dishes like roast pavé of Wield Wood venison, creamed
celeriac, buttered Savoy cabbage, pancetta crisp and
rosemary jus. The fresh seafood menu is available all
day and changes following daily deliveries from the
markets. An extensive wine list recommends what to
drink with your food, while the bar stocks draught
Burton Bitter and a good selection of bottled beers. As
we went to press we learned of a change of hands here.

Open all day all wk **Bar Meals** food served all day
Restaurant food served all day ⊕ FREE HOUSE
◀ Burton Bitter, Marstons, Guinness, Guest ales.
Facilities Children welcome Children's portions Garden
Parking

NORTHUMBERLAND

ALNWICK   Map 21 NU11

The Masons Arms

Stamford, Nr Rennington NE66 3RX
☎ 01665 577275   📠 01665 577894
e-mail: bookings@masonsarms.net
dir: *NE of Alnwick on B1340, 0.5m past Rennington*

A tastefully modernised 200-year-old coaching inn,
known by the local community as Stamford Cott. It is a
useful staging post for visitors to Hadrian's Wall,
Lindisfarne and the large number of nearby golf courses.
There is a great range of beers to enjoy, including Farne
Island and Secret Kingdom. The substantial home-cooked
food is available in the bar and the restaurant, and is
made using the best of local produce. Typical examples
include lemon sole with prawns and parsley sauce, or
Northumbrian game casserole.

Open all wk noon-2 6.30-11pm (Sun noon-2
6.30-10.30pm) ⊕ FREE HOUSE ◀ John Smiths,
Theakston Best, Secret Kingdom, Gladiator, Farne Island.
Facilities Children welcome Children's menu Children's
portions Family room Garden Parking

BELFORD   Map 21 NU13

Blue Bell Hotel

Market Place NE70 7NE
☎ 01668 213543   📠 01668 213787
e-mail: enquiries@bluebellhotel.com
dir: *Off A1, 15m N of Alnwick, 15m S of
Berwick-upon-Tweed*

Halfway between Alnwick and Berwick on the old London
to Edinburgh road, this independently-run, creeper-
covered 17th-century coaching inn stands in the heart of
the village in fine gardens, beyond which, through the
trees, rises Belford church tower. Local meats, game, fish
and cheeses are employed to good effect in the Garden
Restaurant, Tavern Bar and Bistro, whose menus present
the tastes of Northumbria and beyond. The perfect spot to
unwind after a day of walking, cycling, watersports or
golf.

Open all day all wk 11am-mdnt **Bar Meals** L served all
wk 12-2.30 D served all wk 6-9 Av main course £11.95
Restaurant L served Sun 12-2.30 booking required
D served all wk 6-9 booking required Fixed menu price fr
£19.95 ⊕ FREE HOUSE ◀ Calders, Tetleys Smooth, Black
Sheep, Guinness. **Facilities** Children welcome Children's
menu Children's portions Play area Garden Parking Wi-fi

BLANCHLAND   Map 18 NY95

The Lord Crewe Arms ♥

DH8 9SP ☎ 01434 675251   📠 01434 675337
e-mail: reception@lordcrewehotel.co.uk
dir: *10m S of Hexham via B6306*

Set amongst the honey coloured buildings in the heart of
one of England's prettiest villages, this 12th-century free
house is one of the oldest inns in the country. Formerly
part of Blanchland Abbey, it was originally built as the
abbot's lodge, guest house and kitchens. The priest's
hiding hole can still be seen high inside the chimney. The
antique furniture, barrel-vaulted bar, blazing log fires
and flagstone floors create an atmospheric setting. The
wide-ranging bar and restaurant menus offer sandwiches
and salads, as well as traditional British main course
dishes. The cloister gardens are a stunning setting for
summer eating and drinking. The pub held its first beer
festival in August 2011.

Open all day all wk 11-11 (Sun noon-10.30)
Bar Meals L served all wk 12-9 D served all wk 7-9 food
served all day **Restaurant** L served Sun 12-3 D served all
wk 7-9 booking required ⊕ FREE HOUSE ◀ Black Sheep,
John Smith's, Guinness, Guest ales. ♥ 10
Facilities Children welcome Children's menu Children's
portions Family room Dogs allowed Garden Beer festival
Parking Wi-fi

PICK OF THE PUBS

The Pheasant Inn ★★★★ INN

FALSTONE   Map 21 NY78

Stannersburn NE48 1DD
☎ **01434 240382**   📠 **01434 240382**
e-mail: stay@thepheasantinn.com
web: www.thepheasantinn.com
dir: *A69, B6079, B6320, follow signs for Kielder Water*

Byroads thread this particularly pretty part of the Northumberland National Park, meandering between verdant valleys, high moors and tranquil woodlands at the edge of the Cheviot Hills. Here too are England's largest man-made forest and biggest reservoir, Kielder Water. Ideally sited to take full advantage is the ivy-clad Pheasant Inn, secluded at the forest's edge beside a lane heading towards the cycle tracks, sculpture trail, observatory, endless walks and superb wildlife watching (lots of red squirrels here) that set Kielder apart. Long before forest or lake existed, farmers visited a beer house at Stannersburn; from such beginnings as long ago as 1624 has developed today's archetypical old country inn; effortlessly welcoming, endlessly satisfying and with eight individually styled bedrooms to tempt travellers to tarry-a-while. Photos of yesteryear's locals and trades festoon the exposed stone walls that support blackened beams; light from winter log fires flickers across antique artefacts and furniture whilst summer guests use a

stream-side garden of utter tranquillity. There's also a tasteful, terracotta-hued dining room, where the daily-changing menu makes the most of Northumberland's generous larder, creatively cooked by Irene and Robin Kershaw. Twice baked Northumberland Kielder cheese soufflé or roast tomato and red pepper soup starters set the scene for a Stilton and vegetable crumble, a slab of hearty home-made game and mushroom pie or perhaps slow roasted Northumberland lamb with a rosemary and redcurrant jus appeals. A good range of fish fresh from North Shields fish quay add to the choice. Excellent beers from Wylam Brewery satisfy guests eager to get their fill of Northumberland's bounty.

Open 12-3 6.30-11 Closed: 25-27 Dec, Mon-Tue (Nov-Mar) **Bar Meals** L served Mon-Sat noon-2.30 **Restaurant** L served Mon-Sat 12-2.30 booking required D served Mon-Sat 6.30-8.30 booking required ⊕ FREE HOUSE 🍺 Timothy Taylor Landlord, Wylam Gold, Wylam Rocket, Wylam Red Kite, Wylam Angel. **Facilities** Children's menu Children's portions Play area Family room Dogs allowed Garden Parking **Rooms** 8

Save on hotels. Book at **theAA.com/hotel**

NORTHUMBERLAND 337 ENGLAND

PICK OF THE PUBS

The Manor House Inn ▼

DH8 9LX ☎ 01207 255268
dir: *A69 W from Newcastle, left onto A68 then S for 8m. Inn on right*

Just 30 minutes from both Newcastle and Durham, this small family-run free house is an ideal base for exploring the region. Occupying an elevated position on the A68, overlooking open moorland and the stunning Derwent valley, the pub was built around 1760. The stone-walled bar, with log fires, low-beamed ceiling and massive timber support, serves five real ales all year, among which are Theakstons Best and Workie Ticket from the Mordue brewery in North Shields. The bar and lounge are good for a snack, while the restaurant is divided into two dining areas, the larger of which welcomes families with children. The focus on fresh local produce is typified by dishes such as supreme of chicken breast with sautéed leeks and Northumbrian nettle cheese sauce, or slow-braised oxtail with black pudding mash and Guinness gravy. The specials board is aptly named, bringing you wild Scottish venison and local braised squirrel. Ideally situated for visiting the Roman wall, Durham and Slaley Hall.

Open all day all wk 11-11 (Sun noon-10.30)
Bar Meals food served all day **Restaurant** food served all day ⊕ FREE HOUSE ◀ Theakstons Best, Mordue Workie Ticket, Greene King Ruddles County, Courage Directors, Old Speckled Hen ♂ Westons Old Rosie Scrumpy. ▼ 8 **Facilities** Children welcome Children's menu Children's portions Dogs allowed Garden Parking Wi-fi

The Percy Arms Hotel

Main Rd NE66 5PS ☎ 01668 215244 ▤ 01668 215277
dir: *From Alnwick take A1 N, then B6348 to Chatton*

Traditional 19th-century former coaching inn, situated in the heart of rural Northumberland. Expect a warm, traditional pub welcome, as well as a selection of fine beers, wines and tempting food. Bar menu includes deep fried Brie wedges with cranberry salsa; risotto of king prawn tails risotto with lardons and asparagus spears; home-made steak and kidney pudding, bubble and squeak; pan-fried duck breast with honey, soy and Chinese five spice glaze. Bar games include snooker, pool and darts, but those who wish to can still enjoy a quiet pint in comfort.

Open all wk **Bar Meals** L served all wk 12-3 booking required D served all wk 6-9 booking required **Restaurant** L served all wk 12-3 booking required D served all wk 6-9 booking required ⊕ JENNINGS BROTHERS PLC ◀ Jennings Cumberland Cream, Guest ales. **Facilities** Children welcome Garden Parking

The Angel of Corbridge

Main St NE45 5LA ☎ 01434 632119 ▤ 01434 633496
e-mail: info@theangelofcorbridge.com
dir: *0.5m off A69, signed Corbridge*

Stylish 18th-century coaching inn overlooking the River Tyne. Relax with a pint and the daily papers in the wood-panelled lounge, attractive split-level lounge bar, or the refurbished bar, and enjoy a home-made dish or two in the new oak-beamed restaurant hung with local artists' work. Plenty of choices on the menu range from starters of chilled poached salmon, to mains of stir-fried beef fillet, and sweets such as chocolate brownie with deep-fried vanilla ice cream.

Open all day all wk Closed: 25 Dec ⊕ FREE HOUSE ◀ Timothy Taylor Landlord, local ales. **Facilities** Children welcome Children's menu Children's portions Garden Parking Wi-fi

Black Bull

TD12 4TL ☎ 01890 820200 ▤ 07092 367733
dir: *Off A697, left at junct for 1m then left into Etal*

The Black Bull stands by the ruins of Etal Castle, not far from the River Till, with the grand walking country of the Cheviots on the doorstep. The only thatched pub in Northumberland, it serves traditional pub food such as mince and dumpling with potatoes and vegetables; or home-made steak and ale pie. Lighter options include soup, sandwiches, and toasted teacakes.

Open 12-3 6-11 (Summer 11-11) Closed: Tue (winter) ⊕ PUBMASTER ◀ Deuchars, John Smith's Smooth. **Facilities** Children welcome Children's menu Garden Parking

PICK OF THE PUBS

The Pheasant Inn ★★★★ INN

See Pick of the Pubs on opposite page

Milecastle Inn

Military Rd, Cawfields NE49 9NN ☎ 01434 321372
e-mail: clarehind@aol.com
dir: *From A69 into Haltwhistle. Pub approx 2m at junct with B6318*

In a wonderfully remote and peaceful location high on the moorland edge, one horizon is serrated by the line of Hadrian's Wall; easy walks up the lane pass Roman camps to reach Milecastle 42 beside the Wall at Cawfield Crags. Tasty beers from Newcastle's Big Lamp Brewery are ample reward for a breezy stroll, accompanied by home-cooked meals and ever-changing specials covering

bases such as rabbit casserole or beer-battered haddock. A roaring winter fire takes the chill, or sit out and enjoy the curlew-haunted countryside.

Open all day noon-11 (noon-3 6-10 Nov-Mar) Closed: Sun eve in Jan-Mar **Bar Meals** L served all wk 12-2.30 winter, 12-8.45 summer D served all wk 6-8.30 winter, 12-8.45 summer **Restaurant** L served all wk 12-2.30 winter, 12-8.45 summer D served all wk 6-8.30 winter, 12-8.45 summer ⊕ FREE HOUSE ◀ Big Lamp, Prince Bishop, Castle Eden. **Facilities** Children welcome Children's menu Children's portions Garden Parking Wi-fi

The General Havelock Inn ▼

Ratcliffe Rd NE47 6ER
☎ 01434 684376 ▤ 01434 684283
e-mail: info@generalhavelock.co.uk
web: www.generalhavelock.co.uk
dir: *On A69, 7m W of Hexham*

Built in around 1766, this riverside free house is named after a 19th-century British Army officer. The pub, with its restaurant in a converted stone barn overlooking the River Tyne, is a favourite with local show business personalities. Owner/chef Gary Thompson makes everything by hand, including bread and ice cream. Local ingredients are the foundation of his menus, which may feature rabbit or venison burgers; smoked bacon, leek and Cheddar pie; and North Shields fish in dishes such as fillet of cod with parsley liquor.

Open 12-2.30 7-mdnt Closed: Mon **Bar Meals** L served Tue-Sun 12-2 D served Tue-Sun 7-9 Av main course £8 **Restaurant** L served Tue-Sun 12-2 booking required D served Tue-Sun 7-9 booking required Fixed menu price fr £13.50 Av 3 course à la carte fr £21 ⊕ FREE HOUSE ◀ Hesket Newmarket Helvellyn Gold, Wylam Magic, High House Nel's Best, Durham Brewery Magus, Allendale Best Bitter. ▼ 15 **Facilities** Children welcome Children's portions Dogs allowed Garden

PICK OF THE PUBS

The Feathers Inn ▼

See Pick of the Pubs on page 338

PICK OF THE PUBS

Battlesteads Hotel & Restaurant

See Pick of the Pubs on page 339

PICK OF THE PUBS

The Feathers Inn 🍷

HEDLEY ON THE HILL   Map 19 NZ05

NE43 7SW
☎ **01661 843607** 📠 **01661 843607**
e-mail: info@thefeathers.net
web: www.thefeathers.net
dir: *Telephone for directions*

Rhian Cradock and Helen Greer's unassuming three-roomed pub is worth the detour for its tip-top Northumbrian micro-brewery ales, some cracking pub food and the splendid views across the Cheviot Hills. The small stone-built free house is well patronised locally, but strangers are frequently charmed by its friendly and relaxed atmosphere. Old oak beams, stone walls decorated with local photographs, coal fires and rustic settles set the informal scene, and there's a good selection of traditional pub games like shove ha'penny and bar skittles. Rhian's impressive daily menu makes sound use of the freshest local ingredients - including game from local shoots, rare breed local cattle and Longhorn beef - to create great British classics as well as regional dishes from the North East. Expect starters such as Greenside mutton and lentil broth with home-made bread, or potted shrimps with watercress and lemon. Follow with local roe deer burger with sourdough bun, celeriac coleslaw and chunky chips; casserole of gurnard, mullet, crab and mussels with rouille; or braised mutton shoulder with mint and nettle sauce, braised red cabbage and dauphinoise potatoes. Leave room for desserts like ginger burnt Northumbrian cream (best accompanied with a glass of black Muscat), and dark chocolate brownie. Relax and sup one of the cask ales, perhaps Wylam Red Kite or Mordue Workie Ticket, beside a real open fire and dip into one of the many cookery books that spill over the place. The Feathers is the perfect location to enjoy a relaxing lunch with beautiful Northumbrian views, or meet with friends for an intimate dinner. Families are welcome, and a small side room can be booked in advance if required. The Feathers annual beer and food festival takes place over Easter and includes a barrel race, egg jarping, farmers' market and a barbecue.

Open all wk noon-11pm (Mon 6-11pm Sun 12-10.30pm) Closed: No food served 1st 2wks Jan **Bar Meals** L served Tue-Sat 12-2, Sun 12-2.30 booking required D served Tue-Sat 6-8.30 booking required Av main course £12 ⊕ FREE HOUSE ◼ Mordue Workie Ticket, Fuller's London Pride, Northumberland Pit Pony, Orkney Red McGreggor, Hadrian Gladiator, Wylam Red Kite, Consett Red Dust ○ Westons 1st Quality, Westons Old Rosie.
Facilities Children's portions Beer festival Parking Wi-fi

PICK OF THE PUBS

Battlesteads Hotel & Restaurant

HEXHAM   Map 21 NY96

Wark NE48 3LS
☎ **01434 230209** 📠 **01434 230039**
e-mail: info@battlesteads.com
web: www.battlesteads.com
dir: 10m N of Hexham on B6320 (Kielder road)

Situated in Wark, near Hexham, Battlesteads is renowned for its superb food, warm and welcoming Northumbrian hospitality and outstanding 'green' credentials that include an electric car charging point.

Converted from an 18th-century farmhouse, Battlesteads is now a hugely popular, award-winning, family-run pub, hotel and restaurant standing just a few miles north of Hadrian's Wall and close to Kielder and Border Riever country.

Battlesteads offers three dining options – a more relaxed affair in the bar area with the jolly banter of bar manager Mike entertaining customers; views of the secret walled garden and some wildlife-spotting from a great vantage point in the conservatory; or a more formal, intimate experience in the main restaurant area with its dark wood furnishings and low lighting.

Food served in the 80-seater restaurant is either grown on-site in the two acre gardens and two polytunnels or sourced within 25 miles of the village, so it's truly local and wholesome. Chef Eddie Shilton favours traditional dishes with a modern twist and his innovative approach makes for a few interesting culinary surprises. Anyone with a sweet tooth will love the award-winning desserts made by Dee Slade.

Battlesteads oozes charm and character – from the flower tubs and hanging baskets ablaze with colour in the spring and summer to Gilroy the cat, who has adopted the hotel as his home, and the daily tours of the hotel's green installations run by owner Richard Slade.

Open all day all wk **Bar Meals** L served all wk 12-3 booking required D served all wk 6.30-9.30 booking required Av main course £10.75 **Restaurant** L served all wk 12-3 booking required D served all wk 6.30-9.30 booking required Fixed menu price fr £21.50 Av 3 course à la carte fr £27.75 ⊕ FREE HOUSE ◪ Wylam Gold Tankard, Durham Magus, Black Sheep Bitter, High House Nell's Best, Guest ales ♉ Thatchers Gold. **Facilities** Children's portions Dogs allowed Garden Parking Wi-fi Electric car charging point

HEXHAM continued

PICK OF THE PUBS

Dipton Mill Inn ♥

Dipton Mill Rd NE46 1YA ☎ 01434 606577
e-mail: ghb@hexhamshire.co.uk
dir: 2m S of Hexham on HGV route to Blanchland, B6306, Dipton Mill Rd

A former farmhouse, with the millstream running right through the gardens, the pub has recently celebrated its rebuilding 400 years ago. It is surrounded by farms and woodland with footpaths for pleasant country walks, and there is Hadrian's Wall and an assortment of other Roman sites in the area to explore. The Dipton Mill is home to Hexhamshire Brewery ales, including Devil's Water and Old Humbug. Food is served evenings and lunchtimes and all dishes are freshly prepared from local produce where possible. Start with home-made soup, such as carrot and celery served with a warm roll, followed by hearty dishes like mince and dumplings, lamb leg steak in wine and mustard sauce, or tomato, bean and vegetable casserole. Traditional desserts include bread and butter pudding or syrup sponge and custard. Salads, sandwiches and ploughman's are also always available.

Open noon-2.30 6-11 (Sun noon-3) Closed: 25 Dec, Sun eve **Bar Meals** L served all wk 12-2 D served Mon-Sat 6.30-8 ⊕ FREE HOUSE ◀ Hexhamshire Shire Bitter, Old Humbug, Devil's Water, Devil's Elbow, Whapweasel, Blackhall English Stout ♂ Westons Old Rosie. ♥ 17 **Facilities** Children welcome Children's portions Garden **Notes** ⊜

Miners Arms Inn

Main St, Acomb NE46 4PW ☎ 01434 603909
e-mail: info@theminersacomb.com
dir: 17m W of Newcastle on A69. 2m W of Hexham

In a peaceful spot near Hadrian's Wall, this family-run village pub dates from 1746. Three top local real ales are always available, with guest deliveries from further afield every weekend. Mainly locally sourced dishes, including vegetable or beef chilli; Cumberland sausage casserole; and wholetail scampi typify the traditional pub food. Visitors can enjoy the open hearth fire, the sun-trap of a beer garden, or sitting out front absorbing village life. Beer festivals are held occasionally.

Open all wk Mon-Fri 5-mdnt (Sat-Sun noon-mdnt) **Bar Meals** L served Sat 12-2.30 booking required D served Thu-Sat 5-8.30 booking required **Restaurant** L served Sun 12-2.30 booking required D served Thu-Sat 5-8.30 booking required ⊕ FREE HOUSE ◀ Wylam Bitter, Pilsner Urquell, Yates Bitter ♂ Perry's Farmhouse Cider. **Facilities** Children welcome Dogs allowed Garden Beer festival

PICK OF THE PUBS

Rat Inn ♥

NE46 4LN ☎ 01434 602814
e-mail: info@theratinn.com
dir: 2m from Hexham, Bridge End (A69) rdbt, take 4th exit signed Oakwood. Inn 500yds on right

Pick a sunny day and soak up the views of the Tyne Valley from the glorious hillside garden at this old drovers' inn by the green in picture-book Anick. On cooler days retreat into the classic bar, where you'll find crackling log fires, a stone-flagged floor, old pews and benches and an impressive oak bar dispensing six local micro-brewery ales, including beers from Allendale, Geltsdale and Northumberland breweries. Peruse the papers over a pint, then order a plate of food from an interesting daily menu that bristles with locally sourced ingredients – a blackboard in the bar details the farms where the day's meats have come from. In addition, herbs are grown in the pub garden and the cheeseboard features only Northumbrian cheeses. Typically, tuck into local game terrine with fig chutney, rack of lamb with olives, rosemary and oven-fried tomatoes, confit duck leg with dauphinoise potatoes, and roast rib of beef (for two) with béarnaise. Leave room for chocolate and coconut bread-and-butter pudding.

Open all day all wk **Bar Meals** L served Tue-Sat 12-2, Sun 12-3 booking required D served Tue-Sat 6-9 booking required Av main course £12 **Restaurant** L served Tue-Sat 12-2, Sun 12-3 booking required D served Tue-Sat 6-9 booking required Av 3 course à la carte fr £18-£30 ⊕ FREE HOUSE ◀ 6 changing guest ales. **Facilities** Children welcome Children's portions Garden Parking Wi-fi

LONGFRAMLINGTON   Map 21 NU10

PICK OF THE PUBS

The Anglers Arms

Weldon Bridge NE65 8AX ☎ 01665 570271 & 570655
e-mail: johnyoung@anglersarms.fsnet.co.uk
dir: From N, 9m S of Alnwick right Weldon Bridge sign. From S, A1 to by-pass Morpeth, left onto A697 for Wooler & Coldstream. 7m, left to Weldon Bridge

Commanding the picturesque Weldon Bridge over the River Coquet since the 1760s, this part-battlemented, former coaching inn on the road to Scotland is full of knick-knacks and curios, pictures and fishing memorabilia. Timothy Taylor Landlord and Theakstons Best Bitter are among the real ales to accompany bar meals like Whitby wholetail scampi and Northumbrian sausage with bacon and onion bubble and squeak. An old Pullman railway carriage provides a different dining experience, with silver service as standard, and dishes such as tournedos Flodden, which is prime fillet stuffed with Applewood cheese wrapped in bacon and coated in garlic sauce; grilled fillet of salmon with new potatoes, baby corn, green beans, rocket and chilli

sauce; and stir-fried vegetable sizzler. The carefully tended half-acre of garden is perfect for alfresco dining and includes a children's play park. You can fish on the pub's own mile of River Coquet.

Open all day all wk 11-11 (Sun 12-10.30) **Bar Meals** L served all wk 12-9.30 D served all wk 12-9.30 food served all day **Restaurant** L served all wk 12-9.30 booking required D served all wk 12-9.30 booking required food served all day ⊕ FREE HOUSE ◀ Timothy Taylor Landlord, Old Speckled Hen, Abbot Ale, Theakstons Best Bitter. **Facilities** Children welcome Play area Family room Garden Parking

LONGHORSLEY   Map 21 NZ19

Linden Tree ★★★★ HL ⊛⊛

Linden Hall NE65 8XF
☎ 01670 500033 📄 01670 500001
e-mail: lindenhall@macdonald-hotels.co.uk
dir: Off A1 on A697, 1m N of Longhorsley

This popular pub was originally two large cattle byres. It takes its name from the linden trees near Linden Hall, the impressive Georgian mansion (now hotel) in whose grounds it stands. The brasserie-style menu might include a ham and pease pudding sandwich; a traditional Caesar salad; home-made Craster kipper pâté with brown bread, butter and lemon; spaghetti carbonara; and (from its Taste of Northumberland selection) home-made steak and suet pudding. Change of hands.

Open all wk Mon-Sat 11am-11pm (Sun 11am-10.30pm) ◀ Worthington, Greene King IPA, Caffreys, Guinness. **Facilities** Children welcome Play area Garden Parking **Rooms** 50

LOW NEWTON BY THE SEA   Map 21 NU22

The Ship Inn

The Square NE66 3EL ☎ 01665 576262
e-mail: forsythchristine@hotmail.com
dir: NE from A1 at Alnwick towards Seahouses

The beach is only a stroll away from this pretty inn, which overlooks the green. Low Newton was purpose-built as a fishing village in the 18th century and remains wonderfully unspoilt. Bustling in summer and a peaceful retreat in winter, The Ship offers plenty of fresh, locally caught fish and free-range meats, along with interesting vegetarian food and old fashioned puddings. The pub now has its own micro-brewery, so expect some cracking real ales.

Open all wk ⊕ FREE HOUSE ◀ Micro-brewery - Sea Coal, Dolly Day Dream, Sea Wheat, Ship Hop Ale, Sandcastles at Dawn. **Facilities** Children welcome Dogs allowed Garden **Notes** ⊜

MILFIELD   Map 21 NT93

The Red Lion Inn

Main Rd NE71 6JD ☎ **01668 216224**
e-mail: redlioninn@fsmail.net
web: www.redlionmilfield.co.uk
dir: *On A697, 9m S of Coldstream (6m N of Wooler)*

Three hundred years ago this stone building was a sheep drover's pub. Later it became a stagecoach inn, then during WWII it was popular with fighter pilots based nearby. Situated on the edge of Northumberland National Park, it is within easy reach of fishing on both the Till and Tweed, walking routes in the Cheviot Hills, and the battle site of Flodden Field (AD1513). Locally sourced ingredients feature in dishes such as honey roast pork belly, home-made steak and ale pie, and pan-fried salmon fillet with garlic king prawns, and there's a choice of excellent guest beers to wash it all down with.

Open all wk 11-2 5-11 **Bar Meals** L served Mon-Fri 11-2, Sat-Sun 11-9 D served Mon-Fri 5-9, Sat-Sun 11-9 booking required Av main course £9 ⊕ FREE HOUSE ◀ Deuchars IPA, Black Sheep, Guinness, Guest ales ♂ Thatchers Gold. **Facilities** Children welcome Children's menu Children's portions Garden Parking

See advert below

NETHERTON   Map 21 NT90

The Star Inn

NE65 7HD ☎ **01669 630238**
dir: *7m from Rothbury*

This place is a real find - owned by the same family since 1917, and situated in superb remote countryside, The Star retains many period features. The bar is a bit like someone's living room, comfortable and quiet, with no fruit machines or piped music – no food is served and there's nothing fancy about it - just cask ales in the peak of condition, served from a hatch in the entrance hall.

Open 7.30-11 Closed: Mon, Thu ⊕ FREE HOUSE ◀ Camerons Strongarm, guest beers. **Facilities** Parking **Notes** ⊗

NEWTON-ON-THE-MOOR   Map 21 NU10

PICK OF THE PUBS

The Cook and Barker Inn ★★★★ INN ♥

NE65 9JY ☎ **01665 575234** 📄 **01665 575887**
e-mail: info@cookandbarkerinn.co.uk
dir: *0.5m from A1 S of Alnwick*

Enjoy outstanding views of the Cheviot Hills and the Northumbrian coast from this traditional country inn set in an elevated position in a picturesque village. The Cook and Barker is a long-established family business run by Phil Farmer, who has set his sights well above the conventional 'pub grub with rooms'. To this end, highly skilled kitchen staff strive to prepare quality dishes that give value for money, while the front-of-house team looks after guests with expertise and finesse. The bar and lounge menu offers a dazzling array of dishes, from a deluxe prawn open sandwich to confit roast duck with fine beans, olive oil crushed potatoes and hoi sin sauce. With seafood from North Shields fish quay, excellent fresh fish and seafood dishes might include pan-fried lemon sole with shrimp

and lemon butter sauce, while restaurant dishes typically include Northumbrian beef fillet stuffed with Stilton and wrapped in back bacon with a red wine jus. There are 18 smartly furnished en suite bedrooms if you would like to stay over.

Open all day all wk noon-11 **Bar Meals** food served all day **Restaurant** L served Mon-Sat 12-2, Sun all day booking required D served Mon-Sat 7-9, Sun all day booking required ⊕ FREE HOUSE ◀ Timothy Taylor Landlord, Theakstons Best Bitter, Fuller's London Pride, Batemans XXXB, Black Sheep. ♥ 12 **Facilities** Children welcome Children's menu Family room Garden Parking Wi-fi **Rooms** 18

SEAHOUSES   Map 21 NU23

The Bamburgh Castle Inn ★★★ INN ♥ NEW

NE68 7SQ ☎ **01665 720283**
e-mail: enquiries@bamburghcastleinn.co.uk
dir: *A1 onto B1341 to Bamburgh, B1340 to Seahouses, follow signs to harbour*

From its prime location on the quayside you can see the Farne Islands, surely making this one of the best positions for a pub anywhere along Northumberland's stunning coast. Dating back to the 18th century, the inn has been transformed in recent years and has superb bar and dining areas, with outside seating. Cajun chicken and king prawn stir-fry; liver, bacon and onions; roast duck breast; and wild mushroom risotto are among items on the core menu, while lighter meals and a Sunday carvery are also available. Smart, comfortable bedrooms are arranged over three floors, some having harbour views. There is an annual beer festival.

Open all day all wk **Bar Meals** Av main course £9.95 food served all day **Restaurant** Fixed menu price fr £8.95 food served all day ⊕ FREE HOUSE ◀ Farne Island, Black Sheep. ♥ 11 **Facilities** Children welcome Children's menu Children's portions Family room Dogs allowed Garden Beer festival Parking Wi-fi **Rooms** 29

SEAHOUSES *continued*

PICK OF THE PUBS

The Olde Ship Inn ★★★★ INN ♈

9 Main St NE68 7RD
☎ 01665 720200 ☐ 01665 721383
e-mail: theoldeship@seahouses.co.uk
dir: *Lower end of main street above harbour*

Set comfortably above the bustling old harbour of Seahouses, this stone-built free house reflects the fishing heritage of this tiny port. Built as a farm around 1745, it has been in the present owners' family for 100 years. These days it is a residential inn with a long established reputation for good food and drink in relaxing surroundings. The main saloon bar is full of character, with its wooden floor made from pine ships' decking and lit by stained glass windows, offers a selection of real ales. The inn's corridors and boat gallery are an Aladdin's cave of antique nautical artefacts and seafaring mementoes, ranging from a figurehead to all manner of ship's brasses and dials. Popular bar foods include locally caught seafood, freshly made sandwiches and home-made soups. In the evenings, starters like moules marinière or traditional prawn cocktail are followed by bosun's fish stew; chicken and mushroom casserole; and steak and ale pie. The tastefully decorated bedrooms are well appointed, and some have views to the bird and seal sanctuary on the Farne Islands.

Open all day all wk 11-11 (Sun noon-11)
Bar Meals L served all wk 12-2.30 D served all wk 7-8.30 (no D late Nov-late Jan) booking required Av main course £8 **Restaurant** L served Sun 12-2 booking required D served all wk 7-8.30 (no D late Nov-late Jan) booking required Fixed menu price fr £10 Av 3 course à la carte fr £10.50 ⊕ FREE HOUSE ◀ Black Sheep, Theakstons, Best Scotch, Ruddles. ♈ 10
Facilities Children welcome Children's portions Family room Garden Parking **Rooms** 18

SLAGGYFORD   Map 18 NY65

The Kirkstyle Inn

CA8 7PB ☎ 01434 381559
dir: *Just off A689, 6m N of Alston*

With enviable views of the South Tyne river and in an Area of Outstanding Natural Beauty, The Kirkstyle Inn takes its name from the stile into the adjacent churchyard of St Jude's. A real log fire heats the pub in winter, but there's a warm seafood welcome here all the year round. Among the beers are real ales from local breweries including Yates' Bitter and in summer a special Kirkstyle ale is available. Expect lunchtime snacks and specials, including local sausages served with local honey mustard and either eggs and hand-cut chips, or mash and gravy. This dog-friendly pub is handy for both the Pennine Way and the South Tyne trail.

Open all wk noon-3 6-11 Closed: Mon in winter
Bar Meals L served all wk 12-2 D served Mon-Sat 6-8.30
Restaurant L served all wk 12-2 D served Mon-Sat 6-8.30 ⊕ FREE HOUSE ◀ Kirkstyle Ale, Yates Bitter, Guinness.
Facilities Children welcome Children's portions Dogs allowed Garden Parking

---

WARDEN   Map 21 NY96

The Boatside Inn ♈

NE46 4SQ ☎ 01434 602233
e-mail: sales@theboatsideinn.com
web: www.theboatsideinn.com
dir: *Off A69 W of Hexham, follow signs to Warden Newborough & Fourstones*

The name of this stone-built country free house harks back to the days when a rowing boat ferried people across the river before the bridge was built. Standing beneath Warden Hill at the confluence of the North and South Tyne rivers, The Boatside welcomes children, walkers and cyclists; the inn also has fishing rights on the river. Local produce is used for main courses such as beef and Guinness cobbler; chicken breast stuffed with sun-dried tomatoes; and creamy vegetarian lasagne.

Open all day all wk 11-11 (Sun 11-10.30)
Bar Meals L served Mon-Sat 11-9, Sun 12-8 D served Mon-Sat 11-9, Sun 12-8 Av main course £9.30 food served all day **Restaurant** L served Mon-Sat 12-2.30, Sun 12-8 D served Mon-Sat 6-9, Sun 12-8 ⊕ FREE HOUSE ◀ Black Sheep, John Smith's, Mordue, Wylam. ♈ 15
Facilities Children welcome Children's menu Children's portions Dogs allowed Garden Parking Wi-fi

---

WARENFORD   Map 21 NU12

PICK OF THE PUBS

The White Swan

NE70 7HY ☎ 01668 213453
e-mail: dianecuthbert@yahoo.com
dir: *100yds E of A1, 10m N of Alnwick*

This 200-year-old coaching inn stands near the original toll bridge over the Waren Burn. Formerly on the Great North Road, the building is now just a stone's throw from the A1. Inside, you'll find thick stone walls and an open fire for colder days; in summer, there's a small sheltered seating area, with further seats in the adjacent field. The Dukes of Northumberland once owned the pub, and its windows and plasterwork still bear the family crests. Visitors and locals alike enjoy the atmosphere and Northumbrian dishes: try Seahouses kippers with creamy horseradish sauce; venison pudding with lemon suet crust and fresh vegetables; or roast pork hock with wine and herbs. Vegetarians are well catered for, with interesting dishes like beetroot and potato gratin; artichoke and leek pancakes; and celeriac pan Haggarty with fresh tomato sauce.

Open all day all wk noon-mdnt **Bar Meals** L served all wk 12-2.30 D served all wk 6-9 **Restaurant** L served all wk 12-2.30 D served all wk 6-9 ⊕ FREE HOUSE ◀ Black Sheep, John Smith's, Guest ales.
Facilities Children welcome Children's menu Children's portions Dogs allowed Garden Parking

---

NOTTINGHAMSHIRE

BEESTON   Map 11 SK53

Victoria Hotel ♈

Dovecote Ln NG9 1JG
☎ 0115 925 4049 ☐ 0115 922 3537
e-mail: victoriabeeston@btconnect.com
dir: *M1 junct 25, A52 E. Turn right at Nurseryman PH, right opp Rockaway Hotel into Barton St 1st left, next to railway station*

The Victoria dates from 1899 when it was built next to Beeston Railway Station, and the large, heated patio garden is still handy for a touch of train-spotting. It offers an excellent range of traditional ales (up to 14 at a time), continental beers and lagers, traditional ciders, a good choice of wines by the glass and single malt whiskies. Home-cooked dishes on the menu might include chargrilled swordfish loin marinated in lemon, chilli and oregano; chicken arrabiata; or vegetable and lentil moussaka. Check out the dates of the beer festivals – end of January, Easter, last two weeks in July and October.

Open all day all wk 10.30am-11pm (Sun 12-11) Closed: 26 Dec **Bar Meals** L served Sun-Tue 12-8.45, Wed-Sat 12-9.30 food served all day **Restaurant** L served Sun-Tue 12-8.45, Wed-Sat 12-9.30 booking required food served all day ⊕ FREE HOUSE ◀ Batemans XB, Castle Rock Harvest Pale, Castle Rock Hemlock, Everards Tiger, Holdens Black Country Bitter, Blue Monkey, Holdens Black Country, 6 guest ales Ŏ Thatchers Traditional, Broadoak Medium, Biddendens Bushels. ❡ 25 **Facilities** Dogs allowed Garden Beer festival Parking

BLIDWORTH   Map 16 SK55

Fox & Hounds ❡

Blidworth Bottoms NG21 0NW ☎ 01623 792383
e-mail: info@foxandhounds-pub.com
dir: *Right off B6020 between Ravenshead & Blidworth*

A traditional country pub, extensively refurbished a few years ago to create a series of attractive rooms in which to eat and drink. The building dates to the early 19th century, but exactly when it became a pub is not known. For nearly 100 years the locals have performed a 'Plough Play' in the pub every January, recalling the days when Blidworth Bottoms was a much larger community with shops and a post office. Good pub food comes in the form of home-made soups, pies, blackened salmon in Cajun spices, hot chilli con carne, and giant Yorkshire puddings with sausages.

Open all day all wk 11.30am-11.30pm (Fri-Sat 11.30am-mdnt) **Bar Meals** L served all wk 11.30-9 D all wk 11.30-9 food served all day **Restaurant** food served all day ⊕ GREENE KING ◀ H&H Cask Bitter, Old Speckled Hen, Olde Trip H&H, Seasonal guest ales. ❡ 9 **Facilities** Children welcome Children's menu Play area Dogs allowed Garden Parking

CAUNTON   Map 17 SK76

PICK OF THE PUBS

Caunton Beck ❡

NG23 6AB ☎ 01636 636793 ▤ 01636 636828
e-mail: email@cauntonbeck.com
dir: *6m NW of Newark on A616 to Sheffield*

This civilised village pub-restaurant is built around a beautifully restored 16th-century cottage, with herb gardens and a colourful rose arbour that reflects a tradition started by Samuel Reynolds Hole, the vicar of Caunton. Like its sister establishment the Wig and Mitre in Lincoln (see entry), Caunton Beck opens daily for breakfast and carries on serving food throughout the day. Real ales complement a worthy international wine list, including a wide choice by the glass. The extensive breakfast menu features Bucks Fizz and a selection of Champagnes alongside more traditional teas and coffees, whilst the main menu changes with the seasons. To start you might choose Portobello mushroom and sage risotto with Pecorino shavings, followed by crisp coley tempura with tartare sauce, mushy peas and hand-cut chips. Rum and raisin crème brûlée is a typical dessert. A sandwich and light meal menu is also available, with home-made chocolates and fudge on offer.

Open all day all wk 8am-mdnt **Bar Meals** L served all wk 8am-10pm D served all wk 8am-10pm Av main course £16 food served all day **Restaurant** L served all wk 8am-10pm booking required D served all wk 8am-10pm booking required Fixed menu price fr £12.75 Av 3 course à la carte fr £26.25 food served all day ⊕ FREE HOUSE ◀ Batemans GHA, Marston's Pedigree, Black Sheep, Guinness Ŏ Thatchers. ❡ 24 **Facilities** Children welcome Children's menu Children's portions Dogs allowed Garden Parking

CAYTHORPE   Map 11 SK64

Black Horse Inn

NG14 7ED ☎ 0115 966 3520
dir: *12m from Nottingham off A612 towards Southwell*

Old-fashioned hospitality is guaranteed in this small, beamed country pub which has been run by the same family for three generations. It has its own brewery, producing Caythorpe Dover Beck bitter (named after the stream that runs past the pub), a coal fire in the bar, and delicious home-cooked food prepared from seasonal ingredients. Fresh fish dishes such as mussels or fish and chips are a speciality. Enjoy a pint of Dover Beck Bitter in the garden in the warmer weather. Good local walks.

Open noon-2.30 6-11 (Sun noon-5 8-10.30) Closed: Mon L (ex BH) & every 3rd Tue L **Bar Meals** L served Tue-Sat 12-1.45 booking required D served Tue-Sat 6.30-8.30 booking required **Restaurant** L served Tue-Sat 12-1.45 booking required D served Tue-Fri 6.30-8.30 booking required ⊕ FREE HOUSE ◀ Greene King Abbot Ale, Dover Beck Bitter, Batemans XB, Adnams Ŏ Westons Stowford Press. **Facilities** Dogs allowed Garden Parking **Notes** ⊚

The Old Volunteer ❡ NEW

Caythorpe Rd NG14 7EB ☎ 0115 966 5967
e-mail: manager@theoldvounteercaythorpe.co.uk
dir: *From Nottingham take A612 signed Southwell. At Lowdham right onto A6097 (signed Leicester & Newark). Left into Gunthorpe Rd (signed Caythorpe). Right into Caythorpe Rd*

At the fringe of a village in the Trent Valley, this old local has been upgraded and transformed into a chic destination dining pub with imposing contemporary furniture and decor. A series of comfy, airy, open spaces with a rustic terrace overlooking open meadows, diners may indulge in a notable menu that covers all the bases, including rabbit stew with carrot purée and honey-roast Chantenay carrots. Locals are still at the heart of the pub, enjoying a lively social calendar and beers from a range of micro-breweries.

Open all day all wk **Bar Meals** Av main course £5.50 food served all day **Restaurant** Fixed menu price fr £10.50 Av 3 course à la carte fr £25 food served all day ⊕ GREENE KING ◀ Greene King IPA, Yorkshire Brewery Yorkshire Terrier, Springhead Brewery Robin Hood Bitter. ❡ 17 **Facilities** Children welcome Children's portions Dogs allowed Garden Parking

COLSTON BASSETT   Map 11 SK73

PICK OF THE PUBS

The Martin's Arms ❡

See Pick of the Pubs on page 344

EDWINSTOWE   Map 16 SK66

Forest Lodge ★★★★ INN

4 Church St NG21 9QA
☎ 01623 824443 ▤ 01623 824686
e-mail: reception@forestlodgehotel.co.uk
web: www.forestlodgehotel.co.uk
dir: *A614 towards Edwinstowe, turn onto B6034. Inn opposite church*

This 18th-century coaching inn stands right on the edge of Sherwood Forest opposite the church where Robin Hood reputedly married Maid Marion. Sympathetically restored by the Thompson family over the past seven years, it includes stylish accommodation and a comfortable restaurant and bar. Five cask ales are always on tap in two beamed bars, both warmed by open fires. An impressive baronial-style dining hall is an ideal setting for appetising plates of wholesome fare such as pan-seared scallops with cauliflower purée and fennel seed bhaji, followed by loin of English mutton Wellington with wild garlic and mushroom stuffing wrapped in a nettle pancake. Also available is a selection of light bites – sandwiches, jacket potatoes and omelettes.

Open all wk 11.30-3 5.30-11 (Fri 11.30-3 5-11, Sun noon-3 6-10.30) Closed: 1 Jan **Bar Meals** L served all wk 12-2.30 booking required D served all wk 6-9.30 booking required Av main course £10 **Restaurant** L served all wk 12-2.30 booking required D served all wk 6-9.30 booking required Av 3 course à la carte fr £25 ⊕ FREE HOUSE ◀ Bombardier, Kelham Island Pale Rider, Kelham Island Easy Rider, Acorn Pale Ale, Eagle IPA. **Facilities** Children welcome Children's menu Children's portions Dogs allowed Garden Parking Wi-fi **Rooms** 13

PICK OF THE PUBS

The Martin's Arms ♉

COLSTON BASSETT Map 11 SK73

School Ln NG12 3FD
☎ **01949 81361** 📠 **01949 81039**
e-mail: martins_arms@hotmail.co.uk
web: www.themartinsarmsinn.co.uk
dir: *Off A46 between Leicester & Newark*

Over the centuries the estate village of Colston Bassett slumbered in the service and protection of the local lords of the manor; a colourful bunch whose number included one who led Charles I to his execution before himself being hung for treason. Estate workers took respite at the beerhouse beside the 13th century village cross, long a market-place in the secluded Vale of Belvoir. In the 18th century it was expanded into an inn named after the landowners, and today's Martin's Arms began to take shape. Much of the interior harks back to those heady days; with Jacobean fireplaces holding crackling log fires warming rooms that shout country-house parlour, brimming with rural prints and lovingly furnished with period pieces. Balmy summer days can be enjoyed in the tranquil setting of the one-acre garden (with croquet lawn) which backs on to a National Trust estate. Time passes easily sipping beer from Castle Rock or Timothy Taylor, or perhaps trying local Belvoir elderflower pressé. Muse over the tantalising menu choices that rely heavily on produce of the parish, local estates and artisan providers to tempt the palates of discerning diners who appreciate the

finer cuisines created on the premises by the new team of chefs headed by Valentin Petiteau. Bar snacks could weigh in with cheeses made in the Vale of Belvoir, accompanied by Melton Mowbray pork pie with breads and preserves made on site; more filling starters include estate smoked pheasant breast with celeriac remoulade. Mains appeal to all tastes, with leek and fennel tartlet topped with mature Cheddar cheese, tomato and basil sauce and a side salad tempting non-meat eaters, whilst carnivores may be enticed by game pie, pomme purée, tartare sauce and lemon salad, or fillet of sea bream on a bed of winter ratatouille bisque. Among the puddings is pear and cranberry tartlet. A good selection of fine wines cap the visit.

Open all wk noon-3.30 6-11 Closed: 25-26 Dec & 1 Jan eve **Bar Meals** L served Mon-Sat 12-2, Sun 12-2.30 D served Mon-Sat 7-9.30 Av main course £15 **Restaurant** L served all wk 12-2 booking required D served Mon-Sat 7-9.30 booking required Fixed menu price fr £16.50 Av 3 course à la carte fr £28 ◀ Marston's Pedigree, Interbrew Bass, Greene King Abbot Ale, Timothy Taylor Landlord, Black Sheep Best, IPA, Castle Rock Harvest Pale, Spitfire. **Facilities** Children's portions Family room Garden Parking

ELKESLEY   Map 17 SK67

Robin Hood Inn

High St DN22 8AJ ☎ 01777 838259
e-mail: a1robinhood@aol.com
dir: *5m SE of Worksop off A1 towards Newark-on-Trent*

Parts of this unassuming village inn date back to the
14th century. Ceilings and floors are deep red, while the
green walls are adorned with pictures of food. The
comprehensive choice is served in both the bar and
restaurant, and includes a fixed price menu, carte and
daily specials board. Typical dishes include soups such
as smoked haddock and leek or celery with blue cheese
croutons, and home-made pies like steak and kidney,
lamb and mint or chicken and leek. Kids eat free every
day.

Open 11.30-2.30 6-11 Closed: Sun eve & Mon
Bar Meals L served Tue-Sun 12-2 D served Tue-Sat
6-8.30 Av main course £7.50 **Restaurant** L served
Tue-Sun 12-2 D served Tue-Sat 6-8.30 Av 3 course à la
carte fr £17.50 ⊕ ENTERPRISE INNS ◀ John Smith's
Extra Smooth, Black Sheep Best Bitter, Guest ale.
Facilities Children welcome Children's menu Children's
portions Play area Dogs allowed Garden Parking

FARNDON   Map 17 SK75

PICK OF THE PUBS

The Farndon Boathouse ◉ ♀

Riverside NG24 3SX
☎ 01636 676578 📠 01636 673911
e-mail: info@farndonboathouse.co.uk
dir: *From Newark-on-Trent take A46 to Farndon x-rds,
turn right, continue to river. Boathouse on riverside*

Clad in wood, with chunky exposed roof trusses, stone
floors, warehouse-style lighting, and an abundance of
glass, this modern bar and eatery, in the style of an old
boathouse, sits wonderfully well on the banks of the
River Trent. Just how well you'll realise if you approach
from the river in your cruiser, or watch a sunset
through the extensively glazed frontage of the bar and
restaurant. With the award of an AA Rosette, the food
philosophy champions local sourcing and home
preparation, with home-smoked meats, fish, spices
and cheeses, for example, and herbs and leaves grown
in the kitchen garden. Exciting dishes include smoked
haddock on a kedgeree style risotto; Thai fish bowl;
seared duck breast on a frittata of potato and Iberico
Belota chorizo; and chargrilled Scotch steaks. Cask-
conditioned real ales change frequently, and live music
is played every Sunday evening.

Open all day all wk 10am-11pm **Bar Meals** L served
Mon-Fri 12-2.30, Sat-Sun 12-3 D served all wk 6-9.30
Restaurant L served Mon-Fri 12-2.30, Sat-Sun 12-3
D served all wk 6-9.30 ⊕ FREE HOUSE ◀ Greene King
IPA, Guest ales ♻ Aspall. ♀46 **Facilities** Children
welcome Children's menu Children's portions Garden
Parking Wi-fi

HARBY   Map 17 SK87

Bottle & Glass ♀

High St NG23 7EB ☎ 01522 703438 📠 01522 703436
e-mail: email@bottleandglassharby.com
dir: *S of A57 (Lincoln to Markham Moor road)*

This compact, convivial free house with its flagged floors
and heavy beams dates back to at least the 13th century.
Edward the First's wife Eleanor reputedly died here in
1290. Today it's a reassuring civilised pub restaurant,
offering great food and drink in a tranquil village at the
edge of the Vale of Trent. Food service begins with
breakfast, whilst sandwiches and light meals are
available all day. Seasonal main course dishes include
beef fillet with mustard mash, and grilled mackerel with
cauliflower cream. There is a sunny terrace for the
warmer months.

Open all day all wk 10am-11pm **Bar Meals** L served
Mon-Fri & Sun 10am-9.30pm, Sat 10am-10pm D served
Mon-Fri & Sun 10am-9.30pm, Sat 10am-10pm Av main
course £17 food served all day **Restaurant** L served
Mon-Fri & Sun 10am-9.30pm, Sat 10am-10pm booking
required D served Mon-Fri & Sun 10am-9.30pm, Sat
10am-10pm booking required Fixed menu price fr £12.75
Av 3 course à la carte fr £25 food served all day ⊕ FREE
HOUSE ◀ Young's Bitter, Young's Gold, Black Sheep,
Guinness ♻ Thatchers Gold. ♀22 **Facilities** Children
welcome Children's menu Children's portions Dogs
allowed Garden Parking

KIMBERLEY   Map 11 SK44

The Nelson & Railway Inn

12 Station Rd NG16 2NR
☎ 0115 938 2177 📠 0115 938 2179
dir: *1m N of M1 junct 26*

Perhaps as the same family has been here for over 40
years, this pub, dating from the 17th century, has its own
distinctive personality. Next door is the Hardy & Hanson
Brewery that supplies many of the beers, but the two
nearby railway stations that once made it a railway inn
are now sadly derelict. A hearty menu of pub favourites
includes soup, ploughman's and hot rolls, as well as
grills and hot dishes like home-made steak and kidney
pie; gammon steak; and mushroom Stroganoff.

Open all day all wk 11am-mdnt **Bar Meals** L served
Mon-Fri 12-2.30, Sat 12-9, Sun 12-6 D served Mon-Fri
5.30-9, Sat 12-9, Sun 12-6 **Restaurant** L served Mon-Fri
12-2.30, Sat 12-9, Sun 12-6 D served Mon-Fri 5.30-9,
Sat 12-9, Sun 12-6 ⊕ GREENE KING ◀ Hardys, Hansons
Best Bitter, Cool & Dark, Olde Trip, Morlands, Ruddles.
Facilities Children welcome Children's menu Children's
portions Family room Dogs allowed Garden Parking Wi-fi

LAXTON   Map 17 SK76

The Dovecote Inn ♀

Cross Hill NG22 0SX ☎ 01777 871586
e-mail: dovecote_inn@btconnect.com
dir: *Exit A1 at Tuxford through Egmanton to Laxton*

Like most of the village of Laxton, this family-run,
18th-century pub is Crown Estate property belonging to
the Royal Family. Outside is a delightful beer garden with
views of the church. The interior includes a bar and three
cosy wining and dining rooms. Here the seasonal, home-
cooked dishes could include blade of beef braised in
stout with sautéed wild mushrooms, spinach, and potato
and onion cake, or grilled fillet of salmon with Puy lentils
in spicy tomato sauce. The village still practises the
Medieval strip field farming method – there is a visitor
centre in the pub car park. A beer festival is held on the
last weekend in August.

Open all wk 11.30-3 6.30-11 (Sun noon-10.30)
Restaurant L served Mon-Sat 12-2, Sun 12.30-6 booking
required D served Mon-Sat 6.30-9.30 booking required
⊕ FREE HOUSE ◀ Mansfield Smooth, John Smith's
Smooth, Black Sheep, Greene King Old Speckled Hen,
Adnams. ♀9 **Facilities** Children welcome Children's
menu Children's portions Garden Beer festival Parking
Wi-fi

MORTON   Map 17 SK75

PICK OF THE PUBS

The Full Moon Inn ♀

Main St NG25 0UT
☎ 01636 830251 📠 01636 830554
e-mail: info@thefullmoonmorton.co.uk
dir: *Newark A617 to Mansfield. Past Kelham, turn left
to Rolleston & follow signs to Morton*

Once upon a time this was a dark and dated pub, but
when William and Rebecca White arrived they
transformed it into the contemporary, comfortable and
friendly Trent-side free house you see today. They
exposed the old beams and brickwork from the original
18th-century cottages and brought in reclaimed
panelling and furniture. The resulting year-round
appeal includes a charming garden for the summer,
and two log fires for wintertime. Five hand-pulls prove
that William White takes his real ales seriously.
Rebecca's forte is cooking, her kitchen producing farm-
fresh food, mostly locally sourced, with specials
running in tandem with the pub menu at lunchtime
and in the evenings. There's plenty on offer, beginning
early with breakfast. Fish dishes include fresh haddock
in beer batter with minted pea purée, and salmon fillet
with Parmesan, tomato and pesto sauce. Pies come
filled with beef and roast vegetables; chicken, leeks
and Stilton; or lentil and roast squash. There are fish
nights and vegetarian evenings too.

Open all wk fr 10.30am **Bar Meals** L served all wk
12-2.30 booking required D served all wk 5.30-9
booking required Av main course £10
Restaurant L served all wk 12-2.30 booking required
D served all wk 5.30-9 booking required Av 3 course à
la carte fr £25 ⊕ FREE HOUSE ◀ Bombardier, Dover
Beck, Moonshine, Guest ales. ♀8 **Facilities** Children
welcome Children's menu Children's portions Play area
Family room Dogs allowed Garden Parking Wi-fi

NOTTINGHAM — Map 11 SK53

Fellows Morton & Clayton

54 Canal St NG1 7EH ☎ 0115 950 6795
e-mail: office@fellowsmortonandclayton.co.uk
dir: *Telephone for directions*

Converted from a former warehouse in 1979, FMC sits in the heart of the impressive Castle Wharf complex, with a cobbled courtyard overlooking the Nottingham canal. The pub is a regular Nottingham in Bloom award winner. Inside, the giant plasma screen shows all the major sporting events, so there is no need to miss a goal while tucking into simple food ranging from a double decker chicken toasted sandwich to bangers with mash and onion gravy or hand-made faggots with champ. For alternative dining, there is the charming Gallery Restaurant.

Open all day all wk **Bar Meals** L served all wk 10-3 D served Thu-Sun 3-9 food served all day ⊕ ENTERPRISE INNS ◖ Timothy Taylor Landlord, Fuller's London Pride, Nottingham EPA, Deuchars IPA, Mallard Bitter. **Facilities** Children's portions Garden Parking Wi-fi

PICK OF THE PUBS

Ye Olde Trip to Jerusalem ⏺

1 Brewhouse Yard, Castle Rd NG1 6AD
☎ 0115 947 3171
e-mail: 4925@greeneking.co.uk
dir: *In town centre*

Castle Rock, upon which stands Nottingham Castle, is riddled with caves and passageways cut into the sandstone. The builders of this unusual pub made the most of this, incorporating some of the caves into the design of the inn, one of Britain's oldest, founded in 1189AD. The name recalls that soldiers, clergy and penitents gathered here before embarking on the Crusade to The Holy Land – doubtless they drank to their quest at the castle's beer-house before their trip to Jerusalem. Centuries of service and piecemeal renovations over the years give the Trip instant appeal, from the magpie collection of furnishings in the warren of rooms to the unique Rock Lounge (look for the Ring the Bull game), spooky alcoves (several ghosts here) and quirks such as the cursed galleon and the fertility chair. Beers from the Nottingham Brewery feature strongly, accompanying a reliable menu of old favourites (sausage and mash, steak and ale pie) and innovative new bites (cauliflower and Cheddar cheese tart). There is a beer festival two or three times a year.

Open all day all wk 11am-11pm (Fri-Sat 11am-mdnt) **Bar Meals** D served all wk 11am-10pm Av main course £7.50 food served all day ⊕ GREENE KING ◖ Ye Olde Trip Ale, Nottingham Brewery guest ales, Greene King IPA, Abbot Ale, Old Speckled Hen ♉ Aspall. ⏺ 13 **Facilities** Children welcome Garden Beer festival

THURGARTON — Map 17 SK64

The Red Lion

Southwell Rd NG14 7GP ☎ 01636 830351
dir: *On A612 between Nottingham & Southwell*

This 16th-century inn was originally the alehouse for the monks at the nearby Thurgarton Priory, and in 1936 it was the scene of the murder of the landlady by her niece. Today, the warren of rooms with original beams and welcoming open fires is a peaceful haven. Outside there is a delightful tree-shaded terraced beer garden. Pub food can be enjoyed in the bar, restaurant or garden. Main courses include the chef's home-made steak and kidney pie; Red Lion beef and Guinness casserole; or chicken breast with a creamy cheese and bacon sauce. For a lighter option, there's a choice of salads.

Open all wk 11.30-2.30 6.30-11 (Sat-Sun & BH 11.30-11) **Bar Meals** L served all wk 12-2 D served Sun-Fri 6.30-9, Sat 6.30-9.30 **Restaurant** L served all wk 12-2 D served Sun-Fri 6.30-9, Sat 6.30-9.30 ⊕ FREE HOUSE ◖ Black Sheep, Blue Monkey, Bass. **Facilities** Children welcome Children's menu Children's portions Garden Parking

TUXFORD — Map 17 SK77

The Mussel & Crab ⏺

Sibthorpe Hill NG22 0PJ
☎ 01777 870491 📄 01777 872302
e-mail: musselandcrab1@hotmail.com
web: www.musselandcrab.com
dir: *From Ollerton/Tuxford junct of A1 & A57. N on B1164 to Sibthorpe Hill. Pub 800yds on right*

Beautifully fresh fish and seafood dominate the menu at this quirky pub with a multitude of rooms, all decked out in inimitable style. The piazza room is styled as an Italian courtyard, with murals by artist Tony Cooke; the beamed restaurant is big on rustic charm; and the gents' toilets is brightened with a tank of fish! Countless blackboards offer ever-changing dishes such as Pacific oysters from Mersey Island; fillet of sea bass and seared king scallop as well as non-fishy dishes like braised brisket in Guinness.

Open all wk 11-3 6-11 **Bar Meals** L served Mon-Sat 11-2.30, Sun 11-3 booking required D served Mon-Sat 6-10, Sun 6-9 booking required Av main course £15 **Restaurant** L served Mon-Sat 11-2.30, Sun 11-3 booking required D served Mon-Sat 6-10, Sun 6-9 booking required Av 3 course à la carte fr £25 ⊕ FREE HOUSE ◖ Tetley Smooth, Tetley Cask, Guinness. ⏺ 16 **Facilities** Children welcome Children's menu Family room Dogs allowed Garden Parking

UPTON — Map 17 SK75

The Cross Keys NEW

43 Main St NG23 5SY ☎ 01636 813269
e-mail: info@crosskeysupton.co.uk
dir: *From Newark-on-Trent take B6326 signed 'All Other Routes'. A617 signed Mansfield. Left onto A612 to Upton*

In November 2010 experienced publicans Roy and Laura Wood left the Waggon & Horses at Halam and migrated a couple of miles east across Southwell to restore the fortunes of the 17th-century Cross Keys. It looks every inch the traditional village inn plus it has a beamed, warren-like interior with open log fires, and a good range of real ales on tap, including local Blue Monkey ales. Fans of Roy's imaginative cooking soon followed, keen to sample the likes of blade of beef with bubble-and-squeak and crisp pancetta, sea bream with spinach and lemon risotto, and rhubarb and custard crème brûlée. Open from 8am for breakfast.

Open all day all wk **Bar Meals** Av main course £6 food served all day **Restaurant** Fixed menu price fr £16 Av 3 course à la carte fr £24 food served all day ⊕ FREE HOUSE ◖ Fuller's London Pride, Timothy Taylor Landlord, Blue Monkey BG Sips. **Facilities** Children welcome Children's portions Dogs allowed Garden Parking Wi-fi

OXFORDSHIRE

ADDERBURY — Map 11 SP43

Red Lion ★★★ INN

The Green OX17 3LU
☎ 01295 810269 📄 01295 811906
e-mail: 6496@greeneking.co.uk
dir: *Off M40, 3m from Banbury*

A fine stone-built coaching inn on the Banbury to Oxford road, overlooking the village green. Established in 1669, the Red Lion was once known as the King's Arms, and had a tunnel in the cellar used by Royalists in hiding during the Civil War. Enter the rambling, beamed interior to find daily newspapers, real ales, good wines, accommodation and a varied menu, with plenty of fish choices like home-made Thai salmon fish cakes, chargrilled tuna steaks, and salmon steak parcels. Change of hands in 2010.

Open all day all wk 7am-11pm (Sat 8am-11.30pm, Sun 8am-11pm) ◖ Greene King IPA, Abbot Ale, Old Speckled Hen, Guest ales. **Facilities** Children welcome Garden Parking **Rooms** 12

ARDINGTON — Map 5 SU48

PICK OF THE PUBS

The Boar's Head ★★★★ INN ☺☺⏺

See Pick of the Pubs on opposite page

Save on hotels. Book at **theAA.com/hotel**

OXFORDSHIRE 347 ENGLAND

PICK OF THE PUBS

The Boar's Head ★★★★ INN ◉◉ 🍷

ARDINGTON   Map 5 SU48

Church St OX12 8QA
☎ **01235 833254** 📄 **01235 833254**
e-mail: info@boarsheadardington.co.uk
web: www.boarsheadardington.co.uk
dir: *Off A417 E of Wantage, next to village
church*

Ardington and its twin community,
Lockinge, lie within the estate laid out in
the 19th century by Lord Wantage, who
would no doubt be delighted that it
remains very much as he left it. The half-
timbered Boar's Head has been serving
the local community for over 150 years,
today as pub, first-class restaurant and
provider of three attractive en suite guest
rooms, converted from the original barns
and outbuildings. Its scrubbed pine
tables, candles, fresh flowers and blazing
log fires create just the atmosphere that
so many pubgoers love.

Local breweries, including Best Mates (in
Ardington itself), Butts and West
Berkshire, are given a good share of the
bar action. Everything, from bread to ice
cream, and from pasta to pastries, is
made on the premises. In the two-AA
Rosette restaurant, the regularly changing
menu is well known for its fish
specialities, featuring whatever is sent up
daily from Cornish ports.

A typical meal might begin with scallop
tempura with chilli jam or artichoke
velouté; to be followed by roast tranche of
Newlyn cod with red wine vinaigrette and
wild garlic; roast squab pigeon with black
pudding and port wine sauce; or roast
rack of spring lamb with herb crust and
garlic confit. Finish with a praline soufflé
and iced nougat, or toffee banana
croustade with vanilla ice cream.
A seven-course tasting menu is available.

Ardington is surrounded by footpaths and
cycle routes winding through nearby
villages and running up to the ancient
Ridgeway. Golfers will find several
excellent courses nearby, while fly-fishers
can obtain a day-pass for the area's well-
stocked trout lakes.

Open all wk **Bar Meals** L served
all wk 12-2 D served all wk 7-9.30
Restaurant L served all wk 12-2 D served
all wk 7-9.30 🍺 FREE HOUSE ◼ West
Berkshire Brewery Dr Hexter's, Butts
Brewery, Barbus Barbus, Best Mates
Brewery, Ardington Ale ♂ Stowford Press.
Facilities Children's portions Dogs
allowed Garden Parking Wi-fi **Rooms** 3

BAMPTON
Map 5 SP30

The Romany

Bridge St OX18 2HA ☎ 01993 850237
e-mail: theromanyinnbampton@yahoo.co.uk
dir: *Telephone for directions*

This 18th-century building of Cotswold stone was a shop until 20 years ago. Now a pretty inn, The Romany counts a beamed bar, log fires and intimate dining room among its many charms. The choice of food ranges from bar snacks and bar meals to a full carte restaurant menu, with home-made specials like lasagne, chicken Romany, or chilli and chips. There is a good range of vegetarian choices. The garden might be just the spot to enjoy a pint of Hooky Bitter or Westons Stowford Press cider. Regional singers provide live entertainment a couple of times a month.

Open all day all wk 12-12 **Bar Meals** L served Fri-Sat 12-9, Sun 12-3 D served Tue-Thu 4-9, Fri-Sat 12-9 Av main course £10 **Restaurant** L served Fri-Sat 12-9, Sun 12-3 D served Tue-Thu 4-9, Fri-Sat 12-9 Fixed menu price fr £7.50 ⊕ PUNCH ◄ Hooky Bitter, London Pride, Guest ales Ŏ Westons Stowford Press. **Facilities** Children welcome Children's menu Children's portions Play area Garden Wi-fi

BANBURY
Map 11 SP44

The Wykham Arms ♥

Temple Mill Rd, Sibford Gower OX15 5RX
☎ 01295 788808
e-mail: info@wykhamarms.co.uk
web: www.wykhamarms.co.uk
dir: *Between Banbury & Shipston-on-Stour off B4035. 15m S of Stratford-upon-Avon*

Once part of William of Wykham's estate, hence the name, Damian and Debbie Bradley, both classically trained chefs, have run this thatched, Cotswold-stone free house with ever-increasing success since 2005. All credit then to their well-kept ales – Hook Norton among them – good wines, and impressive food, typically Malaysian-style chicken satay; classic kedgeree; grilled aged sirloin steaks; and South Coast sea bass with pad Thai-style noodles. As a press reviewer once observed, the loudest sound here is likely to be a passing tractor.

Open 12-3 6-11 Closed: Mon **Bar Meals** L served Tue-Sun 12-2.30 D served Tue-Sat 6-9.30 Av main course £15 **Restaurant** L served Tue-Sun 12-2.30 D served Tue-Sat 6-9.30 Av 3 course à la carte fr £28 ⊕ FREE HOUSE ◄ Hook Norton Best, Guinness, St Austell Tribute, Adnams Broadside, Fuller's London Pride. ♥ 20 **Facilities** Children welcome Children's portions Family room Dogs allowed Garden Parking Wi-fi

See advert below

Ye Olde Reindeer Inn

47 Parsons St OX16 5NA ☎ 01295 264031
e-mail: tonypuddifoot@aol.com
dir: *1m from M40 junct 11, in town centre just off market square*

The oldest pub in Banbury, the Reindeer dates back to 1570. During the Civil War, Oliver Cromwell met his men here in the magnificent Globe Room, which still has its original wood panelling. A great range of cask ales is kept (usually 5 at any one time) and a large selection of malt whiskies. Mulled wines are another house speciality. Menu favourites are bubble and squeak with honey roast ham, baked beans and fried egg; Yorkshire pudding filled with sausage, onion and gravy; and home-made beef and Hooky ale pie.

Open all day all wk **Bar Meals** L served Mon-Sat 11-2.30 Av main course £6.20 ⊕ HOOK NORTON BREWERY
◀ Hook Norton, Best, Hook Norton Haymaker, Old Hooky, 12 Days, Dark & Gold. **Facilities** Children welcome Children's menu Children's portions Family room Dogs allowed Garden Parking

---

BARNARD GATE	Map 5 SP41

PICK OF THE PUBS

The Boot Inn ♟

OX29 6XE ☎ 01865 881231
e-mail: info@theboot-inn.com
dir: *Off A40 between Witney & Eynsham*

The Boot is set in beautiful countryside on the edge of the Cotswolds, near the ancient village of Eynsham, just a few miles west of Oxford. Renowned for its celebrity boot collection - the Bee Gees, George Best and Jeremy Irons to name a few – exposed beams, stone-flagged floors and two fabulous open fires set the scene at the inn, which has a pleasant garden for summer use, a welcoming bar and secluded dining areas. Beers from well known and reliable brewers are on tap, and the wine list would satisfy the most cosmopolitan of oenophiles. The lunch menu offers salads, doorstop sandwiches and a selection from the chargrill: burgers, sausages and steaks. Dinner options are along the lines of roasted chicken breast with Puy lentils and Savoy cabbage; duo of pheasant, braised red cabbage and three root mash and port jus; chocolate fondant with vanilla ice cream.

Open all wk Mon-Sat 12-3 6-11 (Sun all day)
Bar Meals L served Mon-Sat 12-2.30, Sun 12-9
D served Mon-Sat 7-9.30, Sun 12-9
Restaurant L served Mon-Sat 12-2.30, Sun 12-9
D served Mon-Sat 7-9.30, Sun 12-9 ⊕ CHARLES WELLS
◀ Young's, Charles Wells Eagle IPA, Guest ales. ♟ 10
Facilities Children welcome Children's portions Garden Parking Wi-fi

---

BECKLEY	Map 5 SP51

The Abingdon Arms

High St OX3 9UU ☎ 01865 351311
e-mail: chequers89@hotmail.com
dir: *M40 junct 8, follow signs at Headington rdbt for Beckley*

Expect a warm welcome at this cosy, traditional pub set in a pretty village to the north of Oxford. It has been smartly updated, and good food is also helping to put it on the map, backed by excellent beers from Brakspear. A range of sandwiches and bar snacks is available at lunchtime, while dinner could feature whole grilled sea bass; liver and bacon; or a chicken and ham pie. There are opportunities for many pleasant walks in the area. Recent change of hands.

Open all wk 12-3 6-11 (Sat-Sun all day)
Bar Meals L served Mon-Fri 12-2.30, Sat 12-9.30, Sun all day D served Mon-Fri 6-9.30, Sat 12-9.30, Sun all day
Restaurant L served Mon-Fri 12-2.30, Sat 12-9.30, Sun all day D served Mon-Fri 6-9.30, Sat 12-9.30, Sun all day
⊕ BRAKSPEAR ◀ Brakspear Bitter, Brakspear Special, Brakspear guest, Hobgoblin, Marston Pedigree, Oxford Gold ♻ Simmons. **Facilities** Children welcome Children's menu Children's portions Play area Dogs allowed Garden Parking Wi-fi

See advert below

BLACK BOURTON · Map 5 SP20

PICK OF THE PUBS

The Vines

Burford Rd OX18 2PF
☎ 01993 843559 📄 01993 840080
e-mail: info@vineshotel.com
web: www.vinesblackbourton.co.uk
dir: *From A40 Witney, take A4095 to Faringdon, then 1st right after Bampton to Black Bourton*

A beautiful Cotswold village within easy reach of Burford, Witney and the Thames Path is the setting for The Vines, a traditional stone-built inn with an elegant, contemporary feel and surrounded by delightful gardens. The BBC's *Real Rooms* team famously designed and transformed the restaurant and bar, so expect a surprisingly stylish interior for a Cotswold pub, with murals, wooden floors, big plants in pots, and leather sofas fronting open log fires. Relax with a pint of Hooky or linger over lunch or dinner; the menus listing an imaginative choice of modern British dishes with an international twist, all freshly prepared using locally sourced produce. Typical examples from the carte include Thai chicken salad; pan-fried scallops with balsamic dressing; slow cooked lamb shank; pork tenderloin with cider sauce; glazed red onion and goats' cheese tart; and sausage, mash and rich gravy. There's always a Sunday roast and a raft of Old and New World wines by the glass. On sunny days, dine alfresco on the sun-trap patio or play a nostalgic game of Aunt Sally.

Open all wk **Bar Meals** L served Tue-Sun 12-2 D served Mon-Sat 6-9, Sun 7-9 **Restaurant** L served Sat-Sun 12-2 D served Mon-Sat 6-9, Sun 7-9 ⊕ FREE HOUSE ◀ Old Hooky, Tetley Smooth. **Facilities** Children welcome Children's menu Children's portions Garden Parking Wi-fi

BLOXHAM · Map 11 SP43

The Elephant & Castle

OX15 4LZ ☎ 0845 873 7358
e-mail: bloxhamelephant1@btconnect.com
dir: *M40 junct 11, pub just off A361, in village centre. 3m from Banbury*

The arch of this family-run 15th-century Cotswold-stone coaching inn used to straddle the former Banbury to Chipping Norton turnpike. At night the gates of the pub were closed, and no traffic could get over the toll bridge. Locals play Aunt Sally or shove-ha'penny in the big wood-floored bar, whilst the two-roomed lounge boasts a bar-billiards table and a large inglenook fireplace. The menu offers favourites like roast chicken breast with stuffing, crispy battered cod and lasagne verdi, and the bar serves seasonal and guest ales. Beer festival in May.

Open all wk 10-3 6-12 (Fri 10-3 5-2am, Sat 10am-2am, Sun 10am-mdnt) **Bar Meals** L served Mon-Sat 12-2 Av main course £6 **Restaurant** L served Mon-Sat 12-2 ⊕ HOOK NORTON BREWERY ◀ Hook Norton Best Bitter, Hook Norton seasonal ales, Guest ales ◐ Westons Old Rosie Scrumpy. **Facilities** Children welcome Children's menu Children's portions Family room Dogs allowed Garden Beer festival Parking Wi-fi

BRIGHTWELL BALDWIN · Map 5 SU69

PICK OF THE PUBS

The Lord Nelson Inn ♀

See Pick of the Pubs on opposite page

BRIGHTWELL-CUM-SOTWELL · Map 5 SU59

The Red Lion

The Street OX10 0RT ☎ 01491 837373
e-mail: enquiries@redlion.biz
web: www.redlion.biz
dir: *From A4130 (Didcot to Wallingford road) follow Brightwell-cum-Sotwell signs. Pub in village centre*

A picture-postcard thatched and timbered 16th-century village pub that's not only pretty but also a cracking community local, playing host to charity quiz nights, French and painting classes, various cuisine nights and an annual festival. Hearty, traditional pub food is freshly prepared from local produce. Look to the chalkboard for their famous short-crust pastry pie, lamb ragout, home-made fishcakes, and the popular ginger pudding, then

wash it down with a pint of West Berkshire Good Old Boy. Don't miss the Sunday roast lunches. The pub holds a beer festival (with live music) for two days every summer.

Open all wk 12-3 6-11 **Bar Meals** L served all wk 12-2 D served all wk 6.30-9 **Restaurant** L served all wk 12-2 D served Tue-Sat 6.30-9 ⊕ FREE HOUSE ◀ Good Old Boy, Hoppit, Brightwell Gold ◐ Stowford Press, Tutts Clump. **Facilities** Children welcome Children's menu Children's portions Dogs allowed Garden Beer festival Parking

BROUGHTON · Map 11 SP43

Saye and Sele Arms ♀

Main Rd OX15 5ED ☎ 01295 263348
e-mail: mail@sayeandselearms.co.uk
dir: *3m from Banbury Cross*

This pretty, 16th-century free house is just a few minute's walk from Broughton Castle, home to Lord and Lady Saye and Sele, a barony dating back to 1447. Adnams is the pub's resident beer, plus three ever-changing guest ales such as Sharp's Doom Bar, Hook Norton Bitter and Cottage Brewery Jack Frost. The extensive menu includes chef/proprietor Danny McGeehan's 'wholesome proper pies', such as lamb and apricot or beefsteak, kidney and ale, and the home-made desserts like his popular bread and butter pudding or sticky toffee pudding are not to be missed. There is a spacious well-stocked garden to enjoy in summer.

Open 11.30-2.30 7-11 (Sat 11.30-3 7-11 Sun 12-5) Closed: 25 Dec, Sun eve **Bar Meals** L served Mon-Sat 12-2 booking required D served Mon-Sat 7-9.30 booking required **Restaurant** L served Mon-Sat 12-2, Sun 12-3 booking required D served Mon-Sat 7-9.30 booking required ⊕ FREE HOUSE ◀ Adnams Southwold, Sharp's Doom Bar, 2 guest ales ◐ Westons Stowford Press, Thatchers Dry. ♀ 8 **Facilities** Children welcome Children's portions Garden Parking

BURCOT · Map 5 SU59

The Chequers ♀

OX14 3DP ☎ 01865 407771 📄 01865 407771
e-mail: enquiries@thechequers-burcot.co.uk
dir: *On A415 (Dorchester to Abingdon road) between Clifton Hampden & Dorchester*

An impressive thatched roof straddles this 400-year-old timber-framed pub, once a staging post for boats on the Thames, or Isis, to give it its local name. On winter days the fire-warmed sofas are the favoured spots, especially for toasting marshmallows, although on warm days the enclosed beer garden wins hands down. The home-prepared food is serious but far from pretentious - imagine roasted rump of Oxfordshire lamb; grilled cod fillet with vine tomatoes and garlic butter sauce; and wild mushroom and herb pancakes.

Open all day all wk 12-11 (Sun 12-4) **Bar Meals** L served all wk 12-3 D served Mon-Sat 6.30-9.30 Av main course £15 **Restaurant** L served all wk 12-3 booking required D served Mon-Sat 6.30-9.30 booking required Fixed menu price fr £14.50 Av 3 course à la carte fr £30 ⊕ FREE HOUSE ◀ Young's, Tribute, Guest ales ◐ Westons Stowford Press. ♀ 12 **Facilities** Children welcome Children's portions Garden Parking Wi-fi

PICK OF THE PUBS

The Lord Nelson Inn ♀

BRIGHTWELL BALDWIN   Map 5 SU69

OX49 5NP ☎ **01491 612497**
e-mail: ladyhamilton1@hotmail.co.uk
web: www.lordnelson-inn.co.uk
dir: *Off B4009 between Watlington & Benson*

Originally constructed as a thatched cottage, later additions to this 300 year-old stone-built inn include 18th-century gables and a quaint veranda facing the village church. In Nelson's day the pub was simply known as the Admiral Nelson; but when, in 1797, the great man was elevated to the peerage, the pub's name was elevated too. For more than a century after that, villagers slaked their thirst here until, in 1905, the inn was closed following complaints about over-indulgent estate workers. That could have been the end of the story – but, a generation later, the building was bought by a couple who just liked the look of it. They gave it a complete makeover, and the Lord Nelson finally re-opened on Trafalgar Day, 1971.

Now full of fresh flowers, candlelight and a splendid inglenook fireplace, it's just the place to relax after a country walk or a day at the office. And, during the summer, the pretty terraced garden with its weeping willow is popular for alfresco eating and drinking.

All the food is freshly cooked, using local produce where possible. The house menu begins with a complimentary basket of bread and olives. Starters might include home-made smoked haddock and salmon fishcake with watercress and sweet chilli dressing, or French black pudding with smoked bacon and apple salad. For light main course options, try a smoked salmon and prawn platter, or the house special salad of mixed leaves, asparagus spears, tuna and boiled egg. Other main courses include half a slow-roast duck with orange sauce, and leek and morel mushroom risotto topped with parmesan shavings.

Look out for red kites while you're in the area; the RSPB reintroduced them onto the nearby Chiltern escarpment in the early 1990s.

Open all wk 12-3 6-11 (Sun 12-10.30) (Summer 11-3, 6-11) Closed: 25 Dec **Bar Meals** L served Mon-Sat 12-3, Sun 12-3.30 D served Mon-Sat 6-10, Sun 7-9.30 **Restaurant** L served Mon-Sat 12-3, Sun 12-3.30 D served Mon-Sat 6-10, Sun 7-9.30 ⊞ FREE HOUSE ◀ Brakspear Bitter, Adnam's Bitter, Black Sheep ♂ Stowford Press. ♀ 20 **Facilities** Children welcome Dogs allowed Garden Parking

PICK OF THE PUBS

The Inn for All Seasons ★★★ RR ♦

BURFORD   Map 5 SP21

The Barringtons OX18 4TN
☎ 01451 844324 📠 01451 844375
e-mail: sharp@innforallseasons.com
web: www.innforallseasons.com
dir: 3m W of Burford on A40

The inn's humble beginnings were as two quarry cottages, where Cotswold stone was brought to the roadside destined for buildings such as Blenheim Palace and St Paul's Cathedral. As ale was probably dispensed to thirsty workers from the day the cottages were built, their transition to a coaching inn was inevitable. The New Inn, as it was then, was one of three coaching inns at which they could have stopped, all owned by the Barrington Park Estate. It remained estate-owned until the 1950s when, along with the nearby garage, it was bought by Shell; then in 1964 it was sold to Jeremy Taylor who choreographed horses for films such as *Lawrence of Arabia* and *A Man For All Seasons* (hence the change of name). In the mid-1980s the Sharp family took over and have been here ever since. Within its solid Cotswold stone walls you will find a treasure trove of ancient oak beams, leather wing-back chairs and interesting memorabilia, giving it that true country pub feel. The well-stocked bar offers draught ales from Devizes, Wiltshire and guest beers like Doom Bar from Sharp's Brewery, Cornwall. There is an extensive wine list as well as a fine malt whisky

selection, soft drinks and liqueurs. Matthew Sharp is a classically trained chef with a string of prestigious postings behind him. He selects seasonal local produce for his British Continental cuisine, including game from the Barrington Park Estate and local Gloucester pork and ham. The Inn also specialises in fresh fish and shellfish. The guaranteed daily supply of excellent fish makes the fresh fish board the best in the area. Look out for a pair of red mullet lightly pan-fried; seared scallops with crisp smoked streaky bacon; and whole cock crabs freshly cooked and served with garlic mayonnaise, fresh oysters, mussels, fish soup and other favourites. Meat lovers can enjoy grilled sirloin of Aberdeen Angus beef with fat chips, and roasted rump of Cornish lamb with dauphinoise potatoes. There is a more formal restaurant, as well as the bar area, to enjoy your meal, plus a beer

garden. There are ten comfortable en suite bedrooms. Dogs are welcome.

Open Sun-Thu 11-2.30 6-11, Fri-Sat 11-11 **Bar Meals** L served all wk 12-2.30 D served all wk 6.30-9.30 Av main course £12.50 **Restaurant** L served all wk 12-2.30 D served all wk 6.30-9.30 booking required Av 3 course à la carte fr £24.50 🍺 Wadworth 6X, Sharp's Doom Bar 🍏 Sharp's Orchard. ♦ 30 **Facilities** Children's portions Dogs allowed Garden Parking Wi-fi **Rooms** 10

Save on hotels. Book at **theAA.com/hotel**

OXFORDSHIRE 353 **ENGLAND**

BURFORD   Map 5 SP21

PICK OF THE PUBS

The Inn for All Seasons ★★★ RR ♣

See Pick of the Pubs on opposite page

PICK OF THE PUBS

The Lamb Inn ★★★ SHL ◉◉

Sheep St OX18 4LR
☎ 01993 823155 ▤ 01993 822228
e-mail: info@lambinn-burford.co.uk
dir: *M40 junct 8, follow A40 & Burford signs, 1st turn, down hill into Sheep St*

It's difficult to exaggerate the mellow charm of the 15th-century Lamb Inn, tucked down a quiet side street in this most attractive Cotswolds town. It has a welcoming atmosphere in the bar, with its stone-flagged floor, log fire, fine wines and traditional real ales. Throughout, the inn combines old world charm with stylish interiors. The spacious, two-AA Rosette restaurant looks out to a gorgeous walled cottage garden through mullioned windows. The regularly-changing menus present contemporary English cooking based entirely on local produce. Lunch in the bar may take in a meat deli board to share, lamb burger, open sandwiches and main dishes like crayfish and chive risotto, and rib-eye steak with blue cheese butter. Cooking moves up a gear at dinner, the dining room menu offering chicken and foie gras terrine with truffle oil ice cream, turbot with parsley risotto and chilli caramel, and rhubarb and vanilla pannacotta. Comfortable bedrooms are the icing on the cake at this civilised Cotswolds bolthole.

Open all day all wk **Bar Meals** L served all wk 12-2.30 D served all wk 6.30-9.30 Av main course £12 **Restaurant** L served all wk 12-2.30 D served all wk 7-9.30 ⊕ FREE HOUSE ◂ Hook Norton Best, Brakspear. **Facilities** Children welcome Children's menu Children's portions Dogs allowed Garden Wi-fi **Rooms** 17

CASSINGTON   Map 5 SP41

The Chequers Inn ♣

6 The Green OX29 4DG ☎ 01865 882620
dir: *From Oxford take A40 towards Witney. Right to Cassington*

Turn off the busy A40, and you'll find this imposing Cotswold stone inn next to the church at the end of the village road. The refurbished interior is cosy yet stylish, with polished flagstone floors, winter log fires and wooden furniture adorned by pretty candles. Freshly prepared meals include starters of chicken liver parfait with pear chutney, or mussels, chorizo with arrabiata sauce; followed by main courses of beef cobbler, cheese scones and jacket potato, or chilli con carne. There is a beautiful orangery, perfect for private parties and functions.

Open all day all wk **Bar Meals** L served Mon-Fri 12-2.30, Sat-Sun 12-3 D served all wk 6.30-9.30 Av main course £9.95 **Restaurant** L served Mon-Fri 12-2.30, Sat-Sun 12-3 D served all wk 6.30-9.30 ⊕ YOUNG'S ◂ Young's Bombardier. ♣ 10 **Facilities** Children welcome Children's menu Children's portions Dogs allowed Garden Parking Wi-fi

CAULCOTT   Map 11 SP52

Horse & Groom NEW

Lower Heyford Rd OX25 4ND ☎ 01869 343257
web: www.horseandgroomcaulcott.co.uk
dir: *From Bicester take B3040 signed Witney. Through Middleton Stoney. Approx 2.3m to Caulcott*

The perfect mix of character and quality; a picture-perfect thatched village tavern with a great taproom, all wavy beams, settles, inglenook and a bar well-supplied with beer-wickets dispensing local and guest beers, and real cider. An elegant marriage is made with the weekly-changing top-drawer menu, taken in the snug or the cosy little dining room; modern English style prepared by the French chef/patron with a finger firmly on the pulse of the freshest, locally sourced produce - wild boar and pistachio terrine, or a plate of O'Hagan's Drunken Duck sausages anyone? A beer festival is held in July.

Open all wk 12-3 6-11 **Bar Meals** L served Tue-Sun booking required D served Tue-Sat booking required Av main course £15 **Restaurant** L served Tue-Sun booking required D served Tue-Sat booking required Av 3 course à la carte fr £25 ⊕ FREE HOUSE ◂ Hook Norton Bitter, Sharp's Doom Bar, Vale Brewery Gravitas, St Austell Proper Job, White Horse Bitter ♨ Westons Old Rosie, Stowford Press, Moles Black Rat. **Facilities** Children's portions Garden Beer festival Parking Wi-fi

See advert on page 354

CHALGROVE   Map 5 SU69

PICK OF THE PUBS

The Red Lion Inn

The High St OX44 7SS ☎ 01865 890625
web: www.redlionchalgrove.co.uk
dir: *B480 from Oxford ring road, through Stadhampton, left then right at mini-rdbt. At Chalgrove Airfield right into village*

The stream-side beer garden (which you may share with the village's inquisitive ducks) of this old inn overlooks the compact green at the heart of the medieval village, where thatched cottages slumber not far from the village church which is, unusually, owner of the pub. Peaceful now, the village was rocked by a skirmish during the First Civil War in 1643 when Prince Rupert clashed with John Hampden's Parliamentarian forces. Battle lines today are drawn up when selecting from the great range of draught beers; Landlord is a favourite, complementing the attractive menu created from the finest local ingredients by chef-patron Raymond Sexton. A specials board highlights ever-changing mains, where the rump of the choice may include fresh king prawns cooked in shellfish oil, an appetiser for a rustic, warming home-made rabbit stew with white wine sauce, herb dumplings and root vegetables, or fillet of pork wrapped in pancetta and sliced over a rich wild mushroom sauce. Finish with a light mango and passionfruit cheesecake courtesy of Suzanne Sexton, an accomplished pastry chef, then retiring to the cosy bar with a wine from the well balanced list of bins.

Open all wk 11.30-3 6-mdnt (Sat 11.30-3 6-1am Sun all day) Closed: 25 Dec **Bar Meals** L served Mon-Sat 12-2, Sun 12-3 D served Mon-Sat 6-9 **Restaurant** L served Mon-Sat 12-2, Sun 12-3 D served Mon-Sat 6-9 ⊕ FREE HOUSE ◂ Fuller's London Pride, Timothy Taylor Landlord, Guest ale ♨ Aspall, Westons Stowford Press. **Facilities** Children welcome Children's menu Children's portions Play area Dogs allowed Garden

CHARLBURY
Map 11 SP31

PICK OF THE PUBS

The Bull Inn ♥

Sheep St OX7 3RR ☎ **01608 810689**
e-mail: info@bullinn-charlbury.com
dir: *M40 junct 8, A40, A44 follow Woodstock/Blenheim Palace signs. Through Woodstock take B4437 to Charlbury, pub at x-rds in town*

The mellow stone frontage of this fine 16th-century free house presides over Charlbury's main street, within easy reach of Woodstock, Blenheim Palace and other Cotswold attractions. The beamed interior is full of period character, with log fires burning in the inglenook fireplaces in winter. The traditional bar with wooden floors serves delectable Cotswold ales by Goffs and Loddon. A tastefully furnished lounge and dining room add to the relaxing space, while outside the vine-covered terrace is a delightful spot to sit and enjoy a drink or a meal in summer. Sandwiches served at lunchtime from Tuesday to Saturday may suffice when they contain Cotswold rump, prosciutto ham, tomato and garlic mayonnaise, served with house chips and dressed salad. Typical of the starters is soused Cornish mackerel and sardines with crushed Pink Fir Apple potato salad and rocket, follow with loin of Charlbury lamb with a mini shepherd's pie and hand-picked Scottish wild mushrooms.

Open 12-2.30 6-11 Closed: Sun eve & Mon **Bar Meals** L served Tue-Fri 12-2, Sat-Sun 12-2.30 D served Tue-Sat 6.30-9 Av main course £13 **Restaurant** L served Tue-Fri 12-2, Sat-Sun 12-2.30 booking required D served Tue-Sat 6.30-9 booking required Av 3 course à la carte fr £20.50 ⊕ FREE HOUSE ◀ Goffs Loddon ♂ Thatchers Gold. ♥ 10 **Facilities** Children welcome Children's portions Garden Parking

CHECKENDON
Map 5 SU68

PICK OF THE PUBS

The Highwayman ◉

Exlade St RG8 0UA ☎ **01491 682020**
dir: *On A4074 (Reading to Wallingford road)*

Tucked away in a secluded hamlet, overlooking open fields on the edge of the wooded Chiltern Hills, this rambling, beautifully refurbished 17th-century inn makes the perfect destination following a glorious walk through the surrounding beech woods. Traditional low beams, wooden floors and open fireplaces blend effortlessly with the smart, contemporary decor, providing a comfortable atmosphere in which to savour a pint of London Pride and interesting seasonal menus that offer good modern pub food prepared from locally-sourced produce. Typically, order braised pork belly on mashed swede and carrot with thyme sauce, lamb stew with black pudding, root vegetables and mash, and bread-and-butter pudding with ginger cream and orange sauce. A peaceful rear garden and sun-trap terrace make for laid back summer drinking.

Open 12-3 6-11 (Sun 12-10) Closed: Mon **Bar Meals** L served 12-2 (Sun 12-3) D served 6-9 (not Sun eve) Av main course £9.95 **Restaurant** L served 12-2 (Sun 12-3) D served 6-9 (not Sun eve) Fixed menu price fr £10 Av 3 course à la carte fr £24.95 ⊕ FREE HOUSE ◀ Fuller's London Pride, Loddon Ferryman's Gold, Butlers Brewers, guest ale. **Facilities** Children welcome Children's portions Dogs allowed Garden Parking Wi-fi

The Horse & Groom

The Horse & Groom is renowned for its locally sourced produce, homemade and quality fresh food. And of course the famous Sausage menu!

A Grade II listed property of local limestone beneath a thatched roof, dating back from the early 18th century makes the Horse and Groom the epitome of a classic English country pub.

The Horse & Groom remains a popular destination for real ale. Hook Norton ale is a resident at the *Horse & Groom*, starring next to three guest ales from all over the UK, which change weekly (or sometimes within a few days dependent on how popular they are with the locals!).

The dining areas are cosy and intimate with a capacity up to 26 in the dining room and 14 in and around the bar area. Chef Owner Jerome has over 20 years experience in the industry, and creates a weekly menu using locally-sourced produce. Jerome also creates dishes to suit all dietary requirements.

A good-sized beer garden to the front of the pub is perfect for a summer's day, and ample parking can be found opposite.

Well-behaved children are welcome, and dogs are welcome in the beer garden.

CAMRA Pub of the Year 2010 North Oxfordshire

"A cosy pub with a warm welcome. A gem." – *Good Beer Guide 2011*

Lower Heyford Road, Caulcott, Oxfordshire OX25 4ND
Tel: 01869 343 257
www.horseandgroomcaulcott.co.uk
Booking is advised.
Please inform us of any dietary requirements in advance.

Save on hotels. Book at **theAA.com/hotel**

OXFORDSHIRE 355 ENGLAND

CHINNOR — Map 5 SP70

PICK OF THE PUBS

The Sir Charles Napier ◎◎ ♥

Spriggs Alley OX39 4BX
☎ 01494 483011 📄 01494 485311
web: www.sircharlesnapier.co.uk
dir: M40 junct 6 to Chinnor. Turn right at rdbt, up hill to Spriggs Alley

High amidst the beech woods of the Chiltern Hills in an Area of Outstanding Natural Beauty, elegant red kites soar over this sublime flint-and-brick dining inn, which is also just 10 minutes from the M40. Making the most of this secluded locale, seasonal forays to the hedgerows and woods (customers can join in) produce herbs, fungi and berries used in the inventive menus, whilst the plump local game finds its way into some of the extraordinary AA 2-Rosette winning dishes here. Diners distribute themselves amidst a most eclectically furnished suite of rooms; Michael Cooper's memorable sculptures and comfy sofas set near warming winter log fires. Confit mallard and blood orange salad gives a flavour of things to come; roast pheasant with bubble and squeak and cavolo nero or lemon sole with crushed potatoes and mussel chowder for example, accompanied by a choice from over 200 wines. Digestive time may be spent appreciating the superb grounds, where more sculptures are displayed.

Open noon-4 6-mdnt (Sun noon-6) Closed: 25-26 Dec, Mon, Sun eve **Bar Meals** L served Tue-Fri 12-2.30 D served Tue-Fri 6.30-9 Av main course £15.50 **Restaurant** L served Tue-Sat 12-2.30, Sun 12-3.30 booking required D served Tue-Sat 6.30-10 booking required Fixed menu price fr £15 Av 3 course à la carte fr £35 ⊕ FREE HOUSE ◀ Wadworth 6X, Wadworth IPA. ♥ 12 **Facilities** Children welcome Children's menu Children's portions Dogs allowed Garden Parking Wi-fi

CHIPPING NORTON — Map 10 SP32

See also Nether Westcote, Gloucestershire

The Chequers ♥

Goddards Ln OX7 5NP
☎ 01608 644717 📄 01608 646237
e-mail: info@chequers-pub.com
dir: In town centre, next to theatre

This traditional English pub stands next to Chipping Norton's popular theatre, making it ideal for pre-show drinks and suppers. The name dates back to 1750, but it's thought that an alehouse has stood on this site since the 16th century. Besides the cosy bar, there's a conservatory restaurant serving locally sourced home-made dishes such as rabbit casserole in cider, mustard and tarragon; a daily shortcrust pie; and roast pumpkin, sundried tomato and olive risotto. Recent change of hands.

Open all day all wk 11am-11pm (Fri-Sat 11am-mdnt Sun 11am-10.30pm) Closed: 25 Dec **Bar Meals** L served Mon-Sat 12-2.30, Sun 12-4 D served Mon-Sat 6-9.30 **Restaurant** L served Mon-Sat 12-2.30, Sun 12-4 D served Mon-Sat 6-9.30 ⊕ FULLER'S BREWERY ◀ Fuller's Chiswick Bitter, London Pride & ESB, Gales HSB. ♥ 12 **Facilities** Children welcome Children's menu Children's portions Dogs allowed Wi-fi

CHISELHAMPTON — Map 5 SU59

PICK OF THE PUBS

Coach & Horses Inn ★★★★ INN ♥

Watlington Rd OX44 7UX
☎ 01865 890255 📄 01865 891995
e-mail: enquiries@coachhorsesinn.co.uk
dir: From Oxford on B480 towards Watlington, 5m

This delightful 16th-century inn is set in peaceful countryside six miles south-east of Oxford. Inside you'll find roaring log fires, original exposed beams, an old bread oven and furniture styles that enhance the character of the building. A wide range of imaginative food is served, including a daily specials fish board. Grills, poultry and game are also perennial favourites. There are nine chalet-style en suite bedrooms available, all with lovely rural views.

Open all day all wk 11am-11pm (Sun 12-3.30 7-10.30) **Bar Meals** L served Mon-Sun 12-2 booking required **Restaurant** L served Mon-Sun 12-2 booking required D served Mon-Sat 7-9.30 booking required ⊕ FREE HOUSE ◀ Hook Norton Best, London Pride, Old Hooky. ♥ 10 **Facilities** Children's menu Children's portions Dogs allowed Garden Parking Wi-fi **Rooms** 9

CHRISTMAS COMMON — Map 5 SU79

The Fox and Hounds

OX49 5HL ☎ 01491 612599
e-mail: hello@thetopfox.co.uk
dir: M40 junct 5, 2.5m to Christmas Common, on road towards Henley

Renovations have transformed this charming 500-year-old inn into a stylish dining pub with an immaculate interior, a large restaurant complete with open-plan kitchen, and four cosy bar areas. Changing special and an imaginative menu that places a clear emphasis on quality ingredients, local where possible. Recent change of hands.

Open all day all wk Mon-Sat noon-11 (Sun noon-10.30) Closed: 25-26 Dec eve, 1 Jan eve, BHs eve ⊕ BRAKSPEAR ◀ Brakspear Bitter, seasonal ales. **Facilities** Children's portions Dogs allowed Garden Parking

CHURCH ENSTONE — Map 11 SP32

PICK OF THE PUBS

The Crown Inn ♥

Mill Ln OX7 4NN ☎ 01608 677262
dir: Off A44, 15m N of Oxford

Award-winning chef Tony Warburton runs this stone-built 17th-century free house on the eastern edge of the Cotswolds with his wife Caroline. During the summer season you can while away the long evenings eating or drinking in the quiet and secluded rear garden, which is sheltered from the wind but enjoys the best of the late sunshine. Inside you'll find a traditional rustic bar with an open fire, a spacious slate floored conservatory, and a richly decorated beamed dining room. All meals are prepared on the premises using fresh produce, including, fish and shellfish, pork, beef and game from the local farms and estates. Starters may include cream of mushroom and basil soup or duck and smoked pheasant terrine. Main course choices range from steak and Hooky pie to braised rabbit with Dijon mustard and roast potatoes or poached smoked haddock and Cheddar mash. A home-made dessert such as ginger sponge and custard will round things off nicely.

Open all wk noon-3 6-11 (Sun noon-4) Closed: 26 Dec, 1 Jan **Bar Meals** L served all wk 12-2 D served Mon-Sat 7-9 Av main course £10 **Restaurant** L served all wk 12-2 D served Mon-Sat 7-9 Fixed menu price fr £14.95 ⊕ FREE HOUSE ◀ Hook Norton Best Bitter, Timothy Taylor Landlord, Wychwood Hobgoblin ♂ Cotswold Cider. ♥ 8 **Facilities** Children welcome Children's portions Dogs allowed Garden Parking

CLIFTON   Map 11 SP43

Duke of Cumberland's Head

OX15 0PE ☎ 01869 338534 🖹 **01869 338643**
e-mail: info@thecliftonduke.com
dir: A4260 from Banbury, then B4031 from Deddington.
7m from Banbury

Built in 1645, this thatched and beamed stone pub was named to honour Rupert of the Rhine, whose forces fought for his uncle, Charles I, at the nearby Battle of Edge Hill; important strategic decisions may well have been made around the pub's inglenook fireplace. Today it offers a choice of real ales, two dining rooms, and a wonderful garden in summer. The menu is based on traditional pub favourites like sausages and mash, with changing chef's specials and a large selection of fish and game in season.

Open all wk 11-3 6-11 Closed: 25 Dec ⊕ CLIFTON PUBLIC HOUSE MANAGEMENT LTD ◀ Hook Norton, Adnams, Deuchars, Black Sheep, Cotswold Ales ♂ Stowford Press. **Facilities** Children welcome Dogs allowed Garden Parking Wi-fi

CRAY'S POND   Map 5 SU68

The White Lion ♀ NEW

Goring Rd, Goring Heath RG8 7SH ☎ 01491 680471
e-mail: enquiries@thewhitelioncrayspond.com
dir: From M4 junct 11 follow signs to Pangbourne, through toll on bridge to Whitchurch. N for 3m into Cray's Pond

Reopened in 2010 after a thorough make-over, this 250 year old local slumbers high in the Chilterns Area of Outstanding Natural Beauty adjoining lovely woodland, inviting ramblers (it's handily open for breakfast) and diners to relax in the easy mix of contemporary and traditional interior; thoughtfully furnished and with open fires to take away a winter chill. Good, sturdy pub meals like braised lamb shank or Thai green chicken curry also warm the cockles, taken in the conservatory restaurant or on summer evenings in the secluded garden.

Open all day all wk (No food Sun eve) **Bar Meals** Av main course £9.95 food served all day **Restaurant** Fixed menu price fr £9.95 Av 3 course à la carte fr £16.40 food served all day ⊕ GREENE KING ◀ IPA, Speckled Hen. **Facilities** Children welcome Children's menu Children's portions Play area Dogs allowed Garden Parking Wi-fi

CUMNOR   Map 5 SP40

PICK OF THE PUBS

Bear & Ragged Staff ♀

See Pick of the Pubs on opposite page

The Vine Inn

11 Abingdon Rd OX2 9QN
☎ 01865 862567 🖹 **01865 862567**
dir: A420 from Oxford, right onto B4017

Set in the quiet location of Cumnor, this 18th-century village pub has a name that needs no explanation when you see its frontage. Nearby Cumnor Place, built by the monks of Abingdon Abbey in the early 14th century, was the scene of the suspicious death of the wife of Lord Robert Dudley, favourite of Elizabeth I, in 1560. Today, with a selection of real ales to chose from, a typical menu could include Cajun spiced chicken; beer-battered haddock with chips; or pan-fried fillet steak with brandy and mushroom sauce. The seasonal menu is complemented by blackboard specials. Children love the huge garden.

Open all wk (Sat-Sun all day) **Bar Meals** L served Mon-Fri 12-2, Sat 12-3, Sun 12-4 booking required **Restaurant** L served Mon-Fri 12-2, Sat 12-3, Sun 12-4 D served Mon-Sat 6-9.15 booking required ⊕ PUNCH TAVERNS ◀ Brakspear, Adnams Bitter, Guest ales. **Facilities** Children welcome Children's menu Children's portions Play area Dogs allowed Garden Parking

DEDDINGTON   Map 11 SP43

PICK OF THE PUBS

Deddington Arms ★★★ HL ◉ ♀

Horsefair OX15 0SH
☎ 01869 338364 🖹 **01869 337010**
e-mail: deddarms@oxfordshire-hotels.co.uk
dir: M40 junct 11 to Banbury. Follow signs for hospital, then towards Adderbury & Deddington, on A4260

This attractive, 16th-century former coaching inn overlooks the market square in pretty Deddington on the edge of the Cotswolds. It boasts a wealth of timbering, flagstone floors, numerous nooks and crannies, crackling winter log fires and sought-after window seats in the beamed bar, where you can savour a pint of Black Sheep or Adnams while perusing the great value set lunch menu or the imaginative carte. Eat in the bar or head for the elegant dining room and kick off a good meal with duck terrine with fig chutney, followed by pan-fried sea bass with chive beurre blanc, and chocolate St Emilion with vanilla Chantilly cream. From the market lunch menu perhaps choose garlic mushrooms with brioche, rocket and Parmesan and lambs' liver and bacon with spring onion mash – two courses £11.95. Accommodation includes 27 en suite bedrooms with cottage suites and four-poster luxury.

Open all day all wk Mon-Sat 11am-mdnt (Sun 11-11) **Bar Meals** L served all wk 12-2.30 D served all wk 6.30-9.30 Av main course £10 **Restaurant** L served all wk 12-2.30 D served all wk 6.30-9.30 Fixed menu price fr £11.95 Av 3 course à la carte fr £29.50 ⊕ FREE HOUSE ◀ Black Sheep, Adnams, 2 Guest ales ♂ Stowford Press. ♀ 8 **Facilities** Children welcome Children's menu Children's portions Parking Wi-fi **Rooms** 27

DORCHESTER (ON THAMES)   Map 5 SU59

Fleur De Lys

9 High St OX10 7HH ☎ 01865 340502 🖹 **01865 341360**
e-mail: info@fleurdorchester.co.uk
web: www.fleurdelys-dorchester.co.uk
dir: Telephone for directions

One of the Thames valley's hidden gems; the remarkable old abbey church here, and the village, regularly crop up in *Midsomer Murders*. Lovely riverside and country walks work up a thirst and appetite to be sated at this charming ancient inn at the heart of the old village, where regular beers like Hook Norton are boosted by the annual beer festival at Easter. Meals at the cosy bar or in the tranquil dining room are a good mix of pub classics and enticing specials making full use of the fine produce available locally - sweet chilli duck and bacon salad, followed by slow roasted shoulder of lamb with bubble and squeak, green beans and honey jus.

Open all wk noon-3 6-12.30am (Sat-Sun all day) **Bar Meals** L served all wk 12-2.30, Sun 12.30-3 booking required D served Mon-Sat 6.30-9.30 booking required **Restaurant** L served all wk 12-2.30, Sun 12.30-3 booking required D served Mon-Sat 6.30-9.30 booking required ⊕ FREE HOUSE ◀ Brakspear, Hooky, Guinness, Tribute, Guest ale ♂ Stowford Press. **Facilities** Children welcome Children's portions Dogs allowed Garden Beer festival Parking Wi-fi

Save on hotels. Book at **theAA.com/hotel**

OXFORDSHIRE 357 ENGLAND

PICK OF THE PUBS

Bear & Ragged Staff ♀

CUMNOR Map 5 SP40

28 Appleton Rd OX2 9QH
☎ **01865 862329** 📄 **01865 862048**
e-mail:
enquiries@bearandraggedstaff.com
web: www.bearandraggedstaff.com
dir: *A420 from Oxford, right onto B4017
signed Cumnor*

In typically tranquil Oxfordshire countryside, this 16th-century, stone-built dining pub has a rich history, not least having served as a billet for troops during the English Civil War. While the soldiers were here, Richard Cromwell, son of Oliver and Lord Protector of England, allegedly chiselled away the Royal Crest that once adorned the lintel above one of the doors in the bar, and Sir Walter Scott mentions this very Bear & Ragged Staff in his novel, *Kenilworth*. The chefs here take full advantage of the fresh, seasonal game available from local estates and shoots, since the surrounding woods and farmland teem with pheasant, partridge, deer, muntjac, rabbit, duck and pigeon. From the microwave-free kitchen (in other words, everything is cooked with fresh ingredients) come hearty, country-style casseroles, stews, steaks, bangers and mash and other pub classics. Install yourself in one of the traditional bar rooms, all dressed stone and warmed by log fires, relax on the stone-flagged patio, or settle in the comfortable restaurant and ask for the eminently manageable menu. Start with meze, charcuterie, crispy duck leg pancakes or home-made soup; then choose vegetable tagine; pork and wild boar faggots; chargrilled venison steak; market fish of the day; or butternut squash, brown cap mushrooms and spinach risotto. Pizzas from an authentic oven are another option. If, to follow, upside-down apple pudding with Calvados crème anglaise, or creamy rice pudding with red plum compote fail to tick the right box, call for the cheeseboard, full of British classics with crackers, celery, chutney and grapes. The Bear has a climbing frame for children and dogs are welcome in the bar area.

Open all day all wk **Bar Meals** L served Mon-Fri 12-2.30, Sat 12-3 D served Mon-Fri 6.30-9.30, Sat 6.30-10 **Restaurant** L served Mon-Fri 12-2.30, Sat 12-3, Sun 12-8 D served Mon-Fri 6.30-9.30, Sat 6.30-10 Fixed menu price fr £7.50 Av 3 course à la carte fr £20 ⊕ GREENE KING ◖ IPA, Abbot Ale. ♀ 14 **Facilities** Children's menu Children's portions Play area Dogs allowed Garden Parking Wi-fi

DORCHESTER (ON THAMES) *continued*

PICK OF THE PUBS

The George ★★ HL

25 High St OX10 7HH
☎ 01865 340404 📠 01865 341620
e-mail: georgedorchester@relaxinnz.co.uk
dir: From M40 junct 7, A329 S to A4074 at Shillingford. Follow Dorchester signs. From M4 junct 13, A34 to Abingdon then A415 E to Dorchester

The George stands at the centre of the picturesque village of Dorchester-on-Thames, opposite the famous Dorchester Abbey and museum. A 15th-century coaching inn, believed to be one of the oldest public houses in Britain, its welcoming atmosphere has attracted the likes of DH Lawrence in the past. Oak beams and inglenook fireplaces characterise the interior, while the elevated restaurant offers a secret garden with waterfall. The Potboys bar is a traditional taproom – just the spot to enjoy a pint of Brakspear while tucking into a grilled rump steak in a mushroom sauce flambéed in brandy; or a lamb shank braised in red wine and rosemary and served with parsnip purée, red cabbage and roasted vegetables. If you're just passing through at lunchtime, stop by for a fresh baguette, a ploughman's, or bangers and mash with red onion gravy. Expect crumbles, cheesecakes and ice creams on the dessert list.

Open all wk 11am-mdnt **Bar Meals** L served all wk 12-3 D served all wk 6-9 **Restaurant** L served all wk 12-3 booking required D served all wk 6-9 booking required ⊕ CHAPMANS GROUP ◀ Wadworth 6X, Brakspear ♻ Stowford Press. **Facilities** Children welcome Children's menu Children's portions Garden Parking Wi-fi **Rooms** 17

PICK OF THE PUBS

The White Hart ★★★ HL ❀ ♟

High St OX10 7HN
☎ 01865 340074 📠 01865 341082
e-mail: whitehart@oxfordshire-hotels.co.uk
dir: A4074 (Oxford to Reading), 5m from M40 junct 7/ A329 to Wallingford

If this picture-perfect hotel looks familiar, that could be because it has played a starring role in the TV series *Midsomer Murders*. Set seven miles from Oxford in heart of historic Dorchester-on-Thames, it has welcomed travellers for around 400 years, and the bars attract locals, residents and diners alike. There is a great choice of real beers available. Log fires and candlelight create an intimate atmosphere for the enjoyment of innovative dishes prepared from fresh ingredients. A good-value fixed-price lunch is available Monday to Saturday, with a choice of three starters, mains and desserts. The carte menu doubles your choice and includes imaginative dishes such as pumpkin risotto or Thai-style fish cakes, followed by

roasted loin of pork with braised red cabbage, caramelised apple and sweet potato crisps; fish and chips in beer batter with crushed minted peas and hand cut chips; or grilled peppered rump steak.

Open all day all wk Mon-Sat 11am-mdnt (Sun 11-11) **Bar Meals** L served all wk 12-2.30 D served all wk 6.30-9.30 **Restaurant** L served all wk 12-2.30 D served all wk 6.30-9.30 ⊕ FREE HOUSE ◀ Adnams, Black Sheep. ♟ 12 **Facilities** Children welcome Children's portions Garden Parking **Rooms** 26

FARINGDON   Map 5 SU29

PICK OF THE PUBS

The Lamb at Buckland ♟

Lamb Ln, Buckland SN7 8QN ☎ 01367 870484
e-mail: thelambatbuckland@googlemail.com
web: www.lambatbuckland.co.uk
dir: Just off A420, 3m E of Faringdon

Built in Cotswold stone, The Lamb enjoys a tucked away location in the beautiful village of Buckland in the Vale of the White Horse. Dating from the 18th century, the pub is now run by husband and wife Richard and Shelley Terry and Christopher Green. All three are trained chefs, but you'll find Shelley running front of house while the two men work in the kitchen. The trio are united in their objective: to proffer good food in a pub atmosphere, with relaxed and friendly service. To this end local producers of both ales and food are called upon to stock the bar and larder and many of the vegetables are grown in the kitchen garden next to the suntrap patio. Typical dishes plucked from the menu might be grilled fillet of mackerel with tomato and fennel compote, followed by locally shot pheasant with fondant potato and red cabbage, or pan-fried fillet of sea bass on a smoked haddock and chive risotto.

Open all wk 11.30-3 6-11 Closed: Sun eve, Mon **Bar Meals** L served Tue-Sat 12-2, Sun 12-3 booking required D served Tue-Sat 7-9 booking required **Restaurant** L served Tue-Sat 12-2, Sun 12-3 booking required D served Tue-Sat 7-9 booking required ⊕ FREE HOUSE ◀ Brakspear Bitter, Ramsbury Gold, West Berks Good Old Boy. ♟ 12 **Facilities** Children welcome Children's portions Dogs allowed Garden Parking Wi-fi

PICK OF THE PUBS

The Trout at Tadpole Bridge
★★★★ INN ❀ ♟

Buckland Marsh SN7 8RF ☎ 01367 870382
e-mail: info@troutinn.co.uk
dir: From A420 (between Oxford & Swindon) take A417 into Faringdon, onto A4095 signed Bampton, pub approx 2m

Once a riverside toll house, this 17th-century free house has a classic Wind in the Willows name and setting on the banks of the Thames, just twenty minutes from Oxford. Log fires welcome the locals who come in every night for the fine range of regional beers such as Ramsbury Bitter and White Horse, while in summer there is an extensive riverside garden to enjoy. Owners Gareth and Helen Pugh have run several fine-dining restaurants and take food seriously. The kitchen makes good use of the best local ingredients: typical menu choices include roast loin of wild rabbit with red lentils and coriander, or cutlet of veal with sweet potato gnocchi and cherry tomato confit. The couple also understand that families need toys and a decent children's menu. Chosen as the AA's Pub of the Year for England in 2009-2010, the refurbished pub has six luxurious bedrooms.

Open 11.30-3 6-11 Closed: 25-26 Dec, Sun eve (Nov-Apr) **Bar Meals** L served all wk 12-2 booking required D served all wk 7-9 booking required Av main course £12.95 **Restaurant** L served all wk 12-2 booking required D served all wk 7-9 booking required Av 3 course à la carte fr £25 ⊕ FREE HOUSE ◀ Ramsbury Bitter, Young's, PA Bitter, White Horse ♻ Stowford Press. ♟ 12 **Facilities** Children welcome Children's menu Children's portions Dogs allowed Garden Parking Wi-fi **Rooms** 6

FERNHAM   Map 5 SU29

The Woodman Inn **NEW**

SN7 7NX ☎ 01367 820643
e-mail: enquiries@thewoodmaninn.net
dir: M4 junct 15, A419 towards Swindon. Right onto A420 signed Oxford/Shrivenham. Straight on at next 2 rdbts. At x-rds left onto B4508 to Fernham

Regulars at this picturesque, 17th-century pub in a hamlet in the Vale of the White Horse praise it for its well-kept real ales and ciders. Log fires burn throughout the pub in winter, while friendly staff provide excellent table service on the terrace in summer. The restaurant, a medieval banqueting hall with minstrels' gallery, provides a great atmosphere for lunch and dinner, with a wide choice of mains, including home-cooked honey-roast ham; locally made sausages and mash; breaded haddock goujons; and tomato, herb and goat's cheese tart. A beer festival is held once a year.

Save on hotels. Book at **theAA**.com/hotel

OXFORDSHIRE 359 ENGLAND

Open all day all wk **Bar Meals** L served all wk 12-2 D served all wk 6.30-9.30 Av main course £12 **Restaurant** L served all wk 12-2 D served all wk 6.30-9.30 Fixed menu price fr £21.95 Av 3 course à la carte fr £26.95 ⊞ FREE HOUSE ◀ Timothy Taylor Landlord, Oakham Ales, Wadworth 6X, Wychwood Hobgoblin Ở Aspall, Thatchers Cheddar Valley. **Facilities** Children welcome Children's menu Children's portions Family room Dogs allowed Garden Beer festival Parking Wi-fi

FRINGFORD   Map 11 SP62

The Butchers Arms

OX27 8EB ☎ **01869 277363**
dir: *4m from Bicester on A4421 towards Buckingham*

The village of Fringford is the model for Candleford in *Lark Rise to Candleford*, and its author, Flora Thompson, worked in the local post office and lived on Juniper Hill. This pretty, creeper clad pub offers a good selection of traditional British food such as liver and bacon, succulent fillet and rump steaks, duck breast in orange sauce, and steak and kidney pie. Pumps display Adnams Broadside and Hooky Bitter. From the patio watch the cricket during the summer or visit when the beer festival takes place in June.

Open all day all wk **Bar Meals** L served all wk 12-2.30 D served all wk 6.30-9 Av main course £9.95 **Restaurant** L served Mon-Sat 12-2.30, Sun 12-3.30 D served all wk 6.30-9 Fixed menu price fr £9.95 ⊞ PUNCH TAVERNS ◀ Adnams Broadside, Hooky Bitter, Spitfire Ale Ở Thatchers Katy. **Facilities** Children welcome Dogs allowed Beer festival Parking

FULBROOK   Map 10 SP21

The Carpenters Arms

Fulbrook Hill OX18 4BH ☎ **01993 823275**
dir: *From rdbt on A40 at Burford take A361 signed Chipping Norton. Pub on right 150mtrs from mini rdbt just after bridge*

This 17th-century stone pub oozes charm and character; the warren of cosy, beautifully decorated and furnished rooms draw a cosmopolitan crowd for the civilised atmosphere and the modern British cooking. Look to the chalkboard and perhaps find fresh Colchester oysters with shallot vinegar, pea and ham soup, pan-seared mackerel with cucumber and cockle vinaigrette, or braised ox cheek with suet dumpling. Recent change of hands.

Open 11.30-3.30 6-11 Closed: 25-26 Dec, Sun eve, Mon ⊞ GREENE KING ◀ Greene King IPA, Abbot Ale Ở Aspall. **Facilities** Children welcome Children's portions Dogs allowed Garden Parking

FYFIELD   Map 5 SU49

PICK OF THE PUBS

The White Hart ◉◉ ♀

Main Rd OX13 5LW ☎ **01865 390585**
e-mail: info@whitehart-fyfield.com
dir: *6m S of Oxford just off A420 (Oxford to Swindon road)*

The White Hart is a 15th-century converted chantry house steeped in history. The original soaring eaves and beams, huge stone-flanked windows and flagstones are overlooked by a minstrels' gallery, now the main restaurant. With over 50 wines on the list, sixteen of which are sold by the glass, there's something for everyone. A good range of cask-conditioned ales always includes something from Hook Norton. Awarded two AA Rosettes for their food, owners Mark and Kay Chandler are steadfast in their pursuit of fresh, seasonal food from trusted local suppliers and their own garden, which provides a regular supply of fruit, vegetables and herbs. Mark changes his menus daily to offer smoked duck, fennel and blood orange salad; slow-roasted belly of Kelmscott pork, apple, celeriac purée and cider jus; plum and almond tart and Armagnac ice cream. Other attractions are May and August Bank Holiday beer festivals, and takeaway fish and chips on Thursdays.

Open noon-3 5.30-11 (Sat noon-11 Sun noon-10.30) Closed: Mon ex BH **Bar Meals** L served Tue-Sat 12-2.30, Sun 12-3.30 booking required D served Tue-Sat 7-9.30 booking required Av main course £16 **Restaurant** L served Tue-Sat 12-2.30, Sun 12-3.30 booking required D served Tue-Sat 7-9.30 booking required Fixed menu price fr £15 Av 3 course à la carte fr £25 ⊞ FREE HOUSE ◀ Hooky Bitter, Doom Bar, Hullabaloo, Guest ales Ở Thatchers Cheddar Valley. ♀ 16 **Facilities** Children welcome Children's menu Children's portions Play area Garden Beer festival Parking Wi-fi

GORING   Map 5 SU68

PICK OF THE PUBS

Miller of Mansfield   RR ◉

High St RG8 9AW ☎ **01491 872829** 🖹 **01491 873100**
e-mail: reservations@millerofmansfield.com
dir: *From Pangbourne take A329 to Streatley. Right on B4009, 0.5m to Goring*

The beautiful Grade II-listed redbrick building has been stylishly renovated and includes sumptuous accommodation with distinctive and individual style. An 18th-century coaching inn in an Area of Outstanding Natural Beauty, The Miller of Mansfield is highly rated as a restaurant with rooms, but nonetheless remains a focal point for the village. It welcomes local and visiting real ale drinkers, and wine lovers too; indeed, refreshments extend to triple-certified origin coffees and organic teas. The kitchen focuses on freshness of ingredients, so expect

seasonality in its take on modern British cooking. Suppliers are carefully sourced, and just about everything that can be is home made. In the Philippe Starck-influenced dining room, each dish is awash with flavours: roast butternut squash cannelloni with Parmesan and Amaretto, tomato and basil oil; oven-baked red mullet with crushed herbed potatoes and tarragon beurre blanc; blood orange and Cointreau steamed pudding are just a selection. Yet you can order a pork pie, cheese ploughman's or a club sandwich in the bar with a pint of Rebellion IPA - ample demonstration of the lack of ostentation within this welcoming hostelry.

Open all day all wk 8am-11pm **Bar Meals** L served all wk 12-10 D served all wk 12-10 food served all day **Restaurant** L served all wk 12-4.30 D served all wk 6.30-10 booking required ⊞ FREE HOUSE ◀ Good Old Boy, Rebellion IPA, Organic Jester. **Facilities** Children welcome Dogs allowed Garden Parking **Rooms** 13

GREAT TEW   Map 11 SP42

PICK OF THE PUBS

The Falkland Arms ♀

OX7 4DB ☎ **01608 683653**
e-mail: falklandarms@wadworth.co.uk
dir: *Off A361, 1.25m, signed Great Tew*

This 500-year-old inn takes its name from Lucius Carey, 2nd Viscount Falkland, who inherited the manor of Great Tew in 1629. Nestling at the end of a charming row of Cotswold stone cottages, the Falkland Arms is a classic: flagstone floors, high-backed settles and an inglenook fireplace characterise the intimate bar, where a huge collection of beer and cider mugs and jugs hangs from the ceiling. Home-made specials such as spiced lamb burger with salsa and sautéed potatoes; or smoked haddock kedgeree topped with a poached egg supplement the lunchtime menu of filled baguettes and ploughman's; these can be enjoyed in the bar or the pub garden. In the evening, booking is essential for dinner in the small dining room. Expect a pint of shell-on prawns with crusty bread; Falkland Arms fish pie; or whole roasted partridge with Puy lentils and roast vegetables. Being a genuine English pub, clay pipes and snuff are always on sale.

Open all wk Mon-Sat 11.30am-11pm (Sun noon-10.30) **Bar Meals** L served all wk 12-2.30 D served all wk 6.30-9 **Restaurant** L served all wk 12-2.30 D served all wk 6.30-9 booking required ⊞ WADWORTH & CO LTD ◀ Wadworth 6X, Henry's IPA, Horizon, Guest ales Ở Westons Traditional Scrumpy, Westons Perry. ♀ 18 **Facilities** Children welcome Children's portions Dogs allowed Garden

HAILEY Map 11 SP31

Bird in Hand ★★★★ INN ☻

Whiteoak Green OX29 9XP
☎ 01993 868321 ▤ 01993 868702
e-mail: welcome@birdinhandinn.co.uk
dir: From Witney N onto B4022 through Hailey to Whiteoak Green for 3m. At Charlbury S onto B4022 for 4m

Set in the Oxfordshire countryside and ideal for Burford and Blenheim Palace, this classic 17th-century stone free house has a beamed interior with huge inglenook fireplaces and winter log fires. Imaginative seasonal menus in the large restaurant are founded on local produce, and might include sea bass with Kelmscott bacon; summer pea risotto with mint and truffle oil; or stuffed saddle of lamb. Modern accommodation is available and there's free Wi-fi access in the public areas.

Open all day all wk **Bar Meals** L served Mon-Sat 12-2.30, Sun 12-3 D served Mon-Sat 6.30-9.30, Sun 6-9 Av main course £8 **Restaurant** L served Mon-Sat 12-2.30, Sun 12-3 D served Mon-Sat 6.30-9.30, Sun 6-9 Av 3 course à la carte fr £22 ⊕ FREE HOUSE ◾ Ramsbury Ŏ Thatchers Gold. ☻ 10 **Facilities** Children welcome Children's menu Children's portions Dogs allowed Garden Parking Wi-fi **Rooms** 16

HAMPTON POYLE Map 11 SP51

PICK OF THE PUBS

The Bell ★★★★★ INN

OX5 2QD ☎ 01865 376242
e-mail: contactus@thebelloxford.co.uk
dir: From N: exit A34 signed Kidlington, over bridge. At mini rdbt turn right, left to Hampton Poyle (before slip road to rejoin A34). From Kidlington: at Oxford rd rdbt (junct of A4260 & A4165), take Bicester Rd (Sainsbury's on left & towards A34). Left to Hampton Poyle

This welcoming dining inn with boutique-style rooms nestles close to the Cherwell to the north of Oxford. The addition of a contemporary restaurant has done nothing to harm the historic heart of the old village pub, where limestone flagged floors, oak beams and comfortable leather armchairs still greet the bar regulars. Well behaved dogs are welcome here too, or out on the delightful south-facing terrace which has seating for 60. An eye-catching feature is a wood-burning oven where some dishes from the open kitchen are prepared, including legendary rustic pizzas. These, along with burgers and salads, can be served in the bar at any time. If a memorable meal is what you have in mind, head for the restaurant where you could start with warm pigeon breast and chorizo with green bean and shallot vinaigrette. Next, what could be better than the 'Gentleman's Lunch' – a plate of thinly sliced cold rare beef with string chips and salad? Grilled fish and great steaks are also recommended. There is contemporary accommodation available.

Open all wk (Sat-Sun all day) **Bar Meals** L served Mon-Fri 12-2.30, Sat-Sun all day D served Mon-Fri 6-9.30, Sat-Sun 6-10 Av main course £12 **Restaurant** L served Mon-Fri 12-2.30, Sat-Sun all day D served Mon-Fri 6-9.30, Sat-Sun 6-10 Fixed menu price fr £14 Av 3 course à la carte fr £20 ⊕ FREE HOUSE ◾ Fuller's London Pride, Wadworth Ŏ Stowford Press. **Facilities** Dogs allowed Garden Parking Wi-fi **Rooms** 9

HENLEY-ON-THAMES Map 5 SU78

PICK OF THE PUBS

The Cherry Tree Inn ☻

Stoke Row RG9 5QA
☎ 01491 680430 ▤ 01491 682168
e-mail: info@thecherrytreeinn.com
dir: B481 towards Reading & Sonning Common 2m, follow Stoke Row sign

There's a confident blend of ancient and modern inside this 400-year-old listed building. Originally three flint cottages, the Cherry Tree has been comprehensively re-fitted, mixing the original flagstone floors, beamed ceilings and fireplaces with contemporary decor, strong colours and comfortable modern furnishings. The contemporary theme continues throughout the pub, which offers Brakspear real ales, fine malt whiskies and over 40 different wines, including 12 served by the glass. Service is informal, with a variety of classic European dishes prepared from fresh local ingredients. Lunchtime choices include grilled focaccia with goat's cheese, peppers and pesto; as well as more substantial dishes like belly of pork with black pudding and creamy mash. À la carte options range from chargrilled rib-eye steak, to grilled squid and chorizo salad. Outside, the large south-facing garden is perfect for alfresco summer dining.

Open Mon-Sat noon-11 (Sun noon-8) Closed: Sun eve **Bar Meals** L served Mon-Fri 12-3, Sat-Sun 12-4 D served Mon-Sat 7-10 **Restaurant** L served Mon-Fri 12-3, Sat-Sun 12-4 D served Mon-Sat 7-10 ⊕ BRAKSPEAR ◾ Brakspear Bitter, Brakspear Oxford Gold, Seasonal guest ales Ŏ Symonds. ☻ 12 **Facilities** Children welcome Children's menu Dogs allowed Garden Parking

PICK OF THE PUBS

The Five Horseshoes

Maidensgrove RG9 6EX
☎ 01491 641282 ▤ 01491 641086
e-mail: admin@thefivehorseshoes.co.uk
dir: From Henley-on-Thames take A4130, in 1m take B480 to right, signed Stonor. In Stonor left, through woods, over common, pub on left

This traditional 16th-century pub enjoys far-reaching views across the surrounding countryside from its two large beer gardens. Once inside, old pub games, log

fires, heavy beams and brasses set the scene; there are two snug bar areas serving real ales, wines and Champagnes by the glass, as well as a large conservatory restaurant. Food focuses on the freshest produce, locally sourced where possible, and the menu begins with wild mushroom and sherry soup; home smoked rainbow trout; and wood pigeon salad. Other choices include roast haunch of muntjac for two; and ox cheek and oyster pudding; plus pub favourites such as doorstep sandwiches, and prime minced beef or venison burger. Puddings range from apricot soufflé to steamed ginger pudding with butterscotch sauce. Walkers, cyclists and dogs are all welcome in this Area of Outstanding Natural Beauty. Summer weekend barbecues and bank holiday hog roasts are held in one of the gardens.

Open all wk noon-3.30 6-11 (Sat noon-11 Sun noon-6) ⊕ BRAKSPEAR ◾ Brakspear Ordinary, Oxford Gold. **Facilities** Children welcome Children's portions Dogs allowed Garden Parking

The Little Angel ☻

Remenham Ln RG9 2LS ☎ 01491 411008
e-mail: enquiries@thelittleangel.co.uk
web: www.thelittleangel.co.uk
dir: From Henley-on-Thames take A4130 (White Hill) towards Maidenhead. Pub on left

This engaging, listed, country-style three-storey pub hides a very contemporary and chic interior, retaining a tantalising hint of bygone days when trade from boatmen on the nearby Thames would have been the mainstay. Recreational boaters moored near Henley's famous bridge still flock here, as do patrons keen to sample the exceptional modern menu, described as English-with-a-twist; witness starters such as carpaccio of smoked halibut, a prelude to wild mushroom crumble. There's a very generous wine list and a range of real ales such as Brakspears Oxford Gold.

Open all day all wk 11am-11pm (Fri-Sat 11am-mdnt Sun noon-10) Closed: 1 Jan **Bar Meals** L served Mon-Fri 12-3, Sat-Sun all day D served Mon-Fri 7-10, Sat-Sun all day **Restaurant** L served Mon-Fri 12-3, Sat-Sun all day booking required D served Mon-Fri 7-10, Sat-Sun all day booking required ⊕ BRAKSPEAR ◾ Brakspear, Oxford Gold Organic, seasonal ales, Guinness. ☻ 11 **Facilities** Children welcome Children's portions Dogs allowed Garden Parking

See advert opposite

The Little Angel

Henley On Thames, Remenham Lane, Henley On Thames, Berks RG9 2LS
Tel: 01491 411 008
E-mail: enquiries@thelittleangel.co.uk   Web: www.thelittleangel.co.uk

"This is the busiest pub in Henley. When entering The Little Angel, those paying their inaugural visit might be pleasantly surprised by not only the unique style and sophisticated ambience of this historic pub but at its size and clever use of space. From the outside, this lovely, traditional white pub, a stones throw from Henley Bridge and the river Thames is perfectly positioned in every respect and with its interior showing you a modern, creative and comfortable personality – it has something for everyone.

This is a foodhouse pub but is still a great pub with well kept real Ales. A beautiful and tempting bar with comfy chairs and a welcoming smile, The Little Angel is a draw for locals and visitors afar and is not to be missed on any of the many annual social events throughout Henley's calendar (during Henley Royal Regatta, Music & Arts Festival in June/July to the huge 80's Rewind Festival in August). The pub is firmly established as a main destination for corporate and private groups and individuals to meet, eat, drink and be seen throughout the year.

It is unique in its positioning and is garnering an increasing following for excellent food (emphasis heavily on local, fresh and seasonal produce), service and flexibility and is as happy catering for wedding receptions as it is a quiet lunch or dinner for two. Being open all day, every day (even Christmas Day) with seasonally changing menus of locally sourced produce; it is perfect for any occasion.

On a summer's day, there's no better place to be than in the large patio garden, enjoying a three course lunch, or maybe a jug of Pimms, whilst watching the quintessential English cricket game on the Henley lawns.

Those that know The Little Angel have seen it evolve over the years and are loyal to it. This is a smooth operation that adds that special touch!"

HENLEY-ON-THAMES continued

The Three Tuns ♥ NEW

5 The Market Place RG9 2AA
☎ 01491 411588 & 07969 780766
e-mail: info@thethreetuns.com
dir: In town centre. Parking nearby

Since reopening in 2010, Simon Bonwick has sprinkled magic dust over the ancient Brakspear's pub. The resident ghost hovers benignly over the rustic chic style of the place, all white beamed and matchboarded ceilings, bare and carpeted floors richly furnished by scrubbed or antique tables, with a magpie mix of artefacts, posters and prints. Firmly in the gastro-pub stable, produce is sourced from across the south – and indeed, across The Channel for truffles and poultry – to service a small but intense, ever-changing menu: Herefordshire Middlewhite pig or South Devon seafood for example.

Open Tue-Sat 12-3 6-10.45 last orders Closed: Sun & Mon Bar Meals L served Tue-Sat 12-2 D served Tue-Sat 6-9 Av main course £12.50 Restaurant L served Tue-Sat 12-2 D served Tue-Sat 6-9 Fixed menu price fr £10 Av 3 course à la carte fr £28.50 ⊕ BRAKSPEAR ◀ Brakspear Special, Gold ♂ Weston Premier. Facilities Garden

PICK OF THE PUBS

WhiteHartNettlebed ♥

High St, Nettlebed RG9 5DD
☎ 01491 641245 📄 01491 649018
e-mail: info.hart@tmsteaks.co.uk
dir: On A4130 between Henley-on-Thames & Wallingford

Royalist and parliamentary soldiers made a habit of lodging in local taverns during the English Civil War; this 15th-century inn reputedly billeted troops loyal to the King. During the 17th and 18th centuries the area was plagued by highwaymen, including the notorious Isaac Darkin, who was eventually caught, tried and hung at Oxford Gaol. These days the beautifully restored property is favoured by a stylish crowd who appreciate the chic bar and restaurant. Heading the beer list is locally-brewed Brakspear backed by popular internationals and a small selection of cosmopolitan bottles. A typical three-course meal selection could comprise sweet potato and Gruyère tartlet with rocket; spinach, feta and cumin spanakopita with babaganouche; and lemon and thyme pannacotta with red wine poached pear.

Open all day all wk 7am-11pm (Sun 8am-10pm) Bar Meals L served Mon-Sat 12-3, Sun 12-8 booking required D served Mon-Sat 6-10 booking required Restaurant L served Mon-Sat 12-3, Sun 12-8 booking required D served Mon-Sat 6-10 booking required ⊕ BRAKSPEAR ◀ Brakspear, Guinness ♂ Symonds. ♥ 12 Facilities Children welcome Children's menu Children's portions Play area Family room Dogs allowed Garden Parking

---

HIGHMOOR   Map 5 SU78

Rising Sun ♥ NEW

Witheridge Hill RG9 5PF ☎ 01491 640856
e-mail: info@risingsunwitheridgehill.co.uk
dir: From Henley-on-Thames take A4130 towards Wallingford. Take B481, turn right to Highmoor

Nestling adjacent to the green in a small hamlet in the Chilterns, the path to this 17th-century pub passes through the garden. Its idyllic setting is matched by an interior rich in low beamed ceilings, wood-boarded floors, and richly coloured walls adorned with chalk boards listing guest ales, wines and forthcoming events. The thoughtfully decorated restaurant is divided in three sections, making for cosy tables. Here are served dishes such as boneless shin of beef with sweet potatoes and roasted peppers. A 'snacks and nibbles' menu in the bar includes boiled eggs with soldiers.

Open all wk Mon-Fri 12-3 5-11 (Sat 12-11 Sun 12-7) Bar Meals L served Mon-Fri 12-2, Sat-Sun 12-3 D served Mon-Sat 6.30-9 Av main course £8.50 Restaurant L served Mon-Fri 12-2, Sat-Sun 12-3 D served Mon-Sat 6.30-9 Av 3 course à la carte fr £23 ⊕ BRAKSPEAR ◀ Brakspear Ordinary, Oxford Gold ♂ Westons Organic. ♥ 10 Facilities Children welcome Children's menu Children's portions Family room Dogs allowed Garden Parking Wi-fi

---

HOOK NORTON   Map 11 SP33

PICK OF THE PUBS

The Gate Hangs High

Whichford Rd OX15 5DF ☎ 01608 737387
e-mail: gatehangshigh@btconnect.com
dir: Off A361 SW of Banbury, left into village & left again within village towards Sibford Ferris to next junction

This rural pub is on the old drovers' road from Wales to Banbury surrounded by beautiful countryside. It is close to the mystical Rollright Stones and Hook Norton, where the cask-conditioned, dry-hopped ales served in the pub are brewed. A tollgate once stood outside that was said to hang high enough for small creatures to pass under, but owners of larger beasts had to pay. The low-beamed bar has a welcoming atmosphere with polished horse brasses, candles, pretty wall lights and roaring log fire. The menu features good old-fashioned dishes: expect field mushrooms topped with Stilton on a pink peppercorn sauce or fresh sardines in garlic butter to start, followed by braised lamb shank with root vegetables and creamy mash; pork tenderloin with a sherry and mushroom sauce; or trout fillets with garlic prawns. There is also a specials board that changes regularly. Recent change of hands.

Open all wk 11-3 6-close Closed: 25 Dec eve Bar Meals L served Mon-Fri 12-2.30, Sat-Sun 12-2.30 D served Mon-Fri 6-9.30, Sat-Sun 6-9.30 Av main course £8.95 Restaurant L served Mon-Fri 12-2.30, Sat-Sun 12-2.30 D served Mon-Fri 6-9.30, Sat-Sun 6-9.30 Fixed menu price fr £11.95 Av 3 course à la carte fr £17.95 ⊕ HOOK NORTON BREWERY ◀ Hook Norton - Best, Old Hooky, Gold ♂ Stowford Press. Facilities Children welcome Children's portions Dogs allowed Garden Parking Wi-fi

---

KELMSCOTT   Map 5 SU29

The Plough Inn

GL7 3HG ☎ 01367 253543
dir: From M4 junct 15 onto A419 towards Cirencester then right onto A361 to Lechlade. A417 towards Faringdon, follow signs to Kelmscott

Dating from 1631, this attractive Cotswold stone inn stands on the Thames Path midway between Radcot and Lechlade, making it a haven for walkers and boaters. It's also just a short walk from Kelmscott Manor, once home to William Morris. Exposed stone walls and flagstone floors set the scene for real ales and an extensive, hearty menu. Dishes range from mussels cooked in cider, thyme and smoked bacon to pork and apple burger, plum relish and hand-cut chips. The pub holds a beer festival (please contact for dates).

Open all day all wk Bar Meals L served all wk 12-3 D served all wk 7-10 Av main course £8.50 Restaurant L served all wk 12-3 D served all wk 7-10 ⊕ FREE HOUSE ◀ Thames Tickler, Old Lech, Brakspear, Wye Valley ♂ Thatchers Gold. Facilities Children welcome Children's menu Children's portions Dogs allowed Garden Beer festival Wi-fi

---

KINGHAM   Map 10 SP22

PICK OF THE PUBS

The Kingham Plough   INN ☺☺

The Green OX7 6YD ☎ 01608 658327
e-mail: book@thekinghamplough.co.uk
dir: From Chipping Norton, take B4450 to Churchill. Take 2nd right to Kingham, left at T junct in Kingham. Pub on right.

Situated on the village green in what was once described as 'England's favourite village' by Country Life magazine, The Kingham Plough was extensively refurbished in 2007. This quintessential Cotswold inn has a relaxing bar where you can enjoy one of the real ales and daily-changing bar snacks like scotched quail eggs or snails and mushrooms on toast. In the restaurant chef/proprietor Emily Watkins, who worked under Heston Blumenthal at The Fat Duck, changes the short menu daily to accommodate the deliveries from local farms, smallholdings and game estates. Expect dishes like twice-baked smoked haddock and Double Gloucester soufflé; Scottish langoustine, leek and

Save on hotels. Book at **theAA.com/hotel**

OXFORDSHIRE 363 ENGLAND

Cornish shellfish chowder; Evenlode lamb pudding with curly kale; chocolate and salted caramel terrine with pecan fudge ice cream; and an exemplary local cheeseboard. Look out for A Taste of the Cotswolds menu along with other events such as the annual farmers' market, quiz nights and food tasting evenings. There are elegantly furnished bedrooms, all newly refurbished.

Open all day all wk Closed: 25 Dec **Bar Meals** L served all wk 12-9.30 D served all wk 12-9.30 Av main course £7 food served all day **Restaurant** L served Mon-Sat 12-2, Sun 12-2.30 D served Mon-Sat 7-9 Av 3 course à la carte fr £30 ⊕ FREE HOUSE ◀ Cotswold Premium, Hook Norton, Mad Goose, Hereford Pale Ale, Cotswold Wheat Beer ♂ Stowford Press. **Facilities** Children welcome Children's menu Children's portions Dogs allowed Garden Parking Wi-fi **Rooms** 7

LANGFORD   Map 5 SP20

The Bell at Langford ♀ NEW

GL7 3LF ☎ 01367 860249
dir: *From Swindon take A361 towards Lechlade & Burford. Through Lechlade, at rdbt right onto B4477 signed Carterton. Turn right for Langford*

Jacqui and Paul Wynne's busy little dining pub in a charming village has polished flagstones, an inglenook fireplace and simple, low-key furnishings. People like it this way, which is why they enjoy eating here. Paul is the chef and Jacqui runs front of house and is equally passionate about the beers and wines. There's a lot to choose from, including Kelmscott pork and herb sausages, wholegrain mustard and leek mash and onion gravy; seared king scallops with chorizo; Thai green chicken curry; and nut roast with tomato and basil sauce.

Open 12-3 7-11 (Fri 7-12 Sat 7-11.30) Closed: Sun eve & Mon **Bar Meals** L served Tue-Sun 12-1.45 D served Mon-Sat 7-9 Av main course £10.95 **Restaurant** L served Tue-Sun 12-1.45 D served Mon-Sat 7-9 Av 3 course à la carte fr £18.95 ⊕ FREE HOUSE ◀ Hook Norton, Sharp's Doom Bar, St Austell Tribute ♂ Stowford Press. ♀12 **Facilities** Children welcome Children's menu Children's portions Play area Dogs allowed Garden Parking

---

LOWER SHIPLAKE   Map 5 SU77

PICK OF THE PUBS

The Baskerville ★★★★ INN ♀

See Pick of the Pubs on page 364

LOWER WOLVERCOTE   Map 5 SP40

PICK OF THE PUBS

The Trout Inn ♀

195 Godstow Rd OX2 8PN ☎ 01865 510930
dir: *From A40 at Wolvercote rdbt (N of Oxford) follow signs for Wolvercote, through village to pub*

This utterly captivating waterside inn is threaded into the structure of one of Oxford's oldest buildings. A favourite with undergraduates, its renown was assured when Morse and Lewis sat on the terrace below the weir, supping local beers in several episodes of the iconic television detective series filmed here. It was already ancient when Lewis Carroll, and later CS Lewis took inspiration here; centuries before them it was a hospice for Godstow Nunnery, on the opposite bank of The Thames. With leaded windows, great oak beams, flagged floors and fireplaces glowing in winter, it is arguably Oxford's most atmospheric inn, enhanced by modern comforts. The comprehensive, top-notch menu has a distinct Italian lineage, with starters of baked mushrooms, spinach, Dolcelatte and Stiratta Romagna or Mediterranean mezze setting the scene for a wide range of freshly made pastas and pizzas, backed up by reliable modern British fare like whole baked trout with pancetta, leek white wine sauce and watercress salad, or roast rump of lamb, sauce soubise, asparagus, pancetta, button onions and baby potatoes.

Open all day all wk 10.45am-close **Bar Meals** Av main course £13 food served all day **Restaurant** Av 3 course à la carte fr £23 food served all day ⊕ FREE HOUSE ◀ Brakspear Oxford Gold, Timothy Taylor Landlord, Adnams Best Bitter ♂ Aspall Suffolk Draught. ♀21 **Facilities** Children welcome Garden Parking

---

MIDDLETON STONEY   Map 11 SP52

Best Western Jersey Arms Hotel ★★ HL ♀

OX25 4AD ☎ 01869 343234   📄 01869 343565
e-mail: jerseyarms@bestwestern.co.uk
dir: *3m from junct 9/10 of M4. 3m from A34 on B430*

This family-run free house was built as an ale house in the 13th century, on what used to be the estate of Lord Jersey. Combining old fashioned charm with contemporary elegance, food can be taken in the bar and grill with the British menu supplemented by daily blackboard specials. Start with creamy garlic mushrooms and herbs, then try steak and kidney pudding; Scottish rib-eye steak; braised shank of English lamb; or savoury pancake stuffed with spinach and cream cheese; followed by chocolate and hazelnut brownie and chocolate sauce.

Open all day all wk **Bar Meals** L served all wk 12-2 D served all wk 6.30-9 Av main course £11.50 **Restaurant** L served all wk 12-2 booking required D served all wk 6.30-9 booking required Av 3 course à la carte fr £25 ⊕ FREE HOUSE ◀ Interbrew Flower. ♀9 **Facilities** Children welcome Children's menu Garden Parking Wi-fi **Rooms** 20

MURCOTT   Map 11 SP51

PICK OF THE PUBS

The Nut Tree Inn ◉◉ ♀

Main St OX5 2RE ☎ 01865 331253
dir: *M40 junct 9, A34 towards Oxford. Left onto B4027 signed Islip. At Red Lion turn left. Right signed Murcott, Fencott & Charlton-on-Otmoor. Pub on right in village*

A thatched, whitewashed 15th-century free house overlooking the village pond, The Nut Tree stands in four acres including a vegetable garden that supplies the pub kitchen. Still very much a pub, you can stop here for a relaxing pint of Vale Best Bitter at the end of a hard day's work - but step into the newly refurbished dining room, and you'll discover great modern British food and attentive service. Mike North grew up locally and always dreamed of owning The Nut Tree. In 2006 he made those dreams a reality when he and his then fiancée Imogen bought the pub with its oak beams, wood-burning stoves and unusual carvings. Often using produce bartered from the locals, at the bar and in the garden, the chalkboard menu might include daily soups; sandwiches on home-made bread (loaves of which you can pre-order and take home, along with home-made sausages made from the pub's own pigs); and a good old-fashioned ploughman's. A typical restaurant selection starts with crispy English calves' sweetbreads, celeriac remoulade and black truffle, followed by torte of braised Oxfordshire lamb shoulder and potato, and rounded off with warm chocolate fondant with cardamom ice cream.

Open all day Closed: Mon & Sun eve **Bar Meals** L served Tue-Sat 12-2.30, Sun 12-3 D served Tue-Sat 7-9 Av main course £9 **Restaurant** L served Tue-Sat 12-2.30, Sun 12-3 booking required D served Tue-Sat 7-9 booking required Fixed menu price fr £18 Av 3 course à la carte fr £37.50 ⊕ FREE HOUSE ◀ Vale Hadda's Winter Solstice, Fuller's London Pride, Brains Rev James, Wickwar Bob, Vale Best Bitter, Spitfire, Vale Wychert. ♀16 **Facilities** Children welcome Children's portions Dogs allowed Garden Parking

PICK OF THE PUBS

The Baskerville ★★★★ INN ♀

LOWER SHIPLAKE — Map 5 SU77

Station Rd RG9 3NY ☎ **0118 940 3332**
e-mail: enquiries@thebaskerville.com
web: www.thebaskerville.com
dir: *Just off A4155, 1.5m from Henley*

Behind its rather plain exterior lies a pub of real quality on the popular Thames Path, close to Shiplake station and just a few minutes from historic Henley-on-Thames. Brick-built on the outside, modern-rustic within, it boasts an attractive garden where summer Sunday barbecues are a common fixture, plus comfortable accommodation. Walkers remove their muddy boots at the door before heading to the bar adorned with sporting memorabilia, where pints of Loddon Hoppit, brewed two miles away, are served with welcoming smiles. Variety and choice for the customer is a top priority here, as witnessed by award-winning menus covering breakfast, lunch, evening, Sunday lunch and children's choices; a bar snacks blackboard menu proffers buck rarebit, crispy Cornish Brie and cajun fried whitebait. The objective is to serve really good food at a reasonable price in a relaxed and unpretentious atmosphere. Modern British describes the kitchen's approach, with continental and eastern influences. All produce is delivered daily, and all dishes, including the bread, are prepared on the premises; organic, sustainably sourced ingredients travel as few miles as possible, and a special fish menu runs throughout the summer months. Lunchtime open sandwiches

include smoked English bacon grilled with Cornish brie. Alternatively you could savour spring lamb Barnsley chop with black pudding and thyme hash, Puy lentils and whole grain mustard sauce, and English spinach and minted peas. A typical evening choice could start with pan-fried Cornish scallops with tiger prawns, minted cucumber and radish salad, and Pimms and lemon vinaigrette, followed by pan-fried sea bass fillets glazed with smoked harissa and oven-dried tomato and olive cous cous. The wine list extends to 50 bins, and owner Allan Hannah betrays his origins with his range of 40 malt whiskies.

Open all day all wk 9.30am-11pm (Sun noon-4.30 7-10) Closed: 1 Jan
Restaurant Breakfast served Mon-Sat 9.30-12, L served Mon-Sat 12-6, Sun 12-3.30 booking required, D served Mon-Thu 6-9.30, Fri-Sat 6-10 booking required Av main course £15 Fixed menu price L fr £15.95 D fr £20.95 Av 3 course à la carte fr £27.50. Food served all day. ◾ London Pride, Loddon Hoppit, Timothy Taylor Landlord. ♀ 12 **Facilities** Children's menu Children's portions Play area Dogs allowed Garden Parking Wi-fi **Rooms** 4

Save on hotels. Book at **theAA.com/hotel**

OXFORDSHIRE 365 ENGLAND

The Fishes ♥ NEW

OX2 0NA ☎ 01865 249796
e-mail: fishes@peachpubs.com
dir: From A34 S'bound (dual carriageway) left at
junct after Botley Interchange, signed North Hinksey
& Oxford Rugby Club. From A34 N'bound exit at Botley
Interchange & return to A34 S'bound, then follow as
above

A short walk from the centre of Oxford, The Fishes is an
attractive, tile-hung Victorian pub in three acres of
wooded grounds running down to a stream – an ideal
place for a picnic ordered at the bar. Real ales can be
enjoyed in the cosy snug, but you may well be tempted by
the modern British food: mussels with cider cream and
parsley sauce; braised blade of beef bourguignon with
sweet potato mash; steamed chocolate pudding.

Open all day all wk Closed: 25 Dec **Bar Meals** L served all
wk 12-6.30, Sat-Sun brunch 10am-noon D served all wk
6.30-9.30 Av main course £13.50 food served all day
Restaurant L served all wk 12-2.30 D served all wk
6.30-9.30 Av 3 course à la carte fr £25 food served all
day ⊕ PEACH PUBS ◀ Greene King IPA, Old Specked Hen
Ö Aspall. ♥ 13 **Facilities** Children welcome Children's
portions Play area Garden Parking Wi-fi

The Anchor

2 Hayfield Rd, Walton Manor OX2 6TT
☎ 01865 510282
dir: A34 (Oxford ring road N), exit Peartree rdbt, 1.5m
down the Woodstock road, then right at Polstead Rd,
follow road to end, pub on right

Records show a pub on this site since 1752, but the
current Anchor was built in 1933 by Hall's Brewery.
Many of its original art deco features have been left
untouched, including the large central bar. Very much
a community pub, it's a base for coffee mornings, the
book club, and charity fund-raising efforts. It's off the
beaten track – but, for all that, remains firmly on the
map for its well-kept Wadworth ales and small but
carefully chosen wine list. The relaxed and comfortable
surroundings extend to log fires and daily newspapers.
Lunchtime bar snacks embrace merguez sausages with
honey and yogurt dip, or scrambled eggs with smoked
salmon. A typical lunch dish would be spiced smoked
haddock fishcakes. The short but sweet dinner carte
selection tempts with steamed Fowey mussels; grilled
lamb steaks with salsa verde; and caramelised lemon
tart with crème fraîche. There's a garden for alfresco
dining, and major sporting events are shown in the Oak
Bar.

Open all day all wk Closed: 25 & 26 Dec
Bar Meals L served all wk 12-2.30 D served Mon-Sat
6-9.30, Sun 6.30-8.30 Av main course £13
Restaurant L served all wk 12-2.30 booking required
D served Mon-Sat 6-9.30, Sun 6.30-8.30 booking
required Av 3 course à la carte fr £22 ⊕ WADWORTH
◀ Wadworth 6X, Henrys IPA, Bishops Tipple Ö Westons
Stowford Press. **Facilities** Children welcome Children's
menu Children's portions Dogs allowed Garden Parking
Wi-fi

The Oxford Retreat

1-2 Hythe Bridge St OX1 2EW ☎ 01865 250309
e-mail: info@theoxfordretreat.com
dir: In city centre. 200mtrs from rail station towards
centre

Set at the heart of the University city and right next to the
Isis, the decked, tree-shaded waterside garden is the
place to be seen at this chic boutique pub, an imposing,
gabled building where cocktails are de rigueur and diners
can look forward to wild boar bangers and mash or
marinated wood pigeon from an eclectic, finely tuned
menu prepared in the open kitchen. In winter huddle
round the log fire with a real ale, a cosy retreat from the
dreaming spires.

Open all day all wk ⊕ FREE HOUSE ◀ Fuller's London
Pride, Guinness, Staropramen Ö Westons Organic.
Facilities Children welcome Children's portions Garden
Wi-fi

Turf Tavern

4 Bath Place, off Holywell St OX1 3SU ☎ 01865 243235
e-mail: 8004@greeneking.co.uk
dir: Telephone for directions

A jewel of a pub, and consequently one of Oxford's most
popular. It's not easy to find either as it is approached
through hidden alleyways, which, if anything, adds to its
allure. Previously called the Spotted Cow, it became the
Turf in 1842 probably in deference to its gambling
clientele; it has also had brushes with literature, film and
politics. It's certainly one of Oxford's oldest, with some
13th-century foundations and a 17th-century low-
beamed front bar. Three beer gardens help ease
overcrowding, but the eleven real ales and reasonably
priced pub grub keep the students, locals and visitors
flowing in.

Open all day all wk Closed: 25-26 Dec, 1 Jan ⊕ GREENE
KING ◀ Traditional ales, changing daily Ö Westons Old
Rosie Scrumpy. **Facilities** Children welcome Dogs allowed
Garden Wi-fi

The Crown Inn

See Pick of the Pubs on page 366

The Royal Oak ♥

See Pick of the Pubs on page 367

The Lamb at Satwell ♥ NEW

Rotherfield Greys RG9 4QZ ☎ 01491 628482
e-mail: eatanddrink@thelambpub.net
dir: 50mtrs off B481 (Reading to Nettlebed road)
approx 3m from Henley-on-Thames

Chris and Emma Smith have breathed new live into
this charming 16th-century cottage since taking over
in 2009. Set in a large garden, replete with barbecue,
boules pitch and roaming chickens (children can feed
them and collect their eggs), the Lamb is just three
miles from Henley-on-Thames, and is popular with
walkers exploring the surrounding Chilterns footpaths.
The draw, especially in winter, is the cosy candlelit bar
and adjoining dining room, which oozes period charm
and character. Expect head-cracking low beams, worn
tiled floors, a blazing log fire in the grate, foaming
pints of Loddon Leaping Lamb, and fat candles on
scrubbed pine tables. Arrive early for a fireside seat
and follow smoked haddock chowder or a crab tart
starter with braised ox cheeks with celeriac purée and
thyme jus, or skate wing with brown butter, lemon and
capers. Leave room for coconut pannacotta with lime
syrup or a plate of cheese with Emma's chutney.

Open all day all wk **Bar Meals** L served Mon-Fri 12-3,
Sat-Sun 12-6 D served all wk 6-10 Av main course
£12.75 **Restaurant** L served Mon-Fri 12-3, Sat-Sun
12-6 booking required D served all wk 6-10 booking
required Fixed menu price fr £15 Av 3 course à la carte
fr £19.40 ⊕ FREE HOUSE ◀ Loddon Leaping Lamb,
Black Sheep, Timothy Taylor Landlord, Adnams,
Jennings, Ringwood Ö Aspall. ♥ 11 **Facilities** Children
welcome Children's menu Children's portions Play area
Dogs allowed Garden Beer festival Parking Wi-fi

PICK OF THE PUBS

The Crown Inn

PISHILL · Map 5 SU78

RG9 6HH
☎ 01491 638364
e-mail:
enquiries@thecrowninnpishill.co.uk
web: www.thecrowninnpishill.co.uk
dir: *On B480 off A4130, 8m NW of Henley-on-Thames*

As it is bound to come up in conversation, perhaps we should first deal with the name of the village. Old maps show a second 's' in Pishill, which is why some people insist on separating the two syllables. Furthermore, in pre-combustion engine days waggon drivers would stop at the inn for a swift half after the stiff, six-mile climb from Henley-on-Thames, and their horses would relieve themselves while their masters were inside. (Quite why the horses waited so long isn't recorded.) On the other hand, maybe the word evolved from Peashill, because peas used to be grown round here. Take your pick, depending on whether Great Aunt Gertrude is with you.

This pretty, 15th-century brick and flint coaching inn contains a priest's hole (reputably the largest in the country), which was used extensively when Henry VIII was busy persecuting Catholics. Indeed, one of the many clerics who were smuggled in from the big house at nearby

Stonor met a sticky end while hiding out at The Crown and his ghost still haunts the pub on the anniversary of his death. The bar is supplied by mostly local breweries, including Marlow.

The menus and specials are revised daily, typically to provide steak and ale pie; whole grilled lemon sole with herb butter and seasonal vegetables; breast of chicken stuffed with brie and wrapped in smoked bacon; goat's cheese and onion marmalade tart; or The Crown Inn pork pie. On a fine day, enjoy the picturesque gardens overlooking the valley and watch the red kites circling overhead. In winter experience the warmth and cosy atmosphere of the three log fires.

Open all wk 11.30-3 6-11 (Sun noon-3 7-10) Closed: 25-26 Dec
Bar Meals L served all wk 12-2.30 D served all wk 7-9.30 **Restaurant** L served all wk 12-2.30 D served all wk 7-9.30
⊕ FREE HOUSE ◀ Brakspears, West Berkshire Brewery, Loddon Brewery, Marlow Brewery. **Facilities** Children's portions Dogs allowed Garden Parking

PICK OF THE PUBS

The Royal Oak ⏲

RAMSDEN　　　　　Map 11 SP31

High St OX7 3AU
☎ **01993 868213**
web: www.royaloakramsden.com
dir: *From Witney take B4022 towards Charlbury, then right before Hailey, through Poffley End*

This 17th-century former coaching inn was once the stopping off point for the London to Hereford stagecoach. These days, it is more popular with walkers using it as a base to explore the fabulous countryside that surrounds the pretty Cotswold village of Ramsden. Whether you are walking or not, the inn makes a fine place to stop for refreshment, and its old beams, warm fires and stone walls provide a very cosy welcome. The Royal Oak is a free house with beers sourced from local breweries, such as Hook Norton Old Hooky, and Wye Valley from neighbouring Herefordshire. Somerset's Original Cider Company supplies the bar with Pheasant Plucker cider, alongside Weston's Old Rosie from Herefordshire.

With a strong kitchen team, the main menu, built on the very best of fresh local and seasonal ingredients, regularly features a pie of the week topped with puff pastry or the popular suet pudding; there are other pub favourites such as Italian-style meatballs served on linguine

with tomato sauce, fresh crab and smoked salmon fishcakes with tomato and sweet pepper sauce, home-made bacon cheeseburger with French fries. Aberdeen Angus beef is available in the form of sirloin and rump steaks, cooked to your liking on the char-grill. Other popular options include half-shoulder of new season lamb with rosemary and garlic jus; baked fillet of cod with tapenade crust served with mash; chargrilled vegetable lasagne. Every Thursday evening there is a special offer of steak, with a glass of wine and dessert included. Carefully selected by the owner, the wine list has over 200 wines, specialising in those from Bordeaux and Languedoc, with 30 of them served by the glass.

Open all wk 11.30-3 6.30-11 (Sun 11.30-3 7.00-10.30) Closed: 25 Dec
Bar Meals L served all wk 12-2 D served Mon-Sat 7-9.45 Sun 7-9 Av main course £12 **Restaurant** L served all wk 12-2 D served Mon-Sat 7-9.45 Sun 7-9 Fixed menu price fr £21.95 Av 3 course à la carte fr £21 ⊕ FREE HOUSE ◣ Hook Norton Old Hooky, Best, Adnams Broadside, Youngs Special, Hook Norton Bitter, Wye Valley ◌ Old Rosie, Pheasant Plucker. ⏲ 30 **Facilities** Dogs allowed Garden Parking

SHILTON   Map 5 SP20

Rose & Crown ♥ NEW

OX18 4AB ☎ 01993 842280

dir: From A40 at Burford take A361 towards Lechlade on Thames. Right, follow Shilton signs on left. Or from A40 E of Burford take B4020 towards Carteton

A traditional Cotswold stone inn dating back to the 17th century, two miles south of Burford. Each of the two rooms has original beams and a log fire, helping to meld seamlessly its twin functions of friendly village local and destination food pub. Two mainstay real ales are augmented by a regularly changing guest and Westons vintage organic cider. Chef/landlord Martin Coldicott and head chef Jamie Webber are both classically trained (the Connaught and the Ivy respectively), so expect way above average dishes featuring locally sourced produce – pork and duck cassoulet or game pie.

Open all wk Mon-Thu 11.30-3 6-11 (Fri-Sun & BHs 11.30-11) **Bar Meals** L served Mon-Fri 12-2, wknds & BH 12-2.45 D served all wk 7-9 Av main course £12 ⊕ FREE HOUSE ◀ Hook Norton Old Hooky Ö Westons Organic Vintage. ♥ 10 **Facilities** Children welcome Dogs allowed Garden Parking

SHIPTON-UNDER-WYCHWOOD   Map 10 SP21

PICK OF THE PUBS

The Shaven Crown Hotel ♥

High St OX7 6BA ☎ 01993 830330
e-mail: relax@theshavencrown.co.uk
dir: On A361, halfway between Burford & Chipping Norton opposite village green & church

This 14th-century coaching inn is among the ten oldest in England. As its name suggests, The Shaven Crown was built by the monks of Bruern Abbey as a hospice for the poor. Following the Dissolution of the monasteries, Elizabeth I used it as a hunting lodge before giving it to the village in 1580, when it became the Crown Inn. It was not until 1930 that a brewery with a sense of humour changed the name to reflect the hairstyle favoured by monks. A 700-year-old honey-coloured Cotswold stone building set around a medieval courtyard, its interior is full of charm and character, brimming with original features, plus warming winter fires. Light meals and real ales from breweries such as Hook Norton and Goffs are served in the bar, while the restaurant offers a more serious style of dining. Begin with drinks in the impressive Great Hall, then settle down to starters of home-made salmon fritters with sweet chilli sauce, followed perhaps by braised lamb shank with root vegetable gravy and mashed potato. Chalkboard menus also offer pie of the week and sausage of the week. In warmer weather, dine in the courtyard or gardens.

Open all wk 11-3 5-11 (Sat-Sun 11-11)
Bar Meals L served Mon-Fri 12-2, Sat 12-9.30, Sun 12-9 booking required D served Mon-Fri 6-9.30, Sat 12-9.30, Sun 12-9 booking required Av main course £12.95 **Restaurant** L served Mon-Fri 12-2, Sat 12-9.30, Sun 12-9 booking required D served Mon-Fri 6-9.30, Sat 12-9.30, Sun 12-9 booking required Fixed menu price fr £12.95 ⊕ FREE HOUSE ◀ Hook Norton Ales, Wye Valley, Goffs, Cottage Brewery Ö Westons Stowford Press. ♥ 10 **Facilities** Children welcome Children's menu Children's portions Dogs allowed Garden Parking Wi-fi

SHUTFORD   Map 11 SP34

PICK OF THE PUBS

The George & Dragon ♥

See Pick of the Pubs on opposite page

SOUTH STOKE   Map 5 SU58

The Perch and Pike ★★★ INN ♥

RG8 0JS ☎ 01491 872415   🖷 01491 871001
e-mail: info@perchandpike.co.uk
dir: On Ridgeway Hiking Trail. 1.5m N of Goring & 4m S of Wallingford on B4009

The Perch and Pike, just two minutes' walk from the River Thames, was the village's foremost beer house back in the 17th century. There is a welcoming atmosphere in the original pub and in the adjoining barn conversion, which houses the 42-seater restaurant. Food ranges from a selection of salads, baguettes and ploughman's to the likes of avocado tower with summer green salad and honey and mustard dressing to start, followed by roasted breast of duck bigarade flamed with Cointreau with an orange and lemon sauce. Four comfortable bedrooms are available.

Open all wk 11.30-3 5.30-11 (Sat-Sun 11.30-11)
Bar Meals L served Mon-Sat 12-2.30 booking required D served Mon-Sat 7-9.30 booking required Av main course £9.50 **Restaurant** L served Sun 12-2.30 booking required D served Mon-Sat 7-9.30 booking required Av 3 course à la carte fr £27 ⊕ BRAKSPEAR ◀ Brakspear, 1 guest ale. ♥ 10 **Facilities** Children welcome Children's portions Dogs allowed Garden Parking **Rooms** 4

STEEPLE ASTON   Map 11 SP42

The Red Lion NEW

South Side OX25 4RY ☎ 01869 340225
e-mail: redlionsa@aol.com
dir: 0.5m off A4260 (Oxford Rd). Follow brown tourist signs for pub

Situated high in the beautiful North Oxfordshire village of Steeple Aston, this unspoilt 18th-century pub has a majestic view of the Cherwell Valley from its pretty floral sun-trap terrace. Close to Blenheim Palace and Banbury Cross, the pub is a popular place for thirsty walkers to

enjoy a pint of local Hook Norton beer and dogs are welcome. The new conservatory-style oak dining room offers home-made pies, stone-baked pizzas, local game and sirloin steaks carved from the strip to order.

Open all wk 12-3 5.30-11 (Sat 12-11, Sun 12-5) Closed: Sun eve from 5pm **Bar Meals** L served all wk 12-2.30 booking required D served Mon-Sat 6-9 booking required Av main course £11 **Restaurant** L served all wk 12-2.30 booking required D served Mon-Sat 6-9 booking required Av 3 course à la carte fr £17.95 ⊕ HOOK NORTON ◀ Hooky Bitter, Double Stout, seasonal ales Ö Stowford Press. **Facilities** Children welcome Children's portions Dogs allowed Garden Parking Wi-fi

STOKE ROW   Map 5 SU68

PICK OF THE PUBS

Crooked Billet ♥

RG9 5PU ☎ 01491 681048   🖷 01491 682231
dir: From Henley towards Oxford on A4130. Left at Nettlebed for Stoke Row

Built in 1642, The Crooked Billet was once the hideout of notorious highwayman Dick Turpin. Tucked away down a single track lane in deepest Oxfordshire, this charmingly rustic pub is now a popular hideaway for the well-heeled and the well known. Many of its finest features are unchanged, including the low beams, tiled floors and open fires that are so integral to its character. Local produce and organic fare are the mainstays of the kitchen, to the extent that the chef/proprietor will even exchange a lunch or dinner for the locals' excess vegetables. A la carte offerings include starters like smoked eel, warm potato and mustard seed salad. To follow, there's a good range of fish mains, including grilled halibut, langoustine tails, broad beans and Champagne cream. Other alternatives include Moroccan spiced rump of lamb, harissa, chargrilled Mediterranean vegetables, couscous. The pub hosts music nights, wine tastings and other events.

Open all wk noon-3 7-mdnt (Sat-Sun noon-mdnt) Closed: 25 Dec **Bar Meals** L served Mon-Fri 12-2.30, Sat 12-10.30, Sun 12-10 booking required D served Mon-Fri 7-10, Sat 12-10.30, Sun 12-10 booking required **Restaurant** L served Mon-Fri 12-2.30, Sat 12-10.30, Sun 12-10 booking required D served Mon-Fri 7-10, Sat 12-10.30, Sun 12-10 booking required ⊕ BRAKSPEAR ◀ Brakspear Bitter. ♥ 10 **Facilities** Children welcome Children's portions Garden Parking

PICK OF THE PUBS

The George & Dragon ♟

SHUTFORD   Map 11 SP34

Church Ln OX15 6PG ☎ 01295 780320
web: www.thegeorgeanddragon.com
dir: *Take A422 from Banbury. After 4m*
turn left at sign for Shutford, follow
directly to pub

A favourite rest stop for ramblers, this
attractive Cotswold stone country pub is
built into the side of a hill, with the village
church directly above. Dating back to the
13th century, the pub is conveniently
located at the start of the popular
Shutford Walk and is a favourite rest stop
for ramblers who congregate in the beer
garden overlooking the picturesque
village. Legend has it that several ghosts
haunt the pub, and that a secret tunnel
links it to the manor house. The bar (where
dogs are welcome, and where in winter the
locals play dominoes by the roaring fire) is
probably unique in that it is actually
twelve feet underground. That's surely
something to think about while ordering
one of the five real ales, or a refreshing
glass of wine. Everything on the seasonal
menus, except for the locally baked bread,
is made from scratch; villagers bring in
game and vegetables from their
allotments. In the recently refurbished
restaurant, look to the specials list to find
pan-roasted cod steak, green Puy lentils
and red wine sauce or cep and confit
garlic risotto with Parmesan crisp. The à
la carte menu will tempt with slow-
braised ox cheeks, gratin dauphinoise and
roasted vegetables; pan-fried sea bass
fillet, steamed spinach, sautéed king
scallop and cauliflower purée; or venison
Wellington, red cabbage, duxelle confit,
baby onions and port wine sauce. To
finish, lemon posset with plum compote
and citrus biscotti, and apple and thyme
tarte Tatin with vanilla mascarpone cream
cannot be resisted. If you just want a bar
snack before heading off round the
ancient tracks of the Shutford Walk, try a
mature Cheddar ploughman's with apple
and celery salad, or warm steak and onion
sandwich with chips and salad.
Alternatively, forget the walk and time
your visit for a Sunday — you'll be choosing
from the likes of roast rib of Oxfordshire
beef with roast potatoes and mixed
vegetables, followed by spiced apple and
raspberry crumble.

Open all wk 6-11 (Sat-Sun all day)
Bar Meals L served Sat-Sun 12-2.30
D served Mon-Sat 6.30-9 Av main course
£8 **Restaurant** L served Sat-Sun 12-2.30
D served Mon-Sat 6.30-9 Fixed menu price
fr £10 Av 3 course à la carte fr £20
🛢 FREE HOUSE ◀ Hooky Bitter, London
Pride, Old Peculier, Pedigree, Bombardier.
♟ 8 **Facilities** Children's portions Dogs
allowed Garden

SWERFORD
Map 11 SP33

PICK OF THE PUBS

The Mason's Arms ◉

Banbury Rd OX7 4AP
☎ **01608 683212** 📠 **01608 683105**
e-mail: admin@masons-arms.com
dir: *Between Banbury & Chipping Norton on A361*

A 300-year-old, stone-built former Masonic lodge, this award-winning pub in the Cotswolds has retained its traditional, informal feel. Owners Jude and Vicky Kelly took over in summer 2010. The modern British cooking concentrates on local produce where possible with great attention paid to sourcing and seasonality. You might begin with a Bloody Mary sorbet with black pepper jelly and celery sticks, or pickled fillet of black bream, with pickled samphire and orange oil, followed perhaps by confit of Gloucester Old Spot pork belly glazed with maple syrup, pancetta lardons and cardamon bubble and squeak, or poached loin of rabbit wrapped in Parma ham with roast new potatoes. They also offer Pub Classics - dishes like home baked ham, duck egg and chips, or faggots with mash, Hooky gravy and peas.

Open all wk 10-3 6-11 Closed: 25-26 Dec ⊕ FREE HOUSE ◀ Hook Norton Best, Theakstons Best. **Facilities** Children welcome Children's menu Garden Parking Wi-fi

SWINBROOK
Map 5 SP21

PICK OF THE PUBS

The Swan Inn
INN ◉◉ ♀

OX18 4DY ☎ **01993 823339** 📠 **01993 823167**
e-mail: info@theswanswinbrook.co.uk
dir: *A40 towards Cheltenham, left towards Swinbrook, pub 1 mile before Burford*

Hidden in the Windrush Valley you will find the idyllic village of Swinbrook where time stands still. Owners Archie and Nicola Orr-Ewing took on the lease of this dreamy, wisteria-clad stone pub from Dowager Duchess of Devonshire, the last surviving Mitford sister, in 2007. The Swan is the perfect English country pub - it stands by the River Windrush near the village cricket pitch, overlooking unspoilt Cotswold countryside. It gets even better inside, the two cottage-style front rooms, replete with worn flagstones, crackling log fires, low beams and country furnishings, leading through to a cracking bar and classy conservatory extension. First-class pub food ranges from simple bar snacks like hot salt beef and horseradish cream sandwiches to more substantial main courses of roast pork belly with a warm salad of gnocchi, bok choi and chorizo. You won't want to leave, so book one of the stunning en suite rooms in the restored barn.

Open all wk (Closed afternoons Nov-15 Mar) Closed: 25 Dec **Bar Meals** L served all wk 12-2 booking required D served all wk 7-9 booking required **Restaurant** L served all wk 12-2 booking required D served all wk 7-9 booking required ⊕ FREE HOUSE ◀ Hook Norton, Wadworths 6X, Purity ♂ Addlestones, Westons Organic. ♀ 9 **Facilities** Children welcome Children's menu Children's portions Dogs allowed Garden Parking Wi-fi **Rooms** 6

SYDENHAM
Map 5 SP70

PICK OF THE PUBS

The Crown Inn

Sydenham Rd OX39 4NB ☎ **01844 351634**
dir: *M40 junct 6 take B4009 towards Chinnor. Left onto A40. At Postcombe turn right to Sydenham*

In a small village below the scarp slopes of the Chilterns, this pretty 16th-century inn shows how careful refurbishment can successfully incorporate both traditional and modern styles. Old photographs, for example, hang contentedly alongside contemporary paintings. The menu is short – barely a dozen items are featured – but expect good things of those that are, such as main courses of slow-roasted Moroccan spiced lamb shank with baked potato mash; barbecued Jack Daniel's-glazed rack of pork ribs; grilled Cornish sea bass fillet with king prawn, ginger, chilli and spring onion salsa; and spinach and wild mushroom risotto. In the bar, a pint of Brakspear would go well with a ploughman's, omelette, baguette or pizza. Treasure Hunts starting and finishing at The Crown take you through some of the prettiest villages in this part of Oxfordshire.

Open 12-3 5.30-11 (Sat noon-11 Sun noon-3) Closed: 1 wk Jan, 1 wk Aug, Sun eve, Mon **Bar Meals** L served Tue-Sun 12-2.30 D served Tue-Sat 7-9.30 **Restaurant** L served Tue-Sun 12-2.30 D served Tue-Sat 7-9.30 ⊕ THE SYDENHAM PUB CO ◀ Brakspear, London Pride, Guinness, Guest ale ♂ Stowford Press, Thatchers Gold. **Facilities** Children welcome Children's portions Dogs allowed Garden

TETSWORTH
Map 5 SP60

The Old Red Lion ♀

40 High St OX9 7AS ☎ **01844 281274**
e-mail: info@theoldredliontetsworth.co.uk
dir: *Oxford Service area, turn right onto A40. At T-junct turn left then right onto A40 signed Stokenchurch, via Milton Common to Tetsworth*

This pink-washed pub is right on the village green, which conveniently has a large enclosed children's play area. In the relaxing bar area real ales change seasonally. Food can be enjoyed in Nemards restaurant behind the bar, or in the quieter Library room for private dining. Dishes might be beef and ale pie; liver, onions and bacon; jumbo cod and chips; sticky toffee pudding; and home-made fruit crumble. There is also a Sunday carvery with three meats to choose from. Head outside to the patio area on warmer days from where red kites can be spotted.

Open all wk 12-3 5.30-11 **Bar Meals** L served all wk 12-2.30 D served all wk 6-9 Av main course £6.99 **Restaurant** L served all wk 12-2.30 D served all wk 6-9 ⊕ FREE HOUSE ♀ 8 **Facilities** Children welcome Children's portions Dogs allowed Garden Parking Wi-fi

THAME
Map 5 SP70

PICK OF THE PUBS

The James Figg NEW

21 Cornmarket OX9 2BL ☎ **01844 260166**
e-mail: info@thejamesfiggthame.co.uk
dir: *In town centre*

An attractive 18th-century pub close to Thame's market place, The James Figg celebrates one of the town's most famous sons – England's first undisputed champion boxer who lived in the pub 300 years ago before moving to London to run a school teaching the gentry the noble art of self-defence. The pub has a traditional look with dark wood floors, Ercol Windsor chairs, a double-sided open fire and a curving bar dispensing three real ales including the locally brewed Brill Vale Best Bitter. The kitchen keeps to the classics, from roast meat rolls dripping with gravy to pies made by a local award-winning butcher. There are sandwiches, bar snacks and old favourites such as scampi, chips and tartare sauce; honey roast ham with egg and chips; spaghetti and meat balls with spicy tomato sauce. Beyond The Stables function room, you'll find the pub's secret garden.

Open all day 10am-mdnt Closed: 25 Dec **Bar Meals** L served all wk 12-2.30 D served all wk 6-9.30 Av main course £7.50 ⊕ PEACH PUBS ◀ Vale Best Bitter, Purity Mad Goose. **Facilities** Children welcome Children's portions Dogs allowed Garden Parking Wi-fi

The Thatch ♀ NEW

29-30 Lower High St OX9 2AA ☎ **01844 214340**
e-mail: thatch@peachpubs.com
dir: *In town centre*

Originally a row of 16th-century cottages, this thatched pub is a warren of rooms with inglenook fireplaces and antique furniture. If you make it past the bar without being tempted by coffee, cakes or a pint of Old Hooky, you'll find yourself in the restaurant overlooking the sunny courtyard garden. The kitchen focuses on the best seasonal ingredients - clams, chorizo and white wine herb linguine might be followed by beef, mushroom and ale pie.

Open all day all wk 10am-mdnt Closed: 25 Dec **Bar Meals** L served all wk 12-6 D served all wk 6-9.30 Av main course £8.50 food served all day **Restaurant** L served all wk 12-2.45 D served all wk 6-9.30 Av 3 course à la carte fr £22.50 ⊕ PEACH PUBS ◀ Wychert Ale, Old Hooky ♂ Aspall. ♀ 13 **Facilities** Children welcome Children's portions Dogs allowed Garden Parking Wi-fi

TOOT BALDON   Map 5 SP50

PICK OF THE PUBS

The Mole Inn @@ ⬥

OX44 9NG ☎ **01865 340001** 📠 **01865 343011**
e-mail: info@themoleinn.com
dir: *5m SE from Oxford city centre off B480*

It's abundantly clear that those refurbishing this
300-year-old country pub knew exactly what they
wanted to achieve. And achieve it they did, as made
clear by discerning customers who now happily travel
to this amusingly named village to relax with pints of
Hook Norton in leather sofas amid stripped beams,
solid white walls and terracotta floors, or enjoy the
exciting, two AA Rosette awarded culinary output of
award-winning chef/host Gary Witchalls and the front-
of-house professionalism of his wife, Jenny. Gary is big
on provenance: his 28-day dry-aged steaks are from
Aberdeenshire; lamb comes from Cornish flocks; free-
range, rare-breed Blythburgh pigs provide the pork;
and fish arrives daily from Devon and Cornwall. Clues
aplenty there, and then there are the grilled pavé of
salmon with honey and sage roasted vegetables,
pancetta and horseradish mash; the slow-cooked
shoulder of marsh lamb with minted pea mash and
curly kale; and the fettuccine, wild mushrooms and
spinach.

Open all day all wk 12-12 (Sun 12-11) Closed: 25 Dec
Restaurant L served Mon-Sat 12-2.30, Sun 12-4
booking required D served Mon-Sat 7-9.30, Sun 6-9
booking required ⊕ FREE HOUSE ◀ Hook Norton,
London Pride, Spitfire, Guinness. ⬥ 11
Facilities Children welcome Children's
menu Children's portions Garden Parking

WALLINGFORD   Map 5 SU68

The Partridge @@ ⬥ NEW

32 Saint Mary St OX10 0ET
☎ **01491 825005** 📠 **01491 837153**
e-mail: contact@partridge-inn.com
dir: *From M40 junct 6, B4009, follow Wallingford signs
through Watlington to Benson. A4074 to rdbt. Right
through Crowmarsh Gifford to Wallingford*

Leather chairs, wood fires and lovely mirrors form the
background to a menu of modern British and French
rustic dishes at this recently updated Wallingford venue.
New owner and chef José Cau has created a foodie's
haven where the Market Menu might feature local
pheasant with artichoke and onion purée; English belly
pork with braised red cabbage; or roast butternut squash
risotto with truffle broth. Good ales, a formidable wine
list and a pleasant garden complete the picture.

Open all wk 12-3 5-11 **Bar Meals** L served all wk 12-2.30
D served all wk 6-9.30 Av main course £12
Restaurant L served all wk 12-2.30 D served all wk
6-9.30 Fixed menu price fr £13.95 Av 3 course à la carte
fr £30 ⊕ GREENE KING ◀ Abbot Ale, Old Speckled Hen.
⬥ 12 **Facilities** Children welcome Children's
menu Children's portions Garden

WANTAGE   Map 5 SU38

The Hare

Reading Rd, West Hendred OX12 8RH
☎ **01235 833249** 📠 **01235 833268**
dir: *At West Hendred on A417 between Wantage & Didcot*

A late 19th-century inn mid-way between Wantage and
Didcot, modernised in the 1930s by local brewers,
Morland. The building's exterior features a colonial-style
veranda and colonnade, while inside are original wood
floors, beams and an open fire. Steaks, the house
speciality, can be cut to any size to order. Jackets,
baguettes, sandwiches and salads at lunchtime are
superseded by more adventurous fare in the evening –
the fish mixed grill, for example, includes marlin and
barramundi.

Open all day all wk ⊕ GREENE KING ◀ Morland Original,
Guest ales Ⓒ Stowford Press, St Heliers.
Facilities Children welcome Children's portions Dogs
allowed Garden Parking

WEST HANNEY   Map 5 SU49

Plough Inn ⬥ NEW

Church St OX12 0LN ☎ **01235 868674**
e-mail: info@ploughwesthanney.co.uk
dir: *From Wantage take A338 towards Oxford. Inn in 1m*

A pub for 'only' 180 years, although the building dates
back to around 1525. In their seven years here, in which
time they became a free house, Trevor and Ann Cooper
have created a friendly village inn, with log fires, roast
chestnuts, mulled wine and their own damson gin. From
the kitchen comes toad-in-the-hole; Aberdeen Angus
burger; Windrush trout pasta salad; and asparagus and
wild mushroom pie, as well as daily specials and snacks.
Barbecues are hosted in the pretty walled garden in
summer and beer festivals take place on May and August
Bank Holidays.

Open all wk 12-3 6-12 (Sat-Sun all day)
Bar Meals L served all wk 12-3 D served all wk 6-9 Av
main course £9 **Restaurant** L served all wk 12-2 booking
required D served all wk 6-9 booking required Fixed menu
price fr £12.50 Av 3 course à la carte fr £20 ⊕ FREE
HOUSE ◀ West Berkshire Ales, Loddon Ales, Vale Brewery
Ales, Wychwood Ales Ⓒ Westons Scrumpy, Thatchers
Gold. ⬥ 10 **Facilities** Children welcome Children's
menu Children's portions Play area Dogs allowed Garden
Beer festival Parking Wi-fi

WESTON-ON-THE-GREEN   Map 11 SP51

The Ben Jonson ⬥ NEW

OX25 3RA ☎ **01869 351153**
e-mail: dine@thebenjonsonpub.co.uk
web: www.thebenjonsonpub.co.uk
dir: *M40 junct 9, A34 towards Oxford. 1st exit onto B430.
At rdbt right into village. Pub on left*

Dating from 1742, the pub was named after the English
Renaissance dramatist, poet and actor, who would visit
the pub on his way to visit William Shakespeare in
Stratford. The pub has a separate bar and dining area,
as well as a secluded terrace garden. The food is sourced
as locally as possible and all real ales are from
Oxfordshire, as are a number of wines. Simple, seasonal
dishes include lamb stew, smoked haddock fishcakes
and braised pigs' cheeks and mash.

Open all day all wk 12-11 **Bar Meals** L served all wk 12-9
booking required D served all wk 12-9 booking required
food served all day **Restaurant** L served all wk 12-9
booking required D served all wk 12-9 booking required
food served all day ⊕ PUNCH TAVERNS ◀ Brakspear,
Hobgoblin, Old Hooky, White Horse. ⬥ 14
Facilities Children welcome Children's menu Children's
portions Dogs allowed Garden Parking Wi-fi

WHEATLEY   Map 5 SP50

Bat & Ball Inn

28 High St OX44 9HJ
☎ **01865 874379** 📠 **01865 873363**
e-mail: info@batball.co.uk
dir: *Through Wheatley towards Garsington, turn left
signed Cuddesdon*

No surprise that the bar here is packed to the gunnels
with cricketing memorabilia, but the charm of this former
coaching inn extends to beamed ceilings, flagstone floors
and solid wood furniture warmed by an open log fire. The
house ale 'LBW' is flanked by interesting and well-kept
guests. A comprehensive seasonal menu, supplemented
by daily specials, is likely to include the Bat burger, home
made from steak and with a choice of toppings, and
slow-braised shoulder of lamb. Look out for clay pigeon
shoots, pig roasts, steak nights and sausage and mash
evenings. The pub is in an ideal spot for walkers.

Open all day all wk **Bar Meals** L served Mon-Fri 12-2.30,
Sat-Sun all day booking required D served Mon-Fri
6-9.30, Sat-Sun all day booking required Av main course
£10 **Restaurant** L served Mon-Fri 12-2.30, Sat-Sun all
day booking required D served Mon-Fri 6-9.30, Sat-Sun
all day booking required Av 3 course à la carte fr £20
⊕ MARSTONS ◀ Marston's Pedigree, House LBW Bitter,
Guinness Ⓒ Thatchers Gold. **Facilities** Children
welcome Children's menu Children's portions Dogs
allowed Garden Parking Wi-fi

WITNEY
Map 5 SP31

The Fleece ★★★ INN ♀ NEW

11 Church Green OX28 4AZ ☎ 01993 892270
e-mail: fleece@peachpubs.com
dir: *In town centre*

Overlooking the village's beautiful church green in the heart of picturesque Witney, this fine Georgian building was once the home of Clinch's brewery. Nowadays, it serves food and drink all day, from bacon sarnies to dinner, with well-kept ales attracting locals and visitors alike. The appealing modern British menu might include salmon and leek fishcake with beetroot and spring onion salad or slow-roast Cornish lamb with rosemary dauphinoise, creamed leeks and redcurrant jus. Spacious accommodation is available.

Open all day all wk **Bar Meals** L served all wk 12-6.30 D served all wk 6.30-10 Av main course £13.50 food served all day **Restaurant** L served all wk 12-2.30 booking required D served all wk 6.30-10 booking required Av 3 course à la carte fr £22-£25 food served all day ⊕ PEACH PUBS ◀ Old Speckled Hen, Greene King IPA, guest ale Ò Aspall. **Facilities** Children welcome Children's portions Dogs allowed Parking Wi-fi **Rooms** 10

The Three Horseshoes ♀

78 Corn St OX28 6BS ☎ 01993 703086
e-mail: thehorseshoeswitney@hotmail.co.uk
dir: *From Oxford on A40 towards Cheltenham take 2nd turn to Witney. At rdbt take 5th exit to Witney. Over flyover, through lights. At next rdbt take 5th exit into Corn St. Pub on left*

Built of Cotswold stone, the historic Grade II listed building sits on Witney's original main street. A traditional family-run pub, it has a charming and stylish interior with stone walls, low ceilings, wood and flagstone floors, and blazing log fires in winter. An impressive selection of ales includes Ringwood Fortyniner and Wychwood Green Goblin; there's an annual beer festival on August Bank Holiday. Dishes range from simple sandwiches and a grill menu through to dishes such as Cornish crab cake with vanilla and lime mayonnaise, followed by Gressingham duck breast with fondant potato.

Open all day all wk 11am-12.30am **Bar Meals** L served all wk 12-3 D served all wk 6-10 Av main course £12 **Restaurant** L served all wk 12-3 D served all wk 6-10 Fixed menu price fr £12 Av 3 course à la carte fr £14 ⊕ ADMIRAL TAVERNS ◀ White Horse, Ringwood Fortyniner, Wychwood Hobgoblin, Brakspears Bitter, Hook Norton Ò Wychwood Green Goblin, Westons Stowford Press. ♀ 10 **Facilities** Children welcome Children's portions Dogs allowed Garden Beer festival Wi-fi

WOODSTOCK
Map 11 SP41

The Kings Arms ★★★ HL ◉ ♀ NEW

19 Market St OX20 1SU
☎ 01993 813636 📠 01993 813737
e-mail: stay@kingshotelwoodstock.co.uk
dir: *In town centre, on corner of Market St & A44*

An imposing Georgian building at the heart of historic Woodstock, just a short stroll to England's largest private residence, Blenheim Palace. Such grand heritage is reflected in the very British menu here - braised skirt of beef in stout; baked smoked haddock or roast beetroot, thyme and Oxford Blue cheese tart, partnered with beers from the Brakspear stable, taken in the comfortable bar areas with their stripped wooden floors, log burning stove and marble top bars, or stylish Atrium Restaurant. One AA Rosette for the cuisine complements the contemporary accommodation here.

Open all day all wk **Bar Meals** L served Mon-Fri 12-2.30, Sat 12-3, Sun all day D served Mon-Sat 6.30-9, Sun all day **Restaurant** L served Mon-Fri 12-2.30, Sat 12-3, Sun all day booking required D served Mon-Sat 6.30-9, Sun all day booking required ⊕ FREE HOUSE ◀ Brakspear Bitter, Oxford Gold Bitter Ò Thatchers Green Goblin. ♀ 11 **Facilities** Children welcome Children's portions Garden Wi-fi **Rooms** 15

The King's Head

11 Park Ln OX20 1UD ☎ 01993 812164
e-mail: mail@kingsheadwoodstock.co.uk
dir: *Off A44, between Oxford & Chipping Norton. Turn left at pharmacy onto Park Lane*

Close to the World Heritage Site of Blenheim Palace, this pub dates from 1801. To the front its cosy bar with original stone walls and open fireplace stocks at least two Oxfordshire ales; to the rear are a large dining room and attractive courtyard. Well known locally for being a 'spud pub', it celebrates the best of British food by using as much local produce as possible. The ploughman's features Oxford Blue, while main dishes may include honey-roast Callow Farm ham with double egg and chips. Change of hands.

Open all day all wk ⊕ PUNCH TAVERNS ◀ Brakspear, Hobgoblin. **Facilities** Children welcome Children's menu Children's portions Dogs allowed Garden Wi-fi

WOOLSTONE
Map 5 SU28

The White Horse

SN7 7QL ☎ 01367 820726 📠 01367 820566
dir: *Off A420 at Watchfield onto B4508 towards Longcot signed Woolstone*

Unusual windows add to the appeal of this black-and-white-timbered, thatched, Elizabethan village pub, which is perfect for those who enjoy walking and exploring nearby White Horse Hill, the Ridgeway and other ancient monuments. Upholstered stools line the traditional bar, where a fireplace conceals two priest holes, visible to those who don't mind getting their knees dirty. For lunch, there is a choice of starters, light bites and larger snacks. In the oak-beamed restaurant, the evening menu might include pan-fried rare breed pork fillet and spinach mash served with black pudding and devilled herb cream sauce, or Thai roasted monkfish and salmon served with chilli potatoes and coconut curry. Recent change of hands.

Open all day all wk 11am-11pm **Bar Meals** L served Mon-Sat 12-2.30, Sun 12-3 booking required D served Mon-Sat 6-9 booking required Av main course £12 **Restaurant** L served Mon-Sat 12-2.30, Sun 12-3 booking required D served Mon-Sat 6-9 booking required ⊕ ARKELLS BREWERY ◀ Arkells, Moonlight Summer Ale, Guinness Ò Stowford Press. **Facilities** Children welcome Children's portions Dogs allowed Garden Parking Wi-fi

WYTHAM
Map 5 SP40

White Hart ♀

OX2 8QA ☎ 01865 244372
e-mail: whitehartwytham@btconnect.com
dir: *Just off A34 NW of Oxford*

In a sleepy hamlet west of Oxford, this Cotswold stone pub, now under new ownership, was featured in the *Inspector Morse* TV series. The pub is more 'smart gastro-pub' than traditional village local, the bold interior blending flagged floors and big stone fireplaces with a contemporary style. You can pop in for a pint but this is predominantly a place to eat, and boasts an extensive wine list. In summer, dine alfresco on the Mediterranean-style terrace.

Open all wk Mon-Fri 12-4 6-11 (Sat-Sun noon-11) **Bar Meals** L served Mon-Sun 12-4 D served Mon-Fri 6-10, Sat-Sun 6-11 **Restaurant** L served Mon-Sun 12-4 D served Mon-Fri 6-10, Sat-Sun 6-11 ⊕ WADWORTH & COMPANY ◀ Henry IPA, Wadworth 6X, Guest ales Ò Stowford Press. ♀ 15 **Facilities** Children welcome Children's menu Garden Parking Wi-fi

RUTLAND

BARROWDEN   Map 11 SK90

PICK OF THE PUBS

Exeter Arms ♥

LE15 8EQ ☎ 01572 747247 🖷 **01572 747247**
e-mail: enquiries@exeterarmrutland.co.uk
dir: *From A47 turn at landmark windmill, village 0.75m S. 6m E of Uppingham & 17m W of Peterborough*

Overlooking the green and duck pond in a pretty village not far from Rutland Water, this 17th-century pub-restaurant offers half an acre of garden with a pétanque court for lazy summer days. The attractive stone building has seen many roles in its long life, including a smithy, a dairy and a postal collection point. Landlord Martin Allsopp brews ales such as Beech, Bevin, Hopgear and Attitude Two in the on-site micro-brewery, and also offers a range of wines by the glass. Lunchtime sandwiches might include roast ham with wholegrain mustard; or mature Cheddar and chutney, whilst larger appetites can choose from hot dishes like beefburger with hand-cut chips; or slow-cooked lamb shank with kale colcannon. A typical dinner could begin with smoked haddock fishcake on spinach and green beans, followed by chicken breast with Parma ham and mushroom sauce.

Open 12-2.30 6-11 Closed: Sun eve, Mon L **Bar Meals** L served Tue-Sat 12-2 Av main course £10.95 **Restaurant** L served Tue-Sat 12-2 D served Tue-Sat 6.30-9 Fixed menu price fr £11.25 ⊕ FREE HOUSE ◀ Beech, Bevin, Owngear, Hopgear, Attitude Two, Pilot, Blackadder. ♥ 10 **Facilities** Dogs allowed Garden Parking

CLIPSHAM   Map 11 SK91

PICK OF THE PUBS

The Olive Branch ★★★★ INN ⑩⑩ ♥

Main St LE15 7SH
☎ 01780 410355 🖷 **01780 410000**
e-mail: info@theolivebranchpub.com
dir: *2m off A1 at B664 junct, N of Stamford*

The Olive Branch shows what can be done with careful thought and determined effort. The building was originally three farm labourers' cottages, knocked together to make a pub in 1890. It closed in 1997, before a revival which began two years later. Outside is an attractive front garden and terrace where home-made lemonade is served in summer. Inside, the beautifully refurbished interior has bookshelves and an eclectic mix of antique and pine furniture, with log fires and roasted chestnuts in winter. The bar serves local ales including Grainstore 1050, Olive Oil and Fenland, and Sheppy's real cider. From the two-AA Rosette kitchen come classics like braised shoulder of lamb with vegetable tumbet and herb crust; and loin of fallow buck venison, with juniper fondant, celeriac purée and red cabbage. If you time your visit for a

Sunday, the set lunch menu may start with pea and ham soup with black pudding fritters; continue with roast topside of beef with all the trimmings; and finish with treacle tart and yogurt ice cream. Elegant accommodation is available.

Open all wk noon-3.30 6-11 (Sat noon-11, Sun noon-10.30) Closed: 25 Dec eve **Bar Meals** L served Mon-Fri 12-2, Sat 12-2 2.30-5.30, Sun 12-3 D served Mon-Sat 7-9.30, Sun 7-9 Av main course £14.50 **Restaurant** L served Mon-Sat 12-2, Sun 12-3 booking required D served Mon-Sat 7-9.30, Sun 7-9 booking required Fixed menu price fr £16.95 Av 3 course à la carte fr £31 ⊕ RUTLAND INN COMPANY LTD ◀ Grainstore 1050 & Olive Oil, Fenland, Brewster's, VPA Ŏ Sheppy's Dabinett Apple, Oakwood Special, Cider with Honey. ♥ 13 **Facilities** Children welcome Children's menu Children's portions Dogs allowed Garden Parking Wi-fi **Rooms** 6

EMPINGHAM   Map 11 SK90

The White Horse Inn ★★★ INN ♥

Main St LE15 8PS ☎ 01780 460221 🖷 **01780 460521**
e-mail: info@whitehorserutland.co.uk
dir: *From A1 take A606 signed Oakham & Rutland Water. From Oakham take A606 to Stamford*

This stone-built former 17th-century courthouse has lost none of its period charm. The open fire, beamed bar, great selection of real ales and friendly staff makes it an ideal place to relax after a walk or cycle around Rutland Water. The menu begins with home-made soup, sandwiches and baguettes, whilst the specials board might feature hake fillet with lemon butter sauce; or lamb's liver with mash, smoked bacon and onion gravy. A choice of comfortable en suite bedrooms is also available.

Open all day all wk Closed: 25 Dec **Bar Meals** L served all wk 12-9 D served all wk 12-9 Av main course £10 food served all day **Restaurant** L served all wk 12-9 D served all wk 12-9 Av 3 course à la carte fr £20 food served all day ⊕ ENTERPRISE INNS ◀ John Smith's, Adnams Best Bitter, Oakham Ales JHB, Timothy Taylor Landlord, Black Sheep Bitter. ♥ 10 **Facilities** Children welcome Children's menu Children's portions Dogs allowed Garden Parking **Rooms** 13

EXTON   Map 11 SK91

PICK OF THE PUBS

Fox & Hounds ♥

19, The Green LE15 8AP ☎ 01572 812403
e-mail: sandra@foxandhoundsrutland.co.uk
dir: *Take A606 from Oakham towards Stamford, at Barnsdale turn left, after 1.5m turn right towards Exton. Pub in village centre*

Traditional English and Italian food is the hallmark of this imposing 17th-century free house, which stands opposite the green amid the charming stone and thatched cottages in the village centre. There's a

delightful walled garden, making this former coaching inn a perfect spot for a sunny day. The pub has a reputation for good food and hospitality, and is an ideal stopping-off point for walkers and cyclists exploring nearby Rutland Water and the surrounding area. Its menu is the work of Italian chef/proprietor Valter Floris and his team, and in the evenings there's an impressive list of authentic, thin-crust pizzas. In addition, the main menu features coq au vin with bacon, chestnut mushrooms, Savoy cabbage and new potatoes; roasted pumpkin and goat's cheese filo tartlets; and calves' liver with mash and onion gravy. Good beers include Grain Store Rutland Bitter.

Open 11-3 6-11 Closed: Mon ex BH **Bar Meals** L served all wk 12-2 booking required D served Tue-Sat 6-9 booking required Av main course £12 **Restaurant** L served all wk 12-2 booking required D served Tue-Sat 6-9 booking required ⊕ FREE HOUSE ◀ Greene King IPA, Grainstore 1050, Grainstore Rutland PGI Ŏ St Helier Pear, Aspall. ♥ 10 **Facilities** Children welcome Children's menu Children's portions Family room Dogs allowed Garden Parking Wi-fi

LYDDINGTON   Map 11 SP89

The Marquess of Exeter ★★★★ INN ♥
NEW

52 Main St LE15 9LT
☎ 01572 822477 🖷 **08082 801159**
e-mail: info@marquessexeter.co.uk
dir: *A1(N) exit towards Leicester/A4. At rdbt onto A47 towards Leicester. At Uppingham rdbt onto A6003/ Ayston Rd. Through Uppingham to Stoke Rd. Left into Lyddington, left onto Main St. Pub on left*

A tasteful mix of contemporary design and ultra-traditional village inn essentials (beams, flagstoned floor, crackling winter fires) distinguish this award-winning, ironstone-built thatched inn set in very picturesque Lyddington, close to the fascinating Bede House. An invigorating menu covers all the bases — braised oxtail or oven-roasted tart of mushroom — whilst the sharing dish, for example grilled rib of Derbyshire beef, is chef Brian Baker's signature dish; modern British comfort food at its best. Add a chic restaurant, shady beer garden and individually-designed comfortable bedrooms, and the mix is there for a memorable stay.

Open all day all wk **Bar Meals** L served Mon-Sat 12-2.30, Sun 12-3 D served Mon-Sat 6.30-10, Sun 6-9 Av main course £12.95 **Restaurant** L served Mon-Sat 12-2.30, Sun 12-3 D served Mon-Sat 6.30-10, Sun 6-9 Fixed menu price fr £11 Av 3 course à la carte fr £21.45 ⊕ MARSTONS ◀ Brakspear, Pedigree Ŏ Thatchers. ♥ 14 **Facilities** Children welcome Children's menu Children's portions Dogs allowed Garden Parking Wi-fi **Rooms** 18

LYDDINGTON *continued*

Old White Hart ★★★★ INN ♥

51 Main St LE15 9LR
☎ 01572 821703 📄 01572 821978
e-mail: mail@oldwhitehart.co.uk
dir: *From A6003 between Uppingham & Corby take B672. Pub on main street opp village green*

The honey-coloured sandstone cottages of rural Lyddington surround this 17th-century free house opposite the village green. It has retained its original beamed ceilings, stone walls and open fires, but in summer you can take a pint to the well-stocked gardens and listen to bell-ringing practice at the nearby church. Aspall's cider sits alongside a good choice of ales in the bar, a range expanded in summer by a beer festival. Week-day lunch menus are particularly good value: a starter of duck liver parfait could be followed by the White Hart's own sausages with bubble and squeak. Accommodation is available in converted cottages alongside the pub.

Open all wk 12-3 6.30-11 (Sun 12-3 7-10.30) Closed: 25 Dec, 26 Dec eve **Bar Meals** L served Mon-Sat 12-2, Sun 12-2.30 booking required D served all wk 6.30-9 booking required Av main course £11.95 **Restaurant** L served Mon-Sat 12-2, Sun 12-2.30 booking required D served all wk 6.30-9 booking required Fixed menu price fr £10.95 Av 3 course à la carte fr £18.65 ⊕ FREE HOUSE ◀ Greene King IPA, Timothy Taylor Landlord, Timothy Taylor Golden Best, Grainstore, Great Oakley Ŏ Aspall Suffolk Cider. ♥ 10 **Facilities** Children welcome Children's portions Play area Garden Beer festival Parking Wi-fi **Rooms** 10

OAKHAM | Map 11 SK80

Barnsdale Lodge Hotel ★★★ HL ☺

The Avenue, Rutland Water, North Shore LE15 8AH
☎ 01572 724678 📄 01572 724961
e-mail: enquiries@barnsdalelodge.co.uk
dir: *A1 onto A606. Hotel 5m on right, 2m E of Oakham*

This former farmhouse has been in the proprietor's family since 1760 and is part of the adjoining Exton Estate. It overlooks Rutland Water in the heart of this picturesque little county. There's a cosy bar with comfortable chairs and a courtyard with outdoor seating. The bistro-style menu draws on local produce and offers dishes such as tiger prawns with Caesar salad followed by seared spring lamb rump with chorizo, new potatoes and pea and mint jus. Accommodation comprises 44 stylish en suite rooms.

Open all day all wk ⊕ FREE HOUSE ◀ Rutland Grainstore, Tetley, Guinness. **Facilities** Children welcome Children's menu Children's portions Play area Dogs allowed Garden Parking Wi-fi **Rooms** 44

The Finch's Arms ★★★★ INN ♥ NEW

Oakham Rd, Hambleton LE15 8TL ☎ 01572 756575
e-mail: finchsarms@talk21.com
dir: *From Oakham take A606 signed Stamford. Turn right signed Upper Hambleton. Pub on left*

Beamed ceilings, cask ales and a small bustling bar characterise this traditional 17th-century free house, with magnificent views overlooking Rutland Water. Log fires warm the snug seating areas in winter, whilst in summer months there's an appealing outside terrace. Typical dishes in the Garden Room restaurant might include roast chicken with pea, smoked bacon and Parmesan risotto; or baked Cornish cod with buttered cabbage and hazelnut crust. Ten recently refurbished en suite bedrooms complete the picture.

Open all day all wk **Bar Meals** L served Mon-Sat 12-2.30, Sun 12-8 D served Mon-Sat 6.30-9.30 Av main course £13 **Restaurant** L served Mon-Sat 12-2.30, Sun 12-8 D served Mon-Sat 6.30-9.30 Fixed menu price fr £12.50-£19.95 Av 3 course à la carte fr £28 ⊕ PROPER PUB COMPANY ◀ Timothy Taylor Landlord, Black Sheep. ♥ 9 **Facilities** Children welcome Children's portions Garden Parking Wi-fi **Rooms** 10

The Grainstore Brewery

Station Approach LE15 6RE
☎ 01572 770065 📄 01572 770068
e-mail: enquiries@grainstorebrewery.com
dir: *Next to Oakham rail station*

Founded in 1995, Davis's Brewing Company is housed in the three-storey Victorian grain store next to Oakham railway station. Finest quality hops and ingredients are used to make the beers that can be sampled in the pub's Tap Room. Food is wholesome and straightforward, with the ales playing an important part in recipes for steamed fresh mussels; Cheddar and ale soup; Quenby Hall Stilton and Rutland Panther pâté; and beef and Panther stew. A full diary of events includes live music and the annual August Bank Holiday beer festival. Change of hands.

Open all day all wk 11am-1am ⊕ FREE HOUSE ◀ Rutlands Panther, Triple B, Ten Fifty, Silly Billy, Rutland Beast, Nip, seasonal beers Ŏ Sheppy's. **Facilities** Dogs allowed Garden Parking Wi-fi

SOUTH LUFFENHAM | Map 11 SK90

The Coach House Inn

3 Stamford Rd LE15 8NT
☎ 01780 720166 📄 01780 720866
e-mail: thecoachhouse123@aol.com
dir: *On A6121, off A47 between Morcroft & Stamford*

Horses were once stabled here while weary travellers enjoyed a drink in what is now a private house next door. Now elegantly refurbished, it offers a comfortable 40-cover dining room and a cosy bar. A short, appealing menu in the Ostler's Restaurant might feature cassoulet of chorizo with garlic Parmesan bread; hazelnut-crusted pork fillet with dauphinoise potatoes; or traditional oven baked lasagne.

Open noon-2 5-11 (Sat all day) Closed: 25 Dec, 1 Jan, Sun eve, Mon morning **Bar Meals** L served Tue-Sat 12-2 booking required D served Mon-Sat 6.30-9 booking required Av main course £8 **Restaurant** L served Tue-Sun 12-2 booking required D served Mon-Sat 6.30-9 booking required Fixed menu price fr £12 Av 3 course à la carte fr £25 ⊕ FREE HOUSE ◀ IPA, Adnams, Timothy Taylor Landlord, Guinness Ŏ Aspall. **Facilities** Children welcome Children's portions Dogs allowed Garden Parking Wi-fi

STRETTON | Map 11 SK91

PICK OF THE PUBS

The Jackson Stops Country Inn

See Pick of the Pubs on opposite page

Ram Jam Inn

The Great North Rd LE15 7QX ☎ 01780 410776
e-mail: enquiries@ramjaminn.com
dir: *On A1 S'bound carriageway, take B668 for Oakham, turn right at rdbt, then left at next rdbt & another left to car park*

The inn was originally a humble ale house called the Winchelsea Arms, and belonged to the Earl of that title who lived nearby. It is thought that its current name stems from a home-brew invented by a resident publican during the 18th century, when the pub sign advertised 'Fine Ram Jam'. Sadly no recipe survives, so its ingredients remain a mystery. Today's informal café-bar and bistro, with a patio overlooking orchard and paddock, welcomes visitors with its comprehensive daily-changing menu. Dishes might be potted smoked mackerel; spicy crayfish and Thai style salad; chicken Caesar salad; lasagne; finishing off with crème brûlée or apple and blackberry crumble.

Open all day all wk 7am-9pm Closed: 25 Dec **Bar Meals** L served all wk 11.30-9 D served all wk 11.30-9 Av main course £6-12 **Restaurant** L served all wk 11.30-9 D served all wk 11.30-9 Av 3 course à la carte fr £12.20 ⊕ OXFORD HOTEL & INNS MANAGEMENT LIMITED ◀ John Smith's Smooth, Fuller's London Pride. **Facilities** Children welcome Children's menu Children's portions Garden Parking Wi-fi

Save on hotels. Book at **theAA.com/hotel**

RUTLAND 375 ENGLAND

PICK OF THE PUBS

The Jackson Stops Country Inn

STRETTON MAP 11 SK91

Rookery Rd LE15 7RA
☎ **01780 410237**
web: www.thejacksonstops.com
dir: 1m off A1 (pass Little Chef). Follow Stretton sign at B668 for Oakham

David and Laura Graveling took over the running of this pretty country inn in January 2011. It is owned by Robert Reid, a chef born in South Africa whose reputation was assured after leaving his homeland to train in the kitchens of France, most notably with Roger Vergé; this was followed by nearly eight years with Marco Pierre White's Oak Room restaurant. The menu at the Jackson Stops is currently being developed, but you can be certain the new team's emphasis on quality and warm hospitality will embrace every aspect of your visit.

The long, low, stone-built partly thatched building actually dates from 1721, and has plenty of appeal: stone fireplaces with log fires, exposed stone and quarry tiled floors, scrubbed wood tables and no fewer than five intimate dining rooms. In the timeless and beamed snug bar, the choice of real ales lifts the heart, boding well for the excellent value to be had from the carte's dishes, all freshly prepared and cooked by the kitchen staff. Children are well looked after too, as they can select either from their own menu or take smaller portions from the adult choice.

So order a pint of Oakham and settle outside in the garden if it's a sunny day; plans are in place to host a beer festival here in future – telephone for more details. Back inside you can play the ancient pub game of nurdling. The Annual Nurdling World Championships are held here each June. And, just in case you were wondering about the origin of the pub's title, you would be right: there can be few pubs in the country that have acquired their name by virtue of a 'For Sale' sign. One was planted outside the pub for so long during a previous change of ownership, that the locals dispensed with the old name – the White Horse – in favour of the name of the estate agent on the board. Attractive gardens complete the picture.

Open 12-4 6-11 Closed: Sun eve, Mon **Bar Meals** L served all wk 12-3 D served all wk 6.30-9.30 Av main course £7-£10 **Restaurant** L served all wk 12-3 booking required D served all wk 6.30-9.30 booking required Fixed menu price fr £12 Av 2 course à la carte fr £17 ⊕ FREE HOUSE ◀ Oakham Ales JHB, Oakham Grainstore Cooking, Rutland Bitter. **Facilities** Children's menu Children's portions Dogs allowed (in bar) Garden Beer festival Parking

WING
Map 11 SK80

PICK OF THE PUBS

Kings Arms ★★★★ INN ◉◉ ⚑

Top St LE15 8SE ☎ 01572 737634 📠 01572 737255
e-mail: info@thekingsarms-wing.co.uk
dir: *1m off B6003 between Uppingham & Oakham*

Dating from 1649, this attractive free house is run by David and Gisa Goss, whilst their son James looks after the kitchen. The bar, with its flagstone floors, low beamed ceilings, nooks, crannies and two open fires is the oldest part of the building, and offers a wide selection of traditional cask ales and guest beers. Popular bar meals and lunchtime sandwiches are supplemented by an à la carte menu and daily specials. A selection from the two-Rosetted main menu might begin with Rutland crayfish risotto or smoked air-dried mutton with elderberry jelly; followed by roast woodcock, pâté de campagne croûte, red cabbage, kale and rösti potato; or grilled plaice bouillabaisse with sea bass, tiger prawns, mussels and brown shrimp. Finish with sticky toffee Rutland Ale pudding, butterscotch sauce, Grainstore Ale ice cream. Eight spacious en suite letting rooms are set away from the pub with their own private entrance, and guests are welcome to use the large car park for light boats and motorised campers.

Open Tue-Sun (seasonal times) Closed: Sun eve, Mon, Tue L (Oct-Mar), Sun eve, Mon L, (Apr-Sep)
Bar Meals L served Tue-Sun 12-2.30 booking required D served Tue-Sat 6.30-8.30 booking required
Restaurant L served Tue-Sun 12-2.30 booking required D served Mon-Sat 6.30-8.30 booking required ⊕ FREE HOUSE ◀ Shepherd Neame Spitfire, Grainstore Cooking, Bass Ö Sheppey's. ⚑ 20 **Facilities** Children welcome Children's menu Children's portions Dogs allowed Garden Parking Wi-fi **Rooms** 8

SHROPSHIRE

ADMASTON
Map 10 SJ61

The Pheasant Inn at Admaston ⚑

TF5 0AD ☎ 01952 251989
e-mail: info@thepheasantadmaston.co.uk
web: www.thepheasantadmaston.co.uk
dir: *M54 junct 6 follow A5223 towards Whitchurch then follow B5063 towards Shawbirch & Admaston. Pub is on left of main rd*

This lovely old country pub dates from the 19th century and is renowned for its well kept beers and food. Its stylish interior decor and real fire add character to the dining areas, whilst the large enclosed garden is ideal for families. Using the best of local produce, expect steak and ale pie; grilled Gloucester Old Spot pork chop with apple and sage mash, cider sauce. There is also a good menu for 'Little People'.

Open all day all wk 11am-11pm (Thu 11am-11.30pm, Fri-Sat 11am-mdnt) **Bar Meals** L served Mon-Fri 12-2, Sat 12-9.15, Sun 12-7 booking required
Restaurant L served Mon-Fri 12-2, Sat 12-9.15, Sun 12-7 ⊕ ENTERPRISE INNS ◀ Shropshire Gold, Greene King IPA, Guinness. ⚑ 10 **Facilities** Children welcome Children's menu Children's portions Play area Dogs allowed Garden Parking

BASCHURCH
Map 15 SJ42

The New Inn

Church Rd SY4 2EF ☎ 01939 260335
e-mail: eat@thenewinnbaschurch.co.uk
dir: *8m from Shrewsbury, 8m from Oswestry*

This stylishly modernised old whitewashed village pub near the medieval church is a focal point for all things Welsh Marches; with beers from nearby Oswestry's Stonehouse brewery amongst five ales stocked, meats from the village's Moor Farm or Shrewsbury's renowned market, and cheeses from a Cheshire supplier. Chef-patron Marcus and his team transform these into tempting fare such as rump of lamb with mini shepherd's pie, rosemary fondant and mint sauce; and fillet of Cornish coley with slow roasted cherry tomatoes, artichoke purée and basil beignets. The fish specials change daily, and there is a beer festival each year.

Open all wk 11-3 6-11 (Sat 11am-mdnt Sun noon-11) Closed: 26 Dec, 1 Jan **Bar Meals** L served all wk 12-2 D served all wk 6.30-9.30 **Restaurant** L served all wk 12-2 booking required D served all wk 6.30-9.30 booking required ⊕ FREE HOUSE ◀ Greene King Abbot Ale, Banks Bitter, Stonehouse Station, Hobsons Best Bitter Ö Thatchers Gold. **Facilities** Children welcome Children's menu Children's portions Dogs allowed Garden Beer festival Parking Wi-fi

BISHOP'S CASTLE
Map 15 SO38

PICK OF THE PUBS

The Sun at Norbury ★★★★ INN

SY9 5DX ☎ 01588 650680
dir: *10m from Church Stretton, 3m from Bishop's Castle off A489*

Time has stood still in this secret corner of Shropshire. Full of antiques and atmosphere, The Sun lies deep in the valley of the Long Mynd, where you can discover the 'blue remembered hills' that the poet A E Housman wrote about in *A Shropshire Lad*. Enjoy a drink before dinner in the delightful garden, or head straight for the bar with its wealth of unusual artefacts; there is also an 18th-century sitting room and an elegant dining room. The chef/proprietors Charles and Carol Cahan have established a restaurant with a reputation for good, unpretentious food produced from quality ingredients. Starters include smoked trout salad with English watercress, and warm salsa of tomato, anchovy and olives. Main courses may feature grilled cutlets of local lamb with redcurrant, orange and mint jus, and chicken provençal fillets with wild mushrooms and fresh thyme. This is glorious walking and cycling country, so why not stay overnight in one of the comfortable en suite guest rooms?

Open 7pm-11pm (Sun 12-3) Closed: Sun eve, Mon **Bar Meals** L served Sat-Sun (summer) 12-2 D served Tue-Sat 7-9 booking required **Restaurant** L served Sun 12-2 booking required D served Tue-Sat 7-9 booking required ◀ Wye Valley Bitter, Woods Shropshire Lad Ö Westons Stowford Press. **Facilities** Children welcome Children's portions Dogs allowed Garden Parking **Rooms** 6

PICK OF THE PUBS

The Three Tuns Inn ⚑

Salop St SY9 5BW ☎ 01588 638797
e-mail: timce@talk21.com
dir: *From Ludlow take A49 through Craven Arms, then left onto A489 to Lydham, then A488 to Bishop's Castle, inn at top of the town*

The Three Tuns Inn and Brewery were established in 1642, with the brewery being possibly the oldest in the country – records show that King Charles I issued the first brewing licences in that year to raise funds to pay for his army fighting the civil war. Today the wondrous array of Three Tuns ales - including Tuns XXX, Solstice and Clerics Cure - can be enjoyed more or less in

Save on hotels. Book at theAA.com/hotel

SHROPSHIRE 377 ENGLAND

peace: there's no piped music or fruit machines, just occasional live music or Morris dancing in the restored function room, as well as a beer festival in July. The public bar, snug bar and lounge bar have been joined by a classy oak framed, glass sided dining room. Lunch menus offer sandwiches, light bites and main courses such as beer-battered fish and hand cut chips; beef burger with smoked bacon, cheese, salsa, chips and cabbage slaw. In the evening, menus seduce with Moroccan style lamb casserole and cous cous; spaghetti with king prawns, sundried tomatoes, olives and capers; chargrilled 28-day hung rib-eye steak with peppercorn sauce and chips.

Open all day all wk **Bar Meals** L served all wk 12-3 D served Mon-Sat 7-9 Av main course £10 **Restaurant** L served all wk 12-3 booking required D served Mon-Sat 7-9 booking required ⊕ FREE HOUSE ◀ Tuns XXX, Solstice, Scrooge, Clerics Cure, 1642. ♟ 12 **Facilities** Children welcome Children's menu Children's portions Dogs allowed Garden Beer festival

---

BRIDGNORTH   Map 10 SO79

Halfway House Inn ★★★ INN ♟

Cleobury Rd, Eardington WV16 5LS
☎ 01746 762670 📠 01746 768063
e-mail: info@halfwayhouseinn.co.uk
dir: M54 junct 4, A442 to Bridgnorth. Or M5 junct 4, A491 towards Stourbridge. A458 to Bridgnorth. Follow tourist signs on B4363

A 17th-century coaching inn originally called the Old Red Lion. Its name was changed in 1823 after a young Princess Victoria and her entourage paid a visit en route between Shrewsbury and Worcester. An original Elizabethan wall mural has been preserved behind glass for all to enjoy, and the pub is renowned for a good selection of real ales, 40 malts, and around 100 wines. Locally sourced, home-cooked dishes range from light lunchtime bites to Welsh lamb leg steak cooked with rosemary and garlic; and warm chocolate fudge cake with cream or ice cream. Why not stay over and join in one of the activity breaks provided by the inn.

Open 5-11.30 (Fri & Sat 11am-11.30pm Sun 11-6) Closed: Sun eve ex BH **Bar Meals** L served Fri-Sun 12-2 D served Mon-Sat 6-9 Av main course £9 **Restaurant** L served Sat-Sun 12-3 D served Mon-Sat 6-9 Fixed menu price fr £20 Av 3 course à la carte fr £20 ⊕ FREE HOUSE ◀ Holden's Golden Glow, Wood's Shropshire Lad, Draught Guinness ♂ Westons Stowford Export. ♟ 10 **Facilities** Children welcome Children's menu Children's portions Play area Dogs allowed Garden Parking Wi-fi **Rooms** 10

Pheasant Inn

Linley Brook WV16 4TA ☎ 01746 762260
e-mail: pheasant-inn@talktalk.net
dir: From Bridgnorth take B4373 towards Broseley. At junct of B4373 & Briton's Ln follow brown tourist sign pub in 400yds

Run by a husband and wife team for over 25 years, this is a perfect, traditional country pub in a pretty location. Birds in the garden and sheep in the adjacent fields provide the soundtrack – piped music and gaming machines have no place here. Open fires and wood burners heat its two rooms, where locals play bar billiards, dominoes and card games. Various small breweries, usually local, furnish the two pumps, and simple pub food is prepared by the landlord's wife: rump steaks and gammon from a local butcher are popular, in addition to home-made lasagne, curries, and at least one vegetarian option. Local walks include one leading down to the River Severn.

Open 12-2 6.30-11 (Sat & Sun 12-3) Closed: Sun-Mon eve Nov-Mar **Bar Meals** L served all wk 12-2 D served all wk 7-9 Av main course £8 ⊕ FREE HOUSE ◀ Hobson Bitter, Hobson Town Crier, Wye Valley HPA, Salopian Shropshire Gold, Cannon Royall Arrowhead ♂ Westons. **Facilities** Children's portions Garden Parking **Notes** ☺

BURLTON   Map 15 SJ42

PICK OF THE PUBS

The Burlton Inn ★★★★ INN

SY4 5TB ☎ 01939 270284
e-mail: enquiries@burltoninn.com
dir: 10m N of Shrewsbury on A528 towards Ellesmere

Standing on the road between Shrewsbury and Ellesmere, this pretty old building has been transformed into a classy, contemporary interpretation of an 18th-century inn. There's a fresh looking dining area, a soft furnished space for relaxation, and a traditional bar - the perfect place to enjoy a pint of Robinson's Unicorn and other seasonal bitters. Behind the main building are en suite guest rooms and the terrace, ideal for alfresco summer dining. Hosts Lindsay and Paul serve an appealing menu that begins with starters like tempura courgette flower with goat's cheese and soft herbs; and smoked ham hock soup with shiitake mushroom broth and a mirepoix of vegetables. Main course dishes such as spring pea risotto with toasted pine nuts, and roast gilt-head bream with steamed asparagus are representative choices. Home-made desserts include lychee and white peach parfait, and coffee crème brûlée.

Open all wk Mon-Sat noon-3 6-11 (Sun noon-5) Closed: 25 Dec **Bar Meals** L served Mon-Sat 12-2, Sun 12-3 D served Mon-Sat 6-9 **Restaurant** L served Mon-Sat 12-2, Sun 12-3 booking required D served Mon-Sat 6-9 booking required ⊕ ROBINSONS ◀ Robinsons Unicorn, Cumbria Way, seasonal bitters ♂ Stowford Press. **Facilities** Children welcome Children's menu Children's portions Garden Parking Wi-fi **Rooms** 6

CHURCH STRETTON   Map 15 SO49

The Bucks Head ★★★★ INN

42 High St SY6 6BX ☎ 01694 722898
e-mail: lnutting@btinternet.com
dir: 12m from Shrewsbury & Ludlow

At the heart of the local community, The Bucks Head is a charming old building, parts of which may have been built as a hunting lodge for the Marquis of Bath. A tunnel is rumoured to run from the cellar under the beer garden. The pub is known for its well kept Marston and guest ales, its steaks and specials board, and four nicely welcoming letting rooms. So bring your boots, ramble along the Long Mynd, and return to a sizzling rump steak and chips; Cajun chicken with soured cream; or maybe roasted vegetable lasagne.

Open all day all wk **Bar Meals** L served all wk 12-2.30 D served all wk 6-9 **Restaurant** L served all wk 12-2.30 D served all wk 6-9 ⊕ MARSTON'S PUB COMPANY ◀ Banks Original, Banks Bitter, Marston's Pedigree, Guinness, Guest Ale. **Facilities** Children welcome Children's menu Children's portions Garden Wi-fi **Rooms** 4

The Royal Oak

Cardington SY6 7JZ
☎ 01694 771266 📠 01694 771685
e-mail: inntoxicated@gmail.com
dir: Turn right off A49 N of Church Stretton; 2m off B4371 (Church Stretton-Much Wenlock road)

Said to be the oldest continuously licensed pub in Shropshire, this free house in a conservation village can trace its roots to the 15th century. The rambling low-beamed bar with vast inglenook and comfortable beamed dining room are refreshingly undisturbed by music, TV or games machines. Choose from the excellent cask ales and join in the locals' banter or ponder your choice of sustenance: good value home-made fare includes 'fidget pie', a Shropshire recipe of gammon, apples and cider.

Open 12-2.30 (Sun 12-3.30) Tue-Wed 6.30-11 (Thu-Sat 6.30-mdnt Sun 7-mdnt) Closed: Mon (ex BH Mon L) **Bar Meals** L served Tue-Sat & BH Mon 12-2, Sun 12-2.30 D served Tue-Sat 6.30-9, Sun 7-9 **Restaurant** L served Tue-Sat & BH Mon 12-2, Sun 12-2.30 D served Tue-Sat 6.30-9, Sun 7-9 ⊕ FREE HOUSE ◀ Hobsons Best Bitter, Three Tuns XXX, Wye Valley Butty Bach, Bass, Six Bells 1859. **Facilities** Children welcome Children's menu Garden Parking

CLAVERLEY   Map 10 SO79

The Woodman ♥ NEW

Danford Ln WV5 7DG ☎ 01746 710553
dir: *On B4176 (Bridgnorth to Dudley road)*

Village farms, butcher and baker supply much of the produce used in the well respected dishes here at this sibling-run, three-storey Victorian inn outside a very picturesque settlement deep in the east Shropshire countryside. The beer, too, comes from just down the lane in Enville, whilst the notable wine list spreads its wings worldwide to source some bins unique in England to The Woodman. The contemporary interior is a comfy mix of village local and bistro, where breast of Shropshire pheasant with chestnuts and smoked bacon, sautéed scallops, or the very popular honeycomb ice cream show the quality of the fare here. Alfresco dining is a popular summer option, indulging in grand rural views to the ridge of Abbot's Castle Hill.

Open all day Closed: Sun eve **Bar Meals** Av main course £9.95 **Restaurant** L served Mon-Sat 12-2.30, Sun 12-3 booking required D served Mon-Thu 6-9, Fri-Sat 6-9.45 booking required Av 3 course à la carte fr £25 ⊕ PUNCH TAVERNS ◀ Black Sheep, Enville Ale. ♥ 10
Facilities Children welcome Children's portions Garden Parking Wi-fi

CLEOBURY MORTIMER   Map 10 SO67

PICK OF THE PUBS

The Crown Inn ♥

Hopton Wafers DY14 0NB
☎ 01299 270372 ▤ 01299 271127
dir: *On A4117 8m E of Ludlow, 2m W of Cleobury Mortimer*

Situated in the small village of Hopton Wafers, this 16th-century creeper-clad inn retains much of its original character. It has an enviable reputation for good food and the ingredients are all sourced from regional producers. Eat in one of three eating areas: in the Shropshire Restaurant overlooking the countryside; in Poachers, with exposed beams, stonework and large inglenook fireplace; and in the Rent Room, which offers daily menus, light bites and specials - and more of those rural views. In Poachers, typical starters are pan-seared scallops and asparagus with lemon dressing, followed by main courses of salmon steak with rocket, roasted cherry tomatoes, herb oil and balsamic syrup. The wine list has been selected by a local merchant and includes a wide range of fine ports, Armagnacs and Cognacs. The Crown is in an ideal spot for walking in the lush surrounding countryside.

Open all day all wk **Bar Meals** L served all wk 12-2.30 D served all wk 6-9 Av main course £12.95 **Restaurant** L served Mon-Fri 12.30-2, Sat 12-2.30, Sun 12-8 D served Mon-Fri 6-9, Sat 6-9.30, Sun 12-8 Fixed menu price fr £9.95 Av 3 course à la carte fr £29.95 ⊕ FREE HOUSE ◀ Hobsons Best, Guest ales. ♥ 25
Facilities Children welcome Children's menu Children's portions Play area Dogs allowed Garden Parking

CLUN   Map 9 SO38

The White Horse Inn NEW

The Square SY7 8JA ☎ 01588 640305
e-mail: pub@whi-clun.co.uk
web: www.whi-clun.co.uk
dir: *On A488 in village centre*

Gloriously unspoilt and unpretentious, a great survival of a village inn oozing character, beams, wizened wood and slab floors upon which may be spilled beers brewed in their own micro-brewery, together with others selected from Shropshire's many craft breweries. Heart-warming pub grub derived from very local suppliers awaits visitors drawn to AE Housman's 'Quietest place under the sun'. Regular events take place here, including the Clun Valley beer festival each October.

Open all day all wk **Bar Meals** L served Mon-Sat 12-2, Sun 12.30-2.30 D served all wk 6.30-8.30 Av main course £8.50 **Restaurant** L served Mon-Sat 12-2, Sun 12.30-2.30 D served all wk 6.30-8.30 Fixed menu price fr £8.75 Av 3 course à la carte fr £15.95 ⊕ FREE HOUSE ◀ Wye Valley Butty Bach, Hobsons Best Bitter, Salopian Brewery Shropshire Gold Ď Westons First Quality & Perry, Robinson's Flagon. **Facilities** Children welcome Children's portions Dogs allowed Garden Beer festival Wi-fi

COCKSHUTT   Map 15 SJ42

The Leaking Tap

Shrewsbury Rd SY12 0JQ
☎ 01939 270636 ▤ 01939 270746
e-mail: lesley@theleakingtap.org
dir: *On A528 (Shrewsbury to Ellesmere road)*

Saved from closure in 2009 and now privately owned, this traditional old coaching inn is in the heart of beautiful Shropshire countryside on the road from Shrewsbury to Ellesmere. The Leaking Tap has a unique atmosphere and charm and features oak beams and log fires, along with a selection of ales and food cooked from local produce. Regularly changing lunchtime or evening menus are available and might include chicken breast wrapped in bacon in a brandy and Stilton sauce, or leek and parsnip cheese bake.

Open all wk 12-2 5.30-11.30 ⊕ FREE HOUSE ◀ Worthington, Guest ales. **Facilities** Children welcome Children's menu Children's portions Parking

CRAVEN ARMS   Map 9 SO48

The Sun Inn ♥

Corfton SY7 9DF ☎ 01584 861239
e-mail: normanspride@btconnect.com
dir: *On B4368, 7m N of Ludlow*

First licensed in 1613, this historic pub has a public bar with pool table, jukebox and dartboard, along with a lounge and restaurant. Landlord Norman Pearce brews the Corvedale ales in what was the pub's old chicken and lumber shed, using local borehole water; Mahorall cider, from just down the road, is another drinks option. Teresa Pearce uses local produce in a delicious array of traditional dishes – lamb hotpot, chicken curry, pork and apple in cider - served with up to six fresh vegetables and a choice of chips or new potatoes. The pub has historic connection with the transportation of criminals to Australia.

Open all wk 12-2.30 6-11 (Sun 12-3 7-11)
Bar Meals L served all wk 12-2 D served all wk 6-9 Av main course £8.90 **Restaurant** L served all wk 12-2 D served all wk 6-9 ⊕ FREE HOUSE ◀ Corvedale Normans Pride, Dark & Delicious, Katie's Pride, Farmer Rays Ď Mahorall. ♥ 8 **Facilities** Children welcome Children's menu Children's portions Play area Dogs allowed Garden Beer festival Parking Wi-fi

CRESSAGE   Map 10 SJ50

The Riverside Inn ♥

Cound SY5 6AF ☎ 01952 510900 ▤ 01952 510926
dir: *On A458 7m from Shrewsbury, 1m from Cressage*

A haven for fishermen, this inn sits in three acres of gardens alongside the River Severn, offering customers delightful river views both outdoors and from a modern conservatory. Originally a vicarage for St Peter's church in the village, the building also housed a girls' school and a railway halt before becoming a pub in 1878. The monthly-changing menu might open with Welsh rarebit or a curried beef pancake, followed perhaps by lamb and leek pie or game casserole and dumplings. Comforting desserts include home-made marmalade roll with whisky sauce. Their own brew, Riverside Inn Bitter, is available in the cosy bar.

Open all wk all day Sat-Sun May-Sep **Bar Meals** L served all wk 12-2.30 D served all wk 6.30-9.30 Av main course £11 **Restaurant** L served all wk 12-2.30 D served all wk 6.30-9.30 Av 3 course à la carte fr £19 ⊕ FREE HOUSE ◀ Riverside Inn Bitter, Guest ales. **Facilities** Dogs allowed Garden Parking Wi-fi

HODNET — Map 15 SJ62

The Bear at Hodnet

TF9 3NH ☎ 01630 685214 🖨 01630 685787
e-mail: reception@bearathodnet.co.uk
dir: At junct of A53 & A442 turn right at rdbt. Inn in village centre

With its old beams and fireplaces, secret passages and medieval banquets, this 16th-century coaching inn is steeped in history. Standing opposite Hodnet Hall Gardens, the pub has a bar that is full of character with plenty of real ales, and secret passages leading to the parish church. Famous for medieval banquets in the newly refurbished hall, food in the bar includes rare breed meats (Black Mountain Farm Dexter beef lasagne) and pub classics like grilled Maynard's gammon steak, egg and hand-cut chips, and traditional pork sausage mash with spicy apricot chutney.

Open 11-11 Closed: Sun eve **Bar Meals** L served Mon-Sat 12-2.30 D served Mon-Sat 6-9.30 **Restaurant** L served all wk 12-2.30 D served Mon-Sat 6-9.30 ⊕ FREE HOUSE ◀ Shropshire Gold, Guinness, Guest ales Ö Stowford Press. **Facilities** Children welcome Children's portions Dogs allowed Garden Parking

IRONBRIDGE — Map 10 SJ60

The Malthouse ♀

The Wharfage TF8 7NH ☎ 01952 433712
e-mail: mcdonald740@msn.com
dir: Telephone for directions

Overlooking the River Severn in the Ironbridge Gorge, birthplace of the Industrial Revolution, the 18th-century Malthouse is known locally for its lively bar which, at weekends, offers "the best live music in town". The restaurant is rather different, with candlelit tables, low music and extensive menus of pub grub, vegetarian and vegan meals and main meals featuring minted lamb casserole; seafood tagliatelle; poached loin of cod; 16oz porterhouse steaks; and tempura battered vegetables.

Open all wk **Bar Meals** Av main course £8.95 food served all day **Restaurant** Av 3 course à la carte fr £30 food served all day ⊕ FREE HOUSE ◀ Hobgoblin, Brakspear, Shropshire Lad, Titanic Ö Thatchers Gold, Thatchers Pear. ♀ 10 **Facilities** Children welcome Children's menu Children's portions Dogs allowed Garden Parking Wi-fi

LEEBOTWOOD — Map 15 SO49

Pound Inn NEW

SY6 6ND ☎ 01694 751477
e-mail: info@thepound.org.uk
dir: On A49, 9m S of Shrewsbury

An eye-catching pub in a memorable location; this thatched, 15th century drovers' inn lies at the foot of the jagged, whaleback hills of mid-Shropshire, with The Lawley thrusting steeply up beyond the garden. Recently refurbished in a contemporary airy style, a happy mix of

traditional village pub (it's the oldest building in the village) and smart dining destination draws in ramblers to sup Salopian brewery beers and browsers to try a taste of grilled ox tongue cauliflower cheese fritter to start, followed by Shropshire sausages with Cheddar mash or roast venison with butternut squash.

Open all wk 12-2.30 6-10.30 **Bar Meals** L served Mon-Sat 12-2 Av main course £5.95 **Restaurant** L served all wk 12-2.30 D served Sun-Thu 6-9, Fri-Sat 6.30-9 Fixed menu price fr £10 Av 3 course à la carte fr £18.90 ◀ Wye Valley, Butty Bach, Salopian Brewery Shropshire Gold Ö Stowford Press. **Facilities** Children welcome Children's portions Garden Parking

LITTLE STRETTON — Map 15 SO49

The Ragleth Inn NEW

Ludlow Rd SY6 6RB ☎ 01694 722711
e-mail: wendyjd65@hotmail.com
dir: From Shrewsbury take A49 towards Leominster. At lights in Church Stretton turn right. 3rd left into High St. Continue to Little Stretton. Inn on right

A classic country inn in beautiful countryside at the foot of the Long Mynd hills, which dates back to the 1660s. The pretty, traditional exterior includes a beer garden with wooden benches and large children's play area, matched within by two bars and a restaurant with oak beams, antiques and glowing inglenook fireplaces. A good range of ales accompanies classic pub dishes from baguettes on the bar menu to a chalk board for chef's specials. All diets can be catered for, and food is served all day on Sundays.

Open all wk **Bar Meals** L served Mon-Sat 12-2.15, Sun all day D served Mon-Sat 6.30-9, Sun all day Av main course £10 **Restaurant** L served Mon-Sat 12-2.15, Sun all day D served Mon-Sat 6.30-9, Sun all day Fixed menu price fr £11.50 Av 3 course à la carte fr £15 ⊕ FREE HOUSE ◀ Hobsons Brewery, Wye Valley Butty Bach, Abbot's Reserve, Three Tuns Ö Stowford Press. **Facilities** Children welcome Children's menu Children's portions Play area Dogs allowed Garden Beer festival Parking

LLANFAIR WATERDINE — Map 9 SO27

PICK OF THE PUBS

The Waterdine

LD7 1TU ☎ 01547 528214
e-mail: info@waterdine.com
dir: 4.5m W of Knighton off B4355, turn right opposite Lloyney Inn, 0.5m into village, last on left opp church

You might come across this peacefully located pub by sheer chance or, with the help of this Guide, head straight there. Either way, this low-slung, whitewashed former drover's inn dating from the late 16th-century, with original timber floors and leaded windows, is worth visiting. The old parish church stands opposite, the River Teme flows through the bottom of the lovely garden with wonderful views, and Isabel and Ken Adams (the chef) run it in the same highly professional manner as they have for twelve years. There are two

dining rooms: the Garden Room looking out over the river, and the Tap Room, where a massive oak mantle displays burn marks from long-extinguished candles. The concise menus are based on home-grown, locally supplied organic produce, and offer dishes such as roast Cornish monkfish on tomato tart with fennel sauce, and Mortimer Forest roe deer saddle with mushrooms and celeriac. Popular with walkers, there are woodburners creating a cosy atmosphere in the winter. Lord Hunt used to live in the village and the famous Everest Expedition was planned in the lounge bar where an excellent range of real ales and ciders are served.

Open 12-3 7-11 Closed: 1wk winter, 1wk spring, Sun eve & Mon (ex BH) **Bar Meals** L served Thu-Sun 12.15-1.30 booking required **Restaurant** L served Thu-Sun 12.15-1.30 booking required D served Tue-Sat 7-8.30 booking required Fixed menu price fr £32.50 ⊕ FREE HOUSE ◀ Wood Shropshire Legends, Parish Bitter, Shropshire Lad Ö Brook Farm, Wigmore, Westons Oakland. **Facilities** Children welcome Children's portions Garden Parking

LUDLOW — Map 10 SO57

The Church Inn ★★★★ INN

Buttercross SY8 1AW
☎ 01584 872174 🖨 01584 877146
web: www.thechurchinn.com
dir: In town centre, behind Buttercross

The inn stands on one of the oldest sites in Ludlow town centre, dating back some seven centuries, and through the ages has been occupied by a blacksmith, saddler, druggist and barber-surgeon. These days it enjoys a reputation for providing a good range of ales in the cosy bar areas alongside traditional pub food, including cod in beer batter and locally made faggots. There are eight comfortable en suite bedrooms with smart modern bathrooms.

Open all day all wk **Bar Meals** L served Mon-Fri 12-2.30, Sat-Sun 12-3 D served Mon-Sat 6.30-9, Sun 6.30-8.30 ⊕ FREE HOUSE ◀ Hobsons Town Crier, Weetwood, Wye Valley Bitter, Ludlow Gold, Boilingwell Mild Ö Stowford, Aspall. **Facilities** Children welcome Dogs allowed **Rooms** 8

LUDLOW *continued*

The Clive Bar & Restaurant with Rooms ★★★★★ RR ⊚⊚ ♥

Bromfield SY8 2JR
☎ 01584 856565 📠 01584 856661
e-mail: info@theclive.co.uk
web: www.theclive.co.uk
dir: *2m N of Ludlow on A49, between Hereford & Shrewsbury*

This classy bar and restaurant with rooms is situated two miles north of Ludlow on the Earl of Plymouth's estate. Built as a farmhouse in the 18th century, it was home to Robert Clive, who laid the foundation of British rule in India. Inside the handsome Georgian building, traditional and contemporary looks blend well. The bar is bright and modern, with glass-topped tables and contemporary artwork; here local real ales and ciders are dispensed, along with light snacks. An 18th-century lounge in traditional style with beams and brick and stone walls is where you can relax on sofas by an enormous fireplace, and admire Clive's original coat of arms on one wall. A more contemporary upper area leads to a sheltered non-smoking courtyard with tables and parasols for the warmer months. Expect high quality cuisine built around the best of local and seasonal produce: a salad starter of Wenlock Edge Farm air-dried beef, Ludlow Blue cheese and poached pear says it all. Tastefully converted contemporary accommodation is available in period outbuildings.

Open all day all wk Closed: 25-26 Dec
Bar Meals L served Mon-Fri 12-3, Sat-Sun 12-6.30 booking required D served Mon-Sat 6.30-10, Sun 6.30-9.30 booking required Av main course £10.25
Restaurant L served all wk 12-3 booking required D served Mon-Sat 6.30-10, Sun 6.30-9.30 booking required Av 3 course à la carte fr £28 ⊕ FREE HOUSE ◀ Hobsons Best Bitter, Ludlow Gold Bitter ♻ Dunkertons Original, Mahorall Farm, Thatchers Old Rascal Oak Aged. ♥ 9 **Facilities** Children welcome Children's portions Garden Parking **Rooms** 15

The Unicorn ♥

Corve St SY8 1DU
☎ 01584 873555 📠 01584 876268
e-mail: graham-unicorn@btconnect.com
dir: *A49 to Ludlow. From town centre down Corve St towards river*

This low, attractive, timber-framed building backs on to the once flood-prone River Corve. During the great flood of 1885 a photograph was taken of men sitting drinking around a table in the bar while water lapped the doorway. Apparently it wasn't unusual for empty beer barrels to float out of the cellar and down the river. These days, all is warm and dry: log fires in winter and the sunny riverside terrace in summer prove very appealing. The impressive food offerings run from sandwiches (Brie and cranberry; home-cooked ham) to full meals such as home-made Shropshire pâté with sweet onion marmalade followed by the likes of fish pie – a house speciality – or braised local lamb shanks with proper gravy and fresh vegetables. For those seeking pub classics, there are home-made faggots, home-made rare breed steak burger and ale-battered fish with home-made chips. Home-made desserts include sticky toffee pudding and dark chocolate torte.

Open all day all wk 11am-mdnt **Bar Meals** L served all wk 12-2.30 D served all wk 6-9.15 **Restaurant** L served all wk 12-2.30 D served all wk 6-9.15 ◀ Ludlow Best Ale, Butty Bach, Guinness. ♥ 15 **Facilities** Children welcome Children's portions Dogs allowed Garden

Map 10 SJ60

All Nations Inn

20 Coalport Rd TF7 5DP
☎ 01952 585747 📠 01952 585747
dir: *On Coalport Rd, overlooking Blists Hill Museum*

Opened as a brewhouse in 1831, this friendly and largely unspoilt free house has a relaxed and friendly atmosphere. And a brewhouse it remains, with a real fire and outside seating overlooking Blists Hill open air museum. You'll search in vain for a jukebox, pool or fruit machine, although Six Nations rugby matches are shown on a TV propped up on barrels. There's no restaurant either, but quality pork pies and rolls are always available.

Open all day all wk noon-mdnt **Bar Meals** food served all day ⊕ FREE HOUSE ◀ Dabley Ale, Dabley Gold, Coalport Dodger Mild, Guest ales ♻ Westons Scrumpy.
Facilities Children welcome Dogs allowed Garden Parking **Notes** ⊛

The New Inn

Blists Hill Victorian Town, Legges Way TF7 5DU
☎ 01952 601018 📠 01785 252247
e-mail: sales@jenkinsonscaterers.co.uk
dir: *Between Telford & Broseley*

Here's something different - a Victorian pub that was moved brick by brick from the Black Country and re-erected at the Ironbridge Gorge Open Air Museum. The building remains basically as it was in 1890, and customers can buy traditionally brewed beer at five-pence farthing per pint - roughly £2.10 in today's terms - using pre-decimal currency bought from the bank. The mainly traditional menu includes home-made soup, steak and kidney pudding, and ham and leek pie. Tea and coffee are served from 10-2.30, and afternoon tea from 2.30-3.30. There has been a change of hands.

Open all wk 10-4 winter, 10-5 summer Closed: 25 Dec, 1 Jan ⊕ IRONBRIDGE GORGE MUSEUMS ◀ Banks Bitter, Banks Original, Pedigree. **Facilities** Children welcome Garden Parking

Map 15 SJ20

The Lowfield Inn ♥

SY21 8JX ☎ 01743 891313
e-mail: lowfieldinn@tiscali.co.uk
dir: *From Shrewsbury take B4386 towards Montgomery. Through Westbury & Brockton. Pub on right in 13m just before Marton*

A new-ish pub on the Shropshire/Powys border, The Lowfield was built on the site of its demolished predecessor; the views from the large garden are stunning. Inside, the atmosphere is relaxed and informal, with mix and match tables and chairs, comfy sofas and walls displaying local artworks. While locally brewed real ales and ciders quench the thirst, the kitchen produces modern British dishes with ingredients sourced from the surrounding Shropshire countryside whenever possible. You could try the Welsh cockle cake to start, followed by pan-roasted lamb rump and garlic mash. There is live music every Friday night.

Open all day all wk **Bar Meals** L served all wk 12-9.30 D served all wk 12-9.30 Av main course £10.75 food served all day **Restaurant** L served all wk 12-9.30 D served all wk 12-9.30 Fixed menu price fr £13.75 Av 3 course à la carte fr £21 food served all day ⊕ FREE HOUSE ◀ Three Tuns XXX, Three Tuns 1642, Monty's Moonrise, Monty's Mojo, Wood's Shropshire Lad ♻ Inch's Stonehouse, Weston Old Rosie. ♥ 18 **Facilities** Children welcome Children's menu Children's portions Dogs allowed Garden Parking Wi-fi

The Sun Inn ♥

SY21 8JP ☎ **01938 561211**
e-mail: suninnmarton@googlemail.com
dir: On B4386 (Shrewsbury to Montgomery road), in centre of Marton opp village shop

Tucked away in a small hamlet in stunning Shropshire countryside, The Sun Inn is a classic stone free house dating back to 1760. Run by the Gartell family, it's very much a convivial local, with darts, dominoes, regular quiz nights and local Hobsons ale on tap, as well a respected dining venue offering a modern Mediterranean inspired menu in the contemporary restaurant. Typically, follow pheasant and mushroom ravioli in a game sauce, with whole megrim sole with lemon butter, and sticky toffee pudding.

Open 12-3 7-mdnt Closed: Sun eve, Mon, Tue L
Bar Meals L served Wed-Sat 12-2.30 booking required D served Tue-Fri from 7pm booking required
Restaurant L served Wed-Sun 12-2.30 booking required D served Tue-Sat from 7pm booking required ⊕ FREE HOUSE ◀ Hobsons Best Bitter, Guest ales. ♥ 8
Facilities Children welcome Children's portions Garden Parking

MUCH WENLOCK　　　　Map 10 SO69

The George & Dragon

2 High St TF13 6AA ☎ **01952 727312**
e-mail: thegeorge.dragon@btinternet.com
dir: On A458 halfway between Shrewsbury & Bridgnorth, on right of the High Street

A traditional black and white 17th-century inn at the heart of Much Wenlock, The George & Dragon oozes history, charm and character and has many a spooky tale attached. Sited next to the market square, Guildhall and ruined priory, the inn welcomes everyone, from locals to celebrities - John Cleese, Tony Robinson, Jennifer Jones and George Cole are among those who have popped in for refreshment. Run by locals Bev and James, it offers five traditional cask ales and home-cooked food such as Welsh rarebit, home-made pie of the day, or pan-fried Gressingham duck breast with black cherry sauce.

Open all day all wk 11-11 (Fri-Sat 11am-mdnt)
Bar Meals L served all wk 12-2.30 D served Mon-Tue, Thu-Sat 6-9 Av main course £7.95 **Restaurant** L served all wk 12-2.30 D served Mon-Tue, Thu-Sat 6-9 Fixed menu price fr £8.95 ⊕ PUNCH RETAIL ◀ Greene King Abbot Ale, Wadworth 6X, Tribute, Guest ales ♂ Westons Organic. **Facilities** Children welcome Children's menu Children's portions Dogs allowed Wi-fi

Longville Arms

Longville in the Dale TF13 6DT
☎ **01694 771206**　▤ **01694 771742**
dir: From Shrewsbury take A49 to Church Stretton, then B4371 to Longville

Prettily situated in an Area of Outstanding Natural Beauty in Shropshire, this welcoming country inn is ideally placed for walking and touring. Solid elm or cast-iron-framed tables, oak panelling and wood-burning stoves are among the features that help to generate a warm, friendly ambience. Favourite main courses on the bar menu and specials board include steak and ale pie, mixed fish platter, and a range of steaks. Portions can be adapted for children and they have their own menu. There are tethering facilities for horses and dogs are welcome.

Open all day all wk ⊕ FREE HOUSE ◀ Local guest ales.
Facilities Children welcome Children's menu Children's portions Play area Dogs allowed Garden Parking

The Talbot Inn ♥

High St TF13 6AA ☎ **01952 727077**　▤ **01952 728436**
e-mail: the_talbot_inn@hotmail.com
dir: M54 junct 4, follow Ironbridge Gorge Museum signs, then Much Wenlock signs. Much Wenlock on A458, 11m from Shrewsbury, 9m from Bridgnorth

Thought to have been the Almoner's House, The Talbot has been refreshing travellers ever since 1360. Through an archway you can see its delightful old courtyard, while inside are the oak beams and log fires so indicative of great age. Most of the food is freshly prepared from local produce for extensive, regularly changing menus featuring sandwiches, salads, jacket potatoes, steaks, fish and large filled Yorkshire puds. Bread and butter pudding is a fixture.

Open all day all wk 11am-2am **Bar Meals** L served all wk 12-2.30 D served Mon-Sat 6-9, Sun 6-8.30 ⊕ FREE HOUSE ◀ Bass, Guest ales. **Facilities** Children welcome Children's portions Garden Parking

PICK OF THE PUBS

Wenlock Edge Inn ♥

Hilltop, Wenlock Edge TF13 6DJ
☎ **01746 785678**　▤ **01746 785285**
e-mail: info@wenlockedgeinn.co.uk
dir: 4.5m from Much Wenlock on B4371

Perched at one of the highest points of Wenlock Edge's dramatic wooded ledge, this traditional Shropshire pub plays host to walkers and horse riders as well locals, farmers and business folk after work. Originally a row of 17th-century quarrymen's cottages, its cosy interior contains a small country-style dining room and several bars, one with a wood-burning stove. The enclosed patio enjoys views stretching across Apedale to Caer Caradoc and the Long Mynd. It even has its own fishpond fed from the Wenlock Edge fresh water spring. Traditional British pub food is served alongside Hobsons real ales, continental lagers and an exciting wine list, many by the glass. Local and regional

produce is used and favourite dishes include roasted breast of local pheasant and sausage with Parma ham, woodland mushroom and garlic cream sauce. There is also a daily fish board and special fish nights with items such as lobster and beer-battered scallops on the menu.

Open all day all wk 11-11 **Bar Meals** L served all wk 12-3 D served all wk 6-9 Av main course £9 **Restaurant** L served all wk 12-3 D served all wk 6-9 Fixed menu price fr £25 ⊕ FREE HOUSE ◀ Hobsons Best & Town Crier, Three Tuns, Enville Ale ♂ Thatchers Gold. ♥ 8 **Facilities** Children welcome Children's portions Dogs allowed Garden Parking

MUNSLOW　　　　Map 10 SO58
PICK OF THE PUBS

The Crown Country Inn
★★★★ INN ⑧⑨

See Pick of the Pubs on page 382

NORTON　　　　Map 10 SJ70
PICK OF THE PUBS

The Hundred House Hotel
★★ HL ⑧⑨ ♥

Bridgnorth Rd TF11 9EE
☎ **01952 580240**　▤ **01952 580260**
e-mail: reservations@hundredhouse.co.uk
dir: On A442, 6m N of Bridgnorth, 5m S of Telford centre

Close to Ironbridge, Bridgnorth and Telford, parts of this family-run pub date back to the 14th-century. The mainly Georgian hotel has been lovingly run by the Phillips family for more than a quarter of a century and the minute you push through the swing doors with stained glass panels stating 'Temperance Hall', you realise they have created somewhere special. Downstairs is an amazing interconnecting warren of lavishly decorated bars and dining rooms with old quarry-tiled floors, exposed brickwork, beamed ceilings and oak panelling. Younger son Stuart Phillips continues to head kitchen operations, producing a mix of innovative new dishes and pub favourites. The à la carte might offer tea smoked duck breast with warm pancake of confit duck salad, sesame and orange, which might be followed by grilled beef fillet with smoked bacon and blue cheese risotto. Master chef school classes are also available.

Open all day all wk Closed: 25-26 Dec eve
Bar Meals L served all wk 12-2.30 D served all wk 6-9.30 Av main course £10 **Restaurant** L served all wk 12-2.30 D served all wk 6-9.30 Fixed menu price fr £13 Av 3 course à la carte fr £30 ⊕ FREE HOUSE ◀ Heritage Bitter, Marstons Oyster Stout, Ironbridge Steam, Three Tuns Bitter. ♥ 10 **Facilities** Children welcome Children's menu Children's portions Garden Parking Wi-fi **Rooms** 10

PICK OF THE PUBS

The Crown Country Inn ★★★★ INN 🏵🏵

MUNSLOW Map 10 SO58

SY7 9ET ☎ 01584 841205
e-mail: info@crowncountryinn.co.uk
web: www.crowncountryinn.co.uk
dir: *On B4368 between Craven Arms & Much Wenlock*

The Grade II listed Crown has stood in a lovely setting below the rolling hills of Wenlock Edge in the Vale of the River Corve since it was built in Tudor times. The impressive, three-storey building was formerly a Hundred House, where courts – sometimes presided over by the infamous Judge Jeffreys – dished out punishment to local miscreants; these may have included the black-swathed Charlotte whose ghost is sometimes seen in the pub. The main bar retains its sturdy oak beams, flagstone floors and prominent inglenook fireplace, whilst free house status means Mahorall Farm ciders and a good range of ales, including Holden's Golden Glow, are served. Owners Richard and Jane Arnold are perhaps best known for their strong commitment to good food. Richard is not only head chef but is Shropshire's only Master Chef of Great Britain, a title he has held for more than a decade. Meals are served in the main bar, the Bay dining area, and the Corvedale restaurant. Top quality local produce is acquired from trusted sources and proudly featured in Richard's dishes. These may include starters such as a crostini of home-made black pudding and tomato fondue with award-winning Wenlock Edge dry cure bacon. Main courses may

embrace the pub's own smoked breast of Shropshire farm chicken with pearl barley and wild mushroom risotto; or roast local Gloucester Old Spot sausages with a fricassée of vegetables and chorizo sausage. Sunday lunches here are deservedly popular, when a typical choice may start with crisp gingered vegetable and crayfish spring roll; continue with roast loin of pork with mustard mash; and finish with a trio of chocolate desserts. Three large bedrooms are located in a converted Georgian stable block.

Open Tue-Sat 12-3.30 6.45-11 (Sun 12-3.30) Closed: Xmas, Sun eve, Mon
Bar Meals L served Tue-Sun 12-2 booking required D served Tue-Sat 6.45-8.45 booking required Av main course £15
Restaurant L served Tue-Sun 12-2 booking required D served Tue-Sat 6.45-8.45 booking required Fixed menu

price fr £20 Av 3 course à la carte fr £27 🌐 FREE HOUSE 🍺 Holden's Black Country Bitter, Holden's Golden Glow, Holden's Special Bitter, Three Tuns Brewery XXX 🍏 Mahorall.
Facilities Children's portions Play area Garden Parking **Rooms** 3

Save on hotels. Book at **theAA.com/hotel**

SHROPSHIRE 383 | ENGLAND

OSWESTRY | Map 15 SJ22

The Bradford Arms ★★★★ INN

Llanymynech SY22 6EJ
☎ 01691 830582 📄 01691 839009
e-mail: robinbarsteward@tesco.net
dir: 5.5m S of Oswestry on A483 in Llanymynech

Once part of the Earl of Bradford's estate, close to Powis
and Chirk Castles on the Welsh border, this coaching inn
is ideally situated for golfing, fishing and walking. It has
also won an award as a community pub serving first-
class real ales. Eating in the spotless, quietly elegant
bar, dining rooms and conservatory is a rewarding
experience, with every taste catered for. Start by choosing
from the array of menus – for children, senior citizens,
mid-week specials, tapas and special occasions, not to
mention comprehensive lunch and dinner cartes too.
Comfortable accommodation is available.

Open all wk 11.30-3 6-mdnt **Bar Meals** L served all wk
11.30-2 Av main course £9.95 **Restaurant** L served all wk
11.30-2 D served all wk 6.30-9 Fixed menu price fr £7.95
Av 3 course à la carte fr £16.95 ⊕ FREE HOUSE ◼ Black
Sheep Best, Tetley Smooth, Guinness, 2 Guest ales.
Facilities Children welcome Children's menu Children's
portions Dogs allowed Garden Parking Wi-fi **Rooms** 5

PAVE LANE | Map 10 SJ71

The Fox ♟

TF10 9LQ ☎ 01952 815940 📄 01952 815941
e-mail: fox@brunningandprice.co.uk
dir: 1m S of Newport, just off A41

One of the Brunning & Price pub family, The Fox is a
grand Edwardian building with spacious rooms and little
nooks wrapped around a busy central bar, where plenty of
Shropshire real ales demand attention. The menu offers
sandwiches and light meals, as well as chicken,
mushroom, tomato and tarragon pie; grilled mackerel
fillets with gnocchi, crayfish and pea salad; and mixed
bean and vegetable chilli. Enjoy the gently rolling
countryside and wooded hills from the south-facing
terrace.

Open all day all wk noon-11 (Sun noon-10.30)
Bar Meals food served all day **Restaurant** food served all
day ⊕ BRUNNING & PRICE ◼ Timothy Taylor Landlord,
Woods Shropshire Lad, Thwaites Original, Titanic Mild,
Hobsons Golden Glow. **Facilities** Children welcome
Children's portions Dogs allowed Garden Parking

PICKLESCOTT | Map 15 SO49

Bottle & Glass Inn

SY6 6NR ☎ 01694 751345
dir: Exit A49 at Dorrington (between Shrewsbury &
Church Stretton)

The hamlet of Pickelscott lies in the northern foothills of
the Long Mynd, or Mountain. The landlord of this 16th-
century pub, who has been here for 30-odd years,
occasionally hears the ghost of a wooden-legged
predecessor tap-tapping around, somehow upsetting the
pub's electrics. A typical starter is Roquefort-stuffed pear
with green mayonnaise: homity pie; game and red wine
casserole; and haddock with cheese sauce on spinach
are among the main courses.

Open all wk 12-3 6-12 (Sat-Sun noon-mdnt) ⊕ FREE
HOUSE ◼ Hobsons, Three Tuns XXX, Wye Valley Butty
Bach Ö Stowford Press. **Facilities** Dogs allowed Parking

SHIFNAL | Map 10 SJ70

Odfellows Wine Bar ♟

Market Place TF11 9AU
☎ 01952 461517 📄 01952 463855
e-mail: reservations@odley.co.uk
web: www. odleyinns.co.uk
dir: M54 junct 4, 3rd exit at rdbt, at next rdbt take 3rd
exit, past petrol station, round bend under rail bridge.
Bar on left

The 'od' spelling refers to Odley Inns, who own this
quirky, popular wine bar. The bar and outdoor area serve
regional real ales and ciders, as well as a great wine
selection including eleven by the glass. The carefully
prepared food, served in an elevated dining area and
attractive conservatory, is ethically sourced from local
suppliers. Along with two-course specials, seasonal
menus might offer wild rabbit and ham fricassée; beef
and ale pie; and free-range chicken and cashew nut
curry. Look out for monthly theme nights.

Open all day all wk noon-mdnt Closed: 25-26 Dec, 1 Jan
Bar Meals L served all wk 12-2.30 Av main course £9.50
Restaurant L served all wk 12-2.30 D served all wk 6-10
Fixed menu price fr £10 Av 3 course à la carte fr £17
⊕ FREE HOUSE ◼ Salopian, Slater's Ale, Hobsons, Joule's
& Titanic Ö Thatchers, Addlestones. ♟ 11
Facilities Children welcome Children's menu Children's
portions Garden Parking Wi-fi

SHREWSBURY | Map 15 SJ41

The Armoury ♟

Victoria Quay, Victoria Av SY1 1HH
☎ 01743 340525 📄 01743 340526
e-mail: armoury@brunningandprice.co.uk
dir: Telephone for directions

The converted Armoury building makes an impressive,
large scale pub, just over the bridge on the opposite bank
of the river from the new Theatre Severn. Large
warehouse windows and huge bookcases dominate the
interior of the bar and restaurant area. There is a
comprehensive menu accompanied by a great range of
real ales, local cider and comprehensive wine list. Typical
dishes are grilled fresh mackerel with Caesar potato
salad; Welsh rarebit with a poached egg; pan-fried
chicken breast with fragrant rice, pak choi and Thai
green curry sauce.

Open all day all wk Closed: 25 Dec drinks only
Bar Meals food served all day **Restaurant** food served all
day ⊕ BRUNNING & PRICE ◼ Roosters APA, Salopian
Shropshire Gold, Deuchars IPA, Woods Shropshire Lad,
Three Tuns Steamer Ö Stowford Press, Ludlow Cider.
Facilities Children welcome Children's portions Dogs
allowed

PICK OF THE PUBS

The Mytton & Mermaid Hotel ★★★ HL 🏅🏅 ♟

Atcham SY5 6QG ☎ 01743 761220 📄 01743 761292
e-mail: reception@myttonandmermaid.co.uk
dir: From M54 junct 7 signed Shrewsbury, at 2nd rdbt
take 1st left signed Ironbridge/Atcham. In 1.5m hotel
on right after bridge

Reputedly linked by a secret tunnel to nearby St Eata's
church and situated opposite Attingham Park (National
Trust), this Grade II listed hotel dates from 1735 and
enjoys spectacular views over the River Severn.
Tastefully decorated throughout, the interior recalls the
atmosphere of its coaching days. There's a relaxed
gastro-pub feel about the place, especially in Mad
Jack's Bar, which is named after a colourful local
squire and features a wood floor, scrubbed tables,
comfy sofas and an open log fire. Here you can quaff a
pint of local Shropshire Lad and tuck into some
appetising dishes. Top-notch Shropshire ingredients
drive the seasonal, modern British menu with its two
AA Rosettes. Starters like split pea and ham soup
herald main course options that might encompass
lamb tagine with lemon and herb cous cous, or roasted
winter vegetable hotpot with grain mustard dumplings.
Leave space for dessert; blood orange and Champagne
jelly is a typical choice.

Open all day all wk 7am-11pm Closed: 25 Dec
Bar Meals L served Mon-Sat 12-2.30, Sun 12-9
D served Mon-Sat 6.30-10, Sun 12-9
Restaurant L served Mon-Sat 12-2.30, Sun 12-9
booking required D served Mon-Sat 7-10, Sun 12-9
booking required ⊕ FREE HOUSE ◼ Shropshire Lad,
Shropshire Gold, Hobsons Best. ♟ 12
Facilities Children welcome Children's menu Garden
Parking Wi-fi **Rooms** 18

SHREWSBURY *continued*

The Plume of Feathers ⏺

Harley SY5 6LP ☎ 01952 727360 📠 **01952 728542**
e-mail: feathersatharley@aol.com
dir: *Telephone for directions*

Nestling under Wenlock Edge, this beamed 16th-century country inn has stunning views across the valley, particularly from the garden. Look for the Charles I oak bedhead, full size cider press and inglenook fireplace. Food reflects the seasons and is served in the bar and restaurant. Real ales from local breweries feature strongly along with an extensive wine list served by the glass. A popular spot for anyone fond of outdoor pursuits, including fishing, shooting, walking and golf.

Open all wk **Bar Meals** L served all wk 11.30-2.30
D served all wk 5.30-9 Av main course £5
Restaurant L served all wk 12-2.30 D served all wk 6-9
Fixed menu price fr £7.95 Av 3 course à la carte fr £7.50
⊕ FREE HOUSE ◀ Guinness, Directors, Enville Ale, Guest
ales. **Facilities** Children welcome Children's menu
Children's portions Play area Garden Parking Wi-fi

STOTTESDON Map 10 SO68

Fighting Cocks

1 High St DY14 8TZ ☎ 01746 718270 📠 **01746 718270**
e-mail: sandrafc_5@hotmail.com
dir: *11m from Bridgnorth off B4376*

According to a framed newspaper cutting on the pub wall, 'Nipper Cook' drank 30 pints of cider each night at this unassuming 18th-century rural free house. Today, this lively local hosts regular music nights, as well as an apple day each October and an annual beer festival in November. The owners' neighbouring shop supplies local meats, home-made pies, sausages, and produce from the gardens. Expect home-made pâtés, curries, pies and puddings.

Open all wk 6-mdnt (Fri 5pm-1am Sat noon-mdnt Sun noon-10.30) **Bar Meals** L served Sat-Sun 12-2.30 booking required Av main course £9 **Restaurant** L served Sat-Sun 12-2.30 booking required D served Mon-Sat 7-9 booking required ⊕ FREE HOUSE ◀ Hobsons Best, Hobsons Town Crier, Hobsons Mild, Wye Valley HPA, Wye Valley Bitter ⓣ Stowford Press, Flagon. **Facilities** Children welcome Children's menu Garden Beer festival Parking Wi-fi

WELLINGTON Map 10 SJ61

The Old Orleton Inn ⏺

Holyhead Rd TF1 2HA ☎ 01952 255011
e-mail: aapub@theoldorleton.com
dir: *From M54 junct 7 take B5061 (Holyhead Rd), 400yds on left on corner of Haygate Rd & Holyhead Rd*

The old and new blend effortlessly throughout this refurbished 17th-century former coaching inn. Overlooking the famous Wrekin Hill, it is popular with walkers exploring the Shropshire countryside. Expect a relaxed and informal atmosphere, local Hobson ales on tap and modern British food, with lunch in the brasserie

taking in soup, sandwiches, salad platters and ham, egg and chips. Evening extras include Shropshire lamb, seared sea bass, and rib-eye steak with Stilton sauce.

Open noon-3 5-11 Closed: 1st 2wks Jan, Sun eve
Bar Meals L served Mon-Sat 12-2.30, Sun 12-4 D served Mon-Sat 6-9.30 Av main course £12.95
Restaurant L served Mon-Sat 12-2.30, Sun 12-4 booking required D served Mon-Sat 6-9.30 booking required Av 3 course à la carte fr £24.95 ⊕ FREE HOUSE ◀ Hobsons Best, Hobsons Town Crier ⓣ Stowford Press. ⏺ 10
Facilities Garden Parking Wi-fi

WENTNOR Map 15 SO39

The Crown Inn

SY9 5EE ☎ 01588 650613 📠 **01588 650436**
e-mail: thecrowninn@wentnor.com
dir: *From Shrewsbury A49 to Church Stretton, follow signs over Long Mynd to Asterton, right to Wentnor*

Winter walkers warm up beside wood-burning stoves in this inviting 16th-century timbered inn deep in the Shropshire Hills, whilst summer visitors relax on the covered decking, indulging in Three Tuns bitter and gazing at the Long Mynd's lofty ridge. Its homely atmosphere, enhanced by beams, wood burners and horse brasses, makes eating and drinking here a pleasure. Meals are served in the bar or separate restaurant. Typical daily changing, traditional home-made dishes include at least three vegetarian options, or spoil yourself with a famous Crown Pie.

Open all wk noon-3 6-11 (Sat noon-mdnt Sun noon-10) Closed: 25 Dec ⊕ FREE HOUSE ◀ Hobsons, Old Speckled Hen, Three Tuns, Wye Valley ⓣ Westons Scrumpy.
Facilities Children welcome Children's menu Children's portions Play area Garden Parking

WHITCHURCH Map 15 SJ54

Willeymoor Lock Tavern ⏺

Tarporley Rd SY13 4HF ☎ 01948 663274
dir: *2m N of Whitchurch on A49 (Warrington to Tarporley road)*

A much-extended former lock-keeper's cottage by the busy Llangollen Canal, so there are usually narrowboats to watch. In the bar, Shropshire Gold represents the county, teapots hang from low beams and there are open log fires. Competitively priced food includes grills; steak and onion pie; chicken curry; vegetable chilli; and salads. A children's play area and large beer garden make this an ideal warm weather location. A popular spot with walkers as the pub is near the Sandstone Trail and the Bishop Bennett Way.

Open all wk 12-2.30 6-11 (Sun 12-2.30 6-10.30) Closed: 25 Dec **Bar Meals** L served all wk 12-2 D served all wk 6-9 Av main course £7.50 **Restaurant** L served all wk 12-2 D served all wk 6-9 ⊕ FREE HOUSE ◀ Weetwood Eastgate, Timothy Taylor Landlord, Greene King IPA, Old Speckled Hen, Shropshire Gold, Stonehouse. ⏺ 9 **Facilities** Children welcome Children's menu Play area Garden Parking

SOMERSET

APPLEY Map 3 ST02

The Globe Inn ⏺

TA21 0HJ ☎ 01823 672327
e-mail: globeinnappley@btconnect.com
dir: *From M5 junct 26 take A38 towards Exeter. Village signed in 5m*

Known for its large collection of Corgi and Dinky cars, Titanic memorabilia, old advertising posters and enamel signs, this Grade II listed inn dates back 500 years and is hidden in a maze of lanes on the Somerset-Devon border. Its smart beer gardens have lovely views over rolling hills, and it makes a perfect refreshment stop for walkers and cyclists. Local seasonal produce is used in the baguettes, burgers, bar meals and main courses such as oven-baked chicken breast topped with melted Brie and red onion marmalade, lamb, almond and butternut squash tagine, or venison pie. A beer festival is held the first weekend in September.

Open Tue-Sun Closed: Mon (ex BH) Sun eve Nov-Apr
Bar Meals L served Tue-Sun 12-2 booking required D served Tue-Sun 7-9.30 booking required Av main course £10 **Restaurant** L served Tue-Sun 12-2 booking required D served Tue-Sun 7-9.30 booking required Fixed menu price fr £10 Av 3 course à la carte fr £24 ⊕ FREE HOUSE ◀ Exmoor Ales, Appleys Ale, Doom Bar, Tribute, Cotleigh Harrier, Otter Ale, O'Hanlon's Yellow Hammer ⓣ Thatchers Gold, Rattlers. ⏺ 8 **Facilities** Children welcome Children's menu Children's portions Play area Garden Beer festival Parking

ASHCOTT Map 4 ST43

Ring O'Bells ⏺

High St TA7 9PZ ☎ 01458 210232
e-mail: info@ringobells.com
dir: *M5 junct 23 follow A39 & Glastonbury signs. In Ashcott turn left, at post office follow church & village hall signs*

An independent free house successfully run by the same family for 24 years. Parts of the building date from 1750, so the traditional village pub interior has beams, split-level bars, an old fireplace and a collection of bells and horse brasses. Close to the Somerset Levels, RSPB reserve at Ham Wall and National Nature Reserve at Shapwick Heath. Local ales and ciders are a speciality, while all food is made on the premises. Expect good value dishes and daily specials such as fresh grilled sardines with granary bread; pork escalope with apricot and brandy sauce; whole grilled sea bream; Moroccan tagine of lamb; and pineapple meringue pie.

Open all wk noon-3 7-11 (Sun 7-10.30pm) Closed: 25 Dec **Bar Meals** L served all wk 12-2 D served all wk 7-10 Av main course £9-£10 **Restaurant** L served all wk 12-2 D served all wk 7-10 Av 3 course à la carte fr £17 ⊕ FREE HOUSE ◀ Guest ales ⓣ Wilkins Farmhouse Cider. ⏺ 8 **Facilities** Children welcome Children's menu Children's portions Play area Dogs allowed Garden Parking Wi-fi

ASHILL — Map 4 ST31

Square & Compass ★★★★ INN

Windmill Hill TA19 9NX ☎ 01823 480467
e-mail: squareandcompass@tiscali.co.uk
dir: Exit A358 at Stewley Cross service station onto Wood Rd. 1m to pub in Windmill Hill

There's been a pub at Windmill Hill for over 200 years. Beautifully located overlooking the Blackdown Hills in the heart of rural Somerset, this traditional, family-owned country pub has lovely gardens that make the most of the views. Inside there's a warm, friendly atmosphere with the bar area featuring hand-made settles and tables. There is a good choice of home-cooked food (prepared in the state-of-the-art large kitchen). Dishes might include sweet and sour pork, and mixed grill. The barn next door was built by the owners from reclaimed materials for use as a wedding and village events venue, and 'the stables' housing eight four-star bedrooms was built in 2010.

Open 12-3 6.30-late (Sun 7-late) Closed: Tue, Wed, Thu L **Bar Meals** L served Fri-Mon 12-2 D served all wk 7-9.30 **Restaurant** L served Fri-Mon 12-2 D served all wk 7-9.30 ⊕ FREE HOUSE ◀ Exmoor Ale, Tribute, Tinners. **Facilities** Children welcome Children's menu Children's portions Dogs allowed Garden Parking Wi-fi **Rooms** 8

AXBRIDGE — Map 4 ST45

Lamb Inn

The Square BS26 2AP ☎ 01934 732253
dir: 10m from Wells & Weston-Super-Mare on A370

Parts of this rambling 15th-century inn were once the guildhall, but it was licensed in 1830 when the new town hall was built. Standing across the medieval square from King John's hunting lodge, the pub's comfortable bars have log fires and offer Butcombe ales; there's also a skittle alley and large terraced garden. Snacks and pub favourites support contemporary home-made dishes like trio of lambs chops, Mexican spicy chicken, curry of the day, and home-made lasagne.

Open all wk Mon-Wed 11-3 6-11 Thu-Sat 11am-11.30pm Sun 12-10.30 **Bar Meals** L served all wk 12-2.30 booking required D served Mon-Sat 6-9 booking required Av main course £10.25 ⊕ BUTCOMBE ◀ Butcombe, Butcombe Gold, Guest ales Ŏ Thatchers, Ashton Press. **Facilities** Children's menu Dogs allowed Garden Wi-fi

BABCARY — Map 4 ST52

Red Lion ♛

TA11 7ED ☎ 01458 223230 📄 01458 224510
e-mail: redlionbabcary@btinternet.com
dir: Please telephone for directions

A beautifully refurbished, multi-gabled, stone-built free house with rich colour-washed walls, heavy beams and simple wooden furniture. Granary sandwiches, ciabattas and pub favourites like fish pie and honey-glazed Somerset ham, egg and chips are served in the bar along with a great selection of real ales. French doors lead out into the garden from the restaurant, where the daily menus tend to feature dishes such as spiced Marrakesh vegetable tagine with couscous; pan-fried hake fillet; and Belgian-style mussels and frites.

Open all wk **Bar Meals** L served all wk 12-2.30 D served Mon-Sat 7-9.30 Av main course £11.50 **Restaurant** L served all wk 12-2.30 D served Mon-Sat 7-9.30 Av 3 course à la carte fr £23 ⊕ FREE HOUSE ◀ Teignworthy Ale, O'Hanlons, Otter, Bath Ales Ŏ Stowford Press. ♛ 12 **Facilities** Children welcome Play area Dogs allowed Garden Parking Wi-fi

BACKWELL — Map 4 ST46

The New Inn ♛ NEW

86 West Town Rd BS48 3BE ☎ 01275 462199
e-mail: info@newinn-backwell.co.uk
dir: From Bristol A370 towards Weston-Super-Mare. Pub on right just after Backwell in West Town. Or from M5 junct 21, A370 towards Bristol

This 18th-century country pub has a relaxed and welcoming atmosphere inside, and a rear garden perfect for summertime Sunday evening barbecues. A good selection of draught beers and ciders is sold at the bar, while attentive staff look after diners tucking in to French and English inspired dishes that range from the traditional to the contemporary: potato and roasted garlic soup, for example, could be followed by pan-roasted Gressingham duck breast with celeriac purée. Dogs are allowed in the bar and garden, and there is plenty of parking.

Open all day all wk Closed: 25 Dec **Bar Meals** Av main course £15 food served all day **Restaurant** L served Mon-Sat 12-2.30, Sun 12-3.30 D served Mon-Thu 6-9.30, Fri-Sat 6.30-10 Fixed menu price fr £15 Av 3 course à la carte fr £23.50 ⊕ ENTERPRISE INNS ◀ Sharp's Doom Bar, Timothy Taylor Landlord, Butcombe Brunel Ŏ Stowford Press, Westons Organic. ♛ 15 **Facilities** Children welcome Children's portions Dogs allowed Garden Parking

BATH — Map 4 ST76

The Chequers NEW

50 Rivers St BA1 2QA ☎ 01225 360017
e-mail: info@thechequersbath.com
dir: In city centre, near the Royal Crescent

A short walk from Bath's most famous landmarks, this pub opened as the New Inn around 1776 to serve weary sedan chairmen. The name changed to The Chequers in the 1950s and was recently taken over by the team behind the nearby Marlborough Tavern (see entry). The bar offers a range of pub classics, whilst the upstairs restaurant is the place to enjoy à la carte choices like loin of veal with Bolognese ravioli, celeriac cream and horseradish.

Open all day all wk Closed: 25 Dec **Bar Meals** L served all wk 12-2.30 D served all wk 6-9.30 Av main course £13 **Restaurant** D served all wk 6-9.30 Av 3 course à la carte fr £25 ◀ Butcombe Bitter, Bath Ales Gem Ŏ Westons Organic. **Facilities** Children welcome Children's portions

PICK OF THE PUBS

The Hop Pole ♛

7 Albion Buildings, Upper Bristol Rd BA1 3AR
☎ 01225 446327
e-mail: hoppole@bathales.co.uk
dir: On A4 from city centre towards Bristol. Pub opposite Royal Victoria Park

Opposite the Royal Victoria Park and just off the canal path, this is a great spot for quaffing summer ales. One of just ten pubs belonging to Bath Ales, a fresh young micro-brewery, the beers rejoice in names such as Gem, Spa, Wild Hare and Barnstormer. Described as a country pub in the heart of a city, The Hop Pole has a stripped-down, stylish interior, and the lovingly restored, spacious beer garden to the rear is complete with patio heaters and pétanque pitch. The atmospheric old skittle alley has been transformed into a large restaurant, which can accommodate coach parties if pre-booked. Home-cooked food ranges from imaginative bar snacks and sandwiches through to full meals. Children are served smaller portions from the main menu. You could start with pork and foie gras sausage roll with piccalilli before moving on to a slowly braised chuck and shin steak stew, mash and onion gravy, or basil risotto and buffalo mozzarella. Monday night is quiz night.

Open all day all wk noon-11 (Fri-Sat noon-mdnt) **Bar Meals** L served Mon-Fri 12-3, Sat 12-9.30, Sun 12-4 D served Mon-Fri 6-9 **Restaurant** L served Mon-Fri 12-3, Sat 12-9.30, Sun 12-4 D served Mon-Fri 6-9 ◀ Bath Ales: Gem, Spa, Barnstormer, Festivity, Wild Hare Ŏ Bounders. ♛ 14 **Facilities** Children welcome Children's menu Children's portions Garden Wi-fi

BATH *continued*

PICK OF THE PUBS

King William ☆

36 Thomas St BA1 5NN ☎ 01225 428096
e-mail: info@kingwilliampub.com
dir: *At junct of Thomas St & A4 (London Rd), on left from Bath towards London. 15 mins walk from Bath Spa main line station*

Handy for all of Bath's attractions, yet away from the hurly-burly of the often-crowded city centre this appealing end-of-terrace, Bath stone, street-corner local exudes the charm and character that other places can only yearn for. It's a happy mix of destination dining inn and local's pub, effortlessly catering for both these markets, with a cosy snug and traditional bar and a memorable dining room upstairs. Beer-tickers are in seventh heaven, with changing beers from the like of Box Steam and Stonehenge breweries and some presidential-strength real Somerset ciders. Chow down with bar snacks such as cider-steamed mussels and triple-cooked chips, or dine in restaurant style with pigeon and mallard terrine, medlar syrup and leaves starter followed by braised shin of beef with beetroot and horseradish dumplings; the inspiring menu changes daily, ending maybe with hot chocolate pot with Guinness ice cream. Easy eating, with a good wine list for a bracing accompaniment.

Open noon-3 5-close (Sat-Sun noon-close) Closed: Mon-Tue L **Bar Meals** L served Wed-Sun 12-3 D served Mon-Sat 6-10, Sun 6-9 **Restaurant** L served Sun 12-3 booking required D served Wed-Sat 6-10 booking required ⊕ FREE HOUSE ◀ Danish Dynamite, Dorset Gold, Sharp's Doom Bar, Tunnel Vision, Funky Monkey ♻ Pheasant Plucker, Westons Organic, Orchard Pig. ☘ 14 **Facilities** Children welcome Children's portions Dogs allowed Wi-fi

PICK OF THE PUBS

The Marlborough Tavern ◉◉ ☘

35 Marlborough Buildings BA1 2LY ☎ 01225 423731
e-mail: joe@marlborough-tavern.com
dir: *200mtrs from W end of Royal Crescent, on corner of Marlborough Buildings. 10m from M4 junct 18*

'Great tasting food with excellent service in a friendly pub atmosphere' is the admirable promise of this 18th-century corner pub. Revamped from a dreary boozer to a contemporary dining pub in 2006, it stands just a stone's throw away from Bath's famous Royal Crescent. Once a favoured resting place for foot-weary sedan chair carriers, today's shoppers and visitors – probably foot-weary from following the city's tourist trail – seek refreshment in the rustic-chic bars or the attractive courtyard garden. Since acquiring the freehold in 2009, Joe Cussens has added Butcombe and Otter ales to the cellar, and upped the number of wines sold by the glass to 16. The classy menu delivers gutsy, full-flavoured dishes prepared from local seasonal and

organic produce. Typical of the starters is a confit Chew Valley rainbow trout with beetroot purée, trout tartare and almonds. This could be followed by a spice-crusted loin of Brixham ling with clams, Bath pig chorizo and chickpea casserole. Round off with warm pistachio sponge, blood orange pannacotta and pistachio coulis.

Open all day all wk noon-11 (Fri-Sat noon-12.30am) Closed: 25 Dec **Restaurant** L served Mon-Sat 12.30-2.30, Sun 12.30-4 booking required D served Mon-Sat 6-10, Sun 6-9 booking required Av 3 course à la carte fr £25 ⊕ FREE HOUSE ◀ Butcombe Bitter, Timothy Taylor Landlord, Otter ♻ Addlestones. ☘ 16 **Facilities** Children welcome Children's portions Dogs allowed Garden Wi-fi

---

The Star Inn

23 Vineyards BA1 5NA ☎ 01225 425072
e-mail: landlord@star-inn-bath.co.uk
dir: *On A4, 300mtrs from centre of Bath*

One of Bath's oldest pubs and of outstanding historic interest, The Star was first licensed in 1760. Set amid glorious Georgian architecture, it is an impressive building in its own right, with original features including 19th-century Gaskell and Chambers bar fittings, a barrel lift from the cellar, and even complimentary pinches of snuff found in tins in the smaller bar! Long famous for its pints of Bass served from the jug, these days Abbey Ales from Bath's only brewery are also popular. Fresh filled rolls are available and free snacks on Sundays. A beer festival is held twice a year.

Open all wk noon-2.30 5.30-mdnt (Fri noon-2.30 5.30-1am Sat noon-1am Sun noon-mdnt) ⊕ PUNCH TAVERNS ◀ Bellringer, Bass, Bath Star, Twelfth Night, White Friar ♻ Hells Bells. **Facilities** Children welcome Dogs allowed Beer festival Wi-fi

BAWDRIP   Map 4 ST33

The Knowle Inn

TA7 8PN ☎ 01278 683330
e-mail: peter@matthews3.wanadoo.co.uk
dir: *M5 junct 23 or A39 from Bridgwater towards Glastonbury*

A mile off the M5, this 16th-century pub nestles beneath the Polden Hills on the edge of the Somerset levels – a great place for walking and cycling. A true community pub, with live music, skittles and darts, it also specialises in fresh seafood, with sea bass and John Dory often among the catch delivered from Plymouth. A full range of sandwiches and light meals is backed by pub favourites such as home-made lasagne, home-cooked ham, and the butcher's choice mixed grill. A Mediterranean-style garden, complete with fish pond, is ideal for summer alfresco meals.

Open all day all wk ⊕ ENTERPRISE INNS ◀ Otter, Guest ales ♻ Thatchers. **Facilities** Children welcome Children's menu Children's portions Dogs allowed Garden Parking

BECKINGTON   Map 4 ST85

Woolpack Inn ★★★ INN

BA11 6SP ☎ 01373 831244 📠 01373 831223
e-mail: 6534@greeneking.co.uk
dir: *Just off A36 near junct with A361*

Standing in the middle of the village, this charming, stone-built coaching inn dates back to the 1500s. Inside there's an attractive, flagstone floor in the bar and outside at the back, a delightful terraced garden. The lunch menu offers soup and sandwich platters, and larger dishes such as home-made sausages and mash; fresh herb and tomato omelette; steak and ale pie; and beer-battered cod and chips. Some of these are also listed on the evening bar menu. Eleven en suite bedrooms, including one four poster room and one family room, are available. Change of hands.

Open all day all wk 11am-11pm (Sun 11am-10pm) ⊕ OLD ENGLISH INNS & HOTELS ◀ Greene King IPA, Abbot Ale, guest ale ♻ Moles Black Rat. **Facilities** Children welcome Children's menu Children's portions Dogs allowed Garden Parking Wi-fi **Rooms** 11

BLUE ANCHOR   Map 3 ST04

The Smugglers ☘

TA24 6JS ☎ 01984 640385
e-mail: info@take2chefs.co.uk
dir: *Off A3191, midway between Minehead & Watchet*

'Fresh food, cooked well' is the simple philosophy at this friendly 300-year-old inn, standing just yards from Blue Anchor's sandy bay with a backdrop of the Exmoor Hills. Food, using fresh produce locally sourced, can be enjoyed in The Cellar Bar. Sandwiches, filled jacket potatoes, pizzas, wraps, pastas, grills, salads, speciality sausages and fish and seafood are available. Specials might include skate fillet, red peppers, crushed potatoes, capers and smoked ham; and triple-decker thyme marinated steak sandwich. In fine weather diners can eat in the large walled garden, where children will enjoy the animals at the nearby farm and bouncy castle. The pub also offers a take-away menu.

Open Mon-Fri noon-3 6-11 (Sat-Sun 12-11) Closed: Nov-Etr, Sun eve, Mon-Tue **Bar Meals** L served all wk 12-2.15 D served all wk 6-9 **Restaurant** L served all wk 12-2.15 D served all wk 6-9 ⊕ FREE HOUSE ◀ Smuggled Otter, Otter Ale, John Smith's ♻ Western Traditional. ☘ 8 **Facilities** Children welcome Children's menu Children's portions Play area Dogs allowed Garden Parking Wi-fi

BRADFORD-ON-TONE   Map 4 ST12

White Horse Inn

Regent St TA4 1HF ☎ 01823 461239

e-mail: glenwhitehorse@googlemail.com

dir: N of A38 between Taunton & Wellington

Dating back over 300 years, this stone-built inn stands opposite the church in the heart of a delightful thatched village. Very much a community pub, it has a bar area, restaurant, outdoor skittle lane or boules pitch, garden and patio. Real ales brewed in the south west include guests, and home-cooked food favours tried and tested popular dishes: Somerset pork with scrumpy apple and rustic vegetable sauce; steak and ale pie; and fillets of sea bass with red onion marmalade. There's a pasta menu on Tuesdays evenings and a curry on Wednesdays.

Open all day all wk Bar Meals L served all wk 12-2 D served all wk 6-9 Av main course £6
Restaurant L served all wk 12-2 D served all wk 6-9 Fixed menu price fr £8.50 Av 3 course à la carte fr £16 ⊞ ENTERPRISE INNS ◀ Cotleigh Tawney, John Smith's, Whitbread Best, Sharp's Doom Bar, Exmoor ale, Guest ales. Facilities Children welcome Children's menu Children's portions Dogs allowed Garden Parking Wi-fi

CATCOTT   Map 4 ST33

The Crown Inn ₹

1 The Nydon TA7 9HQ ☎ 01278 722288

e-mail: catcottcrownin@aol.com

dir: M5 junct 23, A39 towards Glastonbury. Turn left to Catcott

Perhaps 400 years old, this low-beamed, flagstone-floored pub in the Somerset levels originated as a beer house serving local peat-cutters. The winter log fire takes the chill off Bristol Channel winds; in summer the half-acre beer garden is great for families and sun worshippers. Food is plentiful, imaginative and home made, with highlights including well matured local steaks, fresh fish, and local game when in season. A good range of cask ales and ciders from regional suppliers completes the picture.

Open 12-2.30 6-late Closed: Mon L Bar Meals L served Tue-Sun 12-2 (booking advisable Sun) D served all wk 6-9 Av main course £7.95 Restaurant L served Tue-Sun 12-2 (booking advisable Sun) D served Sun-Thu 6-9, Fri-Sat 6-9.30 (booking advisable Fri-Sat) Fixed menu price fr £9.95 Av 3 course à la carte fr £17.95 ⊞ FREE HOUSE ◀ Butcombe, Sharp's Doom Bar ♻ Ashton Press. ₹ 10 Facilities Children welcome Children's menu Children's portions Play area Dogs allowed Garden Parking

CHEW MAGNA   Map 4 ST56

PICK OF THE PUBS

The Bear and Swan ₹

South Pde BS40 8SL ☎ 01275 331100

e-mail: bearandswan@fullers.co.uk

dir: A37 from Bristol. Turn right signed Chew Magna onto B3130. Or from A38 turn left on B3130

Behind the Victorian frontage of this early 18th-century, oak-beamed pub lies a light, fresh-feeling interior with scrubbed wooden floorboards and a hotchpotch of reclaimed tables and chairs, plus a warm and cosy atmosphere. Real ales include Fuller's London Pride and Butcombe Bitter, real ciders come from around and about and the wines have been well selected. The restaurant offers a daily menu and a carte with good choices of fish, game, seafood, meats and vegetarian dishes. In the bar, 'Bear Basics' include Cumberland sausage with mash and gravy, and char-grilled rib eye steak with salad, fries and herb butter. In the restaurant, you might start with moules marinière or warm goat's cheese tart with red onion jam and mixed leaves before moving on to char-grilled tuna steak with coriander salsa and crème fraîche or duck breast on hoi sin poached pear with passionfruit sauce. For dessert, maybe try chocolate brownies with white and dark chocolate sauce.

Open all day Closed: 25 Dec, Sun eve Bar Meals L served Mon-Sat 12-2.30, Sun 12-3 D served Mon-Sat 6.30-9.30 Av main course £9 Restaurant L served Mon-Sat 12-2.30, Sun 12-3 booking required D served Mon-Sat 6.30-9.30 booking required Av 3 course à la carte fr £24 ⊞ FULLER'S ◀ London Pride, Butcombe Bitter ♻ Ashton Press, Aspall, Symonds. ₹ 12 Facilities Children welcome Children's portions Dogs allowed Garden Parking Wi-fi

The Pony and Trap ₹ NEW

Knowle Hill, Newton BS40 8TQ ☎ 01275 332627

e-mail: josh@theponyandtrap.co.uk

dir: Take A37 S from Bristol. After Pensfold turn right at rdbt onto A368 towards Weston-Super-Mare. In 1.5m right signed Chew Magna & Winford. Pub 1m on right

After working with top chefs around the world, what next? Obvious - return to your native Chew Valley and run a 200-year-old country cottage pub/restaurant, as ex-Gordon Ramsay scholar Josh Eggleton does. Committed to sourcing all ingredients as locally as possible, everything on the menu is freshly cooked and all accompaniments and desserts are hand made. From his impressive menu, try steamed mussels and clams; merguez sausages, roast pigeon breast and red onion jam; chargrilled fillet and pressed belly of pork with cauliflower purée and black pudding; or whole roasted plaice with garlic butter. Fine wines, real ales and ciders complete the picture.

Open 11.30-3 6.30-mdnt Closed: Mon, Sun eve in Winter Bar Meals L served all wk 12-2.30 booking required D served all wk 7-9.30 booking required Av main course £9-£16 Restaurant L served all wk 12-2.30 booking required D served all wk 7-10 booking required Av 3 course à la carte fr £25-£27 ⊞ FREE HOUSE ◀ Butcombe Bitter, Sharp's Doom Bar, Guest ale ♻ Ashton Press, Orchard Pig. ₹ 12 Facilities Children welcome Children's portions Dogs allowed Garden Parking Wi-fi

CHISELBOROUGH   Map 4 ST41

The Cat Head Inn

Cat St TA14 6TT ☎ 01935 881231

e-mail: info@thecatheadinn.co.uk

dir: Leave A303 onto A356 towards Crewkerne, take 3rd left turn (at 1.4m) signposted Chiselborough, then after 0.2m turn left

Once a farmhouse, and probably creeper-clad back then too, the Cat Head's flagstoned, open fire-warmed interior is furnished with light wooden tables and chairs, and high-backed settles. New owners have introduced seasonal menus with a strong commitment to using local produce - roe deer on rösti potato with wild berry sauce; scallops with cream chilli sauce; and pork tenderloin on celeriac mash. Doom Bar and Butcombe are the resident real ales in the picturesque bar, alongside Cheddar Valley cider. Outside are attractive gardens and play area.

Open all wk 12-2.30 6-11 Closed: Mon in winter Bar Meals L served Mon-Sat 12-2.30 booking required D served Tue-Sat 6-9.30 booking required Av main course £8-£10 food served all day Restaurant L served Mon-Sat 12-2.30 booking required D served Mon-Sat 6-9.30 booking required Fixed menu price fr £15 Av 3 course à la carte fr £25 food served all day ⊞ ENTERPRISE INNS ◀ Butcombe, Doom Bar ♻ Cheddar Valley. Facilities Children welcome Children's menu Children's portions Play area Family room Dogs allowed Garden Wi-fi

CHURCHILL   Map 4 ST45

The Crown Inn

The Batch BS25 5PP ☎ 01934 852995

dir: From Bristol take A38 S. Right at Churchill lights, left in 200mtrs, up hill to pub

It's hard to believe that this gem of a pub could once have been a stop on what was then the Bristol to Exeter coach road. Ten real ales are served straight from the cask in the two flagstone-floored bars, where open fires blaze on cold days. Freshly prepared bar lunches, including sandwiches, filled jacket potatoes, sausages and mash and pork casserole, are made from the best local ingredients. Enjoy a meal in the beautiful gardens.

Open all day all wk 11-11 (Fri 11-mdnt) Bar Meals L served all wk 12-2.30 Av main course £5.95 ⊞ FREE HOUSE ◀ Palmers IPA, Draught Bass, P G Steam, Butcombe, Batch Bitter ♻ Thatchers. Facilities Children welcome Children's portions Dogs allowed Garden Parking Notes ⊛

PICK OF THE PUBS

The Hunters Rest ★★★★ INN ♊

CLUTTON — Map 4 ST65

King Ln, Clutton Hill BS39 5QL
☎ **01761 452303** 📠 **01761 453308**
e-mail: info@huntersrest.co.uk
web: www.huntersrest.co.uk
dir: *On A37 follow signs for Wells through Pensford, at large rdbt left towards Bath, 100mtrs right into country lane, pub 1m up hill*

From this popular old free house there's a choice of commanding views – over the Cam Valley to the Mendip Hills, or across the Chew Valley towards Bristol: both are well worth the trip. It was built around 1750 as a hunting lodge for the Earl of Warwick – a man who clearly knew how to pick the perfect site – but when the estate was sold in 1872, the building became a tavern serving the growing number of coal miners working in the area. Mining finished long ago and the inn has been transformed into an attractive place to eat and stay, with five individually decorated bedrooms, including two four-poster suites.

Paul Thomas has been running the place for over 20 years and has established a great reputation for good home-made food, real ales, typically Butcombe, Bath Gem and Otter, and a reasonably priced wine list, with a fair number by the glass. The menu includes local smoked trout and prawn salad; bakehouse rolls with fillings like cold baked ham or rump steak; giant pastries called oggies, which might come filled with casseroled beef, fiery chillies, peppers and tomatoes – that's the one Paul calls, not unreasonably, the Welsh Dragon – or perhaps with cauliflower cheese. Other hot dishes include Somerset faggots with onion gravy; deep-fried wholetail scampi; chicken Madras; breaded vegetable parcels; and from the specials blackboard a selection of daily-delivered Brixham fish and more. There's also a children's menu (battered haddock; beef burger; ham and free-range egg), and a dozen popular desserts such as banana and caramel cheesecake, and blackberry and clotted cream ice cream. In summer you can sit out in the landscaped grounds or take a ride on the 500-yard miniature railway.

Open all day all wk **Bar Meals** L served all wk 12-9.45 D served all wk 12-9.45 Av main course £10 food served all day **Restaurant** L served all wk 12-9.45 D served all wk 12-9.45 Av 3 course à la carte fr £22.50 food served all day ⊕ FREE HOUSE ◀ Butcombe, Bath Gem, Otter Ale ⌚ Broadoak Thatchers. ♊ 10 **Facilities** Children's menu Children's portions Play area Family room Dogs allowed Garden Parking Wi-fi **Rooms** 5

CLAPTON-IN-GORDANO   Map 4 ST47

PICK OF THE PUBS

The Black Horse ♀

Clevedon Ln BS20 7RH ☎ 01275 842105
e-mail: theblackhorse@talktalkbusiness.net
dir: *M5 junct 19, 3m to village. 2m from Portishead, 10m from Bristol*

The pretty, whitewashed Black Horse was built in the 14th century and the small Snug Bar was once the village lock up, as the surviving bars on one of the windows testify. The traditional bar features low beams, flagstone floors, wooden settles and old guns above the big open fireplace. The kitchen in this listed building is tiny, which limits its output to traditional pub food served lunchtimes only (Monday to Saturday). The repertoire includes hot and cold filled baguettes; home-made soup of the day; beef cooked in Guinness; corned beef hash; as well as seasonal specials. The large rear garden includes a children's play area, and there's a separate family room.

Open all day all wk **Bar Meals** L served Mon-Sat 12-2 Av main course £6.50 ⊕ ENTERPRISE ◀ Courage Best, Wadworth 6X, Shepherd Neame Spitfire, Butcombe Best, Exmoor Gold, Otter Bitter Ŏ Thatchers Dry, Moles Black Rat. ♀ 8 **Facilities** Children welcome Play area Family room Dogs allowed Garden Parking

CLUTTON   Map 4 ST65

PICK OF THE PUBS

The Hunters Rest   INN ♀

See Pick of the Pubs on opposite page

COMBE HAY   Map 4 ST75

PICK OF THE PUBS

The Wheatsheaf Inn ♀

See Pick of the Pubs on page 390

COMPTON DANDO   Map 4 ST66

The Compton Inn ♀ NEW

Court Hill BS39 4JZ ☎ 01761 490321
e-mail: paul@huntersrest.co.uk
dir: *From A368 between Chelwood & Marksbury follow Hunstrete & Compton Dando signs*

With its imposing church and hump-backed bridge crossing the River Chew, Compton Dando is a tranquil, picturesque location seven miles from the bustling city of Bristol. A Grade II-listed former farmhouse, The Compton Inn has only been a pub since WWII but it has been sympathetically restored. It's an ideal bolthole to enjoy local ale and cider, and well-cooked dishes like ham and free-range eggs with chips or Somerset faggots with cider and onion gravy.

Open all day all wk **Bar Meals** L served Mon-Sat 12-2.15, Sun 12-6 D served Mon-Sat 6.15-9.15 Av main course £10 **Restaurant** L served Mon-Sat 12-2.15, Sun 12-6 D served Mon-Sat 6.15-9.15 Av 3 course à la carte fr £20 ⊕ PUNCH TAVERNS ◀ Butcombe, Bath Gem, Sharp's Doom Bar Ŏ Thatchers Traditional. ♀ 10 **Facilities** Children welcome Children's menu Children's portions Dogs allowed Garden Parking Wi-fi

CONGRESBURY   Map 4 ST46

The Ship and Castle ★★★★ INN ◉

High St BS49 5JA ☎ 01934 833535
e-mail: info@shipandcastle.com
dir: *M5 junct 21, A370 towards Bristol for 4m. Pub in village centre at lights*

New life has been breathed into this 500-year-old inn close to Bristol Airport and the M5, with six boutique-style bedrooms and a stylish refurbishment of the cosy bar and dining areas. Expect to find log fires in old stone fireplaces, fat church candles on chunky tables, deep sofas to sink into, Greene King ales on handpump and seasonal menus that champion local produce. Try the seafood chowder, followed by braised lamb shank, and chocolate brownie with clotted cream.

Open all day all wk ⊕ GREENE KING ◀ Greene King IPA, Abbot Ale, Old Speckled Hen Ŏ Stowford Press, Aspall. **Facilities** Children welcome Children's menu Children's portions Dogs allowed Garden Parking Wi-fi **Rooms** 6

CORTON DENHAM   Map 4 ST62

PICK OF THE PUBS

The Queens Arms ♀

See Pick of the Pubs on page 391

CRANMORE   Map 4 ST64

Strode Arms

BA4 4QJ ☎ 01749 880450
dir: *S of A361, 3.5m E of Shepton Mallet, 7.5m W of Frome*

Just up the road from the East Somerset Railway, this rambling old coaching inn boasts a splendid front terrace overlooking the village duck pond. Spacious bar areas are neatly laid out with comfortable country furnishings and warmed by winter log fires; the perfect setting to enjoy a pint of Bishop's Tipple or Strong in the Arm. Expect dishes such as grilled lamb cutlets with Indian spiced rice and lime pickle; home-cooked Huntingdon fidget pie; smoked chicken and asparagus tagliatelli; warm sweet red onion tart with Somerset goat's cheese and fresh figs.

Open all wk 11.30-3 6-11 **Bar Meals** L served all wk 12-2 D served Mon-Sat 6-9 Av main course £9.25 **Restaurant** L served all wk 12-2 D served Mon-Sat 6-9 ⊕ WADWORTH ◀ Henry's IPA, Wadworth 6X, Bishop's Tipple, Strong In The Arm. **Facilities** Children welcome Children's menu Children's portions Family room Dogs allowed Garden Parking Wi-fi

CREWKERNE   Map 4 ST40

The George Inn ★★★ INN ♀

Market Square TA18 7LP
☎ 01460 73650   📄 01460 72974
e-mail: georgecrewkerne@btconnect.com
web: www.thegeorgehotelcrewkerne.co.uk
dir: *Telephone for directions*

Situated in the heart of Crewkerne, The George has been welcoming travellers since 1541, though the present ham stone building dates from 1832. Thatchers ciders sit alongside four real ales in the bar, while the kitchen produces an array of popular dishes for bar snacks and more substantial meals from the daily specials board. Vegetarian and vegan meals are always available. Thirteen comfortable en suite bedrooms are traditionally styled and include four-poster rooms.

Open all day all wk **Bar Meals** L served all wk 12-2 D served all wk 7-9 **Restaurant** L served all wk 12-2 D served all wk 7-9 ⊕ FREE HOUSE ◀ Old Speckled Hen, Doom Bar, Tribute, Boddington's Ŏ Thatchers Dry, Thatchers Gold. ♀ 8 **Facilities** Children welcome Wi-fi **Rooms** 13

The Manor Arms

North Perrott TA18 7SG ☎ 01460 72901
dir: *From A30 (Yeovil/Honiton) take A3066 towards Bridport. North Perrott 1.5m*

On the Dorset-Somerset border, this 16th-century Grade II listed pub and its neighbouring hamstone cottages overlook the village green. The popular River Parrett trail runs by the door. The inn has been lovingly restored and an inglenook fireplace, flagstone floors and oak beams are among the charming features inside. With ales like Exmoor, and Thatchers Gold cider, expect simple traditional food such as grilled steaks and chicken dishes, with bar snacks like sandwiches, baguettes and jacket potatoes.

Open all wk noon-11 **Bar Meals** L served all wk 12-2.30 D served all wk 6.30-9 Av main course £8.95 **Restaurant** L served all wk 12-2.30 D served all wk 6.30-9 Av 3 course à la carte fr £13.95 ⊕ ENTERPISE INNS ◀ Butcombe, Sharp's Doom Bar, Exmoor Ŏ Thatchers Gold. **Facilities** Children welcome Children's menu Children's portions Dogs allowed Garden Parking

PICK OF THE PUBS

The Wheatsheaf Inn ♀

COMBE HAY
Map 4 ST75

BA2 7EG ☎ 01225 833504
e-mail: info@wheatsheafcombehay.com
web: www.wheatsheafcombehay.co.uk
dir: *From Bath take A369 (Exeter road) to Odd Down, left at park towards Combe Hay. 2m to thatched cottage, turn left*

A pretty black and white timbered free house, nestling on a peaceful hillside just off the A367 south of Bath and close to the route of the former Somerset Coal Canal. The canal and the railway have come and gone, but the valley and its people survive; in fact, a newspaper recently named Combe Hay as one of England's most desirable villages. The Wheatsheaf was originally built as a farmhouse in 1576, and parts of the present building date back to the 16th century. It began opening its doors as a public house in the 18th century, and has been welcoming locals and travellers alike ever since. Today, real ales, local cider and an amazing European wine list (thanks to the passion of the owner) are available in the stylishly decorated, rambling bar with its massive wooden tables, sporting prints and open fires. The building is decorated with flowers in summer, when the gorgeous south-facing garden makes an ideal spot for alfresco dining. The daily menus feature ploughman's lunches and an impressive selection of freshly cooked hot dishes. Lunch or dinner might begin with Brixham

crab, lemongrass and ginger risotto; terrine of Creedy Carver duck and Sandridge streaky, with Cumberland jam; or seared Lulworth Bay scallops, black pudding and cauliflower purée. Follow with Wheatsheaf chicken and mushroom pie with spring greens; rump of spring lamb, braised belly, gribiche, and garlic purée; sweet peppered loin of Sandridge Farm pork, ham hock hash and spring onions. Don't miss dessert options like vanilla and rhubarb crème brûlée; milk chocolate and honeycomb mousse; Valrhona chocolate fondant, malted milk ice cream; or Alphanso Mando rice pudding with mango sorbet. Polite dogs are welcome to join the pub's own spaniels, Milo and Brie.

Open 11-3.30, 6-11 (Sun 11-5.30) Closed: 25-27 Dec & 1st 2wks Jan, Sun eve, Mon

(ex BH) **Bar Meals** L served Tue-Sat 12-2.30 D served Tue-Sat 6.30-9.30 **Restaurant** L served Tue-Sun 12-2 D served Tue-Sat 6.30-9.30 ⊕ FREE HOUSE ◖ Butcombe Bitter, Bath Ales, Guest ales ⚘ Cheddar Valley, Ashton Press. ♀ 13 **Facilities** Children's menu Dogs allowed Garden Parking Wi-fi

PICK OF THE PUBS

The Queens Arms ♟

CORTON DENHAM　　Map 4 ST62

DT9 4LR
☎ **01963 220317**　📠 **01963 220797**
e-mail: relax@thequeensarms.com
web: www.thequeensarms.com
dir: *From A30 (Sherborne) take B3145 signed Wincanton. Approx 1.5m left at red sign to Corton Denham. 1.5m, left down hill, right at bottom into village. Pub on left*

The tower of the church in this ancient, secluded village peeks through the trees near to this solid, stone-built Georgian inn, lost in a web of lanes in stunning countryside on the Somerset/Dorset border. Footpaths slink up onto grassy downs and alongside gurgling trout streams; it's the idea place to chill out after a good ramble. The engagingly furnished bar and separate dining room feature old scrubbed tables beside grand fireplaces, bucket chairs tucked into quiet corners of the gently colourwashed walls, barrel seats and sofas dotting wood and flagstoned floors, with high beams adding a flourish. Outside, a sheltered terrace against creeper-clad walls and sunny garden tick all the right boxes. Voted AA Pub of the Year in 2009, the inn continues to exude the warmth, character and quiet sophistication that drew this accolade. Owners Gordon and Jeanette Reid are totally committed to the local area's galaxy of micro-breweries (Moor brewery at Pitney being a particular favourite) and

wealth of fine food producers. They champion low food miles and animal welfare; pork is from their own (beer fed!) pigs, poultry and eggs via their own free-range chickens, whilst stringent quality control ensures that visitors will enjoy only the best farm ciders. There's a great wine list, too. Food is simple, high quality and seasonal; earthy British dishes such as a starter of seared wood pigeon breast on mushroom and leek hash or a thick home-made beef and lentil soup set the tone for mains including lamb loin with black pudding crumble, or home-made faggots with creamy mash and red onion gravy, whilst the veggie Wellington is something of a signature dish.

Open all wk **Bar Meals** L served all wk 12-3 D served Mon-Sat 6-10, Sun 6-9.30 Av main course £11 **Restaurant** L served all wk 12-3 booking required D served Mon-Sat 6-10, Sun 6-9.30 booking required ⊕ FREE HOUSE ◀ Moor Revival, Moor Northern Star, changing guest ales wkly ♂ Thatchers Gold, Hecks, Wilkins, Burrow Hill, Orchard Pig. ♟ 23 **Facilities** Children welcome Children's menu Children's portions Dogs allowed Garden Parking Wi-fi

CROSCOMBE
Map 4 ST54

The Bull Terrier ★★★ INN ♀

Long St BA5 3QJ ☎ 01749 343658
e-mail: barry.vidler@bullterrierpub.co.uk
dir: *Halfway between Wells & Shepton Mallet on A371*

First licensed in 1612, this unspoiled village free house is one of Somerset's oldest pubs. With three bars and a dining room, the building itself dates from the late 15th century, though the fireplace and ceiling in the inglenook bar are 16th-century additions. The name was changed from the 'Rose and Crown' in 1976. The pretty walled garden overlooks the surrounding hills. One menu is offered throughout, including chicken in tarragon sauce, lasagne and chilli con carne. Accommodation consists of two brightly decorated bedrooms.

Open all wk 12-2.45 7-late **Bar Meals** L served all wk 12-2 D served all wk 7-9 **Restaurant** L served all wk 12-2 D served all wk 7-9 ⊕ FREE HOUSE ◀ Butcombe, Courage Directors, Marston's Pedigree, Greene King Old Speckled Hen, Ruddles County ♂ Thatchers Cheddar Valley, Thatchers Gold. ♀ 8 **Facilities** Children welcome Children's menu Children's portions Family room Dogs allowed Garden Parking **Rooms** 2

The George Inn ♀ NEW

Long St BA5 3QH ☎ 01749 342306 & 345189
e-mail: pg@thegeorgeinn.co.uk
dir: *On A371 midway between Shepton Mallet & Wells*

The softly lit bar of this 17th-century family-owned pub contains a large inglenook fireplace, the family grandfather clock and some giraffes (it's best you ask when you're there). Peter and Veryan Graham have worked tirelessly on converting and renovating The George. One of the four real ales is King George 'the Thirst', brewed solely for this pub; there are real ciders too. Diners enjoy locally sourced quality food, with organic, vegetarian, game and fish specials complementing regular menus. The garden terrace incorporates an all-weather patio and children's area.

Open all wk 12-2.30 6-11 **Bar Meals** L served all wk 12-2 D served all wk 6-9 Av main course £8.95 **Restaurant** L served all wk 12-2 D served all wk 6-9 Av 3 course à la carte fr £17.95 ⊕ FREE HOUSE ◀ Butcombe Bitter, Moor Revival, Blindmans Brewery ♂ Thatchers Cheddar Valley, Orchard Pig. ♀ 9 **Facilities** Children welcome Children's menu Children's portions Play area Family room Dogs allowed Garden Beer festival Parking Wi-fi

DINNINGTON
Map 4 ST41

Dinnington Docks

TA17 8SX ☎ 01460 52397 📄 01460 52397
e-mail: hilary@dinningtondocks.co.uk
dir: *S of A303 between South Petherton & Ilminster*

Formerly known as the Rose & Crown, this traditional village pub on the old Fosse Way has been licensed for over 250 years and has no loud music, pool tables or fruit machines to drown out the conversation. Inside you will find pictures, signs and memorabilia of its rail and maritime past. Good quality cask ales and farmhouse cider are served, and freshly prepared food including the likes of crab cakes, faggots, snapper, steak, and lamb shank for two. With quiz night every Sunday, the pub is located in an ideal place for cycling and walking.

Open all wk 11.30-3 6-mdnt (Sat-Sun all day) **Bar Meals** L served all wk 12-2 D served all wk 7-9 Av main course £7.50 **Restaurant** L served all wk 12-2 D served all wk 7-9 ⊕ FREE HOUSE ◀ Butcombe Bitter, Guest ales ♂ Burrow Hill, Stowford Press, Thatchers Gold. **Facilities** Children welcome Children's portions Play area Family room Dogs allowed Garden Parking

DITCHEAT
Map 4 ST63

PICK OF THE PUBS

The Manor House Inn ♀

BA4 6RB ☎ 01749 860276 📄 0870 286 3379
e-mail: landlord@manorhouseinn.co.uk
dir: *From Shepton Mallet take A371 towards Castle Cary, in 3m turn right to Ditcheat*

Tucked away in the pretty Mendip village of Ditcheat, this attractive 17th-century free house belonged to the lord of the manor about 150 years ago and was known as the White Hart. It is within easy reach of the Royal Bath and West showground, and the East Somerset steam railway. Built from Ditcheat red brick, it has flagstone floors and roaring log fires in winter. The bar serves Butcombe Bitter and regular guest ales, local cider, apple brandies and up to nine wines by the glass. The seasonal menu may offer starters such as smoked salmon parcel, stuffed egg and chive mayonnaise with citrus dressing, or ham hock and pear terrine wrapped in bacon, followed by main courses of chef's rustic rabbit casserole with root vegetables or winter vegetable risotto with balsamic dressing. The fish of the day is shown on the specials board.

Open all day all wk Mon-Sat (Sun noon-9) **Bar Meals** L served Mon-Sat 12-2.30, Sun 12-5 D served Mon-Thu 6.30-9, Fri-Sat 6.30-9.30 Av main course £10 **Restaurant** L served Mon-Sat 12-2.30, Sun 12-5 booking required D served Mon-Thu 6.30-9, Fri-Sat 6.30-9.30 booking required Av 3 course à la carte fr £20.45 ⊕ FREE HOUSE ◀ Butcombe, John Smith's, Guest ales ♂ Ashton Press, Natch. ♀ 9 **Facilities** Children welcome Children's portions Dogs allowed Garden Parking Wi-fi

DULVERTON
Map 3 SS92

Woods Bar & Dining Room ◉ NEW

4 Bank Square TA22 9BU ☎ 01398 324007
e-mail: woodsdulverton@hotmail.com
dir: *From Tiverton take A396 N. At Machine Cross take B3222 to Dulverton. Establishment adjacent to church*

Situated on the edge of Exmoor in the rural town of Dulverton, this is a bar and dining room where food and drink is taken very seriously indeed. Run by owners with a passion for wine – everything on the list is available by the glass – the cosy bar crackles with conversation whilst the restaurant delivers modern British cooking with a heavy French accent - coarse pork pâté with prune chutney, garlic marinated lamb steak with sauté potatoes.

Open all wk 11-3 6-11.30 (Sun 12-3 7-11) **Bar Meals** L served all wk 12-2 D served all wk 6-9.30 **Restaurant** L served all wk 12-2 booking required D served all wk 7-9.30 booking required ⊕ FREE HOUSE ◀ Dartmoor, Tribute, HSD ♂ Thatchers, Cornish Rattler. **Facilities** Children welcome Children's menu Children's portions Dogs allowed Garden

DUNSTER
Map 3 SS94

PICK OF THE PUBS

The Luttrell Arms ★★★ HL

High St TA24 6SG ☎ 01643 821555 📄 01643 821567
e-mail: info@luttrellarms.fsnet.co.uk
dir: *From A39 (Bridgwater to Minehead), left onto A396 to Dunster (2m from Minehead)*

Built in the 15th century this beguiling hotel was used as a guest house by the Abbots of Cleeve. Oozing history and charm, the building also served as a headquarters for Cromwell during his siege of Dunster Castle. Its open fires and oak beams make the bar a welcoming place in winter, while the garden in summer offers delightful views of the surrounding medieval village and Exmoor National Park. Pick up a pint of the guest ale or Thatchers Cheddar Valley cider and ponder your choice from the menu, which can be eaten in the bar, in the more formal restaurant, or outside. Flavoursome lunchtime sandwiches and baguettes include warm salt beef with dill pickles. Main courses range from a full rack of pork ribs in a smokey barbecue sauce served with coleslaw and chips to a deep-fried wedge of Somerset Brie with a sweet chilli dip and mixed salad. The bedrooms are period pieces complete with leather armchairs and four-poster beds.

Open all wk 8am-11pm **Bar Meals** L served all wk 11.30-3, all day summer D served all wk 7-10 **Restaurant** L served Sun 12-3 booking required D served all wk 7-10 booking required ⊕ FREE HOUSE ◀ Exmoor Gold Fox, Guest ale ♂ Cheddar Valley Cider. **Facilities** Children welcome Children's menu Children's portions Family room Dogs allowed Garden **Rooms** 28

Save on hotels. Book at **theAA.com/hotel**

SOMERSET 393 ENGLAND

EAST COKER   Map 4 ST51

PICK OF THE PUBS

The Helyar Arms ★★★★ INN ◉

Moor Ln BA22 9JR
☎ **01935 862332**   📄 **01935 864129**
e-mail: info@helyar-arms.co.uk
dir: *3m from Yeovil. Take A57 or A30, follow East Coker signs*

This Grade II listed building dates back in part to 1468 and reputedly takes its name from Archdeacon Helyar, a chaplain to Queen Elizabeth I. Log fires warm the charming old world bar, where Butcombe, Black Sheep and Hobgoblin ales are backed by Stowford Press and Taunton Traditional ciders. There's a skittle alley, comfortable accommodation and a separate restaurant occupying an original apple loft. The kitchen makes full use of local produce, including wood pigeon, rabbit, venison, pheasant and fish from the south Devon coast. There's plenty of choice, from sandwiches and lighter bites (maybe tagliatelle with smoked haddock, saffron and prawns) to starters such as game terrine with winter chutney and walnut bread followed by toad in the hole with bubble and squeak and a jug of gravy. Succulent steaks can be cut to order and grilled, plus their steak sandwich is award winning. All puddings are home made, and coffees and teas come with home-made petits fours.

Open all wk 11-3 6-11 **Bar Meals** L served all wk 12-2.30 D served all wk 6.30-9.30 Av main course £9 **Restaurant** L served all wk 12-2.30 D served all wk 6.30-9.30 Av 3 course à la carte fr £30 ◉ PUNCH TAVERNS ◀ Butcombe Bitter, Black Sheep, Hobgoblin Ö Stowford Press, Taunton Traditional.
Facilities Children welcome Family room Dogs allowed Garden Parking Wi-fi **Rooms** 6

EXFORD   Map 3 SS83

PICK OF THE PUBS

The Crown Hotel ★★★ HL ◉ ♚

TA24 7PP ☎ **01643 831554**   📄 **01643 831665**
e-mail: info@crownhotelexmoor.co.uk
web: www.crownhotelexmoor.co.uk
dir: *From M5 junct 25 follow Taunton signs. Take A358 then B3224 via Wheddon Cross to Exford*

The family-run 17th-century Crown Hotel was the first purpose-built coaching inn on Exmoor; today's incarnation, a comfy mix of elegance and tradition, recalls such stalwart service. Right at the heart of the National Park, it's no surprise that outdoor pursuits enthusiasts make a bee-line for the village, with rambling, horse-riding, fishing and shooting all popular. With three acres of grounds and a tributary of the infant River Exe flowing through its own woodland, it's a country lover's idyll. The cosy bar is very much the social heart of the village, many of whose patrons enjoy the Exmoor Ales from Wiveliscombe just down the road. Guests staying in the appealing accommodation relax on the terrace or tree-shaded beer garden, perusing the impressive menu which has gained an AA Rosette award. With the benefit of Exmoor's profuse organic produce, on the doorstep there are superb dishes to accompany the comprehensive wine list. The bar menu could tempt with home-cured dill and tarragon salmon gravadlax with garlic and herb potato salad, or the more filling beef and Exmoor Ale pie with buttered mash and red wine gravy. The restaurant selection offers a starter of slow braised pig's cheek in ginger beer, leading to braised shoulder of Exmoor venison and pan-fried haunch with crispy polenta cake.

Open all day all wk noon-11pm **Bar Meals** L served all wk 12-2.30 D served all wk 5.30-9.30 **Restaurant** D served all wk 7-9 ◉ FREE HOUSE ◀ Exmoor Ale, Exmoor Gold, Guest ales Ö Thatchers Gold, Cornish Rattler. ♚ 10 **Facilities** Children welcome Children's portions Dogs allowed Garden Parking Wi-fi **Rooms** 16

FAULKLAND   Map 4 ST75

Tuckers Grave

BA3 5XF ☎ **01373 834230**
dir: *From Bath take A36 towards Warminster. Turn right on A366, through Norton St Philip towards Faulkland. In Radstock, left at x-rds, pub on left*

Situated in the heart of the countryside, tapped ales and farm cider are served at Somerset's smallest pub, a tiny atmospheric bar with old settles but no counter, or music, television or juke box either. Lunchtime sandwiches and ploughman's lunches are available, and a large lawn with flower borders makes an attractive outdoor seating area, with the countryside adjacent. The 'grave' in the pub's name is the unmarked one of Edward Tucker, who hung himself here in 1747.

Open 11.30-3 6-11 (Sun noon-3 7-10.30) Closed: 25 Dec, Mon L ◉ FREE HOUSE ◀ London Pride, Butcombe Bitter Ö Cheddar Valley, Farmhouse Gold. **Facilities** Children welcome Family room Garden Parking **Notes** ◉

FRESHFORD   Map 4 ST76

The Inn at Freshford ♚

The Hill BA2 7WG ☎ **01225 722250**
e-mail: landlord@theinnatfreshford.co.uk
web: www.theinnatfreshford.co.uk
dir: *1m from A36 between Beckington & Limpley Stoke*

This popular family run 15th-century inn in the Limpley Stoke valley is ideally placed for walking, especially along the nearby Kennet & Avon Canal. There are extensive gardens, whilst inside the wooden floors, original beams and log fires add to its charm in winter. The varied and contemporary menu changes weekly, but choices might include locally made sausages with mash and onion gravy; or salmon steak with new potatoes, lemon and herb cream sauce.

Open all wk 10.30-3 6-11 (all day Fri-Sun & spring/ summer) **Bar Meals** L served Mon-Sat 12-2.30, Sun 12-5 D served Mon-Sat 6.30-9, Sun 6-8 Av main course £9 **Restaurant** Av 3 course à la carte fr £17.22 ◀ Butcombe Bitter, Courage Best, guest ale. ♚ 12 **Facilities** Children welcome Children's menu Children's portions Dogs allowed Garden Parking

See advert on page 394

FROME
Map 4 ST74

PICK OF THE PUBS

The Horse & Groom ♥

East Woodlands BA11 5LY ☎ 01373 462802
e-mail: kathybarrett@btconnect.com
dir: *A361 towards Trowbridge, over B3092 rdbt, take immediate right towards East Woodlands, pub 1m on right*

Located at the end of a single track lane, this attractive 17th-century building is adorned with colourful hanging baskets in summer and surrounded by lawns fronted by severely pollarded lime trees. The bar, furnished with pine pews and settles on a flagstone floor and a large inglenook fireplace, offers shove ha'penny, cribbage, dominoes and a selection of daily newspapers for your diversion. There's also a carpeted lounge, including three dining tables in addition to the conservatory-style garden room with 32 covers. A great choice of drinks includes smoothies and milkshakes, and designated drivers are provided with free soft drinks. The lunch and bar menu is offered at lunchtime along with baguettes, salads and daily specials. In the evening, the bar and baguette menus are complemented by a full carte served in all areas. Typical dishes are smoked salmon roulade followed by peppered venison with Cumberland sauce.

Open all wk Mon-Sat 11.30-2 6.30-11 (Sun 12-2 7-10.30) **Bar Meals** L served Mon-Sat 11.30-2, Sun 12-2 D served Mon-Sat 6.30-9, Sun 7-9 **Restaurant** L served Mon-Sat 11.30-2, Sun 12-2 D served Mon-Sat 6.30-9, Sun 7-9 ⊕ FREE HOUSE ◀ Wadworth 6X, Butcombe Bitter, Timothy Taylor Landlord, Blindmans Brewery, Blindmans Buff, Yeovil Star Gazer ♂ Stowford Press, Westons Bounds Scrumpy, Westons Old Rosie. ♥ 9 **Facilities** Children welcome Dogs allowed Garden Parking

HASELBURY PLUCKNETT
Map 4 ST41

PICK OF THE PUBS

The White Horse at Haselbury ♥

North St TA18 7RJ ☎ 01460 78873
e-mail: haselbury@btconnect.com
dir: *Just off A30 between Crewkerne & Yeovil on B3066*

Set in the peaceful village of Haselbury Plucknett, the building started life as a rope works and flax store, later becoming a cider house. Its interior feels fresh and warm, but retains the original character of exposed stone and open fires. Patrick and Jan Howard have run the hostelry for over ten years, with the explicit promise to provide the best food, service and value for money possible. This is confirmed by the lunchtime set menu served from Tuesday to Saturday, when vegetable soup could be followed by poached smoked hake with creamy spinach sauce, and rounded off with spiced fruit sponge and brandy sauce. The eclectic carte might include pork and three mustard Stroganoff, or roasted breast of Aylesbury duck with plum sauce, plus an excellent selection of fish specials. Enjoy your meal with a glass of Otter ale, Burrow Hill cider or one of the ten wines by the glass.

Open noon-2.30 6.30-11 Closed: Sun eve, Mon **Bar Meals** L served Tue-Sun 12-2 D served Tue-Sat 6.30-9.30 **Restaurant** L served Tue-Sun 12-2 D served Tue-Sat 6.30-9.30 ⊕ FREE HOUSE ◀ Palmers IPA, Otter Ale ♂ Thatchers Dry, Burrow Hill. ♥ 10 **Facilities** Children welcome Children's menu Children's portions Garden Parking

HINTON BLEWETT
Map 4 ST55

Ring O'Bells ♥

BS39 5AN ☎ 01761 452239 📄 01761 451245
e-mail: jonjenssen@btinternet.com
dir: *11m S of Bristol on A37 towards Wells. Turn right from either Clutton or Temple Cloud to Hinton Blewett*

On the edge of the Mendips, this 200-year-old inn describes itself as the 'archetypal village green pub' and offers good views of the Chew Valley. An all-year-round cosy atmosphere is boosted by a log fire in winter, and a wide choice of well kept real ales. An extra dining area/function room has recently been added. There's always something going on, whether it's a tour of the brewery, pig racing night or fishing competitions! Good value dishes include beer-battered haddock fillet with chips, Cumberland sausages on mashed potato, or Ashton cider braised pork belly and pork cheek on a black pudding mash. Baguettes, sandwiches, jacket potatoes and ploughman's also available. There has been a change of hands.

Open all wk Mon-Thu 12-3 5-11 (Fri-Sun all day) **Bar Meals** L served Fri-Sat 12-2.30, Sun 12-3 D served Fri-Sat 6-9 booking required **Restaurant** L served Fri-Sat 12-2.30, Sun 12-3 booking required D served Fri-Sat 6-9 booking required ⊕ BUTCOMBE ◀ Butcombe, Fuller's London Pride, Butcombe Gold, Guest ales ♂ Ashton Press, Ashton Still. ♥ 8 **Facilities** Children welcome Children's menu Children's portions Dogs allowed Garden Parking Wi-fi

---

HINTON ST GEORGE · Map 4 ST41

PICK OF THE PUBS

The Lord Poulett Arms ♥

High St TA17 8SE ☎ 01460 73149
e-mail: reservations@lordpoulettarms.com
dir: *2m N of Crewkerne, 1.5m S of A303*

There's a hint of France in the secluded garden of this stylish village inn; the click of boules drifts across tumbled spreads of lavender, whilst a wisteria-shrouded pergola is tucked in next to an old fives wall. Within, sheltered by a thatched roof, all is firmly English, with a marvellous magpie-mix of antique furniture sprinkled liberally across timeworn boarded floors, polished old flagstones and a vast fireplace where demi-trees burn for winter warmth, pumping out the heat into tastefully decorated rooms. And what could be more English than gravity-served beers and ciders from West Country producers. The same geographical spot supplies much of the produce featured in the gastro-pub menu; a spring starter may be local asparagus and edamame with yuzu dressing, pea shoots and konbu crème, an exotic precursor to crispy fillet of sea bass with new potato and chorizo salad; or chargrilled Barnsley chop with asparagus, white bean houmous, soprasada and jus.

Open all day all wk noon-11 Closed: 26 Dec, 1 Jan **Bar Meals** L served all wk 12-2.30 booking required D served all wk 7-9.15 booking required Av main course £7.95 **Restaurant** L served all wk 12-2.30 booking required D served all wk 7-9.15 booking required Av 3 course à la carte fr £19 ⊕ FREE HOUSE ◀ Hopback, Branscombe, Cotleigh, Archers, Otter Ö Thatchers Gold, Burrow Hill. ♥ 14 **Facilities** Children welcome Children's portions Dogs allowed Garden Parking

HOLCOMBE · Map 4 ST64

The Holcombe Inn ♥

Stratton Rd BA3 5EB
☎ 01761 232478 ▤ 01761 233979
e-mail: bookings@holcombeinn.co.uk
dir: *On A367 to Stratton-on-the-Fosse, take concealed left turn opposite Downside Abbey signed Holcombe, take next right, pub 1.5m on left*

Under new ownership from February 2011, this smart, Grade II listed 17th-century country inn boasts a large garden with panoramic views of nearby Downside Abbey and the Somerset countryside. The kitchen sources top-notch local produce for an appealing menu that might include Cornish red mullet, confit fennel, chargrilled courgette, aubergine, olive oil mash; or duck breast, spinach and parsnips, mash, vanilla and brandy jus. The pub is ideally situated between Bath, and Wells, and is close to the National Trust Stourhead Estate.

Open all day all wk **Bar Meals** L served all wk 12-2.30 D served all wk 6.30-9.30 Av main course £11 **Restaurant** L served all wk 12-2.30 D served all wk 6.30-9.30 ⊕ FREE HOUSE ◀ Otter Ale, Gem Ö Thatchers. ♥ 17 **Facilities** Children welcome Children's menu Children's portions Dogs allowed Garden Parking Wi-fi

ILCHESTER · Map 4 ST52

Ilchester Arms ♥

The Square BA22 8LN
☎ 01935 840220 ▤ 01935 841353
e-mail: mail@ilchesterarms.com
dir: *From A303 take A37 signed Ilchester/Yeovil, left at 2nd Ilchester sign. Hotel 100yds on right*

An elegant Georgian fronted house with lots of character, this establishment was first licensed in 1686; attractive features include open fires and a lovely walled garden. Between 1962 and 1985 it was owned by the man who developed Ilchester cheese, and its association with good food continues: chef proprietor Brendan McGee takes pride in producing modern British dishes such as breast of chicken filled with wild mushroom mousse; pan-fried medallions of pork tenderloin on a bed of baked sweet potato purée; and wild and forest mushroom casserole. The McGees now own the Inn opposite and hold a beer festival there.

Open all day all wk 7am-11pm Closed: 26 Dec **Bar Meals** L served Mon-Sat 12-2.30 D served Mon-Sat 7-9 Av main course £8.50 **Restaurant** L served all wk 12-2.30 D served Mon-Sat 7-9 Av 3 course à la carte fr £24.50 ⊕ FREE HOUSE ◀ Butcombe, Flowers IPA, Bass, local ales Ö Thatchers Gold, Thatchers Pear. ♥ 14 **Facilities** Children welcome Children's menu Children's portions Play area Family room Garden Beer festival Parking Wi-fi

ILMINSTER · Map 4 ST31

New Inn ★★★★ INN ♥

Dowlish Wake TA19 0NZ ☎ 01460 52413
dir: *From Ilminster follow Kingstone & Perry's Cider Museum signs, in Dowlish Wake follow pub signs*

Deep in rural Somerset, this 350-year-old stone-built pub is tucked away in the village of Dowlish Wake, a stone's throw away from Perry's thatched Cider Mill and Museum. Inside are two bars with wood-burning stoves and a restaurant, where menus of home-cooked food capitalise on the quality and freshness of local produce. You could opt for a signature dish such as Stilton chicken topped with a generous helping of smoked bacon; or stick to pub favourites such as West Country crab cakes with chips, salad and garlic mayonnaise. There are four guest rooms situated in the pleasant garden.

Open all wk 11.30-3 6-11 **Bar Meals** L served all wk 12-2.30 D served all wk 6-8.45 Av main course £7 **Restaurant** L served all wk 12-2.30 D served all wk 6-8.45 Fixed menu price fr £9 Av 3 course à la carte fr £16 ⊕ FREE HOUSE ◀ Butcombe Bitter, Otter Ale, Otter Bitter Ö Thatcher's Gold. ♥ 10 **Facilities** Children welcome Children's menu Children's portions Dogs allowed Garden Parking Wi-fi **Rooms** 4

KILVE · Map 3 ST14

The Hood Arms ♥

TA5 1EA ☎ 01278 741210 ▤ 01278 741477
e-mail: info@thehoodarms.com
dir: *From M5 junct 23/24 follow A39 to Kilve. Village between Bridgwater & Minehead*

Set at the foot of the Quantock Hills close to a spectacular fossil beach, this traditional, family-run 17th-century coaching inn provides thirsty walkers with real ales in the charming beamed character bar or wonderful garden with lovely views. A good range of dishes can be found on the menu, especially local game and fish, and might include sea bream fillets on a bed of crayfish risotto, or braised belly of pork with celeriac purée and apple and cider creamed sauce. At lunchtime, try the warm filled foccacia rolls, jackets and daily specials.

Open all day all wk **Bar Meals** L served Mon-Sat 12-2, Sun 12-3 booking required D served Mon-Sat 6-9, Sun 6-8 booking required Av main course £10 **Restaurant** L served Mon-Sat 12-2, Sun 12-3 booking required D served Mon-Sat 6-9, Sun 6-8 booking required Fixed menu price fr £15 Av 3 course à la carte fr £25 ⊕ FREE HOUSE ◀ Guinness, Otter Head, Palmers Copperdale, Fuller's London Pride, Guest ales Ö Thatchers Gold. ♥ 12 **Facilities** Children welcome Children's menu Children's portions Play area Family room Dogs allowed Garden Parking Wi-fi

KINGSDON · Map 4 ST52

Kingsdon Inn ♥

TA11 7LG ☎ 01935 840543
e-mail: enquiries@kingsdoninn.co.uk
dir: *A303 onto A372, right onto B3151, right into village, right at post office*

Once a cider house, the three charmingly decorated, saggy-beamed rooms in this pretty thatched pub create a relaxed and friendly feel. Stripped pine tables and cushioned farmhouse chairs are judiciously placed throughout, and there are enough open fires to keep everywhere well warmed. Traditional country cooking includes game in season – perhaps saddle of rabbit braised in mustard and thyme. Other choices might be warm crab and prawn tart; Cajun fried chicken with lime and coconut rice; orange and caramel baked cheesecake. There is always a wide selection of guest beers provided by local micro-breweries as well as more traditional ales.

Open all wk noon-3 6-11 (Sun noon-3 7-10.30) **Bar Meals** L served all wk 12-2 booking required D served all wk 6.30-9 booking required Av main course £9.80 ⊕ FREE HOUSE ◀ Butcombe Cask, Otter Cask, Guest ale Ö Burrow Hill. ♥ 10 **Facilities** Children welcome Garden Parking

LANGLEY MARSH — Map 3 ST02

The Three Horseshoes

TA4 2UL ☎ 01984 623763
e-mail: mark_jules96@hotmail.com
dir: M5 junct 25 take B3227 to Wiveliscombe. Turn right up hill at lights. From square, turn right, follow Langley Marsh signs, pub in 1m

Surrounded by beautiful countryside, this handsome 17th-century red sandstone pub has had only four landlords during the last century. It remains a free house, with traditional opening hours, a good choice of ales straight from the barrel and a warm, friendly welcome. The landlord's wife prepares home-cooked meals, incorporating local ingredients and vegetables from the pub garden. Popular with locals, walkers and cyclists, there's an enclosed garden with outdoor seating to enjoy in warmer weather.

Open noon-2.30 7-11 Closed: Sun eve, Mon, Tue-Fri L Bar Meals L served Sat-Sun 12-1.45 D served Tue-Sat 7-9 ⊕ FREE HOUSE ◀ Otter Ale, Exmoor Ale, Cotleigh 25, Tribute. Facilities Children welcome Garden Parking

LANGPORT — Map 4 ST42

The Old Pound Inn ★★★ INN

Aller TA10 0RA ☎ 01458 250469 📠 01458 250469
e-mail: oldpoundinn@btconnect.com
dir: 2.5m N of Langport on A372. 8m SE of Bridgwater on A372

With parts dating from 1571 and 1756, this cider house was originally known as the White Lion. It was renamed in 1980 to commemorate the fact that its garden was once the village pound. Plenty of historic character has been retained with oak beams and open fires. Locally it has a reputation as a friendly pub selling a range of real ales, whiskies, and good home-cooked food: Somerset beef features in burgers and prime steaks, while vegetarians will enjoy the Mediterranean vegetable tart. There is also a skittle alley and accommodation.

Open all wk 11.30-2.30 5-11 (Sat 11.30-mdnt Sun noon-10) Bar Meals L served all wk 12-2 D served all wk 6-9 Av main course £8.95 Restaurant D served Fri-Sun 6-9 Fixed menu price fr £12 Av 3 course à la carte fr £14 ⊕ FREE HOUSE ◀ Tribute, Sharp's, Cotleigh, Branscombe, Glastonbury, Teignworthy, Butcombe ♂ Thatchers Gold. Facilities Children welcome Children's menu Children's portions Dogs allowed Garden Parking Wi-fi Rooms 8

Rose & Crown

Huish Episcopi TA10 9QT ☎ 01458 250494
dir: M5 junct 25, A358 towards Ilminster. Left onto A378. Village in 14m (1m from Langport). Pub near church in village

Now run by the fourth generation of the Pittard family, Eli's (named after the current landlord's grandfather) is an old thatched inn with no counter, just a flagstoned taproom where customers congregate among the ale and farmhouse cider casks. In a side room are a sit-up-and-beg piano, old photos and fairly basic furniture. Home-made food includes popular steak and ale pie, sandwiches, jacket potatoes or pork cobbler. Monthly folk-singing evenings are fun.

Open all wk 11.30-3 5.30-11 (Fri-Sat 11.30-11.30 Sun noon-10.30) Bar Meals L served all wk 12-2 D served Mon-Sat 5.30-7.30 Av main course £7.25 ⊕ FREE HOUSE ◀ Teignworthy Reel Ale, Mystery Tor, Hop Back Summer Lightning, Butcombe Bitter, Summathat ♂ Burrow Hill Farmhouse. Facilities Children welcome Play area Family room Dogs allowed Garden Parking Notes ⊛

LONG SUTTON — Map 4 ST42

PICK OF THE PUBS

The Devonshire Arms ★★★★ INN ⊛ ▾

TA10 9LP ☎ 01458 241271 📠 01458 241037
e-mail: mail@thedevonshirearms.com
dir: Exit A303 at Podimore rdbt onto A372. Continue for 4m, left onto B3165

A fine-looking, stone-built former hunting lodge on a pretty village green. Step through its imposing portico, decorated with the Devonshire family crest, to discover unexpectedly contemporary styling complementing the large open fire and other original features. Refreshments come in the form of increasingly popular regional brews and ciders, and the pub is also renowned for its daily changing menu based whenever possible on locally sourced produce. Maybe try the Cornish mussels steamed in Burrow Hill cider, garlic, chilli and thyme; or Dorset crab crème brûlée, followed by spicy pork stew with apricots and walnuts; or Quantock duck confit with mash and mixed vegetables. Desserts may include chocolate clafoutis with praline ice cream; and ginger sticky toffee pudding with lime leaf ice cream. Your can drink and dine alfresco in the courtyard, large walled garden or overlooking the green at the front. To complete the picture, nine en suite bedrooms, each with wide-screen TV, are designed in a fresh modern style, and benefit from the personal touch of hosts Philip and Sheila Mepham.

Open all wk noon-3 6-11 Closed: 25-26 Dec, 1 Jan Bar Meals L served all wk 12-2.30 booking required D served all wk 7-9.30 booking required Restaurant D served all wk 7-9.30 booking required ⊕ FREE HOUSE ◀ Bath Spa, Cheddar Potholer, Moor Revival, Moor Merlins Magic ♂ Burrow Hill, Olde Harry's. ▾ 10 Facilities Children welcome Children's menu Play area Dogs allowed Garden Parking Wi-fi Rooms 9

LOVINGTON — Map 4 ST53

PICK OF THE PUBS

The Pilgrims ★★★★ INN ⊛ ▾

BA7 7PT ☎ 01963 240597
e-mail: jools@thepilgrimsatlovington.co.uk
dir: A303 onto A37 to Lyford, right at lights, 1.5m to The Pilgrims on B3153

Restaurant quality food in an atmosphere as relaxed as a pub. That's the aim of owners Sally and Jools Mitchison – who, with disarming honesty, admit that The Pilgrims will never be pretty from the outside. Step inside, however, and it's another story. Wicker and leather seating characterise the bar, whilst locals' pewter mugs hang ready for the next pint of Orchard Pig cider or Cottage Brewing Champflower ale. Herbs and vegetables are grown in the pub's own garden, and every effort is made to source produce nearby, especially cheeses. Starters and light lunches might include spiced parsnip soup with home-made bread, or hot potted smoked pollock in cheese sauce with tomato salsa. More substantial dishes range from prime beef goulash with golden saffron rice to penne pasta with roasted vegetables and pesto. Desserts include Somerset apple crumble. Five highly individual king size guest rooms tempt you to linger, and the breakfast is excellent.

Open noon-3 7-11 Closed: Oct, Sun eve, Mon, Tue L Bar Meals L served Wed-Sun 12-2.30 booking required D served Tue-Sat 7-9 booking required Av main course £16 Restaurant L served Wed-Sun 12.30-2.30 booking required D served Tue-Sat 7-9 booking required Av 3 course à la carte fr £31 ⊕ FREE HOUSE ◀ Cottage Brewing Champflower ♂ Burrow Hill, Orchard Pig. ▾ 12 Facilities Children welcome Children's portions Dogs allowed Garden Parking Rooms 5

LOWER LANGFORD — Map 4 ST46

The Langford Inn ★★★★ INN ▾

BS40 5BL ☎ 01934 863059 📠 01934 863539
e-mail: langfordinn@aol.com
web: www.langfordinn.com
dir: M5 junct 21, A370 towards Bristol. At Congresbury turn right onto B3133 to Lower Langford. Village on A38

Displays of local memorabilia feature in this award-winning country pub and restaurant below the Mendips. Somerset's Butcombe brewery supplies one of the resident real ales; another comes from Brains across the Bristol Channel in Cardiff. Carefully prepared, daily-changing traditional food includes plenty of fresh fish, especially lobster, crab, trout and mussels, and there's a good choice of carefully sourced wines to accompany your chosen dish. Stay overnight in one of the converted 17th-century barns.

The Langford Inn

Open all day all wk **Bar Meals** L served 12-9 Av main course £9 food served all day **Restaurant** L served 12-9 D served Fri-Sat 12-9.30 Fixed menu price fr £7.95 Av 3 course à la carte fr £15 food served all day ⊕ BRAINS ◀ Butcombe, Brains SA, Guinness ♂ Thatchers Gold, Thatchers Katy. ♥ 24 **Facilities** Children welcome Children's menu Children's portions Dogs allowed Garden Parking Wi-fi **Rooms** 7

LOWER VOBSTER	Map 4 ST74

PICK OF THE PUBS

Vobster Inn　　　INN ◉◉ ♥

See Pick of the Pubs on page 398

MARTOCK	Map 4 ST41

The Nag's Head Inn

East St TA12 6NF ☎ 01935 823432
dir: *Telephone for directions*

This 16th-century former cider house is set in a lovely hamstone street in a picturesque south Somerset village. The large rear garden is partly walled and has pretty borders and trees. Ales, wines and home-cooked food are served in both the public and lounge/diner bars, where crib, dominoes, darts and pool are available. The pub also has a separate skittle alley.

Open all wk noon-3 6-11 (Fri-Sun noon-mdnt) **Bar Meals** L served all wk 12-2 D served Mon-Tue 6-8, Wed-Sat 6-9 Av main course £9 **Restaurant** L served all wk 12-2 D served Mon-Tue 6-8, Wed-Sat 6-9 Av 3 course à la carte fr £16 ◀ Guinness, Worthington, Toby. **Facilities** Children welcome Children's menu Children's portions Family room Dogs allowed Garden Parking

MILVERTON	Map 3 ST12

PICK OF THE PUBS

The Globe　⚬⚬　INN ◉ ♥

See Pick of the Pubs on page 399

MONTACUTE	Map 4 ST41

The Kings Arms Inn

49 Bishopston TA15 6UU ☎ 01935 822255
e-mail: info@thekingsarmsinn.co.uk
dir: *From A303 onto A3088 at rdbt signed Montacute. Hotel in village centre*

The hamstone-built, freshly refurbished Kings Arms has stood in this picturesque village, at the foot of Mons Acutus (thus, supposedly, Montacute) since 1632. Along with cask ales and fine wines, you can eat in the fire-warmed bar or lounge, in the large beer garden, or in the restaurant. Starters include deep-fried whitebait, or duck and orange pâté, with main courses of chicken supreme with bacon, mushroom and shallot cream sauce; or battered cod and chips. A bar favourite is the succulent salt beef sandwich. There are plenty of events to watch out for. Change of hands September 2010.

Open all wk 7.30am-11pm **Bar Meals** L served all wk 12-3 D served all wk 6-9 **Restaurant** L served all wk 12-3 D served all wk 6-9 booking required ⊕ GREENE KING ◀ Ruddles Best, Greene King IPA, Old Speckled Hen ♂ Aspall, Thatchers. **Facilities** Children welcome Dogs allowed Garden Parking Wi-fi

The Phelips Arms

The Borough TA15 6XB ☎ 01935 822557
e-mail: phelipsarmsmontacute@talktalk.net
dir: *From Cartgate rdbt on A303 follow signs for Montacute*

A 17th-century listed ham stone building overlooking the village square and close to historic Montacute House (NT). The emphasis is on the well kept Palmers beers and quality of the food, and everything is prepared on the premises using the best local and West Country produce. The menu features dishes such as home-made beef lasagne; smoked haddock and mozzarella fishcakes; and chicken breast with brandy and mushroom sauce.

Open all wk noon-2.30 6-11 Closed: 25 Dec **Bar Meals** L served all wk 12-2 D served all wk 6.30-9 Av main course £5 **Restaurant** L served all wk 12-2 booking required D served all wk 6.30-9 booking required Fixed menu price fr £7.95 ⊕ PALMERS ◀ Palmers IPA & 200 Premium Ale, Copper Ale ♂ Thatchers Gold. **Facilities** Children welcome Children's menu Children's portions Dogs allowed Garden Parking Wi-fi

NORTH CURRY	Map 4 ST32

The Bird in Hand

1 Queen Square TA3 6LT ☎ 01823 490248
dir: *M5 junct 25, A358 towards Ilminster, left onto A378 towards Langport. Left to North Curry*

Cheerful staff provide a warm welcome to this friendly 300-year-old village inn, which boasts large inglenook fireplaces, flagstone floors, exposed beams and studwork. The place is very atmospheric at night by candlelight, and blackboard menus feature local produce including vegetarian options and steak dishes, while the constantly changing seafood is supplied by a Plymouth fishmonger.

Open all wk ⊕ FREE HOUSE ◀ Badger Tanglefoot, Exmoor Gold, Otter Ale, Cotleigh Barn Owl, Hop Back Thunderstorm, Butcombe Gold, Teignworthy Old Moggie ♂ Parsons Farm. **Facilities** Children welcome Dogs allowed Parking

NORTON ST PHILIP	Map 4 ST75

PICK OF THE PUBS

George Inn ♥

High St BA2 7LH ☎ 01373 834224
e-mail: georgeinn@wadworth.co.uk
dir: *From Bath take A36 to Warminster, after 6m take A366 on right to Radstock, village 1m*

With more than 700 years under its belt, this Grade I listed building is one of the country's oldest continuously licensed inns. Just over a decade ago, the Wadworth brewery meticulously restored it, and during the process uncovered medieval wall paintings, now preserved. Other noteworthy features are the stone-slated roof, massive doorway, cobbled courtyard and impressive timbered galleries. The new owners strive to source all the ingredients for their two menus locally, so expect the bar menu to feature Cornish crab and salmon bake, or Masala-style chicken curry. For a lighter option, a choice of ciabattas is served until 6pm. In the beamed restaurant, choose from roast monkfish wrapped in Parma ham, minted pea purée with roast pepper and cream sauce; lamb rump, crispy fried leek and parsnip with rosemary and whisky gravy; or an individual local venison Wellington. Outside you can eat in the ancient and atmospheric courtyard and from the beer garden watch cricket on the Mead.

Open all day all wk **Bar Meals** Av main course £9.95 food served all day **Restaurant** booking required booking required Av 3 course à la carte fr £19.95 food served all day ⊕ WADWORTH ◀ Wadworth 6X, Henrys IPA, Wadworth Bishops Tipple ♂ Stowford Press, Thatchers Gold. **Facilities** Children welcome Children's menu Children's portions Play area Dogs allowed Garden Parking Wi-fi

PICK OF THE PUBS

Vobster Inn ★★★★ INN ❀❀ ♇

LOWER VOBSTER　Map 4 ST74

BA3 5RJ
☎ 01373 812920　🖨 01373 812247
e-mail: info@vobsterinn.co.uk
web: www.vobsterinn.co.uk
dir: *4m W of Frome*

Set in four acres of glorious countryside in the pretty hamlet of Lower Vobster, this long stone building dates back to the 17th century, though there was probably an inn here even before that. It is believed the inn originated a century before that and was used by King James II and his army of Royalists prior to the battle of Sedgemoor in 1685.

Raf and Peta Davila have been making their mark here ever since they arrived, a process that includes being awarded two AA Rosettes for the quality of their food and ingredients. The simple bar menu makes choosing easy with inexpensive suggestions such as fried whitebait with aïoli; seared beef sandwich, granary bloomer, goat's cheese glaze and caramelized onions; and grilled mushrooms with smoked ham and Welsh rarebit. On the main menu you'll find echoes of Raf's origins on Galicia's wild coast, including a selection of Spanish cured and smoked meats with salad, olives, houmous and crusty bread. Typical among the mains options are fillet of West Country beef and oyster pie, goose fat chips and purple sprouting broccoli, and pot-roasted boned quail, ox tongue, Puy lentils, roast garlic and foie gras.

Fish lovers will want to see what has come up fresh from St Mawes in Cornwall: fillet of bass, perhaps, with crushed herb potatoes, beetroot syrup, olive oil, tomato and olive dressing, or pan-fried monkfish, crayfish ravioli, vegetable spaghetti and red pepper relish. All desserts are home made, with choices like apple tart with spiced fruit ice cream and Catalan crème brûlée with black cracked pepper strawberries and orange and mango sorbet. Children are particularly welcome and have their own menu, plus there is a great cheese menu too. Three individually furnished bedrooms are available.

Open 12-3 6.30-11 (Open BH Mon for L only) Closed: Sun eve & Mon
Bar Meals L served 12-2 booking required D served Tue-Sat 6.30-9 booking required
Restaurant L served 12-2 booking required D served Tue-Sat 6.30-9 booking required ⊕ FREE HOUSE ◀ Butcombe Blonde, Butcombe Bitter Ö Ashton Press, Orchard Pig. ♇ 10 **Facilities** Children's menu Children's portions Family room Garden Parking Wi-fi **Rooms** 3

PICK OF THE PUBS

The Globe ★★★ INN 🌹 🍷

MILVERTON   Map 3 ST12

Fore St TA4 1JX ☎ 01823 400534
e-mail: info@theglobemilverton.co.uk
web: www.theglobemilverton.co.uk
dir: *On B3187*

The Globe is a free house that is clearly very much part of the village and local community, thanks to husband and wife team, Mark and Adele Tarry. They've been presiding over this old coaching inn for over five years, its clean-lined, contemporary interior sitting comfortably within the Grade II-listed structure. Local artists display their paintings on the walls of the restaurant and bar area, whilst a wood-burning stove and a sun terrace provide for all seasons. One of Mark's passions is local ales; Exmoor and Cotleigh are the regulars, while guest ales come from other Somerset brewers. Sheppy's local cider and English wines are also available.

An extensive menu ranges from traditional steak and kidney pie and home-made burgers at lunchtime, to the main menu with slow-roasted Gloucester Old Spot belly pork, and a wide selection of fish specials, among them sea trout, scallops and River Fowey mussels. Everything is home made, including the bread. For a quick and easy lunch option there are baguettes and ciabattas with fillings like Parma ham, brie and rocket; and roasted vegetables with feta cheese.

The kitchen uses West Country produce extensively in the production of sea bass fillets with chorizo pesto and rocket; chargrilled rib-eye steak with brandy and green peppercorn sauce and home-made fat chips; roasted Barbary duck breast with celeriac purée and spiced orange sauce; and wild mushroom and Gruyère cheese tart with red onion jam. Home-made (with a little help from Mark's mum) desserts include classic crème brûlée; mascarpone and Amaretto tiramisu; and lemon tart with raspberry cream. There is a carefully thought out children's menu too.

Stay over in one of the comfortable bedrooms because Milverton is a good base from which to explore the Quantock Hills and Exmoor.

Open noon-3 6-11 (Fri-Sat 12-3 6-11.30) Closed: Sun eve, Mon L **Bar Meals** L served Tue-Sun 12-2 D served Mon-Sat 6.30-9 booking required **Restaurant** L served Tue-Sun 12-2 D served Mon-Sat 6.30-9 booking required ⊕ FREE HOUSE ◀ Exmoor Ale, Cotleigh 25, Butcombe Bitter, Otter Bitter, Guest ales ♂ Sheppy's. 🍷 8 **Facilities** Children's menu Parking Wi-fi **Rooms** 3

NUNNEY
Map 4 ST74

The George at Nunney ☻

Church St BA11 4LW
☎ 01373 836458 📠 01373 836565
e-mail: info@thegeorgeatnunney.co.uk
dir: 0.5m N off A361, Frome/Shepton Mallet

Set in a classic English village complete with moated castle ruins, this rambling inn has established itself as the hub of the village's lively community. Run by Fraser Carruth and head chef Wayne Carnegie, it serves a choice of real ales, ciders and imported beers in the comfortable beamed bar. Lunch and dinner menus change every few weeks and the specials change weekly. A typical selection could comprise twice baked goat's cheese soufflé with baby leaf spinach and crushed hazelnuts, followed by veal schnitzel served with coleslaw and purple truffle potatoes, and vanilla pannacotta with blueberry and honey sauce to finish.

Open all wk 12-3 6-11 (Sun 7-10.30) **Bar Meals** L served all wk 12-2 D served all wk 7-9 Av main course £9.95 **Restaurant** L served all wk 12-2 D served all wk 7-9 booking required Av 3 course à la carte fr £39.75 ⊕ FREE HOUSE ◀ 6X, Hobgoblin Ruby ♂ Stowford Press. ☻ 8 **Facilities** Dogs allowed Garden Parking Wi-fi

OAKHILL
Map 4 ST64

PICK OF THE PUBS

The Oakhill Inn ★★★★ INN ☻

Fosse Rd BA3 5HU ☎ 01749 840442
e-mail: info@theoakhillinn.com
dir: On A367 between Stratton-on-the-Fosse & Shepton Mallet

Why not pop in to this pub, borrow a map and discover some of the many paths and bridleways around Oakhill? Then, having earned your refreshment, you can repair to this spacious but cosy country inn with warming winter fires and comfy sofas, or stay over in one of the comfortable rooms. If the weather permits, the landscaped garden is a lovely spot, with views to the village and the Mendip Hills. The inn helps to support the county's increasingly prolific brewing industry by serving three rotating real ales from nearby micro-breweries. If cider is your preference, there are three of those too, all on draught and all local; festivals celebrating these drinks are held twice per year. Head chef Neil Creese insists on free range and organic produce for his menus; everything is made on the premises except bread, butter and cheese. So settle back with the menu and go for three courses: venison and bacon terrine with apple and pear chutney could be followed by new season's lamb chops with peas and baby carrots; round things off with a hot chocolate pot and Midway Farm cream.

Open all wk Mon-Fri noon-3 5-11 (Sat-Sun all day) **Bar Meals** L served all wk 12-3 booking required D served all wk 5-9.30 booking required Av main course £12 **Restaurant** Fixed menu price fr £11.95 Av 3 course à la carte fr £26 ⊕ FREE HOUSE ◀ Sharp's Doom Bar, Butcombe ♂ Orchard Pig, Pheasant Plucker. **Facilities** Children welcome Children's menu Children's portions Dogs allowed Garden Beer festival Parking Wi-fi **Rooms** 5

OVER STRATTON
Map 4 ST41

The Royal Oak

TA13 5LQ ☎ 01460 240906
e-mail: info@the-royal-oak.net
dir: Exit A303 at Hayes End rdbt (South Petherton). 1st left after Esso garage signed Over Stratton

Blackened beams, flagstones, log fires, pews and settles set the scene in this welcoming old thatched inn built from warm ham stone. Originally built in the 1600s as a farmhouse, it received its licence around 1850. Expect real ales served in the bar, including Tanglefoot from the Badger Brewery in Blandford Forum. Dishes on the home-cooked menu range from Thai fish curry to slow roasted and stuffed belly pork, or roasted mushroom and asparagus risotto. Many dishes have a small and normal appetite price. Added attractions are the beer garden, children's play area and barbecue.

Open Tue-Sun Closed: Mon **Bar Meals** L served Tue-Sun 12-2 booking required D served Tue-Sun 6-9 booking required **Restaurant** L served Tue-Sun 12-2 booking required D served Tue-Sun 6-9 booking required ⊕ HALL & WOODHOUSE ◀ Badger Best, Tanglefoot, Sussex Best Bitter. **Facilities** Children welcome Children's menu Children's portions Play area Family room Dogs allowed Garden Parking

PITNEY
Map 4 ST42

The Halfway House ☻

TA10 9AB ☎ 01458 252513
dir: On B3153, 2m from Langport & Somerton

Now in new hands, this pub is largely dedicated to the promotion of real ale, and there are always six to ten available in tip-top condition, including Moore Northern Star and Teignworthy. This delightfully old-fashioned rural pub has three homely rooms boasting open fires, books and games, but no music or electronic games. Home-cooked rustic food made using local ingredients (except Sundays when it is too busy with drinkers) include soups, local sausages, sandwiches and a good selection of curries and casseroles.

Open all wk 11.30-3 5.30-11 (Fri-Sat 5.30-mdnt Sun noon-3 7-11) Closed: 25 Dec **Bar Meals** L served Mon-Sat 12-2.30 D served Mon-Sat 7-9.30 Av main course £8.95 ⊕ FREE HOUSE ◀ Butcombe Bitter, Teignworthy, Otter Ale, Hop Back Summer Lightning, Moore Northern Star ♂ Kingstone Black, Burrow Hill, Wilkins Medium. ☻ 8 **Facilities** Children welcome Children's portions Play area Dogs allowed Garden Parking

PORLOCK
Map 3 SS84

The Bottom Ship

Porlock Weir TA24 8PB ☎ 01643 863288
e-mail: info@thebottomship.co.uk
dir: Telephone for directions

At the water's edge on the southern bank of the Bristol Channel, this thatched pub's outside seats offer superb views over to south Wales, but there's plenty of space inside if the weather is inclement. Exmoor ales are the mainstay in the beamed bar, with a couple of real ciders also on tap. Home-made food using fresh local produce includes most pub favourites, from deep-fried whitebait to steak and ale pie. Children have their own menu and dogs are welcome.

Open all day all wk ⊕ FREE HOUSE ◀ Exmoor Ale, Exmoor Stag, Otter Bright, Proper Job, St Austell IPA ♂ Pear & Apple Rattler, Cheddar Valley. **Facilities** Children welcome Children's menu Children's portions Dogs allowed Garden Parking

The Ship Inn

High St TA24 8QD ☎ 01643 862507
e-mail: enquiries@shipinnporlock.co.uk
dir: A358 to Williton, then A39 to Porlock. 6m from Minehead

Many travellers have been welcomed to this 13th-century inn, one of the oldest on Exmoor, including Wordsworth, Coleridge and even Nelson's press gang. Nestling at the foot of Porlock's notorious hill, where Exmoor tumbles into the sea, its thatched roof and traditional interior provide an evocative setting for a meal or drink. Regularly changing menus include ploughman's, light bites and dishes such as sausage and mash and beer battered cod and chips. There's a beer garden with children's play area.

Open all day all wk ⊕ FREE HOUSE ◀ Tribute, Exmoor Ale, Otter, Proper Job, Tawny ♂ Cheddar Valley, Thatchers. **Facilities** Children welcome Children's menu Children's portions Play area Dogs allowed Garden Parking Wi-fi

RODE
Map 4 ST85

The Mill at Rode ☻

BA11 6AG ☎ 01373 831100 📠 01373 831144
e-mail: info@themillatrode.co.uk
dir: 6m S of Bath

A converted grist mill on the banks of the beautiful river Frome, this magnificent multi-storeyed Georgian building sits in its own landscaped grounds in the rural hinterland south of Bath. The dining-terrace overhangs the rushing waters, a great location in which to indulge in local beers or select from the West Country based menu; maybe terrine of local game with apple chutney and warm toast followed by fillets of Cornish plaice stuffed with mushrooms and spinach and topped with a vintage Cheddar sauce. A children's playroom offers grown-ups the chance of escape and a peaceful chinwag.

Open all day all wk noon–11 Closed: 25 Dec
Bar Meals L served all wk 12–7 booking required D served all wk 7–10 booking required food served all day
Restaurant L served all wk 12–7 booking required D served all wk 7–10 booking required food served all day
⊕ FREE HOUSE ◀ Butcombe Bitter, Pedigree, Guinness, Guest ales ♂ Black Rat, Ashton Press. ♟ 35
Facilities Children welcome Children's menu Children's portions Play area Family room Garden Parking Wi-fi

RUDGE   Map 4 ST85

The Full Moon at Rudge ★★★ INN

BA11 2QF ☎ 01373 830936 📄 01373 831366
e-mail: info@thefullmoon.co.uk
dir: From A36 (Bath to Warminster road) follow Rudge signs

Just seven miles from Longleat, this venerable 16th-century old cider house is located at the crossing of two old drove roads and enjoys great views of Westbury White Horse. Sympathetically updated, the pub retains its stone-floored rooms furnished with scrubbed tables. The modern menus change to reflect the seasons, with Barnsley lamb chop with rosemary jus or Somerset sirloin steak being examples of the fare. There is a large garden with play area and 17 comfortable bedrooms for those wishing to stay longer.

Open all day all wk 11.30–11 (Sun noon–10.30)
Bar Meals L served all wk 12–2 D served all wk 6–9 Av main course £5 **Restaurant** L served all wk 12–2 D served all wk 6–9 Fixed menu price fr £15 Av 3 course à la carte fr £20 ◀ Butcombe Bitter, London Pride, Guest ale ♂ Thatchers Cheddar Valley, Richs Farmhouse.
Facilities Children welcome Children's menu Play area Dogs allowed Garden Parking Wi-fi **Rooms** 17

SHEPTON BEAUCHAMP   Map 4 ST41

Duke of York ♟

North St TA19 0LW ☎ 01460 240314
e-mail: sheptonduke@tiscali.co.uk
dir: M5 junct 25 Taunton or A303

Run by husband and wife team Paul and Hayley Rowlands, and Purdy, the 'famous' pub dog, this 17th-century free house occupies a lovely spot in the pretty village of Shepton Beauchamp. The bar stocks some good West Country real ales and the restaurant has a varied menu: smoked salmon and prawn roulade might be followed by pan-fried sea bass or sirloin steak and chips. Food and drink can also be enjoyed in the pub garden.

Open all day noon–mdnt (Mon 5.30–11) Closed: Mon L
Bar Meals L served Tue–Sun 12–2 D served Tue–Sat 6.45–9 booking required Av main course £8.50
Restaurant L served Sun 12–2.30 booking required D served Tue–Sat 6.45–9 booking required ⊕ FREE HOUSE ◀ Teignworthy Reel Ale, Otter Bright ♂ Thatchers Gold.
♟ 9 **Facilities** Children welcome Children's menu Children's portions Family room Dogs allowed Garden Beer festival Parking Wi-fi

SHEPTON MALLET   Map 4 ST64

PICK OF THE PUBS

The Three Horseshoes Inn ★★★★ INN ♟

Batcombe BA4 6HE
☎ 01749 850359 📄 01749 850615
e-mail: info@thethreehorseshoesinn.com
dir: Take A359 from Frome to Bruton. Batcombe signed on right. Pub by church

This honey-coloured stone inn enjoys a peaceful position squirreled away in the very rural Batcombe Vale, and the lovely rear garden overlooks the old parish church. The long and low-ceilinged main bar has exposed stripped beams, a huge stone inglenook with log fire, and is warmly and tastefully decorated, with pale blue walls hung with old paintings, creating a homely atmosphere. From gleaming handpumps on the bar come foaming pints of locally brewed Cheddar Potholer. Menus draw on the wealth of fresh seasonal produce available locally, with lunches taking in cumin spiced lamb salad with new potatoes and fine beans, or Somerset ham and local eggs with chips. Choice at dinner extends to pan-fried bream with fennel and creamed leeks, or a more classic rib-eye steak and chips. Desserts include boozy orange parfait or a board of local cheeses. There are three stylishly decorated letting bedrooms available.

Open all wk Mon–Fri 11–3 6–11 (Sun 11am–11pm, Sun noon–10.30pm) **Bar Meals** L served all wk 12–2.30 booking required D served Mon–Sat 6–9.30, Sun 6–9 booking required **Restaurant** L served all wk 12–2.30 booking required D served Mon–Sat 6–9.30, Sun 6–9 booking required ⊕ FREE HOUSE ◀ Butcombe Bitter, Moor Revival, Cheddar Potholer ♂ Orchard Pig, Butcombe Blond, Ashton Press. ♟ 8 **Facilities** Children welcome Children's menu Children's portions Dogs allowed Garden Parking Wi-fi **Rooms** 3

PICK OF THE PUBS

The Waggon and Horses

Frome Rd, Doulting Beacon BA4 4LA
☎ 01749 880302
e-mail: waggon.horses09@googlemail.com
dir: 1.5m N of Shepton Mallet at x-roads with Old Wells-Frome road, 1m off A37

This friendly family-run, 18th-century coaching inn is a pretty, whitewashed building with leaded windows, situated high up on the Mendips with views over Glastonbury. There is a large enclosed garden and drinks and meals can be enjoyed outside in fine weather. A varying range of local real beers and ciders are served alongside traditional home cooked dishes. Expect the likes of steak and ale pie; mushroom and spinach lasagne; fillet of salmon in dill sauce; and home-made faggots and onion gravy. Baguettes, jacket potatoes, ploughman's and other 'lite bites' are available at lunchtime. Children and dogs are most

welcome, and the building is accessible for wheelchairs. Other facilities include the skittle alley and a function room, plus there are bike nights, steak nights and Italian chefs' nights.

Open all wk Mon–Sat 12–2.30 6–11 (Sun 12–3 6–10)
Bar Meals L served Mon–Sat 12–2.30, Sun 12–3 D served Mon–Sat 6–9, Sun 6–8 **Restaurant** L served Mon–Sat 12–2.30, Sun 12–3 D served Mon–Sat 6–9, Sun 6–8 ⊕ FREE HOUSE ◀ Wadworth 6X, Butcombe ♂ Wilkins, Addlestones, Ashton Press.
Facilities Children welcome Children's menu Children's portions Dogs allowed Garden Parking

SHEPTON MONTAGUE   Map 4 ST63

PICK OF THE PUBS

The Montague Inn ♟

BA9 8JW ☎ 01749 813213 📄 01749 813213
e-mail: themontagueinn@aol.com
dir: From Wincanton & Castle Cary turn right off A371

Nestling in rolling unspoilt Somerset countryside on the edge of sleepy Shepton Montague, this award-winning 18th-century stone-built village inn is hidden down winding country lanes close to Castle Cary. Tastefully decorated throughout, with the homely bar featuring old dark pine and an open log fire, and a cosy, yellow-painted dining room, the focus and draw of this rural dining pub is the careful sourcing of local foods from artisan producers and the kitchen's imaginative seasonal menus. Expect to find cask ales from Bath Ales, salads, fruit and vegetables from local farms, and free-range eggs from Blackacre Farm. This translates to lunchtime dishes like duck liver parfait and orange jelly; smoked haddock soufflé; and devilled chicken livers on toast. Evening specials might include rump of lamb, roasted garlic and parsley mash, ending with strawberry parfait and berry compote. The attractive rear terrace with rural views is perfect for summer sipping. Families and dogs are most welcome.

Open noon–3 6–11.30 Closed: Sun eve
Bar Meals L served all wk 12–2.30 booking required D served Mon–Sat 7–9.30 booking required Av main course £8.50 – £14.50 **Restaurant** L served all wk 12–2.30 booking required D served Mon–Sat 7–9.30 booking required Fixed menu price fr £10 Av 3 course à la carte fr £21 ⊕ FREE HOUSE ◀ Bath Ale, Wadworth 6X, Strongarm, Guest ales ♂ Local cider, Thatchers Gold, Addlestones Cloudy. **Facilities** Children welcome Children's portions Family room Dogs allowed Garden Parking Wi-fi

STANTON WICK Map 4 ST66

PICK OF THE PUBS

The Carpenters Arms ♥

See Pick of the Pubs on opposite page

STOGUMBER Map 3 ST03

The White Horse

High St TA4 3TA ☎ 01984 656277
e-mail: info@whitehorsestogumber.co.uk
dir: *From Taunton take A358 to Minehead. In 8m left to Stogumber, 2m into village centre. Right at T-junct & right again. Pub opp church*

Situated in the village of Stogumber on the edge of the Quantock Hills, this traditional free house is ideally situated for walkers and visitors to the nearby West Somerset Steam Railway. The dining room was once the village's Market Hall and Reading Room. Home-cooked menus change daily; deep-fried whitebait might be followed by whole local rainbow trout cooked with sherry and almonds, or Mediterranean-style chicken casserole. Enjoy local ales in the courtyard garden.

Open all day all wk 11-11 (Sun 12-11)
Bar Meals L served all wk 12-2 D served all wk 7-9 Av main course £8.50 **Restaurant** L served all wk 12-2 D served all wk 7-9 ⊕ FREE HOUSE ◄ Cotleigh Tawny Bitter, Local West Country, Proper Job, Guest ales Ở Thatchers Cheddar Valley. **Facilities** Children welcome Children's menu Family room Dogs allowed Garden Parking

STOKE ST GREGORY Map 4 ST32

Rose & Crown

Woodhill TA3 6EW ☎ 01823 490296
e-mail: info@browningpubs.com
dir: *M5 junct 25, A358 towards Langport, left at Thornfalcon, left again, follow signs to Stoke St Gregory*

Run by the same family for over 30 years, this pub enjoys a well deserved reputation for good food (both sons are the chefs), local produce and a warm reception. A chatty newsletter gives diary dates and reminders of special offers such as fish on Fridays, charity events, and take-away dishes at reduced cost. Following a fire in 2008, internal changes have been introduced gradually and focus on maximising customer comfort. All the bread, sausages and desserts are home made. Expect dishes like a trio of prime pork and scrumpy sausages with onion gravy and mash, or steak and kidney pie cooked in red wine.

Open all wk 11-3 6-11 **Bar Meals** L served all wk 12-2 booking required D served all wk 7-9 booking required **Restaurant** L served all wk 12-2 booking required D served all wk 7-9 booking required ⊕ FREE HOUSE ◄ Exmoor Fox, Stag, Butcombe, Otter Ale, Exmoor Ale, Guest ales Ở Thatchers Gold, local country cider. **Facilities** Children welcome Children's menu Children's portions Garden Parking Wi-fi

STREET Map 4 ST43

The Two Brewers ★★★★ INN NEW

38 Leigh Rd BA16 0HB ☎ 01458 442421
e-mail: richard@thetwobrewers.co.uk
dir: *In town centre*

Festooned with creeper and dazzling hanging baskets in summer, this stone inn successfully achieves a balance between town local and country pub. Both alley skittles and boules in the enclosed garden are taken seriously. Guests staying over in the converted stable accommodation may plan visits to nearby Glastonbury Tor over a glass of St Austell Tribute or a galaxy of guest beers, and look forward to freshly home-cooked goodies such as the filling Ohio meat pie or one of the regularly-changing blackboard specials.

Open all wk Mon-Sat 11-3 6-11 (Sun 11.30-3 6-10.30) Closed: 25-26 Dec **Bar Meals** L served all wk 12-2 D served all wk 6-9 **Restaurant** L served all wk 12-2 D served all wk 6-9 ⊕ FREE HOUSE ◄ St Austell Brewery Tribute, 3 Guest ales. **Facilities** Children welcome Children's menu Children's portions Garden Parking Wi-fi **Rooms** 3

TAUNTON Map 4 ST22

The Hatch Inn ♥

Village Rd, Hatch Beauchamp TA3 6SG ☎ 01823 480245
e-mail: nytram62@msn.com
dir: *M5 junct 25, S on A358 for 3m. Left to Hatch Beauchamp, pub in 1m*

Surrounded by splendid Somerset countryside, this family-run pub dates back to the mid 1800s and has its share of ghostly occupants. The inn prides itself on its friendly atmosphere and the quality of its wines and beers – there are always four real ales available, rotating regularly via local brewers. Wholesome home-made food is served, prepared from local produce, with a good choice of snacks and meals served in the both the bar and restaurant. A children's menu is also offered. Recent change of hands.

Open all day all wk noon-3 5-11 (Thu noon-3 5-12, Fri-Sat noon-mdnt, Sun noon-10.30) **Bar Meals** L served all wk 12-3 D served all wk 6-9 **Restaurant** L served all wk 12-3 D served all wk 6-9 ⊕ FREE HOUSE ◄ Four real ales rotated regularly via local brewers Ở Thatchers, Stowford Press. ♥ 20 **Facilities** Children welcome Children's menu Children's portions Family room Dogs allowed Beer festival Parking Wi-fi

Queens Arms

Pitminster TA3 7AZ ☎ 01823 421529 📄 01823 451068
e-mail: enquiries@queensarms-taunton.co.uk
dir: *4m from town centre. On entering Corfe, turn right signed Pitminster. 0.75m, pub on left*

This ancient building was once a mill and even gets a mention in the Domesday Book of 1086. Situated in the heart of Pitminster, its present day incarnation is as a stylish country pub that combines the traditional welcome of a classic country inn with a touch of continental sophistication. Oak and slate floors and roaring log fires in winter add to the appeal, while in summer the patio garden is the perfect spot for a cold drink or after-dinner coffee. The chef uses only the finest locally produced ingredients. Meat and game are produced in Somerset, and the vegetables are grown locally. As we went to press a change of hands was taking place.

Open 12-3 6-12 Closed: Sun eve & Mon ⊕ ENTERPRISE INNS ◄ Otter Ale, Exmoor Ale, Sharp's Doom Bar Ở Thatchers Gold. **Facilities** Children welcome Children's menu Children's portions Dogs allowed Garden Parking Wi-fi

TINTINHULL Map 4 ST41

PICK OF THE PUBS

The Crown and Victoria Inn ★★★★ INN ❀ ♥

14 Farm St BA22 8PZ ☎ 01935 823341 📄 01935 825786
e-mail: info@thecrownandvictoria.co.uk
dir: *Next to the National Trust gardens at Tintinhull House*

This 300-year-old inn occupies an enviable rural setting amidst sweeping willow trees. Now a friendly family-orientated pub with a peaceful beer garden, Mark Hilyard and Isabel Thomas have worked wonders since taking it over in 2006. Along with award-winning beers and a good selection of wines, the locally sourced food, much of it organic and free-range, has built up a following of its own. Typical dishes on the extensive menu might include Yeovil Marsh free-range chicken, ham and leek pie with mustard sauce, Savoy cabbage and mash; butternut squash and parsnip risotto with sage and truffle oil and Parmesan crackling; chargrilled rib-eye steak with grilled beef tomato, Portobello mushroom, onion rings and Dorset red watercress with triple-cooked chips. Finish with lemon posset with Garibaldi biscuits or hot chocolate fondant with hazelnut ice cream and sesame wafer. The five spacious, well-equipped bedrooms complete the package.

Open all wk 10-4 5.30-late **Bar Meals** L served all wk 12-2.30 D served Mon-Sat 6.30-9.30 **Restaurant** L served all wk 12-2.30 D served Mon-Sat 6.30-9.30 booking required ⊕ FREE HOUSE ◄ Butcombe, Cheddar Ales, Sharp's Doom Bar, Cotleigh, Yeovil Ales Ở Ashton Press. ♥ 10 **Facilities** Children welcome Children's menu Children's portions Dogs allowed Garden Beer festival Parking Wi-fi **Rooms** 5

Save on hotels. Book at **theAA.com/hotel**

SOMERSET 403 ENGLAND

PICK OF THE PUBS

The Carpenters Arms ♜

STANTON WICK   Map 4 ST66

BS39 4BX
☎ **01761 490202** 📠 **01761 490763**
e-mail: carpenters@buccaneer.co.uk
web: www.the-carpenters-arms.co.uk
dir: *A37 to Chelwood rdbt, then A368. Pub 8m S of Bath*

Tucked away in the Chew Valley, this charming stone-built free house is centrally placed for Bath, Bristol and the tiny city of Wells. Converted from a row of miners' cottages, the inn has become a popular retreat over the years for anyone appreciating good food, fine wines and real ales. Outside you'll find an attractively landscaped patio for alfresco drinks or meals, while behind the flower-bedecked façade squashy sofas and old pews offer a relaxed welcome in the rustic bar. Low beams and neatly stacked logs frame the large fireplace and add to the appeal of the chatty, music-free atmosphere, and the range of real ales includes locally brewed Butcombe Bitter from Wrington. The extensive menus are changed regularly to make the best of local and seasonal produce and keep the chefs on their toes. There are dishes to suit most tastes; among them you might see a Thai chicken curry; sea bass fillet on crispy vegetable stir fry, egg noodles and Thai dressing; or a hearty belly of pork on creamed potato, braised Savoy cabbage

and black pudding with sage and mustard sauce. Vegetarians may find a linguini with spinach, pine nuts, sun blushed tomatoes and garlic with seasoned olive oil; or a mushroom, roasted red pepper and spinach risotto with freshly grated Parmesan. Leave space for some delicious home-made desserts - glazed pannetone bread and butter pudding, or treacle tart with lemon curd ice cream are typical choices. Lighter snacks include baguettes and sandwiches. To complement the food, the extensive wine list combines New and Old World favourites.

Open all day all wk 11-11 (Sun 12-10.30) Closed: 25-26 Dec **Bar Meals** L served Mon-Sat 12-2, Sun 12-9 booking required D served Mon-Thu 6-9.30, Fri-Sat 6-10,

Sun 12-9 booking required Av main course £13.95 **Restaurant** L served Mon-Sat 12-2, Sun 12-9 booking required D served Mon-Thu 6-9.30, Fri-Sat 6-10, Sun 12-9 booking required Av 3 course à la carte fr £25 🛢 FREE HOUSE ◀ Butcombe Bitter, Sharp's Doom Bar, Otter Ale. 🍷 10 **Facilities** Children's menu Children's portions Garden Parking

PICK OF THE PUBS

The Rock Inn ★★★★ INN 🍷

WATERROW **Map 3 ST02**

TA4 2AX
☎ 01984 623293 **📠 01984 623293**
e-mail: lnp@rockinn.co.uk
web: www.rockinn.co.uk
dir: *From Taunton take B3227. Waterrow approx 14m W. Or from M5 junct 27, A361 towards Tiverton, then A396 N, right to Bampton, then B3227 to Waterrow*

True to its name, a third of this 400-year-old half-timbered former smithy and coaching inn is carved out of the rock, with parts visible in the bar next to the open fire. Set in a lovely green valley beside the babbling River Tone on the southern fringe of Exmoor, the inn has been comfortably upgraded by Matt Harvey and Joanna Oldman, who also own a farm in the valley. Expect a laid-back feel in the rustic bar, with its worn floors, scrubbed tables and local farmers downing pints of Exmoor Gold. Steps lead up to the small dining room, a cosy space with chunky tables topped with church candles.

Everything served here is locally sourced, freshly prepared and cooked to order, the ever-changing blackboard menu featuring the best and most succulent cuts of West Country meat (Aberdeen Angus beef comes from the their own farm), fish delivered daily from Brixham, and game from Exmoor shoots. Lunch may include prawn cocktail or pan-fried wood pigeon breasts with black pudding and leaf salad, followed by steak and kidney pie or home-cooked ham, local free-range eggs and home-made chips. Dinner options are more inventive, perhaps sweet potato, chilli and coriander soup, followed by roast duck breast with honey and soy reduction; Fitzhead venison steak, dauphinoise potato, red wine and port sauce; or lamb chump with onion and rosemary purée and a red wine and redcurrant jus. And finally, the indulgent puddings - try warm chocolate brownie or bread and butter pudding or a plate of West Country cheeses. Miles of wonderful walking and fishing country make this region much cherished by outdoor types. Stop off for a night or two in one of the cosy bedrooms.

Open all wk **Bar Meals** L served all wk 12-2.30 D served all wk 6.30-9.30 Av main course £13.50 **Restaurant** L served all wk 12-2.30 D served all wk 6.30-9.30 Av 3 course à la carte fr £25 ⊕ FREE HOUSE ◀ Cotleigh Tawny, Exmoor Gold, Otter Ale, Cotleigh Barn Owl, Exmoor Antler 🍏 Sheppy's. 🍷 9 **Facilities** Children's menu Children's portions Dogs allowed Parking Wi-fi **Rooms** 8

TRISCOMBE   Map 4 ST13

PICK OF THE PUBS

The Blue Ball ♥

TA4 3HE ☎ 01984 618242
e-mail: enq@blueballinn.info
dir: *From Taunton take A358 past Bishops Lydeard towards Minehead*

A public house since 1608, The Blue Ball is hidden away down a narrow lane in the Quantock Hills. Beneath the A-frame wooden ceilings of the converted 18th-century thatched barn you'll find solid beech furniture and log fires, as well as windows that offer superb southerly views to the Brendon Hills. A range of West Country ales including Cotleigh Tawny, Exmoor Gold and Otter Head accompanies a solid selection of hot and cold sandwiches like Exmoor blue cheese with home-made red onion marmalade; and north Atlantic prawns with lime crème fraîche. Other light bites range from cauliflower cheese to smoked salmon with pickled gherkin, caper berries and brown bread. Typical main meals are a trio of sausages with creamy mash and red onion gravy; kipper kedgeree; and Thai yellow potato and spinach curry with naan bread and Basmati rice.

Open noon-3 6-11 (Fri-Sat 12-11 Sun 12-7) Closed: 25 Dec, 26 Dec eve, 1 Jan eve, Mon, Sun eve (winter only) **Bar Meals** L served Tue-Sat 12-2, Sun 12-3 D served Tue-Sat 7-9 **Restaurant** L served Tue-Sat 12-2, Sun 12-3 booking required D served Tue-Sun 7-9 booking required ⊕ FREE HOUSE ◀ Cotleigh Tawny, Exmoor Gold & Stag, Tribute, Otter Head Ale Ŏ Thatchers, Mad Apple. ♥ 11 **Facilities** Children welcome Dogs allowed Garden Parking

WATERROW   Map 3 ST02

PICK OF THE PUBS

The Rock Inn ★★★★ INN ♥

See Pick of the Pubs on opposite page

WELLS   Map 4 ST54

The City Arms ♥

69 High St BA5 2AG ☎ 01749 673916
e-mail: cityofwellspubcoltd@hotmail.com
dir: *On corner of Queen St & Lower High St*

This building was once the city gaol (Judge Jeffreys passed sentence here) and original features include barred windows, a solitary cell, chains and locks. The pub offers traditional standards of quality and service, and its choice of seven real ales, draught ciders and menus of fresh local produce. The bar menu might offer toasted goat's cheese salad with roasted tomatoes on garlic ciabatta with balsamic glaze followed by pan-fried liver and bacon with creamy mash. Typical specials include spicy Swedish meatballs and red Thai chicken curry. There are monthly live music evenings.

Open all wk 9am-11pm (Fri-Sat 9-mdnt Sun 10am-11pm) **Bar Meals** food served all day **Restaurant** L served all wk 12-3 booking required D served all wk 6-10.30 (May-Sep Fri-Sun 7-10) booking required ⊕ FREE HOUSE ◀ Butcombe, Sharp's, Potholer, Barbus, Hedge Monkey, George Best Ŏ Ashton Press, Aspall. ♥ 10 **Facilities** Children welcome Children's menu Children's portions Family room Dogs allowed Garden

The Crown at Wells ★★★★ INN NEW

Market Place BA5 2RP
☎ 01749 673457   📠 01749 679792
e-mail: eat@crownatwells.co.uk
dir: *On entering Wells follow signs for Hotels & Deliveries, in Market Place*

Set in the Market Place at the heart of England's smallest city, this 15th-century coaching inn is within a stone's throw of the magnificent Cathedral and moated Bishop's Palace. The Penn bar, named after the Quaker William Penn who preached here in 1695, is full of character with three original fireplaces, and is comfortably furnished. Bar menu choices include battered haddock and chips; slow-braised belly of pork with bubble and squeak; and pasta with wild mushrooms and pesto. There are 15 charming bedrooms available, including some four-posters.

Open all day all wk Closed: 25 Dec **Bar Meals** L served Mon-Fri & Sun 12-2, Sat fr 12, D served all wk 6-9 Av main course £6.95 **Restaurant** L served Mon-Sat 12-2, Sun 12-2.30 booking required D served all wk 6-9.30 booking required Fixed menu price fr £10.50 Av 3 course à la carte fr £23 **Facilities** Children welcome Children's menu Children's portions Garden Parking **Rooms** 15

PICK OF THE PUBS

The Fountain Inn & Boxer's Restaurant ♥

1 Saint Thomas St BA5 2UU
☎ 01749 672317   📠 01749 670825
e-mail: eat@fountaininn.co.uk
dir: *In city centre, at A371 & B3139 junct. Follow signs for The Horringtons. Inn on junct of Tor St & Saint Thomas St*

An attractive gastro-pub, yellow-painted with blue shutters and pretty window boxes; car parking is available opposite. It was built during the 18th century to accommodate men working on nearby Wells Cathedral. A family-run business since Adrian and Sarah Lawrence took it over in 1981, front of house is now managed by their eldest daughter Kateley (who was born at the pub) and her husband Andrew Kinnersley. A large open fire in winter, interesting bric-a-brac, unobtrusive music and board games, and customers popping in and out confirm the bar's friendly character. Boxer's restaurant upstairs is run by head chef Julie Pearce, who uses the finest local produce to create an impressive selection of quality home-cooked food for both the restaurant and the bar below. Among the favourites are 'Priddy Good' steaks and sausages: the beef is served with hand-cut chips, onion rings and your choice of sauce, while the sausages come with classic creamy mash and rich onion gravy.

Open all wk Mon-Sat noon-2.30 6-11 (Sun 7-11) Closed: 25-26 Dec **Bar Meals** L served all wk 12-2 D served all wk 6-9 Av main course £9.50 **Restaurant** L served all wk 12-2 D served all wk 6-9 Av 3 course à la carte fr £23 ⊕ PUNCH ◀ Butcombe Bitter, Sharp's Doom Bar. ♥ 23 **Facilities** Children welcome Children's menu Children's portions Parking

WEST BAGBOROUGH   Map 4 ST13

The Rising Sun Inn ♥

TA4 3EF ☎ 01823 432575
e-mail: jon@risingsuninn.info
dir: *Telephone for directions*

A traditional, 16th-century village pub serving West Country ales, in the picturesque Quantock Hills. Rebuilt around the cob walls and magnificent door, because of a fire, the decor is both bold and smart. A good choice of food at lunch and dinner includes main courses such as prime fillet of Somerset beef with black peppercorn sauce; duo of Creedy Carver duckling with onion marmalade jus; whole roasted lemon sole with crayfish tails; and warm goat's cheese with walnut and mulled wine plum salad. A gallery restaurant above the bar is ideal for private functions.

Open all wk 10.30-3 6-11 **Bar Meals** L served all wk 12-2 D served all wk 6.30-9.30 Av main course £10 **Restaurant** L served all wk 12-2 D served all wk 6.30-9.30 Av 3 course à la carte fr £30 ⊕ FREE HOUSE ◀ Exmoor Ale, Butcombe, St Austell Brewery Proper Job IPA. **Facilities** Children welcome Children's portions Dogs allowed

WEST CAMEL — Map 4 ST52

PICK OF THE PUBS

The Walnut Tree ★★ HL ⊛ ♀

Fore St BA22 7QW
☎ 01935 851292 🖹 01935 851292
e-mail: info@thewalnuttreehotel.com
dir: Off A303 between Sparkford & Yeovilton Air Base

A smartly modernised and extended family-run village inn located half a mile off the A303 between Sparkford and Ilchester. It's named after its magnificent walnut tree whose dappled shade can be enjoyed on summer days when the new terrace comes into its own. A popular pit-stop for weary A303 travellers, the friendly, family-run inn is also favoured by walkers exploring the Leyland Trail that passes through the village. Flagstone floors, red leather bucket chairs and black beams set the relaxing scene in the contemporary-styled bar. Here, Otter ale is dispensed along with dishes from the lunch menu: perhaps smoked haddock, prawn and potato bake served with crusty bread, or warm Capricorn goat's cheese and sun blushed tomato tartlets. The evening menu, served in the Rosewood restaurant, changes with the seasons and offers starters such as local scallops with pasta, bacon, chorizo and a coral sauce; followed perhaps by a main course of cod fillet on wilted spinach served with a mild curry sauce.

Open 11-3 5.30-11 Closed: 25-26 Dec, 1 Jan, Sun eve Mon L **Bar Meals** L served Tue-Sun 12-2 D served Mon-Sat 6-9 **Restaurant** L served Tue-Sun 12-2 booking required D served Mon-Sat 6-9 booking required ⊕ FREE HOUSE ◖ Otter Ale & Bitter. ♀ 9 **Facilities** Children welcome Children's portions Garden Parking Wi-fi **Rooms** 13

WEST HUNTSPILL — Map 4 ST34

PICK OF THE PUBS

Crossways Inn ♀

Withy Rd TA9 3RA ☎ 01278 783756
e-mail: info@crosswaysinn.com
dir: On A38 3.5m from M5

This characterful 17th century, tile-hung inn is a popular haunt for locals practising the art of alley skittles and visitors to the Somerset Levels which stretch away to the distant Mendip Hills. Sympathetically renovated, the cosy, wavy-beamed interior with fine old photos of the area is warmed on winter days by grand log fires, enough to take the chill off the winds whipping in from nearby Bridgwater Bay. Draw close to the bar to inspect the panoply of excellent beers, often from micro-breweries in Somerset (and generously supplemented at their August Bank Holiday beer festival); here too may be Richs Cider created at a local farm just a couple of miles distant. The classic food here also tends to be very locally sourced; settle in with button mushrooms and lardons of smoky bacon in a garlic and white wine cream sauce

before indulging in a Somerset steak or a choice of pie of the day, a home-made West Country treat using the freshest ingredients which may change daily. There is a large enclosed beer garden and children's play area.

Open all day all wk Closed: 25 Dec **Bar Meals** food served all day **Restaurant** food served all day ⊕ FREE HOUSE ◖ Fuller's London Pride, Exmoor Stag, Cotleigh Snowy, Butcombe, Doom Bar, Otter Ale Ö Thatchers Gold, Thatchers Dry, Richs. ♀ 16 **Facilities** Children welcome Children's menu Children's portions Play area Family room Dogs allowed Garden Beer festival Parking Wi-fi

WEST MONKTON — Map 4 ST22

PICK OF THE PUBS

The Monkton Inn

Blundells Ln TA2 8NP ☎ 01823 412414
dir: M5 junct 25 to Taunton, right at Creech Castle for 1m, left into West Monkton

This village pub was given a new lease of life when Eddie Street and Guy Arnold took over in 2006. A significant sum of money has been invested in refurbishing the interior and kitchen, and adding a stylish patio area to the garden in this convivial country pub located two miles from Taunton. A mission statement requires staff to greet customers within 30 seconds of entering, to 'go the extra mile', and to have fun at work. Hear, hear! By serving freshly prepared, reasonably priced food they have built a loyal following, while taking good care of the drinks-only community too. Served in the restaurant or private dining room, lunch and dinner menus change daily, which makes for a great many possibilities. Randomly selected are starters of cold poached salmon with mayonnaise dressing or 'really creamy' fresh mushroom soup; main courses of grilled local gammon steak with pineapple, peaches, coleslaw and home-made chips, or flash-fried liver and bacon with colcannon, and desserts such as oaty apple and rhubarb crumble or bread, butter, marmalade and apricot pudding.

Open noon-3 6-11 (Sat noon-11) Closed: Sun eve, Mon L **Bar Meals** L served Tue-Sun 12-2 **Restaurant** L served Tue-Sun 12-2 D served Mon-Sat 6.30-9.30 booking required Fixed menu price fr £15 ⊕ ENTERPRISE INNS ◖ Butcombe Bitter, Cotleigh Tawny, Exmoor Ale, Exmoor Gold. **Facilities** Children welcome Children's portions Play area Garden Parking Wi-fi

WHEDDON CROSS — Map 3 SS93

The Rest and Be Thankful Inn ★★★★ INN ♀

TA24 7DR ☎ 01643 841222 🖹 01643 841813
e-mail: stay@restandbethankful.co.uk
web: www.restandbethankful.co.uk
dir: 5m S of Dunster

Almost 1,000 feet up in Exmoor National Park's highest village, this early 19th-century coaching inn blends old world charm with friendly hospitality, and where years ago travellers were grateful for a break. A range of sandwiches, baguettes and jacket potatoes will fill the odd corner, supported by hot dishes like salmon with mustard and dill sauce; steak and Exmoor ale pie; and roasted vegetable moussaka. Eight en suite bedrooms provide comfortable accommodation, and there's a beer festival in September.

Open all wk 10-3 6-close **Bar Meals** L served all wk 12-2 D served all wk 6.30-9 booking required **Restaurant** L served all wk 12-2 booking required D served all wk 6.30-9 booking required ⊕ FREE HOUSE ◖ Exmoor Ale, Proper Job, Tribute, Guinness, Sharp's Own Ö Thatchers Gold, Rattler. ♀ 9 **Facilities** Children welcome Children's menu Children's portions Dogs allowed Garden Beer festival Parking Wi-fi **Rooms** 8

WINSFORD — Map 3 SS93

Royal Oak Inn NEW

TA24 7JE ☎ 01643 851455
e-mail: enquiries@royaloakexmoor.co.uk
dir: Off A396 (Minehead to Tiverton road)

A breathtaking, thatched, cream-washed ancient inn in one of Exmoor's prettiest villages, huddled beneath the rising moors beside the River Exe. Inside its all big fires, comfy chairs, restrained paraphernalia and restful decor, all the better to enjoy the twin treats of good honest Exmoor beers and rich local produce, including their own air-cured hams and beef; braised lamb suet pudding and Heidi Pie (sweet potato, spinach, goat's cheese and red onion).

Open all wk 11-3 6-11 **Bar Meals** L served all wk 12-2.30 D served all wk 6.30-9.30 booking required Av main course £11 **Restaurant** L served all wk 12-2.30 D served all wk 6.30-9.30 booking required Av 3 course à la carte fr £25 ⊕ ENTERPRISE INNS ◖ Exmoor Ale, Stag & Gold Ö Thatchers. **Facilities** Children welcome Children's menu Children's portions Dogs allowed Garden Parking Wi-fi

PICK OF THE PUBS

White Hart ★★★★ INN ♀

WIVELISCOMBE   Map 3 ST02

West St TA4 2JP
☎ **01984 623344** 📄 **01984 624748**
e-mail: reservations@
whitehartwiveliscombe.co.uk
web: www.whitehartwiveliscombe.co.uk
dir: *M5 junct 26. Pub in town centre*

Located at the foot of the Brendon Hills and nearby Quantocks, the White Hart offers an attractive gateway to Exmoor. Facing the square in Wiveliscombe, this former coaching inn dates back some 350 years. Now completely transformed after a major renovation, it offers high standards and modern comforts, whilst still retaining its traditional appeal. Wiveliscombe has been described as Somerset's capital of brewing and, with its rich history dating back over two hundred years, it is now home to both the Cotleigh and Exmoor Breweries. Both companies' products are regularly on offer in the vibrant, friendly bar, beside a variety of other regional and award-winning guest ales. Meanwhile, head chef Dave Gaughan's reputation for high quality, freshly cooked food using locally sourced produce has led to a number of prestigious accolades for his pub classics, such as fresh battered Brixham pollock and home-made chips; organic roasted vegetable lasagne; and a choice of ploughman's with home-made bread, chutney and salad. Other favourites include starters like slow roasted organic tomato and basil soup; and honey roast

ham with local free range poached egg, home-made bruschetta and chutney. Main course dishes like grilled Exe Valley trout with local herbs, sautéed potatoes and local organic salad; Gloucester Old Spot pork belly in local cider sauce with apple mash and seasonal organic vegetables; or oven roasted rack of local lamb with new potatoes; might precede profiteroles with strawberry cream filling and warm chocolate sauce. Bar snacks are available from 5-11 Monday to Saturday. Each of the sixteen en suite bedrooms has its own individual character, with a blend of original and contemporary features.

Open all day all wk 10.30am-11pm (Fri-Sat 9am-mdnt) **Bar Meals** L served Mon-Sat 12-2, Sun 12-2.30 booking required D served Mon-Fri 6.30-9, Sat-Sun 6.30-9.30 booking required

Restaurant L served Tue-Sat 12-2, Sun 12-2.30 D served Mon-Fri 6.30-9, Sat-Sun 6.30-9.30 booking required ⊞ FREE HOUSE ◼ Exmoor Beers, Cotleigh Beers, guest ales ♀ 8 **Facilities** Children welcome Children's menu Children's portions Dogs allowed Garden Parking Wi-fi **Rooms** 16

WIVELISCOMBE — Map 3 ST02

PICK OF THE PUBS

White Hart ★★★★ INN ♀

See Pick of the Pubs on page 407

WOOKEY — Map 4 ST54

The Burcott Inn

Wells Rd BA5 1NJ ☎ 01749 673874
e-mail: ian@burcottinn.co.uk
dir: *2m from Wells on B3139*

The 300-year-old stone building is set on the edge of a charming village with views of the Mendip Hills from the large enclosed garden. The inn features low beamed ceilings, flagstone floor, log fires and a copper topped bar. Meals are served in the restaurant, and snacks and daily specials in the bar alongside quality local ales. Typical dishes include salmon and dill fishcakes; oven roasted lamb rump; trout and almond salad; and home-made steak and ale pie. There are also special board choices.

Open all wk 11.30-2.30 6-11 (Sun 12-3 7-10.30) Closed: 25-26 Dec, 1 Jan **Bar Meals** L served all wk 12-2 D served Tue-Sat 6.30-9 **Restaurant** L served all wk 12-2 D served Tue-Sat 6.30-9 ⊕ FREE HOUSE ◀ Teignworthy Old Moggie, RCH Pitchfork, Hop Back Summer Lightning, Cotleigh 25, Cheddar Potholer ♂ Addlestones. **Facilities** Children welcome Children's menu Children's portions Family room Garden Parking

YARLINGTON — Map 4 ST62

The Stags Head Inn

Pound Ln BA9 8DG ☎ 01963 440393 📄 01963 440393
e-mail: mrandall1960@tiscali.co.uk
dir: *Exit A303 at Wincanton onto A37 signed Castle Carey. In 3m turn left signed Yarlington, take 2nd right into village. Pub opposite church*

Halfway between Wincanton and Castle Cary lies this completely unspoilt country inn with flagstones and real fires, its authentic atmosphere undisturbed by electronic intrusions. The annual fair in the village of Yarlington is reputedly the one referred to by Thomas Hardy in *The Mayor of Casterbridge* – although wives and children are no longer sold to visiting sailors as far as anyone knows. Real ales include Greene King and guests, backed by Thatchers and Aspall ciders; food revolves around home-cooked favourites served in the restaurant, the snug bar, or alfresco in fine weather.

Open Mon-Sun L Closed: 25 Dec, Sun (eve) **Bar Meals** L served all wk 12-2 booking required D served Mon-Sat 6-9 booking required Av main course £10.25 **Restaurant** L served all wk 12-2 booking required D served Mon-Sat 6-9 booking required Av 3 course à la carte fr £20 ⊕ FREE HOUSE ◀ Greene King, IPA, Bass, Guest ales ♂ Thatchers Gold, Aspall. **Facilities** Children welcome Children's menu Dogs allowed Garden Parking Wi-fi

YEOVIL — Map 4 ST51

The Half Moon Inn ★★★ INN ♀ NEW

Main St, Mudford BA21 5TF
☎ 01935 850289 📄 01935 850842
e-mail: enquiries@thehalfmoon.co.uk
dir: *A303 at Sparkford onto A359 to Yeovil, 3.5m on left*

Situated north of Yeovil in the small village of Mudford, this charming pub dates from the 17th century but has been painstakingly restored. The original exposed beams and flagstone floors retain the pub's character, as does the large cobbled courtyard ideal for alfresco dining in warmer months. The extensive menu of home-cooked food includes old favourites like ham, egg and chips; steaks and fish dishes, all of it washed down with local Pitchfork ale or real ciders. Spacious, well-equipped bedrooms are available.

Open all day all wk Closed: 25-26 Dec **Bar Meals** L served all wk 12-6 D served all wk 12-9.30 Av main course £10.50 food served all day **Restaurant** L served all wk 12-9.30 D served all wk 6-9.30 food served all day ⊕ FREE HOUSE ◀ RCH Brewery Pitchfork & East Street Cream ♂ Westons Cider Old Rosie, Perry & Scrumpy. ♀ 10 **Facilities** Children welcome Children's menu Children's portions Garden Parking Wi-fi **Rooms** 14

PICK OF THE PUBS

The Masons Arms INN ♀

41 Lower Odcombe BA22 8TX
☎ 01935 862591 📄 01935 862591
e-mail: paula@masonsarmsodcombe.co.uk
dir: *A3088 to Yeovil, right to Montacute, through village, 3rd right after petrol station to Lower Odcombe*

Believed to be the oldest building in the village, this 16th century inn has a thatched roof and four thatched 'eyebrows' above its upper windows. Originally a traditional cider house comprising three cottages, it had a small parlour where thirsty masons from the local quarry were served. These days, the bar serves pints from the pub's own micro-brewery. Proprietors Drew and Paula Read have built strong green credentials, recycling anything and everything and growing many of their own vegetables and fruit. The wine list reflects this commitment, with organic, vegetarian, biodynamic and fairly-traded choices. Drew also runs the kitchen, producing freshly prepared dishes for seasonal and daily-changing menus. 'Pub grub' might include ham, free range duck egg and chips; the main menu might offer Thai fried beef with sweet chilli sauce followed by oxtail casserole with garlic and herb dumplings and roast potatoes. The comfortable en suite letting rooms are set back from the road and overlook the garden.

Open all wk noon-3 6-mdnt **Bar Meals** L served all wk 12-2 booking required D served all wk 6.30-9.30 booking required Av main course £7 **Restaurant** L served all wk 12-2 booking required D served all wk 6.30-9.30 booking required Av 3 course à la carte fr £24 ⊕ FREE HOUSE ◀ Odcombe No1,

Odcombe Spring, Odcombe Roly Poly, Odcombe Winters Tail, Odcombe Half Jack ♂ Thatchers Gold, Thatchers Heritage. ♀ 8 **Facilities** Children welcome Children's menu Children's portions Dogs allowed Garden Parking Wi-fi **Rooms** 6

STAFFORDSHIRE

ALSTONEFIELD — Map 16 SK15

PICK OF THE PUBS

The George ♀

DE6 2FX ☎ 01335 310205
e-mail: emily@thegeorgeatalstonefield.com
dir: *7m N of Ashbourne, signed Alstonefield to left off A515*

The nearby valley is a famous haunt for ramblers and many seek well-earned refreshment at this friendly 18th-century coaching inn. Run by three generations of the same family, the current landlady warmly welcome all-comers, as long as muddy boots are left at the door. The appeal of this fine pub, other than the wonderful location and welcome, includes the cracking range of real ales and wines by the glass, and the fantastic home-cooked food. The emphasis is on seasonal, regional and traditional dishes: at lunch start with juniper-cured Scottish salmon with celeriac remoulade and beetroot; chicken liver parfait, toasted brioche and chutney; followed by shin of beef, red wine and root vegetable casserole; and nutmeg bread and butter pudding and custard. By night, tuck into ox tongue terrine; duo of venison – pan roasted haunch and braised shoulder pudding, or pan-fried sea bass fillet, crayfish cassoulet and gnocchi dumplings. There is a farm shop and wedding venue in the Grade II listed coach house.

Open all wk Mon-Fri 11.30-3 6-11 (Sat 11.30-11 Sun 12-9.30) Closed: 25 Dec **Bar Meals** L served all wk 12-2.30 booking required D served Mon-Sat 7-9, Sun 6.30-8 booking required **Restaurant** L served all wk 12-2.30 booking required D served Mon-Sat 7-9, Sun 6.30-8 booking required ⊕ MARSTONS ◀ Marston's Bitter & Pedigree, Jennings Cumberland Ale, Brakspear Oxford Gold, Guest ale ♂ Thatchers. ♀ 10 **Facilities** Children welcome Children's portions Dogs allowed Garden Parking

PICK OF THE PUBS

The Watts Russell Arms ♀

See Pick of the Pubs on opposite page

PICK OF THE PUBS

The Watts Russell Arms ♍

ALSTONEFIELD   Map 16 SK15

Alstonefield DE6 2GD ☎ 01335 310126
e-mail: contact@wattsrussell.co.uk
web: www.wattsrussell.co.uk
dir: *Take A515 N towards Buxton. In 6.5m left to Alstonefield & Mildale. Cross River Dove, take left fork to Mildale. 1.5m to pub*

Husband and wife team Bruce and Chris Elliott run this picture-postcard pub, originally a homestead dating from the 17th century. Later it became a beer-house called the New Inn, which was renamed in 1851 in honour of the wife of Jesse Watts-Russell; her family owned Ilam Hall down the road, the surviving part of which is now a youth hostel. Perhaps the dear lady wasn't that grateful, as her ghost reputedly still roams the area. Dogs are welcome in the terraced gardens and courtyard, while the cosy interior is welcoming for all the family, with a bar made from old oak barrels. Here Chris holds sway, serving perfectly kept pints of three changing range of real ales including local craft beers, single malts from a selection of fifteen, or eight wines by the glass. In the kitchen, Bruce prepares everything from scratch, using mostly locally supplied produce and ingredients – nothing comes from a packet or a tin. Salt beef is cured on the premises, and dishes such as hand-rolled six-hour pork allow the kitchen time to cater for special dietary demands. At

lunchtime there are tempting sandwiches, wraps, soups, hand-made pizzas and hot plates such as beef and ale casserole or fillet of salmon, while typical evening selections could comprise olive and artichoke heart salad, lobby (Staffordshire's own beef and vegetable casserole) or drunken duck cooked in cider and Calvados. Vegetarian dishes, of which there are usually at least three, such as vegetable whim, reflect the latest neighbourly donation. Popular Sunday lunches include prime topside of beef served pink, and leg of lamb slow-roasted with garlic, rosemary and orange. Once a month, Bruce hosts an evening devoted to food from other countries. A short walk from the pub is the River Dove and the beginning of Dovedale, one of the country's most beautiful walks.

Open Mon 12-2.30 Tue-Fri 12-10 (Sat 12-11, Sun 12-8) Closed: Mon eve **Bar Meals** L served Mon 12-2, Tue-Sat 12-4, Sun 12-7 D served Tue-Sat 7-9 booking required Av main course £10 **Restaurant** Av 3 course à la carte fr £20 🍴 FREE HOUSE ◀ Guest ales. ♍ 8 **Facilities** Children's portions Dogs allowed Garden Parking

| ALTON | Map 10 SK04 |

Bulls Head Inn ♟

High St ST10 4AQ ☎ 01538 702307 ▤ 01538 702065
e-mail: janet@thebullsheadalton.co.uk
dir: *M6 junct 14, A518 to Uttoxeter. Follow Alton Towers signs. Onto B5030 to Rocester, then B5032 to Alton. Pub in village centre*

This family-run 17th-century coaching inn is situated less than a mile from Alton Towers theme park. Oak beams and an inglenook fireplace set the scene for the old world bar, and the country-style dining room with its pine furniture and slate floor. Serving a selection of real ales from three handpumps, the main courses on the menu might include baked chicken supreme with wild mushroom and white wine sauce, home-made cottage pie, and curry or pie of the day, plus succulent steaks.

Open all wk 11am-11pm **Bar Meals** L served all wk 12-3 D served all wk 6-9 booking required **Restaurant** L served all wk 12-3 D served all wk 6-9 booking required ⊕ FREE HOUSE ◀ Bass, Abbot Ale, Hancocks, London Pride, Doom Bar, Ruddles County, Bombardier ♂ Crabbies, Kopparberg. ♟ 8 **Facilities** Children welcome Children's menu Children's portions Garden Parking

---

| ANSLOW | Map 10 SK22 |

The Burnt Gate at Anslow

Hopley Rd DE13 9PY ☎ 01283 563664
e-mail: info@burntgate.co.uk
dir: *From Burton take B5017 towards Abbots Bromley. At top of Henhurst Hill turn right Inn on Hopley Rd, 2m from town centre*

There's a country house feel to this hanging-basket bedecked village inn, set in pleasant countryside near Tutbury. Named after a tollhouse that was burned to the ground centuries ago; light oak beams and colourwashed walls brighten the interior, where patrons can look forward to locally brewed real ale and a generous menu crafted largely from Staffordshire sourced materials; chicken breast stuffed with fresh spinach and mushrooms in Madeira sauce hits the spot. Vegans, vegetarians and coeliacs will be particularly pleased with the choices available here.

Open all day all wk Closed: 31 Dec **Bar Meals/ Restaurant** L served Mon-Thu 12-2.30, Fri-Sat 12-9, Sun 12-4 D served Mon-Thu 6-9, Fri-Sat 12-9 ⊕ FREE HOUSE ◀ Pedigree, Guest ales. **Facilities** Children's menu Dogs allowed Parking Wi-fi

---

| BARTON-UNDER-NEEDWOOD | Map 10 SK11 |

The Waterfront ♟ NEW

Barton Marina DE13 8DZ
☎ 01283 711500 ▤ 01283 711155
e-mail: waterfront@bartonmarina.co.uk
web: www.bartonmarina.co.uk
dir: *Off A38, 1st left signed Barton-under-Needwood*

Purpose-built with reclaimed canal heritage materials as a part of an impressive marina complex just outside Barton-under-Needwood, the terrace overlooks busy moorings. It is the ideal place to sup on beers specially brewed for the pub, contemplate just how to turn-round a 70ft boat and indulge in the very fulsome menu, from snacks to mains including chicken breast and black pudding mash, with specials to swell the choice. A walk along the Trent and Mersey towpath links to paths to the nearby National Memorial Arboretum.

Open all day all wk **Bar Meals** food served all day
Restaurant L served Mon-Sat 12-4, Sun 12-8 booking
required D served Mon-Sat 6-9.30 booking required
⊕ FREE HOUSE ◀ Waterfront Barton Pale, Waterfront
Marina Bitter, Tribute, Pedigree Ō Thatchers. ▲ 20
Facilities Children welcome Children's menu Children's
portions Garden Parking Wi-fi

See advert opposite

Burton Bridge Inn ▲

24 Bridge St DE14 1SY ☎ 01283 536596
dir: *Telephone for directions*

The oldest pub in the historic brewing town of Burton,
this former coaching inn has its own brewery at the back
in an old stable block. Now in new hands, the old-
fashioned interior has oak panelling, feature fireplaces,
and a distinct lack of electronic entertainment. A full
range of Burton Bridge ales is available on tap, as well
as the locally produced Freedom Four lager. The menu
offers straightforward dishes, sandwiches and jacket
potatoes and the pub hosts beer festivals twice a year. A
skittle alley is also available for hire.

Open all wk 11.30-2.30 5-11 (Sun noon-3 7-10.30)
Bar Meals L served all wk 12-2 ⊕ BURTON BRIDGE
BREWERY ◀ Burton Bridge - Gold Medal Ale, Festival Ale,
Golden Delicious, Bridge Bitter. ▲ 15 **Facilities** Dogs
allowed Garden Beer festival Wi-fi

Yew Tree Inn

ST10 3EJ ☎ 01538 308348   📠 01782 212064
dir: *Between A52 & A523. 4.5m from Alton Towers*

The Yew Tree is so well known that people come from all
over the world to see it. The pub dates back 300 years
and has plenty of character and lots of fascinating
artefacts, including Victorian music boxes, pianolas,
grandfather clocks, a crank handle telephone, and a pub
lantern. A varied snack menu offers locally made, hand-
raised pork pies, sandwiches, baps, quiche and desserts,
and can be washed down with a pint of Burton Bridge or
Rudgate Ruby Mild.

Open all wk 10.30-2.30 6-12 (Sun 12-3 7-12) ⊕ FREE
HOUSE ◀ Burton Bridge, Bass, Rudgate Ruby Mild.
Facilities Children welcome Family room Dogs allowed
Parking **Notes** ⊗

The Queens At Freehay

Counslow Rd, Freehay ST10 1RF
☎ 01538 722383   📠 01538 723748
e-mail: mail@queensatfreehay.co.uk
dir: *4m from Alton Towers*

Surrounded by mature trees and well tended gardens,
this tucked-away 18th century pub is very much a family-
run establishment and boasts a refreshingly modern
interior. The pub has established a good reputation for
food, and dishes from the menu are supplemented by
chef's specials from the fish or meat boards. Expect pan-
fried duck breast with stir-fried vegetables and plum
sauce; Barnsley lamb chops with minted gravy; leeks,
goat's cheese and oatcake gratin. Local beer Alton Abbey
is another plus.

Open all wk noon-3 6-11 (Sun noon-4 6.30-11) Closed:
25-26, 31 Dec-1 Jan **Bar Meals** L served Mon-Sat 12-2,
Sun 12-2.30 booking required D served Mon-Sat 6-9.30,
Sun 6.30-9.30 booking required Av main course £10.95
Restaurant L served Mon-Sat 12-2, Sun 12-2.30 booking
required D served Mon-Sat 6-9.30, Sun 6.30-9.30
booking required Av 3 course à la carte fr £20.95 ⊕ FREE
HOUSE ◀ Draught Burton, Peakstones Alton Abbey,
Guinness. **Facilities** Children welcome Children's
portions Garden Parking

PICK OF THE PUBS

The Yorkshireman ▲

See Pick of the Pubs on page 412

The George

Castle St ST21 6DF ☎ 01785 850300   📠 01785 851452
e-mail: vicki@slatersales.co.uk
dir: *From M6 junct 14 take A5013 to Eccleshall (6m)*

A 17th-century former coaching inn, The George has been
in the Slater's hands for over 20 years. It's the brewery
tap for the other part of the family business – the micro-
brewery a few miles away in Stafford where the owners'
son produces award-winning ales. The traditional bar
features a large open fireplace, and proffers a good
selection of malt whiskies and wines in addition to the
family brews. A wide variety of dishes, including Wexford
mushroom crostini and Eccleshall-reared lamb steak,
can be eaten either in the bar or in the appealing
restaurant.

Open all day all wk Mon-Thu 11am-1.30am (Fri-Sat
11am-2.30am Sun noon-mdnt) Closed: 25 Dec ⊕ FREE
HOUSE ◀ Slaters Ales. **Facilities** Children
welcome Children's menu Dogs allowed Parking Wi-fi

Three Horseshoes Inn ★★★ HL ⊛⊛ ▲

Buxton Rd, Blackshaw Moor ST13 8TW
☎ 01538 300296   📠 01538 300320
e-mail: enquiries@threeshoesinn.co.uk
dir: *On A53, 3m N of Leek*

A family-run inn and country hotel in the Peak National
Park, the Three Horseshoes offers breathtaking views of
the moorlands, Tittesworth reservoir and rock formations
from the attractive gardens. Inside this creeper-covered
inn are ancient beams, gleaming brass, rustic furniture
and wood fires in the winter, with a good selection of real
ales. Using the best Staffordshire produce, visitors can
choose from three dining options: locally-reared roast
meat in the bar carvery, the relaxed atmosphere of the
brasserie offering two-Rosetted modern British and Thai
dishes, or Kirks Restaurant. Delicious afternoon teas are
also available.

Open all day all wk **Bar Meals** food served all day
Restaurant L served Sun 12.15-1.30 booking required
D served Mon-Sat 6.30-9 booking required ⊕ FREE
HOUSE ◀ Theakstons XB, Courage Directors, Morland Old
Speckled Hen, John Smith's. ▲ 12 **Facilities** Children
welcome Children's menu Children's portions Play area
Garden Parking **Rooms** 26

The Junction Inn

ST20 0PN ☎ 01785 284288
e-mail: enquiries@norburyjunction.co.uk
dir: *From M6 junct 14 take A5013 for Eccleshall, left at
Great Bridgeford onto B5405 towards Woodseaves, left
onto A519 towards Newport, left for Norbury Junction*

Situated on a beautiful stretch of waterway where the
Shropshire Union Canal meets the disused Newport arm,
the inn's large beer garden has a ringside view of
everything happening on the canal. Famous for its
Junction steak pie, the pub also serves other home-made
dishes such as pork faggots and beef lasagne; there's a
Sunday carvery with local meat and barbecues in the
garden in summer. There are cosy open fires in winter
and plenty of real ales include a choice of guest ales.

Open all wk 11-3 6-11 (Fri 11-11 Sat 11am-mdnt Sun
noon-10.30 open all day in summer) Closed: afternoon in
winter **Bar Meals** L served Mon-Fri 12-2.45, Sat-Sun all
day D served Mon-Fri 6-8.45, Sat-Sun all day
Restaurant L served Mon-Fri 12-2.45, Sat-Sun all day
D served Mon-Fri 6-8.45, Sat-Sun all day ⊕ FREE HOUSE
◀ Banks Mild, Banks Bitter, Junction Ale, Guest ales.
Facilities Children welcome Children's menu Children's
portions Play area Family room Garden Parking

PICK OF THE PUBS

The Yorkshireman 🍷

COLTON   Map 10 SK02

Colton Rd WS15 3HB ☎ 01889 583977
e-mail: theyorkshireman@btconnect.com
web: www.wine-dine.co.uk
dir: *10m from Stafford; 10m from Lichfield*

The heritage of this edge-of-town pub opposite Rugeley's Trent Valley railway station is lost in the mists of time, or possibly lost in steam billowing from express engines as it may have been established as a tavern to serve the new railway in Victorian times. It's seen a lot of life since those days, including a boisterous period as a local known as 'Wilf and Rosa's Tavern' and as a meeting place for farmers and soldiers when the sawdust and straw on the floor was doubtless put to good use.

It's rather more sedate these days, emerging from a complete refurbishment just a few years ago as a panelled, wood-floored dining pub specialising in dishes using the best of Staffordshire produce and offering beers from a local micro-brewery including, unusually, a lager. The eclectic furnishings are part of the charm, and the Stubbs' paintings attract much comment. Just as much part of the furnishings is the pub's greyhound, Dahl.

The menu is updated regularly, as season and supply allow, but a good range covering all the bases is assured. Starters may encompass mushroom and spinach

parcel with Shropshire Blue cheese sauce, or pan-fried pigeon breast on black pudding and caramelised apple salad with balsamic vinegar. Such treats continue with mains such as Staffordshire asparagus risotto topped with roast peppers and mozzarella, or saffron-marinated cod on roasted vine tomato with a courgette and watercress salad. Staffordshire-reared steaks are a speciality, as are dishes featuring rare-breed Gloucester Old Spot pork. There's a special Sunday menu at the Yorkshireman Deli. And the pub's name comes from a scion of the White Rose county who was once landlord here!

Open all wk noon-2.30 5.30-11 (Sat noon-11pm Sun noon-6)
Bar Meals L served Mon-Sat 12-2.30, Sun 12-6 D served Mon-Fri 6-9.30, Sat 6-11

Restaurant L served Mon-Sat 12-2.30, Sun 12-6 booking required D served Mon-Sat 6-9.30 booking required ⊕ FREE HOUSE ◼ Local Blythe Brewery Ŏ Stowford Press. 🍷 10
Facilities Children's portions Dogs allowed Garden Parking Wi-fi

Save on hotels. Book at theAA.com/hotel

STAFFORDSHIRE 413 ENGLAND

ONNELEY
Map 15 SJ74

The Wheatsheaf Inn ★★★★ INN
NEW

Bar Hill Rd CW3 9QF ☎ 01782 751581
e-mail: pub@wheatsheafpub.co.uk
web: www.wheatsheafpub.co.uk
dir: On A525 between Madeley & Woore

The Wheatsheaf opened as a coaching inn in 1769 and
although it has been modernised in recent years, the old
beams and fires are still in place, making for a cosy
setting to enjoy real ales or a meal in the restaurant.
Meat from the local farm appears on the menu, which
includes beef lasagne, seafood risotto and curry of the
week. The pub adjoins a golf course so don't forget to
pack your clubs and maybe stay over in the guest rooms
situated in converted stables.

Open all day all wk **Bar Meals** L served Mon-Sat 12-9
D served Mon-Sat 12-9 food served all day
Restaurant L served Mon-Sat 12-9 D served Mon-Sat
12-9 food served all day ⊕ FREE HOUSE ◀ Wells
Bombardier, Timothy Taylor Landlord, Guest ales.
Facilities Children welcome Children's menu Children's
portions Play area Family room Garden Parking Wi-fi
Rooms 10

STAFFORD
Map 10 SJ92

PICK OF THE PUBS

The Holly Bush Inn ♀
See Pick of the Pubs on page 414

PICK OF THE PUBS

The Moat House ★★★★ HL ◉◉ ♀

Lower Penkridge Rd, Acton Trussell ST17 0RJ
☎ 01785 712217 📄 01785 715344
e-mail: info@moathouse.co.uk
dir: M6 junct 13 towards Stafford, 1st right to Acton
Trussell

Along with the nearby church, this moated manor
house has been the focal point of the village since the
early part of the medieval period. A Grade II listed
mansion dating back to the 14th century, the house
stands on a Norman mound, scheduled as an Ancient
Monument, beside the Staffordshire and Worcestershire
Canal. Inside are oak beams and an inglenook
fireplace, the stylish Brasserie Bar and the

Conservatory Restaurant. The food, for which the AA
has awarded two Rosettes, is listed on a variety of
menus offering, for example, fillet of Cornish mackerel,
frisée and apple salad, beetroot salsa and horseradish
mascarpone; slow-cooked belly of Tamworth pork,
swede and honey pureé, black pudding bon bon,
buttered spinach and peppered jus; and fillet of plaice,
saffron potatoes, tomato chervil and mustard nage
with a spaghetti of vegetables. Finish, perhaps, with
warm poached white peach with thyme ice cream and
raspberry compote. There is also a tasting menu.
Quality bedrooms, conference facilities and corporate
events are big attractions, and with four honeymoon
suites, two with four-posters, the Moat House is a
popular venue for weddings.

Open all day all wk Mon-Sun 10am-11pm Closed:
25 Dec **Bar Meals** L served all wk 12-2.15 D served
Sun-Fri 6-9.30 **Restaurant** L served all wk 12-2
booking required D served all wk 6.30-9.30 booking
required ⊕ FREE HOUSE ◀ Old Speckled Hen, Greene
King IPA, Guinness. ♀ 16 **Facilities** Children welcome
Children's menu Children's portions Family room
Garden Parking **Rooms** 41

STOCKTON BROOK
Map 16 SJ95

The Hollybush ♀

1 Stanley Rd ST9 9NL ☎ 01782 502116
e-mail: mail@thehollybush.info
web: www.thehollybush.info
dir: Just off A53 between Stoke-on-Trent & Leek

The beer garden of this very stylish food-led village inn
stretches towards the peaceful, tree-shrouded Caldon
Canal, where a lock offers fascinating entertainment for
onlookers. Staffordshire's wealthy larder is plundered
generously here and prepared in contemporary fashion;
duo of pan-roast pork fillet and home-made pork, sage
and apple parcel wrapped in Serrano ham, or slow-
cooked shin of beef pie just two of the many appealing
dishes, accompanied by beers from, perhaps, Wincle
Brewery in the nearby Peak District hills.

Open all wk noon-11pm (Sun noon-10.30)
Bar Meals L served Mon-Fri 12-2.30, Sat 12-9.30, Sun
12-8 D served Mon-Fri 5-9.30 **Restaurant** L served
Mon-Fri 12-2.30, Sat 12-9.30, Sun 12-8 booking required
D served Mon-Fri 5-9.30 booking required ⊕ MOYO LTD
◀ Greene King IPA, Black Sheep Original, rotating guest
ales. ♀ 12 **Facilities** Children welcome Children's
menu Children's portions Garden Parking

STOURTON
Map 10 SO88

The Fox Inn

Bridgnorth Rd DY7 5BL
☎ 01384 872614 & 872123   📄 01384 877771
e-mail: fox-inn-stourton@dial.pipex.com
dir: 5m from Stourbridge town centre. On A458
(Stourbridge to Bridgnorth road)

The Fox is a late 18th-century inn on an estate once
owned by Lady Jane Grey. In the forty years Stefan Caron
has been running it, he has built its reputation for quality
and value for money, but his customers also enjoy the
warm atmosphere and historic surroundings. Typical
evening meal choices could include chef's own ham hock
terrine with piccalilli, followed by half a boneless duck on
a bed of stir-fry vegetables. A large garden with weeping
willow, gazebo and attractive patio area completes the
picture.

Open all wk 10.30-3 5-11 (Sat-Sun 10.30am-11pm)
Bar Meals L served Mon-Sat 12-2.30 D served Tue-Sat
7-9.30 **Restaurant** L served Tue-Sat 12-2.30, Sun
12.30-5 D served Tue-Sat 7-9.30 booking required
⊕ FREE HOUSE ◀ Bathams Ale, Hereford Pale Ale,
Guinness. **Facilities** Children welcome Children's
menu Children's portions Garden Parking

SUMMERHILL
Map 10 SK00

Oddfellows in the Boat ♀ NEW

The Boat, Walsall Rd WS14 0BU ☎ 01543 361692
e-mail: info@oddfellowsintheboat.com
dir: A461 (Lichfield towards Walsall). At rdbt junct with
A5 (Muckley Corner) continue on A461. In 600mtrs
establishment is visible. Continue 500mtrs, U-turn on
dual carriageway back to establishment

The Boat once served bargees on the adjacent, now-
disused Curly Wyrley, the Wyrley & Essington canal. Real
ale lovers enjoy what amounts to a rolling beer festival,
thanks to owner Gary's ever-changing micro-brewery
choice. Locally sourced dishes are prepared in an open
kitchen and chalked up daily, with tried and tested
entries including duck breast with plum and ginger
compote; sea bass with mussel sauce and saffron mash;
and vegetarian pear and blue cheese tart.

Open all wk 11-3 6-11 (Sun 12-11) Closed: 25 Dec
Bar Meals L served Mon-Sat 12-2.15, Sun 12-8.15
D served Mon-Sat 6-9.30, Sun 12-8.15 Av main course
£11 **Restaurant** L served Mon-Sat 12-2.15, Sun 12-8.15
D served Mon-Sat 6-9.30, Sun 12-8.15 Fixed menu price
fr £10.95 Av 3 course à la carte fr £18.95 ⊕ FREE HOUSE
◀ 3 changing guest ales. ♀ 13 **Facilities** Children
welcome Dogs allowed Garden Beer festival Parking Wi-fi

PICK OF THE PUBS

The Holly Bush Inn ♀

Map 10 SJ92

Salt ST18 0BX
☎ **01889 508234** 📄 **01889 508058**
e-mail: geoff@hollybushinn.co.uk
web: www.hollybushinn.co.uk
dir: *Telephone for directions*

This thatched inn is situated in the village of Salt, probably a settlement originating from the Saxon period due to its sheltered position and proximity to the river Trent. Believed to be only the second pub in the country to receive, back in Charles II's reign, a licence to sell alcohol, although the building itself possibly dates from as long ago as 1190. And when landlord Geoff Holland's son became a joint licensee at the age of 18 years and 6 days, he was the youngest person ever to be granted a licence.

The pub's comfortably old-fashioned interior contains all the essential ingredients: heavy carved beams, open fires, attractive prints and cosy alcoves. In the kitchen there's a strong commitment to limiting food miles by supporting local producers, and to ensuring that animals supplying meat have lived stress-free lives.

The main menu features traditional dishes such as steak and kidney pudding; battered cod with mushy peas; and mixed grill, but also included are the still-traditional-but-less-well-known, such as braised venison with chestnuts; and slow-cooked lamb and barley stew. The specials board changes every session, but will usually include Staffordshire oatcakes stuffed with bacon and cheese; hand-made pork, leek and Stilton sausages with fried eggs and chips; and a roast meat, perhaps topside of beef; or ham with sweet Madeira gravy. The evening specials board may offer home-smoked fillet of Blythe Field trout with creamy horseradish sauce; warm pan-fried duck and pear salad; Scottish mussels steamed with cider and cream; rabbit casserole with dumplings; or slow-cooked mutton with caper sauce.

Cheeses are all hand-made to old English recipes, while seasonal puddings include the unquestionably traditional bread and butter pudding, and apple crumble with cinnamon and nutmeg dusting.

Handmade pizzas are cooked in a wood-fired brick oven; in addition to the usual favourites, try the surf and turf, or seafood special.

Open all day all wk noon–11 (Sun noon–10.30) **Meals** Mon-Sat 12-9.30, Sun 12-9 food served all day ⊕ FREE HOUSE ◖ Adnams, Pedigree, guest ales. ♀ 12 **Facilities** Children's menu Children's portions Garden Parking

PICK OF THE PUBS

The Crown Inn ♟

WRINEHILL   Map 15 SJ74

Den Ln CW3 9BT ☎ 01270 820472
e-mail: info@thecrownatwrinehill.co.uk
web: www.thecrownatwrinehill.co.uk
dir: *Village on A531, 1m S of Betley. 6m S of Crewe; 6m N of Newcastle-under-Lyme*

Charles Davenhill (probably the longest-serving licensee in Staffordshire) and his wife Sue have owned this 19th-century free house for more than thirty years; their daughter and son-in-law, Anna and Mark Condliffe, joined them eleven years ago, the two men being the current licensees. Open plan in layout, it nevertheless retains its oak beams and large inglenook fireplace, a welcome feature on chilly days. The bar does a good line in well-kept real ales; there is always a choice of six traditional cask ales, two of which are regularly-changing regional guest beers. Food is a major reason for the success of The Crown, which is famed locally not just for its consistent quality, but for the generosity of the portions it serves. The regularly changing menus are jam-packed with choices, from modestly priced light meals, such as warm salad of jalapeno peppers, oak-smoked bacon and olives, to the more expensive, such as a 10oz sirloin steak, which arrives with Stilton, cream and port topping in addition to the regular grilled tomato, mushrooms, petits pois, onion rings and chips. In between comes, my, where to start! Well, as good a place

as any is oven-baked organic salmon fillet with herb, lemon and Parmesan crust and creamy garlic sauce; free-range chicken with bell and chilli peppers in jalfrezi sauce; head chef Steve's piri piri chicken and the 'legendary' shortcrust pastry pie filled with beef simmered in Marston's Pedigree gravy. Sue and Anna's disaffection for 'the typical mushroom Stroganoff found in lots of pubs' inspires the vegetarian selection – for example, burritos filled with courgettes, mushrooms, baby corn and mixed peppers; and Cheshire cheese sausages with wholegrain mustard mash and caramelised onion gravy. From the puddings menu, try home-made apple and sultana crumble with custard; or Snugbury's vanilla ice cream with chocolate sauce and whipped cream. Children have their own menu.

Open noon-3 6-11 (Sun noon-4 6-10.30) Closed: 25-26 Dec, Mon L (except for BHs) **Bar Meals** L served Tue-Fri 12-2, Sat-Sun 12-3 D served Mon-Fri 6-9, Sat 6-10 Sun 6-9 ⊞ FREE HOUSE ◄ Marstons Pedigree & Bitter, Cumberland Ale, Sneck Lifter, Salopian Ale, guest ales. ♟ 10 **Facilities** Children's menu Children's portions Garden Parking

TAMWORTH — Map 10 SK20

The Globe Inn ★★★ INN

Lower Gungate B79 7AT
☎ 01827 60455 📠 01827 63575
e-mail: info@theglobetamworth.com
dir: Telephone for directions

A popular meeting place in the 19th century, The Globe was completely rebuilt in 1901. More recently, the building has been extended and refurbished to offer 18 en suite bedrooms and air conditioning in the public areas. Nonetheless decoration has followed design styles of the era, and the elegant carved bar and fireplaces reinforce its period character. Breakfast, lunch, dinner and children's menus are all served from the well-equipped kitchen; the three-course Sunday lunch is a particular favourite.

Open all day all wk 11-11 (Thu-Sat 11am-mdnt Sun 11-4 7-11) Closed: 25 Dec, 1 Jan **Bar Meals** L served all wk 11-2 D served Mon-Sat 6-9 Av main course £7 **Restaurant** L served all wk 11-2 D served Mon-Sat 6-9 Fixed menu price fr £16 Av 3 course à la carte fr £16 ⊕ FREE HOUSE ◼ Bass, Worthington. **Facilities** Children welcome Children's menu Children's portions Parking **Rooms** 18

TUTBURY — Map 10 SK22

Ye Olde Dog & Partridge Inn ♀

High St DE13 9LS ☎ 01283 813030 📠 01283 816159
dir: From A38 in Burton upon Trent take A511 signed Utoxter at Derby Turn rdbt. Tutbury approx 4.5m

The oldest building on what is a quaint and traditional High Street close to Tutbury Castle, this medieval half-timbered pub dates back to the 15th century. The heavily beamed interior shelters nooks and alcoves where you can tuck into a menu that covers the whole gamut, from classics such as grilled gammon and egg or venison pie to chorizo chicken or aromatic duck, all washed down with real ales and a good list of wines.

Open all day all wk **Bar Meals** L served all wk 12-10 Av main course £9 food served all day **Restaurant** L served all wk 12-10 Fixed menu price fr £9.99 Av 3 course à la carte fr £17 food served all day ⊕ PUNCH PUB COMPANY ◼ Marston's Pedigree, Courage Directors. ♀ 12 **Facilities** Children welcome Children's menu Children's portions Garden Parking Wi-fi

WETTON — Map 16 SK15

Ye Olde Royal Oak

DE6 2AF ☎ 01335 310287
e-mail: royaloakwetton@live.co.uk
dir: A515 towards Buxton, left in 4m to Manifold Valley-Alstonfield, follow signs to Wetton

The stone-built inn dates back over 400 years and features wooden beams recovered from oak ships at Liverpool Docks. It was formerly part of the Chatsworth Estate, and the Tissington walking and cycling trail is close by. Guest ales are served along with dishes such as home-made soup, large battered cod, and treacle sponge. Separate vegetarian and children's menus are available. The pub's moorland garden includes a campsite with showers and toilets.

Open 12-2 7-closing Closed: Mon-Tue in winter **Bar Meals** L served Wed-Sun 12-2 D served Wed-Sun 7-9 Av main course £8 ⊕ FREE HOUSE ◼ Hartington, Old Speckled Hen. **Facilities** Children welcome Children's menu Family room Dogs allowed Garden Parking

WOODSEAVES — Map 15 SJ72

The Plough Inn

Newport Rd ST20 0NP ☎ 01785 284210
dir: From Stafford take A5013 towards Eccleshall. Turn left onto B4505. Woodseaves at junct with A519. 5m from Eccleshall on A519 towards Newport

This mid-18th century inn, which was built for workers constructing the nearby canal, has returned to its roots as a traditional country pub. The restored large inglenook fireplace gives a warm, welcoming feel, there's a good selection of real ales, and home-cooked, traditional pub dishes are served. Expect beef lasagne with salad; home-made pie; or plaice, chips and peas. Pie night is every third Tuesday of the month, steak night every first Tuesday, and an Italian gourmet night is held every three months.

Open all wk Mon 5-11 Tue-Thu 12-3 5-11 (Fri-Sat noon-mdnt Sun noon-10pm, all day BHs) **Bar Meals** L served all wk 12-2.30 D served all wk 5-8 Av main course £6.50 **Restaurant** L served Sat 12-8, Sun 12-6 ⊕ FREE HOUSE ◼ Banks Bitter, Banks Mild, Pedigree, Jennings, Cumberland Ale ♂ Thatchers Gold. **Facilities** Children welcome Children's menu Children's portions Family room Dogs allowed Garden Parking Wi-fi

WRINEHILL — Map 15 SJ74

PICK OF THE PUBS

The Crown Inn ♀

See Pick of the Pubs on page 415

The Hand & Trumpet ♀

Main Rd CW3 9BJ ☎ 01270 820048 📠 01270 821911
e-mail: hand.and.trumpet@brunningandprice.co.uk
dir: M6 junct 16, A351, follow Keele signs, 7m, pub on right in village

A relaxed country pub, The Hand & Trumpet has a comfortable interior with original floors, old furniture, open fires and rugs. A deck to the rear overlooks the sizeable grounds, which include a large pond. Six cask ales including guests and over 70 malt whiskies are served, along with a locally sourced menu. Typical dishes are potted smoked mackerel, crab and crayfish with pickled vegetables; rump steak sandwich with fried onion and tomato chutney; bouillabaisse; Thai chicken with noodle broth and coriander dumplings. There is a beer and food festival in the last week of January.

Open all day all wk 11.30-11 (Sun 11.30-10.30) Closed: 25 Dec **Bar Meals** L served all wk 12-10 D served all wk 12-10 Av main course £11.95 food served all day **Restaurant** L served all wk 12-10 D served all wk 12-10 ⊕ FREE HOUSE ◼ Deuchars IPA, Hawkshead Lakeland Gold, Guest ales ♂ Thatchers Gold. ♀ 12 **Facilities** Children welcome Children's portions Dogs allowed Garden Beer festival Parking

SUFFOLK

ALDEBURGH — Map 13 TM45

The Mill Inn ★★★ INN

Market Cross Place IP15 5BJ ☎ 01728 452563
e-mail: peeldennisp@aol.com
dir: Follow Aldeburgh signs from A12 on A1094. Pub last building on left before sea

A genuine fisherman's inn located less than 100 metres from the seafront, and a short walk from the town and bird sanctuaries. Seafood bought fresh from the fishermen on the beach is a speciality here, backed by pub favourites such as sirloin steak, ham and eggs, and lamb shank. Well-kept Adnams Bitter, Broadside, Regatta and Fisherman can all be enjoyed at this favourite haunt of the local lifeboat crew. There are four bedrooms available, some with sea views.

Open all wk 11-11 ◼ Adnams Bitter, Broadside, Regatta & Fisherman, OLD ♂ Aspall. **Facilities** Dogs allowed Garden **Rooms** 4

ALDRINGHAM — Map 13 TM46

The Parrot and Punchbowl Inn & Restaurant

Aldringham Ln IP16 4PY ☎ 01728 830221
dir: On B1122, 1m from Leiston, 3m from Aldeburgh, on x-rds to Thorpeness

Originally called The Case is Altered, it became the Parrot in 1604 and as such enjoyed considerable notoriety, particularly during the 17th century, as the haunt of Aldringham's smuggling gangs. Don't ask if there's any contraband rum on offer; just study the menu and try and decide between slowly braised lamb's liver with onion and bacon and mashed potato; steak and kidney pie with short crust pastry top; or pan seared duck breast with a raspberry jus. 'Parrot sandwiches' are generously overfilled.

Open all wk 12-2.30 6-11 ⊕ ENTERPRISE INNS ◼ Adnams, Guest ale ♂ Aspall. **Facilities** Children welcome Children's portions Play area Family room Dogs allowed Garden Parking Wi-fi

BRANDESTON — Map 13 TM26

PICK OF THE PUBS

The Queens Head ◉

The Street IP13 7AD ☎ 01728 685307
e-mail: thequeensheadinn@btconnect.com
dir: From A14 take A1120 to Earl Soham, then S to Brandeston

Alan Randall's smartened up Adnams pub, created from four cottages and first opened in 1811, stands slightly off the beaten track in a sleepy village deep in peaceful Suffolk countryside, and is well worth the detour for cracking ale and food, and its lovely summer garden. Inside, expect a warm and richly coloured decor that complements the traditional homely features of wood panelling, quarry-tiled floors and open log fires. The modern British menu bristles with interest and locally sourced ingredients and typical starters may include ham terrine with home-made piccalilli, and mushroom ravioli with braised oxtail, pickled mushrooms and shallot purée. For main course, try the pork belly with Savoy cabbage and bacon and truffle cream, or roast hake with pak choi, and round off with chocolate tart with rhubarb sorbet, or tiramisu with Amaretto jelly. Wash down with a pint of Broadside or a refreshing glass of Aspall's cider.

Open noon-3 5-mdnt (Sun noon-5) Closed: Sun eve, Mon **Bar Meals** L served Tue-Sun 12-2 booking required D served Tue-Sat 6.30-9 booking required **Restaurant** L served Tue-Sun 12-2 booking required D served Tue-Sat 6.30-9 booking required ⊕ ADNAMS ◄ Adnams Broadside & Bitter, Explorer, seasonal ales Ö Aspall. **Facilities** Children welcome Children's menu Children's portions Dogs allowed Garden Parking Wi-fi

BURY ST EDMUNDS — Map 13 TL86

The Linden Tree

7 Out Northgate IP33 1JQ ☎ 01284 754600
e-mail: lindentree@live.com
dir: Opposite railway station

Built to serve the railway station, this is a large, friendly Victorian pub, with stripped pine bar, dining area, conservatory and charming garden. Along with real ales and regular guests, the family-orientated menu ranges from Stilton and leek tart or chicken pesto pasta to stout braised beef and wild mushrooms casserole, pie of the week or grilled Suffolk gammon. Leave room for one of the desserts like banoffi cream slice or pecan and maple waffles.

Open all wk noon-11 (Fri-Sat 11-11 Sun noon-10) Closed: 25 Dec **Bar Meals** L served Mon-Fri 12-2.30, Sat-Sun all day D served Mon-Fri 6-9.30, Sat-Sun all day **Restaurant** L served Mon-Fri 12-2.30, Sat-Sun all day booking required D served Mon-Fri 6-9.30, Sat-Sun all day booking required ⊕ GREENE KING ◄ Greene King, IPA & Old Speckled Hen, Guest ale Ö Aspall. **Facilities** Children welcome Children's menu Children's portions Play area Dogs allowed Garden

The Nutshell

17 The Traverse IP33 1BJ ☎ 01284 764867
dir: Telephone for directions

Unique pub measuring just 15ft by 7ft, and has been confirmed as Britain's smallest by the Guinness Book of Records; and somehow more than 100 people and a dog managed to fit inside in the 1980s. It has certainly become a tourist attraction and there's lots to talk about while you enjoy a drink – a mummified cat and the bar ceiling is covered with paper money; and there have been regular sightings of ghosts around the building, including a nun and a monk who apparently weren't praying! No food is available, though the pub jokes about its dining area for parties of two or fewer.

Open all day all wk ⊕ GREENE KING ◄ Greene King IPA, Abbot Ale, Guest ales. **Facilities** Dogs allowed **Notes** ◉

PICK OF THE PUBS

The Old Cannon Brewery — INN ♀

86 Cannon St IP33 1JR ☎ 01284 768769
e-mail: info@oldcannonbrewery.co.uk
dir: From A14 (junct 43) follow signs to Bury St Edmunds town centre, at 1st rdbt take 1st left onto Northgate St, then 1st right onto Cadney Ln, left at end onto Cannon St, pub 100yds on left

Two giant stainless steel brewing vessels dominate the bar of the only independent brewpub in Bury St Edmunds. Beers made here use East Anglian grown and malted barley, choice hops and the special house yeast. So ale lovers have at least four to choose between at the bar, sometimes augmented by a brew for a special occasion such as Hornblower which celebrated the recent royal wedding. In true brasserie style, the Brewery Kitchen serves 'cannon fodder', freshly prepared from great local produce. Some starters and light bites can be upped in size. Of the main courses, Smoked Orford ham hock, bacon and Suffolk Gold cheese salad; shin of Lavenham beef, Suffolk chorizo and carrots braised in red wine with parsley mash; and fresh Lowestoft cod in beer batter with chips and peas are typical choices; Thai curries and local estate game appear on the seasonal specials board. Overnight guests are catered for in the converted Brewery Rooms, just across the courtyard from the bar.

Open all wk noon-3 5-11 (Sat noon-11 Sun & BHs noon-10.30) Closed: 25-26 Dec, 1 Jan **Restaurant** L served Tue-Sun 12-3 booking required D served Tue-Sat 6-11 booking required ⊕ FREE HOUSE ◄ Old Cannon Best Bitter, Old Cannon Gunner's Daughter, Old Cannon Blonde Bombshell, Adnams Bitter, seasonal Old Cannon ales, Guest ales Ö Aspall. ♀ 12 **Facilities** Garden Parking Wi-fi **Rooms** 7

The Three Kings ★★★★ INN ♀

Hengrave Rd, Fornham All Saints IP28 6LA ☎ 01284 766979
e-mail: thethreekings@keme.co.uk
dir: Bury St Edmunds (2m), A14 junct 42 (1m)

An 18th-century coaching inn in a pretty village setting, reputedly named from three Saxon kings buried in the area. Expect a warm reception at this family-run establishment, which has all the classic pub features – wood panelled bars, a conservatory, restaurant and courtyard. Menus comprise traditional bar food at lunchtimes, while à la carte dining in the evening offers dishes such as haddock and Cheddar cheese fishcake, and chicken breast in a smoked bacon, leek and Stilton sauce. Comfortable accommodation is available in converted outbuildings.

Open all day all wk noon-mdnt **Bar Meals** L served Mon-Fri 12-2, Sat-Sun 12-2.30 D served Sun-Mon 6-8, Tue-Sat 5.30-9 Av main course £10 **Restaurant** Av 3 course à la carte fr £18 ⊕ GREENE KING ◄ Greene King IPA, Abbot, Guest ales. ♀ 14 **Facilities** Children welcome Children's menu Children's portions Garden Parking **Rooms** 9

BUTLEY — Map 13 TM35

The Butley Oyster ♀

Woodbridge Rd IP12 3NZ ☎ 01394 450790
dir: On B1084 (Woodbridge to Orford road)

This informal inn, dating back to the 12th century, offers a warm welcome and retains the essential, timeless character of the village local it truly is. Adnams beers from the coast a few miles away, live music and community events draw in dedicated regulars. The menus feature steaks, calves' liver and bacon, gammon, burgers and fish dishes, all created from locally sourced, seasonal produce. Daily specials and vegetarians options are also available. Now under new ownership.

Open all wk 11-3 6-11 (Sat 11-11 Sun 11-6 (winter) 11-11 (summer)) **Bar Meals** L served Mon-Fri 12-2, Sat 12-3, Sun 12-6 D served Mon-Sat 6.30-9 ⊕ ADNAMS ◄ Adnams Bitter, Broadside, Explorer Ö Aspall. ♀ 9 **Facilities** Children welcome Children's menu Children's portions Dogs allowed Garden Parking

CAVENDISH — Map 13 TL84

Bull Inn

High St CO10 8AX ☎ 01787 280245
e-mail: knaffton@aol.com
dir: A134 (Bury St Edmunds to Long Melford), then right at green, pub 3m on right

A Victorian pub set in one of Suffolk's most beautiful villages, with an unassuming façade hiding a splendid 15th-century beamed interior. Expect a good atmosphere and decent food, with the daily-changing blackboard menu listing perhaps curries, shank of lamb, fresh fish and shellfish, and a roast on Sundays. Enjoy food and drink outside in the pleasant garden. Change of hands.

Open all wk 11-3 6.30-11 ⊕ ADNAMS ◄ Adnams Bitter, Broadside, Guest ales Ö Aspall. **Facilities** Children welcome Children's menu Children's portions Dogs allowed Parking

CHILLESFORD — Map 13 TM35

The Froize Inn ⓦ ⓣ

The Street IP12 3PU ☎ 01394 450282
e-mail: dine@froize.co.uk
dir: On B1084 between Woodbridge (8m) & Orford (3m)

Built on the site of Chillesford Friary and originally a pair of gamekeeper's cottages, this distinctive red-brick building dates from 1490 and stands on today's popular Suffolk Coastal Path. Chef-owner David Grimwood may operate The Froize as more of a restaurant than a pub, but the atmosphere is informal and there's always a decent pint of Adnams on tap. Daily menus champion East Anglian growers and suppliers and excellent dishes are served buffet-style on a groaning hot table, perhaps pheasant breast stuffed with pumpkin and redcurrants, and Suffolk red Poll beef olives with mushrooms and caramelised onions.

Open Tue-Sun Closed: Mon **Restaurant** L served Tue-Sun 12-2 booking required D served Thu-Sat from 7pm booking required Fixed menu price fr £15 ⓕ FREE HOUSE ◀ Adnams Ö Aspall. ⓣ 12 **Facilities** Children welcome Garden Parking

CRATFIELD — Map 13 TM37

The Poacher

Bell Green IP19 0BL ☎ 01986 798206
e-mail: cratfieldpoacher@yahoo.co.uk
dir: From Halesworth take B1117 towards Eye. At Laxfield turn right, follow Cratfield signs (3m). Or, from Diss, take A143 towards Bungay. Right at Harleston onto B1123 towards Halesworth. Through Metfield, 1m, turn right & follow Cratfield signs (2m)

Off the beaten track in a sleepy village deep in rural Suffolk countryside, the 350-year-old Poacher is an attractive longhouse featuring some beautiful exterior plasterwork pargeting. Equally charming and unspoilt inside, with low beams, tiled floors and a welcoming atmosphere, the pub is the hub of the community, hosting musical evenings, bridge and book clubs, and bank holiday classic car rallies. There's always eight draught beers available at weekends from the Adnams and Earl Soham breweries, plus local Aspall cider. Home-cooked food, especially the haddock and chips, with three changing specials complete the pleasing picture at this proper village local.

Open noon-2.30, 6-mdnt (Sat-Sun all day) Closed: Mon, Tue L **Bar Meals** L served 12-2.30 (Sat-Sun all day) D served 6-9 (Sat-Sun all day) Av main course £8.75 **Restaurant** L served 12-2.30 (Sat-Sun all day) D served 6-9 (Sat-Sun all day) Fixed menu price fr £8.50 Av 3 course à la carte fr £15.95 ⓕ FREE HOUSE ◀ Adnams, Brewers Gold, Oakham JHB, Earl Soham Victoria, Earl Soham Mild Ö Aspall (draught and bottled). **Facilities** Children welcome Children's menu Children's portions Dogs allowed Garden Parking

DENNINGTON — Map 13 TM26

The Queens Head

The Square IP13 8AB ☎ 01728 638241
e-mail: denningtonqueen@yahoo.co.uk
dir: From Ipswich A14 to exit for Lowestoft (A12). then B1116 to Framlingham then follow signs to Dennington

It may be refurbished, but this 500-year-old inn retains bags of old world charm including open fires, a resident ghost, a coffin hatch and a bricked-up tunnel to the neighbouring church. Locally brewed Aspall cider is available alongside real ales from Adnams, St Austells Tribute and Earl Soham's Victoria. The modern British menu centres around fresh food made with local produce and ingredients - perhaps cottage pie or fillet of plaice parcels.

Open all wk 12-3 6-10.30 Closed: 25-26 Dec
Bar Meals L served all wk 12-2 booking required D served all wk 6.30-9 booking required **Restaurant** L served all wk 12-2 booking required D served all wk 6.30-9 booking required ⓕ FREE HOUSE ◀ Adnams, Black Sheep, Tribute, Victoria Ö Aspall. **Facilities** Children welcome Children's menu Children's portions Garden Parking

DUNWICH — Map 13 TM47

PICK OF THE PUBS

The Ship Inn ★★ SHL ⓦ ⓣ

Saint James St IP17 3DT
☎ 01728 648219   📠 01728 648675
e-mail: info@shipatdunwich.co.uk
web: www.shipatdunwich.co.uk
dir: N on A12 from Ipswich through Yoxford, right signed Dunwich

Dunwich was at one time a medieval port of some size and importance, then the original village was virtually destroyed by a terrible storm in 1326. Further storms and erosion followed and now the place is little more than a hamlet beside a shingle beach. Two minutes stroll from the beach, The Ship is a well-loved old smugglers' inn overlooking the salt marshes and sea, and is popular with walkers and birdwatchers visiting the nearby RSPB Minsmere reserve. The delightful unspoilt public bar offers nautical bric-a-brac, a wood-burning stove in a huge fireplace, flagged floors and simple wooden furnishings. Sympathetically spruced up in recent years, with the addition of clean, comfortable and contemporary-styled bedrooms, it is

locally renowned for its fish and chips. Other favourites that make good use of fresh local produce include smoked haddock, tomato and basil gratin, roast Blythburgh pork chop with caramelised apple gravy, and Colin's classic Bakewell tart. Look for the ancient fig tree in the garden.

Open all day all wk 11am-11pm (Sun noon-10.30pm) **Bar Meals** L served all wk 12-3 D served all wk 6-9 Av main course £11.50 **Restaurant** L served all wk 12-3 D served all wk 6-9 ⓕ FREE HOUSE ◀ Adnams Bitter, Green Jack Gone Fishing, Humpty Dumpty Little Sharpie Ö Aspall. ⓣ 9 **Facilities** Children welcome Children's menu Children's portions Family room Dogs allowed Garden Parking **Rooms** 15

EARL SOHAM — Map 13 TM26

Victoria

The Street IP13 7RL ☎ 01728 685758
dir: From A14 at Stowmarket take A1120 towards Yoxford

This friendly, down to earth free house is a showcase for Earl Soham beers, which for many years were produced from a micro-brewery behind the pub. Some ten years ago the brewery moved to the Old Forge building a few yards away, where production still continues. Inside this traditional pub, simple furnishings, bare floorboards and an open fire set the scene for traditional home-cooked pub fare, including ploughman's, jacket potatoes and macaroni cheese. Heartier meals include a variety of casseroles and curries, followed by home-made desserts. A specials board and vegetarian dishes add to the choices.

Open all wk 11.30-3 6-11 **Bar Meals** L served all wk 12-2 D served all wk 7-10 Av main course £9 ⓕ FREE HOUSE ◀ Earl Soham Victoria Bitter, Albert Ale, Brandeston Gold, Earl Soham Porter Ö Aspall. **Facilities** Children welcome Children's portions Dogs allowed Garden Parking

EYE — Map 13 TM17

The White Horse Inn ★★★★ INN

Stoke Ash IP23 7ET ☎ 01379 678222   📠 01379 678800
e-mail: mail@whitehorse-suffolk.co.uk
dir: On A140 between Ipswich & Norwich

A 17th-century coaching inn set amid lovely Suffolk countryside. The heavily-timbered interior accommodates an inglenook fireplace, two bars and a restaurant. An extensive menu is supplemented by lunchtime snacks, grills and daily specials from the blackboard. Try pan-fried lamb's liver and crispy bacon; Cantonese style lemon chicken; or lamb and mint burger. There are eleven spacious motel bedrooms in the grounds, as well as a patio and secluded grassy area.

Open all day all wk 7am-11pm (Sat 8am-11pm Sun 8am-10.30pm) **Bar Meals** food served all day **Restaurant** food served all day ⓕ FREE HOUSE ◀ Adnams, Greene King Abbot Ö Aspall. **Facilities** Children welcome Children's menu Children's portions Garden Parking Wi-fi **Rooms** 11

FRAMLINGHAM   Map 13 TM26

The Station Hotel

Station Rd IP13 9EE ☎ 01728 723455
e-mail: framstation@btinternet.com
dir: *Bypass Ipswich towards Lowestoft on A12. Approx 6m left onto B1116 towards Framlingham*

Built as part of the local railway in the 19th century, The Station Hotel has been a pub since the 1950s, outliving the railway which closed in 1962. You will find scrubbed tables and an eclectic mix of furniture. During the last decade it has established a fine reputation for its gutsy and earthy food, such as garlic and herb escargots; local venison with herb mash, celeriac remoulade and kale; braised ham hock; and smoked haddock kedgeree. Try ales such as Earl Soham Victoria and Albert & Mild, supplied by the Earl Soham Brewery. There is a beer festival in mid July.

Open all wk noon-2.30 5-11 (Sun noon-3 7-10.30)
Bar Meals L served all wk 12-2 D served Sun-Thu 6.30-9, Fri-Sat 6.30-9.30 booking required ⊕ FREE HOUSE
◀ Earl Soham Victoria, Albert & Mild, Veltins, Crouch Vale, Guinness Ŏ Aspall. **Facilities** Children welcome Children's portions Family room Dogs allowed Garden Beer festival Parking

FRAMSDEN   Map 13 TM15

The Dobermann Inn

The Street IP14 6HG ☎ 01473 890461
dir: *S off A1120 (Stowmarket to Yoxford road) 10m from Ipswich on B1077 towards Debenham*

Previously called The Greyhound, the pub was renamed by its current proprietor, a prominent breeder and judge of Dobermanns. The thatched roofing, gnarled beams, open fire and assorted furniture reflect its 16th-century origins. With a selection of Adnams ales on offer and Mauldons Dickens Bitter, food ranges from sandwiches, ploughman's and salads to main courses featuring game from a local estate when in season, and plenty of fish choices. Reliable favourites include sirloin steak with sautéed mushrooms, and chicken and mushroom pie.

Open noon-3 7-11 Closed: 25-26 Dec, Sun eve, Mon
Bar Meals L served Tue-Sun 12-2 D served Tue-Sat 7-9
⊕ FREE HOUSE ◀ Adnams Bitter & Broadside, Mauldons Dickens Bitter, Adnams Old WA Ŏ Aspall, Bitburger.
Facilities Garden Parking **Notes** ⊛

GREAT BRICETT   Map 13 TM05

PICK OF THE PUBS

The Veggie Red Lion

Green Street Green IP7 7DD ☎ 01473 657799
e-mail: janwise@fsmail.net
dir: *4.5m from Needham Market on B1078*

In an inspired move a few years ago, Jan Wise re-invented the old 17th century village pub at Great Bricett as a ground-breaking vegetarian and vegan destination dining inn. Re-invigorated and instantly popular, the Veggie continues to gain accolades for the quality of the food and Jan's unfailing commitment to developing the most exquisite dishes with no hint of anything that once grazed, swam or nibbled. Set in large, peaceful grounds amidst pocket woodland, settle down in the rustic, beamed, colourwashed interior and experience delightful difficulty deciding just what treats to try. Start with roasted shiitake and oyster mushroom skewers with a spicy satay sauce or perhaps spicy red lentil, coconut and coriander dhal and then push the boat out with porcini risotto fritters stuffed with Gruyère or roasted mushroom Wellington. Fresh whipped cream could accompany a closing salvo of dark chocolate truffle torte. Weekend booking is strongly recommended.

Open all wk 12-3 6-11 Closed: Sun eve & Mon
Bar Meals L served Tue-Sun 12-2 D served Tue-Sat 6-9
Av main course £10 ⊕ GREENE KING ◀ Greene King IPA, Old Speckled Hen Ŏ Aspall. **Facilities** Children welcome Children's menu Children's portions Play area Dogs allowed Garden Parking

GREAT GLEMHAM   Map 13 TM36

The Crown Inn

IP17 2DA ☎ 01728 663693
e-mail: crown-i.cottle@btconnect.com
dir: *A12 (Ipswich to Lowestoft), in Stratford-St-Andrew left at Shell garage. Pub 1.5m*

A warm welcome, open fires and excellent food and ales make this cosy 17th-century village pub an appealing prospect. Set in Great Glemham, it overlooks the Great Glemham Estate, where some of the fine produce is sourced, and is within easy reach of the Suffolk Heritage Coast. You can eat in the extensively renovated bars with their wooden pews, sofas and inglenook fireplace, and large flower-filled garden. Smoked haddock and pea fishcake with lemon crème fraîche, and slow-roasted belly pork with crunchy crackling and dauphinoise potatoes might appear on the menu.

Open 11.30-3 6.30-11.30 Closed: Mon (ex BH) ⊕ FREE HOUSE ◀ Adnams Bitter, Tribute, Hobgoblin, Old Ale
Ŏ Aspall. **Facilities** Children welcome Children's menu Children's portions Dogs allowed Garden Parking

HALESWORTH   Map 13 TM37

PICK OF THE PUBS

The Queen's Head ♥

The Street, Bramfield IP19 9HT ☎ 01986 784214
e-mail: qhbfield@aol.com
dir: *2m from A12 on A144 towards Halesworth*

A lovely old building in the centre of Bramfield on the edge of the Suffolk Heritage Coast near historic Southwold. The enclosed garden, ideal for children, is overlooked by the thatched village church which has an unusual separate round bell tower. The pub's interior welcomes with scrubbed pine tables, exposed beams, a vaulted ceiling in the bar and enormous fireplaces. In the same capable hands for over 15 years, the landlord enthusiastically supports the 'local and organic' movement – reflected by a menu which proudly names the farms and suppliers from which the carefully chosen ingredients are sourced. There is nonetheless a definite cosmopolitan twist in dishes such as curried local parsnip soup, and 'Emmerdale Farm' Darsham minced beef lasagne served with salad. Children are treated to Suffolk Red Poll beefburgers or Moat Farm sausages. Amanda's home-made desserts are tempting, as is the platter of three local cheeses with celery – Lincolnshire Poacher, Suffolk Blue and Norfolk White Lady.

Open all wk 10.30-2.30 6.30-11 (Sun noon-3 7-10.30)
Closed: 25 Dec **Bar Meals** L served all wk 12-2
D served Mon-Fri 6.30-9.15, Sat 6.30-10, Sun 7-9
⊕ ADNAMS ◀ Adnams Bitter, Broadside Ŏ Aspall. ♥ 8
Facilities Children welcome Children's menu Children's portions Family room Dogs allowed Garden Parking Wi-fi

HITCHAM   Map 13 TL95

The White Horse Inn ♥

The Street IP7 7NQ ☎ 01449 740981 🖩 01449 740981
e-mail: lewis@thewhitehorse.wanadoo.co.uk
dir: *13m from Ipswich & Bury St Edmunds, 7m Stowmarket, 7m Hadleigh*

Parts of the Grade II listed building are estimated to be around 400 years old, making a perfect setting for traditional pub games and regular live entertainment. Inside this family-run free house you'll find Adnams ales, a warm, friendly atmosphere and freshly-prepared meals – perhaps traditional prawn cocktail followed by duck with Cumberland sauce, or a ploughman's from the bar menu. In summer, the beer garden is open for barbecues.

Open all wk 12-3 6-11 **Bar Meals** L served all wk 12-2.30 D served all wk 6-9 **Restaurant** L served all wk 12-2.30 D served all wk 6-9 booking required ⊕ FREE HOUSE
◀ IPA, Adnams Best Bitter, Rattlesden Best, Stowmarket Porter, Adnams Fisherman Ŏ Aspall. **Facilities** Children welcome Children's menu Children's portions Dogs allowed Garden Parking

HOLBROOK — Map 13 TM13

The Compasses ♟

Ipswich Rd IP9 2QR
☎ 01473 328332 📠 01473 327403
e-mail: compasses.holbrook@virgin.net
dir: *From A137 S of Ipswich, take B1080 to Holbrook, pub on left. From Ipswich take B1456 to Shotley. At Freston Water Tower right onto B1080 to Holbrook. Pub 2m right*

A traditional country pub dating from the 17th century, The Compasses sits in Holbrook on the Shotley peninsula, a spectacular area bordered by the rivers Orwell and Stour. The simple, good value menu includes ploughman's, salads and jacket potatoes; pub favourites such as pie or roast of the day, or home-made traditional or seafood lasagne; and a fish and vegetarian selection. Party bookings are a speciality, and look out for Wine of the Week deals. A monthly quiz night and pensioners' weekday lunches complete this pub's honest offerings.

Open 11.30-2.30 6-11 (Sun noon-3 6-10.30) Closed: 26 Dec-1 Jan, Tue eve **Bar Meals** L served all wk 12-2.15 booking required D served Wed-Mon 6-9.15 booking required Av main course £9.95 **Restaurant** L served all wk 12-2.15 booking required D served Wed-Mon 6-9.15 booking required ⊕ PUNCH TAVERNS ◀ Greene King IPA, Adnams Bitter Ò Aspall. ♟ 12 **Facilities** Children welcome Children's menu Children's portions Play area Garden Parking Wi-fi

HONEY TYE — Map 13 TL93

The Lion

CO6 4NX ☎ 01206 263434 📠 01206 263434
e-mail: enquiries@lionhoneytye.co.uk
dir: *On A134 midway between Colchester & Sudbury*

A traditional country dining pub, located in an Area of Outstanding Natural Beauty, The Lion has low-beamed ceilings and an open log fire inside, plus a patio with tables and umbrellas for outside eating and drinking. The menu offers a good choice of fish (pan seared mackerel fillets with warm horseradish potato salad), pub favourites (chargrilled gammon steak with fried egg and chips), and main dishes such as pressed pork belly and apple terrine. Recent change of hands.

Open all wk 11.30-3 6-11 (Sun noon-10) ◀ Greene King IPA, guest ale. **Facilities** Children welcome Children's menu Children's portions Garden Parking

HOXNE — Map 13 TM17

The Swan ♟

Low St IP21 5AS ☎ 01379 668275
e-mail: info@hoxneswan.co.uk
web: www.hoxneswan.co.uk
dir: *Telephone for directions*

This 15th-century Grade II listed lodge, reputedly built for the Bishop of Norwich, has large gardens running down to the River Dove, with a vast willow tree. Inside, the restaurant and front bar boast a 10ft inglenook fireplace, ornate beamed ceilings and old planked floors. Food includes starters like pan-fried pigeon breast with celeriac and apple gratin or smoked mackerel fishcakes, followed by silverside and oxtail braise with horseradish mash, millefeuille of pork, apricot and almonds, or aubergine, chickpea and sweet potato tagine.

Open all wk **Bar Meals** L served all wk 12-2 booking required D served all wk 6.30-9 booking required **Restaurant** L served all wk 12-2 booking required D served all wk 6.30-9 booking required ⊕ ENTERPRISE INNS ◀ Adnams Best Bitter, 4 other real ales Ò Aspall. ♟ 9 **Facilities** Children welcome Children's portions Dogs allowed Garden Parking

ICKLINGHAM — Map 13 TL77

The Plough Inn ♟

The Street IP28 6PL
☎ 01638 711770 📠 01638 640002
e-mail: suerocke@btconnect.com
dir: *Telephone for directions*

Set in the picturesque village of Icklingham, this old, flint-built village pub is surrounded by beautiful countryside but is close to Bury St Edmunds, Newmarket, Thetford, the US air base at Mildenhall, and the rebuilt Saxon village at West Stow Country Park. All the food is cooked on the premises by chef-proprietor Rocke, while his wife Sue manages front of house. Expect main courses like honey roast duck; beef fillet pie; and home-cooked ham on the bone with egg and chips. Accompany your meal with one of the constantly changing six real ales on offer or wine; there are 27 by the glass to choose from.

Open all day all wk 11am-11pm Closed: 26 Dec, 1 Jan **Bar Meals** L served all wk 11am-8.30pm booking required D served all wk 11am-8.30pm booking required Av main course £9.95 food served all day **Restaurant** L served all wk 11am-11.30pm booking required D served all wk 11am-8.30pm booking required Av 3 course à la carte fr £20 food served all day ⊕ FREE HOUSE ◀ IPA, Woodforde's Wherry, London Pride, Adnams. ♟ 27 **Facilities** Garden Parking Wi-fi

INGHAM — Map 13 TL87

The Cadogan ★★★★ INN ⊛ ♟ **NEW**

The Street IP31 1NG ☎ 01284 728443
e-mail: info@thecadogan.co.uk
dir: *A14 junct 42, 1st exit onto B1106. At rdbt take 1st exit (A134). 3m to Ingham. Pub on left*

Just four miles from the centre of Bury St Edmunds, The Cadogan is a friendly and inviting pub with seven en suite bedrooms for those who want to stay longer. The emphasis on the food is seasonality and local produce, with vegetables from the garden and even sausages made on the premises. Lunchtime sandwiches and light bites are complemented by dinner options such as chicken and Portobello mushroom pie or ale braised shin of Suffolk beef. Open all day, there is a large garden perfect for alfresco dining.

Open all day all wk Closed: 25-26 Dec **Bar Meals** L served all wk 12-2.30 D served all wk 6-9.30 Av main course £12 **Restaurant** L served all wk 12-2.30 D served all wk 6-9.30 ⊕ GREENE KING ◀ Greene King IPA, Abbot Ale Ò Aspall. ♟ 12 **Facilities** Children welcome Children's menu Children's portions Play area Garden Parking Wi-fi **Rooms** 7

IPSWICH — Map 13 TM14

The Fat Cat ♟ **NEW**

288 Spring Rd IP4 5NL ☎ 01473 726524
e-mail: fatcatipswich@btconnect.com
dir: *rom A12 take A1214 towards town centre, becomes A1071 (Woodbridge Road East). At mini rdbt 2nd left into Spring Rd*

Mecca for Ipswich beer aficionados, the Fat Cat is a no-frills free house with a friendly atmosphere in two homely bars and a raft of real ales served in tip-top condition from the taproom behind the bar. The mind-boggling choice – up to 20 every day – come from Crouch Vale, Woodforde's, Adnams and a host of local micro-breweries, perhaps Green Jack and Mauldons. Mop the beer up with simple bar snacks like baguettes, pasties and home-made Scotch eggs.

Open all day all wk **Bar Meals** food served all day ⊕ FREE HOUSE ◀ Adnams Old Ale, Dark Star Hophead, Elgoods Mild, Black Dog, Green Jack, Gone Fishing, rotating beers. ♟ 8 **Facilities** Garden **Notes** ⊛

Save on hotels. Book at **theAA.com/hotel**

SUFFOLK 421 ENGLAND

IXWORTH
Map 13 TL97

Pykkerell Inn

38 High St IP31 2HH
☎ 01359 230398 📄 01359 234019
dir: *On A143 from Bury St Edmunds towards Diss*

A former coaching inn whose name can be traced to around 1500; in the late 15th century an Ixworth family named Pykerel probably owned the land upon which the inn would be built only a few years later. Today it retains most of its original beams, inglenook fireplace and other features in the lounge and public bars; it is surrounded by Grade I listed buildings too. The menu includes popular starters, and main courses such as Suffolk ham, egg and chips, or half a roasted duck coated in hoi sin sauce. However it is the choice of seven real ales at the bar that will test your decision-making skills.

Open all day all wk **Bar Meals** L served Mon-Fri 12-2 booking required D served all wk 5-9 booking required **Restaurant** L served Mon-Fri 12-2, Sat-Sun 12-4 booking required D served all wk 5-9 booking required ⊕ GREENE KING ◀ Greene King IPA, Abbot Ale, IPA, St Edmunds, 3 guest ales ♂ Aspall. **Facilities** Children welcome Children's menu Children's portions Dogs allowed Garden Parking Wi-fi

LAVENHAM
Map 13 TL94

PICK OF THE PUBS

The Angel ★★★★ RR ◉ ♥

Market Place CO10 9QZ
☎ 01787 247388 📄 01787 248344
e-mail: angel@maypolehotels.com
dir: *7m from Sudbury on A1141 between Sudbury & Bury St Edmunds*

Recently acquired by celebrity chef Marco Pierre White, The Angel overlooks the medieval market place and famous timbered Guildhall and was first licensed in 1420. Believed to be Lavenham's oldest inn, it was originally a 'high hall' house, and smoke from a central fire would drift out through vents in the roof. The ventilation improved in around 1500, when two wings with brick chimneys were added to the building, along with a first-floor solar room, which is now the residents' lounge. The historic character of this famous inn can still be seen in the beamed dining room and adjoining bar, with its huge inglenook fireplace and attractive plasterwork. Expect starters like salted ox cheek salad with mayonnaise and main courses of whole grilled plaice with Jersey Royals, leeks and brown shrimp and butter sauce. You could finish with a selection of English cheeses, or pear and ginger steamed pudding with custard. The en suite bedrooms are full of character, with old beams and sloping floors.

Open all day all wk Mon-Sat 11am-11pm (Sun noon-10.30) **Bar Meals** L served all wk 12-2.15 booking required D served all wk 6.45-9.15 booking required **Restaurant** L served all wk 12-2.15 booking required D served all wk 6.45-9.15 booking required ⊕ FREE HOUSE ◀ Adnams Bitter, Greene King IPA, Speckled Hen, Guest Ales ♂ Aspall. ♥ 9 **Facilities** Children welcome Children's menu Children's portions Dogs allowed Garden Parking Wi-fi **Rooms 8**

LAXFIELD
Map 13 TM27

PICK OF THE PUBS

The Kings Head (The Low House) ♥

Gorams Mill Ln IP13 8DW ☎ 01986 798395
e-mail: lowhouse@keme.co.uk
dir: *On B1117*

Beer festivals in May and September are unforgettable occasions thanks to the beautiful situation of this thatched 16th-century alehouse overlooking the river; its grounds, now with rose gardens and an arbour, were formerly the village bowling green. For the rest of the year ales are served straight from the cask in the original tap room – this is one of the few pubs in Britain which has no bar. Choose the ale you fancy and retire to an ancient fireplace with a horseshoe of high-backed settles with an oak table in the middle. Another room, also called the tap room, has a similar layout and the same abundance of charm. Traditional lunchtime fare includes sandwiches and baguettes, perhaps a BLT or a roast beef and horseradish. Home-cooked dishes vary from the familiar – Creasey's chicken liver pâté – to the more unusual: baked banana in a creamy Stilton sauce, or fresh Lowestoft smoked grilled kippers.

Open all wk **Bar Meals** L served all wk 12-2 D served Mon-Sat 7-9 Av main course £9.95 **Restaurant** L served all wk 12-2 D served Mon-Sat 7-9 Av 3 course à la carte fr £18.50 ⊕ ADNAMS ◀ Adnams Best & Broadside, Adnams seasonal, Guest ales ♂ Aspall. ♥ 11 **Facilities** Children welcome Children's portions Play area Family room Dogs allowed Garden Beer festival Parking

LEVINGTON
Map 13 TM23

PICK OF THE PUBS

The Ship Inn ♥

Church Ln IP10 0LQ
☎ 01473 659573 📄 01473 659151
e-mail: theshipinnlevington@hotmail.co.uk
dir: *Off A14 towards Felixstowe. Nr Levington Marina*

The timbers of this 13th-century thatched inn overlooking the River Orwell are impregnated with the salt of the sea, and ghosts of bygone smugglers still occupy the many nooks and crannies. The Ship Inn stands within sight of the Suffolk marshes, where the hulks of beached sailing vessels were broken up for their precious beams. Indeed, families are welcome to enjoy the estuary views outside on the attractive front seats or on the rear patio. The interior walls and surfaces, however, are so full of maritime lamps, compasses and keepsakes that it's deemed an unsafe environment for children. There are two log-burning stoves in wintertime to keep things cosy. The service is informal, friendly and attentive. The sophisticated menu changes daily and focuses on executing a select number of dishes well. Starters may include pan-fried

sardines with tomato and coriander salsa and might be followed by a main course confit of duck leg with red wine-braised cabbage and sweet potato fries.

Open all wk 11.30-3 6-11 (Sat 11.30-11pm Sun noon-10.30) **Bar Meals** L served Mon-Sat 12-2.30, Sun 12-3 D served Mon-Sat 6.30-9 Av main course £10.95 **Restaurant** L served Mon-Sat 12-2.30, Sun 12-3 D served Mon-Sat 6.30-9 Av 3 course à la carte fr £22 ⊕ ADNAMS ◀ Adnams Best, Broadside, Guest ale ♂ Aspall. ♥ 10 **Facilities** Children welcome Dogs allowed Garden Parking Wi-fi

LIDGATE
Map 12 TL75

PICK OF THE PUBS

The Star Inn

The Street CB8 9PP
☎ 01638 500275 📄 01638 500275
e-mail: tonyaxon@aol.com
dir: *From Newmarket clocktower in High St follow signs towards Clare on B1063. Lidgate 7m*

Although this quintessentially English pub dates back to the 14th-century, step inside and the aromas are more reminiscent of a modern Spanish tapas bar. An important meeting place for local residents, the pub is popular with Newmarket trainers on race days, and with dealers and agents from all over the world during bloodstock sales. Originally two cottages, the two traditionally furnished bars still fit the old world bill with heavy oak beams, log fires, pine tables and antique furniture, but the food is unashamedly Spanish, Catalan and Mediterranean. The menu offers appealingly hearty food: starters like whole baby squid with garlic and chilli or fish soup might be followed by bean and chorizo stew. English tastes are also catered for, with dishes such as warm chicken liver salad; venison steaks in port; and pigs' cheeks. There's an extensive wine list, too, with a number of well-priced Riojas jostling for position alongside the real ales on tap.

Open noon-3 6-mdnt Closed: 25-26 Dec, 1 Jan, Mon **Bar Meals** L served Tue-Sat 12-3 booking required D served Tue-Sat 7-10 booking required Av main course £8 **Restaurant** L served Tue-Sun 12-3 booking required D served Tue-Sat 7-10 booking required Fixed menu price fr £10 Av 3 course à la carte fr £25 ⊕ GREENE KING ◀ Greene King IPA, Ruddles County, Abbot Ale ♂ Aspall. **Facilities** Children welcome Children's portions Dogs allowed Garden Parking

LINDSEY TYE — Map 13 TL94

The Lindsey Rose NEW

IP7 6PP ☎ **01449 741424**
e-mail: thelindseyrose@hotmail.co.uk
dir: *From A12 between Ipswich & Sudbury take A1141 signed Lavenham. Ignore 1st sign for Lindsey, follow 2nd sign and pub sign*

Set in the beautiful Suffolk countryside between Ipswich and Sudbury, The Lindsey Rose has been the village local for over 500 years. Local ales are stocked in the bar and also take centre stage at the pub's annual beer festival. The region's produce is also celebrated on the menu which might include venison hot pot; beer battered haddock and chips; warm treacle tart. Children are very welcome here and get their own menu and activity area outside.

Open all wk 11-3 5.30-11 (Sun all day)
Bar Meals L served Mon-Sat 12-2.30, Sun 12-3 D served Mon-Sat 6.30-9.30, Sun 7-9 Av main course £12.50
Restaurant L served Mon-Sat 12-2.30, Sun 12-3 D served Mon-Sat 6.30-9.30, Sun 7-9 booking required ⊕ FREE HOUSE ◖ Adnams Bitter, Mauldons Brewery Ò Aspall.
Facilities Children welcome Children's menu Children's portions Play area Dogs allowed Garden Beer festival Parking Wi-fi

MELTON — Map 13 TM25

Wilford Bridge ♀

Wilford Bridge Rd IP12 2PA
☎ **01394 386141** 🖷 **01394 386141**
e-mail: wilfordbridge@debeninns.com
dir: *From A12 towards coast, follow signs to Bawdsey & Orford, cross rail lines, next pub on left*

Just down the road from the famous Sutton Hoo treasure ship, Mike and Anne Lomas have been running the free house at Wilford Bridge for the last 19 years. As a former West End chef, Mike specialises in classic English dishes, especially seafood dishes; look out for local game, mussels and sprats in season, as well as crab, lobster, cod, salmon, trout, sea bass and others as available. At the bar, guest ales supplement the regular choice of beers.

Open all day all wk **Bar Meals** L served all wk 11-9.30 D served all wk 11-9.30 Av main course £12 food served all day **Restaurant** D served all wk 11-9.30 Av 3 course à la carte fr £19 food served all day ⊕ FREE HOUSE ◖ Adnams Best, Broadside, John Smith's, Guest ales Ò Aspall. ♀ 9 **Facilities** Children welcome Children's menu Dogs allowed Garden Parking

MILDENHALL — Map 12 TL77

PICK OF THE PUBS

The Olde Bull Inn ★★★ HL ☺ ♀

The Street, Barton Mills IP28 6AA
☎ **01638 711001** 🖷 **01638 712003**
e-mail: bookings@bullinn-bartonmills.com
web: www.bullinn-bartonmills.com
dir: *Off A11 between Newmarket & Mildenhall, signed Barton Mills*

Thetford Chase and Forest and the memorable cathedral at Ely are equidistant, just a few miles away from this long-established coaching inn. All gables and dormer windows, coaching courtyard and home comforts, past visitors who've tarried overnight include Good Queen Bess; today's individually styled boutique accommodation reflects such august patronage. The village inn has been beautifully refurbished in contemporary fashion over five years, whilst retaining the charm and character associated with scrubbed pine tables and reclaimed oak flooring. Gleaming hand-pumps dispense tip-top East Anglian ales, so order a pint of Humpty Dumpty Brewery's finest and settle by the fire to peruse menus of AA Rosette standard food. The owners are determined to reduce their 'food miles'; thus the ingredients in the freshly prepared meals are locally sourced as far as is possible. Witness the Suffolk ham hock terrine with sauce gribiche and honey mustard dressed leaves starter; the Bull's team of chefs specialise in modern British with a twist. Evolving with the seasons, mains may tempt with chicken breast with ship dock Cheddar gratin potato, caramelised red cabbage, red wine and thyme jus, taken at the bar or in the intimate Oak Room restaurant.

Open all day all wk 8am-11pm **Bar Meals** L served all wk 12-9 (bkfst 8-noon) D served all wk 12-9 Av main course £10 food served all day **Restaurant** L served Sun 12-3 D served all wk 6-9 ⊕ FREE HOUSE ◖ Adnams Broadside, Greene King IPA, Brandon Brewery Rusty Bucket, Humpty Dumpty, Wolf Ò Aspall. ♀ 11 **Facilities** Children welcome Children's menu Children's portions Family room Garden Parking Wi-fi **Rooms** 14

MONKS ELEIGH — Map 13 TL94

PICK OF THE PUBS

The Swan Inn ☺☺ ♀

The Street IP7 7AU ☎ **01449 741391**
e-mail: carol@monkseleigh.com
dir: *On B1115 between Sudbury & Hadleigh*

This definitive village inn snuggles near to the church and green in one of Suffolk's lovely little thatched villages. Wealth came from the wool trade and the original inn may have been the manorial court before affluent wool merchants first dined out here. Vestiges of the original building remain, including the old smoke hole and some fine beams supporting the thatched roof. Woodcock, teal and courgette flowers are amongst the more unusual delicacies that may feature on the menu here; a season for everything, and everything in its season is a guiding principal followed by chef/proprietor Nigel Ramsbottom, who honed his considerable skills at The Walnut Tree, Abergavenny, explaining the Italian influence to some dishes. Settle in with mussels steamed in coconut milk with green chilli, lemon grass, coriander and spring onions before taking time over a monumental choice of mains; perhaps pan-fried guinea fowl breast with wild mushrooms, grapes and tarragon sauce, or Vincigrassi - a lasagne of Parma ham, porcini mushrooms and Parmesan. Pannacotta with red fruits and grappa is a fitting final flourish.

Open noon-2.30 7-11 Closed: 25-26 Dec, 2wks in summer, Sun eve & Mon **Bar Meals** L served Tue-Sun 12-2 D served Tue-Sat 7-9 Av main course £15 **Restaurant** L served Tue-Sun 12-2 D served Tue-Sat 7-9 Fixed menu price fr £13.75 Av 3 course à la carte fr £25 ⊕ FREE HOUSE ◖ Greene King IPA, Adnams Bitter, Broadside Ò Aspall, Thatchers Katy. **Facilities** Children welcome Children's portions Garden Parking

NAYLAND — Map 13 TL93

PICK OF THE PUBS

Anchor Inn

26 Court St CO6 4JL
☎ **01206 262313** 🖷 **01206 264166**
e-mail: enquiries@anchornayland.co.uk
dir: *Follow A134 Colchester to Sudbury for 3.5m through Gt Horkesley, bottom of hill turn right to Nayland, Horkesley Road. Pub on right after bridge*

The Anchor Inn Heritage Farm delivers a wealth of fresh produce to this 15th-century pub's kitchen, and the menu reflects this close relationship. The farm, which welcomes visitors, is run on traditional lines, with working Suffolk Punch horses helping produce good old-fashioned food in the time-honoured way (they appear at the inn every Tuesday and Thursday lunchtime during the summer). Starters include a smoked platter fish, meat and cheeses from their own smokehouse; wild boar goulash with steamed dumpling bread served with home-baked rolls; and country pâté with quince and apple chutney. Classic mains include home-made traditional pork sausages; mussels in white wine cream sauce; and broccoli and Stilton tartlet, as well as a choice of roasts on Sunday. Ales from Greene King and Adnams are drawn, and wines include an award-winner from their own vineyard just three miles away. Beer festivals are held on Father's Day and in October. Set on the banks of the River Stour, the Anchor is reputedly the last remaining place from which press-gangs recruited their 'volunteers'.

Open all wk 11-3 5-11 (all day spring & summer) **Bar Meals** L served Mon-Fri 12-2, Sat 12-2.30, Sun 12-3 booking required D served Mon-Fri 6.30-9, Sat 6.30-9.30, Sun 5-8.30 booking required Av main course £15 **Restaurant** L served Mon-Fri 12-2, Sat 12-2.30, Sun 12-3 booking required D served Mon-Fri 6.30-9, Sat 6.30-9.30, Sun 5-8.30 booking required Av 3 course à la carte fr £12.95 ⊕ FREE HOUSE ◀ Adnams, IPA, Mild, Local ales ♂ Aspall, Carters. **Facilities** Children welcome Children's menu Children's portions Garden Beer festival Parking

---

ORFORD   Map 13 TM45

Jolly Sailor Inn ♥

Quay St IP12 2NU ☎ 01394 450243 📠 0870 128 7874
e-mail: hello@thejollysailor.net
web: www.thejollysailor.net
dir: On B1084 E of Woodbridge, Orford signed from A12 approx 10m

This timber-framed 16th century quayside inn draws yachtsmen to moor and landlubbers to dream of long-gone smuggling practices here on the Suffolk coast. Fishermen still use the sheltered anchorage protected by Orford Ness's shingle bank, and the pub relies on their catches for its seasonal menu - skate wing, lobster or roasted cod may feature – alongside the hearty, red-blooded pub fare such as grilled venison steak with port and cranberry sauce or inventive vegetarian options such as fig, walnut and Stilton tart. Sup Adnams beers in the orchard with great views to the saltings and marshes where avocets nest.

Open all wk 11-3 6-mdnt (Sat 11am-1am Sun noon-11 summer all wk 11am-mdnt) **Bar Meals** L served Mon-Fri 12-3, Sat-Sun 11-11 D served Mon-Fri 6-9.30, Sat-Sun 11-11 **Restaurant** L served Mon-Fri 12-3, Sat-Sun 11-11 D served Mon-Fri 6-9.30, Sat-Sun 11-11 ⊕ ADNAMS ◀ Adnams Bitter, Broadside, Explorer ♂ Aspall. ♥ 14 **Facilities** Children welcome Children's menu Children's portions Play area Family room Dogs allowed Garden Parking Wi-fi

---

REDE   Map 13 TL85

The Plough ♥

IP29 4BE ☎ 01284 789208
dir: On A143 between Bury St Edmunds & Haverhill

With the same landlord for 29 years, this picture-postcard, half-thatched, 16th-century pub has an old plough outside. The building has a cream exterior with restored beams, and a fresh, open feel to the interior. Dishes in the form of South African bobotie, local game vol-au-vents, braised shoulder of lamb, and oxtail casserole are backed by an adventurous array of blackboard-listed dishes including fresh fish options. Menus change with the seasons and availability of fresh local produce. The bar serves a range of ales and up to ten wines by the glass.

Open all wk 11-3 6-12 (Sun 12-3) **Bar Meals** L served all wk 12-2 D served Mon-Sat 6-9 Av main course £15.95 **Restaurant** L served all wk 12-2 D served Mon-Sat 6-9 ⊕ ADMIRAL TAVERNS ◀ London Pride, Adnams, Ringwood Best, Sharp's Cornish Coaster ♂ Aspall. ♥ 10 **Facilities** Children welcome Children's portions Garden Parking

---

ST PETER SOUTH ELMHAM   Map 13 TM38

PICK OF THE PUBS

Wicked at St Peter's Hall ♥

NR35 1NQ ☎ 01986 782288
e-mail: mail@wickedlygoodfoodltd.co.uk
dir: From A143/A144 follow brown signs to St Peter's Brewery

Located in the Saints region of Suffolk, St Peter's Hall is now home to one of the county's most unusual and romantic pub/restaurants. This magnificent 13th-century moated hall was enlarged in 1539 using materials salvaged from nearby Flixton Priory, and the stunning conversion features period furnishings that make the most of original stone floors, Gothic windows and lofty ceilings. St Peter's brewery was established in 1996 in an adjacent range of former agricultural buildings, and now produces traditional ales as well as some more unusual varieties like honey porter and fruit beer including grapefruit ale. The full range of cask and bottled beers is available alongside local Aspall cider in the bar. You can dine in the traditionally furnished library bar and private dining room upstairs or the elegant great hall. Wherever you dine, locally sourced free range and organic produce is the mainstay of the menus, which range through dishes like poached pear, Stilton and walnut salad; Suffolk pork chop with grilled black pudding and cider cream sauce; steamed sponge of the day served with custard. Children get to choose from their own menu.

Open noon-3 6-11 (Sun noon-4) Closed: 1-12 Jan, Mon **Bar Meals** L served Tue-Sat 12-3 booking required Av main course £9 **Restaurant** L served Sun 12-4 booking required D served Tue-Sat 6-10 booking required Av 3 course à la carte fr £28 ⊕ ST PETER'S BREWERY ◀ Golden Ale, Organic Ale, Grapefruit ale, Cream Stout, Organic Best Bitter ♂ Aspall. ♥ 12 **Facilities** Children welcome Children's menu Children's portions Garden Parking Wi-fi

---

SIBTON   Map 13 TM36

PICK OF THE PUBS

Sibton White Horse Inn
★★★★ INN ❀ ♥

See Pick of the Pubs on page 424

SNAPE   Map 13 TM35

PICK OF THE PUBS

The Crown Inn ♥

Bridge Rd IP17 1SL ☎ 01728 688324
e-mail: snapecrown@tiscali.co.uk
dir: A12 N to Lowestoft, right to Aldeburgh, then right again in Snape at x-rds by church, pub at bottom of hill

First-time visitors to this 15th-century former smugglers' inn are often astonished by the adjoining smallholding where a veritable menagerie of livestock is lovingly reared by Teresa and Garry Cook. It pays not to become too attached however, as these are destined for the table at this marvellously atmospheric pub (no gaming machines or background music here), with abundant old beams, log fire, brick floors and, around the large inglenook, a very fine double Suffolk settle. Fish from Orford fishermen and locally raised beef feature in the strong British menus, with daily specials adding to the tally. The menus are forever changing but dishes such as crab spring roll with chilli crème fraîche; pork terrine with piccalilli (both home made of course); Orford smoked fish platter with lemon mayonnaise; and chicken breast with beansprouts, shiitake mushrooms and lemongrass broth might appear, all helped along with Adnams beers or a choice from 12 wines by the glass. There is a spacious garden for summer dining. Being close to Snape Maltings Concert Hall, pre- and post-concert dining is available.

Open all wk **Bar Meals** L served all wk 12-2.30 booking required D served all wk 6-9.30 booking required **Restaurant** L served all wk 12-2.30 booking required D served all wk 6-9.30 booking required ⊕ ADNAMS ◀ Adnams Bitter, Broadside, Adnams Seasonal Ales ♂ Aspall. ♥ 12 **Facilities** Children welcome Children's portions Dogs allowed Garden Parking

---

PICK OF THE PUBS

Sibton White Horse Inn ★★★★ INN

SIBTON Map 13 TM36

Halesworth Rd IP17 2JJ ☎ 01728 660337
e-mail: info@sibtonwhitehorseinn.co.uk
web: www.sibtonwhitehorseinn.co.uk
*dir: From A12 at Yoxford take A1120
signed Sibton & Peasonhall (ignore all
Sibton signs). Turn right opposite
Creaseys (butcher), signed White Horse/
Pouy Street/Walpole. 1m to inn*

In the heart of the Suffolk countryside, yet five minutes from the A12 at Yoxford, this 16th-century free house is off the beaten track on the edge of a pretty village. This rustic pub retains its Tudor charm and incorporates stone floors, exposed brickwork and ships' timbers believed to have come from Woodbridge shipyard. A genuine free house, the bar is the place to enjoy pints of Adnams Bitter or Woodforde's Wherry, with a choice of dining areas to sample the award-winning food. Owners Neil and Gill Mason are committed to producing high quality food from fresh local ingredients - and, to prove it, they grow many of their vegetables in the raised beds behind the pub. In the buzzy restaurant, you can order old favourites like smoked haddock fish cake, salad Niçoise and hard-boiled egg; honey and mustard home-roasted ham with twice-cooked chips and two fried duck eggs; ox liver with bacon, creamed potato and broccoli. For those diners in search of something a little more special, pan-seared Suffolk wood pigeon breast with confit shallot, fine beans, dried cherry tomato and redcurrant jus might be followed by trio of Chapel Farm rare-breed pork (fillet, confit belly, boudin blanc) with fondant potato, braised red cabbage, roast apples and red wine jus, or pan-seared Gressingham duck with tomato and thyme rösti, winter greens, roast griottine cherries and kirsch jus. Finish, perhaps, with pistachio tart, white chocolate ice cream and chocolate sauce, or vanilla cheesecake, hazelnut praline, vanilla syrup, cranberry ice cream. A secluded courtyard has a Mediterranean feel when the sun comes out.

Open all wk 12-2.30 6.30-11 (winter) 6-11 (summer) Sun 12-3.30 Closed: 26-27 Dec **Bar Meals** L served Mon-Sat 12-2, Sun 12-2.30 booking required D served all wk 7-9 booking required Av main course £13 **Restaurant** L served Mon-Sat 12-2, Sun 12-2.30 booking required D served all wk 7-9 booking required Av 3 course à la carte fr £25 ⊕ FREE HOUSE ◀ Adnams Bitter, Greene King Abbot Ale, Woodforde's Wherry ♂ Aspall. ♀ 9 **Facilities** Children's portions Dogs allowed Garden Parking Wi-fi **Rooms** 6

Save on hotels. Book at theAA.com/hotel

SUFFOLK 425 ENGLAND

SNAPE continued

PICK OF THE PUBS

The Golden Key ♟

Priory Ln IP17 1SQ ☎ 01728 688510
dir: Telephone for directions

This award-winning village pub dates back to the 1600s and some aspects of the interior recall those days, particularly the fabulous fireplaces beside which winter visitors warm by grand log fires. There's a cottagey feel to the place, with a run of rooms and alcoves popular both with locals enjoying the Adnams beers and discerning diners who travel far to sample the well-balanced menu that draws strongly on ultra-local produce. Fish is fresh daily from nearby Aldeburgh beach; organic vegetables come from the parson's garden, game from a nearby shoot and lamb from a neighbouring farm. The wine list stretches to 43 bins; on good days enjoy a glass outside beside the boules pitch.

Open all wk 12-3 6-11 (Sat 12-4 6-11 Sun 12-4 7-11)
Bar Meals L served Mon-Sat 12-2, Sun 12-3 booking required D served Mon-Sat 6.30-9, Sun 7-9 booking required **Restaurant** L served Mon-Sat 12-2, Sun 12-3 booking required D served Mon-Sat 6.30-9, Sun 7-9 booking required ⊕ ADNAMS ◀ Adnams Bitter, Broadside, Explorer, Old, Oyster Stout Ŏ Aspall. ♟ 15
Facilities Children welcome Children's portions Dogs allowed Garden Parking Wi-fi

Plough & Sail

Snape Maltings IP17 1SR
☎ 01728 688413 ▤ 01728 688930
e-mail: ploughandsail@debeninns.co.uk
dir: Snape Maltings on B1069 S of Snape. Signed from A12

A pink, pantiled old inn at the heart of the renowned Snape Maltings complex, handy for the cultural and shopping opportunities here and close to splendid coastal walks. The interior is a comfy mix of dining and avant-garde destination pub; local ales and a good bin of wines accompany a solid menu, featuring an Orford smoked fish platter or slow roast belly of pork with Suffolk cider apple chutney, plus a wide range of starters, nibbles and sandwiches. Change of hands.

Open all day all wk ⊕ FREE HOUSE ◀ Adnams Broadside, Adnams Bitter, Explorer, Woodforde's Wherry Ŏ Aspall Suffolk Cyder. **Facilities** Children welcome Children's menu Children's portions Dogs allowed Garden Parking Wi-fi

PICK OF THE PUBS

The Crown Hotel ★★ HL ◉ ♟

The High St IP18 6DP
☎ 01502 722275 ▤ 01502 727263
e-mail: crown.hotel@adnams.co.uk
dir: A12 onto A1095 to Southwold. Into town centre, pub on left

Once a posting inn dating from 1750, this pub, wine bar, eatery and small hotel is now the flagship operation for Adnams Brewery, so expect plenty of excellent ales on tap. The whole place buzzes with lively informality as waiting staff attend to customers installed on green leather cushioned settles or at the green-washed oak-panelled bar. It's a popular place, especially in summer when customers can enjoy a pint or a meal outside. The high standard of cooking is recognised with an AA rosette. The seaside location brings impressive seafood options such as pan-fried North Sea plaice, crushed celeriac, spring cabbage and pickled mushrooms, or home-made fish pie with a cheesy mash top and greens. Other options might include curried Suffolk mutton with braised rice, mango chutney and raita, or Suffolk rose veal, tomato and lemon stew with herb dumpling. Excellent puddings include rhubarb and custard trifle. The Crown's bedrooms have been built around twisting corridors and staircases.

Open all wk 8am-11pm (Sun 8am-10.30pm)
Bar Meals L served Sun-Fri 12-2, Sat 12-2.30 D served Sun-Fri 6-9, Sat 6-9.30 (5.30-9.30 summer)
Restaurant L served Sun-Fri 12-2, Sat 12-2.30 D served Sun-Fri 6-9, Sat 6-9.30 (5.30-9.30 summer) ⊕ ADNAMS ◀ Adnams Ales Ŏ Aspall. ♟ 20
Facilities Children welcome Children's menu Children's portions Dogs allowed Garden Parking Wi-fi
Rooms 14

PICK OF THE PUBS

The Randolph

41 Wangford Rd, Reydon IP18 6PZ
☎ 01502 723603 ▤ 01502 722194
e-mail: reception@therandolph.co.uk
dir: A1095 from A12 at Blythburgh 4m, Southwold 9m from Darsham train station

Built by Southwold brewery Adnams, this grand, late-Victorian, family-run, award-winning community pub, hotel and restaurant is named after Sir Winston Churchill's father. It is a fifteen minute stroll from the centre of picturesque Southwold and is the perfect place for exploring the Suffolk Heritage Coast. The lounge bar is light and airy and has contemporary furnishings including high-backed chairs and comfortable sofas. The same brewer's beers are sold today, alongside real cider from another Suffolk maker, Aspall. Sandwiches and lighter meals are served in the bar, whereas in the large dining area the cooking style is modern British. Locally sourced ingredients produce starters and light meals such as cod and salmon terrine with cucumber raita or warm Gruyère and tomato tart with onion marmalade, and main courses ranging from char-grilled rib eye steak with all the trimmings to Thai green curry. To one side of the building lies a large enclosed garden.

Open all day all wk **Bar Meals** L served all wk 12-2 D served all wk 6.30-9 Av main course £12
Restaurant L served all wk 12-2 D served all wk 6.30-9 Av 3 course à la carte fr £22 ⊕ ADNAMS PLC ◀ Adnams Bitter, Adnams Broadside, Explorer, Old Ale Ŏ Aspall. **Facilities** Children welcome Children's menu Children's portions Garden Parking Wi-fi

The Rose & Crown

Bury Rd IP31 2BZ ☎ 01359 250236
e-mail: roseandcrownstanton@btconnect.com
dir: On A413 from Bury St Edmunds towards Diss

Under new ownership since October 2010, this former coaching inn is surrounded by three acres of landscaped grounds. Settle on one of the comfy sofas in the split-level bar for a pint of Southwold-brewed Adnams Bitter, before tucking into a classic haddock in batter made with that very beer; sausage bubble and squeak; pie of the day; or a special such as pork medallions in Aspall's cider sauce. Monday curry nights mean a free pint and the Sunday carvery is served all day. In warmer weather there are large gardens and an enclosed decking area to enjoy.

Open all day all wk **Bar Meals** L served Mon-Thu 12-3, Fri-Sat 12-9.30, Sun 12-8.30 D served Mon-Thu 5-9, Fri-Sat 12-9.30 Av main course £8.50 **Restaurant** L served Mon-Thu 12-3, Fri-Sat 12-9.30, Sun 12-8.30 D served Mon-Thu 5-9, Fri-Sat 12-9.30 Fixed menu price fr £8.50 Av 3 course à la carte fr £16 ◀ Greene King IPA, Adnams Broadside, Guinness, Tribute, Timothy Taylor Landlord. **Facilities** Children welcome Children's menu Children's portions Play area Dogs allowed Garden Beer festival Parking Wi-fi

STOKE-BY-NAYLAND Map 13 TL93

PICK OF THE PUBS

The Angel Inn ♥

CO6 4SA ☎ 01206 263245 📠 01206 264145
e-mail: info@angelinnsuffolk.co.uk
dir: *From Colchester take A134 towards Sudbury, 5m to Nayland. Or from A12 between juncts 30 & 31 take B1068, then B1087 to Nayland*

Set in a landscape immortalised in the paintings of local artist, John Constable, The Angel is a 16th-century inn with beamed bars, log fires and a long tradition of hospitality. The relaxed, modern feel extends to the air-conditioned conservatory, the patio and sun terrace. Tables for lunch and dinner may be reserved in The Well Room, which has a high ceiling open to the rafters, a gallery leads to rough brick and timber studded walls, and the well itself, fully 52 feet deep. Eating in the bar, by comparison, is on a strictly first-come, first-served basis but the same menu is served throughout. Main courses offer a range of meat, seafood and vegetarian options, typically including griddled whole plaice served with salad and French fries. There is an extensive wine list. Recent change of hands.

Open all day all wk Mon-Sat 11am-11pm (Sun 11am-10.30pm) **Bar Meals** L served Mon-Fri 12-3.30, Sat 12-9.45, Sun 12-9.30 D served Mon-Fri 6-9.45, Sat 12-9.45, Sun 12-9.30 **Restaurant** L served Mon-Fri 12-3.30, Sat 12-9.45, Sun 12-9.30 D served Mon-Fri 6-9.45, Sat 12-9.45, Sun 12-9.30 ⊕ FREE HOUSE ◄ Adnams Best, 2 Guest ales. ♥ 9 **Facilities** Children welcome Children's menu Family room Dogs allowed Garden Parking

PICK OF THE PUBS

The Crown ★★★ SHL ◉◉ ♥

CO6 4SE ☎ 01206 262001 📠 01206 264026
e-mail: info@crowninn.net
dir: *Exit A12 signed Stratford St Mary/Dedham. Through Stratford St Mary 0.5m, left, follow signs to Higham. At village green turn left, left again 2m, pub on right*

The timeless villages of Lavenham, Kersey and Long Melford are all within easy reach of this 16th-century free house. The building has been stylishly updated to create a contemporary bar and informal dining areas, with smart soft furnishings and pastel colours. Meanwhile, the eye-catching glass wine cellar-cum-shop offers some cracking wines to take away. Local produce underpins the modern British menu, with dishes freshly prepared to order. Lunch brings full meals and lighter options, or look to the chalkboard for the daily east coast fish selection. An evening meal might begin with haggis Scotch egg and celeriac remoulade, followed by rabbit, field mushroom and sage pie with new potatoes and spring greens, or roast rib of beef on Sunday. A locally produced sorbet makes a refreshing end to the meal. Every dish is given a wine

match and a decent selection of ales complements the superb wine list. Eleven luxury en suite bedrooms complete the picture.

Open all day all wk 7.30am-11pm (Sun 8am-10.30pm) Closed: 25-26 Dec **Bar Meals** L served Mon-Sat 12-2.30, Sun 12-9 D served Mon-Thu 6-9.30, Fri-Sat 6-10, Sun 12-9 **Restaurant** L served Mon-Sat 12-2.30, Sun 12-9 D served Mon-Thu 6-9.30, Fri-Sat 6-10, Sun 12-9 ⊕ FREE HOUSE ◄ Adnams Best Bitter, Brewers Gold, Woodforde's Wherry, Guest ales ♂ Aspall. ♥ 32 **Facilities** Children welcome Children's menu Children's portions Dogs allowed Garden Parking Wi-fi **Rooms** 11

STOWMARKET Map 13 TM05

PICK OF THE PUBS

The Buxhall Crown ♥

Mill Rd, Buxhall IP14 3DW ☎ 01449 736521
e-mail: thebuxhallcrown@hotmail.co.uk
dir: *3m from Stowmarket and A14*

A 17th-century building, The Buxhall Crown has a classic old bar with intimate corners and an open fire, and a second bar with a lighter, more modern feel. The owners and staff pride themselves on the friendly family feel of the pub, and the high quality of the food they serve. Dishes are prepared from locally sourced produce, and breads, biscuits, ice creams and sorbets are all freshly made on the premises. Anything from a bar snacks to a full four-course meal is catered for, and the menu changes regularly to suit the weather and the availability of ingredients. To start, spiced parsnip soup with apple crème fraîche and pressed ham hock terrine with redcurrants, Russet apple salad and piccalilli; followed by Suffolk chicken breast, chanterelle mushroom mousse, fondant potatoes and smoked mushroom velouté; St Edmunds beer battered haddock fillet, triple cooked chips and minted crushed peas; and woodland mushroom and vegetable nage risotto all appeared on a winter menu.

Open noon-3 7-11 (Sat noon-3 6.30-11) Closed: 25 & 26 Dec, Sun eve **Bar Meals** L served all wk 12-2 D served Mon-Fri 7-9.30, Sat 6.30-9.30 Av main course £12 **Restaurant** L served all wk 12-2 D served Mon-Fri 7-9.30, Sat 6.30-9.30 Fixed menu price fr £10 Av 3 course à la carte fr £19.15 ⊕ GREENE KING ◄ Greene King IPA, Olde Trip, Old Speckled Hen, Guest Ale ♂ Aspall. ♥ 12 **Facilities** Children welcome Children's menu Children's portions Dogs allowed Garden Parking Wi-fi

STRADBROKE Map 13 TM27

The Ivy House ♥

Wilby Rd IP21 5JN ☎ 01379 384634
e-mail: stensethhome@aol.com
dir: *Telephone for directions*

A Grade II listed thatched pub just off the main street in Stradbroke. The comfortable bar offers real ales and wine from Adnams wine cellar. The remodelled restaurant has beech tables and chairs, and white china. The weekly-changing menu makes good use of local and seasonal produce, some grown on the premises. Typical dishes include pan-fried calves' liver with Suffolk dry-cured bacon, mash and onion gravy, and seared tuna steak with salad niçoise. In warmer weather you can sit outside at the front or in the garden.

Open all wk **Restaurant** L served all wk 12-2 booking required D served all wk 6.30-9 booking required ⊕ FREE HOUSE ◄ Adnams, Woodforde's, Buffy's ♂ Aspall. ♥ 12 **Facilities** Dogs allowed Garden Parking

SWILLAND Map 13 TM15

Moon & Mushroom Inn

High Rd IP6 9LR ☎ 01473 785320
e-mail: themoonandmusroom@live.co.uk
dir: *Take B1077 (Westerfield road) from Ipswich. Approx 6m right to Swilland*

'Home-cooked food at its very best' is the promise at this award-winning 400-year-old free house, but that statement makes no mention of the lip-smacking array of East Anglian real ales served here straight from the barrel. The pub was reputedly a staging post for the despatch of convicts to Australia, and the records at Ipswich Assizes do indeed show that a previous landlord was deported for stealing two ducks and pig. A point to ponder as you tuck into your slow-roast pork belly with apple sauce…

Open Tue-Sun L & Mon L Closed: Sun eve & Mon eve **Bar Meals** L served all wk 12-2 D served Tue-Sat 6-9 Av main course £9.95 **Restaurant** L served all wk 12-2 D served Tue-Sat 6-9 Fixed menu price fr £9.95 ⊕ FREE HOUSE ◄ Nethergate Suffolk County, Woodforde's Wherry, Buffy's Hopleaf, Wolf Ale, Golden Jackal, Lavender Honey ♂ Aspall. **Facilities** Children welcome Children's portions Dogs allowed Garden Parking

THORPENESS
Map 13 TM45

The Dolphin Inn ♥

Peace Place IP16 4NA ☎ 01728 454994
e-mail: dolphininn@hotmail.co.uk
dir: A12 onto A1094 & follow Thorpeness signs

In 1910, local landowner Stuart Ogilvie started building a seaside holiday village in Aldringham-cum-Thorpe; Ogilvie renamed his creation Thorpeness. The original pub predated all this, but unfortunately it burnt down. This 1995 rebuild stocks real ales from independent local breweries, and serves locally sourced produce such as baked Lowestoft skate wing; slow-cooked Dingley Dell pork belly; and leek and mushroom tarte Tatin. Very much a community pub, the kitchen also supplies preserves, pies and pastries to the attached village store.

Open Mon-Sun L Closed: Sun eve & Mon in winter
Bar Meals L served all wk 12-2.30 booking required D served all wk 6.30-9.30 booking required Av main course £12.50 **Restaurant** L served all wk 12-2.30 booking required D served all wk 6.30-9.30 booking required Fixed menu price fr £12.95 Av 3 course à la carte fr £22 ⊕ FREE HOUSE ◀ Adnams Best, Adnams Broadside, Rusty Bucket, Nautilus, Mid Summer Gold Ö Aspall. ♥ 16 **Facilities** Children welcome Children's menu Children's portions Dogs allowed Garden Parking Wi-fi

TUDDENHAM
Map 13 TM14

The Fountain ♥ NEW

The Street IP6 9BT ☎ 01473 785377
e-mail: fountainpub@btconnect.com
dir: From Ipswich take B1077 (Westerfield Rd) signed Debenham. At Westerfield turn right for Tuddenham

Located in the lovely village of Tuddenham St Martin, only three miles north of Ipswich, this 16th-century country pub combines old fashioned pub hospitality with an informal bistro-style restaurant. The menu changes frequently and there is an emphasis on local produce in dishes such as chargrilled Dingley Dell pork loin with whole grain mustard sauce, or mint-crusted Suffolk lamb rump with red wine sauce. Wash it all down with pints of Adnams ale or Aspalls cider.

Open 12-3 6-11 Closed: Sun eve **Bar Meals** L served all wk 12-2 booking required D served Mon-Fri 6-9, Sat 6-9.30 booking required Av main course £12.15 **Restaurant** L served all wk 12-2 booking required D served Mon-Fri 6-9, Sat 6-9.30 booking required Fixed menu price fr £13.25 Av 3 course à la carte fr £9.15 ⊕ FREE HOUSE ◀ Adnams Ö Aspall. ♥ 9 **Facilities** Children welcome Children's portions Garden Parking

WALBERSWICK
Map 13 TM47

PICK OF THE PUBS

The Anchor ◉ ♥

Main St IP18 6UA
☎ 01502 722112 📠 01502 724464
e-mail: info@anchoratwalberswick.com
dir: From A12 turn at B1387. Follow signs for Walberswick. Continue on Main St, pub on right

An eye-catchingly striking Arts and Crafts building close to the seashore in trendy Walberswick; patrons dabbling in the exceptional choice of dishes here are in for an education as well as a gastronomic treat as each meal is twinned with a recommended beer or award-winning wine. Thus seared scallops, pancetta and white bean purée comes with a suggested Westmalle Tripel bottled lager or Chateau Le Chec Graves 2008 vintage; whilst roast cod fillet, gnocchi, leeks and capers is matched with a glass of Meantime Helles beer (from Greenwich) or a Saint Veran 2008. Good conversation, food and drink is the mission statement of licensees Mark and Sophie Dorber; Mark oversees the drinks side of the business whilst Sophie continually invents culinary treats; she cut her chef-teeth catering for cast and crew of the *Star Wars* films, so expect some very unusual dishes! Chinese water deer, slip soles and snipe may feature on her award-winning menu; the rule-of-thumb is to use only the freshest, most local produce available, so the salt marsh lamb or rabbit may have matured as near-neighbours on the coastal strip outside the village, stretching away from the sheltered terrace and wildflower meadow beside the pub. A mid-August beer festival is something to look forward to.

Open all day all wk **Bar Meals** L served all wk 12-3 booking required D served all wk 6-9 **Restaurant** L served all wk 12-3 booking required D served all wk 6-9 booking required Fixed menu price fr £23.95 ⊕ ADNAMS ◀ Adnams Bitter, Broadside, Seasonal, Meantime Helles, Meantime Pale Ale, Bitburger, Guest ales Ö Aspall. ♥ 22 **Facilities** Children welcome Children's menu Children's portions Family room Dogs allowed Garden Beer festival Parking Wi-fi

PICK OF THE PUBS

Bell Inn ♥

Ferry Rd IP18 6TN ☎ 01502 723109
dir: From A12 take B1387, follow to beyond village green, bear right down track

The inn dates back 600 years and is located near the village green, beach and the ancient fishing harbour on the River Blyth. The large garden has beach and sea views, while the building's great age is evident from the interior's low beams, stone-flagged floors, high wooden settles and open fires. Adnams furnishes the bar with Broadside and Spindrift among others, while Suffolk cyder maker Aspall is also well represented.

(Aspall has spelt its cyder with a 'y' since the 1920s, reputedly to reflect the refined quality of the family firm's multi-award-winning product.) Food is all home cooked with local produce featuring strongly, particularly fresh fish. Specialities include starters of locally smoked sprats or Suffolk smokies – flaked smoked haddock in a creamy cheese sauce – both served with granary toast and a salad garnish. There are non-fish dishes too, like baked Suffolk ham or lamb burger in toasted ciabatta. Change of hands.

Open all wk 11-11 **Bar Meals** L served all wk 12-2.30 D served all wk 6-9 **Restaurant** L served all wk 12-2.30 D served all wk 6-9 ⊕ ADNAMS ◀ Adnams Bitter, Broadside, Explorer, Spindrift Ö Aspall. ♥ 15 **Facilities** Children welcome Children's menu Family room Dogs allowed Garden Parking

WESTLETON
Map 13 TM46

PICK OF THE PUBS

The Westleton Crown ★★★ HL ◉ ◉ ♥

See Pick of the Pubs on page 428

WHEPSTEAD
Map 13 TL85

PICK OF THE PUBS

The White Horse ◉ ♥

Rede Rd IP29 4SS ☎ 01284 735760
dir: From Bury St Edmunds take A143 towards Haverhill. Left onto B1066 to Whepstead. In Whepstead right into Church Hill, leads into Rede Rd

Built in the 17th century as a farmhouse and extended during the reign of Victoria, this pub was on the verge of extinction in 2009. Owners Gary and Di Kingshott recognised its potential, succeeded in buying it from the brewery, closed it for a few months while it was being refurbished, and reopened it to the great delight of the locals and tremendously loyal staff. The clean and uncluttered interior makes it a great space for the display and sale of artworks by local painters. The open fire and comfortable wooden chairs make you feel instantly at home, whilst nostalgic touches like the Tuck Shop appeal to adults and children alike. As well as reliable Suffolk ales and real cider, the AA rosette awarded food presents the likes of smoked haddock chowder served with crusty bread; slow-braised shoulder of Ickworth lamb, with black olives, fresh herbs and creamy mash; and chocolate truffle torte.

Open 11.30-3 7-11 Closed: 25-26 Dec, Sun eve **Bar Meals** L served all wk 12-2 D served Mon-Sat 7-9.30 **Restaurant** L served all wk 12-2 D served Mon-Sat 7-9.30 ⊕ FREE HOUSE ◀ Adnams Bitter, Adnams Broadside, Guest Ale Ö Aspall. ♥ 10 **Facilities** Children welcome Children's portions Dogs allowed Garden Parking

PICK OF THE PUBS

The Westleton Crown ★★★ HL   ♓

WESTLETON Map 13 TM46

The Street IP17 3AD
☎ **01728 648777** 📄 **01728 648239**
e-mail: info@westletoncrown.co.uk
web: www.westletoncrown.co.uk
dir: *A12 N, turn right for Westleton just after Yoxford. Hotel opposite on entering Westleton*

Dating back to the 12th century, this traditional Suffolk coaching inn retains plenty of character and rustic charm, but with all the comforts of contemporary living. Standing opposite the parish church in a peaceful village close to the RSPB's Minsmere Reserve, it provides a comfortable base for exploring Suffolk's glorious Heritage Coast. On winter days you'll find three crackling log fires, local real ales including Purity UBU and Green Jack, as well as a good list of wines (with 11 available by the glass).

There's also an extensive menu that includes innovative daily specials and classic dishes with a twist, all freshly prepared from the best local produce available. You can eat in the cosy bar, in the elegant dining room, or in the fabulous new garden room, completed as part of a major refurbishment project in 2010. Sandwiches are made with a choice of The Crown's own breads, and served with sea-salted crisps and a dressed salad.

More substantial appetites might choose from starters like slow-cooked Suffolk

chicken, tarragon and lentil terrine with endive salad; or parsnip beignets with blue cheese and walnut cream and beetroot and apple salad. Follow up with main course choices such as pan-fried local venison with shallow-fried sweet potato polenta, buttered curly kale, sautéed girolles and prune sauce; or pan-fried gilthead bream with boulangère potatoes and winter vegetable broth. Save some space for accomplished desserts like pannacotta with spiced autumn fruit compote; or chocolate soufflé tart with fig ice cream and fig syrup.

Retire to one of the 34 comfortably refurbished and individually styled bedrooms, complete with flat screen TV. Outside, the large terraced gardens are floodlit in the evening.

Open all day all wk 7am-11pm (Sun 7.30am-10.30pm) **Bar Meals** L served all wk 12-2.30 D served all wk 7-9.30 **Restaurant** L served all wk 12-2.30 D served all wk 7-9.30 ⊕ FREE HOUSE 🍺 Adnams Bitter, Purity UBU, Green Jack, Brandeston Gold Ö Aspall. ♓ 11 **Facilities** Children's menu Children's portions Dogs allowed Garden Parking Wi-fi **Rooms** 34

Save on hotels. Book at **theAA.com/hotel**

SURREY 429 ENGLAND

SURREY

ABINGER
Map 6 TQ14

PICK OF THE PUBS

The Stephan Langton
See Pick of the Pubs page 430

The Volunteer ☻

Water Ln, Sutton RH5 6PR ☎ 01306 730985
e-mail: volunteer247@btinternet
dir: *Between Guildford & Dorking, 1m S of A25*

Enjoying a delightful rural setting with views over the River Mole, this popular village pub was originally farm cottages and first licensed about 1870. Under the ownership of Hall & Woodhouse, it remains an ideal watering hole for walkers who want to relax over a pint in the attractive three-tier pub garden or in the bustling bar with its two fireplaces. Typical dishes include red Thai curry; chicken and asparagus pie; and the renowned Volunteer fish pie. Sandwiches, baguettes, melts, toasted sandwiches and jacket potatoes are all available too. Recent change of hands.

Open all day all wk 11.30-11 (Sat 11-11 Sun noon-11) **Bar Meals** L served all wk noon-11pm **Restaurant** L served all wk noon-2.30 D served all wk 6.30-9.30 ⊕ HALL & WOODHOUSE ◀ Badger Tanglefoot, King & Barns Sussex, Guest ales Ö Stowford Press. ☻ 9 **Facilities** Children welcome Children's menu Children's portions Dogs allowed Garden Parking Wi-fi

ALBURY
Map 6 TQ04

The Drummond at Albury ★★★ INN ☻

The Street GU5 9AG
☎ 01483 202039 📇 01483 205361
e-mail: drummondarms@aol.com
dir: *6m from Guildford*

A comforting mix of great local real ales from the like of Surrey Hills and Hogs Back breweries with the best of modern and traditional British cooking — local lake trout or slow roast belly pork - mark out this eye-catching Victorian village inn, recently officially re-opened and renamed by the Duke of Northumberland whose family has historic links. A grassy, tree-shaded beer garden slopes to the lively River Tillingbourne at the heart of the Surrey Hills Area of Outstanding Natural Beauty close to the North Downs; ample excuse to stay over at the individually appointed letting rooms here.

Open all day all wk 11-11 (Fri-Sat 11-mdnt, Sun noon-10.30) **Bar Meals** L served Mon-Fri 12-3, Sat 12-6, Sun 12-8 D served Mon-Sat 6-9.30, Sun 12-8 Av main course £11.50 **Restaurant** L served Mon-Fri 12-3, Sat 12-6, Sun 12-8 D served Mon-Sat 6-9.30, Sun 12-8 Av 3 course à la carte fr £21 ⊕ FREE HOUSE ◀ Courage Best, London Pride, Shere Drop, Hogs Back TEA, Adnams. ☻ 10 **Facilities** Children welcome Children's portions Dogs allowed Garden Parking Wi-fi **Rooms** 9

William IV

Little London GU5 9DG ☎ 01483 202685
dir: *Just off A25 between Guildford & Dorking. Near Shere*

Deep in the Surrey Hills yet only a stone's throw from Guildford, this 16th-century free house provides 'proper pub food' made from mostly local produce. Sometimes it's the free-range pork raised by landlord Giles written on the blackboards, but more usually it's steak and chips, battered cod, sticky toffee pudding, all served in the bar and dining room. Young's and two Surrey breweries supply the real ales. It is great walking and riding country, and the attractive garden is ideal for post-ramble relaxation.

Open all wk 11-3 5.30-11 (Sat 11-11, Sun noon-11) Closed: 25 Dec **Bar Meals** L served all wk 12-2 booking required D served Mon-Sat 7-9 booking required ⊕ FREE HOUSE ◀ Young's, Hogs Back, Surrey Hills Brewery Ö Westons Stowford Press, Bounds Brand Scrumpy. **Facilities** Children welcome Children's portions Dogs allowed Garden Parking

BETCHWORTH
Map 6 TQ25

The Red Lion ★★★ INN ☻

Old Rd, Buckland RH3 7DS
☎ 01737 843336 📇 01737 845242
e-mail: info@redlionbetchworth.co.uk
dir: *Telephone for directions*

The family-run Red Lion dates back to 1795 and is set in 18 acres with a cricket ground, a 230-year-old wisteria and rolling countryside views, all just 15 minutes from Gatwick Airport. A vaulted cellar accommodates a function room, and six en suite bedrooms are available in a separate self-contained block. The menu offers a meat pie of the week; curry of the week; ham, egg and chips; home-made fish pie; or a sharing meat platter. The area is ideal for walkers.

Open all day all wk 11am-11.30pm (Fri-Sat 11am-mdnt) **Bar Meals** L served Sun-Fri 12-2.30, Sat 12-4 Av main course £12 **Restaurant** L served Mon-Fri 12-2.30, Sat-Sun 12-4 D served Mon-Thu 6.30-9, Fri-Sat 6.30-9.30, Sun 6.30-8 ⊕ PUNCH TAVERNS ◀ Adnams Bitter, Doom Bar, Hogs Back TEA Ö Addlestones, Stowford Press. ☻ 9 **Facilities** Children welcome Children's menu Children's portions Dogs allowed Garden Parking **Rooms** 6

BRAMLEY
Map 6 TQ04

Jolly Farmer Inn ☻

High St GU5 0HB ☎ 01483 893355 📇 01483 890484
e-mail: enquiries@jollyfarmer.co.uk
dir: *From Guildford take A281 (Horsham road). Bramley 3.5m S of Guildford*

There's a passion for cask ales at this friendly 16th-century family-run traditional free house. Besides the impressive range of Belgian bottled beers, you'll always find up to eight constantly-changing real ales on the counter. Originally a coaching inn steeped in character and history, the Jolly Farmer offers a high

standard of food all freshly cooked, with daily specials board featuring beef Wellington with port and red wine sauce, or baked rainbow trout with lemon and dill.

Open all day all wk 11-11 **Bar Meals** L served all wk 12-2.30 D served all wk 6-9.30 Av main course £10 **Restaurant** L served all wk 12-2.30 D served all wk 6-9.30 Av 3 course à la carte fr £22 ⊕ FREE HOUSE ◀ 8 continually changing cask ales Ö Westons Stowford Press. ☻ 16 **Facilities** Children welcome Children's menu Dogs allowed Garden Parking Wi-fi

BUCKLAND
Map 6 TQ25

The Jolly Farmers Deli Pub & Restaurant ☻ NEW

Reigate Rd RH3 7BG ☎ 01737 221355
e-mail: info@thejollyfarmersreigate.co.uk
dir: *On A25 approx 2m from Reigate & 4m from Dorking*

A unique free house beside the A25 between Reigate and Dorking. It may look like a traditional pub but step inside and you'll find a cracking deli/farmshop that showcases local foods and artisan producers smack next to the comfortable, wood-floored bar and restaurant. What's more, it is open all day, serving breakfast (at weekends), lunch, cream teas and dinner, or you can just pop in for some deli produce. Typical dishes include warm salad of pork belly, chorizo and new potatoes, lamb and wild mushroom suet pudding, calves' liver with herb and garlic butter, and sticky toffee pudding. Local ales, farmers' markets and beer festivals are added attractions.

Open all day all wk **Bar Meals** L served all wk all day D served all wk all day Av main course £10.95 food served all day **Restaurant** L served Mon-Fri 12-3, Sat 12-9.30, Sun 12-8.30 D served Sat 12-9.30, Sun 12-8.30 Av 3 course à la carte fr £24 ⊕ FREE HOUSE ◀ Dark Star Hophead, W J King Horsham Best Bitter. ☻ 14 **Facilities** Children welcome Children's menu Children's portions Garden Beer festival Parking Wi-fi

CHIDDINGFOLD
Map 6 SU93

The Crown Inn ★★★★★ INN

The Green GU8 4TX ☎ 01428 682255 📇 01428 685736
e-mail: enquiries@thecrownchiddingfold.com
dir: *On A283 between Milford & Petworth*

Historic inn, dating back over 700 years, with lots of charming features, including ancient panelling, open fires, distinctive carvings, huge beams, and eight comfortable bedrooms. Reliable food ranges from pork and leek sausages served with mash and onion gravy or home made chicken and mushroom pie on the bar menu; to monkfish wrapped in Parma ham served with confit tomato and pepper salad or cumin spiced rump of lamb on butternut squash with spinach and a rosemary jus on the à la carte.

Open all day all wk ⊕ FGH INNS ◀ London Pride, Moon Dance, Crown Bitter, Summer Lightning. **Facilities** Children welcome Children's menu Children's portions Dogs allowed Garden Wi-fi **Rooms** 8

PICK OF THE PUBS

The Stephan Langton

ABINGER Map 6 TQ14

Friday St RH5 6JR
☎ **01306 730775 & 737129**
e-mail: info@stephanlangtonpub.co.uk
web: www.stephanlangtonpub.co.uk
dir: *Exit A25 between Dorking & Guildford at Hollow Lane, W of Wootton. 1.5m then left into Friday St. At end of hill right at pond*

Undulating mixed woodland surrounds this secluded hamlet at the base of Leith Hill, which is nothing more than a tranquil hammer pond and a handful of stone and timber cottages. This is prime Surrey walking country and a popular pit-stop is The Stephan Langton, a 1930s building named after the first archbishop of Canterbury, who was supposedly born in Friday Street. He helped draw up the Magna Carta and a copy of the document is pinned to a wall in the rustic, bare-boarded bar.

Equally unpretentious is the adjoining dining room, with its cream-washed walls, simple wooden tables and chairs, and open fires. Having conquered Leith Hill, the highest summit in south-east England, relax on the sun-trap patio and savour a thirst-quenching pint of locally-brewed Hog's Back TEA or Shere Drop.

Peruse the short, inviting menu that hits the spot with lunchtime sandwiches and starters like smoked chicken and leek

risotto, and local smoked trout with potato scones, mixed leaves and walnut pesto dressing. Typical hearty main dishes take in grilled cod with Tuscan bean broth; beef slow-braised in beer with root vegetables, bashed neeps and tatties; seared venison with roasted beetroot, local watercress and crème de cassis jus; and thyme and sage roasted rack of lamb with sweet potato gratin, cavalo nero and red wine jus. Changing daily specials make the most of local produce, much of it sourced from the surrounding Wooton Estate. Mathew Granger and Marissa Waters took over the pub in November 2009 and are gradually upgrading the place and developing the food side of the operation.

Open all wk 11-3 5-10.30 (Sat 11-11 Sun 12-9) **Bar Meals** L served Tue-Sat 12-2.30, Sun 12-4 booking required D served Tue-Sat 6.30-9.30 booking required **Restaurant** L served Tue-Sat 12-2.30, Sun 12-4 booking required D served Tue-Sat 6.30-9.30 booking required ⊕ FREE HOUSE ◀ Fuller's London Pride, Hog's Back TEA, Shere Drop, Ringwood Best ♂ Rough Old Wife. **Facilities** Children's portions Dogs allowed Garden Parking Wi-fi

Save on hotels. Book at theAA.com/hotel

SURREY 431 ENGLAND

CHURT
Map 5 SU83

PICK OF THE PUBS

Pride of the Valley ♥

Tilford Rd GU10 2LH
☎ 01428 605799 📠 01428 605875
e-mail: reservations@prideofthevalleyhotel.com
dir: *4m from Farnham on outskirts of Churt. 3m from Haslemere*

Built in 1867, the Pride of the Valley has always been a coaching inn. Once a watering hole for former Prime Minister David Lloyd George, who retired locally in the 1920s, the house is set in some of Surrey's most picturesque countryside, close to Devil's Jumps beauty spot and Frensham Common with its sculpture park spread across hillsides, vales and woodlands. Now a comfortable country house hotel, the building is distinguished by some fine art nouveau touches and wonderful wood panelling. The owner is an enthusiastic supporter of the local Hogs Back Brewery and maintains a first class wine list, all of which complements a regularly refreshed menu reflecting seasonal, locally sourced produce. A typical day may find pan-seared fillet of trout with warm winter salad, mandarin vinaigrette and smoked salmon beignet, or slow braised belly of lamb, roasted lamb cutlet, wild mushroom bread pudding, pea and mint purée and rosemary sauce, finishing off with mandarin and blood orange cheesecake or orange and date sticky pudding with orange butterscotch sauce and pink peppercorn ice cream.

Open all wk **Bar Meals** L served Mon-Sat 12-2.30, Sun 12-3 D served all wk 6.30-9.30 Av main course £10 **Restaurant** L served Sun 12-3 booking required D served Mon-Sat 6.30-9.30 booking required Av 3 course à la carte fr £19.25 ⊕ FREE HOUSE ◀ Hogs Back TEA, Hogs Back Bitter, Doom Bar. ♥ 8 **Facilities** Children welcome Children's menu Children's portions Dogs allowed Garden Parking Wi-fi

CLAYGATE
Map 6 TQ16

Swan Inn & Lodge

2 Hare Ln KT10 9BS ☎ 01372 462582
e-mail: info@theswaninn.net
dir: *At Esher/Oxshott junct of A3 take A244 towards Esher. Right at 1st lights, pub 300yds on right*

Rebuilt in 1905 overlooking the village green and cricket pitch, yet barely 15 miles from Charing Cross. There's an attractively furnished Continental-style bar and a Thai restaurant offering nearly 75 starters, soups, curries, stir-fries, and seafoods. The Thai menu is available at lunchtime and in the evenings, as are calamari, Cajun chicken burgers, scampi, roast beef and lamb, and paninis. Dishes of the day appear on the specials board. Recent change of hands.

Open all day all wk noon-11 ⊕ WELLINGTON PUB COMPANY ◀ London Pride, Old Speckled Hen, Woodforde's Wherry Ö Aspall. **Facilities** Children's menu Play area Family room Dogs allowed Garden Parking

COBHAM
Map 6 TQ16

The Cricketers

Downside KT11 3NX
☎ 01932 862105 📠 01932 868186
e-mail: info@thecricketersdownside.co.uk
dir: *M25 junct 10, A3 towards London. 1st exit signed Cobham. Straight over 1st rdbt, right at 2nd. In 1m right opposite Waitrose into Downside Bridge Rd*

Traditional, family-run pub, parts of which date back to 1540, with beamed ceilings and log fires. The inn's charming rural setting makes it popular with walkers, and the pretty River Mole is close by. The main menu offers dishes like best end of lamb served with herb crust, ratatouille and rosemary jus; or confit duck leg served with mashed potato, Savoy cabbage with raisins, honey and port sauce.

Open all day all wk ◀ Old Speckled Hen, London Pride, IPA. **Facilities** Children welcome Children's portions Play area Dogs allowed Garden Parking

COLDHARBOUR
Map 6 TQ14

PICK OF THE PUBS

The Plough Inn

Coldharbour Ln RH5 6HD
☎ 01306 711793 📠 01306 710055
e-mail: ploughinn@btinternet.com
dir: *M25 junct 9, A24 to Dorking. A25 towards Guildford. Coldharbour signed from one-way system*

At 965 feet above sea level, nearby Leith Hill is the highest point in south-eastern England – it's one of the reasons why walkers and cyclists head for this 17th-century former coaching inn. Earlier visitors were smugglers en route from the South Coast to London, which may explain why the resident ghost is a sailor. Another high point is the inn's own micro-brewery, which produces Tallywhacker porter, Crooked Furrow bitter and The Beautiful South, a lighter beer, while Biddenden cider kicks in at a hefty eight per cent ABV. Long-term refurbishment has produced a family-friendly place with big winter fires, a pretty garden and, the latest addition, an evening steakhouse serving 21-day, dry-aged local award-winning steaks, as well as chargrilled marinated langoustines, chicken supreme with Applewood-smoked Cheddar and leek sauce, and caramelised macaroni cheese and red onion wholemeal tart. The Plough has a new single malt whisky collection in conjunction with the steakhouse.

Open all day all wk 11.30am-mdnt Closed: 25 Dec **Bar Meals** L served Mon-Fri 12-2.30, Sat-Sun 12-3 D served Mon 7-9.30 Av main course £9.95 **Restaurant** D served Tue-Sun 7-10 booking required Av 3 course à la carte fr £23.85 ⊕ FREE HOUSE ◀ Crooked Furrow, Tallywhacker, Beautiful South, Shepherd Neame Spitfire Ö Biddenden. **Facilities** Children welcome Children's menu Children's portions Dogs allowed Garden Parking Wi-fi

COMPTON
Map 6 SU94

The Withies Inn

Withies Ln GU3 1JA ☎ 01483 421158 📠 01483 425904
dir: *Telephone for directions*

Set amid unspoiled country on Compton Common just below the Hog's Back, this low-beamed 16th-century pub has been carefully modernised to incorporate a small restaurant. There is also a splendid garden where meals and drinks can be served under the pergola. Snacks available in the bar range from sandwiches and jackets to fisherman's broth or a seafood platter. In the restaurant dishes include paw paw with fresh crab; Arbroath smokies; roast rack of lamb with rosemary; beef Stroganoff; and steak Diane flambé.

Open 11-3 6-11 (Fri 11-11) Closed: Sun eve **Bar Meals** L served all wk 12-2.30 D served Mon-Sat 7-10 **Restaurant** L served all wk 12-2.30 D served Mon-Sat 7-10 ⊕ FREE HOUSE ◀ TEA, Adnams, Young's, Greene King IPA Ö Addlestones. **Facilities** Children welcome Dogs allowed Garden Parking Wi-fi

CRANLEIGH
Map 6 TQ03

The Richard Onslow ♥ NEW

113-117 High St GU6 8AU ☎ 01483 274922
e-mail: hello@therichardonslow.co.uk
dir: *From A281 between Guildford & Horsham take B2130 to Cranleigh, pub in village centre*

At the heart of Cranleigh village, the former Onslow Arms reopened in 2009 after a major refurbishment. A grand old tile-hung pub with original brick inglenook, the pub has retained its character whilst benefiting from a contemporary decor and new dining room. Now, you can enjoy pints of local Surrey Hills ale and tuck into all-day menus offering tempting sandwiches, roasts, salads and main courses such as roast cod with champ mash and parsley sauce or 8oz onglet steak with bubble and squeak and soft boiled egg.

Open all day all wk **Bar Meals** L served all wk 12-3 D served all wk 6-10 Av main course £12.50 **Restaurant** L served all wk 12-3 D served all wk 6-10 Av 3 course à la carte fr £25 ⊕ PEACH PUBS ◀ Surrey Hills Shere Drop, Dark Star Hop Head Ö Aspall Blush. ♥ 12 **Facilities** Children welcome Children's portions Dogs allowed Garden Parking Wi-fi

DUNSFOLD
Map 6 TQ03

The Sun Inn ♥

The Common GU8 4LE
☎ 01483 200242 📠 01483 201141
e-mail: suninn@dunsfold.net
dir: *A281 through Shalford & Bramley, take B2130 to Godalming. Dunsfold on left after 2m*

A traditional 500-year-old family-run inn in a chocolate box village, set opposite the cricket green and village pond. Inside the welcome is warm, with blazing fires and an array of real ales including Adnams and Harveys. The

continued

DUNSFOLD *continued*

award-winning, home-made healthy eating dishes, use produce from the inn's own vegetable garden, includes hearty minestrone soup; coarse farmhouse pâté with red onion and apricot relish and walnut bread; a choice of burgers (including the very popular Aberdeen Angus steakburger) hand-made from locally sourced meat accompanied by a topping of your choosing; or classic coq au vin. There is a great menu for children too. Enjoy the quiz every Sunday evening.

Open all wk 11-3 5-mdnt (Fri-Sun 11am-1am) **Bar Meals** L served all wk 12-2.30 D served Tue-Sat 7-9.15, Sun 7-8.30 **Restaurant** L served all wk 12-2.30 D served Tue-Sat 7-9.15, Sun 7-8.30 ⊕ PUNCH TAVERNS ◀ Harveys Sussex, Adnams, Old Speckled Hen, Tribute, Guinness ♂ Westons Old Rosie. ♟ 10 **Facilities** Children welcome Children's menu Children's portions Dogs allowed Garden Parking Wi-fi

---

EAST CLANDON   Map 6 TQ05

The Queens Head ♟

The Street GU4 7RY ☎ 01483 222332
e-mail: mark.williams@redmistleisure.co.uk
dir: *4m E of Guildford on A246. Signed*

A haven for ramblers and locals seeking the best local produce, this charming brick-built village pub nestles in the Surrey Hills just a short step from the North Downs Way. Beer is courtesy of the nearby Surrey Hills Brewery, while the food focuses on locally sourced fresh, seasonal produce with meat from a 100-acre working farm. Steak, ale and mushroom pie with chunky chips and roasted vegetables will revive after a winter walk, or share a charcuterie platter, including chorizo and Parma ham, in the tree-shaded garden.

Open all wk noon-3 6-11 (Sat noon-11 Sun noon-9) **Bar Meals** L served Mon-Fri 12-2.30, Sat 12-9.30, Sun 12-8 booking required D served Mon-Thu 6-9, Fri 6-9.30, Sat 12-9.30, Sun 12-8 booking required Av main course £13 **Restaurant** L served Mon-Fri 12-2.30, Sat 12-9.30, Sun 12-8 booking required D served Mon-Thu 6-9, Fri 6-9.30, Sat 12-9.30, Sun 12-8 booking required ⊕ FREE HOUSE ◀ Shere Drop, TEA, Oxford Gold, Spitfire, Doom Bar. ♟ 13 **Facilities** Children welcome Children's menu Children's portions Dogs allowed Garden Parking Wi-fi

---

EFFINGHAM   Map 6 TQ15

The Plough

Orestan Ln KT24 5SW
☎ 01372 458121   📄 01372 458121
dir: *Between Guildford & Leatherhead on A246*

A peaceful retreat on a no-through road in a picturesque village close to Polesden Lacey National Trust property. It was redecorated and recarpeted throughout in 2010, while the exterior saw the addition of a new orchard and herb garden. Regulars enjoy the well-kept ales and freshly prepared food at reasonable prices. The monthly changing menus feature half a dozen starters, a dozen main courses and four specials. Sunday roasts include rib of beef and loin of pork with crackling and apple sauce.

Open all wk 11.30-3 5.30-11 (Sun noon-3 7-10.30) Closed: 25-26 Dec & 31 Dec eve **Bar Meals** L served all wk 12-2.30 D served Mon-Sat 7-10, Sun 7-9 Av main course £11.95 **Restaurant** L served all wk 12-2.30 D served Mon-Sat 7-10, Sun 7-9 ⊕ YOUNG & CO BREWERY PLC ◀ Young's IPA, Special, Winter Warmer, Bombardier, Courage Directors, Tribute. **Facilities** Children welcome Children's menu Children's portions Garden Parking

---

ELSTEAD   Map 6 SU94

The Golden Fleece ♟ NEW

Farnham Rd GU8 6DB ☎ 01252 702349
e-mail: sheilapride@aol.com
dir: *From A3 at Milford follow Elstead signs on B3001. Pub past village green on left*

Situated in the tranquil village of Elstead, surrounded by beautiful countryside, this family-run pub offers a warm and traditional welcome with real log fire and hand-pulled ales. What sets it apart, however, is the extensive and authentic Thai menu that runs alongside more traditional pub classics. The pub also offers a Thai takeaway service during opening hours, and an enclosed beer garden is ideal for families with children.

Open all wk 11.30-3.30 5.30-11.30 (Fri-Sun all day) **Bar Meals** L served Tue-Thu 12-2.30, Fri-Sat 12-10, Sun 12-9 D served Mon-Thu 6-10, Fri-Sat 12-10, Sun 12-9 Av main course £8.50 **Restaurant** L served Tue-Thu 12-2.30, Fri-Sat 12-10, Sun 12-9 D served Mon-Thu 6-10, Fri-Sat 12-10, Sun 12-9 Fixed menu price fr £9.95 Av 3 course à la carte fr £16.95 ⊕ ENTERPRISE INNS ◀ Otter Ale, Shere Drop, Adnams Broadside, Ringwood Fortyniner ♂ Thatchers. ♟ 9 **Facilities** Children welcome Children's menu Children's portions Family room Dogs allowed Garden Parking Wi-fi

---

The Woolpack

The Green, Milford Rd GU8 6HD ☎ 01252 703106
e-mail: info@woolpackelstead.co.uk
dir: *A3 S, take Milford exit, follow signs for Elstead on B3001*

The Woolpack was originally a wool exchange dating back to the 17th century. The surrounding common land attracts ramblers galore, especially at lunchtime. In the carpeted bar, weaving shuttles and other remnants of the wool industry make appealing features, as do the open log fires, low beams, high-backed settles, window seats and spindle-backed chairs. A good range of cask-conditioned beers is offered.

Open all wk noon-3 5.30-11 (Sat-Sun noon-11) ⊕ PUNCH TAVERNS ◀ Greene King Abbot Ale, Hobgoblin, Deuchars, Spitfire, London Pride. **Facilities** Children welcome Children's menu Children's portions Family room Dogs allowed Garden Parking Wi-fi

---

FARNHAM   Map 5 SU84

PICK OF THE PUBS

The Bat & Ball Freehouse ♟

15 Bat & Ball Ln, Boundstone GU10 4SA
☎ 01252 792108
e-mail: info@thebatandball.co.uk
web: www.thebatandball.co.uk
dir: *From A31 Farnham bypass follow signs for Birdworld. Left at Bengal Lounge into School Hill. At top over staggered x-rds into Sandrock Hill Rd. After 0.25m left into Upper Bourne Lane, signed*

Tucked down a lane in a wooded valley south of Farnham, this 150-year-old inn is not that easy to find, but well worth hunting out. Hops for the local breweries in Farnham and Alton were grown in the valley, and originally the hop pickers were paid in the building that eventually became the pub. An enterprising tenant grasped the business opportunity that presented itself, and began to provide the pickers with ale, relieving them of some of their hard earned cash! Very much a community pub, the interior features terracotta floors, oak beams, a roaring fire and plenty of cricketing memorabilia. The lovely garden has a terrace with vine-topped pergola and a children's play fort. Expect six regularly changing cask-conditioned ales, a range of wines and home-cooked food. Starters and light meals might include mushrooms in creamy Welsh rarebit sauce, and a Spanish platter to share. The mains take in rich beef and ale casserole with horseradish dumplings; Calcutta lamb jalfrezi; venison Stroganoff; and roast vegetable moussaka. There's live music on the last Sunday of the month, and a Beer, Cider and Music Festival every June.

Open all day all wk 11-11 (Sun noon-10.30) **Bar Meals** L served Mon-Sat 12-2.15, Sun 12-3 booking required D served Mon-Sat 7-9.30, Sun 6-8.30 booking required ⊕ FREE HOUSE ◀ Young's Bitter, Tongham TEA, Triple fff, Bowmans, Ballards. ♟ 8 **Facilities** Children welcome Children's menu Children's portions Play area Family room Dogs allowed Garden Beer festival Parking Wi-fi

See advert on opposite page

Save on hotels. Book at **theAA.com/hotel**

SURREY 433 **ENGLAND**

The Bat and Ball Freehouse

Bat and Ball Lane, Boundstone, Farnham, Surrey GU10 4SA
www.thebatandball.co.uk

Tel: 01252 792108
E-mail: info@thebatandball.co.uk

The Bat and Ball Freehouse nestles in the bottom of the Bourne valley in Boundstone near Farnham. Over 150 years old, the Pub has a relaxed, rural feel, surrounded by woodland and wildlife, and is the focal point of 5 footpaths which connect to local villages. Customers can eat or drink throughout the Pub, patio area and the large south-facing garden (which backs onto the Bourne stream and has a popular children's play structure). All the food is cooked in-house and this is very much a pub that serves restaurant quality food and not a restaurant that sells beer! The bar area has both a traditional and modern style to it to provide for our differing customer tastes, both young and old, and we have a tempting selection of 6 well-kept Cask Ales.

FARNHAM *continued*

The Spotted Cow at Lower Bourne NEW

Bourne Grove, Lower Bourne GU10 3QT
☎ 01252 726541
e-mail: thespottedcow@btinternet.com
web: www.thespottedcowpub.com
dir: *From Farnham Station left into Approach Rd. Left onto A287, continue onto Vicarage Hill. Left into Bourne Grove.*

Secluded in four acres of woodland shaded gardens, there's ample space to let the kids play whilst you indulge in some of the great TEA beer from nearby Hogs Back brewery and consider the ever-changing menu of tried and tested favourites. Lamb shank, steak and ale pie and beer-battered fish all have a place here, or keep an eye out for seasonal specials or unusual dishes like pan-fried pangasius on sweet potato mash.

Open all wk 12-3 5.30-11 (Sat 12-11 Sun 12-10.30)
Bar Meals L served Mon-Sat 12-2.30 D served Mon-Sat 6-9.15 **Restaurant** L served Mon-Sat 12-2.30, Sun 12-7 D served Mon-Sat 6-9.15 ◀ Timothy Taylor Landlord, Otter, Hogs Back TEA. **Facilities** Children welcome Children's menu Children's portions Play area Dogs allowed Garden Parking

FETCHAM   Map 6 TQ15

The Bell ⬤ NEW

Bell Ln KT22 9ND ☎ 01372 372624
e-mail: bellfetcham@youngs.co.uk
dir: *From A245 in Leatherhead take Waterway Rd (B2122). At rdbt 2nd exit into Guildford Rd (B2122). At mini-rdbt right into Cobham Rd. Straight on at next 2 mini-rdbts. Left into School Lane, left into Bell Lane*

The striking 1930s building in the heart of Fetcham village in the pretty Mole Valley has been stylishly spruced up by Young's Brewery and is one of the 'flagship' dining pubs. Expect a smart terrace for alfresco drinking and dining, a light and airy wood-panelled restaurant, and a comfortable bar, replete with leather sofas and chairs, where tip-top Young's and Wells ales are offered. Using local and seasonal produce, menus are

a cut above the norm, with the likes of duck confit with red onion marmalade, sea bass with spinach and chive velouté, and sweet potato curry on the main menu. Classic bar food, Sunday roasts and an autumn beer festival complete the picture.

Open all day all wk **Bar Meals** Av main course £10 food served all day **Restaurant** Av 3 course à la carte fr £25-£30 food served all day ⬤ YOUNG'S ◀ Young's, Young's Special, Wells Bombardier, Guest ale. ⬤ 22
Facilities Children welcome Children's portions Dogs allowed Garden Beer festival Parking Wi-fi

FOREST GREEN   Map 6 TQ14

PICK OF THE PUBS

The Parrot Inn ⬤

RH5 5RZ ☎ 01306 621339   ⬛ 01306 621255
e-mail: drinks@theparrot.co.uk
dir: *B2126 from A29 at Ockley, signed Forest Green*

With its oak beams and huge fire, this attractive 17th-century building is in many ways the archetypal English inn, right down to its location opposite the village green and cricket pitch. But in addition to the expected features, it has its own butchery, bakery, charcuterie and farm shop called The Butcher's Hall and Country Grocer. The owners have a farm just a couple of miles away where they raise shorthorn cattle, Middle White pigs, Dorset sheep and Black Rock hens. The pub makes its own sausages, preserves and chutneys, and much of the menu uses these home-grown or home-made products. The restaurant is eclectic – a bit 'churchy', yet modern, inviting and comforting. Here, dishes blend modern, traditional and European. Not to be forgotten is a good range of real ales, which can be enjoyed in the bar or one of the gardens or on the terrace.

Open all day all wk **Bar Meals** L served Mon-Sat 12-3, Sun 12-5 D served Mon-Sat 6-10 Av main course £12.50 **Restaurant** L served Mon-Sat 12-3, Sun 12-5 booking required D served Mon-Sat 6-10 booking required Av 3 course à la carte fr £22.50 ⬤ FREE HOUSE ◀ Ringwood Best, Young's PA, Timothy Taylor Landlord, Ringwood Old Thumper, Dorking Brewery DB1. ⬤ 14 **Facilities** Dogs allowed Garden Parking Wi-fi

GUILDFORD   Map 6 SU94

The Boatman ⬤ NEW

Millbrook GU1 3XJ ☎ 01483 568024
e-mail: contact@boatman-guildford.co.uk
web: www.boatman-guildford.co.uk
dir: *From Guildford take A281 towards Shalford. Pub on right*

Set on the banks of the River Wey, with views across the river to parkland, it's hard to believe this pub is only half a mile from Guildford's bustling shops. Extensive terraced seating leads down to the river where you can enjoy a pint of Otter Bitter or one of the 14 wines by the glass, or there's a covered garden area if the weather is being unkind. Food served throughout the day is freshly prepared, and centres on the usual pub favourites: salmon and dill fishcakes; Mediterranean chicken supreme; and burgers, chips and salad. The Boatman's platter features a selection of meats, cheese, pickles, salad and crusty bread.

Open all wk 12-11 (Sun 12-10.30) **Bar Meals** L served Mon-Sat 12-9.30, Sun 12-8 D served Mon-Sat 12-9.30, Sun 12-8 **Restaurant** L served Mon-Sat 12-9.30, Sun 12-8 D served Mon-Sat 12-9.30, Sun 12-8 ⬤ FREE HOUSE ◀ Otter Bitter, Hogs Back TEA. ⬤ 14 **Facilities** Children welcome Children's menu Garden Parking Wi-fi

The Keystone ⬤

3 Portsmouth Rd GU2 4BL ☎ 01483 575089
e-mail: drink@thekeystone.co.uk
web: www.thekeystone.co.uk
dir: *From Guildford rail station turn right. Cross 2nd pedestrian crossing, follow road downhill, past Savills Estate Agents. Pub 200yds on left*

Just off the bottom of Guildford's bustling High Street, this easy-going and unpretentious pub features squashy leather sofas, pub art and a secluded outdoor terrace. Live music and an annual July cider festival are amongst the things to look out for. Along with real ales and cider,

Save on hotels. Book at **theAA.com/hotel**

SURREY 435 **ENGLAND**

expect fairly priced, modern pub food including salads, steaks and award-winning pies. Main course options range from sweet potato, chick pea and red pepper curry to lime and coriander chicken breast with wild rice.

Open all day all wk noon–11 (Fri-Sat noon-mdnt Sun noon-5) Closed: 25-26 Dec, 1 Jan **Bar Meals** L served all wk 12-3 D served Mon-Sat 6-9 Av main course £8 ⊕ PUNCH TAVERNS ◀ 6X, Alton's, Pride fff, Guest ales Ö Westons Organic, Addlestones. ♟ 10 **Facilities** Children welcome Children's menu Children's portions Garden Beer festival

---

HASCOMBE   Map 6 TQ03

The White Horse ♟

The Street GU8 4JA ☎ **01483 208258** ▤ **01483 208200**
e-mail: pub@whitehorsehascombe.co.uk
dir: *From Godalming take B2130. Pub on left 0.5m after Hascombe*

Surrounded by picturesque walking country and a short drive from Winkworth Arboretum, this 16th-century building is unmissable in summer thanks to its flower-filled garden. Its pristine, traditional interior, the fine beers, a popular family room and ample outdoor seating are some of the selling points; another is the high standard of food – all meat is from organic pedigree breeds. A meal might embrace fritto misto of seafood with aïoli and lemon; roast Hascombe pheasant with root vegetables; and apple and oatmeal crumble with custard.

Open all day all wk **Bar Meals** food served all day **Restaurant** food served all day ⊕ PUNCH TAVERNS ◀ Harveys, Tribute, Altons Pride, Doom Bar, Adnams Best Bitter, Hogs Back TEA, Guest ales Ö Old Rosie, Green Goblin, Kopparberg Pear, Westons Organic. ♟ 11 **Facilities** Children welcome Children's menu Children's portions Play area Family room Dogs allowed Garden Parking Wi-fi

---

HASLEMERE   Map 6 SU93

The Wheatsheaf Inn ★★★ INN

Grayswood Rd, Grayswood GU27 2DE
☎ **01428 644440** ▤ **01428 641285**
e-mail: thewheatsheaf@aol.com
dir: *Exit A3 at Milford, A286 to Haslemere. Grayswood approx 7.5m N*

A stunning display of hanging baskets takes the eye at this friendly, award-winning village inn set in the tranquil Surrey Hills; the magnificent viewpoint at Black Down, beloved of Alfred, Lord Tennyson, is nearby. You may be tempted to book B&B here by this or by the inviting menus of classics and specials – warmed Brie with toasted almonds or deep-fried whitebait; followed by lambs' liver and bacon with red wine gravy; chicken tikka masala; prawn, smoked salmon and dill fusilli before perhaps relaxing with Sharp's Doom Bar beer or Aspall cider in the peaceful garden.

Open all wk 11-3 6-11 (Sun noon-3 7-10.30)
Bar Meals L served all wk 12-2 booking required D served all wk 7-9.45 booking required **Restaurant** L served all wk 12-2 booking required D served all wk 7-9.45 booking required ⊕ FREE HOUSE ◀ London Pride, Sharp's Doom Bar, Abbot Ale Hip Hop Ö Aspall. **Facilities** Children welcome Children's menu Children's portions Dogs allowed Garden Parking Wi-fi **Rooms** 7

LEIGH   Map 6 TQ24

The Plough ♟

Church Rd RH2 8NJ ☎ **01306 611348** ▤ **01306 611299**
e-mail: sarah@theploughleigh.wanadoo.co.uk
dir: *Telephone for directions*

On the village green opposite the church, this white-painted, featherboarded, family-run country pub has low beams (helpfully padded) in the lounge bar that date from the late 15th century. The public bar, where you can play traditional pub games and enjoy mulled wine during the winter, is positively new by comparison, being only 111 years old. Run by the same landlady for 20 years, it offers home cooked food such as pie of the day, hot pot, and bacon and onion roly-poly. A popular destination for walkers.

Open all wk 11-11 (Sun noon-11) **Bar Meals** Av main course £9.50 food served all day **Restaurant** Av 3 course à la carte fr £22.50 food served all day ⊕ HALL & WOODHOUSE ◀ Badger Best, Tanglefoot, Sussex Bitter. ♟ 11 **Facilities** Children welcome Children's menu Children's portions Dogs allowed Garden Parking Wi-fi

---

The Seven Stars ♟ NEW

Bunce Common Rd, Dawes Green RH2 8NP
☎ **01306 611254**
e-mail: davepellen@aol.com
web: www.thesevenstarsleigh.co.uk
dir: *S of A25 (Dorking to Reigate road)*

A 17th-century tavern tucked away in the rural southern reaches of the Mole Valley. Plenty of parking, two gardens and a secluded patio area characterise the exterior. Inside it prides itself on a worldly ambience created by an absence of music and the exclusion of under-14s; the buzz of friendly chatter is the only background noise. Home-smoked products such as ribs or salmon often appear on the specials board, along with the likes of John Dory fillet on a creamy prawn, coconut and coriander risotto.

Open all wk 12-3 5.30-11 (Sun 12-8) Closed: 25-26 Dec, 1 Jan **Bar Meals** L served Mon-Sat 12-3, Sun 12-4 booking required D served Mon-Thu 6-9, Fri-Sat 6.30-9.30 booking required Av main course £10.95 **Restaurant** L served Mon-Sat 12-3, Sun 12-4 booking required D served Mon-Thu 6-9, Fri-Sat 6.30-9.30 booking required ⊕ PUNCH TAVERNS ◀ Young's Ordinary, Old Speckled Hen, Fuller's London Pride. ♟ 12 **Facilities** Dogs allowed Garden Parking

See advert on page 436

LINGFIELD   Map 6 TQ34
PICK OF THE PUBS

Hare and Hounds

Common Rd RH7 6BZ ☎ **01342 832351**
e-mail: info@hareandhoundspublichouse.co.uk
dir: *From A22 follow signs for Lingfield Racecourse into Common Rd*

Just a short drive from Lingfield Park racecourse, this charming 18th-century country pub has a welcoming atmosphere for propping up the bar with a pint of real ale or cider or a glass of wine from the carefully considered list, sitting by the fire, or relaxing in the candlelit snug. The pub has a good name for its modern and classic food, the owners having worked in the UK and France and developed some great seasonal recipes. Using local produce where possible, the menu may start with smoked chicken liver parfait, toasted brioche and fig jam, or deep-fried squid, tartare mousseline, chickpea and pickled cauliflower, followed by pan-fried calves' liver with a bacon crust, mashed potato and parsley dressing, or slow-cooked cod with black olive oil, potato croquette and caramelised turnips. Desserts might include black cherry and vanilla trifle; sticky toffee pudding with vanilla ice cream; and baked lemon curd, warm buttered cake and raspberry coulis. On a sunny day, the split-level decked garden is a good spot for a drink.

Open all day Closed: 1-5 Jan, Sun eve
Bar Meals L served Mon-Sat 12-2.30, Sun 12-3 D served Mon-Sat 7-9.30 **Restaurant** L served Mon-Sat 12-2.30, Sun 12-3 D served Mon-Sat 7-9.30 ⊕ PUNCH TAVERNS ◀ Greene King IPA, Flowers Original, Guinness, London Pride, Harvey Sussex Ö Stowford Press. **Facilities** Children welcome Children's portions Dogs allowed Garden Parking

THE SEVEN STARS

Bunce Common Road, Dawes Green, Leigh, Reigate, Surrey RH2 8NP   *Tel: 01306 611254*
www.thesevenstarsleigh.co.uk

Located in the Southern reaches of the Mole Valley between the old Market Towns of Reigate and Dorking can be found The Seven Stars, a truly traditional inn dating back to early 1600. The Seven Stars GRADE II listed building can be found in a tiny hamlet called Dawes Green. 'Dawes Green' lies within The Seven Stars boundary and is the grassed area of land at the front which has picnic tables set aside for drinkers. To the side of the pub can be found a separate garden and patio which is available for drinkers and diners during the summer months.

Children are very welcome during the warmer months when food is served outside but unfortunately cannot be accommodated inside. The Premises Licence allowing only young adults over the age of fourteen to dine with their parents indeed indicates the real meaning of the word 'traditional' pub.

The Seven Stars concentrates on serving quality beer and food, which is freshly prepared by a team of chefs and home smoked meat and fish can often be found on the Specials Board. Music, machines and TV will not be found all the time Dave and Rebecca are at the helm and strongly feel that customers need no other entertainment than the pub itself. Dogs are welcome in the Bar.

LONG DITTON
Map 6 TQ16

The Ditton ☕

64 Ditton Hill Rd KT6 5JD ☎ 020 8339 0785
e-mail: goodfood@theditton.co.uk
dir: *Telephone for directions*

Whilst at heart this rambling village pub remains a community local with beers from the likes of Sharp's and Young's, the main ambience leans towards a contemporary dining pub where families are particularly welcome. Expect pub classics such as home-made puff pastry pie of the day, and sweet chilli and soy chicken, noodles and stir-fry vegetables. Also here is Long's Brasserie offering dishes like fillet of sea bass on fragrant Thai seafood and potato broth. There is a large enclosed beer garden with barbecues in the summer.

Open all day all wk noon–11 **Bar Meals** L served all wk 12-9 D served all wk 12-9 food served all day **Restaurant** L served Wed-Sun 12-9 booking required D served Wed-Sat 12-9 booking required ⊕ ENTERPRISE INNS ◀ Bombardier, Young's, Tanglefoot, Sharp's Doom Bar. ☕ 10 **Facilities** Children welcome Children's menu Children's portions Play area Dogs allowed Garden Parking Wi-fi

MICKLEHAM
Map 6 TQ15

King William IV ☕

Byttom Hill RH5 6EL ☎ 01372 372590
dir: *From M25 junct 9, A24 signed to Dorking, pub just before Mickleham*

The King Billy, built in 1790 for local estate workers, has a panelled snug and larger back bar with an open fire, cast-iron tables and grandfather clock. The terraced garden is ideal for summer socialising and offers panoramic views of the Mole Valley, where you might earlier have been walking. Hogs Back TEA and Shere Drop are in the bar, with food such as tournedos Rossini; Thai-spiced free-range chicken; and Scottish fillet steak.

Open 11.30-3, 6-11 (Sun 12-4, 7-10.30) Closed: 25 Dec, Sun, Mon eve **Bar Meals** L served 12-2 D served 7-9 Av main course £12 **Restaurant** L served 12-2 D served 7-9 Fixed menu price fr £20 Av 3 course à la carte fr £23 ⊕ FREE HOUSE ◀ Hogs Back TEA, Shere Drop ♂ Stowford Press. ☕ 11 **Facilities** Children welcome Children's portions Garden Parking

The Running Horses ☕

Old London Rd RH5 6DU
☎ 01372 372279 📠 01372 363004
e-mail: info@therunninghorses.co.uk
dir: *1.5m from M25 junct 9. Off A24 between Leatherhead & Dorking*

Set amid lovely National Trust countryside near the foot of Box Hill, The Running Horses has been welcoming travellers for more than 400 years. The interior still resonates with history, right down to the bare beams and real fires, and a history of sheltering highwaymen. Lunchtime brings chunky sandwiches and innovative

dishes like herb-stuffed beef tomato with crusted pumpkin wedges. Restaurant choices are also available on the bar and might include game casserole with herb dumplings, and black bream fillet on crab and parsley risotto.

Open all day all wk 11.30-11 (Sun noon-10.30) Closed: 25-26 Dec, 31 Dec-1 Jan eve **Bar Meals** L served Mon-Fri 12-2.30, Sat-Sun 12-3 D served Mon-Sat 7-9.30, Sun 6.30-9 Av main course £9 **Restaurant** L served Mon-Fri 12-2.30, Sat-Sun 12-3 booking required D served Mon-Sat 7-9.30, Sun 6.30-9 booking required Av 3 course à la carte fr £30 ⊕ FREE HOUSE ◀ Fuller's London Pride, Young's Bitter, HSB, Chiswick ♂ Aspall. ☕ 9 **Facilities** Children welcome Children's portions Dogs allowed Garden Wi-fi

NEWDIGATE
Map 6 TQ14

The Surrey Oaks

Parkgate Rd RH5 5DZ
☎ 01306 631200 📠 01306 631200
e-mail: ken@surreyoaks.co.uk
dir: *From A24 follow signs to Newdigate, at T-junct turn left, pub 1m on left*

Picturesque oak-beamed pub located one mile outside the village of Newdigate. Parts of the building date back to 1570, and it became an inn around the middle of the 19th century. There are two bars, one with an inglenook fireplace, as well as a restaurant area, patio and beer garden with boules pitch. The great selection of beers is mainly from micro-breweries. A typical specials board features Barnsley lamb chop with minted gravy, or grilled plaice with parsley butter. This family-friendly pub also has a children's menu and play area, plus a skittle alley and dart board in the barn at the rear. Beer festivals are held at Whitsun and August Bank Holiday.

Open all wk 11.30-2.30 5.30-11 (Sat 11.30-3 6-11 Sun noon-10.30) **Bar Meals** L served Mon-Sat 12-2, Sun 12-2.30 D served Tue-Sat 6.30-9.30 Av main course £9 **Restaurant** L served Mon-Sat 12-2, Sun 12-2.30 D served Tue-Sat 6.30-9.30 Av 3 course à la carte fr £18 ⊕ ADMIRAL TAVERNS ◀ Harveys Sussex Best, Surrey Hills Ranmore Ale, rotating guest ales ♂ Moles Black Rat, Westons Country Perry. **Facilities** Children welcome Children's menu Children's portions Play area Dogs allowed Garden Beer festival Parking Wi-fi

OCKHAM
Map 6 TQ05

The Black Swan

Old Ln KT11 1NG ☎ 01932 862364
e-mail: enquiries@blackswanockham.com
dir: *M25 junct 10, A3 towards Guildford. Approx 2m turn left to Ockham*

Pubs with this name tend to get called the Mucky Duck, but after Geronimo Inns bought this one locals became more respectful. Inside are rough sawn timbers, wooden rafters, unusual antique furnishings, great beers and wine, and good food at affordable prices. Using the best of local produce, dishes include Dexter rump or sirloin steak with hand-cut chips, field mushroom and

peppercorn sauce; prawn and salmon penne pasta with white wine sauce; and aubergine and vegetable stack with tomato sauce. Change of hands.

Open all day all wk ⊕ FREE HOUSE ◀ Shere Drop, Doom Bar, Bitburger, Guinness, Hogs Back TEA ♂ Aspall. **Facilities** Children welcome Children's menu Children's portions Dogs allowed Garden Parking Wi-fi

OCKLEY
Map 6 TQ14

PICK OF THE PUBS

Bryce's at The Old School House ⊛ ☕

RH5 5TH ☎ 01306 627430 📠 01306 628274
e-mail: fish@bryces.co.uk
web: www.bryces.co.uk
dir: *8m S of Dorking on A29*

Formerly a boarding school, this Grade II listed building dates back to 1750 and was bought by Bill Bryce nearly 20 years ago. He's passionate about fresh fish and offers a huge range, despite the location in rural Surrey. It's more of a restaurant than a pub, although there is a bar with its own interesting menu (cullen skink and salmon, prawn and Avruga linguini).The dishes on the restaurant menu are nearly all fish, with some non-fish daily specials. Options to start include chilli salted soft shell crab with chilli and passionfruit sauce; Bryce's langoustine bisque; and warm salad of confit duck. Main course examples are sea bass fillets, chive potato cake and baby artichokes; pan-fried south coast lemon sole meunière; and roast supreme of Scottish halibut with garlic mash. Look to the blackboard for the home-made desserts. You can even take home fish and chips.

Open noon-3 6-11 Closed: 25-26 Dec, 1 Jan, (Sun pm Nov, Jan-Feb) **Bar Meals** L served all wk 12-2.30 D served all wk 6-9.30 Av main course £15 **Restaurant** L served all wk 12-2.30 D served all wk 7-9.30 Fixed menu price fr £10 Av 3 course à la carte fr £34 ⊕ FREE HOUSE ◀ London Pride, Horsham Bitter, John Smith's Smooth. ☕ 15 **Facilities** Children welcome Children's portions Dogs allowed Parking

OCKLEY continued

The Kings Arms Inn ?

Stane St RH5 5TS ☎ **01306 711224**
e-mail: enquiries@thekingsarmsockley.co.uk
dir: From M25 junct 9 take A24 through Dorking towards
Horsham, A29 to Ockley

Welcoming log fires, a priest hole, a friendly ghost and an
award-winning garden are just a few charms of this
heavily-beamed 16th-century inn. Set in the picturesque
village of Ockley and overlooked by the tower of Leith Hill,
it's an ideal setting in which to enjoy a pint and home-
cooked food prepared by new chef-proprietor David
Wickenden. Choices include crusty baguette sandwiches;
chargrilled steaks; and more adventurous dishes such as
Cornish crab ravioli followed by butter-roasted chicken
with pumpkin and sage mash and mushroom and
Parmesan sauce.

Open all wk noon-2.30 5-11 **Bar Meals** L served all wk
12-2.30 D served all wk 6.30-9.30 Av main course £11
Restaurant L served all wk 12-2.30 D served all wk
6.30-9.30 Fixed menu price fr £12 Av 3 course à la carte
fr £25 ⊕ CROSSOAK INNS ◀ Horsham Best, Doom Bar,
TEA ♂ Stowford Press. ♥ 10 **Facilities** Children
welcome Children's menu Children's portions Dogs
allowed Garden Parking

| RIPLEY | Map 6 TQ05 |

PICK OF THE PUBS

The Talbot Inn ★★★★ INN ◉ ?

High St GU23 6BB
☎ **01483 225188** 📠 **01483 211332**
e-mail: thetalbot@bespokehotels.com
dir: Telephone for directions

One of England's finest 15th-century coaching inns,
The Talbot is said to have provided the stage for Lord
Nelson and Lady Hamilton's love affair in 1798.
Recently refurbished, but retaining its impressive
historic features, the cosy beamed bar boasts open
fires and real ales. In contrast, the chic dining room
has a copper ceiling and modern glass conservatory
extension. Good food blends pub classics like fish and
chips or local sausages and mash with more
innovative dishes like venison loin with chestnut purée
and spiced pears, or brill paupiettes with creamed
leeks and shellfish sauce. Finish with hot apple and
rhubarb crumble and crème Anglaise. The 39 stylish
bedrooms are smart and contemporary, ranging from
beamed rooms in the inn to new-build rooms
overlooking the garden. The pub is conveniently
positioned just 20 minutes from Heathrow and Gatwick
International airports.

Open all day all wk noon-11 (Sun noon-10) **Bar Meals**
booking required food served all day **Restaurant** booking
required food served all day ⊕ BESPOKE HOTELS ◀ Shere
Drop, IPA, Abbot Ale ♂ Stowford Press. ♥ 27 **Facilities**
Children welcome Children's menu Children's portions Dogs
allowed Garden Parking Wi-fi **Rooms** 39

| SOUTH GODSTONE | Map 6 TQ34 |

Fox & Hounds

Tilburstow Hill Rd RH9 8LY ☎ **01342 893474**
dir: 4m from M25 junct 6

A large inglenook in the restaurant and a real fire in the
lower bar add to the old world charm of this building,
which dates in part to 1368 and has been a pub since
1601. Food-wise there's plenty to choose from, including
a starter of mussels cooked with garlic, cream and white
wine; and mains ranging from home-cooked ham with
egg and chips to spicy three bean bake and fresh local
meat cooked on the grill. Other imaginative choices
include specials like swordfish steak or chicken stuffed
with Brie and dates. Outside, the large garden offers
rural views.

Open all wk noon-3 6-11 (Fri-Sun noon-11pm)
Bar Meals L served Mon-Thu 12-3, Fri-Sun all day
D served Mon-Thu 6-9, Fri-Sun all day
Restaurant L served Mon-Thu 12-3, Fri-Sun all day
D served Mon-Thu 6-9, Fri-Sun all day ⊕ GREENE KING
◀ All Greene King. **Facilities** Children welcome
Children's menu Dogs allowed Garden Parking

| WEST END | Map 6 SU96 |

PICK OF THE PUBS

The Inn @ West End ?

See Pick of the Pubs on opposite page

| WEST HORSLEY | Map 6 TQ05 |

PICK OF THE PUBS

The King William IV ?

83 The Street KT24 6BG
☎ **01483 282318** 📠 **01483 282318**
e-mail: kingbilly4th@aol.com
dir: On The Street off A246 (Leatherhead to Guildford)

Situated in a leafy Surrey village, this popular gastro-
pub was named in honour of the monarch who relaxed
England's brewing laws. The business was started by a
miller, Edmund Collins, who knocked two cottages
together to create an alehouse. Many of the original
Georgian features have been preserved, but there is
also an airy conservatory restaurant and a large
garden and terrace to the rear, with colourful tubs and
floral baskets. It's popular with walkers as it is close to
the Royal Horticultural Society's Wisley Gardens and
many other places of interest. Local beers include
Shere Drop and Courage Directors, plus a guest ale of
the month, and a dozen wines are offered by the glass.
The specials boards are hand written and the well-
priced menu ranges from sandwiches, salads, burgers
and jacket potatoes, to home-made steak and kidney
pie, and line-caught haddock in beer batter with
mushy peas and chips. Leave room for cheesecake to
finish.

Open all day all wk 11.30am-mdnt (Sun noon-10.30)
Bar Meals L served all wk 12-3 D served Mon-Fri 6-9,
Sat all day Av main course £8.95 **Restaurant** L served
all wk 12-3 D served Mon-Fri 6-9, Sat all day
⊕ ENTERPRISE INNS ◀ Shere Drop, Courage Best,
Courage Directors, Guest ales. ♥ 12 **Facilities** Children
welcome Children's menu Children's portions Family
room Dogs allowed Garden Parking Wi-fi

| WITLEY | Map 6 SU93 |

The White Hart ?

Petworth Rd GU8 5PH ☎ **01428 683695**
e-mail: sarawhitehart@hotmail.co.uk
dir: From A3 follow signs to Milford, then A283 towards
Petworth. Pub 2m on left

This delightfully warm and welcoming pub, now under
new ownership, was built in 1380 as a hunting lodge for
Richard II; the white hart became his personal emblem.
Licensed since 1700, the three log fires, oak beams,
Young's ales and hearty portions of good value home-
cooked food continue to attract. Soups, sandwiches,
salads and pastas make a light lunch; steak and kidney
pudding, venison casserole, and sausages and mash are
some of the main course options. Said to be haunted,
George Eliot used the pub to write some of her best-
selling books.

Open 11.30-3 5.30-11 (Fri-Sat 11.30am-11pm) Closed:
Sun eve **Bar Meals** L served Mon-Sat 12-2.30, Sun 12-3
D served Tue-Sat 6-9 **Restaurant** L served Mon-Sat
12-2.30, Sun 12-3 D served Tue-Sat 6-9 ⊕ YOUNG'S
◀ Young's Bitter, Young's Special, Guinness ♂ Stowford
Press. ♥ 10 **Facilities** Children welcome Children's menu
Children's portions Play area Dogs allowed Garden
Parking Wi-fi

PICK OF THE PUBS

The Inn @ West End 🍷

WEST END   Map 6 SU96

42 Guildford Rd GU24 9PW
☎ **01276 858652**
e-mail: greatfood@the-inn.co.uk
web: www.the-inn.co.uk
dir: On A322 towards Guildford. 3m from M3 junct 3, just beyond Gordon Boys rdbt

The people of Surrey certainly know a good dining pub, as several years of county-wide awards testify. But this doesn't preclude anyone from simply enjoying a pint of Timothy Taylor Landlord or Fuller's London Pride with the newspaper in the bar, or a fine evening on the clematis-hung terrace overlooking the garden and boules pitch. In their eleven years here, Gerry and Ann Price have created an establishment that out-manoeuvres many a competitor with events like fish and game cooking presentations and wine/food-matching evenings. In that regard, their guests in 2010 included eminent winemakers from New Zealand, Portugal and Spain.

The modern interior is open plan, with wooden floors, yellow walls, tasteful check fabrics, crisp linen-clothed tables and an open fire. The kitchen makes good use of home-grown herbs and vegetables and other locally sourced ingredients, game shot by Gerry himself, and fresh fish collected in the pub's own chiller van from whichever port it is freshest and best.

While the accomplished kitchen team guarantees no shortage of ideas for new dishes, they make sure old favourites don't fall off the seasonal menus, so expect typical mains of braised brisket of beef, caramelised onions and balsamic mushroom; pan-fried rib of English veal with brandy and stock cream; a selection of British fish served with tomato and dill risotto and poached duck egg; pan-roasted loin and slow-cooked haunch of wild hare with chocolate and juniper sauce; and poached egg on celeriac with mushroom hash and spiced aubergine.

Gerry's knowledge of wines is not only reflected in the contents of his extensive cellar, but in the new wine shop, where you can also buy whiskies, Cognacs and grappa, as well as decanters and giftware.

Open all wk noon-3, 5-11 (Sat noon-11, Sun noon-10.30) **Bar Meals** L served all wk 12-2.30 D served all wk 6-9.30 Av main course £17 **Restaurant** L served all wk 12-2.30 booking required D served all wk 6-9.30 booking required Fixed menu price fr £18.75 Av 3 course à la carte fr £30 ⊕ ENTERPRISE INNS ◧ Timothy Taylor Landlord, Fuller's London Pride, Exmoor. 🍷 15 **Facilities** Dogs allowed Garden Parking Wi-fi

SUSSEX, EAST

ALCISTON   Map 6 TQ50

PICK OF THE PUBS

Rose Cottage Inn ▼

BN26 6UW ☎ 01323 870377 📠 **01323 871440**
e-mail: ian@alciston.freeserve.co.uk
dir: Off A27 between Eastbourne & Lewes

Expect a warm welcome at this traditional Sussex pub, complete with roses round the door, in the village of Alciston in the heart of the South Downs National Park. Ramblers will find it a good base for long walks in unspoilt countryside, especially along the old traffic-free coach road to the south. The inn has been in the same family for over 40 years, and is well known for its good, home-cooked meats, poultry and game, served in rambling dining rooms, in the bar or in the patio garden. Try home-cooked honey-roast ham with poached eggs and chips, Sussex recipe pork sausages with mash and gravy or a tempting ploughman's. From the choices on the restaurant menu you might opt for pan-fried escalope of local free-range pork with a blue cheese sauce; or roasted breast of free-range chicken with spinach, mushrooms and bacon wrapped in pancetta with red wine sauce.

Open all wk 11.30-3 6.30-11 Closed: 25-26 Dec
Bar Meals L served all wk 12-2 D served all wk 7-9.30
Av main course £10 **Restaurant** L served all wk 12-2
D served all wk 7-9.30 booking required Av 3 course à
la carte fr £19.50 ⊕ FREE HOUSE ◀ Harveys Best, Dark
Star ⌀ Biddenden. ▼ 8 **Facilities** Dogs allowed Garden
Parking

ALFRISTON   Map 6 TQ50

George Inn

High St BN26 5SY ☎ 01323 870319
e-mail: info@thegeorge-alfriston.com
dir: Telephone for directions

Splendid 14th-century, Grade II listed flint and half-timbered inn set in a magical South Downs village. The George boasts heavy oak beams, an ancient inglenook fireplace and a network of smugglers' tunnels leading from its cellars. The team of three chefs create delights such as rustic boards to share; potted crab with gremolata butter; game pâté with chestnuts and cranberry; braised lamb shank in spiced red wine, root vegetables and mash; linguine with mussels, king prawns, chilli and garlic in a white wine and cream sauce; and Sardinian spiced vegetable casserole.

Open all day all wk Closed: 25-26 Dec **Bar Meals** food
served all day **Restaurant** booking required Av 3 course à
la carte fr £24 food served all day ⊕ GREENE KING
◀ Greene King IPA, Abbot Ale, 2 guests.
Facilities Children welcome Children's menu Children's
portions Dogs allowed Garden Wi-fi

ASHBURNHAM PLACE   Map 6 TQ61

Ash Tree Inn

Brownbread St TN33 9NX ☎ 01424 892104
dir: From Eastbourne take A271 at Boreham Bridge
towards Battle. Next left, follow pub signs

The Ash Tree is a 400-year old pub with four fireplaces (two of them inglenooks), exposed beams and a friendly local atmosphere. With a choice of real ales and ciders, bar food includes ploughman's, salads and sandwiches, while the restaurant serves steaks, local sausages and ham, and dishes such as home-made chicken and mushroom pie, mushroom and bacon tagliatelle, and beer-battered haddock. Daily specials chalked on the blackboard add to the choice, and there's always a roast on Sundays.

Open noon-4 7-11 (Sat-Sun 11.30am-mdnt) Closed: Mon
Bar Meals L served Tue-Sun 12-3 booking required
D served Tue-Sat 7-9 booking required
Restaurant L served Tue-Sun 12-3 booking required
D served Tue-Sat 7-9 booking required ⊕ FREE HOUSE
◀ Harveys Best, Guest ales ⌀ Stowford Press.
Facilities Children welcome Children's portions Dogs
allowed Garden Parking

BERWICK   Map 6 TQ50

PICK OF THE PUBS

The Cricketers Arms ▼

BN26 6SP ☎ 01323 870469 📠 **01323 871411**
e-mail: pbthecricketers@aol.com
dir: Off A27 between Polegate & Lewes, follow signs for
Berwick Church

Nestling below the South Downs, this Grade II listed flintstone pub sits in beautiful cottage gardens close to many popular walks, including the South Downs Way running along the crest of the chalk scarp to the south. Originally, in the 16th century, it was two farmworkers' cottages, then it became an alehouse for 200 years, until around 50 years ago Harveys of Lewes, Sussex's oldest brewery, bought it and turned it into a 'proper' pub. Three beamed, music-free rooms with stone floors and open fires are simply furnished with old pine furniture. Home-made food includes starters such as smoked mackerel and apple pâté, and chicken goujons with sweet chilli dip. Main courses include steak and Harveys ale pie, and hunter's chicken with crispy bacon. Nearby is Charleston Farmhouse, the country rendezvous of the London writers, painters and intellectuals known as the Bloomsbury Group, and scene of an annual literary festival.

Open all wk Closed: 25 Dec **Bar Meals** L served all wk
12-2.15 (Etr-Sep 12-9) booking required D served all
wk 6-9 (Etr-Sep 12-9) booking required Av main course
£9.95 food served all day ⊕ HARVEYS OF LEWES
◀ Harveys Best Bitter, Pale, Armada ⌀ Thatchers.
▼ 12 **Facilities** Children welcome Children's portions
Family room Dogs allowed Garden Parking

BLACKBOYS   Map 6 TQ52

The Blackboys Inn ▼

Lewes Rd TN22 5LG ☎ 01825 890283 📠 **01825 890283**
e-mail: blackboys-inn@btconnect.com
dir: From A22 at Uckfield take B2102 towards Cross in
Hand. Or from A267 at Esso service station in Cross in
Hand take B2102 towards Uckfield. Village in 1.5m at
junct of B2102 & B2192

Fourteenth century, part-weatherboarded and architecturally very Sussex, this pub was once a favourite with local charcoal-burners, or blackboys, whose soot-caked skin can just about be imagined. Today's well-scrubbed visitors enjoy beers from Harveys of Lewes, vegetables from the garden, game from local shoots, and fish from Rye and Hastings. Pan-fried halibut with prawn, crab and brandy cream sauce, and fillet steak, mushrooms and onions are typical. Outside are rambling grounds and an orchard.

Open all day all wk noon-mdnt **Bar Meals** L served Mon-Fri 12-3, Sat 12-10, Sun 12-9 D served Sun-Mon 6-9,
Tue-Sat 6-10 **Restaurant** L served Mon-Fri 12-3, Sat
12-10, Sun 12-9 D served Sun-Mon 6-9, Tue-Sat 6-10
⊕ HARVEYS OF LEWES ◀ Harveys Sussex Best Bitter,
Sussex Hadlow, Sussex XXXX Old Ale, seasonal. ▼ 15
Facilities Children welcome Children's portions Dogs
allowed Garden Parking Wi-fi

BRIGHTON & HOVE   Map 6 TQ30

The Basketmakers Arms

12 Gloucester Rd BN1 4AD
☎ 01273 689006 📠 **01273 682300**
e-mail: bluedowd@hotmail.co.uk
dir: From Brighton station main entrance 1st left
(Gloucester Rd). Pub on right at bottom of hill

This Victorian corner pub in the North Laine area of the city has been run with pride by the same landlord for nearly 25 years. Peter Dowd rings the changes with eight real ales, around 100 malt whiskies and large selections of vodka, gin, and bourbon. Menus too are all cooked in-house, prepared from locally sourced produce. Fish is bought daily straight from the local fishermen, so specials may include a seafood platter with calamari, tiger prawns, cod goujons and mussels accompanied by a full salad.

Open all day all wk 11-11 (Fri-Sat 11am-mdnt Sun noon-
11) **Bar Meals** L served Mon-Fri 12-8.30, Sat 12-7, Sun
12-6 D served Mon-Fri 12-8.30, Sat 12-7, Sun 12-6 Av
main course £8.50 food served all day ⊕ FULLER'S
BREWERY ◀ Gales HSB, London Pride, ESB, Discovery,
Bengal Lancer, Seafarers, Guest ales. **Facilities** Children
welcome Dogs allowed

Save on hotels. Book at theAA.com/hotel

SUSSEX, EAST 441 ENGLAND

The Chimney House ♥

28 Upper Hamilton Rd BN1 5DF ☎ **01273 556708**
e-mail: info@chimneyhousebrighton.co.uk
dir: *Telephone for directions*

This is primarily a family-friendly pub serving the local community, but word of mouth has spread its popularity beyond the neighbourhood. In addition to reliable Harveys ales, the food is fresh, seasonal, and bought locally if possible. You'll find different menus for lunch and dinner, children have their own selections, and Sunday roasts feature prime Sussex pork, lamb and beef. Choices in the evening might include carrot and coriander soup, followed by pork tenderloin, creamy mash, choucroute of Savoy cabbage, and finishing with lemon and vanilla posset with blackberry sorbet.

Open noon-3 5-11 (Fri-Sat noon-11 Sun noon-8) Closed: 25 Dec 1 Jan, Mon **Bar Meals** L served Tue-Fri 12-2.30, Sat 12-4, Sun 12-6 D served Tue-Sat 6-9.45 **Restaurant** L served Tue-Fri 12-2.30, Sat 12-4, Sun 12-6 booking required D served Tue-Sat 6-9.45 booking required ⊕ FREE HOUSE ◀ Harvey's Sussex Best Bitter, Guinness, Staropramen, Kirin Ichiban ♂ Aspall, Westons. ♥ 22 **Facilities** Children welcome Children's menu Children's portions Dogs allowed Wi-fi

PICK OF THE PUBS

The Greys

105 Southover St BN2 9UA ☎ **01273 680734**
e-mail: chris@greyspub.com
dir: *0.5m from St Peters Church in Hanover area of Brighton*

Painted an eye-catching turquoise and described by the landlord as a 'shoebox', The Greys delights in its role as a thriving community pub in the bohemian area of Hanover in central Brighton. A compact back-street local, stripped wood and flagstone floors and timber panelled walls give the sense of a country pub in the town, and with the wood-burning stove glowing in the fireplace, there is no finer place to relax with a pint of Harveys bitter or a Breton cider. There is a great selection of Belgian beers, too, and annual Sussex and Belgian beer festival on August Bank Holiday weekend. Former Claridge's chef Roz Batty tantalises the tastebuds with an eclectic, ever-changing menu based on local, seasonal produce, so expect anything from South Downs rabbit pâté with toasted home-made apple bread to meatballs with buttered mash, root vegetable and bean stew with herb dumplings, or game dishes when in season. The Greys is also known for its live country/folk/bluegrass music on Monday nights, featuring many leading artistes.

Open all wk 4-11 (Sat noon-12.30, Sun noon-11) **Bar Meals** L served Sun 12-4.30 D served Tue-Thu & Sat 6-9 Av main course £11.50 **Restaurant** L served Sun 12-4.30 D served Tue-Thu & Sat 6-9 booking required Av 3 course à la carte fr £21 ⊕ ENTERPRISE INNS ◀ Timothy Taylor Landlord, Harveys Best Bitter ♂ Stowford Press, Westons Organic, Cidre Breton. **Facilities** Dogs allowed Beer festival Parking Wi-fi

The Market Inn ★★★ INN

1 Market St BN1 1HH
☎ **01273 329483** ▯ **01273 777227**
e-mail: marketinn@reallondonpubs.com
dir: *In The Lanes area, 50mtrs from junct of North St & East St*

Set in the historic Lanes area, this fine traditional English pub is located a short walk from the Brighton Pavilion, seafront and pier. A traditional English menu is served all day along with local and regional ales, and a good range of wines; a wide-screen television shows all the major sporting events. Food is made on the premises from locally sourced produce. To stay over and enjoy this famous seaside city, two attractively decorated en suite rooms are available, with a separate guest entrance.

Open all wk 11-11 (Fri-Sat 11am-mdnt Sun noon-10.30) **Bar Meals** L served Mon-Sat 11-9, Sun 12-6 D served Mon-Sat 11-9, Sun 12-6 Av main course £7 food served all day ⊕ SCOTTISH COURAGE ◀ Harveys, Wells Bombardier, Spitfire. **Facilities** Children welcome Children's menu Children's portions Dogs allowed Wi-fi **Rooms** 2

Preston Park Tavern ♥ NEW

88 Havelock Rd BN1 6GF ☎ **01273 542271**
e-mail: info@prestonparktavern.co.uk
dir: *From N towards Brighton on A23, at Mill Rd rdbt take 2nd exit, continue on A23 (follow Brighton, then Town Centre signs). Left (one-way) onto Stanford Ave (A23), left into Havelock Rd*

Since it opened four years ago, Preston Park Tavern has become a must-visit family-friendly food pub. Tucked away in the residential backstreets of Brighton, this light and airy gastro-pub with its open kitchen offers lunchtime sandwiches and main courses of guinea fowl stew, with the evening menu moving up a gear with slow-braised pork belly with Puy lentils or pan-fried sea bream fillets with braised fennel and chicory. Sunday lunches are worth booking for and children have their own menus.

Open all day all wk Closed: 25 Dec & 1 Jan **Bar Meals** L served Mon-Fri 12-2.30, Sat 12-4, Sun 12-6 booking required D served Mon-Sat 6-9.45 booking required **Restaurant** L served Mon-Fri 12-2.30, Sat 12-4, Sun 12-6 booking required D served Mon-Sat 6-9.45 booking required ⊕ FREE HOUSE ◀ Harveys Bitter. ♥ 22 **Facilities** Children welcome Children's menu Children's portions Dogs allowed Garden Wi-fi

The Five Bells Restaurant and Bar ♥

East Grinstead Rd BN8 4DA ☎ **01825 722259**
e-mail: info@fivebellschailey.co.uk
dir: *5m N of Lewes on A275*

This 500-year-old pub retains many original features, including a large inglenook fireplace. It is run now by the Fisher family, who have created a homely, relaxed atmosphere in the snug with its log fires and in the restaurant. All the dishes are made on the premises. Friday evenings host live music, with plans to extend this to Saturdays. In summer, the large bar terrace and secluded restaurant garden come into their own and barbecues are held there. Car and motor cycle clubs are welcomed and it is a venue for car events, plus it's handy for Sheffield Park, the Bluebell Railway, Plumpton racecourse and walks around Chailey.

Open all wk noon-3 6-12 (Sat-Sun all day) **Bar Meals** L served Mon-Fri 12-2.30, Sat-Sun all day D served Mon-Fri 6.30-9.30, Sat-Sun all day **Restaurant** L served Mon-Fri 12-2.30, Sat-Sun all day D served Mon-Fri 6.30-9.30, Sat-Sun all day ⊕ ENTERPRISE INNS ◀ Harvey's Best, Sharp's Doom Bar ♂ Aspall. ♥ 13 **Facilities** Children welcome Children's portions Dogs allowed Garden Parking Wi-fi

The Six Bells

BN8 6HE ☎ **01825 872227**
dir: *E of A22 between Hailsham & Uckfield. Turn opp Golden Cross PH*

Inglenook fireplaces and plenty of bric-a-brac are to be found at this large free house which is where various veteran car and motorbike enthusiasts meet on club nights. The jury in the famous Onion Pie Murder trial sat and deliberated in the bar before finding the defendant guilty. Exceptionally good value bar food includes green lip mussels with salad and French bread; cauliflower and broccoli bake; rack of ribs; chicken curry; and spicy ravioli with salad. Enjoy the fortnightly popular folk and blues evenings.

Open all wk 10-3 6-11 (Fri-Sun all day) **Bar Meals** L served all wk 12-2.30 (Fri-Sun all day) D served all wk 6-10 (Fri-Sun all day) Av main course £6.70 **Restaurant** L served all wk 12-2.30 (Fri-Sun all day) D served all wk 6-10 (Fri-Sun all day) ⊕ FREE HOUSE ◀ Courage Directors, Harveys Best. **Facilities** Children welcome Family room Dogs allowed Garden Parking

COOKSBRIDGE
Map 6 TQ41

PICK OF THE PUBS

The Rainbow Inn ♀

Resting Oak Hill BN8 4SS
☎ 01273 400334 📠 01273 401667
e-mail: enquires@rainbowsussex.co.uk
dir: *3m outside Lewes on A275 towards Haywards Heath*

A long history of providing hospitality continues in the hands of Tarquin Gorst, determined to maintain his 18th-century, flint-built pub not only as an important local amenity, but also as an appealing place to visit from further afield. There is a rustic bar and three warmly decorated dining areas, creating a relaxing atmosphere. It helps, of course, that Harveys Bitter is always available, alongside a regularly-changing guest ale, and that the extensive wine list includes a fine selection from Burgundy and Bordeaux. Further backing comes from a kitchen proud of its ability to source almost all its fresh, organic and free range ingredients from within Sussex. Thus, on a typical menu you might find slow-cooked Tottingworth Farm beef cheek with creamy mash, pancetta, baby mushrooms and baby onions; pan-fried sea bream with salsify, grapefruit, broccoli and beurre noisette; and spinach and ricotta ravioli with red pepper coulis. There is a suntrap enclosed rear terrace and grassy beer garden with views to the South Downs.

Open all day all wk noon–11 **Bar Meals** L served all wk 12-3 D served all wk 6.30-10 Av main course £13.50 **Restaurant** L served all wk 12-3 D served all wk 6.30-10 Fixed menu price fr £13 ⊕ STERLING PUB COMPANY ◀ Harveys Best Bitter, Guinness, Dark Star, Guest ale ♂ Stowford Press. ♀ 10 **Facilities** Children welcome Children's menu Children's portions Dogs allowed Garden Parking Wi-fi

COWBEECH
Map 6 TQ61

PICK OF THE PUBS

The Merrie Harriers ♀

BN27 4JQ ☎ 01323 833108 📠 01323 833108
e-mail: ben@sussexcountrytaverns.co.uk
dir: *Off A271, between Hailsham & Herstmonceux*

Built in 1624, this white clapboarded village inn is a fine-looking building. A former coachhouse, its good looks continue inside, where there's a wealth of oak beams, and a huge inglenook fireplace takes centre stage. Look out for the harmless female ghost who wanders around and likes looking out of the kitchen window. Outside, the terrace overlooks an acre of the Weald where the pub's tug-of-war team practises; here too is the kitchen's fruit and vegetable patch. Guests sampling a Harveys, Timothy Taylor or W J King real ale, or one of the 10 wines by the glass can study the modern British, daily changing and seasonal menu that reflects a commitment to cook with locally grown ingredients; the fish, for example, is freshly caught off

the South Coast and is very popular, especially on the regular seafood nights. Other options include twice-cooked Sussex pork belly, grilled tiger prawn spaghetti with chilli, and chargrilled aubergine and halloumi lasagne. A beer and music festival is held over the August Bank Holiday.

Open all wk Mon-Thur 11.30-3 6-12 (Fri-Sun all day) **Bar Meals** L served all wk 12-2.30 D served all wk 6.30-9 Av main course £8 **Restaurant** L served all wk 12-2.30 D served all wk 6.30-9 Fixed menu price fr £10 Av 3 course à la carte fr £25 ⊕ FREE HOUSE ◀ Harveys, Timothy Taylor, W J King ♂ Stowford Press. ♀ 10 **Facilities** Children welcome Children's menu Children's portions Play area Dogs allowed Garden Beer festival Parking Wi-fi

DANEHILL
Map 6 TQ42

PICK OF THE PUBS

The Coach and Horses ♀

RH17 7JF ☎ 01825 740369 📠 01825 740369
e-mail: coachandhorses@danehill.biz
dir: *From East Grinstead, S through Forest Row on A22 to junct with A275 (Lewes road), right on A275, 2m to Danehill, left onto School Lane, 0.5m, pub on left*

The cough of a distant steam engine on the Bluebell Railway may drift across the lovely countryside in which The Coach and Horses is set. The Victorian landed gentry hereabouts built an alehouse and stabling to serve local estates; from this has developed a welcoming food-oriented pub which also strives successfully to be the village local. It's a popular place to sit in the tranquil gardens (one is 'adults only') and drink in both local beers and views to Ashdown Forest and the South Downs; inside, vaulted ceilings, panelling and stone and wood flooring add to the charm. The menu is strong on surf, turf and game, with fish fresh daily from Seaford, pheasant, rabbit and venison from local estates and lamb from a neighbouring farm. Typical choices may be smoked Rye Bay whiting and saffron tagliatelle with sweet chilli and Parmesan, or slow-braised Ashdown venison with confit celeriac, baby turnips and mashed potatoes.

Open all wk 11.30-3 6-11 (Sat-Sun 12-11) Closed: 26 Dec **Bar Meals** L served Mon-Fri 12-2.30, Sun 12-3 D served Mon-Fri 7-9, Sat 7-9.30 **Restaurant** L served Mon-Fri 12-2.30, Sun 12-3 D served Mon-Fri 7-9, Sat 7-9.30 ⊕ FREE HOUSE ◀ Harveys, Guest ales ♂ Stowford Press, Black Rat Scrumpy, Thatcher Heritage. ♀ 8 **Facilities** Children welcome Children's menu Children's portions Play area Dogs allowed Garden Parking Wi-fi

DITCHLING
Map 6 TQ31

PICK OF THE PUBS

The Bull ★★★★ INN ♀

See Pick of the Pubs on opposite page

EAST CHILTINGTON
Map 6 TQ31

The Jolly Sportsman ♀

Chapel Ln BN7 3BA ☎ 01273 890400 📠 01273 890400
e-mail: thejollysportsman@mistral.co.uk
dir: *From Lewes take A275, left at Offham onto B2166 towards Plumpton, take Novington Ln, after approx 1m left into Chapel Ln*

Set within the South Downs National Park, this sympathetically upgraded dining inn is tucked away down a quiet no-through road. The bar retains some of the character of a Victorian ale house, with guest ales and a selection of malts, while the dining room strikes a cool, modern pose. Typical à la carte dishes are pork rillette and caramelised apples; grilled skate wing with warm cauliflower and caper salad. Fixed-price and children's menus are also available.

Open all wk (Sat & Summer all day) Closed: 25-26 Dec **Bar Meals** L served Mon-Sat 12-2.30, Sun 12.15-3.30 D served Mon-Thu & Sun 6.30-9.30, Fri-Sat 6.30-10 Av main course £15.85 **Restaurant** L served Mon-Sat 12.15-2.30, Sun 12.15-3.30 booking required D served all wk 7-9.30, Fri-Sat 7-10, Sun 7-9 booking required Fixed menu price fr £12.50 Av 3 course à la carte fr £26 ⊕ FREE HOUSE ◀ Dark Star Hophead, Harveys Best ♂ Gwynt-y-Ddraig. ♀ 14 **Facilities** Children welcome Children's menu Children's portions Play area Dogs allowed Garden Parking Wi-fi

Save on hotels. Book at theAA.com/hotel

SUSSEX, EAST 443 ENGLAND

PICK OF THE PUBS

The Bull ★★★★ INN ♉

2 High St BN6 8TA
☎ 01273 843147   📠 01273 843147
e-mail: info@thebullditchling.com
web: www.thebullditchling.com
dir: *S on M23/A23 5m. N of Brighton follow signs to Pyecombe/Hassocks then signs to Ditchling, 3m*

A venerable 450 year old inn which started out as monks' lodgings; today's cosy retreat is a far cry from those spartan days, with a memorable interior pushing all the right buttons — open fires, wavy beams, leather sofas, cosy corners, candlelight, bare floorboards, scrubbed tables and a local's bar brimming with good Sussex beers from Harveys and Dark Star. Over the past nine years, Dominic and Vanessa Worral have toiled tirelessly to create the archetypical English village inn with a refreshing contemporary edge; those monks' draughty lodgings have been replaced with individually designed guest rooms, very popular with visitors to the South Downs National Park within which The Bull stands. The rounded tops of the Downs rise steeply beyond the village to the commanding Ditchling Beacon (there's a self-guided walk from the pub, whilst the South Downs Way National Trail crosses the Beacon); views from the sheltered terrace and garden stretch towards the grassy ridges which protect pretty Ditchling from the sea breezes at Brighton, just 15 minutes away by car.

Sussex farms and estates provide the chefs with a panoply of delights with which to create their staunchly modern gourmet British dishes; a typical 'small plates' starter may be moules marinière with warm sour dough, graduating then to the luxury of a 'large plates' main of pan-fried sea bream, spring onion crushed new potatoes, wilted spinach, dill and crab cream; or honey-glazed pheasant with celeriac purée, sautéed Savoy cabbage, bacon and chestnuts. Flavoursome vegetarian options include butternut squash and crème fraîche risotto with crispy sage leaves, whilst children have their own menu. Wine lovers will delight in a generous list of bins, including sparkling wines from the Ridgeview Estate just outside the village.

Open all day all wk 11-11 (Sun 11-10.30) **Bar Meals** L served Mon-Fri 12-2.30, Sat 12-9.30, Sun 12-9 D served Mon-Sat 6-9.30, Sun 12-9 ⊕ FREE HOUSE
🍺 Harveys Best, Timothy Taylor Landlord, Hop Back Summer Lightning, Dark Star. ♉ 21 **Facilities** Children welcome Children's menu Children's portions Play area Dogs allowed Garden Parking Wi-fi **Rooms** 4

EAST DEAN
Map 6 TV59

PICK OF THE PUBS

The Tiger Inn 🍷 NEW

The Green BN20 0DA ☎ 01323 423209
e-mail: tiger@beachyhead.org.uk
dir: *From A259 between Eastbourne & Seaford. Pub 0.5m in village centre*

If you fancy a stroll around Beachy Head followed by a pint at The Tiger, chances are you will not be alone. Even in mid winter, such are the charms of this estate-owned pub that its popularity is growing as word spreads. It sits beside a village green lined with picture postcard cottages and enjoys wonderful downland views. The interior is quintessentially English too, with log fires, beams, stone floors and ancient settles. Its own micro-brewery supplies award-winning ales such as Legless Rambler. Happily The Tiger's popularity is not reflected in hiked prices on the menu. Good value and high quality home-cooked dishes stream out of the new kitchen, built to meet demand. Lunchtime choices include salads, open-faced sandwiches, hand-baked baps, and classics such as The Tiger burger or sausage of the day. In the evening relax and enjoy sweet roasted garlic and caramelised onion ham hock terrine, followed by honey and pepper crusted breast of duck, or pan-fried sea bream.

Open all day all wk **Bar Meals** L served all wk 12-3 D served all wk 6-9 Av main course £8.50 ⊕ FREE HOUSE ◀ Beachyhead Legless Rambler & Original Ale, Harveys. 🍷 10 **Facilities** Children welcome Children's portions Dogs allowed Garden Parking Wi-fi

FLETCHING
Map 6 TQ42

PICK OF THE PUBS

The Griffin Inn 🍷

TN22 3SS ☎ 01825 722890 ▤ 01825 722810
e-mail: info@thegriffininn.co.uk
dir: *M23 junct 10 to East Grinstead, then A22, then A275. Village signed on left, 15m from M23*

Don't be surprised if you hear a steam whistle drifting across The Griffin's huge landscaped gardens, for this imposing Grade II listed inn is little more than a mile from the heritage Bluebell Railway at Sheffield Park. There are views to Ashdown Forest and the Sussex Downs from the landscaped gardens, whilst the 16th-century interior simply oozes charm from its beams, panelling, settles and log fires. The bar boasts handpumps dispensing the best of local ales, and there's a generous wine list, too. Walkers and cyclists arriving to join destination diners will revel in the terrific menu, created from the freshest of local produce. There are two menus which change daily. In the bar, starters might include pan-fried Rye Bay scallops with aubergine caviar, crispy pancetta and truffle oil, followed by main course options such as roast Sussex lamb rump with Puy lentils, braised salsify and salsa verde. Round off, perhaps, with praline parfait and honey roasted pear.

Open all wk noon-11 Closed: 25 Dec
Bar Meals L served Mon-Fri 12-2.30, Sat-Sun 12-3 D served all wk 7-9.30 Av main course £14
Restaurant L served Mon-Fri 12-2.30, Sat-Sun 12-3 booking required D served Mon-Sat 7-9.30 booking required Fixed menu price fr £30 Av 3 course à la carte fr £30 ⊕ FREE HOUSE ◀ Harveys Best, Kings of Horsham, Hepworths. 🍷 16 **Facilities** Children welcome Children's menu Children's portions Play area Dogs allowed Garden Parking Wi-fi

GUN HILL
Map 6 TQ51

PICK OF THE PUBS

The Gun 🍷

TN21 0JU ☎ 01825 872361
e-mail: enquiries@thegunhouse.co.uk
dir: *5m S of Heathfield, 1m off A267 towards Gun Hill. 4m off A22 between Uckfield & Hailsham*

Tucked away in the heart of the East Sussex countryside, yet easily accessible, this lovely 17th-century pub provides the perfect opportunity to enjoy first class food in beautiful surroundings. Once the main courthouse serving the neighbouring towns and villages, now it has wooden floors and beams, and lots of hideaway places for quiet eating and drinking. A separate beautifully panelled dining room with a stunning fireplace is ideal for private parties. Food is seasonal and sourced from local suppliers. Three deli board selections can be shared by a gathering of friends - the antipasti board, for example, includes honey-roast ham, chorizo, houmous, Sicilian olives, Scottish smoked salmon, mayonnaise, gherkins and sourdough bread. Main courses might include slow-cooked English lamb shank with honey-roasted root vegetables; wild sea bass fillets with steamed jasmine rice; or wild mushroom and ricotta cheese risotto. Dine alfresco in the large garden or on the terrace on sunny days. The Old Coach House behind The Gun has been transformed into a farmer's market selling local fruits and vegetables, organic foods, fish and meats.

Open 11.30-3 5.30-11 (Sun noon-10.30)
Bar Meals L served Mon-Sat 12-2.30, Sun 12-9 D served Mon-Sat 6-9.30, Sun 12-9 Av main course £12 **Restaurant** L served Mon-Sat 12-2.30, Sun 12-9 D served Mon-Sat 6-9.30, Sun 12-9 Av 3 course à la carte fr £22 ⊕ FREE HOUSE ◀ Harveys, Guinness, Young's Ö Biddenden. 🍷 14 **Facilities** Children welcome Children's menu Children's portions Play area Dogs allowed Garden Parking Wi-fi

HARTFIELD
Map 6 TQ43

Anchor Inn

Church St TN7 4AG ☎ 01892 770424
dir: *On B2110*

A 14th-century, Grade II listed inn at the heart of 'Winnie the Pooh' country, deep within the scenic Ashdown Forest. In 1924 AA Milne bought a nearby farm which inspired the setting for the stories of his son Christopher Robin and his loveable bear. Inside are stone floors enhanced by a large inglenook fireplace and heavy beams. Sandwiches and salads are among the bar snacks, while for something more substantial the menu offers traditional pub food including steaks and curries. There is a verandah at the front and large garden to enjoy in the warmer weather.

Open all day all wk **Bar Meals** L served all wk 12-2 booking required D served all wk 6-10 booking required **Restaurant** L served all wk 12-2 booking required D served all wk 6-10 booking required ⊕ FREE HOUSE ◀ Harveys Sussex Best Bitter, Larkins. **Facilities** Children welcome Family room Dogs allowed Garden Parking

PICK OF THE PUBS

The Hatch Inn 🍷

See Pick of the Pubs on opposite page

ICKLESHAM
Map 7 TQ81

The Queen's Head 🍷

**Parsonage Ln TN36 4BL
☎ 01424 814552 ▤ 01424 814766**
dir: *Between Hastings & Rye on A259. Pub in village on x-rds near church*

Recently dubbed a 'must visit' in the national press, this award-winning 17th-century tile-hung pub enjoys a magnificent view across the Brede valley to Rye. The traditional atmosphere has been preserved, with vaulted ceilings, large inglenook fireplaces, church pews, antique farm implements, and a bar from the old Midland Bank in Eastbourne. Landlord Ian Mitchell keeps his customers happy with at least six real ales, an annual beer festival on the first weekend in October, and menus ranging from pub favourites to specials featuring fresh fish or game — game pudding, venison casserole, moules marinière.

Open all wk 11-11 (Sun 11-10.30) **Bar Meals** L served Mon-Fri 12-2.30, Sat-Sun 12-9.30 D served Mon-Fri 6-9.30, Sat-Sun 12-9.30 Av main course £9.50 ⊕ FREE HOUSE ◀ Rother Valley Level Best, Greene King Abbot Ale, Harveys Best, Dark Star, Ringwood Fortyniner Ö Biddenden, Westons Old Rosie. 🍷 12 **Facilities** Children welcome Children's menu Children's portions Play area Dogs allowed Garden Beer festival Parking Wi-fi

PICK OF THE PUBS

The Hatch Inn ♀

HARTFIELD   **Map 6 TQ43**

Coleman's Hatch TN7 4EJ
☎ 01342 822363   📄 01342 822363
e-mail: nickad@bigfoot.com
web: www.hatchinn.co.uk
dir: *A22, 14m, left at Forest Row rdbt, 3m
to Colemans Hatch, right by church.
Straight on at next junct, pub on right*

After a therapeutic walk with llamas at
the nearby llama park, a ramble through
the heritage of Ashdown Forest or a flutter
on the progress of your stick beneath the
nearby Poohsticks Bridge, a favoured
pastime of characters in AA Milne's
famous *Winnie the Pooh* books, home in on
this eyecatching inn. It stands at the site
of one of the medieval gates into the then
closely guarded woodland preserve, where
valuable iron and timber reserves drew in
industrialists. The inn's 1430 origin may
be as cottages to house iron workers;
today's building has been a pub for
approaching 300 years. White Sussex
weatherboarding features here, whilst a
tranquil grassy beer garden to the rear
has fine views across the Forest. Classic
beams and open fires draw an
appreciative crowd to sample beers from
the likes of Larkins and Harveys and head
chef Greg Palmer's eclectic menu, a fusion
of classic and modern approaches. With a
generous raft of local suppliers to draw
on, fresh seasonal produce features in
dishes that may range across appetisers
such as goat's cheese and leek tartlet,
baked ciabatta with melted brie, bacon
and cranberry sauce, or a traditional
ploughman's. Lunchtime mains include a
risotto of baby crayfish tails, leeks and
spinach with white wine, cream and
Parmesan, or maybe steak, Guinness and
field mushroom pie. Evening dining needs
a reservation, securing which leads to
choices including roast fillet of pork
wrapped in filo pastry and oven roasted,
served with a cream of sweet mustard
seed sauce; or breast of chicken filled with
a Roquefort duxelle, wrapped in smoked
bacon and oven roasted, served with chive
creamed potatoes and cream of wild
mushroom sauce. Finish with pear tart
Tatin, Chantilly cream and berries.

Open all wk 11.30-3 5.30-11 (Sat-Sun all
day) **Bar Meals** L served all wk 12-2.15
D served Mon-Thu 7-9.15, Fri-Sat 7-9.30
booking required Av main course £12
Restaurant L served all wk 12-2.15
D served Mon-Thu 7-9.15, Fri-Sat 7-9.30
booking required 🍺 FREE HOUSE
🍺 Harveys, Fuller's London Pride, Larkins,
Harvey's Old. ♀ 10 **Facilities** Children's
portions Play area Dogs allowed Garden

PICK OF THE PUBS

The Middle House ♟

MAYFIELD Map 6 TQ52

High St TN20 6AB
☎ 01435 872146 📄 01435 873423
e-mail: kirsty@middle-house.com
web: www.middlehousemayfield.co.uk
dir: *E of A267, S of Tunbridge Wells*

This Grade I listed 16th-century village inn dominates Mayfield's High Street. Described as 'one of the finest examples of a timber-framed building in Sussex', it has survived since 1575, when it was built for Sir Thomas Gresham, Elizabeth I's Keeper of the Privy Purse and founder of the London Stock Exchange. A private residence until the 1920s, the entrance hall features a large ornately-carved wooden fireplace by master carver Grinling Gibbons; records show it originally came from the Royal College of Physicians in London. A family-run business from start to finish, The Middle House rewards real ale lovers with a handsome choice ranging from the local Harveys to Sharp's Doom Bar. It's well known too for good, hand-made food – the kitchen uses meats, poultry, game and vegetables from local farms and producers. The bar menu comprises over 40 dishes including traditional classics such as pan-fried lamb's liver with crispy smoked bacon; home-made lasagne with side salad; and nachos – spicy chilli con carne topped with cheese nacho chips and sour cream. Fresh salads, vegetarian options and a children's healthy eating

menu are augmented by lunchtime main courses of pan-seared loin of local rabbit, and tempura of cod cheeks with home-made tartare sauce. If something out of the ordinary takes your fancy, try the fanned rump of kangaroo on a bed of Asian vegetables and noodle stir-fry. The beautiful oak-panelled restaurant, which incorporates a private chapel, has been described as 'one of the most magnificent in England'. The carte is shorter than it used to be, with half a dozen options at each course. But the quality shines through in dishes such as duo of duck: an Earl Grey smoked duck breast with cucumber salad and duck confit spring roll with celeriac remoulade. Vegetarians will relish the Cajun-roasted organic squash risotto with village leek fondue. Head outside to the lovely garden in the summer.

Open all wk **Bar Meals** L served Mon-Fri 12-2, Sat 12-2.30 D served Mon-Sat 6.30-9.30, Sun all day **Restaurant** L served Tue-Sun 12-2 booking required D served Tue-Sat 6.30-9 booking required ⊕ **FREE HOUSE** ◼ Harveys Best, Greene King Abbot Ale, Black Sheep Best, Theakston Best, Adnams Bitter, Sharp's Doom Bar, London Pride Ŏ Thatchers Gold. ♟ 9 **Facilities** Children's menu Children's portions Play area Garden Parking

MAYFIELD   Map 6 TQ52

PICK OF THE PUBS

The Middle House ♟

See Pick of the Pubs on opposite page

MILTON STREET   Map 6 TQ50

The Sussex Ox ♟

BN26 5RL ☎ **01323 870840**
e-mail: mail@thesussexox.co.uk
dir: *Off A27 between Wilmington & Drusillas. Follow brown signs to pub*

Drink deeply of old Sussex here, with the wonderful, match-boarded old bar rooms, wood and sealed-brick floors oozing character and a lawned beer garden looking out to that famous Sussex character, the Long Man of Wilmington. Dine in the bar, the Garden Room, or the more formal Dining Room; the daily-changing menu relies on the best local ingredients; perhaps braised oxtail with winter vegetables and mash; or Huntingdon Fidget pie. Bar snacks and smoked Applewood Cheddar ploughman's are also available, perhaps washed down with the pub's own Oxhead Bitter from Dark Star Brewery.

Open all wk 11.30-3 6-11 Closed: 25-31 Dec
Bar Meals L served all wk 12-2 booking required D served all wk 6-9 booking required **Restaurant** L served all wk 12-2 booking required D served all wk 6-9 booking required ⊕ FREE HOUSE ◀ Harveys Best, Dark Star Oxhead, Golden Gate, Hop Back Summer Lightning, Crouch Vale Brewers Gold Ò Westons Perry. ♟ 17
Facilities Children welcome Children's portions Family room Dogs allowed Garden Parking Wi-fi

OFFHAM   Map 6 TQ41

The Blacksmiths Arms ★★★★ INN ♟

London Rd BN7 3QD ☎ **01273 472971**
e-mail: blacksmithsarms@shineadsl.co.uk
web: www.theblacksmithsarms-offham.co.uk
dir: *2m N of Lewes on A275*

An attractive, mid-18th-century free house in an Area of Outstanding Natural Beauty that now has national park status. A hostelry since it was built, with charming, high quality accommodation available, today's ales hale from Harveys and log fires still burn in the inglenook. Bernard and Sylvia Booker aim to provide high quality dishes using the best of local produce, sustainably sourced and simply presented. The seafood platter, Bernard's own steak and kidney pie, and Newhaven whole grilled plaice 'on the bone' all meet these worthy objectives.

The Blacksmiths Arms

Open 12-3 6.30-10.30 Closed: Mon **Bar Meals** L served Tue-Sun 12-2 **Restaurant** L served Tue-Sun 12-2 booking required D served Tue-Sun 6.30-9 booking required ⊕ FREE HOUSE ◀ Harveys Ales, Bitburger. ♟ 10
Facilities Children welcome Children's portions Garden Parking **Rooms** 4

RINGMER
Map 6 TQ41

The Cock ♀

Uckfield Rd BN8 5RX
☎ 01273 812040 📠 01273 812040
e-mail: matt@cockpub.co.uk
web: www.cockpub.co.uk
dir: *Just off A26 approx 2m N of Lewes just outside Ringmer*

Built in the 16th century, The Cock takes its name from a bygone era when a spare horse (the cock horse) was kept to help another horse pull its heavy load to the top of a steep hill. Original oak beams, flagstone floors and a blazing fire in the inglenook set a cosy scene. Harveys ales and guest beers accompany the extensive menu of favourites and specials among which dishes of grilled sardines; steak and kidney pie; lamb tagine; home-made treacle tart may be found. Ask about the two women born here who married famous men.

Open all wk 11-3 6-11.30 (Sun 11-11) Closed: 26 Dec
Bar Meals L served Mon-Fri 12-2, Sat 12-2.30 D served Mon-Sat 6-9.30, Sun 12-9.30 Av main course £10
Restaurant L served Mon-Fri 12-2, Sat 12-2.30 booking required D served Mon-Sat 6-9.30, Sun 12-9.30 booking required Av 3 course à la carte fr £17 ⊕ FREE HOUSE
◀ Harveys Sussex Best Bitter, Sussex XXXX Old Ale, Fuller's London Pride, Dark Star Hophead ♂ Westons 1st Quality. ♀ 10 **Facilities** Children welcome Children's portions Play area Dogs allowed Garden Parking

See advert on page 447

RUSHLAKE GREEN
Map 6 TQ61

PICK OF THE PUBS

Horse & Groom

TN21 9QE ☎ 01435 830320 📠 01435 830310
e-mail: chappellhatpeg@aol.com
dir: *Telephone for directions*

An appealing pub-restaurant at the edge of the enormous green that gives the village its name. Residents have supped here for over 230 years and the pub retains much rustic character, with heavy beams, hearth, lots of brass and copper, and a cosy Gun Room restaurant complete with antique firearms. Outside a huge garden offers a grand prospect over the pretty East Sussex countryside, a much sought-after spot for summertime refreshment. Drinkers delight in Harveys ales all year round, whilst diners are rewarded by a fulfilling menu of home-cooked fare, including blackboard specials. Typical choices include starters of deep-fried whitebait dusted with cayenne pepper, and glazed goat's cheese and caramelised onion tartlet. Main courses may feature a fresh fillet of Hastings cod in chef's beer batter with thick-cut chips, mushy peas and home-produced tartare sauce; or a marinated duck breast, oven-roasted and served on a bed of stir-fried vegetables.

Open all wk 11.30-3 6-11 (Sun all day)
Bar Meals L served Mon-Fri 12-2.15, Sat-Sun 12-2.30 booking required D served all wk 7-9.30 booking required Av main course £10 **Restaurant** L served Mon-Fri 12-2.15, Sat-Sun 12-2.30 booking required D served all wk 7-8.30 booking required Av 3 course à la carte fr £25 ⊕ SHEPHERD NEAME ◀ Master Brew, Spitfire, Kent Best, Late Red, Bishop's Finger, Harveys Best ♂ Thatchers Gold. **Facilities** Children welcome Children's portions Dogs allowed Garden Parking Wi-fi

---

RYE
Map 7 TQ92

The George Tap ★★★★ HL ⊛ ♀ **NEW**

98 High St TN31 7JT
☎ 01797 222114 📠 01797 224065
e-mail: stay@thegeorgeinrye.com
dir: *M20 junct 10, A2070 to Brenzett, A259 to Rye*

The smart Georgian facade of this town centre inn hides an older genesis dating back to 1575. Such heritage promises a fascinating mix, and the comfortable blend of old and new certainly delivers; the original Georgian ballroom is exquisite. Antique and contemporary furnishings and locally produced art draw in clients to sample the Sussex beers from Dark Star and Harveys with a tasty, light bar menu. Diners taking the AA one Rosette meals relish fruits of the sea from Rye's boats, perhaps pan roast hake with white bean and pancetta cassoulet; or tackle a leg of Romney Marsh lamb, clearing the palate with Kentish or Sussex wines. Luxury en suite accommodation allows time to fully explore this historic old port.

Open all day all wk **Bar Meals** L served all wk 12-6 booking required D served all wk 6-10 Av main course £10 food served all day **Restaurant** L served all wk 12-3 D served all wk 6-10 Fixed menu price fr £12.50 Av 3 course à la carte fr £25 ⊕ FREE HOUSE ◀ Chilly Willy, Dark Star American Pale Ale, Harveys Best ♂ Biddenden, Bushell. ♀ 15 **Facilities** Children welcome Children's menu Children's portions Dogs allowed Garden Wi-fi
Rooms 34

The Globe Inn ♀

10 Military Rd TN31 7NX ☎ 01797 227918
e-mail: info@theglobe-inn.com
dir: *M20 junct 10 onto A2070, A259 & A268*

A small, informal free house just outside the ancient town walls. An absence of gaming machines, jukeboxes and TV screens encourages conversation over drinks, or while enjoying contemporary food in the modern, wood-floored bar and restaurant area. Using local produce, the menu kicks off with dishes that can either be eaten as tapas or individually as starters. The mains range from spiced chickpea stew, harissa chicken supreme with red pepper and apricot couscous and baba ghanouch; grilled sea bass fillet with braised endive and artichoke and citrus fruits. Wash down your meal with a glass of British Bulldog.

Open 12-3.30 6-11 (BHs all day) Closed: Mon, Sun eve
Bar Meals L served Tue-Sun 12-3 D served Tue-Sat 6-9 booking required Av main course £12 **Restaurant** L served Tue-Sun 12-3 D served Tue-Sat 6-9 booking required Av 3 course à la carte fr £20 ⊕ FREE HOUSE ◀ ESB, Harveys, British Bulldog. ♀ 10 **Facilities** Children welcome Children's portions Dogs allowed Garden Parking

PICK OF THE PUBS

Mermaid Inn ★★★ HL ⊛ ♀

Mermaid St TN31 7EY
☎ 01797 223065 📠 01797 225069
e-mail: info@mermaidinn.com
dir: *A259, follow signs to town centre, then into Mermaid St*

Although the main building is nearly 600 years old, the wine cellars here date back to 1156, the year that Rye became one of Edward the Confessor's confederation of Cinque Ports. It stands supreme in its ancient cobbled street, with ships' timbers for beams, and huge open fireplaces carved from French stone ballast dredged from the harbour. In the bar the infamous Hawkhurst Gang of smugglers once met, their insolently displayed loaded pistols providing immunity from interference by magistrates; there is also a priest's hole in the chimney breast. British and French-style food is served in both the bar and award-winning, linenfold-panelled restaurant, or under sunshades on the patio. Salmon en croute and roast pheasant may be on the lunch menu, while dinner choices include pan-fried monkfish; grilled lobster Thermidor; pork fillet in pancetta; plus a separate vegetarian menu. The Elizabethan Chamber is one of the eight delightfully furnished bedrooms with a four-poster.

Save on hotels. Book at **theAA.com/hotel**

SUSSEX, EAST 449 ENGLAND

Open all wk noon-11 **Bar Meals** L served all wk 12-2.30 D served all wk 6-9 Av main course £10.95 **Restaurant** L served all wk 12-2.30 booking required D served all wk 7-9.30 booking required Fixed menu price fr £20 Av 3 course à la carte fr £45.50 ⊕ FREE HOUSE ◀ Greene King Old Speckled Hen, Fuller's London Pride, Harveys ⟳ Kingstone Press. ⬤15 **Facilities** Children welcome Children's menu Children's portions Garden Parking Wi-fi **Rooms** 31

PICK OF THE PUBS

The Ypres Castle Inn ⬤

See Pick of the Pubs on page 450

| SALEHURST | Map 7 TQ72 |

PICK OF THE PUBS

Salehurst Halt NEW

Church Ln TN32 5PH ☎ 01580 880620
dir: *0.5m from A21 (Tunbridge Wells to Hastings road). Exit at Robertsbridge rdbt to Salehurst*

So named because it was a stop on the hop-picking steam railway line between Robertsbridge and Tenterden. This very highly regarded hostelry boasts a traditional cellar, much prized for maintaining real ales in top condition. The landscaped garden has a wonderful terrace with beautiful views over the Rother Valley; it also has a wood-fired pizza oven which runs almost continually during the summer, with orders taken at the garden counter. But don't assume this is a fast-food joint. It easily qualifies as a gastro-pub, such is the attention given to sourcing as many ingredients as possible from neighbouring farms. Fish comes from Hastings and Rye, vegetables from Icklesham, ales and cider from Kent and Sussex. Dishes such as tongue and mushroom crumble; pork pie ploughman's; and mutton tagine all reflect genuine focus on real seasonal dishes, and prices are reasonable too. Before leaving, have a stroll around this picturesque hamlet and take a look at the 12th-century church.

Open Tue-Wed 12-3 6-11 (Thu-Sun 12-11) Closed: Mon **Bar Meals** L served Tue-Sun 12-2.30 D served Wed-Sat 7-9 booking required Av main course £8.50-£10 ⊕ FREE HOUSE ◀ Harveys Best, Dark Star, Old Dairy, Guest ales ⟳ Biddenden Bushells, East Stour. **Facilities** Children welcome Children's portions Dogs allowed Garden

| SHORTBRIDGE | Map 6 TQ42 |

PICK OF THE PUBS

The Peacock Inn

TN22 3XA ☎ 01825 762463 ▤ 01825 762463
e-mail: enquiries@peacock-inn.co.uk
dir: *Just off A272 (Haywards Heath to Uckfield road) & A26 (Uckfield to Lewes road)*

Mentioned in Samuel Pepys' diary, this traditional inn dates from 1567 and is full of old world charm, both inside and out. Today it is renowned for its food (created by no fewer than three chefs), and also the resident ghost of Mrs Fuller. The large rear patio garden is a delightful spot in summer. Food choices include toasted ciabatta and toasted foccacia with a variety of fillings. For the hungry there are starters such as chicken and duck liver pâté, or crayfish tails and smoked salmon, followed by seafood crêpe, pan-fried sea bass fillets; steak, Guinness and mushroom pie or fillet steak with garlic and Stilton butter. For the non-meat eaters there's Mediterranean vegetable and mozzarella tartlet, or vegetarian tagine. Look out for chefs' specials.

Open all wk 11-3 6-11 Closed: 25-26 Dec ⊕ FREE HOUSE ◀ Harveys Best Bitter, Fuller's London Pride, Marlets. **Facilities** Children welcome Dogs allowed Garden Parking

| THREE LEG CROSS | Map 6 TQ63 |

The Bull

Dunster Mill Ln TN5 7HH
☎ 01580 200586 ▤ 01580 201289
e-mail: enquiries@thebullinn.co.uk
dir: *From M25 exit at Sevenoaks toward Hastings, right at x-rds onto B2087, right onto B2099 through Ticehurst, right for Three Legged Cross*

The Bull started life as a 14th-century Wealden Hall House, reputedly one of the oldest dwelling places in the country, and is set in a hamlet close to Bewl Water. The interior features oak beams, inglenook fireplaces, quarry tiled floors, and a mass of small intimate areas in the bar. The extensive gardens are popular with families who enjoy the duck pond, petanque pitch, aviary and children's play area. Menus offer pub favourites ranging from freshly baked baguettes and bar snacks to hearty dishes full of comfort, such as bangers and mash and treacle tart.

Open all wk noon-mdnt Closed: 25-26 Dec eve ⊕ FREE HOUSE ◀ Harveys, Sussex Best, Harveys Armada, Timothy Taylor, Guest ales ⟳ Stowford Press. **Facilities** Children welcome Play area Dogs allowed Garden Parking

| WADHURST | Map 6 TQ63 |

PICK OF THE PUBS

The Best Beech Inn

Mayfield Ln TN5 6JH ☎ 01892 782046
e-mail: info@bestbeechinn.co.uk
dir: *7m from Tunbridge Wells. On A246 at lights turn left onto London Rd (A26), left at mini rdbt onto A267, left then right onto B2100. At Mark Cross signed Wadhurst, 3m on right*

Once a coaching house dating back to 1680, the Best Beech Inn is in the perfect country pub setting in an Area of Outstanding Natural Beauty near the Kent and Sussex border. The pub has been sympathetically refurbished to preserve the essentially Victorian character of its heyday, with comfy chairs, exposed brickwork and open fireplaces. Now in new capable and experienced hands, dine in the recently refurbished rooms with a decor combining old and new. The seasonal menus offer the freshest, most dynamic ingredients sourced from local suppliers. Starters might include crayfish cocktail with lettuce, avocado purée and toasted flutes, and baked Brie wrapped in filo pastry with red onion marmalade, followed by main courses such as grilled rib-eye steak with red wine and shallot sauce, and boneless chicken leg filled with apricot and thyme stuffing. The award-winning ales and great selection of wines can be enjoyed by the fire in winter or out on the terrace in summer.

Open all day Mon-Fri noon-3, 6-11 (Sat noon-11, Sun noon-6) Closed: Sun eve **Bar Meals** L served Mon-Fri 12-2.30, Sat all day, Sun 12-5 booking required D served Tue-Fri 6-9.30, Sat all day booking required Av main course £13.95 **Restaurant** L served Mon-Fri noon-3 6-11 (Sat noon-11, Sun noon-6) booking required D served Tue-Fri 6-9.30, Sat all day booking required Fixed menu price fr £12.50 Av 3 course à la carte fr £25 ⊕ SHEPHERD NEAME ◀ Kent Best, Master Brew, Spitfire. **Facilities** Children welcome Children's menu Children's portions Family room Dogs allowed Garden Parking Wi-fi

PICK OF THE PUBS

The Ypres Castle Inn ♀

RYE Map 7 TQ92

Gun Garden TN31 7HH ☎ **01797 223248**
e-mail: info@yprescastleinn.co.uk
web: www.yprescastleinn.co.uk
dir: *Behind church & adjacent to Ypres Tower*

Hidden below the ramparts of the Ypres Tower, thought to have been built in 1249 as part of the town's defences, stands the white weather-boarded free house known locally as 'The Wipers'. Providing hospitality since 1640, but with its 17th-century origins masked by Victorian additions, it stands close to Rye harbour and was once the haunt of smugglers. Nowadays, the colourful art and interior furnishings give the building a warm and friendly atmosphere, and from the garden – the only one belonging to a pub in the citadel area – there are delightful views not just of the Tower, but of Romney Marsh and the River Rother, with its working fishing fleet, which provides most of the seafood offered in the restaurant, including the famous Rye Bay scallop, plaice, sea bass, gurnard, John Dory and skate. Other local produce on the ever-changing menu includes Winchelsea pork and home-cooked Biddenden cider-soaked ham. Lunchtime brings daily soups, as well as a selection of freshly baked filled baguettes; avocado and crayfish tail salad; traditional beer-battered cod and

chips; and spring onion and sun-blushed tomato risotto. In the evenings, dinner might begin with game and chestnut terrine with grape compote, or crab, coriander and sweetcorn spring roll with chilli dip. To follow, Romney Marsh lamb shank in red wine sauce; pot-roasted partridge with smoked bacon and honeygrain mustard dressing; oven-baked cod fillet on creamed leeks; or Mediterranean vegetable tower with grilled goat's cheese. Desserts are listed on the blackboard. Booking is especially advisable in the summer, on Friday nights, when the pub comes alive with a varied programme of contemporary rock, jazz and blues bands, and always at weekends.

Open all day all wk **Bar Meals** L served all wk 12-3 D served Mon-Sat 6-9

Restaurant L served all wk 12-3 booking required D served Mon-Sat 6-9 booking required ⊞ FREE HOUSE ◀ Harveys Best, Adnams Broadside, Timothy Taylor Landlord, Fuller's London Pride, Fuller's ESB Ŏ Biddenden Bushels. ♀ 12 **Facilities** Children's menu Children's portions Garden Wi-fi

PICK OF THE PUBS

The Dorset Arms

WITHYHAM   Map 6 TQ43

TN7 4BD
☎ **01892 770278**   📄 **01892 770195**
e-mail: pete@dorset-arms.co.uk
web www.dorset-arms.co.uk
dir: *4m W of Tunbridge Wells on B2110 between Groombridge & Hartfield*

For over six centuries a building here has gradually settled to become an integral part of the landscape. Its picture postcard perfection is a jigsaw of ages and styles; slender chimneystacks, sharp gables and the finest, gleaming white weatherboarding slumber beneath careworn tiles at the northern fringe of Ashdown Forest, where a medieval hall house first took shape when the Wars of the Roses were being fought out. Licensed some 200 years ago when it took the name of the local landowning family, once Earls of Dorset, the interior doesn't disappoint, with a comfy, period mix of flagstoned and oak-boarded floors, vast open fireplace, undulating beams, magpie furniture and decor, and that indefinable character that develops only with maturity. It remains at heart a true village local, with darts, good Sussex ales from Harveys and a vibrant community atmosphere; the village church and cricket ground are near neighbours. Quite apart from the social conviviality, the produce of the kitchen is a major draw, with an extensive, daily-changing specials board complementing the respectable carte menu. Starters range from the simple comfort of home-made soup to pan-seared pigeon breast with blackberry, cardamom and chilli dressing, or ham hock terrine. The main event might include a large lamb chop in Shrewsbury sauce, half a roast duckling with stuffing and Amaretto and cherry sauce, or the signature dish of half shoulder of English lamb with red wine gravy; there's also a great range of fish dishes such as pan-fried fillet of brill in parsley butter. The choice will vary with the availability of raw ingredients; the owners pride themselves in sourcing their produce from the local area. Tables on the green outside allow summertime alfresco dining.

Open all wk 11.30-3 6-11 (Sat-Sun all day) **Bar Meals** L served all wk 12-2, Sat-Sun all day D served all wk 7.30-9, Sat-Sun all day **Restaurant** L served all wk 12-2, Sat-Sun all day D served all wk 7.30-9, Sat-Sun all day 🍺 HARVEYS OF LEWES ◖◗ Harveys Sussex Best, seasonal ales. **Facilities** Dogs allowed Garden Parking Wi-fi

WARTLING
Map 6 TQ60

PICK OF THE PUBS

The Lamb Inn ☻

BN27 1RY ☎ 01323 832116
dir: *A259 from Polegate to Pevensey rdbt. Take 1st left to Wartling & Herstmonceux Castle. Pub 3m on right*

Set in the East Sussex countryside near the Pevensey levels, this family-run, 16th-century country pub and restaurant is a welcome rest stop for birdwatchers, walkers and locals. Draw up one of the comfortable cream sofas to the fire and enjoy a real ale from Sussex breweries or a glass of wine. Aside from liquid refreshment, the pub is well known for its food. Everything is made on the premises, including the bread, and, as far as possible, makes use of top quality produce sourced locally from places like Chilley Farm, which specialises in raising Gloucester Old Spot pigs, Southdown and Kent Cross lamb, and Sussex beef. The menu offers plenty of variety, and a meal might begin with seafood pancake in cheese sauce, followed by fillet of pork Stroganoff finished with brandy, French mustard and soured cream. Home-made desserts are represented by apple and cinnamon Pavlova with butterscotch sauce.

Open Tue-Sat 11-3 6-11 (Sun 12-3) Closed: Sun eve, Mon **Bar Meals** L served Tue-Sun 12-2.15 booking required D served Tue-Sat 7-9 booking required **Restaurant** L served Tue-Sun 12-2.15 booking required D served Tue-Sat 7-9 booking required ⊕ FREE HOUSE ◀ Harveys, guest beers ♻ Stowford Press. ☻ 8 **Facilities** Children welcome Children's menu Children's portions Dogs allowed Garden Parking

WILMINGTON
Map 6 TQ50

The Giants Rest

The Street BN26 5SQ
☎ 01323 870207 📠 01323 870207
e-mail: abecjane@aol.com
dir: *2m from Polegate on A27 towards Brighton*

With the famous chalk figure of the Long Man of Wilmington standing guard further up the lane, this family-owned Victorian free house can properly claim to be one of the most Druid-friendly pubs in Sussex. The rustic wooden-floored bar is decorated with Beryl Cook prints. Take a seat at a pine table, each with its own wooden puzzle, and order some home-prepared food: garlic mushrooms with crusty bread; spicy Mexican lamb; African spinach, sweet potato and peanut stew; or a simple jacket potato or ploughman's.

Open all wk 11am-3 6-11pm (Sat-Sun all day) **Bar Meals** L served Mon-Fri 11.30-2, Sat-Sun all day booking required D served Mon-Fri 6.30-9, Sat-Sun all day booking required Av main course £10.50 **Restaurant** L served Mon-Fri 11.30-2, Sat-Sun all day booking required D served Mon-Fri 6.30-9, Sat-Sun all day booking required ⊕ FREE HOUSE ◀ Harveys Best, Timothy Taylor Landlord, Summer Lightning, Harveys Best ♻ Stowford Press. **Facilities** Children welcome Children's portions Dogs allowed Garden Parking

WINCHELSEA
Map 7 TQ91

The New Inn ☻

German St TN36 4EN ☎ 01797 226252
e-mail: thenewinnwinchelsea@sky.com
dir: *Telephone for directions*

It may not be a thriving seaport any more but Winchelsea boasts one of the finest collections of heritage medieval buildings in Britain and the historic 18th-century New Inn welcomes visitors and locals alike. Known today for its comfort, hospitality and excellent cuisine, it offers a light bite menu (moules marinière, local sausages and mash) or a dining menu that features the likes of Rye Bay seafood linguine, rack of Sussex lamb and hot Thai red chicken curry. The lovely walled garden is a delight on a sunny day.

Open all day all wk **Bar Meals** L served Mon-Fri 12-3, Sat-Sun all day D served Mon-Fri 6-9, Sat-Sun all day Av main course £10.95 **Restaurant** L served Mon-Fri 12-3, Sat-Sun all day D served Mon-Fri 6-9, Sat-Sun all day Av 3 course à la carte fr £17.95 ◀ Morlands Original, Abbots Ale, Greene King IPA, Old Speckled Hen ♻ Stowford Press. ☻ 10 **Facilities** Children welcome Children's menu Children's portions Family room Dogs allowed Garden Parking Wi-fi

WITHYHAM
Map 6 TQ43

PICK OF THE PUBS

The Dorset Arms

See Pick of the Pubs on page 451

SUSSEX, WEST

AMBERLEY
Map 6 TQ01

Black Horse

High St BN18 9NL ☎ 01798 831700
dir: *Telephone for directions*

This lively 17th-century tavern sits in the heart of Amberley, deep in the South Downs. Look out for the display of sheep bells donated by the last shepherd to have a flock on the local hills. Food is served in the large restaurant and bar or in the beer garden complete with pond, and there's plenty of choice for everyone, including a specials board and children's menu. Great beer, good local walks and nice views of the South Downs completes the picture. Dogs (on leads) are welcome in the bar.

Open all day all wk **Bar Meals** L served all wk 12-3 D served Mon-Thu 6.30-9, Fri-Sat 6-9.30, Sun 12-8 Av main course £9.95 **Restaurant** L served Sun only booking required D served Mon & Wed-Thu 6.30-9, Fri-Sat 6-9.30, Sun 12-8 booking required ⊕ ADMIRAL TAVERNS ◀ Greene King IPA, Harveys Sussex, Guest ale. **Facilities** Children welcome Children's menu Dogs allowed Garden Wi-fi

The Bridge Inn

Houghton Bridge BN18 9LR ☎ 01798 831619
e-mail: bridgeamberley@btinternet.com
dir: *5m N of Arundel on B2139. Next to Amberley main line station*

Standing alongside the River Arun at the mid-point of the South Downs Way National Trail, this traditional free house dates from 1650. The pretty pub garden and patio are summer favourites, whilst the candle-lit bar and log fires come into their own on cold winter evenings. Drinkers will find Westons ciders and a good range of real ales like Betty Stogs and King's Old Ale, whilst daily chalkboard specials and an extensive range of pub classics sustain the heartiest appetites.

Open all day all wk noon-11 (Sun noon-10.30) **Bar Meals** L served Mon-Fri 12-2.30, Sat-Sun 12-4 D served Mon-Sat 6-9, Sun 5.30-8 Av main course £9.95 ⊕ FREE HOUSE ◀ Harveys Sussex, Skinner's Betty Stogs, Hopback Summer Lightning, Sharp's Cornish Coaster, Kings Old Ale ♻ Westons Stowford Press, Westons Old Rosie. **Facilities** Children welcome Children's menu Children's portions Dogs allowed Garden Parking

ASHURST
Map 6 TQ11

PICK OF THE PUBS

The Fountain Inn ☻

BN44 3AP ☎ 01403 710219
dir: *On B2135 N of Steyning*

The South Downs loom as the southern horizon visible from the pretty gardens - there's a great duck pond, too - of this 16th-century Sussex inn where Paul McCartney once played; he filmed his *Wonderful Christmas Time* video here back in 1979. A huge brick chimneystack vents the capacious inglenook, just one of the period features that run to flagstone floors, wonky walls, rustic furnishings and old beams whilst, for the sporty, a traditional skittles alley is a must. Local beers from Harveys and other regional breweries accompany the good, solid pub food that attracts walkers, cyclists and locals. At lunchtime there are ploughman's, salads and freshly cut sandwiches. The menu runs to favourites like steak, mushroom and ale pie as well as chunky steaks, chicken breast or perhaps a choice of fresh fish straight from the English Channel.

Open all day all wk 11.30am-11pm (Sun noon-10.30pm) **Bar Meals** L served Mon-Sat 11.30-2.30, Sun 12-3 booking required D served Mon-Sat 6-9.30, Sun 6-8.30 booking required Av main course £8.95 **Restaurant** L served Mon-Sat 11.30-2.30, Sun 12-3 booking required D served Mon-Sat 6-9.30, Sun 6-8.30 booking required Fixed menu price fr £19.95 Av 3 course à la carte fr £19.95 ⊕ FREE HOUSE ◀ Harveys Sussex, Fuller's London, Seasonal ales, Guest ales ♻ Stowford Press. ☻ 11 **Facilities** Dogs allowed Garden Parking

Save on hotels. Book at **theAA.com/hotel**

SUSSEX, WEST 453 ENGLAND

BALCOMBE
Map 6 TQ33

The Cowdray ♀

RH17 6QD ☎ **01444 811280**
e-mail: alexandandy@hotmail.co.uk
dir: *From M23 junct 10a take the B2036 towards
Balcombe*

Just a mile from Junction 10a of the M23, this once run-
down village boozer has been transformed into a plushly-
upholstered dining pub. Expect wood floors, a fresh, crisp
decor, and a pub menu that's a cut above average. Alex
and Andy Owen, who previously worked for Gordon
Ramsay, specialise in sourcing ingredients within Sussex
if possible. Notable exceptions are the Scottish Angus
and Longhorn beef cuts which appear on the recently
introduced rare-breeds steak menu.

Open all day all wk Closed: 25 Dec eve
Bar Meals L served Mon-Sat 12-3, Sun 12-4 D served
Mon-Thu 6-9, Fri-Sat 6-10 Av main course £14
Restaurant L served Mon-Sat 12-3, Sun 12-4 booking
required D served Mon-Thu & Sun 5.30-9.30, Fri-Sat 6-10
booking required Fixed menu price fr £11.95 Av 3 course
à la carte fr £28 ⊕ GREENE KING ◀ Morland Original,
IPA, Guinness. ♀ 11 **Facilities** Children welcome
Children's menu Children's portions Play area Family
room Dogs allowed Garden Parking Wi-fi

BOSHAM
Map 5 SU80

The Anchor Bleu ♀ NEW

High St PO18 8LS ☎ **01243 573956**
dir: *From A27 SW of Chichester take A259. Follow
Fishbourne signs, then Bosham signs*

If you park your car at The Anchor Bleu, check the tide
times as this 17th century harbourside inn as it floods
during most high tides. Flagstone floors, low beams, open
log fire and two terraces, one overlooking the waterfront,
add to the charm of this popular pit stop for walkers and
cyclists. With five real ales on offer, local seafood is
showcased on the menu, which might also include Thai
crab cakes or smoked haddock, prawn and leek pie.

Open all wk 12-3 5.30-11 (Etr-Oct 11-11)
Bar Meals L served all wk 12-3 D served all wk 6.30-9.30
booking required Av main course £7.95
Restaurant L served all wk 12-3 D served all wk
6.30-9.30 booking required Fixed menu price fr £6.95
⊕ ENTERPRISE INNS ◀ Sharp's Cornish Coaster,
Ringwood Fortyniner, Hogs Back TEA, Otter Ale, Hopback
Summer Lightning ♻ Stowford Press. ♀ 10
Facilities Children welcome Children's menu Children's
portions Dogs allowed

BURGESS HILL
Map 6 TQ31

The Oak Barn ♀

Cuckfield Rd RH15 8RE
☎ **01444 258222** 🖨 **01444 258388**
e-mail: enquiries@oakbarnrestaurant.co.uk
web: www.oakbarnrestaurant.co.uk
dir: *Telephone for directions*

As its name suggests, this popular pub-restaurant
occupies a 250-year-old barn that has been lovingly
restored using salvaged timbers from wooden ships.
Brimming with charm and atmosphere, the interior is rich
in oak flooring, authentic wagon wheel chandeliers, and
fine stained glass. Lofty raftered ceilings, a galleried
restaurant, and leather chairs fronting a huge fireplace
are an idyllic setting for supping a pint of Harvey's and
tucking into Thai-style mussels, followed by pan-fried
mallard breast with dauphinoise potatoes, port and

continued

BURGESS HILL *continued*

redcurrant sauce. Outside is an enclosed courtyard and patios, with water features.

Open all day all wk 10am-11pm (Sun 11-11)
Bar Meals L served all wk 12-2.30 D served all wk 6-9.30
Restaurant L served all wk 12-2.30 booking required
D served all wk 6-9.30 booking required ⊕ FREE HOUSE
◀ Guinness, Harveys. ♈ 8 **Facilities** Children welcome
Children's portions Garden Parking Wi-fi

See advert on page 453

BURPHAM	Map 6 TQ00

PICK OF THE PUBS

George & Dragon ◎

BN18 9RR ☎ 01903 883131
e-mail: sara.cheney@btinternet.com
dir: *Off A27 1m E of Arundel, signed Burpham, 2.5m pub on left*

Tucked away down a long 'no through road', Burpham looks across the Arun valley to the mighty Arundel Castle. There are excellent riverside and downland walks on the doorstep of this 300 year-old free house, and walkers and their dogs are welcome in the bar. Step inside and you'll find beamed ceilings and modern prints on the walls, with worn stone flags on the floor. The original rooms have been opened out to form a large space that catches the late sunshine, but there are still a couple of alcoves with tables for an intimate drink. You'll also discover a small bar hidden around a corner. This is very much a dining pub, attracting visitors from far and wide. The à la carte menu and specials board offer a good choice of dishes between them: for starters you could try ravioli of braised oxtail or assiette of trout. Main courses might include orange-roasted partridge with thyme fondant root vegetables, or cannon of lamb with white and black pudding. There are tables outside, ideal for whiling away an afternoon or evening in summer, listening to the cricket being played on the green.

Open all wk 12-3 6-11 **Bar Meals** L served Mon-Fri 12-2, Sat-Sun 12-3 booking required D served all wk 6-9 booking required **Restaurant** L served Mon-Fri 12-2, Sat 12-2.30, Sun 12-3 booking required D served all wk 6-9 booking required ⊕ FREE HOUSE ◀ Arundel Ales, Guest ales ♂ Aspall. **Facilities** Children welcome Children's menu Dogs allowed Garden Parking

---

BURY	Map 6 TQ01

The Squire & Horse ♈

Bury Common RH20 1NS
☎ 01798 831343 🖷 01798 831904
e-mail: squireandhorse@btconnect.com
dir: *On A29, 4m S of Pulbrough, 4m N of Arundel*

The original 16th-century building was extended a few years ago, with old wooden beams and country fireplaces throughout. All the food is freshly cooked to order and sourced locally wherever possible. With the head chef originating from Australia there are innovative gastro-pub style dishes on offer here. These could include barbecued barracuda fillet on a bed of prawn risotto, or calves' liver with bacon and red wine glaze. Thai food is a speciality too. You can also dine outside in the stylish seating area. There is a members' dining club to join with discounts throughout the year.

Open all wk 11-3 6-11 **Bar Meals** L served all wk 12-2 D served all wk 6-9 **Restaurant** L served all wk 12-2 D served all wk 6-9 ⊕ FREE HOUSE ◀ Greene King IPA, Harveys Sussex, Guest ales. ♈ 10 **Facilities** Children welcome Children's menu Garden Parking

---

CHARLTON	Map 6 SU81

PICK OF THE PUBS

The Fox Goes Free ★★★★ INN

See Pick of the Pubs on opposite page

CHICHESTER	Map 5 SU80

The Bull's Head ★★★★ INN ♈ **NEW**

99 Fishbourne Road West PO19 3JP ☎ 01243 839895
e-mail: julie@bullsheadfishbourne.net
dir: *A27 onto A259, 0.5m on left*

Proud holder of a Fuller's Master Cellarman certificate, The Bull's Head serves five real ales all in tip-top condition. This traditional roadside pub with large open fire dates to the 17th century. Its position just outside Chichester is perfect for visiting Fishbourne Roman Palace and Bosham harbour. Live jazz is played every month, special events are hosted throughout the year, and four en suite bedrooms in a converted barn offer contemporary comforts. Home-cooked food is based on locally-sourced ingredients.

Open all wk Mon-Fri 11-3 5.30-11 (Sat-Sun all day)
Bar Meals L served Mon-Fri 12-2, Sat 12-9.30, Sun 12-3 booking required D served Mon-Fri 6-9, Sat 12-9.30, Sun 6-8.30 booking required **Restaurant** L served Mon-Fri 12-2, Sat 12-9.30, Sun 12-3 booking required D served Mon-Fri 6-9, Sat 12-9, Sun 6-8.30 booking required ⊕ FULLER'S ◀ London Pride, Seafarers ♂ Aspall. ♈ 10 **Facilities** Children welcome Children's portions Dogs allowed Parking Wi-fi **Rooms** 4

PICK OF THE PUBS

The Earl of March ◎◎ ♈

Lavant Rd, Lavant PO18 0BQ ☎ 01243 533993
e-mail: info@theearlofmarch.com
dir: *On A286, 1m N of Chichester*

Handy for Goodwood's racecourse and nestling at the foot of the South Downs National Park, The Earl – named after the local landowning dynasty - is an inspirational place to stay awhile. William Blake wrote the words to Jerusalem whilst sitting in the east-facing bay window here in 1803; today's visitors can enjoy much the same views that prompted his outpourings whilst sharing in the bounty of local estates and the nearby Channel used in the preparation of a sublime choice of dishes, gaining 2 AA Rosettes. Local butternut squash soup with Sussex Blue cheese and toasted pumpkin seeds whets the appetite, then fully sated with roast loin of Funtington pork with onion bread, apple sauce and roast juices or maybe fillet of sea bass, linguini, champagne sauce and mixed leaves. Such top-notch dishes are crafted by Giles Thompson, former Executive Chef at London's Ritz Hotel and now proprietor of this delightful old 18th century coaching inn, rescued in 2005 from five years of closure and refurbished in 'country plush' style.

Open all day all wk **Bar Meals** L served all wk 12-2.30 (winter) 12-9 (summer) D served all wk 12-9 (summer) Av main course £16.50 **Restaurant** L served all wk 12-2.30 (winter) booking required D served all wk 5.30-9.30 (winter) 12-9 (summer) booking required Fixed menu price fr £18.50 Av 3 course à la carte fr £30 ⊕ ENTERPRISE INNS ◀ Summer Lightning, Harveys, Fuller's London Pride, Ringwood ♂ Stowford Press. ♈ 16 **Facilities** Children welcome Children's menu Children's portions Dogs allowed Garden Parking Wi-fi

PICK OF THE PUBS

The Fox Goes Free ★★★★ INN

CHARLTON   Map 6 SU81

PO18 0HU
☎ **01243 811461** 📄 **01243 811712**
e-mail: enquiries@thefoxgoesfree.com
web: www.thefoxgoesfree.com
dir: *A286, 6m from Chichester towards
Midhurst. 1m from Goodwood racecourse*

Standing in unspoiled countryside at the
foot of the South Downs, this lovely old
brick and flint free house was a favoured
hunting lodge of William III. With its three
huge fireplaces, old pews and brick floors,
the 15th-century building simply exudes
charm and character. The pub, which
hosted the first Women's Institute meeting
in 1915, lies close to the rambling Weald
and Downland open-air museum, where
fifty historic buildings from around
southern England have been reconstructed
to form a unique collection. Goodwood
Estate is also close by, and The Fox
attracts many customers during the
racing season and the annual Festival of
Speed. Comfortable accommodation is
available here if you would like to stay
over. Away from the high life, you can
watch the world go by from the solid
timber benches and tables to the front, or
relax under the apples trees in the lawned
rear garden. Lest all this sounds rather
extravagant, you'll find that The Fox is a
friendly and welcoming drinkers' pub with
a good selection of real ales that includes
the eponymous Fox Goes Free bitter.
Everything from the chips to the ice cream

is home made and, whether you're looking
for a quick bar snack or something more
substantial, the daily-changing menus
offer something for every taste. Bar meals
include fresh butcher's sausages and
mash with vegetables and onion gravy,
and battered cod and chips with side
salad. À la carte choices may start with
home-baked bread and marinated olives,
or game terrine with quince jelly and
toasted brioche. Continue with meat and
fish main courses such as confit duck leg
with cabbage, bacon and a plum jus, or
grilled salmon with basil mash and chive
velouté. Salads can be prepared for both
small and large appetites, and there are
some appealing vegetarian options, too.

Open all day all wk 11-11 (Sun noon-11)
Closed: 25 Dec eve **Bar Meals** L served
Mon-Fri 12-2.30, Sat-Sun 12-10 booking
required D served Mon-Fri 6.30-10,

Sat-Sun 12-10 booking required Av main
course £10.95-£16.95 **Restaurant**
L served all wk 12-2.30 booking required
D served all wk 6.30-10 booking required
Av 3 course à la carte fr £25
🍺 FREE HOUSE 🍺 Ballards Best, The Fox
Goes Free, Otter. **Facilities** Children's
menu Children's portions Dogs allowed
Garden Parking Wi-fi **Rooms** 5

CHICHESTER *continued*

PICK OF THE PUBS

Royal Oak Inn ★★★★★ INN ◉ ☂

Pook Ln, East Lavant PO18 0AX ☎ 01243 527434
e-mail: info@royaloakeastlavant.co.uk
dir: *A286 from Chichester signed Midhurst, 2m then right at mini-rdbt, pub over bridge on left*

East Lavant nestles at the foot of the South Downs within the boundary of the National Park, just a short drive from Glorious Goodwood, Chichester's medieval attractions and the grand walking at The Trundle hillfort. Two centuries old, the little Georgian inn is at the heart of the historic village; verdant creepers adorn the door, behind which lies a smart dining pub blessed with luxury accommodation. The brick-lined restaurant and beamed bar achieve a crisp, rustic brand of chic: details include open fires, fresh flowers, candles, and wine attractively displayed in alcoves set into the walls; Arundel ale and Gospel Green champagne cider are among the thirst-quenchers on offer. The seasonal menu is an easy mix of English classics and modern Mediterranean dishes; pace yourself with a starter of pigeon breast, Stilton and walnut salad with port dressing prior to setting to baked hake with walnut and herb crust, orange caramelised salsify and scallop ravioli, or pan roast partridge with creamed Savoy cabbage and sweet potato fondant; a specials board adds to the enviable fray.

Open all day all wk 7am-11.30pm Closed: 25 Dec **Bar Meals** L served Mon-Sat 12-5.30 D served all wk 6-9 Av main course £7 **Restaurant** L served all wk 12-2.30 booking required D served all wk 6-9 booking required Av 3 course à la carte fr £25 ⊕ FREE HOUSE ◀ Otter Amber, Betty Stogs, Doom Bar, Arundel Gold, Horsham Best Ở Gospel Green Champagne Cider, Thatchers Gold, Westons Organic. ☂ 16 **Facilities** Children welcome Children's portions Dogs allowed Garden Parking **Rooms** 8

COMPTON   Map 5 SU71

Coach & Horses

The Square PO18 9HA ☎ 023 9263 1228
dir: *On B2146 S of Petersfield, to Emsworth, in centre of Compton*

A 17th-century coaching inn and Victorian bar are comfortably combined here to make a charming village pub. Set in a pretty Downland village, it's a popular spot for walkers and cyclists. In the same hands for over a quarter of a century, the front bar features two open fires and a bar billiards table, while the restaurant is in the oldest part of the pub, with many exposed beams. Up to five guest beers from independent breweries are usually available. Expect proper cooking such as steak and kidney pudding, slow-roasted belly pork, and pheasant braised in red wine.

Open all wk 11.30-3 6-11 **Bar Meals** L served all wk 12-2 D served all wk 7-9 **Restaurant** L served all wk 12-2 booking required D served all wk 7-9 booking required ⊕ FREE HOUSE ◀ Fuller's ESB, Ballard's Best, Dark Star Golden Gate, Oakleaf Brewery Nuptu'ale, Dark Star Hophead Ở Thatchers Dry. **Facilities** Children welcome Children's portions Dogs allowed

DIAL POST   Map 6 TQ11

The Crown Inn NEW

Worthing Rd RH13 8NH ☎ 01403 710902
e-mail: crowninndialpost@aol.com
dir: *8m S of Horsham, off A24*

Overlooking the village green, this family-owned free-house offers a relaxed pub atmosphere for those who just want a pint of Harveys Best or those who want to tuck in to the excellent home-made food. Local sourcing doesn't get much better than lamb and pork from the family farm, and everything is made on the premises, from home-made faggots with seasonal greens to steak burgers topped with local bacon and Sussex Charmer cheese.

Open all wk Mon-Sat 11-3 6-11 (Sun 12-4) **Bar Meals** L served all wk 12-2.15 booking required D served Mon-Sat 6-9.15 booking required **Restaurant** L served all wk 12-2.15 booking required D served Mon-Sat 6-9.15 booking required ⊕ FREE HOUSE ◀ Harveys Best, Guest Ale, Dark Star Ở Thatchers Gold. **Facilities** Children welcome Children's portions Dogs allowed Garden Parking Wi-fi

DUNCTON   Map 6 SU91

The Cricketers

GU28 0LB ☎ 01798 342473
e-mail: info@thecricketersduncton.co.uk
dir: *On A285, 3m from Petworth, 8m from Chichester*

Dating back to the 16th century, this attractive white-painted pub is situated in spectacular South Downs walking country. The inn, little changed over the years, is named to commemorate its one-time owner John Wisden, the first-class cricketer and creator of the famous sporting almanac. The menu offers good hearty meals like trio of Old English sausages on mash with onion gravy; sizzling pork, pear and parsnip skillet; and whole lemon sole meunière with new potatoes. Children are welcome in the dining areas and gardens, with a menu catering to younger tastes.

Open all day all wk **Bar Meals** L served Mon-Fri 12-2.30, Sat-Sun 12-6 D served Mon-Fri 6-9, Sat-Sun 12-9 **Restaurant** L served Mon-Fri 12-2.30, Sat-Sun 12-6 D served Mon-Fri 6-9, Sat-Sun 12-9 ⊕ FREE HOUSE ◀ Betty Stogs, Horsham Best, Arundel Gold, Guest ale Ở Thatchers Heritage, Thatchers Draught. **Facilities** Children welcome Children's menu Play area Dogs allowed Garden Parking

EAST ASHLING   Map 5 SU80

Horse and Groom ★★★★ INN

East Ashling PO18 9AX
☎ 01243 575339   🖷 01243 575560
e-mail: info@thehorseandgroomchichester.co.uk
web: www.thehorseandgroomchichester.co.uk
dir: *3m from Chichester on B1278 between Chichester & Rowland's Castle. 2m off A27 at Fishbourne*

With Bosham Harbour's creeks and anchorages just to the south and the countryside of the South Downs National Park immediately to the north, this 400-year-old village inn is popular with visitors touring the sights and sites. The inn retains much of its heritage; timber frames, cooking range, oak beams and flagstoned floors a comfy retreat in which to try traditional ales from the likes of Hopback and Dark Star. On a summer day the beer garden, fringed by the flint-dressed restaurant and old barns converted into AA 4 star accommodation, is a suntrap in which to enjoy the extensive menu of mains and specials; seared aubergine layered with courgette, or line-caught fish such as John Dory take the eye here.

Open noon-3 6-11 (Sun noon-6) Closed: Sun eve **Bar Meals** L served Mon-Sat 12-2.15, Sun 12-2.30 D served Mon-Sat 6.30-9.15 **Restaurant** L served Mon-Sat 12-2.15, Sun 12-2.30 D served Mon-Sat 6.30-9.15 booking required ⊕ FREE HOUSE ◀ Young's, Harveys, Summer Lightning, Hop Head Ở Stowford Press, Addlestones. **Facilities** Children welcome Children's menu Children's portions Dogs allowed Garden Parking **Rooms** 11

Save on hotels. Book at theAA.com/hotel

SUSSEX, WEST 457 ENGLAND

EAST DEAN — Map 6 SU91

PICK OF THE PUBS

The Star & Garter ☻

PO18 0JG ☎ 01243 811318 ☒ 01243 811826
e-mail: thestarandgarter@hotmail.com
dir: On A286 between Chichester & Midhurst. Exit A286 at Singleton. Village in 2m

Built as a pub from traditional Sussex flint in about 1740, The Star & Garter stands close to the village pond in the pretty downland village of East Dean. The interior has been opened out to give a light and airy atmosphere with original brickwork, antique panelling, scrubbed tables and a wood-burning stove. In the bar, three locally brewed real ales are served from the barrel alongside two ciders and a range of wines by the glass. Locally renowned for an excellent selection of fish and shellfish, the menu also includes fine meat and vegetarian dishes, plus sharing platters. Typical choices include roasted guinea fowl with creamy Shropshire blue sauce; cous cous crusted goat's cheese with red onion salad; and pan-seared scallops with crispy pancetta and salad. A sunny sheltered patio, an original well and attractive lawned gardens complete the picture. Goodwood racecourse and motor racing venues are just a short hop in the car.

Open all wk 11-3 6-11 (Sat-Sun all day)
Bar Meals L served Mon-Fri 12-2.30, Sat-Sun all day D served Mon-Fri 6.30-11, Sat-Sun all day Av main course £13 Restaurant L served Mon-Fri 12-2.30, Sat-Sun all day booking required D served Mon-Fri 6.30-10, Sat-Sun all day booking required Fixed menu price fr £16.50 Av 3 course à la carte fr £25 ⊕ FREE HOUSE ◀ Ballards Best, Guinness, Arundel Castle, Gold ☼ Westons 1st Quality, Aspall. ☻11 Facilities Children welcome Children's menu Children's portions Dogs allowed Garden Parking Wi-fi

ELSTED — Map 5 SU81

PICK OF THE PUBS

The Three Horseshoes

GU29 0JY ☎ 01730 825746
dir: A272 from Midhurst towards Petersfield, after 2m left to Harting & Elsted, after 3m pub on left

Tucked below the steep scarp slope of the South Downs National Park in the peaceful village of Elsted, this 16th-century former drovers' ale house is one of those quintessential English country pubs that Sussex specialises in, full of rustic charm. Expect unspoilt cottage style bars, worn stone-flagged floors, low beams, latch doors, a vast inglenook, and a mix of antique furnishings. On fine days the extensive rear garden, with roaming chickens and stunning southerly views, is hugely popular. Tip-top real ales, including Bowman's and Flowerpots from across the Hampshire border, are drawn from the cask, and a daily-changing blackboard menu offers classic country cooking. Game such as pheasant is abundant in season; alternatively fish of the day comes with dauphinoise potatoes.

Open all wk Bar Meals L served all wk 12-2 D served Mon-Sat 6.30-9, Sun 7-8.30 Restaurant L served all wk 12-2 D served Mon-Sat 6.30-9, Sun 7-8.30 ⊕ FREE HOUSE ◀ Flowerpots Ale, Ballard's Best, Fuller's London Pride, Timothy Taylor Landlord, Hop Back Summer Lightning, Bowman Ales Wallops Wood. Facilities Dogs allowed Garden Parking

FERNHURST — Map 6 SU82

The Red Lion ☻

The Green GU27 3HY
☎ 01428 643112 ☒ 01428 643939
dir: Just off A286 midway between Haslemere & Midhurst

Renowned for its warm welcome and friendly atmosphere, this attractive 16th-century inn with oak beams and open fires is set in its own lovely gardens on the village green. The good choice of beers includes Fuller's ESB, Chiswick and London Pride along with seasonal guest ales. Freshly cooked, traditional English food is offered from a regularly changing specials menu featuring the likes of deep-fried whitebait; sautéed calves' liver and bacon; Jamaican chicken; and wild game poacher's pot casserole.

Open all day all wk 11.30am-11pm (Sun 11.30-10.30)
Bar Meals L served all wk 12-3 booking required D served all wk 6-9.30 booking required Restaurant L served all wk 12-3 booking required D served all wk 6-9.30 booking required ⊕ FULLER SMITH TURNER PLC ◀ Fuller's ESB, Chiswick, London Pride, Guest Ale ☼ Aspall. ☻8 Facilities Children welcome Children's menu Children's portions Dogs allowed Garden Parking

GRAFFHAM — Map 6 SU91

PICK OF THE PUBS

The Foresters Arms ☻

The Street GU28 0QA ☎ 01798 867202
e-mail: info@forestersgraffham.co.uk
dir: Telephone for directions

New landlords are reinvigorating this 17th-century pub tucked away in a cul-de-sac village at the foot of the South Downs. It's ideally placed for post walking and biking refreshments, and it's handy for Goodwood racing or polo at Cowdray Park. In the bar you'll find old beams, exposed stone walls and a large smoke-blackened fireplace, as well as a real ale choice likely to embrace Harvey's Best and Langhams Hip Hop, or there are 12 wines served by the glass. Freshly prepared food uses local produce where possible, but no corners are cut in the pub's objective to offer the best in quality and value: watercress, baby spinach and rosemary soup, followed by courgette and pea risotto with Barkham Blue cheese and rocket, slow-roasted lamb shank with redcurrant gravy, or Sussex pork loin with lemon and garlic risotto. Leave room for chocolate and orange iced parfait or baked vanilla and raisin cheesecake, then walk it all off with a downland stroll.

Open all wk noon-3 6-late (all day Sat-Sun in summer)
Bar Meals L served all wk 12-2.30 booking required D served Mon-Sat 6-9.15, Sun 6-8 booking required Restaurant L served all wk 12-2.30 booking required D served Mon-Sat 6-9.15, Sun 6-8 booking required ⊕ FREE HOUSE ◀ Langham Hip Hop, Harveys Best, Hog Back TEA ☼ Thatchers Gold. ☻12 Facilities Children welcome Children's menu Children's portions Dogs allowed Garden Parking Wi-fi

HALNAKER — Map 6 SU90

PICK OF THE PUBS

The Anglesey Arms at Halnaker ☻

PO18 0NQ ☎ 01243 773474 ☒ 01243 530034
e-mail: info@angleseyarms.co.uk
dir: From centre of Chichester 4m E on A285 (Petworth road)

Whether you pop in for a quick drink or a full meal, you'll find a warm welcome at this charmingly old-fashioned Georgian inn. Standing in two acres of landscaped grounds on the Goodwood Estate, head to the wood-floored bar to enjoy hand-pulled ales such as Bowman Swift One or choose from the extensive list of unusual wines from small vineyards. Hand-cut sandwiches, ploughman's, local sausages, and other traditional pub favourites will fill the odd corner, or you could sample something from the carte. The kitchen team makes skilful use of meat from fully traceable and organically raised animals, as well as locally caught fish from sustainable stocks. The Anglesey has built a special reputation for its steaks, cut from British beef and hung for at least 21 days. Dinner might begin with garlic wild mushrooms on toasted brioche, followed by seafood vol-au-vent with light thermidor sauce.

Open all wk 11-3 5.30-11 (Sat-Sun 11am-11pm)
Bar Meals L served Mon-Sat 12-2.30, Sun 12-3 D served Mon-Sat 6.30-9.30 Restaurant L served Mon-Sat 12-2.30, Sun 12-3 booking required D served Mon-Sat 6.30-9.30 booking required ⊕ PUNCH TAVERNS ◀ Young's Bitter, Bowman Swift One, Black Sheep Bitter ☼ Stowford Press. ☻14 Facilities Children welcome Children's portions Dogs allowed Garden Parking Wi-fi

HENLEY   Map 6 SU82

Duke of Cumberland Arms ▼ NEW

GU27 3HQ ☎ 01428 652280
e-mail: info@thedukeofcumberland.com
dir: *Between Haslemere & Midhurst, just off A286 near Fernhurst*

Deeply secluded amidst magnificent grounds in the wooded hills of the South Downs National Park, this rambling, red-roofed inn dates back, in parts, over 500 years. Recalling these centuries of service are brick, tile and flagstoned floors, matchboarded bar room, capacious fireplace and, totally in keeping, local beers served straight from the wood. The first rate menu is built to impress; carpaccio of local wild venison or whole roast partridge just a snapshot of the home-cooked meals much appreciated by enthusiastic clientele. The gardens have fine views and fresh trout can be found in many of the garden ponds.

Open all day all wk **Bar Meals** L served Mon-Sat 12-2 booking required Av main course £13.95
Restaurant L served all wk 12-2 booking required D served Tue-Sat 7-9 booking required Av 3 course à la carte fr £35 ⊕ FREE HOUSE ◀ Harveys Sussex, Langham Best & Hip Hop ♂ Stowford Press. **Facilities** Children welcome Children's portions Dogs allowed Garden Beer festival Parking

HEYSHOTT   Map 6 SU81

PICK OF THE PUBS

Unicorn Inn

GU29 0DL ☎ 01730 813486 📠 01730 814896
e-mail: unicorninnheyshott@hotmail.co.uk
dir: *Telephone for directions*

The location of this mid-18th-century free house lends much to its appeal, with super views of the South Downs from its beautiful, south-facing rear gardens. The bar, with beams and a large log fire, is particularly atmospheric. Since the Unicorn was first licensed in 1839, many publicans have left their mark; today's landlady is Jenni Halpin, whose wine list owes quite a bit to her native Oz, and her manager is Sally Carter. Being within the South Downs National Park, it's a fair bet that you'll share the pub with walkers and cyclists (and, of course, some locals) taking a much-needed break to knock back some Horsham Best Bitter or Arundel Sussex Gold. The subtly lit, cream-painted restaurant is strong on locally sourced food, such as fresh fish from Selsey – try wild sea bass fillet with white wine and chive sauce; other possibilities are chicken breast wrapped in bacon, and Mediterranean vegetable risotto.

Open 11.30-3 6-11 (Sun 12-4) Closed: Sun eve & Mon **Bar Meals** L served Tue-Sat 12-2, Sun 12-2.30 booking required D served Tue-Sat 7-9 booking required **Restaurant** L served Tue-Sat 12-2, Sun 12-2.30 booking required D served Tue-Sat 7-9 ⊕ FREE HOUSE ◀ Horsham Best Bitter, Fuller's London Pride, Arundel Sussex Gold ♂ Stowford Press. **Facilities** Children welcome Children's menu Children's portions Dogs allowed Garden Parking

HORSHAM   Map 6 TQ13

The Black Jug ▼

31 North St RH12 1RJ
☎ 01403 253526 📠 01403 217821
e-mail: black.jug@brunningandprice.co.uk
dir: *Telephone for directions*

Set close to the railway station, this busy town centre pub is a lovely old city-style pub. You'll find a congenial atmosphere with friendly staff, plenty of ales, an open fire, large conservatory and walled garden. All-day meals are freshly prepared using local ingredients wherever possible; light bites include lost churdle pie – a 17th century creation using bacon and lamb's liver; or smoked haddock and leek risotto, whilst for larger appetites there's ham, free-range egg and chips; and fish pie with green beans and almonds.

Open all day all wk 11.30am-11pm (Sun 12-10.30)
Bar Meals L served Mon-Sat 12-10, Sun 12-9.30 booking required D served Mon-Sat 12-10, Sun 12-9.30 booking required Av main course £11.95 food served all day **Restaurant** L served Mon-Sat 12-10, Sun 12-9.30 booking required D served Mon-Sat 12-10, Sun 12-9.30 booking required food served all day ⊕ BRUNNING & PRICE ◀ Harveys, Deuchars IPA, Guest Ales ♂ Westons. ▼ 20 **Facilities** Children welcome Children's portions Dogs allowed Garden

KINGSFOLD   Map 6 TQ13

The Dog and Duck

Dorking Rd RH12 3SA ☎ 01306 627295
e-mail: info@thedogandduck.fsnet.co.uk
dir: *On A24, 3m N of Horsham*

A 16th-century family-run and family-friendly country pub. There's plenty of children's play equipment in the huge garden, and three very large fields encourage dogs and energetic owners to stretch their legs. In the summer a native American camp is set up, complete with tepees and camp fire. The rest of the year sees the diary chock-full of celebratory and fundraising events; the royal wedding, for example, started with breakfast and continued with family party games and free buffet.

Open all wk Mon-Thu 12-3 6-11 (Fri 12-3 6-12 Sat noon-mdnt Sun noon-10pm) **Bar Meals** L served all wk 12-2.30 (3pm Sun) D served Mon-Sat 6-9 **Restaurant** L served all wk 12-2.30 (3pm Sun) D served Mon-Sat 6-9 ⊕ HALL & WOODHOUSE ◀ King & Barnes Sussex, Badger Best, seasonal variations, Guest ales ♂ Stowford Press. **Facilities** Children welcome Children's menu Children's portions Play area Dogs allowed Garden Beer festival Parking

The Owl at Kingsfold ▼ NEW

Dorking Rd RH12 3SA ☎ 01306 628499
e-mail: info@theowl-kingsfold.co.uk
web: www.theowl-kingsfold.co.uk
dir: *On A24, 4m N of Horsham*

Nigel and Jean White took over The Owl in October 2010 after moving from the Cotswolds. They have given it a stylish makeover but it remains a traditional country free house, with wooden beams, flagstone floors and log burners. It occupies a prominent roadside site in the village, with plenty of parking and a garden with views to the Surrey Hills; composer Ralph Vaughan Williams reputedly arranged the Kingsfold Hymn here. There are three real ales to choose from, while the menu of pub classics is backed by a chalk board for specials, plus sharing platters.

Open all day **Bar Meals** food served all day **Restaurant** food served all day ◀ Otter Ale, Hogs Back TEA, Hepworth Pullman ♂ Westons Scrumpy. ▼ 12 **Facilities** Children welcome Children's menu Children's portions Garden Parking Wi-fi

KIRDFORD   Map 6 TQ02

PICK OF THE PUBS

The Half Moon Inn

RH14 0LT ☎ 01403 820223
web: www.halfmoonkirdford.co.uk
dir: *Off A272 between Billingshurst & Petworth. At Wisborough Green follow Kirdford signs*

Set directly opposite the church in this quiet unspoilt Sussex village near the River Arun, this picturesque, red-tiled 16th-century village inn is covered in climbing roses. A bit off the beaten track, the pub is made up of cottages that were once craftsmen's workshops. Although drinkers are welcome, The Half Moon is mainly a dining pub. The interior consists of an attractive bar with adjoining wooden-floored restaurant area. The furniture and paintings charmingly reflect the oak beams, tiled floors, open fireplaces and log fires in winter. The chef serves honest wholesome food, locally sourced from healthy well-reared stock. The à la carte, daily set menus and lunchtime snacks reflect the best of the season's ingredients. At dinner, the atmosphere changes, with candlelight, linen tablecloths and polished glassware. Private dining is available. Well tended gardens at the front and rear are an added draw in the summer. Look out for the monthly themed music-to-dine-to evenings. There are also a number of walks and cycle routes in the area if you want to work up an appetite.

Open 11-3 6-11 Closed: Sun eve, Mon eve
Bar Meals L served all wk 12-2.30 D served Tue-Sat 6-9.15 **Restaurant** D served Tue-Sat 6-9.15 Local ale, Ballards. **Facilities** Children welcome Children's portions Garden Parking

LAMBS GREEN　　　Map 6 TQ23

The Lamb Inn ♥

RH12 4RG
☎ 01293 871336 & 871933 　 01293 871933
e-mail: lambinnrusper@yahoo.co.uk
dir: 6m from Horsham between Rusper & Faygate. 5m from Crawley

Public footpaths pass by the The Lamb's front door, making it an ideal place for a country walk. It remains an unchanged traditional country pub, with a patio to side and front, a bar with inglenook fire, and a conservatory. A good selection of real ales is sourced from local micro-breweries, and as much local produce as possible is used in the kitchen - everything from starters to puddings is home made. Typical dishes include steak and Sussex ale pie; half a roasted Suffolk duck with orange and green peppercorn sauce; and chargrilled steak with all the trimmings. Annual beer festival in October.

Open all wk Mon-Thu 11.30am-3 5.30-11pm (Fri-Sat 11.30am-11pm Sun noon-10.30pm) Closed: 25-26 Dec **Bar Meals** L served Mon-Thu 12-2, Fri-Sat 12-9.30, Sun 12-9 D served Mon-Thu 6.30-9.30, Fri-Sat 12-9.30, Sun 12-9 Av main course £11 **Restaurant** L served Mon-Thu 12-2, Fri-Sat 12-9.30, Sun 12-9 D served Mon-Thu 6.30-9.30, Fri-Sat 12-9.30, Sun 12-9 ⊕ FREE HOUSE Kings Old Ale, Weltons Old Cocky, Langham LSD, Dark Star Hop Head, Dark Star Best Ö Stowford Press, Biddenden Cider, Rekorderlig. ♥ 12 **Facilities** Children welcome Children's menu Children's portions Dogs allowed Beer festival Parking Wi-fi

LODSWORTH　　　Map 6 SU92

PICK OF THE PUBS

The Halfway Bridge Inn ♥

Halfway Bridge GU28 9BP ☎ 01798 861281
e-mail: enquiries@halfwaybridge.co.uk
dir: Between Petworth & Midhurst, next to Cowdray Estate & Golf Club on A272

You'll find this red brick 18th-century coaching inn beside the A272 midway between Petworth and Midhurst, close to Cowdray Park polo ground, Petworth House and the South Downs. It's a delightful mix of traditional pub and contemporary dining inn; log fires, beams, blackened iron stove and wooden floors characterise the tastefully furnished series of rooms, whilst modern touches added by Paul and Sue Carter add an airy, cutting-edge atmosphere. Weary travellers will find a great welcome, tip-top ales — try a pint of

local Langham's Halfway to Heaven — and an appealing menu listing traditional British dishes that are given a uniquely modern twist. Start with scallops, chorizo and black pudding potato cake with sauce vièrge before indulging in calves' liver, pancetta crisps, basil mash and caramelised shallot jus, or baked whole sea bass with lemongrass and coriander butter. Squeeze in a chocolate fondant with home-made vanilla ice cream before rewarding yourself with a seat in the peaceful patio and garden.

Open all wk Mon-Sat 11-11 (Sun 12-10.30) Closed: 25 Dec **Bar Meals** L served all wk 12-2.30 D served all wk 6.30-9.15 **Restaurant** L served all wk 12-2.30 D served all wk 6.30-9.15 ⊕ FREE HOUSE Skinner's Betty Stogs Sharp's Doom Bar, Langhams Halfway to Heaven. ♥ 12 **Facilities** Children welcome Children's menu Children's portions Dogs allowed Garden Parking Wi-fi

PICK OF THE PUBS

The Hollist Arms

The Street GU28 9BZ ☎ 01798 861310
e-mail: george@thehollistarms.co.uk
dir: 0.5m between Midhurst & Petworth, 1m N of A272, adjacent to Country Park

The Hollist Arms, a pub since 1823, is full of traditional charm and character. The 15th-century building overlooks a lawn where a grand old tree stands ringed by a bench. Step through the pretty entrance porch and you'll find open fires in winter, leather sofas and a blissful absence of fruit machines. The atmospheric dining room has a popular window table, but if that's occupied you can head for the snug or one of a number of small intimate rooms in which to drink or eat with family and friends. All the dishes served here are prepared by chefs using traditional methods and fresh local ingredients whenever possible. Summer sees everyone heading for the wonderful garden and terraced area clutching pints of Horsham Best or Stowford Press cider. Well behaved children and dogs are welcome, all looked after by smiling staff who contribute greatly to this hostelry's warm and friendly ambience.

Open all day all wk 11am-11pm ⊕ FREE HOUSE Langham, Timothy Taylor Landlord, Horsham Best Ö Stowford Press. **Facilities** Children welcome Children's menu Children's portions Dogs allowed Garden Parking Wi-fi

LURGASHALL　　　Map 6 SU92

The Noah's Ark

The Green GU28 9ET ☎ 01428 707346
e-mail: amy@noahsarkinn.co.uk
dir: B2131 from Haslemere follow signs to Petworth/Lurgashall. A3 from London towards Portsmouth. At Milford take A283 signed Petworth. Follow signs to Lurgashall

In a picturesque village beneath Blackdown Hill, this attractive 16th-century inn overlooks the cricket green. The revitalised interior is full of warmth thanks to the charm of old beams, a large inglenook fireplace, and the enthusiasm of its owners. Ales include a regularly changing guest, and traditional British food with a contemporary twist uses ingredients carefully sourced from the best local suppliers: gammon and cauliflower terrine, cornichons and English mustard may precede main courses such as creamy crab and prawn spaghetti, chilli and parsley crumbs with Parmesan.

Open all wk 11-3.30 5.30-11 (Sat-Sun all day) **Bar Meals** L served all wk 12-2.30 booking required D served all wk 7-9.30 booking required **Restaurant** L served all wk 12-2.30 booking required D served all wk 7-9.30 booking required ⊕ GREENE KING Greene King IPA , Abbot, Guest ale Ö Stowford Press. **Facilities** Children welcome Children's portions Family room Dogs allowed Garden Parking Wi-fi

MAPLEHURST　　　Map 6 TQ12

The White Horse ♥

Park Ln RH13 6LL ☎ 01403 891208
dir: 5m SE of Horsham, between A281 & A272

This award-winning rural free house lies deep in the Sussex countryside and offers a welcome haven free from music and fruit machines. Hearty home-cooked pub food and an enticing selection of five real ales are served over what is reputed to be the widest bar counter in Sussex. Sip a pint of Harveys Best or Station Pullman Ale whilst admiring the rolling countryside from the large, quiet, south-facing garden. Village-brewed cider is a speciality.

Open all wk 12-2.30 6-11 (Sun 12-3 7-11) **Bar Meals** L served all wk 12-2 D served all wk 6-9 ⊕ FREE HOUSE Harvey's Best, Welton's Pride & Joy, Dark Star Espresso Stout, King's Red River, Station Pullman ale Ö Local cider, JB Cider. ♥ 11 **Facilities** Children welcome Children's menu Children's portions Play area Family room Dogs allowed Garden Parking **Notes** ⊛

MIDHURST
Map 6 SU82

The Angel Hotel ♥

North St GU29 9DN ☎ 01730 812421 📠 **01730 815928**
e-mail: info@theangelmidhurst.co.uk
dir: Telephone for directions

The true Tudor origins of this historic former coaching inn are hidden behind an imposing and well-proportioned late-Georgian façade. Its frontage overlooks the town's main street, while at the rear attractive gardens give way to meadowland and the ruins of Cowdray Castle. A reliable pint of Fuller's could be followed by dinner in the new Bentley's Grill, where a range of the finest Argentinean steaks can be cut to suit appetites large and small. Other choices include sautéed Bignor Park pheasant with wild mushroom risotto. A recent sympathetic refurbishment has retained and enhanced original features.

Open all day all wk **Bar Meals** L served all wk 12-2 D served all wk 7-10 Av main course £9.50 **Restaurant** L served all wk 12-2 D served all wk 7-10 Av 3 course à la carte fr £28.40 ⊕ FREE HOUSE ◀ Fuller's HSB, Best, London Pride, Guinness Ŏ Aspall. ♥ 12 **Facilities** Children welcome Children's menu Children's portions Garden Parking Wi-fi

NUTHURST
Map 6 TQ12

PICK OF THE PUBS

Black Horse Inn

Nuthurst St RH13 6LH ☎ 01403 891272
e-mail: enquiries@theblackhorseinn.com
dir: 4m S of Horsham, off A281, A24 & A272

The Black Horse's 18th-century features – stone-flagged floors, exposed wattle and daub walls, inglenook fire – have been combined with touches of contemporary style to create a truly relaxing dining pub. The lovely old building, half masked by impressive window boxes in summer, was originally part of a row of workers' cottages on the Sedgwick Park estate; it was first recorded as an inn in 1817. Today the award-winning hostelry's real ales and ciders are backed by a concise but complete menu of dishes from the kitchen. Lunch sees a range of open sandwiches competing with classic hot plates (Sussex bangers and mash) and specials (pan-fried salmon with creamed leeks and new potatoes). In the evening expect more complex fare such as rump of lamb provençal; or loin of pork with roast peppers. Home-made puddings follow simple but classic lines such as vanilla crème brûlée. On sunny days you can sit out on the terraces at the front and rear, or take drinks across the stone bridge over a stream into the delightful back garden.

Open all wk 12-3 6-11 (Sat noon-11pm Sun noon-9pm BHs all day) **Bar Meals** L served Mon-Sat 12-2.30, Sun 12-6 booking required D served all wk 6-9.30 booking required **Restaurant** L served Mon-Sat 12-2.30, Sun 12-6 booking required D served all wk 6-9.30 booking required ⊕ MR SMITHS PUBS ◀ Harveys Sussex, W J King, Hepworths, Dark Star Hophead, Guest ales Ŏ Westons, Stowford Press. **Facilities** Children welcome Children's menu Children's portions Dogs allowed Garden Parking

OVING
Map 6 SU90

The Gribble Inn ♥

PO20 2BP ☎ 01243 786893 📠 **01243 786893**
dir: From A27 take A259. After 1m left at rdbt, 1st right to Oving, 1st left in village

This charming 16th-century inn is a peaceful spot to quietly sup any of the eight real ales from its on-site micro-brewery plus a choice of five or six seasonal extras; takeaway polypins are also sold. Named after local schoolmistress Rose Gribble, it has large open fireplaces, wood burners, low beams and no background music. Enjoy traditional pub food with a twist: rabbit and Stowford Press cider with mustard mash, West Sussex rump of lamb with rosemary roasted potatoes and red wine jus, or savoury baked four-cheese cheesecake with roasted tomatoes and kale. The inn hosts summer and winter beer festivals, and there is also a skittle alley, enjoyed by parties and works' social functions.

Open all wk 11-3 5.30-11 (Fri-Sun 11-11) **Bar Meals** L served all wk 12-2 D served all wk 6.30-9.30 Av main course £9.95 **Restaurant** L served all wk 12-2 booking required D served all wk 6.30-9.30 booking required ⊕ HALL & WOODHOUSE ◀ Gribble Ale, Reg's Tipple, Badger First Gold, Pigs Ear, Fuzzy Duck, Plucking Pheasant, Mocha Mole, Sussex Quad Hopper, Flints Full Glory Ŏ Stowford Press. ♥ 20 **Facilities** Children welcome Children's menu Children's portions Family room Dogs allowed Garden Beer festival Parking

PETWORTH
Map 6 SU92

The Black Horse

Byworth GU28 0HL ☎ 01798 342424
dir: A285 from Petworth, 2m, turn right signed Byworth, pub 50yds on right

An unspoilt 16th-century village pub, once part of the old tanneries, The Black Horse retains a rustic feel with exposed beams, flagstone floors, pew seating, scrubbed wooden tables, period photographs and open fires. It is a great place for enjoying a glass of well kept ale. The former kitchen has been transformed into a snug dining area including the original Aga, whilst the large garden offers views to the South Downs. Expect lunchtime baguettes, jacket potatoes, light dishes and ploughman's, and in the evening maybe seared king scallops with crispy bacon and aged balsamic reduction, followed by honey and mustard glazed pork steak with oven roasted vegetables.

Open all day all wk 11-11 (Sun 12-11) ⊕ FREE HOUSE ◀ Fuller's London Pride, TEA, Flowerpots, Hophead. **Facilities** Children welcome Children's menu Dogs allowed Garden Parking

PICK OF THE PUBS

The Grove Inn

Grove Ln GU28 0HY ☎ 01798 343659
e-mail: steveandvaleria@tiscali.co.uk
dir: On outskirts of town, just off A283 between Pulborough & Petworth. 0.5m from Petworth Park

A 17th-century free house a stone's throw south of historic Petworth. Idyllically sited, it nestles in beautiful gardens with views to the South Downs; a patio area with shady pergola is ideal for alfresco drinks. Inside is a bar with oak-beamed ceilings and large fireplace, while the conservatory restaurant is the place to sample a seasonal menu revised every six to eight weeks. The pub is hosted by a husband and wife partnership: Valeria looks after front of house, warmly welcoming locals and visitors alike, while husband Stephen runs the kitchen operation. His simple objective is to serve quality dishes at prices that do not detract from their enjoyment. Typical starters include deep fried calamari with garlic mayonnaise; followed by South Downs venison fillet medallions with port jus; or poached smoked haddock topped with cheese sauce and a poached egg. Expect desserts along the lines of toffee and banana pancake with vanilla ice cream or rhubarb crumble.

Open Tue-Sat 12-3 6-11 (Sun 12-3) Closed: Sun eve & Mon (ex BH) **Bar Meals** L served Tue-Sun 12-2.30 D served Tue-Sat 6-9.15 **Restaurant** L served Tue-Sun 12-2.30 D served Tue-Sat 6-9.15 ⊕ FREE HOUSE ◀ Young's, Betty Stogs, Sharp's Doom Bar, Halfway to Heaven. **Facilities** Children welcome Children's portions Dogs allowed Garden Parking

POYNINGS
Map 6 TQ21

PICK OF THE PUBS

Royal Oak ♥

See Pick of the Pubs on opposite page

Save on hotels. Book at **theAA.com/hotel**

SUSSEX, WEST 461 ENGLAND

PICK OF THE PUBS

Royal Oak ♀

POYNINGS   Map 6 TQ21

The Street BN45 7AQ
☎ **01273 857389** 📠 **01273 857202**
e-mail: ropoynings@aol.com
web: www.royaloakpoynings.biz
dir: *N on A23 just outside Brighton, take A281 signed Henfield & Poynings, then follow signs into Poynings*

Set in a pretty village below the South Downs and miles of glorious downland walks, a wonderful summer garden with barbecue facilities, serene rural views, and all-day food that utilises local produce are the major attractions at Paul Day and Lewis Robinson's award-winning, late 19th-century pub. The eye-catching window blinds and cream-painted exterior draw customers into a building with solid oak floors, where old beams hung with hop bines blend effortlessly with contemporary decor and comfy sofas. In the bar, Sussex-brewed Harveys Bitter sit alongside Sharp's Doom Bar, and a decent wine list includes new and old world wines with up to 14 available by the glass.

The menu changes seasonally, bristles with local produce and offers a range of meals to suit most appetites. A fish sharing platter comes laden with smoked halibut, crayfish tails, 'Springs' smoked salmon, marinated anchovies and warm ciabatta bread, or you can opt for a classic bacon, lettuce and tomato ciabatta sandwich. Moving up the scale,

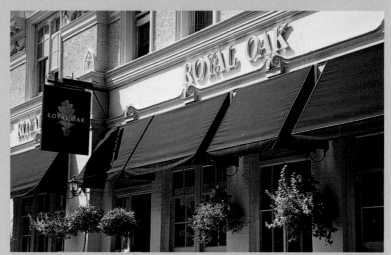

good old fashioned pub favourites like Harvey's beer battered haddock with fat chips, mushy peas and caper mayonnaise, or a classic fish pie with Cheddar mash rub shoulders with more ambitious dishes. For starters, try the pressed Sussex game with apple and raisin compôte, or the caramelised red onion and Gruyère tartlet with sticky apple. Main course options might include steak, oxtail and kidney pie with truffled mash, and Old Spot pork belly with Savoy cabbage and Cheddar and bacon cream. Local beef from the pedigree Sussex herd from the neighbouring farm is often featured on the menus and some puddings (sticky toffee pudding) are served with hand-made ice cream from local dairy herd. In summer months the barbecue menu is very popular as are the winter themed menu events.

Open all day all wk 11-11 (Sun noon-10.30) **Bar Meals** food served all day **Restaurant** food served all day ⊕ FREE HOUSE ◀ Harveys Sussex, Sharp's Doom Bar ♂ Westons Herefordshire Country Perry, Westons Scrumpy. ♀ 14 **Facilities** Children welcome Children's menu Children's portions Play area Dogs allowed Garden Parking Wi-fi

ROWHOOK   Map 6 TQ13

PICK OF THE PUBS

The Chequers Inn ◉ ♀

RH12 3PY ☎ 01403 790480 ▤ 01403 790480
e-mail: thechequersrowhook@googlemail.com
dir: Off A29 NW of Horsham

A striking, higgledy-piggledy pub, at least 400 years
old and on the line of the Roman Stane Street. A classic
interior of flagstone floor, low beams, inglenook fire and
all the trimmings is a fine welcome to a country inn
masterminded by the accomplished chef Tim Neal,
member of the prestigious Master Chefs of Great
Britain and holder of an AA Rosette. Harveys Sussex
beers and a very impressive wine list partner an
extensive bar menu which may also be taken in the
inn's restaurant. Tim delights in using only the best
local produce, taking this to the extreme by going
native and sourcing seasonal wild mushrooms and
even truffles from the generous woodlands near the
hamlet of Rowhook. From the local shoot may come the
bird used in the sauté pigeon, roasted Jerusalem
artichoke, lardons, croutes and hazelnut dressing
starter; a precursor to pan-fried halibut with buttered
spinach, asparagus, brown shrimp and chive cream,
whilst Sussex cheeses feature on the dessert menu.

Open 11.30-3.30 6-11.30 Closed: 25 Dec, Sun & BH
eve **Bar Meals** L served all wk 12-2 booking required
D served Mon-Fri 7-9 booking required Av main course
£8.50 **Restaurant** L served all wk 12-2 booking
required D served Mon-Sat 7-9 booking required Av 3
course à la carte fr £28.50 ⊕ FREE HOUSE ◀ Harveys
Sussex Ale, Fuller's London Pride, Guest ale
♂ Thatchers Gold. ♀ 30 **Facilities** Children's portions
Dogs allowed Garden Parking

SHIPLEY   Map 6 TQ12

PICK OF THE PUBS

The Countryman Inn ♀

See Pick of the Pubs on opposite page

George & Dragon ♀

Dragons Green RH13 8GE ☎ 01403 741320
e-mail: marlenegrace@googlemail.com
dir: Signed from A272 between Coolham & A24

Set amid beautiful Sussex countryside, this 17th-century
cottage is a haven of peace and quiet, especially on
balmy summer evenings when the garden is a welcome
retreat. Its interior is all head-banging beams and
inglenook fireplaces, with an excellent choice of real ales
at the bar. Food-wise, expect pub classics such as
sausage, mash and onion gravy, seared salmon fillet with
new potatoes, and pesto chicken and bacon salad.
Shipley is famous for its smock mill.

Open all wk 12-3 6-11 (Sat-Sun all day)
Bar Meals L served all wk 12-2 booking required D served
Tue-Sat 6-9 booking required **Restaurant** L served all wk
12-2 booking required D served Tue-Sat 6-9 booking
required ⊕ HALL & WOODHOUSE ◀ Badger Best, Sussex
Best, Hall and Woodhouse Fursty Ferret & Pickled
Partridge, Guest ale ♂ Westons Stowford Press. ♀ 8
Facilities Children welcome Children's portions Play area
Family room Dogs allowed Garden Parking Wi-fi

SINGLETON   Map 5 SU81

The Partridge Inn ♀

PO18 0EY ☎ 01243 811251
e-mail: info@thepartridgeinn.co.uk
dir: Telephone for directions

Set within the picturesque Goodwood estate in the South
Downs village of Singleton, this pub, formerly called the
Fox and Hounds, dates back to the 16th century when it
was part of a huge hunting park owned by the Fitzalan
Earls of Arundel. Today, it is popular with walkers
enjoying the rolling Sussex countryside and visitors to
Goodwood for motor and horse-racing. Now run by Giles
Thompson, former executive head chef of The Ritz, you
can expect a friendly welcome and great food, from
tempting sandwiches, salads and light bites to main
courses of O'Hagan's sausages and mash with red onion
gravy; steak, mushroom and ale pie; or salmon, smoked
haddock and chive fishcakes.

Open all wk all day Sat-Sun **Bar Meals** L served all wk
12-2, Sat-Sun 12-3 D served all wk 6-9, Fri-Sat 6-9.30 Av
main course £9.50 **Restaurant** L served all wk 12-2, Sat-
Sun 12-3 booking required D served all wk 6-9, Fri-Sat
6-9.30 booking required Av 3 course à la carte fr £20
⊕ ENTERPRISE INNS ◀ London Pride, Harvey's Sussex,
Summer Lightening ♂ Stowford Press. ♀ 10
Facilities Children welcome Children's menu Children's
portions Dogs allowed Garden Parking

SLINDON   Map 6 SU90

The Spur ♀

BN18 0NE ☎ 01243 814216
e-mail: thespurslindon@btinternet.com
dir: Off A27 on A29 outside Slindon

Set just outside the village of Slindon on top of the rolling
South Downs, this 17th-century pub is a an ideal
stopping-off point on a day out in the country. It has been
praised for its friendly atmosphere and for generous
portions of food. Outside are large pub gardens and a
courtyard, inside is an open-plan bar and restaurant,
warmed by crackling log fires and offering regularly
changing menus. If you book in advance you can use the
skittle alley, or enjoy a game of pool or other pub games.
There has been a change of hands at The Spur.

Open all wk 11.30-3 6-11 (Sun noon-3 7-10.30)
Bar Meals L served all wk 12-2 D served Sun-Tue 7-9,
Wed-Sat 7-9.30 **Restaurant** L served all wk 12-2 booking
required D served Sun-Tue 7-9, Wed-Sat 7-9.30 booking
required ⊕ FREE HOUSE ◀ Sharp's Doom Bar, Directors
♂ Thatchers Gold. ♀ 10 **Facilities** Children welcome
Children's portions Dogs allowed Garden Parking

SOUTH HARTING   Map 5 SU71

The Ship Inn

GU31 5PZ ☎ 01730 825302
dir: From Petersfield take B2146 towards Chichester.
Inn in 5m

A 17th-century inn made from a ship's timbers, hence the
name. There is a great selection of real ales and
Thatchers Gold cider available. Home-made pies are a
feature, and other popular dishes include fish pie, mussel
chowder, calves' liver and rack of lamb, all washed down
with a pint of Palmer IPA. A range of vegetarian dishes
and bar snacks is also available. In warmer months there
is a pleasant garden and outdoor seating to enjoy. Recent
change of hands.

Open all day all wk noon-11 (Sun noon-10.30)
Bar Meals L served all wk 12-2.30 D served Mon-Sat 6-9
Av main course £8.95 **Restaurant** Av 3 course à la carte
fr £17.95 ⊕ FREE HOUSE ◀ Palmer IPA, Dark Star
Brewery Hop Head, Ballards Best, Palmers Copper Ale
♂ Thatchers Gold. **Facilities** Children welcome Children's
menu Children's portions Dogs allowed Garden Parking

STEDHAM   Map 5 SU82

Hamilton Arms/Nava Thai Restaurant ♀

Hamilton Arms School Ln GU29 0NZ
☎ 01730 812555 ▤ 01730 817459
e-mail: hamiltonarms@hotmail.com
web: www.thehamiltonarms.co.uk
dir: Off A272 between Midhurst & Petersfield

Standing opposite the village common amid beautiful
South Downs countryside, this whitewashed free house is
one of the first country pubs to serve authentic Thai food.
It's also the home of the Mudita Trust, dedicated to
helping abused and underprivileged children in Thailand.
The pub serves English bar snacks and a good selection
of real ales alongside Thai beer and Thai dishes such as
fried Thai noodles with shrimps, crabmeat, egg and
beansprouts. The Nava Thai restaurant offers an
extensive range of Thai dishes, and there is also a
takeaway service.

Open all day Closed: Mon (ex BH) **Bar Meals** L served
Tue-Sun 12-2.30 D served Tue-Sun 6-10
Restaurant L served Tue-Sun 12-2.30 D served Tue-Sun
6-10 booking required ⊕ FREE HOUSE ◀ Fuller's London
Pride, Alton Pride, Hamilton Armless ♂ Westons Vintage,
Stowford Press. ♀ 8 **Facilities** Children welcome
Children's menu Children's portions Play area Dogs
allowed Garden Parking Wi-fi

Save on hotels. Book at **theAA.com/hotel**

SUSSEX, WEST 463 ENGLAND

PICK OF THE PUBS

The Countryman Inn 🍷

SHIPLEY   Map 6 TQ12

Countryman Ln RH13 8PZ
☎ 01403 741383   📠 01403 741115
e-mail: countrymaninn@btinternet.com
web: www.countrymanshipley.co.uk
dir: *From A272 at Coolham into Smithers
Hill Ln. 1m to junct with Countryman Ln*

The Vaughan family has run this
traditional rural free house, just outside
the village of Shipley, since 1986. It
stands surrounded by 3,500 acres of
farmland owned by the Knepp Castle
Estate, where fallow deer, Tamworth pigs,
Exmoor ponies and longhorn cattle roam
free, and wild grasses have been planted
to attract birds. In the welcoming, open
log fire-warmed bar, you'll find cask-
conditioned Harveys and Organic
Hailsham ales, and more than thirty wines
from around the world. Out in the garden
a newly installed polytunnel enables the
Vaughans to grow vegetables and herbs,
entitling them to be a little self-righteous
in any food miles debate; in any event,
most of the other produce is locally
sourced too, game, for example, coming
from the Estate, and fish direct from boats
working out of Shoreham and Newhaven.
All this helps to ensure day-to-day menus
change frequently, though classics such
as Cumberland sausages and mash, and
scampi and chips are usually always
available, as are lunchtime baguettes and

salads. Typical main menu starters
include pan-seared scallops, and minced
beef and pork meatballs, with main
courses of roast belly of Saddleback pork;
plaice and Serrano ham paupiettes; and
mixed bean tabouleh. Please note that
very young children are not permitted in
the restaurant, but when the weather
permits some meals are served in the
garden, where the outdoor barbecue is
likely to be fired up for grills. In the
Countryman Farm Shop you can buy a
wide range of foods, including free-range
eggs, and home-made preserves, pickles
and relishes. Shipley's historic eight-sided
smock mill is worth a visit, and is just a
mile's walk along a woodland bridle path
from The Countryman.

Open all wk 10-4 6-11
Bar Meals L served all wk 11.30-3.30 D
served all wk 6-10 **Restaurant** L served all
wk 11.30-3.30 D served all wk 6-10
🍺 FREE HOUSE ◨ Harveys, London Pride,
Dark Star Ö Thatchers Gold. 🍷 18
Facilities Dogs allowed Garden Parking

SUTTON — Map 6 SU91

PICK OF THE PUBS

The White Horse Inn

The Street RH20 1PS
☎ 01798 869221 📄 01798 869221
e-mail: mail@whitehorse-sutton.co.uk
dir: From Petworth follow signs for Roman villa then to Sutton village

Set in the beautiful village of Sutton in the heart of the West Sussex countryside, this erstwhile run-down boozer was transformed into a pub in the modern country style when new owners took it over in 2008. Being so handy for polo at Cowdray Park and racing at Goodwood, it makes a great watering hole at the end of a hard day's entertainment. Hand pumps at the bar dispense the likes of Fuller's ales, while menus use produce from local suppliers in the creation of modern dishes to suit today's sophisticated palates. With prices so reasonable, a full three-course affair may not be out of the question: start with grilled sardines on garlic ciabatta, with sunblush tomato and herb salad. Next could come belly of pork in cider sauce with gratin potatoes, Savoy cabbage and baby carrots. To finish, blueberry ice cream on meringue with fruit coulis is both delicious and manageable.

Open all wk 11-3 6-11 Bar Meals L served all wk 11.30-2.30 D served all wk 6.30-9.30 Restaurant L served all wk 11.30-2.30 booking required D served all wk 6.30-9.30 booking required ⊕ ENTERPRISE INNS ◀ Sharp's Doom Bar, Harveys, Adnams, London Pride ♂ Stowford Press. Facilities Children welcome Children's portions Dogs allowed Garden Parking Wi-fi

TILLINGTON — Map 6 SU92

PICK OF THE PUBS

The Horseguards Inn

★★★★ INN ◉ ♥

GU28 9AF ☎ 01798 342332 📄 01798 345126
e-mail: info@thehorseguardsinn.co.uk
dir: From Petworth towards Midhurst on A272. In 1m turn right signed Tillington. Inn 300mtrs up hill opposite church

The Horseguards is a charming 300-year-old inn peacefully positioned opposite the parish church on the edge of the National Trust's Petworth Park. Raised up from the village lane it was originally three cottages and enjoys good views across the Rother Valley towards the South Downs. Inside, expect to find a rambling series of relaxing and tastefully refurbished rooms that ooze period charm, with sagging beams, original pine panelling, four glowing fires (one in an old black range), antique and pine furnishings, fresh flowers and candles. Cosy, intimate and friendly it certainly is and Sam and Misa Beard run the pub with passion and flair, sourcing ingredients from local farms and artisan producers. Chalkboards announce where the day's

meats have come from, perhaps hand-reared veal from Cranfields Farm at Rudgwick, or game from the Barlavington Estate. From the interesting modern menu, order potted rabbit and toast, fish stew with tomato, chorizo and fennel, and vanilla pannacotta with stewed plums. Three bright, airy bedrooms and a secluded garden provide a quiet, homely location for an overnight stay.

Open all day all wk Bar Meals L served Mon-Fri 12-2.30, Sat 12-3, Sun 12-3.30 D served Mon-Sat 6.30-9 Restaurant L served Mon-Fri 12-2.30, Sat 12-3, Sun 12-3.30 booking required D served Mon-Sat 6.30-9 booking required ⊕ ENTERPRISE INNS ◀ Harveys Sussex Best, Skinner's Betty Stogs, Staropramen, Guinness ♂ Stowford Press. ♥ 11 Facilities Children welcome Children's menu Children's portions Dogs allowed Garden Wi-fi Rooms 3

TROTTON — Map 5 SU82

PICK OF THE PUBS

The Keepers Arms ◉ ♥

GU31 5ER ☎ 01730 813724
e-mail: nick@keepersarms.co.uk
dir: 5m from Petersfield on A272, pub on right just after narrow bridge

This well-groomed and charming 17th-century free house sits up above the A272 just above the river Rother, in an Area of Outstanding Natural Beauty. A log fire provides a warm welcome in the lovely, low-ceilinged bar, and the stylish dining room is also a treat with its warm colours, modern oak dining tables, comfortable upholstered chairs and tartan fabrics. By day, there are fabulous views over the South Downs from the alfresco terrace. Food is taken seriously, with real efforts made to source local and seasonal produce. Blackboard menus offer pub favourites such as tiger prawn and crayfish cocktail; cod in beer batter with chips and mushy peas; calves' liver and bacon with foie gras sauce, while the frequently changing à la carte menu features starters such as seared scallops on cauliflower purée and main courses of fillet of line-caught Solent sea bass with saffron and crayfish risotto or roasted Cowdray Estate sirloin steak on root vegetable dauphinoise and red wine sauce.

Open all wk 12-3.30 6-11 Bar Meals L served all wk 12-2 D served all wk 7-9.30 Restaurant L served all wk 12-2 D served all wk 7-9.30 ⊕ FREE HOUSE ◀ Dark Star Hophead, Ringwood Best, Ballards Best, Ringwood Fortyniner, Otter Ale. ♥ 8 Facilities Children's portions Dogs allowed Garden Parking

WALDERTON — Map 5 SU71

The Barley Mow ♥

PO18 9ED ☎ 023 9263 1321 📄 023 9263 1403
e-mail: info@thebarleymowpub.co.uk
dir: B2146 from Chichester towards Petersfield. Turn right signed Walderton, pub 100yds on left

Popular with walkers, cyclists and horse-riders out exploring the Kingley Vale nature reserve, this ivy-clad 18th-century pub was used by the local Home Guard as its HQ in World War II; it's famous locally for its skittle alley. The secluded, stream-bordered garden is a real sun trap, perfect for a pint of Fortyniner; in winter months the log fires crackle. The menu covers the usual favourites such as lightly fried breaded whitebait; chef's mixed grill; sausage and mash; and curry of the day. Look out for jazz and country folk nights.

Open all wk 11-3 6-11 (Sun 12-10.30) Bar Meals L served Mon-Sat 12-2.30 (Sun all day) D served all wk 6-9.30 Av main course £7.50 Restaurant L served all wk 12-2.30 D served all wk 6-9.30 ⊕ FREE HOUSE ◀ Ringwood Old Thumper & Fortyniner, Fuller's London Pride, Harveys Best, Sharp's Doom Bar ♂ Stowford Press. ♥ 10 Facilities Children welcome Children's menu Children's portions Dogs allowed Garden Parking

WARNINGLID — Map 6 TQ22

The Half Moon

The Street RH17 5TR ☎ 01444 461227
e-mail: info@thehalfmoonwarninglid.co.uk
dir: 1m from Warninglid/Cuckfield junct of A23 & 6m from Haywards Heath

This picture perfect Grade II listed building dates from the 18th century and has been sympathetically extended to preserve its traditional feel. Enjoy a pint of Harveys or a real cider while perusing the menu in this picturesque pub with its friendly atmosphere. The menu offers snacks, specials and pub classics. Try beer-battered halloumi with tomato fondue and pea purée at lunchtime, or guinea fowl, pork and apricot terrine followed by confit pork belly with creamed leeks, black pudding and mash in the evening.

Open all wk 11.30-2.30 5.30-11 (Sun 11.30-11) ⊕ FREE HOUSE ◀ Harveys Sussex, Black Sheep, Ringwood Best, Dark Star, Harvey's Old Ale ♂ Westons Stowford Press, Sheppy's Dabinett, Oakwood Special. Facilities Children's portions Dogs allowed Garden Parking

WEST CHILTINGTON   Map 6 TQ01

The Queens Head

The Hollow RH20 2JN ☎ **01798 812244**
e-mail: enquiries@thequeenshead.info
dir: *Telephone for directions*

The pub is named after Anne of Cleves who was given an estate nearby in her divorce settlement. This is a textbook country pub, from its beams, low ceilings and open fire to the bar serving a good selection of well-kept real ales. The building is mostly 17th-century, and houses two bars plus a restaurant. Meals range from traditional sirloin steak with chips, mushrooms and tomato to spicy bean and lentil casserole, or grilled sea bass with salsa verde. There are also sharing platters, including the fish option of whole king prawns, rollmop herrings and smoked salmon with ciabatta; and pizzas, stonebaked or deep pan, with many topping combinations.

Open all day all wk noon–11 (Mon 5–11 ex BHs noon–11 Sun noon–10.30) **Bar Meals** L served Tue–Sat 12–2.30, Sun & BH 12–4 D served Tue–Sat 6–9.30 Av main course £10 **Restaurant** L served Tue–Sat 12–2.30, Sun & BH 12–4 D served Tue–Sat 6–9.30 Av 3 course à la carte fr £20 ⊕ ENTERPRISE INNS PLC ◀ Harveys Sussex Best Bitter, Fuller's London Pride, Ballards Best Bitter, Itchen Valley Godfathers, Langhams Halfway to Heaven. **Facilities** Children welcome Children's portions Dogs allowed Garden Parking Wi-fi

WEST HOATHLY   Map 6 TQ33

PICK OF THE PUBS

The Cat Inn ☻ NEW

North Ln RH19 4PP ☎ **01342 810369**
e-mail: thecatinn@googlemail.com
dir: *From East Grinstead centre take A22 towards Forest Row. Into left lane, into B2110 (Beeching Way) signed Turners Hill. Left into Vowels Lane signed Kingscote & West Hoathly. Left into Selsfield Rd, forward into Chapel Row, right into North Lane*

The 16th-century Cat Inn commands a prime spot opposite the church in picturesque West Hoathly, a hilltop village on the edge of the Ashdown Forest. Landlord Andrew Russell swapped grand Gravetye Manor for this working free house in 2009, then placed local chef Max Leonard in the kitchen and hasn't looked back since. Step inside the character old bar to find an enormous fireplace, oak beams, fine wooden panelling and floors, and a buzzy atmosphere. Beyond are the light and airy garden room and the sun-trap terrace for summer alfresco dining at smart teak tables. Max draws on fresh, seasonal produce, including local South Downs lamb, Rye Bay fish and seafood, estate game and locally foraged ingredients. This translates to lamb chops with dauphinoise, greens and jus, sand dabs with brown shrimp and caper butter, and a classic steak, mushroom and ale pie. Puddings may include Valrhona chocolate brownie with honeycomb ice cream. Super local walks.

Open 12–3.30 6–11.30 Closed: Sun eve **Bar Meals** L served Mon–Thu 12–2, Fri–Sun 12–2.30 booking required D served Mon–Thu 6–9, Fri–Sat 6–9.30 booking required Av main course £13 **Restaurant** L served Mon–Thu 12–2, Fri–Sun 12–2.30 booking required D served Mon–Thu 6–9, Fri–Sat 6–9.30 booking required Av 3 course à la carte fr £25.25 ⊕ FREE HOUSE ◀ Harveys Best, Larkins ♂ Stowford Press. ☻ 10 **Facilities** Children welcome Children's portions Dogs allowed Garden Parking Wi-fi

WINEHAM   Map 6 TQ22

The Royal Oak ☻

BN5 9AY ☎ **01444 881252**
e-mail: theroyaloakwineham@sky.com
dir: *Wineham between A272 (Cowfold to Bolney) & B2116 (Hurst to Henfield)*

Well worth seeking out, this part-tiled, black-and-white timbered cottage dates back to the 14th century and stands tucked away on a quiet country lane between the A272 and B2116 near Henfield. It's a classic ale house, a true rural survivor that has been serving the locals for 300 years and is delightfully traditional and unspoilt in every way. Head-cracking low beams, huge inglenook with warming winter fire, brick and stone-flagged floors, rustic furnishings and time-honoured pub games (no music or machines) characterise the charming bar and tiny rear room. Harvey's and Dark Star ales are drawn straight from the drum and home-cooked pub food ranges from rare roast beef ploughman's and cauliflower cheese to roast duck with green beans and an orange and Grand Marnier sauce and cracking Sunday roasts. Extensive gardens for summer alfresco drinking.

Open all wk 11–3 5.30–close (Sat 6pm–close Sun 7pm–close) **Bar Meals** L served all wk 12–2.30 booking required D served all wk 7–9.30 booking required Av main course £12 **Restaurant** L served all wk 12–2.30 booking required D served all wk 7–9.30 booking required ⊕ FREE HOUSE ◀ Harveys Best, Darkstar Hop Head ♂ Thatchers Gold, Weston Old Rosie. ☻ 20 **Facilities** Children welcome Children's portions Dogs allowed Garden Beer festival Parking Wi-fi

WISBOROUGH GREEN   Map 6 TQ02

Cricketers Arms

Loxwood Rd RH14 0DG ☎ **01403 700369**
e-mail: craig@cricketersarms.com
dir: *On A272 between Billingshurst & Petworth. In centre of Wisborough Green turn at junct next to village green, pub 100yds on right*

A traditional village pub dating from the 16th century with oak beams, wooden floors and open fires. Fans of extreme sports should be aware that the Cricketers is the home of the British Lawn Mower Racing Association. Alongside real ales there are many wines by the glass in the bar, with a menu ranging from snacks to three course meals and Sunday roasts, with plenty of specials. Typical dishes include steak pie, sea bass in a prawn and oyster sauce, game dishes in season, and 'mega' salads. Thursday is live music night.

Open all day all wk ⊕ ENTERPRISE INNS ◀ Harveys Sussex, Fuller's London Pride, Swift One. **Facilities** Children welcome Children's menu Children's portions Dogs allowed Garden Parking Wi-fi

TYNE & WEAR

NEWCASTLE UPON TYNE   Map 21 NZ26

Shiremoor House Farm ☻

Middle Engine Ln, New York NE29 8DZ
☎ **0191 257 6302**   🖹 **0191 257 8602**
dir: *Telephone for directions*

A swift pint of Jarrow River Catcher or Mordue Workie Ticket in New York? Since that's the name of the village, it's eminently feasible at this popular north Tyneside pub, brilliantly converted from old farm buildings and in the same hands for 23 years. Particularly appealing is the glazed former granary where a wide range of traditional, home cooked pub food is served, from a daily-changing blackboard menu - perhaps steak, ale and mushroom casserole, or fillet of salmon with prawn and dill sauce. The fish on the menus has been caught and landed locally.

Open all day all wk **Bar Meals** L served all wk 11–10 D served all wk 11–10 Av main course £8.95 food served all day ⊕ FREE HOUSE ◀ Timothy Taylor Landlord, Mordue Workie Ticket, Theakston BB, John Smith's, Jarrow River Catcher ♂ Rosie Nosey. ☻ 12 **Facilities** Children's menu Family room Garden Parking

TYNEMOUTH   Map 21 NZ36

Copperfields ★★★ HL

Grand Hotel, Grand Pde NE30 4ER
☎ 0191 293 6666 📠 0191 293 6665
e-mail: info30@grandhotel-uk.com
dir: *On NE coast, 10m from Newcastle upon Tyne*

Copperfields bar is at the rear of the imposing Grand
Hotel away from the hustle and bustle, where Stan Laurel
and Oliver Hardy always stayed when they played
Newcastle's Theatre Royal. Worth a visit for the great
views up and down the coast, as well as an extensive bar
menu that includes butternut squash and sage risotto,
chicken tagine, lamb stew, beer-battered haddock and
ciabatta steak sandwich. A blackboard lists daily
specials. A change of hands has taken place.

Open all day all wk **Bar Meals** L served all wk 12-9.45
D served all wk 12-9.45 Av main course £7.50 food served
all day **Restaurant** L served all wk 12-3 D served all wk
6-9.45 Av 3 course à la carte fr £30 ⊕ FREE HOUSE
◀ Black Sheep, Deuchars. **Facilities** Children welcome
Children's menu Garden Parking Wi-fi **Rooms** 45

WHITLEY BAY   Map 21 NZ37

The Waterford Arms

Collywell Bay Rd, Seaton Sluice NE26 4QZ
☎ 0191 237 0450
e-mail: les47@bt.connect.com
dir: *From A1 N of Newcastle take A19 at Seaton Burn then
follow signs for A190 to Seaton Sluice*

The building dates back to 1899 and is located close to
the small local fishing harbour, overlooking the North
Sea. Splendid beaches and sand dunes are within easy
reach, and the pub is very popular with walkers. Seafood
dishes are the speciality, including seared swordfish,
lemon sole, halibut, crab-stuffed plaice, and the
famously large portions of fish and chips. The pub
changed hands in 2010.

Open all wk noon-11.30 (Thu-Sat noon-mdnt Sun noon-
10.30) ⊕ PUNCH ◀ Tetleys, John Smith's, Scotch,
Guinness. **Facilities** Children welcome Children's menu
Parking Wi-fi

WARWICKSHIRE

ALCESTER   Map 10 SP05

PICK OF THE PUBS

The Holly Bush

37 Henley St B49 5QX ☎ 01789 762482
e-mail: thehollybushpub@btconnect.com
dir: *M40 junct 15 for Warwick/Stratford, take A46 to
Stratford. From Stratford take A46 to Redditch, follow
Alcester signs*

Tracey-Jane Deffley has transformed the 17th-century
Holly Bush from a one-bar boozer into a cracking town
centre pub run with passion and panache – and there's
an award-winning garden too. Two bars serve eight
regional brews and a local cider, supped cheerfully in
five characterful rooms along with plates of
contemporary and traditional food from the kitchen:
asparagus, Parma ham and Parmesan tartlet, and
crispy confit of duck with crushed new potatoes give a
flavour of the treats in store. Specials continue the
focus on flavoursome ingredients in such dishes as
smoked haddock and Applewood cheese fishcake with
rocket and Chardonnay cream sauce; and pan-fried red
snapper with coriander rice. Accompanying wines from
a well-priced selection are easily chosen thanks to the
succinct guidance on the list. Come here to enjoy not
just the food and drink but also the exceptional friendly
service. Watch out for regular live music nights, as well
as beer festivals in June and October.

Open all day all wk noon-mdnt (Fri-Sat noon-1am)
Bar Meals L served Mon-Sat 12-2.30, Sun 12-4
D served Tue-Sat 6.30-9.30 Av main course £13
Restaurant L served Mon-Sat 12-2.30, Sun 12-4
D served Tue-Sat 6.30-9.30 Av 3 course à la carte fr
£24 ⊕ FREE HOUSE ◀ Sharp's Doom Bar, Black Sheep,
Purity Gold, Purity Mad Goose, Uley Bitter ♂ Local farm
cider, Hogans. **Facilities** Children welcome Children's
menu Children's portions Dogs allowed Garden Beer
festival Parking

ALDERMINSTER   Map 10 SP24

PICK OF THE PUBS

The Bell ♀

CV37 8NY ☎ 01789 450414 📠 01789 450998
e-mail: info@thebellald.co.uk
dir: *On A3400 3.5m S of Stratford-upon-Avon*

Judicious upgrading and refurbishment of this
Georgian coaching inn between Stratford and Shipston
has produced a refreshing mix of contemporary
comforts and rustic charm, with the core beamed
ceilings, fires and flagged floors the counterpoint to a
modern dining courtyard beside a grassy garden and
pastures rippling down to the nearby River Stour. The
restaurant is cunningly designed into zones, each with
its own distinct atmosphere. Time to enjoy a pint of the
inn's locally-brewed Alscot Ale and nibble on a self-
selected grazing platter before considering the

indulgent menu - Alscot reared lamb tagine with cider
and herb dumplings, or Warwickshire turkey, honey-
roast ham and sweet potato Wellington - that changes
daily with the availability of local produce.

Open Mon-Thu 9.30-3 6-11 (Fri-Sun 9.30am-11pm)
Closed: Mon Jan-Mar **Bar Meals** L served Mon-Fri 12-2,
Sat 12-2.30, Sun 12-3 booking required D served Mon-
Thu 7-9, Fri-Sat 6-9 booking required
Restaurant L served Mon-Fri 12-2, Sat 12-2.30, Sun
12-3 booking required D served Mon-Thu 7-9, Fri-Sat
6-9 booking required ⊕ FREE HOUSE ◀ Hook Norton,
Lady Godiva, Alscot Ale ♂ Hogans Cider. ♀ 14
Facilities Children welcome Children's menu Children's
portions Dogs allowed Garden Parking Wi-fi

ALVESTON   Map 10 SP25

PICK OF THE PUBS

The Baraset Barn

1 Pimlico Ln CV37 7RJ
☎ 01789 295510 📠 01789 292961
e-mail: barasetbarn@lovelypubs.co.uk
web: www.barasetbarn.co.uk
dir: *Telephone for directions*

Although the original flagstones reflect the age of this
200-year-old converted barn, it is now a light and
modern gastro-pub with a dramatic interior styled from
granite, pewter and oak. Stone steps lead from the bar
to the main dining area with its brick walls and high
oak beams, whilst the open mezzanine level makes for
a perfect vantage point of the glass-fronted kitchen.
There's also a luxurious lounge with comfortable sofas
for whiling away a relaxing morning coffee with the
papers. The crowd-pleasing menu successfully blends
classic British dishes with an eclectic Mediterranean
choice, offering sharing plates of Greek mezze
alongside conventional starters like devilled lambs'
kidneys with wilted spinach and garlic croute. Follow
on with rack of lamb and shepherd's pie with creamed
cabbage and leeks. Leave room for hot chocolate
fondant with coconut ice cream. The continental-style
patio garden is just right for summer alfresco dining.

Open all day noon-mdnt Closed: 25 Dec & 1 Jan, Sun
eve, Mon (Jan-Feb) **Bar Meals** L served all wk 12-3.30
D served Mon-Sat 6.30-9.30 **Restaurant** L served Mon-
Sat 12-2.30, Sun 12-3.30 booking required D served
Mon-Sat 6.30-9.30 booking required ⊕ FREE HOUSE
◀ UBU. **Facilities** Children welcome Children's
portions Dogs allowed Garden Parking

See advert on opposite page

ARDENS GRAFTON — Map 10 SP15

PICK OF THE PUBS

The Golden Cross

Wixford Rd B50 4LG
☎ 01789 772420 📠 01789 773697
e-mail: info@thegoldencross.net
dir: *Telephone for directions*

Inside this beautiful 18th-century building you'll find a rug-strewn bar with flagstone floors, massive beams and open fires. Wells Bombardier and Purity Brewing ales are amongst the beers on offer here, together with regular guest ales. The light, airy dining room presents a complete contrast, with its soft pastel decor and elegant plaster ceiling. The same menu is served throughout the pub; traditional favourites are always available, and the blackboards reflect an ever-changing selection of specials. Starters and light bites include caramelised onion and Stilton tart; oven baked boxed Camembert studded with garlic and thyme with onion marmalade, pear chutney. In addition to pub classics, the other main course choices are just as appealing; choose chargrilled Cajun chicken with hand-cut chips; herb gnocchi with Mediterranean vegetable and roasted tomato ragout; or pan-roasted duck breast with dauphinoise potatoes. For warmer days there's a large safe garden which also boasts a covered, heated patio. Thursday night is song and steak night – both local.

Open all wk **Bar Meals** L served all wk 12-2.30 D served all wk 5-9 Av main course £11
Restaurant L served all wk 12-2.30 D served all wk 5-9 Fixed menu price fr £12 Av 3 course à la carte fr £25 ⊕ CHARLES WELLS ◀ Wells Bombardier, Purity Brewing, Guest ales ⊘ Thatchers Heritage.
Facilities Children welcome Children's menu Children's portions Garden Parking Wi-fi

BARFORD — Map 10 SP26

PICK OF THE PUBS

The Granville @ Barford ⚑

52 Wellesbourne Rd CV35 8DS ☎ 01926 624236
e-mail: info@granvillebarford.co.uk
web: www.granvillebarford.co.uk
dir: *1m from M40 junct 15. Take A429 signed Stow. Located at furthest end of Barford village*

Situated in the heart of Shakespeare country, this impressive brick building dates back to Georgian times. Now owned and run by Val Kersey, this comfortable dining pub benefits from stylish decor and warm, friendly service, which has made it a firm favourite with locals and visitors alike. Relax on the leather sofas in the lounge with a drink - a pint of Purity Gold perhaps, or choose from the accessible wine list. The Granville's ever-changing seasonal menus offer varied, interesting choices and good value. At lunch, the offering ranges from doorstep sandwiches and wraps to starters like linguine in a lightly spiced crab broth with spring onion, lime and coriander. An evening meal might begin with salmon and haddock fishcakes, wilted spinach, lemon and butter sauce, followed by North African spiced lamb patties, winter fruit saffron cous cous, mint and cucumber yoghurt. Enjoy alfresco dining in the spacious patio garden. There is a calendar of events to entertain customers.

Open all wk noon-3 5.30-11 (Fri-Sat noon-11.30 Sun noon-11) **Bar Meals** L served Mon-Fri 12-2.30 D served Mon-Thu 6-9, Fri 6-10, Sat noon-10, Sun noon-5 Av main course £11 **Restaurant** L served Mon-Fri 12-2.30 D served Mon-Thu 6-9, Fri 6-10, Sat noon-10, Sun noon-5 Fixed menu price fr £11 Av 3 course à la carte fr £25 ⊕ ENTERPRISE INNS PLC ◀ Hooky Bitter, Purity Gold, Purity UBU. ⚑ 17 **Facilities** Children welcome Children's portions Play area Dogs allowed Garden Parking Wi-fi

BROOM — Map 10 SP05

Broom Tavern

High St B50 4HL ☎ 01789 773656 📠 01789 773656
e-mail: sdsmngmnt@btinternet.com
dir: *N of B439 W of Stratford-upon-Avon*

Once a haunt of William Shakespeare, this 16th-century brick and timber inn is smartly furnished, with a large beer garden where barbecues are held in summer. Very much at the heart of village life, it is home to the Broom Tavern Golf Society, and fun days, charity events and outings are a feature. The menu offers a large selection of vegetarian dishes and seafood specials, which can be accompanied with a good choice of ales.

Open all wk noon-3 5.30-11 ⊕ PUNCH TAVERNS ◀ Greene King IPA, Black Sheep, Timothy Taylor Landlord, Wells Bombardier, Hook Norton.
Facilities Children welcome Dogs allowed Garden Parking Wi-fi

---

EDGEHILL
Map 11 SP34

The Castle Inn

OX15 6DJ ☎ **01295 670255** 📠 **01295 670521**
e-mail: castleinnedgehill@gmail.com
dir: *M40 junct 11 then A422 towards Stratford-upon-Avon. 6m to Upton House, next right, 1.5m to Edgehill*

On the summit of Edgehill, 700 feet above sea level, this fascinating property was built as a copy of Warwick Castle in 1742 to commemorate the centenary of the Battle of Edgehill. Its castellated tower marks the spot where King Charles raised the standard before the two sides clashed. Tales of ghostly soldiers abound. It opened on the anniversary of Cromwell's death in 1750, was first licensed in 1822, and acquired by Hook Norton a hundred years later; its still serves their fine ales in the two bars today. A selection of hearty, traditional food includes gammon, egg and chips, and a lengthy selection of home-made pies. There has been a change of hands.

Open all day all wk 11.30am-close **Bar Meals** Av main course £8 food served all day ⊕ HOOK NORTON ◀ Hook Norton Best, Old Hooky & Generation, Hooky Dark, Guest ales Ö Old Rosie. **Facilities** Children welcome Children's portions Garden Beer festival Parking

ETTINGTON
Map 10 SP24

PICK OF THE PUBS

The Chequers Inn

91 Banbury Rd CV37 7SR ☎ **01789 740387**
e-mail: hello@the-chequers-ettington.co.uk
dir: *Take A422 from Stratford-upon-Avon towards Banbury. Ettington in 5m, after junction with A429*

With its subtle French undertones, beautiful tapestries and comfy armchairs, this sumptuously appointed country dining inn radiates a welcoming, homely feel. Whilst its origins are uncertain, the pub may have been named after the ancient Chequers tree that once stood in front of the building. Today, you can choose between the relaxed setting of the bar, the well-appointed restaurant, and the large garden overlooking the chef's vegetable patch. Cooking is modern European with a nod to traditional English favourites, and there's a very popular monthly fish night. Lunchtime brings sandwiches and light meals like Scotch duck egg and mustard mayonnaise, whilst main menu selections might start with cauliflower cheese, rocket salad and garlic bread. Main course options include rabbit and mustard rigatoni with peas, broad beans and spinach, and chilli-crusted salmon with noodles and stir-fried vegetables. A good selection of real ales and ciders, plus a wine list with descriptions completes the package.

Open noon-3 5-11 (Sat noon-11 Sun noon-6) Closed: Sun eve, Mon **Bar Meals** L served Tue-Sat 12-2.30, Sun 12.30-3.30 booking required D served Tue-Sat 6.30-9.30 booking required Av main course £12 **Restaurant** L served Tue-Sat 12-2.30, Sun 12.30-3.30 booking required D served Tue-Sat 6.30-9.30 booking required Av 3 course à la carte fr £22 ⊕ INDEPENDENT ◀ Greene King IPA, London Pride, St Austell Tribute Ö Stowford Press, Hogans. **Facilities** Children welcome Children's menu Children's portions Dogs allowed Garden Parking

The Houndshill

Banbury Rd CV37 7NS
☎ **01789 740267** 📠 **01789 740075**
e-mail: info@thehoundshill.co.uk
dir: *On A422 SE of Stratford-upon-Avon*

Family-run for over 30 years, this inn is set in twelve acres of garden and woodland in the beautiful Warwickshire countryside, and a perfect base for exploring popular tourist attractions such as Oxford, Blenheim, Stratford and the Cotswolds. The pleasant tree-lined garden is especially popular with families. Typical dishes include grilled sirloin steak with fries, tomatoes, mushrooms and peas; chilli con carne; home-made chicken curry; baked lasagne; or The Houndshill platter – smoked salmon, avocado, prawns, melon and cold poached salmon.

Open all wk 12-3 6-11 Closed: 25-28 Dec **Bar Meals** L served all wk 12-2 D served all wk 7-9.30 Av main course £9.95 **Restaurant** L served all wk 12-2 D served all wk 7-9.30 ⊕ FREE HOUSE ◀ Purity Gold, Purity UBU. **Facilities** Children welcome Children's menu Children's portions Play area Dogs allowed Garden Parking Wi-fi

FARNBOROUGH
Map 11 SP44

PICK OF THE PUBS

The Inn at Farnborough ☕

OX17 1DZ ☎ **01295 690615**
e-mail: enquiries@innatfarnborough.co.uk
dir: *M40 junct 11 towards Banbury. Right at 3rd rdbt onto A423 signed Southam. 4m & onto A423. Left onto single track road signed Farnborough. Approx 1m turn right into village, pub on right*

An ale house for at least 200 years, this Grade II listed 16th-century property enjoys a picturesque setting in a National Trust village. Built of Hornton stone, it was formerly known as the Butcher's Arms, having once belonged to the butcher on the Farnborough Estate; original features include a fine inglenook fireplace. At the bar there are real ales, Hogan's cider, and plenty of wines served by the glass. The menu is concise, but the kitchen's focus on quality ingredients and preparing everything from scratch lifts its dishes way above the average. Starters include seared scallops with toasted hazelnuts, tarragon and plum tomato dressing. Main courses embrace slow-cooked Moroccan spiced lamb with roasted vegetables and coriander couscous. Ask about special offers in the evenings – they may range from moules frites with a cut-price bottle of wine, to half price à la carte if booked before 7pm. The Inn has a glorious terraced garden and a heated and covered decking area.

Open all wk 10-3 6-11 (Sat-Sun all day) Closed: 25 Dec **Bar Meals** L served all wk 12-3 booking required D served all wk 6-10 booking required Av main course £7.95 **Restaurant** L served all wk 12-3 booking required D served Mon-Fri 6-10, wknd 10am-mdnt booking required Fixed menu price fr £11.95 Av 3 course à la carte fr £25 ⊕ FREE HOUSE ◀ Hook Norton Hooky Ö Hogan's Ciders, Local. ☕ 14 **Facilities** Children welcome Children's menu Children's portions Play area Dogs allowed Garden Parking Wi-fi

GAYDON
Map 11 SP35

The Malt Shovel ☕ NEW

Church Rd CV35 0ET ☎ **01926 641221**
e-mail: malt.shovel@btconnect.com
dir: *M40 junct 12 follow B4451 to Gaydon*

Little is known about the history of the Malt Shovel, except that it dates from the 16th century; its original entrance door has been incorporated into a unique dining area. Richard and Debi Morisot have been in charge for over ten years, serving 'real food and real ale' in a simple but successful formula. The ales include Hook Norton, and hand-made soups and pies appear on the specials board. Other delights include Brixworth pâté (a medium coarse Northamptonshire recipe), smoked haddock Welsh rarebit and wild boar and apple sausages. Well-behaved children and dogs are welcome.

Save on hotels. Book at theAA.com/hotel

WARWICKSHIRE 469 ENGLAND

Open all wk Mon-Thu 11-3 5-11 (Fri-Sat 11-11, Sun 12-10.30) **Bar Meals** L served all wk 12-2 D served all wk 6.30-9 Av main course £9 **Restaurant** L served all wk 12-2 booking required D served all wk 6.30-9 booking required ⊕ ENTERPRISE INNS ◀ Hook Norton, Fuller's London Pride, Timothy Taylor Landlord. ♀ 10 **Facilities** Children welcome Children's portions Dogs allowed Parking

GREAT WOLFORD
Map 10 SP23

PICK OF THE PUBS

The Fox & Hounds Inn

CV36 5NQ ☎ **01608 674220**
e-mail: enquiries@thefoxandhoundsinn.com
dir: Off A44 NE of Moreton-in-Marsh

Nestled in the heart of Warwickshire on the edge of the Cotswolds, this family-run village inn is as unspoilt as the wonderful countryside around it. The quintessential English inn ambience - settles, log fires and beams festooned with hops – is an ideal place to sup pints of Hook Norton or Purity ales. The busy kitchen uses local produce such as Dexter beef and seasonal game from local shoots. Herbs and vegetables come from the productive kitchen garden, and mushrooms are wild; only fresh fish comes from further afield, with deliveries from Scotland and Cornwall. Even the bread is baked using fresh yeast and organic flour milled in the Cotswolds. A typical selection from the modern British menu could include baked Kitebrook egg with chard, crispy capers and sourdough soldiers; oxtail risotto with horseradish, tarragon, carrots and crispy Parmesan; slow-roast belly pork, home-made black pudding, roast Cox's pippins, cider and juices. There is a daily-changing menu on the blackboard.

Open 12-2.30 6-11.30 (Sun 12-10.30) Closed: 1st 2wks Jan, Mon **Bar Meals** L served Tue-Sun 12-2 D served Tue-Sat 6.30-9 ⊕ FREE HOUSE ◀ Hook Norton Best, Purity, Guest ales ♂ Stowford Press. **Facilities** Children welcome Children's portions Dogs allowed Garden Parking

HATTON
Map 10 SP26

The Case is Altered

Case Ln, Five Ways CV35 7JD ☎ **01926 484206**
dir: Telephone for directions

A very traditional whitewashed free house of great charm and character, this is a true old-style pub. It serves no food and does not accept children or dogs. That aside, it's a thoroughly welcoming spot for adults who appreciate the pleasures of a quiet pint. Local and independent brewery beers are always available, and there is a guest or two ales to sup while enjoying lively conversation, or just relaxing and appreciating the atmosphere.

Open all wk noon-2.30 6-11 (Sun 12-2 7-10.30) ⊕ FREE HOUSE ◀ Greene King IPA, Wye Vally Butty Bach, 2 Guest ales. **Facilities** Parking **Notes** ✆

HENLEY-IN-ARDEN
Map 10 SP16

The Bluebell ♀ NEW

93 High St B95 5AT ☎ **01564 793049**
e-mail: info@bluebellhenley.co.uk
dir: Opposite police station on A3400 in town centre

The 500-year-old former coaching inn on the High Street has been boldly updated by Leigh and Duncan Taylor. Be wowed by the swanky interior design, which cleverly combines original old beams, worn flagstones and open fireplaces with bold colours and an eclectic mix of furnishings and fabrics. Bar and dining room oozes style and atmosphere and both throng with drinkers (good wine and local ales) and diners (booking essential), with seasonal menus brimming with local or home-grown produce. Typically, tuck into potted confit salmon followed by roast venison with Cognac and peppercorn cream.

Open all day Closed: Mon L **Bar Meals** L served Tue-Sat 12-2.30, Sun 12-3.30 booking required D served Tue-Sat 6-9.30 booking required Av main course £17 **Restaurant** L served Tue-Sat 12-2.30, Sun 12-3.30 booking required D served Tue-Sat 6-9.30 booking required Fixed menu price fr £19.95 Av 3 course à la carte fr £21.40 ⊕ FREE HOUSE ◀ Church End What the Fox's Hat, Hook Norton Hooky Bitter, Wye Valley HPA ♂ Hogan's. ♀ 16 **Facilities** Children welcome Children's portions Dogs allowed Garden Parking Wi-fi

HUNNINGHAM
Map 11 SP36

The Red Lion, Hunningham ♀ NEW

Main St CV33 9DY ☎ **01926 632715** ⎙ **01926 633703**
e-mail: sam@redlionhunningham.co.uk
dir: From Leamington Spa take B4453, through Cubbington to Weston under Wetherby. Follow Hunningham signs (turn sharp right as road bends left towards Princethorpe)

Accessed by a 14th century bridge, this quirky country pub's beer garden leads down to the River Leam and offers splendid views of local livestock. Set in the heart of rural Warwickshire, this delightful pub's real fires and original features are enhanced by contemporary touches such as framed vintage comic book covers. Local produce drives an appealing, well-executed menu of sandwiches, light bites, sharing dishes and mains such as local ham, egg and chips, and chicken with pearl barley and black pudding stew. There is a film and beer festival on August Bank Holiday.

Open all day all wk **Bar Meals** Av main course £9.95 food served all day **Restaurant** Av 3 course à la carte fr £19.85 food served all day ⊕ GREENE KING ◀ Greene King IPA, Abbot Ale, Hook Norton Old Hooky, Brewdog Alpha Dog, Guest ales. ♀ 28 **Facilities** Children welcome Children's portions Dogs allowed Garden Beer festival Parking Wi-fi

ILMINGTON
Map 10 SP24

PICK OF THE PUBS

The Howard Arms ♀

See Pick of the Pubs on page 470

KENILWORTH
Map 10 SP27

The Almanack ♀ NEW

Abbey End North CV8 1QJ ☎ **01926 353637**
e-mail: hello@thealmanack-kenilworth.co.uk
dir: Exit A46 at Kenilworth & brown Castle sign, towards town centre. Turn left onto Abbey Hill (B4104) signed Balsall Common. At rdbt into Abbey End. Opposite Holiday Inn

Stylish and contemporary, this award-winning modern British gastro-pub was inspired by the 1960s Kinks' hit 'Autumn Almanac'. With its retro Danish teak furniture, original album covers and a huge island bar separating the lounge from the eatery and open kitchen, the pub is open all day for breakfast, coffee and cake, lunch and dinner. Menu choices include sustainable fishcakes, free-range coq au vin, spiced lentil cake, plus great Sunday lunches. There's a special kids' menu, too.

Open all day all wk 8am-11pm (Thu-Sat 8am-mdnt) Closed: 25 Dec **Bar Meals** Av main course £11.50 food served all day **Restaurant** Av 3 course à la carte fr £25 food served all day ⊕ PEACH PUBS ◀ Purity UBU, Purity Gold. ♀ 10 **Facilities** Children welcome Children's menu Children's portions Dogs allowed Garden Beer festival Wi-fi

PICK OF THE PUBS

The Howard Arms ♟

ILMINGTON　　　　　Map 10 SP24

Lower Green CV36 4LT
☎ 01608 682226　📠 01608 682874
e-mail: info@howardarms.com
web: www.howardarms.com
dir: *Off A429 or A3400, 9m from Stratford-upon-Avon*

On the picturesque village green of Ilmington, set in the crook of the Cotswold Hills, lies The Howard Arms, a stunning 400-year-old Cotswold stone inn at the centre of village life. The flagstoned bar and open-plan dining room create a civilised look without sacrificing period charm, and it is all imbued with an informal atmosphere and a log fire that burns for most of the year. The breadth of choice among pumps and bottles in the bar indicates a serious approach to meeting the wide and various demands of locals and visitors. Half a dozen award-winning ales feature famous names such as Lady Godiva and Jouster, while wine drinkers can choose from a list of over thirty served by the glass. Equally serious are the inn's efforts to source excellent ingredients for the kitchen and many of the suppliers are named on the menu. While mulling it over you can warm to the task ahead with home-made houmous and olive tapenade with warm pitta bread or hot garlic ciabatta. Why not begin with smoked Bibury trout fillet, horseradish crème fraîche and cucumber ribbons, or

carpaccio of beetroot with North Cerney goat's cheese, watercress and pine nuts? The pub's favourite main dishes include The Howards fish pie with a mature Cheddar and potato crust and minted peas or honey and mustard baked ham, two Ilmington fried eggs and hand-cut chips. Alternatively, choose spiced Aylesbury duck breast with a fricassee of butternut squash and mushrooms, or fillet of hake with tomato and chorizo cassoulet. And so to desserts: will it be the apple pie with custard or Malibu marinated pineapple with coconut ice cream? Notably, The Howard Arms is the start and finish to a number of local walks, a detailed guide can be bought at the bar for a small donation, with all the monies going to the church funds. There is a lovely garden to enjoy in summer.

Open all day all wk Closed: 25 Dec eve-26 Dec eve **Bar Meals** L served Mon-Sat 12-2.30, Sun 12-3 booking required D served Mon-Sun 6.30-9.30 booking required **Restaurant** L served Mon-Sat 12-2.30, Sun 12-3 booking required D served Mon-Sun 6.30-9.30 booking required ⊕ FREE HOUSE ◼ Old Hooky, Warwickshire Beer Co Lady Godiva, Wye Valley Bitter, Hook Norton, Goffs Brewery Jouster, Tournament. ♟ 32
Facilities Children's portions Dogs allowed Garden Parking Wi-fi

Save on hotels. Book at **theAA.com/hotel**

WARWICKSHIRE 471 ENGLAND

LAPWORTH
Map 10 SP17

PICK OF THE PUBS

The Boot Inn ☻

Old Warwick Rd B94 6JU
☎ **01564 782464** 🖨 **01564 784989**
e-mail: bootinn@hotmail.com
web: www.bootinnlapworth.co.uk
dir: *Telephone for directions*

Beside the Grand Union Canal in the unspoilt village of Lapworth, this lively and convivial 16th-century former coaching inn is well worth seeking out. Apart from its smart interior with its soft modern furnishings complementing the old world feel, the attractive garden is a great place to relax on warm days, while a canopy and patio heaters make it a comfortable place to sit even on cooler evenings; barbecues are a speciality. Being a free house, there is a good choice of real ales to enjoy – Fuller's London Pride or Purity UBU maybe. But the main draw is the modern brasserie-style food, with wide-ranging menus that deliver home-produced dishes. Children and 'well natured' dogs are welcome.

Open all day all wk 11-11 (Thu-Sat 11am-mdnt Sun 11-10.30) **Bar Meals** L served all wk 12-2.30 D served Mon-Fri 7-9.30, Sat 6.30-9.30, Sun 7-9 Av main course £10 **Restaurant** L served all wk 12-2.30 D served Mon-Fri 7-9.30, Sat 6.30-9.30, Sun 7-9 Fixed menu price fr £12.50 Av 3 course à la carte fr £20 ⊕ FREE HOUSE ◀ Fuller's London Pride, Speckled Hen, Purity UBU. ☻ 9 **Facilities** Children welcome Children's menu Children's portions Dogs allowed Garden Parking

See advert below

LONG COMPTON
Map 10 SP23

PICK OF THE PUBS

The Red Lion ★★★★ INN ◉ ☻

Main St CV36 5JS
☎ **01608 684221** 🖨 **01608 684968**
e-mail: info@redlion-longcompton.co.uk
web: www.redlion-longcompton.co.uk
dir: *On A3400 between Shipston on Stour & Chipping Norton*

Originally built as a coaching inn in 1748, The Red Lion makes a good base from which to explore the Cotswolds and the fascinating towns of Stratford-upon-Avon and Warwick. Although still very much the village local, it appeals equally to those seeking a decent meal or stay, with oak beams, wood-burning stoves and open fires in the stone-flagged bar and the cosy, well-decorated dining areas. The menu and blackboards cater for all tastes, beginning with interesting sandwiches like hot steak, tomato and horseradish on ciabatta, or battered cod and chips served on the 'Red Lion Times'. Serious diners might start with pork and chicken liver terrine, before moving on to rib-eye steak with Café de Paris butter, followed by rhubarb and ginger crumble tart with crème Anglaise. Children have their own menu. Five elegant en suite bedrooms feature such modern luxuries as Egyptian cotton bed linen, fluffy towels and flat-screen televisions.

Open all wk Mon-Thu 10-2.30 6-11 (Fri-Sun all day) **Bar Meals** L served Mon-Thu 12-2.30, Fri-Sun 12-9.30 D served Mon-Thu 6-9, Fri-Sun 12-9.30 Av main course £14 **Restaurant** L served Mon-Thu 12-2.30, Fri-Sun 12-9.30 D served Mon-Thu 6-9, Fri-Sun 12-9.30 Fixed menu price fr £11.95 ⊕ FREE HOUSE ◀ Hook Norton Best, Adnams, Timothy Taylor. ☻ 11 **Facilities** Children welcome Children's menu Children's portions Play area Dogs allowed Garden Parking Wi-fi **Rooms** 5

LONG ITCHINGTON
Map 11 SP46

The Duck on the Pond ☻

The Green CV47 9QJ ☎ **01926 815876**
dir: *On A423 in village centre, 1m N of Southam*

Children will be delighted to discover that the name of this attractive village inn does indeed indicate the presence of a pond complete with drakes and mallards. Winter fires light an intriguing interior, crammed with fascinating bric-a-brac, while the menu offers a selection of pub favourites including battered fish, gammon and steaks, as well as vegetarian choices like aubergine and walnut bake or spinach and ricotta cannelloni. There is a lovely outdoor area for alfresco dining and a beer festival on May Bank Holiday.

Open all day all wk **Bar Meals** Av main course £8.95 ⊕ CHARLES WELLS ◀ Wells Bombardier, Young's Best, Guinness, Eagle IPA. ☻ 15 **Facilities** Children welcome Children's menu Children's portions Dogs allowed Beer festival Parking

MONKS KIRBY · Map 11 SP48

The Bell Inn

Bell Ln CV23 0QY ☎ 01788 832352 ▤ 01788 832352
e-mail: belindagb@aol.com
dir: *Village off B4455 (Fosse Way)*

The Spanish owners of this quaint, timbered inn, once a Benedictine priory gatehouse and then a brewhouse cottage, describe it as "a corner of Spain in the heart of England". The pine bar top came from a tree grown in Leire churchyard nearby. Mediterranean and traditional cuisine play an important role on the extensive menu. Enjoy a glass of Ruddles while taking you time to make your choices. Fillet steak Rossini; tuna à la Carzuela; lobster mornay; and beef Stroganoff all make a showing.

Open Tue-Sun Closed: 26 Dec, 1 Jan, Mon ⊕ FREE HOUSE ◀ IPA, Ruddles. **Facilities** Children welcome Garden Parking

OFFCHURCH · Map 11 SP36

The Stag at Offchurch ♀ NEW

Welsh Rd CV33 9AQ
☎ 01926 425801 ▤ 01926 886158
e-mail: info@thestagatoffchurch.com
dir: *From Leamington Spa take A425 towards Southam. At Radford Semele turn left onto Offchurch Lane to Offchurch*

A 16th-century thatched pub in the centre of the picturesque village of Offchurch, The Stag has recently been refurbished but has retained its character. Walkers and locals mingle in the bar with its oak floor and open fires, while diners can choose between two comfortable restaurant areas. The menu offers plenty of choice and meat from local farms – blue cheese soufflé might be followed by Jimmy Butler's free-range pork belly, sauté wild mushrooms and artichokes and mash.

Open all day all wk **Bar Meals** L served all wk 12-2.30 booking required D served all wk 6-9.30 booking required Av main course £13 **Restaurant** L served all wk 12-2.30 booking required D served all wk 6-9.30 booking required Av 3 course à la carte fr £21 ⊕ FREE HOUSE ◀ Warwickshire Beer Co, Purity Ò Hogan's Dry Cider. **Facilities** Children welcome Children's menu Children's portions Dogs allowed Garden Parking Wi-fi

OXHILL · Map 10 SP34

The Peacock

Main St CV35 0QU ☎ 01295 688060
e-mail: info@thepeacockoxhill.co.uk
dir: *From Stratford-upon-Avon take A422 towards Banbury. Turn right to Oxhill*

Meander down leafy lanes between Stratford and Banbury to locate Oxhill and this 16th-century stone-built pub. Recently spruced up and successfully combining traditional old-world charm with a contemporary feel, it focuses on sourcing local meats and vegetables from local farms and the seasonal menus and chalkboard specials have found favour with local diners. Typical choices may include smoked salmon ravioli with pesto cream, slow-roasted Paddock Farm pork belly with cider gravy, and zesty lemon bread and butter pudding.

Open all day all wk noon-11 ◀ Timothy Taylor Golden Best, Guest ales Ò Thatchers Pear, Thatchers Gold, Rattler. **Facilities** Children welcome Children's menu Children's portions Dogs allowed Garden Parking Wi-fi

PRESTON BAGOT · Map 10 SP16

The Crabmill ♀

B95 5EE ☎ 01926 843342
e-mail: thecrabmill@lovelypubs.co.uk
web: www.thecrabmill.co.uk
dir: *M42 junct 8, A3400 towards Stratford-upon-Avon. Take A4189 Henley-in-Arden lights. Left, pub 1.5m on left*

The name is a reminder that crab apple cider was once made at this 15th-century hostelry, which is set in beautiful rural surroundings. Restored to create an upmarket venue, the pub has a comfortable, light, open feel. Even the menu is fresh and exciting, with a lunchtime sharing platter or New York deli bagel to evening dishes such as ostrich fillet in cured ham with creamed potato, curly kale, lardons and red wine jus; and Gressingham duck breast with noodles, Asian vegetables, coconut and chilli sauce and pineapple salsa.

Open all day 11-11 Closed: 25 Dec, Sun eve **Bar Meals** L served Mon-Thu 12-2.30, Fri-Sat 12-5 D served all wk 6.30-9.30 Av main course £13.95 **Restaurant** L served Mon-Sat 12-2.30 D served Mon-Sat 6.30-9.30 Fixed menu price fr £13.50-£16 Av 3 course à la carte fr £25 ⊕ FREE HOUSE ◀ Wadworth 6X, Tetleys, Greene King Abbot Ale. ♀ 9 **Facilities** Children welcome Children's menu Children's portions Dogs allowed Garden Parking Wi-fi

See advert below

PRIORS MARSTON   Map 11 SP45

PICK OF THE PUBS

The Hollybush Inn ☻

Hollybush Ln CV47 7RW ☎ 01327 260934
e-mail: enquiries@hollybushatpriorsmarston.co.uk
dir: *From Southam A425, off bypass, 1st right, 6m*
to Priors Marston. Left after war memorial, next left,
150yds left again

The Hollybush started life as a farmhouse and only
became a fully licensed pub in 1947. Set in the
beautiful village of Priors Marston in the heart of
Warwickshire, it's a warm hub of village social activity
with a very relaxed atmosphere and real fires; people
can eat and/or drink wherever they choose. The menus
range from open sandwiches and sharing boards to a
comprehensive main menu selection. Perhaps a starter
of ham hock and black pudding terrine or trout
fishcakes followed by roast supreme of salmon with
braised fennel and confit shallots, or slow cooked belly
of pork with Savoy cabbage and smoked bacon. For
those in search of pub classics, corned beef hash and
beef stew and dumplings are also on offer. Desserts
could include profiteroles or sticky toffee pudding.
Smaller portions can be ordered for most of the
grown-up dishes. Look out for live music and other
events during the year.

Open all wk Mon-Fri 12-3 5.30-11 (Sat-Sun 12-11)
Bar Meals L served all wk 12-2.30 booking required
D served Mon-Sat 6.30-9.30 booking required
Restaurant L served Mon-Sat 12-2.30, Sun 12-4
D served Mon-Sat 6-9.30, Sun 12-4 ⊕ PUNCH TAVERNS
◀ Hook Norton, Fuller's, Old Speckled Hen ♂ Stowford
Press. ☻ 12 **Facilities** Children welcome Children's
portions Dogs allowed Garden Parking Wi-fi

RATLEY   Map 11 SP34

The Rose and Crown

OX15 6DS ☎ 01295 678148
e-mail: k.marples@btinternet.com
dir: *Follow Edgehill signs, 7m N of Banbury (13m SE of*
Stratford-upon-Avon) on A422

First, a grisly tale: following the Battle of Edge Hill in
1642, a Roundhead was discovered hiding in the chimney
of this 12th-century pub and promptly beheaded. His
ghost now reputedly haunts the building, but don't let
that spoil your enjoyment of the peaceful village location,
the fine ales and the home-made pub meals, perhaps
cottage pie; ham, eggs and chips; haddock and spring
onion fishcakes; vegetarian options; as well as one of the
Sunday roasts.

Open all wk 12-2.30 6-11 **Bar Meals** L served Mon-Sun
12-2.30 booking required D served Mon-Sat 6.30-9
booking required Av main course £9.95 ◀ Wells
Bombardier, Eagle IPA, Greene King Old Speckled Hen,
Guest ale. **Facilities** Children welcome Children's
portions Family room Dogs allowed Garden Parking

RED HILL   Map 10 SP15

PICK OF THE PUBS

The Stag at Redhill ☻

Alcester Rd B49 6NQ
☎ 01789 764634 📄 01789 764431
e-mail: info@thestagatredhill.co.uk
dir: *On A46 between Stratford-upon-Avon & Alcester*

Sitting proudly on the A46 between Stratford-upon-
Avon and Alcester, the Stag was originally Stratford's
courthouse and jail in the 17th century; the interior
features a preserved cell door and windows in cast iron
frames. Today it's a family-run business, satisfying
popular demand for Greene King ales such as Abbot
and Morland Original; a rotating selection of guests
adds to the choice. Food service begins with breakfast
from 7.30am and runs right through to dinner, every
day of the year. On Sundays the popular traditional
carvery offers three joints, one of which is always beef
– and two beef joints ensure you can choose between
rare or more cooked meat. Wednesday night is pie-and-
a-pint night, Friday night is grill night accompanied by
the pub's piano player, and there's usually a good
value prix fixe lunch menu running during the week.
Specials change regularly, sometimes daily, and often
feature fresh seafood such as tempura battered
prawns, whole plaice, or red mullet fillets with stir-
fried vegetables.

Open all day all wk 7am-11pm **Bar Meals** L served all
wk 12-5 D served all wk 5-9 food served all day
Restaurant L served all wk 12-5 D served all wk 5-9
food served all day ⊕ GREENE KING ◀ Greene King IPA,
Abbot Ale, Old Speckled Hen, Ruddles, Morland Original
♂ Stowford Press. **Facilities** Children welcome
Children's menu Garden Parking Wi-fi

RUGBY   Map 11 SP57

PICK OF THE PUBS

Golden Lion ★★★ HL

Easenhall CV23 0JA
☎ 01788 832265 📄 01788 832878
e-mail: reception@goldenlionhotel.org
dir: *From Rugby take A426, take 1st exit Newbold road*
B4112. Through Newbold. At Harborough Parva follow
brown sign, turn left, pub in 1m

Set in idyllic Warwickshire countryside, this charming
free house has its bar and award-winning restaurant
in the original 16th-century building, which retains
many original features, including log fires, low beams
and wattle and daub walls. The adjoining
contemporary hotel has 20 well equipped bedrooms.
Run by the Austin family since 1931, you'll find real
ales such as Young's Bitter and Wells Bombardier in
the bar, as well as excellent food and service, with a
wide choice of sandwiches, baguettes and
ploughman's; a Sunday lunch carvery and speciality
nights. The restaurant menu may feature loin of cod
wrapped in pancetta with white wine, mushroom and

prawn sauce; chef's hearty steak, mushroom and
Stilton pie; or lamb's liver black pudding and bacon
with creamy mash. Finish with sticky toffee pudding
with toffee sauce and vanilla ice cream or fruits of the
forest pancakes with raspberry pannacotta ice cream.

Open all day all wk 11-11 (Sun noon-11)
Bar Meals L served Mon-Sat 12-2, Sun 12-2.30
D served Mon-Sat 4.30-9.30, Sun 3-8.45
Restaurant L served Mon-Sat 12-2, Sun 12-2.30
D served Mon-Sat 4.30-9.30, Sun 3-8.45 ⊕ FREE
HOUSE ◀ Young's, Directors, UBU, Bombardier
♂ Stowford Press, Brothers. **Facilities** Children
welcome Children's menu Children's portions Garden
Parking Wi-fi **Rooms** 20

Old Smithy ☻

1 Green Ln, Church Lawford CV23 9EF
☎ 02476 542333
e-mail: smithy@king-henrys-taverns.co.uk
dir: *From Rugby take A428 (Lawford Rd) towards*
Coventry. Turn right to Church Lawford

A prettier building is hard to imagine. There is an inviting
interior too with huge logs fires to add to the atmosphere
in the winter, a modern conservatory-style dining area,
and outside a garden and patio much frequented in the
warmer weather. The menu of freshly prepared dishes
has choices for small and large appetites alike. Choose
from steaks, fish and seafood, rumpburgers, traditional
favourites, and international and vegetarian dishes.

Open all day all wk 11.30am-11pm **Bar Meals** food
served all day **Restaurant** food served all day ⊕ FREE
HOUSE ◀ Guinness, IPA, Marstons Pedigree. ☻ 16
Facilities Children welcome Children's menu Children's
portions Garden Parking

SALFORD PRIORS   Map 10 SP05

The Bell at Salford Priors ☻

Evesham Rd WR11 8UU ☎ 01789 772112
e-mail: info@thebellatsalfordpriors.com
web: www.thebellatsalfordpriors.com
dir: *From A46 (Bidford Island) towards Salford Priors.*
Through village. Pub on left

Refurbished to a high standard not long ago, this country
pub glows with open fires and welcoming hospitality. On
offer at the bar are at least three cask ales, and a
draught cider too. The daily-changing menus offer plenty
of choice. Sample starters are home-made spiced
pumpkin soup; and pan-fried calves' liver in bacon and

continued

SALFORD PRIORS *continued*

brandy cream served on farmhouse toast. Game lovers will not resist a main course trio of partridge, pheasant and duck breasts with a rich port and berry sauce.

The Bell at Salford Priors

Open all day all wk **Bar Meals** food served all day **Restaurant** L served Mon-Fri 12-3, Sat-Sun all day booking required D served Mon-Fri fr 6, Sat-Sun all day booking required ⊕ ENTERPRISE INNS ◀ Wye Valley HPA, Sharp's Doom Bar, Wickwar Bob ♂ Westons Old Rosie. ☕ 10 **Facilities** Children welcome Children's menu Children's portions Dogs allowed Garden Parking Wi-fi

---

SHIPSTON ON STOUR   Map 10 SP24

White Bear Hotel ☕

High St CV36 4AJ ☎ 01608 661558
e-mail: whitebearshipton@hotmail.com
dir: *From M40 junct 15, follow signs to Stratford-upon-Avon, then take A3400 to Shipston on Stour*

Situated in the market town square and providing the hub of the local community, the refurbished bars of this Georgian hotel have a comfortable, timeless appeal, with open fires and wooden settles. You'll find a range of real ales and keg beers, with up to ten wines available by the glass. Food-wise, expect simple offerings such as filled jacket potatoes, fresh salads or pie of the day. Visit in the afternoon and you can enjoy a scone with clotted cream and jam.

Open all day all wk **Bar Meals** L served all wk 9-9 D served all wk 9-9 Av main course £9.95 food served all day **Restaurant** L served all wk 9-9 D served all wk 9-9 Fixed menu price fr £6.95 Av 3 course à la carte fr £12.95 food served all day ⊕ PUNCH TAVERNS ◀ London Pride, Deuchars IPA, Hooky Bitter, Adnams, Tribute, Black Sheep, 3 Guest ales ♂ Scrumpy, Old Rosie. ☕ 10 **Facilities** Children welcome Children's menu Children's portions Dogs allowed Garden Beer festival Parking Wi-fi

---

SHREWLEY   Map 10 SP26

PICK OF THE PUBS

The Durham Ox Restaurant and Country Pub

Shrewley Common CV35 7AY ☎ 01926 842283
e-mail: enquiries@durham-ox.co.uk
dir: *M40 junct 15 onto A46 towards Coventry. 1st exit signed Warwick, turn left onto A4177. After Hatton Country World, pub signed 1.5m*

An award-winning pub/restaurant in a peaceful village just four miles from Warwick and Leamington. Warm and inviting, its old beams, roaring fire and traditional hospitality combine with a city chic that give it a competitive edge. Success is in no small measure due to the restaurant, where Master Chef Simon Diprose prepares impressive, seasonally changing classic and contemporary dishes. A meal might consist of deep-fried Boursin with ratatouille and basil sorbet; roast fillet of five-spice salmon with sweetcorn, pak choi and coriander dressing; and hot chocolate and Snickers fondant with vanilla ice cream. For more examples of his style, consider roast vegetables with North African spices, couscous and yoghurt dressing; and fresh plaice fillet in crispy Cajun coating with buttered peas and chunky chips. Children are offered penne pasta, and home-made fishcakes from their own menu. Extensive gardens incorporate a safe children's play area.

Open all wk 11-11 (Sun 12-10) ⊕ GREENE KING ◀ Ruddles, IPA, Guest ales ♂ Stowford Press. **Facilities** Children welcome Play area Dogs allowed Garden Parking

---

STRATFORD-UPON-AVON   Map 10 SP25

PICK OF THE PUBS

The Fox & Goose Inn ☕

CV37 8DD ☎ 01608 682635   📠 01608 682635
e-mail: mail@foxandgoosecountryinn.co.uk
dir: *1m off A3400, between Shipston on Stour & Stratford-upon-Avon*

This ivy-clad inn sits tucked away in an unspoilt country village south of Stratford-upon-Avon and makes an ideal base for exploring the Cotswolds. Converted from cottages and a blacksmith's forge and recently refurbished, the rustic-chic interior comprises a cosy locals bar with squishy velvet cushions on benches and pews, and a stylish dining room with open log fire and an eclectic mix of furnishings on flagstone floors. Expect to find local Hooky or London Pride on tap, or coincide your visit with the champagne happy hour in the early evening from Monday to Saturday and enjoy a glass (or bottle) of fizz. For more solid sustenance, look to the country-style menu: scallops wrapped in Parma ham with pea guacamole could be followed by salmon and chive fishcakes with creamy watercress sauce, or roast lamb with Cajun spiced lentils and rosemary jus. There's alfresco decking for dining under the vines, and lovely countryside views.

Open all day all wk Bar Meals booking required Av main course £11 food served all day **Restaurant** Fixed menu price fr £12.95 Av 3 course à la carte fr £15 food served all day ⊕ FREE HOUSE ◀ local guest ales, 6X, Hooky, Fuller's London Pride ♂ Thatchers Gold. ☕ 10 **Facilities** Children welcome Children's menu Children's portions Dogs allowed Garden Parking Wi-fi

---

PICK OF THE PUBS

The One Elm ☕

1 Guild St CV37 6QZ ☎ 01789 404919
e-mail: theoneelm@peachpubs.com
dir: *In town centre*

In a prime location in the town centre, a stroll from the river and theatre, The One Elm mirrors the chic, contemporary look and style of menus to be found at other Peach Pubs, the innovative small pub group founded by Lee Cash and Hamish Stoddart nearly a decade ago. Opening at 9.30am for coffee and breakfast, there's an informal, almost continental feel about the place, especially in the stylish front lounge area with its wood floor, bright painted walls, leather sofas and low tables displaying the day's newspapers. Beyond the central, open-to-view kitchen is the more formal dining area, while the upstairs seating area has an even grander feel. From deli boards offering tapas-style starters or nibbles of charcuterie, cheese, and rustic breads, the menu is an eclectic list of modern pub food. Enjoy starter or main course size moules marinière or begin with chicken liver pâté with apple chutney, then follow with pan-fried cod with creamy chorizo, butter beans and leeks, and dark chocolate tart. The secluded terrace induces a feeling of being abroad.

Open all day all wk Mon-Wed 11-11 Thu 11am-11.30pm Fri-Sat 11am-mdnt Sun 11-10.30 Closed: 25 Dec Bar Meals L served all wk 12-6 D served all wk 6-10 Av main course £12 food served all day **Restaurant** L served all wk 12-2.30 booking required D served all wk 6-10 booking required Av 3 course à la carte fr £25 food served all day ⊕ PEACH PUB CO ◀ UBU Purity, Purity Gold, London Pride ♂ Addlestones. ☕ 8 **Facilities** Children welcome Children's menu Children's portions Dogs allowed Garden Parking Wi-fi

Save on hotels. Book at **theAA.com/hotel**

WARWICKSHIRE 475 **ENGLAND**

STRETTON ON FOSSE
Map 10 SP23

The Plough Inn ♥

GL56 9QX ☎ 01608 661053
e-mail: saravol@aol.com
dir: *From Moreton-in-Marsh, 4m on A429 N. From Stratford-upon-Avon, 10m on A429 S*

A classic award-winning village pub built from mellow Cotswold stone, The Plough has the requisite exposed beams and real fire, plus a friendly resident cat, Alfie, to add to the welcome. Four real ales are usually on tap, ciders include Black Rat from Moles, and there's a good range of wines too. It's a family-run affair, with French chef and co-owner Jean-Pierre in charge of the kitchen; so expect traditional French dishes on the specials board. With a spit roast in the inglenook fireplace in winter and spring, entertainment on Sunday evenings ranges from quizzes to folk music.

Open 11.30-2.30 6-11.30 (Sun noon-3) Closed: 25 Dec eve, Sun eve Oct-Apr **Bar Meals** L served all wk 12-2 D served Mon-Sat 7-9 Av main course £10 ⊕ FREE HOUSE ◀ Hook Norton, Ansells Mild, Spitfire, Purity, local ales ♂ Old Katy, Black Rat, Thatchers Traditional. ♥ 9 **Facilities** Children welcome Children's portions Play area Garden Parking Wi-fi

TEMPLE GRAFTON
Map 10 SP15

The Blue Boar Inn ♥

B49 6NR ☎ 01789 750010 📠 01789 750635
e-mail: info@thebluebaor.co.uk
dir: *From A46 (Stratford to Alcester) turn left to Temple Grafton. Pub at 1st x-rds*

An alehouse from the outset, the oldest part of this village inn dates from the early 1600s. Water from the glass-covered well was once used for brewing, but nowadays it's a home for goldfish. Warmth in the bar and restaurant comes from four open fires, while in the summer there is a patio garden with views of the Cotswold Hills. Regularly-changing menus include lamb kofta; pan-seared lamb's liver; griddled tuna steak; and Mediterranean vegetable and tomato risotto. Try food from different countries on the first Friday of every month.

Open all day all wk **Bar Meals** L served all wk 12-3 D served all wk 6-10 **Restaurant** L served Mon-Fri 12-3, Sat 12-10, Sun 12-9 D served Mon-Fri 6-10, Sat 12-10, Sun 12-9 ⊕ MARSTONS ◀ Marstons Banks Original, Pedigree, Hobgoblin, Jennings ♂ Thatchers Gold. **Facilities** Children welcome Children's menu Children's portions Dogs allowed Garden Parking Wi-fi

WARWICK
Map 10 SP26

PICK OF THE PUBS

The Rose & Crown ♥

30 Market Place CV34 4SH
☎ 01926 411117 📠 01926 492117
e-mail: roseandcrown@peachpubs.com
dir: *M40 junct 15 follow signs to Warwick. Pass castle car park entrance up hill to West Gate, left into Bowling Green St, 1st right, then turn right into Market Square*

A decade on since Lee Cash and Hamish Stoddart created the innovative Peach Pub Company and their flagship Rose & Crown, a vibrant and stylish gastro-pub in the heart of Warwick, continues to thrive. One of the main draws is the contemporary look that complements period features and inspired touches such as leather sofas, coffee tables with the day's newspapers, and a laid-back vibe, plus a policy of opening early for breakfast (free toast), and a modern pub menu that's served all day. Deli boards offer small tapas-style portions of cheeses, charcuterie and fish and the seasonal menu also offers a wide selection of dishes to suit the occasion and time of day, with breakfast sarnies, small or large plates of risotto (pea, broad bean and mint), pancakes and salads, then main dishes like sea bass with salsa verde, and 28-day dry aged rump steak with green peppercorn butter. Puddings may include rhubarb fool and hot chocolate brownie.

Open all day all wk Closed: 25 Dec **Bar Meals** Av main course £8 food served all day **Restaurant** Av 3 course à la carte fr £23 food served all day ⊕ PEACH PUBS ◀ Purity UBU, Purity Gold, Guest ales ♂ Addlestones. ♥ 10 **Facilities** Children welcome Children's menu Children's portions Dogs allowed Wi-fi

WELFORD-ON-AVON
Map 10 SP15

PICK OF THE PUBS

The Bell Inn ♥

Binton Rd CV37 8EB
☎ 01789 750353 📠 01789 750893
e-mail: info@thebellwelford.co.uk
dir: *Please telephone for directions*

Dating from the early 16th century, this is reputedly one of the oldest pubs in the Warwickshire Cotswolds. Handy for Stratford, legend has it that William Shakespeare contracted fatal pneumonia after stumbling home from here in the pouring rain. Although it is now a contemporary restaurant, the historic bar with its limestone flagged floors, beams, oak furniture and open fires still serves at least five real ales. Owners Colin and Teresa Ombler have always aimed to proffer a warm welcome and a simple pint, with dishes of quality food and outstanding service when desired. These are certainly hard to resist, the menu proudly listing all the local suppliers of fresh and seasonal produce. Starters and light meals include avocado and crispy bacon salad, or breaded chicken

goujons with a dipping pot of spiced crème fraîche; specials range from deep-fried squid to Lashford's pork and leek sausages. There are sharing deli plates and hot sandwich of the week too.The pub's busy diary includes themed evenings such as fish and chip suppers, and nights of spice.

Open all wk Mon-Sat 11.30-11 (Sun noon-10.30) **Bar Meals** L served Mon-Fri 11.30-2.30, Sat 11.30-3, Sun all day booking required D served Mon-Thu 6-9.30, Fri-Sat 6-10, Sun all day booking required Av main course £11.95 **Restaurant** L served Mon-Sat 11.30-2.30, Sun all day booking required D served Mon-Thu 6-9.30, Fri-Sat 6-10, Sun all day booking required Fixed menu price fr £15 Av 3 course à la carte fr £20 ⊕ ENTERPRISE INNS ◀ Hook Norton (various), Flowers Original, Hobsons Best, Wadworth 6X, Flowers Best, Purity Gold, UBU. ♥ 14 **Facilities** Children welcome Children's menu Children's portions Garden Parking Wi-fi

WITHYBROOK
Map 11 SP48

The Pheasant ♥

Main St CV7 9LT ☎ 01455 220480 📠 01455 221296
e-mail: thepheasant01@hotmail.com
web: www.thepheasanteatinghouse.com
dir: *7m NE of Coventry, on B4112*

This popular 17th-century free house stands beside the brook where withies were once cut for fencing, hence the village's name, Withybrook. Under the same ownership since 1981, the inn is full of character with an inglenook fireplace, farm implements and horse-racing photographs on display. There's a wealth of food choices - a typical menu includes chicken and mushroom pie, T-bone steak garni, and Japanese breaded king prawns, and there is also a specials blackboard. Outside, the benches overlooking the Withy Brook can accommodate 100 people. There are lots of walks nearby and walkers can quench their thirst with one of the great real ales on offer.

Open all wk 11-3 6-11.30 (Sun & BH 11-11) Closed: 25-26 Dec (unless falling at wknd) **Bar Meals** L served Mon-Sat 12-2, Sun 12-9 booking required D served Mon-Sat 6-10, Sun 12-9 booking required Av main course £11.75 **Restaurant** L served Mon-Sat 12-2, Sun 12-9 booking required D served Mon-Sat 6-10, Sun 12-9 booking required Fixed menu price fr £18 Av 3 course à la carte fr £21.95 ⊕ FREE HOUSE ◀ Courage Directors, Theakstons Best, John Smith's Smooth, Theakstons Dark, Young's Bitter. ♥ 16 **Facilities** Children welcome Children's menu Children's portions Garden Parking

WOOTTON WAWEN Map 10 SP16

PICK OF THE PUBS

The Bulls Head ♥

Stratford Rd B95 6BD ☎ 01564 792511
e-mail: info@thebullsheadwootonwawen.co.uk
dir: *On B3400, 4m N of Stratford-upon-Avon, 1m S of Henley-in-Arden*

A smart, black-and-white timber-framed pub, just one of the notable old buildings in Wootton Wawen, just a mile or so from the picturesque village of Henley-in-Arden and ideally placed for touring and exploring Warwickshire and the Cotswolds. Originally two separate cottages, it displays a stone with the date 1317, and the bar and snug areas feature rug-strewn flagstone floors, low, gnarled oak beams, old church pews, and leather sofas fronting log fires. Ale drinkers will find Marston's Pedigree, Banks Original and Hobgoblin ales on tap in the bar, while the food offering here takes in ham, egg and chips, classic fish and chips, and the hearty Bull's Head club sandwich filled with bacon, chicken, lettuce, tomato and egg mayonnaise. The same tone and style are maintained in the magnificent 'great hall' restaurant, with its vaulted ceiling and yet more exposed beams. Here you can tuck into braised lamb shank with caramelised onion gravy or roast salmon with watercress sauce, followed by sticky toffee pudding.

Open all day all wk **Bar Meals** Av main course £11 food served all day **Restaurant** L served Mon-Sat 12-2.30, Sun 12-5 D served all wk 6-9.30 Fixed menu price fr £11.50 ⊕ BILLESLEY PUB COMPANY ◀ Marston's Pedigree, Banks Bitter, Banks Original, Hobgoblin, Guest ales. ♥ 8 **Facilities** Children welcome Children's portions Dogs allowed Garden Parking Wi-fi

WEST MIDLANDS

BARSTON Map 10 SP27

PICK OF THE PUBS

The Malt Shovel at Barston ◉

Barston Ln B92 0JP
☎ 01675 443223   📠 01675 443223
web: www.themaltshovelatbarston.com
dir: *M42 junct 5, take turn towards Knowle. 1st left on Jacobean Ln, right at T-junct (Hampton Ln). Sharp left into Barston Ln. Restaurant 0.5m*

A neat village pub a short hop from Birmingham, The Malt Shovel is a bustling, award-winning free house with modern soft furnishings and interesting artefacts. Natural wood and pastel colours characterise the interiors of this stylishly converted early 20th-century mill building. The bar is cosy and relaxed with winter log fires, and the restaurant is housed in an adjacent converted barn. The imaginative, modern British dishes make the best of seasonal ingredients. The menu includes starters of seared Scottish scallops on pea purée with Colnakilty black pudding and crisp bacon; mildly spiced king prawns, passionfruit and chilli sauce; grilled line-caught mackerel, free-range slow roast pork belly and buttered Savoy cabbage. These may be followed by grilled plaice, roast sweet potato, crab and black Tuscan olive oil dressing; Cornish wild turbot with shelled mussels, crayfish, samphire and saffron broth; or lamb noisette on hazelnut and merlot risotto, rosemary and mint gremolata. There's a super rear garden for summer alfresco dining.

The Malt Shovel at Barston

Open all day all wk **Bar Meals** L served Mon-Sat 12-2.30, Sun 12-4 booking required D served Mon-Sat 6-9.30 booking required Av main course £12.95 **Restaurant** L served Sun 12-4 booking required D served Mon-Sat 7-9.30 booking required Av 3 course à la carte fr £23.95 ⊕ FREE HOUSE ◀ Tribute, Brew XI, Timothy Taylor Landlord. **Facilities** Garden Parking

See advert below

BIRMINGHAM   Map 10 SP08

The Old Joint Stock ♥ NEW

4 Temple Row West B2 5NY
☎ 0121 200 1892   🖷 0121 200 0948
e-mail: oldjointstock@fullers.co.uk
dir: *Opposite main entrance to St Philip's Cathedral, just off Colmore Row*

An architecturally astonishing, colonnaded pub that is an integral part of a theatre and functions complex at the heart of the city centre. Its cathedral-like interior assaults the senses; high Victorian Gothic with immense domed ceiling, stately-home fittings and towering mahogany island bar, at which Fuller's beers are dispensed. A bank until the 1990's, take a chance to withdraw to the widely dispersed tables and snack down on a speciality range of home-made pies – pork, Fuller's organic honeydew, pear and sage hits the right notes.

Open all wk all day (Sun 12-5) **Bar Meals** L served all wk 12-5 D served Mon-Sat 5-10 Av main course £9.50 food served all day **Restaurant** L served all wk 12-5 D served Mon-Sat 5-10 food served all day ⊕ FULLER SMITH TURNER PLC ◀ Fuller's London Pride, ESB, Discovery. ♥ 16 **Facilities** Children welcome Family room Garden Beer festival Wi-fi

Penny Blacks ♥

132-134 Wharfside St, The Mailbox B1 1RQ
☎ 0121 632 1460   🖷 0121 632 1463
e-mail: info@penny-blacks.com
dir: *In Mailbox district in city centre. Nearest station: Birmingham New Street*

Part of the regenerated Mailbox area of Birmingham, a short walk from the National Indoor Arena and Symphony Hall, this large canalside bar has a traditional pub feel with a warm and welcoming atmosphere. With five to seven real ales on tap and a vast range of wines, it has become a popular meeting place for locals and tourists

alike. The bar menu is a mix of pub classics and modern British dishes, from bar bites, sharing plates, pies or speciality sausages with a choice of mash, to steaks, fish and chips and vegetarian options. There is also a restaurant, a wine bar, sporting events on TV, and a DJ on Thursday, Friday and Saturday night.

Open all day all wk Closed: 25-26 Dec, 1 Jan
Bar Meals L served Mon-Thu 10-10, Fri-Sat 10am-10.30pm, Sun 10-8.30 D served Mon-Thu 10-10, Fri-Sat 10am-10.30pm, Sun 10-8.30 Av main course £9.95 food served all day **Restaurant** Av 3 course à la carte fr £20 food served all day ⊕ CROPTHORNE INNS ◀ Wyre Piddle, Hook Norton, St Austell, Church End, Cottage Brewery, Wentworth Brewery, Slater's. ♥ 15 **Facilities** Children welcome Children's menu Children's portions Dogs allowed Garden Wi-fi

CHADWICK END   Map 10 SP27

PICK OF THE PUBS

The Orange Tree ♥

Warwick Rd B93 0BN ☎ 01564 785364
e-mail: theorangetree@lovelypubs.co.uk
web: www.theorangetreepub.co.uk
dir: *3m from Knowle towards Warwick*

One of a small and select chain of comfy, chic pubs in the West Midlands owned by Paul Salisbury and Paul Hales, The Orange Tree is a destination dining pub that ticks all the right boxes. Chunky wooden furniture, airy

interiors dappled with prints on thick walls supporting old beams all meld easily with a labyrinth of more traditional rustic, pubby corners with leather sofas in quiet alcoves, log fires, antique-style mirrors and colourwashed walls creating a great ambience. The dining experience is summed up as 'simple but up-to-the-minute' and encapsulates a good range such as sharing plates, pizzas and pastas from the stone-fired ovens together with modern European and global dishes. Expect asparagus, proscuitto, poached egg and hollandaise sauce as an appetiser. From the stove comes pork belly, chorizo, watercress, apple, spring onion and coriander mash. Summer diners can indulge in a feast on the sunny patio or amidst landscaped gardens in the tranquil Warwickshire countryside.

Open all day all wk 11-11 Closed: 25 Dec
Bar Meals L served Mon-Sat 12-2.30, Sun 12-7
D served Mon-Sat 6-9.30 **Restaurant** L served Mon-Sat 12-2.30, Sun 12-7 booking required D served Mon-Sat 6-9.30 booking required ⊕ FREE HOUSE ◀ IPA, London Pride, UBU. ♥ 10 **Facilities** Children welcome Children's portions Play area Dogs allowed Garden Parking Wi-fi

See advert below

HAMPTON IN ARDEN   Map 10 SP28

PICK OF THE PUBS

The White Lion Inn

10 High St B92 0AA ☎ 01675 442833
e-mail: info@thewhitelioninn.com
dir: Opposite church

This charming village inn, now under new ownership, is situated at the heart of the picturesque village of Hampton in Arden, yet is in close proximity to major road, rail and air links. Originally a farmhouse, this 17th-century timber-framed village pub has been licensed since at least 1836. The new owners have based their philosophy for running this pub from managing (and visiting) many restaurants, bistros and gastro-pubs in England and France. There's a bright and modern interior with wooden floors, fresh flowers and wicker chairs. The simple bistro-style menu, with a definite nod towards France, features foie gras maison; whitebait with fresh mayonnaise; Mediterranean vegetable goat's cheese tart; and tiger prawns in garlic butter to start with. The main courses include calves' liver, bacon, mash and roast vegetables; moules and frites; scallop and bacon brochettes; boeuf bourguignon. For smaller appetites, there are sandwiches (toasted if preferred) and jacket potatoes. Traditional Sunday lunches are a must.

Open all wk noon-12.30am (Sun noon-10.30)
Bar Meals L served all wk 12-2.30 D served all wk 6.30-9.30 Av main course £11 Restaurant L served all wk 12-2.30 D served all wk 6.30-9.30 Av 3 course à la carte fr £15 ⊕ PUNCH TAVERNS ◀ Brew XI, Black Sheep, Adnams, Mad Goose, Tribute, Doom Bar ☼ Aspall, Stowford Press. Facilities Children welcome Children's menu Children's portions Dogs allowed Garden Parking Wi-fi

OLDBURY   Map 10 SO98

PICK OF THE PUBS

Waggon & Horses

17a Church St B69 3AD ☎ 0121 552 5467
e-mail: andrew.gale.17a@hotmail.com
dir: Telephone for directions

Tucked away in the remnants of the old town centre and popular with shoppers and office workers, the Waggon & Horses is a Grade II listed Victorian pub and firmly on CAMRA's National Inventory of Historic Pub Interiors. Come to see the ornate tiled walls, the lovely copper-panelled ceiling, the fine Holts Brewery etched windows, and the huge tie collection in the splendid back bar. The side room has big old tables and high-backed settles, where you can also enjoy freshly prepared hot and cold pub food and bar snacks at lunch and in the evening. Ale drinkers can sup contentedly as the choice is good, including Brains Rev James, Enville White, Salopian Shropshire Gold and guest ales.

Open all wk Closed: Sun eve in winter Bar Meals L served Mon-Sat 12-2.30 D served Tue-Fri 5.30-7.30 Av main course £4.99 ⊕ S A BRAIN ◀ Enville White, Brains, Salopian Shropshire Gold, Salopian Oracle, Guest ale. Facilities Children welcome Children's portions Family room Parking

SEDGLEY   Map 10 SO99

PICK OF THE PUBS

Beacon Hotel & Sarah Hughes Brewery

129 Bilston St DY3 1JE
☎ 01902 883380   📄 01902 884020
dir: Telephone for directions

Home of the Sarah Hughes Brewery and the famous Dark Ruby Mild, the Beacon Hotel is a restored Victorian tap house that has barely changed in 150 years. Proprietor John Hughes reopened the adjoining Sarah Hughes Brewery in 1987, 66 years after his grandmother became the licensee. The rare snob-screened island bar serves a simple taproom, with its old wall benches and a fine blackened range, a super cosy snug replete with a green-tiled marble fireplace, dark woodwork, velvet curtains and huge old tables, and a large smoke-room with an adjoining, plant-festooned conservatory. Like the pub, it remains totally unchanged and on a tour of the brewery you can see the original grist case and rare open-topped copper that add to the Victorian charm and give unique character to the brews. Flagship beers are Sarah Hughes Dark Ruby, Surprise and Pale Amber, with seasonal bitter also available and two guest beers from small micro-breweries. Food in the pub is limited to filled cob rolls but there is a designated children's room and play area, as well as a large garden.

Open all wk noon-2.30 5.30-11 (Fri 12-3 Sat-12-3 6-11 Sun 12-3 7-10.30) Bar Meals food served all day ⊕ FREE HOUSE ◀ Sarah Hughes Dark Ruby, Surprise & Pale Amber, plus guest, seasonal ales. Facilities Children welcome Play area Family room Dogs allowed Garden Parking Notes ☺

WEST BROMWICH   Map 10 SP09

The Vine

Roebuck St B70 6RD ☎ 0121 553 2866
e-mail: bharat@thevine.co.uk
dir: 0.5m from M5 junct 1.2m from town centre

Well-known, family-run business renowned for its excellent curries and cheap drinks. Since 1978 the typically Victorian alehouse has provided the setting for Suresh 'Suki' Patel's eclectic menu. Choose from a comprehensive range of Indian dishes (chicken balti, lamb saag), a barbecue menu and Thursday spit roast, offered alongside traditional pub fare. The Vine boasts the Midlands' only indoor tandoori barbeque, plus it is a stone's throw from The Hawthorns, West Bromwich Albion's football ground.

Open all wk (Fri-Sun all day) Bar Meals L served Mon-Fri 11.30-2.30, Sat-Sun 12-10.30 D served Mon-Fri 5-10.30, Sat-Sun 12-10.30 Av main course £6 Restaurant L served Mon-Fri 11.30-2.30, Sat-Sun 12-10.30 D served Mon-Fri 5-10.30, Sat-Sun 12-10.30 Av 3 course à la carte fr £12 ⊕ FREE HOUSE ◀ Banks Mild, Brew XI, John Smith's. Facilities Children welcome Garden

WIGHT, ISLE OF

ARRETON   Map 5 SZ58

The White Lion

PO30 3AA ☎ 01983 528479
e-mail: chrisandkateiow@hotmail.co.uk
web: www.white-lion-arreton.com
dir: B3056 (Newport to Sandown road)

Situated in the old part of the village in an outstandingly beautiful conservation area, this 300-year-old former coaching inn offers a warm welcome with its oak beams, polished brass and open fires. An outside seating area enjoys views of the Arreton scenery. Well-kept ales and pub grub are served all day, ranging from traditional ploughman's and sandwiches to dishes like home-made lasagne, pork steak with a creamy green peppercorn sauce, or smoked haddock and spring onion fishcakes. Ask about the small window in the corner of the bar and the Arreton ghost walk.

Open all day all wk Bar Meals L served all wk 12-9 D served all wk 12-9 Av main course £8.50 food served all day Restaurant L served all wk 12-9 D served all wk 12-9 Fixed menu price fr £10 Av 3 course à la carte fr £12.50 food served all day ⊕ ENTERPRISE INNS ◀ John Smith's Smooth, Flowers Best, Doom Bar, 6X, Ruddles, Wells Eagle IPA ☼ Stowford Press, Westons Scrumpy. Facilities Children welcome Children's menu Children's portions Play area Family room Dogs allowed Garden Parking

BEMBRIDGE   Map 5 SZ68

The Crab & Lobster Inn ★★★★ INN ☗

32 Forelands Field Rd PO35 5TR
☎ 01983 872244   📄 01983 873495
e-mail: info@crabandlobsterinn.co.uk
dir: From Bembridge village, 1st left after Boots onto Forelands Rd to Windmill Hotel. Left onto Lane End Rd, 2nd right onto Egerton Rd, left onto Howgate Rd & immediately right onto Forelands Field Rd

Smothered by summer flower baskets and troughs, this Victorian spirit merchant's inn sports a fine beamed interior, whilst the stunning coastal location beside Bembridge Ledge means the raised deck and patio is the place to sup Wight brewed Goddard's Fuggle-Dee-Dum bitter, idly watch yachts and fishing boats. Locally caught seafood is one of the pub's great attractions, with dishes such as local seafood tagliatelli or home-made crab cakes, and guarantees repeat visits from the inn's many admirers. Mixed grills and steaks cater for meat-eaters. Some of the light and airy bedrooms have memorable sea views.

Open all day all wk 11-11 (Sun 11-10.30) **Bar Meals** L served all wk 12-2.30 (summer Sat-Sun & BHs 2.30-5.30 limited menu) booking required D served Sun-Thu 6-9, Fri-Sat 6-9.30 booking required Av main course £8 **Restaurant** L served all wk 12-2.30 (summer Sat-Sun & BHs 2.30-5.30 limited menu) booking required D served Sun-Thu 6-9, Fri-Sat 6-9.30 booking required ⊕ ENTERPRISE INNS ◀ Sharp's Doom Bar, Goddards Fuggle-Dee-Dum, Greene King IPA, John Smith's ○ Stowford Press. ♀ 12 **Facilities** Children welcome Children's menu Children's portions Dogs allowed Garden Parking Wi-fi **Rooms** 5

The Windmill Inn ♀

1 Steyne Rd PO35 5UH ☎ 01983 872875 📄 01983 874760

e-mail: enquiries@windmill-inn.com
dir: From Sandown take B3395 (Sandown Rd) Straight on at rdbt into Steyne Rd in Bembridge. Inn on right

Ideally placed for walking and cycling and near the beach in the quiet village of Bembridge, this is a relaxing place to chat and look at paintings by local artists and yachts in the harbour, while enjoying a drink and a bite to eat. Enjoy home-made food from a light snack of chicken liver pâté with red onion marmalade to fresh lobster and fish from the blackboards, washed down with a pint of Fuggle-Dee-Dum from Goddards in Ryde. Recent change of hands.

Open all day all wk **Bar Meals** L served all wk 11.30-2 D served all wk 5-9 Av main course £8 **Restaurant** L served all wk 12-2 D served all wk 5-9 Av 3 course à la carte fr £9 ⊕ FREE HOUSE ◀ Ringwood Best, Goddards Fuggle-Dee-Dum, Goddards Special Bitter, Greene King IPA ○ Stowford Press. ♀ 12 **Facilities** Children welcome Children's menu Children's portions Play area Dogs allowed Garden Parking Wi-fi

BONCHURCH   Map 5 SZ57

The Bonchurch Inn

Bonchurch Shute PO38 1NU
☎ 01983 852611 📄 01983 856657
e-mail: gillian@bonchurch-inn.co.uk
dir: Off A3055 in Bonchurch

In its quiet off the road location, this small family-run free house inn lies tucked away in a secluded Dickensian-style courtyard. You won't be disturbed by juke boxes or gaming machines, for little has changed here since this former coaching inn and stables was granted its first licence in the 1840s. Food is available lunchtime and evenings in the bar; choices range from sandwiches and ploughman's to plenty of fresh fish dishes, chicken dishes, juicy steaks and Italian specialities. Desserts also have an Italian bias – perhaps zabaglione, cassata or tiramisu.

Open all wk 11-3 6.30-11 Closed: 25 Dec **Bar Meals** L served all wk 12-2 D served all wk 6.30-9 booking required Av main course £9.95 **Restaurant** D served all wk 7-8.45 booking required ⊕ FREE HOUSE ◀ Courage Directors, Best. **Facilities** Children welcome Children's portions Family room Dogs allowed Garden Parking Wi-fi

COWES   Map 5 SZ49

Duke of York Inn ★★★ INN NEW

Mill Hill Rd PO31 7BT
☎ 01983 295171 📄 01983 295047
e-mail: bookings@dukeofyorkcowes.co.uk
dir: In town centre

Family run by the same landlord for 43 years, this former coaching inn is situated close to the centre of Cowes and marina. A nautical theme runs throughout this friendly inn where everyone is welcome, even soggy, wet yachtsmen. Quality home-cooked food is available in the bar and restaurant and includes fresh seafood especially crab, and roast lunches on Sunday. Real ales include Goddards Fuggle Dee Dum with real ciders too. Comfortable, individually decorated bedrooms are available.

Open all day all wk **Bar Meals** L served all wk 12-2.30 D served all wk 6-10 Av main course £10-£15 **Restaurant** L served all wk 12-2.30 booking required D served all wk 6-10 booking required ⊕ ENTERPRISE INNS ◀ Goddards Fuggle-Dee-Dum, Sharp's Doom Bar, Ringwood Best ○ Westons 1st Quality, Old Rosie. **Facilities** Children welcome Children's menu Children's portions Dogs allowed Parking Wi-fi **Rooms** 13

The Fountain Inn ★★★ INN ♀ NEW

High St PO31 7AW ☎ 01983 292397 📄 01983 299554
e-mail: 6447@greeneking.co.uk
dir: Adjacent to Red Jet passenger ferry in town centre

American president Thomas Jefferson once stayed at this inn, which was built in 1771. In the heart of Cowes, with a decked area overlooking the harbour, The Fountain makes a great base for the town's many annual sailing events. In the restaurant, enjoy pints of local Goddards ale with an extensive menu of traditional English dishes, steaks, gourmet burgers and chef's specials such as ham hock and broad bean pie. There is live music every Friday and Saturday night, and accommodation is available.

Open all day all wk **Bar Meals** L served all wk 12-9 D served all wk 12-9 Av main course £6-£9 food served all day **Restaurant** L served all wk 12-9 D served all wk 12-9 Fixed menu price fr £9.99 food served all day ⊕ GREENE KING ◀ Greene King IPA, Goddards. **Facilities** Children welcome Children's menu Children's portions Dogs allowed Garden Wi-fi **Rooms** 20

FRESHWATER   Map 5 SZ38

PICK OF THE PUBS

The Red Lion

Church Place PO40 9BP
☎ 01983 754925 📄 01983 754483
dir: In Old Freshwater follow signs for All Saints Church

There's been a pub on this island site since the 11th century, although today's charming, climber-clad red brick building is clearly more recent. Situated in the centre of the village, a short walk from Yarmouth harbour, it's a popular drinking spot for visiting yachtsmen, as well as walkers and golfers. A garden at the rear is well furnished with hardwood chairs and tables, and a canvas dome comes into its own for candlelit alfresco dinners. The bar is comfortable with settles and chairs around scrubbed pine tables, the log fire burns throughout the winter, and peace and quiet is preferred to music as regulars settle down with a pint of Goddards or Spitfire. Much of the produce used in Lorna Mence's filling meals comes from the Island and is detailed on the daily-changing blackboard menu. The light lunch menu includes pub favourites like Welsh rarebit and bacon, and ham, eggs and chips, as well as sandwiches, baguettes, panini, ploughman's, and salads. Add to this main course specials of braised lamb shank with minted gravy, pan-fried scallops wrapped in bacon, and beef Stroganoff. Round off the meal with jam roly-poly, spotted Richard, bread and butter pudding, or chocolate roulade.

Open all wk 11.30-3 5.30-11 (Sun noon-3 7-10.30) **Bar Meals** L served all wk 12-2 booking required D served all wk 6.30-9 booking required **Restaurant** L served all wk 12-2 booking required D served all wk 6.30-9 booking required ⊕ ENTERPRISE INNS ◀ Interbrew Flowers Original, Spitfire, Goddards, Sharp's Doom Bar. **Facilities** Dogs allowed Garden Parking

GODSHILL
Map 5 SZ58

PICK OF THE PUBS

The Taverners ▾

High St PO38 3HZ ☎ 01983 840707
dir: *Please telephone for directions*

The Taverners has filled many roles in its history, including village bakehouse, post office, general store and tea room, reputedly graced by a visit from Queen Victoria. Today's pub is run by islanders Roger Serjent and Lisa Choi, who are committed to producing a high-quality menu while keeping their food and drink miles as low as possible. To this end they source as much as they can from the island; meat, poultry, eggs and dairy produce all come from within a couple of miles' radius, whilst seafood arrives from nearby Ventnor and Bembridge. An in-pub shop sells home-made food items from the kitchen, handicrafts, and some of their suppliers' produce. Traditional choices from the menu could be shepherd's pie or macaroni cheese, while the specials board branches out with slow-roast Moor Farm pork cheek with faggot and mash, or Briddlesford veal wrapped in pancetta. In the garden is a toddlers' play area, and a run for the pub's two pet chickens, Sam and Ella.

Open all day all wk Closed: 1st 2wks Jan
Bar Meals L served all wk 12-3 D served all wk summer 6-9.30, Mon-Sat winter 6-9 Av main course £12
Restaurant L served all wk 12-3 booking required D served Sun-Thu 6-9, Fri-Sat 6-9.30 booking required Av 3 course à la carte fr £22 ⊕ PUNCH ◀ Undercliff, London Pride, John Smith's, Taverners Own, Sharp's Doom Bar, Black Sheep ♂ Stowford Press, Old Rosie. ▾ 9 **Facilities** Children welcome Children's menu Children's portions Play area Dogs allowed Garden Parking

HULVERSTONE
Map 5 SZ38

The Sun Inn at Hulverstone NEW

Main Rd PO30 4EH ☎ 01983 741124
e-mail: lesleyblanchard@btconnect.com
dir: *Between Mottistone & Brook on B3399*

Set in beautiful National Trust countryside near Brook Chine, with spectacular views of Freshwater Cliffs and beyond, this traditional thatched pub is 600 years old. Once a haunt for smugglers, it is now a family-run pub and restaurant showcasing local produce on a menu that includes rare-breed pork, beef and lamb from an adjoining farm and plenty of local fish. The huge beer garden has outstanding views.

Open all day all wk **Bar Meals** L served all wk 12-9 D served all wk 12-9 Av main course £9.95 food served all day **Restaurant** L served all wk 12-9 booking required D served all wk 12-9 booking required food served all day ⊕ ENTERPRISE INNS ◀ Ringwood Fortyniner, Goddards Fuggle-Dee-Dum, Adnams Best, Otter Ale ♂ Stowford Press. **Facilities** Children welcome Children's portions Dogs allowed Garden Parking Wi-fi

NINGWOOD
Map 5 SZ38

Horse & Groom ▾

Main Rd PO30 4NW ☎ 01983 760672   🖹 01983 874760
e-mail: info@horse-and-groom.com
dir: *On A3054 (Yarmouth to Newport road)*

A couple of miles west of Yarmouth, this large family pub is a landmark on the Newport road. There's a nice garden with a large children's play area, and four-footed family members are also welcome on the stone and wood floored indoor areas. Food is served daily from noon until 9pm, and the offering ranges from baguettes and light bites to pub favourites like braised lamb shank, battered fish and chips, and Mediterranean vegetable lasagne, plus a specials board offering seasonal specialities. There is a real ale festival each September.

Open all day all wk **Bar Meals** L served all wk 12-9 booking required D served all wk 12-9 booking required Av main course £9 food served all day ⊕ ENTERPRISE INNS ◀ Ringwood, Goddards. ▾ 16 **Facilities** Children welcome Children's menu Children's portions Play area Dogs allowed Garden Beer festival Parking Wi-fi

NITON
Map 5 SZ57

Buddle Inn

St Catherines Rd PO38 2NE ☎ 01983 730243
dir: *Take A3055 from Ventnor. In Niton take 1st left signed 'to the lighthouse'*

A stone's throw from the English Channel one way and the Coastal Path the other, this 16th-century, former cliff-top farmhouse is one of the island's oldest hostelries. Popular with hikers and ramblers (and their muddy boots and dogs), the interior has the full traditional complement - stone flags, oak beams and large open fire, as well as great real ales on tap. Hearty home-made food is served, along with specials like fresh lemon sole with hot crab, and chargrilled duck breast with plum sauce.

Open all day all wk 11-11 (Fri-Sat 11-mdnt Sun noon-10.30) ⊕ ENTERPRISE INNS ◀ Adnams, Buddle Best, London Pride ♂ Stowford Press. **Facilities** Children welcome Children's menu Children's portions Family room Dogs allowed Garden Parking

NORTHWOOD
Map 5 SZ49

Travellers Joy

85 Pallance Rd PO31 8LS ☎ 01983 298024
e-mail: tjoy@globalnet.co.uk
dir: *Telephone for directions*

Ruth, Derek and Andy run this 300-year-old alehouse, just a little way inland from Cowes. They keep eight real ales on hand pump all year round. Don't expect dishes described on the menu as 'drizzled' or 'pan-roasted' here because the food is home cooked and uncomplicated but with all the trimmings – steak and kidney pie; cottage pie; lamb shank; chicken goujons. Outside is a pétanque terrain, pets' corner and play area.

Open all wk Mon-Thu 12-2.30 5-11 (Fri-Sat noon-11.30, Sun noon-3 7-11) **Bar Meals** L served all wk 12-2 D served all wk 6.30-9.30 Av main course £7.25 ⊕ FREE HOUSE ◀ Goddards Special Bitter, Courage Directors, Ventnor Golden Bitter, Deuchars IPA, St Austell Tribute. **Facilities** Children welcome Children's menu Children's portions Family room Dogs allowed Garden Parking

ROOKLEY
Map 5 SZ58

The Chequers ▾

Niton Rd PO38 3NZ ☎ 01983 840314   🖹 01983 840820
e-mail: richard@chequersinn-iow.co.uk
dir: *Telephone for directions*

Surrounded by farms in the centre of the island, this 250-year-old family-friendly country free house has a reputation for good food at reasonable prices. Choose from jackets, sandwiches, ploughman's, salads or the main menu. Fish, naturally, features prominently, and other favourites are pan-fried breast of duck with orange and cranberry sauce or pork chop with apple and cider sauce. There are also plenty of choices for children, who get their own menu. Check out the date for the next beer festival.

Open all day all wk **Bar Meals** food served all day **Restaurant** food served all day ⊕ FREE HOUSE ◀ Ringwood Best, Ringwood Fortyniner, Guest ales ♂ Thatchers. **Facilities** Children welcome Children's menu Children's portions Play area Family room Dogs allowed Garden Beer festival Parking Wi-fi

RYDE   Map 5 SZ59

Ryde Castle ★★★ INN ♥ NEW

The Esplanade PO33 1JA
☎ **01983 563755** 📠 **01983 566906**
e-mail: 6506@greeneking.co.uk
dir: B3331 from Fishbourne ferry port to lights. Left onto A3054 to Binstead. At next lights left into Queens Rd to Esplanade. Ryde Castle at rdbt

Originally a large, spacious home overlooking Ryde Harbour, this impressive building has stunning views across the Solent and is claimed to have been commissioned by Henry VIII to defend the Spithead and Solent from invasion by the Spanish Armada. It is now a popular place where locally brewed Goddards ale can be enjoyed with dishes from the extensive menu of pub classics, steaks and chef's specials. Accommodation is available.

Open all day all wk **Bar Meals** L served all wk 12-10 D served all wk 12-10 food served all day **Restaurant** L served all wk 12-10 D served all wk 12-10 food served all day ⊕ GREENE KING ◀ Greene King IPA, Goddards. ♥ 10 **Facilities** Children welcome Children's menu Children's portions Play area Garden Beer festival Parking Wi-fi **Rooms** 18

SEAVIEW   Map 5 SZ69

The Boathouse ♥

Springvale Rd PO34 5AW ☎ **01983 810616**
e-mail: info@theboathouseiow.co.uk
dir: From Ryde take A3055. Left onto A3330, left into Puckpool Hill. Pub 0.25m on right

In a spectacular promenade setting overlooking the Solent, The Boathouse was tastefully refurbished in 2010. Well-kept ales and an extensive wine selection now complement exciting specials boards that make the most of freshly landed local fish. Other choices include lunchtime baguettes, pub favourites and hot dishes like pan-roasted pumpkin salad with ricotta and croutons, and locally made sausages on chef's special mash.

Open all wk 9-3 6-11 (Sat-Sun 9am-10.30pm) all day every day May-Sep **Bar Meals** L served May-Sep 12-9.30, Oct-Apr 12-2.30 D served May-Sep 12-9.30, Oct-Apr 6-9.30 Av main course £10 **Restaurant** L served May-Sep 12-9.30, Oct-Apr 12-2.30 D served May-Sep 12-9.30, Oct-Apr 6-9.30 Av 3 course à la carte fr £25 ⊕ PUNCH TAVERNS ◀ Ringwood Best, Sharp's Doom Bar, Bass, Greene King IPA ♂ Stowford Press. ♥ 11 **Facilities** Children welcome Children's menu Children's portions Dogs allowed Garden Parking Wi-fi

PICK OF THE PUBS

The Seaview Hotel & Restaurant

High St PO34 5EX
☎ **01983 612711** 📠 **01983 613729**
e-mail: reception@seaviewhotel.co.uk
dir: B3330 (Ryde to Seaview road), left via Puckpool along seafront road, hotel on left

Its quiet location just a short stroll from the seafront means that from selected vantage points, particularly The Terrace, this rather special establishment enjoys fantastic views of the Solent. In the Pump Bar, real ales from Goddards Brewery in Ryde are complemented by an extensive menu of traditional and innovative dishes, including locally caught fresh fish specials. The Front Bar, modelled on a naval wardroom, is home to a magnificent collection of naval pictures, photographs, lobster pots, oars, masts and other nautical artefacts. The hotel offers a choice of dining venues; there's the small Victorian dining room, and the more contemporary Sunshine restaurant and conservatory. Both offer the same menu, which reflects the hotel's close relationship with local farmers and fishermen. For a main course, choose from New Close Farm venison Wellington or poached fillet of herb-crusted cod with spiced tomato and courgette chutney.

Open all wk ⊕ FREE HOUSE ◀ Goddards, Ventnor Bitter, guest ale. **Facilities** Children welcome Dogs allowed

SHALFLEET   Map 5 SZ48

PICK OF THE PUBS

The New Inn ♥

Mill Ln PO30 4NS ☎ **01983 531314** 📠 **01983 531314**
e-mail: info@thenew-inn.co.uk
web: www.thenew-inn.co.uk
dir: 6m from Newport to Yarmouth on A3054

This charming whitewashed pub's location on the National Trust-owned Newtown River estuary makes it an absolute mecca for yachties. One of the island's best-known dining pubs, its name reflects how it rose phoenix-like from the charred remains of an older inn, which burnt down in 1743; original inglenook fireplaces, flagstone floors and low-beamed ceilings give it bags of character. The waterside location helps explain its reputation for excellent seafood dishes, with lobster and cracked local crab usually featuring on the specials carte; other fish options may include fillet of

hake with lemon, thyme and honey; or seafood royale – a mammoth mixed platter of fish and seafood on a bed of salad. For meat lovers there are local hand-made sausages with mash; prime steaks; and gammon with double egg and chips. The excellent vegetarian section of the menu may offer grilled goat's cheese salad with tomato, thyme and red onion chutney. At the bar you'll find Goddards Special and Greene King among others, and over 60 worldwide wines comprise one of the island's most extensive selections.

Open all day all wk **Bar Meals** L served all wk 12-2.30 booking required D served all wk 6-9.30 booking required Av main course £12 **Restaurant** L served all wk 12-2.30 booking required D served all wk 6-9.30 booking required Av 3 course à la carte fr £22 ⊕ ENTERPRISE INNS ◀ Interbrew Bass, Goddards Special Bitter, Greene King IPA, Marston's Pedigree. ♥ 11 **Facilities** Children welcome Children's menu Children's portions Dogs allowed Garden Parking Wi-fi

SHORWELL   Map 5 SZ48

PICK OF THE PUBS

The Crown Inn ♥

Walkers Ln PO30 3JZ
☎ **01983 740293** 📠 **01983 740293**
e-mail: karen@crowninnshorwell.co.uk
dir: Turn left at top of Carisbrooke High Street, Shorwell approx 6m

Set in a pretty village, this traditional country pub dates partly from the 17th century, although its different floor levels suggest many subsequent alterations. The picture is completed by log fires, antique furniture and a friendly female ghost who seems to disapprove of customers playing cards. Outside are a children's play area and a beautiful stream, whose trout grow fat exclusively for the herons it seems. Six real ales include island brew, Goddards. Good use is made of locally sourced lamb, beef, game and fish on the bi-annually revised menus offering pub staples like sausage and mash, lasagne, chicken curry, and pie of the day, while further study reveals a good selection of grills, fisherman's pie, smoked haddock and crayfish risotto, beef goulash (a winter warmer), pizzas and mixed nut roast. Add award-winning specials, such as roast duck breast, sea bass and salmon, and you'll see why choosing a meal might take a while.

Open all day all wk **Bar Meals** L served all day 12-9.30 booking required D served all day 12-9.30 booking required Av main course £8.95 food served all day **Restaurant** L served all day 12-9.30 booking required D served all day 12-9.30 booking required food served all day ⊕ ENTERPRISE INNS ◀ Goddards (local), Ringwood Fortyniner, Ringwood Best, Sharp's Doom Bar, Adnams Broadside ♂ Stowford Press. ♥ 12 **Facilities** Children welcome Children's menu Children's portions Play area Family room Dogs allowed Garden Parking Wi-fi

The Folly ☻

Folly Ln PO32 6NB ☎ 01983 297171
dir: Telephone for directions

The Folly stands beside the River Medina and you can, if you wish, travel here from Cowes on the pub's own waterbus. In the bar are timbers from the hull of an old barge, and even the restaurant tables are named after boats. The menus offer a wide choice of sandwiches and wraps; jacket potatoes; gourmet burgers; and classics like beef and ale pie; breaded wholetail Scottish scampi; pan-seared Barbary duck; and spinach and ricotta cannelloni. There is a large beer garden and patio, and a new sheltered area.

Open all day all wk **Bar Meals** L served all wk 12-5 D served all wk 5-10 food served all day **Restaurant** L served all wk 12-5 D served all wk 5-10 food served all day ⊕ GREENE KING ◄ Greene King IPA, Old Speckled Hen, Goddards Best Bitter ○ Aspall. ☻ 11 **Facilities** Children welcome Children's menu Children's portions Dogs allowed Garden Parking

The Blue Boar NEW

20 The Green SN8 2EN ☎ 01672 540237
e-mail: bluebear.green@btconnect.com
dir: From Salisbury take B4192 to Aldbourne. Or M4 junct 14 take A338 to Hungerford, B4192 to Aldbourne & follow brown signs

A traditional, 16th-century pub serving Wadworth and regularly-changing guest ales from a perfect location on the village green. Eating outside is a joy, with views of beautiful houses, the church and a Celtic cross. Typical home-prepared food includes minted lamb casserole, beer-battered haddock, and Stilton-stuffed field mushrooms. Beer festivals are held in April and October. Enthusiasts periodically relive the days of the American 'Screaming Eagles', who were billeted in Aldbourne from 1941 to 1945.

Open all wk Mon-Thu 11.30-3 5.30-11 (Fri-Sun 11.30-11) **Bar Meals** L served all wk 12-2 D served all wk 6.30-9.30 Av main course £9 **Restaurant** L served Mon-Fri 12-2, Sat-Sun 12-2.30 booking required D served all wk 6.30-9.30 booking required Fixed menu price fr £10 ⊕ WADWORTH ◄ Wadworth's 6X, IPA, Guest ales ○ Westons Scrumpy, Stowford Press. **Facilities** Children welcome Children's portions Dogs allowed Garden Beer festival Wi-fi

The Crown Inn

The Square SN8 2DU ☎ 01672 540214
dir: M4 junct 15, N on A419, signed to Aldbourne

Overlooking the village square and duck pond, the Crown is a spick-and-span 18th-century inn with a cosy, traditional beamed bar and a comfortable, wooden-floored dining room. Very much the village inn, smartly refurbished and with local Ramsbury Gold on tap, it offers a good selection of home-cooked dishes, from soup and sandwiches to Sunday roasts and a popular tapas menu. The courtyard is a pleasant spot for summer sipping. Change of hands.

Open all wk noon-3 6-11 (Sat-Sun noon-11) ⊕ ENTERPRISE INNS ◄ Spitfire Shepherds Neame, Ramsbury Gold ○ Westons Stowford Press. **Facilities** Children welcome Children's menu Play area Dogs allowed Garden Parking

PICK OF THE PUBS

Red Lion Inn

See Pick of the Pubs on opposite page

The Talbot Inn NEW

The Cross SP7 0HA ☎ 01747 828222
dir: From Shaftesbury take A30 towards Salisbury. Right to Berwick St John. Pub 1.5m

A typical old English country pub nestling in the beautiful Chalke Valley; the building dates from the 17th century and has the beams, low ceilings and huge inglenook fireplace so typical of its kind. It used to be three cottages, one of them the village shop, before becoming an alehouse in 1835. Real ales and good home-cooked food are on offer: why not plump for a reasonably priced main course? Pies include steak and kidney; steak and ale; and chicken, ham and leek.

Open 12-2.30 6.30-11 (Sun 12-4) Closed: Sun eve & Mon **Bar Meals** L served Tue-Sun 12-2 D served Tue-Sat 6.30-9 booking required Av main course £11 ⊕ FREE HOUSE ◄ Ringwood Best & Fortyniner, Wadworth 6X ○ Stowford Press. **Facilities** Children welcome Children's portions Dogs allowed Garden Parking

The Northey ☻

Bath Rd SN13 8AE ☎ 01225 742333
e-mail: thenorthey@ohhcompany.co.uk
dir: 4m from Bath on A4 towards Chippenham. Between M4 juncts 17 & 18

This former station hotel was built by Brunel for his workers who were building a box tunnel when stone was sent by train up North to build houses. These days this stylishly transformed pub is now a favourite in the area for eating and drinking. Designed throughout by owner Sally Warburton, the interior makes good use of wood and flagstone flooring, high-backed oak chairs, leather loungers and handcrafted tables around the bar, where inviting sandwiches, ciabattas and Italian platters hold sway. The main menu ranges from calves' liver and bacon; rack of spring lamb; pan-fried gnocchi; to the pub's speciality fish dishes and great steaks.

Open all day all wk Closed: 25-26 Dec **Bar Meals** L served all wk 11-6 D served all wk 6-10 Av main course £10 food served all day **Restaurant** L served all wk 11-6 D served all wk 6-10 Av 3 course à la carte fr £28 food served all day ⊕ WADWORTH ◄ 6X, Warburtons ○ Stowford Press, Thatchers Gold. ☻ 14 **Facilities** Children welcome Children's menu Children's portions Garden Parking Wi-fi

The Quarrymans Arms ☻

Box Hill SN13 8HN ☎ 01225 743569
e-mail: pub@quarrymans-arms.co.uk
dir: Telephone for directions

When Brunel built his Great Western Railway, he tunnelled through the solid limestone beneath this 300-year-old pub, as witnessed by its exceptional display of quarrying memorabilia. Superb views from the restaurant and pub garden over the Box Valley are enjoyed by visiting walkers, cavers and cyclists, but it's a great community pub too, with quizzes, fishing trips and charity fund-raising events. Local ales wash down light meals such as scampi or Boxhill bangers. Options for the truly hungry include the Quarryman's pie, home made to traditional recipes, and lots of fish and game. Look out for mini-ale weeks throughout the year.

Open all day all wk 11am-11.30pm **Bar Meals** L served all wk 11-3 booking required D served all wk fr 6 booking required Av main course £10 **Restaurant** L served all wk fr 11 booking required D served all wk fr 6 booking required Av 3 course à la carte fr £16 ⊕ FREE HOUSE ◄ Butcombe Bitter, Wadworth 6X, Moles Best, Local guest ales ○ Stowford Press, Black Rat. ☻ 13 **Facilities** Children welcome Children's menu Children's portions Family room Dogs allowed Garden Beer festival Parking Wi-fi

PICK OF THE PUBS

Red Lion Inn

AXFORD   Map 5 SU27

SN8 2HA ☎ 01672 520271
e-mail: info@redlionaxford.com
web: www.redlionaxford.com
dir: *M4 junct 15, A246 Marlborough
centre. Follow Ramsbury signs. Inn 3m*

For over 400 years, this eye-catching old inn has welcomed travellers on lanes threading along the Kennet valley just outside the stirring Georgian town of Marlborough. From the flower-bedecked terrace (perfect for alfresco summer dining), divine views percolate to the river and this most peaceful stretch of countryside. It's located in the North Wessex Downs Area of Outstanding Natural Beauty and close to the popular walks in the remarkable, ancient Savernake Forest; ample opportunity to work up an appetite to dine at one of Wiltshire's finest dining inns. Tables and chairs cunningly constructed from half-barrels and squashy, all-too comfortable sofas dot the timeworn parquet flooring of the convivial bar, all beams and boards focussed on a huge inglenook fireplace.

Elsewhere, brick and flint feature walls are the backdrop for the well-appointed lounges and Garden Restaurant, offering a choice of dining areas. Settle in with a vintage from the extensive wine list or a glass of own-label Axford Ale from the nearby Ramsbury micro-brewery and

consider a menu which is strong on seasonal game and fish dishes with a contemporary European flavour. In the restaurant, start with twice-baked goat's cheese soufflé with beetroot or perhaps tempura of king prawns in beer batter and chilli dip. Mains that make the most of Wiltshire's larder include braised rabbit with prunes and Madeira, flash-fried calves' liver with caramelised onions and bacon, or slowly braised lamb shank with a rosemary jus. Vegetarian options include home-made caramelised onion and fig tart with smoked Cheddar and tomato. Completing the calorie top-up is a daily-changing dessert choice. The bar menu offers steak and Ramsbury ale pie, fish pie and Red Lion Aberdeen Angus burger with French fries, plus a variety of Caesar salads.

Open 12-3 6-11 Closed: Sun eve, Mon eve
Bar Meals L served Tue-Sat 12-2
D served Tue-Fri 6-9
Restaurant L served Tue-Sun 12-2
D served Tue-Sat 6-9 ⊕ FREE HOUSE
◀ Axford Ale, Ramsbury Gold, Guest
ales ○ Stowford Press.
Facilities Children's portions Garden
Parking

BRADFORD-ON-AVON Map 4 ST86

The Dandy Lion ☿

35 Market St BA15 1LL ☎ **01225 863433**
e-mail: Dandylion35@aol.com
dir: *Telephone for directions*

Over the years this property has been a boot and shoe shop, a medicine and wine shop, and a grocery shop, but the spirit of the original 18th century inn lives on through its well-kept ales and continental lagers, together with a mix of traditional English and rustic European food. The café-bar menu offers grazing boards for sharing, and hot filled flatbreads alongside favourites like chicken Kiev or home-made burger with melting mozzarella. The restaurant menu changes weekly and might include seafood pie of salmon, white fish and tiger prawns, or balsamic marinated hanger steak on pan-fried mushrooms and onions with triple-cooked chips. Desserts are home made and are shown on the blackboard.

Open all wk 11-3 6-11 (Fri-Sat 11-11 Sun 11.30-10.30)
Bar Meals L served all wk 12-2.30 D served all wk 6-9
Restaurant D served Fri-Sat 7-9.30 booking required
⊕ WADWORTH ◼ Wadworth 6X, Henrys IPA, Wadworth Seasonal, Butcombe Ŏ Stowford Press, Westons Organic.
☿ 21 **Facilities** Children welcome Children's portions Dogs allowed

PICK OF THE PUBS

The Kings Arms ☿

Monkton Farleigh BA15 2QH ☎ **01225 858705**
e-mail: enquiries@kingsarms-bath.co.uk
web: www.kingsarms-bath.co.uk
dir: *Off A363 (Bath to Bradford-on-Avon road), follow brown tourist signs to pub*

This stunning Bath-stone village inn oozes history and character, with origins in the 1100's as a Cluniac Priory and much to remind visitors of later medieval times, including wonderful mullioned windows, stone doorways and a vast inglenook fireplace. Past residents find it hard to leave; the inn is said to be one of the most haunted in the country, with a practical joker monk regularly reported. Patrons were first able to share his love for the place in 1881 when it became a beerhouse for quarrymen, since when villagers and visitors have enjoyed local beers and food here; Butcombe Bitter is today's tipple of choice, maybe enjoyed in the secluded gardens behind the pub, bordering fields that ripple towards the nearby Avon Valley. The menus here are locally sourced, seasonal

and unpretentious; perhaps a roast butternut squash and rosemary risotto to start, trumped by a beef cobbler; ale-battered Cornish pollack with chips and marrowfat peas; Wiltshire pork sausages and mash; or a Torbay crab linguini.

Open all wk 12-3 6-11 (Sat-Sun 12-11.30)
Bar Meals L served Mon-Fri 12-3, Sat 12-10, Sun 12-9
D served Mon-Fri 6-10, Sat 12-10, Sun 12-9 ⊕ PUNCH TAVERNS ◼ Butcombe Bitter, Tribute, Guest ale. ☿ 8
Facilities Children welcome Dogs allowed Garden Parking

The Swan ★★★★ INN

1 Church St BA15 1LN
☎ **01225 868686** 📠 **01225 868681**
e-mail: theswan-hotel@btconnect.com
dir: *From train station turn left, over bridge, on left adjacent to river*

Smack beside the medieval bridge that spans the River Avon, the Swan is a striking, 15th-century honey-stoned inn that is appointed with style and flair. Bar and dining areas exude an elegant, contemporary feel, with rugs on stripped boards and flagged floors and comfy sofas fronting blazing log fires. Modern touches extend to the short menus, from a lunchtime deli board to braised lamb shank on buttered mash with mint and port gravy. There is a very good children's menu too. A sunny terrace and comfortable accommodation completes the picture. Change of hands.

Open all day all wk 7am-11pm (Sun 7am-10.30pm)
⊕ GREENE KING ◼ Old Speckled Hen, IPA Ŏ Stowford Press. **Facilities** Children welcome Children's menu Children's portions Garden Parking Wi-fi **Rooms** 12

PICK OF THE PUBS

The Tollgate Inn ★★★★ INN ☻☻ ☿

See Pick of the Pubs on opposite page

BRINKWORTH Map 4 SU08

PICK OF THE PUBS

The Three Crowns ☿

SN15 5AF ☎ **01666 510366**
dir: *From Swindon take A3102 to Wootton Bassett, then B4042, 5m to Brinkworth*

Lots of greenery inside and out here, with the conservatory restaurant festooned with potted plants, a tree-shaded patio, peaceful garden and the little village green fronting this traditional old inn set in rich farming countryside on a low ridge above the River Avon. Amiable staff greet you in the beamed, fire-warmed old bar, where beers from Abbey Ales in Bath are the pick of the generous bunch enjoyed by locals at this thriving community pub that doubles as a destination gastro-pub. Expect the unexpected here on the ambitious menu which features 28 day aged local

beef as prime cuts of steak. Delve more deeply into the choice to reveal home-made game pie created with pieces of venison, kangaroo, ostrich and wild boar in a shiraz wine gravy flavoured with a hint of Stilton; or local pheasant breast filled with a fruit stuffing, roasted and served with sweet peppers, asparagus and mushroom. The wide seafood selection features supreme of coley steam-fried with champagne, whilst the generously calorific puddings have an accompanying wine suggested.

Open all day all wk 10am-mdnt Closed: 25-26 Dec
Bar Meals L served Mon-Sat 12-2, Sun 12-9 D served Mon-Sat 6-9.30, Sun 12-9 Av main course £13
Restaurant L served Mon-Sat 12-2, Sun 12-9 D served Mon-Sat 6-9.30, Sun 12-9 booking required
⊕ ENTERPRISE INNS ◼ Greene King IPA, Abbey Ales Bellringer, London Pride, Timothy Taylor Ŏ Stowford Press. ☿ 27 **Facilities** Children welcome Children's menu Children's portions Play area Dogs allowed Garden Parking Wi-fi

BROAD CHALKE Map 5 SU02

The Queens Head Inn

1 North St SP5 5EN ☎ **01722 780344**
e-mail: ryan.prince@btinternet.com
dir: *A354 from Salisbury towards Blandford Forum, at Coombe Bissett right towards Bishopstone, pub in 4m*

First recorded as a cottage in the 1730s, the building became the village pub in 1865. It was rebuilt following a disastrous fire in 1887, and subsequent alterations have created a cosy environment with low beams and a wood burning stove. Fresh, locally sourced produce is used to create a traditional and seasonal range of dishes such as hot pork curry with rice and poppadoms, and poached smoked haddock in cheese and herb sauce. Head out to the courtyard in warmer weather. Recent change of hands.

Open all wk Mon-Thu 11-3 6-11 (Fri 11-3 6-mdnt, Sat 11-11.30, Sun 12-8) **Bar Meals** L served all wk 12-2.30 booking required D served Mon-Sat 7-9.30 Av main course £11.45 **Restaurant** L served all wk 12-2.30 booking required D served Mon-Sat 7-9.30 (Sun 7-9 summer only) Av 3 course à la carte fr £12.95 ⊕ HALL & WOODHOUSE ◼ Badger Best, Badger Tanglefoot, Hopping Hare, Pickled Partridge, Lemony Cricket (seasonal) Ŏ Stowford Press. **Facilities** Children welcome Children's menu Children's portions Family room Dogs allowed Garden Beer festival Parking Wi-fi

Save on hotels. Book at **theAA.com/hotel**

WILTSHIRE 485 ENGLAND

PICK OF THE PUBS

The Tollgate Inn ★★★★ INN 🏵🏵 🍷

Holt BA14 6PX
☎ 01225 782326   📄 01225 782805
e-mail: alison@tollgateholt.co.uk
web: www.tollgateholt.co.uk
dir: *M4 junct 18, A46 towards Bath, then
A363 to Bradford-on-Avon, then B3107
towards Melksham, pub on right*

Standing just off the green in the homely
village of Holt, this characterful old inn,
parts of which go back nearly 500 years,
grew from an amalgamation of a weaving
shed and a former Baptist chapel. This
unusual forced marriage produced a
building which has seen use as a
reputedly bawdy cider house and a school.
The education and experience enjoyed by
today's discerning guest draws a veil over
this eclectic past; instead think top-notch
two AA Rosette cuisine and elegant
accommodation. The bar, richly diverse in
its furnishings and fittings, serves a
rotating selection of guest ales, mostly
from small West Country micro-breweries,
while diners can eat in a small adjoining
room with a wood-burning stove and
country-style decoration. The restaurant
proper is up wooden stairs in what was
originally the chapel for the weavers
working below. Chef-proprietor Alexander
Venables manages to mix the best of
modern British cooking with an
undercurrent of Mediterranean influence,
producing original, essentially simple
dishes with locally sourced ingredients;
hand-reared beef comes from Broughton
Gifford, lamb from Limpley Stoke, and
pork from Woolley Farm. Village shoots
provide the game, whilst vegetables are
grown on surrounding farms. Seafood is
fresh sourced from the south coast, so
kick in with a starter of pan-fried skate
wing with a caper and herb brown butter
sauce or a bowl of Cornish mussels before
indulging in pheasant breast wrapped in
bacon, with braised red cabbage and a
miniature game pie. Traditionalists may
prefer the signature beef Wellington dish
- Church Farm beef fillet topped with
mushroom duxelle and chicken liver
parfait wrapped in rich puff pastry. Set
lunches and a gourmet dinner menu are
also prepared. The extensive grounds have
a flock of sheep and goats; views stretch
across the Avon Valley. Seasons deli and
farm shop has now opened in the barn,
promoting the best in local produce, meat,
fish and cheeses.

Open 11.30-3 5.30-11 (Sun 11.30-3)
Closed: Mon **Bar Meals** L served Tue-Sun
12-2 D served Tue-Sat 7-9 Av main course
£14.50 **Restaurant** L served Tue-Sun 12-2
D served Tue-Sat 7-9 Fixed menu lunch fr
£17.95 Fixed menu dinner fr £19.95 Av 3
course à la carte fr £23 ⊕ FREE HOUSE
◀ Tunnel Vision, Moles Best, Sharp's
Own, Tor, St Austell ales, Sharp's Doom
Bar Ö Thatchers Scrumpy, Ashton Press,
Bee Sting Pear. 🍷 10 **Facilities** Children's
portions Garden Parking **Rooms** 4

BROUGHTON GIFFORD — Map 4 ST86

The Fox ♥ NEW

The Street SN12 8PN ☎ 01225 782949
e-mail: alexgeneen@gmail.com
dir: *From Melksham take B3107 towards Holt. Turn right to Broughton Gifford. Pub in village centre*

Real ales from Bath, Otter and Butcombe breweries keep the beer drinkers happy, although the owners of this village pub consider it food led. Since they raise their own chickens, ducks and pigs, tend an extensive vegetable and herb garden, and barter with villagers for wild fowl and other produce, you can see why that might be. Main courses include braised oxtail pie; sea bream and mussel broth with butter mash and samphire; and pan-fried polenta with vegetable caponata. With a strong emphasis on community ties, the pub sponsors the local football team and raises money for the school.

Open all day Closed: 25 Dec, 1 Jan, Mon
Bar Meals L served Tue-Sun 12-2.30 D served Tue-Sun 6.30-9.30 **Restaurant** L served Tue-Sun 12-2.30 D served Tue-Sun 6.30-9.30 Fixed menu price fr £13.95 Av 3 course à la carte fr £24 ⊕ FREE HOUSE ◀ Bath Ales Gem, Otter Bitter, Butcombe Bitter. ♥10 **Facilities** Children welcome Children's menu Children's portions Dogs allowed Garden Parking

BURCOMBE — Map 5 SU03

The Ship Inn ♥

Burcombe Ln SP2 0EJ
☎ 01722 743182   📠 01722 743182
e-mail: theshipburcombe@mail.com
web: www.theshipburcombe.co.uk
dir: *In Burcombe, off A30, 1m from Wilton & 5m W of Salisbury*

A 17th-century village pub with low ceilings, oak beams and a large open fire. In summer the riverside garden is a great place to enjoy a leisurely meal in the company of the resident ducks. Seasonal menu examples include smoked pigeon breast on polenta crouton, winter berry coulis; smoked salmon and brown shrimp roulade; Gloucester Old Spot pork belly, sage mash, braised cabbage and gravy; potato gnocchi with rabbit, spinach and grain mustard cream sauce.

Open all wk 11-3 6-11 **Bar Meals** L served all wk 12-2.30 D served all wk 6-9 Av main course £10 **Restaurant** L served all wk 12-2.30 D served all wk 6-9 Av 3 course à la carte fr £24 ⊕ ENTERPRISE INNS ◀ Wadworth 6X, Ringwood Best, Butcombe. ♥9 **Facilities** Children welcome Children's menu Children's portions Dogs allowed Garden Parking Wi-fi

BURTON — Map 4 ST87

The Old House at Home ★★★★★ INN ♥

SN14 7LT ☎ 01454 218227
e-mail: office@ohhcompany.co.uk
dir: *On B4039 NW of Chippenham*

This early 19th-century, ivy-clad stone free house is one of three run by the Warburton family; dad David has been here nearly three decades and still happily pulls pints of Maiden Voyage and Wadworth 6X in the low-beamed bar. Impressive menu favourites include Mexican chilli; griddled sea bass; woodland duck; fillet steak chasseur; and goat's cheese risotto. The gardens are not only beautifully landscaped but also feature a waterfall. Six high quality bedrooms are available in a stylish annexe.

Open all day all wk **Bar Meals** L served all wk 12-2.30 D served all wk 6.30-10 **Restaurant** L served all wk 12-2.30 D served all wk 6.30-10 ⊕ FREE HOUSE ◀ Maiden Voyage, Doom Bar, Wadworth Ale ☼ Stowford Press. ♥12 **Facilities** Children welcome Dogs allowed Garden Parking Wi-fi **Rooms** 6

COLLINGBOURNE DUCIS — Map 5 SU25

The Shears Inn ♥

The Cadley Rd SN8 3ED ☎ 01264 850304
e-mail: info@theshears.co.uk
dir: *Just off A338 between Marlborough & Salisbury*

Dating from the 18th century, this traditional family-run country inn was once a shearing shed for market-bound sheep. The original part of the building is thatched. Inside you'll find wooden and slate floors, low beamed ceilings and a large inglenook dominates the restaurant. Now a thriving country inn, the inn serves pub classics and modern British dishes such as pork terrine with toasted brioche and pickles followed by pan-fried duck breast with duck liver, beetroot and celeriac purée. To finish, maybe try crème brûlée with chocolate ice cream.

Open 11-3 6-11 (Sat 11-11 summer, Sun fr noon) Closed: Sun eve **Bar Meals** L served Mon-Sat 12-2, Sun 12-3.30 D served Mon-Sat 6-9.30 Av main course £10 **Restaurant** L served Mon-Sat 12-2, Sun 12-3.30 booking required D served Mon-Fri 7-9.15, Sat 7-9.30 booking required Av 3 course à la carte fr £24.50 ⊕ BRAKSPEAR ◀ Brakspear Bitter, Hobgoblin, Guest ales ☼ Westons Organic. ♥12 **Facilities** Children welcome Children's portions Dogs allowed Garden Parking Wi-fi

CORSHAM — Map 4 ST87

PICK OF THE PUBS

The Flemish Weaver ♥

63 High St SN13 0EZ ☎ 01249 701929
e-mail: profmac@yahoo.com
dir: *Next to town hall on Corsham High St*

Standing opposite the historic Corsham Court, this stone-built town centre inn takes its name from a nearby row of original Flemish weavers' cottages. Drinkers and diners are all welcome to enjoy the winter log fires and candlelit interior - though it's advisable to book a table. Thatchers Gold and Stowford Press ciders complement a good range of real ales, some of which are served straight from the barrel. There's also an extensive wine list, with many choices available by the glass. Menus are changed daily, and you might start with hand-crumbed Somerset Brie and cranberry compote before making the choice between tagliatelle in Dolcelatte cream sauce with spinach and toasted pine nuts; and cod with leek and potato gratin. Typical desserts include bread and butter pudding laced with Bailey's; and summer fruits and jelly terrine. Enjoy them in the large outdoor eating area on warmer days. Change of hands in 2010.

Open 12-3 6-11 (Sun noon-5) Closed: Sun eve **Bar Meals** L served Mon-Sat 12-2.30, Sun 12-4.30 D served Mon-Sat 6-9 **Restaurant** L served Mon-Sat 12-2.30, Sun 12-4.30 D served Mon-Sat 6-9 ⊕ ENTERPRISE INNS ◀ Bath Spa, Doom Bar, Bath Gem ☼ Thatchers Gold, Stowford Press. ♥10 **Facilities** Children welcome Children's portions Dogs allowed Garden Parking

CORTON — Map 4 ST94

PICK OF THE PUBS

The Dove Inn ★★★ INN ◉

See Pick of the Pubs on opposite page

Save on hotels. Book at **theAA.com/hotel**

WILTSHIRE 487 **ENGLAND**

PICK OF THE PUBS

The Dove Inn ★★★ INN ❀

CORTON   Map 4 ST94

BA12 0SZ
☎ **01985 850109**   📠 **01985 851041**
e-mail: info@thedove.co.uk
web: www.thedove.co.uk
dir: *A36 (Salisbury towards Warminster),*
in 14m turn left signed Corton & Boyton.
Cross rail line, right at T-junct. Corton
approx 1.5m, turn right into village

Squirreled away in the delightful Wylye Valley in the heart of Wiltshire, this bustling 19th-century pub guarantees a warm welcome for locals or visitors alike. A striking central fireplace is a feature of the refurbished bar with a wood-burning stove and flagstone and oak floors, and the spacious garden is the perfect spot for barbecues or a drink on long summer days.

The appealing menu is based firmly on West Country produce, with many ingredients coming from within just a few miles of the kitchen. Popular lunchtime bar snacks and ciabattas give way to a full evening carte featuring well-made and hearty pub classics. Typical starters include steamed Shetland Isle mussels, chorizo and Stowford Press cider sauce or an Italian-style salad of Parma ham, sweet peaches, shaved Parmesan, wild rocket and basil dressing. These might be followed by whole grilled Cornish lemon sole, new potatoes, anchovy, caper and parsley butter, or local rabbit, pancetta, wild mushroom and cider pie with short crust pastry. Hot chocolate fondant pot with vanilla ice cream, and apple and blackberry crumble with vanilla mascarpone are crowd-pleasing desserts.

Five en suite bedrooms arranged around a courtyard make The Dove an ideal touring base - Bath, Longleat, Salisbury and Stonehenge are all close by. And for those visitors who haven't got time to stay for lunch or dinner, beer-battered fish and chips and the famous Dove burger and chips are available to takeaway wrapped traditionally in newspaper.

Open all wk noon-3 6-11.30 **Bar Meals** L served all wk 12-2.30 D served all wk 6.30-9 **Restaurant** L served all wk 12-2.30 D served all wk 6.30-9 🛢 FREE HOUSE 🍺 London Pride, Sharp's Doom Bar, Hop Back GFB ⟳ Stowford Press. **Facilities** Children welcome Children's portions Dogs allowed Garden Parking Wi-fi **Rooms** 5

DEVIZES   Map 4 SU06

The Bear Hotel ★★★ HL

The Market Place SN10 1HS
☎ 01380 722444   📄 01380 722450
e-mail: info@thebearhotel.net
dir: *In town centre, follow Market Place signs*

Dating from at least 1559, this old coaching inn lists
Judge Jeffreys, George III and Harold Macmillan amongst
its notable former guests. Right in the centre of Devizes,
it has plentiful old beams, log fires and fresh flowers
inside. Outside is a courtyard for sunny days. A meal
might include chicken terrine with hazelnut dressing,
followed by cider braised pork belly with glazed apple and
braised fennel. Music fans should check out the weekly
jazz sessions in the cellar.

Open all day all wk 9.30am-11pm Closed: 25-26 Dec
⊕ WADWORTH ◀ Wadworth 6X, Wadworth IPA, Old Timer,
Malt & Hops, Wadworths Strong in the Arm, Horizon,
seasonal ales. **Facilities** Children welcome Children's
menu Children's portions Dogs allowed Garden Parking
Rooms 25

The Raven Inn

Poulshot Rd SN10 1RW
☎ 01380 828271   📄 01380 828271
e-mail: theraveninnpoulshot@yahoo.co.uk
dir: *A361 from Devizes towards Trowbridge, left at
Poulshot sign*

A characterful half-timbered 18th-century pub in an
attractive village - an easy walk to the Kennet and Avon
Canal and the towpath by the famous Caen Hill flight of
locks. The weekly-changing menu is a mixture of modern
pub classics and restaurant dishes. From burgers, pizzas
and fish and chips to confit of duck, slow roasted belly
pork and pan-fried venison, everyone should find
something to suit their palate and budget. The pub is dog
friendly and there are plenty of local walks to build up a
healthy appetite. Change of hands.

Open 11.30-2.30 6.30-9 (Sun 12-3 7-10.30) Closed: Mon
◀ Wadworth 6X, Wadworth IPA, Wadworth Horizon,
Wadworth Old Timer ☼ Thatchers Gold.
Facilities Children's menu Children's portions Dogs
allowed Garden Parking

DONHEAD ST ANDREW   Map 4 ST92

PICK OF THE PUBS

The Forester 🍷

Lower St SP7 9EE ☎ 01747 828038
e-mail: possums1@btinternet.com
dir: *4.5m from Shaftesbury off A30 towards Salisbury*

Located in the Donheads close to Wardour Castle, this
lovely old country pub is a perfect place to finish a
country walk. Traditional in style, it has warm stone
walls, a thatched roof, original beams and an
inglenook fireplace. An extension provides a restaurant
plus a restaurant/meeting room, with double doors
opening on to the lower patio area. The garden and
large terrace are furnished with hardwood chairs and
tables as well as bench seating. The restaurant has a
good reputation for freshly cooked meals and
specialises in Cornish seafood, with deliveries five
times a week. These quality ingredients are treated
with a mix of traditional and cosmopolitan flavours to
create dishes such as moules marinière; fresh crab
spaghetti with chilli, garlic and parsley; traditional
roast partridge with bread sauce and game chips; and
prime West Country venison Wellington with pickled red
cabbage, potato purée, sloe gin and loganberry sauce.
To finish, maybe try classic crème brûlée with cassis
sorbet.

Open noon-2 6.30-11 Closed: 25-26 Dec, Sun eve
Bar Meals L served all wk 12-2 booking required
D served Mon-Sat 7-9 booking required Av main course
£15 **Restaurant** L served all wk 12-2 D served Mon-Sat
7-9 booking required Fixed menu price fr £15.50 Av 3
course à la carte fr £25 ⊕ FREE HOUSE ◀ Ringwood,
Butcombe, Butts, Otter ☼ Stowford Press, Ashton
Press, Westons Organic. 🍷 15 **Facilities** Children
welcome Children's menu Children's portions Dogs
allowed Garden Parking Wi-fi

EAST CHISENBURY   Map 5 SU15

Red Lion 🍷 NEW

SN9 6AQ ☎ 01980 671124
e-mail: enquiries@redlionfreehouse.com
dir: *From A303 take A345 N. Exit at Enford. Left at
T-junct towards East Chisenbury. Pub 1m on right*

The Red Lion backs directly onto Salisbury Plain where
there are many horse riding and walking trails, plus the
best chalk-stream fishing. Why has the Red Lion become
so popular? Well, if you look into the background of chef,
Guy Manning, and his co-owner wife Brittany, you'll soon
understand. Guy's locally sourced home-made food
appears on a daily-changing menu of traditional British
dishes, with some American, Spanish and French thrown
in. Then there's the home-cured meats and charcuterie,
the wines from Stone, Vine and Sun, two guest beers and
the real ciders.

Open all day all wk **Bar Meals** L served Mon-Sat 12-2,
Sun 12-3 booking required D served all wk 6.30-9
booking required Av main course £15 **Restaurant** Fixed
menu price fr £15 Av 3 course à la carte fr £28 ⊕ FREE
HOUSE ◀ Guest ales ☼ Stowford Press, Westons Organic,
Aspall. 🍷 10 **Facilities** Children welcome Children's
portions Dogs allowed Garden Parking Wi-fi

EAST KNOYLE   Map 4 ST83

PICK OF THE PUBS

The Fox and Hounds 🍷

See Pick of the Pubs on opposite page

EBBESBOURNE WAKE   Map 4 ST92

PICK OF THE PUBS

The Horseshoe

Handley St SP5 5JF ☎ 01722 780474
dir: *Telephone for directions*

A genuine old English pub in a pretty village, The
Horseshoe dates from the 17th century. The original
building has not changed much, except for a necessary
conservatory extension to accommodate more diners,
and there's a pretty, flower-filled garden. Beyond the
climbing roses are two rooms filled with simple
furniture, old farming implements and country
bygones, linked to a central servery where well-kept
cask-conditioned ales are dispensed straight from
their barrels – Bowmans Swift One, Otter Best Bitter
and Palmers Copper – plus real ciders too. Good value
traditional bar food is offered from a varied menu.
Freshly prepared from local produce, dishes are
generous and favourites include the home-made pies –
steak and kidney, wild boar and apricot - and Sunday
roasts. There are some great home-made desserts:
seasonal fruit crumble, Bakewell tart, and crème
brûlée among them.

Open all wk 12-3 6.30-11 (Sun 12-4) Closed: 26 Dec,
Sun eve & Mon L **Bar Meals** L served Tue-Sat 12-2
booking required D served Tue-Sat 7-9 booking
required **Restaurant** L served Sun 12-2.30 booking
required D served Tue-Sat 7-9 booking required
⊕ FREE HOUSE ◀ Otter Best bitter, Bowmans Swift
One, Palmers Copper ☼ Hecks Farm Cider, Thatchers
Gold. **Facilities** Children welcome Children's portions
Play area Dogs allowed Garden Parking

Save on hotels. Book at **theAA.com/hotel**

WILTSHIRE 489 ENGLAND

PICK OF THE PUBS

The Fox and Hounds 🍷

EAST KNOYLE   Map 4 ST83

The Green SP3 6BN
☎ **01747 830573** 📄 **01747 830865**
e-mail:
pub@foxandhounds-eastknoyle.co.uk
web: www.foxandhounds-eastknoyle.co.uk
dir: *1.5m off A303 at the A350 turn off,*
follow brown signs

Hidden in a timeless village on a
greensand ridge, this partly thatched and
half-timbered, rustic old inn makes the
most of its location in the stunning
Blackmore Vale. There are exceptional
views from the patio beer garden and
nearby East Knoyle village green across
these Wiltshire and Dorset boundary-
lands, where Sir Christopher Wren was
born and the family of Jane Seymour
(Henry VIII's third wife) were based.

The engaging exterior is well matched by
the atmospheric interior, with lots of
flagstone flooring, wood-burning fires and
restful stripped wood furniture. Locals
eager to partake of Thatchers Cheddar
Valley cider or Palmers Dorset Gold rub
shoulders with diners keen to make the
acquaintance of the eclectic menu.

Blackboard menus increase the choice,
dependant entirely on the availability of
the freshest local fare; catch of the day is
a local favourite. Good, wholesome pub
grub like a traditional steak and kidney
pudding with chunky chips and peas or
chicken Caesar salad share the board
with beef and mushroom casserole in red
wine with mash and vegetables; North
Indian-style mutton curry with basmati
rice; South coast lemon sole, new potatoes
and salad. Vegetarians can look forward
to grilled Somerset soft goat's cheese
salad with grilled ciabatta or onion,
Parmesan and ricotta tart with fresh pesto
and salad. Stone-baked pizzas from a clay
oven add to the fray, whilst afters include
jam sponge and custard or a selection of
local Purbeck ice creams.

Open all wk 11.30-3 5.30-11 **Bar Meals**
L served all wk 12-2.30 D served all wk
6-9 Av main course £11 **Restaurant**
L served all wk 12-2.30 D served all wk
6-9 🍺 FREE HOUSE 🍴 Plain Innocence,
Butcombe, Summer Lightning, Wickwar
'BOB', Adnams Broadside, Palmers Dorset
Gold ♂ Thatchers Cheddar Valley. 🍷 15
Facilities Children welcome Children's
menu Dogs allowed Garden Parking Wi-fi

FONTHILL GIFFORD — Map 4 ST93

PICK OF THE PUBS

The Beckford Arms ☺

SP3 6PX ☎ **01747 870385**
e-mail: info@beckfordarms.com
dir: *From A303 (E of Wincanton) take turn to Fonthill Bishop. At T-junct in village turn right, 1st left signed Fonthill Gifford & Tisbury. Through Fonthill Estate arch (lake on left) to pub*

Situated close to Stonehenge, this Georgian country coaching inn is approached in style through a Triumphal Arch on the edge of the 10,000-acre Fonthill Estate. The ex-Soho House owners had given the inn an extensive but sympathetic refurbishment before a major fire in 2010 resulted in re-building work. The parquet-floored bar serves interesting real ales and ciders, the restaurant's glass wall opens on to the terrace, and outside, the large garden is 'ridiculously pretty' with hammocks in the trees. Choose from excellent pub food, day-boat landed fish, locally grown salads and home-smoked wild salmon or locally caught trout on the daily-changing menus: try pan-fried wild black sea bream, roasted fennel, mussels and lemon butter sauce; or poached leg of mutton with creamed leeks and caper sauce.

Open all day all wk **Bar Meals** L served all wk 12-2.30 D served all wk 6-9.30 Av main course £10 **Restaurant** L served Mon-Sat 12-2.30, Sun 12-3 D served all wk 6-9.30 Av 3 course à la carte fr £25 ⊕ FREE HOUSE ◀ Butcombe, Keystone Large One, Piddle's Jimmy Riddle, Erdinger Wheat, Veltins Ô Ashton Press, Westons Organic, Sheppy's. ♀ 12 **Facilities** Children welcome Children's menu Children's portions Play area Dogs allowed Garden Parking Wi-fi

FROXFIELD — Map 5 SU26

The Pelican Inn ☺ NEW

Bath Rd SN8 3JY ☎ **01488 682479**
e-mail: enquiries@pelicaninn.co.uk
dir: *On A4 midway between Marlborough & Hungerford*

Standing prominently beside the road between Marlborough and Hungerford, this 17th-century inn has recently been transformed. Beyond the baby grand piano, subtle lighting complements the flagstone floors, leather sofas and rustic furniture, whilst outside you can stroll around the large garden with its busy duck pond. The menu features traditional dishes with a modern twist,

and also has a children's section; there are Sunday roasts, as well as seasonal treats from the specials board. Real ales are chosen from micro and regional breweries.

Open all wk 11.30-11 (Sun 12-10.30) **Bar Meals** L served Mon-Sat 12-2.30, Sun 12-7 D served Mon-Thu 6-9, Fri-Sat 6-9.30, Sun 12-7 **Restaurant** L served Mon-Sat 12-2.30, Sun 12-7 D served Mon-Thu 6-9, Fri-Sat 6-9.30, Sun 12-7 ⊕ FREE HOUSE ◀ Otter Bitter, Butcombe Bitter. ♀ 11 **Facilities** Children welcome Children's menu Children's portions Garden Parking Wi-fi

GREAT BEDWYN — Map 5 SU26

PICK OF THE PUBS

The Three Tuns ☺

High St SN8 3NU ☎ **01672 870280**
e-mail: jan.carr2@btinternet.com
dir: *Off A4 between Marlborough & Hungerford*

Just a short walk from the bustling Kennet and Avon Canal, boaters join a dedicated local trade basking in the warmth of the huge inglenook fire or chilling out in the attractive beer garden. Based on the old village bakery – the bread oven is a restaurant feature – trading started in 1756; the cellar was also the village morgue and unquiet spirits are rumoured to be abroad! This great community pub (with a renowned Sunday meat raffle) overflows with rustic artefacts and continues to shine, with rare local beers a perfect accompaniment to the enticing menu created largely from Wiltshire goodies; what the owners casually refer to as 'peasant food'. The rillette of pork served with ciabatta starter is a good entrée before pushing out the boat with, perhaps, home-made salmon fishcakes served on a bed of buttered leeks with fresh tomato and basil sauce and shoestring fries, or local rabbit Normandy style cooked in cider – the landlord knows his stuff here, he was gamekeeper to the Prince of Wales. Rarely have peasants been so well-catered for!

Open 12-3 6-11 (Sun 12-6) Closed: Sun eve **Bar Meals** L served Mon-Sat 12-2, Sun 12-2.30 D served Mon-Sat 7-9 **Restaurant** L served Mon-Sat 12-2, Sun 12-2.30 D served Mon-Sat 7-9 ⊕ FREE HOUSE ◀ Ramsbury Gold, Three Tuns Bitter, Local guest ales Ô Pheasant Plucker. ♀ 9 **Facilities** Children welcome Children's menu Children's portions Dogs allowed Garden Parking

GREAT CHEVERELL — Map 4 ST95

PICK OF THE PUBS

The Bell Inn ☺

High St SN10 5TH ☎ **01380 813277**
e-mail: gary06weston@aol.com
dir: *From Salisbury take A360 towards Devizes, through West Lavington, 1st left after black & yellow striped bridge onto B3098. Right to Great Cheverell*

Mentioned in the Domesday Book, this property became a drovers' inn in the 18th century. The Grade II listed building has achieved more recent fame featuring on the television programme *Location, Location, Location*. Sharp's Doom Bar and 6X are among the ales on offer in the bar with its welcoming log fire. Home-cooked West Country food is served in the elegantly styled, oak beamed restaurant. The imaginative and varied menu makes use of top quality ingredients which you'll find in starters such as creamy garlic and mushroom tart, smoked trout pâté, and prawn and Brixham crab cocktail. Main courses extend to beef Stroganoff, sea bass fillets served with chilli and soy noodles, and hunters' chicken. Pub classics like home-made steak and ale pie, and venison casserole also have a place on the menu. The sunny, secluded garden is set in tranquil surroundings with lots of wooden benches and a patio area, enjoyed by families and locals long into the evening.

Open all wk **Bar Meals** L served all wk 12-2.30 D served all wk 6-9 **Restaurant** L served all wk 12-2.30 D served all wk 6-9 ⊕ FREE HOUSE ◀ 6X, IPA, Doom Bar, guest ale Ô Stowford Press. ♀ 16 **Facilities** Children welcome Children's menu Children's portions Dogs allowed Garden Parking Wi-fi

HANNINGTON — Map 5 SU19

The Jolly Tar ☺

Queens Rd SN6 7RP
☎ **01793 762245** 🖹 **01793 765159**
e-mail: jolly.tar@sky.com
dir: *M4 junct 15, A419 towards Cirencester. At Bunsdon/Highworth sign follow B4109. Towards Highworth, left at Freke Arms, follow Hannington & Jolly Tar pub signs*

Although far from the sea, there's a nautical reason for this former farmhouse's name – a retired sea captain married into the Freke family, who once owned it. Old timbers and locally brewed Arkells ales are served in its two bars, making this pretty inn an appealing prospect. All food is freshly prepared, with daily menu changes. The conservatory restaurant overlooks the sun terrace patio and spacious grounds with a children's play area

Open 12-3 6-11 Closed: Mon L (except BHs) **Restaurant** L served Tue-Sun 12-2 booking required D served Mon-Sat 6.30-9, Sun 6.30-7 booking required ⊕ ARKELLS ◀ Arkells 3B, Noel Ale, Kingsdown. ♀ 9 **Facilities** Children welcome Children's menu Play area Garden Parking

HEYTESBURY   Map 4 ST94

PICK OF THE PUBS

The Angel Coaching Inn ♉

High St BA12 0ED
☎ **01985 840330**   🖹 **01985 840931**
e-mail: admin@angelheytesbury.co.uk
dir: *From A303 take A36 towards Bath, 8m, Heytesbury on left*

Surrounded by stunning countryside, this 16th-century inn by the River Wylye retains the traditional charm and character of a coaching inn past, although these days it is more of a dining destination. Original features and modern comforts blend well: the beamed bar, for instance, has scrubbed pine tables, sofas, warmly decorated walls and a wood-burning stove in an attractive fireplace. You may eat here, or in the restaurant, furnished with antiques and various objects of interest or, during the summer, in the secluded courtyard garden. Menus change daily to offer starters of devilled lambs' kidneys, toast and watercress. Among a good selection of mains, look for slow-roasted belly pork in cider with creamed potato or a more classic cottage pie. Ham, egg and chips, and grilled rib-eye sandwiches are served at lunchtime. Wash it all down with a pint of Morlands or a glass of house wine from the extensive list.

Open all day all wk **Bar Meals** L served all wk 12-2.30 D served all wk 6.30-9.30 **Restaurant** L served all wk 12-2.30 D served all wk 6.30-9.30 ⊕ GREENE KING ◀ Morlands, Greene King IPA, 6X ♂ Stowford Press. ♉ 8 **Facilities** Children welcome Children's portions Dogs allowed Garden Parking Wi-fi

HINDON   Map 4 ST93

PICK OF THE PUBS

Angel Inn ♉

High St SP3 6DJ ☎ 01747 820696
e-mail: info@theangelathindon.com
dir: *1.5m from A303, on B3089 towards Salisbury*

In the heart of rural Wiltshire, minutes from the ancient mounds and henges of Salisbury Plain, this beautifully restored 18th-century coaching inn offers many original features, wooden floors, beams and a huge stone fireplace. An elegant gastro-pub where rustic charm meets urbane sophistication, outside is an attractive paved courtyard and garden furniture, where food can be served in fine weather. The interior is characterised by natural wood flooring, beams, large stone fireplace and comfortable leather seating. Behind the bar can be found Brakspear and Timothy Taylor ales; pine country-style tables and chairs, together with the day's newspapers, lend a friendly and relaxed atmosphere. An eclectic mix of traditional and modern dishes characterise the brasserie-style menu, based on quality seasonal ingredients. Typical starters are warm pigeon, lentil and bacon salad, and warm brown shrimps, caper butter and toasted crumpet. The

main courses could be slow cooked blade of beef with oxtail faggot and horseradish mash; smoked haddock and salmon fishcakes; roasted pork fillet, barley risotto, caramelised turnips and apple compote. Desserts are on the blackboard, as are the day's set menu and specials.

Open all day all wk 11-11 (Sun noon-4) **Bar Meals** L served all wk 12-2.30 D served Mon-Sat 6-9.30 Av main course £11 **Restaurant** L served all wk 12-2.30 booking required D served Mon-Sat 6-9.30 Fixed menu price fr £10 Av 3 course à la carte fr £20 ⊕ FREE HOUSE ◀ Sharp's, Timothy Taylor Landlord, Brakspear ♂ Thatchers Gold. ♉ 14 **Facilities** Children welcome Children's portions Dogs allowed Garden Parking Wi-fi

PICK OF THE PUBS

The Lamb at Hindon ★★★★ INN ⊛ ♉

High St SP3 6DP ☎ 01747 820573   🖹 **01747 820605**
e-mail: info@lambathindon.co.uk
dir: *From A303 follow signs to Hindon. At Fonthill Bishop right onto B3089 to Hindon. Pub on left*

A Lamb Inn was trading in this charming Wiltshire village 800 years ago. Today's wisteria smothered Georgian building continues this selfless service to locals and visitors, who perhaps retire here after an exhausting game of boules on the village green opposite. The interior of the stone-built inn is divided into several cosy areas and oozes olde-worlde charm, with sturdy period furnishings, flagstone floors, and terracotta walls hung with old prints and paintings; the splendid old stone fireplace with crackling log fire adds the finishing touch to the warm, homely atmosphere. Where better to enjoy Wiltshire's largest selection of malt whiskies? And just to confirm its position as a bon viveur's kind of place, you can purchase a Cuban cigar and puff away merrily on the heated and awning-covered terrace. Better to eat first of course, and the menu, recognised with an AA Rosette, brings its own pleasures: Godminster Cheddar rarebit made with Young's ale with local dry-cured bacon makes an excellent starter. Follow perhaps with roast chicken breast with wild mushrooms and bubble and squeak. There is accommodation here with some four-poster bedrooms.

Open all day all wk 7.30am-mdnt **Bar Meals** L served all wk 12-2.30 D served all wk 6.30-9.30 booking required Av main course £10 **Restaurant** L served all wk 12-2.30 D served all wk 6.30-9.30 booking required Fixed menu price fr £25 ⊕ BOISDALE ◀ Young's Bitter, St Austell Tribute, Young's London Gold ♂ Stowford Press. ♉ 10 **Facilities** Children welcome Children's menu Children's portions Dogs allowed Garden Parking Wi-fi **Rooms** 19

HORNINGSHAM   Map 4 ST84

PICK OF THE PUBS

The Bath Arms at Longleat
★★★★ INN ⊛⊛ ♉

BA12 7LY ☎ 01985 844308   🖹 **01985 845187**
e-mail: enquiries@batharms.co.uk
dir: *Off B3092 S of Frome*

Built in the 17th century, The Bath Arms occupies a prime position at one of the entrances to Longleat Estate and the famous Safari Park. The building became a public house with rooms in 1732 called the New Inn; it was later renamed the Weymouth Arms, and became the Marquess of Bath Arms in 1850. An ivy-clad stone inn, it has been comfortably refurbished and features two fine beamed bars — one traditional with settles, old wooden tables and an open fire, and a bar for dining. The Wessex Brewery furnishes the public bar with its much-cherished Horningsham Pride ale, while most food is sourced within 50 miles of the pub. Simple menus focus on quality produce, with minimal use of international influences and an emphasis on traditional preserving methods — smoking, curing, potting and pickling. The lunchtime menu has traditional favourites such as traditional fish and chips, chicken Caesar salad and rib-eye steak, but these belie the kitchen team's culinary expertise which has won two AA Rosettes - revealed in dinner dishes such as pan-fried fillet of sea bass, brown shrimps and white wine sauce, and slow roasted belly pork, crackling, roasted apple, mashed potato. Stylish accommodation is available.

Open all day all wk **Bar Meals** L served all wk 12-2.30 D served all wk 7-9 **Restaurant** L served all wk 12-2.30 booking required D served all wk 7-9 booking required ⊕ HILLBROOKE HOTELS ◀ Horningsham Pride, P.I.G, Guest ales ♂ Stowford Press. ♉ 9 **Facilities** Children welcome Children's menu Children's portions Dogs allowed Garden Parking Wi-fi **Rooms** 15

HORTON   Map 5 SU06

The Bridge Inn

Horton Rd SN10 2JS ☎ 01380 860273
e-mail: adrian@bridgeinnhorton.co.uk
dir: *A361 from Devizes, right at 3rd rdbt. Follow brown signs*

Built as a farm in about 1800, the buildings that are now the Bridge Inn were later used as a flour mill. Today, this attractive waterside pub boasts a cosy interior with open fires, and a delightful garden bordering the Kennet and Avon canal. The extensive menu ranges from freshly filled rolls and boatman's lunches to hot dishes like braised chicken breast with bacon and cheese sauce; mixed fish pie; pub favourite steak and 6X ale pie and Bargee's all-day breakfast. An ideal destination for boaters, cyclists, walkers and anglers. As we went to press a change of hands was taking place.

continued

HORTON continued

Open 12-3 6-11 Closed: Mon ex BHs ⊕ WADWORTH
◀ Wadworth Henry's Original IPA, 6X, Old Father Timer,
Horizon ☼ Stowford Press. **Facilities** Children
welcome Children's menu Children's portions Dogs
allowed Garden Parking Wi-fi

The Red Lion Inn

BA12 6RP ☎ 01985 844263
dir: B3092 off A303 N towards Frome. Pub 2.5m from
A303 on right on B3092 just after turn to Stourhead
Gardens

This 15th-century former coaching inn once provided
spare horses to assist coaches in the climb up nearby
White Sheet Hill. A lane from the pub garden leads to the
hill. Chris Gibbs has been landlord for 32 years and
provides a friendly, convivial meeting place with
flagstone floors, beams, antique settles and blazing log
fires. With a large beer garden to enjoy in warmer months,
the inn is popular for the well-kept real ales and good
value snacks and lunches, including home-made
casseroles, pies and pasties as well as jacket potatoes
and ploughman's.

Open all wk 11.30-2.30 6.30-11 (Sun noon-3 7-11)
Bar Meals L served all wk 12-1.50 booking required Av
main course £7.50 ⊕ FREE HOUSE ◀ Butcombe Bitter,
Jester, Guest ale ☼ Thatchers Cheddar Valley, Ashton
Press. **Facilities** Children welcome Dogs allowed Garden
Parking **Notes** ⊛

The George Inn ♟

4 West St SN15 2LH
☎ 01249 730263 📄 01249 730186
e-mail: thegeorge01@btconnect.com
dir: M4 junct 17 take A350, S, between Chippenham and
Melksham

Steeped in history and much used as a film and television
location, the beautiful National Trust village of Lacock
includes this atmospheric inn. The George dates from
1361 and boasts a medieval fireplace, a low-beamed
ceiling, mullioned windows, flagstone floors, plenty of
copper and brass, and an old tread wheel by which a dog
would drive the spit. Locals and visitors discuss the
merits of the ale selection at the bar, while menus proffer
a selection of steaks and flavoursome pies, with fish
options among the summertime specials; finish with
home-made bread and butter pudding.

Open all wk Mon-Thu 9-2.30 5-11 (Fri-Sat 9am-11pm
Sun 9am-10.30pm) Closed: 25 Dec **Bar Meals** L served
all wk 12-2 D served all wk 6-9 **Restaurant** L served all
wk 12-2 D served all wk 6-9 ⊕ WADWORTH ◀ Wadworth
6X, Henrys IPA, J.C.B, Henrys Smooth ☼ Stowford Press.
♟ 9 **Facilities** Children welcome Children's menu
Children's portions Play area Dogs allowed Garden
Parking

Red Lion Inn ♟

1 High St SN15 2LQ ☎ 01249 730456 📄 01249 730766
e-mail: redlionlacock@wadworth.co.uk
dir: Just off A350 between Chippenham & Melksham.
Follow Lacock signs

An historic 18th-century inn at the heart of the National
Trust village of Lacock, whose famous abbey has featured
in many films. The pub's Georgian interior with large open
fireplace and flagstone floors creates an atmosphere
conducive to the enjoyment of Wadworth ales and a
wondrous choice of real ciders — many of which can be
tasted during the pub's annual cider festival. Home-
cooked food follows traditional lines, from sharing boards
of meats, fish or cheeses to main plates of wild boar and
apple sausages; free-range chicken breast with a Stilton
and bacon cream; or a Red Lion beefburger topped with
red onion marmalade and goat's cheese.

Open all day all wk Mon-Fri 8am-11pm (Sat 9am-11pm
Sun 9am-10.30pm) **Bar Meals** L served all wk 12-2.30
D served all wk 6-9 Av main course £8.95
Restaurant L served all wk 12-2.30 D served all wk 6-9
Fixed menu price fr £9.95 ⊕ WADWORTH ◀ Wadworth 6X,
Henrys IPA, Wadworth Horizon, Swordfish ☼ Stowford
Press, Thatchers Gold. ♟ 15 **Facilities** Children
welcome Children's menu Children's portions Dogs
allowed Garden Beer festival Parking Wi-fi

The Hop Pole Inn

Woods Hill, Lower Limpley Stoke BA2 7FS
☎ 01225 723134 📄 01225 723199
dir: Telephone for directions

Set in the beautiful Limpley Stoke valley, the Hop Pole
dates from 1580 and takes its name from the hop plant
that still grows outside the pub. Eagle-eyed film fans may
recognise it as the hostelry in the 1992 film Remains of
the Day. A hearty menu includes Thai vegetable curry;
home-made pies; fresh local trout; and steaks. Food can
be enjoyed with one of the many ales, or one of the wines
served by the glass.

Open all wk 11-2.30 6-11 (Sun noon-3 7-10.30) Closed:
25 Dec ⊕ FREE HOUSE ◀ Courage Best, Butcombe Bitter,
Sharp's Doom Bar, Guest ales ☼ Ashton Press.
Facilities Children welcome Children's menu Children's
portions Family room Dogs allowed Garden Parking

Compasses Inn ★★★★ INN ⊛ ♟

SP3 6NB ☎ 01722 714318
e-mail: thecompasses@aol.com
dir: On A30 (1.5m W of Fovant) take 3rd right to Lower
Chicksgrove. In 1.5m turn left into Lagpond Lane, pub
1m on left

Amid rolling countryside in a tiny hamlet on the old
drovers' track from Poole to Birmingham, this picture-
perfect 14th-century thatched inn is bursting with
character. An old cobbled path leads to the low latched
door which opens into a charming bar with worn
flagstones, old beams and stone walls. Snuggle up to
the large inglenook fireplace or relax in the intimate
booth seating, with soft candlelight on winter evenings.
You can be certain to find three or four real ales on tap,
and the wine list is comprehensive. Be sure to try the
food: the kitchen team has won an AA Rosette for their
freshly made seasonal dishes; these are written on a
blackboard because they change so frequently.
Examples are starters of ham hock and prune terrine,
or and devilled kidneys. Main dishes may feature
Marleycombe Farm calves' liver with bacon and bean
casserole, or whole baked sea bream with tomato
roasted potatoes. Five bedrooms are available,
providing an ideal base for exploring the beautiful
surrounding countryside.

Open noon-3 6-11 (Sun noon-3 7-10.30) Closed: 25-26
Dec, & Mon Jan-Mar **Bar Meals** L served all wk 12-2
D served all wk 6.30-9 Av main course £13 ⊕ FREE
HOUSE ◀ Keystone Large One, Butcombe, Stonehenge
Spire, Bristol Seven ☼ Thatchers Gold. ♟ 8
Facilities Children welcome Children's menu Children's
portions Dogs allowed Garden Parking Wi-fi **Rooms** 5

The Horse & Groom Inn ♟

The Street, Charlton SN16 9DL ☎ 01666 823904
e-mail: info.horseandgroominn@bespokehotels.com
dir: M4 junct 17 follow signs to Cirencester on A429.
Through Corston & Malmesbury. Straight on at Priory
rdbt, at next rdbt take 3rd exit to Cricklade, then to
Charlton

Fronted by a tree-sheltered lawn and surrounded by its
own paddock, this 16th-century, Cotswold-stone
coaching inn has all the charm and character you'd
expect from original stone flags, open fires, solid oak
tables and rug-strewn wooden floors. In the dog-
friendly Charlton Bar, Wadworth 6X house beer is
joined by guest ales, while outside, there's plenty of space,
including a lovely walled garden and separate play
area. In the kitchen, almost all the ingredients come
from within 40 miles of the pub. Beef, for example,
comes from Jesse Smith's, a local family butcher. Their
rib-eye steaks are hung for 28 days and are delivered

Save on hotels. Book at **theAA.com/hotel**

WILTSHIRE 493 ENGLAND

on the bone when required; pork belly and bacon comes from nearby Bromham; free range chickens from a farm in Stroud; and lamb from the Cotswolds. Sausage and mash, and home-made pies are among the traditional dishes, while the modern British are represented by lamb rump with garlic mash and broad beans, or pheasant with fondant potato, cabbage and bacon. Recent change of hands.

Open all wk 9am-11pm (Sun 11-10.30) **Bar Meals** L served Mon-Sat 12-2, Sun 12-3 D served Mon-Thu 6.30-9, Fri-Sat 6.30-9.30, Sun 6.30-8.30 **Restaurant** L served Mon-Sat 12-2, Sun 12-3 D served Mon-Thu 6.30-9, Fri-Sat 6.30-9.30, Sun 6.30-8.30 ⊕ FREE HOUSE ◀ Wadworth 6X, Guest ales ♻ Stowford Press. **Facilities** Children welcome Children's menu Children's portions Play area Dogs allowed Garden Parking Wi-fi

The Smoking Dog

62 The High St SN16 9AT ☎ 01666 825823 e-mail: smokingdog@sabrain.com dir: *5m N of M4 junct 17*

Right in the heart of Malmesbury, this refined 17th-century stone-built pub has a warm and cosy atmosphere enhanced by log fires and wooden floors. Local produce underpins an imaginative, ever-changing menu. Guest ales also change regularly. A renowned beer and sausage festival over Spring Bank Holiday weekend is the time to sample over 30 brews and 15 banger varieties.

Open all day all wk noon-11 (Fri-Sat noon-mdnt, Sun noon-10.30) **Bar Meals** L served Mon-Fri 12-2.30, Sat-Sun 12-3 D served Mon-Sat 6.30-9.30, Sun 6.30-8.30 **Restaurant** L served Mon-Fri 12-2.30, Sat-Sun 12-3 D served Mon-Sat 6.30-9.30, Sun 6.30-8.30 ⊕ S A BRAIN ◀ Reverend James, Butcombe Best, 3 guest bitters. **Facilities** Children welcome Children's menu Children's portions Dogs allowed Garden Beer festival Wi-fi

PICK OF THE PUBS

The Vine Tree ♥

Foxley Rd, Norton SN16 0JP ☎ 01666 837654 e-mail: tiggi@thevinetree.co.uk dir: *M4 junct 17, A429 towards Malmesbury. Turn left for village*

The Vine Tree used to be a mill, and workers apparently passed beverages out through front windows to passing carriages - an early drive-through it would seem. These days, it is well worth seeking out for its interesting modern pub food and memorable outdoor summer dining. In the central bar a large open fireplace burns wood all winter, and there's a wealth of old beams, flagstone and oak floors. Ramblers and cyclists exploring Wiltshire's charms are frequent visitors, and the inn is situated on the official county cycle route. Cooking is modern British in style, with menus changing daily in response to local produce availability. Dishes include salads, light bites and vegetarian options, local game and well-sourced fish and meats. Perhaps start with skewer of Moroccan

chargrilled boned quail with minted couscous and tzatziki; followed by pan-fried wild sea bass from Looe, rustic ratatouille and cannellini beans. There are also great real ales and a terrific stock of wines with 40 by the glass. In addition to the suntrap terrace, there's a two-acre garden with two boules pitches.

Open all wk noon-3 6-12 (Sun noon-4 6-11) **Bar Meals** L served Mon-Sat 12-2.30, Sun 12-3.30 D served Mon-Thu & Sun 7-9.30, Fri-Sat 7-10 **Restaurant** L served Mon-Sat 12-2.30, Sun 12-3.30 D served Mon-Thu & Sun 7-9.30 Fri-Sat 7-10 ⊕ FREE HOUSE ◀ Tinners, Tribute, Uley Bitter, Pigswill, Guest ales ♻ Stowford Press. ♟ 40 **Facilities** Children welcome Children's menu Children's portions Play area Dogs allowed Garden Parking Wi-fi

MARLBOROUGH   Map 5 SU16

The Lamb Inn ★★★ INN ♥

The Parade SN8 1NE **☎ 01672 512668** ▤ 01672 512668 e-mail: thelambinnmarlboro@fsmail.net dir: *E along High St (A4) turn right into The Parade, pub 50yds on left*

Overlooking Marlborough's impressively wide main street, this 17th-century coaching inn offers plenty of traditional pub dishes and daily specials to enjoy in the bar or smartly renovated former stables. Landlady Jackie uses prime ingredients - trout and crayfish come from the nearby River Kennet, meat from local butchers and there's locally shot game in season. Sample dishes include baked goat's cheese with honey, walnuts, pickled baby beetroot and salad followed by duck confit with thyme-crushed potatoes and braised red cabbage. Finish with home-made chocolate brownies and wash it down with Wadworth 6X straight from the barrel. Six en suite bedrooms complete the picture.

Open all day all wk **Bar Meals** L served all wk 12-2.30 booking required D served Mon-Thu 6.30-9 booking required ⊕ WADWORTH ◀ Wadworth 6X, Guest ales. ♟ 10 **Facilities** Children welcome Children's portions Dogs allowed Garden Wi-fi **Rooms** 6

MINETY   Map 5 SU09

PICK OF THE PUBS

Vale of the White Horse Inn ♥

SN16 9QY ☎ 01666 860175 dir: *On B4040 (3m W of Cricklade, 6m & E of Malmesbury)*

An eye-catching and beautifully restored inn overlooking a large pond. Built in the early 1800s, the building's true history is something of a mystery, but it was registered by its current name in the 1881 census. It closed in 1999, but was rescued and reopened in 2002. Today, sitting under a parasol on the large raised terrace, it's hard to think of a better spot. The village bar is popular with the local community, drawn by a good selection of real ales and events such as

skittles evenings, live music and quizzes. Upstairs, lunch and dinner are served in the stone-walled restaurant with its polished tables and bentwood chairs. The ethos is to serve good home-cooked food at sensible prices. The bar menu has a range of baguettes; nachos topped with cheese, guacamole, salsa and jalapeños; and specials that change with the day of the week. Most pub favourites will be found on the main menu, ranging from prawn and crayfish cocktail to deep-fried scampi and chips; grills include a half-pound burger.

Open all wk 11.45-2.45 4.45-11 (Thu-Sat 11.45am-11.30pm, Sun 11.45am-10.30pm) **Bar Meals** L served all wk 12-2.30 D served all wk 6-9.15 **Restaurant** L served all wk 12-2.30 D served all wk 6-9.15 ⊕ FREE HOUSE ◀ Three Castle Vale Ale, Saxon Archer, Hancocks, Braydon Ales ♻ Stowford Press. ♟ 14 **Facilities** Children welcome Children's menu Children's portions Family room Dogs allowed Garden Parking Wi-fi

NEWTON TONY   Map 5 SU24

PICK OF THE PUBS

The Malet Arms ♥

SP4 0HF ☎ 01980 629279 ▤ 01980 629459 e-mail: info@maletarms.com web: www.maletarms.com dir: *8m N of Salisbury on A338, 2m from A303*

Off the beaten track, in a quiet village on the River Bourne, this 17th-century inn was originally built as a dwelling house. Much later it became The Three Horseshoes, named after a nearby smithy. An earlier Malet Arms, owned by lord of the manor Sir Henry Malet, closed in the 1890s and its name was transferred. It's not just the village that's quiet: the pub is too, as fruit machines and piped music are banned. There is a good range of real ales and whiskies, and all the food on the ever-changing blackboard menu is home cooked. Game is plentiful in season, often courtesy of the landlord who shoots pheasant and deer. The landlady makes all the puddings, often sourced from obscure old English recipes. In fine weather you can sit outside in the garden, where there is a children's play area. Dogs are also welcome. Look out for the beer festival in July.

Open all wk 11-3 6-11 (Sun 12-3 6-10.30) Closed: 25-26 Dec, 1 Jan **Bar Meals** L served all wk 12-2.30 D served all wk 6.30-10 booking required Av main course £10.50 **Restaurant** L served all wk 12-2.30 D served all wk 6.30-10 booking required Av 3 course à la carte fr £22 ⊕ FREE HOUSE ◀ Ramsbury, Stonehenge, Triple fff, Palmers, Andwell ♻ Old Rosie, Stowford Press, Ashton Press. ♟ 9 **Facilities** Children welcome Children's menu Play area Dogs allowed Garden Beer festival Parking

NUNTON   Map 5 SU12

The Radnor Arms

SP5 4HS ☎ 01722 329722
dir: *From Salisbury ring road take A338 to Ringwood. Nunton signed on right*

Not far from Salisbury this is a popular pub in the centre of Nunton dating from around 1750. In 1855 it was owned by the local multi-talented brewer/baker/grocer, and bought by Lord Radnor in 1919. Bar snacks are supplemented by an extensive fish choice and daily specials, which might include braised lamb shank, wild mushroom risotto, turbot with spinach or Scotch rib-eye fillet, all freshly prepared. There is a summer garden with rural views to enjoy, and the pub hosts an annual pumpkin competition in October.

Open all wk 11-3.30 6-11.30 **Bar Meals** L served all wk 12-2 D served all wk 6-9 Av main course £9 **Restaurant** L served all wk 12-2 D served all wk 6-9 Av 3 course à la carte fr £25 ⊕ HALL & WOODHOUSE ◀ Badger Tanglefoot, Best, Hopping Hare ♂ Stowford Press. **Facilities** Children welcome Children's portions Play area Family room Dogs allowed Garden Parking

OAKSEY   Map 4 ST99

PICK OF THE PUBS

The Wheatsheaf at Oaksey ◉◉ ♀

Wheatsheaf Ln SN16 9TB ☎ 01666 577348
e-mail: info@thewheatsheafatoaksey.co.uk
dir: *Off A419, 6m S of Cirencester, through waterparks, follow signs for Oaksey*

An easy mix of sophisticated dining pub (with two AA Rosettes) and old-world charm characterise this mellow stone Cotswold inn, the origins of which go back over 700 years. The huge old fireplace, beams, parquet floor and comfortably lived-in bar furniture are instantly welcoming, whilst in the restaurant area, Elizabethan England is replaced by inspiring, contemporary decor, light wood and striking prints. Handy for the Cotswold Water Park and Roman Cirencester, explorers chancing on The Wheatsheaf are rewarded with top-notch dishes created by chef-patron Tony Robson-Burrell and his Ritz Hotel-trained son Jack. From simple bar snacks to 32-day hung beef, all appetites can be sated. Enjoy a starter of home-smoked salmon and then stretch to mains of slow-roast Middlewhite pork, black pudding cake and

smoked apple sauce or English spinach and Isle of Mull Cheddar pie, aiding the digestion with a good list of bins. The pub has a dedicated band of locals who revel in the choice of beers from the likes of Bath Brewery.

Open Tue-Sat 12-2 6-11 (Mon 6-11 Sun 12-6) Closed: Sun eve, Mon L **Bar Meals** L served Tue-Sun 12-2 D served Tue-Sat 6.30-9 Av main course £12 **Restaurant** L served Tue-Sun 12-2 D served Tue-Sat 6.30-9 ⊕ FREE HOUSE ◀ Sharp's Doom Bar, Hook Norton, Bath Gem, Butcombe Bitter. ♀ 10 **Facilities** Children welcome Children's menu Children's portions Dogs allowed Garden Parking

OGBOURNE ST ANDREW   Map 5 SU17

Silks on the Downs ♀ NEW

Main Rd SN8 1RZ ☎ 01672 841229
e-mail: silks@silksonthedowns.co.uk
dir: *M4 junct 15, A346 towards Marlborough. Approx 6m to Ogbourne St Andrew. Pub on A346*

Framed silks of leading racehorse owners and jockeys adorning the walls reflect the racing heritage and name of this award-winning village pub. Located one mile outside the bustling market town of Marlborough and 15 minutes of Barbary Castle Estate, the pub offers real ales, fine wines and an informal dining experience, whether it's filled freshly baked organic baguettes at lunchtime or classics such as haddock in beer batter, local rib-eye steaks or Silks Thai fishcakes. There are two outdoor dining areas to enjoy in warmer weather.

Open all wk 12-3 6.30-11 **Bar Meals** Av main course £12.50 **Restaurant** L served all wk 12-3 booking required D served all wk 7-9.30 booking required Av 3 course à la carte fr £25 ⊕ FREE HOUSE ◀ Ramsbury Gold, Wadworth 6X, Adnams ♂ Aspall. **Facilities** Children welcome Children's menu Children's portions Garden Parking Wi-fi

PEWSEY   Map 5 SU16

The Seven Stars

Bottlesford SN9 6LW ☎ 01672 851325
e-mail: info@thesevenstars.co.uk
dir: *Off A345*

Just a 15 minute drive from the stone circles of Avebury and five minutes from two of Wiltshire's famous white horses, this thatched 16th-century free house is a delightful old building set in a splendid seven-acre garden. Its front door opens straight onto the low-beamed, oak-panelled bar, now tastefully refurbished. Expect well-kept ales and hearty meals with occasional international touches: perhaps chilli-lime squid followed by pork belly and mash or spicy sausage tagliatelle.

Open noon-3 6-11 Closed: Mon & Tue L **Bar Meals** food served all day **Restaurant** food served all day ⊕ FREE HOUSE ◀ Wadworth 6X, Ramsbury Gold, Timothy Taylor Landlord, Guest ales ♂ Stowford Press, Lilleys Cider Barn, Apples & Pears. **Facilities** Children welcome Children's menu Children's portions Dogs allowed Garden Parking Wi-fi

PITTON   Map 5 SU23

PICK OF THE PUBS

The Silver Plough

White Hill SP5 1DU
☎ 01722 712266 ▤ 01722 712262
e-mail: info@silverplough.co.uk
dir: *From Salisbury take A30 towards Andover, Pitton signed. Approx 3m*

Rather deceptive from the outside; inside the pub is all country character; wood-burning stoves pumping out the heat into thickly beamed rooms full of collectable containers and artefacts of all sorts (including glass rolling pins), country prints festoon the walls (as does footballing memorabilia from the landlord's professional career) and an eclectic range of dark-wood furnishings and old settles tempt drinkers sampling King and Barnes or Badger bitter to linger a while before challenging locals to a session on the alley skittles. Diners may anticipate a menu based on seasonally, locally available ingredients, including locally smoked Cheddar and leek tart, honey roast duck or pan-fried scallops. Lunchtime snacks include a good range of baguettes, or indulge in a home-made steak and kidney pie at one of the tables on the lawns, appreciating the views across thatched cottages to the tree-feathered ridge tops marking the adjacent Salisbury Downs.

Open all wk 11-3 6-11 **Bar Meals** L served all wk 12-2 D served all wk 6-9 Av main course £10.50 **Restaurant** L served all wk 12-2 D served all wk 6-9 ⊕ HALL & WOODHOUSE ◀ Badger Tanglefoot, Badger Gold, King & Barnes Sussex, guest ale. **Facilities** Children welcome Children's menu Children's portions Family room Dogs allowed Garden Parking

ROWDE   Map 4 ST96

PICK OF THE PUBS

The George & Dragon

★★★★ RR ◉◉ ♀

High St SN10 2PN ☎ 01380 723053
e-mail: thegandd@tiscali.co.uk
dir: *1m from Devizes, take A342 towards Chippenham*

Elizabeth I was tackling the Spanish problem when this solid old inn first opened its doors; a carved Tudor rose in a wavy beam recalls these early times. Today's incarnation is an appealing mix of olde worlde nostalgia, beamed rooms dotted with antique rugs and dark-wood period furniture, near blistering log fires, and innovative gastro-pub where fish dishes take pride of place, enhancing a diverse, daily-changing menu that is also strong on local meat and game dishes. Fruits of the sea arrive daily from St Mawes harbour in Cornwall, but you may instead be tempted to a starter of River Kennet crayfish, fresh from the nearby chalk river, prior to setting about a main such as grilled skate wing with caper butter or roast rack of lamb with mint pea purée and red wine jus. It's largely a

Save on hotels. Book at **theAA.com/hotel**

WILTSHIRE 495 **ENGLAND**

destination dining inn, with quality accommodation to match, but locals and boaters using the nearby Kennet & Avon Canal pop in for a jar of real ale from the likes of Bath Ales, mixing easily with guests eating at the candlelit tables in the main room or tranquil restaurant.

Open Mon-Sun L Closed: Sun eve **Bar Meals** L served Mon-Fri 12-3, Sun-Sun 12-4 booking required D served Mon-Fri 7-10, Sat 6.30-10 booking required Av main course £13 **Restaurant** L served Mon-Fri 12-3, Sat-Sun 12-4 booking required D served Mon-Fri 7-10, Sat 6.30-10 booking required Fixed menu price fr £9.95 Av 3 course à la carte fr £24 ⊕ FREE HOUSE ◀ Butcombe Bitter, Sharp's Doom Bar, Bath Ales Gem, ESB, London Pride, Ringwood Fortyniner ♂ Ashton Press. ♀ 10 **Facilities** Children welcome Children's menu Children's portions Dogs allowed Garden Parking **Rooms** 3

SALISBURY   Map 5 SU12

The Cloisters ♀ NEW

83 Catherine St SP1 2DH ☎ 01722 338102
dir: *In city centre, near cathedral*

A mid-18th-century building with Victorian windows that look into a beamed interior warmed by a pair of open fires. A weekly changing choice of ales includes Hop Back's Summer Lightning. The Cloisters has a good reputation for food in the city, thanks to a well-qualified chef who makes and bakes products from scratch, including bread and sausages. Nonetheless the menu comprises popular pub plates, from toasted sandwiches at lunchtime to all-day duck spring rolls and specials such as pan-seared fillet of pork with herb crust.

Open all day all wk **Bar Meals** L served Mon-Fri 11-3, Sat 11-9, Sun 12-9 D served Mon-Fri 6-9, Sat 11-9, Sun 12-9 **Restaurant** L served Mon-Fri 11-3, Sat 11-9, Sun 12-9 D served Mon-Fri 6-9, Sat 11-9, Sun 12-9 ⊕ ENTERPRISE INNS ◀ Sharp's Doom Bar, Hop Back Summer Lightning. **Facilities** Children welcome Children's menu Children's portions

PICK OF THE PUBS

The Haunch of Venison ♀

See Pick of the Pubs on page 496

Old Mill ★★★ INN ♀ NEW

Town Path SP2 8EU
☎ 01722 327517   🖳 01722 333367
e-mail: theoldmill@simonandsteve.com
dir: *From A338 onto A3094, take 3rd right*

Set on an acre of land within the Harnham water meadows Site of Special Scientific Interest with views to the cathedral, this pub is so called because its 16th-century restaurant was England's first paper mill; through a glass panel water can be seen passing beneath the building. The bar, along with

accommodation, is housed in a part dating from the 19th century. Here you can order a pint of Abbot Ale, and perhaps retire to one of the largest beer gardens in the city, which straddles the River Nadder. Choose your favourite pub food from the menu, which includes a variety of ploughman's. A beer festival is held during October.

Open all day all wk **Bar Meals** Av main course £9 **Restaurant** L served all wk 12-2.30 D served all wk 7-8.45 Av 3 course à la carte fr £20 ⊕ GREENE KING ◀ Greene King IPA, Old Speckled Hen, Abbot Ale ♂ Aspall. ♀ 10 **Facilities** Children welcome Children's menu Children's portions Dogs allowed Garden Beer festival Parking Wi-fi **Rooms** 11

The Wig and Quill ♀

1 New St SP1 2PH ☎ 01722 335665
e-mail: tricia@wigandquill.co.uk
dir: *On approach to Salisbury follow brown Old George Mall Car Park signs. Pub opposite car park*

New Street is very close to the cathedral, whose superlative spire soars skywards just behind this traditional city pub. In the roomy, beamed bar with its open fires, flagstone and wooden floored, enjoy a pint of Bishop's Tipple or a guest cider. From the menu choose between trio of Wiltshire lamb cutlets; rump steak and chips; and local ham, egg and chips. Lying behind is a sheltered courtyard garden for the summer months. There are Sunday roasts, music and quiz nights, and winter mulled wine and chestnut evenings.

Open all wk 11-4 5-2.30am (Sat-Sun all day) **Bar Meals** L served all wk 12-3.30 D served all wk 6.30-8.45 Av main course £6.95 **Restaurant** L served all wk 12-3.30 D served all wk 6.30-8.45 ⊕ WADWORTHS ◀ 6X, Bishop's Tipple, IPA, Horizon, Guest ales ♂ Stowford Press, Westons, Guest ciders. ♀ 14 **Facilities** Children welcome Children's menu Children's portions Dogs allowed Garden

---

SEEND   Map 4 ST96

Bell Inn

Bell Hill SN12 6SA ☎ 01380 828338
e-mail: fgfdevizes@aol.com
dir: *On A361 between Devizes & Semington*

Oliver Cromwell and his troops reputedly enjoyed breakfast at this inn, quite possibly on 18 September 1645 when he was advancing from Trowbridge to attack Devizes Castle. Its other claim to fame is that John Wesley opened the chapel next door and preached against the 'evils' of drink outside the pub. The restaurant of this newly refurbished barn conversion has lovely valley views and offers a tempting menu of home-cooked fare using locally sourced organic meats and produce.

Open all wk 12-2.30 5.30-11.30 **Bar Meals** L served all wk 12-2.30 D served all wk 5.30-10 Av main course £4.95 **Restaurant** L served all wk 12-2.30 D served all wk 5.30-10 Av 3 course à la carte fr £18 ⊕ WADWORTH ◀ Wadworth 6X, Henry's IPA, Bishop's Tipple ♂ Stowford Press. **Facilities** Children welcome Children's menu Children's portions Play area Dogs allowed Garden Parking

---

SEMINGTON   Map 4 ST86

The Lamb on the Strand

99 The Strand BA14 6LL
☎ 01380 870263 & 870815   🖳 01380 871203
e-mail: lamb@cipubs.com
dir: *1.5m E on A361 from junct with A350*

An 18th-century farmhouse that later became a beer and cider house. Today it is a popular dining pub serving real ales such as Bath Gem and Moles Best, plus plenty of wines by the glass. Expect starters of smoked salmon and pea risotto, and wild mushrooms and garlic on toast; followed by lamb, mint and chilli burger with chips; slow roast local lamb for two; or pan-seared fillet of bream with sauce verte. Old favourites such as Downland Farm sausages and mash, and home-made steak and ale pie are sure to make an appearance. Take a look at the daily-changing chalkboard specials too. Recent change of hands.

Open noon-3 6.30-11 Closed: Sun eve, Mon ⊕ FREE HOUSE ◀ Butcombe Bitter, Moles Best, Bath Gem, Guinness. **Facilities** Children welcome Children's portions Dogs allowed Garden Parking Wi-fi

PICK OF THE PUBS

The Somerset Arms ★★★★ INN ♀

High St BA14 6JR ☎ 01380 870067
dir: *From Devizes towards Trowbridge on A361 (approx 8m) turn right at rdbt after rdbt junct with A350. Pub in village*

This 17th-century coaching inn is located in the quiet village of Semington, within strolling distance of the Kennet and Avon Canal. Recently refurbished, it sports tiled floors in the bar and lounge, roaring log fires in brick fireplaces, squashy leather sofas, exposed beams, and warm heritage hues on the walls. The stylish design extends to the contemporary dining room, with its modern light wood furniture and jazzy wall coverings, and upstairs to the three boutique-style en suite bedrooms. Ales from within a 50-mile radius are selected for the bar and the pub holds a beer festival every May Bank Holiday. The seasonal menu features locally-sourced meat and vegetables and is accompanied by a comprehensive wine menu. Typical dishes include pigeon breast with black pudding and sautéed chicken livers with Brussels sprout and chestnut salad for starters, while mains might feature sea bass fillet with crab risotto, venison haunch steak with dauphinoise potatoes or vegetable Wellington with vine tomatoes and salsa verdi.

Open all day all wk **Bar Meals** L served all wk 12-3 D served all wk 6.30-9 Av main course £8 **Restaurant** L served all wk 12-3 booking required D served Sun-Thu 6.30-9, Fri-Sat 6.30-9.30 booking required Av 3 course à la carte fr £16.95 ⊕ FREE HOUSE ◀ Gem, Summer Lightning, Golden Bolt, Danish Dynamite, Summerset ♂ Broadoak Perry, Cheddar Valley, Old Bristolian. ♀ 16 **Facilities** Children welcome Children's menu Children's portions Family room Dogs allowed Garden Beer festival Parking Wi-fi **Rooms** 3

PICK OF THE PUBS

The Haunch of Venison ♀

SALISBURY   Map 5 SU12

1-5 Minster St SP1 1TB ☎ 01722 411313
e-mail: oneminsterst@aol.com
web: www.haunchofvenison.uk.com
dir: *In city centre. Opposite Poultry Cross Monument, adjacent to market place*

Dating from 1320, this is probably Salisbury's oldest hostelry. Heavily beamed, it once housed craftsmen working on the cathedral spire, although it is closer to St Thomas's Church, whose clergy used to visit via a tunnel to avoid the unseemly goings on in some of the rooms. The arrangement of floor levels is supposed to reflect an ecclesiastical hierarchy, the so-called House of Lords room being for the higher orders. The bar has a small, intimate 'Horsebox', originally for ladies, which was reputedly used by Churchill and Eisenhower when planning the D-Day landings. Charming details include what is believed to be the country's only surviving complete pewter bar top, as well as original gravity-fed spirit taps. Real ales served here are as local as you would wish, with Salisbury's Hop Back Brewery having a major presence. Which leads us nicely to another type of presence – the resident ghosts. Most talked about is the one-handed Demented Whist Player whose hand, severed for cheating at cards, was found mummified in the 19th century and is on display to this day; he is usually seen in the private bar, which has the only

licensed landing in England. Another ghost, this time female, takes the form of the Grey Lady searching for her child; if seen, you may need to refer to the pub's list of 80 whiskies. In the main dining room is a working fireplace dating back to 1588. Here, lunchtime sees fresh hot paninis and baguettes, backed by a short list of starters such as breaded Camembert with home-made cranberry sauce, and main courses such as steak and kidney pudding. In the evening, the menu continues to focus on quality of flavour at affordable prices: home-made fishcakes with red cabbage coleslaw could be followed by roast sweet chilli chicken with spring ribboned vegetables and sauté potatoes; or, of course, haunch of venison with basil mash and rosemary and onion gravy.

Open all day all wk 11am-11pm Closed: 25 Dec eve **Bar Meals** L served all wk 12-2.30 D served Sun-Wed 6-9.30 Thu-Sat 6-10 **Restaurant** L served all wk 12-2.30 booking required D served Sun-Wed 6-9.30 Thu-Sat 6-10 booking required ⊕ ENTERPRISE INNS ◀ Courage Best, Summer Lightning, Greene King IPA, Hopback guest ale Ö Stowford Press. ♀ 13 **Facilities** Children's menu Children's portions Dogs allowed Wi-fi

Save on hotels. Book at theAA.com/hotel

WILTSHIRE 497 ENGLAND

SHERSTON
Map 4 ST88

The Rattlebone Inn ☻

Church St SN16 0LR ☎ 01666 840871
e-mail: eat@therattlebone.co.uk
dir: M4 junct 17, A429 to Malmesbury. 2m after passing
petrol station at Stanton St Quentin, turn left signed
Sherston

Named after the legendary Saxon warrior John Rattlebone,
this lovely 16th-century pub boasts roaring winter fires
and bags of character. A lively drinkers' pub serving real
ales and organic cider, it hosts regular live music and
other events in the public bar. Outside are three boules
pistes, two gardens and a beautiful skittle alley. Its
menus, best described as 'country bistro', proffer such
delights as a sharing plate of Serrano and Parma ham,
olives and bread; Malmesbury Gold pork sausages with
onion gravy and mash; and a seriously tempting
cheeseboard.

Open all wk noon-3 5-11 (Fri noon-3 5-mdnt Sat noon-
mdnt Sun noon-11) Bar Meals L served Mon-Sat 12-2.30,
Sun 12-3 D served Mon-Sat 6-9.30 Av main course £9
Restaurant L served Mon-Sat 12-2.30, Sun 12-3 D served
Mon-Sat 6-9.30 Fixed menu price fr £10.95 Av 3 course à
la carte fr £20 ◀ Young's Bitter, Bombardier, St Austell
Tribute ♻ Stowford Press, Westons Organic. ☻ 14
Facilities Children welcome Children's portions Dogs
allowed Garden

STOFORD
Map 5 SU03

The Swan Inn ★★★★ INN

Warminster Rd SP2 0PR
☎ 01722 790236 📄 01722 444972
e-mail: info@theswanatstoford.co.uk
dir: From Salisbury take A36 towards Warminster. Stoford
on right 4m from Wilton

The Swan is a landmark coaching inn, close to the
cathedral city of Salisbury, with attractive gardens
overlooking the River Wylye to meadow and farmland.
There is a welcoming log fire, great real ales, many wines
by the glass and traditional home cooked food. Dishes
might include slow braised duck, baby pearl onions,
sautéed oyster mushrooms and Wiltshire bacon lardons;
steamed Scottish rope mussels with a choice of sauce;
and shredded smoked chicken and chorizo sausage
linguine. As well as lovely riverside gardens, there are
comfortable guest rooms available.

Open all day all wk 8am-11pm (Sun 8am-10.30pm)
⊕ ENTERPRISE INNS ◀ Hopback Odyssey, Timothy Taylor
Landlord, Guest ale. Facilities Children welcome
Children's portions Dogs allowed Garden Parking Wi-fi
Rooms 8

STOURTON
Map 4 ST73

PICK OF THE PUBS

Spread Eagle Inn ★★★★ INN ☻

BA12 6QE ☎ 01747 840587 📄 01747 840954
e-mail: enquiries@spreadeagleinn.com
dir: N of A303 off B3092

This charming 19th-century inn is in an enviable
position right at the heart of the 2,650-acre Stourhead
Estate, one of the country's most loved National Trust
properties. Before or after a walk through the
magnificent gardens and landscapes, there is plenty
on offer here, including real ales brewed in a nearby
village and traditional countryside cooking using
produce from local specialists in and around North
Dorset, West Wiltshire and South Somerset. Even the
simple ploughman's is prepared with local bread with
a Dorset Blue cheese or Keene's mature Cheddar
served with home-made chutney. In the restaurant,
expect oven-baked Cornish sea bass fillets on a bed of
Parmesan rice; free-range tarragon-stuffed chicken
suprême with Parmentier potatoes; and chef's crème
brûlée to finish. The interior is smartly traditional, and
in the bedrooms, antiques sit side by side with modern
comforts.

Open all day all wk 9.30am-11pm Bar Meals L served
all wk 12-3 D served all wk 7-9 Av main course £10
Restaurant L served all wk 12-3 D served all wk 7-9 Av
3 course à la carte fr £25 ⊕ FREE HOUSE
◀ Kilmington, Butcombe, Guest ales ♻ Ashton Press.
☻ 8 Facilities Children welcome Garden Parking
Rooms 5

TOLLARD ROYAL
Map 4 ST91

King John Inn ☻

SP5 5PS ☎ 01725 516207
e-mail: info@kingjohninn.co.uk
dir: On B3081 (7m E of Shaftesbury)

Rescued and revamped with style and flair by Alex and
Gretchen Boon in 2008, this attractive Victorian pub
stands in idyllic Tollard Royal, deep in unspoilt downland
on the Wiltshire/Dorset border. The airy, open-plan bar
and dining areas are stylishly uncluttered and have an
upmarket feel, featuring rugs on terracotta tiles, old pine
tables, snug alcoves, warming winter log fires, and a
solid oak bar. Peruse the daily papers, sup a pint of
Ringwood Best or delve in Alex's impressive list of wines
by the glass, then tuck into some hearty, modern British
food from the delicious daily menu that brims with local
produce. Perhaps start with squid in lemonade batter
with clams and chorizo, follow with roast partridge with
beets and cabbage, and round off with dark chocolate
and orange terrine. Super summer terrace for alfresco
meals and don't miss Alex's wine shop across the car
park.

Open all wk noon-3 6-11 Bar Meals L served Mon-Fri
12-2.30, Sat-Sun 12-3 booking required D served all wk
7-9.30 booking required Av main course £12
Restaurant L served Mon-Fri 12-2.30, Sat-Sun 12-3
booking required D served all wk 7-9.30 booking required
⊕ FREE HOUSE ◀ Ringwood Best, Fuller's London Pride,
Summer Lightning, Guest ales ♻ Stowford Press. ☻ 16
Facilities Children's portions Dogs allowed Garden
Parking Wi-fi

UPPER CHUTE
Map 5 SU25

The Cross Keys Inn ☻ NEW

SP11 9ER ☎ 01264 730295
e-mail: crosskeysinn@upperchute.com
dir: From Andover take A342 towards Ludgershall signed
Devizes. Turn right for Upper Chute

If you are heading to the South West on the second
weekend in August, take time out to enjoy the beer
festival held at this family- and dog-friendly traditional
country pub. Gardens front and back enjoy fabulous
views over farmland, and a multitude of old tracks for
enthusiastic walkers and cyclists lead away from the pub
in all directions. Food, all prepared on the premises,
includes a dedicated pie menu, probably featuring beef
and Stilton, or chicken, ham and leek.

Open all wk Bar Meals L served Mon-Fri 12-2, Sat-Sun
12-2.30 D served Mon-Sat 6-9 booking required Av main
course £10.95 Restaurant L served Mon-Fri 12-2, Sat-
Sun 12-2.30 D served Mon-Sat 6-9 booking required
⊕ FREE HOUSE ◀ London Pride, Hopback G.F.B
♻ Stowford Press. ☻ 9 Facilities Children welcome
Children's menu Children's portions Play area Dogs
allowed Beer festival Parking Wi-fi

UPPER WOODFORD
Map 5 SU13

The Bridge Inn ☻

SP4 6NU ☎ 01722 782323
e-mail: enquiries@thebridgewoodford.co.uk
web: www.thebridgewoodford.co.uk
dir: From Salisbury take A360. Turn right for Middle
Woodford & Upper Woodford. (Village between A360 &
A345 5m N of Salisbury)

Hidden away on a quiet lane beside the Wiltshire Avon
just north of Salisbury, this charming pub has been
completely refurbished to include a modern, theatre-style
kitchen. As well as a riverside garden and winter fires,
you'll find flowers and candles on the tables at any time
of year. Seasonal menu choices might include deep fried

continued

UPPER WOODFORD *continued*

baby goat's cheese, tomato and chilli chutney; sticky BBQ chicken wings; fish pie, cheesy mash and minted peas; pot roast lamb shank, colcannon and gravy.

Open all wk 11-3 6-11 **Bar Meals** L served all wk 12-2.30 D served all wk 6-9 Av main course £10
Restaurant L served all wk 12-2.30 D served all wk 6-9 Av 3 course à la carte fr £24 ⊕ ENTERPRISE INNS
◀ Summer Lightning, Wadworth 6X, Ringwood Best. ☂ 10 **Facilities** Children welcome Children's menu Children's portions Dogs allowed Garden Parking Wi-fi

---

UPTON LOVELL   Map 4 ST94

Prince Leopold Inn ☂

BA12 0JP ☎ 01985 850460
e-mail: princeleopold@live.co.uk
dir: *From Warminster take A36 after 4.5m turn left into Upton Lovell*

Built in 1887 as the local shop, post office and store, the Prince Leopold (named after Queen Victoria's popular youngest son, who died tragically young) enjoys an idyllic setting overlooking the River Wylye and the water meadows beyond. The panelled bar serves three hand-pumped ales, perhaps to be enjoyed in the Victorian snug, complete with a log fire but updated with the creature comforts of modern sofas and the day's papers. Lunchtime classics include beef and ale pie, while saddle of Longleat venison may feature on the dinner menu. Recent change of hands.

Open all wk 11-3 6-11 **Bar Meals** L served all wk 12-2.30 D served all wk 6.30-9.30 Av main course £9.50
Restaurant L served all wk 12-2.30 D served all wk 6.30-9.30 Av 3 course à la carte fr £20 ⊕ FREE HOUSE
◀ Wadworth 6X, Butcombe Keystone ales, Guest ales
Ö Stowford Press. ☂ 30 **Facilities** Children welcome Children's menu Children's portions Dogs allowed Garden Beer festival Parking Wi-fi

---

WARMINSTER   Map 4 ST84

PICK OF THE PUBS

The Angel Inn ☂

Upton Scudamore BA12 0AG
☎ 01985 213225   📠 01985 218182
e-mail: mail@theangelinn.co.uk
dir: *From Warminster take A350 towards Westbury or A36 towards Bath*

This restored 16th-century coaching inn is extraordinarily well placed - Longleat is five miles away, and Bath and Salisbury are within easy reach, albeit in opposite directions. Access to the pub is via a walled garden and terrace, where meals and drinks can be served, while inside, open fires, natural wood flooring and regular and guest ales help to create a welcoming feel. Lunchtime choices and specials might include venison casserole with root vegetables and thyme; tempura-battered plaice; and mushroom risotto with roasted shallots and Parmesan. The modern British theme continues at dinner with loin of local lamb with potatoes dauphinoise, ratatouille, and pea

and mint jus: supreme of wild sea bass with red pepper purée, spiced aubergine and pine-nut and coriander ragoût; and breast of maize-fed chicken with braised leg terrine, potato rösti and wilted greens. The Angel showcases the work of contemporary Wessex artists four times a year.

Open all wk 11-3 6-11 **Bar Meals** L served all wk 12-2 booking required D served all wk 6-9 booking required Av main course £14 **Restaurant** L served all wk 12-3 booking required D served all wk 6-9.30 booking required Av 3 course à la carte fr £25 ⊕ FREE HOUSE
◀ Wadworth 6X, Butcombe, John Smith's Smooth, Guest ales. ☂ 10 **Facilities** Children welcome Children's menu Children's portions Dogs allowed Garden Parking Wi-fi

---

The Bath Arms

Clay St, Crockerton BA12 8AJ
☎ 01985 212262   📠 01985 218670
e-mail: batharms@aol.com
dir: *From Warminster on A36 take A350 towards Shaftesbury then left to Crockerton, follow signs for Shearwater*

Set on the Longleat Estate close to the Shearwater Lake, this well known free house attracts locals, walkers and tourists. The garden has been landscaped to provide a pleasant spot for outdoor drinking and dining, and the Garden Suite, with views across the lawn, provides additional seating on busy weekends. Expect stylish food such as pan-roasted quail with hazelnut dressing; Jerusalem artichoke risotto; and slow roasted pork belly, crackling, roasted apple and mash. A vegetarian menu is available.

Open all wk **Bar Meals** L served all wk 12-2 D served all wk 6.30-9 **Restaurant** L served all wk 12-2 D served all wk 6.30-9 ⊕ FREE HOUSE ◀ Crockerton Classic, Naughty Ferrit, Guest ales. **Facilities** Children welcome Play area Dogs allowed Garden Parking

---

The George Inn ★★★★ INN ☂

BA12 7DG ☎ 01985 840396   📠 01985 841333
e-mail: info@the-georgeinn.co.uk
dir: *Telephone for directions*

A 17th-century coaching inn at the heart of the pretty village of Longbridge Deverill. Customers can enjoy a pint of real ale by the fire in the oak-beamed Longbridge bar, or sit outside in the two-acre garden on the banks of the River Wylye. Food is served in a choice of two restaurants, and there is a Sunday carvery in the Wylye Suite. Function facilities are available, plus accommodation in 12 en suite bedrooms. Beer festival in August.

Open all day all wk 11-11 (Sun noon-10.30) Closed: 25 Dec fr 3, 26 Dec (1 Jan open 11-3) **Bar Meals** L served Mon-Thu 12-2.30, Fri-Sat 12-9.30, Sun 12-9 D served Mon-Thu 6-9.30 Av main course £9.95
Restaurant L served Mon-Thu 12-2.30, Fri-Sat 12-9.30, Sun 12-9 D served Mon-Thu 6-9.30 ⊕ POWDER TRAIN
◀ John Smith's, Wadworth 6X, Hobdens Deverill's Advocate Ö Thatchers Cheddar Valley. ☂ 11
Facilities Children welcome Children's menu Children's portions Play area Garden Beer festival Parking Wi-fi
Rooms 12

WEST LAVINGTON   Map 4 SU05

PICK OF THE PUBS

The Bridge Inn ☂

26 Church St SN10 4LD ☎ 01380 813213
e-mail: portier@btopenworld.com
dir: *Approx 7m S of Devizes on A360 towards Salisbury. On edge of village, beyond church*

The Bridge is an attractive food-led pub in a village setting on the edge of Salisbury Plain. Inside you'll find a beamed bar with a log fire and displays of local paintings for sale, while outside is a large garden and boule pitch. The pub is owned by Cyrille and Paula Portier. Cyrille heads up the kitchen, bringing a French accent to the menu whether it's a bowl of pommes frites on the side, or oven-baked snails served in their shell with garlic and herb butter. Look to the baguettes for a lighter lunch; alternatively, for the same price, Cyrille will turn the contents of a baguette (smoked salmon with crème fraîche, for example, or warm striploin of beef with onions and strong horseradish) into a bowl of delicious salad with mixed leaves, tomatoes, spring onions and cucumber. Washed down with a pint of Plain Ales' Innocence, who could want for more? If it sounds like your kind of place, there's a charity beer festival every August Bank Holiday weekend.

Open noon-3 6.30-11 Closed: 2wks Feb, Sun eve & Mon **Bar Meals** L served Tue-Sun 12-2 booking required D served Tue-Sat 7-9 booking required Av main course £12 **Restaurant** L served Tue-Sun 12-2 booking required D served Tue-Sat 7-9 booking required Av 3 course à la carte fr £20 ⊕ ENTERPRISE INNS
◀ Wadworth 6X, Ringwood Best Bitter, Plain Ale Innocence. ☂ 12 **Facilities** Children's portions Garden Beer festival Parking

---

WHITLEY   Map 4 ST86

PICK OF THE PUBS

The Pear Tree Inn

Top Ln SN12 8QX ☎ 01225 709131   📠 01225 702276
e-mail: peartreeinn@maypolehotels.com
dir: *A365 from Melksham towards Bath, at Shaw right onto B3353 into Whitley, 1st left in lane, pub at end*

This sublime, wisteria-clad stone pub surveys tranquil farmland between the Cotswolds and the Marlborough Downs, recalling its genesis as a yeoman's farmhouse centuries ago. Much rustic, rural character remains, from the flagstone floors to the grand open fires and eclectic collection of agricultural artefacts. Like other establishments in the Maypole Group, it cares deeply about its real ales and a carefully selected worldwide wine list. The home-made food on its popular menu of hearty, traditional dishes has won praise for the obvious attention paid to the quality, selection and cooking of ingredients. Indeed, everything comes from locally based suppliers - meats from nearby farms and top quality fruit and vegetables from village growers.

Taken in the characterful bar, airy restaurant or alfresco in the peaceful gardens, the fruits of the chefs' labours also extend to a modern fusion of British and European dishes. Being close to Bath, Lacock Abbey and the remarkable Avebury stones, it's the ideal place for a refreshment break.

Open all day all wk bkfst–11pm **Bar Meals** L served all wk 12–2.30 D served all wk 6.30–9.30
Restaurant L served all wk 12–2.30 D served all wk 6.30–9.30 Av 3 course à la carte fr £25 ⊕ MAYPOLE GROUP PLC ◀ Wadworth 6X, Sharp's Doom Bar, London Pride ♂ Thatchers Gold. **Facilities** Children welcome Children's menu Dogs allowed Garden Parking Wi-fi

WINTERBOURNE BASSETT   Map 5 SU07

The White Horse Inn

SN4 9QB ☎ 01793 731257   📠 01793 739030
e-mail: ckstone@btinternet.com
dir: *5m S of Swindon on A4361 (Devizes road)*

Just two miles north of the mysterious Avebury stone circle, this is an ideal base for walks on the historic Ridgeway path. Along with fine traditional ales from Wadworth Brewery, food is served in the bar and conservatory restaurant, as well as in the safe, lawned garden. Budget lunches and snacks are supported by a full menu and daily specials: look out for tiger prawn provençale; chicken Sorrento; or honey roasted vegetable Wellington.

Open all wk 11.30–3 6–11 ⊕ WADWORTH ◀ Wadworth 6X, IPA, Hophouse Brews ♂ Stowford Press.
Facilities Children welcome Children's menu Garden Parking Wi-fi

WOOTTON RIVERS   Map 5 SU16

PICK OF THE PUBS

Royal Oak 🍷

SN8 4NQ ☎ 01672 810322   📠 01672 811168
e-mail: royaloak35@hotmail.com
dir: *3m S from Marlborough*

Only 100 yards from the Kennet and Avon Canal and the Mid-Wilts Way, this much expanded 16th Century thatched and timbered pub is perfectly situated for Stonehenge, Bath and Winchester, and for exploring the ancient oaks of Savernake Forest. The interior is as charming as the setting, with low, oak-beamed ceilings, exposed brickwork and wide open fireplaces. In the bar you'll find Wadworth 6X and guest ales, including local Ramsbury Bitter. As well as the carte, snacks, sandwiches and meat, fish and poultry dishes, there are daily specials. To give you an idea of what may be available, items taken from a sample menu include warm potted shrimps with wholemeal toast or home-made chicken liver and brandy pâté with caramelised onion marmalade as starters; and main meals of local game and claret pie; English lamb cassoulet with rosemary; or oven-baked lemon sole with sea salt.

Open all wk 10–3 6–11 (Sat–Sun all day)
Bar Meals L served Mon–Sat 12–2.30, Sun 12–8.30
D served Mon–Sat 6–9.30, Sun 12–8.30
Restaurant L served Mon–Sat 12–2.30, Sun 12–8.30
D served Mon–Sat 6–9.30, Sun 12- 8.30 ⊕ FREE HOUSE ◀ Wadworth 6X, Guest ales inc local Ramsbury Bitter.
🍷 9 **Facilities** Children welcome Children's menu Children's portions Family room Dogs allowed Garden Parking Wi-fi

WORCESTERSHIRE

BECKFORD   Map 10 SO93

The Beckford ★★★★ INN 🍷

Cheltenham Rd GL20 7AN ☎ 01386 881532
e-mail: enquiries@thebeckford.com
dir: *On A46 (Evesham to Cheltenham road) 5m from M5 junct 9*

A rambling Georgian country inn set mid-way between Tewkesbury and Evesham, with the Cotswolds beckoning just to the east and shapely Bredon Hill rising immediately to the north. Painstakingly upgraded and refurbished over recent years, the result is an enticing mix of contemporary comforts and traditional fixtures throughout including the comfortable bedrooms, local beers and the very best produce from this most productive of locales. Dine informally or alfresco in the stream-side gardens, choosing from a superb menu featuring Hereford steaks and Gloucester Old Spot pork, attractive vegetarian options and a good range of artisan local cheeses. Look out for a summer beer festival.

Open all day all wk **Bar Meals** L served Mon–Fri 12–2.30, Sat–Sun 12–9.30 D served Mon–Fri 6.30–9.30, Sat–Sun 12–9.30 Av main course £15.95 **Restaurant** L served Mon–Fri 12–2.30, Sat–Sun 12–9.30 D served Mon–Fri 6.30–9.40, Sat–Sun 12–9.30 Av 3 course à la carte fr £27.95 ⊕ FREE HOUSE ◀ London Pride, Greene King Abbot, St Austell, Tribute, Perscott Hill Climb, Timothy Taylor Landlord ♂ Stowford Press. 🍷 22
Facilities Children welcome Children's menu Children's portions Dogs allowed Garden Beer festival Parking Wi-fi **Rooms** 13

BEWDLEY   Map 10 SO77

Little Pack Horse 🍷

31 High St DY12 2DH
☎ 01299 403762   📠 01299 403762
e-mail: enquires@littlepackhorse.co.uk
dir: *From Kidderminster follow ring road & Safari Park signs. Then follow Bewdley signs over bridge, turn left, then right, right at top of Lax Ln. Pub in 20mtrs*

This historic timber-framed inn is warmed by cosy log fires and lit by candles at night. There are low beams, an elm bar, and a small outside patio for alfresco summer dining. Expect a great selection of real ales and ciders, and a menu built on local, seasonal produce. A meal might include Stilton and port mushrooms, followed by chicken and bacon linguini or roasted breast of pheasant. Home-made pies are a speciality, especially Desperate Dan cow pie, and can be purchased at the Sunday pie shop.

Open all wk 12–2.30 6–11.30 (Sat–Sun noon–mdnt)
Bar Meals L served Mon–Fri 12–2.15, Sat–Sun 12–4 booking required D served Mon–Thu 6–9, Fri 6–9.30, Sat–Sun 5.30–9.30, booking required Av main course £9.50
Restaurant L served Mon–Fri 12–2.15, Sat–Sun 12–4 booking required D served Mon–Thu 6–9, Fri 6–9.30, Sat–Sun 5.30–9.30 booking required Fixed menu price fr £4.50 Av 3 course à la carte fr £18.95 ⊕ PUNCH TAVERNS ◀ St Austells Tribute, Greene King IPA, Abbot Ale, Worcestershire Way ♂ Stowford Press, Westons Organic, Thatchers Katy. 🍷 10 **Facilities** Children welcome Children's menu Children's portions Family room Dogs allowed Garden

PICK OF THE PUBS

The Mug House Inn & Angry Chef Restaurant   INN ◉ 🍷

12 Severnside North DY12 2EE ☎ 01299 402543
e-mail: drew@mughousebewdley.co.uk
web: www.mughousebewdley.co.uk
dir: *A456 from Kidderminster to Bewdley. Pub in town on river*

Nestling beside the River Severn in picturesque Bewdley, this inn's riverside seating is popular on warmer days. The unusual name dates back to the 17th century when 'mug house' was a popular term for an alehouse. Nowadays you'll find at least two guest ales at the bar, alongside regulars such as Hereford Pale Ale and Westons traditional scrumpy. The inn holds an annual beer festival on May Day Bank Holiday weekend. This is when the rear garden comes into its own. It's a wonderful sun trap, there are regular barbecues, and a glass-covered patio with heaters can be used if rain or chilly winds threaten. Food follows pub favourite lines, but quality is not sacrificed and prices are reasonable: chunky crusty bread sarnies or jacket potatoes overflowing with the likes of chicken and smoked bacon with garlic mayonnaise; AA Rosette-standard options from the short restaurant carte may proffer pan-seared scallops on a sweet potato purée, and poached monkfish wrapped in smoked salmon with pan-fried king prawns. Accommodation is comfortable and thoughtfully furnished.

Open all wk noon–11 **Bar Meals** L served Mon–Sat 12–2.30, Sun 12–5 **Restaurant** L served Mon–Sat 12.2.30, Sun 12–5 D served Mon–Sat 6.30–9 booking required ⊕ PUNCH TAVERNS ◀ Timothy Taylor Landlord, Hereford Pale Ale, 2 guest ales ♂ Westons Traditional Scrumpy. 🍷 9 **Facilities** Dogs allowed Garden Beer festival Wi-fi **Rooms** 7

BEWDLEY *continued*

Woodcolliers Arms ★★★ INN ♀

76 Welch Gate DY12 2AU ☎ 01299 400589
e-mail: roger@woodcolliers.co.uk
dir: *3m from Kidderminster. 2 mins walk from No 2 bus stop*

Russian trained chef Boris Rumba serves a unique blend of pub favourites and authentic Russian dishes at this 17th-century family-run free house built into a hillside, close to the centre of Bewdley and just across the river from the Severn Valley steam railway. There is always a good range of well kept real ales and ciders on offer. In the railway-themed restaurant, the regularly-changing specials board might feature rack of lamb, cauliflower cheese in a Stilton sauce, or the traditional Russian atbivnaya, prepared from an old family recipe. Comfortable accommodation is available.

Open all wk 5-12.30 (Sat 12.30pm-12.30am, Sun 12.30-11) **Bar Meals** L served Sat-Sun 12.30-3 D served all wk 6-9.30 booking required Av main course £11.25 **Restaurant** L served Sat-Sun 12.30-3 booking required D served all wk 6-9.30 booking required Av 3 course à la carte fr £16 ⊕ OLIVERS INNS LTD ◀ Ludlow Gold, Three Tuns 1642, Hobsons Twisted Spire ♂ Thatchers Gold, Westons Old Rosie. ♀ 24 **Facilities** Children welcome Children's portions Dogs allowed Garden Parking Wi-fi **Rooms** 5

BRANSFORD   Map 10 SO75

The Bear & Ragged Staff ♀

Station road WR6 5JH ☎ 01886 833399
📠 **01886 833106**
e-mail: mail@bear.uk.com
dir: *3m from Worcester or Malvern, clearly signed from A4103 or A449*

This lovely old free house was built in 1861 as an estate rent office and stables, and the original stable doors still survive. Just minutes from both Malvern and Worcester, the pub is also handy for the Malvern Hills and fishing on the River Teme. These days it has a reputation for good beers and food. A meal might take in local pheasant with thyme, brandy and satsuma, or butternut squash and courgette risotto. Desserts include white chocolate and cranberry crème brûlée.

Open all wk 11.30-2 6-11 Closed: 25 Dec eve, 1 Jan eve, Sun eve **Bar Meals** L served all wk 12-2 D served Mon-Fri 6.30-9 Av main course £12 **Restaurant** L served all wk 12-2 D served Mon-Sat 6.30-9.30 Av 3 course à la carte fr £28 ⊕ FREE HOUSE ◀ Hobsons Twisted Spire, Fuller's London Pride ♂ Robinsons. ♀ 10 **Facilities** Children welcome Children's portions Dogs allowed Garden Parking

BRETFORTON   Map 10 SP04

PICK OF THE PUBS

The Fleece Inn ♀

The Cross WR11 7JE ☎ 01386 831173
e-mail: nigel@thefleeceinn.co.uk
dir: *From Evesham follow signs for B4035 towards Chipping Campden. Through Badsey into Bretforton. Right at village hall, past church, pub in open parking area*

Originally built in the time of Chaucer, The Fleece Inn remained in the ownership of a single family for most of its six-century history. A quintessential English pub, now owned by the National Trust, the beautiful timbered building was originally a longhouse whose last private owner, Lola Taplin, died in front of the fire in the snug in 1977; she was a direct descendant of the man who built it. The pub was nearly lost in a tragic fire in 2004; a massive renovation followed, when its features and integrity were restored. Real ale devotees will admire one of England's oldest pewter collections as they order a pint of Pig's Ear, and cider lovers too over their Prior's Tipple. Families can enjoy the summer sunshine in the apple orchard while children use the play area. There are regular music evenings too. Typical dishes include slow roasted belly pork with haricot cassoulet topped with grilled apple slices and smoked Applewood cheese; steak and mushroom pie with braised red cabbage, curly kale and new potatoes; and local faggots with chive mash. A beer festival is held in October.

Open all wk Mon-Tue 11-3 6-11, Wed-Sun 11-11 **Bar Meals** L served Mon-Sat 12-2.30, Sun 12-4 D served Mon-Sat 6.30-9, Sun 6.30-8.30 **Restaurant** Fixed menu price fr £7.95 ⊕ FREE HOUSE ◀ Buckle Street no 1 Bitter, Pig's Ear, Dog in the Fog, Pandora's Box ♂ Thatchers, Prior's Tipple. ♀ 12 **Facilities** Children welcome Children's menu Children's portions Play area Garden Beer festival

CLENT   Map 10 SO97

PICK OF THE PUBS

The Bell & Cross ♀

Holy Cross DY9 9QL
☎ **01562 730319** 📠 **01562 731733**
dir: *Telephone for directions*

This award-winning pub is run by the chef to the England football team, so you can be sure that the food here hits the spot. Dating from the early 19th century, the pub has been refurbished in recent years but retained its character. Head for the bar for traditional hand-pulled beers and an inviting log fire in winter, or the covered and heated patio for comfortable alfresco dining on cooler nights. Expect modern British food in a traditional setting; light bar lunches include a range of sandwiches, pasta and risotto, as well as classic mains like Scotch minced beef and onion pie, chilli and mint crushed peas with mash, or the Bell & Cross

burger with melted cheese, onion rings, fries and mayo. The evening dinner might kick off with oak-smoked Scottish salmon, quail egg and caper salad, followed by slow cooked shoulder of Cornish lamb, red onion confit, wilted spinach, mousseline potatoes and pimento jus. Sticky rum baba with winter red berry compote and Cornish clotted cream is a typical dessert.

Open all wk noon-3 6-11 Closed: 25 Dec, 26 Dec eve, 31 Dec & 1 Jan eve **Bar Meals** L served all wk 12-2 D served Mon-Sat 6.30-9.15 booking required Av main course £12.50 **Restaurant** L served Mon-Sat 12-2, Sun 12-7 booking required D served Mon-Sat 6.30-9.15, Sun 12-7 booking required Fixed menu price fr £13.95 Av 3 course à la carte fr £19.60 ⊕ ENTERPRISE INNS ◀ Pedigree, Mild, Bitter, Timothy Taylor Landlord, Guest ales. ♀ 15 **Facilities** Children welcome Children's menu Children's portions Dogs allowed Garden Parking

CLOWS TOP   Map 10 SO77

PICK OF THE PUBS

The Colliers Arms ♀

Tenbury Rd DY14 9HA ☎ 01299 832242
e-mail: thecolliersarms@aol.com
dir: *On A456.11 Pub 4m from Bewdley & 7m from Kidderminster*

With its great old tap room, comfy lounge and restaurant, this convivial country free house simply oozes character. The pub is just a stone's throw from the glades of Wyre Forest, whilst from the outside patio and beer garden you can enjoy the views of the largest Norman church in England at nearby Rock. Closer to hand is the pub's own vegetable, herb and fruit garden, from which the chefs source many of the ingredients for their oft-changing modern British menu. Consider a starter of beer-battered cod cheeks with tartare sauce and lemon, before launching into roast belly pork with rapeseed oil mash and creamed cabbage, or sweet potato, pumpkin and forest mushroom lasagne. A growing proportion of the food is sourced from local farms and estates; in a similar vein, local breweries are well represented at The Colliers, with Hobsons beers a regular favourite.

Open noon-3 6-11 (Sat 11-11 Sun noon-4) Closed: Sun eve **Bar Meals** L served Mon-Fri 12-2, Sat 12-2.30, Sun 12-3 booking required D served Mon-Fri 6.30-9, Sat 6.30-9.30 booking required Av main course £9.95 **Restaurant** L served Tue-Fri 12-2, Sat 12-2.30, Sun 12-3 booking required D served Tue-Fri 6.30-9, Sat 6.30-9.30 booking required Fixed menu price fr £15 Av 3 course à la carte fr £18.95 ⊕ FREE HOUSE ◀ Hobsons Best, Town Crier, Guinness, Malvern Hills Black Pear, Wye Valley Butty Bach, guest ale ♂ Stowford Press. ♀ 14 **Facilities** Children welcome Children's portions Dogs allowed Garden Parking

DROITWICH
Map 10 SO86

PICK OF THE PUBS

The Chequers ♥

Kidderminster Rd, Cutnall Green WR9 0PJ
☎ 01299 851292 📠 01299 851744
dir: Telephone for directions

Run by Roger Narbett, chef to the England football team, it's not just the memorabilia on the bar wall that's in the premier league at this charming village pub. Roger runs The Chequers with his wife Joanne, and they have retained its traditional pub atmosphere with open fire, church panel bar and richly coloured furnishings after a recent makeover. A goodly range of real ales includes Hook Norton and Ruddles. Next to the bar is the modern country style Garden Room with warmly painted walls, a plush sofa and hanging tankards. Popular Sunday lunches here may start with sautéed lamb's kidneys and baby onions on toasted brioche with mustard and chive cream, continue with roast loin of free-range pork, honey-glazed parsnips and cider apple sauce, and finish with warm treacle sponge pudding with lemon meringue ice cream. Children are well catered for, with their own menu or portions from the main menu. You'll also find light bites such as fish cakes with white wine, prawn and chive sauce, mains like grilled fillet of sea bass with crayfish, leek and butterbean fricassee, mousseline potatoes and Champagne sauce, with pub classics such as beef and onion pie or beer-battered cod and chips.

Open all wk 12-3 6-11 (Sun 12-4 6-10.30) Closed: 25 Dec, 1 Jan eve Bar Meals L served Mon-Sat 12-2, Sun 12-2.30 D served Mon-Sun 6.30-9.15 Av main course £12.50 Restaurant L served Mon-Sat 12-2, Sun 12-2.30 booking required D served Mon-Sun 6.30-9.15 booking required Fixed menu price fr £13.95 Av 3 course à la carte fr £19.60 ⊕ ENTERPRISE INNS ◀ Timothy Taylor, Enville Ale, Hook Norton, Ruddles, Hereford Pale Ale. ♥ 15 Facilities Children welcome Children's menu Children's portions Family room Dogs allowed Garden Parking

The Honey Bee ♥

Doverdale Ln, Doverdale WR9 0QB ☎ 01299 851620
e-mail: honey@king-henrys-taverns.co.uk
dir: From Droitwich take A442 towards Kidderminster. Left into Dovedale Lane to Dovedale

'It's buzzin' at The Honey Bee but you won't get stung!' say King Henry's Taverns. This spacious, modern and friendly pub has a garden and a play area for children. There are plenty of areas, inside or out, to enjoy a drink or the freshly prepared dishes which will satisfy small and large appetites alike. Choose from steaks, fish and seafood, rumpburgers, traditional favourites, and international and vegetarian dishes. The pub is set in four and half acres with two fishing lakes that are stocked with carp.

Open all day all wk 11.30am-11pm Bar Meals food served all day Restaurant food served all day ⊕ KING HENRY'S TAVERNS ◀ Guinness, Greene King IPA, Marstons Pedigree. ♥ 15 Facilities Children welcome Children's menu Children's portions Play area Garden Parking

The Old Cock Inn

Friar St WR9 8EQ ☎ 01905 774233
dir: M5 junct 5, A449 in Droitwich town centre opposite theatre

Three stained-glass windows, rescued from a church destroyed during the Civil War, are a feature of this charming pub, first licensed during the reign of Queen Anne. The stone carving above the front entrance is believed to portray Judge Jeffreys, who presided over the local magistrates' court. A varied menu, including snacks and more substantial dishes - beer battered fish and chips, vegetarian risotto, and local sausages and mash - is supplemented by the daily specials. Change of hands.

Open 12-3 6-11 Closed: Sun eve ◀ Jennings Ales, 3 guest ales. Facilities Children welcome Children's menu Dogs allowed Garden Wi-fi

FLADBURY
Map 10 SO94

Chequers Inn

Chequers Ln WR10 2PZ ☎ 01386 860276
e-mail: chequersinn@btinternet.com
dir: Off A44 between Evesham & Pershore

The Chequers is a 14th-century inn with plenty of beams and an open fire, tucked away in a pretty village with views of the glorious Bredon Hills. Local produce from the Vale of Evesham provides the basis for home-cooked dishes offered from the monthly-changing menu, plus a choice of daily specials. There is also a traditional Sunday carvery. The pretty walled garden enjoys outstanding views, a great setting for drinking or dining, and the nearby River Avon is ideal for walking. Change of hands in September 2010.

Open all wk 11.30-2.30 6-11 (Sun 11.30-3.30) ⊕ ENTERPRISE INNS ◀ Purity, Bombardier Real Ales. Facilities Children welcome Children's menu Children's portions Garden Parking Wi-fi

FLYFORD FLAVELL
Map 10 SO95

PICK OF THE PUBS

The Boot Inn
INN ♥

See Pick of the Pubs on page 502

GUARLFORD
Map 10 SO84

Plough and Harrow NEW

Rhydd Rd WR13 6NY ☎ 01684 310453
e-mail: info@theploughandharrow.co.uk
dir: From Great Malvern take B4211 (Guarlford Rd). Through Guarlford, pub on left

With views of the Malvern Hills from its back garden, this charming country pub was formerly a dray house and stable. Today you'll find Wadworths beers and freshly cooked meals in comfortable surroundings, with winter fires and alfresco summer dining. Seasonal produce from the pub's own kitchen garden drives menu options that graduate from lunchtime light bites and salads to evening choices like twice-baked spinach and Cheddar soufflé, and Cotswold venison with braised red cabbage.

Open 11-3 6-11.30 Closed: 25 Dec, 1 Jan, 1wk spring, 1wk autumn, Sun eve & Mon Bar Meals L served Tue-Sat 12-2, Sun 12-2.15 D served Tue-Sat 6.30-9 Av main course £10.95 Restaurant L served Tue-Sat 12-2, Sun 12-2.15 D served Tue-Sat 6.30-9 Fixed menu price fr £13.95 Av 3 course à la carte fr £29.95 ⊕ WADWORTHS ◀ Wadworths IPA, 6X. Facilities Children welcome Children's portions Dogs allowed Garden Parking Wi-fi

KEMPSEY
Map 10 SO84

PICK OF THE PUBS

Walter de Cantelupe Inn ★★★ INN

Main Rd WR5 3NA ☎ 01905 820572
dir: 4m S of Worcester city centre on A38. Pub in village centre

Situated in the village of Kempsey, just 4 miles from Worcester city centre, this privately owned and run free house commemorates a 13th-century Bishop of Worcester, who was strongly against his parishioners' habit of brewing and selling ales as a way to raise church funds. With its whitewashed walls bedecked with flowers, parts of the pub date from the 17th century. Outside, a walled and paved garden has been fragrantly planted with clematis, roses and honeysuckle, and its south-facing position can be a real sun-trap. The menu is written up each day on a blackboard, with choices to appeal to both traditionalists and those seeking something more contemporary. You could begin with Worcestershire rare titbit and follow with Malvern Victorian sausages and mash or the pie of the day. Three or four cask ales are usually on offer, including Mayfields Copper Fox. The pub also has accommodation.

Open 12-2.30 6-11 (Sun 12-3 6-10.30) Closed: 25-26 Dec, 1 Jan, Mon (ex BH) Bar Meals L served Tue-Sat 12-2, Sun 12-3 D served Tue-Sat 6.30-9, Sun 6.30-8 Restaurant L served Tue-Sat 12-2, Sun 12-3 D served Tue-Sat 6.30-9 booking required ⊕ FREE HOUSE ◀ Timothy Taylor Landlord, Cannon Royal Kings Shilling, Mayfields Copper Fox ♻ Stowford Press. Facilities Children welcome Children's portions Dogs allowed Garden Parking Wi-fi Rooms 3

PICK OF THE PUBS

The Boot Inn ★★★★ INN 🍷

FLYFORD FLAVELL Map 10 SO95

Radford Rd WR7 4BS
☎ 01386 462658 📠 01386 462547
e-mail: enquiries@thebootinn.com
web: www.thebootinn.com
dir: *From Worcester take A422 towards Stratford. Turn right to village*

Parts of this family-run, award-winning, traditional coaching inn can be traced back to the 13th century, and for evidence you need only to look at the heavy beams and slanting doorways. Keep an eye out too for the friendly ghost, age uncertain. The large bar area is comfortable, the pool table and TV having been banished to a separate room, and regulars like Old Speckled Hen, London Pride and Black Sheep, and an extensive wine list complements the varied and imaginative menus which change every six weeks.

You can eat from the lunchtime sandwich and bar snack menu, from the extensive specials board, or from the full à la carte, but no matter which you choose, or indeed where – including the conservatory – only the best and freshest, mostly county-sourced, produce is used.

A sample menu therefore may include starters of Portobello mushroom stuffed with crispy bacon and goat's cheese, and mango and crayfish salad; followed by something from the griddle, such as English steaks hung for 21 days; sea bass fillets with sizzled ginger, chilli, spring onion and hoi sin; pork ribeye steak with walnut crust and cider apple sauce; roasted lamb shank with redcurrant and rosemary gravy; or chive savoury pancakes filled with roasted vegetables and melted Brie. Roasts – beef, pork and turkey - are served on Sundays, along with the specials menu.

Gardens and a shaded patio area are especially suited to summer dining. The comfortable en suite bedrooms in the converted coach house are furnished in antique pine and equipped with practical goodies.

Open all day all wk **Bar Meals** L served all wk 12-2 D served all wk 6.30-10 **Restaurant** L served all wk 12-2 D served all wk 6.30-10 PUNCH TAVERNS Old Speckled Hen, London Pride, Black Sheep Stowford Press. 🍷 8 **Facilities** Children's menu Children's portions Dogs allowed (bar area only) Garden Parking Wi-fi **Rooms** 5

Save on hotels. Book at **theAA.com/hotel**

WORCESTERSHIRE 503 ENGLAND

KINGTON
Map 10 SO95

PICK OF THE PUBS

The Red Hart

Stratford Rd WR7 4DD ☎ 01386 792559
e-mail: redhartpub@yahoo.co.uk
dir: *M5 junct 6, A4538. Then A422 towards Stratford-upon-Avon, approx 4m. From Redditch A441, right onto A422, approx 3m*

This beautiful, easy-going country pub and restaurant was created from a derelict shell by a team of local craftsmen. The interior has been stripped to reveal its original looks, while some stunning contemporary touches have been added. The main bar is furnished in wine bar style, while the secondary bar area boasts deep leather sofas surrounding a log burner. The restaurant is also smart and full of atmosphere. You could start with duck and pork terrine with watercress and apple salad, and move on to lime crusted sea bass and Thai scented crab risotto; or crispy pork belly with leek and bacon mash, cider and vegetable jus. Lunch brings home-made soup, lasagne, baguettes and perhaps whole tail scampi and chips.

Open all wk Mon-Thu 12-3 (Fri-Sun all day) ⊕ MARSTONS ◼ Banks, Marstons, Cocker Hoop, Hobgoblin. **Facilities** Children welcome Children's menu Children's portions Dogs allowed Garden Parking Wi-fi

---

KNIGHTWICK
Map 10 SO75

PICK OF THE PUBS

The Talbot ♥

WR6 5PH ☎ 01886 821235 📄 01886 821060
e-mail: admin@the-talbot.co.uk
dir: *A44 (Leominster road) through Worcester, 8m W right onto B4197 at River Teme bridge*

The Teme Valley's traditions and produce are firmly rooted in this late 14th-century coaching inn. Annie Clift and her team have run it for over 25 years, and nearly everything is made in-house, including bread, preserves, black pudding and raised pies. Salads, herbs and vegetables are grown in the large organic kitchen garden, and wild foods are gathered from the fields and hedgerows; anything they cannot produce themselves comes from a local source with the exception of fish, which comes from Cornwall and Wales. The Talbot is also home to the Teme Valley Brewery, which uses locally grown hops in a range of curiously named cask conditioned ales called This, That, T'Other and Wot. The pub hosts a produce market on the second Sunday of the month and a beer festival is held the second weekend in October. The bar menu offers ploughman's, filled rolls and hot dishes, whilst in the restaurant starters might include venison carpaccio or potted duck jazzier, followed by black bream with mixed pepper and red onion couscous and wild garlic pesto. Leave space for garden berry millefeuille and cream. There are day fishing tickets available as Talbot Waters runs the length of the garden.

Open all day all wk 7.30am-11.30pm
Bar Meals L served all wk 12-9 D served all wk 12-9 food served all day **Restaurant** D served all wk 6.30-9 booking required ⊕ FREE HOUSE ◼ Teme Valley This, That , T'Other & Wot, Hobsons Best Bitter Choice ♂ Kingstone Press, Kingston Rosy, Robinson's. ♥ 12 **Facilities** Children welcome Children's portions Dogs allowed Garden Beer festival Parking Wi-fi

---

LOWER BROADHEATH
Map 10 SO85

The Dewdrop Inn ★★★★ INN

Bell Ln WR2 6RR ☎ 01905 640012 📄 01905 640265
e-mail: enquiries@thedewdrop-inn.co.uk
dir: *From Worcester take A443 towards Kidderminster. left onto B4202 towards Martley. Left into Bell Ln on entering Lower Broadheath. Pub 400yds on left*

This painstakingly refurbished country inn reopened in 2009 under chef-patron Tim Hoare, whose menus offers interest, quality and genuine value for money. Typical choices include home 'tea smoked' duck breast with roasted red onions, rocket and walnut dressing, and a whole boned poussin stuffed with lemon, apricot and thyme stuffing and dauphinoise potatoes. B&B guests can enjoy breakfast in the lee of the pretty Malvern and Abberley Hills. All this and beer from the local St George's micro-brewery too! Sir Edward Elgar hailed from Lower Broadheath; his birthplace museum is an easy stroll away.

Open all day all wk **Bar Meals** L served all wk 12-2.30 D served all wk 6-9.30 Av main course £9.50 **Restaurant** L served all wk 12-2.30 booking required D served all wk 6.30-9.30 booking required Fixed menu price fr £8.95 Av 3 course à la carte fr £21.50 ⊕ FREE HOUSE ◼ Fuller's London Pride, St George's, Guinness. **Facilities** Children welcome Children's menu Children's portions Play area Garden Parking Wi-fi **Rooms** 7

MALVERN
Map 10 SO74

The Inn at Welland ♥

Drake St, Welland WR13 6LN ☎ 01684 592317
e-mail: info@theinnatwelland.co.uk
dir: *M50 junct 1, A38 follow signs for Upton upon Severn. Left onto A4104, through Upton upon Severn, 2.5m. Pub on right*

This attractive 17th-century country inn, formerly known as the Anchor Inn, changed hands in 2011 and has been recently renovated. With spectacular views of the Malvern Hills and close to the Three Counties Showground, there is a stylish alfresco terrace for the warmer months and a wood burner and open fire for the winter. Food centres around seasonal local produce, with daily classic rotisserie specialties, accompanied by local Wye Valley ale plus guests. A separate deli offers take-home or eat-in snacks.

Open Tue-Sun 9am-11.30pm Closed: Mon (ex BH)
Bar Meals Av main course £12.50 ⊕ FREE HOUSE ◼ Wye Valley, Malvern Hills, Hobson's, Guest ales ♂ Stowford Press. ♥ 20 **Facilities** Children welcome Children's menu Garden Parking

---

Nags Head NEW

19-21 Bank St WR14 2JG ☎ 01684 574373
e-mail: enquiries@nagsheadmalvern.co.uk
dir: *Off A449 in Malvern*

From the garden the looming presence of North Hill, northernmost top of the stunning Malvern Hills takes the eye, if only momentarily, away from the panoply of beery delights that mark out this enterprising free house. Up to 14 micro-brewery marvels (including the pub's own St George's and a beer festival on St George's Day) adorn the bar, with an interior dotted with snugs, log fires and a magpie's nest of artefacts. With a marvellous menu (try fruity Moroccan lamb) to enjoy, the hills can wait!

Open all day all wk **Bar Meals** L served all wk 12-2 **Restaurant** D served all wk 6.30-8.30 ⊕ FREE HOUSE ◼ St George's Brewery Friar Tuck, Charger, Dragons Blood, Sharp's Doom Bar ♂ Thatchers Heritage, Westons 1st Quality. **Facilities** Children welcome Children's portions Dogs allowed Garden Beer festival Parking

---

The Wyche Inn ★★★★ INN ♥ NEW

74 Wyche Rd WR14 4EQ ☎ 01684 575396
e-mail: thewycheinn@googlemail.com
dir: *1.5m S of Malvern. On B4218 towards Malvern & Colwall. Off A449 (Worcester to Ross/Ledbury road)*

High up in the Malvern Hills, with paths from the door curling to the spectacular ridge walk linking Worcestershire Beacon with the stunning hillfort on Herefordshire Beacon, small wonder that this is a popular spot for ramblers to rest awhile, enjoying beers from a wide variety of micro-breweries. The inner-man can be satisfied with good, solid pub fare; home-made pies and thick steaks are a favourite. Views to the distant Cotswold Hills are part of the draw for visitors staying at the comfortable accommodation.

Open all day all wk **Bar Meals** L served Mon-Fri 12-2.30, Sat 12-8.30, Sun 12-6 D served Mon-Fri 6-8.30, Sat 12-8.30, Sun 12-6 **Restaurant** L served Mon-Fri 12-2.30, Sat 12-8.30, Sun 12-6 D served Mon-Fri 6-8.30, Sat 12-8.30, Sun 12-6 ⊕ FREE HOUSE ◼ Hobsons Bitter, Wye Valley HPA. ♥ 9 **Facilities** Children welcome Children's menu Children's portions Dogs allowed Garden Parking Wi-fi **Rooms** 5

MARTLEY
Map 10 SO76

Admiral Rodney Inn ★★★★ INN

Berrow Green, WR6 6PL ☎ 01886 821375
e-mail: rodney@admiral.fslife.co.uk
dir: *M5 junct 7, A44 signed Leominster. Approx 7m at Knightwick right onto B4197. Inn 2m on left at Berrow Green*

This early 17th-century farmhouse/alehouse stands in the heart of the countryside on the Worcester Way footpath. The stylishly traditional interior includes a split-level restaurant housed in an old barn. Traditional pub fare includes Rodney sausages with Yorkshire pudding; surf and turf; beer battered or grilled fish of the day; and a vegetarian choice that might include

continued

MARTLEY *continued*

courgette and mushroom gratin; all washed down with a pint of Wye Valley Bitter. En suite bedrooms and a skittle alley are also available.

Open all wk noon-3 5-11 (Mon 5-11 Sat noon-11 Sun noon-10.30) **Bar Meals** L served Tue-Sat 12.15-2.15, Sun 12.30-3.30 D served all wk 6.30-9 **Restaurant** L served Tue-Sat 12.15-2.15, Sun 12.30-3.30 D served all wk 6.30-9 ⊕ FREE HOUSE ◀ Wye Valley Bitter, HPA, Local guest ales (Black Pear, Malvern Hills Brewery, Kinver, Hobsons) ♻ Westons Stowford Press, Robinsons Cask Cider. **Facilities** Children welcome Children's menu Dogs allowed Garden Parking Wi-fi **Rooms** 3

The Crown Inn

Berrow Green Rd WR6 6PA ☎ 01886 888840
e-mail: thecrowninnmartley@yahoo.co.uk
dir: *7m W of Worcester on B4204*

A Victorian village pub with a large extension formed from redundant outbuildings, The Crown was once the scene of an unlikely gig by Eric Clapton. Set on the Worcester Way, it is popular with walkers and locals. In one bar is an open fire, Sky TV, pool table and jukebox, while the other has dining tables and French windows to the garden. Locally sourced, freshly cooked food runs from steak and ale pie to curry. There is also a pizza and take away menu. Change of hands.

Open all wk noon-11 (Fri-Sat noon-mdnt Sun noon-10.30) ⊕ MARSTONS ◀ Banks Bitter, Banks Mild. **Facilities** Children welcome Children's menu Children's portions Play area Dogs allowed Garden Parking

PICK OF THE PUBS

Crown & Sandys Arms ⚲

Main Rd WR9 0EW ☎ 01905 620252
e-mail: enquiries@crownandsandys.co.uk
web: www.crownandsandys.co.uk
dir: *3m from Droitwich, off A449, 6m off junct 6 & junct 5 of M5*

Run with close care and attention by Richard and Rachael Everton, this smartly refurbished former coaching inn has bang up-to-date decor, yet the original beams and fireplaces blend effortlessly with the trendy furnishings. Set in the picturesque black and white village of Ombersley, the inn prides itself on well kept real ales and ciders, a smoothly managed

food operation and excellent service. The modern menus burst with the latest flavours. The full carte is backed by a weekly specials list, and customers can choose between three dining areas: the Orangery, the Bistro and the Bar. Lunch brings sandwiches (perhaps roasted beef and horseradish or smoked salmon and chive crème fraîche), and at lunch or dinner you can enjoy a selection from the char grill or full meals such as smoked salmon and spring onion fish cake with chive beurre blanc followed by tempura-battered fresh fish with triple cooked chips, mushy peas and home-made tartare sauce. Daily specials might be moules 'Normandes' or red Thai king prawn curry.

Open all day all wk 11-11 (Sun 11-10.30) **Bar Meals** L served all wk 12-2.30 D served all wk 6-9.30 booking required Av main course £12.50 **Restaurant** L served all wk 12-2.30 booking required D served all wk 6-9.30 booking required Fixed menu price fr £11.95 Av 3 course à la carte fr £20 ⊕ FREE HOUSE ◀ Wye Valley H.P.A, Shropshire Lad, Timothy Taylor Landlord, Jacks Ale IPA. ⚲ 15 **Facilities** Children welcome Children's menu Children's portions Garden Parking Wi-fi

The Defford Arms

Upton Rd, Defford WR8 9BD ☎ 01386 750378
dir: *From Pershore take A4104 towards Upton upon Severn. Pub on left in village*

Neil and Sue Overton rescued the Defford from dereliction in 2007. They have worked hard to make it the success that it is today, eschewing music, gambling machines and TV in favour of the old fashioned values of a family pub. It's in a great location too, so days out at Croome Park, the three counties showground at Malvern, Cheltenham racecourse or Pershore plum festival could all include a welcome break here. The reasonably priced home-cooked food includes all the pub favourites, including a great range of grills.

Open all wk Mon 5.30-9 Tue-Wed 12-2.30 5.30-11 Thu 12-2.30 5.30-10 Fri 12-2.30 5.30-11 Sat noon-mdnt Sun noon-4 **Bar Meals** L served Tue-Sun D served all wk Av main course £6.95 food served all day **Restaurant** L served Tue-Sun D served all wk Fixed menu price fr £7.95 food served all day ⊕ FREE HOUSE ◀ Wye Valley Brewery, Three Tuns, Otter, Doom Bar, Prescott ♻ Stowford Press. **Facilities** Children welcome Children's menu Children's portions Dogs allowed Garden Parking

The Halfway House Inn

Bastonford WR2 4SL
☎ 01905 831098   📠 01905 831704
dir: *From M5 junct 7 take A4440 then A449*

Situated between Worcester and Malvern, this imposing and attractive Georgian property is an ideal destination for a great pint and a plate of something home-cooked, almost certainly featuring local produce. If you feel like seafood or steaks, you're in luck, because it specialises in them; otherwise, perhaps pork tenderloin with black pudding; roasted Mediterranean and goat's cheese lasagne; or a spicy tortilla. Sit on the Worcester side of the two-section restaurant for the log fire. Mature trees and foliage shade the garden.

Open noon-3 6-11 Closed: Mon-Tue **Bar Meals** L served Wed-Sun 12-2 D served Wed-Sun 6-9 Av main course £12.95 **Restaurant** L served Wed-Sun 12-2 D served Wed-Sun 6-9 Av 3 course à la carte fr £25 ⊕ FREE HOUSE ◀ Abbot Ale, St Georges Bitter, Fuller's London Pride, Timothy Taylor ♻ Stowford Press. **Facilities** Children welcome Children's menu Children's portions Garden Parking Wi-fi

PICK OF THE PUBS

The Inn at Stonehall ◉

Stonehall Common WR5 3QG ☎ 01905 820462
e-mail: info@theinnatstonehall.com
dir: *2m from M5 junct 7. Stonehall Common 1.5m from St Peters Garden Centre Norton*

Known as The Fruiterer's Arms until 2007, the year Joanna Coull arrived to completely transform it. Now basking in the glow of an AA Rosette, her inn clearly places more emphasis on food than when the local agricultural workers patronised it. The bar is furnished with dark-wood tables and leather seats, the restaurant has that clean-cut look, and there are great views from outside. In his open kitchen, Dwight Clayton produces French-influenced modern British cooking like his signature home-made pork faggots; braised blade of beef with mash, roasted root vegetables and red wine sauce; beer-battered haddock with thrice-cooked chips and pea purée; and red onion tarte Tatin with Ragstone goat's cheese tomato vinaigrette. An occasional, but unusual, ingredient is the black pear, after which the Malvern Hills Brewery bitter is named. The fruit comes from trees in the car park, but steer clear – only cooking makes the pears edible.

Open noon-5 6-11 (Sun 12-3) Closed: 26-30 Dec, 1-8 Jan, Sun eve & Mon **Bar Meals** L served Tue-Sat 12-2.30, Sun 12-3 Av main course £14 **Restaurant** L served Tue-Sat 12-2.30, Sun 12-3 D served Tue-Sat 6.30-9.30 Av 3 course à la carte fr £25 ⊕ FREE HOUSE ◀ Malvern Hills, Black Pear ♻ Stowford Press. **Facilities** Children welcome Children's menu Children's portions Play area Dogs allowed Garden Parking Wi-fi

TENBURY WELLS   Map 10 SO56

PICK OF THE PUBS

The Peacock Inn

WR15 8LL ☎ 01584 810506
dir: *On A456 (Kidderminster to Tenbury Wells)*

A 14th-century coaching inn with a sympathetic extension overlooking the River Teme. A pleasant patio eating area means you can relax outside and enjoy the views over the valley in summer. The inviting bars and oak-panelled restaurant are enhanced by oak beams, dried hops and open log fires, while upstairs the ghost of Mrs Brown, a former landlady, does her best to make her presence felt. Produce from local markets and specialist suppliers is used for the menus, which cover an eclectic mix of reasonably priced dishes. The bar menu ranges from a three-egg omelette with choice of fillings and served with chips; to chilli con carne; or rendang pedis - a home-made Indonesian beef curry made to a traditional family recipe. Other main courses tend towards the more usual: spicy meatballs; wholetail scampi; creamy pasta bake; and barbecued chicken fillet are among the choices.

Open all wk noon-3 6-11 Closed: 25 Dec eve **Bar Meals** L served all wk 12-2.30 **Restaurant** L served all wk 12-2.30 D served Tue-Sat 7-8.30 ⊕ FREE HOUSE ◀ Hobsons Best Bitter, Brakspear Oxford Gold, Banks's Mild, guest ale ♂ Thatcher's Gold. **Facilities** Children welcome Children's menu Children's portions Garden Parking

UPTON SNODSBURY   Map 10 SO95

Bants ★★★★ INN ♟

Worcester Rd WR7 4NN
☎ 01905 381282 ▤ 01905 381173
e-mail: info@bants.co.uk
dir: *Exit M5 junct 6, follow Evesham signs. At 2nd rdbt left onto A422 towards Stratford. Bants 2m on left*

Bants takes its name from its owners, Sue and Steve Bant, who have been running the pub for 25 years. A 16th-century free house serving traditional ales, it has real fires in winter warming an eclectic mix of ancient beams and modern furnishings. Traditional dishes with a modern twist and are served in three lounge bars and the dedicated conservatory restaurant. The food has a high comfort factor: typical choices include sea bass fillets on creamy dauphinoise potatoes and steak in a rich Stroganoff sauce. There are nine en suite rooms.

Open all day all wk **Bar Meals** food served all day **Restaurant** food served all day ⊕ FREE HOUSE ◀ London Pride, 6X. ♟ 12 **Facilities** Children welcome Children's menu Children's portions Dogs allowed Garden Parking Wi-fi **Rooms** 9

YORKSHIRE, EAST RIDING OF

BARMBY ON THE MARSH   Map 17 SE62

The King's Head

High St DN14 7HT ☎ 01757 630705 ▤ 01757 630957
e-mail: rainderpubcoltd@tiscali.co.uk
dir: *M62 junct 37 follow A614/Bridlington/York/Howden signs. Left at A63. At rdbt 1st exit onto A614/Booth Ferry Rd towards Goole. At rdbt 4th exit on B1228/Booth Ferry Rd. Left, through Asselby to Barmby on the Marsh*

Originating in the 17th century as a pub serving a ferry that crossed the local rivers Ouse and Derwent, this white-painted, pantiled old village local was painstakingly refurbished in 2008, producing a place for all tastes; from the flagged, beamed bar through a bright, modern lounge to the cosy, intimate restaurant. Several members of the family-run concern are trained chefs and make the most of Yorkshire's burgeoning larder; a chicken and leek pudding with tarragon gravy and vegetables just one of the tempting mains here. Another approach is via their innovative Yorkshire tapas menu; great open sandwiches, too, all washed down with a pint of Black Sheep or one of the regularly-changing guest beers. There's a take-away deli menu available, including ice creams!

Open Mon-Tue 5-11, Wed-Thu noon-2 5-11, Fri noon-2 5-mdnt, Sat noon-mdnt, Sun noon-11 Closed: Mon L, Tue L **Bar Meals** L served Wed-Fri 12-2, Sat-Sun all day D served Mon-Thu 5-8.30, Fri 5-9, Sat-Sun all day Av main course £8.25 **Restaurant** L served Sat-Sun all day booking required D served Mon-Thu 5-8.30, Fri 5-9, Sat-Sun all day booking required Av 3 course à la carte fr £21.95 ⊕ FREE HOUSE ◀ Black Sheep Bitter, 3 Guest ales (changed weekly). **Facilities** Children welcome Children's menu Children's portions Garden Parking

BEVERLEY   Map 17 TA03

The Ferguson Fawsitt Arms & Country Lodge ♟ NEW

East End, Walkington HU17 8RX
☎ 01482 882665 ▤ 01482 882665
e-mail: admin@fergusonfawsitt.com
web: www.fergusonfawsitt.co.uk
dir: *M62 junct 38 onto B1230, left on A1034, right onto B1230, on left in centre of Walkington*

Step back in time here, where little has changed since Victorian villagers first enjoyed hospitality in the 1860s; until the 1950s part of the inn was the village smithy.

Open fires, dark-wood panelling, carved settles and beams welcome those set on sampling a pint of Copper Dragon Golden Pippin, or diners intent on a good Sunday roast, steak pie from the carvery or a poached fish duo of salmon wrapped with pangasius fish. Accommodation is available.

The Ferguson Fawsitt Arms & Country Lodge

Open all day all wk Closed: 25 Dec **Bar Meals** L served all wk 12-5 D served Mon-Thu 5-9, Fri-Sat 5-9.30, Sun 12-9 Av main course £8.20 food served all day **Restaurant** L served Sun 12-2 booking required Fixed menu price fr £14.95 Av 3 course à la carte fr £22.50 ⊕ FREE HOUSE ◀ Abbot Ale, Old Speckled Hen, Golden Pippin. ♟ 10 **Facilities** Children welcome Children's menu Children's portions Garden Parking Wi-fi

DRIFFIELD   Map 17 TA05

Best Western The Bell ★★★ HL ♟

46 Market Place YO25 6AN
☎ 01377 256661 ▤ 01377 253228
e-mail: bell@bestwestern.co.uk
dir: *Enter town from A164, right at lights. Car park 50yds on left behind black railings*

A delightful 18th-century coaching inn, tastefully furnished with antiques and fine art. The Oak Bar limits beer miles by sticking to Driffield's Wold Top and an interesting selection of other local breweries; collectively, the 300 whiskies may have knocked up a higher tally. After an overnight stay, start the day with coffee and cream scones; then lunch, maybe a salad, in the bar; and dinner – oven-roasted breast of English duckling with spicy plum sauce, perhaps – in the oak-panelled dining room.

Open all day all wk Closed: 25 Dec, 1 Jan **Bar Meals** L served Mon-Sat 12-1.30 D served all wk 5-8.30 Av main course £8.50 **Restaurant** L served Sun 12-1.30 booking required D served Mon-Sat 6.30-8.30 booking required Fixed menu price fr £18.50 ⊕ FREE HOUSE ◀ Wold Top, Falling Stones, Mars Magic, Hambleton Stallion & Stud, Tom Wood Shepherds Delight. ♟ 10 **Facilities** Children welcome Children's portions Parking Wi-fi **Rooms** 16

FLAMBOROUGH — Map 17 TA27

The Seabirds Inn ▼

Tower St YO15 1PD ☎ 01262 850242 📠 **01262 851874**
dir: On B1255 E of Bridlington, 6m from train station

Head westwards from famous Flamborough Head and its lighthouse, and you'll swiftly arrive at this village pub which is over 200 years old. Good eating is the emphasis here, with a daily-changing specials board. Fresh fish dishes include grilled lemon sole and haddock fillet mornay; while meat options include steaks, gammon with egg or pineapple or both; and grilled butterfly chicken breast with garlic butter. There are headland walks and a golf course close by.

Open noon-3 6-11 Closed: Mon (winter)
Bar Meals L served all wk 12-2 D served Sun-Fri 6-8.30, Sat 6-9.30 Av main course £6.50 **Restaurant** L served all wk 12-2 D served Sun-Fri 6-8.30, Sat 6-9.30 booking required Av 3 course à la carte fr £25 ⊕ FREE HOUSE ◀ John Smith's, Interbrew, Tetleys Creamflow, Guest ales. ▼ 9 **Facilities** Children's menu Children's portions Dogs allowed Garden Parking

HUGGATE — Map 19 SE85

The Wolds Inn ★★★ INN

YO42 1YH ☎ 01377 288217
e-mail: huggate@woldsinn.freeserve.co.uk
dir: S off A166 between York & Driffield

Probably the highest inn on the Yorkshire Wolds, this family-run hostelry is 16th century in origin, with tiled roofs and white-painted chimneys, and a wood-panelled interior with open fires and gleaming brassware. The robust menu includes dishes such as smoked haddock and spring onion fishcakes; home-made chicken goujons; rack of lamb; or a selection of jackets, baguettes and sandwiches. For a 'mixed grill to remember', try the Wolds Topper.

Open noon-2 6-11 (Sun noon-10.30) (May-Sep Mon 6-11) Closed: Mon (Oct-Apr ex BH) **Bar Meals** L served Tue-Sun 12-2 D served Tue-Sun 6-9 (also Mon May-Sep) booking required Av main course £10 **Restaurant** L served Tue-Sat 12-2, Sun 12-6 booking required D served Tue-Sun 6-9 (also Mon May-Sep) booking required Fixed menu price fr £13.90 Av 3 course à la carte fr £17.70 ⊕ FREE HOUSE ◀ Tetley Bitter, Timothy Taylor Landlord.
Facilities Children welcome Children's menu Children's portions Garden Parking **Rooms** 3

KILHAM — Map 17 TA06

The Old Star Inn

Church St YO25 4RG ☎ 01262 420619
e-mail: oldstarkilham@hotmail.com
dir: Between Driffield & Bridlington on A164. 6m from Driffield. 9m from Bridlington

Standing opposite the village church, this pantiled, multi-roomed old village pub with open fires is handy for the Wolds, the spectacular Flamborough Head and the old fishing port of Filey. Home-cooked food is sourced from local suppliers, with particular attention to reducing the travelling time of ingredients. Special diets are catered for, and children have half price portions. The licensee is a dedicated supporter of Yorkshire beers, with regulars such as Daleside and Copper Dragon complemented by a popular annual beer and cider festival each September.

Open all wk 5-11 (Mon 6-11, Fri (Summer only) 12-2 4-12, Sat noon-mdnt, Sun noon-10.30)
Bar Meals L served Fri (Summer only) 12-2, Sat 12-2, Sun 12-4 D served Mon-Sat 6-9 **Restaurant** L served Sun 12-4.30 booking required D served Sat 6-8.30 booking required ⊕ ENTERPRISE INNS ◀ John Smith's, Black Sheep, Theakston, Copper Dragon, Timothy Taylor, Daleside. **Facilities** Children welcome Children's portions Dogs allowed Garden Beer festival Parking Wi-fi

LOW CATTON — Map 17 SE75

The Gold Cup Inn ▼

YO41 1EA ☎ 01759 371354
dir: 1m S of A166 or 1m N of A1079, E of York

Solid tables and pews - reputedly made from a single oak tree - feature in the restaurant of this 300-year-old, family-run free house. There's a large beer garden, for just enjoying a pint of Black Bull perhaps, plus an adjoining paddock that runs down to the River Derwent. On the menu expect to find mermaid's basket (seafood in filo); venison steak slowly braised in wine; half a crispy roast duckling with cherry and brandy sauce; and spinach and cream cheese cannelloni.

Open noon-2.30 6-11 (Sat-Sun noon-11) Closed: Mon L **Bar Meals** L served Tue-Fri 12-2.30, Sat-Sun 12-6 D served all wk 6-9 Av main course £10 **Restaurant** L served Sun 12-8.30 booking required D served all wk 6-9 booking required Fixed menu price fr £14 Av 3 course à la carte fr £20 ⊕ FREE HOUSE ◀ Theakston Black Bull. ▼ 13 **Facilities** Children welcome Children's menu Children's portions Play area Dogs allowed Garden Parking

LUND — Map 17 SE94

The Wellington Inn ▼

19 The Green YO25 9TE
☎ 01377 217294 📠 **01377 217192**
e-mail: tellmemore@thewellingtoninn.co.uk
dir: On B1248 NE of Beverley

Nicely situated opposite the picture-postcard village green in a stunning rural location, this country pub is popular with locals and visitors alike, whether for a pint of real ale, a glass of wine, or a plate of decent food. Inside is a unique blend of old and new where you can choose from the traditional pub menu or from the carte in the more formal restaurant. Expect mouthwatering dishes like Godminster Cheddar and cumin seed twice baked soufflé; pea and honey roast ham hock risotto; pan fried lambs' liver and sautéed lambs kidney with potato and bacon hotpot; or grilled Cornish mackerel fillets on paella risotto.

Open 12-3 6.30-11 Closed: Mon L **Bar Meals** L served Tue-Sun 12-2 D served Tue-Sat 6.30-9
Restaurant D served Tue-Sat 7-9 booking required ⊕ FREE HOUSE ◀ Timothy Taylor Landlord, Black Sheep Best, John Smith's, Copper Dragon, regular guest ale. ▼ 11 **Facilities** Children welcome Children's menu Children's portions Garden Parking Wi-fi

SOUTH CAVE — Map 17 SE93

The Fox and Coney Inn ▼

52 Market Place HU15 2AT
☎ 01430 424044 📠 **01430 425281**
e-mail: info@foxandconey.co.uk
dir: 4m E of M62 on A63. 4m N of Brough mainline railway

Right in the heart of South Cave, this former coaching inn dates from 1739 and is probably the oldest building in the village. With a new landlord, the inn, which is handy for walkers on the nearby Wolds Way, was known simply as The Fox until William Goodlad added the Coney (rabbit) in 1788. The bar area has two original fireplaces which are lit on cold days, original beams, and very popular lunchtime sandwiches. In the restaurant area, with tables set with crisp white tablecloths and napkins, expect a daily menu with seasonal specials. Food is sourced locally, especially the meat, which is all free range.

Open all wk 11.30-11 **Bar Meals** L served Mon-Sat 12-3, Sun 12-8 D served Mon-Sat 4.30-9, Sun 12-8 **Restaurant** L served Mon-Sat 12-3, Sun 12-8 D served Mon-Sat 4.30-9, Sun 12-8 ◀ Timothy Taylor Landlord, John Smith's, Theakston Cool Cask, Deuchars IPA, Guest ales. ▼ 10 **Facilities** Children welcome Family room Dogs allowed Garden Parking

SOUTH DALTON   Map 17 SE94

PICK OF THE PUBS

The Pipe & Glass Inn ◉◉ ♟

West End HU17 7PN ☎ 01430 810246
e-mail: email@pipeandglass.co.uk
dir: *Just off B1248 (Beverley to Malton road). 7m from Beverley*

James and Kate Mackenzie's part-15th, part 17th-century inn stands on the site of the original gatehouse to Dalton Hall in the pretty village of South Dalton. The Mackenzie's may have transformed it into a destination dining pub, earning it two AA Rosettes, but it maintains a local pub atmosphere, with Wold Top, Black Sheep and York ales on tap in the pubby bar. The restaurant has a more contemporary look and the large conservatory, which houses a magnificent 24-seater table, looks out over the garden. James sources top-notch local and seasonal produce for his innovative modern British menus, which may feature baked hare and juniper pasty for starters, followed by slow-cooked lamb with mutton and kidney faggot, butternut squash purée and soubise sauce, and ginger burnt cream with stewed Yorkshire rhubarb for pudding. On the lunch and specials menu you'll find sandwiches and ploughman's, fish pie and sausages with bubble-and-squeak and onion gravy. The wines are sourced entirely from small producers. A new private dining room is planned for 2011 and James is writing a cookery book.

Open noon-3 6.30-11 (Sun noon-10.30) Closed: 2wks Jan, Mon (ex BH) **Bar Meals** L served Tue-Sat 12-2, Sun 12-4 D served Tue-Sat 6.30-9.30 **Restaurant** L served Tue-Sat 12-2, Sun 12-4 booking required D served Tue-Sat 6.30-9.30 booking required ⊕ FREE HOUSE ◀ Wold Top, Copper Dragon, Black Sheep, Cropton, John Smith's, York Brewery ♂ Old Rosie. ♟ 15 **Facilities** Children welcome Children's menu Children's portions Garden Parking

SUTTON UPON DERWENT   Map 17 SE74

St Vincent Arms ♟

Main St YO41 4BN ☎ 01904 608349
e-mail: enquiries@stvincentarms.co.uk
dir: *From A64 follow signs for A1079. Turn right, follow signs for Elvington on B1228. Through Elvington to Sutton upon Derwent*

The name comes from John Jervis, mentor to Admiral Lord Nelson and created the first Earl of St Vincent in the 18th century. This is a warm family-run pub with an old-fashioned welcoming atmosphere, minus music or gaming machines but plus great food and an excellent selection of beers. Food options include tempting sandwiches, hot ciabatta, salads and steaks at lunch, and in the evening dishes such as fillet of plaice with brown shrimp and caper butter and parsley mash, or venison steak with a port wine sauce and a mini venison pie.

Open all wk 11.30-3 6-11 (Sun 12-3 6.30-10.30) **Bar Meals** L served all wk 12-2 D served all wk 6.30-9.30 Av main course £11 **Restaurant** L served all wk 12-2 D served all wk 6.30-9.30 ⊕ FREE HOUSE ◀ Timothy Taylor Landlord, Fuller's ESB, Yorkshire Terrier, Wells Bombardier, Fuller's London Pride, Old Mill Bitter, York Brewery Terrier. ♟ 16 **Facilities** Children welcome Garden Parking

YORKSHIRE, NORTH

AKEBAR   Map 19 SE19

The Friar's Head ♟

Akebar Park DL8 5LY
☎ 01677 450201 & 450591   ▤ 01677 450046
e-mail: info@akebarpark.com
dir: *From A1 at Leeming Bar onto A684, 7m towards Leyburn. Entrance at Akebar Park*

At the entrance to a stunning, peaceful holiday park, this typical stone-built Dales pub overlooks beautiful countryside and grounds, where bowls or croquet can be played on the lawn. Inside you'll find exposed beams and stonework and a roaring fire in winter. The large south-facing conservatory dining room called The Cloister is a stunning feature, particularly by candlelight, with its stone flags, lush planting and fruiting vines. Hand-pulled local ales are served, and typical dishes include Thai stir-fried prawns with egg noodles and Yorkshire venison steak with port wine jus.

Open all wk 10-3 6-11.30 (Fri-Sun 10am-11.30pm Jul-Sep) Closed: 25 Dec, 26 Dec eve & 1 Jan **Bar Meals** L served all wk 12-2.30 D served all wk 6-9.30 **Restaurant** L served all wk 12-2.30 booking required D served all wk 6-9.30 booking required ⊕ FREE HOUSE ◀ John Smith's & Theakston Best Bitter, Black Sheep Best, Timothy Taylor Landlord. ♟ 12 **Facilities** Children welcome Children's portions Garden Parking

ALDWARK   Map 19 SE46

The Aldwark Arms ♟ NEW

YO61 1UB ☎ 01347 838324
e-mail: enquiries@aldwarkarms.co.uk
dir: *From York ring road take A19 N. Left into Warehill Lane signed Tollerton & Helperby. Through Tollerton, follow Aldwark signs*

From near-closure as the Bulls Head, this handsome pub has risen phoenix-like under its new guise as a dining inn dedicated to supporting farms and estates in the Hambleton area of Yorkshire. Sofas, open fires, wooden floors all draw locals to indulge in a jar of perhaps Great Heck White Rabbit guest bitter, whilst diners travel considerable distances to sample chef/patron Chris Hill's exceptional menu – think assiette of rabbit starter followed by braised venison suet pudding and roast sirloin with claret wine gravy, taken in the airy restaurant or cosy bar.

Open 12-3 5-11 (Sat-Sun 12-11) Closed: Mon **Bar Meals** Av main course £13 **Restaurant** L served Tue-Sun 12-2 booking required D served Tue-Sun 6-9 booking required Fixed menu price fr £16.50 Av 3 course à la carte fr £25 food served all day ⊕ FREE HOUSE ◀ Timothy Taylor Landlord, Black Sheep, Guest ales ♂ Thatchers Gold. ♟ 12 **Facilities** Children welcome Children's menu Children's portions Garden Parking Wi-fi

APPLETON-LE-MOORS   Map 19 SE78

The Moors Inn

YO62 6TF ☎ 01751 417435
e-mail: enquiries@moorsinn.co.uk
dir: *On A170 between Pickering & Kirbymoorside*

Whether you're interested in walking or sightseeing by car, this inn is a good choice for its location and good home-cooked food. Set in a small moors village with lovely scenery in every direction, in summer you can sit in the large garden and enjoy the splendid views. Dishes include beef brisket, mash and red wine gravy; and twice baked sun blush tomato and Stilton soufflé, and in addition to hand-pumped Black Bull and Black Sheep, there is a selection of 50 malt whiskies and a good choice of wines by the glass.

Open all day all wk ⊕ FREE HOUSE ◀ Black Sheep, Black Bull, Landlords ♂ Stowford Press. **Facilities** Children welcome Children's menu Children's portions Dogs allowed Garden Parking Wi-fi

APPLETREEWICK   Map 19 SE06

The Craven Arms

BD23 6DA ☎ 01756 720270
e-mail: info@craven-cruckbarn.co.uk
dir: *2m E of Burnsall off B6160*

Enjoy spectacular views of the River Wharfe and Simon's Seat from this 16th-century Dales pub, which was originally a farm and later used as a weaving shed and courthouse. The village stocks are still outside. The building retains its original beams, flagstone floors, gas lighting and magnificent fireplace. Traditional real ales are served and there's a beer festival every October. The menu, on a blackboard on the wall, offers a choice of around 12 mains that change daily, using locally-sourced food. A heather-thatched cruck barn to the rear serves as restaurant and function room.

Open all day all wk **Bar Meals** L served Mon-Thu 12-2, Fri-Sun 12-2.30 D served Mon-Sat 6.30-9, Sun 6.30-8.30 Av main course £11.50 **Restaurant** L served all wk 12-2.30 D served Mon-Sat 6.30-9, Sun 6.30-8.30 Av 3 course à la carte fr £18.50 ⊕ FREE HOUSE ◀ Hetton Cruck Barn Bitter, Hetton Pale Ale, Saltaire Raspberry Blonde, Moorhouses Blonde, Black Witch ♂ Kingstone Press. **Facilities** Children welcome Children's menu Children's portions Play area Dogs allowed Garden Beer festival Parking Wi-fi

ASENBY Map 19 SE37

PICK OF THE PUBS

Crab & Lobster ◉◉

Dishforth Rd YO7 3QL
☎ **01845 577286** 📄 **01845 577109**
e-mail: reservations@crabandlobster.co.uk
dir: *From A1(M) take A168 towards Thirsk, follow signs for Asenby*

In the heart of the North Yorkshire countryside, this unique 17th-century thatched pub with its friendly bar and adjacent small hotel is set amid seven acres of garden, lake and streams. Inside and out it is festooned with everything from old advertising signs to fishing nets, an Aladdin's cave of antiques and artefacts from around the world. Equally famous for its innovative cuisine and special gourmet extravaganzas, the menus show influences from France and Italy. Starters leave no doubt you are in seafood heaven: steamed Shetland mussels in a light curry cream sauce; grilled half shell queenie scallops, garlic butter, Cheddar and Gruyère; Loch Fyne smoked salmon, whipped horseradish and warm blinis. The theme continues into main courses with the likes of roast monkfish tail, fricassee of lentils with brown shrimp sauce; grilled fresh local halibut, cauliflower and almond purée, seared king scallops and lobster bisque. For those who prefer meat, the range of locally-sourced ingredients will not disappoint: hazelnut-crusted loin of Yorkshire venison with apple tarragon rösti; or honey-spiced breast of Barbary duck with oriental vegetable stir fry. There are outside areas for eating and drinking.

Open all day all wk **Bar Meals** L served all wk 12-2.30 D served Sun-Fri 7-9, Sat 6.30-9.30 ⊕ FREE HOUSE 🍺 John Smith's, Scots 1816, Golden Pippin, Guinness. **Facilities** Children welcome Children's portions Garden Parking

AUSTWICK Map 18 SD76

The Game Cock Inn

The Green LA2 8BB ☎ **015242 51226**
e-mail: eric.coupey@hotmail.co.uk
dir: *Follow the A65 from Skipton or Kendal, then follow signs for Austwick*

Expect a warm welcome at this traditional, award-winning pub, set in the limestone village of Austwick. There's a large garden and children's play area, with winter log fires in the cosy bar and a restaurant. Expect real ales and an imaginative menu including traditional English, French and Mediterranean dishes. The beef, rabbit and majority of the lamb is sourced from a farm just three miles away. There are savoury galettes and sweet crêpes, plus main courses such as boeuf bourguignon, Milanese chicken and lapin à la moutarde. There are regular specials nights – Breton, French and steak.

Open 11.30-3, from 5 Mon-Fri (Sat-Sun from 11.30am) **Bar Meals** L served Mon-Fri 11.30-2, Sat-Sun 11.30-9 D served Mon-Fri 5-9 Av main course £10.99 **Restaurant** L served Mon-Fri 11.30-2, Sat-Sun 11.30-9 booking required D served Mon-Fri 5-9 booking required Av 3 course à la carte fr £20 ⊕ THWAITES 🍺 Original, Bomber, Wainwright, Nutty Black, Guest ales ♻ Kingstone. **Facilities** Children welcome Children's menu Children's portions Play area Dogs allowed Garden Parking

AYSGARTH Map 19 SE08

PICK OF THE PUBS

The George & Dragon Inn 🍷

DL8 3AD ☎ **01969 663358** 📄 **01969 663773**
e-mail: info@georgeanddragonaysgarth.co.uk
dir: *On A684 midway between Leyburn & Hawes. Pub in village centre*

The George & Dragon Inn is a 17th-century Grade II listed building in a superb location in the Yorkshire Dales National Park, near the beautiful Aysgarth Falls. The area is perfect for walking, touring and visiting local attractions, including Forbidden Corner, the Wensleydale Railway, and the cheese factory. The owners are proud to continue a centuries-long tradition of Yorkshire hospitality at the inn, with customers keeping cosy in winter by the fireside, and in summer enjoying their drinks and meals out on the furnished flower-filled patio. Well-kept real ales are served, and the inn has a great reputation for its traditional food including steak pie and fish and chips. In the early evening a fixed-price menu meets the needs of ravenous walkers, while a broader à la carte choice comes into force after 7pm. Choices could be home-made chicken liver pâté with apple chutney; Wensleydale pork sausages and mash; or braised pork belly, mash, choucroute and cider reduction.

Open all wk noon-close Closed: 2wks Jan **Bar Meals** L served all wk 12-2 D served all wk 6-8.30, May-Sep 5.30-8.30 ⊕ FREE HOUSE 🍺 Black Sheep Best, John Smith's Cask, Yorkshire Dales ales, Guest ales ♻ Thatchers Gold. 🍷 16 **Facilities** Children welcome Dogs allowed Garden Parking

BAGBY Map 19 SE48

The Bagby Inn

Main St YO7 2PF ☎ **01845 597315**
e-mail: thebagbyinn@hotmail.com
dir: *2m SE of Thirsk. Easily accessed from A19 & A170. Follow signs for Bagby, Balk & Kilburn*

Yorkshire flavours predominate in this 18th century whitewashed free house - a hub for the local community. Formerly The Roebuck Inn, expect a welcoming and friendly atmosphere and a menu of great home-made food. There's a good selection from the grill plus traditional choices such as home-made steak and ale pie, lamb Henry or beer-battered haddock with home-cut chips. Finish with home-made fruit crumble and custard. Look out for summer barbecues. Change of hands.

Open noon-3 5-11 (Fri 12-3 5-mdnt Sat noon-mdnt Sun 11am-11pm) Closed: Mon ⊕ FREE HOUSE 🍺 John Smith's Cask, Black Sheep Best, Theakston Black Bull Cask, Guest ales. **Facilities** Children welcome Children's menu Children's portions Dogs allowed Garden Parking

BEDALE Map 19 SE28

The Castle Arms Inn
★★★★ INN **NEW**

Meadow Ln, Snape DL8 2TB ☎ **01677 470270**
e-mail: castlearms@aol.com
dir: *From A1 (M) at Leeming Bar take A684 to Bedale. A x-roads in town centre take B6268 to Masham. Approx 2m, turn left to Thorp Perrow Arboretum. In 0.5m left for Snape*

Expect a warm welcome at this family-run Grade II listed 14th century inn, set in the sleepy village of Snape. With comfortable accommodation available, it makes a perfect base for walking the Yorkshire Dales and North York Moors, or visiting nearby Thorp Perrow arboretum. The homely interior is all exposed beams and horse brasses, with a real fire in the bar where you can sample a fine range of traditional ales. A meal in the cosy restaurant might take in roast parsnip and sweet potato followed by Yorkshire game casserole with apple and thyme dumplings, finishing with tangy lemon posset.

Open all wk 12-3 6-12 **Bar Meals** L served all wk 12-2 D served all wk 7-9 (ex Sun winter) Av main course £9.50 **Restaurant** L served all wk 12-2 D served all wk 7-9 (ex Sun winter) Av 3 course à la carte fr £22.50 ⊕ MARSTON'S 🍺 Marston's Pedigree, Jennings Bitter, Banks's Bitter. **Facilities** Children welcome Children's menu Children's portions Dogs allowed Garden Parking **Rooms** 9

BILBROUGH Map 16 SE54

The Three Hares Country Inn & Restaurant

Main St YO23 3PH ☎ **01937 832128**
dir: *Off A64 between A659 Tadcaster & A1237 York junct*

This charming 18th-century country pub is situated in the lovely village of Bilbrough, just outside York, and draws race-goers and locals alike. A light and smartly turned-out brick-walled dining room provides an elegant setting for the food; Sunday evening is now steak night. Any day of the week you'll find an excellent selection of real ales, such as Copper Dragon. A heated terrace completes the package.

Open all day all wk noon-11.30 **Bar Meals** L served Mon-Sat 12-9, Sun 12-3 booking required D served Mon-Sat 12-9, Sun 6-8 booking required food served all day **Restaurant** L served Mon-Sat 12-9, Sun 12-3 booking required D served Mon-Sat 12-9, Sun 6-8 booking required food served all day ⊕ FREE HOUSE 🍺 Copper Dragon, Tetley's. **Facilities** Children welcome Children's portions Garden Parking Wi-fi

PICK OF THE PUBS

The Black Bull Inn ♛

BOROUGHBRIDGE　　　　　Map 19 SE36

6 St James Square YO51 9AR
☎ 01423 322413　📠 01423 323915
web: www.blackbullboroughbridge.co.uk
dir: *From A1(M) junct 48 take B6265
E for 1m*

Using a false name, highwayman Dick
Turpin stayed at this ancient inn which
stands in a quiet corner of the market
square and was one of the main stopping
points for travellers on the long road
between London and the North. Today you
have to turn off the A1(M), but it's well
worth it to discover an inn built in 1258
that retains its ancient beams, low ceilings
and roaring open fires, not to mention one
that also gives houseroom to the supposed
ghosts of a monk, a blacksmith, a cavalier
and a small boy.

Tony Burgess is the landlord and the man
responsible for high standards that exclude
anything electronic which makes a noise.
The hot and cold sandwich selection in the
bar is wide, while in the dining room expect
a good choice of traditional pub food on
menus offering lamb shank on creamy
mash in port and honey gravy; salmon
steak on fried noodles with spicy oriental
sauce; Barnsley chop and other grills; and
Sizzlers, such as Mexican spiced vegetables
in a hot sweet salsa sauce; and pan-fried
duck breast topped with peppers,
mushrooms, bamboo shoots and sweet and
sour sauce.

Frequently changing blackboard specials
widen the choice to include halibut steak
with smoked salmon and fresh prawns in
white wine sauce; and wild button
mushroom ragout with garlic slices and
fresh salad. Possible followers are apple
pie and custard; citrus lemon tart; or mixed
ice creams, brandy snaps and fruit purées.

In the bar, real ale drinkers will find
favourites from Timothy Taylor, Cottage
Brewery and Theakston's, while the wine
list shows all the signs of careful
compilation.

Open all day all wk 11-11 (Fri-Sat 11am-
mdnt, Sun noon-11) **Bar Meals** L served
all wk 12-2 D served all wk 6-9 food
served all day **Restaurant** L served all wk
12-2 booking required D served all wk 6-9
booking required ⬛ FREE HOUSE

🍺 John Smith's, Timothy Taylor Best
Bitter, Cottage Brewing, Wells Bombardier
Premium Bitter, Theakston, guest ale.
♛ 11 **Facilities** Children's menu Children's
portions Dogs allowed Parking

BOROUGHBRIDGE — Map 19 SE36

PICK OF THE PUBS

The Black Bull Inn ⚑

See Pick of the Pubs on page 509

PICK OF THE PUBS

Crown Inn Roecliffe
★★★★★ INN ⊛ ⚑ NEW

Roecliffe YO51 9LY ☎ 01423 322300
e-mail: info@crowninnroecliffe.co.uk
dir: A1(M) junct 48, follow signs for Boroughbridge. At rdbt exit towards Roecliffe & brown tourist signs

Karl and Amanda Mainey have worked wonders since taking over this handsome 16th-century former coaching inn in 2007. Just minutes from the A1M (junction 48) and smack beside pretty Roecliffe's neatly trimmed green, the striking green-painted pub has been restored to its former glory, with stone-flagged floors, old oak beams and crackling log fires featuring prominently in the civilised and smartly furnished bar and dining rooms. Local produce is name-checked – farm meats, game shoots, Whitby fish and crab, and kippers, salmon and haddock are smoked in-house – and put to fine use on a clearly-focused modern British menu, backed up by daily chalkboard specials. Everything is home-made, from pork belly and confit duck terrine with cranberry jelly and pear chutney for a starter, to Cold Kirby Farm lamb shank with red wine, garlic mash and lavender jus, or lemon sole grilled with rock shrimps, samphire and beurre noisette for main course. Delicious puddings may include dark chocolate terrine, or why not try a plate of hand-made Yorkshire cheeses. The four elegant bedrooms, each with sleigh beds, authentic antiques and free-standing baths, are the icing on the cake.

Open all wk 12-3.30 5-12 **Bar Meals** L served Mon-Sat 12-2.30, Sun 12-7 D served Mon-Sat 6-9.30, Sun 12-7 Av main course £15 **Restaurant** L served Mon-Sat 12-2.30, Sun 12-7 D served Mon-Sat 6-9.30, Sun 12-7 Fixed menu price fr £15.95 Av 3 course à la carte fr £25 ⊕ FREE HOUSE ◀ Four weekly changing ales. ⚑ 30 **Facilities** Children welcome Children's menu Children's portions Dogs allowed Garden Parking **Rooms** 4

BREARTON — Map 19 SE36

PICK OF THE PUBS

Malt Shovel Inn ⚑

See Pick of the Pubs on page 512

BROMPTON-BY-SAWDON — Map 17 SE98

The Cayley Arms ⚑

YO13 9DA ☎ 01723 859372
e-mail: joannabou@hotmail.co.uk
dir: On A170 in Brompton-by-Sawdon between Pickering & Scarborough

Named after pioneering aviator Sir George Cayley, this pub stands in the heart of picturesque Brompton-by-Sawdon. Its cosy log fire and friendly atmosphere have been the centre of village life for over a century. All food is sourced locally and specials include crab, lobster and mussels. Chunky lunchtime sandwiches with home-made crisps and hot baguettes are supplemented by hot dishes such as warm chicken and bacon salad or fisherman's pie. Outside is an award-winning garden and decked area where you can enjoy a pint of Black Sheep or Hobgoblin.

Open noon-3 5-close (Mon 6-close) Closed: Mon L **Bar Meals** L served Tue-Sun 12-2 D served Mon-Sat 6-9 Av main course £8 **Restaurant** L served Tue-Sat 12-2 D served Mon-Sat 6-9 ⊕ PUNCH TAVERNS ◀ Tetley Cask, Black Sheep Cask, Hobgoblin. ⚑ 10 **Facilities** Children welcome Children's menu Children's portions Play area Dogs allowed Garden Parking Wi-fi

---

BROUGHTON — Map 18 SD95

PICK OF THE PUBS

The Bull ⊛

See Pick of the Pubs on page 513

BURNSALL — Map 19 SE06

PICK OF THE PUBS

The Devonshire Fell
★★★★ RR ⊛⊛ ⚑ NEW

BD23 6BT ☎ 01756 729000 📠 01756 729009
e-mail: manager@devonshirefell.co.uk
dir: On B6160, 6m from Bolton Abbey rdbt, A59 junct

The former Victorian club for gentlemen mill-owners stands perched on a hillside on the edge of the Duke of Devonshire's estate. Given the lineage and the stunning Yorkshire Dales setting, one would expect polished antiques and a classic country-house feel, but the decor is bright and lively, with vibrant colours, polished floorboards, and bold, contemporary works of art throughout the relaxing, open-plan lounge bar and conservatory restaurant, and the quirky, hugely individual boutique-style bedrooms. Equally bang up-to-date is Daniel Birk's modern repertoire of Mediterranean-inspired dishes, which may take in ham hock and foie gras terrine with cep purée, roast cod with confit potato, curly kale and a caper and shallot beurre blanc, and glazed lemon tart in the restaurant. Simpler, more traditional dishes like smoked salmon and scrambled egg, the Fell burger and fish and chips are served in the bar, alongside local Copper Dragon

---

ales. Overnight guests have use of the luxury Health and Beauty Therapy Spa at Devonshire Arms at nearby Bolton Abbey.

Open all day all wk **Bar Meals** Av main course £14.95 **Restaurant** Av 3 course à la carte fr £26 ⊕ FREE HOUSE ◀ Copper Dragon Scotts 1816, Golden Pippin, Trueman. ⚑ 10 **Facilities** Children welcome Children's menu Children's portions Garden Parking Wi-fi **Rooms** 12

PICK OF THE PUBS

The Red Lion ★★ HL ⚑

By the Bridge BD23 6BU
☎ 01756 720204 📠 01756 720292
e-mail: info@redlion.co.uk
dir: From Skipton take A59 E, take B6160 towards Bolton Abbey, Burnsall 7m

This 16th-century ferryman's inn overlooks the River Wharfe as it gently curves under a magnificent five-arch bridge. Large gardens and terraces make it an ideal spot for sunny days. The Grayshon family have sympathetically upgraded the interior, retaining its beamed ceilings and creaky sloping floors. The original 'one-up, one-down' structure, now the oak-panelled and floored main bar, is the focal point of the hotel. Bar food includes lunchtime sandwiches and light meals such as ham hock terrine with shallot compote; and shepherd's pie or pork belly with a spring vegetable and smoked bacon jardinière in the evening. The main menu ups the ante with the likes of Thai style fish fritters, followed by oxtail and potato pie. If you are staying over in one of the bedrooms look out for the horse trough – it was easier to build the steps around it.

Open all day all wk 8am-11.30pm **Bar Meals** L served Mon-Sat 12-2.30, Sun 12-9 D served all wk 7-9 **Restaurant** L served Mon-Sat 12-2.30, Sun 12-9 ⊕ FREE HOUSE ◀ Timothy Taylor Golden Best, Theakston Best Bitter, Copper Dragon. ⚑ 14 **Facilities** Children welcome Play area Family room Dogs allowed Garden Parking **Rooms** 25

CALDWELL — Map 19 NZ11

Brownlow Arms ⚑

DL11 7QH ☎ 01325 718471 📠 01325 718471
e-mail: brownlowarms@mail.com
dir: From A1 at Scotch Corner take A66 towards Bowes. Right onto B6274 to Caldwell. Or from A1 junct 56 take B6275 N. 1st left through Mesonby to junct with B6274. Right to Caldwell

Set in delightful, rolling countryside between Barnard Castle and Darlington, fine food is to the fore at this updated stone inn in the tiny, delightful village of Caldwell. A blend of traditional and modern rooms is the setting for unpicking a phenomenal menu of game, fish, fowl and meat; try the king scallops on black pudding with pea purée and oyster sauce; individual suet steak and kidney pudding; roast partridge in Madeira sauce. With 10 wines by the glass, plenty more bins and reliable Yorkshire real ales, time passes easily here.

Open all wk 5.30-10.30 (Sat-Sun noon-11) Closed: 25 Dec **Bar Meals** L served Sat-Sun all day fr 12 booking required D served Mon-Fri 5.30-9 booking required **Restaurant** L served Sat-Sun all day fr 12 booking required D served Mon-Fri 5.30-9, Sat-Sun 5-9.30 booking required ⊕ FREE HOUSE ◄ Timothy Taylor Landlord, Black Sheep, John Smith's, Guinness. ♀ 10 **Facilities** Children welcome Children's menu Children's portions Garden Parking

---

CARTHORPE   Map 19 SE38

PICK OF THE PUBS

The Fox & Hounds

DL8 2LG ☎ 01845 567433
dir: Off A1, signed on both N'bound & S'bound carriageways

The Fox and Hounds has been serving its locals in the sleepy village of Carthorpe for over 200 years. A family-run pub with a warm welcome, Helen Taylor (whose parents bought the pub in 1983) and her husband Vincent take pride in the quality of their refreshments and food, and have won many awards to prove it. Beers include Black Sheep brewed nearby at Masham, while the wine choice is plentiful and global in scope. The restaurant was once the village smithy, and the old anvil and other tools of the trade are still on display, giving a nice sense of history to the place. The pub's excellent reputation for food is built on named suppliers and daily fresh fish deliveries; home-made products such as jams and chutneys are available for sale at the bar. A typical dinner choice could begin with duck filled filo parcels, and continue with a chicken breast stuffed with Coverdale cheese. A warm chocolate, pear and almond tart brings a happy conclusion.

Open Tue-Sun 12-3 7-11 Closed: 25-26 Dec eve & 1st wk Jan, Mon **Bar Meals** L served Tue-Sun 12-2 D served Tue-Sun 7-9.30 **Restaurant** L served Tue-Sun 12-2 D served Tue-Sun 7-9.30 ⊕ FREE HOUSE ◄ Black Sheep Best, Worthington's Bitter ♂ Thatchers Gold. **Facilities** Children welcome Children's portions Parking

---

CHAPEL LE DALE   Map 18 SD77

The Old Hill Inn

LA6 3A4 ☎ 015242 41256
dir: From Ingleton take B6255 4m, on right

Built as a farm, this inn dates in part to 1615 and once served passing drovers. It is run by a family of chefs, one of whom is renowned for his spectacular sugar sculptures. You'll find beautiful views of the Dales and many walks on the doorstep, and some of Yorkshire's most famous ales behind the bar. Lunchtime snacks embrace sandwiches, home-cooked ham (hot or cold) and

home-made sausages. Larger plates may include lamb shanks, confit of duck or venison steaks.

Open Tue-Sun Closed: 24-25 Dec, Mon (ex BH) **Bar Meals** L served Tue-Sat 12-2.30, Sun 12-3 booking required D served Tue-Fri & Sun 6.30-8.45, Sat 6-8.45 booking required Av main course £11.95 **Restaurant** L served Tue-Sat 12-2.30, Sun 12-3 booking required D served Tue-Fri & Sun 6.30-8.45, Sat 6-8.45 booking required ⊕ FREE HOUSE ◄ Black Sheep Best & Ale, Theakstons Best, Dent Aviator, Guest beer ♂ Thatchers Gold, Aspall. **Facilities** Children welcome Children's menu Children's portions Dogs allowed Garden Parking

---

CLAPHAM   Map 18 SD76

New Inn

LA2 8HH ☎ 01524 251203   📄 01524 251496
e-mail: info@newinn-clapham.co.uk
dir: On A65 in Yorkshire Dales National Park

Set in the charming village of Clapham beneath the famous summit of Ingleborough in Three Peaks country, this 18th-century inn offers a delightful blend of old and new. The honest, wholesome food uses local produce, particularly lamb and beef. Dishes range from a starter of black pudding fritters with mustard sauce, to main courses such as poached sea bream with caper butter; risotto with wild mushrooms, smoked chicken and chorizo; or crusty steak pie. Naturally, this is a popular base for walking holidays.

Open all day all wk 11am-mdnt (Fri-Sat 11am-1am) ⊕ ENTERPRISE INNS ◄ Black Sheep Best, Timothy Taylor Landlord, Copper Dragon Pippin, Copper Dragon Best, Bowland Hen Harrier. **Facilities** Children welcome Children's menu Dogs allowed Garden Parking Wi-fi

---

COLTON   Map 16 SE54

PICK OF THE PUBS

Ye Old Sun Inn ♀

Main St LS24 8EP
☎ 01904 744261   📄 01904 744261
e-mail: info@yeoldsuninn.co.uk
dir: 3-4m from York, off A64

This 17th-century coaching inn sits in an idyllic country setting. It has undergone major refurbishment, increasing the dining area and making a dedicated bar area for local drinkers. A marquee in the garden, overlooking rolling countryside, is used for large functions. The award-winning pub holds a beer festival in the summer, and prides itself on serving fine local seasonal food and ales. Lunches include light bites such as sandwiches, salads and wraps; or there is Sunday lunch of locally sourced roasted meats; chef's specials and a dinner menu. Expect Yorkshire-style main courses such as pot-roasted chicken cooked with red wine, mushroom, tomato, smoked bacon and tarragon; Kirby Malzeard rib-eye steak with creamy Yorkshire Blue or garlic and herb butter; or stone bass

steak with goat's cheese crust and tomato ratatouille-style sauce. All dishes come with a wine recommendation. Desserts include a platter of chef's 'dinky' desserts, a collection of home-made desserts all on one plate.

Open all wk 12-2.30 6-11 (Sun 12-10.30) **Bar Meals** L served Mon-Sat 12-2.30, Sun 12-7 booking required D served Mon-Sat 6-9.30 booking required Av main course £15 **Restaurant** Av 3 course à la carte fr £25 ⊕ FREE HOUSE ◄ Timothy Taylor Landlord, Timothy Taylor Golden Best, Black Sheep, Rudgate Battle Axe, Ossett Brewery, Moorhouse's, Guest ale ♂ Aspall. ♀ 18 **Facilities** Children welcome Children's menu Children's portions Garden Beer festival Parking Wi-fi

---

CRAY   Map 18 SD97

PICK OF THE PUBS

The White Lion Inn ♀

Cray BD23 5JB ☎ 01756 760262
e-mail: admin@whitelioncray.com
dir: B6265 from Skipton to Grassington, then B6160 towards Aysgarth. Or from Leyburn take A684 towards Hawes. At Aysgarth take B6160 towards Grassington. Cray in 10m

Nestling beneath Buckden Pike, The White Lion is Wharfedale's highest inn. It also boasts some spectacular scenery, since it's set right at the heart of the Yorkshire Dales. Indeed, the celebrated fell-walker Wainwright once described this former drovers' hostelry as a 'tiny oasis', a claim that's just as accurate today. All the qualities of a traditional Yorkshire inn have been maintained here, from warm hospitality to oak beams, log fire and flagstone floors. A good choice of hand-pulled real ales is offered and 20-plus malt whiskies. You can eat and drink in the bar or dining room, though the sight of the cascading Cray Gill, which runs past the inn, is sure to entice children out to the garden. Before or after a meal, you can also make your way across the stepping-stones in the gill to the open fells and many walks, long and short. In the bar, lunchtime options include filled baguettes, ploughman's, and plate-sized Yorkshire puddings with a choice of fillings. Also available, lunchtime and evenings, is a variety of substantial dishes such as pork fillet in a honey and mustard cream sauce; whole steamed Kilnsey trout, or steak and mushroom casserole.

Open all day all wk 10am-11pm **Bar Meals** L served all wk 12-2 D served all wk 6-8.30 **Restaurant** L served all wk 12-2 D served all wk 6-8.30 ⊕ FREE HOUSE ◄ Timothy Taylor Golden Best, Copper Dragon Golden Pippin, Copper Dragon Best Bitter, John Smith's Cask ♂ Stowford Press. ♀ 9 **Facilities** Children welcome Family room Dogs allowed Garden Parking

PICK OF THE PUBS

Malt Shovel Inn ♗

BREARTON Map 19 SE36

HG3 3BX ☎ 01423 862929
e-mail:
bleikers@themaltshovelbrearton.co.uk
web: www.themaltshovelbrearton.co.uk
dir: *From A61 (Ripon/Harrogate) onto*
B6165 towards Knaresborough. Left &
follow Brearton signs. In 1m right into
village

Tiny Brearton lies secluded down a no through road in the rolling countryside between Ripon and Harrogate. Footpaths diverge across rich farmland, parts of estates from which much of the pub's widely-renowned fare is sourced. For four centuries a beer house has served lucky locals; parts of the original structure form eye-catching detail in the busy interior of today's rustic retreat, where log fires and reclaimed church panelling draw guests into the jigsaw of spaces and corners that characterise the place. Wingback leather chairs and pianos dot stone-flagged floors of the bar, curiously named The Monkey; more intimate settings in the Red Room or the elegant Green Room all meld together at this destination gastro-pub; a modern conservatory is a striking counterpoint. Licensee Jurg Bleiker is also the head chef; front-of house is run by other family members, two of whom are renowned opera singers and who host regular operatic evenings at this most unlikely location. Wine fans will appreciate the well balanced list of bins, whilst beer lovers can indulge in Rudgate Brewery ales whilst considering the startling menu, which is strong on fish dishes: salt and chilli squid with fine herb salad and sweet chilli dip starter just one example. Jurg has established a smokery here; salmon, pollock, duck, chicken and home-made Toulouse sausages may populate the signature 'Smoking Kiln' special. From a local estate comes marinated venison haunch on a bed of red cabbage and apple, with rich red wine, port and juniper sauce served with spätzli (Swiss crispy pancake) and a mini gamekeepers' pie. Ever-changing specials draw on the fish theme; perhaps fillet of east coast bream with a lobster bisque and hollandaise sauce will hit the spot. To accompany, organic vegetables are sourced from the pub's own smallholding. There's jazz playing on Sunday lunchtimes.

Open Wed-Sun L Closed: Sun eve, Mon, Tue **Bar Meals** L served Wed-Sat 12-2, Sun 12-3 booking required D served Wed-Sat 6-9 booking required Av main course £14.95 **Restaurant** L served Wed-Sat 12-2, Sun 12-3 booking required D served Wed-Sat 6-9 booking required Fixed menu price fr £13.95 Av 3 course à la carte fr £24.85 ⊕ FREE HOUSE ◧ Black Sheep Best, Timothy Taylor Landlord, guest beer. ♟ 14 **Facilities** Children's portions Garden Parking

PICK OF THE PUBS

The Bull

BROUGHTON   Map 18 SD95

BD23 3AE ☎ 01756 792065
e-mail:
enquiries@thebullatbroughton.com
web: www.thebullatbroughton.com
dir: *3m from Skipton on A59, on right*

Tucked away off a busy main road, The Bull belongs to another, less frantic era; the unhurried, relaxed atmosphere of this Ribble Valley Inns dining pub eases you seamlessly into this lost world. The setting helps, of course; The Bull is part of the historic Broughton Estate, 3,000 acres of prime Yorkshire turf owned by the Tempest family for 900 years. The stunning mansion is close by and the pedigree shorthorn cattle, after which the pub is named, graze pastures skirting the Aire Valley. A dining pub it may be, but The Bull welcomes beer drinkers with plenty of choice: try Saltaire Raspberry Blonde for a change, a refreshing ale delicately infused with raspberry flavours; another option is Hetton's Dark Horse, a golden ale made with a blend of four different hops which give a spicy flavour with mild bitterness. Award-winning chefs make the most of the largesse offered by carefully selected producers across Yorkshire and Lancashire; provenance and traceability are key to the ingredients used in the extensive modern English menus here. By welcoming children with their own menu scaled down from the adult version, The Bull hopes to widen kiddies'

understanding of fine and fresh local food; there are fun sheets and competitions for them too. How better to start than with red deer faggots with butternut squash and juniper berry sauce; or boiled onions, Wensleydale cheese and an organic boiled egg. Main courses and grills feature the famous beef – perhaps in the form of a burger in an English muffin, served with real chips cooked in dripping, battered onion rings and tomato relish. Alternatively you'll find a North Sea fish pie stuffed with good things and topped with Wensleydale mash, and Yorkshire game pudding with roasted root vegetables. Round off with traditional pancakes and choose your filling – hazelnut and chocolate is very popular.

Open all day all wk noon–11pm (Sun noon–10.30pm) Closed: 25 Dec

Bar Meals/Restaurant L served Mon-Sat 12-2, Sun 12-8 Afternoon Bites Mon-Sat 2-5.30 D served Mon-Thu 5.30-8.30, Fri-Sat 5.30-9, Sun 12-8 Av main course £12 Av 3 course à la carte fr £25 ⊕ FREE HOUSE ◀ Timothy Taylor, Copper Dragon, Saltaire Raspberry Blonde.
Facilities Children welcome Children's menu Dogs allowed Garden Parking

CRAYKE — Map 19 SE57

PICK OF THE PUBS

The Durham Ox ♀

See Pick of the Pubs on opposite page

CROPTON — Map 19 SE78

The New Inn

YO18 8HH ☎ 01751 417330 📠 01751 417582
e-mail: info@croptonbrewery.com
dir: *Telephone for directions*

Home of the award-winning Cropton micro-brewery, this family-run free house on the edge of the North York Moors National Park is popular with locals and visitors alike. Meals are served in the restored village bar and in the elegant Victorian restaurant: choices could include Whitby cod with mushy peas and home-made chips; three cheese and roasted vegetable frittata; an extensive range from the grill; plus lunchtime sandwiches and ciabatta rolls. The New Inn holds a beer festival in November.

Open all day all wk 11-11 (Sun 11-10.30)
Bar Meals L served all wk 12-2 D served all wk 6-9 Av main course £11 **Restaurant** D served all wk 6-9 ⊕ FREE HOUSE ◀ Cropton Two Pints, Monkmans Slaughter, Yorkshire Moors Bitter, Honey Gold Bitter.
Facilities Children welcome Children's menu Children's portions Play area Family room Dogs allowed Garden Beer festival Parking

---

EAST WITTON — Map 19 SE18

PICK OF THE PUBS

The Blue Lion ♀

DL8 4SN ☎ 01969 624273 📠 01969 624189
e-mail: enquiries@thebluelion.co.uk
web: www.thebluelion.co.uk
dir: *From Ripon take A6108 towards Leyburn*

Once frequented by drovers and travellers journeying through Wensleydale, this stylishly refurbished 18th-century coaching inn, tucked away in an unspoilt estate village close to Jervaulx Abbey, has been transformed into one of North Yorkshire's finest inns by Paul and Helen Klein. An extensive but sympathetic refurbishment has created rural chic interiors with stacks of atmosphere and charm. The classic bar with its open fire and flagstone floor is a beer drinker's

haven, where the best of North Yorkshire's breweries present a pleasant dilemma for the real ale lover. A blackboard displays imaginative but unpretentious bar meals, while diners in the candlelit restaurant can expect culinary treats incorporating a variety of Yorkshire ingredients, notably seasonal game. A memorable meal may comprise game terrine or smoked haddock, leek and broad bean risotto; followed by turbot with roast king scallop and tomato compôte, or cassoulet of duck leg, Toulouse sausage and pork belly; and sticky toffee pudding with banana ice cream to finish.

Open all day all wk 11-11 Closed: 25 Dec
Bar Meals L served all wk 12-2.15 D served all wk 7-9.30 **Restaurant** L served Sun 12-2.15 D served all wk 7-9.30 ⊕ FREE HOUSE ◀ Black Sheep Bitter, Theakston Best Bitter, Black Sheep Riggwelter, Worthingtons Ö Thatchers Gold. ♀ 12
Facilities Children welcome Children's portions Dogs allowed Garden Parking Wi-fi

---

The Cover Bridge Inn NEW

DL8 4SQ ☎ 01969 623250
e-mail: enquiries@thecoverbridgeinn.co.uk
dir: *On A6108 between Middleham & East Witton*

A cunning door-latch befuddles many a first-time visitor to this magnificent little pub, snuggled beside the lively River Cover at one end of a memorable arched bridge, at the fringe of the Dales National Park close to Jervaulx Abbey. The timeless interior promises wrinkled beams, vast hearth and open fires, settles and fulfilling fodder, including grand home-made pies and a huge ham and eggs. Take to the riverside beer garden with a choice from eight ales and keep a wary eye out for the supernatural river kelpie, said to stalk the waters here.

Open all day all wk **Bar Meals** L served all wk 12-2 D served all wk 6-9 Av main course £8.75 ⊕ FREE HOUSE ◀ 5 real ales, 3 rotating guest ales Ö Westons Old Rosie.
Facilities Children welcome Children's menu Children's portions Play area Dogs allowed Garden Parking

---

EGTON — Map 19 NZ80

PICK OF THE PUBS

The Wheatsheaf Inn

YO21 1TZ ☎ 01947 895271
e-mail: info@wheatsheafegton.com
dir: *Off A169 NW of Grosmont*

This unassuming old pub sits back from the wide main road, so be careful not to miss it. The main bar is cosy and traditional, with low beams, dark green walls and comfy settles. There's a locals' bar too, but it only holds about twelve, so get there early. The pub is very popular with fishermen, as the River Esk runs along at the foot of the hill, and is a big draw for fly-fishers in particular. The menu offers white nut and artichoke heart roast with mushroom Stroganoff, and chicken and smoked bacon puff pastry pie among others.

Open 11.30-3 5.30-11.30 (Sat 11.30-11.30 Sun 11.30-11) Closed: Mon **Bar Meals** L served Tue-Sun 12-2 D served Tue-Sat 6-9 ⊕ FREE HOUSE ◀ Black Sheep Bitter, Black Sheep Golden, John Smith's, Timothy Taylor Landlord, Guest ales Ö Thatchers Gold.
Facilities Children welcome Dogs allowed Garden Parking

EGTON BRIDGE — Map 19 NZ80

Horseshoe Hotel

YO21 1XE ☎ 01947 895245
e-mail: paul@thehorseshoehotel.co.uk
dir: *From Whitby take A171 towards Middlesborough. Village signed in 5m*

An 18th-century country house set in beautiful grounds by the River Esk, handy for visiting the North Yorkshire Moors Railway and TV's *Heartbeat* country. Inside are oak settles and tables, local artists' paintings, and plates around the picture rails. Along with some great beers, lunchtime bar food consists of granary bread sandwiches and hot baguettes, while the main menu includes crab cakes with sweet chilli dip, lasagne, scampi, and pie of the day. There's a specials board too.

Open all wk 11.30-3 6.30-11 (Sat 11.30-11 Sun noon-10.30) **Bar Meals** L served all wk 12-2 D served all wk 7-9 Av main course £10 **Restaurant** L served all wk 12-2 D served all wk 7-9 ⊕ FREE HOUSE ◀ John Smith's Cask, Durham, Black Sheep, Guest ales. **Facilities** Children welcome Children's menu Children's portions Family room Dogs allowed Garden Parking

---

GIGGLESWICK — Map 18 SD86

Black Horse Hotel

32 Church St BD24 0BE
☎ 01729 822506 📠 01729 822506
e-mail: theblackhorse-giggle@tiscali.co.uk
dir: *Telephone for directions*

Set next to the church and behind the market cross in the 17th-century main street, this traditional free house is as charming as Giggleswick itself. Down in the warm and friendly bar you'll find a range of hand-pulled ales, with local guest beer sometimes available. The menu of freshly-prepared pub favourites ranges from hot sandwiches, home-made pizzas or giant filled Yorkshire puddings to main course dishes like traditional lamb hotpot or horseshoe of local gammon.

Open noon-2.30 5.30-11 (Sat-Sun noon-11) Closed: Mon L **Bar Meals** L served Tue-Sun 12-1.45 D served all wk 7-8.45 **Restaurant** L served Sun 12-1.45 booking required D served all wk 7-8.45 booking required ⊕ FREE HOUSE ◀ Timothy Taylor Landlord, John Smith's, Timothy Taylor Golden Best. **Facilities** Children's menu Children's portions Garden Parking

PICK OF THE PUBS

The Durham Ox ♟

CRAYKE Map 19 SE57

Westway YO61 4TE
☎ 01347 821506 📄 01347 823326
e-mail: enquiries@thedurhamox.com
web: www.thedurhamox.com
dir: *Off A19 from York to Thirsk, then to Easingwold. From market place to Crayke, turn left up hill, pub on right*

A former AA Pub of The Year, The Durham Ox is named after an eponymous ox that was born in 1796 and grew to massive proportions. A print hanging in the bottom bar is dedicated to the ox's first owner, the Rt Hon Lord Somerville. Another claim to fame is that the Grand Old Duke of York is said to have marched his men up and down the hill outside the inn. But whether you march in, arrive by helicopter or take a break on a ramble, the finest of Yorkshire welcomes awaits you at this hilltop pub.

The pretty pantiled free house is set in the beautiful Howardian Hills Area of Outstanding Natural Beauty just a 20-minute drive from York, whilst Herriot country and the sublime Castle Howard are nearby. With its flagstone floors, exposed beams, oak panelling and roaring winter fires in the main bar, The Durham Ox ticks all the right boxes. The White Rose County provides real ales and the produce for many of the award-winning meals produced in the kitchen, with fish and game being especially well regarded.

Sandwiches and pub classics like Black Sheep beer-battered haddock and chunky chips; or gammon and eggs with mushroom, tomato and fries provide everyday fare, whilst more discerning palates will also find plenty of choice.

Start your meal, maybe, with Yellison goat's cheese fritters with fig, honey and walnut dressing, before moving on to confit duck leg with cassoulet of Toulouse sausage and pork belly served with sticky red cabbage. Desserts are no less appealing, with rich chocolate mousse with Cointreau cream and honeycomb a typical choice.

Open all wk 12-2.30 6-11 Closed: 25 Dec **Bar Meals** L served Mon-Sat 12-2.30, Sun 12-3 booking required D served Mon-Sat 6-9.30, Sun 6-8.30 booking required **Restaurant** L served Mon-Sat 12-2.30, Sun 12-3 booking required D served Mon-Sat 6-9.30, Sun 6-8.30 booking required ⊕ FREE HOUSE ◼ John Smith's, Theakstons, Timothy Taylor Landlord, Black Sheep Best. ♟ 10 **Facilities** Dogs allowed Garden Parking Wi-fi

GOATHLAND Map 19 NZ80

Birch Hall Inn

Beck Hole YO22 5LE ☎ 01947 896245
e-mail: glenys@birchhallinn.fsnet.co.uk
dir: 9m from Whitby on A169

Beck Hole is a tiny hamlet of nine cottages and a pub hidden in the steep Murk Esk valley close to the North York Moors steam railway. This delightful little free house has just two tiny rooms separated by a sweet shop. The main bar offers well kept local ales to sup beside an open fire in winter, including the pub's house ale, Beckwater. In warm weather, food and drink can be enjoyed in the large garden, which has peaceful views of the local walks. The local quoits team play on the village green on summer evenings. The pub has been in the same ownership for 25 years and the simple menu features the local butcher's pies, old-fashioned flatcakes filled with ham, cheese, corned beef or farmhouse pâté, and home-made scones and buttered beer cake.

Open 11-3 7.30-11 (11-11 summer) Closed: Mon eve & Tue in winter **Bar Meals** food served all day ⊕ FREE HOUSE ◀ Black Sheep Best, Cropton Yorkshire Moors Bitter, Daleside Brewery Legover, Durhams Black Velvet, Beckwater. **Facilities** Children welcome Family room Dogs allowed Garden **Notes** ⊕

GREAT AYTON Map 19 NZ51

The Royal Oak ★★★ INN ♥

123 High St TS9 6BW
☎ 01642 722361 📠 01642 724047
e-mail: info@royaloak-hotel.co.uk
dir: Telephone for directions

Real fires and a relaxed atmosphere are part of the attraction at this traditional 18th-century former coaching inn now corner pub, run by the Monaghan family since 1978. The public bar and restaurant retain many original features and offer a good selection of real ales such as Theakston, and an extensive range of food is available all day. There are five comfortable bedrooms if you would like to stay over.

Open all day all wk Closed: 25 Dec **Bar Meals** food served all day **Restaurant** food served all day ⊕ SCOTTISH & NEWCASTLE BREWERIES ◀ Theakstons, John Smith's Smooth, Directors. ♥ 10 **Facilities** Children welcome Children's menu Children's portions Dogs allowed Garden Wi-fi **Rooms** 5

GREEN HAMMERTON Map 19 SE45

The Bay Horse Inn

York Rd YO26 8BN ☎ 01423 330338
e-mail: enquiry@bayhorsegreenhammerton.co.uk
dir: A1 junct 47 follow signs for A59 towards York. After 3m, turn left into village, on right opposite post office

Set at the village centre crossroads beside the old coach road between York and Harrogate, the inn has served travellers and villagers for over 200 years; many original features remain in the beamed, fire-warmed interior, up steps behind the pleasing shrubbery shaded frontage. Reliable Yorkshire cask beers (there's a spring beer festival, too) accompany home prepared meals strong on local produce; pork fillet with cider and apple sauce or a snack of garlic mushrooms with Jervaulx blue cheese may feature on the daily-changing menu, or plump for traditional fish and chips on Tuesdays and Fridays.

Open all wk 11.30-2.30 5.30-12 (Sat 11.30am-mdnt, Sun 11.30-8) **Bar Meals** L served all wk 12-2.30 D served Mon-Fri 6-9, Sat 12-9 Av main course £9.95 **Restaurant** L served all wk 12-2.30 D served Mon-Fri 6-9, Sat 12-9, Sun 12-7.30 ⊕ GREENE KING ◀ Timothy Taylor, Black Sheep, Guest ale, Abbot Ale. **Facilities** Children welcome Children's portions Dogs allowed Garden Beer festival Parking Wi-fi

GRINTON Map 19 SE09

PICK OF THE PUBS

The Bridge Inn

See Pick of the Pubs on opposite page

HAROME Map 19 SE68

PICK OF THE PUBS

The Star Inn ◎◎ ♥

YO62 5JE ☎ 01439 770397 📠 01439 771833
e-mail: reservations@thestarinnatharome.co.uk
dir: From Helmsley take A170 towards Kirkbymoorside 0.5m. Turn right for Harome

This astounding gastro-pub huddles in a tiny village on the fringe of the North Yorks Moors National Park. The seemingly endless, rippling purple heather moors are succour for some of the game that may feature on the ever-changing menu, available in bar or restaurant. In fact the pubby bar of this 14th-century thatched gem is well worth seeking out in order to get your eye in trying to spot the trademark carved mouse which decorates the classic oak furniture created by 'Mouseman' Thompson's works in nearby Kilburn. Locals and guests can glory in Hambleton Ales from the local village of that name, eagerly awaiting the call to dine on Andrew Pern's jaw-dropping menu crafted largely from North Yorkshire produce. Treat yourself to marinated grilled Golden Cross goat's cheese before tackling pot roasted wood pigeon Rossini with pan-fried duck foie gras and yellow chanterelle mushrooms, tailing off with poached quince and damson crumble.

Open all wk 11.30-3 6-11 (Sun noon-11) Closed: 1 Jan, Mon L **Bar Meals** L served Tue-Sat 11.30-2, Sun 12-6 D served Mon-Sat 6-9.30, Sun 12-6 Av main course £19 **Restaurant** L served Tue-Sat 11.30-2, Sun 12-6 booking required D served Mon-Sat 6-9.30, Sun 12-6 booking required Av 3 course à la carte fr £45 ⊕ FREE HOUSE ◀ Black Sheep Special, Copper Dragon, Hambleton Ales, John Smith's, Theakstons Best Ö Stowford Press, Ampleforth. ♥ 24 **Facilities** Children welcome Children's portions Garden Parking

HAWES Map 18 SD88

The Moorcock Inn

Garsdale Head LA10 5PU
☎ 01969 667488 📠 01969 667488
e-mail: admin@moorcockinn.com
dir: On A684 5m from Hawes, 10m from Sedbergh at junct for Kirkby Stephen (10m). Garsdale Station 1m

At the tip of Wensleydale, this lonely 18th-century inn's old white walls are a welcome sight, although only three-quarters of a mile from Garsdale station on the Settle/Carlisle line. Inside is a traditional blend of stonework and bright colours, comfortable sofas and wooden chairs. Savour a local real ale or one of the 50 malt whiskies around the wood-burning stove, and enjoy the spectacular views from the garden. Home cooked dishes include lamb and root vegetable hotpot; guinea fowl stuffed with haggis and cranberries; and chicken Wensleydale.

Open all day all wk noon-mdnt **Bar Meals** food served all day **Restaurant** D served all wk 6.30-9 ⊕ FREE HOUSE ◀ Black Sheep, Copper Dragon, Theakstons, Guest ales Ö Thatchers. **Facilities** Children welcome Children's menu Children's portions Family room Dogs allowed Garden Parking Wi-fi

HAWNBY Map 19 SE58

PICK OF THE PUBS

The Inn at Hawnby

★★★★★ INN ◎ ♥ **NEW**

YO62 5QS ☎ 01439 798202 📠 01439 798344
e-mail: info@innathawnby.co.uk
dir: Off B1257 between Stokesley & Helmsley

A charming 19th-century village pub with rooms set in the heart of the North Yorkshire Moors, this peaceful former drovers' inn offers panoramic views of the surrounding countryside. With hands-on and welcoming proprietors, Kathryn and David Young, the award-winning food majors on local produce. Dishes such as potted Whitby crab; pan-sautéed pigeon breast with roast beetroot, garlic and shallot chutney; locally shot breast of grouse with purple sprouting broccoli, sautéed girolles and glazed shallot sauce; and Holme Farm venison steak with bubble and squeak cake and red wine sauce can be enjoyed with a pint of light and quaffable Hawnby Hops ale brewed especially for the pub. Classic puddings include apple and berry pie; glazed lemon tart with Yorkshire lemon tart; sticky toffee pudding with butterscotch sauce. For designated drivers, there's even free water from the inn's own spring. If you would like to stay over, there are comfortable rooms: indeed, Kathryn was a finalist for AA Landlady of the Year 2010.

Open 10-3 6-11 (Fri-Sun all day) Closed: 25 Dec, Mon-Tue in Feb & Mar **Bar Meals** L served all wk 12-2 D served all wk 7-9 Av main course £13 **Restaurant** L served all wk 12-2 D served all wk 7-9 Av 3 course à la carte fr £22 ⊕ FREE HOUSE ◀ Timothy Taylor Landlord, Black Sheep, Hawnby Hops Ö Stowford Press. ♥ 8 **Facilities** Children welcome Children's menu Children's portions Garden Parking Wi-fi **Rooms** 9

Save on hotels. Book at **theAA.com/hotel**

YORKSHIRE, NORTH 517 ENGLAND

PICK OF THE PUBS

The Bridge Inn

GRINTON Map 19 SE09

DL11 6HH ☎ **01748 884224**
e-mail: atkinbridge@btinternet.com
web: www.bridgeinngrinton.co.uk
dir: *Exit A1 at Scotch Corner onto A6108 towards Richmond. Through Richmond. Left onto B6270 towards Grinton & Reeth*

Two of the Yorkshire Dales' wildest and prettiest dales meet at Grinton; Arkengarthdale and Swaledale collide in a symphony of fells, moors, waterfalls and cataracts, at the heart of which Grinton has stood for nearly 1000 years. The inn is just a tad younger; a 13th-century building at the riverside and close to one of Yorkshire's finest old churches, known as the Cathedral of the Dales. Lanes and tracks slope down from the heights, bringing ramblers and riders to appreciate the good range of northern beers that Andrew Atkin matches with his fine foods; York Brewery's Yorkshire Terrier being a case in point. It's a happy mix of village pub and dining inn, with locals enjoying the bustling games room and beamed old bar whilst a more tranquil restaurant area caters for those after a more intimate meal experience. Resident chef John Scott is in charge of the food, his menu inspired by carefully chosen seasonal local game, meats, fish and other produce, including

herbs plucked from the garden. Traditional English dishes with a modern twist offer a flavour of the fare, which is enhanced by daily-changing specials. Ham hock terrine or smoked haddock fishcakes ease you into the spirit of the inn as flavoursome starters; the main event will draw on dishes such as Bedale belly pork (garlic and sage roasted belly pork on a stew of lentils, smoked bacon, tomato, onions and white wine); cod in cider and dill batter; or wholewheat pasta with butternut squash, red onion and spinach finished with tomato, Stilton and cream. Finish with Liz's ginger pudding or a selection of Swaledale cheeses with savoury biscuits and chutney. For entertainment there is musicians' night every Thursday.

Open all day all wk **Bar Meals** Av main course £8.75-£16.95 food served all day **Restaurant** Av 3 course à la carte fr £25 food served all day ⊕ JENNINGS BROTHERS PLC ◼ Cumberland Ale, Cocker Hoop, Deuchars IPA, Adnams, Yorkshire Terrier. **Facilities** Children's menu Children's portions Dogs allowed Garden Parking Wi-fi

HETTON
Map 18 SD95

PICK OF THE PUBS

The Angel ★★★★★ RR ☺☺ ♥

BD23 6LT ☎ **01756 730263** 📠 **01756 730363**
e-mail: info@angelhetton.co.uk
dir: *A59 onto B6265 towards Grassington. Left at
Rylstone Pond (signed) then left at T-junct*

Once a drovers' inn, this ancient Dales pub became a
landmark gastro-pub when Denis and Juliet Watkins
took the reins in 1985, and Juliet and her team have
built on that success since Denis' death in 2004. The
interior is all oak beams, nooks and crannies, and
winter log fires; in summer you can sit on the flagged
forecourt and enjoy views of Cracoe Fell. Chef Bruce
Elsworth has stayed true to Denis' vision of 'good food
and great value' with locally sourced meats, seasonal
game and fresh Fleetwood fish the foundation of the
varied menus. The bar brasserie winter menu might
offer yapas (Yorkshire tapas) to nibble while you peruse
the menu. Starters include duo of mackerel and trout
terrine, or wild mushroom risotto, followed by suckling
pig braised then roasted with black pudding mash, or
venison haunch steak, celeriac purée and roast
beetroot. Vegetarians have their own menu with
perhaps twice baked Yellisons goat's cheese soufflé;
and parsnip, leek, sage and walnut Wellington. Large
and stylish bedrooms are located across the road in a
converted barn.

Open all wk Mon-Thu noon-3 6-11 (Fri-Sun all day
summer) Closed: 25 Dec & 1wk Jan **Bar Meals** L served
Mon-Sat 12-2.15, Sun all day D served all wk 6-9.30
(6-9 in winter) Av main course £15 **Restaurant** L served
Sun 12-1.45 booking required D served Mon-Fri 6-9,
Sat 6-9.30 booking required Fixed menu price fr £11.50
Av 3 course à la carte fr £27 ⊕ FREE HOUSE ◀ Black
Sheep Bitter, Timothy Taylor Landlord, Hetton Pale Ale.
♥ 26 **Facilities** Children welcome Children's menu
Children's portions Garden Parking Wi-fi **Rooms** 9

HOVINGHAM
Map 19 SE67

The Malt Shovel

Main St YO62 4LF ☎ **01653 628264** 📠 **01653 628264**
e-mail: info@themaltshovelhovingham.co.uk
dir: *18m NE of York, 5m from Castle Howard*

Tucked away in the Duchess of Kent's home village, the
stone-built 18th-century Malt Shovel offers a friendly
atmosphere with well kept ales and food prepared from
quality local ingredients. There are two dining rooms
where you can enjoy starters of shallow fried whitebait
with lime and chilli mayonnaise, smoked haddock, leek
and Gruyère tartlet or black pudding and apple fritters,
followed by wholegrain mustard chicken; steak pie; or
chickpea curry. There is a large beer garden at the rear of
the pub where you can sit and enjoy a pint or two in lovely
surroundings.

Open all wk 11.30-2 6-11 (winter), 11.30-2.30 5.30-11
(summer) **Bar Meals** L served Mon-Sat 11.30-2 (winter)
11.30-2.30 (summer), Sun 12-2.30 D served Mon-Sat 6-9
(winter) 5.30-9 (summer), Sun 5.30-8
Restaurant L served Mon-Sat 11.30-2 (winter)
11.30-2.30 (summer), Sun 12-2.30 booking required
D served Mon-Sat 6-9 (winter) 5.30-9 (summer), Sun
5.30-8 booking required ⊕ PUNCH TAVERNS ◀ Tetley's,
Black Sheep, Guest Ale. **Facilities** Children welcome
Children's menu Children's portions Garden Parking

PICK OF THE PUBS

The Worsley Arms Hotel ★★★ HL ♥

Main St YO62 4LA
☎ **01653 628234** 📠 **01653 628130**
e-mail: enquiries@worsleyarms.co.uk
dir: *On B1257 between Malton & Helmsley*

The Worsley Arms has been welcoming guests to the
village of Hovingham since 1841, when Sir William
Worsley built a spa house and a hotel. The spa failed,
but the hotel survived and, together with the separate
pub, forms part of the Worsley family's historic
Hovingham Hall estate, birthplace of the Duchess of
Kent, and currently home to her nephew. You can eat in
the restaurant or the Cricketer's Bar (the local team
has played on the village green for over 150 years).
Hambleton beers from nearby Thirsk are on tap, and
food choices in the pub include home-made chicken
liver parfait flavoured with port and Armagnac; steak,
ale and button mushroom pie with puff pastry lid;
classic Caesar salad and a range of ciabatta
sandwiches. A short drive from Pickering and Thirsk,
the pub is a magnificent base for exploring North
Yorkshire.

Open all day all wk 11-11 **Bar Meals** L served all wk
12-2 booking required D served all wk 6.30-9 booking
required Av main course £13 **Restaurant** L served Sun
12-2 booking required D served all wk 6.30-9 booking
required Av 3 course à la carte fr £27.50 ⊕ FREE
HOUSE ◀ Tetleys, Hambleton Ales. ♥ 20
Facilities Children welcome Dogs allowed Garden
Parking **Rooms** 20

HUBBERHOLME
Map 18 SD97

The George Inn

BD23 5JE ☎ **01756 760223**
dir: *From Skipton take B6265 to Threshfield. B6160 to
Buckden. Follow signs for Hubberholme*

To check if the bar is open, look for a lighted candle in
the window. Another old tradition is the annual land-
letting auction on the first Monday night of the year, when
local farmers bid for 16 acres of land owned by the
church. Stunningly located beside the River Wharfe in the
Yorkshire Dales National Park, this pub has flagstone
floors, stone walls, mullioned windows, an open fire and
an inviting summer terrace. With beers from Black Sheep
and Yorkshire Dales breweries, evening menus include
poached Scottish salmon fillet with creamy peppercorn
sauce, and Dales lamb chops with rich gravy.

Open noon-3 7-11 Closed: 1st 2wks Dec, Mon
Bar Meals L served Tue-Sun 12-2 D served Tue-Sun
6.30-8 booking required Av main course £9 ⊕ FREE
HOUSE ◀ Black Sheep Special, Yorkshire Dales Brewery
Ŏ Thatchers Gold. **Facilities** Children welcome Children's
menu Garden Parking

KETTLEWELL
Map 18 SD97

The Kings Head NEW

The Green BD23 5RD ☎ **01756 760242**
e-mail: info@kingsheadkettlewell.co.uk
dir: *Take B6160 to Kettlewell from either A684, or A59 at
Bolton Bridge*

Set in the picturesque village of Kettlewell in the heart of
the Yorkshire Dales, The Kings Head is a perfect base to
explore the area's breathtaking scenery. A traditional pub
with inglenook fireplace and fabulous views, expect to
find local cask ales and an appealing menu of home-
cooked favourites such as gammon, egg and chips, steak
and ale pie or beer-battered cod goujons with chips. The
pub welcomes children and dogs.

Open all day all wk **Bar Meals** L served all wk 12-2.30
D served all wk 5-8.30 Av main course £9.95 ⊕ FREE
HOUSE ◀ Black Sheep Bitter, Timothy Taylor Landlord,
Yorkshire Dales Brewery Butter Tubs Ŏ Thatchers Gold,
Thatchers Pear. **Facilities** Children welcome Children's
menu Children's portions Dogs allowed Garden Parking
Wi-fi

KILBURN
Map 19 SE57

The Forresters Arms Inn

The Square YO61 4AH ☎ **01347 868386**
e-mail: admin@forrestersarms.com
dir: *From Thirsk take A170, after 3m turn right signed
Kilburn. At Kilburn Rd junct, turn right, Inn on left in
village square*

A sturdy stone-built former coaching inn still catering for
travellers passing close by the famous White Horse of
Kilburn on the North York Moors. Next door is the famous
Robert Thompson workshop; fine examples of his early
work, with the distinctive mouse symbol on every piece,
can be seen in both bars. Visiting coachmen would
undoubtedly have enjoyed the log fires, cask ales and
good food as much as today's visitors. Dishes include
smoked mackerel mousse or belly pork and black pudding
warm salad to start, followed by steak and ale pie or slow
braised lamb shank with mash and vegetables. There's a
beer festival on St George's Day (23rd April).

Open all day all wk 9am-11pm **Bar Meals** L served Mon-
Fri 12-3, off season 12-2.30, Sat-Sun all day booking
required D served all wk 6-9, off season 6-8 booking
required Av main course £8.95 **Restaurant** L served Mon-
Fri 12-3, off season 12-2.30, Sat-Sun all day booking
required D served all wk 6-9, off season 6-8 booking
required ⊕ ENTERPRISE INNS ◀ John Smith's Cask,
Hambleton Bitter, Guest ales Ŏ Symonds Reserve.
Facilities Children welcome Children's menu Children's
portions Dogs allowed Garden Beer festival Parking Wi-fi

KILNSEY Map 18 SD96

The Tennant Arms 🍷 NEW

BD23 5PS ☎ 01756 752301
e-mail: tennant-arms@intrepid-leisure.co.uk
dir: *From Skipton take B6265 to Grassington. Left onto B6160 to Kilnsey. Pub approx 400mtrs after trout farm*

Dramatic Kilnsey Crag, one of the wonders of Wharfedale, looms over this homely inn deep in the Yorkshire Dales National Park. Sit in the suntrap garden, admiring the climbers as you contemplate the highly traditional comfort menu – treat yourself to Aunt Betty's brisket or slow-roasted belly pork and black pudding – or, warmed by a roaring winter log fire, reflect on the craft of the micro-brewers' whose beers take centre stage at this rural idyll; an Easter beer festival adds to the choice.

Open all day all wk **Bar Meals** L served all wk 12-2 D served Mon-Sat 6-9, Sun 6-8 Av main course £10.80 **Restaurant** L served all wk 12-2 D served Mon-Sat 6-9, Sun 6-8 booking required Fixed menu price fr £15.95 Av 3 course à la carte fr £15.95 ◀ Black Sheep Best, Thwaites Wainwright Ale, Salamander Brewery. 🍷 10 **Facilities** Children welcome Children's menu Children's portions Dogs allowed Garden Beer festival Parking Wi-fi

KIRBY HILL Map 19 NZ10

The Shoulder of Mutton Inn

DL11 7JH ☎ 01748 822772
e-mail: info@shoulderofmutton.net
dir: *From A1 Scotch Corner junct take A66. Approx 6m follow signs for Kirby Hill on left*

With panoramic views over Holmedale and beyond, this ivy-clad 18th-century inn boasts two open log fires in the bar, where you can enjoy the excellent locally brewed ales, especially micro-breweries. The separate stone-walled restaurant, replete with original beams and white linen, sets the tone for renowned daily-changing home-cooked dishes. A typical selection could comprise smoked haddock, spinach and blue cheese pancakes, followed by roast rump of lamb topped with tomato fondue and garlic herb and Parmesan crust.

Open all wk 6-11 (Sat-Sun noon-3 6-11) **Bar Meals** L served Sat-Sun 12-2 booking required D served Wed-Sun 6.30-9 booking required Av main course £9.50 **Restaurant** L served Sun 12-2 booking required D served Wed-Sun 6.30-9 booking required Av 3 course à la carte fr £25.95 ⊕ FREE HOUSE ◀ Daleside, Black Sheep, Copper Dragon, Yorkshire Dales, Guest ales. **Facilities** Children welcome Garden Beer festival Parking

KIRKBY FLEETHAM Map 19 SE29

The Black Horse Inn 🍷 NEW

Lumley Ln DL7 0SH ☎ 01609 749010
e-mail: gm@blackhorsekirkbyfleetham.com
dir: *Village signed from A1 between Catterick & Leeming Bar*

Local gossip has it that Dick Turpin eloped with his ladyfriend from the village pub in Kirkby Fleetham; it was renamed the Black Horse after the outlaw's steed to celebrate this particular theft of valuables. Today's locals and visitors find it pays to tarry a while longer at the inn just off the vast village green, spiriting away pints of grand Yorkshire beers from Timothy Taylors and Copper Dragon and stealing a glance at an accomplished menu covering all the bases, including oxtail casserole, wild mushroom pappardelle or Yorkshire caviar with fish and chips. Settle in with these goodies in the stylishly remodelled interior, a pleasing mix of tradition and comfort, or in a garden adjoining fields here in the Swale valley.

Open all day all wk **Bar Meals** L served Mon-Sat 12-2.30, Sun 12-7 booking required D served Mon-Sat 5-9.30, Sun 12-7 booking required Av main course £10.95-£17.95 **Restaurant** L served Mon-Sat 12-2.30, Sun 12-7 booking required D served Mon-Sat 5-9.30, Sun 12-7 booking required Av 3 course à la carte fr £20-£30 ⊕ FREE HOUSE ◀ Black Sheep, Copper Dragon, Timothy Taylor Landlord. 🍷 10 **Facilities** Children welcome Children's menu Children's portions Dogs allowed Garden Parking Wi-fi

KIRKBYMOORSIDE Map 19 SE68

PICK OF THE PUBS

George & Dragon Hotel 🍷

17 Market Place YO62 6AA
☎ 01751 433334 ▤ 0870 706 0004
e-mail: reception@georgeanddragon.net
dir: *Just off A170 between Scarborough & Thirsk. In town centre*

Lanes thread north from compact Kirkbymoorside to engage with Farndale's famous daffodils, remote Bransdale, Rosedale's rich heritage and the heather expanses of the enfolding North Yorks Moors National Park. This long-established, town-centre coaching inn oozes charm, from the log fire in the bar and sheltered courtyard with fountain to the eclectic collection of cricketing, golf and rugby paraphernalia adorning the nooks and crannies where may also be enjoyed some of Yorkshire's great beers. Sit tight here, or in the adjoining bistro and restaurant, and sample a haggis and black pudding gateau with whisky mustard sauce, an inventive starter prior to Whitby beer-battered haddock with chips and Yorkshire caviar, steak and Stilton pie with fresh seasonal vegetables, or Yorkshire venison steak with bitter chocolate wine sauce, carved onto black pudding with dauphinoise potatoes. The traditional Sunday carvery is immensely popular here.

Open all day all wk 10.30am-11pm **Bar Meals** L served all wk 12-2 D served all wk 6-9 Av main course £8.50 **Restaurant** L served all wk 12-2 D served all wk 6-9 Fixed menu price fr £10 Av 3 course à la carte fr £25 ⊕ FREE HOUSE ◀ Copper Dragon, Daleside, Black Sheep, Abbot Ale, Guest ales. 🍷 12 **Facilities** Children welcome Children's menu Children's portions Dogs allowed Garden Beer festival Parking

KIRKHAM Map 19 SE76

PICK OF THE PUBS

Stone Trough Inn 🍷

Kirkham Abbey YO60 7JS ☎ 01653 618713
e-mail: timstonetroughinn@live.co.uk
dir: *1.5m off A64, between York & Malton*

Set amongst the Howardian Hills in a stunning location overlooking Kirkham Priory and the River Derwent, this free house has a great reputation for fine food and a great selection of real ales. Stone Trough Cottage was converted to an inn during the early 1980s, and took its name from the base of a 12th-century cross erected by a French knight to commemorate a son killed in a riding accident. The cross has long since disappeared, but its hollowed-out base now stands at the entrance to the car park. A real fire, bare beams and wooden settles make for a pleasingly traditional interior. Food-wise, the menu includes salmon fillet on champ mashed potato with a saffron, leek and prawn sauce; potato, chick pea and spinach curry with tomato, fresh ginger and yoghurt; and chicken fillet in bacon with saffron rice and lightly curried coconut cream.

Open all day all wk 11-11 (Sun noon-11pm) **Bar Meals** L served Mon-Thu 12-2.30, Fri-Sat 12-9.30, Sun 12-8 D served Mon-Fri 6-9.30, Sat 12-9.30, Sun 12-8 Av main course £9.95 **Restaurant** L served Mon-Thu 12-2.30, Fri-Sat 12-9.30, Sun 12-8 D served Mon-Fri 6-9.30, Sat 12-9.30, Sun 12-8 ⊕ FREE HOUSE ◀ Tetley Cask, Timothy Taylor Landlord, Black Sheep Best, York Brewery, Cropton Brewery, Wold Top Brewery, Cropton Brewery, Guest ales. 🍷 14 **Facilities** Children welcome Children's menu Children's portions Dogs allowed Garden Parking

KNARESBOROUGH — Map 19 SE35

PICK OF THE PUBS

The General Tarleton Inn
★★★★★ RR ◉◉ ♀

See Pick of the Pubs on opposite page

LANGTHWAITE — Map 19 NZ00

The Red Lion Inn ♀

DL11 6RE ☎ 01748 884218 📠 01748 884133
e-mail: rlionlangthwaite@aol.com
web: www.redlionlangthwaite.co.uk
dir: *Through Reeth into Arkengarthdale, 18m from A1*

The Red Lion is a traditional country pub owned by the same family for 46 years. It hosts two darts teams in winter, a quoits team in summer and bar snacks are served all year round. There are some wonderful walks in this part of the Dales and relevant books and maps are on sale in the bar. In the tiny snug there are photographs relating to the various films and TV programmes filmed at this unusually photogenic pub (including *All Creatures Great and Small*, *A Woman of Substance* and *Hold the Dream*). Ice cream, chocolates and sweets are available as well.

Open all wk 11-3 7-11 **Bar Meals** L served all wk 11-3 Av main course £3 ⊕ FREE HOUSE ◀ Black Sheep Bitter, Riggwelter, Worthington Cream Flow, Guinness ○ Thatchers Gold. ♀ 9 **Facilities** Family room Garden Parking

LASTINGHAM — Map 19 SE79

Blacksmiths Arms

YO62 6TN ☎ 01751 417247 📠 01751 417247
e-mail: pete.hils@blacksmithslastingham.co.uk
dir: *7m from Pickering & 4m from Kirkbymoorside. A170 (Pickering to Kirbymoorside road), follow Lastingham & Appleton-le-Moors signs*

This stone-built free house stands opposite St Mary's Church (renowned for its Saxon crypt) in the National Park area. Inside it retains its original 17th-century low-beamed ceilings and open range fireplace, and outside there's a cottage garden and decked seating area. Home-cooked dishes prepared from locally supplied ingredients are served in the recently re-decorated dining areas, and include lamb casserole with Yorkshire pudding, and beer-battered jumbo cod; there is a takeaway service too. Enjoy the food with a pint of Theakston Best Bitter or one of the guest ales.

Open all day Closed: Tue L (Nov-May) **Bar Meals** L served all wk 12-5 (not Tue Nov-May) D served all wk 6.30-8.45 Av main course £9.50 **Restaurant** L served all wk 12-5 (not Tue Nov-May) D served all wk 6.30-8.45 booking required ⊕ FREE HOUSE ◀ Theakston Best Bitter, 2 rotating guest ales. **Facilities** Children welcome Children's menu Children's portions Family room Garden Wi-fi

LEVISHAM — Map 19 SE89

Horseshoe Inn ★★★★ INN ♀

Main St YO18 7NL ☎ 01751 460240 📠 01751 460052
e-mail: info@horseshoelevisham.co.uk
dir: *A169, 5m from Pickering. 4m, pass Fox & Rabbit Inn on right. In 0.5m left to Lockton. Follow steep winding road to village*

This welcoming country inn sits at the head of a tranquil village on the edge of the North York Moors National Park. It makes an ideal base for walking, cycling and touring the moors – don't miss a trip on the nearby steam railway. Charles and Toby Wood have created an inviting atmosphere in the beamed bar, with its polished plank floor and roaring log fire, offering tip-top ales and hearty country cooking - maybe venison suet pudding; seafood platter; Whitby haddock with home-made chips and mushy peas; or duck breast with sweet potato mash. There are nine comfortable bedrooms available.

Open all day all wk **Bar Meals** L served all wk 12-2 booking required D served all wk 6-8.30 booking required **Restaurant** L served all wk 12-2 booking required D served all wk 6-8.30 booking required ⊕ FREE HOUSE ◀ Black Sheep Best, Cropton Brewery Yorkshire Moors, Yorkshire Warrior & Endeavour ○ Thatchers Gold. ♀ 12 **Facilities** Children welcome Children's menu Children's portions Dogs allowed Garden Parking Wi-fi **Rooms** 9

LEYBURN — Map 19 SE19

The Old Horn Inn

Spennithorne DL8 5PR ☎ 01969 622370
dir: *From Leyburn on A684 approx 1.5m E. Turn right signed Spennithorne. From Bedale & A1 on A684 approx 9m W. Turn left signed Spennithorne*

Low beams and open log fires characterise this traditional 17th-century free house. The former farmhouse, which has been a pub for at least 100 years, is named after the horn that summoned the farmer's workers to lunch. Today's customers enjoy good home-made dishes produced from local meat and from fish fetched from Whitby by the owners. Expect chicken breast filled with home-cooked ham served with cheese and mustard sauce; trio of sausages with mashed potato and rich gravy; or baked cod with cherry tomatoes, basil and mozzarella.

Open Tue-Sat 12-3 6-11 (Sun 12-3 7-11) Closed: Mon (ex BH) **Bar Meals** L served Tue-Sun 12-2 booking required D served Tue-Sat 6-8.30 booking required Av main course £9.50 **Restaurant** L served Tue-Sun 12-2 D served Tue-Sat 6-8.30 ⊕ FREE HOUSE ◀ Marstons, Jennings Cumberland, Mansfield Cask, Banks's Mild, Guest ales. **Facilities** Children welcome Children's menu Children's portions Dogs allowed Garden **Notes** ⬚

The Queens Head ★★★★ INN ♀ NEW

Westmoor Ln, Finghall DL8 1QZ ☎ 01677 450259
e-mail: enquiries@queensfinghall.co.uk
dir: *From Bedale follow A684 W towards Leyburn, just after pub & caravan park turn left signed to Finghall. Follow road, on left*

From its hillside terrace above Wensleydale, drinkers quaffing Masham's finest beers here can gaze over woodland that inspired Kenneth Grahame to create the Wild Wood in *Wind in the Willows*. Fires have glowed in the grates since the 18th century, seasoning beams that today shelter diners keen to share in the freshly prepared food, from great sandwiches and pub classics to confident, modern dishes like medallions of beef fillet and haggis, or crab and ginger risotto. Bedrooms are spacious and located in an adjacent annexe.

Open all wk 12-3 6-close Closed: 26 Dec & 1 Jan **Bar Meals** L served all wk 12-2 D served all wk 6-9 Av main course £6.95 **Restaurant** L served all wk 12-2 D served all wk 6-9 Fixed menu price fr £12.95 Av 3 course à la carte fr £16 ◀ Black Sheep Bitter & Ale, Theakston Best Bitter. ♀ 10 **Facilities** Children welcome Children's menu Children's portions Garden Parking **Rooms** 3

PICK OF THE PUBS

Sandpiper Inn ♀

Market Place DL8 5AT
☎ 01969 622206 📠 01969 625367
e-mail: hsandpiper99@aol.com
dir: *From A1 take A684 to Leyburn*

Handy for Wensleydale and many other Yorkshire attractions, this 17th-century, ivy-clad inn occupies the oldest building in Leyburn, but has only been a pub for only 30 years. Inside is a bar and snug where you can enjoy a pint of Copper Dragon, or your pick from 100 single malts. Chef/proprietor Jonathan Harrison has been at the helm for 12 years now, during which time he has established an excellent reputation for preparing modern British food using the finest ingredients. Head for the dining room to peruse the list of exciting and varied traditional and international dishes such as roasted halibut with mushy peas, tartare sauce and chips, or wild mushroom and spinach risotto. Lunch brings sandwiches such as smoked salmon and Whitby crab. Children are not only welcome - they get to choose from their own menu of home-made dishes, perhaps crispy battered chicken strips followed by Knickerbocker Glory.

Open 11.30-3 6.30-11 (Sun noon-2.30 7-10.30) Closed: Mon & occasionally Tue **Bar Meals** L served all wk 12-2.30 Av main course £15 **Restaurant** L served all wk 12-2.30 booking required D served all wk 6.30-9.30 booking required Av 3 course à la carte fr £28 ⊕ FREE HOUSE ◀ Black Sheep Best, Black Sheep Special, Daleside, Copper Dragon, Archers, Yorkshire Dales Brewing Co Ltd ○ Thatcher's Gold. **Facilities** Children welcome Children's menu Family room Dogs allowed Garden Wi-fi

PICK OF THE PUBS

The General Tarleton Inn ★★★★★RR   ♍

KNARESBOROUGH   Map 19 SE35

Boroughbridge Rd, Ferrensby HG5 0PZ
☎ **01423 340284**   📠 **01423 340288**
e-mail: gti@generaltarleton.co.uk
web: www.generaltarleton.co.uk
dir: *A1(M) junct 48 at Boroughbridge, take A6055 to Knaresborough. Inn 4m on right*

Ferrensby stands in pleasant surroundings just north of Harrogate, mid-way between the protected Area of Outstanding Natural Beauty countryside of Nidderdale and the Howardian Hills and handy for the Dales. Close to the A1, the village inn, The General Tarleton (re-named at the time in honour of a somewhat notorious British general in the American War of Independence) originated as a coaching inn drawing on the trade using this ever-busy road. Vestiges of its genesis remain in the much renovated interior, where feature beams reflect flickering log fires, whilst sofas encourage guests to flop down with newspapers in cosy corners, awaiting the call to experience choices from the distinguished menu, which has garnered the award of two AA Rosettes for John Topham and his very capable team. Menus entitled 'Food with Yorkshire Roots' change daily to reflect the pick of the crop or catch, thus the chef usually gets a call from fishing boat skippers returning to Yorkshire's wealth of fishing ports and the catch is whisked to Ferrensby within hours. All those telephone calls are good news for seafood lovers: Little Moneybags, the chef's signature starter dish of seafood parcels in lobster

sauce, is widely renowned. Taken in the Bar Brasserie, the Tarleton fine-dining restaurant or alfresco in the terrace garden and courtyard, other tempting starters may run to Vale of York wood pigeon with salt-baked beetroot, Mrs Bells Yorkshire Blue cheese and hazelnuts; or Swaledale ewe's cheese soufflé. Startling mains include Taste of Rabbit: roast loin and best end, herb stuffed leg wrapped in bacon, mini rabbit pie, celeriac purée and truffle jus. Alternatively, Yorkshire rare breed pork – crisp slowly braised belly, roast fillet, black pudding, mock goose pie, plum purée and cider glaze - would equally leave little room for a trio of Yorkshire rhubarb pudding. To accompany it's possible to select from a list of 150 bins of wines selected both from smaller producers and memorable vineyards. Well appointed accommodation available.

Open all wk 12-3 6-11
Bar Meals L served all wk 12-2 booking required D served all wk 6-9.15 booking required Av main course £14 **Restaurant** L served Sun 12-1.45 booking required D served Mon-Sat 6-9.15 booking required Av 3 course à la carte fr £35 ⊕ FREE HOUSE ◀ Black Sheep Best, Timothy Taylor Landlord ♂ Aspall Suffolk. ♍ 11
Facilities Children's menu Children's portions Garden Parking Wi-fi **Rooms** 14

LITTON   Map 18 SD97

Queens Arms ☖

BD23 5QJ ☎ **01756 770208**
e-mail: queens.litton@gmail.com
dir: N of Skipton

Dating from the 18th century, this drover's inn is full of original features including flagstones and beams. The open fire offers a warm winter welcome to outdoor enthusiasts and their dogs, fresh from enjoying the Yorkshire Dales countryside. Cask-conditioned ales from the on-site micro-brewery accompany home-cooked dishes like local lamb chops, beer-battered haddock or chef's veggie tart. There are stunning views from the bars and garden.

Open noon-3 6.30-11.30 (Sun 7-11) Closed: Mon
Bar Meals L served Tue-Sun 12-2.30 booking required D served Tue-Sat 6.30-9, Sun 7-9 Av main course £9.95 **Restaurant** L served Tue-Sun 12-2.30 D served Tue-Sat 6.30-9, Sun 7-9 ⊕ FREE HOUSE ◧ Litton Ale, Tetley Cask, Guest ales ♻ Stowford Press. ☖ 12 **Facilities** Children welcome Children's portions Family room Dogs allowed Garden Parking

LONG PRESTON   Map 18 SD85

Maypole Inn ☖

Maypole Green BD23 4PH ☎ **01729 840219**
e-mail: robert@maypole.co.uk
dir: On A65 between Settle & Skipton

In 1695, Ambrose Wigglesworth first threw open the doors of his inn on the edge of what is now the Yorkshire Dales National Park. Today, its commitment to real ale and cider has earned it top honours, while its traditional home cooking ensures eminently satisfying food. Enjoy Yorkshire ham and eggs, Kilnsey trout or Thai green vegetable curry in the beamed dining room or cosy bars. The maypole stands on the green outside and seating provides great views of Long Preston Moor.

Open all day all wk **Bar Meals** L served Sun-Thu 12-9, Fri-Sat 12-9.30 Av main course £9 food served all day **Restaurant** L served Mon-Fri 12-2.30, Sat-Sun all day D served Mon-Fri 6-9, Sat-Sun all day ⊕ ENTERPRISE INNS ◧ Timothy Taylor Landlord, Moorhouses Premier, Jennings, Cumberland, Copper Dragon, Bowland Beers ♻ Westons Vintage Organic. ☖ 11 **Facilities** Children welcome Children's menu Children's portions Dogs allowed Garden Parking Wi-fi

LOW ROW   Map 18 SD99

The Punch Bowl Inn ★★★★ INN ☖

DL11 6PF ☎ **01748 886233** 🖷 **01748 886945**
e-mail: info@pbinn.co.uk
web: www.pbinn.co.uk
dir: A1 from Scotch Corner take A6108 to Richmond. Through Richmond then right onto B6270 to Low Row

Located in Swaledale with Wainwright's Coast to Coast Walk on the doorstep, this Grade II listed pub dates back to the 17th century. During a refurbishment a couple of years ago, the bar and bar stools were hand-crafted by Robert 'The Mouseman' Thompson (see if you can spot the mice around the bar). Typical food choices include game terrine; parsnip and butternut risotto; pan-fried chicken with ham, pea and cream linguini; and Amaretto crème brûlée. Local cask conditioned ales also feature. If you would like to stay over for the Swaledale festivals, there are stylish bedrooms available, all with spectacular views.

Open all day all wk 11am-mdnt Closed: 25 Dec
Bar Meals L served all wk 12-2 booking required D served all wk 6.30-9 booking required Av main course £13.50 **Restaurant** L served all wk 12-2 booking required D served all wk 6.30-9 booking required Av 3 course à la carte fr £22.50 ⊕ FREE HOUSE ◧ Theakston Best Bitter, Black Sheep Best Bitter, Timothy Taylor Landlord, Black Sheep Riggwelter ♻ Thatchers Gold. ☖ 13 **Facilities** Children welcome Children's menu Children's portions Parking Wi-fi **Rooms** 11

MALHAM   Map 18 SD96

PICK OF THE PUBS

The Lister Arms ★★★★ INN ☖

BD23 4DB ☎ **01729 830330**
e-mail: relax@listerarms.co.uk
web: www.listerarms.co.uk
dir: In town centre

Muddy boots, dogs and bikes are all welcome at this 17th-century ivy-clad coaching inn, which stands on the village green in the heart of picture-postcard Malham, just a short stroll beside the River Aire to

Malham's magnificent cove and limestone pavement. Glorious Dales countryside and fabulous walks (the Pennine Way cuts through the village) surround the village, so explore and return at night in winter to hunker down by the wood-burning stove in the friendly, stone-walled bar or the cosy dining rooms. In summer, spill out onto the cobbled terrace and refuel with a pint of Thwaites Lancaster Bomber and hearty meal from the seasonal menu. Using local suppliers, dishes on the daytime menu take in hot sandwiches, oak-smoked salmon pâté, Yorkshire rarebit, imaginative deli boards, or classic main courses like ham, egg and thick-cut chips. Evening extras may include Dales shepherd's pie, roast pork belly with apple sauce, and 28-day aged sirloin steak. In addition, you'll find nine refurbished en suite rooms, with pretty fabrics, old pine and cast-iron beds, and village or country views, plus activity breaks.

Open all day all wk **Bar Meals** Av main course £10 food served all day **Restaurant** Av 3 course à la carte fr £20 food served all day ⊕ THWAITES INNS ◀ Thwaites Wainwright, Original ♻ Kingstone Press. ☗ 8 **Facilities** Children welcome Children's menu Children's portions Dogs allowed Garden Parking Wi-fi **Rooms** 9

See advert opposite

MASHAM   Map 19 SE28

The Black Sheep Brewery

Wellgarth HG4 4EN
☎ 01765 680101 & 680100   ▤ 01765 689746
e-mail: sue.dempsey@blacksheep.co.uk
web: www.blacksheepbrewery.co.uk
dir: *Off A6108, 9m from Ripon & 7m from Bedale*

The Black Sheep Brewery was founded in the early nineties by Paul Theakston, of Masham's famous brewing family. The complex boasts a visitor centre where you can enjoy a 'shepherded' tour of the brewhouse, before popping into the cosy bistro and 'baa...r' to sample a freshly-made pint. With wonderful views over the River Ure and surrounding countryside, settle down to snack on a speciality ciabatta, or go the whole hog with a gammon steak cured in the famous ale.

Open all wk 10.30-4.30 (Thu-Sat 10.30-late)
Bar Meals food served all day **Restaurant** food served all day ⊕ BLACK SHEEP BREWERY ◀ Black Sheep Best Bitter, Riggwelter, Black Sheep Ale, Golden Sheep. **Facilities** Children welcome Children's menu Children's portions Garden Parking Wi-fi

Kings Head Hotel ★★ HL ☗

Market Place HG4 4EF
☎ 01765 689295   ▤ 01765 689070
dir: *B6267 towards Masham, 7m from A1*

Overlooking Masham's large market square with its cross and maypole, this tastefully renovated Georgian inn boasts open fires in the public rooms and a pleasant terrace for summer dining. Unwind over a pint of Theakstons or one of the popular long drinks in the bar, or sample a range of traditional and contemporary dishes in the wood panelled restaurant. Options might include Thai fish cakes, fillet steak bourguignon, or grilled swordfish with gremolata. The pub has vegetarian nights, curry nights and fish nights every week and traditional roasts on Sunday.

Open all day all wk 10.30am-1am **Bar Meals** Av main course £8 food served all day **Restaurant** Fixed menu price fr £9.99 food served all day ⊕ PUNCH PUB COMPANY ◀ Theakston Best Bitter, Black Sheep Bitter, Black Sheep Riggwelter. ☗ 14 **Facilities** Children welcome Children's menu Children's portions Garden Wi-fi **Rooms** 27

MIDDLEHAM   Map 19 SE18

Black Swan Hotel

Market Place DL8 4NP
☎ 01969 622221   ▤ 01969 625086
dir: *Telephone for directions*

Backing onto Middleham Castle, home of Richard III, this historic 17th-century pub is at the heart of Yorkshire's racing country. Horses can be seen passing outside every morning on their way to the gallops. The emphasis here is on good food cooked by a skilled continental chef. Choices run from bangers and mash to Kilnsey trout roasted with parsley and thyme dressing. Fish and seafood are a speciality. As we went to press a change of hands was taking place.

Open all wk (all day summer & all wknds) ⊕ ENTERPRISE INNS ◀ John Smith's, Theakstons Best Bitter, Old Peculier, Black Sheep, Hambleton Stud. **Facilities** Children welcome Children's menu Children's portions Dogs allowed Garden Wi-fi

The White Swan ☗

Market Place DL8 4PE
☎ 01969 622093   ▤ 01969 624551
e-mail: enquiries@whiteswanhotel.co.uk
dir: *From A1, take A684 towards Leyburn then A6108 to Ripon, 1.5m to Middleham*

Middleham is within an hour's drive of five top racecourses. No surprise then that this picturesque inn overlooking the town's market square is steeped in the history of the turf. A range of hand-pulled Yorkshire ales, Thatchers cider and quality wines are served in the cosy bar, all complementing brasserie cuisine: shredded confit crispy duck leg with bacon salad; chicken breast stuffed with mozzarella and sundried tomato and pesto risotto; and iced liquorice terrine with caramel sauce.

Open all day all wk 10.30am-11pm (mdnt at wknds)
Restaurant L served all wk 8am-9.30pm booking

required D served all wk 8am-9.30pm booking required food served all day ⊕ FREE HOUSE ◀ Black Sheep Best, John Smith's, Theakstons ♻ Thatchers Gold. ☗ 9 **Facilities** Children welcome Children's portions Family room Dogs allowed Parking Wi-fi

MIDDLESMOOR   Map 19 SE07

Crown Hotel

HG3 5ST ☎ 01423 755204
dir: *Telephone for directions*

There are great views towards Gouthwaite Reservoir from this breezy 900ft hilltop village with its cobbled streets. This family-run traditional free house dates back to the 17th century and is in an ideal spot for anyone following the popular Nidderdale Way. Visitors can enjoy a good pint of local beer and food by the cosy, roaring log fire, or in the sunny pub garden. A large selection of malt whisky is also on offer.

Open Tue-Sun (ex Wed & Thu L in winter) Closed: all day Mon, Wed & Thu L (winter) **Bar Meals** L served 12-2 D served 7-8.30 ⊕ FREE HOUSE ◀ Black Sheep Best, Guinness, Wensleydale Bitter. **Facilities** Children welcome Dogs allowed Garden Parking

MOULTON   Map 19 NZ20

PICK OF THE PUBS

Black Bull Inn ☺ ☗

DL10 6QJ ☎ 01325 377289   ▤ 01325 377422
e-mail: info@blackbullmoulton.com
dir: *1m S of Scotch Corner off A1, 5m from Richmond*

The entrance to this traditional old free house introduces customers directly to the bar. Here beams, whitewashed walls, antique curios and fresh flowers generate an effortless atmosphere of well-being, aided by friendly and efficient staff. With a pint of Theakston's or glass of wine in hand, it's time to peruse the menu. It's the pub's reputation for fresh seafood that brings most people here — seafood, and the prospect of eating it in an immaculate Pullman dining carriage. Built in 1932 for service on the Brighton Belle, it is called 'Hazel' and lends the elegance of a bygone age to dishes of rock oysters from Cork, Dublin Bay prawns, and lobster — all served as fresh as can be thanks to the pub's holding tanks. If seafood is not for you, meat and vegetarian options may include mixed game presse with toasted brioche; salad of endive, Roquefort, sweet beetroot and pickled walnuts; and classic boeuf bourguignon, with smoked bacon and garlic toast. Comfortable accommodation is available.

Open noon-3 6-mdnt Closed: Sun eve
Bar Meals L served Mon-Fri 12-2.30, Sat 12-2 Sun 12-4 D served 6.30-9 Av main course £8.50
Restaurant L served Mon-Fri 12-2.30, Sun 12-4 booking required D served Mon-Thu 6.30-9.30, Fri-Sat 6.30-10 booking required Fixed menu price fr £19.95 Av 3 course à la carte fr £29.50 ⊕ FREE HOUSE ◀ Theakstons Best, John Smith's Smooth. **Facilities** Children welcome Children's portions Garden Parking **Rooms** 9

PICK OF THE PUBS

The Black Swan at Oldstead ★★★★★ RR

OLDSTEAD   Map 19 SE57

Main St YO61 4BL ☎ 01347 868387
e-mail:
enquiries@blackswanoldstead.co.uk
web: www.blackswanoldstead.co.uk
dir: *A1 junct 49, A168, A19S, after 3m left*
to Coxwold then Byland Abbey. In 2m left
for Oldstead, pub 1m on left

Dating back to the 16th century and set in
a sleepy hamlet below the North York
Moors, The Black Swan is owned and run
by the Banks family, generations of whom
have farmed in the village. In the bar
you'll find a stone-flagged floor, an open
log fire, antique furniture window seats,
soft cushions and fittings by Robert
'Mousey' Thompson, in the 1930s a prolific
maker of traditional handcrafted English
oak furniture. Expect tip-top real ales,
cracking wines by the glass, malt whiskies
and vintage port, while the food on offer is
first class, changing with seasons and
sourced mainly from local farms. Expect a
pub classic, such as fish and chips and a
hot steak and balsamic onion sandwich.
Cooking really moves up several gears in
the comfortable restaurant (3 Rosettes),
with its oak floor, Persian rugs, antique
furniture and soft light from traditional
candles in old brass holders. The
innovative modern country menu bristles
with great ideas and combinations, from
classic pairings to the most delicate and
ambitious flavours and textures. Start,
perhaps, with game terrine with game

pâté, Cumberland jelly and date and
walnut bread; move on to moist, perfectly
seasoned roast pork belly with apple
purée, fondant potatoes and Thatcher's
cider foam; and finish with crème Catalan
with rhubarb and orange, accompanied by
a glass of late harvest Tokaji Ats Cuvée.
The bedrooms have solid oak floors and
are furnished with quality antiques,
stylish soft fabrics and paintings.
Bathrooms include iron roll-top baths and
walk-in wet room shower areas. This place
oozes style and quality in a superb country
setting - wonderful walks radiate from the
front door and route details are available
at the bar.

Open noon-3 6-11 Closed: 1st 2wks Jan,
Mon L, Tue L, Wed L **Bar Meals** L served
Thu-Sun 12-2 D served all wk 6-9 Av main
course £12 **Restaurant** L served Thu-Sun

12-2 booking required D served all wk 6-9
booking required Fixed menu price fr £20
Av 3 course à la carte fr £37 ⊕ FREE
HOUSE ◼ Black Sheep, Copper Dragon.
♟ 19 **Facilities** Children welcome
Children's menu Children's portions
Garden Parking Wi-fi **Rooms** 4

MUKER   Map 18 SD99

The Farmers Arms ☺

DL11 6QG ☎ 01748 886297
e-mail: enquiries@farmersarmsmuker.co.uk
dir: From Richmond take A6108 towards Leyburn, turn right onto B6270

Dave and Sheila Alderson took over this 19th-century inn at the end of 2010 and have injected new life into the village's last remaining pub. Located at the head of beautiful Swaledale, the pub is understandably popular with walkers and in summer the south facing patio is a relaxing place to enjoy a pint of Black Sheep. The menu includes home-made giant Yorkshire puddings filled with local sausages and gravy, or chilli con carne.

Open all day all wk **Bar Meals** L served all wk 12-2.30 D served all wk 6-8.30 ⊕ FREE HOUSE ◀ Theakstons Best, Old Peculier, John Smith's, Black Sheep, Guest ales ♂ Thatchers Gold. ☺ 9 **Facilities** Children welcome Children's menu Children's portions Dogs allowed Garden Parking

NUNNINGTON   Map 19 SE67

The Royal Oak Inn ☺

Church St YO62 5US ☎ 01439 748271
dir: Village centre, close to Nunnington Hall

This Grade II listed solid stone country inn welcomes with an open plan bar furnished with scrubbed pine and decorated with farming memorabilia, open fires in winter and fresh flowers in summer. The sign on the front door says it all: 'Real ale, real food, real people'. True to this promise you'll find hearty home-cooked meals made with locally reared meats, game from nearby estates, and fresh vegetables. Typical dishes include pork fillet in barbecue sauce; ham and mushroom tagliatelle; crispy roast duckling; and steak and kidney casserole.

Open 11.45-2.30 6.30-11 (Sun noon-2.30 7-11) Closed: Mon (ex BHs 12-2) **Bar Meals** L served Tue-Sun 12-2 (booking required Sun) **Restaurant** D served Tue-Sun 6.30-9 ⊕ FREE HOUSE ◀ Black Sheep, Wold Top, John Smith's. ☺ 10 **Facilities** Children welcome Children's menu Children's portions Dogs allowed Garden Parking

OLDSTEAD   Map 19 SE57

PICK OF THE PUBS

The Black Swan at Oldstead

XXXXX RR ●●● ☺

See Pick of the Pubs on opposite page

OSMOTHERLEY   Map 19 SE49

PICK OF THE PUBS

The Golden Lion

6 West End DL6 3AA ☎ 01609 883526
e-mail: goldenlionosmotherley@yahoo.co.uk
dir: Telephone for directions

The Golden Lion is a cosy sandstone building of some 250 years standing. The atmosphere is warm and welcoming, with open fires and wooden flooring on one side of the downstairs area. Furnishings are simple with a wooden bar, bench seating and tables, whitewashed walls, mirrors and fresh flowers. The extensive menu ranges through basic pub grub to more refined dishes. The starters are divided between fish, soups, vegetarian, pastas and risottos, meat and salads, and might include smoked salmon; buffalo mozzarella with tomato and basil; spicy pork ribs; and avocado and king prawn salad. Mains are along the lines of grilled sea bass with new potatoes and peas; coq au vin; calves' liver with fried onions and mash; home-made beef burger with Mexican salsa; and spicy chilladas with fresh tomato sauce. Also interesting are specials like pork Stroganoff and rice, or lamb and feta lasagne. Sherry trifle, and bread and butter pudding with cream, are popular desserts.

Open 12-3 6-11 Closed: 25 Dec, Mon L, Tue L ⊕ FREE HOUSE ◀ Timothy Taylor Landlord, Yorkshire Dales Brewery, York Guzzler ♂ Herefordshire Cider. **Facilities** Children welcome Children's menu Dogs allowed Garden

PATELEY BRIDGE   Map 19 SE16

PICK OF THE PUBS

The Sportsmans Arms Hotel ☺

Wath-in-Nidderdale HG3 5PP
☎ 01423 711306   ▤ 01423 712524
e-mail: sportsmansarms@btconnect.com
dir: A59/B6451, hotel 2m N of Pateley Bridge

Wath is a conservation village, picturesque and unspoilt, set in beautiful Nidderdale, one of the loveliest of the Yorkshire Dales. Ray and June Carter have been running their 17th-century restaurant, reached by a packhorse bridge across the Nidd, for over 30 years, although son Jamie and daughter Sarah have leading roles too these days. Enter the hallway and find open log fires, comfortable chairs, a warm and welcoming bar and a calm, softly lit restaurant, dominated at one end by a Victorian sideboard and substantial wine rack. As much of the food as possible is locally sourced: fish arrives daily from Whitby and other East Coast harbours. Always a good choice are the Nidderdale lamb, pork, beef, fresh trout and especially game (season permitting) from the moors. The wine list offers a wide selection of styles and prices to complement any dish. The Sportsmans Arms stands on the 53-mile, circular Nidderdale Way, hard by the dam over the River Nidd (some fishing rights belong to the hotel) that creates Gouthwaite Reservoir.

Open all wk noon-2.30 6.30-11 Closed: 25 Dec **Bar Meals** L served all wk 12-2 D served all wk 7-9 **Restaurant** L served Sun 12-2 D served Mon-Sat 7-9 ⊕ FREE HOUSE ◀ Black Sheep, Worthingtons, Timothy Taylor ♂ Thatchers Gold. ☺ 12 **Facilities** Children's portions Garden Parking Wi-fi

PICKERING   Map 19 SE78

PICK OF THE PUBS

Fox & Hounds Country Inn ★★ HL ●

Sinnington YO62 6SQ
☎ 01751 431577   ▤ 01751 432791
e-mail: fox.houndsinn@btconnect.com
dir: 3m W of town, off A170 between Pickering & Helmsley

Proprietors Andrew and Catherine Stephens and friendly, efficient staff ensure a warm welcome at this handsome 18th-century coaching inn. Situated in Sinnington, on a quiet road between Pickering and Kirkbymoorside, a gentle walk from the pub passes the village green to the pretty riverside where ducks swim in the shallows and an ancient packhorse bridge leads to more footpaths through the woods. As you settle down with a pint of Theakstons or Black Sheep, you can relax and enjoy the oak-beamed ceilings, old wood panelling and open fires. The inn has ten well-equipped en suite bedrooms, and a residents' lounge where guests can relax by the fire before dinner in the recently refurbished restaurant with its comfortable, contemporary design. The menu is full of locally farmed produce, and many of the starters are also available as main courses. Expect the likes of roasted king scallops wrapped in pancetta, crab and Pernod risotto, apple and ginger purée; trio of guinea fowl; roast duck leg caramelised with sweet chilli and orange, soy noodles; ginger baked Alaska and poached Yorkshire rhubarb.

Open all wk 12-2 6-11 (Sun 12-2 6-10.30) Closed: 25-26 Dec **Bar Meals** L served all wk 12-2 booking required D served all wk 6.30-9 booking required Av main course £14.95 **Restaurant** L served all wk 12-2 booking required D served all wk 6.30-9 booking required Av 3 course à la carte fr £20 ⊕ FREE HOUSE ◀ Theakstons Best, Black Sheep Special, Copper Dragon ♂ Thatchers Gold. **Facilities** Children welcome Children's menu Children's portions Dogs allowed Garden Parking **Rooms** 10

The Fox & Rabbit Inn ☺

Whitby Rd, Lockton YO18 7NQ
☎ 01751 460213   ▤ 01751 460052
e-mail: info@foxandrabbit.co.uk
dir: From Pickering take A169 towards Whitby. Lockton in 5m

Dating from the 18th century and originally known as Keld House, the pub sits at the edge of Dalby Forest with panoramic views over the North York Moors. Brothers Charles and Toby Wood run a welcoming operation — bar and restaurant food is available all day to accommodate

continued

PICKERING *continued*

weary walkers whenever they arrive. Order a pint of Black Sheep and tuck in to plates of Dalby sausages and mash, or deep-fried Whitby haddock with home-made chips and mushy peas.

Open all day all wk **Bar Meals** food served all day **Restaurant** food served all day ⊕ FREE HOUSE ◀ Black Sheep Best, Cropton Brewery Beers ☼ Thatchers Gold. ♙ 11 **Facilities** Children welcome Children's menu Children's portions Dogs allowed Garden Parking

PICK OF THE PUBS

The White Swan Inn
★★★ HL ◉ ♙ **NEW**

Market Place YO18 7AA
☎ 01751 472288 🖷 01751 475554
e-mail: welcome@white-swan.co.uk
dir: *From N: A19 or A1 to Thirsk, A170 to Pickering, left at lights, 1st right onto Market Place. Pub on left. From S: A1 or A1(M) to A64 to Malton rdbt, A169 to Pickering*

The award-winning White Swan is the inn every market town wishes it had. Two miles from the North Yorkshire Moors National Park in the middle of 'Heartbeat Country', this stylish inn offers great food and comfortable accommodation, with York and its magnificent Minster only half an hour away. Close links with top London butcher The Ginger Pig, whose farm is seven miles from the pub, means that rare-breed meat gets star billing on a seasonal menu that has wowed critics and visitors. Tempting dishes include the likes of honey and mustard glazed Tamworth belly pork with apple and radish relish or chargrilled rib-eye of Longhorn beef with sautéed potatoes, Bordelaise sauce and creamed parsley, which may follow Whitby fishcakes, tartare sauce and herbed shrimp salad. Make room for comforting puddings: spiced Ampleforth apple and bramble crumble and custard; glazed lemon tart, prune and treacle ice cream. Fine ales and carefully chosen wines complete the picture.

Open all day all wk **Bar Meals** L served all wk 12-2 D served all wk 6.45-9 Av main course £16.95 **Restaurant** L served all wk 12-2 booking required D served all wk 6.45-9 booking required Av 3 course à la carte fr £25 ⊕ FREE HOUSE ◀ Black Sheep, Timothy Taylor Landlord. ♙ 13 **Facilities** Children welcome Children's menu Children's portions Dogs allowed Garden Parking Wi-fi **Rooms** 21

PICK OF THE PUBS

Nags Head Country Inn
★★★★ INN ◉◉ ♙

YO7 4JG ☎ 01845 567391 🖷 01845 567212
e-mail: enquiries@nagsheadpickhill.co.uk
dir: *1m E of A1. 4m N of A1/A61 junct*

The Boynton family have been welcoming visitors to their extended, former 17th-century coaching inn, situated in a peaceful village just off the A1 north of Thirsk, for nearly 40 years. Synonymous with Yorkshire hospitality at its best, notably among weary A1 travellers and the local racing fraternity, you can retreat to the traditional tap-room bar, with its flagged and tiled floors, beams adorned with ties, and a magpie selection of tables and chairs tucked around open fires, or the beamed lounge, or stay overnight in one of the comfortably furnished bedrooms. A terrific menu is the icing on the cake here; a small but perfectly formed tap-room menu offers smoked salmon and scrambled eggs, or great pizzas and sandwiches. In the lounge or elegant restaurant, order Lindisfarne oysters to start, then follow with seafood pancake, wild venison with juniper sauce, or confit duck leg with wild mushrooms, potato rösti and duck jus. Tempting, calorific puddings seal the deal, perhaps spiced ginger bread with pear mousse and ginger ice cream.

Open all wk 11-11 (Sun 11-10.30) Closed: 25 Dec **Bar Meals** L served Mon-Sat 12-2, Sun 12-8 booking required D served Mon-Sat 6-9.30, Sun 6-8 booking required Av main course £13.95 **Restaurant** L served Mon-Sat 12-2, Sun 12-5 booking required D served Mon-Sat 6-9.30, Sun 6-8 booking required ⊕ FREE HOUSE ◀ Black Sheep Best, Old Peculier, Theakstons Best Bitter, Black Bull, York Brewery Guzzler ☼ Thatchers Gold. ♙ 8 **Facilities** Children welcome Children's portions Garden Parking Wi-fi **Rooms** 14

The Station Hotel

TS15 0AE ☎ 01642 700067
dir: *1.5m from A19*

This family-run and family-friendly village pub is adjacent to the village play area, making it ideal for children. Parents can relax in front of the open fire or in the beer garden with a pint of Black Sheep. Enjoying the same ownership for over 20 years, all the food is locally sourced from the village farm shop, local farmers and butcher. Everything on the extensive specials board is home made, including real hand-cut chips.

Open all wk 6-11.30 (Sat noon-2.30 6-11.30 Sun noon-4 6-11.30) **Bar Meals** L served Sat 12-2.30, Sun 12-4 D served all wk Av main course £11 **Restaurant** L served Sat 12-2.30, Sun 12-4 booking required D served all wk booking required Fixed menu price fr £20 ⊕ FREE HOUSE ◀ Black Sheep Cask, Tetleys Smooth, Guinness, Timothy Taylor, Guest ales. **Facilities** Children welcome Children's menu Children's portions Play area Garden Parking Wi-fi

PICK OF THE PUBS

Charles Bathurst Inn ★★★★ INN ♙

Arkengarthdale DL11 6EN
☎ 01748 884567 🖷 01748 884599
e-mail: info@cbinn.co.uk
web: www.cbinn.co.uk
dir: *From A1 exit at Scotch Corner onto A6108, through Richmond, left onto B6270 to Reeth. At Buck Hotel right signed Langthwaite, pass church on right, inn 0.5m on right*

Nestling in the spectacular scenery of the most rugged and remote of the Yorkshire Dales, Arkengarthdale, this country inn caters for serious ramblers tackling The Pennine Way and the Coast-to-Coast route. The inn takes its name from the 18th-century lord of the manor and son of Oliver Cromwell's physician who built it for his workers. In winter, it offers a welcome escape from the rigours of the moors. The 19 bedrooms overlooking beautiful dales scenery may tempt other visitors to linger and enjoy the attractions of the area, including locations used in the television series *All Creatures Great and Small*. The daily menu – a happy mix of old English and modern European – is written up on an imposing mirror hanging above a stone fireplace. Choose from a selection of real ales and enjoy crab spring roll with crisp noodle salad or spicy lamb kofta and tomato salsa to start, followed by supreme of corn-fed chicken with smoked bacon filo parcel or smoked haddock fillet with a leek and Cheddar tart, poached egg and hollandaise sauce. A decent bin of wines includes 12 by the glass. For private dining, there is the Terrace Room complete with handcrafted tables and chairs by Robert Thompson.

Open all wk 11am-mdnt Closed: 25 Dec **Bar Meals** L served all wk 12-2 booking required D served all wk 6.30-9 booking required Av main course £13.50 **Restaurant** L served all wk 12-2 booking required D served all wk 6.30-9 booking required Av 3 course à la carte fr £22.50 ⊕ FREE HOUSE ◀ Theakstons, Timothy Taylor Landlord, John Smith's Smooth, Black Sheep Best, Riggwelter. ♙ 12 **Facilities** Children welcome Children's menu Children's portions Play area Garden Parking **Rooms** 19

RIPON   Map 19 SE37

The George at Wath
★★★★ INN ♥ **NEW**

Main St, Wath HG4 5EN ☎ 01765 641324
e-mail: richard@thegeorgeatwath.co.uk
dir: *From A1 (dual carriageway) N'bound turn left signed Melmerby & Wath. From A 1 S'bound exit at slip road signed A61. At T-junct right (signed Ripon). Approx 0.5m turn right for Melmerby & Wath*

The George at Wath lies only 3 miles from the cathedral city of Ripon, making it a perfect base for exploring the Yorkshire Dales. Refurbished in 2009, the pub retains its flagstone floors, log-burning fires and cosy atmosphere. Seasonal, locally sourced produce drives a tempting menu of pub classics and bistro-style dishes. Typical main courses are beer-battered haddock fillet, chips and mushy peas, or venison steak with home-made black pudding, port and Madeira jus. Accommodation is available.

Open all wk 12-3 5-11 (Sat-Sun all day)
Bar Meals L served Mon-Sat 12-3, Sun 12-7 D served Mon-Sat fr 5.30 Av main course £15 **Restaurant** L served Mon-Sat 12-3, Sun 12-7 D served Mon-Sat 5.30-9 Fixed menu price fr £15 Av 3 course à la carte fr £25 ◀ Copper Dragon, Black Sheep. **Facilities** Children welcome Children's menu Children's portions Dogs allowed Garden Beer festival Parking **Rooms** 5

The Royal Oak ★★★★ INN ◉ ♥ **NEW**

36 Kirkgate HG4 1PB ☎ 01765 602284
e-mail: info@royaloakripon.co.uk
dir: *In town centre*

Built as a coaching inn, this refurbished city centre venue now has a clean, modern and open feel, with wooden floorboards in the bright, spacious bar and comfortable leather settees in the AA one-Rosette restaurant. Owned by Timothy Taylor brewery you can obviously expect excellent ales. Lunchtime brings 'knife and fork' sandwiches with hand-cut chips, and there's also a good range of pub classics like pie and mash. Other mains include line caught bass with peanut and lime risotto, prawns and Thai red curry sauce. Regular food and wine tasting events and modern accommodation completes the package.

Open all day all wk **Bar Meals** L served Mon-Fri 12-2.30, Sat 12-9, Sun 12-7 D served all wk 5.30-9 Av main course £12 **Restaurant** L served Mon-Fri 12-2.30, Sat 12-9, Sun 12-7 D served all wk 5.30-9 Av 3 course à la carte fr £20 ⊕ TIMOTHY TAYLOR & CO LTD ◀ Timothy Taylor Landlord, Best Bitter, Golden Best, Ram Tam. ♥ 14 **Facilities** Children welcome Children's menu Children's portions Garden Parking Wi-fi **Rooms** 6

ROBIN HOOD'S BAY   Map 19 NZ90

Laurel Inn

New Rd YO22 4SE ☎ 01947 880400
dir: *Telephone for directions*

Given its location it's hardly surprising that this was once the haunt of smugglers who used a network of underground tunnels and secret passages to bring the booty ashore. Nowadays it's the haunt of holidaymakers and walkers and the setting for this small, traditional pub which retains lots of character features, including beams and an open fire. The bar is decorated with old photographs, and an international collection of lager bottles. This popular free house serves Old Peculier, Theakstons Best and Deuchars IPA.

Open all wk ⊕ FREE HOUSE ◀ Old Peculier, Theakstons Best, Deuchars IPA. **Facilities** Children welcome Family room Dogs allowed **Notes** ⊜

SAWDON   Map 17 SE98

PICK OF THE PUBS

The Anvil Inn ♥

Main St YO13 9DY ☎ 01723 859896
e-mail: info@theanvilinnsawdon.co.uk
dir: *1.5m N of Brompton-by-Sawdon, on A170 8m E of Pickering & 6m W of Scarborough*

Off the beaten track in a sleepy village on the edge of Dalby Forest, a popular walking and mountain biking area, The Anvil was a working forge for over 200 years before becoming a pub in the mid 1980s. The bar was once the blacksmith's workshop and is crammed with old artefacts, from the original furnace to bellows, tools and, of course, the anvil. Parched walkers and bikers fresh from the trails will find cracking ales from Daleside, Northumberland and Great Newsome micro-breweries, but the real draw is modern European cooking conjured up by chef-patron Mark Wilson. Typically, tuck into a bowl of mussels with garlic, parsley, white wine and cream, followed by roast pork belly with apple and sage mash and cider and pork jus, and iced pistachio parfait with pear Tatin and cider syrup for pudding.

Open 12-2.30 6.30-11 Closed: 26 Dec & 1 Jan, Mon-Tue **Bar Meals** L served Wed-Sat 12-2, Sun 12-2.30 booking required D served Wed-Sat 6.30-9, Sun 6-8 booking required **Restaurant** L served Wed-Sat 12-2, Sun 12-3 booking required D served Wed-Sat 6.30-9, Sun 6-8 booking required ⊕ FREE HOUSE ◀ Daleside, Wold Top, Northumberland Brewery, Great Newsome Brewery ♂ Stowford Press. ♥ 11 **Facilities** Children welcome Children's portions Dogs allowed Garden Parking

SAWLEY   Map 19 SE26

The Sawley Arms

HG4 3EQ ☎ 01765 620642
e-mail: junehawes1@aol.co.uk
dir: *A1(M) junct 47, A59 to Knaresborough, B6165 to Ripley, A61 towards Ripon, left for Sawley. Or from Ripon B6265 towards Pateley Bridge, left to Sawley. Pub 1m from Fountains Abbey*

Just a mile from Fountains Abbey, this delightful 200-year-old pub was a frequent haunt of the late author and vet James Herriot. Run by the same owners for 41 years, it is big on old world charm and is surrounded by its own stunning award-winning gardens. The menu is modern British yet varied, with dishes ranging from salmon three ways to pork, sage and apricot cassoulet with cider, leeks, smoked bacon, mushrooms and cannellini beans. Look out for various promotions and offers.

Open 11.30-3 6-10.30 Closed: 25 Dec, Mon eve in winter ⊕ FREE HOUSE ◀ Theakston Best, John Smith's. **Facilities** Children welcome Children's portions Garden Parking

SCAWTON   Map 19 SE58

PICK OF THE PUBS

The Hare Inn ◉ ♥

YO7 2HG ☎ 01845 597769
e-mail: info@thehareinn.co.uk
dir: *Telephone for directions*

Built in the 13th century and allegedly used as a brewhouse by the monks who built Rievaulx Abbey, the Hare also boasts a friendly ghost! Later, in the 17th century, ale was brewed here for local iron workers. Inside, you'll find low-beamed ceilings and flagstone floors, a wood-burning stove offering a warm welcome in the bar, and an old-fashioned kitchen range in the dining area. Eating here promises food of AA Rosette standard, with the kitchen ringing the changes according to availability of locally sourced ingredients. The full à la carte menu is complemented by light lunch and early bird options, offering quality dining at value prices. A representative choice might start with roast goat's cheese in filo pastry with pine nuts and basil dressing; continuing with pan-fried breast of guinea fowl with tarragon mousse and wild mushrooms; and finishing with passionfruit crème brûlée.

Open Tue-Sat 12-2 6-9.30 (Sun 12-4) Closed: Mon, Sun eve (ex BHs) **Bar Meals** L served Tue-Sat 12-2, Sun 12-4 **Restaurant** L served Tue-Sat 12-2, Sun 12-4 booking required D served Tue-Sat 6-9 booking required ⊕ FREE HOUSE ◀ Black Sheep, Timothy Taylor Landlord, Guest ales ♂ Thatchers. ♥ 10 **Facilities** Children welcome Children's portions Garden Parking

SETTLE   Map 18 SD86

The Lion at Settle ★★★★ INN ☂

Duke St BD24 9DU ☎ 01729 822203   📄 01729 824103
e-mail: relax@thelionsettle.co.uk
web: thelionsettle.co.uk
dir: Telephone for directions

New life has been breathed into this traditional Dales
coaching inn situated in the heart of Settle's
17th-century market place. Owner Thwaites Brewery
completely refurbished the inn early in 2011, sprucing up
the bedrooms and revamping the cosy bars and the
spacious restaurant, which ooze history and atmosphere
with original inglenook fireplaces, wooden floors and a
grand staircase lined with pictures that trace back
through the town's history. It's now a comfortable base for
exploring the Dales and meets the needs of travellers
experiencing the spectacular Settle to Carlisle railway line.
In addition, expect decent cask ales and a classic pub
menu offering freshly prepared pub favourites with a
strong Yorkshire influence and sound use of local,
seasonal produce. Typically, tuck into warm Blue Pig black
pudding, bacon and potato salad, haddock in beer batter
or beef and ale suet pudding, and toffee apple crumble.

Open all day all wk 11-11 (Sun noon-10.30)
Bar Meals L served all wk 9-9 D served all wk 9-9 food
served all day Restaurant L served all wk 9-9 food served
all day ⊕ DANIEL THWAITES PLC ◀ Thwaites Bitter,
Bomber, Guest ales ♂ Kingstone Press. ☂ 9
Facilities Children welcome Children's menu Children's
portions Dogs allowed Garden Parking Rooms 14

See advert below

SKIPTON   Map 18 SD95

Devonshire Arms

Grassington Rd, Cracoe BD23 6LA ☎ 01756 730237
e-mail: info@devonshirecracoe.co.uk
dir: Telephone for directions

This convivial, caringly renovated 17th-century inn was
the original setting for the Rhylstone Ladies WI calendar.
Conveniently located for the Three Peaks, it has excellent
views of Rhylstone Fell. In the hands of experienced
licensees, your will find character, quality and service
here. A wide range of cask ales plus extensive wine list
will wash down a menu that runs from local sausages
with baby Yorkshire puddings and home-made gravy to
fillet of monkfish finished with a grapefruit and star anise
cream.

Open all wk ⊕ MARSTONS ◀ Jennings, Jennings
Cumberland, Pedigree. Facilities Children welcome
Children's menu Children's portions Play area Dogs
allowed Garden Parking Wi-fi

SNAINTON   Map 17 SE98

The Coachman Inn ★★★★ RR ⊛ ☂

Pickering Road West YO13 9PL
☎ 01723 859231   📄 01723 850008
e-mail: info@coachmaninn.co.uk
web: www.coachmaninn.co.uk
dir: 5m from Pickering, off A170 onto B1258, 9m from
Scarborough off the A170 onto B1258

This imposing Grade II listed Georgian coaching inn on
the road between York and Scarborough offers award-
winning food and holds the coveted AA Rosette for
culinary excellence. Food is served in the romantic
candlelit Carriages Restaurant, cosy lounge or rustic
Coachman Bar with its blazing log fire. Traditional beers
are available and a wide selection of wines by the glass.
Typical dishes include dressed crab and smoked salmon
tian, herb salad and guacamole followed by pan-roast
Goosnargh duck, potato terrine, spiced carrots, honey and
black pepper jus. Outside, the tranquil gardens with large
lawn and courtyard offer alfresco dining. Comfortable
accommodation is available.

Open all wk noon-mdnt Bar Meals L served all wk 12-3
D served all wk 6.30-9 Restaurant L served all wk 12-3
D served all wk 6.30-9 booking required Av 3 course à la
carte fr £25 ⊕ FREE HOUSE ◀ John Smith's, Wold Top,
Guinness. ☂ 15 Facilities Children welcome Children's
menu Children's portions Garden Parking Wi-fi Rooms 6

Save on hotels. Book at **theAA.com/hotel**

YORKSHIRE, NORTH 529 ENGLAND

PUB GUIDE 2012

STARBOTTON — Map 18 SD97

Fox & Hounds Inn ⚲

BD23 5HY ☎ 01756 760269 & 760367
e-mail: starbottonfox@aol.com
dir: *Telephone for directions*

Built as a private house some 400 years ago, but since the 1840s a pub serving this picturesque limestone Yorkshire Dales village. Make for the bar, with its large stone fireplace, oak beams and flagged floor to enjoy a pint of Black Sheep or Timothy Taylor Landlord, or one of the wide selection of malts. Head to the dining room for home-cooked pork medallions in brandy and mustard sauce; Thai cod and prawn fishcakes; or broccoli and Stilton quiche. The area is renowned for its spectacular walks.

Open noon-3 6-11 (Sun noon-3.30 5.30-10.30) Closed: 1-22 Jan, Mon **Bar Meals** L served Tue-Sun 12-2.30 D served Tue-Sat 6-9, Sun 5.30-8 ⊕ FREE HOUSE ◀ Black Sheep, Timothy Taylor Landlord, Moorhouse, Guest ales Ⓧ Thatchers Gold. ⚲ 10 **Facilities** Children welcome Garden Parking

SUTTON-ON-THE-FOREST — Map 19 SE56

PICK OF THE PUBS

The Blackwell Ox Inn
INN ⊛ ⚲

Huby Rd YO61 1DT
☎ 01347 810328 ▤ 01347 812738
e-mail: enquiries@blackwelloxinn.co.uk
dir: *A1237 onto B1363 to Sutton-on-the-Forest. Left at T-junct, 50yds on right*

Named after a magnificent beast weighing 2,278 pounds and slaughtered in 1779, some 40 years before the building, a house for a Mrs Mary Shepherd, was started. Today's Blackwell Ox blends modern elegance with period charm; visitors will find hand-pulled ales and an open fire in the bar, as well as a terrace for the warmer months. The chef believes in simple, honest cooking, and sources local North Yorkshire produce to create his dishes. Substantial 'knife and fork' sandwiches appear at lunchtime, alongside a short but well-considered menu that might include starters of duck scotch egg with warm bread and fruit chutney; sautéed mushrooms on toast with a soft poached egg; and seared pigeon breast with beetroot salsa. Half a dozen main courses may offer venison rack served pink; pheasant breast wrapped in bacon; and braised leek and blue cheese tart with grape and walnut salad. Just seven miles from the centre of York, the inn also offers comfortable, individually designed bedrooms.

Open all wk noon-3 5.30-11 (Sun noon-10.30) Closed: 25 Dec, 1 Jan **Bar Meals** L served all wk 12-2 D served all wk 6-9.30 **Restaurant** L served all wk 12-2 D served all wk 6-9.30 ⊕ FREE HOUSE ◀ Black Sheep, John Smith's Cask, Guinness, Timothy Taylor Landlord, Copper Dragon. ⚲ 14 **Facilities** Children welcome Children's menu Children's portions Garden Parking Wi-fi **Rooms** 7

TERRINGTON — Map 19 SE67

The Bay Horse Inn (The Storyteller Brewery) ⚲

Main St YO60 6PP ☎ 01653 648416
e-mail: info@bayhorseinterrington.co.uk
dir: *From Malton take unclassified road W (8m) through Coneysthorpe, pass Castle Howard, on to Terrington*

Located in the Howardian Hills, at the edge of the North York Moors in an unspoiled village, this 17th-century pub is home to The Storyteller Brewery, set up by landlord Robert Frankin in 2008. Expect to sup a tip-top pint of Genesis by the crackling log fire in the cosy lounge bar, or in the conservatory dining, which is adorned with old farm tools. If tempted to sample the Full Moon ale, then accompany it with a plate of traditional Yorkshire food, perhaps chicken and ham pie, or sirloin steak served with oven-roasted tomatoes and hand-cut chips.

Open Tue 6-11, Wed-Fri noon-3 6-11, Sat noon-11, Sun noon-7.30 Closed: Mon, Tue L **Bar Meals** L served Wed-Sun 12-3 D served Wed-Sun 6-10 **Restaurant** booking required ⊕ THE STORYTELLER BREWERY ◀ Storyteller Genesis, 1402, Full Moon, Golden Lily, Nepenthe. ⚲ 8 **Facilities** Children welcome Children's menu Children's portions Dogs allowed Garden Parking Wi-fi

THORNTON LE DALE — Map 19 SE88

The New Inn

Maltongate YO18 7LF ☎ 01751 474226
e-mail: enquire@the-new-inn.com
dir: *A64 N from York towards Scarborough. At Malton take A169 to Pickering. At Pickering rdbt right onto A170, 2m, pub on right*

An old Georgian coaching house dating back to 1720, this attractive family-run pub stands at the heart of a picturesque village complete with stocks and a market cross. The old world charm of the location is echoed inside the bar and restaurant, with real log fires and exposed beams. Enjoy well kept Theakston Black Bull and guest ales, bitters, lagers and wines and tuck into battered Whitby haddock, chunky vegetable curry or pheasant, mushroom and bacon casserole.

Open all wk 12-2.30 5-11 (summer all day) **Bar Meals** L served Mon-Sat 12-2, Sun 12-2.30 (winter Tue-Sat) D served Mon-Sat 6-8.30, Sun 6.30-8.30 (winter Mon-Sat) **Restaurant** L served Mon-Sat 12-2, Sun 12-2.30 (winter Tue-Sat) D served Mon-Sat 6-8.30, Sun 6.30-8.30 (winter Mon-Sat) ⊕ SCOTTISH & NEWCASTLE ◀ Theakston Black Bull, Guest ales. **Facilities** Children welcome Children's menu Children's portions Dogs allowed Garden Parking Wi-fi

THORNTON WATLASS — Map 19 SE28

PICK OF THE PUBS

The Buck Inn ★★★ INN

See Pick of the Pubs on page 530

WASS — Map 19 SE57

PICK OF THE PUBS

Wombwell Arms ⚲

YO61 4BE ☎ 01347 868280
e-mail: wombwellarms@btconnect.com
dir: *From A1 take A168 to A19 junct. Take York exit, then left after 2.5m, left at Coxwold to Ampleforth. Wass 2m*

Ian and Eunice Walker's whitewashed village inn dates from 1620, when it was built as a granary using stones from the ruins of nearby Byland Abbey, and it sits in the shadow of the Hambleton Hills. There are two oak-beamed, flagstone-floored bars, one with a huge inglenook fireplace, the other with a wood-burning stove, and the atmosphere is relaxed and informal - dogs are welcome to sprawl contentedly across the floor, while locals, walkers and cyclists quaff pints of Timothy Taylor Landlord. High quality, freshly prepared meals are prepared from local produce as far as possible. Tuck into decent sandwiches, salads and ploughman's, or choose one of the Wombwell classics, perhaps the Wass steak, Guinness and mushroom pie. Look to the week's specials for scallops with a prawn and saffron sauce, or pan-fried beef with a creamy mushroom and mustard sauce, and leave room for apple and pear crumble or a plate of local cheeses.

Open noon-3 6-11 (Sat noon-11 Sun noon-4 6-10.30) Closed: Sun eve-Mon Nov-Mar **Bar Meals** L served Mon-Thu 12-2, Fri-Sat 12-2.30, Sun 12-3 D served Mon-Thu 6.30-9, Fri-Sat 6.30-9.30, Sun 6.30-8.30 Av main course £11 **Restaurant** L served Mon-Thu 12-2, Fri-Sat 12-2.30, Sun 12-3 booking required D served Mon-Thu 6.30-9, Fri-Sat 6.30-9.30, Sun 6.30-8.30 booking required Av 3 course à la carte fr £19.20 ⊕ FREE HOUSE ◀ Timothy Taylor Landlord, Theakston Best Ⓧ Galtres Gold. ⚲ 9 **Facilities** Children welcome Children's menu Children's portions Dogs allowed Garden Parking Wi-fi

PICK OF THE PUBS

The Buck Inn ★★★ INN

THORNTON WATLASS   Map 19 SE28

HG4 4AH
☎ **01677 422461** 🖹 **01677 422447**
e-mail: innwatlass1@btconnect.com
web: www.buckwatlass.co.uk
dir: *From A1 at Leeming Bar take A684 to Bedale, then B6268 towards Masham. Village 2m on right, by cricket green*

A traditional, well run, friendly institution that has been in experienced hands of Michael and Margaret Fox for over 20 years, who have no trouble in maintaining its welcoming and relaxed atmosphere. The inn doesn't just overlook the village green and cricket pitch; players score four runs for hitting the pub wall, and six if the ball goes over the roof! Very much the quintessential village scene in beautiful Thornton Watlass, Bedale is where Wensleydale, gateway to the Yorkshire Dales National Park, begins, and this glorious area is where much of the television programme *Heartbeat* was filmed. There are three separate dining areas - the bar for informality, the restaurant for dining by candlelight, and on busy days the large function room is opened. The menu ranges from traditional, freshly prepared pub fare to exciting modern cuisine backed by daily changing blackboard specials. Typical bar favourites are Masham rarebit (Wensleydale cheese with local ale topped with bacon and served with pear chutney); steak and ale pie; oven-baked lasagne;

lamb cutlets with rosemary and redcurrant sauce; and beer-battered fish and chips. Hearty and wholesome daily specials may take in seared scallops with frizzy salad and five spice sauce; prawn and crab tian with a herb and lemon mayonnaise; or smoked duck salad. Main courses include dishes like grilled smoked haddock with buttery mash, saffron cream and crisp onion rings; salmon fillet with buttered noodles and tomato and garlic sauce; venison sausages with Lyonnaise potatoes and rosemary gravy; or pan-fried duck breast with stir fry vegetables and hoi sin sauce. Beer drinkers have a choice of five real ales pulled from handpumps, including Masham-brewed Black Sheep, while whisky drinkers have a selection of some forty different malts to try, ideal when relaxing by the real coal fire, and there's live jazz music most Sunday

lunchtimes. Cottage-style bedrooms provide a comfortable night's sleep.

Open all wk 11-mdnt Closed: 25 Dec eve **Bar Meals** L served Mon-Sat 12-2, Sun 12-3 D served all wk 6.30-9 **Restaurant** L served Mon-Sat 12-2, Sun 12-3 D served all wk 6.30-9 ⊕ FREE HOUSE ◀ Black Sheep Best, 4 guest ales ♂ Thatchers Gold. **Facilities** Children's menu Children's portions Play area Family room Dogs allowed Garden Parking **Rooms** 7

WEST BURTON Map 19 SE08

Fox & Hounds

DL8 4JY ☎ 01969 663111 📄 01969 663279
e-mail: the_fox_hounds@unicombox.co.uk
web: www.fhinn.co.uk
dir: *A468 between Hawes & Leyburn, 0.5m E of Aysgarth*

In a beautiful Dales setting, this is a traditional pub overlooking the large village green, which has swings and football goals, and its own hidden waterfalls. Parents can happily sit at the front and enjoy a drink while keeping an eye on their children. A proper local, the pub hosts men's and women's darts teams and a dominoes team. In summer customers play quoits out on the green. Real ales, some from The Black Sheep Brewery down the road, and home-made food prepared from fresh ingredients are served. In addition to the pizzas cooked in the pizza oven, dishes include chicken curry, steak and kidney pie, lasagne, steaks and other pub favourites.

Open all day all wk **Bar Meals** L served all wk 12-2 D served all wk 6-8.30 Av main course £8.95 **Restaurant** L served all wk 12-2 booking required D served all wk 6-8.30 booking required ⊕ FREE HOUSE ◀ Black Sheep, John Smith's, Theakstons Best, Copper Dragon. **Facilities** Children welcome Children's menu Children's portions Dogs allowed Parking

WEST TANFIELD Map 19 SE27

PICK OF THE PUBS

The Bruce Arms ♟

Main St HG4 5JJ ☎ 01677 470325
e-mail: brucefarms1@btconnect.com
dir: *On A6108 between Ripon & Masham*

Set in the pretty riverside village of West Tanfield, this 18th century stone-built pub is a great base for exploring the Yorkshire Dales. Owners David Stead and Hugh Carruthers have really made their mark over the last two years – David with his art studio and Hugh with his cooking. The pub's bistro-style interior exudes charm with traditional exposed beams, log fires and candles on the tables. Expect a good wine list, real ales from the local Black Sheep brewery, and heartfelt cooking from Hugh using the best of local produce. Choices include home-cured ham, egg and chips and contemporary British and European cuisine. There is a lovely alfresco dining area for summer. A handy base for visiting the races at both Ripon and Thirsk, and famous sights such as Fountains Abbey.

Open 12-2.30 6-9.30 (Sun 12-3.30) Closed: Mon **Bar Meals** L served Tue-Sat 12-2.30 D served Tue-Sat 6-7.30 Av main course £9.50 **Restaurant** L served Tue-Sat 12-2.30, Sun 12-3 D served Tue-Sat 6-9.30 Fixed menu price fr £12.95 Av 3 course à la carte fr £25 ⊕ FREE HOUSE ◀ Black Sheep Bitter Ale, Guest ales ♦ Aspall. ♟ 10 **Facilities** Children welcome Dogs allowed Garden Parking

WEST WITTON Map 19 SE08

PICK OF THE PUBS

The Wensleydale Heifer
RR ◉◉ ♟ NEW

Main St DL8 4LS ☎ 01969 622322
dir: *A1 to Leeming Bar junct, A684 towards Bedale for approx 10m to Leyburn, then towards Hawes, 3.5m to West Witton*

Located in the heart of the Yorkshire Dales, this traditional 17th-century coaching inn has been fully refurbished and retains many of the original features whilst offering guests modern comfort in the 13 Dales-themed bedrooms. As well as an inviting lounge with roaring log fires and real ales, the pub offers two different dining experiences. The fish bar is less formal with seagrass flooring, wooden tables and rattan chairs, whilst the light and airy restaurant has a much more contemporary and casually formal atmosphere. In the kitchen, fresh fish and seafood and locally sourced meats are handled with simplicity. Whitby crab and brown shrimp tian might be followed by herb-crusted cod with buttered spinach and mustard seed and chive cream. Leave room for desserts of chocolate and hazelnut knickerbocker glory or sticky toffee pudding with butterscotch sauce and clotted cream ice cream. There is a great Little Heifer menu.

Open all day all wk **Bar Meals** L served all wk 12.30-2.30 D served all wk 6-9.30 Av main course £17 **Restaurant** L served all wk 12.30-2.30 D served all wk 6-9.30 Fixed menu price fr £18.75 Av 3 course à la carte fr £35 ⊕ FREE HOUSE ◀ Black Sheep, Heifer Ale ♦ Aspall. **Facilities** Children welcome Children's portions Dogs allowed Garden Parking Wi-fi **Rooms** 13

WHASHTON Map 19 NZ10

Hack & Spade

DL11 7JL ☎ 01748 823721
e-mail: info@hackandspade.com
dir: *From Scotch Corner A66 W towards Penrith for 5m. Left exit towards Ravensworth, follow for 2m. Left at x-rds for Whashton*

There are fantastic views over Holmedale and the surrounding area from this popular free house which sits amid rolling hills in the heart of North Yorkshire. Its name relates to the quarry that used to be opposite; nowadays it has been filled in to form part of the village green. The menu is built on local ingredients and is chalked on the board every day and might include local venison and Swaledale lamb. Desserts are all home made including the ice cream.

Open all wk 6.30-11.30 **Restaurant** D served all wk 6.30-8.45 ⊕ FREE HOUSE ◀ John Smith's Smooth, Theakstons. **Facilities** Children welcome Children's portions Parking Wi-fi

WHITBY Map 19 NZ81

The Magpie Café

14 Pier Rd YO21 3PU
☎ 01947 602058 📄 01947 601801
e-mail: ian@magpiecafe.co.uk
dir: *Telephone for directions*

More a licensed restaurant than a pub, the award-winning Magpie has been the home of North Yorkshire's best-ever fish and chips since the late 1930s. You could pop in for a pint of Cropton, but the excellent views of the harbour from the dining room, together with the prospect of fresh seafood, could prove too much of a temptation. Up to ten fish dishes are served daily, perhaps including Whitby cuckoo skink; and Scarborough woof (a type of catfish) with chips.

Open all day all wk Closed: 1-21 Jan ⊕ FREE HOUSE ◀ Cropton, Scoresby Bitter, Tetley Bitter. **Facilities** Children welcome Children's menu Children's portions

WIGGLESWORTH Map 18 SD85

The Plough Inn

BD23 4RJ ☎ 01729 840243 📄 01729 840638
e-mail: plough.inn.wigglesworth@gmail.com
dir: *From A65 between Skipton & Long Preston take B6478 to Wigglesworth*

Dating back to 1720, the bar of this traditional country free house features oak beams and an open fire. There are fine views of the surrounding hills from the conservatory restaurant, where the pub's precarious position on the Yorkshire/Lancashire border is reflected in a culinary 'War of the Roses'. Yorkshire pudding with beef casserole challenges Lancashire hotpot and pickled red cabbage - the latest score is published beside the daily blackboard specials!

Open Tue-Sun Closed: Mon ⊕ FREE HOUSE **Facilities** Children welcome Children's portions Parking

YORK
Map 16 SE65

PICK OF THE PUBS

Blue Bell

53 Fossgate YO1 9TF ☎ 01904 654904
e-mail: robsonhardie@aol.com
dir: In city centre

Its narrow frontage makes it easy to miss, but don't walk past this charming pub – the smallest in York – which has been serving customers in the ancient heart of the city for 200 years. In 1903 it was given a typical Edwardian makeover, and since then almost nothing has changed - this includes the varnished wall and ceiling panelling, the two cast-iron tiled fireplaces, and the old settles. The layout is original too, with the taproom at the front and the snug down a long corridor at the rear, both with servery hatches. Quite fittingly, the whole interior is now Grade II listed. The only slight drawback is that the pub's size leaves no room for a kitchen, so don't expect anything more complicated than lunchtime sandwiches. However, there's a good selection of real ales: no fewer than six are usually on tap, including rotating guests. The pub has won awards for its efforts in fund-raising.

Open all day all wk **Bar Meals** L served Mon-Sat 12-2.30 ⊕ PUNCH TAVERNS ◀ Deuchars IPA, Timothy Taylor Landlord, Adnams Bitter, Greene King Abbot, Tetleys Dark Mild ♻ Westons Traditional.
Facilities Dogs allowed **Notes** ⊛

Lamb & Lion Inn

★★★★ INN ⊚ ♥ **NEW**

2-4 High Petergate YO1 7EH ☎ 01904 612078
e-mail: gm@lambandlionyork.com
dir: From York Station, turn left. Stay in left lane, over Lendal Bridge. At lights left (Theatre Royal on right). At next lights pub on right under Bootham Bar (medieval gate)

Few places can equal the views of nearby York Minster gained from the elevated beer garden here at this rambling Georgian inn, conjoined to the medieval Bootham Bar gateway. Furnished and styled in keeping with its grand heritage, a warren of snugs and corridors radiate from a bar offering a challenging array of beers, including Golden Mane, brewed for the inn. Equally enticing is the menu, fielding Yorkshire dishes ranging from Dales lamb hotpot to hay-baked Nidderdale chicken, backed by some great pubby specials like a fish butty.

Open all day all wk **Bar Meals** Av main course £9 food served all day **Restaurant** food served all day ⊕ FREE HOUSE ◀ Great Heck Golden Mane, Black Sheep Bitter. ♥ 10 **Facilities** Children's portions Dogs allowed Garden Wi-fi **Rooms** 12

Lysander Arms ♥

Manor Ln, Shipton Rd YO30 5TZ ☎ 01904 640845
e-mail: christine@lysanderarms.co.uk
dir: Telephone for directions

The former RAF airfield on which this recently built pub stands was where No. 4 Squadron's Westland Lysander aircraft were based early in World War II. Still relatively modern, which accounts for the contemporary feel of the interior, it has a long, fully air-conditioned bar with modern furnishings, brick-built fireplace and large-screen TV. Brasserie restaurant meals include chargrills; Mediterranean oven-baked chicken; steak and Yorkshire Guzzler Ale pie; paper-wrapped beer-battered fish and chips; and vegetable filo tartlet.

Open all day all wk **Bar Meals** L served Tue-Sun 12-2 D served Tue-Sat 5-9 **Restaurant** L served Tue-Sun 12-2 D served Tue-Sat 5-9 booking required ⊕ FREE HOUSE ◀ John Smith's Cask, John Smith's Smooth, Yorkshire Guzzler, Copper Dragon, Leeds Best ♻ Kopparberg. ♥ 8 **Facilities** Children welcome Children's menu Children's portions Play area Dogs allowed Garden Parking Wi-fi

YORKSHIRE, SOUTH

BRADFIELD
Map 16 SK29

The Strines Inn ♥

Bradfield Dale S6 6JE ☎ 0114 285 1247
dir: N off A57 between Sheffield & Manchester

Overlooking Strines Reservoir and with seven others dotted around it (strines is an old English word meaning 'the meeting of waters'), this popular free house feels a world away from nearby Sheffield. Although it was built as a manor house in the 13th century, most of the present building is 16th century. It has been an inn since 1771. Traditional home-made fare ranges from sandwiches and salads, to liver and onions and mammoth mixed grills. Enclosed play area; peacocks, geese and chickens roam freely.

Open all wk 10.30-3 5.30-11 (Sat-Sun 10.30am-11pm all day Apr-Oct) Closed: 25 Dec **Bar Meals** L served Mon-Fri 12-2.30 Sat-Sun 12-9 (summer 12-9) D served Mon-Fri 5.30-9 Sat-Sun 12-9 (summer 12-9) Av main course £8.75 ⊕ FREE HOUSE ◀ Marston's Pedigree, Jennings Cocker Hoop, Bradfield Bitter, Wychwood Hobgoblin. ♥ 10 **Facilities** Children welcome Children's menu Children's portions Play area Dogs allowed Garden Parking

CADEBY
Map 16 SE50

PICK OF THE PUBS

Cadeby Inn

Main St DN5 7SW ☎ 01709 864009
e-mail: info@cadebyinn.co.uk
web: www.cadebyinn.co.uk
dir: In the centre of village

The date on the gable is 1751, but records of a pub on the site in this peaceful Yorkshire village go a lot further back. Standing behind a tree-shaded beer garden at the edge of the village, this Georgian gem fuses the welcome of a village local with the quiet sophistication of a destination dining pub. Beers from Yorkshire breweries take the eye at the bar (a changing beer from the local Wentworth micro is a favourite), whilst the extensive regular menu, with mains such as slow roast lamb shank or a trio of Marr Grange Farm pork sausages (local produce is enthusiastically sourced by the team here) is enhanced by a good specials board that may reveal venison steak with parsnip purée and red wine sauce, or seared, marinated line-caught Cornish tuna with a tropical mango, papaya and pineapple salsa. Bread and butter pudding or winterberry pannacotta complete the feast.

Open all wk noon-11 **Bar Meals** L served all wk 12-2.30 D served all wk 5.30-9.30 **Restaurant** L served Mon-Thu 12-2.30, Fri-Sat 12-5.30, Sun 12-8 D served Mon-Sat 5.30-9.30, Sun 12-8 ⊕ FREE HOUSE ◀ John Smith's Cask, Black Sheep Best Bitter, Guest ales. **Facilities** Children welcome Children's menu Children's portions Garden Parking Wi-fi

DONCASTER
Map 16 SE50

Waterfront Inn

Canal Ln, West Stockwith DN10 4ET ☎ 01427 891223
e-mail: keithescreet@gmail.com
dir: From Gainsborough take either A159 N, then minor road to village. Or A631 towards Bawtry/Rotherham, right onto A161, then onto minor road

Now under new ownership, this 19th-century pub is located at the end of the Chesterfield canal and overlooks the picturesque marina at West Stockwith. Walkers and visitors to this lovely spot beat a path here, lured by the promise of real ales and good value food. The restaurant has views on all sides of the marina and large beer garden. The pub welcomes families and offers a children's menu and a play area.

Open noon-2.30 6-11 (Sat noon-11 Sun noon-9) Closed: Mon (ex BH) **Bar Meals** L served Tue-Sun 12-2.30 D served Tue-Sun 6.30-9 **Restaurant** L served Tue-Sun 12-2.30 D served Tue-Sun 6.30-9 ⊕ ENTERPRISE INNS ◀ John Smith's Cask, Greene King, Old Speckled Hen ♻ Stowford Press. **Facilities** Children welcome Children's menu Children's portions Play area Dogs allowed Garden Parking

PENISTONE   Map 16 SE20

PICK OF THE PUBS

Cubley Hall

Mortimer Rd, Cubley S36 9DF
☎ 01226 766086   📠 01226 767335
e-mail: info@cubleyhall.co.uk
dir: *M1 junct 37, A628 towards Manchester, or M1 junct 35a, A616. Hall just S of Penistone*

On the edge of the Peak District National Park, Cubley Hall was built as a farm in the 1700s, by Queen Victoria's reign and on into the 20th century it was a gentleman's residence, and later a children's home before becoming a pub in 1982. In 1990 the massive, oak-beamed bar was converted into the restaurant and furnished with old pine tables, chairs and church pews, and the building was extended to incorporate the hotel, which was designed to harmonise with the original mosaic floors, ornate plaster ceilings, oak panelling and stained glass. Food ranges from light bites, chalkboard specials and Sunday carvery roasts to an extensive main menu listing pub classics and home-made pizzas. Typically, choose from a Crawshaw beef burger with all the trimmings, fish and chips, pork and leek sausages, mash and onion gravy, and chicken and mushroom carbonara. The hotel, particularly its garden pavilion, is a popular wedding venue.

Open all day all wk **Bar Meals** L served all wk 12-9.30 D served Mon-Fri until 9.30, Sat-Sun until 10 food served all day **Restaurant** L served Sun 12.30-3.30 booking required D served Sun, last orders at 5.45 booking required ⊕ FREE HOUSE ◀ Tetley Bitter, Burton Ale, Greene King Abbot Ale, Young's Special. **Facilities** Children welcome Children's menu Children's portions Play area Family room Garden Parking Wi-fi

The Fountain Inn Hotel

Wellthorne Ln, Ingbirchworth S36 7GJ
☎ 01226 763125   📠 01226 761336
dir: *M1 junct 37, A628 to Manchester then A629 to Huddersfield*

Parts of this former coaching inn date from the 17th century; it is attractively located by Ingbirchworth Reservoir in the foothills of the southern Pennines. The interior is cosy and stylish, the locals' bar has real log fires and traditional games, and the food focus is on quality with value for money: expect the likes of prawn cocktail, roast sirloin of local beef, and apple and blackberry crumble with custard. Garden with large decking and seating area. Change of hands.

Open all day all wk 11.30-11 ⊕ INTREPID LEISURE ◀ Black Sheep, John Smith's Smooth, Timothy Taylor Landlord. **Facilities** Children welcome Children's menu Play area Dogs allowed Garden Parking

SHEFFIELD   Map 16 SK38

PICK OF THE PUBS

The Fat Cat

23 Alma St S3 8SA
☎ 0114 249 4801   📠 0114 249 4803
e-mail: info@thefatcat.co.uk
dir: *Telephone for directions*

This reputedly haunted three-storey, back street pub was built in 1832, and is Grade II listed. Beer-wise, it's hard to imagine anywhere better: a constantly changing range of guest beers from across the country, especially from micro-breweries, makes for a real ale heaven. Two hand-pumped ciders, unusual bottled beers and 21 country wines (the likes of elderberry and cowslip) are also sold, while the Kelham Island Brewery, owned by the pub, accounts for at least four of the ten traditional draught real ales on offer. The number of different beers sold since the concept was introduced now exceeds 4,500. The smart interior is very much that of a traditional, welcoming city pub; outside there's an attractive walled garden complete with Victorian-style lanterns, bench seating and shrubbery. Real fires in winter complete the cosy feel. Home-cooked food from a simple weekly menu is available except on Sunday evenings – nutty mushroom pie or Mexican chicken casserole. Look out for special events such as Monday curry night, beer and food evenings.

Open all wk noon-11 (Fri-Sat noon-mdnt Sun noon-11pm) Closed: 25 Dec **Bar Meals** L served Mon-Fri & Sun 12-3, Sat 12-8 D served Mon-Fri 6-8 ⊕ FREE HOUSE ◀ Timothy Taylor Landlord, Kelham Island Bitter, Pale Rider, Guest ales ♻ Stowford Press, Guest ciders. **Facilities** Children welcome Children's portions Family room Dogs allowed Garden Parking

PICK OF THE PUBS

Kelham Island Tavern

62 Russell St S3 8RW ☎ 0114 272 2482
e-mail: kelhamislandtav@aol.com
dir: *Just off A61 (inner ring road). Follow brown tourist signs for Kelham Island*

This 1830s back-street pub was built to quench the thirst of steelmakers who lived and worked nearby. Now it's in a conservation and popular walking area, with old buildings converted into stylish apartments, and The Kelham Island Museum round the corner in Alma Street telling the story of the city's industrial heritage. The semi-derelict pub was rescued in 2001 by Lewis Gonda and Trevor Wraith, who transformed it into an award-winning 'small gem'. The real ale list is formidable: residents Barnsley Bitter, Brewers Gold and Farmers Blonde are joined by ten ever-changing

guests, as well as Westons Old Rosie cider, and it holds a mid-summer beer festival every year. Constantly updated blackboards typically offer beef bourguignon; chicken fillet in mushroom and Stilton sauce; steak and ale pie; fish pie; broccoli and cheese pie; soups, pâtés and various bar snacks; and a small selection of desserts. Great in the summer, the pub has won awards for its beer garden and floral displays.

Open all day all wk noon-mdnt **Bar Meals** L served Mon-Sat 12-3 Av main course £5.50 ⊕ FREE HOUSE ◀ Barnsley Bitter, Brewers Gold, Farmers Blonde, 10 changing guest ales ♻ Westons Old Rosie. **Facilities** Children welcome Children's portions Family room Dogs allowed Garden Beer festival Parking

TOTLEY   Map 16 SK37

PICK OF THE PUBS

The Cricket Inn ♥

Penny Ln, Totley Bents S17 3AZ ☎ 0114 236 5256
e-mail: info@brewkitchen.co.uk
dir: *Follow A621 from Sheffield 8m. Turn right onto Hillfoot Rd, 1st left onto Penny Ln*

The scenery around Sheffield, especially as you head towards the Peak District, is glorious, which helps to explain why this much-praised, seafood- and game-led pub appeals to outdoor types – their muddy running shoes, walking boots, children and dogs are all welcome. Originally a farmhouse, it later sold beer to navvies building the nearby Totley Tunnel on the Sheffield to Manchester railway. Thornbridge Brewery in Bakewell owns it, so expect to find four of its ales on tap as well as a small selection of bottled Belgian beers. Snacks include devilled whitebait with tartare sauce and home-roasted pork scratchings, or go for a good portion of scallops of the day; lamb hotpot with home-made pickled red cabbage; bangers and mash with black pudding, crispy bacon and caramelised onion gravy; whole roast sea bass with chorizo and olive ragoût, and salsa verdi; or try one of the boards – butcher's, ploughman's or fisherman's.

Open all wk 11-11 **Bar Meals** L served Mon-Fri 12-2.30, Sat-Sun all day D served Mon-Fri 5-8.30, Sat-Sun all day **Restaurant** L served Mon-Fri 12-2.30, Sat-Sun all day D served Mon-Fri 5-8.30, Sat-Sun all day ⊕ BREWKITCHEN LTD ◀ Wild Swan, Lord Marples, Jaipur. ♥ 10 **Facilities** Children welcome Children's menu Children's portions Dogs allowed Garden Parking

The Black Horse Inn

Clifton Village, Brighouse, West Yorkshire HD6 4HJ
Tel: 01484 713862   Fax: 01484 400582
E-mail: mail@blackhorseclifton.co.uk   Web: www.blackhorseclifton.co.uk

The Black Horse is a family owned village Inn, bubbling with country charm. It is located half a mile from junction 25 of the M62, but Clifton village is a real oasis and easily accessible. It has a great bar, an outstanding restaurant, fantastic function room, 21 individually designed boutique bedrooms and a lovely flower filled outdoor courtyard, perfect to relax and enjoy that well earned pint.

Luscious local food is at the heart of *The Black Horse Inn*, and the seasonal menu, sourced from Yorkshire's ambrosial larder, has won a loyal following. With great food comes great drink – cask conditioned ales such as championship bitter Timothy Taylor are served and also their own beer – *Black Horse Brew*, made exclusively for them by a small micro brewery from Sowerby Bridge; guest ales feature regularly too.

Why not take advantage of The Black Horse's 'Booze n Snooze' nights and enjoy a delicious combination of great food and drink, excellent service and first class accommodation.

Save on hotels. Book at **theAA.com/hotel**

YORKSHIRE, WEST 535 ENGLAND

YORKSHIRE, WEST

ADDINGHAM — Map 19 SE04

PICK OF THE PUBS

The Fleece ▾

154 Main St LS29 0LY ☎ **01943 830491**
dir: *Between Ilkley & Skipton*

Situated at the intersection of several well-tramped footpaths, this 17th-century coaching inn is a popular refreshment stop for walkers. Food and drink can be served on the front terrace in summer. At other times you can cosy up in the stone-flagged interior with its enormous fireplace, wooden settles and friendly bunch of locals. A pint of Copper Dragon might be all you're seeking, but if you feel peckish, be sure to consult the daily chalkboard. Much of the produce is local and organic, with beef and lamb coming from a nearby farm, surplus vegetables brought along by allotment holders, and seasonal game delivered straight from the shoot. Simple flavoursome dishes are the speciality here. The lunchtime offerings include sandwiches (maybe roast rump of beef with dripping and home-made pickled onions), omelettes and traditional plates such as Wharfedale shepherd's pie with mint relish or local bangers and mash with onion gravy. For a full meal, try Shetland mussels with white wine, tarragon and cream ahead of hearty mains such as honey-glazed ham hock with mash, mushy peas and piccalilli.

Open all day all wk noon-11 (Sun noon-10.30) **Bar Meals** L served Mon-Sat 12-2.15, Sun 12-8 D served Mon-Sat 6-9.15, Sun 12-8 booking required Av main course £13 **Restaurant** L served Mon-Sat 12-2.15, Sun 12-8 booking required D served Mon-Sat 6-9.15, Sun 12-8 booking required Fixed menu price fr £30 Av 3 course à la carte fr £20 ⊕ PUNCH TAVERNS ◀ Black Sheep, Copper Dragon, Timothy Taylor Landlord, Tetleys ♂ Stowford Press. ▾ 15 **Facilities** Children welcome Children's menu Children's portions Dogs allowed Parking

BRADFORD — Map 19 SE13

New Beehive Inn

171 Westgate BD1 3AA
☎ **01274 721784** 📠 **01274 735092**
e-mail: newbeehiveinn+21@btinternet.com
dir: *A606 into Bradford, A6161 200yds B6144, left after lights, pub on left*

Dating from 1901 and centrally situated with many tourist attractions nearby, this classic Edwardian inn retains its period atmosphere with separate bars and gas lighting. It is on the national inventory list of historic pubs. Outside, with a complete change of mood, you can relax in the Mediterranean-style courtyard. The pub offers a good range of unusual real ales, such as Salamander Mudpuppy and Abbeydale Moonshine, and a selection of over 100 malt whiskies, served alongside some simple bar snacks.

Open all day all wk ⊕ FREE HOUSE ◀ Timothy Taylor Landlord, Kelham Island Bitter, Abbeydale Moonshine, Salamander Mudpuppy ♂ Westons Old Rosie. **Facilities** Children welcome Family room Dogs allowed Garden Parking Wi-fi

CLIFTON — Map 16 SE12

The Black Horse Inn ◉ ▾

HD6 4HJ ☎ **01484 713862** 📠 **01484 400582**
e-mail: mail@blackhorseclifton.co.uk
web: www.blackhorseclifton.co.uk
dir: *1m from Brighouse town centre. 0.5m from M62 junct 25*

Past guests at this pretty, 17th century inn tucked away in a quiet village above the Calder Valley included Roy Orbison, who spent his second honeymoon here, and Shirley Bassey. There's plenty to sing the praises about here, with the finest Yorkshire gastro-pub fare gaining one AA Rosette; look forward to accompanying a pint of own-label Black Horse Brew (from Sowerby Bridge) with smoked haddock kedgeree with coconut foam starter, leading to a main of assiette of Pateley Bridge pork with black pudding terrine. *Last of the Summer Wine* was filmed here; with over 100 bins to choose from, it's a minor miracle that they're not still here.

Open all day all wk noon-mdnt **Bar Meals** L served Mon-Sat 12-2.30, Sun 12-8 D served Mon-Sat 5.30-9.30, Sun 12-8 Av main course £15 **Restaurant** L served Mon-Sat 12-2.30, Sun 12-8 D served Mon-Sat 5.30-9.30, Sun 12-8 Fixed menu price fr £14.75 Av 3 course à la carte fr £28 ⊕ FREE HOUSE ◀ Timothy Taylor Landlord, Black Horse Brew. ▾ 18 **Facilities** Children welcome Children's menu Children's portions Garden Parking Wi-fi

See advert opposite

EMLEY — Map 16 SE21

The White Horse ▾

2 Chapel Ln HD8 9SP ☎ **01924 849823**
dir: *M1 junct 38, A637 towards Huddersfield. At rdbt left onto A636, then right to Emley*

On the old coaching route to Huddersfield and Halifax, this 18th-century pub's bar is warmed by a working Yorkshire range; the restaurant has a fire too. Of the eight cask ales, four are permanent, four are ever-rotating guests, featuring micro-breweries and their own Ossett Brewery ales. Both the carte and blackboard specials offer the likes of black pudding and scallops, pea purée and balsamic reduction; tenderloin of pork

sautéed with shallots, cider and mint sauce; Gressingham duck breast on mustard and spring onion mash with a red wine jus. The pub is popular with walkers and cyclists and locals, of course.

Open all wk Mon-Thu 4-11, Fri 3-11.30, Sat noon-11.30, Sun noon-11 **Bar Meals** L served Sat 12-3 D served Wed-Fri 4-6 **Restaurant** L served Sun 12-5 booking required D served Wed-Sat 5-9 booking required ⊕ OSSETT BREWERY PUB CO ◀ London Pride, Ossett Excelsior, Ossett Emley Cross, Ossett Pale Gold, Ossett Treacle Stout. ▾ 9 **Facilities** Children welcome Children's portions Family room Dogs allowed Garden Parking

HALIFAX — Map 19 SE02

PICK OF THE PUBS

The Old Bore ◉ ▾

Oldham Rd, Rishworth HX6 4QU ☎ **01422 822291**
dir: *M62 junct 22, A672 towards Halifax, 3m on left after reservoir*

If ever a pub name lent itself to jokes, it's this one. Of course, there's nothing at all boring about this family-run, 19th-century converted coaching inn, because it's packed with the sort of period features that give British pubs their unique character — flagged floors, oak beams, antique furniture. The bar is popular with real ale lovers attracted by the well-kept Black Sheep, Timothy Taylor Landlord and, yes, even Bore Bitter. Front of house is Lisa Hessel, whose husband/chef, Scott, has an impressive CV that began with a Roux Brothers scholarship in 1990. From him and his team today come modern British dishes using seasonal produce from committed suppliers, typically a starter of pan-seared Shetland scallops with slow-cooked pork confit, cauliflower purée, capers and raisins; followed by roast Yorkshire veal with wild mushroom risotto, roast squash and citrus juices with a little shin stew; and, to finish, pineapple tarte Tatin with rum and raisin ice cream.

Open noon-2.15 6-9.30 (Sun noon-7.30) Closed: 2wks Jan, Mon-Tue **Bar Meals** L served Wed-Sat 12-2.15, Sun 12-7.30 booking required D served Wed-Sat 6-9.30, Sun 12-7.30 booking required Av main course £10.95 **Restaurant** L served Wed-Sat 12-2.15, Sun 12-7.30 booking required D served Wed-Sat 6-9.30, Sun 12-7.30 booking required Av 3 course à la carte fr £35 ⊕ FREE HOUSE ◀ Timothy Taylor, Black Sheep Best, Bore Bitter. ▾ 12 **Facilities** Children welcome Children's menu Children's portions Dogs allowed Garden Parking

The Rock Inn Hotel

Holywell Green HX4 9BS
☎ **01422 379721** 📠 **01422 379110**
e-mail: enquiries@therockhotel.co.uk
dir: *From M62 junct 24 follow Blackley signs, left at x-rds, approx 0.5m on left*

Substantial modern extensions have transformed this attractive 17th-century wayside inn into a thriving hotel and conference venue in the scenic valley of Holywell

continued

HALIFAX *continued*

Green. All-day dining in the brasserie-style conservatory is truly cosmopolitan; kick off with freshly prepared parsnip and apple soup or crispy duck and seaweed, followed by liver and bacon, Thai-style steamed halibut, or vegetables jalfrezi. The bar serves a choice of beers and plenty of wines by the glass.

Open all day all wk noon–11 ⊞ FREE HOUSE ◀ Timothy Taylor Landlord, John Smith's. **Facilities** Children welcome Children's menu Children's portions Garden Parking Wi-fi

PICK OF THE PUBS

Shibden Mill Inn ★★★★ INN ◉◉ ♈

See Pick of the Pubs on opposite page

The Three Pigeons NEW

1 Sun Fold, South Pde HX1 2LX ☎ 01422 347001
e-mail: threepigeons@ossett-brewery.co.uk
dir: *From A629 (Skircoat Rd) in Halifax turn into Hunger Hill. Left into Union St, right into Heath View St, left into South Parade, right into Sun Fold*

When Ossett Brewery took over this great little real ale pub they restored its period features to their former glory; it has an English Heritage Conservation Award. Divided into four small rooms or snugs each with their own character and charm, there is an amazing painted ceiling in the central bar along with a great ambience throughout. Good ales are the draw here, with Three Pigeon ale and three other beers always available. Expect live jamming sessions every Sunday night.

Open all wk 4–11 (Fri-Sat noon-mdnt, Sun noon–11) ⊞ OSSETT BREWERY PUB CO LTD ◀ Pale Gold, 3 Pigeons Ale, Silver King, Excelsior, Yorkshire Blonde Ō Westons Traditional Scrumpy, Perry, Old Rosie. **Facilities** Dogs allowed **Notes** ◉

The Gray Ox ♈ NEW

15 Hartshead Ln WF15 8AL ☎ 01274 872845
e-mail: grayox@hotmail.co.uk
dir: *M62 junct 25, A644 signed Dewsbury. Take A62, then branch left signed Hartshead & Moor Top B6119. Left again to Hartshead*

Originally a farmhouse dating back to 1709, The Gray Ox has a commanding position overlooking Brighouse, Huddersfield and the surrounding countryside. Booking is strongly recommended in the award-winning restaurant, where regional produce drives the menu and suppliers even appear on a 'local heroes' board. Typical dishes are lightly curried Whitby crab cocktail; Yorkshire Dales lamb cutlets with garlic and rosemary dauphinoise; loin of Holme Farm venison with haggis mash and Madeira jus; and 'posh' fish pie.

Open all wk 12–3.30 6–12 Closed: 1 Jan
Bar Meals L served Mon-Sat 12-2, Sun 12-7 booking required D served Mon-Fri 6-9, Sat 6-9.30, Sun 12-7

booking required Av main course £15
Restaurant L served Mon-Sat 12-2, Sun 12-7 booking required D served Mon-Fri 6-9, Sat 6-9.30, Sun 12-7 booking required Fixed menu price fr £10.95 Av 3 course à la carte fr £25 ⊞ MARSTON'S ◀ Cumberland, Cocker Hoop, Sneck Lifter. ♈ 12 **Facilities** Children welcome Children's portions Garden Parking Wi-fi

The Old White Lion Hotel ♈

Main St BD22 8DU ☎ 01535 642313 📄 01535 646222
e-mail: enquiries@oldwhitelionhotel.com
dir: *A629 onto B6142, 0.5m past Haworth Station*

Set in the famous Brontë village of Haworth, this traditional family-run 300-year-old coaching inn looks down onto the famous cobbled Main Street. In the charming bar the ceiling beams are held up by timber posts. Bar food includes a wide range of all the usual favourites plus filled giant Yorkshire puddings. A meal in the Gimmerton Restaurant might start with pork terrine or teriyaki beef salad, followed by perhaps braised game pie of rabbit, pheasant and pigeon in rich Guinness gravy; grilled ostrich fillet; or monkfish linguine.

Open all day all wk 11-11 (Sun noon-10.30)
Bar Meals L served Mon-Fri 12-2.30, Sat-Sun all day D served Mon-Fri 6-9.30, Sat-Sun all day Av main course £9.20 **Restaurant** L served Sun 12-2.30 booking required D served all wk 7-9.30 booking required Fixed menu price fr £17.50 Av 3 course à la carte fr £26 ⊞ FREE HOUSE ◀ Theakstons Best, Tetley Bitter, John Smith's, guest beer. ♈ 9 **Facilities** Children welcome Children's menu Children's portions Parking Wi-fi

The Woodman Inn ★★★★ INN

Thunderbridge HD8 0PX
☎ 01484 605778 📄 01484 604110
e-mail: thewoodman@connectfree.co.uk
dir: *Approx 5m S of Huddersfield, just off A629*

Lovely old stone-built inn set in the wooded hamlet of Thunderbridge. One menu is offered throughout, but customers can eat in the bar downstairs or the more sophisticated ambience of the restaurant upstairs. Dishes include daily fresh fish (grilled brill with chilli), and the likes of wild boar and apple sausages. Wine is selected by the owners, whose family has been in the licensed trade since 1817. Accommodation is provided in adjacent converted weavers' cottages.

Open all day all wk 12-11 (Fri-Sat noon-mdnt Sun 12-10.30) ⊞ FREE HOUSE ◀ Timothy Taylor Best Bitter, Black Sheep, Guest ales Ō Aspall. **Facilities** Parking **Rooms** 12

PICK OF THE PUBS

The Cross Keys ♈

107 Water Ln LS11 5WD ☎ 0113 243 3711
e-mail: info@the-crosskeys.com
dir: *0.5m from Leeds Station: right onto Neville St, right onto Water Lane. Pass Globe Rd, pub on left*

Legend has it that James Watt, famed inventor of the steam engine, hired a room here to spy on his competitor Matthew Murray; to learn his trade secrets Watt simply bought drinks for Murray's foundry workers relaxing here shortly after the pub was built in 1802. Incredibly, this historic landmark from the peak of Leeds' industrial history was closed in the 1980s; when the current owners discovered it, it was a tyre storage depot for a local garage. Today, the pub proudly combines a city centre restaurant with a country pub atmosphere, serving hand-pulled pints from local micro-breweries, and dishes of food recreated from long lost recipes for traditional British dishes. Well-trained staff will happily talk you through the menus, which use the best of seasonal produce in starters such as home-smoked mussels with sweetcorn purée, and pigeon breast with apple, chicory and hazelnut dressing. Main dishes may proffer New Moor rose veal liver with celeriac mash, or grey mullet with bacon and bean stew.

Open all wk noon-11 (Fri-Sat noon-mdnt, Sun noon-10.30) **Bar Meals** L served Mon-Sat 12-4, Sun 12-5 D served Mon-Sat 6-10 Av main course £12 **Restaurant** L served Mon-Sat 12-4, Sun 12-5 D served Mon-Sat 6-10 Av 3 course à la carte fr £25 ⊞ FREE HOUSE ◀ Roosters, Saltaire, Wensleydale Ō Westons Organic, Westons Pear, Aspall Suffolk. ♈ 13 **Facilities** Children welcome Children's menu Children's portions Dogs allowed Garden Wi-fi

Whitelocks

Turks Head Yard, Briggate LS1 6HB
☎ 0113 245 3950 📄 0113 242 3368
e-mail: whitelocks@live.co.uk
dir: *Next to Marks & Spencer in Briggate*

First licensed in 1715 as the Turks Head, this is the oldest pub in Leeds. Restoration has highlighted its classic long bar with polychrome tiles, stained-glass windows, advertising mirrors and a mid-Victorian-style Top Bar known as Ma'Gamps. Food is along the lines of home-made soup; roast of the day; ham, egg and chips; home-made tray pie (steak; steak and Stilton or vegetable); treacle sponge and apple pie. There is a children's menu too. Guest ales are on a weekly rotation – sometimes daily.

Open all wk 11-11 (Sun noon-6 winter Sun noon-10.30 summer) Closed: 25-26 Dec, 1 Jan ⊞ CHENNEL & ARMSTRONG ◀ Theakston Best, Old Peculier, John Smith's, Deuchars, Leeds & York Brewery Ales, Guest ales.

PICK OF THE PUBS

Shibden Mill Inn ★★★★ INN

HALIFAX   Map 19 SE02

Shibden Mill Fold HX3 7UL
☎ **01422 365840** 📄 **01422 362971**
e-mail: enquiries@shibdenmillinn.com
web: www.shibdenmillinn.com
dir: *From A58 turn into Kell Ln. After 0.5m left into Blake Hill*

Hard to imagine that this rural enclave is but a short distance from the heart of Halifax. Tucked away in a wooded glen, the inn itself is barely a century old, but draws on a heritage stretching back to medieval times when a cornmill harnessed the power of Red Beck. It saw time as a spinning mill in Victorian times; then burned down before being licensed in 1890. This chequered history has delivered a charming inn, refurbished over the years to make the most of the open fires, oak beams and 17th century shell, with small windows and heavy tiles slumbering below overhanging trees. The beer garden is an extremely popular place in clement weather, when beer fans make the pilgrimage to sample Shibden Mill, brewed for the inn as well as a clutch of guest ales. It's the food that draws in the crowds here too, with a notable menu that changes with the seasons and dares to experiment, with inspirational dishes cheek-by-jowl with old favourites (with a twist) meaning there's something for everyone. Ingredients are sourced from local growers and suppliers whose input is vital in serving up the region's finest fish, poultry, game, meat and vegetables — food is a real 'local affair' here. Kick in with rolled crispy Yorkshire lamb breast with asparagus and Woodall's ham salad, or duo of Calderdale rabbit; filling starters in themselves before sampling roast cod chunk with chorizo and white bean stuffed pork belly, or braised English veal breast with white polenta mash, oven-dried tomatoes, game jus and gremolata crust. Individually designed luxury bedrooms let you linger before a full Yorkshire breakfast sets up the next day in style.

Open all wk noon-2.30 5.30-11 (Sat-Sun noon-11) Closed: 25-26 Dec eve & 1 Jan eve **Bar Meals** L served Mon-Sat 12-2, Sun all day D served Mon-Sat 6-9.30 Av main course £16 **Restaurant** L served Sun 12-7.30 D served Fri-Sat 6-9.30 Av 3 course à la carte fr £30 ⊕ FREE HOUSE ◀ John Smith's, Theakston XB, Shibden Mill, 3 guest ales. ♚ 12 **Facilities** Children's menu Children's portions Dogs allowed Garden Parking Wi-fi **Rooms** 11

LINTHWAITE
Map 16 SE11

The Sair Inn

Hoyle Ing HD7 5SG ☎ 01484 842370
dir: From Huddersfield take A62 (Oldham road) for 3.5m. Left just before lights at bus stop (in centre of road) into Hoyle Ing & follow sign

You won't be able to eat here, but this old hilltop ale house has enough character in its four small rooms to make up for that. Three are heated by hot (landlord Ron Crabtree's word) Yorkshire ranges in winter. Ron has brewed his own beers for 25 years and much sought after they are by real ale aficionados. Imported German and Czech lagers are available too. In summer the outside drinking area catches the afternoon sun and commands views across the Colne Valley.

Open all wk 5-11 (Sat noon-11 Sun noon-10.30) ⊕ FREE HOUSE ◗ Linfit Special Bitter, Linfit Bitter, Linfit Gold Medal, Autumn Gold, Old Eli Ô Westons First Quality. **Facilities** Children welcome Dogs allowed **Notes** ⊜

LINTON
Map 16 SE34

The Windmill Inn ⬤

Main St LS22 4HT ☎ 01937 582209 📠 01937 587518
dir: From A1 exit at Tadcaster/Otley junct, follow Otley signs. In Collingham follow Linton signs

The small beamed rooms in this pleasant village pub, once the home of the long-disappeared miller, have been stripped back to bare stone, presumably the original 14th-century walls. A coaching inn since the 18th century, polished antique settles, log fires, oak beams and copper-topped cast-iron tables set the scene in which to enjoy good food in the bar or Pear Tree restaurant. While you're there, ask to take a look at the local history scrapbook. A beer festival is held in July.

Open all wk 11-3 5.30-11 (Sat 11-11 Sun noon-10.30) Closed: 1 Jan **Bar Meals** L served Mon-Fri 12-2, Sat 12-2.30, Sun 12-5.45 **Restaurant** L served Mon-Fri 12-2, Sat 12-2.30, Sun 12-5.45 D served Mon-Tue 5.30-8.30, Wed-Sat 5.30-9, Sun 12-5.45 ⊕ SCOTTISH COURAGE ◗ John Smith's, Theakston Best, Daleside, Greene King Ruddles County. ⬤ 12 **Facilities** Children welcome Children's portions Dogs allowed Garden Beer festival Parking

MARSDEN
Map 16 SE01

The Olive Branch ★★★★ RR ⊛ ⬤

Manchester Rd HD7 6LU ☎ 01484 844487
e-mail: eat@olivebranch.uk.com
dir: On A62 between Marsden & Slaithwaite, 6m from Huddersfield

Set on a former packhorse route, the interior of this traditional 19th-century inn comprises a rambling series of rooms warmed by real fires in winter. The restaurant has a strong reputation for its brasserie-style food. Expect modern French-style cooking fuelled by seasonal ingredients. The choice is wide, with starters of gratin of

queen scallops followed by the likes of confit leg of Barbary duck. Local real ales are always available and can be enjoyed on the sun deck in warmer weather. Three designer bedrooms are available.

Open all wk Mon-Sat 6.30-11 (Sun 12.30-10.30) Closed: 1st 2wks Jan **Bar Meals** L served Sun 1-8.30 Av main course £17 **Restaurant** L served Sun 1-8.30 D served Mon-Sat 6.30-9.30, Sun 1-8 booking required Fixed menu price fr £15.95 Av 3 course à la carte fr £30 ⊕ FREE HOUSE ◗ Dogcross Bitter, Greenfield Red Ale. ⬤ 12 **Facilities** Children welcome Children's menu Garden Parking Wi-fi **Rooms** 3

PICK OF THE PUBS

The Riverhead Brewery Tap & Dining Room NEW

2 Peel St HD7 6BR ☎ 01484 841270 & 844324
e-mail: riverhead@ossett-brewery.co.uk
dir: In town centre

The lively River Colne cascades through the centre of this engaging little mill town, beside which stands a modest, stone built Victorian former co-op building. Re-emerging in 1995 as a micro-brewery and thriving pub, its beers, named after reservoirs nestling in the enfolding high South Pennine moors, are a major draw on the popular Trans-Pennine Rail Ale Trail. Now owned by Ossett Brewery, the beers are still brewed in the brewery just off the bar; it's an immensely popular spot for ramblers, rail-alers and locals, a genuine melting pot. Enjoy a pint of March Haigh in the bare-boarded, wood-rich bar, dappled with great local photos, or pop upstairs to the dining room for some classic lunchtime pub grub, enhanced in the evenings by tip-top modern dishes such as starter of black pudding and chestnut spring roll with slowly roasted belly pork, preceding medallion of turkey with spatchcock quail and a herb, leek and smoked cheese polenta, crispy skin and port sauce.

Open all day all wk **Bar Meals** Av main course £14 **Restaurant** L served all wk 12-2.30 D served all wk 6-9 Av 3 course à la carte fr £28 ⊕ OSSETT BREWERY PUB CO LTD ◗ Riverhead March Haigh, Butterley Bitter, Redbrook, Black Moss Stout. **Facilities** Children welcome Children's portions Dogs allowed

MYTHOLMROYD
Map 19 SE02

Shoulder of Mutton ⬤

New Rd HX7 5DZ ☎ 01422 883165
e-mail: shoulder@tesco.net
dir: A646 Halifax to Todmorden, in Mytholmroyd on B6138, opposite rail station

This award-winning Pennines' pub is the birthplace of Ted Hughes, Poet Laureate from 1984 to 1998, and has been under the same ownership for 35 years. Popular with walkers, cyclists and families, it has a good reputation for real ales, snacks and home-cooked meals of filled giant Yorkshire pudding, beef in ale and golden fried scampi, as well as a vegetarian blackboard. An interesting collection

of counterfeit gold coins made by the Cragg Vale Coiners in the late-18th century is on display. There is a streamside beer garden for the warmer months.

Open all wk 11.30-3 7-11 (Sat-Sun 11.30am-11pm) Closed: Tue L **Bar Meals** L served Wed-Mon 11.30-2 D served Wed-Sun 7-8.15 Av main course £4.50 ⊕ ENTERPRISE INNS ◗ Black Sheep, Copper Dragon, Timothy Taylor Landlord. ⬤ 12 **Facilities** Children welcome Children's portions Play area Family room Dogs allowed Garden Parking **Notes** ⊜

OSSETT
Map 16 SE22

Ossett Brewery Tap NEW

2 The Green WF5 8JS ☎ 01924 272215
e-mail: ossetttap@ossett-brewery.co.uk
dir: M1 junct 40, A638 signed Wakefield. At lights right into Queens Dr, right into Station Rd (B6128), left into Southdale Rd, right into The Green

Taking on the mantle from the original brewery pub in the adjacent Calder Valley; the Tap fires on all cylinders with a great range of Ossett's award-winning beers (plus guests) always available over the ornately-moulded wooden bar of this local's pub with a heart of gold. Recent updating has spruced up the traditional interior, with real fires warming flag-floored and oak-boarded rooms liberally spread with Britannia tables, and upholstered wall-benches threaded amongst tastefully decorated stone and colourwashed rooms.

Open all wk 3-12 (Fri-Sat noon-1am, Sun 12-12) ⊕ OSSETT BREWERY PUB CO LTD ◗ Pale Gold, Silver King, Excelsior, Yorkshire Blonde, Fuller's London Pride. **Facilities** Dogs allowed Garden Parking **Notes** ⊜

RIPPONDEN
Map 16 SE01

Old Bridge Inn ⬤

Priest Ln HX6 4DF ☎ 01422 822595
web: www.theoldbridgeinn.co.uk
dir: 5m from Halifax in village centre by church, over a pack horse bridge

This ancient inn has changed very little over the last 700 years. Approached by an old packhorse bridge in a Pennine conservation village, the whitewashed, award-winning pub has three traditional bars, with antique furniture and open fires. In addition to Timothy Taylor ales, they always offer two guest beers and are currently the only outlet in the UK offering Westmalle Dubbel Trappist ale on draught. Tranquil landscaped seating

continued on page 540

PICK OF THE PUBS

Ring O'Bells Country Pub & Restaurant ♟

THORNTON   Map 19 SE03

212 Hilltop Rd BD13 3QL
☎ **01274 832296**   📄 **01274 831707**
e-mail: enquiries@theringobells.com
web: www.theringobells.com
dir: *From M62 take A58 for 5m, right onto A644. 4.5m follow Denholme signs, onto Well Head Rd into Hilltop Rd*

Thornton is the village where the Brontë Sisters, whose father was the rector, were born, christened and lived. Originally, the Ring O' Bells, high above the village, was a Wesleyan chapel overlooking the dramatic Yorkshire Pennines where, on a clear day, the views stretch for over 40 miles. Ann and Clive Preston have successfully run the pub for over 19 years, and their cuisine, service and professionalism have been recognised with accolades from the trade and visitors from far and wide. Their refurbishment of the bar and dining area in 2010 has done nothing to dilute its traditional, historical feel, enhanced by prints of the village in the 1920s on the wood-panelled walls, although contemporary art is displayed in the restaurant. The fully air-conditioned Brontë restaurant, once two mill workers' cottages, now has a conservatory running its whole length that rewards diners with stunning valley views. Local farmers and suppliers of meat, fish, game and vegetables know that everything will be carefully prepared and cooked by a team of award-winning chefs, whose à la carte menu and daily specials board offer traditional British dishes with European influences. Expect starters such as Cajun battered king prawns with sweet chilli mayonnaise; apple and endive salad with crumbled Roquefort with apple dressing; and lamb, cumin and spinach meatballs with mint and cucumber yoghurt. Main courses may include steamed smoked haddock with poached egg, crushed new potatoes, and wholegrain mustard and chive sauce; slow-cooked marinated belly pork and roasted pork fillet with black pudding mash and cider gravy; and a choice of award-winning traditional pies. Imaginative vegetarian options are on the blackboard. Among the desserts, all made to order, are steamed roly-poly with vanilla custard; and espresso chocolate mousse with white chocolate pannacotta.

Open all wk 11.30-4 5.30-11.30 (Sat-Sun 6.15-11.30) Closed: 25 Dec
Bar Meals L served all wk 12-2 D served all wk 5.30-9.30 **Restaurant** L served all wk 12-2 D served all wk 5.30-9.30 booking required ⊞ FREE HOUSE ◀ John Smith's, Courage Directors, Black Sheep ales, Saltaire ales. ♟ 12 **Facilities** Children welcome Children's menu Children's portions Parking

RIPPONDEN *continued*

outside overlooks the River Ryburn. Expect good old-fashioned dishes like Hinchliffes championship pork pie and mushy peas, lamb and mint sausages with crushed new potatoes, or sea bass fillet with samphire, new potatoes and crab sauce.

Open all wk Mon-Thu noon-3 5.30-11 Fri-Sat noon-11.30 Sun noon-10.30 **Bar Meals** L served all wk 12-2 booking required D served Mon-Sat 6.30-9.30 booking required Av main course £10 **Restaurant** Fixed menu price fr £12.95 Av 3 course à la carte fr £18 ⊕ FREE HOUSE ◀ Timothy Taylor Landlord, Golden Best & Best Bitter, Guest ales. ♀ 12 **Facilities** Children's portions Garden Parking Wi-fi

---

SHELLEY Map 16 SE21

PICK OF THE PUBS

The Three Acres Inn

HD8 8LR ☎ 01484 602606 📱 01484 608411
e-mail: info@3acres.com
dir: *From Huddersfield take A629 then B6116, turn left for village*

Just ten minutes from the M1, this old drovers' inn is an ideal stopping off place for travellers heading north to the Yorkshire Dales. Well into their fourth decade here, Brian Orme and Neil Truelove have built a reputation for good quality food, and a welcoming atmosphere. The inn's spacious interior is lavishly traditional with exposed beams and large fireplaces. On summer evenings, sit out on the deck with a pint of Black Sheep (to remind you of the drovers), or a glass of wine and soak up the fabulous views. The food served in both bar and restaurant successfully fuses traditional English with international influences. A starter of 'posh' prawn and crayfish cocktail might be followed by braised oxtail and shin beef suet pudding, winter vegetables and buttery mashed potatoes, or creamy fish pie. A generous range of sandwiches and light meals makes a great lunchtime choice.

Open all wk noon-2 6.30-9.30 Closed: 25-26 Dec eve, 1 Jan eve **Bar Meals** L served all wk 12-2 D served all wk 6.30-9.30 booking required **Restaurant** L served all wk 12-2 D served all wk 6.30-9.30 booking required ⊕ FREE HOUSE ◀ Timothy Taylor Landlord, Black Sheep, Tetley's Smooth, Tetley's Bitter. **Facilities** Children welcome Garden Parking

---

SOWERBY Map 16 SE02

PICK OF THE PUBS

The Travellers Rest

Steep Ln HX6 1PE
☎ 01422 832124 📱 01422 831365
dir: *M62 junct 22 or 24*

The 17th-century former coaching inn sits high on a steep hillside with stunning views, a dining terrace for savouring the sunsets, a duck pond, space for camping, and a helipad. Restored and refurbished with

style a decade ago by Caroline Lumley, it continues to draw the crowds despite its rural location. The appeal is the cosy stone-flagged bar, which boasts fresh flowers, a blazing winter log fire and Little Valley Brewery beers on tap, and the comfortable restaurant, with its exposed stone wall and beams, animal print sofas and eclectic pub menus. Dishes cooked to order from local produce are rooted in Yorkshire tradition yet refined with French flair, yielding an immaculate and happy mix of classic and contemporary cooking, overseen by head chef, Mark Lilley. Start with a warm salad of black pudding and bacon or chicken liver pâté, continue with minted lamb Henry with rosemary mash, beef bourguignon with Parmesan risotto, or a classic beer battered cod and chips. Resist the rhubarb crumble if you can and don't miss the summer barbecues.

Open Wed-Sat (Sun all day) Closed: Mon-Tue ⊕ FREE HOUSE ◀ Timothy Taylor Landlord, Timothy Taylor Best Bitter, Little Valley Brewery. **Facilities** Children welcome Dogs allowed Garden Parking Wi-fi

---

SOWERBY BRIDGE Map 16 SE02

The Alma Inn & Fresco Italian Restaurant

Cotton Stones HX6 4NS ☎ 01422 823334
e-mail: info@almainn.com
dir: *Exit A58 at Triangle between Sowerby Bridge & Ripponden. Follow signs for Cotton Stones*

This old stone inn is set in a dramatically beautiful location at Cotton Stones and enjoys stunning views of the Ryburn Valley. Inside there are stone-flagged floors and real fires, while the cosy bar serves Timothy Taylor Landlord and Golden Best plus Tetley Bitter, as well as a range of cool-serve lagers and over 50 Belgian bottled beers (each served with its own individual glass). Fresco Italian Restaurant features a wood-burning pizza oven and a fantastic fish display counter which is very popular with diners. Start with shell roasted queen scallops cooked in the wood-burning oven with fresh herbs, Parmesan and parma ham, or mango and smoked chicken salad with mustard dressing, followed by a steak, pasta or pizza from a wide selection. There's also a good choice of vegetarian dishes such as sun blushed tomato and leek capellini. A private function/dining room is available, and in fine weather there's outside seating for 200 people.

Open all day all wk noon-10.30 ⊕ FREE HOUSE ◀ Tetley Bitter, Timothy Taylor Landlord, Timothy Taylor Golden Best. **Facilities** Children welcome Children's portions Dogs allowed Garden Parking

---

THORNTON Map 19 SE03

PICK OF THE PUBS

Ring O'Bells Country Pub & Restaurant ♀

See Pick of the Pubs on page 539

WIDDOP Map 18 SD93

Pack Horse Inn

HX7 7AT ☎ 01422 842803 📱 01422 842803
dir: *Off A646 & A6033*

The Pack Horse is a converted Laithe farmhouse dating from the 1600s, complete with welcoming open fires. A beautiful location just 300 yards from the Pennine Way makes it popular with walkers, but equally attractive are the home-cooked meals, good range of real ales and fabulous choice of 130 single malt whiskies. Please note that from October to Easter the pub is only open in the evening.

Open Summer noon-3 7-11 Closed: Mon & Tue-Fri lunch (Oct-Etr) ⊕ FREE HOUSE ◀ Thwaites, Theakston XB, Black Sheep Bitter, Golden Pippin, Lancaster Bomber. **Facilities** Children welcome Dogs allowed Parking

---

CHANNEL ISLANDS

GUERNSEY

CASTEL Map 24

PICK OF THE PUBS

Fleur du Jardin ♀

Kings Mills GY5 7JT
☎ 01481 257996 📱 01481 256834
e-mail: info@fleurdujardin.com
dir: *2.5m from town centre*

Guernsey's finest sandy beaches are but a short stroll from this friendly hotel, bar and restaurant, named after one of the island's most famous breeds of cow. Dating from the 15th century, it has been restyled with a modern shabby chic appeal, but historical features such as granite walls, wood beams and fireplaces remain untouched. The low bar might require some to stoop, but that needn't hamper the enjoyment of a pint of Jersey-brewed Sunbeam. Kitchen watchwords are seasonality and freshness - it isn't unusual to see a local fisherman delivering a 10lb sea bass. Expect steaks, lasagne and burgers; confit of salmon teriyaki; pot-roast barbecue pork; Thai chicken curry; and, of course, seafood. Sunday lunch could be roast sirloin of beef; chicken and leek pasta bake; or steamed haddock mornay. Desserts along traditional lines include warm chocolate fudge cake with Guernsey cream.

Open all day all wk **Bar Meals** L served all wk 12-2 D served all wk 6-9 booking required Av main course £10 **Restaurant** L served all wk 12-2 D served all wk 6-9 booking required Fixed menu price fr £15 Av 3 course à la carte fr £19.50 ⊕ FREE HOUSE ◀ Sunbeam, Guernsey Special, London Pride, Guest ales ○ Roquette cider. ♀ 12 **Facilities** Children welcome Children's menu Children's portions Dogs allowed Garden Parking Wi-fi

Hotel Hougue du Pommier

Hougue du Pommier Rd GY5 7FQ
☎ 01481 256531   📠 01481 256260
e-mail: hotel@houguedupommier.guernsey.net
dir: *Telephone for directions*

An 18th-century Guernsey farmhouse with the only feu du bois (literally 'cooking on the fire') in the Channel Islands. Eat in the beamed Tudor Bar with its open fire or the more formal restaurant. Menu options may include chargrilled fillet of pork with stir-fried vegetables; asparagus and Stilton cheese tartlet; home-made seafood pie; or grilled fillet of lemon sole with crab and tarragon cream. The 8-acre gardens have a swimming pool, barbecue and medieval area, where banquets are held.

Open all day all wk **Bar Meals** L served all wk 12-2 booking required D served all wk 6.30-9 booking required Av main course £9 **Restaurant** Fixed menu price fr £19 Av 3 course à la carte fr £17 ⊕ FREE HOUSE ◀ John Smith's, Guinness ○ Roquette. **Facilities** Children welcome Dogs allowed Garden Parking

ST PETER PORT   Map 24

The Admiral de Saumarez ★★★ HL

Duke of Normandie Hotel, Lefebvre St GY1 2JP
☎ 01481 721431   📠 01481 711763
e-mail: dukeofnormandie@cwgsy.net
dir: *From harbour rdbt St Julians Ave, 3rd left into Anns Place, continue to right, up hill, then left into Lefebvre St, archway entrance on right*

As part of the Duke of Normandie Hotel, this thoughtfully restored bar attracts a mix of Guernsey locals and hotel residents. It is full of architectural salvage, including old timbers (now painted with well-known amusing sayings), and maritime memorabilia. Details of the great naval victories of the Admiral himself are engraved on the tables. On the menu at lunch and dinner are traditional English pub meals: Cumberland sausage with spring onion mash and rich onion gravy; fish, chips and mushy peas; shepherd's pie; and thyme and lemon chicken. Head out to the sun-trap beer garden in warmer weather.

Open all day all wk 11am-11.30pm **Bar Meals** L served all wk 12-2 D served all wk 6-9 Av main course £8 **Restaurant** Fixed menu price fr £12.50 ⊕ FREE HOUSE ◀ Guinness, Tetley's. **Facilities** Children welcome Children's menu Children's portions Garden Parking Wi-fi **Rooms** 37

JERSEY

GOREY   Map 24

Castle Green Gastropub ▾

La Route de la Cote JE3 6DR
☎ 01534 840218   📠 01534 840229
e-mail: enquiries@jerseypottery.com
dir: *Opposite main entrance of Gorey Castle*

This stylish pub overlooks Gorey harbour and is, in turn, overlooked by dramatic Mont Orgueil Castle. The views from this pub's sun terrace are, not surprisingly,

breathtaking. Genuine Jersey produce is used on the seasonally evolving menu. Naturally fish dishes feature strongly and fresh fish and shellfish is purchased daily. Choices range from sushi and sashimi through tempura-battered catch of the day to seafood risotto. For meat eaters there are home-made beef burgers and grilled steak and chips. Round it off with comforting desserts such as spotted dick or local ice cream.

Open 11.30-3 6-11 (all day in summer) Closed: Sun eve & Mon **Bar Meals** L served Tue-Sun 12-2.30 D served Tue-Sat 6-9 Av main course £11.95 **Restaurant** L served Tue-Sun 12-2.30 D served Tue-Sat 6-9 Av 3 course à la carte fr £25 ◀ Directors, John Smith's Extra Smooth, Theakstons. ▾ 8 **Facilities** Children welcome Children's menu Children's portions Garden Wi-fi

ST AUBIN   Map 24

Old Court House Inn

St Aubin's Harbour JE3 8AB
☎ 01534 746433   📠 01534 745103
e-mail: info@oldcourthousejersey.com
dir: *From Jersey Airport, right at exit, left at lights, 0.5m to St Aubin*

The original courthouse at the rear of the property dates from 1450 and was first restored in 1611. Beneath the front part are enormous cellars where privateers stored their plunder. Three bars offer food, and there are two restaurants with terrific views over the harbour, plus an attractive courtyard. There's lots of locally caught fish on the menus of course, plus hand-dived scallops, moules marinière and Jersey lobster. Real ales include some from the Jersey Brewery; they can be enjoy in the courtyard or deck over the harbour in warmer weather.

Open all wk Closed: 25 Dec, Mon Jan-Feb **Bar Meals** L served all wk 12.30-2.30 D served Mon-Sat 7.30-10 Av main course £9 **Restaurant** L served all wk 12.30-2.30 D served all wk 7.30-10 Fixed menu price fr £25 Av 3 course à la carte fr £40 ⊕ FREE HOUSE ◀ Directors, Theakstons, John Smith's, Jersey Brewery. **Facilities** Children welcome Children's menu Children's portions Dogs allowed Wi-fi

ST MARTIN   Map 24

Royal Hotel ▾

La Grande Route de Faldouet JE3 6UG
☎ 01534 856289   📠 01534 857298
e-mail: johnbarker@jerseymail.co.uk
dir: *2m from Five Oaks rdbt towards St Martin. Pub on right next to St Martin's Church*

A friendly local in the heart of St Martin, this former coaching inn prides itself on offering quality food and drink. Landlord John Barker has been welcoming guests for over 23 years. A roaring log fire in the spacious lounge warm winter visitors, and there's a sunny beer garden to enjoy during the summer months. On the menu are traditional home-made favourites such as steak and ale pie, fresh grilled trout, monkfish and prawn Thai curry, and vegetarian lasagne. Ploughman's lunches, filled jacket potatoes, grills and children's choices are also on offer.

Open all day all wk **Bar Meals** L served all wk 12-2.15 D served all wk 6-8.30 **Restaurant** L served all wk 12-2.15 D served all wk 6-8.30 ◀ John Smith's Smooth, Theakstons Cool, Guinness, Ringwood Real Ale. ▾ 9 **Facilities** Children welcome Children's menu Children's portions Play area Garden Parking

ISLE OF MAN

PEEL   Map 24 SC28

The Creek Inn ▾

Station Place IM5 1AT
☎ 01624 842216   📠 01624 843359
e-mail: thecreekinn@manx.net
dir: *On quayside opposite House of Mannanan Museum*

On the quayside, overlooked by Peel Hill, the family-run Creek Inn is a real ale drinkers' paradise, with locally brewed Okells ales and up to five changing guests. Bands play every weekend, and nightly during the TT and Manx Grand Prix, when the pub becomes the town's focal point. Fish, such as Manx queenies; pan-fried sea bass and hot fish platter, accounts for most of the main courses, alongside sandwiches, hot baguettes, toasties and Manx burgers.

Open all day all wk **Bar Meals** L served all wk 11-9.30 D served all wk 11-9.30 Av main course £8 food served all day **Restaurant** L served all wk 11-9.30 D served all wk 11-9.30 food served all day ⊕ FREE HOUSE ◀ Okells Bitter, Okells Seasonal, Bushy's Bitter, 4 guest ales ○ Green Goblin, St Heliers. ▾ 12 **Facilities** Children welcome Children's menu Children's portions Dogs allowed Garden Parking Wi-fi

PORT ERIN   Map 24 SC26

Falcon's Nest Hotel ★★ HL

The Promenade, Station Rd IM9 6AF
☎ 01624 834077   📠 01624 835370
e-mail: falconsnest@enterprise.net
dir: *Follow coast road, S from airport or ferry. Hotel on seafront, immediately after steam railway station*

A magnificent pub-hotel overlooking a beautiful sheltered harbour and beach. Head for the saloon bar, 'Ophidian's Lair', for the pool table, jukebox and live sports via satellite; alternatively the residents' lounge, also open to the public, serves the same local ales from Okells and Bushy's, among others, and over 80 whiskies. The former ballroom has been restored and turned into a Victorian-style dining room, where local seafood dishes include crab, prawns, sea bass, marlin, lobster and local scallops known as 'queenies'; the carvery here is also very popular.

Open all wk **Bar Meals** L served all wk 12-2 D served all wk 6-9 Av main course £10 **Restaurant** L served all wk 12-2 D served all wk 6-9 Av 3 course à la carte fr £17.50 ⊕ FREE HOUSE ◀ Manx guest ale, Guinness, John Smith's, Okells, Bushy's, Guest ales. **Facilities** Children welcome Children's menu Children's portions Family room Dogs allowed Parking Wi-fi **Rooms** 39

Scotland

Glen Muick, Cairngorms National Park

SCOTLAND

ABERDEEN, CITY OF

ABERDEEN
Map 23 NJ90

Old Blackfriars ♥

52 Castle St AB11 5BB
☎ 01224 581922 📠 01224 582153
e-mail: oldblackfriars.aberdeen@belhavenpubs.net
dir: *From train station turn right along Guild St then left into Market St, at end turn right onto Union St. Pub on right at end of road*

Situated in Aberdeen's historic Castlegate, this traditional split-level city centre pub stands on the site of property owned by Blackfriars Dominican monks, hence the name. Inside you'll find stunning stained glass, plus well kept real ales (nine handpumps) and a large selection of malt whiskies. The pub is also renowned for excellent food and an unobtrusive atmosphere (no background music and no television). The wide ranging menu has all the pub favourites and more – chicken Balmoral, chicken tikka makhani, sweet potato curry and baked lasagne. There is a weekly quiz and live music every Friday.

Open all day all wk Mon-Thu 11am-mdnt (Fri-Sat 11am-1am Sun 11am-11pm) Closed: 25 Dec, 1 Jan
Bar Meals L served all wk 12-9.30 D served all wk 12-9.30 food served all day **Restaurant** L served all wk 12-9.30 D served all wk 12-9.30 food served all day ⊕ BELHAVEN ◀ Deuchars IPA, Inveralmond, Ossian, Ruddles County, Guest ales. ♥ 9 **Facilities** Children welcome Children's menu Family room Wi-fi

ABERDEENSHIRE

BALMEDIE
Map 23 NJ91

The Cock & Bull Bar & Restaurant ◉

Ellon Rd, Blairton AB23 8XY
☎ 01358 743249 📠 01358 742466
e-mail: info@thecockandbull.co.uk
web: www.thecockandbull.co.uk
dir: *11m N of city centre, on left of A90 between Balmedie junct & Foveran*

This intimate coaching inn still retains its original character as well as gaining a good reputation for its honest food at affordable prices. The bar area is warmed by a cast-iron range and has big sofas and a hotchpotch of hanging items, from a ship's lifebelt to a trombone. The AA one Rosette menu ranges from bar dishes to restaurant fare like confit belly pork with potato and black pudding terrine and apple purée or halibut with dauphinoise potatoes and pancetta cream.

Open all day all wk 10am-11.30pm (Sun 12-6.30) Closed: 26-27 Dec, 2-3 Jan **Bar Meals** L served Mon-Sat 10-8.45, Sun 12-6.30 D served Mon-Sat 10-8.45, Sun 12-6.30 Av main course £12.95 food served all day **Restaurant** L served Mon-Sat 10-8.45, Sun 12-6.30 D served Mon-Sat 10-8.45, Sun 12-6.30 Av 3 course à la carte fr £32.50 food served all day ⊕ FREE HOUSE ◀ Caledonian 80/-, Guinness. **Facilities** Children welcome Children's menu Play area Dogs allowed Garden Parking

MARYCULTER
Map 23 NO89

Old Mill Inn

South Deeside Rd AB12 5FX
☎ 01224 733212 📠 01224 732884
e-mail: info@oldmillinn.co.uk
dir: *5m W of Aberdeen on B9077*

This delightful family-run 200-year-old country inn stands on the edge of the River Dee, five miles from Aberdeen city centre. A former mill house, the 18th-century granite building has been tastefully modernised to include a restaurant where the finest Scottish ingredients feature on the menu: black pudding parcel, seafood chowder, warm salad of monkfish and chicken and ham shank terrine are typical. Food and drink can be enjoyed in the garden in warmer months.

Open all day all wk **Bar Meals** L served all wk 12-2 D served all wk 5.30-9 Av main course £10.50 **Restaurant** L served all wk 12-2 D served all wk 5.30-9 Av 3 course à la carte fr £18.50 ⊕ FREE HOUSE ◀ Caledonian Deuchars IPA, Timothy Taylor Landlord, London Pride. **Facilities** Children welcome Children's menu Children's portions Garden Parking

NETHERLEY
Map 23 NO89

PICK OF THE PUBS

The Lairhillock Inn

AB39 3QS ☎ 01569 730001 📠 01569 731175
e-mail: info@lairhillock.co.uk
dir: *From Aberdeen take A90. Right towards Durris on B9077 then left onto B979 to Netherley*

Standing alone surrounded by fields in beautiful rural Deeside, the Lairhillock is easily spotted from the B979. Formerly a farmhouse and then a coaching inn, the original building is 17th century and the interior is full of old rustic atmosphere, most notably the fine old bar with its exposed stone, panelling, old settles, and crackling log fires. Here you can quaff Deuchars IPA, Timothy Taylor Landlord or a choice of guest ales. Food is robust and dishes make good use of fresh, quality, local and regional produce such as langoustines from Gourdon, mussels from Shetland, scallops from Orkney, wild boar and venison from the Highlands and salmon from the Dee and Don, not forgetting certified Aberdeen Angus beef. In the bar and conservatory, try the Cullen

skink or peat smoked salmon with citrus dressing; followed by seafood pie or braised beef olives with red wine gravy. For a more formal dining option, the atmospheric Crynoch Restaurant menu might offer chicken liver and bacon parfait to start, followed by saddle of venison with a tomato and cannellini bean ragout and thyme jus, or rib-eye steak with wild mushroom sauce.

Open all day all wk Closed: 25-26 Dec, 1-2 Jan **Bar Meals** L served all wk 12-2 booking required D served all wk 6-9.30 booking required **Restaurant** L served Sun 12-2 booking required D served Tue-Sat 7-9.30 booking required ⊕ FREE HOUSE ◀ Timothy Taylor Landlord, Deuchars IPA, Guest ales. **Facilities** Children welcome Children's menu Children's portions Dogs allowed Garden Parking

OLDMELDRUM
Map 23 NJ82

The Redgarth

Kirk Brae AB51 0DJ ☎ 01651 872353 📠 01651 873763
e-mail: redgarth1@aol.com
dir: *From A947 (Oldmeldrum bypass) follow signs to Golf Club/Pleasure Park. Establishment E of bypass*

Built as a house in 1928, this friendly family-run inn has been in the same hands for the past 20 years. It is situated in a small village with an attractive garden that offers magnificent views of Bennachie and the surrounding countryside. Cask-conditioned ales, such as Orkney Scapa and Inveralmond Thrappledouser, and interesting wines are served along with dishes prepared on the premises using fresh local produce. A typical selection might include duo of hot and cold salmon with horseradish mayonnaise, or pork fillet stuffed with black pudding.

Open all wk 11-3 5-11 (Fri-Sat 11-3 5-11.45) Closed: 25-26 Dec, 1-3 Jan **Bar Meals** L served all wk 12-2 D served Sun-Thu 5-9, Fri-Sat 5-9.30 Av main course £9 **Restaurant** L served all wk 12-2 booking required D served Sun-Thu 5-9, Fri-Sat 5-9.30 booking required Av 3 course à la carte fr £20 ⊕ FREE HOUSE ◀ Inveralmond Thrappledouser, Timothy Taylor Landlord, Orkney Scapa & Best, Pivo Estivo. **Facilities** Children welcome Children's menu Children's portions Garden Parking Wi-fi

STRATHDON   Map 23 NJ31

PICK OF THE PUBS

The Glenkindie Arms ★★★ INN ◉◉

Glenkindie AB33 8SX ☎ 01975 641288
e-mail: iansimpson.glenkindiearms@gmail.com
web: www.theglenkindiearmshotel.com
dir: On A97 between Alford & Strathdon

Set in Upper Donsdale, close to Balmoral and the Malt
Whisky Trail, and enjoying breathtaking views of the
Highlands, this 400-year-old traditional drovers' inn
has been spruced-up with style and panache by chef/
patron Ian Simpson and Aneta Olechno. They injected
their passion for good food and drink into the place,
offering local real ales from Cairngorm and Deeside
breweries and menus that bristle with meat, eggs and
vegetables from local farms. Expect sound modern
Scottish cooking, with dishes kept unfussy and put
together with attention to detail and well balanced
flavours. Typically, tuck into such Wark Farm Black
Spot pork terrine with spiced pear purée and home-
baked bread for a starter, then choose roast rump of
Dexter beef with thyme Yorkshire pudding and beef jus,
or poached Scrabster bream with cockle fricassee and
sauce vièrge for a main course. Round off with bitter
chocolate tart or spiced rice pudding with apple
compôte. Comfortable accommodation is also
available. The inn is remote so do book ahead to ensure
a table and then why not stay over.

Open all day all wk Bar Meals Av main course £15 food
served all day Restaurant Fixed menu price fr £23.50
Av 3 course à la carte fr £27.50 food served all day
⊕ FREE HOUSE ◀ Houston Brewing Company Peters
Well, Cairngorm Brewery Company Trade Winds,
Deeside Brewery. Facilities Children welcome
Children's menu Children's portions Garden Parking
Wi-fi Rooms 3

ARGYLL & BUTE

ARDUAINE   Map 20 NM71

PICK OF THE PUBS

Loch Melfort Hotel ★★★ HL ◉◉ ♟

PA34 4XG ☎ 01852 200233
e-mail: reception@lochmelfort.co.uk
dir: On A816, midway between Oban & Lochgilphead

Perfect for garden enthusiasts, sailors or simply those
looking for tranquility, the Chartroom II is part of the
Loch Melfort Hotel, previously the Campbell family
home, and located on the path to the NTS Arduaine
Gardens with spectacular views over Asknish Bay
towards Jura and beyond. The relaxed atmosphere of
this modern bar and bistro is the place to enjoy all-day
drinks and home baking, as well as light lunches and
suppers. It has the finest views on the West Coast and
serves home-made Scottish fare including plenty of
locally landed seafood including fantastic
langoustines, scallops, crabs, lobsters and mussels,
Highland beef burgers and steak and ale pies. You can
sit outside and enjoy a drink in warmer weather
watching magical sunsets or sit around the cosy fire in
winter and watch the waves crashing against the
rocks. The Chartroom II is family friendly and serves
children's meals or smaller portions from the main
menu, plus there is a playground. There are also four
free moorings from April to October.

Open all wk 11-10 Bar Meals L served all wk 12-2.30
booking required D served all wk 6-9 booking required
Av main course £9.95 ⊕ FREE HOUSE ◀ Caledonian
80/- Ale, Belhaven, Fyne Ale. ♟ 8 Facilities Children
welcome Children's menu Children's portions Play area
Dogs allowed Garden Parking Rooms 25

CAIRNDOW   Map 20 NN11

Cairndow Stagecoach Inn ★★★ INN NEW

PA26 8BN ☎ 01499 600286 🖹 01499 600220
e-mail: enq@cairndowinn.com
dir: N of Glasgow take A82, left on A83 at Arrochar.
Through Rest and be Thankful to Cairndow. Follow signs
for inn

On the upper reaches of Loch Fyne, this old coaching inn
offers plenty of fine views of mountains, magnificent
woodlands and rivers. Sample one of many malt whiskies
in the friendly bar by the fire, or idle away the time in the
loch-side garden watching the oyster-catchers while
sipping the local Loch Fyne ales. The menu in the
candlelit Stables Restaurant offers sautéed haunch of
venison in red wine sauce; salmon from the loch; and
home-made mushroom Stroganoff. Meals are also served
all day in the bar and lounges. Accommodation is
available if you would like to stay over and explore the
area.

Open all day all wk Bar Meals L served all wk 12-6
D served all wk 6-9 food served all day
Restaurant L served all wk 12-6 booking required
D served all wk 6-9 booking required food served all day
⊕ FREE HOUSE ◀ Fyne Ales Hurricane Jack, Avalanche,
Piper's Gold, Maverick, Jarl. Facilities Children welcome
Children's menu Children's portions Dogs allowed Garden
Parking Wi-fi Rooms 18

CLACHAN-SEIL   Map 20 NM71

PICK OF THE PUBS

Tigh an Truish Inn

PA34 4QZ ☎ 01852 300242
web: www.tighantruish.co.uk
dir: 12m S of Oban take A816. Onto B844 towards
Atlantic Bridge

Popular with tourists and members of the yachting
fraternity, the inn's waterfront beer garden is much in
demand on summer days, when the tides can be
watched as they swirl around the famous Bridge over
the Atlantic. The inn's name has quite a tale attached:
following the Battle of Culloden in 1746, kilts were
outlawed on pain of death. The Seil islanders defied
this edict at home but, on excursions to the mainland,
they would stop at the Tigh an Truish - the 'house of
trousers' - to change into the hated trews. These days
people pause here for single malts, regularly changing
ales from local brewers, and a menu that includes
plenty of seafood: salmon and mussels from Argyll
producers, and lobster and prawns caught by local
fishermen working the Firth of Lorne. Fish-free options
include macaroni cheese, chef's beefburger and home-
made steak and ale pie. For families, a separate
lounge off the main bar is furnished with children's
books - another indication of the pub's genuinely warm
welcome.

Open all wk 11-11 (Mon-Fri 11-2.30 5-11 Oct-Mar)
Closed: 25 Dec & 1 Jan Bar Meals L served all wk 12-2
D served all wk 6-8.30 (Apr-Oct) ⊕ FREE HOUSE
◀ Local guest ales, changing regularly.
Facilities Children welcome Children's menu
Children's portions Family room Dogs allowed Garden
Parking

CONNEL — Map 20 NM93

PICK OF THE PUBS

The Oyster Inn

PA37 1PJ ☎ 01631 710666 📠 01631 710042
e-mail: stay@oysterinn.co.uk
dir: Telephone for directions

A comfortable, informal hotel overlooking the tidal whirlpools and white water of the Falls of Lora, and enjoying glorious views of the mountains of Mull. It was built in the 18th century to serve ferry passengers, but the ferry has long since been superseded by the modern road bridge. Ferryman's Bar in the pub next door was, and still is, known as the Glue Pot. Years ago canny locals knew they could be 'stuck' here between ferries and evade Oban's Sunday licensing laws; additionally, a blacksmith's shop behind the pub melted down horses hooves for glue – the pots hang from the bar ceiling. Food is served all day in the bar and in the evenings in the restaurant. Using locally sourced quality produce, particularly from the sea and lochs, West Coast mussels marinière and ocean pie (smoked haddock, salmon, mussels, prawns and squid) might appear on the menu. Meaty alternatives may include medallions of Scottish venison fillet with a mild Stornoway black pudding and port and redcurrant jus

Open all day all wk noon-mdnt **Bar Meals** L served all wk 12-6 D served all wk 6-9.30 Av main course £8 food served all day **Restaurant** D served all wk 6-9.30 Av 3 course à la carte fr £27 ⊕ FREE HOUSE ◀ Guinness, John Smith's. **Facilities** Children welcome Children's menu Children's portions Family room Dogs allowed Garden Parking Wi-fi

CRINAN — Map 20 NR79

PICK OF THE PUBS

Crinan Hotel

PA31 8SR ☎ 01546 830261 📠 01546 830292
e-mail: reservations@crinanhotel.com
dir: From M8, at end of bridge take A82, at Tarbert left onto A83. At Inveraray follow Campbeltown signs to Lochgilphead, follow signs for A816 to Oban. 2m, left to Crinan on B841

At the north end of the Crinan Canal which connects Loch Fyne to the Atlantic Ocean, the Crinan is a romantic retreat enjoying fabulous views across the sound of Jura. It's a long-standing place of welcome at the heart of community life in this tiny fishing village. The hotel dates back some 200 years and has been run by owners Nick and Frances Ryan for around 40 of them. Eat in the Crinan Seafood Bar or the Westward Restaurant. The cuisine is firmly based on the freshest of seafood – it's landed daily just 50 metres from the hotel. Starters could include brochettes of Loch Fyne scallops with organic salad leaves and balsamic reduction. For a main course perhaps choose grilled fillet of monkfish with caper lemon butter, or roast rack

of Argyll Hill lamb. Boat trips can be arranged to the islands, and there is a classic boats regatta in the summer. Look for the 'secret garden' just behind the hotel.

Open all day all wk 11am-11pm Closed: 25 Dec **Bar Meals** L served all wk 12-2.30 D served all wk 6-8.30 **Restaurant** D served all wk 7-9 booking required ◀ Worthington Bitter, Tennent's Velvet, Guinness, Loch Fyne Ales. **Facilities** Children welcome Children's menu Children's portions Dogs allowed Garden Parking Wi-fi

DUNOON — Map 20 NS17

Coylet Inn

Loch Eck PA23 8SG ☎ 01369 840426
e-mail: info@coyletinn.co.uk
dir: N of Dunoon on A815

A blissful hideaway with no television or games machines to disturb the peace, this charming, beautifully refurbished 17th-century coaching inn overlooks the shores of Loch Eck. You may relax and drink your pint of Pipers Gold or Highlander in peace by one of three log fires. Impressive menus are derived from fully traceable produce – from haggis fritters to ham 'n' haddy wi' a drappit egg, there's plenty to choose from. A perfect spot for walking, fishing, cycling or stalking.

Open all day Closed: 3-26 Jan, Mon & Tue (Oct-Mar) **Bar Meals** L served all wk 12-2.30 D served all wk 6-8.30 Av main course £10.95 **Restaurant** L served all wk 12-2.30 D served all wk 6-8.30 ⊕ FREE HOUSE ◀ Highlander, Pipers Gold, Guest ales. **Facilities** Children welcome Children's menu Children's portions Dogs allowed Garden Parking

KILFINAN — Map 20 NR97

Kilfinan Hotel Bar

PA21 2EP ☎ 01700 821201 📠 01700 821205
e-mail: info@kilfinan.com
dir: 8m N of Tighnabruaich on B8000

On the eastern shore of Loch Fyne, set amid spectacular Highland scenery on a working estate, this hotel has been welcoming travellers since the 1760s. The bars are cosy with log fires in winter, and offer a fine selection of malts. There are two intimate dining rooms, with the Lamont room for larger parties. Menus change daily and offer the best of local produce: Loch Fyne langoustines grilled in garlic and butter; pan seared Loch Fyne scallops with crispy bacon and sage; or Isle of Bute venison steak. Enjoy the views from the garden on warmer days.

Open all wk Closed: winter ⊕ FREE HOUSE ◀ McEwens 80/-, Fyne Ales. **Facilities** Children welcome Children's menu Children's portions Family room Dogs allowed Garden Parking

LOCHGILPHEAD — Map 20 NR88

PICK OF THE PUBS

Cairnbaan Hotel ★★★ HL ⊛ ▾

Cairnbaan PA31 8SJ
☎ 01546 603668 📠 01546 606045
e-mail: info@cairnbaan.com
dir: 2m N, take A816 from Lochgilphead, hotel off B841

Built in 1801 to coincide with the opening of the Crinan Canal, which it overlooks, this historic hotel has been run by Darren and Christine Dobson for the past decade. Lighter meals are served from the bistro-style menu in the relaxed atmosphere of the bar, conservatory lounge, or alfresco. For a more formal occasion dine in the serene, AA Rosetted restaurant, where the carte specialises in the use of fresh local produce, notably seafood and game. Look for starters of Tarbet landed langoustine with bread, salad and mayonnaise. Mains might include Sound of Jura scallops wrapped in pancetta with garlic butter and new potatoes. Round off, perhaps, with sticky toffee pudding with vanilla ice cream. From nearby Oban there are sailings to the islands of Mull, Coll and Tiree. Inveraray Castle is also well worth a visit, as is Dunadd Fort where the ancient kings of Scotland were crowned.

Open all wk 8am-11pm Closed: 25 Dec **Bar Meals** L served all wk 12-2.30 D served all wk 6-9.30 **Restaurant** L served all wk 12-2.30 D served all wk 6-9.30 ⊕ FREE HOUSE ◀ Local ales. ▾ 8 **Facilities** Children welcome Children's menu Children's portions Garden Parking Wi-fi **Rooms** 12

LUSS — Map 20 NS39

PICK OF THE PUBS

The Inn at Inverbeg — INN ▾

G83 8PD ☎ 01436 860678 📠 01436 860203
e-mail: inverbeg.reception@loch-lomond.co.uk
dir: 12m N of Balloch

Set in glorious scenery with stunning views of Loch Lomond and Ben Lomond, this inn blends contemporary and rustic styles, making it the perfect stop for visitors exploring the West Highlands. Comfortable, individually styled rooms are split between the inn and, right by the loch, a sumptuous beach house featuring wooden floors, hand-crafted furniture, crisp linen, and a hot tub. Mr C's Fish & Whisky Restaurant/Bar celebrates two things Scotland is famous for: fresh fish and fantastic whisky. Try a starter of smoke house salmon pâté or West Coast steamed mussels, a main of Inverbeg traditional fish supper or home-made fishcakes. Meat dishes include skillet of sirloin with chips and home-made steak pie. Choose from more than 200 malts and real ales, such as Deuchars IPA and Highlander. There is traditional, live folk music every night throughout the summer. This was AA Pub of the Year for Scotland 2009-2010.

Open all day all wk Mon-Thu & Sun 11-11 (Fri-Sat 11am-mdnt) **Bar Meals** L served all wk 12-9 D served all wk 12-9 Av main course £9.95 food served all day **Restaurant** L served all wk 12-9 D served all wk 12-9 food served all day ⊕ FREE HOUSE ◀ Killellan, Highlander, Deuchars IPA. ♀ 30 **Facilities** Children welcome Children's menu Children's portions Parking Wi-fi **Rooms** 20

PORT APPIN   Map 20 NM94

PICK OF THE PUBS

The Pierhouse Hotel & Seafood Restaurant ★★★ SHL ⊛

PA38 4DE ☎ 01631 730302   📄 01631 730509
e-mail: reservations@pierhousehotel.co.uk
dir: *A828 from Ballachulish to Oban. In Appin right at Port Appin & Lismore ferry sign. After 2.5m left after post office, hotel at end of road by pier*

With breathtaking views to the islands of Lismore and Mull, it would be hard to imagine a more spectacular setting for this family-run 12-bedroom hotel and renowned seafood restaurant. Once home to the piermaster, the distinctive building now houses a popular bar, pool room, terrace and dining area, and offers a selection of menus featuring the finest seasonal Scottish seafood, meat, game and vegetables. Lunches in the Ferry bar range from freshly-filled ciabattas and baked potatoes to burgers, pastas and fish dishes. Meanwhile a typical three-course restaurant meal might start with velvet crab bisque, seafood medley and lemon oil; before progressing to roast loin of Kingairloch venison with truffle mashed potato, creamy Savoy cabbage and venison jus. The tempting desserts include Pierhouse sorbets and chocolate fondant with clotted cream. Twelve individually designed bedrooms include two with four-poster beds and superb loch views, and three triple family rooms.

Open all wk 11am-11pm Closed: 25-26 Dec **Bar Meals** L served all wk 12.30-2.30 D served all wk 6.30-9.30 **Restaurant** L served all wk 12.30-2.30 booking required D served all wk 6.30-9.30 booking required ⊕ FREE HOUSE ◀ Calders 80/-, Belhaven Best, Guinness. **Facilities** Children welcome Family room Dogs allowed Garden Parking **Rooms** 12

STRACHUR   Map 20 NN00

PICK OF THE PUBS

Creggans Inn ★★★ HL ⊛⊛

PA27 8BX ☎ 01369 860279   📄 01369 860637
e-mail: info@creggans-inn.co.uk
dir: *A82 from Glasgow, at Tarbet take A83 towards Cairndow, left onto A815 to Strachur*

Standing on the shores of Loch Fyne and a coaching inn since the days of Mary, Queen of Scots, this small, informal and very comfortable inn enjoys glorious vistas across the Mull of Kintyre to the Western Isles. A good range of Scottish ales, including Atlas Latitude and Harviestoun Bitter and Twisted, and some fine malt whiskies are all served at the bar. Regional produce plays a key role in the seasonal menus: the famed Loch Fyne oysters of course, but also salmon from the same waters, perhaps a gravadlax starter served with rocket, cream cheese and mustard vinaigrette. Robust main courses may feature rib-eye steak with confit tomato, roast shallots and baked mushrooms in garlic butter, battered haddock and chips, and lamb loin with port and basil jus. Dark chocolate and coffee torte with mint ice cream makes a fulfilling conclusion. There's a formal terraced garden and patio for alfresco summer enjoyment – both make the most of the view.

Open all day all wk 11am-mdnt **Bar Meals** L served all wk 12-2.30 D served all wk 6-8.30 Av main course £11 **Restaurant** D served all wk 7-8.30 booking required Av 3 course à la carte fr £21 ⊕ FREE HOUSE ◀ Fyne Ales Highlander, Atlas Latitude, Deuchars IPA, Harviestoun Bitter & Twisted. **Facilities** Children welcome Children's menu Children's portions Dogs allowed Garden Parking Wi-fi **Rooms** 14

TAYVALLICH   Map 20 NR78

Tayvallich Inn ♀

PA31 8PL ☎ 01546 870282
dir: *From Lochgilphead take A816 then B841/B8025*

The inn stands by a natural harbour at the head of Loch Sween with stunning views over the anchorage, particularly from the outside area of decking, where food and a great selection of real ales can be enjoyed. Not surprisingly given the location, fresh seafood features strongly – the catch is landed from the boats right outside the front door! There's always lobster, crab and langoustine available in the summer and other typical dishes might be line-caught haddock served with chips; fish pie; beef and ale pie; and home-made burgers.

Open all wk all day in summer (closed 3-6 Mon-Fri in winter) Closed: 25-26 Dec, Mon (Nov-Mar) **Bar Meals** L served all wk 12-2.30 D served all wk 6-9 Av main course £9.95 **Restaurant** L served all wk 12-2.30 booking required D served all wk 6-9 booking required Av 3 course à la carte fr £17.95 ⊕ FREE HOUSE ◀ Guinness, Loch Fyne Ales, Belhaven Best, Maverick, Avalanche, Pipers Gold. ♀ 8 **Facilities** Children welcome Children's menu Children's portions Garden Parking

CLACKMANNANSHIRE

DOLLAR   Map 21 NS99

Castle Campbell Hotel

11 Bridge St FK14 7DE
☎ 01259 742519   📄 01259 743742
e-mail: bookings@castle-campbell.co.uk
dir: *A91 (Stirling to St Andrews road). In Dollar centre by bridge overlooking clock tower*

Handy for Dollar Glen's spectacular gorges, this 19th-century coaching inn offers a real taste of Scotland. Built in 1821, pictures on the walls date back to that period. Recognised as a Whisky Ambassador, the hotel has over 50 malts; local ale is always on tap and the wine list runs to several pages. Prime Scottish produce features on the menus, with options ranging from fish and chips in the bar to seared rack of lamb with red wine and rosemary in the restaurant. Change of hands.

Open all wk ⊕ FREE HOUSE ◀ Harviestoun Bitter & Twisted, Deuchars IPA (guest), McEwans 70/-. **Facilities** Children welcome Children's menu Children's portions Dogs allowed Parking

DUMFRIES & GALLOWAY

ISLE OF WHITHORN   Map 20 NX43

PICK OF THE PUBS

The Steam Packet Inn ♀

Harbour Row DG8 8LL
☎ 01988 500334   📄 01988 500627
e-mail: steampacketinn@btconnect.com
dir: *From Newton Stewart take A714, then A746 to Whithorn, then Isle of Whithorn*

This lively quayside pub stands in a picturesque village at the tip of the Machars peninsula. Personally run by the Scoular family for over 20 years, it is the perfect place to escape from the pressures of modern living. Sit in one of the comfortable bars, undisturbed by television, fruit machines or piped music, and enjoy one of the real ales, a malt whisky from the great selection, or a glass of wine. Glance out of the picture windows and watch the fishermen at work, then look to the menu for a chance to sample the fruits of their labours. Extensive seafood choices - perhaps a kettle of mussels cooked in a cream and white wine sauce, isle-landed monkfish tail or fillet of bream - are supported by the likes of haggis-stuffed mushroom; and braised Galloway lamb shank.

Open all wk 11am-11pm (Sun noon-11) Closed: 25 Dec, winter Tue-Thu 2.30-6 **Bar Meals** L served all wk 12-2 D served all wk 6.30-9 **Restaurant** L served all wk 12-2 D served all wk 6.30-9 ⊕ FREE HOUSE ◀ Timothy Taylor Landlord, Guest ales. ♀ 12 **Facilities** Children welcome Children's menu Children's portions Dogs allowed Garden Parking

Selkirk Arms Hotel ♀

Old High St DG6 4JG
☎ 01557 330402 📄 01557 331639
e-mail: reception@selkirkarmshotel.co.uk
dir: M74 & M6 to A75, halfway between Dumfries & Stranraer on A75

On one of his Galloway tours Robert Burns reputedly stopped at this privately owned hotel and wrote the *Selkirk Grace*. The hotel's Selkirk Grace ale was produced in conjunction with Sulwath Brewers to celebrate the fact. The public rooms include two bars, and a great choice of dishes is offered in The Bistro or more intimate Artistas Restaurant, including local specialities like scallops, fish and chips and Galloway beef steaks.

Open all day all wk **Bar Meals** L served all wk 12-2 D served all wk 6-9 Av main course £10.50
Restaurant L served Sun 12-2 booking required D served all wk 7-9 booking required Fixed menu price fr £26 Av 3 course à la carte fr £29 ◀ Youngers Tartan, John Smith's Bitter, Criffel, Timothy Taylor Landlord, The Selkirk Grace. ♀ 8 **Facilities** Children welcome Children's menu Children's portions Dogs allowed Garden Parking

Annandale Arms ★★★ HL ◉

High St DG10 9HF ☎ 01683 220013 📄 01683 221395
e-mail: margaret@annandalearmshotel.co.uk
dir: A74(M) junct 15. Take A701, Moffat 1m

A major Moffat landmark for over 250 years, it used to be a matter of pride that this hostelry could change a coach and four in less than a minute, in which time the driver would down a pint of ale; today, Broughton's Merlin deserves much more time and appreciation. The award-winning food, a mix of traditional Scottish and international dishes, is also worth pondering over: choose between monkfish thermidor in a shallot, white wine tarragon and cream sauce, or pan-fried pigeon breast set on grilled Stornoway black pudding and a tattie scone with a sloe berry sauce. Besides the à la carte menu, there are daily specials.

Open all day all wk **Bar Meals** L served all wk 12-2 D served all wk 5-9 Av main course £9
Restaurant L served all wk 12-2 booking required D served all wk 6-9 Av 3 course à la carte fr £30 ⊕ FREE HOUSE ◀ Broughton ♂ Stowford Press.
Facilities Children welcome Children's menu Children's portions Dogs allowed Parking Wi-fi **Rooms** 16

Black Bull Hotel

Churchgate DG10 9EG
☎ 01683 220206 📄 01683 220483
e-mail: hotel@blackbullmoffat.co.uk
dir: Telephone for directions

This historic pub was the headquarters of Graham of Claverhouse during the 17th-century Scottish rebellion, and was frequented by Robert Burns around 1790. The Railway Bar, in former stables across the courtyard, houses a collection of railway memorabilia and traditional pub games. Food is served in the lounge, Burns Room or restaurant. Dishes include Black Bull sizzlers (steak, chicken fillets, gammon) served on a cast iron platter; the daily roast, and deep-fried breaded haddock fillet. Recent change of hands.

Open all day all wk 11-11 (Thu-Sat 11am-mdnt Sun 12-11) ⊕ FREE HOUSE ◀ McEwans, John Smith's.
Facilities Children welcome Children's menu Children's portions Dogs allowed Garden Parking

Cross Keys Hotel ♀

High St DG7 3RN ☎ 01644 420494 📄 01644 701071
e-mail: enquiries@thecrosskeys-newgalloway.co.uk
dir: At N end of Loch Ken, 10m from Castle Douglas on A712

This 17th-century former coaching inn sits in a stunning location at the top of Loch Ken and on the edge of Galloway Forest Park, a superb area for walking, fishing, birdwatching, golf, watersports, painting and photography. Part of the hotel was once the police station and in the beamed period bar the food is served in restored, stone-walled cells. The à la carte restaurant offers hearty food with a Scottish accent, such as home-made Galloway steak pie, fish in cider batter, and minted shoulder of lamb. Real ales are a speciality, and there's a good choice of malts in the whisky bar.

Open 6-11.30 Closed: Sun & Mon eve winter
Bar Meals D served all wk 6.30-8.30 **Restaurant** D served all wk 6.30-8.30 ⊕ FREE HOUSE ◀ Houston, Sulwarth, Guest ales ♂ Stowford Press. ♀ 9 **Facilities** Children's menu Dogs allowed Garden Wi-fi

PICK OF THE PUBS

Creebridge House Hotel

Minnigaff DG8 6NP
☎ 01671 402121 📄 01671 403258
e-mail: info@creebridge.co.uk
dir: From A75 into Newton Stewart, turn right over river bridge, hotel 200yds on left

A listed building dating from 1760, this family-run, country house hotel stands in three acres of tranquil gardens and woodland at the foot of Kirroughtree forest. Taking its name from the River Cree, the hotel used to be the Earl of Galloway's shooting lodge and the grounds part of his estate. The bar and brasserie offer malt whiskies and real ales, including Deuchars. For lunch or candlelit dinner in the restaurant, the well-filled menu offers plenty of dishes with Scottish credentials, such as grilled locally made haggis with melted Cheddar and rich whisky cream sauce; pan-fried haunch of Highland venison; Galloway wholetail scampi; and West Coast prawn and salmon penne pasta. Home-made desserts include pear and almond tart with custard, and lemon posset with shortbread. If you're an outdoor sort, this is the place to be as there is fishing, golf, cycling, horse riding walking and deer stalking.

Open all wk noon-2 6-11.30 (Fri-Sat noon-2 6-1am) Closed: 1st 3wks Jan **Bar Meals** L served all wk noon-2 D served all wk 6-9 **Restaurant** L served all wk noon-2 D served all wk 6-9 ⊕ FREE HOUSE ◀ Deuchars, Guinness, Guest ales. **Facilities** Children welcome Dogs allowed Garden Parking

The Galloway Arms Hotel ♀

54-58 Victoria St DG8 6DB
☎ 01671 402653 📄 01671 401202
e-mail: info@gallowayarmshotel.com
web: www.gallowayarmshotel.com
dir: In town centre, opposite clock

Founded 260 years ago by 6th Earl of Galloway, the hotel acted as the focus for developing the 'planted' market town of Newton Stewart, first established in the 1650's. On the banks of the River Cree, the town is well sited to explore Galloway Forest or the Machars of Whithorn, working up an appetite for traditional Scottish dishes such as chicken, leek and Highland crowdie or the prosaically-named Bonnie Prince Charlie's Balls (deep-fried haggis in Drambuie-based sauce), accompanied by a dram from the most extensive selection of malts in Galloway.

Open all day all wk 11am-mdnt (Fri-Sat 11am-1am) **Bar Meals** L served all wk 12-2 D served all wk 6-9 **Restaurant** D served all wk 6-9 ⊕ FREE HOUSE ◀ Belhaven Best, Guinness, Caledonian Deuchars IPA, 70/- Shilling. ₹11 **Facilities** Children welcome Children's menu Children's portions Dogs allowed Garden Parking

See advert below

SANDHEAD	Map 20 NX04

Tigh Na Mara Hotel

Main St DG9 9JF ☎ 01776 830210 ▤ 01776 830432 e-mail: tighnamara@btconnect.com **dir:** *A75 from Dumfries towards Stranraer. Left onto B7084 to Sandhead. Hotel in village centre*

A family-run village hotel at the western end of the Gulf Stream-washed Sands of Luce, with an extensive menu of dishes created from top quality local ingredients. Stornoway black pudding accompanies duo of pheasant and pigeon; roast rib of Galloway beef shares its plate with Yorkshire pudding; and the seafood in the pancakes comes from Scotland's West Coast waters. Relax in the beer garden, comfortable lounge or beside the fire in the public bar. By the way, Tigh na Mara means 'house by the sea'.

Open all day all wk **Bar Meals** L served all wk 12-2.30 D served all wk 6-9 **Restaurant** L served all wk 12-2.30 D served all wk 6-9 booking required Fixed menu price fr £10.95 ⊕ BELHAVEN ◀ Belhaven Best, Morland Old Speckled Hen. **Facilities** Children welcome Children's menu Children's portions Family room Dogs allowed Garden Parking Wi-fi

---

DUNDEE, CITY OF	

BROUGHTY FERRY	Map 21 NO43

The Royal Arch Bar ☕

285 Brook St DD5 2DS ☎ 01382 779741 ▤ 01382 739174 **dir:** *3m from Dundee. 0.5 min from Broughty Ferry rail station*

Handy for the Tay-side esplanade and sandy beach at Broughty Ferry, the pub's striking, tile-hung exterior hides a superb art deco lounge (note the stools, table legs and vivid stained glass) off a fine Victorian panelled, turned-wood bar. Its name derives from the Masonic Arch, its logo from a now-demolished monument to Queen Victoria. At this popular community local, sup Carnoustie-brewed beers and chow on robust pub food (maybe haddock Kiev); the pavement café here is busy in good weather.

Open all day all wk **Bar Meals** L served Mon-Fri 12-2.15, Sat-Sun 12-5 booking required D served all wk 5-7.30 booking required Av main course £7 ⊕ FREE HOUSE ◀ McEwans 80/-, Belhaven Best, Caledonian Deuchars IPA, Angus Mashie Niblick Cask. ₹30 **Facilities** Children welcome Children's portions Family room Dogs allowed Garden Beer festival Wi-fi

---

DUNDEE	Map 21 NO43

Speedwell Bar ☕

165-167 Perth Rd DD2 1AS ☎ 01382 667783 **dir:** *From A92 (Tay Bridge), A991 signed Perth/A85/ Coupar Angus/A923. At Riverside rdbt 3rd exit (A991). At lights left into Nethergate signed Parking/South Tay St. Forward into Perth Rd. Pass university. Bar on right*

This fine example of an unspoiled Edwardian bar is worth visiting for its interior alone; all the fitments in the bar and sitting rooms are beautifully crafted mahogany – gantry, drink shelves, dado panelling and fireplace.

The same family owned it for 90 years, until the present landlord's father bought it in 1995. As well as the cask-conditioned ales, 157 whiskies and imported bottles are offered. A kitchen would be good, but since the pub is listed this is impossible. This community pub is home to several clubs and has live Scottish music from time to time on a Tuesday.

Open all day all wk ⊕ FREE HOUSE ◀ McEwans, Belhaven Best, Caledonian, Deuchars IPA. ₹18 **Facilities** Dogs allowed Wi-fi **Notes** ⊛

EAST AYRSHIRE	

DALRYMPLE	Map 20 NS31

The Kirkton Inn

1 Main St KA6 6DF ☎ 01292 560241 e-mail: kirkton@cqm.co.uk **dir:** *6m SE from centre of Ayr just off A77*

In the heart of the village of Dalrymple, this inn was built in 1879 as a coaching inn and has been providing sustenance to travellers ever since; the welcoming atmosphere makes it easy to feel at home. It's a stoutly traditional setting, with open fires and polished brasses. Eat traditional and wholesome dishes in the Coach Room in the oldest part of the building, and perhaps choose chicken and leek pie, or Kirkton burger, followed by hot chocolate fudge cake. Lighter options are soup and sandwiches.

Open all day all wk **Bar Meals** L served all wk 12-2.30 D served all wk 5-8 Av main course £7.50 **Restaurant** L served all wk 12-2.30 D served all wk 5-9 Fixed menu price fr £5.95 Av 3 course à la carte fr £15 ⊕ SCOTTISH & NEWCASTLE ◀ John Smith's, Guinness. **Facilities** Children welcome Children's menu Children's portions Play area Family room Dogs allowed Garden Parking Wi-fi

---

THE GALLOWAY ARMS

Enjoy the comfort, atmosphere and excellent food of Bonnie Galloway at The Galloway Arms Hotel. All our food is fresh and our menu is extensive. The perfect base for touring. Enjoy the wonderful scenery, the World class bike trails in the town that has become the Gateway to the Galloway Hills. We could not be easier to find, in the town centre, opposite the town clock. Private parking and garage. Secluded hotel garden, real ales and great food.

54–58 Victoria Street
Newton Stewart   DG8 6DB
Tel: 01671 402653   Fax: 01671 401202
Website: www.gallowayarmshotel.com   Email: info@gallowayarmshotel.com

The Cochrane Inn

45 Main Rd KA2 0AP ☎ 01563 570122
dir: *From Glasgow A77 to Kilmarnock, then A759 to Gatehead*

There's a friendly, bustling atmosphere inside this traditional ivy-covered village centre pub, which sits just a short drive from the Ayrshire coast. The interior has natural stone walls adorned with gleaming brasses and log fires in winter. The menus combine British and international flavours in hearty, wholesome food. This might translate as salt and pepper squid with jalapeño salsa or smoked duck breast with apple salad, walnuts and orange dressing; then haggis, neeps and tatties; chicken stuffed with cream cheese, chorizo and garlic; or steak and sausage pie.

Open all wk noon-2.30 5.30 onwards (Sun noon-9)
Bar Meals food served all day **Restaurant** food served all day ⊕ FREE HOUSE ◀ John Smith's. **Facilities** Children welcome Children's menu Children's portions Garden Parking Wi-fi

PICK OF THE PUBS

The Sorn Inn ★★★★ RR ◉◉ ❦

35 Main St KA5 6HU
☎ 01290 551305 📠 01290 553470
e-mail: craig@sorninn.com
dir: *A70 from S; or A76 from N onto B743 to Sorn*

Dating back to the 18th century when it was a coaching inn on the old Edinburgh to Kilmarnock route, The Sorn is now a smart gastro-pub with comfortably refurbished rooms. Along with award-winning real ales from Renfrewshire's Houston Brewery, twelve wines are served by the glass. Menus in both the Chop House and Restaurant offer a fusion of fine dining and brasserie-style food using the best of seasonal ingredients. Some starters, such as crisp pork belly with spiced Puy lentils and apple salad, or mussels cooked in fennel with Pernod and shallots, can be ordered in main course size. Pasta dishes too, such as penne with meatballs in a rich tomato and basil sauce, can be a starter or a main. Grills are a favourite, with aged Scotch beef naturally the star of the show. For a seafood option, pan-fried sea bass with artichokes, wild mushrooms, braised shallots and saffron gnocchi will fit the bill. The table d'hôte lunch from Tuesday to Friday represents superb value, especially as this standard of cuisine has attained two AA Rosettes for the last nine years.

Open noon-2.30 6-10 (Fri noon-2.30 6-mdnt Sat noon-mdnt Sun 12-10) Closed: 2wks Jan, Mon
Bar Meals L served Tue-Fri 12-2.30, Sat 12-9, Sun 12-8 D served Tue-Fri 6-9, Sat 12-9, Sun 12.30-8 Av main course £12.50 **Restaurant** L served Tue-Fri 12-2.30, Sat 12-9, Sun 12-8 booking required D served Tue-Fri 6-9, Sat 12-9, Sun 12-8 booking required Av 3 course à la carte fr £25 ⊕ FREE HOUSE ◀ John Smith's, Real Ale Texas, Houston Brewery, Guinness. ❦ 12 **Facilities** Children welcome Children's menu Children's portions Dogs allowed Parking Wi-fi
Rooms 4

The Longniddry Inn

Main St EH32 0NF ☎ 01875 852401
e-mail: info@longniddryinn.com
dir: *On A198 (Main St), near rail station*

Formerly a blacksmith's forge and four cottages on Longniddry's main street, this inviting looking pub is noted locally for good food and friendly service. From the extensive menu, start with haggis, neeps and tatties, deep-fried Brie with redcurrant jelly, or pâté with Cumberland sauce, then follow with chicken and mushroom pie, lambs' liver, bacon and onion gravy, or a rib-eye steak from the grill. In warmer weather why not sit outside with a pint of Belhaven Best.

Open all day all wk ⊕ PUNCH TAVERNS ◀ Belhaven Best, Deuchars IPA. **Facilities** Children welcome Children's menu Children's portions Garden Parking Wi-fi

Bennets Bar ❦

8 Leven St EH3 9LG ☎ 0131 229 5143
e-mail: bennetsbar@hotmail.co.uk
dir: *Next to Kings Theatre. Please phone for more detailed directions*

Bennets is a listed property dating from 1839 with hand-painted tiles and murals on the walls, original stained glass windows, intricate wood carving on bar fitments and brass beer taps. It's a friendly pub, popular with performers from the adjacent Kings Theatre. The traditional bar has some contemporary twists and serves real ales, over 120 malt whiskies and a decent selection of wines. The home-made food, at a reasonable price, ranges from toasties, burgers and salads to stovies, steak pie, and Scottish fare. There's also a daily roast and traditional puddings. Coffee and tea are served all day.

Open all day all wk 11am-1am Closed: 25 Dec
Bar Meals L served Mon-Sat 12-2, Sun 11-8 D served Mon-Sat 5-8.30, Sun 11-8 Av main course £7.55 **Restaurant** L served Mon-Sat 12-2 D served Mon-Sat 5-8.30 ⊕ IONA PUB ◀ Caledonian Deuchars IPA, Guinness, Caledonian 80/-. ❦ 10 **Facilities** Children welcome Children's menu Children's portions Family room Wi-fi

The Bow Bar

80 The West Bow EH1 2HH ☎ 0131 226 7667
dir: *Telephone for directions*

This free house in the heart of Edinburgh's old town reflects the history and traditions of the area. Tables are from decommissioned railway carriages, and a gantry reclaimed from an old church is used to house around 200 malt whiskies. Eight real ales from micro-breweries across the UK, along with some keg beers, are dispensed from antique Aitken founts driven by air pressure. Such is the focus on liquid refreshment that bar snacks are the only solids served. Conversation is highly prized too – there are no gaming machines or music to detract from the agreeable ambience.

Open all day all wk Closed: 25-26 Dec, 1-2 Jan
Bar Meals L served Mon-Sat 12-2 ⊕ FREE HOUSE ◀ Deuchars IPA, Stewarts 80/-, Timothy Taylor Landlord, Harviestoun Bitter & Twisted, Atlas Latitude, Trade Winds, Stewarts Pentland IPA ☼ Stowford Press, Thistly Cross. **Facilities** Dogs allowed Beer festival Wi-fi

PICK OF THE PUBS

The Café Royal ◉ ❦ NEW

AA PUB OF THE YEAR FOR SCOTLAND 2011-2012

19 West Register St EH2 2AA ☎ 0131 556 1884
e-mail: info@caferoyal.org.uk
dir: *Off Princes St, in city centre*

A glorious example of Victorian and Baroque, little has changed at the Café Royal since it moved across the road from its original site in 1863. A stylish Parisian building designed by local architect Robert Paterson, entering the Café Royal is like stepping back in time. Elegant stained glass and fine late Victorian plasterwork dominate the building, as do irreplaceable Doulton ceramic murals in the bar and restaurant. The whole building and its interior were listed in 1970 so future generations will enjoy the unique building which still sticks to its early 19th century roots by serving local ales, wine, coffee and fresh oysters in the bar and restaurant. Scottish produce dominates the menu, from starters of Stornoway black pudding and apple gratin or Scottish smoked salmon with lemon mayonnaise to main courses of fish stew or haggis and whisky cream pie with chips.

Open all day all wk **Bar Meals** Av main course £9 food served all day **Restaurant** L served all wk 12-2.30 booking required D served all wk 5-9.30 booking required Av 3 course à la carte fr £30 ⊕ PUNCH PUB CO ◀ Deuchars IPA, Kelburn Ca'Canny & Goldihops, Harviestoun Bitter & Twisted. ❦ 10 **Facilities** Children welcome Children's portions

PICK OF THE PUBS

Doric Tavern

15-16 Market St EH1 1DE ☎ 0131 225 1084
e-mail: info@the-doric.com
dir: *In city centre opp Waverly Station & Edinburgh Dungeons*

Built in the 17th-century, The Doric claims to be Edinburgh's oldest gastro-pub. It became a pub in the mid-1800s and takes its name from a language that used to be spoken in north-east Scotland, mainly in Aberdeenshire. Conveniently located for Waverley Station, the pub is just a short walk from Princes Street and Edinburgh Castle. Public rooms include a refurbished ground-floor bar, and a wine bar and bistro upstairs. In these pleasantly informal surroundings, a wide choice of fresh, locally sourced food is prepared by the chefs on site. While sipping a pint of Deuchars IPA or Edinburgh Pale Ale, you can nibble on traditional Cullen skink or slow roasted barbecue ribs. Starter options include steamed Scottish mussels, smoked salmon or deep-fried Brie with cranberry and orange jelly. Main dishes range from linguine with fresh clams sautéed with garlic, chilli and white wine to roast lamb rump served on a garlic and rosemary mash with butternut squash, plum tomato stuffed with ratatouille. Haggis, neeps and tatties covered with a whisky jus will also satisfy traditionalists.

Open all day all wk 11.30am-mdnt (Thu-Sat 11.30am-1am) Closed: 25-26 Dec, 1 Jan **Bar Meals** Av main course £13 food served all day **Restaurant** Fixed menu price fr £12 Av 3 course à la carte fr £22 food served all day ⊕ FREE HOUSE ◄ Deuchars IPA, Guinness, Stewarts 80/, Edinburgh Gold, Edinburgh Pale Ale. **Facilities** Children welcome Children's portions Family room

The Shore Bar & Restaurant ☶

3 Shore, Leith EH6 6QW
☎ 0131 553 5080 ▤ 0131 553 5080
e-mail: info@theshore.biz
dir: *Telephone for directions*

Part of this historic pub was a 17th-century lighthouse and, as befits its location beside the Port of Leith, it has a fine reputation for fish and seafood. Both restaurant and bar serve food all day from noon, with the carte changing as and when fresh produce arrives. Typical of the snacks are smoked mackerel pâté, and ham hash cake with free-range poached egg and hollandaise. For a main course expect the likes of the Shore Bar's fish pie, or pork belly with snail scampi and boulangère potatoes.

Open all wk noon-1am (Sun 12.30pm-1am) Closed: 25-26 Dec, 1 Jan **Bar Meals** L served all wk 12-6 booking required D served all wk 6-10.30 booking required Av main course £15 **Restaurant** L served all wk 12-6 booking required D served all wk 6-10.30 booking required Av 3 course à la carte fr £25 ⊕ FREE HOUSE ◄ Belhaven 80/-, Deuchars IPA, Guinness. ☶ 14 **Facilities** Children welcome Dogs allowed

---

PICK OF THE PUBS

The Bridge Inn ☶

27 Baird Rd EH28 8RA ☎ 0131 333 1320
e-mail: info@bridgeinn.com
dir: *From Newbridge at B7030 junct, follow signs for Ratho and Edinburgh Canal Centre*

Just to the west of Edinburgh, this canal-side inn makes the most of its idyllic waterside location, catering for boaters, cyclists and ramblers using this popular waterway and basing two floating restaurants on renovated barges which ply the canal most weekends, a diverting trip on the tree-lined Edinburgh and Glasgow Union Canal first opened in 1820. The waterside beer garden is a popular summertime venue, where a grand selection of beers from Scotland's burgeoning micro-brewery sector is the order of the day. Inside, the Pop Inn or a brand new bar attract locals to regular quiz nights, whilst the bistro restaurant, with its equally strong commitment to Scottish produce, may include on the menu pork from the inn's own herd of saddleback pigs. Starters cover pan-seared pigeon breast and breaded Camembert, whilst mains include courgette and blue cheese fritters with chickpea salsa.

Open all day all wk 11-11 (Fri-Sat 11am-mdnt) Closed: 25-26 Dec, 2 Jan **Bar Meals** L served Mon-Fri 12-3, Sat 12-9, Sun 12.30-8.30 D served Mon-Fri 5.30-9, Sat 12-9, Sun 12-30-8.30 Av main course £9.95 **Restaurant** L served Mon-Fri 12-3, Sat 12-9, Sun 12.30-8.30 booking required D served Mon-Fri 5.30-9, Sat 12-9, Sun 12.30-8.30 booking required Fixed menu price fr £17.95 Av 3 course à la carte fr £17.95 ⊕ FREE HOUSE ◄ Belhaven, Deuchars IPA, Guest ales ♻ Aspall. ☶ 21 **Facilities** Children welcome Children's menu Children's portions Dogs allowed Garden Beer festival Parking Wi-fi

---

FIFE

The Dreel Tavern

16 High Street West KY10 3DL
☎ 01333 310727 ▤ 01333 310577
e-mail: thedreeltavern@btconnect.com
dir: *From Anstruther centre take A917 towards Pittenweem*

Complete with a local legend concerning an amorous encounter between James V and a local gypsy woman, the welcoming 17th-century Dreel Tavern has plenty of atmosphere. Its oak beams, open fire and stone walls retain much of the distant past, while home-cooked food and cask-conditioned ales are served to hungry visitors of the present. Peaceful gardens overlook Dreel Burn.

Open all day all wk 11am-mdnt (Sun 12.30-mdnt) ⊕ SCOTTISH & NEWCASTLE ◄ Deuchars IPA, 2 guest ales. **Facilities** Children welcome Family room Dogs allowed Garden Parking

---

Burntisland Sands Hotel

Lochies Rd KY3 9JX ☎ 01592 872230 ▤ 01592 872230
e-mail: mail@burntlandsands.co.uk
dir: *Towards Kirkcaldy, Burntisland on A921. Hotel on right before Kinghorn*

Once a highly regarded girls' boarding school, this small, family-run hotel stands just 50 yards from an award-winning sandy beach. Visitors can expect reasonably priced breakfasts, snacks, lunches and evening meals, including internationally themed evenings. Typical choices range from Mexican-style chicken to haggis, neeps and tatties. Relax and enjoy a drink in the bar and lounge area or in the courtyard.

Open all day all wk **Bar Meals** L served Mon-Fri 12-2.30, Sat-Sun all day booking required D served Mon-Fri 5-8.30 booking required Av main course £8.20 **Restaurant** L served Mon-Fri 12-2.30, Sat-Sun all day booking required D served Mon-Fri 5-8.30 booking required Fixed menu price fr £22 Av 3 course à la carte fr £26 ⊕ FREE HOUSE ◄ Scottish Courage ales, Guinness, Guest ales. **Facilities** Children welcome Children's menu Children's portions Play area Dogs allowed Garden Parking Wi-fi

---

The Ship Inn

The Toft KY9 1DT ☎ 01333 330246 ▤ 01333 330864
e-mail: info@ship-elie.com
dir: *Follow A915 & A917 to Elie. From High Street follow signs to Watersport Centre & The Toft*

A pub since 1838, this lively free house sits right on the waterfront at Elie Bay. It has been run by the enthusiastic Philip family for over 20 years. The cricket team plays regular fixtures on the beach, live music is regularly staged, and a full programme of charity and celebratory events runs throughout the year, including a barbecue on New Year's Day. The best of local produce features on the concise menu which offers the likes of deep-fried haddock in beer batter, and baguettes of chicken mayonnaise and spicy chorizo sausage.

Open all wk Closed: 25 Dec ⊕ FREE HOUSE ◄ Caledonian Deuchars IPA, Belhaven Best, Caledonian 80/-, Tartan Special. **Facilities** Children welcome Children's menu Children's portions Play area Family room Dogs allowed Garden

KINCARDINE
Map 21 NS98

The Unicorn

15 Excise St FK10 4LN ☎ 01259 739129
e-mail: info@theunicorn.co.uk
dir: *Exit M9 junct 7 towards Kincardine Bridge. Cross bridge, bear left. 1st left, then sharp left at rdbt*

This 17th-century pub-restaurant in the heart of the historic port of Kincardine used to be a coaching inn. And it was where, in 1842, Sir James Dewar, inventor of the vacuum flask, was born. There is a comfortable lounge bar, a grillroom, and a more formal dining room upstairs. Leather sofas and modern decor blend in well with the older parts of the building; relax and enjoy a pint of Old Engine Oil by the open fire in the bar.

Open noon-2.30 5.30-mdnt (Sun 12.30-mdnt) Closed: 3rd wk Jul, Mon ⊕ FREE HOUSE ◀ Bitter & Twisted, Schiehavillion, Old Engine Oil. **Facilities** Children welcome Children's menu Children's portions Parking

ST ANDREWS
Map 21 NO51

PICK OF THE PUBS

The Inn at Lathones
★★★★ INN ◉◉ ♀

Largoward KY9 1JE
☎ 01334 840494 📄 01334 840694
e-mail: lathones@theinn.co.uk
dir: *5m from St Andrews on A915*

Although many people associate St Andrews purely with golf, this 400-year-old coaching inn with rooms is the exception to the rule as it doubles up as an award-winning live music venue. Lindisfarne and Curtis Stigers are among the many luminaries who perform here and the walls display one of the best collections of music memorabilia in the country. Ancient meets modern here and guests can relax in deep sofas and enjoy excellent ales from Orkney Brewery around log-burners. For the past 13 years the chefs here have been awarded two AA Rosettes; their innovative cooking of well sourced local ingredients can be judged from starters that include game spiced terrine or leek and Dunsyre Blue tart with mixed leaves and hazelnut dressing. Mains come up trumps, too, with roasted sea bass with mussels and prawns, lemon and fennel sauce, or slow-roasted belly of pork with sautéed wild mushrooms and pak choi. Smart, contemporary accommodation is available.

Open all day all wk Closed: 2wks Jan **Bar Meals** Av main course £10.50 food served all day **Restaurant** L served all wk 12-2.30 D served all wk 6-9.30 Av 3 course à la carte fr £32.95 ⊕ FREE HOUSE ◀ Dark Island, Three Sisters, Belhaven Best. ♀ 11 **Facilities** Children welcome Dogs allowed Garden Parking **Rooms** 21

PICK OF THE PUBS

The Jigger Inn ♀

The Old Course Hotel KY16 9SP
☎ 01334 474371 📄 01334 477688
e-mail: reservations@oldcoursehotel.co.uk
dir: *M90 junct 8, A91 to St Andrews*

Steeped in history, The Jigger was a stationmaster's lodge in the 1800s on a railway line that disappeared many years ago. Located in the grounds of The Old Course Hotel, its close proximity to the world famous St Andrew's golf course means that it is home to some impressive golfing memorabilia. Don't be surprised if you are sharing the bar with a caddy or a golfing legend fresh from a game. Crackling open-hearth fires, traditional Scottish pub hospitality and plenty of golfing gossip are the backdrop for a selection of Scottish beers, including St Andrew's Best and Jigger Ale. All-day availability is one advantage of a short, simple menu that lists soups, inviting sandwiches and quenelles of haggis, neeps and tatties as starters, and continues with Jigger burger with Mull Cheddar, Ayrshire bacon and fries; shepherd's pie with roasted root vegetables; pork and honey sausages on colcannon mash; and desserts such as apple and pear crumble.

Open all day all wk 11-11 (Sun noon-11) Closed: 25 Dec **Bar Meals** L served all wk 12-9.30 food served all day **Restaurant** D served all wk 12-9.30 booking required ⊕ FREE HOUSE ◀ Guinness, St Andrews Best, Jigger Ale. ♀ 8 **Facilities** Children welcome Garden Parking

GLASGOW, CITY OF

GLASGOW
Map 20 NS56

Bon Accord ♀ NEW

153 North St G3 7DA ☎ 0141 248 4427
e-mail: paul.bonaccord@ntlbusiness.com
dir: *M8 junct 19 merge onto A804 (North Street) signed Charing Cross*

Paul and Thomas McDonagh run this award-winning ale house and malt whisky bar, patronised by tourists from all over the world, their taste buds primed for some of the annual tally of a thousand-plus different beers (perhaps at one of the four beer festivals), the 240-strong malts collection, or over 40 ciders. To line the stomach are all-day breakfasts, baguettes, jacket potatoes, burgers, fish dishes, grills and chicken salad, with Glamorgan sausage and macaroni cheese for vegetarians.

Open all day all wk **Bar Meals** L served all wk 12-8 D served all wk 12-8 Av main course £4.95 food served all day **Restaurant** food served all day ⊕ FREE HOUSE ◀ Over 1000 real ales per year ♂ Over 40 ciders per year. ♀ 11 **Facilities** Children welcome Garden Beer festival Wi-fi

Rab Ha's

83 Hutchieson St G1 1SH
☎ 0141 572 0400 📄 0141 572 0402
e-mail: management@rabhas.com
dir: *Telephone for directions*

In the heart of Glasgow's revitalised Merchant City, Rab Ha's takes its name from Robert Hall, a local 19th-century character known as 'The Glasgow Glutton'. This hotel, restaurant and bar blend Victorian character with contemporary Scottish decor. Pre-theatre and set menus show extensive use of carefully sourced Scottish produce in starters like poached egg on grilled Stornoway black pudding, and pan-seared Oban scallops, followed by roast saddle of Rannoch Moor venison. Change of hands.

Open all day all wk noon-mdnt (Sun 12.30pm-mdnt) ⊕ FREE HOUSE ◀ Tennent's, Deuchars IPA. **Facilities** Children welcome Children's portions

PICK OF THE PUBS

Stravaigin ◉◉ ♀

28 Gibson St G12 8NX
☎ 0141 334 2665 📄 0141 334 4099
e-mail: stravaigin@btinternet.com
dir: *Telephone for directions*

This popular café bar close to the university has picked up several awards for its food and design recently. Located in a busy street, the modern split-level basement restaurant continues to pull the crowds with its contemporary decor, stone and leather-covered walls, modern art and quirky antiques. The award-winning bar was intended to be where diners had pre-dinner drinks but it now has a life and clientele of its own, offering real ales like Fyne Ales Chip 71 and Belhaven Best to casual drinkers. Expect innovative and exciting fusion food cooked from top notch Scottish ingredients. The wide range of eclectic dishes may include Jerusalem artichoke and Arbroath smokie arrancini with pea purée and bacon crisps; seared sea bream, fondant potato, crab and mussel chowder, green beans and chilli crushed sweetcorn; mustard and thyme pork belly, Brussels sprouts and ham hock spiked barley risotto, apple compote; and pear and caramel custard trifle, sherry granita and almond biscuits for dessert (wines are recommended with each dessert).

Open all day all wk Closed: 25 Dec, 1 Jan **Bar Meals** L served all wk 11-5 D served all wk 5-11 Av main course £16 food served all day **Restaurant** L served Sat-Sun 12-11 D served all wk 5-11 Fixed menu price fr £13.95 Av 3 course à la carte fr £25 ⊕ FREE HOUSE ◀ Deuchars IPA, Belhaven Best, Chip 71 ♂ Westons Premium Organic. ♀ 18 **Facilities** Children welcome Children's menu Children's portions Dogs allowed Wi-fi

Save on hotels. Book at theAA.com/hotel

GLASGOW, CITY OF – HIGHLAND 553 SCOTLAND

PICK OF THE PUBS

Ubiquitous Chip ◉◉ ⚲

12 Ashton Ln G12 8SJ
☎ **0141 334 5007** ▤ **0141 337 6417**
e-mail: mail@ubiquitouschip.co.uk
dir: *In West End of Glasgow, off Byres Rd. Beside Hillhead subway station*

A West End stalwart for four decades, the Ubiquitous Chip is one of Glasgow's most famous eateries. Set at the end of a cobbled mews; the main dining area opens into a beautiful, vine-covered courtyard, at mezzanine level is a new dining space for private dining, while upstairs is the brasserie-style, two-AA Rosette restaurant. There are three drinking areas: the traditional pub, serving real ales, nearly 30 wines by the glass, more than 150 malt whiskies; the Wee Bar, which is indeed quite 'wee', possibly the wee-est in Scotland; and the Corner Bar, which serves cocktails across a granite slab reclaimed from a mortuary. The kitchen showcases the very best of Scotland's produce on the menu in the shape of marinated haunch and loin of Galloway venison, potato and onion rosti cake with rhubarb, red cabbage, green peppercorn and Drambuie sauce; Troon landed halibut fillet with herb and pine nut crust, braised fennel, red wine and Belgian chocolate sauce; Perthshire wood pigeon wrapped in bacon, pearl barley risotto, wild mushroom sauce and rich game sauce.

Open all wk 11am-mdnt Closed: 25 Dec, 1 Jan
Bar Meals L served all wk 12-11 D served all wk 12-11 Av main course £15 food served all day
Restaurant L served Mon-Sat 12.30-2.30, Sun 12.30-3.30 booking required D served all wk 5.30-11 booking required Fixed menu price fr £39.95 food served all day ⊕ FREE HOUSE ◼ Deuchars IPA, The Chip 71 Ale. ⚲ 29 **Facilities** Children welcome Children's menu Children's portions Wi-fi

HIGHLAND

ACHILTIBUIE   Map 22 NC00

PICK OF THE PUBS

Summer Isles Hotel & Bar ◉◉

IV26 2YG ☎ **01854 622282** ▤ **01854 622251**
e-mail: info@summerisleshotel.com
dir: *Take A835 N from Ullapool for 10m, Achiltibuie signed on left, 15m to village. Hotel 1m on left*

Located in a stunningly wild and untouched landscape, the hotel is a favourite destination for food lovers, outdoor adventurers and those simply looking for peace and fresh air. The all-year bar at the side of the hotel is open all day, serving fresh ground coffee, snacks, lunch, afternoon tea and evening meals in an informal setting. (Note that the pub restaurant only serves food from April until October.) This is where the local crofters gathered to drink well over a century ago. Today they would probably ask for the list, such is the choice of ales and bottled beers available. Chief

among these are the An Teallach Brewery draught ales, but multi-award-winning bottles from the Orkney Brewing Company are well worth trying too. The short menu is based on fine fresh Scottish ingredients, especially seafood – will it be a platter of langoustines, or freshly cooked mussels with pancetta?

Open all wk noon-11 **Bar Meals** L served all wk 12-2.30, soup & snacks till 5 D served all wk 5-8.30 Av main course £13 food served all day
Restaurant L served Apr-Oct 12.30-2.30 D served Apr-Oct all wk till 8 ⊕ FREE HOUSE ◼ An Teallach, Crofters Pale, Beinn Deorg. **Facilities** Children welcome Children's menu Children's portions Garden Parking Wi-fi

AVIEMORE   Map 23 NH81

The Old Bridge Inn

Dalfaber Rd PH22 1PU ☎ **01479 811137**
e-mail: sayhello@oldbridgeinn.co.uk
dir: *Exit A9 to Aviemore, 1st right to Ski Rd, then 1st left again 200mtrs*

Overlooking the River Spey, this friendly pub is in an area popular for outdoor pursuits and now with a new landlord. Drink in the attractive riverside garden or in the relaxing bars warmed by a roaring log fire. Here malt whiskies naturally have their place, but not to the exclusion of excellent real ales. In winter try a warming seasonal cocktail while perusing the après-ski menu in the comfortable restaurant. After an active day, a Dalfour brown trout starter could easily be followed by a Geddes Farm chicken with braised cabbage and Puy lentils.

Open all day all wk Mon-Thu 11am-mdnt (Fri-Sat 11am-1am Sun 12.30-mdnt) **Bar Meals** L served Mon-Sat 12-3, Sun 12.30-3 booking required D served Mon-Thu 6-9, Fri-Sat 6-10 booking required Av main course £13
Restaurant L served Mon-Sat 12-3, Sun 12.30-3 booking required D served Mon-Sat 12-3, Fri-Sat 6-10 booking required Fixed menu price fr £23 Av 3 course à la carte fr £25 ⊕ FREE HOUSE ◼ Deuchars IPA, Cairngorm Trade Winds, Cairngorm Black Gold, Atlas Nimbus, Schiehallion ♂ Thistly Cross Cider. **Facilities** Children welcome Children's portions Dogs allowed Garden Parking Wi-fi

BADACHRO   Map 22 NG77

The Badachro Inn

IV21 2AA ☎ **01445 741255** ▤ **01445 741319**
e-mail: Lesley@badachroinn.com
dir: *From Kinlochewe A832 towards Gairloch. Onto B8056, right to Badachro after 3.25m, towards quay*

Expect great views from one of Scotland's finest anchorages at this convivial waterside pub, which has two moorings for visitors. Decking, with nautical-style sails and rigging, runs right down to the water overlooking Loch Gairloch. Interesting photographs and collages adorn the bar walls, where there is a dining area by a log fire. Friendly staff serve beers from the An Teallach or Caledonian breweries. A further dining conservatory overlooks the bay. Excellent fresh fish is the speciality of the house, along with dishes such as local venison terrine and chicken breast on crushed haggis, neeps and tatties.

Open all wk Closed: 25-26 Dec ⊕ FREE HOUSE ◼ Red Cullen, An Teallach, Blaven, 80/-, Guinness.
Facilities Children welcome Children's portions Dogs allowed Garden Parking Wi-fi

CARRBRIDGE   Map 23 NH92

The Cairn

PH23 3AS ☎ **01479 841212** ▤ **01479 841362**
e-mail: info@cairnhotel.co.uk
dir: *In village centre*

The Highland village of Carrbridge and this family-run inn make the perfect base for exploring the Cairngorms, the Moray coast and the Malt Whisky Trail. In the homely, tartan-carpeted bar, you'll find cracking Isle of Skye and Cairngorm ales on handpump, blazing winter log fires, all-day sandwiches, and hearty bar meals, including sweet marinated herring with oatcakes, venison sausage casserole, and sticky toffee pudding. Change of hands.

Open all day all wk 11-11 (Fri-Sat 11am-1am) ⊕ FREE HOUSE ◼ Cairngorm, Black Isle, Guest ales.
Facilities Children welcome Children's menu Children's portions Dogs allowed Garden Parking Wi-fi

CAWDOR   Map 23 NH85

PICK OF THE PUBS

Cawdor Tavern 🍷

The Lane IV12 5XP
☎ 01667 404777   📠 01667 404584
e-mail: enquiries@cawdortavern.co.uk
web: www.cawdortavern.co.uk
dir: *From A96 (Inverness-Aberdeen) take B9006 &*
follow Cawdor Castle signs. Tavern in village centre

Tucked away in the heart of Cawdor's pretty village, the
Tavern's near neighbour is the castle where Macbeth
held court. Nairn's pretty wooded countryside slides
away from the pub, offering umpteen opportunities for
easy rambles before retiring to consider the welcoming
mix of fine Scottish food and island micro-brewery ales
that makes the pub a destination in its own right.
There's an almost baronial feel to the bars, created
from the Cawdor Estate's joinery workshop and
featuring wonderful panelling which originated in the
castle; log fires and stoves add winter warmth, as does
the impressive list of Highland and Island malts. A
highly accomplished menu balances meat, fish, game
and vegetarian options, prepared in a modern Scottish
style with first class Scottish produce. Settle in with a
pint of Raven Ale from the respected Orkney Brewery
and contemplate a starter of seafood platter,
appetizers for mains covering pan-fried fillet of sea
bream served on spinach crayfish-tail risotto, fillet of
Moray pork encased in a sage and onion mousse, or
local Brie, cranberry and chestnut risotto.

Open all wk 11-3 5-11 (Sat 11am-mdnt Sun 12.30-11)
all day in summer Closed: 25 Dec, 1 Jan, 2wks mid Jan
Bar Meals L served Mon-Sat 12-2, Sun 12.30-3
D served all wk 5.30-9 **Restaurant** L served Mon-Sat
12-2, Sun 12.30-3 booking required D served all wk
5.30-9 booking required ⊕ FREE HOUSE ◀ Red
MacGregor, Three Sisters, Orkney Dark Island, Raven
Ale, Latitude Highland Pilsner, Nimbus Ö Thatchers
Gold. 🍷 9 **Facilities** Children welcome Children's menu
Children's portions Dogs allowed Garden Parking

FORTROSE   Map 23 NH75

PICK OF THE PUBS

The Anderson 🍷 NEW

Union St IV10 8TD ☎ 01381 620236
e-mail: info@theanderson.co.uk
dir: *From Inverness take A9 N signed Wick. Right onto*
B9161 signed Munlochy, Cromarty A832. At T-junct
right onto A832 to Fortrose

In a tranquil seaside setting on the beautiful Black Isle
to the north of Inverness; a short walk from the striking
black-and-white painted pub passes the gaunt, ruined
cathedral before happening on the picturesque harbour
at Fortrose, with sweeping views across the Moray
Firth. Nearby Chanonry Point lighthouse is renowned as
one of the best places from which to watch the
dolphins of the Firth. But why leave an inn famed for
its classic range of finest Scottish micro-brewery beers,
vast array of Belgian beers and 230 single malts
selected by American proprietor and head mop slinger
Jim Anderson?! The 'Global cuisine' created with
freshest Scottish produce is equally comprehensive.
Aberdeen beef, West Coast seafood and Highland game
are amongst dishes that may inhabit the daily-
changing menu: Manhattan seafood chowder or peat-
smoked haddock fritters an opening indulgence to be
followed by Stornoway guinea fowl stuffed with local
white pudding with a creamy leek and Somerset cider
sauce, or baby beef stew cooked in Timmerman's
Lambicus beer. Co-owner Anne Anderson trained as a
chef in New Orleans, so expect unexpected twists to
add spice.

Open all wk 4pm-11.30pm (Sun 12.30-11.30) Closed:
10 Nov-18 Dec **Bar Meals** L served Sun fr 1pm D served
all wk fr 6pm booking required Av main course £11
Restaurant L served Sun fr 1pm D served all wk fr 6pm
booking required Av 3 course à la carte fr £21 ⊕ FREE
HOUSE ◀ Rotating ales Ö Westons 1st Quality, Gwynt
y Ddraig Black Dragon. 🍷 13 **Facilities** Children
welcome Children's menu Dogs allowed Garden Beer
festival Parking Wi-fi

FORT WILLIAM   Map 22 NN17

Moorings Hotel ★★★ HL ◉

Banavie PH33 7LY ☎ 01397 772797   📠 01397 772441
e-mail: reservations@moorings-fortwilliam.co.uk
dir: *From A82 in Fort William follow signs for Mallaig,*
then left onto A830 for 1m. Cross canal bridge then 1st
right signed Banavie

Smack beside the historic Caledonian Canal and
Neptune's Staircase, the famous flight of eight locks, the
Moorings is a modern hotel and pub that enjoys
panoramic views on clear days towards Ben Nevis and
the surrounding mountains. The view is best savoured
from the Upper Deck lounge bar and the bedrooms. Food,
served in the nautically themed Mariners cellar bar, the
lounge and the fine-dining Jacobean Restaurant features
local fish and seafood. Dishes in the bar and lounge

include haddock in beer batter, haggis, neeps and tatties,
Mallaig mussels, and seafood linguini. There is access to
the canal tow path from the gardens.

Open all day all wk Closed: 24-26 Dec **Bar Meals** Av main
course £9.95 food served all day **Restaurant** D served all
wk 7-9.30 booking required Fixed menu price fr £30
⊕ FREE HOUSE ◀ Calders 70/-, Tetley Bitter, Guinness.
Facilities Children welcome Children's menu Dogs
allowed Garden Parking Wi-fi **Rooms** 27

GAIRLOCH   Map 22 NG87

PICK OF THE PUBS

The Old Inn

IV21 2BD ☎ 01445 712006   📠 01445 712933
e-mail: info@theoldinn.net
web: www.theoldinn.net
dir: *Just off A832, near harbour at south end of village*

This former changing house for horses enjoys a
wonderful setting at the foot of the Flowerdale valley.
Built in 1750, Gairloch's oldest hostelry boasts views of
Outer Hebrides and attracts many outdoor enthusiasts
especially walkers. Long established as a real ale pub,
owner Alastair Pearson has now opened the pub's very
own on-site micro-brewery so expect the pints of
Slattadale and Flowerdale to be in tip-top condition at
the bar; more ales are planned. Fresh local seafood
features prominently on the menu, which also includes
home-made pies, oven bakes and casseroles. Typical
choices include Highland lamb pie; West Coast seafood
platter; grilled or steamed local mussels; and braised
beef ribs. Picnic tables on the large grassy area by the
stream make an attractive spot for eating and enjoying
the views. Dogs are welcomed with bowls, baskets and
rugs to help them feel at home.

Open all day all wk 11am-mdnt (Sun noon-mdnt)
Bar Meals L served all wk 12-2.30 (summer 12-4.30)
D served all wk 5-9.30 Av main course £12
Restaurant D served all wk 6-9.30 booking required
Fixed menu price fr £27.50 ⊕ FREE HOUSE ◀ Adnams
Bitter, An Teallach, Deuchars IPA, Wildcat, Erradale,
Flowerdale, Crofters, Trade Winds, Slattadale, Three
Sisters. **Facilities** Children welcome Children's menu
Children's portions Play area Family room Dogs allowed
Garden Parking Wi-fi

Save on hotels. Book at **theAA.com/hotel**

HIGHLAND 555   SCOTLAND

INVERGARRY	Map 22 NH30

The Invergarry Inn

PH35 4HJ ☎ **01809 501206** 🖹 **01809 501400**
e-mail: info@invergarryhotel.co.uk
dir: At junct of A82 & A87

A real Highland atmosphere pervades this refurbished roadside inn set in glorious mountain scenery between Fort William and Fort Augustus. Spruced-up bars make it a great base from which to explore Loch Ness, Glencoe and the West Coast. Relax by the crackling log fire with a wee dram or a pint of Garry Ale, then tuck into a good meal. Perhaps try Lochaber haggis, bashit neeps and tatties to start; followed by sea bream en papiette or a succulent 10oz rib-eye Scottish beef and hand-cut chips. Good lunches and excellent walks from the front door.

Open all day all wk Closed: Dec-Jan **Bar Meals** L served all day 8am-9.30pm booking required for D Av main course £14 food served all day **Restaurant** L served all day 8am-9.30pm booking required for D food served all day ⊕ FREE HOUSE ◀ Garry Ale, Timothy Taylor, Guinness. **Facilities** Children welcome Children's menu Children's portions Family room Garden Parking

INVERIE	Map 22 NG70

The Old Forge

PH41 4PL ☎ **01687 462267** 🖹 **01687 462267**
e-mail: info@theoldforge.co.uk
dir: From Fort William take A830 (Road to the Isles) towards Mallaig. Take ferry from Mallaig to Inverie (boat details on website)

Accessible only by boat, The Old Forge is Britain's most remote mainland pub. It stands literally between heaven and hell; Loch Nevis is Gaelic for heaven and Loch Hourn is Gaelic for hell. It's popular with everyone from locals to hill walkers, and is renowned for its impromptu ceilidhs. It is also the ideal place to sample local fish and seafood and there's no better way than choosing the seafood platter of rope mussels, langoustines, oak-smoked salmon and smoked trout; other specialities include slow roasted belly of Scottish pork with a home-made brandy and apple sauce; and slow-cooked lamb shank with clapshot. There are twelve boat moorings and a daily ferry from Mallaig.

Open all day all wk **Bar Meals** L served all wk 12-3 D served all wk 6-9.30 Av main course £10 **Restaurant** L served all wk 12-3 D served all wk 6-9.30 ⊕ FREE HOUSE ◀ Guinness, Calders 80/, Guest ales. **Facilities** Children welcome Children's menu Children's portions Play area Family room Dogs allowed Garden Parking Wi-fi

KYLESKU	Map 22 NC23

PICK OF THE PUBS

Kylesku Hotel

See Pick of the Pubs on page 556

LYBSTER	Map 23 ND23

Portland Arms ★★★★ INN

KW3 6BS ☎ **01593 721721** 🖹 **01593 721722**
e-mail: manager.portlandarms@ohiml.com
dir: Exit A9 signed Latheron, take A99 to Wick. Then 4m to Lybster

Just half a mile from the North Sea coastline, this former coaching inn has evolved into a comfortable modern inn. The bar and dining areas serve fresh local produce and menus cater for all tastes, with everything from home-made soup with freshly baked baguette to flash-fried langoustine in garlic and brandy butter. Look out for delicious desserts and home baking with morning coffee and afternoon tea. Sunday lunch is a speciality. Take time for a nostalgic walk around this historic fishing town, or why not stay over in one of the bedrooms to explore the marvellous area further.

Open all day all wk 7am-11pm ⊕ FREE HOUSE ◀ McEwans 70/-, Guinness, Belhaven Best, John Smith's. **Facilities** Children welcome Children's menu Children's portions Family room Garden Parking **Rooms** 23

PICK OF THE PUBS

Kylesku Hotel

KYLESKU Map 22 NC23

IV27 4HW ☎ 01971 502231
e-mail: info@kyleskuhotel.co.uk
web: www.kyleskuhotel.co.uk
dir: *A835, then A837 & A894 into Kylesku.*
Hotel at end of road at Old Ferry Pier

Bypassed by the new bridge over Loch Glencoul in the early 80s, the former 17th-century coaching inn enjoys a glorious location down by the old ferry slipway where boats land the local seafood that forms the backbone of the daily chalkboard menu. It's a delightful spot on the shores of Loch Glendhu and Glencoul and the views from the bar and restaurant are truly memorable. Legendary fell-walking writer Alfred Wainwright once wrote of this village: 'Anyone with an eye for impressive beauty will not regard time spent at Kylesku as wasted.' You can understand why as the hotel is at the centre of the North West Highlands Global Geopark, 2,000-square kilometres of lochs, mountains and wild coast. The day's catch - langoustines, spineys, lobster, crab, hand-dived scallops, haddock, monkfish, John Dory and rope-grown mussels certainly don't have far to travel before ending up in the kitchen. Salmon is hot- and cold-smoked in-house, beef and lamb fillets are from animals reared in the Highlands, and all the venison is wild. The bar menu offers

starters of cullen skink (smoked haddock, potato and chive crème fraîche chowder); hand-dived scallops with garlic butter; whole cracked crab straight from the loch; and a pint of langoustines with Marie Rose dressing. Main courses may include mussels in a Thai coconut broth with lime and coriander (also available as a starter); fishcakes in a mussel sauce; grilled langoustine; John Dory with colcannon, lemongrass and dill butter sauce; and monkfish with sun-dried tomato risotto. The Kylesku signature dish is the local seafood platter. Puddings range from lime cheesecake to sticky toffee pudding to platters of Isle of Mull Cheddar with celery and spicy apricot sauce. To drink, there are two An Teallach real ales on tap, bottled beers from the Isle of Skye, 40 wines and 50 malt whiskies.

Open all day all wk Closed: Nov-Feb **Bar Meals** L served all wk 12-6 D served all wk 6-9 Av main course £13 food served all day **Restaurant** D served all wk 7-9 booking required Fixed menu price fr £28 Av 3 course à la carte fr £33 ⊕ FREE HOUSE ◼ A selection of Black Isle Brewery and Skye Cuillin bottled ales, An Teallach Real Ales **Facilities** Children welcome Children's menu Children's portions Dogs allowed Garden Wi-fi

PICK OF THE PUBS

The Plockton Hotel ★★★ SHL

PLOCKTON   Map 22 NG83

Harbour St IV52 8TN
☎ **01599 544274**   📠 **01599 544475**
e-mail: info@plocktonhotel.co.uk
web: www.plocktonhotel.co.uk
dir: *On A87 to Kyle of Lochalsh take turn at Balmacara. Plockton 7m N*

The Pearson family – Dorothy, Tom, Alan and Ann-Mags – have been running this award-winning harbourside hotel for more than twenty years. It's easy to see why they stay (and indeed why so many guests return again and again) because as you walk down the main street a surprising panorama opens up: to one side the watchful mountains, to the other the deep blue waters of Loch Carron lapping at the edge of a sweep of whitewashed Highland cottages. There are palm trees too, courtesy of the Gulf Stream. The building dates from 1827 and later became a ship's chandlery, from which it was converted into a hotel in 1913.

In the dining room and hotel bar the speciality is seafood, including locally caught langoustines and fresh fish landed at Gairloch and Kinlochbervie. Succulent Highland steaks and locally reared beef also add to the wealth of other tempting Scottish produce. Example starters from a recent menu are Talisker whisky pâté and Plockton mackerel smokies, while from among the mains there might be pan-fried

medallions of pork with brandied apricots in cream sauce; casserole of Highland venison in red wine, juniper berries and redcurrant jelly; supreme of chicken stuffed with Argyle smoked ham in sun-dried tomato, garlic and basil sauce; and chargrilled Plockton prawns. Vegetarian dishes are detailed on the blackboard. Basket meals, such as beer-battered fish and chips and breaded scampi tails, are served nightly. Well kept ales and a fine range of malts is available to round off that perfect Highland day.

All bedrooms are en suite and many look out across the loch to the mountains beyond. Two family suites are also available along with a cottage annexe nearby.

Open all day all wk 11am-mdnt (Sun 12.30pm-11pm) Closed: 25 Dec, 1 Jan
Bar Meals L served all wk 12-2.15 D served all wk 6-10 Av main course £14
Restaurant L served all wk 12-2.15 D served all wk 6-10 booking required Av 3 course à la carte fr £20 ⊕ FREE HOUSE ◀ Plockton Bay, Crags Ale, Trade Winds.
Facilities Children's menu Children's portions Family room Garden Wi-fi
Rooms 15

PICK OF THE PUBS

Plockton Inn & Seafood Restaurant

PLOCKTON   Map 22 NG83

Innes St IV52 8TW
☎ **01599 544222** 📠 **01599 544487**
e-mail: info@plocktoninn.co.uk
web: www.plocktoninn.co.uk
dir: *On A87 to Kyle of Lochalsh take turn at Balmacara. Plockton 7m N*

Just 100 metres from the harbour, this attractive stone-built free house is run by Mary Gollan, her brother Kenny and his partner, Susan Trowbridge. Mary and Kenny's great-grandfather built it as a manse, and they themselves were born and bred in Plockton. Since buying the business in 1997, Mary, Susan and Kenny have turned it into an inveterate award-winner, the ladies sharing the role of chef, while Kenny runs the bar. An easygoing atmosphere is apparent throughout, with winter fires in both bars, and a selection of over 50 malt whiskies. A meal in the reasonably formal Dining Room, or the more relaxed Lounge Bar, is a must, with a wealth of freshly caught local fish and shellfish, West Highland beef, lamb, game and home-made vegetarian dishes on the set menu, plus daily specials. Martin, the barman, lands the Plockton prawns (langoustines here) himself, then Kenny takes them and other seafood off to his smokehouse, to feature later in the seafood platter, perhaps. Starters include a vegetable or fish-based soup; oysters with vodka, tomato juice and herbs; edamame (baby soya beans), asparagus

and pea salad; and both meat and vegetarian antipasti. Among the main dishes are those langoustines Martin caught in Loch Carron, served hot with garlic, or cold with Marie Rose sauce; Scottish salmon fillet; hand-dived king scallops; lamb shank; Moorish pork kebabs; chicken and bacon salad; and spinach and ricotta gnocchi. Desserts include lemon and ginger crunch pie; cranachan ice cream; and Scottish cheeses served with Orkney oatcakes. The public bar is alive on Tuesdays and Thursdays with music from local musicians, who are often joined by talented youngsters from the National Centre of Excellence in Traditional Music.

Open all day all wk **Bar Meals** L served all wk 12-2.30 D served all wk 6-9 booking required Av main course £12

Restaurant D served all wk 6-9 booking required Av 3 course à la carte fr £20
🌐 **FREE HOUSE** ◀ Greene King Abbot Ale, Fuller's London Pride, Young's Special, Plockton Crag Ale, Plockton Bay.
Facilities Children's menu Children's portions Play area Dogs allowed Garden Parking Wi-fi

PICK OF THE PUBS

Shieldaig Bar & Coastal Kitchen ★ SHL

SHIELDAIG	Map 22 NG85

IV54 8XN
☎ **01520 755251** 📠 **01520 755321**
e-mail: tighaneilean@keme.co.uk
web:
www.shieldaigbarandcoastalkitchen.co.uk
dir: *Off A896, in village centre*

In an utterly stunning location beside Loch Shieldaig; the bulk of Upper Loch Torridon and its astonishing mountains are literally just round the corner, whilst the lane to the remote Applecross Peninsula curves round the bay from the inn. Patrons have been left speechless by the abundance of wildlife visible from this extraordinary waterside setting; otters and seals abound and there's a nesting pair of white-tailed sea eagles here too. Tipples of choice here are beers from the respected brewery across the Sounds on Skye or maybe from the Black Isle to the north of Inverness; equally intoxicating are the sunsets viewed from the terrace of the Coastal Kitchen restaurant upstairs, and from the traditional bar, where live music and certainly ceilidhs add a weekend buzz to the village. Part of the award-winning Tigh an Eilean Hotel, the Coastal Kitchen majors on the bountiful fruits of the sea; in particular the local shellfish which are landed daily by small boats operated by village fishermen and sourced by environmentally-responsible methods such as creel-fishing or hand-diving.

Razor clam fritters or langoustines à la plancha are a great introduction to the menu and specials choices cooked in the open kitchen here. The wood-burning oven gives a flavoursome edge to the hand-made pizzas like the 'from the sea' feast of crayfish, squid, shrimps, wood-fired langoustines, onion and orange-braised fennel; or try a trio of hand-dived scallops, oven-seared and served on a bed of dressed leaves with lemon and chilli butter. Sustainable fish such as pollack and sea bream also feature, whilst meat lovers can indulge in wood-fired rib-eye steaks, outdoor-reared pork chops or civet of hare. There is a lochside courtyard with benches and tables.

Open all day all wk **Bar Meals** L served all wk 12-9 D served all wk 6-9 Av main course £7 **Restaurant** L served all wk 12-9 booking required D served all wk 6-8.30 Av 3 course à la carte fr £17.50 ⊕ FREE HOUSE ◀ Isle of Skye Brewery Ales, Black Isle. ♟ 8 **Facilities** Children's menu Children's portions Parking Wi-fi **Rooms** 11

PICK OF THE PUBS

The Torridon Inn ★★★ INN

TORRIDON Map 22 NG95

IV22 2EY

☎ 01445 791242 📠 01445 712253

e-mail: Inn@thetorridon.com

web: www.thetorridon.com/inn

dir: *From Inverness take A9 N, then follow signs to Ullapool. Take A835 then A832. In Kinlochewe take A896 to Annat. Pub 200yds on right after village*

Set in 58 acres of parkland and created by converting the stable block, buttery and farm buildings on the Torridon Estate, this informal inn stands in an idyllic location overlooking Loch Torridon and surrounded by lofty mountains on all sides. In the convivial bar you can replay the day's adventures – climbing, walking, mountain biking, canoeing - over one of the 60 malt whiskies, including local favourites Talisker and Glen Ord, or a pint of real ale from the An Teallach, Isle of Skye or Cairngorm breweries. The restaurant is separate from the inn with its comfortable, spacious and well equipped bedrooms, where at any time you can sample the high quality, locally sourced food in which it specialises. During the day you can tuck into hearty soups, sandwiches and bar meals, while in the evening you can linger over a delicious choice of starters, main courses and desserts on menus likely to feature salmon and other local fish, venison, haggis and a variety of home-made specials. Dinner could therefore begin with seared scallops with celeriac purée, rocket salad and balsamic dressing; smoked salmon with caper and shallot dressing; or Strathdon blue cheese, pear and walnut salad. Next, consider ordering fish pie; gammon steak, pineapple and chips; braised lamb shank with red cabbage, roast potatoes and mint gravy; or chargrilled sirloin steak with pepper sauce and all the trimmings. Round off with sticky toffee pudding with butterscotch sauce and vanilla ice cream. Live traditional music is laid on regularly and there is a beer festival late September. This remote location offers marvellous walking opportunities.

Open all day all wk Closed: Jan **Bar Meals** food served all day Av main course £10 **Restaurant** food served all day Av 3 course à la carte fr £24 ⊕ FREE HOUSE ◀ Isle of Skye Brewery - Red Cuillin, Torridon Ale, Cairngorm Brewery Tradewinds, An Teallach, Crofters Pale Ale. **Facilities** Children's menu Children's portions Play area Dogs allowed Garden Beer festival Parking Wi-fi **Rooms** 12

NORTH BALLACHULISH — Map 22 NN06

Loch Leven Hotel

Old Ferry Rd PH33 6SA
☎ 01855 821236   📄 01855 821550
e-mail: reception@lochlevenhotel.co.uk
web: www.lochlevenhotel.co.uk
dir: Off A82, N of Ballachulish Bridge

The slipway into Loch Leven at the foot of the garden recalls the origins of this 17th century inn as one staging point on the old ferry linking the Road to The Isles. This extraordinary location, at the foot of Glencoe and with horizons peppered by Munro peaks rising above azure sea lochs, is also gifted with superb seafood from the local depths; such as scampi and haddock, or indulge in a chunky lamb Celtic casserole. Sip beers from Cairngorm Brewery or a wee dram from a choice of over 75 malts, making the best of the sun terrace which must have one of Scotland's most idyllic views.

Open all day all wk 11-11 (Thu-Sat 11am-mdnt Sun 12.30-11) **Bar Meals** L served all wk 12-3 D served all wk 6-9 Av main course £12 **Restaurant** L served all wk 12-3 D served all wk 6-9 Fixed menu price fr £25 Av 3 course à la carte fr £25 ⊕ FREE HOUSE ◀ Cairngorm Brewery, Atlas Brewery, small micro-brewery. **Facilities** Children welcome Children's menu Children's portions Play area Family room Dogs allowed Garden Parking Wi-fi

See Advert on page 555

PLOCKTON — Map 22 NG83

PICK OF THE PUBS

The Plockton Hotel ★★★ SHL

See Pick of the Pubs on page 557

PICK OF THE PUBS

Plockton Inn & Seafood Restaurant

See Pick of the Pubs on page 558

SHIELDAIG — Map 22 NG85

PICK OF THE PUBS

Shieldaig Bar & Coastal Kitchen
★ SHL ◎◎ ♥

See Pick of the Pubs on page 559

TORRIDON — Map 22 NG95

PICK OF THE PUBS

The Torridon Inn ★★★ INN

See Pick of the Pubs on opposite page

MIDLOTHIAN

DALKEITH — Map 21 NT36

PICK OF THE PUBS

The Sun Inn ★★★★ INN ◎ ♥

Lothianbridge EH22 4TR ☎ 0131 663 2456
e-mail: thesuninn@live.co.uk
web: www.thesuninnedinburgh.co.uk
dir: On A7 towards Galashiels, opposite Newbattle Viaduct

A former AA Pub of the Year for Scotland, this family-run refurbished gastro-pub with boutique rooms continues to impress. Modern creature comforts sit comfortably alongside log fires, oak beams, exposed stone and wood panelling. In the bar, local cask ales have pride of place, while the extensive wine list has been put together by host Bernie MacCarron and Craig Minto. Food in the more formal restaurant is modern British, emphasised by seafood and pub classics. Ian is the head chef here with son Craig running front of house to exacting standards. Lunch would get off to a great start with queenie scallops, Gruyère cheese and garlic butter; followed by Borders lamb's liver with creamy mash, crispy bacon, spinach, sage and white onion cream. At dinner, pig's cheek slow braised with black pudding, apple purée and crisp Parma ham might precede a main of Balquidder Estate loin of venison, haggis, Parisienne potatoes, turnip fondant and red wine jus. Modestly priced puddings include honey and walnut tart with honey ice cream or raspberry Eton Mess.

Open all day all wk Closed: 26 Dec, 1 Jan **Bar Meals** L served Mon-Sat 12-2, Sun 12-7 booking required D served Mon-Sat 6-9, Sun 12-7 booking required Av main course £9 **Restaurant** L served Mon-Sat 12-2, Sun 12-7 booking required D served Mon-Sat 6-9, Sun 12-7 booking required Fixed menu price fr £10.95 Av 3 course à la carte fr £22 ⊕ FREE HOUSE ◀ Deuchars, Timothy Taylor, Belhaven Best. ♥ 10 **Facilities** Children welcome Children's menu Children's portions Garden Parking Wi-fi **Rooms** 5

See Advert on page 562

PENICUIK — Map 21 NT25

The Howgate Restaurant ♥

Howgate EH26 8PY ☎ 01968 670000   📄 01968 670000
e-mail: peter@howgate.com
dir: 10m N of Peebles. 3m E of Penicuik on A6094 between Leadburn junct & Howgate

This beautifully converted farm building was formerly the home of Howgate cheeses. Its fire-warmed bar offers bistro-style meals, while the candle-lit restaurant serves a full carte. Executive and head chefs, Steven Worth and Sean Blake, respectively, use the finest Scottish produce, especially beef, with steaks from the charcoal grill, and lamb; other options might include Cullen skink; a filo 'moneybag' of haggis with a mustard and whisky jus; braised lamb shank with chive mash, honey roasted vegetables and onion gravy; or penne with asparagus and basil cream sauce. There are fine beers to enjoy and an impressively produced wine list roams the globe.

Open all wk Closed: 25-26 Dec, 1 Jan **Bar Meals** L served all wk 12-2 D served all wk 6-9.30 Av main course £9.95 **Restaurant** L served all wk 12-2 booking required D served all wk 6-9.30 booking required Fixed menu price fr £15 Av 3 course à la carte fr £30 ⊕ FREE HOUSE ◀ Belhaven Best, Hoegaarden Wheat Biere. ♥ 14 **Facilities** Children welcome Children's portions Garden Parking

ROSLIN — Map 21 NT26

The Original Rosslyn Inn
★★★★ INN ♥ **NEW**

2-4 Main St EH25 9LE
☎ 0131 440 2384   📄 0131 440 2514
e-mail: enquiries@theoriginalhotel.co.uk
dir: Off city bypass at Straiton for A703 (inn near Rosslyn Chapel)

Just 8 miles from central Edinburgh, this family-run village inn has been in the Harris family for 37 years. A short walk from the famous Rosslyn Chapel, Robert Burns, the famous Scottish poet, once stayed here and wrote a small poem about his stay. Catch up with the locals in the village bar, or relax by the fire in the lounge whilst choosing from the menu. Soups, jackets and paninis are supplemented by main course options like haggis with tatties and neeps; breaded haddock and chips; and vegetarian harvester pie. Alternatively, the Grail Restaurant offers more comprehensive dining options. There are well-equipped bedrooms, four with four-posters.

continued

ROSLIN *continued*

Open all day all wk **Bar Meals** L served all wk 12-9.15 D served all wk 12-9.15 Av main course £9.50 food served all day **Restaurant** L served all wk 12-9.15 D served all wk 12-9.15 Fixed menu price fr £12.50 Av 3 course à la carte fr £20 ⊕ FREE HOUSE ◀ Belhaven Best. ☕ 14 **Facilities** Children welcome Children's menu Children's portions Dogs allowed Garden Parking Wi-fi **Rooms** 6

MORAY

FOCHABERS   Map 23 NJ35

Gordon Arms Hotel

80 High St IV32 7DH
☎ 01343 820508   📠 01343 829059
e-mail: gordonarmsfochabers@live.co.uk
dir: *A96 approx halfway between Aberdeen & Inverness, 9m from Elgin*

This 200-year-old former coaching inn, close to the River Spey and within easy reach of Speyside's whisky distilleries, is understandably popular with salmon fishers, golfers and walkers. Its public rooms have been carefully refurbished, and the hotel makes an ideal base from which to explore this scenic corner of Scotland. The cuisine makes full use of local produce: venison, lamb and game from the uplands, fish and seafood from the Moray coast, beef from Aberdeenshire and salmon from the Spey - barely a stone's throw from the kitchen! Change of hands.

Open all day all wk 11-11 (Thu 11-mdnt Fri-Sat 11am-12.30am) **Bar Meals** L served all wk 12-2 D served all wk 5-8.30 **Restaurant** L served all wk 12-2 D served all wk 5-8.30 ⊕ FREE HOUSE ◀ Caledonian Deuchars IPA, John Smith's Smooth, Guest ales. **Facilities** Children welcome Dogs allowed Parking

NORTH LANARKSHIRE

CUMBERNAULD   Map 21 NS77

Castlecary House Hotel ☕

Castlecary Rd G68 0HD
☎ 01324 840233   📠 01324 841608
e-mail: enquiries@castlecaryhotel.com
dir: *A80 onto B816 between Glasgow & Stirling. 7m from Falkirk, 9m from Stirling*

Run by the same family for over 30 years, this friendly hotel is located close to the historic Antonine Wall and Forth and Clyde Canal. Meals in the lounge bars plough a traditional furrow with options such as venison and port terrine; chicken tourneo (chicken stuffed with haggis and served with traditional clapshot and Arran mustard sauce); roast salmon fillet with prawn bisque and rumbledethumps. There is an excellent selection of real ales on offer, and more formal fare is available in Camerons Restaurant. A beer festival is held twice a year – contact the hotel for details of the dates.

Open all day all wk Closed: 1 Jan **Bar Meals** L served 12-9 D served 12-9 food served all day **Restaurant** L served Sun 12.30-3 D served Mon-Sat 6-9.30 booking required Fixed menu price fr £10 ⊕ FREE HOUSE ◀ Arran Blonde, Harviestoun Brooker's Bitter & Twisted, Inveralmond Ossian's Ale, Houston Peter's Well, Caledonian Deuchars IPA. ☕ 8 **Facilities** Children welcome Children's menu Children's portions Garden Beer festival Parking Wi-fi

PERTH & KINROSS

GLENDEVON   Map 21 NN90

An Lochan Tormaukin Country Inn and Restaurant

FK14 7JY ☎ 01259 781252   📠 01259 781526
e-mail: info@anlochan.co.uk
dir: *M90 junct 6 onto A977 to Kincardine, follow signs to Stirling. Exit at Yelts of Muckhard onto A823/Crieff*

This attractive whitewashed building was built in 1720 as a drovers' inn, at a time when Glendevon was frequented by cattlemen making their way from the Tryst of Crieff to the market place at Falkirk, the name Tormaukin is Gaelic for 'hill of the mountain hare', which reflects its serene, romantic location in the midst of the Ochil Hills. Sympathetically refurbished throughout, it still bristles with real Scottish character and charm. Original features like stone walls, exposed beams and

Save on hotels. Book at **theAA.com/hotel**

PERTH & KINROSS 563 SCOTLAND

blazing winter fires in the cosy public rooms ensure a warm and welcoming atmosphere. This inn changed hands in 2010.

Open all day all wk ◧ Bitter & Twisted, Thrappledouser Ō Aspall. **Facilities** Children welcome Dogs allowed Garden Parking

---

GLENFARG   Map 21 NO11

The Famous Bein Inn

PH2 9PY ☎ **01577 830216** 🖹 01577 830211
e-mail: enquiries@beininn.com
dir: *From S: M90 junct 8, A91 towards Cupar. Left onto B996 to Bein Inn. From N: M90 junct 9, A912 towards Gateside*

In a wooded glen overlooking the river, the inn is owned by a local farming family, well known for the quality of their beef. While enjoying a refreshing pint of Inveralmond ale by the log fire or out on the sundeck, choose from the list of locally sourced and freshly prepared food served all day from midday. The Balvaird Restaurant is the place to taste the famous beef, while plates in the bistro range from snacks to Balmoral chicken – roast chicken supreme stuffed with haggis.

Open all day all wk Closed: 25-26 Dec **Bar Meals** Av main course £10.95 food served all day **Restaurant** food served all day ⊕ FREE HOUSE ◧ Belhaven Best, Inveralmond Ale, Guinness. **Facilities** Children welcome Children's menu Children's portions Garden Parking Wi-fi

---

GUILDTOWN   Map 21 NO13

PICK OF THE PUBS

Anglers Inn   INN

Main Rd PH2 6BS ☎ **01821 640329**
e-mail: info@theanglersinn.co.uk
dir: *6m N of Perth on A93*

A contemporary gastro-pub completely renovated and refurbished by Shona and Jeremy Wares since they took it over in 2007. With its six en suite bedrooms, the Anglers is popular for small fishing and shooting parties; it's also only two miles from Perth racecourse. Comfortable leather chairs and a log fire induce a relaxed and homely atmosphere, ideal surroundings in which to sample one of the Inveralmond Brewery ales on offer at the bar. Expect food prepared to an award-winning standard: typical choices for a three-course dinner from the carte could include starters of potted Morecambe brown shrimps and Skye prawns, or fried herb and tomato risotto cake. Main courses could comprise roast herb marinated rump of lamb with haggis hack, or free-range chicken breast stuffed with black pudding. Banana and rum crème brûlée or sticky toffee pudding with butterscotch sauce are typical of the desserts.

Open 11-3 5.30-mdnt Closed: Mon **Bar Meals** L served all wk 12.15-2.30 D served all wk 6.15-9 **Restaurant** L served all wk 12.15-2.30 booking required D served all wk 6.15-9 booking required ⊕ FREE HOUSE ◧ Ossian, LiaFail. **Facilities** Children welcome Children's menu Children's portions Dogs allowed Garden Parking Wi-fi **Rooms** 6

KILLIECRANKIE   Map 23 NN96

PICK OF THE PUBS

Killiecrankie House Hotel
★★★ SHL ֎ ֎ ♟

See Pick of the Pubs on page 564

KINNESSWOOD   Map 21 NO10

PICK OF THE PUBS

Lomond Country Inn ♟

KY13 9HN ☎ **01592 840253** 🖹 01592 840693
e-mail: enquires@lomondinn.co.uk
dir: *M90 junct 5, follow signs for Glenrothes then Scotlandwell. Kinnesswood next village*

Gliders from Scotland's oldest club swoop above this characterful small hotel, benefiting from the updraught created by the spectacular Lomond Hills below which the inn nestles. Take advantage of the capacious terrace for views across nearby Loch Leven to the shapely summits of the Ochill Hills, a glorious summer sunset panorama. Under new ownership since late 2010, the inn continues to champion Scottish real ales, with beers from Perth's Inveralmond brewery going down well in the friendly, log fire warmed village bar. Dine with a view in the homely restaurant, where large windows make full use of the panorama to the loch; meals are exceptional value and offer a choice of good, pubby food like pies and curries with local favourites such as game stew, enhanced by a daily-changing specials board. This is an ideal stop-off point for visitors following the local heritage trail or exploring the Kingdom of Fife.

Open all day all wk 7am-1am **Bar Meals** L served all wk 7am-9pm D served all wk 5-9 booking required Av main course £5 food served all day **Restaurant** L served all wk 7am-9pm D served all wk 5-9 booking required food served all day ⊕ FREE HOUSE ◧ Deuchars IPA, Calders Cream, Tetley's, Orkney Dark Island, Ossian Lia Fail. ♟ 12 **Facilities** Children welcome Children's menu Children's portions Play area Family room Dogs allowed Garden Parking Wi-fi

---

MEIKLEOUR   Map 21 NO13

Meikleour Hotel NEW

PH2 6EB ☎ **01250 883206**
e-mail: visitus@meikleourhotel.co.uk
dir: *From A93 (between Perth & Blairgowrie) take A984 into village centre*

In the shadow of the famously vast Beech Hedge of Meikleour, this attractive old creeper-clad, gabled coach and posting house ticks all the boxes for country sports enthusiasts (with fishing on the local River Tay and shoots nearby), whilst ale fans will revel in the house beer, brewed at the nearby Inveralmond brewery. Add top-notch Scottish provender (Arbroath smokies, local estate venison) to the mix; it's little wonder that visitors touring the nearby Angus Glens or skiing at Glenshee are amongst the dedicated aficionados of this welcoming inn.

Open all wk 11-3 6-11 Closed: 25-30 Dec **Bar Meals** L served all wk 12.15-2.30 booking required D served all wk 6.30-9 booking required Av main course £12 **Restaurant** L served all wk 12.15-2.30 booking required D served all wk 6.30-9 booking required Av 3 course à la carte fr £23 ⊕ FREE HOUSE ◧ Lure of Meikleour. **Facilities** Children welcome Children's menu Children's portions Dogs allowed Garden Beer festival Parking Wi-fi

---

PITLOCHRY   Map 23 NN95

PICK OF THE PUBS

Moulin Hotel ★★★ HL ♟

11-13 Kirkmichael Rd, Moulin PH16 5EH
☎ **01796 472196** 🖹 01796 474098
e-mail: enquiries@moulinhotel.co.uk
dir: *From A924 at Pitlochry take A923. Moulin 0.75m*

Built in 1695 at the foot of Ben Vrackie on an old drovers' road, this great all-round inn is popular as a walking and touring base. Locals are drawn to the bar for the excellent home-brewed beers, with Ale of Atholl, Braveheart, Moulin Light, and Old Remedial served on handpump. The interior boasts beautiful stone walls and lots of cosy niches, with blazing log fires in winter; while the courtyard garden is lovely in summer. Menus offer the opportunity to try something local such as mince and tatties; Skye mussels; venison pan-fried in Braveheart beer; and Vrackie Grostel – sautéed potatoes with smoked bacon topped with a fried egg. You might then round off your meal with Highland honey sponge and custard, or raspberry crumble. A specials board broadens the choice further. Over 20 wines by the glass and more than 30 malt whiskies are available.

Open all day all wk 11-11 (Fri-Sat 11am-11.45pm Sun noon-11) **Bar Meals** L served all wk 12-9.30 D served all wk 12-9.30 food served all day **Restaurant** D served all wk 6-9 booking required ⊕ FREE HOUSE ◧ Moulin Braveheart, Old Remedial, Ale of Atholl, Moulin Light, Belhaven Best. ♟ 25 **Facilities** Children welcome Children's menu Children's portions Dogs allowed Garden Parking Wi-fi **Rooms** 15

PICK OF THE PUBS

Killiecrankie House Hotel ★★★ SHL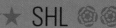

KILLIECRANKIE   Map 23 NN96

PH16 5LG
☎ 01796 473220   📄 01796 472451
e-mail: enquiries@killiecrankiehotel.co.uk
web: www.killiecrankiehotel.co.uk
dir: *Take B8079 N from Pitlochry. Hotel in 3m after NT Visitor Centre*

This white-painted Victorian manse gleams amidst woodland at the Pass of Killiecrankie, the gateway to The Highlands. This magnificent gorge, famed for the battle in 1689 when the Jacobites routed the forces of King William III, is a stronghold for red squirrels and a renowned birdwatching area. The hotel's logo shows Royalist soldier Donald McBean leaping the gorge to escape pursuing Highlanders; today's visitor can be equally energised, with countless walks climbing into the hills, including majestic Ben Vrackie rising directly behind the hotel, riverside walks and the nearby lochs in the Tummel Valley, with a garland of shapely mountains. Less active guests explore the area's distilleries, including that at Edradour, outside nearby Pitlochry, which is Scotland's smallest. Standing in a four-acre estate, the hotel retains much of the character of old combined with modern comforts. The cosy, wood-panelled bar is a popular haunt of both locals and visitors, while the snug sitting room (with a grand fire for winter days) opens on to a small patio and a fine herbaceous border. Arm yourself with a beer from the likes of Orkney or Belhaven breweries and relax

beside the tranquil rose garden, studying an uplifting menu that makes the most of Scotland's diverse produce and which has gained head chef Mark Easton two AA Rosettes. Creative starters range from terrine of scallop and twice-baked goat's cheese brûlée to fulfilling home-made soups; the ever-evolving mains selection could see pan-fried fillet of Highland venison and breast of woodpigeon; or pan-seared fillet of Ayrshire pork in black peppercorn and herb crust with roast garlic mash, vegetables and Lochaber smoked cheese sauce. Each main is matched on the menu with a specific wine suggestion from the hotel's notable list of quality bins. Finish with a traditional Cranachan - toasted oatmeal and Drambuie cream with raspberries and shortbread. Lighter lunchtime meals may be taken in the conservatory.

Open all day all wk Closed: Jan & Feb
Bar Meals L served all wk 12.30-2
D served all wk 6.30-8.30
Restaurant D served all wk 6.30-8.30
🍺 FREE HOUSE ◀ Red MacGregor, Deuchars IPA, Belhaven Best
🍏 Kopperberg. ☐ 8 **Facilities** Children's menu Dogs allowed Garden Parking
Rooms 10

RENFREWSHIRE

HOUSTON   Map 20 NS46

Fox & Hounds ♥

South St PA6 7EN
☎ 01505 612448 & 612991   📠 01505 614133
e-mail: jonathon.wengel@btconnect.com
web: www.foxandhoundshouston.co.uk
dir: *A737, W from Glasgow. Take Johnstone Bridge off Weir exit, follow signs for Houston. Pub in village centre*

At the heart of the attractive village of Houston, this welcoming old coaching inn pulls in the plaudits for the beers which flow from the micro-brewery here; beer festivals in May and August add spice. One fan is singer Neil Diamond, who treated his chords to glasses of Peter's Well bitter whilst staying locally in 2011, and indulged in fare from the homely menu, which mixes pub favourites with some inspired dishes; haggis with bashed neeps, champ and whisky cream or baked aubergine pie amongst them. A list of around 150 whiskies, including some rare ones, is the icing on the cake here.

Open all day all wk 11am-mdnt (Fri-Sat 11am-1am Sun from 12.30) **Bar Meals** Av main course £9 food served all day **Restaurant** Fixed menu price fr £20 Av 3 course à la carte fr £22 food served all day ⊕ FREE HOUSE ◀ Killelan, Warlock Stout, Texas, Jock Frost, Peter's Well. ♥ 10 **Facilities** Children welcome Children's menu Children's portions Dogs allowed Garden Beer festival Parking

SCOTTISH BORDERS

ALLANTON   Map 21 NT85

Allanton Inn ♥

TD11 3JZ ☎ 01890 818260
e-mail: info@allantoninn.co.uk
dir: *From A1 at Berwick take A6105 for Chirnside (5m). At Chirnside Inn take Coldstream Rd for 1m to Allanton*

A perfect base to explore the Borders, this family-run 18th-century coaching inn has built up a formidable reputation for its local ales and excellent food. A large lawned area with fruit trees overlooking open countryside is an ideal spot to sup on a pint of Bitter & Twisted or tuck into locally-sourced dishes such as house cured and smoked pork fillet, or Peelham Farm rack of lamb with rosemary and garlic butter. Barbecues are held in the summer.

Open all day all wk 11am-11pm Closed: 2 wks Feb (dates vary) **Bar Meals** L served Mon-Sun 12-3 D served Mon-Sun 6-9 booking required Av main course £10 **Restaurant** L served Mon-Sun 12-3 D served Mon-Sun 6-9 booking required Av 3 course à la carte fr £23 ⊕ FREE HOUSE ◀ Ossian, Trade Winds, Pentland IPA, Game Bird, Bitter & Twisted, Piper's Gold. ♥ 10 **Facilities** Children welcome Children's menu Children's portions Dogs allowed Garden Wi-fi

ETTRICK   Map 21 NT21

Tushielaw Inn

TD7 5HT ☎ 01750 62205   📠 01750 62205
e-mail: robin@tushielaw-inn.co.uk
dir: *At junct of B709 & B711(W of Hawick)*

An 18th-century former toll house and drovers' halt on the banks of Ettrick Water, making a good base for touring the Borders, trout fishing (salmon fishing can be arranged), wildlife and bird watching, and those tackling the Southern Upland Way. An extensive menu is always available with daily-changing specials. Fresh produce is used according to season, with local lamb and Aberdeen Angus beef regular specialities. Local haggis smothered in melted Lockerbie Cheddar and steak and ale pie are popular choices.

Open all wk ⊕ FREE HOUSE **Facilities** Children welcome Dogs allowed Parking

GALASHIELS   Map 21 NT43

Kingsknowes Hotel ★★★ HL

1 Selkirk Rd TD1 3HY
☎ 01896 758375   📠 01896 750377
e-mail: enquiries@kingsknowes.co.uk
dir: *Off A7 at Galashiels/Selkirk rdbt*

In over three acres of grounds on the banks of the Tweed, a splendid baronial mansion built in 1869 for a textile magnate. There are lovely views of the Eildon Hills and Abbotsford House, Sir Walter Scott's ancestral home. Meals are served in two restaurants and the Courtyard Bar, where fresh local or regional produce is used as much as possible. The impressive glass conservatory is the ideal place to enjoy a drink.

Open all day all wk Mon-Wed noon-11 (Thu-Sat noon-1pm Sun noon-11) ⊕ FREE HOUSE ◀ McEwans 70/-, John Smith's. **Facilities** Children welcome Children's menu Play area Dogs allowed Garden Parking **Rooms** 12

INNERLEITHEN   Map 21 NT33

Traquair Arms Hotel NEW

Traquair Rd EH44 6PD ☎ 01896 830229
e-mail: info@traquairarmshotel.co.uk
dir: *From A72 (Peebles to Galashiels road) take B709 for St Mary's Loch & Traquair*

Amidst the heather-covered hills of the Scottish Borders stands this imposing pub, hotel and tranquil beer garden. It's one of only two places where you can drink Traquair Bear ale, brewed a stone's throw away at Traquair House. Scottish and Italian food includes roast haunch of Tweed Valley venison; local Borders lamb; tiger prawns with spaghetti, white wine and flat leaf parsley; and Italian sausage with borlotti beans, cherry tomatoes, toasted focaccia and salad. There are downhill and cross country mountain bike trails right on the doorstep.

Open all day all wk Closed: 25 Dec **Bar Meals** L served Mon-Fri 12-2.30, Sat-Sun all day D served Mon-Fri 5-9, Sat-Sun all day Av main course £9-£12 **Restaurant** L served Mon-Fri 12-2.30, Sat-Sun all day booking required D served Mon-Fri 5-9, Sat-Sun all day booking required ⊕ FREE HOUSE ◀ Deuchars IPA, Timothy Taylor Landlord, Traquair Bear Ale. **Facilities** Children welcome Children's menu Children's portions Dogs allowed Garden Parking Wi-fi

KELSO   Map 21 NT73

PICK OF THE PUBS

The Cobbles Inn NEW

7 Bowmont St TD5 7JH ☎ 01573 223548
e-mail: info@thecobblesinn.co.uk
dir: *In town centre*

In the cobbled town square in the heart of picturesque Kelso, this modernised 19th-century coaching inn has character and atmosphere in abundance. Sit by the roaring log fire in winter and enjoy single malts, continental beers or the pub's own ales from their local Tempest Brewing Co (they have a craft brewery in town). The well-established restaurant offers a frequently changing menu dominated by local fish and shellfish, Border lamb, beef and pork or game in season. This excellent local produce makes an appearance on an eclectic menu that takes in British classics, Pacific Rim dishes and modern European cuisine. A starter of fried haggis balls in pinhead oatmeal with whisky cream sauce might be followed by slow-cooked belly of Border pork, Stornoway black pudding, apple, roasties, cider sauce and crackling. Comforting puddings include sticky ginger and date pudding with toffee sauce and vanilla ice cream or a trio of Overlangshaw Farmhouse ice creams. Every Friday night there is folk and live music.

Open 11.30-3 5-late (Sat-Sun & summer all day) Closed: 2wks Jan, Mon in autumn/winter **Bar Meals** L served Tue-Sun 12-2 D served Tue-Sun 5-9 Av main course £10.95 **Restaurant** L served Tue-Sun 12-2 Av 3 course à la carte fr £24.95 ⊕ FREE HOUSE ◀ Tempest Brewing Co Ŏ Thistly Cross. **Facilities** Children welcome Children's menu Parking Wi-fi

KIRK YETHOLM
Map 21 NT82

The Border Hotel ♀

The Green TD5 8PQ ☎ 01573 420237
e-mail: borderhotel@aol.com
dir: From A698 in Kelso take B6352 for 7m to Kirk Yetholm

Just a mile from the border between Scotland and England, this 18th-century former coaching inn stands at the end of the famous Pennine Way long-distance walking trail. Naturally, this updated inn is the first port of call for weary walkers, who can expect a warm and friendly welcome in the character bar. Cracking pints of Pennine Way Bitter or Orkney Raven Ale will slake parched throats and the traditional British menu, which features local game and farm meats, will satisfy healthy appetites. Follow Cullen skink with marinated Border lamb, peppered saddle of local venison, or Eyemouth haddock and chips, leaving room for a hearty pudding.

Open all day all wk Closed: 25 Dec **Bar Meals** L served all wk 12-2 booking required D served all wk 6-8.45 booking required Av main course £9.95 **Restaurant** L served all wk 12-2 booking required D served all wk 6-8.45 booking required ⊕ FREE HOUSE ◀ Pennine Way Bitter, Game Bird-Border Brewery, Raven Ale Orkney Brewery ♂ Westons Old Rosie. ♀ 10 **Facilities** Children welcome Children's menu Children's portions Play area Dogs allowed Garden Parking Wi-fi

LAUDER
Map 21 NT54

PICK OF THE PUBS

The Black Bull ★★★★ INN ♀

Market Place TD2 6SR
☎ 01578 722208 ▤ 01578 722419
e-mail: enquiries@blackbull-lauder.com
dir: In centre of Lauder on A68

In the heart of the Scottish Borders, on the edge of the Lammermuir Hills, this whitewashed, three-storey coaching inn dates from 1750. After a day of walking in the hills, visiting Thirlestane Castle, playing golf or checking out the Princes Street bargains in nearby Edinburgh, enjoy a gastro-pub-style lunch in the relaxed Harness Room bar or the more formal lounge bar. A light lunch menu of snacks and sandwiches is served from midday, while a typical supper menu might lead you to begin with Cullen skink or terrine of pheasant, hare and mallard. Follow with Border beef, Guinness and mushroom pie or something from the grill might appeal. To finish, there is brioche bread and butter pudding; or a selection of Scottish cheeses - Cooleeney, Gubbeens and Dunsyre Blue - with oatcakes. The inn has eight superb en suite rooms.

Open all day all wk **Bar Meals** L served Mon-Fri 12-2.30, Sat-Sun 12-9 booking required D served Mon-Thu 5-9, Fri-Sun 12-9 **Restaurant** L served Mon-Fri 12-2.30, Sat-Sun 12-9 D served Mon-Thu 5-9, Fri-Sun 12-9 ⊕ BLACKBULL HOTEL (LAUDER) LTD ◀ Guinness, Landlord, Tetley, Deuchars IPA, Old Speckled Hen, Marstons Pedigree ♂ Olde English. ♀ 27 **Facilities** Children welcome Children's menu Children's portions Dogs allowed Parking Wi-fi **Rooms** 8

LEITHOLM
Map 21 NT74

The Plough Hotel

Main St TD12 4JN ☎ 01890 840252 ▤ 01890 840252
e-mail: theplough@leitholm.wanadoo.co.uk
web: www.bordersteakhouse.com
dir: 5m N of Coldstream on A697. Take B6461, Leitholm in 1m

Set in a small village in rich farming country south of the Lammermuir Hills, this compact old coaching inn specialises in Aberdeen Angus steaks. The beef is sourced by the local butcher from the foremost livestock market in the Borders and well aged before preparation. The wide ranging menu also features chicken and haggis stack in Drambuie sauce; hand-pulled beers draw in the locals, whilst the beer garden is a tranquil retreat.

Open all day all wk Mon-Tue 4-12 Wed-Thu & Sun noon-mdnt Fri-Sat noon-1am **Bar Meals** L served Sun 12-4 D served Tue-Sun 6-9 **Restaurant** L served Sun 12-4 D served Tue-Sun 6-9 ⊕ FREE HOUSE ◀ Guinness, Real Ale. **Facilities** Children welcome Dogs allowed Garden Parking

MELROSE
Map 21 NT53

PICK OF THE PUBS

Burts Hotel ★★★ HL ☺☺ ♀

Market Square TD6 9PL
☎ 01896 822285 ▤ 01896 822870
e-mail: enquiries@burtshotel.co.uk
dir: A6091, 2m from A68 3m S of Earlston

For four decades the Henderson family have cared for this eye-catching former temperance hotel at the heart of old Melrose. Practice evidently pays off, with 2 AA Rosettes being held for 15 consecutive years and the comfy accommodation. Melrose lies in the shadow of the Eildon Hills amidst rich countryside from which comes much of the produce used both in the bar menu and the table d'hôte in the formal restaurant. After a day's rambling or exploring Sir Walter Scott's Elysian backyard, settle down with a dram (choice of 80) or a jar of Deuchars finest and consider the dishes, prime amongst the starters of which may be Teviot Smokery smoked salmon. Progress to Eyemouth scampi tails from the coast a few miles distant or go straight to the local game, button mushroom, baby onion and red wine casserole with creamy mash. Finish with local cheeses before an evening constitutional along the banks of the nearby River Tweed.

Open all wk noon-2.30 5-11 **Bar Meals** L served all wk 12-2 D served all wk 6-9.30 Av main course £11.50 **Restaurant** L served all wk 12-2 booking required D served all wk 7-9 booking required Fixed menu price fr £35 Av 3 course à la carte fr £35 ⊕ FREE HOUSE ◀ Caledonian 80/-, Deuchars IPA, Timothy Taylor Landlord, Fuller's London Pride. ♀ 10 **Facilities** Children welcome Children's portions Dogs allowed Garden Parking Wi-fi **Rooms** 20

ST BOSWELLS
Map 21 NT53

PICK OF THE PUBS

Buccleuch Arms Hotel ♀

The Green TD6 0EW
☎ 01835 822243 ▤ 01835 823965
e-mail: info@buccleucharms.com
dir: On A68, 10m N of Jedburgh. Hotel on village green

Dating from the 16th century, this smart and friendly country-house hotel was originally an inn for the fox-hunting aristocracy. Set beside the village cricket pitch, it's an attractive brick and stone building with an immaculate garden. Inside, a large and comfortable lounge is warmed by a log fire in winter, while the spacious enclosed garden comes into its own during the warmer months. The bar serves one real ale at a time, but turnover is high so locals keep coming back to find out what's on offer - the Stewart Brewery, Broughton Ales, and the Hadrian and Border Brewery are just three of the regular suppliers. Menus change seasonally, but the specials may well change twice daily to reflect the availability of ingredients from the Scottish Borders countryside. Typical dishes include pressed ham hock with caramelised onions and parsley; fillet of Eyemouth haddock in crispy beer batter with chips, garden peas and home-made tartare sauce; and slow-cooked lamb casserole with pearl barley and red cabbage. 2011 is the 175th year anniversary of the hotel.

Open all day all wk 7am-11pm Closed: 25 Dec **Bar Meals** L served all wk 12-2 D served all wk 6-9 Av main course £10 **Restaurant** D served all wk 6-9 booking required ⊕ FREE HOUSE ◀ McEwan's 70/-, Stewarts Ales, Atlas, Orkney, Northumberland, Broughton, Guest ales. ♀ 8 **Facilities** Children welcome Children's menu Children's portions Play area Dogs allowed Garden Parking

SWINTON
Map 21 NT84

PICK OF THE PUBS

The Wheatsheaf at Swinton ♀

Main St TD11 3JJ ☎ 01890 860257 ▤ 01890 860688
e-mail: reception@wheatsheaf-swinton.co.uk
dir: From Edinburgh A697 onto B6461. From East Lothian A1 onto B6461

In the past few years, the Wheatsheaf has built up an impressive reputation as a dining destination. Run by husband and wife team Chris and Jan Winson, this popular venue is tucked away in the picturesque village of Swinton. The Wheatsheaf's secret is to use carefully sourced local ingredients in imaginative combinations. In addition to wild mushrooms and organic vegetables, wild salmon, venison, partridge, pheasant, woodcock and duck are all likely menu contenders subject to seasonal availability. Lunchtime offers the likes of sautéed Paris brown mushrooms and bacon in a tarragon crêpe with a Mull Cheddar glaze; and open omelette of Dunsyre Blue cheese and confit cherry tomatoes. In the evening settle back, enjoy the friendly service, and tuck into plates of seared scallops with a lemon and chive butter sauce; and braised shank of Border lamb, gratin dauphinoise and creamed Savoy.

Open Mon-Fri 5-11 Sat noon-mdnt Sun noon-11 Closed: 24-26 Dec, Mon-Fri L **Bar Meals** L served Sat-Sun 12-2 D served Mon-Sat 6-9, Sun 6-8.30 **Restaurant** L served Sat-Sun 12-2 booking required D served Mon-Sat 6-9, Sun 6-8.30 booking required ⊕ FREE HOUSE ◀ Deuchars IPA, Belhaven Best, Guinness. ♥ 12 **Facilities** Children welcome Parking

---

TIBBIE SHIELS INN | Map 21 NT22

PICK OF THE PUBS

Tibbie Shiels Inn

St Mary's Loch TD7 5LH
☎ 01750 42231 📄 01750 42302
dir: *From Moffat take A708. Inn 14m on right*

This friendly waterside hostelry positioned between St Mary's Loch and the Loch of the Lowes, is named after the woman who first opened it in 1826. Isabella 'Tibbie' Shiels expanded the inn from a small cottage to a hostelry which could sleep around 35 people - many of them on the floor! Famous visitors during her time included Walter Scott, Thomas Carlyle and Robert Louis Stevenson. Tibbie Shiels herself is rumoured to keep watch over the bar, where the selection of over 50 malt whiskies helps sustain long periods of ghost watching. Food from the traditional pub menu can be enjoyed in either the bar or the dining room. The majority of the ingredients are local, including the famous hill-farmed lamb, game and even herbs grown in the garden. Sandwiches, salads, ploughman's, toasties, paninis, burgers and jackets are all on offer, while the straightforward carte may tempt with chicken liver pâté followed by steak and ale pie, five-bean chilli or Scottish wholetail scampi served with home-made tartare sauce. There are plenty of evening events throughout the year.

Open all day all wk 10am-mdnt **Bar Meals** food served all day **Restaurant** food served all day ⊕ FREE HOUSE ◀ Broughton Greenmantle Ale, Belhaven 80/- Ö Stowford Press. **Facilities** Children welcome Children's menu Children's portions Play area Dogs allowed Garden Parking Wi-fi

---

SOUTH AYRSHIRE

SYMINGTON | Map 20 NS33

Wheatsheaf Inn

Main St KA1 5QB ☎ 01563 830307 📄 01563 830307
dir: *In Symington, off A77 between Ayr & Kilmarnock*

Martin and Marnie Thompson have run this charming 17th-century former coaching inn close to Royal Troon Golf Course for over 25 years. Log fires burn in every room and the work of local artists adorns the walls. Seafood dominates the menu, perhaps sea bass with tomato, basil and balsamic, while meaty options may include lamb shank with redcurrant and mint jus, and braised beef olive with a rich ale gravy. Leave room for cranachan – whipped cream and oats with raspberries soaked in honey and whisky.

Open all day all wk 11-11 (Fri-Sat 11am-mdnt) Closed: 25 Dec, 1 Jan **Bar Meals** L served all wk all day D served all wk all day **Restaurant** L served all wk 12-2 D served all wk 5-9 ⊕ FREE HOUSE ◀ Belhaven Best, Old Speckled Hen, Guinness. **Facilities** Children welcome Children's menu Children's portions Garden Parking

---

STIRLING

CALLANDER | Map 20 NN60

The Lade Inn ♥

Kilmahog FK17 8HD ☎ 01877 330152
e-mail: info@theladeinn.com
dir: *From Stirling take A84 to Callander. 1m N of Callander, left at Kilmahog Woollen Mills onto A821 towards Aberfoyle. Pub immediately on left*

Standing 200 yards fro the River Teith in the heart of the Trossachs National Park, the stone built Lade Inn is part of the surrounding Leny Estate and was built as a tearoom in 1935. First licensed in the 1960s, the traditional bar is noted for its real ales – try a pint of Belhaven Best – and home-cooked food. Typical dishes include smoked venison with spiced fruit chutney, beer-battered haddock, and sticky toffee pudding. There's a superb beer garden with three ponds and Scottish folk music is played every Friday and Saturday. Don't miss the pub's real ale shop, which stocks over 130 Scottish bottled beers from 30 micro-breweries, and the week-long beer festival in late August.

Open all day all wk noon-11 (Fri-Sat noon-1am Sun 12.30-10.30) **Bar Meals** L served Mon-Fri 12-3, Sat 12-9, Sun 12.30-9 D served Mon-Fri 5-9, Sat 12-9, Sun 12.30-9 booking required Av main course £10 **Restaurant** L served Mon-Fri 12-3, Sat 12-9, Sun 12.30-9 D served Mon-Fri 5-9, Sat 12-9, Sun 12.30-9 booking required Fixed menu price fr £14.50 Av 3 course à la carte fr £14 ⊕ FREE HOUSE ◀ Waylade, LadeBack, LadeOut, Belhaven Best, Tennent's Ö Thistly Cross. ♥ 9 **Facilities** Children welcome Children's menu Children's portions Play area Family room Dogs allowed Garden Beer festival Parking Wi-fi

---

DRYMEN | Map 20 NS48

The Clachan Inn

2 Main St G63 0BG ☎ 01360 660824
e-mail: info@clachaninndrymen.co.uk
dir: *Telephone for directions*

Believed to be the oldest licensed pub in Scotland, this quaint, white-painted cottage sits in a small village on the West Highland Way, and was once owned by Rob Roy's sister. In the bar, guest ales are changed often and there is a warming log fire to keep things cosy. Locate the appealing lounge bar for freshly-made food using the best of local produce, where the specials menu changes daily.

Open all day all wk Closed: 25 Dec & 1 Jan ⊕ FREE HOUSE ◀ Guinness. **Facilities** Children welcome Children's menu Children's portions Dogs allowed

---

KIPPEN | Map 20 NS69

Cross Keys Hotel ♥

Main St FK8 3DN ☎ 01786 870293
e-mail: info@kippencrosskeys.co.uk
dir: *10m W of Stirling, 20m from Loch Lomond off A811*

Now run by Debby and Brian, this cosy inn is over 300 years old and offers seasonally changing menus and a good pint of Harviestoun Bitter and Twisted. The pub's welcoming interior, warmed by three log fires, is perfect for resting your feet after walk on the nearby Burnside Wood nature trails, or you can sit in the garden when the weather permits. The menu takes in game, apricot and chicken terrine with Cross Keys chutney; pork belly and loin of pork, roast celeriac fondant, apple and thyme sauce; confit duck leg and venison sausage casserole, cannellini beans and rhubarb sauce. Lighter lunches are available at lunchtime. Dogs are welcome in the top bar.

Open all wk Mon-Thu noon-3 5-11, Fri noon-3 5-1am, Sat noon-1am, Sun noon-mdnt Closed: 1 Jan **Bar Meals** L served Mon-Fri 12-3, Sat 12-9, Sun 12-8 D served Mon-Fri 5-9, Sat 12-9, Sun 12-8 **Restaurant** L served Mon-Fri 12-3, Sat 12-9, Sun 12-8 D served Mon-Fri 5-9, Sat 12-9, Sun 12-8 ⊕ FREE HOUSE ◀ Belhaven Best, Harviestoun Bitter & Twisted, Guinness Ö Addlestones. ♥ 10 **Facilities** Children welcome Children's menu Children's portions Family room Dogs allowed Garden Parking Wi-fi

KIPPEN *continued*

PICK OF THE PUBS

The Inn at Kippen ♥ NEW

Fore Rd FK8 3DT ☎ **01786 870500** 🖹 **01786 871011**
e-mail: info@theinnatkippen.co.uk
dir: *From Stirling take A811 to Loch Lomond. 1st left at Kippen station rdbt, 1st right onto Fore Rd. Inn on left*

Located in a picturesque village at the foot of the Campsie Hills, this traditional whitewashed free house enjoys views across the Forth valley to the Highlands. The stylish bar is a relaxing place to sample the extensive range of cask ales and wines, as well as a superb selection of spirits that reflects the proprietor's long career in the Scotch whisky business. Two separate areas offer a choice of casual or more formal dining from a menu driven by seasonal, locally sourced ingredients. Traditional and contemporary dishes reveal British, European and Oriental influences. Start, perhaps, with a twice-baked Parmesan soufflé before moving on to steak pie with seasonal vegetables; Thai seafood broth with sea bass, mussels and king prawns; or butternut squash, sage and Parmesan risotto. Tempting desserts include treacle and stem ginger pudding with coconut ice cream. There's a pretty garden area for summer dining, and a heated smoking deck.

Open all day all wk noon-11 Fri & Sat noon-1am
Bar Meals L served all wk 12-5 D served all wk 5-9 booking required Av main course £16 food served all day **Restaurant** L served Sat-Sun 12-5 booking required D served Fri-Sun 5-9 booking required Fixed menu price fr £14 Av 3 course à la carte fr £20 food served all day ⊕ FREE HOUSE ◄ Killians. ♥ 9
Facilities Children welcome Children's menu Children's portions Dogs allowed Garden Parking Wi-fi

---

WEST LOTHIAN

LINLITHGOW   Map 21 NS97

PICK OF THE PUBS

Champany Inn - The Chop and Ale House ◉◉

Champany EH49 7LU
☎ **01506 834532** 🖹 **01506 834302**
e-mail: reception@champany.com
web: www.champany.com
dir: *2m NE of Linlithgow on corner of A904 & A803*

Several 16th-century buildings and an ancient watermill comprise this unusual little hotel, which has two splendid restaurants. The more informal is the easy chair and couch-strewn Chop and Ale House, a converted farmer's bothy which was once the public bar of an inn here. With a pint of Belhaven in hand, or a glass of the Champany's own-label South African wine, settle in your chosen spot with the bistro-style menu. Beef is the big thing here – Aberdeen Angus of course – whether it be steaks or the same steak minced and formed in half-pound burgers. The 'keep fit' version comes without bun or fries, just salad; but it would seem a shame to miss the top of the range: steak with thick cut slices of Brie topped with bacon from their own smokehouse. Scottish best end of lamb chops make an altogether acceptable alternative. If you can manage a dessert, cranachan is on the carte, or brandy snap basket with griotte cherries.

Open all wk noon-2 6.30-10 (Fri-Sun noon-10) Closed: 25-26 Dec, 1 Jan **Bar Meals** L served all wk 12-2 D served all wk 6.30-10 **Restaurant** L served all wk 12.30-2 booking required D served all wk 6.30-10 booking required ⊕ FREE HOUSE ◄ Belhaven.
Facilities Children welcome Children's portions Garden Parking

---

The Four Marys ♥ NEW

65/67 High St EH49 7ED
☎ **01506 842171** 🖹 **01506 844410**
dir: *M9 junct 3 or 4 take A803 to Linlithgow. Pub in town centre*

Named after one of the four ladies-in-waiting of Mary, Queen of Scots, who was born in nearby Linlithgow Palace, this town house dates from 1500, but it remained unlicensed until 1981 having previously been a chemists, newsagents and printers. It now thrives as one of Scotland top real ale pubs, serving predominantly Scottish brews and hosting popular beer festivals in May and October. Soak up the ale with a steak pie, a classic beef burger, or St Andrew's ale pork and herb sausages.

Open all day all wk **Bar Meals** L served all wk 12-5 D served all wk 5-9 Av main course £7.99 food served all day **Restaurant** L served all wk 12-5 D served all wk 5-9 Fixed menu price fr £14.99 food served all day ⊕ BELHAVEN, GREENE KING ◄ Belhaven 80/-, Greene King Old Speckled Hen, Caledonian Deuchars IPA, Stewart Edinburgh Gold. ♥ 9 **Facilities** Children welcome Children's menu Children's portions Garden Beer festival

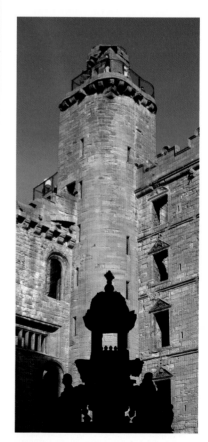

Save on hotels. Book at **theAA.com/hotel**

SCOTTISH ISLANDS 569 **SCOTLAND**

SCOTTISH ISLANDS
COLL, ISLE OF

ARINAGOUR	Map 22 NM25

PICK OF THE PUBS

Coll Hotel

PA78 6SZ ☎ 01879 230334 🖹 01879 230317
e-mail: info@collhotel.com
dir: *Ferry from Oban. Hotel at head of Arinagour Bay, 1m from Pier (collections by arrangement)*

Being the only inn on the Isle of Coll, it's no surprise that the bar of this award-winning hotel is the hub of the island community. Come here to meet the locals, soak in the atmosphere, and enjoy stunning views over the sea to Jura and Mull. The most popular drinks are pints of Loch Fyne ale and malt whiskies from the list, but there is a good wine selection too. In the summer months the fabulous garden acts as an extension to the bar or the Gannet restaurant; watch the yachts coming and going while enjoying a glass of Pimms. Fresh produce is landed and delivered from around the island every day and features on the specials board. Famed for its seafood, you'll find it in dishes such as seared scallops in garlic and lemon butter, and a platter of Coll langoustines that can be served hot or cold, with seasonal salad or fried potatoes. Among the non-fish options, try the chicken topped with haggis in a whisky sauce.

Open all day all wk **Bar Meals** L served all wk 12-2 D served all wk 6-9 Av main course £12 **Restaurant** L served all wk 12-2 D served all wk 6-9 booking required Av 3 course à la carte fr £28 ⊕ FREE HOUSE ◀ Loch Fyne Ale, Pipers Gold, Guinness. **Facilities** Children welcome Children's menu Children's portions Play area Family room Garden Parking Wi-fi

ISLAY, ISLE OF

PORT CHARLOTTE	Map 20 NR25

The Port Charlotte Hotel ♥ NEW

Main St PA48 7TU ☎ 01496 850360 🖹 01496 850361
e-mail: info@portcharlottehotel.co.uk
dir: *From Port Askaig take A846 towards Bowmore. Right onto A847, through Blackrock. Take unclassified road to Port Charlotte*

On the west shore of Loch Indaal is the attractive conservation village of Port Charlotte, whose pretty whitewashed stone buildings include this completely restored hotel. A large comfortable conservatory opens out into the beer garden, which overlooks the sea. Warmed by open fires, the lounge and public bar are convivial gathering points for lovers of Scottish art displayed on the walls and the traditional music sometimes played here. Islay ales and whiskies make great aperitifs before tucking in to beef, lamb or game from local farms and estates; or scallops, lobster and crab landed by the Islay fishing fleet.

Open all day all wk Closed: 24-26 Dec
Bar Meals L served all wk 12-2 D served all wk 6-9 Av main course £11.95 **Restaurant** D served all wk 6-9 Av 3 course à la carte fr £32 ⊕ FREE HOUSE ◀ Islay Ales. **Facilities** Children welcome Children's menu Children's portions Play area Family room Dogs allowed Garden Parking Wi-fi

SKYE, ISLE OF

ARDVASAR	Map 22 NG60

Ardvasar Hotel ★★★ SHL

IV45 8RS ☎ 01471 844223 🖹 01471 844495
e-mail: richard@ardvasar-hotel.demon.co.uk
web: www.ardvasarhotel.com
dir: *From ferry terminal, 50yds & turn left*

Beside the road towards the southern tip of Skye, sit out front to drink in the extraordinary views to the rocky foreshore, Sound of Sleat and the mountains of the Knoydart Peninsula, a ferry ride away via Mallaig. Once you've sipped your Skye-brewed beer or local malt, retire to the comfy lounge bar or dining room to indulge in some of Skye's most renowned seafood meals; the local boats may land salmon, crab, lobster or scallops. Estate venison and Aberdeen Angus beef extend the choice. Residents in the individually designed rooms can look to a fine Scottish breakfast to set another day in paradise going.

Open all day all wk 11am-mdnt (Sun noon-11pm)
Bar Meals L served all wk 12-2.30 D served all wk 5.30-9 ⊕ FREE HOUSE ◀ IPA, Isle of Skye Red Cuillin.
Facilities Children welcome Children's menu Children's portions Dogs allowed Garden Parking **Rooms** 10

CARBOST	Map 22 NG33

The Old Inn

IV47 8SR ☎ 01478 640205 🖹 01478 640205
e-mail: enquiries@theoldinnskye.co.uk
web: www.theoldinnskye.co.uk
dir: *From Skye Bridge follow A87 north. Take A863, then B8009 to inn*

On the shores of Loch Harport and near the Talisker distillery, The Old Inn is a charming, 200-year-old island cottage and is very popular among the walking and climbing fraternity. Arrive early for a table on the waterside patio and savour the breathtaking views of the Cuillin Hills with a pint of Hebridean Ale in hand. Inside, open fires welcome winter visitors, and live music is a regular feature. With a great selection of real ales, the menu includes daily home-cooked specials, with numerous fresh fish dishes, including local prawns and oysters and mackerel from the loch.

Open all day all wk 11am-mdnt **Bar Meals** L served all wk 12-9.30 D served all wk food served all day **Restaurant** D served all wk food served all day ⊕ FREE HOUSE ◀ Red Cuillin, Black Cuillin, Hebridean Ale, Cuillin Skye Ale, Pinnacle Ale. **Facilities** Children welcome Children's portions Family room Dogs allowed Garden Parking Wi-fi

ISLEORNSAY   Map 22 NG71

PICK OF THE PUBS

Hotel Eilean Iarmain ★★★ SHL ◎◎

IV43 8QR ☎ 01471 833332 🖷 **01471 833275**
e-mail: hotel@eilean-iarmain.co.uk
dir: A851, A852 right to Isleornsay harbour front

This award-winning Hebridean hotel with its own pier,
overlooks the Isle of Ornsay harbour and Sleat Sound.
The old-fashioned character of the hotel remains
intact, and decor is mainly cotton and linen chintzes
with traditional furniture. More a small private hotel
than a pub, the bar and restaurant ensure that the
standards of food and drinks served here are exacting.
The head chef declares: 'We never accept second best,
it shines through in the standard of food served in our
restaurant'. Here you can try dishes like Eilean Iarmain
estate venison casserole, pan-seared sirloin steak, or
grilled fillet of cod with hollandaise sauce. If you call in
at lunchtime, a range of baked potatoes, sandwiches
and toasties is also available. Half portions are served
for children.

Open all day all wk Sun-Wed 11am-11.30pm, Thurs
11am-mdnt, Fri 11am-1am, Sat 11am-12.30am
Bar Meals L served 12-2 D served 5.30-9
Restaurant D served 6.30-8.30 booking required
⊕ FREE HOUSE ◀ McEwans 80/-, Guinness, Isle of
Skye real ale. **Facilities** Children welcome Dogs allowed
Garden Parking **Rooms** 16

STEIN   Map 22 NG25

Stein Inn ♀

Macleod's Ter IV55 8GA ☎ 01470 592362
e-mail: angus.teresa@steininn.co.uk
dir: A87 from Portree. In 5m take A850 for 15m. Right
onto B886, 3m to T-junct. Turn left

The seas around Skye abound with fish while the land
supports sheep, wild venison and highland cattle. This
inn, the oldest on the island, offers fine food, and an
impressive selection of drinks: fine wines, real ales and
no fewer than a hundred malt whiskies. Highland meat,
game and local seafood feature strongly on the daily-
changing menu, in dishes such as Skye scallops in
oatmeal, steak braised in Skye ale, and Highland venison
pie. Lunchtime bar food includes local crab sandwiches,
smoked salmon platter and haggis toastie.

Open all day all wk 11am-mdnt Closed: 25 Dec, 1 Jan
Bar Meals L served all wk 12-4 D served all wk 6-9.30 Av
main course £8 **Restaurant** D served all wk 6-9.30 Av 3
course à la carte £17.90 ⊕ FREE HOUSE ◀ Red Cuillin,
Trade Winds, Reeling Deck, Deuchars IPA, Dark Island.
♀ 9 **Facilities** Children welcome Children's menu
Children's portions Play area Family room Dogs allowed
Garden Parking Wi-fi

SOUTH UIST

LOCHBOISDALE   Map 22 NF71

The Polochar Inn

Polochar HS8 5TT ☎ 01878 700215 🖷 **01878 700768**
e-mail: polocharinn@aol.com
dir: W from Lochboisdale, take B888. Hotel at end of road

By the water's edge in a beautiful location at the tip of
South Uist, this mid-18th-century inn was once the
change-house, where travellers caught the island's ferry.
Sibling owners Morag MacKinnon and Margaret Campbell
specialise in local seafood, meats and pastas, which are
served in a dining room with outstanding views of the
sea, the islands of Barra and Eriskay, and even dolphins
playing. On summer Saturday nights the public bar
echoes to live music.

Open all day all wk 11-11 (Fri-Sat 11am-1am Sun
12.30pm-1am) **Bar Meals** L served Mon-Sat 12.30-8.30,
Sun 1-8.30 (winter all wk 12-2.30) D served Mon-Sat
12.30-8.30, Sun 1-8.30 (winter all wk 5-8.30) food served
all day ⊕ FREE HOUSE ◀ Hebridean ales, Guest ales.
Facilities Children welcome Children's menu Children's
portions Family room Garden Parking Wi-fi

Wales

Harlech Castle, Gwynedd

WALES

ANGLESEY, ISLE OF

BEAUMARIS Map 14 SH67

PICK OF THE PUBS

Ye Olde Bulls Head Inn
★★★★★ INN ◉◉ ♟

See Pick of the Pubs on page 576

RED WHARF BAY Map 14 SH58

PICK OF THE PUBS

The Ship Inn
LL75 8RJ ☎ 01248 852568 📠 01248 851013
dir: *Telephone for directions*

The pub faces east on the lee side of a hill, sheltered from prevailing winds and catching the morning and afternoon sun perfectly. Wading birds flock here to feed on the extensive sands of Red Wharf Bay, making The Ship's waterside beer garden a birdwatcher's paradise on warm days. Before the age of steam, sailing ships landed cargoes here from all over the world; now the boats bring fresh Conwy Bay fish and seafood to the kitchens of this traditional free house. In the Kenneally family's hands for around 40 years, real ales are carefully tended and a single menu, on which dishes are given refreshingly light-hearted titles, applies to both bars and restaurant; specials always include a catch of the day. So expect to see starters such as smoky sunrise salmon; and main course titles like 'Force 10 from Red Wharf' – shoulder of Welsh lamb, mint forcemeat stuffing, white onion cream, mash and vegetables.

Open all wk **Bar Meals** L served all wk 12-2.30 D served all wk 6-9 booking required **Restaurant** D served Sat-Sun booking required ⊕ FREE HOUSE ◀ Brains SA, Adnams, Guest ales. **Facilities** Children welcome Children's menu Play area Family room Garden Parking

BRIDGEND

KENFIG Map 9 SS88

Prince of Wales Inn
CF33 4PR ☎ 01656 740356
e-mail: prince-of-wales@btconnect.com
dir: *M4 junct 37 into North Cornelly. Left at x-rds, follow signs for Kenfig & Porthcaw. Pub 600yds on right*

A 16th-century property, this stone-built inn has been many things in its time: a school, town hall and courtroom among others. This is thought to be one of the most haunted pubs in Wales and only pub in Britain to hold a Sunday school continuously from 1857 to 2000. Local fare on the menu could include award-winning sausages, Welsh minted lamb chops and Welsh braised faggots. Also worth attention are the daily specials on the blackboard and traditional Sunday lunches.

Open all wk **Bar Meals** L served all wk 12-2.30 D served all wk 6-8.30 Av main course £8.50 **Restaurant** L served all wk 12-2.30 D served all wk 6-8.30 ⊕ FREE HOUSE ◀ Bass Triangle, Worthington Best, Guest ales ♻ Taffy Apples. **Facilities** Children welcome Children's menu Children's portions Dogs allowed Garden Parking

CARDIFF

CREIGIAU Map 9 ST08

PICK OF THE PUBS

Caesars Arms

See Pick of the Pubs on page 577

GWAELOD-Y-GARTH Map 9 ST18

Gwaelod-y-Garth Inn
Main Rd CF15 9HH ☎ 029 2081 0408 & 07855 313247
e-mail: gwaelo-dinn@btconnect.com
web: www.gwaelodinn.co.uk
dir: *From M4 junct 32, N on A470, left at next exit, at rdbt turn right 0.5m. Right into village*

This stone built hillside cottage hugs lanes striking across the thickly wooded flank of Garth Hill, high above Taffs Well. Across the vale is the fairytale Castell Coch Victorian sham castle; one diversion amongst many in this pretty corner of the Taff Valley just north of Cardiff. Three Cliffs Gold from Swansea Brewery, guest ales and farm cider from Pontypridd slake the thirst of cyclists,

ramblers and locals; solid fare is a pleasing mix of sturdy pub grub and tasty specials such as duck breast with kumquat and cassis sauce.

Open all wk 11am-mdnt (Sun noon-11) **Bar Meals** L served Mon-Thu 12-2, Fri-Sat 11am-9pm, Sun 12-3 **Restaurant** L served Mon-Thu 12-2, Fri-Sat 11am-9pm, Sun 12-3 booking required D served Mon-Sat 6.30-9 booking required ⊕ FREE HOUSE ◀ HPA (Wye Valley), Three Cliffs Gold, Gower, RCH Pitchfork, Vale of Glamorgan, Crouch Vale Brewers Gold ♻ Local cider. **Facilities** Children welcome Children's menu Children's portions Family room Dogs allowed Garden Parking

See also opposite page

CARMARTHENSHIRE

ABERGORLECH Map 8 SN53

The Black Lion
SA32 7SN ☎ 01558 685271
e-mail: georgerashbrook@hotmail.com
dir: *A40 E from Carmarthen, then B4310 signed Brechfa & Abergorlech*

The pretty village of Abergorlech is one of the lesser-known jewels of Carmarthenshire; its 16th-century pub is run by George and Louise Rashbrook, with Mrs R doing all the cooking. The award-winning beer garden overlooks an ancient Roman bridge, the bar has flagstone floors, while the dining room is newly refurbished and more modern. Menus offer sandwiches, jacket potatoes, salads, curries, fish and chips, Welsh steaks, pies and Moroccan lamb casserole. The area is popular with walkers and mountain bikers.

Open 12-3 7-11 (Sat-Sun & BH all day) Closed: Mon (ex BH) **Bar Meals** L served Tue-Sun 12-2.30 D served Tue-Sun 7-9 booking required Av main course £6.50 **Restaurant** D served Tue-Sun 7-9 booking required Av 3 course à la carte fr £15 ⊕ FREE HOUSE ◀ Rhymney ♻ Stowford Press. **Facilities** Children welcome Children's menu Children's portions Dogs allowed Garden Parking Wi-fi

Gwaelod y Garth Inn

It's just a short ride out of the city, but here, above the valley, in the shelter of the Garth, the pace of life is slower. The welcome at the Gwaelod y Garth Inn is a genuine one, so we're a much favoured watering-hole for walkers, cyclists, hang-gliders, and our colourful locals, too.

The village and the pub have exceptional views of the Taff Vale and the Bristol Channel beyond, and our terrace is a marvellous place just to meet and watch the world go by. Inside, in the cosy bar and in the pool-room, you'll find plenty of choice of drinks, including good real ales, tasty bar-food, friendly company and, when it's cold outside, open fires. Upstairs, Chef ensures that our comfortable award-winning restaurant serves a fine extensive menu with wines to match, and on Sundays there is always a traditional roast.

The pub has recently been given a Highly Commended Award from CAMRA. B&B is also available (awaiting rating - see website for up to date information). The rest is up to you.

Licenced restaurant

CAMRA Commended bar

Open fires

Main Rd, Gwaelod y Garth, Cardiff, CF15 9HH

Tel: 029 20810408   **Email:** gwaelo-dinn@btconnect.com   **Website:** www.gwaelodinn.co.uk

PICK OF THE PUBS

Ye Olde Bulls Head Inn ★★★★★ INN

BEAUMARIS Map 14 SH67

Castle St LL58 8AP
☎ **01248 810329** 📠 **01248 811294**
e-mail: info@bullsheadinn.co.uk
web: www.bullsheadinn.co.uk
dir: *From Britannia Road Bridge follow A545. Inn in town centre*

The Bull first appears in the records in 1472 as a staging post and inn on the vital route between London and Ireland. The horses pulling the mail coaches and official conveyances were changed here after tackling the exhausting route across the sands of the Menai Strait. Its near neighbour is even older; Beaumaris Castle was started in 1295 but never completed, its looks make it a favourite of castle-lovers and it is a listed World Heritage Site. A short way up the coast is Penmon Priory, a secluded retreat with connections to the medieval Welsh Princes. Today's imposing establishment retains much of the character of Georgian and Victorian times, underscored by tasteful contemporary additions. The light and airy Brasserie has been moulded from the former stables; the Welsh slate floor, oak tables and open fire a relaxing location at any time. The bar itself transports drinkers back to Dickensian times (the man himself stayed here), with settles, antique furnishings and artefacts, including the town's old ducking stool and remarkable

old weaponry; Bass and Hancocks are supplemented by regularly changing guest ales. The Bull's happy location in the midst of a rich larder of seafood and Welsh livestock farms means that the menus here are exceptional; this potential has been realised and recognised by the award of two AA Rosettes. The popular Brasserie offers a children's menu and portions and a good range of modern global dishes; Thai spiced fish or tagliatelli with wilted spinach and braised leeks a sample, but it is the intimate Loft Restaurant where the boat is pushed out. Start with seared Anglesey king scallop, potato, kohlrabi, confit lemon, and crème fraîche, leading to pan-seared sea trout, roast quail, herb risotto, asparagus, and béarnaise sauce. The exceptional accommodation here comes with a full

Welsh breakfast, ample repast before exploring the treasure trove that is Ynys Môn, the Isle of Anglesey.

Open all day all wk Closed: 25 Dec **Bar Meals** L served Mon-Sat 12-2, Sun 12-3 D served Mon-Sun 6-9 Av main course £12 **Restaurant** D served Tue-Sun 7-9.30 Av 3 course à la carte fr £41 ⊕ FREE HOUSE ◼ Bass, Hancocks, Guest ales. ♟ 20 **Facilities** Children welcome Children's menu Children's portions Parking Wi-fi **Rooms** 26

Save on hotels. Book at **theAA.com/hotel**

CARDIFF 577 WALES

PICK OF THE PUBS

Caesars Arms

CREIGIAU Map 9 ST08

Cardiff Rd CF15 9NN
☎ **029 2089 0486** 📠 **029 2089 2176**
e-mail: info@caesarsarms.co.uk
web: www.caesarsarms.co.uk
dir: *M4 junct 34, A4119 towards
Llantrisant/Rhondda. Approx 0.5m right at
lights signed Groesfaen. Through
Groesfaen, past Dynevor Arms pub. Next
left, signed Creigiau. 1m, left at T-junct,
pass Creigiau Golf Course. Pub in 1m on
left*

An upmarket country dining pub and farm
shop tucked away down winding lanes
just ten miles from Cardiff. The
whitewashed building is older than it
looks, but inside you'll find an appealing
bar and dining area, and fine views over
extensive gardens and surrounding
countryside from the heated patio and
terrace. There's so much more here than
the excellent ales from Llanelli's Felinfoel
Brewery and the award-winning wine list,
which extends to more than 100 bottles
and is probably one of the best selections
in Wales. The pub has its own beehives
and makes its own honey, vegetables,
herbs and salads from its own gardens
are grown organically and used in the
kitchen, and there's an in-house smokery,
giving a truly local flavour. The excellent
farm shop is well stocked with free-range
eggs, rare breed pork products, honey
from their hives, Welsh cheeses, home-
baked bread and chef's ready prepared
meals to take away. The inn prides itself
on the vast selection of fresh fish,
seafood, meat and game displayed on
shaven ice in display cabinets. Fresh
seafood is an undoubted strength, with
deliveries taken twice daily. Start with
Pembrokeshire dressed crab, tiger prawns
cooked in garlic, or scallops with leek and
bacon, then follow with hake, salmon,
John Dory, Dover sole or lobster in season.
For a real showstopper, order sea bass
baked in rock salt – it will be theatrically
cracked open and filleted at your table.
Carnivores can choose from slow-reared,
dry-aged Welsh Black beef, plus mountain
lamb, venison from the Brecon Beacons,
and free-range chickens from the Wye
Valley. Bajan fishcakes, scallops with leek
julienne, or cherry-smoked duck breast
with organic beetroot give an indication of
the flavours that await in this much
favoured hostelry. There is private parking
for over 100 cars.

Open noon-2.30 6-10 (Sun noon-4)
Closed: 25 Dec, 1 Jan, Sun eve
Bar Meals L served Mon-Sat 12-2.30
Restaurant L served Mon-Sat 12-2.30,
Sun 12-4 D served Mon-Sat 6-10 Fixed
menu price fr £7.95 Av 3 course à la carte
fr £19.95 🍺 FREE HOUSE 🍺 Felinfoel
Double Dragon, Brains Smooth, Guinness
🍏 Orchard Gold. **Facilities** Children
welcome Children's portions Dogs allowed
Garden Parking

PICK OF THE PUBS

White Hart Thatched Inn & Brewery

LLANDDAROG   **MAP 8 SN51**

SA32 8NT ☎ 01267 275395
e-mail: bestpubinwales@aol.com
web: www.thebestpubinwales.co.uk
dir: *6m E of Carmarthen towards Swansea, just off A48 on B4310, signed Llanddarog*

Interesting legends surround this family-run, ancient thatched building, thought to be built to house stone masons who built the first church next door. Dylan Thomas often visited on his way west. Llanddarog is famous for its fair cakes, which were made at the inn using the cask beer from the adjoining micro-brewery. 'Cwrw Blasus' (meaning tasty ale) is always available along with different cask conditioned ales, made from top quality ingredients – malted barley, whole hop cones and yeast - including water from 300 feet beneath the inn.

The pub's 14th-century origins can be seen in the thick stone walls, heavy beams and cosy log fire. The restaurant is situated in a converted barn, and has views to the open-plan kitchen where the chefs can be seen preparing your food.

The family-run business is now a member of Prince Charles' exclusive Welsh lamb club as they use only best Welsh lamb. They also serve pedigree Welsh Black beef on the menu.

The specials board is likely to include beef and ale pie and beef and ale with cauliflower cheese double pie; trio of Welsh pork sausages, peas and mash; half duckling sizzling in orange sauce; and home-made lasagne.

In summer, the flower-filled patio garden is perfect for alfresco dining. Children will enjoy the play area and seeing the pigs, chickens, ducks and turkeys on the small home farm.

Open 11.30-3 6.30-11 (Sun noon-3 7-10.30) Closed: Jan, Wed
Bar Meals L served Thu-Tue 11.30-3 inc wknd D served Thu-Tue 6.30-11 inc wknd
Restaurant L served Thu-Tue 11.30-3 inc wknd D served Thu-Tue 6.30-11 inc wknd Av 3 course à la carte fr £20
🌐 FREE HOUSE 🍺 Roasted Barley Stout, Llanddarog Ale, Bramling Cross, Cwrw Blasus, Swn y Dail 🍏 First Choice.
Facilities Children welcome Children's menu Children's portions Play area Garden Parking

LLANDDAROG   Map 8 SN51

PICK OF THE PUBS

White Hart Thatched Inn & Brewery

See Pick of the Pubs on opposite page

LLANDEILO   Map 8 SN62

The Angel Hotel ☕

Rhosmaen St SA19 6EN
☎ 01558 822765 📠 01558 824346
e-mail: capelbach@hotmail.com
dir: *In town centre next to post office*

Just a short step from the bridge over the glorious River Towy and in the shadow of the Black Mountain, this angel at the heart of bustling Llandeilo incorporates many flights of fancy. Locals rest easy in the café bar with its choice of four real ales and lively events calendar; diners favour taking a place in the thriving Y Capel Bach (the little chapel) bistro, where multiple menus feature a specialist hot buffet every week, whilst the daily menus leave you spoilt for choice; Venezuelan pork ragout or mushroom and lentil loaf with cracked pepper cream just scratching the surface. The upstairs function room features memorable Sistine Chapel-like frescoes, whilst a secluded walled garden offers the ultimate escape.

Open 11.30-3 6-11 Closed: Sun **Bar Meals** L served Mon-Sat 11.30-2.30 D served Mon-Sat 6-9 Av main course £6.50 **Restaurant** L served Mon-Sat 11.30-2.30 booking required D served Mon-Sat 6-9 booking required Fixed menu price fr £9.50 Av 3 course à la carte fr £18 ⊕ FREE HOUSE ◀ Evan Evans Ales, Tetleys, Butty Bach. ☕ 10 **Facilities** Children welcome Children's menu Children's portions Garden

The Castle Hotel

113 Rhosmaen St SA19 6EN ☎ 01558 824714
dir: *Telephone for directions*

A 19th-century hotel within easy reach of Dinefwr Castle and wonderful walks through classic parkland. A charming, tiled and partly green-painted back bar attracts plenty of locals, while the front bar and side area offer smart furnishings and the chance to relax in comfort over a drink. A good range of real ales is available and quality bar and restaurant food is prepared with the finest of fresh local ingredients.

Open all day all wk ⊕ ENTERPRISE INNS ◀ Hancocks HB, Courage Directors, Timothy Taylor Landlord, Exmoor Gold, Adnams Broadside. **Facilities** Children welcome Children's portions Dogs allowed Garden Parking **Notes** 🖵

LLANLLWNI   Map 8 SN43

Belle @ Llanllwni ☕

SA40 9SQ ☎ 01570 480495
e-mail: mail@bellevueinn.co.uk
dir: *Midway between Carmarthen & Lampeter on A485*

Surrounded by countryside and with stunning views, this cosy and welcoming roadside inn sits on the A485 between Carmarthen and Lampeter. Head this way on a sunny day and dine alfresco in the garden, perhaps on sausages and champ mash with shallot gravy from the lunch menu. There are two rotating ales here to enjoy along with local bottled Welsh ciders. In the dining room, slow-roasted pork belly with Calvados red onion jus and colcannon mash, might be followed by chocolate truffle torte. Expect excellent ingredients including free-range local meats. There is a nine-course menu gastronomies and monthly themed menus too.

Open 12-3 5.30-11 Closed: Mon (ex BHs) **Bar Meals** L served Wed-Sat 12-3 D served Tue-Sun 6-9.30 Av main course £10 **Restaurant** L served Sun 12-3 D served Tue-Sun 6-9.30 Av 3 course à la carte fr £20 ⊕ FREE HOUSE ◀ Guinness, Guest ales ♂ Stowford Press, Gwynt y Ddraig. **Facilities** Children welcome Children's menu Children's portions Parking

NANTGAREDIG   Map 8 SN42

PICK OF THE PUBS

Y Polyn ◉◉ ☕

SA32 7LH ☎ 01267 290000
e-mail: ypolyn@hotmail.com
dir: *From A48 follow signs to National Botanic Garden of Wales. Then follow brown signs to Y Polyn*

With a trout fishery nearby, bracing walks in the Towy Valley just down the hill and the inspiring National Botanic Garden of Wales a mile or so up the road, this rambling former tollhouse outside the attractive county town of Carmarthen is an established destination pub for lovers of Welsh food. West Wales is rapidly becoming one of the hotspots for organic and homespun cuisine, and the largesse of the local area is to the forefront in the tempting dishes that tumble from the modest kitchen here. Treats include Carmarthen ham and celeriac rémoulade capped by duck shepherd's pie; Ferryside salt marsh lamb daube or, with an eye to sustainable resources, roast Pembrokeshire pollock with cannellini beans and chorizo. Home-made gooseberry ripple or honey and almond ice-cream seal the deal. These, and the enticing fillet of coracle-caught Towy Sewin (sea-trout), have gained the inn 2 AA Rosettes for the fare. Oddly, the beers come from Yorkshire, but damn good ones at that.

Open all wk 12-4 7-11 Closed: Mon, Sun eve **Restaurant** L served Tue-Sun 12-2 D served Tue-Sat 7-9 Fixed menu price fr £29 Av 3 course à la carte fr £21 ⊕ FREE HOUSE ◀ Otley 03 Boss. ☕ 12 **Facilities** Children welcome Children's portions Garden Parking

CEREDIGION

ABERAERON   Map 8 SN46

PICK OF THE PUBS

The Harbourmaster

INN ◉ ☕

Pen Cei SA46 0BA ☎ 01545 570755
e-mail: info@harbour-master.com
dir: *From A487. In Aberaeron follow Tourist Information Centre signs. Pub next door*

Originally the harbourmaster's house and flanked by pretty pastel-coloured buildings of similar age, the inn has been the focal point on Aberaeron's Georgian quayside since 1811. In 2008 the former grain store next door was converted into a relaxing bar overlooking the harbour – the perfect spot for a pint of HM Best or one of the dozen or so wines sold by the glass. The cobalt blue interior is complemented by original features like the Welsh slate masonry and a spiral staircase. The kitchen's AA Rosette rated dishes feature carefully sourced produce, cooked with pride and thoughtfully presented. Typical of starters could be half a dozen Carlingford oysters with shallot and red wine vinegar, or deep-fried Perl Wen cheese with cherry mustard and watercress. Among the main courses may be found the Harbourmaster's côte de boeuf – a rib of Welsh beef on the bone, served with skinny fries and béarnaise. The bedrooms are delightfully furnished and comfortable, and the breakfast is a treat.

Open all day all wk 10am-11.30pm Closed: 25 Dec **Bar Meals** L served Mon-Sun 12-2.30 D served Mon-Sun 6-9 Av main course £10.50 **Restaurant** L served Mon-Sun 12-2.30 booking required D served Mon-Sun 6.30-9 booking required Av 3 course à la carte fr £30 ⊕ FREE HOUSE ◀ Glaslyn, HM Best Bitter. ☕ 14 **Facilities** Children welcome Children's menu Children's portions Parking Wi-fi Rooms 13

LLWYNDAFYDD   Map 8 SN35

The Crown Inn & Restaurant ☕

SA44 6BU ☎ 01545 560396
e-mail: thecrowninnandrestaurant@hotmail.co.uk
dir: *Off A487 NE of Cardigan*

A traditional Welsh longhouse dating from 1799, with original beams, open fireplaces and a pretty restaurant. There's a carvery every Sunday and a varied menu with a good selection of dishes, including lambs' liver cooked in port, bacon and red onion gravy; cashew nut and apricot roast; or beef lasagne with chips and salad. Blackboard specials, a children's menu, light snacks and bar food are also available. Outside is a delightful, award-winning garden, while an easy walk down the lane leads to a cove with caves and National Trust cliffs.

Open all day all wk **Bar Meals** L served all wk 12-3 D served all wk 6-9 **Restaurant** L served all wk 12-3 D served all wk 6-9 ⊕ FREE HOUSE ◀ Flowers IPA, Old Speckled Hen, Cottage Brewery ales, Guest ales. ☕ 12 **Facilities** Children welcome Children's menu Play area Family room Dogs allowed Garden Parking

CONWY

BETWS-Y-COED Map 14 SH75

PICK OF THE PUBS

Ty Gwyn Inn INN

LL24 0SG
☎ **01690 710383 & 710787** 📠 **01690 710383**
e-mail: mratcl1050@aol.com
dir: At junct of A5 & A470, 100yds S of Waterloo Bridge

A coaching inn on the old London to Holyhead road long before Thomas Telford built his impressive cast iron Waterloo Bridge over the River Conwy opposite in 1815. Much of the original 17th-century character is evident inside. The Ratcliffe family has owned and run it for the past 28 years, and now Martin (the chef for all that time) and his wife Nicola are in charge. Real ales come from as near as Conwy's Great Orme brewery, as well as from much further afield. Martin relies heavily on quality Welsh produce for a mostly international cooking style that results in breast of chicken, goat's cheese and asparagus marinated in Chardonnay, garlic and lime cream; rosemary-scented roast rack of Snowdon lamb with onion and peppercorn marmalade; and fresh fillet of line-caught wild sea bass with king prawns, saffron and garlic. Some of Nicola's own-designed en suite rooms have four-posters.

Open all wk noon-2 6.30-11 Closed: 1wk Jan
Bar Meals L served all wk 12-2 D served all wk 6.30-9 booking required **Restaurant** L served all wk 12-2 D served all wk 6.30-9 booking required ⊕ FREE HOUSE ◀ Adnams Broadside, Reverend James, Old Speckled Hen, Orme Best. **Facilities** Children welcome Children's menu Children's portions Parking **Rooms** 13

BETWS-YN-RHOS Map 14 SH97

The Wheatsheaf Inn

LL22 8AW ☎ **01492 680218**
e-mail: wheatsheafinn@hotmail.co.uk
dir: A55 to Abergele, take A548 to Llanrwst from High Street. 2m turn right B5381, 1m to Betws-yn-Rhos

Although the building dates back to the 1200s, The Wheatsheaf was licensed as a coaching inn in the 17th-century, serving the mail route between Conwy and Chester. The pub oozes old world character with oak beams and stone pillars. Bar snacks are served in addition to the restaurant menu, which makes good use of local produce. A starter of mussels in garlic and white wine might be followed by Welsh Black steak and ale pie.

Open noon-11 (Tue & Sun noon-10 Fri-Sat noon-mdnt Winter closed Mon-Fri 2.30-5) Closed: Mon
Bar Meals L served Tue-Sun 12-2 D served Tue-Sun 5-9 **Restaurant** L served Tue-Sun 12-2 booking required D served Tue-Sun 6-9 booking required ⊕ ENTERPRISE INNS ◀ Old Speckled Hen, Guinness, Deuchars, Black Sheep, Doom Bar ☼ Kopparberg. **Facilities** Children welcome Children's menu Children's portions Family room Dogs allowed Garden Parking

CAPEL CURIG Map 14 SH75

Cobdens Hotel ★★ SHL

LL24 0EE ☎ **01690 720243** 📠 **01690 720354**
e-mail: info@cobdens.co.uk
dir: On A5, 5m W of Betws-y-Coed

Situated in a beautiful mountain village in the heart of Snowdonia, this 250-year-old inn sits at the foot of Moel Siabod, with Snowdon itself a couple of miles down the valley. No surprise then that it's a haven for outdoor pursuit enthusiasts of all descriptions, taking refreshment, rebuilding their strength or enjoying live music in the famous Mountain Bar built into the rock face. It offers wholesome, locally sourced food and real ales. Children are welcome too, and have their own menu to choose from.

Open all day all wk noon-11pm (Sun noon-10.30pm)
Closed: 6-26 Jan **Bar Meals** L served all wk 12-2 D served all wk 6-9 Av main course £12.95 **Restaurant** Av 3 course à la carte fr £20 ⊕ FREE HOUSE ◀ Conwy Rampart, Cobdens Ale, Honey Fayre, Guest ales ☼ Rosie's Perry. **Facilities** Children welcome Children's menu Children's portions Dogs allowed Garden Parking Wi-fi **Rooms** 17

COLWYN BAY Map 14 SH87

PICK OF THE PUBS

Pen-y-Bryn ☼

Pen-y-Bryn Rd LL29 6DD ☎ **01492 533360**
e-mail: pen.y.bryn@brunningandprice.co.uk
dir: 1m from A55. Follow signs to Welsh Mountain Zoo. Establishment at top of hill

Behind the simple exterior of this 1970s building you'll find a friendly and chatty atmosphere with local ales, Taffy Apples cider, and good, straightforward food cooked and served throughout the day. The interior has character in spades, with oak floors, open fires, rugs and old furniture, whilst the stunning rear garden and terrace enjoy panoramic views over the sea and the Great Orme headland. The modern British menu offers a great choice of sandwiches and lighter meals: the steak open sandwich is served on toast with chutney and a few chips, for instance, or you might opt for Chinese chicken pancakes with hoi-sin sauce. Main course options range from lamb Wellington with fondant potatoes, red wine and rosemary sauce, to smoked haddock and salmon fishcakes with tomato and spring onion salad. Vanilla pannacotta with rhubarb compote is typical of the appetising pudding selection.

Open all day all wk **Bar Meals** L served Mon-Sat 12-9.30, Sun 12-9 D served Mon-Sat 12-9.30, Sun 12-9 Av main course £12.95 food served all day **Restaurant** food served all day ⊕ BRUNNING & PRICE ◀ Great Orme 'Ormes Best', Snowdonia Ale, Brunning and Price original ☼ Aspall's suffolk cider. ☼ 14 **Facilities** Children welcome Children's portions Garden Parking

CONWY Map 14 SH77

PICK OF THE PUBS

The Groes Inn INN ⊛ ☼

LL32 8TN ☎ **01492 650545** 📠 **01492 650855**
e-mail: reception@groesinn.com
web: www.groesinn.com
dir: Exit A55 to Conwy, left at mini rdbt by Conwy Castle onto B5106, 2.5m inn on right

One of Wales's oldest pubs (first licensed in 1573), the creeper-clad inn nestles between the easternmost summits of the Carneddau mountain range and the rich riverside pastures of the verdant Conwy Valley; Snowdonia at its most benign, with extraordinary views from the flowery gardens one good reason to linger, another is the range luxuriously appointed yet ultra traditional bedroom suites. Rambling rooms, beamed ceilings, careworn settles, military hats (there's a connection to the Duke of Wellington here), historic cooking utensils, a stag's head over an open fire – this inn has plenty to point out and even snigger over (namely, the saucy Victorian postcards) – but don't expect a jukebox, gaming machines or pool table. Naturally there's a distinctly Welsh tilt to the menu, awarded one AA Rosette, with lamb and game from nearby estates and an infinitely varied selection of fruits of the sea brought in through Conwy's quay or Anglesey's boats; try the seafood pie, a medley of fresh market fish, or perhaps some renowned Conwy mussels. The chalk board specials denote the ever-changing quality dishes of the day, whilst the beers are mostly from the Great Orme micro-brewery.

Open all wk 12-3 6-11 **Bar Meals** L served all wk 12-2 D served all wk 6.30-9 Av main course £12 **Restaurant** L served all wk 12-2 D served all wk 6.30-9 ⊕ FREE HOUSE ◀ Burton Ale, Groes Ale, Ormes Best, Great Orme, Welsh Black, Tetley's ☼ Stowford Press. ☼ 14 **Facilities** Children's menu Children's portions Family room Dogs allowed Garden Parking Wi-fi **Rooms** 14

DOLWYDDELAN — Map 14 SH75

Elen's Castle Hotel

LL25 0EJ ☎ 01690 750207
e-mail: stay@hotelinsnowdonia.co.uk
dir: 5m S of Betws-Y-Coed, follow A470

Elen's Castle was originally owned by Baron Gwydyr, Earl of Ancaster, who sold it to his gamekeeper who opened it as a coaching inn around 1880, specialising in hunting parties. Now a family-run free house, it boasts an old world bar with a wood-burning stove and an intimate restaurant with breathtaking views of the mountains and Lledr River. Sample dishes include Welsh Black beef pie and fillet of sea bass with dill and cucumber sauce.

Open vary by season Closed: 1st 2wks Jan, wk days in quiet winter periods **Bar Meals** D served 6.30-9 Av main course £8.95 **Restaurant** D served 6.30-9 Av 3 course à la carte fr £20 ⊕ FREE HOUSE ◀ Brains, Worthington, Black Sheep, Spitfire ♨ Stowford Press.
Facilities Children welcome Children's menu Children's portions Play area Family room Dogs allowed Garden Parking Wi-fi

LLANDUDNO JUNCTION — Map 14 SH77

PICK OF THE PUBS

The Queens Head ♀

Glanwydden LL31 9JP
☎ 01492 546570 ▤ 01492 546487
e-mail: enquiries@queensheadglanwydden.co.uk
dir: From A55 take A470 towards Llandudno. At 3rd rdbt right towards Penrhyn Bay, then 2nd right into Glanwydden, pub on left

Just a five-minute drive from the Victorian seaside town of Llandudno, this charming free house is perfectly situated for country walks, cycling, or a day on the beach. A smart country pub in a pretty rural village, the Queen's Head has previously been awarded AA Pub of the Year for Wales, and continues to attract discerning customers with its warm welcome, effortless charm and excellent service. The stylish terrace is great for summer evenings, whilst on colder nights the relaxed atmosphere in the bar is perfect for a pre-dinner drink by the log fire; real ales include Great Orme brews, and the lip-smacking wine list with description notes on the back of the menu has plenty of choice. The dedicated kitchen makes excellent use of local produce in varied menus that might include grilled loin pork steak with a prune and Armagnac jus, or chargrilled marinated chicken breast with Moroccan couscous.

Open all wk 11.30-3 6-10.30 (Sat-Sun 11.30-10.30)
Bar Meals L served Mon-Fri 12-2, Sat-Sun 12-9 D served Mon-Fri 6-9, Sat-Sun 12-9
Restaurant L served Mon-Fri 12-2, Sat-Sun 12-9 D served Mon-Fri 6-9, Sat-Sun 12-9 ⊕ FREE HOUSE ◀ Weetwood Ales, Great Orme Brewery. ♀ 10
Facilities Children's portions Garden Parking

LLANELIAN-YN-RHÔS — Map 14 SH87

The White Lion Inn ♀ NEW

LL29 8YA ☎ 01492 515807
e-mail: info@whitelioninn.co.uk
dir: A55 junct 22, left signed Old Colwyn, A547. At rdbt 2nd exit onto B5383 signed Betwys-yn-Rhos. In 1m turn right into Llanelian Rd, follow to village. Pub on right

This traditional family-run village inn stands on the crossroads of the hamlet of Llanelian, a village with plenty of history concerning St Elian's well. It still retains its original slate floor and oak beamed ceiling, and there is an old salt cellar by the inglenook fireplace. Indeed the Cole Family have restored and preserved many aspects of traditional village life including reinstating the snug next to the bar. The food is traditional home cooked, wherever possible locally sourced, including of course shoulder of Welsh lamb. Other dishes on the comprehensive main menu and specials board include White Lion smokie, based on natural smoked haddock, and pork and leek sausages from Edwards of Conwy.

Open Tue-Fri 11.30-3 6-11 (Sat 11.30-4 6-11.30 Sun 12-11) Closed: Mon (ex BHs) **Bar Meals** L served Tue-Fri 2-9, Sat 2.30-9, Sun 12-9 D served Tue-Fri 2-9, Sat 2.30-9, Sun 12-9 Av main course £10
Restaurant L served Tue-Fri 2-9, Sat 2.30-9, Sun 12-9 D served Tue-Fri 2-9, Sat 2.30-9, Sun 12-9 booking required Av 3 course à la carte fr £20 ⊕ FREE HOUSE ◀ Marston's, Marston's Pedigree, Mansfield Smooth, Mansfield Mild, 1 guest ale. ♀ 11 **Facilities** Children welcome Children's menu Children's portions Garden Parking Wi-fi

LLANNEFYDD — Map 14 SH97

The Hawk & Buckle Inn

LL16 5ED ☎ 01745 540249
e-mail: enquiries@hawkandbuckleinn.com
dir: Telephone for directions

This lovingly restored 17th-century coaching inn sits 200 metres up in the North Wales hills, with wonderful views to the sea beyond. There is a great choice of real ales in the bar of this free house – Purple Moose Glaslyn. Fresh local produce is used in traditional dishes such as slow-roasted shank of Welsh lamb, chicken breast stuffed with Welsh cheese, or Celtic loin of pork, and pub favourites like rib-eye steak; beef or mushroom Stroganoff; and gammon, fried egg, pineapple and chips.

Open all wk winter 6-11, Sat-Sun noon-mdnt (summer 12-3 6-11 Sat-Sun noon-mdnt) **Bar Meals** L served winter Sat-Sun 12-9, summer Mon-Fri 12-3, Sat-Sun 12-9 booking required D served Mon-Fri 6-9, Sat-Sun 12-9 booking required ⊕ FREE HOUSE ◀ Reverend James, Purple Moose Glaslyn, Conwy Celebration, Brains SA. **Facilities** Dogs allowed Parking Wi-fi

DENBIGHSHIRE

PRESTATYN — Map 15 SJ08

Nant Hall Restaurant & Bar ♀

Nant Hall Rd LL19 9LD
☎ 01745 886766 ▤ 01745 886998
e-mail: mail@nanthall.com
dir: E towards Chester, 1m on left opposite large car garage

Nant Hall, a Grade II listed Victorian country house in seven acres of grounds, operates as a gastro-pub with a great variety of food, beers and wines. The menu offers local and regional dishes alongside recipes from around the world: Thai green chicken curry, pan-seared fillet of salmon with a creamy herb risotto, chargrilled steaks, Chinese chicken and vegetable satay, or creamy fish pie in a parsley sauce. The large outdoor eating area is great in summer.

Open all day all wk noon-11pm **Bar Meals** Av main course £6.95 food served all day **Restaurant** Fixed menu price fr £9.95 Av 3 course à la carte fr £15.95 ◀ Bass Smooth. ♀ 14 **Facilities** Children welcome Children's menu Children's portions Play area Family room Garden Parking

RHEWL — Map 15 SJ16

The Drovers Arms, Rhewl

Denbigh Rd LL15 2UD
☎ 01824 703163 ▤ 01824 703163
dir: 1.3m from Ruthin on A525

A small countryside village pub whose name recalls a past written up and illustrated on storyboards displayed inside. Main courses are divided on the menu into poultry, traditional meat, fish, grills and vegetarian; examples from each section are chicken tarragon; Welsh lamb's liver and onions; Vale of Clwyd sirloin steak; home-made fish pie; and mushroom Stroganoff. Ales are from JW Lees, including Coronation Street, and can be enjoyed in the garden in summer.

Open all wk noon-3 5.30-11 (Sat noon-3 5.30-mdnt Sun noon-11pm Jun-Sep all day) Closed: Tue L ⊕ J W LEES ◀ J W Lees bitter, Coronation Street Premium Ale.
Facilities Children welcome Children's menu Children's portions Play area Family room Garden Parking Wi-fi

RUTHIN
Map 15 SJ15

PICK OF THE PUBS

The Wynnstay Arms ★★★★ INN

Well St LL15 1AN ☎ 01824 703147 📠 01824 705428
e-mail: reservations@wynnstayarms.com
dir: In town centre

It was in this 460-year-old, timber-framed inn that wandering 19th-century author George Borrow, after walking from Llangollen, treated his trusty guide, John Jones, to "the best duck he had ever tasted". Today it's a popular gastro-pub with comfortable accommodation serving award-winning Welsh ales and cuisine based on ingredients sourced within the Principality; bread, pâtés and desserts are all made in-house. For a quiet lunchtime pint of Madog and a read of the papers, Bar W is the place to be. You can eat here too, or settle in to Fusions brasserie – the menu is the same for both. Typical of the starters are a baked field mushroom filled with traditional Welsh rarebit, and salad of smoked trout with pesto dressed cherry tomatoes. Prime Welsh beef steaks make a hearty main course, or a slow-roast shank of Welsh lamb with bubble and squeak. Professional and attentive service from the young team is the icing on the cake.

Open all day all wk **Bar Meals** L served all wk 12-2 booking required D served Mon-Sat 5.30-9.30, Sun 12-7 booking required Av main course £13.50 **Restaurant** L served Sun booking required D served Tue-Sat booking required Av 3 course à la carte fr £21 ⊕ FREE HOUSE ◀ Old Speckled Hen, Tetleys, Conwy Welsh Pride, Madog Ales. **Facilities** Children welcome Children's menu Children's portions Parking Wi-fi **Rooms** 7

ST ASAPH
Map 15 SJ07

The Plough Inn

The Roe LL17 0LU ☎ 01745 585080 📠 01745 585363
e-mail: ploughsa@gmail.com
dir: Exit A55 at Rhyl/St Asaph signs, left at rdbt, pub 200yds on left

An 18th-century former coaching inn, The Plough has been transformed. The ground floor retains the traditional pub concept, cosy with open fires and rustic furniture plus ales from local breweries, while upstairs is a modern restaurant, once a vaulted ceiling ballroom, with a wine shop. There's even a cocktail bar. The kitchen is open so you can see the food being prepared – from oriental and Tex-Mex sharing platters to braised lamb shank with dauphinoise potatoes, sticky roasted vegetables and a rich redcurrant and rosemary jus. There is a great children's menu and live music twice monthly.

Open all day all wk **Bar Meals** L served 12-9 D served 12-9 Av main course £8.25 food served all day **Restaurant** L served 12-9 booking required D served 7-11 booking required Fixed menu price fr £14.95 Av 3 course à la carte fr £18 ⊕ FREE HOUSE ◀ Conwy Brewery, Great Orme Brewery, Plassey. **Facilities** Children welcome Children's menu Children's portions Garden Parking Wi-fi

FLINTSHIRE

BABELL
Map 15 SJ17

Black Lion Inn ♥

CH8 8PZ ☎ 01352 720239
e-mail: theblacklioninn@btinternet.com
dir: A55 junct 31 to Caerwys. Left at x-roads signed Babell. In 3m turn right

Like many ancient inns, this 13th-century coaching inn is steeped in history and stories of ghosts, but modern day travellers are more likely to see the views across the surrounding Area of Outstanding Natural Beauty. Expect an excellent range of locally brewed cask ales, including the pub's own Black Lion Bitter. Families are welcome, offering a children's menu and play area. Food for the restaurant is sourced locally and cooked to order.

Open 6pm-close (Fri-Sun noon-close) Closed: Mon, Tue **Bar Meals** L served Fri-Sun 12-9 D served Wed-Sun 6-9 Av main course £12.95 **Restaurant** L served Fri-Sun 12-9 D served Wed-Sun 6-9 Av 3 course à la carte fr £22 ⊕ FREE HOUSE ◀ Thwaites Smooth Bitter, Purple Moose Brewery Traeth Mawr, Thirstquencher Spitting Feathers, Black Lion Bitter. ♥ 8 **Facilities** Children welcome Children's menu Children's portions Play area Garden Parking

CILCAIN
Map 15 SJ16

White Horse Inn

CH7 5NN ☎ 01352 740142 📠 01352 740142
e-mail: christine.jeory@btopenworld.com
dir: From Mold take A541 towards Denbigh. After approx 6m turn left

This 400-year-old pub is the last survivor of five originally to be found in this lovely hillside village, probably because it was the centre of the local gold-mining industry in the 19th century. Today, the White Horse is popular with walkers, cyclists and horse-riders. Food here is home made by the landlord's wife using the best quality local ingredients, and is accompanied by a good range of real ales. Curries, fish dishes and Welsh beef steaks are popular.

Open all wk noon-3 6.30-11 (Sat noon-11 Sun noon-10.30) **Bar Meals** L served Mon-Sat 12-2, Sun 12-9 D served all wk 7-9 Av main course £8.50 ⊕ FREE HOUSE ◀ Marston's Pedigree, Banks Bitter, Timothy Taylor Landlord, Draught Bass, Archers Golden, London Pride. **Facilities** Dogs allowed Garden Parking

MOLD
Map 15 SJ26

PICK OF THE PUBS

Glasfryn ♥

Raikes Ln, Sychdyn CH7 6LR
☎ 01352 750500 📠 01352 751923
e-mail: glasfryn@brunningandprice.co.uk
dir: From Mold follow signs to Theatr Clwyd, 1m from town centre

Built as a Judge's residence in about 1900, Glasfryn was rescued by the present owners at the end of the last century and transformed into a busy pub. Today, this North Wales pub attracts a varied clientele, from holidaymakers to farmers and business people. Inside is a bright open space with lots of polished wooden tables and chairs, whilst outside you'll find an attractively landscaped garden. A good choice of beers and ciders complements the comprehensive daily menu, which runs from interesting sandwiches like Mediterranean vegetables with goat's cheese and pesto ciabatta; and crispy lamb wrap with hoi sin sauce; to three course meals. Start, perhaps, with beetroot, goat's cheese, orange and pomegranate salad; before moving on to steak, ale and mushroom suet pudding with creamed potatoes and vegetables. Leave space for dessert – bread and butter pudding with apricot sauce and clotted cream is a typical choice.

Open all day all wk noon-11 **Bar Meals** L served all day 12-9.30 D served all day 12-9.30 booking required Av main course £11.95 food served all day **Restaurant** L served all day 12-9.30 D served all day 12-9.30 booking required Av 3 course à la carte fr £16 food served all day ⊕ BRUNNING & PRICE ◀ Timothy Taylor, Thwaites, Snowdonia Ale, Greene King IPA, Flowers Original, Weetwood Cheshire Cat, Great Drue Celtica Ö Organic Westons Vintage, Inch's Cider, Aspall. ♥ 20 **Facilities** Children welcome Children's portions Dogs allowed Garden Parking

NORTHOP
Map 15 SJ26

Stables Bar Restaurant ♥

CH7 6AB ☎ 01352 840577 📠 01352 840382
e-mail: info@soughtonhall.co.uk
dir: From A55, take A119 through Northop

This unusual free house dates from the 18th century and was created from Soughton Hall's original stable block; the magnificent main house was built as a bishop's palace, and original features like the cobbled floors and roof timbers remain intact. The selection of real ales includes Stables Bitter while diners can browse the wine shop for a bottle to accompany their meal. Lunch choices range from hot and cold light dishes and open sandwiches, with a seasonal à la carte dinner menu featuring perhaps slow-roasted pork belly with sage and onion mash, apple, black pudding and a spiced honey and orange sauce. Enjoy the gardens in summer.

Open all day all wk **Bar Meals** L served all wk 12-9.30
D served all wk 12-9.30 Av main course £8.95 food
served all day **Restaurant** L served Sun 1-3 booking
required D served all wk 7-9.30 booking required Fixed
menu price fr £12.95 Av 3 course à la carte fr £22.95
⊕ FREE HOUSE ◀ Coach House Honeypot, Dick Turpin,
Plassey Bitter, Stables Bitter. ♥ 8 **Facilities** Children
welcome Children's menu Children's portions Family
room Garden Parking Wi-fi

GWYNEDD

ABERDYFI   Map 14 SN69

PICK OF THE PUBS

Penhelig Arms Hotel & Restaurant ♥

Terrace Rd LL35 0LT
☎ 01654 767215   📠 01654 767690
e-mail: info@penheligarms.com
dir: *On A493 W of Machynlleth*

Step out of the front door of this late-18th century inn
and the tidal Dyfi estuary is across the road. Indeed, in
the summer months many customers sit on the sea
wall opposite the pub. The wood-panelled and log-fire-
warmed Fisherman's Bar, where Brains real ales, and
bar meals such as chargrilled rib-eye steaks are
served, is TV and music free. Or you might prefer a
brasserie-style meal in the award-winning waterfront
restaurant, where a strong dependency on local
suppliers results in plenty of seafood and Welsh beef
and lamb. A cosmopolitan menu offers cod and king
prawns grilled with chilli, ginger and garlic butter;
pan-fried chicken breast with creamy vegetable risotto,
pancetta and herb dressing; and mushroom, Brie,
hazelnut and cranberry Wellington with salad and
chips. The short wine list is attractively priced. Cader
Idris, the Snowdonia National Park and historic castles
are within easy reach.

Open all day all wk Closed: 25-26 Dec
Bar Meals L served all wk 12-2 (Jun-Sep 12-9)
D served all wk 6-9 booking required
Restaurant L served all wk 12-2 booking required
D served all wk 7-9 booking required ⊕ S A BRAIN & CO
LTD ◀ Brains Reverend James, Brains Bitter, Guest ale
Ŏ Stowford Press, Thatchers Katy. ♥ 20
Facilities Children welcome Children's portions Dogs
allowed Parking Wi-fi

BEDDGELERT   Map 14 SH54

Tanronnen Inn ★★★★ INN **NEW**

LL55 4YB ☎ 01766 890347   📠 01766 890606
e-mail: guestservice@tanronnen.co.uk
dir: *In village centre opposite river bridge*

Originally part of the Beddgelert estate, this stone-built
building was the stables for the passing coach trade in
1809; after conversion to a cottage, it opened as a beer
house in 1830. By the end of the 19th century, it had two
letting bedrooms and was serving meals for visitors.
Badly damaged by flooding in 1906, the shop at the back
was incorporated to provide more accommodation.
Today's inn has two attractive small bars serving
Robinsons ales, a large lounge with open fire, and a
dining room open to non-residents in which to enjoy
home-cooked meals, and attractive accommodation.

Open all day all wk **Bar Meals** L served all wk 12.30-2
D served all wk 7-8 Av main course £8
Restaurant L served all wk 12.30-2 D served all wk 7-8
Av 3 course à la carte fr £25 ⊕ FREDERIC ROBINSON
◀ Unicorn Bitter, Dizzy Blonde. **Facilities** Children
welcome Children's menu Children's portions Parking
Rooms 7

BLAENAU FFESTINIOG   Map 14 SH74

The Miners Arms

Llechwedd Slate Caverns LL41 3NB
☎ 01766 830306   📠 01766 831260
e-mail: quarrytours@aol.com
dir: *From Llandudno take A470 south. Through Betwys-y-
Coed, 16m to Blaenau Ffestiniog*

Experience the life of a Victorian slate quarryman on a
spectacular underground tour of the Llechwedd Slate
Caverns, then surface for a pint of local Purple Moose ale
at this welcoming pub, which is housed in original
buildings on the quarry site. Slate floors, open fires and
staff in Victorian costume emphasise the heritage theme
and you can expect steak and ale casserole, pork pie and
salad, various ploughman's lunches, and hot apple pie,
as well as afternoon tea with scones and cream on the
varied menu.

Open all wk 11-5 Closed: Oct-Etr **Bar Meals** L served all
wk 11-4 ⊕ FREE HOUSE ◀ Purple Moose Ales.
Facilities Children welcome Children's portions Play area
Family room Dogs allowed Garden Parking

CAERNARFON   Map 14 SH46

Black Boy Inn ★★★★ INN **NEW**

Northgate St LL55 1RW
☎ 01286 673604   📠 01286 674955
e-mail: office@black-boy-inn.com
web: www.black-boy-inn.com
dir: *A55 junct 9 onto A487, follow signs for Caernarfon.
Within town walls between castle & Victoria Dock*

Character oozes from the very fabric of this ancient inn,
one of the oldest in Wales (built 1522) and standing
within the town walls in the shadow of the unforgettable
Caernarfon Castle. Outside all gables and flower
displays; within are restful real-fire warmed, low-
ceilinged rooms sewn amidst beams and struts rescued
from old ships. On the bar beers from the likes of Purple
Moose; whilst dishes include a plate of Menai mussels
from the nearby Strait, cassoulet of duck, or Caernarfon
lob scouse, made with shin of Welsh Black beef. The well-
proportioned bedrooms are an ideal base from which to
explore the Lleyn Peninsula or catch the newly re-opened
Welsh Highland Railway.

Open all day all wk **Bar Meals** Av main course £6
food served all day **Restaurant** Fixed menu price fr £5
food served all day ⊕ FREE HOUSE ◀ Snowdonia Ale,
Hancock's, Brains Brewery The Rev. James.
Facilities Children welcome Children's menu Children's
portions Play area Garden Parking Wi-fi **Rooms** 15

LLANBEDR
Map 14 SH52

Victoria Inn ★★★★ INN ☻

LL45 2LD ☎ 01341 241213 ▤ 01341 241644
e-mail: junevicinn@aol.com
dir: On A496 between Barmouth and Harlech

Fascinating features for pub connoisseurs are the circular wooden settle, ancient stove, grandfather clock and flagged floors in the atmospheric bar of the Victoria. Home-made food is served in the lounge bar and restaurant, complemented by a range of Robinsons traditional ales. A children's play area has been incorporated into the well-kept garden, with a playhouse, slides and swings. Situated beside the River Artro, the Rhinog mountain range and the famous Roman Steps are right on the doorstep. If you would like to explore the area, there are five spacious and thoughtfully furnished bedrooms.

Open all day all wk 11-11 (Sun noon-10.30)
Bar Meals L served Mon-Fri 12-3, Sat-Sun 12-9 D served Mon-Fri 5-9 ⊕ FREDERIC ROBINSON ◖ Robinsons Best Bitter, guest bitters ♂ Stowford Press. ☻ 10
Facilities Children welcome Children's menu Children's portions Play area Dogs allowed Garden Parking **Rooms** 5

TUDWEILIOG
Map 14 SH23

Lion Hotel

LL53 8ND ☎ 01758 770244
e-mail: martlee.lion@gmail.com
dir: A487 from Caernarfon onto A499 towards Pwllheli. Right onto B4417 to Nefyn, onto Edern then onto Tudweiliog

The beach is only a mile away from this friendly inn, run by the Lee family for over 30 years. The large garden and children's play area makes the pub especially popular with the cyclists, walkers and families who flock to the Lleyn Peninsula. The bar features an extensive list of over 80 malt whiskies alongside ale from Purple Moose Brewery. A typical menu might consist of country chicken liver pâté; Pysgod Llyns crab and spinach cannelloni; and home-made Bakewell tart.

Open all wk 11-3 6-11 (summer all day)
Bar Meals L served all wk 12-2 D served all wk 6-9 ⊕ FREE HOUSE ◖ Purple Moose Brewery Ale, Guinness.
Facilities Children welcome Children's menu Children's portions Play area Family room Garden Parking

WAUNFAWR
Map 14 SH55

Snowdonia Parc Brewpub & Campsite

LL55 4AQ ☎ 01286 650409 & 650218
e-mail: info@snowdonia-park.co.uk
dir: Telephone for directions

This pub stands 400 feet above sea level at Waunfawr Station on the Welsh Highland Railway. There are steam trains on site (the building was originally the stationmaster's house), plus a micro-brewery and campsite. The foot of Mount Snowdon is four miles away. Expect home-cooked food based on locally produced and traditionally reared beef, lamb, chicken and pork. Naturally the pub serves its own Welsh Highland Bitter along with other ales. The Welsh Highland Railway Rail Ale Festival is held in mid May.

Open all day all wk 11-11 (Fri-Sat 11am-11.30pm)
Bar Meals food served all day **Restaurant** food served all day ⊕ FREE HOUSE ◖ Welsh Highland Bitter, Summer Ale, Carmensutra, Gwyrfai. **Facilities** Children welcome Children's menu Play area Family room Dogs allowed Garden Beer festival Parking Wi-fi

MONMOUTHSHIRE

ABERGAVENNY
Map 9 SO21

PICK OF THE PUBS

Clytha Arms ☻

Clytha NP7 9BW ☎ 01873 840206
e-mail: theclythaarms@tiscali.co.uk
dir: From A449/A40 junction (E of Abergavenny) follow signs for 'Old Road Abergavenny/Clytha'

Tucked away off the old road between Abergavenny and Raglan, this eye-catching old dower house stands at the edge of parkland dappled with pocket woods and the occasional folly. Enchanting views from the large garden splay across the verdant Vale of Gwent towards Blorenge Mountain and the shapely Skirrid hill, whilst the Usk Valley Walk skips along the lovely valley nearby; stately Raglan Castle is a little way up the road. The extremely characterful main bar, with old pews, tables and rustic furnishing, posters and wood-burning stove, is renowned for its range of real ales, with Wye Valley Bitter and guests from local micros accompanying great artisan ciders and perrys; the Clytha hosts the annual Welsh Cider Festival each May and the Welsh Beer, Cheese and Music festival in August. Widely feted for the exceptional gastro-pub menu created by Andrew Canning and his team, grazers can have a simple tapas, perhaps fried Penclawdd cockles and laverbread or fried cheese-stuffed peppers; or tuck in to mains like wild boar and duck cassoulet, shellfish and fish stew with hazelnut romesco sauce, or stuffed loin of lamb with sweetbreads and wild garlic. Wine lovers will appreciate the choice from over 100 bins, including a white from Monnow Valley vineyard in nearby Monmouth.

Open noon-3 6-mdnt (Fri-Sun noon-mdnt) Closed: 25 Dec, Mon L **Bar Meals** L served Tue-Sun 12.30-2.30 D served Mon-Sat 7-9.30 Av main course £10 **Restaurant** L served Tue-Sun 12.30-2.30 D served Mon-Sat 7-9.30 Fixed menu price fr £18.50 Av 3 course à la carte fr £28 ⊕ FREE HOUSE ◖ Felinfoel Double Dragon, Rhymney Bitter, 4 guest ales (300+ per year), Wye Valley Bitter ♂ Black Dragon, Ragan Perry, Clytha Perry. ☻ 12 **Facilities** Children welcome Children's menu Children's portions Play area Dogs allowed Garden Beer festival Parking Wi-fi

CHEPSTOW
Map 4 ST59

Castle View Hotel ★★★ HL

16 Bridge St NP16 5EZ
☎ 01291 620349 ▤ 01291 627397
e-mail: castleviewhotel@btconnect.com
dir: Opposite Chepstow Castle

Standing opposite Chepstow Castle and built as a private house in the 17th-century, the inn boasts walls that are five feet thick and a delightful secluded walled garden. There is a cosy bar area and small restaurant, plus comfortable accommodation. Using quality ingredients from local suppliers the menus may list moules marinière, braised lamb shank with redcurrant and rosemary jus, wild mushroom risotto, and traditional bar snacks like sandwiches, ploughman's lunches and omelettes.

Open all wk ◖ Wye Valley Real Ale, Double Dragon, Felinfoel Best Bitter ♂ Stowford Press. **Facilities** Children welcome Dogs allowed Garden Parking **Rooms** 13

LLANGYBI
Map 9 ST39

PICK OF THE PUBS

The White Hart Village Inn ◉◉ ☻

See Pick of the Pubs on opposite page

Save on hotels. Book at **theAA.com/hotel**

MONMOUTHSHIRE 585 WALES

PICK OF THE PUBS

The White Hart Village Inn

AA PUB OF THE YEAR FOR WALES 2011-2012

LLANGYBI
Map 9 ST39

NP15 1NP ☎ 01633 450258
e-mail:
enquiries@thewhitehartvillageinn.com
web: www.thewhitehartvillageinn.com
dir: *M4 junct 25 onto B4596 (Caerleon road) through town centre on High St, straight over rdbt onto Usk Rd, continue to Llangybi*

Situated in the beautiful Usk Valley, in the pretty village of Llangybi, a warm welcome awaits at this picturesque, lovingly restored historic inn where no less than eleven fireplaces can be found. Henry VIII became owner-by-default upon receiving it in the dowry of Jane Seymour, whilst arch-republican Oliver Cromwell based himself here during local Civil War campaigns. Add a priest hole, a wealth of exposed beams, precious Tudor plasterwork and a mention in a TS Eliot poem *Usk* and you've a destination to savour. Chef patron Michael Bates, formerly at Celtic Manor, is at the helm, offering village drinkers reliable beers from the likes of Tomos Watkins and Taffy Apple cider. It's the AA 2 Rosette menu that keeps visitors returning time-and-time again, though. Using fresh local produce, and combining exciting ingredients and complementary flavours, head chef Adam Whittle prepares and presents dishes with the utmost care and attention to detail. Lunchtime menus suggest Jerusalem artichoke soup followed by beetroot and chestnut open tart, whilst the broader dinner menu may include roast pigeon leg and liver with carrot, cocoa and juniper, pan-roasted monkfish tail, braised white beans, mussels and brown bread, or parsnip, truffle and button mushroom tagliatelle, finishing with lime and pineapple caramel carpaccio or white chocolate and rhubarb pannacotta with rhubarb sorbet. In summer, head outside to the extensive seating area.

Open all day 12-11 (Sun 12-10) Closed: Mon **Bar Meals** Av main course £9.95 food served all day **Restaurant** L served Tue-Sun 12-3 D served Tue-Sat 6-10 Fixed menu price fr £18 Av 3 course à la carte fr £26 ⊕ FREE HOUSE ◀ Marstons Pedigree, Tomos Watkins Cwrw Braf & Tomos Watkins Guest ♂ Taffy Apple, Thatcher's Gold, Ty-Gwyn. ♛ 10 **Facilities** Children welcome Children's menu Children's portions Garden Parking

LLANTRISANT — Map 9 ST39

PICK OF THE PUBS

The Greyhound Inn ☂

NP15 1LE
☎ 01291 672505 & 673447 📠 01291 673255
e-mail: enquiry@greyhound-inn.com
web: www.greyhound-inn.com
dir: M4 junct 24, A449 towards Monmouth, exit at
1st junct signed Usk. 2nd left for Llantrisant. Or from
Monmouth A40, A449 exit for Usk. In Usk left into Twyn
Sq follow Llantrisant signs. 2.5m under A449 bridge.
Inn on right

Established as a country inn in 1845, The Greyhound
Inn was originally a 17th-century Welsh longhouse and
part of a 400-acre farm. In the same family's hands for
the past three decades, the pub has two acres of
award-winning beautiful gardens, a four-acre paddock,
and an array of restored outbuildings. The lounges are
served by one bar with a range of real ales including a
monthly guest, and ciders such as Wales' own Gwynt y
Ddraig. Owner Nick Davies heads the kitchen team,
serving customers in the four eating areas, one of
which is a candlelit dining room. Dishes, in traditional
home-cooked style, range from old favourites such as
gammon with egg or pineapple, or fresh battered cod,
garden peas and chips to fillet of salmon in white wine,
Pernod, onions and prawn sauce, or chicken with
cream, white wine, onions, asparagus and garlic.
Finish with peach Melba or banana split.

Open all day 11-11 Closed: 25 & 31 Dec, 1 Jan, Sun eve
Bar Meals L served all wk 12-2.15 D served Mon-Sat
6-10 Av main course £9 **Restaurant** L served all wk
12-2.15 booking required D served Mon-Sat 6-10
booking required Av 3 course à la carte fr £22 ⊕ FREE
HOUSE ◀ Flowers Original & Bass, Greene King Abbot
Ale, guest ale ♂ Gwynt y Ddraig, Kingstone Press. ☂ 10
Facilities Children welcome Children's menu Family
room Dogs allowed Garden Parking Wi-fi

LLANVAIR DISCOED — Map 9 ST49

PICK OF THE PUBS

The Woodlands Tavern Country Pub & Dining ☂

NP16 6LX ☎ 01633 400313 📠 01633 400313
e-mail: info@thewoodlandstavern.co.uk
dir: 5m from Caldicot & Magor

Set at the foot of Gray Hill, close to the Roman fortress
town of Caerwent and the walking trails through
Wentwood forest, the Woodland Tavern is a friendly,
family-run village free house. Not only is the pub
popular with walkers, cyclists and fishermen looking for
refreshment with pints of Felinfoel, Butcombe and
Bevans, it draws diners from far and wide for its
modern British menu and daily chalkboard specials.
Typically, you can tuck into chicken livers with Cognac
and cream, followed by roast venison with braised red
cabbage and red wine sauce, rack of Welsh lamb with
mash and creamed leek tartlet, or line-caught Severn
sea bass with hollandaise, with white chocolate
pannacotta for pudding. Bar meals include filled
baguettes, ploughman's lunches and sausage and
mash. A patio area with seating ensures that food and
drink can be served outside in fine weather.

Open noon-3 6-mdnt Closed: 1 Jan, Sun eve, Mon
Bar Meals L served Tue-Fri 12-2, Sat 12-2.30, Sun
12-4 D served Tue-Fri 6-9, Sat 6-9.30
Restaurant L served Tue-Fri 12-2, Sat 12-2.30, Sun
12-4 booking required D served Tue-Fri 6-9, Sat 6-9.30
booking required Fixed menu price fr £9.95 ⊕ FREE
HOUSE ◀ Felinfoel, Butcombe, Bevans. ☂ 10
Facilities Children welcome Children's menu Children's
portions Dogs allowed Parking Wi-fi

PANTYGELLI — Map 9 SO31

The Crown

Old Hereford Rd NP7 7HR ☎ 01873 853314
e-mail: crown@pantygelli.com
web: www.thecrownatpantygelli.com
dir: Telephone for directions

Dating from the 16th century, this charming family-run
free house, with fine views of Skirrid Mountain, attracts
its fair share of walkers and cyclists, but it's a genuine
community pub too; charity and fund-raising events are
happy and well-supported affairs. Local real ales and
ciders accompany lunchtime baguettes and ciabattas

(gluten-free bread available upon request), while the
specials menu may tempt with smoked mackerel and
horseradish cream; halibut poached in red wine; and a
home-made caramel crème brûlée with shortbread.

Open noon-2.30 6-11 (Sat-Sun noon-3 Sun 6-10.30)
Closed: Mon L **Bar Meals** L served Tue-Sun 12-2 booking
required D served Tue-Sat 7-9 booking required
Restaurant L served Tue-Sun 12-2 booking required
D served Tue-Sat 7-9 booking required ⊕ FREE HOUSE
◀ Rhymney Best, Wye Valley HPA, Bass, Guest ales
♂ Westons Stowford Press, Gwatkin Yarlington Mill.
Facilities Children welcome Children's portions Dogs
allowed Garden Parking

PENALLT — Map 4 SO51

The Boat Inn

Lone Ln NP25 4AJ ☎ 01600 712615 📠 01600 719120
dir: From Monmouth take A466. In Redbrook, pub car park
signed. Access by foot across rail bridge over River Wye

Dating back over 360 years, this riverside pub has served
as a hostelry for quarry, mill, paper and tin mine workers,
and even had a landlord operating a ferry across the Wye
at shift times. The unspoilt slate floor is testament to the
age of the place. The excellent selection of real ales
complements the menu well, with choices ranging from
various ploughman's to lamb stifado or the charmingly-
named pan haggerty. Ideal for walkers taking the Offa's
Dyke or Wye Valley walks.

Open all wk Mon-Sat noon-11 (Sun 12-10.30 summer all
day) ⊕ FREE HOUSE ◀ Wye Valley Beers, Guest ales
♂ Stowford Press. **Facilities** Children welcome Dogs
allowed Garden Parking

The Inn at Penallt NEW

NP25 4SE ☎ 01600 772765
e-mail: enquiries@theinnatpenallt.co.uk
dir: From Monmouth take B4293 to Trellech. Up hill, in
approx 2m left signed Penallt. In village at x-roads, turn
left. Inn approx 0.3m on right

Built as a farmhouse in the 16th century, Bush Farm
started serving cider, ale and perry in the early 1800s
before becoming the Bush Inn in the 1890s. Spruced up
and renamed in 2010 by new owners Jackie and Andrew
Murphy, the pub maintains its time-honoured reputation
for serving quality local ales (Kingstone & Celt Brewery)
and ciders (Ty Gwyn), alongside good bar food. Tuck into
Usk Valley beef and vegetable stew with herb dumplings
in the bar, or Brecon venison with port and redcurrant
sauce in the restaurant.

Open Tue-Thu 6-11, Fri-Sun 12-11 winter (Tue-Fri 12-3
6-11, Sat-Sun 12-11 summer) Closed: Mon
Bar Meals L served Fri-Sun 12-2.30 D served Tue-Sat 6-9
Av main course £9.95-£15.95 **Restaurant** D served Tue-
Sat 6-9 booking required Av 3 course à la carte fr £30
⊕ FREE HOUSE ◀ Wye Valley Butty Bach, Kingstone
Brewery Classic, Wolvers Ale ♂ Ty Gwyn, Wernddu Black
Dingle, Gwatkin. **Facilities** Children welcome Children's
menu Children's portions Play area Dogs allowed Garden
Parking Wi-fi

Save on hotels. Book at **theAA.com/hotel**

MONMOUTHSHIRE 587 WALES

RAGLAN
Map 9 SO40

PICK OF THE PUBS

The Beaufort Arms Coaching Inn & Brasserie ★★★ HL ⍟ ♟

High St NP15 2DY
☎ 01291 690412 📠 01291 690935
e-mail: enquiries@beaufortraglan.co.uk
dir: *0.5m from junct of A40 & A449 Abergavenny/Monmouth*

It's not unusual to see men in full medieval armour tucking into a full Welsh breakfast in the brasserie at this former coaching inn. The Beaufort Arms has always had strong links with nearby Raglan Castle and during the Civil War Roundhead soldiers frequented the bar during the siege of 1646. Nowadays, the place is equally popular when re-enactments are held at the castle. The inn has been beautifully refurbished with many delightful design features, while holding strong to its traditional roots. A handsome display of fishing trophies dominates the country bar, where locals and visitors gather and chat over pints of Reverend James. The inn offers well-kept real ales, ciders, and Belgian and German beers. Food is served in the lounge, with its carved bar, deep leather settees, and large stone fireplace ('lifted', some say, from the castle), as well as in the private dining room and brasserie. Enjoy skilfully presented modern dishes like Bayonne ham, quail eggs and rocket and Parmesan salad to start; and mains such as treacle duck breast, creamy date parsnip and Madeira jus. All breads, pastas, desserts and ice creams are home made. The weekly-changing specials board includes fresh fish from Devon.

Open all day all wk **Bar Meals** L served Mon-Thu 12-3, Fri-Sat 12-5 D served all wk 6-9.30 **Restaurant** L served Mon-Thu 12-3, Fri-Sat 12-5, Sun 12-4 D served Mon-Sat 6-9.30, Sun 6-8.30 booking required ⊕ FREE HOUSE ◀ London Pride, Reverend James, Old Speckled Hen ⌀ Stowford Press, Thatchers Gold. ♟ 16 **Facilities** Children welcome Children's menu Children's portions Garden Parking Wi-fi **Rooms** 15

RHYD-Y-MEIRCH
Map 9 SO30

Goose and Cuckoo Inn NEW

Upper Llanover NP7 9ER ☎ 01873 880277
e-mail: gooseandcuckoo@lineone.net
dir: *From Abergavenny take A4042 towards Pontypool. Turn left after Llanover, follow signs for inn*

Located within the Brecon National Park and so popular with walkers, this friendly pub has a traditional flagstoned bar area, and wood-burning stove in a stone fireplace flanked by original wooden cupboards. So, the perfect setting for a pint of well kept Rhymney Bitter or one of the 85 single malt whiskies. Home-made, Aga-cooked food includes soups, pies, lasagnes, quiches and Sunday roasts. The beer garden, with goats, geese, ducks and chickens to amuse the children, looks towards the Malvern Hills. The pub hosts two beer festivals – May and August.

Open Mon-Thu 11.30-3 7-11 (Fri-Sun all day) Closed: Mon (ex BH) **Bar Meals** L served all wk 11.30-3 Av main course £7.50 ⊕ FREE HOUSE ◀ Rhymney Bitter, Red Stag. **Facilities** Children welcome Children's portions Family room Dogs allowed Garden Beer festival Parking **Notes** ⍟

SHIRENEWTON
Map 9 ST49

The Carpenters Arms ♟

Usk Rd NP16 6BU ☎ 01291 641231
dir: *M48 junct 2, A48 to Chepstow then A4661, B4235. Village 3m on left*

A 400-year-old traditional country pub in a wooded location in the valley of the Mounton Brook between the rivers Wye and Usk. Formerly a smithy and carpenter's shop, today's four bars have flagstone floors, open fires, church pew seating and lots of old chamber pots. Home-made food is typified by rainbow trout with sage and bacon butter; chef's steak pie; Welsh faggots, mash and mushy peas; lasagne with hand-cut chips; and, for vegetarians, a special vegetable shepherd's pie with goat's cheese mash. Traditional Sunday roasts are popular.

Open all wk Mon-Fri 12-3 5.30-mdnt (Sat all day Sun noon-4.30) **Bar Meals** L served all wk 12-2.30 D served Mon-Sat 6.30-9.30 Av main course £4.95 **Restaurant** L served all wk 12-2.30 D served Mon-Sat 6.30-9.30 Fixed menu price fr £7.95 ⊕ PUNCH TAVERNS ◀ Fuller's London Pride, Spitfire, Gem (Bath Ales) ⌀ Thatchers Traditional. **Facilities** Children welcome Children's menu Children's portions Family room Dogs allowed Parking Wi-fi

SKENFRITH
Map 9 SO42

PICK OF THE PUBS

The Bell at Skenfrith
RR ⍟ ⍟ ♟

NP7 8UH ☎ 01600 750235 📠 01600 750525
e-mail: enquiries@skenfrith.co.uk
dir: *M4 junct 24 onto A449. Exit onto A40, through tunnel & lights. At rdbt take 1st exit, right at lights onto A466 towards Hereford road. Left onto B4521 towards Abergavenny, 3m on left*

Occupying an enviable rural location on the banks of the River Monnow, this award-winning, fully restored 17th-century coaching inn boasts splendid views of Skenfrith Castle. Character oozes from the oak bar, flagstone floors, comfortable sofas and old settles, while eleven individually decorated and well-equipped bedrooms, some with four-posters, provide high quality accommodation. On draught are Wye Valley Bitter, Hereford Pale Ale, Kingstone Bitter, and Ty Gwyn local cider. The AA two-Rosette restaurant uses produce from its fully certified organic kitchen garden in its regularly changing menus, from which a good lunch could be confit Madgett's Farm duck leg with lentils and potato galette, followed by hot pot of Talgarth lamb with curly kale and carrots. For a thoroughly

satisfying three-course dinner, perhaps ham hock ravioli with spinach, tomato and poached egg; roasted monkfish wrapped in bacon with blanquette of butter beans, pointy cabbage, bacon lardons and white wine cream sauce; hot chocolate fondant with Seville orange marmalade ice cream. The award-winning wine list offers a well-chosen world selection.

Open all day Closed: last wk Jan & 1st wk Feb, Tue Nov-Mar **Bar Meals** L served all wk 12-2.30 booking required D served Mon-Sat 7-9.30, Sun 7-9 booking required Av main course £14 **Restaurant** L served all wk 12-2.30 booking required D served Mon-Sat 7-9.30, Sun 7-9 booking required Fixed menu price fr £21 Av 3 course à la carte fr £33 ⊕ FREE HOUSE ◀ Wye Valley Bitter, Hereford Pale Ale, Kingstone Bitter ⌀ Stowford Press, Local cider, Ty Gwyn. ♟ 13 **Facilities** Children welcome Children's menu Dogs allowed Garden Parking Wi-fi **Rooms** 11

TINTERN PARVA
Map 4 SO50

Fountain Inn ♟

Trellech Grange NP16 6QW ☎ 01291 689303
e-mail: fountaininntintern@btconnect.com
dir: *From M48 junct 2 follow Chepstow then A466/Tintern signs. In Tintern turn by George Hotel for Raglan. Bear right, inn at top of hill, 2m from A466*

A fire failed to destroy this fine old early 17th-century inn, and its charming character remains unspoilt. Set in the middle of lovely countryside, it enjoys views of the Wye Valley from the garden, and is close to Tintern Abbey. Expect home-cooked dishes which can be washed down with a pint of one of the many real ales or ciders such as Thatchers Gold or Spinning Dog! There is a beer festival around Easter and in September. The pub is now under new ownership.

Open all day all wk **Bar Meals** L served Tue-Sun 12-2.30 D served all wk 6-9 **Restaurant** L served Tue-Sun 12-2.30 D served all wk 6-9 ⊕ FREE HOUSE ◀ Hook Norton, Spinning Dog, Ring of Bells, Interbrew Bass, Hobgoblin, Rev James, Kingstone Classic, Cats Whiskers, Butcombe, Mayfield, Rhymney ⌀ Thatchers Gold, Broad Oak Traditional. ♟ 9 **Facilities** Children welcome Children's menu Children's portions Family room Dogs allowed Garden Beer festival Parking

TREDUNNOCK
Map 9 ST39

PICK OF THE PUBS

The Newbridge ★★★★ RR ◉ ♟

NP15 1LY ☎ 01633 451000
e-mail: newbridgeonusk@celtic-manor.com
dir: M4 junct 24 follow Newport signs. Right at Toby Carvery, B4236 to Caerleon. Right over bridge, through Caerleon to mini rdbt. Straight ahead onto Llangibby/Usk road

Set above a bend in the river in the verdant Vale of Usk, this smart residential (six en suite rooms) gastro-pub is the latest incarnation of a hostelry that has served passers by for 200 years. With medieval Usk and Roman Caerleon on the doorstep and myriad sporting opportunities locally (including golf at the Ryder Cup venue Celtic Manor, owners of the inn), the pub offers a relaxing end to a busy day. Cosy, rustic, old world fittings meld seamlessly with contemporary comforts; on summer evenings the riverside garden is a winning place to sup a glass of Reverend James and contemplate the sunset illuminating Wentwood and the beautiful Monmouthshire hills. Head chef Ian Sampson has gained an AA Rosette for his skilful and creative use of Welsh produce, resulting in a superb choice of dishes with tasters like free range saddleback ham hock cured in Welsh cider a prelude to mains such as sewin (sea trout) with lyonnaise potatoes, samphire, Penclawdd cockles and pastis beurre blanc; Preseli Blue Mountain Welsh lamb rump with wild garlic crust; or perhaps home-made local duck burger.

Open all wk 11am-mdnt **Bar Meals** L served all wk 12-2.30, River Bites menu 12-6 D served all wk 7-10 Av main course £14.95 **Restaurant** L served all wk 12-2.30, River Bites menu 12-6 D served all wk 7-10pm Fixed menu price fr £13.95 ⊕ FREE HOUSE ◄ Brains Rev James, Brains Smooth, Guest ale ♂ Taffy Apple Cider. ♟ 12 **Facilities** Children welcome Children's menu Children's portions Garden Parking **Rooms** 6

TRELLECH
Map 4 SO50

PICK OF THE PUBS

The Lion Inn

NP25 4PA ☎ 01600 860322 ▤ 01600 860060
e-mail: debs@globalnet.co.uk
web: www.lioninn.co.uk
dir: From A40 S of Monmouth take B4293, follow signs for Trellech. From M8 junct 2, straight across rdbt, 2nd left at 2nd rdbt, B4293 to Trellech

When a naval captain, presumably retired, built this former brewhouse and inn in 1580, he used ships' timbers for the main structural beams to remind himself of the sea. Now in the same hands for sixteen years, its many awards reflect everything it offers, from the real fires to the wholesome food, real ales and local ciders. The extensive menu embraces bar snacks, basket meals, ideas for small appetites and numerous

specials – one blackboard each for steaks and sauces, Thai curries, fish and the rest. Regularly featured are trio of sausages; chicken in tarragon; beef in black bean sauce; pan-fried kangaroo steak; South African game grill; Russian-style monkfish; swordfish steak; and mushroom Stroganoff. Children have plenty of favourites to choose from, while dogs are fussed over with biscuits and fresh water. The pub garden features a stream and an aviary, and the suntrap courtyard has beautiful views. Check dates for summer and winter beer festivals.

Open 12-3 6-11 (Fri-Sat noon-mdnt Sun 12-4.30 Mon eve 7-11pm Thu eve 6-mdnt) Closed: Sun eve **Bar Meals** L served Mon-Fri 12-2, Sat-Sun 12-2.30 D served Mon 7-9.30, Tue-Sat 6-9.30 booking required Av main course £10 **Restaurant** L served Mon-Fri 12-2, Sat-Sun 12-2.30 D served Mon 7-9.30, Tue-Sat 6-9.30 booking required Av 3 course à la carte fr £28 ⊕ FREE HOUSE ◄ Bath Ales, Wye Valley Butty Bach, Sharp's Cornish Coaster, Rhymney Best, Butcombe Gold. **Facilities** Children welcome Children's portions Dogs allowed Garden Beer festival Parking

USK
Map 9 SO30

The Nags Head Inn ♟

Twyn Square NP15 1BH
☎ 01291 672820 ▤ 01291 672720
e-mail: keynags@tiscali.co.uk
dir: On A472

Owned by the Key family for over 40 years, this 15th-century coaching inn overlooks the square just a short stroll from the River Usk, and boasts magnificent hanging flower baskets. The traditional bar is furnished with polished tables and chairs, and decorated with collections of horse brasses, farming tools and lanterns hanging from exposed oak beams plus a good range of beers is available. Game in season figures strongly among the speciality dishes, including whole stuffed partridge, pheasant in port, home-made rabbit pie and brace of quails.

Open all wk 10.30-2.30 5-11 Closed: 25 Dec **Bar Meals** L served all wk 11.45-1.45 D served all wk 5.30-9.30 **Restaurant** L served all wk 11.45-1.45 D served all wk 5.30-9.30 ⊕ FREE HOUSE ◄ Brains Bitter, Dark, Buckleys Best, Reverend James, Bread of Heaven, Doom Bar ♂ Stowford Press. ♟ 9 **Facilities** Children welcome Children's portions Dogs allowed Garden Parking

PICK OF THE PUBS

Raglan Arms ◉ ♟

Llandenny NP15 1DL
☎ 01291 690800 ▤ 01291 690155
e-mail: raglanarms@gmail.com
dir: From Monmouth take A449 to Raglan, left in village. From M4 take A449 exit. Signposted to Llandenny on right

Tucked away in a small, attractive village, this mid 19th-century stone-built pub puts a firm emphasis on locally sourced food and its restaurant holds an AA Rosette. Its daily-changing menu will prove easy to assimilate, with everything well chosen. Dine on mostly modern British dishes at rustic tables around the bar, where you'll find Wye Valley Bitter and Butty Bach, or in the conservatory. In summer, head for the decked area and enjoy a crab platter with a glass of real ale, cider or one of the wines by the glass including champagne. Some dishes, such as rotolo of organic pumpkin, piquillo peppers and Ragstone cheese, are Italian influenced; expect too, locally bred longhorn rib-eye of beef; Black Mountain smoked salmon; grilled Loch Fyne langoustines; and, in a category all of its own, a Middle Eastern dish called imam bayaldi, featuring spiced aubergine and tomato, a particular favourite with locals. Maybe to follow, try a delicious Llandenny damson Bakewell tart, accompanied by one of the dessert wines. A Raglan hallmark is its excellent selection of Welsh and English cheeses. Look out for the special events with tasting menus.

Open noon-2.30 6.30-9.30 (Sun noon-3) Closed: 25-27 Dec, Sun eve & Mon **Bar Meals** L served Tue-Sat 12-2.30, Sun 12-3 D served Tue-Sat 6.30-9.30 Av main course £11 **Restaurant** L served Tue-Sat 12-2.30, Sun 12-3 booking required D served Tue-Sat 6.30-9.30 booking required Av 3 course à la carte fr £25 ⊕ FREE HOUSE ◄ Wye Valley Bitter, Butty Bach, Guinness ♂ Thatchers Gold. ♟ 12 **Facilities** Children welcome Children's portions Dogs allowed Garden Parking

PEMBROKESHIRE

ABERCYCH
Map 8 SN24

Nags Head Inn

SA37 0HJ ☎ 01239 841200
dir: On B4332 (Carmarthen to Newcastle Emlyn road)

Situated at the entrance to the enchanted valley in the famous Welsh folk tales of Mabinogion, this famous old inn is the first building you see over the county boundary when crossing into Pembrokeshire from the Teifi Falls at Cenarth. In one of the out-buildings the old forge still remains where the blacksmith crafted the first horse drawn ploughs to export to America. Old Emrys ale is brewed on the premises ready for consuming in the beamed bars and riverside gardens. The fine fare includes home-made cawl with cheese and crusty bread; steak, Guinness and mushroom pie; garlic king prawns with crusty bread; and Cardigan Island crab salad.

Save on hotels. Book at theAA.com/hotel

PEMBROKESHIRE 589 WALES

Open Tue-Sun Closed: Mon **Bar Meals** L served Tue-Sun 12-2 D served Tue-Sun 6-9 **Restaurant** L served Tue-Sun 12-2 D served Tue-Sun 6-9 ⊕ FREE HOUSE ◀ Old Emrys. **Facilities** Children welcome Play area Dogs allowed Garden Parking

---

AMROTH Map 8 SN10

The New Inn

SA67 8NW ☎ 01834 812368
dir: A48 to Carmarthen, A40 to St Clears, A477 to Llanteg then left, follow road to sea front, turn left. 0.25m on left

A 16th century inn, originally a farmhouse, belonging to Amroth Castle Estate and family run for some 36 years. It has old world charm with beamed ceilings, a Flemish chimney, a flagstone floor and an inglenook fireplace. It is close to the beach with views towards Saundersfoot and Tenby from the dining room upstairs. Locally caught fish and shellfish are specialities along with Welsh beef; home-made dishes include soup, pies and curries. Enjoy food or drink outside on the large lawn complete with picnic benches.

Open all day all wk Mar-Oct 11am-11pm (Oct-Mar eve & wknds) **Bar Meals** food served all day **Restaurant** food served all day ⊕ FREE HOUSE ◀ Brains, Old Speckled Hen, Guinness, Guest ales. **Facilities** Children welcome Children's menu Children's portions Family room Dogs allowed Garden Parking

---

CAREW Map 8 SN00

Carew Inn

SA70 8SL ☎ 01646 651267
e-mail: mandy@carewinn.co.uk
dir: From A477 take A4075. Inn 400yds opp castle & Celtic cross

A traditional stone-built country inn situated opposite the Carew Celtic cross and Norman castle. Enjoy the one-mile circular walk around the castle and millpond. A good range of bar meals includes Welsh Black steak and kidney pie; chilli con carne; Thai red chicken curry; and seafood pancakes. Fruit crumble and old favourite jam roly poly feature among the puddings. Live music every Thursday night under the marquee.

Open all day all wk Mon-Sat 11am-mdnt (Sun noon-mdnt) Closed: 25 Dec ⊕ FREE HOUSE ◀ Worthington Best, SA Brains Reverend James, Guest ales. **Facilities** Children welcome Children's menu Children's portions Play area Dogs allowed Garden Parking

---

LETTERSTON Map 8 SM92

The Harp Inn

31 Haverfordwest Rd SA62 5UA
☎ 01348 840061 📄 01348 840812
e-mail: info@theharpatletterston.co.uk
dir: On A40, 10m from Haverfordwest, 4m from Fishguard ferry.

This 15th-century family-owned free house was once a working farm, as well as home to a weekly market. After remaining largely unchanged for 500 years, it is now completely up-to-date with a conservatory restaurant, where menu of freshly prepared dishes include crispy whitebait; liver and bacon casserole; hickory chicken; and prime Welsh steak. Enjoy lunch with your children (and dog) in the fenced garden.

Open all day all wk Jul-Sep (ex Sun) **Bar Meals** Av main course £9 food served all day **Restaurant** Av 3 course à la carte fr £25 ⊕ FREE HOUSE ◀ Tetleys, Greene King, Abbot Ale. **Facilities** Children welcome Children's menu Children's portions Play area Garden Parking

---

LITTLE HAVEN Map 8 SM81

St Brides Inn NEW

St Brides Rd SA62 3UN ☎ 01437 781266
e-mail: kgardham@btinternet.com
dir: From Haverfordwest take B4341 signed Broad Haven. Through Broad Haven to Little Haven

Situated in the seaside village of Little Haven in the Pembrokeshire National Park, St Brides Inn is an ideal stop for walkers on the nearby coastal path. The pub has the added attraction of an indoor ancient well, as well as a pretty floral beer garden. The menu changes with the seasons but excellent fresh fish landed locally is the big seller in summer. Children get to choose from their own menu. Look out for themed evenings throughout the year.

Open all wk 11.30-3 5.30-11.30 (all day summer) **Bar Meals** L served all wk 12-2.30 D served all wk 6-9 Av main course £10 **Restaurant** L served all wk 12-2.30 D served all wk 6-9 ⊕ MARSTONS ◀ Marstons Pedigree, Banks's Bitter. **Facilities** Children welcome Children's menu Children's portions Dogs allowed Garden

---

PICK OF THE PUBS

The Swan Inn

Point Rd SA62 3UL
☎ 01437 781880 📄 04137 781880
e-mail: enquiries@theswanlittlehaven.co.uk
dir: From Haverfordwest take B4341 (Broad Haven road). In Broad Haven follow signs for seafront & Little Haven, 0.75m

Just a few years ago The Swan was boarded up; now, thanks to Paul and Tracey Morris, it buzzes with chatter and contented diners. Perched above a rocky cove overlooking St Bride's Bay, this award-winning 200-year-old free house (AA Pub of the Year for Wales 2010-2011) dispenses well kept real ales and a decent choice of wines from the pewter-topped bar, furnished

---

with rustic old settles, polished oak tables and leather armchairs beside the fireplace. There's also an intimate dining room, with an elegant contemporary-style restaurant upstairs; cooking is modern British, with a commitment to seasonal and local produce. Choose from open sandwiches and pub favourites like pie of the day and peas, or treat yourself to the full works. A typical selection might start with grilled halloumi and sesame seeds on puff pastry; followed by whole roasted grey mullet with lemon potatoes en papillote; and finishing with marmalade and whisky bread and butter pudding with custard.

Open all day 11am-mdnt Closed: 3 Jan-18 Feb, Mar-Etr & Oct-Nov wknd only **Bar Meals** L served all wk 12-2 D served all wk 6-9 (closed Sun out of season) **Restaurant** L served all wk 12-2 booking required D served all wk 6-9 (closed Sun out of season) booking required ⊕ FREE HOUSE ◀ Worthington Best Bitter, Old Speckled Hen, Guinness, S A Brains, Penlon, Rev James. **Facilities** Children welcome Children's menu Children's portions Dogs allowed Garden Wi-fi

---

NEWPORT Map 8 SN03

Salutation Inn

Felindre Farchog, Crymych SA41 3UY
☎ 01239 820564 📄 01239 820355
e-mail: johndenley@aol.com
web: www.salutationcountryhotel.co.uk
dir: On A487 between Cardigan & Fishguard

Ideal for walkers on the coastal path, this 16th-century coaching inn is set right on the banks of the River Nevern in the heart of the Pembrokeshire Coast National Park. The oak-beamed bars are full of old world charm and country atmosphere. There is an emphasis on fresh local produce on the varied menu, including local butchers' sausages with mash and onion gravy, and fillet of haddock in butter and black pepper.

Open all day Closed: Tue in winter **Bar Meals** L served all wk 12.30-2.30 D served all wk 6.30-9 Av main course £9.50 **Restaurant** L served Sun 12.30-2.30 booking required D served Sat-Sun 7-9 booking required ⊕ FREE HOUSE ◀ Felinfoel, Brains, Local guest ales ♂ Thatchers Gold. **Facilities** Children welcome Children's menu Children's portions Dogs allowed Garden Parking

PORTHGAIN — Map 8 SM83

The Sloop Inn

SA62 5BN ☎ 01348 831449 ⌨ 01348 831388
e-mail: matthew@sloop-inn.freeserve.co.uk
dir: Take A487 NE from St David's for 6m. Left at Croesgooch for 2m to Porthgain

Possibly the most famous pub on the North Pembrokeshire Coast, The Sloop Inn is located in beautiful quarrying village of Porthgain and is especially welcome on a cold winter's day. The walls and ceilings are packed with pictures and memorabilia from nearby shipwrecks. The harbour is less than 100 metres from the door and there is a village green to the front and a large south-facing patio. With ales like Reverend James on the pump, a varied menu includes breakfasts, snacks, pub favourites, steaks and home-caught fish. The menu might offer home-made Thai chicken green curry or roast saddle of Welsh lamb stuffed with apricots, sausage meat and capers.

Open all day all wk 9.30am-11pm Closed: 25 Dec **Bar Meals** L served all wk 12-2.30 D served all wk 6-9.30 **Restaurant** L served all wk 12-2.30 D served all wk 6-9.30 ⊕ B.G. BETTERSPOONS ◀ Reverend James, Brains Draught, Felinfoel, IPA. **Facilities** Children welcome Children's menu Garden Parking

ROSEBUSH — Map 8 SN02

Tafarn Sinc

Preseli SA66 7QT ☎ 01437 532214
dir: Telephone for directions

The looming presence of this large red corrugated-iron free house stands testament to its rapid construction in 1876. Now deserted by the railway it was built to serve, this idiosyncratic establishment that refuses to be modernised boasts wood-burning stoves, a sawdust floor, and a charming garden. Set high in the Preseli Hills amid stunning scenery, it is popular with walkers, who can stoke up on traditional favourites like Preseli lamb burgers; prime Welsh sirloin steak; faggots and onion gravy; and vegetable lasagne.

Open all day noon-11 Closed: Mon (ex BH & summer) **Bar Meals** L served Tue-Sat 12-2 D served Tue-Sat 6-9 **Restaurant** L served Tue-Sat 12-2 D served Tue-Sat 6-9 ⊕ FREE HOUSE ◀ Worthington, Tafarn Sinc, Guest ale. **Facilities** Children welcome Children's menu Garden Parking

ST DAVID'S — Map 8 SM72

Farmers Arms **NEW**

14-16 Goat St SA62 6RF ☎ 01437 721666
dir: A487 to St David's. From Cross Sq in city centre take 1st left (signed Porth Clais & St Justinian) pub 100yds on right

Exposed dressed stone, beams and thick pillars characterise the inside of this village pub at the heart of Wales' smallest city. Opposite the old cross and just yards from the fabulous Cathedral, locals make a bee-line for the Gluepot bar and its wickets dispensing traditional Welsh real ales. It's popular too with visitors keen to sample good pubby fare with a local twist, such as a bowl of cawl, a hearty Welsh broth. There is a sun-trap patio and a seasonal outside bar.

Open all day all wk **Bar Meals** L served all wk 12-2.30 D served all 6-9 **Restaurant** L served all wk 12-2.30 D served all wk 6-9 ⊕ FREE HOUSE ◀ Rhymney, Hancocks, Felinfoel. **Facilities** Children welcome Children's menu Children's portions Dogs allowed Garden Wi-fi

ST DOGMAELS — Map 8 SN14

Webley Waterfront Inn & Hotel ♀

Poppit Sands SA43 3LN
☎ 01239 612085 ⌨ 01267 600000
e-mail: enquiries@webleyhotel.co.uk
dir: A484 from Carmarthen to Cardigan, then to St Dogmaels, right in village centre to Poppit Sands on B4546

With easy access to Cardigan and St Dogmaels, this long-established family business is spectacularly situated at the start of the Pembrokeshire Coast National Park. The inn offers outstanding views across the River Teifi and Poppit Sands to Cardigan Bay. Not surprisingly, local seafood and fish dominate the menu, with specialties such as seared scallops and Cardigan Bay lobster cocktail; plus crispy confit chicken wings, and pan-fried fillet of salmon with braised fennel, asparagus and hollandaise. Welsh lamb and beef comes from nearby farms.

Open all day all wk **Bar Meals** L served all wk 12-2.30 D served all wk 6-8.30 **Restaurant** D served all wk 6-9 booking required ⊕ FREE HOUSE ◀ Brains Buckleys Bitter, Worthington, Rev James, DSB, Guest ales. ♀ 8 **Facilities** Children welcome Children's menu Dogs allowed Garden Parking

SOLVA — Map 8 SM82

The Cambrian Inn ♀

Main St SA62 6UU ☎ 01437 721210 ⌨ 01437 720661
e-mail: thecambrianinn@btconnect.com
dir: 13m from Haverfordwest on A487 towards St David's

This Grade II listed inn is something of an institution in this pretty fishing village, and attracts local and returning visitors alike. Full of charm and character, a major refurbishment was completed a few years ago. A sample bar menu offers local Welsh lamb cutlets, gammon steak or Welsh sirloin steak, while the carte dinner menu offers lots of fresh fish dishes. Local and Welsh real ales are served and can be enjoyed in the outside seating area in warmer weather.

Open all day all wk **Bar Meals** food served all day **Restaurant** food served all day ⊕ FREE HOUSE ◀ Tomos Watkins OSB & Cwrw Braf/Haf, Butty Bach, Guest ales. ♀ 15 **Facilities** Children welcome Children's menu Children's portions Garden Parking

STACKPOLE — Map 8 SR99

PICK OF THE PUBS

The Stackpole Inn ♀

See Pick of the Pubs on opposite page

WOLF'S CASTLE — Map 8 SM92

The Wolfe Inn

SA62 5LS ☎ 01437 741662
dir: On A40 between Haverfordwest & Fishguard. 7m from both towns

The Wolfe, now with new owners, is an oak-beamed, stone-built property in a lovely village setting. The building has three-foot walls and despite being recently refurbished in neutral tones it still has an olde worlde feel. The bar-brasserie and restaurant comprise four interconnecting but distinctly different rooms: the Victorian Parlour, Hunters' Lodge, the Brasserie and a conservatory. There is a bar menu (perhaps Texan barbeque chicken or Chinese crispy beef) and full à la carte - roast duck with fresh orange Cointreau and ginger sauce or a mixed grill. Desserts could be lemon lush pie or strawberry trifle.

Open all wk all day in summer **Bar Meals** L served all wk 12-2.30 D served all wk 6-9 booking required **Restaurant** D served all wk 7-9 booking required ⊕ BRAINS ◀ Interbrew Worthington Bitter, guest ale. **Facilities** Children welcome Children's menu Garden Parking Wi-fi

PICK OF THE PUBS

The Stackpole Inn ♀

STACKPOLE   Map 8 SR99

nr Pembroke, SA71 5DF
☎ 01646 672324   🖹 01646 672716
e-mail: info@stackpoleinn.co.uk
web: www.stackpoleinn.co.uk
dir: *From Pembroke take B4319 & follow
signs for Stackpole, approx 4m*

This traditional inn is a walker's delight,
set in pristine gardens at the heart of the
National Trust's Stackpole estate and
close to the spectacular Pembrokeshire
coastal path. There's a rare George V post
box in the mellow stone wall outside, a
survival from the time when one of the two
original stone cottages was a post office.
Nowadays the pub offers facilities for
walkers, cyclists, fishermen and climbers,
as well as those who simply prefer to relax
and do nothing.

Once inside, you'll find a slate bar, ceiling
beams made from ash trees grown on the
estate, and a wood-burning stove set
within the stone fireplace. The pub's free
house status means that there's always a
guest beer from around the UK to
accompany three Welsh ales, a couple of
real ciders and a varied wine list.

Local produce from the surrounding
countryside and fish from the coast play a
major part in the home-cooked menu. A
lighter lunch menu offers freshly-baked
Couronne loaves with an appetising
selection of fillings that includes Welsh
brie with locally cured bacon, and tuna
with tarragon mayonnaise. Three-course
appetites might begin with creamy Welsh
blue cheese on bitter leaf salad with
pickled walnuts and poached grapes, or
smoked salmon on potato blini with herb
crème fraîche. Main course options range
from seared Welsh lamb with Moroccan
couscous and tomato jus with seasonal
vegetables; to wild sea bass fillet with
fennel and saffron risotto. Round things
off with caramelised lemon tart and
passionfruit sorbet, or creamy rice
pudding with cinnamon and apple.

Open 12-3 6-11 Closed: Sun eve (winter)
Bar Meals L served Mon-Sat 12-2, Sun
12-2.30 booking required D served all wk
6.30-9 booking required Av main course
£11 **Restaurant** L served Mon-Sat 12-2,
Sun 12-2.30 booking required

D served all wk 6.30-9 booking required
Av 3 course à la carte fr £25 ⊞ FREE
HOUSE ◼ Brains Reverend James, Double
Dragon, Best Bitter, Guest ale ○ Stowford
Press, Westons Old Rosie. ♀ 12
Facilities Children's menu Children's
portions Dogs allowed Garden Parking
Wi-fi

POWYS

BERRIEW
Map 15 SJ10

The Lion Hotel

SY21 8PQ ☎ 01686 640452 📄 01686 640604
e-mail: trudi.jones@btconnect.com
dir: 5m from Welshpool on A483, right to Berriew. In village centre next to church

Behind the black and white timbered exterior of this 17th-century family-run coaching inn lie bars and dining areas where yet more old timbers testify to its age. Menus, based on local produce, include a starter of ballotine of mackerel, potato and chive salad, coriander and lemon mayo; then mains might be loin of Welsh lamb with boulangère potatoes, or dill gnocchi with white wine cream sauce. Yoghurt pannacotta with candied orange or a selection of Welsh farmhouse cheese finish things off nicely. There is a separate bar area where you can enjoy a pint of real ale from the selection on tap including Banks, Pedigree and Old Empire.

Open all wk noon-3 5-11 (Fri-Sat noon-11 Sun noon-3 6-10.30) Bar Meals L served all wk 12-2 D served all wk 6-9 Av main course £10 Restaurant L served all wk 12-2 D served all wk 6-9 booking required Av 3 course à la carte fr £22 ⊕ MARSTONS ◀ Banks Bitter, Pedigree, Old Empire, Guest ales. Facilities Children welcome Children's portions Dogs allowed Parking Wi-fi

BRECON
Map 9 SO02

PICK OF THE PUBS

The Felin Fach Griffin
★★★★ INN ⊛⊛ ♀

Felin Fach LD3 0UB ☎ 01874 620111
e-mail: enquiries@felinfachgriffin.co.uk
dir: 4.5m N of Brecon on A470 (Brecon to Hay-on-Wye road)

This much-feted country inn exemplifies owner Charles Inkin's passion for 'the simple things, done well'. The ethos is applied to food, wines, beers and en suite bedrooms. In the bar are deep leather sofas surrounding a newspaper-strewn table and open fire. Food is served in rambling bare-floored rooms where original features, including an Aga, are teamed with tasteful modern touches. Set on the edge of the Brecon Beacons, the Griffin draws much of its ingredients from the surrounding area, while the garden keeps up a steady flow of organic produce. The all important lunchtime menu includes Gorwydd Caerphilly ploughman's with home-made soda bread and pickles, or Welsh pork and leek sausages. The freshest seafood could feature wild halibut fillet with young spring vegetables and fresh creamed morels. Other mains include rack of Herdwick lamb, shepherd's pie and carrot purée, and oak roast salmon on crushed Witchill potato and spinach. Quality draught beers, 20 wines by the glass and beer tasting with the breweries complete the experience.

Open all day all wk 11.30am-11pm (Sun 11am-10.30pm) Closed: 24-25 Dec Bar Meals L served Mon-Thu 12-2, Fri-Sun 12-2.30 & BHs booking required D served Sun-Thu 6-9, Fri-Sat 6-9.30 Restaurant L served Mon-Thu 12-2, Fri-Sun 12-2.30 & BHs booking required D served Sun-Thu 6-9, Fri-Sat 6-9.30 ⊕ FREE HOUSE ◀ Breconshire Breweries, Wye Valley Bitter, Pontypridd, Otley, Tomos Watkins ♂ Stowford Press, Ty Gwyn, Pips. ♀ 20 Facilities Children welcome Children's menu Children's portions Dogs allowed Garden Parking Rooms 7

The Old Ford Inn

Llanhamlach LD3 7YB
☎ 01874 665391 📄 01874 665391
e-mail: lynxcymru@aol.com
dir: 2.5m from Brecon on A40 towards Abergavenny

The family-run Old Ford is a 900-year-old inn set in the foothills of the Brecon Beacons, affording outstanding views over the mountains, the River Usk and the canal. There are cosy beamed bars and a cottage-style restaurant serving home-cooked food using local produce. Chef's specials might include Old Ford cow pie, with beef, vegetables and ale under a puffed pastry lid; and braised Welsh lamb shank with mint and rosemary sauce. There is a beer garden to relax in when the weather permits.

Open 12-3 6-11 Closed: 25 Dec, 3-6 months winter, Mon in winter ⊕ FREE HOUSE ◀ Worthington, Guinness. Facilities Children welcome Children's menu Children's portions Garden Parking

PICK OF THE PUBS

The Usk Inn ★★★★ INN ♀

Talybont-on-Usk LD3 7JE
☎ 01874 676251 📄 01874 676392
e-mail: stay@uskinn.co.uk
web: www.uskinn.co.uk
dir: 6m E of Brecon, just off A40 towards Abergavenny & Crickhowell

The inn was established in the 1840s, just as the Brecon to Merthyr Railway arrived. In 1878 the locomotive Hercules failed to stop at the former station opposite and crashed into the street, seriously disrupting conversations and beer consumption in the bar. These days, locals and visitors to the Brecon Beacons National Park can expect a choice of guest ales and real ciders, along with a menu of wholesome food. Start with melon with pink grapefruit sorbet,

followed by pork escalope filled with apple and black pudding and served with cider jus, or fillet of salmon with saffron and herb sauce. The Brecon to Monmouth Canal runs through the village, in some places at rooftop level, and walking, fishing or cruising on the canal is popular. Enjoy a stay in one of the en suite bedrooms; one room has a four-poster bed.

Open all day all wk 11am-11.30pm (Sun 11-10.30) Closed: 25-26 Dec eve Bar Meals L served all wk 12-2.30 Restaurant L served Sun 12-2.30 D served all wk 6.30-9.30 ⊕ FREE HOUSE ◀ Guinness, Guest ales ♂ Thatchers, Robinson. ♀ 11 Facilities Children welcome Garden Parking Rooms 10

PICK OF THE PUBS

The White Swan Inn ♀

Llanfrynach LD3 7BZ
☎ 01874 665276 📄 01874 665362
e-mail: lee.harward@hotmail.co.uk
dir: 3m E of Brecon off A40, take B4558, follow Llanfrynach signs

Set opposite the ancient church of St Brynach, this smartly-converted row of white-painted stone cottages enjoys the awesome backdrop of the Brecon Beacons. Originally a coaching inn in the 17th century, it is now an unpretentious gastro-pub with character and atmosphere, featuring stone walls, exposed oak beams, stone-flagged floors, wooden furniture and bar counter, plus log fires, leather sofas, atmospheric lighting, and a warm and cosy feel. Eat in the spacious Flagstone Restaurant, or more informally in the bar, which also offers a lighter snack menu and Brains Bitter on handpump. With imaginative menus changing monthly, enjoy crisp, honest dishes in the unpretentious gastro-pub mould, all freshly prepared using locally sourced produce, with daily fish specials listed on the chalkboard. Lunch might be a crispy Thai style spring roll with tempura battered scallops, sweet and sour apple and Thai dressing followed by traditional Welsh lamb cawl with Welsh cheese and freshly baked bread. Typical evening dishes include Chinese spiced Gressingham duck breast with spiced sweet potatoes, roast plums and sweet and sour sauce, and peppered local venison haunch with potato and celeriac mash and red wine jus. There's also a selection from the grill.

Open 11.30-3 6.30-11.30 Closed: 25-26 Dec, 1st 2wks Jan, Mon & Tue (ex summer, Dec & BH) Bar Meals L served Wed-Sat 12-2, Sun 12-2.30 D served Wed-Sun 7-9 Av main course £10.95 Restaurant L served Wed-Sat 12-2, Sun 12-2.30 D served Wed-Sun 7-9 Av 3 course à la carte fr £25 ⊕ FREE HOUSE ◀ HB, Brains SA, Brains Smooth, Guinness, Rev James. ♀ 8 Facilities Children welcome Children's menu Garden Parking

Save on hotels. Book at **theAA.com/hotel**

POWYS 593 | WALES

COEDWAY — Map 15 SJ31

The Old Hand and Diamond Inn

SY5 9AR ☎ 01743 884379 🖩 01743 884379
e-mail: moz123@aol.com
web: www.oldhandanddiamond.co.uk
dir: *9m from Shrewsbury*

On the Powys/Shropshire border and providing refreshment to travellers for hundreds of years, this 17th-century inn retains much of its original character, with exposed beams and inglenook fireplace. This is the place to enjoy a pint of local Woods ale, whilst choosing from an extensive menu that uses the best from local suppliers. Dishes might include steak and ale pie with chips and gravy or grilled gammon steak with fried egg. The beer garden has plenty of seating and a children's play area.

Open all day all wk 11am-1am **Bar Meals** L served Mon-Thu 12-2.30, Fri-Sun 12-9.30 D served Mon-Thu 6-9.30, Fri-Sun 12-9.30 **Restaurant** L served Mon-Thu 12-2.30, Fri-Sun 12-9.30 D served Mon-Thu 6-9.30, Fri-Sun 12-9.30 ⊕ FREE HOUSE ◀ Worthington, Shropshire Lad, Guest ales. **Facilities** Children welcome Children's portions Play area Dogs allowed Garden Parking

CRICKHOWELL — Map 9 SO21

PICK OF THE PUBS

The Bear Hotel ★★★ HL ⊛ ♀

Brecon Rd NP8 1BW
☎ 01873 810408 🖩 01873 811696
e-mail: bearhotel@aol.com
dir: *On A40 between Abergavenny & Brecon*

This extremely imposing inn has surveyed the heart of Crickhowell for nearly 600 years, and retains oodles of the character derived from successive generations, with a superb old bar brimming with antique furnishings on the rug-strewn floor, sheltered cobbled courtyard and memorable hanging baskets. With the lovely Usk Valley walk, nearby canal and the tops of the Black Mountains and Brecon Beacons looming large, visitor wanting peace, tranquillity and adventure seek out the comfortably appointed bedrooms, whilst the cuisine has gained an AA Rosette for the skilled chef and kitchen team. Taken in the bar or in two restaurant areas, the fare is strongly influenced by availability of local produce for which the area is widely renowned. Welsh Black beef features in several dishes (try the

home-made cottage pie), or sample roasted lamb shank on aubergine and tomato crushed new potatoes, with bread and butter pudding with rum and bananas to follow.

Open all wk 11-3 6-11 Closed: 25 Dec
Bar Meals L served all wk 12-2 D served Mon-Sat 6-10, Sun 7-9.30 **Restaurant** L served Sun 12-2 booking required ⊕ FREE HOUSE ◀ Interbrew Bass, Ruddles Best, Brains Reverend James, John Smith's. ♀ 10 **Facilities** Children welcome Children's menu Children's portions Family room Dogs allowed Garden Parking Wi-fi **Rooms** 34

PICK OF THE PUBS

Nantyffin Cider Mill Inn ♀

Brecon Rd NP8 1SG ☎ 01873 810775
e-mail: info@cidermill.co.uk
dir: *At junct of A40 & A479, 1.5m W of Crickhowell*

Tucked above the River Usk, views from the inn's garden sweep across to wooded hills beneath Llangattock Mountain and the distant Brecon Beacons, whilst behind rise the shapely summits of the secluded Black Mountains. For centuries, drovers driving cattle, sheep or geese to market stopped here to sample the home-made cider; pressing ceased in the 1960's, although excellent local cider still flies the flag at this colourwashed old cider mill where the original press, still fully usable, can be seen in the Mill Room Restaurant. Dressed stone walls, precarious beams and vast fireplace fit the scene to a tee, whilst the stunning restaurant is a destination dining favourite. Welsh produce is to the fore, with cobbler of local lamb or chargrilled dry-aged rib-eye steak hitting the spot; the specials board updates the daily catch available from local rivers and harbours, perhaps hake, leek and pancetta thermidor. Splendid beers from breweries in the Welsh Valleys, and a good bin of wines seal the deal.

Open noon-3 6-11 Closed: Mon (ex BH), Sun eve Oct-Mar **Bar Meals** L served Tue-Sun 12-2.30 D served Tue-Sun 6.30-9.30 Av main course £10 **Restaurant** L served Sun 12-2.30 booking required D served Fri-Sat 6.30-9.30 booking required Av 3 course à la carte fr £25 ⊕ FREE HOUSE ◀ Reverend James, Rhymney Best Bitter, Felinfoel Best Bitter ♂ Thatchers Gold, Green Goblin, Kingstone Press. ♀ 10 **Facilities** Children welcome Children's portions Dogs allowed Garden Parking

DYLIFE — Map 14 SN89

Star Inn

SY19 7BW ☎ 01650 521345 🖩 01650 521345
e-mail: starinn365@aol.com
dir: *Between Llanidloes & Machynlleth on mountain road*

Dating from 1640 and set at 1300 feet amid breathtaking countryside, the Star Inn is in an area favoured by Dylan Thomas and Wynford Vaughn Thomas. Red kites swoop overhead, and the magnificent Clywedog reservoir is close by. This family-run inn is the perfect setting for getting away from it all. For a more active break, fishing, golf, sailing, walking and pony trekking are just some of the activities nearby. A varied choice of wholesome pub fare and great real ales complete the picture.

Open 12-2.30 6.30-11 Closed: Mon-Fri lunch (winter) ⊕ FREE HOUSE ◀ Brains Smooth, Rev James. **Facilities** Children welcome Children's menu Children's portions Family room Dogs allowed Parking

GLADESTRY — Map 9 SO25

The Royal Oak Inn

HR5 3NR ☎ 01544 370669 & 370342
e-mail: brianhall@btinternet.com
dir: *4m W of Kington, 10m from Hay-on-Wye on B4594*

This 400-year-old inn once welcomed drovers taking store cattle from Wales to England. The huge inglenook fireplace, heavily beamed ceilings and a flagstone floor set the scene for the home-made fare served in the lounge bar/dining area, including bar snacks, soups, jacket potatoes, sandwiches and salads. A roast is served every Sunday. Offa's Dyke footpath is nearby, and there's an exhilarating four-mile walk from Kington along Hergest Ridge with its breathtaking views.

Open all day all wk Etr-Aug (Oct-Mar reduced hrs) Closed: Thu eve in winter ⊕ FREE HOUSE ◀ Brains Reverend James, Butty Bach, Worthingtons, Guest ales ♂ Stowford Press. **Facilities** Children welcome Children's portions Dogs allowed Garden Parking **Notes** ⊛

HAY-ON-WYE — Map 9 SO24

PICK OF THE PUBS

The Old Black Lion ★★★★ INN ® ♥

HR3 5AD ☎ 01497 820841 📄 01497 822960
e-mail: info@oldblacklion.co.uk
dir: In town centre

Parts of this charming whitewashed inn date from the 1300s, although structurally most of it is 17th century. It is situated close to what was known as the Lion Gate, one of the original entrances to the old walled town of Hay-on-Wye. The oak-timbered bar is furnished with scrubbed pine tables, comfy armchairs and a log-burning stove – perfect for savouring a pint of Old Black Lion Ale. The inn has a long-standing reputation for its food – witness the AA Rosette – and the pretty dining room overlooking the garden terrace is where to enjoy bar favourites of baked loin of cod with fennel, leeks and cheese sauce. In the restaurant the menu typically offers supreme of guinea fowl with spinach, sun-blushed tomatoes and Madeira sauce; and herb-crusted rack of local lamb with sweet potatoes and rosemary and port jus. Guest rooms all accommodate a live-in teddy bear. Hay, of course, has bookshops at every turn, and it is also home to a renowned annual literary festival.

Open all day all wk 8am-11pm Closed: 24-26 Dec Bar Meals L served Mon-Fri 12-2, Sat-Sun 12-2.30 D served Sun-Thu 6.30-9, Fri-Sat 6.30-9.30 Restaurant L served Mon-Fri 12-2, Sat-Sun 12-2.30 D served Sun-Thu 6.30-9, Fri-Sat 6.30-9.30 ⊕ FREE HOUSE ◀ Old Black Lion Ale, Doom Bar Ò Stowford Press. ♥ 8 Facilities Garden Parking Wi-fi Rooms 10

LLANDRINDOD WELLS — Map 9 SO06

The Bell Country Inn

Llanyre LD1 6DY ☎ 01597 823959 📄 01597 825618
e-mail: info@bellcountryinn.co.uk
dir: 1.5m NW of Llandrindod Wells on A4081

Sitting high in the hills above Llandrindod Wells, this smartly refurbished former drovers' inn is now a pleasing mix of old and new. Two bars and a restaurant serve a range of beers and seasonally changing menus. Local ingredients are used with meat coming from neighbouring farms and woodland. A meal might include seared scallops on cauliflower purée and black pudding followed by breast of Gressingham duck with honey glazed onions, minted pea purée, chateau potato and a Madeira sauce. Finish with home-made lemon tart.

Open noon-3 6-11.30 Closed: Sun eve ⊕ FREE HOUSE ◀ Guinness, Guest ales, HB. Facilities Children welcome Children's menu Children's portions Garden Parking Wi-fi

The Laughing Dog

Howey LD1 5PT ☎ 01597 822406
dir: From A483 between Builth Wells & Llandrindod Wells follow Howey signs. Pub in village centre

A traditional country pub comprising a public bar, snug, games room, restaurant and dog-friendly beer garden. The original part of the building dates back to the 17th century when it was used as a stop for drovers. Wye Valley and Wood's Parish bitters are the resident real ales, while Westons provides the ciders. Locally sourced, home-made British food is the order of the day (perhaps shoulder of Welsh lamb pot roasted with rosemary, beer and honey), but sometimes with other influences, like Indonesian roast chicken in yellow sauce; and Malaysian Basa Masak Lemak (fish in coconut sauce).

Open all wk Mon-Thurs 6-11 (Fri 5.30-11 Sat-Sun all day) Bar Meals L served Sun 12-2 D served Fri-Sat 6.30-9 Av main course £9.95 Restaurant L served Sun 12-2 booking required D served Fri-Sat 6.30-9 booking required ⊕ FREE HOUSE ◀ Wye Valley Bitter, Newman's Wolver's Ale, Celt Experience Celt Bronze, Felinfoel Double Dragon, Wood's Parish Bitter Ò Westons First Quality, Westons Traditional Scrumpy, Westons Country Perry. Facilities Children welcome Children's menu Children's portions Dogs allowed Garden

LLANFYLLIN — Map 15 SJ11

Cain Valley Hotel ★★ HL

High St SY22 5AQ ☎ 01691 648366 📄 01691 648307
e-mail: info@cainvalleyhotel.co.uk
dir: From Shrewsbury & Oswestry follow signs for Lake Vyrnwy & onto A490 to Llanfyllin. Hotel on right

This family-run, Grade II listed coaching inn dates from the 17th century, with a stunning Jacobean staircase, oak-panelled lounge bar and a heavily beamed restaurant with exposed hand-made bricks. A full bar menu is available at lunchtime and in the evening. Typical meals include grilled Welsh lamb 'double' chop with redcurrant, port and rosemary sauce; and baked salmon fillet with white wine, cream and leek sauce. The comfortable accommodation includes family rooms.

Open all day all wk 11.30am-mdnt (Sun noon-11pm) Closed: 25 Dec Bar Meals L served all wk 12-2 booking required D served all wk 7-9 booking required Restaurant D served all wk 7-9 booking required ⊕ FREE HOUSE ◀ Worthington's, Ansells Mild, Guinness. Facilities Children welcome Children's menu Children's portions Dogs allowed Parking Wi-fi Rooms 13

LLANGYNIDR — Map 9 SO11

The Coach & Horses

Cwmcrawnon Rd NP8 1LS ☎ 01874 730245
e-mail: info@coachandhorses.org
dir: A40 from Brecon to Abergavenny, 12m from Brecon. Through Bwlch, pub after bend turn right

Just two minutes' walk from the nearby canal moorings, this free house is also a popular meeting place for car club members. The car park can accommodate over 70 vehicles. Three real ales change more or less daily sourced usually from a 25-mile radius, and local spirits are available. The talented chefs prepare the likes of tempura battered squid rings with sweet chilli sauce followed by home-made beef and ale stew with horseradish dumplings, finishing with marmalade bread and butter pudding with custard. The garden has lovely views.

Open all day noon-mdnt Closed: Mon in winter Bar Meals L served all wk 12-2 booking required D served all wk 6-9 booking required Av main course £8 Restaurant L served Mon-Sat 12-2, Sun 12-3 booking required D served Sun 6-9 booking required ⊕ FREE HOUSE ◀ Guest ales Ò Stowford Press. Facilities Children welcome Children's menu Children's portions Dogs allowed Garden Beer festival Parking Wi-fi

MACHYNLLETH — Map 14 SH70

PICK OF THE PUBS

Wynnstay Hotel ♥

SY20 8AE ☎ 01654 702941 📄 01654 703884
e-mail: info@wynnstay-hotel.com
dir: At junct A487 & A489. 5m from A470

'Mach', as the locals call it, is a vibrant market town where, in the late 18th century, Sir Watcyn Williams-Wynne built his pied-à-terre. Now The Wynnstay, Herbert Arms and Unicorn Hotel (to give it its full title) it's run by Gareth Johns, a Master Chef of Great Britain, and his brother Paul. For their attractive, award-winning restaurant Gareth sources what he cooks from within 50 miles, as Welsh place names on the menu testify, but European influences are also discernable (wood-fired pizzas, for instance). Lunch then could be fillet of Aberdyfi pollack or Welsh Black rump steak; and for dinner, haunch of Marches venison; loin and slow-roast belly of Y Durn pork; or wild mushroom risotto. Drop in for tea, coffee and cakes, or a Welsh-brewed real ale in the bar, where piped music is right out, although you might hear the occasional impromptu rendition by a visiting choir.

Open all wk 12-2.30 6-11 Closed: 1wk over New Year Bar Meals Av main course £11 Restaurant L served all wk 12-2 booking required D served all wk 6.30-9 booking required Av 3 course à la carte fr £27.50 ⊕ FREE HOUSE ◀ Greene King IPA, Celt Golden, Guinness, Montys Moss. ♥ 10 Facilities Children welcome Children's portions Dogs allowed Parking

Save on hotels. Book at **theAA.com/hotel**

POWYS 595 | WALES

MONTGOMERY — Map 15 SO29

PICK OF THE PUBS

Dragon Hotel ★★ HL ⊚

SY15 6PA ☎ 01686 668359 🖹 0870 011 8227
e-mail: reception@dragonhotel.com
web: www.dragonhotel.com
dir: *A483 towards Welshpool, right onto B4386 then B4385. Behind town hall*

Husband and wife team Mark and Sue Michaels oversee the bar and kitchen respectively of this black and white timber-framed coaching inn set in the stunning Welsh Marches. Dating back to the 1600s, an unusual feature is the enclosed patio which has been created from the former coach entrance; the bar, lounge and most bedrooms include beams and masonry allegedly removed from Montgomery Castle after its destruction by Oliver Cromwell. Ales from the Montgomery Brewery, wines from the Wroxeter Roman Vineyard and whisky from the Penderyn Distillery are among the refreshments on offer. Awarded an AA Rosette for its fine food for over ten years, Sue personally oversees the preparation of ingredients in such starters as mushrooms in Shropshire Blue cheese sauce, and hot chicken and bacon roulade. Main courses may proffer a casserole of local beef in Montgomery ale, or a roast shoulder of Welsh lamb. Twenty en suite rooms make the Dragon an ideal base for touring and fishing on the Wye and the Severn.

Open all wk noon-2 6-11 **Bar Meals** L served all wk 12-2 D served all wk 7-9 Av main course £9 **Restaurant** L served all wk 12-2 booking required D served all wk 7-9 booking required Fixed menu price fr £26.25 Av 3 course à la carte fr £30 ⊕ FREE HOUSE ◀ Wood Special, Interbrew Bass, Montgomery Brew Ö Old Monty. **Facilities** Children welcome Children's menu Children's portions Dogs allowed Garden Parking Wi-fi **Rooms** 20

NEW RADNOR — Map 9 SO26

PICK OF THE PUBS

Red Lion Inn

Llanfihangel-nant-Melan LD8 2TN
☎ 01544 350220 🖹 01544 350220
e-mail: theredlioninn@yahoo.co.uk
dir: *A483 to Crossgates then right onto A44, 6m to pub. 3m W of New Radnor on A44*

Here in the wild landscape of mid-Wales is an ancient drover's inn that still provides water, though nowadays it's for hosing down muddy bikes, rather than for livestock to drink. There's a beamed lounge bar and a locals' bar offering guest real ales, two small restaurants and a sun-trap garden. Traditional and modern cookery is based on fresh, local produce, some of the most popular dishes being Welsh Black sirloin steaks, Welsh lamb and organic salmon. Other main courses include game terrine with Cognac and grape preserve; and leek, wild mushroom and chestnut gâteau. Add imaginative vegetarian dishes, a children's menu and traditional Sunday roasts. Round off with Welsh cheeses and home-made walnut bread. Welsh cream teas are served during the afternoon. Next door is St Michael's church, one of four so named encircling the burial place of the last Welsh dragon. According to legend, should anything happen to them the dragon will rise again.

Open noon-11.30 (Sun noon-7.30) Closed: Tue **Bar Meals** L served Mon-Sat 12-2, Sun 12-7.30 D served Mon-Sat 6-9, Sun 12-7.30 **Restaurant** L served Mon-Sat 12-2, Sun 12-7.30 D served Mon-Sat 6-9, Sun 12-7.30 ⊕ FREE HOUSE ◀ Guest Ales Ö Stowford Press. **Facilities** Children welcome Family room Dogs allowed Garden Parking

OLD RADNOR — Map 9 SO25

PICK OF THE PUBS

The Harp

LD8 2RH ☎ 01544 350655
e-mail: mail@harpinnradnor.co.uk
dir: *Old Radnor signed from A44 between Kington & New Radnor*

The Harp is a 15th-century Welsh longhouse, made from local stone and slate. When you open the simple wooden door you step into a cosy lounge and bars with oak beams, log fires, semi-circular wooden settles and flagstone floors. Through the windows are glorious countryside views. Two real ales from Shropshire are kept on hand-pump. When finished, the next one is ready, ensuring a huge variety during the year; the pub has run an annual mid-summer beer festival now for over five years. A change of hands in 2010 and the appointment of a new chef in 2011 signalled a serious intent by the new owners to raise the food stakes. The focus is on fresh and seasonal: when the daffs are out, for example, you can expect starters such as ale and

spring leek Welsh rarebit, or spring onion and watercress soup. Follow with slow-cooked shoulder of Welsh lamb with Victoria potato, home-cured pancetta boxty and spring greens.

Open 6-11 (Sat-Sun noon-3 6-11) Closed: Mon **Bar Meals** L served Sat-Sun 12-2.30 booking required D served Tue-Sun 6-9 booking required **Restaurant** L served Sat-Sun 12-2.30 booking required D served Tue-Sun 6-9 booking required Av 3 course à la carte fr £18.85 ⊕ FREE HOUSE ◀ Three Tuns, Wye Valley, Hobsons, Ludlow Ö Kingstone Rosie, Dunkertons, Stowford Press. **Facilities** Children welcome Children's portions Dogs allowed Garden Beer festival Parking

TALGARTH — Map 9 SO13

Castle Inn

Pengenffordd LD3 0EP
☎ 01874 711353 🖹 01874 711353
e-mail: info@thecastleinn.co.uk
dir: *4m S of Talgarth on A479*

This welcoming inn enjoys a spectacular location in the heart of the Black Mountains, in the Brecon Beacons National Park. It is named after the Iron Age hill fort that tops the hill behind it – Castell Dinas. Numerous walks and mountain bike routes begin and end at its door, making it popular with outdoor enthusiasts. With a good selection of real local ales, substantial pub food includes steaks, beef, lamb, venison swordfish and tuna cooked on hot rocks; chicken and leek pie; and vegetable chilli. Look out for the Black Mountains' Beast – a large black cat that has been seen by several customers!

Open Wed-Fri 6-11 (Sat-Sun noon-11) Closed: Mon-Tue **Bar Meals** L served Sat-Sun 12-2 D served Wed-Sun 6-9 Av main course £9.50 **Restaurant** L served Sat-Sun 12-2 D served Wed-Sun 6-9 ⊕ FREE HOUSE ◀ Butty Bach, Rhymney Bitter, Rev James, Hobby Horse, Evan Evans, Guest ales Ö Stowford Press, Thatchers Gold, Westons Vintage Cider. **Facilities** Children welcome Children's portions Garden Parking Wi-fi

PICK OF THE PUBS

The Castle Coaching Inn

TRECASTLE   MAP 9 SN82

LD3 8UH
☎ **01874 636354**   📄 **01874 636457**
e-mail:
reservations@castle-coaching-inn.co.uk
web: www.castle-coaching-inn.co.uk
dir: *On A40 W of Brecon*

Owned and run by John and Val Porter and their son Andrew, this Georgian coaching inn on the old London to Carmarthen coaching route, in the northern part of the Brecon Beacons National Park, has been carefully restored in recent years. There are lovely old fireplaces and a remarkable bow-fronted bar window, and the inn also offers a peaceful terrace and garden. An open log fire burns in the bar throughout the winter, where with a pint of one of the weekly changing real ales or a glass of wine in your hand, you may savour the pub's great atmosphere.

Some guests prefer to stay in the bar to eat, where the menu is the same as in the restaurant, but which additionally offers fresh sandwiches, ploughman's, hot filled baguettes and filled jackets. Thus in both locations there might be minestrone or leek and potato soup; smoked haddock topped with ham and tomato in Cheddar cheese sauce; and Japanese-style prawns with sweet chilli dip as starters. Main courses typically include fillet steak with melted Stilton and roasted red onions; supreme of chicken with mushroom, Gruyère and white wine sauce; Welsh lamb chops with rosemary and redcurrant sauce; steak and Guinness pie; chilli con carne with rice and garlic bread; chicken curry served with rice; pan-fried salmon with orange and tarragon; and Mediterranean vegetable bake.

Finally, desserts include favourites like Dutch apple flan; cool mint fling; banana and amaretto cheesecake; and treacle sponge pudding and custard.

Open Wed-Sun noon-3, Mon-Sat 6-11 **Bar Meals** L served Wed-Sun 12-2 D served Mon-Sat 6.30-9, Sun 7-9 Av main course £12 **Restaurant** L served Wed-Sun 12-2 D served Mon-Sat 6.30-9, Sun 7-9 🛢 FREE HOUSE ◀ Fuller's London Pride, Timothy Taylor Landlord, Spitfire, Rhymney, Evan Evans.
Facilities Children's menu Children's portions Dogs allowed Garden Parking Wi-fi

TALYBONT-ON-USK — Map 9 SO12

Star Inn

LD3 7YX ☎ **01874 676635**
e-mail: anna@starinntalybont.co.uk
dir: *6m off A40 from Brecon towards Crickhowell*

Standing where the River Caerfanell runs under the Brecon & Monmouth Canal, this unmodernised 250-year-old inn is known, indeed revered, for its huge selection of well-kept real ales and hearty bar food. Dishes are typically traditional Welsh cawl; steak and ale pie; fresh fish and chips; and Mediterranean vegetable parcels. Mondays are quiz nights, live music is Wednesdays, beer festivals are in June and October, and special events will celebrate the canal's bicentenary in 2012.

Open all wk 11.30-3 5-11 (summer Mon-Fri 11.30-11 Sat-Sun 11-11) **Bar Meals** L served Mon-Fri 12-2, Sat-Sun 12-2.30 D served all wk 6-9 **Restaurant** L served Mon-Fri 12-2, Sat-Sun 12-2.30 D served all wk 6-9 ⊕ FREE HOUSE ◖ Felinfoel Double Dragon, Theakston Old Peculier, Hancock's HB, Bullmastiff Best, Wadworth 6X, regular guest ales. **Facilities** Children welcome Children's menu Children's portions Dogs allowed Garden Beer festival

TRECASTLE — Map 9 SN82

PICK OF THE PUBS

The Castle Coaching Inn

See Pick of the Pubs on opposite page

RHONDDA CYNON TAFF

PONTYPRIDD — Map 9 ST08

Bunch of Grapes NEW

Ynysangharad Rd CF37 4DA
☎ **01443 402934** 🖷 **01443 407357**
e-mail: info@bunchofgrapes.org.uk
dir: *From A470 onto A4054 (Pentrebach Rd/Merthyr Rd) into Ynysangharad Rd*

The Bunch of Grapes backs on to one of the last remnants of the Glamorganshire canal, built in 1792. Now tastefully and sympathetically refurbished, Otley ales are among the excellent refreshments on offer at the bar. Head for the separate dining room to choose from the list of modern British dishes which uses sustainably farmed ingredients: wood pigeon and oxtail faggots, with swede and turnip purée; devilled Welsh lamb's kidneys on toasted focaccia; and chargrilled 'Breconshire' sirloin steak are some examples. If you enjoy the signature dessert of sticky toffee pudding, you can buy the butterscotch sauce from the pub's deli.

Open all day all wk **Bar Meals** Av main course £7.95 food served all day **Restaurant** L served all wk 12-2.30 D served all wk 6.30-9.30 booking required Av 3 course à la carte fr £23 ⊕ FREE HOUSE ◖ Otley O1, 6 guest ales ⚘ Gwynt y Ddraig, Blaengawney Farm. **Facilities** Children welcome Children's menu Children's portions Dogs allowed Garden Beer festival Parking

SWANSEA

LLANGENNITH — Map 8 SS49

Kings Head ★★★★ INN

SA3 1HX ☎ **01792 386212** 🖷 **01792 386477**
e-mail: info@kingsheadgower.co.uk
dir: *M4 junct 47, follow signs for Gower A483, 2nd exit at rdbt, right at lights onto B495 towards Old Walls, left at fork to Llangennith, pub on right*

Originally three 17th-century buildings, this inn retains its old beams, exposed stonework and large winter fire. Just down the road the sands of Llangennith beach stretch to Rhosilli – one of the most beautiful views in Britain. Take a stroll here before enjoying carefully tended real ales including a local brew from the Felinfoel Brewery. The Stevens family have run this pub for over 20 years and enjoy a good reputation for home-cooked food using local produce. Examples include home-made venison and blueberry pie, Penclawdd pizza (topped with laverbread, bacon and cockles), and Welsh steak and chips. Comfortable accommodation is available.

Open all day all wk 9am-11pm (Sun 9am-10.30pm) **Bar Meals** L served all wk 9am-9.30pm D served all wk 9am-9.30pm Av main course £7.75 food served all day **Restaurant** L served all wk 9am-9.30pm D served all wk 9am-9.30pm food served all day ⊕ COORS ◖ Tomos Watkins, Guinness, Rhymney. **Facilities** Children welcome Children's menu Children's portions Dogs allowed Garden Beer festival Parking **Rooms** 27

REYNOLDSTON — Map 8 SS48

King Arthur Hotel ?

Higher Green SA3 1AD
☎ **01792 390775** 🖷 **01792 391075**
e-mail: info@kingarthurhotel.co.uk
dir: *Just N of A4118 SW of Swansea*

Set opposite the green in a pretty village at the heart of the beautiful Gower Peninsula, this traditional country inn has real log fires, bare wood floors and walls decorated with nautical memorabilia. Eat in the restaurant, main bar or family room, where choices range from bar snacks such as burgers and baguettes through to pub classics including a pint of shell-on prawns; home-made lasagne; pie of the day; and sausages, mash and gravy. Enjoy the food with a choice of well kept local ales, or one of 11 wines served by the glass.

Open all day all wk Closed: 25 Dec **Bar Meals** food served all day **Restaurant** L served all wk 12-2.30 booking required D served Sun-Thu 6-9, Fri-Sat 6-9.30 booking required ⊕ FREE HOUSE ◖ Felinfoel Double Dragon, Worthington Bitter & Bass, Tomos Watkins OSB, King Arthur Ale. ? 11 **Facilities** Children welcome Children's menu Children's portions Family room Garden Parking

VALE OF GLAMORGAN

COWBRIDGE — Map 9 SS97

The Cross Inn

Church Rd, Llanblethian CF71 7JF ☎ **01446 772995**
e-mail: enquiry@crossinncowbridge.co.uk
web: www.crossinncowbridge.com
dir: *Telephone for directions*

First licensed as a coaching inn in 1671, The Cross is tucked away in a peaceful corner of the Vale of Glamorgan just a few miles from the splendid Heritage Coast. It was not long ago that father and son Liam and Arthur O'Leary took over the reins, breathing new life into it with a careful refurbishment that left all its charm intact. Fresh produce is sourced as locally as possible, for dishes such as steak and dark ale pie or pan-seared duck breast with confit of butternut squash and plum and apple compôte. Look out for the mini beer and cider festivals in April and September.

Open all day all wk 10am-11pm **Bar Meals** L served Mon-Fri 12-2.30, Sat 12-9, Sun 12-3.30 D served Mon-Fri 5.30-9, Sat 12-9, Sun 5-8.30 Av main course £8.30 **Restaurant** L served Mon-Fri 12-2.30, Sat 12-9, Sun 12-3.30 D served Mon-Fri 5.30-9, Sat 12-9, Sun 5-8.30 Av 3 course à la carte fr £21 ⊕ FREE HOUSE ◖ Hancocks HB, Wye Valley Butty Bach, Evan Evans, Crwr, Bishop's Finger, Thornbridge Jaipur ⚘ Westons, Stowford Press. **Facilities** Children welcome Children's menu Children's portions Dogs allowed Garden Beer festival Parking Wi-fi

COWBRIDGE continued

Victoria Inn

Sigingstone CF71 7LP ☎ 01446 773943
e-mail: aleary445@aol.com
dir: *Off B4270 in Sigingstone*

A much-loved village inn whose beamed interior is absolutely stuffed with photographs, prints and antiques, and whose reputation for good quality home-prepared food has spread throughout the Vale of Glamorgan. The daily breakfast, lunchtime and evening menus are extensive, with dishes including hearty roasts, slow-braised lamb shank, traditional pies and faggots, fish pancake, or a juicy steak, or beautifully fresh fish from the blackboard. Thursday is curry night. The cosy snug is the perfect place to relax and enjoy a pint.

Open all wk 9.30-3 5.30-11.30 **Bar Meals** L served 11.45-2.30 D served 5.30-9 Av main course £7.95 **Restaurant** L served 11.45-2.30 D served 5.30-9 Fixed menu price fr £7.95 ⊕ FREE HOUSE ◀ Hancocks HB, Worthington Creamflow, Wadworths 6X, Brains SA Smooth. **Facilities** Children welcome Children's menu Dogs allowed Garden Parking

---

EAST ABERTHAW   Map 9 ST06

PICK OF THE PUBS

Blue Anchor Inn

CF62 3DD ☎ 01446 750329
e-mail: blueanchor@gmail.com
dir: *From Barry take A4226, then B4265 towards Llantwit Major. Follow signs, turn left for East Aberthaw. 3m W of Cardiff Airport*

The Blue Anchor Inn has been trading almost continuously since 1380, the only break being in 2004 when a serious fire destroyed the top half of the building, forcing its closure for restoration. The grandfather of the present owners, Jeremy and Andrew Coleman, acquired this pretty, stone-built and heavily thatched inn in 1941, when he bought it from a large local estate. Inside, a warren of small rooms are separated by thick walls, low, beamed ceilings and open fires, including a large inglenook. A selection of well-kept real ales, including Wye Valley plus guests, is always on tap. An enticing range of food is offered in both the bar and the upstairs restaurant. Expect a starter such as smoked haddock fishcakes with mustard and tarragon sauce to be followed by fillet of bream with saffron fondant potato and sweet and sour peppers. A good choice is offered for Sunday lunch.

Open all day all wk 11-11 (25 Dec noon-2) **Bar Meals** L served Mon-Sat 12-2 D served Mon-Sat 6-9 Av main course £8.75 **Restaurant** L served Sun 12.30-2.30 booking required D served Mon-Sat 7-9.30 booking required Fixed menu price fr £19.75 Av 3 course à la carte fr £23 ⊕ FREE HOUSE ◀ Theakston Old Peculier, Wadworth 6X, Wye Valley Hereford Pale Ale, Brains Bitter. **Facilities** Children welcome Dogs allowed Garden Parking

---

MONKNASH   Map 9 SS97

The Plough & Harrow

CF71 7QQ ☎ 01656 890209
e-mail: info@theploughmonknash.com
dir: *M4 junct 35 take dual carriageway to Bridgend. At rdbt follow St Brides sign, then brown tourist signs. Pub 3m NW of Llantwit Major*

Set in peaceful countryside on the edge of a small village with views across the fields to the Bristol Channel, this area is great for walkers attracted to the coastline. Dating back to 1383, the low, slate-roofed building was originally built as the chapter house of a monastery, although it has been a pub for 500 years. Expect an atmospheric interior, open fires, real ciders, up to eight guest ales on tap, and home-cooked food.

Open all day all wk **Bar Meals** L served Mon-Fri 12-2.30, Sat-Sun 12-5 D served all wk 6-8.30 Av main course £8.50 **Restaurant** L served Mon-Fri 12-2.30, Sat-Sun 12-5 D served Mon-Sat 6-9 ⊕ FREE HOUSE ◀ Otley O1, Shepherd Neame Spitfire, Hereford Pale ale, Sharp's IPA, Bass, Guest ales Ŏ Happy Daze, Fiery Fox, Barnstormer. **Facilities** Children welcome Children's menu Children's portions Garden Parking

---

WREXHAM

ERBISTOCK   Map 15 SJ34

Cross Foxes ♥ NEW

Overton Bridge LL13 0DR ☎ 01978 780380
e-mail: cross.foxes@brunningandprice.co.uk
dir: *From Wrexham take A525 S. At Marchwiel take A528 signed Ellesmere to Erbistock*

Smack beside the River Dee close to the Shropshire border, this spruced-up 18th-century former coaching inn offers great river views from its raised terrace and through picture-windows in the one of the light and airy dining rooms. In typical Brunning and Price style, the interior is smart and comfortable, the choice of ales wines and spirits is impressive, and the all-day food operation is not only good value but a cut above the norm. Take potted salmon and crab, lamb shank with bubble-and-squeak and rosemary sauce, and sticky toffee pudding.

Open all day all wk Closed: 25 Dec **Bar Meals** L served Mon-Sat 12-9.30, Sun 12-9 D served Mon-Sat 12-9.30, Sun 12-9 Av main course £9.25 food served all day **Restaurant** L served Mon-Sat 12-9.30, Sun 12-9 D served Mon-Sat 12-9.30, Sun 12-9 Av 3 course à la carte fr £22.95 food served all day ⊕ BRUNNING & PRICE ◀ Brakspear, Cumberland Ale, Ringwood Bitter, Riding Bitter Ŏ Westons Scrumpy. ♥ 24 **Facilities** Children welcome Children's portions Play area Dogs allowed Garden Parking

---

GRESFORD   Map 15 SJ35

PICK OF THE PUBS

Pant-yr-Ochain ♥

Old Wrexham Rd LL12 8TY
☎ 01978 853525   🖷 01978 853505
e-mail: pant.yr.ochain@brunningandprice.co.uk
dir: *From Chester take exit for Nantwich. Holt off A483. Take 2nd left, also signed Nantwich Holt. Turn left at 'The Flash' sign. Pub 500yds on right*

There has been a building on this site since the 13th-century and today's structure originally dates from the 1530s, as you can see from the Tudor wattle and daub walls and timber in the snug. A sweeping drive lined by majestic trees leads to this 16th-century, decoratively gabled manor house overlooking a lake and award-winning gardens. The interior fulfils this initial promise, with an inglenook fireplace and a host of nooks and crannies. The bar dispenses well-kept real ales such as Snowdonia Purple Moose, with Taffy Apples cider in support. Wine lovers too will not be disappointed by having to choose between over two dozen options. A daily-changing menu may offer a starter of smoked chicken, ham hock and baby leek terrine; a light bite such as crab linguine with ginger, red chilli and coriander; and main courses such as baked gilt head bream with lemon, chilli and pine nut crust, or coq au vin with mustard mash and greens. Custard, clotted cream and ice cream are all to be found supporting desserts such as cherry Bakewell, bread and butter pudding, or apple and berry crumble.

Open all wk noon-11.30 (Sun noon-11) Closed: 25 Dec **Bar Meals** Av main course £11.50 food served all day **Restaurant** food served all day ⊕ FREE HOUSE ◀ Flowers Original, Weetwood Cheshire Cat, Brunning & Price Original, Snowdonia Purple Moose Brewery Ŏ Taffy Apples, Westons, Stowford Press, Aspall. ♥ 22 **Facilities** Children welcome Children's portions Play area Dogs allowed Garden Parking

HANMER   Map 15 SJ43

The Hanmer Arms ★★★★ INN ♥

SY13 3DE ☎ **01948 830532** 📄 **01948 830740**
e-mail: info@hanmerarms.co.uk
dir: *Between Wrexham & Whitchurch on A539, off A525*

Locals fill the beamed and wooden floored bars of this traditional free house, set beside the parish church in a peaceful, rural location on the Welsh border. The daily set dinner for two includes a glass of house wine, whilst the menu options include starters such as chicken liver pâté with toasted brioche and house chutney, followed by roast lamb rump with boulangère potatoes or fresh fillet of salmon with a champagne herb sauce. Comfortable en suite rooms make the Hanmer Arms a good touring base.

Open all day all wk **Bar Meals** L served all wk 12-2.30 D served all wk 6-9.30 Av main course £10 **Restaurant** L served Mon-Sat 12-2.30, Sun 12-9 D served all wk 6-9.30 Fixed menu price fr £16 Av 3 course à la carte fr £20 ⊕ FREE HOUSE ◀ Timothy Taylor, Adnams, Stonehouse Ò Stowford Press. ♥ 22 **Facilities** Children welcome Children's menu Children's portions Dogs allowed Garden Parking Wi-fi **Rooms** 12

LLANARMON DYFFRYN CEIRIOG   Map 15 SJ13

PICK OF THE PUBS

The Hand at Llanarmon

INN ⊛

LL20 7LD ☎ **01691 600666** 📄 **01691 600262**
e-mail: reception@thehandhotel.co.uk
dir: *Exit A5 at Chirk follow B4500 for 11m. Through Ceiriog Valley to Llanarmon D C. Pub straight ahead*

Built beside the old drovers' road from London to Anglesey, this 16th-century farmhouse was a natural stopping place for drovers and their flocks. Yet The Hand only became a fully-fledged inn as recently as the late 1950s, and it still retains its original oak beams and large fireplaces. Make the journey up the remote Ceiriog Valley, and you'll find a classic country inn with a unique dining room and 13 comfortable en suite bedrooms. Chef Grant Mulholland has built a strong reputation for superb cuisine, and the pub menu includes traditional favourites such as ploughman's with Welsh cheeses and home-made bread; as well as hot dishes like gammon, eggs and chips. Restaurant diners can expect starters like grilled red mullet with celeriac and ginger purée; followed, perhaps, by leg of Welsh lamb with cranberries and red wine. Desserts are just as inviting; try sticky date pudding, or honey and cranberry pannacotta.

Open all day all wk 11-11 (Sun 12-10.30) ⊕ FREE HOUSE ◀ Worthington Cream Flow, Guinness, Guest ale Ò Stowford Press. **Facilities** Children welcome Dogs allowed Garden Parking **Rooms** 13

PICK OF THE PUBS

West Arms ★★★★ INN ⊛⊛

See Pick of the Pubs on page 600

MARFORD   Map 15 SJ35

Trevor Arms Hotel

LL12 8TA ☎ **01244 570436** 📄 **01244 570273**
e-mail: thetrevorarmshotel@live.co.uk
dir: *Off A483 onto B5102 then right onto B5445 into Marford*

The early 19th-century coaching inn takes its name from Lord Trevor of Trevallin, who was killed in a duel; public executions, both by beheading and hanging, took place in the village. Grisly history notwithstanding, today's Trevor Arms is a charming hostelry, offering a selection of real ales and a varied menu of home cooked dishes. Starters may include chicken liver pâté or prawn cocktail; then a main course of a mixed grill; beer battered fish; or crispy Chinese glazed pork belly. Lite bites could be a duck wrap or salmon fish cakes.

Open all day all wk ⊕ HEINEKEN ◀ John Smith's, Guinness, Guest Ales. **Facilities** Children welcome Children's menu Children's portions Garden Parking

PICK OF THE PUBS

West Arms ★★★★ INN ❀❀

LLANARMON DYFFRYN CEIRIOG Map 15 SJ13

LL20 7LD
☎ 01691 600665 📄 01691 600622
e-mail: gowestarms@aol.com
web: www.thewestarms.co.uk
dir: Off A483/A5 at Chirk, take B4500 to Ceiriog Valley

The twentieth-century Prime Minister David Lloyd George described the Ceiriog Valley as 'A little piece of Heaven on Earth'. Secluded way off the beaten track in this secret valley in the shadow of the lofty, little known Berwyn Mountains is the village of Llanarmon Dyffryn Ceiriog; where once drovers gathered together their geese, sheep and cattle, now ramblers and adventurers assemble to challenge the moors and mountains. The West Arms is a direct link to those heady days; the old bridge-side inn, all gables, creepers and tall chimneys remains a favourite with visitors, and drovers would probably recognise the timeless Wayfarers Bar and memorable adjoining lounge with its vast fireplace and quirky furniture. Add the undulating stone floors, wizened beams and solid timberwork dating back 350 years and the scene is set for an idyllic break in the attractive accommodation here. World-travelled, award-winning Chef Grant Williams makes the most of the Ceiriog Valley's abundant produce, including home-grown produce from the vast hotel garden, with local trout featuring on the thoughtful menu that also draws on lamb - pan-fried fillet of Welsh lamb with a mint and rosemary crust. Other mains include breast of herb crusted chicken roasted with chorizo, leek, bacon and peas; there's also a wonderful choice of fish dishes - grilled fillet of line caught Anglesey bay sea bass with home-smoked salmon in champagne butter sauce; all come together perfectly, gaining Grant the award of two AA Rosettes. From the inn's door, superb walks thread along the valley, offering extraordinary views of the countryside that was, in the 1920s, threatened with being drowned under a reservoir to supply Warrington. The beautiful lawned gardens drift down to the bank of the lively River Ceiriog, so secure a table, and a pint of beer from Oswestry's excellent Stonehouse Brewery, and gaze upstream into the mountains.

Open all day all wk **Bar Meals** L served Mon-Fri 12-2.30, Sat-Sun 12-9 D served all wk 6.30-9 Av main course £12 **Restaurant** L served Sun 12-2.30 booking required D served all wk 7-9 Fixed menu price fr £27.95 Av 3 course à la carte fr £32.90 ⊕ FREE HOUSE ◀ Flowers IPA, Cambrian Gold, XXX Three Tuns, Guinness, Guest ales ☼ Welsh Dragon.
Facilities Children's menu Children's portions Dogs allowed Garden Parking Wi-fi **Rooms** 15

Save on hotels. Book at **theAA.com/hotel**

WREXHAM 601 WALES

How to Find a Pub in the Atlas Section

Pubs are located in the gazetteer under the name of the nearest town or village. If a pub is in a small village or rural area, it may appear under a town within five miles of its actual location. The black dots and town names shown in the atlas refer to the gazetteer location in the guide. Please use the directions in the pub entry to find the pub on foot or by car. If directions are not given, or are not clear, please telephone the pub for details.

Key to County Map

The county map shown here will help you identify the counties within each country. You can look up each county in the guide using the county names at the top of each page. Towns featured in the guide use the atlas pages and index following this map.

England

1 Bedfordshire
2 Berkshire
3 Bristol
4 Buckinghamshire
5 Cambridgeshire
6 Greater Manchester
7 Herefordshire
8 Hertfordshire
9 Leicestershire
10 Northamptonshire
11 Nottinghamshire
12 Rutland
13 Staffordshire
14 Warwickshire
15 West Midlands
16 Worcestershire

Scotland

17 City of Glasgow
18 Clackmannanshire
19 East Ayrshire
20 East Dunbartonshire
21 East Renfrewshire
22 Perth & Kinross
23 Renfrewshire
24 South Lanarkshire
25 West Dunbartonshire

Wales

26 Blaenau Gwent
27 Bridgend
28 Caerphilly
29 Denbighshire
30 Flintshire
31 Merthyr Tydfil
32 Monmouthshire
33 Neath Port Talbot
34 Newport
35 Rhondda Cynon Taff
36 Torfaen
37 Vale of Glamorgan
38 Wrexham

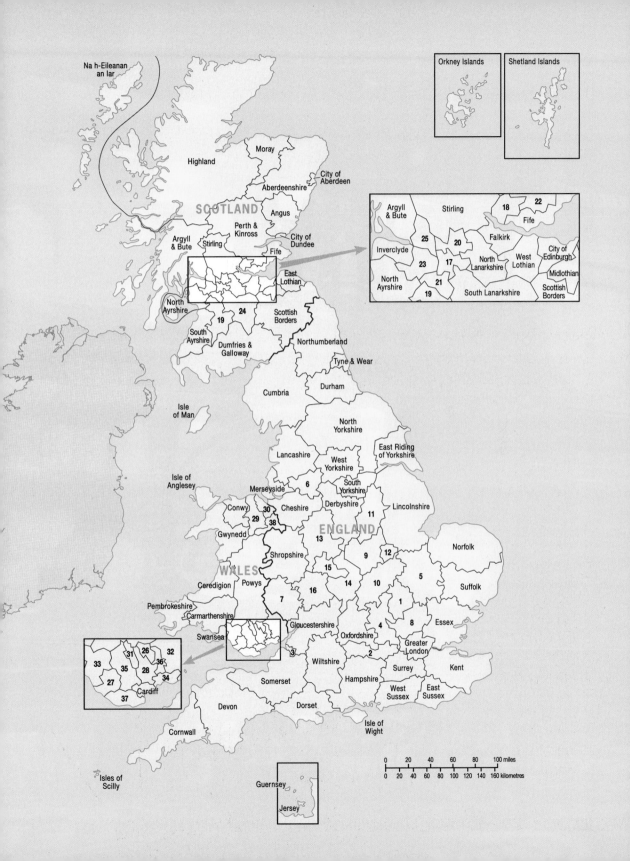

Na h-Eileanan
an Iar

Orkney Islands

Shetland Islands

Highland

Moray

Aberdeenshire

City of
Aberdeen

SCOTLAND

Angus

Perth &
Kinross

City of
Dundee

Argyll
& Bute

Stirling

Fife

Argyll
& Bute

Stirling

18

22

Fife

25

20

Falkirk

East
Lothian

Inverclyde

17

North
Lanarkshire

West
Lothian

City of
Edinburgh

North
Ayrshire

23

21

Midlothian

North
Ayrshire

19

South Lanarkshire

Scottish
Borders

19

24

South
Ayrshire

Dumfries &
Galloway

Scottish
Borders

Northumberland

Tyne & Wear

Cumbria

Durham

Isle
of Man

North
Yorkshire

Lancashire

West
Yorkshire

East Riding
of Yorkshire

Isle of
Anglesey

Merseyside

6

South
Yorkshire

Lincolnshire

Conwy

30

Cheshire

Derbyshire

29

38

ENGLAND

11

Gwynedd

13

Norfolk

Shropshire

9

12

WALES

15

5

Ceredigion

Powys

16

14

10

Suffolk

Pembrokeshire

7

Essex

Carmarthenshire

Gloucestershire

8

Swansea

4

Oxfordshire

Greater
London

3

31

26

32

Wiltshire

2

33

36

Swansea

35

28

34

Somerset

Hampshire

Surrey

Kent

27

Cardiff

West
Sussex

East
Sussex

37

Devon

Dorset

Isle of
Wight

Cornwall

Isles of
Scilly

Guernsey

Jersey

| 0 | 20 | 40 | 60 | 80 | 100 miles |

| 0 | 20 | 40 | 60 | 80 | 100 | 120 | 140 | 160 kilometres |

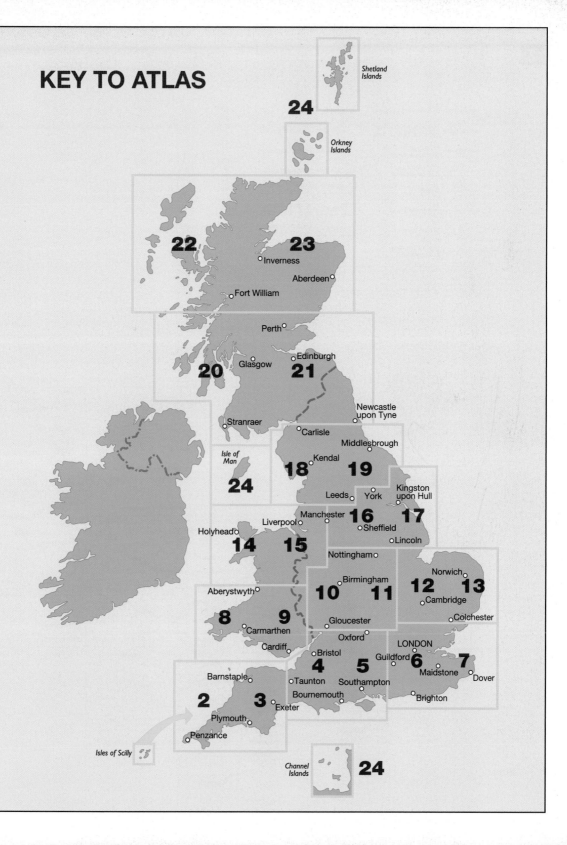

KEY TO ATLAS

Shetland Islands **24**

Orkney Islands

22 **23**
Inverness
Aberdeen
Fort William

Perth
20 Glasgow Edinburgh **21**

Stranraer
Newcastle upon Tyne
Isle of Man Carlisle
Middlesbrough
Kendal
24 **18** **19**
Leeds York Kingston upon Hull
Liverpool Manchester **16** **17**
Holyhead Sheffield
Lincoln
14 **15**
Nottingham
Aberystwyth Birmingham Norwich
10 **11** **12** **13**
Cambridge
8 **9** Gloucester Colchester
Carmarthen Oxford LONDON
Cardiff Bristol Guildford **6** **7**
4 **5** Maidstone Dover
Barnstaple Taunton Southampton Brighton
2 **3** Bournemouth
Exeter
Plymouth
Isles of Scilly Penzance

Channel Islands **24**

2

Map Legend

M6	Motorway/toll motorway
	Motorway junction full/restricted. Service area
A15	Primary route single/dual carriageway
A34	Other A road single/dual carriageway
B3400	B road
	Unclassified road
V	Vehicle ferry
C	Fast vehicle ferry or catamaran
● Oundle	Pub/Inn
● Llangybi	AA Pub of the Year
○ King's Cliffe	Town/Village name
	National boundary
ESSEX	English county name & boundary
CONWY	Welsh county name & boundary
MORAY	Scottish county name & boundary
	National Park

Lundy

Hartland Point
Hartland

Morwenstow

Kilkhampton

Bude
Bay
Bude
Stra

Widemouth Bay

Crackington
Haven
Week
St Mary

Boscastle

Tintagel

Trebarwith

Delabole
Camelford

Port Isaac
Port Gaverne

Polzeath
Pendoggett
St Tudy
St Breward
Bolventor
BODMIN
MOOR
Blisland

ISLES OF SCILLY

Bryher
New Grimsby
Tresco
St Martin's
Higher
Town
Hugh
Town
St Mary's
ISLES OF SCILLY
(ST MARY'S)
Old
Town
Middle
Town
St Agnes

SV

Harlyn
Rock
St Merryn
Padstow
Porthcothan
Wadebridge

Mawgan
Porth
St
Mawgan
Dunmere
Bodmin
St Cleer
CORNWALL

St Columb
Major
Lanivet
Dobwalls

Newquay
West
Pentire
Roche
Lanlivery
St
Keyne
Bugle
Lostwithiel
Pelynt

Cubert
Summercourt
St
Blazey
Par
Bodinnick
Perranporth
Mitchell
Polkerris
Fowey
Polperro
St Agnes
Mithian
Ladock
St
Stephen
Polruan
Marazanvose

Porthtowan
Grampound
Pentewan
Portreath
St Day
Truro
St Ewe
Mevagissey
Carnon
Downs
Malpas
Ruan
Lanihorne
Tregony
Gorran Haven
Redruth
Camborne
Ph- Philleigh
Gwithian
Feock
Veryan
Portloe
St Ives
Zennor
Lelant
Mylor Bridge
St Just-in-
Roseland
Portscatho
Hayle
Penryn
St Mawes
Ludgvan
Falmouth
St Just
Marazion
Goldsithney
Penzance
Constantine
Newlyn
Perranuthnoe
Helston
Mawnan Smith
Land's
End
St Buryan
Praa
Sands
Sennen
Mousehole
Porthleven
Gweek
Manaccan
Lamorna
Porthcurno
Treen
Gunwalloe
St Keverne
Mullion

Coverack

Lizard
Cadgwith
Lizard Point

St Ives Bay

PENZANCE

LAND'S
END

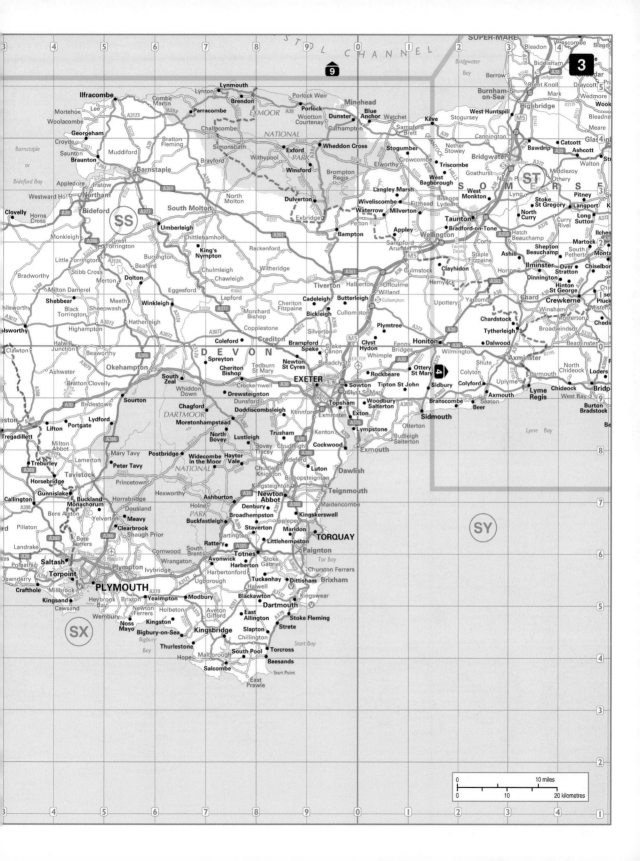

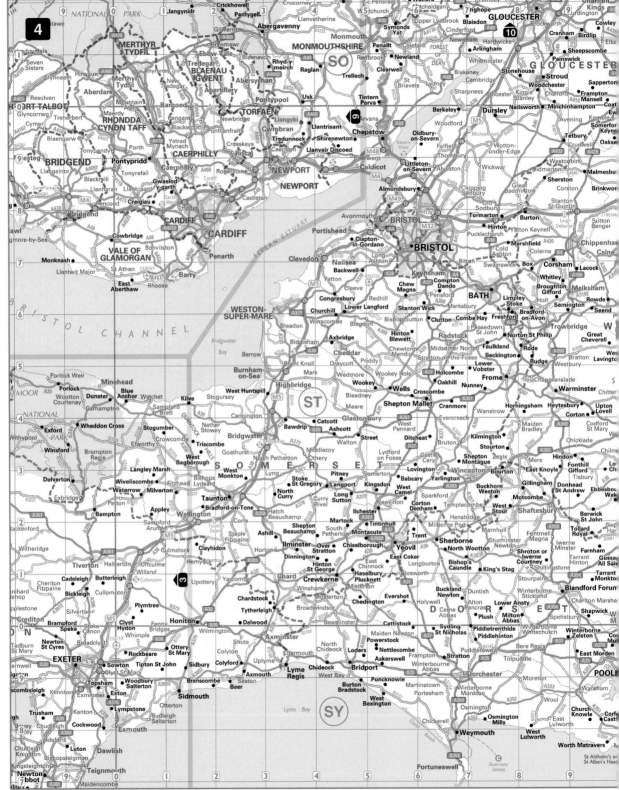

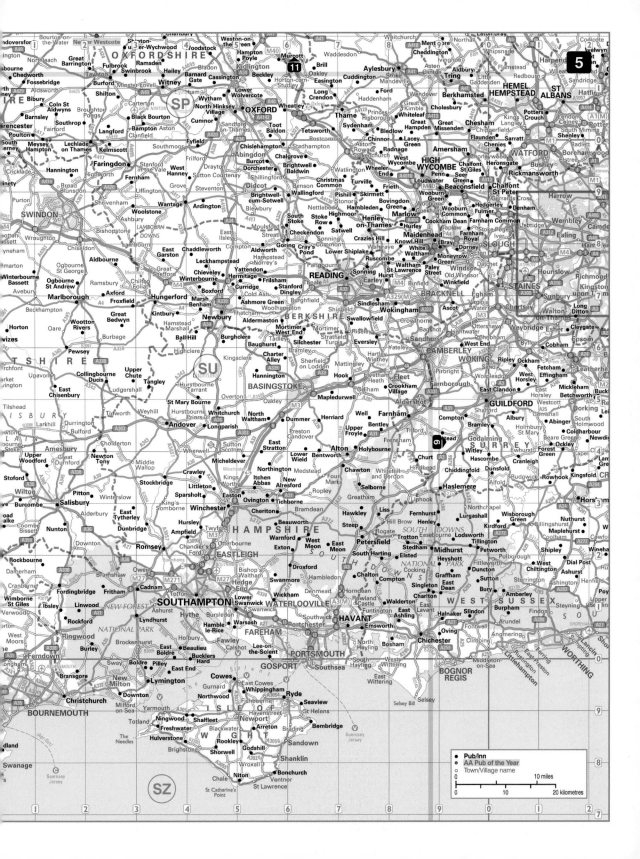

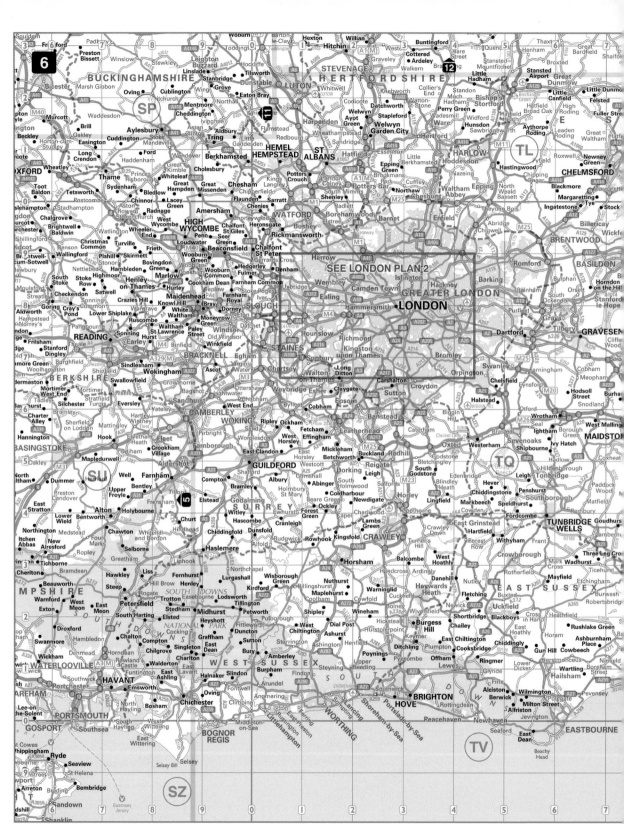

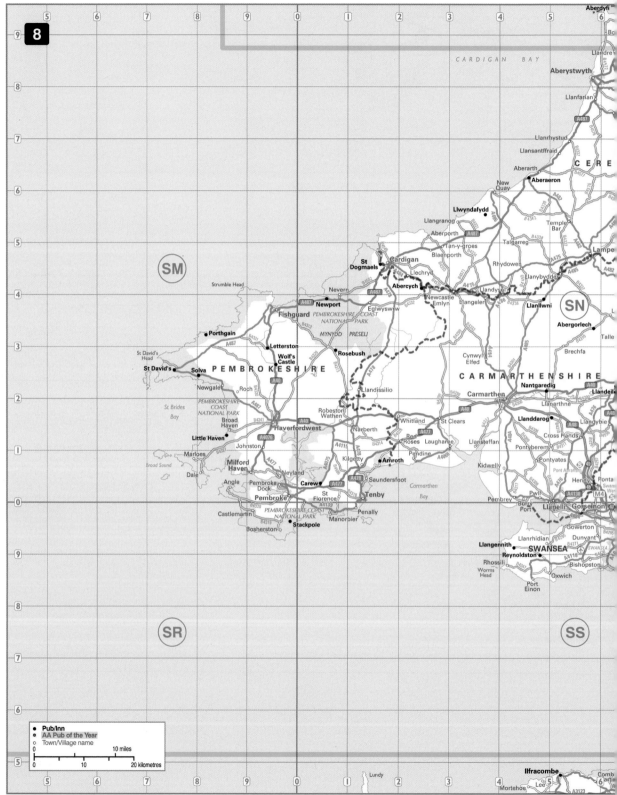

CARDIGAN BAY

Aberystwyth

CERE

SM

SN

SR

SS

Pub/Inn
AA Pub of the Year
Town/Village name
0   10 miles
0   10   20 kilometres

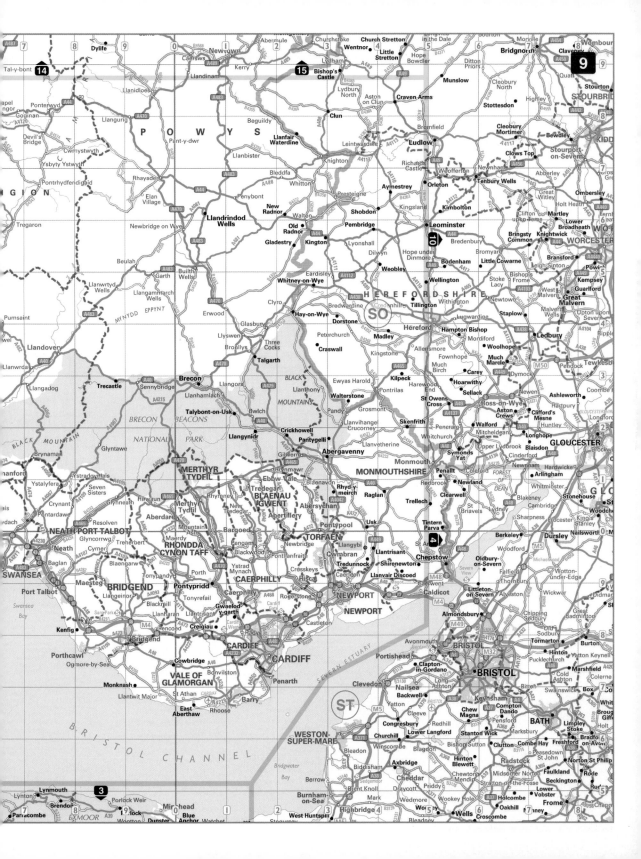

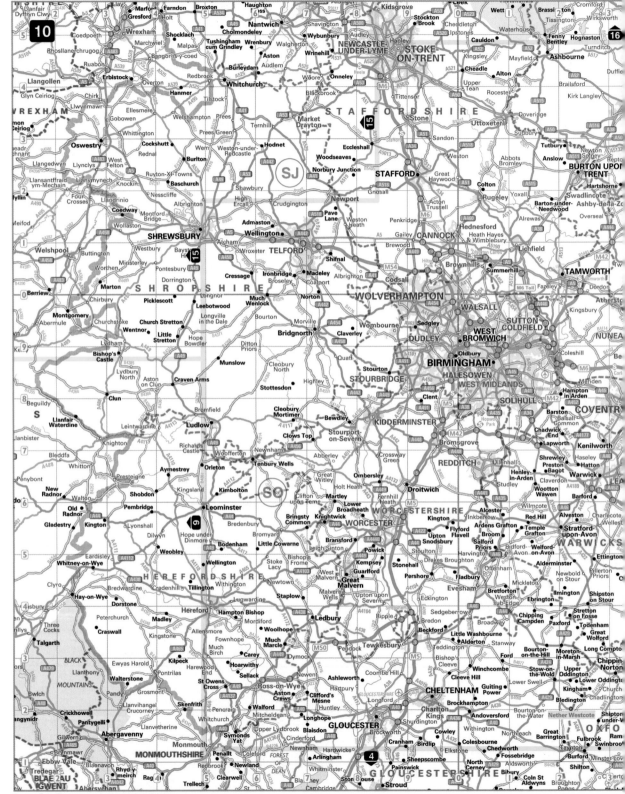

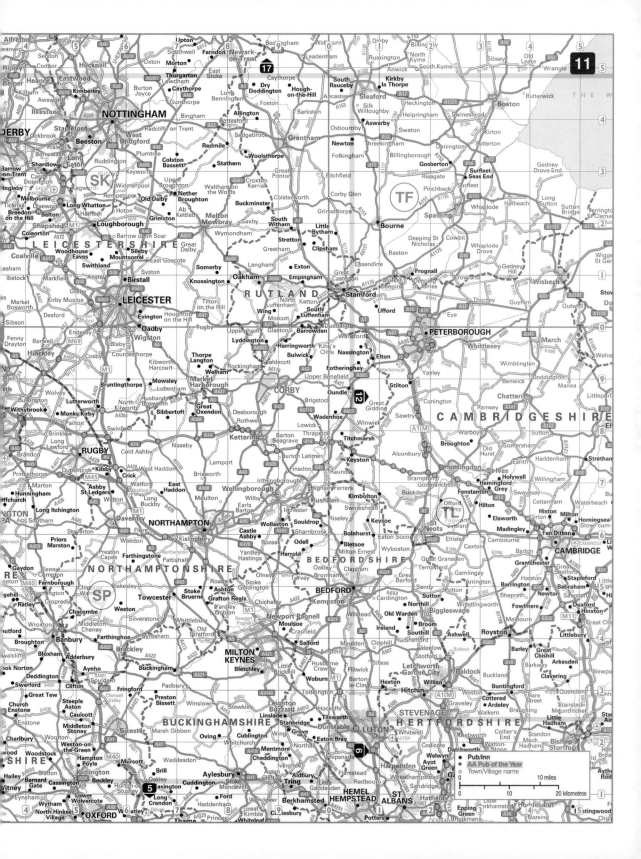

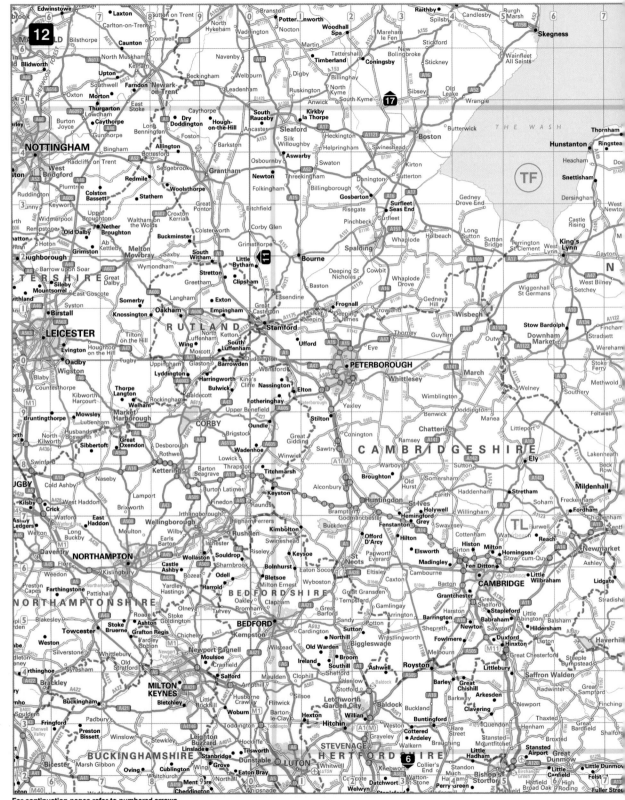

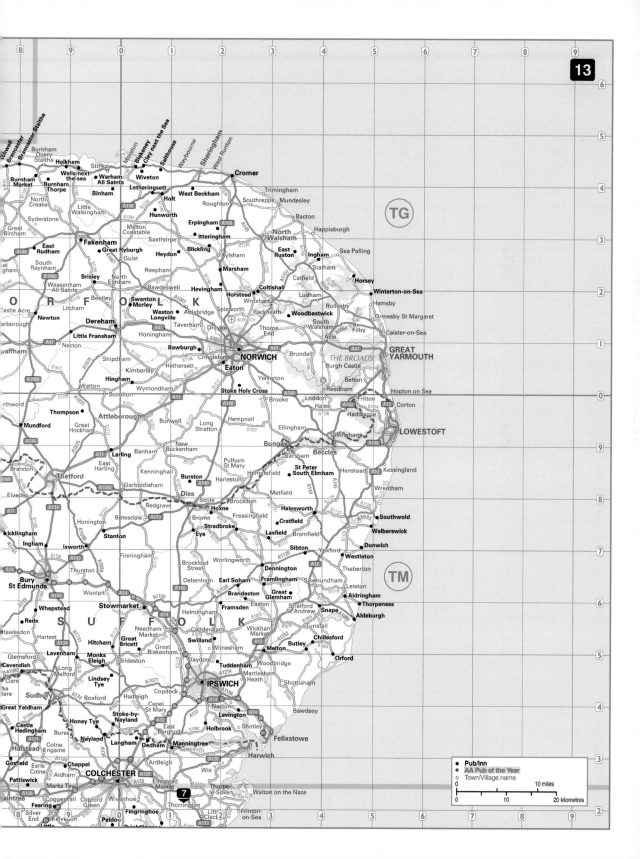

ISLE OF
ANGLESEY
Llanerchymedd

Cemaes
Amlwch

Holyhead

Llanfachraeth
Benllech

**Red
Wharf Bay**
Llangoed
Pentraeth

Llandudno
Deganwy

Rhôs-
on-Sea
Colwyn Bay
Aberg

Trearddur Bay

Holy
Island

Rhosneigr

Llangefni

Penmaenmawr

Llandudno Junction

Conwy
Llansanffraid
Glan Conwy

Llanddulas
**Llanelian-
yn-Rhôs**

**Betws-
yn-Rhôs**
Llannefy

Menai
Bridge
Bangor
Beaumaris
Llanfairfechan

Llanfair
P.G.
Llanllechid
Bethesda

Tal-y-Cain

Llanfair
Talhaiarn
Llansanna

Aberffraw
Y Felinheli

Newborough

Caernarfon
Llanrug
Llanberis
Tal-y-Bont
Langernyw

Bontnewydd

Waunfawr
Trefriw
Llanrwst

Bylchau

Llandwrog
Llanwnda

Caernarfon
Bay

Capel Curig

Betws-y-Coed

C O N W Y

He

Penygroes
Rhyd Ddu

Dolwyddelan
Penmachno

Pentrefoelas

Cerrigydrudion

Clynnog-fawr

SH
Beddgelert
S N O W D O N I A

A9

Y Ganl

Llanaelhaearn

Blaenau Ffestiniog

Prenteg
Ffestiniog

Morfa Nefyn
Nefyn
Bodfuan
PENINSULA
Tremadog
Maentwrog

Llanystumdwy
Porthmadog
Penrhyndeudraeth

N A T I O N A L
Llandde

Tudweiliog
LLEYN
Criccieth
Borth-y-Gest
Talsarnau
Trawsfynydd

A4212

Bala

Sarn
Harlech

G W Y N E D D

Llanbedrog
Pwllheli

Y Rhiw

Aberdaron

Abersoch

Llanbedr
Dyffryn Ardudwy

Ganllwyd
P A R K

Llanuwchllyn

Llanw

Bardsey
Island

Tal-y-bont

Barmouth
Fairbourne

Dolgellau
Dinas-Mawddwy

Mallwyd
Llangad

Llwyngwril

Cemmaes
Road
Corris
Llanbrynmair

Bryncrug

Tywyn
Pennal
Machynlleth
Carno

SN
Aberdyfi
Dylife

Borth
Tal-y-bont

Llandre
Llanidloes

CARDIGAN BAY
Aberystwyth
Capel
Bangor
Ponterwyd

• Pub/Inn
◉ AA Pub of the Year
○ Town/Village name

0 ────────── 10 miles
0 ───── 10 ───── 20 kilometres

For continuation pages refer to numbered arrows

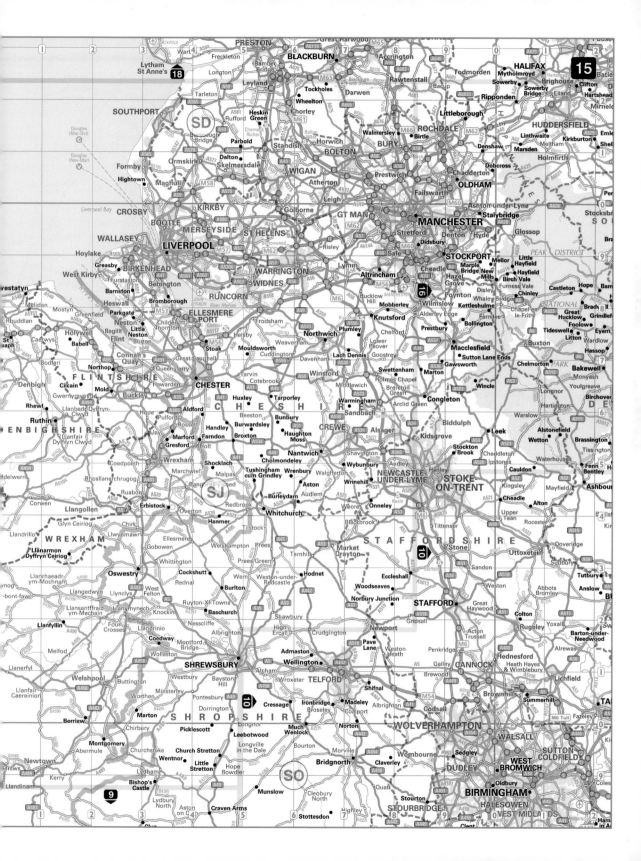

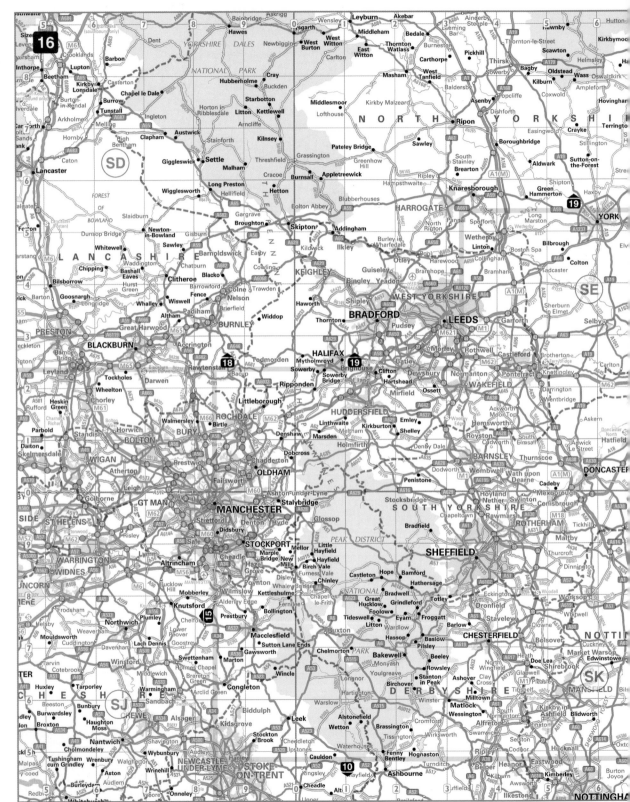

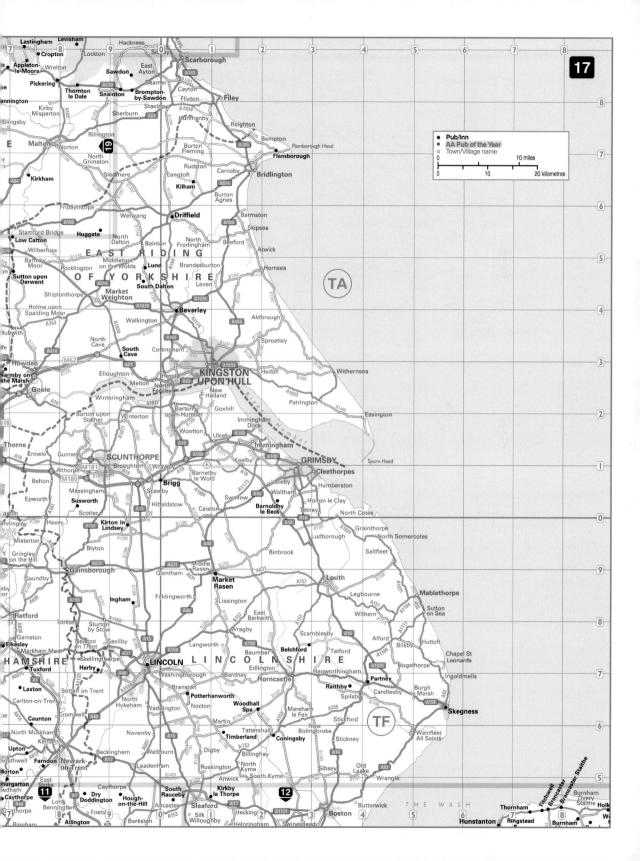

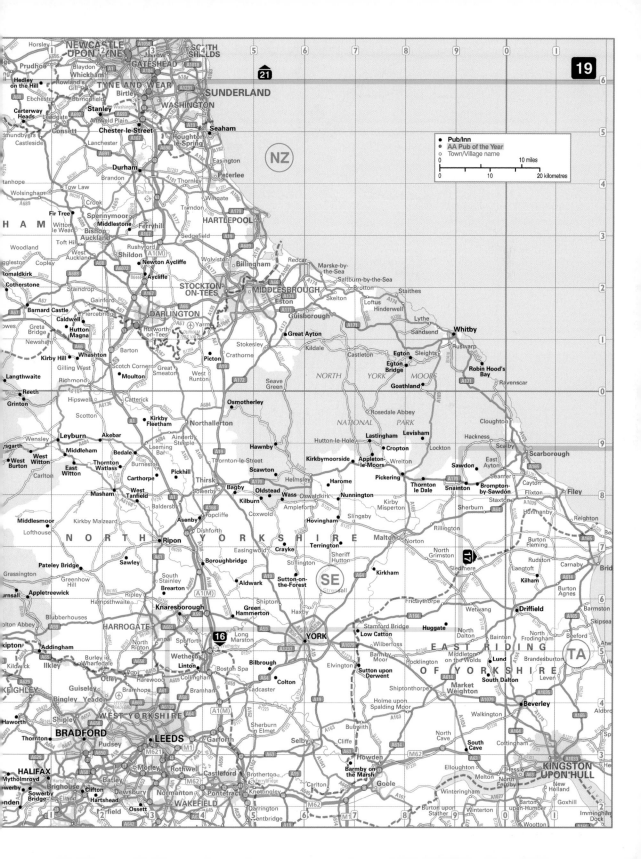

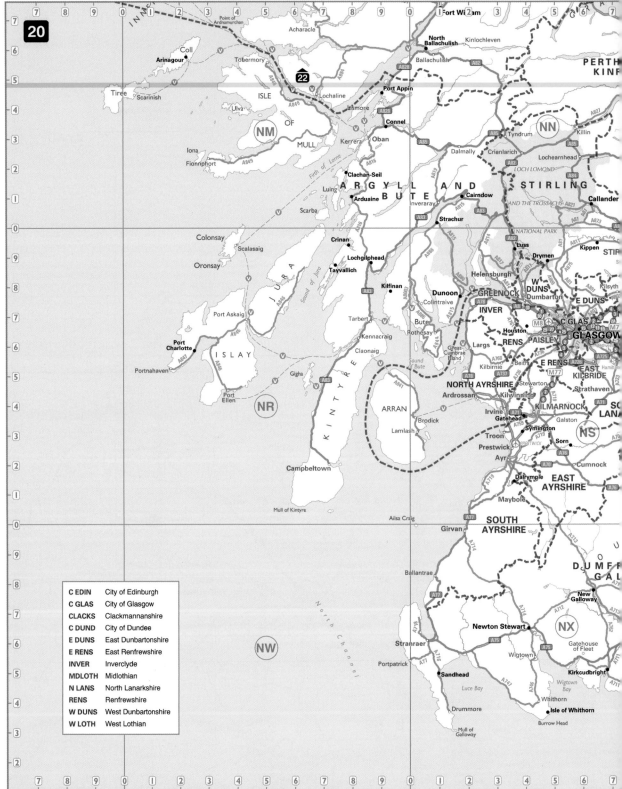

20

22

C EDIN   City of Edinburgh
C GLAS   City of Glasgow
CLACKS   Clackmannanshire
C DUND   City of Dundee
E DUNS   East Dunbartonshire
E RENS   East Renfrewshire
INVER   Inverclyde
MDLOTH   Midlothian
N LANS   North Lanarkshire
RENS   Renfrewshire
W DUNS   West Dunbartonshire
W LOTH   West Lothian

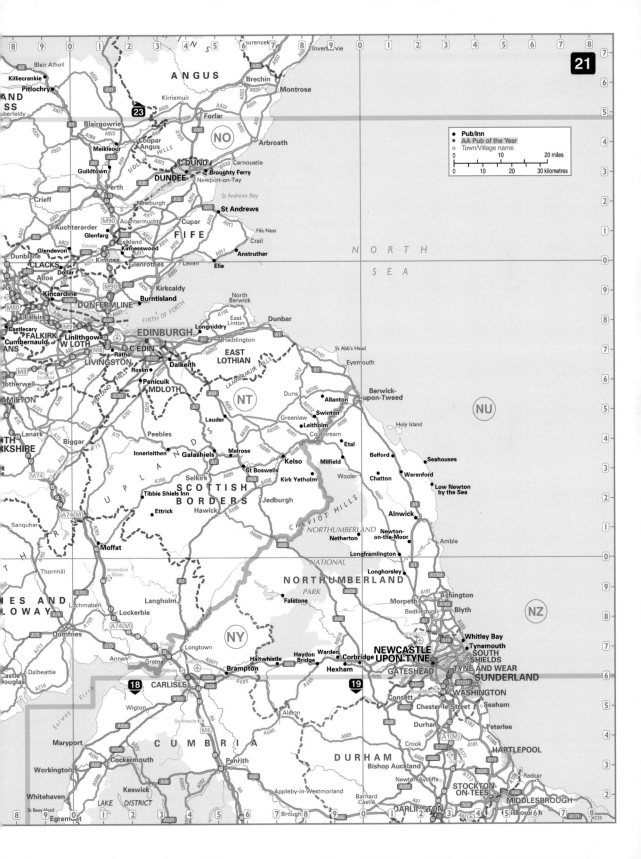

Cape Wrath

Rudha Rhobhanais
(Butt of Lewis)
Port Nis
(Port of Ness)

Cellar
Head

LEWIS

Handa Island
Scourie

Kylesku

A894

NA

A857

A858

Great
Bernera

Carlabhagh
(Carloway)

OF

Tiumpan
Head

NB

A837

Inchnadamp

Lochinver

A858

Steornabhagh
(Stornoway)

STORNOWAY

A857

A859

A858

Scarp

ISLE

NA H-EILEANAN
AN IAR

Achiltibuie

A835

Taransay

Tairbeart
(Tarbert)

Scalpay

Gruinard
Bay

Ullapool

A832

HARRIS

Pabbay

A859

Boreray

Berneray

A865

NORTH UIST

Loch nam Madadh
(Lochmaddy)

Ronay

THE LITTLE MINCH

Uig

A855

A87

Stein

Gairloch

Badachro

Kinlochewe

A832

Torridon

Shieldaig

NG

A896

Achnasheen

HIGHLANDS

A832

A890

Benbecula

A865

Wiay

Dunvegan

ISLE

A863

Portree

Raasay

Inner Sound

Plockton

A890

Cannich

WEST

NF

SOUTH
UIST

A865

OF

A87

Carbost

Drynoch

Scalpay

Kyle of
Lochalsh

A87

A87

SKYE

Loch Baghasdail
(Lochboisdale)

Eriskay

Soay

A851

Isleornsay

A87

NORTH

Invergarry

A82

A887

BARRA

A888

Canna

Cuillin Sound

Ardvasar

Sound of Sleat

Inverie

Bàgh a Chaisteil
(Castlebay)

Rùm

Mallaig

Sandray

Eigg

A830

Spean
Bridge

A82

Mingulay

Muck

A861

A830

Fort William

INNER HEBRIDES

Point of
Ardnamurchan

Acharacle

NM

North
Ballachulish

Kinlochleven

Coll

Arinagour

Tobermory

Ballachulish

A82

A828

NL

A884

20

Tiree

Scarinish

ISLE

Lochaline

A849

Port Appin

A828

Ulva

Lismore

Connel

OF

Kerrera

Oban

A85

Iona

Dalmally

Fionnphort

A849

MULL

A816

Crianlaric

A85

For continuation pages refer to numbered arrows

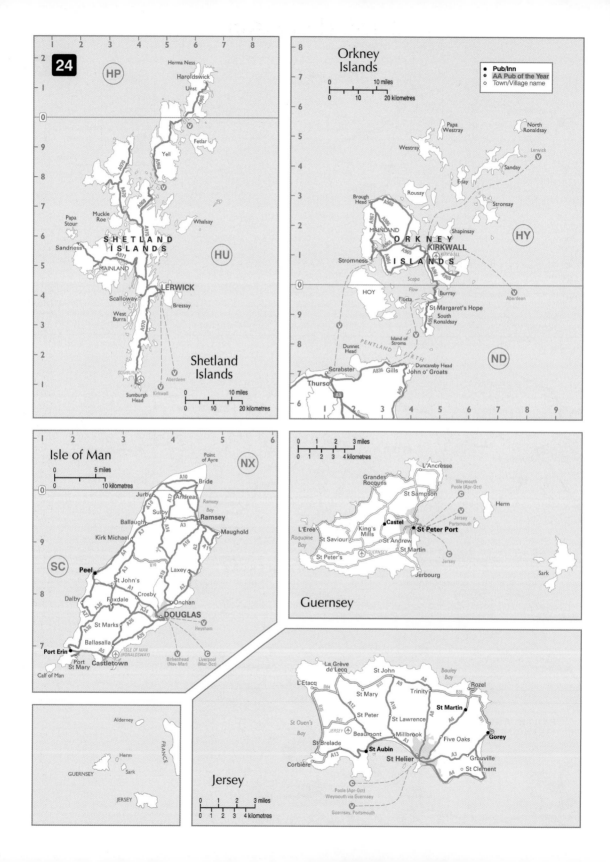

24

HP

Herma Ness
Haroldswick
Unst
A968

Fetlar

Yell
A968
A970
A968

Whalsay
Muckle Roe
Papa Stour
SHETLAND
ISLANDS
A971
Sandness
HU
MAINLAND
A970
Scalloway
LERWICK
Bressay
West Burra
A970

SUMBURGH
Sumburgh Head
Aberdeen
Kirkwall

Shetland Islands

10 miles
20 kilometres

Orkney Islands

- ● Pub/Inn
- ● AA Pub of the Year
- ○ Town/Village name

10 miles
20 kilometres

Papa Westray
North Ronaldsay
Westray
Sanday
Lerwick
Eday
Stronsay
Rousay
Brough Head
A966
Shapinsay
A967
HY
MAINLAND
ORKNEY
A986
KIRKWALL
A965
Stromness
ISLANDS
A964
A961
A960

Scapa
Flow
HOY
Burray
Flotta
St Margaret's Hope
South Ronaldsay
A961

Island of Stroma
PENTLAND FIRTH
Dunnet Head
Duncansby Head
John o' Groats
Scrabster
A836
Gills
Thurso
A9
Aberdeen
ND

Isle of Man

5 miles
10 miles

Point of Ayre
NX
A10
Bride
Jurby
A17
Andreas
Ramsey Bay
Sulby
A18
Ballaugh
A3
Ramsey
Kirk Michael
A14
A3
Maughold
A4
A18
A2
A15
SC
Peel
B10
Laxey
A1
St John's
A2
Dalby
Foxdale
Crosby
Onchan
A3
A24
DOUGLAS
St Marks
A25
A26
Heysham
A36
A5
Ballasalla
ISLE OF MAN (RONALDSWAY)
Port Erin
Castletown
Birkenhead (Nov-Mar)
Port St Mary
Liverpool (Mar-Oct)
Calf of Man

Guernsey

3 miles
4 kilometres

L'Ancresse
Grandes Rocques
St Sampson
Weymouth Poole (Apr-Oct)
Herm
L'Erée
King's Mills
Castel
St Peter Port
Jersey Portsmouth
Roquaine Bay
St Saviour
St Andrew
St Peter's
GUERNSEY
St Martin
Jersey
Jerbourg
Sark

Jersey

Alderney
Herm
FRANCE
GUERNSEY
Sark
JERSEY

La Grève de Lecq
St John
Bouley Bay
Rozel
L'Etacq
B84
B33
A9
A8
St Mary
Trinity
B31
A12
St Peter
A10
St Lawrence
St Martin
A8
St Ouen's Bay
B41
JERSEY
Beaumont
Millbrook
Five Oaks
Gorey
St Brelade
St Aubin
St Helier
A3
Grouville
Corbière
A13
A4
St Clement
Poole (Apr-Oct)
Weymouth via Guernsey
Guernsey, Portsmouth

3 miles
4 kilometres

Central London

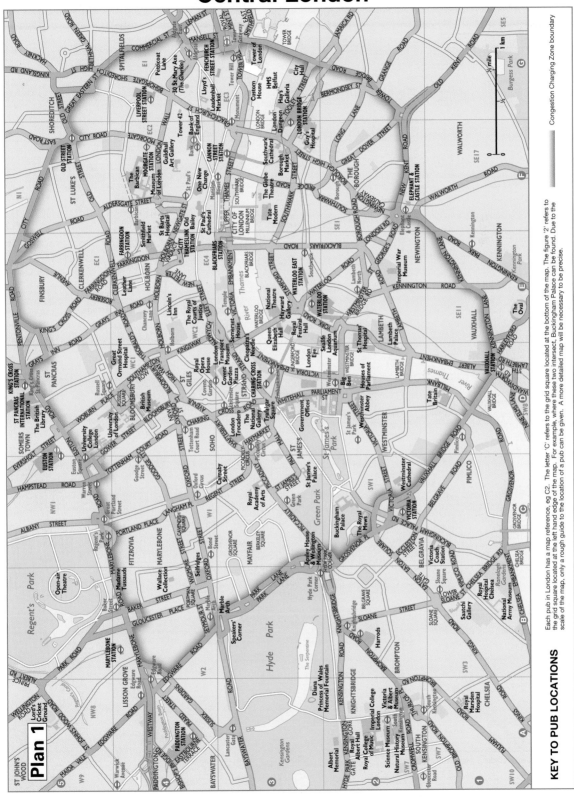

Plan 1

KEY TO PUB LOCATIONS

Each pub in London has a map reference, eg C2. The letter 'C' refers to the grid square located at the bottom of the map. The figure '2' refers to the grid square located at the left hand edge of the map. For example, where these two intersect, Buckingham Palace can be found. Due to the scale of the map, only a rough guide to the location of a pub can be given. A more detailed map will be necessary to be precise.

Congestion Charging Zone boundary

Index

Red entries are Pick of the Pubs

H

Save on hotels. Book at theAA.com/hotel

INDEX 651

AA Media Limited would like to thank the following photographers and companies for their assistance in the preparation of this book.

Abbreviations for the picture credits are as follows: (t) top; (b) bottom; (l) left; (r) right; (c) centre (AA) AA World Travel Library.

1 The Fox and Hounds, East Knoyle; 2 Andy Abbott; 3 The Pheasant Inn, Burwardsley; 4 The Coachman Inn, Snainton; 5bc Winyards Gap Inn, Chedington; 5br The Cock & Bull Bar & Restaurant, Balmedie; 6 The Seaview Hotel and Restaurant, Isle of Wight; 7t Killiecrankie House Hotel, Pitlochry; 7c The Three Fishes, Whalley; 8 The Feathered Nest Inn, Nether Westcote; 9t The Café Royal, Edinburgh; 9b The White Hart Village Inn, Llangybi; 10 The Boatman, Guildford; 11 The Black Swan, Ravenstonedale; 12 Ange/Alamy; 13 The Beer Engine, Newton St Cyres; 14 brinkstock/Alamy; 15t The Old Inn, Gairloch; 15b Black Sheep Brewery, Masham; 16/17 The Bush, Ovington; 18t Brackenrigg Inn, Watermillock; 18c The Fox Goes Free, Charlton; 18b Old Hall Inn, Chinley; 19t Kerry Dunstone/Alamy; 19b Shieldaig Bar & Coastal Kitchen, Shieldaig; 20 Bear of Rodborough Hotel, Stroud; 21t The Middle House, Mayfield; 21b Andy Brining; 26/27 AA/M Kipling; 28/29 AA/J Smith; 30/31 AA/M Bauer; 568 AA/K Blackwell; 570 AA/S Whitehorne; 571 AA/S Whitehorne; 599 AA/D Croucher; 601 AA/S Lewis; 604 The John Thompson Inn & Brewery, Ingleby

Every effort has been made to trace the copyright holders, and we apologise in advance for any accidental errors. We would be happy to apply the corrections in the following edition of this publication.

Readers' Report Form

Please send this form to:–
Editor, The Pub Guide,
Lifestyle Guides,
AA Publishing,
13th Floor, Fanum House,
Basingstoke RG21 4EA

or fax: 01256 491647
or e-mail: lifestyleguides@theAA.com

Please use this form to tell us about any pub or inn you have visited, whether it is in the guide or not currently listed. We are interested in the quality of food, the selection of beers and the overall ambience of the establishment.

Feedback from readers helps us to keep our guide accurate and up to date. However, if you have a complaint to make during a visit, we do recommend that you discuss the matter with the pub management there and then, so that they have a chance to put things right before your visit is spoilt.

Please note that the AA does not undertake to arbitrate between you and the pub management, or to obtain compensation or engage in protracted correspondence.

Date

Your name (BLOCK CAPITALS)

Your address (BLOCK CAPITALS)

Post code

E-mail address

Name of pub

Location

Comments

(please attach a separate sheet if necessary)

Please tick here ☐ if you DO NOT wish to receive details of AA offers or products

PTO

Readers' Report Form *continued*

Have you bought this guide before? ☐ YES ☐ NO

Do you regularly use any other pub, accommodation or food guides? ☐ YES ☐ NO
If YES, which ones?

_____

_____

What do you find most useful about The AA Pub Guide?

_____

_____

_____

_____

Do you read the editorial features in the guide? ☐ YES ☐ NO

Do you use the location atlas? ☐ YES ☐ NO

Is there any other information you would like to see added to this guide?

_____

_____

_____

_____

What are your main reasons for visiting pubs (tick all that apply)
food ☐   business ☐   accommodation ☐
beer ☐   celebrations ☐   entertainment ☐
atmosphere ☐   leisure ☐
other

How often do you visit a pub for a meal?
more than once a week ☐
once a week ☐
once a fortnight ☐
once a month ☐
once in six months ☐

Readers' Report Form

Please send this form to:–
Editor, The Pub Guide,
Lifestyle Guides,
AA Publishing,
13th Floor, Fanum House,
Basingstoke RG21 4EA

or fax: 01256 491647
or e-mail: lifestyleguides@theAA.com

Please use this form to tell us about any pub or inn you have visited, whether it is in the guide or not currently listed. We are interested in the quality of food, the selection of beers and the overall ambience of the establishment.

Feedback from readers helps us to keep our guide accurate and up to date. However, if you have a complaint to make during a visit, we do recommend that you discuss the matter with the pub management there and then, so that they have a chance to put things right before your visit is spoilt.

Please note that the AA does not undertake to arbitrate between you and the pub management, or to obtain compensation or engage in protracted correspondence.

Date

Your name (BLOCK CAPITALS)

Your address (BLOCK CAPITALS)

Post code

E-mail address

Name of pub

Location

Comments

(please attach a separate sheet if necessary)

Please tick here ☐ if you DO NOT wish to receive details of AA offers or products

PTO

Readers' Report Form *continued*

Have you bought this guide before? ☐ YES ☐ NO

Do you regularly use any other pub, accommodation or food guides? ☐ YES ☐ NO
If YES, which ones?

What do you find most useful about The AA Pub Guide?

Do you read the editorial features in the guide? ☐ YES ☐ NO

Do you use the location atlas? ☐ YES ☐ NO

Is there any other information you would like to see added to this guide?

What are your main reasons for visiting pubs (tick all that apply)
food ☐   business ☐   accommodation ☐
beer ☐   celebrations ☐   entertainment ☐
atmosphere ☐   leisure ☐
other

How often do you visit a pub for a meal?
more than once a week ☐
once a week ☐
once a fortnight ☐
once a month ☐
once in six months ☐